CRC Handbook of Mathematical Sciences

5th Edition

Editor

William H. Beyer, Ph.D.

Chairman
Department of Mathematics and Statistics
University of Akron
Akron, Ohio

CRC Press, Inc.
Boca Raton, Florida

Library of Congress Cataloging in Publication Data

Main entry under title:

CRC handbook of mathematical sciences.

   5th ed. published under title: Handbook of tables for mathematics.

   Bibliography: p.
   Includes index.
   1. Mathematics — — Tables, etc. I. Beyer, William H. II. Title: Handbook of tables for
mathematics.
QA47.H324   1978   510'.21'2   78-10602
ISBN 0-8493-0655-8

PREFACE

In spite of the rapid change in the mathematics environment today, it is clear that there is wide spread, if not universal, acceptance and satisfaction with the base of reference material that has been provided in handbooks published by CRC Press, Inc. There is no clearer evidence of the vitality of prior editions than the fact that, as this handbook celebrates 16 years of growth and achievement, much of the celebration takes the form of planning for the future. The final result of a complete review and examination of the reference material that has appeared in predecessor editions is that this fifth edition has been restructured in content and format, and has been retitled *CRC Handbook of Mathematical Sciences*. It is hoped that this fifth edition will receive the same excellent reception and wide use as have earlier editions.

Advancements in the mathematical sciences are all around us. The rapid development of statistics, applied mathematics, and computer technology, and the wide spread availability and use of hand-held calculators have certainly had their effect on the nature of published reference material. It has long been the established policy of CRC Press, Inc. to publish, in handbook form, the most up-to-date, authoritative, and logically arranged reference material available. This fifth edition continues to follow this policy. The material is presented in a multi-sectional format in order to maintain a usefulness of reference data for the present and the future. The format is such that existing sections can be expanded as needed, and new sections can be developed as warranted. Each section contains a valuable collection of fundamental reference material — both expository and tabular — necessary for usage by mathematicians, scientists, and students. A vast improvement is provided in the presentation of new material throughout this fifth edition, on such topics as Theory of Numbers, Differential Equations, Special Functions, Complex Variables, Numerical Methods, and Astrodynamics.

The Editor gratefully acknowledges the participation of the Advisory Board and the many users of CRC Handbooks for their constructive suggestions and contributions toward the preparation of this new fifth edition of the *CRC Handbook of Mathematical Sciences*. The Editor is particularly grateful to our Coordinating Editor, Paul Gottehrer, for his handling of the detail work which is so essential in the final production of this edition. And finally, the Editor is especially indebted to Dr. Samuel M. Selby, Editor Emeritus of CRC Mathematics, whose untimely death in the summer of 1976 will be felt by all in the mathematical community. This edition is conceived in line with the tradition he set.

As in the past, CRC Press, Inc. and the Editorial Staff invite and welcome constructive comments from its users, as this is a most effective means for keeping the editions of handbooks updated and abreast of the times.

MATHEMATICS ADVISORY BOARD

ACKNOWLEDGMENTS

Acknowledgment is made to the following authors, editors, and publishers whose material has been used in the Handbook of Mathematical Sciences and for which permission has been received.

AMERICAN SOCIETY FOR TESTING MATERIALS STP-15C;
  ASTM Manual on Quality Control of Materials (1951)
    Factors for Computing Control Limits

BARGMANN, ROLF E., PH.D.
  Matrices and Determinants

BIOMETRIKA TRUSTEES, E. S. PEARSON
  Cambridge University Press
    Biometrika Tables for Statisticians and Biometrika, Vol. 32,
      Percentage Points, Chi-Square Distribution
      Percentage Points, F-Distribution

E. RICHARD COHEN, A. B., M. S., PH.D.
  Fundamental Physical Constants

DESKINS, W. E., PH.D.
  Basic Concepts in Algebra

EVES, HOWARD, PH.D.
  Analytic Geometry
  Curves and Surfaces
  Mensuration Formula
  Trigonometry
GASKELL, R. E., PH. D.
  The Laplace Transform

GIRLING, BRIAN, M.Sc., F.I.M.A.
  Differentiation Formulas
  Finite Differences
  Sine, Cosine, and Exponential Integrals
  The Z Transforms

GUPTA, MADHU-SUDAN, M.Sc. TECH., M.S., A.M.
  Inverse Hyperbolic Function Tables

HARPER & ROWE, NEW YORK, N.Y.
  Concepts of Calculus by A. H. Lighston
    Bessel Function J_0, J_1

HERRICK, SAMUEL, B. A., Sc.D., PH.D.
  Astrodynamics: Basic Orbital Equations
  Astrodynamical Terminology. Notation, and Usage
    Condensed from Astrodynamics: N.Y. Van Nostrand Reinhold, 1970

INTERNATIONAL BUSINESS MACHINES CORPORATION
  IBM Brochure "360 Principles of Operation," Form A 22-6821-3
    Hexadecimal-Direct Conversion Table

MCGRAW-HILL, NEW YORK
  Lazenga Diagram-Interpolation Coefficients for Orthogonal Polynomials
    and for x^n in Terms of Orthogonal Polynomials
      Table of Real and Imaginary Parts, Zeros, and Singularities
      Table of Transformations of Regions

OLIVER AND BOYD, LTD., EDINBURGH, SCOTLAND
    Statistical Tables for Biological, Agricultural and Medical Research of Fisher & Yates
    Percentage Points, Student's t-Distribution

PRATT, RICHARD, A. M.
    Explanations to Tables
    Use of Logarithms (Law of Exponents)
    Integral Tables

THE ROYAL SOCIETY, LONDON, ENGLAND
    Vol. 3 (1954) 2 Royal Society Mathematical Tables
    Number of Combinations

SICKAFUS, E. N. and Mackie, N. A.
    The Interstitial Sphere

SPRINGER-VERLAG NEW YORK, INC.
    Funfstellige Funktionentafeln (1930), Hayashi, K.
    Number of Permutations

TABLE OF CONTENTS

Greek letter	Greek name	English equivalent	Greek letter	Greek name	English equivalent
A α	Alpha	a	N ν	Nu	n
B β	Beta	b	Ξ ξ	Xi	x
Γ γ	Gamma	g	O o	Omicron	ŏ
Δ δ	Delta	d	Π π	Pi	p
E ε	Epsilon	ĕ	P ρ	Rho	r
Z ζ	Zeta	z	Σ σ ς	Sigma	s
H η	Eta	ē	T τ	Tau	t
Θ θ ϑ	Theta	th	Υ υ	Upsilon	u
I ι	Iota	i	Φ φ φ	Phi	ph
K κ	Kappa	k	X χ	Chi	ch
Λ λ	Lambda	l	Ψ ψ	Psi	ps
M μ	Mu	m	Ω ω	Omega	ō

THE NUMBER OF EACH DAY OF THE YEAR

Day of Mo.	Jan.	Feb.	Mar.	Apr.	May	Jun.	Jul.	Aug.	Sep.	Oct.	Nov.	Dec.	Day of Mo.
1	1	32	60	91	121	152	182	213	244	274	305	335	1
2	2	33	61	92	122	153	183	214	245	275	306	336	2
3	3	34	62	93	123	154	184	215	246	276	307	337	3
4	4	35	63	94	124	155	185	216	247	277	308	338	4
5	5	36	64	95	125	156	186	217	248	278	309	339	5
6	6	37	65	96	126	157	187	218	249	279	310	340	6
7	7	38	66	97	127	158	188	219	250	280	311	341	7
8	8	39	67	98	128	159	189	220	251	281	312	342	8
9	9	40	68	99	129	160	190	221	252	282	313	343	9
10	10	41	69	100	130	161	191	222	253	283	314	344	10
11	11	42	70	101	131	162	192	223	254	284	315	345	11
12	12	43	71	102	132	163	193	224	255	285	316	346	12
13	13	44	72	103	133	164	194	225	256	286	317	347	13
14	14	45	73	104	134	165	195	226	257	287	318	348	14
15	15	46	74	105	135	166	196	227	258	288	319	349	15
16	16	47	75	106	136	167	197	228	259	289	320	350	16
17	17	48	76	107	137	168	198	229	260	290	321	351	17
18	18	49	77	108	138	169	199	230	261	291	322	352	18
19	19	50	78	109	139	170	200	231	262	292	323	353	19
20	20	51	79	110	140	171	201	232	263	293	324	354	20
21	21	52	80	111	141	172	202	233	264	294	325	355	21
22	22	53	81	112	142	173	203	234	265	295	326	356	22
23	23	54	82	113	143	174	204	235	266	296	327	357	23
24	24	55	83	114	144	175	205	236	267	297	328	358	24
25	25	56	84	115	145	176	206	237	268	298	329	359	25
26	26	57	85	116	146	177	207	238	269	299	330	360	26
27	27	58	86	117	147	178	208	239	270	300	331	361	27
28	28	59	87	118	148	179	209	240	271	301	332	362	28
29	29	*	88	119	149	180	210	241	272	302	333	363	29
30	30		89	120	150	181	211	242	273	303	334	364	30
31	31		90		151		212	243		304		365	31

* In leap years, after February 28, add 1 to the tabulated number.

SI SYSTEM OF MEASUREMENT

SI, which is the abbreviation of the French words "Système Internationale d'Unites," is the accepted abbreviation for the International Metric System, which has seven base units, as shown below.

UNITS FOR A SYSTEM OF MEASURES AS USED INTERNATIONALLY

Quantity measured	Unit	Abbreviation
Length	meter	m
Mass	kilogram	kg
Time	second	s
Electric current	ampere	A
Temperature	degree Kelvin	K
Luminous intensity	candela	cd
Amount of substance	mole	mol

Supplementary and Derived Units From Base Units as used Internationally

Supplementary Units

Plane angle	radian	rad
Solid angle	steradian	sr

Derived Units

Area	square meter	m^2	
Volume	cubic meter	m^3	
Frequency	hertz	Hz	(s^{-1})
Density	kilogram per cubic meter	kg/m^3	
Velocity	meter per second	m/s	
Angular velocity	radian per second	rad/s	
Acceleration	meter per second squared	m/s^2	
Angular acceleration	radian per second squared	rad/s^2	
Force	newton	N	$(kg \cdot m/s^2)$
Pressure	newton per sq meter	N/m^2	
Kinematic viscosity	sq meter per second	m^2/s	
Dynamic viscosity	newton-second per sq meter	$N \cdot s/m^2$	
Work, energy, quantity of heat	joule	J	$(N \cdot m)$
Power	watt	W	(J/s)
Electric charge	coulomb	C	$(A \cdot s)$
Voltage, potential difference, electromotive force	volt	V	(W/A)
Electric field strength	volt per meter	V/m	
Electric resistance	ohm	Ω	(V/A)
Electric capacitance	farad	F	$(A \cdot s/V)$
Magnetic flux	weber	Wb	$(V \cdot s)$
Inductance	henry	H	$(V \cdot s/A)$
Magnetic flux density	tesla	T	(Wb/m^2)
Magnetic field strength	ampere per meter	A/m	
Magnetomotive force	ampere	A	
Luminous flux	lumen	lm	$(cd \cdot sr)$
Luminance	candela per sq meter	cd/m^2	
Illumination	lux	lx	(lm/m^2)

RECOMMENDED UNIT PREFIXES

Multiples and submultiples	Prefixes	Symbols
10^{18}	exa	E
10^{15}	pecta	P
10^{12}	tera	T
10^{9}	giga	G
10^{6}	mega	M
10^{3}	kilo	k
10^{2}	hecto	h
10	deka	da
10^{-1}	deci	d
10^{-2}	centi	c
10^{-3}	milli	m
10^{-6}	micro	μ (greek mu)
10^{-9}	nano	n
10^{-12}	pico	p
10^{-15}	femto	f
10^{-18}	atto	a

DEFINED VALUES AND EQUIVALENTS

Meter................................(m)	1 650 763.73 wave lengths in vacuo of the unperturbed transition $2p_{10} - 5d_5$ in ^{86}Kr
Kilogram.............................(kg)	mass of the international kilogram at Sèvres, France
Second...............................(s)	1/31 556 925.974 7 of the tropical year at 12^{h} ET, 0 January 1900
Degree Kelvin ....(°K)	defined in the thermodynamic scale by assigning 273.16°K to the triple point of water (freezing point, 273.15°K = 0°C)
Unified atomic mass unit ....(u)	1/12 the mass of an atom of the ^{12}C nuclide
Mole ....(mol)	amount of substance containing the same number of atoms as 12 g of pure ^{12}C
Standard acceleration of free fall........(g_n)	9.806 65 M s^{-2}, 980.665 cm s^{-2}
Normal atmospheric pressure ....(atm)	101 325 N m^{-2}, 1 013 250 dyn cm^{-2}
Thermochemical calorie.................(cal_{th})	4.1840 J, 4.1840 × 10^{7} erg
International Steam Table calorie........(cal_{IT})	4.1868 J, 4.1868 × 10^{7} erg
Liter.................................(l)	0.001 000 028 m^{3}, 1 000.028 cm^{3} (recommended by CIPM, 1950) 0.001 m^{3}, 1000 cm^{3} (recommended by GCWM 1964)
Inch ....(in)	0.0254 m, 2.54 cm
Pound (avdp) ....(lb)	0.453 592 37 kg, 453.592 37 g

CONVERSION FACTORS

Conversion Factors – Metric to English

To obtain	Multiply	By
Inches	Centimeters	0.3937007874
Feet	Meters	3.280839895
Yards	Meters	1.093613298
Miles	Kilometers	0.6213711922
Ounces	Grams	$3.527396195 \times 10^{-2}$
Pounds	Kilograms	2.204622622
Gallons	Liters	0.2641720524
Fluid ounces	Milliliters (cc)	$3.381402270 \times 10^{-2}$
Square inches	Square centimeters	0.1550003100
Square feet	Square meters	10.76391042
Square yards	Square meters	1.195990046
Cubic inches	Milliliters (cc)	$6.102374409 \times 10^{-2}$
Cubic feet	Cubic meters	35.31466672
Cubic yards	Cubic meters	1.307950619

Conversion Factors – English to Metric*

To obtain	Multiply	By
Microns	Mils	**25.4**
Centimeters	Inches	**2.54**
Meters	Feet	**0.3048**
Meters	Yards	**0.9144**
Kilometers	Miles	**1.609344**
Grams	Ounces	28.34952313
Kilograms	Pounds	**0.45359237**
Liters	Gallons	**3.785411784**
Milliliters (cc)	Fluid ounces	29.57352956
Square centimeters	Square inches	**6.4516**
Square meters	Square feet	**0.09290304**
Square meters	Square yards	**0.83612736**
Milliliters (cc)	Cubic inches	**16.387064**
Cubic meters	Cubic feet	$2.831684659 \times 10^{-2}$
Cubic meters	Cubic yards	0.764554858

Conversion Factors – General*

To obtain	Multiply	By
Atmospheres	Feet of water @ 4°C	2.950×10^{-5}
Atmospheres	Inches of mercury @ 0°C	3.342×10^{-2}
Atmospheres	Pounds per square inch	6.804×10^{-2}
BTU	Food-pounds	1.285×10^{-3}
BTU	Joules	9.480×10^{-4}
Cords	Cubic feet	**128**

*Boldface numbers are exact; others are given to ten significant figures where so indicated by the multiplier factor.

Conversion Factors – General (Continued)

To obtain	Multiply	By
Degree (angle)	Radians	57.2958
Ergs	Foot-pounds	1.356×10^7
Feet	Miles	**5280**
Feet of water @ 4°C	Atmospheres	33.90
Foot-pounds	Horsepower-hours	1.98×10^6
Foot-pounds	Kilowatt-hours	2.655×10^6
Food-pounds per min	Horsepower	3.3×10^4
Horsepower	Foot-pounds per sec	1.818×10^{-3}
Inches of mercury @ 0°C	Pounds per square inch	2.036
Joules	BTU	1054.8
Joules	Foot-pounds	1.35582
Kilowatts	BTU per min	1.758×10^{-2}
Kilowatts	Foot-pounds per min	2.26×10^{-5}
Kilowatts	Horsepower	0.745712
Knots	Miles per hour	0.86897624
Miles	Feet	1.894×10^{-4}
Nautical miles	Miles	0.86897624
Radians	Degrees	1.745×10^{-2}
Square feet	Acres	**43560**
Watts	BTU per min	17.5796

Temperature Factors

$$°F = 9/5 \ (°C) + 32$$

Fahrenheit temperature = 1.8 (temperature in kelvins) −459.67

$$°C = 5/9 \ [(°F) - 32]$$

Celsius temperature = temperature in kelvins −273.15
Fahrenheit temperature = 1.8 (Celsius temperature) +32

CONVERSION FACTORS
U. S. AND METRIC UNITS

Each unit in bold face type is followed by its equivalent in other units of the same quantity.

Acre—0.0015625 square mile (statute); 4.3560 × 10⁴ square feet; 0.40468564 hectare.

Bushel—(U.S.)—1.244456 cubic feet; 2150.42 cubic inches; 0.035239 cubic meter; 35.23808 liters.

Centimeter—0.0328084 foot; 0.393701 inch.

Circular Mil—7.853982 × 10⁻⁷ square inches; 5.067075 × 10⁻⁸ square centimeters.

Cubic Centimeter—0.061024 cubic inch; 0.270512 dram (U. S. fluid); 16.230664 minims (U. S.); 0.999972 milliliter.

Cubic Foot—0.803564 bushel (U. S.); 7.480520 gallons (U. S. liquid); 0.028317 cubic meter; 28.31605 liters.

Cubic Inch—16.387064 cubic centimeters.

Cubic Meter—35.314667 cubic feet; 264.17205 gallons (U. S. liquid).

Foot—0.3048 meter.

Gallon (U. S. liquid)—0.1336816 cubic foot; 0.832675 gallon (British); 231 cubic inches; 0.0037854 cubic meter; 3.785306 liters.

Grain—0.06479891 gram.

Gram—0.00220462 pound (avoirdupois); 0.035274 ounce (avoirdupois); 15.432358 grains.

Hectare—2.471054 acres; 1.07639 × 10⁵ square feet.

Inch—2.54 centimeters.

Kilogram—2.204623 pounds (avoirdupois).

Kilometer—0.621371 mile (statute).

Liter—0.264179 gallon (U. S. liquid); 0.0353157 cubic foot; 1.056718 quarts (U. S. liquid).

Meter—1.093613 yards; 3.280840 feet; 39.37008 inches.

Mile (statute)—1.609344 kilometers.

Ounce (U. S. fluid)—1.804688 cubic inches; 29.573730 cubic centimeters.

Ounce (avoirdupois)—28.349523 grams.

Ounce (apothecary or troy)—31.103486 grams.

Pint (U. S. liquid)—0.473163 liter; 473.17647 cubic centimeters.

Pound (avoirdupois)—0.453592 kilogram; 453.59237 grams.

Pound (apothecary or troy)—0.3732417 kilogram, 373.24172 grams.

Quart (U. S. dry)—1.10119 liters.

Quart (liquid)—0.946326 liter.

Radian—57.295779 degrees.

Rod—5.0292 meters.

Square Centimeter—0.155000 square inch.

Square Foot—0.09290304 square meter.

Square Inch—645.16 square millimeters.

Square Meter—10.763910 square feet.

Square Yard—0.836127 square meter.

Ton (short)—907.18474 kilograms.

Yard—0.9144 meter.

See Index for extensive Conversion Factors.

METRIC CONVERSION TABLE

Inches	Centimeters	Centimeters	Inches
1	2.54	1	0.393701
2	5.0	2	0.787402
3	7.62	3	1.181103
4	10.16	4	1.574804
5	12.70	5	1.968505
6	15.24	6	2.362206
7	17.78	7	2.755907
8	20.32	8	3.149608
9	22.86	9	3.543309

Feet	Meters	Meters	Feet
1	0.3048	1	3.280840
2	0.6096	2	6.561680
3	0.9144	3	9.842520
4	1.2192	4	13.123360
5	1.5240	5	16.404200
6	1.8288	6	19685040
7	2.1336	7	22.965880
8	2.4384	8	26.246720
9	2.7432	9	29.527560

Yards	Meters	Meters	Yards
1	0.9144	1	1.0936133
2	1.8288	2	2.1872266
3	2.7432	3	3.2808399
4	3.6576	4	4.3744532
5	4.5720	5	5.4680665
6	5.4864	6	6.5616798
7	6.4008	7	7.6552931
8	7.3152	8	8.7489064
9	8.2296	9	9.8425197

Miles (statute)	Kilometers	Kilometers	Miles
1	1.609344	1	0.6213712
2	3.218688	2	1.2427424
3	4.828032	3	1.8641136
4	6.437376	4	2.4854848
5	8.046720	5	3.1068560
6	9.656064	6	3.7282272
7	11.265408	7	4.3495984
8	12.874752	8	4.9709696
9	14.484096	9	5.5923408

Square inches	Square centimeters	Square centimeters	Square inches
1	6.45	1	0.155
2	12.90	2	0.310
3	19.36	3	0.465
4	25.81	4	0.620
5	32.26	5	0.775
6	38.71	6	0.930
7	45.16	7	1.085
8	51.61	8	1.240
9	58.06	9	1.395

METRIC CONVERSION TABLE (continued)

Square feet	Square meters	Square meters	Square feet
1	0.0929	1	10.76
2	0.1858	2	21.53
3	0.2787	3	32.29
4	0.3716	4	43.06
5	0.4645	5	53.82
6	0.5574	6	64.58
7	0.6503	7	75.35
8	0.7432	8	86.11
9	0.8361	9	96.88

Cubic inches	Cubic centimeters	Cubic centimeters	Cubic Inches
1	16.39	1	0.0610
2	32.77	2	0.1221
3	49.16	3	0.1831
4	65.55	4	0.2441
5	81.94	5	0.3051
6	98.32	6	0.3661
7	114.71	7	0.4272
8	131.10	8	0.4882
9	147.48	9	0.5492

Cubic feet	Cubic meters	Cubic meters	Cubic feet
1	0.0283	1	35.3
2	0.0566	2	70.6
3	0.0850	3	105.9
4	0.1133	4	141.3
5	0.1416	5	176.6
6	0.1699	6	211.9
7	0.1982	7	247.2
8	0.2265	8	282.5
9	0.2549	9	317.8

Cubic feet	Liters	Liters	Cubic feet
1	28.32	1	0.0353
2	56.63	2	0.0706
3	84.95	3	0.1060
4	113.26	4	0.1413
5	141.58	5	0.1766
6	169.90	6	0.2119
7	198.21	7	0.2472
8	226.53	8	0.2825
9	254.84	9	0.3178

U.S. gallons	Liters	Liters	U.S. gallons
1	3.785306	1	0.264179
2	7.570612	2	0.528358
3	11.355918	3	0.792537
4	15.141224	4	1.056716
5	18.926530	5	1.320895
6	22.711836	6	1.585074
7	26.497142	7	1.849253
8	30.282448	8	2.113432
9	34.067754	9	2.377611

British or Imperial gallons	Liters	Liters	British or Imperial gallons
1	4.546	1	0.220
2	9.092	2	0.440
3	13.638	3	0.660
4	18.184	4	0.880
5	22.730	5	1.100
6	27.276	6	1.320
7	31.822	7	1.540
8	36.368	8	1.760
9	40.914	9	1.980

Pounds (av)	Kilograms	Kilograms	Pounds (av)
1	0.45359237	1	2.2046226
2	0.90718474	2	4.4092452
3	1.36077711	3	6.6138678
4	1.81436948	4	8.8184904
5	2.26796185	5	11.0231130
6	2.72155422	6	13.2277356
7	3.17514659	7	15.4323582
8	3.62873896	8	17.6369808
9	4.08233133	9	19.8416034

Ounces Avoirdupois	Grams	Grams	Ounces Avoirdupois
1	28.350	1	0.035274
2	56.699	2	0.070548
3	85.049	3	0.10582
4	113.40	4	0.14110
5	141.75	5	0.17637
6	170.10	6	0.21164
7	198.45	7	0.24692
8	226.80	8	0.28219
9	255.15	9	0.31747

Pounds per foot	Kilograms per meter	Kilograms per meter	Pounds per foot
1	1.4882	1	0.6720
2	2.9763	2	1.3439
3	4.4645	3	2.0159
4	5.9527	4	2.6879
5	7.4408	5	3.3598
6	8.9290	6	4.0318
7	10.4171	7	4.7038
8	11.9053	8	5.3758
9	13.3935	9	6.0477

Pounds per square inch	Kilograms per square centimeter	Kilograms per square centimeter	Pounds per square inch
1	0.0703	1	14.22
2	0.1406	2	28.45
3	0.2109	3	42.67
4	0.2812	4	56.89
5	0.3515	5	71.12
6	0.4218	6	85.34
7	0.4922	7	99.96
8	0.5625	8	113.79
9	0.6328	9	128.01

Pounds per square inch	Kilonewtons per square meter	Kilonewtons per square meter	Pounds per square inch
1	6.895	1	0.145
2	13.790	2	0.290
3	20.684	3	0.435
4	27.579	4	0.580
5	34.474	5	0.725
6	41.369	6	0.870
7	48.263	7	1.015
8	55.158	8	1.160
9	62.053	9	1.305

Pounds per square foot	Kilograms per square meter	Kilograms per square meter	Pounds per square foot
1	4.88	1	0.2048
2	9.77	2	0.4096
3	14.65	3	0.6144
4	19.53	4	0.8193
5	24.41	5	1.0241
6	29.30	6	1.2289
7	34.18	7	1.4337
8	39.06	8	1.6385
9	43.94	9	1.8433

Pound feet	Kilogram meters	Kilogram meters	Pound feet
1	0.138	1	7.23
2	0.277	2	14.47
3	0.415	3	21.70
4	0.553	4	28.93
5	0.691	5	36.17
6	0.830	6	43.40
7	0.968	7	50.63
8	1.106	8	57.87
9	1.244	9	65.10

Foot pounds force	Joules	Joules	Foot pounds force
1	1.356	1	0.7376
2	2.712	2	1.4751
3	4.068	3	2.2127
4	5.423	4	2.9502
5	6.779	5	3.6878
6	8.135	6	4.4254
7	9.491	7	5.1629
8	10.847	8	5.9005
9	12.202	9	6.6381

British thermal units	Kilojoules	Kilojoules	British thermal units
1	105.51	1	94.78
2	211.01	2	189.56
3	316.52	3	284.35
4	422.02	4	379.13
5	527.53	5	473.91
6	633.03	6	568.69
7	738.54	7	663.47
8	844.04	8	758.25
9	949.55	9	853.04

METRIC CONVERSION TABLE (continued)

Horsepower	Kilowatts	Kilowatts	Horsepower
1	0.746	1	1.341
2	1.491	2	2.682
3	2.237	3	4.023
4	2.983	4	5.364
5	3.729	5	6.705
6	4.474	6	8.046
7	5.220	7	9.387
8	5.966	8	10.728
9	6.711	9	12.069

Pounds force	Newtons	Newtons	Pounds force
1	4.448	1	0.22481
2	8.896	2	0.44962
3	13.345	3	0.67443
4	17.793	4	0.89924
5	22.241	5	1.12404
6	26.689	6	1.34885
7	31.138	7	1.57366
8	35.586	8	1.79847
9	40.034	9	2.02328

CONVERSION FACTORS

(From various U. S. Government and IUPAC publications and from calculations based on values given in these publications)

To convert from	To	Multiply by	To convert from	To	Multiply by
Amperes	Amperes	10	Acre-inches	Gallons (U.S.)	27154.286
"	E.M. cgs. units of current	1	Amperes	Abamperes	0.1
"	E.S. cgs. units	2.997930×10^{10}	"	Amperes (Int.)	1.000165
"	Faradays (chem.)/sec	1.036377×10^{-4}	"	Cgs. units of current	1
"	Faradays (phys.)/sec	1.036086×10^{-4}	"	Mks. units of current	1
"	Statamperes	2.997930×10^{10}	"	Coulombs/sec	1
Amperes/cm	E.M. cgs. units of surface charge density	1	"	Coulombs (Int.)/sec	1.000165
"	E.S. cgs. units	2.997930×10^{10}	"	Faradays (chem.)/sec	1.036377×10^{-5}
Amperes/sq. cm	Amperes/circ. mil	5.0670748×10^{-5}	"	Faradays (phys.)/sec	1.036086×10^{-5}
"	Amperes/sq. cm	10	"	Statamperes	2.997930×10^{9}
"	Amperes/sq. inch	64.516	Amperes (Int.)	Amperes	0.999835
Ampere-turns	Ampere-turns	10	"	Coulombs/sec	0.999835
Ampere-turns/cm	Ampere-turns/cm	10	"	Coulombs (Int.)/sec	1
Coulombs	Ampere-hours	0.0027777	"	Faradays (chem.)/sec	1.03623×10^{-5}
"	Coulombs	10	"	Faradays (phys.)/sec	1.03592×10^{-5}
"	Electronic charges	6.24196×10^{19}	Amperes/meter	Cgs. units of surface current density	0.01
"	E.M. cgs. units of charge	1	"	E.M. cgs. units	0.001
"	E.S. cgs. units	2.997930×10^{10}	"	E.S. cgs. units	2.997930×10^{7}
"	Faradays (chem.)	1.036377×10^{-4}	"	Mks. units	1
"	Faradays (phys.)	1.036086×10^{-4}	Amperes/sq. meter	Cgs. units of volume current density	0.0001
"	Statcoulombs	2.997930×10^{10}	"	E.M. cgs. units	1×10^{-5}
Farads	E.M. cgs. units of capacitance	1	"	E.S. cgs. units	299793.0
"	E.S. cgs. units	8.987584×10^{20}	"	Mks. units	1
"	Farads	1×10^{9}	Amperes/sq. mil	Abamperes/sq. cm	15500.031
"	Microfarads	1×10^{15}	"	Amperes/sq. cm	1.5500031×10^{5}
"	Statfarads	8.987584×10^{20}	Ampere-hours	Abcoulombs	360
Henries	E.M. cgs. units of induction	1	"	Coulombs	3600
"	E.S. cgs. units	1.112646×10^{-21}	"	Faradays (chem.)	0.373096
"	Henries	1×10^{-9}	"	Faradays (phys.)	0.372991
Mhos	E.M. cgs. units of conductance	1	Ampere-turns	Cgs. units of magnetomotive force	1.2566371
"	E.S. cgs. units	8.987584×10^{20}	"	E.M. cgs. units	1.2566371
"	Megamhos	1000	"	E.S. cgs. units	3.767310×10^{10}
"	Mhos	1×10^{9}	"	Gilberts	1.2566371
"	Statmhos	8.987584×10^{20}	Ampere-turns/weber	Cgs. units of reluctance	1.256637×10^{-8}
Ohms	E.M. cgs. units of resistance	1	"	E.M. cgs. units	1.256637×10^{-8}
"	Megohms	1×10^{-15}	"	E.S. cgs. units	1.129413×10^{11}
"	Microhms	0.001	"	Gilberts/maxwell	1.256637×10^{-8}
"	Ohms	1×10^{-9}	Ångström units	Centimeters	1×10^{-8}
"	Statohms	1.112646×10^{-21}	"	Inches	3.9370079×10^{-9}
Ohm-cm	Circ. mil-ohms/ft	0.0060153049	"	Microns	0.0001
"	E.M. cgs. units of resistivity	1	"	Millimicrons	0.1
"	Microhm-inches	0.00039370079	"	Wave length of orange-red line of krypton 86	0.000165076373
"	Ohm-cm	1×10^{-9}	"	Wave length of red line of cadmium	0.000155316413
Volts	Microvolts	0.01	Ares	Acres	0.024710538
"	Millivolts	1×10^{-5}	"	Sq. dekameters	1
"	Volts	1×10^{-8}	"	Sq. feet	1076.3910
"	Volts (Int.)	9.99670×10^{-9}	"	Sq. ft. (U.S. Survey)	1076.3867
Volts/cm	E.M. cgs. units of electric field intensity	1	"	Sq. meters	100
"	E.S. cgs. units	3.335635×10^{-11}	"	Sq. miles	3.8610216×10^{-5}
"	Volts/cm	1×10^{-8}	Atmospheres	Bars	1.01325
"	Volts/inch	2.54×10^{-8}	"	Cm. of Hg (0°C.)	76
"	Volts/meter	1×10^{-6}	"	Cm. of H₂O (4°C.)	1033.26
Acres	Sq. cm	40468564	"	Dynes/sq. cm	1.01325×10^{6}
"	Sq. ft	43560	"	Ft. of H₂O (39.2°F.)	33.8995
"	Sq. ft. (U.S. Survey)	43559.826	"	Grams/sq. cm	1033.23
"	Sq. inches	6272640	"	In. of Hg (32°F.)	29.9213
"	Sq. kilometers	0.0040468564	"	Kg./sq. cm	1.03323
"	Sq. links (Gunter's)	1×10^{5}	"	Mm. of Hg (0°C.)	760
"	Sq. meters	4046.8564	"	Pounds/sq. inch	14.6960
"	Sq. miles (statute)	0.0015625	"	Tons (short)/sq. ft.	1.05811
"	Sq. perches	160	"	Torrs	760
"	Sq. rods	160	Atomic mass units (chem.)*	Electron volts	9.31395×10^{8}
"	Sq. yards	4840	"	Grams	1.66024×10^{-24}
Acre-feet	Cu. feet	43560	Atomic mass units (phys.)*	Electron volts	9.31141×10^{8}
"	Cu. meters	1233.4818	"	Grams	1.65979×10^{-24}
"	Cu. yards	1613.333			
Acre-inches	Cu. feet	3630			
"	Cu. meters	102.79033			

CONVERSION FACTORS (Continued)

To convert from	To	Multiply by
Bags (Brit.)	Bushels (Brit.)	3
Barns	Sq. cm.	1×10^{-24}
Barrels (Brit.)	Bags (Brit.)	1.5
"	Barrels (U.S., dry)	1.415404
"	Barrels (U.S., liq.)	1.372513
"	Bushels (Brit.)	4.5
"	Bushels (U.S.)	4.644253
"	Cu. feet	5.779568
"	Cu. meters	0.1636591
"	Gallons (Brit.)	36
"	Liters	163.6546
Barrels (petroleum, U.S.)	Cu. feet	5.614583
"	Gallons (U.S.)	42
"	Liters	158.98284
Barrels (U.S., dry)	Barrels (U.S. liq.)	0.969696
"	Bushels (U.S.)	3.2812195
"	Cu. feet	4.083333
"	Cu. inches	7056
"	Cu. meters	0.11562712
"	Quarts (U.S., dry)	105
Barrels (U.S., liq.)	Barrels (U.S., dry)	1.03125
"	Barrels (wine)	1
"	Cu. feet	4.2109375
"	Cu. inches	7276.5
"	Cu. meters	0.11924047
"	Gallons (Brit.)	26.22925
"	Gallons (U.S., liq.)	31.5
"	Liters	119.23713
Bars	Atmospheres	0.986923
"	Baryes	1×10^{6}
"	Cm. of Hg (0°C.)	75.0062
"	Dynes/sq. cm.	1×10^{6}
"	Ft. of H₂O (60°F.)	33.4883
"	Grams/sq. cm.	1019.716
"	In. of Hg (32°F.)	29.5300
"	Kg./sq. cm.	1.019716
"	Millibars	1000
"	Pounds/sq. inch	14.5038
Baryes	Atmospheres	9.86923×10^{-7}
"	Bars	1×10^{-6}
"	Dynes/sq. cm.	1
"	Grams/sq. cm.	0.001019716
"	Millibars	0.001
Bels	Decibels	10
Board feet	Cu. cm	2359.7372
"	Cu. feet	0.083333
"	Cu. inches	144
Bolts of cloth	Linear feet	120
"	Meters	36.576
Bougie decimales	Candles (Int.)	1.00
B.t.u.	B.t.u. (IST.)**	0.999346
"	B.t.u. (mean)	0.998563
"	B.t.u. (39°F.)	0.994982
"	B.t.u. (60°F.)	0.999689
"	Cal. *gm.*	251.99576
"	Cal., *gm.* (IST.)	251.831
"	Cal., *gm.* (mean)	251.634
"	Cal., *gm.* (20°C.)	252.122
"	Cu. cm.-atm.	10405.6
"	Ergs	1.05435×10^{10}
"	Foot-poundals	25020.1
"	Foot-pounds	777.649
"	Gram-cm.	1.07514×10^{7}
"	Hp.-hours	0.000392752
"	Hp.-years	4.48347×10^{-8}
"	Joules	1054.35
"	Joules (Int.)	1054.18
"	Kg.-meters	107.514
"	Kw.-hours	0.000292875

To convert from	To	Multiply by
B.t.u.	Kw.-hours (Int.)	0.000292827
"	Liter-atm	10.4053
"	Tons of refrig. (U.S. std.)	3.46995×10^{-6}
"	Watt-seconds	1054.35
"	Watt-seconds (Int.)	1054.18
B.t.u. (IST.)	B.t.u.	1.00065
B.t.u. (mean)	B.t.u.	1.00144
"	B.t.u. (IST.)	1.00078
"	B.t.u. (39°F.)	0.996415
"	B.t.u. (60°F.)	1.00113
"	Hp.-hours	0.000393317
"	Joules	1055.87
"	Kg.-meters	107.669
"	Kw.-hours	0.000293297
"	Kw.-hours (Int.)	0.000293248
"	Liter-atm	10.4203
"	Watt-hours	0.293297
"	Watt-hours (Int.)	0.293248
B.t.u. (39°F.)	B.t.u.	1.00504
"	B.t.u. (IST.)	1.00439
"	B.t.u. (mean)	1.00360
"	B.t.u. (60°F)	1.00473
"	Joules	1059.67
B.t.u. (60°F.)	B.t.u.	1.00031
"	B.t.u. (IST.)	0.999657
"	B.t.u. (mean)	0.998873
"	B.t.u. (39°F.)	0.995291
B.t.u./hr.	Cal., *kg.*/hr.	0.251996
"	Ergs/sec.	2.928751×10^{6}
"	Foot-pounds/hr.	777.649
"	Horsepower	0.000392752
"	Horsepower (boiler)	2.98563×10^{-5}
"	Horsepower (electric)	0.000392594
"	Horsepower (metric)	0.000398199
"	Kilowatts	0.000292875
"	Lb. ice melted/hr.	0.0069714
"	Tons of refrig. (U.S. comm.)	8.32789×10^{-5}
"	Watts	0.292875
B.t.u./min.	Cal., *kg.*/min.	0.251996
"	Ergs/sec.	1.75725×10^{8}
"	Foot-pounds/min.	777.649
"	Horsepower	0.0235651
"	Horsepower (boiler)	0.00179138
"	Horsepower (electric)	0.0235556
"	Horsepower (metric)	0.0238920
"	Joules/sec.	17.5725
"	Kg.-meters/min.	107.514
"	Kilowatts	0.0175725
"	Lb. ice melted/hr.	0.41828
"	Tons of refrig. (U.S. comm.)	0.00499673
"	Watts	17.5725
B.t.u. (mean)/min.	B.t.u. (mean)/hr.	60
"	Cal., *kg.* (mean)/hr.	15.1197
"	Cal., *kg.* (mean)/min.	0.251996
"	Ergs/sec.	1.75978×10^{8}
"	Foot-pounds/min.	778.768
"	Horsepower	0.0235990
"	Horsepower (boiler)	0.00179396
"	Horsepower (electric)	0.0235895
"	Horsepower (metric)	0.0239264
"	Joules/sec.	17.5978
"	Kg.-meters/min.	107.669
"	Kilowatts	0.0175978
"	Lb. ice-melted/hr.	0.41888
B.t.u./lb.	Cal., *gm.*/gram	0.555555
"	Cu. cm.-atm./gram	22.9405
"	Cu. ft.-atm./lb.	0.367471
"	Cu. ft.-(lb./sq. in.)/lb.	5.40034
"	Foot-pounds/lb.	777.649
"	Hp.-hr./lb.	0.000392752

* Barrel (Brit., liq.) = Barrel (Brit., dry)
** International Steam Table.

CONVERSION FACTORS (Continued)

To convert from	To	Multiply by	To convert from	To	Multiply by
..u./lb	Joules/gram	2.32444	Calories, *gm.***	B.t.u.	0.0039683207
..u. (mean)/lb	Cal., *gm.* (mean)/gram	0.555555	"	B.t.u. (IST.)	0.00396573
"	Cu. cm.-atm./gram	22.9735	"	B.t.u. (mean)	0.00396262
"	Foot-pounds/lb	778.768	"	B.t.u. (39°F.)	0.00394841
"	Hp.-hr./lb	0.000393317	"	B.t.u. (60°F.)	0.00396709
"	Joules/gram	2.32779	"	Cal., *gm.* (IST.)	0.999346
..u./sec	B.t.u./hr	3600	"	Cal., *gm.* (mean)	0.998563
"	B.t.u./min	60	"	Cal., *gm.* (15°C.)	0.999570
"	Cal., *kg.*/hr	907.185	"	Cal., *gm.* (20°C.)	1.00050
"	Cal., *kg.*/min	15.1197	"	Cal., *kg*	0.001
"	Cheval-vapeur	1.43352	"	Cal., *kg.* (IST.)	0.000999346
"	Ergs/sec	1.05435 × 10¹⁰	"	Cal., *kg.* (mean)	0.000998563
"	Foot-pounds/sec	777.649	"	Cal., *kg.* (15°C.)	0.000999570
"	Horsepower	1.41391	"	Cal., *kg.* (20°C.)	0.00100050
"	Horsepower (boiler)	0.107483	"	Cu. cm.-atm	41.2929
"	Horsepower (electric)	1.41334	"	Cu. ft.-atm	0.00145824
"	Horsepower (metric)	1.43352	"	Ergs	4.184 × 10⁷
"	Kg.-meters/sec	107.514	"	Foot-poundals	99.2878
"	Kilowatts	1.05435	"	Foot-pounds	3.08596
"	Kilowatts (Int.)	1.05418	"	Gram-cm	42664.9
"	Watts	1054.35	"	Hp.-hours	1.55857 × 10⁻⁶
"	Watts (Int.)	1054.18	"	Joules	4.184
.t.u. (mean)/sec	Ergs/sec	1.05587 × 10¹⁰	"	Joules (Int.)	4.18331
"	Foot-pounds/sec	778.768	"	Kg.-meters	0.426649
"	Horsepower	1.41594	"	Kw.-hours	1.162222 × 10⁻⁶
"	Horsepower (boiler)	0.107637	"	Liter-atm	0.0412917
"	Horsepower (electric)	1.41537	"	Watt-hours	0.001162222
"	Horsepower (metric)	1.43558	"	Watt-hours (Int.)	0.00116203
"	Watts	1055.87	"	Watt-seconds	4.184
.t.u./sq. ft	Cal., *gm.*/sq. cm	0.271246	Calories, *gm.* (mean)	B.t.u.	0.00397403
.t.u./sq.ft. × min.)	Hp./sq. ft	0.0235651	"	Cal., *gm*	1.00144
"	Kw./sq. ft	0.0175725	"	Cal., *gm.* (IST.)	1.00078
"	Watts/sq. in	0.122031	"	Cal., *gm.* (20°C.)	1.00194
uckets (Brit.)	Cu. cm	18184.35	"	Cal., *kg.* (mean)	0.001
"	Gallons (Brit.)	4	"	Cu. cm.-atm	41.3523
ushels (Brit.)	Bags (Brit.)	0.333333	"	Cu. ft.-atm	0.00146034
"	Bushels (U.S.)	1.032056	"	Ergs	4.19002 × 10⁷
"	Cu. cm	36368.70	"	Foot-poundals	99.4308
"	Cu. feet	1.284348	"	Foot-pounds	3.09040
"	Cu. inches	2219.354	"	Hp.-hours	1.56081 × 10⁻⁶
"	Dekaliters	3.636768	"	Joules	4.19002
"	Gallons (Brit.)	8	"	Joules (Int.)	4.18933
"	Hectoliters	0.3636768	"	Kg.-meters	0.427263
"	Liters	36.36768	"	Kw.-hours	1.16390 × 10⁻⁶
ushels (U.S.)*	Barrels (U.S.), dry	0.3047647	"	Liter-atm	0.0413511
"	Bushels (Brit.)	0.9689395	"	Watt-seconds	4.19002
"	Cu. cm	35239.07	Calories, *gm.* (15°C.)	B.t.u.	0.00397003
"	Cu. feet	1.244456	"	Cal., *gm*	1.00043
"	Cu. inches	2150.42	"	Cal., *gm.* (IST.)	0.999776
"	Cu. meters	0.03523907	"	Cal., *gm.* (mean)	0.998992
"	Cu. yards	0.04609096	"	Cal., *gm.* (20°C.)	1.00093
"	Gallons (U.S., dry)	8	"	Joules	4.18580
"	Gallons (U.S., liq.)	9.309177	"	Joules (Int.)	4.18511
"	Liters	35.23808	Calories, *gm.* (20°C.)	B.t.u.	0.00396633
"	Ounces (U.S., fluid)	1191.575	"	Cal., *gm*	0.999498
"	Pecks (U.S.)	4	"	Cal., *gm.* (IST.)	0.998845
"	Pints (U.S., dry)	64	"	Cal., *gm.* (mean)	0.998061
"	Quarts (U.S., dry)	32	"	Cal., *gm.* (15°C.)	0.999068
"	Quarts (U.S., liq.)	37.23671	"	Joules	4.18190
utts (Brit.)	Bushels (U.S.)	13.53503	"	Joules (Int.)	4.18121
"	Cu. feet	16.84375	Calories, *kg*	B.t.u.	3.9683207
"	Cu. meters	0.4769619	"	B.t.u. (IST.)	3.96573
"	Gallons (U.S.)	126	"	B.t.u. (mean)	3.96262
			"	B.t.u. (60°F.)	3.96709
			"	Cal., *gm*	1000
able lengths	Fathoms	120	"	Cal., *kg.* (mean)	0.998563
"	Feet	720	"	Cal., *kg.* (15°C.)	0.999570
"	Meters	219.456	"	Cal., *kg.* (20°C.)	1.00050
			"	Cu. cm.-atm	41292.86

* Stricken or struck bushel. A heaped bushel for apples of 2747.715 cu. inches was established by the U.S. Court of Customs Appeals on Feb. 15, 1912. heaped bushel equal to 1¼ stricken bushels is also known.

** This is the calorie as defined by the U.S. National Bureau of Standards and is equal to 4.18400 joules.

CONVERSION FACTORS (Continued)

To convert from	To	Multiply by
Calories, *kg*	Ergs	4.184×10^{10}
"	Foot-poundals	99287.8
"	Foot-pounds	3085.96
"	Gram-cm	4.26649×10^{7}
"	Hp.-hours	0.00155857
"	Joules	4184
"	Kw.-hours	0.001162222
"	Liter-atm	41.2917
"	Watt-hours	1.162222
Calories, *kg.* (mean)	B.t.u.	3.97403
"	B.t.u. (IST.)	3.97144
"	B.t.u. (mean)	3.9683207
"	B.t.u. (60°F.)	3.97280
"	Cal., *gm*	1001.44
"	Cal., *gm.* (IST.)	1000.78
"	Cal., *gm.* (mean)	1000
"	Cal., *gm.* (15°C.)	1000.10
"	Cal., *gm.* (20°C.)	1001.94
"	Ergs	4.19002×10^{10}
"	Foot-poundals	99430.8
"	Foot-pounds	3090.40
"	Gram-cm	4.27263×10^{7}
"	Hp.-hours	0.00156081
"	Joules	4190.02
"	Kg.-meters	427.263
"	Kw.-hours (Int.)	0.00116370
"	Liter-atm	41.3511
"	Watt-hours	1.16390
Cal., *gm.*/°C	B.t.u./°F	0.00220462
"	Joules/°F	2.324444
"	Joules (Int.)/°F	2.32406
Cal., *gm.*/gram	B.t.u./lb	1.8
"	Foot-pounds/lb	1399.77
"	Joules/gram	4.184
"	Watt-hours/gram	0.001162222
Cal., *gm.*/(gram × °C)	B.t.u./(lb. × °C.)	1.8
"	B.t.u./(lb. × °F.)	1
"	Cal., *kg.*/(kg. × °C.)	1
"	Joules/(gram × °C.)	4.184
"	Joules/(lb. × °F.)	1054.35
Cal., *gm.*/hr	B.t.u./hr	0.0039683207
"	Ergs/sec	11622.222
"	Watts	0.00116222
Cal., *gm.* (mean)/hr	B.t.u. (mean)/hr	0.0039683207
"	Ergs/sec	11639.0
"	Watts	0.00116390
Cal., *kg.*/hr	Watts	1.162222
Cal., *gm.*/min	B.t.u./min	0.0039683207
"	Ergs/sec	697333.3
"	Watts	0.069733
Cal., *gm.* (mean)/min	B.t.u. (mean)/min	0.0039683207
"	Ergs/sec	698337
"	Joules/sec	0.0698337
"	Watts	0.0698337
Cal., *kg.*/min	Kg. ice melted/min	0.012548
"	Lb. ice melted/min	0.027665
"	Watts	69.7333
Cal., *gm.*/sec	B.t.u./sec	0.0039683207
"	Ergs/sec	4.184×10^{7}
"	Foot-pounds/sec	3.08596
"	Horsepower	0.00561084
"	Watts	4.184
Cal., *gm.* (mean)/sec	Ergs/sec	4.19002×10^{7}
"	Watts	4.19002
Cal., *gm.*/(sec. × sq. cm.)	B.t.u./(hr. × sq. ft.)	13272.1
"	Cal., *gm.*/(hr. × sq. cm.)	3600
"	Watts/sq. cm	4.184
Cal., *gm.*/(sec. × sq. cm. × °C.)	B.t.u./(hr. × sq. ft. × °F.)	7373.38
Cal., *gm.*/sq. cm	B.t.u./sq. ft	3.68669
$\dfrac{\text{Cal., } gm\text{.-cm.}}{(\text{hr.} \times \text{sq. cm.} \times °\text{C.})}$	$\dfrac{\text{B.t.u.-ft.}}{(\text{hr.} \times \text{sq. ft.} \times °\text{F.})}$	0.0671969
"	$\dfrac{\text{B.t.u.-inch}}{(\text{hr.} \times \text{sq. ft.} \times °\text{F.})}$	0.806363
Cal., *gm.*-cm./sq. cm	B.t.u.-inch/sq. ft	1.4514530
Cal., *gm.*-sec.	Planck's constant	6.31531×10^{33}
Cal., *gm.*-sec./Avog. No. (chem.)*	Planck's constant	1.04849×10^{10}
Cal., *gm.*-sec./Avog. No. (phys.)*	Planck's constant	1.04821×10^{10}
Candles (English)	Candles (Int.)	1.04
"	Hefner units	1.16
Candles (German)	Candles (English)	1.01
"	Candles (Int.)	1.05
"	Hefner units	1.17
Candles (Int.)	Candles (English)	0.96
"	Candles (German)	0.95
"	Candles (pentane)	1.00
"	Hefner units	1.11
"	Lumens (Int.)/steradian	1
Candles (pentane)	Candles (Int.)	1.00
Candles/sq. cm	Candles/sq. inch	6.4516
"	Candles/sq. meter	10000
"	Foot-lamberts	2918.6351
"	Lamberts	3.1415927
Candles/sq. ft	Candles/sq. inch	0.0069444
"	Candles/sq. meter	10.763910
"	Foot-lamberts	3.1415927
"	Lamberts	0.0033815822
Candles/sq. inch	Candles/sq. cm	0.15500031
"	Candles/sq. foot	144
"	Foot-lamberts	452.38934
"	Lamberts	0.48694784
Candle power (spher.)	Lumens	12.566370
Carats (parts of gold per 24 of mixture)	Milligrams/gram	41.6666
Carats (1877)	Grains	3.168
"	Milligrams	205.3
Carats (metric)	Grains	3.08647
"	Grams	0.2
"	Milligrams	200
Carcel units	Candles (Int.)	9.61
Centals	Kilograms	45.359237
"	Pounds	100
Centares	Ares	0.01
"	Sq. feet	10.763910
"	Sq. inches	1550.0031
"	Sq. meters	1
"	Sq. yards	1.1959900
Centigrams	Grains	0.15432358
"	Grams	0.01
Centiliters	Cu. cm	10.00028
"	Cu. inches	0.6102545
"	Liters	0.01
"	Ounces (U.S., fluid)	0.3381497
Centimeters	Ångström units	1×10^{8}
"	Feet	0.032808399
"	Feet (U.S. Survey)	0.032808333
"	Hands	0.098425197
"	Inches	0.39370079
"	Links (Gunter's)	0.049709695
"	Links (Ramden's)	0.032808399
"	Meters	0.01
"	Microns	10000
"	Miles (naut., Int.)	5.3995680×10^{-6}
"	Miles (statute)	6.2137119×10^{-6}
"	Millimeters	10
"	Millimicrons	1×10^{7}
"	Mils	393.70079
"	Picas (printer's)	2.3710630
"	Points (printer's)	28.452756

* For factors for C = 12 scale or those which can be derived from same table on Values for General Physical Constants.

CONVERSION FACTORS (Continued)

To convert from	To	Multiply by
timeters	Rods	0.0019883878
"	Wave length of orange-red line of krypton 86	16507.6373
"	Wave length of red line of cadmium	15531.6413
"	Yards	0.010936133
of Hg (0°C.)	Atmospheres	0.013157895
"	Bars	0.0133322
"	Dynes/sq. cm	13332.2
"	Ft. of H_2O (4°C.)	0.446050
"	Ft. of H_2O (60°F.)	0.446474
"	In. of Hg (0°C.)	0.39370079
"	Kg./sq. meter	135.951
"	Pounds/sq. ft	27.8450
"	Pounds/sq. inch	0.193368
"	Torrs	10
. of H_2O (4°C.)	Atmospheres	0.000967814
"	Dynes/sq. cm	980.638
"	Pounds/sq. inch	0.0142229
ntimeters/sec	Feet/min	1.9685039
"	Feet/sec	0.032808399
"	Kilometers/hr	0.036
"	Kilometers/min	0.0006
"	Knots (Int.)	0.019438445
"	Meters/min	0.6
"	Miles/hr	0.022369363
"	Miles/min	0.00037282272
n./(sec. × sec.)	Kilometers/(hr. × sec.)	0.036
"	Miles/(hr. × sec.)	0.022369363
ntimeters/year	Inches/year	0.39370079
ntipoises	Grams/(cm. × sec.)	0.01
"	Poises	0.01
"	Pound/(ft. × hr.)	2.4190883
"	Pounds/(ft. × sec.)	0.00067196898
ntistokes	Stokes	0.01
hains (Gunter's)	Centimeters	2011.68
"	Chains (Ramden's)	0.66
"	Feet	66
"	Feet (U.S. Survey)	65.999868
"	Furlongs	0.1
"	Inches	792
"	Links (Gunter's)	100
"	Links (Ramden's)	66
"	Meters	20.1168
"	Miles (statute)	0.0125
"	Rods	4
"	Yards	22
Chains (Ramden's)	Centimeters	3048
"	Chains (Gunter's)	1.515151
"	Feet	100
"	Feet (U.S. Survey)	99.999800
Cheval-vapeur	Horsepower (metric)	1
Cheval-vapeur-heures	Joules	2647795
Circles	Degrees	360
"	Grades	400
"	Minutes	21600
"	Radians	6.2831853
"	Signs	12
Circular inches	Circular mm	645.16
"	Sq. cm	5.0670748
"	Sq. inches	0.78539816
Circular mm	Sq. cm	0.0078539816
"	Sq. inches	0.0012173696
"	Sq. mm	0.78539816
Circular mils	Circular inches	1×10^{-6}
"	Sq. cm	5.0670748×10^{-6}
"	Sq. inches	7.8539816×10^{-7}
"	Sq. mm	0.00050670748
"	Sq. mils	0.78539816
Circumferences	Degrees	360
"	Grades	400

To convert from	To	Multiply by
Circumferences	Minutes	21600
"	Radians	6.2831853
"	Seconds	1296000
Cords	Cord-feet	8
"	Cu. feet	128
"	Cu. meters	3.6245734
Cord-feet	Cords	0.125
"	Cu. feet	16
Coulombs	Abcoulombs	0.1
"	Ampere-hours	0.0002777
"	Ampere-seconds	1
"	Coulombs (Int.)	1.000165
"	Electronic charge	6.24196×10^{18}
"	E.M. cgs. units of electric charge	0.1
"	E.S. cgs. units of electric charge	2.997930×10^{9}
"	Faradays (chem.)	1.036377×10^{-5}
"	Faradays (phys.)	1.036086×10^{-5}
"	Mks. units of electric charge	1
"	Statcoulombs	2.997930×10^{9}
Coulombs/cu. meter	E.M. cgs. units of volume charge density	1×10^{-7}
"	E.S. cgs. units	2997.930
Coulombs/sq. cm	Abcoulombs/sq. cm	0.1
"	Cgs. units of polarization, *and* surface charge density	1
Cubic centimeters	Board feet	0.00042377600
"	Bushels (Brit.)	2.749617×10^{-5}
"	Bushels (U.S.)	2.837759×10^{-5}
"	Cu. feet	3.5314667×10^{-5}
"	Cu. inches	0.061023744
"	Cu. meters	1×10^{-6}
"	Cu. yards	1.3079506×10^{-6}
"	Drachms (Brit., fluid)	0.28156080
"	Drams (U.S., fluid)	0.27051218
"	Gallons (Brit.)	0.0002199694
"	Gallons (U.S., dry)	0.00022702075
"	Gallons (U.S., liq.)	0.00026417205
"	Gills (Brit.)	0.007039020
"	Gills (U.S.)	0.0084535058
"	Liters	0.000999972
"	Ounces (Brit., fluid)	0.03519510
"	Ounces (U.S., fluid)	0.033814023
"	Pints (U.S., dry)	0.0018161660
"	Pints (U.S., liq.)	0.0021133764
"	Quarts (Brit.)	0.0008798775
"	Quarts (U.S., dry)	0.00090808298
"	Quarts (U.S., liq.)	0.0010566882
Cu. cm./gram	Cu. ft./lb	0.016018463
Cu. cm./sec	Cu. ft./min	0.0021188800
"	Gal. (U.S.)/min	0.015850323
"	Gal. (U.S.)/sec	0.00026417205
Cu. cm.-atm	B.t.u.	9.61019×10^{-5}
"	B.t.u. (mean)	9.59637×10^{-5}
"	Cal., *gm*	0.0242173
"	Cal., *gm* (mean)	0.0241824
"	Cu. ft.-atm	3.5314667×10^{-5}
"	Joules	0.101325
"	Watt-hours	2.81458×10^{-5}
Cu. cm.-atm./gram	B.t.u./lb	0.0435911
"	Cal., *gm*/gram	0.0242173
"	Cu. ft.-(lb./sq. in.)/lb	0.235406
"	Ft.-lb./lb	33.8985
"	Joules/gram	0.101325
"	Kg.-meters/gram	0.0103323
"	Kw.-hr./gram	2.81458×10^{-5}
Cubic decimeters	Cu. cm	1000
"	Cu. feet	0.035316667
"	Cu. inches	61.023744
"	Cu. meters	0.001

CONVERSION FACTORS (Continued)

To convert from	To	Multiply by
Cubic decimeters	Cu. yards	0.0013079506
"	Liters	0.999972
Cubic dekameters	Cu. decimeters	1×10^6
"	Cu. feet	35314.667
"	Cu. inches	6.1023744×10^7
"	Cu. meters	1000
"	Liters	999972
Cubic feet	Acre-feet	2.2956841×10^{-5}
"	Board feet	12
"	Bushels (Brit.)	0.7786049
"	Bushels (U.S.)	0.80356395
"	Cords (wood)	0.0078125
"	Cord-feet	0.0625
"	Cu. centimeters	28316.847
"	Cu. meters	0.028316847
"	Gallons (U.S., dry)	6.4285116
"	Gallons (U.S., liq.)	7.4805195
"	Liters	28.31605
"	Ounces (Brit., fluid)	996.6143
"	Ounces (U.S., fluid)	957.50649
"	Pints (U.S., liq.)	59.844156
"	Quarts (U.S., dry)	25.714047
"	Quarts (U.S., liq.)	29.922078
Cu. ft. of H$_2$O (39.2°F.)	Pounds of H$_2$O	62.4262
Cu. ft. of H$_2$O (60°F.)	Pounds of H$_2$O	62.3663
Cu. ft./hr	Acre-feet/hr	2.2956841×10^{-5}
"	Cu. cm./sec.	7.8657907
"	Cu. ft./day	24
"	Gal. (U.S.)/hr	7.4805195
"	Liters/hr	28.31605
Cu. ft./min	Acre-feet/hr	0.0013774105
"	Acre-feet/min	2.2956841×10^{-5}
"	Cu. cm./sec.	471.94744
"	Cu. ft./hr	60
"	Gal. (U.S.)/min	7.4805195
"	Liters/sec.	0.4719342
Cu. ft./lb	Cu. cm./gram	62.427961
"	Millimeters/gram	62.42621
Cu. ft./sec.	Acre-inches/hr	0.99173553
"	Cu. cm./sec.	28316.847
"	Cu. yards/min	2.222222
"	Gal. (U.S.)/min	448.83117
"	Liters/min	1698.963
"	Liters/sec.	28.31605
Cu. ft. of H$_2$O (60°F.)/sec.	Lb. of H$_2$O/min	3741.98
Cu. ft.-atm	B.t.u.	2.72130
"	Cal., gm	685.756
"	Cu. cm.-atm	28316.847
"	Cu. ft.-(lb/sq. in.)	14.6960
"	Foot-pounds	2116.22
"	Hp.-hours	0.00106880
"	Joules	2869.20
"	Kg.-meters	292.577
"	Kw.-hours	0.000797001
Cubic inches	Barrels (Brit.)	0.0001001292
"	Barrels (U.S., dry)	0.00014172336
"	Board feet	0.0069444
"	Bushels (Brit.)	0.0004505815
"	Bushels (U.S.)	0.00046502544
"	Cu. cm	16.387064
"	Cu. feet	0.00057870370
"	Cu. meters	1.6387064×10^{-5}
"	Cu. yards	2.1433470×10^{-5}
"	Drams (U.S., fluid)	4.4329004
"	Gallons (Brit.)	0.003604652
"	Gallons (U.S., dry)	0.0037202035
"	Gallons (U.S., liq.)	0.0043290043
"	Liters	0.01638661
"	Milliliters	16.38661
"	Ounces (Brit., fluid)	0.5767444
Cubic inches	Ounces (U.S., fluid)	0.55411255
"	Pecks (U.S.)	0.0018601017
"	Pints (U.S., dry)	0.029761628
"	Pints (U.S., liq.)	0.034632035
"	Quarts (U.S., dry)	0.014880814
"	Quarts (U.S., liq.)	0.017316017
Cu. in. of H$_2$O (4°C.)	Pounds of H$_2$O	0.0361263
Cu. in. of H$_2$O (60°F.)	Pounds of H$_2$O	0.0360916
Cubic meters	Acre-feet	0.00081071319
"	Barrels (Brit.)	6.110261
"	Barrels (U.S., dry)	8.648490
"	Barrels (U.S., liq.)	8.3864145
"	Bushels (Brit.)	27.49617
"	Bushels (U.S.)	28.377593
"	Cu. cm	1×10^6
"	Cu. feet	35.314667
"	Cu. inches	61023.74
"	Cu. yards	1.3079506
"	Gallons (Brit.)	219.9694
"	Gallons (U.S., liq.)	264.17205
"	Hogshead	4.1932072
"	Liters	999.972
"	Pints (U.S., liq.)	2113.3764
"	Quarts (U.S., liq.)	1056.6882
"	Steres	1
Cu. meters/min	Gal. (Brit.)/min	219.9694
"	Gal. (U.S.)/min	264.1721
"	Liters/min	999.972
Cu. millimeters	Cu. cm	0.001
"	Cu. inches	6.1023744×10^{-5}
"	Cu. meters	1×10^{-9}
"	Minims (Brit.)	0.01689365
"	Minims (U.S.)	0.016230731
Cu. yards	Bushels (Brit.)	21.02233
"	Bushels (U.S.)	21.696227
"	Cu. cm	764554.86
"	Cu. feet	27
"	Cu. inches	46.656
"	Cu. meters	0.76455486
"	Gallons (Brit.)	168.1787
"	Gallons (U.S., dry)	173.56981
"	Gallons (U.S., liq.)	201.97403
"	Liters	764.5335
"	Quarts (Brit.)	672.7146
"	Quarts (U.S., dry)	694.27926
"	Quarts (U.S., liq.)	807.89610
Cu. yd./min	Cu. ft./sec.	0.45
"	Gal. (U.S.)/sec.	3.3662338
"	Liters/sec.	12.74222
Cubits	Centimeters	45.72
"	Feet	1.5
"	Inches	18
Daltons (chem.)	Grams	1.66024×10^{-24}
Daltons (phys.)	Grams	1.65979×10^{-24}
Days (mean solar)	Days (sidereal)	1.00273791
"	Hours (mean solar)	24
"	Hours (sidereal)	24.065710
"	Years (calendar)	0.0027397260
"	Years (sidereal)	0.0027378031
"	Years (tropical)	0.0027379093
Days (sidereal)	Days (mean solar)	0.99726957
"	Hours (mean solar)	23.934470
"	Hours (sidereal)	24
"	Minutes (mean solar)	1436.0682
"	Minute (sidereal)	1440
"	Second (sidereal)	86400
"	Years (calendar)	0.0027322454
"	Years (sidereal)	0.0027303277
"	Years (tropical)	0.0027304336
Decibels	Bels	0.1
Decimeters	Centimeters	10

CONVERSION FACTORS (Continued)

To convert from	To	Multiply by
imeters	Feet	0.32808399
"	Feet (U.S. Survey)	0.328083333
"	Inches	3.9370079
"	Meters	0.1
isteres	Cu. meters	0.1
grees	Circles	0.0027777
"	Minutes	60
"	Quadrants	0.0111111
"	Radians	0.017453293
"	Seconds	3600
grees/cm	Radians/cm	0.017453293
grees/foot	Radians/cm	0.00057261458
grees/inch	Radian/cm	0.0068713750
grees/min	Degrees/sec	0.0166666
"	Radians/sec	0.00029088821
"	Revolutions/sec	4.629629×10^{-5}
grees/sec	Radians/sec	0.017453293
"	Revolutions/min	0.166666
"	Revolutions/sec	0.0027777
kaliters	Pecks (U.S.)	1.135136
"	Pints (U.S., dry)	18.16217
kameters	Centimeters	1000
"	Feet	32.808399
"	Feet (U.S. Survey)	32.808333
"	Inches	393.70079
"	Kilometers	0.01
"	Meters	10
"	Yards	10.93613
emals	Gram-equiv./cu. decimeter	1
rachms (Brit., fluid)	Cu. cm	3.551631
"	Cu. inches	0.2167338
"	Drams (U.S., fluid)	0.9607594
"	Milliliters	3.551531
rams (apoth. or troy)	Drams (avdp.)	2.1942857
"	Grains	60
"	Grams	3887.9346
"	Ounces (apoth. or troy)	0.125
"	Ounces (avdp.)	0.13714286
"	Scruples (apoth.)	3
rams (avdp.)	Drams (apoth. or troy)	0.455729166
"	Grains	27.34375
"	Grams	1.7718452
"	Ounces (apoth. or troy)	0.056966146
"	Ounces (avdp.)	0.0625
"	Pennyweights	1.1393229
"	Pounds (apoth. or troy)	0.0047471788
"	Pounds (avdp.)	0.00390625
"	Scruples (apoth.)	1.3671875
rams (U.S., fluid)	Cu. cm	3.6967162
"	Cu. inches	0.22558594
"	Drachms (Brit., fluid)	1.040843
"	Gills (U.S.)	0.03125
"	Milliliters	3.696588
"	Minims (U.S.)	60
"	Ounces (U.S., fluid)	0.125
"	Pints (U.S., liq.)	0.0078125
ynes	Grains	0.01573663
"	Grams	0.001019716
"	Newtons	0.00001
"	Poundals	7.2330138×10^{-5}
"	Pounds	2.248089×10^{-6}
ynes/cm	Ergs/sq. cm	1
"	Ergs/sq. mm	0.01
"	Grams/cm	0.001019716
"	Poundals/inch	0.00018371855
ynes/cu. cm	Grams/cu. cm	0.001019716
"	Poundals/cu. inch	0.0011852786
ynes/sq. cm	Atmospheres	9.86923×10^{-7}
"	Bars	1×10^{-6}
"	Baryes	1
"	Cm. of Hg (0°C.)	7.50062×10^{-5}

To convert from	To	Multiply by
Dynes/sq. cm	Cm. of H_2O (4°C.)	0.001019745
"	Grams/sq. cm	0.001019716
"	In. of Hg (32°F.)	2.95300×10^{-5}
"	In. of H_2O (4°C.)	0.000401474
"	Kg./sq. meter	0.01019716
"	Poundals/sq. in	0.00046664510
"	Pounds/sq. in.	1.450377×10^{-5}
Dyne-centimeters	Ergs	1
"	Foot-poundals	2.3730360×10^{-6}
"	Foot-pounds	7.37562×10^{-8}
"	Gram-cm	0.001019716
"	Inch-pounds	8.85075×10^{-7}
"	Kg.-meters	1.019716×10^{-8}
"	Newton-meters	1×10^{-7}
Electron volts	Ergs	1.60209×10^{-12}
"	Grams	1.78253×10^{-33}
Electronic charges	Abcoulombs	1.60209×10^{-20}
"	Coulombs	1.60209×10^{-19}
"	Statcoulombs	4.80296×10^{-10}
Electronic charges/kg.	Statcoulombs/dyne	4.89766×10^{-16}
E.S. cgs. units of induction flux	E.M. cgs. units	2.997930×10^{10}
E.S. cgs. units of magnetic charge	E.M. cgs. units	2.997930×10^{10}
E.S. cgs. units of magnetic field intensity	E.M. cgs. units	3.335635×10^{-11}
Ells	Centimeters	114.3
"	Inches	45
Ergs	B.t.u.	9.48451×10^{-11}
"	Cal., *gm*	2.39006×10^{-8}
"	Cal., *kg*	2.39006×10^{-11}
"	Cal., *kg.* (20°C.)	2.39126×10^{-11}
"	Cu. cm.-atm	9.86923×10^{-7}
"	Cu. ft.-atm	3.48529×10^{-11}
"	Cu. ft.-(lb./sq. in.)	5.12196×10^{-10}
"	Dyne-cm	1
"	Electron volts	6.24196×10^{11}
"	Foot-poundals	2.3730360×10^{-6}
"	Foot-pounds	7.37562×10^{-8}
"	Gram-cm	0.001019716
"	Joules	1×10^{-7}
"	Joules (Int.)	9.99835×10^{-8}
"	Kw.-hours	2.777777×10^{-14}
"	Kg.-meters	1.019716×10^{-8}
"	Liter-atm	9.86895×10^{-10}
"	Watt-sec	1×10^{-7}
Ergs/(gram-mol. × °C.)	Foot-pounds/(lb.-mol. × °F.)	1.85863×10^{-5}
Ergs/sec	B.t.u./min	5.69071×10^{-9}
"	Cal., *gm.*/min	1.43403×10^{-6}
"	Dyne-cm./sec	1
"	Foot-pounds/min	4.42537×10^{-6}
"	Gram-cm./sec	0.001019716
"	Horsepower	1.34102×10^{-10}
"	Joules/sec	1×10^{-7}
"	Kilowatts	1×10^{-10}
"	Watts	1×10^{-7}
Ergs/sq. cm	Dynes/cm	1
"	Ergs/sq. mm	0.01
Ergs/sq. mm	Dynes/cm	100
"	Ergs/sq. cm	100
Erg-sec	Planck's constant	1.50932×10^{26}
Farads	Abfarads	1×10^{-9}
"	E.M. cgs. units	1×10^{-9}
"	E.S. cgs. units	8.987584×10^{11}
"	Farads (Int.)	1.000495
"	Microfarads	1×10^{6}
"	Statfarads	8.98758×10^{11}
Farads (Int.)	Farads	0.999505
Fathoms	Centimeters	182.88

CONVERSION FACTORS (Continued)

To convert from	To	Multiply by	To convert from	To	Multiply by
Fathoms..........	Feet..............	6	Feet/(sec. × sec.)....	Meters/(sec. × sec.)......	0.3048
"	Inches............	72	"	Miles/(hr. × sec.)........	0.68181818
"	Meters............	1.8288	Firkins (Brit.)......	Bushels (Brit.)........	1.125
"	Miles (naut., Int.)...	0.00098747300	"	Cu. cm.............	40914.79
"	Miles (statute).......	0.001136363	"	Cu. feet...........	1.444892
"	Yards.............	2	"	Firkins (U.S.)......	1.200949
Feet.............	Centimeters........	30.48	"	Gallons (Brit.)..........	9
"	Chains (Gunter's)........	0.01515151	"	Liters............	40.91364
"	Fathoms...........	0.166666	"	Pints (Brit.)......	72
"	Feet (U.S. Survey)......	0.99999800	Firkins (U.S.)......	Barrels (U.S., dry)....	0.29464286
"	Furlongs..........	0.00151515	"	Barrels (U.S., liq.)....	0.28571429
"	Inches............	12	"	Bushels (U.S.)......	0.96678788
"	Meters............	0.3048	"	Cu. feet...........	1.203125
"	Microns...........	304800	"	Firkins (Brit.)......	0.8326747
"	Miles (naut., Int.)...	0.00016457883	"	Liters............	34.06775
"	Miles (statute).......	0.000189393	"	Pints (U.S., liq.)....	72
"	Rods.............	0.060606	Foot-candles.......	Lumens/sq. ft.......	1
"	Ropes (Brit.)......	0.05	"	Lumens/sq. meter.......	10.763910
"	Yards.............	0.333333	"	Lux.............	10.763910
Feet (U.S. Survey)...	Centimeters........	30.480061	"	Milliphots........	1.0763910
"	Chains (Gunter's)........	0.015151545	Foot-lamberts.......	Candles/sq. cm.......	0.00034262591
"	Chains (Ramden's)........	0.010000020	"	Candles/sq. ft.......	0.31830989
"	Feet..............	1.0000020	"	Millilamberts........	1.0763910
"	Inches............	12.000024	"	Lamberts..........	0.0010763910
"	Links (Gunter's)........	1.5151545	"	Lumens/sq. ft.......	1
"	Links (Ramden's)........	1.0000020	Foot-poundals......	B.t.u............	3.99678×10^{-5}
"	Meters............	0.30480061	"	B.t.u. (IST.)......	3.99417×10^{-5}
"	Miles (statute).......	0.00018939432	"	B.t.u. (mean)......	3.99104×10^{-5}
"	Rods.............	0.060606182	"	Cal., *gm*........	0.0100717
"	Yards.............	0.33333400	"	Cal., *gm*. (IST.)....	0.0100651
Feet of air (1 atm., 60°F.)..........	Atmospheres........	3.6083×10^{-5}	"	Cal., *gm*. (mean)....	0.0100573
"	Ft. of Hg (32°F.)......	0.00089970	"	Cu. cm.-atm.......	0.415890
"	Ft. of H$_2$O (60°F.)......	0.0012244	"	Cu. ft.-atm.......	1.46870×10^{-5}
"	In. of Hg (32°F.)......	0.0010796	"	Dyne-cm..........	4.2140110×10^{5}
"	Pounds/sq. inch.......	0.00053027	"	Ergs............	4.2140110×10^{5}
Feet of Hg (32°F.)....	Cm. of Hg (0°C.)......	30.48	"	Foot-pounds........	0.0310810
"	Ft. of H$_2$O (60°F.)......	13.6085	"	Hp.-hours.........	1.56974×10^{-8}
"	In. of H$_2$O (60°F.)......	163.302	"	Joules...........	0.042140110
"	Ounces/sq. inch.......	94.3016	"	Joules (Int.)......	0.0421332
"	Pounds/sq. inch.......	5.89385	"	Kg.-meters........	0.00429710
Feet of H$_2$O (4°C.)...	Atmospheres........	0.0294990	"	Kw.-hours.........	1.17056×10^{-8}
"	Cm. of Hg (0°C.)......	2.24192	"	Liter-atm.........	0.000415879
"	Dynes/sq. cm.......	29889.8	Foot-pounds.......	B.t.u............	0.00128593
"	Grams/sq. cm.......	30.4791	"	B.t.u. (IST.)......	0.00128509
"	In. of Hg (32°F.)......	0.882646	"	B.t.u. (mean)......	0.00128408
"	Kg./sq. meter.......	304.791	"	Cal., *gm*........	0.324048
"	Pounds/sq. inch.......	0.433515	"	Cal., *gm*. (IST.)....	0.323836
Feet/hour.......	Cm./hr............	30.48	"	Cal., *gm*. (mean)....	0.323582
"	Cm./min............	0.508	"	Cal., *gm*. (20°C.)....	0.324211
"	Cm./sec............	0.0084666	"	Cal., *kg*........	0.000324048
"	Feet/min..........	0.0166666	"	Cal., *kg*. (IST.)....	0.000323836
"	Inches/hr..........	12	"	Cal., *kg*. (mean)....	0.000323582
"	Kilometers/hr........	0.0003048	"	Cu. ft.-atm.......	0.000472541
"	Kilometers/min........	5.08×10^{-6}	"	Dyne-cm..........	1.35582×10^{7}
"	Knots (Int.)......	0.0001645788	"	Ergs............	1.35582×10^{7}
"	Miles/hr..........	0.000189393	"	Foot-poundals......	32.1740
"	Miles/min.........	3.156565×10^{-6}	"	Gram-cm..........	13825.5
"	Miles/sec.........	5.2609428×10^{-8}	"	Hp.-hours.........	5.05050×10^{-7}
Feet/minute.......	Cm./sec............	0.508	"	Joules...........	1.35582
"	Feet/sec..........	0.0166666	"	Kg.-meters........	0.138255
"	Kilometers/hr........	0.018288	"	Kw.-hours.........	3.76616×10^{-7}
"	Meters/min.........	0.3048	"	Kw.-hours (Int.)........	3.76554×10^{-7}
"	Meters/sec.........	0.00508	"	Liter-atm.........	0.0133805
"	Miles/hr..........	0.01136363	"	Newton-meters........	1.3558180
Feet/second......	Cm./sec............	30.48	"	Lb. H$_2$O evap. from and at 212°F............	1.3245×10^{-6}
"	Kilometers/hr........	1.09728	"	Watt-hours.........	0.000376616
"	Kilometers/min........	0.018288	Foot-pounds/hr......	B.t.u./min.........	2.14321×10^{-5}
"	Meters/min.........	18.288	"	B.t.u. (mean)/min....	2.14013×10^{-5}
"	Miles/hr..........	0.68181818	"	Cal., gm./min......	0.00540080
"	Miles/min.........	0.01136363	"	Cal., *gm*. (mean)/min....	0.00539304
Feet/(sec. × sec.)....	Kilometers/(hr. × sec.)....	1.09728	"	Ergs/min..........	2.25970×10^{5}

CONVERSION FACTORS (Continued)

To convert from	To	Multiply by
ot-pounds/hr	Foot-pounds/min	0.0166666
"	Horsepower	5.050505 × 10⁻⁷
"	Horsepower (metric)	5.12055 × 10⁻⁷
"	Kilowatts	3.76616 × 10⁻⁷
"	Watts	0.000376616
"	Watts (Int.)	0.000376554
ot-pounds/min	B.t.u./sec	2.14321 × 10⁻⁵
"	B.t.u. (mean)/sec	2.14013 × 10⁻⁵
"	Cal., gm./sec	0.00540080
"	Cal., gm. (mean)/sec	0.00539304
"	Ergs/sec	2.25970 × 10⁵
"	Foot-pounds/sec	0.0166666
"	Horsepower	3.030303 × 10⁻⁵
"	Horsepower (metric)	3.07233 × 10⁻⁵
"	Joules/sec	0.0225970
"	Joules (Int.)/sec	0.0225932
"	Kilowatts	2.25970 × 10⁻⁵
"	Watts	0.0225970
oot-pounds/lb	B.t.u./lb	0.00128593
"	B.t.u. (IST.)/lb	0.00128509
"	B.t.u. (mean)/lb	0.00128408
"	Cal., gm./gm	0.000714404
"	Cal., gm. (IST.)/gram	0.000713937
"	Cal., gm. (mean)/gram	0.000713377
"	Hp.-hr./lb	5.05050 × 10⁻⁷
"	Joules/gram	0.00298907
"	Kg.-meters/gram	0.000304800
"	Kw.-hr./gram	8.30296 × 10⁻¹⁰
oot-pounds/sec	B.t.u./min	0.0771556
"	B.t.u. (mean)/min	0.0770447
"	B.t.u./sec	0.00128593
"	B.t.u. (mean)/sec	0.00128408
"	Cal., gm./sec	0.324048
"	Cal., gm. (mean)/sec	0.323582
"	Ergs/sec	1.35582 × 10⁷
"	Gram-cm./sec	13825.5
"	Horsepower	0.00181818
"	Joules/sec	1.35582
"	Kilowatts	0.00135582
"	Watts	1.35582
"	Watts (Int.)	1.35559
urlongs	Centimeters	20116.8
"	Chains (Gunter's)	10
"	Chains (Ramden's)	6.6
"	Feet	660
"	Inches	7920
"	Meters	201.168
"	Miles (naut., Int.)	0.10862203
"	Miles (statute)	0.125
"	Rods	40
"	Yards	220
Gallons (Brit.)	Barrels (Brit.)	0.027777
"	Bushels (Brit.)	0.125
"	Cu. centimeters	4546.087
"	Cu. feet	0.1605436
"	Cu. inches	277.4193
"	Drachms (Brit. fluid)	1280
"	Firkins (Brit.)	0.111111
"	Gallons (U.S., liq.)	1.200949
"	Gills (Brit.)	32
"	Liters	4.545960
"	Minims (Brit.)	76800
"	Ounces (Brit., fluid)	160
"	Ounces (U.S., fluid)	153.7215
"	Pecks (Brit.)	0.5
"	Lb. of H₂O (62°F.)	10
Gallons (U.S., dry)	Barrels (U.S., dry)	0.038095592
"	Barrels (U.S., liq.)	0.036941181
"	Bushels (U.S.)	0.125
"	Cu. centimeters	4404.8828
"	Cu. feet	0.15555700

To convert from	To	Multiply by
Gallons (U.S., dry)	Cu. inches	268.8025
"	Gallons (U.S., liq.)	1.16364719
"	Liters	4.404760
Gallons (U.S., liq.)	Acre-feet	3.0688833 × 10⁻⁶
"	Barrels (U.S., liq.)	0.031746032
"	Barrels (petroleum, U.S.)	0.023809524
"	Bushels (U.S.)	0.10742088
"	Cu. centimeters	3785.4118
"	Cu. feet	0.133680555
"	Cu. inches	231
"	Cu. meters	0.0037854118
"	Cu. yards	0.0049511317
"	Gallons (Brit.)	0.8326747
"	Gallons (U.S., dry)	0.85936701
"	Gallons (wine)	1
"	Gills (U.S.)	32
"	Liters	3.785306
"	Minims (U.S.)	61440
"	Ounces (U.S., fluid)	128
"	Pints (U.S., liq.)	8
"	Quarts (U.S., liq.)	4
Gallons (U.S.) of H₂O (4°C.)	Lb. of H₂O	8.34517
Gallons (U.S.) of H₂O (60°F.)	Lb. of H₂O	8.33717
Gallons (U.S.)/day	Cu. ft./hr	0.0055700231
Gallons (Brit.)/hr	Cu. meters/min	7.576812 × 10⁻⁵
Gallons (U.S.)/hr	Acre-feet/hr	3.0688833 × 10⁻⁶
"	Cu. ft./hr	0.1336805
"	Cu. meters/min	6.3090197 × 10⁻⁵
"	Cu. yd./min	8.2518861 × 10⁻⁵
"	Liters/hr	3.785306
Gal. (Brit.)/sec	Cu. cm./sec	4546.087
Gal. (U.S.)/sec	Cu. cm./sec	3785.4118
"	Cu. ft./min	8.020833
"	Cu. yd./min	0.29706790
"	Liters/min	227.1183
Gammas	Grams	1 × 10⁻⁶
"	Micrograms	1
Gausses	E.M. cgs. units of magnetic flux density	1
"	E.S. cgs. units	3.335635 × 10⁻¹¹
"	Gausses (Int.)	0.999670
"	Maxwells/sq. cm.	1
"	Lines/sq. cm	1
"	Lines/sq. inch	6.4516
Gausses (Int.)	Gausses	1.000330
Gausses/oersted	E.M. cgs. units of permeability	1
"	E.S. cgs. units	1.112646 × 10⁻²¹
Geepounds	Slugs	1
"	Kilograms	14.5939
Gigameters	Meters	1 × 10⁹
Gilberts	Abampere-turns	0.079577472
"	Ampere-turns	0.79577472
"	E.M. cgs. units of mmf., or magnetic potential	1
"	E.S. cgs. units	2.997930 × 10¹⁰
"	Gilberts (Int.)	1.000165
Gilberts (Int.)	Gilberts	0.999835
Gilberts/cm	Ampere-turns/cm	0.79577472
"	Ampere-turns/in	2.0212678
"	Oersteds	1
Gilberts/maxwell	Ampere-turns/weber	7.957747 × 10⁷
"	E.M. cgs. units of reluctance	1
"	E.S. cgs. units	8.987584 × 10²⁰
Gills (Brit.)	Cu. cm	142.0652
"	Gallons (Brit.)	0.03125
"	Gills (U.S.)	1.200949
"	Liters	0.1420613
"	Ounces (Brit., fluid)	5

CONVERSION FACTORS (Continued)

To convert from	To	Multiply by
Gills (Brit.)	Ounces (U.S., fluid)	4.803764
"	Pints (Brit.)	0.25
Gills (U.S.)	Cu. cm	118.29412
"	Cu. inches	7.21875
"	Drams (U.S., fluid)	32
"	Gallons (U.S., liq.)	0.03125
"	Gills (Brit.)	0.8326747
"	Liters	0.1182908
"	Minims (U.S.)	1920
"	Ounces (U.S., fluid)	4
"	Pints (U.S., liq.)	0.25
"	Quarts (U.S., liq.)	0.125
Grades	Circles	0.0025
"	Circumferences	0.0025
"	Degrees	0.9
"	Minutes	54
"	Radians	0.015707963
"	Revolutions	0.0025
"	Seconds	3240
Grains	Carats (metric)	0.32399455
"	Drams (apoth. or troy)	0.016666
"	Drams (avdp.)	0.036571429
"	Dynes	63.5460
"	Grams	0.06479891
"	Milligrams	64.79891
"	Ounces (apoth. or troy)	0.0020833
"	Ounces (avdp.)	0.0022857143
"	Pennyweights	0.041666
"	Pounds (apoth. or troy)	0.000173611
"	Pounds (avdp.)	0.00014285714
"	Scruples (apoth.)	0.05
"	Tons (metric)	6.479891×10^{-8}
Grains/cu. ft.	Grams/cu. meter	2.2883519
Grains/gal. (U.S.)	Parts/million*	17.11854
"	Pounds/million gal	142.8571
Grams	Carats (metric)	5
"	Decigrams	10
"	Dekagrams	0.1
"	Drams (apoth. or troy)	0.25720597
"	Drams (avdp.)	0.56438339
"	Dynes	980.665
"	Grains	15.432358
"	Kilograms	0.001
"	Micrograms	1×10^{6}
"	Myriagrams	0.0001
"	Ounces (apoth. or troy)	0.032150737
"	Ounces (avdp.)	0.035273962
"	Pennyweights	0.64301493
"	Poundals	0.0709316
"	Pounds (apoth. or troy)	0.0026792289
"	Pounds (avdp.)	0.0022046226
"	Scruples (apoth.)	0.77161792
"	Tons (metric)	1×10^{-6}
Grams/cm	Dynes/cm	980.665
"	Grams/inch	2.54
"	Kg./km	100
"	Kg./meter	0.1
"	Poundals/inch	0.180166
"	Pounds/ft	0.067196898
"	Pounds/inch	0.0055997415
"	Tons (metric)/km	0.1
Grams/(cm. × sec.)	Poises	1
"	Lb./(ft. × sec.)	0.06719690
Grams/cu. cm	Dynes/cu. cm	980.665
"	Grains/milliliter	15.43279
"	Grams/milliliter	1.000028
"	Poundals/cu. inch	1.16236
"	Pounds/circ. mil-ft	3.4049170×10^{-7}
"	Pounds/cu. ft	62.427961
"	Pounds/cu. inch	0.036127292
"	Pounds/gal. (Brit.)	10.02241
Grams/cu. cm	Pounds/gal. (U.S., dry)	9.7111064
"	Pounds/gal. (U.S., liq.)	8.3454044
Grams/cu. meter	Grains/cu. ft.	0.43699572
Grams/liter	Parts/million*	1000
"	Lb./cu. ft.	0.06242621
"	Lb./gal. (U.S.)	8.345171
Grams/milliliter	Grams/cu. cm	0.999972
"	Pounds/cu. ft.	62.42621
"	Pounds/gallon (U.S.)	8.345171
Grams/sq. cm	Atmospheres	0.000967841
"	Bars	0.000980665
"	Cm. of Hg. (0°C.)	0.0735559
"	Dynes/sq. cm.	980.665
"	In. of Hg (32°F.)	0.0289590
"	Kg./sq. meter	10
"	Mm. of Hg (0°C.)	0.735559
"	Poundals/sq. inch	0.457623
"	Pounds/sq. inch	0.014223343
Grams/ton (long)	Milligrams/kg.	0.98420653
Grams/ton (short)	Milligrams/kg.	1.1023113
Grams-cm	B.t.u.	9.30113×10^{-8}
"	B.t.u. (IST.)	9.29505×10^{-8}
"	B.t.u. (mean)	9.28776×10^{-8}
"	Cal., *gm*	2.34385×10^{-5}
"	Cal., *gm.* (IST.)	2.34231×10^{-5}
"	Cal., *gm.* (mean)	2.34048×10^{-5}
"	Cal., *gm.* (15°C.)	2.34284×10^{-5}
"	Cal., *gm,* (20°C.)	2.34502×10^{-5}
"	Cal., *kg*	2.34385×10^{-8}
"	Cal., *kg.* (IST.)	2.34231×10^{-8}
"	Cal., *kg.* (mean)	2.34048×10^{-8}
"	Dyne-cm	980.665
"	Ergs	980.665
"	Foot-poundals	0.00232715
"	Foot-pounds	7.2330138×10
"	Hp.-hours	3.65303×10^{-11}
"	Joules	9.80665×10^{-5}
"	Kw.-hours	2.72407×10^{-11}
"	Kw.-hours (Int.)	2.72362×10^{-11}
"	Newton-meters	9.80665×10^{-5}
"	Watt-hours	2.72407×10^{-8}
Gram-cm./sec.	B.t.u./sec.	9.30113×10^{-8}
"	Cal., *gm.*/sec.	2.34385×10^{-5}
"	Ergs-sec.	980.665
"	Foot-pounds/sec.	7.2330138×10
"	Horsepower	1.31509×10^{-7}
"	Joules/sec.	9.80665×10^{-5}
"	Kilowatts	9.80665×10^{-8}
"	Kilowatts (Int.)	9.80503×10^{-8}
"	Watts	9.80665×10^{-5}
Gram/sq. cm	Pounds/sq. inch	0.000341717
Gram wt.-sec./sq. cm.	Poises	980.665
Gravitational con- stants	Cm./(sec. × sec.)	980.621
"	Ft./(sec. × sec.)	32.1725
Hands	Centimeters	10.16
"	Inches	4
Hectares	Acres	2.4710538
"	Ares	100
"	Sq. cm	1×10^{8}
"	Sq. feet	107639.10
"	Sq. meters	10000
"	Sq. miles	0.0038610216
"	Sq. rods	395.36861
Hectograms	Grams	100
"	Poundals	7.09316
"	Pounds (apoth or troy)	0.26792289
"	Pounds (avdp.)	0.22046226
Hectoliters	Bushels (Brit.)	2.749694
"	Bushels (U.S.)	2.837839

* Based on density of 1 gram/ml.

CONVERSION FACTORS (Continued)

To convert from	To	Multiply by	To convert from	To	Multiply by
toliters	Cu. cm	1.00028×10^5	Horsepower (boiler)	Horsepower (metric)	13.3372
"	Cu. feet	3.531566	"	Horsepower (water)	13.1487
"	Gallons (U.S., liq.)	26.41794	"	Joules/sec	9809.50
"	Liters	100	"	Kilowatts	9.80950
"	Ounces (U.S.) fluid	3381.497	"	Lb. H_2O evap. per hr. from	
"	Pecks (U.S.)	11.35136		and at 212°F	34.5
tometers	Centimeters	10000	Horsepower (electric)	B.t.u./hr	2547.16
"	Decimeters	1000	"	B.t.u. (IST.)/hr	2545.50
"	Dekameters	10	"	B.t.u. (mean)/hr	2543.50
"	Feet	328.08399	"	Cal., *gm.*/sec	178.298
"	Meters	100	"	Cal., *kg.*/hr	641.874
"	Rods	19.883878	"	Ergs/sec	7.46×10^9
"	Yards	109.3613	"	Foot-pounds/min	33013.3
ctowatts	Watts	100	"	Foot-pounds/sec	550.221
ner units	Candles (English)	0.86	"	Horsepower	1.00040
"	Candles (German)	0.85	"	Horsepower (boiler)	0.0760487
"	Candles (Int.)	0.90	"	Horsepower (metric)	1.0142777
"	10-cp. pentane candles	0.090	"	Horsepower (water)	0.999942
nries	Abhenries	1×10^9	"	Joules/sec	746
"	E.M. cgs. units	1×10^9	"	Kilowatts	0.746
"	E.S. cgs. units	1.112646×10^{-12}	"	Watts	746
"	Henries (Int.)	0.999505	Horsepower (metric)	B.t.u./hr	2511.31
"	Millihenries	1000	"	B.t.u. (IST.)/hr	2509.66
"	Mks. (r *or* nr) units	1	"	B.t.u. (mean)/hr	2507.70
"	Stathenries	1.112646×10^{-12}	"	Cal., *gm.*/hr	6.32838×10^5
nries (Int.)	Henries	1.000495	"	Cal., *gm.* (IST.)/hr	6.32425×10^5
nries/meter	Cgs. units of permeability	795774.72	"	Cal., *gm.* (mean)/hr	6.31929×10^5
"	E.M. cgs. units	795774.72	"	Ergs/sec	7.35499×10^9
"	E.S. cgs. units	8.854156×10^{-16}	"	Foot-pounds/min	32548.6
"	Gausses/oersted	795774.72	"	Foot-pounds/sec	542.476
"	Mks. (nr) units	0.079577472	"	Horsepower	0.986320
"	Mks. (r) units	1	"	Horsepower (boiler)	0.0749782
gsheads	Butts (Brit.)	0.5	"	Horsepower (electric)	0.985923
"	Cu. feet	8.421875	"	Horsepower (water)	0.985866
"	Cu. inches	14553	"	Kg.-meters/sec	75
"	Cu. meters	0.23848094	"	Kilowatts	0.735499
"	Gallons (Brit.)	52.458505	"	Watts	735.499
"	Gallons (U.S.)	63	Horsepower (water)	Foot-pounds/min	33015.2
"	Gallons (wine)	63	"	Horsepower	1.00046
"	Liters	238.47427	"	Horsepower (boiler)	0.0760531
rsepower*	B.t.u. (mean)/hr	2542.48	"	Horsepower (electric)	1.00006
"	B.t.u./min	42.4356	"	Horsepower (metric)	1.01434
"	B.t.u. (mean)/sec	0.706243	"	Kilowatts	0.746043
"	Cal., *gm.*/hr	6.41616×10^5	Horsepower-hours	B.t.u	2546.14
"	Cal., *gm.* (IST.)/hr	6.41196×10^5	"	B.t.u. (IST.)	2544.47
"	Cal., *gm.* (mean)/hr	6.40693×10^5	"	B.t.u. (mean)	2542.48
"	Cal., *gm.*/min	10693.6	"	Cal., *gm.*	641616
"	Cal., *gm.* (IST.)/min	10686.6	"	Cal., *gm.* (IST.)	641196
"	Cal., *gm.* (mean)/min	10678.2	"	Cal., *gm.* (mean)	640693
"	Ergs/sec	7.45700×10^9	"	Foot-pounds	1.98×10^6
"	Foot-pounds/hr	1980000	"	Joules	2.68452×10^6
"	Foot-pounds/min	33000	"	Kg.-meters	273745
"	Foot-pounds/sec	550	"	Kw.-hours	0.745700
"	Horsepower (boiler)	0.0760181	"	Watt-hours	745.700
"	Horsepower (electric)	0.999598	Hp.-hr./lb	B.t.u./lb	2546.14
"	Horsepower (metric)	1.01387	"	Cal., *gm.*/gram	1414.52
"	Joules/sec	745.700	"	Cu. ft.-(lb./sq. in.)/lb	13750
"	Kilowatts	0.745700	"	Foot-pounds/lb	1980000
"	Kilowatts (Int.)	0.745577	"	Joules/gram	5918.35
"	Tons of refrig. (U.S., comm.)	0.21204	Hours (mean solar)	Days (mean solar)	0.0416666
"	Watts	745.700	"	Days (sidereal)	0.041780746
orsepower (boiler)	B.t.u. (mean)/hr	33445.7	"	Hours (sidereal)	1.00273791
"	Cal., *gm.*/min	140671.6	"	Minutes (mean solar)	60
"	Cal., *gm.* (mean)/min	140469.4	"	Minutes (sidereal)	60.164275
"	Cal., *gm.* (15°C.)/min	140611.1	"	Seconds (mean solar)	3600
"	Cal., *gm.*, (20°C.)/min	140742.2	"	Seconds (sidereal)	3609.8565
"	Ergs/sec	9.80950×10^{10}	"	Weeks (mean calendar)	0.0059523809
"	Foot-pounds/min	434107	Hours (sidereal)	Days (mean solar)	0.41552899
"	Horsepower	13.1548	"	Days (sidereal)	0.0416666
"	Horsepower (electric)	13.1495	"	Hours (mean solar)	0.99726957
			"	Minutes (mean solar)	59.836174

* Mechanical horsepower, equal to 550 ft.-lb./sec.

CONVERSION FACTORS (Continued)

To convert from	To	Multiply by
Hours (sidereal)	Minutes (sidereal)	60
Hundredweights (long)	Kilograms	50.802345
"	Pounds	112
"	Quarters (Brit., long)	4
"	Quarters (U.S., long)	0.2
"	Tons (long)	0.05
Hundredweights (short)	Kilograms	45.359237
"	Pounds (advp.)	100
"	Quarters (Brit., short)	4
"	Quarters (U.S., short)	0.2
"	Tons (long)	0.044642857
"	Tons (metric)	0.045359237
"	Tons (short)	0.05
Inches	Ångström units	2.54×10^8
"	Centimeters	2.54
"	Chains (Gunter's)	0.00126262
"	Cubits	0.055555
"	Fathoms	0.013888
"	Feet	0.083333
"	Feet (U.S. Survey)	0.083333167
"	Links (Gunter's)	0.126262
"	Links (Ramden's)	0.083333
"	Meters	0.0254
"	Mils	1000
"	Picas (printer's)	6.0225
"	Points (printer's)	72.27000
"	Wave length of orange-red line of krypton 86	41929.399
"	Wave length of the red line of cadmium	39450.369
"	Yards	0.027777
Inches of Hg (32°F.)	Atmospheres	0.0334211
"	Bars	0.0338639
"	Dynes/sq. cm.	33863.9
"	Ft. of air (1 atm., 60°F.)	926.24
"	Ft. of H_2O (39.2°F.)	1.132957
"	Grams/sq. cm.	34.5316
"	Kg./sq. meter	345.316
"	Mm. of Hg (60°C.)	25.4
"	Ounces/sq. inch	7.85847
Inches of Hg (32°F.)	Pounds/sq. ft.	70.7262
Inches of Hg (60°F.)	Atmospheres	0.0333269
"	Dynes/sq. cm.	39768.5
"	Grams/sq. cm.	34.4343
"	Mm. of Hg (60°F.)	25.4
"	Ounces/sq. inch	7.83633
"	Pounds/sq. ft.	70.5269
Inches of H_2O(4°C.)	Atmospheres	0.0024582
"	Dynes/sq. cm.	2490.82
"	In. of Hg (32°F.)	0.0735539
"	Kg./sq. meter	25.3993
"	Ounces/sq. ft.	83.2350
"	Ounces/sq. inch	0.578020
"	Pounds/sq. ft.	5.20218
"	Pounds/sq. inch	0.03612628
Inches/hr.	Cm./hr.	2.54
"	Feet/hr.	0.0833333
"	Miles/hr.	1.578282×10^{-5}
Inches/min.	Cm./hr.	152.4
"	Feet/hr.	5
"	Miles/hr.	0.000946969
Joules (abs.)	B.t.u.	0.000948451
"	B.t.u. (IST.)	0.000947831
"	B.t.u. (mean)	0.000947088
"	Cal., gm.	0.239006
"	Cal., gm. (IST.)	0.238849
"	Cal., gm. (mean)	0.238662
"	Cal., gm. (15°C.)	0.238903
"	Cal., gm. (20°C.)	0.239126

To convert from	To	Multiply by
Joules (abs.)	Cal., kg. (mean)	0.000238662
" "	Cu. ft.-atm.	0.000348529
" "	Ergs	1×10^7
" "	Foot-poundals	23.730360
" "	Foot-pounds	0.737562
" "	Gram-cm	10197.16
" "	Hp.-hours	3.72506×10^{-7}
" "	Joules (Int.)	0.999835
" "	Kg.-meters	0.1019716
" "	Kw.-hours	2.7777×10^{-7}
" "	Liter-atm.	0.00986895
" "	Volt-coulombs (Int.)	0.999835
" "	Watt-hours (abs.)	0.0002777777
" "	Watt-hours (Int.)	0.000277732
" "	Watt-sec.	1
" "	Watt-sec. (Int.)	0.999835
Joules (Int.)	B.t.u.	0.000948608
"	B.t.u. (IST.)	0.000947988
"	B.t.u. (mean)	0.000947244
"	Cal. gm.	0.239045
"	Cal., gm. (IST.)	0.238888
"	Cal., gm. (mean)	0.238702
"	C.h.u.	0.000527004
"	C.h.u. (IST.)	0.000526660
"	C.h.u. (mean)	0.000526247
"	Cu. cm.-atm.	9.87086
"	Cu. ft.-atm.	0.000348586
"	Dyne-cm.	1.000165×10^7
"	Ergs.	1.000165×10^7
"	Foot-poundals.	23.73428
"	Foot-pounds.	0.737684
"	Gram-cm.	10198.8
"	Joules (abs.).	1.000165
"	Kw.-hours.	2.77824×10^{-7}
"	Liter-atm.	0.00987058
"	Volt-coulombs.	1.000165
"	Volt-coulombs (Int.)	1
"	Watt-sec.	1.000165
"	Watt-sec. (Int.).	1
Joules/(abcoulomb × °F.)	Joules/(coulomb × °C.)	0.18
Joules/amp.-hr.	Joules/abcoulomb	0.002777
"	Joules/statcoulomb	9.265653×10^{-16}
Joules/coulomb	Joules/abcoulomb	10
"	Volts	1
Joules/(coulomb × °F.)	Joules/(coulomb × °C.)	1.8
Joules/°C.	B.t.u./°F.	0.000526917
"	Cal., gm./°C.	0.239006
"	Cal., gm. (mean)/°C.	0.238662
Joules/electronic charge	Joules/abcoulomb	6.24196×10^{19}
Joules/(electronic charge × °C.)	Joules/(coulomb × °C.)	6.24196×10^{18}
Joules/(gram × °C.)	B.t.u./(lb. × °F.)	0.239006
"	Cal., gm./(gram × °C.)	0.239006
Joules (Int.)/(gram °C.)	B.t.u./(lb. × °F.)	0.239045
"	Cal., gm. (mean)/(gram × °C.)	0.238702
Joules/sec. (abs.)	B.t.u./min.	0.0569071
"	Cal., gm./min.	14.3403
"	Cal., kg./min.	0.0143403
"	Cal., kg. (mean)/min.	0.0143197
"	Dyne-cm./sec.	1×10^7
"	Ergs/sec.	1×10^7
"	Foot-pounds/sec.	0.737562
"	Gram-cm./sec.	10197.16
"	Horsepower	0.00134102
"	Watts	1
"	Watts (Int.)	0.999835
Joules (Int.)/sec.	B.t.u./min.	0.0569165

CONVERSION FACTORS (Continued)

To convert from	To	Multiply by	To convert from	To	Multiply by
es (Int.)/sec......	B.t.u. (mean)/min........	0.0568347	Kilogram-meters.....	Hp.-hours...............	3.65304 × 10⁻⁶
"	Cal., gm./min...........	14.3427	"	Joules..................	9.80665
"	Cal., kg./min...........	0.0143427	"	Joules (Int.)............	9.80503
"	Dyne-cm./sec...........	1.000165 × 10⁷	"	Kw.-hours..............	2.72407 × 10⁻⁶
"	Ergs/sec................	1.000165 × 10⁷	"	Liter-atm..............	0.0967814
"	Foot-pounds/min........	44.2610	"	Newton-meters.........	9.80665
"	Foot-pounds/sec........	0.737684	"	Watt-hours.............	0.00272407
"	Gram-cm./sec...........	10198.8	"	Watt-hours (Int.).......	0.00272362
"	Horsepower.............	0.00134124	Kilogram-meters/sec..	Watts.................	9.80665
"	Watts..................	1.000165	Kilolines.............	Maxwells..............	1000
"	Watts (Int.)...........	1	"	Webers................	1 × 10⁻⁵
erkins (Brit.).....	Cu. cm.................	81829.57	Kiloliters............	Cu. centimeters........	1.000028 × 10⁶
"	Cu. feet...............	2.889784	"	Cu. feet..............	35.31566
"	Cu. inches.............	4993.55	"	Cu. inches............	61025.45
"	Cu. meters.............	0.08182957	"	Cu. meters............	1.000028
"	Gallons (Brit.)........	18	"	Cu. yards.............	1.307987
grams...........	Drams (apoth. or troy)....	257.20597	"	Gallons (Brit.)........	219.9755
"	Drams (avdp.).........	564.38339	"	Gallons (U.S., dry).....	227.0271
"	Dynes.................	980665	"	Gallons (U.S., liq.).....	264.1794
"	Grains................	15432.358	"	Liters................	1000
"	Hundredweights (long)....	0.019684131	Kilometers...........	Astronomical units.....	6.68878 × 10⁻⁹
"	Hundredweights (short)...	0.022046226	"	Centimeters...........	100000
"	Ounces (apoth. or troy)....	32.150737	"	Feet..................	3280.8399
"	Ounces (avdp.).........	35.273962	"	Feet (U.S. Survey).....	3280.833
"	Pennyweights..........	643.01493	"	Light years...........	1.05702 × 10⁻¹¹
"	Poundals..............	70.931635	"	Meters................	1000
"	Pounds (apoth. or troy)....	2.6792289	"	Miles (naut., Int.).....	0.53995680
"	Pounds (avdp.).........	2.2046226	"	Miles (statute)........	0.62137119
"	Quarters (Brit., long)....	0.078736522	"	Myriameters...........	0.1
"	Quarters (U.S. long)......	0.0039368261	"	Rods..................	198.83878
"	Scruples (apoth.)........	771.61792	"	Yards.................	1093.6133
"	Slugs.................	0.06852177	Kilometers/hr.......	Cm./sec...............	27.7777
"	Tons (long)............	0.00098420653	"	Feet/hr...............	3280.8399
"	Tons (metric).........	0.001	"	Feet/min..............	54.680665
"	Tons (short)..........	0.0011023113	"	Knots (Int.)..........	0.53995680
grams/cu. meter..	Grams/cu. cm..........	0.001	"	Meters/sec............	0.277777
"	Lb./cu. ft............	0.062427961	"	Miles (statute)/hr.....	0.62137119
"	Lb./cu. inch..........	3.6127292 × 10⁻⁵	Kilometers/(hr. ×		
"	Tons of refrig. (U.S., comm.)....	0.026336	sec.)..............	Cm./(sec. × sec.)......	27.7777
grams/sq. cm....	Atmospheres...........	0.967841	"	Ft./(sec. × sec.)......	0.91134442
"	Bars..................	0.980665	"	Meters/(sec. × sec.)......	0.277777
"	Cm. of Hg (0°C.)........	73.5559	Kilometers/min.....	Cm./sec...............	1666.666
"	Dynes/sq. cm..........	980665	"	Feet/min..............	3280.8399
"	Ft. of H₂O (39.2°F.)......	32.8093	"	Kilometers/hr.........	60
"	In. of Hg (32°F.)........	28.9590	"	Knots (Int.)..........	32.397408
"	Pounds/sq. inch........	14.223343	"	Miles/hr..............	37.282272
grams/sq. meter..	Atmospheres...........	9.67841 × 10⁻⁵	"	Miles/min.............	0.62137119
"	Bars..................	9.80665 × 10⁻⁵	Kilovolts/cm........	Abvolts/cm............	1 × 10¹¹
"	Dynes/sq. cm..........	98.0665	"	Microvolts/meter.......	1 × 10¹¹
"	Ft. of H₂O (39.2°F.)......	0.00328093	"	Millivolts/meter.......	1 × 10⁸
"	Grams/sq. cm..........	0.1	"	Statvolts/cm..........	3.335635
"	In. of Hg. (32°F.)......	0.00289590	"	Volts/inch............	2540
"	Mm. of Hg (0°C.).......	0.0735559	Kilowatts...........	B.t.u./hr.............	3414.43
"	Pounds/sq. ft.........	0.20481614	"	B.t.u. (IST.)/hr.......	3412.19
"	Pounds/sq. in.........	0.0014223343	"	B.t.u. (mean)/hr.......	3409.52
grams/sq. mm...	Pounds/sq. ft.........	204816.14	"	B.t.u. (mean)/min......	56.8253
"	Pounds/sq. in.........	1422.3343	"	B.t.u. (mean)/sec......	0.947088
"	Tons (short)/sq. in.....	0.71116716	"	Cal., gm. (mean)/hr.....	859184
gram sq. cm....	Pounds sq. ft.........	0.0023730360	"	Cal., gm. (mean)/min....	14319.7
"	Pounds sq. in.........	0.34171719	"	Cal., gm. (mean)/sec....	238.662
gram-meters....	B.t.u. (mean).........	0.00928776	"	Cal., kg. (mean)/hr.....	859.184
"	Cal., gm. (mean)......	2.34048	"	Cal., kg. (mean)/min....	14.3197
"	Cal., kg. (mean)......	0.00234048	"	Cal., kg. (mean)/sec....	0.238662
"	Cu. ft.-atm...........	0.00341790	"	Cu. ft.-atm./hr........	1254.70
"	Dynes-cm..............	9.80665 × 10⁷	"	Ergs/sec..............	1 × 10¹⁰
"	Ergs..................	9.80665 × 10⁷	"	Foot-poundals/min......	1.42382 × 10⁶
"	Foot-poundals.........	232.715	"	Foot-poundals/sec......	2.65522 × 10⁴
"	Foot-pounds...........	7.23301	"	Foot-pounds/min.......	44253.7
"	Gram-cm...............	100000	"	Foot-pounds/sec.......	737.562
			"	Gram-cm./sec..........	1.019716 × 10⁷
			"	Horsepower............	1.34102

CONVERSION FACTORS (Continued)

To convert from	To	Multiply by	To convert from	To	Multiply by
Kilowatts............	Horsepower (boiler)......	0.101942	Lamberts............	Candles/sq. cm..........	0.31830989
"	Horsepower (electric).....	1.34048	"	Candles/sq. ft..........	295.71956
"	Horsepower (metric).....	1.35962	"	Candles/sq. inch..........	2.0536081
"	Joules/hr..............	3.6×10^6	"	Foot-lamberts..........	929.0304
"	Joules (IST.)/hr........	3.59941×10^6	"	Lumens/sq. cm..........	1
"	Joules/sec............	1000	Lasts (Brit.)...........	Liters..........	2909.414
"	Kg.-meters/hr..........	3.67098×10^5	Leagues (naut., Brit.).	Feet..........	18240
"	Kilowatts (Int.)........	0.999835	"	Kilometers..........	5.559552
"	Watts (Int.)...........	999.835	"	Leagues (naut., Int.)....	1.0006393
Kilowatts (Int.).....	B.t.u./hr..............	3414.99	"	Leagues (statute)..........	1.151515
"	B.t.u. (IST.)/hr........	3412.76	"	Miles (statute)..........	3.454545
"	B.t.u. (mean)/hr........	3410.08	Leagues (naut., Int.)...	Fathoms..........	3038.0577
"	B.t.u. (mean)/min.......	56.8347	"	Feet..........	18228.346
"	B.t.u. (mean)/sec.......	0.947244	"	Kilometers..........	5.556
"	Cal., *gm.* (mean)/hr......	859326	"	Leagues (statute)..........	1.1507794
"	Cal., *gm.* (mean)/min.....	14322.1	"	Miles (statute)..........	3.4523383
"	Cal., *kg.*/hr...........	860.563	Leagues (statute)....	Fathoms..........	2640
"	Cal., *kg.* (IST.)/hr.......	860	"	Feet..........	15840
"	Cal., *kg.* (mean)/hr......	859.326	"	Kilometers..........	4.828032
"	Cu. cm.-atm./hr.......	3.55351×10^7	"	Leagues (naut., Int.).....	0.86897625
"	Cu. ft.-atm./hr.......	1254.91	"	Miles (naut., Int.).....	2.6069287
"	Ergs/sec...........	1.000165×10^{10}	"	Miles (statute)..........	3
"	Foot-poundals/min......	1.42406×10^6	Light years.........	Astronomical units.......	63279.5
"	Foot-pounds/min......	44261.0	"	Kilometers..........	9.46055×10^{12}
"	Foot-pounds/sec.......	737.684	"	Miles (statute)..........	5.87851×10^{12}
"	Gram-cm./sec.......	1.01988×10^7	Lines...............	Maxwells..........	1
"	Horsepower...........	1.34124	Lines (Brit.)........	Centimeters..........	0.211666
"	Horsepower (boiler).....	0.101959	"	Inches..........	0.083333
"	Horsepower (electric).....	1.34070	Lines/sq. cm........	Gausses..........	1
"	Horsepower (metric).....	1.35985	Lines/sq. inch.......	Gausses..........	0.15500031
"	Joules/hr..............	3.60059×10^6	"	Webers/sq. inch.......	1×10^{-8}
"	Joules (Int.)/hr........	3.6×10^6	Links (Gunter's).....	Chains (Gunter's).......	0.01
"	Kg.-meters/hr........	367158	"	Feet..........	0.66
"	Kilowatts...........	1.000165	"	Feet (U.S. Survey).....	0.65999868
Kilowatt-hours......	B.t.u. (mean).........	3409.52	"	Inches..........	7.92
"	Cal., *gm.* (mean)........	859184	"	Meters..........	0.201168
"	Foot-pounds........	2.65522×10^6	"	Miles (statute)..........	0.000125
"	Hp.-hours..........	1.34102	"	Rods..........	0.04
"	Joules.............	3.6×10^6	Links (Ramden's)....	Centimeters..........	30.48
"	Kg.-meters..........	367098	"	Chains (Ramdens).......	0.01
"	Lb. H_2O evap. from and at 212°F.............	3.5168	"	Feet..........	1
"	Watt-hours.........	1000	"	Inches..........	12
"	Watt-hours (Int.)......	999.835	Liters.............	Bushels (Brit.)..........	0.02749694
Kilowatt-hours (Int.).	B.t.u. (mean).........	3410.08	"	Bushels (U.S.)..........	0.02837839
"	Cal., *gm.* (IST.).........	860000	"	Cu. centimeters..........	1000
"	Cal., *gm.* (mean)........	859326	"	Cu. feet..........	0.03531566
"	Cu. cm.-atm........	3.55351×10^7	"	Cu. inches..........	61.02545
"	Cu. ft.-atm........	1254.91	"	Cu. meters..........	0.001000028
"	Foot-pounds........	2.65566×10^6	"	Cu. yards..........	0.001307987
"	Hp.-hours..........	1.34124	"	Drams (U.S., fluid)......	270.5198
"	Joules.............	3.60059×10^6	"	Gallons (Brit.)......	0.2199755
"	Joules (Int.)........	3.6×10^6	"	Gallons (U.S., dry)......	0.2270271
"	Kg.-meters..........	367158	"	Gallons (U.S., liq.)......	0.2641794
Kw.-hr./gram.......	B.t.u./(lb..........	1.54876×10^6	"	Gills (Brit.)..........	7.039217
"	B.t.u. (IST.)/lb........	1.54774×10^6	"	Gills (U.S.)..........	8.453742
"	B.t.u. (mean)/lb........	1.54653×10^6	"	Hogsheads..........	0.004193325
"	Cal., *gm.*/gram........	860421	"	Minims (U.S.)..........	16231.19
"	Cal., *gm.* (mean)/gram.....	859184	"	Ounces (Brit., fluid)......	35.19609
"	Cu. cm.-atm./gram......	3.55292×10^7	"	Ounces (U.S., fluid)......	33.81497
"	Cu. ft.-atm./lb........	569124	"	Pecks (Brit.)..........	0.1099878
"	Hp.-hr./lb..........	608.277	"	Pecks (U.S.)..........	0.1135136
"	Joules/gram........	3.6×10^6	"	Pints (Brit.)..........	1.759804
Knots (Int.)........	Cm./sec...........	51.4444	"	Pints (U.S., dry)..........	1.816251
"	Feet/hr............	6076.1155	"	Pints (U.S., liq.)..........	2.113436
"	Feet/min..........	101.26859	"	Quarts. (Brit.)..........	0.8799021
"	Feet/sec...........	1.6878099	"	Quarts (U.S., dry)........	0.9081084
"	Kilometers/hr........	1.852	"	Quarts (U.S., liq.)........	1.056718
"	Meters/min.........	30.8666	Liters/min.........	Cu. ft./min..........	0.03531566
"	Meters/sec.........	0.514444	"	Cu. ft./sec..........	0.0005885943
"	Miles (naut., Int.)/hr......	1	"	Gal. (U.S., liq.)/min......	0.2641794
"	Miles (statute)/hr........	1.1507794	Liters/sec..........	Cu. ft./min..........	2.118939
			"	Cu. ft./sec..........	0.03531566

CONVERSION FACTORS (Continued)

To convert from	To	Multiply by	To convert from	To	Multiply by
ers/sec	Cu. yards/min	0.07847923	Meters	Links (Ramden's)	3.2808399
"	Gal. (U.S., liq.)/min	15.85077	"	Megameters	1×10^{-6}
"	Gal. (U.S., liq.)/sec	0.2641794	"	Miles (naut., Brit.)	0.00053961182
er-atm	B.t.u.	0.0961045	"	Miles (naut., Int.)	0.00053995680
"	B.t.u. (IST.)	0.0960417	"	Miles (statute)	0.00062137119
"	B.t.u. (mean)	0.0959664	"	Millimeters	1000
"	Cal., $gm.$	24.2179	"	Millimicrons	1×10^{9}
"	Cal., $gm.$ (IST.)	24.2021	"	Mils	39370.079
"	Cal., $gm.$ (mean)	24.1831	"	Rods	0.19883878
"	Cu. ft.-atm	0.0353157	"	Yards	1.0936133
"	Foot-poundals	2404.55	Meters of Hg (0°C.)	Atmospheres	1.3157895
"	Foot-pounds	74.7356	"	Ft. of H_2O (60°F.)	44.6474
"	Hp.-hours	3.77452×10^{-5}	"	In. of Hg (32°F.)	39.370079
"	Joules	101.328	"	Kg./sq. cm	1.35951
"	Joules (Int.)	101.311	"	Pounds/sq. inch	19.3368
"	Kg.-meters	10.3326	Meters/hr	Feet/hr	3.2808399
"	Kw.-hours	2.81466×10^{-5}	"	Feet/min	0.054680665
er-atm. (lat. 45°)	Joules	101.323	"	Knots (Int.)	0.00053995680
mens	Candle power (spher.)	0.079577472	"	Miles (statute)/hr	0.00062137119
mens (at 5550 Å)	Watts	0.0014705882	Meters/min	Cm./sec	1.666666
mens/sq. cm	Lamberts	1	"	Feet/min	3.2808399
"	Phots	1	"	Feet/sec	0.054680665
mens/(sq. cm. × teradian)	Lamberts	3.1415927	"	Kilometers/hr	0.06
mens/sq. ft	Foot-candles	1	"	Knots (Int.)	0.032397408
"	Foot-lamberts	1	"	Miles (statute)/hr	0.037282272
"	Lumens/sq. meter	10.763910	Meters/sec	Feet/min	196.85039
mens/(sq. ft. × teradian)	Millilamberts	3.3815822	"	Feet/sec	3.2808399
mens/sq. meter	Foot-candles	0.09290304	"	Kilometers/hr	3.6
"	Lumens/sq. ft	0.09290304	"	Kilometers/min	0.06
"	Phots	0.0001	"	Miles (statute)/hr	2.2369363
x	Foot-candles	0.09290304	Meters/(sec. × sec.)	Kilometers/(hr. × sec.)	3.6
"	Lumens/sq. meter	1	"	Miles/(hr. × sec.)	2.2369363
"	Phots	0.0001	Meter-candles	Lumens/sq. meter	1
xwells	E.M. cgs. units of induction flux	1	Mhos	Abmhos	1×10^{-9}
"	E.S. cgs. units	3.335635×10^{-11}	"	Cgs. units of conductance	1
"	Gauss-sq. cm	1	"	E.M. cgs. units	1×10^{-9}
"	Lines	1	"	E.S. cgs. units	8.987584×10^{11}
"	Maxwells (Int.)	0.999670	"	Mhos (Int.)	1.000495
"	Volt-seconds	1×10^{-8}	"	Mks. (r or nr) units	1
"	Webers	1×10^{-8}	"	Ohms⁻¹	1
xwells (Int.)	Maxwells	1.000330	"	Siemen's units	1
xwells/sq. cm	Maxwells/sq. in	6.4516	"	Statmhos	8.987584×10^{11}
"	Maxwells (Int.)/sq. cm	0.999670	Mhos (Int.)	Abmhos	9.99505×10^{-10}
xwells (Int.)/sq. m	Maxwells/sq. cm	1.000330	"	Mhos	0.999505
xwells/sq. inch	Maxwells/sq. cm	0.15500031	Mhos/meter	Abmhos/cm	1×10^{-11}
galines	Maxwells	1×10^{8}	"	Mhos (Int.)/meter	1.000495
gmhos/cm	Abmhos/cm	0.001	Mho-ft./circ. mil	Mhos/cm	6.0153049×10^{6}
"	Megmhos/inch cube	2.54	Microfarads	Abfarads	1×10^{-15}
"	(Microhm-cm.)⁻¹	1	"	Farads	1×10^{-6}
gmhos/inch	Megmhos/cm	0.39370079	"	Statfarads	8.987584×10^{5}
"	(Microhm-inches)⁻¹	1	Micrograms	Grams	1×10^{-6}
gohms	Microhms	1×10^{12}	"	Milligrams	0.001
"	Ohms	1×10^{6}	Microhenries	Henries	1×10^{-6}
"	Statohms	1.112646×10^{-6}	"	Stathenries	1.112646×10^{-18}
gohms⁻¹	Micromhos	1	Microhms	Abohms	1000
ters	Ångström units	1×10^{10}	"	Megohms	1×10^{-12}
"	Centimeters	100	"	Ohms	1×10^{-6}
"	Chains (Gunter's)	0.049709695	"	Statohms	1.112646×10^{-18}
"	Chains (Ramden's)	0.032808399	Microhm-cm	Abohm-cm	1000
"	Fathoms	0.54680665	"	Circ. mil-ohms/ft	6.0153049
"	Feet	3.2808399	"	Microhm-inches	0.39370079
"	Feet (U.S. Survey)	3.280833	"	Ohm-cm	1×10^{-6}
"	Furlongs	0.0049709695	Microhm-inches	Circ. mil-ohms/ft	15.278875
"	Inches	39.370079	"	Michrom-cm	2.54
"	Kilometers	0.001	Micromicrofarads	Farads	1×10^{-12}
"	Links (Gunter's)	4.9709695	Micromicrons	Ångström units	0.01
			"	Centimeters	1×10^{-10}
			"	Inches	$3.9370079 \times 10^{-11}$
			"	Meters	1×10^{-12}
			"	Microns	1×10^{-6}
			Microns	Ångström units	10000

CONVERSION FACTORS (Continued)

To convert from	To	Multiply by	To convert from	To	Multiply by
Microns	Centimeters	0.0001	Milligrams	Grains	0.015432358
"	Feet	3.2808399×10^{-6}	"	Grams	0.001
"	Inches	3.9370079×10^{-5}	"	Ounces (apoth. *or* troy)	3.2150737×10
"	Meters	1×10^{-6}	"	Ounces (avdp.)	3.5273962×10
"	Millimeters	0.001	"	Pennyweights	0.00064301493
"	Millimicrons	1000	"	Pounds (apoth. *or* troy)	2.6792289×10
Miles (naut., Brit.)	Cable lengths (Brit.)	8.4444	"	Pounds (avdp.)	2.2046226×10
"	Fathoms	1013.333	"	Scruples (apoth.)	0.00077161792
"	Feet	6080	Milligrams/assay ton	Milligrams/kg	34.285714
"	Meters	1853.184	"	Ounces (troy)/ton (avdp.)	1
"	Miles (Adm., Brit.)	1	Milligrams/gm	Dynes/cm	0.980665
"	Miles (naut., Int.)	1.0006393	"	Pounds/inch	$5.5997415 \times$
"	Miles (statute)	1.151515	Milligrams/gram	Carats (parts gold per 24 of mixture)	0.024
Miles (naut., Int.)	Cable lengths	8.4390493	"	Grams/ton (short)	907.18474
"	Fathoms	1012.6859	"	Milligrams/assay ton	29.166666
"	Feet	6076.1155	"	Ounces (avdp.)/ton (long)	35.84
"	Feet (U.S. Survey)	6076.1033	"	Ounces (avdp.)/ton (short)	32
"	Kilometers	1.852	"	Ounces (troy)/ton (long)	32.6666
"	Leagues (naut., Int.)	0.333333	"	Ounces (troy)/ton (short)	29.1666
"	Meters	1852	Milligrams/inch	Dynes/cm	0.386089
"	Miles (geographical)	1	"	Dynes/inch	0.980665
"	Miles (naut. Brit.)	0.99936110	"	Grams/cm	0.00039370079
"	Miles (statute)	1.1507794	"	Grams/inch	0.0001
Miles (statute)	Centimeters	160934.4	Milligrams/kg	Pounds (avdp.)/ton (short)	0.002
"	Chains (Gunter's)	80	Milligrams/liter	Grains/gal. (U.S.)	0.05841620
"	Chains (Ramden's)	52.8	"	Grams/liter	0.001
"	Feet	5280	"	Parts/million*	1
"	Feet (U.S. Survey)	5279.9894	"	Lb./cu. ft.	6.242621×10
"	Furlongs	8	Milligrams/mm	Dynes/cm	9.80665
"	Inches	63360	Millihenries	Abhenries	1×10^{6}
"	Kilometers	1.609344	"	Henries	0.001
"	Light years	1.70111×10^{-13}	"	Stathenries	1.112646×10
"	Links (Gunter's)	8000	Millilamberts	Candles/sq. cm.	0.00031830989
"	Meters	1609.344	"	Candles/sq. inch	0.0020536081
"	Miles (naut., Brit.)	0.86842105	"	Foot-lamberts	0.9290304
"	Miles (naut., Int.)	0.86897624	"	Lamberts	0.001
"	Myriameters	0.1609344	"	Lumens/sq. cm.	0.001
"	Rods	320	"	Lumens/sq. ft.	0.9290304
"	Yards	1760	Milliliters	Cu. cm	1.000028
Miles/hr	Cm./sec	44.704	"	Cu. inches	0.06102545
"	Feet/hr	5280	"	Drams (U.S., fluid)	0.2705198
"	Feet/min	88	"	Gills (U.S.)	0.008453742
"	Feet/sec	1.466666	"	Liters	0.001
"	Kilometers/hr	1.609344	"	Minims (U.S.)	16.23119
"	Knots (Int.)	0.86897624	"	Ounces (Brit., fluid)	0.03519609
"	Meters/min	26.8224	"	Ounces (U.S., fluid)	0.03381497
"	Miles/min	0.0166666	"	Pints (Brit.)	0.001759804
Miles/(hr. $\times$ min.)	Cm./(sec. $\times$ sec.)	0.7450666	"	Pints (U.S., liq.)	0.002113436
Miles/(hr. $\times$ sec.)	Cm./(sec. $\times$ sec.)	44.704	Millimeters	Ångström units	1×10^{7}
"	Ft./(sec. $\times$ sec.)	1.466666	"	Centimeters	0.1
"	Kilometers/(hr. $\times$ sec.)	1.609344	"	Decimeters	0.01
"	Meters/(sec. $\times$ sec.)	0.44704	"	Dekameters	0.0001
Miles/min	Cm./sec	2682.24	"	Feet	0.0032808399
"	Feet/hr	316800	"	Inches	0.039370079
"	Feet/sec	88	"	Meters	0.001
"	Kilometers/min	1.609344	"	Microns	1000
"	Knots (Int.)	52.138574	"	Mils	39.370079
"	Meters/min	1609.344	"	Wave length of orange-red line of krypton 86	1650.76373
"	Miles/hr	60	"	Wave length of red line of cadmium	1553.16413
Millibars	Atmospheres	0.000986923	Millimeters of Hg (0°C.)	Atmospheres	0.0013157895
"	Bars	0.001	"	Bars	0.00133322
"	Baryes	1000	"	Dynes/sq. cm	1333.224
"	Dynes/sq. cm	1000	"	Grams/sq. cm	1.35951
"	Grams/sq. cm	1.019716	"	Kg./sq. meter	13,5951
"	In. of Hg (32°F.)	0.0295300	"	Pounds/sq. ft.	2.78450
"	Pounds/sq. ft	2.088543	"	Pounds/sq. inch	0.0193368
"	Pounds/sq. inch	0.0145038	"	Torrs	1
Milligrams	Carats (1877)	0.004871			
"	Carats (metric)	0.005			
"	Drams (apoth. *or* troy)	0.00025720597			
"	Drams (advp.)	0.00056438339			

* Density of 1 gram per milliliter of solvent.

CONVERSION FACTORS (Continued)

To convert from	To	Multiply by	To convert from	To	Multiply by
Millimicrons	Ångström units	10	Oersteds	Gilberts/cm	1
"	Centimeters	1×10^{-7}	"	Oersteds (Int.)	1.000165
"	Inches	3.9370079×10^{-8}	Oersteds (Int.)	Oersteds	0.999835
"	Microns	0.001	Ohms	Abohms	1×10^{9}
"	Millimeters	1×10^{-6}	"	Cgs. units of resistance	1
Milliphots	Foot-candles	0.9290304	"	Megohms	1×10^{-6}
"	Lumens/sq. ft	0.9290304	"	Microhms	1×10^{6}
"	Lumens/sq. meter	10	"	Ohms (Int.)	0.999505
"	Lux	10	"	Statohms	1.112646×10^{-12}
"	Phots	0.001	Ohms (Int.)	Ohms	1.000495
Millivolts	Statvolts	3.335635×10^{-6}	Ohms (mil, foot)	Circ. mil-ohms/ft	1
"	Volts	0.001	"	Ohm-cm	1.6624261×10^{-7}
Minims (Brit.)	Cu. cm	0.05919385	Ohm-cm	Circ. mil-ohms/ft	6.0153049×10^{6}
"	Cu. inches	0.003612230	"	Microhm-cm	1×10^{6}
"	Milliliters	0.05919219	"	Ohm-inches	0.39370079
"	Ounces (Brit., fluid)	0.0020833333	Ohm-inches	Ohm-cm	2.54
"	Scruples (Brit., fluid)	0.05	Ohm-meters	Abohm-cm	1×10^{11}
Minims (U.S.)	Cu. cm	0.061611520	"	E.M. cgs. units	1×10^{11}
"	Cu. inches	0.0037597656	"	E.S. cgs. units	1.112646×10^{-10}
"	Drams (U.S., fluid)	0.0166666	"	Mks. units	1
"	Gallons (U.S., liq.)	1.6276042×10^{-5}	"	Statohm-cm	1.112646×10^{-10}
"	Gills (U.S.)	0.0005208333	Ounces (apoth. or troy)	Dekagrams	1.7554286
"	Liters	6.160979×10^{-5}	"	Drams (apoth. or troy)	8
"	Milliliters	0.06160937	"	Drams (avdp.)	17.554286
"	Ounces (U.S., fluid)	0.002083333	"	Grains	480
"	Pints (U.S., liq.)	0.0001302083	"	Grams	31.103486
Minutes (angular)	Degrees	0.0166666	"	Milligrams	31103.486
"	Quadrants	0.000185185	"	Ounces (avdp.)	1.0971429
"	Radians	0.00029088821	"	Pennyweights	20
"	Seconds (angular)	60	"	Pounds (apoth. or troy)	0.0833333
Minutes (mean solar)	Days (mean solar)	0.0006944444	"	Pounds (avdp.)	0.068571429
"	Days (sidereal)	0.00069634577	"	Scruples (apoth.)	24
"	Hours (mean solar)	0.0166666	"	Tons (short)	3.4285714×10^{-5}
"	Hours (sidereal)	0.016712298	Ounces (avdp.)	Drams (apoth. or troy)	7.291666
"	Minutes (sidereal)	1.00273791	"	Drams (avdp.)	16
Minutes (sidereal)	Days (mean solar)	0.00069254831	"	Grains	437.5
"	Minutes (mean solar)	0.99726957	"	Grams	28.349523
"	Months (mean calendar)	2.2768712×10^{-5}	"	Hundredweights (long)	0.00055803571
"	Seconds (sidereal)	60	"	Hundredweights (short)	0.000625
Minutes/cm	Radians/cm	0.00029088821	"	Ounces (apoth. or troy)	0.9114583
Months (lunar)	Days (mean solar)	29.530588	"	Pennyweights	18.229166
"	Hours (mean solar)	708.73411	"	Pounds (apoth. or troy)	0.075954861
"	Minutes (mean solar)	42524.047	"	Pounds (avdp.)	0.0625
"	Second (mean solar)	2.5514428×10^{6}	"	Scruples (apoth.)	21.875
"	Weeks (mean calendar)	4.2186554	"	Tons (long)	2.7901786×10^{-5}
Months (mean calendar)	Days (mean solar)	30.416666	"	Tons (metric)	2.8349527×10^{-5}
"	Hours (mean solar)	730	"	Tons (short)	3.125×10^{-5}
"	Months (lunar)	1.0300055	Ounces (Brit., fluid)	Cu. cm	28.41305
"	Weeks (mean calendar)	4.3452381	"	Cu. inches	1.733870
"	Years (calendar)	0.08333333	"	Drachms (Brit., fluid)	8
"	Years (sidereal)	0.083274845	"	Drams (U.S., fluid)	7.686075
"	Years (tropical)	0.083278075	"	Gallons (Brit.)	0.00625
Myriagrams	Grams	10000	"	Milliliters	28.41225
"	Kilograms	10	"	Minims (Brit.)	480
"	Pounds (avdp.)	22.046226	"	Ounces (U.S., fluid)	0.9607594
Newtons	Dynes	100000	Ounces (U.S., fluid)	Cu. cm	29.573730
"	Pounds	0.22480894	"	Cu. inches	1.8046575
Newton-meters	Dyne-cm	1×10^{7}	"	Cu. meters	2.9573730×10^{-5}
"	Gram-cm	10197.162	"	Drams (U.S., fluid)	8
"	Kg.-meters	0.10197162	"	Gallons (U.S., dry)	0.0067138047
"	Pound-feet	0.73756215	"	Gallons (U.S., liq.)	0.0078125
Noggins (Brit.)	Cu. cm	142.0652	"	Gills (U.S.)	0.25
"	Gallons (Brit.)	0.03125	"	Liters	0.029572702
"	Gills (Brit.)	1	"	Minims (U.S.)	480
Oersteds	Ampere-turns/inch	2.0212678	"	Ounces (Brit., fluid)	1.040843
"	Ampere-turns/meter	79.577472	"	Pints (U.S., liq.)	0.0625
"	E.M. cgs. units of magnetic field intensity	1	"	Quarts (U.S., liq.)	0.03125
"	E.S. cgs. units	2.997930×10^{10}	Ounces/sq. inch	Dynes/sq. cm	4309.22
			"	Grams/sq. cm	4.3941849
			"	In. of H_2O (39.2°F.)	1.73004
			"	In. of H_2O (60°F.)	1.73166

CONVERSION FACTORS (Continued)

To convert from	To	Multiply by	To convert from	To	Multiply by
Ounces/sq. inch	Pounds/sq. ft	9	Pints (Brit.)	Minims (Brit.)	9600
"	Pounds/sq. inch	0.0625	"	Ounces (Brit., fluid)	20
Ounces (avdp.)/ton (long)	Milligrams/kg	27.901786	"	Pints (U.S., dry)	1.032056
Ounces (avdp.)/ton (short)	Milligrams/kg	31.25	"	Pints (U.S., liq.)	1.200949
			"	Quarts (Brit.)	0.5
Paces	Centimeters	76.2	"	Scruples (Brit., fluid)	480
"	Chains (Gunter's)	0.0378788	Pints (U.S., dry)	Bushels (U.S.)	0.015625
"	Chains (Ramden's)	0.025	"	Cu. cm	550.61047
"	Feet	2.5	"	Cu. inches	33.6003125
"	Hands	7.5	"	Gallons, (U.S., dry)	0.125
"	Inches	30	"	Gallons (U.S., liq.)	0.14545590
"	Ropes (Brit.)	0.125	"	Liters	0.5505951
Palms	Centimeters	7.62	"	Pecks (U.S.)	0.0625
"	Chains (Ramden's)	0.0025	"	Quarts (U.S., dry)	0.5
"	Cubits	0.1666666	Pints (U.S., liq.)	Cu. cm	473.17647
"	Feet	0.25	"	Cu. feet	0.016710069
"	Hands	0.75	"	Cu. inches	28.875
"	Inches	3	"	Cu. yards	0.00061889146
Parsecs	Kilometers	3.08374×10^{13}	"	Drams (U.S., fluid)	128
"	Miles (statute)	1.91615×10^{13}	"	Gallons (U.S., liq.)	0.125
Parts/million*	Grains/gal. (Brit.)	0.07015488	"	Gills (U.S.)	4
"	Grains/gal. (U.S.)	0.05841620	"	Liters	0.4731632
"	Grams/liter	0.001	"	Milliliters	473.1632
"	Milligrams/liter	1	"	Minims (U.S.)	7680
Pecks (Brit.)	Bushels (Brit.)	0.25	"	Ounces (U.S., fluid)	16
"	Coombs (Brit.)	0.0625	"	Pints (Brit.)	0.8326747
"	Cu. cm	9092.175	"	Quarts (U.S., liq.)	0.5
"	Cu. inches	554.8385	Planck's constant	Erg-seconds	6.6255×10^{-27}
"	Gallons (Brit.)	2	"	Joule-seconds	6.6255×10^{-34}
"	Gills (Brit.)	64	"	Joule-sec./Avog. No. (chem.)	3.9905×10^{-10}
"	Hogsheads	0.03812537	Points (printer's)	Centimeters	0.03514598
"	Kilderkins (Brit.)	0.111111	"	Inches	0.013837
"	Liters	9.091920	"	Picas	0.0833333
"	Pints (Brit.)	16	Poises	Cgs. units of absolute viscosity	1
"	Quarterns (Brit., dry)	4	"	Grams/(cm. × sec.)	1
"	Quarters (Brit., dry)	0.03125	Poise-cu. cm./gram	Sq. cm./sec.	1
"	Quarts (Brit.)	8	Poise-cu. ft./lb	Sq. cm./sec.	62.427960
"	Quarts (U.S., dry)	8.256449	Poise-cu. in./gram	Sq. cm./sec.	16.387064
Pecks (U.S.)	Barrels (U.S., dry)	0.076191185	Poles/sq. cm	E.M. cgs. units of magnetization	1
"	Bushels (U.S.)	0.25	Pottles (Brit.)	Gallons (Brit.)	0.5
"	Cu. cm	8809.7675	"	Liters	2.272980
"	Cu. feet	0.311114005	Poundals	Dynes	13825.50
"	Cu. inches	537.605	"	Grams	14.09808
"	Gallons (U.S., dry)	2	"	Pounds (avdp.)	0.0310810
"	Gallons (U.S., liq.)	2.3272944	Pounds (apoth. or troy)	Drams (apoth. or troy)	96
"	Liters	8.809521	"	Drams (avdp.)	210.65143
"	Pints (U.S., dry)	16	"	Grains	5760
"	Quarts (U.S., dry)	8	"	Grams	373.24172
Pennyweights	Drams (apoth. or troy)	0.4	"	Kilograms	0.37324172
"	Drams (avdp.)	0.87771429	"	Ounces (apoth. or troy)	12
"	Grains	24	"	Ounces (avdp.)	13.165714
"	Grams	1.55517384	"	Pennyweights	240
"	Ounces (apoth. or troy)	0.05	"	Pounds (avdp.)	0.8228571
"	Ounces (avdp.)	0.054857143	"	Scruples (apoth.)	288
"	Pounds (apoth. or troy)	0.0041666	"	Tons (long)	0.00036734694
"	Pounds (avdp.)	0.0034285714	"	Tons (metric)	0.00037324172
Perches (masonry)	Cu. feet	24.75	"	Tons (short)	0.00041142857
Phots	Foot-candles	929.0304	Pounds (avdp.)	Drams (apoth. or troy)	116.6666
"	Lumens/sq. cm	1	"	Drams (avdp.)	256
"	Lumens/sq. meter	10000	"	Grains	7000
"	Lux	10000	"	Grams	453.59237
Picas (printer's)	Centimeters	0.42175176	"	Hundredweights (long)	0.00892857
"	Inches	0.166044	"	Hundredweights (short)	0.01
Pints (Brit.)	Cu. cm	568.26092	"	Kilograms	0.45359237
"	Gallons (Brit.)	0.125	"	Ounces (apoth. or troy)	14.583333
"	Gills (Brit.)	4	"	Ounces (avdp.)	16
"	Gills (U.S.)	4.803797			
"	Liters	0.5682450			

* Based on density of 1 gram/ml. for the solvent.

CONVERSION FACTORS (Continued)

To convert from	To	Multiply by	To convert from	To	Multiply by
...nds (avdp.).....	Pennyweights............	291.6666	Quarterns (Brit., liq.).	Gallons (Brit.)...........	0.03125
"	Poundals................	32.1740	"	Liters....................	0.1420613
"	Pounds (apoth. *or* troy)...	1.215277	Quarters (U.S., long)..	Kilograms................	254.0117272
"	Scruples (apoth.)........	350	" ...	Pounds (avdp.)..........	560
"	Slugs...................	0.0310810	Quarters (U.S., short).	Kilograms................	226.796185
"	Tons (long).............	0.00044642857	"	Pounds.................	500
"	Tons (metric)..........	0.00045359237	Quarts (Brit.)........	Cu. cm................	1136.522
"	Tons (short)...........	0.0005	"	Cu. inches.............	69.35482
...nds of H₂O			"	Gallons (Brit.).........	0.25
vap. from and			"	Gallons (U.S., liq.)....	0.3002373
...t 212°F.........	B.t.u.................	970.9	"	Liters..................	1.136490
"	B.t.u. (IST.)...........	970.2	"	Quarts (U.S., dry)......	1.032056
"	B.t.u. (mean)...........	969.4	"	Quarts (U.S., liq.).....	1.200949
"	Joules.................	1.0237×10^6	Quarts (U.S., dry)....	Bushels (U.S.).........	0.03125
"	Joules (Int.)...........	1.0234×10^6	" ...	Cu. cm................	1101.2209
...nds/cu. ft.......	Grams/cu. cm..........	0.016018463	"	Cu. feet...............	0.038889251
"	Kg./cu. meter..........	16.018463	"	Cu. inches.............	67.200625
...nds/cu. inch......	Grams/cu. cm..........	27.679905	"	Gallons (U.S., dry).....	0.25
"	Grams/liter...........	27.68068	"	Gallons (U.S., liq.)....	0.29091180
"	Kg./cu. meter..........	27679.905	"	Liters..................	1.1011901
...nds/gal. (Brit.).	Pounds/cu. ft..........	6.228839	"	Pecks (U.S.)...........	0.125
...nds/gal. (U.S.,			"	Pints (U.S., dry).......	2
...q.)...............	Grams/cu. cm..........	0.11982643	Quarts (U.S., liq.)....	Cu. cm................	946.35295
"	Pounds/cu. ft..........	7.4805195	"	Cu. feet...............	0.033420136
...nds/inch.........	Grams/cm..............	178.57967	"	Cu. inches.............	57.75
"	Grams/ft..............	5443.1084	"	Drams (U.S., fluid).....	256
"	Grams/inch............	453.59237	"	Gallons (U.S., dry).....	0.21484175
"	Ounces/cm.............	6.2992	"	Gallons (U.S., liq.)....	0.25
"	Ounces/inch...........	16	"	Gills (U.S.)...........	8
"	Pounds/meter..........	39.370079	"	Liters..................	0.9463264
...nds/minute......	Kilograms/hr..........	27.2155422	"	Ounces (U.S., fluid)....	32
"	Kilograms/min.........	0.45359237	"	Pints (U.S., liq.)......	2
...nds of H₂O			"	Quarts (Brit.).........	0.8326747
...39.2°F.)/min.....	Cu. ft./min...........	0.01601891	"	Quarts (U.S., dry).....	0.8593670
"	Gal. (U.S.)/min.......	0.1198298	Quintals (metric)....	Grams.................	100000
"	Liters/min............	0.45359237	"	Hundredweights (long)....	1.9684131
...nds/sq. ft.......	Atmospheres...........	0.000472541	"	Kilograms..............	100
"	Bars..................	0.000478803	"	Pounds (avdp.).........	220.46226
"	Cm. of Hg (0°C.)......	0.0359131			
"	Dynes/sq. cm..........	478.803	Radians..............	Circumferences.........	0.15915494
"	Ft. of air (1 atm., 60°F.).	13.096	"	Degrees................	57.295779
"	Grams/sq. cm..........	0.48824276	"	Minutes................	3437.7468
"	In. of Hg (32°F.)......	0.0141390	"	Quadrants..............	0.63661977
"	In. of H₂O (39.2°F.)......	0.192227	"	Revolutions............	0.15915494
"	Kg./sq. meter..........	4.8824276	"	Seconds................	206264.81
"	Mm. of Hg (0°C.)......	0.359131	Radians/cm...........	Degrees/cm............	57.295779
...nds/sq. inch.....	Atmospheres...........	0.0680460	"	Degrees/ft.............	1746.3754
"	Bars..................	0.0689476	"	Degrees/inch...........	145.53128
"	Cm. of Hg (0°C.)......	5.17149	"	Minutes/cm............	3437.7468
"	Cm. of H₂O (4°C.)......	70.3089	Radians/sec..........	Degrees/sec............	57.295779
"	Dynes/sq. cm..........	68947.6	"	Revolutions/min........	9.5492966
"	Grams/sq. cm..........	70.306958	"	Revolutions/sec........	0.15915494
"	In. of Hg (32°F.)......	2.03602	Radians/(sec. × sec.).	Revolutions/(min. × min.)	572.95779
"	In. of H₂O (39.2°F.)....	27.6807	" ..	Revolutions/(min. × sec.).	9.5492966
"	Kg./sq. cm............	0.070306958	"	Revolutions/(sec. × sec.).	0.15915494
"	Mm. of Hg (0°C.)......	51.7149	Register tons........	Cu. feet...............	100
...nd wt.-sec./sq. ft..	Poises................	478.803	"	Cu. meters.............	2.8316847
...nd wt.-sec./sq. in..	Poises................	68947.6	Revolutions..........	Degrees................	360
...ncheons (Brit.)..	Cu. meters............	0.31797510	"	Grades................	400
"	Gallons (Brit.)........	69.94467	"	Quadrants..............	4
"	Gallons (U.S.).........	84	"	Radians................	6.2831853
			Reyns	Centipoises............	6.89476×10^6
...adrants...........	Minutes...............	5400	Rhes................	Poises⁻¹...............	1
"	Radians...............	1.5707963	Rods................	Centimeters............	502.92
...arterns (Brit., dry).	Buckets (Brit.)........	0.125	"	Chains (Gunter's)......	0.25
"	Bushels (Brit.)........	0.0625	"	Chains (Ramden's)......	0.165
"	Cu. cm................	2273.044	"	Feet..................	16.5
"	Gallons (Brit.)........	0.5	"	Feet (U.S. Survey).....	16.499967
"	Liters.................	2.272980	"	Furlongs...............	0.025
"	Pecks (Brit.)..........	0.25	"	Inches................	198
...arterns (Brit., liq.).	Cu. cm................	142.0652	"	Links (Gunter's).......	25

CONVERSION FACTORS (Continued)

To convert from	To	Multiply by
Rods	Links (Ramden's)	16.5
"	Meters	5.0292
"	Miles (statute)	0.003125
"	Perches	1
"	Yards	5.5
Rods (Brit., volume)	Cu. feet	1000
"	Cu. meters	28.316847
Roods (Brit.)	Acres	0.25
"	Ares	10.117141
"	Sq. perches	40
"	Sq. yards	1210
Ropes (Brit.)	Feet	20
"	Meters	6.096
"	Yards	6.6666666
Scruples (apoth.)	Drams (apoth. or troy)	0.333333
"	Drams (avdp.)	0.73142857
"	Grains	20
"	Grams	1.2959782
"	Ounces (apoth. or troy)	0.041666
"	Ounces (avdp.)	0.045714286
"	Pennyweights	0.833333
"	Pounds (apoth. or troy)	0.003472222
"	Pounds (avdp.)	0.0028571429
Scruples (Brit., fluid)	Minims (Brit.)	20
Seams (Brit.)	Bushels (Brit.)	8
"	Cu. feet	10.27479
"	Liters	290.9414
Seconds (angular)	Degrees	0.000277777
"	Minutes	0.0166666
"	Radians	4.8481368×10^{-6}
Seconds (mean solar)	Days (mean solar)	1.1574074×10^{-5}
"	Days (sidereal)	1.1605763×10^{-5}
"	Hours (mean solar)	0.0002777777
"	Hours (sidereal)	0.00027853831
"	Minutes (mean solar)	0.0166666
"	Minutes (sidereal)	0.016712298
"	Seconds (sidereal)	1.00273791
Seconds (sidereal)	Days (mean solar)	1.1542472×10^{-5}
"	Days (sidereal)	1.1574074×10^{-5}
"	Hours (mean solar)	0.00027701932
"	Hours (sidereal)	0.000277777
"	Minutes (mean solar)	0.016621159
"	Minutes (sidereal)	0.0166666
"	Seconds (mean solar)	0.99726957
Siemen's units	*Same as Mhos*	
Skeins	Feet	360
"	Meters	109.728
Slugs	Geepounds	1
"	Kilograms	14.5939
"	Pounds (avdp.)	32.1740
Slugs/cu. ft.	Grams/cu. cm.	0.515379
Space (entire)	Hemispheres	2
"	Steradians	12.566371
Spans	Centimeters	22.86
"	Fathoms	0.125
"	Feet	0.75
"	Inches	9
"	Quarters (Brit. linear)	1
Spherical right angles	Hemispheres	0.25
"	Spheres	0.125
"	Steradians	1.5707963
Sq. centimeters	Ares	1×10^{-6}
"	Circ. mm	127.32395
"	Circ. mils	197352.52
"	Sq. chains (Gunter's)	2.4710538×10^{-7}
"	Sq. chains (Ramden's)	1.0763910×10^{-7}
"	Sq. decimeters	0.01
"	Sq. feet	0.0010763910
"	Sq. ft. (U.S. Survey)	0.0010763867
"	Sq. inches	0.15500031
"	Sq. meters	0.0001

To convert from	To	Multiply by
Sq. centimeters	Sq. mm	100
"	Sq. mils	155000.31
"	Sq. rods	3.9536861×10^{-6}
"	Sq. yards	0.00011959900
Sq. chains (Gunter's)	Acres	0.1
"	Sq. feet	4356
"	Sq. ft. (U.S. Survey)	4355.9826
"	Sq. inches	627264
"	Sq. links (Gunter's)	10000
"	Sq. meters	404.68564
"	Sq. miles	0.00015625
"	Sq. rods	16
"	Sq. yards	484
Sq. chains (Ramden's)	Acres	0.22956841
"	Sq. feet	10000
"	Sq. ft. (U.S. Survey)	9999.9600
"	Sq. inches	1.44×10^{6}
"	Sq. links (Ramden's)	10000
"	Sq. meters	929.0304
"	Sq. miles	0.00035870064
"	Sq. rods	36.730946
"	Sq. yards	1111.111
Sq. decimeters	Sq. cm	100
"	Sq. inches	15.500031
Square degrees	Steradians	0.00030461742
Sq. dekameters	Acres	0.024710538
"	Ares	1
"	Sq. meters	100
"	Sq. yards	119.59900
Sq. feet	Acres	2.295684×10^{-5}
"	Ares	0.0009290304
"	Sq. cm	929.0304
"	Sq. chains (Gunter's)	0.00022956841
"	Sq. ft. (U.S. Survey)	0.99999600
"	Sq. inches	144
"	Sq. links (Gunter's)	2.2956841
"	Sq. meters	0.09290304
"	Sq. miles	3.5870064×10^{-8}
"	Sq. rods	0.0036730946
"	Sq. yards	0.111111
Sq. feet (U.S. Survey)	Acres	$2.29569330 \times 10^{-5}$
"	Sq. centimeters	929.03412
"	Sq. chains (Ramden's)	0.00010000040
"	Sq. feet	1.0000040
Sq. hectometers	Sq. meters	10000
Sq. inches	Circ. mils	1273239.5
"	Sq. cm	6.4516
"	Sq. chains (Gunter's)	1.5942251×10^{-6}
"	Sq. decimeters	0.064516
"	Sq. feet	0.0069444
"	Sq. ft. (U.S. Survey)	0.0069444167
"	Sq. links (Gunter's)	0.01594225
"	Sq. meters	0.00064516
"	Sq. miles	$2.4909767 \times 10^{-10}$
"	Sq. mm	645.16
"	Sq. mils	1×10^{6}
Sq. inches/sec	Sq. cm./hr	23225.76
"	Sq. cm./sec	6.4516
"	Sq. ft./min	0.416666
Sq. kilometers	Acres	247.10538
"	Sq. feet	1.0763910×10^{7}
"	Sq. ft. (U.S. Survey)	1.0763867×10^{7}
"	Sq. inches	1.5500031×10^{9}
"	Sq. meters	1×10^{6}
"	Sq. miles	0.38610216
"	Sq. yards	1.1959900×10^{6}
Sq. links (Gunter's)	Acres	1×10^{-5}
"	Sq. cm	404.68564
"	Sq. chains (Gunter's)	0.0001
"	Sq. feet	0.4356
"	Sq. ft. (U.S. Survey)	0.43559826
"	Sq. Inches	62.7264

CONVERSION FACTORS (Continued)

To convert from	To	Multiply by
links (Ramden's)..	Acres..................	2.2956841×10^{-5}
" " ..	Sq. feet..................	1
meters..........	Acres..................	0.00024710538
"	Ares..................	0.01
"	Hectares..................	0.0001
"	Sq. cm..................	10000
"	Sq. feet..................	10.763910
"	Sq. inches..................	1550.0031
"	Sq. kilometers..................	1×10^{-6}
"	Sq. links (Gunter's)......	24.710538
"	Sq. links (Ramden's)......	10.763910
"	Sq. miles..................	3.8610216×10^{-7}
"	Sq. mm..................	1×10^{6}
"	Sq. rods..................	0.039536861
"	Sq. yards..................	1.1959900
miles..........	Acres..................	640
"	Hectares..................	258.99881
"	Sq. chains (Gunter's).....	6400
"	Sq. feet..................	2.7878288×10^{7}
"	Sq. ft. (U.S. Survey).....	2.78288×10^{7}
"	Sq. kilometers..................	2.5899881
"	Sq. meters..................	2589988.1
"	Sq. rods..................	102400
"	Sq. yards..................	3.0976×10^{6}
millimeters.....	Circ. mm..................	1.2732395
"	Circ. mils..................	1973.5252
"	Sq. cm..................	0.01
"	Sq. inches..................	0.0015500031
"	Sq. meters..................	1×10^{-6}
mils.....	Circ. mils..................	1.2732395
"	Sq. cm..................	6.4516×10^{-6}
"	Sq. inches..................	1×10^{-6}
"	Sq. mm..................	0.00064516
rods.....	Acres..................	0.00625
"	Ares..................	0.2529285264
"	Hectares..................	0.002529285264
"	Sq. cm..................	252928.5264
"	Sq. feet..................	272.25
"	Sq. ft. (U.S. Survey).....	272.24891
"	Sq. inches..................	39204
"	Sq. links (Gunter's)......	625
"	Sq. links (Ramden's)......	272.25
"	Sq. meters..................	25.29285264
"	Sq. miles..................	9.765625×10^{-6}
"	Sq. yards..................	30.25
yards.....	Acres..................	0.00020661157
"	Ares..................	0.0083612736
"	Hectares..................	8.3612736×10^{-5}
"	Sq. cm..................	8361.2736
"	Sq. chains (Gunter's).....	0.0020661157
"	Sq. chains (Ramden's).....	0.0009
"	Sq. feet..................	9
"	Sq. ft. (U.S. Survey)....	8.9999640
"	Sq. inches..................	1296
"	Sq. links (Gunter's)......	20.661157
"	Sq. links (Ramden's)......	9
"	Sq. meters..................	0.83612736
"	Sq. miles..................	$3.228305785 \times 10^{-7}$
"	Sq. perches (Brit.).....	0.033057851
"	Sq. rods..................	0.033057851
atamperes.....	Abamperes..................	3.335635×10^{-11}
"	Amperes..................	3.335635×10^{-10}
"	E.M. cgs. units of current.	3.335635×10^{-11}
"	E.S. cgs. units..................	1
atcoulombs.....	Ampere-hours..................	9.265653×10^{-14}
"	Coulombs..................	3.335635×10^{-10}
"	Electronic charges..................	2.082093×10^{9}
"	E.M. cgs. units of electric charge..................	3.335635×10^{-11}
atfarads.....	E.M. cgs. units of capacitance..................	1.112646×10^{-21}
"	E.S. cgs. units..................	1

To convert from	To	Multiply by
Statfarads	Farads..................	1.112646×10^{-19}
"	Microfarads..................	1.112646×10^{-6}
Stathenries	Abhenries..................	8.987584×10^{20}
"	E.M. cgs. units of inductance..................	8.987584×10^{20}
"	E.S. cgs. units..................	1
"	Henries..................	8.987584×10^{11}
"	Millihenries..................	8.987584×10^{14}
Statohms..........	Abohms..................	8.987584×10^{20}
"	E.S. cgs. units..................	1
"	Ohms..................	8.987584×10^{11}
Statvolts	Abvolts..................	2.997930×10^{10}
"	Volts..................	299.7930
Statvolts/cm	Volts/cm..................	299.7930
"	Volts/inch..................	761.4742
Statvolts/inch....	Volts/cm..................	118.0287
Steradians..........	Hemispheres..................	0.15915494
"	Solid angles..................	0.079577472
"	Spheres..................	0.079577472
"	Spher. right angles..................	0.63661977
"	Square degrees..................	3282.8063
Steres..........	Cubic meters..................	1
"	Decisteres..................	10
"	Dekasteres..................	0.1
"	Liters..................	999.972
Stilbs..........	Candles/sq. cm..................	1
"	Candles/sq. inch..................	6.4516
"	Lamberts..................	3.1415927
Stokes	Cgs. units of kinematic viscosity..................	1
"	Sq. cm./sec..................	1
"	Sq. inches/sec..................	0.15500031
"	Poise cu. cm./gram......	1
Stones (Brit., legal)...	Centals (Brit.)..................	0.14
Tons (long)..........	Dynes..................	9.96402×10^{8}
"	Hundredweights (long)....	20
"	Hundredweights (short)...	22.4
"	Kilograms..................	1016.0469
"	Ounces (avdp.)..................	35840
"	Pounds (apoth. or troy).	2722.22
"	Pounds (avdp.)..................	2240
"	Tons (metric)..................	1.0160469
"	Tons (short)..................	1.12
Tons (metric)..........	Dynes..................	9.80665×10^{8}
"	Grams..................	1×10^{6}
"	Hundredweights (short)..	22.046226
"	Kilograms..................	1000
"	Ounces (avdp.)..................	35273.962
"	Pounds (apoth. or troy)..	2679.2289
"	Pounds (avdp.)..................	2204.6226
"	Tons (long)..................	0.98420653
"	Tons (short)..................	1.1023113
Tons (short)..........	Dynes..................	8.89644×10^{8}
"	Hundredweights (short)..	20
"	Kilograms..................	907.18474
"	Ounces (avdp.)..................	32000
"	Pounds (apoth. or troy).	2430.555
"	Pounds (avdp.)..................	2000
"	Tons (long)..................	0.89285714
"	Tons (metric)..................	0.90718474
Tons of refrig. (U.S., comm.)..................	B.t.u. (IST.)/hr..	12000
"	B.t.u. (IST.)/min..	200
"	Cal., kg. (IST.)/hr..	3023.949
"	Horsepower..................	4.71611
"	Kg. of ice melted/hr.....	37.971
"	Lb. of ice melted/hr......	83.711
Tons of refrig. (U.S., std.)..................	B.t.u. (IST.)..................	288000
"	B.t.u. (mean)..................	287774
"	Cal., kg. (IST.)..................	72574.8

CONVERSION FACTORS (Continued)

To convert from	To	Multiply by
Tons of refrig. (U.S., std.)	Cal., kg. (mean)	72517.9
"	Lb. of ice melted	2009.1
Tons (long)/sq. ft	Atmospheres	1.05849
"	Dynes/sq. cm	1.07252×10^6
"	Grams/sq. cm	1093.6638
"	Pounds/sq. ft	2240
Tons (short)/sq. ft	Atmospheres	0.945082
"	Dynes/sq. cm	957.605
"	Grams/sq. cm	976.486
"	Pounds/sq. inch	13.8888
Tons (long)/sq. in	Atmospheres	152.423
"	Dynes/sq. cm	1.54443×10^8
"	Grams/sq. cm	157487.59
Tons (short)/sq. in	Dynes/sq. cm	1.37895×10^8
"	Kg./sq. mm	1406.139
"	Pounds/sq. inch	2000
Torrs (or Tors)	Millimeters of Hg (0°C.)	1
Townships (U.S.)	Acres	23040
"	Sections	36
"	Sq. miles	36
Tuns	Gallons (U.S.)	252
"	Hogsheads	4
Volts	Abvolts	1×10^8
"	Mks. (r or nr) units	1
"	Statvolts	0.003335635
"	Volts (Int.)	0.999670
Volts (Int.)	Volts	1.000330
Volts/°C.	Joules/(coulomb $\times$ °C.)	1
Volt-coulombs	Joules (Int.)	0.999835
Volt-coulombs (Int.)	Joules	1.000165
Volt-electronic charge-seconds	Planck's constant*	2.41814×10^{14}
Volt-faraday (chem.)-seconds	Planck's constant*	1.45650×10^{38}
Volt-faraday (phys.)-seconds	Planck's constant	1.45690×10^{38}
Volt-seconds	Maxwells	1×10^8
Watts	B.t.u./hr	3.41443
"	B.t.u. (mean)/hr	3.40952
"	B.t.u. (mean)/min	0.0568253
"	B.t.u./sec	0.000948451
"	B.t.u. (mean)/sec	0.000947088
"	Cal., gm./hr	860.421
"	Cal., gm. (mean)/hr	859.184
"	Cal., gm. (20°C.)/hr	860.853
"	Cal., gm./min	14.3403
"	Cal., gm. (IST.)/min	14.3310
"	Cal., gm. (mean)/min	14.3197
"	Cal., kh./min	0.0143403
"	Cal., kg. (IST.)/min	0.0143310
"	Cal., kg. (mean)/min	0.0143197
"	Ergs/sec	1×10^7
"	Foot-pounds/min	44.2537
"	Horsepower	0.00134102
"	Horsepower (boiler)	0.000101942
"	Horsepower (elec.)	0.00134048
"	Horsepower (metric)	0.00135962
"	Joules/sec	1
"	Kilowatts	0.001
"	Liter-atm./hr	35.5282
Watts (Int.)	B.t.u./hr	3.41499
"	B.t.u. (mean)/hr	3.41008
"	B.t.u./min	0.569165
"	B.t.u. (mean)/min	0.0568347
"	Cal., gm./hr	860.563
"	Cal., gm. (mean)/hr	859.326
"	Cal., kg./min	0.0143427
"	Cal., kg. (IST.)/min	0.0143333
"	Cal., kg. (mean)/min	0.0143221

To convert from	To	Multiply by
Watts (Int.)	Ergs/sec	1.000165×10^7
"	Joules (Int.)/sec	1
"	Watts	1.000165
Watts/sq. cm	B.t.u./(hr. $\times$ sq. ft.)	3172.10
"	Cal., gm./(hr. $\times$ sq. cm.)	860.421
"	Ft.-lb./(min. $\times$ sq. ft.)	41113.1
Watts/sq. in	B.t.u./(hr. $\times$ sq. ft.)	491.677
"	Cal., gm./(hr. $\times$ sq. cm.)	133.365
"	Ft.-lb./(min. $\times$ sq. ft.)	6372.54
Watt-hours	B.t.u.	3.41443
"	B.t.u. (mean)	3.40952
"	Cal., gm.	860.421
Watt-hours	Cal., kg.	0.859184
"	Cal., gm. (mean)	859.184
"	Foot-pounds	2655.22
"	Hp.-hours	0.00134102
"	Joules	3600
"	Joules (Int.)	3599.41
"	Kg.-meters	367.098
"	Kw.-hours	0.001
"	Watt-hours (Int.)	0.999835
Watt-sec	Foot-pounds	0.737562
"	Gram-cm	10197.16
"	Joules	1
"	Liter-atm	0.00986895
"	Volt-coulombs	1
Wave length of orange-red line of krypton 86	Ångström units	6057.80211
"	Millimeters	0.000605780211
Wave length of red line of cadmium	Ångström units	6438.4696
"	Millimeters	0.00064384696
Webers	Cgs. units of induction flux	1×10^8
"	E.M. cgs. units of induction flux	1×10^8
"	Lines	1×10^8
"	Maxwells	1×10^8
"	Mks. units of induction flux	1
"	Mks. units of magnetic charge	0.079577472
"	Mks. units of magnetic charge	1
"	Volt-seconds	1
Webers/sq. cm	Gausses	1×10^8
"	Lines	1×10^8
"	Lines/sq. inch	6.4516×10^8
Webers/sq. in	Gausses	1.5500031×10^7
Weeks (mean calendar)	Days (mean solar)	7
"	Days (sidereal)	7.0191654
"	Hours (mean solar)	168
"	Hours (sidereal)	168.45997
"	Minutes (mean solar)	10080
"	Minutes (sidereal)	10107.598
"	Months (lunar)	0.23704235
"	Months (mean calendar)	0.23013699
"	Years (calendar)	0.019178082
"	Years (sidereal)	0.019164622
"	Years (tropical)	0.019165365
Weys (Brit., mass.)	Pounds (avdp.)	252
Yards	Centimeters	91.44
"	Chains (Gunter's)	0.4545454
"	Chains (Ramden's)	0.03
"	Cubits	2
"	Fathoms	0.5
"	Feet	3
"	Feet (U.S. Survey)	2.9999940
"	Furlongs	0.00454545
"	Inches	36
"	Meters	0.9144
"	Poles (Brit.)	0.181818

* For factors for C = 12 scale or those which can be derived from same see table on Values for General Physical Constants.

CONVERSION FACTORS (Continued)

To convert from	To	Multiply by	To convert from	To	Multiply by
rds............	Quarters (Brit., linear)....	4	Years (sidereal)......	Days (sidereal)...........	366.25640
"	Rods...................	0.181818	"	Years (calendar)..........	1.0007024
"	Spans..................	4	"	Years (tropical)..........	1.0000388
ars (calendar).....	Days (mean solar).......	365	Years (tropical)......	Days (mean solar).......	365.24219
"	Hours (mean solar)......	8760	"	Days (sidereal)...........	366.24219
"	Minutes (mean solar).....	525600	"	Hours (mean solar).......	8765.8126
"	Months (lunar)..........	12.360065	"	Hours (sidereal)..........	8789.8126
"	Months (mean calendar)...	12	"	Months (mean calendar)...	12.007963
"	Seconds (mean solar).....	3.1536×10^7	"	Seconds (mean solar).....	3.1556926×10^7
"	Weeks (mean calendar)....	52.142857	"	Seconds (sidereal)........	3.1643326×10^7
"	Years (sidereal)..........	0.99929814	"	Weeks (mean calendar)....	52.177456
"	Years (tropical)..........	0.99933690	"	Years (calendar)..........	1.0006635
ars (leap)........	Days (mean solar).......	366	"	Years (sidereal)..........	0.99996121
ars (sidereal)......	Days (mean solar).......	365.25636			

DECIMAL EQUIVALENTS OF COMMON FRACTIONS

		1/64	= 0.015 625		11/32	22/64	= 0.343 75				43/64	= 0.671 875
	1/32	2/64	= .031 25			23/64	= .359 375	11/16	22/32	44/64	= .687 5
		3/64	= .046 875	3/8	12/32	24/64	= .375			45/64	= .703 125
1/16	2/32	4/64	= .062 5			25/64	= .390 625		23/32	46/64	= .718 75
		5/64	= .078 125		13/32	26/64	= .406 25			47/64	= .734 375
	3/32	6/64	= .093 75			27/64	= .421 875	3/4	24/32	48/64	= .75
		7/64	= .109 375	7/16	14/32	28/64	= .437 5			49/64	= .765 625
1/8	4/32	8/64	= .125			29/64	= .453 125		25/32	50/64	= .781 25
		9/64	= .140 625		15/32	30/64	= .468 75			51/64	= .796 875
	5/32	10/64	= .156 25			31/64	= .484 375	13/16	26/32	52/64	= .812 5
		11/64	= .171 875	1/2	16/32	32/64	= .50			53/64	= .828 125
3/16	6/32	12/64	= .187 5			33/64	= .515 625		27/32	54/64	= .843 75
		13/64	= .203 125		17/32	34/64	= .531 25			55/64	= .859 375
	7/32	14/64	= .218 75			35/64	= .546 875	7/8	28/32	56/64	= .875
		15/64	= .234 375	9/16	18/32	36/64	= .562 5			57/64	= .890 625
1/4	8/32	16/64	= .25			37/64	= .578 125		29/32	58/64	= .906 25
		17/64	= .265 625		19/32	38/64	= .593 75			59/64	= .921 875
	9/32	18/64	= .281 25			39/64	= .609 375	15/16	30/32	60/64	= .937 5
		19/64	= .296 875	5/8	20/32	40/64	= .625			61/64	= .953 125
5/16	10/32	20/64	= .312 5			41/64	= .640 625		31/32	62/64	= .968 75
		21/64	= .328 125		21/32	42/64	= .656 25			63/64	= .984 375

FUNDAMENTAL PHYSICAL CONSTANTS

Dr. E. Richard Cohen

The following table contains data which are a tentative revision of the 1963 values of the fundamental physical constants.

It has become increasingly clear in the last several years that the 1963 analysis of the fundamental physical constants by Cohen and DuMond must be revised and that the values recommended at the time are in error by as much as 100 ppm. The strongest evidence for this revision came from the measurement in 1967 of macroscopic phase coherence in superconductors by Langenberg, Parker and Taylor at the University of Pennsylvania. Their measured value of the quantum of magnetic flux ($h/2e$), measured with an accuracy of 4 ppm, was inconsistent with the 1963 recommendation by 10 times that amount. This verified the growing evidence from spectroscopic and microwave data that the value of the fine structure constant needed a revision of 20 ppm.

It is therefore clear that a complete revision of the 1963 recommendation is necessary. Such a revision will of course include experimental data in addition to that on the fine structure constant, including careful attention to the electrical standards maintained by each national standards laboratory as recalibrated with respect to BIPM in 1968, effective January 1, 1969.

The following table of numerical values of the physical constants is intended as a general indication of the extent of the revision required in the 1963 values. Because of the tentative nature, and since the full effect of experimental correlations between data have not been calculated, no errors are quoted for these values. The numerical values, although tentative, and not representing a full reassessment of the available data are believed to be more reliable than the 1963 values. A more recent discussion of the status of the physical constants as of approximately January, 1969, is given by B. N. Taylor, W. H. Parker, and D. N. Langenberg in Reviews of Modern Physics, July 1969.

FUNDAMENTAL PHYSICAL CONSTANTS

Constant	Symbol	Old value	New value		*Correction ppm
Speed of light in vacuum	c	2.997925_1	2.997925	$\times 10^8$ ms^{-1}	0
Gravitational constant	G	6.670_5	6.670	10^{-11} Nm^{2}kg^{-2}	0
Elementary charge	e	1.60210_2	1.6022	10^{-19}C	$+60$
		4.80298_7	4.8032	10^{-10} esu	$+60$
Avogadro constant	N_A	6.02252_9	6.0222	10^{26} kmole^{-1}	-60
Mass unit	u	1.66043_2	1.66053	10^{-27} kg	$+60$
Electron rest mass	m_e	9.10908_{13}	9.1096	10^{-31} kg	$+60$
		5.48597_3	5.48593	10^{-4} u	0
Proton rest mass	m_p	1.67252_3	1.67262	10^{-27} kg	$+60$
		1.00727663_8	1.00727661	u	0
Neutron rest mass	m_n	1.67482_3	1.67492	10^{-27} kg	$+60$
		1.0086654_4	1.0086652	u	0
Faraday constant	F	9.64870_5	9.6487	10^4C mole^{-1}	0
		2.8926_{125}	2.8926	10^{14} esu	0
Planck constant	h	6.62559_{16}	6.6262	10^{-34} Js	$+100$
	$h/2\pi$	1.054494_{25}	1.05459	10^{-34} Js	$+100$
Fine-structure constant	α	7.29720_3	7.29735	10^{-3}	$+20$
$2\pi e^2/hc$	$1/\alpha$	137.0388_6	137.0360		-20
Charge-to-mass ratio	e/m_e	1.758796_6	1.75880	10^{11}C kg^{-1}	0
for electron		5.27274_2	5.27276	10^{17} esu	0
Quantum of magnetic flux	hc/e	4.13556_4	4.13571	10^{-11} Wb	$+40$
		1.379474_{13}	1.37952	10^{-17} esu	$+40$
Rydberg constant	R_∞	1.0973731_1	1.0973731	10^7 m^{-1}	0
Bohr radius	a_0	5.29167_2	5.29177	10^{-11} m	$+20$
Compton wavelength of	$\lambda_c = h/m_ec$	2.42621_2	2.42631	10^{-12} m	$+40$
electron	$\lambda_c/2\pi$	3.86144_3	3.86159	10^{-13} m	$+40$
Gyromagnetic ratio of	γ	2.675192_7	2.67519	10^8 rad s^{-1}T^{-1}	0
proton	$\gamma/2\pi$	4.25770_1	4.2577	10^7 Hz T^{-1}	0
(Uncorrected for	γ'	2.675123_7	$\dagger 2.67512$	10^8 s^{-1}T^{-1}	0
diamagnetism H$_2$O)	$\gamma'/2\pi$	4.25759_1	$\dagger 4.257586$	10^7 Hz T^{-1}	0
Bohr magneton	μ_B	9.2732_2	9.2741	10^{-24} J T^{-1}	$+100$
Nuclear magneton	μ_N	5.05050_{13}	5.0510	10^{-27} J T^{-1}	$+100$
Proton Moment	μ_p	1.41049_4	1.4106	10^{-26} J T^{-1}	$+80$
	μ_p/μ_N	2.79276_2	2.79278		0
(Uncorrected for diamagnetism in H$_2$O sample)		2.79268_2	2.79271		0
Gas constant	R_0	8.31434_{35}	8.3143	J deg^{-1} mole^{-1}	0
Boltzmann constant	k	1.38054_6	1.3806	10^{-23} J deg^{-1}	$+60$
First radiation constant $(2\pi hc^2)$	c_1	3.74150_9	3.7418	10^{-16} W m^2	$+80$
Second radiation constant (hc/k)	c_2	1.43879_6	1.4388	10^{-2} m deg	0
Stephan-Boltzmann constant	σ	5.6697_{10}	5.6696	10^{-8} W m^{-2} deg^{-4}	-20

* This column gives the correction resulting only from the increase of 20 ppm in the value of the fine structure constant, not the total change from 1963 to the tentative new value.

† The value for the gyromagnetic ratio of the proton has been recommended by the Comité International des Poids et Mesures in their meeting of 14–17 October 1968 for international metrological usage. This value is based on the 1969 BIPM scales of resistance and electromotive force which are in agreement, as exactly as is possible, with the (absolute) definitions of electrical units adopted by the Conférence Generale des Poids et Mesures.

CONSTANTS AND CONVERSION FACTORS
MISCELLANEOUS CONSTANTS

PHYSICAL CONSTANTS

Equatorial radius of the earth = 6378.388 km = 3963.34 miles (statute).
Polar radius of the earth, 6356.912 km = 3949.99 miles (statute).
1 degree of latitude at $40°$ = 69 miles.
1 international nautical mile = 1.15078 miles (statute) = 1852 m = 6076.115 ft.
Mean density of the earth = 5.522 g/cm^3 = 344.7 lb/ft^3.
Constant of gravitation, $(6.673 \pm 0.003) \times 10^3$ cm^3 gm^{-1} s^{-2}.
Acceleration due to gravity at sea level, latitude $45°$ = 980.665cm/s^2 = 32.1740 ft/sec^2
Length of seconds pendulum at sea level, latitude $45°$ = 99.3574 cm = 39.1171 in.
1 knot (international) = 101.269 ft/min = 1.6878 ft/sec = 1.1508 miles (statute)/hr.
1 micron = 10^{-4} cm.
1 angstrom = 10^{-8} cm.
Mass of hydrogen atom = $(1.67339 \pm 0.0031) \times 10^{-24}$ g.
Density of mercury at $0°C$ = 13.5955 g/ml.
Density of water at $3.98°C$ = 1.000000 g/ml.
Density, maximum, of water, at $3.98°C$ = 0.999973 g/cm^3.
Density of dry air at $0°C$, 760 mm = 1.2929 g/liter.
Velocity of sound in dry air at $0°C$ = 331.36 m/s - 1087.1 ft/sec.
Velocity of light in vacuum = $(2.997925 \pm 0.000002) \times 10^{10}$ cm/s.
Heat of fusion of water $0°C$ = 79.71 cal/g.
Heat of vaporization of water $100°C$ = 539.55 cal/g.
Electrochemical equivalent of silver 0.001118 g/sec international amp.
Absolute wave length of red cadmium light in air at $15°C$, 760 mm pressure = 6438.4696 A.
Wave length of orange-red line of krypton 86 = 6057.802 A.

π CONSTANTS

$$\pi = 3.14159\ 26535\ 89793\ 23846\ 26433\ 83279\ 50288\ 41971\ 69399\ 37511$$
$$1/\pi = 0.31830\ 98861\ 83790\ 67153\ 77675\ 26745\ 02872\ 40689\ 19291\ 48091$$
$$\pi^2 = 9.86960\ 44010\ 89358\ 61883\ 44909\ 99876\ 15113\ 53136\ 99407\ 24079$$
$$\log_e \pi = 1.14472\ 98858\ 49400\ 17414\ 34273\ 51353\ 05871\ 16472\ 94812\ 91531$$
$$\log_{10} \pi = 0.49714\ 98726\ 94133\ 85435\ 12682\ 88290\ 89887\ 36516\ 78324\ 38044$$
$$\log_{10} \sqrt{2\pi} = 0.39908\ 99341\ 79057\ 52478\ 25035\ 91507\ 69595\ 02099\ 34102\ 92128$$

CONSTANTS INVOLVING e

$$e = 2.71828\ 18284\ 59045\ 23536\ 02874\ 71352\ 66249\ 77572\ 47093\ 69996$$
$$1/e = 0.36787\ 94411\ 71442\ 32159\ 55237\ 70161\ 46086\ 74458\ 11131\ 03177$$
$$e^2 = 7.38905\ 60989\ 30650\ 22723\ 04274\ 60575\ 00781\ 31803\ 15570\ 55185$$
$$M = \log_{10} e = 0.43429\ 44819\ 03251\ 82765\ 11289\ 18916\ 60508\ 22943\ 97005\ 80367$$
$$1/M = \log_e 10 = 2.30258\ 50929\ 94045\ 68401\ 79914\ 54684\ 36420\ 76011\ 01488\ 62877$$
$$\log_{10} M = 9.63778\ 43113\ 00536\ 78912\ 29674\ 98645 - 10$$

π^e AND e^π CONSTANTS

$$\pi^e = 22.45915\ 77183\ 61045\ 47342\ 71522$$
$$e^\pi = 23.14069\ 26327\ 79269\ 00572\ 90864$$
$$e^{-\pi} = 0.04321\ 39182\ 63772\ 24977\ 44177$$
$$e^{\frac{1}{2}\pi} = 4.81047\ 73809\ 65351\ 65547\ 30357$$
$$i^i = e^{-\frac{1}{2}\pi} = 0.20787\ 95763\ 50761\ 90854\ 69556$$

NUMERICAL CONSTANTS

$$\sqrt{2} = 1.41421\ 35623\ 73095\ 04880\ 16887\ 24209\ 69807\ 85696\ 71875\ 37695$$
$$\sqrt[3]{2} = 1.25992\ 10498\ 94873\ 16476\ 72106\ 07278\ 22835\ 05702\ 51464\ 70151$$
$$\log_e 2 = 0.69314\ 71805\ 59945\ 30941\ 72321\ 21458\ 17656\ 80755\ 00134\ 36026$$
$$\log_{10} 2 = 0.30102\ 99956\ 63981\ 19521\ 37388\ 94724\ 49302\ 67681\ 89881\ 46211$$
$$\sqrt{3} = 1.73205\ 08075\ 68877\ 29352\ 74463\ 41505\ 87236\ 69428\ 05253\ 81039$$
$$\sqrt[3]{3} = 1.44224\ 95703\ 07408\ 38232\ 16383\ 10780\ 10958\ 83918\ 69253\ 49935$$
$$\log_e 3 = 1.09861\ 22886\ 68109\ 69139\ 52452\ 36922\ 52570\ 46474\ 90557\ 82275$$
$$\log_{10} 3 = 0.47712\ 12547\ 19662\ 43729\ 50279\ 03255\ 11530\ 92001\ 28864\ 19070$$

OTHER CONSTANTS

$$\text{Euler's Constant } \gamma = 0.57721\ 56649\ 01532\ 86061$$
$$\log_e \gamma = -0.54953\ 93129\ 81644\ 82234$$
$$\text{Golden Ratio } \phi = 1.61803\ 39887\ 49894\ 84820\ 45868\ 34365\ 63811\ 77203\ 09180$$

NUMBERS CONTAINING π

	Number	Logarithm		Number	Logarithm
π	3.1415 927	0.4971 499	$2\pi^2$	19.7392 088	1.2953 297
2π	6.2831 853	0.7981 799	$\pi/180$	0.0174 533	8.2418 774 − 10
3π	9.4247 780	0.9742 711	$180/\pi$	57.2957 795	1.7581 226
4π	12.5663 706	1.0992 099	$4\pi^2$	39.4784 176	1.5963 597
8π	25.1327 412	1.4002 399	$1/\pi^2$	0.1013 212	9.0057 003 − 10
$\pi/2$	1.5707 963	0.1961 199	$1/(2\pi^2)$	0.0506 606	8.7046 703 − 10
$\pi/3$	1.0471 976	0.0200 286	$1/(4\pi^2)$	0.0253 303	8.4036 403 − 10
$\pi/4$	0.7853 982	9.8950 899 − 10	$\sqrt{\pi}$	1.7724 539	0.2485 749
$\pi/6$	0.5235 988	9.7189 986 − 10	$\sqrt{\frac{\pi}{2}}$	0.8862 269	9.9475 449 − 10
$\pi/8$	0.3926 991	9.5940 599 − 10	$\sqrt{\frac{\pi}{4}}$	0.4431 135	9.6465 149 − 10
$2\pi/3$	2.0943 951	0.3210 586	$\sqrt{\frac{\pi}{2}}$	1.2533 141	0.0980 599
$4\pi/3$	4.1887 902	0.6220 886	$\frac{\sqrt{2}}{\pi}$	0.7978 846	9.9019 401 − 10
$1/\pi$	0.3183 099	9.5028 501 − 10		31.0062 767	1.4914 496
$2/\pi$	0.6366 198	9.8038 801 − 10	π^3	1.4645 919	0.1657 166
$4/\pi$	1.2732 395	0.1049 101	$\sqrt[3]{\pi}$	0.6827 841	9.8342 834 − 10
$1/(2\pi)$	0.1591 549	9.2018 201 − 10	$1/\sqrt[3]{\pi}$	2.1450 294	0.3314 332
$1/(4\pi)$	0.0795 775	8.9007 901 − 10	$1/\sqrt[3]{\pi^2}$	0.5641 896	9.7514 251 − 10
$1/(6\pi)$	0.0530 516	8.7246 989 − 10	$1/\sqrt{\pi}$	0.3989 423	9.6009 101 − 10
$1/(8\pi)$	0.0397 887	8.5997 601 − 10	$1/\sqrt{2\pi}$		
π^2	9.8696 044	0.9942 997	$2/\sqrt{\pi}$	1.1283 792	0.0524 551

MULTIPLES OF $\frac{\pi}{2}$

n	$n\frac{\pi}{2}$	n	$n\frac{\pi}{2}$	n	$n\frac{\pi}{2}$	n	$n\frac{\pi}{2}$
1	1.57079 63268	26	40.84070 44967	51	80.11061 26665	76	119.38502 08364
2	3.14159 26536	27	42.41150 08235	52	81.68140 89933	77	120.95131 71632
3	4.71238 89804	28	43.98229 71503	53	83.25220 53201	78	122.52211 34900
4	6.28318 53072	29	45.55309 34771	54	84.82300 16469	79	124.09290 98168
5	7.85398 16340	30	47.12388 98038	55	86.39379 79737	80	125.66370 61436
6	9.42477 79608	31	48.69468 61306	56	87.96459 43005	81	127.23450 24704
7	10.99557 42876	32	50.26548 24574	57	89.53539 06273	82	128.80529 87972
8	12.56637 06144	33	51.83627 87842	58	91.10618 69541	83	130.37609 51240
9	14.13716 69412	34	53.40707 51110	59	92.67698 32809	84	131.94689 14508
10	15.70796 32679	35	54.97787 14378	60	94.24777 96077	85	133.51768 77776
11	17.27875 95947	36	56.54866 77646	61	95.81857 59345	86	135.08848 41044
12	18.84955 59215	37	58.11946 40914	62	97.38937 22613	87	136.65928 04312
13	20.42035 22483	38	59.69026 04182	63	98.96016 85881	88	138.23007 67580
14	21.99114 85751	39	61.26105 67450	64	100.53096 49149	89	139.80087 30847
15	23.56194 49019	40	62.83185 30718	65	102.10176 12417	90	141.37166 94115
16	25.13274 12287	41	64.40264 93986	66	103.67255 75685	91	142.94246 57383
17	26.70533 75555	42	65.97344 57254	67	105.24335 38953	92	144.51326 20651
18	28.27433 38823	43	67.54424 20522	68	106.81415 02221	93	146.08405 83919
19	29.84513 02091	44	69.11503 83790	69	108.38494 65488	94	147.65485 47187
20	31.41592 65359	45	70.68583 47058	70	109.95574 28765	95	149.22565 10455
21	32.98672 28627	46	72.25663 10326	71	111.52653 92024	96	150.79644 73723
22	34.55751 91895	47	73.82742 73594	72	113.09733 55292	97	152.36724 36991
23	36.12831 55163	48	75.39822 36862	73	114.66813 18560	98	153.93804 00259
24	37.69911 18431	49	76.96902 00129	74	116.23892 81828	99	155.50883 63527
25	39.26990 81699	50	78.53981 63397	75	117.80972 45096	100	157.07963 26795

FACTORS AND EXPANSIONS

$$(a \pm b)^2 = a^2 \pm 2ab + b^2.$$

$$(a \pm b)^3 = a^3 \pm 3a^2b + 3ab^2 \pm b^3.$$

$$(a \pm b)^4 = a^4 \pm 4a^3b + 6a^2b^2 \pm 4ab^3 + b^4.$$

$$a^2 - b^2 = (a - b)(a + b).$$

$$a^2 + b^2 = (a + b\sqrt{-1})(a - b\sqrt{-1}).$$

$$a^3 - b^3 = (a - b)(a^2 + ab + b^2).$$

$$a^3 + b^3 = (a + b)(a^2 - ab + b^2).$$

$$a^4 + b^4 = (a^2 + ab\sqrt{2} + b^2)(a^2 - ab\sqrt{2} + b^2).$$

$$a^n - b^n = (a - b)(a^{n-1} + a^{n-2}b + \ldots + b^{n-1}).$$

$$a^n - b^n = (a + b)(a^{n-1} - a^{n-2}b + \ldots - b^{n-1}),$$

for even values of n.

$$a^n + b^n = (a + b)(a^{n-1} - a^{n-2}b + \ldots + b^{n-1}),$$

for odd values of n.

$$a^4 + a^2b^2 + b^4 = (a^2 + ab + b^2)(a^2 - ab + b^2).$$

$$(a + b + c)^2 = a^2 + b^2 + c^2 + 2ab + 2ac + 2bc.$$

$$(a + b + c)^3 = a^3 + b^3 + c^3 + 3a^2(b + c) + 3b^2(a + c) + 3c^2(a + b) + 6abc.$$

$$(a + b + c + d + \ldots)^2 = a^2 + b^2 + c^2 + d^2 + \ldots +$$
$$2a(b + c + d + \ldots) + 2b(c + d + \ldots) + 2c(d + \ldots) + \ldots$$

See also under Series.

POWERS AND ROOTS

$$a^x \times a^y = a^{(x+y)}. \qquad a^0 = 1 \,[\text{if } a \neq 0] \qquad (ab)^x = a^x b^x.$$

$$\frac{a^x}{a^y} = a^{(x-y)}. \qquad a^{-x} = \frac{1}{a^x}. \qquad \left(\frac{a}{b}\right)^x = \frac{a^x}{b^x}.$$

$$(a^x)^y = a^{xy}. \qquad a^{\frac{1}{x}} = \sqrt[x]{a}. \qquad \sqrt[x]{ab} = \sqrt[x]{a}\,\sqrt[x]{b}.$$

$$\sqrt[x]{\sqrt[y]{a}} = \sqrt[xy]{a}. \qquad a^{\frac{x}{y}} = \sqrt[y]{a^x}. \qquad \sqrt[x]{\frac{a}{b}} = \frac{\sqrt[x]{a}}{\sqrt[x]{b}}.$$

PROPORTION

If $\quad \dfrac{a}{b} = \dfrac{c}{d}, \qquad$ then $\qquad \dfrac{a + b}{b} = \dfrac{c + d}{d},$

$$\frac{a - b}{b} = \frac{c - d}{d}, \qquad \frac{a - b}{a + b} = \frac{c - d}{c + d}.$$

*ARITHMETIC PROGRESSION

An arithmetic progression is a sequence of numbers such that each number differs from the previous number by a constant amount, called the *common difference*.

If a_1 is the first term; a_n the nth term; d the common difference; n the number of terms; and s_n the sum of n terms—

$$a_n = a_1 + (n - 1)d, \quad s_n = \frac{n}{2}[a_1 + a_n].$$

$$s_n = \frac{n}{2}[2a_1 + (n - 1)d].$$

The arithmetic mean between a and b is given by $\dfrac{a + b}{2}$.

*GEOMETRIC PROGRESSION

A geometric progression is a sequence of numbers such that each number bears a constant ratio, called the *common ratio*, to the previous number.

If a_1 is the first term; a_n the nth term; r the common ratio; n the number of terms; and s_n the sum of n terms

$$a_n = a_1 r^{n-1}; \quad s_n = a_1 \frac{1 - r^n}{1 - r}$$

$$= a_1 \frac{r^n - 1}{r - 1}, \quad r \neq 1.$$

$$= \frac{a_1 - r a_n}{1 - r}$$

$$= \frac{r a_n - a_1}{r - 1}$$

If $|r| < 1$, then the sum of an infinite geometrical progression converges to the limiting value

$$\frac{a_1}{1 - r}, \quad \left[s_\infty = \lim_{n \to \infty} \frac{a_1(1 - r^n)}{1 - r} = \frac{a_1}{1 - r} \right]$$

The geometric mean between a and b is given by $\sqrt{ab}$.

*It is customary to represent a_n by l in a finite progression and refer to it as the last term.

HARMONIC PROGRESSION

A sequence of numbers whose reciprocals form an arithmetic progression is called an harmonic progression. Thus

$$\frac{1}{a_1}, \quad \frac{1}{a_1 + d}, \quad \frac{1}{a_1 + 2d}, \cdots, \frac{1}{a_1 + (n - 1)d}, \cdots,$$

where

$$\frac{1}{a_n} = \frac{1}{a_1 + (n - 1)d}$$

forms an harmonic progression. The harmonic mean between a and b is given by $\dfrac{2ab}{a + b}$.

If A, G, H respectively represent the arithmetic mean, geometric mean, and harmonic mean between a and b, then $G^2 = AH$.

QUADRATIC EQUATIONS

Any quadratic equation may be reduced to the form,—

$$ax^2 + bx + c = 0.$$

Then

$$x = \frac{-b \pm \sqrt{b^2 - 4ac}}{2a}.$$

If a, b, and c are real then:

If $b^2 - 4ac$ is positive, the roots are real and unequal;

If $b^2 - 4ac$ is zero, the roots are real and equal;

If $b^2 - 4ac$ is negative, the roots are imaginary and unequal.

CUBIC EQUATIONS

A cubic equation, $y^3 + py^2 + qy + r = 0$ may be reduced to the form,—

$$x^3 + ax + b = 0$$

by substituting for y the value, $x - \dfrac{p}{3}$. Here

$$a = \tfrac{1}{3}(3q - p^2) \text{ and } b = \tfrac{1}{27}(2p^3 - 9pq + 27r).$$

For solution let,—

$$A = \sqrt[3]{-\frac{b}{2} + \sqrt{\frac{b^2}{4} + \frac{a^3}{27}}}, \qquad B = \sqrt[3]{+\frac{b}{2} + \sqrt{\frac{b^2}{4} + \frac{a^3}{27}}},$$

then the values of x will be given by,

$$x = A + B, \quad -\frac{A + B}{2} + \frac{A - B}{2}\sqrt{-3}, \quad -\frac{A + B}{2} - \frac{A - B}{2}\sqrt{-3}.$$

If p, q, r are real, then:

If $\dfrac{b^2}{4} + \dfrac{a^3}{27} > 0$, there will be one real root and two conjugate complex roots;

If $\dfrac{b^2}{4} + \dfrac{a^3}{27} = 0$, there will be three real roots of which at least two are equal;

If $\dfrac{b^2}{4} + \dfrac{a^3}{27} < 0$, there will be three real and unequal roots.

Trignometric Solution of the Cubic Equation

The form $x^3 + ax + b = 0$ with $ab \neq 0$ can always be solved by transforming it to the trignometric identity

$$4 \cos^3 \theta - 3 \cos \theta - \cos (3\theta) \equiv 0.$$

Let $x = m \cos \theta$, then

$$x^3 + ax + b \equiv m^3 \cos^3 \theta + am \cos \theta + b \equiv 4 \cos^3 \theta - 3 \cos \theta - \cos (3\theta) \equiv 0.$$

Hence

$$\frac{4}{m^3} = -\frac{3}{am} = \frac{-\cos(3\theta)}{b},$$

from which follows that

$$m = 2 \sqrt{-\frac{a}{3}}, \quad \cos (3\theta) = \frac{3b}{am}.$$

Any solution θ_1 which satisfies $\cos (3\theta) = \dfrac{3b}{am}$, will also have the solutions

$$\theta_1 + \frac{2\pi}{3} \quad \text{and} \quad \theta_1 + \frac{4\pi}{3}.$$

The roots of the cubic $x^3 + ax + b = 0$ are

$$2 \sqrt{-\frac{a}{3}} \cos \theta_1, \quad 2 \sqrt{-\frac{a}{3}} \cos \left(\theta_1 + \frac{2\pi}{3}\right), \quad 2 \sqrt{-\frac{a}{3}} \cos \left(\theta_1 + \frac{4\pi}{3}\right).$$

Example where hyperbolic functions are necessary for solution with latter procedure

The roots of the equation $x^3 - x + 2 = 0$ may be found as follows:

Here

$$a = -1, \quad b = 2, \quad m = 2 \sqrt{\tfrac{1}{3}} = 1.155$$

$$\cos (3\theta) = \frac{6}{-1.155} = -5.196$$

$$\cos (3\theta) = -\cos (3\theta - \pi) = -\cosh [i(3\theta - \pi)] = -5.196.$$

Using hyperbolic function tables for cosh $[i(3\theta - \pi)] = 5.196$, it is found that

$$i(3\theta - \pi) = 2.332.$$

Thus

$$3\theta - \pi = -i(2.332).$$
$$3\theta = \pi - i(2.332)$$
$$\theta_1 = \frac{\pi}{3} - i(0.777)$$
$$\theta_1 + \frac{2\pi}{3} = \pi - i(0.777)$$
$$\theta_1 + \frac{4\pi}{3} = \frac{5\pi}{3} - i(0.777)$$

$$\cos \theta_1 = \cos \left[\frac{\pi}{3} - i(0.777) \right]$$

$$= \left(\cos \frac{\pi}{3} \right) [\cos i(0.777)] + \left(\sin \frac{\pi}{3} \right) [\sin i(0.777)]$$

$$= \left(\cos \frac{\pi}{3} \right) (\cosh 0.777) + i \left(\sin \frac{\pi}{3} \right) (\sinh 0.777)$$

$$= (0.5)(1.317) + i(0.866)(0.858) = 0.659 + i(0.743).$$

Note that

$$\cos \mu = \cosh (i\mu) \quad \text{and} \quad \sin \mu = -i \sinh (i\mu).$$

Similarly

$$\cos \left(\theta_1 + \frac{2\pi}{3} \right) = \cos [\pi - i(0.777)]$$

$$= (\cos \pi)(\cosh 0.777) + i(\sin \pi)(\sinh 0.777)$$

$$= -1.317,$$

and

$$\cos \left(\theta_1 + \frac{4\pi}{3} \right) = \cos \left[\frac{5\pi}{3} - i(0.777) \right]$$

$$= \left(\cos \frac{5\pi}{3} \right) (\cosh 0.777) + i \left(\sin \frac{5\pi}{3} \right) (\sinh 0.777)$$

$$= (0.5)(1.317) - i(0.866)(0.858) = 0.659 - i(0.743).$$

The required roots are

$$1.155[0.659 + i(0.743)] = 0.760 + i(0.858)$$
$$(1.155)(-1.317) = -1.520$$
$$(1.155)[0.659 - i(0.743)] = 0.760 - i(0.858).$$

QUARTIC OR BIQUADRATIC EQUATION

A quartic equation,

$$x^4 + ax^3 + bx^2 + cx + d = 0,$$

has the *resolvent cubic equation*

$$y^3 - by^2 + (ac - 4d)y - a^2d + 4bd - c^2 = 0.$$

Let y be any root of this equation, and

$$R = \sqrt{\frac{a^2}{4} - b + y}.$$

If $R \neq 0$, then let

$$D = \sqrt{\frac{3a^2}{4} - R^2 - 2b + \frac{4ab - 8c - a^3}{4R}}$$

and

$$E = \sqrt{\frac{3a^2}{4} - R^2 - 2b - \frac{4ab - 8c - a^3}{4R}}$$

If $R = 0$, then let

$$D = \sqrt{\frac{3a^2}{4} - 2b + 2\sqrt{y^2 - 4d}}$$

and

$$E = \sqrt{\frac{3a^2}{4} - 2b - 2\sqrt{y^2 - 4d}}.$$

Then the four roots of the original equation are given by

$$x = -\frac{a}{4} + \frac{R}{2} \pm \frac{D}{2}$$

and

$$x = -\frac{a}{4} - \frac{R}{2} \pm \frac{E}{2}.$$

EQUATION $x^n = c$

Using DeMoivre's theorem:

$$(\cos \theta + i \sin \theta)^n = \cos n\theta + i \sin n\theta; \; i = \sqrt{-1},$$

the equation $x^n = c$ has n roots given by

$$x = \sqrt[n]{c}\left(\cos \frac{2m\pi}{n} + i \sin \frac{2m\pi}{n}\right) \text{if } c > 0,$$

or

$$x = \sqrt[n]{-c}\left(\cos \frac{(2m + 1)\pi}{n} + i \sin \frac{(2m + 1)\pi}{n}\right) \text{if } c < 0,$$

where m takes the n values 0,1,2, . . . $(n - 1)$ giving n roots.

PARTIAL FRACTIONS

This section applies only to rational algebraic fractions with numerator of lower degree than the denominator. Improper fractions can be reduced to proper fractions by long division.

Every fraction may be expressed as the sum of component fractions whose denominators are factors of the denominator of the original fraction.

Let $N(x)$ = numerator, a polynomial of the form

$$n_0 + n_1 x + n_2 x^2 + \cdots + n_i x^i$$

I. *Non-repeated Linear Factors*

$$\frac{N(x)}{(x - a)G(x)} = \frac{A}{x - a} + \frac{F(x)}{G(x)}$$

$$A = \left[\frac{N(x)}{G(x)}\right]_{x = a}$$

$F(x)$ determined by methods discussed in the following sections.

Example:

$$\frac{x^2 + 3}{x(x - 2)(x^2 + 2x + 4)} = \frac{A}{x} + \frac{B}{x - 2} + \frac{F(x)}{x^2 + 2x + 4}$$

$$A = \left[\frac{x^2 + 3}{(x - 2)(x^2 + 2x + 4)}\right]_{x = 0} = -\frac{3}{8}$$

$$B = \left[\frac{x^2 + 3}{x(x^2 + 2x + 4)}\right]_{x = 2} = \frac{4 + 3}{2(4 + 4 + 4)} = \frac{7}{24}$$

II. *Repeated Linear Factors*

$$\frac{N(x)}{x^m G(x)} = \frac{A_0}{x^m} + \frac{A_1}{x^{m-1}} + \cdots + \frac{A_{m-1}}{x} + \frac{F(x)}{G(x)}$$

$$F(x) = f_0 + f_1 x + f_2 x^2 + \cdots, \quad G(x) = g_0 + g_1 x + g_2 x^2 + \cdots$$

$$A_0 = \frac{n_0}{g_0}, \quad A_1 = \frac{n_1 - A_0 g_1}{g_0}, \quad A_2 = \frac{n_2 - A_0 g_2 - A_1 g_1}{g_0}$$

General term:

$$A_k = \frac{1}{g_0}\left[n_k - \sum_{i=0}^{k-1} A_i g_{k-i}\right]$$

$$*m = 1 \begin{cases} f_0 = n_1 - A_0 g_1 \\ f_1 = n_2 - A_0 g_2 \\ f_j = n_{j+1} - A_0 g_{j+1} \end{cases}$$

$$m = 2 \begin{cases} f_0 = n_2 - A_0 g_2 - A_1 g_1 \\ f_1 = n_3 - A_0 g_3 - A_1 g_2 \\ f_j = n_{j+2} - [A_0 g_{j+2} + A_1 g_{j+1}] \end{cases}$$

$$m = 3 \begin{cases} f_0 = n_3 - A_0 g_3 - A_1 g_2 - A_2 g_1 \\ f_1 = n_3 - A_0 g_4 - A_1 g_3 - A_2 g_2 \\ f_j = n_{j+3} - [A_0 g_{j+3} + A_1 g_{j+2} + A_2 g_{j+1}] \end{cases}$$

$$\text{any } m: \; f_j = n_{m+j} - \sum_{i=0}^{m-1} A_i g_{m+j-i}$$

Example:

$$\frac{x^2 + 1}{x^3(x^2 - 3x + 6)} = \frac{A_0}{x^3} + \frac{A_1}{x^2} + \frac{A_2}{x} + \frac{f_1 x + f_0}{x^2 - 3x + 6}$$

$$A_0 = \frac{1}{6}, \quad A_1 = \frac{0 - (\frac{1}{6})(-3)}{6} = \frac{1}{12},$$

$$A_2 = \frac{1 - (\frac{1}{6})(1) - (\frac{1}{12})(-3)}{6} = \frac{13}{72},$$

$$m = 3 \begin{cases} f_0 = 0 - \frac{1}{6}(0) + \frac{1}{12}(1) - \frac{13}{72}(-3) = \frac{11}{24} \\ f_1 = 0 - \frac{1}{6}(0) - \frac{1}{12}(0) - \frac{13}{72}(1) = -\frac{13}{72} \end{cases}$$

*Note: If $G(x)$ contains linear factors, $F(x)$ may be determined by previous section I.

III. *Repeated Linear Factors*

$$\frac{N(x)}{(x - a)^m G(x)} = \frac{A_0}{(x - a)^m} + \frac{A_1}{(x - a)^{m-1}} + \cdots + \frac{A_{m-1}}{(x - a)} + \frac{F(x)}{G(x)}$$

Change to form $\dfrac{N'(y)}{y^m G'(y)}$ by substitution of $x = y + a$. Resolve into partial fractions in terms of y as described in Section II. Then express in terms of x by substitution $y = x - a$.

Example:

$$\frac{x - 3}{(x - 2)^2(x^2 + x + 1)}$$

Let $x - 2 = y$, $x = y + 2$

$$\frac{(y + 2) - 3}{y^2[(y + 2)^2 + (y + 2) + 1]} = \frac{y - 1}{y^2(y^2 + 5y + 7)} = \frac{A_0}{y^2} + \frac{A_1}{y} + \frac{f_1 y + f_0}{y^2 + 5y + 7}$$

$$A_0 = -\frac{1}{7}, \quad A_1 = \frac{1 - (-\frac{1}{7})(5)}{7} = \frac{12}{49},$$

$$m = 2 \begin{cases} f_0 = 0 - (-\frac{1}{7})(1) - (\frac{12}{49})(5) = -\frac{53}{49} \\ f_1 = 0 - (-\frac{1}{7})(0) - (\frac{12}{49})(1) = -\frac{12}{49} \end{cases}$$

$$\therefore \quad \frac{y - 1}{y^2(y^2 + 5y + 7)} = \frac{-\frac{1}{7}}{y^2} + \frac{\frac{12}{49}}{y} + \frac{-\frac{12}{49} y - \frac{53}{49}}{y^2 + 5y + 7}$$

Let $y = x - 2$, then

$$\frac{x - 3}{(x - 2)^2(x^2 + x + 1)} = \frac{-\frac{1}{7}}{(x - 2)^2} + \frac{\frac{12}{35}}{(x - 2)} + \frac{-\frac{12}{49}(x - 2) - \frac{53}{49}}{x^2 + x + 1}$$

$$= -\frac{1}{7(x - 2)^2} + \frac{12}{35(x - 2)} + \frac{-12x - 29}{49(x^2 + x + 1)}$$

IV. *Repeated Linear Factors*

Alternative method of determining coefficients:

$$\frac{N(x)}{(x-a)^m G(x)} = \frac{A_0}{(x-a)^m} + \cdots + \frac{A_k}{(x-a)^{m-k}} + \cdots + \frac{A_{m-1}}{x-a} + \frac{F(x)}{G(x)}$$

$$A_k = \frac{1}{k!}\left\{D_x^k\left[\frac{N(x)}{G(x)}\right]\right\}_{x=a}$$

where D_x^k is the differentiating operator, and the derivative of zero order is defined as:

$$D_x^0 u = u.$$

V. *Factors of Higher Degree*

Factors of higher degree have the corresponding numerators indicated.

$$\frac{N(x)}{(x^2+h_1x+h_0)G(x)} = \frac{a_1x+a_0}{x^2+h_1x+h_0} + \frac{F(x)}{G(x)}$$

$$\frac{N(x)}{(x^2+h_1x+h_0)^2 G(x)} = \frac{a_1x+a_0}{(x^2+h_1x+h_0)^2} + \frac{b_1x+b_0}{(x^2+h_1x+h_0)} + \frac{F(x)}{G(x)}$$

$$\frac{N(x)}{(x^3+h_2x^2+h_1x+h_0)G(x)} = \frac{a_2x^2+a_1x+a_0}{x^3+h_2x^2+h_1x+h_0} + \frac{F(x)}{G(x)}$$

etc.

Problems of this type are determined first by solving for the coefficients due to linear factors as shown above, and then determining the remaining coefficients by the general methods given below.

VI. *General Methods for Evaluating Coefficients*

1. $$\frac{N(x)}{D(x)} = \frac{N(x)}{G(x)H(x)L(x)} = \frac{A(x)}{G(x)} + \frac{B(x)}{H(x)} + \frac{C(x)}{L(x)} + \cdots$$

Multiply both sides of equation by $D(x)$ to clear fractions. Then collect terms, equate like powers of x, and solve the resulting simultaneous equations for the unknown coefficients.

2. Clear fractions as above. Then let x assume certain convenient values ($x = 1, 0, -1, \ldots$). Solve the resulting equations for the unknown coefficients.

3. $$\frac{N(x)}{G(x)H(x)} = \frac{A(x)}{G(x)} + \frac{B(x)}{H(x)}$$

Then

$$\frac{N(x)}{G(x)H(x)} - \frac{A(x)}{G(x)} = \frac{B(x)}{H(x)}$$

If $A(x)$ can be determined, such as by Method I, then $B(x)$ can be found as above.

BASIC CONCEPTS IN ALGEBRA

Dr. W. E. Deskins

I. ALGEBRA OF SETS

1. Intuitively a set is a collection of objects called the elements of the set. Set and set membership are generally accepted as basic, undefined terms used to define and construct mathematical systems.

   The notation $a \in A$ indicates that a is an element of the set A. The notation $a \notin A$ means that a is not a member of A.

   A set is sometimes specified by listing its elements within a set of braces: $\{a\}$ is the set containing only the element a.

2. Set A is a subset of set B provided $a \in A$ implies $a \in B$. This is denoted by $A \subseteq B$. Every set has as a subset the empty or null set, denoted by ϕ, which has no elements.

3. Set A equals set B, written $A = B$, if and only if $A \subseteq B$ and $B \subseteq A$. A is a proper subset of B, sometimes indicated by $A \subset B$, if and only if $A \subseteq B$ and $A \neq B$; then B has at least one element which does not belong to A.

4. The Cartesian product of sets A and B, denoted by $A \times B$, is the set of all ordered pairs (a, b) where $a \in A$ and $b \in B$. A subset R of $A \times A$ is a binary relation on A, and this is an equivalence relation on A provided (i) $(a, a) \in R$ for every $a \in A$, (ii) $(a, b) \in R$ implies $(b, a) \in R$, and (iii) $(a, b) \in R$ and $(b, c) \in R$ imply $(a, c) \in R$. Ordinary equality of numbers, equality of sets, and congruence of plane figures are examples of equivalence relations.

5. A subset F of $A \times B$ is a *function* from A to B provided each element of A appears exactly once as the first element of a pair in F. A function F from A to B is *onto* provided each element of B appears at least once as the second element of a pair in F. It is *one-to-one* provided each element of B appears at most once as the second element of a pair in F. A function from $A \times A$ to A is a *binary operation* on A. Addition and multiplication of ordinary numbers are examples of binary operations.

6. If consideration is restricted to elements and subsets of a particular set I, then I is the universal set.

7. Common binary operations on subsets of I are: $A \cup B$, the union or join of sets A and B, is the set of all elements of I which belong to either A or B or both A and B.

   $A \cap B$, the intersection or meet of sets A and B, is the set of all elements of I which belong to both A and B.

   $A \setminus B$, the difference of sets A and B, is the set of elements of I which belong to A but not B.

   The difference $I \setminus A$ is denoted by A' and called the complement of A (relative to I). Except in dealing with the concept of complementation the use of a universal set is not essential to the above ideas.

8. Some theorems basic to the Algebra of Sets:

   Let A, B, and C be arbitrary subsets of a universal set I.
   (a) (Commutativity) $A \cup B = B \cup A$ and $A \cap B = B \cap A$.
   (b) (Associativity) $(A \cup B) \cup C = A \cup (B \cup C)$ and
                            $(A \cap B) \cap C = A \cap (B \cap C)$.

(c) (Distributivity) $A \cap (B \cup C) = (A \cap B) \cup (A \cap C)$ and
                               $A \cup (B \cap C) = (A \cup B) \cap (A \cup C)$.

(d) (Idempotency) $A \cup A = A \cap A = A$.

(e) Properties of I and ϕ: $A \cap I = A \cup \phi = A$,
                               $A \cup I = I$, and
                               $A \cap \phi = \phi$.

(f) $(A \cap B) \cup (A \setminus B) = A$.

(g) $(A \setminus B) \cup B = A \cup B$.

(h) $A \subseteq A \cup B$.

(i) $A \cap B \subseteq A$.

(j) $A \cup B = A$ if and only if $B \subseteq A$.

(k) $A \cap B = A$ if and only if $A \subseteq B$.

(m) $A \setminus B = A \setminus (A \cap B)$.

(n) (DeMorgan's Theorem) $(A \setminus B) \cap (A \setminus C) = A \setminus (B \cup C)$ and
                               $(A \setminus B) \cup (A \setminus C) = A \setminus (B \cap C)$.

(o) $(A \cup B)' = A' \cap B'$ and $(A \cap B)' = A' \cup B'$.

(p) $A \cup A' = I$ and $A \cap A' = \phi$.

9. A mathematical system S is a set $S = \{E, O, A\}$ where E is a nonempty set of elements, O is a set of relations and operations on E, and A is a set of axioms, postulates, or assumptions concerning the elements of E and O.

10. The Algebra of Sets provides an example of a mathematical system called a Boolean Algebra (or Boolean Ring) which is defined as:

Set E of elements $a, b, c, \ldots$;

Set O of 2 binary operations $\oplus$ and $\otimes$; (Here $a \oplus b$ denotes the image of (a, b) under the binary operation.)

Set A of axioms for all a, b, c of E:

A_1.   The binary operations are commutative; i.e.,

$$a \oplus b = b \oplus a \quad \text{and} \quad a \otimes b = b \otimes a.$$

A_2.   Each binary operation is distributive over the other; i.e.,

$$a \oplus (b \otimes c) = (a \oplus b) \otimes (a \oplus c) \quad \text{and} \quad a \otimes (b \oplus c) = (a \otimes b) + (a \otimes c).$$

A_3.   There exist elements e and z in E such that for each $a \in E$, $a \oplus z = a$ and $a \otimes e = a$.

A_4.   For each $a \in E$ there exists an element $a' \in E$ such that $a \otimes a' = e$ and $a \oplus a' = z$.

In the algebra of subsets of a (universal) set I, ϕ plays the role of z, I that of e, $\cup$ that of $\oplus$, and $\cap$ that of $\otimes$.

11. A Boolean Algebra has the Principle of Duality: If the interchanges of $\begin{Bmatrix} \oplus \text{ and } \otimes \\ e \text{ and } z \end{Bmatrix}$ are made in a correct statement, then the result is also a correct statement.

12. In addition to the Algrebra of Sets which is a Boolean Algebra, other representations of Boolean Algebra that are interesting of themselves and valuable for their applications are:

(a) The Algebra of Symbolic Logic

(b) The Algebra of Switching Currents

Algebra of Sets	Binary Operator	Symbolic Logic	Binary Operator	Switching Circuits	Binary Operator
Union of 2 sets	$\cup$	Disjunction of 2 propositions	$\vee$	2 switches in $\parallel$	$+$
Intersection of 2 sets	$\cap$	Conjunction of 2 propositions	$\wedge$	2 switches in series	$\times$
Complement of a set A		Negation of a proposition T, F	$\sim$	on-off, or 1, 0	1 or $^-$

Both in symbolic logic and in switching circuits, we can consider "0" and "1" as the elements, in the former representing "False" and "True"; in the latter, "Off" and "On", satisfying the following "rules":

$$\left.\begin{array}{l} 0 + 0 = 0 \\ 1 + 1 = 1 \end{array}\right\} \text{ i.e. } a + a = a$$

$$\left.\begin{array}{l} 0 \times 0 = 0 \\ 1 \times 1 = 1 \end{array}\right\} \text{ i.e. } a \times a = a$$

$$0' = 1$$
$$1' = 0$$

$$\left.\begin{array}{l} 0 + 0' = 0 + 1 = 1 \\ 1 + 1' = 1 + 0 = 1 \end{array}\right\} \text{ i.e. } a + a' = 1$$

$$\left.\begin{array}{l} 0 \times 0' = 0 \times 1 = 0 \\ 1 \times 1' = 1 \times 0 = 0 \end{array}\right\} a \times a' = 0$$

In switching circuits:

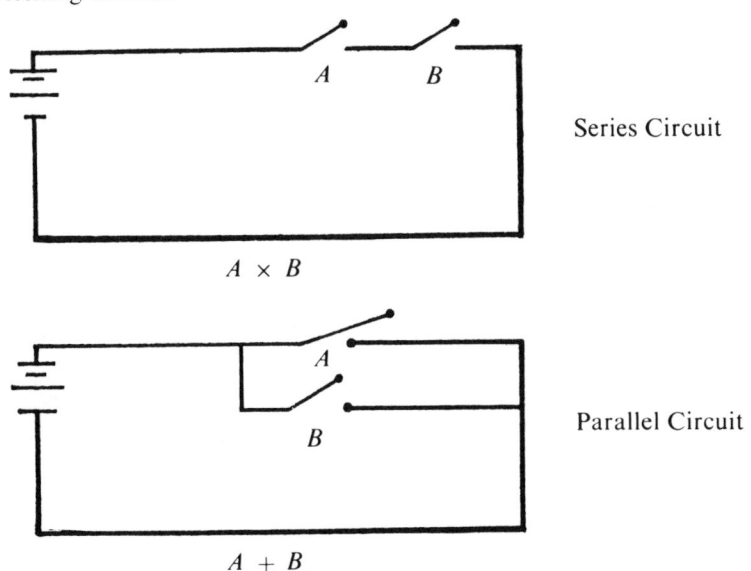

Series Circuit

$$A \times B$$

Parallel Circuit

$$A + B$$

here, "0" represents an open circuit: ●——⚬ ●——● and "1"
$$A = 0$$

a closed circuit: ●——⚬ ●——●
$$A = 1$$

In the Algebra of Symbolic Logic, we use *Truth Tables* to define the operations $\wedge$, $\vee$, $\sim$ as follows:

					Other Operators Used	
p	q	$p \wedge q$	$p \vee q$	$\sim p$	$p \to q$	$p \leftrightarrow q$
T	T	T	T	F	T	T
T	F	F	T	F	F	F
F	T	F	T	T	T	F
F	F	F	F	T	T	T

13. In order to re-emphasize the use of switching circuits and their relation to truth tables the following is included. Conventionally a "1" represents "True" and a "0" represents "False." The switching circuit symbols are $-$, $\cdot$, $+$, $\to$, $\equiv$ representing "Not," "And," "Or," "Implies," "Equivalent" respectively and their Truth Table Definitions are

p	q	$p \cdot q$	$p + q$	p	$p \to q$	$p \equiv q$
0	0	0	0	1	1	1
0	1	0	1	1	1	0
1	0	0	1	0	0	0
1	1	1	1	0	1	1

The comparison with the Algebra of Symbolic Logic being obvious. The "rules" for these circuits are as follows:

$$0 + 0 = 0$$
$$1 + 1 = 1$$
$$1 + 0 = 0 + 1 = 1$$
$$0 \cdot 0 = 0$$
$$1 \cdot 1 = 1$$
$$0 \cdot 1 = 1 \cdot 0 = 0$$
$$\bar{0} = 1$$
$$\bar{1} = 0$$

Mechanical switches or relays are represented by

the former indicating that the circuit is closed, i.e. the switch is made, when $p = 1$ and the latter indicating the converse namely that the circuit is closed when $\bar{p} = 1$ or, what amounts to the same thing, when $p = 0$.

Electronic switches or gates are represented by more complex symbols—four in all, three of which are independent and can stand alone

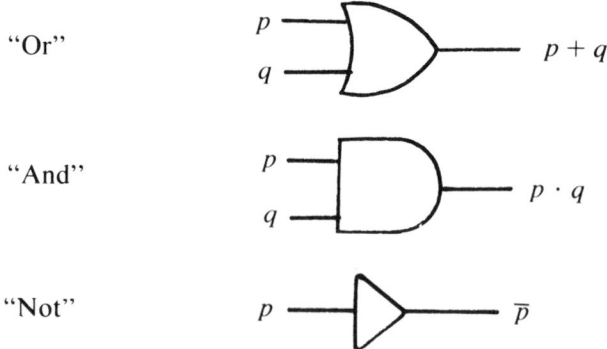

and one which represents the negation of an input or an output and is used with one of the above

"Not"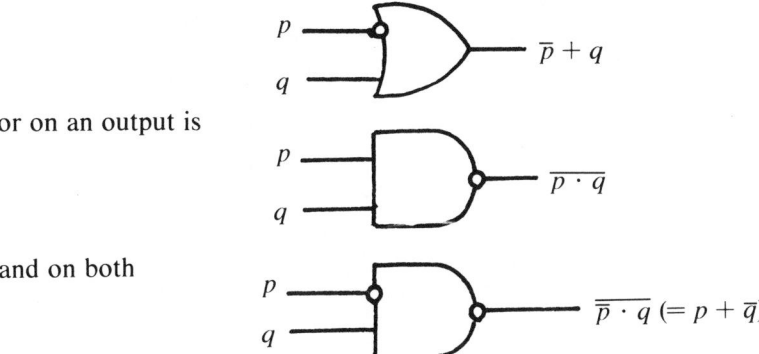

An example of its use on an input line is

$$\bar{p} + q$$

or on an output is

$$\overline{p \cdot q}$$

and on both

$$\overline{\bar{p} \cdot q}\ (= p + \bar{q})$$

The basic functions obtained from the two types of switching circuits are

1 —— p —— p p ———————— p

1 —— $\bar{p}$ —— $\bar{p}$ p ———▷——— $\bar{p}$

1 —— p —— q —— $p \cdot q$ $p \cdot q$

1 —— $p + q$ $p + q$

1 —— $p \rightarrow q$ $p \rightarrow q$

1 —— $p \equiv q$ $p \equiv q$

All the above electronic circuits can be negated by simply adding a negating circle to the output as for example in

Alternative circuits however, which are direct analogues of their relay switching counterparts, are

The operation $+$ is sometimes referred to as the "Inclusive Or" and $\not\equiv$ as the "Exclusive Or", the former having the value "True" when both the inputs are "True"—see the truth table.   Note that $p \not\equiv q$ is a shorthand for $\overline{p \equiv q}$.

14. Two sets A and B are equivalent (have same cardinal) if and only if there exists a one-to-one correspondence between the elements of the two sets.   This is an equivalence relation on the collection of subsets of set I.

A set is infinite if and only if it is equivalent with a proper subset of itself.

A set is called countably (denumerably) infinite if it is equivalent with the set of all positive integers.   The set of all rational numbers is countably infinite but the set of all real numbers is noncountably infinite.   The cardinal of the set of all rational numbers is denoted by (aleph null); the cardinal of the set of reals is denoted by (aleph).

II. ABSTRACT ALGEBRAIC SYSTEMS

1. *Semigroup.*   A semigroup is a system $\{S, 0, A\}$; S is a nonempty set $\{a, b, c, \ldots\}$, θ consists of one binary operation on S, denoted by $*$, and A consists of the axiom

A_1.   Associativity: $a * (b * c) = (a * b) * c$ for all $a, b \circ c \in S$.

Basic Theorem.   (*Generalized Associativity*).   If $a_1, a_2, \ldots, a_n$ are elements of S then all associations of the n elements yield the same "product". (For example,

$$a * ((b * c) * d) = a * (b * (c * d)) = (a * b) * (c * d), \text{etc.}$$

2. *Group.* A group is a system $\{G, 0, A\}$; G is a nonempty set $\{a, b, c, \ldots\}$, θ consists of one binary operation denoted by $\circ$, and A consists of the axioms:

A_1. Associativity: $a \circ (b \circ c) = (a \circ b) \circ c$ for all $a, b, c \in G$.

A_2. Identity Element: G contains an element e having the property, $a \circ e = e \circ a = a$ for every $a \in G$.

A_3. Inverse Element: For each $a \in G$ there is an element $a' \in G$ with the property, $a \circ a' = a' \circ a = e$.

If the following additional axiom belongs to A,

A_4. Commutativity: $a \circ b = b \circ a$ for all $a, b \in G$. Then the group is called Abelian (after Niels Henrik Abel). Some basic theorems:

(a) The element e (Axiom A_2) is unique. Then e is *the* identity element of G.

(b) The element a' (Axiom A_3) is unique for each $a \in G$. Then a' is *the* inverse of a in G.

(c) The equation $a \circ x = b$ has a unique solution in G, viz., $x = a' \circ b$.

(d) $(a')' = a$ and $(a \circ b)' = b' \circ a'$.

(e) $a \circ b = a \circ c$ if and only if $b = c$.

If a nonempty subset H of G satisfies the two conditions:

H_1. $a \circ b \in H$ whenever $a, b \in H$. (Closure)

H_2. $a \in H$ if and only if $a' \in H$.

then H is a *subgroup* of G.

(Lagrange). If G is a finite set then the number of elements in H divides the number of elements in G.

Example of group. Let G be the set of all one-to-one functions from a nonempty S onto itself. For any $f, g \in G$, define the function $f \circ g$ as the function which maps s onto $f(g(s))$, for each $s \in S$. Relative to this binary operation G is a group, the *symmetric group* of all permutations on S.

Each group is essentially a subgroup of the symmetric group of some set S.

3. *Ring.* A ring is a system $\{R, \theta, A\}$; R is a nonempty set $\{a, b, c, \ldots\}$, θ consists of two binary operations denoted by $+$ and $\times$, and A consists of the axioms:

A_0. Relative to addition (i.e., $+$) R is an Abelian group in which the identity element is denoted by z and the inverse of a is denoted by $-a$.

M_0. Relative to multiplication (i.e., $\times$) R is a semigroup.

D_1. Left distributive: $a \times (b + c) = (a \times b) + (a \times c)$, all $a, b, c \in R$.

D_2. Right distributive: $(b + c)a = (b \times a) + (c \times a)$, all $a, b, c \in R$.

EXAMPLE 1. The set of all integers (whole numbers) and ordinary addition and multiplication.

EXAMPLE 2. The set of all real functions continuous on the interval $0 \leq y \leq 1$, with addition and multiplication defined by $(f + g)(y) = f(y) + g(y)$, sum of real numbers, and $(f \times g)(y) = f(y) \times g(y)$, product of real numbers.

Special types of rings have been studied extensively.

3.1 *Integral Domain.* An integral domain is a ring R in which multiplication ($\times$) satisfies the additional assumptions:

M_1. Commutativity: $a \times b = b \times a$ for all a and b in R.

M_2. Multiplicative identity: R contains an element $e \neq z$ with the property $a \times e = e \times a = a$ for all a in R.

M_3. Cancellation: $a \times b = a \times c$ if and only if $b = c$.

An element u of integral domain R is a *unit* provided R contains v such that $u \times v = e$.

An element p of integral domain R is a *prime* (irreducible element) provided $p = a \times b$ implies that exactly one of the elements a or b is a unit.

The elements of integral domain R which differ from z and are neither units nor primes are *composites*.

In some integral domains (such as the ring of integers) each composite can be factored uniquely (up to unit factors) as the product of a finite set of primes. However in the integral domain of all entire functions this is not true.

3.2   *Field.*   A field is an integral domain in which every element except z is a unit. In other words, the non-z elements form an Abelian group relative to multiplication ($\times$).

EXAMPLE 1.   The rational field consisting of ordinary fractions, addition, and multiplication.

EXAMPLE 2.   The set of all real numbers $a + b\sqrt{2}$, a and b rational. Then

$$(a + b\sqrt{2}) + (c + d\sqrt{2}) = (a + c) + (b + d)\sqrt{2} \text{ and}$$
$$(a + b\sqrt{2}) \times (c + d\sqrt{2}) = (ac + 2bd) + (ad + bc)\sqrt{2}.$$

Besides these well-known examples there exist finite fields (sometimes called Galois fields).

EXAMPLE 3.   Let p be a prime integer.   Denote by $GF(p)$ the p integers $0, 1, \ldots, p - 1$.   Define addition($\oplus$) of two of these elements a and b as the remainder of $a + b$ (ordinary addition) after division by p.   (Thus $1 \oplus (p - 1) = 0$.)

Define $a \otimes b$, the product, to be the remainder of ab (ordinary multiplication) after division by p.   (Thus, when $p = 3$, $2 \otimes 2 = 1$.)   The resulting system $\{GF(p), \oplus, \otimes\}$ is the (modular) field of integers modulo p.

3.3   *Skew Field or Division Ring.*   A skew field is a ring in which the non-z elements form a group relative to multiplication ($\times$).

The classical example of a skew field is the ring of real *quaternions*, first described by W. R. Hamilton. A quaternion is expressible in the form $ae + bi + cj + dk$ where a, b, c, and d are real numbers and e, i, j, and k are elements which commute with all real numbers and multiply as follows:

$$e \times e = e, \quad e \times i = i \times e = i, \quad e \times j = j \times e = j, \quad e \times k = k \times e = k;$$
$$i \times i = -e, \quad i \times j = k, \quad j \times i = -k, \quad i \times k = -j, \quad k \times i = j,$$
$$j \times j = -e, \quad j \times k = i, \quad k \times j = -i, \quad k \times k = -e.$$

These elements distribute over addition. e is generally identified with and written as the real number 1.

3.4   *Matric Ring.*   The matric ring $M_n(R)$ over the ring R, where n is a positive integer, consists of all doubly-ordered sets of n^2 elements of R, written as an array

$$\begin{pmatrix} a_{1,1} & a_{1,2} \cdots a_{1,n} \\ a_{2,1} & a_{2,2} \cdots a_{2,n} \\ \vdots & \\ a_{n,1} & \cdot \cdot \quad\quad a_{n,n} \end{pmatrix} = (a_{i,j})$$

with addition and multiplication defined as follows:

$$(a_{i,j}) + (b_{i,j}) = (a_{i,j} + b_{i,j})$$
$$(a_{i,j}) \times (b_{i,j}) = (c_{i,j})$$

where

$$c_{i,j} = \sum_{k=1}^{n} a_{i,k} b_{k,j}, \quad i = 1,\ldots,n \quad \text{and} \quad j = 1,\ldots,n.$$

If $n > 1$, then multiplication is noncommutative in general; i.e., $(a_{i,j}) \times (b_{i,j})$ can differ from $(b_{i,j}) \times (a_{i,j})$. Moreover, the product of two nonzero matrices can be the zero matrix (which consists of only the element z in all n^2 positions).

A similar useful method for forming a new ring from a known ring utilizes sequences.

3.5 *Power Series and Polynomial Ring.* Let R be a ring in which multiplication ($\times$) is commutative. The set $PS(R)$ of all sequences $(a_0,a_1,\ldots)$ with $a_i \in R$ is the power series ring of R, with addition and multiplication defined as

$$(a_0,a_1,\ldots) \oplus (b_0,b_1,\ldots) = (a_0 + b_0, \quad a_1 + b_1,\ldots) \text{ and}$$
$$(a_0,a_1,\ldots) \oplus (b_0,b_1,\ldots) = (c_0,c_1,\ldots)$$

where

$$c_0 = a_0 \times b_0, \quad c_1 = a_0 \times b_1 + a_1 \times b_0,\ldots, \text{ and,}$$

generally,

$$c_n = a_0 \times b_n + a_1 \times b_{n-1} + \cdots + a_n \times b_0.$$

The subset $P(R)$ of $PS(R)$ consisting of those sequences $(a_0,a_1,\ldots)$ in which at most only finitely many of the a_i differ from z, form a ring relative to the addition and multiplication just defined. This ring $\{P(R),\oplus,\otimes\}$, is the polynomial ring of R.

Some theorems for rings, fields, etc.

(a) In a ring R, if $a = b$ and $c = d$, then $a + c = b + d$ and $a \times c = b \times d$.

(b) In a ring R, $-(-a) = a$; $(-a) \times b = a \times (-b) = -(a \times b)$; and $(-a) \times (-b) = a \times b$, for all $a,b \in R$.

(c) In a ring R, $a \times z = z \times a = z$, for all $a \in R$.

(d) In a ring R the equation $a + x = b$ has a unique solution, viz., $x = -a + b$.

(f) In a field, skew field, or integral domain, $a \times b = z$ if and only if a and/or b equals z.

(g) A finite integral domain is a field.

(h) The polynomial ring of an integral domain is also an integral domain.

(i) The power series ring of an integral domain is also an integral domain.

(j) A ring is a field provided it is both an integral domain and a skew field.

(k) If R is a (skew) field, then the equation $a \times y = b, a \neq z$, has a unique solution $y = a' \times b$.

(l) The polynomial ring and the power series ring of a field are unique factorization domains.

4. *Vector Space.* A vector space $V(F)$ over a field F consists of a nonempty set V (the vectors), a binary operation ($\oplus$) on V, a function (called *scalar multiplication*) from the product set $F \times V$ onto V with the image of (a,v) denoted by $a \circ v$, and the following axioms:

A_0. Relative to addition ($\oplus$) V is an Abelian group in which the identity element (vector) is denoted by z and the inverse of v is denoted by $-v$.

M_1. $a \circ (b \circ v) = (ab) \circ v$ for all $a,b \in F$ and $v \in F$. (Here ab denotes the product of a and b in F.)

M_2. $1 \circ v = v$ for all $v \in V$. (Here 1 denotes the multiplicative indentity element of F.)

D_1. $a \circ (\mu \oplus \nu) = (a \circ \mu) \oplus (a \circ \nu)$ for all $a \in F, \mu, \nu \in V$.

D_2. $(a + b) \circ \nu = (a \circ \nu) \oplus (b \circ \nu)$ for all $a, b \in F, \nu \in V$. (Here + denotes addition in the field F.)

The elements of F are referred to as *scalars*.

EXAMPLE 1.   The polynomial ring $P(F)$ of a field F is a vector space over F. In this example scalar multiplication is a special case of the multiplication defined for $P(F)$.

EXAMPLE 2.   Denote by $C_n(F)$ the set of all n-tuples, $(a_1, a_2, \ldots, a_n), n$ a positive integer, with all $a_i \in F$. Define

$$(a_1, \ldots, a_n) \oplus (b_1, \ldots, b_n) = (a_1 + b_1, \ldots, a_n + b_n) \quad \text{and}$$
$$c \circ (a_1, \ldots, a_n) = (c \times a_1, \ldots, c \times a_n),$$

where + and × denote the addition and multiplication, respectively, of the field F. Relative to $\oplus$ and $\circ$, $C_n(F)$ is a vector space, called the *n-dimensional coordinate space* over F.

A vector space $V(F)$ is *n-dimensional* over F provided V contains n elements $\nu_1, \nu_2, \ldots, \nu_n$ such that each element $\nu \in V$ is uniquely expressible in the form

$$\nu = a_1 \circ \nu_1 \oplus a_2 \circ \nu_2 \oplus \cdots \oplus a_n \circ \nu_n$$

for some $a_1, a_2, \ldots, a_n \in F$.

Two vector spaces $V(F)$ and $W(F)$ over the field of scalars F are *isomorphic* provided there is a one-to-one correspondence between the elements of V and the elements of W which is preserved under the arithmetic of the two spaces.

Basic Theorem.   An *n*-dimensional vector space $V(F)$ is isomorphic with the coordinate space $C_n(F)$ (of Example 2, above).

MATRICES AND DETERMINANTS

Dr. R. E. Bargmann

1. GENERAL DEFINITIONS

1.1. A matrix is an array of numbers, consisting of m rows and n columns. It is usually denoted by a bold-face capital letter, e.g.,

$$\mathbf{A} \qquad \mathbf{\Sigma} \qquad \mathbf{M}$$

1.2. The (i,j) element of a matrix is the element occurring in row i and column j. It is usually denoted by a lower-case letter with subscripts, e.g.,

$$a_{ij} \qquad \sigma_{ij} \qquad m_{ij}$$

Exceptions to this convention will be stated where required.

1.3. A matrix is called rectangular if m (number of rows) $\neq n$ (number of columns).

1.4. A matrix is called square if $m = n$.

1.5a. In the transpose of a matrix $\mathbf{A}$, denoted by $\mathbf{A}'$, the element in the j'th row and i'th column of $\mathbf{A}$ is equal to the element in the i'th row and j'th column of $\mathbf{A}'$. Formally $(\mathbf{A}')_{ij} = (\mathbf{A})_{ji}$ where the symbol $(\mathbf{A}')_{ij}$ denotes the (i,j) element of $\mathbf{A}'$.

1.5b. The Hermitian conjugate of a matrix $\mathbf{A}$, denoted by $\mathbf{A}^H$ or $\mathbf{A}^\dagger$ is obtained by transposing $\mathbf{A}$ and replacing each element by its conjugate complex. Hence if

$$a_{kl} = u_{kl} + iv_{kl}$$

then

$$(\mathbf{A}^H)_{kl} = u_{lk} - iv_{lk}$$

where typical elements have been denoted by (k,l) to avoid confusion with $i = \sqrt{-1}$.

1.6a. A square matrix is called symmetric if $\mathbf{A} = \mathbf{A}'$.

1.6b. A square matrix is called Hermitian if $\mathbf{A} = \mathbf{A}^H$.

1.7. A matrix with m rows and 1 column is called a column vector and is usually denoted by bold faced, lower-case letters, e.g.,

$$\boldsymbol{\beta} \qquad \mathbf{x} \qquad \mathbf{a}$$

1.8. A matrix with one row and n columns is called a row vector and is usually denoted by a primed, bold faced, lower-case letter, e.g.,

$$\mathbf{a}' \qquad \mathbf{c}' \qquad \boldsymbol{\mu}'$$

1.9. A matrix with one row and one column is called a scalar, and is usually denoted by a lower-case letter, occasionally italicized.

1.10. The diagonal extending from upper left (NW) to lower right (SE) is called the principal diagonal of a square matrix.

1.11a. A matrix with all elements above the principal diagonal equal to zero is called a lower triangular matrix.

Example

$$\mathbf{T} = \begin{bmatrix} t_{11} & 0 & 0 \\ t_{21} & t_{22} & 0 \\ t_{31} & t_{32} & t_{33} \end{bmatrix} \text{ is lower triangular}$$

1.11b. The transpose of a lower triangular matrix is called an upper triangular matrix.

1.12. A square matrix with all off-diagonal elements equal to zero is called a diagonal matrix, denoted by the letter **D** with subscript indicating the typical element in the principal diagonal.

Example

$$\mathbf{D}_a = \begin{bmatrix} a_1 & 0 & 0 \\ 0 & a_2 & 0 \\ 0 & 0 & a_3 \end{bmatrix} \text{ is diagonal}$$

2. ADDITION, SUBTRACTION, AND MULTIPLICATION

2.1. Two matrices **A** and **B** can be added (subtracted) if the number of rows (columns) in **A** equals the number of rows (columns) in **B**.

$$\mathbf{A} \pm \mathbf{B} = \mathbf{C}$$

implies

$$a_{ij} \pm b_{ij} = c_{ij} \qquad \begin{aligned} i &= 1, 2, \ldots m \\ j &= 1, 2, \ldots n \end{aligned}$$

2.2. Multiplication of a matrix or vector by a scalar implies multiplication of each element by the scalar. If

$$\mathbf{B} = \gamma \mathbf{A}$$

then

$$b_{ij} = \gamma a_{ij}$$

for all elements.

2.3a. Two matrices, **A** and **B**, can be multiplied if the number of columns in **A** equals the number of rows in **B**.

2.3b. Let **A** be of order $(m \times n)$ (have m rows and n columns) and **B** of order $(n \times p)$. Then the product of two matrices $\mathbf{C} = \mathbf{AB}$, is a matrix of order $(m \times p)$ with elements

$$c_{ij} = \sum_{k=1}^{n} a_{ik} b_{kj}$$

This states that c_{ij} is the scalar product of the i'th row vector of **A** and the j'th column vector of **B**.

Example

$$\begin{bmatrix} 3 & 4 & 2 \\ 2 & 3 & -1 \end{bmatrix} \begin{bmatrix} 1 & -2 & -4 \\ 0 & -1 & 2 \\ 6 & -3 & 9 \end{bmatrix} = \begin{bmatrix} 15 & -16 & 14 \\ -4 & -4 & -11 \end{bmatrix}$$

e.g.,

$$c_{23} = \begin{bmatrix} 2 & 3 & -1 \end{bmatrix} \begin{bmatrix} -4 \\ 2 \\ 9 \end{bmatrix}$$

$$= 2 \times (-4) + 3 \times 2 + (-1) \times 9 = -11$$

2.3c. In general, matrix multiplication is not commutative

$$\mathbf{AB} \neq \mathbf{BA}$$

2.3d. Matrix multiplication is associative

$$\mathbf{A(BC)} = \mathbf{(AB)C}$$

2.3e. The distributive law for multiplication and addition holds as in the case of scalars,

$$\mathbf{(A + B)C} = \mathbf{AC} + \mathbf{BC}$$
$$\mathbf{C(A + B)} = \mathbf{CA} + \mathbf{CB}$$

2.4. In some applications, the term-by-term product of two matrices **A** and **B** of identical order is defined as

$$\mathbf{C} = \mathbf{A} * \mathbf{B}$$

where

$$c_{ij} = a_{ij}b_{ij}$$

2.5. $(\mathbf{ABC})' = \mathbf{C'B'A'}$
2.6. $(\mathbf{ABC})^H = \mathbf{C^H B^H A^H}$
2.7. If both **A** and **B** are symmetric, then $(\mathbf{AB})' = \mathbf{BA}$. Note that the product of two symmetric matrices is generally not symmetric.

3. RECOGNITION RULES AND SPECIAL FORMS

3.1. A column (row) vector with all elements equal to zero is called a null vector, and usually denoted by the symbol **0**.

3.2. A null matrix has all elements equal to zero.

3.3a. A diagonal matrix with all elements equal to one in the principal diagonal is called the identity matrix **I**.

3.3b. $\gamma\mathbf{I}$, i.e., a diagonal matrix with all diagonal elements equal to a constant γ, is called a scalar matrix.

3.4. A matrix which has only one element equal to one and all others equal to zero is called an elementary matrix $(\mathbf{EL})_{ij}$.

Example

$$(\mathbf{EL})_{23} = \begin{bmatrix} 0 & 0 & 0 & 0 & 0 \\ 0 & 0 & 1 & 0 & 0 \\ 0 & 0 & 0 & 0 & 0 \\ 0 & 0 & 0 & 0 & 0 \end{bmatrix}$$

The order of the matrix is usually implicit.

3.5a. The symbol **j** is reserved for a column vector with all elements equal to 1.
3.5b. The symbol **j'** is reserved for a row vector with all elements equal to 1.
3.6. An expression ending with a column vector is a column vector.

Example

$$\mathbf{ABx} = \mathbf{y}$$

(It is assumed that rule 2.3a is satisfied, else matrix multiplication would not be defined.)

3.7. An expression beginning with a row vector is a row vector.

Example

$$\mathbf{y'(A + BC)} = \mathbf{d'}$$

3.8. An expression beginning with a row vector and ending with a column vector, is a scalar.

Example

$$\mathbf{a'Bc} = \gamma$$

3.9a. If $\mathbf{Q}$ is a square matrix, the scalar $\mathbf{x'Qx}$ is called a quadratic form. If $\mathbf{Q}$ is non-symmetric, one can always find a symmetric matrix $\mathbf{Q}^*$ such that

$$\mathbf{x'Qx} = \mathbf{x'Q^*x}$$

where

$$(\mathbf{Q}^*)_{ij} = \tfrac{1}{2}(q_{ij} + q_{ji})$$

3.9b. If $\mathbf{Q}$ is a square matrix the scalar $\mathbf{x}^H\mathbf{Qx}$ is called a Hermitian form.

3.10. A scalar $\mathbf{x'Qy}$ is called a bilinear form.

3.11. The scalar $\mathbf{x'x} = \Sigma x_i^2$, i.e., the sum of squares of all elements of $\mathbf{x}$.

3.12. The scalar $\mathbf{x'y} = \Sigma x_i y_i$, i.e., the sum of products of elements in $\mathbf{x}$ by those in $\mathbf{y}$. $\mathbf{x}$ and $\mathbf{y}$ have the same number of elements.

3.13. The scalar $\mathbf{x'D_wx} = \Sigma w_i x_i^2$ is called a weighted sum of squares.

3.14. The scalar $\mathbf{x'D_wy} = \Sigma w_i x_i y_i$ is called a weighted sum of products.

3.15a. The vector $\mathbf{Aj}$ is a column vector whose elements are the row sums of $\mathbf{A}$.

3.15b. The vector $\mathbf{j'A}$ is a row vector whose elements are the column sums of $\mathbf{A}$.

3.15c. The scalar $\mathbf{j'Aj}$ is the sum of all elements in $\mathbf{A}$. Schematically

$\mathbf{A}$	$\mathbf{Aj}$
$\mathbf{j'A}$	$\mathbf{j'Aj}$

3.16a. If $\mathbf{B} = \mathbf{D_wA}$; then $b_{ij} = w_i a_{ij}$.

3.16b. If $\mathbf{B} = \mathbf{AD_w}$; then $b_{ij} = a_{ij} w_j$.

3.17. Interchanging summation and matrix notation:

If

$$\mathbf{ABCD} = \mathbf{E}$$

then

$$e_{ij} = \sum_k \sum_l \sum_m a_{ik} b_{kl} c_{lm} d_{mj}$$

The second subscript of an element must coincide with the first of the next one. Reordering and transposing may be required.

Example

If

$$e_{ij} = \sum_k \sum_l \sum_m a_{kl} b_{ki} c_{jm} d_{ml}$$

$$= \sum_k \sum_l \sum_m b_{ki} a_{kl} d_{ml} c_{jm}$$

Then

$$\mathbf{E} = \mathbf{B'AD'C'}$$

3.18a. $\mathbf{A'A}$ is a symmetric matrix whose (i, j) element is the scalar product of the i'th column vector and the j'th column vector of $\mathbf{A}$.

3.18b. $\mathbf{AA'}$ is a symmetric matrix whose (i, j) element is the scalar product of the i'th row vector and the j'th row vector of $\mathbf{A}$.

4. DETERMINANTS

4.1a. A determinant $|\mathbf{A}|$ or $\det(\mathbf{A})$ is a scalar function of a square matrix defined in such a way that

$$|\mathbf{A}|\,|\mathbf{B}| = |\mathbf{AB}|$$

and

$$\begin{vmatrix} a_{11} & a_{12} \\ a_{21} & a_{22} \end{vmatrix} = a_{11}a_{22} - a_{12}a_{21}$$

4.1b. $|\mathbf{A}| = |\mathbf{A}'|$

4.2.

$$\begin{vmatrix} a_{11} & a_{12} & a_{13} \\ a_{21} & a_{22} & a_{23} \\ a_{31} & a_{32} & a_{33} \end{vmatrix} = \begin{aligned} & a_{11}a_{22}a_{33} + a_{12}a_{23}a_{31} + a_{13}a_{21}a_{32} \\ & - a_{13}a_{22}a_{31} - a_{11}a_{23}a_{32} - a_{12}a_{21}a_{33} \end{aligned}$$

4.3.

$$\begin{vmatrix} a_{11} & a_{12} & \cdots & a_{1n} \\ a_{21} & a_{22} & \cdots & a_{2n} \\ \cdot & & \cdots & \cdot \\ a_{n1} & a_{n2} & \cdots & a_{nm} \end{vmatrix} = \sum (-1)^{\delta} a_{1i_1} a_{2i_2} \cdots a_{ni_n}$$

where the sum is over all permutations

$$i_1 \neq i_2 \neq \cdots i_n$$

and δ denotes the number of exchanges necessary to bring the sequence $(i_1, i_2, \ldots i_n)$ back into the natural order $(1, 2, \ldots n)$.

4.4. If two rows (columns) in a matrix are exchanged, the determinant will change its sign.

4.5. A determinant does not change its value if a linear combination of other rows (columns) is added to any given row (column).

Example

$$\begin{vmatrix} a_{11} & a_{12} & a_{13} & a_{14} \\ b_{21} & b_{22} & b_{23} & b_{24} \\ a_{31} & a_{32} & a_{33} & a_{34} \\ a_{41} & a_{42} & a_{43} & a_{44} \end{vmatrix} = \begin{vmatrix} a_{11} & a_{12} & a_{13} & a_{14} \\ a_{21} & a_{22} & a_{23} & a_{24} \\ a_{31} & a_{32} & a_{33} & a_{34} \\ a_{41} & a_{42} & a_{43} & a_{44} \end{vmatrix}$$

where

$$b_{2i} = a_{2i} + \gamma_1 a_{1i} + \gamma_3 a_{3i} + \gamma_4 a_{4i}$$
$$i = 1, 2, 3, 4$$

$\gamma_1, \gamma_3, \gamma_4$ arbitrary.

4.6. If the i'th row (column) equals (a constant times) the j'th row (column) of a matrix, its determinant is equal to zero, $(i \neq j)$.

4.7. If, in a matrix $\mathbf{A}$, each element of a row (column) is multiplied by a constant γ, the determinant is multiplied by γ.

4.8. $|\gamma\mathbf{A}| = \gamma^n |\mathbf{A}|$ assuming that $\mathbf{A}$ is of order $(n \times n)$.

4.9. The cofactor of a square matrix $\mathbf{A}$, $\text{cof}_{ij}(\mathbf{A})$ is the determinant of a matrix obtained by striking the i'th row and j'th column of $\mathbf{A}$ and choosing positive (negative) sign if $i + j$ is even (odd).

Example

$$\mathrm{cof}_{23}\begin{bmatrix} 2 & 4 & 3 \\ 6 & 1 & 5 \\ -2 & 1 & 3 \end{bmatrix} = -\begin{vmatrix} 2 & 4 \\ -2 & 1 \end{vmatrix}$$

$$= -(2 + 8) = -10$$

4.10. (Laplace Development)

$$|\mathbf{A}| = a_{i1}\mathrm{cof}_{i1}(\mathbf{A}) + a_{i2}\mathrm{cof}_{i2}(\mathbf{A}) + \cdots + a_{in}\mathrm{cof}_{in}(\mathbf{A})$$

$$= a_{1j}\mathrm{cof}_{1j}(\mathbf{A}) + a_{2j}\mathrm{cof}_{2j}(\mathbf{A}) + \cdots + a_{nj}\mathrm{cof}_{nj}(\mathbf{A})$$

for any row i or any column j.

4.11. Numerical Evaluation of the determinant of a symmetric matrix.

Note: If $\mathbf{A}$ is non-symmetric, form $\mathbf{A'A}$ or $\mathbf{AA'}$ by rule 3.18, obtain its determinant, and take the square root.

("Forward Doolittle Scheme", "left side")

Let

$$p_{11} = a_{11}, \quad p_{12} = a_{12} = a_{21},\ldots p_{1n} = a_{1n}$$

$$
\begin{array}{cccc}
p_{11} & p_{12} & p_{13} & \cdots & p_{1n} \\
1 & u_{12} & u_{13} & \cdots & u_{1n} \\
\hline
 & a_{22} & a_{23} & \cdots & a_{2n} \\
 & p_{22} & p_{23} & \cdots & p_{2n} \\
 & 1 & u_{23} & \cdots & u_{2n} \\
\hline
 & & a_{33} & \cdots & a_{3n} \\
 & & p_{33} & \cdots & p_{3n} \\
 & & 1 & \cdots & u_{3n} \\
 & & \cdot & \cdots & \cdot \\
 & & & & a_{nn} \\
 & & & & p_{nn} \\
 & & & & 1
\end{array}
$$

$$u_{1i} = p_{1i}/p_{11} \qquad\qquad\qquad\qquad\qquad i = 1,2,\ldots n$$

$$p_{2i} = a_{2i} - u_{12}p_{1i} \qquad\qquad\qquad\qquad i = 2,3,\ldots n$$

$$u_{2i} = p_{2i}/p_{22}$$

$$p_{3i} = a_{3i} - u_{13}p_{1i} - u_{23}p_{2i} \qquad\qquad i = 3,4,\ldots n$$

$$u_{3i} = p_{3i}/p_{33}$$

$$p_{ki} = a_{ki} - u_{1k}p_{1i} - u_{2k}p_{2i} - \cdots - u_{k-1,k}p_{k-1,i} \qquad i = k, k+1,\ldots n$$

$$k = 2,3,\ldots n$$

$$u_{ki} = p_{ki}/p_{kk}$$

If, at some stage, $p_{kk} = 0$, reordering of rows and columns may be required. If the matrix is positive-definite (see 8.16) (always true for $\mathbf{AA'}$ or $\mathbf{A'A}$, see rule 10.24), none of the

p_{kk} will be zero. The p_{ii} are called pivots. Then

$$|\mathbf{A}| = \prod_{i=1}^{n} p_{ii}$$

Further, if $\mathbf{A}$ is partitioned

$$\mathbf{A} = \begin{bmatrix} \mathbf{A}_{11} & \mathbf{A}_{12} \\ \mathbf{A}'_{12} & \mathbf{A}_{22} \end{bmatrix}$$

where $\mathbf{A}_{11}$ is of order $(k \times k)$, then

$$|\mathbf{A}_{11}| = \prod_{i=1}^{k} p_{ii}$$

(Numerical Examples: see 6.14.)

5. SINGULARITY AND RANK

5.1. A matrix $\mathbf{A}$ is called singular if there exists a vector $\mathbf{x} \neq \mathbf{0}$ such that $\mathbf{Ax} = \mathbf{0}$ or $\mathbf{A'x} = \mathbf{0}$. Note $\mathbf{x} \neq \mathbf{0}$ if a single element of $\mathbf{x}$ is unequal 0. If a matrix is not singular, it is called non-singular.

5.2. If a matrix $\mathbf{A}_1$ can be formed by selection of r rows and columns of $\mathbf{A}$ such that $\mathbf{A}_1 \mathbf{x} \neq \mathbf{0}$ or $\mathbf{A}'_1 \mathbf{x} \neq \mathbf{0}$ for every $\mathbf{x} \neq \mathbf{0}$, and if addition of an $(r + 1)st$ row and column would produce a singular matrix, r is called the rank of $\mathbf{A}$.

Example

$$\mathbf{A} = \begin{bmatrix} 2 & 4 & 6 \\ 1 & 3 & 7 \\ 3 & 7 & 13 \\ 1 & 1 & -1 \end{bmatrix}$$

Note that

$$[1, \quad 1, \quad -1] \begin{bmatrix} 2 & 4 & 6 \\ 1 & 3 & 7 \\ 3 & 7 & 13 \end{bmatrix} = [0 \quad 0 \quad 0]$$

and

$$[1, \quad -1, \quad -1] \begin{bmatrix} 2 & 4 & 6 \\ 1 & 3 & 7 \\ 1 & 1 & -1 \end{bmatrix} = [0 \quad 0 \quad 0]$$

but

$$\begin{bmatrix} 2 & 4 \\ 1 & 3 \end{bmatrix} \begin{bmatrix} x_1 \\ x_2 \end{bmatrix} \neq \begin{bmatrix} 0 \\ 0 \end{bmatrix}$$

or

$$[x_1 \quad x_2] \begin{bmatrix} 2 & 4 \\ 1 & 3 \end{bmatrix} \neq [0, \quad 0]$$

for any arbitrary

$$[x_1, \quad x_2] \neq [0, \quad 0].$$

Hence the matrix has rank 2.

5.3. If **A** has rank *r* and if **A₁** is a non-singular submatrix consisting of *r* rows and columns of **A**, then **A₁** is called a basis of **A**.

5.4a. The determinant of a square singular matrix is 0.

5.4b. The determinant of a non-singular matrix is $\neq 0$.

5.5. rank **(AB)** ≤ min [rank **(A)**, rank **(B)**].

5.6. rank **(AA′)** = rank **(A′A)** = rank **(A)**.

5.7. $|\mathbf{A'A}| = |\mathbf{AA'}| = |\mathbf{A}|^2$ if **A** is square.

5.8. $|\mathbf{A'A}| = |\mathbf{AA'}| \geq 0$ for every **A** with real elements.

6. INVERSION

(Regular Case, non-singular matrices)

6.1. If **A** is square and non-singular ($|\mathbf{A}| \neq 0$) there exists a unique matrix $\mathbf{A}^{-1}$ such that $\mathbf{AA}^{-1} = \mathbf{A}^{-1}\mathbf{A} = \mathbf{I}$.

6.2. $(\mathbf{ABC})^{-1} = \mathbf{C}^{-1}\mathbf{B}^{-1}\mathbf{A}^{-1}$ (provided that all inverses exist).

6.3. $(\mathbf{A}^{-1})' = (\mathbf{A}')^{-1}$

6.4. **Ax** = **b** is a system of linear equations. If **A** is square and non-singular, there exists a unique solution

$$\mathbf{x} = \mathbf{A}^{-1}\mathbf{b}$$

6.5. $(\gamma\mathbf{A})^{-1} = (1/\gamma)\mathbf{A}^{-1}$

6.6. $|\mathbf{A}^{-1}| = 1/|\mathbf{A}|$

6.7. $\mathbf{D}_w^{-1} = \mathbf{D}_{1/w}$ where **D** is a diagonal matrix.

6.8. If

$$\mathbf{A} = \mathbf{B} + \mathbf{uv}'$$

then

$$\mathbf{A}^{-1} = \mathbf{B}^{-1} - \lambda\mathbf{yz}'$$

where

$$\mathbf{y} = \mathbf{B}^{-1}\mathbf{u}, \quad \mathbf{z}' = \mathbf{v}'\mathbf{B}^{-1},$$

and

$$\lambda = 1/(1 + \mathbf{z}'\mathbf{u})$$

Example 6.8.1

$$\mathbf{A} = \begin{bmatrix} 4 & 2 & 4 & 5 \\ 3 & 9 & 12 & 15 \\ 2 & 4 & 11 & 10 \\ 1 & 2 & 4 & 10 \end{bmatrix}$$

This matrix can be written as

$$\begin{bmatrix} 3 & 0 & 0 & 0 \\ 0 & 3 & 0 & 0 \\ 0 & 0 & 3 & 0 \\ 0 & 0 & 0 & 5 \end{bmatrix} + \begin{bmatrix} 1 \\ 3 \\ 2 \\ 1 \end{bmatrix} \begin{bmatrix} 1 & 2 & 4 & 5 \end{bmatrix} = \mathbf{B} + \mathbf{uv}'$$

$$\mathbf{B}^{-1} = \begin{bmatrix} 1/3 & 0 & 0 & 0 \\ 0 & 1/3 & 0 & 0 \\ 0 & 0 & 1/3 & 0 \\ 0 & 0 & 0 & 1/5 \end{bmatrix}$$

$$\mathbf{y} = \mathbf{B}^{-1}\mathbf{u} = \begin{bmatrix} 1/3 \\ 1 \\ 2/3 \\ 1/5 \end{bmatrix}$$

$$\mathbf{z}' = \mathbf{v}'\mathbf{B}^{-1} = [1/3 \quad 2/3 \quad 4/3 \quad 1]$$

$$\mathbf{z}'\mathbf{u} = 1/3 \times 1 + 2/3 \times 3 + 4/3 \times 2 + 1 \times 1 = 6$$

$$\lambda = 1/7$$

$$\mathbf{A}^{-1} = \begin{bmatrix} 1/3 & 0 & 0 & 0 \\ 0 & 1/3 & 0 & 0 \\ 0 & 0 & 1/3 & 0 \\ 0 & 0 & 0 & 1/5 \end{bmatrix} - (1/7) \begin{bmatrix} 1/3 \\ 1 \\ 2/3 \\ 1/5 \end{bmatrix} [1/3 \quad 2/3 \quad 4/3 \quad 1]$$

$$= (1/315) \begin{bmatrix} 100 & -10 & -20 & -15 \\ -15 & 75 & -60 & -45 \\ -10 & -20 & 65 & -30 \\ -3 & -6 & -12 & 54 \end{bmatrix}$$

(This rule is especially useful if all off-diagonal elements are equal, then $\mathbf{u} = k\mathbf{j}$ and $\mathbf{v}' = \mathbf{j}'$ and $\mathbf{B}$ is diagonal.)

6.9. Let $\mathbf{B}$ (elements b_{ij}) have a known inverse, $\mathbf{B}^{-1}$ (elements b^{ij}). Let $\mathbf{A} = \mathbf{B}$ except for one element $a_{rs} = b_{rs} + k$. Then the elements of $\mathbf{A}^{-1}$ are

$$a^{ij} = b^{ij} - \frac{kb^{ir}b^{sj}}{1 + kb^{sr}}.$$

6.10. (Partitioning)

Let

$$\begin{matrix} & (p) & (q) \\ \mathbf{A} = \begin{matrix} (p) \\ (q) \end{matrix} & \begin{bmatrix} \mathbf{B} & \mathbf{C} \\ \mathbf{D} & \mathbf{E} \end{bmatrix} \end{matrix}$$

(letters in parentheses denote order of the submatrices)

Let $\mathbf{B}^{-1}$ and $\mathbf{E}^{-1}$ exist. Then

$$\mathbf{A}^{-1} = \begin{bmatrix} \mathbf{X} & \mathbf{Y} \\ \mathbf{Z} & \mathbf{U} \end{bmatrix}$$

where

$$\mathbf{X} = (\mathbf{B} - \mathbf{C}\mathbf{E}^{-1}\mathbf{D})^{-1}$$
$$\mathbf{U} = (\mathbf{E} - \mathbf{D}\mathbf{B}^{-1}\mathbf{C})^{-1}$$
$$\mathbf{Y} = -\mathbf{B}^{-1}\mathbf{C}\mathbf{U}$$
$$\mathbf{Z} = -\mathbf{E}^{-1}\mathbf{D}\mathbf{X}$$

6.11. (Partitioning of Determinants)

Let

$$|\mathbf{A}| = \begin{vmatrix} \mathbf{B} & \mathbf{C} \\ \mathbf{D} & \mathbf{E} \end{vmatrix} \qquad \text{(same structure as in 6.10)}$$

Then

$$|\mathbf{A}| = |\mathbf{E}|\,|(\mathbf{B} - \mathbf{C}\mathbf{E}^{-1}\mathbf{D})| = |\mathbf{B}|\,|(\mathbf{E} - \mathbf{D}\mathbf{B}^{-1}\mathbf{C})|$$

6.12. Let

$$\mathbf{A} = \mathbf{B} + \mathbf{U}\mathbf{V}$$

where $\mathbf{B}(n \times n)$ has an inverse

$\qquad$ U is of order $(n \times k)$, with k usually very small

$\qquad$ V is of order $(k \times n)$

(the special case for $k = 1$ is treated in 6.8).

Then
$$\mathbf{A}^{-1} = \mathbf{B}^{-1} - \mathbf{Y}\mathbf{\Lambda}\mathbf{Z}$$

where

$$\mathbf{Y} = \mathbf{B}^{-1}\mathbf{U}(n \times k)$$
$$\mathbf{Z} = \mathbf{V}\mathbf{B}^{-1}(k \times n)$$

and

$$\mathbf{\Lambda}(k \times k) = [\mathbf{I} + \mathbf{Z}\mathbf{U}]^{-1}$$

6.13. Let a_{ij} denote the elements of $\mathbf{A}$ and a^{ij} those of $\mathbf{A}^{-1}$. Then

$$a^{ij} = \text{cof}_{ji}(\mathbf{A})/|\mathbf{A}|$$

where cof is the determinant defined in 4.9.

6.14. "Doolittle" Method of inverting symmetric matrices (see also 4.11). Let

$$p_{11} = a_{11}, \quad p_{12} = a_{12} = a_{21}, \ldots p_{1n} = a_{1n} = a_{n1}$$

Forward Solution

p_{11}	p_{12}	p_{13}	$\cdots$	p_{1n}	1				
1	u_{12}	u_{13}	$\cdots$	u_{1n}	u_{11}				
	a_{22}	a_{23}	$\cdots$	a_{2n}	0	1			
	p_{22}	p_{23}	$\cdots$	p_{2n}	p_{21}	$p_{2\text{II}}$			
	1	u_{23}	$\cdots$	u_{2n}	u_{21}	$u_{2\text{II}}$			
		a_{33}	$\cdots$	a_{3n}	0	0	1		
		p_{33}	$\cdots$	p_{3n}	p_{31}	$p_{3\text{II}}$	$p_{3\text{III}}$		
		1	$\cdots$	u_{3n}	u_{31}	$u_{3\text{II}}$	$u_{3\text{III}}$		
		$\cdot$	$\cdots$	$\cdot$	$\cdot$	$\cdots$	$\cdot$		
				a_{nn}	0	0	0	$\cdots$	1
				p_{nn}	p_{n1}	$p_{n\text{II}}$	$p_{n\text{III}}$	$\cdots$	p_{nN}
				1	u_{n1}	$u_{n\text{II}}$	$u_{n\text{III}}$	$\cdots$	u_{nN}

$$u_{1i} = p_{1i}/p_{11} \qquad\qquad i = 1, 2, \ldots n, \text{I}$$

$$p_{2i} = a_{2i} - u_{12}\,p_{1i} \qquad\qquad i = 2, 3, \ldots n, \text{I}, \text{II}$$

$$u_{2i} = p_{2i}/p_{22}$$

$$p_{3i} = a_{3i} - u_{13}\,p_{1i} - u_{23}\,p_{2i} \qquad\qquad i = 3, 4, \ldots n, \text{I}, \text{II}, \text{III}$$

$$u_{3i} = p_{3i}/p_{33}$$

$$p_{ki} = a_{ki} - u_{1k}\,p_{1i} - u_{2k}\,p_{2i} - \cdots - u_{k-1,k}\,p_{k-1,i} \qquad i = k, k+1, \ldots n, \text{I}, \text{II}, \ldots K$$
$$k = 2, 3, \ldots n$$

$$u_{ki} = p_{ki}/p_{kk}$$

Backward Solution

(j refers to Arabic, J refers to Roman numerals)

The elements of $\mathbf{A}^{-1}$ are a^{ij}

$$a^{nj} = u_{nJ} \qquad\qquad \begin{aligned} &j = 1, 2, \ldots n; \\ &J = \text{I}, \text{II}, \ldots N \end{aligned}$$

$$a^{n-1,j} = u_{n-1,J} - u_{n-1,n}\,a^{nj} \qquad\qquad \begin{aligned} &j = 1, 2, \ldots (n-1); \\ &J = \text{I}, \text{II}, \ldots (N-1) \end{aligned}$$

$$a^{n-2,j} = u_{n-2,J} - u_{n-2,n}\,a^{nj} - u_{n-2,n-1}\,a^{n-1,j} \qquad\qquad \begin{aligned} &j = 1, 2, \ldots (n-2); \\ &J = \text{I}, \text{II}, \ldots (N-2) \end{aligned}$$

$$a^{n-k,j} = u_{n-k,J} - u_{n-k,n}\,a^{nj} - u_{n-k,n-1}\,a^{n-1,j} - \cdots - u_{n-k,n-k+1}\,a^{n-k+1,j} \qquad \begin{aligned} &j = 1, 2, \ldots (n-k); \\ &J = \text{I}, \text{II}, \ldots (N-k); \\ &k = 1, 2, \ldots (n-1), \end{aligned}$$

and $a^{ji} = a^{ij}$.

Numerical Example 6.14.1.

Invert the Matrix

$$\begin{bmatrix} 25 & 30 & -10 \\ 30 & 40 & -6 \\ -10 & -6 & 17 \end{bmatrix}$$

a_1	25	30	-10	1		
u_1	1	1.2	-0.4	0.04		
	a_2	40	-6	0	1	
	p_2	4	6	-1.2	1	
	u_2	1	1.5	-0.3	0.25	
		a_3	17	0	0	1
		p_3	4	2.2	-1.5	1
		u_3	1	0.55	-0.375	0.25

1.61	-1.125	0.55
-1.125	0.8125	-0.375
0.55	-0.375	0.25

Enter row a_1.

Elements in u_1 = Elements in a_1 divided by $a_{11}(=25)$.

Enter row a_2.

$$p_{22} = 40 - 1.2 \times 30 = 4$$
$$p_{23} = -6 - 1.2 \times (-10) = 6$$
$$p_{21} = 0 - 1.2 \times 1 = -1.2$$
$$p_{211} = 1$$

Elements in u_2 = Elements in p_2 divided by $p_{22}(=4)$.

Enter row a_3.

$$p_{33} = 17 - (-0.4) \times (-10) - 1.5 \times 6 = 4$$
$$p_{31} = 0 - (-0.4) \times 1 - 1.5 \times (-1.2) = 2.2$$
$$p_{311} = 0 - 1.5 \times 1 = -1.5$$
$$p_{3111} = 1$$

Elements in u_3 = Elements in p_3 divided by $p_{33}(=4)$.

Copy the right-hand side of the last (third) u – row as the last column below the double line.

$$a^{21} = -0.3 - 1.5 \times 0.55 = -1.125$$
$$a^{22} = 0.25 - 1.5 \times (-0.375) = 0.8125$$
$$a^{23} = 0 - 1.5 \times 0.25 = -0.375 \quad \text{(check against } a^{32}\text{)}.$$

These are entered in the next to last (second) column below.

$$a^{11} = 0.04 - (-0.4) \times 0.55 - 1.2 \times (-1.125) = 1.61$$
$$a^{12} = 0 - (-0.4) \times (-0.375) - 1.2 \times 0.8125 = -1.125 \quad \text{(check against } a^{21}\text{)}$$
$$a^{13} = 0 - (-0.4) \times (0.25) - 1.2 \times (-0.375) = 0.55 \quad \text{(check against } a^{31}\text{)}.$$

6.15. A matrix is called orthogonal if $\mathbf{A'} = \mathbf{A}^{-1}$ (or $\mathbf{AA'} = \mathbf{I}$).

7. TRACES

7.1. If $\mathbf{A}$ is a square matrix then the trace of $\mathbf{A}$ is $tr\ \mathbf{A} = \sum_i a_{ii}$, i.e., the sum of the diagonal elements.

7.2. If $\mathbf{A}$ is of order $(m \times k)$ and $\mathbf{B}$ of order $(k \times m)$ then $tr(\mathbf{AB}) = tr(\mathbf{BA})$.

7.3. If $\mathbf{A}$ is of order $(m \times k)$, $\mathbf{B}$ of order $(k \times r)$ and $\mathbf{C}$ of order $(r \times m)$, then

$$tr(\mathbf{ABC}) = tr(\mathbf{BCA}) = tr(\mathbf{CAB}).$$

7.3a. If $\mathbf{b}$ is a column vector and $\mathbf{c'}$ a row vector, then

$$tr(\mathbf{Abc'}) = tr(\mathbf{bc'A}) = \mathbf{c'Ab}$$

since the trace of a scalar is the scalar.

7.4. $tr(\mathbf{A} + \gamma\mathbf{B}) = tr\mathbf{A} + \gamma tr\mathbf{B}$; where γ is a scalar.

7.5. $tr(\mathbf{EL})_{ij}\mathbf{A} = tr\mathbf{A}(\mathbf{EL})_{ij} = a_{ji}$; where $(\mathbf{EL})_{ij}$ is an elementary matrix as defined in 3.4.

7.6. $tr(\mathbf{EL})_{ij}\mathbf{A}(\mathbf{EL})_{rs}\mathbf{B} = a_{jr}b_{si}$

(These rules are useful in matrix differentiation)

7.7. The trace of the second order of a square matrix $\mathbf{A}$ is the sum of the determinants of all $\binom{n}{2}$ matrices of order (2×2) which can be formed by intersecting rows i and j with columns i and j.

$$tr_2\mathbf{A} = \begin{vmatrix} a_{11} & a_{12} \\ a_{21} & a_{22} \end{vmatrix} + \begin{vmatrix} a_{11} & a_{13} \\ a_{31} & a_{33} \end{vmatrix}$$

$$+ \cdots + \begin{vmatrix} a_{11} & a_{1n} \\ a_{n1} & a_{nn} \end{vmatrix} + \begin{vmatrix} a_{22} & a_{23} \\ a_{32} & a_{33} \end{vmatrix}$$

$$+ \cdots + \begin{vmatrix} a_{22} & a_{2n} \\ a_{n2} & a_{nn} \end{vmatrix} + \cdots + \begin{vmatrix} a_{n-1,n-1} & a_{n-1,n} \\ a_{n,n-1} & a_{nn} \end{vmatrix}$$

7.8. The trace of the k'th order of a square matrix is the sum of the determinants of all $\binom{n}{k}$ matrices of order $(k \times k)$ which can be formed by intersecting any k rows of $\mathbf{A}$ with the same k columns.

$$tr_k\mathbf{A} = \sum \begin{vmatrix} a_{i_1 i_1} & a_{i_1 i_2} & \cdots & a_{i_1 i_k} \\ a_{i_2 i_1} & a_{i_2 i_2} & \cdots & a_{i_2 i_k} \\ \cdot & \cdot & \cdots & \cdot \\ a_{i_k i_1} & a_{i_k i_2} & \cdots & a_{i_k i_k} \end{vmatrix}$$

where the sum extends over all combinations of n elements taken k at a time in order

$$i_1 < i_2 < \cdots < i_k.$$

7.9. Rules 7.2 and 7.3 (cyclic exchange) are valid for trace of k'th order.

7.10. $tr_n\mathbf{A} = |\mathbf{A}|$ if $\mathbf{A}$ is of order $(n \times n)$.

8. CHARACTERISTIC ROOTS AND VECTORS

8.1. If $\mathbf{A}$ is a square matrix of order $(n \times n)$, then $|\mathbf{A} - \lambda\mathbf{I}| = 0$ is called the characteristic equation of the matrix $\mathbf{A}$. It is a polynomial of the n'th degree in λ.

8.2. The n roots of the characteristic equation (not necessarily distinct) are called the characteristic roots of $\mathbf{A}$

$$ch(\mathbf{A}) = \lambda_1, \lambda_2, \ldots \lambda_n$$

8.3. The characteristic equation of $\mathbf{A}$ can be obtained by the relation

$$\lambda^n - (tr\mathbf{A})\lambda^{n-1} + (tr_2\mathbf{A})\lambda^{n-2} - (tr_3\mathbf{A})\lambda^{n-3} \cdots - (-1)^n(tr_{n-1}\mathbf{A})\lambda + (-1)^n|\mathbf{A}| = 0$$

where tr_k is defined in 7.8.

Example 8.3.1

$$\mathbf{A} = \begin{bmatrix} 25 & 30 & -10 \\ 30 & 40 & -6 \\ -10 & -6 & 17 \end{bmatrix}$$

$tr\mathbf{A} = 25 + 40 + 17 = 82$

$tr_2\mathbf{A} = (25 \times 40 - 30 \times 30) + (25 \times 17 - 10 \times 10) + (40 \times 17 - 6 \times 6) = 1069$

$tr_3\mathbf{A} = |\mathbf{A}| = 25 \times 4 \times 4 = 400$

(cf. 6.14 and procedure stated in 4.11)

Hence

$$\lambda^3 - 82\lambda^2 + 1069\lambda - 400 = 0$$

The solutions (by Newton iteration) are

$$\lambda_1 = 65.86108$$
$$\lambda_2 = 15.75339$$
$$\lambda_3 = 0.38553$$

These are the characteristic roots of $\mathbf{A}$.

8.4. $ch(\mathbf{A} + \gamma\mathbf{I}) = \gamma + ch(\mathbf{A})$

8.5. $ch(\mathbf{AB}) = ch(\mathbf{BA})$

  (except that $\mathbf{AB}$ or $\mathbf{BA}$ may have additional roots equal to zero).

8.6. $ch(\mathbf{A}^{-1}) = 1/ch(\mathbf{A})$

8.7. If $\lambda_1, \lambda_2, \ldots \lambda_n$ are the roots of $\mathbf{A}$ then

$$\sum_i \lambda_i = tr\mathbf{A}$$

$$\sum_{i<j} \lambda_i\lambda_j = tr_2\mathbf{A}$$

$$\sum_{i<j<k} \lambda_i\lambda_j\lambda_k = tr_3\mathbf{A}$$

$$\prod_i \lambda_i = |\mathbf{A}|$$

8.8. If $\mathbf{x}'$ denotes the radius vector (running coordinates $[x, y, z]$) and if a matrix $\mathbf{Q}$ is positive-definite, then

$$(\mathbf{x}' - \mathbf{x}_0')\mathbf{Q}^{-1}(\mathbf{x} - \mathbf{x}_0) = 1$$

is the equation of an ellipsoid with center at $[x_0, y_0, z_0] = \mathbf{x}_0'$ and semi-axes equal to the square roots of the characteristic roots of $\mathbf{Q}$.

8.9. The characteristic roots of a triangular (or diagonal) matrix are the diagonal elements of the matrix.

8.10. If $\mathbf{A}$ is a real matrix with positive roots, then

$$ch_{min}(\mathbf{AA}') \leq [ch_{min}(\mathbf{A})]^2 \leq [ch_{max}(\mathbf{A})]^2 \leq ch_{max}(\mathbf{AA}')$$

where ch_{min} denotes the smallest and ch_{max} the largest root.

8.11. The ratio of two quadratic forms ($\mathbf{B}$ non-singular)

$$u = \frac{\mathbf{x}'\mathbf{A}\mathbf{x}}{\mathbf{x}'\mathbf{B}\mathbf{x}}$$

attains stationary values at the roots of $\mathbf{B}^{-1}\mathbf{A}$. In particular

$$u_{max} = ch_{max}(\mathbf{B}^{-1}\mathbf{A}) \qquad \text{and} \qquad u_{min} = ch_{min}(\mathbf{B}^{-1}\mathbf{A})$$

8.12. The equation system

$$\mathbf{A}\mathbf{x} = \lambda\mathbf{x}$$

permits non-zero solutions only if λ is one of the characteristic roots of $\mathbf{A}$. Such a solution $\mathbf{x}$ is called a characteristic vector.

8.13. If $\mathbf{x}$ is a solution to 8.12, so is $\gamma\mathbf{x}$ for an arbitrary scalar γ.

8.14. A solution $\mathbf{x}$ which has unit length ($\mathbf{x}'\mathbf{x} = 1$) is called the eigenvector associated with the characteristic root λ of $\mathbf{A}$. The vector is frequently denoted by $\mathbf{e}$.

8.15. A real symmetric matrix has real roots.

8.16. A matrix $\mathbf{A}$ is called positive-definite (abbreviated p.d.) if the quadratic form $\mathbf{x}'\mathbf{A}\mathbf{x} > 0$ for every $\mathbf{x} \neq \mathbf{0}$.

8.17. A matrix **A** is called positive-semidefinite (abbreviated p.s.d.) if the quadratic form $\mathbf{x'Ax} > 0$ and/or $\mathbf{x'Ax} = 0$ for some $\mathbf{x} \neq \mathbf{0}$.

8.18. A positive-definite real symmetric matrix has only positive characteristic roots.

8.19. If a real symmetric matrix is positive-semidefinite, it has no negative roots. The number of non-zero roots equals the rank of the matrix.

8.20. If all roots of a real symmetric matrix are distinct, the associated eigenvectors are distinct.

8.21. The matrix of eigenvectors

$$\mathbf{E} = [\mathbf{e}_1, \mathbf{e}_2, \ldots \mathbf{e}_n]$$

of a real symmetric matrix is (or can be chosen to be) orthogonal.

8.22. $\mathbf{AE} = \mathbf{ED}_\lambda$.

8.23. For a real symmetric matrix, $\mathbf{A} = \mathbf{ED}_\lambda \mathbf{E'}$ (decomposition into matrices of unit rank)

$$\mathbf{E'AE} = \mathbf{D}_\lambda$$

where $\mathbf{D}_\lambda$ denotes the diagonal matrix of characteristic roots ordered in the same way as the eigenvector columns in $\mathbf{E}$.

8.24. If $f(\lambda)$ is a polynomial in λ, then

$$f(\mathbf{A}) = \mathbf{ED}_{f(\lambda)}\mathbf{E}^{-1}$$

where λ are the characteristic roots of **A** and **E** is the matrix of associated eigenvectors. If **A** is symmetric, $\mathbf{E}^{-1} = \mathbf{E'}$.

Example 8.24.1

Consider the matrix in 8.3 (and 6.14).

$$\mathbf{A} = \begin{bmatrix} 25 & 30 & -10 \\ 30 & 40 & -6 \\ -10 & -6 & 17 \end{bmatrix}$$

The characteristic roots were found in Example 8.3.1,

$$\lambda_1 = 65.86108 \qquad \lambda_2 = 15.75339 \qquad \lambda_3 = 0.38553.$$

To find some **x** such that $\mathbf{Ax} = \lambda_1 \mathbf{x}$, we arbitrarily set the first element of **x** equal to 1. Using only the first two rows of **A** we solve the equation system

$$25 + 30x_2 - 10x_3 = 65.86108$$
$$30 + 40x_2 - 6x_3 = 65.86108x_2$$

which yields $x_2 = 1.24294$ and $x_3 = -0.35729$. Substitution of these values into the third equation

$$-10 - 6x_2 + 17x_3 = 65.86108x_3$$

yields zero to five decimal places, indicating the accuracy of the first characteristic root. To reduce to unit length the characteristic vector

$$[1 \qquad 1.24294 \qquad -0.35729]$$

we divide each element by

$$\sqrt{1 + 1.24294^2 + 0.35729^2}$$

and thus obtain the first eigenvector

$$[0.61170 \qquad 0.76030 \qquad -0.21855]$$

This, written as a column vector, is e_1. Repeating the same process for the second and third eigenvectors we obtain

$$e_2 = \begin{bmatrix} -0.08659 \\ 0.33896 \\ 0.93681 \end{bmatrix} \qquad e_3 = \begin{bmatrix} 0.78634 \\ -0.55412 \\ 0.27318 \end{bmatrix}$$

The three vectors can be placed into the eigenvector matrix E, which is easily seen to be orthogonal.

9.   CONDITIONAL INVERSES

9.1. Any matrix A (singular or non-singular, rectangular or square) has some conditional or generalized inverse $A^{(-1)}$ defined by the relation

$$AA^{(-1)}A = A.$$

9.2. If (and only if) A is square and non-singular, $A^{(-1)}$ is unique and equals A^{-1}. Otherwise there will be infinitely many matrices $A^{(-1)}$ which satisfy the defining relation 9.1.

9.3a. If A is rectangular ($n \times m$) of rank m, with $m < n$, then $A^{(-1)}$ is of order ($m \times n$) and $A^{(-1)}A = I(m \times m)$. Then $A^{(-1)}$ is called an inverse from the left. $AA^{(-1)} \neq I$ in this case.

9.3b. If A is rectangular ($n \times m$) of rank n, with $m > n$, then $A^{(-1)}$ is of order ($m \times n$) and $AA^{(-1)} = I(n \times n)$. Then $A^{(-1)}$ is called an inverse to the right. In this case,

$$A^{(-1)}A \neq I.$$

9.3c. For a square, singular matrix, $AA^{(-1)} \neq I$ and $A^{(-1)}A \neq I$.

Example 9.3.1

$$A = \begin{bmatrix} 3 \\ 2 \\ 1 \end{bmatrix}$$

The row vector $[1/3 \quad 0 \quad 0]$ is an inverse from the left. The row vector

$$[x \quad y \quad (1 - 3x - 2y)]$$

is a conditional inverse of the above matrix A for any values of x and y. It is called the generalized inverse of A.

Example 9.3.2

$$A = \begin{bmatrix} 1 & 2 & 3 \\ 2 & 5 & 6 \\ 3 & 7 & 9 \end{bmatrix}$$

A conditional inverse is

$$A^{(-1)} = \begin{bmatrix} 5 & -2 & 0 \\ -2 & 1 & 0 \\ 0 & 0 & 0 \end{bmatrix}$$

Here it was obtained by inversion of the basis (the 2×2 matrix in the upper left-hand corner) and replacement of the other elements by zeros.

9.4. A square matrix $\mathbf{A}$ is called idempotent if $\mathbf{AA} = \mathbf{A}^2 = \mathbf{A}$.

9.5. $\mathbf{AA}^{(-1)}$ and $\mathbf{A}^{(-1)}\mathbf{A}$ are idempotent.

9.6. All characteristic roots of idempotent matrices are either zero or one.

9.7. A system of linear equations (m equations in n unknowns)

$$\mathbf{Ax} = \mathbf{b}$$

is called consistent if there exists some solution $\mathbf{x}$ which satisfies the equation system.

Example 9.7.1

The system

$$x + y = 2$$
$$2x + 2y = 4 \qquad \text{is consistent.}$$

Example 9.7.2

The system

$$x + y = 2$$
$$2x + 2y = 5 \qquad \text{is inconsistent,}$$

for no pair of values (x, y) will satisfy this system.

9.8. If, in a system of equations (rectangular or square)

$$\mathbf{Ax} = \mathbf{b}$$

$\mathbf{AA}^{(-1)}\mathbf{b} = \mathbf{b}$ for some conditional inverse $\mathbf{A}^{(-1)}$, then $\mathbf{AA}^{(-1)}\mathbf{b} = \mathbf{b}$ for every conditional inverse of $\mathbf{A}$, and $\mathbf{Ax} = \mathbf{b}$ is consistent. Conversely, if $\mathbf{AA}^{(-1)}\mathbf{b} \neq \mathbf{b}$ for some conditional inverse $\mathbf{A}^{(-1)}$ then $\mathbf{AA}^{(-1)}\mathbf{b} \neq \mathbf{b}$ for every conditional inverse of $\mathbf{A}$, and $\mathbf{Ax} = \mathbf{b}$ is inconsistent.

9.9. If $\mathbf{Ax} = \mathbf{b}$ is consistent, then $\mathbf{x} = \mathbf{A}^{(-1)}\mathbf{b}$ is a solution (generally a different one for each $\mathbf{A}^{(-1)}$).

9.10. Let $\mathbf{y}$ ($p \times 1$) be a set of linear functions of the solutions $\mathbf{x}$ ($n \times 1$) of a consistent system of equations $\mathbf{Ax} = \mathbf{b}$, given by the relation $\mathbf{y} = \mathbf{Cx}$. Then $\mathbf{y} = \mathbf{Cx}$ is called unique if the same values of $\mathbf{y}$ will result regardless which solution $\mathbf{x}$ is used.

Example 9.10.1

$$3x + 4y + 5z = 22$$
$$x + y + z = 6$$

is a consistent system. One solution would be

$$x = 3 \quad y = 2 \quad z = 1$$

Another solution is

$$x = 2 \quad y = 4 \quad z = 0$$

The linear function

$$[7 \quad 9 \quad 11] \begin{bmatrix} x \\ y \\ z \end{bmatrix} = u$$

($7x + 9y + 11z = u$) will have the same value (50) regardless which of the two (or any other) solutions is substituted. Thus u is unique.

9.11. Let $\mathbf{Ax} = \mathbf{b}$ be a consistent system of equations. For $\mathbf{Cx} = \mathbf{y}$ to be a unique linear combination of the solution $\mathbf{x}$, it is necessary and sufficient that $\mathbf{CA}^{(-1)}\mathbf{A} = \mathbf{C}$. If this relation holds for some $\mathbf{A}^{(-1)}$ it will hold for every conditional inverse of $\mathbf{A}$. If it is violated for some $\mathbf{A}^{(-1)}$ it will be violated for every $\mathbf{A}^{(-1)}$, and $\mathbf{y}$ will be non-unique.

9.12. Let $\mathbf{A}$ be of rank r and select r rows and r columns which form a basis of $\mathbf{A}$. Then a conditional inverse of $\mathbf{A}$ can be obtained as follows: Invert the $(r \times r)$ matrix, place the inverse (without transposing) into the r rows corresponding to the column numbers and the r columns corresponding to the row numbers of the basis, and place zero into all remaining elements. Thus, if $\mathbf{A}$ is of order (5×4) and rank 3, and if rows $1, 2, 4$ and columns $2, 3, 4$ are selected as a basis, $\mathbf{A}^{(-1)}$, of order (4×5) will contain the inverse elements of the basis in rows $2, 3, 4$ and columns $1, 2, 4$, and zeros elsewhere. (See example 9.3.2)

9.13. If $\mathbf{A}$ is a square, singular matrix of order $(n \times n)$ and rank r, let $\mathbf{M}$ be a matrix of order $[n \times (n - r)]$ and $\mathbf{K}$ another matrix of order $[(n - r) \times n]$ chosen in such a way that $\mathbf{A} + \mathbf{MK}$ is non-singular. Then $(\mathbf{A} + \mathbf{MK})^{-1}$ is a conditional inverse of $\mathbf{A}$.

Example 9.13.1

$$\mathbf{A} = \begin{bmatrix} 3 & -1 & -1 & -1 \\ -1 & 3 & -1 & -1 \\ -1 & -1 & 3 & -1 \\ -1 & -1 & -1 & 3 \end{bmatrix}$$

is of order (4×4) and rank 3. Take $\mathbf{M} = \mathbf{j}$ (column vector of ones) and $\mathbf{K} = \mathbf{j}'$ (row vector of ones). Then $\mathbf{A} + \mathbf{MK} = \mathbf{A} + \mathbf{jj}' = 4\mathbf{I}$. Hence $(1/4)\,\mathbf{I}$ is a conditional inverse of $\mathbf{A}$.

9.14. The "Doolittle" method (see 6.14) can be employed to obtain a conditional inverse of a symmetric matrix. If, at any stage, the leading element of the p-row is zero, that cycle is disregarded.

Example 9.14.1

Invert, conditionally, the matrix

$$\mathbf{A} = \begin{bmatrix} 4 & 2 & -2 & 4 \\ 2 & 17 & 11 & 6 \\ -2 & 11 & 10 & 1 \\ 4 & 6 & 1 & 30 \end{bmatrix}$$

4	2	-2	4	1			
1	.5	-.5	1	.25			
	17	11	6	0	1		
	16	12	4	-.5	1		
	1	.75	.25	-.03125	.0625		
		10	1	0	0	1	
		0					
			30	0	0	0	1
			25	-.875	-.25	0	1
			1	-.035	-.01	0	.04

$$\begin{bmatrix} .29625 & -.0225 & 0 & -.035 \\ -.0225 & .065 & 0 & -.01 \\ 0 & 0 & 0 & 0 \\ -.035 & -.01 & 0 & .04 \end{bmatrix} = \mathbf{A}^{(-1)}$$

10. MATRIX DIFFERENTIATION

10.1a. If the elements of a matrix $\mathbf{Y}$ $(m \times n)$ are functions of a scalar, x, the expression

$$\partial \mathbf{Y}/\partial x$$

denotes a matrix of order $(m \times n)$ with elements $\partial y_{ij}/\partial x$.

10.1b. If the elements of a column (row) vector $\mathbf{y}$ ($\mathbf{y}'$) are functions of a scalar, x, the expression

$$\partial \mathbf{y}/\partial x \quad (\partial \mathbf{y}'/\partial x)$$

denotes a column (row) vector with elements $\partial y_i/\partial x$.

10.2a. If y is a scalar function of $m \times n$ variables, x_{ij}, arranged into a matrix $\mathbf{X}$, the expression

$$\partial y/\partial \mathbf{X}$$

denotes a matrix with elements $\partial y/\partial x_{ij}$.

(Note: Partial differentiation is performed with respect to the element in row i and column j of $\mathbf{X}$. If the same x-variable occurs in another place as, e.g., in a symmetric matrix, differentiation with respect to the distinct (repeated) variable is performed in two stages.)

Example 10.2.1

If $y = \mathbf{j}'\mathbf{X}\mathbf{j}$ (sum of all elements of a square matrix), $\partial y/\partial \mathbf{X}$ is a matrix of ones. If $\mathbf{X}$ is symmetric, one can introduce a new notation $x_{ij} = x_{ji} = z_{ij}$. Then

$$\begin{aligned} \partial y/\partial z_{ij} &= (\partial y/\partial x_{ij})(\partial x_{ij}/\partial z_{ij}) \\ &\quad + (\partial y/\partial x_{ji})(\partial x_{ji}/\partial z_{ij}) \\ &= 1 + 1 = 2 \quad (\text{if } i \neq j) \\ &= 1 \qquad\qquad (\text{if } i = j). \end{aligned}$$

10.2b. If y is a scalar function of n variables, x_i, arranged into a column (row) vector $\mathbf{x}$ ($\mathbf{x}'$), the expression

$$\partial y/\partial \mathbf{x} \quad (\partial y/\partial \mathbf{x}')$$

denotes a column (row) vector with elements $\partial y/\partial x_i$.

10.3. If $\mathbf{y}$ is a column vector with m elements, each a function of n variables, x_i, arranged into a row vector $\mathbf{x}'$, the expression $\partial \mathbf{y}/\partial \mathbf{x}'$ denotes a matrix with m rows and n columns, with elements $\partial y_i/\partial x_j$.

10.4. $\partial \mathbf{Y}/\partial y_{ij} = (\mathbf{EL})_{ij}$ (see definition of $(\mathbf{EL})$ in 3.4).

10.5. $\partial \mathbf{UV}/\partial x = (\partial \mathbf{U}/\partial x)\mathbf{V} + \mathbf{U}(\partial \mathbf{V}/\partial x)$.

10.6. $\partial \mathbf{AY}/\partial x = \mathbf{A}(\partial \mathbf{Y}/\partial x)$ (if elements of $\mathbf{A}$ are not functions of x).

10.7. $\partial \mathbf{Y}'/\partial y_{ij} = (\mathbf{EL})_{ji}$

10.8. $\partial \mathbf{A}'\mathbf{YA}/\partial x = \mathbf{A}'(\partial \mathbf{Y}/\partial x)\mathbf{A}$

10.9. $\partial \mathbf{Y}'\mathbf{AY}/\partial x = (\partial \mathbf{Y}'/\partial x)\mathbf{AY} + \mathbf{Y}'\mathbf{A}(\partial \mathbf{Y}/\partial x)$

10.10. $\partial \mathbf{a}'\mathbf{x}/\partial \mathbf{x} = \mathbf{a}$

10.11. $\partial \mathbf{x}'\mathbf{x}/\partial \mathbf{x} = 2\mathbf{x}$

10.12. $\partial \mathbf{x}' \mathbf{A} \mathbf{x} / \partial \mathbf{x} = \mathbf{A} \mathbf{x} + \mathbf{A}' \mathbf{x}$

10.13. (Chain Rule No. 1) $\partial \mathbf{y} / \partial \mathbf{x}' = (\partial \mathbf{y} / \partial \mathbf{z}')(\partial \mathbf{z} / \partial \mathbf{x}')$

10.14. $\partial \mathbf{A} \mathbf{x} / \partial \mathbf{x}' = \mathbf{A}$

10.15. $\partial tr \mathbf{X} / \partial \mathbf{X} = \mathbf{I}$

10.16. $\partial tr \mathbf{A} \mathbf{X} / \partial \mathbf{X} = \partial tr \mathbf{X} \mathbf{A} / \partial \mathbf{X} = \mathbf{A}'$

10.17. $\partial tr \mathbf{A} \mathbf{X} \mathbf{B} / \partial \mathbf{X} = \mathbf{A}' \mathbf{B}'$

10.18. $\partial tr \mathbf{X}' \mathbf{A} \mathbf{X} / \partial \mathbf{X} = \mathbf{A} \mathbf{X} + \mathbf{A}' \mathbf{X}$

10.19. $\partial \log | \mathbf{X} | / \partial \mathbf{X} = (\mathbf{X}')^{-1}$ (log to base e).

10.20. $\partial \mathbf{Y}^{-1} / \partial x = -\mathbf{Y}^{-1}(\partial \mathbf{Y} / \partial x) \mathbf{Y}^{-1}$

10.21. (Chain Rule No. 2)

$$\partial y / \partial x = tr(\partial y / \partial \mathbf{Z})(\partial \mathbf{Z}' / \partial x)$$

where y and x are scalars. The scalar y is a function of $m \times n$ variables z_{ij}, and each of the z_{ij} is a function of x.

Example 10.21.1

Obtain $\log | \mathbf{R} - \mathbf{F} \mathbf{F}' | / \partial \mathbf{F}$, where $\mathbf{R}$ is symmetric.

By Chain Rule No. 2:

$\partial \log | \mathbf{R} - \mathbf{F} \mathbf{F}' | / \partial f_{ij}$

$\quad = tr[\partial \log | \mathbf{R} - \mathbf{F} \mathbf{F}' | / \partial (\mathbf{R} - \mathbf{F} \mathbf{F}')][\partial (\mathbf{R} - \mathbf{F} \mathbf{F}') / \partial f_{ij}]$ (since $\mathbf{R}$ and $\mathbf{F} \mathbf{F}'$ are symmetric)

$\quad = tr(\mathbf{R} - \mathbf{F} \mathbf{F}')^{-1}[\partial (\mathbf{R} - \mathbf{F} \mathbf{F}') / \partial f_{ij}]$ (by 10.19)

$\quad = tr(\mathbf{R} - \mathbf{F} \mathbf{F}')^{-1}[-(\partial \mathbf{F} / \partial f_{ij}) \mathbf{F}' - \mathbf{F}(\partial \mathbf{F}' / \partial f_{ij})]$ (by 10.5)

$\quad = tr(\mathbf{R} - \mathbf{F} \mathbf{F}')^{-1}[-(\mathbf{E} \mathbf{L})_{ij} \mathbf{F}' - \mathbf{F}(\mathbf{E} \mathbf{L})_{ji}]$ (by 10.4 and 10.7)

$\quad = -tr(\mathbf{R} - \mathbf{F} \mathbf{F}')^{-1}(\mathbf{E} \mathbf{L})_{ij} \mathbf{F}' - tr(\mathbf{R} - \mathbf{F} \mathbf{F}')^{-1} \mathbf{F}(\mathbf{E} \mathbf{L})_{ji}$

$\quad = -tr(\mathbf{E} \mathbf{L})_{ij} \mathbf{F}'(\mathbf{R} - \mathbf{F} \mathbf{F}')^{-1} - tr(\mathbf{E} \mathbf{L})_{ji}(\mathbf{R} - \mathbf{F} \mathbf{F}')^{-1} \mathbf{F}$ (by 7.3)

$\quad = -[\mathbf{F}'(\mathbf{R} - \mathbf{F} \mathbf{F}')^{-1}]_{ji} - [(\mathbf{R} - \mathbf{F} \mathbf{F}')^{-1} \mathbf{F}]_{ij},$

where $[\ ]_{ij}$ denotes the (i, j) element of the matrix in brackets (by 7.5),

$\quad = -[(\mathbf{R} - \mathbf{F} \mathbf{F}')^{-1} \mathbf{F}]_{ij} - [(\mathbf{R} - \mathbf{F} \mathbf{F}')^{-1} \mathbf{F}]_{ij}$ (since $\mathbf{R} - \mathbf{F} \mathbf{F}'$ is symmetric)

$\quad = -2[(\mathbf{R} - \mathbf{F} \mathbf{F}')^{-1} \mathbf{F}]_{ij}.$

Hence, by definition 10.2a

$$\partial \log | \mathbf{R} - \mathbf{F} \mathbf{F}' | / \partial \mathbf{F} = -2(\mathbf{R} - \mathbf{F} \mathbf{F}')^{-1} \mathbf{F}.$$

10.22. $| \partial \mathbf{y} / \partial \mathbf{x}' | = J(\mathbf{y}; \mathbf{x})$ is called the Jacobian or Functional Determinant used in variable transformation of multiple integrals. Formally, if $\mathbf{y}$ is a column vector with m elements, each a function of m variables x_i arranged into a row vector $\mathbf{x}'$,

$$dx_1 dx_2 \ldots dx_m = | \partial \mathbf{y} / \partial \mathbf{x}' |^{-1} dy_1 dy_2 \ldots dy_m.$$

10.23. For a scalar y (a function of m variables x_i) to attain a stationary value, it is necessary that

$$\partial y / \partial \mathbf{x} = \mathbf{0}.$$

10.24. For a stationary value to be a minimum (maximum) it is necessary that

$$\partial (\partial y / \partial \mathbf{x}) / \partial \mathbf{x}'   (-\partial (\partial y / \partial \mathbf{x}) / \partial \mathbf{x}')$$

be a positive-definite matrix for the value of $\mathbf{x}$ satisfying 10.23.

Example 10.24.1

Find the values of $\boldsymbol{\beta}$ which minimize $u = \mathbf{x}' \mathbf{x}$ (the sum of squares of x_i) where $\mathbf{x} = \mathbf{y} - \mathbf{A} \boldsymbol{\beta}$ (with $\mathbf{y}$ and $\mathbf{A}$ known and fixed).

$$\partial u/\partial \beta' = (\partial u/\partial \mathbf{x}')(\partial \mathbf{x}/\partial \beta') \quad \text{(by Chain Rule No. 1)}$$
$$= -2\mathbf{x}'\mathbf{A} \quad \text{(by 10.11 and 10.14)}$$

Hence

$$\partial u/\partial \beta = -2\mathbf{A}'\mathbf{x}$$
$$= -2\mathbf{A}'(\mathbf{y} - \mathbf{A}\beta).$$

Hence, for a stationary value, by 10.23, it is necessary that

$$\mathbf{A}'\mathbf{A}\hat{\beta} = \mathbf{A}'\mathbf{y}$$

where $\hat{\beta}$ denotes the values which make u stationary. Now,

$$\partial(\partial u/\partial \beta)/\partial \beta' = 2\partial(\mathbf{A}'\mathbf{A}\beta)/\partial \beta' = 2\mathbf{A}'\mathbf{A}.$$

If $\mathbf{A}$ has real elements, and if $\mathbf{A}'\mathbf{A}$ is non-singular, then it is positive-definite (since, given an arbitrary real $\mathbf{x} \neq \mathbf{0}$, $\mathbf{x}'\mathbf{A}'\mathbf{A}\mathbf{x} = \mathbf{z}'\mathbf{z}$, with $\mathbf{z} = \mathbf{A}\mathbf{x}$; thus this is a sum of squares). Hence $\hat{\beta}$ minimizes u.

10.25. (Generalized Newton Iteration)

Let $\mathbf{x}_0'$ be an initial estimate (m elements) of the roots of the m equations

$$\mathbf{f}(\mathbf{x}') = \mathbf{0}$$

where the m elements of the column vector $\mathbf{f}$ are each functions of $x_1, x_2, \ldots x_m$. Then an improved root is

$$\mathbf{x}_1 = \mathbf{x}_0 - \mathbf{Q}_0^{-1}\mathbf{f}(\mathbf{x}_0'),$$

where $\mathbf{Q}_0$ is the matrix of derivatives $\partial \mathbf{f}/\partial \mathbf{x}'$ evaluated at $\mathbf{x} = \mathbf{x}_0$. The usual procedure consists of evaluating $\mathbf{f}(\mathbf{x}_0')$, then solving $\mathbf{Q}_0\mathbf{u} = \mathbf{f}(\mathbf{x}_0')$ for $\mathbf{u}$. Then $\mathbf{x}_1 = \mathbf{x}_0 - \mathbf{u}$.

Example 10.25.1

Solve

$$f_1(x,y) = x^3 - x^2y + y^2 - 3.526 = 0$$
$$f_2(x,y) = x^3 + y^3 - 14.911 = 0$$

$$\mathbf{Q} = \begin{bmatrix} 3x^2 - 2xy & 2y - x^2 \\ 3x^2 & 3y^2 \end{bmatrix}$$

Take $x_0 = 1, \quad y_0 = 2$

$$f_1(x_0, y_0) = -0.526$$
$$f_2(x_0, y_0) = -5.911$$

$$\mathbf{Q}_0 = \begin{bmatrix} -1 & 3 \\ 3 & 12 \end{bmatrix}$$

$$-u + 3v = -0.526$$
$$3u + 12v = -5.911$$

yields $u = -0.55, \quad v = -0.36.$

Then,

$$x_1 = x_0 - u = 1.55$$
$$y_1 = y_0 - v = 2.36$$
$$f_1(x_1, y_1) = 0.0976$$
$$f_2(x_1, y_1) = 1.9572$$

$$\mathbf{Q}_1 = \begin{bmatrix} -0.1085 & 2.3175 \\ 7.2075 & 16.7088 \end{bmatrix}$$

$$-0.1085u + 2.3175v = 0.0976$$
$$7.2075u + 16.7088v = 1.9572$$

yields $u = 0.157, \quad v = 0.049.$

Then

$$x_2 = x_1 - u = 1.393$$
$$y_2 = y_1 - v = 2.311$$
$$f_1(x_2, y_2) = 0.03337$$
$$f_2(x_2, y_2) = 0.13443$$

$$\mathbf{Q}_2 = \begin{bmatrix} -0.61710 & 2.68155 \\ 5.82135 & 16.02216 \end{bmatrix}$$

$$-0.61710u + 2.68155v = 0.03337$$
$$5.82135u + 16.02216v = 0.13443$$

yields $u = -0.0068, \quad v = 0.0109.$

Then,

$$x_3 = x_2 - u = 1.3998$$

$$y_3 = y_2 - v = 2.3001$$

(The exact roots are $x = 1.4$ and $y = 2.3$).

11. STATISTICAL MATRIX FORMS

11.1. Let E denote the expectation operator, and let $\mathbf{y}$ be a set of p random variables. Then

$$E(\mathbf{y}) = \boldsymbol{\mu}$$

states that $E(y_i) = \mu_i \quad (i = 1, 2, \ldots p)$.

11.2. Let var denote variance. Then

$$\text{var}(\mathbf{y}) = \boldsymbol{\Sigma}$$

denotes a $p \times p$ symmetric matrix whose elements are $\text{cov}(y_i, y_j)$, and whose diagonal elements are $\text{var}(y_i)$, where cov denotes covariance.

11.3. $E(\mathbf{AY} + \mathbf{b}) = \mathbf{A}E(\mathbf{y}) + \mathbf{b} = \mathbf{A}\boldsymbol{\mu} + \mathbf{b}$

11.4. $\text{var}(\mathbf{Ay} + \mathbf{b}) = \mathbf{A} \text{var}(\mathbf{y}) \mathbf{A}' = \mathbf{A}\boldsymbol{\Sigma}\mathbf{A}'$

11.5. $\text{cov}(\mathbf{y}, \mathbf{z}')$ denotes a matrix with elements $\text{cov}(y_i, z_j)$.
       $\text{cov}(\mathbf{z}, \mathbf{y}') = [\text{cov}(\mathbf{y}, \mathbf{z}')]'.$

11.6. $\text{cov}(\mathbf{Ay} + \mathbf{b}, \mathbf{z}'\mathbf{C} + \mathbf{d}') = \mathbf{A} \text{cov}(\mathbf{y}, \mathbf{z}') \mathbf{C}$

11.7. $\text{var}(\mathbf{y}) = E(\mathbf{yy}') - E(\mathbf{y})E(\mathbf{y}')$

11.8. $\text{cov}(\mathbf{y}, \mathbf{z}') = E(\mathbf{yz}') - E(\mathbf{y})E(\mathbf{z}')$

11.9. (Expected "sum of squares")

$$E(\mathbf{y}'\mathbf{Q}\mathbf{y}) = tr[\mathbf{Q} \text{ var } (\mathbf{y})] + E(\mathbf{y}')\mathbf{Q}E(\mathbf{y}).$$

11.10. If a matrix $\mathbf{Q}$ is symmetric and positive-definite, one can find a lower triangular matrix $\mathbf{T}$ (with positive diagonal terms, for uniqueness) such that $\mathbf{TT}' = \mathbf{Q}$. The matrices $\mathbf{T}$ and $\mathbf{T}^{-1}$ can be obtained from the Doolittle pattern (6.14) (Gauss elimination or square-root method) as follows: In each cycle, divide the p-row (left and right hand side) by $\sqrt{p_{ii}}$ (instead of p_{ii} for the u-row). Thus obtain rows designated as t-rows. The left-hand side (Arabic subscripts) is $\mathbf{T}'$, and the right-hand side (Roman subscripts) is $\mathbf{T}^{-1}$

11.11. If a coordinate system $\mathbf{x}$ is oblique, and if the cosines between reference vectors (scalar products of basis vectors of unit length) are stated in a symmetric matrix $\mathbf{Q}$, then $\mathbf{T}^{-1}\mathbf{x} = \mathbf{y}$ is an orthogonal system, where $\mathbf{T}$ is obtained from $\mathbf{Q}$ by 11.10.

11.12. The likelihood function of a sample of size n from a multivariate normal distribution (p responses), with common variance-covariance matrix $\Sigma(p \times p)$, and with means or main effects replaced by maximum-likelihood or least-squares estimates, can be written as

$$\log L = -\frac{np}{2} \log 2\pi - \frac{n}{2} \log |\Sigma| - \frac{n}{2} tr\, \Sigma^{-1}\mathbf{S}$$

where $\Sigma(p \times p)$ is the common variance-covariance matrix, and $\mathbf{S}$ is its maximum-likelihood estimate (matrix of sums of squares and products due to error, divided by sample size n).

11.13. If Σ has a structure under a model or null hypothesis, and if elements of Σ are to be estimated, by maximum-likelihood, two cases can be distinguished: (11.14) Σ^{-1} has the same structure (intraclass correlation, mixed model, compound symmetry, factor analysis). (11.15) Σ^{-1} has a different structure (autocorrelation, Simplex structure).

11.14. If the structure of Σ and Σ^{-1} is identical, and if u and v are elements (or functions of elements) of Σ^{-1} then estimates of Σ can be obtained from the relations (usually requiring Newton iteration, see 10.25):

$$\partial \log L/\partial u = \frac{n}{2} tr\, \mathbf{A}(\Sigma - \mathbf{S})$$

where $\mathbf{A} = \partial\Sigma^{-1}/\partial u$, is frequently an elementary matrix (see 3.4 and, especially, the rules 7.5 and 7.6).

$$\partial^2 \log L/\partial u \partial v = \frac{n}{2} tr(\partial \mathbf{A}/\partial v)(\Sigma - \mathbf{S}) + \frac{n}{2} tr\, \mathbf{A}\Sigma^{-1}\mathbf{B}\Sigma^{-1}$$

where $\mathbf{B} = \partial\Sigma^{-1}/\partial v$. These rules are useful to obtain Newton iterations and asymptotic variance-covariance matrices of the estimates.

11.15. If the structures of Σ and Σ^{-1} are different, then an estimate of Σ can be obtained from the relations

$$\partial \log L/\partial x = -\frac{n}{2} tr\, \mathbf{A}(\Sigma^{-1} - \mathbf{Q}),$$

where

$$\mathbf{Q} = \Sigma^{-1}\mathbf{S}\Sigma^{-1}$$

and

$$\mathbf{A} = \partial\Sigma/\partial x \qquad \text{(see comments in 11.14).}$$

$$\partial^2 \log L/\partial x \partial y = -\frac{n}{2} tr(\partial \mathbf{A}/\partial y)(\Sigma^{-1} - \mathbf{Q}) + \frac{n}{2} tr\, \mathbf{A}\Sigma^{-1}\mathbf{B}(\Sigma^{-1} - \mathbf{Q}) - \frac{n}{2} tr\, \mathbf{A}\mathbf{Q}\mathbf{B}\Sigma^{-1},$$

where

$$\mathbf{B} = \partial\Sigma/\partial y$$

x and y are elements (or functions of elements) of Σ. The comments of 11.14 apply, but the iterative procedure is considerably more complex.

Suggestions for further reading:

A. S. Householder, *The Theory of Matrices in Numerical Analysis*, Blaisdell, 1964.

S. R. Searle, *Matrix Algebra for the Biological Sciences*, Wiley, 1966.

P. H. Schonemann, Matrix differentiation of traces and determinants, *Psychometrika*, 1966.

SQUARES, SQUARE ROOT, CUBES AND CUBE ROOT

The squares and cubes from 1 to 1000 are given exactly. The roots are given to seven significant figures. Since the square roots of $10n$ are given, values of the square roots from 1 to 10 000 may be found directly. For the square roots of numbers below and above this range, use may be made of the following relations: $\sqrt{100n} = 10\sqrt{n}$; $\sqrt{1000n} = 10\sqrt{10n}$; $\sqrt{\frac{1}{10}n} = \frac{1}{10}\sqrt{10n}$; $\sqrt{\frac{1}{100}n} = \frac{1}{10}\sqrt{n}$; $\sqrt{\frac{1}{1000}n} = \frac{1}{100}\sqrt{10n}$. For example, the square root of 0.268 may be found by using the form $\sqrt{0.268} = \frac{1}{100}\sqrt{10 \times 268}$. The tabular value for the square root of $10n$ for 268 is 51.76872. Hence, the desired root is 0.5176872.

Values of cube roots for all numbers from 1 to 100 000 will be found directly in the table. Cube roots for numbers above or below this range will be found from the following relations: $\sqrt[3]{1000n} = 10\sqrt[3]{n}$; $\sqrt[3]{10\,000n} = 10\sqrt[3]{10n}$; $\sqrt[3]{100\,000n} = 10\sqrt[3]{100n}$; $\sqrt[3]{\frac{1}{10}n} = \frac{1}{10}\sqrt[3]{100n}$; $\sqrt[3]{\frac{1}{100}n} = \frac{1}{10}\sqrt[3]{10n}$; $\sqrt[3]{\frac{1}{1000}n} = \frac{1}{10}\sqrt[3]{n}$. For example, the cube root of 731 000 may be found by using the form, $\sqrt[3]{731\,000} = 10\sqrt[3]{731}$. The tabular value of the root for 731 is 9.008 223. The desired root is, therefore, 90.08223.

For higher integral powers of numbers, see table "Powers of Numbers," page 101.

SQUARES, SQUARE ROOT, CUBES AND CUBE ROOT

n	n^2	$\sqrt{n}$	$\sqrt{10n}$	n^3	$\sqrt[3]{n}$	$\sqrt[3]{10n}$	$\sqrt[3]{100n}$
1	1	1.000 000	3.162 278	1	1.000 000	2.154 435	4.641 589
2	4	1.414 214	4.472 136	8	1.259 921	2.714 418	5.848 035
3	9	1.732 051	5.477 226	27	1.442 250	3.107 233	6.694 330
4	16	2.000 000	6.324 555	64	1.587 401	3.419 952	7.368 063
5	25	2.236 068	7.071 068	125	1.709 976	3.684 031	7.937 005
6	36	2.449 490	7.745 967	216	1.817 121	3.914 868	8.434 327
7	49	2.645 751	8.366 600	343	1.912 931	4.121 285	8.879 040
8	64	2.828 427	8.944 272	512	2.000 000	4.308 869	9.283 178
9	81	3.000 000	9.486 833	729	2.080 084	4.481 405	9.654 894
10	100	3.162 278	10.00000	1 000	2.154 435	4.641 589	10.00000
11	121	3.316 625	10.48809	1 331	2.223 980	4.791 420	10.32280
12	144	3.464 102	10.95445	1 728	2.289 428	4.932 424	10.62659
13	169	3.605 551	11.40175	2 197	2.351 335	5.065 797	10.91393
14	196	3.741 657	11.83216	2 744	2.410 142	5.192 494	11.18689
15	225	3.872 983	12.24745	3 375	2.466 212	5.313 293	11.44714
16	256	4.000 000	12.64911	4 096	2.519 842	5.428 835	11.69607
17	289	4.123 106	13.03840	4 913	2.571 282	5.539 658	11.93483
18	324	4.242 641	13.41641	5 832	2.620 741	5.646 216	12.16440
19	361	4.358 899	13.78405	6 859	2.668 402	5.748 897	12.38562
20	400	4.472 136	14.14214	8 000	2.714 418	5.848 035	12.59921
21	441	4.582 576	14.49138	9 261	2.758 924	5.943 922	12.80579
22	484	4.690 416	14.83240	10 648	2.802 039	6.036 811	13.00591
23	529	4.795 832	15.16575	12 167	2.843 867	6.126 926	13.20006
24	576	4.898 979	15.49193	13 824	2.884 499	6.214 465	13.38866
25	625	5.000 000	15.81139	15 625	2.924 018	6.299 605	13.57209
26	676	5.099 020	16.12452	17 576	2.962 496	6.382 504	13.75069
27	729	5.196 152	16.43168	19 683	3.000 000	6.463 304	13.92477
28	784	5.291 503	16.73320	21 952	3.036 589	6.542 133	14.09460
29	841	5.385 165	17.02939	24 389	3.072 317	6.619 106	14.26043
30	900	5.477 226	17.32051	27 000	3.107 233	6.694 330	14.42250
31	961	5.567 764	17.60682	29 791	3.141 381	6.767 899	14.58100
32	1 024	5.656 854	17.88854	32 768	3.174 802	6.839 904	14.73613
33	1 089	5.744 563	18.16590	35 937	3.207 534	6.910 423	14.88806
34	1 156	5.830 952	18.43909	39 304	3.239 612	6.979 532	15.03695
35	1 225	5.916 080	18.70829	42 875	3.271 066	7.047 299	15.18294
36	1 296	6.000 000	18.97367	46 656	3.301 927	7.113 787	15.32619
37	1 369	6.082 763	19.23538	50 653	3.332 222	7.179 054	15.46680
38	1 444	6.164 414	19.49359	54 872	3.361 975	7.243 156	15.60491
39	1 521	6.244 998	19.74842	59 319	3.391 211	7.306 144	15.74061
40	1 600	6.324 555	20.00000	64 000	3.419 952	7.368 063	15.87401
41	1 681	6.403 124	20.24846	68 921	3.448 217	7.428 959	16.00521
42	1 764	6.480 741	20.49390	74 088	3.476 027	7.488 872	16.13429
43	1 849	6.557 439	20.73644	79 507	3.503 398	7.547 842	16.26133
44	1 936	6.633 250	20.97618	85 184	3.530 348	7.605 905	16.38643
45	2 025	6.708 204	21.21320	91 125	3.556 893	7.663 094	16.50964
46	2 116	6.782 330	21.44761	97 336	3.583 048	7.719 443	16.63103
47	2 209	6.855 655	21.67948	103 823	3.608 826	7.774 980	16.75069
48	2 304	6.928 203	21.90890	110 592	3.634 241	7.829 735	16.86865
49	2 401	7.000 000	22.13594	117 649	3.659 306	7.883 735	16.98499
50	2 500	7.071 068	22.36068	125 000	3.684 031	7.937 005	17.09976

SQUARES, SQUARE ROOT, CUBES AND CUBE ROOT (Continued)

n	n^2	$\sqrt{n}$	$\sqrt{10n}$	n^3	$\sqrt[3]{n}$	$\sqrt[3]{10n}$	$\sqrt[3]{100n}$
50	2 500	7.071 068	22.36068	125 000	3.684 031	7.937 005	17.09976
51	2 601	7.141 428	22.58318	132 651	3.708 430	7.989 570	17.21301
52	2 704	7.211 103	22.80351	140 608	3.732 511	8.041 452	17.32478
53	2 809	7.280 110	23.02173	148 877	3.756 286	8.092 672	17.43513
54	2 916	7.348 469	23.23790	157 464	3.779 763	8.143 253	17.54411
55	3 025	7.416 198	23.45208	166 375	3.802 952	8.193 213	17.65174
56	3 136	7.483 315	23.66432	175 616	3.825 862	8.242 571	17.75808
57	3 249	7.549 834	23.87467	185 193	3.848 501	8.291 344	17.86316
58	3 364	7.615 773	24.08319	195 112	3.870 877	8.339 551	17.96702
59	3 481	7.681 146	24.28992	205 379	3.892 996	8.387 207	18.06969
60	3 600	7.745 967	24.49490	216 000	3.914 868	8.434 327	18.17121
61	3 721	7.810 250	24.69818	226 981	3.936 497	8.480 926	18.27160
62	3 844	7.874 008	24.89980	238 328	3.957 892	8.527 019	18.37091
63	3 969	7.937 254	25.09980	250 047	3.979 057	8.572 619	18.46915
64	4 096	8.000 000	25.29822	262 144	4.000 000	8.617 739	18.56636
65	4 225	8.062 258	25.49510	274 625	4.020 726	8.662 391	18.66256
66	4 356	8.124 038	25.69047	287 496	4.041 240	8.706 588	18.75777
67	4 489	8.185 353	25.88436	300 763	4.061 548	8.750 340	18.85204
68	4 624	8.246 211	26.07681	314 432	4.081 655	8.793 659	18.94536
69	4 761	8.306 624	26.26785	328 509	4.101 566	8.836 556	19.03778
70	4 900	8.366 600	26.45751	343 000	4.121 285	8.879 040	19.12931
71	5 041	8.426 150	26.64583	357 911	4.140 818	8.921 121	19.21997
72	5 184	8.485 281	26.83282	373 248	4.160 168	8.962 809	19.30979
73	5 329	8.544 004	27.01851	389 017	4.179 339	9.004 113	19.39877
74	5 476	8.602 325	27.20294	405 224	4.198 336	9.045 042	19.48695
75	5 625	8.660 254	27.38613	421 875	4.217 163	9.085 603	19.57434
76	5 776	8.717 798	27.56810	438 976	4.235 824	9.125 805	19.66095
77	5 929	8.774 964	27.74887	456 533	4.254 321	9.165 656	19.74681
78	6 084	8.831 761	27.92848	474 552	4.272 659	9.205 164	19.83192
79	6 241	8.888 194	28.10694	493 039	4.290 840	9.244 335	19.91632
80	6 400	8.944 272	28.28427	512 000	4.308 869	9.283 178	20.00000
81	6 561	9.000 000	28.46050	531 441	4.326 749	9.321 698	20.08299
82	6 724	9.055 385	28.63564	551 368	4.344 481	9.359 902	20.16530
83	6 889	9.110 434	28.80972	571 787	4.362 071	9.397 796	20.24694
84	7 056	9.165 151	28.98275	592 704	4.379 519	9.435 388	20.32793
85	7 225	9.219 544	29.15476	614 125	4.396 830	9.472 682	20.40828
86	7 396	9.273 618	29.32576	636 056	4.414 005	9.509 685	20.48800
87	7 569	9.327 379	29.49576	658 503	4.431 048	9.546 403	20.56710
88	7 744	9.380 832	29.66479	681 472	4.447 960	9.582 840	20.64560
89	7 921	9.433 981	29.83287	704 969	4.464 745	9.619 002	20.72351
90	8 100	9.486 833	30.00000	729 000	4.481 405	9.654 894	20.80084
91	8 281	9.539 392	30.16621	753 571	4.497 941	9.690 521	20.87759
92	8 464	9.591 663	30.33150	778 688	4.514 357	9.725 888	20.95379
93	8 649	9.643 651	30.49590	804 357	4.530 655	9.761 000	21.02944
94	8 836	9.695 360	30.65942	830 584	4.546 836	9.795 861	21.10454
95	9 025	9.746 794	30.82207	857 375	4.562 903	9.830 476	21.17912
96	9 216	9.797 959	30.98387	884 736	4.578 857	9.864 848	21.25317
97	9 409	9.848 858	31.14482	912 673	4.594 701	9.898 983	21.32671
98	9 604	9.899 495	31.30495	941 192	4.610 436	9.932 884	21.39975
99	9 801	9.949 874	31.46427	970 299	4.626 065	9.966 555	21.47229
100	10 000	10.00000	31.62278	1 000 000	4.641 589	10.00000	21.54435

SQUARES, SQUARE ROOT, CUBES AND CUBE ROOT (Continued)

n	n^2	$\sqrt{n}$	$\sqrt{10n}$	n^3	$\sqrt[3]{n}$	$\sqrt[3]{10n}$	$\sqrt[3]{100n}$
100	10 000	10.00000	31.62278	1 000 000	4.641 589	10.00000	21.54435
101	10 201	10.04988	31.78050	1 030 301	4.657 010	10.03322	21.61592
102	10 404	10.09950	31.93744	1 061 208	4.672 329	10.06623	21.68703
103	10 609	10.14889	32.09361	1 092 727	4.687 548	10.09902	21.75767
104	10 816	10.19804	32.24903	1 124 864	4.702 669	10.13159	21.82786
105	11 025	10.24695	32.40370	1 157 625	4.717 694	10.16396	21.89760
106	11 236	10.29563	32.55764	1 191 016	4.732 623	10.19613	21.96689
107	11 449	10.34408	32.71085	1 225 043	4.747 459	10.22809	22.03575
108	11 664	10.39230	32.86335	1 259 712	4.762 203	10.25986	22.10419
109	11 881	10.44031	33.01515	1 295 029	4.776 856	10.29142	22.17220
110	12 100	10.48809	33.16625	1 331 000	4.791 420	10.32280	22.23980
111	12 321	10.53565	33.31666	1 367 631	4.805 896	10.35399	22.30699
112	12 544	10.58301	33.46640	1 404 928	4.820 285	10.38499	22.37378
113	12 769	10.63015	33.61547	1 442 897	4.834 588	10.41580	22.44017
114	12 996	10.67708	33.76389	1 481 544	4.848 808	10.44644	22.50617
115	13 225	10.72381	33.91165	1 520 875	4.862 944	10.47690	22.57179
116	13 456	10.77033	34.05877	1 560 896	4.876 999	10.50718	22.63702
117	13 689	10.81665	34.20526	1 601 613	4.890 973	10.53728	22.70189
118	13 924	10.86278	34.35113	1 643 032	4.904 868	10.56722	22.76638
119	14 161	10.90871	34.49638	1 685 159	4.918 685	10.59699	22.83051
120	14 400	10.95445	34.64102	1 728 000	4.932 424	10.62659	22.89428
121	14 641	11.00000	34.78505	1 771 561	4.946 087	10.65602	22.95770
122	14 884	11.04536	34.92850	1 815 848	4.959 676	10.68530	23.02078
123	15 129	11.09054	35.07136	1 860 867	4.973 190	10.71441	23.08350
124	15 376	11.13553	35.21363	1 906 624	4.986 631	10.74337	23.14589
125	15 625	11.18034	35.35534	1 953 125	5.000 000	10.77217	23.20794
126	15 876	11.22497	35.49648	2 000 376	5.013 298	10.80082	23.26967
127	16 129	11.26943	35.63706	2 048 383	5.026 526	10.82932	23.33107
128	16 384	11.31371	35.77709	2 097 152	5.039 684	10.85767	23.39214
129	16 641	11.35782	35.91657	2 146 689	5.052 774	10.88587	23.45290
130	16 900	11.40175	36.05551	2 197 000	5.065 797	10.91393	23.51335
131	17 161	11.44552	36.19392	2 248 091	5.078 753	10.94184	23.57348
132	17 424	11.48913	36.33180	2 299 968	5.091 643	10.96961	23.63332
133	17 689	11.53256	36.46917	2 352 637	5.104 469	10.99724	23.69285
134	17 956	11.57584	36.60601	2 406 104	5.117 230	11.02474	23.75208
135	18 225	11.61895	36.74235	2 460 375	5.129 928	11.05209	23.81102
136	18 496	11.66190	36.87818	2 515 456	5.142 563	11.07932	23.86966
137	18 769	11.70470	37.01351	2 571 353	5.155 137	11.10641	23.92803
138	19 044	11.74734	37.14835	2 628 072	5.167 649	11.13336	23.98610
139	19 321	11.78983	37.28270	2 685 619	5.180 101	11.16019	24.04390
140	19 600	11.83216	37.41657	2 744 000	5.192 494	11.18689	24.10142
141	19 881	11.87434	37.54997	2 803 221	5.204 828	11.21346	24.15867
142	20 164	11.91638	37.68289	2 863 288	5.217 103	11.23991	24.21565
143	20 449	11.95826	37.81534	2 924 207	5.229 322	11.26623	24.27236
144	20 736	12.00000	37.94733	2 985 984	5.241 483	11.29243	24.32881
145	21 025	12.04159	38.07887	3 048 625	5.253 588	11.31851	24.38499
146	21 316	12.08305	38.20995	3 112 136	5.265 637	11.34447	24.44092
147	21 609	12.12436	38.34058	3 176 523	5.277 632	11.37031	24.49660
148	21 904	12.16553	38.47077	3 241 792	5.289 572	11.39604	24.55202
149	22 201	12.20656	38.60052	3 307 949	5.301 459	11.42165	24.60719
150	22.500	12.24745	38.72983	3 375 000	5.313 293	11.44714	24.66212

SQUARES, SQUARE ROOT, CUBES AND CUBE ROOT (Continued)

n	n^2	$\sqrt{n}$	$\sqrt{10n}$	n^3	$\sqrt[3]{n}$	$\sqrt[3]{10n}$	$\sqrt[3]{100n}$
150	22 500	12.24745	38.72983	3 375 000	5.313 293	11.44714	24.66212
151	22 801	12.28821	38.85872	3 442 951	5.325 074	11.47252	24.71680
152	23 104	12.32883	38.98718	3 511 808	5.336 803	11.49779	24.77125
153	23 409	12.36932	39.11521	3 581 577	5.348 481	11.52295	24.82545
154	23 716	12.40967	39.24283	3 652 264	5.360 108	11.54800	24.87942
155	24 025	12.44990	39.37004	3 723 875	5.371 685	11.57295	24.93315
156	24 336	12.49000	39.49684	3 796 416	5.383 213	11.59778	24.98666
157	24 649	12.52996	39.62323	3 869 893	5.394 691	11.62251	25.03994
158	24 964	12.56981	39.74921	3 944 312	5.406 120	11.64713	25.09299
159	25 281	12.60952	39.87480	4 019 679	5.417 502	11.67165	25.14581
160	25 600	12.64911	40.00000	4 096 000	5.428 835	11.69607	25.19842
161	25 921	12.68858	40.12481	4 173 281	5.440 122	11.72039	25.25081
162	26 244	12.72792	40.24922	4 251 528	5.451 362	11.74460	25.30298
163	26 569	12.76715	40.37326	4 330 747	5.462 556	11.76872	25.35494
164	26 896	12.80625	40.49691	4 410 944	5.473 704	11.79274	25.40668
165	27 225	12.84523	40.62019	4 492 125	5.484 807	11.81666	25.45822
166	27 556	12.88410	40.74310	4 574 296	5.495 865	11.84048	25.50954
167	27 889	12.92285	40.86563	4 657 463	5.506 878	11.86421	25.56067
168	28 224	12.96148	40.98780	4 741 632	5.517 848	11.88784	25.61158
169	28 561	13.00000	41.10961	4 826 809	5.528 775	11.91138	25.66230
170	28 900	13.03840	41.23106	4 913 000	5.539 658	11.93483	25.71282
171	29 241	13.07670	41.35215	5 000 211	5.550 499	11.95819	25.76313
172	29 584	13.11488	41.47288	5 088 448	5.561 298	11.98145	25.81326
173	29 929	13.15295	41.59327	5 177 717	5.572 055	12.00463	25.86319
174	30 276	13.19091	41.71331	5 268 024	5.582 770	12.02771	25.91292
175	30 625	13.22876	41.83300	5 359 375	5.593 445	12.05071	25.96247
176	30 976	13.26650	41.95235	5 451 776	5.604 079	12.07362	26.01183
177	31 329	13.30413	42.07137	5 545 233	5.614 672	12.09645	26.06100
178	31 684	13.34166	42.19005	5 639 752	5.625 226	12.11918	26.10999
179	32 041	13.37909	42.30839	5 735 339	5.635 741	12.14184	26.15879
180	32 400	13.41641	42.42641	5 832 000	5.646 216	12.16440	26.20741
181	32 761	13.45362	42.54409	5 929 741	5.656 653	12.18689	26.25586
182	33 124	13.49074	42.66146	6 028 568	5.667 051	12.20929	26.30412
183	33 489	13.52775	42.77850	6 128 487	5.677 411	12.23161	26.35221
184	33 856	13.56466	42.89522	6 229 504	5.687 734	12.25385	26.40012
185	34 225	13.60147	43.01163	6 331 625	5.698 019	12.27601	26.44786
186	34 596	13.63818	43.12772	6 434 856	5.708 267	12.29809	26.49543
187	34 969	13.67479	43.24350	6 539 203	5.718 479	12.32009	26.54283
188	35 344	13.71131	43.35897	6 644 672	5.728 654	12.34201	26.59006
189	35 721	13.74773	43.47413	6 751 269	5.738 794	12.36386	26.63712
190	36 100	13.78405	43.58899	6 859 000	5.748 897	12.38562	26.68402
191	36 481	13.82027	43.70355	6 967 871	5.758 965	12.40731	26.73075
192	36 864	13.85641	43.81780	7 077 888	5.768 998	12.42893	26.77732
193	37 249	13.89244	43.93177	7 189 057	5.778 997	12.45047	26.82373
194	37 636	13.92839	44.04543	7 301 384	5.788 960	12.47194	26.86997
195	38 025	13.96424	44.15880	7 414 875	5.798 890	12.49333	26.91606
196	38 416	14.00000	44.27189	7 529 536	5.808 786	12.51465	26.96199
197	38 809	14.03567	44.38468	7 645 373	5.818 648	12.53590	27.00777
198	39 204	14.07125	44.49719	7 762 392	5.828 477	12.55707	27.05339
199	39 601	14.10674	44.60942	7 880 599	5.838 272	12.57818	27.09886
200	40 000	14.14214	44.72136	8 000 000	5.848 035	12.59921	27.14418

SQUARES, SQUARE ROOT, CUBES AND CUBE ROOT (Continued)

n	n^2	$\sqrt{n}$	$\sqrt{10n}$	n^3	$\sqrt[3]{n}$	$\sqrt[3]{10n}$	$\sqrt[3]{100n}$
200	40 000	14.14214	44.72136	8 000 000	5.848 035	12.59921	27.14418
201	40 401	14.17745	44.83302	8 120 601	5.857 766	12.62017	27.18934
202	40 804	14.21267	44.94441	8 242 408	5.867 464	12.64107	27.23436
203	41 209	14.24781	45.05552	8 365 427	5.877 131	12.66189	27.27922
204	41 616	14.28286	45.16636	8 489 664	5.886 765	12.68265	27.32394
205	42 025	14.31782	45.27693	8 615 125	5.896 369	12.70334	27.36852
206	42 436	14.35270	45.38722	8 741 816	5.905 941	12.72396	27.41295
207	42 849	14.38749	45.49725	8 869 743	5.915 482	12.74452	27.45723
208	43 264	14.42221	45.60702	8 998 912	5.924 992	12.76501	27.50138
209	43 681	14.45683	45.71652	9 129 329	5.934 472	12.78543	27.54538
210	44 100	14.49138	45.82576	9 261 000	5.943 922	12.80579	27.58924
211	44 521	14.52584	45.93474	9 393 931	5.953 342	12.82609	27.63296
212	44 944	14.56022	46.04346	9 528 128	5.962 732	12.84632	27.67655
213	45 369	14.59452	46.15192	9 663 597	5.972 093	12.86648	27.72000
214	45 796	14.62874	46.26013	9 800 344	5.981 424	12.88659	27.76331
215	46 225	14.66288	46.36809	9 938 375	5.990 726	12.90663	27.80649
216	46 656	14.69694	46.47580	10 077 696	6.000 000	12.92661	27.84953
217	47 089	14.73092	46.58326	10 218 313	6.009 245	12.94653	27.89244
218	47 524	14.76482	46.69047	10 360 232	6.018 462	12.96638	27.93522
219	47 961	14.79865	46.79744	10 503 459	6.027 650	12.98618	27.97787
220	48 400	14.83240	46.90416	10 648 000	6.036 811	13.00591	28.02039
221	48 841	14.86607	47.01064	10 793 861	6.045 944	13.02559	28.06278
222	49 284	14.89966	47.11688	10 941 048	6.055 049	13.04521	28.10505
223	49 729	14.93318	47.22288	11 089 567	6.064 127	13.06477	28.14718
224	50 176	14.96663	47.32864	11 239 424	6.073 178	13.08427	28.18919
225	50 625	15.00000	47.43416	11 390 625	6.082 202	13.10371	28.23108
226	51 076	15.03330	47.53946	11 543 176	6.091 199	13.12309	28.27284
227	51 529	15.06652	47.64452	11 697 083	6.100 170	13.14242	28.31448
228	51 984	15.09967	47.74935	11 852 352	6.109 115	13.16169	28.35600
229	52 441	15.13275	47.85394	12 008 989	6.118 033	13.18090	28.39739
230	52 900	15.16575	47.95832	12 167 000	6.126 926	13.20006	28.43867
231	53 361	15.19868	48.06246	12 326 391	6.135 792	13.21916	28.47983
232	53 824	15.23155	48.16638	12 487 168	6.144 634	13.23821	28.52086
233	54 289	15.26434	48.27007	12 649 337	6.153 449	13.25721	28.56178
234	54 756	15.29706	48.37355	12 812 904	6.162 240	13.27614	28.60259
235	55 225	15.32971	48.47680	12 977 875	6.171 006	13.29503	28.64327
236	55 696	15.36229	48.57983	13 144 256	6.179 747	13.31386	28.68384
237	56 169	15.39480	48.68265	13 312 053	6.188 463	13.33264	28.72430
238	56 644	15.42725	48.78524	13 481 272	6.197 154	13.35136	28.76464
239	57 121	15.45962	48.88763	13 651 919	6.205 822	13.37004	28.80487
240	57 600	15.49193	48.98979	13 824 000	6.214 465	13.38866	28.84499
241	58 081	15.52417	49.09175	13 997 521	6.223 084	13.40723	28.88500
242	58 564	15.55635	49.19350	14 172 488	6.231 680	13.42575	28.92489
243	59 049	15.58846	49.29503	14 348 907	6.240 251	13.44421	28.96468
244	59 536	15.62050	49.39636	14 526 784	6.248 800	13.46263	29.00436
245	60 025	15.65248	49.49747	14 706 125	6.257 325	13.48100	29.04393
246	60 516	15.68439	49.59839	14 886 936	6.265 827	13.49931	29.08339
247	61 009	15.71623	49.69909	15 069 223	6.274 305	13.51758	29.12275
248	61 504	15.74802	49.79960	15 252 992	6.282 761	13.53580	29.16199
249	62 001	15.77973	49.89990	15 438 249	6.291 195	13.55397	29.20114
250	62 500	15.81139	50.00000	15 625 000	6.299 605	13.57209	29.24018

SQUARES, SQUARE ROOT, CUBES AND CUBE ROOT (Continued)

n	n^2	$\sqrt{n}$	$\sqrt{10n}$	n^3	$\sqrt[3]{n}$	$\sqrt[3]{10n}$	$\sqrt[3]{100n}$
250	62 500	15.81139	50.00000	15 625 000	6.299 605	13.57209	29.24018
251	63 001	15.84298	50.09990	15 813 251	6.307 994	13.59016	29.27911
252	63 504	15.87451	50.19960	16 003 008	6.316 360	13.60818	29.31794
253	64 009	15.90597	50.29911	16 194 277	6.324 704	13.62616	29.35667
254	64 516	15.93738	50.39841	16 387 064	6.333 026	13.64409	29.39530
255	65 025	15.96872	50.49752	16 581 375	6.341 326	13.66197	29.43383
256	65 536	16.00000	50.59644	16 777 216	6.349 604	13.67981	29.47225
257	66 049	16.03122	50.69517	16 974 593	6.357 861	13.69760	29.51058
258	66 564	16.06238	50.79370	17 173 512	6.366 097	13.71534	29.54880
259	67 081	16.09348	50.89204	17 373 979	6.374 311	13.73304	29.58693
260	67 600	16.12452	50.99020	17 576 000	6.382 504	13.75069	29.62496
261	68 121	16.15549	51.08816	17 779 581	6.390 677	13.76830	29.66289
262	68 644	16.18641	51.18594	17 984 728	6.398 828	13.78586	29.70073
263	69 169	16.21727	51.28353	18 191 447	6.406 959	13.80337	29.73847
264	69 696	16.24808	51.38093	18 399 744	6.415 069	13.82085	29.77611
265	70 225	16.27882	51.47815	18 609 625	6.423 158	13.83828	29.81366
266	70 756	16.30951	51.57519	18 821 096	6.431 228	13.85566	29.85111
267	71 289	16.34013	51.67204	19 034 163	6.439 277	13.87300	29.88847
268	71 824	16.37071	51.76872	19 248 832	6.447 306	13.89030	29.92574
269	72 361	16.40122	51.86521	19 465 109	6.455 315	13.90755	29.96292
270	72 900	16.43168	51.96152	19 683 000	6.463 304	13.92477	30.00000
271	73 441	16.46208	52.05766	19 902 511	6.471 274	13.94194	30.03699
272	73 984	16.49242	52.15362	20 123 648	6.479 224	13.95906	30.07389
273	74 529	16.52271	52.24940	20 346 417	6.487 154	13.97615	30.11070
274	75 076	16.55295	52.34501	20 570 824	6.495 065	13.99319	30.14742
275	75 625	16.58312	52.44044	20 796 875	6.502 957	14.01020	30.18405
276	76 176	16.61325	52.53570	21 024 576	6.510 830	14.02716	30.22060
277	76 729	16.64332	52.63079	21 253 933	6.518 684	14.04408	30.25705
278	77 284	16.67333	52.72571	21 484 952	6.526 519	14.06096	30.29342
279	77 841	16.70329	52.82045	21 717 639	6.534 335	14.07780	30.32970
280	78 400	16.73320	52.91503	21 952 000	6.542 133	14.09460	30.36589
281	78 961	16.76305	53.00943	22 188 041	6.549 912	14.11136	30.40200
282	79 524	16.79286	53.10367	22 425 768	6.557 672	14.12808	30.43802
283	80 089	16.82260	53.19774	22 665 187	6.565 414	14.14476	30.47395
284	80 656	16.85230	53.29165	22 906 304	6.573 138	14.16140	30.50981
285	81 225	16.88194	53.38539	23 149 125	6.580 844	14.17800	30.54557
286	81 796	16.91153	53.47897	23 393 656	6.588 532	14.19456	30.58126
287	82 369	16.94107	53.57238	23 639 903	6.596 202	14.21109	30.61686
288	82 944	16.97056	53.66563	23 887 872	6.603 854	14.22757	30.65238
289	83 521	17.00000	53.75872	24 137 569	6.611 489	14.24402	30.68781
290	84 100	17.02939	53.85165	24 389 000	6.619 106	14.26043	30.72317
291	84 681	17.05872	53.94442	24 642 171	6.626 705	14.27680	30.75844
292	85 264	17.08801	54.03702	24 897 088	6.634 287	14.29314	30.79363
293	85 849	17.11724	54.12947	25 153 757	6.641 852	14.30944	30.82875
294	86 436	17.14643	54.22177	25 412 184	6.649 400	14.32570	30.86378
295	87 025	17.17556	54.31390	25 672 375	6.656 930	14.34192	30.89873
296	87 616	17.20465	54.40588	25 934 336	6.664 444	14.35811	30.93361
297	88 209	17.23369	54.49771	26 198 073	6.671 940	14.37426	30.96840
298	88 804	17.26268	54.58938	26 463 592	6.679 420	14.39037	31.00312
299	89 401	17.29162	54.68089	26 730 899	6.686 883	14.40645	31.03776
300	90 000	17.32051	54.77226	27 000 000	6.694 330	14.42250	31.07233

SQUARES, SQUARE ROOT, CUBES AND CUBE ROOT (Continued)

n	n^2	$\sqrt{n}$	$\sqrt{10n}$	n^3	$\sqrt[3]{n}$	$\sqrt[3]{10n}$	$\sqrt[3]{100n}$
300	90 000	17 32051	54.77226	27 000 000	6.694 330	14.42250	31.07233
301	90 601	17.34935	54.86347	27 270 901	6.701 759	14.43850	31.10681
302	91 204	17.37815	54.95453	27 543 608	6.709 173	14.45447	31.14122
303	91 809	17.40690	55.04544	27 818 127	6.716 570	14.47041	31.17556
304	92 416	17.43560	55.13620	28 094 464	6.723 951	14.48631	31.20982
305	93 025	17.46425	55.22681	28 372 625	6.731 315	14.50218	31.24400
306	93 636	17.49286	55.31727	28 652 616	6.738 664	14.51801	31.27811
307	94 249	17.52142	55.40758	28 934 443	6.745 997	14.53381	31.31214
308	94 864	17.54993	55.49775	29 218 112	6.753 313	14.54957	31.34610
309	95 481	17.57840	55.58777	29 503 629	6.760 614	14.56530	31.37999
310	96 100	17.60682	55.67764	29 791 000	6.767 899	14.58100	31.41381
311	96 721	17.63519	55.76737	30 080 231	6.775 169	14.59666	31.44755
312	97 344	17.66352	55.85696	30 371 328	6.782 423	14.61229	31.48122
313	97 969	17.69181	55.94640	30 664 297	6.789 661	14.62788	31.51482
314	98 596	17.72005	56.03570	30 959 144	6.796 884	14.64344	31.54834
315	99 225	17.74824	56.12486	31 255 875	6.804 092	14.65897	31.58180
316	99 856	17.77639	56.21388	31 554 496	6.811 285	14.67447	31.61518
317	100 489	17.80449	56.30275	31 855 013	6.818 462	14.68993	31.64850
318	101 124	17.83255	56.39149	32 157 432	6.825 624	14.70536	31.68174
319	101 761	17.86057	56.48008	32 461 759	6.832 771	14.72076	31.71492
320	102 400	17.88854	56.56854	32 768 000	6.839 904	14.73613	31.74802
321	103 041	17.91647	56.65686	33 076 161	6.847 021	14.75146	31.78106
322	103 684	17.94436	56.74504	33 386 248	6.854 124	14.76676	31.81403
323	104 329	17.97220	56.83309	33 698 267	6.861 212	14.78203	31.84693
324	104 976	18.00000	56.92100	34 012 224	6.868 285	14.79727	31.87976
325	105 625	18.02776	57.00877	34 328 125	6.875 344	14.81248	31.91252
326	106 276	18.05547	57.09641	34 645 976	6.882 389	14.82766	31.94522
327	106 929	18.08314	57.18391	34 965 783	6.889 419	14.84280	31.97785
328	107 584	18.11077	57.27128	35 287 552	6.896 434	14.85792	32.01041
329	108 241	18.13836	57.35852	35 611 289	6.903 436	14.87300	32.04291
330	108 900	18.16590	57.44563	35 937 000	6.910 423	14.88806	32.07534
331	109 561	18.19341	57.53260	36 264 691	6.917 396	14.90308	32.10771
332	110 224	18.22087	57.61944	36 594 368	6.924 356	14.91807	32.14001
333	110 889	18.24829	57.70615	36 926 037	6.931 301	14.93303	32.17225
334	111 556	18.27567	57.79273	37 259 704	6.938 232	14.94797	32.20442
335	112 225	18.30301	57.87918	37 595 375	6.945 150	14.96287	32.23653
336	112 896	18.33030	57.96551	37 933 056	6.952 053	14.97774	32.26857
337	113 569	18.35756	58.05170	38 272 753	6.958 943	14.99259	32.30055
338	114 244	18.38478	58.13777	38 614 472	6.965 820	15.00740	32.33247
339	114 921	18.41195	58.22371	38 958 219	6.972 683	15.02219	32.36433
340	115 600	18.43909	58.30952	39 304 000	6.979 532	15.03695	32.39612
341	116 281	18.46619	58.39521	39 651 821	6.986 368	15.05167	32.42785
342	116 964	18.49324	58.48077	40 001 688	6.993 191	15.06637	32.45952
343	117 649	18.52026	58.56620	40 353 607	7.000 000	15.08104	32.49112
344	118 336	18.54724	58.65151	40 707 584	7.006 796	15.09568	32.52267
345	119 025	18.57418	58.73670	41 063 625	7.013 579	15.11030	32.55415
346	119 716	18.60108	58.82176	41 421 736	7.020 349	15.12488	32.58557
347	120 409	18.62794	58.90671	41 781 923	7.027 106	15.13944	32.61694
348	121 104	18.65476	58.99152	42 144 192	7.033 850	15.15397	32.64824
349	121 801	18.68154	59.07622	42 508 549	7.040 581	15.16847	32.67948
350	122 500	18.70829	59.16080	42 875 000	7.047 299	15.18294	32.71066

COMBINATORIAL ANALYSIS

SQUARES, SQUARE ROOT, CUBES AND CUBE ROOT (Continued)

n	n^2	$\sqrt{n}$	$\sqrt{10n}$	n^3	$\sqrt[3]{n}$	$\sqrt[3]{10n}$	$\sqrt[3]{100n}$
350	122 500	18.70829	59.16080	42 875 000	7.047 299	15.18294	32.71066
351	123 201	18.73499	59.24525	43 243 551	7.054 004	15.19739	32.74179
352	123 904	18.76166	59.32959	43 614 208	7.060 697	15.21181	32.77285
353	124 609	18.78829	59.41380	43 986 977	7.067 377	15.22620	32.80386
354	125 316	18.81489	59.49790	44 361 864	7.074 044	15.24057	32.83480
355	126 025	18.84144	59.58188	44 738 875	7.080 699	15.25490	32.86569
356	126 736	18.86796	59.66574	45 118 016	7.087 341	15.26921	32.89652
357	127 449	18.89444	59.74948	45 499 293	7.093 971	15.28350	32.92730
358	128 164	18.92089	59.83310	45 882 712	7.100 588	15.29775	32.95801
359	128 881	18.94730	59.91661	46 268 279	7.107 194	15.31198	32.98867
360	129 600	18.97367	60.00000	46 656 000	7.113 787	15.32619	33.01927
361	130 321	19.00000	60.08328	47 045 881	7.120 367	15.34037	33.04982
362	131 044	19.02630	60.16644	47 437 928	7.126 936	15.35452	33.08031
363	131 769	19.05256	60.24948	47 832 147	7.133 492	15.36864	33.11074
364	132 496	19.07878	60.33241	48 228 544	7.140 037	15.38274	33.14112
365	133 225	19.10497	60.41523	48 627 125	7.146 569	15.39682	33.17144
366	133 956	19.13113	60.49793	49 027 896	7.153 090	15.41087	33.20170
367	134 689	19.15724	60.58052	49 430 863	7.159 599	15.42489	33.23191
368	135 424	19.18333	60.66300	49 836 032	7.166 096	15.43889	33.26207
369	136 161	19.20937	60.74537	50 243 409	7.172 581	15.45286	33.29217
370	136 900	19.23538	60.82763	50 653 000	7.179 054	15.46680	33.32222
371	137 641	19.26136	60.90977	51 064 811	7.185 516	15.48073	33.35221
372	138 384	19.28730	60.99180	51 478 848	7.191 966	15.49462	33.38215
373	139 129	19.31321	61.07373	51 895 117	7.198 405	15.50849	33.41204
374	139 876	19.33908	61.15554	52 313 624	7.204 832	15.52234	33.44187
375	140 625	19.36492	61.23724	52 734 375	7.211 248	15.53616	33.47165
376	141 376	19.39072	61.31884	53 157 376	7.217 652	15.54996	33.50137
377	142 129	19.41649	61.40033	53 582 633	7.224 045	15.56373	33.53105
378	142 884	19.44222	61.48170	54 010 152	7.230 427	15.57748	33.56067
379	143 641	19.46792	61.56298	54 439 939	7.236 797	15.59121	33.59024
380	144 400	19.49359	61.64414	54 872 000	7.243 156	15.60491	33.61975
381	145 161	19.51922	61.72520	55 306 341	7.249 505	15.61858	33.64922
382	145 924	19.54482	61.80615	55 742 968	7.255 842	15.63224	33.67863
383	146 689	19.57039	61.88699	56 181 887	7.262 167	15.64587	33.70800
384	147 456	19.59592	61.96773	56 623 104	7.268 482	15.65947	33.73731
385	148 225	19.62142	62.04837	57 066 625	7.274 786	15.67305	33.76657
386	148 996	19.64688	62.12890	57 512 456	7.281 079	15.68661	33.79578
387	149 769	19.67232	62.20932	57 960 603	7.287 362	15.70014	33.82494
388	150 544	19.69772	62.28965	58 411 072	7.293 633	15.71366	33.85405
389	151 321	19.72308	62.36986	58 863 869	7.299 894	15.72714	33.88310
390	152 100	19.74842	62.44998	59 319 000	7.306 144	15.74061	33.91211
391	152 881	19.77372	62.52999	59 776 471	7.312 383	15.75405	33.94107
392	153 664	19.79899	62.60990	60 236 288	7.318 611	15.76747	33.96999
393	154 449	19.82423	62.68971	60 698 457	7.324 829	15.78087	33.99885
394	155 236	19.84943	62.76942	61 162 984	7.331 037	15.79424	34.02766
395	156 025	19.87461	62.84903	61 629 875	7.337 234	15.80759	34.05642
396	156 816	19.89975	62.92853	62 099 136	7.343 420	15.82092	34.08514
397	157 609	19.92486	63.00794	62 570 773	7.349 597	15.83423	34.11381
398	158 404	19.94994	63.08724	63 044 792	7.355 762	15.84751	34.14242
399	159 201	19.97498	63.16645	63 521 199	7.361 918	15.86077	34.17100
400	160 000	20.00000	63.24555	64 000 000	7.368 063	15.87401	34.19952

SQUARES, SQUARE ROOT, CUBES AND CUBE ROOT (Continued)

n	n^2	$\sqrt{n}$	$\sqrt{10n}$	n^3	$\sqrt[3]{n}$	$\sqrt[3]{10n}$	$\sqrt[3]{100n}$
400	160 000	20.00000	63.24555	64 000 000	7.368 063	15.87401	34.19952
401	160 801	20.02498	63.32456	64 481 201	7.374 198	15.88723	34.22799
402	161 604	20.04994	63.40347	64 964 808	7.380 323	15.90042	34.25642
403	162 409	20.07486	63.48228	65 450 827	7.386 437	15.91360	34.28480
404	163 216	20.09975	63.56099	65 939 264	7.392 542	15.92675	34.31314
405	164 025	20.12461	63.63961	66 430 125	7.398 636	15.93988	34.34143
406	164 836	20.14944	63.71813	66 923 416	7.404 721	15.95299	34.36967
407	165 649	20.17424	63.79655	67 419 143	7.410 795	15.96607	34.39786
408	166 464	20.19901	63.87488	67 917 312	7.416 860	15.97914	34.42601
409	167 281	20.22375	63.95311	68 417 929	7.422 914	15.99218	34.45412
410	168 100	20.24846	64.03124	68 921 000	7.428 959	16.00521	34.48217
411	168 921	20.27313	64.10928	69 426 531	7.434 994	16.01821	34.51018
412	169 744	20.29778	64.18723	69 934 528	7.441 019	16.03119	34.53815
413	170 569	20.32240	64.26508	70 444 997	7.447 034	16.04415	34.56607
414	171 396	20.34699	64.34283	70 957 944	7.453 040	16.05709	34.59395
415	172 225	20.37155	64.42049	71 473 375	7.459 036	16.07001	34.62178
416	173 056	20.39608	64.49806	71 991 296	7.465 022	16.08290	34.64956
417	173 889	20.42058	64.57554	72 511 713	7.470 999	16.09578	34.67731
418	174 724	20.44505	64.65292	73 034 632	7.476 966	16.10864	34.70500
419	175 561	20.46949	64.73021	73 560 059	7.482 924	16.12147	34.73266
420	176 400	20.49390	64.80741	74 088 000	7.488 872	16.13429	34.76027
421	177 241	20.51828	64.88451	74 618 461	7.494 811	16.14708	34.78783
422	178 084	20.54264	64.96153	75 151 448	7.500 741	16.15986	34.81535
423	178 929	20.56696	65.03845	75 686 967	7.506 661	16.17261	34.84283
424	179 776	20.59126	65.11528	76 225 024	7.512 572	16.18534	34.87027
425	180 625	20.61553	65.19202	76 765 625	7.518 473	16.19806	34.89766
426	181 476	20.63977	65.26868	77 308 776	7.524 365	16.21075	34.92501
427	182 329	20.66398	65.34524	77 854 483	7.530 248	16.22343	34.95232
428	183 184	20.68816	65.42171	78 402 752	7.536 122	16.23608	34.97958
429	184 041	20.71232	65.49809	78 953 589	7.541 987	16.24872	35.00680
430	184 900	20.73644	65.57439	79 507 000	7.547 842	16.26133	35.03398
431	185 761	20.76054	65.65059	80 062 991	7.553 689	16.27393	35.06112
432	186 624	20.78461	65.72671	80 621 568	7.559 526	16.28651	35.08821
433	187 489	20.80865	65.80274	81 182 737	7.565 355	16.29906	35.11527
434	188 356	20.83267	65.87868	81 746 504	7.571 174	16.31160	35.14228
435	189 225	20.85665	65.95453	82 312 875	7.576 985	16.32412	35.16925
436	190 096	20.88061	66.03030	82 881 856	7.582 787	16.33662	35.19618
437	190 969	20.90454	66.10598	83 453 453	7.588 579	16.34910	35.22307
438	191 844	20.92845	66.18157	84 027 672	7.594 363	16.36156	35.24991
439	192 721	20.95233	66.25708	84 604 519	7.600 139	16.37400	35.27672
440	193 600	20.97618	66.33250	85 184 000	7.605 905	16.38643	35.30348
441	194 481	21.00000	66.40783	85 766 121	7.611 663	16.39883	35.33021
442	195 364	21.02380	66.48308	86 350 888	7.617 412	16.41122	35.35689
443	196 249	21.04757	66.55825	86 938 307	7.623 152	16.42358	35.38354
444	197 136	21.07131	66.63332	87 528 384	7.628 884	16.43593	35.41014
445	198 025	21.09502	66.70832	88 121 125	7.634 607	16.44826	35.43671
446	198 916	21.11871	66.78323	88 716 536	7.640 321	16.46057	35.46323
447	199 809	21.14237	66.85806	89 314 623	7.646 027	16.47287	35.48971
448	200 704	21.16601	66.93280	89 915 392	7.651 725	16.48514	35.51616
449	201 601	21.18962	67.00746	90 518 849	7.657 414	16.49740	35.54257
450	202 500	21.21320	67.08204	91 125 000	7.663 094	16.50964	35.56893

SQUARES, SQUARE ROOT, CUBES AND CUBE ROOT (Continued)

n	n^2	$\sqrt{n}$	$\sqrt{10n}$	n^3	$\sqrt[3]{n}$	$\sqrt[3]{10n}$	$\sqrt[3]{100n}$
450	202 500	21.21320	67.08204	91 125 000	7.663 094	16.50964	35.56893
451	203 401	21.23676	67.15653	91 733 851	7.668 766	16.52186	35.59526
452	204 304	21.26029	67.23095	92 345 408	7.674 430	16.53406	35.62155
453	205 209	21.28380	67.30527	92 959 677	7.680 086	16.54624	35.64780
454	206 116	21.30728	67.37952	93 576 664	7.685 733	16.55841	35.67401
455	207 025	21.33073	67.45369	94 196 375	7.691 372	16.57056	35.70018
456	207 936	21.35416	67.52777	94 818 816	7.697 002	16.58269	35.72632
457	208 849	21.37756	67.60178	95 443 993	7.702 625	16.59480	35.75242
458	209 764	21.40093	67.67570	96 071 912	7.708 239	16.60690	35.77848
459	210 681	21.42429	67.74954	96 702 579	7.713 845	16.61897	35.80450
460	211 600	21.44761	67.82330	97 336 000	7.719 443	16.63103	35.83048
461	212 521	21.47091	67.89698	97 972 181	7.725 032	16.64308	35.85642
462	213 444	21.49419	67.97058	98 611 128	7.730 614	16.65510	35.88233
463	214 369	21.51743	68.04410	99 252 847	7.736 188	16.66711	35.90820
464	215 296	21.54066	68.11755	99 897 344	7.741 753	16.67910	35.93404
465	216 225	21.56386	68.19091	100 544 625	7.747 311	16.69108	35.95983
466	217 156	21.58703	68.26419	101 194 696	7.752 861	16.70303	35.98559
467	218 089	21.61018	68.33740	101 847 563	7.758 402	16.71497	36.01131
468	219 024	21.63331	68.41053	102 503 232	7.763 936	16.72689	36.03700
469	219 961	21.65641	68.48357	103 161 709	7.769 462	16.73880	36.06265
470	220 900	21.67948	68.55655	103 823 000	7.774 980	16.75069	36.08826
471	221 841	21.70253	68.62944	104 487 111	7.780 490	16.76256	36.11384
472	222 784	21.72556	68.70226	105 154 048	7.785 993	16.77441	36.13938
473	223 729	21.74856	68.77500	105 823 817	7.791 488	16.78625	36.16488
474	224 676	21.77154	68.84766	106 496 424	7.796 975	16.79807	36.19035
475	225 625	21.79449	68.92024	107 171 875	7.802 454	16.80988	36.21578
476	226 576	21.81742	68.99275	107 850 176	7.807 925	16.82167	36.24118
477	227 529	21.84033	69.06519	108 531 333	7.813 389	16.83344	36.26654
478	228 484	21.86321	69 13754	109 215 352	7.818 846	16.84519	36.29187
479	229 441	21.88607	69.20983	109 902 239	7.824 294	16.85693	36.31716
480	230 400	21.90890	69 28203	110 592 000	7.829 735	16.86865	36.34241
481	231 361	21.93171	69.35416	111 284 641	7.835 169	16.88036	36.36763
482	232 324	21.95450	69.42622	111 980 168	7.840 595	16.89205	36.39282
483	233 289	21.97726	69 49820	112 678 587	7.846 013	16.90372	36.41797
484	234 256	22.00000	69.57011	113 379 904	7.851 424	16.91538	36.44308
485	235 225	22.02272	69.64194	114 084 125	7.856 828	16.92702	36.46817
486	236 196	22.04541	69.71370	114 791 256	7.862 224	16.93865	36.49321
487	237 169	22.06808	69.78539	115 501 303	7.867 613	16.95026	36.51822
488	238 144	22.09072	69.85700	116 214 272	7.872 994	16.96185	36.54320
489	239 121	22.11334	69.92853	116 930 169	7.878 368	16.97343	36.56815
490	240 100	22.13594	70.00000	117 649 000	7.883 735	16.98499	36.59306
491	241 081	22.15852	70.07139	118 370 771	7.889 095	16.99654	36.61793
492	242 064	22.18107	70.14271	119 095 488	7.894 447	17.00807	36.64278
493	243 049	22.20360	70.21396	119 823 157	7.899 792	17.01959	36.66758
494	244 036	22.22611	70.28513	120 553 784	7.905 129	17.03108	36.69236
495	245 025	22.24860	70.35624	121 287 375	7.910 460	17.04257	36.71710
496	246 016	22.27106	70.42727	122 023 936	7.915 783	17.05404	36.74181
497	247 009	22.29350	70.49823	122 763 473	7.921 099	17.06549	36.76649
498	248 004	22.31591	70.56912	123 505 992	7.926 408	17.07693	36.79113
499	249 001	22.33831	70.63993	124 251 499	7.931 710	17.08835	36.81574
500	250 000	22.36068	70.71068	125 000 000	7.937 005	17.09976	36.84031

SQUARES, SQUARE ROOT, CUBES AND CUBE ROOT (Continued)

n	n^2	$\sqrt{n}$	$\sqrt{10n}$	n^3	$\sqrt[3]{n}$	$\sqrt[3]{10n}$	$\sqrt[3]{100n}$
500	250 000	22.36068	70.71068	125 000 000	7.937 005	17.09976	36.84031
501	251 001	22.38303	70.78135	125 751 501	7.942 293	17.11115	36.86486
502	252 004	22.40536	70.85196	126 506 008	7.947 574	17.12253	36.88937
503	253 009	22.42766	70.92249	127 263 527	7.952 848	17.13389	36.91385
504	254 016	22.44994	70.99296	128 024 064	7.958 114	17.14524	36.93830
505	255 025	22.47221	71.06335	128 787 625	7.963 374	17.15657	36.96271
506	256 036	22.49444	71.13368	129 554 216	7.968 627	17.16789	36.98709
507	257 049	22.51666	71.20393	130 323 843	7.973 873	17.17919	37.01144
508	258 064	22.53886	71.27412	131 096 512	7.979 112	17.19048	37.03576
509	259 081	22.56103	71.34424	131 872 229	7.984 344	17.20175	37.06004
510	260 100	22.58318	71.41428	132 651 000	7.989 570	17.21301	37.08430
511	261 121	22.60531	71.48426	133 432 831	7.994 788	17.22425	37.10852
512	262 144	22.62742	71.55418	134 217 728	8.000 000	17.23548	37.13271
513	263 169	22.64950	71.62402	135 005 697	8.005 205	17.24669	37.15687
514	264 196	22.67157	71.69379	135 796 744	8.010 403	17.25789	37.18100
515	265 225	22.69361	71.76350	136 590 875	8.015 595	17.26908	37.20509
516	266 256	22.71563	71.83314	137 388 096	8.020 779	17.28025	37.22916
517	267 289	22.73763	71.90271	138 188 413	8.025 957	17.29140	37.25319
518	268 324	22.75961	71.97222	138 991 832	8.031 129	17.30254	37.27720
519	269 361	22.78157	72.04165	139 798 359	8.036 293	17.31367	37.30117
520	270 400	22.80351	72.11103	140 608 000	8.041 452	17.32478	37.32511
521	271 441	22.82542	72.18033	141 420 761	8.046 603	17.33588	37.34902
522	272 484	22.84732	72.24957	142 236 648	8.051 748	17.34696	37.37290
523	273 529	22.86919	72.31874	143 055 667	8.056 886	17.35804	37.39675
524	274 576	22.89105	72.38784	143 877 824	8.062 018	17.36909	37.42057
525	275 625	22.91288	72.45688	144 703 125	8.067 143	17.38013	37.44436
526	276 676	22.93469	72.52586	145 531 576	8.072 262	17.39116	37.46812
527	277 729	22.95648	72.59477	146 363 183	8.077 374	17.40218	37.49185
528	278 784	22.97825	72.66361	147 197 952	8.082 480	17.41318	37.51555
529	279 841	23.00000	72.73239	148 035 889	8.087 579	17.42416	37.53922
530	280 900	23.02173	72.80110	148 877 000	8.092 672	17.43513	37.56286
531	281 961	23.04344	72.86975	149 721 291	8.097 759	17.44609	37.58647
532	283 024	23.06513	72.93833	150 568 768	8.102 839	17.45704	37.61005
533	284 089	23.08679	73.00685	151 419 437	8.107 913	17.46797	37.63360
534	285 156	23.10844	73.07530	152 273 304	8.112 980	17.47889	37.65712
535	286 225	23.13007	73.14369	153 130 375	8.118 041	17.48979	37.68061
536	287 296	23.15167	73.21202	153 990 656	8.123 096	17.50068	37.70407
537	288 369	23.17326	73.28028	154 854 153	8.128 145	17.51156	37.72751
538	289 444	23.19483	73.34848	155 720 872	8.133 187	17.52242	37.75091
539	290 521	23.21637	73.41662	156 590 819	8.138 223	17.53327	37.77429
540	291 600	23.23790	73.48469	157 464 000	8.143 253	17.54411	37.79763
541	292 681	23.25941	73.55270	158 340 421	8.148 276	17.55493	37.82095
542	293 764	23.28089	73.62065	159 220 088	8.153 294	17.56574	37.84424
543	294 849	23.30236	73.68853	160 103 007	8.158 305	17.57654	37.86750
544	295 936	23.32381	73.75636	160 989 184	8.163 310	17.58732	37.89073
545	297 025	23.34524	73.82412	161 878 625	8.168 309	17.59809	37.91393
546	298 116	23.36664	73.89181	162 771 336	8.173 302	17.60885	37.93711
547	299 209	23.38803	73.95945	163 667 323	8.178 289	17.61959	37.96025
548	300 304	23.40940	74.02702	164 566 592	8.183 269	17.63032	37.98337
549	301 401	23.43075	74.09453	165 469 149	8.188 244	17.64104	38.00646
550	302 500	23.45208	74.16198	166 375 000	8.193 213	17.65174	38.02952

SQUARES, SQUARE ROOT, CUBES AND CUBE ROOT (Continued)

n	n^2	$\sqrt{n}$	$\sqrt{10n}$	n^3	$\sqrt[3]{n}$	$\sqrt[3]{10n}$	$\sqrt[3]{100n}$
550	302 500	23.45208	74.16198	166 375 000	8.193 213	17.65174	38.02952
551	303 601	23.47339	74.22937	167 284 151	8.198 175	17.66243	38.05256
552	304 704	23.49468	74.29670	168 196 608	8.203 132	17.67311	38.07557
553	305 809	23.51595	74.36397	169 112 377	8.208 082	17.68378	38.09854
554	306 916	23.53720	74.43118	170 031 464	8.213 027	17.69443	38.12149
555	308 025	23.55844	74.49832	170 953 875	8.217 966	17.70507	38.14442
556	309 136	23.57965	74.56541	171 879 616	8.222 899	17.71570	38.16731
557	310 249	23.60085	74.63243	172 808 693	8.227 825	17.72631	38.19018
558	311 364	23.62202	74.69940	173 741 112	8.232 746	17.73691	38.21302
559	312 481	23.64318	74.76630	174 676 879	8.237 661	17.74750	38.23584
560	313 600	23.66432	74.83315	175 616 000	8.242 571	17.75808	38.25862
561	314 721	23.68544	74.89993	176 558 481	8.247 474	17.76864	38.28138
562	315 844	23.70654	74.96666	177 504 328	8.252 372	17.77920	38.30412
563	316 969	23.72762	75.03333	178 453 547	8.257 263	17.78973	38.32682
564	318 096	23.74868	75.09993	179 406 144	8.262 149	17.80026	38.34950
565	319 225	23.76973	75.16648	180 362 125	8.267 029	17.81077	38.37215
566	320 356	23.79075	75.23297	181 321 496	8.271 904	17.82128	38.39478
567	321 489	23.81176	75.29940	182 284 263	8.276 773	17.83177	38.41737
568	322 624	23.83275	75.36577	183 250 432	8.281 635	17.84224	38.43995
569	323 761	23.85372	75.43209	184 220 009	8.286 493	17.85271	38.46249
570	324 900	23.87467	75.49834	185 193 000	8.291 344	17.86316	38.48501
571	326 041	23.89561	75.56454	186 169 411	8.296 190	17.87360	38.50750
572	327 184	23.91652	75.63068	187 149 248	8.301 031	17.88403	38.52997
573	328 329	23.93742	75.69676	188 132 517	8.305 865	17.89444	38.55241
574	329 476	23.95830	75.76279	189 119 224	8.310 694	17.90485	38.57482
575	330 625	23.97916	75.82875	190 109 375	8.315 517	17.91524	38.59721
576	331 776	24.00000	75.89466	191 102 976	8.320 335	17.92562	38.61958
577	332 929	24.02082	75.96052	192 100 033	8.325 148	17.93599	38.64191
578	334 084	24.04163	76.02631	193 100 552	8.329 954	17.94634	38.66422
579	335 241	24.06242	76.09205	194 104 539	8.334 755	17.95669	38.68651
580	336 400	24.08319	76.15773	195 112 000	8.339 551	17.96702	38.70877
581	337 561	24.10394	76.22336	196 122 941	8.344 341	17.97734	38.73100
582	338 724	24.12468	76.28892	197 137 368	8.349 126	17.98765	38.75321
583	339 889	24.14539	76.35444	198 155 287	8.353 905	17.99794	38.77539
584	341 056	24.16609	76.41989	199 176 704	8.358 678	18.00823	38.79755
585	342 225	24.18677	76.48529	200 201 625	8.363 447	18.01850	38.81968
586	343 396	24.20744	76.55064	201 230 056	8.368 209	18.02876	38.84179
587	344 569	24.22808	76.61593	202 262 003	8.372 967	18.03901	38.86387
588	345 744	24.24871	76.68116	203 297 472	8.377 719	18.04925	38.88593
589	346 921	24.26932	76.74634	204 336 469	8.382 465	18.05947	38.90796
590	348 100	24.28992	76.81146	205 379 000	8.387 207	18.06969	38.92996
591	349 281	24.31049	76.87652	206 425 071	8.391 942	18.07989	38.95195
592	350 464	24.33105	76.94154	207 474 688	8.396 673	18.09008	38.97390
593	351 649	24.35159	77.00649	208 527 857	8.401 398	18.10026	38.99584
594	352 836	24.37212	77.07140	209 584 584	8.406 118	18.11043	39.01774
595	354 025	24.39262	77.13624	210 644 875	8.410 833	18.12059	39.03963
596	355 216	24.41311	77.20104	211 708 736	8.415 542	18.13074	39.06149
597	356 409	24.43358	77.26578	212 776 173	8.420 246	18.14087	39.08332
598	357 604	24.45404	77.33046	213 847 192	8.424 945	18.15099	39.10513
599	358 801	24.47448	77.39509	214 921 799	8.429 638	18.16111	39.12692
600	360 000	24.49490	77.45967	216 000 000	8.434 327	18.17121	39.14868

SQUARES, SQUARE ROOT, CUBES AND CUBE ROOT (Continued)

n	n^2	$\sqrt{n}$	$\sqrt{10n}$	n^3	$\sqrt[3]{n}$	$\sqrt[3]{10n}$	$\sqrt[3]{100n}$
600	360 000	24.49490	77.45967	216 000 000	8.434 327	18.17121	39.14868
601	361 201	24.51530	77.52419	217 081 801	8.439 010	18.18130	39.17041
602	362 404	24.53569	77.58866	218 167 208	8.443 688	18.19137	39.19213
603	363 609	24.55606	77.65307	219 256 227	8.448 361	18.20144	39.21382
604	364 816	24.57641	77.71744	220 348 864	8.453 028	18.21150	39.23548
605	366 025	24.59675	77.78175	221 445 125	8.457 691	18.22154	39.25712
606	367 236	24.61707	77.84600	222 545 016	8.462 348	18.23158	39.27874
607	368 449	24.63737	77.91020	223 648 543	8.467 000	18.24160	39.30033
608	369 664	24.65766	77.97435	224 755 712	8.471 647	18.25161	39.32190
609	370 881	24.67793	78.03845	225 866 529	8.476 289	18.26161	39.34345
610	372 100	24.69818	78.10250	226 981 000	8.480 926	18.27160	39.36497
611	373 321	24.71841	78.16649	228 099 131	8.485 558	18.28158	39.38647
612	374 544	24.73863	78.23043	229 220 928	8.490 185	18.29155	39.40795
613	375 769	24.75884	78.29432	230 346 397	8.494 807	18.30151	39.42940
614	376 996	24.77902	78.35815	231 475 544	8.499 423	18.31145	39.45083
615	378 225	24.79919	78.42194	232 608 375	8.504 035	18.32139	39.47223
616	379 456	24.81935	78.48567	233 744 896	8.508 642	18.33131	39.49362
617	380 689	24.83948	78.54935	234 885 113	8.513 243	18.34123	39.51498
618	381 924	24.85961	78.61298	236 029 032	8.517 840	18.35113	39.53631
619	383 161	24.87971	78.67655	237 176 659	8.522 432	18.36102	39.55763
620	384 400	24.89980	78.74008	238 328 000	8.527 019	18.37091	39.57892
621	385 641	24.91987	78.80355	239 483 061	8.531 601	18.38078	39.60018
622	386 884	24.93993	78.86698	240 641 848	8.536 178	18.39064	39.62143
623	388 129	24.95997	78.93035	241 804 367	8.540 750	18.40049	39.64265
624	389 376	24.97999	78.99367	242 970 624	8.545 317	18.41033	39.66385
625	390 625	25.00000	79.05694	244 140 625	8.549 880	18.42016	39.68503
626	391 876	25.01999	79.12016	245 314 376	8.554 437	18.42998	39.70618
627	393 129	25.03997	79.18333	246 491 883	8.558 990	18.43978	39.72731
628	394 384	25.05993	79.24645	247 673 152	8.563 538	18.44958	39.74842
629	395 641	25.07987	79.30952	248 858 189	8.568 081	18.45937	39.76951
630	396 900	25.09980	79.37254	250 047 000	8.572 619	18.46915	39.79057
631	398 161	25.11971	79.43551	251 239 591	8.577 152	18.47891	39.81161
632	399 424	25.13961	79.49843	252 435 968	8.581 681	18.48867	39.83263
633	400 689	25.15949	79.56130	253 636 137	8.586 205	18.49842	39.85363
634	401 956	25.17936	79.62412	254 840 104	8.590 724	18.50815	39.87461
635	403 225	25.19921	79.68689	256 047 875	8.595 238	18.51788	39.89556
636	404 496	25.21904	79.74961	257 259 456	8.599 748	18.52759	39.91649
637	405 769	25.23886	79.81228	258 474 853	8.604 252	18.53730	39.93740
638	407 044	25.25866	79.87490	259 694 072	8.608 753	18.54700	39.95829
639	408 321	25.27845	79.93748	260 917 119	8.613 248	18.55668	39.97916
640	409 600	25.29822	80.00000	262 144 000	8.617 739	18.56636	40.00000
641	410 881	25.31798	80.06248	263 374 721	8.622 225	18.57602	40.02082
642	412 164	25.33772	80.12490	264 609 288	8.626 706	18.58568	40.04162
643	413 449	25.35744	80.18728	265 847 707	8.631 183	18.59532	40.06240
644	414 736	25 37716	80.24961	267 089 984	8.635 655	18.60495	40.08316
645	416 025	25.39685	80.31189	268 336 125	8.640 123	18.61458	40.10390
646	417 316	25.41653	80.37413	269 586 136	8.644 585	18.62419	40.12461
647	418 609	25.43619	80.43631	270 840 023	8.649 044	18.63380	40.14530
648	419 904	25.45584	80.49845	272 097 792	8.653 497	18.64340	40.16598
649	421 201	25.47548	80.56054	273 359 449	8.657 947	18.65298	40.18663
650	422 500	25.49510	80.62258	274 625 000	8.662 391	18.66256	40.20726

SQUARES, SQUARE ROOT, CUBES AND CUBE ROOT (Continued)

n	n^2	$\sqrt{n}$	$\sqrt{10n}$	n^3	$\sqrt[3]{n}$	$\sqrt[3]{10n}$	$\sqrt[3]{100n}$
650	422 500	25.49510	80.62258	274 625 000	8.662 391	18.66256	40.20726
651	423 801	25.51470	80.68457	275 894 451	8.666 831	18.67212	40.22787
652	425 104	25.53429	80.74652	277 167 808	8.671 266	18.68168	40.24845
653	426 409	25.55386	80.80842	278 445 077	8.675 697	18.69122	40.26902
654	427 716	25.57342	80.87027	279 726 264	8.680 124	18.70076	40.28957
655	429 025	25.59297	80.93207	281 011 375	8.684 546	18.71029	40.31009
656	430 336	25.61250	80.99383	282 300 416	8.688 963	18.71980	40.33059
657	431 649	25.63201	81.05554	283 593 393	8.693 376	18.72931	40.35108
658	432 964	25.65151	81.11720	284 890 312	8.697 784	18.73881	40.37154
659	434 281	25.67100	81.17881	286 191 179	8.702 188	18.74830	40.39198
660	435 600	25.69047	81.24038	287 496 000	8.706 588	18.75777	40.41240
661	436 921	25.70992	81.30191	288 804 781	8.710 983	18.76724	40.43280
662	438 244	25.72936	81.36338	290 117 528	8.715 373	18.77670	40.45318
663	439 569	25.74879	81.42481	291 434 247	8.719 760	18.78615	40.47354
664	440 896	25.76820	81.48620	292 754 944	8.724 141	18.79559	40.49388
665	442 225	25.78759	81.54753	294 079 625	8.728 519	18.80502	40.51420
666	443 556	25.80698	81.60882	295 408 296	8.732 892	18.81444	40.53449
667	444 889	25.82634	81.67007	296 740 963	8.737 260	18.82386	40.55477
668	446 224	25.84570	81.73127	298 077 632	8.741 625	18.83326	40.57503
669	447 561	25.86503	81.79242	299 418 309	8.745 985	18.84265	40.59526
670	448 900	25.88436	81.85353	300 763 000	8.750 340	18.85204	40.61548
671	450 241	25.90367	81.91459	302 111 711	8.754 691	18.86141	40.63568
672	451 584	25.92296	81.97561	303 464 448	8.759 038	18.87078	40.65585
673	452 929	25.94224	82.03658	304 821 217	8.763 381	18.88013	40.67601
674	454 276	25.96151	82.09750	306 182 024	8.767 719	18.88948	40.69615
675	455 625	25.98076	82.15838	307 546 875	8.772 053	18.89882	40.71626
676	456 976	26.00000	82.21922	308 915 776	8.776 383	18.90814	40.73636
677	458 329	26.01922	82.28001	310 288 733	8.780 708	18.91746	40.75644
678	459 684	26.03843	82.34076	311 665 752	8.785 030	18.92677	40.77650
679	461 041	26.05763	82.40146	313 046 839	8.789 347	18.93607	40.79653
680	462 400	26.07681	82.46211	314 432 000	8.793 659	18.94536	40.81655
681	463 761	26.09598	82.52272	315 821 241	8.797 968	18.95465	40.83655
682	465 124	26.11513	82.58329	317 214 568	8.802 272	18.96392	40.85653
683	466 489	26.13427	82.64381	318 611 987	8.806 572	18.97318	40.87649
684	467 856	26.15339	82.70429	320 013 504	8.810 868	18.98244	40.89643
685	469 225	26.17250	82.76473	321 419 125	8.815 160	18.99169	40.91635
686	470 596	26.19160	82.82512	322 828 856	8.819 447	19.00092	40.93625
687	471 969	26.21068	82.88546	324 242 703	8.823 731	19.01015	40.95613
688	473 344	26.22975	82.94577	325 660 672	8.828 010	19.01937	40.97599
689	474 721	26.24881	83.00602	327 082 769	8.832 285	19.02858	40.99584
690	476 100	26.26785	83.06624	328 509 000	8.836 556	19.03778	41.01566
691	477 481	26.28688	83.12641	329 939 371	8.840 823	19.04698	41.03546
692	478 864	26.30589	83.18654	331 373 888	8.845 085	19.05616	41.05525
693	480 249	26.32489	83.24662	332 812 557	8.849 344	19.06533	41.07502
694	481 636	26.34388	83.30666	334 255 384	8.853 599	19.07450	41.09476
695	483 025	26.36285	83.36666	335 702 375	8.857 849	19.08366	41.11449
696	484 416	26.38181	83.42661	337 153 536	8.862 095	19.09281	41.13420
697	485 809	26.40076	83.48653	338 608 873	8.866 338	19.10195	41.15389
698	487 204	26.41969	83.54639	340 068 392	8.870 576	19.11108	41.17357
699	488 601	26.43861	83.60622	341 532 099	8.874 810	19.12020	41.19322
700	490 000	26.45751	83.66600	343 000 000	8.879 040	19.12931	41.21285

SQUARES, SQUARE ROOT, CUBES AND CUBE ROOT (Continued)

n	n^2	$\sqrt{n}$	$\sqrt{10n}$	n^3	$\sqrt[3]{n}$	$\sqrt[3]{10n}$	$\sqrt[3]{100n}$
700	490 000	26.45751	83.66600	343 000 000	8.879 040	19.12931	41.21285
701	491 401	26.47640	83.72574	344 472 101	8.883 266	19.13842	41.23247
702	492 804	26.49528	83.78544	345 948 408	8.887 488	19.14751	41.25207
703	494 209	26.51415	83.84510	347 428 927	8.891 706	19.15660	41.27164
704	495 616	26.53300	83.90471	348 913 664	8.895 920	19.16568	41.29120
705	497 025	26.55184	83.96428	350 402 625	8.900 130	19.17475	41.31075
706	498 436	26.57066	84.02381	351 895 816	8.904 337	19.18381	41.33027
707	499 849	26.58947	84.08329	353 393 243	8.908 539	19.19286	41.34977
708	501 264	26.60827	84.14274	354 894 912	8.912 737	19.20191	41.36926
709	502 681	26.62705	84.20214	356 400 829	8.916 931	19.21095	41.38873
710	504 100	26.64583	84.26150	357 911 000	8.921 121	19.21997	41.40818
711	505 521	26.66458	84.32082	359 425 431	8.925 308	19.22899	41.42761
712	506 944	26.68333	84.38009	360 944 128	8.929 490	19.23800	41.44702
713	508 369	26.70206	84.43933	362 467 097	8.933 669	19.24701	41.46642
714	509 796	26.72078	84.49852	363 994 344	8.937 843	19.25600	41.48579
715	511 225	26.73948	84.55767	365 525 875	8.942 014	19.26499	41.50515
716	512 656	26.75818	84.61678	367 061 696	8.946 181	19.27396	41.52449
717	514 089	26.77686	84.67585	368 601 813	8.950 344	19.28293	41.54382
718	515 524	26.79552	84.73488	370 146 232	8.954 503	19.29189	41.56312
719	516 961	26.81418	84.79387	371 694 959	8.958 658	19.30084	41.58241
720	518 400	26.83282	84.85281	373 248 000	8.962 809	19.30979	41.60168
721	519 841	26.85144	84.91172	374 805 361	8.966 957	19.31872	41.62093
722	521 284	26.87006	84.97058	376 367 048	8.971 101	19.32765	41.64016
723	522 729	26.88866	85.02941	377 933 067	8.975 241	19.33657	41.65938
724	524 176	26.90725	85.08819	379 503 424	8.979 377	19.34548	41.67857
725	525 625	26.92582	85.14693	381 078 125	8.983 509	19.35438	41.69775
726	527 076	26.94439	85.20563	382 657 176	8.987 637	19.36328	41.71692
727	528 529	26.96294	85.26429	384 240 583	8.991 762	19.37216	41.73606
728	529 984	26.98148	85.32292	385 828 352	8.995 883	19.38104	41.75519
729	531 441	27.00000	85.38150	387 420 489	9.000 000	19.38991	41.77430
730	532 900	27.01851	85.44004	389 017 000	9.004 113	19.39877	41.79339
731	534 361	27.03701	85.49854	390 617 891	9.008 223	19.40763	41.81247
732	535 824	27.05550	85.55700	392 223 168	9.012 329	19.41647	41.83152
733	537 289	27.07397	85.61542	393 832 837	9.016 431	19.42531	41.85056
734	538 756	27.09243	85.67380	395 446 904	9.020 529	19.43414	41.86959
735	540 225	27.11088	85.73214	397 065 375	9.024 624	19.44296	41.88859
736	541 696	27.12932	85.79044	398 688 256	9.028 715	19.45178	41.90758
737	543 169	27.14774	85.84870	400 315 553	9.032 802	19.46058	41.92655
738	544 644	27.16616	85.90693	401 947 272	9.036 886	19.46938	41.94551
739	546 121	27.18455	85.96511	403 583 419	9.040 966	19.47817	41.96444
740	547 600	27.20294	86.02325	405 224 000	9.045 042	19.48695	41.98336
741	549 081	27.22132	86.08136	406 869 021	9.049 114	19.49573	42.00227
742	550 564	27.23968	86.13942	408 518 488	9.053 183	19.50449	42.02115
743	552 049	27.25803	86.19745	410 172 407	9.057 248	19.51325	42.04002
744	553 536	27.27636	86.25543	411 830 784	9.061 310	19.52200	42.05887
745	555 025	27.29469	86.31338	413 493 625	9.065 368	19.53074	42.07771
746	556 516	27.31300	86.37129	415 160 936	9.069 422	19.53948	42.09653
747	558 009	27.33130	86.42916	416 832 723	9.073 473	19.54820	42.11533
748	559 504	27.34959	86.48699	418 508 992	9.077 520	19.55692	42.13411
749	561 001	27.36786	86.54479	420 189 749	9.081 563	19.56563	42.15288
750	562 500	27.38613	86.60254	421 875 000	9.085 603	19.57434	42.17163

SQUARES, SQUARE ROOT, CUBES AND CUBE ROOT (Continued)

n	n^2	$\sqrt{n}$	$\sqrt{10n}$	n^3	$\sqrt[3]{n}$	$\sqrt[3]{10n}$	$\sqrt[3]{100n}$
750	562 500	27.38613	86.60254	421 875 000	9.085 603	19.57434	42.17163
751	564 001	27.40438	86.66026	423 564 751	9.089 639	19.58303	42.19037
752	565 504	27.42262	86.71793	425 259 008	9.093 672	19.59172	42.20909
753	567 009	27.44085	86.77557	426 957 777	9.097 701	19.60040	42.22779
754	568 516	27.45906	86.83317	428 661 064	9.101 727	19.60908	42.24647
755	570 025	27.47726	86.89074	430 368 875	9.105 748	19.61774	42.26514
756	571 536	27.49545	86.94826	432 081 216	9.109 767	19.62640	42.28379
757	573 049	27.51363	87.00575	433 798 093	9.113 782	19.63505	42.30243
758	574 564	27.53180	87.06320	435 519 512	9.117 793	19.64369	42.32105
759	576 081	27.54995	87.12061	437 245 479	9.121 801	19.65232	42.33965
760	577 600	27.56810	87.17798	438 976 000	9.125 805	19.66095	42.35824
761	579 121	27.58623	87.23531	440 711 081	9.129 806	19.66957	42.37681
762	580 644	27.60435	87.29261	442 450 728	9.133 803	19.67818	42.39536
763	582 169	27.62245	87.34987	444 194 947	9.137 797	19.68679	42.41390
764	583 696	27.64055	87.40709	445 943 744	9.141 787	19.69538	42.43242
765	585 225	27.65863	87.46428	447 697 125	9.145 774	19.70397	42.45092
766	586 756	27.67671	87.52143	449 455 096	9.149 758	19.71256	42.46941
767	588 289	27.69476	87.57854	451 217 663	9.153 738	19.72113	42.48789
768	589 824	27.71281	87.63561	452 984 832	9.157 714	19.72970	42.50634
769	591 361	27.73085	87.69265	454 756 609	9.161 687	19.73826	42.52478
770	592 900	27.74887	87.74964	456 533 000	9.165 656	19.74681	42.54321
771	594 441	27.76689	87.80661	458 314 011	9.169 623	19.75535	42.56162
772	595 984	27.78489	87.86353	460 099 648	9.173 585	19.76389	42.58001
773	597 529	27.80288	87.92042	461 889 917	9.177 544	19.77242	42.59839
774	599 076	27.82086	87.97727	463 684 824	9.181 500	19.78094	42.61675
775	600 625	27.83882	88.03408	465 484 375	9.185 453	19.78946	42.63509
776	602 176	27.85678	88.09086	467 288 576	9.189 402	19.79797	42.65342
777	603 729	27.87472	88.14760	469 097 433	9.193 347	19.80647	42.67174
778	605 284	27.89265	88.20431	470 910 952	9.197 290	19.81496	42.69004
779	606 841	27.91057	88.26098	472 729 139	9.201 229	19.82345	42.70832
780	608 400	27.92848	88.31761	474 552 000	9.205 164	19.83192	42.72659
781	609 961	27.94638	88.37420	476 379 541	9.209 096	19.84040	42.74484
782	611 524	27.96426	88.43076	478 211 768	9.213 025	19.84886	42.76307
783	613 089	27.98214	88.48729	480 048 687	9.216 950	19.85732	42.78129
784	614 656	28.00000	88.54377	481 890 304	9.220 873	19.86577	42.79950
785	616 225	28.01785	88.60023	483 736 625	9.224 791	19.87421	42.81769
786	617 796	28.03569	88.65664	485 587 656	9.228 707	19.88265	42.83586
787	619 369	28.05352	88.71302	487 443 403	9.232 619	19.89107	42.85402
788	620 944	28.07134	88.76936	489 303 872	9.236 528	19.89950	42.87216
789	622 521	28.08914	88.82567	491 169 069	9.240 433	19.90791	42.89029
790	624 100	28.10694	88.88194	493 039 000	9.244 335	19.91632	42.90840
791	625 681	28.12472	88.93818	494 913 671	9.248 234	19.92472	42.92650
792	627 264	28.14249	88.99438	496 793 088	9.252 130	19.93311	42.94458
793	628 849	28.16026	89.05055	498 677 257	9.256 022	19.94150	42.96265
794	630 436	28.17801	89.10668	500 566 184	9.259 911	19.94987	42.98070
795	632 025	28.19574	89.16277	502 459 875	9.263 797	19.95825	42.99874
796	633 616	28.21347	89.21883	504 358 336	9.267 680	19.96661	43.01676
797	635 209	28.23119	89.27486	506 261 573	9.271 559	19.97497	43.03477
798	636 804	28.24889	89.33085	508 169 592	9.275 435	19.98332	43.05276
799	638 401	28.26659	89.38680	510 082 399	9.279 308	19.99166	43.07073
800	640 000	28.28427	89.44272	512 000 000	9.283 178	20.00000	43.08869

SQUARES, SQUARE ROOT, CUBES AND CUBE ROOT (Continued)

n	n^2	$\sqrt{n}$	$\sqrt{10n}$	n^3	$\sqrt[3]{n}$	$\sqrt[3]{10n}$	$\sqrt[3]{100n}$
800	640 000	28.28427	89.44272	512 000 000	9.283 178	20.00000	43.08869
801	641 601	28.30194	89.49860	513 922 401	9.287 044	20.00833	43.10664
802	643 204	28.31960	89.55445	515 849 608	9.290 907	20.01665	43.12457
803	644 809	28.33725	89.61027	517 781 627	9.294 767	20.02497	43.14249
804	646 416	28.35489	89.66605	519 718 464	9.298 624	20.03328	43.16039
805	648 025	28.37252	89.72179	521 660 125	9.302 477	20.04158	43.17828
806	649 636	28.39014	89.77750	523 606 616	9.306 328	20.04988	43.19615
807	651 249	28.40775	89.83318	525 557 943	9.310 175	20.05816	43.21400
808	652 864	28.42534	89.88882	527 514 112	9.314 019	20.06645	43.23185
809	654 481	28.44293	89.94443	529 475 129	9.317 860	20.07472	43.24967
810	656 100	28.46050	90.00000	531 441 000	9.321 698	20.08299	43.26749
811	657 721	28.47806	90.05554	533 411 731	9.325 532	20.09125	43.28529
812	659 344	28.49561	90.11104	535 387 328	9.329 363	20.09950	43.30307
813	660 969	28.51315	90.16651	537 367 797	9.333 192	20.10775	43.32084
814	662 596	28.53069	90.22195	539 353 144	9.337 017	20.11599	43.33859
815	664 225	28.54820	90.27735	541 343 375	9.340 839	20.12423	43.35633
816	665 856	28.56571	90.33272	543 338 496	9.344 657	20.13245	43.37406
817	667 489	28.58321	90.38805	545 338 513	9.348 473	20.14067	43.39177
818	669 124	28.60070	90.44335	547 343 432	9.352 286	20.14889	43.40947
819	670 761	28.61818	90.49862	549 353 259	9.356 095	20.15710	43.42715
820	672 400	28.63564	90.55385	551 368 000	9.359 902	20.16530	43.44481
821	674 041	28.65310	90.60905	553 387 661	9.363 705	20.17349	43.46247
822	675 684	28.67054	90.66422	555 412 248	9.367 505	20.18168	43.48011
823	677 329	28.68798	90.71935	557 441 767	9.371 302	20.18986	43.49773
824	678 976	28.70540	90.77445	559 476 224	9.375 096	20.19803	43.51534
825	680 625	28.72281	90.82951	561 515 625	9.378 887	20.20620	43.53294
826	682 276	28.74022	90.88454	563 559 976	9.382 675	20.21436	43.55052
827	683 929	28.75761	90.93954	565 609 283	9.386 460	20.22252	43.56809
828	685 584	28.77499	90.99451	567 663 552	9.390 242	20.23066	43.58564
829	687 241	28.79236	91.04944	569 722 789	9.394 021	20.23880	43.60318
830	688 900	28.80972	91.10434	571 787 000	9.397 796	20.24694	43.62071
831	690 561	28.82707	91.15920	573 856 191	9.401 569	20.25507	43.63822
832	692 224	28.84441	91.21403	575 930 368	9.405 339	20.26319	43.65572
833	693 889	28.86174	91.26883	578 009 537	9.409 105	20.27130	43.67320
834	695 556	28.87906	91.32360	580 093 704	9.412 869	20.27941	43.69067
835	697 225	28.89637	91.37833	582 182 875	9.416 630	20.28751	43.70812
836	698 896	28.91366	91.43304	584 277 056	9.420 387	20.29561	43.72556
837	700 569	28.93095	91.48770	586 376 253	9.424 142	20.30370	43.74299
838	702 244	28.94823	91.54234	588 480 472	9.427 894	20.31178	43.76041
839	703 921	28 96550	91.59694	590 589 719	9.431 642	20.31986	43.77781
840	705 600	28.98275	91.65151	592 704 000	9.435 388	20.32793	43.79519
841	707 281	29.00000	91.70605	594 823 321	9.439 131	20.33599	43.81256
842	708 964	29.01724	91.76056	596 947 688	9.442 870	20.34405	43.82992
843	710 649	29.03446	91.81503	599 077 107	9.446 607	20.35210	43.84727
844	712 336	29.05168	91.86947	601 211 584	9.450 341	20.36014	43.86460
845	714 025	29.06888	91.92388	603 351 125	9.454 072	20.36818	43.88191
846	715 716	29.08608	91.97826	605 495 736	9.457 800	20.37621	43.89922
847	717 409	29.10326	92.03260	607 645 423	9.461 525	20.38424	43.91651
848	719 104	29.12044	92.08692	609 800 192	9.465 247	20.39226	43.93378
849	720 801	29.13760	92.14120	611 960 049	9.468 966	20.40027	43.95105
850	722 500	29.15476	92.19544	614 125 000	9.472 682	20.40828	43.96830

SQUARES, SQUARE ROOT, CUBES AND CUBE ROOT (Continued)

n	n^2	$\sqrt{n}$	$\sqrt{10n}$	n^3	$\sqrt[3]{n}$	$\sqrt[3]{10n}$	$\sqrt[3]{100n}$
850	722 500	29.15476	92.19544	614 125 000	9.472 682	20.40828	43.96830
851	724 201	29.17190	92.24966	616 295 051	9.476 396	20.41628	43.98553
852	725 904	29.18904	92.30385	618 470 208	9.480 106	20.42427	44.00275
853	727 609	29.20616	92.35800	620 650 477	9.483 814	20.43226	44.01996
854	729 316	29.22328	92.41212	622 835 864	9.487 518	20.44024	44.03716
855	731 025	29.24038	92.46621	625 026 375	9.491 220	20.44821	44.05434
856	732 736	29.25748	92.52027	627 222 016	9.494 919	20.45618	44.07151
857	734 449	29.27456	92.57429	629 422 793	9.498 615	20.46415	44.08866
858	736 164	29.29164	92.62829	631 628 712	9.502 308	20.47210	44.10581
859	737 881	29.30870	92.68225	633 839 779	9.505 998	20.48005	44.12293
860	739 600	29.32576	92.73618	636 056 000	9.509 685	20.48800	44.14005
861	741 321	29.34280	92.79009	638 277 381	9.513 370	20.49593	44.15715
862	743 044	29.35984	92.84396	640 503 928	9.517 052	20.50387	44.17424
863	744 769	29.37686	92.89779	642 735 647	9.520 730	20.51179	44.19132
864	746 496	29.39388	92.95160	644 972 544	9.524 406	20.51971	44.20838
865	748 225	29.41088	93.00538	647 214 625	9.528 079	20.52762	44.22543
866	749 956	29.42788	93.05912	649 461 896	9.531 750	20.53553	44.24246
867	751 689	29.44486	93.11283	651 714 363	9.535 417	20.54343	44.25949
868	753 424	29.46184	93.16652	653 972 032	9.539 082	20.55133	44.27650
869	755 161	29.47881	93.22017	656 234 909	9.542 744	20.55922	44.29349
870	756 900	29.49576	93.27379	658 503 000	9.546 403	20.56710	44.31048
871	758 641	29.51271	93.32738	660 776 311	9.550 059	20.57498	44.32745
872	760 384	29.52965	93.38094	663 054 848	9.553 712	20.58285	44.34440
873	762 129	29.54657	93.43447	665 338 617	9.557 363	20.59071	44.36135
874	763 876	29.56349	93.48797	667 627 624	9.561 011	20.59857	44.37828
875	765 625	29.58040	93.54143	669 921 875	9.564 656	20.60643	44.39520
876	767 376	29.59730	93.59487	672 221 376	9.568 298	20.61427	44.41211
877	769 129	29.61419	93.64828	674 526 133	9.571 938	20.62211	44.42900
878	770 884	29.63106	93.70165	676 836 152	9.575 574	20.62995	44.44588
879	772 641	29.64793	93.75500	679 151 439	9.579 208	20.63778	44.46275
880	774 400	29.66479	93.80832	681 472 000	9.582 840	20.64560	44.47960
881	776 161	29.68164	93.86160	683 797 841	9.586 468	20.65342	44.49644
882	777 924	29.69848	93.91486	686 128 968	9.590 094	20.66123	44.51327
883	779 689	29.71532	93.96808	688 465 387	9.593 717	20.66904	44.53009
884	781 456	29.73214	94.02127	690 807 104	9.597 337	20.67684	44.54689
885	783 225	29.74895	94.07444	693 154 125	9.600 955	20.68463	44.56368
886	784 996	29.76575	94.12757	695 506 456	9.604 570	20.69242	44.58046
887	786 769	29.78255	94.18068	697 864 103	9.608 182	20.70020	44.59723
888	788 544	29.79933	94.23375	700 227 072	9.611 791	20.70798	44.61398
889	790 321	29.81610	94.28680	702 595 369	9.615 398	20.71575	44.63072
890	792 100	29.83287	94.33981	704 969 000	9.619 002	20.72351	44.64745
891	793 881	29.84962	94.39280	707 347 971	9.622 603	20.73127	44.66417
892	795 664	29.86637	94.44575	709 732 288	9.626 202	20.73902	44.68087
893	797 449	29.88311	94.49868	712 121 957	9.629 797	20.74677	44.69756
894	799 236	29.89983	94.55157	714 516 984	9.633 391	20.75451	44.71424
895	801 025	29.91655	94.60444	716 917 375	9.636 981	20.76225	44.73090
896	802 816	29.93326	94.65728	719 323 136	9.640 569	20.76998	44.74756
897	804 609	29.94996	94.71008	721 734 273	9.644 154	20.77770	44.76420
898	806 404	29.96665	94.76286	724 150 792	9.647 737	20.78542	44.78083
899	808 201	29.98333	94.81561	726 572 699	9.651 317	20.79313	44.79744
900	810 000	30.00000	94.86833	729 000 000	9.654 894	20.80084	44.81405

SQUARES, SQUARE ROOT, CUBES AND CUBE ROOT (Continued)

n	n^2	$\sqrt{n}$	$\sqrt{10n}$	n^3	$\sqrt[3]{n}$	$\sqrt[3]{10n}$	$\sqrt[3]{100n}$
900	810 000	30.00000	94.86833	729 000 000	9.654 894	20.80084	44.81405
901	811 801	30.01666	94.92102	731 432 701	9.658 468	20.80854	44.83064
902	813 604	30.03331	94.97368	733 870 808	9.662 040	20.81623	44.84722
903	815 409	30.04996	95.02631	736 314 327	9.665 610	20.82392	44.86379
904	817 216	30.06659	95.07891	738 763 264	9.669 176	20.83161	44.88034
905	819 025	30.08322	95.13149	741 217 625	9.672 740	20.83929	44.89688
906	820 836	30.09983	95.18403	743 677 416	9.676 302	20.84696	44.91341
907	822 649	30.11644	95.23655	746 142 643	9.679 860	20.85463	44.92993
908	824 464	30.13304	95.28903	748 613 312	9.683 417	20.86229	44.94644
909	826 281	30.14963	95.34149	751 089 429	9.686 970	20.86994	44.96293
910	828 100	30.16621	95.39392	753 571 000	9.690 521	20.87759	44.97941
911	829 921	30.18278	95.44632	756 058 031	9.694 069	20.88524	44.99588
912	831 744	30.19934	95.49869	758 550 528	9.697 615	20.89288	45.01234
913	833 569	30.21589	95.55103	761 048 497	9.701 158	20.90051	45.02879
914	835 396	30.23243	95.60335	763 551 944	9.704 699	20.90814	45.04522
915	837 225	30.24897	95.65563	766 060 875	9.708 237	20.91576	45.06164
916	839 056	30.26549	95.70789	768 575 296	9.711 772	20.92338	45.07805
917	840 889	30.28201	95.76012	771 095 213	9.715 305	20.93099	45.09445
918	842 724	30.29851	95.81232	773 620 632	9.718 835	20.93860	45.11084
919	844 561	30.31501	95.86449	776 151 559	9.722 363	20.94620	45.12721
920	846 400	30.33150	95.91663	778 688 000	9.725 888	20.95379	45.14357
921	848 241	30.34798	95.96874	781 229 961	9.729 411	20.96138	45.15992
922	850 084	30.36445	96.02083	783 777 448	9.732 931	20.96896	45.17626
923	851 929	30.38092	96.07289	786 330 467	9.736 448	20.97654	45.19259
924	853 776	30.39737	96.12492	788 889 024	9.739 963	20.98411	45.20891
925	855 625	30.41381	96.17692	791 453 125	9.743 476	20.99168	45.22521
926	857 476	30.43025	96.22889	794 022 776	9.746 986	20.99924	45.24150
927	859 329	30.44667	96.28084	796 597 983	9.750 493	21.00680	45.25778
928	861 184	30.46309	96.33276	799 178 752	9.753 998	21.01435	45.27405
929	863 041	30.47950	96.38465	801 765 089	9.757 500	21.02190	45.29030
930	864 900	30.49590	96.43651	804 357 000	9.761 000	21.02944	45.30655
931	866 761	30.51229	96.48834	806 954 491	9.764 497	21.03697	45.32278
932	868 624	30.52868	96.54015	809 557 568	9.767 992	21.04450	45.33900
933	870 489	30.54505	96.59193	812 166 237	9.771 485	21.05203	45.35521
934	872 356	30.56141	96.64368	814 780 504	9.774 974	21.05954	45.37141
935	874 225	30.57777	96.69540	817 400 375	9.778 462	21.06706	45.38760
936	876 096	30.59412	96.74709	820 025 856	9.781 946	21.07456	45.40377
937	877 969	30.61046	96.79876	822 656 953	9.785 429	21.08207	45.41994
938	879 844	30.62679	96.85040	825 293 672	9.788 909	21.08956	45.43609
939	881 721	30.64311	96.90201	827 936 019	9.792 386	21.09706	45.45223
940	883 600	30.65942	96.95360	830 584 000	9.795 861	21.10454	45.46836
941	885 481	30.67572	97.00515	833 237 621	9.799 334	21.11202	45.48448
942	887 364	30.69202	97.05668	835 896 888	9.802 804	21.11950	45.50058
943	889 249	30.70831	97.10819	838 561 807	9.806 271	21.12697	45.51668
944	891 136	30.72458	97.15966	841 232 384	9.809 736	21.13444	45.53276
945	893 025	30.74085	97.21111	843 908 625	9.813 199	21.14190	45.54883
946	894 916	30.75711	97.26253	846 590 536	9.816 659	21.14935	45.56490
947	896 809	30.77337	97.31393	849 278 123	9.820 117	21.15680	45.58095
948	898.704	30.78961	97.36529	851 971 392	9.823 572	21.16424	45.59698
949	900 601	30.80584	97.41663	854 670 349	9.827 025	21.17168	45.61301
950	902 500	30.82207	97.46794	857 375 000	9.830 476	21.17912	45.62903

SQUARES, SQUARE ROOT, CUBES AND CUBE ROOT (Continued)

n	n^2	$\sqrt{n}$	$\sqrt{10n}$	n^3	$\sqrt[3]{n}$	$\sqrt[3]{10n}$	$\sqrt[3]{100n}$
950	902 500	30.82207	97.46794	857 375 000	9.830 476	21.17912	45.62903
951	904 401	30.83829	97.51923	860 085 351	9.833 924	21.18655	45.64503
952	906 304	30.85450	97.57049	862 801 408	9.837 369	21.19397	45.66102
953	908 209	30.87070	97.62172	865 523 177	9.840 813	21.20139	45.67701
954	910 116	30.88689	97.67292	868 250 664	9.844 254	21.20880	45.69298
955	912 025	30.90307	97.72410	870 983 875	9.847 692	21.21621	45.70894
956	913 936	30.91925	97.77525	873 722 816	9.851 128	21.22361	45.72489
957	915 849	30.93542	97.82638	876 467 493	9.854 562	21.23101	45.74082
958	917 764	30.95158	97.87747	879 217 912	9.857 993	21.23840	45.75675
959	919 681	30.96773	97.92855	881 974 079	9.861 422	21.24579	45.77267
960	921 600	30.98387	97.97959	884 736 000	9.864 848	21.25317	45.78857
961	923 521	31.00000	98.03061	887 503 681	9.868 272	21.26055	45.80446
962	925 444	31.01612	98.08160	890 277 128	9.871 694	21.26792	45.82035
963	927 369	31.03224	98.13256	893 056 347	9.875 113	21.27529	45.83622
964	929 296	31.04835	98.18350	895 841 344	9.878 530	21.28265	45.85208
965	931 225	31.06445	98.23441	898 632 125	9.881 945	21.29001	45.86793
966	933 156	31.08054	98.28530	901 428 696	9.885 357	21.29736	45.88376
967	935 089	31.09662	98.33616	904 231 063	9.888 767	21.30470	45.89959
968	937 024	31.11270	98.38699	907 039 232	9.892 175	21.31204	45.91541
969	938 961	31.12876	98.43780	909 853 209	9.895 580	21.31938	45.93121
970	940 900	31.14482	98.48858	912 673 000	9.898 983	21.32671	45.94701
971	942 841	31.16087	98.53933	915 498 611	9.902 384	21.33404	45.96279
972	944 784	31.17691	98.59006	918 330 048	9.905 782	21.34136	45.97857
973	946 729	31.19295	98.64076	921 167 317	9.909 178	21.34868	45.99433
974	948 676	31.20897	98.69144	924 010 424	9.912 571	21.35599	46.01008
975	950 625	31.22499	98.74209	926 859 375	9.915 962	21.36329	46.02582
976	952 576	31.24100	98.79271	929 714 176	9.919 351	21.37059	46.04155
977	954 529	31.25700	98.84331	932 574 833	9.922 738	21.37789	46.05727
978	956 484	31.27299	98.89388	935 441 352	9.926 122	21.38518	46.07298
979	958 441	31.28898	98.94443	938 313 739	9.929 504	21.39247	46.08868
980	960 400	31.30495	98.99495	941 192 000	9.932 884	21.39975	46.10436
981	962 361	31.32092	99.04544	944 076 141	9.936 261	21.40703	46.12004
982	964 324	31.33688	99.09591	946 966 168	9.939 636	21.41430	46.13571
983	966 289	31.35283	99.14636	949 862 087	9.943 009	21.42156	46.15136
984	968 256	31.36877	99.19677	952 763 904	9.946 380	21.42883	46.16700
985	970 225	31.38471	99.24717	955 671 625	9.949 748	21.43608	46.18264
986	972 196	31.40064	99.29753	958 585 256	9.953 114	21.44333	46.19826
987	974 169	31.41656	99.34787	961 504 803	9.956 478	21.45058	46.21387
988	976 144	31.43247	99.39819	964 430 272	9.959 839	21.45782	46.22948
989	978 121	31.44837	99.44848	967 361 669	9.963 198	21.46506	46.24507
990	980 100	31.46427	99.49874	970 299 000	9.966 555	21.47229	46.26065
991	982 081	31.48015	99.54898	973 242 271	9.969 910	21.47952	46.27622
992	984 064	31.49603	99.59920	976 191 488	9.973 262	21.48674	46.29178
993	986 049	31.51190	99.64939	979 146 657	9.976 612	21.49396	46.30733
994	988 036	31.52777	99.69955	982 107 784	9.979 960	21.50117	46.32287
995	990 025	31.54362	99.74969	985 074 875	9.983 305	21.50838	46.33840
996	992 016	31.55947	99.79980	988 047 936	9.986 649	21.51558	46.35392
997	994 009	31.57531	99.84989	991 026 973	9.989 990	21.52278	46.36943
998	996 004	31.59114	99.89995	994 011 992	9.993 329	21.52997	46.38492
999	998 001	31.60696	99.94999	997 002 999	9.996 666	21.53716	46.40041
1000	1 000 000	31.62278	100.00000	1 000 000 000	10.000 000	21.54435	46.41589

POWERS OF NUMBERS

The larger numbers are expressed exponentially to at least seven significant figures.

The approximate value written as a whole number may be obtained by shifting the decimal point to the right by the number of places indicated in the exponent of 10 shown at the head of each group of values. For example: the approximate value of 33^8 is found in the table as 14.064086×10^{11}. Written as a whole number it is 1 406 408 600 000.

n	n^4	n^5	n^6	n^7	n^8	n^9
1	1	1	1	1	1	1
2	16	32	64	128	256	512
3	81	243	729	2187	6561	19683
4	256	1024	4096	16384	65536	262144
5	625	3125	15625	78125	390625	1953125
6	1296	7776	46656	279936	1679616	10077696
7	2401	16807	117649	823543	5764801	40353607
8	4096	32768	262144	2097152	16777216	134217728
9	6561	59049	531441	4782969	43046721	387420489
					$\times 10^8$	$\times 10^9$
10	10000	100000	1000000	10000000	1.000000	1.000000
11	14641	161051	1771561	19487171	2.143589	2.357948
12	20736	248832	2985984	35831808	4.299817	5.159780
13	28561	371293	4826809	62748517	8.157307	10.604499
14	38416	537824	7529536	105413504	14.757891	20.661047
15	50625	759375	11390625	170859375	25.628906	38.443359
16	65536	1048576	16777216	268435456	42.949673	68.719477
17	83521	1419857	24137569	410338673	69.757574	118.587876
18	104976	1889568	34012224	612220032	110.199606	198.359290
19	130321	2476099	47045881	893871739	169.835630	322.687698
				$\times 10^9$	$\times 10^{10}$	$\times 10^{11}$
20	160000	3200000	64000000	1.280000	2.560000	5.120000
21	194481	4084101	85766121	1.801089	3.782286	7.942800
22	234256	5153632	113379904	2.494358	5.487587	12.072692
23	279841	6436343	148035889	3.404825	7.831099	18.011527
24	331776	7962624	191102976	4.586471	11.007531	26.418075
25	390625	9765625	244140625	6.103516	15.258789	38.146973
26	456976	11881376	308915776	8.031810	20.882706	54.295037
27	531441	14348907	387420489	10.460353	28.242954	76.255975
28	614656	17210368	481890304	13.492929	37.780200	105.784560
29	707281	20511149	594823321	17.249876	50.024641	145.071460
			$\times 10^8$	$\times 10^{10}$	$\times 10^{11}$	$\times 10^{13}$
30	810000	24300000	7.290000	2.187000	6.561000	1.968300
31	923521	28629151	8.875037	2.751261	8.528910	2.643962
32	1048576	33554432	10.737418	3.435974	10.995116	3.518437
33	1185921	39135393	12.914680	4.261844	14.064086	4.641148
34	1336336	45435424	15.448044	5.252335	17.857939	6.071699
35	1500625	52521875	18.382656	6.433930	22.518754	7.881564
36	1679616	60466176	21.767823	7.836416	28.211099	10.155996
37	1874161	69343957	25.657264	9.493188	35.124795	12.996174
38	2085136	79235168	30.109364	11.441558	43.477921	16.521610
39	2313441	90224199	35.187438	13.723101	53.520093	20.872836
			$\times 10^9$	$\times 10^{10}$	$\times 10^{12}$	$\times 10^{14}$
40	2560000	102400000	4.096000	16.384000	6.553600	2.621440
41	2825761	115856201	4.750104	19.475427	7.984925	3.273819
42	3111696	130691232	5.489032	23.053933	9.682652	4.066714
43	3418801	147008443	6.321363	27.181861	11.688200	5.025926
44	3748096	164916224	7.256314	31.927781	14.048224	6.181218
45	4100625	184528125	8.303766	37.366945	16.815125	7.566806
46	4477456	205962976	9.474297	43.581766	20.047612	9.221902
47	4879681	229345007	10.779215	50.662312	23.811287	11.191305
48	5308416	254803968	12.230590	58.706834	28.179280	13.526055
49	5764801	282475249	13.841287	67.822307	33.232931	16.284136
50	6250000	312500000	15.625000	78.125000	39.062500	19.531250

POWERS OF NUMBERS (Continued)

n	n^4	n^5	n^6	n^7	n^8	n^9
			$\times 10^9$	$\times 10^{11}$	$\times 10^{13}$	$\times 10^{14}$
50	6250000	312500000	15.625000	7.812500	3.906250	19.531250
51	6765201	345025251	17.596288	8.974107	4.576794	23.341652
52	7311616	380204032	19.770610	10.280717	5.345973	27.799059
53	7890481	418195493	22.164361	11.747111	6.225969	32.997636
54	8503056	459165024	24.794911	13.389252	7.230196	39.043059
55	9150625	503284375	27.680641	15.224352	8.373394	46.053666
56	9834496	550731776	30.840979	17.270948	9.671731	54.161694
57	10556001	601692057	34.296447	19.548975	11.142916	63.514620
58	11316496	656356768	38.068693	22.079842	12.806308	74.276587
59	12117361	714924299	42.180534	24.886515	14.683044	86.629958
		$\times 10^8$	$\times 10^{10}$	$\times 10^{11}$	$\times 10^{13}$	$\times 10^{16}$
60	12960000	7.776000	4.665600	27.993600	16.796160	1.007770
61	13845841	8.445963	5.152037	31.427428	19.170731	1.169415
62	14776336	9.161328	5.680024	35.216146	21.834011	1.353709
63	15752961	9.924365	6.252350	39.389806	24.815578	1.563381
64	16777216	10.737418	6.871948	43.980465	28.147498	1.801440
65	17850625	11.602906	7.541889	49.022279	31.864481	2.071191
66	18974736	12.523326	8.265395	54.551607	36.004061	2.376268
67	20151121	13.501251	9.045838	60.607116	40.606768	2.720653
68	21381376	14.539336	9.886748	67.229888	45.716324	3.108710
69	22667121	15.640313	10.791816	74.463533	51.379837	3.545209
		$\times 10^8$	$\times 10^{10}$	$\times 10^{12}$	$\times 10^{14}$	$\times 10^{16}$
70	24010000	16.807000	11.764900	8.235430	5.764801	4.035361
71	25411681	18.042294	12.810028	9.095120	6.457535	4.584850
72	26873856	19.349176	13.931407	10.030613	7.222041	5.199870
73	28398241	20.730716	15.133423	11.047399	8.064601	5.887159
74	29986576	22.190066	16.420649	12.151280	8.991947	6.654041
75	31640625	23.730469	17.797852	13.348389	10.011292	7.508469
76	33362176	25.355254	19.269993	14.645195	11.130348	8.459064
77	35153041	27.067842	20.842238	16.048523	12.357363	9.515169
78	37015056	28.871744	22.519960	17.565569	13.701144	10.686892
79	38950081	30.770564	24.308746	19.203909	15.171088	11.985160
		$\times 10^8$	$\times 10^{10}$	$\times 10^{12}$	$\times 10^{14}$	$\times 10^{16}$
80	40960000	32.768000	26.214400	20.971520	16.777216	13.421773
81	43046721	34.867844	28.242954	22.876792	18.530202	15.009464
82	45212176	37.073984	30.400667	24.928547	20.441409	16.761955
83	47458321	39.390406	32.694037	27.136051	22.522922	18.694026
84	49787136	41.821194	35.129803	29.509035	24.787589	20.821575
85	52200625	44.370531	37.714952	32.057709	27.249053	23.161695
86	54700816	47.042702	40.456724	34.792782	29.921793	25.732742
87	57289761	49.842092	43.362620	37.725479	32.821167	28.554415
88	59969536	52.773192	46.440409	40.867560	35.963452	31.647838
89	62742241	55.840594	49.698129	44.231335	39.365888	35.035640
		$\times 10^9$	$\times 10^{11}$	$\times 10^{13}$	$\times 10^{15}$	$\times 10^{17}$
90	65610000	5.904900	5.314410	4.782969	4.304672	3.874205
91	68574961	6.240321	5.678693	5.167610	4.702525	4.279298
92	71639296	6.590815	6.063550	5.578466	5.132189	4.721614
93	74805201	6.956884	6.469902	6.017009	5.595818	5.204111
94	78074896	7.339040	6.898698	6.484776	6.095689	5.729948
95	81450625	7.737809	7.350919	6.983373	6.634204	6.302494
96	84934656	8.153727	7.827578	7.514475	7.213896	6.925340
97	88529281	8.587340	8.329720	8.079828	7.837434	7.602311
98	92236816	9.039208	8.858424	8.681255	8.507630	8.337478
99	96059601	9.509900	9.414801	9.320653	9.227447	9.135172
100	100000000	10.000000	10.000000	10.000000	10.000000	10.000000

POSITIVE POWERS OF TWO

n	2^n			
1	2			
2	4			
3	8			
4	16			
5	32			
6	64			
7	128			
8	256			
9	512			
10	1024			
11	2048			
12	4096			
13	8192			
14	16384			
15	32768			
16	65536			
17	13107	2		
18	26214	4		
19	52428	8		
20	10485	76		
21	20971	52		
22	41943	04		
23	83886	08		
24	16777	216		
25	33554	432		
26	67108	864		
27	13421	7728		
28	26843	5456		
29	53687	0912		
30	10737	41824		
31	21474	83648		
32	42949	67296		
33	85899	34592		
34	17179	86918	4	
35	34359	73836	8	
36	68719	47673	6	
37	13743	89534	72	
38	27487	79069	44	
39	54975	58138	88	
40	10995	11627	776	
41	21990	23255	552	
42	43980	46511	104	
43	87960	93022	208	
44	17592	18604	4416	
45	35184	37208	8832	
46	70368	74417	7664	
47	14073	74883	55328	
48	28147	49767	10656	
49	56294	99534	21312	
50	11258	99906	84262	4

n	2^n						
51	22517	99813	68524	8			
52	45035	99627	37049	6			
53	90071	99254	74099	2			
54	18014	39850	94819	84			
55	36028	79701	89639	68			
56	72057	59403	79279	36			
57	14411	51880	75855	872			
58	28823	03761	51711	744			
59	57646	07523	03423	488			
60	11529	21504	60684	6976			
61	23058	43009	21369	3952			
62	46116	86018	42738	7904			
63	92233	72036	85477	5808			
64	18446	74407	37095	51616			
65	36893	48814	74191	03232			
66	73786	97629	48382	06464			
67	14757	39525	89676	41292	8		
68	29514	79051	79352	82585	6		
69	59029	58103	58705	65171	2		
70	11805	91620	71741	13034	24		
71	23611	83241	43482	26068	48		
72	47223	66482	86964	52136	96		
73	94447	32965	73929	04273	92		
74	18889	46593	14785	80854	784		
75	37778	93186	29571	61709	568		
76	75557	86372	59143	23419	136		
77	15111	57274	51828	64683	8272		
78	30223	14549	03657	29367	6544		
79	60446	29098	07314	58735	3088		
80	12089	25819	61462	91747	06176		
81	24178	51639	22925	83494	12352		
82	48357	03278	45851	66988	24704		
83	96714	06556	91703	33976	49408		
84	19342	81311	38340	66795	29881	6	
85	38685	62622	76681	33590	59763	2	
86	77371	25245	53362	67181	19526	4	
87	15474	25049	10672	53436	23905	28	
88	30948	50098	21345	06872	47810	56	
89	61897	00196	42690	13744	95621	12	
90	12379	40039	28538	02748	99124	224	
91	24758	80078	57076	05497	98248	448	
92	49517	60157	14152	10995	96496	896	
93	99035	20314	28304	21991	92993	792	
94	19807	04062	85660	84398	38598	7584	
95	39614	08125	71321	68796	77197	5168	
96	79228	16251	42643	37593	54395	0336	
97	15845	63250	28528	67518	70879	00672	
98	31691	26500	57057	35037	41758	01344	
99	63382	53001	14114	70074	83516	02688	
100	12676	50600	22822	94014	96703	20537	6
101	25353	01200	45645	88029	93406	41075	2

NEGATIVE POWERS OF TWO

n	2^{-n}							
0	1.0							
1	0.5							
2	0.25							
3	0.125							
4	0.0625							
5	0.03125							
6	0.01562	5						
7	0.00781	25						
8	0.00390	625						
9	0.00195	3125						
10	0.00097	65625						
11	0.00048	82812	5					
12	0.00024	41406	25					
13	0.00012	20703	125					
14	0.00006	10351	5625					
15	0.00003	05175	78125					
16	0.00001	52587	89062	5				
17	0.00000	76293	94531	25				
18	0.00000	38146	97265	625				
19	0.00000	19073	48632	8125				
20	0.00000	09536	74316	40625				
21	0.00000	04768	37158	20312	5			
22	0.00000	02384	18579	10156	25			
23	0.00000	01192	09289	55078	125			
24	0.00000	00596	04644	77539	0625			
25	0.00000	00298	02322	38769	53125			
26	0.00000	00149	01161	19384	76562	5		
27	0.00000	00074	50580	59692	38281	25		
28	0.00000	00037	25290	29846	19140	625		
29	0.00000	00018	62645	14923	09570	3125		
30	0.00000	00009	31322	57461	54785	15625		
31	0.00000	00004	65661	28730	77392	57812	5	
32	0.00000	00002	32830	64365	38696	28906	25	
33	0.00000	00001	16415	32182	69348	14453	125	
34	0.00000	00000	58207	66091	34674	07226	5625	
35	0.00000	00000	29103	83045	67337	03613	28125	
36	0.00000	00000	14551	91522	83668	51806	64062	5
37	0.00000	00000	07275	95761	41834	25903	32031	25
38	0.00000	00000	03637	97880	70917	12951	66015	625
39	0.00000	00000	01818	98940	35458	56475	83007	8125
40	0.00000	00000	00909	49470	17729	28237	91503	90625
41	0.00000	00000	00454	74735	08864	64118	95751	95312 5
42	0.00000	00000	00227	37367	54432	32059	47875	97656 25
43	0.00000	00000	00113	68683	77216	16029	73937	98828 125
44	0.00000	00000	00056	84341	88608	08014	86968	99414 0625
45	0.00000	00000	00028	42170	94304	04007	43484	49707 03125
46	0.00000	00000	00014	21085	47152	02003	71742	24853 51562 5
47	0.00000	00000	00007	10542	73576	01001	85871	12426 75781 25
48	0.00000	00000	00003	55271	36788	00500	92935	56213 37890 625
49	0.00000	00000	00001	77635	68394	00250	46467	78106 68945 3125
50	0.00000	00000	00000	88817	84197	00125	23233	89053 34472 65625

SUMS OF POWERS OF INTEGERS, $\sum_{k=1}^{n} k^m$

$(m = 1, 2, 3, 4); 1 \leq n \leq 40$

n	Σk	Σk^2	Σk^3	Σk^4
1	1	1	1	1
2	3	5	9	17
3	6	14	36	98
4	10	30	100	354
5	15	55	225	979
6	21	91	441	2275
7	28	140	784	4676
8	36	204	1296	8772
9	45	285	2025	15333
10	55	385	3025	25333
11	66	506	4356	39974
12	78	650	6084	60710
13	91	819	8281	89271
14	105	1015	11025	127687
15	120	1240	14400	178312
16	136	1496	18496	243848
17	153	1785	23409	327369
18	171	2109	29241	432345
19	190	2470	36100	562666
20	210	2870	44100	722666
21	231	3311	53361	917147
22	253	3795	64009	1151403
23	276	4324	76176	1431244
24	300	4900	90000	1763020
25	325	5525	105625	2153645
26	351	6201	123201	2610621
27	378	6930	142884	3142062
28	406	7714	164836	3756718
29	435	8555	189225	4463999
30	465	9455	216225	5273999
31	496	10416	246016	6197520
32	528	11440	278784	7246096
33	561	12529	314721	8432017
34	595	13685	354025	9768353
35	630	14910	396900	11268978
36	666	16206	443556	12948594
37	703	17575	494209	14822755
38	741	19019	549081	16907891
39	780	20540	608400	19221332
40	820	22140	672400	21781332

SUMS OF POWERS OF THE FIRST n INTEGERS*

$$\sum_{k=1}^{n} k = 1 + 2 + 3 + \cdots + n = \frac{n(n+1)}{2}$$

$$\sum_{k=1}^{n} k^2 = 1^2 + 2^2 + 3^2 + \cdots + n^2 = \frac{n(n+1)(2n+1)}{6}$$

$$\sum_{k=1}^{n} k^3 = \frac{n^2(n+1)^2}{4}$$

$$\sum_{k=1}^{n} k^4 = \frac{n}{30}(n+1)(2n+1)(3n^2+3n-1).$$

$$\sum_{k=1}^{n} k^5 = \frac{n^2}{12}(n+1)^2(2n^2+2n-1).$$

$$\sum_{k=1}^{n} k^6 = \frac{n}{42}(n+1)(2n+1)(3n^4+6n^3-3n+1).$$

$$\sum_{k=1}^{n} k^7 = \frac{n^2}{24}(n+1)^2(3n^4+6n^3-n^2-4n+2).$$

$$\sum_{k=1}^{n} k^8 = \frac{n}{90}(n+1)(2n+1)(5n^6+15n^5+5n^4-15n^3-n^2+9n-3).$$

$$\sum_{k=1}^{n} k^9 = \frac{n^2}{20}(n+1)^2(2n^6+6n^5+n^4-8n^3+n^2+6n-3).$$

$$\sum_{k=1}^{n} k^{10} = \frac{n}{66}(n+1)(2n+1)(3n^8+12n^7+8n^6-18n^5$$
$$-10n^4+24n^3+2n^2-15n+5).$$

Note that

$$\sum_{k=1}^{n} k^p = 1^p + 2^p + 3^p + \cdots + n^p \text{ is a function of } n \text{ which can be conveniently generated}$$

by use of the *following proposition*

If
$$\sum_{k=1}^{n} k^p = a_1 n^{p+1} + a_2 n^p + a_3 n^{p-1} + \cdots + a_{p+1} n$$

then

$$\sum_{k=1}^{n} k^{p+1} = \frac{p+1}{p+2} a_1 n^{p+2} + \frac{p+1}{p+1} a_2 n^{p+1} + \frac{p+1}{p} a_3 n^p$$
$$+ \cdots + \frac{p+1}{2} a_{p+1} n^2 + \left[1 - (p+1) \sum_{k=1}^{p+1} \frac{a_k}{(p+3-k)} \right] n$$

Example Since $\displaystyle\sum_{k=1}^{n} k = \frac{1}{2}n^2 + \frac{1}{2}n$, then

$$\sum_{k=1}^{n} k^2 = \frac{1}{3}n^3 + \frac{1}{2}n^2 + \frac{1}{6}n \text{ and from this result}$$

$$\sum_{k=1}^{n} k^3 = \frac{1}{4}n^4 + \frac{1}{2}n^3 + \frac{1}{4}n^2 \quad \text{etc.}$$

This proposition is extracted from a paper written by Michael A. Budin and Arnold J. Cantor entitled "Simplified Computation of Sums of Powers of Integers."

COMBINATORIAL ANALYSIS
*SUMS OF RECIPROCAL POWERS

n	$\zeta(n) = \sum\limits_{k=1}^{\infty} k^{-n}$			$\sum\limits_{k=1}^{\infty} (-1)^{k-1} k^{-n}$		
1	∞			0.69314	71805 59945	30942
2	1.64493	40668 48226	43637	0.82246	70334 24113	21824
3	1.20205	69031 59594	28540	0.90154	26773 69695	71405
4	1.08232	32337 11138	19152	0.94703	28294 97245	91758
5	1.03692	77551 43369	92633	0.97211	97704 46909	30594
6	1.01734	30619 84449	13971	0.98555	10912 97435	10410
7	1.00834	92773 81922	82684	0.99259	38199 22830	28267
8	1.00407	73561 97944	33938	0.99623	30018 52647	89923
9	1.00200	83928 26082	21442	0.99809	42975 41605	33077
10	1.00099	45751 27818	08534	0.99903	95075 98271	56564
11	1.00049	41886 04119	46456	0.99951	71434 98060	75414
12	1.00024	60865 53308	04830	0.99975	76851 43858	19085
13	1.00012	27133 47578	48915	0.99987	85427 63265	11549
14	1.00006	12481 35058	70483	0.99993	91703 45979	71817
15	1.00003	05882 36307	02049	0.99996	95512 13099	23808
16	1.00001	52822 59408	65187	0.99998	47642 14906	10644
17	1.00000	76371 97637	89976	0.99999	23782 92041	01198
18	1.00000	38172 93264	99984	0.99999	61878 69610	11348
19	1.00000	19082 12716	55394	0.99999	80935 08171	67511
20	1.00000	09539 62033	87280	0.99999	90466 11581	52212
21	1.00000	04769 32986	78781	0.99999	95232 58215	54282
22	1.00000	02384 50502	72773	0.99999	97616 13230	82255
23	1.00000	01192 19925	96531	0.99999	98808 01318	43950
24	1.00000	00596 08189	05126	0.99999	99403 98892	39463
25	1.00000	00298 03503	51465	0.99999	99701 98856	96283
26	1.00000	00149 01554	82837	0.99999	99850 99231	99657
27	1.00000	00074 50711	78984	0.99999	99925 49550	48496
28	1.00000	00037 25334	02479	0.99999	99962 74753	40011
29	1.00000	00018 62659	72351	0.99999	99981 37369	41811
30	1.00000	00009 31327	43242	0.99999	99990 68682	28145
31	1.00000	00004 65662	90650	0.99999	99995 34340	33145
32	1.00000	00002 32831	18337	0.99999	99997 67169	89595
33	1.00000	00001 16415	50173	0.99999	99998 83584	85805
34	1.00000	00000 58207	72088	0.99999	99999 41792	39905
35	1.00000	00000 29103	85044	0.99999	99999 70896	18953
36	1.00000	00000 14551	92189	0.99999	99999 85448	09143
37	1.00000	00000 07275	95984	0.99999	99999 92724	04461
38	1.00000	00000 03637	97955	0.99999	99999 96362	02193
39	1.00000	00000 01818	98965	0.99999	99999 98181	01084
40	1.00000	00000 00909	49478	0.99999	99999 99090	50538
41	1.00000	00000 00454	74738	0.99999	99999 99545	25268
42	1.00000	00000 00227	37368	0.99999	99999 99772	62633

For $n > 42$, $\sum\limits_{k=1}^{\infty} k^{-(n+1)} = \dfrac{1}{2}\left[1 + \sum\limits_{k=1}^{\infty} k^{-n}\right]$, $\sum\limits_{k=1}^{\infty} (-1)^{k-1} k^{-(n+1)} = \dfrac{1}{2}\left[1 + \sum\limits_{k=1}^{\infty} (-1)^{k-1} k^{-n}\right]$

*Note: By definition, Riemann's Zeta Function is

$$\zeta(p) = \text{Zeta}(p) = 1 + \frac{1}{2^p} + \frac{1}{3^p} + \frac{1}{4^p} + \cdots$$

n	$\displaystyle\sum_{k=0}^{\infty} (2k + 1)^{-n}$				$\displaystyle\sum_{k=0}^{\infty} (-1)^k (2k + 1)^{-n}$			
1		∞			0.78539	81633	97448	310
2	1.23370	05501	36169	82735	0.91596	55941	77219	015
3	1.05179	97902	64644	99972	0.96894	61462	59369	380
4	1.01467	80316	04192	05455	0.98894	45517	41105	336
5	1.00452	37627	95139	61613	0.99615	78280	77088	064
6	1.00144	70766	40942	12191	0.99868	52222	18438	135
7	1.00047	15486	52376	55476	0.99955	45078	90539	909
8	1.00015	51790	25296	11930	0.99984	99902	46829	657
9	1.00005	13451	83843	77259	0.99994	96841	87220	090
10	1.00001	70413	63044	82549	0.99998	31640	26196	877
11	1.00000	56660	51090	10935	0.99999	43749	73823	699
12	1.00000	18858	48583	11958	0.99999	81223	50587	882
13	1.00000	06280	55421	80232	0.99999	93735	83771	841
14	1.00000	02092	40519	21150	0.99999	97910	87248	735
15	1.00000	00697	24703	12929	0.99999	99303	40842	624
16	1.00000	00232	37157	37916	0.99999	99767	75950	903
17	1.00000	00077	44839	45587	0.99999	99922	57782	104
18	1.00000	00025	81437	55666	0.99999	99974	19086	745
19	1.00000	00008	60444	11452	0.99999	99991	39660	745
20	1.00000	00002	86807	69746	0.99999	99997	13213	274
21	1.00000	00000	95601	16531	0.99999	99999	04403	029
22	1.00000	00000	31866	77514	0.99999	99999	68134	064
23	1.00000	00000	10622	20241	0.99999	99999	89377	965
24	1.00000	00000	03540	72294	0.99999	99999	96459	311
25	1.00000	00000	01180	23874	0.99999	99999	98819	768
26	1.00000	00000	00393	41247	0.99999	99999	99606	589
27	1.00000	00000	00131	13740	0.99999	99999	99868	863
28	1.00000	00000	00043	71245	0.99999	99999	99956	288
29	1.00000	00000	00014	57081	0.99999	99999	99985	429
30	1.00000	00000	00004	85694	0.99999	99999	99995	143
31	1.00000	00000	00001	61898	0.99999	99999	99998	381
32	1.00000	00000	00000	53966	0.99999	99999	99999	460
33	1.00000	00000	00000	17989	0.99999	99999	99999	820
34	1.00000	00000	00000	05996	0.99999	99999	99999	940
35	1.00000	00000	00000	01999	0.99999	99999	99999	980
36	1.00000	00000	00000	00666	0.99999	99999	99999	993
37	1.00000	00000	00000	00222	0.99999	99999	99999	998
38	1.00000	00000	00000	00074	0.99999	99999	99999	999
39	1.00000	00000	00000	00025				
40	1.00000	00000	00000	00008				
41	1.00000	00000	00000	00003				
42	1.00000	00000	00000	00001				

*This table is related to Riemann's Zeta Function, where

$$1 + \frac{1}{2^p} + \frac{1}{3^p} + \frac{1}{4^p} + \cdots = \zeta(p) = \text{Zeta}(p)$$

Factorials, Exact Values

n	$n!$
0	1 (by definition)
1	1
2	2
3	6
4	24
5	120
6	720
7	5040
8	40,320
9	362,880
10	3,628,800
11	39,916,800
12	479,001,600
13	6,227,020,800
14	87,178,291,200
15	1,307,674,368,000
16	20,922,789,888,000
17	355,687,428,096,000
18	6,402,373,705,728,000
19	121,645,100,408,832,000
20	2,432,902,008,176,640,000
21	51,090,942,171,709,440,000
22	1,124,000,727,777,937,680,000
23	25,852,016,738,892,566,840,000
24	620,448,401,733,421,599,360,000
25	15,511,210,043,335,539,984,000,000
26	403,291,461,126,724,039,584,000,000
27	10,888,869,450,421,459,068,768,000,000
28	304,888,344,511,803,373,925,504,000,000
29	8,841,761,993,742,297,843,839,616,000,000
30	265,252,859,812,268,935,315,188,480,000,000
31	8.22284×10^{33}
32	2.63131×10^{35}
33	8.68332×10^{36}
34	2.95233×10^{38}
35	1.03331×10^{40}
36	3.71993×10^{41}
37	1.37638×10^{43}
38	5.23023×10^{44}
39	2.03979×10^{46}

$\lfloor n = n! = e^{-n} n^n \sqrt{2\pi n}.$ approximately, known as Stirling's formula

$\log_e n! = n \log_e n - n$, approximately.

FACTORIALS AND THEIR COMMON LOGARITHMS

n	$n!$	$\log n!$	n	$n!$	$\log n!$
			50	3.0414×10^{64}	64.48307
1	1.0000	0.00000	51	1.5511×10^{66}	66.19065
2	2.0000	0.30103	52	8.0658×10^{67}	67.90665
3	6.0000	0.77815	53	4.2749×10^{69}	69.63092
4	2.4000×10	1.38021	54	2.3084×10^{71}	71.36332
5	1.2000×10^{2}	2.07918	55	1.2696×10^{73}	73.10368
6	7.2000×10^{2}	2.85733	56	7.1100×10^{74}	74.85187
7	5.0400×10^{3}	3.70243	57	4.0527×10^{76}	76.60774
8	4.0320×10^{4}	4.60552	58	2.3506×10^{78}	78.37117
9	3.6288×10^{5}	5.55976	59	1.3868×10^{80}	80.14202
10	3.6288×10^{6}	6.55976	60	8.3210×10^{81}	81.92017
11	3.9917×10^{7}	7.60116	61	5.0758×10^{83}	83.70550
12	4.7900×10^{8}	8.68034	62	3.1470×10^{85}	85.49790
13	6.2270×10^{9}	9.79428	63	1.9826×10^{87}	87.29724
14	8.7178×10^{10}	10.94041	64	1.2689×10^{89}	89.10342
15	1.3077×10^{12}	12.11650	65	8.2477×10^{90}	90.91633
16	2.0923×10^{13}	13.32062	66	5.4434×10^{92}	92.73587
17	3.5569×10^{14}	14.55107	67	3.6471×10^{94}	94.56195
18	6.4024×10^{15}	15.80634	68	2.4800×10^{96}	96.39446
19	1.2165×10^{17}	17.08509	69	1.7112×10^{98}	98.23331
20	2.4329×10^{18}	18.38612	70	1.1979×10^{100}	100.07841
21	5.1091×10^{19}	19.70834	71	8.5048×10^{101}	101.92966
22	1.1240×10^{21}	21.05077	72	6.1234×10^{103}	103.78700
23	2.5852×10^{22}	22.41249	73	4.4701×10^{105}	105.65032
24	6.2045×10^{23}	23.79271	74	3.3079×10^{107}	107.51955
25	1.5511×10^{25}	25.19065	75	2.4809×10^{109}	109.39461
26	4.0329×10^{26}	26.60562	76	1.8855×10^{111}	111.27543
27	1.0889×10^{28}	28.03698	77	1.4518×10^{113}	113.16192
28	3.0489×10^{29}	29.48414	78	1.1324×10^{115}	115.05401
29	8.8418×10^{30}	30.94654	79	8.9462×10^{116}	116.95164
30	2.6525×10^{32}	32.42366	80	7.1569×10^{118}	118.85473
31	8.2228×10^{33}	33.91502	81	5.7971×10^{120}	120.76321
32	2.6313×10^{35}	35.42017	82	4.7536×10^{122}	122.67703
33	8.6833×10^{36}	36.93869	83	3.9455×10^{124}	124.59610
34	2.9523×10^{38}	38.47016	84	3.3142×10^{126}	126.52038
35	1.0333×10^{40}	40.01423	85	2.8171×10^{128}	128.44980
36	3.7199×10^{41}	41.57054	86	2.4227×10^{130}	130.38430
37	1.3764×10^{43}	43.13874	87	2.1078×10^{132}	132.32382
38	5.2302×10^{44}	44.71852	88	1.8548×10^{134}	134.26830
39	2.0398×10^{46}	46.30959	89	1.6508×10^{136}	136.21769
40	8.1592×10^{47}	47.91165	90	1.4857×10^{138}	138.17194
41	3.3453×10^{49}	49.52443	91	1.3520×10^{140}	140.13098
42	1.4050×10^{51}	51.14768	92	1.2438×10^{142}	142.09476
43	6.0415×10^{52}	52.78115	93	1.1568×10^{144}	144.06325
44	2.6583×10^{54}	54.42460	94	1.0874×10^{146}	146.03638
45	1.1962×10^{56}	56.07781	95	1.0330×10^{148}	148.01410
46	5.5026×10^{57}	57.74057	96	9.9168×10^{149}	149.99637
47	2.5862×10^{59}	59.41267	97	9.6193×10^{151}	151.98314
48	1.2414×10^{61}	61.09391	98	9.4269×10^{153}	153.97437
49	6.0828×10^{62}	62.78410	99	9.3326×10^{155}	155.97000
50	3.0414×10^{64}	64.48307	100	9.3326×10^{157}	157.97000

$$n! = \left(\frac{n}{e}\right)^{n}\sqrt{2\pi n} + h; \; n = 1, 2, 3, \ldots \left[0 < \frac{h}{n!} < \frac{1}{12n}\right]$$

$$\lim_{n \to \infty} \frac{n! e^{n}}{n^{n+\frac{1}{2}}} = \sqrt{2\pi} \qquad \lim_{n \to \infty} \frac{(n!)^{\frac{1}{n}}}{n} = \frac{1}{e}$$

RECIPROCALS OF FACTORIALS AND THEIR COMMON LOGARITHMS

n	$1/n!$	$\log (1/n!)$	n	$1/n!$	$\log (1/n!)$
1	1.	.00000	51	$.64470 \times 10^{-66}$	$\overline{67}.80935$
2	0.5	$\overline{1}.69897$	52	$.12398 \times 10^{-67}$	$\overline{68}.09335$
3	.16667	$\overline{1}.22185$	53	$.23392 \times 10^{-69}$	$\overline{70}.36908$
*4	$.41667 \times 10^{-1}$	$\overline{2}.61979$	54	$.45282 \times 10^{-71}$	$\overline{72}.63668$
5	$.83333 \times 10^{-2}$	$\overline{3}.92082$	55	$.78765 \times 10^{-73}$	$\overline{74}.89632$
6	$.13889 \times 10^{-2}$	$\overline{3}.14267$	56	$.14065 \times 10^{-74}$	$\overline{75}.14813$
7	$.19841 \times 10^{-3}$	$\overline{4}.29757$	57	$.24675 \times 10^{-76}$	$\overline{77}.39226$
8	$.24802 \times 10^{-4}$	$\overline{5}.39448$	58	$.42542 \times 10^{-78}$	$\overline{79}.62883$
9	$.27557 \times 10^{-5}$	$\overline{6}.44024$	59	$.72108 \times 10^{-80}$	$\overline{81}.85798$
10	$.27557 \times 10^{-6}$	$\overline{7}.44024$	60	$.12018 \times 10^{-81}$	$\overline{82}.07983$
11	$.25052 \times 10^{-7}$	$\overline{8}.39884$	61	$.19701 \times 10^{-83}$	$\overline{84}.29450$
12	$.20877 \times 10^{-8}$	$\overline{9}.31966$	62	$.31776 \times 10^{-85}$	$\overline{86}.50210$
13	$.16059 \times 10^{-9}$	$\overline{10}.20572$	63	$.50439 \times 10^{-87}$	$\overline{88}.70276$
14	$.11471 \times 10^{-10}$	$\overline{11}.05959$	64	$.78808 \times 10^{-89}$	$\overline{90}.89658$
15	$.76472 \times 10^{-12}$	$\overline{13}.88350$	65	$.12125 \times 10^{-90}$	$\overline{91}.08367$
16	$.47795 \times 10^{-13}$	$\overline{14}.67938$	66	$.18371 \times 10^{-92}$	$\overline{93}.26413$
17	$.28115 \times 10^{-14}$	$\overline{15}.44893$	67	$.27419 \times 10^{-94}$	$\overline{95}.43805$
18	$.15619 \times 10^{-15}$	$\overline{16}.19365$	68	$.40323 \times 10^{-96}$	$\overline{97}.60554$
19	$.82206 \times 10^{-17}$	$\overline{18}.91491$	69	$.58439 \times 10^{-98}$	$\overline{99}.76668$
20	$.41103 \times 10^{-18}$	$\overline{19}.61388$	70	$.83479 \times 10^{-100}$	$\overline{101}.92159$
21	$.19573 \times 10^{-19}$	$\overline{20}.29165$	71	$.11758 \times 10^{-101}$	$\overline{102}.07034$
22	$.88968 \times 10^{-21}$	$\overline{22}.94923$	72	$.16331 \times 10^{-103}$	$\overline{104}.21300$
23	$.38682 \times 10^{-22}$	$\overline{23}.58751$	73	$.22371 \times 10^{-105}$	$\overline{106}.34968$
24	$.16117 \times 10^{-23}$	$\overline{24}.20728$	74	$.30231 \times 10^{-107}$	$\overline{108}.48045$
25	$.64470 \times 10^{-25}$	$\overline{26}.80935$	75	$.40308 \times 10^{-109}$	$\overline{110}.60538$
26	$.24796 \times 10^{-26}$	$\overline{27}.39438$	76	$.53036 \times 10^{-111}$	$\overline{112}.72457$
27	$.91836 \times 10^{-28}$	$\overline{29}.96302$	77	$.68880 \times 10^{-113}$	$\overline{114}.83808$
28	$.32799 \times 10^{-29}$	$\overline{30}.51586$	78	$.88308 \times 10^{-115}$	$\overline{116}.94599$
29	$.11310 \times 10^{-30}$	$\overline{31}.05346$	79	$.11178 \times 10^{-116}$	$\overline{117}.04836$
30	$.37644 \times 10^{-32}$	$\overline{33}.57634$	80	$.13973 \times 10^{-118}$	$\overline{119}.14527$
31	$.12161 \times 10^{-33}$	$\overline{34}.08498$	81	$.17250 \times 10^{-120}$	$\overline{121}.23679$
32	$.38004 \times 10^{-35}$	$\overline{36}.57983$	82	$.21037 \times 10^{-122}$	$\overline{123}.32297$
33	$.11516 \times 10^{-36}$	$\overline{37}.06131$	83	$.25345 \times 10^{-124}$	$\overline{125}.40390$
34	$.33872 \times 10^{-38}$	$\overline{39}.52984$	84	$.30173 \times 10^{-126}$	$\overline{127}.47962$
35	$.96775 \times 10^{-40}$	$\overline{41}.98577$	85	$.35497 \times 10^{-128}$	$\overline{129}.55020$
36	$.26882 \times 10^{-41}$	$\overline{42}.42946$	86	$.41276 \times 10^{-130}$	$\overline{131}.61570$
37	$.72653 \times 10^{-43}$	$\overline{44}.86126$	87	$.47443 \times 10^{-132}$	$\overline{133}.67618$
38	$.19120 \times 10^{-44}$	$\overline{45}.28148$	88	$.53914 \times 10^{-134}$	$\overline{135}.73170$
39	$.49024 \times 10^{-46}$	$\overline{47}.69041$	89	$.60577 \times 10^{-136}$	$\overline{137}.78231$
40	$.12256 \times 10^{-47}$	$\overline{48}.08835$	90	$.67308 \times 10^{-138}$	$\overline{139}.82806$
41	$.29893 \times 10^{-49}$	$\overline{50}.47557$	91	$.73964 \times 10^{-140}$	$\overline{141}.86902$
42	$.71174 \times 10^{-51}$	$\overline{52}.85232$	92	$.80399 \times 10^{-142}$	$\overline{143}.90524$
43	$.16552 \times 10^{-52}$	$\overline{53}.21885$	93	$.86445 \times 10^{-144}$	$\overline{145}.93675$
44	$.37618 \times 10^{-54}$	$\overline{55}.57540$	94	$.91962 \times 10^{-146}$	$\overline{147}.96362$
45	$.83598 \times 10^{-56}$	$\overline{57}.92219$	95	$.96805 \times 10^{-148}$	$\overline{149}.98590$
46	18173×10^{-57}	$\overline{58}.25943$	96	$.10084 \times 10^{-149}$	$\overline{150}.00363$
47	$.38667 \times 10^{-59}$	$\overline{60}.58733$	97	$.10396 \times 10^{-151}$	$\overline{152}.01686$
48	$.80554 \times 10^{-61}$	$\overline{62}.90609$	98	$.10608 \times 10^{-153}$	$\overline{154}.02563$
49	$.16440 \times 10^{-62}$	$\overline{63}.21590$	99	$.10715 \times 10^{-155}$	$\overline{156}.03000$
50	$.32880 \times 10^{-64}$	$\overline{65}.51693$	100	$.10715 \times 10^{-157}$	$\overline{158}.03000$

* For example $\log \dfrac{1}{4!} = \overline{2}.61979 = .61979 - 2 = 8.61979 - 10.$

NUMBER OF PERMUTATIONS $P(n,m)$

This table contains the number of permutations of n distinct things taken m at a time, given by

$$P(n,m) = \frac{n!}{(n-m)!} = n(n-1) \cdots (n-m+1)$$

n \ m	0	1	2	3	4	5	6	7	8	9	10
1	1										
1	1	1									
1	1	2	2								
1	1	3	6	6							
1	1	4	12	24	24						
1	1	5	20	60	120	120					
1	1	6	30	120	360	720	720				
1	1	7	42	210	840	2520	5040	5040			
1	1	8	56	336	1680	6720	20160	40320	40320		
1	1	9	72	504	3024	15120	60480	1 81440	3 62880	3 62880	
1	1	10	90	720	5040	30240	1 51200	6 04800	18 14400	36 28800	36 28800
1	1	11	110	990	7920	55440	3 32640	16 63200	66 52800	199 58400	399 16800
1	1	12	132	1320	11880	95040	6 65280	39 91680	199 58400	798 33600	2395 00800
1	1	13	156	1716	17160	1 54440	12 35520	86 48640	518 91840	2594 59200	10378 36800
1	1	14	182	2184	24024	2 40240	21 62160	172 97280	1210 80960	7264 85760	36324 28800
1	1	15	210	2730	32760	3 60360	36 03600	324 32400	2594 59200	18162 14400	1 08972 86400

n \ m	11	12	13	14	15
8					
9					
10					
11	399 16800				
12	4790 01600	4790 01600			
13	31135 10400	62270 20800	62270 20800		
14	1 45297 15200	4 35891 45600	8 71782 91200	8 71782 91200	
15	5 44864 32000	21 79457 28000	65 38371 84000	130 76743 68000	130 76743 68000

NUMBER OF COMBINATIONS

$$\binom{n}{m} = C(n, m)$$

Properties of Binomial Coefficients

$$(1 + x)^n = \binom{n}{0} x^0 + \binom{n}{1} x^n + \binom{n}{2} x^2 + \ldots + \binom{n}{n} x^n$$

$$\binom{n}{m} + \binom{n}{m+1} = \binom{n+1}{m+1}, \binom{n}{m} = \binom{n}{n-m}$$

This leads to Pascal's triangle

$$\binom{n}{0} + \binom{n}{1} + \binom{n}{2} + \ldots + \binom{n}{n} = 2^n$$

$$\binom{n}{0} - \binom{n}{1} + \binom{n}{2} - \ldots (-1)^n \binom{n}{n} = 0$$

$$\binom{n}{n} + \binom{n+1}{n} + \binom{n+2}{n} + \ldots + \binom{n+m}{n} = \binom{n+m+1}{n+1}$$

$$\binom{n}{0} + \binom{n}{2} + \binom{n}{4} + \ldots = 2^{n-1}$$

$$\binom{n}{1} + \binom{n}{3} + \binom{n}{5} + \ldots = 2^{n-1}$$

$$\binom{n}{0}^2 + \binom{n}{1}^2 + \binom{n}{2}^2 + \ldots + \binom{n}{n}^2 = \binom{2n}{n}$$

$$\binom{m}{0}\binom{n}{p} + \binom{m}{1}\binom{n}{p-1} + \ldots + \binom{m}{p}\binom{n}{0} = \binom{m+n}{p}$$

$$(1)\binom{n}{1} + (2)\binom{n}{2} + (3)\binom{n}{3} + \ldots + (n)\binom{n}{n} = n2^{n-1}$$

$$(1)\binom{n}{1} - (2)\binom{n}{2} + (3)\binom{n}{3} - \ldots (-1)^{n+1}(n)\binom{n}{n} = 0$$

NUMBER OF COMBINATIONS $C(n,m)$

This table contains the number of combinations of n distinct things taken m at a time, given by

$$\binom{n}{m} = C(n,m) = \frac{n!}{m!(n-m)!} = \frac{P(n,r)}{m!} \; .$$

For values missing from the above table, use the relation $\binom{n}{m} = \binom{n}{n-m}$, e.g. $\binom{20}{12} = \binom{20}{8} = 125970$. $\binom{n}{m}$ is also referred to as a binomial coefficient. A recursion relation for the binomial coefficients is

$$\binom{n+1}{m+1} = \binom{n}{m} + \binom{n}{m+1}$$

NUMBER OF COMBINATIONS

$$\binom{n}{m} = C(n,m)$$

n \ m	0	1	2	3	4	5	6	7	8
1	1	1							
2	1	2	1						
3	1	3	3	1					
4	1	4	6	4	1				
5	1	5	10	10	5	1			
6	1	6	15	20	15	6	1		
7	1	7	21	35	35	21	7	1	
8	1	8	28	56	70	56	28	8	1
9	1	9	36	84	126	126	84	36	9
10	1	10	45	120	210	252	210	120	45
11	1	11	55	165	330	462	462	330	165
12	1	12	66	220	495	792	924	792	495
13	1	13	78	286	715	1287	1716	1716	1287
14	1	14	91	364	1001	2002	3003	3432	3003
15	1	15	105	455	1365	3003	5005	6435	6435
16	1	16	120	560	1820	4368	8008	11440	12870
17	1	17	136	680	2380	6188	12376	19448	24310
18	1	18	153	816	3060	8568	18564	31824	43758
19	1	19	171	969	3876	11628	27132	50388	75582
20	1	20	190	1140	4845	15504	38760	77520	1 25970
21	1	21	210	1330	5985	20349	54264	1 16280	2 03490
22	1	22	231	1540	7315	26334	74613	1 70544	3 19770
23	1	23	253	1771	8855	33649	1 00947	2 45157	4 90314
24	1	24	276	2024	10626	42504	1 34596	3 46104	7 35471
25	1	25	300	2300	12650	53130	1 77100	4 80700	10 81575
26	1	26	325	2600	14950	65780	2 30230	6 57800	15 62275
27	1	27	351	2925	17550	80730	2 96010	8 88030	22 20075
28	1	28	378	3276	20475	98280	3 76740	11 84040	31 08105
29	1	29	406	3654	23751	1 18755	4 75020	15 60780	42 92145
30	1	30	435	4060	27405	1 42506	5 93775	20 35800	58 52925
31	1	31	465	4495	31465	1 69911	7 36281	26 29575	78 88725
32	1	32	496	4960	35960	2 01376	9 06192	33 65856	105 18300
33	1	33	528	5456	40920	2 37336	11 07568	42 72048	138 84156
34	1	34	561	5984	46376	2 78256	13 44904	53 79616	181 56204
35	1	35	595	6545	52360	3 24632	16 23160	67 24520	235 35820
36	1	36	630	7140	58905	3 76992	19 47792	83 47680	302 60340
37	1	37	666	7770	66045	4 35897	23 24784	102 95472	386 08020
38	1	38	703	8436	73815	5 01942	27 60681	126 20256	489 03492
39	1	39	741	9139	82251	5 75757	32 62623	153 80937	615 23748
40	1	40	780	9880	91390	6 58008	38 38380	186 43560	769 04685
41	1	41	820	10660	101270	7 49398	44 96388	224 81940	955 48245
42	1	42	861	11480	111930	8 50668	52 45786	269 78328	1180 30185
43	1	43	903	12341	123410	9 62598	60 96454	322 24114	1450 08513
44	1	44	946	13244	135751	10 86008	70 59052	383 20568	1772 32627
45	1	45	990	14190	148995	12 21759	81 45060	453 79620	2155 53195
46	1	46	1035	15180	163185	13 70754	93 66819	535 24680	2609 32815
47	1	47	1081	16215	178365	15 33939	107 37573	628 91499	3144 57495
48	1	48	1128	17296	194580	17 12304	122 71512	736 29072	3773 48994
49	1	49	1176	18424	211876	19 06884	139 83816	859 00584	4509 78066
50	1	50	1225	19600	230300	21 18760	158 90700	998 84400	5368 78650

NUMBER OF COMBINATIONS

$$\binom{n}{m} = C(n, m)$$

n \ m	9	10	11	12	13
9	1				
10	10	1			
11	55	11	1		
12	220	66	12	1	
13	715	286	78	13	1
14	2002	1001	364	91	14
15	5005	3003	1365	455	105
16	11440	8008	4368	1820	560
17	24310	19448	12376	6188	2380
18	48620	43758	31824	18564	8568
19	92378	92378	75582	50388	27132
20	1 67960	1 84756	1 67960	1 25970	77520
21	2 93930	3 52716	3 52716	2 93930	2 03490
22	4 97420	6 46646	7 05432	6 46646	4 97420
23	8 17190	11 44066	13 52078	13 52078	11 44066
24	13 07504	19 61256	24 96144	27 04156	24 96144
25	20 42975	32 68760	44 57400	52 00300	52 00300
26	31 24550	53 11735	77 26160	96 57700	104 00600
27	46 86825	84 36285	130 37895	173 83860	200 58300
28	69 06900	131 23110	214 74180	304 21755	374 42160
29	100 15005	200 30010	345 97290	518 95935	678 63915
30	143 07150	300 45015	546 27300	864 93225	1197 59850
31	201 60075	443 52165	846 72315	1411 20525	2062 53075
32	280 48800	645 12240	1290 24480	2257 92840	3474 73600
33	385 67100	925 61040	1935 36720	3548 17320	5731 66440
34	524 51256	1311 28140	2860 97760	5483 54040	9279 83760
35	706 07460	1835 79396	4172 25900	8344 51800	14763 37800
36	941 43280	2541 86856	6008 05296	12516 77700	23107 89600
37	1244 03620	3483 30136	8549 92152	18524 82996	35624 67300
38	1630 11640	4727 33756	12033 22288	27074 75148	54149 50296
39	2119 15132	6357 45396	16760 56044	39107 97436	81224 25444
40	2734 38880	8476 60528	23118 01440	55868 53480	1 20332 22880
41	3503 43565	11210 99408	31594 61968	78986 54920	1 76200 76360
42	4458 91810	14714 42973	42805 61376	1 10581 16888	2 55187 31280
43	5639 21995	19173 34783	57520 04349	1 53386 78264	3 65768 48168
44	7098 30508	24812 56778	76693 39132	2 10906 82613	5 19155 26432
45	8861 63135	31901 87286	1 01505 95910	2 87600 21745	7 30062 09045
46	11017 16330	40763 50421	1 33407 83196	3 89106 17655	10 17662 30790
47	13626 49145	51780 66751	1 74171 33617	5 22514 00851	14 06768 48445
48	16771 06640	65407 15896	2 25952 00368	6 96685 34468	19 29282 49296
49	20544 55634	82178 22536	2 91359 16264	9 22637 34836	26 25967 83764
50	25054 33700	1 02722 78170	3 73537 38800	12 13996 51100	35 48605 18600

NUMBER OF COMBINATIONS

$$\binom{n}{m} = C(n,m)$$

m \ n	14	15	16	17	18	19
14	1					
15	15	1				
16	120	16	1			
17	680	136	17	1		
18	3060	816	153	18	1	
19	11628	3876	969	171	19	1
20	38760	15504	4845	1140	190	20
21	1 16280	54264	20349	5985	1330	210
22	3 19770	1 70544	74613	26334	7315	1540
23	8 17190	4 90314	2 45157	1 00947	33649	8855
24	19 61256	13 07504	7 35471	3 46104	1 34596	42504
25	44 57400	32 68760	20 42975	10 81575	4 80700	1 77100
26	96 57700	77 26160	53 11735	31 24550	15 62275	6 57800
27	200 58300	173 83860	130 37895	84 36285	46 86825	22 20075
28	401 16600	374 42160	304 21755	214 74180	131 23110	69 06900
29	775 58760	775 58760	678 63915	518 95935	345 97290	200 30010
30	1454 22675	1551 17520	1454 22675	1197 59850	864 93225	546 27300
31	2651 82525	3005 40195	3005 40195	2651 82525	2062 53075	1411 20525
32	4714 35600	5657 22720	6010 80390	5657 22720	4714 35600	3473 73600
33	8188 09200	10371 58320	11668 03110	11668 03110	10371 58320	8188 09200
34	13919 75640	18559 67520	22039 61430	23336 06220	22039 61430	18559 67520
35	23199 59400	32479 43160	40599 28950	45375 67650	45375 67650	40599 28950
36	37962 97200	55679 02560	73078 72110	85974 96600	90751 35300	85974 96600
37	61070 86800	93641 99760	1 28757 74670	1 59053 68710	1 76726 31900	1 76726 31900
38	96695 54100	1 54712 86560	2 22399 74430	2 87811 43380	3 35780 00610	3 53452 63800
39	1 50845 04396	2 51408 40660	3 77112 60990	5 10211 17810	6 23591 43990	6 89232 64410
40	2 32069 29840	4 02253 45056	6 28521 01650	8 87323 78800	11 33802 61800	13 12824 08400
41	3 52401 52720	6 34322 74896	10 30774 46706	15 15844 80450	20 21126 40600	24 46626 70200
42	5 28602 29080	9 86724 27616	16 65097 21602	25 46619 27156	35 36971 21050	44 67753 10800
43	7 83789 60360	15 15326 56696	26 51821 49218	42 11716 48758	60 83590 48206	80 04724 31850
44	11 49558 08528	22 99116 17056	41 67148 05914	68 63537 97976	102 95306 96964	140 88314 80056
45	16 68713 34960	34 48674 25584	64 66264 22970	110 30686 03890	171 58844 94940	243 83621 77020
46	23 98775 44005	51 17387 60544	99 14938 48554	174 96950 26860	281 89530 98830	415 42466 71960
47	34 16437 74795	75 16163 04549	150 32326 09098	274 11888 75414	456 86481 25690	697 31997 70790
48	48 23206 23240	109 32600 79344	225 48489 13647	424 44214 84512	730 98370 01104	1154 18478 96480
49	67 52488 72536	157 55807 02584	334 81089 92991	649 92703 98159	1155 42584 85616	1885 16848 97584
50	93 78456 56300	225 08295 75120	492 36896 95575	984 73793 91150	1805 35288 83775	3040 59433 83200

NUMBER OF COMBINATIONS

$$\binom{n}{m} = C(n,m)$$

m \ n	20	21	22	23	24	25
20	1					
21	21	1				
22	231	22	1			
23	1771	253	23	1		
24	10626	2024	276	24	1	
25	53130	12650	2300	300	25	1
26	2 30230	65780	14950	2600	325	26
27	8 88030	2 96010	80730	17550	2925	351
28	31 08105	11 84040	3 76740	98280	20475	3276
29	100 15005	42 92145	15 60780	4 75020	1 18755	23751
30	300 45015	143 07150	58 52925	20 35800	5 93775	1 42506
31	846 72315	443 52165	201 60075	78 88725	26 29575	7 36281
32	2257 92840	1290 24480	645 12240	280 48800	105 18300	33 65856
33	5731 66440	3548 17320	1935 36720	925 61040	385 67100	138 84156
34	13919 75640	9279 83760	5483 54040	2860 97760	1311 28140	524 51256
35	32479 43160	23199 59400	14763 37800	8344 51800	4172 25900	1835 79396
36	73078 72110	55679 02560	37962 97200	23107 89600	12516 77700	6008 05296
37	1 59053 68710	1 28757 74670	93641 99760	61070 86800	35624 67300	18524 82996
38	3 35786 00610	2 87811 43380	2 22399 74430	1 54712 86560	96695 54100	54149 50296
39	6 89232 64410	6 23591 43990	5 10211 17810	3 77112 60990	2 51408 40660	1 50845 04396
40	13 78465 28820	13 12824 08400	11 33802 61800	8 87323 78800	6 28521 01650	4 02253 45056
41	26 91289 37220	26 91289 37220	24 46626 70200	20 21126 40600	15 15844 80450	10 30774 46706
42	51 37916 07420	53 82578 74440	51 37916 07420	44 67753 10800	35 36971 21050	25 46619 27156
43	96 05669 18220	105 20494 81860	105 20494 81860	96 05669 18220	80 04724 31850	60 83590 48206
44	176 10393 50070	201 26164 00080	210 40989 63720	201 26164 00080	176 10393 50070	140 88314 80056
45	316 98708 30126	377 36557 50150	411 67153 63800	411 67153 63800	377 36557 50150	316 98708 30126
46	560 82330 07146	694 35265 80276	789 03711 13950	823 34307 27600	789 03711 13950	694 35265 80276
47	976 24796 79106	1255 17595 87422	1483 38976 94226	1612 38018 41550	1612 38018 41550	1483 38976 94226
48	1673 56794 49896	2231 42392 66528	2738 56572 81648	3095 76995 35776	3224 76036 83100	3095 76995 35776
49	2827 75273 46376	3904 99187 16424	4969 98965 48176	5834 33568 17424	6320 53032 18876	6320 53032 18876
50	4712 92122 43960	6732 74460 62800	8874 98152 64600	10804 32533 65600	12154 86600 36300	12641 06064 37752

LOGARITHMS OF THE BINOMIAL COEFFICIENTS

This table contains the logarithms of the binomial coefficients $\binom{n}{m}$; also referred to as the number of combinations of n distinct things taken m at a time. For values missing from the table, use the relation

$$\binom{n}{m} = \frac{n!}{m!(n-m)!} = \binom{n}{n-m}$$

m	n = 1	n = 2	n = 3	n = 4	n = 5	n = 6	n = 7	n = 8	n = 9	n = 10
1	.0000	.3010	.4771	.6021	.6990	.7782	.8451	.9031	.9542	1.0000
2			.4771	.7782	1.0000	1.1761	1.3222	1.4472	1.5563	1.6532
3					1.0000	1.3010	1.5441	1.7482	1.9243	2.0792
4							1.5441	1.8451	2.1004	2.3222
5									2.1004	2.4014

m	n = 11	n = 12	n = 13	n = 14	n = 15	n = 16	n = 17	n = 18	n = 19	n = 20
1	1.0414	1.0792	1.1139	1.1461	1.1761	1.2041	1.2304	1.2553	1.2788	1.3010
2	1.7404	1.8195	1.8921	1.9590	2.0212	2.0792	2.1335	2.1847	2.2330	2.2788
3	2.2175	2.3424	2.4564	2.5611	2.6580	2.7482	2.8325	2.9117	2.9863	3.0569
4	2.5185	2.6946	2.8543	3.0004	3.1351	3.2601	3.3766	3.4857	3.5884	3.6853
5	2.6646	2.8987	3.1096	3.3015	3.4776	3.6403	3.7916	3.9329	4.0655	4.1904
6	2.6646	2.9657	3.2345	3.4776	3.6994	3.9035	4.0926	4.2687	4.4335	4.5884
7			3.2345	3.5355	3.8085	4.0584	4.2889	4.5028	4.7023	4.8894
8					3.8085	4.1096	4.3858	4.6411	4.8784	5.1003
9							4.3858	4.6868	4.9656	5.2252
10									4.9656	5.2666

m	n = 21	n = 22	n = 23	n = 24	n = 25	n = 26	n = 27	n = 28	n = 29	n = 30
1	1.3222	1.3424	1.3617	1.3802	1.3979	1.4150	1.4314	1.4472	1.4624	1.4771
2	2.3222	2.3636	2.4031	2.4409	2.4771	2.5119	2.5453	2.5775	2.6085	2.6385
3	3.1239	3.1875	3.2482	3.3062	3.3617	3.4150	3.4661	3.5153	3.5628	3.6085
4	3.7771	3.8642	3.9472	4.0264	4.1021	4.1746	4.2443	4.3112	4.3757	4.4378
5	4.3085	4.4205	4.5270	4.6284	4.7253	4.8181	4.9070	4.9925	5.0747	5.1538
6	4.7345	4.8728	5.0041	5.1290	5.2482	5.3622	5.4713	5.5760	5.6767	5.7736
7	5.0655	5.2318	5.3894	5.5392	5.6819	5.8181	5.9484	6.0734	6.1933	6.3087
8	5.3085	5.5048	5.6905	5.8666	6.0341	6.1938	6.3464	6.4925	6.6327	6.7674
9	5.4682	5.6967	5.9123	6.1164	6.3103	6.4948	6.6709	6.8393	7.0007	7.1556
10	5.5474	5.8107	6.0585	6.2925	6.5144	6.7252	6.9262	7.1180	7.3017	7.4778
11	5.5474	5.8485	6.1310	6.3973	6.6491	6.8880	7.1152	7.3319	7.5390	7.7374
12			6.1310	6.4320	6.7160	6.9849	7.2401	7.4832	7.7151	7.9370
13					6.7160	7.0171	7.3023	7.5734	7.8316	8.0783
14							7.3023	7.6033	7.8896	8.1626
15									7.8896	8.1907

LOGARITHMS OF THE BINOMIAL COEFFICIENTS

m	n = 31	n = 32	n = 33	n = 34	n = 35	n = 36	n = 37	n = 38	n = 39	n = 40
1	1.4914	1.5052	1.5185	1.5315	1.5441	1.5563	1.5682	1.5798	1.5911	1.6021
2	2.6675	2.6955	2.7226	2.7490	2.7745	2.7993	2.8235	2.8470	2.8698	2.8921
3	3.6527	3.6955	3.7369	3.7770	3.8159	3.8537	3.8904	3.9261	3.9609	3.9948
4	4.4978	4.5558	4.6119	4.6663	4.7190	4.7702	4.8198	4.8681	4.9151	4.9609
5	5.2302	5.3040	5.3754	5.4444	5.5114	5.5763	5.6394	5.7007	5.7602	5.8182
6	5.8670	5.9572	6.0444	6.1287	6.2104	6.2895	6.3664	6.4410	6.5136	6.5841
7	6.4199	6.5271	6.6306	6.7308	6.8277	6.9216	7.0126	7.1011	7.1870	7.2705
8	6.8970	7.0219	7.1425	7.2590	7.3717	7.4809	7.5867	7.6893	7.7890	7.8860
9	7.3045	7.4479	7.5862	7.7198	7.8489	7.9738	8.0948	8.2122	8.3262	8.4369
10	7.6469	7.8096	7.9664	8.1177	8.2638	8.4052	8.5420	8.6746	8.8033	8.9282
11	7.9277	8.1107	8.2868	8.4565	8.6204	8.7787	8.9320	9.0804	9.2243	9.3640
12	8.1496	8.3537	8.5500	8.7391	8.9214	9.0975	9.2678	9.4326	9.5923	9.7472
13	8.3144	8.5408	8.7583	8.9675	9.1692	9.3638	9.5518	9.7336	9.9097	10.0804
14	8.4235	8.6734	8.9132	9.1436	9.3655	9.5794	9.7858	9.9854	10.1785	10.3656
15	8.4779	8.7526	9.0158	9.2686	9.5116	9.7457	9.9715	10.1895	10.4004	10.6045
16	8.4779	8.7789	9.0670	9.3432	9.6085	9.8638	10.1098	10.3471	10.5765	10.7983
17			9.0670	9.3680	9.6568	9.9344	10.2015	10.4591	10.7078	10.9481
18					9.6568	9.9579	10.2473	10.5261	10.7949	11.0545
19							10.2473	10.5483	10.8384	11.1182
20									10.8384	11.1394

m	n = 41	n = 42	n = 43	n = 44	n = 45	n = 46	n = 47	n = 48	n = 49	n = 50
1	1.6128	1.6232	1.6335	1.6435	1.6532	1.6628	1.6721	1.6812	1.6902	1.6990
2	2.9138	2.9350	2.9557	2.9759	2.9956	3.0149	3.0338	3.0523	3.0704	3.0881
3	4.0278	4.0599	4.0914	4.1220	4.1520	4.1813	4.2099	4.2379	4.2654	4.2923
4	5.0055	5.0489	5.0914	5.1327	5.1732	5.2127	5.2513	5.2891	5.3261	5.3623
5	5.8747	5.9298	5.9834	6.0358	6.0870	6.1370	6.1858	6.2336	6.2803	6.3261
6	6.6529	6.7198	6.7851	6.8487	6.9109	6.9716	7.0309	7.0889	7.1456	7.2011
7	7.3518	7.4310	7.5082	7.5834	7.6569	7.7286	7.7986	7.8670	7.9340	7.9995
8	7.9802	8.0720	8.1614	8.2485	8.3336	8.4165	8.4976	8.5767	8.6542	8.7299
9	8.5445	8.6492	8.7512	8.8506	8.9475	9.0421	9.1344	9.2246	9.3127	9.3989
10	9.0496	9.1677	9.2827	9.3947	9.5038	9.6103	9.7142	9.8156	9.9148	10.0117
11	9.4996	9.6315	9.7598	9.8848	10.0065	10.1252	10.2410	10.3540	10.4644	10.5723
12	9.8976	10.0437	10.1858	10.3241	10.4588	10.5901	10.7181	10.8430	10.9650	11.0842
13	10.2460	10.4069	10.5632	10.7153	10.8634	11.0076	11.1482	11.2854	11.4193	11.5501
14	10.5470	10.7231	10.8942	11.0605	11.2224	11.3800	11.5336	11.6833	11.8295	11.9721
15	10.8023	10.9942	11.1805	11.3616	11.5377	11.7090	11.8760	12.0387	12.1974	12.3523
16	11.0132	11.2214	11.4235	11.6198	11.8107	11.9963	12.1770	12.3531	12.5248	12.6923
17	11.1807	11.4060	11.6245	11.8365	12.0426	12.2430	12.4379	12.6278	12.8129	12.9933
18	11.3056	11.5486	11.7842	12.0126	12.2345	12.4501	12.6598	12.8639	13.0627	13.2566
19	11.3886	11.6501	11.9033	12.1489	12.3871	12.6185	12.8434	13.0623	13.2754	13.4830
20	11.4300	11.7108	11.9825	12.2458	12.5010	12.7488	12.9896	13.2236	13.5916	13.6733
21	11.4300	11.7310	12.0220	12.3038	12.5768	12.8416	13.0987	13.3486	13.5916	13.8282
22		12.0220	12.3231	12.6146	12.8971	13.1713	13.4375	13.6964	13.9482
23					12.6146	12.9156	13.2075	13.4908	13.7660	14.0336
24							13.2075	13.5085	13.8008	14.0848
25									13.8008	14.1018

LOGARITHMS OF THE BINOMIAL COEFFICIENTS

m	$n = 51$	$n = 52$	$n = 53$	$n = 54$	$n = 55$	$n = 56$	$n = 57$	$n = 58$	$n = 59$	$n = 60$
1	1.7076	1.7160	1.7243	1.7324	1.7404	1.7482	1.7559	1.7634	1.7709	1.7782
2	3.1055	3.1225	3.1392	3.1556	3.1717	3.1875	3.2030	3.2183	3.2333	3.2480
3	4.3186	4.3444	4.3697	4.3945	4.4189	4.4428	4.4663	4.4893	4.5120	4.5343
4	5.3978	5.4325	5.4666	5.5000	5.5328	5.5650	5.5966	5.6276	5.6581	5.6881
5	6.3709	6.4148	6.4578	6.5000	6.5414	6.5820	6.6219	6.6611	6.6995	6.7373
6	7.2555	7.3087	7.3609	7.4121	7.4622	7.5115	7.5598	7.6072	7.6538	7.6995
7	8.0636	8.1264	8.1879	8.2482	8.3073	8.3653	8.4222	8.4781	8.5329	8.5868
8	8.8040	8.8765	8.9476	9.0172	9.0855	9.1524	9.2181	9.2826	9.3459	9.4080
9	9.4832	9.5657	9.6466	9.7257	9.8033	9.8794	9.9541	10.0273	10.0992	10.1698
10	10.1065	10.1992	10.2900	10.3790	10.4661	10.5515	10.6353	10.7175	10.7982	10.8773
11	10.6778	10.7811	10.8821	10.9810	11.0779	11.1729	11.2660	11.3573	11.4470	11.5349
12	11.2007	11.3147	11.4262	11.5353	11.6422	11.7469	11.8496	11.9503	12.0490	12.1459
13	11.6778	11.8028	11.9250	12.0446	12.1617	12.2764	12.3889	12.4991	12.6072	12.7132
14	12.1115	12.2477	12.3809	12.5113	12.6388	12.7638	12.8862	13.0062	13.1238	13.2392
15	12.5036	12.6514	12.7959	12.9372	13.0755	13.2109	13.3436	13.4735	13.6009	13.7259
16	12.8558	13.0155	13.1716	13.3242	13.4735	13.6196	13.7627	13.9029	14.0403	14.1750
17	13.1694	13.3413	13.5093	13.6735	13.8341	13.9912	14.1450	14.2957	14.4433	14.5880
18	13.4456	13.6301	13.8104	13.9864	14.1586	14.3270	14.4918	14.6532	14.8113	14.9662
19	13.6854	13.8829	14.0757	14.2640	14.4481	14.6280	14.8041	14.9765	15.1453	15.3107
20	13.8895	14.1004	14.3061	14.5070	14.7033	14.8952	15.0829	15.2665	15.4463	15.6224
21	14.0586	14.2833	14.5024	14.7163	14.9252	15.1293	15.3289	15.5241	15.7152	15.9022
22	14.1933	14.4322	14.6651	14.8924	15.1142	15.3309	15.5427	15.7499	15.9525	16.1509
23	14.2940	14.5476	14.7948	15.0358	15.2710	15.5007	15.7251	15.9444	16.1590	16.3689
24	14.3610	14.6298	14.8917	15.1470	15.3960	15.6390	15.8764	16.1083	16.3351	16.5569
25	14.3944	14.6790	14.9561	15.2261	15.4894	15.7462	15.9969	16.2418	16.4812	16.7153
26	14.3944	14.6954	14.9883	15.2736	15.5515	15.8226	16.0871	16.3454	16.5977	16.8444
27			14.9883	15.2894	15.5826	15.8683	16.1471	16.4192	16.6849	16.9445
28					15.5826	15.8836	16.1771	16.4634	16.7429	17.0159
29							16.1771	16.4781	16.7718	17.0586
30									16.7718	17.0729

m	$n = 61$	$n = 62$	$n = 63$	$n = 64$	$n = 65$	$n = 66$	$n = 67$	$n = 68$	$n = 69$	$n = 70$
1	1.7853	1.7924	1.7993	1.8062	1.8129	1.8195	1.8261	1.8325	1.8388	1.8451
2	3.2625	3.2767	3.2907	3.3045	3.3181	3.3314	3.3446	3.3576	3.3703	3.3829
3	4.5562	4.5777	4.5989	4.6198	4.6403	4.6605	4.6804	4.7000	4.7193	4.7383
4	5.7175	5.7465	5.7750	5.8030	5.8306	5.8578	5.8845	5.9108	5.9368	5.9623
5	6.7745	6.8110	6.8469	6.8822	6.9170	6.9512	6.9849	7.0180	7.0507	7.0829
6	7.7445	7.7887	7.8322	7.8749	7.9170	7.9584	7.9991	8.0392	8.0787	8.1177
7	8.6398	8.6918	8.7429	8.7932	8.8427	8.8914	8.9393	8.9865	9.0330	9.0787
8	9.4691	9.5291	9.5880	9.6460	9.7031	9.7592	9.8144	9.8688	9.9223	9.9750
9	10.2391	10.3072	10.3742	10.4400	10.5047	10.5684	10.6310	10.6927	10.7534	10.8131
10	10.9551	11.0315	11.1066	11.1803	11.2529	11.3242	11.3944	11.4635	11.5315	11.5985
11	11.6213	11.7061	11.7894	11.8713	11.9519	12.0310	12.1089	12.1856	12.2610	12.3352
12	12.2411	12.3345	12.4263	12.5164	12.6051	12.6922	12.7779	12.8623	12.9452	13.0269
13	12.8173	12.9195	13.0199	13.1185	13.2154	13.3107	13.4044	13.4965	13.5872	13.6764
14	13.3524	13.4636	13.5727	13.6799	13.7853	13.8888	13.9906	14.0907	14.1892	14.2861
15	13.8484	13.9687	14.0868	14.2028	14.3168	14.4287	14.5388	14.6470	14.7535	14.8582
16	14.3071	14.4367	14.5640	14.6889	14.8116	14.9322	15.0507	15.1672	15.2818	15.3945
17	14.7298	14.8690	15.0056	15.1397	15.2714	15.4007	15.5278	15.6527	15.7756	15.8964
18	15.1180	15.2670	15.4131	15.5565	15.6973	15.8356	15.9715	16.1050	16.2363	16.3654
19	15.4727	15.6317	15.7875	15.9405	16.0907	16.2381	16.3829	16.5253	16.6651	16.8027
20	15.7950	15.9641	16.1300	16.2927	16.4524	16.6092	16.7632	16.9144	17.0631	17.2092

LOGARITHMS OF THE BINOMIAL COEFFICIENTS

m	n = 61	n = 62	n = 63	n = 64	n = 65	n = 66	n = 67	n = 68	n = 69	n = 70
21	16.0855	16.2651	16.4412	16.6139	16.7834	16.9497	17.1130	17.2734	17.4311	17.5860
22	16.3452	16.5355	16.7220	16.9050	17.0844	17.2605	17.4334	17.6031	17.7699	17.9337
23	16.5745	16.7758	16.9731	17.1665	17.3562	17.5422	17.7249	17.9042	18.0802	18.2532
24	16.7741	16.9867	17.1949	17.3991	17.5992	17.7955	17.9881	18.1772	18.3628	18.5451
25	16.9443	17.1685	17.3881	17.6032	17.8140	18.0208	18.2236	18.4227	18.6181	18.8099
26	17.0857	17.3217	17.5529	17.7793	18.0011	18.2186	18.4319	18.6412	18.8465	19.0482
27	17.1984	17.4467	17.6897	17.9277	18.1608	18.3893	18.6133	18.8330	19.0486	19.2603
28	17.2827	17.5436	17.7989	18.0487	18.2935	18.5332	18.7682	18.9987	19.2247	19.4466
29	17.3388	17.6127	17.8805	18.1426	18.3993	18.6506	18.8969	19.1383	19.3751	19.6074
30	17.3668	17.6541	17.9349	18.2096	18.4784	18.7417	18.9996	19.2523	19.5001	19.7431
31	17.3668	17.6679	17.9620	18.2497	18.5311	18.8066	19.0764	19.3407	19.5998	19.8538
32			17.9620	18.2631	18.5575	18.8455	19.1275	19.4038	19.6744	19.9397
33					18.5575	18.8585	19.1531	19.4415	19.7241	20.0010
34							19.1531	19.4541	19.7489	20.0377
35									19.7489	20.0499

m	n = 71	n = 72	n = 73	n = 74	n = 75	n = 76	n = 77	n = 78	n = 79	n = 80
1	1.8513	1.8573	1.8633	1.8692	1.8751	1.8808	1.8865	1.8921	1.8976	1.9031
2	3.3953	3.4076	3.4196	3.4315	3.4433	3.4548	3.4663	3.4776	3.4887	3.4997
3	4.7571	4.7755	4.7938	4.8117	4.8295	4.8470	4.8642	4.8812	4.8981	4.9147
4	5.9875	6.0123	6.0368	6.0609	6.0847	6.1082	6.1314	6.1542	6.1768	6.1991
5	7.1146	7.1459	7.1767	7.2071	7.2370	7.2666	7.2957	7.3245	7.3529	7.3809
6	8.1560	8.1938	8.2310	8.2678	8.3040	8.3397	8.3749	8.4097	8.4440	8.4778
7	9.1238	9.1682	9.2120	9.2552	9.2977	9.3397	9.3811	9.4219	9.4622	9.5020
8	10.0269	10.0781	10.1285	10.1782	10.2271	10.2754	10.3231	10.3701	10.4165	10.4622
9	10.8720	10.9300	10.9871	11.0435	11.0990	11.1537	11.2077	11.2609	11.3135	11.3653
10	11.6644	11.7293	11.7933	11.8564	11.9185	11.9798	12.0402	12.0998	12.1586	12.2166
11	12.4083	12.4803	12.5513	12.6212	12.6900	12.7579	12.8249	12.8909	12.9560	13.0203
12	13.1073	13.1865	13.2645	13.3413	13.4170	13.4917	13.5652	13.6378	13.7094	13.7799
13	13.7642	13.8507	13.9359	14.0198	14.1024	14.1839	14.2642	14.3434	14.4215	14.4985
14	14.3815	14.4754	14.5679	14.6590	14.7487	14.8371	14.9243	15.0102	15.0949	15.1784
15	14.9613	15.0628	15.1626	15.2610	15.3579	15.4534	15.5475	15.6403	15.7317	15.8219
16	15.5054	15.6145	15.7220	15.8278	15.9320	16.0346	16.1358	16.2355	16.3338	16.4307
17	16.0153	16.1322	16.2474	16.3607	16.4724	16.5823	16.6907	16.7974	16.9027	17.0064
18	16.4924	16.6173	16.7403	16.8613	16.9805	17.0979	17.2136	17.3275	17.4398	17.5505
19	16.9379	17.0710	17.2019	17.3308	17.4576	17.5826	17.7057	17.8269	17.9464	18.0641
20	17.3529	17.4942	17.6333	17.7701	17.9048	18.0374	18.1680	18.2967	18.4235	18.5484
21	17.7382	17.8880	18.0353	18.1803	18.3230	18.4634	18.6017	18.7379	18.8721	19.0044
22	18.0948	18.2532	18.4089	18.5621	18.7129	18.8613	19.0075	19.1514	19.2931	19.4328
23	18.4233	18.5904	18.7547	18.9164	19.0755	19.2320	19.3861	19.5378	19.6873	19.8345
24	18.7243	18.9004	19.0735	19.2438	19.4113	19.5761	19.7383	19.8980	20.0553	20.2102
25	18.9984	19.1837	19.3568	19.5448	19.7209	19.8941	20.0646	20.2324	20.3977	20.5604
26	19.2462	19.4408	19.6320	19.8200	20.0049	20.1867	20.3657	20.5417	20.7151	20.8858
27	19.4681	19.6722	19.8728	20.0699	20.2637	20.4543	20.6419	20.8264	21.0080	21.1868
28	19.6644	19.8783	20.0884	20.2948	20.4978	20.6974	20.8937	21.0868	21.2769	21.4639
29	19.8354	20.0593	20.2792	20.4952	20.7075	20.9162	21.1215	21.3234	21.5220	21.7175
30	19.9816	20.2157	20.4455	20.6713	20.8931	21.1112	21.3256	21.5364	21.7439	21.9480
31	20.1030	20.3475	20.5876	20.8234	21.0550	21.2826	21.5063	21.7263	21.9427	22.1556
32	20.1999	20.4552	20.7057	20.9517	21.1933	21.4307	21.6639	21.8933	22.1188	22.3406
33	20.2725	20.5387	20.8000	21.0564	21.3082	21.5556	21.7986	22.0375	22.2724	22.5034
34	20.3208	20.5983	20.8706	21.1377	21.4000	21.6576	21.9106	22.1592	22.4037	22.6440
35	20.3449	20.6340	20.9176	21.1957	21.4687	21.7368	22.0000	22.2586	22.5128	22.7627

LOGARITHMS OF THE BINOMIAL COEFFICIENTS

m	n = 71	n = 72	n = 73	n = 74	n = 75	n = 76	n = 77	n = 78	n = 79	n = 80
36	20.3449	20.6459	20.9410	21.2305	21.5145	21.7932	22.0670	22.3358	22.6000	22.8596
37			20.9410	21.2421	21.5374	21.8271	22.1115	22.3908	22.6652	22.9348
38					21.5374	21.8384	22.1338	22.4238	22.7087	22.9885
39							22.1338	22.4348	22.7304	23.0207
40									22.7304	23.0314

m	n = 81	n = 82	n = 83	n = 84	n = 85	n = 86	n = 87	n = 88	n = 89	n = 90
1	1.9085	1.9138	1.9191	1.9243	1.9294	1.9345	1.9395	1.9445	1.9494	1.9542
2	3.5105	3.5213	3.5319	3.5423	3.5527	3.5629	3.5730	3.5830	3.5928	3.6026
3	4.9311	4.9472	4.9632	4.9790	4.9946	5.0100	5.0253	5.0403	5.0552	5.0700
4	6.2211	6.2428	6.2643	6.2854	6.3064	6.3271	6.3475	6.3677	6.3877	6.4074
5	7.4086	7.4359	7.4629	7.4896	7.5159	7.5419	7.5676	7.5930	7.6181	7.6430
6	8.5113	8.5443	8.5769	8.6090	8.6408	8.6722	8.7033	8.7339	8.7643	8.7942
7	9.5412	9.5800	9.6182	9.6560	9.6934	9.7302	9.7667	9.8027	9.8382	9.8734
8	10.5074	10.5520	10.5960	10.6394	10.6824	10.7248	10.7667	10.8081	10.8490	10.8894
9	11.4165	11.4669	11.5168	11.5660	11.6146	11.6626	11.7100	11.7569	11.8032	11.8490
10	12.2738	12.3303	12.3860	12.4411	12.4954	12.5491	12.6021	12.6545	12.7063	12.7574
11	13.0837	13.1462	13.2080	13.2689	13.3291	13.3885	13.4472	13.5052	13.5625	13.6191
12	13.8496	13.9183	13.9861	14.0531	14.1191	14.1844	14.2489	14.3125	14.3754	14.4376
13	14.5745	14.6494	14.7234	14.7964	14.8685	14.9397	15.0100	15.0794	15.1480	15.2157
14	15.2609	15.3422	15.4224	15.5016	15.5797	15.6569	15.7331	15.8083	15.8827	15.9561
15	15.9108	15.9986	16.0851	16.1706	16.2549	16.3381	16.4203	16.5015	16.5816	16.6608
16	16.5263	16.6205	16.7135	16.8053	16.8959	16.9853	17.0735	17.1607	17.2468	17.3318
17	17.1087	17.2096	17.3092	17.4074	17.5043	17.5999	17.6943	17.7876	17.8796	17.9705
18	17.6596	17.7673	17.8734	17.9782	18.0815	18.1835	18.2842	18.3836	18.4817	18.5786
19	18.1802	18.2947	18.4076	18.5190	18.6288	18.7373	18.8443	18.9499	19.0542	19.1572
20	18.6716	18.7930	18.9127	19.0308	19.1473	19.2623	19.3757	19.4877	19.5983	19.7074
21	19.1347	19.2632	19.3899	19.5148	19.6380	19.7596	19.8796	19.9980	20.1149	20.2303
22	19.5704	19.7061	19.8398	19.9717	20.1018	20.2301	20.3567	20.4817	20.6050	20.7267
23	19.9795	20.1225	20.2634	20.4024	20.5394	20.6746	20.8079	20.9395	21.0693	21.1975
24	20.3628	20.5131	20.6614	20.8075	20.9516	21.0937	21.2339	21.3722	21.5087	21.6434
25	20.7207	20.8786	21.0343	21.1877	21.3390	21.4882	21.6353	21.7804	21.9236	22.0650
26	21.0539	21.2195	21.3827	21.5436	21.7022	21.8585	22.0127	22.1648	22.3148	22.4629
27	21.3629	21.5364	21.7073	21.8757	22.0416	22.2053	22.3667	22.5258	22.6828	22.8377
28	21.6481	21.8296	22.0083	22.1844	22.3579	22.5290	22.6977	22.8640	23.0280	23.1899
29	21.9100	22.0996	22.2862	22.4702	22.6514	22.8300	23.0061	23.1797	23.3510	23.5199
30	22.1489	22.3467	22.5415	22.7334	22.9225	23.1088	23.2924	23.4735	23.6520	23.8281
31	22.3651	22.5714	22.7744	22.9744	23.1715	23.3656	23.5569	23.7455	23.9315	24.1149
32	22.5589	22.7738	22.9853	23.1936	23.3987	23.6008	23.8000	23.9963	24.1898	24.3806
33	22.7306	22.9542	23.1743	23.3911	23.6045	23.8147	24.0218	24.2259	24.4271	24.6255
34	22.8804	23.1130	23.3418	23.5671	23.7890	24.0075	24.2227	24.4348	24.6438	24.8499
35	23.0084	23.2501	23.4880	23.7220	23.9525	24.1794	24.4029	24.6231	24.8401	25.0540
36	23.1149	23.3659	23.6129	23.8559	24.0952	24.3307	24.5626	24.7911	25.0162	25.2381
37	23.1999	23.4605	23.7168	23.9690	24.2172	24.4615	24.7020	24.9389	25.1723	25.4023
38	23.2635	23.5339	23.7998	24.0613	24.3186	24.5719	24.8212	25.0667	25.3085	25.5468
39	23.3060	23.5863	23.8619	24.1330	24.3996	24.6620	24.9203	25.1746	25.4250	25.6717
40	23.3271	23.6177	23.9033	24.1841	24.4603	24.7321	24.9995	25.2627	25.5219	25.7772
41	23.3271	23.6828	23.9240	24.2148	24.5008	24.7821	25.0588	25.3312	25.5994	25.8634
42		23.9240	24.2250	24.5210	24.8120	25.0983	25.3801	25.6573	25.9303
43				24.5210	24.8220	25.1181	25.4093	25.6960	25.9781
44						25.1181	25.4191	25.7153	26.0068
45								25.7153	26.0163

LOGARITHMS OF THE BINOMIAL COEFFICIENTS

m	n = 91	n = 92	n = 93	n = 94	n = 95	n = 96	n = 97	n = 98	n = 99	n = 100
1	1.9590	1.9638	1.9685	1.9731	1.9777	1.9823	1.9868	1.9912	1.9956	2.0000
2	3.6123	3.6218	3.6312	3.6406	3.6498	4.6590	3.6680	3.6770	3.6858	3.6946
3	5.0845	5.0989	5.1132	5.1272	5.1412	5.1550	5.1686	5.1821	5.1955	5.2087
4	6.4269	6.4463	6.4653	6.4842	6.5029	6.5214	6.5397	6.5578	6.5757	6.5934
5	7.6675	7.6918	7.7158	7.7395	7.7630	7.7862	7.8092	7.8319	7.8544	7.8767
6	8.8238	8.8531	8.8821	8.9107	8.9391	8.9671	8.9948	9.0223	9.0494	9.0763
7	9.9082	9.9425	9.9765	10.0101	10.0434	10.0762	10.1088	10.1410	10.1728	10.2043
8	10.9294	10.9689	11.0079	11.0466	11.0848	11.1225	11.1599	11.1969	11.2335	11.2697
9	11.8942	11.9389	11.9831	12.0268	12.0700	12.1128	12.1551	12.1969	12.2383	12.2793
10	12.8080	12.8580	12.9074	12.9562	13.0045	13.0523	13.0996	13.1463	13.1925	13.2383
11	13.6751	13.7304	13.7851	13.8391	13.8926	13.9454	13.9977	14.0494	14.1005	14.1512
12	14.4990	14.5597	14.6197	14.6790	14.7377	14.7956	14.8530	14.9097	14.9658	15.0214
13	15.2827	15.3488	15.4142	15.4789	15.5428	15.6060	15.6685	15.7303	15.7914	15.8519
14	16.0287	16.1003	16.1712	16.2412	16.3105	16.3789	16.4466	16.5136	16.5798	16.6453
15	16.7391	16.8163	16.8927	16.9682	17.0429	17.1167	17.1896	17.2618	17.3331	17.4037
16	17.4157	17.4987	17.5807	17.6617	17.7418	17.8210	17.8993	17.9767	18.0533	18.1290
17	18.0604	18.1491	18.2368	18.3234	18.4090	18.4937	18.5773	18.6601	18.7419	18.8228
18	18.6743	18.7689	18.8623	18.9546	19.0458	19.1360	19.2252	19.3133	19.4005	19.4866
19	19.2589	19.3594	19.4586	19.5567	19.6536	19.7494	19.8440	19.9376	20.0302	20.1217
20	19.8152	19.9216	20.0268	20.1307	20.2334	20.3348	20.4351	20.5342	20.6322	20.7292
21	20.3442	20.4568	20.5679	20.6777	20.7862	20.8934	20.9994	21.1041	21.2076	21.3100
22	20.8469	20.9656	21.0828	21.1986	21.3130	21.4261	21.5378	21.6482	21.7573	21.8652
23	21.3240	21.4490	21.5723	21.6942	21.8146	21.9336	22.0511	22.1673	22.2821	22.3956
24	21.7763	21.9076	22.0372	22.1653	22.2917	22.4167	22.5401	22.6621	22.7827	22.9019
25	22.2045	22.3422	22.4781	22.6124	22.7450	22.8761	23.0055	23.1334	23.2598	23.3847
26	22.6090	22.7533	22.8957	23.0363	23.1752	23.3123	23.4479	23.5818	23.7141	23.8448
27	22.9906	23.1415	23.2904	23.4374	23.5827	23.7261	23.8678	24.0077	24.1460	24.2827
28	23.3496	23.5072	23.6628	23.8164	23.9680	24.1178	24.2657	24.4118	24.5562	24.6989
29	23.6865	23.8510	24.0133	24.1735	24.3317	24.4879	24.6421	24.7945	24.9451	25.0938
30	24.0018	24.1732	24.3423	24.5093	24.6741	24.8368	24.9975	25.1563	25.3130	25.4679
31	24.2958	24.4742	24.6503	24.8241	24.9957	25.1650	25.3322	25.4974	25.6605	25.8217
32	24.5688	24.7544	24.9376	25.1183	25.2967	25.4728	25.6466	25.8183	25.9879	26.1554
33	24.9211	25.0141	25.2044	25.3922	25.5775	25.7604	25.9410	26.1194	26.2954	26.4694
34	25.0531	25.2534	25.4511	25.6460	25.8384	26.0283	26.2157	26.4008	26.5835	26.7640
35	25.2649	25.4728	25.6778	25.8801	26.0797	26.2766	26.4710	26.6629	26.8524	27.0394
36	25.4568	25.6724	25.8850	26.0947	26.3015	26.5057	26.7071	26.9059	27.1022	27.2961
37	25.6289	25.8523	26.0726	26.2899	26.5042	26.7156	26.9242	27.1301	27.3334	27.5340
38	25.7815	26.0129	26.2410	26.4660	26.6878	26.9067	27.1226	27.3357	27.5460	27.7536
39	25.9147	26.1543	26.3903	26.6231	26.8526	27.0790	27.3024	27.5228	27.7402	27.9549
40	26.0287	26.2765	26.5207	26.7614	26.9988	27.2329	27.4638	27.6916	27.9163	28.1382
41	26.1235	26.3797	26.6322	26.8810	27.1264	27.3683	27.6068	27.8422	28.0744	28.3036
42	26.1992	26.4640	26.7249	26.9820	27.2355	27.4854	27.7318	27.9748	28.2146	28.4512
43	26.2559	26.5295	26.7990	27.0646	27.3263	27.5843	27.8387	28.0895	28.3370	28.5811
44	26.2937	26.5763	26.8545	27.1287	27.3989	27.6651	27.9276	28.1865	28.4417	28.6935
45	26.3126	26.6043	26.8915	27.1745	27.4532	27.7279	27.9987	28.2656	28.5289	28.7885
46	26.3126	26.6136	26.9100	27.2019	27.3894	27.7727	28.0519	28.3272	28.5985	28.8661
47			26.9100	27.2110	27.5075	27.7996	28.0874	28.3711	28.6507	28.9264
48					27.5075	27.8086	28.1051	28.3974	28.6855	28.9694
49							28.1051	28.4062	28.7028	28.9953
50									28.7028	29.0039

POSITIONAL NOTATION

In our ordinary system of writing numbers, the value of any digit depends on its position in the number. The value of a digit in any position is ten times the value of the same digit one position to the right, or one-tenth the value of the same digit one position to the left. Thus, for example,

$$173.246 = 1 \times 10^2 + 7 \times 10^1 + 3 + 2 \times \frac{1}{10} + 4 \times \frac{1}{10^2} + 6 \times \frac{1}{10^3}.$$

There is no reason that a number other than 10 cannot be used as the *base*, or *radix*, of the number system. In fact, bases of 2, 8, and 16 are commonly used in working with digital computers. When the base used is not clear from the context, it is usually indicated as a parenthesized subscript or merely as a subscript. Thus

$$743_{(8)} = 7 \times 8^2 + 4 \times 8 + 3 = 7 \times 64 + 4 \times 8 + 3 = 448 + 32 + 3 = 483_{(10)}$$

$$1011.101_{(2)} = 1 \times 2^3 + 0 \times 2^2 + 1 \times 2 + 1 + 1 \times \tfrac{1}{2} + 0 \times \tfrac{1}{4} + 1 \times \tfrac{1}{8} = 11.625_{(10)}$$

CHANGE OF BASE

In this section, it is assumed that all calculations will be performed in base 10, since this is the only base in which most people can easily compute. However, there is no logical reason that some other base could not be used for the computations.

To convert a number from another base into base 10:

Simply write down the digits of the number, with each one multiplied by its appropriate positional value. Then perform the indicated computations in base 10, and write down the answer.

For examples, see the two examples in the previous section.

To convert a number from base 10 into another base:

The part of the number to the left of the point and the part to the right must be operated on separately. For the integer part (the part to the left of the point):

   a. Divide the number by the new base, getting an integer quotient and remainder.
   b. Write down the remainder as the last digit of the number in the new base.
   c. Using the quotient from the last division in place of the original number, repeat the above two steps until the quotient becomes zero.

For the fractional part (the part to the right of the point):

   a. Multiply the number by the new base.
   b. Write down the integral part of the product as the first digit of the fractional part in the new base.
   c. Using the fractional part of the last product in place of the original number, repeat the above two steps until the product becomes an integer, or until the desired number of places have been computed.

Examples:

These examples show a convenient method of arranging the computations.

1. Convert $103.118_{(10)}$ to base 8.

					.118
8	$\lfloor 103 \rfloor$	7			8
8	$\lfloor 12 \rfloor$	4			.944
	1			147.074324 ...	8
					7.552
					8

The calculation of the fractional part could be carried out as far as desired. It is a non-terminating fraction which will eventually repeat itself.

$$4.416$$
$$8$$
$$3.328$$
$$8$$
$$2.624$$
$$8$$

$$103.118_{(10)} = 147.074324 \ldots_{(8)} \qquad 4.992$$

The calculations may be further shortened by not writing down the multiplier and divisor at each step of the algorithm, as shown in the next example.

2. Convert $275.824_{(10)}$ to base 5.

				.824
5	$\lfloor 275 \rfloor$	0		4.120
	$\lfloor 55 \rfloor$	0		0.600
	$\lfloor 11 \rfloor$	1		3.000
	2			

$$275.824_{(10)} = 2100.403_{(5)}$$

To convert from one base to another (neither of which is 10):

The easiest procedure is usually to convert first to base 10, and then to the desired base. However, there are two exceptions to this:

1. If computational facility is possessed in either of the bases, it may be used instead of base 10, and the appropriate one of the above methods applied.

2. If the two bases are different powers of the same number, the conversion may be done digit-by-digit to the base which is the common root of both bases, and then digit-by-digit back to the other base.

Example: Convert $127.653_{(8)}$ to base 16. (For base 16, the letters A–F are used for the digits $10_{(10)}-15_{(10)}$.)

The first step is to convert the number to base 2, simply by converting each digit to its binary equivalent:

$$127.653_{(8)} = 001 \ 010 \ 111 \cdot 110 \ 101 \ 011_{(2)}$$

Now by simply regrouping the binary number into groups of four binary digits, starting at the point, we convert to base 16:

$$127.653_{(8)} = 101 \ 0111 \cdot 1101 \ 0101 \ 1_{(2)} = 57.D58_{(16)}$$

$10^{\pm n}$ IN OCTAL SCALE

10^n	n	10^{-n}	10^n	n	10^{-n}
1	0	1.000 000 000 000 000	112 402 762 000	10	0.000 000 000 006 676
12	1	0.063 146 314 631 463	1 351 035 564 000	11	0.000 000 000 000 538
144	2	0.005 075 341 217 270	16 432 451 210 000	12	0.000 000 000 000 043
1 750	3	0.000 406 111 564 571	221 441 634 520 000	13	0.000 000 000 000 003
23 420	4	0.000 032 155 613 531	2 657 142 036 440 000	14	0.000 000 000 000 000
303 240	5	0.000 002 476 132 611	34 327 724 461 500 000	15	0.000 000 000 000 000
3 641 100	6	0.000 000 206 157 364	434 157 115 760 200 000	16	0.000 000 000 000 000
46 113 200	7	0.000 000 015 327 745	5 432 127 413 542 400 000	17	0.000 000 000 000 000
575 360 400	8	0.000 000 001 257 144	67 405 553 164 731 000 000	18	0.000 000 000 000 000
7 346 545 000	9	0.000 000 000 104 560			

2^n IN DECIMAL SCALE

n	2^n	n	2^n	n	2^n
0.001	1.00069 33874 62581	0.01	1.00695 55500 56719	0.1	1.07177 34625 36293
0.002	1.00138 72557 11335	0.02	1.01395 94797 90029	0.2	1.14869 83549 97035
0.003	1.00208 16050 79633	0.03	1.02101 21257 07193	0.3	1.23114 44133 44916
0.004	1.00277 64359 01078	0.04	1.02811 38266 56067	0.4	1.31950 79107 72894
0.005	1.00347 17485 09503	0.05	1.03526 49238 41377	0.5	1.41421 35623 73095
0.006	1.00416 75432 38973	0.06	1.04246 57608 41121	0.6	1.51571 65665 10398
0.007	1.00486 38204 23785	0.07	1.04971 66836 23067	0.7	1.62450 47927 12471
0.008	1.00556 05803 98468	0.08	1.05701 80405 61380	0.8	1.74110 11265 92248
0.009	1.00625 78234 97782	0.09	1.06437 01824 53360	0.9	1.86606 59830 73615

$n \log_{10} 2$, $n \log_2 10$ IN DECIMAL SCALE

n	$n \log_{10} 2$	$n \log_2 10$	n	$n \log_{10} 2$	$n \log_2 10$
1	0.30102 99957	3.32192 80949	6	1.80617 99740	19.93156 85693
2	0.60205 99913	6.64385 61898	7	2.10720 99696	23.25349 66642
3	0.90308 99870	9.96578 42847	8	2.40823 99653	26.57542 47591
4	1.20411 99827	13.28771 23795	9	2.70926 99610	29.89735 28540
5	1.50514 99783	16.60964 04744	10	3.01029 99566	33.21928 09489

ADDITION AND MULTIPLICATION TABLES

Addition   Multiplication

Binary Scale

$$0 + 0 = 0 \qquad\qquad 0 \times 0 = 0$$
$$0 + 1 = 1 + 0 = 1 \qquad 0 \times 1 = 1 \times 0 = 0$$
$$1 + 1 = 10 \qquad\qquad 1 \times 1 = 1$$

Octal Scale

Addition   Multiplication

0	01	02	03	04	05	06	07
1	02	03	04	05	06	07	10
2	03	04	05	06	07	10	11
3	04	05	06	07	10	11	12
4	05	06	07	10	11	12	13
5	06	07	10	11	12	13	14
6	07	10	11	12	13	14	15
7	10	11	12	13	14	15	16

1	02	03	04	05	06	07
2	04	06	10	12	14	16
3	06	11	14	17	22	25
4	10	14	20	24	30	34
5	12	17	24	31	36	43
6	14	22	30	36	44	52
7	16	25	34	43	52	61

MATHEMATICAL CONSTANTS IN OCTAL SCALE

$\pi = (3.11037\ 552421)_{(8)}$ $e = (2.55760\ 521305)_{(8)}$ $\gamma = (0.44742\ 147707)_{(8)}$

$\pi^{-1} = (0.24276\ 301556)_{(8)}$ $e^{-1} = (0.27426\ 530661)_{(8)}$ $\log_e \gamma = -(0.43127\ 233602)_{(8)}$

$\sqrt{\pi} = (1.61337\ 611067)_{(8)}$ $\sqrt{e} = (1.51411\ 230704)_{(8)}$ $\log_2 \gamma = -(0.62573\ 030645)_{(8)}$

$\log_e \pi = (1.11206\ 404435)_{(8)}$ $\log_{10} e = (0.33626\ 754251)_{(8)}$ $\sqrt{2} = (1.32404\ 746320)_{(8)}$

$\log_2 \pi = (1.51544\ 163223)_{(8)}$ $\log_2 e = (1.34252\ 166245)_{(8)}$ $\log_e 2 = (0.54271\ 027760)_{(8)}$

$\sqrt{10} = (3.12305\ 407267)_{(8)}$ $\log_2 10 = (3.24464\ 741136)_{(8)}$ $\log_e 10 = (2.23273\ 067355)_{(8)}$

OCTAL-DECIMAL INTEGER CONVERSION TABLE

	0	1	2	3	4	5	6	7
0000	0000	0001	0002	0003	0004	0005	0006	0007
0010	0008	0009	0010	0011	0012	0013	0014	0015
0020	0016	0017	0018	0019	0020	0021	0022	0023
0030	0024	0025	0026	0027	0028	0029	0030	0031
0040	0032	0033	0034	0035	0036	0037	0038	0039
0050	0040	0041	0042	0043	0044	0045	0046	0047
0060	0048	0049	0050	0051	0052	0053	0054	0055
0070	0056	0057	0058	0059	0060	0061	0062	0063
0100	0064	0065	0066	0067	0068	0069	0070	0071
0110	0072	0073	0074	0075	0076	0077	0078	0079
0120	0080	0081	0082	0083	0084	0085	0086	0087
0130	0088	0089	0090	0091	0092	0093	0094	0095
0140	0096	0097	0098	0099	0100	0101	0102	0103
0150	0104	0105	0106	0107	0108	0109	0110	0111
0160	0112	0113	0114	0115	0116	0117	0118	0119
0170	0120	0121	0122	0123	0124	0125	0126	0127
0200	0128	0129	0130	0131	0132	0133	0134	0135
0210	0136	0137	0138	0139	0140	0141	0142	0143
0220	0144	0145	0146	0147	0148	0149	0150	0151
0230	0152	0153	0154	0155	0156	0157	0158	0159
0240	0160	0161	0162	0163	0164	0165	0166	0167
0250	0168	0169	0170	0171	0172	0173	0174	0175
0260	0176	0177	0178	0179	0180	0181	0182	0183
0270	0184	0185	0186	0187	0188	0189	0190	0191
0300	0192	0193	0194	0195	0196	0197	0198	0199
0310	0200	0201	0202	0203	0204	0205	0206	0207
0320	0208	0209	0210	0211	0212	0213	0214	0215
0330	0216	0217	0218	0219	0220	0221	0222	0223
0340	0224	0225	0226	0227	0228	0229	0230	0231
0350	0232	0233	0234	0235	0236	0237	0238	0239
0360	0240	0241	0242	0243	0244	0245	0246	0247
0370	0248	0249	0250	0251	0252	0253	0254	0255

	0	1	2	3	4	5	6	7
0400	0256	0257	0258	0259	0260	0261	0262	0263
0410	0264	0265	0266	0267	0268	0269	0270	0271
0420	0272	0273	0274	0275	0276	0277	0278	0279
0430	0280	0281	0282	0283	0284	0285	0286	0287
0440	0288	0289	0290	0291	0292	0293	0294	0295
0450	0296	0297	0298	0299	0300	0301	0302	0303
0460	0304	0305	0306	0307	0308	0309	0310	0311
0470	0312	0313	0314	0315	0316	0317	0318	0319
0500	0320	0321	0322	0323	0324	0325	0326	0327
0510	0328	0329	0330	0331	0332	0333	0334	0335
0520	0336	0337	0338	0339	0340	0341	0342	0343
0530	0344	0345	0346	0347	0348	0349	0350	0351
0540	0352	0353	0354	0355	0356	0357	0358	0359
0550	0360	0361	0362	0363	0364	0365	0366	0367
0560	0368	0369	0370	0371	0372	0373	0374	0375
0570	0376	0377	0378	0379	0380	0381	0382	0383
0600	0384	0385	0386	0387	0388	0389	0390	0391
0610	0392	0393	0394	0395	0396	0397	0398	0399
0620	0400	0401	0402	0403	0404	0405	0406	0407
0630	0408	0409	0410	0411	0412	0413	0414	0415
0640	0416	0417	0418	0419	0420	0421	0422	0423
0650	0424	0425	0426	0427	0428	0429	0430	0431
0660	0432	0433	0434	0435	0436	0437	0438	0439
0670	0440	0441	0442	0443	0444	0445	0446	0447
0700	0448	0449	0450	0451	0452	0453	0454	0455
0710	0456	0457	0458	0459	0460	0461	0462	0463
0720	0464	0465	0466	0467	0468	0469	0470	0471
0730	0472	0473	0474	0475	0476	0477	0478	0479
0740	0480	0481	0482	0483	0484	0485	0486	0487
0750	0488	0489	0490	0491	0492	0493	0494	0495
0760	0496	0497	0498	0499	0500	0501	0502	0503
0770	0504	0505	0506	0507	0508	0509	0510	0511

0000	0000
to	to
0777	0511
(Octal)	(Decimal)

Octal	Decimal
10000-	4096
20000-	8192
30000-	12288
40000-	16384
50000-	20480
60000-	24576
70000-	28672

	0	1	2	3	4	5	6	7
1000	0512	0513	0514	0515	0516	0517	0518	0519
1010	0520	0521	0522	0523	0524	0525	0526	0527
1020	0528	0529	0530	0531	0532	0533	0534	0535
1030	0536	0537	0538	0539	0540	0541	0542	0543
1040	0544	0545	0546	0547	0548	0549	0550	0551
1050	0552	0553	0554	0555	0556	0557	0558	0559
1060	0560	0561	0562	0563	0564	0565	0566	0567
1070	0568	0569	0570	0571	0572	0573	0574	0575
1100	0576	0577	0578	0579	0580	0581	0582	0583
1110	0584	0585	0586	0587	0588	0589	0590	0591
1120	0592	0593	0594	0595	0596	0597	0598	0599
1130	0600	0601	0602	0603	0604	0605	0606	0607
1140	0608	0609	0610	0611	0612	0613	0614	0615
1150	0616	0617	0618	0619	0620	0621	0622	0623
1160	0624	0625	0626	0627	0628	0629	0630	0631
1170	0632	0633	0634	0635	0636	0637	0638	0639
1200	0640	0641	0642	0643	0644	0645	0646	0647
1210	0648	0649	0650	0651	0652	0653	0654	0655
1220	0656	0657	0658	0659	0660	0661	0662	0663
1230	0664	0665	0666	0667	0668	0669	0670	0671
1240	0672	0673	0674	0675	0676	0677	0678	0679
1250	0680	0681	0682	0683	0684	0685	0686	0687
1260	0688	0689	0690	0691	0692	0693	0694	0695
1270	0696	0697	0698	0699	0700	0701	0702	0703
1300	0704	0705	0706	0707	0708	0709	0710	0711
1310	0712	0713	0714	0715	0716	0717	0718	0719
1320	0720	0721	0722	0723	0724	0725	0726	0727
1330	0728	0729	0730	0731	0732	0733	0734	0735
1340	0736	0737	0738	0739	0740	0741	0742	0743
1350	0744	0745	0746	0747	0748	0749	0750	0751
1360	0752	0753	0754	0755	0756	0757	0758	0759
1370	0760	0761	0762	0763	0764	0765	0766	0767

	0	1	2	3	4	5	6	7
1400	0768	0769	0770	0771	0772	0773	0774	0775
1410	0776	0777	0778	0779	0780	0781	0782	0783
1420	0784	0785	0786	0787	0788	0789	0790	0791
1430	0792	0793	0794	0795	0796	0797	0798	0799
1440	0800	0801	0802	0803	0804	0805	0806	0807
1450	0808	0809	0810	0811	0812	0813	0814	0815
1460	0816	0817	0818	0819	0820	0821	0822	0823
1470	0824	0825	0826	0827	0828	0829	0830	0831
1500	0832	0833	0834	0835	0836	0837	0838	0839
1510	0840	0841	0842	0843	0844	0845	0846	0847
1520	0848	0849	0850	0851	0852	0853	0854	0855
1530	0856	0857	0858	0859	0860	0861	0862	0863
1540	0864	0865	0866	0867	0868	0869	0870	0871
1550	0872	0873	0874	0875	0876	0877	0878	0879
1560	0880	0881	0882	0883	0884	0885	0886	0887
1570	0888	0889	0890	0891	0892	0893	0894	0895
1600	0896	0897	0898	0899	0900	0901	0902	0903
1610	0904	0905	0906	0907	0908	0909	0910	0911
1620	0912	0913	0914	0915	0916	0917	0918	0919
1630	0920	0921	0922	0923	0924	0925	0926	0927
1640	0928	0929	0930	0931	0932	0933	0934	0935
1650	0936	0937	0938	0939	0940	0941	0942	0943
1660	0944	0945	0946	0947	0948	0949	0950	0951
1670	0952	0953	0954	0955	0956	0957	0958	0959
1700	0960	0961	0962	0963	0964	0965	0966	0967
1710	0968	0969	0970	0971	0972	0973	0974	0975
1720	0976	0977	0978	0979	0980	0981	0982	0983
1730	0984	0985	0986	0987	0988	0989	0990	0991
1740	0992	0993	0994	0995	0996	0997	0998	0999
1750	1000	1001	1002	1003	1004	1005	1006	1007
1760	1008	1009	1010	1011	1012	1013	1014	1015
1770	1016	1017	1018	1019	1020	1021	1022	1023

1000	0512
to	to
1777	1023
(Octal)	(Decimal)

OCTAL-DECIMAL INTEGER CONVERSION TABLE (Continued)

	0	1	2	3	4	5	6	7
2000	1024	1025	1026	1027	1028	1029	1030	1031
2010	1032	1033	1034	1035	1036	1037	1038	1039
2020	1040	1041	1042	1043	1044	1045	1046	1047
2030	1048	1049	1050	1051	1052	1053	1054	1055
2040	1056	1057	1058	1059	1060	1061	1062	1063
2050	1064	1065	1066	1067	1068	1069	1070	1071
2060	1072	1073	1074	1075	1076	1077	1078	1079
2070	1080	1081	1082	1083	1084	1085	1086	1087
2100	1088	1089	1090	1091	1092	1093	1094	1095
2110	1096	1097	1098	1099	1100	1101	1102	1103
2120	1104	1105	1106	1107	1108	1109	1110	1111
2130	1112	1113	1114	1115	1116	1117	1118	1119
2140	1120	1121	1122	1123	1124	1125	1126	1127
2150	1128	1129	1130	1131	1132	1133	1134	1135
2160	1136	1137	1138	1139	1140	1141	1142	1143
2170	1144	1145	1146	1147	1148	1149	1150	1151
2200	1152	1153	1154	1155	1156	1157	1158	1159
2210	1160	1161	1162	1163	1164	1165	1166	1167
2220	1168	1169	1170	1171	1172	1173	1174	1175
2230	1176	1177	1178	1179	1180	1181	1182	1183
2240	1184	1185	1186	1187	1188	1189	1190	1191
2250	1192	1193	1194	1195	1196	1197	1198	1199
2260	1200	1201	1202	1203	1204	1205	1206	1207
2270	1208	1209	1210	1211	1212	1213	1214	1215
2300	1216	1217	1218	1219	1220	1221	1222	1223
2310	1224	1225	1226	1227	1228	1229	1230	1231
2320	1232	1233	1234	1235	1236	1237	1238	1239
2330	1240	1241	1242	1243	1244	1245	1246	1247
2340	1248	1249	1250	1251	1252	1253	1254	1255
2350	1256	1257	1258	1259	1260	1261	1262	1263
2360	1264	1265	1266	1267	1268	1269	1270	1271
2370	1272	1273	1274	1275	1276	1277	1278	1279

	0	1	2	3	4	5	6	7
2400	1280	1281	1282	1283	1284	1285	1286	1287
2410	1288	1289	1290	1291	1292	1293	1294	1295
2420	1296	1297	1298	1299	1300	1301	1302	1303
2430	1304	1305	1306	1307	1308	1309	1310	1311
2440	1312	1313	1314	1315	1316	1317	1318	1319
2450	1320	1321	1322	1323	1324	1325	1326	1327
2460	1328	1329	1330	1331	1332	1333	1334	1335
2470	1336	1337	1338	1339	1340	1341	1342	1343
2500	1344	1345	1346	1347	1348	1349	1350	1351
2510	1352	1353	1354	1355	1356	1357	1358	1359
2520	1360	1361	1362	1363	1364	1365	1366	1367
2530	1368	1369	1370	1371	1372	1373	1374	1375
2540	1376	1377	1378	1379	1380	1381	1382	1383
2550	1384	1385	1386	1387	1388	1389	1390	1391
2560	1392	1393	1394	1395	1396	1397	1398	1399
2570	1400	1401	1402	1403	1404	1405	1406	1407
2600	1408	1409	1410	1411	1412	1413	1414	1415
2610	1416	1417	1418	1419	1420	1421	1422	1423
2620	1424	1425	1426	1427	1428	1429	1430	1431
2630	1432	1433	1434	1435	1436	1437	1438	1439
2640	1440	1441	1442	1443	1444	1445	1446	1447
2650	1448	1449	1450	1451	1452	1453	1454	1455
2660	1456	1457	1458	1459	1460	1461	1462	1463
2670	1464	1465	1466	1467	1468	1469	1470	1471
2700	1472	1473	1474	1475	1476	1477	1478	1479
2710	1480	1481	1482	1483	1484	1485	1486	1487
2720	1488	1489	1490	1491	1492	1493	1494	1495
2730	1496	1497	1498	1499	1500	1501	1502	1503
2740	1504	1505	1506	1507	1508	1509	1510	1511
2750	1512	1513	1514	1515	1516	1517	1518	1519
2760	1520	1521	1522	1523	1524	1525	1526	1527
2770	1528	1529	1530	1531	1532	1533	1534	1535

Side reference (left):

```
2000 | 1024
 to  |  to
2777 | 1535
(Octal)|(Decimal)

Octal  Decimal
10000-  4096
20000-  8192
30000- 12288
40000- 16384
50000- 20480
60000- 24576
70000- 28672
```

	0	1	2	3	4	5	6	7
3000	1536	1537	1538	1539	1540	1541	1542	1543
3010	1544	1545	1546	1547	1548	1549	1550	1551
3020	1552	1553	1554	1555	1556	1557	1558	1559
3030	1560	1561	1562	1563	1564	1565	1566	1567
3040	1568	1569	1570	1571	1572	1573	1574	1575
3050	1576	1577	1578	1579	1580	1581	1582	1583
3060	1584	1585	1586	1587	1588	1589	1590	1591
3070	1592	1593	1594	1595	1596	1597	1598	1599
3100	1600	1601	1602	1603	1604	1605	1606	1607
3110	1608	1609	1610	1611	1612	1613	1614	1615
3120	1616	1617	1618	1619	1620	1621	1622	1623
3130	1624	1625	1626	1627	1628	1629	1630	1631
3140	1632	1633	1634	1635	1636	1637	1638	1639
3150	1640	1641	1642	1643	1644	1645	1646	1647
3160	1648	1649	1650	1651	1652	1653	1654	1655
3170	1656	1657	1658	1659	1660	1661	1662	1663
3200	1664	1665	1666	1667	1668	1669	1670	1671
3210	1672	1673	1674	1675	1676	1677	1678	1679
3220	1680	1681	1682	1683	1684	1685	1686	1687
3230	1688	1689	1690	1691	1692	1693	1694	1695
3240	1696	1697	1698	1699	1700	1701	1702	1703
3250	1704	1705	1706	1707	1708	1709	1710	1711
3260	1712	1713	1714	1715	1716	1717	1718	1719
3270	1720	1721	1722	1723	1724	1725	1726	1727
3300	1728	1729	1730	1731	1732	1733	1734	1735
3310	1736	1737	1738	1739	1740	1741	1742	1743
3320	1744	1745	1746	1747	1748	1749	1750	1751
3330	1752	1753	1754	1755	1756	1757	1758	1759
3340	1760	1761	1762	1763	1764	1765	1766	1767
3350	1768	1769	1770	1771	1772	1773	1774	1775
3360	1776	1777	1778	1779	1780	1781	1782	1783
3370	1784	1785	1786	1787	1788	1789	1790	1791

	0	1	2	3	4	5	6	7
3400	1792	1793	1794	1795	1796	1797	1798	1799
3410	1800	1801	1802	1803	1804	1805	1806	1807
3420	1808	1809	1810	1811	1812	1813	1814	1815
3430	1816	1817	1818	1819	1820	1821	1822	1823
3440	1824	1825	1826	1827	1828	1829	1830	1831
3450	1832	1833	1834	1835	1836	1837	1838	1839
3460	1840	1841	1842	1843	1844	1845	1846	1847
3470	1848	1849	1850	1851	1852	1853	1854	1855
3500	1856	1857	1858	1859	1860	1861	1862	1863
3510	1864	1865	1866	1867	1868	1869	1870	1871
3520	1872	1873	1874	1875	1876	1877	1878	1879
3530	1880	1881	1882	1883	1884	1885	1886	1887
3540	1888	1889	1890	1891	1892	1893	1894	1895
3550	1896	1897	1898	1899	1900	1901	1902	1903
3560	1904	1905	1906	1907	1908	1909	1910	1911
3570	1912	1913	1914	1915	1916	1917	1918	1919
3600	1920	1921	1922	1923	1924	1925	1926	1927
3610	1928	1929	1930	1931	1932	1933	1934	1935
3620	1936	1937	1938	1939	1940	1941	1942	1943
3630	1944	1945	1946	1947	1948	1949	1950	1951
3640	1952	1953	1954	1955	1956	1957	1958	1959
3650	1960	1961	1962	1963	1964	1965	1966	1967
3660	1968	1969	1970	1971	1972	1973	1974	1975
3670	1976	1977	1978	1979	1980	1981	1982	1983
3700	1984	1985	1986	1987	1988	1989	1990	1991
3710	1992	1993	1994	1995	1996	1997	1998	1999
3720	2000	2001	2002	2003	2004	2005	2006	2007
3730	2008	2009	2010	2011	2012	2013	2014	2015
3740	2016	2017	2018	2019	2020	2021	2022	2023
3750	2024	2025	2026	2027	2028	2029	2030	2031
3760	2032	2033	2034	2035	2036	2037	2038	2039
3770	2040	2041	2042	2043	2044	2045	2046	2047

Side reference (lower left):

```
3000 | 1536
 to  |  to
3777 | 2047
(Octal)|(Decimal)
```

OCTAL-DECIMAL INTEGER CONVERSION TABLE (Continued)

	0	1	2	3	4	5	6	7
4000	2048	2049	2050	2051	2052	2053	2054	2055
4010	2056	2057	2058	2059	2060	2061	2062	2063
4020	2064	2065	2066	2067	2068	2069	2070	2071
4030	2072	2073	2074	2075	2076	2077	2078	2079
4040	2080	2081	2082	2083	2084	2085	2086	2087
4050	2088	2089	2090	2091	2092	2093	2094	2095
4060	2096	2097	2098	2099	2100	2101	2102	2103
4070	2104	2105	2106	2107	2108	2109	2110	2111
4100	2112	2113	2114	2115	2116	2117	2118	2119
4110	2120	2121	2122	2123	2124	2125	2126	2127
4120	2128	2129	2130	2131	2132	2133	2134	2135
4130	2136	2137	2138	2139	2140	2141	2142	2143
4140	2144	2145	2146	2147	2148	2149	2150	2151
4150	2152	2153	2154	2155	2156	2157	2158	2159
4160	2160	2161	2162	2163	2164	2165	2166	2167
4170	2168	2169	2170	2171	2172	2173	2174	2175
4200	2176	2177	2178	2179	2180	2181	2182	2183
4210	2184	2185	2186	2187	2188	2189	2190	2191
4220	2192	2193	2194	2195	2196	2197	2198	2199
4230	2200	2201	2202	2203	2204	2205	2206	2207
4240	2208	2209	2210	2211	2212	2213	2214	2215
4250	2216	2217	2218	2219	2220	2221	2222	2223
4260	2224	2225	2226	2227	2228	2229	2230	2231
4270	2232	2233	2234	2235	2236	2237	2238	2239
4300	2240	2241	2242	2243	2244	2245	2246	2247
4310	2248	2249	2250	2251	2252	2253	2254	2255
4320	2256	2257	2258	2259	2260	2261	2262	2263
4330	2264	2265	2266	2267	2268	2269	2270	2271
4340	2272	2273	2274	2275	2276	2277	2278	2279
4350	2280	2281	2282	2283	2284	2285	2286	2287
4360	2288	2289	2290	2291	2292	2293	2294	2295
4370	2296	2297	2298	2299	2300	2301	2302	2303

	0	1	2	3	4	5	6	7
4400	2304	2305	2306	2307	2308	2309	2310	2311
4410	2312	2313	2314	2315	2316	2317	2318	2319
4420	2320	2321	2322	2323	2324	2325	2326	2327
4430	2328	2329	2330	2331	2332	2333	2334	2335
4440	2336	2337	2338	2339	2340	2341	2342	2343
4450	2344	2345	2346	2347	2348	2349	2350	2351
4460	2352	2353	2354	2355	2356	2357	2358	2359
4470	2360	2361	2362	2363	2364	2365	2366	2367
4500	2368	2369	2370	2371	2372	2373	2374	2375
4510	2376	2377	2378	2379	2380	2381	2382	2383
4520	2384	2385	2386	2387	2388	2389	2390	2391
4530	2392	2393	2394	2395	2396	2397	2398	2399
4540	2400	2401	2402	2403	2404	2405	2406	2407
4550	2408	2409	2410	2411	2412	2413	2114	2415
4560	2416	2417	2418	2419	2420	2421	2422	2423
4570	2424	2425	2426	2427	2428	2429	2430	2431
4600	2432	2433	2434	2435	2436	2437	2438	2439
4610	2440	2441	2442	2443	2444	2445	2446	2447
4620	2448	2449	2450	2451	2452	2453	2454	2455
4630	2456	2457	2458	2459	2460	2461	2462	2463
4640	2464	2465	2466	2467	2468	2469	2470	2471
4650	2472	2473	2474	2475	2476	2477	2478	2479
4660	2480	2481	2482	2483	2484	2485	2486	2487
4670	2488	2489	2490	2491	2492	2493	2494	2495
4700	2496	2497	2498	2499	2500	2501	2502	2503
4710	2504	2505	2506	2507	2508	2509	2510	2511
4720	2512	2513	2514	2515	2516	2517	2518	2519
4730	2520	2521	2522	2523	2524	2525	2526	2527
4740	2528	2529	2530	2531	2532	2533	2534	2535
4750	2536	2537	2538	2539	2540	2541	2542	2543
4760	2544	2545	2546	2547	2548	2549	2550	2551
4770	2552	2553	2554	2555	2556	2557	2558	2559

4000	2048
to	to
4777	2559
(Octal)	(Decimal)

Octal	Decimal
10000-	4096
20000-	8192
30000-	12288
40000-	16384
50000-	20480
60000-	24576
70000-	28672

	0	1	2	3	4	5	6	7
5000	2560	2561	2562	2563	2564	2565	2566	2567
5010	2568	2569	2570	2571	2572	2573	2574	2575
5020	2576	2577	2578	2579	2580	2581	2582	2583
5030	2584	2585	2586	2587	2588	2589	2590	2591
5040	2592	2593	2594	2595	2596	2597	2598	2599
5050	2600	2601	2602	2603	2604	2605	2606	2607
5060	2608	2609	2610	2611	2612	2613	2614	2615
5070	2616	2617	2618	2619	2620	2621	2622	2623
5100	2624	2625	2626	2627	2628	2629	2630	2631
5110	2632	2633	2634	2635	2636	2637	2638	2639
5120	2640	2641	2642	2643	2644	2645	2646	2647
5130	2648	2649	2650	2651	2652	2653	2654	2655
5140	2656	2657	2658	2659	2660	2661	2662	2663
5150	2664	2665	2666	2667	2668	2669	2670	2671
5160	2672	2673	2674	2675	2676	2677	2678	2679
5170	2680	2681	2682	2683	2684	2685	2686	2687
5200	2688	2689	2690	2691	2692	2693	2694	2695
5210	2696	2697	2698	2699	2700	2701	2702	2703
5220	2704	2705	2706	2707	2708	2709	2710	2711
5230	2712	2713	2714	2715	2716	2717	2718	2719
5240	2720	2721	2722	2723	2724	2725	2726	2727
5250	2728	2729	2730	2731	2732	2733	2734	2735
5260	2736	2737	2738	2739	2740	2741	2742	2743
5270	2744	2745	2746	2747	2748	2749	2750	2751
5300	2752	2753	2754	2755	2756	2757	2758	2759
5310	2760	2761	2762	2763	2764	2765	2766	2767
5320	2768	2769	2770	2771	2772	2773	2774	2775
5330	2776	2777	2778	2779	2780	2781	2782	2783
5340	2784	2785	2786	2787	2788	2789	2790	2791
5350	2792	2793	2794	2795	2796	2797	2798	2799
5360	2800	2801	2802	2803	2804	2805	2806	2807
5370	2808	2809	2810	2811	2812	2813	2814	2815

	0	1	2	3	4	5	6	7
5400	2816	2817	2818	2819	2820	2821	2822	2823
5410	2824	2825	2826	2827	2828	2829	2830	2831
5420	2832	2833	2834	2835	2836	2837	2838	2839
5430	2840	2841	2842	2843	2844	2845	2846	2847
5440	2848	2849	2850	2851	2852	2853	2854	2855
5450	2856	2857	2858	2859	2860	2861	2862	2863
5460	2864	2865	2866	2867	2868	2869	2870	2871
5470	2872	2873	2874	2875	2876	2877	2878	2879
5500	2880	2881	2882	2883	2884	2885	2886	2887
5510	2888	2889	2890	2891	2892	2893	2894	2895
5520	2896	2897	2898	2899	2900	2901	2902	2903
5530	2904	2905	2906	2907	2908	2909	2910	2911
5540	2912	2913	2914	2915	2916	2917	2918	2919
5550	2920	2921	2922	2923	2924	2925	2926	2927
5560	2928	2929	2930	2931	2932	2933	2934	2935
5570	2936	2937	2938	2939	2940	2941	2942	2943
5600	2944	2945	2946	2947	2948	2949	2950	2951
5610	2952	2953	2954	2955	2956	2957	2958	2959
5620	2960	2961	2962	2963	2964	2965	2966	2967
5630	2968	2969	2970	2971	2972	2973	2974	2975
5640	2976	2977	2978	2979	2980	2981	2982	2983
5650	2984	2985	2986	2987	2988	2989	2990	2991
5660	2992	2993	2994	2995	2996	2997	2998	2999
5670	3000	3001	3002	3003	3004	3005	3006	3007
5700	3008	3009	3010	3011	3012	3013	3014	3015
5710	3016	3017	3018	3019	3020	3021	3022	3023
5720	3024	3025	3026	3027	3028	3029	3030	3031
5730	3032	3033	3034	3035	3036	3037	3038	3039
5740	3040	3041	3042	3043	3044	3045	3046	3047
5750	3048	3049	3050	3051	3052	3053	3054	3055
5760	3056	3057	3058	3059	3060	3061	3062	3063
5770	3064	3065	3066	3067	3068	3069	3070	3071

5000	2560
to	to
5777	3071
(Octal)	(Decimal)

OCTAL-DECIMAL INTEGER CONVERSION TABLE (Continued)

6000 | 3072
to | to
6777 | 3583
(Octal) | (Decimal)

Octal Decimal
10000- 4096
20000- 8192
30000-12288
40000-16384
50000-20480
60000-24576
70000-28672

	0	1	2	3	4	5	6	7
6000	3072	3073	3074	3075	3076	3077	3078	3079
6010	3080	3081	3082	3083	3084	3085	3086	3087
6020	3088	3089	3090	3091	3092	3093	3094	3095
6030	3096	3097	3098	3099	3100	3101	3102	3103
6040	3104	3105	3106	3107	3108	3109	3110	3111
6050	3112	3113	3114	3115	3116	3117	3118	3119
6060	3120	3121	3122	3123	3124	3125	3126	3127
6070	3128	3129	3130	3131	3132	3133	3134	3135
6100	3136	3137	3138	3139	3140	3141	3142	3143
6110	3144	3145	3146	3147	3148	3149	3150	3151
6120	3152	3153	3154	3155	3156	3157	3158	3159
6130	3160	3161	3162	3163	3164	3165	3166	3167
6140	3168	3169	3170	3171	3172	3173	3174	3175
6150	3176	3177	3178	3179	3180	3181	3182	3183
6160	3184	3185	3186	3187	3188	3189	3190	3191
6170	3192	3193	3194	3195	3196	3197	3198	3199
6200	3200	3201	3202	3203	3204	3205	3206	3207
6210	3208	3209	3210	3211	3212	3213	3214	3215
6220	3216	3217	3218	3219	3220	3221	3222	3223
6230	3224	3225	3226	3227	3228	3229	3230	3231
6240	3232	3233	3234	3235	3236	3237	3238	3239
6250	3240	3241	3442	3243	3244	3245	3246	3247
6260	3248	3249	3250	3251	3252	3253	3254	3255
6270	3256	3257	3258	3259	3260	3261	3262	3263
6300	3264	3265	3266	3267	3268	3269	3270	3871
6310	3272	3273	3274	3275	3276	3277	3278	3279
6320	3280	3281	3282	3283	3284	3285	3286	3287
6330	3288	3289	3290	3291	3292	3293	3294	3295
6340	3296	3297	3298	3299	3300	3301	3302	3003
6350	3304	3305	3306	3307	3308	3309	3310	3311
6360	3312	3313	3314	3315	3316	3317	3318	3319
6370	3320	3321	3322	3323	3324	3325	3326	3327

	0	1	2	3	4	5	6	7
6400	3328	3329	3330	3331	3332	3333	3334	3335
6410	3336	3337	3338	3339	3340	3341	3342	3343
6420	3344	3345	3346	3347	3348	3349	3350	3351
6430	3352	3353	3354	3355	3356	3357	3358	3359
6440	3360	3361	3362	3363	3364	3365	3366	3367
6450	3368	3369	3370	3371	3372	3373	3374	3375
6460	3376	3377	3378	3379	3380	3381	3382	3383
6470	3384	3385	3386	3387	3388	3389	3390	3391
6500	3392	3393	3394	3395	3396	3397	3398	3399
6510	3400	3401	3402	3403	3404	3405	3406	3407
6520	3408	3409	3410	3411	3412	3413	3414	3415
6530	3416	3417	3418	3419	3420	3421	3422	3423
6540	3424	3425	3426	3427	3428	3429	3430	3431
6550	3432	3433	3434	3435	3436	3437	3438	3439
6560	3440	3441	3442	3443	3444	3445	3446	3447
6570	3448	3449	3450	3451	3452	3453	3454	3455
6600	3456	3457	3458	3459	3460	3461	3462	3463
6610	3464	3465	3466	3467	3468	3469	3470	3471
6620	3472	3473	3474	3475	3476	3477	3478	3479
6630	3480	3481	3482	3483	3484	3485	3486	3487
6640	3488	3489	3490	3491	3492	3493	3494	3495
6650	3496	3497	3498	3499	3500	3501	3502	3503
6660	3504	3505	3506	3507	3508	3509	3510	3511
6670	3512	3513	3514	3515	3516	3517	3518	3519
6700	3520	3521	3522	3523	3524	3525	3526	3527
6710	3528	3529	3530	3531	3532	3533	3534	3535
6720	3536	3537	3538	3539	3540	3541	3542	3543
6730	3544	3545	3546	3547	3548	3549	3550	3551
6740	3552	3553	3554	3555	3556	3557	3558	3559
6750	3560	3561	3562	3563	3564	3565	3566	3567
6760	3568	3569	3570	3571	3572	3573	3574	3575
6770	3576	3577	3578	3579	3580	3581	3582	3583

7000 | 3584
to | to
7777 | 4095
(Octal) | (Decimal)

	0	1	2	3	4	5	6	7
7000	3584	3585	3586	3587	3588	3589	3590	3591
7010	3592	3593	3594	3595	3596	3597	3598	3599
7020	3600	3601	3602	3603	3604	3605	3606	3607
7030	3608	3609	3610	3611	3612	3613	3614	3615
7040	3616	3617	3618	3619	3620	3621	3622	3623
7050	3624	3625	3626	3627	3628	3629	3630	3631
7060	3632	3633	3634	3635	3636	3637	3638	3639
7070	3640	3641	3642	3643	3644	3645	3646	3647
7100	3648	3649	3650	3651	3652	3653	3654	3655
7110	3656	3657	3658	3659	3660	3661	3662	3663
7120	3664	3665	3666	3667	3668	3669	3670	3671
7130	3672	3673	3674	3675	3676	3677	3678	3679
7140	3680	3681	3682	3683	3684	3685	3686	3687
7150	3688	3689	3690	3691	3692	3693	3694	3695
7160	3696	3697	3698	3699	3700	3701	3702	3703
7170	3704	3705	3706	3707	3708	3709	3710	3711
7200	3712	3713	3714	3715	3716	3717	3718	3719
7210	3720	3721	3722	3723	3724	3725	3726	3727
7220	3728	3729	3730	3731	3732	3733	3734	3735
7230	3736	3737	3738	3739	3740	3741	3742	3743
7240	3744	3745	3746	3747	3748	3749	3750	3751
7250	3752	3753	3754	3755	3756	3757	3758	3759
7260	3760	3761	3762	3763	3764	3765	3766	3767
7270	3768	3769	3770	3771	3772	3773	3774	3775
7300	3776	3777	3778	3779	3780	3781	3782	3783
7310	3784	3785	3786	3787	3788	3789	3790	3791
7320	3792	3893	3794	3795	3796	3797	3798	3799
7330	3800	3801	3802	3803	3804	3805	3806	3807
7340	3808	3809	3810	3811	3812	3813	3814	3815
7350	3816	3817	3818	3819	3820	3821	3822	3823
7360	3824	3825	3826	3827	3828	3829	3830	3831
7370	3832	3833	3834	3835	3836	3837	3838	3839

	0	1	2	3	4	5	6	7
7400	3840	3841	3482	3843	3844	3845	3846	3847
7410	3848	3849	3850	3851	3852	3853	3854	3855
7420	3856	3857	3858	3859	3860	3861	3862	3863
7430	3864	3865	3866	3867	3868	3869	3870	3871
7440	3872	3873	3874	3875	3876	3877	3878	3879
7450	3880	3881	3882	3883	3884	3885	3886	3887
7460	3888	3889	3890	3891	3892	3893	3894	3895
7470	3896	3897	3898	3899	3900	3901	3902	3903
7500	3904	3905	3906	3907	3908	3909	3910	3911
7510	3912	3913	3914	3915	3916	3917	3918	3919
7520	3920	3921	3922	3923	3924	3925	3926	3927
7530	3928	3929	3930	3931	3932	3933	3934	3935
7540	3936	3937	3938	3939	3940	3941	3942	3943
7550	3944	3945	3946	3947	3948	3949	3950	3951
7560	3952	3953	3954	3955	3956	3957	3958	3959
7570	3960	3961	3962	3963	3964	3965	3966	3967
7600	3968	3969	4970	3971	3972	3973	3974	3975
7610	3976	3977	3978	3979	3980	3981	3982	3983
7620	3984	3985	3986	3987	3988	3989	3990	3991
7630	3992	3993	3994	3995	3996	3997	3998	3999
7640	4000	4001	4002	4003	4004	4005	4006	4007
7650	4008	4009	4010	4011	4012	4013	4014	4015
7660	4016	4017	4018	4019	4020	4021	4022	4023
7670	4024	4025	4026	4027	4028	4029	4030	4031
7700	4032	4033	4034	4035	4036	4037	4038	4039
7710	4040	4041	4042	4043	4044	4045	4046	4047
7720	4048	4049	4050	4051	4052	4053	4054	4055
7730	4056	4057	4058	4059	4060	4061	4062	4063
7740	4064	4065	4066	4067	4068	4069	4070	4071
7750	4072	4073	4074	4075	4076	4077	4078	4079
7760	4080	4081	4082	4083	4084	4085	4086	4087
7770	4088	4089	4090	4091	4092	4093	4094	4095

OCTAL-DECIMAL FRACTION CONVERSION TABLE

This table covers the entries from $(.000)_8$ to $(.377)_8$. For entries from $(.400)_8$ to $(.777)_8$, cognizance should be made of the fact that $(.400)_8$ is $(.500)_{10}$. Hence if $(.637)_8$ is desired, find $(.237)_8$ in table, namely, $(.310456)_{10}$ and add $(.50000)_{10}$ for $(.400)_8$. Thus

$(.637)_8$ = $(.237)_8$ + $(.400)_8$

    = $(.310456)_{10}$ + $(.50000)_{10}$

    = $(.810456)_{10}$.

OCTAL	DEC.	OCTAL	DEC.	OCTAL	DEC.	OCTAL	DEC.
.000	.000000	.100	.125000	.200	.250000	.300	.375000
.001	.001953	.101	.126953	.201	.251953	.301	.376953
.002	.003906	.102	.128906	.202	.253906	.302	.378906
.003	.005859	.103	.130859	.203	.255859	.303	.380859
.004	.007812	.104	.132812	.204	.257812	.304	.382812
.005	.009765	.105	.134765	.205	.259765	.305	.384765
.006	.011718	.106	.136718	.206	.261718	.306	.386718
.007	.013671	.107	.138671	.207	.263671	.307	.388671
.010	.015625	.110	.140625	.210	.265625	.310	.390625
.011	.017578	.111	.142578	.211	.267578	.311	.392578
.012	.019531	.112	.144531	.212	.269531	.312	.394531
.013	.021484	.113	.146484	.213	.271484	.313	.396484
.014	.023437	.114	.148437	.214	.273437	.314	.398437
.015	.025390	.115	.150390	.215	.275390	.315	.400490
.016	.027343	.116	.152343	.216	.277343	.316	.402343
.017	.029296	.117	.154296	.217	.279296	.317	.404296
.020	.031250	.120	.156250	.220	.281250	.320	.406250
.021	.033203	.121	.158203	.221	.283203	.321	.408203
.022	.035156	.122	.160156	.222	.285156	.322	.410156
.023	.037109	.123	.162109	.223	.287109	.323	.412109
.024	.039062	.124	.164062	.224	.289062	.324	.414062
.025	.041015	.125	.166015	.225	.291015	.325	.416015
.026	.042968	.126	.167968	.226	.292968	.326	.417968
.027	.044921	.127	.169921	.227	.294921	.327	.419921
.030	.046875	.130	.171875	.230	.294875	.330	.421875
.031	.048828	.131	.173828	.231	.298828	.331	.423828
.032	.050781	.132	.175781	.232	.300781	.332	.425781
.033	.052734	.133	.177734	.233	.302734	.333	.427734
.034	.054687	.134	.179687	.234	.304687	.334	.429687
.035	.056640	.135	.181640	.235	.306640	.335	.431640
.036	.058593	.136	.183593	.236	.308593	.336	.433593
.037	.060546	.137	.185546	.237	.310546	.337	.435546
.040	.062500	.140	.187500	.240	.312500	.340	.437500
.041	.064453	.141	.189453	.241	.314453	.341	.439453
.042	.066406	.142	.191406	.242	.316406	.342	.441406
.043	.068359	.143	.193359	.243	.318359	.343	.443359
.044	.070312	.144	.195312	.244	.320312	.344	.445312
.045	.072265	.145	.197265	.245	.322265	.345	.447265
.046	.074218	.146	.199218	.246	.324218	.346	.449218
.047	.076171	.147	.201171	.247	.326171	.347	.451171
.050	.078125	.150	.203125	.250	.328125	.350	.453125
.051	.080078	.151	.205078	.251	.330078	.351	.455078
.052	.082031	.152	.207031	.252	.332031	.352	.457031
.053	.083984	.153	.208984	.253	.333984	.353	.458984
.054	.085937	.154	.210937	.254	.335937	.354	.460937
.055	.087890	.155	.212890	.255	.337890	.355	.462890
.056	.089843	.156	.214843	.256	.339843	.356	.464843
.057	.091796	.157	.216796	.257	.341796	.357	.466796
.060	.093750	.160	.218750	.260	.343750	.360	.468750
.061	.095703	.161	.220703	.261	.345703	.361	.470703
.062	.097656	.162	.222656	.262	.347656	.362	.472656
.063	.099609	.163	.224609	.263	.349609	.363	.474609
.064	.101562	.164	.226562	.264	.351562	.364	.476562
.065	.103515	.165	.228515	.265	.353515	.365	.478515
.066	.105468	.166	.230468	.266	.355468	.366	.480468
.067	.107421	.167	.232421	.267	.357421	.367	.482421
.070	.109375	.170	.234375	.270	.359375	.370	.484375
.071	.111328	.171	.236328	.271	.361328	.371	.486328
.072	.113281	.172	.238281	.272	.363281	.372	.488281
.073	.115234	.173	.240234	.273	.365234	.373	.490234
.074	.117187	.174	.242187	.274	.367187	.374	.492187
.075	.119140	.175	.244140	.275	.369140	.375	.494140
.076	.121093	.176	.246093	.276	.371093	.376	.496093
.077	.123046	.177	.248046	.277	.373046	.377	.498046

OCTAL-DECIMAL FRACTION CONVERSION TABLE (Continued)

OCTAL	DEC.	OCTAL	DEC.	OCTAL	DEC.	OCTAL	DEC.
.000000	.000000	.000100	.000244	.000200	.000488	.000300	.000732
.000001	.000004	.000101	.000247	.000201	.000492	.000301	.000736
.000002	.000007	.000102	.000251	.000202	.000495	.000302	.000740
.000003	.000011	.000103	.000255	.000203	.000499	.000303	.000743
.000004	.000015	.000104	.000259	.000204	.000503	.000304	.000747
.000005	.000019	.000105	.000263	.000205	.000507	.000305	.000751
.000006	.000022	.000106	.000267	.000206	.000511	.000306	.000755
.000007	.000026	.000107	.000270	.000207	.000514	.000307	.000759
.000010	.000030	.000110	.000274	.000210	.000518	.000310	.000762
.000011	.000034	.000111	.000278	.000211	.000522	.000311	.000766
.000012	.000038	.000112	.000282	.000212	.000526	.000312	.000770
.000013	.000041	.000113	.000286	.000213	.000530	.000313	.000774
.000014	.000045	.000114	.000289	.000214	.000534	.000314	.000778
.000015	.000049	.000115	.000293	.000215	.000537	.000315	.000782
.000016	.000053	.000116	.000297	.000216	.000541	.000316	.000785
.000017	.000057	.000117	.000301	.000217	.000545	.000317	.000789
.000020	.000061	.000120	.000305	.000220	.000549	.000320	.000793
.000021	.000064	.000121	.000308	.000221	.000553	.000321	.000797
.000022	.000068	.000122	.000312	.000222	.000556	.000322	.000801
.000023	.000072	.000123	.000316	.000223	.000560	.000323	.000805
.000024	.000076	.000124	.000320	.000224	.000564	.000324	.000808
.000025	.000080	.000125	.000324	.000225	.000568	.000325	.000812
.000026	.000083	.000126	.000328	.000226	.000572	.000326	.000816
.000027	.000087	.000127	.000331	.000227	.000576	.000327	.000820
.000030	.000091	.000130	.000335	.000230	.000579	.000330	.000823
.000031	.000095	.000131	.000339	.000231	.000583	.000331	.000827
.000032	.000099	.000132	.000343	.000232	.000587	.000332	.000831
.000033	.000102	.000133	.000347	.000233	.000591	.000333	.000835
.000034	.000106	.000134	.000350	.000234	.000595	.000334	.000839
.000035	.000110	.000135	.000354	.C00235	.000598	.000335	.000843
.000036	.000114	.000136	.000358	.000236	.000602	.000336	.000846
.000037	.000118	.000137	.000362	.000237	.000606	.000337	.000850
.000040	.000122	.000140	.000366	.000240	.000610	.000340	.000854
.000041	.000125	.000141	.000370	.000241	.000614	.000341	.000858
.000042	.000129	.000142	.000373	.000242	.000617	.000342	.000862
.000043	.000133	000143	.000377	.000243	.000621	.000343	.000865
.000044	.000137	.000144	.000381	.000244	.000625	.000344	.000869
.000045	.000141	.000145	.000385	.000245	.000629	.000345	.000873
.000046	.000144	.000146	.000389	.000246	.000633	.000346	.000877
.000047	.000148	.000147	.000392	.000247	.000637	.000347	.000881
.000050	.000152	.000150	.000396	.000250	.000640	.000350	.000885
.000051	.000156	.000151	.000400	.000251	.000644	.000351	.000888
.000052	.000160	.000152	.000404	.000252	.000648	.000352	.000892
.000053	.000164	.000153	.000408	.000253	.000652	.000353	.000896
.000054	.000167	.000154	.000411	.000254	.000656	.000354	.000900
.000055	.000171	.000155	.000415	.000255	.000659	.000355	.000904
.000056	.000175	.000156	.000419	.000256	.000663	.000356	.000907
.000057	.000179	.000157	.000423	.000257	.000667	.000357	.000911
.000060	.000183	.000160	.000427	.000260	.000671	.000360	.000915
.000061	.000186	.000161	.000431	.000261	.000675	.000361	.000919
.000062	.000190	.000162	.000434	.000262	.000679	.000362	.000923
.000063	.000194	.000163	.000438	.000263	.000682	.000363	.000926
.000064	.000198	.000164	.000442	.000264	.000686	.000364	.000930
.000065	.000202	.000165	.000446	.000265	.000690	.000365	.000934
.000066	.000205	.000166	.000450	.000266	.000694	.000366	.000938
.000067	.000209	.000167	.000453	.000267	.000698	.000367	.000942
.000070	.000213	.000170	.000457	.000270	.000701	.000370	.000946
.000071	.000217	.000171	.000461	.000271	.000705	.000371	.000949
.000072	.000221	.000172	.000465	.000272	.000709	.000372	.000953
.000073	.000225	.000173	.000469	.000273	.000713	.000373	.000957
.000074	.000228	.000174	.000473	.000274	.000717	.000374	.000961
.000075	.000232	.000175	.000476	.000275	.000720	.000375	.000965
.000076	.000326	.000176	.000480	.000276	.000724	.000376	.000968
.000077	.000240	.000177	.000484	.000277	.000728	.000377	.000972

OCTAL-DECIMAL FRACTION CONVERSION TABLE (Continued)

OCTAL	DEC.	OCTAL	DEC.	OCTAL	DEC.	OCTAL	DEC.
.000400	.000976	.000500	.001220	.000600	.001464	.000700	.001708
.000401	.000980	.000501	.001224	.000601	.001468	.000701	.001712
.000402	.000984	.000502	.001228	.000602	.001472	.000702	.001716
.000403	.000988	.000503	.001232	.000603	.001476	.000703	.001720
.000404	.000991	.000504	.001235	.000604	.001480	.000704	.001724
.000405	.000995	.000505	.001239	.000605	.001483	.000705	.001728
.000406	.000999	.000506	.001243	.000606	.001487	.000706	.001731
.000407	.001003	.000507	.001247	.000607	.001491	.000707	.001735
.000410	.001007	.000510	.001251	.000610	.001495	.000710	.001739
.000411	.001010	.000511	.001255	.000611	.001499	.000711	.001743
.000412	.001014	.000512	.001258	.000612	.001502	.000712	.001747
.000413	.001018	.000513	.001262	.000613	.001506	.000713	.001750
.000414	.001022	.000514	.001266	.000614	.001510	.000714	.001754
.000415	.001026	.000515	.001270	.000615	.001514	.000715	.001758
.000416	.001029	.000516	.001274	.000616	.001518	.000716	.001762
.000417	.001033	.000517	.001277	.000617	.001522	.000717	.001766
.000420	.001037	.000520	.001281	.000620	.001525	.000720	.001770
.000421	.001041	.000521	.001285	.000621	.001529	.000721	.001733
.000422	.001045	.000522	.001289	.000622	.001533	.000722	.001777
.000423	.001049	.000523	.001293	.000623	.001537	.000723	.001781
.000424	.001052	.000524	.001296	.000624	.001541	.000724	.001785
.000425	.001056	.000525	.001300	.000625	.001544	.000725	.001789
.000426	.001060	.000526	.001304	.000626	.001548	.000726	.001792
.000427	.001064	.000527	.001308	.000627	.001552	.000727	.001796
.000430	.001068	.000530	.001312	.000630	.001556	.000730	.001800
.000431	.001071	.000531	.001316	.000631	.001560	.000731	.001804
.000432	.001075	.000532	.001319	.000632	.001564	.000732	.001808
.000433	.001079	.000533	.001323	.000633	.001567	.000733	.001811
.000434	.001083	.000534	.001327	.000634	.001571	.000734	.001815
.000435	.001087	.000535	.001331	.000635	.001575	.000735	.001819
.000436	.001091	.000536	.001335	.000636	.001579	.000736	.001823
.000437	.001094	.000537	.001338	.000637	.001583	.000737	.001827
.000440	.001098	.000540	.001342	.000640	.001586	.000740	.001831
.000441	.001102	.000541	.001346	.000641	.001590	.000741	.001834
.000442	.001106	.000542	.001350	.000642	.001594	.000742	.001838
.000443	.001110	.000543	.001354	.000643	.001598	.000743	.001842
.000444	.001113	.000544	.001358	.000644	.001602	.000744	.001846
.000445	.001117	.000545	.001361	.000645	.001605	.000745	.001850
.000446	.001121	.000546	.001365	.000646	.001609	.000746	.001853
.000447	.001125	.000547	.001369	.000647	.001613	.000747	.001857
.000450	.001129	.000550	.001373	.000650	.001617	.000750	.001861
.000451	.001132	.000551	.001377	.000651	.001621	.000751	.001865
.000452	.001136	.000552	.001380	.000652	.001625	.000752	.001869
.000453	.001140	.000553	.001384	.000653	.001628	.000753	.001873
.000454	.001144	.000554	.001388	.000654	.001632	.000754	.001876
.000455	.001148	.000555	.001392	.000655	.001636	.000755	.001880
.000456	.001152	.000556	.001396	.000656	.001640	.000756	.001884
.000457	.001155	.000557	.001399	.000657	.001644	.000757	.001888
.000460	.001159	.000560	.001403	.000660	.001647	.000760	.001892
.000461	.001163	.000561	.001407	.000661	.001651	.000761	.001895
.000462	.001167	.000562	.001411	.000662	.001655	.000762	.001899
.000463	.001171	.000563	.001415	.000663	.001659	.000763	.001903
.000464	.001174	.000564	.001419	.000664	.001663	.000764	.001907
.000465	.001178	.000565	.001422	.000665	.001667	.000765	.001911
.000466	.001182	.000566	.001426	.000666	.001670	.000766	.001914
.000467	.001186	.000567	.001430	.000667	.001674	.000767	.001918
.000470	.001190	.000570	.001434	.000670	.001678	.000770	.001922
.000471	.001194	.000571	.001438	.000671	.001682	.000771	.001926
.000472	.001197	.000572	.001441	.000672	.001686	.000772	.001930
.000473	.001201	.000573	.001445	.000673	.001689	.000773	.001934
.000474	.001205	.000574	.001449	.000674	.001693	.000774	.001937
.000475	.001209	.000575	.001453	.000675	.001697	.000775	.001941
.000476	.001213	.000576	.001457	.000676	.001701	.000776	.001945
.000477	.001216	.000577	.001461	.000677	.001705	.000777	.001949

I. HEXADECIMAL AND DECIMAL DIRECT CONVERSION TABLE

The following tables aid in converting hexadecimal (base 16) numbers to decimal, and the reverse. Note that the base 16 digits for the decimal values 10–15 are represented by the letters A–F, respectively.

This table provides direct conversion of decimal and hexadecimal numbers in these ranges:

HEXADECIMAL	DECIMAL
1000	4096
2000	8192
3000	12288
4000	16384
5000	20480
6000	24576
7000	28672
8000	32768
9000	36864
A000	40960
B000	45056
C000	49152
D000	53248
E000	57344
F000	61440

HEXADECIMAL 000 to FFF   DECIMAL 0000 to 4095

For numbers outside the range of the table, add the following values to the table figures:

	0	1	2	3	4	5	6	7	8	9	A	B	C	D	E	F
00_	0000	0001	0002	0003	0004	0005	0006	0007	0008	0009	0010	0011	0012	0013	0014	0015
01_	0016	0017	0018	0019	0020	0021	0022	0023	0024	0025	0026	0027	0028	0029	0030	0031
02_	0032	0033	0034	0035	0036	0037	0038	0039	0040	0041	0042	0043	0044	0045	0046	0047
03_	0048	0049	0050	0051	0052	0053	0054	0055	0056	0057	0058	0059	0060	0061	0062	0063
04_	0064	0065	0066	0067	0068	0069	0070	0071	0072	0073	0074	0075	0076	0077	0078	0079
05_	0080	0081	0082	0083	0084	0085	0086	0087	0088	0089	0090	0091	0092	0093	0094	0095
06_	0096	0097	0098	0099	0100	0101	0102	0103	0104	0105	0106	0107	0108	0109	0110	0111
07_	0112	0113	0114	0115	0116	0117	0118	0119	0120	0121	0122	0123	0124	0125	0126	0127
08_	0128	0129	0130	0131	0132	0133	0134	0135	0136	0137	0138	0139	0140	0141	0142	0143
09_	0144	0145	0146	0147	0148	0149	0150	0151	0152	0153	0154	0155	0156	0157	0158	0159
0A_	0160	0161	0162	0163	0164	0165	0166	0167	0168	0169	0170	0171	0172	0173	0174	0175
0B_	0176	0177	0178	0179	0180	0181	0182	0183	0184	0185	0186	0187	0188	0189	0190	0191
0C_	0192	0193	0194	0195	0196	0197	0198	0199	0200	0201	0202	0203	0204	0205	0206	0207
0D_	0208	0209	0210	0211	0212	0213	0214	0215	0216	0217	0218	0219	0220	0221	0222	0223
0E_	0224	0225	0226	0227	0228	0229	0230	0231	0232	0233	0234	0235	0236	0237	0238	0239
0F_	0240	0241	0242	0243	0244	0245	0246	0247	0248	0249	0250	0251	0252	0253	0254	0255
10_	0256	0257	0258	0259	0260	0261	0262	0263	0264	0265	0266	0267	0268	0269	0270	0271
11_	0272	0273	0274	0275	0276	0277	0278	0279	0280	0281	0282	0283	0284	0285	0286	0287
12_	0288	0289	0290	0291	0292	0293	0294	0295	0296	0297	0298	0299	0300	0301	0302	0303
13_	0304	0305	0306	0307	0308	0309	0310	0311	0312	0313	0314	0315	0316	0317	0318	0319
14_	0320	0321	0322	0323	0324	0325	0326	0327	0328	0329	0330	0331	0332	0333	0334	0335
15_	0336	0337	0338	0339	0340	0341	0342	0343	0344	0345	0346	0347	0348	0349	0350	0351
16_	0352	0353	0354	0355	0356	0357	0358	0359	0360	0361	0362	0363	0364	0365	0366	0367
17_	0368	0369	0370	0371	0372	0373	0374	0375	0376	0377	0378	0379	0380	0381	0382	0383
18_	0384	0385	0386	0387	0388	0389	0390	0391	0392	0393	0394	0395	0396	0397	0398	0399
19_	0400	0401	0402	0403	0404	0405	0406	0407	0408	0409	0410	0411	0412	0413	0414	0415
1A_	0416	0417	0418	0419	0420	0421	0422	0423	0424	0425	0426	0427	0428	0429	0430	0431
1B_	0432	0433	0434	0435	0436	0437	0438	0439	0440	0441	0442	0443	0444	0445	0446	0447
1C_	0448	0449	0450	0451	0452	0453	0454	0455	0456	0457	0458	0459	0460	0461	0462	0463
1D_	0464	0465	0466	0467	0468	0469	0470	0471	0472	0473	0474	0475	0476	0477	0478	0479
1E_	0480	0481	0482	0483	0484	0485	0486	0487	0488	0489	0490	0491	0492	0493	0494	0495
1F_	0496	0497	0498	0499	0500	0501	0502	0503	0504	0505	0506	0507	0508	0509	0510	0511

DIRECT CONVERSION TABLE (Continued)

	0	1	2	3	4	5	6	7	8	9	A	B	C	D	E	F
20__	0512	0513	0514	0515	0516	0517	0518	0519	0520	0521	0522	0523	0524	0525	0526	0527
21__	0528	0529	0530	0531	0532	0533	0534	0535	0536	0537	0538	0539	0540	0541	0542	0543
22__	0544	0545	0546	0547	0548	0549	0550	0551	0552	0553	0554	0555	0556	0557	0558	0559
23__	0560	0561	0562	0563	0564	0565	0566	0567	0568	0569	0570	0571	0572	0573	0574	0575
24__	0576	0577	0578	0579	0580	0581	0582	0583	0584	0585	0586	0587	0588	0589	0590	0591
25__	0592	0593	0594	0595	0596	0597	0598	0599	0600	0601	0602	0603	0604	0605	0606	0607
26__	0608	0609	0610	0611	0612	0613	0614	0615	0616	0617	0618	0619	0620	0621	0622	0623
27__	0624	0625	0626	0627	0628	0629	0630	0631	0632	0633	0634	0635	0636	0637	0638	0639
28__	0640	0641	0642	0643	0644	0645	0646	0647	0648	0649	0650	0651	0652	0653	0654	0655
29__	0656	0657	0658	0659	0660	0661	0662	0663	0664	0665	0666	0667	0668	0669	0670	0671
2A__	0672	0673	0674	0675	0676	0677	0678	0679	0680	0681	0682	0683	0684	0685	0686	0687
2B__	0688	0689	0690	0691	0692	0693	0694	0695	0696	0697	0698	0699	0700	0701	0702	0703
2C__	0704	0705	0706	0707	0708	0709	0710	0711	0712	0713	0714	0715	0716	0717	0718	0719
2D__	0720	0721	0722	0723	0724	0725	0726	0727	0728	0729	0730	0731	0732	0733	0734	0735
2E__	0736	0737	0738	0739	0740	0741	0742	0743	0744	0745	0746	0747	0748	0749	0750	0751
2F__	0752	0753	0754	0755	0756	0757	0758	0759	0760	0761	0762	0763	0764	0765	0766	0767
30__	0768	0769	0770	0771	0772	0773	0774	0775	0776	0777	0778	0779	0780	0781	0782	0783
31__	0784	0785	0786	0787	0788	0789	0790	0791	0792	0793	0794	0795	0796	0797	0798	0799
32__	0800	0801	0802	0803	0804	0805	0806	0807	0808	0809	0810	0811	0812	0813	0814	0815
33__	0816	0817	0818	0819	0820	0821	0822	0823	0824	0825	0826	0827	0828	0829	0830	0831
34__	0832	0833	0834	0835	0836	0837	0838	0839	0840	0841	0842	0843	0844	0845	0846	0847
35__	0848	0849	0850	0851	0852	0853	0854	0855	0856	0857	0858	0859	0860	0861	0862	0863
36__	0864	0865	0866	0867	0868	0869	0870	0871	0872	0873	0874	0875	0876	0877	0878	0879
37__	0880	0881	0882	0883	0884	0885	0886	0887	0888	0889	0890	0891	0892	0893	0894	0895
38__	0896	0897	0898	0899	0900	0901	0902	0903	0904	0905	0906	0907	0908	0909	0910	0911
39__	0912	0913	0914	0915	0916	0917	0918	0919	0920	0921	0922	0923	0924	0925	0926	0927
3A__	0928	0929	0930	0931	0932	0933	0934	0935	0936	0937	0938	0939	0940	0941	0942	0943
3B__	0944	0945	0946	0947	0948	0949	0950	0951	0952	0953	0954	0955	0956	0957	0958	0959
3C__	0960	0961	0962	0963	0964	0965	0966	0967	0968	0969	0970	0971	0972	0973	0974	0975
3D__	0976	0977	0978	0979	0980	0981	0982	0983	0984	0985	0986	0987	0988	0989	0990	0991
3E__	0992	0993	0994	0995	0996	0997	0998	0999	1000	1001	1002	1003	1004	1005	1006	1007
3F__	1008	1009	1010	1011	1012	1013	1014	1015	1016	1017	1018	1019	1020	1021	1022	1023
40__	1024	1025	1026	1027	1028	1029	1030	1031	1032	1033	1034	1035	1036	1037	1038	1039
41__	1040	1041	1042	1043	1044	1045	1046	1047	1048	1049	1050	1051	1052	1053	1054	1055
42__	1056	1057	1058	1059	1060	1061	1062	1063	1064	1065	1066	1067	1068	1069	1070	1071
43__	1072	1073	1074	1075	1076	1077	1078	1079	1080	1081	1082	1083	1084	1085	1086	1087
44__	1088	1089	1090	1091	1092	1093	1094	1095	1096	1097	1098	1099	1100	1101	1102	1103
45__	1104	1105	1106	1107	1108	1109	1110	1111	1112	1113	1114	1115	1116	1117	1118	1119
46__	1120	1121	1122	1123	1124	1125	1126	1127	1128	1129	1130	1131	1132	1133	1134	1135
47__	1136	1137	1138	1139	1140	1141	1142	1143	1144	1145	1146	1147	1148	1149	1150	1151
48__	1152	1153	1154	1155	1156	1157	1158	1159	1160	1161	1162	1163	1164	1165	1166	1167
49__	1168	1169	1170	1171	1172	1173	1174	1175	1176	1177	1178	1179	1180	1181	1182	1183
4A__	1184	1185	1186	1187	1188	1189	1190	1191	1192	1193	1194	1195	1196	1197	1198	1199
4B__	1200	1201	1202	1203	1204	1205	1206	1207	1208	1209	1210	1211	1212	1213	1214	1215
4C__	1216	1217	1218	1219	1220	1221	1222	1223	1224	1225	1226	1227	1228	1229	1230	1231
4D__	1232	1233	1234	1235	1236	1237	1238	1239	1240	1241	1242	1243	1244	1245	1246	1247
4E__	1248	1249	1250	1251	1252	1253	1254	1255	1256	1257	1258	1259	1260	1261	1262	1263
4F__	1264	1265	1266	1267	1268	1269	1270	1271	1272	1273	1274	1275	1276	1277	1278	1279
50__	1280	1281	1282	1283	1284	1285	1286	1287	1288	1289	1290	1291	1292	1293	1294	1295
51__	1296	1297	1298	1299	1300	1301	1302	1303	1304	1305	1306	1307	1308	1309	1310	1311
52__	1312	1313	1314	1315	1316	1317	1318	1319	1320	1321	1322	1323	1324	1325	1326	1327
53__	1328	1329	1330	1331	1332	1333	1334	1335	1336	1337	1338	1339	1340	1341	1342	1343
54__	1344	1345	1346	1347	1348	1349	1350	1351	1352	1353	1354	1355	1356	1357	1358	1359
55__	1360	1361	1362	1363	1364	1365	1366	1367	1368	1369	1370	1371	1372	1373	1374	1375
56__	1376	1377	1378	1379	1380	1381	1382	1383	1384	1385	1386	1387	1388	1389	1390	1391
57__	1392	1393	1394	1395	1396	1397	1398	1399	1400	1401	1402	1403	1404	1405	1406	1407
58__	1408	1409	1410	1411	1412	1413	1414	1415	1416	1417	1418	1419	1420	1421	1422	1423
59__	1424	1425	1426	1427	1428	1429	1430	1431	1432	1433	1434	1435	1436	1437	1438	1439
5A__	1440	1441	1442	1443	1444	1445	1446	1447	1448	1449	1450	1451	1452	1453	1454	1455
5B__	1456	1457	1458	1459	1460	1461	1462	1463	1464	1465	1466	1467	1468	1469	1470	1471
5C__	1472	1473	1474	1475	1476	1477	1478	1479	1480	1481	1482	1483	1484	1485	1486	1487
5D__	1488	1489	1490	1491	1492	1493	1494	1495	1496	1497	1498	1499	1500	1501	1502	1503
5E__	1504	1505	1506	1507	1508	1509	1510	1511	1512	1513	1514	1515	1516	1517	1518	1519
5F__	1520	1521	1522	1523	1524	1525	1526	1527	1528	1529	1530	1531	1532	1533	1534	1535

COMBINATORIAL ANALYSIS

DIRECT CONVERSION TABLE (Continued)

	0	1	2	3	4	5	6	7	8	9	A	B	C	D	E	F
60__	1536	1537	1538	1539	1540	1541	1542	1543	1544	1545	1546	1547	1548	1549	1550	1551
61__	1552	1553	1554	1555	1556	1557	1558	1559	1560	1561	1562	1563	1564	1565	1566	1567
62__	1568	1569	1570	1571	1572	1573	1574	1575	1576	1577	1578	1579	1580	1581	1582	1583
63__	1584	1585	1586	1587	1588	1589	1590	1591	1592	1593	1594	1595	1596	1597	1598	1599
64__	1600	1601	1602	1603	1604	1605	1606	1607	1608	1609	1610	1611	1612	1613	1614	1615
65__	1616	1617	1618	1619	1620	1621	1622	1623	1624	1625	1626	1627	1628	1629	1630	1631
66__	1632	1633	1634	1635	1636	1637	1638	1639	1640	1641	1642	1643	1644	1645	1646	1647
67__	1648	1649	1650	1651	1652	1653	1654	1655	1656	1657	1658	1659	1660	1661	1662	1663
68__	1664	1665	1666	1667	1668	1669	1670	1671	1672	1673	1674	1675	1676	1677	1678	1679
69__	1680	1681	1682	1683	1684	1685	1686	1687	1688	1689	1690	1691	1692	1693	1694	1695
6A__	1696	1697	1698	1699	1700	1701	1702	1703	1704	1705	1706	1707	1708	1709	1710	1711
6B__	1712	1713	1714	1715	1716	1717	1718	1719	1720	1721	1722	1723	1724	1725	1726	1727
6C__	1728	1729	1730	1731	1732	1733	1734	1735	1736	1737	1738	1739	1740	1741	1742	1743
6D__	1744	1745	1746	1747	1748	1749	1750	1751	1752	1753	1754	1755	1756	1757	1758	1759
6E__	1760	1761	1762	1763	1764	1765	1766	1767	1768	1769	1770	1771	1772	1773	1774	1775
6F__	1776	1777	1778	1779	1780	1781	1782	1783	1784	1785	1786	1787	1788	1789	1790	1791
70__	1792	1793	1794	1795	1796	1797	1798	1799	1800	1801	1802	1803	1804	1805	1806	1807
71__	1808	1809	1810	1811	1812	1813	1814	1815	1816	1817	1818	1819	1820	1821	1822	1823
72__	1824	1825	1826	1827	1828	1829	1830	1831	1832	1833	1834	1835	1836	1837	1838	1839
73__	1840	1841	1842	1843	1844	1845	1846	1847	1848	1849	1850	1851	1852	1853	1854	1855
74__	1856	1857	1858	1859	1860	1861	1862	1863	1864	1865	1866	1867	1868	1869	1870	1871
75__	1872	1873	1874	1875	1876	1877	1878	1879	1880	1881	1882	1883	1884	1885	1886	1887
76__	1888	1889	1890	1891	1892	1893	1894	1895	1896	1897	1898	1899	1900	1901	1902	1903
77__	1904	1905	1906	1907	1908	1909	1910	1911	1912	1913	1914	1915	1916	1917	1918	1919
78__	1920	1921	1922	1923	1924	1925	1926	1927	1928	1929	1930	1931	1932	1933	1934	1935
79__	1936	1937	1938	1939	1940	1941	1942	1943	1944	1945	1946	1947	1948	1949	1950	1951
7A__	1952	1953	1954	1955	1956	1957	1958	1959	1960	1961	1962	1963	1964	1965	1966	1967
7B__	1968	1969	1970	1971	1972	1973	1974	1975	1976	1977	1978	1979	1980	1981	1982	1983
7C__	1984	1985	1986	1987	1988	1989	1990	1991	1992	1993	1994	1995	1996	1997	1998	1999
7D__	2000	2001	2002	2003	2004	2005	2006	2007	2008	2009	2010	2011	2012	2013	2014	2015
7E__	2016	2017	2018	2019	2020	2021	2022	2023	2024	2025	2026	2027	2028	2029	2030	2031
7F__	2032	2033	2034	2035	2036	2037	2038	2039	2040	2041	2042	2043	2044	2045	2046	2047
80__	2048	2049	2050	2051	2052	2053	2054	2055	2056	2057	2058	2059	2060	2061	2062	2063
81__	2064	2065	2066	2067	2068	2069	2070	2071	2072	2073	2074	2075	2076	2077	2078	2079
82__	2080	2081	2082	2083	2084	2085	2086	2087	2088	2089	2090	2091	2092	2093	2094	2095
83__	2096	2097	2098	2099	2100	2101	2102	2103	2104	2105	2106	2107	2108	2109	2110	2111
84__	2112	2113	2114	2115	2116	2117	2118	2119	2120	2121	2122	2123	2124	2125	2126	2127
85__	2128	2129	2130	2131	2132	2133	2134	2135	2136	2137	2138	2139	2140	2141	2142	2143
86__	2144	2145	2146	2147	2148	2149	2150	2151	2152	2153	2154	2155	2156	2157	2158	2159
87__	2160	2161	2162	2163	2164	2165	2166	2167	2168	2169	2170	2171	2172	2173	2174	2175
88__	2176	2177	2178	2179	2180	2181	2182	2183	2184	2185	2186	2187	2188	2189	2190	2191
89__	2192	2193	2194	2195	2196	2197	2198	2199	2200	2201	2202	2203	2204	2205	2206	2207
8A__	2208	2209	2210	2211	2212	2213	2214	2215	2216	2217	2218	2219	2220	2221	2222	2223
8B__	2224	2225	2226	2227	2228	2229	2230	2231	2232	2233	2234	2235	2236	2237	2238	2239
8C__	2240	2241	2242	2243	2244	2245	2246	2247	2248	2249	2250	2251	2252	2253	2254	2255
8D__	2256	2257	2258	2259	2260	2261	2262	2263	2264	2265	2266	2267	2268	2269	2270	2271
8E__	2272	2273	2274	2275	2276	2277	2278	2279	2280	2281	2282	2283	2284	2285	2286	2287
8F__	2288	2289	2290	2291	2292	2293	2294	2295	2296	2297	2298	2299	2300	2301	2302	2303
90__	2304	2305	2306	2307	2308	2309	2310	2311	2312	2313	2314	2315	2316	2317	2318	2319
91__	2320	2321	2322	2323	2324	2325	2326	2327	2328	2329	2330	2331	2332	2333	2334	2335
92__	2336	2337	2338	2339	2340	2341	2342	2343	2344	2345	2346	2347	2348	2349	2350	2351
93__	2352	2353	2354	2355	2356	2357	2358	2359	2360	2361	2362	2363	2364	2365	2366	2367
94__	2368	2369	2370	2371	2372	2373	2374	2375	2376	2377	2378	2379	2380	2381	2382	2383
95__	2384	2385	2386	2387	2388	2389	2390	2391	2392	2393	2394	2395	2396	2397	2398	2399
96__	2400	2401	2402	2403	2404	2405	2406	2407	2408	2409	2410	2411	2412	2413	2414	2415
97__	2416	2417	2418	2419	2420	2421	2422	2423	2424	2425	2426	2427	2428	2429	2430	2431
98__	2432	2433	2434	2435	2436	2437	2438	2439	2440	2441	2442	2443	2444	2445	2446	2447
99__	2448	2449	2450	2451	2452	2453	2454	2455	2456	2457	2458	2459	2460	2461	2462	2463
9A__	2464	2465	2466	2467	2468	2469	2470	2471	2472	2473	2474	2475	2476	2477	2478	2479
9B__	2480	2481	2482	2483	2484	2485	2486	2487	2488	2489	2490	2491	2492	2493	2494	2495
9C__	2496	2497	2498	2499	2500	2501	2502	2503	2504	2505	2506	2507	2508	2509	2510	2511
9D__	2512	2513	2514	2515	2516	2517	2518	2519	2520	2521	2522	2523	2524	2525	2526	2527
9E__	2528	2529	2530	2531	2532	2533	2534	2535	2536	2537	2538	2539	2540	2541	2542	2543
9F__	2544	2545	2546	2547	2548	2549	2550	2551	2552	2553	2554	2555	2556	2557	2558	2559

DIRECT CONVERSION TABLE (Continued)

	0	1	2	3	4	5	6	7	8	9	A	B	C	D	E	F
A0__	2560	2561	2562	2563	2564	2565	2566	2567	2568	2569	2570	2571	2572	2573	2574	2575
A1__	2576	2577	2578	2579	2580	2581	2582	2583	2584	2585	2586	2587	2588	2589	2590	2591
A2__	2592	2593	2594	2595	2596	2597	2598	2599	2600	2601	2602	2603	2604	2605	2606	2607
A3__	2608	2609	2610	2611	2612	2613	2614	2615	2616	2617	2618	2619	2620	2621	2622	2623
A4__	2624	2625	2626	2627	2628	2629	2630	2631	2632	2633	2634	2635	2636	2637	2638	2639
A5__	2640	2641	2642	2643	2644	2645	2646	2647	2648	2649	2650	2651	2652	2653	2654	2655
A6__	2656	2657	2658	2659	2660	2661	2662	2663	2664	2665	2666	2667	2668	2669	2670	2671
A7__	2672	2673	2674	2675	2676	2677	2678	2679	2680	2681	2682	2683	2684	2685	2686	2687
A8__	2688	2689	2690	2691	2692	2693	2694	2695	2696	2697	2698	2699	2700	2701	2702	2703
A9__	2704	2705	2706	2707	2708	2709	2710	2711	2712	2713	2714	2715	2716	2717	2718	2719
AA__	2720	2721	2722	2723	2724	2725	2726	2727	2728	2729	2730	2731	2732	3733	2734	2735
AB__	2736	2737	2738	2739	2740	2741	2742	2743	2744	2745	2746	2747	2748	2749	2750	2751
AC__	2752	2753	2754	2755	2756	2757	2758	2759	2760	2761	2762	2763	2764	2765	2766	2767
AD__	2768	2769	2770	2771	2772	2773	2774	2775	2776	2777	2778	2779	2780	2781	2782	2783
AE__	2784	2785	2786	2787	2788	2789	2790	2791	2792	2793	2794	2795	2796	2797	2798	2799
AF__	2800	2801	2802	2803	2804	2805	2806	2807	2808	2809	2810	2811	2812	2813	2814	2815
B0__	2816	2817	2818	2819	2820	2821	2822	2823	2824	2825	2826	2827	2828	2829	2830	2831
B1__	2832	2833	2834	2835	2836	2837	2838	2839	2840	2841	2842	2843	2844	2845	2846	2847
B2__	2848	2849	2850	2851	2852	2853	2854	2855	2856	2857	2858	2859	2860	2861	2862	2863
B3__	2864	2865	2866	2867	2868	2869	2870	2871	2872	2873	2874	2875	2876	2877	2878	2879
B4__	2880	2881	2882	2883	2884	2885	2886	2887	2888	2889	2890	2891	2892	2893	2894	2895
B5__	2896	2897	2898	2899	2900	2901	2902	2903	2904	2905	2906	2907	2908	2909	2910	2911
B6__	2912	2913	2914	2915	2916	2917	2918	2919	2920	2921	2922	2923	2924	2925	2926	2927
B7__	2928	2929	2930	2931	2932	2933	2934	2935	2936	2937	2938	2939	2940	2941	2942	2943
B8__	2944	2945	2946	2947	2948	2949	2950	2951	2952	2953	2954	2955	2956	2957	2958	2959
B9__	2960	2961	2962	2963	2964	2965	2966	2967	2968	2969	2970	2971	2972	2973	2974	2975
BA__	2976	2977	2978	2979	2980	2981	2982	2983	2984	2985	2986	2987	2988	2989	2990	2991
BB__	2992	2993	2994	2995	2996	2997	2998	2999	3000	3001	3002	3003	3004	3005	3006	3007
BC__	3008	3009	3010	3011	3012	3013	3014	3015	3016	3017	3018	3019	3020	3021	3022	3023
BD__	3024	3025	3026	3027	3028	3029	3030	3031	3032	3033	3034	3035	3036	3037	3038	3039
BE__	3040	3041	3042	3043	3044	3045	3046	3047	3048	3049	3050	3051	3052	3053	3054	3055
BF__	3056	3057	3058	3059	3060	3061	3062	3063	3064	3065	3066	3067	3068	3069	3070	3071
C0__	3072	3073	3074	3075	3076	3077	3078	3079	3080	3081	3082	3083	3084	3085	3086	3087
C1__	3088	3089	3090	3091	3092	3093	3094	3095	3096	3097	3098	3099	3100	3101	3102	3103
C2__	3104	3105	3106	3107	3108	3109	3110	3111	3112	3113	3114	3115	3116	3117	3118	3119
C3__	3120	3121	3122	3123	3124	3125	3126	3127	3128	3129	3130	3131	3132	3133	3134	3135
C4__	3136	3137	3138	3139	3140	3141	3142	3143	3144	3145	3146	3147	3148	3149	3150	3151
C5__	3152	3153	3154	3155	3156	3157	3158	3159	3160	3161	3162	3613	3164	3165	3166	3167
C6__	3168	3169	3170	3171	3172	3173	3174	3175	3176	3177	3178	3179	3180	3181	3182	3183
C7__	3184	3185	3186	3187	3188	3189	3190	3191	3192	3193	3194	3195	3196	3197	3198	3199
C8__	3200	3201	3202	3203	3204	3205	3206	3207	3208	3209	3210	3211	3212	3213	3214	3215
C9__	3216	3217	3218	3219	3220	3221	3222	3223	3224	3225	3226	3227	3228	3229	3230	3231
CA__	3232	3233	3234	3235	3236	3237	3238	3239	3240	3241	3242	3243	3244	3245	3246	3247
CB__	3248	3249	3250	3251	3252	3253	3254	3255	3256	3257	3258	3259	3260	3261	3262	3263
CC__	3264	3265	3266	3267	3268	3269	3270	3271	3272	3273	3274	3275	3276	3277	3278	3279
CD__	3280	3281	3282	3283	3284	3285	3286	3287	3288	3289	3290	3291	3292	3293	3294	3295
CE__	3296	3297	3298	3299	3300	3301	3302	3303	3304	3305	3306	3307	3308	3309	3310	3311
CF__	3312	3313	3314	3315	3316	3317	3318	3319	3320	3321	3322	3323	3324	3325	3326	3327
D0__	3328	3329	3330	3331	3332	3333	3334	3335	3336	3337	3338	3339	3340	3341	3342	3343
D1__	3344	3345	3346	3347	3348	3349	3350	3351	3352	3353	3354	3355	3356	3357	3358	3359
D2__	3360	3361	3362	3363	3364	3365	3366	3367	3368	3369	3370	3371	3372	3373	3374	3375
D3__	3376	3377	3378	3379	3380	3381	3382	3383	3384	3385	3386	3387	3388	3389	3390	3391
D4__	3392	3393	3394	3395	3396	3397	3398	3399	3400	3401	3402	3403	3404	3405	3406	3407
D5__	3408	3409	3410	3411	3412	3413	3414	3415	3416	3417	3418	3419	3420	3421	3422	3423
D6__	3424	3425	3426	3427	3428	3429	3430	3431	3432	3433	3434	3435	3436	3437	3438	3439
D7__	3440	3441	3442	3443	3444	3445	3446	3447	3448	3449	3450	3451	3452	3453	3454	3455
D8__	3456	3457	3458	3459	3460	3461	3462	3463	3464	3465	3466	3467	3468	3469	3470	3471
D9__	3472	3473	3474	3475	3476	3477	3478	3479	3480	3481	3482	3483	3484	3485	3486	3487
DA__	3488	3489	3490	3491	3492	3493	3494	3495	3496	3497	3498	3499	3500	3501	3502	3503
DB__	3504	3505	3506	3507	3508	3509	3510	3511	3512	3513	3514	3515	3516	3517	3518	3519
DC__	3520	3521	3522	3523	3524	3525	3526	3527	3528	3529	3530	3531	3532	3533	3534	3535
DD__	3536	3537	3538	3539	3540	3541	3542	3543	3544	3545	3546	3547	3548	3549	3550	3551
DE__	3552	3553	3554	3555	3556	3557	3558	3559	3560	3561	3562	3563	3564	3565	3566	3567
DF__	3568	3569	3570	3571	3572	3573	3574	3575	3576	3577	3578	3579	3580	3581	3582	3583

DIRECT CONVERSION TABLE (Continued)

	0	1	2	3	4	5	6	7	8	9	A	B	C	D	E	F
E0__	3584	3585	3586	3587	3588	3589	3590	3591	3592	3593	3594	3595	3596	3597	3598	3599
E1__	3600	3601	3602	3603	3604	3605	3606	3607	3608	3609	3610	3611	3612	3613	3614	3615
E2__	3616	3617	3618	3619	3620	3621	3622	3623	3624	3625	3626	3627	3628	3629	3630	3631
E3__	3632	3633	3634	3635	3636	3637	3638	3639	3640	3641	3642	3643	3644	3645	3646	3647
E4__	3648	3649	3650	3651	3652	3653	3654	3655	3656	3657	3658	3659	3660	3661	3662	3663
E5__	3664	3665	3666	3667	3668	3669	3670	3671	3672	3673	3674	3675	3676	3677	3678	3679
E6__	3680	3681	3682	3683	3684	3685	3686	3687	3688	3689	3690	3691	3692	3693	3694	3695
E7__	3696	3697	3698	3699	3700	3701	3702	3703	3704	3705	3706	3707	3708	3709	3710	3711
E8__	3712	3713	3714	3715	3716	3717	3718	3719	3720	3721	3722	3723	3724	3725	3726	3727
E9__	3728	3729	3730	3731	3732	3733	3734	3735	3736	3737	3738	3739	3740	3741	3742	3743
EA__	3744	3745	3746	3747	3748	3749	3750	3751	3752	3753	3754	3755	3756	3757	3758	3759
EB__	3760	3761	3762	3763	3764	3765	3766	3767	3768	3769	3770	3771	3772	3773	3774	3775
EC__	3776	3777	3778	3779	3780	3781	3782	3783	3784	3785	3786	3787	3788	3789	3790	3791
ED__	3792	3793	3794	3795	3796	3797	3798	3799	3800	3801	3802	3803	3804	3805	3806	3807
EE__	3808	3809	3810	3811	3812	3813	3814	3815	3816	3817	3818	3819	3820	3821	3822	3823
EF__	3824	3825	3826	3827	3828	3829	3830	3831	3832	3833	3834	3835	3836	3837	3838	3839
F0__	3840	3841	3842	3843	3844	3845	3846	3847	3848	3849	3850	3851	3852	3853	3854	3855
F1__	3856	3857	3858	3859	3860	3861	3862	3863	3864	3865	3866	3867	3868	3869	3870	3871
F2__	3872	3873	3874	3875	3876	3877	3878	3879	3880	3881	3882	3883	3884	3885	3886	3887
F3__	3888	3889	3890	3891	3892	3893	3894	3895	3896	3897	3898	3899	3900	3901	3902	3903
F4__	3904	3905	3906	3907	3908	3909	3910	3911	3912	3913	3914	3915	3916	3917	3918	3919
F5__	3920	3921	3922	3923	3924	3925	3926	3927	3928	3929	3930	3931	3932	3933	3934	3935
F6__	3936	3937	3938	3939	3940	3941	3942	3943	3944	3945	3946	3947	3948	3949	3950	3951
F7__	3952	3953	3954	3955	3956	3957	3958	3959	3960	3961	3962	3963	3964	3965	3966	3967
F8__	3968	3969	3970	3971	3972	3973	3974	3975	3976	3977	3978	3979	3980	3981	3982	3983
F9__	3984	3985	3986	3987	3988	3989	3990	3991	3992	3993	3994	3995	3996	3997	3998	3999
FA__	4000	4001	4002	4003	4004	4005	4006	4007	4008	4009	4010	4011	4012	4013	4014	4015
FB__	4016	4017	4018	4019	4020	4021	4022	4023	4024	4025	4026	4027	4028	4029	4030	4031
FC__	4032	4033	4034	4035	4036	4037	4038	4039	4040	4041	4042	4043	4044	4045	4046	4047
FD__	4048	4049	4050	4051	4052	4053	4054	4055	4056	4057	4058	4059	4060	4061	4062	4063
FE__	4064	4065	4066	4067	4068	4069	4070	4071	4072	4073	4074	4075	4076	4077	4078	4079
FF__	4080	4081	4082	4083	4084	4085	4086	4087	4088	4089	4090	4091	4092	4093	4094	4095

II. HEXADECIMAL AND DECIMAL INTEGER CONVERSION TABLE

	8		7		6		5		4		3		2		1
Hex	Decimal	Hex	Decimal	Hex	Decimal	Hex	Decimal	Hex	Decimal	Hex	Decimal	Hex	Decimal	Hex	Decimal
0	0	0	0	0	0	0	0	0	0	0	0	0	0	0	0
1	268,435,456	1	16,777,216	1	1,048,576	1	65,536	1	4,096	1	256	1	16	1	1
2	536,870,912	2	33,554,432	2	2,097,152	2	131,072	2	8,192	2	512	2	32	2	2
3	805,306,368	3	50,331,648	3	3,145,728	3	196,608	3	12,288	3	768	3	48	3	3
4	1,073,741,824	4	67,108,864	4	4,194,304	4	262,144	4	16,384	4	1,024	4	64	4	4
5	1,342,177,280	5	83,886,080	5	5,242,880	5	327,680	5	20,480	5	1,280	5	80	5	5
6	1,610,612,736	6	100,663,296	6	6,291,456	6	393,216	6	24,576	6	1,536	6	96	6	6
7	1,879,048,192	7	117,440,512	7	7,340,032	7	458,752	7	28,672	7	1,792	7	112	7	7
8	2,147,483,648	8	134,217,728	8	8,388,608	8	524,288	8	32,768	8	2,048	8	128	8	8
9	2,415,919,104	9	150,994,944	9	9,437,184	9	589,824	9	36,864	9	2,304	9	144	9	9
A	2,684,354,560	A	167,772,160	A	10,485,760	A	655,360	A	40,960	A	2,560	A	160	A	10
B	2,952,790,016	B	184,549,376	B	11,534,336	B	720,896	B	45,056	B	2,816	B	176	B	11
C	3,221,225,472	C	201,326,592	C	12,582,912	C	786,432	C	49,152	C	3,072	C	192	C	12
D	3,489,660,928	D	218,103,808	D	13,631,488	D	851,968	D	53,248	D	3,328	D	208	D	13
E	3,758,096,384	E	234,881,024	E	14,680,064	E	917,504	E	57,344	E	3,584	E	224	E	14
F	4,026,531,840	F	251,658,240	F	15,728,640	F	983,040	F	61,440	F	3,840	F	240	F	15
	8		7		6		5		4		3		2		1

INTEGER CONVERSION TABLE (Continued)

TO CONVERT HEXADECIMAL TO DECIMAL

1. Locate the column of decimal numbers corresponding to the left-most digit or letter of the hexadecimal; select from this column and record the number that corresponds to the position of the hexadecimal digit or letter.

2. Repeat step 1 for the next (second from the left) position.

3. Repeat step 1 for the units (third from the left) position.

4. Add the numbers selected from the table to form the decimal number.

To convert integer numbers greater than the capacity of table, use the techniques below:

HEXADECIMAL TO DECIMAL

Successive cumulative multiplication from left to right, adding units position.

Example: $D34_{16} = 3380_{10}$

$$
\begin{array}{rr}
D = & 13 \\
& \times 16 \\
\hline
& 208 \\
3 = & +3 \\
\hline
& 211 \\
& \times 16 \\
\hline
& 3376 \\
4 = & +4 \\
\hline
& 3380
\end{array}
$$

EXAMPLE	
Conversion of Hexadecimal Value	D34
1. D	3328
2. 3	48
3. 4	4
4. Decimal	3380

TO CONVERT DECIMAL TO HEXADECIMAL

1. (a) Select from the table the highest decimal number that is equal to or less than the number to be converted.
(b) Record the hexadecimal of the column containing the selected number.
(c) Subtract the selected decimal from the number to be converted.

2. Using the remainder from step 1(c) repeat all of step 1 to develop the second position of the hexadecimal (and a remainder).

3. Using the remainder from step 2 repeat all of step 1 to develop the units position of the hexadecimal.

4. Combine terms to form the hexadecimal number.

EXAMPLE	
Conversion of Decimal Value	3380
1. D	-3328
	52
2. 3	-48
	4
3. 4	-4
4. Hexadecimal	D34

DECIMAL TO HEXADECIMAL

Divide and collect the remainder in reverse order.

Example: $3380_{10} = X_{16}$

$$
\begin{array}{ll}
16\ \underline{|\ 3380} & \text{remainder} \\
16\ \underline{|\ 211} & 4 \\
16\ \underline{|\ 13} & 3 \\
& D
\end{array}
$$

$$3380_{10} = D34_{16}$$

INTEGER CONVERSION TABLE (Continued)

POWERS OF 16 TABLE

Example: $268,435,456_{10} = (2.68435456 \times 10^8)_{10} = 1000\ 0000_{16} = (10^7)_{16}$

16^n	n
1	0
16	1
256	2
4 096	3
65 536	4
1 048 576	5
16 777 216	6
268 435 456	7
4 294 967 296	8
68 719 476 736	9
1 099 511 627 776	10 = A
17 592 186 044 416	11 = B
281 474 976 710 656	12 = C
4 503 599 627 370 496	13 = D
72 057 594 037 927 936	14 = E
1 152 921 504 606 846 976	15 = F

Decimal Values

III. HEXADECIMAL AND DECIMAL FRACTION CONVERSION TABLE

1		2			3				4				
Hex	Decimal	Hex	Decimal		Hex	Decimal			Hex	Decimal Equivalent			
.0	.0000	.00	.0000	0000	.000	.0000	0000	0000	.0000	.0000	0000	0000	0000
.1	.0625	.01	.0039	0625	.001	.0002	4414	0625	.0001	.0000	1525	8789	0625
.2	.1250	.02	.0078	1250	.002	.0004	8828	1250	.0002	.0000	3051	7578	1250
.3	.1875	.03	.0117	1875	.003	.0007	3242	1875	.0003	.0000	4577	6367	1875
.4	.2500	.04	.0156	2500	.004	.0009	7656	2500	.0004	.0000	6103	5156	2500
.5	.3125	.05	.0195	3125	.005	.0012	2070	3125	.0005	.0000	7629	3945	3125
.6	.3750	.06	.0234	3750	.006	.0014	6484	3750	.0006	.0000	9155	2734	3750
.7	.4375	.07	.0273	4375	.007	.0017	0898	4375	.0007	.0001	0681	1523	4375
.8	.5000	.08	.0312	5000	.008	.0019	5312	5000	.0008	.0001	2207	0312	5000
.9	.5625	.09	.0351	5625	.009	.0021	9726	5625	.0009	.0001	3732	9101	5625
.A	.6250	.0A	.0390	6250	.00A	.0024	4140	6250	.000A	.0001	5258	7890	6250
.B	.6875	.0B	.0429	6875	.00B	.0026	8554	6875	.000B	.0001	6784	6679	6875
.C	.7500	.0C	.0468	7500	.00C	.0029	2968	7500	.000C	.0001	8310	5468	7500
.D	.8125	.0D	.0507	8125	.00D	.0031	7382	8125	.000D	.0001	9836	4257	8125
.E	.8750	.0E	.0546	8750	.00E	.0034	1796	8750	.000E	.0002	1362	3046	8750
.F	.9375	.0F	.0585	9375	.00F	.0036	6210	9375	.000F	.0002	2888	1835	9375
1		2			3				4				

TO CONVERT .ABC HEXADECIMAL TO DECIMAL

Find .A   in position 1   .6250
Find .0B   in position 2   .0429 6875
Find .00C in position 3   .0029 2968 7500
  .ABC Hex is equal to   .6708 9843 7500

FRACTION CONVERSION TABLE (Continued)

TO CONVERT .13 DECIMAL TO HEXADECIMAL

1. Find .i250 next lowest to	.1300	
subtract	− .1250	= .2 Hex
2. Find .0039 0625 next lowest to	.0050 0000	
	− .0039 0625	= .01
3. Find .0009 7656 2500	.0010 9375 0000	
	− .0009 7656 2500	= .004
4. Find .0001 0681 1523 4375	.0001 1718 7500 0000	
	− .0001 0681 1523 4375	= .0007
	.0000 1037 5976 5625	= .2147 Hex

5. 13 Decimal is approximately equal to ⟶

To convert fractions beyond the capacity of table, use techniques below:

HEXADECIMAL FRACTION TO DECIMAL

Convert the hexadecimal fraction to its decimal equivalent using the same technique as for integer numbers.
Divide the results by 16^n (n is the number of fraction
positions).

Example: $.8A7_{16} = .540771_{10}$

$$8A7_{16} = 2215_{10}$$
$$16^3 = 4096$$

$$4096 \overline{)2215.000000} = .540771$$

DECIMAL FRACTION TO HEXADECIMAL

Collect integer parts of product in the order of calculation.

Example: $.5408_{10} = .8A7_{16}$

$$
\begin{array}{r}
.5408 \\
\times 16 \\
\hline
8 \leftarrow \boxed{8}\,.6528 \\
\times 16 \\
\hline
A \leftarrow \boxed{10}\,.4448 \\
\times 16 \\
\hline
7 \leftarrow \boxed{7}\,.1168 \\
\end{array}
$$

HEXADECIMAL ADDITION AND SUBTRACTION TABLE

Example: $6 + 2 = 8$, $8 - 2 = 6$, and $8 - 6 = 2$

	1	2	3	4	5	6	7	8	9	A	B	C	D	E	F
1	02	03	04	05	06	07	08	09	0A	0B	0C	0D	0E	0F	10
2	03	04	05	06	07	08	09	0A	0B	0C	0D	0E	0F	10	11
3	04	05	06	07	08	09	0A	0B	0C	0D	0E	0F	10	11	12
4	05	06	07	08	09	0A	0B	0C	0D	0E	0F	10	11	12	13
5	06	07	08	09	0A	0B	0C	0D	0E	0F	10	11	12	13	14
6	07	08	09	0A	0B	0C	0D	0E	0F	10	11	12	13	14	15
7	08	09	0A	0B	0C	0D	0E	0F	10	11	12	13	14	15	16
8	09	0A	0B	0C	0D	0E	0F	10	11	12	13	14	15	16	17
9	0A	0B	0C	0D	0E	0F	10	11	12	13	14	15	16	17	18
A	0B	0C	0D	0E	0F	10	11	12	13	14	15	16	17	18	19
B	0C	0D	0E	0F	10	11	12	13	14	15	16	17	18	19	1A
C	0D	0E	0F	10	11	12	13	14	15	16	17	18	19	1A	1B
D	0E	0F	10	11	12	13	14	15	16	17	18	19	1A	1B	1C
E	0F	10	11	12	13	14	15	16	17	18	19	1A	1B	1C	1D
F	10	11	12	13	14	15	16	17	18	19	1A	1B	1C	1D	1E

HEXADECIMAL MULTIPLICATION TABLE

Example: $2 \times 4 = 08$, $F \times 2 = 1E$

	1	2	3	4	5	6	7	8	9	A	B	C	D	E	F
1	01	02	03	04	05	06	07	08	09	0A	0B	0C	0D	0E	0F
2	02	04	06	08	0A	0C	0E	10	12	14	16	18	1A	1C	1E
3	03	06	09	0C	0F	12	15	18	1B	1E	21	24	27	2A	2D
4	04	08	0C	10	14	18	1C	20	24	28	2C	30	34	38	3C
5	05	0A	0F	14	19	1E	23	28	2D	32	37	3C	41	46	4B
6	06	0C	12	18	1E	24	2A	30	36	3C	42	48	4E	54	5A
7	07	0E	15	1C	23	2A	31	38	3F	46	4D	54	5B	62	69
08	08	10	18	20	28	30	38	40	48	50	58	60	68	70	78
9	09	12	1B	24	2D	36	3F	48	51	5A	63	6C	75	7E	87
A	0A	14	1E	28	32	3C	46	50	5A	64	6E	78	82	8C	96
B	0B	16	21	2C	37	42	4D	58	63	6E	79	84	8F	9A	A5
C	0C	18	24	30	3C	48	54	60	6C	78	84	90	9C	A8	B4
D	0D	1A	27	34	41	4E	5B	68	75	82	8F	9C	A9	B6	C3
E	0E	1C	2A	38	46	54	62	70	7E	8C	9A	A8	B6	C4	D2
F	0F	1E	2D	3C	4B	5A	69	78	87	96	A5	B4	C3	D2	E1

TOTIENT FUNCTION $\phi(n)$

Introductory facts

$\phi(n)$ is the number of integers not exceeding and relatively prime to n.

σ_k is the sum of the k'th powers of divisors of n.

σ_0 is usually denoted by $d(n)$ and specifies the number of divisors of n.

For example if $n = 10$, then the divisors are 1, 2, 5, 10 and the sum of the first powers is 18, i.e. $\sigma_0 = d(10) = 4$; $\sigma_1 = 18$; $\phi(10) = 4$.

n	$\phi(n)$	σ_0	σ_1	n	$\phi(n)$	σ_0	σ_1	n	$\phi(n)$	σ_0	σ_1	n	$\phi(n)$	σ_0	σ_1
1	1	1	1	41	40	2	42	81	54	5	121	121	110	3	133
2	1	2	3	42	12	8	96	82	40	4	126	122	60	4	186
3	2	2	4	43	42	2	44	83	82	2	84	123	80	4	168
4	2	3	7	44	20	6	84	84	24	12	224	124	60	6	224
5	4	2	6	45	24	6	78	85	64	4	108	125	100	4	156
6	2	4	12	46	22	4	72	86	42	4	132	126	36	12	312
7	6	2	8	47	46	2	48	87	56	4	120	127	126	2	128
8	4	4	15	48	16	10	124	88	40	8	180	128	64	8	255
9	6	3	13	49	42	3	57	89	88	2	90	129	84	4	176
10	4	4	18	50	20	6	93	90	24	12	234	130	48	8	252
11	10	2	12	51	32	4	72	91	72	4	112	131	130	2	132
12	4	6	28	52	24	6	98	92	44	6	168	132	40	12	336
13	12	2	14	53	52	2	54	93	60	4	128	133	108	4	160
14	6	4	24	54	18	8	120	94	46	4	144	134	66	4	204
15	8	4	24	55	40	4	72	95	72	4	120	135	72	8	240
16	8	5	31	56	24	8	120	96	32	12	252	136	64	8	270
17	16	2	18	57	36	4	80	97	96	2	98	137	136	2	138
18	6	6	39	58	28	4	90	98	42	6	171	138	44	8	288
19	18	2	20	59	58	2	60	99	60	6	156	139	138	2	140
20	8	6	42	60	16	12	168	100	40	9	217	140	48	12	336
21	12	4	32	61	60	2	62	101	100	2	102	141	92	4	192
22	10	4	36	62	30	4	96	102	32	8	216	142	70	4	216
23	22	2	24	63	36	6	104	103	102	2	104	143	120	4	168
24	8	8	60	64	32	7	127	104	48	8	210	144	48	15	403
25	20	3	31	65	48	4	84	105	48	8	192	145	112	4	180
26	12	4	42	66	20	8	144	106	52	4	162	146	72	4	222
27	18	4	40	67	66	2	68	107	106	2	108	147	84	6	228
28	12	6	56	68	32	6	126	108	36	12	280	148	72	6	266
29	28	2	30	69	44	4	96	109	108	2	110	149	148	2	150
30	8	8	72	70	24	8	144	110	40	8	216	150	40	12	372
31	30	2	32	71	70	2	72	111	72	4	152	151	150	2	152
32	16	6	63	72	24	12	195	112	48	10	248	152	72	8	300
33	20	4	48	73	72	2	74	113	112	2	114	153	96	6	234
34	16	4	54	74	36	4	114	114	36	8	240	154	60	8	288
35	24	4	48	75	40	6	124	115	88	4	144	155	120	4	192
36	12	9	91	76	36	6	140	116	56	6	210	156	48	12	392
37	36	2	38	77	60	4	96	117	72	6	182	157	156	2	158
38	18	4	60	78	24	8	168	118	58	4	180	158	78	4	240
39	24	4	56	79	78	2	80	119	96	4	144	159	104	4	216
40	16	8	90	80	32	10	186	120	32	16	360	160	64	12	378

TOTIENT FUNCTION $\phi(n)$ (Continued)

n	$\phi(n)$	σ_0	σ_1	n	$\phi(n)$	σ_0	σ_1	n	$\phi(n)$	σ_0	σ_1	n	$\phi(n)$	σ_0	σ_1
161	132	4	192	211	210	2	212	261	168	6	390	311	310	2	312
162	54	10	363	212	104	6	378	262	130	4	396	312	96	16	840
163	162	2	164	213	140	4	288	263	262	2	264	313	312	2	314
164	80	6	294	214	106	4	324	264	80	16	720	314	156	4	474
165	80	8	288	215	168	4	264	265	208	4	324	315	144	12	624
166	82	4	252	216	72	16	600	266	108	8	480	316	156	6	560
167	166	2	168	217	180	4	256	267	176	4	360	317	316	2	318
168	48	16	480	218	108	4	330	268	132	6	476	318	104	8	648
169	156	3	183	219	144	4	296	269	268	2	270	319	280	4	360
170	64	8	324	220	80	12	504	270	72	16	720	320	128	14	762
171	108	6	260	221	192	4	252	271	270	2	272	321	212	4	432
172	84	6	308	222	72	8	456	272	128	10	558	322	132	8	576
173	172	2	174	223	222	2	224	273	144	8	448	323	288	4	360
174	56	8	360	224	96	12	504	274	136	4	414	324	108	15	847
175	120	6	248	225	120	9	403	275	200	6	372	325	240	6	434
176	80	10	372	226	112	4	342	276	88	12	672	326	162	4	492
177	116	4	240	227	226	2	228	277	276	2	278	327	216	4	440
178	88	4	270	228	72	12	560	278	138	4	420	328	160	8	630
179	178	2	180	229	228	2	230	279	180	6	416	329	276	4	384
180	48	18	546	230	88	8	432	280	96	16	720	330	80	16	864
181	180	2	182	231	120	8	384	281	280	2	282	331	330	2	332
182	72	8	336	232	112	8	450	282	92	8	576	332	164	6	588
183	120	4	248	233	232	2	234	283	282	2	284	333	216	6	494
184	88	8	360	234	72	12	546	284	140	6	504	334	166	4	504
185	144	4	228	235	184	4	288	285	144	8	480	335	264	4	408
186	60	8	384	236	116	6	420	286	120	8	504	336	96	20	992
187	160	4	216	237	156	4	320	287	240	4	336	337	336	2	338
188	92	6	336	238	96	8	432	288	96	18	819	338	156	6	549
189	108	8	320	239	238	2	240	289	272	3	307	339	224	4	456
190	72	8	360	240	64	20	744	290	112	8	540	340	128	12	756
191	190	2	192	241	240	2	242	291	192	4	392	341	300	4	384
192	64	14	508	242	110	6	399	292	144	6	518	342	108	12	780
193	192	2	194	243	162	6	364	293	292	2	294	343	294	4	400
194	96	4	294	244	120	6	434	294	84	12	684	344	168	8	660
195	96	8	336	245	168	6	342	295	232	4	360	345	176	8	576
196	84	9	399	246	80	8	504	296	144	8	570	346	172	4	522
197	196	2	198	247	216	4	280	297	180	8	480	347	346	2	348
198	60	12	468	248	120	8	480	298	148	4	450	348	112	12	840
199	198	2	200	249	164	4	336	299	264	4	336	349	348	2	350
200	80	12	465	250	100	8	468	300	80	18	868	350	120	12	744
201	132	4	272	251	250	2	252	301	252	4	352	351	216	8	560
202	100	4	306	252	72	18	728	302	150	4	456	352	160	12	756
203	168	4	240	253	220	4	288	303	200	4	408	353	352	2	354
204	64	12	504	254	126	4	384	304	144	10	620	354	116	8	720
205	160	4	252	255	128	8	432	305	240	4	372	355	280	4	432
206	102	4	312	256	128	9	511	306	96	12	702	356	176	6	630
207	132	6	312	257	256	2	258	307	306	2	308	357	192	8	576
208	96	10	434	258	84	8	528	308	120	12	672	358	178	4	540
209	180	4	240	259	216	4	304	309	204	4	416	359	358	2	360
210	48	16	576	260	96	12	588	310	120	8	576	360	96	24	1170

TOTIENT FUNCTION $\phi(n)$ (Continued)

n	$\phi(n)$	σ_0	σ_1	n	$\phi(n)$	σ_0	σ_1	n	$\phi(n)$	σ_0	σ_1	n	$\phi(n)$	σ_0	σ_1
361	342	3	381	411	272	4	552	461	460	2	462	511	432	4	592
362	180	4	546	412	204	6	728	462	120	16	1152	512	256	10	1023
363	220	6	532	413	348	4	480	463	462	2	464	513	324	8	800
364	144	12	784	414	132	12	936	464	224	10	930	514	256	4	774
365	288	4	444	415	328	4	504	465	240	8	768	515	408	4	624
366	120	8	744	416	192	12	882	466	232	4	702	516	168	12	1232
367	366	2	368	417	276	4	560	467	466	2	468	517	460	4	576
368	176	10	744	418	180	8	720	468	144	18	1274	518	216	8	912
369	240	6	546	419	418	2	420	469	396	4	544	519	344	4	696
370	144	8	684	420	96	24	1344	470	184	8	864	520	192	16	1260
371	312	4	432	421	420	2	422	471	312	4	632	521	520	2	522
372	120	12	896	422	210	4	636	472	232	8	900	522	168	12	1170
373	372	2	374	423	276	6	624	473	420	4	528	523	522	2	524
374	160	8	648	424	208	8	810	474	156	8	960	524	260	6	924
375	200	8	624	425	320	6	558	475	360	6	620	525	240	12	992
376	184	8	720	426	140	8	864	476	192	12	1008	526	262	4	792
377	336	4	420	427	360	4	496	477	312	6	702	527	480	4	576
378	108	16	960	428	212	6	756	478	238	4	720	528	160	20	1488
379	378	2	380	429	240	8	672	479	478	2	480	529	506	3	553
380	144	12	840	430	168	8	792	480	128	24	1512	530	208	8	972
381	252	4	512	431	430	2	432	481	432	4	532	531	348	6	780
382	190	4	576	432	144	20	1240	482	240	4	726	532	216	12	1120
383	382	2	384	433	432	2	434	483	264	8	768	533	480	4	588
384	128	16	1020	434	180	8	768	484	220	9	931	534	176	8	1080
385	240	8	576	435	224	8	720	485	384	4	588	535	424	4	648
386	192	4	582	436	216	6	770	486	162	12	1092	536	264	8	1020
387	252	6	572	437	396	4	480	487	486	2	488	537	356	4	720
388	192	6	686	438	144	8	888	488	240	8	930	538	268	4	810
389	388	2	390	439	438	2	440	489	324	4	656	539	420	6	684
390	96	16	1008	440	160	16	1080	490	168	12	1026	540	144	24	1680
391	352	4	432	441	252	9	741	491	490	2	492	541	540	2	542
392	168	12	855	442	192	8	756	492	160	12	1176	542	270	4	816
393	260	4	528	443	442	2	444	493	448	4	540	543	360	4	728
394	196	4	594	444	144	12	1064	494	216	8	840	544	256	12	1134
395	312	4	480	445	352	4	540	495	240	12	936	545	432	4	660
396	120	18	1092	446	222	4	672	496	240	10	992	546	144	16	1344
397	396	2	398	447	296	4	600	497	420	4	576	547	546	2	548
398	198	4	600	448	192	14	1016	498	164	8	1008	548	272	6	966
399	216	8	640	449	448	2	450	499	498	2	500	549	360	6	806
400	160	15	961	450	120	18	1209	500	200	12	1092	550	200	12	1116
401	400	2	402	451	400	4	504	501	332	4	672	551	504	4	600
402	132	8	816	452	224	6	798	502	250	4	756	552	176	16	1440
403	360	4	448	453	300	4	608	503	502	2	504	553	468	4	640
404	200	6	714	454	226	4	684	504	144	24	1560	554	276	4	834
405	216	10	726	455	288	8	672	505	400	4	612	555	288	8	912
406	168	8	720	456	144	16	1200	506	220	8	864	556	276	6	980
407	360	4	456	457	456	2	458	507	312	6	732	557	556	2	558
408	128	16	1080	458	228	4	690	508	252	6	896	558	180	12	1248
409	408	2	410	459	288	8	720	509	508	2	510	559	504	4	616
410	160	8	756	460	176	12	1008	510	128	16	1296	560	192	20	1488

COMBINATORIAL ANALYSIS
TOTIENT FUNCTION $\phi(n)$ (Continued)

n	$\phi(n)$	σ_0	σ_1	n	$\phi(n)$	σ_0	σ_1	n	$\phi(n)$	σ_0	σ_1	n	$\phi(n)$	σ_0	σ_1
561	320	8	864	611	552	4	672	661	660	2	662	711	468	6	1040
562	280	4	846	612	192	18	1638	662	330	4	996	712	352	8	1350
563	562	2	564	613	612	2	614	663	384	8	1008	713	660	4	768
564	184	12	1344	614	306	4	924	664	328	8	1260	714	192	16	1728
565	448	4	684	615	320	8	1008	665	432	8	960	715	480	8	1008
566	282	4	852	616	240	16	1440	666	216	12	1482	716	356	6	1260
567	324	10	968	617	616	2	618	667	616	4	720	717	476	4	960
568	280	8	1080	618	204	8	1248	668	332	6	1176	718	358	4	1080
569	568	2	570	619	618	2	620	669	444	4	896	719	718	2	720
570	144	16	1440	620	240	12	1344	670	264	8	1224	720	192	30	2418
571	570	2	572	621	396	8	960	671	600	4	744	721	612	4	832
572	240	12	1176	622	310	4	936	672	192	24	2016	722	342	6	1143
573	380	4	768	623	528	4	720	673	672	2	674	723	480	4	968
574	240	8	1008	624	192	20	1736	674	336	4	1014	724	360	6	1274
575	440	6	744	625	500	5	781	675	360	12	1240	725	560	6	930
576	192	21	1651	626	312	4	942	676	312	9	1281	726	220	12	1596
577	576	2	578	627	360	8	960	677	676	2	678	727	726	2	728
578	272	6	921	628	312	6	1106	678	224	8	1368	728	288	16	1680
579	384	4	776	629	576	4	684	679	576	4	784	729	486	7	1093
580	224	12	1260	630	144	24	1872	680	256	16	1620	730	288	8	1332
581	492	4	672	631	630	2	632	681	452	4	912	731	672	4	792
582	192	8	1176	632	312	8	1200	682	300	8	1152	732	240	12	1736
583	520	4	648	633	420	4	848	683	682	2	684	733	732	2	734
584	288	8	1110	634	316	4	954	684	216	18	1820	734	366	4	1104
585	288	12	1092	635	504	4	768	685	544	4	828	735	336	12	1368
586	292	4	882	636	208	12	1512	686	294	8	1200	736	352	12	1512
587	586	2	588	637	504	6	798	687	456	4	920	737	660	4	816
588	168	18	1596	638	280	8	1080	688	336	10	1364	738	240	12	1638
589	540	4	640	639	420	6	936	689	624	4	756	739	738	2	740
590	232	8	1080	640	256	16	1530	690	176	16	1728	740	288	12	1596
591	392	4	792	641	640	2	642	691	690	2	692	741	432	8	1120
592	288	10	1178	642	212	8	1296	692	344	6	1218	742	312	8	1296
593	592	2	594	643	642	2	644	693	360	12	1248	743	742	2	744
594	180	16	1440	644	264	12	1344	694	346	4	1044	744	240	16	1920
595	384	8	864	645	336	8	1056	695	552	4	840	745	592	4	900
596	296	6	1050	646	288	8	1080	696	224	16	1800	746	372	4	1122
597	396	4	800	647	646	2	648	697	640	4	756	747	492	6	1092
598	264	8	1008	648	216	20	1815	698	348	4	1050	748	320	12	1512
599	598	2	600	649	580	4	720	699	464	4	936	749	636	4	864
600	160	24	1860	650	240	12	1302	700	240	18	1736	750	200	16	1872
601	600	2	602	651	360	8	1024	701	700	2	702	751	750	2	752
602	252	8	1056	652	324	6	1148	702	216	16	1680	752	368	10	1488
603	396	6	884	653	652	2	654	703	648	4	760	753	500	4	1008
604	300	6	1064	654	216	8	1320	704	320	14	1524	754	336	8	1260
605	440	6	798	655	520	4	792	705	368	8	1152	755	600	4	912
606	200	8	1224	656	320	10	1302	706	352	4	1062	756	216	24	2240
607	606	2	608	657	432	6	962	707	600	4	816	757	756	2	758
608	288	12	1260	658	276	8	1152	708	232	12	1680	758	378	4	1140
609	336	8	960	659	658	2	660	709	708	2	710	759	440	8	1152
610	240	8	1116	660	160	24	2016	710	280	8	1296	760	288	16	1800

TOTIENT FUNCTION $\phi(n)$ (Continued)

n	$\phi(n)$	σ_0	σ_1	n	$\phi(n)$	σ_0	σ_1	n	$\phi(n)$	σ_0	σ_1	n	$\phi(n)$	σ_0	σ_1
761	760	2	762	811	810	2	812	861	480	8	1344	911	910	2	912
762	252	8	1536	812	336	12	1680	862	430	4	1296	912	288	20	2480
763	648	4	880	813	540	4	1088	863	862	2	864	913	820	4	1008
764	380	6	1344	814	360	8	1368	864	288	24	2520	914	456	4	1374
765	384	12	1404	815	648	4	984	865	688	4	1044	915	480	8	1488
766	382	4	1152	816	256	20	2232	866	432	4	1302	916	456	6	1610
767	696	4	840	817	756	4	880	867	544	6	1228	917	780	4	1056
768	256	18	2044	818	408	4	1230	868	360	12	1792	918	288	16	2160
769	768	2	770	819	432	12	1456	869	780	4	960	919	918	2	920
770	240	16	1728	820	320	12	1764	870	224	16	2160	920	352	16	2160
771	512	4	1032	821	820	2	822	871	792	4	952	921	612	4	1232
772	384	6	1358	822	272	8	1656	872	432	8	1650	922	460	4	1386
773	772	2	774	823	822	2	824	873	576	6	1274	923	840	4	1008
774	252	12	1716	824	408	8	1560	874	396	8	1440	924	240	24	2688
775	600	6	992	825	400	12	1488	875	600	8	1248	925	720	6	1178
776	384	8	1470	826	348	8	1440	876	288	12	2072	926	462	4	1392
777	432	8	1216	827	826	2	828	877	876	2	878	927	612	6	1352
778	388	4	1170	828	264	18	2184	878	438	4	1320	928	448	12	1890
779	720	4	840	829	828	2	830	879	584	4	1176	929	928	2	930
780	192	24	2352	830	328	8	1512	880	320	20	2232	930	240	16	2304
781	700	4	864	831	552	4	1112	881	880	2	882	931	756	6	1140
782	352	8	1296	832	384	14	1778	882	252	18	2223	932	464	6	1638
783	504	8	1200	833	672	6	1026	883	882	2	884	933	620	4	1248
784	336	15	1767	834	276	8	1680	884	384	12	1764	924	466	4	1404
785	624	4	948	835	664	4	1008	885	464	8	1440	935	640	8	1296
786	260	8	1584	836	360	12	1680	886	442	4	1332	936	288	24	2730
787	786	2	788	837	540	8	1280	887	886	2	888	937	936	2	938
788	392	6	1386	838	418	4	1260	888	288	16	2280	938	396	8	1632
789	524	4	1056	839	838	2	840	889	756	4	1024	939	624	4	1256
790	312	8	1440	840	192	32	2880	890	352	8	1620	940	368	12	2016
791	672	4	912	841	812	3	871	891	540	10	1452	941	940	2	942
792	240	24	2340	842	420	4	1266	892	444	6	1568	942	312	8	1896
793	720	4	868	843	560	4	1128	893	828	4	960	943	880	4	1008
794	396	4	1194	844	420	6	1484	894	296	8	1800	944	464	10	1860
795	416	8	1296	845	624	6	1098	895	712	4	1080	945	432	16	1920
796	396	6	1400	846	276	12	1872	896	384	16	2040	946	420	8	1584
797	796	2	798	847	660	6	1064	897	528	8	1344	947	946	2	948
798	216	16	1920	848	416	10	1674	898	448	4	1350	948	312	12	2240
799	736	4	864	849	564	4	1136	899	840	4	960	949	864	4	1036
800	320	18	1953	850	320	12	1674	900	240	27	2821	950	360	12	1860
801	528	6	1170	851	792	4	912	901	832	4	972	951	632	4	1272
802	400	4	1206	852	280	12	2016	902	400	8	1512	952	384	16	2160
803	720	4	888	853	852	2	854	903	504	8	1408	953	952	2	954
804	264	12	1904	854	360	8	1488	904	448	8	1710	954	312	12	2106
805	528	8	1152	855	432	12	1560	905	720	4	1092	955	760	4	1152
806	360	8	1344	856	424	8	1620	906	300	8	1824	956	476	6	1680
807	536	4	1080	857	856	2	858	907	906	2	908	957	560	8	1440
808	400	8	1530	858	240	16	2016	908	452	6	1596	958	478	4	1440
809	808	2	810	859	858	2	860	909	600	6	1326	959	816	4	1104
810	216	20	2178	860	336	12	1848	910	288	16	2016	960	256	28	3048

COMBINATORIAL ANALYSIS

TOTIENT FUNCTION $\phi(n)$ (Continued)

n	$\phi(n)$	σ_0	σ_1	n	$\phi(n)$	σ_0	σ_1	n	$\phi(n)$	σ_0	σ_1	n	$\phi(n)$	σ_0	σ_1
961	930	3	993	971	970	2	972	981	648	6	1430	991	990	2	992
962	432	8	1596	972	324	18	2548	982	490	4	1476	992	480	12	2016
963	636	6	1404	973	828	4	1120	983	982	2	984	993	660	4	1328
964	480	6	1694	974	486	4	1464	984	320	16	2520	994	420	8	1728
965	768	4	1164	975	480	12	1736	985	784	4	1188	995	792	4	1200
966	264	16	2304	976	480	10	1922	986	448	8	1620	996	328	12	2352
967	966	2	968	977	976	2	978	987	552	8	1536	997	996	2	998
968	440	12	1995	978	324	8	1968	988	432	12	1960	998	498	4	1500
969	576	8	1440	979	880	4	1080	989	924	4	1056	999	648	8	1520
970	384	8	1764	980	336	18	2394	990	240	24	2808	1000	400	16	2340

From British Association for the Advancement of Science, Mathematical Tables, vol. VIII, Number-divisor tables, by permission of Cambridge University Press.

TABLES OF INDICES AND POWER RESIDUES

H. C. Williams, Ph.D.

1. Introduction

Let a and b be any two positive integers. If the largest integer that divides both a and b is unity, a and b are said to be *relatively prime*. If m is any positive integer, the *totient of m*, denoted by $\phi(m)$, is defined to be the number of positive integers less than m and relatively prime to m. If one writes

$$m = p_1^{\alpha_1} p_2^{\alpha_2} \ldots p_n^{\alpha_n},$$

where $p_1, p_2, \ldots, p_n$ are distinct primes, it can be shown that

$$\phi(m) = p_1^{\alpha_1 - 1} p_2^{\alpha_2 - 1} \ldots p_n^{\alpha_n - 1}(p_1 - 1)(p_2 - 1) \ldots (p_n - 1).$$

Two integers a and b are said to be *congruent modulo* an integer m if m is an integer divisor of $a - b$. This relation between a and b is denoted by

$$a \equiv b \pmod{m}.$$

If a is congruent to b modulo m and $0 \le b < m$, b is called the residue of a modulo m. a and b are said to be distinct modulo m if m is not an integer divisor of $a - b$. A well-known result is the

Theorem. If a and m ($\geqslant 0$) are relatively prime integers, then

$$a^{\phi(m)} \equiv 1 \pmod{m}.$$

Corollary. If p is a prime which is not a divisor of an integer a, then

$$a^{p-1} \equiv 1 \pmod{p}.$$

If a and m (> 0) are relatively prime integers, and μ is the least positive integer for which

$$a^\mu \equiv 1 \pmod{m},$$

μ is called the *exponent* to which a belongs modulo m. If the exponent to which a belongs modulo m is $\phi(m)$, a is defined to be a *primitive root* modulo m (or a primitive root of m).
Theorem. The only integers which possess primitive roots are 2, 4, p^n, $2p^n$, where p is an odd prime.

If m does have a primitive root, it has $\phi(\phi(m))$ distinct primitive roots modulo m.

Let p be any prime, and let g be any primitive root of p. To each integer a relatively prime to p there corresponds a unique integer i such that

$$a \equiv g^i \pmod{p} \qquad (0 < i < p-1).$$

i is called the *index* to base g of a modulo p. This is written

$$i = \text{ind}_g a.$$

For example, consider the prime 11 which has a primitive root $g = 2$. Construct the table below, where

$$r_i \equiv g^i \pmod{p} \qquad (0 < r_i < p).$$

i	0	1	2	3	4	5	6	7	8	9	10
r_i	1	2	4	8	5	10	9	7	3	6	1

Note that the bottom row runs through all possible residues modulo 11, except zero. The index, then, of any number in this row is the corresponding entry in the top row. That is, $\text{ind}_2 1 = 0$, $\text{ind}_2 2 = 1$, $\text{ind}_2 3 = 8$, $\text{ind}_2 4 = 2$, $\text{ind}_2 5 = 4$, $\text{ind}_2 6 = 9$, etc. Indices possess the following important properties (analogous to those of logarithms).

TABLES OF INDICES AND POWER RESIDUES (Continued)

(1) $\text{ind}_g 1 = 0$

(2) $\text{ind}_g(-1) = (p-1)/2$

(3) $\text{ind}_g(ab) \equiv \text{ind}_g a + \text{ind}_g b \pmod{p-1}$

(4) $\text{ind}_g a^n \equiv n \, \text{ind}_g a \pmod{p-1}$

(5) $\text{ind}_g a \equiv \text{ind}_g g' \cdot \text{ind}_{g'} a \pmod{p-1}$,

where g' is any other primitive root of p.

The *power residue* of an integer b to base g is simply the integer r such that

$$r \equiv g^b \pmod{p} \qquad (0 < r < p).$$

Since the power residue of $\text{ind}_g a$ is congruent to a modulo p, it is clear that the concept of indices and power residues is analogous to that of logarithms and antilogarithms.

2. Use of the tables

In the tables that follow, the indices and power residues are given for all primes less than 100. (A table of indices and power residues for all primes and prime powers less than 2000 is given in [1].) In the tables which follow, the base g for the indices and power residues is chosen as the smallest primitive root of p.

To determine the index or power residue of an integer a modulo p, look at the appropriate table for prime p and select the entry in the column under j and in the row under i, where

$$a \equiv 10i + j \pmod{p} \qquad (0 \le i, j \le 9).$$

For example, the index modulo 97 of 134 ($\equiv 37 \pmod{97}$) is the entry under the number 7 and across from the number 3. This is found to be 91.

Indices and power residues can be used to simplify number-theoretic calculations. The following two examples illustrate the use of indices and power residues.

Example. Find an integer congruent to

$$(134)^{92} (54)^{67} \quad \text{modulo (97)}.$$

Let

$$a \equiv (134)^{92} (54)^{67} \pmod{97};$$

then

$$\text{ind}_g a \equiv 92 \, \text{ind}_g 37 + 67 \, \text{ind}_g 54 \pmod{96}$$

$$\equiv 92\,(91) + 67\,(52) \pmod{96}$$

$$\equiv 48 \pmod{96}.$$

Hence

$$a \equiv g^{48} \equiv 96 \pmod{97}.$$

This is obtained by looking in the body of the table of indices under $p = 97$ and locating the index 48, and then reading the appropriate quadratic residue from the first column and top row.

Example. Find an integer x such that

$$44x^{21} \equiv 53 \pmod{73}.$$

If we take indices of both sides, we get

$$\text{ind}_g 44 + 21 \, \text{ind}_g x \equiv \text{ind}_g 53 \pmod{72}$$

$$71 + 21 \, \text{ind}_g x \equiv 53 \pmod{72}$$

$$21 \, \text{ind}_g x \equiv 54 \pmod{72}$$

$$7 \, \text{ind}_g x \equiv 18 \pmod{24}$$

TABLES OF INDICES AND POWER RESIDUES (Continued)

Multiplying by 7, we get

$$\text{ind}_g x \equiv 7(18) \equiv 6 \quad (\text{mod } 24).$$

Hence

$$x \equiv g^6, g^{30}, g^{54} \quad (\text{mod } 73)$$

and

$$x \equiv 3, 24, 46 \quad (\text{mod } 73).$$

REFERENCE

1. *A Table of Indices and Power Residues,* University of Oklahoma Mathematical Tables Project, W. W. Norton and Co., New York, N.Y., 1962.

INDICES FOR PRIMES 3 to 97

Prime 3
$g = 2$

	0	1	2	3	4	5	6	7	8	9
0		0	1							

Prime 5
$g = 2$

	0	1	2	3	4	5	6	7	8	9
0		0	1	3	2					

Prime 7
$g = 3$

	0	1	2	3	4	5	6	7	8	9
0		0	2	1	4	5	3			

Prime 11
$g = 2$

	0	1	2	3	4	5	6	7	8	9
0		0	1	8	2	4	9	7	3	6
1	5									

Prime 13
$g = 2$

	0	1	2	3	4	5	6	7	8	9
0		0	1	4	2	9	5	11	3	8
1	10	7	6							

Prime 17
$g = 3$

	0	1	2	3	4	5	6	7	8	9
0		0	14	1	12	5	15	11	10	2
1	3	7	13	4	9	6	8			

Prime 19
$g = 2$

	0	1	2	3	4	5	6	7	8	9
0		0	1	13	2	16	14	6	3	8
1	17	12	15	5	7	11	4	10	9	

Prime 23
$g = 5$

	0	1	2	3	4	5	6	7	8	9
0		0	2	16	4	1	18	19	6	10
1	3	9	20	14	21	17	8	7	12	15
2	5	13	11							

Prime 29
$g = 2$

	0	1	2	3	4	5	6	7	8	9
0		0	1	5	2	22	6	12	3	10
1	23	25	7	18	13	27	4	21	11	9
2	24	17	26	20	8	16	19	15	14	

Prime 31
$g = 3$

	0	1	2	3	4	5	6	7	8	9
0		0	24	1	18	20	25	28	12	2
1	14	23	19	11	22	21	6	7	26	4
2	8	29	17	27	13	10	5	3	16	9
3	14									

Prime 37
$g = 2$

	0	1	2	3	4	5	6	7	8
0		0	1	26	2	23	27	32	3
1	24	30	28	11	33	13	4	7	17
2	25	22	31	15	29	10	12	6	34
3	14	9	5	20	8	19	18		

Prime 41
$g = 6$

	0	1	2	3	4	5	6	7	8
0		0	26	15	12	22	1	39	38
1	8	3	27	31	25	37	24	33	16
2	34	14	29	36	13	4	17	5	11
3	23	28	10	18	19	21	2	32	35
4	20								

Prime 43
$g = 3$

	0	1	2	3	4	5	6	7	8
0		0	27	1	12	25	28	35	39
1	10	30	13	32	20	26	24	38	29
2	37	36	15	16	40	8	17	3	5
3	11	34	9	31	23	18	14	7	4
4	22	6	21						

Prime 47
$g = 5$

	0	1	2	3	4	5	6	7	8
0		0	18	20	36	1	38	32	8
1	19	7	10	11	4	21	26	16	12
2	37	6	25	5	28	2	29	14	22
3	39	3	44	27	34	33	30	42	17
4	9	15	24	13	43	41	23		

Prime 53
$g = 2$

	0	1	2	3	4	5	6	7	8
0		0	1	17	2	47	18	14	3
1	48	6	19	24	15	12	4	10	35
2	49	31	7	39	20	42	25	51	16
3	13	33	5	23	11	9	36	30	38
4	50	45	32	22	8	29	40	44	21
5	43	27	26						

Prime 59
$g = 2$

	0	1	2	3	4	5	6	7	8
0		0	1	50	2	6	51	18	3
1	7	25	52	45	19	56	4	40	43
2	8	10	26	15	53	12	46	34	20
3	57	49	5	17	41	24	44	55	39
4	9	14	11	33	27	48	16	23	54
5	13	32	47	22	35	31	21	30	29

Prime 61
$g = 2$

	0	1	2	3	4	5	6	7	8
0		0	1	6	2	22	7	49	3
1	23	15	8	40	50	28	4	47	13
2	24	55	16	57	9	44	41	18	51
3	29	59	5	21	48	11	14	39	27
4	25	54	56	43	17	34	58	20	10
5	45	53	42	33	19	37	52	32	36
6	30								

INDICES FOR PRIMES 3 to 97 (Continued)

Prime 67
$g = 2$

Indices

	0	1	2	3	4	5	6	7	8	9
0		0	1	39	2	15	40	23	3	12
1	16	59	41	19	24	54	4	64	13	10
2	17	62	60	28	42	30	20	51	25	44
3	55	47	5	32	65	38	14	22	11	58
4	18	53	63	9	61	27	29	50	43	46
5	31	37	21	57	52	8	26	49	45	36
6	56	7	48	35	6	34	33			

Prime 71
$g = 7$

Indices

	0	1	2	3	4	5	6	7	8	9
0		0	6	26	12	28	32	1	18	52
1	34	31	38	39	7	54	24	49	58	16
2	40	27	37	15	44	56	45	8	13	68
3	60	11	30	57	55	29	64	20	22	65
4	46	25	33	48	43	10	21	9	50	2
5	62	5	51	23	14	59	19	42	4	3
6	66	69	17	53	36	67	63	47	61	41
7	35									

Prime 73
$g = 5$

Indices

	0	1	2	3	4	5	6	7	8	9
0		0	8	6	16	1	14	33	24	12
1	9	55	22	59	41	7	32	21	20	62
2	17	39	63	46	30	2	67	18	49	35
3	15	11	40	61	29	34	28	64	70	65
4	25	4	47	51	71	13	54	31	38	66
5	10	27	3	53	26	56	57	68	43	5
6	23	58	19	45	48	60	69	50	37	52
7	42	44	36							

Prime 79
$g = 3$

Indices

	0	1	2	3	4	5	6	7	8	9
0		0	4	1	8	62	5	43	12	2
1	66	68	9	34	57	63	16	21	6	32
2	70	54	72	26	13	46	38	3	61	11
3	67	56	20	69	25	37	10	19	36	35
4	74	75	58	49	76	64	30	59	17	28
5	50	22	42	77	7	52	65	33	15	31
6	71	45	60	55	24	18	73	48	29	27
7	41	51	14	44	23	47	40	43	39	

Prime 83
$g = 2$

Indices

	0	1	2	3	4	5	6	7	8	9
0		0	1	72	2	27	73	8	3	62
1	28	24	74	77	9	17	4	56	63	47
2	29	80	25	60	75	54	78	52	10	12
3	18	38	5	14	57	35	64	20	48	67
4	30	40	81	71	26	7	61	23	76	16
5	55	46	79	59	53	51	11	37	3	34
6	19	66	39	70	6	22	15	45	58	50
7	36	33	65	69	21	44	49	32	68	43
8	31	42	41							

Prime 89
$g = 3$

Indices

	0	1	2	3	4	5	6	7	8	9
0		0	16	1	32	70	17	81	48	2
1	86	84	33	23	9	71	64	6	18	35
2	14	82	12	57	49	52	39	3	25	59
3	87	31	80	85	22	63	34	11	51	24
4	30	21	10	29	28	72	73	54	65	74
5	68	7	55	78	19	66	41	36	75	43
6	15	69	47	83	8	5	13	56	38	58
7	79	62	50	20	27	53	67	77	40	42
8	46	4	37	61	26	76	45	60	44	

Prime 97
$g = 5$

Indices

	0	1	2	3	4	5	6	7	8	9
0		0	34	70	68	1	8	31	6	44
1	35	86	42	25	65	71	40	89	78	81
2	69	5	24	77	76	2	59	18	3	13
3	9	46	74	60	27	32	16	91	19	95
4	7	85	39	4	58	45	15	84	14	62
5	36	63	93	10	52	87	37	55	47	67
6	43	64	80	75	12	26	94	57	61	51
7	66	11	50	28	29	72	53	21	33	30
8	41	88	23	17	73	90	38	83	92	54

PRIMITIVE ROOTS FOR PRIMES 3 to 5003

In this table

    g denotes the least primitive root of p

    G denotes the least negative primitive root of p

    ϵ denotes whether 10, -10 both or neither are primitive roots of p

Introductory Facts

As noted in the preceding Totient and Indices Tables, the number of integers not exceeding and relatively prime to a fixed integer n is represented by $\phi(n)$. These integers form a group; the group is cyclic if and only if $n = 2$, 4, or n is of the form p^k or $2p^k$ where p is an odd prime. We refer to g as a primitive root of n if it generates that group i.e. if g, g^2, ..., $g^{\phi(n)}$ are distinct modulo n. There are $\phi(\phi(n))$ primitive roots of n. If g is a primitive root of p and $g^{p-1} \not\equiv 1 \pmod{p^2}$, then g is a primitive root of p^k for all k. If $g^{p-1} \equiv 1 \pmod{p^2}$ then $g + p$ is a primitive root of p^k for all k.

If g is a primitive root of p^k then either g or $g + p^k$, whichever is odd, is a primitive root of $2p^k$.

If g is a primitive root of n, then g^k is a primitive root of n if and only if k and $\phi(n)$ are relatively prime, and each primitive root of n is of this form, i.e. $(k, \phi(n)) = 1$.

p	$p-1$	g	$-G$	ϵ	p	$p-1$	g	$-G$	ϵ
3	2	2	1	-10	167	$2 \cdot 83$	5	2	10
5	2^2	2	2	—	173	$2^2 \cdot 43$	2	2	—
7	$2 \cdot 3$	3	2	10	179	$2 \cdot 89$	2	3	10
11	$2 \cdot 5$	2	3	—	181	$2^2 \cdot 3^2 \cdot 5$	2	2	± 10
13	$2^2 \cdot 3$	2	2	—	191	$2 \cdot 5 \cdot 19$	19	2	-10
17	2^4	3	3	± 10	193	$2^6 \cdot 3$	5	5	± 10
19	$2 \cdot 3^2$	2	4	10	197	$2^2 \cdot 7^2$	2	2	—
23	$2 \cdot 11$	5	2	10	199	$2 \cdot 3^2 \cdot 11$	3	2	-10
29	$2^2 \cdot 7$	2	2	± 10	211	$2 \cdot 3 \cdot 5 \cdot 7$	2	4	—
31	$2 \cdot 3 \cdot 5$	3	7	-10	223	$2 \cdot 3 \cdot 37$	3	9	10
37	$2^2 \cdot 3^2$	2	2	—	227	$2 \cdot 113$	2	3	-10
41	$2^3 \cdot 5$	6	6	—	229	$2^2 \cdot 3 \cdot 19$	6	6	± 10
43	$2 \cdot 3 \cdot 7$	3	9	-10	233	$2^3 \cdot 29$	3	3	± 10
47	$2 \cdot 23$	5	2	10	239	$2 \cdot 7 \cdot 17$	7	2	—
53	$2^2 \cdot 13$	2	2	—	241	$2^4 \cdot 3 \cdot 5$	7	7	—
59	$2 \cdot 29$	2	3	10	251	$2 \cdot 5^3$	6	3	—
61	$2^2 \cdot 3 \cdot 5$	2	2	± 10	257	2^8	3	3	± 10
67	$2 \cdot 3 \cdot 11$	2	4	-10	263	$2 \cdot 131$	5	2	10
71	$2 \cdot 5 \cdot 7$	7	2	-10	269	$2^2 \cdot 67$	2	2	± 10
73	$2^3 \cdot 3^2$	5	5	—	271	$2 \cdot 3^3 \cdot 5$	6	2	—
79	$2 \cdot 3 \cdot 13$	3	2	—	277	$2^2 \cdot 3 \cdot 23$	5	5	—
83	$2 \cdot 41$	2	3	-10	281	$2^3 \cdot 5 \cdot 7$	3	3	—
89	$2^3 \cdot 11$	3	3	—	283	$2 \cdot 3 \cdot 47$	3	6	-10
97	$2^5 \cdot 3$	5	5	± 10	293	$2^2 \cdot 73$	2	2	—
101	$2^2 \cdot 5^2$	2	2	—	307	$2 \cdot 3^2 \cdot 17$	5	7	-10
103	$2 \cdot 3 \cdot 17$	5	2	—	311	$2 \cdot 5 \cdot 31$	17	2	-10
107	$2 \cdot 53$	2	3	-10	313	$2^3 \cdot 3 \cdot 13$	10	10	± 10
109	$2^2 \cdot 3^3$	6	6	± 10	317	$2^2 \cdot 79$	2	2	—
113	$2^4 \cdot 7$	3	3	± 10	331	$2 \cdot 3 \cdot 5 \cdot 11$	3	5	—
127	$2 \cdot 3^2 \cdot 7$	3	9	—	337	$2^4 \cdot 3 \cdot 7$	10	10	± 10
131	$2 \cdot 5 \cdot 13$	2	3	10	347	$2 \cdot 173$	2	3	-10
137	$2^3 \cdot 17$	3	3	—	349	$2^2 \cdot 3 \cdot 29$	2	2	—
139	$2 \cdot 3 \cdot 23$	2	4	—	353	$2^5 \cdot 11$	3	3	—
149	$2^2 \cdot 37$	2	2	± 10	359	$2 \cdot 179$	7	2	-10
151	$2 \cdot 3 \cdot 5^2$	6	5	-10	367	$2 \cdot 3 \cdot 61$	6	2	10
157	$2^2 \cdot 3 \cdot 13$	5	5	—	373	$2^2 \cdot 3 \cdot 31$	2	2	—
163	$2 \cdot 3^4$	2	4	-10	379	$2 \cdot 3^3 \cdot 7$	2	4	10

PRIMITIVE ROOTS FOR PRIMES 3 to 5003 (Continued)

p	$p-1$	g	$-G$	ϵ	p	$p-1$	g	$-G$	ϵ
383	$2 \cdot 191$	5	2	10	769	$2^8 \cdot 3$	11	11	—
389	$2^2 \cdot 97$	2	2	± 10	773	$2^2 \cdot 193$	2	2	—
397	$2^2 \cdot 3^2 \cdot 11$	5	5	—	787	$2 \cdot 3 \cdot 131$	2	4	-10
401	$2^4 \cdot 5^2$	3	3	—	797	$2^2 \cdot 199$	2	2	—
409	$2^3 \cdot 3 \cdot 17$	21	21	—	809	$2^3 \cdot 101$	3	3	—
419	$2 \cdot 11 \cdot 19$	2	3	10	811	$2 \cdot 3^4 \cdot 5$	3	5	10
421	$2^2 \cdot 3 \cdot 5 \cdot 7$	2	2	—	821	$2^2 \cdot 5 \cdot 41$	2	2	± 10
431	$2 \cdot 5 \cdot 43$	7	5	-10	823	$2 \cdot 3 \cdot 137$	3	2	10
433	$2^4 \cdot 3^3$	5	5	± 10	827	$2 \cdot 7 \cdot 59$	2	3	-10
439	$2 \cdot 3 \cdot 73$	15	5	-10	829	$2^2 \cdot 3^2 \cdot 23$	2	2	—
443	$2 \cdot 13 \cdot 17$	2	3	-10	839	$2 \cdot 419$	11	2	-10
449	$2^6 \cdot 7$	3	3	—	853	$2^2 \cdot 3 \cdot 71$	2	2	—
457	$2^3 \cdot 3 \cdot 19$	13	13	—	857	$2^3 \cdot 107$	3	3	± 10
461	$2^2 \cdot 5 \cdot 23$	2	2	± 10	859	$2 \cdot 3 \cdot 11 \cdot 13$	2	4	—
463	$2 \cdot 3 \cdot 7 \cdot 11$	3	2	—	863	$2 \cdot 431$	5	2	10
467	$2 \cdot 233$	2	3	-10	877	$2^2 \cdot 3 \cdot 73$	2	2	—
479	$2 \cdot 239$	13	2	-10	881	$2^4 \cdot 5 \cdot 11$	3	3	—
487	$2 \cdot 3^5$	3	2	10	883	$2 \cdot 3^2 \cdot 7^2$	2	4	-10
491	$2 \cdot 5 \cdot 7^2$	2	4	10	887	$2 \cdot 443$	5	2	10
499	$2 \cdot 3 \cdot 83$	7	5	10	907	$2 \cdot 3 \cdot 151$	2	4	—
503	$2 \cdot 251$	5	2	10	911	$2 \cdot 5 \cdot 7 \cdot 13$	17	3	-10
509	$2^2 \cdot 127$	2	2	± 10	919	$2 \cdot 3^3 \cdot 17$	7	5	-10
521	$2^3 \cdot 5 \cdot 13$	3	3	—	929	$2^5 \cdot 29$	3	3	—
523	$2 \cdot 3^2 \cdot 29$	2	4	-10	937	$2^3 \cdot 3^2 \cdot 13$	5	5	± 10
541	$2^2 \cdot 3^3 \cdot 5$	2	2	± 10	941	$2^2 \cdot 5 \cdot 47$	2	2	± 10
547	$2 \cdot 3 \cdot 7 \cdot 13$	2	4	—	947	$2 \cdot 11 \cdot 43$	2	3	-10
557	$2^2 \cdot 139$	2	2	—	953	$2^3 \cdot 7 \cdot 17$	3	3	± 10
563	$2 \cdot 281$	2	3	-10	967	$2 \cdot 3 \cdot 7 \cdot 23$	5	2	—
569	$2^3 \cdot 71$	3	3	—	971	$2 \cdot 5 \cdot 97$	6	3	10
571	$2 \cdot 3 \cdot 5 \cdot 19$	3	5	10	977	$2^4 \cdot 61$	3	3	± 10
577	$2^6 \cdot 3^2$	5	5	± 10	983	$2 \cdot 491$	5	2	10
587	$2 \cdot 293$	2	3	-10	991	$2 \cdot 3^2 \cdot 5 \cdot 11$	6	2	-10
593	$2^4 \cdot 37$	3	3	± 10	997	$2^2 \cdot 3 \cdot 83$	7	7	—
599	$2 \cdot 13 \cdot 23$	7	2	-10	1009	$2^4 \cdot 3^2 \cdot 7$	11	11	—
601	$2^3 \cdot 3 \cdot 5^2$	7	7	—	1013	$2^2 \cdot 11 \cdot 23$	3	3	—
607	$2 \cdot 3 \cdot 101$	3	2	—	1019	$2 \cdot 509$	2	3	10
613	$2^2 \cdot 3^2 \cdot 17$	2	2	—	1021	$2^2 \cdot 3 \cdot 5 \cdot 17$	10	10	± 10
617	$2^3 \cdot 7 \cdot 11$	3	3	—	1031	$2 \cdot 5 \cdot 103$	14	2	—
619	$2 \cdot 3 \cdot 103$	2	4	10	1033	$2^3 \cdot 3 \cdot 43$	5	5	± 10
631	$2 \cdot 3^2 \cdot 5 \cdot 7$	3	9	-10	1039	$2 \cdot 3 \cdot 173$	3	2	-10
641	$2^7 \cdot 5$	3	3	—	1049	$2^3 \cdot 131$	3	3	—
643	$2 \cdot 3 \cdot 107$	11	7	—	1051	$2 \cdot 3 \cdot 5^2 \cdot 7$	7	5	10
647	$2 \cdot 17 \cdot 19$	5	2	10	1061	$2^2 \cdot 5 \cdot 53$	2	2	—
653	$2^2 \cdot 163$	2	2	—	1063	$2 \cdot 3^2 \cdot 59$	3	2	10
659	$2 \cdot 7 \cdot 47$	2	3	10	1069	$2^2 \cdot 3 \cdot 89$	6	6	± 10
661	$2^2 \cdot 3 \cdot 5 \cdot 11$	2	2	—	1087	$2 \cdot 3 \cdot 181$	3	2	10
673	$2^5 \cdot 3 \cdot 7$	5	5	—	1091	$2 \cdot 5 \cdot 109$	2	4	10
677	$2^2 \cdot 13^2$	2	2	—	1093	$2^2 \cdot 3 \cdot 7 \cdot 13$	5	5	—
683	$2 \cdot 11 \cdot 31$	5	10	-10	1097	$2^3 \cdot 137$	3	3	± 10
691	$2 \cdot 3 \cdot 5 \cdot 23$	3	6	—	1103	$2 \cdot 19 \cdot 29$	5	3	10
701	$2^2 \cdot 5^2 \cdot 7$	2	2	± 10	1109	$2^2 \cdot 277$	2	2	± 10
709	$2^2 \cdot 3 \cdot 59$	2	2	± 10	1117	$2^2 \cdot 3^2 \cdot 31$	2	2	—
719	$2 \cdot 359$	11	2	-10	1123	$2 \cdot 3 \cdot 11 \cdot 17$	2	4	-10
727	$2 \cdot 3 \cdot 11^2$	5	7	10	1129	$2^3 \cdot 3 \cdot 47$	11	11	—
733	$2^2 \cdot 3 \cdot 61$	6	6	—	1151	$2 \cdot 5^2 \cdot 23$	17	2	-10
739	$2 \cdot 3^2 \cdot 41$	3	6	—	1153	$2^7 \cdot 3^2$	5	5	± 10
743	$2 \cdot 7 \cdot 53$	5	2	10	1163	$2 \cdot 7 \cdot 83$	5	3	-10
751	$2 \cdot 3 \cdot 5^3$	3	2	—	1171	$2 \cdot 3^2 \cdot 5 \cdot 13$	2	4	10
757	$2^2 \cdot 3^3 \cdot 7$	2	2	—	1181	$2^2 \cdot 5 \cdot 59$	7	7	± 10
761	$2^3 \cdot 5 \cdot 19$	6	6	—	1187	$2 \cdot 593$	2	3	-10

PRIMITIVE ROOTS FOR PRIMES 3 to 5003 (Continued)

p	$p-1$	g	$-G$	ϵ	p	$p-1$	g	$-G$	ϵ
1193	$2^3 \cdot 149$	3	3	± 10	1619	$2 \cdot 809$	2	3	10
1201	$2^4 \cdot 3 \cdot 5^2$	11	11	—	1621	$2^2 \cdot 3^4 \cdot 5$	2	2	± 10
1213	$2^2 \cdot 3 \cdot 101$	2	2	—	1627	$2 \cdot 3 \cdot 271$	3	6	—
1217	$2^6 \cdot 19$	3	3	± 10	1637	$2^2 \cdot 409$	2	2	—
1223	$2 \cdot 13 \cdot 47$	5	2	10	1657	$2^3 \cdot 3^2 \cdot 23$	11	11	—
1229	$2^2 \cdot 307$	2	2	± 10	1663	$2 \cdot 3 \cdot 277$	3	2	10
1231	$2 \cdot 3 \cdot 5 \cdot 41$	3	2	—	1667	$2 \cdot 7^2 \cdot 17$	2	3	-10
1237	$2^2 \cdot 3 \cdot 103$	2	2	—	1669	$2^2 \cdot 3 \cdot 139$	2	2	—
1249	$2^5 \cdot 3 \cdot 13$	7	7	—	1693	$2^2 \cdot 3^2 \cdot 47$	2	2	—
1259	$2 \cdot 17 \cdot 37$	2	3	10	1697	$2^5 \cdot 53$	3	3	± 10
1277	$2^2 \cdot 11 \cdot 29$	2	2	—	1699	$2 \cdot 3 \cdot 283$	3	6	—
1279	$2 \cdot 3^2 \cdot 71$	3	2	-10	1709	$2^2 \cdot 7 \cdot 61$	3	3	± 10
1283	$2 \cdot 641$	2	3	-10	1721	$2^3 \cdot 5 \cdot 43$	3	3	—
1289	$2^3 \cdot 7 \cdot 23$	6	6	—	1723	$2 \cdot 3 \cdot 7 \cdot 41$	3	6	—
1291	$2 \cdot 3 \cdot 5 \cdot 43$	2	4	10	1733	$2^2 \cdot 433$	2	2	—
1297	$2^4 \cdot 3^4$	10	10	± 10	1741	$2^2 \cdot 3 \cdot 5 \cdot 29$	2	2	± 10
1301	$2^2 \cdot 5^2 \cdot 13$	2	2	± 10	1747	$2 \cdot 3^2 \cdot 97$	2	4	—
1303	$2 \cdot 3 \cdot 7 \cdot 31$	6	2	10	1753	$2^3 \cdot 3 \cdot 73$	7	7	—
1307	$2 \cdot 653$	2	3	-10	1759	$2 \cdot 3 \cdot 293$	6	2	-10
1319	$2 \cdot 659$	13	2	-10	1777	$2^4 \cdot 3 \cdot 37$	5	5	± 10
1321	$2^3 \cdot 3 \cdot 5 \cdot 11$	13	13	—	1783	$2 \cdot 3^4 \cdot 11$	10	2	10
1327	$2 \cdot 3 \cdot 13 \cdot 17$	3	9	10	1787	$2 \cdot 19 \cdot 47$	2	3	-10
1361	$2^4 \cdot 5 \cdot 17$	3	3	—	1789	$2^2 \cdot 3 \cdot 149$	6	6	± 10
1367	$2 \cdot 683$	5	2	10	1801	$2^3 \cdot 3^2 \cdot 5^2$	11	11	—
1373	$2^2 \cdot 7^3$	2	2	—	1811	$2 \cdot 5 \cdot 181$	6	3	10
1381	$2^2 \cdot 3 \cdot 5 \cdot 23$	2	2	± 10	1823	$2 \cdot 911$	5	2	10
1399	$2 \cdot 3 \cdot 233$	13	5	-10	1831	$2 \cdot 3 \cdot 5 \cdot 61$	3	9	—
1409	$2^7 \cdot 11$	3	3	—	1847	$2 \cdot 13 \cdot 71$	5	2	10
1423	$2 \cdot 3^2 \cdot 79$	3	9	—	1861	$2^2 \cdot 3 \cdot 5 \cdot 31$	2	2	± 10
1427	$2 \cdot 23 \cdot 31$	2	3	-10	1867	$2 \cdot 3 \cdot 311$	2	4	-10
1429	$2^2 \cdot 3 \cdot 7 \cdot 17$	6	6	± 10	1871	$2 \cdot 5 \cdot 11 \cdot 17$	14	2	-10
1433	$2^3 \cdot 179$	3	3	± 10	1873	$2^4 \cdot 3^2 \cdot 13$	10	10	± 10
1439	$2 \cdot 719$	7	2	-10	1877	$2^2 \cdot 7 \cdot 67$	2	2	—
1447	$2 \cdot 3 \cdot 241$	3	2	10	1879	$2 \cdot 3 \cdot 313$	6	2	—
1451	$2 \cdot 5^2 \cdot 29$	2	3	—	1889	$2^5 \cdot 59$	3	3	—
1453	$2^2 \cdot 3 \cdot 11^2$	2	2	—	1901	$2^2 \cdot 5^2 \cdot 19$	2	2	—
1459	$2 \cdot 3^6$	3	6	—	1907	$2 \cdot 953$	2	3	-10
1471	$2 \cdot 3 \cdot 5 \cdot 7^2$	6	5	-10	1913	$2^3 \cdot 239$	3	3	± 10
1481	$2^3 \cdot 5 \cdot 37$	3	3	—	1931	$2 \cdot 5 \cdot 193$	2	3	—
1483	$2 \cdot 3 \cdot 13 \cdot 19$	2	4	—	1933	$2^2 \cdot 3 \cdot 7 \cdot 23$	5	5	—
1487	$2 \cdot 743$	5	2	10	1949	$2^2 \cdot 487$	2	2	± 10
1489	$2^4 \cdot 3 \cdot 31$	14	14	—	1951	$2 \cdot 3 \cdot 5^2 \cdot 13$	3	2	—
1493	$2^2 \cdot 373$	2	2	—	1973	$2^2 \cdot 17 \cdot 29$	2	2	—
1499	$2 \cdot 7 \cdot 107$	2	3	—	1979	$2 \cdot 23 \cdot 43$	2	3	10
1511	$2 \cdot 5 \cdot 151$	11	2	-10	1987	$2 \cdot 3 \cdot 331$	2	4	—
1523	$2 \cdot 761$	2	3	-10	1993	$2^3 \cdot 3 \cdot 83$	5	5	—
1531	$2 \cdot 3^2 \cdot 5 \cdot 17$	2	4	10	1997	$2^2 \cdot 499$	2	2	—
1543	$2 \cdot 3 \cdot 257$	5	2	10	1999	$2 \cdot 3^3 \cdot 37$	3	5	-10
1549	$2^2 \cdot 3^2 \cdot 43$	2	2	± 10	2003	$2 \cdot 7 \cdot 11 \cdot 13$	5	3	-10
1553	$2^4 \cdot 97$	3	3	± 10	2011	$2 \cdot 3 \cdot 5 \cdot 67$	3	5	—
1559	$2 \cdot 19 \cdot 41$	19	2	-10	2017	$2^5 \cdot 3^2 \cdot 7$	5	5	± 10
1567	$2 \cdot 3^3 \cdot 29$	3	2	10	2027	$2 \cdot 1013$	2	3	-10
1571	$2 \cdot 5 \cdot 157$	2	3	10	2029	$2^2 \cdot 3 \cdot 13^2$	2	2	± 10
1579	$2 \cdot 3 \cdot 263$	3	5	10	2039	$2 \cdot 1019$	7	2	-10
1583	$2 \cdot 7 \cdot 113$	5	2	10	2053	$2^2 \cdot 3^3 \cdot 19$	2	2	—
1597	$2^2 \cdot 3 \cdot 7 \cdot 19$	11	11	—	2063	$2 \cdot 1031$	5	2	10
1601	$2^6 \cdot 5^2$	3	3	—	2069	$2^3 \cdot 11 \cdot 47$	2	2	± 10
1607	$2 \cdot 11 \cdot 73$	5	2	10	2081	$2^5 \cdot 5 \cdot 13$	3	3	—
1609	$2^3 \cdot 3 \cdot 67$	7	7	—	2083	$2 \cdot 3 \cdot 347$	2	4	-10
1613	$2^2 \cdot 13 \cdot 31$	3	3	—	2087	$2 \cdot 7 \cdot 149$	5	2	—

PRIMITIVE ROOTS FOR PRIMES 3 to 5003 (Continued)

p	$p-1$	g	$-G$	ϵ	p	$p-1$	g	$-G$	ϵ
2089	$2^3 \cdot 3^2 \cdot 29$	7	7	—	2579	$2 \cdot 1289$	2	3	10
2099	$2 \cdot 1049$	2	3	10	2591	$2 \cdot 5 \cdot 7 \cdot 37$	7	2	—
2111	$2 \cdot 5 \cdot 211$	7	2	-10	2593	$2^5 \cdot 3^4$	7	7	± 10
2113	$2^6 \cdot 3 \cdot 11$	5	5	± 10	2609	$2^4 \cdot 163$	3	3	—
2129	$2^4 \cdot 7 \cdot 19$	3	3	—	2617	$2^3 \cdot 3 \cdot 109$	5	5	± 10
2131	$2 \cdot 3 \cdot 5 \cdot 71$	2	4	—	2621	$2^2 \cdot 5 \cdot 131$	2	2	± 10
2137	$2^3 \cdot 3 \cdot 89$	10	10	± 10	2633	$2^3 \cdot 7 \cdot 47$	3	3	± 10
2141	$2^2 \cdot 5 \cdot 107$	2	2	± 10	2647	$2 \cdot 3^3 \cdot 7^2$	3	2	—
2143	$2 \cdot 3^2 \cdot 7 \cdot 17$	3	9	10	2657	$2^5 \cdot 83$	3	3	± 10
2153	$2^3 \cdot 269$	3	3	± 10	2659	$2 \cdot 3 \cdot 443$	2	4	—
2161	$2^4 \cdot 3^3 \cdot 5$	23	23	—	2663	$2 \cdot 11^3$	5	2	10
2179	$2 \cdot 3^2 \cdot 11^2$	7	5	10	2671	$2 \cdot 3 \cdot 5 \cdot 89$	7	5	-10
2203	$2 \cdot 3 \cdot 367$	5	7	-10	2677	$2^2 \cdot 3 \cdot 223$	2	2	—
2207	$2 \cdot 1103$	5	2	10	2683	$2 \cdot 3^2 \cdot 149$	2	4	—
2213	$2^2 \cdot 7 \cdot 79$	2	2	—	2687	$2 \cdot 17 \cdot 79$	5	3	10
2221	$2^2 \cdot 3 \cdot 5 \cdot 37$	2	2	± 10	2689	$2^7 \cdot 3 \cdot 7$	19	19	—
2237	$2^2 \cdot 13 \cdot 43$	2	2	—	2693	$2^2 \cdot 673$	2	2	—
2239	$2 \cdot 3 \cdot 373$	3	2	-10	2699	$2 \cdot 19 \cdot 71$	2	3	10
2243	$2 \cdot 19 \cdot 59$	2	3	-10	2707	$2 \cdot 3 \cdot 11 \cdot 41$	2	4	-10
2251	$2 \cdot 3^2 \cdot 5^3$	7	5	10	2711	$2 \cdot 5 \cdot 271$	7	2	-10
2267	$2 \cdot 11 \cdot 103$	2	3	-10	2713	$2^3 \cdot 3 \cdot 113$	5	5	± 10
2269	$2^2 \cdot 3^4 \cdot 7$	2	2	± 10	2719	$2 \cdot 3^2 \cdot 151$	3	2	-10
2273	$2^5 \cdot 71$	3	3	± 10	2729	$2^3 \cdot 11 \cdot 31$	3	3	—
2281	$2^3 \cdot 3 \cdot 5 \cdot 19$	7	7	—	2731	$2 \cdot 3 \cdot 5 \cdot 7 \cdot 13$	3	5	10
2287	$2 \cdot 3^2 \cdot 127$	19	7	—	2741	$2^2 \cdot 5 \cdot 137$	2	2	± 10
2293	$2^2 \cdot 3 \cdot 191$	2	2	—	2749	$2^2 \cdot 3 \cdot 229$	6	6	—
2297	$2^3 \cdot 7 \cdot 41$	5	5	± 10	2753	$2^6 \cdot 43$	3	3	± 10
2309	$2^2 \cdot 577$	2	2	± 10	2767	$2 \cdot 3 \cdot 461$	3	9	10
2311	$2 \cdot 3 \cdot 5 \cdot 7 \cdot 11$	3	2	—	2777	$2^3 \cdot 347$	3	3	± 10
2333	$2^2 \cdot 11 \cdot 53$	2	2	—	2789	$2^2 \cdot 17 \cdot 41$	2	2	± 10
2339	$2 \cdot 7 \cdot 167$	2	3	10	2791	$2 \cdot 3^2 \cdot 5 \cdot 31$	6	7	—
2341	$2^2 \cdot 3^2 \cdot 5 \cdot 13$	7	7	± 10	2797	$2^2 \cdot 3 \cdot 233$	2	2	—
2347	$2 \cdot 3 \cdot 17 \cdot 23$	3	6	-10	2801	$2^4 \cdot 5^2 \cdot 7$	3	3	—
2351	$2 \cdot 5^2 \cdot 47$	13	3	-10	2803	$2 \cdot 3 \cdot 467$	2	4	-10
2357	$2^2 \cdot 19 \cdot 31$	2	2	—	2819	$2 \cdot 1409$	2	3	10
2371	$2 \cdot 3 \cdot 5 \cdot 79$	2	4	10	2833	$2^4 \cdot 3 \cdot 59$	5	5	± 10
2377	$2^3 \cdot 3^3 \cdot 11$	5	5	—	2837	$2^2 \cdot 709$	2	2	—
2381	$2^2 \cdot 5 \cdot 7 \cdot 17$	3	3	—	2843	$2 \cdot 7^2 \cdot 29$	2	4	-10
2383	$2 \cdot 3 \cdot 397$	5	13	10	2851	$2 \cdot 3 \cdot 5^2 \cdot 19$	2	4	10
2389	$2^2 \cdot 3 \cdot 199$	2	2	± 10	2857	$2^3 \cdot 3 \cdot 7 \cdot 17$	11	11	—
2393	$2^3 \cdot 13 \cdot 23$	3	3	—	2861	$2^2 \cdot 5 \cdot 11 \cdot 13$	2	2	± 10
2399	$2 \cdot 11 \cdot 109$	11	2	-10	2879	$2 \cdot 1439$	7	2	-10
2411	$2 \cdot 5 \cdot 241$	6	3	10	2887	$2 \cdot 3 \cdot 13 \cdot 37$	5	2	10
2417	$2^4 \cdot 151$	3	3	± 10	2897	$2^4 \cdot 181$	3	3	± 10
2423	$2 \cdot 7 \cdot 173$	5	2	10	2903	$2 \cdot 1451$	5	2	10
2437	$2^2 \cdot 3 \cdot 7 \cdot 29$	2	2	—	2909	$2^2 \cdot 727$	2	2	± 10
2441	$2^3 \cdot 5 \cdot 61$	6	6	—	2917	$2^2 \cdot 3^6$	5	5	—
2447	$2 \cdot 1223$	5	2	10	2927	$2 \cdot 7 \cdot 11 \cdot 19$	5	2	10
2459	$2 \cdot 1229$	2	3	10	2939	$2 \cdot 13 \cdot 113$	2	3	10
2467	$2 \cdot 3^2 \cdot 137$	2	4	—	2953	$2^3 \cdot 3^2 \cdot 41$	13	13	—
2473	$2^3 \cdot 3 \cdot 103$	5	5	± 10	2957	$2^2 \cdot 739$	2	2	—
2477	$2^2 \cdot 619$	2	2	—	2963	$2 \cdot 1481$	2	3	-10
2503	$2 \cdot 3^2 \cdot 139$	3	2	—	2969	$2^3 \cdot 7 \cdot 53$	3	3	—
2521	$2^3 \cdot 3^2 \cdot 5 \cdot 7$	17	17	—	2971	$2 \cdot 3^3 \cdot 5 \cdot 11$	10	5	10
2531	$2 \cdot 5 \cdot 11 \cdot 23$	2	3	—	2999	$2 \cdot 1499$	17	2	-10
2539	$2 \cdot 3^3 \cdot 47$	2	4	10	3001	$2^3 \cdot 3 \cdot 5^3$	14	14	—
2543	$2 \cdot 31 \cdot 41$	5	2	10	3011	$2 \cdot 5 \cdot 7 \cdot 43$	2	3	10
2549	$2^2 \cdot 7^2 \cdot 13$	2	2	± 10	3019	$2 \cdot 3 \cdot 503$	2	4	10
2551	$2 \cdot 3 \cdot 5^2 \cdot 17$	6	2	—	3023	$2 \cdot 1511$	5	2	10
2557	$2^2 \cdot 3^2 \cdot 71$	2	2	—	3037	$2^2 \cdot 3 \cdot 11 \cdot 23$	2	2	—

PRIMITIVE ROOTS FOR PRIMES 3 to 5003 (Continued)

p	$p-1$	g	$-G$	ϵ	p	$p-1$	g	$-G$	ϵ
304.	$2^5 \cdot 5 \cdot 19$	3	3	—	3541	$2^2 \cdot 3 \cdot 5 \cdot 59$	7	7	—
3049	$2^3 \cdot 3 \cdot 127$	11	11	—	3547	$2 \cdot 3^2 \cdot 197$	2	4	-10
3061	$2^2 \cdot 3^2 \cdot 5 \cdot 17$	6	6	—	3557	$2^2 \cdot 7 \cdot 127$	2	2	—
3067	$2 \cdot 3 \cdot 7 \cdot 73$	2	4	-10	3559	$2 \cdot 3 \cdot 593$	3	2	-10
3079	$2 \cdot 3^4 \cdot 19$	6	2	-10	3571	$2 \cdot 3 \cdot 5 \cdot 7 \cdot 17$	2	4	10
3083	$2 \cdot 23 \cdot 67$	2	3	-10	3581	$2^2 \cdot 5 \cdot 179$	2	2	± 10
3089	$2^4 \cdot 193$	3	3	—	3583	$2 \cdot 3^2 \cdot 199$	3	2	—
3109	$2^2 \cdot 3 \cdot 7 \cdot 37$	6	6	—	3593	$2^3 \cdot 449$	3	3	± 10
3119	$2 \cdot 1559$	7	2	-10	3607	$2 \cdot 3 \cdot 601$	5	11	10
3121	$2^4 \cdot 3 \cdot 5 \cdot 13$	7	7	—	3613	$2^2 \cdot 3 \cdot 7 \cdot 43$	2	2	—
3137	$2^6 \cdot 7^2$	3	3	± 10	3617	$2^5 \cdot 113$	3	3	± 10
3163	$2 \cdot 3 \cdot 17 \cdot 31$	3	6	-10	3623	$2 \cdot 1811$	5	2	10
3167	$2 \cdot 1583$	5	2	10	3631	$2 \cdot 3 \cdot 5 \cdot 11^2$	15	10	-10
3169	$2^5 \cdot 3^2 \cdot 11$	7	7	—	3637	$2^2 \cdot 3^2 \cdot 101$	2	2	—
3181	$2^2 \cdot 3 \cdot 5 \cdot 53$	7	7	—	3643	$2 \cdot 3 \cdot 607$	2	4	-10
3187	$2 \cdot 3^3 \cdot 59$	2	4	—	3659	$2 \cdot 31 \cdot 59$	2	3	10
3191	$2 \cdot 5 \cdot 11 \cdot 29$	11	5	—	3671	$2 \cdot 5 \cdot 367$	13	2	—
3203	$2 \cdot 1601$	2	3	-10	3673	$2^3 \cdot 3^3 \cdot 17$	5	5	± 10
3209	$2^3 \cdot 401$	3	3	—	3677	$2^2 \cdot 919$	2	2	—
3217	$2^4 \cdot 3 \cdot 67$	5	5	—	3691	$2 \cdot 3^2 \cdot 5 \cdot 41$	2	4	—
3221	$2^2 \cdot 5 \cdot 7 \cdot 23$	10	10	± 10	3697	$2 \cdot 43^2$	5	5	—
3229	$2^2 \cdot 3 \cdot 269$	6	6	—	3701	$2^2 \cdot 5^2 \cdot 37$	2	2	± 10
3251	$2 \cdot 5^3 \cdot 13$	6	3	10	3709	$2^2 \cdot 3^2 \cdot 103$	2	2	± 10
3253	$2^2 \cdot 3 \cdot 271$	2	2	—	3719	$2 \cdot 11 \cdot 13^2$	7	2	-10
3257	$2^3 \cdot 11 \cdot 37$	3	3	± 10	3727	$2 \cdot 3^4 \cdot 23$	3	2	10
3259	$2 \cdot 3^2 \cdot 181$	3	5	10	3733	$2^2 \cdot 3 \cdot 311$	2	2	—
3271	$2 \cdot 3 \cdot 5 \cdot 109$	3	5	-10	3739	$2 \cdot 3 \cdot 7 \cdot 89$	7	5	—
3299	$2 \cdot 17 \cdot 97$	2	3	10	3761	$2^4 \cdot 5 \cdot 47$	3	3	—
3301	$2^2 \cdot 3 \cdot 5^2 \cdot 11$	6	6	± 10	3767	$2 \cdot 7 \cdot 269$	5	2	10
3307	$2 \cdot 3 \cdot 19 \cdot 29$	2	4	-10	3769	$2^3 \cdot 3 \cdot 157$	7	7	—
3313	$2^4 \cdot 3^2 \cdot 23$	10	10	± 10	3779	$2 \cdot 1889$	2	3	10
3319	$2 \cdot 3 \cdot 7 \cdot 79$	6	2	—	3793	$2^4 \cdot 3 \cdot 79$	5	5	—
3323	$2 \cdot 11 \cdot 151$	2	3	-10	3797	$2^2 \cdot 13 \cdot 73$	2	2	—
3329	$2^8 \cdot 13$	3	3	—	3803	$2 \cdot 1901$	2	3	-10
3331	$2 \cdot 3^2 \cdot 5 \cdot 37$	3	5	10	3821	$2^2 \cdot 5 \cdot 191$	3	3	± 10
3343	$2 \cdot 3 \cdot 557$	5	11	10	3823	$2 \cdot 3 \cdot 7^2 \cdot 13$	3	9	—
3347	$2 \cdot 7 \cdot 239$	2	3	-10	3833	$2^3 \cdot 479$	3	3	± 10
3359	$2 \cdot 23 \cdot 73$	11	2	-10	3847	$2 \cdot 3 \cdot 641$	5	2	10
3361	$2^5 \cdot 3 \cdot 5 \cdot 7$	22	22	—	3851	$2 \cdot 5^2 \cdot 7 \cdot 11$	2	4	—
3371	$2 \cdot 5 \cdot 337$	2	3	10	3853	$2^2 \cdot 3^2 \cdot 107$	2	2	—
3373	$2^2 \cdot 3 \cdot 281$	5	5	—	3863	$2 \cdot 1931$	5	2	10
3389	$2^2 \cdot 7 \cdot 11^2$	3	3	± 10	3877	$2^2 \cdot 3 \cdot 17 \cdot 19$	2	2	—
3391	$2 \cdot 3 \cdot 5 \cdot 113$	3	5	-10	3881	$2^3 \cdot 5 \cdot 97$	13	13	—
3407	$2 \cdot 13 \cdot 131$	5	2	10	3889	$2^4 \cdot 3^5$	11	11	—
3413	$2^2 \cdot 853$	2	2	—	3907	$2 \cdot 3^2 \cdot 7 \cdot 31$	2	4	-10
3433	$2^3 \cdot 3 \cdot 11 \cdot 13$	5	5	± 10	3911	$2 \cdot 5 \cdot 17 \cdot 23$	13	2	-10
3449	$2^3 \cdot 431$	3	3	—	3917	$2^2 \cdot 11 \cdot 89$	2	2	—
3457	$2^7 \cdot 3^3$	7	7	—	3919	$2 \cdot 3 \cdot 653$	3	2	—
3461	$2^2 \cdot 5 \cdot 173$	2	2	± 10	3923	$2 \cdot 37 \cdot 53$	2	3	-10
3463	$2 \cdot 3 \cdot 577$	3	9	10	3929	$2^3 \cdot 491$	3	3	—
3467	$2 \cdot 1733$	2	3	-10	3931	$2 \cdot 3 \cdot 5 \cdot 131$	2	4	—
3469	$2^2 \cdot 3 \cdot 17^2$	2	2	± 10	3943	$2 \cdot 3^3 \cdot 73$	3	9	10
3491	$2 \cdot 5 \cdot 349$	2	3	—	3947	$2 \cdot 1973$	2	3	-10
3499	$2 \cdot 3 \cdot 11 \cdot 53$	2	4	—	3967	$2 \cdot 3 \cdot 661$	6	2	10
3511	$2 \cdot 3^3 \cdot 5 \cdot 13$	7	2	-10	3989	$2^2 \cdot 997$	2	2	± 10
3517	$2^2 \cdot 3 \cdot 293$	2	2	—	4001	$2^5 \cdot 5^3$	3	3	—
3527	$2 \cdot 41 \cdot 43$	5	2	10	4003	$2 \cdot 3 \cdot 23 \cdot 29$	2	4	—
3529	$2^3 \cdot 3^2 \cdot 7^2$	17	17	—	4007	$2 \cdot 2003$	5	2	10
3533	$2^2 \cdot 883$	2	2	—	4013	$2^2 \cdot 17 \cdot 59$	2	2	—
3539	$2 \cdot 29 \cdot 61$	2	3	10	4019	$2 \cdot 7^2 \cdot 41$	2	4	10

PRIMITIVE ROOTS FOR PRIMES 3 to 5003 (Continued)

p	$p-1$	g	$-G$	ϵ	p	$p-1$	g	$-G$	ϵ
4021	$2^2 \cdot 3 \cdot 5 \cdot 67$	2	2	—	4519	$2 \cdot 3^2 \cdot 251$	3	9	—
4027	$2 \cdot 3 \cdot 11 \cdot 61$	3	6	-10	4523	$2 \cdot 7 \cdot 17 \cdot 19$	5	3	-10
4049	$2^4 \cdot 11 \cdot 23$	3	3	—	4547	$2 \cdot 2273$	2	3	-10
4051	$2 \cdot 3^4 \cdot 5^2$	10	5	10	4549	$2^2 \cdot 3 \cdot 379$	6	6	—
4057	$2^3 \cdot 3 \cdot 13^2$	5	5	± 10	4561	$2^4 \cdot 3 \cdot 5 \cdot 19$	11	11	—
4073	$2^3 \cdot 509$	3	3	± 10	4567	$2 \cdot 3 \cdot 761$	3	7	10
4079	$2 \cdot 2039$	11	2	-10	4583	$2 \cdot 29 \cdot 79$	5	2	10
4091	$2 \cdot 5 \cdot 409$	2	3	10	4591	$2 \cdot 3^3 \cdot 5 \cdot 17$	11	2	-10
4093	$2^2 \cdot 3 \cdot 11 \cdot 31$	2	2	—	4597	$2^2 \cdot 3 \cdot 383$	5	5	—
4099	$2 \cdot 3 \cdot 683$	2	4	10	4603	$2 \cdot 3 \cdot 13 \cdot 59$	2	4	-10
4111	$2 \cdot 3 \cdot 5 \cdot 137$	12	2	-10	4621	$2^2 \cdot 3 \cdot 5 \cdot 7 \cdot 11$	2	2	—
4127	$2 \cdot 2063$	5	2	10	4637	$2^2 \cdot 19 \cdot 61$	2	2	—
4129	$2^5 \cdot 3 \cdot 43$	13	13	—	4639	$2 \cdot 3 \cdot 773$	3	2	-10
4133	$2^2 \cdot 1033$	2	2	—	4643	$2 \cdot 11 \cdot 211$	5	3	-10
4139	$2 \cdot 2069$	2	3	10	4649	$2^3 \cdot 7 \cdot 83$	3	3	—
4153	$2^3 \cdot 3 \cdot 173$	5	5	± 10	4651	$2 \cdot 3 \cdot 5^2 \cdot 31$	3	5	10
4157	$2^2 \cdot 1039$	2	2	—	4657	$2^4 \cdot 3 \cdot 97$	15	15	—
4159	$2 \cdot 3^3 \cdot 7 \cdot 11$	3	2	—	4663	$2 \cdot 3^2 \cdot 7 \cdot 37$	3	9	—
4177	$2^4 \cdot 3^2 \cdot 29$	5	5	± 10	4673	$2^6 \cdot 73$	3	3	± 10
4201	$2^3 \cdot 3 \cdot 5^2 \cdot 7$	11	11	—	4679	$2 \cdot 2339$	11	2	-10
4211	$2 \cdot 5 \cdot 421$	6	3	10	4691	$2 \cdot 5 \cdot 7 \cdot 67$	2	3	10
4217	$2^3 \cdot 17 \cdot 31$	3	3	± 10	4703	$2 \cdot 2351$	5	2	10
4219	$2 \cdot 3 \cdot 19 \cdot 37$	2	4	10	4721	$2^4 \cdot 5 \cdot 59$	6	6	—
4229	$2^2 \cdot 7 \cdot 151$	2	2	± 10	4723	$2 \cdot 3 \cdot 787$	2	4	-10
4231	$2 \cdot 3^2 \cdot 5 \cdot 47$	3	2	-10	4729	$2^3 \cdot 3 \cdot 197$	17	17	—
4241	$2^4 \cdot 5 \cdot 53$	3	3	—	4733	$2^2 \cdot 7 \cdot 13^2$	5	5	—
4243	$2 \cdot 3 \cdot 7 \cdot 101$	2	4	-10	4751	$2 \cdot 5^3 \cdot 19$	19	3	-10
4253	$2^2 \cdot 1063$	2	2	—	4759	$2 \cdot 3 \cdot 13 \cdot 61$	3	5	-10
4259	$2 \cdot 2129$	2	3	10	4783	$2 \cdot 3 \cdot 797$	6	2	10
4261	$2^2 \cdot 3 \cdot 5 \cdot 71$	2	2	± 10	4787	$2 \cdot 2393$	2	3	-10
4271	$2 \cdot 5 \cdot 7 \cdot 61$	7	3	-10	4789	$2^2 \cdot 3^2 \cdot 7 \cdot 19$	2	2	—
4273	$2^4 \cdot 3 \cdot 89$	5	5	—	4793	$2^3 \cdot 599$	3	3	± 10
4283	$2 \cdot 2141$	2	3	-10	4799	$2 \cdot 2399$	7	2	-10
4289	$2^6 \cdot 67$	3	3	—	4801	$2^6 \cdot 3 \cdot 5^2$	7	7	—
4297	$2^3 \cdot 3 \cdot 179$	5	5	—	4813	$2^2 \cdot 3 \cdot 401$	2	2	—
4327	$2 \cdot 3 \cdot 7 \cdot 103$	3	2	10	4817	$2^4 \cdot 7 \cdot 43$	3	3	± 10
4337	$2^4 \cdot 271$	3	3	± 10	4831	$2 \cdot 3 \cdot 5 \cdot 7 \cdot 23$	3	2	—
4339	$2 \cdot 3^2 \cdot 241$	10	5	10	4861	$2^2 \cdot 3^5 \cdot 5$	11	11	—
4349	$2^2 \cdot 1087$	2	2	± 10	4871	$2 \cdot 5 \cdot 487$	11	3	-10
4357	$2^2 \cdot 3^2 \cdot 11^2$	2	2	—	4877	$2^2 \cdot 23 \cdot 53$	2	2	—
4363	$2 \cdot 3 \cdot 727$	2	4	-10	4889	$2^3 \cdot 13 \cdot 47$	3	3	—
4373	$2^2 \cdot 1093$	2	2	—	4903	$2 \cdot 3 \cdot 19 \cdot 43$	3	2	—
4391	$2 \cdot 5 \cdot 439$	14	2	-10	4909	$2^2 \cdot 3 \cdot 409$	6	6	—
4397	$2^2 \cdot 7 \cdot 157$	2	2	—	4919	$2 \cdot 2459$	13	2	-10
4409	$2^3 \cdot 19 \cdot 29$	3	3	—	4931	$2 \cdot 5 \cdot 17 \cdot 29$	6	3	10
4421	$2^2 \cdot 5 \cdot 13 \cdot 17$	3	3	± 10	4933	$2^2 \cdot 3^2 \cdot 137$	2	2	—
4423	$2 \cdot 3 \cdot 11 \cdot 67$	3	7	10	4937	$2^3 \cdot 617$	3	3	± 10
4441	$2^3 \cdot 3 \cdot 5 \cdot 37$	21	21	—	4943	$2 \cdot 7 \cdot 353$	7	2	10
4447	$2 \cdot 3^2 \cdot 13 \cdot 19$	3	2	10	4951	$2 \cdot 3^2 \cdot 5^2 \cdot 11$	6	2	-10
4451	$2 \cdot 5^2 \cdot 89$	2	3	10	4957	$2^2 \cdot 3 \cdot 7 \cdot 59$	2	2	—
4457	$2^3 \cdot 557$	3	3	± 10	4967	$2 \cdot 13 \cdot 191$	5	2	10
4463	$2 \cdot 23 \cdot 97$	5	2	10	4969	$2^3 \cdot 3^3 \cdot 23$	11	11	—
4481	$2^7 \cdot 5 \cdot 7$	3	3	—	4973	$2^2 \cdot 11 \cdot 113$	2	2	—
4483	$2 \cdot 3^3 \cdot 83$	2	4	—	4987	$2 \cdot 3^2 \cdot 277$	2	4	-10
4493	$2^2 \cdot 1123$	2	2	—	4993	$2^7 \cdot 3 \cdot 13$	5	5	—
4507	$2 \cdot 3 \cdot 751$	2	4	—	4999	$2 \cdot 3 \cdot 7^2 \cdot 17$	3	9	—
4513	$2^5 \cdot 3 \cdot 47$	7	7	—	5003	$2 \cdot 41 \cdot 61$	2	3	-10
4517	$2^2 \cdot 1129$	2	2	—					

From Applied Mathematics Series—55, Primitive Roots, Factorization of $p-1$, pages 864, 866, 867. By permission of United States Department of Commerce, National Bureau of Standards, Washington, D.C.

PRIMES

The following table contains all primes from 1 to 100,000. Taken from the Handbook of Mathematical Functions, Applied Mathematics Series 55, Permission received from National Bureau of Standards, Washington, D. C.

PRIMES (side heading)

	24	23	22	21	20	19	18	17	16	15	14	13	12	11	10	9	8	7	6	5	4	3	2	1	0
1	21391	20359	19427	18329	17393	16411	15413	14533	13513	12569	11677	10663	9739	8837	7927	7001	6143	5281	4421	3581	2749	1993	1229	547	2
2	21397	20369	19429	18341	17401	16417	15427	14537	13523	12577	11681	10667	9743	8839	7933	7013	6151	5297	4423	3583	2753	1997	1231	557	3
3	21401	20389	19433	18353	17417	16421	15439	14543	13537	12583	11689	10687	9749	8849	7937	7019	6163	5303	4441	3593	2767	1999	1237	563	5
4	21407	20393	19441	18367	17419	16427	15443	14549	13553	12589	11699	10691	9767	8861	7949	7027	6173	5309	4447	3607	2777	2003	1249	569	7
5	21419	20399	19447	18371	17431	16433	15451	14551	13567	12601	11701	10709	9769	8863	7951	7039	6197	5323	4451	3613	2789	2011	1259	571	11
6	21433	20407	19457	18379	17443	16447	15461	14557	13577	12611	11717	10711	9781	8867	7963	7043	6199	5333	4457	3617	2791	2017	1277	577	13
7	21467	20411	19463	18397	17449	16451	15467	14561	13591	12613	11719	10723	9787	8887	7993	7057	6203	5347	4463	3623	2797	2027	1279	587	17
8	21481	20431	19469	18401	17467	16453	15473	14563	13597	12619	11731	10729	9791	8893	8009	7069	6211	5351	4481	3631	2801	2029	1283	593	19
9	21487	20441	19471	18413	17471	16477	15493	14591	13613	12637	11743	10733	9803	8923	8011	7079	6217	5381	4483	3637	2803	2039	1289	599	23
10	21491	20443	19477	18427	17477	16481	15497	14593	13619	12641	11777	10739	9811	8929	8017	7103	6221	5387	4493	3643	2819	2053	1291	601	29
11	21493	20477	19483	18433	17483	16487	15511	14621	13627	12647	11779	10753	9817	8933	8039	7109	6229	5393	4507	3659	2833	2063	1297	607	31
12	21499	20479	19489	18439	17489	16493	15527	14627	13633	12653	11783	10771	9829	8941	8053	7121	6247	5399	4513	3671	2837	2069	1301	613	37
13	21503	20483	19501	18443	17491	16519	15541	14629	13649	12659	11789	10781	9833	8951	8059	7127	6257	5407	4517	3673	2843	2081	1303	617	41
14	21517	20507	19507	18451	17497	16529	15551	14633	13669	12671	11801	10789	9839	8963	8069	7129	6263	5413	4519	3677	2851	2083	1307	619	43
15	21521	20509	19531	18457	17509	16547	15559	14639	13679	12689	11807	10799	9851	8969	8081	7151	6269	5417	4523	3691	2857	2087	1319	631	47
16	21523	20521	19541	18461	17519	16553	15569	14653	13681	12697	11813	10831	9857	8971	8087	7159	6271	5419	4547	3697	2861	2089	1321	641	53
17	21529	20533	19543	18481	17539	16561	15581	14657	13687	12703	11821	10837	9859	8999	8089	7177	6277	5431	4549	3701	2879	2099	1327	643	59
18	21557	20543	19553	18493	17551	16567	15583	14669	13691	12713	11827	10847	9871	9001	8093	7187	6287	5437	4561	3709	2887	2111	1361	647	61
19	21559	20549	19559	18503	17569	16573	15601	14683	13693	12721	11831	10853	9883	9007	8101	7193	6299	5441	4567	3719	2897	2113	1367	653	67
20	21563	20551	19571	18517	17573	16603	15607	14699	13697	12739	11833	10859	9887	9011	8111	7207	6301	5443	4583	3727	2903	2129	1373	659	71
21	21569	20563	19577	18521	17579	16607	15619	14713	13709	12743	11839	10861	9901	9013	8117	7211	6311	5449	4591	3733	2909	2131	1381	661	73
22	21577	20593	19583	18523	17581	16619	15629	14717	13711	12757	11863	10867	9907	9029	8123	7213	6317	5471	4597	3739	2917	2137	1399	673	79
23	21587	20599	19597	18539	17597	16631	15641	14723	13721	12763	11867	10883	9923	9041	8147	7219	6323	5477	4603	3761	2927	2141	1409	677	83
24	21589	20611	19603	18541	17599	16633	15643	14731	13723	12781	11887	10889	9929	9043	8161	7229	6329	5479	4621	3767	2939	2143	1423	683	89
25	21599	20627	19609	18553	17609	16649	15647	14737	13729	12791	11897	10891	9931	9049	8167	7237	6337	5483	4637	3769	2953	2153	1427	691	97
26	21601	20639	19661	18583	17623	16651	15649	14741	13751	12799	11903	10903	9941	9059	8171	7243	6343	5501	4639	3779	2957	2161	1429	701	101
27	21611	20641	19681	18587	17627	16657	15661	14747	13757	12809	11909	10909	9949	9067	8179	7247	6353	5503	4643	3793	2963	2179	1433	709	103
28	21613	20663	19687	18593	17657	16661	15667	14753	13759	12821	11923	10937	9967	9091	8191	7253	6359	5507	4649	3797	2969	2203	1439	719	107
29	21617	20681	19697	18617	17659	16673	15671	14759	13763	12823	11927	10939	9973	9103	8209	7283	6361	5519	4651	3803	2971	2207	1447	727	109
30	21647	20693	19699	18637	17669	16691	15679	14767	13781	12829	11933	10949	10007	9109	8219	7297	6367	5521	4657	3821	2999	2213	1451	733	113
31	21649	20707	19709	18661	17681	16693	15683	14771	13789	12841	11939	10957	10009	9127	8221	7307	6373	5527	4663	3823	3001	2221	1453	739	127
32	21661	20717	19717	18671	17683	16699	15727	14779	13799	12853	11941	10973	10037	9133	8231	7309	6379	5531	4673	3833	3011	2237	1459	743	131
33	21673	20719	19727	18679	17707	16703	15731	14783	13807	12889	11953	10979	10039	9137	8233	7321	6389	5557	4679	3847	3019	2239	1471	751	137
34	21683	20731	19739	18691	17713	16729	15733	14797	13829	12893	11959	10987	10061	9151	8237	7331	6397	5563	4691	3851	3023	2243	1481	757	139
35	21701	20743	19751	18701	17729	16741	15737	14813	13831	12899	11969	10993	10067	9157	8243	7333	6421	5569	4703	3853	3037	2251	1483	761	149
36	21713	20747	19753	18713	17737	16747	15739	14821	13841	12907	11971	11003	10069	9161	8263	7349	6427	5573	4721	3863	3041	2267	1487	769	151
37	21727	20749	19759	18719	17747	16759	15749	14827	13859	12911	11981	11027	10079	9173	8269	7351	6449	5581	4723	3877	3049	2269	1489	773	157
38	21737	20753	19763	18731	17749	16763	15761	14831	13873	12917	11987	11047	10091	9181	8273	7369	6451	5591	4729	3881	3061	2273	1493	787	163
39	21739	20759	19777	18743	17761	16787	15767	14843	13877	12919	12007	11057	10093	9187	8287	7393	6469	5623	4733	3889	3067	2281	1499	797	167
40	21751	20771	19793	18749	17783	16811	15773	14851	13879	12923	12011	11059	10099	9199	8291	7411	6473	5639	4751	3907	3079	2287	1511	809	173
41	21757	20773	19801	18757	17789	16823	15787	14867	13883	12941	12037	11069	10103	9203	8293	7417	6481	5641	4759	3911	3083	2293	1523	811	179
42	21767	20789	19813	18773	17791	16829	15791	14869	13901	12953	12041	11071	10111	9209	8297	7433	6491	5647	4783	3917	3089	2297	1531	821	181
43	21773	20807	19819	18787	17807	16831	15797	14879	13903	12959	12043	11083	10133	9221	8311	7451	6521	5651	4787	3919	3109	2309	1543	823	191
44	21787	20809	19841	18793	17827	16843	15803	14887	13907	12967	12049	11087	10139	9227	8317	7457	6529	5653	4789	3923	3119	2311	1549	827	193
45	21799	20849	19843	18797	17837	16871	15809	14891	13913	12973	12071	11093	10141	9239	8329	7459	6547	5657	4793	3929	3121	2333	1553	829	197
46	21803	20857	19853	18803	17839	16879	15817	14897	13921	12979	12073	11113	10151	9241	8353	7477	6551	5659	4799	3931	3137	2339	1559	839	199
47	21817	20873	19861	18839	17851	16883	15823	14923	13931	12983	12097	11117	10159	9257	8363	7481	6553	5669	4801	3943	3163	2341	1567	853	211
48	21821	20879	19867	18859	17863	16889	15859	14929	13933	13001	12101	11119	10163	9277	8369	7487	6563	5683	4813	3947	3167	2347	1571	857	223
49	21839	20887	19889	18869	17881	16901	15877	14939	13963	13003	12107	11131	10169	9281	8377	7489	6569	5689	4817	3967	3169	2351	1579	859	227
50	21841	20897	19891	18899	17891	16903	15881	14947	13967	13007	12109	11149	10177	9283	8387	7499	6571	5693	4831	3989	3181	2357	1583	863	229

PRIMES (continued)

	24	23	22	21	20	19	18	17	16	15	14	13	12	11	10	9	8	7	6	5	4	3	2	1	0
51	21851	20899	19913	18911	17903	16921	15887	14951	13997	13009	12113	11159	10181	9293	8389	7507	6577	5701	4861	4001	3187	2371	1597	877	233
52	21859	20903	19919	18913	17909	16927	15889	14957	13999	13033	12119	11161	10193	9311	8419	7517	6581	5711	4871	4003	3191	2377	1601	881	239
53	21863	20921	19927	18917	17911	16931	15901	14969	14009	13037	12143	11171	10211	9319	8423	7523	6599	5717	4877	4007	3203	2381	1607	883	241
54	21871	20929	19937	18919	17921	16937	15907	14983	14011	13043	12149	11173	10223	9323	8429	7529	6607	5737	4889	4013	3209	2383	1609	887	251
55	21881	20939	19949	18947	17923	16943	15913	15013	14029	13049	12157	11177	10243	9337	8431	7537	6619	5741	4903	4019	3217	2389	1613	907	257
56	21893	20947	19961	18959	17929	16963	15919	15017	14033	13063	12161	11197	10247	9341	8443	7541	6637	5743	4909	4021	3221	2393	1619	911	263
57	21911	20959	19963	18973	17939	16979	15923	15031	14051	13093	12163	11213	10253	9343	8447	7547	6653	5749	4919	4027	3229	2399	1621	919	269
58	21929	20963	19973	18979	17957	16981	15937	15053	14057	13099	12197	11239	10259	9349	8461	7549	6659	5779	4931	4049	3251	2411	1627	929	271
59	21937	20981	19979	19001	17959	16987	15959	15061	14071	13103	12203	11243	10267	9371	8467	7559	6661	5783	4933	4051	3253	2417	1637	937	277
60	21943	20983	19991	19009	17971	16993	15971	15073	14081	13109	12211	11251	10271	9377	8501	7561	6673	5791	4937	4057	3257	2423	1657	941	281
61	21961	21001	19993	19013	17977	17011	15973	15077	14083	13121	12227	11257	10273	9391	8513	7573	6679	5801	4943	4073	3259	2437	1663	947	283
62	21977	21011	19997	19031	17981	17021	15991	15083	14087	13127	12239	11261	10289	9397	8521	7577	6689	5807	4951	4079	3271	2441	1667	953	293
63	21991	21013	20011	19037	17987	17027	16001	15091	14107	13147	12241	11273	10301	9403	8527	7583	6691	5813	4957	4091	3299	2447	1669	967	307
64	21997	21017	20021	19051	17989	17029	16007	15101	14143	13151	12251	11279	10303	9413	8537	7589	6701	5821	4967	4093	3301	2459	1693	971	311
65	22003	21019	20023	19069	18013	17033	16033	15107	14149	13159	12253	11287	10313	9419	8539	7591	6703	5827	4969	4099	3307	2467	1697	977	313
66	22013	21023	20029	19073	18041	17041	16057	15121	14153	13163	12263	11299	10321	9421	8543	7603	6709	5839	4973	4111	3313	2473	1699	983	317
67	22027	21031	20047	19079	18043	17047	16061	15131	14159	13171	12269	11311	10331	9431	8563	7607	6719	5843	4987	4127	3319	2477	1709	991	331
68	22031	21059	20051	19081	18047	17053	16063	15137	14173	13177	12277	11317	10333	9433	8573	7621	6733	5849	4993	4129	3323	2503	1721	997	337
69	22037	21061	20063	19087	18049	17077	16067	15139	14177	13183	12281	11321	10337	9437	8581	7639	6737	5851	4999	4133	3329	2521	1723	1009	347
70	22039	21067	20071	19121	18059	17093	16069	15149	14197	13187	12289	11329	10343	9439	8597	7643	6761	5857	5003	4139	3331	2531	1733	1013	349
71	22051	21089	20089	19139	18061	17099	16073	15161	14207	13217	12301	11351	10357	9461	8599	7649	6763	5861	5009	4153	3343	2539	1741	1019	353
72	22063	21101	20101	19141	18077	17107	16087	15173	14221	13219	12323	11353	10369	9463	8609	7669	6779	5867	5011	4157	3347	2543	1747	1021	359
73	22067	21107	20107	19157	18089	17117	16091	15187	14243	13229	12329	11369	10391	9467	8623	7673	6781	5869	5021	4159	3359	2549	1753	1031	367
74	22073	21121	20113	19163	18097	17123	16097	15193	14249	13241	12343	11383	10399	9473	8627	7681	6791	5879	5023	4177	3361	2551	1759	1033	373
75	22079	21139	20117	19181	18119	17137	16103	15199	14251	13249	12347	11393	10427	9479	8629	7687	6793	5881	5039	4201	3371	2557	1777	1039	379
76	22091	21143	20123	19183	18121	17159	16111	15217	14281	13259	12373	11399	10429	9491	8641	7691	6803	5897	5051	4211	3373	2579	1783	1049	383
77	22093	21149	20129	19207	18127	17167	16127	15227	14293	13267	12377	11411	10433	9497	8647	7699	6823	5903	5059	4217	3389	2591	1787	1051	389
78	22109	21157	20143	19211	18131	17183	16139	15233	14303	13291	12379	11423	10453	9511	8663	7703	6827	5923	5077	4219	3391	2593	1789	1061	397
79	22111	21163	20147	19213	18133	17189	16141	15241	14321	13297	12391	11437	10457	9521	8669	7717	6829	5927	5081	4229	3407	2609	1801	1063	401
80	22123	21169	20149	19219	18143	17191	16183	15259	14323	13309	12401	11443	10459	9533	8677	7723	6833	5939	5087	4231	3413	2617	1811	1069	409
81	22129	21179	20161	19231	18149	17203	16187	15263	14327	13313	12409	11447	10463	9539	8681	7727	6841	5953	5099	4241	3433	2621	1823	1087	419
82	22133	21187	20173	19237	18169	17207	16189	15269	14341	13327	12413	11467	10477	9547	8689	7741	6857	5981	5101	4243	3449	2633	1831	1091	421
83	22147	21191	20177	19249	18181	17209	16193	15271	14347	13331	12421	11471	10487	9551	8693	7753	6863	5987	5107	4253	3457	2647	1847	1093	431
84	22153	21193	20183	19259	18191	17231	16217	15277	14369	13337	12433	11483	10499	9587	8699	7757	6869	6007	5113	4259	3461	2657	1861	1097	433
85	22157	21211	20201	19267	18199	17239	16223	15287	14387	13339	12437	11489	10501	9601	8707	7759	6871	6011	5119	4261	3463	2659	1867	1103	439
86	22159	21221	20219	19273	18211	17257	16229	15289	14389	13367	12451	11491	10513	9613	8713	7789	6883	6029	5147	4271	3467	2663	1871	1109	443
87	22171	21227	20231	19289	18217	17291	16231	15299	14401	13381	12457	11497	10529	9619	8719	7793	6899	6037	5153	4273	3469	2671	1873	1117	449
88	22189	21247	20233	19301	18223	17293	16249	15307	14407	13397	12473	11503	10531	9623	8731	7817	6907	6043	5167	4283	3491	2677	1877	1123	457
89	22193	21269	20249	19309	18229	17299	16253	15313	14411	13399	12479	11519	10559	9629	8737	7823	6911	6047	5171	4289	3499	2683	1879	1129	461
90	22229	21277	20261	19319	18233	17317	16267	15319	14419	13411	12487	11527	10567	9631	8741	7829	6917	6053	5179	4297	3511	2687	1889	1151	463
91	22247	21283	20269	19333	18251	17321	16273	15329	14423	13417	12491	11549	10589	9643	8747	7841	6947	6067	5189	4327	3517	2689	1901	1153	467
92	22259	21313	20287	19373	18253	17327	16301	15331	14431	13421	12497	11551	10597	9649	8753	7853	6949	6073	5197	4337	3527	2693	1907	1163	479
93	22271	21317	20297	19379	18257	17333	16319	15349	14437	13441	12503	11579	10601	9661	8761	7867	6959	6079	5209	4339	3529	2699	1913	1171	487
94	22273	21319	20323	19381	18269	17341	16333	15359	14447	13451	12511	11587	10607	9677	8779	7873	6961	6089	5227	4349	3533	2707	1931	1181	491
95	22277	21323	20327	19387	18287	17351	16339	15361	14449	13457	12517	11593	10613	9679	8783	7877	6967	6091	5231	4357	3539	2711	1933	1187	499
96	22279	21341	20333	19391	18289	17359	16349	15373	14461	13463	12527	11597	10627	9689	8803	7879	6971	6101	5233	4363	3541	2713	1949	1193	503
97	22283	21347	20341	19403	18301	17377	16361	15377	14479	13469	12539	11617	10631	9697	8807	7883	6977	6113	5237	4373	3547	2719	1951	1201	509
98	22291	21377	20347	19417	18307	17383	16363	15383	14489	13477	12541	11621	10639	9719	8819	7901	6983	6121	5261	4391	3557	2729	1973	1213	521
99	22303	21379	20353	19421	18311	17387	16369	15391	14503	13487	12547	11633	10651	9721	8821	7907	6991	6131	5273	4397	3559	2731	1979	1217	523
100	22307	21383	20357	19423	18313	17389	16381	15401	14519	13499	12553	11657	10657	9733	8831	7919	6997	6133	5279	4409	3571	2741	1987	1223	541

PRIMES (continued)

PRIMES (continued)

	25	26	27	28	29	30	31	32	33	34	35	36	37	38	39	40	41	42	43	44	45	46	47	48	49
1	22343	23327	24317	25409	26407	27457	28513	29453	30577	31607	32611	33617	34651	35771	36787	37831	38917	39979	41113	42083	43063	44203	45317	46451	47533
2	22349	23333	24329	25411	26417	27479	28517	29473	30593	31627	32621	33619	34667	35797	36791	37847	38933	39983	41117	42089	43067	44207	45319	46457	47543
3	22367	23339	24337	25423	26423	27481	28537	29483	30631	31643	32633	33623	34673	35801	36793	37853	38953	39989	41131	42101	43093	44221	45329	46471	47563
4	22369	23357	24359	25439	26431	27487	28541	29501	30637	31649	32647	33629	34679	35803	36809	37861	38959	40009	41141	42131	43103	44249	45337	46477	47569
5	22381	23369	24371	25447	26437	27509	28547	29527	30643	31657	32653	33637	34687	35809	36821	37871	38971	40013	41143	42139	43117	44257	45341	46489	47581
6	22391	23371	24373	25453	26449	27527	28549	29531	30649	31663	32687	33641	34693	35831	36833	37879	38977	40031	41149	42157	43133	44263	45343	46499	47591
7	22397	23399	24379	25457	26459	27529	28559	29537	30661	31667	32693	33647	34703	35837	36847	37889	38993	40037	41161	42169	43151	44267	45361	46507	47599
8	22409	23417	24391	25463	26479	27539	28571	29567	30671	31687	32707	33679	34721	35851	36857	37897	39019	40039	41177	42179	43159	44269	45377	46511	47609
9	22433	23431	24407	25469	26489	27541	28573	29569	30677	31699	32713	33703	34729	35863	36871	37907	39023	40063	41179	42181	43177	44273	45389	46523	47623
10	22441	23447	24413	25471	26497	27551	28579	29573	30689	31721	32717	33713	34739	35869	36877	37951	39041	40087	41183	42187	43189	44279	45403	46549	47629
11	22447	23459	24419	25523	26501	27581	28591	29581	30697	31723	32719	33721	34747	35879	36887	37957	39043	40093	41189	42193	43201	44281	45413	46559	47639
12	22453	23473	24421	25537	26513	27583	28597	29587	30703	31727	32749	33739	34757	35897	36899	37963	39047	40099	41201	42197	43207	44293	45427	46567	47653
13	22469	23497	24439	25541	26539	27611	28603	29599	30707	31729	32771	33749	34759	35899	36901	37967	39079	40111	41203	42209	43223	44351	45433	46573	47657
14	22481	23509	24443	25561	26557	27617	28607	29611	30713	31741	32779	33751	34763	35911	36913	37987	39089	40123	41213	42221	43237	44357	45439	46589	47659
15	22483	23531	24469	25577	26561	27631	28619	29629	30727	31751	32783	33757	34781	35923	36919	37991	39097	40127	41221	42223	43261	44371	45481	46591	47681
16	22501	23537	24473	25579	26573	27647	28621	29633	30757	31769	32789	33767	34807	35933	36923	37993	39103	40129	41227	42227	43271	44381	45491	46601	47699
17	22511	23539	24481	25583	26591	27653	28627	29641	30763	31771	32797	33769	34819	35951	36929	37997	39107	40151	41231	42239	43283	44383	45497	46619	47701
18	22531	23549	24499	25589	26597	27673	28631	29663	30773	31793	32801	33773	34841	35963	36931	38011	39113	40153	41233	42257	43291	44389	45503	46633	47711
19	22541	23557	24509	25601	26627	27689	28643	29669	30781	31799	32803	33791	34843	35969	36943	38039	39119	40163	41243	42281	43313	44417	45523	46639	47713
20	22543	23561	24517	25603	26633	27691	28649	29671	30803	31817	32831	33797	34847	35977	36947	38047	39133	40169	41257	42283	43319	44449	45533	46643	47717
21	22549	23563	24527	25609	26641	27697	28657	29683	30809	31847	32833	33809	34849	35983	36973	38053	39139	40177	41263	42293	43321	44453	45541	46649	47737
22	22567	23567	24533	25621	26647	27701	28661	29717	30817	31849	32839	33811	34871	35993	36979	38069	39157	40189	41269	42299	43331	44483	45553	46663	47741
23	22571	23581	24547	25633	26669	27733	28663	29723	30829	31859	32843	33827	34877	35999	36997	38083	39161	40193	41281	42307	43391	44491	45557	46679	47743
24	22573	23593	24551	25639	26681	27737	28669	29741	30839	31873	32869	33829	34883	36007	37003	38113	39163	40213	41299	42323	43397	44497	45569	46681	47777
25	22613	23599	24571	25643	26683	27739	28687	29753	30841	31883	32887	33851	34897	36011	37013	38119	39181	40231	41333	42331	43399	44501	45587	46687	47779
26	22619	23603	24593	25657	26687	27743	28697	29759	30851	31891	32909	33857	34913	36013	37019	38149	39191	40237	41341	42337	43403	44507	45589	46691	47791
27	22621	23609	24611	25667	26693	27749	28703	29761	30853	31907	32911	33863	34919	36017	37021	38153	39199	40241	41351	42349	43411	44519	45599	46703	47797
28	22637	23623	24623	25673	26699	27751	28711	29789	30859	31957	32917	33871	34939	36037	37039	38167	39209	40253	41357	42359	43427	44531	45613	46723	47807
29	22639	23627	24631	25679	26701	27763	28723	29803	30869	31963	32933	33889	34949	36061	37049	38177	39217	40277	41381	42373	43441	44533	45631	46727	47809
30	22643	23629	24659	25693	26711	27767	28729	29819	30871	31973	32939	33893	34961	36067	37057	38183	39227	40283	41387	42379	43451	44537	45641	46747	47819
31	22651	23633	24671	25703	26713	27773	28751	29833	30881	31981	32941	33911	34963	36073	37061	38189	39229	40289	41389	42391	43457	44543	45659	46751	47837
32	22669	23663	24677	25717	26717	27779	28753	29837	30893	31991	32957	33923	34981	36083	37087	38197	39233	40343	41399	42397	43481	44549	45667	46757	47843
33	22679	23669	24683	25733	26723	27791	28759	29851	30911	32003	32969	33931	35023	36097	37097	38201	39239	40351	41411	42403	43487	44563	45673	46769	47857
34	22691	23671	24691	25741	26729	27799	28771	29863	30931	32009	32971	33937	35027	36107	37117	38219	39241	40357	41413	42407	43499	44579	45677	46771	47869
35	22697	23677	24697	25747	26731	27803	28789	29867	30937	32027	32983	33941	35051	36109	37123	38231	39251	40361	41443	42409	43517	44587	45691	46807	47881
36	22699	23687	24709	25759	26737	27809	28793	29873	30941	32029	32987	33961	35053	36131	37139	38237	39293	40387	41453	42433	43541	44617	45697	46811	47903
37	22709	23689	24733	25763	26759	27817	28807	29879	30949	32051	32993	33967	35059	36151	37159	38239	39301	40423	41467	42437	43543	44621	45707	46817	47911
38	22717	23719	24749	25771	26777	27823	28813	29881	30971	32057	32999	33997	35069	36161	37171	38261	39313	40427	41479	42443	43573	44623	45737	46819	47917
39	22721	23741	24763	25793	26783	27827	28817	29917	30977	32059	33013	34019	35081	36187	37181	38273	39317	40429	41491	42451	43577	44633	45751	46829	47933
40	22727	23743	24767	25799	26801	27847	28837	29921	30983	32063	33023	34031	35083	36191	37189	38281	39323	40433	41507	42457	43579	44641	45757	46831	47939
41	22739	23747	24781	25801	26813	27851	28843	29927	31013	32069	33029	34033	35089	36209	37199	38287	39341	40459	41513	42461	43591	44647	45763	46853	47947
42	22741	23753	24793	25819	26821	27883	28859	29947	31019	32077	33037	34039	35099	36217	37201	38299	39343	40471	41519	42463	43597	44651	45767	46861	47951
43	22751	23761	24799	25841	26833	27893	28867	29959	31033	32083	33049	34057	35107	36229	37217	38303	39359	40483	41521	42467	43607	44657	45779	46867	47963
44	22769	23767	24809	25847	26839	27901	28871	29983	31039	32089	33053	34061	35111	36241	37223	38317	39367	40487	41539	42473	43609	44683	45817	46877	47969
45	22777	23773	24821	25849	26849	27917	28879	29989	31051	32099	33071	34123	35117	36251	37243	38321	39371	40493	41543	42487	43613	44687	45821	46889	47977
46	22783	23789	24841	25867	26861	27919	28901	30011	31063	32117	33073	34127	35129	36263	37253	38327	39373	40499	41549	42491	43627	44699	45823	46901	47981
47	22787	23801	24847	25873	26863	27941	28909	30013	31069	32119	33083	34129	35141	36277	37273	38329	39383	40507	41579	42499	43633	44701	45827	46919	48017
48	22807	23813	24851	25889	26879	27943	28921	30029	31079	32141	33091	34141	35149	36293	37277	38333	39397	40519	41593	42509	43649	44711	45833	46933	48023
49	22811	23819	24859	25903	26881	27947	28927	30047	31081	32143	33107	34147	35153	36299	37307	38351	39409	40529	41597	42533	43651	44729	45841	46957	48029
50	22817	23827	24877	25913	26891	27953	28933	30059	31091	32159	33113	34157	35159	36307	37309	38371	39419	40531	41603	42557	43661	44741	45853	46993	48049

PRIMES (continued)

	25	26	27	28	29	30	31	32	33	34	35	36	37	38	39	40	41	42	43	44	45	46	47	48	49
51	22853	23831	24889	25919	26893	27953	28949	30071	31121	32173	33119	34159	35171	36293	37313	38377	39439	40543	41609	42569	43669	44753	45863	46997	48073
52	22859	23833	24907	25931	26903	27961	28961	30089	31123	32183	33149	34171	35201	36299	37321	38393	39443	40559	41611	42577	43691	44771	45869	47017	48079
53	22861	23857	24917	25933	26921	27967	28979	30091	31139	32189	33151	34183	35221	36307	37337	38431	39451	40577	41617	42583	43711	44773	45887	47041	48091
54	22871	23869	24919	25939	26927	27983	29009	30097	31147	32191	33161	34211	35227	36313	37339	38447	39461	40583	41621	42589	43717	44777	45893	47051	48109
55	22877	23873	24923	25943	26947	27997	29017	30103	31151	32203	33179	34213	35251	36319	37357	38449	39499	40591	41627	42611	43721	44789	45943	47057	48119
56	22901	23879	24943	25951	26951	28001	29021	30109	31153	32213	33181	34217	35257	36341	37361	38453	39503	40597	41641	42641	43753	44797	45949	47059	48121
57	22907	23887	24953	25969	26959	28019	29023	30113	31159	32233	33191	34231	35267	36343	37363	38459	39509	40609	41647	42643	43759	44809	45953	47087	48131
58	22921	23893	24967	25981	26981	28027	29027	30119	31177	32237	33199	34253	35279	36353	37369	38461	39511	40627	41651	42649	43777	44819	45959	47093	48157
59	22937	23899	24971	25997	26987	28031	29033	30133	31181	32251	33203	34259	35281	36373	37379	38501	39521	40637	41659	42667	43781	44839	45971	47111	48163
60	22943	23909	24977	25999	26993	28051	29059	30137	31183	32257	33211	34261	35291	36383	37397	38543	39541	40639	41669	42677	43783	44843	45979	47119	48179
61	22961	23911	24979	26003	27011	28057	29063	30139	31189	32261	33223	34267	35311	36389	37409	38557	39551	40693	41681	42683	43787	44851	45989	47123	48187
62	22963	23917	24989	26017	27017	28069	29077	30161	31193	32297	33247	34273	35317	36433	37423	38561	39563	40697	41687	42689	43789	44867	46021	47129	48193
63	22973	23929	25013	26021	27031	28081	29101	30169	31219	32299	33287	34283	35323	36451	37441	38567	39569	40699	41719	42697	43793	44879	46027	47137	48197
64	22993	23957	25031	26029	27043	28087	29123	30181	31223	32303	33289	34297	35327	36457	37447	38569	39581	40709	41729	42701	43801	44887	46049	47143	48221
65	23003	23971	25033	26041	27059	28097	29129	30187	31231	32309	33301	34301	35339	36467	37463	38593	39607	40739	41737	42703	43853	44893	46051	47147	48239
66	23011	23977	25037	26053	27061	28099	29131	30197	31237	32321	33311	34303	35353	36469	37483	38603	39619	40751	41759	42709	43867	44909	46061	47149	48247
67	23017	23981	25057	26083	27067	28109	29137	30203	31247	32323	33317	34313	35363	36473	37489	38609	39623	40759	41761	42719	43889	44917	46073	47161	48259
68	23021	23993	25073	26099	27073	28111	29147	30211	31249	32327	33329	34319	35381	36479	37493	38611	39631	40763	41771	42727	43891	44927	46091	47189	48271
69	23027	24001	25087	26107	27077	28123	29153	30223	31253	32341	33331	34327	35393	36493	37501	38629	39659	40771	41777	42737	43913	44939	46093	47207	48281
70	23029	24007	25097	26111	27091	28151	29167	30241	31259	32353	33343	34337	35401	36497	37507	38639	39667	40787	41801	42743	43933	44953	46099	47221	48299
71	23039	24019	25111	26113	27103	28163	29173	30253	31267	32359	33347	34351	35407	36523	37511	38651	39671	40801	41809	42751	43943	44959	46103	47237	48311
72	23041	24023	25117	26119	27107	28181	29179	30259	31271	32363	33349	34361	35419	36527	37517	38653	39679	40813	41813	42767	43951	44963	46133	47251	48313
73	23053	24029	25121	26141	27109	28183	29191	30269	31277	32369	33353	34367	35423	36529	37529	38669	39703	40819	41843	42773	43961	44971	46141	47269	48337
74	23057	24043	25127	26153	27127	28201	29201	30271	31307	32371	33359	34369	35437	36541	37537	38671	39709	40823	41849	42787	43963	44983	46147	47279	48341
75	23059	24049	25147	26161	27143	28211	29207	30293	31319	32377	33377	34381	35447	36551	37547	38677	39719	40829	41851	42793	43969	44987	46153	47287	48353
76	23063	24061	25153	26171	27179	28219	29209	30307	31379	32381	33391	34403	35449	36559	37549	38693	39727	40841	41863	42797	43973	45007	46171	47293	48371
77	23071	24071	25163	26177	27191	28229	29221	30313	31387	32401	33403	34421	35461	36563	37561	38699	39733	40847	41879	42821	43987	45013	46181	47297	48383
78	23081	24077	25169	26183	27197	28277	29231	30319	31391	32411	33409	34429	35491	36571	37567	38707	39749	40849	41887	42829	43991	45053	46183	47303	48397
79	23087	24083	25171	26189	27211	28307	29243	30323	31393	32413	33413	34439	35507	36583	37571	38711	39761	40853	41893	42839	43997	45061	46187	47309	48407
80	23099	24091	25183	26203	27239	28319	29251	30341	31397	32423	33427	34457	35509	36587	37573	38713	39769	40867	41897	42841	44017	45077	46199	47317	48409
81	23117	24097	25189	26209	27241	28349	29269	30347	31469	32429	33457	34469	35521	36599	37579	38723	39779	40879	41903	42853	44021	45083	46219	47339	48413
82	23131	24103	25219	26227	27253	28351	29287	30367	31477	32441	33461	34471	35527	36607	37589	38737	39791	40883	41911	42859	44027	45119	46229	47351	48437
83	23143	24107	25229	26237	27259	28387	29297	30389	31481	32443	33469	34483	35531	36629	37591	38747	39799	40897	41927	42863	44029	45121	46237	47353	48449
84	23159	24109	25237	26249	27271	28393	29303	30391	31489	32467	33479	34487	35533	36637	37607	38749	39821	40903	41941	42899	44041	45127	46261	47363	48463
85	23167	24113	25243	26251	27277	28403	29311	30403	31511	32479	33487	34499	35537	36643	37619	38767	39827	40927	41947	42901	44053	45131	46271	47381	48473
86	23173	24121	25247	26261	27281	28409	29327	30427	31513	32491	33493	34501	35543	36653	37633	38783	39829	40933	41953	42923	44059	45137	46273	47387	48479
87	23189	24133	25253	26263	27283	28411	29333	30431	31517	32497	33503	34511	35569	36671	37643	38791	39839	40939	41957	42929	44071	45139	46279	47389	48481
88	23197	24137	25261	26293	27299	28429	29339	30449	31531	32503	33521	34513	35573	36677	37649	38803	39841	40949	41959	42937	44087	45161	46301	47407	48487
89	23201	24151	25301	26297	27329	28433	29347	30467	31541	32507	33529	34519	35591	36683	37657	38821	39847	40961	41969	42943	44089	45179	46307	47417	48491
90	23203	24169	25303	26309	27337	28439	29363	30469	31543	32531	33533	34537	35593	36691	37663	38833	39857	40973	41981	42953	44101	45181	46309	47419	48497
91	23209	24179	25307	26317	27361	28447	29383	30491	31547	32533	33547	34543	35597	36697	37691	38839	39863	40993	41983	42961	44111	45191	46327	47431	48523
92	23227	24181	25309	26321	27367	28463	29387	30493	31567	32537	33563	34549	35603	36709	37693	38851	39869	41011	41999	42967	44119	45197	46337	47441	48527
93	23251	24197	25321	26339	27397	28477	29389	30497	31573	32561	33569	34583	35617	36713	37699	38861	39877	41017	42013	42979	44123	45233	46349	47459	48533
94	23269	24203	25339	26347	27407	28493	29399	30509	31583	32563	33577	34589	35671	36721	37717	38867	39883	41023	42017	42989	44129	45247	46351	47491	48539
95	23279	24223	25343	26357	27409	28499	29401	30517	31601	32569	33581	34591	35677	36739	37747	38873	39887	41039	42019	43003	44131	45259	46381	47497	48541
96	23291	24229	25349	26371	27427	28513	29411	30529	31607	32573	33587	34603	35729	36749	37781	38891	39901	41047	42023	43013	44159	45263	46399	47501	48563
97	23293	24239	25357	26387	27431	28517	29423	30539	31627	32579	33589	34607	35731	36761	37783	38903	39929	41051	42043	43019	44171	45281	46411	47507	48571
98	23297	24247	25367	26393	27437	28537	29429	30553	31643	32587	33599	34613	35747	36767	37799	38917	39937	41057	42061	43037	44179	45289	46439	47513	48589
99	23311	24251	25373	26399	27449	28541	29437	30557	31649	32603	33601	34631	35753	36779	37811	38921	39953	41077	42071	43049	44189	45293	46447	47521	48593
100	23321	24281	25391	26407	27457	28547	29443	30559	31657	32609	33613	34649	35759	36781	37813	38933	39971	41081	42073	43051	44201	45307	46457	47527	48611

PRIMES (continued)

#	50	51	52	53	54	55	56	57	58	59	60	61	62	63	64	65	66	67	68	69	70	71	72	73	74
1	48619	49667	50767	51817	52937	54001	55109	56197	57193	58243	59369	60509	61637	62791	63823	65071	66107	67247	68389	69497	70663	71719	72859	73999	75083
2	48623	49669	50773	51827	52951	54011	55117	56207	57203	58271	59377	60521	61643	62801	63839	65089	66109	67261	68399	69499	70667	71741	72869	74017	75109
3	48647	49681	50777	51829	52957	54013	55127	56209	57221	58309	59387	60527	61651	62819	63841	65099	66137	67271	68437	69539	70687	71761	72871	74021	75133
4	48649	49697	50789	51839	52963	54037	55147	56237	57223	58313	59393	60539	61657	62827	63853	65101	66161	67273	68443	69557	70709	71777	72883	74027	75149
5	48661	49711	50821	51853	52967	54049	55163	56239	57241	58321	59399	60589	61667	62851	63857	65111	66169	67289	68447	69593	70717	71789	72889	74047	75161
6	48673	49727	50833	51859	52973	54059	55171	56249	57251	58337	59407	60601	61673	62861	63863	65119	66173	67307	68449	69623	70729	71807	72893	74051	75167
7	48677	49739	50839	51869	52981	54083	55201	56263	57259	58363	59417	60607	61681	62869	63901	65123	66179	67339	68473	69653	70753	71809	72901	74071	75169
8	48679	49747	50849	51871	52999	54091	55207	56267	57269	58367	59419	60611	61687	62873	63907	65129	66191	67343	68477	69661	70769	71821	72907	74077	75181
9	48731	49757	50857	51893	53003	54101	55213	56269	57271	58369	59441	60617	61703	62897	63913	65141	66221	67349	68483	69677	70783	71837	72911	74093	75193
10	48733	49783	50867	51899	53017	54121	55217	56299	57283	58379	59443	60623	61717	62903	63929	65147	66239	67369	68489	69691	70793	71843	72923	74099	75209
11	48751	49787	50873	51907	53047	54133	55219	56311	57287	58391	59447	60631	61723	62921	63949	65167	66271	67391	68491	69697	70823	71849	72931	74101	75211
12	48757	49789	50891	51913	53051	54139	55229	56333	57301	58393	59453	60637	61729	62929	63997	65173	66293	67399	68501	69709	70841	71861	72937	74131	75217
13	48761	49801	50893	51929	53069	54151	55243	56359	57329	58403	59467	60647	61751	62939	64007	65179	66301	67409	68507	69737	70843	71867	72949	74143	75223
14	48767	49807	50909	51941	53077	54163	55249	56369	57331	58411	59471	60649	61757	62969	64013	65183	66337	67411	68521	69739	70849	71879	72953	74149	75227
15	48779	49811	50923	51949	53087	54167	55259	56377	57347	58417	59473	60659	61781	62971	64019	65203	66343	67421	68531	69761	70853	71881	72959	74159	75239
16	48781	49823	50929	51971	53089	54181	55291	56383	57349	58427	59497	60661	61813	62981	64033	65213	66347	67427	68539	69763	70867	71887	72973	74161	75253
17	48787	49831	50951	51973	53093	54193	55313	56393	57367	58439	59509	60679	61819	62987	64037	65239	66359	67429	68543	69767	70877	71899	72977	74167	75269
18	48799	49843	50957	51977	53101	54217	55331	56401	57373	58441	59513	60689	61837	62989	64063	65257	66361	67433	68567	69779	70879	71909	72997	74177	75277
19	48809	49853	50969	51991	53113	54251	55333	56417	57383	58451	59539	60703	61843	63029	64067	65267	66373	67447	68581	69809	70891	71917	73009	74189	75289
20	48817	49871	50971	52009	53117	54269	55337	56431	57389	58453	59557	60719	61861	63031	64081	65269	66377	67453	68597	69821	70901	71933	73013	74197	75307
21	48821	49877	50989	52021	53129	54277	55339	56437	57397	58477	59561	60727	61871	63059	64091	65287	66383	67477	68611	69827	70913	71941	73019	74201	75323
22	48823	49891	50993	52027	53147	54287	55343	56443	57413	58481	59567	60733	61879	63067	64109	65293	66403	67481	68633	69829	70919	71947	73037	74203	75329
23	48847	49919	51001	52051	53149	54293	55351	56453	57427	58511	59581	60737	61909	63073	64123	65309	66413	67489	68639	69833	70921	71963	73039	74209	75337
24	48857	49921	51031	52057	53161	54311	55373	56467	57457	58537	59611	60757	61927	63079	64151	65323	66431	67493	68659	69847	70937	71971	73043	74219	75347
25	48859	49927	51043	52067	53171	54319	55381	56473	57467	58543	59617	60761	61933	63097	64153	65327	66449	67499	68669	69857	70949	71983	73061	74231	75353
26	48869	49937	51047	52069	53173	54323	55399	56477	57487	58549	59621	60763	61949	63103	64157	65353	66457	67511	68683	69859	70951	71987	73063	74257	75367
27	48871	49939	51059	52081	53189	54331	55411	56479	57493	58567	59627	60773	61961	63113	64171	65357	66463	67523	68687	69877	70957	71993	73079	74279	75377
28	48883	49943	51061	52103	53197	54347	55439	56489	57503	58573	59629	60779	61967	63127	64187	65371	66467	67531	68699	69899	70969	71999	73091	74287	75389
29	48889	49957	51071	52121	53201	54361	55457	56501	57527	58579	59651	60793	61979	63131	64189	65381	66491	67547	68711	69911	70979	72019	73121	74293	75391
30	48907	49991	51109	52127	53231	54367	55469	56503	57529	58601	59659	60811	61981	63149	64217	65393	66499	67559	68713	69929	70981	72031	73127	74297	75401
31	48947	49993	51131	52147	53233	54371	55487	56509	57557	58603	59663	60821	61987	63179	64223	65407	66509	67567	68729	69931	70991	72043	73133	74311	75403
32	48953	49999	51137	52153	53239	54377	55501	56519	57571	58613	59669	60859	61991	63197	64231	65413	66523	67577	68737	69941	70997	72047	73141	74317	75407
33	48973	50021	51151	52163	53267	54401	55511	56527	57587	58631	59671	60869	62003	63199	64237	65419	66529	67579	68743	69959	70999	72053	73181	74323	75431
34	48989	50023	51157	52177	53269	54403	55529	56531	57593	58657	59693	60887	62017	63211	64271	65423	66533	67589	68749	69991	71011	72073	73189	74353	75437
35	48991	50033	51169	52181	53279	54409	55541	56533	57601	58661	59699	60889	62039	63241	64279	65437	66541	67601	68767	69997	71023	72077	73237	74357	75479
36	49003	50047	51193	52183	53281	54413	55547	56543	57637	58679	59707	60899	62047	63247	64283	65447	66553	67607	68771	70001	71039	72089	73243	74363	75503
37	49009	50051	51197	52189	53299	54419	55579	56569	57641	58687	59723	60901	62053	63277	64301	65479	66569	67619	68777	70003	71059	72091	73259	74377	75511
38	49019	50053	51199	52201	53309	54421	55589	56591	57649	58693	59729	60913	62057	63281	64303	65497	66571	67631	68791	70009	71069	72101	73277	74381	75521
39	49031	50069	51203	52223	53323	54437	55603	56597	57653	58699	59743	60917	62071	63299	64319	65519	66587	67651	68813	70019	71081	72103	73291	74383	75527
40	49033	50077	51217	52237	53327	54443	55609	56599	57667	58711	59747	60919	62081	63311	64327	65521	66593	67679	68819	70039	71089	72109	73303	74411	75533
41	49037	50087	51229	52249	53353	54449	55619	56611	57679	58727	59753	60923	62099	63313	64333	65537	66601	67699	68821	70051	71119	72139	73309	74413	75539
42	49043	50093	51239	52253	53359	54469	55621	56629	57689	58733	59771	60937	62119	63331	64373	65539	66617	67709	68863	70061	71129	72161	73327	74419	75541
43	49057	50101	51241	52259	53377	54493	55631	56633	57697	58741	59779	60943	62129	63337	64381	65543	66629	67723	68879	70067	71143	72167	73331	74441	75553
44	49069	50111	51257	52267	53381	54497	55633	56659	57709	58757	59791	60953	62131	63347	64399	65551	66653	67733	68881	70079	71147	72169	73351	74449	75557
45	49081	50119	51263	52289	53401	54499	55639	56663	57713	58763	59797	60961	62137	63353	64403	65557	66683	67741	68891	70099	71153	72173	73361	74453	75571
46	49103	50123	51283	52291	53407	54503	55661	56671	57719	58771	59809	61001	62141	63361	64433	65563	66697	67757	68897	70111	71161	72211	73363	74471	75577
47	49109	50129	51287	52301	53411	54517	55663	56681	57727	58787	59833	61007	62143	63367	64439	65579	66701	67759	68899	70117	71167	72221	73369	74489	75583
48	49117	50131	51307	52313	53419	54521	55667	56687	57731	58789	59863	61027	62171	63377	64451	65581	66713	67763	68903	70121	71171	72223	73379	74507	75611
49	49121	50147	51329	52321	53437	54539	55673	56701	57737	58831	59879	61031	62189	63389	64453	65587	66721	67777	68909	70123	71191	72227	73387	74509	75617
50	49123	50159	51341	52361	53441	54541	55681	56711	57751	58889	59887	61043	62191	63391	64483	65599	66733	67783	68917	70139	71209	72229	73417	74521	75619

PRIMES (continued)

	50	51	52	53	54	55	56	57	58	59	60	61	62	63	64	65	66	67	68	69	70	71	72	73	74
51	49139	50153	51341	52363	53453	54547	55681	56713	57751	58897	59929	61057	62191	63377	64483	65587	66733	67777	68927	70141	71233	72251	73421	74527	75629
52	49157	50159	51343	52369	53479	54559	55691	56731	57773	58901	59951	61091	62201	63391	64489	65599	66749	67783	68947	70157	71237	72253	73433	74531	75641
53	49169	50177	51347	52379	53503	54563	55697	56737	57781	58907	59957	61099	62207	63397	64499	65609	66751	67789	68963	70163	71249	72269	73453	74551	75653
54	49171	50207	51349	52387	53507	54577	55711	56747	57787	58909	59971	61121	62213	63409	64513	65617	66763	67801	68993	70177	71257	72271	73459	74561	75659
55	49177	50221	51361	52391	53527	54581	55717	56767	57791	58913	59981	61129	62219	63419	64553	65629	66791	67807	69001	70181	71261	72277	73471	74567	75679
56	49193	50227	51383	52433	53549	54583	55721	56773	57793	58921	59999	61141	62233	63421	64567	65633	66797	67819	69011	70183	71263	72287	73477	74573	75683
57	49199	50231	51407	52453	53551	54601	55733	56779	57803	58937	60013	61151	62273	63439	64577	65647	66809	67829	69019	70199	71287	72307	73483	74587	75689
58	49201	50261	51413	52457	53569	54617	55763	56783	57809	58943	60017	61153	62297	63443	64579	65651	66821	67843	69029	70201	71293	72313	73517	74597	75703
59	49207	50263	51419	52489	53591	54623	55787	56807	57829	58963	60029	61169	62299	63463	64591	65657	66841	67853	69031	70207	71317	72337	73523	74609	75707
60	49211	50273	51421	52501	53593	54629	55793	56809	57839	58967	60037	61211	62303	63467	64601	65677	66851	67867	69061	70223	71327	72341	73529	74611	75709
61	49223	50287	51427	52511	53597	54631	55799	56813	57847	58979	60041	61223	62311	63473	64609	65687	66853	67891	69067	70229	71329	72353	73547	74623	75721
62	49253	50291	51431	52517	53609	54647	55807	56821	57853	58991	60077	61231	62323	63487	64613	65699	66863	67901	69073	70237	71333	72367	73553	74653	75731
63	49261	50311	51437	52529	53611	54667	55813	56827	57859	58997	60083	61253	62327	63493	64621	65701	66877	67927	69109	70241	71339	72379	73561	74687	75743
64	49277	50321	51439	52541	53617	54673	55817	56843	57881	59009	60089	61261	62347	63499	64627	65707	66883	67931	69119	70249	71341	72383	73571	74699	75767
65	49279	50329	51449	52543	53623	54679	55819	56857	57899	59011	60091	61283	62351	63521	64633	65713	66889	67933	69127	70271	71347	72421	73583	74707	75773
66	49297	50333	51461	52553	53629	54709	55823	56873	57901	59021	60101	61291	62383	63527	64661	65717	66919	67939	69143	70289	71353	72431	73589	74713	75781
67	49307	50341	51473	52561	53633	54713	55829	56891	57917	59023	60103	61297	62401	63533	64667	65719	66923	67943	69149	70297	71359	72461	73597	74717	75787
68	49331	50359	51479	52567	53639	54721	55837	56893	57923	59029	60107	61331	62417	63541	64679	65729	66931	67957	69151	70309	71363	72467	73607	74719	75793
69	49333	50363	51481	52571	53653	54727	55843	56897	57943	59051	60127	61333	62423	63559	64693	65731	66943	67961	69163	70313	71387	72469	73609	74729	75797
70	49339	50377	51487	52579	53657	54751	55849	56909	57947	59053	60133	61339	62459	63577	64709	65761	66947	67967	69191	70321	71389	72481	73613	74731	75821
71	49363	50383	51503	52583	53681	54767	55871	56911	57973	59063	60139	61343	62467	63587	64717	65777	66949	67979	69193	70327	71399	72493	73637	74747	75833
72	49367	50387	51511	52609	53693	54773	55889	56921	57977	59069	60149	61357	62473	63589	64747	65789	66959	67987	69197	70351	71411	72497	73643	74759	75853
73	49369	50411	51517	52627	53699	54779	55897	56923	57991	59077	60161	61363	62477	63599	64763	65809	66973	67993	69203	70373	71413	72503	73651	74761	75869
74	49391	50417	51521	52631	53717	54787	55901	56929	58013	59083	60167	61379	62483	63601	64781	65827	66977	68023	69221	70379	71419	72533	73673	74771	75883
75	49393	50423	51539	52639	53719	54799	55903	56941	58027	59093	60169	61381	62497	63607	64783	65831	67003	68041	69233	70381	71429	72547	73679	74779	75913
76	49409	50441	51551	52667	53731	54829	55921	56951	58031	59107	60209	61403	62501	63611	64793	65837	67021	68053	69239	70393	71437	72551	73681	74797	75931
77	49411	50459	51563	52673	53759	54833	55927	56957	58043	59113	60217	61409	62507	63629	64811	65839	67033	68059	69247	70423	71443	72559	73693	74821	75937
78	49417	50461	51577	52691	53773	54851	55931	56963	58049	59119	60223	61417	62533	63647	64817	65843	67043	68071	69257	70429	71453	72577	73699	74827	75941
79	49429	50497	51581	52697	53777	54869	55933	56983	58057	59123	60251	61441	62539	63649	64849	65851	67049	68087	69259	70439	71471	72613	73709	74831	75967
80	49433	50503	51593	52709	53783	54877	55949	56989	58061	59141	60257	61463	62549	63659	64853	65867	67057	68099	69263	70451	71473	72617	73721	74843	75979
81	49451	50513	51599	52711	53791	54881	55967	56993	58067	59149	60259	61469	62563	63667	64871	65881	67061	68111	69313	70457	71479	72623	73727	74857	75983
82	49459	50527	51607	52721	53813	54907	55987	56999	58073	59159	60271	61471	62581	63671	64877	65899	67073	68113	69317	70459	71483	72643	73751	74861	75989
83	49463	50539	51613	52727	53819	54917	55997	57037	58099	59167	60289	61483	62591	63689	64891	65921	67079	68141	69337	70481	71503	72647	73757	74869	75991
84	49477	50543	51631	52733	53831	54919	56003	57041	58109	59183	60293	61487	62597	63691	64901	65927	67103	68147	69341	70487	71527	72649	73771	74873	75997
85	49481	50549	51637	52747	53849	54941	56009	57047	58111	59197	60317	61493	62603	63697	64919	65929	67121	68161	69371	70489	71537	72661	73783	74887	76001
86	49499	50551	51647	52757	53857	54949	56039	57059	58129	59207	60331	61511	62617	63703	64921	65951	67129	68171	69379	70501	71549	72671	73819	74891	76003
87	49523	50581	51659	52769	53861	54959	56041	57073	58147	59209	60337	61519	62627	63709	64927	65957	67139	68207	69383	70507	71551	72673	73823	74897	76031
88	49529	50587	51673	52783	53881	54973	56053	57077	58151	59219	60343	61543	62633	63719	64937	65963	67141	68209	69389	70529	71563	72679	73847	74903	76039
89	49537	50591	51679	52807	53887	54979	56081	57089	58153	59221	60353	61547	62639	63727	64951	65981	67153	68213	69401	70537	71569	72689	73849	74923	76079
·90	49547	50593	51683	52813	53891	54983	56087	57097	58169	59233	60373	61553	62653	63737	64969	65983	67157	68219	69403	70549	71593	72701	73859	74929	76081
91	49549	50599	51691	52817	53897	55001	56093	57107	58171	59239	60383	61559	62659	63743	64997	65993	67169	68227	69427	70571	71597	72707	73867	74933	76091
92	49559	50627	51713	52837	53899	55009	56099	57119	58189	59243	60397	61561	62683	63761	65003	66029	67181	68239	69431	70573	71633	72719	73877	74941	76099
93	49597	50647	51719	52859	53917	55021	56101	57131	58193	59263	60413	61583	62687	63773	65011	66037	67187	68261	69439	70583	71647	72727	73883	74959	76103
94	49603	50651	51721	52861	53923	55049	56113	57139	58199	59273	60427	61603	62701	63781	65027	66041	67189	68279	69457	70589	71663	72733	73897	75011	76123
95	49613	50671	51749	52879	53927	55051	56123	57143	58207	59281	60443	61609	62723	63793	65029	66047	67211	68281	69463	70607	71671	72739	73907	75013	76129
96	49627	50683	51767	52883	53939	55057	56131	57149	58211	59333	60449	61613	62731	63799	65033	66067	67213	68311	69467	70619	71693	72763	73939	75017	76147
97	49633	50707	51769	52889	53951	55061	56149	57163	58217	59341	60457	61627	62743	63803	65053	66071	67217	68329	69473	70621	71699	72767	73943	75029	76157
98	49639	50723	51787	52901	53959	55073	56167	57173	58229	59351	60493	61631	62753	63809	65063	66083	67219	68351	69481	70627	71707	72797	73951	75037	76159
99	49663	50741	51797	52903	53987	55079	56171	57179	58231	59357	60497	61637	62761	63823	65071	66089	67231	68371	69491	70639	71711	72817	73961	75041	76163
100	49667	50753	51803	52919	53993	55103	56179	57191	58237	59359	60509	61643	62773	63839	65089	66103	67247	68389	69493	70657	71713	72823	73973	75079	76207

PRIMES (continued)

PRIMES (continued)

	75	76	77	78	79	80	81	82	83	84	85	86	87	88	89	90	91	92	93	94	95
1	76213	77359	78487	79627	80737	81817	82903	84131	85243	86381	87557	88807	89867	90989	92177	93187	94351	95443	96587	97829	98953
2	76231	77369	78497	79631	80747	81839	82913	84137	85247	86389	87559	88811	89891	90997	92179	93199	94379	95461	96589	97841	98963
3	76243	77377	78509	79633	80749	81847	82939	84143	85259	86399	87583	88813	89897	91009	92189	93229	94397	95467	96601	97843	98981
4	76249	77383	78511	79657	80761	81853	82963	84163	85297	86413	87587	88817	89899	91019	92203	93239	94399	95471	96643	97847	98993
5	76253	77417	78517	79669	80777	81869	82981	84179	85303	86423	87589	88819	89909	91033	92219	93241	94421	95479	96661	97849	98999
6	76259	77419	78539	79687	80779	81883	82997	84181	85313	86441	87613	88843	89917	91079	92221	93251	94427	95483	96667	97859	99013
7	76261	77431	78541	79691	80783	81899	83003	84191	85331	86453	87623	88853	89923	91081	92227	93253	94433	95507	96671	97861	99017
8	76283	77447	78553	79693	80789	81901	83009	84199	85333	86461	87629	88861	89939	91097	92233	93257	94439	95527	96697	97871	99023
9	76289	77471	78569	79697	80803	81919	83023	84211	85361	86467	87631	88867	89959	91099	92237	93263	94441	95531	96703	97879	99041
10	76303	77477	78571	79699	80809	81929	83047	84221	85363	86477	87641	88873	89963	91121	92243	93281	94447	95539	96731	97883	99053
11	76333	77479	78577	79757	80819	81931	83059	84223	85369	86491	87643	88883	89977	91127	92251	93283	94463	95549	96737	97919	99079
12	76343	77489	78583	79769	80831	81937	83063	84229	85381	86501	87649	88897	89983	91129	92269	93287	94477	95561	96739	97927	99083
13	76367	77491	78593	79777	80833	81943	83071	84239	85411	86509	87671	88903	89989	91139	92297	93307	94483	95569	96749	97931	99089
14	76369	77509	78607	79801	80849	81953	83077	84247	85427	86531	87679	88919	89999	91141	92311	93319	94513	95581	96757	97943	99103
15	76379	77513	78623	79811	80863	81967	83089	84263	85429	86533	87683	88937	90001	91151	92317	93323	94529	95597	96763	97961	99109
16	76387	77521	78643	79813	80897	81971	83093	84299	85439	86539	87691	88951	90007	91153	92333	93329	94531	95603	96769	97967	99119
17	76403	77527	78649	79817	80909	81973	83101	84307	85447	86561	87697	88969	90011	91159	92347	93337	94541	95617	96779	97973	99131
18	76421	77543	78653	79823	80911	82003	83117	84313	85451	86573	87701	88993	90017	91163	92353	93371	94543	95621	96787	97987	99133
19	76423	77549	78691	79829	80917	82007	83137	84317	85453	86579	87719	88997	90019	91183	92357	93377	94547	95629	96797	98009	99137
20	76441	77551	78697	79841	80923	82009	83177	84319	85469	86587	87721	89003	90023	91193	92363	93383	94559	95633	96799	98011	99139
21	76463	77557	78707	79843	80929	82013	83203	84347	85487	86599	87739	89009	90031	91199	92369	93407	94561	95651	96821	98017	99149
22	76471	77563	78713	79847	80933	82021	83207	84349	85513	86627	87743	89017	90053	91229	92377	93419	94573	95701	96823	98041	99173
23	76481	77569	78721	79861	80953	82031	83219	84377	85517	86629	87751	89021	90059	91237	92381	93427	94583	95707	96827	98047	99181
24	76487	77573	78737	79867	80963	82037	83221	84389	85523	86677	87767	89041	90067	91243	92383	93463	94597	95713	96847	98057	99191
25	76493	77587	78779	79873	80989	82039	83227	84391	85531	86689	87793	89051	90071	91249	92387	93479	94603	95717	96851	98081	99223
26	76507	77591	78781	79889	81001	82051	83231	84401	85549	86693	87797	89057	90089	91253	92399	93481	94613	95723	96857	98101	99233
27	76511	77611	78787	79901	81013	82067	83233	84407	85571	86711	87803	89069	90107	91283	92401	93487	94621	95731	96893	98123	99241
28	76519	77617	78791	79903	81017	82073	83243	84421	85577	86719	87811	89071	90121	91291	92413	93491	94649	95737	96907	98129	99251
29	76537	77621	78797	79907	81019	82129	83257	84431	85597	86729	87833	89083	90127	91297	92419	93493	94651	95747	96911	98143	99257
30	76541	77641	78803	79939	81023	82139	83267	84437	85601	86743	87853	89087	90149	91303	92431	93497	94687	95773	96931	98179	99259
31	76543	77647	78809	79943	81031	82141	83269	84443	85607	86753	87869	89101	90163	91309	92459	93503	94693	95783	96953	98207	99277
32	76561	77659	78823	79967	81041	82153	83273	84449	85619	86767	87877	89107	90173	91331	92461	93523	94709	95789	96959	98213	99289
33	76579	77681	78839	79973	81043	82163	83299	84457	85621	86771	87881	89113	90187	91367	92467	93529	94723	95791	96973	98221	99317
34	76597	77687	78853	79979	81047	82171	83311	84463	85627	86783	87887	89119	90191	91369	92479	93553	94727	95801	96979	98227	99347
35	76603	77689	78857	79987	81049	82183	83339	84467	85639	86813	87911	89123	90197	91373	92489	93557	94747	95803	96989	98251	99349
36	76607	77699	78877	79997	81071	82189	83341	84481	85643	86837	87917	89137	90199	91381	92503	93559	94771	95813	96997	98257	99367
37	76631	77711	78887	79999	81077	82193	83357	84499	85661	86843	87931	89153	90203	91387	92507	93563	94777	95819	97001	98269	99371
38	76649	77713	78889	80021	81083	82207	83383	84503	85667	86851	87943	89189	90217	91393	92551	93581	94781	95857	97003	98297	99377
39	76651	77719	78893	80039	81097	82217	83389	84509	85669	86857	87959	89203	90227	91397	92557	93601	94789	95869	97007	98299	99391
40	76667	77723	78901	80051	81101	82219	83399	84521	85691	86861	87961	89209	90239	91411	92567	93607	94793	95873	97021	98317	99397
41	76673	77731	78919	80071	81119	82223	83407	84523	85703	86869	87973	89213	90247	91423	92569	93629	94811	95881	97039	98321	99401
42	76679	77743	78929	80077	81131	82231	83417	84533	85711	86923	87977	89227	90263	91433	92581	93637	94819	95891	97073	98323	99409
43	76697	77747	78941	80107	81157	82237	83423	84551	85717	86929	87991	89231	90271	91453	92593	93683	94823	95911	97081	98327	99431
44	76717	77761	78977	80111	81163	82241	83431	84559	85733	86939	88001	89237	90281	91457	92623	93701	94837	95917	97103	98347	99439
45	76733	77773	78979	80141	81173	82261	83437	84589	85751	86959	88003	89261	90289	91459	92627	93703	94841	95923	97117	98369	99469
46	76753	77783	78989	80147	81181	82267	83443	84629	85781	86969	88007	89269	90313	91463	92639	93719	94847	95929	97127	98377	99487
47	76757	77797	79031	80149	81197	82279	83449	84631	85793	86981	88019	89273	90353	91493	92641	93739	94849	95947	97151	98387	99497
48	76771	77801	79039	80153	81199	82301	83459	84649	85817	86993	88037	89293	90359	91499	92647	93761	94873	95957	97157	98389	99523
49	76777	77813	79043	80167	81203	82307	83471	84653	85819	87011	88069	89303	90371	91513	92657	93763	94889	95959	97159	98407	99527
50	76781	77839	79063	80173	81223	82339	83477	84659	85829	87013	88079	89317	90373	91529	92669	93787	94903	95971	97169	98411	99529

PRIMES (continued)

PRIMES (continued)

	95	94	93	92	91	90	89	88	87	86	85	84	83	82	81	80	79	78	77	76	75
51	99551	98419	97171	95987	94907	93809	92671	91541	90379	89329	88093	87011	85831	84673	83477	82349	81233	80177	79087	77849	76801
52	99559	98429	97177	95989	94933	93811	92681	91571	90397	89363	88117	87013	85837	84691	83497	82351	81239	80191	79103	77863	76819
53	99563	98443	97187	96001	94949	93827	92683	91573	90401	89381	88129	87037	85843	84697	83537	82361	81281	80207	79111	77867	76829
54	99571	98453	97213	96013	94951	93851	92693	91577	90403	89387	88169	87041	85847	84701	83557	82373	81283	80209	79133	77893	76831
55	99577	98459	97231	96017	94961	93871	92699	91583	90407	89393	88177	87049	85853	84713	83561	82387	81293	80221	79139	77899	76843
56	99581	98467	97241	96043	94993	93887	92707	91591	90437	89399	88211	87071	85889	84719	83563	82393	81299	80231	79147	77929	76871
57	99607	98473	97259	96053	94999	93889	92717	91621	90439	89413	88223	87083	85903	84731	83579	82421	81307	80233	79151	77933	76873
58	99611	98479	97283	96059	95003	93893	92723	91631	90469	89417	88237	87103	85909	84737	83591	82457	81331	80239	79153	77951	76883
59	99623	98491	97301	96079	95009	93901	92737	91639	90473	89431	88241	87107	85931	84751	83597	82463	81343	80251	79159	77969	76907
60	99643	98507	97303	96097	95021	93911	92753	91673	90481	89443	88259	87119	85933	84761	83609	82469	81349	80263	79181	77977	76913
61	99661	98519	97327	96137	95027	93913	92761	91691	90499	89449	88261	87121	85991	84787	83617	82471	81353	80273	79187	77983	76919
62	99667	98533	97367	96149	95063	93923	92767	91703	90511	89459	88289	87133	85999	84793	83621	82483	81371	80279	79193	77999	76943
63	99679	98543	97369	96157	95071	93937	92779	91711	90523	89477	88301	87149	86011	84809	83639	82487	81373	80287	79201	78007	76949
64	99689	98561	97373	96167	95083	93941	92789	91733	90527	89491	88321	87151	86017	84811	83641	82493	81401	80309	79229	78017	76961
65	99707	98563	97379	96179	95087	93949	92791	91753	90529	89501	88327	87179	86027	84827	83653	82499	81409	80317	79231	78031	76963
66	99709	98573	97381	96181	95089	93967	92801	91757	90533	89513	88337	87181	86029	84857	83663	82507	81421	80329	79241	78041	76991
67	99713	98597	97387	96199	95093	93971	92809	91771	90547	89519	88339	87187	86069	84859	83689	82529	81439	80341	79259	78049	77003
68	99719	98621	97397	96211	95101	93979	92821	91781	90583	89521	88379	87211	86077	84869	83701	82531	81457	80347	79273	78059	77017
69	99721	98627	97423	96221	95107	93983	92831	91801	90599	89527	88397	87221	86083	84871	83717	82549	81463	80363	79279	78079	77023
70	99733	98639	97429	96223	95111	93997	92849	91807	90617	89533	88411	87223	86111	84913	83719	82559	81509	80369	79283	78101	77029
71	99761	98641	97441	96233	95131	94007	92857	91811	90619	89561	88423	87251	86113	84919	83737	82561	81517	80387	79301	78121	77041
72	99767	98663	97453	96259	95143	94009	92861	91813	90631	89563	88427	87253	86117	84947	83761	82567	81527	80407	79309	78137	77047
73	99787	98669	97459	96263	95153	94033	92863	91823	90641	89567	88463	87257	86137	84961	83773	82571	81533	80429	79319	78139	77069
74	99793	98689	97463	96269	95177	94049	92867	91837	90647	89591	88469	87277	86143	84967	83777	82591	81547	80447	79333	78157	77081
75	99809	98711	97499	96281	95189	94057	92893	91841	90659	89597	88471	87281	86161	84977	83791	82601	81551	80449	79337	78163	77093
76	99817	98713	97501	96289	95191	94063	92899	91867	90677	89599	88493	87293	86171	84979	83813	82609	81553	80471	79349	78167	77101
77	99823	98717	97511	96293	95203	94079	92921	91873	90679	89603	88499	87299	86179	84991	83833	82613	81559	80473	79357	78173	77137
78	99829	98729	97523	96323	95213	94099	92927	91909	90697	89611	88513	87313	86183	85009	83843	82619	81563	80489	79367	78179	77141
79	99833	98731	97547	96329	95219	94109	92941	91921	90703	89627	88523	87317	86197	85021	83857	82633	81569	80491	79379	78191	77153
80	99839	98737	97549	96331	95231	94111	92951	91939	90709	89633	88547	87323	86201	85027	83869	82651	81611	80513	79393	78193	77167
81	99859	98773	97553	96337	95233	94117	92957	91943	90731	89653	88589	87337	86209	85037	83873	82657	81619	80527	79397	78203	77171
82	99871	98779	97561	96353	95239	94121	92959	91951	90749	89657	88591	87359	86239	85049	83891	82699	81629	80537	79411	78229	77191
83	99877	98801	97571	96377	95257	94151	92987	91957	90787	89659	88607	87383	86243	85061	83903	82721	81637	80557	79423	78233	77201
84	99881	98807	97577	96401	95261	94153	92993	91961	90793	89669	88609	87403	86249	85081	83911	82723	81647	80567	79427	78241	77213
85	99901	98809	97579	96419	95267	94169	93001	91967	90803	89671	88643	87407	86257	85087	83921	82727	81649	80599	79433	78259	77237
86	99907	98837	97583	96431	95273	94201	93047	91969	90821	89681	88651	87421	86263	85091	83933	82729	81667	80603	79451	78277	77239
87	99923	98849	97607	96443	95279	94207	93053	91997	90823	89689	88657	87427	86269	85093	83939	82757	81671	80611	79481	78283	77243
88	99929	98867	97609	96451	95287	94219	93059	92003	90833	89753	88661	87433	86287	85103	83969	82759	81677	80621	79493	78301	77249
89	99961	98869	97613	96457	95311	94229	93077	92009	90841	89759	88663	87443	86291	85109	83983	82763	81689	80627	79531	78307	77261
90	99971	98873	97649	96461	95317	94253	93083	92033	90863	89767	88667	87473	86293	85121	83987	82781	81701	80629	79537	78311	77263
91	99989	98887	97651	96469	95327	94261	93089	92041	90887	89779	88681	87481	86297	85133	84011	82787	81703	80651	79549	78317	77267
92	99991	98893	97673	96479	95339	94273	93097	92051	90901	89783	88721	87491	86311	85147	84017	82793	81707	80657	79559	78341	77269
93		98897	97687	96487	95369	94291	93103	92077	90907	89797	88729	87509	86323	85159	84047	82799	81727	80669	79561	78347	77279
94		98899	97711	96493	95383	94307	93113	92083	90911	89809	88741	87511	86341	85193	84053	82811	81737	80671	79579	78367	77291
95		98909	97729	96497	95393	94309	93131	92107	90917	89819	88747	87517	86351	85199	84059	82813	81749	80677	79589	78401	77317
96		98911	97771	96517	95401	94321	93133	92111	90931	89821	88771	87523	86353	85201	84061	82837	81761	80681	79601	78427	77323
97		98927	97777	96527	95413	94327	93139	92119	90947	89833	88789	87539	86357	85213	84067	82847	81769	80683	79609	78437	77339
98		98929	97787	96553	95419	94331	93151	92143	90971	89839	88793	87541	86369	85223	84089	82883	81773	80687	79613	78439	77347
99		98939	97789	96557	95429	94343	93169	92153	90977	89849	88799	87547	86371	85229	84121	82889	81799	80701	79621	78467	77351
100		98947	97813	96581	95441	94349	93179	92173	90989	89867	88801	87553	86381	85237	84127	82891	81817	80713	79627	78479	77359

FACTORS AND PRIMES

This table presents the prime factors of all factorable numbers and the mantissas of the common logarithms of all prime numbers from 1 to 2,000. The table runs across two facing pages. Thus, the factors of 258 are found on a line with 25 and under vertical column 8 to be $2 \cdot 3 \cdot 43$. If n is prime, the mantissa of its common logarithm is given. If n is not prime its prime factors are given.

n	0	1	2	3	4
0	....	0000000	3010300	4771213	2^3
1	$2 \cdot 5$	0413927	$2^2 \cdot 3$	1139434	$2 \cdot 7$
2	$2^2 \cdot 5$	$3 \cdot 7$	$2 \cdot 11$	3617278	$2^3 \cdot 3$
3	$2 \cdot 3 \cdot 5$	4913617	2^5	$3 \cdot 11$	$2 \cdot 17$
4	$2^3 \cdot 5$	6127839	$2 \cdot 3 \cdot 7$	6334685	$2^2 \cdot 11$
5	$2 \cdot 5^2$	$3 \cdot 17$	$2^2 \cdot 13$	7242759	$2 \cdot 3^3$
6	$2^2 \cdot 3 \cdot 5$	7853298	$2 \cdot 31$	$3^2 \cdot 7$	2^6
7	$2 \cdot 5 \cdot 7$	8512583	$2^3 \cdot 3^2$	8633229	$2 \cdot 37$
8	$2^4 \cdot 5$	3^4	$2 \cdot 41$	9190781	$2^2 \cdot 3 \cdot 7$
9	$2 \cdot 3^2 \cdot 5$	$7 \cdot 13$	$2^2 \cdot 23$	$3 \cdot 31$	$2 \cdot 47$
10	$2^2 \cdot 5^2$	0043214	$2 \cdot 3 \cdot 17$	0128372	$2^3 \cdot 13$
11	$2 \cdot 5 \cdot 11$	$3 \cdot 37$	$2^4 \cdot 7$	0530784	$2 \cdot 3 \cdot 19$
12	$2^3 \cdot 3 \cdot 5$	11^2	$2 \cdot 61$	$3 \cdot 41$	$2^2 \cdot 31$
13	$2 \cdot 5 \cdot 13$	1172713	$2^2 \cdot 3 \cdot 11$	$7 \cdot 19$	$2 \cdot 67$
14	$2^2 \cdot 5 \cdot 7$	$3 \cdot 47$	$2 \cdot 71$	$11 \cdot 13$	$2^4 \cdot 3^2$
15	$2 \cdot 3 \cdot 5^2$	1789769	$2^3 \cdot 19$	$3^2 \cdot 17$	$2 \cdot 7 \cdot 11$
16	$2^5 \cdot 5$	$7 \cdot 23$	$2 \cdot 3^4$	2121876	$2^2 \cdot 41$
17	$2 \cdot 5 \cdot 17$	$3^2 \cdot 19$	$2^2 \cdot 43$	2380461	$2 \cdot 3 \cdot 29$
18	$2^2 \cdot 3^2 \cdot 5$	2576786	$2 \cdot 7 \cdot 13$	$3 \cdot 61$	$2^3 \cdot 23$
19	$2 \cdot 5 \cdot 19$	2810334	$2^4 \cdot 3$	2855573	$2 \cdot 97$
20	$2^3 \cdot 5^2$	$3 \cdot 67$	$2 \cdot 101$	$7 \cdot 29$	$2^2 \cdot 3 \cdot 17$
21	$2 \cdot 3 \cdot 5 \cdot 7$	3242825	$2^2 \cdot 53$	$3 \cdot 71$	$2 \cdot 107$
22	$2^2 \cdot 5 \cdot 11$	$13 \cdot 17$	$2 \cdot 3 \cdot 37$	3483049	$2^5 \cdot 7$
23	$2 \cdot 5 \cdot 23$	$3 \cdot 7 \cdot 11$	$2^2 \cdot 29$	3673559	$2 \cdot 3^2 \cdot 13$
24	$2^4 \cdot 3 \cdot 5$	3820170	$2 \cdot 11^2$	3^5	$2^2 \cdot 61$
25	$2 \cdot 5^3$	3996737	$2^2 \cdot 3^2 \cdot 7$	$11 \cdot 23$	$2 \cdot 127$
26	$2^2 \cdot 5 \cdot 13$	$3^2 \cdot 29$	$2 \cdot 131$	4199557	$2^3 \cdot 3 \cdot 11$
27	$2 \cdot 3^3 \cdot 5$	4329693	$2^4 \cdot 17$	$3 \cdot 7 \cdot 13$	$2 \cdot 137$
28	$2^3 \cdot 5 \cdot 7$	4487063	$2 \cdot 3 \cdot 47$	4517864	$2^3 \cdot 71$
29	$2 \cdot 5 \cdot 29$	$3 \cdot 97$	$2^2 \cdot 73$	4668676	$2 \cdot 3 \cdot 7^2$
30	$2^2 \cdot 3 \cdot 5^2$	$7 \cdot 43$	$2 \cdot 151$	$3 \cdot 101$	$2^4 \cdot 19$
31	$2 \cdot 5 \cdot 31$	4927604	$2^3 \cdot 3 \cdot 13$	4955443	$2 \cdot 157$
32	$2^6 \cdot 5$	$3 \cdot 107$	$2 \cdot 7 \cdot 23$	$17 \cdot 19$	$2^2 \cdot 3^4$
33	$2 \cdot 3 \cdot 5 \cdot 11$	5198280	$2^2 \cdot 83$	$3^2 \cdot 37$	$2 \cdot 167$
34	$2^2 \cdot 5 \cdot 17$	$11 \cdot 31$	$2 \cdot 3^2 \cdot 19$	7^3	$2^3 \cdot 43$
35	$2 \cdot 5^2 \cdot 7$	$3^3 \cdot 13$	$2^5 \cdot 11$	5477747	$2 \cdot 3 \cdot 59$
36	$2^3 \cdot 3^2 \cdot 5$	19^2	$2 \cdot 181$	$3 \cdot 11^2$	$2^2 \cdot 7 \cdot 13$
37	$2 \cdot 5 \cdot 37$	$7 \cdot 53$	$2^2 \cdot 3 \cdot 31$	5717088	$2 \cdot 11 \cdot 17$
38	$2^2 \cdot 5 \cdot 19$	$3 \cdot 127$	$2 \cdot 191$	5831988	$2^7 \cdot 3$
39	$2 \cdot 3 \cdot 5 \cdot 13$	$17 \cdot 23$	$2^3 \cdot 7^2$	$3 \cdot 131$	$2 \cdot 197$
40	$2^4 \cdot 5^2$	6031444	$2 \cdot 3 \cdot 67$	$13 \cdot 31$	$2^2 \cdot 101$
41	$2 \cdot 5 \cdot 41$	$3 \cdot 137$	$2^2 \cdot 103$	$7 \cdot 59$	$2 \cdot 3^2 \cdot 23$
42	$2^2 \cdot 3 \cdot 5 \cdot 7$	6242821	$2 \cdot 211$	$3^2 \cdot 47$	$2^3 \cdot 53$
43	$2 \cdot 5 \cdot 43$	6344773	$2^4 \cdot 3^3$	6364879	$2 \cdot 7 \cdot 31$
44	$2^3 \cdot 5 \cdot 11$	$3^2 \cdot 7^2$	$2 \cdot 13 \cdot 17$	6464037	$2^2 \cdot 3 \cdot 37$
45	$2 \cdot 3^2 \cdot 5^2$	$11 \cdot 41$	$2^2 \cdot 113$	$3 \cdot 151$	$2 \cdot 227$
46	$2^2 \cdot 5 \cdot 23$	6637009	$2 \cdot 3 \cdot 7 \cdot 11$	6655810	$2^4 \cdot 29$
47	$2 \cdot 5 \cdot 47$	$3 \cdot 157$	$2^3 \cdot 59$	$11 \cdot 43$	$2 \cdot 3 \cdot 79$
48	$2^5 \cdot 3 \cdot 5$	$13 \cdot 37$	$2 \cdot 241$	$3 \cdot 7 \cdot 23$	$2^2 \cdot 11^2$
49	$2 \cdot 5 \cdot 7^2$	6910815	$2^3 \cdot 3 \cdot 41$	$17 \cdot 29$	$2 \cdot 13 \cdot 19$

FACTORS AND PRIMES (Continued)

n	5	6	7	8	9
0	6989700	$2 \cdot 3$	8450980	2^3	3^2
1	$3 \cdot 5$	2^4	2304489	$2 \cdot 3^2$	2787536
2	5^2	$2 \cdot 13$	3^3	$2^2 \cdot 7$	4623980
3	$5 \cdot 7$	$2^2 \cdot 3^2$	5682017	$2 \cdot 19$	$3 \cdot 13$
4	$3^2 \cdot 5$	$2 \cdot 23$	6720979	$2^4 \cdot 3$	7^2
5	$5 \cdot 11$	$2^3 \cdot 7$	$3 \cdot 19$	$2 \cdot 29$	7708520
6	$5 \cdot 13$	$2 \cdot 3 \cdot 11$	8260748	$2^2 \cdot 17$	$3 \cdot 23$
7	$3 \cdot 5^2$	$2^2 \cdot 19$	$7 \cdot 11$	$2 \cdot 3 \cdot 13$	8976271
8	$5 \cdot 17$	$2 \cdot 43$	$3 \cdot 29$	$2^3 \cdot 11$	9493900
9	$5 \cdot 19$	$2^5 \cdot 3$	9867717	$2 \cdot 7^2$	$3^2 \cdot 11$
10	$3 \cdot 5 \cdot 7$	$2 \cdot 53$	0293838	$2^2 \cdot 3^3$	0374265
11	$5 \cdot 23$	$2^2 \cdot 29$	$3^2 \cdot 13$	$2 \cdot 59$	$7 \cdot 17$
12	5^3	$2 \cdot 3^2 \cdot 7$	1038037	2^7	$3 \cdot 43$
13	$3^3 \cdot 5$	$2^3 \cdot 17$	1367206	$2 \cdot 3 \cdot 23$	1430148
14	$5 \cdot 29$	$2 \cdot 73$	$3 \cdot 7^2$	$2^2 \cdot 37$	1731863
15	$5 \cdot 31$	$2^2 \cdot 3 \cdot 13$	1958997	$2 \cdot 79$	$3 \cdot 53$
16	$3 \cdot 5 \cdot 11$	$2 \cdot 83$	2227165	$2^3 \cdot 3 \cdot 7$	13^2
17	$5^2 \cdot 7$	$2^4 \cdot 11$	$3 \cdot 59$	$2 \cdot 89$	2528530
18	$5 \cdot 37$	$2 \cdot 3 \cdot 31$	$11 \cdot 17$	$2^2 \cdot 47$	$3^3 \cdot 7$
19	$3 \cdot 5 \cdot 13$	$2^2 \cdot 7^2$	2944662	$2 \cdot 3^2 \cdot 11$	2988531
20	$5 \cdot 41$	$2 \cdot 103$	$3^2 \cdot 23$	$2^4 \cdot 13$	$11 \cdot 19$
21	$5 \cdot 43$	$2^3 \cdot 3^3$	$7 \cdot 31$	$2 \cdot 109$	$3 \cdot 73$
22	$3^2 \cdot 5^2$	$2 \cdot 113$	3560259	$2^2 \cdot 3 \cdot 19$	3598355
23	$5 \cdot 47$	$2^2 \cdot 59$	$3 \cdot 79$	$2 \cdot 7 \cdot 17$	3783979
24	$5 \cdot 7^2$	$2 \cdot 3 \cdot 41$	$13 \cdot 19$	$2^3 \cdot 31$	$3 \cdot 83$
25	$3 \cdot 5 \cdot 17$	2^8	4099331	$2 \cdot 3 \cdot 43$	$7 \cdot 37$
26	$5 \cdot 53$	$2 \cdot 7 \cdot 19$	$3 \cdot 89$	$2^2 \cdot 67$	4297523
27	$5^2 \cdot 11$	$2^2 \cdot 3 \cdot 23$	4424798	$2 \cdot 139$	$3^2 \cdot 31$
28	$3 \cdot 5 \cdot 19$	$2 \cdot 11 \cdot 13$	$7 \cdot 41$	$2^5 \cdot 3^2$	17^2
29	$5 \cdot 59$	$2^3 \cdot 37$	$3^3 \cdot 11$	$2 \cdot 149$	$13 \cdot 23$
30	$5 \cdot 61$	$2 \cdot 3^2 \cdot 17$	4871384	$2^2 \cdot 7 \cdot 11$	$3 \cdot 103$
31	$3^2 \cdot 5 \cdot 7$	$2^2 \cdot 79$	5010593	$2 \cdot 3 \cdot 53$	$11 \cdot 29$
32	$5^2 \cdot 13$	$2 \cdot 163$	$3 \cdot 109$	$2^3 \cdot 41$	$7 \cdot 47$
33	$5 \cdot 67$	$2^4 \cdot 3 \cdot 7$	5276299	$2 \cdot 13^2$	$3 \cdot 113$
34	$3 \cdot 5 \cdot 23$	$2 \cdot 173$	5403295	$2^2 \cdot 3 \cdot 29$	5428254
35	$5 \cdot 71$	$2^3 \cdot 89$	$3 \cdot 7 \cdot 17$	$2 \cdot 179$	5550944
36	$5 \cdot 73$	$2 \cdot 3 \cdot 61$	5646661	$2^4 \cdot 23$	$3^2 \cdot 41$
37	$3 \cdot 5^3$	$2^3 \cdot 47$	$13 \cdot 29$	$2 \cdot 3^3 \cdot 7$	5786392
38	$5 \cdot 7 \cdot 11$	$2 \cdot 193$	$3^3 \cdot 43$	$2^2 \cdot 97$	5899496
39	$5 \cdot 79$	$2^3 \cdot 3^2 \cdot 11$	5987905	$2 \cdot 199$	$3 \cdot 7 \cdot 19$
40	$3^4 \cdot 5$	$2 \cdot 7 \cdot 29$	$11 \cdot 37$	$2^3 \cdot 3 \cdot 17$	6117233
41	$5 \cdot 83$	$2^6 \cdot 13$	$3 \cdot 139$	$2 \cdot 11 \cdot 19$	6222140
42	$5^2 \cdot 17$	$2 \cdot 3 \cdot 71$	$7 \cdot 61$	$2^2 \cdot 107$	$3 \cdot 11 \cdot 13$
43	$3 \cdot 5 \cdot 29$	$2^2 \cdot 109$	$19 \cdot 23$	$2 \cdot 3 \cdot 73$	6424645
44	$5 \cdot 89$	$2 \cdot 223$	$3 \cdot 149$	$2^6 \cdot 7$	6522463
45	$5 \cdot 7 \cdot 13$	$2^3 \cdot 3 \cdot 19$	6599162	$2 \cdot 229$	$3^3 \cdot 17$
46	$3 \cdot 5 \cdot 31$	$2 \cdot 233$	6693169	$2^2 \cdot 3^2 \cdot 13$	$7 \cdot 67$
47	$5^2 \cdot 19$	$2^2 \cdot 7 \cdot 17$	$3^2 \cdot 53$	$2 \cdot 239$	6803355
48	$5 \cdot 97$	$2 \cdot 3^5$	6875290	$2^3 \cdot 61$	$3 \cdot 163$
49	$3^2 \cdot 5 \cdot 11$	$2^4 \cdot 31$	$7 \cdot 71$	$2 \cdot 3 \cdot 83$	6981005

FACTORS AND PRIMES (Continued)

n	0	1	2	3	4
50	$2^2 \cdot 5^3$	$3 \cdot 167$	$2 \cdot 251$	**7015680**	$2^3 \cdot 3^2 \cdot 7$
51	$2 \cdot 3 \cdot 5 \cdot 17$	$7 \cdot 73$	2^9	$3^3 \cdot 19$	$2 \cdot 257$
52	$2^3 \cdot 5 \cdot 13$	**7168377**	$2 \cdot 3^2 \cdot 29$	**7185017**	$2^2 \cdot 131$
53	$2 \cdot 5 \cdot 53$	$3^2 \cdot 59$	$2^2 \cdot 7 \cdot 19$	$13 \cdot 41$	$2 \cdot 3 \cdot 89$
54	$2^2 \cdot 3^3 \cdot 5$	**7331973**	$2 \cdot 271$	$3 \cdot 181$	$2^5 \cdot 17$
55	$2 \cdot 5^2 \cdot 11$	$19 \cdot 29$	$2^3 \cdot 3 \cdot 23$	$7 \cdot 79$	$2 \cdot 277$
56	$2^4 \cdot 5 \cdot 7$	$3 \cdot 11 \cdot 17$	$2 \cdot 281$	**7505084**	$2^2 \cdot 3 \cdot 47$
57	$2 \cdot 3 \cdot 5 \cdot 19$	**7566361**	$2^2 \cdot 11 \cdot 13$	$3 \cdot 191$	$2 \cdot 7 \cdot 41$
58	$2^2 \cdot 5 \cdot 29$	$7 \cdot 83$	$2 \cdot 3 \cdot 97$	$11 \cdot 53$	$2^3 \cdot 73$
59	$2 \cdot 5 \cdot 59$	$3 \cdot 197$	$2^4 \cdot 37$	**7730547**	$2 \cdot 3^3 \cdot 11$
60	$2^3 \cdot 3 \cdot 5^2$	**7788745**	$2 \cdot 7 \cdot 43$	$3^2 \cdot 67$	$2^2 \cdot 151$
61	$2 \cdot 5 \cdot 61$	$13 \cdot 47$	$2^2 \cdot 3^2 \cdot 17$	**7874605**	$2 \cdot 307$
62	$2^2 \cdot 5 \cdot 31$	$3^3 \cdot 23$	$2 \cdot 311$	$7 \cdot 89$	$2^4 \cdot 3 \cdot 13$
63	$2 \cdot 3^2 \cdot 5 \cdot 7$	**8000294**	$2^3 \cdot 79$	$3 \cdot 211$	$2 \cdot 317$
64	$2^7 \cdot 5$	**8068580**	$2 \cdot 3 \cdot 107$	**8082110**	$2^2 \cdot 7 \cdot 23$
65	$2 \cdot 5^2 \cdot 13$	$3 \cdot 7 \cdot 31$	$2^2 \cdot 163$	**8149132**	$2 \cdot 3 \cdot 109$
66	$2^2 \cdot 3 \cdot 5 \cdot 11$	**8202015**	$2 \cdot 331$	$3 \cdot 13 \cdot 17$	$2^3 \cdot 83$
67	$2 \cdot 5 \cdot 67$	$11 \cdot 61$	$2^5 \cdot 3 \cdot 7$	**8280151**	$2 \cdot 337$
68	$2^3 \cdot 5 \cdot 17$	$3 \cdot 227$	$2 \cdot 11 \cdot 31$	**8344207**	$2^2 \cdot 3^2 \cdot 19$
69	$2 \cdot 3 \cdot 5 \cdot 23$	**8394780**	$2^2 \cdot 173$	$3^2 \cdot 7 \cdot 11$	$2 \cdot 347$
70	$2^2 \cdot 5^2 \cdot 7$	**8457180**	$2 \cdot 3^3 \cdot 13$	$19 \cdot 37$	$2^6 \cdot 11$
71	$2 \cdot 5 \cdot 71$	$3^2 \cdot 79$	$2^3 \cdot 89$	$23 \cdot 31$	$2 \cdot 3 \cdot 7 \cdot 17$
72	$2^4 \cdot 3^2 \cdot 5$	$7 \cdot 103$	$2 \cdot 19^2$	$3 \cdot 241$	$2^2 \cdot 181$
73	$2 \cdot 5 \cdot 73$	$17 \cdot 43$	$2^2 \cdot 3 \cdot 61$	**8651040**	$2 \cdot 367$
74	$2^2 \cdot 5 \cdot 37$	$3 \cdot 13 \cdot 19$	$2 \cdot 7 \cdot 53$	**8709888**	$2^3 \cdot 3 \cdot 31$
75	$2 \cdot 3 \cdot 5^3$	**8756399**	$2^4 \cdot 47$	$3 \cdot 251$	$2 \cdot 13 \cdot 29$
76	$2^3 \cdot 5 \cdot 19$	**8813847**	$2 \cdot 3 \cdot 127$	$7 \cdot 109$	$2^2 \cdot 191$
77	$2 \cdot 5 \cdot 7 \cdot 11$	$3 \cdot 257$	$2^2 \cdot 193$	**8881795**	$2 \cdot 3^2 \cdot 43$
78	$2^2 \cdot 3 \cdot 5 \cdot 13$	$11 \cdot 71$	$2 \cdot 17 \cdot 23$	$3^3 \cdot 29$	$2^4 \cdot 7^2$
79	$2 \cdot 5 \cdot 79$	$7 \cdot 113$	$2^3 \cdot 3^2 \cdot 11$	$13 \cdot 61$	$2 \cdot 397$
80	$2^5 \cdot 5^2$	$3^2 \cdot 89$	$2 \cdot 401$	$11 \cdot 73$	$2^2 \cdot 3 \cdot 67$
81	$2 \cdot 3^4 \cdot 5$	**9090209**	$2^2 \cdot 7 \cdot 29$	$3 \cdot 271$	$2 \cdot 11 \cdot 37$
82	$2^2 \cdot 5 \cdot 41$	**9143432**	$2 \cdot 3 \cdot 137$	**9153998**	$2^3 \cdot 103$
83	$2 \cdot 5 \cdot 83$	$3 \cdot 277$	$2^6 \cdot 13$	$7^2 \cdot 17$	$2 \cdot 3 \cdot 139$
84	$2^3 \cdot 3 \cdot 5 \cdot 7$	29^2	$2 \cdot 421$	$3 \cdot 281$	$2^2 \cdot 211$
85	$2 \cdot 5^2 \cdot 17$	$23 \cdot 37$	$2^2 \cdot 3 \cdot 71$	**9309490**	$2 \cdot 7 \cdot 61$
86	$2^2 \cdot 5 \cdot 43$	$3 \cdot 7 \cdot 41$	$2 \cdot 431$	**9360108**	$2^5 \cdot 3^3$
87	$2 \cdot 3 \cdot 5 \cdot 29$	$13 \cdot 67$	$2^3 \cdot 109$	$3^2 \cdot 97$	$2 \cdot 19 \cdot 23$
88	$2^4 \cdot 5 \cdot 11$	**9449759**	$2 \cdot 3^2 \cdot 7^2$	**9459607**	$2^2 \cdot 13 \cdot 17$
89	$2 \cdot 5 \cdot 89$	$3^4 \cdot 11$	$2^2 \cdot 223$	$19 \cdot 47$	$2 \cdot 3 \cdot 149$
90	$2^2 \cdot 3^2 \cdot 5^2$	$17 \cdot 53$	$2 \cdot 11 \cdot 41$	$3 \cdot 7 \cdot 43$	$2^3 \cdot 113$
91	$2 \cdot 5 \cdot 7 \cdot 13$	**9595184**	$2^4 \cdot 3 \cdot 19$	$11 \cdot 83$	$2 \cdot 457$
92	$2^3 \cdot 5 \cdot 23$	$3 \cdot 307$	$2 \cdot 461$	$13 \cdot 71$	$2^3 \cdot 3 \cdot 7 \cdot 11$
93	$2 \cdot 3 \cdot 5 \cdot 31$	$7^2 \cdot 19$	$2^2 \cdot 233$	$3 \cdot 311$	$2 \cdot 467$
94	$2^2 \cdot 5 \cdot 47$	**9735896**	$2 \cdot 3 \cdot 157$	$23 \cdot 41$	$2^4 \cdot 59$
95	$2 \cdot 5^2 \cdot 19$	$3 \cdot 317$	$2^3 \cdot 7 \cdot 17$	**9790929**	$2 \cdot 3^2 \cdot 53$
96	$2^6 \cdot 3 \cdot 5$	31^2	$2 \cdot 13 \cdot 37$	$3^2 \cdot 107$	$2^3 \cdot 241$
97	$2 \cdot 5 \cdot 97$	**9872192**	$2^2 \cdot 3^5$	$7 \cdot 139$	$2 \cdot 487$
98	$2^2 \cdot 5 \cdot 7^2$	$3^2 \cdot 109$	$2 \cdot 491$	**9925535**	$2^3 \cdot 3 \cdot 41$
99	$2 \cdot 3^2 \cdot 5 \cdot 11$	**9960737**	$2^5 \cdot 31$	$3 \cdot 331$	$2 \cdot 7 \cdot 71$

FACTORS AND PRIMES (Continued)

n	5	6	7	8	9
50	$5 \cdot 101$	$2 \cdot 11 \cdot 23$	$3 \cdot 13^2$	$2^2 \cdot 127$	7067178
51	$5 \cdot 103$	$2^3 \cdot 3 \cdot 43$	$11 \cdot 47$	$2 \cdot 7 \cdot 37$	$3 \cdot 173$
52	$3 \cdot 5^2 \cdot 7$	$2 \cdot 263$	$17 \cdot 31$	$2^4 \cdot 3 \cdot 11$	23^2
53	$5 \cdot 107$	$2^3 \cdot 67$	$3 \cdot 179$	$2 \cdot 269$	$7^2 \cdot 11$
54	$5 \cdot 109$	$2 \cdot 3 \cdot 7 \cdot 13$	7379873	$2^2 \cdot 137$	$3^2 \cdot 61$
55	$3 \cdot 5 \cdot 37$	$2^2 \cdot 139$	7458552	$2 \cdot 3^2 \cdot 31$	$13 \cdot 43$
56	$5 \cdot 113$	$2 \cdot 283$	$3^4 \cdot 7$	$2^3 \cdot 71$	7551123
57	$5^2 \cdot 23$	$2^6 \cdot 3^2$	7611758	$2 \cdot 17^2$	$3 \cdot 193$
58	$3^2 \cdot 5 \cdot 13$	$2 \cdot 293$	7686381	$2^3 \cdot 3 \cdot 7^2$	$19 \cdot 31$
59	$5 \cdot 7 \cdot 17$	$2^2 \cdot 149$	$3 \cdot 199$	$2 \cdot 13 \cdot 23$	7774268
60	$5 \cdot 11^2$	$2 \cdot 3 \cdot 101$	7831887	$2^5 \cdot 19$	$3 \cdot 7 \cdot 29$
61	$3 \cdot 5 \cdot 41$	$2^3 \cdot 7 \cdot 11$	7902852	$2 \cdot 3 \cdot 103$	7916906
62	5^4	$2 \cdot 313$	$3 \cdot 11 \cdot 19$	$2^2 \cdot 157$	$17 \cdot 37$
63	$5 \cdot 127$	$2^2 \cdot 3 \cdot 53$	$7^2 \cdot 13$	$2 \cdot 11 \cdot 29$	$3^2 \cdot 71$
64	$3 \cdot 5 \cdot 43$	$2 \cdot 17 \cdot 19$	8109043	$2^3 \cdot 3^4$	$11 \cdot 59$
65	$5 \cdot 131$	$2^4 \cdot 41$	$3^2 \cdot 73$	$2 \cdot 7 \cdot 47$	8188854
66	$5 \cdot 7 \cdot 19$	$2 \cdot 3^2 \cdot 37$	$23 \cdot 29$	$2^2 \cdot 167$	$3 \cdot 223$
67	$3^3 \cdot 5^2$	$2^2 \cdot 13^2$	8305887	$2 \cdot 3 \cdot 113$	$7 \cdot 97$
68	$5 \cdot 137$	$2 \cdot 7^2$	$3 \cdot 229$	$2^4 \cdot 43$	$13 \cdot 53$
69	$5 \cdot 139$	$2^3 \cdot 3 \cdot 29$	$17 \cdot 41$	$2 \cdot 349$	$3 \cdot 233$
70	$3 \cdot 5 \cdot 47$	$2 \cdot 353$	$7 \cdot 101$	$2^2 \cdot 3 \cdot 59$	8506462
71	$5 \cdot 11 \cdot 13$	$2^2 \cdot 179$	$3 \cdot 239$	$2 \cdot 359$	8567289
72	$5^2 \cdot 29$	$2 \cdot 3 \cdot 11^2$	8615344	$2^3 \cdot 7 \cdot 13$	3^6
73	$3 \cdot 5 \cdot 7^2$	$2^5 \cdot 23$	$11 \cdot 67$	$2 \cdot 3^2 \cdot 41$	8686444
74	$5 \cdot 149$	$2 \cdot 373$	$3^2 \cdot 83$	$2^2 \cdot 11 \cdot 17$	$7 \cdot 107$
75	$5 \cdot 151$	$2^2 \cdot 3^3 \cdot 7$	8790959	$2 \cdot 379$	$3 \cdot 11 \cdot 23$
76	$3^2 \cdot 5 \cdot 17$	$2 \cdot 383$	$13 \cdot 59$	$2^8 \cdot 3$	8859263
77	$5^2 \cdot 31$	$2^3 \cdot 97$	$3 \cdot 7 \cdot 37$	$2 \cdot 389$	$19 \cdot 41$
78	$5 \cdot 157$	$2 \cdot 3 \cdot 131$	8959747	$2^2 \cdot 197$	$3 \cdot 263$
79	$3 \cdot 5 \cdot 53$	$2^3 \cdot 199$	9014583	$2 \cdot 3 \cdot 7 \cdot 19$	$17 \cdot 47$
80	$5 \cdot 7 \cdot 23$	$2 \cdot 13 \cdot 31$	$3 \cdot 269$	$2^3 \cdot 101$	9079485
81	$5 \cdot 163$	$2^4 \cdot 3 \cdot 17$	$19 \cdot 43$	$2 \cdot 409$	$3^2 \cdot 7 \cdot 13$
82	$3 \cdot 5^2 \cdot 11$	$2 \cdot 7 \cdot 59$	9175055	$2^2 \cdot 3^2 \cdot 23$	9185545
83	$5 \cdot 167$	$2^3 \cdot 11 \cdot 19$	$3^3 \cdot 31$	$2 \cdot 419$	9237620
84	$5 \cdot 13^2$	$2 \cdot 3^2 \cdot 47$	$7 \cdot 11^2$	$2^4 \cdot 53$	$3 \cdot 283$
85	$3^2 \cdot 5 \cdot 19$	$2^3 \cdot 107$	9329808	$2 \cdot 3 \cdot 11 \cdot 13$	9339932
86	$5 \cdot 173$	$2 \cdot 433$	$3 \cdot 17^2$	$2^2 \cdot 7 \cdot 31$	$11 \cdot 79$
87	$5^3 \cdot 7$	$2^2 \cdot 3 \cdot 73$	9429996	$2 \cdot 439$	$3 \cdot 293$
88	$3 \cdot 5 \cdot 59$	$2 \cdot 443$	9479236	$2^3 \cdot 3 \cdot 37$	$7 \cdot 127$
89	$5 \cdot 179$	$2^7 \cdot 7$	$3 \cdot 13 \cdot 23$	$2 \cdot 449$	$29 \cdot 31$
90	$5 \cdot 181$	$2 \cdot 3 \cdot 151$	9576073	$2^2 \cdot 227$	$3^2 \cdot 101$
91	$3 \cdot 5 \cdot 61$	$2^2 \cdot 229$	$7 \cdot 131$	$2 \cdot 3^3 \cdot 17$	9633155
92	$5^2 \cdot 37$	$2 \cdot 463$	$3^2 \cdot 103$	$2^5 \cdot 29$	9680157
93	$5 \cdot 11 \cdot 17$	$2^3 \cdot 3^2 \cdot 13$	9717396	$2 \cdot 7 \cdot 67$	$3 \cdot 313$
94	$3^3 \cdot 5 \cdot 7$	$2 \cdot 11 \cdot 43$	9763500	$2^2 \cdot 3 \cdot 79$	$13 \cdot 73$
95	$5 \cdot 191$	$2^2 \cdot 239$	$3 \cdot 11 \cdot 29$	$2 \cdot 479$	$7 \cdot 137$
96	$5 \cdot 193$	$2 \cdot 3 \cdot 7 \cdot 23$	9854265	$2^3 \cdot 11^2$	$3 \cdot 17 \cdot 19$
97	$3 \cdot 5^2 \cdot 13$	$2^4 \cdot 61$	9898946	$2 \cdot 3 \cdot 163$	$11 \cdot 89$
98	$5 \cdot 197$	$2 \cdot 17 \cdot 29$	$3 \cdot 7 \cdot 47$	$2^2 \cdot 13 \cdot 19$	$23 \cdot 43$
99	$5 \cdot 199$	$2^2 \cdot 3 \cdot 83$	9986952	$2 \cdot 499$	$3^3 \cdot 37$

FACTORS AND PRIMES (Continued)

n	0	1	2	3	4
100	$2^3 \cdot 5^3$	$7 \cdot 11 \cdot 13$	$2 \cdot 3 \cdot 167$	$17 \cdot 59$	$2^2 \cdot 251$
101	$2 \cdot 5 \cdot 101$	$3 \cdot 337$	$2^2 \cdot 11 \cdot 23$	**0056094**	$2 \cdot 3 \cdot 13^2$
102	$2^2 \cdot 3 \cdot 5 \cdot 17$	**0090257**	$2 \cdot 7 \cdot 73$	$3 \cdot 11 \cdot 31$	2^{10}
103	$2 \cdot 5 \cdot 103$	**0132587**	$2^3 \cdot 3 \cdot 43$	**0141003**	$2 \cdot 11 \cdot 47$
104	$2^4 \cdot 5 \cdot 13$	$3 \cdot 347$	$2 \cdot 521$	$7 \cdot 149$	$2^3 \cdot 3^2 \cdot 29$
105	$2 \cdot 3 \cdot 5^2 \cdot 7$	**0216027**	$2^2 \cdot 263$	$3^4 \cdot 13$	$2 \cdot 17 \cdot 31$
106	$2^2 \cdot 5 \cdot 53$	**0257154**	$2 \cdot 3^2 \cdot 59$	**0265333**	$2^3 \cdot 7 \cdot 19$
107	$2 \cdot 5 \cdot 107$	$3^2 \cdot 7 \cdot 17$	$2^4 \cdot 67$	$29 \cdot 37$	$2 \cdot 3 \cdot 179$
108	$2^3 \cdot 3^3 \cdot 5$	$23 \cdot 47$	$2 \cdot 541$	$3 \cdot 19^2$	$2^2 \cdot 271$
109	$2 \cdot 5 \cdot 109$	**0378248**	$2^2 \cdot 3 \cdot 7 \cdot 13$	**0386202**	$2 \cdot 547$
110	$2^2 \cdot 5^2 \cdot 11$	$3 \cdot 367$	$2 \cdot 19 \cdot 29$	**0425755**	$2^4 \cdot 3 \cdot 23$
111	$2 \cdot 3 \cdot 5 \cdot 37$	$11 \cdot 101$	$2^3 \cdot 139$	$3 \cdot 7 \cdot 53$	$2 \cdot 557$
112	$2^5 \cdot 5 \cdot 7$	$19 \cdot 59$	$2 \cdot 3 \cdot 11 \cdot 17$	**0503798**	$2^2 \cdot 281$
113	$2 \cdot 5 \cdot 113$	$3 \cdot 13 \cdot 29$	$2^2 \cdot 283$	$11 \cdot 103$	$2 \cdot 3^4 \cdot 7$
114	$2^2 \cdot 3 \cdot 5 \cdot 19$	$7 \cdot 163$	$2 \cdot 571$	$3^2 \cdot 127$	$2^3 \cdot 11 \cdot 13$
115	$2 \cdot 5^2 \cdot 23$	**0610753**	$2^7 \cdot 3^2$	**0618293**	$2 \cdot 577$
116	$2^3 \cdot 5 \cdot 29$	$3^3 \cdot 43$	$2 \cdot 7 \cdot 83$	**0655797**	$2^2 \cdot 3 \cdot 97$
117	$2 \cdot 3^2 \cdot 5 \cdot 13$	**0685569**	$2^2 \cdot 293$	$3 \cdot 17 \cdot 23$	$2 \cdot 587$
118	$2^2 \cdot 5 \cdot 59$	**0722499**	$2 \cdot 3 \cdot 197$	$7 \cdot 13^2$	$2^5 \cdot 37$
119	$2 \cdot 5 \cdot 7 \cdot 17$	$3 \cdot 397$	$2^3 \cdot 149$	**0766404**	$2 \cdot 3 \cdot 199$
120	$2^4 \cdot 3 \cdot 5^2$	**0795430**	$2 \cdot 601$	$3 \cdot 401$	$2^2 \cdot 7 \cdot 43$
121	$2 \cdot 5 \cdot 11^2$	$7 \cdot 173$	$2^2 \cdot 3 \cdot 101$	**0838608**	$2 \cdot 607$
122	$2^2 \cdot 5 \cdot 61$	$3 \cdot 11 \cdot 37$	$2 \cdot 13 \cdot 47$	**0874265**	$2^3 \cdot 3^2 \cdot 17$
123	$2 \cdot 3 \cdot 5 \cdot 41$	**0902581**	$2^4 \cdot 7 \cdot 11$	$3^2 \cdot 137$	$2 \cdot 617$
124	$2^3 \cdot 5 \cdot 31$	$17 \cdot 73$	$2 \cdot 3^3 \cdot 23$	$11 \cdot 113$	$2^2 \cdot 311$
125	$2 \cdot 5^4$	$3^2 \cdot 139$	$2^2 \cdot 313$	$7 \cdot 179$	$2 \cdot 3 \cdot 11 \cdot 19$
126	$2^2 \cdot 3^2 \cdot 5 \cdot 7$	$13 \cdot 97$	$2 \cdot 631$	$3 \cdot 421$	$2^4 \cdot 79$
127	$2 \cdot 5 \cdot 127$	$31 \cdot 41$	$2^3 \cdot 3 \cdot 53$	$19 \cdot 67$	$2 \cdot 7^2 \cdot 13$
128	$2^8 \cdot 5$	$3 \cdot 7 \cdot 61$	$2 \cdot 641$	**1082267**	$2^2 \cdot 3 \cdot 107$
129	$2 \cdot 3 \cdot 5 \cdot 43$	**1109262**	$2^2 \cdot 17 \cdot 19$	$3 \cdot 431$	$2 \cdot 647$
130	$2^2 \cdot 5^2 \cdot 13$	**1142773**	$2 \cdot 3 \cdot 7 \cdot 31$	**1149444**	$2^3 \cdot 163$
131	$2 \cdot 5 \cdot 131$	$3 \cdot 19 \cdot 23$	$2^5 \cdot 41$	$13 \cdot 101$	$2 \cdot 3^2 \cdot 73$
132	$2^3 \cdot 3 \cdot 5 \cdot 11$	**1209028**	$2 \cdot 661$	$3^3 \cdot 7^2$	$2^2 \cdot 331$
133	$2 \cdot 5 \cdot 7 \cdot 19$	11^3	$2^2 \cdot 3^2 \cdot 37$	$31 \cdot 43$	$2 \cdot 23 \cdot 29$
134	$2^2 \cdot 5 \cdot 67$	$3^2 \cdot 149$	$2 \cdot 11 \cdot 61$	$17 \cdot 79$	$2^6 \cdot 3 \cdot 7$
135	$2 \cdot 3^3 \cdot 5^2$	$7 \cdot 193$	$2^3 \cdot 13^2$	$3 \cdot 11 \cdot 41$	$2 \cdot 677$
136	$2^4 \cdot 5 \cdot 17$	**1338581**	$2 \cdot 3 \cdot 227$	$29 \cdot 47$	$2^2 \cdot 11 \cdot 31$
137	$2 \cdot 5 \cdot 137$	$3 \cdot 457$	$2^2 \cdot 7^3$	**1376705**	$2 \cdot 3 \cdot 229$
138	$2^2 \cdot 3 \cdot 5 \cdot 23$	**1401937**	$2 \cdot 691$	$3 \cdot 461$	$2^3 \cdot 173$
139	$2 \cdot 5 \cdot 139$	$13 \cdot 107$	$2^4 \cdot 3 \cdot 29$	$7 \cdot 199$	$2 \cdot 17 \cdot 41$
140	$2^3 \cdot 5^2 \cdot 7$	$3 \cdot 467$	$2 \cdot 701$	$23 \cdot 61$	$2^2 \cdot 3^3 \cdot 13$
141	$2 \cdot 3 \cdot 5 \cdot 47$	$17 \cdot 83$	$2^2 \cdot 353$	$3^2 \cdot 157$	$2 \cdot 7 \cdot 101$
142	$2^2 \cdot 5 \cdot 71$	$7^2 \cdot 29$	$2 \cdot 3^2 \cdot 79$	**1532049**	$2^4 \cdot 89$
143	$2 \cdot 5 \cdot 11 \cdot 13$	$3^3 \cdot 53$	$2^3 \cdot 179$	**1562462**	$2 \cdot 3 \cdot 239$
144	$2^5 \cdot 3^2 \cdot 5$	$11 \cdot 131$	$2 \cdot 7 \cdot 103$	$3 \cdot 13 \cdot 37$	$2^2 \cdot 19^2$
145	$2 \cdot 5^2 \cdot 29$	**1616674**	$2^2 \cdot 3 \cdot 11^2$	**1622656**	$2 \cdot 727$
146	$2^2 \cdot 5 \cdot 73$	$3 \cdot 487$	$2 \cdot 17 \cdot 43$	$7 \cdot 11 \cdot 19$	$2^3 \cdot 3 \cdot 61$
147	$2 \cdot 3 \cdot 5 \cdot 7^2$	**1676127**	$2^6 \cdot 23$	$3 \cdot 491$	$2 \cdot 11 \cdot 67$
148	$2^3 \cdot 5 \cdot 37$	**1705551**	$2 \cdot 3 \cdot 13 \cdot 19$	**1711412**	$2^2 \cdot 7 \cdot 53$
149	$2 \cdot 5 \cdot 149$	$3 \cdot 7 \cdot 71$	$2^3 \cdot 373$	**1740598**	$2 \cdot 3^2 \cdot 83$

FACTORS AND PRIMES (Continued)

n	5	6	7	8	9
100	$3 \cdot 5 \cdot 67$	$2 \cdot 503$	$19 \cdot 53$	$2^4 \cdot 3^2 \cdot 7$	0038912
101	$5 \cdot 7 \cdot 29$	$2^3 \cdot 127$	$3^2 \cdot 113$	$2 \cdot 509$	0081742
102	$5^2 \cdot 41$	$2 \cdot 3^2 \cdot 19$	$13 \cdot 79$	$2^2 \cdot 257$	$3 \cdot 7^3$
103	$3^2 \cdot 5 \cdot 23$	$2^3 \cdot 7 \cdot 37$	$17 \cdot 61$	$2 \cdot 3 \cdot 173$	0166155
104	$5 \cdot 11 \cdot 19$	$2 \cdot 523$	$3 \cdot 349$	$2^3 \cdot 131$	0207755
105	$5 \cdot 211$	$2^5 \cdot 3 \cdot 11$	$7 \cdot 151$	$2 \cdot 23^2$	$3 \cdot 353$
106	$3 \cdot 5 \cdot 71$	$2 \cdot 13 \cdot 41$	$11 \cdot 97$	$2^2 \cdot 3 \cdot 89$	0289777
107	$5^2 \cdot 43$	$2^2 \cdot 269$	$3 \cdot 359$	$2 \cdot 7^2 \cdot 11$	$13 \cdot 83$
108	$5 \cdot 7 \cdot 31$	$2 \cdot 3 \cdot 181$	0362295	$2^6 \cdot 17$	$3^2 \cdot 11^2$
109	$3 \cdot 5 \cdot 73$	$2^3 \cdot 137$	0402066	$2 \cdot 3^2 \cdot 61$	$7 \cdot 157$
110	$5 \cdot 13 \cdot 17$	$2 \cdot 7 \cdot 79$	$3^3 \cdot 41$	$2^2 \cdot 277$	0449315
111	$5 \cdot 223$	$2^2 \cdot 3^2 \cdot 31$	0480532	$2 \cdot 13 \cdot 43$	$3 \cdot 373$
112	$3^2 \cdot 5^3$	$2 \cdot 563$	$7^2 \cdot 23$	$2^3 \cdot 3 \cdot 47$	0526939
113	$5 \cdot 227$	$2^4 \cdot 71$	$3 \cdot 379$	$2 \cdot 569$	$17 \cdot 67$
114	$5 \cdot 229$	$2 \cdot 3 \cdot 191$	$31 \cdot 37$	$2^2 \cdot 7 \cdot 41$	$3 \cdot 383$
115	$3 \cdot 5 \cdot 7 \cdot 11$	$2^2 \cdot 17^2$	$13 \cdot 89$	$2 \cdot 3 \cdot 193$	$19 \cdot 61$
116	$5 \cdot 233$	$2 \cdot 11 \cdot 53$	$3 \cdot 389$	$2^4 \cdot 73$	$7 \cdot 167$
117	$5^2 \cdot 47$	$2^3 \cdot 3 \cdot 7^2$	$11 \cdot 107$	$2 \cdot 19 \cdot 31$	$3^2 \cdot 131$
118	$3 \cdot 5 \cdot 79$	$2 \cdot 593$	0744507	$2^2 \cdot 3^2 \cdot 11$	$29 \cdot 41$
119	$5 \cdot 239$	$2^3 \cdot 13 \cdot 23$	$3^2 \cdot 7 \cdot 19$	$2 \cdot 599$	$11 \cdot 109$
120	$5 \cdot 241$	$2 \cdot 3^2 \cdot 67$	$17 \cdot 71$	$2^3 \cdot 151$	$3 \cdot 13 \cdot 31$
121	$3^5 \cdot 5$	$2^6 \cdot 19$	0852906	$2 \cdot 3 \cdot 7 \cdot 29$	$23 \cdot 53$
122	$5^2 \cdot 7^2$	$2 \cdot 613$	$3 \cdot 409$	$2^2 \cdot 307$	0895519
123	$5 \cdot 13 \cdot 19$	$2^2 \cdot 3 \cdot 103$	0923697	$2 \cdot 619$	$3 \cdot 7 \cdot 59$
124	$3 \cdot 5 \cdot 83$	$2 \cdot 7 \cdot 89$	$29 \cdot 43$	$2^5 \cdot 3 \cdot 13$	0965624
125	$5 \cdot 251$	$2^3 \cdot 157$	$3 \cdot 419$	$2 \cdot 17 \cdot 37$	1000257
126	$5 \cdot 11 \cdot 23$	$2 \cdot 3 \cdot 211$	$7 \cdot 181$	$2^2 \cdot 317$	$3^3 \cdot 47$
127	$3 \cdot 5^2 \cdot 17$	$2^2 \cdot 11 \cdot 29$	1061909	$2 \cdot 3^2 \cdot 71$	1068705
128	$5 \cdot 257$	$2 \cdot 643$	$3^2 \cdot 11 \cdot 13$	$2^3 \cdot 7 \cdot 23$	1102529
129	$5 \cdot 7 \cdot 37$	$2^4 \cdot 3^4$	1129400	$2 \cdot 11 \cdot 59$	$3 \cdot 433$
130	$3^2 \cdot 5 \cdot 29$	$2 \cdot 653$	1162756	$2^2 \cdot 3 \cdot 109$	$7 \cdot 11 \cdot 17$
131	$5 \cdot 263$	$2^2 \cdot 7 \cdot 47$	$3 \cdot 439$	$2 \cdot 659$	1202448
132	$5^2 \cdot 53$	$2 \cdot 3 \cdot 13 \cdot 17$	1228709	$2^4 \cdot 83$	$3 \cdot 443$
133	$3 \cdot 5 \cdot 89$	$2^3 \cdot 167$	$7 \cdot 191$	$2 \cdot 3 \cdot 223$	$13 \cdot 103$
134	$5 \cdot 269$	$2 \cdot 673$	$3 \cdot 449$	$2^2 \cdot 337$	$19 \cdot 71$
135	$5 \cdot 271$	$2^2 \cdot 3 \cdot 113$	$23 \cdot 59$	$2 \cdot 7 \cdot 97$	$3^2 \cdot 151$
136	$3 \cdot 5 \cdot 7 \cdot 13$	$2 \cdot 683$	1357685	$2^3 \cdot 3^2 \cdot 19$	37^2
137	$5^2 \cdot 11$	$2^5 \cdot 43$	$3^4 \cdot 17$	$2 \cdot 13 \cdot 53$	$7 \cdot 197$
138	$5 \cdot 277$	$2 \cdot 3^2 \cdot 7 \cdot 11$	$19 \cdot 73$	$2^2 \cdot 347$	$3 \cdot 463$
139	$3^2 \cdot 5 \cdot 31$	$2^2 \cdot 349$	$11 \cdot 127$	$2 \cdot 3 \cdot 233$	1458177
140	$5 \cdot 281$	$2 \cdot 19 \cdot 37$	$3 \cdot 7 \cdot 67$	$2^7 \cdot 11$	1489110
141	$5 \cdot 283$	$2^3 \cdot 3 \cdot 59$	$13 \cdot 109$	$2 \cdot 709$	$3 \cdot 11 \cdot 43$
142	$3 \cdot 5^2 \cdot 19$	$2 \cdot 23 \cdot 31$	1544240	$2^2 \cdot 3 \cdot 7 \cdot 17$	1550322
143	$5 \cdot 7 \cdot 41$	$2^3 \cdot 359$	$3 \cdot 479$	$2 \cdot 719$	1580608
144	$5 \cdot 17^2$	$2 \cdot 3 \cdot 241$	1604685	$2^3 \cdot 181$	$3^2 \cdot 7 \cdot 23$
145	$3 \cdot 5 \cdot 97$	$2^4 \cdot 7 \cdot 13$	$31 \cdot 47$	$2 \cdot 3^6$	1640553
146	$5 \cdot 293$	$2 \cdot 733$	$3^2 \cdot 163$	$2^2 \cdot 367$	$13 \cdot 113$
147	$5^2 \cdot 59$	$2^2 \cdot 3^2 \cdot 41$	$7 \cdot 211$	$2 \cdot 739$	$3 \cdot 17 \cdot 29$
148	$3^2 \cdot 5 \cdot 11$	$2 \cdot 743$	1723110	$2^4 \cdot 3 \cdot 31$	1728947
149	$5 \cdot 13 \cdot 23$	$2^3 \cdot 11 \cdot 17$	$3 \cdot 499$	$2 \cdot 7 \cdot 107$	1758016

FACTORS AND PRIMES (Continued)

n	0	1	2	3	4
150	$2^2 \cdot 3 \cdot 5^3$	$19 \cdot 79$	$2 \cdot 751$	$3^2 \cdot 167$	$2^5 \cdot 47$
151	$2 \cdot 5 \cdot 151$	**1792645**	$2^3 \cdot 3^3 \cdot 7$	$17 \cdot 89$	$2 \cdot 757$
152	$2^4 \cdot 5 \cdot 19$	$3^2 \cdot 13^2$	$2 \cdot 761$	**1826999**	$2^2 \cdot 3 \cdot 127$
153	$2 \cdot 3^2 \cdot 5 \cdot 17$	**1849752**	$2^2 \cdot 383$	$3 \cdot 7 \cdot 73$	$2 \cdot 13 \cdot 59$
154	$2^2 \cdot 5 \cdot 7 \cdot 11$	$23 \cdot 67$	$2 \cdot 3 \cdot 257$	**1883659**	$2^3 \cdot 193$
155	$2 \cdot 5^2 \cdot 31$	$3 \cdot 11 \cdot 47$	$2^4 \cdot 97$	**1911715**	$2 \cdot 3 \cdot 7 \cdot 37$
156	$2^3 \cdot 3 \cdot 5 \cdot 13$	$7 \cdot 223$	$2 \cdot 11 \cdot 71$	$3 \cdot 521$	$2^2 \cdot 17 \cdot 23$
157	$2 \cdot 5 \cdot 157$	**1961762**	$2^2 \cdot 3 \cdot 131$	$11^2 \cdot 13$	$2 \cdot 787$
158	$2^2 \cdot 5 \cdot 79$	$3 \cdot 17 \cdot 31$	$2 \cdot 7 \cdot 113$	**1994809**	$2^4 \cdot 3^2 \cdot 11$
159	$2 \cdot 3 \cdot 5 \cdot 53$	$37 \cdot 43$	$2^3 \cdot 199$	$3^3 \cdot 59$	$2 \cdot 797$
160	$2^6 \cdot 5^2$	**2043913**	$2 \cdot 3^2 \cdot 89$	$7 \cdot 229$	$2^2 \cdot 401$
161	$2 \cdot 5 \cdot 7 \cdot 23$	$3^2 \cdot 179$	$2^2 \cdot 13 \cdot 31$	**2076344**	$2 \cdot 3 \cdot 269$
162	$2^2 \cdot 3^4 \cdot 5$	**2097830**	$2 \cdot 811$	$3 \cdot 541$	$2^3 \cdot 7 \cdot 29$
163	$2 \cdot 5 \cdot 163$	$7 \cdot 233$	$2^5 \cdot 3 \cdot 17$	$23 \cdot 71$	$2 \cdot 19 \cdot 43$
164	$2^3 \cdot 5 \cdot 41$	$3 \cdot 547$	$2 \cdot 821$	$31 \cdot 53$	$2^2 \cdot 3 \cdot 137$
165	$2 \cdot 3 \cdot 5^2 \cdot 11$	$13 \cdot 127$	$2^2 \cdot 7 \cdot 59$	$3 \cdot 19 \cdot 29$	$2 \cdot 827$
166	$2^2 \cdot 5 \cdot 83$	$11 \cdot 151$	$2 \cdot 3 \cdot 277$	**2208922**	$2^7 \cdot 13$
167	$2 \cdot 5 \cdot 167$	$3 \cdot 557$	$2^3 \cdot 11 \cdot 19$	$7 \cdot 239$	$2 \cdot 3^3 \cdot 31$
168	$2^4 \cdot 3 \cdot 5 \cdot 7$	41^2	$2 \cdot 29^2$	$3^2 \cdot 11 \cdot 17$	$2^2 \cdot 421$
169	$2 \cdot 5 \cdot 13^2$	$19 \cdot 89$	$2^2 \cdot 3^2 \cdot 47$	**2286570**	$2 \cdot 7 \cdot 11^2$
170	$2^2 \cdot 5^2 \cdot 17$	$3^5 \cdot 7$	$2 \cdot 23 \cdot 37$	$13 \cdot 131$	$2^3 \cdot 3 \cdot 71$
171	$2 \cdot 3^2 \cdot 5 \cdot 19$	$29 \cdot 59$	$2^4 \cdot 107$	$3 \cdot 571$	$2 \cdot 857$
172	$2^3 \cdot 5 \cdot 43$	**2357809**	$2 \cdot 3 \cdot 7 \cdot 41$	**2362853**	$2^2 \cdot 431$
173	$2 \cdot 5 \cdot 173$	$3 \cdot 577$	$2^2 \cdot 433$	**2387986**	$2 \cdot 3 \cdot 17^2$
174	$2^2 \cdot 3 \cdot 5 \cdot 29$	**2407988**	$2 \cdot 13 \cdot 67$	$3 \cdot 7 \cdot 83$	$2^4 \cdot 109$
175	$2 \cdot 5^3 \cdot 7$	$17 \cdot 103$	$2^3 \cdot 3 \cdot 73$	**2437819**	$2 \cdot 877$
176	$2^5 \cdot 5 \cdot 11$	$3 \cdot 587$	$2 \cdot 881$	$41 \cdot 43$	$2^2 \cdot 3^2 \cdot 7^2$
177	$2 \cdot 3 \cdot 5 \cdot 59$	$7 \cdot 11 \cdot 23$	$2^2 \cdot 443$	$3^2 \cdot 197$	$2 \cdot 887$
178	$2^2 \cdot 5 \cdot 89$	$13 \cdot 137$	$2 \cdot 3^4 \cdot 11$	**2511513**	$2^3 \cdot 223$
179	$2 \cdot 5 \cdot 179$	$3^2 \cdot 199$	$2^8 \cdot 7$	$11 \cdot 163$	$2 \cdot 3 \cdot 13 \cdot 23$
180	$2^3 \cdot 3^2 \cdot 5^2$	**2555137**	$2 \cdot 17 \cdot 53$	$3 \cdot 601$	$2^2 \cdot 11 \cdot 41$
181	$2 \cdot 5 \cdot 181$	**2579185**	$2^2 \cdot 3 \cdot 151$	$7^2 \cdot 37$	$2 \cdot 907$
182	$2^2 \cdot 5 \cdot 7 \cdot 13$	$3 \cdot 607$	$2 \cdot 911$	**2607867**	$2^5 \cdot 3 \cdot 19$
183	$2 \cdot 3 \cdot 5 \cdot 61$	**2626883**	$2^3 \cdot 229$	$3 \cdot 13 \cdot 47$	$2 \cdot 7 \cdot 131$
184	$2^4 \cdot 5 \cdot 23$	$7 \cdot 263$	$2 \cdot 3 \cdot 307$	$19 \cdot 97$	$2^2 \cdot 461$
185	$2 \cdot 5^2 \cdot 37$	$3 \cdot 617$	$2^2 \cdot 463$	$17 \cdot 109$	$2 \cdot 3^2 \cdot 103$
186	$2^2 \cdot 3 \cdot 5 \cdot 31$	**2697464**	$2 \cdot 7^2 \cdot 19$	$3^4 \cdot 23$	$2^3 \cdot 233$
187	$2 \cdot 5 \cdot 11 \cdot 17$	**2720738**	$2^4 \cdot 3^2 \cdot 13$	**2725378**	$2 \cdot 937$
188	$2^3 \cdot 5 \cdot 47$	$3^2 \cdot 11 \cdot 19$	$2 \cdot 941$	$7 \cdot 269$	$2^2 \cdot 3 \cdot 157$
189	$2 \cdot 3^3 \cdot 5 \cdot 7$	$31 \cdot 61$	$2^2 \cdot 11 \cdot 43$	$3 \cdot 631$	$2 \cdot 947$
190	$2^2 \cdot 5^2 \cdot 19$	**2789821**	$2 \cdot 3 \cdot 317$	$11 \cdot 173$	$2^4 \cdot 7 \cdot 17$
191	$2 \cdot 5 \cdot 191$	$3 \cdot 7^2 \cdot 13$	$2^3 \cdot 239$	**2817150**	$2 \cdot 3 \cdot 11 \cdot 29$
192	$2^7 \cdot 3 \cdot 5$	$17 \cdot 113$	$2 \cdot 31^2$	$3 \cdot 641$	$2^2 \cdot 13 \cdot 37$
193	$2 \cdot 5 \cdot 193$	**2857823**	$2^2 \cdot 3 \cdot 7 \cdot 23$	**2862319**	$2 \cdot 967$
194	$2^2 \cdot 5 \cdot 97$	$3 \cdot 647$	$2 \cdot 971$	$29 \cdot 67$	$2^3 \cdot 3^5$
195	$2 \cdot 3 \cdot 5^2 \cdot 13$	**2902573**	$2^5 \cdot 61$	$3^2 \cdot 7 \cdot 31$	$2 \cdot 977$
196	$2^3 \cdot 5 \cdot 7^2$	$37 \cdot 53$	$2 \cdot 3^2 \cdot 109$	$13 \cdot 151$	$2^2 \cdot 491$
197	$2 \cdot 5 \cdot 197$	$3^3 \cdot 73$	$2^2 \cdot 17 \cdot 29$	**2951271**	$2 \cdot 3 \cdot 7 \cdot 47$
198	$2^2 \cdot 3^2 \cdot 5 \cdot 11$	$7 \cdot 283$	$2 \cdot 991$	$3 \cdot 661$	$2^6 \cdot 31$
199	$2 \cdot 5 \cdot 199$	$11 \cdot 181$	$2^3 \cdot 3 \cdot 83$	**2995073**	$2 \cdot 997$

FACTORS AND PRIMES (Continued)

n	5	6	7	8	9
150	$5 \cdot 7 \cdot 43$	$2 \cdot 3 \cdot 251$	$11 \cdot 137$	$2^2 \cdot 13 \cdot 29$	$3 \cdot 503$
151	$3 \cdot 5 \cdot 101$	$2^2 \cdot 379$	$37 \cdot 41$	$2 \cdot 3 \cdot 11 \cdot 23$	$7^2 \cdot 31$
152	$5^2 \cdot 61$	$2 \cdot 7 \cdot 109$	$3 \cdot 509$	$2^3 \cdot 191$	$11 \cdot 139$
153	$5 \cdot 307$	$2^9 \cdot 3$	$29 \cdot 53$	$2 \cdot 769$	$3^4 \cdot 19$
154	$3 \cdot 5 \cdot 103$	$2 \cdot 773$	$7 \cdot 13 \cdot 17$	$2^2 \cdot 3^2 \cdot 43$	1900514
155	$5 \cdot 311$	$2^2 \cdot 389$	$3^2 \cdot 173$	$2 \cdot 19 \cdot 41$	1928461
156	$5 \cdot 313$	$2 \cdot 3^3 \cdot 29$	1950690	$2^5 \cdot 7^2$	$3 \cdot 523$
157	$3^2 \cdot 5^2 \cdot 7$	$2^2 \cdot 197$	$19 \cdot 83$	$2 \cdot 3 \cdot 263$	1983821
158	$5 \cdot 317$	$2 \cdot 13 \cdot 61$	$3 \cdot 23^2$	$2^2 \cdot 397$	$7 \cdot 227$
159	$5 \cdot 11 \cdot 29$	$2^2 \cdot 3 \cdot 7 \cdot 19$	2033049	$2 \cdot 17 \cdot 47$	$3 \cdot 13 \cdot 41$
160	$3 \cdot 5 \cdot 107$	$2 \cdot 11 \cdot 73$	2060159	$2^3 \cdot 3 \cdot 67$	2065560
161	$5 \cdot 17 \cdot 19$	$2^4 \cdot 101$	$3 \cdot 7^2 \cdot 11$	$2 \cdot 809$	2092468
162	$5^3 \cdot 13$	$2 \cdot 3 \cdot 271$	2113876	$2^2 \cdot 11 \cdot 37$	$3^2 \cdot 181$
163	$3 \cdot 5 \cdot 109$	$2^2 \cdot 409$	2140487	$2 \cdot 3^2 \cdot 7 \cdot 13$	$11 \cdot 149$
164	$5 \cdot 7 \cdot 47$	$2 \cdot 823$	$3^3 \cdot 61$	$2^4 \cdot 103$	$17 \cdot 97$
165	$5 \cdot 331$	$2^2 \cdot 3^2 \cdot 23$	2193225	$2 \cdot 829$	$3 \cdot 7 \cdot 79$
166	$3^2 \cdot 5 \cdot 37$	$2 \cdot 7^2 \cdot 17$	2219356	$2^2 \cdot 3 \cdot 139$	2224563
167	$5^2 \cdot 67$	$2^2 \cdot 419$	$3 \cdot 13 \cdot 43$	$2 \cdot 839$	$23 \cdot 73$
168	$5 \cdot 337$	$2 \cdot 3 \cdot 281$	$7 \cdot 241$	$2^3 \cdot 211$	$3 \cdot 563$
169	$3 \cdot 5 \cdot 113$	$2^5 \cdot 53$	2296818	$2 \cdot 3 \cdot 283$	2301934
170	$5 \cdot 11 \cdot 31$	$2 \cdot 853$	$3 \cdot 569$	$2^2 \cdot 7 \cdot 61$	2327421
171	$5 \cdot 7^3$	$2^2 \cdot 3 \cdot 11 \cdot 13$	$17 \cdot 101$	$2 \cdot 859$	$3^2 \cdot 191$
172	$3 \cdot 5^2 \cdot 23$	$2 \cdot 863$	$11 \cdot 157$	$2^6 \cdot 3^3$	$7 \cdot 13 \cdot 19$
173	$5 \cdot 347$	$2^2 \cdot 7 \cdot 31$	$3^2 \cdot 193$	$2 \cdot 11 \cdot 79$	$37 \cdot 47$
174	$5 \cdot 349$	$2 \cdot 3^2 \cdot 97$	2422929	$2^2 \cdot 19 \cdot 23$	$3 \cdot 11 \cdot 53$
175	$3^2 \cdot 5 \cdot 13$	$2^2 \cdot 439$	$7 \cdot 251$	$2 \cdot 3 \cdot 293$	2452658
176	$5 \cdot 353$	$2 \cdot 883$	$3 \cdot 19 \cdot 31$	$2^3 \cdot 13 \cdot 17$	$29 \cdot 61$
177	$5^2 \cdot 71$	$2^4 \cdot 3 \cdot 37$	2496874	$2 \cdot 7 \cdot 127$	$3 \cdot 593$
178	$3 \cdot 5 \cdot 7 \cdot 17$	$2 \cdot 19 \cdot 47$	2521246	$2^2 \cdot 3 \cdot 149$	2526103
179	$5 \cdot 359$	$2^2 \cdot 449$	$3 \cdot 599$	$2 \cdot 29 \cdot 31$	$7 \cdot 257$
180	$5 \cdot 19^2$	$2 \cdot 3 \cdot 7 \cdot 43$	$13 \cdot 139$	$2^4 \cdot 113$	$3^3 \cdot 67$
181	$3 \cdot 5 \cdot 11^2$	$2^2 \cdot 227$	$23 \cdot 79$	$2 \cdot 3^2 \cdot 101$	$17 \cdot 107$
182	$5^2 \cdot 73$	$2 \cdot 11 \cdot 83$	$3^2 \cdot 7 \cdot 29$	$2^2 \cdot 457$	$31 \cdot 59$
183	$5 \cdot 367$	$2^2 \cdot 3^2 \cdot 17$	$11 \cdot 167$	$2 \cdot 919$	$3 \cdot 613$
184	$3^2 \cdot 5 \cdot 41$	$2 \cdot 13 \cdot 71$	2664669	$2^2 \cdot 3 \cdot 7 \cdot 11$	43^2
185	$5 \cdot 7 \cdot 53$	$2^6 \cdot 29$	$3 \cdot 619$	$2 \cdot 929$	$11 \cdot 13^2$
186	$5 \cdot 373$	$2 \cdot 3 \cdot 311$	2711443	$2^2 \cdot 467$	$3 \cdot 7 \cdot 89$
187	$3 \cdot 5^4$	$2^2 \cdot 7 \cdot 67$	2734643	$2 \cdot 3 \cdot 313$	2739268
188	$5 \cdot 13 \cdot 29$	$2 \cdot 23 \cdot 41$	$3 \cdot 17 \cdot 37$	$2^5 \cdot 59$	2762320
189	$5 \cdot 379$	$2^2 \cdot 3 \cdot 79$	$7 \cdot 271$	$2 \cdot 13 \cdot 73$	$3^2 \cdot 211$
190	$3 \cdot 5 \cdot 127$	$2 \cdot 953$	2803507	$2^2 \cdot 3^2 \cdot 53$	$23 \cdot 83$
191	$5 \cdot 383$	$2^2 \cdot 479$	$3^3 \cdot 71$	$2 \cdot 7 \cdot 137$	$19 \cdot 101$
192	$5^2 \cdot 7 \cdot 11$	$2 \cdot 3^2 \cdot 107$	$41 \cdot 47$	$2^3 \cdot 241$	$3 \cdot 643$
193	$3^2 \cdot 5 \cdot 43$	$2^4 \cdot 11^2$	$13 \cdot 149$	$2 \cdot 3 \cdot 17 \cdot 19$	$7 \cdot 277$
194	$5 \cdot 389$	$2 \cdot 7 \cdot 139$	$3 \cdot 11 \cdot 59$	$2^2 \cdot 487$	2898118
195	$5 \cdot 17 \cdot 23$	$2^2 \cdot 3 \cdot 163$	$19 \cdot 103$	$2 \cdot 11 \cdot 89$	$3 \cdot 653$
196	$3 \cdot 5 \cdot 131$	$2 \cdot 983$	$7 \cdot 281$	$2^4 \cdot 3 \cdot 41$	$11 \cdot 179$
197	$5^2 \cdot 79$	$2^2 \cdot 13 \cdot 19$	$3 \cdot 659$	$2 \cdot 23 \cdot 43$	2964458
198	$5 \cdot 397$	$2 \cdot 3 \cdot 331$	2981979	$2^2 \cdot 7 \cdot 71$	$3^2 \cdot 13 \cdot 17$
199	$3 \cdot 5 \cdot 7 \cdot 19$	$2^2 \cdot 499$	3003781	$2 \cdot 3^2 \cdot 37$	3008128

EXTENDED TABLES OF FACTORS AND PRIMES

The following procedure makes possible the determination of a number between 2009 and 19,949 as being either prime, or if not, what its factors will be. It is herewith included with the kind permission of its author, Professor Leonard Caners.

The following symbols will be used:

N is the number whose factors, if any, are to be determined.

A is N with the last digit dropped. Thus if $N = 17,873$, $A = 1787$.

R is the range and is the integral part of the square root of N with its last two digits dropped. Thus R of $17,873 = 13$.

K is the key number and is found in the table below.

P_1 is a possible factor corresponding to K.

The twin series are given in the table for the sake of completeness but are not written down in actual practice.

There are two steps as outlined below.

Step I

N	K	P_1	Series	Procedure
Any number ending in 1, 3, 7, or 9, within limits stated above	$A - R$	$10R$ + last digit	$K + n; P_1 - 10n$ $n = 0, 1, \ldots, 2R + 1$	Beginning with K read table of Factors and Primes from left to right and look for corresponding possible factors

Step II

N ending in	K	P_1	Series	Procedure
1	$(A - 2) - 3R$	$10R + 7$	$K + 3n; P_1 - 10n$ $n = 0, 1, \ldots, 2R + 1$	Same as in Step I except that only every *third* entry in table of Factors and Primes is examined for corresponding possible factors
3	$A - 3R$	$10R + 1$	$n = 0, 1, \ldots, 2R + 1$	
7	$(A - 2) - 3R$	$10R + 9$	$n = 0, 1, \ldots, 2R + 1$	
9	$A - 3R$	$10R + 3$	$n = 0, 1, \ldots, 2R + 1$	

As an example consider 7519. Using tables on preceding pages proceed as follows:

Step I

From Table $N = 7519$; $A = 751$; $R = 8$, $K = 743$; $P_1 = 89$ and the series obtained:

743	89
744	79
745	69
746	59
—	—
751	9
752	1
753	11
—	—
760	81

EXTENDED TABLES OF FACTORS AND PRIMES (Continued)

Examining the Table of Factors and Primes beginning with 743 note whether 743 has 89 as a factor; whether 744 has 79 as a factor, etc. Then continue to read from left to right keeping in mind the possible factors 69, 59, . . . 81.

Since none are found one concludes that 7519 has no factors within the given range ending in 9 or 1.

Step II

From Table $K = 727$ and $P_1 = 83$; the series obtained is:

727	83
730	73
733	63
—	—
751	3
754	7
—	—
778	87

Proceed exactly as in Step I. Begin with 727 and note whether it has 83 as a factor. Thereafter examine every *third* entry for the remaining corresponding possible factors 73, 63 . . . 3, 7, . . . 87. Since 730 yields the factor 73 one concludes that 73 is the factor of 7519. By division $7519 = 73 \times 103$. Had no factor been found in either Step I or Step II the conclusion would be that the number under consideration was prime.

Proof for Step I

Let N end in 1. Then, if N has a factor ending in 1, write

$$(10a + 1)(10b + 1) = N = 10A + 1$$
$$10ab + a + b = A$$

or

$$b(10a + 1) = (A - a)$$

This proves that any factor $10a + 1$ of N is also a factor of $A - a$. Let $a = (R - n)$, then $(10a + 1)$ becomes $(10R + 1) - 10n$ and $(A - a)$ becomes $(A - R) + n$, i.e., $P_1 - 10n$ and $K + n$ respectively as given in the table. Since $P_1 - 10n$ becomes a number ending in 9 when $P_1 < 10n$, all possible factors ending in 9 are also provided for.

The proof for Step II is similar. For possible factors ending in 3 or 7 write

$$(10a + 7)(10b + 3) = N = 10A + 1.$$

By identical reasoning this results in $P_1 - 10n$ and $K + 3n$ respectively given in the table. This completes the proof for numbers ending in 1.

Identical reasoning establishes the key numbers and series for ending in 3, 7, or 9.

DIOPHANTINE EQUATIONS

H. C. Williams

Let $f(x_1, x_2, \ldots, x_n)$ be a given polynomial in the n variables $x_1, x_2, \ldots, x_n$ with integral coefficients. The equation

(*) $f(x_1, x_2, \ldots, x_n) = 0$

is said to be a *Diophantine equation* when it is to be solved with integral (or rational) values for the unknowns $x_1, x_2, \ldots, x_n$.

The general or complete integral (rational) solution of (*) is that solution which contains all integral (rational) solutions of (*). For the equations that follow, we shall only be concerned with integral solutions. When it is possible, the general solution of these equations will be presented; however, many of these equations have not yet been completely solved. In the course of discussing such equations, some partial results will be given.

Much more information about Diophantine equations can be found in the following works: (1) Z. I. Borevich and I. R. Shafarevich, *Number Theory*, Academic Press, New York and London (1966); (2) R. D. Carmichael, *The Theory of Numbers and Diophantine Analysis*, Dover, New York, N.Y., 1959; (3) B. N. Delone and D. K. Faddeev, *The Theory of Irrationalities of the Third Degree*, Vol. 10, Translations of Mathematical Monographs, American Mathematical Society, Providence, R.I., 1964; (4) L. E. Dickson, *History of the Theory of Numbers*, Vol. II, Chelsea, New York, N.Y., 1952; (5) L. E. Dickson, *Introduction to the Theory of Numbers*, Dover, New York, N.Y., 1957; (6) L. J. Mordell, *Diophantine Equations*, Academic Press, London and New York, 1969. The book by Mordell is especially valuable for modern developments in the theory of Diophantine Equations.

Some Selected Equations

The symbols m,n, will be used exclusively to denote integer parameters.

The linear Diophantine equation

$$ax + by = c$$

and the equation

$$ax^2 - by^2 = c$$

will be dealt with in the following section on continued fractions.

Diophantine Equations of Degree Two

1. All solutions with even y of the Pythagorean Diophantine equation

(1) $x^2 + y^2 = z^2$

are given by

$x = r(m^2 - n^2)$, $y = 2rmn$, $z = r(m^2 + n^2)$,

where r,m,n, are integer parameters.

DIOPHANTINE EQUATIONS

2. All solutions of

(2) $x^2 + y^2 = z^2 + w^2$

are given by

$2x = mn + pq,\ 2z = mp + nq,$
$2y = mp - nq,\ 2w = mn - pq,$

where m,q, are both even; n,p, are both even; or all four are odd.
3. The general integer solution of the equation

(3) $x_1^2 + x_2^2 + \ldots + x_n^2 = x^2$, $(x_1,x_2,\ldots,x_n) = 1$, $x > 0$, is given by
        $dx_i = 2q_i q_n$ $(i = 1,2,\ldots,n-1)$,
        $dx_n = q_n^2 - q_1^2 - \ldots - q_{n-1}^2$,
        $dx = q_n^2 + q_1^2 + \ldots + q_{n-1}^2$,

where the q's are arbitrary integers with $(q_1,q_2,\ldots,q_n) = 1$ and $d > 0$ is chosen so that
$(x_1,x_2,\ldots,x_n) = 1$.
4. If $e \neq 0$ and $d = b^2 - 4ac$ is not the square of an integer, and
if (u,v,w) is a given solution (u, v, w not all zero) of

(4) $ax^2 + bxy + cy^2 = ez^2$,

then all of its integer solutions are

$x = kr,\ y = ks,\ z = kt,$
$r = -(au+bv)m^2 - 2cvmn + cun^2,$
$s = avm^2 - 2aumn - (bu+cv)n^2,\ t = wT,\ T = am^2 + bmn + cn^2$

where m and n are relatively prime and k is an irreducible fraction whose denominator is
gD, where g divides w, and D divides both T and the expression $2aum + 2cvn + b(un+vm)$
and hence also $(b^2 - 4ac)eg^2$.
5. If a,b,c, are square free, $(a,b) = (b,c) = (a,c) = 1$, and
a,b,c, do not have the same sign, then the equation

(5) $ax^2 + by^2 + cz^2 = 0$

has non-trivial solutions if and only if $-bc$, $-ca$, $-ab$, are quadratic residues of a,b,c,
respectively, and if

$$ax^2 + by^2 + cz^2 \equiv 0 \pmod 8$$

is solvable. In fact, if (5) is put in its canonical form, i.e., $a > 0$, $b > 0$, $c < 0$, there exists
a non-trivial solution with

$$|x| < \sqrt{|bc|},\ |y| \leqslant \sqrt{|c|a},\ |z| \leqslant \sqrt{ab},$$

DIOPHANTINE EQUATIONS

and $(x,y) = (z,y) = (z,x) = 1$.

If a,b,c, are coprime in pairs and $abc \neq 0$, and if u,v,w, is a solution of (5) such that $(u,v) = (u,w) = 1$, we may assume that au is even and determine integers r,s,t, such that $aur + bvs + cwt = 1$ (r even). Express abc as a product $k\ell$ of two integers in all ways. Select integers d,m,n, subject to the following conditions:

$$(n,m) = (n,\ell) = (m,k) = 1,$$

and

d is even; or d,m,n, all odd, $k \equiv \ell \pmod 2$.

Put

$t_1 = d\ell m^2$, $t_2 = dkn^2$, $t_3 = dmn$, $h = ar^2 + bs^2 + ct^2$, $U = 2r-hu$,
$V = 2s-hv$, $W = 2t-hw$, $2u_1 = vW-wV$, $2v_1 = wU-uW$, $2w_1 = uV-vU$.

Then

$x = (ut_1 + Ut_2 - 2bcu_1 t_3)/2,$
$y = (vt_1 + Vt_2 - 2cav_1 t_3)/2,$
$z = (wt_1 + Wt_2 - 2baw_1 t_3)/2,$

satisfy (5), and all integer solutions of (5) are so obtained.

Equations of Degree Three

Apart from the trivial solutions $x=y=0$, $u=-w$, $x=z$, $y=w$, the general solution of

(6) $x^3 + y^3 = z^3 + w^3$

is given by

$x = r(HQ-M^2)$, $y = r(GQ+M^2)$,
$z = r(Q^2-MH)$, $w = r(Q^2+MG)$,

where

$M = m^2+3n^2,$
$Q = q^2+3p^2,$
$H = 3mp + 3np - mq + 3nq,$
$G = 3mp - 3np + mq + 3nq$, and r,m,n,p,q, are integer parameters.

7. The complete solution of

(7) $z^2 = x^3 + y^3$

such that y is odd and prime to x is given by

DIOPHANTINE EQUATIONS

$$x = -4p^3q + 4q^3, y = p^4 + 8pq^3,$$
$$x = -p^4 + 6p^2q^2 + 3q^4, y = p^4 + 6p^2q^2 - 3q^4,$$
$$x = p^4 + 6p^2q^2 - 3q^4, y = -p^4 + 6p^2q^2 + 3q^4,$$
$$x = 2p^4 - 4p^3q - 4pq^3 + 2q^4, y = p^4 + 4p^3q - 6p^2q^2 + 4pq^3 + q^4,$$
$$x = 4p^3q + 24p^2q^2 + 48pq^3 + 36q^4, y = p^4 + 8p^3q + 24p^2q^2 + 24pq^3,$$

where p and q are selected so that y is odd and prime to x.

8. The equation

(8) $$x^3 + y^3 = Az^3$$

has no non-trivial integer solutions if

$$A = p, 2p, 9p, p^2, 9p^2, 4p^2, pq, p_1 p_2^2,$$

or if

$$A = q, 4q, 9q, 2q^2, q^2, 9q^2, q_1 q_2^2, p^2 q^2,$$

where p and q are primes with $p \equiv 5 \pmod{18}$ and $q \equiv 11 \pmod{18}$. When (8) does have non-trivial solutions, it can be shown that all of these solutions can be derived by applying certain operations to a finite number of basic solutions. A table of these basic solutions for all $A \leqslant 500$ is given in Selmer [5,6].

9. The equation

(9) $$ax^3 + by^3 = c$$

with $a>b>1$, c=1 or 3, (ab,c) = 1, b=1 if c=3, has at most one integer solution (x,y), and for this solution $c^{-1}(x \, a^{1/3} + y \, b^{1/3})^3$ is either the fundamental unit or its square in the cubic field $Q(d^{1/3})$ defined by $Q(a^{1/3} \, b^{2/3})$. The only exception is the equation $2x^3 + y^3 = 3$, which has the two solutions (1,1) and (4,-5).

10. The equation

(10) $$x^3 + dy^3 = 1 \ (d>1 \ , d \neq 19, 20, 28)$$

has at most one solution with $xy \neq 0$. This is given by the fundamental unit in the cubic field $Q(d^{1/3})$ when it is a binomial unit, i.e., when the unit has the form $x + y \, d^{1/3}$. If d = 19, the only solution of (10) is (-8, 3); if d = 20, the only solution of (10) is (-19, 7); and if d = 28, the only solution of (10) is (-3, 1). A table of fundamental units of pure cubic fields $K(d^{1/3})$, $d \leqslant 1000$, is given in [2].

11. If the equation

(11) $$y^2 = ax^3 + by^2 + cx + d, a \neq 0,$$

has a solution (x,y), then max $(|x|, |y|) < \exp[(AH)^A]$ where $A = 10^6$ and $H = \max(|a|, |b|, |c|, |d|)$ (see Baker [1]).

DIOPHANTINE EQUATIONS

12. The special case of (11)

$$(12) \qquad y^2 - k = x^3$$

is discussed extensively in Mordell's book. A table of all solutions of (12) for $0 < k \leqslant 100$, as well as all (see Coghlan & Stevens [3]) solutions for $0 < -k < 100$, can be found in Hemer.[4]

Equations of Degree Four

13. The equation

$$(13) \qquad x^4 + y^4 = z^4 + w^4$$

has an infinitude of solutions given by

$$x = m^7 + m^5 n^2 - 2m^3 n^4 + 3m^2 n^5 + mn^6,$$
$$y = m^6 n - 3m^5 n^2 - 2m^4 n^3 + m^2 n^5 + n^7,$$
$$z = m^7 + m^5 n^2 - 2m^3 n^4 - 3m^2 n^5 + mn^6,$$
$$w = m^6 n + 3m^5 n^2 - 2m^4 n^3 + m^2 n^5 + n^7.$$

14. The equation

$$(14) \qquad x^4 + y^4 + z^4 = w^4$$

has no solution for $w < 220{,}000$.

15. The equation

$$(15) \qquad x^4 + y^4 + z^4 = 2w^4$$

has an infinitude of solutions given by

$$x = m^2 - n^2, \ y = 2mn + n^2,$$
$$z = m^2 + 2mn, \ w = m^2 + mn + n^2.$$

16. If the equation

$$(16) \qquad x^4 + ay^4 + bz^4 = w^2$$

has a solution x,t,u,v, then a second solution is given by

$$x = s^4 - at^4 - bu^4, \ y = 2stv,$$
$$z = 2suv, \ w = v^4 + 4as^4 t^4 + 4bs^4 u^4.$$

17. The special case

$$(17) \qquad x^4 + y^4 + z^4 = w^2$$

DIOPHANTINE EQUATIONS

of (16) has an infinitude of solutions given by

$$x = 2mn(m^2 - n^2), \quad y = 2mn(m^2 + n^2),$$
$$z = m^4 - n^4, \quad w = m^8 + 14m^4 n^4 + n^8.$$

18. If the equation

(18) $$ax^4 + bx^2 y^2 + cy^4 = ez^2$$

has a solution (r,s,t), it has a second solution given by

$$x = r(4ces^4 t^2 - q^2), \quad y = s(4aer^4 t^2 - q^2),$$
$$z = t[4dr^4 s^4 q^2 - (e^2 t^4 - dr^4 s^4)^2],$$

where

$$q = ar^4 - cs^4, \quad d = b^2 - 4ac.$$

19. The equations

(19) $$x^4 \pm y^4 = z^2$$

have no solutions such that $xyz \neq 0$.
20. The equation

(20) $$ax^4 - by^4 = c$$

has at most one solution in positive integers when $c = 1, 2, 4, 8$.
21. The equations

(21) $$x^4 - dy^4 = \pm 1$$

have at most one solution in positive integers. This will be given by $x=a$, $y=b$, if the fundamental unit of the ring of integers in $Q[(-4d)^{1/4}]$ takes the form $a^2 + ab(-4d)^{1/4} + b^2(-d)^{1/2}$.

Let $\epsilon = a + bd^{1/2}$ be the fundamental unit in the ring $Z[d^{1/2}]$ formed by adjoining $d^{1/2}$ to the rational integers. If $a^2 - db^2 = -1$, the equation $x^4 - dy^4 = 1$ has no solution unless $d=5$. If $d=5$ the equation has the solution $(3,2)$. If $a^2 - db^2 = 1$ and (r,s) is a solution of $x^4 - dy^4 = 1$ $(d \neq 7140)$, than $a=r^2$ and $b=s^2$. If $d = 7140$, the equation has the solution $(239, 26)$.

Equations of Degree Greater than Four
22. The equations

(22) $$y^2 = x^r \pm 1 \quad (r > 3)$$

have no solutions for which $xy \neq 0$.

DIOPHANTINE EQUATIONS

23. The equations

$$(23) \qquad y^3 = x^r \pm 1 \ (r > 2)$$

have no non-trivial solutions.

24. The equation

$$(24) \qquad 1 + x^2 = 2y^n \ (n > 2, n \neq 4)$$

has no solution (r,s) for which $|rs| \neq 1$. When $n=4$, the only solutions of (24) in positive integers are $(1,1)$ and $(239, 13)$.

25. The equations

$$(25) \qquad ax^n - by^n = \pm 1,$$

where $a > 0, b > 0$, and $n \geqslant 5$, have at most two solutions in positive integers.

26. The equations

$$(26) \qquad x^n - dy^n = \pm 1,$$

where $d > 0$ and $n \geqslant 5$, has at most one solution in positive integers x,y, except possibly when $d=2$ or when $n=5$ or 6 and $d = 2^n \pm 1$. If $d > 1250 \cdot 20^{1/6}$, the equation $x^5 + dy^5 = 1$ has at most one solution in non-zero integers.

27. If

$$f(x) = a_0 x^n + a_1 x^{n-1} + \ldots + a_n,$$

has at least three simple zeros, then all integer solutions of

$$(27) \qquad y^2 = f(x)$$

satisfy the inequality

$$\max (|x|,|y|) < \exp \exp \exp (n^{10} n^3 A^{n^2}),$$

where

$$A = \max|a_i| \ (i = 0,1, \ldots ,n).$$

28. The equation

$$(28) \qquad x^n + y^n = z^n \ (n > 2)$$

has no solution x,y,z, where $xyz \neq 0$, if n is a prime $< 25,000$ and n divides z; or if n is a prime $< 253,747,888$ and $(n,z) = 1$.

DIOPHANTINE EQUATIONS

REFERENCES

1. A. Baker, *The Diophantine Equation $y^2 = ax^3 + bx^2 + cx + d$, J. Lond. Math. Soc.,* Vol. 43 (1968), pp. 1-9.
2. B. D. Beach, H. C. Williams, C. R. Zarnke, *Some Computer Results on Units in Quadratic and Cubic Fields,* Proc. 25th Summer Meeting Can. Math. Congress, 1971, pp. 609-648.
3. F. B. Coghlan and N. M. Stevens, *The Diophantine Equation $x^3 - y^2 = k$,* Computers in Number Theory, Academic Press, London and New York, 1971, pp. 199-205.
4. O. Hemer, *Notes on the Diophantine Equation $y^2 - k = x^3$, Arkiv för Math.,* 3, 67, 1954.
5. E. S. Selmer, *The Diophantine Equation $ax^3 + by^3 + cz^3 = 0$, Acta Math.,* 85, 203, 1951.
6. *The Diophantine Equation $ax^3 + by^3 + cz^3 = 0$,* Completion of the tables, *Acta Math.,* 91, 191, 1954.

IV. GEOMETRY

MENSURATION FORMULAS

Dr. Howard Eves

TRIANGLES

In the following: K = area, r = radius of the inscribed circle, R = radius of the circumscribed circle.

Right Triangle

$A + B = C = 90°$
$c^2 = a^2 + b^2$ *(Pythagorean relation)*
$a = \sqrt{(c + b)(c - b)}$
$K = \frac{1}{2}ab$
$r = \dfrac{ab}{a + b + c}$, $R = \frac{1}{2}c$
$h = \dfrac{ab}{c}$, $m = \dfrac{b^2}{c}$, $n = \dfrac{a^2}{c}$

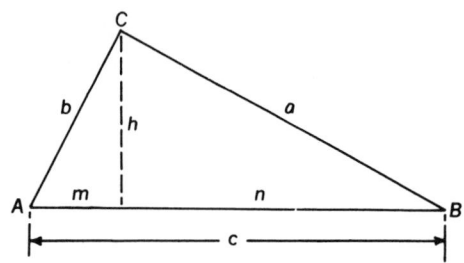

Equilateral Triangle

$A = B = C = 60°$
$K = \frac{1}{4}a^2\sqrt{3}$
$r = \frac{1}{6}a\sqrt{3}$, $R = \frac{1}{3}a\sqrt{3}$
$h = \frac{1}{2}a\sqrt{3}$

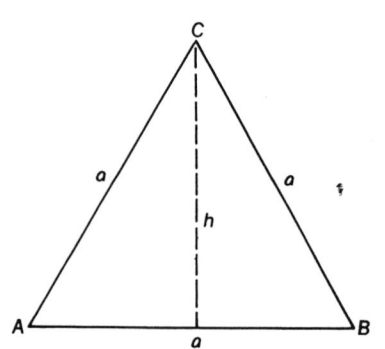

General Triangle

Let $s = \frac{1}{2}(a + b + c)$, h_c = length of altitude on side c, t_c = length of bisector of angle C, m_c = length of median to side c.

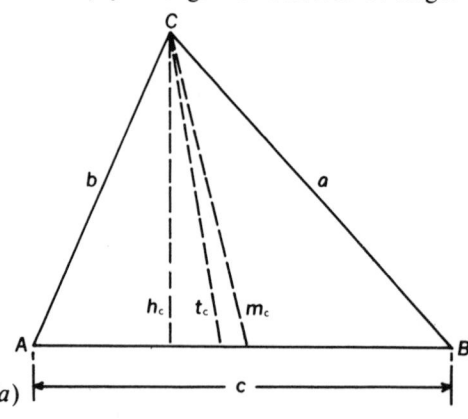

$A + B + C = 180°$
$c^2 = a^2 + b^2 - 2ab \cos C$
$\qquad$ *(law of cosines)*
$K = \frac{1}{2}h_c c = \frac{1}{2}ab \sin C$
$\quad = \dfrac{c^2 \sin A \sin B}{2 \sin C}$
$\quad = rs = \dfrac{abc}{4R}$
$\quad = \sqrt{s(s - a)(s - b)(s - c)}$ *(Heron's formula)*

Mensuration Formulas

$$r = c \sin \frac{A}{2} \sin \frac{B}{2} \sec \frac{C}{2} = \frac{ab \sin C}{2s} = (s - c) \tan \frac{C}{2}$$

$$= \sqrt{\frac{(s - a)(s - b)(s - c)}{s}} = \frac{K}{s} = 4R \sin \frac{A}{2} \sin \frac{B}{2} \sin \frac{C}{2}$$

$$R = \frac{c}{2 \sin C} = \frac{abc}{4 \sqrt{s(s - a)(s - b)(s - c)}} = \frac{abc}{4K}$$

$$h_c = a \sin B = b \sin A = \frac{2K}{c}$$

$$t_c = \frac{2ab}{a + b} \cos \frac{C}{2} = \sqrt{ab\left\{1 - \frac{c^2}{(a + b)^2}\right\}}$$

$$m_c = \sqrt{\frac{a^2}{2} + \frac{b^2}{2} - \frac{c^2}{4}}$$

 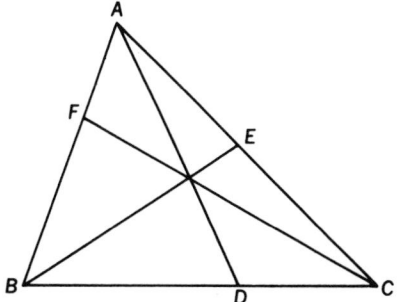

Menelaus' Theorem. A necessary and sufficient condition for points D, E, F on the respective side lines BC, CA, AB of a triangle ABC to be collinear is that

$$BD \cdot CE \cdot AF = - DC \cdot EA \cdot FB,$$

where all segments in the formula are directed segments.

Ceva's Theorem. A necessary and sufficient condition for AD, BE, CF, where D, E, F are points on the respective side lines BC, CA, AB of a triangle ABC, to be concurrent is that

$$BD \cdot CE \cdot AF = + DC \cdot EA \cdot FB,$$

where all segments in the formula are directed segments.

QUADRILATERALS

In the following: K = area, p and q are diagonals.

Rectangle

$A = B = C = D = 90°$

$K = ab, \quad p = \sqrt{a^2 + b^2}$

Parallelogram

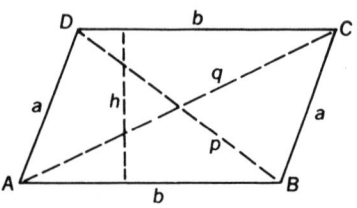

$A = C$, $B = D$, $A + B = 180°$

$K = bh = ab \sin A = ab \sin B$

$h = a \sin A = a \sin B$

$p = \sqrt{a^2 + b^2 - 2ab \cos A}$

$q = \sqrt{a^2 + b^2 - 2ab \cos B} = \sqrt{a^2 + b^2 + 2ab \cos A}$

Rhombus

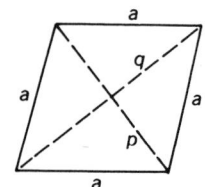

$p^2 + q^2 = 4a^2$

$K = \tfrac{1}{2}pq$

Trapezoid

$m = \tfrac{1}{2}(a + b)$

$K = \tfrac{1}{2}(a + b)h = mh$

General quadrilateral

Let $s = \tfrac{1}{2}(a + b + c + d)$.

$$
\begin{aligned}
K &= \tfrac{1}{2}pq \sin \theta \\
&= \tfrac{1}{4}(b^2 + d^2 - a^2 - c^2) \tan \theta \\
&= \tfrac{1}{4}\sqrt{4p^2q^2 - (b^2 + d^2 - a^2 - c^2)^2} \\
&\qquad (Bretschneider's\ formula) \\
&= \sqrt{(s - a)(s - b)(s - c)(s - d) - abcd \cos^2\left(\frac{A + B}{2}\right)}
\end{aligned}
$$

Theorem.   The diagonals of a quadrilateral with consecutive sides a, b, c, d are perpendicular if and only if $a^2 + c^2 = b^2 + d^2$.

Cyclic Quadrilateral

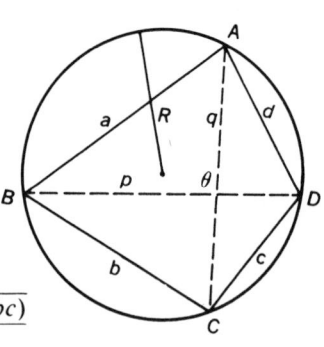

Let R = radius of the circumscribed circle.

$A + C = B + D = 180°$

$K = \sqrt{(s - a)(s - b)(s - c)(s - d)}$

     (*Brahmagupta's formula*)

$ = \dfrac{\sqrt{(ac + bd)(ad + bc)(ab + cd)}}{4R}$

$p = \sqrt{\dfrac{(ac + bd)(ab + cd)}{ad + bc}}$, $q = \sqrt{\dfrac{(ac + bd)(ad + bc)}{ab + cd}}$

$R = \tfrac{1}{2}\sqrt{\dfrac{(ac + bd)(ad + bc)(ab + cd)}{(s - a)(s - b)(s - c)(s - d)}}$, $\sin \theta = \dfrac{2K}{ac + bd}$

Mensuration Formulas

Ptolemy's Theorem. A convex quadrilateral with consecutive sides a, b, c, d and diagonals p and q is cyclic if and only if $ac + bd = pq$.

Cyclic-inscriptable Quadrilateral

Let r = radius of the inscribed circle, R = radius of the circumscribed circle, m = distance between the centers of the inscribed and the circumscribed circles.

$$A + C = B + D = 180°$$
$$a + c = b + d$$
$$K = \sqrt{abcd}$$
$$\frac{1}{(R - m)^2} + \frac{1}{(R + m)^2} = \frac{1}{r^2}$$
$$r = \frac{\sqrt{abcd}}{s}$$
$$R = \tfrac{1}{2} \sqrt{\frac{(ac + bd)(ad + bc)(ab + cd)}{abcd}}$$

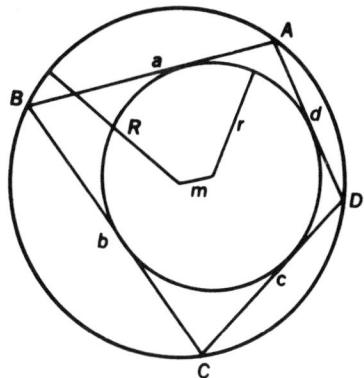

REGULAR POLYGONS

In the following: n = number of sides, s = length of each side, p = perimeter, θ = one of the vertex angles, r = radius of the inscribed circle, R = radius of the circumscribed circle, K = area.

$$\theta = \left(\frac{n - 2}{n}\right) 180°$$
$$s = 2r \tan \frac{180°}{n} = 2R \sin \frac{180°}{n}$$
$$p = ns$$
$$K = \tfrac{1}{4} ns^2 \cot \frac{180°}{n}$$
$$= nr^2 \tan \frac{180°}{n}$$
$$= \tfrac{1}{2} nR^2 \sin \frac{360°}{n}$$
$$r = \tfrac{1}{2} s \cot \frac{180°}{n}, \quad R = \tfrac{1}{2} s \csc \frac{180°}{n}$$

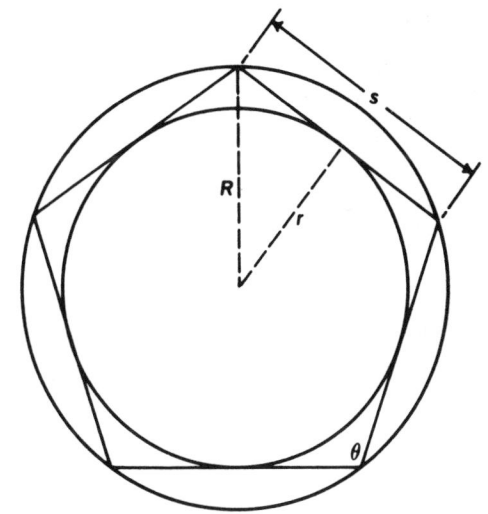

Polygon	n	K	r	R
Triangle (equilateral)	3	$0.43301s^2$	$0.28868s$	$0.57735s$
Square	4	$1.00000s^2$	$0.50000s$	$0.70711s$
Pentagon	5	$1.72048s^2$	$0.68819s$	$0.85065s$
Hexagon	6	$2.59808s^2$	$0.86603s$	$1.00000s$
Heptagon	7	$3.63391s^2$	$1.0383s$	$1.1524s$
Octagon	8	$4.82843s^2$	$1.2071s$	$1.3066s$
Nonagon	9	$6.18182s^2$	$1.3737s$	$1.4619s$
Decagon	10	$7.69421s^2$	$1.5388s$	$1.6180s$
Undecagon	11	$9.36564s^2$	$1.7028s$	$1.7747s$
Dodecagon	12	$11.19615s^2$	$1.8660s$	$1.9319s$

Mensuration Formulas

If s_k denotes the side of a regular polygon of k sides inscribed in a circle of radius R, then

$$s_{2n} = \sqrt{2R^2 - R\sqrt{4R^2 - s_n^2}}$$

If S_k denotes the side of a regular polygon of k sides circumscribed about a circle of radius r, then

$$S_{2n} = \frac{2rS_n}{2r + \sqrt{4r^2 + S_n^2}}$$

If p_k and P_k denote, respectively, the perimeters of regular polygons of k sides inscribed in and circumscribed about the same circle, then

$$P_{2n} = \frac{2p_n P_n}{p_n + P_n} \quad \text{and} \quad p_{2n} = \sqrt{p_n P_{2n}}.$$

If a_k and A_k denote, respectively, the areas of regular polygons of k sides inscribed in and circumscribed about the same circle, then

$$a_{2n} = \sqrt{a_n A_n} \quad \text{and} \quad A_{2n} = \frac{2a_{2n} A_n}{a_{2n} + A_n}.$$

CIRCLES

In the following: R = radius, D = diameter, C = circumference, K = area.

Circumference and Area of a Circle

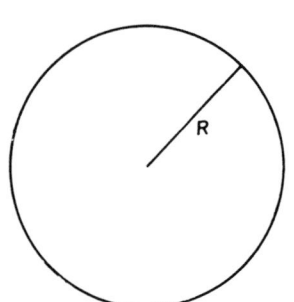

$$C = 2\pi R = \pi D \qquad (\pi = 3.14159\cdots)$$
$$K = \pi R^2 = \tfrac{1}{4}\pi D^2 = 0.7854 D^2$$
$$C = 2\sqrt{\pi K} = \frac{2K}{R}$$
$$K = \frac{C^2}{4\pi} = \tfrac{1}{2}CR$$

Sector and Segment of a Circle

Let the central angle θ be measured in radians ($\theta < \pi$).

$$h = R - d, \quad d = R - h$$
$$s = R\theta$$
$$d = R\cos\frac{\theta}{2} = \tfrac{1}{2}c\cot\frac{\theta}{2}$$
$$\quad = \tfrac{1}{2}\sqrt{4R^2 - c^2}$$
$$c = 2R\sin\frac{\theta}{2} = 2d\tan\frac{\theta}{2}$$
$$\quad = 2\sqrt{R^2 - d^2} = \sqrt{4h(2R - h)}$$
$$\theta = \frac{s}{R} = 2\,\mathrm{Cos}^{-1}\frac{d}{R} = 2\,\mathrm{Tan}^{-1}\frac{c}{2d} = 2\,\mathrm{Sin}^{-1}\frac{c}{2R}$$
$$K \text{ (sector)} = \tfrac{1}{2}Rs = \tfrac{1}{2}R^2\theta$$
$$K \text{ (segment)} = \tfrac{1}{2}R^2(\theta - \sin\theta) = \tfrac{1}{2}(Rs - cd) = R^2\,\mathrm{Cos}^{-1}\frac{d}{R} - d\sqrt{R^2 - d^2}$$
$$\quad = R^2\,\mathrm{Cos}^{-1}\frac{R - h}{R} - (R - h)\sqrt{2Rh - h^2}$$

Sector of an Annulus

$h = R_1 - R_2$

$K = \frac{1}{2}\theta(R_1 + R_2)(R_1 - R_2)$

$\quad = \frac{1}{2}\theta h(R_1 + R_2)$

$\quad = \frac{1}{2}h(s_1 + s_2)$

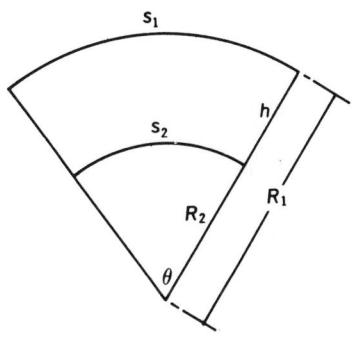

CONIC SECTIONS

Ellipse

Let p = circumference, K = area

$p = 2\pi\sqrt{\dfrac{a^2 + b^2}{2}}$ (approximately)

$\quad = 4aE$ (exactly)   See table of elliptic integral for E, using $k = \sqrt{a^2 - b^2}/a$.

$K = \pi ab$

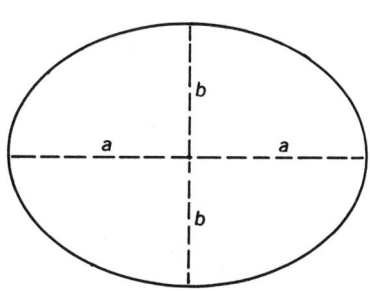

Parabolic Segment

$s = \sqrt{4x^2 + y^2} + \dfrac{y^2}{2x}\log_e\left[\dfrac{2x + \sqrt{4x^2 + y^2}}{y}\right]$

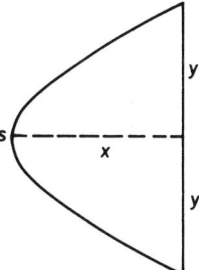

K (right segment) $= \frac{4}{3}xy$

K (oblique segment) $= \frac{4}{3}T$, where T is the area of the triangle with base along the chord of the segment and with opposite vertex at the point on the parabola at which the tangent to the parabola is parallel to the chord of the segment.

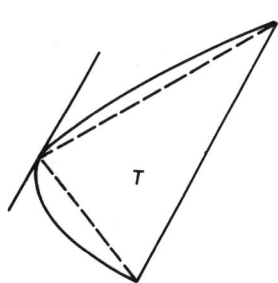

CAVALIERI'S THEOREM FOR THE PLANE

If two planar areas are included between a pair of parallel lines, and if the two segments cut off by the areas on any line parallel to the including lines are equal in length, then the two planar areas are equal.

PLANAR AREAS BY APPROXIMATION

Divide the planar area K into n strips by equidistant parallel chords of lengths $y_0, y_1, y_2, \ldots, y_n$ (where y_0 and/or y_n may be zero), and let h denote the common distance between the chords. Then, approximately:

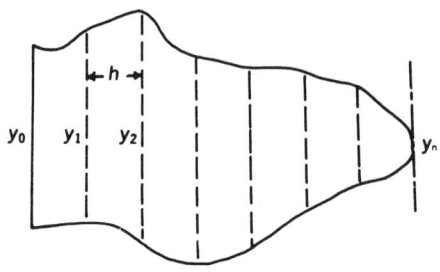

Trapezoidal Rule

$$K = h(\tfrac{1}{2}y_0 + y_1 + y_2 + \cdots + y_{n-1} + \tfrac{1}{2}y_n)$$

Durand's Rule

$$K = h(\tfrac{4}{10}y_0 + \tfrac{11}{10}y_1 + y_2 + y_3 + \cdots + y_{n-2} + \tfrac{11}{10}y_{n-1} + \tfrac{4}{10}y_n)$$

Simpson's rule (n even)

$$K = \tfrac{1}{3}h(y_0 + 4y_1 + 2y_2 + 4y_3 + 2y_4 + \cdots + 2y_{n-2} + 4y_{n-1} + y_n)$$

Weddle's Rule ($n = 6$)

$$K = \tfrac{3}{10}h(y_0 + 5y_1 + y_2 + 6y_3 + y_4 + 5y_5 + y_6)$$

SOLIDS BOUNDED BY PLANES

In the following: S = lateral surface, T = total surface, V = volume.

Cube

Let a = length of each edge.

$$T = 6a^2, \quad \text{diagonal of face} = a\sqrt{2}$$
$$V = a^3, \quad \text{diagonal of cube} = a\sqrt{3}$$

Rectangular Parallelepiped (or box)

Let a, b, c be the lengths of its edges.

$$T = 2(ab + bc + ca), \quad V = abc$$
$$\text{diagonal} = \sqrt{a^2 + b^2 + c^2}$$

Prism

$$S = \text{(perimeter of right section)} \times \text{(lateral edge)}$$
$$V = \text{(area of right section)} \times \text{(lateral edge)}$$
$$= \text{(area of base)} \times \text{(altitude)}$$

Truncated Triangular Prism

$$V = \text{(area of right section)} \times \tfrac{1}{3}\text{(sum of the three lateral edges)}$$

Mensuration Formulas

Pyramid

S of regular pyramid $= \frac{1}{2}$ (perimeter of base) $\times$ (slant height)

$V = \frac{1}{3}$ (area of base) $\times$ (altitude)

Frustum of Pyramid

Let B_1 = area of lower base, B_2 = area of upper base, h = altitude.

S of regular figure $= \frac{1}{2}$ (sum of perimeters of bases) $\times$ (slant height)

$V = \frac{1}{3}h(B_1 + B_2 + \sqrt{B_1 B_2})$

Prismatoid

A *prismatoid* is a polyhedron having for bases two polygons in parallel planes, and for lateral faces triangles or trapezoids with one side lying in one base, and the opposite vertex or side lying in the other base, of the polyhedron. Let B_1 = area of lower base, M = area of midsection, B_2 = area of upper base, h = altitude.

$$V = \frac{1}{6}h(B_1 + 4M + B_2) \quad \text{(the \textit{prismoidal formula})}$$

Note: Since cubes, rectangular parallelepipeds, prisms, pyramids, and frustums of pyramids are all examples of prismatoids, the formula for the volume of a prismatoid subsumes most of the above volume formulae.

Regular Polyhedra

Let v = number of vertices, e = number of edges, f = number of faces, α = each dihedral angle, a = length of each edge, r = radius of the inscribed sphere, R = radius of the circumscribed sphere, A = area of each face, T = total area, V = volume.

$v - e + f = 2$ (the *Euler-Descartes formula*—actually holds for *any* convex polyhedron)

$$T = fA$$
$$V = \frac{1}{3}rfA = \frac{1}{3}rT$$

Name	Nature of Surface	T	V
Tetrahedron	4 equilateral triangles	$1.73205a^2$	$0.11785a^3$
Hexahedron (cube)	6 squares	$6.00000a^2$	$1.00000a^3$
Octahedron	8 equilateral triangles	$3.46410a^2$	$0.47140a^3$
Dodecahedron	12 regular pentagons	$20.64573a^2$	$7.66312a^3$
Icosahedron	20 equilateral triangles	$8.66025a^2$	$2.18169a^3$

Name	v	e	f	α	a	r
Tetrahedron	4	6	4	70° 32′	1.633R	0.333R
Hexahedron	8	12	6	90°	1.155R	0.577R
Octahedron	6	12	8	109° 28′	1.414R	0.577R
Dodecahedron	20	30	12	116° 34′	0.714R	0.795R
Icosahedron	12	30	20	138° 11′	1.051R	0.795R

GEOMETRY

Mensuration Formulas

Name	A	r	R	V
Tetrahedron	$\frac{1}{4}a^2\sqrt{3}$	$\frac{1}{12}a\sqrt{6}$	$\frac{1}{4}a\sqrt{6}$	$\frac{1}{12}a^3\sqrt{2}$
Hexahedron	a^2	$\frac{1}{2}a$	$\frac{1}{2}a\sqrt{3}$	a^3
Octahedron	$\frac{1}{4}a^2\sqrt{3}$	$\frac{1}{6}a\sqrt{6}$	$\frac{1}{2}a\sqrt{2}$	$\frac{1}{3}a^3\sqrt{2}$
Dodecahedron	$\frac{1}{4}a^2\sqrt{25+10\sqrt{5}}$	$\frac{1}{20}a\sqrt{250+110\sqrt{5}}$	$\frac{1}{4}a(\sqrt{15}+\sqrt{3})$	$\frac{1}{4}a^3(15+7\sqrt{5})$
Icosahedron	$\frac{1}{4}a^2\sqrt{3}$	$\frac{1}{12}a\sqrt{42+18\sqrt{5}}$	$\frac{1}{4}a\sqrt{10+2\sqrt{5}}$	$\frac{5}{12}a^3(3+\sqrt{5})$

CYLINDERS AND CONES

In the following: B_1 = area of lower base, B_2 = area of upper base, h = altitude, S = lateral surface, T = total surface, V = volume.

Cylinder

S = (perimeter of right section) × (lateral edge)
V = (area of right section) × (lateral edge)

Right Circular Cylinder

Let R = radius of base.

$$S = 2\pi Rh, \quad T = 2\pi R(R+h), \quad V = \pi R^2 h$$

Cone

$$V = \tfrac{1}{3}B_1 h$$

Right Circular Cone

Let R = radius of base, s = slant height.

$$s = \sqrt{R^2 + h^2}$$
$$S = \pi Rs = \pi R\sqrt{R^2 + h^2}$$
$$T = \pi R(R+s) = \pi R(R + \sqrt{R^2 + h^2})$$
$$V = \tfrac{1}{3}\pi R^2 h$$

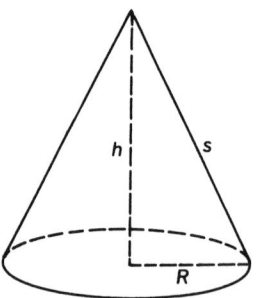

Frustum of Cone

$V = \frac{1}{3}h(B_1 + B_2 + \sqrt{B_1 B_2})$, where B_1 and B_2 are the areas of the bases.

Frustum of Right Circular Cone

Let R_1 = radius of lower base, R_2 = radius of upper base, s = slant height.

Mensuration Formulas

$$s = \sqrt{(R_1 - R_2)^2 + h^2}$$
$$S = \pi(R_1 + R_2)\,s$$
$$\quad = \pi(R_1 + R_2)\sqrt{(R_1 - R_2)^2 + h^2}$$
$$T = \pi[R_1^2 + R_2^2 + (R_1 + R_2)\,s]$$
$$\quad = \pi[R_1^2 + R_2^2 + (R_1 + R_2)\sqrt{(R_1 - R_2)^2 + h^2}]$$
$$V = \tfrac{1}{3}\pi h(R_1^2 + R_2^2 + R_1 R_2)$$

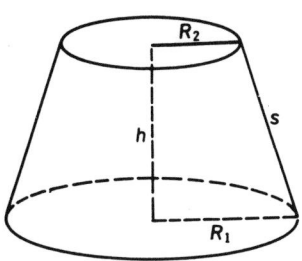

SPHERICAL FIGURES

In the following: R = radius of sphere, D = diameter of sphere, S = surface area, V = volume.

Sphere

$$D = 2R$$
$$S = 4\pi R^2 = \pi D^2 = 12.57R^2$$
$$V = \tfrac{4}{3}\pi R^3 = \tfrac{1}{6}\pi D^3 = 4.189R^3$$

Zone and Segment of One Base

$$S = 2\pi Rh = \pi Dh = \pi p^2$$
$$V = \tfrac{1}{3}\pi h^2(3R - h) = \tfrac{1}{6}\pi h(3a^2 + h^2)$$

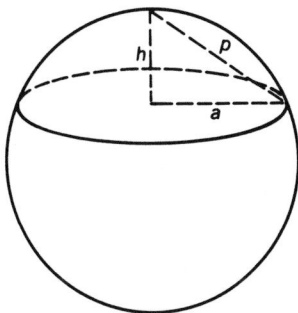

Zone and Segment of Two Bases

$$S = 2\pi Rh = \pi Dh$$
$$V = \tfrac{1}{6}\pi h(3a^2 + 3b^2 + h^2)$$

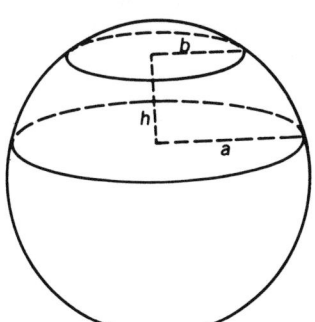

Lune

$$S = 2R^2\theta, \quad \theta \text{ in radians}$$

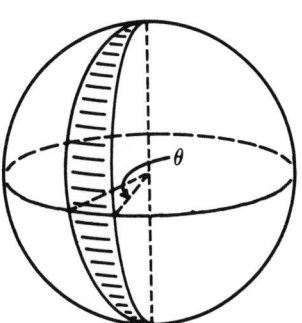

Spherical Sector

$$V = \tfrac{2}{3}\pi R^2 h = \tfrac{1}{6}\pi D^2 h$$

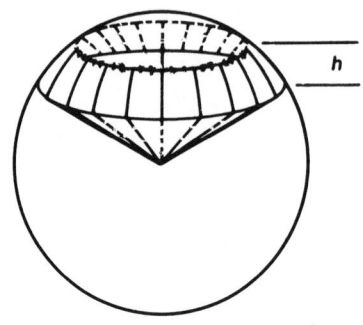

Spherical Triangle and Polygon

Let A, B, C be the angles, in radians, of the triangle; let θ = sum of angles, in radians, of a spherical polygon of n sides.

$$S = (A + B + C - \pi) R^2$$
$$S = [\theta - (n - 2) \pi] R^2$$

SPHEROIDS

Ellipsoid

Let a, b, c be the lengths of the semiaxes.

$$V = \tfrac{4}{3}\pi abc$$

Oblate Spheroid

An *oblate spheroid* is formed by the rotation of an ellipse about its minor axis. Let a and b be the major and minor semiaxes, respectively, and ϵ the eccentricity, of the revolving ellipse.

$$S = 2\pi a^2 + \pi \frac{b^2}{\epsilon} \log_e \frac{1 + \epsilon}{1 - \epsilon}$$
$$V = \tfrac{4}{3}\pi a^2 b$$

Prolate Spheroid

A *prolate spheroid* is formed by the rotation of an ellipse about its major axis. Let a and b be the major and minor semiaxes, respectively, and ϵ the eccentricity, of the revolving ellipse.

$$S = 2\pi b^2 + 2\pi \frac{ab}{\epsilon} \sin^{-1} \epsilon$$
$$V = \tfrac{4}{3}\pi ab^2$$

CIRCULAR TORUS

A *circular torus* is formed by the rotation of a circle about an axis in the plane of the circle and not cutting the circle. Let r be the radius of the revolving circle and let R be the distance of its center from the axis of rotation.

Mensuration Formulas

$$S = 4\pi^2 Rr$$
$$V = 2\pi^2 Rr^2$$

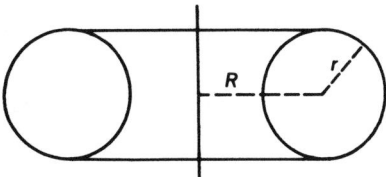

PAPPUS-GULDINUS THEOREMS

1. If a planar arc be revolved about an axis in its plane, but not cutting the arc, the area of the surface of revolution so formed is equal to the product of the length of the arc and the length of the path traced by the centroid of the arc.

2. If a planar area be revolved about an axis in its plane, but not intersecting the area, the volume of the solid of revolution so formed is equal to the product of the area and the length of the path traced by the centroid of the area.

CAVALIERI'S THEOREM FOR SPACE

If two solids are included between a pair of parallel planes, and if the two sections cut by them on any plane parallel to the including planes are equal in area, then the volumes of the solids are equal.

GENERAL PRISMATOID

A *general prismatoid* is a solid such that the area A_y of any section parallel to and distant y from a fixed plane can be expressed as a polynomial in y of degreee not higher than the third. That is,

$$A_y = ay^3 + by^2 + cy + d,$$

where a, b, c, d are constants which may be positive, zero, or negative. Let B_1 = area of lower base, M = area of midsection, B_2 = area of upper base, h = altitude.

$$V = \tfrac{1}{6}h(B_1 + 4M + B_2)$$

Note. All prismatoids, cylinders, cones, spheres, spheroids, and many other solids are general prismatoids.

CENTROIDS

If a geometrical figure possesses a center of symmetry, that point is the centroid of the figure.

If a geometrical figure possesses an axis of symmetry, the centroid of the figure lies on that axis.

GEOMETRY

Mensuration Formulae

Geometrical Figure	Location of Centroid
Perimeter of triangle	Center of the inscribed circle of the triangle whose vertices are the midpoints of the sides of the given triangle.
Arc of semicircle of radius R	Distance from diameter $= \dfrac{2R}{\pi}$
Arc of 2α radians of a circle of radius R	Distance from center of circle $= \dfrac{R \sin \alpha}{\alpha}$
Area of triangle	Intersection of the medians
Area of quadrilateral	Intersection of the diagonals of the parallelogram whose sides pass through adjacent trisection points of pairs of consecutive sides of the quadrilateral
Area of semicircle of radius R	Distance from diameter $= \dfrac{4R}{3\pi}$
Area of circular sector of radius R and central angle 2α radians	Distance from center of circle $= \dfrac{2R \sin \alpha}{3\alpha}$
Area of semiellipse of altitude h	Distance from base $= \dfrac{4h}{3\pi}$
Area of a quadrant of an ellipse of major and minor semiaxes a and b	Distance from minor axis $= \dfrac{4a}{3\pi}$, distance from major axis $= \dfrac{4b}{3\pi}$
Area of right parabolic segment of altitude h	Distance from base $= \frac{2}{5}h$
Lateral area of regular pyramid or right circular cone	Distance from base $= \frac{1}{3}h$
Area of hemisphere of radius R	Distance from base $= \frac{1}{2}R$
Volume of pyramid or cone	One fourth the way from the centroid of the base to the vertex of the pyramid or cone
Volume of frustum of pyramid or cone with d as the distance between the centroids of its bases and k as the ratio of similarity of the upper base to the lower base	On the line joining the centroids of the two bases at a distance from the centroid of the lower base $= \frac{1}{4}d\left(\dfrac{1 + 2k + 3k^2}{1 + k + k^2}\right)$
Volume of hemisphere of radius R	Distance from base $= \frac{3}{8}R$
Volume of revolution of altitude h obtained by revolving a semiellipse about its axis of symmetry	Distance from base $= \frac{3}{8}h$
Volume of paraboloid of revolution of altitude h	Distance from base $= \frac{1}{3}h$

RECIPROCALS, CIRCUMFERENCE AND AREA OF CIRCLES

As a matter of convenience, the values of $1000 \times (1/n)$ are given in the table. To obtain the actual value of the reciprocal, shift the decimal point three places to the left.

Circumferences and areas of circles are given for the values of n as the diameter.

$n = $ dia	$1000\dfrac{1}{n}$	Circum- ference πn	Area $\dfrac{\pi n^2}{4}$	$n = $ dia	$1000\dfrac{1}{n}$	Circum- ference πn	Area $\dfrac{\pi n^2}{4}$
0	∞	0.000000	.0000000	50	20.00000	157.0796	1963.495
1	1000.000	3.141593	.7853982	51	19.60784	160.2212	2042.821
2	500.0000	6.283185	3.141593	52	19.23077	163.3628	2123.717
3	333.3333	9.424778	7.068583	53	18.86792	166.5044	2206.183
4	250.0000	12.56637	12.56637	54	18.51852	169.6460	2290.221
5	200.0000	15.70796	19.63495	55	18.18182	172.7876	2375.829
6	166.6667	18.84956	28.27433	56	17.85714	175.9292	2463.009
7	142.8571	21.99115	38.48451	57	17.54386	179.0708	2551.759
8	125.0000	25.13274	50.26548	58	17.24138	182.2124	2642.079
9	111.1111	28.27433	63.61725	59	16.94915	185.3540	2733.971
10	100.0000	31.41593	78.53982	60	16.66667	188.4956	2827.433
11	90.90909	34.55752	95.03318	61	16.39344	191.6372	2922.467
12	83.33333	37.69911	113.0973	62	16.12903	194.7787	3019.071
13	76.92308	40.84070	132.7323	63	15.87302	197.9203	3117.245
14	71.42857	43.98230	153.9380	64	15.62500	201.0619	3216.991
15	66.66667	47.12389	176.7146	65	15.38462	204.2035	3318.307
16	62.50000	50.26548	201.0619	66	15.15152	207.3451	3421.194
17	58.82353	53.40708	226.9801	67	14.92537	210.4867	3525.652
18	55.55556	56.54867	254.4690	68	14.70588	213.6283	3631.681
19	52.63158	59.69026	283.5287	69	14.49275	216.7699	3739.281
20	50.00000	62.83185	314.1593	70	14.28571	219.9115	3848.451
21	47.61905	65.97345	346.3606	71	14.08451	223.0531	3959.192
22	45.45455	69.11504	380.1327	72	13.88889	226.1947	4071.504
23	43.47826	72.25663	415.4756	73	13.69863	229.3363	4185.387
24	41.66667	75.39822	452.3893	74	13.51351	232.4779	4300.840
25	40.00000	78.53982	490.8739	75	13.33333	235.6194	4417.865
26	38.46154	81.68141	530.9292	76	13.15789	238.7610	4536.460
27	37.03704	84.82300	572.5553	77	12.98701	241.9026	4656.626
28	35.71429	87.96459	615.7522	78	12.82051	245.0442	4778.362
29	34.48276	91.10619	660.5199	79	12.65823	248.1858	4901.670
30	33.33333	94.24778	706.8583	80	12.50000	251.3274	5026.548
31	32.25806	97.38937	754.7676	81	12.34568	254.4690	5152.997
32	31.25000	100.5310	804.2477	82	12.19512	257.6106	5281.017
33	30.30303	103.6726	855.2986	83	12.04819	260.7522	5410.608
34	29.41176	106.8142	907.9203	84	11.90476	263.8938	5541.769
35	28.57143	109.9557	962.1128	85	11.76471	267.0354	5674.502
36	27.77778	113.0973	1017.876	86	11.62791	270.1770	5808.805
37	27.02703	116.2389	1075.210	87	11.49425	273.3186	5944.679
38	26.31579	119.3805	1134.115	88	11.36364	276.4602	6082.123
39	25.64103	122.5221	1194.591	89	11.23596	279.6017	6221.139
40	25.00000	125.6637	1256.637	90	11.11111	282.7433	6361.725
41	24.39024	128.8053	1320.254	91	10.98901	285.8849	6503.882
42	23.80952	131.9469	1385.442	92	10.86957	289.0265	6647.610
43	23.25581	135.0885	1452.201	93	10.75269	292.1681	6792.909
44	22.72727	138.2301	1520.531	94	10.63830	295.3097	6939.778
45	22.22222	141.3717	1590.431	95	10.52632	298.4513	7088.218
46	21.73913	144.5133	1661.903	96	10.41667	301.5929	7238.229
47	21.27660	147.6549	1734.945	97	10.30928	304.7345	7389.811
48	20.83333	150.7964	1809.557	98	10.20408	307.8761	7542.964
49	20.40816	153.9380	1885.741	99	10.10101	311.0177	7697.687
50	20.00000	157.0796	1963.495	100	10.00000	314.1593	7853.982

RECIPROCALS, CIRCUMFERENCE AND AREA OF CIRCLES (Continued)

$n = $ dia	$1000\dfrac{1}{n}$	Circum-ference πn	Area $\dfrac{\pi n^2}{4}$	$n = $ dia	$1000\dfrac{1}{n}$	Circum-ference πn	Area $\dfrac{\pi n^2}{4}$
100	10.00000	314.1593	7853.982	**150**	6.666 667	471.2389	17671.46
101	9.900 990	317.3009	8011.847	151	6.622 517	474.3805	17907.86
102	9.803 922	320.4425	8171.282	152	6.578 947	477.5221	18145.84
103	9.708 738	323.5840	8332.289	153	6.535 948	480.6637	18385.39
104	9.615 385	326.7256	8494.867	154	6.493 506	483.8053	18626.50
105	9.523 810	329.8672	8659.015	155	6.451 613	486.9469	18869.19
106	9.433 962	333.0088	8824.734	156	6.410 256	490.0885	19113.45
107	9.345 794	336.1504	8992.024	157	6.369 427	493.2300	19359.28
108	9.259 259	339.2920	9160.884	158	6.329 114	496.3716	19606.68
109	9.174 312	342.4336	9331.316	159	6.289 308	499.5132	19855.65
110	9.090 909	345.5752	9503.318	**160**	6.250 000	502.6548	20106.19
111	9.009 009	348.7168	9676.891	161	6.211 180	505.7964	20358.31
112	8.928 571	351.8584	9852.035	162	6.172 840	508.9380	20611.99
113	8.849 558	355.0000	10028.75	163	6.134 969	512.0796	20867.24
114	8.771 930	358.1416	10207.03	164	6.097 561	515.2212	21124.07
115	8.695 652	361.2832	10386.89	165	6.060 606	518.3628	21382.46
116	8.620 690	364.4247	10568.32	166	6.024 096	521.5044	21642.43
117	8.547 009	367.5663	10751.32	167	5.988 024	524.6460	21903.97
118	8.474 576	370.7079	10935.88	168	5.952 381	527.7876	22167.08
119	8.403 361	373.8495	11122.02	169	5.917 160	530.9292	22431.76
120	8.333 333	376.9911	11309.73	**170**	5.882 353	534.0708	22698.01
121	8.264 463	380.1327	11499.01	171	5.847 953	537.2123	22965.83
122	8.196 721	383.2743	11689.87	172	5.813 953	540.3539	23235.22
123	8.130 081	386.4159	11882.29	173	5.780 347	543.4955	23506.18
124	8.064 516	389.5575	12076.28	174	5.747 126	546.6371	23778.71
125	8.000 000	392.6991	12271.85	175	5.714 286	549.7787	24052.82
126	7.936 508	395.8407	12468.98	176	5.681 818	552.9203	24328.49
127	7.874 016	398.9823	12667.69	177	5.649 718	556.0619	24605.74
128	7.812 500	402.1239	12867.96	178	5.617 978	559.2035	24884.56
129	7.751 938	405.2655	13069.81	179	5.586 592	562.3451	25164.94
130	7.692 308	408.4070	13273.23	**180**	5.555 556	565.4867	25446.90
131	7.633 588	411.5486	13478.22	181	5.524 862	568.6283	25730.43
132	7.575 758	414.6902	13684.78	182	5.494 505	571.7699	26015.53
133	7.518 797	417.8318	13892.91	183	5.464 481	574.9115	26302.20
134	7.462 687	420.9734	14102.61	184	5.434 783	578.0530	26590.44
135	7.407 407	424.1150	14313.88	185	5.405 405	581.1946	26880.25
136	7.352 941	427.2566	14526.72	186	5.376 344	584.3362	27171.63
137	7.299 270	430.3982	14741.14	187	5.347 594	587.4778	27464.59
138	7.246 377	433.5398	14957.12	188	5.319 149	590.6194	27759.11
139	7.194 245	436.6814	15174.68	189	5.291 005	593.7610	28055.21
140	7.142 857	439.8230	15393.80	**190**	5.263 158	596.9026	28352.87
141	7.092 199	442.9646	15614.50	191	5.235 602	600.0442	28652.11
142	7.042 254	446.1062	15836.77	192	5.208 333	603.1858	28952.92
143	6.993 007	449.2477	16060.61	193	5.181 347	606.3274	29255.30
144	6.944 444	452.3893	16286.02	194	5.154 639	609.4690	29559.25
145	6.896 552	455.5309	16513.00	195	5.128 205	612.6106	29864.77
146	6.849 315	458.6725	16741.55	196	5.102 041	615.7522	30171.86
147	6.802 721	461.8141	16971.67	197	5.076 142	618.8938	30480.52
148	6.756 757	464.9557	17203.36	198	5.050 505	622.0353	30790.75
149	6.711 409	468.0973	17436.62	199	5.025 126	625.1769	31102.55
150	6.666 667	471.2389	17671.46	**200**	5.000 000	628.3185	31415.93

RECIPROCALS, CIRCUMFERENCE AND AREA OF CIRCLES (Continued)

$n = $ dia	$1000\dfrac{1}{n}$	Circumference πn	Area $\dfrac{\pi n^2}{4}$	$n = $ dia	$1000\dfrac{1}{n}$	Circumference πn	Area $\dfrac{\pi n^2}{4}$
200	5.000 000	628.3185	31415.93	**250**	4.000 000	785.3982	49087.39
201	4.975 124	631.4601	31730.87	251	3.984 066	788.5398	49480.87
202	4.950 495	634.6017	32047.39	252	3.968 254	791.6813	49875.92
203	4.926 108	637.7433	32365.47	253	3.952 569	794.8229	50272.55
204	4.901 961	640.8849	32685.13	254	3.937 008	797.9645	50670.75
205	4.878 049	644.0265	33006.36	255	3.921 569	801.1061	51070.52
206	4.854 369	647.1681	33329.16	256	3.906 250	804.2477	51471.85
207	4.830 918	650.3097	33653.53	257	3.891 051	807.3893	51874.76
208	4.807 692	653.4513	33979.47	258	3.875 969	810.5309	52279.24
209	4.784 689	656.5929	34306.98	259	3.861 004	813.6725	52685.29
210	4.761 905	659.7345	34636.06	**260**	3.846 154	816.8141	53092.92
211	4.739 336	662.8760	34966.71	261	3.831 418	819.9557	53502.11
212	4.716 981	666.0176	35298.94	262	3.816 794	823.0973	53912.87
213	4.694 836	669.1592	35632.73	263	3.802 281	826.2389	54325.21
214	4.672 897	672.3008	35968.09	264	3.787 879	829.3805	54739.11
215	4.651 163	675.4424	36305.03	265	3.773 585	832.5221	55154.59
216	4.629 630	678.5840	36643.54	266	3.759 398	835.6636	55571.63
217	4.608 295	681.7256	36983.61	267	3.745 318	838.8052	55990.25
218	4.587 156	684.8672	37325.26	268	3.731 343	841.9468	56410.44
219	4.566 210	688.0088	37668.48	269	3.717 472	845.0884	56832.20
220	4.545 455	691.1504	38013.27	**270**	3.703 704	848.2300	57255.53
221	4.524 887	694.2920	38359.63	271	3.690 037	851.3716	57680.43
222	4.504 505	697.4336	38707.56	272	3.676 471	854.5132	58106.90
223	4.484 305	700.5752	39057.07	273	3.663 004	857.6548	58534.94
224	4.464 286	703.7168	39408.14	274	3.649 635	860.7964	58964.55
225	4.444 444	706.8583	39760.78	275	3.636 364	863.9380	59395.74
226	4.424 779	709.9999	40115.00	276	3.623 188	867.0796	59828.49
227	4.405 286	713.1415	40470.78	277	3.610 108	870.2212	60262.82
228	4.385 965	716.2831	40828.14	278	3.597 122	873.3628	60698.71
229	4.366 812	719.4247	41187.07	279	3.584 229	876.5044	61136.18
230	4.347 826	722.5663	41547.56	**280**	3.571 429	879.6459	61575.22
231	4.329 004	725.7079	41909.63	281	3.558 719	882.7875	62015.82
232	4.310 345	728.8495	42273.27	282	3.546 099	885.9291	62458.00
233	4.291 845	731.9911	42638.48	283	3.533 569	889.0707	62901.75
234	4.273 504	735.1327	43005.26	284	3.521 127	892.2123	63347.07
235	4.255 319	738.2743	43373.61	285	3.508 772	895.3539	63793.97
236	4.237 288	741.4159	43743.54	286	3.496 503	898.4955	64242.43
237	4.219 409	744.5575	44115.03	287	3.484 321	901.6371	64692.46
238	4.201 681	747.6991	44488.09	288	3.472 222	904.7787	65144.07
239	4.184 100	750.8406	44862.73	289	3.460 208	907.9203	65597.24
240	4.166 667	753.9822	45238.93	**290**	3.448 276	911.0619	66051.99
241	4.149 378	757.1238	45616.71	291	3.436 426	914.2035	66508.30
242	4.132 231	760.2654	45996.06	292	3.424 658	917.3451	66966.19
243	4.115 226	763.4070	46376.98	293	3.412 969	920.4866	67425.65
244	4.098 361	766.5486	46759.47	294	3.401 361	923.6282	67886.68
245	4.081 633	769.6902	47143.52	295	3.389 831	926.7698	68349.28
246	4.065 041	772.8318	47529.16	296	3.378 378	929.9114	68813.45
247	4.048 583	775.9734	47916.36	297	3.367 003	933.0530	69279.19
248	4.032 258	779.1150	48305.13	298	3.355 705	936.1946	69746.50
249	4.016 064	782.2566	48695.47	299	3.344 482	939.3362	70215.38
250	4.000 000	785.3982	49087.39	**300**	3.333 333	942.4778	70685.83

RECIPROCALS, CIRCUMFERENCE AND AREA OF CIRCLES (Continued)

$n = $ dia	$1000\frac{1}{n}$	Circum-ference πn	Area $\frac{\pi n^2}{4}$	$n = $ dia	$1000\frac{1}{n}$	Circum-ference πn	Area $\frac{\pi n^2}{4}$
300	3.333 333	942.4778	70685.83	**350**	2.857 143	1099.557	96211.28
301	3.322 259	945.6194	71157.86	351	2.849 003	1102.699	96761.84
302	3.311 258	948.7610	71631.45	352	2.840 909	1105.841	97313.97
303	3.300 330	951.9026	72106.62	353	2.832 861	1108.982	97867.68
304	3.289 474	955.0442	72583.36	354	2.824 859	1112.124	98422.96
305	3.278 689	958.1858	73061.66	355	2.816 901	1115.265	98979.80
306	3.267 974	961.3274	73541.54	356	2.808 989	1118.407	99538.22
307	3.257 329	964.4689	74022.99	357	2.801 120	1121.549	100 098.2
308	3.246 753	967.6105	74506.01	358	2.793 296	1124.690	100 659.8
309	3.236 246	970.7521	74990.60	359	2.785 515	1127.832	101 222.9
310	3.225 806	973.8937	75476.76	**360**	2.777 778	1130.973	101 787.6
311	3.215 434	977.0353	75964.50	361	2.770 083	1134.115	102 353.9
312	3.205 128	980.1769	76453.80	362	2.762 431	1137.257	102 921.7
313	3.194 888	983.3185	76944.67	363	2.754 821	1140.398	103 491.1
314	3.184 713	986.4601	77437.12	364	2.747 253	1143.540	104 062.1
315	3.174 603	989.6017	77931.13	365	2.739 726	1146.681	104 634.7
316	3.164 557	992.7433	78426.72	366	2.732 240	1149.823	105 208.8
317	3.154 574	995.8849	78923.88	367	2.724 796	1152.965	105 784.5
318	3.144 654	999.0265	79422.60	368	2.717 391	1156.106	106 361.8
319	3.134 796	1002.168	79922.90	369	2.710 027	1159.248	106 940.6
320	3.125 000	1005.310	80424.77	**370**	2.702 703	1162.389	107 521.0
321	3.115 265	1008.451	80928.21	371	2.695 418	1165.531	108 103.0
322	3.105 590	1011.593	81433.22	372	2.688 172	1168.672	108 686.5
323	3.095 975	1014.734	81939.80	373	2.680 965	1171.814	109 271.7
324	3.086 420	1017.876	82447.96	374·	2.673 797	1174.956	109 858.4
325	3.076 923	1021.018	82957.68	375	2.666 667	1178.097	110 446.6
326	3.067 485	1024.159	83468.98	376	2.659 574	1181.239	111 036.5
327	3.058 104	1027.301	83981.84	377	2.652 520	1184.380	111 627.9
328	3.048 780	1030.442	84496.28	378	2.645 503	1187.522	112 220.8
329	3.039 514	1033.584	85012.28	379	2.638 522	1190.664	112 815.4
330	3.030 303	1036.726	85529.86	**380**	2.631 579	1193.805	113 411.5
331	3.021 148	1039.867	86049.01	381	2.624 672	1196.947	114 009.2
332	3.012 048	1043.009	86569.73	382	2.617 801	1200.088	114 608.4
333	3.003 003	1046.150	87092.02	383	2.610 966	1203.230	115 209.3
334	2.994 012	1049.292	87615.88	384	2.604 167	1206.372	115 811.7
335	2.985 075	1052.434	88141.31	385	2.597 403	1209.513	116 415.6
336	2.976 190	1055.575	88668.31	386	2.590 674	1212.655	117 021.2
337	2.967 359	1058.717	89196.88	387	2.583 979	1215.796	117 628.3
338	2.958 580	1061.858	89727.03	388	2.577 320	1218.938	118 237.0
339	2.949 853	1065.000	90258.74	389	2.570 694	1222.080	118 847.2
340	2.941 176	1068.142	90792.03	**390**	2.564 103	1225.221	119 459.1
341	2.932 551	1071.283	91326.88	391	2.557 545	1228.363	120 072.5
342	2.923 977	1074.425	91863.31	392	2.551 020	1231.504	120 687.4
343	2.915 452	1077.566	92401.31	393	2.544 529	1234.646	121 304.0
344	2.906 977	1080.708	92940.88	394	2.538 071	1237.788	121 922.1
345	2.898 551	1083.849	93482.02	395	2.531 646	1240.929	122 541.7
346	2.890 173	1086.991	94024.73	396	2.525 253	1244.071	123 163.0
347	2.881 844	1090.133	94569.01	397	2.518 892	1247.212	123 785.8
348	2.873 563	1093.274	95114.86	398	2.512 563	1250.354	124 410.2
349	2.865 330	1096.416	95662.28	399	2.506 266	1253.495	125 036.2
350	2.857 143	1099.557	96211.28	**400**	2.500 000	1256.637	125 663.7

RECIPROCALS, CIRCUMFERENCE AND AREA OF CIRCLES (Continued)

$n = \text{dia}$	$1000\dfrac{1}{n}$	Circumference πn	Area $\dfrac{\pi n^2}{4}$	$n = \text{dia}$	$1000\dfrac{1}{n}$	Circumference πn	Area $\dfrac{\pi n^2}{4}$
400	2.500 000	1256.637	125 663.7	**450**	2.222 222	1413.717	159 043.1
401	2.493 766	1259.779	126 292.8	451	2.217 295	1416.858	159 750.8
402	2.487 562	1262.920	126 923.5	452	2.212 389	1420.000	160 460.0
403	2.481 390	1266.062	127 555.7	453	2.207 506	1423.141	161 170.8
404	2.475 248	1269.203	128 189.5	454	2.202 643	1426.283	161 883.1
405	2.469 136	1272.345	128 824.9	455	2.197 802	1429.425	162 597.1
406	2.463 054	1275.487	129 461.9	456	2.192 982	1432.566	163 312.6
407	2.457 002	1278.628	130 100.4	457	2.188 184	1435.708	164 029.6
408	2.450 980	1281.770	130 740.5	458	2.183 406	1438.849	164 748.3
409	2.444 988	1284.911	131 382.2	459	2.178 649	1441.991	165 468.5
410	2.439 024	1288.053	132 025.4	**460**	2.173 913	1445.133	166 190.3
411	2.433 090	1291.195	132 670.2	461	2.169 197	1448.274	166 913.6
412	2.427 184	1294.336	133 316.6	462	2.164 502	1451.416	167 638.5
413	2.421 308	1297.478	133 964.6	463	2.159 827	1454.557	168 365.0
414	2.415 459	1300.619	134 614.1	464	2.155 172	1457.699	169 093.1
415	2.409 639	1303.761	135 265.2	465	2.150 538	1460.841	169 822.7
416	2.403 846	1306.903	135 917.9	466	2.145 923	1463.982	170 553.9
417	2.398 082	1310.044	136 572.1	467	2.141 328	1467.124	171 286.7
418	2.392 344	1313.186	137 227.9	468	2.136 752	1470.265	172 021.0
419	2.386 635	1316.327	137 885.3	469	2.132 196	1473.407	172 757.0
420	2.380 952	1319.469	138 544.2	**470**	2.127 660	1476.549	173 494.5
421	2.375 297	1322.611	139 204.8	471	2.123 142	1479.690	174 233.5
422	2.369 668	1325.752	139 866.8	472	2.118 644	1482.832	174 974.1
423	2.364 066	1328.894	140 530.5	473	2.114 165	1485.973	175 716.3
424	2.358 491	1332.035	141 195.7	474	2.109 705	1489.115	176 460.1
425	2.352 941	1335.177	141 862.5	475	2.105 263	1492.257	177 205.5
426	2.347 418	1338.318	142 530.9	476	2.100 840	1495.398	177 952.4
427	2.341 920	1341.460	143 200.9	477	2.096 436	1498.540	178 700.9
428	2.336 449	1344.602	143 872.4	478	2.092 050	1501.681	179 450.9
429	2.331 002	1347.743	144 545.5	479	2.087 683	1504.823	180 202.5
430	2.325 581	1350.885	145 220.1	**480**	2.083 333	1507.964	180 955.7
431	2.320 186	1354.026	145 896.3	481	2.079 002	1511.106	181 710.5
432	2.314 815	1357.168	146 574.1	482	2.074 689	1514.248	182 466.8
433	2.309 469	1360.310	147 253.5	483	2.070 393	1517.389	183 224.8
434	2.304 147	1363.451	147 934.5	484	2.066 116	1520.531	183 984.2
435	2.298 851	1366.593	148 617.0	485	2.061 856	1523.672	184 745.3
436	2.293 578	1369.734	149 301.0	486	2.057 613	1526.814	185 507.9
437	2.288 330	1372.876	149 986.7	487	2.053 388	1529.956	186 272.1
438	2.283 105	1376.018	150 673.9	488	2.049 180	1533.097	187 037.9
439	2.277 904	1379.159	151 362.7	489	2.044 990	1536.239	187 805.2
440	2.272 727	1382.301	152 053.1	**490**	2.040 816	1539.380	188 574.1
441	2.267 574	1385.442	152 745.0	491	2.036 660	1542.522	189 344.6
442	2.262 443	1388.584	153 438.5	492	2.032 520	1545.664	190 116.6
443	2.257 336	1391.726	154 133.6	493	2.028 398	1548.805	190 890.2
444	2.252 252	1394.867	154 830.3	494	2.024 291	1551.947	191 665.4
445	2.247 191	1398.009	155 528.5	495	2.020 202	1555.088	192 442.2
446	2.242 152	1401.150	156 228.3	496	2.016 129	1558.230	193 220.5
447	2.237 136	1404.292	156 929.6	497	2.012 072	1561.372	194 000.4
448	2.232 143	1407.434	157 632.6	498	2.008 032	1564.513	194 781.9
449	2.227 171	1410.575	158 337.1	499	2.004 008	1567.655	195 564.9
450	2.222 222	1413.717	159 043.1	**500**	2.000 000	1570.796	196 349.5

RECIPROCALS, CIRCUMFERENCE AND AREA OF CIRCLES (Continued)

$n = $ dia	$1000\dfrac{1}{n}$	Circumference πn	Area $\dfrac{\pi n^2}{4}$	$n = $ dia	$1000\dfrac{1}{n}$	Circumference πn	Area $\dfrac{\pi n^2}{4}$
500	2.000 000	1570.796	196 349.5	**550**	1.818 182	1727.876	237 582.9
501	1.996 008	1573.938	197 135.7	551	1.814 882	1731.018	238 447.7
502	1.992 032	1577.080	197 923.5	552	1.811 594	1734.159	239 314.0
503	1.988 072	1580.221	198 712.8	553	1.808 318	1737.301	240 181.8
504	1.984 127	1583.363	199 503.7	554	1.805 054	1740.442	241 051.3
505	1.980 198	1586.504	200 296.2	555	1.801 802	1743.584	241 922.3
506	1.976 285	1589.646	201 090.2	556	1.798 561	1746.726	242 794.8
507	1.972 387	1592.787	201 885.8	557	1.795 332	1749.867	243 669.0
508	1.968 504	1595.929	202 683.0	558	1.792 115	1753.009	244 544.7
509	1.964 637	1599.071	203 481.7	559	1.788 909	1756.150	245 422.0
510	1.960 784	1602.212	204 282.1	**560**	1.785 714	1759.292	246 300.9
511	1.956 947	1605.354	205 084.0	561	1.782 531	1762.433	247 181.3
512	1.953 125	1608.495	205 887.4	562	1.779 359	1765.575	248 063.3
513	1.949 318	1611.637	206 692.4	563	1.776 199	1768.717	248 946.9
514	1.945 525	1614.779	207 499.1	564	1.773 050	1771.858	249 832.0
515	1.941 748	1617.920	208 307.2	565	1.769 912	1775.000	250 718.7
516	1.937 984	1621.062	209 117.0	566	1.766 784	1778.141	251 607.0
517	1.934 236	1624.203	209 928.3	567	1.763 668	1781.283	252 496.9
518	1.930 502	1627.345	210 741.2	568	1.760 563	1784.425	253 388.3
519	1.926 782	1630.487	211 555.6	569	1.757 469	1787.566	254 281.3
520	1.923 077	1633.628	212 371.7	**570**	1.754 386	1790.708	255 175.9
521	1.919 386	1636.770	213 189.3	571	1.751 313	1793.849	256 072.0
522	1.915 709	1639.911	214 008.4	572	1.748 252	1796.991	256 969.7
523	1.912 046	1643.053	214 829.2	573	1.745 201	1800.133	257 869.0
524	1.908 397	1646.195	215 651.5	574	1.742 160	1803.274	258 769.8
525	1.904 762	1649.336	216 475.4	575	1.739 130	1806.416	259 672.3
526	1.901 141	1652.478	217 300.8	576	1.736 111	1809.557	260 576.3
527	1.897 533	1655.619	218 127.8	577	1.733 102	1812.699	261 481.8
528	1.893 939	1658.761	218 956.4	578	1.730 104	1815.841	262 389.0
529	1.890 359	1661.903	219 786.6	579	1.727 116	1818.982	263 297.7
530	1.886 792	1665.044	220 618.3	**580**	1.724 138	1822.124	264 207.9
531	1.883 239	1668.186	221 451.7	581	1.721 170	1825.265	265 119.8
532	1.879 699	1671.327	222 286.5	582	1.718 213	1828.407	266 033.2
533	1.876 173	1674.469	223 123.0	583	1.715 266	1831.549	266 948.2
534	1.872 659	1677.610	223 961.0	584	1.712 329	1834.690	267 864.8
535	1.869 159	1680.752	224 800.6	585	1.709 402	1837.832	268 782.9
536	1.865 672	1683.894	225 641.8	586	1.706 485	1840.973	269 702.6
537	1.862 197	1687.035	226 484.5	587	1.703 578	1844.115	270 623.9
538	1.858 736	1690.177	227 328.8	588	1.700 680	1847.256	271 546.7
539	1.855 288	1693.318	228 174.7	589	1.697 793	1850.398	272 471.1
540	1.851 852	1696.460	229 022.1	**590**	1.694 915	1853.540	273 397.1
541	1.848 429	1699.602	229 871.1	591	1.692 047	1856.681	274 324.7
542	1.845 018	1702.743	230 721.7	592	1.689 189	1859.823	275 253.8
543	1.841 621	1705.885	231 573.9	593	1.686 341	1862.964	276 184.5
544	1.838 235	1709.026	232 427.6	594	1.683 502	1866.106	277 116.7
545	1.834 862	1712.168	233 282.9	595	1.680 672	1869.248	278 050.6
546	1.831 502	1715.310	234 139.8	596	1.677 852	1872.389	278 986.0
547	1.828 154	1718.451	234 998.2	597	1.675 042	1875.531	279 923.0
548	1.824 818	1721.593	235 858.2	598	1.672 241	1878.672	280 861.5
549	1.821 494	1724.734	236 719.8	599	1.669 449	1881.814	281 801.6
550	1.818 182	1727.876	237 582.9	**600**	1.666 667	1884.956	282 743.3

RECIPROCALS, CIRCUMFERENCE AND AREA OF CIRCLES (Continued)

$n = $ dia	$1000\dfrac{1}{n}$	Circum-ference πn	Area $\dfrac{\pi n^2}{4}$	$n = $ dia	$1000\dfrac{1}{n}$	Circum-ference πn	Area $\dfrac{\pi n^2}{4}$
600	1.666 667	1884.956	282 743.3	**650**	1.538 462	2042.035	331 830.7
601	1.663 894	1888.097	283 686.6	651	1.536 098	2045.177	332 852.5
602	1.661 130	1891.239	284 631.4	652	1.533 742	2048.318	333 875.9
603	1.658 375	1894.380	285 577.8	653	1.531 394	2051.460	334 900.8
604	1.655 629	1897.522	286 525.8	654	1.529 052	2054.602	335 927.4
605	1.652 893	1900.664	287 475.4	655	1.526 718	2057.743	336 955.4
606	1.650 165	1903.805	288 426.5	656	1.524 390	2060.885	337 985.1
607	1.647 446	1906.947	289 379.2	657	1.522 070	2064.026	339 016.3
608	1.644 737	1910.088	290 333.4	658	1.519 757	2067.168	340 049.1
609	1.642 036	1913.230	291 289.3	659	1.517 451	2070.310	341 083.5
610	1.639 344	1916.372	292 246.7	**660**	1.515 152	2073.451	342 119.4
611	1.636 661	1919.513	293 205.6	661	1.512 859	2076.593	343 157.0
612	1.633 987	1922.655	294 166.2	662	1.510 574	2079.734	344 196.0
613	1.631 321	1925.796	295 128.3	663	1.508 296	2082.876	345 236.7
614	1.628 664	1928.938	296 092.0	664	1.506 024	2086.018	346 278.9
615	1.626 016	1932.079	297 057.2	665	1.503 759	2089.159	347 322.7
616	1.623 377	1935.221	298 024.0	666	1.501 502	2092.301	348 368.1
617	1.620 746	1938.363	298 992.4	667	1.499 250	2095.442	349 415.0
618	1.618 123	1941.504	299 962.4	668	1.497 006	2098.584	350 463.5
619	1.615 509	1944.646	300 933.9	669	1.494 768	2101.725	351 513.6
620	1.612 903	1947.787	301 907.1	**670**	1.492 537	2104.867	352 565.2
621	1.610 306	1950.929	302 881.7	671	1.490 313	2108.009	353 618.5
622	1.607 717	1954.071	303 858.0	672	1.488 095	2111.150	354 673.2
623	1.605 136	1957.212	304 835.8	673	1.485 884	2114.292	355 729.6
624	1.602 564	1960.354	305 815.2	674	1.483 680	2117.433	356 787.5
625	1.600 000	1963.495	306 796.2	675	1.481 481	2120.575	357 847.0
626	1.597 444	1966.637	307 778.7	676	1.479 290	2123.717	358 908.1
627	1.594 896	1969.779	308 762.8	677	1.477 105	2126.858	359 970.8
628	1.592 357	1972.920	309 748.5	678	1.474 926	2130.000	361 035.0
629	1.589 825	1976.062	310 735.7	679	1.472 754	2133.141	362 100.8
630	1.587 302	1979.203	311 724.5	**680**	1.470 588	2136.283	363 168.1
631	1.584 786	1982.345	312 714.9	681	1.468 429	2139.425	364 237.0
632	1.582 278	1985.487	313 706.9	682	1.466 276	2142.566	365 307.5
633	1.579 779	1988.628	314 700.4	683	1.464 129	2145.708	366 379.6
634	1.577 287	1991.770	315 695.5	684	1.461 988	2148.849	367 453.2
635	1.574 803	1994.911	316 692.2	685	1.459 854	2151.991	368 528.5
636	1.572 327	1998.053	317 690.4	686	1.457 726	2155.133	369 605.2
637	1.569 859	2001.195	318 690.2	687	1.455 604	2158.274	370 683.6
638	1.567 398	2004.336	319 691.6	688	1.453 488	2161.416	371 763.5
639	1.564 945	2007.478	320 694.6	689	1.451 379	2164.557	372 845.0
640	1.562 500	2010.619	321 699.1	**690**	1.449 275	2167.699	373 928.1
641	1.560 062	2013.761	322 705.2	691	1.447 178	2170.841	375 012.7
642	1.557 632	2016.902	323 712.8	692	1.445 087	2173.982	376 098.9
643	1.555 210	2020.044	324 722.1	693	1.443 001	2177.124	377 186.7
644	1.552 795	2023.186	325 732.9	694	1.440 922	2180.265	378 276.0
645	1.550 388	2026.327	326 745.3	695	1.438 849	2183.407	379 366.9
646	1.547 988	2029.469	327 759.2	696	1.436 782	2186.548	380 459.4
647	1.545 595	2032.610	328 774.7	697	1.434 720	2189.690	381 553.5
648	1.543 210	2035.752	329 791.8	698	1.432 665	2192.832	382 649.1
649	1.540 832	2038.894	330 810.5	699	1.430 615	2195.973	383 746.3
650	1.538 462	2042.035	331 830.7	**700**	1.428 571	2199.115	384 845.1

RECIPROCALS, CIRCUMFERENCE AND AREA OF CIRCLES (Continued)

n = dia	$1000\dfrac{1}{n}$	Circumference πn	Area $\dfrac{\pi n^2}{4}$	n = dia	$1000\dfrac{1}{n}$	Circumference πn	Area $\dfrac{\pi n^2}{4}$
700	1.428 571	2199.115	384 845.1	**750**	1.333 333	2356.194	441 786.5
701	1.426 534	2202.256	385 945.4	751	1.331 558	2359.336	442 965.3
702	1.424 501	2205.398	387 047.4	752	1.329 787	2362.478	444 145.8
703	1.422 475	2208 540	388 150.8	753	1.328 021	2365.619	445 327.8
704	1.420 455	2211.681	389 255.9	754	1.326 260	2368.761	446 511.4
705	1.418 440	2214.823	390 362.5	755	1.324 503	2371.902	447 696.6
706	1.416 431	2217.964	391 470.7	756	1.322 751	2375.044	448 883.3
707	1.414 427	2221.106	392 580.5	757	1.321 004	2378.186	450 071.6
708	1.412 429	2224.248	393 691.8	758	1.319 261	2381.327	451 261.5
709	1.410 437	2227.389	394 804.7	759	1.317 523	2384.469	452 453.0
710	1.408 451	2230.531	395 919.2	**760**	1.315 789	2387.610	453 646.0
711	1.406 470	2233.672	397 035.3	761	1.314 060	2390.752	454 840.6
712	1.404 494	2236.814	398 152.9	762	1.312 336	2393.894	456 036.7
713	1.402 525	2239.956	399 272.1	763	1.310 616	2397.035	457 234.5
714	1.400 560	2243.097	400 392.8	764	1.308 901	2400.177	458 433.8
715	1.398 601	2246.239	401 515.2	765	1.307 190	2403.318	459 634.6
716	1.396 648	2249.380	402 639.1	766	1.305 483	2406.460	460 837.1
717	1.394 700	2252.522	403 764.6	767	1.303 781	2409.602	462 041.1
718	1.392 758	2255.664	404 891.6	768	1.302 083	2412.743	463 246.7
719	1.390 821	2258.805	406 020.2	769	1.300 390	2415.885	464 453.8
720	1.388 889	2261.947	407 150.4	**770**	1.298 701	2419.026	465 662.6
721	1.386 963	2265.088	408 282.2	771	1.297 017	2422.168	466 872.9
722	1.385 042	2268.230	409 415.5	772	1.295 337	2425.310	468 084.7
723	1.383 126	2271.371	410 550.4	773	1.293 661	2428.451	469 298.2
724	1.381 215	2274.513	411 686.9	774	1.291 990	2431.593	470 513.2
725	1.379 310	2277.655	412 824.9	775	1.290 323	2434.734	471 729.8
726	1.377 410	2280.796	413 964.5	776	1.288 660	2437.876	472 947.9
727	1.375 516	2283.938	415 105.7	777	1.287 001	2441.017	474 167.6
728	1.373 626	2287.079	416 248.5	778	1.285 347	2444.159	475 388.9
729	1.371 742	2290.221	417 392.8	779	1.283 697	2447.301	476 611.8
730	1.369 863	2293.363	418 538.7	**780**	1.282 051	2450.442	477 836.2
731	1.367 989	2296.504	419 686.1	781	1.280 410	2453.584	479 062.2
732	1.366 120	2299.646	420 835.2	782	1.278 772	2456.725	480 289.8
733	1.364 256	2302.787	421 985.8	783	1.277 139	2459.867	481 519.0
734	1.362 398	2305.929	423 138.0	784	1.275 510	2463.009	482 749.7
735	1.360 544	2309.071	424 291.7	785	1.273 885	2466.150	483 982.0
736	1.358 696	2312.212	425 447.0	786	1.272 265	2469.292	485 215.8
737	1.356 852	2315.354	426 603.9	787	1.270 648	2472.433	486 451.3
738	1.355 014	2318.495	427 762.4	788	1.269 036	2475.575	487 688.3
739	1.353 180	2321.637	428 922.4	789	1.267 427	2478.717	488 926.9
740	1.351 351	2324.779	430 084.0	**790**	1.265 823	2481.858	490 167.0
741	1.349 528	2327.920	431 247.2	791	1.264 223	2485.000	491 408.7
742	1.347 709	2331.062	432 412.0	792	1.262 626	2488.141	492 652.0
743	1.345 895	2334.203	433 578.3	793	1.261 034	2491.283	493 896.8
744	1.344 086	2337.345	434 746.2	794	1.259 446	2494.425	495 143.3
745	1.342 282	2340.487	435 915.6	795	1.257 862	2497.566	496 391.3
746	1.340 483	2343.628	437 086.6	796	1.256 281	2500.708	497 640.8
747	1.338 688	2346.770	438 259.2	797	1.254 705	2503.849	498 892.0
748	1.336 898	2349.911	439 433.4	798	1.253 133	2506.991	500 144.7
749	1.335 113	2353.053	440 609.2	799	1.251 564	2510.133	501 399.0
750	1.333 333	2356.194	441 786.5	**800**	1.250 000	2513.274	502 654.8

RECIPROCALS, CIRCUMFERENCE AND AREA OF CIRCLES (Continued)

n = dia	$1000\dfrac{1}{n}$	Circumference πn	Area $\dfrac{\pi n^2}{4}$	n = dia	$1000\dfrac{1}{n}$	Circumference πn	Area $\dfrac{\pi n^2}{4}$
800	1.250 000	2513.274	502 654.8	**850**	1.176 471	2670.354	567 450.2
801	1.248 439	2516.416	503 912.2	851	1.175 088	2673.495	568 786.1
802	1.246 883	2519.557	505 171.2	852	1.173 709	2676.637	570 123.7
803	1.245 330	2522.699	506 431.8	853	1.172 333	2679.779	571 462.8
804	1.243 781	2525.840	507 693.9	854	1.170 960	2682.920	572 803.4
805	1.242 236	2528.982	508 957.6	855	1.169 591	2686.062	574 145.7
806	1.240 695	2532.124	510 222.9	856	1.168 224	2689.203	575 489.5
807	1.239 157	2535.265	511 489.8	857	1.166 861	2692.345	576 834.9
808	1.237 624	2538.407	512 758.2	858	1.165 501	2695.486	578 181.9
809	1.236 094	2541.548	514 028.2	859	1.164 144	2698.628	579 530.4
810	1.234 568	2544.690	515 299.7	**860**	1.162 791	2701.770	580 880.5
811	1.233 046	2547.832	516 572.9	861	1.161 440	2704.911	582 232.2
812	1.231 527	2550.973	517 847.6	862	1.160 093	2708.053	583 585.4
813	1.230 012	2554.115	519 123.8	863	1.158 749	2711.194	584 940.2
814	1.228 501	2557.256	520 401.7	864	1.157 407	2714.336	586 296.6
815	1.226 994	2560.398	521 681.1	865	1.156 069	2717.478	587 654.5
816	1.225 490	2563.540	522 962.1	866	1.154 734	2720.619	589 014.1
817	1.223 990	2566.681	524 244.6	867	1.153 403	2723.761	590 375.2
818	1.222 494	2569.823	525 528.8	868	1.152 074	2726.902	591 737.8
819	1.221 001	2572.964	526 814.5	869	1.150 748	2730.044	593 102.1
820	1.219 512	2576.106	528 101.7	**870**	1.149 425	2733.186	594 467.9
821	1.218 027	2579.248	529 390.6	871	1.148 106	2736.327	595 835.2
822	1.216 545	2582.389	530 681.0	872	1.146 789	2739.469	597 204.2
823	1.215 067	2585.531	531 973.0	873	1.145 475	2742.610	598 574.7
824	1.213 592	2588.672	533 266.5	874	1.144 165	2745.752	599 946.8
825	1.212 121	2591.814	534 561.6	875	1.142 857	2748.894	601 320.5
826	1.210 654	2594.956	535 858.3	876	1.141 553	2752.035	602 695.7
827	1.209 190	2598.097	537 156.6	877	1.140 251	2755.177	604 072.5
828	1.207 729	2601.239	538 456.4	878	1.138 952	2758.318	605 450.9
829	1.206 273	2604.380	539 757.8	879	1.137 656	2761.460	606 830.8
830	1.204 819	2607.522	541 060.8	**880**	1.136 364	2764.602	608 212.3
831	1.203 369	2610.663	542 365.3	881	1.135 074	2767.743	609 595.4
832	1.201 923	2613.805	543 671.5	882	1.133 787	2770.885	610 980.1
833	1.200 480	2616.947	544 979.1	883	1.132 503	2774.026	612 366.3
834	1.199 041	2620.088	546 288.4	884	1.131 222	2777.168	613 754.1
835	1.197 605	2623.230	547 599.2	885	1.129 944	2780.309	615 143.5
836	1.196 172	2626.371	548 911.6	886	1.128 668	2783.451	616 534.4
837	1.194 743	2629.513	550 225.6	887	1.127 396	2786.593	617 926.9
838	1.193 317	2632.655	551 541.1	888	1.126 126	2789.734	619 321.0
839	1.191 895	2635.796	552 858.3	889	1.124 859	2792.876	620 716.7
840	1.190 476	2638.938	554 176.9	**890**	1.123 596	2796.017	622 113.9
841	1.189 061	2642.079	555 497.2	891	1.122 334	2799.159	623 512.7
842	1.187 648	2645.221	556 819.0	892	1.121 076	2802.301	624 913.0
843	1.186 240	2648.363	558 142.4	893	1.119 821	2805.442	626 315.0
844	1.184 834	2651.504	559 467.4	894	1.118 568	2808.584	627 718.5
845	1.183 432	2654.646	560 793.9	895	1.117 318	2811.725	629 123.6
846	1.182 033	2657.787	562 122.0	896	1.116 071	2814.867	630 530.2
847	1.180 638	2660.929	563 451.7	897	1.114 827	2818.009	631 938.4
848	1.179 245	2664.071	564 783.0	898	1.113 586	2821.150	633 348.2
849	1.177 856	2667.212	566 115.8	899	1.112 347	2824.292	634 759.6
850	1.176 471	2670.354	567 450.2	**900**	1.111 111	2827.433	636 172.5

RECIPROCALS, CIRCUMFERENCE AND AREA OF CIRCLES (Continued)

$n =$ dia	$1000\dfrac{1}{n}$	Circumference πn	Area $\dfrac{\pi n^2}{4}$	$n =$ dia	$1000\dfrac{1}{n}$	Circumference πn	Area $\dfrac{\pi n^2}{4}$
900	1.111 111	2827.433	636 172.5	**950**	1.052 632	2984.513	708 821.8
901	1.109 878	2830.575	637 587.0	951	1.051 525	2987.655	710 314.9
902	1.108 647	2833.717	639 003.1	952	1.050 420	2990.796	711 809.5
903	1.107 420	2836.858	640 420.7	953	1.049 318	2993.938	713 305.7
904	1.106 195	2840.000	641 839.9	954	1.048 218	2997.079	714 803.4
905	1.104 972	2843.141	643 260.7	955	1.047 120	3000.221	716 302.8
906	1.103 753	2846.283	644 683.1	956	1.046 025	3003.363	717 803.7
907	1.102 536	2849.425	646 107.0	957	1.044 932	3006.504	719 306.1
908	1.101 322	2852.566	647 532.5	958	1.043 841	3009.646	720 810.2
909	1.100 110	2855.708	648 959.6	959	1.042 753	3012.787	722 315.8
910	1.098 901	2858.849	650 388.2	**960**	1.041 667	3015.929	723 822.9
911	1.097 695	2861.991	651 818.4	961	1.040 583	3019.071	725 331.7
912	1.096 491	2865.133	653 250.2	962	1.039 501	3022.212	726 842.0
913	1.095 290	2868.274	654 683.6	963	1.038 422	3025.354	728 353.9
914	1.094 092	2871.416	656 118.5	964	1.037 344	3028.495	729 867.4
915	1.092 896	2874.557	657 555.0	965	1.036 269	3031.637	731 382.4
916	1.091 703	2877.699	658 993.0	966	1.035 197	3034.779	732 899.0
917	1.090 513	2880.840	660 432.7	967	1.034 126	3037.920	734 417.2
918	1.089 325	2883.982	661 873.9	968	1.033 058	3041.062	735 936.9
919	1.088 139	2887.124	663 316.7	969	1.031 992	3044.203	737 458.2
920	1.086 957	2890.265	664 761.0	**970**	1.030 928	3047.345	738 981.1
921	1.085 776	2893.407	666 206.9	971	1.029 866	3050.486	740 505.6
922	1.084 599	2896.548	667 654.4	972	1.028 807	3053.628	742 031.6
923	1.083 424	2899.690	669 103.5	973	1.027 749	3056.770	743 559.2
924	1.082 251	2902.832	670 554.1	974	1.026 694	3059.911	745 088.4
925	1.081 081	2905.973	672 006.3	975	1.025 641	3063.053	746 619.1
926	1.079 914	2909.115	673 460.1	976	1.024 590	3066.194	748 151.4
927	1.078 749	2912.256	674 915.4	977	1.023 541	3069.336	749 685.3
928	1.077 586	2915.398	676 372.3	978	1.022 495	3072.478	751 220.8
929	1.076 426	2918.540	677 830.8	979	1.021 450	3075.619	752 757.8
930	1.075 269	2921.681	679 290.9	**980**	1.020 408	3078.761	754 296.4
931	1.074 114	2924.823	680 752.5	981	1.019 368	3081.902	755 836.6
932	1.072 961	2927.964	682 215.7	982	1.018 330	3085.044	757 378.3
933	1.071 811	2931.106	683 680.5	983	1.017 294	3088.186	758 921.6
934	1.070 664	2934.248	685 146.8	984	1.016 260	3091.327	760 466.5
935	1.069 519	2937.389	686 614.7	985	1.015 228	3094.469	762 012.9
936	1.068 376	2940.531	688 084.2	986	1.014 199	3097.610	763 561.0
937	1.067 236	2943.672	689 555.2	987	1.013 171	3100.752	765 110.5
938	1.066 098	2946.814	691 027.9	988	1.012 146	3103.894	766 661.7
939	1.064 963	2949.956	692 502.1	989	1.011 122	3107.035	768 214.4
940	1.063 830	2953.097	693 977.8	**990**	1.010 101	3110.177	769 768.7
941	1.062 699	2956.239	695 455.2	991	1.009 082	3113.318	771 324.6
942	1.061 571	2959.380	696 934.1	992	1.008 065	3116.460	772 882.1
943	1.060 445	2962.522	698 414.5	993	1.007 049	3119.602	774 441.1
944	1.059 322	2965.663	699 896.6	994	1.006 036	3122.743	776 001.7
945	1.058 201	2968.805	701 380.2	995	1.005 025	3125.885	777 563.8
946	1.057 082	2971.947	702 865.4	996	1.004 016	3129.026	779 127.5
947	1.055 966	2975.088	704 352.1	997	1.003 009	3132.168	780 692.8
948	1.054 852	2978.230	705 840.5	998	1.002 004	3135.309	782 259.7
949	1.053 741	2981.371	707 330.4	999	1.001 001	3138.451	783 828.2
950	1.052 632	2984.513	708 821.8	**1000**	1.000 000	3141.593	785 398.2

TRIGONOMETRY
DR. HOWARD EVES

PLANE TRIGONOMETRY

Angle

That part of a straight line lying entirely to one side of a point O on the line is called a *ray* (or a *half-line*); the point O is called the *origin* of the ray. A ray of origin O is identified by the notation OA, where A is any point of the ray.

If a ray OA is rotated, in a plane, about its origin O onto ray OB, an *angle AOB* is said to be generated. Ray OA is called the *initial side*, ray OB the *terminal side*, and point O the *vertex* of the angle. The angle is said to be *positive* or *negative* according as the generating rotation is counterclockwise or clockwise.

An angle is said to be in *standard position* if its vertex is at the origin O and its initial side is on the positive x-axis of a rectangular Cartesian coordinate system (see p.344). If the terminal side of the angle falls on a coordinate axis, the angle is called a *quadrantal angle*; otherwise the angle is called a *first, second, third,* or *fourth quadrant angle* according as the terminal side falls in the first, second, third, or fourth quadrant of the coordinate system.

An angle of one *degree* is an angle in which the rotation is 1/360 of one complete rotation.

A *straight angle* is an angle of 180° (180 degrees).

A *right angle* is an angle of 90°.

An *acute angle* is an angle between 0° and 90°.

An *obtuse angle* is an angle between 90° and 180°.

A *radian* is an angle subtended at the center of a circle by an arc whose length is equal to that of the radius.

$$180° = \pi \text{ radians}; \quad 1° = \frac{\pi}{180} \text{ radians}; \quad 1 \text{ radian} = \frac{180}{\pi} \text{ degrees}.$$

The Trigonometric Functions of an Acute Angle

In the right triangle ABC,

sine A = $\sin A$ = a/c

cosine A = $\cos A$ = b/c

tangent A = $\tan A$ = a/b

cosecant A = $\csc A$ = c/a

secant A = $\sec A$ = c/b

cotangent A = $\cot A$ = $\text{ctn } A$ = b/a

exsecant A = $\text{exsec } A$ = $\sec A - 1$

versine A = $\text{vers } A$ = $1 - \cos A$

coversine A = $\text{covers } A$ = $1 - \sin A$

haversine A = $\text{hav } A$ = $\frac{1}{2}\text{vers } A$

Formulas for Use in Trigonometry

The Trigonometric Functions of an Arbitrary Angle

Let α be any angle in standard position and let $P(x,y)$ be any point on the terminal side of the angle. Denote the positive distance OP by r. Then

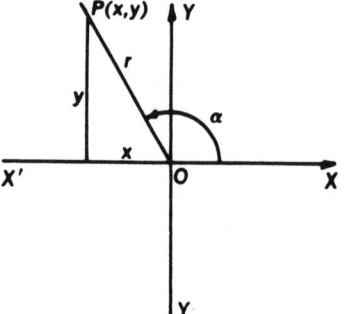

$$\sin \alpha = y/r \qquad \csc \alpha = r/y$$
$$\cos \alpha = x/r \qquad \sec \alpha = r/x$$
$$\tan \alpha = y/x \qquad \cot \alpha = \text{ctn } \alpha = x/y$$
$$\text{exsec } \alpha = \sec \alpha - 1 \qquad \text{covers } \alpha = 1 - \sin \alpha$$
$$\text{vers } \alpha = 1 - \cos \alpha \qquad \text{hav } \alpha = \tfrac{1}{2}\text{vers } \alpha$$
$$\text{cis } \alpha = \cos \alpha + i \sin \alpha = e^{i\alpha}, \alpha \text{ in radians, } i = \sqrt{-1}$$

RELATIONS BETWEEN CIRCULAR (OR INVERSE CIRCULAR) FUNCTIONS

$$\left(0 \leq x \leq \frac{\pi}{2} \right)$$

	$\sin x = a$	$\cos x = a$	$\tan x = a$
$\sin x$	a	$(1 - a^2)^{1/2}$	$a(1 + a^2)^{-1/2}$
$\cos x$	$(1 - a^2)^{1/2}$	a	$(1 + a^2)^{-1/2}$
$\tan x$	$a(1 - a^2)^{-1/2}$	$a^{-1}(1 - a^2)^{1/2}$	a
$\csc x$	a^{-1}	$(1 - a^2)^{-1/2}$	$a^{-1}(1 + a^2)^{1/2}$
$\sec x$	$(1 - a^2)^{-1/2}$	a^{-1}	$(1 + a^2)^{1/2}$
$\cot x$	$a^{-1}(1 - a^2)^{1/2}$	$a(1 - a^2)^{-1/2}$	a^{-1}

	$\csc x = a$	$\sec x = a$	$\cot x = a$
$\sin x$	a^{-1}	$a^{-1}(a^2 - 1)^{1/2}$	$(1 + a^2)^{-1/2}$
$\cos x$	$a^{-1}(a^2 - 1)^{1/2}$	a^{-1}	$a(1 + a^2)^{-1/2}$
$\tan x$	$(a^2 - 1)^{-1/2}$	$(a^2 - 1)^{1/2}$	a^{-1}
$\csc x$	a	$a(a^2 - 1)^{-1/2}$	$(1 + a^2)^{1/2}$
$\sec x$	$a(a^2 - 1)^{-1/2}$	a	$a^{-1}(1 + a^2)^{1/2}$
$\cot x$	$(a^2 - 1)^{1/2}$	$(a^2 - 1)^{-1/2}$	a

Examples:

If $\sec x = a$, then $\tan x = (a^2 - 1)^{1/2}$
$\text{arc tan } a = \text{arc cos } (1 + a^2)^{-1/2}$

Formulas for Use in Trigonometry

SIGNS OF THE TRIGONOMETRIC FUNCTIONS

Quadrant	sin	cos	tan	cot	sec	csc
I	+	+	+	+	+	+
II	+	−	−	−	−	+
III	−	−	+	+	−	−
IV	−	+	−	−	+	−

VARIATIONS OF THE TRIGONOMETRIC FUNCTIONS

Quadrant	sin	cos	tan	cot	sec	csc
I	$0 \to +1$	$+1 \to 0$	$0 \to +\infty$	$+\infty \to 0$	$+1 \to +\infty$	$+\infty \to +1$
II	$+1 \to 0$	$0 \to -1$	$-\infty \to 0$	$0 \to -\infty$	$-\infty \to -1$	$+1 \to +\infty$
III	$0 \to -1$	$-1 \to 0$	$0 \to +\infty$	$+\infty \to 0$	$-1 \to -\infty$	$-\infty \to -1$
IV	$-1 \to 0$	$0 \to +1$	$-\infty \to 0$	$0 \to -\infty$	$+\infty \to +1$	$-1 \to -\infty$

TRIGONOMETRIC FUNCTIONS OF SOME SPECIAL ANGLES

Angle	sin	cos	tan	cot	sec	csc
$0° = 0$	0	1	0	$\cdots$	1	$\cdots$
$15° = \dfrac{\pi}{12}$	$\dfrac{\sqrt{2}}{4}(\sqrt{3}-1)$	$\dfrac{\sqrt{2}}{4}(\sqrt{3}+1)$	$2-\sqrt{3}$	$2+\sqrt{3}$	$\sqrt{2}(\sqrt{3}-1)$	$\sqrt{2}(\sqrt{3}+1)$
$30° = \dfrac{\pi}{6}$	$1/2$	$\sqrt{3}/2$	$\sqrt{3}/3$	$\sqrt{3}$	$2\sqrt{3}/3$	2
$45° = \dfrac{\pi}{4}$	$\sqrt{2}/2$	$\sqrt{2}/2$	1	1	$\sqrt{2}$	$\sqrt{2}$
$60° = \dfrac{\pi}{3}$	$\sqrt{3}/2$	$1/2$	$\sqrt{3}$	$\sqrt{3}/3$	2	$2\sqrt{3}/3$
$75° = \dfrac{5\pi}{12}$	$\dfrac{\sqrt{2}}{4}(\sqrt{3}+1)$	$\dfrac{\sqrt{2}}{4}(\sqrt{3}-1)$	$2+\sqrt{3}$	$2-\sqrt{3}$	$\sqrt{2}(\sqrt{3}+1)$	$\sqrt{2}(\sqrt{3}-1)$
$90° = \dfrac{\pi}{2}$	1	0	$\cdots$	0	$\cdots$	1
$105° = \dfrac{7\pi}{12}$	$\dfrac{\sqrt{2}}{4}(\sqrt{3}+1)$	$-\dfrac{\sqrt{2}}{4}(\sqrt{3}-1)$	$-(2+\sqrt{3})$	$-(2-\sqrt{3})$	$-2(\sqrt{3}+1)$	$\sqrt{2}(\sqrt{3}-1)$
$120° = \dfrac{2\pi}{3}$	$\sqrt{3}/2$	$-1/2$	$-\sqrt{3}$	$-\sqrt{3}/3$	-2	$2\sqrt{3}/3$
$135° = \dfrac{3\pi}{4}$	$\sqrt{2}/2$	$-\sqrt{2}/2$	-1	-1	$-\sqrt{2}$	$\sqrt{2}$
$150° = \dfrac{5\pi}{6}$	$1/2$	$-\sqrt{3}/2$	$-\sqrt{3}/3$	$-\sqrt{3}$	$-2\sqrt{3}/3$	2
$165° = \dfrac{11\pi}{12}$	$\dfrac{\sqrt{2}}{4}(\sqrt{3}-1)$	$-\dfrac{\sqrt{2}}{4}(\sqrt{3}+1)$	$-(2-\sqrt{3})$	$-(2+\sqrt{3})$	$-\sqrt{2}(\sqrt{3}-1)$	$\sqrt{2}(\sqrt{3}+1)$
$180° = \pi$	0	-1	0	$\cdots$	-1	$\cdots$
$270° = \dfrac{3\pi}{2}$	-1	0	$\cdots$	0	$\cdots$	-1

Formulas for Use in Trigonometry

Relations among the Functions

$$\sin x = \frac{1}{\csc x} \qquad\qquad\qquad \csc x = \frac{1}{\sin x}$$

$$\cos x = \frac{1}{\sec x} \qquad\qquad\qquad \sec x = \frac{1}{\cos x}$$

$$\tan x = \frac{1}{\cot x} = \frac{\sin x}{\cos x}$$

$$\sin^2 x + \cos^2 x = 1$$

$$\cot x = \frac{1}{\tan x} = \frac{\cos x}{\sin x} \qquad\qquad 1 + \tan^2 x = \sec^2 x$$
$$1 + \cot^2 x = \csc^2 x$$

$$* \; \sin x = \pm\sqrt{1 - \cos^2 x}$$
$$* \; \tan x = \pm\sqrt{\sec^2 x - 1} \qquad\qquad * \; \cos x = \pm\sqrt{1 - \sin^2 x}$$
$$* \; \cot x = \pm\sqrt{\csc^2 x - 1} \qquad\qquad * \; \sec x = \pm\sqrt{\tan^2 x + 1}$$
$$* \; \csc x = \pm\sqrt{\cot^2 x + 1}$$

$$\sin x = \cos (90° - x) = \sin (180° - x)$$
$$\cos x = \sin (90° - x) = -\cos (180° - x)$$
$$\tan x = \cot (90° - x) = -\tan (180° - x)$$
$$\cot x = \tan (90° - x) = -\cot (180° - x)$$

$$\csc x = \cot \frac{x}{2} - \cot x$$

*The sign in front of radical depends on quadrant in which x falls.

Reduction Formulas

$$\sin \alpha = +\cos(\alpha - 90°) = -\sin(\alpha - 180°) = -\cos(\alpha - 270°)$$
$$\cos \alpha = -\sin(\alpha - 90°) = -\cos(\alpha - 180°) = +\sin(\alpha - 270°)$$
$$\tan \alpha = -\cot(\alpha - 90°) = +\tan(\alpha - 180°) = -\cot(\alpha - 270°)$$
$$\cot \alpha = -\tan(\alpha - 90°) = +\cot(\alpha - 180°) = -\tan(\alpha - 270°)$$
$$\sec \alpha = -\csc(\alpha - 90°) = -\sec(\alpha - 180°) = +\csc(\alpha - 270°)$$
$$\csc \alpha = +\sec(\alpha - 90°) = -\csc(\alpha - 180°) = -\sec(\alpha - 270°)$$

FURTHER REDUCTION FORMULAS

	sin	cos	tan	cot	sec	csc
$-\alpha$	$-\sin \alpha$	$+\cos \alpha$	$-\tan \alpha$	$-\cot \alpha$	$+\sec \alpha$	$-\csc \alpha$
$90° + \alpha$	$+\cos \alpha$	$-\sin \alpha$	$-\cot \alpha$	$-\tan \alpha$	$-\csc \alpha$	$+\sec \alpha$
$90° - \alpha$	$+\cos \alpha$	$+\sin \alpha$	$+\cot \alpha$	$+\tan \alpha$	$+\csc \alpha$	$+\sec \alpha$
$180° + \alpha$	$-\sin \alpha$	$-\cos \alpha$	$+\tan \alpha$	$+\cot \alpha$	$-\sec \alpha$	$-\csc \alpha$
$180° - \alpha$	$+\sin \alpha$	$-\cos \alpha$	$-\tan \alpha$	$-\cot \alpha$	$-\sec \alpha$	$+\csc \alpha$
$270° + \alpha$	$-\cos \alpha$	$+\sin \alpha$	$-\cot \alpha$	$-\tan \alpha$	$+\csc \alpha$	$-\sec \alpha$
$270° - \alpha$	$-\cos \alpha$	$-\sin \alpha$	$+\cot \alpha$	$+\tan \alpha$	$-\csc \alpha$	$-\sec \alpha$
$360° + \alpha$	$+\sin \alpha$	$+\cos \alpha$	$+\tan \alpha$	$+\cot \alpha$	$+\sec \alpha$	$+\csc \alpha$
$360° - \alpha$	$-\sin \alpha$	$+\cos \alpha$	$-\tan \alpha$	$-\cot \alpha$	$+\sec \alpha$	$-\csc \alpha$

Formulas for Use in Trigonometry

The previous table may be summarized and extended by the following easily remembered rule:

$$f(\pm\alpha + n90°) = \pm g(\alpha)$$

where n may be any integer, positive, negative, or zero
          f is any one of the six trigonometric functions: sin, cos, tan, cot, sec, or csc
          α may be any real angle measure
If n is even, then g is the same function as f.   If n is odd, then g is the *cofunction* of f.

(Sine and cosine, tangent and cotangent, secant and cosecant, are cofunctions of each other.)

The second $\pm$ sign is not necessarily the same as the first one, but is determined as follows: For a given function f, a given value of n, and a given choice of the first $\pm$ sign, the second $\pm$ sign will be the same for all values of α.   Thus it is only necessary to check the sign for any one value of α, and the formula will be complete.

EXAMPLES:

$\tan(\alpha + 270°) = \pm\cot\alpha$.   Since $n(=3)$ is odd, we use the cofunction.   To determine the sign, assume a value of α in the first quadrant.   Then $\alpha + 270°$ is in the fourth quadrant, where the tangent is negative, so a minus sign is required.   Thus the formula becomes

$$\tan(\alpha + 270°) = -\cot\alpha, \quad \text{valid for all values of } \alpha.$$

$\cos(\alpha - 450°) = \pm\sin\alpha$.   Again assuming a value of α in the first quadrant, we find that $\alpha - 450°$ is in the fourth quadrant.   Thus $\cos(\alpha - 450°)$ would be positive, and no minus sign is needed.   Hence the formula becomes

$$\cos(\alpha - 450°) = \sin\alpha.$$

$\sec(180° - \alpha) = \pm\sec\alpha$.   Here $n(=2)$ is even, so we use the same function.   To determine the sign, again assume a value of α in the first quadrant.   Then $180° - \alpha$ is in the second quadrant, where the secant is negative.   Thus the formula, valid for all values of α, is

$$\sec(180° - \alpha) = -\sec\alpha.$$

Fundamental Identities

Where a double sign appears in the following, the choice of sign depends upon the quadrant in which the angle terminates.

Reciprocal relations

$$\sin\alpha = \frac{1}{\csc\alpha}, \qquad \cos\alpha = \frac{1}{\sec\alpha}, \qquad \tan\alpha = \frac{1}{\cot\alpha}$$

$$\csc\alpha = \frac{1}{\sin\alpha}, \qquad \sec\alpha = \frac{1}{\cos\alpha}, \qquad \cot\alpha = \frac{1}{\tan\alpha}$$

Product relations

$$\sin\alpha = \tan\alpha\cos\alpha, \qquad \cos\alpha = \cot\alpha\sin\alpha$$
$$\tan\alpha = \sin\alpha\sec\alpha, \qquad \cot\alpha = \cos\alpha\csc\alpha$$
$$\sec\alpha = \csc\alpha\tan\alpha, \qquad \csc\alpha = \sec\alpha\cot\alpha$$

Quotient relations

$$\sin\alpha = \frac{\tan\alpha}{\sec\alpha}, \qquad \cos\alpha = \frac{\cot\alpha}{\csc\alpha}, \qquad \tan\alpha = \frac{\sin\alpha}{\cos\alpha}$$

$$\csc\alpha = \frac{\sec\alpha}{\tan\alpha}, \qquad \sec\alpha = \frac{\csc\alpha}{\cot\alpha}, \qquad \cot\alpha = \frac{\cos\alpha}{\sin\alpha}$$

Pythagorean relations

$$\sin^2\alpha + \cos^2\alpha = 1, \qquad 1 + \tan^2\alpha = \sec^2\alpha, \qquad 1 + \cot^2\alpha = \csc^2\alpha$$

Angle-sum and angle-difference relations

$$\sin(\alpha + \beta) = \sin\alpha\cos\beta + \cos\alpha\sin\beta$$
$$\sin(\alpha - \beta) = \sin\alpha\cos\beta - \cos\alpha\sin\beta$$
$$\cos(\alpha + \beta) = \cos\alpha\cos\beta - \sin\alpha\sin\beta$$
$$\cos(\alpha - \beta) = \cos\alpha\cos\beta + \sin\alpha\sin\beta$$
$$\tan(\alpha + \beta) = \frac{\tan\alpha + \tan\beta}{1 - \tan\alpha\tan\beta}$$
$$\tan(\alpha - \beta) = \frac{\tan\alpha - \tan\beta}{1 + \tan\alpha\tan\beta}$$
$$\cot(\alpha + \beta) = \frac{\cot\beta\cot\alpha - 1}{\cot\beta + \cot\alpha}$$
$$\cot(\alpha - \beta) = \frac{\cot\beta\cot\alpha + 1}{\cot\beta - \cot\alpha}$$
$$\sin(\alpha + \beta)\sin(\alpha - \beta) = \sin^2\alpha - \sin^2\beta = \cos^2\beta - \cos^2\alpha$$
$$\cos(\alpha + \beta)\cos(\alpha - \beta) = \cos^2\alpha - \sin^2\beta = \cos^2\beta - \sin^2\alpha$$

Double-angle relations

$$\sin 2\alpha = 2\sin\alpha\cos\alpha = \frac{2\tan\alpha}{1 + \tan^2\alpha}$$

$$\cos 2\alpha = \cos^2\alpha - \sin^2\alpha = 2\cos^2\alpha - 1 = 1 - 2\sin^2\alpha = \frac{1 - \tan^2\alpha}{1 + \tan^2\alpha}$$

$$\tan 2\alpha = \frac{2\tan\alpha}{1 - \tan^2\alpha}, \qquad \cot 2\alpha = \frac{\cot^2\alpha - 1}{2\cot\alpha}$$

Multiple-angle relations

$$\sin 3\alpha = 3\sin\alpha - 4\sin^3\alpha$$
$$\cos 3\alpha = 4\cos^3\alpha - 3\cos\alpha$$
$$\sin 4\alpha = 4\sin\alpha\cos\alpha - 8\sin^3\alpha\cos\alpha$$
$$\cos 4\alpha = 8\cos^4\alpha - 8\cos^2\alpha + 1$$
$$\sin 5\alpha = 5\sin\alpha - 20\sin^3\alpha + 16\sin^5\alpha$$
$$\cos 5\alpha = 16\cos^5\alpha - 20\cos^3\alpha + 5\cos\alpha$$
$$\sin 6\alpha = 32\cos^5\alpha\sin\alpha - 32\cos^3\alpha\sin\alpha + 6\cos\alpha\sin\alpha$$
$$\cos 6\alpha = 32\cos^6\alpha - 48\cos^4\alpha + 18\cos^2\alpha - 1$$
$$\sin n\alpha = 2\sin(n - 1)\alpha\cos\alpha - \sin(n - 2)\alpha$$
$$\cos n\alpha = 2\cos(n - 1)\alpha\cos\alpha - \cos(n - 2)\alpha$$
$$\tan 3\alpha = \frac{3\tan\alpha - \tan^3\alpha}{1 - 3\tan^2\alpha}$$
$$\tan 4\alpha = \frac{4\tan\alpha - 4\tan^3\alpha}{1 - 6\tan^2\alpha + \tan^4\alpha}$$
$$\tan n\alpha = \frac{\tan(n - 1)\alpha + \tan\alpha}{1 - \tan(n - 1)\alpha\tan\alpha}$$

Formulas for Use in Trigonometry

Function-product relations

$$\sin \alpha \sin \beta = \tfrac{1}{2} \cos(\alpha - \beta) - \tfrac{1}{2} \cos(\alpha + \beta)$$
$$\cos \alpha \cos \beta = \tfrac{1}{2} \cos(\alpha - \beta) + \tfrac{1}{2} \cos(\alpha + \beta)$$
$$\sin \alpha \cos \beta = \tfrac{1}{2} \sin(\alpha + \beta) + \tfrac{1}{2} \sin(\alpha - \beta)$$
$$\cos \alpha \sin \beta = \tfrac{1}{2} \sin(\alpha + \beta) - \tfrac{1}{2} \sin(\alpha - \beta)$$

Function-sum and function-difference relations

$$\sin \alpha + \sin \beta = 2 \sin \tfrac{1}{2}(\alpha + \beta) \cos \tfrac{1}{2}(\alpha - \beta)$$
$$\sin \alpha - \sin \beta = 2 \cos \tfrac{1}{2}(\alpha + \beta) \sin \tfrac{1}{2}(\alpha - \beta)$$
$$\cos \alpha + \cos \beta = 2 \cos \tfrac{1}{2}(\alpha + \beta) \cos \tfrac{1}{2}(\alpha - \beta)$$
$$\cos \alpha - \cos \beta = -2 \sin \tfrac{1}{2}(\alpha + \beta) \sin \tfrac{1}{2}(\alpha - \beta)$$

$$\tan \alpha + \tan \beta = \frac{\sin(\alpha + \beta)}{\cos \alpha \cos \beta}, \qquad \tan \alpha - \tan \beta = \frac{\sin(\alpha - \beta)}{\cos \alpha \cos \beta}$$

$$\cot \alpha + \cot \beta = \frac{\sin(\alpha + \beta)}{\sin \alpha \sin \beta}, \qquad \cot \alpha - \cot \beta = \frac{\sin(\beta - \alpha)}{\sin \alpha \sin \beta}$$

$$\frac{\sin \alpha + \sin \beta}{\sin \alpha - \sin \beta} = \frac{\tan \tfrac{1}{2}(\alpha + \beta)}{\tan \tfrac{1}{2}(\alpha - \beta)}, \qquad \frac{\sin \alpha + \sin \beta}{\cos \alpha - \cos \beta} = \cot \tfrac{1}{2}(\beta - \alpha)$$

$$\frac{\sin \alpha + \sin \beta}{\cos \alpha + \cos \beta} = \tan \tfrac{1}{2}(\alpha + \beta), \qquad \frac{\sin \alpha - \sin \beta}{\cos \alpha + \cos \beta} = \tan \tfrac{1}{2}(\alpha - \beta)$$

Half-angle relations

$$\sin \frac{\alpha}{2} = \pm \sqrt{\frac{1 - \cos \alpha}{2}}, \qquad \cos \frac{\alpha}{2} = \pm \sqrt{\frac{1 + \cos \alpha}{2}}$$

$$\tan \frac{\alpha}{2} = \pm \sqrt{\frac{1 - \cos \alpha}{1 + \cos \alpha}} = \frac{1 - \cos \alpha}{\sin \alpha} = \frac{\sin \alpha}{1 + \cos \alpha}$$

$$\cot \frac{\alpha}{2} = \pm \sqrt{\frac{1 + \cos \alpha}{1 - \cos \alpha}} = \frac{1 + \cos \alpha}{\sin \alpha} = \frac{\sin \alpha}{1 - \cos \alpha}$$

Power relations

$$\sin^2 \alpha = \tfrac{1}{2}(1 - \cos 2\alpha), \qquad \sin^3 \alpha = \tfrac{1}{4}(3 \sin \alpha - \sin 3\alpha)$$
$$\sin^4 \alpha = \tfrac{1}{8}(3 - 4 \cos 2\alpha + \cos 4\alpha)$$
$$\cos^2 \alpha = \tfrac{1}{2}(1 + \cos 2\alpha), \qquad \cos^3 \alpha = \tfrac{1}{4}(3 \cos \alpha + \cos 3\alpha)$$
$$\cos^4 \alpha = \tfrac{1}{8}(3 + 4 \cos 2\alpha + \cos 4\alpha)$$

$$\tan^2 \alpha = \frac{1 - \cos 2\alpha}{1 + \cos 2\alpha}, \qquad \cot^2 \alpha = \frac{1 + \cos 2\alpha}{1 - \cos 2\alpha}$$

Exponential relations (α in radians), Euler's equation

$$e^{i\alpha} = \cos \alpha + i \sin \alpha, \qquad i = \sqrt{-1}$$

$$\sin \alpha = \frac{e^{i\alpha} - e^{-i\alpha}}{2i}, \qquad \cos \alpha = \frac{e^{i\alpha} + e^{-i\alpha}}{2}$$

$$\tan \alpha = -i\left(\frac{e^{i\alpha} - e^{-i\alpha}}{e^{i\alpha} + e^{-i\alpha}}\right) = -i\left(\frac{e^{2i\alpha} - 1}{e^{2i\alpha} + 1}\right)$$

THE TRIGONOMETRIC FUNCTIONS IN TERMS OF ONE ANOTHER

Function	$\sin\alpha$	$\cos\alpha$	$\tan\alpha$	$\cot\alpha$	$\sec\alpha$	$\csc\alpha$
$\sin\alpha$	$\sin\alpha$	$\pm\sqrt{1-\cos^2\alpha}$	$\dfrac{\tan\alpha}{\pm\sqrt{1+\tan^2\alpha}}$	$\dfrac{1}{\pm\sqrt{1+\cot^2\alpha}}$	$\dfrac{\pm\sqrt{\sec^2\alpha-1}}{\sec\alpha}$	$\dfrac{1}{\csc\alpha}$
$\cos\alpha$	$\pm\sqrt{1-\sin^2\alpha}$	$\cos\alpha$	$\dfrac{1}{\pm\sqrt{1+\tan^2\alpha}}$	$\dfrac{\cot\alpha}{\pm\sqrt{1+\cot^2\alpha}}$	$\dfrac{1}{\sec\alpha}$	$\dfrac{\pm\sqrt{\csc^2\alpha-1}}{\csc\alpha}$
$\tan\alpha$	$\dfrac{\sin\alpha}{\pm\sqrt{1-\sin^2\alpha}}$	$\dfrac{\pm\sqrt{1-\cos^2\alpha}}{\cos\alpha}$	$\tan\alpha$	$\dfrac{1}{\cot\alpha}$	$\pm\sqrt{\sec^2\alpha-1}$	$\dfrac{1}{\pm\sqrt{\csc^2\alpha-1}}$
$\cot\alpha$	$\dfrac{\pm\sqrt{1-\sin^2\alpha}}{\sin\alpha}$	$\dfrac{\cos\alpha}{\pm\sqrt{1-\cos^2\alpha}}$	$\dfrac{1}{\tan\alpha}$	$\cot\alpha$	$\dfrac{1}{\pm\sqrt{\sec^2\alpha-1}}$	$\pm\sqrt{\csc^2\alpha-1}$
$\sec\alpha$	$\dfrac{1}{\pm\sqrt{1-\sin^2\alpha}}$	$\dfrac{1}{\cos\alpha}$	$\pm\sqrt{1+\tan^2\alpha}$	$\dfrac{\pm\sqrt{1+\cot^2\alpha}}{\cot\alpha}$	$\sec\alpha$	$\dfrac{\csc\alpha}{\pm\sqrt{\csc^2\alpha-1}}$
$\csc\alpha$	$\dfrac{1}{\sin\alpha}$	$\dfrac{1}{\pm\sqrt{1-\cos^2\alpha}}$	$\dfrac{\pm\sqrt{1+\tan^2\alpha}}{\tan\alpha}$	$\pm\sqrt{1+\cot^2\alpha}$	$\dfrac{\sec\alpha}{\pm\sqrt{\sec^2\alpha-1}}$	$\csc\alpha$

Note. The choice of sign depends upon the quadrant in which the angle terminates.

Principal Values of the Inverse Trigonometric Functions

The notation arcsin x (or $\sin^{-1}x$) is used to denote any angle whose sine is x; Arcsin x (or $\text{Sin}^{-1}x$) is usually used to denote the *principal value*. Similar notation is used for the other inverse trigonometric functions. The principal values of the inverse trigonometric functions are defined as follows:

$$-\pi/2 \le \text{Arcsin } x \le \pi/2, \qquad -1 \le x \le 1$$

$$0 \le \text{Arccos } x \le \pi, \qquad -1 \le x \le 1$$

$$-\pi/2 < \text{Arctan } x < \pi/2, \qquad -\infty < x < \infty$$

$$0 < \text{Arccsc } x \le \pi/2, \qquad x \ge 1$$
$$-\pi < \text{Arccsc } x \le -\pi/2, \qquad x \le -1$$

$$0 \le \text{Arcsec } x < \pi/2, \qquad x \ge 1$$
$$-\pi \le \text{Arcsec } x < -\pi/2, \qquad x \le -1$$

$$0 < \text{Arccot } x < \pi, \qquad -\infty < x < \infty$$

Note. There is no uniform agreement on the definitions of Arccsc x, Arcsec x, Arccot x for negative values of x.

Fundamental Identities Involving Principal Values

$$\text{Arcsin } x + \text{Arccos } x = \pi/2$$
$$\text{Arctan } x + \text{Arccot } x = \pi/2$$

If $\alpha = \text{Arcsin } x$, then

$$\sin\alpha = x, \qquad \cos\alpha = \sqrt{1-x^2}, \qquad \tan\alpha = \frac{x}{\sqrt{1-x^2}}$$

$$\csc\alpha = \frac{1}{x}, \qquad \sec\alpha = \frac{1}{\sqrt{1-x^2}}, \qquad \cot\alpha = \frac{\sqrt{1-x^2}}{x}$$

If $\alpha = \text{Arccos } x$, then

$$\sin \alpha = \sqrt{1 - x^2}, \qquad \cos \alpha = x, \qquad \tan \alpha = \frac{\sqrt{1 - x^2}}{x}$$

$$\csc \alpha = \frac{1}{\sqrt{1 - x^2}}, \qquad \sec \alpha = \frac{1}{x}, \qquad \cot \alpha = \frac{x}{\sqrt{1 - x^2}}$$

If $\alpha = \text{Arctan } x$, then

$$\sin \alpha = \frac{x}{\sqrt{1 + x^2}}, \qquad \cos \alpha = \frac{1}{\sqrt{1 + x^2}}, \qquad \tan \alpha = x$$

$$\csc \alpha = \frac{\sqrt{1 + x^2}}{x}, \qquad \sec \alpha = \sqrt{1 + x^2}, \qquad \cot \alpha = \frac{1}{x}$$

Relations Between Principal Values of Inverse Trigonometric Functions

The following additional relations between principal values of the inverse trigonometric functions are useful:

$$\text{Arcsin } x = \text{Arccos}(-x) - \frac{\pi}{2} = \frac{\pi}{2} - \text{Arccos } x$$

$$= -\text{Arcsin}(-x) = \text{Arctan } \frac{x}{\sqrt{1 - x^2}}$$

$$= \frac{\pi}{2} - \text{Arccot } \frac{x}{\sqrt{1 - x^2}}$$

$$\text{Arctan } x = \text{Arccot}(-x) - \frac{\pi}{2} = \frac{\pi}{2} - \text{Arccot } x$$

$$= -\text{Arctan}(-x) = \text{Arcsin } \frac{x}{\sqrt{x^2 + 1}}$$

$$= \frac{\pi}{2} - \text{Arccos } \frac{x}{\sqrt{x^2 + 1}}$$

$$\text{Arccos } x = \frac{\pi}{2} + \text{Arcsin}(-x) = \frac{\pi}{2} - \text{Arcsin } x$$

$$= \pi - \text{Arccos}(-x) = \text{Arccot } \frac{x}{\sqrt{1 - x^2}}$$

$$= \frac{\pi}{2} - \text{Arctan } \frac{x}{\sqrt{1 - x^2}}$$

$$\text{Arccot } x = \frac{\pi}{2} + \text{Arctan}(-x) = \frac{\pi}{2} - \text{Arctan } x$$

$$= \pi - \text{Arccot}(-x) = \text{Arccos } \frac{x}{\sqrt{x^2 + 1}}$$

$$= \frac{\pi}{2} - \text{Arcsin } \frac{x}{\sqrt{x^2 + 1}}$$

Formulas for Use in Trigonometry

$$\text{Arccsc } x = \text{Arcsec } \frac{x}{\sqrt{x^2 - 1}}$$

$$\text{Arcsec } x = \text{Arccsc } \frac{x}{\sqrt{x^2 - 1}}$$

$$\cos(\text{Arcsin } x) = \sin(\text{Arccos } x) = \sqrt{1 - x^2}$$

$$\sec(\text{Arctan } x) = \csc(\text{Arccot } x) = \sqrt{x^2 + 1}$$

$$\tan(\text{Arcsec } x) = \cot(\text{Arccsc } x) = \sqrt{x^2 - 1}$$

The above are valid for x positive or negative. The following are valid only for $x \geq 0$.

$$\text{Arcsin } x = \text{Arccos } \sqrt{1 - x^2} = \text{Arccot } \frac{\sqrt{1 - x^2}}{x}$$

$$= \text{Arcsec } \frac{1}{\sqrt{1 - x^2}} = \text{Arccsc } \frac{1}{x}$$

$$= \frac{\pi}{2} - \text{Arcsin } \sqrt{1 - x^2}$$

$$\text{Arccos } x = \text{Arcsin } \sqrt{1 - x^2} = \text{Arctan } \frac{\sqrt{1 - x^2}}{x}$$

$$= \text{Arcsec } \frac{1}{x} = \text{Arccsc } \frac{1}{\sqrt{1 - x^2}}$$

$$= \frac{\pi}{2} - \text{Arccos } \sqrt{1 - x^2}$$

$$\text{Arctan } x = \text{Arccot } \frac{1}{x} = \text{Arccos } \frac{1}{\sqrt{x^2 + 1}}$$

$$= \text{Arcsec } \sqrt{x^2 + 1} = \text{Arccsc } \frac{\sqrt{x^2 + 1}}{x}$$

$$= \frac{\pi}{2} - \text{Arctan } \frac{1}{x}$$

$$\text{Arccot } x = \text{Arctan } \frac{1}{x} = \text{Arcsin } \frac{1}{\sqrt{x^2 + 1}}$$

$$= \text{Arcsec } \frac{\sqrt{x^2 + 1}}{x} = \text{Arccsc } \sqrt{x^2 + 1}$$

$$= \frac{\pi}{2} - \text{Arccot } \frac{1}{x}$$

$$\text{Arcsec } x = \text{Arctan } \sqrt{x^2 - 1} = \text{Arccot } \frac{1}{\sqrt{x^2 - 1}}$$

$$= \text{Arcsin } \frac{\sqrt{x^2 - 1}}{x} = \text{Arccos } \frac{1}{x} = \pi + \text{Arcsec}(-x)$$

$$= \frac{\pi}{2} - \text{Arccsc } x = -\frac{\pi}{2} - \text{Arccsc}(-x)$$

Formulas for Use in Trigonometry

$$\text{Arccsc } x = \text{Arctan } \frac{1}{\sqrt{x^2 - 1}} = \text{Arccot } \sqrt{x^2 - 1}$$

$$= \text{Arcsin } \frac{1}{x} = \text{Arccos } \frac{\sqrt{x^2 - 1}}{x} = \pi + \text{Arccsc}(-x)$$

$$= \frac{\pi}{2} - \text{Arcsec } x = -\frac{\pi}{2} - \text{Arcsec}(-x)$$

The following are valid if $x < 0$.

$$\text{Arcsin } x = -\text{Arccos } \sqrt{1 - x^2} = \text{Arccot } \frac{\sqrt{1 - x^2}}{x} - \pi$$

$$= -\pi - \text{Arccsc } \frac{1}{x} = -\text{Arcsec } \frac{1}{\sqrt{1 - x^2}}$$

$$= \text{Arcsin } \sqrt{1 - x^2} - \frac{\pi}{2}$$

$$\text{Arccos } x = \pi - \text{Arcsin } \sqrt{1 - x^2} = \pi + \text{Arctan } \frac{\sqrt{1 - x^2}}{x}$$

$$= \pi - \text{Arccsc } \frac{1}{\sqrt{1 - x^2}} = -\text{Arcsec } \frac{1}{x}$$

$$= \text{Arccos } \sqrt{1 - x^2} + \frac{\pi}{2}$$

$$\text{Arctan } x = \text{Arccot } \frac{1}{x} - \pi = -\text{Arccos } \frac{1}{\sqrt{x^2 + 1}}$$

$$= -\text{Arcsec } \sqrt{x^2 + 1} = -\pi - \text{Arccsc } \frac{\sqrt{x^2 + 1}}{x}$$

$$= -\frac{\pi}{2} - \text{Arctan } \frac{1}{x}$$

$$\text{Arccot } x = \pi + \text{Arctan } \frac{1}{x} = \pi - \text{Arcsin } \frac{1}{\sqrt{x^2 + 1}}$$

$$= -\text{Arcsec } \frac{\sqrt{x^2 + 1}}{x} = \pi - \text{Arccsc } \sqrt{x^2 + 1}$$

$$= \frac{3\pi}{2} - \text{Arccot } \frac{1}{x}$$

$$\text{Arcsec } x = \text{Arctan } \sqrt{x^2 - 1} - \pi = \text{Arccot } \frac{1}{\sqrt{x^2 - 1}} - \pi$$

$$= -\pi - \text{Arcsin } \frac{\sqrt{x^2 - 1}}{x} = -\text{Arccos } \frac{1}{x} = \text{Arcsec}(-x) - \pi$$

$$= -\frac{3\pi}{2} - \text{Arccsc } x = -\frac{\pi}{2} - \text{Arccsc}(-x)$$

Formulas for Use in Trigonometry

$$\text{Arccsc } x = \text{Arctan } \frac{1}{\sqrt{x^2 - 1}} - \pi = \text{Arccot } \sqrt{x^2 - 1} - \pi$$

$$= -\pi - \text{Arcsin } \frac{1}{x} = -\text{Arccos } \frac{\sqrt{x^2 - 1}}{x} = \text{Arccsc}(-x) - \pi$$

$$= -\frac{3\pi}{2} - \text{Arcsec } x = -\frac{\pi}{2} - \text{Arcsec}(-x)$$

Plane Triangle Formulas

In the following, A, B, C denote the angles of any plane triangle, a, b, c the corresponding opposite sides, and $s = \frac{1}{2}(a + b + c)$.

Radius of inscribed circle:

$$r = \sqrt{\frac{(s - a)(s - b)(s - c)}{s}}$$

Radius of circumscribed circle:

$$R = \frac{a}{2 \sin A} = \frac{b}{2 \sin B} = \frac{c}{2 \sin C}$$

Law of sines:

$$\frac{a}{\sin A} = \frac{b}{\sin B} = \frac{c}{\sin C}$$

Law of cosines:

$$a^2 = b^2 + c^2 - 2bc \cos A, \qquad \cos A = \frac{b^2 + c^2 - a^2}{2bc}$$

$$b^2 = c^2 + a^2 - 2ca \cos B, \qquad \cos B = \frac{c^2 + a^2 - b^2}{2ca}$$

$$c^2 = a^2 + b^2 - 2ab \cos C, \qquad \cos C = \frac{a^2 + b^2 - c^2}{2ab}$$

Law of tangents:

$$\frac{b - c}{b + c} = \frac{\tan \frac{1}{2}(B - C)}{\tan \frac{1}{2}(B + C)}, \qquad \frac{c - a}{c + a} = \frac{\tan \frac{1}{2}(C - A)}{\tan \frac{1}{2}(C + A)}$$

$$\frac{a - b}{a + b} = \frac{\tan \frac{1}{2}(A - B)}{\tan \frac{1}{2}(A + B)}$$

Half-angle formulas:

$$\tan \tfrac{1}{2}A = \frac{r}{s - a}, \qquad \tan \tfrac{1}{2}B = \frac{r}{s - b}, \qquad \tan \tfrac{1}{2}C = \frac{r}{s - c}$$

$$\sin \tfrac{1}{2}A = \sqrt{\frac{(s - b)(s - c)}{bc}}, \qquad \cos \tfrac{1}{2}A = \sqrt{\frac{s(s - a)}{bc}}$$

$$\sin \tfrac{1}{2}B = \sqrt{\frac{(s - c)(s - a)}{ca}}, \qquad \cos \tfrac{1}{2}B = \sqrt{\frac{s(s - b)}{ca}}$$

$$\sin \tfrac{1}{2}C = \sqrt{\frac{(s - a)(s - b)}{ab}}, \qquad \cos \tfrac{1}{2}C = \sqrt{\frac{s(s - c)}{ab}}$$

Formulas for Use in Trigonometry

Area:

$$K = \tfrac{1}{2}bc \sin A = \tfrac{1}{2}ca \sin B = \tfrac{1}{2}ab \sin C$$

$$K = \frac{a^2 \sin B \sin C}{2 \sin A} = \frac{b^2 \sin C \sin A}{2 \sin B} = \frac{c^2 \sin A \sin B}{2 \sin C}$$

$$K = \sqrt{s(s-a)(s-b)(s-c)} = rs = \frac{abc}{4R}$$

Mollweide's formulas:

$$\frac{b-c}{a} = \frac{\sin\tfrac{1}{2}(B-C)}{\cos\tfrac{1}{2}A}, \quad \frac{c-a}{b} = \frac{\sin\tfrac{1}{2}(C-A)}{\cos\tfrac{1}{2}B}$$

$$\frac{a-b}{c} = \frac{\sin\tfrac{1}{2}(A-B)}{\cos\tfrac{1}{2}C}$$

Newton's formulas:

$$\frac{b+c}{a} = \frac{\cos\tfrac{1}{2}(B-C)}{\sin\tfrac{1}{2}A}, \quad \frac{c+a}{b} = \frac{\cos\tfrac{1}{2}(C-A)}{\sin\tfrac{1}{2}B}$$

$$\frac{a+b}{c} = \frac{\cos\tfrac{1}{2}(A-B)}{\sin\tfrac{1}{2}C}$$

Solution of Right Triangles

(**a**) Given acute angle A and opposite leg a.

$$B = 90° - A, \quad b = a/\tan A = a \cot A, \quad c = a/\sin A = a \csc A$$

(**b**) Given acute angle A and adjacent leg b.

$$B = 90° - A, \quad a = b \tan A, \quad c = b/\cos A = b \sec A$$

(**c**) Given acute angle A and hypotenuse c.

$$B = 90° - A, \quad a = c \sin A, \quad b = c \cos A$$

(**d**) Given legs a and b.

$$c = \sqrt{a^2 + b^2}, \quad \tan A = a/b, \quad B = 90° - A$$

(**e**) Given hypotenuse c and leg a.

$$b = \sqrt{(c+a)(c-a)}, \quad \sin A = a/c, \quad B = 90° - A$$

Solution of Oblique Triangles

(**a**) Given sides b and c and included angle A.

Nonlogarithmic solution

$$a^2 = b^2 + c^2 - 2bc \cos A, \quad \cos B = (c^2 + a^2 - b^2)/2ca,$$
$$\cos C = (a^2 + b^2 - c^2)/2ab$$

Logarithmic solution

$$\tfrac{1}{2}(B+C) = 90° - \tfrac{1}{2}A, \quad \tan\tfrac{1}{2}(B-C) = \frac{b-c}{b+c}\tan\tfrac{1}{2}(B+C),$$
$$B = \tfrac{1}{2}(B+C) + \tfrac{1}{2}(B-C), \quad C = \tfrac{1}{2}(B+C) - \tfrac{1}{2}(B-C),$$
$$a = (b \sin A)/\sin B, \quad K = \tfrac{1}{2}bc \sin A$$

Formulas for Use in Spherical Trigonometry

Check. $A + B + C = 180°$, or use Newton's formula or law of sines.

(b) Given angles B and C and included side a.

$$A = 180° - (B + C), \quad b = (a \sin B)/\sin A,$$
$$c = (a \sin C)/\sin A, \quad K = \frac{a^2 \sin B \sin C}{2 \sin A}$$

Check. $a = b \cos C + c \cos B$, or use Newton's formula or law of tangents.

(c) Given sides a and c and opposite angle A.

$$\sin C = (c \sin A)/a, \quad B = 180° - (A + C),$$
$$b = (a \sin B)/\sin A, \quad K = \tfrac{1}{2}ac \sin B$$

Check. $a = b \cos C + c \cos B$, or use Newton's formula or law of tangents.
Note. In this case there may be two solutions, for C may have two values:

$C_1 < 90°$ and $C_2 = 180° - C_1 > 90°$. If $A + C_2 > 180°$, use only C_1.

(d) Given the three sides a, b, c.

Nonlogarithmic solution

$$\cos A = (b^2 + c^2 - a^2)/2bc, \quad \cos B = (c^2 + a^2 - b^2)/2ca,$$
$$\cos C = (a^2 + b^2 - c^2)/2ab$$

Logarithmic solution

$$s = \tfrac{1}{2}(a + b + c), \quad r = \sqrt{\frac{(s - a)(s - b)(s - c)}{s}},$$
$$\tan \tfrac{1}{2}A = \frac{r}{s - a}, \quad \tan \tfrac{1}{2}B = \frac{r}{s - b}, \quad \tan \tfrac{1}{2}C = \frac{r}{s - c},$$
$$K = \sqrt{s(s - a)(s - b)(s - c)}$$

Check. $A + B + C = 180°$.

Relations Between Accuracy of Computed Lengths and Angles

When solving a triangle for any of its parts, the following should be observed:

Significant figures for sides	Angles to the nearest
2	degree
3	ten minutes
4	minute
5	tenth of a minute

SPHERICAL TRIGONOMETRY

Right Spherical Triangles

Let a, b, c be the sides of a right spherical triangle with opposite angles $A, B, C = 90°$, respectively, where each side is measured by the angle subtended at the center of the sphere.

$$\sin a = \tan b \cot B, \quad \sin a = \sin A \sin c$$
$$\sin b = \tan a \cot A, \quad \sin b = \sin B \sin c$$
$$\cos A = \tan b \cot c, \quad \cos A = \cos a \sin B$$
$$\cos B = \tan a \cot c, \quad \cos B = \cos b \sin A$$
$$\cos c = \cot A \cot B, \quad \cos c = \cos a \cos b$$

Formulas for Use in Spherical Trigonometry

Napier's Rules of Circular Parts

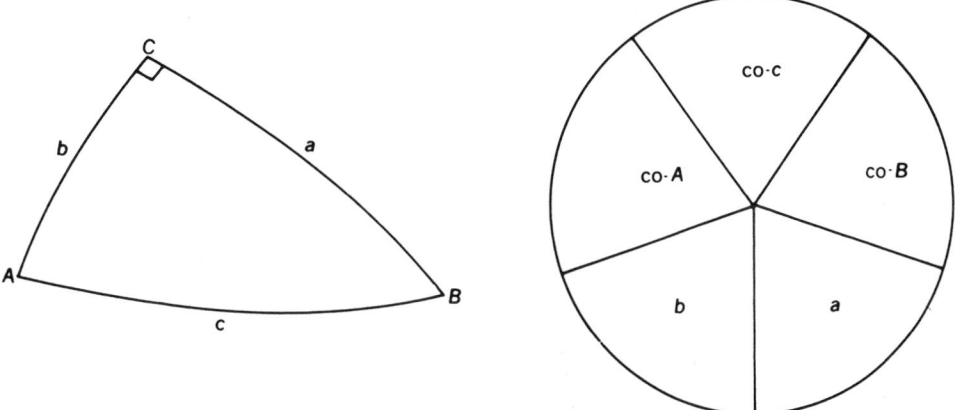

Arrange the five quantities a, b, co-A (complement of A), co-c, co-B of a right spherical triangle right-angled at C in cyclic order as pictured. If any one of these quantities is designated a *middle* part, then two of the other parts are *adjacent* to it, and the remaining two parts are *opposite* to it. The above formulas for a right spherical triangle may be recalled by the following two rules:

(a) The sine of any middle part is equal to the product of the *tangents* of the two *adjacent* parts.

(b) The sine of any middle part is equal to the product of the *cosines* of the two *opposite* parts.

Rules for Determining the Quadrant of a Calculated Part of a Right Spherical Triangle

(a) A leg and the angle opposite it are always of the same quadrant.

(b) If the hypotenuse if less than 90° the legs are of the same quadrant.

(c) If the hypotenuse is greater than 90°, the legs are of unlike quadrants.

Oblique Spherical Triangles

In the following, a, b, c represent the sides of any spherical triangle, A, B, C the corresponding opposite angles, $s = \frac{1}{2}(a + b + c)$, $S = \frac{1}{2}(A + B + C)$, Δ = area of triangle, E = spherical excess of triangle, R = radius of the sphere upon which the triangle lies, and a', b', c', A', B', C' are the corresponding parts of the polar triangle.

$$0° < a + b + c < 360°, \qquad 180° < A + B + C < 540°$$
$$E = A + B + C - 180°, \qquad \Delta = \pi R^2 E / 180$$
$$\tan \tfrac{1}{4}E = \sqrt{\tan \tfrac{s}{2} \tan \tfrac{1}{2}(s - a) \tan \tfrac{1}{2}(s - b) \tan \tfrac{1}{2}(s - c)}$$
$$A = 180° - a', \qquad B = 180° - b', \qquad C = 180° - c'$$
$$a = 180° - A', \qquad b = 180° - B', \qquad c = 180° - C'$$

Law of sines:

$$\frac{\sin a}{\sin A} = \frac{\sin b}{\sin B} = \frac{\sin c}{\sin C}$$

Law of cosines for sides:

$$\cos a = \cos b \cos c + \sin b \sin c \cos A$$
$$\cos b = \cos c \cos a + \sin c \sin a \cos B$$
$$\cos c = \cos a \cos b + \sin a \sin b \cos C$$

TRIGONOMETRY
Formulas for Use in Spherical Trigonometry

Law of cosines for angles:

$$\cos A = -\cos B \cos C + \sin B \sin C \cos a$$
$$\cos B = -\cos C \cos A + \sin C \sin A \cos b$$
$$\cos C = -\cos A \cos B + \sin A \sin B \cos c$$

Law of tangents:

$$\frac{\tan \frac{1}{2}(B - C)}{\tan \frac{1}{2}(B + C)} = \frac{\tan \frac{1}{2}(b - c)}{\tan \frac{1}{2}(b + c)}, \qquad \frac{\tan \frac{1}{2}(C - A)}{\tan \frac{1}{2}(C + A)} = \frac{\tan \frac{1}{2}(c - a)}{\tan \frac{1}{2}(c + a)}$$

$$\frac{\tan \frac{1}{2}(A - B)}{\tan \frac{1}{2}(A + B)} = \frac{\tan \frac{1}{2}(a - b)}{\tan \frac{1}{2}(a + b)}$$

Half-angle formulas:

$$\tan \tfrac{1}{2} A = \frac{k}{\sin(s - a)}, \qquad \tan \tfrac{1}{2} B = \frac{k}{\sin(s - b)}, \qquad \tan \tfrac{1}{2} C = \frac{k}{\sin(s - c)},$$

where

$$k^2 = \frac{\sin(s - a) \sin(s - b) \sin(s - c)}{\sin s} = (\tan r)^2$$

Half-side formulas:

$$\tan \tfrac{1}{2} \alpha = K \cos(S - A), \qquad \tan \tfrac{1}{2} b = K \cos(S - B),$$
$$\tan \tfrac{1}{2} c = K \cos(S - C),$$

where

$$K^2 = \frac{-\cos S}{\cos(S - A) \cos(S - B) \cos(S - C)} = (\tan R)^2$$

Gauss's formulas:

$$\frac{\sin \frac{1}{2}(a - b)}{\sin \frac{1}{2} c} = \frac{\sin \frac{1}{2}(A - B)}{\cos \frac{1}{2} C}, \qquad \frac{\cos \frac{1}{2}(a - b)}{\cos \frac{1}{2} c} = \frac{\sin \frac{1}{2}(A + B)}{\cos \frac{1}{2} C}$$

$$\frac{\sin \frac{1}{2}(a + b)}{\sin \frac{1}{2} c} = \frac{\cos \frac{1}{2}(A - B)}{\sin \frac{1}{2} C}, \qquad \frac{\cos \frac{1}{2}(a + b)}{\cos \frac{1}{2} c} = \frac{\cos \frac{1}{2}(A + B)}{\sin \frac{1}{2} C}$$

Napier's analogies:

$$\frac{\sin \frac{1}{2}(A - B)}{\sin \frac{1}{2}(A + B)} = \frac{\tan \frac{1}{2}(a - b)}{\tan \frac{1}{2} c}, \qquad \frac{\sin \frac{1}{2}(a - b)}{\sin \frac{1}{2}(a + b)} = \frac{\tan \frac{1}{2}(A - B)}{\cot \frac{1}{2} C}$$

$$\frac{\cos \frac{1}{2}(A - B)}{\cos \frac{1}{2}(A + B)} = \frac{\tan \frac{1}{2}(a + b)}{\tan \frac{1}{2} c}, \qquad \frac{\cos \frac{1}{2}(a - b)}{\cos \frac{1}{2}(a + b)} = \frac{\tan \frac{1}{2}(A + B)}{\cot \frac{1}{2} C}$$

Haversine formulas:

$$\operatorname{hav} a = \operatorname{hav}(b - c) + \sin b \sin c \operatorname{hav} A$$

$$\operatorname{hav} A = \frac{\sin(s - b) \sin(s - c)}{\sin b \sin c}$$

$$= \frac{\operatorname{hav} a - \operatorname{hav}(b - c)}{\sin b \sin c}$$

$$= \operatorname{hav}[180° - (B + C)] + \sin B \sin C \operatorname{hav} a$$

Rules for Determining the Quadrant of a Calculated Part of an Oblique Spherical Triangle

(a) If $A > B > C$, then $a > b > c$.

(b) A side (angle) which differs more from 90° than does another side (angle) is in the same quadrant as its opposite angle (side).

(c) Half the sum of any two sides and half the sum of the opposite angles are in the same quadrant.

SUMMARY OF SOLUTION OF OBLIQUE SPHERICAL TRIANGLES

Given	Solution	Check
Three sides	Half-angle formulas.	Law of sines
Three angles	Half-side formulas.	Law of sines
Two sides and included angle	Napier's analogies (to find sum and difference of unknown angles), then law of sines (to find remaining side).	Gauss's formula
Two angles and included side	Napier's analogies (to find sum and difference of unknown sides), then law of sines (to find remaining angle).	Gauss's formula
Two sides and an opposite angle	Law of sines (to find an angle), then Napier's analogies (to find remaining angle and side). Note number of solutions.	Gauss's formula
Two angles and an opposite side	Law of sines (to find a side), then Napier's analogies (to find remaining side and angle). Note number of solutions.	Gauss's formula

TRIGONOMETRY

DEGREES, MINUTES, AND SECONDS TO RADIANS

Units in degrees, minutes *or* seconds	Degrees to Radians	Minutes to Radians	Seconds to Radians
10	0.174 5329	0.002 9089	0.000 0485
20	0.349 0659	0.005 8178	0.000 0970
30	0.523 5988	0.008 7266	0.000 1454
40	0.698 1317	0.011 6355	0.000 1939
50	0.872 6646	0.014 5444	0.000 2424
60	1.047 1976	0.017 4533	0.000 2909
70	1.221 7305	(0.020 3622)	(0.000 3394)
80	1.396 2634	(0.023 2711)	(0.000 3879)
90	1.570 7963	(0.026 1799)	(0.000 4363)
100	1.745 3293	....	....
200	3.490 6585	....	....
300	5.235 9878	....	....

where n = 1, 2, 3, 4, etc. n (100°) = n (1.745 3293)

RADIANS TO DEGREES, MINUTES, AND SECONDS

Radians	1.0	0.1	0.01	0.001	0.0001
1	57° 17' 44.8"	5° 43' 46.5"	0° 34' 22.6"	0° 03' 26.3"	0° 00' 20.6"
2	114° 35' 29.6"	11° 27' 33.0"	1° 08' 45.3"	0° 06' 52.5"	0° 00' 41.3"
3	171° 53' 14.4"	17° 11' 19.4"	1° 43' 07.9'	0° 10' 18.8"	0° 01' 01.9"
4	229° 10' 59.2"	22° 55' 05.9"	2° 17' 30.6"	0° 13' 45.1'	0° 01' 22.5"
5	286° 28' 44.0"	28° 38' 52.4"	2° 51' 53.2"	0° 17' 11.3"	0° 01' 43.1"
6	343° 46' 28.8"	34° 22' 38.9"	3° 26' 15.9"	0° 20' 37.6"	0° 02' 03.8"
7	401° 04' 13.6"	40° 06' 25.4"	4° 00' 38.5"	0° 24' 03.9"	0° 02' 24.4"
8	458° 21' 58.4"	45° 50' 11.8"	4° 35' 01.2"	0° 27' 30.1"	0° 02' 45.0"
9	515° 39' 43.3"	51° 33' 58.3"	5° 09' 23.8"	0° 30' 56.4"	0° 03' 05.6"

Example: If 3.214 is desired in degrees, minutes and seconds it is obtained as follows:

$$
\begin{aligned}
3 &= 171° \ 53' \ 14.4" \\
.2 &= \ \ 11° \ 27' \ 33.0" \\
.01 &= \ \ \ \ 0° \ 34' \ 22.6" \\
.004 &= \ \ \ \ 0° \ 13' \ 45.1" \\
\hline
3.214 &= 184° \ \ 8' \ 55.1"
\end{aligned}
$$

MILS—RADIANS—DEGREES

1 mil = 0.00098175 radians = 0.05625° = 3.375' = 202.5"

1000 mils = 0.98175 radians = 56.25°

6400 mils = 360° = 2π radians

1 radian = 1018.6 mils

1° = 17.777778 mils

1' = 0.296296 mils

1" = 0.0049383 mils

DEGREES—RADIANS

1 radian = 57° 17' 44" .80625

		log
1 radian =	57.29577 95131 degrees	1.75812 26324
1 radian =	3437.74677 07849 minutes	3.53627 38828
1 radian =	206264.80625 seconds	5.31442 51332
1 degree =	0.01745 32925 19943 radians	8.24187 73676—10
1 minute =	0.00029 08882 08666 radians	6.46372 61172—10
1 second =	0.00000 48481 36811 radians	4.68557 48668—10

DEGREES—RADIANS

The table gives in radians the angle which is expressed in degrees and minutes at the side and top. Angles expressed to the nearest minute and second can readily be converted to radians by adding to the equivalent of the whole number of degrees the equivalents of the minutes and seconds found on the third page of this table.

°	00'	10	20	30	40	50
0	0.00000	0.00291	0.00582	0.00873	0.01164	0.01454
1	0.01745	0.02036	0.02327	0.02618	0.02909	0.03200
2	0.03491	0.03782	0.04072	0.04363	0.04654	0.04945
3	0.05236	0.05527	0.05818	0.06109	0.06400	0.06690
4	0.06981	0.07272	0.07563	0.07854	0.08145	0.08436
5	0.08727	0.09018	0.09308	0.09599	0.09890	0.10181
6	0.10472	0.10763	0.11054	0.11345	0.11636	0.11926
7	0.12217	0.12508	0.12799	0.13090	0.13381	0.13672
8	0.13963	0.14254	0.14544	0.14835	0.15126	0.15417
9	0.15708	0.15999	0.16290	0.16581	0.16872	0.17162
10	0.17453	0.17744	0.18035	0.18326	0.18617	0.18908
11	0.19199	0.19490	0.19780	0.20071	0.20362	0.20653
12	0.20944	0.21235	0.21526	0.21817	0.22108	0.22398
13	0.22689	0.22980	0.23271	0.23562	0.23853	0.24144
14	0.24435	0.24725	0.25016	0.25307	0.25598	0.25889
15	0.26180	0.26471	0.26762	0.27053	0.27343	0.27634
16	0.27925	0.28216	0.28507	0.28798	0.29089	0.29380
17	0.29671	0.29961	0.30252	0.30543	0.30834	0.31125
18	0.31416	0.31707	0.31998	0.32289	0.32579	0.32870
19	0.33161	0.33452	0.33743	0.34034	0.34325	0.34616
20	0.34907	0.35197	0.35488	0.35779	0.36070	0.36361
21	0.36652	0.36943	0.37234	0.37525	0.37815	0.38106
22	0.38397	0.38688	0.38979	0.39270	0.39561	0.39852
23	0.40143	0.40433	0.40724	0.41015	0.41306	0.41597
24	0.41888	0.42179	0.42470	0.42761	0.43051	0.43342
25	0.43633	0.43924	0.44215	0.44506	0.44797	0.45088
26	0.45379	0.45669	0.45960	0.46251	0.46542	0.46833
27	0.47124	0.47415	0.47706	0.47997	0.48287	0.48578
28	0.48869	0.49160	0.49451	0.49742	0.50033	0.50324
29	0.50615	0.50905	0.51196	0.51487	0.51778	0.52069
30	0.52360	0.52651	0.52942	0.53233	0.53523	0.53814
31	0.54105	0.54396	0.54687	0.54978	0.55269	0.55560
32	0.55851	0.56141	0.56432	0.56723	0.57014	0.57305
33	0.57596	0.57887	0.58178	0.58469	0.58759	0.59050
34	0.59341	0.59632	0.59923	0.60214	0.60505	0.60796
35	0.61087	0.61377	0.61668	0.61959	0.62250	0.62541
36	0.62832	0.63123	0.63414	0.63705	0.63995	0.64286
37	0.64577	0.64868	0.65159	0.65450	0.65741	0.66032
38	0.66323	0.66613	0.66904	0.67195	0.67486	0.67777
39	0.68068	0.68359	0.68650	0.68941	0.69231	0.69522
40	0.69813	0.70104	0.70395	0.70686	0.70977	0.71268
41	0.71558	0.71849	0.72140	0.72431	0.72722	0.73013
42	0.73304	0.73595	0.73886	0.74176	0.74467	0.74758
43	0.75049	0.75340	0.75631	0.75922	0.76213	0.76504
44	0.76794	0.77085	0.77376	0.77667	0.77958	0.78249
45	0.78540	0.78831	0.79122	0.79412	0.79703	0.79994
46	0.80285	0.80576	0.80867	0.81158	0.81449	0.81740
47	0.82030	0.82321	0.82612	0.82903	0.83194	0.83485
48	0.83776	0.84067	0.84358	0.84648	0.84939	0.85230
49	0.85521	0.85812	0.86103	0.86394	0.86685	0.86976

DEGREES—RADIANS (Continued)

°	00′	10	20	30	40	50
50	0.87266	0.87557	0.87848	0.88139	0.88430	0.88721
51	0.89012	0.89303	0.89594	0.89884	0.90175	0.90466
52	0.90757	0.91048	0.91339	0.91630	0.91921	0.92212
53	0.92502	0.92793	0.93084	0.93375	0.93666	0.93957
54	0.94248	0.94539	0.94830	0.95120	0.95411	0.95702
55	0.95993	0.96284	0.96575	0.96866	0.97157	0.97448
56	0.97738	0.98029	0.98320	0.98611	0.98902	0.99193
57	0.99484	0.99775	1.00066	1.00356	1.00647	1.00938
58	1.01229	1.01520	1.01811	1.02102	1.02393	1.02684
59	1.02974	1.03265	1.03556	1.03847	1.04138	1.04429
60	1.04720	1.05011	1.05302	1.05592	1.05883	1.06174
61	1.06465	1.06756	1.07047	1.07338	1.07629	1.07920
62	1.08210	1.08501	1.08792	1.09083	1.09374	1.09665
63	1.09956	1.10247	1.10538	1.10828	1.11119	1.11410
64	1.11701	1.11992	1.12283	1.12574	1.12865	1.13156
65	1.13446	1.13737	1.14028	1.14319	1.14610	1.14901
66	1.15192	1.15483	1.15774	1.16064	1.16355	1.16646
67	1.16937	1.17228	1.17519	1.17810	1.18101	1.18392
68	1.18682	1.18973	1.19264	1.19555	1.19846	1.20137
69	1.20428	1.20719	1.21009	1.21300	1.21591	1.21882
70	1.22173	1.22464	1.22755	1.23046	1.23337	1.23627
71	1.23918	1.24209	1.24500	1.24791	1.25082	1.25373
72	1.25664	1.25955	1.26245	1.26536	1.26827	1.27118
73	1.27409	1.27700	1.27991	1.28282	1.28573	1.28863
74	1.29154	1.29445	1.29736	1.30027	1.30318	1.30609
75	1.30900	1.31191	1.31481	1.31772	1.32063	1.32354
76	1.32645	1.32936	1.33227	1.33518	1.33809	1.34099
77	1.34390	1.34681	1.34972	1.35263	1.35554	1.35845
78	1.36136	1.36427	1.36717	1.37008	1.37299	1.37590
79	1.37881	1.38172	1.38463	1.38754	1.39045	1.39335
80	1.39626	1.39917	1.40208	1.40499	1.40790	1.41081
81	1.41372	1.41663	1.41953	1.42244	1.42535	1.42826
82	1.43117	1.43408	1.43699	1.43990	1.44281	1.44571
83	1.44862	1.45153	1.45444	1.45735	1.46026	1.46317
84	1.46608	1.46899	1.47189	1.47480	1.47771	1.48062
85	1.48353	1.48644	1.48935	1.49226	1.49517	1.49807
86	1.50098	1.50389	1.50680	1.50971	1.51262	1.51553
87	1.51844	1.52135	1.52425	1.52716	1.53007	1.53298
88	1.53589	1.53880	1.54171	1.54462	1.54753	1.55043
89	1.55334	1.55625	1.55916	1.56207	1.56498	1.56789
90	1.57080	1.57371	1.57661	1.57952	1.58243	1.58534
91	1.58825	1.59116	1.59407	1.59698	1.59989	1.60279
92	1.60570	1.60861	1.61152	1.61443	1.61734	1.62025
93	1.62316	1.62607	1.62897	1.63188	1.63479	1.63770
94	1.64061	1.64352	1.64643	1.64934	1.65225	1.65515
95	1.65806	1.66097	1.66388	1.66679	1.66970	1.67261
96	1.67552	1.67842	1.68133	1.68424	1.68715	1.69006
97	1.69297	1.69588	1.69879	1.70170	1.70460	1.70751
98	1.71042	1.71333	1.71624	1.71915	1.72206	1.72497
99	1.72788	1.73078	1.73369	1.73660	1.73951	1.74242
100	1.74533	1.74824	1.75115	1.75406	1.75696	1.75987
101	1.76278	1.76569	1.76860	1.77151	1.77442	1.77733
102	1.78024	1.78314	1.78605	1.78896	1.79187	1.79478
103	1.79769	1.80060	1.80351	1.80642	1.80932	1.81223
104	1.81514	1.81805	1.82096	1.82387	1.82678	1.82969
105	1.83260	1.83550	1.83841	1.84132	1.84423	1.84714
106	1.85005	1.85296	1.85587	1.85878	1.86168	1.86459
107	1.86750	1.87041	1.87332	1.87623	1.87914	1.88205
108	1.88496	1.88786	1.89077	1.89368	1.89659	1.89950
109	1.90241	1.90532	1.90823	1.91114	1.91404	1.91695
110	1.91986	1.92277	1.92568	1.92859	1.93150	1.93441

DEGREES—RADIANS (Continued)

Deg.	Radians	Deg.	Radians	Min.	Radians	Sec.	Radians
90	1.57080	**150**	2.61799	**0**	0.00000	**0**	0.00000
91	1.58825	151	2.63545	1	0.00029	1	0.00000
92	1.60570	152	2.65290	2	0.00058	2	0.00001
93	1.62316	153	2.67035	3	0.00087	3	0.00001
94	1.64061	154	2.68781	4	0.00116	4	0.00002
95	1.65806	**155**	2.70526	**5**	0.00145	**5**	0.00002
96	1.67552	156	2.72271	6	0.00175	6	0.00003
97	1.69297	157	2.74017	7	0.00204	7	0.00003
98	1.71042	158	2.75762	8	0.00233	8	0.00004
99	1.72788	159	2.77507	9	0.00262	9	0.00004
100	1.74533	**160**	2.79253	**10**	0.00291	**10**	0.00005
101	1.76278	161	2.80998	11	0.00320	11	0.00005
102	1.78024	162	2.82743	12	0.00349	12	0.00006
103	1.79769	163	2.84489	13	0.00378	13	0.00006
104	1.81514	164	2.86234	14	0.00407	14	0.00007
105	1.83260	**165**	2.87979	**15**	0.00436	**15**	0.00007
106	1.85005	166	2.89725	16	0.00465	16	0.00008
107	1.86750	167	2.91470	17	0.00495	17	0.00008
108	1.88496	168	2.93215	18	0.00524	18	0.00009
109	1.90241	169	2.94961	19	0.00553	19	0.00009
110	1.91986	**170**	2.96706	**20**	0.00582	**20**	0.00010
111	1.93732	171	2.98451	21	0.00611	21	0.00010
112	1.95477	172	3.00197	22	0.00640	22	0.00011
113	1.97222	173	3.01942	23	0.00669	23	0.00011
114	1.98968	174	3.03687	24	0.00698	24	0.00012
115	2.00713	**175**	3.05433	**25**	0.00727	**25**	0.00012
116	2.02458	176	3.07178	26	0.00756	26	0.00013
117	2.04204	177	3.08923	27	0.00785	27	0.00013
118	2.05949	178	3.10669	28	0.00814	28	0.00014
119	2.07694	179	3.12414	29	0.00844	29	0.00014
120	2.09440	**180**	3.14159	**30**	0.00873	**30**	0.00015
121	2.11185	190	3.31613	31	0.00902	31	0.00015
122	2.12930	200	3.49066	32	0.00931	32	0.00016
123	2.14675	210	3.66519	33	0.00960	33	0.00016
124	2.16421	220	3.83972	34	0.00989	34	0.00016
125	2.18166	**230**	4.01426	**35**	0.01018	**35**	0.00017
126	2.19911	240	4.18879	36	0.01047	36	0.00017
127	2.21657	250	4.36332	37	0.01076	37	0.00018
128	2.23402	260	4.53786	38	0.01105	38	0.00018
129	2.25147	270	4.71239	39	0.01134	39	0.00019
130	2.26893	**280**	4.88692	**40**	0.01164	**40**	0.00019
131	2.28638	290	5.06145	41	0.01193	41	0.00020
132	2.30383	300	5.23599	42	0.01222	42	0.00020
133	2.32129	310	5.41052	43	0.01251	43	0.00021
134	2.33874	320	5.58505	44	0.01280	44	0.00021
135	2.35619	**330**	5.75959	**45**	0.01309	**45**	0.00022
136	2.37365	340	5.93412	46	0.01338	46	0.00022
137	2.39110	350	6.10865	47	0.01367	47	0.00023
138	2.40855	360	6.28319	48	0.01396	48	0.00023
139	2.42601	370	6.45772	49	0.01425	49	0.00024
140	2.44346	**380**	6.63225	**50**	0.01454	**50**	0.00024
141	2.46091	390	6.80678	51	0.01484	51	0.00025
142	2.47837	400	6.98132	52	0.01513	52	0.00025
143	2.49582	410	7.15585	53	0.01542	53	0.00026
144	2.51327	420	7.33038	54	0.01571	54	0.00026
145	2.53073	**430**	7.50492	**55**	0.01600	**55**	0.00027
146	2.54818	440	7.67945	56	0.01629	56	0.00027
147	2.56563	450	7.85398	57	0.01658	57	0.00028
148	2.58309	460	8.02851	58	0.01687	58	0.00028
149	2.60054	470	8.20305	59	0.01716	59	0.00029
150	2.61799	**480**	8.37758	**60**	0.01745	**60**	0.00029

DEGREES AND DECIMAL FRACTIONS TO RADIANS

The table below facilitates conversion of an angle expressed in degrees and decimal fractions into radians. To convert 25.78 into radians, find the equivalents, successively, of 20°, 5°, 0°.7, 0°.08 and add.

Deg.	Radians	Deg.	Radians	Deg.	Radians	Deg.	Radians	Deg.	Radians
10	0.174533	1	0.017453	0.1	0.001745	0.01	0.000175	0.001	0.000017
20	0.349066	2	.034907	.2	.003491	.02	.000349	.002	.000035
30	0.523599	3	.052360	.3	.005236	.03	.000524	.003	.000052
40	0.698132	4	.069813	.4	.006981	.04	.000698	.004	.000070
50	0.872665	5	.087266	.5	.008727	.05	.000873	.005	.000087
60	1.047198	6	.104720	.6	.010472	.06	.001047	.006	.000105
70	1.221730	7	.122173	.7	.012217	.07	.001222	.007	.000122
80	1.396263	8	.139626	.8	.013963	.08	.001396	.008	.000140
90	1.570796	9	.157080	.9	.015708	.09	.001571	.009	.000157

RADIANS TO DEGREES AND DECIMALS

Radians	Degrees	Radians	Degrees	Radians	Degrees	Radians	Degrees
1	57.2958	0.1	5.7296	0.01	0.5730	0.001	0.0573
2	114.5916	.2	11.4592	.02	1.1459	.002	.1146
3	171.8873	.3	17.1887	.03	1.7189	.003	.1719
4	229.1831	.4	22.9183	.04	2.2918	.004	.2292
5	286.4789	.5	28.6479	.05	2.8648	.005	.2865
6	343.7747	.6	34.3775	.06	3.4377	.006	.3438
7	401.0705	.7	40.1070	.07	4.0107	.007	.4011
8	458.3662	.8	45.8366	.08	4.5837	.008	.4584
9	515.6620	.9	51.5662	.09	5.1566	.009	.5157
10	572.9578	1.0	57.2958	.10	5.7296	.010	.5730

RADIANS—DEGREES

Multiples and Fractions of π Radians in Degrees

Radians	Radians	Deg.	Radians	Radians	Deg.	Radians	Radians	Deg.
π	3.1416	180	$\pi/2$	1.5708	90	$2\pi/3$	2.0944	120
2π	6.2832	360	$\pi/3$	1.0472	60	$3\pi/4$	2.3562	135
3π	9.4248	540	$\pi/4$	0.7854	45	$5\pi/6$	2.6180	150
4π	12.5664	720	$\pi/5$	0.6283	36	$7\pi/6$	3.6652	210
5π	15.7080	900	$\pi/6$	0.5236	30	$5\pi/4$	3.9270	225
6π	18.8496	1080	$\pi/7$	0.4488	25.714	$4\pi/3$	4.1888	240
7π	21.9911	1260	$\pi/8$	0.3927	22.5	$3\pi/2$	4.7124	270
8π	25.1327	1440	$\pi/9$	0.3491	20	$5\pi/3$	5.2360	300
9π	28.2743	1620	$\pi/10$	0.3142	18	$7\pi/4$	5.4978	315
10π	31.4159	1800	$\pi/12$	0.2618	15	$11\pi/6$	5.7596	330

CONVERSION OF ANGLES FROM ARC TO TIME

Arc	Time	Arc	Time	Arc	Time	Arc	Time
°	h m	°	h m	″	s	″	s
′	m s	′	m s				
0	0 00	20	1 20	0	0.00	8	0.53
1	0 04	30	2 00	1	0.07	9	0.60
2	0 08	40	2 40	2	0.13	10	0.67
3	0 12	50	3 20	3	0.20	20	1.33
4	0 16	60	4 00	4	0.27	30	2.00
5	0 20	70	4 40	5	0.33	40	2.67
6	0 24	80	5 20	6	0.40	50	3.33
7	0 28	90	6 00	7	0.47	60	4.00
8	0 32	100	6 40				
9	0 36	200	13 20				
10	0 40	300	20 00				

MINUTES AND SECONDS TO DECIMAL PARTS OF A DEGREE

MINUTES AND SECONDS TO DECIMAL PARTS OF A DEG.				DECIMAL PARTS OF A DEGREE TO MINUTES AND SECONDS					
Min.	Degrees	Sec.	Degrees	Deg.	'	"	Deg.	'	"
0	0.00000	**0**	0.00000	**0.00**	0	00	**0.60**	36	
1	.01667	1	.00028	.01	0	36	.61	36	36
2	.03333	2	.00056	.02	1	12	.62	37	12
3	.05	3	.00083	.03	1	48	.63	37	48
4	.06667	4	.00111	.04	2	24	.64	38	24
5	.08333	5	.00139	.05	3		.65	39	
6	.10	6	.00167	.06	3	36	.66	39	36
7	.11667	7	.00194	.07	4	12	.67	40	12
8	.13333	8	.00222	.08	4	48	.68	40	48
9	.15	9	.0025	.09	5	24	.69	41	24
10	0.16667	**10**	0.00278	**0.10**	6		**0.70**	42	
11	.18333	11	.00306	.11	6	36	.71	42	36
12	.20	12	.00333	.12	7	12	.72	43	12
13	.21667	13	.00361	.13	7	48	.73	43	48
14	.23333	14	.00389	.14	8	24	.74	44	24
15	.25	15	.00417	.15	9		.75	45	
16	.26667	16	.00444	.16	9	36	.76	45	36
17	.28333	17	.00472	.17	10	12	.77	46	12
18	.30	18	.005	.18	10	48	.78	46	48
19	.31667	19	.00528	.19	11	24	.79	47	24
20	0.33333	**20**	0.00556	**0.20**	12		**0.80**	48	
21	.35	21	.00583	.21	12	36	.81	48	36
22	.36667	22	.00611	.22	13	12	.82	49	12
23	.38333	23	.00639	.23	13	48	.83	49	48
24	.40	24	.00667	.24	14	24	.84	50	24
25	.41667	25	.00694	.25	15		.85	51	
26	.43333	26	.00722	.26	15	36	.86	51	36
27	.45	27	.0075	.27	16	12	.87	52	12
28	.46667	28	.00778	.28	16	48	.88	52	48
29	.48333	29	.00806	.29	17	24	.89	53	24
30	0.50	**30**	0.00833	**0.30**	18		**0.90**	54	
31	.51667	31	.00861	.31	18	36	.91	54	36
32	.53333	32	.00889	.32	19	12	.92	55	12
33	.55	33	.00917	.33	19	48	.93	55	48
34	.56667	34	.00944	.34	20	24	94	56	24
35	.58333	35	.00972	.35	21		.95	57	
36	.60	36	.01	.36	21	36	.96	57	36
37	.61667	37	.01028	.37	22	12	.97	58	12
38	.63333	38	.01056	.38	22	48	.98	58	48
39	.65	39	.01083	.39	23	24	.99	59	24
40	0.66667	**40**	0.01111	**0.40**	24		**1.00**	60	
41	.68333	41	.01139	.41	24	36			
42	.70	42	.01167	.42	25	12			
43	.71667	43	.01194	.43	25	48			
44	.73333	44	.01222	.44	26	24			
45	.75	45	.0125	.45	27				
46	.76667	46	.01278	.46	27	36			
47	.78333	47	.01306	.47	28	12			
48	.80	48	.01333	.48	28	48			
49	.81667	49	.01361	.49	29	24			
50	0.83333	**50**	0.01389	**0.50**	30				
51	.85	51	.01417	.51	30	36			
52	.86667	52	.01444	.52	31	12			
53	.88333	53	.01472	.53	31	48			
54	.90	54	.015	.54	32	24			
55	.91667	55	.01528	.55	33				
56	.93333	56	.01556	.56	33	36			
57	.95	57	.01583	.57	34	12			
58	.96667	58	.01611	.58	34	48			
59	.98333	59	.01639	.59	35	24			
60	1.00	**60**	0.01667	**0.60**	36				

Deg.	Sec.
0.000	0.0
.001	3.6
.002	7.2
.003	10.8
.004	14.4
.005	18.
.006	21.6
.007	25.2
.008	28.8
.009	32.4
0.010	36.

TRIGONOMETRY
NATURAL TRIGONOMETRIC FUNCTIONS TO FIVE PLACES

For degrees indicated at the top of the page use the top column headings. For degrees indicated at the bottom use the column indications at the bottom. With degrees at the left of each block (top or bottom), use the minute column at the left;with degrees at the right of each block, use the minute column at the right. Appropriate signs for the functions must be supplied in accordance with the quadrant in which the angle measure belongs. Linear interpolation may be used except in regions where the functions are rapidly changing. See "Use of Logarithm Tables" for further discussion in interpolation practice.

0° (180°)   (359)° 179°

′	Sin	Tan	Cot	Cos	Sec	Csc	′
0	.00000	.00000	————	1.0000	1.0000		60
1	.00029	.00029	3437.7	1.0000	1.0000	3437.7	59
2	.00058	.00058	1718.9	1.0000	1.0000	1718.9	58
3	.00087	.00087	1145.9	1.0000	1.0000	1145.9	57
4	.00116	.00116	859.44	1.0000	1.0000	859.44	56
5	.00145	.00145	687.55	1.0000	1.0000	687.55	55
6	.00175	.00175	572.96	1.0000	1.0000	572.96	54
7	.00204	.00204	491.11	1.0000	1.0000	491.11	53
8	.00233	.00233	429.72	1.0000	1.0000	429.72	52
9	.00262	.00262	381.97	1.0000	1.0000	381.97	51
10	.00291	.00291	343.77	1.0000	1.0000	343.78	50
11	.00320	.00320	312.52	.99999	1.0000	312.52	49
12	.00349	.00349	286.48	.99999	1.0000	286.48	48
13	.00378	.00378	264.44	.99999	1.0000	264.44	47
14	.00407	.00407	245.55	.99999	1.0000	245.55	46
15	.00436	.00436	229.18	.99999	1.0000	229.18	45
16	.00465	.00465	214.86	.99999	1.0000	214.86	44
17	.00495	.00495	202.22	.99999	1.0000	202.22	43
18	.00524	.00524	190.98	.99999	1.0000	190.99	42
19	.00553	.00553	180.93	.99998	1.0000	180.93	41
20	.00582	.00582	171.89	.99998	1.0000	171.89	40
21	.00611	.00611	163.70	.99998	1.0000	163.70	39
22	.00640	.00640	156.26	.99998	1.0000	156.26	38
23	.00669	.00669	149.47	.99998	1.0000	149.47	37
24	.00698	.00698	143.24	.99998	1.0000	143.24	36
25	.00727	.00727	137.51	.99997	1.0000	137.51	35
26	.00756	.00756	132.22	.99997	1.0000	132.22	34
27	.00785	.00785	127.32	.99997	1.0000	127.33	33
28	.00814	.00815	122.77	.99997	1.0000	122.78	32
29	.00844	.00844	118.54	.99996	1.0000	118.54	31
30	.00873	.00873	114.59	.99996	1.0000	114.59	30
31	.00902	.00902	110.89	.99996	1.0000	110.90	29
32	.00931	.00931	107.43	.99996	1.0000	107.43	28
33	.00960	.00960	104.17	.99995	1.0000	104.18	27
34	.00989	.00989	101.11	.99995	1.0000	101.11	26
35	.01018	.01018	98.218	.99995	1.0001	98.223	25
36	.01047	.01047	95.489	.99995	1.0001	95.495	24
37	.01076	.01076	92.908	.99994	1.0001	92.914	23
38	.01105	.01105	90.463	.99994	1.0001	90.469	22
39	.01134	.01135	88.144	.99994	1.0001	88.149	21
40	.01164	.01164	85.940	.99993	1.0001	85.946	20
41	.01193	.01193	83.844	.99993	1.0001	83.849	19
42	.01222	.01222	81.847	.99993	1.0001	81.853	18
43	.01251	.01251	79.943	.99992	1.0001	79.950	17
44	.01280	.01280	78.126	.99992	1.0001	78.133	16
45	.01309	.01309	76.390	.99991	1.0001	76.397	15
46	.01338	.01338	74.729	.99991	1.0001	74.736	14
47	.01367	.01367	73.139	.99991	1.0001	73.146	13
48	.01396	.01396	71.615	.99990	1.0001	71.622	12
49	.01425	.01425	70.153	.99990	1.0001	70.160	11
50	.01454	.01455	68.750	.99989	1.0001	68.757	10
51	.01483	.01484	67.402	.99989	1.0001	67.409	9
52	.01513	.01513	66.105	.99989	1.0001	66.113	8
53	.01542	.01542	64.858	.99988	1.0001	64.866	7
54	.01571	.01571	63.657	.99988	1.0001	63.665	6
55	.01600	.01600	62.499	.99987	1.0001	62.507	5
56	.01629	.01629	61.383	.99987	1.0001	61.391	4
57	.01658	.01658	60.306	.99986	1.0001	60.314	3
58	.01687	.01687	59.266	.99986	1.0001	59.274	2
59	.01716	.01716	58.261	.99985	1.0001	58.270	1
60	.01745	.01746	57.290	.99985	1.0002	57.299	0
′	Cos	Cot	Tan	Sin	Csc	Sec	′

1° (181°)   (358°) 17

′	Sin	Tan	Cot	Cos	Sec	Csc	′
0	.01745	.01746	57.290	.99985	1.0002	57.299	60
1	.01774	.01775	56.351	.99984	1.0002	56.359	59
2	.01803	.01804	55.442	.99984	1.0002	55.451	58
3	.01832	.01833	54.561	.99983	1.0002	54.570	57
4	.01862	.01862	53.709	.99983	1.0002	53.718	56
5	.01891	.01891	52.882	.99982	1.0002	52.892	55
6	.01920	.01920	52.081	.99982	1.0002	52.090	54
7	.01949	.01949	51.303	.99981	1.0002	51.313	53
8	.01978	.01978	50.549	.99980	1.0002	50.558	52
9	.02007	.02007	49.816	.99980	1.0002	49.826	51
10	.02036	.02036	49.104	.99979	1.0002	49.114	50
11	.02065	.02066	48.412	.99979	1.0002	48.422	49
12	.02094	.02095	47.740	.99978	1.0002	47.750	48
13	.02123	.02124	47.085	.99977	1.0002	47.096	47
14	.02152	.02153	46.449	.99977	1.0002	46.460	46
15	.02181	.02182	45.829	.99976	1.0002	45.840	45
16	.02211	.02211	45.226	.99976	1.0002	45.237	44
17	.02240	.02240	44.639	.99975	1.0003	44.650	43
18	.02269	.02269	44.066	.99974	1.0003	44.077	42
19	.02298	.02298	43.508	.99974	1.0003	43.520	41
20	.02327	.02328	42.964	.99973	1.0003	42.976	40
21	.02356	.02357	42.433	.99972	1.0003	42.445	39
22	.02385	.02386	41.916	.99972	1.0003	41.928	38
23	.02414	.02415	41.411	.99971	1.0003	41.423	37
24	.02443	.02444	40.917	.99970	1.0003	40.930	36
25	.02472	.02473	40.436	.99969	1.0003	40.448	35
26	.02501	.02502	39.965	.99969	1.0003	39.978	34
27	.02530	.02531	39.506	.99968	1.0003	39.519	33
28	.02560	.02560	39.057	.99967	1.0003	39.070	32
29	.02589	.02589	38.618	.99966	1.0003	38.631	31
30	.02618	.02619	38.188	.99966	1.0003	38.202	30
31	.02647	.02648	37.769	.99965	1.0004	37.782	29
32	.02676	.02677	37.358	.99964	1.0004	37.371	28
33	.02705	.02706	36.956	.99963	1.0004	36.970	27
34	.02734	.02735	36.563	.99963	1.0004	36.576	26
35	.02763	.02764	36.178	.99962	1.0004	36.191	25
36	.02792	.02793	35.801	.99961	1.0004	35.815	24
37	.02821	.02822	35.431	.99960	1.0004	35.445	23
38	.02850	.02851	35.070	.99959	1.0004	35.084	22
39	.02879	.02881	34.715	.99959	1.0004	34.730	21
40	.02908	.02910	34.368	.99958	1.0004	34.382	20
41	.02938	.02939	34.027	.99957	1.0004	34.042	19
42	.02967	.02968	33.694	.99956	1.0004	33.708	18
43	.02996	.02997	33.366	.99955	1.0004	33.381	17
44	.03025	.03026	33.045	.99954	1.0005	33.060	16
45	.03054	.03055	32.730	.99953	1.0005	32.746	15
46	.03083	.03084	32.421	.99952	1.0005	32.437	14
47	.03112	.03114	32.118	.99952	1.0005	32.134	13
48	.03141	.03143	31.821	.99951	1.0005	31.836	12
49	.03170	.03172	31.528	.99950	1.0005	31.544	11
50	.03199	.03201	31.242	.99949	1.0005	31.258	10
51	.03228	.03230	30.960	.99948	1.0005	30.976	9
52	.03257	.03259	30.683	.99947	1.0005	30.700	8
53	.03286	.03288	30.412	.99946	1.0005	30.428	7
54	.03316	.03317	30.145	.99945	1.0006	30.161	6
55	.03345	.03346	29.882	.99944	1.0006	29.899	5
56	.03374	.03376	29.624	.99943	1.0006	29.641	4
57	.03403	.03405	29.371	.99942	1.0006	29.388	3
58	.03432	.03434	29.122	.99941	1.0006	29.139	2
59	.03461	.03463	28.877	.99940	1.0006	28.894	1
60	.03490	.03492	28.636	.99939	1.0006	28.654	0
′	Cos	Cot	Tan	Sin	Csc	Sec	′

NATURAL TRIGONOMETRIC FUNCTIONS TO FIVE PLACES (continued)

(182°)   (357°) 177°   3° (183°)   (356°) 176°

′	Sin	Tan	Cot	Cos	Sec	Csc	′		′	Sin	Tan	Cot	Cos	Sec	Csc	′
0	.03490	.03492	28.636	.99939	1.0006	28.654	60		0	.05234	.05241	19.081	.99863	1.0014	19.107	60
1	.03519	.03521	28.399	.99938	1.0006	28.417	59		1	.05263	.05270	18.976	.99861	1.0014	19.002	59
2	.03548	.03550	28.166	.99937	1.0006	28.184	58		2	.05292	.05299	18.871	.99860	1.0014	18.898	58
3	.03577	.03579	27.937	.99936	1.0006	27.955	57		3	.05321	.05328	18.768	.99858	1.0014	18.794	57
4	.03606	.03609	27.712	.99935	1.0007	27.730	56		4	.05350	.05357	18.666	.99857	1.0014	18.692	56
5	.03635	.03638	27.490	.99934	1.0007	27.508	55		5	.05379	.05387	18.564	.99855	1.0014	18.591	55
6	.03664	.03667	27.271	.99933	1.0007	27.290	54		6	.05408	.05416	18.464	.99854	1.0015	18.492	54
7	.03693	.03696	27.057	.99932	1.0007	27.075	53		7	.05437	.05445	18.366	.99852	1.0015	18.393	53
8	.03723	.03725	26.845	.99931	1.0007	26.864	52		8	.05466	.05474	18.268	.99851	1.0015	18.295	52
9	.03752	.03754	26.637	.99930	1.0007	26.655	51		9	.05495	.05503	18.171	.99849	1.0015	18.198	51
10	.03781	.03783	26.432	.99929	1.0007	26.451	50		10	.05524	.05533	18.075	.99847	1.0015	18.103	50
11	.03810	.03812	26.230	.99927	1.0007	26.249	49		11	.05553	.05562	17.980	.99846	1.0015	18.008	49
12	.03839	.03842	26.031	.99926	1.0007	26.050	48		12	.05582	.05591	17.886	.99844	1.0016	17.914	48
13	.03868	.03871	25.835	.99925	1.0007	25.854	47		13	.05611	.05620	17.793	.99842	1.0016	17.822	47
14	.03897	.03900	25.642	.99924	1.0008	25.661	46		14	.05640	.05649	17.702	.99841	1.0016	17.730	46
15	.03926	.03929	25.452	.99923	1.0008	25.471	45		15	.05669	.05678	17.611	.99839	1.0016	17.639	45
16	.03955	.03958	25.264	.99922	1.0008	25.284	44		16	.05698	.05708	17.521	.99838	1.0016	17.549	44
17	.03984	.03987	25.080	.99921	1.0008	25.100	43		17	.05727	.05737	17.431	.99836	1.0016	17.460	43
18	.04013	.04016	24.898	.99919	1.0008	24.918	42		18	.05756	.05766	17.343	.99834	1.0017	17.372	42
19	.04042	.04046	24.719	.99918	1.0008	24.739	41		19	.05785	.05795	17.256	.99833	1.0017	17.285	41
20	.04071	.04075	24.542	.99917	1.0008	24.562	40		20	.05814	.05824	17.169	.99831	1.0017	17.198	40
21	.04100	.04104	24.368	.99916	1.0008	24.388	39		21	.05844	.05854	17.084	.99829	1.0017	17.113	39
22	.04129	.04133	24.196	.99915	1.0009	24.216	38		22	.05873	.05883	16.999	.99827	1.0017	17.028	38
23	.04159	.04162	24.026	.99913	1.0009	24.047	37		23	.05902	.05912	16.915	.99826	1.0017	16.945	37
24	.04188	.04191	23.859	.99912	1.0009	23.880	36		24	.05931	.05941	16.832	.99824	1.0018	16.862	36
25	.04217	.04220	23.695	.99911	1.0009	23.716	35		25	.05960	.05970	16.750	.99822	1.0018	16.779	35
26	.04246	.04250	23.532	.99910	1.0009	23.553	34		26	.05989	.05999	16.668	.99821	1.0018	16.698	34
27	.04275	.04279	23.372	.99909	1.0009	23.393	33		27	.06018	.06029	16.587	.99819	1.0018	16.618	33
28	.04304	.04308	23.214	.99907	1.0009	23.235	32		28	.06047	.06058	16.507	.99817	1.0018	16.538	32
29	.04333	.04337	23.058	.99906	1.0009	23.079	31		29	.06076	.06087	16.428	.99815	1.0019	16.459	31
30	.04362	.04366	22.904	.99905	1.0010	22.926	30		30	.06105	.06116	16.350	.99813	1.0019	16.380	30
31	.04391	.04395	22.752	.99904	1.0010	22.774	29		31	.06134	.06145	16.272	.99812	1.0019	16.303	29
32	.04420	.04424	22.602	.99902	1.0010	22.624	28		32	.06163	.06175	16.195	.99810	1.0019	16.226	28
33	.04449	.04454	22.454	.99901	1.0010	22.476	27		33	.06192	.06204	16.119	.99808	1.0019	16.150	27
34	.04478	.04483	22.308	.99900	1.0010	22.330	26		34	.06221	.06233	16.043	.99806	1.0019	16.075	26
35	.04507	.04512	22.164	.99898	1.0010	22.187	25		35	.06250	.06262	15.969	.99804	1.0020	16.000	25
36	.04536	.04541	22.022	.99897	1.0010	22.044	24		36	.06279	.06291	15.895	.99803	1.0020	15.926	24
37	.04565	.04570	21.881	.99896	1.0010	21.904	23		37	.06308	.06321	15.821	.99801	1.0020	15.853	23
38	.04594	.04599	21.743	.99894	1.0011	21.766	22		38	.06337	.06350	15.748	.99799	1.0020	15.780	22
39	.04623	.04628	21.606	.99893	1.0011	21.629	21		39	.06366	.06379	15.676	.99797	1.0020	15.708	21
40	.04653	.04658	21.470	.99892	1.0011	21.494	20		40	.06395	.06408	15.605	.99795	1.0021	15.637	20
41	.04682	.04687	21.337	.99890	1.0011	21.360	19		41	.06424	.06438	15.534	.99793	1.0021	15.566	19
42	.04711	.04716	21.205	.99889	1.0011	21.229	18		42	.06453	.06467	15.464	.99792	1.0021	15.496	18
43	.04740	.04745	21.075	.99888	1.0011	21.098	17		43	.06482	.06496	15.394	.99790	1.0021	15.427	17
44	.04769	.04774	20.946	.99886	1.0011	20.970	16		44	.06511	.06525	15.325	.99788	1.0021	15.358	16
45	.04798	.04803	20.819	.99885	1.0012	20.843	15		45	.06540	.06554	15.257	.99786	1.0021	15.290	15
46	.04827	.04833	20.693	.99883	1.0012	20.717	14		46	.06569	.06584	15.189	.99784	1.0022	15.222	14
47	.04856	.04862	20.569	.99882	1.0012	20.593	13		47	.06598	.06613	15.122	.99782	1.0022	15.155	13
48	.04885	.04891	20.446	.99881	1.0012	20.471	12		48	.06627	.06642	15.056	.99780	1.0022	15.089	12
49	.04914	.04920	20.325	.99879	1.0012	20.350	11		49	.06656	.06671	14.990	.99778	1.0022	15.023	11
50	.04943	.04949	20.206	.99878	1.0012	20.230	10		50	.06685	.06700	14.924	.99776	1.0022	14.958	10
51	.04972	.04978	20.087	.99876	1.0012	20.112	9		51	.06714	.06730	14.860	.99774	1.0023	14.893	9
52	.05001	.05007	19.970	.99875	1.0013	19.995	8		52	.06743	.06759	14.795	.99772	1.0023	14.829	8
53	.05030	.05037	19.855	.99873	1.0013	19.880	7		53	.06773	.06788	14.732	.99770	1.0023	14.766	7
54	.05059	.05066	19.740	.99872	1.0013	19.766	6		54	.06802	.06817	14.669	.99768	1.0023	14.703	6
55	.05088	.05095	19.627	.99870	1.0013	19.653	5		55	.06831	.06847	14.606	.99766	1.0023	14.640	5
56	.05117	.05124	19.516	.99869	1.0013	19.541	4		56	.06860	.06876	14.544	.99764	1.0024	14.578	4
57	.05146	.05153	19.405	.99867	1.0013	19.431	3		57	.06889	.06905	14.482	.99762	1.0024	14.517	3
58	.05175	.05182	19.296	.99866	1.0013	19.322	2		58	.06918	.06934	14.421	.99760	1.0024	14.456	2
59	.05205	.05212	19.188	.99864	1.0014	19.214	1		59	.06947	.06963	14.361	.99758	1.0024	14.395	1
60	.05234	.05241	19.081	.99863	1.0014	19.107	0		60	.06976	.06993	14.301	.99756	1.0024	14.336	0
′	Cos	Cot	Tan	Sin	Csc	Sec	′		′	Cos	Cot	Tan	Sin	Csc	Sec	′

92° (272°)   (267°) 87°   93° (273°)   (266°) 86°

NATURAL TRIGONOMETRIC FUNCTIONS TO FIVE PLACES (continued)

4° (184°) (355°) 175°

′	Sin	Tan	Cot	Cos	Sec	Csc	′
0	.06976	.06993	14.301	.99756	1.0024	14.336	60
1	.07005	.07022	14.241	.99754	1.0025	14.276	59
2	.07034	.07051	14.182	.99752	1.0025	14.217	58
3	.07063	.07080	14.124	.99750	1.0025	14.159	57
4	.07092	.07110	14.065	.99748	1.0025	14.101	56
5	.07121	.07139	14.008	.99746	1.0025	14.044	55
6	.07150	.07168	13.951	.99744	1.0026	13.987	54
7	.07179	.07197	13.894	.99742	1.0026	13.930	53
8	.07208	.07227	13.838	.99740	1.0026	13.874	52
9	.07237	.07256	13.782	.99738	1.0026	13.818	51
10	.07266	.07285	13.727	.99736	1.0027	13.763	50
11	.07295	.07314	13.672	.99734	1.0027	13.708	49
12	.07324	.07344	13.617	.99731	1.0027	13.654	48
13	.07353	.07373	13.563	.99729	1.0027	13.600	47
14	.07382	.07402	13.510	.99727	1.0027	13.547	46
15	.07411	.07431	13.457	.99725	1.0028	13.494	45
16	.07440	.07461	13.404	.99723	1.0028	13.441	44
17	.07469	.07490	13.352	.99721	1.0028	13.389	43
18	.07498	.07519	13.300	.99719	1.0028	13.337	42
19	.07527	.07548	13.248	.99716	1.0028	13.286	41
20	.07556	.07578	13.197	.99714	1.0029	13.235	40
21	.07585	.07607	13.146	.99712	1.0029	13.184	39
22	.07614	.07636	13.096	.99710	1.0029	13.134	38
23	.07643	.07665	13.046	.99708	1.0029	13.084	37
24	.07672	.07695	12.996	.99705	1.0030	13.035	36
25	.07701	.07724	12.947	.99703	1.0030	12.985	35
26	.07730	.07753	12.898	.99701	1.0030	12.937	34
27	.07759	.07782	12.850	.99699	1.0030	12.888	33
28	.07788	.07812	12.801	.99696	1.0030	12.840	32
29	.07817	.07841	12.754	.99694	1.0031	12.793	31
30	.07846	.07870	12.706	.99692	1.0031	12.745	30
31	.07875	.07899	12.659	.99689	1.0031	12.699	29
32	.07904	.07929	12.612	.99687	1.0031	12.652	28
33	.07933	.07958	12.566	.99685	1.0032	12.606	27
34	.07962	.07987	12.520	.99683	1.0032	12.560	26
35	.07991	.08017	12.474	.99680	1.0032	12.514	25
36	.08020	.08046	12.429	.99678	1.0032	12.469	24
37	.08049	.08075	12.384	.99676	1.0033	12.424	23
38	.08078	.08104	12.339	.99673	1.0033	12.379	22
39	.08107	.08134	12.295	.99671	1.0033	12.335	21
40	.08136	.08163	12.251	.99668	1.0033	12.291	20
41	.08165	.08192	12.207	.99666	1.0034	12.248	19
42	.08194	.08221	12.163	.99664	1.0034	12.204	18
43	.08223	.08251	12.120	.99661	1.0034	12.161	17
44	.08252	.08280	12.077	.99659	1.0034	12.119	16
45	.08281	.08309	12.035	.99657	1.0034	12.076	15
46	.08310	.08339	11.992	.99654	1.0035	12.034	14
47	.08339	.08368	11.950	.99652	1.0035	11.992	13
48	.08368	.08397	11.909	.99649	1.0035	11.951	12
49	.08397	.08427	11.867	.99647	1.0035	11.909	11
50	.08426	.08456	11.826	.99644	1.0036	11.868	10
51	.08455	.08485	11.785	.99642	1.0036	11.828	9
52	.08484	.08514	11.745	.99639	1.0036	11.787	8
53	.08513	.08544	11.705	.99637	1.0036	11.747	7
54	.08542	.08573	11.664	.99635	1.0037	11.707	6
55	.08571	.08602	11.625	.99632	1.0037	11.668	5
56	.08600	.08632	11.585	.99630	1.0037	11.628	4
57	.08629	.08661	11.546	.99627	1.0037	11.589	3
58	.08658	.08690	11.507	.99625	1.0038	11.551	2
59	.08687	.08720	11.468	.99622	1.0038	11.512	1
60	.08716	.08749	11.430	.99619	1.0038	11.474	0
′	Cos	Cot	Tan	Sin	Csc	Sec	′

94° (274°) (265°) 85°

5° (185°) (354°) 17°

′	Sin	Tan	Cot	Cos	Sec	Csc	′
0	.08716	.08749	11.430	.99619	1.0038	11.474	60
1	.08745	.08778	11.392	.99617	1.0038	11.436	59
2	.08774	.08807	11.354	.99614	1.0039	11.398	58
3	.08803	.08837	11.316	.99612	1.0039	11.360	57
4	.08831	.08866	11.279	.99609	1.0039	11.323	56
5	.08860	.08895	11.242	.99607	1.0039	11.286	55
6	.08889	.08925	11.205	.99604	1.0040	11.249	54
7	.08918	.08954	11.168	.99602	1.0040	11.213	53
8	.08947	.08983	11.132	.99599	1.0040	11.176	52
9	.08976	.09013	11.095	.99596	1.0041	11.140	51
10	.09005	.09042	11.059	.99594	1.0041	11.105	50
11	.09034	.09071	11.024	.99591	1.0041	11.069	49
12	.09063	.09101	10.988	.99588	1.0041	11.034	48
13	.09092	.09130	10.953	.99586	1.0042	10.998	47
14	.09121	.09159	10.918	.99583	1.0042	10.963	46
15	.09150	.09189	10.883	.99580	1.0042	10.929	45
16	.09179	.09218	10.848	.99578	1.0042	10.894	44
17	.09208	.09247	10.814	.99575	1.0043	10.860	43
18	.09237	.09277	10.780	.99572	1.0043	10.826	42
19	.09266	.09306	10.746	.99570	1.0043	10.792	41
20	.09295	.09335	10.712	.99567	1.0043	10.758	40
21	.09324	.09365	10.678	.99564	1.0044	10.725	39
22	.09353	.09394	10.645	.99562	1.0044	10.692	38
23	.09382	.09423	10.612	.99559	1.0044	10.659	37
24	.09411	.09453	10.579	.99556	1 0045	10.626	36
25	.09440	.09482	10.546	.99553	1.0045	10.593	35
26	.09469	.09511	10.514	.99551	1.0045	10.561	34
27	.09498	.09541	10.481	.99548	1.0045	10.529	33
28	.09527	.09570	10.449	.99545	1.0046	10.497	32
29	.09556	.09600	10.417	.99542	1.0046	10.465	31
30	.09585	.09629	10.385	.99540	1.0046	10.433	30
31	.09614	.09658	10.354	.99537	1.0047	10.402	29
32	.09642	.09688	10.322	.99534	1.0047	10.371	28
33	.09671	.09717	10.291	.99531	1.0047	10.340	27
34	.09700	.09746	10.260	.99528	1.0047	10.309	26
35	.09729	.09776	10.229	.99526	1.0048	10.278	25
36	.09758	.09805	10.199	.99523	1.0048	10.248	24
37	.09787	.09834	10.168	.99520	1.0048	10.217	23
38	.09816	.09864	10.138	.99517	1.0049	10.187	22
39	.09845	.09893	10.108	.99514	1.0049	10.157	21
40	.09874	.09923	10.078	.99511	1.0049	10.128	20
41	.09903	.09952	10.048	.99508	1.0049	10.098	19
42	.09932	.09981	10.019	.99506	1.0050	10.068	18
43	.09961	.10011	9.9893	.99503	1.0050	10.039	17
44	.09990	.10040	9.9601	.99500	1.0050	10.010	16
45	.10019	.10069	9.9310	.99497	1.0051	9.9812	15
46	.10048	.10099	9.9021	.99494	1.0051	9.9525	14
47	.10077	.10128	9.8734	.99491	1.0051	9.9239	13
48	.10106	.10158	9.8448	.99488	1.0051	9.8955	12
49	.10135	.10187	9.8164	.99485	1.0052	9.8672	11
50	.10164	.10216	9.7882	.99482	1.0052	9.8391	10
51	.10192	.10246	9.7601	.99479	1.0052	9.8112	9
52	.10221	.10275	9.7322	.99476	1.0053	9.7834	8
53	.10250	.10305	9.7044	.99473	1.0053	9.7558	7
54	.10279	.10334	9.6768	.99470	1.0053	9.7283	6
55	.10308	.10363	9.6493	.99467	1.0054	9.7010	5
56	.10337	.10393	9.6220	.99464	1.0054	9.6739	4
57	.10366	.10422	9.5949	.99461	1.0054	9.6469	3
58	.10395	.10452	9.5679	.99458	1.0054	9.6200	2
59	.10424	.10481	9.5411	.99455	1.0055	9.5933	1
60	.10453	.10510	9.5144	.99452	1.0055	9.5668	0
′	Cos	Cot	Tan	Sin	Csc	Sec	′

95° (275°) (264°) 84°

NATURAL TRIGONOMETRIC FUNCTIONS TO FIVE PLACES (continued)

186°)   (353°) 173°   7° (187°)   (352°) 172°

'	Sin	Tan	Cot	Cos	Sec	Csc	'
0	.10453	.10510	9.5144	.99452	1.0055	9.5668	60
1	.10482	.10540	9.4878	.99449	1.0055	9.5404	59
2	.10511	.10569	9.4614	.99446	1.0056	9.5141	58
3	.10540	.10599	9.4352	.99443	1.0056	9.4880	57
4	.10569	.10628	9.4090	.99440	1.0056	9.4620	56
5	.10597	.10657	9.3831	.99437	1.0057	9.4362	55
6	.10626	.10687	9.3572	.99434	1.0057	9.4105	54
7	.10655	.10716	9.3315	.99431	1.0057	9.3850	53
8	.10684	.10746	9.3060	.99428	1.0058	9.3596	52
9	.10713	.10775	9.2806	.99424	1.0058	9.3343	51
10	.10742	.10805	9.2553	.99421	1.0058	9.3092	50
11	.10771	.10834	9.2302	.99418	1.0059	9.2842	49
12	.10800	.10863	9.2052	.99415	1.0059	9.2593	48
13	.10829	.10893	9.1803	.99412	1.0059	9.2346	47
14	.10858	.10922	9.1555	.99409	1.0059	9.2100	46
15	.10887	.10952	9.1309	.99406	1.0060	9.1855	45
16	.10916	.10981	9.1065	.99402	1.0060	9.1612	44
17	.10945	.11011	9.0821	.99399	1.0060	9.1370	43
18	.10973	.11040	9.0579	.99396	1.0061	9.1129	42
19	.11002	.11070	9.0338	.99393	1.0061	9.0890	41
20	.11031	.11099	9.0098	.99390	1.0061	9.0652	40
21	.11060	.11128	8.9860	.99386	1.0062	9.0415	39
22	.11089	.11158	8.9623	.99383	1.0062	9.0179	38
23	.11118	.11187	8.9387	.99380	1.0062	8.9944	37
24	.11147	.11217	8.9152	.99377	1.0063	8.9711	36
25	.11176	.11246	8.8919	.99374	1.0063	8.9479	35
26	.11205	.11276	8.8686	.99370	1.0063	8.9248	34
27	.11234	.11305	8.8455	.99367	1.0064	8.9019	33
28	.11263	.11335	8.8225	.99364	1.0064	8.8790	32
29	.11291	.11364	8.7996	.99360	1.0064	8.8563	31
30	.11320	.11394	8.7769	.99357	1.0065	8.8337	30
31	.11349	.11423	8.7542	.99354	1.0065	8.8112	29
32	.11378	.11452	8.7317	.99351	1.0065	8.7888	28
33	.11407	.11482	8.7093	.99347	1.0066	8.7665	27
34	.11436	.11511	8.6870	.99344	1.0066	8.7444	26
35	.11465	.11541	8.6648	.99341	1.0066	8.7223	25
36	.11494	.11570	8.6427	.99337	1.0067	8.7004	24
37	.11523	.11600	8.6208	.99334	1.0067	8.6786	23
38	.11552	.11629	8.5989	.99331	1.0067	8.6569	22
39	.11580	.11659	8.5772	.99327	1.0068	8.6353	21
40	.11609	.11688	8.5555	.99324	1.0068	8.6138	20
41	.11638	.11718	8.5340	.99320	1.0068	8.5924	19
42	.11667	.11747	8.5126	.99317	1.0069	8.5711	18
43	.11696	.11777	8.4913	.99314	1.0069	8.5500	17
44	.11725	.11806	8.4701	.99310	1.0069	8.5289	16
45	.11754	.11836	8.4490	.99307	1.0070	8.5079	15
46	.11783	.11865	8.4280	.99303	1.0070	8.4871	14
47	.11812	.11895	8.4071	.99300	1.0070	8.4663	13
48	.11840	.11924	8.3863	.99297	1.0071	8.4457	12
49	.11869	.11954	8.3656	.99293	1.0071	8.4251	11
50	.11898	.11983	8.3450	.99290	1.0072	8.4047	10
51	.11927	.12013	8.3245	.99286	1.0072	8.3843	9
52	.11956	.12042	8.3041	.99283	1.0072	8.3641	8
53	.11985	.12072	8.2838	.99279	1.0073	8.3439	7
54	.12014	.12101	8.2636	.99276	1.0073	8.3238	6
55	.12043	.12131	8.2434	.99272	1.0073	8.3039	5
56	.12071	.12160	8.2234	.99269	1.0074	8.2840	4
57	.12100	.12190	8.2035	.99265	1.0074	8.2642	3
58	.12129	.12219	8.1837	.99262	1.0074	8.2446	2
59	.12158	.12249	8.1640	.99258	1.0075	8.2250	1
60	.12187	.12278	8.1443	.99255	1.0075	8.2055	0
'	Cos	Cot	Tan	Sin	Csc	Sec	'

5° (276°)   (263°) 83°

'	Sin	Tan	Cot	Cos	Sec	Csc	'
0	.12187	.12278	8.1443	.99255	1.0075	8.2055	60
1	.12216	.12308	8.1248	.99251	1.0075	8.1861	59
2	.12245	.12338	8.1054	.99248	1.0076	8.1668	58
3	.12274	.12367	8.0860	.99244	1.0076	8.1476	57
4	.12302	.12397	8.0667	.99240	1.0077	8.1285	56
5	.12331	.12426	8.0476	.99237	1.0077	8.1095	55
6	.12360	.12456	8.0285	.99233	1.0077	8.0905	54
7	.12389	.12485	8.0095	.99230	1.0078	8.0717	53
8	.12418	.12515	7.9906	.99226	1.0078	8.0529	52
9	.12447	.12544	7.9718	.99222	1.0078	8.0342	51
10	.12476	.12574	7.9530	.99219	1.0079	8.0156	50
11	.12504	.12603	7.9344	.99215	1.0079	7.9971	49
12	.12533	.12633	7.9158	.99211	1.0079	7.9787	48
13	.12562	.12662	7.8973	.99208	1.0080	7.9604	47
14	.12591	.12692	7.8789	.99204	1.0080	7.9422	46
15	.12620	.12722	7.8606	.99200	1.0081	7.9240	45
16	.12649	.12751	7.8424	.99197	1.0081	7.9059	44
17	.12678	.12781	7.8243	.99193	1.0081	7.8879	43
18	.12706	.12810	7.8062	.99189	1.0082	7.8700	42
19	.12735	.12840	7.7882	.99186	1.0082	7.8522	41
20	.12764	.12869	7.7704	.99182	1.0082	7.8344	40
21	.12793	.12899	7.7525	.99178	1.0083	7.8168	39
22	.12822	.12929	7.7348	.99175	1.0083	7.7992	38
23	.12851	.12958	7.7171	.99171	1.0084	7.7817	37
24	.12880	.12988	7.6996	.99167	1.0084	7.7642	36
25	.12908	.13017	7.6821	.99163	1.0084	7.7469	35
26	.12937	.13047	7.6647	.99160	1.0085	7.7296	34
27	.12966	.13076	7.6473	.99156	1.0085	7.7124	33
28	.12995	.13106	7.6301	.99152	1.0086	7.6953	32
29	.13024	.13136	7.6129	.99148	1.0086	7.6783	31
30	.13053	.13165	7.5958	.99144	1.0086	7.6613	30
31	.13081	.13195	7.5787	.99141	1.0087	7.6444	29
32	.13110	.13224	7.5618	.99137	1.0087	7.6276	28
33	.13139	.13254	7.5449	.99133	1.0087	7.6109	27
34	.13168	.13284	7.5281	.99129	1.0088	7.5942	26
35	.13197	.13313	7.5113	.99125	1.0088	7.5776	25
36	.13226	.13343	7.4947	.99122	1.0089	7.5611	24
37	.13254	.13372	7.4781	.99118	1.0089	7.5446	23
38	.13283	.13402	7.4615	.99114	1.0089	7.5282	22
39	.13312	.13432	7.4451	.99110	1.0090	7.5119	21
40	.13341	.13461	7.4287	.99106	1.0090	7.4957	20
41	.13370	.13491	7.4124	.99102	1.0091	7.4795	19
42	.13399	.13521	7.3962	.99098	1.0091	7.4635	18
43	.13427	.13550	7.3800	.99094	1.0091	7.4474	17
44	.13456	.13580	7.3639	.99091	1.0092	7.4315	16
45	.13485	.13609	7.3479	.99087	1.0092	7.4156	15
46	.13514	.13639	7.3319	.99083	1.0093	7.3998	14
47	.13543	.13669	7.3160	.99079	1.0093	7.3840	13
48	.13572	.13698	7.3002	.99075	1.0093	7.3684	12
49	.13600	.13728	7.2844	.99071	1.0094	7.3527	11
50	.13629	.13758	7.2687	.99067	1.0094	7.3372	10
51	.13658	.13787	7.2531	.99063	1.0095	7.3217	9
52	.13687	.13817	7.2375	.99059	1.0095	7.3063	8
53	.13716	.13846	7.2220	.99055	1.0095	7.2909	7
54	.13744	.13876	7.2066	.99051	1.0096	7.2757	6
55	.13773	.13906	7.1912	.99047	1.0096	7.2604	5
56	.13802	.13935	7.1759	.99043	1.0097	7.2453	4
57	.13831	.13965	7.1607	.99039	1.0097	7.2302	3
58	.13860	.13995	7.1455	.99035	1.0097	7.2152	2
59	.13889	.14024	7.1304	.99031	1.0098	7.2002	1
60	.13917	.14054	7.1154	.99027	1.0098	7.1853	0
'	Cos	Cot	Tan	Sin	Csc	Sec	'

97° (277°)   (262°) 82°

NATURAL TRIGONOMETRIC FUNCTIONS TO FIVE PLACES (continued)

8° (188°)   (351°) 171°

′	Sin	Tan	Cot	Cos	Sec	Csc	′
0	.13917	.14054	7.1154	.99027	1.0098	7.1853	60
1	.13946	.14084	7.1004	.99023	1.0099	7.1705	59
2	.13975	.14113	7.0855	.99019	1.0099	7.1557	58
3	.14004	.14143	7.0706	.99015	1.0100	7.1410	57
4	.14033	.14173	7.0558	.99011	1.0100	7.1263	56
5	.14061	.14202	7.0410	.99006	1.0100	7.1117	55
6	.14090	.14232	7.0264	.99002	1.0101	7.0972	54
7	.14119	.14262	7.0117	.98998	1.0101	7.0827	53
8	.14148	.14291	6.9972	.98994	1.0102	7.0683	52
9	.14177	.14321	6.9827	.98990	1.0102	7.0539	51
10	.14205	.14351	6.9682	.98986	1.0102	7.0396	50
11	.14234	.14381	6.9538	.98982	1.0103	7.0254	49
12	.14263	.14410	6.9395	.98978	1.0103	7.0112	48
13	.14292	.14440	6.9252	.98973	1.0104	6.9971	47
14	.14320	.14470	6.9110	.98969	1.0104	6.9830	46
15	.14349	.14499	6.8969	.98965	1.0105	6.9690	45
16	.14378	.14529	6.8828	.98961	1.0105	6.9550	44
17	.14407	.14559	6.8687	.98957	1.0105	6.9411	43
18	.14436	.14588	6.8548	.98953	1.0106	6.9273	42
19	.14464	.14618	6.8408	.98948	1.0106	6.9135	41
20	.14493	.14648	6.8269	.98944	1.0107	6.8998	40
21	.14522	.14678	6.8131	.98940	1.0107	6.8861	39
22	.14551	.14707	6.7994	.98936	1.0108	6.8725	38
23	.14580	.14737	6.7856	.98931	1.0108	6.8589	37
24	.14608	.14767	6.7720	.98927	1.0108	6.8454	36
25	.14637	.14796	6.7584	.98923	1.0109	6.8320	35
26	.14666	.14826	6.7448	.98919	1.0109	6.8186	34
27	.14695	.14856	6.7313	.98914	1.0110	6.8052	33
28	.14723	.14886	6.7179	.98910	1.0110	6.7919	32
29	.14752	.14915	6.7045	.98906	1.0111	6.7787	31
30	.14781	.14945	6.6912	.98902	1.0111	6.7655	30
31	.14810	.14975	6.6779	.98897	1.0112	6.7523	29
32	.14838	.15005	6.6646	.98893	1.0112	6.7392	28
33	.14867	.15034	6.6514	.98889	1.0112	6.7262	27
34	.14896	.15064	6.6383	.98884	1.0113	6.7132	26
35	.14925	.15094	6.6252	.98880	1.0113	6.7003	25
36	.14954	.15124	6.6122	.98876	1.0114	6.6874	24
37	.14982	.15153	6.5992	.98871	1.0114	6.6745	23
38	.15011	.15183	6.5863	.98867	1.0115	6.6618	22
39	.15040	.15213	6.5734	.98863	1.0115	6.6490	21
40	.15069	.15243	6.5606	.98858	1.0116	6.6363	20
41	.15097	.15272	6.5478	.98854	1.0116	6.6237	19
42	.15126	.15302	6.5350	.98849	1.0116	6.6111	18
43	.15155	.15332	6.5223	.98845	1.0117	6.5986	17
44	.15184	.15362	6.5097	.98841	1.0117	6.5861	16
45	.15212	.15391	6.4971	.98836	1.0118	6.5736	15
46	.15241	.15421	6.4846	.98832	1.0118	6.5612	14
47	.15270	.15451	6.4721	.98827	1.0119	6.5489	13
48	.15299	.15481	6.4596	.98823	1.0119	6.5366	12
49	.15327	.15511	6.4472	.98818	1.0120	6.5243	11
50	.15356	.15540	6.4348	.98814	1.0120	6.5121	10
51	.15385	.15570	6.4225	.98809	1.0120	6.4999	9
52	.15414	.15600	6.4103	.98805	1.0121	6.4878	8
53	.15442	.15630	6.3980	.98800	1.0121	6.4757	7
54	.15471	.15660	6.3859	.98796	1.0122	6.4637	6
55	.15500	.15689	6.3737	.98791	1.0122	6.4517	5
56	.15529	.15719	6.3617	.98787	1.0123	6.4398	4
57	.15557	.15749	6.3496	.98782	1.0123	6.4279	3
58	.15586	.15779	6.3376	.98778	1.0124	6.4160	2
59	.15615	.15809	6.3257	.98773	1.0124	6.4042	1
60	.15643	.15838	6.3138	.98769	1.0125	6.3925	0
′	Cos	Cot	Tan	Sin	Csc	Sec	′

9° (189°)   (350°) 1

′	Sin	Tan	Cot	Cos	Sec	Csc	
0	.15643	.15838	6.3138	.98769	1.0125	6.3925	6
1	.15672	.15868	6.3019	.98764	1.0125	6.3807	5
2	.15701	.15898	6.2901	.98760	1.0126	6.3691	5
3	.15730	.15928	6.2783	.98755	1.0126	6.3574	5
4	.15758	.15958	6.2666	.98751	1.0127	6.3458	5
5	.15787	.15988	6.2549	.98746	1.0127	6.3343	5
6	.15816	.16017	6.2432	.98741	1.0127	6.3228	5
7	.15845	.16047	6.2316	.98737	1.0128	6.3113	5
8	.15873	.16077	6.2200	.98732	1.0128	6.2999	5
9	.15902	.16107	6.2085	.98728	1.0129	6.2885	5
10	.15931	.16137	6.1970	.98723	1.0129	6.2772	5
11	.15959	.16167	6.1856	.98718	1.0130	6.2659	4
12	.15988	.16196	6.1742	.98714	1.0130	6.2546	4
13	.16017	.16226	6.1628	.98709	1.0131	6.2434	4
14	.16046	.16256	6.1515	.98704	1.0131	6.2323	4
15	.16074	.16286	6.1402	.98700	1.0132	6.2211	4
16	.16103	.16316	6.1290	.98695	1.0132	6.2100	4
17	.16132	.16346	6.1178	.98690	1.0133	6.1990	4
18	.16160	.16376	6.1066	.98686	1.0133	6.1880	4
19	.16189	.16405	6.0955	.98681	1.0134	6.1770	4
20	.16218	.16435	6.0844	.98676	1.0134	6.1661	4
21	.16246	.16465	6.0734	.98671	1.0135	6.1552	3
22	.16275	.16495	6.0624	.98667	1.0135	6.1443	3
23	.16304	.16525	6.0514	.98662	1.0136	6.1335	3
24	.16333	.16555	6.0405	.98657	1.0136	6.1227	3
25	.16361	.16585	6.0296	.98652	1.0137	6.1120	3
26	.16390	.16615	6.0188	.98648	1.0137	6.1013	3
27	.16419	.16645	6.0080	.98643	1.0138	6.0906	3
28	.16447	.16674	5.9972	.98638	1.0138	6.0800	3
29	.16476	.16704	5.9865	.98633	1.0139	6.0694	3
30	.16505	.16734	5.9758	.98629	1.0139	6.0589	3
31	.16533	.16764	5.9651	.98624	1.0140	6.0483	2
32	.16562	.16794	5.9545	.98619	1.0140	6.0379	2
33	.16591	.16824	5.9439	.98614	1.0141	6.0274	2
34	.16620	.16854	5.9333	.98609	1.0141	6.0170	2
35	.16648	.16884	5.9228	.98604	1.0142	6.0067	2
36	.16677	.16914	5.9124	.98600	1.0142	5.9963	2
37	.16706	.16944	5.9019	.98595	1.0143	5.9860	2
38	.16734	.16974	5.8915	.98590	1.0143	5.9758	2
39	.16763	.17004	5.8811	.98585	1.0144	5.9656	2
40	.16792	.17033	5.8708	.98580	1.0144	5.9554	20
41	.16820	.17063	5.8605	.98575	1.0145	5.9452	19
42	.16849	.17093	5.8502	.98570	1.0145	5.9351	18
43	.16878	.17123	5.8400	.98565	1.0146	5.9250	17
44	.16906	.17153	5.8298	.98561	1.0146	5.9150	16
45	.16935	.17183	5.8197	.98556	1.0147	5.9049	15
46	.16964	.17213	5.8095	.98551	1.0147	5.8950	14
47	.16992	.17243	5.7994	.98546	1.0148	5.8850	13
48	.17021	.17273	5.7894	.98541	1.0148	5.8751	12
49	.17050	.17303	5.7794	.98536	1.0149	5.8652	11
50	.17078	.17333	5.7694	.98531	1.0149	5.8554	10
51	.17107	.17363	5.7594	.98526	1.0150	5.8456	9
52	.17136	.17393	5.7495	.98521	1.0150	5.8358	8
53	.17164	.17423	5.7396	.98516	1.0151	5.8261	7
54	.17193	.17453	5.7297	.98511	1.0151	5.8164	6
55	.17222	.17483	5.7199	.98506	1.0152	5.8067	5
56	.17250	.17513	5.7101	.98501	1.0152	5.7970	4
57	.17279	.17543	5.7004	.98496	1.0153	5.7874	3
58	.17308	.17573	5.6906	.98491	1.0153	5.7778	2
59	.17336	.17603	5.6809	.98486	1.0154	5.7683	1
60	.17365	.17633	5.6713	.98481	1.0154	5.7588	0
′	Cos	Cot	Tan	Sin	Csc	Sec	′

NATURAL TRIGONOMETRIC FUNCTIONS TO FIVE PLACES (continued)

(190°)   (349°) **169°**   **11°** (191°)   (348°) **168°**

	Sin	Tan	Cot	Cos	Sec	Csc	′		′	Sin	Tan	Cot	Cos	Sec	Csc	′
	.17365	.17633	5.6713	.98481	1.0154	5.7588	**60**		0	.19081	.19438	5.1446	.98163	1.0187	5.2408	**60**
	.17393	.17663	5.6617	.98476	1.0155	5.7493	59		1	.19109	.19468	5.1366	.98157	1.0188	5.2330	59
	.17422	.17693	5.6521	.98471	1.0155	5.7398	58		2	.19138	.19498	5.1286	.98152	1.0188	5.2252	58
	.17451	.17723	5.6425	.98466	1.0156	5.7304	57		3	.19167	.19529	5.1207	.98146	1.0189	5.2174	57
	.17479	.17753	5.6329	.98461	1.0156	5.7210	56		4	.19195	.19559	5.1128	.98140	1.0189	5.2097	56
	.17508	.17783	5.6234	.98455	1.0157	5.7117	**55**		5	.19224	.19589	5.1049	.98135	1.0190	5.2019	**55**
	.17537	.17813	5.6140	.98450	1.0157	5.7023	54		6	.19252	.19619	5.0970	.98129	1.0191	5.1942	54
	.17565	.17843	5.6045	.98445	1.0158	5.6930	53		7	.19281	.19649	5.0892	.98124	1.0191	5.1865	53
	.17594	.17873	5.5951	.98440	1.0158	5.6838	52		8	.19309	.19680	5.0814	.98118	1.0192	5.1789	52
	.17623	.17903	5.5857	.98435	1.0159	5.6745	51		9	.19338	.19710	5.0736	.98112	1.0192	5.1712	51
	.17651	.17933	5.5764	.98430	1.0160	5.6653	**50**		10	.19366	.19740	5.0658	.98107	1.0193	5.1636	**50**
	.17680	.17963	5.5671	.98425	1.0160	5.6562	49		11	.19395	.19770	5.0581	.98101	1.0194	5.1560	49
	.17708	.17993	5.5578	.98420	1.0161	5.6470	48		12	.19423	.19801	5.0504	.98096	1.0194	5.1484	48
	.17737	.18023	5.5485	.98414	1.0161	5.6379	47		13	.19452	.19831	5.0427	.98090	1.0195	5.1409	47
	.17766	.18053	5.5393	.98409	1.0162	5.6288	46		14	.19481	.19861	5.0350	.98084	1.0195	5.1333	46
	.17794	.18083	5.5301	.98404	1.0162	5.6198	**45**		15	.19509	.19891	5.0273	.98079	1.0196	5.1258	**45**
	.17823	.18113	5.5209	.98399	1.0163	5.6107	44		16	.19538	.19921	5.0197	.98073	1.0197	5.1183	44
	.17852	.18143	5.5118	.98394	1.0163	5.6017	43		17	.19566	.19952	5.0121	.98067	1.0197	5.1109	43
	.17880	.18173	5.5026	.98389	1.0164	5.5928	42		18	.19595	.19982	5.0045	.98061	1.0198	5.1034	42
	.17909	.18203	5.4936	.98383	1.0164	5.5838	41		19	.19623	.20012	4.9969	.98056	1.0198	5.0960	41
	.17937	.18233	5.4845	.98378	1.0165	5.5749	**40**		20	.19652	.20042	4.9894	.98050	1.0199	5.0886	**40**
	.17966	.18263	5.4755	.98373	1.0165	5.5660	39		21	.19680	.20073	4.9819	.98044	1.0199	5.0813	39
	.17995	.18293	5.4665	.98368	1.0166	5.5572	38		22	.19709	.20103	4.9744	.98039	1.0200	5.0739	38
	.18023	.18323	5.4575	.98362	1.0166	5.5484	37		23	.19737	.20133	4.9669	.98033	1.0201	5.0666	37
	.18052	.18353	5.4486	.98357	1.0167	5.5396	36		24	.19766	.20164	4.9594	.98027	1.0201	5.0593	36
	.18081	.18384	5.4397	.98352	1.0168	5.5308	**35**		25	.19794	.20194	4.9520	.98021	1.0202	5.0520	**35**
	.18109	.18414	5.4308	.98347	1.0168	5.5221	34		26	.19823	.20224	4.9446	.98016	1.0202	5.0447	34
	.18138	.18444	5.4219	.98341	1.0169	5.5134	33		27	.19851	.20254	4.9372	.98010	1.0203	5.0375	33
	.18166	.18474	5.4131	.98336	1.0169	5.5047	32		28	.19880	.20285	4.9298	.98004	1.0204	5.0302	32
	.18195	.18504	5.4043	.98331	1.0170	5.4960	31		29	.19908	.20315	4.9225	.97998	1.0204	5.0230	31
	.18224	.18534	5.3955	.98325	1.0170	5.4874	**30**		30	.19937	.20345	4.9152	.97992	1.0205	5.0159	**30**
	.18252	.18564	5.3868	.98320	1.0171	5.4788	29		31	.19965	.20376	4.9078	.97987	1.0205	5.0087	29
	.18281	.18594	5.3781	.98315	1.0171	5.4702	28		32	.19994	.20406	4.9006	.97981	1.0206	5.0016	28
	.18309	.18624	5.3694	.98310	1.0172	5.4617	27		33	.20022	.20436	4.8933	.97975	1.0207	4.9944	27
	.18338	.18654	5.3607	.98304	1.0173	5.4532	26		34	.20051	.20466	4.8860	.97969	1.0207	4.9873	26
	.18367	.18684	5.3521	.98299	1.0173	5.4447	**25**		35	.20079	.20497	4.8788	.97963	1.0208	4.9803	**25**
	.18395	.18714	5.3435	.98294	1.0174	5.4362	24		36	.20108	.20527	4.8716	.97958	1.0209	4.9732	24
	.18424	.18745	5.3349	.98288	1.0174	5.4278	23		37	.20136	.20557	4.8644	.97952	1.0209	4.9662	23
	.18452	.18775	5.3263	.98283	1.0175	5.4194	22		38	.20165	.20588	4.8573	.97946	1.0210	4.9591	22
	.18481	.18805	5.3178	.98277	1.0175	5.4110	21		39	.20193	.20618	4.8501	.97940	1.0210	4.9521	21
	.18509	.18835	5.3093	.98272	1.0176	5.4026	**20**		40	.20222	.20648	4.8430	.97934	1.0211	4.9452	**20**
	.18538	.18865	5.3008	.98267	1.0176	5.3943	19		41	.20250	.20679	4.8359	.97928	1.0212	4.9382	19
	.18567	.18895	5.2924	.98261	1.0177	5.3860	18		42	.20279	.20709	4.8288	.97922	1.0212	4.9313	18
	.18595	.18925	5.2839	.98256	1.0178	5.3777	17		43	.20307	.20739	4.8218	.97916	1.0213	4.9244	17
	.18624	.18955	5.2755	.98250	1.0178	5.3695	16		44	.20336	.20770	4.8147	.97910	1.0213	4.9175	16
	.18652	.18986	5.2672	.98245	1.0179	5.3612	**15**		45	.20364	.20800	4.8077	.97905	1.0214	4.9106	**15**
	.18681	.19016	5.2588	.98240	1.0179	5.3530	14		46	.20393	.20830	4.8007	.97899	1.0215	4.9037	14
	.18710	.19046	5.2505	.98234	1.0180	5.3449	13		47	.20421	.20861	4.7937	.97893	1.0215	4.8969	13
	.18738	.19076	5.2422	.98229	1.0180	5.3367	12		48	.20450	.20891	4.7867	.97887	1.0216	4.8901	12
	.18767	.19106	5.2339	.98223	1.0181	5.3286	11		49	.20478	.20921	4.7798	.97881	1.0217	4.8833	11
	.18795	.19136	5.2257	.98218	1.0181	5.3205	**10**		50	.20507	.20952	4.7729	.97875	1.0217	4.8765	**10**
	.18824	.19166	5.2174	.98212	1.0182	5.3124	9		51	.20535	.20982	4.7659	.97869	1.0218	4.8697	9
	.18852	.19197	5.2092	.98207	1.0183	5.3044	8		52	.20563	.21013	4.7591	.97863	1.0218	4.8630	8
	.18881	.19227	5.2011	.98201	1.0183	5.2963	7		53	.20592	.21043	4.7522	.97857	1.0219	4.8563	7
	.18910	.19257	5.1929	.98196	1.0184	5.2883	6		54	.20620	.21073	4.7453	.97851	1.0220	4.8496	6
	.18938	.19287	5.1848	.98190	1.0184	5.2804	**5**		55	.20649	.21104	4.7385	.97845	1.0220	4.8429	**5**
	.18967	.19317	5.1767	.98185	1.0185	5.2724	4		56	.20677	.21134	4.7317	.97839	1.0221	4.8362	4
	.18995	.19347	5.1686	.98179	1.0185	5.2645	3		57	.20706	.21164	4.7249	.97833	1.0222	4.8296	3
	.19024	.19378	5.1606	.98174	1.0186	5.2566	2		58	.20734	.21195	4.7181	.97827	1.0222	4.8229	2
	.19052	.19408	5.1526	.98168	1.0187	5.2487	1		59	.20763	.21225	4.7114	.97821	1.0223	4.8163	1
	.19081	.19438	5.1446	.98163	1.0187	5.2408	**0**		60	.20791	.21256	4.7046	.97815	1.0223	4.8097	**0**
	Cos	Cot	Tan	Sin	Csc	Sec	′		′	Cos	Cot	Tan	Sin	Csc	Sec	′

°(280°)   (259°) **79°**   **101°** (281°)   (258°) **78°**

NATURAL TRIGONOMETRIC FUNCTIONS TO FIVE PLACES (continued)

12° (192°)   (347°) 167°

′	Sin	Tan	Cot	Cos	Sec	Csc	′
0	.20791	.21256	4.7046	.97815	1.0223	4.8097	60
1	.20820	.21286	4.6979	.97809	1.0224	4.8032	59
2	.20848	.21316	4.6912	.97803	1.0225	4.7966	58
3	.20877	.21347	4.6845	.97797	1.0225	4.7901	57
4	.20905	.21377	4.6779	.97791	1.0226	4.7836	56
5	.20933	.21408	4.6712	.97784	1.0227	4.7771	55
6	.20962	.21438	4.6646	.97778	1.0227	4.7706	54
7	.20990	.21469	4.6580	.97772	1.0228	4.7641	53
8	.21019	.21499	4.6514	.97766	1.0228	4.7577	52
9	.21047	.21529	4.6448	.97760	1.0229	4.7512	51
10	.21076	.21560	4.6382	.97754	1.0230	4.7448	50
11	.21104	.21590	4.6317	.97748	1.0230	4.7384	49
12	.21132	.21621	4.6252	.97742	1.0231	4.7321	48
13	.21161	.21651	4.6187	.97735	1.0232	4.7257	47
14	.21189	.21682	4.6122	.97729	1.0232	4.7194	46
15	.21218	.21712	4.6057	.97723	1.0233	4.7130	45
16	.21246	.21743	4.5993	.97717	1.0234	4.7067	44
17	.21275	.21773	4.5928	.97711	1.0234	4.7004	43
18	.21303	.21804	4.5864	.97705	1.0235	4.6942	42
19	.21331	.21834	4.5800	.97698	1.0236	4.6879	41
20	.21360	.21864	4.5736	.97692	1.0236	4.6817	40
21	.21388	.21895	4.5673	.97686	1.0237	4.6755	39
22	.21417	.21925	4.5609	.97680	1.0238	4.6693	38
23	.21445	.21956	4.5546	.97673	1.0238	4.6631	37
24	.21474	.21986	4.5483	.97667	1.0239	4.6569	36
25	.21502	.22017	4.5420	.97661	1.0240	4.6507	35
26	.21530	.22047	4.5357	.97655	1.0240	4.6446	34
27	.21559	.22078	4.5294	.97648	1.0241	4.6385	33
28	.21587	.22108	4.5232	.97642	1.0241	4.6324	32
29	.21616	.22139	4.5169	.97636	1.0242	4.6263	31
30	.21644	.22169	4.5107	.97630	1.0243	4.6202	30
31	.21672	.22200	4.5045	.97623	1.0243	4.6142	29
32	.21701	.22231	4.4983	.97617	1.0244	4.6081	28
33	.21729	.22261	4.4922	.97611	1.0245	4.6021	27
34	.21758	.22292	4.4860	.97604	1.0245	4.5961	26
35	.21786	.22322	4.4799	.97598	1.0246	4.5901	25
36	.21814	.22353	4.4737	.97592	1.0247	4.5841	24
37	.21843	.22383	4.4676	.97585	1.0247	4.5782	23
38	.21871	.22414	4.4615	.97579	1.0248	4.5722	22
39	.21899	.22444	4.4555	.97573	1.0249	4.5663	21
40	.21928	.22475	4.4494	.97566	1.0249	4.5604	20
41	.21956	.22505	4.4434	.97560	1.0250	4.5545	19
42	.21985	.22536	4.4373	.97553	1.0251	4.5486	18
43	.22013	.22567	4.4313	.97547	1.0251	4.5428	17
44	.22041	.22597	4.4253	.97541	1.0252	4.5369	16
45	.22070	.22628	4.4194	.97534	1.0253	4.5311	15
46	.22098	.22658	4.4134	.97528	1.0253	4.5253	14
47	.22126	.22689	4.4075	.97521	1.0254	4.5195	13
48	.22155	.22719	4.4015	.97515	1.0255	4.5137	12
49	.22183	.22750	4.3956	.97508	1.0256	4.5079	11
50	.22212	.22781	4.3897	.97502	1.0256	4.5022	10
51	.22240	.22811	4.3838	.97496	1.0257	4.4964	9
52	.22268	.22842	4.3779	.97489	1.0258	4.4907	8
53	.22297	.22872	4.3721	.97483	1.0258	4.4850	7
54	.22325	.22903	4.3662	.97476	1.0259	4.4793	6
55	.22353	.22934	4.3604	.97470	1.0260	4.4736	5
56	.22382	.22964	4.3546	.97463	1.0260	4.4679	4
57	.22410	.22995	4.3488	.97457	1.0261	4.4623	3
58	.22438	.23026	4.3430	.97450	1.0262	4.4566	2
59	.22467	.23056	4.3372	.97444	1.0262	4.4510	1
60	.22495	.23087	4.3315	.97437	1.0263	4.4454	0
′	Cos	Cot	Tan	Sin	Csc	Sec	′

13° (193°)   (346°) 1[66°]

′	Sin	Tan	Cot	Cos	Sec	Csc	′
0	.22495	.23087	4.3315	.97437	1.0263	4.4454	6[0]
1	.22523	.23117	4.3257	.97430	1.0264	4.4398	5[9]
2	.22552	.23148	4.3200	.97424	1.0264	4.4342	5[8]
3	.22580	.23179	4.3143	.97417	1.0265	4.4287	5[7]
4	.22608	.23209	4.3086	.97411	1.0266	4.4231	5[6]
5	.22637	.23240	4.3029	.97404	1.0266	4.4176	5[5]
6	.22665	.23271	4.2972	.97398	1.0267	4.4121	5[4]
7	.22693	.23301	4.2916	.97391	1.0268	4.4066	5[3]
8	.22722	.23332	4.2859	.97384	1.0269	4.4011	5[2]
9	.22750	.23363	4.2803	.97378	1.0269	4.3956	5[1]
10	.22778	.23393	4.2747	.97371	1.0270	4.3901	5[0]
11	.22807	.23424	4.2691	.97365	1.0271	4.3847	4[9]
12	.22835	.23455	4.2635	.97358	1.0271	4.3792	4[8]
13	.22863	.23485	4.2580	.97351	1.0272	4.3738	4[7]
14	.22892	.23516	4.2524	.97345	1.0273	4.3684	4[6]
15	.22920	.23547	4.2468	.97338	1.0273	4.3630	4[5]
16	.22948	.23578	4.2413	.97331	1.0274	4.3576	4[4]
17	.22977	.23608	4.2358	.97325	1.0275	4.3522	4[3]
18	.23005	.23639	4.2303	.97318	1.0276	4.3469	4[2]
19	.23033	.23670	4.2248	.97311	1.0276	4.3415	4[1]
20	.23062	.23700	4.2193	.97304	1.0277	4.3362	4[0]
21	.23090	.23731	4.2139	.97298	1.0278	4.3309	3[9]
22	.23118	.23762	4.2084	.97291	1.0278	4.3256	3[8]
23	.23146	.23793	4.2030	.97284	1.0279	4.3203	3[7]
24	.23175	.23823	4.1976	.97278	1.0280	4.3150	3[6]
25	.23203	.23854	4.1922	.97271	1.0281	4.3098	3[5]
26	.23231	.23885	4.1868	.97264	1.0281	4.3045	3[4]
27	.23260	.23916	4.1814	.97257	1.0282	4.2993	3[3]
28	.23288	.23946	4.1760	.97251	1.0283	4.2941	3[2]
29	.23316	.23977	4.1706	.97244	1.0283	4.2889	3[1]
30	.23345	.24008	4.1653	.97237	1.0284	4.2837	3[0]
31	.23373	.24039	4.1600	.97230	1.0285	4.2785	2[9]
32	.23401	.24069	4.1547	.97223	1.0286	4.2733	2[8]
33	.23429	.24100	4.1493	.97217	1.0286	4.2681	2[7]
34	.23458	.24131	4.1441	.97210	1.0287	4.2630	2[6]
35	.23486	.24162	4.1388	.97203	1.0288	4.2579	2[5]
36	.23514	.24193	4.1335	.97196	1.0288	4.2527	2[4]
37	.23542	.24223	4.1282	.97189	1.0289	4.2476	2[3]
38	.23571	.24254	4.1230	.97182	1.0290	4.2425	2[2]
39	.23599	.24285	4.1178	.97176	1.0291	4.2375	2[1]
40	.23627	.24316	4.1126	.97169	1.0291	4.2324	2[0]
41	.23656	.24347	4.1074	.97162	1.0292	4.2273	1[9]
42	.23684	.24377	4.1022	.97155	1.0293	4.2223	1[8]
43	.23712	.24408	4.0970	.97148	1.0294	4.2173	1[7]
44	.23740	.24439	4.0918	.97141	1.0294	4.2122	1[6]
45	.23769	.24470	4.0867	.97134	1.0295	4.2072	1[5]
46	.23797	.24501	4.0815	.97127	1.0296	4.2022	1[4]
47	.23825	.24532	4.0764	.97120	1.0297	4.1973	1[3]
48	.23853	.24562	4.0713	.97113	1.0297	4.1923	1[2]
49	.23882	.24593	4.0662	.97106	1.0298	4.1873	1[1]
50	.23910	.24624	4.0611	.97100	1.0299	4.1824	1[0]
51	.23938	.24655	4.0560	.97093	1.0299	4.1774	[9]
52	.23966	.24686	4.0509	.97086	1.0300	4.1725	[8]
53	.23995	.24717	4.0459	.97079	1.0301	4.1676	[7]
54	.24023	.24747	4.0408	.97072	1.0302	4.1627	[6]
55	.24051	.24778	4.0358	.97065	1.0302	4.1578	[5]
56	.24079	.24809	4.0308	.97058	1.0303	4.1529	[4]
57	.24108	.24840	4.0257	.97051	1.0304	4.1481	[3]
58	.24136	.24871	4.0207	.97044	1.0305	4.1432	[2]
59	.24164	.24902	4.0158	.97037	1.0305	4.1384	[1]
60	.24192	.24933	4.0108	.97030	1.0306	4.1336	[0]
′	Cos	Cot	Tan	Sin	Csc	Sec	′

NATURAL TRIGONOMETRIC FUNCTIONS TO FIVE PLACES (continued)

14° (194°)   (345°) 165°

'	Sin	Tan	Cot	Cos	Sec	Csc	'
0	.24192	.24933	4.0108	.97030	1.0306	4.1336	60
1	.24220	.24964	4.0058	.97023	1.0307	4.1287	59
2	.24249	.24995	4.0009	.97015	1.0308	4.1239	58
3	.24277	.25026	3.9959	.97008	1.0308	4.1191	57
4	.24305	.25056	3.9910	.97001	1.0309	4.1144	56
5	.24333	.25087	3.9861	.96994	1.0310	4.1096	55
6	.24362	.25118	3.9812	.96987	1.0311	4.1048	54
7	.24390	.25149	3.9763	.96980	1.0311	4.1001	53
8	.24418	.25180	3.9714	.96973	1.0312	4.0954	52
9	.24446	.25211	3.9665	.96966	1.0313	4.0906	51
10	.24474	.25242	3.9617	.96959	1.0314	4.0859	50
11	.24503	.25273	3.9568	.96952	1.0314	4.0812	49
12	.24531	.25304	3.9520	.96945	1.0315	4.0765	48
13	.24559	.25335	3.9471	.96937	1.0316	4.0718	47
14	.24587	.25366	3.9423	.96930	1.0317	4.0672	46
15	.24615	.25397	3.9375	.96923	1.0317	4.0625	45
16	.24644	.25428	3.9327	.96916	1.0318	4.0579	44
17	.24672	.25459	3.9279	.96909	1.0319	4.0532	43
18	.24700	.25490	3.9232	.96902	1.0320	4.0486	42
19	.24728	.25521	3.9184	.96894	1.0321	4.0440	41
20	.24756	.25552	3.9136	.96887	1.0321	4.0394	40
21	.24784	.25583	3.9089	.96880	1.0322	4.0348	39
22	.24813	.25614	3.9042	.96873	1.0323	4.0302	38
23	.24841	.25645	3.8995	.96866	1.0324	4.0256	37
24	.24869	.25676	3.8947	.96858	1.0324	4.0211	36
25	.24897	.25707	3.8900	.96851	1.0325	4.0165	35
26	.24925	.25738	3.8854	.96844	1.0326	4.0120	34
27	.24954	.25769	3.8807	.96837	1.0327	4.0075	33
28	.24982	.25800	3.8760	.96829	1.0327	4.0029	32
29	.25010	.25831	3.8714	.96822	1.0328	3.9984	31
30	.25038	.25862	3.8667	.96815	1.0329	3.9939	30
31	.25066	.25893	3.8621	.96807	1.0330	3.9894	29
32	.25094	.25924	3.8575	.96800	1.0331	3.9850	28
33	.25122	.25955	3.8528	.96793	1.0331	3.9805	27
34	.25151	.25986	3.8482	.96786	1.0332	3.9760	26
35	.25179	.26017	3.8436	.96778	1.0333	3.9716	25
36	.25207	.26048	3.8391	.96771	1.0334	3.9672	24
37	.25235	.26079	3.8345	.96764	1.0334	3.9627	23
38	.25263	.26110	3.8299	.96756	1.0335	3.9583	22
39	.25291	.26141	3.8254	.96749	1.0336	3.9539	21
40	.25320	.26172	3.8208	.96742	1.0337	3.9495	20
41	.25348	.26203	3.8163	.96734	1.0338	3.9451	19
42	.25376	.26235	3.8118	.96727	1.0338	3.9408	18
43	.25404	.26266	3.8073	.96719	1.0339	3.9364	17
44	.25432	.26297	3.8028	.96712	1.0340	3.9320	16
45	.25460	.26328	3.7983	.96705	1.0341	3.9277	15
46	.25488	.26359	3.7938	.96697	1.0342	3.9234	14
47	.25516	.26390	3.7893	.96690	1.0342	3.9190	13
48	.25545	.26421	3.7848	.96682	1.0343	3.9147	12
49	.25573	.26452	3.7804	.96675	1.0344	3.9104	11
50	.25601	.26483	3.7760	.96667	1.0345	3.9061	10
51	.25629	.26515	3.7715	.96660	1.0346	3.9018	9
52	.25657	.26546	3.7671	.96653	1.0346	3.8976	8
53	.25685	.26577	3.7627	.96645	1.0347	3.8933	7
54	.25713	.26608	3.7583	.96638	1.0348	3.8890	6
55	.25741	.26639	3.7539	.96630	1.0349	3.8848	5
56	.25769	.26670	3.7495	.96623	1.0350	3.8806	4
57	.25798	.26701	3.7451	.96615	1.0350	3.8763	3
58	.25826	.26733	3.7408	.96608	1.0351	3.8721	2
59	.25854	.26764	3.7364	.96600	1.0352	3.8679	1
60	.25882	.26795	3.7321	.96593	1.0353	3.8637	0
'	Cos	Cot	Tan	Sin	Csc	Sec	'

15° (195°)   (344°) 164°

'	Sin	Tan	Cot	Cos	Sec	Csc	'
0	.25882	.26795	3.7321	.96593	1.0353	3.8637	60
1	.25910	.26826	3.7277	.96585	1.0354	3.8595	59
2	.25938	.26857	3.7234	.96578	1.0354	3.8553	58
3	.25966	.26888	3.7191	.96570	1.0355	3.8512	57
4	.25994	.26920	3.7148	.96562	1.0356	3.8470	56
5	.26022	.26951	3.7105	.96555	1.0357	3.8428	55
6	.26050	.26982	3.7062	.96547	1.0358	3.8387	54
7	.26079	.27013	3.7019	.96540	1.0358	3.8346	53
8	.26107	.27044	3.6976	.96532	1.0359	3.8304	52
9	.26135	.27076	3.6933	.96524	1.0360	3.8263	51
10	.26163	.27107	3.6891	.96517	1.0361	3.8222	50
11	.26191	.27138	3.6848	.96509	1.0362	3.8181	49
12	.26219	.27169	3.6806	.96502	1.0363	3.8140	48
13	.26247	.27201	3.6764	.96494	1.0363	3.8100	47
14	.26275	.27232	3.6722	.96486	1.0364	3.8059	46
15	.26303	.27263	3.6680	.96479	1.0365	3.8018	45
16	.26331	.27294	3.6638	.96471	1.0366	3.7978	44
17	.26359	.27326	3.6596	.96463	1.0367	3.7937	43
18	.26387	.27357	3.6554	.96456	1.0367	3.7897	42
19	.26415	.27388	3.6512	.96448	1.0368	3.7857	41
20	.26443	.27419	3.6470	.96440	1.0369	3.7817	40
21	.26471	.27451	3.6429	.96433	1.0370	3.7777	39
22	.26500	.27482	3.6387	.96425	1.0371	3.7737	38
23	.26528	.27513	3.6346	.96417	1.0372	3.7697	37
24	.26556	.27545	3.6305	.96410	1.0372	3.7657	36
25	.26584	.27576	3.6264	.96402	1.0373	3.7617	35
26	.26612	.27607	3.6222	.96394	1.0374	3.7577	34
27	.26640	.27638	3.6181	.96386	1.0375	3.7538	33
28	.26668	.27670	3.6140	.96379	1.0376	3.7498	32
29	.26696	.27701	3.6100	.96371	1.0377	3.7459	31
30	.26724	.27732	3.6059	.96363	1.0377	3.7420	30
31	.26752	.27764	3.6018	.96355	1.0378	3.7381	29
32	.26780	.27795	3.5978	.96347	1.0379	3.7341	28
33	.26808	.27826	3.5937	.96340	1.0380	3.7302	27
34	.26836	.27858	3.5897	.96332	1.0381	3.7263	26
35	.26864	.27889	3.5856	.96324	1.0382	3.7225	25
36	.26892	.27921	3.5816	.96316	1.0382	3.7186	24
37	.26920	.27952	3.5776	.96308	1.0383	3.7147	23
38	.26948	.27983	3.5736	.96301	1.0384	3.7108	22
39	.26976	.28015	3.5696	.96293	1.0385	3.7070	21
40	.27004	.28046	3.5656	.96285	1.0386	3.7032	20
41	.27032	.28077	3.5616	.96277	1.0387	3.6993	19
42	.27060	.28109	3.5576	.96269	1.0388	3.6955	18
43	.27088	.28140	3.5536	.96261	1.0388	3.6917	17
44	.27116	.28172	3.5497	.96253	1.0389	3.6879	16
45	.27144	.28203	3.5457	.96246	1.0390	3.6840	15
46	.27172	.28234	3.5418	.96238	1.0391	3.6803	14
47	.27200	.28266	3.5379	.96230	1.0392	3.6765	13
48	.27228	.28297	3.5339	.96222	1.0393	3.6727	12
49	.27256	.28329	3.5300	.96214	1.0394	3.6689	11
50	.27284	.28360	3.5261	.96206	1.0394	3.6652	10
51	.27312	.28391	3.5222	.96198	1.0395	3.6614	9
52	.27340	.28423	3.5183	.96190	1.0396	3.6575	8
53	.27368	.28454	3.5144	.96182	1.0397	3.6539	7
54	.27396	.28486	3.5105	.96174	1.0398	3.6502	6
55	.27424	.28517	3.5067	.96166	1.0399	3.6465	5
56	.27452	.28549	3.5028	.96158	1.0400	3.6427	4
57	.27480	.28580	3.4989	.96150	1.0400	3.6390	3
58	.27508	.28612	3.4951	.96142	1.0401	3.6353	2
59	.27536	.28643	3.4912	.96134	1.0402	3.6316	1
60	.27564	.28675	3.4874	.96126	1.0403	3.6280	0
'	Cos	Cot	Tan	Sin	Csc	Sec	'

NATURAL TRIGONOMETRIC FUNCTIONS TO FIVE PLACES (continued)

16° (196°)　　　　　　　　　　　　　　　　　　　　　　　　　　　　(343°) 163°

′	Sin	Tan	Cot	Cos	Sec	Csc	′
0	.27564	.28675	3.4874	.96126	1.0403	3.6280	60
1	.27592	.28706	3.4836	.96118	1.0404	3.6243	59
2	.27620	.28738	3.4798	.96110	1.0405	3.6206	58
3	.27648	.28769	3.4760	.96102	1.0406	3.6169	57
4	.27676	.28801	3.4722	.96094	1.0406	3.6133	56
5	.27704	.28832	3.4684	.96086	1.0407	3.6097	55
6	.27731	.28864	3.4646	.96078	1.0408	3.6060	54
7	.27759	.28895	3.4608	.96070	1.0409	3.6024	53
8	.27787	.28927	3.4570	.96062	1.0410	3.5988	52
9	.27815	.28958	3.4533	.96054	1.0411	3.5951	51
10	.27843	.28990	3.4495	.96046	1.0412	3.5915	50
11	.27871	.29021	3.4458	.96037	1.0413	3.5879	49
12	.27899	.29053	3.4420	.96029	1.0413	3.5843	48
13	.27927	.29084	3.4383	.96021	1.0414	3.5808	47
14	.27955	.29116	3.4346	.96013	1.0415	3.5772	46
15	.27983	.29147	3.4308	.96005	1.0416	3.5736	45
16	.28011	.29179	3.4271	.95997	1.0417	3.5700	44
17	.28039	.29210	3.4234	.95989	1.0418	3.5665	43
18	.28067	.29242	3.4197	.95981	1.0419	3.5629	42
19	.28095	.29274	3.4160	.95972	1.0420	3.5594	41
20	.28123	.29305	3.4124	.95964	1.0421	3.5559	40
21	.28150	.29337	3.4087	.95956	1.0421	3.5523	39
22	.28178	.29368	3.4050	.95948	1.0422	3.5488	38
23	.28206	.29400	3.4014	.95940	1.0423	3.5453	37
24	.28234	.29432	3.3977	.95931	1.0424	3.5418	36
25	.28262	.29463	3.3941	.95923	1.0425	3.5383	35
26	.28290	.29495	3.3904	.95915	1.0426	3.5348	34
27	.28318	.29526	3.3868	.95907	1.0427	3.5313	33
28	.28346	.29558	3.3832	.95898	1.0428	3.5279	32
29	.28374	.29590	3.3796	.95890	1.0429	3.5244	31
30	.28402	.29621	3.3759	.95882	1.0429	3.5209	30
31	.28429	.29653	3.3723	.95874	1.0430	3.5175	29
32	.28457	.29685	3.3687	.95865	1.0431	3.5140	28
33	.28485	.29716	3.3652	.95857	1.0432	3.5106	27
34	.28513	.29748	3.3616	.95849	1.0433	3.5072	26
35	.28541	.29780	3.3580	.95841	1.0434	3.5037	25
36	.28569	.29811	3.3544	.95832	1.0435	3.5003	24
37	.28597	.29843	3.3509	.95824	1.0436	3.4969	23
38	.28625	.29875	3.3473	.95816	1.0437	3.4935	22
39	.28652	.29906	3.3438	.95807	1.0438	3.4901	21
40	.28680	.29938	3.3402	.95799	1.0439	3.4867	20
41	.28708	.29970	3.3367	.95791	1.0439	3.4833	19
42	.28736	.30001	3.3332	.95782	1.0440	3.4799	18
43	.28764	.30033	3.3297	.95774	1.0441	3.4766	17
44	.28792	.30065	3.3261	.95766	1.0442	3.4732	16
45	.28820	.30097	3.3226	.95757	1.0443	3.4699	15
46	.28847	.30128	3.3191	.95749	1.0444	3.4665	14
47	.28875	.30160	3.3156	.95740	1.0445	3.4632	13
48	.28903	.30192	3.3122	.95732	1.0446	3.4598	12
49	.28931	.30224	3.3087	.95724	1.0447	3.4565	11
50	.28959	.30255	3.3052	.95715	1.0448	3.4532	10
51	.28987	.30287	3.3017	.95707	1.0449	3.4499	9
52	.29015	.30319	3.2983	.95698	1.0450	3.4465	8
53	.29042	.30351	3.2948	.95690	1.0450	3.4432	7
54	.29070	.30382	3.2914	.95681	1.0451	3.4399	6
55	.29098	.30414	3.2879	.95673	1.0452	3.4367	5
56	.29126	.30446	3.2845	.95664	1.0453	3.4334	4
57	.29154	.30478	3.2811	.95656	1.0454	3.4301	3
58	.29182	.30509	3.2777	.95647	1.0455	3.4268	2
59	.29209	.30541	3.2743	.95639	1.0456	3.4236	1
60	.29237	.30573	3.2709	.95630	1.0457	3.4203	0
′	Cos	Cot	Tan	Sin	Csc	Sec	′

17° (197°)　　　　　　　　　　　　　　　　　　　　　　　　　　　　(342°)

′	Sin	Tan	Cot	Cos	Sec	Csc
0	.29237	.30573	3.2709	.95630	1.0457	3.4203
1	.29265	.30605	3.2675	.95622	1.0458	3.4171
2	.29293	.30637	3.2641	.95613	1.0459	3.4138
3	.29321	.30669	3.2607	.95605	1.0460	3.4106
4	.29348	.30700	3.2573	.95596	1.0461	3.4073
5	.29376	.30732	3.2539	.95588	1.0462	3.4041
6	.29404	.30764	3.2506	.95579	1.0463	3.4009
7	.29432	.30796	3.2472	.95571	1.0463	3.3977
8	.29460	.30828	3.2438	.95562	1.0464	3.3945
9	.29487	.30860	3.2405	.95554	1.0465	3.3913
10	.29515	.30891	3.2371	.95545	1.0466	3.3881
11	.29543	.30923	3.2338	.95536	1.0467	3.3849
12	.29571	.30955	3.2305	.95528	1.0468	3.3817
13	.29599	.30987	3.2272	.95519	1.0469	3.3785
14	.29626	.31019	3.2238	.95511	1.0470	3.3754
15	.29654	.31051	3.2205	.95502	1.0471	3.3722
16	.29682	.31083	3.2172	.95493	1.0472	3.3691
17	.29710	.31115	3.2139	.95485	1.0473	3.3659
18	.29737	.31147	3.2106	.95476	1.0474	3.3628
19	.29765	.31178	3.2073	.95467	1.0475	3.3596
20	.29793	.31210	3.2041	.95459	1.0476	3.3565
21	.29821	.31242	3.2008	.95450	1.0477	3.3534
22	.29849	.31274	3.1975	.95441	1.0478	3.3502
23	.29876	.31306	3.1943	.95433	1.0479	3.3471
24	.29904	.31338	3.1910	.95424	1.0480	3.3440
25	.29932	.31370	3.1878	.95415	1.0480	3.3409
26	.29960	.31402	3.1845	.95407	1.0481	3.3378
27	.29987	.31434	3.1813	.95398	1.0482	3.3347
28	.30015	.31466	3.1780	.95389	1.0483	3.3317
29	.30043	.31498	3.1748	.95380	1.0484	3.3286
30	.30071	.31530	3.1716	.95372	1.0485	3.3255
31	.30098	.31562	3.1684	.95363	1.0486	3.3224
32	.30126	.31594	3.1652	.95354	1.0487	3.3194
33	.30154	.31626	3.1620	.95345	1.0488	3.3163
34	.30182	.31658	3.1588	.95337	1.0489	3.3133
35	.30209	.31690	3.1556	.95328	1.0490	3.3102
36	.30237	.31722	3.1524	.95319	1.0491	3.3072
37	.30265	.31754	3.1492	.95310	1.0492	3.3042
38	.30292	.31786	3.1460	.95301	1.0493	3.3012
39	.30320	.31818	3.1429	.95293	1.0494	3.2981
40	.30348	.31850	3.1397	.95284	1.0495	3.2951
41	.30376	.31882	3.1366	.95275	1.0496	3.2921
42	.30403	.31914	3.1334	.95266	1.0497	3.2891
43	.30431	.31946	3.1303	.95257	1.0498	3.2861
44	.30459	.31978	3.1271	.95248	1.0499	3.2831
45	.30486	.32010	3.1240	.95240	1.0500	3.2801
46	.30514	.32042	3.1209	.95231	1.0501	3.2772
47	.30542	.32074	3.1178	.95222	1.0502	3.2742
48	.30570	.32106	3.1146	.95213	1.0503	3.2712
49	.30597	.32139	3.1115	.95204	1.0504	3.2683
50	.30625	.32171	3.1084	.95195	1.0505	3.2653
51	.30653	.32203	3.1053	.95186	1.0506	3.2624
52	.30680	.32235	3.1022	.95177	1.0507	3.2594
53	.30708	.32267	3.0991	.95168	1.0508	3.2565
54	.30736	.32299	3.0961	.95159	1.0509	3.2535
55	.30763	.32331	3.0930	.95150	1.0510	3.2506
56	.30791	.32363	3.0899	.95142	1.0511	3.2477
57	.30819	.32396	3.0868	.95133	1.0512	3.2448
58	.30846	.32428	3.0838	.95124	1.0513	3.2419
59	.30874	.32460	3.0807	.95115	1.0514	3.2390
60	.30902	.32492	3.0777	.95106	1.0515	3.2361
′	Cos	Cot	Tan	Sin	Csc	Sec

NATURAL TRIGONOMETRIC FUNCTIONS TO FIVE PLACES (continued)

(198°)   (341°) 161°   19° (199°)   (340°) 160°

′	Sin	Tan	Cot	Cos	Sec	Csc	′
0	.30902	.32492	3.0777	.95106	1.0515	3.2361	60
1	.30929	.32524	3.0746	.95097	1.0516	3.2332	59
2	.30957	.32556	3.0716	.95088	1.0517	3.2303	58
3	.30985	.32588	3.0686	.95079	1.0518	3.2274	57
4	.31012	.32621	3.0655	.95070	1.0519	3.2245	56
5	.31040	.32653	3.0625	.95061	1.0520	3.2217	55
6	.31068	.32685	3.0595	.95052	1.0521	3.2188	54
7	.31095	.32717	3.0565	.95043	1.0522	3.2159	53
8	.31123	.32749	3.0535	.95033	1.0523	3.2131	52
9	.31151	.32782	3.0505	.95024	1.0524	3.2102	51
10	.31178	.32814	3.0475	.95015	1.0525	3.2074	50
11	.31206	.32846	3.0445	.95006	1.0526	3.2045	49
12	.31233	.32878	3.0415	.94997	1.0527	3.2017	48
13	.31261	.32911	3.0385	.94988	1.0528	3.1989	47
14	.31289	.32943	3.0356	.94979	1.0529	3.1960	46
15	.31316	.32975	3.0326	.94970	1.0530	3.1932	45
16	.31344	.33007	3.0296	.94961	1.0531	3.1904	44
17	.31372	.33040	3.0267	.94952	1.0532	3.1876	43
18	.31399	.33072	3.0237	.94943	1.0533	3.1848	42
19	.31427	.33104	3.0208	.94933	1.0534	3.1820	41
20	.31454	.33136	3.0178	.94924	1.0535	3.1792	40
21	.31482	.33169	3.0149	.94915	1.0536	3.1764	39
22	.31510	.33201	3.0120	.94906	1.0537	3.1736	38
23	.31537	.33233	3.0090	.94897	1.0538	3.1708	37
24	.31565	.33266	3.0061	.94888	1.0539	3.1681	36
25	.31593	.33298	3.0032	.94878	1.0540	3.1653	35
26	.31620	.33330	3.0003	.94869	1.0541	3.1625	34
27	.31648	.33363	2.9974	.94860	1.0542	3.1598	33
28	.31675	.33395	2.9945	.94851	1.0543	3.1570	32
29	.31703	.33427	2.9916	.94842	1.0544	3.1543	31
30	.31730	.33460	2.9887	.94832	1.0545	3.1515	30
31	.31758	.33492	2.9858	.94823	1.0546	3.1488	29
32	.31786	.33524	2.9829	.94814	1.0547	3.1461	28
33	.31813	.33557	2.9800	.94805	1.0548	3.1433	27
34	.31841	.33589	2.9772	.94795	1.0549	3.1406	26
35	.31868	.33621	2.9743	.94786	1.0550	3.1379	25
36	.31896	.33654	2.9714	.94777	1.0551	3.1352	24
37	.31923	.33686	2.9686	.94768	1.0552	3.1325	23
38	.31951	.33718	2.9657	.94758	1.0553	3.1298	22
39	.31979	.33751	2.9629	.94749	1.0554	3.1271	21
40	.32006	.33783	2.9600	.94740	1.0555	3.1244	20
41	.32034	.33816	2.9572	.94730	1.0556	3.1217	19
42	.32061	.33848	2.9544	.94721	1.0557	3.1190	18
43	.32089	.33881	2.9515	.94712	1.0558	3.1163	17
44	.32116	.33913	2.9487	.94702	1.0559	3.1137	16
45	.32144	.33945	2.9459	.94693	1.0560	3.1110	15
46	.32171	.33978	2.9431	.94684	1.0561	3.1083	14
47	.32199	.34010	2.9403	.94674	1.0563	3.1057	13
48	.32227	.34043	2.9375	.94665	1.0564	3.1030	12
49	.32254	.34075	2.9347	.94656	1.0565	3.1004	11
50	.32282	.34108	2.9319	.94646	1.0566	3.0977	10
51	.32309	.34140	2.9291	.94637	1.0567	3.0951	9
52	.32337	.34173	2.9263	.94627	1.0568	3.0925	8
53	.32364	.34205	2.9235	.94618	1.0569	3.0898	7
54	.32392	.34238	2.9208	.94609	1.0570	3.0872	6
55	.32419	.34270	2.9180	.94599	1.0571	3.0846	5
56	.32447	.34303	2.9152	.94590	1.0572	3.0820	4
57	.32474	.34335	2.9125	.94580	1.0573	3.0794	3
58	.32502	.34368	2.9097	.94571	1.0574	3.0768	2
59	.32529	.34400	2.9070	.94561	1.0575	3.0742	1
60	.32557	.34433	2.9042	.94552	1.0576	3.0716	0
′	Cos	Cot	Tan	Sin	Csc	Sec	′

8° (288°)   (251°) 71°

′	Sin	Tan	Cot	Cos	Sec	Csc	′
0	.32557	.34433	2.9042	.94552	1.0576	3.0716	60
1	.32584	.34465	2.9015	.94542	1.0577	3.0690	59
2	.32612	.34498	2.8987	.94533	1.0578	3.0664	58
3	.32639	.34530	2.8960	.94523	1.0579	3.0638	57
4	.32667	.34563	2.8933	.94514	1.0580	3.0612	56
5	.32694	.34596	2.8905	.94504	1.0582	3.0586	55
6	.32722	.34628	2.8878	.94495	1.0583	3.0561	54
7	.32749	.34661	2.8851	.94485	1.0584	3.0535	53
8	.32777	.34693	2.8824	.94476	1.0585	3.0509	52
9	.32804	.34726	2.8797	.94466	1.0586	3.0484	51
10	.32832	.34758	2.8770	.94457	1.0587	3.0458	50
11	.32859	.34791	2.8743	.94447	1.0588	3.0433	49
12	.32887	.34824	2.8716	.94438	1.0589	3.0407	48
13	.32914	.34856	2.8689	.94428	1.0590	3.0382	47
14	.32942	.34889	2.8662	.94418	1.0591	3.0357	46
15	.32969	.34922	2.8636	.94409	1.0592	3.0331	45
16	.32997	.34954	2.8609	.94399	1.0593	3.0306	44
17	.33024	.34987	2.8582	.94390	1.0594	3.0281	43
18	.33051	.35020	2.8556	.94380	1.0595	3.0256	42
19	.33079	.35052	2.8529	.94370	1.0597	3.0231	41
20	.33106	.35085	2.8502	.94361	1.0598	3.0206	40
21	.33134	.35118	2.8476	.94351	1.0599	3.0181	39
22	.33161	.35150	2.8449	.94342	1.0600	3.0156	38
23	.33189	.35183	2.8423	.94332	1.0601	3.0131	37
24	.33216	.35216	2.8397	.94322	1.0602	3.0106	36
25	.33244	.35248	2.8370	.94313	1.0603	3.0081	35
26	.33271	.35281	2.8344	.94303	1.0604	3.0056	34
27	.33298	.35314	2.8318	.94293	1.0605	3.0031	33
28	.33326	.35346	2.8291	.94284	1.0606	3.0007	32
29	.33353	.35379	2.8265	.94274	1.0607	2.9982	31
30	.33381	.35412	2.8239	.94264	1.0608	2.9957	30
31	.33408	.35445	2.8213	.94254	1.0610	2.9933	29
32	.33436	.35477	2.8187	.94245	1.0611	2.9908	28
33	.33463	.35510	2.8161	.94235	1.0612	2.9884	27
34	.33490	.35543	2.8135	.94225	1.0613	2.9859	26
35	.33518	.35576	2.8109	.94215	1.0614	2.9835	25
36	.33545	.35608	2.8083	.94206	1.0615	2.9811	24
37	.33573	.35641	2.8057	.94196	1.0616	2.9786	23
38	.33600	.35674	2.8032	.94186	1.0617	2.9762	22
39	.33627	.35707	2.8006	.94176	1.0618	2.9738	21
40	.33655	.35740	2.7980	.94167	1.0619	2.9713	20
41	.33682	.35772	2.7955	.94157	1.0621	2.9689	19
42	.33710	.35805	2.7929	.94147	1.0622	2.9665	18
43	.33737	.35838	2.7903	.94137	1.0623	2.9641	17
44	.33764	.35871	2.7878	.94127	1.0624	2.9617	16
45	.33792	.35904	2.7852	.94118	1.0625	2.9593	15
46	.33819	.35937	2.7827	.94108	1.0626	2.9569	14
47	.33846	.35969	2.7801	.94098	1.0627	2.9545	13
48	.33874	.36002	2.7776	.94088	1.0628	2.9521	12
49	.33901	.36035	2.7751	.94078	1.0629	2.9498	11
50	.33929	.36068	2.7725	.94068	1.0631	2.9474	10
51	.33956	.36101	2.7700	.94058	1.0632	2.9450	9
52	.33983	.36134	2.7675	.94049	1.0633	2.9426	8
53	.34011	.36167	2.7650	.94039	1.0634	2.9403	7
54	.34038	.36199	2.7625	.94029	1.0635	2.9379	6
55	.34065	.36232	2.7600	.94019	1.0636	2.9355	5
56	.34093	.36265	2.7575	.94009	1.0637	2.9332	4
57	.34120	.36298	2.7550	.93999	1.0638	2.9308	3
58	.34147	.36331	2.7525	.93989	1.0640	2.9285	2
59	.34175	.36364	2.7500	.93979	1.0641	2.9261	1
60	.34202	.36397	2.7475	.93969	1.0642	2.9238	0
′	Cos	Cot	Tan	Sin	Csc	Sec	′

109° (289°)   (250°) 70°

NATURAL TRIGONOMETRIC FUNCTIONS TO FIVE PLACES (continued)

20° (200°) (339°) 159°   **21° (201°)** (338°)

′	Sin	Tan	Cot	Cos	Sec	Csc	′		′	Sin	Tan	Cot	Cos	Sec	Csc
0	.34202	.36397	2.7475	.93969	1.0642	2.9238	60		0	.35837	.38386	2.6051	.93358	1.0711	2.7904
1	.34229	.36430	2.7450	.93959	1.0643	2.9215	59		1	.35864	.38420	2.6028	.93348	1.0713	2.7883
2	.34257	.36463	2.7425	.93949	1.0644	2.9191	58		2	.35891	.38453	2.6006	.93337	1.0714	2.7862
3	.34284	.36496	2.7400	.93939	1.0645	2.9168	57		3	.35918	.38487	2.5983	.93327	1.0715	2.7841
4	.34311	.36529	2.7376	.93929	1.0646	2.9145	56		4	.35945	.38520	2.5961	.93316	1.0716	2.7820
5	.34339	.36562	2.7351	.93919	1.0647	2.9122	55		5	.35973	.38553	2.5938	.93306	1.0717	2.7799
6	.34366	.36595	2.7326	.93909	1.0649	2.9099	54		6	.36000	.38587	2.5916	.93295	1.0719	2.7778
7	.34393	.36628	2.7302	.93899	1.0650	2.9075	53		7	.36027	.38620	2.5893	.93285	1.0720	2.7757
8	.34421	.36661	2.7277	.93889	1.0651	2.9052	52		8	.36054	.38654	2.5871	.93274	1.0721	2.7736
9	.34448	.36694	2.7253	.93879	1.0652	2.9029	51		9	.36081	.38687	2.5848	.93264	1.0722	2.7715
10	.34475	.36727	2.7228	.93869	1.0653	2.9006	50		10	.36108	.38721	2.5826	.93253	1.0723	2.7695
11	.34503	.36760	2.7204	.93859	1.0654	2.8983	49		11	.36135	.38754	2.5804	.93243	1.0725	2.7674
12	.34530	.36793	2.7179	.93849	1.0655	2.8960	48		12	.36162	.38787	2.5782	.93232	1.0726	2.7653
13	.34557	.36826	2.7155	.93839	1.0657	2.8938	47		13	.36190	.38821	2.5759	.93222	1.0727	2.7632
14	.34584	.36859	2.7130	.93829	1.0658	2.8915	46		14	.36217	.38854	2.5737	.93211	1.0728	2.7612
15	.34612	.36892	2.7106	.93819	1.0659	2.8892	45		15	.36244	.38888	2.5715	.93201	1.0730	2.7591
16	.34639	.36925	2.7082	.93809	1.0660	2.8869	44		16	.36271	.38921	2.5693	.93190	1.0731	2.7570
17	.34666	.36958	2.7058	.93799	1.0661	2.8846	43		17	.36298	.38955	2.5671	.93180	1.0732	2.7550
18	.34694	.36991	2.7034	.93789	1.0662	2.8824	42		18	.36325	.38988	2.5649	.93169	1.0733	2.7529
19	.34721	.37024	2.7009	.93779	1.0663	2.8801	41		19	.36352	.39022	2.5627	.93159	1.0734	2.7509
20	.34748	.37057	2.6985	.93769	1.0665	2.8779	40		20	.36379	.39055	2.5605	.93148	1.0736	2.7488
21	.34775	.37090	2.6961	.93759	1.0666	2.8756	39		21	.36406	.39089	2.5583	.93137	1.0737	2.7468
22	.34803	.37123	2.6937	.93748	1.0667	2.8733	38		22	.36434	.39122	2.5561	.93127	1.0738	2.7447
23	.34830	.37157	2.6913	.93738	1.0668	2.8711	37		23	.36461	.39156	2.5539	.93116	1.0739	2.7427
24	.34857	.37190	2.6889	.93728	1.0669	2.8688	36		24	.36488	.39190	2.5517	.93106	1.0740	2.7407
25	.34884	.37223	2.6865	.93718	1.0670	2.8666	35		25	.36515	.39223	2.5495	.93095	1.0742	2.7386
26	.34912	.37256	2.6841	.93708	1.0671	2.8644	34		26	.36542	.39257	2.5473	.93084	1.0743	2.7366
27	.34939	.37289	2.6818	.93698	1.0673	2.8621	33		27	.36569	.39290	2.5452	.93074	1.0744	2.7346
28	.34966	.37322	2.6794	.93688	1.0674	2.8599	32		28	.36596	.39324	2.5430	.93063	1.0745	2.7325
29	.34993	.37355	2.6770	.93677	1.0675	2.8577	31		29	.36623	.39357	2.5408	.93052	1.0747	2.7305
30	.35021	.37388	2.6746	.93667	1.0676	2.8555	30		30	.36650	.39391	2.5386	.93042	1.0748	2.7285
31	.35048	.37422	2.6723	.93657	1.0677	2.8532	29		31	.36677	.39425	2.5365	.93031	1.0749	2.7265
32	.35075	.37455	2.6699	.93647	1.0678	2.8510	28		32	.36704	.39458	2.5343	.93020	1.0750	2.7245
33	.35102	.37488	2.6675	.93637	1.0680	2.8488	27		33	.36731	.39492	2.5322	.93010	1.0752	2.7225
34	.35130	.37521	2.6652	.93626	1.0681	2.8466	26		34	.36758	.39526	2.5300	.92999	1.0753	2.7205
35	.35157	.37554	2.6628	.93616	1.0682	2.8444	25		35	.36785	.39559	2.5279	.92988	1.0754	2.7185
36	.35184	.37588	2.6605	.93606	1.0683	2.8422	24		36	.36812	.39593	2.5257	.92978	1.0755	2.7165
37	.35211	.37621	2.6581	.93596	1.0684	2.8400	23		37	.36839	.39626	2.5236	.92967	1.0757	2.7145
38	.35239	.37654	2.6558	.93585	1.0685	2.8378	22		38	.36867	.39660	2.5214	.92956	1.0758	2.7125
39	.35266	.37687	2.6534	.93575	1.0687	2.8356	21		39	.36894	.39694	2.5193	.92945	1.0759	2.7105
40	.35293	.37720	2.6511	.93565	1.0688	2.8334	20		40	.36921	.39727	2.5172	.92935	1.0760	2.7085
41	.35320	.37754	2.6488	.93555	1.0689	2.8312	19		41	.36948	.39761	2.5150	.92924	1.0761	2.7065
42	.35347	.37787	2.6464	.93544	1.0690	2.8291	18		42	.36975	.39795	2.5129	.92913	1.0763	2.7046
43	.35375	.37820	2.6441	.93534	1.0691	2.8269	17		43	.37002	.39829	2.5108	.92902	1.0764	2.7026
44	.35402	.37853	2.6418	.93524	1.0692	2.8247	16		44	.37029	.39862	2.5086	.92892	1.0765	2.7006
45	.35429	.37887	2.6395	.93514	1.0694	2.8225	15		45	.37056	.39896	2.5065	.92881	1.0766	2.6986
46	.35456	.37920	2.6371	.93503	1.0695	2.8204	14		46	.37083	.39930	2.5044	.92870	1.0768	2.6967
47	.35484	.37953	2.6348	.93493	1.0696	2.8182	13		47	.37110	.39963	2.5023	.92859	1.0769	2.6947
48	.35511	.37986	2.6325	.93483	1.0697	2.8161	12		48	.37137	.39997	2.5002	.92849	1.0770	2.6927
49	.35538	.38020	2.6302	.93472	1.0698	2.8139	11		49	.37164	.40031	2.4981	.92838	1.0771	2.6908
50	.35565	.38053	2.6279	.93462	1.0700	2.8117	10		50	.37191	.40065	2.4960	.92827	1.0773	2.6888
51	.35592	.38086	2.6256	.93452	1.0701	2.8096	9		51	.37218	.40098	2.4939	.92816	1.0774	2.6869
52	.35619	.38120	2.6233	.93441	1.0702	2.8075	8		52	.37245	.40132	2.4918	.92805	1.0775	2.6849
53	.35647	.38153	2.6210	.93431	1.0703	2.8053	7		53	.37272	.40166	2.4897	.92794	1.0777	2.6830
54	.35674	.38186	2.6187	.93420	1.0704	2.8032	6		54	.37299	.40200	2.4876	.92784	1.0778	2.6811
55	.35701	.38220	2.6165	.93410	1.0705	2.8010	5		55	.37326	.40234	2.4855	.92773	1.0779	2.6791
56	.35728	.38253	2.6142	.93400	1.0707	2.7989	4		56	.37353	.40267	2.4834	.92762	1.0780	2.6772
57	.35755	.38286	2.6119	.93389	1.0708	2.7968	3		57	.37380	.40301	2.4813	.92751	1.0782	2.6752
58	.35782	.38320	2.6096	.93379	1.0709	2.7947	2		58	.37407	.40335	2.4792	.92740	1.0783	2.6733
59	.35810	.38353	2.6074	.93368	1.0710	2.7925	1		59	.37434	.40369	2.4772	.92729	1.0784	2.6714
60	.35837	.38386	2.6051	.93358	1.0711	2.7904	0		60	.37461	.40403	2.4751	.92718	1.0785	2.6695
′	Cos	Cot	Tan	Sin	Csc	Sec	′		′	Cos	Cot	Tan	Sin	Csc	Sec

110° (290°) (249°) 69°   **111° (291°)** (248°)

NATURAL TRIGONOMETRIC FUNCTIONS TO FIVE PLACES (continued)

202°)   (337°) 157°   23° (203°)   (336°) 156°

	Sin	Tan	Cot	Cos	Sec	Csc	′
	.37461	.40403	2.4751	.92718	1.0785	2.6695	60
	.37488	.40436	2.4730	.92707	1.0787	2.6675	59
	.37515	.40470	2.4709	.92697	1.0788	2.6656	58
	.37542	.40504	2.4689	.92686	1.0789	2.6637	57
	.37569	.40538	2.4668	.92675	1.0790	2.6618	56
	.37595	.40572	2.4648	.92664	1.0792	2.6599	55
	.37622	.40606	2.4627	.92653	1.0793	2.6580	54
	.37649	.40640	2.4606	.92642	1.0794	2.6561	53
	.37676	.40674	2.4586	.92631	1.0796	2.6542	52
	.37703	.40707	2.4566	.92620	1.0797	2.6523	51
	.37730	.40741	2.4545	.92609	1.0798	2.6504	50
	.37757	.40775	2.4525	.92598	1.0799	2.6485	49
	.37784	.40809	2.4504	.92587	1.0801	2.6466	48
	.37811	.40843	2.4484	.92576	1.0802	2.6447	47
	.37838	.40877	2.4464	.92565	1.0803	2.6429	46
	.37865	.40911	2.4443	.92554	1.0804	2.6410	45
	.37892	.40945	2.4423	.92543	1.0806	2.6391	44
	.37919	.40979	2.4403	.92532	1.0807	2.6372	43
	.37946	.41013	2.4383	.92521	1.0808	2.6354	42
	.37973	.41047	2.4362	.92510	1.0810	2.6335	41
	.37999	.41081	2.4342	.92499	1.0811	2.6316	40
	.38026	.41115	2.4322	.92488	1.0812	2.6298	39
	.38053	.41149	2.4302	.92477	1.0814	2.6279	38
	.38080	.41183	2.4282	.92466	1.0815	2.6260	37
	.38107	.41217	2.4262	.92455	1.0816	2.6242	36
	.38134	.41251	2.4242	.92444	1.0817	2.6223	35
	.38161	.41285	2.4222	.92432	1.0819	2.6205	34
	.38188	.41319	2.4202	.92421	1.0820	2.6186	33
	.38215	.41353	2.4182	.92410	1.0821	2.6168	32
	.38241	.41387	2.4162	.92399	1.0823	2.6150	31
	.38268	.41421	2.4142	.92388	1.0824	2.6131	30
	.38295	.41455	2.4122	.92377	1.0825	2.6113	29
	.38322	.41490	2.4102	.92366	1.0827	2.6095	28
	.38349	.41524	2.4083	.92355	1.0828	2.6076	27
	.38376	.41558	2.4063	.92343	1.0829	2.6058	26
	.38403	.41592	2.4043	.92332	1.0830	2.6040	25
	.38430	.41626	2.4023	.92321	1.0832	2.6022	24
	.38456	.41660	2.4004	.92310	1.0833	2.6003	23
	.38483	.41694	2.3984	.92299	1.0834	2.5985	22
	.38510	.41728	2.3964	.92287	1.0836	2.5967	21
	.38537	.41763	2.3945	.92276	1.0837	2.5949	20
	.38564	.41797	2.3925	.92265	1.0838	2.5931	19
	.38591	.41831	2.3906	.92254	1.0840	2.5913	18
	.38617	.41865	2.3886	.92243	1.0841	2.5895	17
	.38644	.41899	2.3867	.92231	1.0842	2.5877	16
	.38671	.41933	2.3847	.92220	1.0844	2.5859	15
	.38698	.41968	2.3828	.92209	1.0845	2.5841	14
	.38725	.42002	2.3808	.92198	1.0846	2.5823	13
	.38752	.42036	2.3789	.92186	1.0848	2.5805	12
	.38778	.42070	2.3770	.92175	1.0849	2.5788	11
	.38805	.42105	2.3750	.92164	1.0850	2.5770	10
	.38832	.42139	2.3731	.92152	1.0852	2.5752	9
	.38859	.42173	2.3712	.92141	1.0853	2.5734	8
	.38886	.42207	2.3693	.92130	1.0854	2.5716	7
	.38912	.42242	2.3673	.92119	1.0856	2.5699	6
	.38939	.42276	2.3654	92107	1.0857	2.5681	5
	.38966	.42310	2.3635	92096	1.0858	2.5663	4
	.38993	.42345	2.3616	.92085	1.0860	2.5646	3
	.39020	.42379	2.3597	.92073	1.0861	2.5628	2
	.39046	.42413	2.3578	.92062	1.0862	2.5611	1
	.39073	.42447	2.3559	.92050	1.0864	2.5593	0

	Cos	Cot	Tan	Sin	Csc	Sec	′

2° (292°)   (247°) 67°

′	Sin	Tan	Cot	Cos	Sec	Csc	′
0	.39073	.42447	2.3559	.92050	1.0864	2.5593	60
1	.39100	.42482	2.3539	.92039	1.0865	2.5576	59
2	.39127	.42516	2.3520	.92028	1.0866	2.5558	58
3	.39153	.42551	2.3501	.92016	1.0868	2.5541	57
4	.39180	.42585	2 3483	92005	1.0869	2.5523	56
5	.39207	.42619	2.3464	.91994	1.0870	2.5506	55
6	.39234	.42654	2.3445	.91982	1.0872	2.5488	54
7	.39260	.42688	2.3426	.91971	1.0873	2.5471	53
8	.39287	.42722	2.3407	.91959	1.0874	2.5454	52
9	.39314	.42757	2.3388	.91948	1.0876	2.5436	51
10	.39341	.42791	2.3369	.91936	1.0877	2.5419	50
11	.39367	.42826	2.3351	.91925	1.0878	2.5402	49
12	.39394	.42860	2.3332	.91914	1.0880	2.5384	48
13	.39421	.42894	2.3313	.91902	1.0881	2.5367	47
14	.39448	.42929	2.3294	.91891	1.0883	2.5350	46
15	.39474	.42963	2.3276	.91879	1.0884	2.5333	45
16	.39501	.42998	2.3257	.91868	1.0885	2.5316	44
17	.39528	.43032	2.3238	.91856	1.0887	2.5299	43
18	.39555	.43067	2.3220	.91845	1.0888	2.5282	42
19	.39581	.43101	2.3201	.91833	1.0889	2.5264	41
20	.39608	.43136	2.3183	.91822	1.0891	2.5247	40
21	.39635	.43170	2.3164	.91810	1.0892	2.5230	39
22	.39661	.43205	2.3146	.91799	1.0893	2.5213	38
23	.39688	.43239	2.3127	.91787	1.0895	2.5196	37
24	.39715	.43274	2.3109	.91775	1.0896	2.5180	36
25	.39741	.43308	2.3090	.91764	1.0898	2.5163	35
26	.39768	.43343	2.3072	.91752	1.0899	2.5146	34
27	.39795	.43378	2.3053	.91741	1.0900	2.5129	33
28	.39822	.43412	2.3035	.91729	1.0902	2.5112	32
29	.39848	.43447	2.3017	.91718	1.0903	2.5095	31
30	.39875	.43481	2.2998	.91706	1.0904	2.5078	30
31	.39902	.43516	2.2980	.91694	1.0906	2.5062	29
32	.39928	.43550	2.2962	.91683	1.0907	2.5045	28
33	.39955	.43585	2.2944	.91671	1.0909	2.5028	27
34	.39982	.43620	2.2925	.91660	1.0910	2.5012	26
35	.40008	.43654	2.2907	.91648	1.0911	2.4995	25
36	.40035	.43689	2.2889	.91636	1.0913	2.4978	24
37	.40062	.43724	2.2871	.91625	1.0914	2.4962	23
38	.40088	.43758	2.2853	.91613	1.0915	2.4945	22
39	.40115	.43793	2.2835	.91601	1.0917	2.4928	21
40	.40141	.43828	2.2817	.91590	1.0918	2.4912	20
41	.40168	.43862	2.2799	.91578	1.0920	2.4895	19
42	.40195	.43897	2.2781	.91566	1.0921	2.4879	18
43	.40221	.43932	2.2763	.91555	1.0922	2.4862	17
44	.40248	.43966	2.2745	.91543	1.0924	2.4846	16
45	.40275	.44001	2.2727	.91531	1.0925	2.4830	15
46	.40301	.44036	2.2709	.91519	1.0927	2.4813	14
47	.40328	.44071	2.2691	.91508	1.0928	2.4797	13
48	.40355	.44105	2.2673	.91496	1.0929	2.4780	12
49	.40381	.44140	2.2655	.91484	1.0931	2.4764	11
50	.40408	.44175	2.2637	.91472	1.0932	2.4748	10
51	.40434	.44210	2.2620	.91461	1.0934	2.4731	9
52	.40461	.44244	2.2602	.91449	1.0935	2.4715	8
53	.40488	.44279	2.2584	.91437	1.0936	2.4699	7
54	.40514	.44314	2.2566	.91425	1.0938	2.4683	6
55	.40541	.44349	2.2549	.91414	1.0939	2.4667	5
56	.40567	.44384	2.2531	.91402	1.0941	2.4650	4
57	.40594	.44418	2.2513	.91390	1.0942	2.4634	3
58	.40621	.44453	2.2496	.91378	1.0944	2.4618	2
59	.40647	.44488	2.2478	.91366	1.0945	2.4602	1
60	.40674	.44523	2.2460	.91355	1.0946	2.4586	0

′	Cos	Cot	Tan	Sin	Csc	Sec	′

113° (293°)   (246°) 66°

NATURAL TRIGONOMETRIC FUNCTIONS TO FIVE PLACES (continued)

24° (204°)   (335°) 155°   **25° (205°)**   (334°) 15

′	Sin	Tan	Cot	Cos	Sec	Csc	′
0	.40674	.44523	2.2460	.91355	1.0946	2.4586	60
1	.40700	.44558	2.2443	.91343	1.0948	2.4570	59
2	.40727	.44593	2.2425	.91331	1.0949	2.4554	58
3	.40753	.44627	2.2408	.91319	1.0951	2.4538	57
4	.40780	.44662	2.2390	.91307	1.0952	2.4522	56
5	.40806	.44697	2.2373	.91295	1.0953	2.4506	55
6	.40833	.44732	2.2355	.91283	1.0955	2.4490	54
7	.40860	.44767	2.2338	.91272	1.0956	2.4474	53
8	.40886	.44802	2.2320	.91260	1.0958	2.4458	52
9	.40913	.44837	2.2303	.91248	1.0959	2.4442	51
10	.40939	.44872	2.2286	.91236	1.0961	2.4426	50
11	.40966	.44907	2.2268	.91224	1.0962	2.4411	49
12	.40992	.44942	2.2251	.91212	1.0963	2.4395	48
13	.41019	.44977	2.2234	.91200	1.0965	2.4379	47
14	.41045	.45012	2.2216	.91188	1.0966	2.4363	46
15	.41072	.45047	2.2199	.91176	1.0968	2.4348	45
16	.41098	.45082	2.2182	.91164	1.0969	2.4332	44
17	.41125	.45117	2.2165	.91152	1.0971	2.4316	43
18	.41151	.45152	2.2148	.91140	1.0972	2.4300	42
19	.41178	.45187	2.2130	.91128	1.0974	2.4285	41
20	.41204	.45222	2.2113	.91116	1.0975	2.4269	40
21	.41231	.45257	2.2096	.91104	1.0976	2.4254	39
22	.41257	.45292	2.2079	.91092	1.0978	2.4238	38
23	.41284	.45327	2.2062	.91080	1.0979	2.4222	37
24	.41310	.45362	2.2045	.91068	1.0981	2.4207	36
25	.41337	.45397	2.2028	.91056	1.0982	2.4191	35
26	.41363	.45432	2.2011	.91044	1.0984	2.4176	34
27	.41390	.45467	2.1994	.91032	1.0985	2.4160	33
28	.41416	.45502	2.1977	.91020	1.0987	2.4145	32
29	.41443	.45538	2.1960	.91008	1.0988	2.4130	31
30	.41469	.45573	2.1943	.90996	1.0989	2.4114	30
31	.41496	.45608	2.1926	.90984	1.0991	2.4099	29
32	.41522	.45643	2.1909	.90972	1.0992	2.4083	28
33	.41549	.45678	2.1892	.90960	1.0994	2.4068	27
34	.41575	.45713	2.1876	.90948	1.0995	2.4053	26
35	.41602	.45748	2.1859	.90936	1.0997	2.4038	25
36	.41628	.45784	2.1842	.90924	1.0998	2.4022	24
37	.41655	.45819	2.1825	.90911	1.1000	2.4007	23
38	.41681	.45854	2.1808	.90899	1.1001	2.3992	22
39	.41707	.45889	2.1792	.90887	1.1003	2.3977	21
40	.41734	.45924	2.1775	.90875	1.1004	2.3961	20
41	.41760	.45960	2.1758	.90863	1.1006	2.3946	19
42	.41787	.45995	2.1742	.90851	1.1007	2.3931	18
43	.41813	.46030	2.1725	.90839	1.1009	2.3916	17
44	.41840	.46065	2.1708	.90826	1.1010	2.3901	16
45	.41866	.46101	2.1692	.90814	1.1011	2.3886	15
46	.41892	.46136	2.1675	.90802	1.1013	2.3871	14
47	.41919	.46171	2.1659	.90790	1.1014	2.3856	13
48	.41945	.46206	2.1642	.90778	1.1016	2.3841	12
49	.41972	.46242	2.1625	.90766	1.1017	2.3826	11
50	.41998	.46277	2.1609	.90753	1.1019	2.3811	10
51	.42024	.46312	2.1592	.90741	1.1020	2.3796	9
52	.42051	.46348	2.1576	.90729	1.1022	2.3781	8
53	.42077	.46383	2.1560	.90717	1.1023	2.3766	7
54	.42104	.46418	2.1543	.90704	1.1025	2.3751	6
55	.42130	.46454	2.1527	.90692	1.1026	2.3736	5
56	.42156	.46489	2.1510	.90680	1.1028	2.3721	4
57	.42183	.46525	2.1494	.90668	1.1029	2.3706	3
58	.42209	.46560	2.1478	.90655	1.1031	2.3692	2
59	.42235	.46595	2.1461	.90643	1.1032	2.3677	1
60	.42262	.46631	2.1445	.90631	1.1034	2.3662	0
′	Cos	Cot	Tan	Sin	Csc	Sec	′

′	Sin	Tan	Cot	Cos	Sec	Csc	
0	.42262	.46631	2.1445	.90631	1.1034	2.3662	6
1	.42288	.46666	2.1429	.90618	1.1035	2.3647	5
2	.42315	.46702	2.1413	.90606	1.1037	2.3633	5
3	.42341	.46737	2.1396	.90594	1.1038	2.3618	5
4	.42367	.46772	2.1380	.90582	1.1040	2.3603	5
5	.42394	.46808	2.1364	.90569	1.1041	2.3588	5
6	.42420	.46843	2.1348	.90557	1.1043	2.3574	5
7	.42446	.46879	2.1332	.90545	1.1044	2.3559	5
8	.42473	.46914	2.1315	.90532	1.1046	2.3545	5
9	.42499	.46950	2.1299	.90520	1.1047	2.3530	5
10	.42525	.46985	2.1283	.90507	1.1049	2.3515	5
11	.42552	.47021	2.1267	.90495	1.1050	2.3501	4
12	.42578	.47056	2.1251	.90483	1.1052	2.3486	4
13	.42604	.47092	2.1235	.90470	1.1053	2.3472	4
14	.42631	.47128	2.1219	.90458	1.1055	2.3457	4
15	.42657	.47163	2.1203	.90446	1.1056	2.3443	4
16	.42683	.47199	2.1187	.90433	1.1058	2.3428	4
17	.42709	.47234	2.1171	.90421	1.1059	2.3414	4
18	.42736	.47270	2.1155	.90408	1.1061	2.3400	4
19	.42762	.47305	2.1139	.90396	1.1062	2.3385	4
20	.42788	.47341	2.1123	.90383	1.1064	2.3371	4
21	.42815	.47377	2.1107	.90371	1.1066	2.3356	3
22	.42841	.47412	2.1092	.90358	1.1067	2.3342	3
23	.42867	.47448	2.1076	.90346	1.1069	2.3328	3
24	.42894	.47483	2.1060	.90334	1.1070	2.3314	3
25	.42920	.47519	2.1044	.90321	1.1072	2.3299	3
26	.42946	.47555	2.1028	.90309	1.1073	2.3285	3
27	.42972	.47590	2.1013	.90296	1.1075	2.3271	3
28	.42999	.47626	2.0997	.90284	1.1076	2.3257	3
29	.43025	.47662	2.0981	.90271	1.1078	2.3242	3
30	.43051	.47698	2.0965	.90259	1.1079	2.3228	30
31	.43077	.47733	2.0950	.90246	1.1081	2.3214	29
32	.43104	.47769	2.0934	.90233	1.1082	2.3200	28
33	.43130	.47805	2.0918	.90221	1.1084	2.3186	27
34	.43156	.47840	2.0903	.90208	1.1085	2.3172	26
35	.43182	.47876	2.0887	.90196	1.1087	2.3158	25
36	.43209	.47912	2.0872	.90183	1.1089	2.3144	24
37	.43235	.47948	2.0856	.90171	1.1090	2.3130	23
38	.43261	.47984	2.0840	.90158	1.1092	2.3115	22
39	.43287	.48019	2.0825	.90146	1.1093	2.3101	21
40	.43313	.48055	2.0809	.90133	1.1095	2.3088	20
41	.43340	.48091	2.0794	.90120	1.1096	2.3074	19
42	.43366	.48127	2.0778	.90108	1.1098	2.3060	18
43	.43392	.48163	2.0763	.90095	1.1099	2.3046	17
44	.43418	.48198	2.0748	.90082	1.1101	2.3032	16
45	.43445	.48234	2.0732	.90070	1.1102	2.3018	15
46	.43471	.48270	2.0717	.90057	1.1104	2.3004	14
47	.43497	.48306	2.0701	.90045	1.1106	2.2990	13
48	.43523	.48342	2.0686	.90032	1.1107	2.2976	12
49	.43549	.48378	2.0671	.90019	1.1109	2.2962	11
50	.43575	.48414	2.0655	.90007	1.1110	2.2949	10
51	.43602	.48450	2.0640	.89994	1.1112	2.2935	9
52	.43628	.48486	2.0625	.89981	1.1113	2.2921	8
53	.43654	.48521	2.0609	.89968	1.1115	2.2907	7
54	.43680	.48557	2.0594	.89956	1.1117	2.2894	6
55	.43706	.48593	2.0579	.89943	1.1118	2.2880	5
56	.43733	.48629	2.0564	.89930	1.1120	2.2866	4
57	.43759	.48665	2.0549	.89918	1.1121	2.2853	3
58	.43785	.48701	2.0533	.89905	1.1123	2.2839	2
59	.43811	.48737	2.0518	.89892	1.1124	2.2825	1
60	.43837	.48773	2.0503	.89879	1.1126	2.2812	0
′	Cos	Cot	Tan	Sin	Csc	Sce	′

NATURAL TRIGONOMETRIC FUNCTIONS TO FIVE PLACES (continued)

06°)   (333°) **153°**   27° (207°)   (332°) **152°**

Sin	Tan	Cot	Cos	Sec	Csc	′		′	Sin	Tan	Cot	Cos	Sec	Csc	′
.43837	.48773	2.0503	.89879	1.1126	2.2812	60		0	.45399	.50953	1.9626	.89101	1.1223	2.2027	60
.43863	.48809	2.0488	.89867	1.1128	2.2798	59		1	.45425	.50989	1.9612	.89087	1.1225	2.2014	59
.43889	.48845	2.0473	.89854	1.1129	2.2785	58		2	.45451	.51026	1.9598	.89074	1.1227	2.2002	58
.43916	.48881	2.0458	.89841	1.1131	2.2771	57		3	.45477	.51063	1.9584	.89061	1.1228	2.1989	57
.43942	.48917	2.0443	.89828	1.1132	2.2757	56		4	.45503	.51099	1.9570	.89048	1.1230	2.1977	56
.43968	.48953	2.0428	.89816	1.1134	2.2744	55		5	.45529	.51136	1.9556	.89035	1.1232	2.1964	55
.43994	.48989	2.0413	.89803	1.1136	2.2730	54		6	.45554	.51173	1.9542	.89021	1.1233	2.1952	54
.44020	.49026	2.0398	.89790	1.1137	2.2717	53		7	.45580	.51209	1.9528	.89008	1.1235	2.1939	53
.44046	.49062	2.0383	.89777	1.1139	2.2703	52		8	.45606	.51246	1.9514	.88995	1.1237	2.1927	52
.44072	.49098	2.0368	.89764	1.1140	2.2690	51		9	.45632	.51283	1.9500	.88981	1.1238	2.1914	51
.44098	.49134	2.0353	.89752	1.1142	2.2677	50		10	.45658	.51319	1.9486	.88968	1.1240	2.1902	50
.44124	.49170	2.0338	.89739	1.1143	2.2663	49		11	.45684	.51356	1.9472	.88955	1.1242	2.1890	49
.44151	.49206	2.0323	.89726	1.1145	2.2650	48		12	.45710	.51393	1.9458	.88942	1.1243	2.1877	48
.44177	.49242	2.0308	.89713	1.1147	2.2636	47		13	.45736	.51430	1.9444	.88928	1.1245	2.1865	47
.44203	.49278	2.0293	.89700	1.1148	2.2623	46		14	.45762	.51467	1.9430	.88915	1.1247	2.1852	46
.44229	.49315	2.0278	.89687	1.1150	2.2610	45		15	.45787	.51503	1.9416	.88902	1.1248	2.1840	45
.44255	.49351	2.0263	.89674	1.1151	2.2596	44		16	.45813	.51540	1.9402	.88888	1.1250	2.1828	44
.44281	.49387	2.0248	.89662	1.1153	2.2583	43		17	.45839	.51577	1.9388	.88875	1.1252	2.1815	43
.44307	.49423	2.0233	.89649	1.1155	2.2570	42		18	.45865	.51614	1.9375	.88862	1.1253	2.1803	42
.44333	.49459	2.0219	.89636	1.1156	2.2556	41		19	.45891	.51651	1.9361	.88848	1.1255	2.1791	41
.44359	.49495	2.0204	.89623	1.1158	2.2543	40		20	.45917	.51688	1.9347	.88835	1.1257	2.1779	40
.44385	.49532	2.0189	.89610	1.1159	2.2530	39		21	.45942	.51724	1.9333	.88822	1.1259	2.1766	39
.44411	.49568	2.0174	.89597	1.1161	2.2517	38		22	.45968	.51761	1.9319	.88808	1.1260	2.1754	38
.44437	.49604	2.0160	.89584	1.1163	2.2504	37		23	.45994	.51798	1.9306	.88795	1.1262	2.1742	37
.44464	.49640	2.0145	.89571	1.1164	2.2490	36		24	.46020	.51835	1.9292	.88782	1.1264	2.1730	36
.44490	.49677	2.0130	.89558	1.1166	2.2477	35		25	.46046	.51872	1.9278	.88768	1.1265	2.1718	35
.44516	.49713	2.0115	.89545	1.1168	2.2464	34		26	.46072	.51909	1.9265	.88755	1.1267	2.1705	34
.44542	.49749	2.0101	.89532	1.1169	2.2451	33		27	.46097	.51946	1.9251	.88741	1.1269	2.1693	33
.44568	.49786	2.0086	.89519	1.1171	2.2438	32		28	.46123	.51983	1.9237	.88728	1.1270	2.1681	32
.44594	.49822	2.0072	.89506	1.1172	2.2425	31		29	.46149	.52020	1.9223	.88715	1.1272	2.1669	31
.44620	.49858	2.0057	.89493	1.1174	2.2412	30		30	.46175	.52057	1.9210	.88701	1.1274	2.1657	30
.44646	.49894	2.0042	.89480	1.1176	2.2399	29		31	.46201	.52094	1.9196	.88688	1.1276	2.1645	29
.44672	.49931	2.0028	.89467	1.1177	2.2385	28		32	.46226	.52131	1.9183	.88674	1.1277	2.1633	28
.44698	.49967	2.0013	.89454	1.1179	2.2372	27		33	.46252	.52168	1.9169	.88661	1.1279	2.1621	27
.44724	.50004	1.9999	.89441	1.1180	2.2359	26		34	.46278	.52205	1.9155	.88647	1.1281	2.1609	26
.44750	.50040	1.9984	.89428	1.1182	2.2346	25		35	.46304	.52242	1.9142	.88634	1.1282	2.1596	25
.44776	.50076	1.9970	.89415	1.1184	2.2333	24		36	.46330	.52279	1.9128	.88620	1.1284	2.1584	24
.44802	.50113	1.9955	.89402	1.1185	2.2320	23		37	.46355	.52316	1.9115	.88607	1.1286	2.1572	23
.44828	.50149	1.9941	.89389	1.1187	2.2308	22		38	.46381	.52353	1.9101	.88593	1.1288	2.1560	22
.44854	.50185	1.9926	.89376	1.1189	2.2295	21		39	.46407	.52390	1.9088	.88580	1.1289	2.1549	21
.44880	.50222	1.9912	.89363	1.1190	2.2282	20		40	.46433	.52427	1.9074	.88566	1.1291	2.1537	20
.44906	.50258	1.9897	.89350	1.1192	2.2269	19		41	.46458	.52464	1.9061	.88553	1.1293	2.1525	19
.44932	.50295	1.9883	.89337	1.1194	2.2256	18		42	.46484	.52501	1.9047	.88539	1.1294	2.1513	18
.44958	.50331	1.9868	.89324	1.1195	2.2243	17		43	.46510	.52538	1.9034	.88526	1.1296	2.1501	17
.44984	.50368	1.9854	.89311	1.1197	2.2230	16		44	.46536	.52575	1.9020	.88512	1.1298	2.1489	16
.45010	.50404	1.9840	.89298	1.1198	2.2217	15		45	.46561	.52613	1.9007	.88499	1.1300	2.1477	15
.45036	.50441	1.9825	.89285	1.1200	2.2205	14		46	.46587	.52650	1.8993	.88485	1.1301	2.1465	14
.45062	.50477	1.9811	.89272	1.1202	2.2192	13		47	.46613	.52687	1.8980	.88472	1.1303	2.1453	13
.45088	.50514	1.9797	.89259	1.1203	2.2179	12		48	.46639	.52724	1.8967	.88458	1.1305	2.1441	12
.45114	.50550	1.9782	.89245	1.1205	2.2166	11		49	.46664	.52761	1.8953	.88445	1.1307	2.1430	11
.45140	.50587	1.9768	.89232	1.1207	2.2153	10		50	.46690	.52798	1.8940	.88431	1.1308	2.1418	10
.45166	.50623	1.9754	.89219	1.1208	2.2141	9		51.	.46716	.52836	1.8927	.88417	1.1310	2.1406	9
.45192	.50660	1.9740	.89206	1.1210	2.2128	8		52	.46742	.52873	1.8913	.88404	1.1312	2.1394	8
.45218	.50696	1.9725	.89193	1.1212	2.2115	7		53	.46767	.52910	1.8900	.88390	1.1313	2.1382	7
.45243	.50733	1.9711	.89180	1.1213	2.2103	6		54	.46793	.52947	1.8887	.88377	1.1315	2.1371	6
.45269	.50769	1.9697	.89167	1.1215	2.2090	5		55	.46819	.52985	1.8873	.88363	1.1317	2.1359	5
.45295	.50806	1.9683	.89153	1.1217	2.2077	4		56	.46844	.53022	1.8860	.88349	1.1319	2.1347	4
.45321	.50843	1.9669	.89140	1.1218	2.2065	3		57	.46870	.53059	1.8847	.88336	1.1320	2.1336	3
.45347	.50879	1.9654	.89127	1.1220	2.2052	2		58	.46896	.53096	1.8834	.88322	1.1322	2.1324	2
.45373	.50916	1.9640	.89114	1.1222	2.2039	1		59	.46921	.53134	1.8820	.88308	1.1324	2.1312	1
.45399	.50953	1.9626	.89101	1.1223	2.2027	0		60	.46947	.53171	1.8807	.88295	1.1326	2.1301	0
Cos	Cot	Tan	Sin	Csc	Sec	′		′	Cos	Cot	Tan	Sin	Csc	Sec	′

NATURAL TRIGONOMETRIC FUNCTIONS TO FIVE PLACES (continued)

28° (208°)   (331°) 151°

′	Sin	Tan	Cot	Cos	Sec	Csc	′
0	.46947	.53171	1.8807	.88295	1.1326	2.1301	60
1	.46973	.53208	1.8794	.88281	1.1327	2.1289	59
2	.46999	.53246	1.8781	.88267	1.1329	2.1277	58
3	.47024	.53283	1.8768	.88254	1.1331	2.1266	57
4	.47050	.53320	1.8755	.88240	1.1333	2.1254	56
5	.47076	.53358	1.8741	.88226	1.1334	2.1242	55
6	.47101	.53395	1.8728	.88213	1.1336	2.1231	54
7	.47127	.53432	1.8715	.88199	1.1338	2.1219	53
8	.47153	.53470	1.8702	.88185	1.1340	2.1208	52
9	.47178	.53507	1.8689	.88172	1.1342	2.1196	51
10	.47204	.53545	1.8676	.88158	1.1343	2.1185	50
11	.47229	.53582	1.8663	.88144	1.1345	2.1173	49
12	.47255	.53620	1.8650	.88130	1.1347	2.1162	48
13	.47281	.53657	1.8637	.88117	1.1349	2.1150	47
14	.47306	.53694	1.8624	.88103	1.1350	2.1139	46
15	.47332	.53732	1.8611	.88089	1.1352	2.1127	45
16	.47358	.53769	1.8598	.88075	1.1354	2.1116	44
17	.47383	.53807	1.8585	.88062	1.1356	2.1105	43
18	.47409	.53844	1.8572	.88048	1.1357	2.1093	42
19	.47434	.53882	1.8559	.88034	1.1359	2.1082	41
20	.47460	.53920	1.8546	.88020	1.1361	2.1070	40
21	.47486	.53957	1.8533	.88006	1.1363	2.1059	39
22	.47511	.53995	1.8520	.87993	1.1365	2.1048	38
23	.47537	.54032	1.8507	.87979	1.1366	2.1036	37
24	.47562	.54070	1.8495	.87965	1.1368	2.1025	36
25	.47588	.54107	1.8482	.87951	1.1370	2.1014	35
26	.47614	.54145	1.8469	.87937	1.1372	2.1002	34
27	.47639	.54183	1.8456	.87923	1.1374	2.0991	33
28	.47665	.54220	1.8443	.87909	1.1375	2.0980	32
29	.47690	.54258	1.8430	.87896	1.1377	2.0969	31
30	.47716	.54296	1.8418	.87882	1.1379	2.0957	30
31	.47741	.54333	1.8405	.87868	1.1381	2.0946	29
32	.47767	.54371	1.8392	.87854	1.1383	2.0935	28
33	.47793	.54409	1.8379	.87840	1.1384	2.0924	27
34	.47818	.54446	1.8367	.87826	1.1386	2.0913	26
35	.47844	.54484	1.8354	.87812	1.1388	2.0901	25
36	.47869	.54522	1.8341	.87798	1.1390	2.0890	24
37	.47895	.54560	1.8329	.87784	1.1392	2.0879	23
38	.47920	.54597	1.8316	.87770	1.1393	2.0868	22
39	.47946	.54635	1.8303	.87756	1.1395	2.0857	21
40	.47971	.54673	1.8291	.87743	1.1397	2.0846	20
41	.47997	.54711	1.8278	.87729	1.1399	2.0835	19
42	.48022	.54748	1.8265	.87715	1.1401	2.0824	18
43	.48048	.54786	1.8253	.87701	1.1402	2.0813	17
44	.48073	.54824	1.8240	.87687	1.1404	2.0802	16
45	.48099	.54862	1.8228	.87673	1.1406	2.0791	15
46	.48124	.54900	1.8215	.87659	1.1408	2.0779	14
47	.48150	.54938	1.8202	.87645	1.1410	2.0768	13
48	.48175	.54975	1.8190	.87631	1.1412	2.0757	12
49	.48201	.55013	1.8177	.87617	1.1413	2.0747	11
50	.48226	.55051	1.8165	.87603	1.1415	2.0736	10
51	.48252	.55089	1.8152	.87589	1.1417	2.0725	9
52	.48277	.55127	1.8140	.87575	1.1419	2.0714	8
53	.48303	.55165	1.8127	.87561	1.1421	2.0703	7
54	.48328	.55203	1.8115	.87546	1.1423	2.0692	6
55	.48354	.55241	1.8103	.87532	1.1424	2.0681	5
56	.48379	.55279	1.8090	.87518	1.1426	2.0670	4
57	.48405	.55317	1.8078	.87504	1.1428	2.0659	3
58	.48430	.55355	1.8065	.87490	1.1430	2.0648	2
59	.48456	.55393	1.8053	.87476	1.1432	2.0637	1
60	.48481	.55431	1.8040	.87462	1.1434	2.0627	0
′	Cos	Cot	Tan	Sin	Csc	Sec	′

29° (209°)   (330)°

′	Sin	Tan	Cot	Cos	Sec	Csc
0	.48481	.55431	1.8040	.87462	1.1434	2.0627
1	.48506	.55469	1.8028	.87448	1.1435	2.0616
2	.48532	.55507	1.8016	.87434	1.1437	2.0605
3	.48557	.55545	1.8003	.87420	1.1439	2.0594
4	.48583	.55583	1.7991	.87406	1.1441	2.0583
5	.48608	.55621	1.7979	.87391	1.1443	2.0573
6	.48634	.55659	1.7966	.87377	1.1445	2.0562
7	.48659	.55697	1.7954	.87363	1.1446	2.0551
8	.48684	.55736	1.7942	.87349	1.1448	2.0540
9	.48710	.55774	1.7930	.87335	1.1450	2.0530
10	.48735	.55812	1.7917	.87321	1.1452	2.0519
11	.48761	.55850	1.7905	.87306	1.1454	2.0508
12	.48786	.55888	1.7893	.87292	1.1456	2.0498
13	.48811	.55926	1.7881	.87278	1.1458	2.0487
14	.48837	.55964	1.7868	.87264	1.1460	2.0476
15	.48862	.56003	1.7856	.87250	1.1461	2.0466
16	.48888	.56041	1.7844	.87235	1.1463	2.0455
17	.48913	.56079	1.7832	.87221	1.1465	2.0445
18	.48938	.56117	1.7820	.87207	1.1467	2.0434
19	.48964	.56156	1.7808	.87193	1.1469	2.0423
20	.48989	.56194	1.7796	.87178	1.1471	2.0413
21	.49014	.56232	1.7783	.87164	1.1473	2.0402
22	.49040	.56270	1.7771	.87150	1.1474	2.0392
23	.49065	.56309	1.7759	.87136	1.1476	2.0381
24	.49090	.56347	1.7747	.87121	1.1478	2.0371
25	.49116	.56385	1.7735	.87107	1.1480	2.0360
26	.49141	.56424	1.7723	.87093	1.1482	2.0350
27	.49166	.56462	1.7711	.87079	1.1484	2.0339
28	.49192	.56501	1.7699	.87064	1.1486	2.0329
29	.49217	.56539	1.7687	.87050	1.1488	2.0318
30	.49242	.56577	1.7675	.87036	1.1490	2.0308
31	.49268	.56616	1.7663	.87021	1.1491	2.0297
32	.49293	.56654	1.7651	.87007	1.1493	2.0287
33	.49318	.56693	1.7639	.86993	1.1495	2.0276
34	.49344	.56731	1.7627	.86978	1.1497	2.0266
35	.49369	.56769	1.7615	.86964	1.1499	2.0256
36	.49394	.56808	1.7603	.86949	1.1501	2.0245
37	.49419	.56846	1.7591	.86935	1.1503	2.0235
38	.49445	.56885	1.7579	.86921	1.1505	2.0225
39	.49470	.56923	1.7567	.86906	1.1507	2.0214
40	.49495	.56962	1.7556	.86892	1.1509	2.0204
41	.49521	.57000	1.7544	.86878	1.1510	2.0194
42	.49546	.57039	1.7532	.86863	1.1512	2.0183
43	.49571	.57078	1.7520	.86849	1.1514	2.0173
44	.49596	.57116	1.7508	.86834	1.1516	2.0163
45	.49622	.57155	1.7496	.86820	1.1518	2.0152
46	.49647	.57193	1.7485	.86805	1.1520	2.0142
47	.49672	.57232	1.7473	.86791	1.1522	2.0132
48	.49697	.57271	1.7461	.86777	1.1524	2.0122
49	.49723	.57309	1.7449	.86762	1.1526	2.0112
50	.49748	.57348	1.7437	.86748	1.1528	2.0101
51	.49773	.57386	1.7426	.86733	1.1530	2.0091
52	.49798	.57425	1.7414	.86719	1.1532	2.0081
53	.49824	.57464	1.7402	.86704	1.1533	2.0071
54	.49849	.57503	1.7391	.86690	1.1535	2.0061
55	.49874	.57541	1.7379	.86675	1.1537	2.0051
56	.49899	.57580	1.7367	.86661	1.1539	2.0040
57	.49924	.57619	1.7355	.86646	1.1541	2.0030
58	.49950	.57657	1.7344	.86632	1.1543	2.0020
59	.49975	.57696	1.7332	.86617	1.1545	2.0010
60	.50000	.57735	1.7321	.86603	1.1547	2.0000
′	Cos	Cot	Tan	Sin	Csc	Sec

NATURAL TRIGONOMETRIC FUNCTIONS TO FIVE PLACES (continued)

210°)   (329°) 149°

Sin	Tan	Cot	Cos	Sec	Csc	′
.50000	.57735	1.7321	.86603	1.1547	2.0000	60
.50025	.57774	1.7309	.86588	1.1549	1.9990	59
.50050	.57813	1.7297	.86573	1.1551	1.9980	58
.50076	.57851	1.7286	.86559	1.1553	1.9970	57
.50101	.57890	1.7274	.86544	1.1555	1.9960	56
.50126	.57929	1.7262	.86530	1.1557	1.9950	55
.50151	.57968	1.7251	.86515	1.1559	1.9940	54
.50176	.58007	1.7239	.86501	1.1561	1.9930	53
.50201	.58046	1.7228	.86486	1.1563	1.9920	52
.50227	.58085	1.7216	.86471	1.1565	1.9910	51
.50252	.58124	1.7205	.86457	1.1566	1.9900	50
.50277	.58162	1.7193	.86442	1.1568	1.9890	49
.50302	.58201	1.7182	.86427	1.1570	1.9880	48
.50327	.58240	1.7170	.86413	1.1572	1.9870	47
.50352	.58279	1.7159	.86398	1.1574	1.9860	46
.50377	.58318	1.7147	.86384	1.1576	1.9850	45
.50403	.58357	1.7136	.86369	1.1578	1.9840	44
.50428	.58396	1.7124	.86354	1.1580	1.9830	43
.50453	.58435	1.7113	.86340	1.1582	1.9821	42
.50478	.58474	1.7102	.86325	1.1584	1.9811	41
.50503	.58513	1.7090	.86310	1.1586	1.9801	40
.50528	.58552	1.7079	.86295	1.1588	1.9791	39
.50553	.58591	1.7067	.86281	1.1590	1.9781	38
.50578	.58631	1.7056	.86266	1.1592	1.9771	37
.50603	.58670	1.7045	.86251	1.1594	1.9762	36
.50628	.58709	1.7033	.86237	1.1596	1.9752	35
.50654	.58748	1.7022	.86222	1.1598	1.9742	34
.50679	.58787	1.7011	.86207	1.1600	1.9732	33
.50704	.58826	1.6999	.86192	1.1602	1.9722	32
.50729	.58865	1.6988	.86178	1.1604	1.9713	31
.50754	.58905	1.6977	.86163	1.1606	1.9703	30
.50779	.58944	1.6965	.86148	1.1608	1.9693	29
.50804	.58983	1.6954	.86133	1.1610	1.9684	28
.50829	.59022	1.6943	.86119	1.1612	1.9674	27
.50854	.59061	1.6932	.86104	1.1614	1.9664	26
.50879	.59101	1.6920	.86089	1.1616	1.9654	25
.50904	.59140	1.6909	.86074	1.1618	1.9645	24
.50929	.59179	1.6898	.86059	1.1620	1.9635	23
.50954	.59218	1.6887	.86045	1.1622	1.9625	22
.50979	.59258	1.6875	.86030	1.1624	1.9616	21
.51004	.59297	1.6864	.86015	1.1626	1.9606	20
.51029	.59336	1.6853	.86000	1.1628	1.9597	19
.51054	.59376	1.6842	.85985	1.1630	1.9587	18
.51079	.59415	1.6831	.85970	1.1632	1.9577	17
.51104	.59454	1.6820	.85956	1.1634	1.9568	16
.51129	.59494	1.6808	.85941	1.1636	1.9558	15
.51154	.59533	1.6797	.85926	1.1638	1.9549	14
.51179	.59573	1.6786	.85911	1.1640	1.9539	13
.51204	.59612	1.6775	.85896	1.1642	1.9530	12
.51229	.59651	1.6764	.85881	1.1644	1.9520	11
.51254	.59691	1.6753	.85866	1.1646	1.9511	10
.51279	.59730	1.6742	.85851	1.1648	1.9501	9
.51304	.59770	1.6731	.85836	1.1650	1.9492	8
.51329	.59809	1.6720	.85821	1.1652	1.9482	7
.51354	.59849	1.6709	.85806	1.1654	1.9473	6
.51379	.59888	1.6698	.85792	1.1656	1.9463	5
.51404	.59928	1.6687	.85777	1.1658	1.9454	4
.51429	.59967	1.6676	.85762	1.1660	1.9444	3
.51454	.60007	1.6665	.85747	1.1662	1.9435	2
.51479	.60046	1.6654	.85732	1.1664	1.9425	1
.51504	.60086	1.6643	.85717	1.1666	1.9416	0
Cos	Cot	Tan	Sin	Csc	Sec	′

(300°)   (239°) 59°

31° (211°)   (328°) 148°

′	Sin	Tan	Cot	Cos	Sec	Csc	′
0	.51504	.60086	1.6643	.85717	1.1666	1.9416	60
1	.51529	.60126	1.6632	.85702	1.1668	1.9407	59
2	.51554	.60165	1.6621	.85687	1.1670	1.9397	58
3	.51579	.60205	1.6610	.85672	1.1672	1.9388	57
4	.51604	.60245	1.6599	.85657	1.1675	1.9379	56
5	.51628	.60284	1.6588	.85642	1.1677	1.9369	55
6	.51653	.60324	1.6577	.85627	1.1679	1.9360	54
7	.51678	.60364	1.6566	.85612	1.1681	1.9351	53
8	.51703	.60403	1.6555	.85597	1.1683	1.9341	52
9	.51728	.60443	1.6545	.85582	1.1685	1.9332	51
10	.51753	.60483	1.6534	.85567	1.1687	1.9323	50
11	.51778	.60522	1.6523	.85551	1.1689	1.9313	49
12	.51803	.60562	1.6512	.85536	1.1691	1.9304	48
13	.51828	.60602	1.6501	.85521	1.1693	1.9295	47
14	.51852	.60642	1.6490	.85506	1.1695	1.9285	46
15	.51877	.60681	1.6479	.85491	1.1697	1.9276	45
16	.51902	.60721	1.6469	.85476	1.1699	1.9267	44
17	.51927	.60761	1.6458	.85461	1.1701	1.9258	43
18	.51952	.60801	1.6447	.85446	1.1703	1.9249	42
19	.51977	.60841	1.6436	.85431	1.1705	1.9239	41
20	.52002	.60881	1.6426	.85416	1.1707	1.9230	40
21	.52026	.60921	1.6415	.85401	1.1710	1.9221	39
22	.52051	.60960	1.6404	.85385	1.1712	1.9212	38
23	.52076	.61000	1.6393	.85370	1.1714	1.9203	37
24	.52101	.61040	1.6383	.85355	1.1716	1.9194	36
25	.52126	.61080	1.6372	.85340	1.1718	1.9184	35
26	.52151	.61120	1.6361	.85325	1.1720	1.9175	34
27	.52175	.61160	1.6351	.85310	1.1722	1.9166	33
28	.52200	.61200	1.6340	.85294	1.1724	1.9157	32
29	.52225	.61240	1.6329	.85279	1.1726	1.9148	31
30	.52250	.61280	1.6319	.85264	1.1728	1.9139	30
31	.52275	.61320	1.6308	.85249	1.1730	1.9130	29
32	.52299	.61360	1.6297	.85234	1.1732	1.9121	28
33	.52324	.61400	1.6287	.85218	1.1735	1.9112	27
34	.52349	.61440	1.6276	.85203	1.1737	1.9103	26
35	.52374	.61480	1.6265	.85188	1.1739	1.9094	25
36	.52399	.61520	1.6255	.85173	1.1741	1.9084	24
37	.52423	.61561	1.6244	.85157	1.1743	1.9075	23
38	.52448	.61601	1.6234	.85142	1.1745	1.9066	22
39	.52473	.61641	1.6223	.85127	1.1747	1.9057	21
40	.52498	.61681	1.6212	.85112	1.1749	1.9048	20
41	.52522	.61721	1.6202	.85096	1.1751	1.9039	19
42	.52547	.61761	1.6191	.85081	1.1753	1.9031	18
43	.52572	.61801	1.6181	.85066	1.1756	1.9022	17
44	.52597	.61842	1.6170	.85051	1.1758	1.9013	16
45	.52621	.61882	1.6160	.85035	1.1760	1.9004	15
46	.52646	.61922	1.6149	.85020	1.1762	1.8995	14
47	.52671	.61962	1.6139	.85005	1.1764	1.8986	13
48	.52696	.62003	1.6128	.84989	1.1766	1.8977	12
49	.52720	.62043	1.6118	.84974	1.1768	1.8968	11
50	.52745	.62083	1.6107	.84959	1.1770	1.8959	10
51	.52770	.62124	1.6097	.84943	1.1773	1.8950	9
52	.52794	.62164	1.6087	.84928	1.1775	1.8941	8
53	.52819	.62204	1.6076	.84913	1.1777	1.8933	7
54	.52844	.62245	1.6066	.84897	1.1779	1.8924	6
55	.52869	.62285	1.6055	.84882	1.1781	1.8915	5
56	.52893	.62325	1.6045	.84866	1.1783	1.8906	4
57	.52918	.62366	1.6034	.84851	1.1785	1.8897	3
58	.52943	.62406	1.6024	.84836	1.1788	1.8888	2
59	.52967	.62446	1.6014	.84820	1.1790	1.8880	1
60	.52992	.62487	1.6003	.84805	1.1792	1.8871	0
′	Cos	Cot	Tan	Sin	Csc	Sec	′

121° (301°)   (238°) 58°

NATURAL TRIGONOMETRIC FUNCTIONS TO FIVE PLACES (continued)

32° (212°)   **(327°) 147°**

′	Sin	Tan	Cot	Cos	Sec	Csc	′
0	.52992	.62487	1.6003	.84805	1.1792	1.8871	60
1	.53017	.62527	1.5993	.84789	1.1794	1.8862	59
2	.53041	.62568	1.5983	.84774	1.1796	1.8853	58
3	.53066	.62608	1.5972	.84759	1.1798	1.8844	57
4	.53091	.62649	1.5962	.84743	1.1800	1.8836	56
5	.53115	.62689	1.5952	.84728	1.1803	1.8827	55
6	.53140	.62730	1.5941	.84712	1.1805	1.8818	54
7	.53164	.62770	1.5931	.84697	1.1807	1.8810	53
8	.53189	.62811	1.5921	.84681	1.1809	1.8801	52
9	.53214	.62852	1.5911	.84666	1.1811	1.8792	51
10	.53238	.62892	1.5900	.84650	1.1813	1.8783	50
11	.53263	.62933	1.5890	.84635	1.1815	1.8775	49
12	.53288	.62973	1.5880	.84619	1.1818	1.8766	48
13	.53312	.63014	1.5869	.84604	1.1820	1.8757	47
14	.53337	.63055	1.5859	.84588	1.1822	1.8749	46
15	.53361	.63095	1.5849	.84573	1.1824	1.8740	45
16	.53386	.63136	1.5839	.84557	1.1826	1.8731	44
17	.53411	.63177	1.5829	.84542	1.1828	1.8723	43
18	.53435	.63217	1.5818	.84526	1.1831	1.8714	42
19	.53460	.63258	1.5808	.84511	1.1833	1.8706	41
20	.53484	.63299	1.5798	.84495	1.1835	1.8697	40
21	.53509	.63340	1.5788	.84480	1.1837	1.8688	39
22	.53534	.63380	1.5778	.84464	1.1830	1.8680	38
23	.53558	.63421	1.5768	.84448	1.1842	1.8671	37
24	.53583	.63462	1.5757	.84433	1.1844	1.8663	36
25	.53607	.63503	1.5747	.84417	1.1846	1.8654	35
26	.53632	.63544	1.5737	.84402	1.1848	1.8646	34
27	.53656	.63584	1.5727	.84386	1.1850	1.8637	33
28	.53681	.63625	1.5717	.84370	1.1852	1.8629	32
29	.53705	.63666	1.5707	.84355	1.1855	1.8620	31
30	.53730	.63707	1.5697	.84339	1.1857	1.8612	30
31	.53754	.63748	1.5687	.84324	1.1859	1.8603	29
32	.53779	.63789	1.5677	.84308	1.1861	1.8595	28
33	.53804	.63830	1.5667	.84292	1.1863	1.8586	27
34	.53828	.63871	1.5657	.84277	1.1866	1.8578	26
35	.53853	.63912	1.5647	.84261	1.1868	1.8569	25
36	.53877	.63953	1.5637	.84245	1.1870	1.8561	24
37	.53902	.63994	1.5627	.84230	1.1872	1.8552	23
38	.53926	.64035	1.5617	.84214	1.1875	1.8544	22
39	.53951	.64076	1.5607	.84198	1.1877	1.8535	21
40	.53975	.64117	1.5597	.84182	1.1879	1.8527	20
41	.54000	.64158	1.5587	.84167	1.1881	1.8519	19
42	.54024	.64199	1.5577	.84151	1.1883	1.8510	18
43	.54049	.64240	1.5567	.84135	1.1886	1.8502	17
44	.54073	.64281	1.5557	.84120	1.1888	1.8494	16
45	.54097	.64322	1.5547	.84104	1.1890	1.8485	15
46	.54122	.64363	1.5537	.84088	1.1892	1.8477	14
47	.54146	.64404	1.5527	.84072	1.1895	1.8468	13
48	.54171	.64446	1.5517	.84057	1.1897	1.8460	12
49	.54195	.64487	1.5507	.84041	1.1899	1.8452	11
50	.54220	.64528	1.5497	.84025	1.1901	1.8443	10
51	.54244	.64569	1.5487	.84009	1.1903	1.8435	9
52	.54269	.64610	1.5477	.83994	1.1906	1.8427	8
53	.54293	.64652	1.5468	.83978	1.1908	1.8419	7
54	.54317	.64693	1.5458	.83962	1.1910	1.8410	6
55	.54342	.64734	1.5448	.83946	1.1912	1.8402	5
56	.54366	.64775	1.5438	.83930	1.1915	1.8394	4
57	.54391	.64817	1.5428	.83915	1.1917	1.8385	3
58	.54415	.64858	1.5418	.83899	1.1919	1.8377	2
59	.54440	.64899	1.5408	.83883	1.1921	1.8369	1
60	.54464	.64941	1.5399	.83867	1.1924	1.8361	0
′	Cos	Cot	Tan	Sin	Csc	Sec	′

122° (302°)   **(237°) 57°**

33° (213°)   **(326°)**

′	Sin	Tan	Cot	Cos	Sec	Csc
0	.54464	.64941	1.5399	.83867	1.1924	1.8361
1	.54488	.64982	1.5389	.83851	1.1926	1.8353
2	.54513	.65024	1.5379	.83835	1.1928	1.8344
3	.54537	.65065	1.5369	.83819	1.1930	1.8336
4	.54561	.65106	1.5359	.83804	1.1933	1.8328
5	.54586	.65148	1.5350	.83788	1.1935	1.8320
6	.54610	.65189	1.5340	.83772	1.9137	1.8312
7	.54635	.65231	1.5330	.83756	1.1939	1.8303
8	.54659	.65272	1.5320	.83740	1.1942	1.8295
9	.54683	.65314	1.5311	.83724	1.1944	1.8287
10	.54708	.65355	1.5301	.83708	1.1946	1.8279
11	.54732	.65397	1.5291	.83692	1.1949	1.8271
12	.54756	.65438	1.5282	.83676	1.1951	1.8263
13	.54781	.65480	1.5272	.83660	1.1953	1.8255
14	.54805	.65521	1.5262	.83645	1.1955	1.8247
15	.54829	.65563	1.5253	.83629	1.1958	1.8238
16	.54854	.65604	1.5243	.83613	1.1960	1.8230
17	.54878	.65646	1.5233	.83597	1.1962	1.8222
18	.54902	.65688	1.5224	.83581	1.1964	1.8214
19	.54927	.65729	1.5214	.83565	1.1967	1.8206
20	.54951	.65771	1.5204	.83549	1.1969	1.8198
21	.54975	.65813	1.5195	.83533	1.1971	1.8190
22	.54999	.65854	1.5185	.83517	1.1974	1.8182
23	.55024	.65896	1.5175	.83501	1.1976	1.8174
24	.55048	.65938	1.5166	.83485	1.1978	1.8166
25	.55072	.65980	1.5156	.83469	1.1981	1.8158
26	.55097	.66021	1.5147	.83453	1.1983	1.8150
27	.55121	.66063	1.5137	.83437	1.1985	1.8142
28	.55145	.66105	1.5127	.83421	1.1987	1.8134
29	.55169	.66147	1.5118	.83405	1.1990	1.8126
30	.55194	.66189	1.5108	.83389	1.1992	1.8118
31	.55218	.66230	1.5099	.83373	1.1994	1.8110
32	.55242	.66272	1.5089	.83356	1.1997	1.8102
33	.55266	.66314	1.5080	.83340	1.1999	1.8094
34	.55291	.66356	1.5070	.83324	1.2001	1.8086
35	.55315	.66398	1.5061	.83308	1.2004	1.8078
36	.55339	.66440	1.5051	.83292	1.2006	1.8070
37	.55363	.66482	1.5042	.83276	1.2008	1.8062
38	.55388	.66524	1.5032	.83260	1.2011	1.8055
39	.55412	.66566	1.5023	.83244	1.2013	1.8047
40	.55436	.66608	1.5013	.83228	1.2015	1.8039
41	.55460	.66650	1.5004	.83212	1.2018	1.8031
42	.55484	.66692	1.4994	.83195	1.2020	1.8023
43	.55509	.66734	1.4985	.83179	1.2022	1.8015
44	.55533	.66776	1.4975	.83163	1.2025	1.8007
45	.55557	.66818	1.4966	.83147	1.2027	1.8000
46	.55581	.66860	1.4957	.83131	1.2029	1.7992
47	.55605	.66902	1.4947	.83115	1.2032	1.7984
48	.55630	.66944	1.4938	.83098	1.2034	1.7976
49	.55654	.66986	1.4928	.83082	1.2036	1.7968
50	.55678	.67028	1.4919	.83066	1.2039	1.7960
51	.55702	.67071	1.4910	.83050	1.2041	1.7953
52	.55726	.67113	1.4900	.83034	1.2043	1.7945
53	.55750	.67155	1.4891	.83017	1.2046	1.7937
54	.55775	.67197	1.4882	.83001	1.2048	1.7929
55	.55799	.67239	1.4872	.82985	1.2050	1.7922
56	.55823	.67282	1.4863	.82969	1.2053	1.7914
57	.55847	.67324	1.4854	.82953	1.2055	1.7906
58	.55871	.67366	1.4844	.82936	1.2057	1.7898
59	.55895	.67409	1.4835	.82920	1.2060	1.7891
60	.55919	.67451	1.4826	.82904	1.2062	1.7883
′	Cos	Cot	Tan	Sin	Csc	Sec

123° (303°)   **(236°)**

NATURAL TRIGONOMETRIC FUNCTIONS TO FIVE PLACES (continued)

(214°)   (325°) 145°

	Sin	Tan	Cot	Cos	Sec	Csc	′
	.55919	.67451	1.4826	.82904	1.2062	1.7883	60
	.55943	.67493	1.4816	.82887	1.2065	1.7875	59
	.55968	.67536	1.4807	.82871	1.2067	1.7868	58
	.55992	.67578	1.4798	.82855	1.2069	1.7860	57
	.56016	.67620	1.4788	.82839	1.2072	1.7852	56
	.56040	.67663	1.4779	.82822	1.2074	1.7844	55
	.56064	.67705	1.4770	.82806	1.2076	1.7837	54
	.56088	.67748	1.4761	.82790	1.2079	1.7829	53
	.56112	.67790	1.4751	.82773	1.2081	1.7821	52
	.56136	.67832	1.4742	.82757	1.2084	1.7814	51
	.56160	.67875	1.4733	.82741	1.2086	1.7806	50
	.56184	.67917	1.4724	.82724	1.2088	1.7799	49
	.56208	.67960	1.4715	.82708	1.2091	1.7791	48
	.56232	.68002	1.4705	.82692	1.2093	1.7783	47
	.56256	.68045	1.4696	.82675	1.2096	1.7776	46
	.56280	.68088	1.4687	.82659	1.2098	1.7768	45
	.56305	.68130	1.4678	.82643	1.2100	1.7761	44
	.56329	.68173	1.4669	.82626	1.2103	1.7753	43
	.56353	.68215	1.4659	.82610	1.2105	1.7745	42
	.56377	.68258	1.4650	.82593	1.2108	1.7738	41
	.56401	.68301	1.4641	.82577	1.2110	1.7730	40
	.56425	.68343	1.4632	.82561	1.2112	1.7723	39
	.56449	.68386	1.4623	.82544	1.2115	1.7715	38
	.56473	.68429	1.4614	.82528	1.2117	1.7708	37
	.56497	.68471	1.4605	.82511	1.2120	1.7700	36
	.56521	.68514	1.4596	.82495	1.2122	1.7693	35
	.56545	.68557	1.4586	.82478	1.2124	1.7685	34
	.56569	.68600	1.4577	.82462	1.2127	1.7678	33
	.56593	.68642	1.4568	.82446	1.2129	1.7670	32
	.56617	.68685	1.4559	.82429	1.2132	1.7663	31
	.56641	.68728	1.4550	.82413	1.2134	1.7655	30
	.56665	.68771	1.4541	.82396	1.2136	1.7648	29
	.56689	.68814	1.4532	.82380	1.2139	1.7640	28
	.56713	.68857	1.4523	.82363	1.2141	1.7633	27
	.56736	.68900	1.4514	.82347	1.2144	1.7625	26
	.56760	.68942	1.4505	.82330	1.2146	1.7618	25
	.56784	.68985	1.4496	.82314	1.2149	1.7610	24
	.56808	.69028	1.4487	.82297	1.2151	1.7603	23
	.56832	.69071	1.4478	.82281	1.2154	1.7596	22
	.56856	.69114	1.4469	.82264	1.2156	1.7588	21
	.56880	.69157	1.4460	.82248	1.2158	1.7581	20
	.56904	.69200	1.4451	.82231	1.2161	1.7573	19
	.56928	.69243	1.4442	.82214	1.2163	1.7566	18
	.56952	.69286	1.4433	.82198	1.2166	1.7559	17
	.56976	.69329	1.4424	.82181	1.2168	1.7551	16
	.57000	.69372	1.4415	.82165	1.2171	1.7544	15
	.57024	.69416	1.4406	.82148	1.2173	1.7537	14
	.57047	.69459	1.4397	.82132	1.2176	1.7529	13
	.57071	.69502	1.4388	.82115	1.2178	1.7522	12
	.57095	.69545	1.4379	.82098	1.2181	1.7515	11
	.57119	.69588	1.4370	.82082	1.2183	1.7507	10
	.57143	.69631	1.4361	.82065	1.2185	1.7500	9
	.57167	.69675	1.4352	.82048	1.2188	1.7493	8
	.57191	.69718	1.4344	.82032	1.2190	1.7485	7
	.57215	.69761	1.4335	.82015	1.2193	1.7478	6
	.57238	.69804	1.4326	.81999	1.2195	1.7471	5
	.57262	.69847	1.4317	.81982	1.2198	1.7463	4
	.57286	.69891	1.4308	.81965	1.2200	1.7456	3
	.57310	.69934	1.4299	.81949	1.2203	1.7449	2
	.57334	.69977	1.4290	.81932	1.2205	1.7442	1
	.57358	.70021	1.4281	.81915	1.2208	1.7434	0
′	Cos	Cot	Tan	Sin	Csc	Sec	′

(304°)   (235°) 55°

35° (215°)   (324°) 144°

′	Sin	Tan	Cot	Cos	Sec	Csc	′
0	.57358	.70021	1.4281	.81915	1.2208	1.7434	60
1	.57381	.70064	1.4273	.81899	1.2210	1.7427	59
2	.57405	.70107	1.4264	.81882	1.2213	1.7420	58
3	.57429	.70151	1.4255	.81865	1.2215	1.7413	57
4	.57453	.70194	1.4246	.81848	1.2218	1.7406	56
5	.57477	.70238	1.4237	.81832	1.2220	1.7398	55
6	.57501	.70281	1.4229	.81815	1.2223	1.7391	54
7	.57524	.70325	1.4220	.81798	1.2225	1.7384	53
8	.57548	.70368	1.4211	.81782	1.2228	1.7377	52
9	.57572	.70412	1.4202	.81765	1.2230	1.7370	51
10	.57596	.70455	1.4193	.81748	1.2233	1.7362	50
11	.57619	.70499	1.4185	.81731	1.2235	1.7355	49
12	.57643	.70542	1.4176	.81714	1.2238	1.7348	48
13	.57667	.70586	1.4167	.81698	1.2240	1.7341	47
14	.57691	.70629	1.4158	.81681	1.2243	1.7334	46
15	.57715	.70673	1.4150	.81664	1.2245	1.7327	45
16	.57738	.70717	1.4141	.81647	1.2248	1.7320	44
17	.57762	.70760	1.4132	.81631	1.2250	1.7312	43
18	.57786	.70804	1.4124	.81614	1.2253	1.7305	42
19	.57810	.70848	1.4115	.81597	1.2255	1.7298	41
20	.57833	.70891	1.4106	.81580	1.2258	1.7291	40
21	.57857	.70935	1.4097	.81563	1.2260	1.7284	39
22	.57881	.70979	1.4089	.81546	1.2263	1.7277	38
23	.57904	.71023	1.4080	.81530	1.2265	1.7270	37
24	.57928	.71066	1.4071	.81513	1.2268	1.7263	36
25	.57952	.71110	1.4063	.81496	1.2271	1.7256	35
26	.57976	.71154	1.4054	.81479	1.2273	1.7249	34
27	.57999	.71198	1.4045	.81462	1.2276	1.7242	33
28	.58023	.71242	1.4037	.81445	1.2278	1.7235	32
29	.58047	.71285	1.4028	.81428	1.2281	1.7228	31
30	.58070	.71329	1.4019	.81412	1.2283	1.7221	30
31	.58094	.71373	1.4011	.81395	1.2286	1.7213	29
32	.58118	.71417	1.4002	.81378	1.2288	1.7206	28
33	.58141	.71461	1.3994	.81361	1.2291	1.7199	27
34	.58165	.71505	1.3985	.81344	1.2293	1.7192	26
35	.58189	.71549	1.3976	.81327	1.2296	1.7185	25
36	.58212	.71593	1.3968	.81310	1.2299	1.7179	24
37	.58236	.71637	1.3959	.81293	1.2301	1.7172	23
38	.58260	.71681	1.3951	.81276	1.2304	1.7165	22
39	.58283	.71725	1.3942	.81259	1.2306	1.7158	21
40	.58307	.71769	1.3934	.81242	1.2309	1.7151	20
41	.58330	.71813	1.3925	.81225	1.2311	1.7144	19
42	.58354	.71857	1.3916	.81208	1.2314	1.7137	18
43	.58378	.71901	1.3908	.81191	1.2317	1.7130	17
44	.58401	.71946	1.3899	.81174	1.2319	1.7123	16
45	.58425	.71990	1.3891	.81157	1.2322	1.7116	15
46	.58449	.72034	1.3882	.81140	1.2324	1.7109	14
47	.58472	.72078	1.3874	.81123	1.2327	1.7102	13
48	.58496	.72122	1.3865	.81106	1.2329	1.7095	12
49	.58519	.72167	1.3857	.81089	1.2332	1.7088	11
50	.58543	.72211	1.3848	.81072	1.2335	1.7081	10
51	.58567	.72255	1.3840	.81055	1.2337	1.7075	9
52	.58590	.72299	1.3831	.81038	1.2340	1.7068	8
53	.58614	.72344	1.3823	.81021	1.2342	1.7061	7
54	.58637	.72388	1.3814	.81004	1.2345	1.7054	6
55	.58661	.72432	1.3806	.80987	1.2348	1.7047	5
56	.58684	.72477	1.3798	.80970	1.2350	1.7040	4
57	.58708	.72521	1.3789	.80953	1.2353	1.7033	3
58	.58731	.72565	1.3781	.80936	1.2355	1.7027	2
59	.58755	.72610	1.3772	.80919	1.2358	1.7020	1
60	.58779	.72654	1.3764	.80902	1.2361	1.7013	0
′	Cos	Cot	Tan	Sin	Csc	Sec	′

125° (305°)   (234°) 54°

NATURAL TRIGONOMETRIC FUNCTIONS TO FIVE PLACES (continued)

36° (216°)   (323°) **143°**   **37° (217°)**   (322°) l

′	Sin	Tan	Cot	Cos	Sec	Csc	′		′	Sin	Tan	Cot	Cos	Sec	Csc	
0	.58779	.72654	1.3764	.80902	1.2361	1.7013	60		0	.60182	.75355	1.3270	.79864	1.2521	1.6616	6
1	.58802	.72699	1.3755	.80885	1.2363	1.7006	59		1	.60205	.75401	1.3262	.79846	1.2524	1.6610	5
2	.58826	.72743	1.3747	.80867	1.2366	1.6999	58		2	.60228	.75447	1.3254	.79829	1.2527	1.6604	5
3	.58849	.72788	1.3739	.80850	1.2369	1.6993	57		3	.60251	.75492	1.3246	.79811	1.2530	1.6597	5
4	.58873	.72832	1.3730	.80833	1.2371	1.6986	56		4	.60274	.75538	1.3238	.79793	1.2532	1.6591	5
5	.58896	.72877	1.3722	.80816	1.2374	1.6979	55		5	.60298	.75584	1.3230	.79776	1.2535	1.6584	5
6	.58920	.72921	1.3713	.80799	1.2376	1.6972	54		6	.60321	.75629	1.3222	.79758	1.2538	1.6578	5
7	.58943	.72966	1.3705	.80782	1.2379	1.6966	53		7	.60344	.75675	1.3214	.79741	1.2541	1.6572	5
8	.58967	.73010	1.3697	.80765	1.2382	1.6959	52		8	.60367	.75721	1.3206	.79723	1.2543	1.6565	5
9	.58990	.73055	1.3688	.80748	1.2384	1.6952	51		9	.60390	.75767	1.3198	.79706	1.2546	1.6559	5
10	.59014	.73100	1.3680	.80730	1.2387	1.6945	50		10	.60414	.75812	1.3190	.79688	1.2549	1.6553	5
11	.59037	.73144	1.3672	.80713	1.2390	1.6939	49		11	.60437	.75858	1.3182	.79671	1.2552	1.6546	4
12	.59061	.73189	1.3663	.80696	1.2392	1.6932	48		12	.60460	.75904	1.3175	.79653	1.2554	1.6540	4
13	.59084	.73234	1.3655	.80679	1.2395	1.6925	47		13	.60483	.75950	1.3167	.79635	1.2557	1.6534	4
14	.59108	.73278	1.3647	.80662	1.2397	1.6918	46		14	.60506	.75996	1.3159	.79618	1.2560	1.6527	4
15	.59131	.73323	1.3638	.80644	1.2400	1.6912	45		15	.60529	.76042	1.3151	.79600	1.2563	1.6521	4
16	.59154	.73368	1.3630	.80627	1.2403	1.6905	44		16	.60553	.76088	1.3143	.79583	1.2566	1.6515	4
17	.59178	.73413	1.3622	.80610	1.2405	1.6898	43		17	.60576	.76134	1.3135	.79565	1.2568	1.6508	4
18	.59201	.73457	1.3613	.80593	1.2408	1.6892	42		18	.60599	.76180	1.3127	.79547	1.2571	1.6502	4
19	.59225	.73502	1.3605	.80576	1.2411	1.6885	41		19	.60622	.76226	1.3119	.79530	1.2574	1.6496	4
20	.59248	.73547	1.3597	.80558	1.2413	1.6878	40		20	.60645	.76272	1.3111	.79512	1.2577	1.6489	4
21	.59272	.73592	1.3588	.80541	1.2416	1.6871	39		21	.60668	.76318	1.3103	.79494	1.2579	1.6483	3
22	.59295	.73637	1.3580	.80524	1.2419	1.6865	38		22	.60691	.76364	1.3095	.79477	1.2582	1.6477	3
23	.59318	.73681	1.3572	.80507	1.2421	1.6858	37		23	.60714	.76410	1.3087	.79459	1.2585	1.6471	3
24	.59342	.73726	1.3564	.80489	1.2424	1.6852	36		24	.60738	.76456	1.3079	.79441	1.2588	1.6464	3
25	.59365	.73771	1.3555	.80472	1.2427	1.6845	35		25	.60761	.76502	1.3072	.79424	1.2591	1.6458	3
26	.59389	.73816	1.3547	.80455	1.2429	1.6838	34		26	.60784	.76548	1.3064	.79406	1.2593	1.6452	3
27	.59412	.73861	1.3539	.80438	1.2432	1.6832	33		27	.60807	.76594	1.3056	.79388	1.2596	1.6446	3
28	.59436	.73906	1.3531	.80420	1.2435	1.6825	32		28	.60830	.76640	1.3048	.79371	1.2599	1.6439	3
29	.59459	.73951	1.3522	.80403	1.2437	1.6818	31		29	.60853	.76686	1.3040	.79353	1.2602	1.6433	3
30	.59482	.73996	1.3514	.80386	1.2440	1.6812	30		30	.60876	.76733	1.3032	.79335	1.2605	1.6427	3
31	.59506	.74041	1.3506	.80368	1.2443	1.6805	29		31	.60899	.76779	1.3024	.79318	1.2608	1.6421	2
32	.59529	.74086	1.3498	.80351	1.2445	1.6799	28		32	.60922	.76825	1.3017	.79300	1.2610	1.6414	2
33	.59552	.74131	1.3490	.80334	1.2448	1.6792	27		33	.60945	.76871	1.3009	.79282	1.2613	1.6408	2
34	.59576	.74176	1.3481	.80316	1.2451	1.6785	26		34	.60968	.76918	1.3001	.79264	1.2616	1.6402	2
35	.59599	.74221	1.3473	.80299	1.2453	1.6779	25		35	.60991	.76964	1.2993	.79247	1.2619	1.6396	2
36	.59622	.74267	1.3465	.80282	1.2456	1.6772	24		36	.61015	.77010	1.2985	.79229	1.2622	1.6390	2
37	.59646	.74312	1.3457	.80264	1.2459	1.6766	23		37	.61038	.77057	1.2977	.79211	1.2624	1.6383	2
38	.59669	.74357	1.3449	.80247	1.2462	1.6759	22		38	.61061	.77103	1.2970	.79193	1.2627	1.6377	2
39	.59693	.74402	1.3440	.80230	1.2464	1.6753	21		39	.61084	.77149	1.2962	.79176	1.2630	1.6371	2
40	.59716	.74447	1.3432	.80212	1.2467	1.6746	20		40	.61107	.77196	1.2954	.79158	1.2633	1.6365	2
41	.59739	.74492	1.3424	.80195	1.2470	1.6739	19		41	.61130	.77242	1.2946	.79140	1.2636	1.6359	1
42	.59763	.74538	1.3416	.80178	1.2472	1.6733	18		42	.61153	.77289	1.2938	.79122	1.2639	1.6353	1
43	.59786	.74583	1.3408	.80160	1.2475	1.6726	17		43	.61176	.77335	1.2931	.79105	1.2641	1.6346	1
44	.59809	.74628	1.3400	.80143	1.2478	1.6720	16		44	.61199	.77382	1.2923	.79087	1.2644	1.6340	1
45	.59832	.74674	1.3392	.80125	1.2480	1.6713	15		45	.61222	.77428	1.2915	.79069	1.2647	1.6334	1
46	.59856	.74719	1.3384	.80108	1.2483	1.6707	14		46	.61245	.77475	1.2907	.79051	1.2650	1.6328	1
47	.59879	.74764	1.3375	.80091	1.2486	1.6700	13		47	.61268	.77521	1.2900	.79033	1.2653	1.6322	1
48	.59902	.74810	1.3367	.80073	1.2489	1.6694	12		48	.61291	.77568	1.2892	.79016	1.2656	1.6316	1
49	.59926	.74855	1.3359	.80056	1.2491	1.6687	11		49	.61314	.77615	1.2884	.78998	1.2659	1.6310	1
50	.59949	.74900	1.3351	.80038	1.2494	1.6681	10		50	.61337	.77661	1.2876	.78980	1.2661	1.6303	1
51	.59972	.74946	1.3343	.80021	1.2497	1.6674	9		51	.61360	.77708	1.2869	.78962	1.2664	1.6297	9
52	.59995	.74991	1.3335	.80003	1.2499	1.6668	8		52	.61383	.77754	1.2861	.78944	1.2667	1.6291	8
53	.60019	.75037	1.3327	.79986	1.2502	1.6661	7		53	.61406	.77801	1.2853	.78926	1.2670	1.6285	7
54	.60042	.75082	1.3319	.79968	1.2505	1.6655	6		54	.61429	.77848	1.2846	.78908	1.2673	1.6279	6
55	.60065	.75128	1.3311	.79951	1.2508	1.6649	5		55	.61451	.77895	1.2838	.78891	1.2676	1.6273	5
56	.60089	.75173	1.3303	.79934	1.2510	1.6642	4		56	.61474	.77941	1.2830	.78873	1.2679	1.6267	4
57	.60112	.75219	1.3295	.79916	1.2513	1.6636	3		57	.61497	.77988	1.2822	.78855	1.2682	1.6261	3
58	.60135	.75264	1.3287	.79899	1.2516	1.6629	2		58	.61520	.78035	1.2815	.78837	1.2684	1.6255	2
59	.60158	.75310	1.3278	.79881	1.2519	1.6623	1		59	.61543	.78082	1.2807	.78819	1.2687	1.6249	1
60	.60182	.75355	1.3270	.79864	1.2521	1.6616	0		60	.61566	.78129	1.2799	.78801	1.2690	1.6243	0
′	Cos	Cot	Tan	Sin	Csc	Sec	′		′	Cos	Cot	Tan	Sin	Csc	Sec	′

126° (306°)   (233°) **53°**   **127° (307°)**   (232°) 5

NATURAL TRIGONOMETRIC FUNCTIONS TO FIVE PLACES (continued)

(218°)   (321°) 141°   39° (219°)   (320°) 140°

Sin.	Tan	Cot	Cos	Sec	Csc	'		'	Sin	Tan	Cot	Cos	Sec	Csc	'
.61566	.78129	1.2799	.78801	1.2690	1.6243	60		0	.62932	.80978	1.2349	.77715	1.2868	1.5890	60
.61589	.78175	1.2792	.78783	1.2693	1.6237	59		1	.62955	.81027	1.2342	.77696	1.2871	1.5884	59
.61612	.78222	1.2784	.78765	1.2696	1.6231	58		2	.62977	.81075	1.2334	.77678	1.2874	1.5879	58
.61635	.78269	1.2776	.78747	1.2699	1.6225	57		3	.63000	.81123	1.2327	.77660	1.2877	1.5873	57
.61658	.78316	1.2769	.78729	1.2702	1.6219	56		4	.63022	.81171	1.2320	.77641	1.2880	1.5867	56
.61681	.78363	1.2761	.78711	1.2705	1.6213	55		5	.63045	.81220	1.2312	.77623	1.2883	1.5862	55
.61704	.78410	1.2753	.78694	1.2708	1.6207	54		6	.63068	.81268	1.2305	.77605	1.2886	1.5856	54
.61726	.78457	1.2746	.78676	1.2710	1.6201	53		7	.63090	.81316	1.2298	.77586	1.2889	1.5850	53
.61749	.78504	1.2738	.78658	1.2713	1.6195	52		8	.63113	.81364	1.2290	.77568	1.2892	1.5845	52
.61772	.78551	1.2731	.78640	1.2716	1.6189	51		9	.63135	.81413	1.2283	.77550	1.2895	1.5839	51
.61795	.78598	1.2723	.78622	1.1719	1.6183	50		10	.63158	.81461	1.2276	.77531	1.2898	1.5833	50
.61818	.78645	1.2715	.78604	1.2722	1.6177	49		11	.63180	.81510	1.2268	.77513	1.2901	1.5828	49
.61841	.78692	1.2708	.78586	1.2725	1.6171	48		12	.63203	.81558	1.2261	.77494	1.2904	1.5822	48
.61864	.78739	1.2700	.78568	1.2728	1.6165	47		13	.63225	.81606	1.2254	.77476	1.2907	1.5816	47
.61887	.78786	1.2693	.78550	1.2731	1.6159	46		14	.63248	.81655	1.2247	.77458	1.2910	1.5811	46
.61909	.78834	1.2685	.78532	1.2734	1.6153	45		15	.63271	.81703	1.2239	.77439	1.2913	1.5805	45
.61932	.78881	1.2677	.78514	1.2737	1.6147	44		16	.63293	.81752	1.2232	.77421	1.2916	1.5800	44
.61955	.78928	1.2670	.78496	1.2740	1.6141	43		17	.63316	.81800	1.2225	.77402	1.2919	1.5794	43
.61978	.78975	1.2662	.78478	1.2742	1.6135	42		18	.63338	.81849	1.2218	.77384	1.2923	1.5788	42
.62001	.79022	1.2655	.78460	1.2745	1.6129	41		19	.63361	.81898	1.2210	.77366	1.2926	1.5783	41
.62024	.79070	1.2647	.78442	1.2748	1.6123	40		20	.63383	.81946	1.2203	.77347	1.2929	1.5777	40
.62046	.79117	1.2640	.78424	1.2751	1.6117	39		21	.63406	.81995	1.2196	.77329	1.2932	1.5771	39
.62069	.79164	1.2632	.78405	1.2754	1.6111	38		22	.63428	.82044	1.2189	.77310	1.2935	1.5766	38
.62092	.79212	1.2624	.78387	1.2757	1.6105	37		23	.63451	.82092	1.2181	.77292	1.2938	1.5760	37
.62115	.79259	1.2617	.78369	1.2760	1.6099	36		24	.63473	.82141	1.2174	.77273	1.2941	1.5755	36
.62138	.79306	1.2609	.78351	1.2763	1.6093	35		25	.63496	.82190	1.2167	.77255	1.2944	1.5749	35
.62160	.79354	1.2602	.78333	1.2766	1.6087	34		26	.63518	.82238	1.2160	.77236	1.2947	1.5744	34
.62183	.79401	1.2594	.78315	1.2769	1.6082	33		27	.63540	.82287	1.2153	.77218	1.2950	1.5738	33
.62206	.79449	1.2587	.78297	1.2772	1.6076	32		28	.63563	.82336	1.2145	.77199	1.2953	1.5732	32
.62229	.79496	1.2579	.78279	1.2775	1.6070	31		29	.63585	.82385	1.2138	.77181	1.2957	1.5727	31
.62251	.79544	1.2572	.78261	1.2778	1.6064	30		30	.63608	.82434	1.2131	.77162	1.2960	1.5721	30
.62274	.79591	1.2564	.78243	1.2781	1.6058	29		31	.63630	.82483	1.2124	.77144	1.2963	1.5716	29
.62297	.79639	1.2557	.78225	1.2784	1.6052	28		32	.63653	.82531	1.2117	.77125	1.2966	1.5710	28
.62320	.79686	1.2549	.78206	1.2787	1.6046	27		33	.63675	.82580	1.2109	.77107	1.2969	1.5705	27
.62342	.79734	1.2542	.78188	1.2790	1.6040	26		34	.63698	.82629	1.2102	.77088	1.2972	1.5699	26
.62365	.79781	1.2534	.78170	1.2793	1.6035	25		35	.63720	.82678	1.2095	.77070	1.2975	1.5694	25
.62388	.79829	1.2527	.78152	1.2796	1.6029	24		36	.63742	.82727	1.2088	.77051	1.2978	1.5688	24
.62411	.79877	1.2519	.78134	1.2799	1.6023	23		37	.63765	.82776	1.2081	.77033	1.2981	1.5683	23
.62433	.79924	1.2512	.78116	1.2802	1.6017	22		38	.63787	.82825	1.2074	.77014	1.2985	1.5677	22
.62456	.79972	1.2504	.78098	1.2804	1.6011	21		39	.63810	.82874	1.2066	.76996	1.2988	1.5672	21
.62479	.80020	1.2497	.78079	1.2807	1.6005	20		40	.63832	.82923	1.2059	.76977	1.2991	1.5666	20
.62502	.80067	1.2489	.78061	1.2810	1.6000	19		41	.63854	.82972	1.2052	.76959	1.2994	1.5661	19
.62524	.80115	1.2482	.78043	1.2813	1.5994	18		42	.63877	.83022	1.2045	.76940	1.2997	1.5655	18
.62547	.80163	1.2475	.78025	1.2816	1.5988	17		43	.63899	.83071	1.2038	.76921	1.3000	1.5650	17
.62570	.80211	1.2467	.78007	1.2819	1.5982	16		44	.63922	.83120	1.2031	.76903	1.3003	1.5644	16
.62592	.80258	1.2460	.77988	1.2822	1.5976	15		45	.63944	.83169	1.2024	.76884	1.3007	1.5639	15
.62615	.80306	1.2452	.77970	1.2825	1.5971	14		46	.63966	.83218	1.2017	.76866	1.3010	1.5633	14
.62638	.80354	1.2445	.77952	1.2828	1.5965	13		47	.63989	.83268	1.2009	.76847	1.3013	1.5628	13
.62660	.80402	1.2437	.77934	1.2831	1.5959	12		48	.64011	.83317	1.2002	.76828	1.3016	1.5622	12
.62683	.80450	1.2430	.77916	1.2834	1.5953	11		49	.64033	.83366	1.1995	.76810	1.3019	1.5617	11
.62706	.80498	1.2423	.77897	1.2837	1.5948	10		50	.64056	.83415	1.1988	.76791	1.3022	1.5611	10
.62728	.80546	1.2415	.77879	1.2840	1.5942	9		51	.64078	.83465	1.1981	.76772	1.3026	1.5606	9
.62751	.80594	1.2408	.77861	1.2843	1.5936	8		52	.64100	.83514	1.1974	.76754	1.3029	1.5601	8
.62774	.80642	1.2401	.77843	1.2846	1.5930	7		53	.64123	.83564	1.1967	.76735	1.3032	1.5595	7
.62796	.80690	1.2393	.77824	1.2849	1.5925	6		54	.64145	.83613	1.1960	.76717	1.3035	1.5590	6
.62819	.80738	1.2386	.77806	1.2852	1.5919	5		55	.64167	.83662	1.1953	.76698	1.3038	1.5584	5
.62842	.80786	1.2378	.77788	1.2855	1.5913	4		56	.64190	.83712	1.1946	.76679	1.3041	1.5579	4
.62864	.80834	1.2371	.77769	1.2859	1.5907	3		57	.64212	.83761	1.1939	.76661	1.3045	1.5573	3
.62887	.80882	1.2364	.77751	1.2862	1.5902	2		58	.64234	.83811	1.1932	.76642	1.3048	1.5568	2
.62909	.80930	1.2356	.77733	1.2865	1.5896	1		59	.64256	.83860	1.1925	.76623	1.3051	1.5563	1
.62932	.80978	1.2349	.77715	1.2868	1.5890	0		60	.64279	.83910	1 1918	.76604	1.3054	1.5557	0
Cos	Cot	Tan	Sin	Csc	Sec	'		'	Cos	Cot	Tan	Sin	Csc	Sec	'

(308°)   (231°) 51°   129° (309°)   (230°) 50°

NATURAL TRIGONOMETRIC FUNCTIONS TO FIVE PLACES (continued)

40° (220°)   (319°) **139°**   **41° (221°)**   (318°) 1

′	Sin	Tan	Cot	Cos	Sec	Csc	′		′	Sin	Tan	Cot	Cos	Sec	Csc	
0	.64279	.83910	1.1918	.76604	1.3054	1.5557	60		0	.65606	.86929	1.1504	.75471	1.3250	1.5243	6
1	.64301	.83960	1.1910	.76586	1.3057	1.5552	59		1	.65628	.86980	1.1497	.75452	1.3253	1.5237	5
2	.64323	.84009	1.1903	.76567	1.3060	1.5546	58		2	.65650	.87031	1.1490	.75433	1.3257	1.5232	5
3	.64346	.84059	1.1896	.76548	1.3064	1.5541	57		3	.65672	.87082	1.1483	.75414	1.3260	1.5227	5
4	.64368	.84108	1.1889	.76530	1.3067	1.5536	56		4	.65694	.87133	1.1477	.75395	1.3264	1.5222	5
5	.64390	.84158	1.1882	.76511	1.3070	1.5530	55		5	.65716	.87184	1.1470	.75375	1.3267	1.5217	5
6	.64412	.84208	1.1875	.76492	1.3073	1.5525	54		6	.65738	.87236	1.1463	.75356	1.3270	1.5212	5
7	.64435	.84258	1.1868	.76473	1.3076	1.5520	53		7	.65759	.87287	1.1456	.75337	1.3274	1.5207	5
8	.64457	.84307	1.1861	.76455	1.3080	1.5514	52		8	.65781	.87338	1.1450	.75318	1.3277	1.5202	5
9	.64479	.84357	1.1854	.76436	1.3083	1.5509	51		9	.65803	.87389	1.1443	.75299	1.3280	1.5197	5
10	.64501	.84407	1.1847	.76417	1.3086	1.5504	50		10	.65825	.87441	1.1436	.75280	1.3284	1.5192	5
11	.64524	.84457	1.1840	.76398	1.3089	1.5498	49		11	.65847	.87492	1.1430	.75261	1.3287	1.5187	4
12	.64546	.84507	1.1833	.76380	1.3093	1.5493	48		12	.65869	.87543	1.1423	.75241	1.3291	1.5182	4
13	.64568	.84556	1.1826	.76361	1.3096	1.5488	47		13	.65891	.87595	1.1416	.75222	1.3294	1.5177	4
14	.64590	.84606	1.1819	.76342	1.3099	1.5482	46		14	.65913	.87646	1.1410	.75203	1.3297	1.5172	4
15	.64612	.84656	1.1812	.76323	1.3102	1.5477	45		15	.65935	.87698	1.1403	.75184	1.3301	1.5167	4
16	.64635	.84706	1.1806	.76304	1.3105	1.5472	44		16	.65956	.87749	1.1396	.75165	1.3304	1.5162	4
17	.64657	.84756	1.1799	.76286	1.3109	1.5466	43		17	.65978	.87801	1.1389	.75146	1.3307	1.5156	4
18	.64679	.84806	1.1792	.76267	1.3112	1.5461	42		18	.66000	.87852	1.1383	.75126	1.3311	1.5151	4
19	.64701	.84856	1.1785	.76248	1.3115	1.5456	41		19	.66022	.87904	1.1376	.75107	1.3314	1.5146	4
20	.64723	.84906	1.1778	.76229	1.3118	1.5450	40		20	.66044	.87955	1.1369	.75088	1.3318	1.5141	4
21	.64746	.84956	1.1771	.76210	1.3122	1.5445	39		21	.66066	.88007	1.1363	.75069	1.3321	1.5136	3
22	.64768	.85006	1.1764	.76192	1.3125	1.5440	38		22	.66088	.88059	1.1356	.75050	1.3325	1.5131	3
23	.64790	.85057	1.1757	.76173	1.3128	1.5435	37		23	.66109	.88110	1.1349	.75030	1.3328	1.5126	3
24	.64812	.85107	1.1750	.76154	1.3131	1.5429	36		24	.66131	.88162	1.1343	.75011	1.3331	1.5121	3
25	.64834	.85157	1.1743	.76135	1.3135	1.5424	35		25	.66153	.88214	1.1336	.74992	1.3335	1.5116	3
26	.64856	.85207	1.1736	.76116	1.3138	1.5419	34		26	.66175	.88265	1.1329	.74973	1.3338	1.5111	3
27	.64878	.85257	1.1729	.76097	1.3141	1.5413	33		27	.66197	.88317	1.1323	.74953	1.3342	1.5107	3
28	.64901	.85308	1.1722	.76078	1.3144	1.5408	32		28	.66218	.88369	1.1316	.74934	1.3345	1.5102	3
29	.64923	.85358	1.1715	.76059	1.3148	1.5403	31		29	.66240	.88421	1.1310	.74915	1.3348	1.5097	3
30	.64945	.85408	1.1708	.76041	1.3151	1.5398	30		30	.66262	.88473	1.1303	.74896	1.3352	1.5092	3
31	.64967	.85458	1.1702	.76022	1.3154	1.5392	29		31	.66284	.88524	1.1296	.74876	1.3355	1.5087	2
32	.64989	.85509	1.1695	.76003	1.3157	1.5387	28		32	.66306	.88576	1.1290	.74857	1.3359	1.5082	2
33	.65011	.85559	1.1688	.75984	1.3161	1.5382	27		33	.66327	.88628	1.1283	.74838	1.3362	1.5077	2
34	.65033	.85609	1.1681	.75965	1.3164	1.5377	26		34	.66349	.88680	1.1276	.74818	1.3366	1.5072	2
35	.65055	.85660	1.1674	.75946	1.3167	1.5372	25		35	.66371	.88732	1.1270	.74799	1.3369	1.5067	2
36	.65077	.85710	1.1667	.75927	1.3171	1.5366	24		36	.66393	.88784	1.1263	.74780	1.3373	1.5062	2
37	.65100	.85761	1.1660	.75908	1.3174	1.5361	23		37	.66414	.88836	1.1257	.74760	1.3376	1.5057	2
38	.65122	.85811	1.1653	.75889	1.3177	1.5356	22		38	.66436	.88888	1.1250	.74741	1.3380	1.5052	2
39	.65144	.85862	1.1647	.75870	1.3180	1.5351	21		39	.66458	.88940	1.1243	.74722	1.3383	1.5047	2
40	.65166	.85912	1.1640	.75851	1.3184	1.5345	20		40	.66480	.88992	1.1237	.74703	1.3386	1.5042	2
41	.65188	.85963	1.1633	.75832	1.3187	1.5340	19		41	.66501	.89045	1.1230	.74683	1.3390	1.5037	1
42	.65210	.86014	1.1626	.75813	1.3190	1.5335	18		42	.66523	.89097	1.1224	.74664	1.3393	1.5032	1
43	.65232	.86064	1.1619	.75794	1.3194	1.5330	17		43	.66545	.89149	1.1217	.74644	1.3397	1.5027	1
44	.65254	.86115	1.1612	.75775	1.3197	1.5325	16		44	.66566	.89201	1.1211	.74625	1.3400	1.5023	1
45	.65276	.86166	1.1606	.75756	1.3200	1.5320	15		45	.66588	.89253	1.1204	.74606	1.3404	1.5018	1
46	.65298	.86216	1.1599	.75738	1.3203	1.5314	14		46	.66610	.89306	1.1197	.74586	1.3407	1.5013	1
47	.65320	.86267	1.1592	.75719	1.3207	1.5309	13		47	.66632	.89358	1.1191	.74567	1.3411	1.5008	1
48	.65342	.86318	1.1585	.75700	1.3210	1.5304	12		48	.66653	.89410	1.1184	.74548	1.3414	1.5003	1
49	.65364	.86368	1.1578	.75680	1.3213	1.5299	11		49	.66675	.89463	1.1178	.74528	1.3418	1.4998	1
50	.65386	.86419	1.1571	.75661	1.3217	1.5294	10		50	.66697	.89515	1.1171	.74509	1.3421	1.4993	1
51	.65408	.86470	1.1565	.75642	1.3220	1.5289	9		51	.66718	.89567	1.1165	.74489	1.3425	1.4988	
52	.65430	.86521	1.1558	.75623	1.3223	1.5283	8		52	.66740	.89620	1.1158	.74470	1.3428	1.4984	
53	.65452	.86572	1.1551	.75604	1.3227	1.5278	7		53	.66762	.89672	1.1152	.74451	1.3432	1.4979	7
54	.65474	.86623	1.1544	.75585	1.3230	1.5273	6		54	.66783	.89725	1.1145	.74431	1.3435	1.4974	6
55	.65496	.86674	1.1538	.75566	1.3233	1.5268	5		55	.66805	.89777	1.1139	.74412	1.3439	1.4969	
56	.65518	.86725	1.1531	.75547	1.3237	1.5263	4		56	.66827	.89830	1.1132	.74392	1.3442	1.4964	
57	.65540	.86776	1.1524	.75528	1.3240	1.5258	3		57	.66848	.89883	1.1126	.74373	1.3446	1.4959	3
58	.65562	.86827	1.1517	.75509	1.3243	1.5253	2		58	.66870	.89935	1.1119	.74353	1.3449	1.4954	2
59	.65584	.86878	1.1510	.75490	1.3247	1.5248	1		59	.66891	.89988	1.1113	.74334	1.3453	1.4950	
60	.65606	.86929	1.1504	.75471	1.3250	1.5243	0		60	.66913	.90040	1.1106	.74314	1.3456	1.4945	0
′	Cos	Cot	Tan	Sin	Csc	Sec	′		′	Cos	Cot	Tan	Sin	Csc	Sec	

130° (310°)   (229°) **49°**   **131° (311°)**   (228°)

NATURAL TRIGONOMETRIC FUNCTIONS TO FIVE PLACES (continued)

(222°) (317°) 137°

′	Sin	Tan	Cot	Cos	Sec	Csc	′
0	.66913	.90040	1.1106	.74314	1.3456	1.4945	60
1	.66935	.90093	1.1100	.74295	1.3460	1.4940	59
2	.66956	.90146	1.1093	.74276	1.3463	1.4935	58
3	.66978	.90199	1.1087	.74256	1.3467	1.4930	57
4	.66999	.90251	1.1080	.74237	1.3470	1.4925	56
5	.67021	.90304	1.1074	.74217	1.3474	1.4921	55
6	.67043	.90357	1.1067	.74198	1.3478	1.4916	54
7	.67064	.90410	1.1061	.74178	1.3481	1.4911	53
8	.67086	.90463	1.1054	.74159	1.3485	1.4906	52
9	.67107	.90516	1.1048	.74139	1.3488	1.4901	51
10	.67129	.90569	1.1041	.74120	1.3492	1.4897	50
11	.67151	.90621	1.1035	.74100	1.3495	1.4892	49
12	.67172	.90674	1.1028	.74080	1.3499	1.4887	48
13	.67194	.90727	1.1022	.74061	1.3502	1.4882	47
14	.67215	.90781	1.1016	.74041	1.3506	1.4878	46
15	.67237	.90834	1.1009	.74022	1.3510	1.4873	45
16	.67258	.90887	1.1003	.74002	1.3513	1.4868	44
17	.67280	.90940	1.0996	.73983	1.3517	1.4863	43
18	.67301	.90993	1.0990	.73963	1.3520	1.4859	42
19	.67323	.91046	1.0983	.73944	1.3524	1.4854	41
20	.67344	.91099	1.0977	.73924	1.3527	1.4849	40
21	.67366	.91153	1.0971	.73904	1.3531	1.4844	39
22	.67387	.91206	1.0964	.73885	1.3535	1.4840	38
23	.67409	.91259	1.0958	.73865	1.3538	1.4835	37
24	.67430	.91313	1.0951	.73846	1.3542	1.4830	36
25	.67452	.91366	1.0945	.73826	1.3545	1.4825	35
26	.67473	.91419	1.0939	.73806	1.3549	1.4821	34
27	.67495	.91473	1.0932	.73787	1.3553	1.4816	33
28	.67516	.91526	1.0926	.73767	1.3556	1.4811	32
29	.67538	.91580	1.0919	.73747	1.3560	1.4807	31
30	.67559	.91633	1.0913	.73728	1.3563	1.4802	30
31	.67580	.91687	1.0907	.73708	1.3567	1.4797	29
32	.67602	.91740	1.0900	.73688	1.3571	1.4792	28
33	.67623	.91794	1.0894	.73669	1.3574	1.4788	27
34	.67645	.91847	1.0888	.73649	1.3578	1.4783	26
35	.67666	.91901	1.0881	.73629	1.3582	1.4778	25
36	.67688	.91955	1.0875	.73610	1.3585	1.4774	24
37	.67709	.92008	1.0869	.73590	1.3589	1.4769	23
38	.67730	.92062	1.0862	.73570	1.3592	1.4764	22
39	.67752	.92116	1.0856	.73551	1.3596	1.4760	21
40	.67773	.92170	1.0850	.73531	1.3600	1.4755	20
41	.67795	.92224	1.0843	.73511	1.3603	1.4750	19
42	.67816	.92277	1.0837	.73491	1.3607	1.4746	18
43	.67837	.92331	1.0831	.73472	1.3611	1.4741	17
44	.67859	.92385	1.0824	.73452	1.3614	1.4737	16
45	.67880	.92439	1.0818	.73432	1.3618	1.4732	15
46	.67901	.92493	1.0812	.73413	1.3622	1.4727	14
47	.67923	.92547	1.0805	.73393	1.3625	1.4723	13
48	.67944	.92601	1.0799	.73373	1.3629	1.4718	12
49	.67965	.92655	1.0793	.73353	1.3633	1.4713	11
50	.67987	.92709	1.0786	.73333	1.3636	1.4709	10
51	.68008	.92763	1.0780	.73314	1.3640	1.4704	9
52	.68029	.92817	1.0774	.73294	1.3644	1.4700	8
53	.68051	.92872	1.0768	.73274	1.3647	1.4695	7
54	.68072	.92926	1.0761	.73254	1.3651	1.4690	6
55	.68093	.92980	1.0755	.73234	1.3655	1.4686	5
56	.68115	.93034	1.0749	.73215	1.3658	1.4681	4
57	.68136	.93088	1.0742	.73195	1.3662	1.4677	3
58	.68157	.93143	1.0736	.73175	1.3666	1.4672	2
59	.68179	.93197	1.0730	.73155	1.3670	1.4667	1
60	.68200	.93252	1.0724	.73135	1.3673	1.4663	0
′	Cos	Cot	Tan	Sin	Csc	Sec	′

132° (312°) (227°) 47°

43° (223°) (316°) 136°

′	Sin	Tan	Cot	Cos	Sec	Csc	′
0	.68200	.93252	1.0724	.73135	1.3673	1.4663	60
1	.68221	.93306	1.0717	.73116	1.3677	1.4658	59
2	.68242	.93360	1.0711	.73096	1.3681	1.4654	58
3	.68264	.93415	1.0705	.73076	1.3684	1.4649	57
4	.68285	.93469	1.0699	.73056	1.3688	1.4645	56
5	.68306	.93524	1.0692	.73036	1.3692	1.4640	55
6	.68327	.93578	1.0686	.73016	1.3696	1.4635	54
7	.68349	.93633	1.0680	.72996	1.3699	1.4631	53
8	.68370	.93688	1.0674	.72976	1.3703	1.4626	52
9	.68391	.93742	1.0668	.72957	1.3707	1.4622	51
10	.68412	.93797	1.0661	.72937	1.3711	1.4617	50
11	.68434	.93852	1.0655	.72917	1.3714	1.4613	49
12	.68455	.93906	1.0649	.72897	1.3718	1.4608	48
13	.68476	.93961	1.0643	.72877	1.3722	1.4604	47
14	.68497	.94016	1.0637	.72857	1.3726	1.4599	46
15	.68518	.94071	1.0630	.72837	1.3729	1.4595	45
16	.68539	.94125	1.0624	.72817	1.3733	1.4590	44
17	.68561	.94180	1.0618	.72797	1.3737	1.4586	43
18	.68582	.94235	1.0612	.72777	1.3741	1.4581	42
19	.68603	.94290	1.0606	.72757	1.3744	1.4577	41
20	.68624	.94345	1.0599	.72737	1.3748	1.4572	40
21	.68645	.94400	1.0593	.72717	1.3752	1.4568	39
22	.68666	.94455	1.0587	.72697	1.3756	1.4563	38
23	.68688	.94510	1.0581	.72677	1.3759	1.4559	37
24	.68709	.94565	1.0575	.72657	1.3763	1.4554	36
25	.68730	.94620	1.0569	.72637	1.3767	1.4550	35
26	.68751	.94676	1.0562	.72617	1.3771	1.4545	34
27	.68772	.94731	1.0556	.72597	1.3775	1.4541	33
28	.68793	.94786	1.0550	.72577	1.3778	1.4536	32
29	.68814	.94841	1.0544	.72557	1.3782	1.4532	31
30	.68835	.94896	1.0538	.72537	1.3786	1.4527	30
31	.68857	.94952	1.0532	.72517	1.3790	1.4523	29
32	.68878	.95007	1.0526	.72497	1.3794	1.4518	28
33	.68899	.95062	1.0519	.72477	1.3797	1.4514	27
34	.68920	.95118	1.0513	.72457	1.3801	1.4510	26
35	.68941	.95173	1.0507	.72437	1.3805	1.4505	25
36	.68962	.95229	1.0501	.72417	1.3809	1.4501	24
37	.68983	.95284	1.0495	.72397	1.3813	1.4496	23
38	.69004	.95340	1.0489	.72377	1.3817	1.4492	22
39	.69025	.95395	1.0483	.72357	1.3820	1.4487	21
40	.69046	.95451	1.0477	.72337	1.3824	1.4483	20
41	.69067	.95506	1.0470	.72317	1.3828	1.4479	19
42	.69088	.95562	1.0464	.72297	1.3832	1.4474	18
43	.69109	.95618	1.0458	.72277	1.3836	1.4470	17
44	.69130	.95673	1.0452	.72257	1.3840	1.4465	16
45	.69151	.95729	1.0446	.72236	1.3843	1.4461	15
46	.69172	.95785	1.0440	.72216	1.3847	1.4457	14
47	.69193	.95841	1.0434	.72196	1.3851	1.4452	13
48	.69214	.95897	1.0428	.72176	1.3855	1.4448	12
49	.69235	.95952	1.0422	.72156	1.3859	1.4443	11
50	.69256	.96008	1.0416	.72136	1.3863	1.4439	10
51	.69277	.96064	1.0410	.72116	1.3867	1.4435	9
52	.69298	.96120	1.0404	.72095	1.3871	1.4430	8
53	.69319	.96176	1.0398	.72075	1.3874	1.4426	7
54	.69340	.96232	1.0392	.72055	1.3878	1.4422	6
55	.69361	.96288	1.0385	.72035	1.3882	1.4417	5
56	.69382	.96344	1.0379	.72015	1.3886	1.4413	4
57	.69403	.96400	1.0373	.71995	1.3890	1.4409	3
58	.69424	.96457	1.0367	.71974	1.3894	1.4404	2
59	.69445	.96513	1.0361	.71954	1.3898	1.4400	1
60	.69466	.96569	1.0355	.71934	1.3902	1.4396	0
′	Cos	Cot	Tan	Sin	Csc	Sec	′

133° (313°) (226°) 46°

NATURAL TRIGONOMETRIC FUNCTIONS TO FIVE PLACES (continued)

44° (224°)   **(315°) 135°**

′	Sin	Tan	Cot	Cos	Sec	Csc	′
0	.69466	.96569	1.0355	.71934	1.3902	1.4396	60
1	.69487	.96625	1.0349	.71914	1.3906	1.4391	59
2	.69508	.96681	1.0343	.71894	1.3909	1.4387	58
3	.69529	.96738	1.0337	.71873	1.3913	1.4383	57
4	.69549	.96794	1.0331	.71853	1.3917	1.4378	56
5	.69570	.96850	1.0325	.71833	1.3921	1.4374	55
6	.69591	.96907	1.0319	.71813	1.3925	1.4370	54
7	.69612	.96963	1.0313	.71792	1.3929	1.4365	53
8	.69633	.97020	1.0307	.71772	1.3933	1.4361	52
9	.69654	.97076	1.0301	.71752	1.3937	1.4357	51
10	.69675	.97133	1.0295	.71732	1.3941	1.4352	50
11	.69696	.97189	1.0289	.71711	1.3945	1.4348	49
12	.69717	.97246	1.0283	.71691	1.3949	1.4344	48
13	.69737	.97302	1.0277	.71671	1.3953	1.4340	47
14	.69758	.97359	1.0271	.71650	1.3957	1.4335	46
15	.69779	.97416	1.0265	.71630	1.3961	1.4331	45
16	.69800	.97472	1.0259	.71610	1.3965	1.4327	44
17	.69821	.97529	1.0253	.71590	1.3969	1.4322	43
18	.69842	.97586	1.0247	.71569	1.3972	1.4318	42
19	.69862	.97643	1.0241	.71549	1.3976	1.4314	41
20	.69883	.97700	1.0235	.71529	1.3980	1.4310	40
21	.69904	.97756	1.0230	.71508	1.3984	1.4305	39
22	.69925	.97813	1.0224	.71488	1.3988	1.4301	38
23	.69946	.97870	1.0218	.71468	1.3992	1.4297	37
24	.69966	.97927	1.0212	.71447	1.3996	1.4293	36
25	.69987	.97984	1.0206	.71427	1.4000	1.4288	35
26	.70008	.98041	1.0200	.71407	1.4004	1.4284	34
27	.70029	.98098	1.0194	.71386	1.4008	1.4280	33
28	.70049	.98155	1.0188	.71366	1.4012	1.4276	32
29	.70070	.98213	1.0182	.71345	1.4016	1.4271	31
30	.70091	.98270	1.0176	.71325	1.4020	1.4267	30
31	.70112	.98327	1.0170	.71305	1.4024	1.4263	29
32	.70132	.98384	1.0164	.71284	1.4028	1.4259	28
33	.70153	.98441	1.0158	.71264	1.4032	1.4255	27
34	.70174	.98499	1.0152	.71243	1.4036	1.4250	26
35	.70195	.98556	1.0147	.71223	1.4040	1.4246	25
36	.70215	.98613	1.0141	.71203	1.4044	1.4242	24
37	.70236	.98671	1.0135	.71182	1.4048	1.4238	23
38	.70257	.98728	1.0129	.71162	1.4052	1.4234	22
39	.70277	.98786	1.0123	.71141	1.4057	1.4229	21
40	.70298	.98843	1.0117	.71121	1.4061	1.4225	20
41	.70319	.98901	1.0111	.71100	1.4065	1.4221	19
42	.70339	.98958	1.0105	.71080	1.4069	1.4217	18
43	.70360	.99016	1.0099	.71059	1.4073	1.4213	17
44	.70381	.99073	1.0094	.71039	1.4077	1.4208	16
45	.70401	.99131	1.0088	.71019	1.4081	1.4204	15
46	.70422	.99189	1.0082	.70998	1.4085	1.4200	14
47	.70443	.99247	1.0076	.70978	1.4089	1.4196	13
48	.70463	.99304	1.0070	.70957	1.4093	1.4192	12
49	.70484	.99362	1.0064	.70937	1.4097	1.4188	11
50	.70505	.99420	1.0058	.70916	1.4101	1.4183	10
51	.70525	.99478	1.0052	.70896	1.4105	1.4179	9
52	.70546	.99536	1.0047	.70875	1.4109	1.4175	8
53	.70567	.99594	1.0041	.70855	1.4113	1.4171	7
54	.70587	.99652	1.0035	.70834	1.4118	1.4167	6
55	.70608	.99710	1.0029	.70813	1.4122	1.4163	5
56	.70628	.99768	1.0023	.70793	1.4126	1.4159	4
57	.70649	.99826	1.0017	.70772	1.4130	1.4154	3
58	.70670	.99884	1.0012	.70752	1.4134	1.4150	2
59	.70690	.99942	1.0006	.70731	1.4138	1.4146	1
60	.70711	1.0000	1.0000	.70711	1.4142	1.4142	0
′	Cos	Cot	Tan	Sin	Csc	Sec	′

134° (314°)   **(225°) 45°**

NATURAL TRIGONOMETRIC FUNCTIONS

FOR ANGLES IN RADIANS

x	Sin	Tan	Cot	Cos	x	Sin	Tan	Cot	Cos
.00	.00000	.00000	∞	1.00000	**.50**	.47943	.54630	1.8305	.87758
.01	.01000	.01000	99.997	0.99995	.51	.48818	.55936	1.7878	.87274
.02	.02000	.02000	49.993	.99980	.52	.49688	.57256	1.7465	.86782
.03	.03000	.03001	33.323	.99955	.53	.50553	.58592	1.7067	.86281
.04	.03999	.04002	24.987	.99920	.54	.51414	.59943	1.6683	.85771
.05	.04998	.05004	19.983	.99875	.55	.52269	.61311	1.6310	.85252
.06	.05996	.06007	16.647	.99820	.56	.53119	.62695	1.5950	.84726
.07	.06994	.07011	14.262	.99755	.57	.53963	.64097	1.5601	.84190
.08	.07991	.08017	12.473	.99680	.58	.54802	.65517	1.5263	.83646
.09	.08988	.09024	11.081	.99595	.59	.55636	.66956	1.4935	.83094
.10	.09983	.10033	9.9666	.99500	**.60**	.56464	.68414	1.4617	.82534
.11	.10978	.11045	9.0542	.99396	.61	.57287	.69892	1.4308	.81965
.12	.11971	.12058	8.2933	.99281	.62	.58104	.71391	1.4007	.81388
.13	.12963	.13074	7.6489	.99156	.63	.58914	.72911	1.3715	.80803
.14	.13954	.14092	7.0961	.99022	.64	.59720	.74454	1.3431	.80210
.15	.14944	.15114	6.6166	.98877	.65	.60519	.76020	1.3154	.79608
.16	.15932	.16138	6.1966	.98723	.66	.61312	.77610	1.2885	.78999
.17	.16918	.17166	5.8256	.98558	.67	.62099	.79225	1.2622	.78382
.18	.17903	.18197	5.4954	.98384	.68	.62879	.80866	1.2366	.77757
.19	.18886	.19232	5.1997	.98200	.69	.63654	.82534	1.2116	.77125
.20	.19867	.20271	4.9332	.98007	**.70**	.64422	.84229	1.1872	.76484
.21	.20846	.21314	4.6917	.97803	.71	.65183	.85953	1.1634	.75836
.22	.21823	.22362	4.4719	.97590	.72	.65938	.87707	1.1402	.75181
.23	.22798	.23414	4.2709	.97367	.73	.66687	.89492	1.1174	.74517
.24	.23770	.24472	4.0864	.97134	.74	.67429	.91309	1.0952	.73847
.25	.24740	.25534	3.9163	.96891	.75	.68164	.93160	1.0734	.73169
.26	.25708	.26602	3.7591	.96639	.76	.68892	.95045	1.0521	.72484
.27	.26673	.27676	3.6133	.96377	.77	.69614	.96967	1.0313	.71791
.28	.27636	.28755	3.4776	.96106	.78	.70328	.98926	1.0109	.71091
.29	.28595	.29841	3.3511	.95824	.79	.71035	1.0092	.99084	.70385
.30	.29552	.30934	3.2327	.95534	**.80**	.71736	1.0296	.97121	.69671
.31	.30506	.32033	3.1218	.95233	.81	.72429	1.0505	.95197	.68950
.32	.31457	.33139	3.0176	.94924	.82	.73115	1.0717	.93309	.68222
.33	.32404	.34252	2.9195	.94604	.83	.73793	1.0934	.91455	.67488
.34	.33349	.35374	2.8270	.94275	.84	.74464	1.1156	.89635	.66746
.35	.34290	.36503	2.7395	.93937	.85	.75128	1.1383	.87848	.65998
.36	.35227	.37640	2.6567	.93590	.86	.75784	1.1616	.86091	.65244
.37	.36162	.38786	2.5782	.93233	.87	.76433	1.1853	.84365	.64483
.38	.37092	.39941	2.5037	.92866	.88	.77074	1.2097	.82668	.63715
.39	.38019	.41105	2.4328	.92491	.89	.77707	1.2346	.80998	.62941
.40	.38942	.42279	2.3652	.92106	**.90**	.78333	1.2602	.79355	.62161
.41	.39861	.43463	2.3008	.91712	.91	.78950	1.2864	.77738	.61375
.42	.40776	.44657	2.2393	.91309	.92	.79560	1.3133	.76146	.60582
.43	.41687	.45862	2.1804	.90897	.93	.80162	1.3409	.74578	.59783
.44	.42594	.47078	2.1241	.90475	.94	.80756	1.3692	.73034	.58979
.45	.43497	.48306	2.0702	.90045	.95	.81342	1.3984	.71511	.58168
.46	.44395	.49545	2.0184	.89605	.96	.81919	1.4284	.70010	.57352
.47	.45289	.50797	1.9686	.89157	.97	.82489	1.4592	.68531	.56530
.48	.46178	.52061	1.9208	.88699	.98	.83050	1.4910	.67071	.55702
.49	.47063	.53339	1.8748	.88233	.99	.83603	1.5237	.65631	.54869
.50	.47943	.54630	1.8305	.87758	**1.00**	.84147	1.5574	.64209	.54030
x	Sin	Tan	Cot	Cos	x	Sin	Tan	Cot	Cos

NATURAL TRIGONOMETRIC FUNCTIONS
FOR ANGLES IN RADIANS (Continued)

x	Sin	Tan	Cot	Cos	x	Sin	Tan	Cot	Cos
1.00	.84147	1.5574	.64209	.54030	1.50	.99749	14.101	.07091	.07074
1.01	.84683	1.5922	.62806	.53186	1.51	.99815	16.428	.06087	.06076
1.02	.85211	1.6281	.61420	.52337	1.52	.99871	19.670	.05084	.05077
1.03	.85730	1.6652	.60051	.51482	1.53	.99917	24.498	.04082	.04079
1.04	.86240	1.7036	.58699	.50622	1.54	.99953	32.461	.03081	.03079
1.05	.86742	1.7433	.57362	.49757	1.55	.99978	48.078	.02080	.02079
1.06	.87236	1.7844	.56040	.48887	1.56	.99994	92.620	.01080	.01080
1.07	.87720	1.8270	.54734	.48012	1.57	1.00000	1255.8	.00080	.00080
1.08	.88196	1.8712	.53441	.47133	1.58	.99996	−108.65	−.00920	−.00920
1.09	.88663	1.9171	.52162	.46249	1.59	.99982	−52.067	−.01921	−.01920
1.10	.89121	1.9648	.50897	.45360	1.60	.99957	−34.233	−.02921	−.02920
1.11	.89570	2.0143	.49644	.44466	1.61	.99923	−25.495	−.03922	−.03919
1.12	.90010	2.0660	.48404	.43568	1.62	.99879	−20.307	−.04924	−.04918
1.13	.90441	2.1198	.47175	.42666	1.63	.99825	−16.871	−.05927	−.05917
1.14	.90863	2.1759	.45959	.41759	1.64	.99761	−14.427	−.06931	−.06915
1.15	.91276	2.2345	.44753	.40849	1.65	.99687	−12.599	−.07397	−.07912
1.16	.91680	2.2958	.43558	.39934	1.66	.99602	−11.181	−.08944	−.08909
1.17	.92075	2.3600	.42373	.39015	1.67	.99508	−10.047	−.09953	−.09904
1.18	.92461	2.4273	.41199	.38092	1.68	.99404	− 9.1208	−.10964	−.10899
1.19	.92837	2.4979	.40034	.37166	1.69	.99290	− 8.3492	−.11977	−.11892
1.20	.93204	2.5722	.38878	.36236	1.70	.99166	− 7.6966	−.12993	−.12884
1.21	.93562	2.6503	.37731	.35302	1.71	.99033	− 7.1373	−.14011	−.13875
1.22	.93910	2.7328	.36593	.34365	1.72	.98889	− 6.6524	−.15032	−.14865
1.23	.94249	2.8198	.35463	.33424	1.73	.98735	− 6.2281	−.16056	−.15853
1.24	.94578	2.9119	.34341	.32480	1.74	.98572	− 5.8535	−.17084	−.16840
1.25	.94898	3.0096	.33227	.31532	1.75	.98399	− 5.5204	−.18115	−.17825
1.26	.95209	3.1133	.32121	.30582	1.76	.98215	− 5.2221	−.19149	−.18808
1.27	.95510	3.2236	.31021	.29628	1.77	.98022	− 4.9534	−.20188	−.19789
1.28	.95802	3.3413	.29928	.28672	1.78	.97820	− 4.7101	−.21231	−.20768
1.29	.96084	3.4672	.28842	.27712	1.79	.97607	− 4.4887	−.22278	−.21745
1.30	.96356	3.6021	.27762	.26750	1.80	.97385	− 4.2863	−.23330	−.22720
1.31	.96618	3.7471	.26687	.25785	1.81	.97153	− 4.1005	−.24387	−.23693
1.32	.96872	3.9033	.25619	.24818	1.82	.96911	− 3.9294	−.25449	−.24663
1.33	.97115	4.0723	.24556	.23848	1.83	.96659	− 3.7712	−.26517	−.25631
1.34	.97348	4.2556	.23498	.22875	1.84	.96398	− 3.6245	−.27590	−.26596
1.35	.97572	4.4552	.22446	.21901	1.85	.96128	− 3.4881	−.28669	−.27559
1.36	.97786	4.6734	.21398	.20924	1.86	.95847	− 3.3608	−.29755	−.28519
1.37	.97991	4.9131	.20354	.19945	1.87	.95557	− 3.2419	−.30846	−.29476
1.38	.98185	5.1774	.19315	.18964	1.88	.95258	− 3.1304	−.31945	−.30430
1.39	.98370	5.4707	.18279	.17981	1.89	.94949	− 3.0257	−.33051	−.31381
1.40	.98545	5.7979	.17248	.16997	1.90	.94630	− 2.9271	−.34164	−.32329
1.41	.98710	6.1654	.16220	.16010	1.91	.94302	− 2.8341	−.35284	−.33274
1.42	.98865	6.5811	.15195	.15023	1.92	.93965	− 2.7463	−.36413	−.34215
1.43	.99010	7.0555	.14173	.14033	1.93	.93618	− 2.6632	−.37549	−.35153
1.44	.99146	7.6018	.13155	.13042	1.94	.93262	− 2.5843	−.38695	−.36087
1.45	.99271	8.2381	.12139	.12050	1.95	.92896	− 2.5095	−.39849	−.37018
1.46	.99387	8.9886	.11125	.11057	1.96	.92521	− 2.4383	−.41012	−.37945
1.47	.99492	9.8874	.10114	.10063	1.97	.92137	− 2.3705	−.42185	−.38868
1.48	.99588	10.983	.09105	.09067	1.98	.91744	− 2.3058	−.43368	−.39788
1.49	.99674	12.350	.08097	.08071	1.99	.91341	− 2.2441	−.44562	−.40703
1.50	.99749	14.101	.07091	.07074	2.00	.90930	− 2.1850	−.45766	−.41615
x	Sin	Tan	Cot	Cos	x	Sin	Tan	Cot	Cos

NATURAL TRIGONOMETRIC FUNCTIONS
SECANTS AND COSECANTS
FOR ANGLES IN RADIANS

x	sec x	csc x	x	sec x	csc x	x	sec x	csc x
0.00	1.00000	∞	0.55	1.17299	1.91319	1.10	2.20460	1.12207
0.01	1.00005	100.00167	0.56	1.18028	1.88258	1.11	2.24890	1.11645
0.02	1.00020	50.00333	0.57	1.18779	1.85311	1.12	2.29525	1.11099
0.03	1.00045	33.33833	0.58	1.19551	1.82474	1.13	2.34379	1.10569
0.04	1.00080	25.00667	0.59	1.20346	1.79739	1.14	2.39467	1.10055
0.05	1.00125	20.00834	0.60	1.21163	1.77103	1.15	2.44806	1.09557
0.06	1.00180	16.67667	0.61	1.22004	1.74560	1.16	2.50413	1.09075
0.07	1.00246	14.29739	0.62	1.22868	1.72107	1.17	2.56311	1.08607
0.08	1.00321	12.51334	0.63	1.23758	1.69738	1.18	2.62519	1.08154
0.09	1.00406	11.12613	0.64	1.24673	1.67449	1.19	2.69063	1.07716
0.10	1.00502	10.01669	0.65	1.25615	1.65238	1.20	2.75970	1.07292
0.11	1.00608	9.10927	0.66	1.26584	1.63101	1.21	2.83271	1.06881
0.12	1.00724	8.35337	0.67	1.27580	1.61034	1.22	2.90997	1.06485
0.13	1.00851	7.71402	0.68	1.28605	1.59035	1.23	2.99188	1.06102
0.14	1.00988	7.16624	0.69	1.29660	1.57100	1.24	3.07885	1.05732
0.15	1.01136	6.69173	0.70	1.30746	1.55227	1.24	3.17136	1.05376
0.16	1.01294	6.27675	0.71	1.31863	1.53413	1.26	3.26993	1.05032
0.17	1.01463	5.91078	0.72	1.33013	1.51657	1.27	3.37518	1.04701
0.18	1.01642	5.58567	0.73	1.34197	1.49954	1.28	3.48778	1.04382
0.19	1.01833	5.29496	0.74	1.35415	1.48305	1.29	3.60853	1.04076
0.20	1.02034	5.03349	0.75	1.36670	1.46705	1.30	3.73833	1.03782
0.21	1.02246	4.79709	0.76	1.37962	1.45154	1.31	3.87822	1.03500
0.22	1.02470	4.58233	0.77	1.39293	1.43650	1.32	4.02941	1.03230
0.23	1.02705	4.38640	0.78	1.40664	1.42191	1.33	4.19329	1.02971
0.24	1.02951	4.20694	0.79	1.42077	1.40775	1.34	4.37153	1.02724
0.25	1.03209	4.04197	0.80	1.43532	1.39401	1.35	4.56607	1.02488
0.26	1.03478	3.88983	0.81	1.45033	1.38067	1.36	4.77923	1.02264
0.27	1.03759	3.74909	0.82	1.46580	1.36772	1.37	5.01379	1.02050
0.28	1.04052	3.61853	0.83	1.48175	1.35514	1.38	5.27313	1.01848
0.29	1.04358	3.49709	0.84	1.49821	1.34293	1.39	5.56133	1.01657
0.30	1.04675	3.38386	0.85	1.51519	1.33106	1.40	5.88349	1.01477
0.31	1.05005	3.27806	0.86	1.53271	1.31954	1.41	6.24593	1.01307
0.32	1.05348	3.17898	0.87	1.55080	1.30834	1.42	6.65666	1.01148
0.33	1.05704	3.08601	0.88	1.56949	1.29746	1.43	7.12598	1.00999
0.34	1.06072	2.99862	0.89	1.58878	1.28688	1.44	7.66732	1.00862
0.35	1.06454	2.91632	0.90	1.60873	1.27661	1.45	8.29856	1.00734
0.36	1.06849	2.83870	0.91	1.62934	1.26662	1.46	9.04406	1.00617
0.37	1.07258	2.76537	0.92	1.65065	1.25691	1.47	9.93782	1.00510
0.38	1.07682	2.69600	0.93	1.67271	1.24747	1.48	11.02881	1.00414
0.39	1.08119	2.63027	0.94	1.69552	1.23830	1.49	12.39028	1.00327
0.40	1.08570	2.56793	0.95	1.71915	1.22938	1.50	14.13683	1.00251
0.41	1.09037	2.50872	0.96	1.74362	1.22072	1.51	16.45850	1.00185
0.42	1.09518	2.45242	0.97	1.76897	1.21229	1.52	19.69493	1.00129
0.43	1.10015	2.39882	0.98	1.79526	1.20410	1.53	24.51881	1.00083
0.44	1.10528	2.34775	0.99	1.82252	1.19614	1.54	32.47654	1.00047
0.45	1.11056	2.29903	1.00	1.85082	1.18840	1.55	48.08888	1.00022
0.46	1.11601	2.25252	1.01	1.88019	1.18087	1.56	92.62589	1.00006
0.47	1.12162	2.20806	1.02	1.91071	1.17356	1.57	+1255.76599	1.00000
0.48	1.12740	2.16554	1.03	1.94243	1.16645	1.58	− 108.65331	1.00004
0.49	1.13336	2.12483	1.04	1.97542	1.15955	1.59	− 52.07657	1.00018
0.50	1.13949	2.08583	1.05	2.00976	1.15284	1.60	− 34.24714	1.00043
0.51	1.14581	2.04844	1.06	2.04552	1.14632			
0.52	1.15231	2.01256	1.07	2.08279	1.13999			
0.53	1.15901	1.97811	1.08	2.12166	1.13384			
0.54	1.16590	1.94501	1.09	2.16223	1.12787			
0.55	1.17299	1.91319	1.10	2.20460	1.12207			

TRIGONOMETRY

NATURAL TRIGONOMETRIC FUNCTIONS
SINE, TANGENT, COTANGENT, COSINE
FOR ANGLES IN πx RADIANS

x		Sin (πx)	Tan (πx)	Cot (πx)	Cos (πx)
.00 or 1.00		.00000	.00000	inf	1.00000
.01	.99	.03141	.03143	31.821	.99951
.02	.98	.06279	.06291	15.895	.99803
.03	.97	.09411	.09453	10.579	.99556
.04	.96	.12533	.12633	7.9158	.99211
.05	.95	.15643	.15838	6.3138	.98769
.06	.94	.18738	.19076	5.2422	.98229
.07	.93	.21814	.22353	4.4737	.97592
.08	.92	.24869	.25676	3.8947	.96858
.09	.91	.27899	.29053	3.4420	.96029
.10	.90	.30902	.32492	3.0777	.95106
.11	.89	.33874	.36002	2.7776	.94088
.12	.88	.36812	.39593	2.5257	.92978
.13	.87	.39715	.43274	2.3109	.91775
.14	.86	.42578	.47056	2.1251	.90483
.15	.85	.45399	.50953	1.9626	.89101
.16	.84	.48175	.54975	1.8190	.87631
.17	.83	.50904	.59140	1.6909	.86074
.18	.82	.53583	.63462	1.5757	.84433
.19	.81	.56208	.67960	1.4715	.82708
.20	.80	.58779	.72654	1.3764	.80902
.21	.79	.61291	.77568	1.2892	.79016
.22	.78	.63742	.82727	1.2088	.77051
.23	.77	.66131	.88162	1.1343	.75011
.24	.76	.68455	.93906	1.0649	.72897
.25	.75	.70711	1.0000	1.0000	.70711
.26	.74	.72897	1.0649	.93906	.68455
.27	.73	.75011	1.1343	.88162	.66131
.28	.72	.77051	1.2088	.82727	.63742
.29	.71	.79016	1.2892	.77568	.61291
.30	.70	.80902	1.3764	.72654	.58779
.31	.69	.82708	1.4715	.67960	.56208
.32	.68	.84433	1.5757	.63462	.53583
.33	.67	.86074	1.6909	.59140	.50904
.34	.66	.87631	1.8190	.54975	.48175
.35	.65	.89101	1.9626	.50953	.45399
.36	.64	.90483	2.1251	.47056	.42578
.37	.63	.91775	2.3109	.43274	.39715
.38	.62	.92978	2.5257	.39593	.36812
.39	.61	.94088	2.7776	.36002	.33874
.40	.60	.95106	3.0777	.32492	.30902
.41	.59	.96029	3.4420	.29053	.27899
.42	.58	.96858	3.8947	.25676	.24869
.43	.57	.97592	4.4737	.22353	.21814
.44	.56	.98229	5.2422	.19076	.18738
.45	.55	.98769	6.3138	.15838	.15643
.46	.54	.99211	7.9158	.12633	.12533
.47	.53	.99556	10.579	.09453	.09411
.48	.52	.99803	15.895	.06291	.06279
.49	.51	.99951	31.821	.03143	.03141
.50	.50	1.0000	inf	.00000	.00000

These functions are useful in the solution of wave equations such as the displacement equation of a sound wave in the form:

$$y = A \sin 2\pi n x$$

without the necessity of reducing the angular rotation either to radians or to degrees in order to find the value of the function.

The algebraic sign of the function follows the familiar Quadrant Law for the particular function desired. Thus a numerical value of 9.13π radians becomes (by the subtraction of the greatest multiple of 2π radians) 1.13π radians. This is the same as $.13\pi$ radians in the 3rd Quadrant, which would give, from the tables above, a value of the sine function of $-.39715$.

Submitted by J. A. Blythe Jr.

NATURAL TRIGONOMETRIC FUNCTIONS IN x RADIANS

x	$\sin \dfrac{\pi x}{2}$	$\tan \dfrac{\pi x}{2}$	$\cot \dfrac{\pi x}{2}$	$1 - x$
0.00	0.00000	0.00000	∞	1.00
0.01	0.01571	0.01571	63.657	0.99
0.02	0.03141	0.03143	31.821	0.98
0.03	0.04711	0.04716	21.205	0.97
0.04	0.06279	0.06291	15.895	0.96
0.05	0.07846	0.07870	12.706	0.95
0.06	0.09411	0.09453	10.579	0.94
0.07	0.10973	0.11040	9.0579	0.93
0.08	0.12533	0.12633	7.9158	0.92
0.09	0.14090	0.14232	7.0264	0.91
0.10	0.15643	0.15838	6.3138	0.90
0.11	0.17193	0.17453	5.7297	0.89
0.12	0.18738	0.19076	5.2422	0.88
0.13	0.20279	0.20709	4.8288	0.87
0.14	0.21814	0.22353	4.4737	0.86
0.15	0.23345	0.24008	4.1653	0.85
0.16	0.24869	0.25676	3.8947	0.84
0.17	0.26387	0.27357	3.6554	0.83
0.18	0.27899	0.29053	3.4420	0.82
0.19	0.29404	0.30764	3.2506	0.81
0.20	0.30902	0.32492	3.0777	0.80
0.21	0.32392	0.34238	2.9208	0.79
0.22	0.33874	0.36002	2.7776	0.78
0.23	0.35347	0.37787	2.6464	0.77
0.24	0.36812	0.39593	2.5257	0.76
0.25	0.38268	0.41421	2.4142	0.75
0.26	0.39715	0.43274	2.3109	0.74
0.27	0.41151	0.45152	2.2148	0.73
0.28	0.42578	0.47056	2.1251	0.72
0.29	0.43994	0.48989	2.0413	0.71
0.30	0.45399	0.50953	1.9626	0.70
0.31	0.46793	0.52947	1.8887	0.69
0.32	0.48175	0.54975	1.8190	0.68
0.33	0.49546	0.57039	1.7532	0.67
0.34	0.50904	0.59140	1.6909	0.66
0.35	0.55250	0.61280	1.6319	0.65
0.36	0.53583	0.63462	1.5757	0.64
0.37	0.54902	0.65688	1.5224	0.63
0.38	0.56208	0.67960	1.4715	0.62
0.39	0.57501	0.70281	1.4229	0.61
0.40	0.58779	0.72654	1.3764	0.60
0.41	0.60042	0.75082	1.3319	0.59
0.42	0.61291	0.77568	1.2892	0.58
0.43	0.62524	0.80115	1.2482	0.57
0.44	0.63742	0.82727	1.2088	0.56
0.45	0.64945	0.85408	1.1708	0.55
0.46	0.66131	0.88162	1.1343	0.54
0.47	0.67301	0.90993	1.0990	0.53
0.48	0.68455	0.93906	1.0649	0.52
0.49	0.69591	0.96907	1.0319	0.51
0.50	0.70711	1.0000	1.0000	0.50
$1 - x$	$\cos \dfrac{\pi x}{2}$	$\cot \dfrac{\pi x}{2}$	$\tan \dfrac{\pi x}{2}$	x

NATURAL TRIGONOMETRIC FUNCTIONS IN x RADIANS

x	$\cos\dfrac{\pi x}{2}$	$\sec\dfrac{\pi x}{2}$	$\csc\dfrac{\pi x}{2}$	$1-x$
0.00	1.0000	1.0000	∞	1.00
0.01	0.99988	1.0001	63.665	0.99
0.02	0.99951	1.0005	31.836	0.98
0.03	0.99889	1.0011	21.229	0.97
0.04	0.99803	1.0020	15.926	0.96
0.05	0.99692	1.0031	12.745	0.95
0.06	0.99556	1.0045	10.626	0.94
0.07	0.99396	1.0061	9.1129	0.93
0.08	0.99211	1.0079	7.9787	0.92
0.09	0.99002	1.0101	7.0972	0.91
0.10	0.98769	1.0125	6.3925	0.90
0.11	0.98511	1.0151	5.8164	0.89
0.12	0.98229	1.0180	5.3367	0.88
0.13	0.97922	1.0212	4.9313	0.87
0.14	0.97592	1.0247	4.5841	0.86
0.15	0.97237	1.0284	4.2837	0.85
0.16	0.96858	1.0324	4.0211	0.84
0.17	0.96456	1.0367	3.7897	0.83
0.18	0.96029	1.0413	3.5843	0.82
0.19	0.95579	1.0463	3.4009	0.81
0.20	0.95106	1.0515	3.2361	0.80
0.21	0.94609	1.0570	3.0872	0.79
0.22	0.94088	1.0628	2.9521	0.78
0.23	0.93544	1.0690	2.8291	0.77
0.24	0.92978	1.0755	2.7165	0.76
0.25	0.92388	1.0824	2.6131	0.75
0.26	0.91775	1.0896	2.5180	0.74
0.27	0.91140	1.0972	2.4300	0.73
0.28	0.90483	1.1052	2.3486	0.72
0.29	0.89803	1.1136	2.2730	0.71
0.30	0.89101	1.1223	2.2027	0.70
0.31	0.88377	1.1315	2.1371	0.69
0.32	0.87631	1.1412	2.0757	0.68
0.33	0.86863	1.1512	2.0183	0.67
0.34	0.86074	1.1618	1.9645	0.66
0.35	0.85264	1.1728	1.9139	0.65
0.36	0.84433	1.1844	1.8663	0.64
0.37	0.83581	1.1964	1.8214	0.63
0.38	0.82708	1.2091	1.7791	0.62
0.39	0.81815	1.2223	1.7391	0.61
0.40	0.80902	1.2361	1.7013	0.60
0.41	0.79968	1.2505	1.6655	0.59
0.42	0.79016	1.2656	1.6316	0.58
0.43	0.78043	1.2813	1.5994	0.57
0.44	0.77051	1.2978	1.5688	0.56
0.45	0.76041	1.3151	1.5398	0.55
0.46	0.75011	1.3331	1.5121	0.54
0.47	0.73963	1.3520	1.4859	0.53
0.48	0.72897	1.3718	1.4608	0.52
0.49	0.71813	1.3925	1.4370	0.51
0.50	0.70711	1.4142	1.4142	0.50
$1-x$	$\sin\dfrac{\pi x}{2}$	$\csc\dfrac{\pi x}{2}$	$\sec\dfrac{\pi x}{2}$	x

SINE AND COSINE FUNCTIONS FOR SPECIAL MULTIPLES OF π RADIANS

k	$\sin\dfrac{2\pi k}{m}$	$\cos\dfrac{2\pi k}{m}$	$\sin\dfrac{2\pi k}{m}$	$\cos\dfrac{2\pi k}{m}$	$\sin\dfrac{2\pi k}{m}$	$\cos\dfrac{2\pi k}{m}$
	$m = 3$		$m = 4$		$m = 5$	
1	0.86603	−0.50000	1.00000	+0.00000	0.95106	+0.30902
2			0.00000	−1.00000	0.58779	−0.80902
	$m = 6$		$m = 7$		$m = 8$	
1	0.86603	+0.50000	0.78183	+0.62349	0.70711	0.70711
2	0.86603	−0.50000	0.97493	−0.22252	1.00000	+0.00000
3	0.00000	−1.00000	0.43388	−0.90097	0.70711	−0.70711
4					0.00000	−1.00000
	$m = 9$		$m = 10$		$m = 11$	
1	0.64279	0.76604	0.58779	0.80902	0.54064	0.84125
2	0.98481	+0.17365	0.95106	+0.30902	0.90963	+0.41542
3	0.86603	−0.50000	0.95106	−0.30902	0.98982	−0.14231
4	0.34202	−0.93969	0.58779	−0.80902	0.75575	−0.65486
5			0.00000	−1.00000	0.28173	−0.95949
	$m = 12$		$m = 13$		$m = 14$	
1	0.50000	0.86603	0.46472	0.88546	0.43388	0.90097
2	0.86603	0.50000	0.82298	0.56806	0.78183	0.62349
3	1.00000	+0.00000	0.99271	+0.12054	0.97493	+0.22252
4	0.86603	−0.50000	0.93502	−0.35460	0.97493	−0.22252
5	0.50000	−0.86603	0.66312	−0.74851	0.78183	−0.62349
6	0.00000	−1.00000	0.23932	−0.97094	0.43388	−0.90097
7					0.00000	−1.00000
	$m = 15$		$m = 16$		$m = 17$	
1	0.40674	0.91355	0.38268	0.92388	0.36124	0.93247
2	0.74314	0.66913	0.70711	0.70711	0.67370	0.73901
3	0.95106	+0.30902	0.92388	0.38268	0.89516	0.44574
4	0.99452	−0.10453	1.00000	+0.00000	0.99573	+0.09227
5	0.86603	−0.50000	0.92388	−0.38268	0.96183	−0.27366
6	0.58779	−0.80902	0.70711	−0.70711	0.79802	−0.60263
7	0.20791	−0.97815	0.38268	−0.92388	0.52643	−0.85022
8			0.00000	−1.00000	0.18375	−0.98297
	$m = 18$		$m = 19$		$m = 20$	
1	0.34202	0.93969	0.32470	0.94582	0.30902	0.95106
2	0.64279	0.76604	0.61421	0.78914	0.58779	0.80902
3	0.86603	0.50000	0.83717	0.54695	0.80902	0.58779
4	0.98481	+0.17365	0.96940	+0.24549	0.95106	0.30902
5	0.98481	−0.17365	0.99658	−0.08258	1.00000	+0.00000
6	0.86603	−0.50000	0.91577	−0.40170	0.95106	−0.30902
7	0.64279	−0.76604	0.73572	−0.67728	0.80902	−0.58779
8	0.34202	−0.93969	0.47595	−0.87947	0.58779	−0.80902
9	0.00000	−1.00000	0.16459	−0.98636	0.30902	−0.95106
10					0.00000	−1.00000
	$m = 21$		$m = 22$		$m = 23$	
1	0.29476	0.95557	0.28173	0.95949	0.26980	0.96292
2	0.56332	0.82624	0.54064	0.84125	0.51958	0.85442
3	0.78183	0.62349	0.75575	0.65486	0.73084	0.68255
4	0.93087	0.36534	0.90963	0.41542	0.88789	0.46007
5	0.99720	+0.07473	0.98982	+0.14231	0.97908	+0.20346
6	0.97493	−0.22252	0.98982	−0.14231	0.99767	−0.06824
7	0.86603	−0.50000	0.90963	−0.41542	0.94226	−0.33488
8	0.68017	−0.73305	0.75575	−0.65486	0.81697	−0.57668
9	0.43388	−0.90097	0.54064	−0.84125	0.63109	−0.77571
10	0.14904	−0.98883	0.28173	−0.95949	0.39840	−0.91721
11			0.00000	−1.00000	0.13617	−0.99069
	$m = 24$		$m = 25$			
1	0.25882	0.96593	0.24869	0.96858		
2	0.50000	0.86603	0.48175	0.87631		
3	0.70711	0.70711	0.68455	0.72897		
4	0.86603	0.50000	0.84433	0.53583		
5	0.96593	0.25882	0.95106	0.30902		
6	1.00000	+0.00000	0.99803	+0.06279		
7	0.96593	−0.25882	0.98229	−0.18738		
8	0.86603	−0.50000	0.90483	−0.42578		
9	0.70711	−0.70711	0.77051	−0.63742		
10	0.50000	−0.86603	0.58779	−0.80902		
11	0.25882	−0.96593	0.36812	−0.92978		
12	0.00000	−1.00000	0.12533	−0.99211		

RADIX TABLE FOR CIRCULAR SINES AND COSINES IN RADIANS

x	n	$\sin\left[x(10^{-n})\right]$	$\cos\left[x(10^{-n})\right]$
1	10	0.00000 00001 00000 00000 00000	0.99999 99999 99999 99999 50000
2	10	0.00000 00002 00000 00000 00000	0.99999 99999 99999 99998 00000
3	10	0.00000 00003 00000 00000 00000	0.99999 99999 99999 99995 50000
4	10	0.00000 00004 00000 00000 00000	0.99999 99999 99999 99992 00000
5	10	0.00000 00005 00000 00000 00000	0.99999 99999 99999 99987 50000
6	10	0.00000 00006 00000 00000 00000	0.99999 99999 99999 99982 00000
7	10	0.00000 00007 00000 00000 00000	0.99999 99999 99999 99975 50000
8	10	0.00000 00008 00000 00000 00000	0.99999 99999 99999 99968 00000
9	10	0.00000 00009 00000 00000 00000	0.99999 99999 99999 99959 50000
1	9	0.00000 00010 00000 00000 00000	0.99999 99999 99999 99950 00000
2	9	0.00000 00020 00000 00000 00000	0.99999 99999 99999 99800 00000
3	9	0.00000 00030 00000 00000 00000	0.99999 99999 99999 99550 00000
4	9	0.00000 00040 00000 00000 00000	0.99999 99999 99999 99200 00000
5	9	0.00000 00050 00000 00000 00000	0.99999 99999 99999 98750 00000
6	9	0.00000 00060 00000 00000 00000	0.99999 99999 99999 98200 00000
7	9	0.00000 00069 99999 99999 99999	0.99999 99999 99999 97550 00000
8	9	0.00000 00079 99999 99999 99999	0.99999 99999 99999 96800 00000
9	9	0.00000 00089 99999 99999 99999	0.99999 99999 99999 95950 00000
1	8	0.00000 00099 99999 99999 99998	0.99999 99999 99999 95000 00000
2	8	0.00000 00199 99999 99999 99987	0.99999 99999 99999 80000 00000
3	8	0.00000 00299 99999 99999 99955	0.99999 99999 99999 55000 00000
4	8	0.00000 00399 99999 99999 99893	0.99999 99999 99999 20000 00000
5	8	0.00000 00499 99999 99999 99792	0.99999 99999 99998 75000 00000
6	8	0.00000 00599 99999 99999 99640	0.99999 99999 99998 20000 00000
7	8	0.00000 00699 99999 99999 99428	0.99999 99999 99997 55000 00000
8	8	0.00000 00799 99999 99999 99147	0.99999 99999 99996 80000 00000
9	8	0.00000 00899 99999 99999 98785	0.99999 99999 99995 95000 00000
1	7	0.00000 00999 99999 99999 98333	0.99999 99999 99995 00000 00000
2	7	0.00000 01999 99999 99999 86667	0.99999 99999 99980 00000 00000
3	7	0.00000 02999 99999 99999 55000	0.99999 99999 99955 00000 00000
4	7	0.00000 03999 99999 99998 93333	0.99999 99999 99920 00000 00000
5	7	0.00000 04999 99999 99997 91667	0.99999 99999 99875 00000 00000
6	7	0.00000 05999 99999 99996 40000	0.99999 99999 99820 00000 00000
7	7	0.00000 06999 99999 99994 28333	0.99999 99999 99755 00000 00000
8	7	0.00000 07999 99999 99991 46667	0.99999 99999 99680 00000 00000
9	7	0.00000 08999 99999 99987 85000	0.99999 99999 99595 00000 00000
1	6	0.00000 09999 99999 99983 33333	0.99999 99999 99500 00000 00000
2	6	0.00000 19999 99999 99866 66667	0.99999 99999 98000 00000 00007
3	6	0.00000 29999 99999 99550 00000	0.99999 99999 95500 00000 00034
4	6	0.00000 39999 99999 98933 33333	0.99999 99999 92000 00000 00107
5	6	0.00000 49999 99999 97916 66667	0.99999 99999 87500 00000 00260
6	6	0.00000 59999 99999 96400 00000	0.99999 99999 82000 00000 00540
7	6	0.00000 69999 99999 94283 33333	0.99999 99999 75500 00000 01000
8	6	0.00000 79999 99999 91466 66667	0.99999 99999 68000 00000 01707
9	6	0.00000 89999 99999 87850 00000	0.99999 99999 59500 00000 02734

For $n > 10$, $\sin\left[x(10^{-n})\right] = x(10^{-n})$; $\cos\left[x(10^{-n})\right] = 1 - \frac{1}{2}x^2(10^{-2n})$; to 25 decimals.

RADIX TABLE FOR CIRCULAR SINES AND COSINES IN RADIANS

x	n	$\sin [x(10^{-n})]$	$\cos [x(10^{-n})]$
1	5	0.00000 99999 99999 83333 33333	0.99999 99999 50000 00000 04167
2	5	0.00001 99999 99998 66666 66667	0.99999 99998 00000 00000 66667
3	5	0.00002 99999 99995 50000 00002	0.99999 99995 50000 00003 37500
4	5	0.00003 99999 99989 33333 33342	0.99999 99992 00000 00010 66667
5	5	0.00004 99999 99979 16666 66693	0.99999 99987 50000 00026 04167
6	5	0.00005 99999 99964 00000 00065	0.99999 99982 00000 00054 00000
7	5	0.00006 99999 99942 83333 33473	0.99999 99975 50000 00100 04167
8	5	0.00007 99999 99914 66666 66940	0.99999 99968 00000 00170 66667
9	5	0.00008 99999 99878 50000 00492	0.99999 99959 50000 00273 37500
1	4	0.00009 99999 99833 33333 34167	0.99999 99950 00000 00416 66667
2	4	0.00019 99999 98666 66666 93333	0.99999 99800 00000 06666 66666
3	4	0.00029 99999 95500 00002 02500	0.99999 99550 00000 33749 99990
4	4	0.00039 99999 89333 33341 86667	0.99999 99200 00001 06666 66610
5	4	0.00049 99999 79166 66692 70833	0.99999 98750 00002 60416 66450
6	4	0.00059 99999 64000 00064 80000	0.99999 98200 00005 39999 99352
7	4	0.00069 99999 42833 33473 39167	0.99999 97550 00010 00416 65033
8	4	0.00079 99999 14666 66939 73333	0.99999 96800 00017 06666 63026
9	4	0.00089 99998 78500 00492 07499	0.99999 95950 00027 33749 92619
1	3	0.00099 99998 33333 34166 66665	0.99999 95000 00041 66666 52778

For $n > 10$, $\sin [x(10^{-n})] = x(10^{-n})$; $\cos [x(10^{-n})] = 1 - \frac{1}{2} x^2 (10^{-2n})$; to 25 decimals.

HAVERSINES

The table that follows gives —values of $\frac{1}{2}(1 - \cos \theta)$ for angles between 0 and 180° are given to five significant figures. The five-place mantissas of the logarithms of the haversines are also given. The correct characteristic must be provided in each case.

The listed values of the haversines were derived from values which were computed to seven significant figures. The logarithms were independently derived from the more exact value of the haversines and are, therefore, in many cases not the exact value of the logarithm of the haversine as listed. This is notably true at the beginning of the table where the logarithm can be given with more exactness than the function.

HAVERSINES

hav $\theta = \frac{1}{2}$ vers $\theta = \frac{1}{2}(1 - \cos \theta) = \sin^2 \frac{1}{2}\theta$
hav $(-\theta) =$ hav θ
hav $(180° - \theta) =$ hav $(180° + \theta) = 1 -$ hav θ
Characteristics of the logarithms are omitted.

$\theta°$	0' Value	Log	10' Value	Log	20' Value	Log	30' Value	Log	40' Value	Log	50' Value	Log
0	.00000	—	.00000	$\bar{6}$.32539	.00001	$\bar{6}$.92745	.00002	.27963	.00003	.52951	.00005	.72332
1	.00008	.88168	.00010	.01557	.00014	.13155	.00017	.23385	.00021	.32536	.00026	.40814
2	.00030	.48371	.00036	.55323	.00041	.61759	.00048	.67751	.00054	.73355	.00061	.78620
3	.00069	.83584	.00076	.88279	.00085	.92733	.0C093	.96970	.00102	.01009	.00112	.04869
4	.00122	.08564	.00132	.12108	.00143	.15513	.00154	.18790	.00166	.21947	.00178	.24993
5	.00190	.27936	.00203	.30782	.00216	.33538	.00230	.36209	.00244	.38800	.00259	.41315
6	.00274	.43760	.00289	.46138	.00305	.48452	.00321	.50706	.00338	.52902	.00355	.55045
7	.00373	.57135	.00391	.59176	.00409	.61170	.00428	.63120	.00447	.65026	.00467	.66891
8	.00487	.68717	.00507	.70505	.00528	.72257	.00549	.73974	.00571	.75657	.00593	.77308
9	.00616	.78929	.00639	.80519	.00662	.82081	.00686	.83615	.00710	.85122	.00735	.86603
10	.00760	.88059	.00785	.89491	.00811	.90900	.00837	.92286	.00864	.93650	.00891	.94992
11	.90919	.96315	.00947	.97617	.00975	.98899	.01004	.00163	.01033	.01409	.01063	.02636
12	.01093	.03847	.01123	.05041	.01154	.06218	.01185	.07379	.01217	.08525	.01249	.09656
13	.01281	.10772	.01314	.11873	.01348	.12961	.01382	.14035	.01416	.15096	.01450	.16144
14	.01485	.17179	.01521	.18202	.01556	.19212	.01593	.20211	.01629	.21198	.01666	.22175
15	.01704	.23140	.01742	.24094	.01780	.25037	.01818	.25971	.01858	.26894	.01897	.27807
16	.01937	.28711	.01977	.29605	.02018	.30490	.02059	.31366	.02101	.32233	.02142	.33091
17	.02185	.33940	.02227	.34782	.02271	.35614	.02314	.36439	.02358	.37256	.02402	.38065
18	.02447	.38866	.02492	.39660	.02538	.40447	.02584	.41226	.02630	.41998	.02677	.42764
19	.02724	.43522	.02772	.44273	.02820	.45018	.02868	.45757	.02917	.46489	.02966	.47215
20	.03015	.47934	.03065	.48647	.03116	.49355	.03166	.50056	.03218	.50752	.03269	.51442
21	.03321	.52127	.03373	.52805	.03426	.53479	.03479	.54147	.03533	.54810	.03587	.55467
22	.03641	.56120	.03695	.56767	.03751	.57410	.03806	.58047	.03862	.58680	.03918	.59308
23	.03975	.59931	.04032	.60550	.04089	.61164	.04147	.61773	.04205	.62379	.04264	.62979
24	.04323	.63576	.04382	.64168	.04442	.64756	.04502	.65340	.04562	.65920	.04623	.66496
25	.04685	.67067	.04746	.67635	.04808	.68199	.04871	.68759	.04934	.69316	.04997	.69869
26	.05060	.70418	.05124	.70963	.05189	.71505	.05253	.72043	.05318	.72578	.05384	.73109
27	.05450	.73637	.05516	.74162	.05582	.74683	.05649	.75201	.05717	.75715	.05785	.76227
28	.05853	.76735	.05921	.77240	.05990	.77742	.06059	.78241	.06129	.78737	.06199	.79230
29	.06269	.79720	.06340	.80207	.06411	.80691	.06482	.81172	.06554	.81651	.06626	.82126
30	.06699	.82599	.06772	.83069	.06845	.83537	.06919	.84001	.06993	.84464	.07067	.84923
31	.07142	.85380	.07217	.85834	.07292	.86286	.07368	.86735	.07444	.87182	.07521	.87626
32	.07598	.88068	.07675	.88507	.07752	.88944	.07830	.89379	.07909	.89811	.07987	.90241
33	.08066	.90668	.08146	.91094	.08226	.91517	.08306	.91938	.08386	.92356	.08467	.92773
34	.08548	.93187	.08630	.93599	.08711	.94009	.08794	.94417	.08876	.94823	.08959	.95227
35	.09042	.95628	.09126	.96028	.09210	.96426	.09294	.96821	.09379	.97215	.09464	.97607
36	.09549	.97996	.09635	.98384	.09721	.98770	.09807	.99154	.09894	.99536	.09981	.99917
37	.10068	.00295	.10156	.00672	.10244	.01047	.10332	.01420	.10421	.01791	.10510	.02161
38	.10599	.02528	.10689	.02894	.10779	.03259	.10870	.03621	.10960	.03982	.11051	.04341
39	.11143	.04699	.11234	.05055	.11326	.05409	.11419	.05762	.11511	.06113	.11604	.06462
40	.11698	.06810	.11791	.07157	.11885	.07501	.11980	.07845	.12074	.08186	.12169	.08526
41	.12265	.08865	.12360	.09202	.12456	.09538	.12552	.09872	.12649	.10205	.12746	.10536
42	.12843	.10866	.12940	.11194	.13038	.11521	.13136	.11847	.13235	.12171	.13333	.12494
43	.13432	.12815	.13532	.13135	.13631	.13454	.13731	.13771	.13832	.14087	.13932	.14402
44	.14033	.14715	.14134	.15027	.14236	.15338	.14337	.15647	.14440	.15955	.14542	.16262
45	.14645	.16568	.14748	.16872	.14851	.17175	.14955	.17477	.15058	.17778	.15163	.18077
46	.15267	.18376	.15372	.18673	.15477	.18968	.15582	.19263	.15688	.19557	.15794	.19849
47	.15900	.20140	.16007	.20430	.16113	.20719	.16220	.21006	.16328	.21293	.16436	.21578
48	.16543	.21863	.16652	.22146	.16760	.22428	.16869	.22709	.16978	.22989	.17087	.23268
49	.17197	.23545	.17307	.23822	.17417	.24098	.17528	.24372	.17638	.24646	.17749	.24918
50	.17861	.25190	.17972	.25460	.18084	.25729	.18196	.25998	.18308	.26265	.18421	.26532
51	.18534	.26797	.18647	.27061	.18761	.27325	.18874	.27587	.18988	.27848	.19102	.28109
52	.19217	.28368	.19332	.28627	.19447	.28885	.19562	.29141	.19677	.29397	.19793	.29652
53	.19909	.29905	.20026	.30158	.20142	.30410	.20259	.30662	.20376	.30912	.20493	.31161
54	.20611	.31409	.20729	.31657	.20847	.31903	.20965	.32149	.21083	.32394	.21202	.32638
55	.21321	.32881	.21440	.33123	.21560	.33365	.21680	.33605	.21800	.33845	.21920	.34084
56	.22040	.34322	.22161	.34559	.22282	.34795	.22403	.35031	.22525	.35266	.22646	.35500
57	.22768	.35733	.22890	.35965	.23012	.36196	.23135	.36427	.23258	.36657	.23381	.36886
58	.23504	.37114	.23627	.37342	.23751	.37569	.23875	.37794	.23999	.38020	.24124	.38244
59	.24248	.38468	.24373	.38691	.24498	.38913	.24623	.39134	.24749	.39355	.24874	.39575
60	.25000	.39794	.25126	.40012	.25252	.40230	.25379	.40447	.25506	.40663	.25632	.40879

HAVERSINES (Continued)

Characteristics of the logarithms are omitted.

$\theta°$	0' Value	Log	10' Value	Log	20' Value	Log	30' Value	Log	40' Value	Log	50' Value	Log
60	.25000	.39794	.25126	.40012	.25252	.40230	.25379	.40447	.25506	.40663	.25632	.40879
61	.25760	.41094	.25887	.41308	.26014	.41521	.26142	.41734	.26270	.41946	.26398	.42157
62	.26526	.42368	.26655	.42578	.26784	.42787	.26913	.42996	.27042	.43203	.27171	.43411
63	.27300	.43617	.27430	.43823	.27560	.44028	.27690	.44232	.27820	.44436	.27951	.44639
64	.28081	.44842	.28212	.45044	.28343	.45245	.28474	.45446	.28606	.45645	.28737	.45845
65	.28869	.46043	.29001	.46241	.29133	.46439	.29265	.46635	.29398	.46831	.29530	.47027
66	.29663	.47222	.29796	.47416	.29929	.47610	.30063	.47803	.30196	.47995	.30330	.48187
67	.30463	.48378	.30597	.48568	.30732	.48758	.30866	.48948	.31000	.49137	.31135	.49325
68	.31270	.49512	.31405	.49699	.31540	.49886	.31675	.50072	.31810	.50257	.31946	.50442
69	.32082	.50626	.32217	.50809	.32353	.50992	.32490	.51174	.32626	.51356	.32762	.51538
70	.32899	.51718	.33036	.51898	.33173	.52078	.33310	.52257	.33447	.52435	.33584	.52613
71	.33722	.52791	.33859	.52968	.33997	.53144	.34135	.53320	.34273	.53495	.34411	.53670
72	.34549	.53844	.34688	.54017	.34826	.54190	.34965	.54363	.35103	.54535	.35242	.54707
73	.35381	.54878	.35521	.55048	.35660	.55218	.35799	.55387	.35939	.55556	.36078	.55725
74	.36218	.55893	.36358	.56060	.36498	.56227	.36638	.56393	.36778	.56559	.36919	.56725
75	.37059	.56889	.37200	.57054	.37340	.57218	.37481	.57381	.37622	.57544	.37763	.57706
76	.37904	.57868	.38045	.58030	.38186	.58191	.38328	.58351	.38469	.58511	.38611	.58671
77	.38752	.58830	.38894	.58988	.39036	.59147	.39178	.59304	.39320	.59461	.39462	.59618
78	.39604	.59774	.39747	.59930	.39889	.60085	.40032	.60240	.40174	.60395	.40317	.60549
79	.40460	.60702	.40602	.60855	.40745	.61008	.40888	.61160	.41031	.61311	.41174	.61463
80	.41318	.61613	.41461	.61764	.41604	.61914	.41748	.62063	.41891	.62212	.42035	.62361
81	.42178	.62509	.42322	.62657	.42466	.62804	.42610	.62951	.42753	.63097	.42897	.63243
82	.43041	.63389	.43185	.63534	.43330	.63678	.43474	.63823	.43618	.63966	.43762	.64110
83	.43907	.64253	.44051	.64395	.44195	.64538	.44340	.64679	.44484	.64821	.44629	.64962
84	.44774	.65102	.44918	.65242	.45063	.65382	.45208	.65521	.45353	.65660	.45497	.65799
85	.45642	.65937	.45787	.66074	.45932	.66212	.46077	.66348	.46222	.66485	.46367	.66621
86	.46512	.66757	.46657	.66892	.46802	.67027	.46948	.67161	.47093	.67295	.47238	.67429
87	.47383	.67562	.47528	.67695	.47674	.67828	.47819	.67960	.47964	.68092	.48110	.68223
88	.48255	.68354	.48400	.68485	.48546	.68615	.48691	.68745	.48837	.68874	.48982	.69004
89	.49127	.69132	.49273	.69261	.49418	.69389	.49564	.69516	.49709	.69644	.49855	.69770
90	.50000	.69897	.50145	.70023	.50291	.70149	.50436	.70274	.50582	.70399	.50727	.70524
91	.50873	.70648	.51018	.70772	.51163	.70896	.51309	.71019	.51454	.71142	.51600	.71265
92	.51745	.71387	.51890	.71509	.52036	.71630	.52181	.71751	.52326	.71872	.52472	.71992
93	.52617	.72112	.52762	.72232	.52907	.72352	.53052	.72471	.53198	.72589	.53343	.72708
94	.53488	.72825	.53633	.72943	.53778	.73060	.53923	.73177	.54068	.73294	.54213	.73410
95	.54358	.73526	.54503	.73642	.54647	.73757	.54792	.73872	.54937	.73987	.55082	.74101
96	.55226	.74215	.55371	.74328	.55516	.74442	.55660	.74554	.55805	.74667	.55949	.74779
97	.56093	.74891	.56238	.75003	.56382	.75114	.56526	.75225	.56670	.75336	.56815	.75446
98	.56959	.75556	.57103	.75666	.57247	.75775	.57390	.75884	.57534	.75993	.57678	.76101
99	.57822	.76209	.57965	.76317	.58109	.76424	.58252	.76531	.58396	.76638	.58539	.76745
100	.58682	.76851	.58826	.76957	.58969	.77062	.59112	.77167	.59255	.77272	.59398	.77377
101	.59540	.77481	.59683	.77585	.59826	.77689	.59968	.77792	.60111	.77895	.60253	.77998
102	.60396	.78101	.60538	.78203	.60680	.78305	.60822	.78406	.60964	.78507	.61106	.78608
103	.61248	.78709	.61389	.78809	.61531	.78909	.61672	.79009	.61814	.79108	.61955	.79208
104	.62096	.79306	.62237	.79405	.62378	.79503	.62519	.79601	.62660	.79699	.62800	.79796
105	.62941	.79893	.63081	.79990	.63222	.80087	.63362	.80183	.63502	.80279	.63642	.80374
106	.63782	.80470	.63922	.80565	.64061	.80660	.64201	.80754	.64340	.80848	.64479	.80942
107	.64619	.81036	.64758	.81129	.64897	.81222	.65035	.81315	.65174	.81407	.65312	.81500
108	.65451	.81592	.65589	.81683	.65727	.81775	.65865	.81866	.66003	.81956	.66141	.82047
109	.66278	.82137	.66416	.82227	.66553	.82317	.66690	.82406	.66827	.82495	.66964	.82584
110	.67101	.82673	.67238	.82761	.67374	.82849	.67510	.82937	.67647	.83025	.67783	.83112
111	.67918	.83199	.68054	.83285	.68190	.83372	.68325	.83458	.68460	.83544	.68595	.83629
112	.68730	.83715	.68865	.83800	.69000	.83885	.69134	.83969	.69268	.84054	.69403	.84138
113	.69537	.84221	.69670	.84305	.69804	.84388	.69937	.84471	.70071	.84554	.70204	.84636
114	.70337	.84718	.70470	.84800	.70602	.84882	.70735	.84963	.70867	.85044	.70999	.85125
115	.71131	.85206	.71263	.85286	.71394	.85366	.71526	.85446	.71657	.85526	.71788	.85605
116	.71919	.85684	.72049	.85763	.72180	.85841	.72310	.85920	.72440	.85998	.72570	.86076
117	.72700	.86153	.72829	.86230	.72958	.86307	.73087	.86384	.73216	.86461	.73345	.86537
118	.73474	.86613	.73602	.86689	.73730	.86764	.73858	.86840	.73986	.86915	.74113	.86990
119	.74240	.87064	.74368	.87138	.74494	.87212	.74621	.87286	.74748	.87360	.74874	.87433
120	.75000	.87506	.75126	.87579	.75251	.87652	.75377	.87724	.75502	.87796	.75627	.87868

HAVERSINES (Continued)

Characteristics of the logarithms are omitted.

$\theta°$	0' Value	Log	10' Value	Log	20' Value	Log	30' Value	Log	40' Value	Log	50' Value	Log
120	.75000	.87506	.75126	.87579	.75251	.87652	.75377	.87724	.75502	.87796	.75627	.87868
121	.75752	.87939	.75876	.88011	.76001	.88082	.76125	.88153	.76249	.88223	.76373	.88294
122	.76496	.88364	.76619	.88434	.76742	.88503	.76865	.88573	.76988	.88642	.77110	.88711
123	.77232	.88780	.77354	.88848	.77475	.88916	.77597	.88984	.77718	.89052	.77839	.89120
124	.77960	.89187	.78080	.89254	.78200	.89321	.78320	.89387	.78440	.89454	.78560	.89520
125	.78679	.89586	.78798	.89651	.78917	.89717	.79035	.89782	.79153	.89847	.79271	.89912
126	.79389	.89976	.79507	.90040	.79624	.90104	.79741	.90168	.79858	.90232	.79974	.90295
127	.80091	.90358	.80207	.90421	.80323	.90484	.80438	.90546	.80553	.90608	.80668	.90670
128	.80783	.90732	.80898	.90794	.81012	.90855	.81126	.90916	.81239	.90977	.81353	.91037
129	.81466	.91098	.81579	.91158	.81692	.91218	.81804	.91277	.81916	.91337	.82028	.91396
130	.82139	.91455	.82251	.91514	.82362	.91573	.82472	.91631	.82583	.91689	.82693	.91747
131	.82803	.91805	.82913	.91862	.83022	.91919	.83131	.91976	.83240	.92033	.83348	.92090
132	.83457	.92146	.83564	.92202	.83672	.92258	.83780	.92314	.83887	.92369	.83993	.92425
133	.84100	.92480	.84206	.92534	.84312	.92589	.84418	.92643	.84523	.92698	.84628	.92751
134	.84733	.92805	.84837	.92859	.84942	.92912	.85045	.92965	.85149	.93018	.85252	.93071
135	.85355	.93123	.85458	.93175	.85560	.93227	.85663	.93279	.85764	.93331	.85866	.93382
136	.85967	.93433	.86068	.93484	.86168	.93535	.86269	.93585	.86369	.93636	.86468	.93686
137	.86568	.93736	.86667	.93785	.86765	.93835	.86864	.93884	.86962	.93933	.87060	.93982
138	.87157	.94030	.87254	.94079	.87351	.94127	.87448	.94175	.87544	.94223	.87640	.94270
139	.87735	.94318	.87831	.94365	.87926	.94412	.88020	.94458	.88115	.94505	.88209	.94551
140	.88302	.94597	.88396	.94643	.88489	.94689	.88581	.94734	.88674	.94779	.88766	.94824
141	.88857	.94869	.88949	.94914	.89040	.94958	.89130	.95003	.89221	.95047	.89311	.95090
142	.89401	.95134	.89490	.95177	.89579	.95221	.89668	.95264	.89756	.95306	.89844	.95349
143	.89932	.95391	.90019	.95433	.90106	.95475	.90193	.95517	.90279	.95559	.90365	.95600
144	.90451	.95641	.90536	.95682	.90621	.95723	.90706	.95763	.90790	.95804	.90874	.95844
145	.90958	.95884	.91041	.95924	.91124	.95963	.91206	.96002	.91289	.96042	.91370	.96081
146	.91452	.96119	.91533	.96158	.91614	.96196	.91694	.96234	.91774	.96272	.91854	.96310
147	.91934	.96347	.92013	.96385	.92091	.96422	.92170	.96459	.92248	.96495	.92325	.96532
148	.92402	.96568	.92479	.96604	.92556	.96640	.92632	.96676	.92708	.96712	.92783	.96747
149	.92858	.96782	.92933	.96817	.93007	.96852	.93081	.96886	.93155	.96921	.93228	.96955
150	.93301	.96989	.93374	.97023	.93446	.97056	.93518	.97089	.93589	.97123	.93660	.97156
151	.93731	.97188	.93801	.97221	.93871	.97253	.93941	.97285	.94010	.97317	.94079	.97349
152	.94147	.97381	.94215	.97412	.94283	.97443	.94351	.97474	.94418	.97505	.94484	.97536
153	.94550	.97566	.94616	.97597	.94682	.97627	.94747	.97656	.94811	.97686	.94876	.97716
154	.94940	.97745	.95003	.97774	.95066	.97803	.95129	.97831	.95192	.97860	.95254	.97888
155	.95315	.97916	.95377	.97944	.95438	.97972	.95498	.97999	.95558	.98027	.95618	.98054
156	.95677	.98081	.95736	.98108	.95795	.98134	.95853	.98161	.95911	.98187	.95968	.98213
157	.96025	.98239	.96082	.98264	.96138	.98290	.96194	.98315	.96249	.98340	.96305	.98365
158	.96359	.98389	.96413	.98414	.96467	.98438	.96521	.98462	.96574	.98486	.96627	.98510
159	.96679	.98533	.96731	.98557	.96782	.98580	.96834	.98603	.96884	.98625	.96935	.98648
160	.96985	.98670	.97034	.98692	.97083	.98714	.97132	.98736	.97180	.98758	.97228	.98779
161	.97276	.98801	.97323	.98822	.97370	.98842	.97416	.98863	.97462	.98884	.97508	.98904
162	.97553	.98924	.97598	.98944	.97642	.98964	.97686	.98983	.97729	.99003	.97773	.99022
163	.97815	.99041	.97858	.99059	.97899	.99078	.97941	.99096	.97982	.99115	.98023	.99133
164	.98063	.99151	.98103	.99168	.98142	.99186	.98182	.99203	.98220	.99220	.98258	.99237
165	.98296	.99254	.98334	.99270	.98371	.99287	.98407	.99303	.98444	.99319	.98479	.99335
166	.98515	.99350	.98550	.99366	.98584	.99381	.98618	.99396	.98652	.99411	.98686	.99425
167	.98719	.99440	.98751	.99454	.98783	.99468	.98815	.99482	.98846	.99496	.98877	.99509
168	.98907	.99523	.98937	.99536	.98967	.99549	.98996	.99562	.99025	.99574	.99053	.99587
169	.99081	.99599	.99109	.99611	.99136	.99623	.99163	.99635	.99189	.99646	.99215	.99658
170	.99240	.99669	.99265	.99680	.99290	.99691	.99314	.99701	.99338	.99712	.99361	.99722
171	.99384	.99732	.99407	.99742	.99429	.99751	.99451	.99761	.99472	.99770	.99493	.99779
172	.99513	.99788	.99533	.99797	.99553	.99805	.99572	.99814	.99591	.99822	.99609	.99830
173	.99627	.99838	.99645	.99845	.99662	.99853	.99679	.99860	.99695	.99867	.99711	.99874
174	.99726	.99881	.99741	.99887	.99756	.99894	.99770	.99900	.99784	.99906	.99797	.99912
175	.99810	.99917	.99822	.99923	.99834	.99928	.99846	.99933	.99857	.99938	.99868	.99943
176	.99878	.99947	.99888	.99951	.99898	.99956	.99907	.99959	.99915	.99963	.99924	.99967
177	.99931	.99970	.99939	.99973	.99946	.99976	.99952	.99979	.99959	.99982	.99964	.99984
178	.99970	.99987	.99974	.99989	.99979	.99991	.99983	.99993	.99986	.99994	.99990	.99995
179	.99992	.99997	.99995	.99998	.99997	.99999	.99998	.99999	.99999	.00000	1.00000	.00000
180	1.00000	.00000										

VI. LOGARITHMIC, EXPONENTIAL, AND HYPERBOLIC FUNCTIONS

LAWS OF EXPONENTS

For a any real number and m a positive integer, the exponential a^m is defined as

$$\underbrace{a \cdot a \cdot a \cdot \cdots \cdot a}_{m \text{ terms}}$$

Using this definition, it is easy to show that the following three *laws of exponents* hold:

I. $a^m \cdot a^n = a^{m+n}$

II. $\dfrac{a^m}{a^n} = \begin{cases} a^{m-n} & \text{if } m > n \\ 1 & \text{if } m = n \\ \dfrac{1}{a^{n-m}} & \text{if } m < n \end{cases}$

III. $(a^m)^n = a^{mn}$

The n-th root function is defined as the inverse of the n-th power function; that is, if

$$b^n = a, \quad \text{then} \quad b = \sqrt[n]{a}.$$

If n is odd, there will be a unique real number satisfying the above definition for $\sqrt[n]{a}$, for any real value of a. If n is even, for positive values of a there will be two real values for $\sqrt[n]{a}$, one positive and one negative. By convention, the symbol $\sqrt[n]{a}$ is understood to mean the positive value in this case. If n is even and a is negative, there are no real values for $\sqrt[n]{a}$.

If we now attempt to extend the definition of the exponential a^t to all rational values of the exponent t, in such a way that the three laws of exponents continue to hold, it is easily shown that the required definitions are:

$$a^0 = 1$$
$$a^{p/q} = \sqrt[q]{a^p}$$
$$a^{-t} = \frac{1}{a^t}$$

In order to avoid difficulties with imaginary numbers and division by zero, a must now be restricted to be positive.

With this extended definition, it is possible to restate the second law of exponents in a simpler form:

II'. $\dfrac{a^m}{a^n} = a^{m-n}$

It is shown in advanced calculus that this definition may be further extended so that the exponent may be any real number, and the laws of exponents continue to hold. When the quantity a^x thus defined is viewed as a function of the exponent x, with the base a held constant, it is a continuous function. Also, if $a > 1$, the exponential function is monotone increasing, and if $0 < a < 1$, it is monotone decreasing.

LOGARITHMS

Any monotone function has a single-valued inverse function, which is also monotone. Furthermore, if the original function is continuous, so is the inverse. Therefore, the inverse function to the exponential function a^x exists for all positive values of a, except $a = 1$. This function is given the name *logarithm to the base a*, abbreviated $\log_a$. That is, if

$$x = a^y, \quad \text{then} \quad y = \log_a x.$$

This function is defined and continuous for all positive values of x. It is monotone increasing if $a > 1$, and monotone decreasing if $a < 1$.

If the laws of exponents are rewritten in terms of logarithms, they become the *laws of logarithms*:

I. $\log_a(xy) = \log_a x + \log_a y$

II. $\log_a\left(\dfrac{x}{y}\right) = \log_a x - \log_a y$

III. $\log_a(x^n) = n \log_a x$

Logarithms derive their main usefulness in computation from the above laws, since they allow multiplication, division, and exponentiation to be replaced by the simpler operations of addition, subtraction, and multiplication, respectively. See the examples which follow.

Further recourse to the definition of logarithm leads to the following formula for change of base

$$\log_a x = \log_b x/\log_b a = (\log_b x) \cdot (\log_a b)$$

Two numbers are commonly used as bases for logarithms. Logarithms to the base 10 are most convenient for use in computation. These logarithm are called common or Briggsian logarithms.

The other usual base for logarithms is an irrational number denoted by e, whose value is approximately 2.71828 .... These logarithms are called natural, Naperian, or hyperbolic logarithms, and occur in many formulas of higher mathematics. The abbreviation ln is frequently used for the natural logarithm function.

Other bases for logarithms, such as 2 and 3, occur in certain applications. These applications are rather specialized and separate tables for these bases are not given. Instead, the formulas for change of base are applied to common or natural logarithms.

If the formulas for change of base are applied to the two usual bases, the following formulas result:

$$\log_{10} x = \log_e x/\log_e 10 = (\log_{10} e)(\log_e x) = M \log_e x$$
$$= 0.43429\ 44819 \log_e x$$

$$\log_e x = \log_{10} x/\log_{10} e = (\log_e 10)(\log_{10} x) = \frac{1}{M} \log_{10} x$$
$$= 2.30258\ 50930 \log_{10} x$$

The following remarks apply to common logarithms.

Since most numbers are irrational powers of ten, a common logarithm, in general, consists of an integer, which is called the characteristic, and an endless decimal, the mantissa.

It is to be observed that the common logarithms of all numbers expressed by the same figures in the same order with the decimal point in different positions have different characteristics but the same mantissa. To illustrate:—if the decimal point stand after the first figure of a number, counting from the left, the characteristic is 0; if after two figures, it is 1; if after three figures, it is 2; and so forth. If the decimal point stand before the first significant figure the characteristic is -1, usually written $\bar{1}$; if there is one zero between the decimal point and the first significant figure it is $\bar{2}$, and so on. For example: log 256 = 2.408240, log 2.56 = 0.408240, log 0.256 = $\bar{1}$.408240, log 0.00256 = $\bar{3}$.408240. The two latter are often written log 0.256 = 9.408240 − 10, log 0.00256 = 7.408240 − 10.

Notice that, although the common logarithm of a number less than one is a negative number, it is customarily written as a negative characteristic and a *positive* mantissa, since the mantissas are usually given in tables as positive numbers. This is the reason that the negative sign is written above the characteristic, since it does not apply to the mantissa. Thus log 0.00256 = $\bar{3}$.408240 = 7.408240 − 10 = -2.591760.

A method of determining characteristics of logarithms is to write the number with one figure to the left of the decimal point multiplied by the appropriate power of 10. The characteristic is then the exponent used. For example:

$$256\ 000\ 000 = 2.56 \times 10^8 \qquad \log = 8.408240$$
$$0.000\ 000\ 256 = 2.56 \times 10^{-7} \qquad \log = \bar{7}.408240 \quad \text{or} \quad 3.408240 - 10$$

Inasmuch as the characteristic may be determined by inspection, the mantissas only are given in tables of common logarithms.

USE OF LOGARITHM TABLES

To find the common logarithm of a number:

(*Note:* This description and examples refer specifically to the table entitled "Six-Place Mantissas for Common Logarithms." For the other tables, there will be minor differences from this description. Most of these differences are obvious. Notes with the individual tables explain any differences which are not immediately obvious.)

For a number of four figures, take out the tabular mantissa on a line with the first three figures of the number and under its fourth figure. The characteristic is determined as previously explained.

For a number of less than four figures, supply zeros to make a four figure number and take the value of the mantissa from the tables as before. For example: log 2 = log 2.000 = 0.301030.

(Notice that in some of the tables not all of the digits of the logarithm are given for every value. For example, in the table of six-place common logarithms, the first two digits of each mantissa are given only once for each line. The remaining four digits of each mantissa are given in the correct place in the table. When the leading two digits are not given on a line, they should be taken from the last line above it on which they do appear. When a mantissa is marked with an asterisk, it indicates that the value for the leading digits is to be taken from the *next* line instead of the present line. Similar remarks apply to the other tables in which this method of presenting the values are used.)

For a number of more than four figures, interpolation must be used. There are several precautions that must be observed when interpolating:

1. Linear interpolation, as described below, may only be used to add one extra digit to the argument (i.e., in the present case, for a five-digit argument).
2. Even though the mantissas given in the table are accurate to six decimal places, interpolated values are accurate only to the same number of places as in the argument, i.e. five places.
3. Because of the rapidly changing values in this region of the table, interpolation is not accurate if the first two digits of the argument are 11 or 12. For this reason, the table has been extended at the end so that such values may be read directly from

the table with five-digit arguments, without interpolation. (The four-place table is not so extended. If interpolation is required in this section of the four-place table, the value should be read instead from the six-place table without interpolation.)

If the above precautions cannot be observed. then higher order interpolation should be used.

Where applicable, linear interpolation is carried out as follows:

Take the tabular value of the mantissa for the first four figures; find the difference between the mantissa and the next greater tabular mantissa and multiply the difference so found by the remaining figures of the number as a decimal and add the product to the mantissa of the first four figures. For example, to find log 46.762:

$$\log 46.76 = 1.669875$$

Tabular difference between this mantissa and that for 4677 is .000092

$$\therefore \log 46.762 = 1.669875 + .2 \times .000092$$
$$= 1.669875 + .000018$$
$$= 1.669893$$

The last digit is not accurate, so must be rounded out. Thus

$$\log 46.762 = 1.66989$$

The accuracy will not ordinarily be affected by more than 1 in the last place if the mantissas are rounded to five decimal places before interpolation, and this makes the computation somewhat easier.

In the four-place logarithm table, a column of proportional parts is given at the end of each line. The number in the column under the fourth digit of the argument is the amount that must be added to any mantissa in that line to interpolate for the fourth digit. This number is to be added to the last place of the mantissa. These numbers are averages for the entire line, so may be off by 1 in the last place.

For example, to find log 33.74

$$\begin{aligned}
\log 33.7 &= 1.5276 \\
\text{proportional part for } 4 &= \underline{5} \\
\therefore \log 33.74 &= 1.5281
\end{aligned}$$

To find the number corresponding to a given logarithm:

(*Note*: This number is called the antilogarithm, and is denoted by $\log^{-1}$. Since the logarithm function is the inverse of the exponential function, $\log_a^{-1} x = a^x$. Therefore, any procedure or table which calculates antilogarithms may also be used to calculate exponentials, and vice-versa. In particular, tables of e^x may be used to compute antilogarithms to the base e.)

The procedure given below refers to the six-place logarithm table. As before, any significant deviation for other tables will be noted.

If the mantissa is found exactly in the table, join the figure at the top which is directly above the given mantissa to the three figures on the line at the left and place the decimal point according to the characteristic of the logarithm. For example,

$$\log^{-1} 3.399674 = \text{antilog } 3.399674 = 2510.$$

If the mantissa is not found exactly in the table it is necessary to interpolate. For example, to find antilog 3.400280, we find in the table

$$\begin{aligned}
\text{antilog } 3.400192 &= 2513. \\
\text{antilog } \underline{3.400365} &= 2514. \\
\text{tabular difference} \quad\quad 173
\end{aligned}$$

The required difference is 88, so we must add $\frac{88}{173}$ = .5.

$$\therefore \text{ antilog } 3.400280 = 2513.5$$

The same precautions must be observed for interpolation in finding antilogarithms as in finding logarithms.

A four-place antilogarithm table is also provided. When using this table, the mantissa of the logarithm is looked up on the margins of the table, and the significant digits of the antilogarithm are read from the body of the table. Lookup and interpolation are done in the same manner as when looking up logarithms in a table of logarithms.

Tables of natural logarithms are used in the same way as tables of common logarithms, except that they contain both the characteristics and the mantissas of the logarithms.

Examples of the use of logarithms in computation follow. Almost all computation with logarithms is done with common logarithms, since the computation of the characteristic is simpler, and since only the significant digits of the argument need be given in the table, without regard for the decimal point location. These examples all use the table of six-place common logarithms.

1. $52600 \times 0.00381 \times 2.74 = 549.11$

log 52600	=	4.720986
log 0.00381	=	3.580925
log 2.74	=	0.437751
adding	=	2.739662
antilog	=	549.11

The sum is the logarithm of the product, the mantissa of which is 739662. On looking up this mantissa in the logarithm tables we see that it corresponds to the digits 54911. The characteristic is 2, hence there are three figures before the decimal point. The number corresponding to the logarithm, called the antilogarithm, is 549.11.

2. $0.00123 \div 52.7 = 0.000\ 023\ 34$ An alternative method:

log 0.00123 = $\bar{3}$.089905		log 0.00123 =	7.089905 − 10
log 52.7 = 1.721811		log 52.7 =	1.721811
subtracting = $\bar{5}$.368094			5.368094 − 10
antilog = 0.000 023 34			

The characteristic 5(5. − 10) shows four zeros after the decimal point before the first significant figure.

3. $\dfrac{273 \times 780}{292 \times 760} \times 15 \times 0.09 = 1.2954$

log 273	= 2.436163		log 292	= 2.465383
log 780	= 2.892095		log 760	= 2.880814
log 15	= 1.176091		log denominator	= 5.346197
log 0.09	= $\bar{2}$.954243			
log numerator	= 5.458592			

log numerator	= 5.458592
log denominator	= 5.346197
subtracting	= 0.112395
antilog	= 1.2954

As division may be accomplished by multiplying by the reciprocal of a number, the above may be considerably simplified. The logarithm of the reciprocal of a number, called the cologarithm, is readily obtained from the table by subtracting the logarithm of the number from zero. This may be readily read off from the table of mantissas. Change the sign of the characteristic algebraically adding to it -1, then mentally subtract each figure of the mantissa from 9 proceeding from left to right, the last figure being subtracted from 10. The example then is:

$$
\begin{aligned}
\log 273 \quad &= 2.436163 \\
\log 780 \quad &= 2.892095 \\
\log \ \ 15 \quad &= 1.176091 \\
\log \ \ \ 0.09 &= \bar{2}.954243 \\
\text{colog } 292 &= \bar{3}.534617 \\
\text{colog } 760 &= \bar{3}.119186 \\
&\ \ \ \ 0.112395
\end{aligned}
$$

4. $(0.00098)^4 = 9.2237 \times 10^{-13}$ An alternative method:

$$
\begin{array}{lll}
\log 0.00098 \quad = \bar{4}.991226 & \qquad \log 0.00098 = \ \ 6.991226 - 10 \\
\underline{\hspace{2.6cm} 4} & \qquad \underline{\hspace{3.6cm} 4} \\
\hspace{1.5cm} 3.964904 \ (a) & \qquad \hspace{1cm} 27.964904 - 40 \\
\bar{4} \times 4 \hspace{1.3cm} = \overline{16.} \hspace{0.8cm} (b) & \qquad \text{or} \ \ 7.964904 - 20 \\
\log (0.00098)^4 = \overline{13}.964904 \ (c) & \qquad \text{or} \ \ \overline{13}.964904 \\
\text{antilog} \hspace{1.4cm} = \ \ 9.2237 \times 10^{-13} & \qquad \text{antilog} \hspace{0.8cm} = \ \ 9.2237 \times 10^{-13}
\end{array}
$$

In the above it will be noted that the mantissa is always positive, hence the multiplication of the mantissa shown at (a), while (b) shows the multiplication of the characteristic. (c) is the algebraic sum.

5. $\sqrt[5]{492} = 3.4546$
$\log 492 = 2.691965$

Dividing the logarithm by 5 gives as the logarithm of the root 0.538393 the antilogarithm of which is 3.4546 both characteristic and mantissa being positive. When the characteristic is negative and not evenly divisible by the root to be taken, a modification of the logarithm is necessary, as the following example shows:

6. $\sqrt[3]{0.000372} = 0.07192$
$\log 3.72 \times 10^{-4} = \ \ \bar{4}.570543 \hspace{1cm} (a)$
$\hspace{2.6cm} = 26.570543 - 30 \ (b)$

Dividing (b) by 3 gives $8.856848 - 10$ which may be written $\bar{2}.856848$ and is the logarithm of the root sought, the antilogarithm of which is 0.07192.

7. $(0.000 \ 372)^{1.2} = 0.000 \ 076 \ 675$
$\log 0.000 \ 372 = \bar{4}.570543$
$\hspace{2.4cm} \text{or} \ 6.570543 - 10$
$\hspace{4.4cm} \underline{1.2}$
$\hspace{2.4cm} 7.884652 - 12$
$\text{antilog} \hspace{1.4cm} = 0.000 \ 076 \ 675$

8. $(0.000372)^{-1.32} = 33642$
$\text{colog } 0.000372 = 3.429457$
$\hspace{3.5cm} \underline{1.32}$
$\hspace{2.6cm} 4.526883$
$\text{antilog} \hspace{1.3cm} = 33642$

SIX-PLACE MANTISSAS FOR COMMON LOGARITHMS

N	0	1	2	3	4	5	6	7	8	9
100	00 0000	0434	0868	1301	1734	2166	2598	3029	3461	3891
01	4321	4751	5181	5609	6038	6466	6894	7321	7748	8174
02	00 8600	9026	9451	9876	*0300	*0724	*1147	*1570	*1993	*2415
03	01 2837	3259	3680	4100	4521	4940	5360	5779	6197	6616
04	01 7033	7451	7868	8284	8700	9116	9532	9947	*0361	*0775
05	02 1189	1603	2016	2428	2841	3252	3664	4075	4486	4896
06	5306	5715	6125	6533	6942	7350	7757	8164	8571	8978
07	02 9384	9789	*0195	*0600	*1004	*1408	*1812	*2216	*2619	*3021
08	03 3424	3826	4227	4628	5029	5430	5830	6230	6629	7028
09	03 7426	7825	8223	8620	9017	9414	9811	*0207	*0602	*0998
110	04 1393	1787	2182	2576	2969	3362	3755	4148	4540	4932
11	5323	5714	6105	6495	6885	7275	7664	8053	8442	8830
12	04 9218	9606	9993	*0380	*0766	*1153	*1538	*1924	*2309	*2694
13	05 3078	3463	3846	4230	4613	4996	5378	5760	6142	6524
14	05 6905	7286	7666	8046	8426	8805	9185	9563	9942	*0320
15	06 0698	1075	1452	1829	2206	2582	2958	3333	3709	4083
16	4458	4832	5206	5580	5953	6326	6699	7071	7443	7815
17	06 8186	8557	8928	9298	9668	*0038	*0407	*0776	*1145	*1514
18	07 1882	2250	2617	2985	3352	3718	4085	4451	4816	5182
19	5547	5912	6276	6640	7004	7368	7731	8094	8457	8819
120	07 9181	9543	9904	*0266	*0626	*0987	*1347	*1707	*2067	*2426
21	08 2785	3144	3503	3861	4219	4576	4934	5291	5647	6004
22	6360	6716	7071	7426	7781	8136	8490	8845	9198	9552
23	08 9905	*0258	*0611	*0963	*1315	*1667	*2018	*2370	*2721	*3071
24	09 3422	3772	4122	4471	4820	5169	5518	5866	6215	6562
25	09 6910	7257	7604	7951	8298	8644	8990	9335	9681	*0026
26	10 0371	0715	1059	1403	1747	2091	2434	2777	3119	3462
27	3804	4146	4487	4828	5169	5510	5851	6191	6531	6871
28	10 7210	7549	7888	8227	8565	8903	9241	9579	9916	*0253
29	11 0590	0926	1263	1599	1934	2270	2605	2940	3275	3609
130	3943	4277	4611	4944	5278	5611	5943	6276	6608	6940
31	11 7271	7603	7934	8265	8595	8926	9256	9586	9915	*0245
32	12 0574	0903	1231	1560	1888	2216	2544	2871	3198	3525
33	3852	4178	4504	4830	5156	5481	5806	6131	6456	6781
34	12 7105	7429	7753	8076	8399	8722	9045	9368	9690	*0012
35	13 0334	0655	0977	1298	1619	1939	2260	2580	2900	3219
36	3539	3858	4177	4496	4814	5133	5451	5769	6086	6403
37	6721	7037	7354	7671	7987	8303	8618	8934	9249	9564
38	13 9879	*0194	*0508	*0822	*1136	*1450	*1763	*2076	*2389	*2702
39	14 3015	3327	3639	3951	4263	4574	4885	5196	5507	5818
140	6128	6438	6748	7058	7367	7676	7985	8294	8603	8911
41	14 9219	9527	9835	*0142	*0449	*0756	*1063	*1370	*1676	*1982
42	15 2288	2594	2900	3205	3510	3815	4120	4424	4728	5032
43	5336	5640	5943	6246	6549	6852	7154	7457	7759	8061
44	15 8362	8664	8965	9266	9567	9868	*0168	*0469	*0769	*1068
45	16 1368	1667	1967	2266	2564	2863	3161	3460	3758	4055
46	4353	4650	4947	5244	5541	5838	6134	6430	6726	7022
47	16 7317	7613	7908	8203	8497	8792	9086	9380	9674	9968
48	17 0262	0555	0848	1141	1434	1726	2019	2311	2603	2895
49	3186	3478	3769	4060	4351	4641	4932	5222	5512	5802
150	17 6091	6381	6670	6959	7248	7536	7825	8113	8401	8689

N	0	1	2	3	4	5	6	7	8	9

SIX-PLACE MANTISSAS FOR COMMON LOGARITHMS (Continued)

N	0	1	2	3	4	5	6	7	8	9
150	17 6091	6381	6670	6959	7248	7536	7825	8113	8401	8689
51	17 8977	9264	9552	9839	*0126	*0413	*0699	*0986	*1272	*1558
52	18 1844	2129	2415	2700	2985	3270	3555	3839	4123	4407
53	4691	4975	5259	5542	5825	6108	6391	6674	6956	7239
54	18 7521	7803	8084	8366	8647	8928	9209	9490	9771	*0051
55	19 0332	0612	0892	1171	1451	1730	2010	2289	2567	2846
56	3125	3403	3681	3959	4237	4514	4792	5069	5346	5623
57	5900	6176	6453	6729	7005	7281	7556	7832	8107	8382
58	19 8657	8932	9206	9481	9755	*0029	*0303	*0577	*0850	*1124
59	20 1397	1670	1943	2216	2488	2761	3033	3305	3577	3848
160	4120	4391	4663	4934	5204	5475	5746	6016	6286	6556
61	6826	7096	7365	7634	7904	8173	8441	8710	8979	9247
62	20 9515	9783	*0051	*0319	*0586	*0853	*1121	*1388	*1654	*1921
63	21 2188	2454	2720	2986	3252	3518	3783	4049	4314	4579
64	4844	5109	5373	5638	5902	6166	6430	6694	6957	7221
65	21 7484	7747	8010	8273	8536	8798	9060	9323	9585	9846
66	22 0108	0370	0631	0892	1153	1414	1675	1936	2196	2456
67	2716	2976	3236	3496	3755	4015	4274	4533	4792	5051
68	5309	5568	5826	6084	6342	6600	6858	7115	7372	7630
69	22 7887	8144	8400	8657	8913	9170	9426	9682	9938	*0193
170	23 0449	0704	0960	1215	1470	1724	1979	2234	2488	2742
71	2996	3250	3504	3757	4011	4264	4517	4770	5023	5276
72	5528	5781	6033	6285	6537	6789	7041	7292	7544	7795
73	23 8046	8297	8548	8799	9049	9299	9550	9800	*0050	*0300
74	24 0549	0799	1048	1297	1546	1795	2044	2293	2541	2790
75	3038	3286	3534	3782	4030	4277	4525	4772	5019	5266
76	5513	5759	6006	6252	6499	6745	6991	7237	7482	7728
77	24 7973	8219	8464	8709	8954	9198	9443	9687	9932	*0176
78	25 0420	0664	0908	1151	1395	1638	1881	2125	2368	2610
79	2853	3096	3338	3580	3822	4064	4306	4548	4790	5031
180	5273	5514	5755	5996	6237	6477	6718	6958	7198	7439
81	25 7679	7918	8158	8398	8637	8877	9116	9355	9594	9833
82	26 0071	0310	0548	0787	1025	1263	1501	1739	1976	2214
83	2451	2688	2925	3162	3399	3636	3873	4109	4346	4582
84	4818	5054	5290	5525	5761	5996	6232	6467	6702	6937
85	7172	7406	7641	7875	8110	8344	8578	8812	9046	9279
86	26 9513	9746	9980	*0213	*0446	*0679	*0912	*1144	*1377	*1609
87	27 1842	2074	2306	2538	2770	3001	3233	3464	3696	3927
88	4158	4389	4620	4850	5081	5311	5542	5772	6002	6232
89	6462	6692	6921	7151	7380	7609	7838	8067	8296	8525
190	27 8754	8982	9211	9439	9667	9895	*0123	*0351	*0578	*0806
91	28 1033	1261	1488	1715	1942	2169	2396	2622	2849	3075
92	3301	3527	3753	3979	4205	4431	4656	4882	5107	5332
93	5557	5782	6007	6232	6456	6681	6905	7130	7354	7578
94	28 7802	8026	8249	8473	8696	8920	9143	9366	9589	9812
95	29 0035	0257	0480	0702	0925	1147	1369	1591	1813	2034
96	2256	2478	2699	2920	3141	3363	3584	3804	4025	4246
97	4466	4687	4907	5127	5347	5567	5787	6007	6226	6446
98	6665	6884	7104	7323	7542	7761	7979	8198	8416	8635
99	29 8853	9071	9289	9507	9725	9943	*0161	*0378	*0595	*0813
200	30 1030	1247	1464	1681	1898	2114	2331	2547	2764	2980
N	0	1	2	3	4	5	6	7	8	9

SIX-PLACE MANTISSAS FOR COMMON LOGARITHMS (Continued)

N	0	1	2	3	4	5	6	7	8	9
200	30 1030	1247	1464	1681	1898	2114	2331	2547	2764	2980
01	3196	3412	3628	3844	4059	4275	4491	4706	4921	5136
02	5351	5566	5781	5996	6211	6425	6639	6854	7068	7282
03	7496	7710	7924	8137	8351	8564	8778	8991	9204	9417
04	30 9630	9843	*0056	*0268	*0481	*0693	*0906	*1118	*1330	*1542
05	31 1754	1966	2177	2389	2600	2812	3023	3234	3445	3656
06	3867	4078	4289	4499	4710	4920	5130	5340	5551	5760
07	5970	6180	6390	6599	6809	7018	7227	7436	7646	7854
08	31 8063	8272	8481	8689	8898	9106	9314	9522	9730	9938
09	32 0146	0354	0562	0769	0977	1184	1391	1598	1805	2012
210	2219	2426	2633	2839	3046	3252	3458	3665	3871	4077
11	4282	4488	4694	4899	5105	5310	5516	5721	5926	6131
12	6336	6541	6745	6950	7155	7359	7563	7767	7972	8176
13	32 8380	8583	8787	8991	9194	9398	9601	9805	*0008	*0211
14	33 0414	0617	0819	1022	1225	1427	1630	1832	2034	2236
15	2438	2640	2842	3044	3246	3447	3649	3850	4051	4253
16	4454	4655	4856	5057	5257	5458	5658	5859	6059	6260
17	6460	6660	6860	7060	7260	7459	7659	7858	8058	8257
18	33 8456	8656	8855	9054	9253	9451	9650	9849	*0047	*0246
19	34 0444	0642	0841	1039	1237	1435	1632	1830	2028	2225
220	2423	2620	2817	3014	3212	3409	3606	3802	3999	4196
21	4392	4589	4785	4981	5178	5374	5570	5766	5962	6157
22	6353	6549	6744	6939	7135	7330	7525	7720	7915	8110
23	34 8305	8500	8694	8889	9083	9278	9472	9666	9860	*0054
24	35 0248	0442	0636	0829	1023	1216	1410	1603	1796	1989
25	2183	2375	2568	2761	2954	3147	3339	3532	3724	3916
26	4108	4301	4493	4685	4876	5068	5260	5452	5643	5834
27	6026	6217	6408	6599	6790	6981	7172	7363	7554	7744
28	7935	8125	8316	8506	8696	8886	9076	9266	9456	9646
29	35 9835	*0025	*0215	*0404	*0593	*0783	*0972	*1161	*1350	*1539
230	36 1728	1917	2105	2294	2482	2671	2859	3048	3236	3424
31	3612	3800	3988	4176	4363	4551	4739	4926	5113	5301
32	5488	5675	5862	6049	6236	6423	6610	6796	6983	7169
33	7356	7542	7729	7915	8101	8287	8473	8659	8845	9030
34	36 9216	9401	9587	9772	9958	*0143	*0328	*0513	*0698	*0883
35	37 1068	1253	1437	1622	1806	1991	2175	2360	2544	2728
36	2912	3096	3280	3464	3647	3831	4015	4198	4382	4565
37	4748	4932	5115	5298	5481	5664	5846	6029	6212	6394
38	6577	6759	6942	7124	7306	7488	7670	7852	8034	8216
39	37 8398	8580	8761	8943	9124	9306	9487	9668	9849	*0030
240	38 0211	0392	0573	0754	0934	1115	1296	1476	1656	1837
41	2017	2197	2377	2557	2737	2917	3097	3277	3456	3636
42	3815	3995	4174	4353	4533	4712	4891	5070	5249	5428
43	5606	5785	5964	6142	6321	6499	6677	6856	7034	7212
44	7390	7568	7746	7924	8101	8279	8456	8634	8811	8989
45	38 9166	9343	9520	9698	9875	*0051	*0228	*0405	*0582	*0759
46	39 0935	1112	1288	1464	1641	1817	1993	2169	2345	2521
47	2697	2873	3048	3224	3400	3575	3751	3926	4101	4277
48	4452	4627	4802	4977	5152	5326	5501	5676	5850	6025
49	6199	6374	6548	6722	6896	7071	7245	7419	7592	7766
250	39 7940	8114	8287	8461	8634	8808	8981	9154	9328	9501
N	0	1	2	3	4	5	6	7	8	9

SIX-PLACE MANTISSAS FOR COMMON LOGARITHMS (Continued)

N	0	1	2	3	4	5	6	7	8	9
250	39 7940	8114	8287	8461	8634	8808	8981	9154	9328	9501
51	39 9674	9847	*0020	*0192	*0365	*0538	*0711	*0883	*1056	*1228
52	40 1401	1573	1745	1917	2089	2261	2433	2605	2777	2949
53	3121	3292	3464	3635	3807	3978	4149	4320	4492	4663
54	4834	5005	5176	5346	5517	5688	5858	6029	6199	6370
55	6540	6710	6881	7051	7221	7391	7561	7731	7901	8070
56	8240	8410	8579	8749	8918	9087	9257	9426	9595	9764
57	40 9933	*0102	*0271	*0440	*0609	*0777	*0946	*1114	*1283	*1451
58	41 1620	1788	1956	2124	2293	2461	2629	2796	2964	3132
59	3300	3467	3635	3803	3970	4137	4305	4472	4639	4806
260	4973	5140	5307 ·	5474	5641	5808	5974	6141	6308	6474
61	6641	6807	6973	7139	7306	7472	7638	7804	7970	8135
62	8301	8467	8633	8798	8964	9129	9295	9460	9625	9791
63	41 9956	*0121	*0286	*0451	*0616	*0781	*0945	*1110	*1275	*1439
64	42 1604	1768	1933	2097	2261	2426	2590	2754	2918	3082
65	3246	3410	3574	3737	3901	4065	4228	4392	4555	4718
66	4882	5045	5208	5371	5534	5697	5860	6023	6186	6349
67	6511	6674	6836	6999	7161	7324	7486	7648	7811	7973
68	8135	8297	8459	8621	8783	8944	9106	9268	9429	9591
69	42 9752	9914	*0075	*0236	*0398	*0559	*0720	*0881	*1042	*1203
270	43 1364	1525	1685	1846	2007	2167	2328	2488	2649	2809
71	2969	3130	3290	3450	3610	3770	3930	4090	4249	4409
72	4569	4729	4888	5048	5207	5367	5526	5685	5844	6004
73	6163	6322	6481	6640	6799	6957	7116	7275	7433	7592
74	7751	7909	8067	8226	8384	8542	8701	8859	9017	9175
75	43 9333	9491	9648	9806	9964	*0122	*0279	*0437	*0594	*0752
76	44 0909	1066	1224	1381	1538	1695	1852	2009	2166	2323
77	2480	2637	2793	2950	3106	3263	3419	3576	3732	3889
78	4045	4201	4357	4513	4669	4825	4981	5137	5293	5449
79	5604	5760	5915	6071	6226	6382	6537	6692	6848	7003
280	7158	7313	7468	7623	7778	7933	8088	8242	8397	8552
81	44 8706	8861	9015	9170	9324	9478	9633	9787	9941	*0095
82	45 0249	0403	0557	0711	0865	1018	1172	1326	1479	1633
83	1786	1940	2093	2247	2400	2553	2706	2859	3012	3165
84	3318	3471	3624	3777	3930	4082	4235	4387	4540	4692
85	4845	4997	5150	5302	5454	5606	5758	5910	6062	6214
86	6366	6518	6670	6821	6973	7125	7276	7428	7579	7731
87	7882	8033	8184	8336	8487	8638	8789	8940	9091	9242
88	45 9392	9543	9694	9845	9995	*0146	*0296	*0447	*0597	*0748
89	46 0898	1048	1198	1348	1499	1649	1799	1948	2098	2248
290	2398	2548	2697	2847	2997	3146	3296	3445	3594	3744
91	3893	4042	4191	4340	4490	4639	4788	4936	5085	5234
92	5383	5532	5680	5829	5977	6126	6274	6423	6571	6719
93	6868	7016	7164	7312	7460	7608	7756	7904	8052	8200
94	8347	8495	8643	8790	8938	9085	9233	9380	9527	9675
95	46 9822	9969	*0116	*0263	*0410	*0557	*0704	*0851	*0998	*1145
96	47 1292	1438	1585	1732	1878	2025	2171	2318	2464	2610
97	2756	2903	3049	3195	3341	3487	3633	3779	3925	4071
98	4216	4362	4508	4653	4799	4944	5090	5235	5381	5526
99	5671	5816	5962	6107	6252	6397	6542	6687	6832	6976
300	47 7121	7266	7411	7555	7700	7844	7989	8133	8278	8422
N	0	1	2	3	4	5	6	7	8	9

SIX-PLACE MANTISSAS FOR COMMON LOGARITHMS (Continued)

N	0	1	2	3	4	5	6	7	8	9
300	47 7121	7266	7411	7555	7700	7844	7989	8133	8278	8422
01	47 8566	8711	8855	8999	9143	9287	9431	9575	9719	9863
02	48 0007	0151	0294	0438	0582	0725	0869	1012	1156	1299
03	1443	1586	1729	1872	2016	2159	2302	2445	2588	2731
04	2874	3016	3159	3302	3445	3587	3730	3872	4015	4157
05	4300	4442	4585	4727	4869	5011	5153	5295	5437	5579
06	5721	5863	6005	6147	6289	6430	6572	6714	6855	6997
07	7138	7280	7421	7563	7704	7845	7986	8127	8269	8410
08	8551	8692	8833	8974	9114	9255	9396	9537	9677	9818
09	48 9958	*0099	*0239	*0380	*0520	*0661	*0801	*0941	*1081	*1222
310	49 1362	1502	1642	1782	1922	2062	2201	2341	2481	2621
11	2760	2900	3040	3179	3319	3458	3597	3737	3876	4015
12	4155	4294	4433	4572	4711	4850	4989	5128	5267	5406
13	5544	5683	5822	5960	6099	6238	6376	6515	6653	6791
14	6930	7068	7206	7344	7483	7621	7759	7897	8035	8173
15	8311	8448	8586	8724	8862	8999	9137	9275	9412	9550
16	49 9687	9824	9962	*0099	*0236	*0374	*0511	*0648	*0785	*0922
17	50 1059	1196	1333	1470	1607	1744	1880	2017	2154	2291
18	2427	2564	2700	2837	2973	3109	3246	3382	3518	3655
19	3791	3927	4063	4199	4335	4471	4607	4743	4878	5014
320	5150	5286	5421	5557	5693	5828	5964	6099	6234	6370
21	6505	6640	6776	6911	7046	7181	7316	7451	7586	7721
22	7856	7991	8126	8260	8395	8530	8664	8799	8934	9068
23	50 9203	9337	9471	9606	9740	9874	*0009	*0143	*0277	*0411
24	51 0545	0679	0813	0947	1081	1215	1349	1482	1616	1750
25	1883	2017	2151	2284	2418	2551	2684	2818	2951	3084
26	3218	3351	3484	3617	3750	3883	4016	4149	4282	4415
27	4548	4681	4813	4946	5079	5211	5344	5476	5609	5741
28	5874	6006	6139	6271	6403	6535	6668	6800	6932	7064
29	7196	7328	7460	7592	7724	7855	7987	8119	8251	8382
330	8514	8646	8777	8909	9040	9171	9303	9434	9566	9697
31	51 9828	9959	*0090	*0221	*0353	*0484	*0615	*0745	*0876	*1007
32	52 1138	1269	1400	1530	1661	1792	1922	2053	2183	2314
33	2444	2575	2705	2835	2966	3096	3226	3356	3486	3616
34	3746	3876	4006	4136	4266	4396	4526	4656	4785	4915
35	5045	5174	5304	5434	5563	5693	5822	5951	6081	6210
36	6339	6469	6598	6727	6856	6985	7114	7243	7372	7501
37	7630	7759	7888	8016	8145	8274	8402	8531	8660	8788
38	52 8917	9045	9174	9302	9430	9559	9687	9815	9943	*0072
39	53 0200	0328	0456	0584	0712	0840	0968	1096	1223	1351
340	1479	1607	1734	1862	1990	2117	2245	2372	2500	2627
41	2754	2882	3009	3136	3264	3391	3518	3645	3772	3899
42	4026	4153	4280	4407	4534	4661	4787	4914	5041	5167
43	5294	5421	5547	5674	5800	5927	6053	6180	6306	6432
44	6558	6685	6811	6937	7063	7189	7315	7441	7567	7693
45	7819	7945	8071	8197	8322	8448	8574	8699	8825	8951
46	53 9076	9202	9327	9452	9578	9703	9829	9954	*0079	*0204
47	54 0329	0455	0580	0705	0830	0955	1080	1205	1330	1454
48	1579	1704	1829	1953	2078	2203	2327	2452	2576	2701
49	2825	2950	3074	3199	3323	3447	3571	3696	3820	3944
350	54 4068	4192	4316	4440	4564	4688	4812	4936	5060	5183
N	0	1	2	3	4	5	6	7	8	9

SIX-PLACE MANTISSAS FOR COMMON LOGARITHMS (Continued)

N	0	1	2	3	4	5	6	7	8	9
350	54 4068	4192	4316	4440	4564	4688	4812	4936	5060	5183
51	5307	5431	5555	5678	5802	5925	6049	6172	6296	6419
52	6543	6666	6789	6913	7036	7159	7282	7405	7529	7652
53	7775	7898	8021	8144	8267	8389	8512	8635	8758	8881
54	54 9003	9126	9249	9371	9494	9616	9739	9861	9984	*0106
55	55 0228	0351	0473	0595	0717	0840	0962	1084	1206	1328
56	1450	1572	1694	1816	1938	2060	2181	2303	2425	2547
57	2668	2790	2911	3033	3155	3276	3398	3519	3640	3762
58	3883	4004	4126	4247	4368	4489	4610	4731	4852	4973
59	5094	5215	5336	5457	5578	5699	5820	5940	6061	6182
360	6303	6423	6544	6664	6785	6905	7026	7146	7267	7387
61	7507	7627	7748	7868	7988	8108	8228	8349	8469	8589
62	8709	8829	8948	9068	9188	9308	9428	9548	9667	9787
63	55 9907	*0026	*0146	*0265	*0385	*0504	*0624	*0743	*0863	*0982
64	56 1101	1221	1340	1459	1578	1698	1817	1936	2055	2174
65	2293	2412	2531	2650	2769	2887	3006	3125	3244	3362
66	3481	3600	3718	3837	3955	4074	4192	4311	4429	4548
67	4666	4784	4903	5021	5139	5257	5376	5494	5612	5730
68	5848	5966	6084	6202	6320	6437	6555	6673	6791	6909
69	7026	7144	7262	7379	7497	7614	7732	7849	7967	8084
370	8202	8319	8436	8554	8671	8788	8905	9023	9140	9257
71	56 9374	9491	9608	9725	9842	9959	*0076	*0193	*0309	*0426
72	57 0543	0660	0776	0893	1010	1126	1243	1359	1476	1592
73	1709	1825	1942	2058	2174	2291	2407	2523	2639	2755
74	2872	2988	3104	3220	3336	3452	3568	3684	3800	3915
75	4031	4147	4263	4379	4494	4610	4726	4841	4957	5072
76	5188	5303	5419	5534	5650	5765	5880	5996	6111	6226
77	6341	6457	6572	6687	6802	6917	7032	7147	7262	7377
78	7492	7607	7722	7836	7951	8066	8181	8295	8410	8525
79	8639	8754	8868	8983	9097	9212	9326	9441	9555	9669
380	57 9784	9898	*0012	*0126	*0241	*0355	*0469	*0583	*0697	*0811
81	58 0925	1039	1153	1267	1381	1495	1608	1722	1836	1950
82	2063	2177	2291	2404	2518	2631	2745	2858	2972	3085
83	3199	3312	3426	3539	3652	3765	3879	3992	4105	4218
84	4331	4444	4557	4670	4783	4896	5009	5122	5235	5348
85	5461	5574	5686	5799	5912	6024	6137	6250	6362	6475
86	6587	6700	6812	6925	7037	7149	7262	7374	7486	7599
87	7711	7823	7935	8047	8160	8272	8384	8496	8608	8720
88	8832	8944	9056	9167	9279	9391	9503	9615	9726	9838
89	58 9950	*0061	*0173	*0284	*0396	*0507	*0619	*0730	*0842	*0953
390	59 1065	1176	1287	1399	1510	1621	1732	1843	1955	2066
91	2177	2288	2399	2510	2621	2732	2843	2954	3064	3175
92	3286	3397	3508	3618	3729	3840	3950	4061	4171	4282
93	4393	4503	4614	4724	4834	4945	5055	5165	5276	5386
94	5496	5606	5717	5827	5937	6047	6157	6267	6377	6487
95	6597	6707	6817	6927	7037	7146	7256	7366	7476	7586
96	7695	7805	7914	8024	8134	8243	8353	8462	8572	8681
97	8791	8900	9009	9119	9228	9337	9446	9556	9665	9774
98	9883	9992	*0101	*0210	*0319	*0428	*0537	*0646	*0755	*0864
99	60 0973	1082	1191	1299	1408	1517	1625	1734	1843	1951
400	60 2060	2169	2277	2386	2494	2603	2711	2819	2928	3036
N	0	1	2	3	4	5	6	7	8	9

SIX-PLACE MANTISSAS FOR COMMON LOGARITHMS (Continued)

N	0	1	2	3	4	5	6	7	8	9
400	60 2060	2169	2277	2386	2494	2603	2711	2819	2928	3036
01	3144	3253	3361	3469	3577	3686	3794	3902	4010	4118
02	4226	4334	4442	4550	4658	4766	4874	4982	5089	5197
03	5305	5413	5521	5628	5736	5844	5951	6059	6166	6274
04	6381	6489	6596	6704	6811	6919	7026	7133	7241	7348
05	7455	7562	7669	7777	7884	7991	8098	8205	8312	8419
06	8526	8633	8740	8847	8954	9061	9167	9274	9381	9488
07	60 9594	9701	9808	9914	*0021	*0128	*0234	*0341	*0447	*0554
08	61 0660	0767	0873	0979	1086	1192	1298	1405	1511	1617
09	1723	1829	1936	2042	2148	2254	2360	2466	2572	2678
410	2784	2890	2996	3102	3207	3313	3419	3525	3630	3736
11	3842	3947	4053	4159	4264	4370	4475	4581	4686	4792
12	4897	5003	5108	5213	5319	5424	5529	5634	5740	5845
13	5950	6055	6160	6265	6370	6476	6581	6686	6790	6895
14	7000	7105	7210	7315	7420	7525	7629	7734	7839	7943
15	8048	8153	8257	8362	8466	8571	8676	8780	8884	8989
16	61 9093	9198	9302	9406	9511	9615	9719	9824	9928	*0032
17	62 0136	0240	0344	0448	0552	0656	0760	0864	0968	1072
18	1176	1280	1384	1488	1592	1695	1799	1903	2007	2110
19	2214	2318	2421	2525	2628	2732	2835	2939	3042	3146
420	3249	3353	3456	3559	3663	3766	3869	3973	4076	4179
21	4282	4385	4488	4591	4695	4798	4901	5004	5107	5210
22	5312	5415	5518	5621	5724	5827	5929	6032	6135	6238
23	6340	6443	6546	6648	6751	6853	6956	7058	7161	7263
24	7366	7468	7571	7673	7775	7878	7980	8082	8185	8287
25	8389	8491	8593	8695	8797	8900	9002	9104	9206	9308
26	62 9410	9512	9613	9715	9817	9919	*0021	*0123	*0224	*0326
27	63 0428	0530	0631	0733	0835	0936	1038	1139	1241	1342
28	1444	1545	1647	1748	1849	1951	2052	2153	2255	2356
29	2457	2559	2660	2761	2862	2963	3064	3165	3266	3367
430	3468	3569	3670	3771	3872	3973	4074	4175	4276	4376
31	4477	4578	4679	4779	4880	4981	5081	5182	5283	5383
32	5484	5584	5685	5785	5886	5986	6087	6187	6287	6388
33	6488	6588	6688	6789	6889	6989	7089	7189	7290	7390
34	7490	7590	7690	7790	7890	7990	8090	8190	8290	8389
35	8489	8589	8689	8789	8888	8988	9088	9188	9287	9387
36	63 9486	9586	9686	9785	9885	9984	*0084	*0183	*0283	*0382
37	64 0481	0581	0680	0779	0879	0978	1077	1177	1276	1375
38	1474	1573	1672	1771	1871	1970	2069	2168	2267	2366
39	2465	2563	2662	2761	2860	2959	3058	3156	3255	3354
440	3453	3551	3650	3749	3847	3946	4044	4143	4242	4340
41	4439	4537	4636	4734	4832	4931	5029	5127	5226	5324
42	5422	5521	5619	5717	5815	5913	6011	6110	6208	6306
43	6404	6502	6600	6698	6796	6894	6992	7089	7187	7285
44	7383	7481	7579	7676	7774	7872	7969	8067	8165	8262
45	8360	8458	8555	8653	8750	8848	8945	9043	9140	9237
46	64 9335	9432	9530	9627	9724	9821	9919	*0016	*0113	*0210
47	65 0308	0405	0502	0599	0696	0793	0890	0987	1084	1181
48	1278	1375	1472	1569	1666	1762	1859	1956	2053	2150
49	2246	2343	2440	2536	2633	2730	2826	2923	3019	3116
450	65 3213	3309	3405	3502	3598	3695	3791	3888	3984	4080
N	0	1	2	3	4	5	6	7	8	9

SIX-PLACE MANTISSAS FOR COMMON LOGARITHMS (Continued)

N	0	1	2	3	4	5	6	7	8	9
450	65 3213	3309	3405	3502	3598	3695	3791	3888	3984	4080
51	4177	4273	4369	4465	4562	4658	4754	4850	4946	5042
52	5138	5235	5331	5427	5523	5619	5715	5810	5906	6002
53	6098	6194	6290	6386	6482	6577	6673	6769	6864	6960
54	7056	7152	7247	7343	7438	7534	7629	7725	7820	7916
55	8011	8107	8202	8298	8393	8488	8584	8679	8774	8870
56	8965	9060	9155	9250	9346	9441	9536	9631	9726	9821
57	65 9916	*C011	*0106	*0201	*0296	*0391	*0486	*0581	*0676	*0771
58	66 0865	0960	1055	1150	1245	1339	1434	1529	1623	1718
59	1813	1907	2002	2096	2191	2286	2380	2475	2569	2663
460	2758	2852	2947	3041	3135	3230	3324	3418	3512	3607
61	3701	3795	3889	3983	4078	4172	4266	4360	4454	4548
62	4642	4736	4830	4924	5018	5112	5206	5299	5393	5487
63	5581	5675	5769	5862	5956	6050	6143	6237	6331	6424
64	6518	6612	6705	6799	6892	6986	7079	7173	7266	7360
65	7453	7546	7640	7733	7826	7920	8013	8106	8199	8293
66	8386	8479	8572	8665	8759	8852	8945	9038	9131	9224
67	66 9317	9410	9503	9596	9689	9782	9875	9967	*0060	*0153
68	67 0246	0339	0431	0524	0617	0710	0802	0895	0988	1080
69	1173	1265	1358	1451	1543	1636	1728	1821	1913	2005
470	2098	2190	2283	2375	2467	2560	2652	2744	2836	2929
71	3021	3113	3205	3297	3390	3482	3574	3666	3758	3850
72	3942	4034	4126	4218	4310	4402	4494	4586	4677	4769
73	4861	4953	5045	5137	5228	5320	5412	5503	5595	5687
74	5778	5870	5962	6053	6145	6236	6328	6419	6511	6602
75	6694	6785	6876	6968	7059	7151	7242	7333	7424	7516
76	7607	7698	7789	7881	7972	8063	8154	8245	8336	8427
77	8518	8609	8700	8791	8882	8973	9064	9155	9246	9337
78	67 9428	9519	9610	9700	9791	9882	9973	*0063	*0154	*0245
79	68 0336	0426	0517	0607	0698	0789	0879	0970	1060	1151
480	1241	1332	1422	1513	1603	1693	1784	1874	1964	2055
81	2145	2235	2326	2416	2506	2596	2686	2777	2867	2957
82	3047	3137	3227	3317	3407	3497	3587	3677	3767	3857
83	3947	4037	4127	4217	4307	4396	4486	4576	4666	4756
84	4845	4935	5025	5114	5204	5294	5383	5473	5563	5652
85	5742	5831	5921	6010	6100	6189	6279	6368	6458	6547
86	6636	6726	6815	6904	6994	7083	7172	7261	7351	7440
87	7529	7618	7707	7796	7886	7975	8064	8153	8242	8331
88	8420	8509	8598	8687	8776	8865	8953	9042	9131	9220
89	68 9309	9398	9486	9575	9664	9753	9841	9930	*0019	*0107
490	69 0196	0285	0373	0462	0550	0639	0728	0816	0905	0993
91	1081	1170	1258	1347	1435	1524	1612	1700	1789	1877
92	1965	2053	2142	2230	2318	2406	2494	2583	2671	2759
93	2847	2935	3023	3111	3199	3287	3375	3463	3551	3639
94	3727	3815	3903	3991	4078	4166	4254	4342	4430	4517
95	4605	4693	4781	4868	4956	5044	5131	5219	5307	5394
96	5482	5569	5657	5744	5832	5919	6007	6094	6182	6269
97	6356	6444	6531	6618	6706	6793	6880	6968	7055	7142
98	7229	7317	7404	7491	7578	7665	7752	7839	7926	8014
99	8101	8188	8275	8362	8449	8535	8622	8709	8796	8883
500	69 8970	9057	9144	9231	9317	9404	9491	9578	9664	9751
N	0	1	2	3	4	5	6	7	8	9

SIX-PLACE MANTISSAS FOR COMMON LOGARITHMS (Continued)

N	0	1	2	3	4	5	6	7	8	9
500	69 8970	9057	9144	9231	9317	9404	9491	9578	9664	9751
01	69 9838	9924	*0011	*0098	*0184	*0271	*0358	*0444	*0531	*0617
02	70 0704	0790	0877	0963	1050	1136	1222	1309	1395	1482
03	1568	1654	1741	1827	1913	1999	2086	2172	2258	2344
04	2431	2517	2603	2689	2775	2861	2947	3033	3119	3205
05	3291	3377	3463	3549	3635	3721	3807	3893	3979	4065
06	4151	4236	4322	4408	4494	4579	4665	4751	4837	4922
07	5008	5094	5179	5265	5350	5463	5522	5607	5693	5778
08	5864	5949	6035	6120	6206	6291	6376	6462	6547	6632
09	6718	6803	6888	6974	7059	7144	7229	7315	7400	7485
510	7570	7655	7740	7826	7911	7996	8081	8166	8251	8336
11	8421	8506	8591	8676	8761	8846	8931	9015	9100	9185
12	70 9270	9355	9440	9524	9609	9694	9779	9863	9948	*0033
13	71 0117	0202	0287	0371	0456	0540	0625	0710	0794	0879
14	0963	1048	1132	1217	1301	1385	1470	1554	1639	1723
15	1807	1892	1976	2060	2144	2229	2313	2397	2481	2566
16	2650	2734	2818	2902	2986	3070	3154	3238	3323	3407
17	3491	3575	3659	3742	3826	3910	3994	4078	4162	4246
18	4330	4414	4497	4581	4665	4749	4833	4916	5000	5084
19	5167	5251	5335	5418	5502	5586	5669	5753	5836	5920
520	6003	6087	6170	6254	6337	6421	6504	6588	6671	6754
21	6838	6921	7004	7088	7171	7254	7338	7421	7504	7587
22	7671	7754	7837	7920	8003	8086	8169	8253	8336	8419
23	8502	8585	8668	8751	8834	8917	9000	9083	9165	9248
24	71 9331	9414	9497	9580	9663	9745	9828	9911	9994	*0077
25	72 0159	0242	0325	0407	0490	0573	0655	0738	0821	0903
26	0986	1068	1151	1233	1316	1398	1481	1563	1646	1728
27	1811	1893	1975	2058	2140	2222	2305	2387	2469	2552
28	2634	2716	2798	2881	2963	3045	3127	3209	3291	3374
29	3456	3538	3620	3702	3784	3866	3948	4030	4112	4194
530	4276	4358	4440	4522	4604	4685	4767	4849	4931	5013
31	5095	5176	5258	5340	5422	5503	5585	5667	5748	5830
32	5912	5993	6075	6156	6238	6320	6401	6483	6564	6646
33	6727	6809	6890	6972	7053	7134	7216	7297	7379	7460
34	7541	7623	7704	7785	7866	7948	8029	8110	8191	8273
35	8354	8435	8516	8597	8678	8759	8841	8922	9003	9084
36	9165	9246	9327	9408	9489	9570	9651	9732	9813	9893
37	72 9974	*0055	*0136	*0217	*0298	*0378	*0459	*0540	*0621	*0702
38	73 0782	0863	0944	1024	1105	1186	1266	1347	1428	1508
39	1589	1669	1750	1830	1911	1991	2072	2152	2233	2313
540	2394	2474	2555	2635	2715	2796	2876	2956	3037	3117
41	3197	3278	3358	3438	3518	3598	3679	3759	3839	3919
42	3999	4079	4160	4240	4320	4400	4480	4560	4640	4720
43	4800	4880	4960	5040	5120	5200	5279	5359	5439	5519
44	5599	5679	5759	5838	5918	5998	6078	6157	6237	6317
45	6397	6476	6556	6635	6715	6795	6874	6954	7034	7113
46	7193	7272	7352	7431	7511	7590	7670	7749	7829	7908
47	7987	8067	8146	8225	8305	8384	8463	8543	8622	8701
48	8781	8860	8939	9018	9097	9177	9256	9335	9414	9493
49	73 9572	9651	9731	9810	9889	9968	*0047	*0126	*0205	*0284
550	74 0363	0442	0521	0600	0678	0757	0836	0915	0994	1073
N	0	1	2	3	4	5	6	7	8	9

SIX-PLACE MANTISSAS FOR COMMON LOGARITHMS (Continued)

N	0	1	2	3	4	5	6	7	8	9
550	74 0363	0442	0521	0600	0678	0757	0836	0915	0994	1073
51	1152	1230	1309	1388	1467	1546	1624	1703	1782	1860
52	1939	2018	2096	2175	2254	2332	2411	2489	2568	2647
53	2725	2804	2882	2961	3039	3118	3196	3275	3353	3431
54	3510	3588	3667	3745	3823	3902	3980	4058	4136	4215
55	4293	4371	4449	4528	4606	4684	4762	4840	4919	4997
56	5075	5153	5231	5309	5387	5465	5543	5621	5699	5777
57	5855	5933	6011	6089	6167	6245	6323	6401	6479	6556
58	6634	6712	6790	6868	6945	7023	7101	7179	7256	7334
59	7412	7489	7567	7645	7722	7800	7878	7955	8033	8110
560	8188	8266	8343	8421	8498	8576	8653	8731	8808	8885
61	8963	9040	9118	9195	9272	9350	9427	9504	9582	9659
62	74 9736	9814	9891	9968	*0045	*0123	*0200	*0277	*0354	*0431
63	75 0508	0586	0663	0740	0817	0894	0971	1048	1125	1202
64	1279	1356	1433	1510	1587	1664	1741	1818	1895	1972
65	2048	2125	2202	2279	2356	2433	2509	2586	2663	2740
66	2816	2893	2970	3047	3123	3200	3277	3353	3430	3506
67	3583	3660	3736	3813	3889	3966	4042	4119	4195	4272
68	4348	4425	4501	4578	4654	4730	4807	4883	4960	5036
69	5112	5189	5265	5341	5417	5494	5570	5646	5722	5799
570	5875	5951	6027	6103	6180	6256	6332	6408	6484	6560
71	6636	6712	6788	6864	6940	7016	7092	7168	7244	7320
72	7396	7472	7548	7624	7700	7775	7851	7927	8003	8079
73	8155	8230	8306	8382	8458	8533	8609	8685	8761	8836
74	8912	8988	9063	9139	9214	9290	9366	9441	9517	9592
75	75 9668	9743	9819	9894	9970	*0045	*0121	*0196	*0272	*0347
76	76 0422	0498	0573	0649	0724	0799	0875	0950	1025	1101
77	1176	1251	1326	1402	1477	1552	1627	1702	1778	1853
78	1928	2003	2078	2153	2228	2303	2378	2453	2529	2604
79	2679	2754	2829	2904	2978	3053	3128	3203	3278	3353
580	3428	3503	3578	3653	3727	3802	3877	3952	4027	4101
81	4176	4251	4326	4400	4475	4550	4624	4699	4774	4848
82	4923	4998	5072	5147	5221	5296	5370	5445	5520	5594
83	5669	5743	5818	5892	5966	6041	6115	6190	6264	6338
84	6413	6487	6562	6636	6710	6785	6859	6933	7007	7082
85	7156	7230	7304	7379	7453	7527	7601	7675	7749	7823
86	7898	7972	8046	8120	8194	8268	8342	8416	8490	8564
87	8638	8712	8786	8860	8934	9008	9082	9156	9230	9303
88	76 9377	9451	9525	9599	9673	9746	9820	9894	9968	*0042
89	77 0115	0189	0263	0336	0410	0484	0557	0631	0705	0778
590	0852	0926	0999	1073	1146	1220	1293	1367	1440	1514
91	1587	1661	1734	1808	1881	1955	2028	2102	2175	2248
92	2322	2395	2468	2542	2615	2688	2762	2835	2908	2981
93	3055	3128	3201	3274	3348	3421	3494	3567	3640	3713
94	3786	3860	3933	4006	4079	4152	4225	4298	4371	4444
95	4517	4590	4663	4736	4809	4882	4955	5028	5100	5173
96	5246	5319	5392	5465	5538	5610	5683	5756	5829	5902
97	5974	6047	6120	6193	6265	6338	6411	6483	6556	6629
98	6701	6774	6846	6919	6992	7064	7137	7209	7282	7354
99	7427	7499	7572	7644	7717	7789	7862	7934	8006	8079
600	77 8151	8224	8296	8368	8441	8513	8585	8658	8730	8802
N	0	1	2	3	4	5	6	7	8	9

SIX-PLACE MANTISSAS FOR COMMON LOGARITHMS (Continued)

N	0	1	2	3	4	5	6	7	8	9
600	77 8151	8224	8296	8368	8441	8513	8585	8658	8730	8802
01	8874	8947	9019	9091	9163	9236	9308	9380	9452	9524
02	77 9596	9669	9741	9813	9885	9957	*0029	*0101	*0173	*0245
03	78 0317	0389	0461	0533	0605	0677	0749	0821	0893	0965
04	1037	1109	1181	1253	1324	1396	1468	1540	1612	1684
05	1755	1827	1899	1971	2042	2114	2186	2258	2329	2401
06	2473	2544	2616	2688	2759	2831	2902	2974	3046	3117
07	3189	3260	3332	3403	3475	3546	3618	3689	3761	3832
08	3904	3975	4046	4118	4189	4261	4332	4403	4475	4546
09	4617	4689	4760	4831	4902	4974	5045	5116	5187	5259
610	5330	5401	5472	5543	5615	5686	5757	5828	5899	5970
11	6041	6112	6183	6254	6325	6396	6467	6538	6609	6680
12	6751	6822	6893	6964	7035	7106	7177	7248	7319	7390
13	7460	7531	7602	7673	7744	7815	7885	7956	8027	8098
14	8168	8239	8310	8381	8451	8522	8593	8663	8734	8804
15	8875	8946	9016	9087	9157	9228	9299	9369	9440	9510
16	78 9581	9651	9722	9762	9863	9933	*0004	*0074	*0144	*0215
17	79 0285	0356	0426	0496	0567	0637	0707	0778	0848	0918
18	0988	1059	1129	1199	1269	1340	1410	1480	1550	1620
19	1691	1761	1831	1901	1971	2041	2111	2181	2252	2322
620	2392	2462	2532	2602	2672	2742	2812	2882	2952	3022
21	3092	3162	3231	3301	3371	3441	3511	3581	3651	3721
22	3790	3860	3930	4000	4070	4139	4209	4279	4349	4418
23	4488	4558	4627	4697	4767	4836	4906	4976	5045	5115
24	5185	5254	5324	5393	5463	5532	5602	5672	5741	5811
25	5880	5949	6019	6088	6158	6227	6297	6366	6436	6505
26	6574	6644	6713	6782	6852	6921	6990	7060	7129	7198
27	7268	7337	7406	7475	7545	7614	7683	7752	7821	7890
28	7960	8029	8098	8167	8236	8305	8374	8443	8513	8582
29	8651	8720	8789	8858	8927	8996	9065	9134	9203	9272
630	79 9341	9409	9478	9547	9616	9685	9754	9823	9892	9961
31	80 0029	0098	0167	0236	0305	0373	0442	0511	0580	0648
32	0717	0786	0854	0923	0992	1061	1129	1198	1266	1335
33	1404	1472	1541	1609	1678	1747	1815	1884	1952	2021
34	2089	2158	2226	2295	2363	2432	2500	2568	2637	2705
35	2774	2842	2910	2979	3047	3116	3184	3252	3321	3389
36	3457	3525	3594	3662	3730	3798	3867	3935	4003	4071
37	4139	4208	4276	4344	4412	4480	4548	4616	4685	4753
38	4821	4889	4957	5025	5093	5161	5229	5297	5365	5433
39	5501	5569	5637	5705	5773	5841	5908	5976	6044	6112
640	6180	6248	6316	6384	6451	6519	6587	6655	6723	6790
41	6858	6926	6994	7061	7129	7197	7264	7332	7400	7467
42	7535	7603	7670	7738	7806	7873	7941	8008	8076	8143
43	8211	8279	8346	8414	8481	8549	8616	8684	8751	8818
44	8886	8953	9021	9088	9156	9223	9290	9358	9425	9492
45	80 9560	9627	9694	9762	9829	9896	9964	*0031	*0098	*0165
46	81 0233	0300	0367	0434	0501	0569	0636	0703	0770	0837
47	0904	0971	1039	1106	1173	1240	1307	1374	1441	1508
48	1575	1642	1709	1776	1843	1910	1977	2044	2111	2178
49	2245	2312	2379	2445	2512	2579	2646	2713	2780	2847
650	81 2913	2980	3047	3114	3181	3247	3314	3381	3448	3514
N	0	1	2	3	4	5	6	7	8	9

SIX-PLACE MANTISSAS FOR COMMON LOGARITHMS (Continued)

N	0	1	2	3	4	5	6	7	8	9
650	81 2913	2980	3047	3114	3181	3247	3314	3381	3448	3514
51	3581	3648	3714	3781	3848	3914	3981	4048	4114	4181
52	4248	4314	4381	4447	4514	4581	4647	4714	4780	4847
53	4913	4980	5046	5113	5179	5246	5312	5378	5445	5511
54	5578	5644	5711	5777	5843	5910	5976	6042	6109	6175
55	6241	6308	6374	6440	6506	6573	6639	6705	6771	6838
56	6904	6970	7036	7102	7169	7235	7301	7367	7433	7499
57	7565	7631	7698	7764	7830	7896	7962	8028	8094	8160
58	8226	8292	8358	8424	8490	8556	8622	8688	8754	8820
59	8885	8951	9017	9083	9149	9215	9281	9346	9412	9478
660	81 9544	9610	9676	9741	9807	9873	9939	*0004	*0070	*0136
61	82 0201	0267	0333	0399	0464	0530	0595	0661	0727	0792
62	0858	0924	0989	1055	1120	1186	1251	1317	1382	1448
63	1514	1579	1645	1710	1775	1841	1906	1972	2037	2103
64	2168	2233	2299	2364	2430	2495	2560	2626	2691	2756
65	2822	2887	2952	3018	3083	3148	3213	3279	3344	3409
66	3474	3539	3605	3670	3735	3800	3865	3930	3996	4061
67	4126	4191	4256	4321	4386	4451	4516	4581	4646	4711
68	4776	4841	4906	4971	5036	5101	5166	5231	5296	5361
69	5426	5491	5556	5621	5686	5751	5815	5880	5945	6010
670	6075	6140	6204	6269	6334	6399	6464	6528	6593	6658
71	6723	6787	6852	6917	6981	7046	7111	7175	7240	7305
72	7369	7434	7499	7563	7628	7692	7757	7821	7886	7951
73	8015	8080	8144	8209	8273	8338	8402	8467	8531	8595
74	8660	8724	8789	8853	8918	8982	9046	9111	9175	9239
75	9304	9368	9432	9497	9561	9625	9690	9754	9818	9882
76	82 9947	*0011	*0075	*0139	*0204	*0268	*0332	*0396	*0460	*0525
77	83 0589	0653	0717	0781	0845	0909	0973	1037	1102	1166
78	1230	1294	1358	1422	1486	1550	1614	1678	1742	1806
79	1870	1934	1998	2062	2126	2189	2253	2317	2381	2445
680	2509	2573	2637	2700	2764	2828	2892	2956	3020	3083
81	3147	3211	3275	3338	3402	3466	3530	3593	3657	3721
82	3784	3848	3912	3975	4039	4103	4166	4230	4294	4357
83	4421	4484	4548	4611	4675	4739	4802	4866	4929	4993
84	5056	5120	5183	5247	5310	5373	5437	5500	5564	5627
85	5691	5754	5817	5881	5944	6007	6071	6134	6197	6261
86	6324	6387	6451	6514	6577	6641	6704	6767	6830	6894
87	6957	7020	7083	7146	7210	7273	7336	7399	7462	7525
88	7588	7652	7715	7778	7841	7904	7967	8030	8093	8156
89	8219	8282	8345	8408	8471	8534	8597	8660	8723	8786
690	8849	8912	8975	9038	9101	9164	9227	9289	9352	9415
91	83 9478	9541	9604	9667	9729	9792	9855	9918	9981	*0043
92	84 0106	0169	0232	0294	0357	0420	0482	0545	0608	0671
93	0733	0796	0859	0921	0984	1046	1109	1172	1234	1297
94	1359	1422	1485	1547	1610	1672	1735	1797	1860	1922
95	1985	2047	2110	2172	2235	2297	2360	2422	2484	2547
96	2609	2672	2734	2796	2859	2921	2983	3046	3108	3170
97	3233	3295	3357	3420	3482	3544	3606	3669	3731	3793
98	3855	3918	3980	4042	4104	4166	4229	4291	4353	4415
99	4477	4539	4601	4664	4726	4788	4850	4912	4974	5036
700	84 5098	5160	5222	5284	5346	5408	5470	5532	5594	5656
N	0	1	2	3	4	5	6	7	8	9

SIX-PLACE MANTISSAS FOR COMMON LOGARITHMS (Continued)

N	0	1	2	3	4	5	6	7	8	9
700	84 5098	5160	5222	5284	5346	5408	5470	5532	5594	5656
01	5718	5780	5842	5904	5966	6028	6090	6151	6213	6275
02	6337	6399	6461	6523	6585	6646	6708	6770	6832	6894
03	6955	7017	7079	7141	7202	7264	7326	7388	7449	7511
04	7573	7634	7696	7758	7819	7881	7943	8004	8066	8128
05	8189	8251	8312	8374	8435	8497	8559	8620	8682	8743
06	8805	8866	8928	8989	9051	9112	9174	9235	9297	9358
07	84 9419	9481	9542	9604	9665	9726	9788	9849	9911	9972
08	85 0033	0095	0156	0217	0279	0340	0401	0462	0524	0585
09	0646	0707	0769	0830	0891	0952	1014	1075	1136	1197
710	1258	1320	1381	1442	1503	1564	1625	1686	1747	1809
11	1870	1931	1992	2053	2114	2175	2236	2297	2358	2419
12	2480	2541	2602	2663	2724	2785	2846	2907	2968	3029
13	3090	3150	3211	3272	3333	3394	3455	3516	3577	3637
14	3698	3759	3820	3881	3941	4002	4063	4124	4185	4245
15	4306	4367	4428	4488	4549	4610	4670	4731	4792	4852
16	4913	4974	5034	5095	5156	5216	5277	5337	5398	5459
17	5519	5580	5640	5701	5761	5822	5882	5943	6003	6064
18	6124	6185	6245	6306	6366	6427	6487	6548	6608	6668
19	6729	6789	6850	6910	6970	7031	7091	7152	7212	7272
720	7332	7393	7453	7513	7574	7634	7694	7755	7815	7875
21	7935	7995	8056	8116	8176	8236	8297	8357	8417	8477
22	8537	8597	8657	8718	8778	8838	8898	8958	9018	9078
23	9138	9198	9258	9318	9379	9439	9499	9559	9619	9679
24	85 9739	9799	9859	9918	9978	*0038	*0098	*0158	*0218	*0278
25	86 0338	0398	0458	0518	0578	0637	0697	0757	0817	0877
26	0937	0996	1056	1116	1176	1236	1295	1355	1415	1475
27	1534	1594	1654	1714	1773	1833	1893	1952	2012	2072
28	2131	2191	2251	2310	2370	2430	2489	2549	2608	2668
29	2728	2787	2847	2906	2966	3025	3085	3144	3204	3263
730	3323	3382	3442	3501	3561	3620	3680	3739	3799	3858
31	3917	3977	4036	4096	4155	4214	4274	4333	4392	4452
32	4511	4570	4630	4689	4748	4808	4867	4926	4985	5045
33	5104	5163	5222	5282	5341	5400	5459	5519	5578	5637
34	5696	5755	5814	5874	5933	5992	6051	6110	6169	6228
35	6287	6346	6405	6465	6524	6583	6642	6701	6760	6819
36	6878	6937	6996	7055	7114	7173	7232	7291	7350	7409
37	7467	7526	7585	7644	7703	7762	7821	7880	7939	7998
38	8056	8115	8174	8233	8292	8350	8409	8468	8527	8586
39	8644	8703	8762	8821	8879	8938	8997	9056	9114	9173
740	9232	9290	9349	9408	9466	9525	9584	9642	9701	9760
41	86 9818	9877	9935	9994	*0053	*0111	*0170	*0228	*0287	*0345
42	87 0404	0462	0521	0579	0638	0696	0755	0813	0872	0930
43	0989	1047	1106	1164	1223	1281	1339	1398	1456	1515
44	1573	1631	1690	1748	1806	1865	1923	1981	2040	2098
45	2156	2215	2273	2331	2389	2448	2506	2564	2622	2681
46	2739	2797	2855	2913	2972	3030	3088	3146	3204	3262
47	3321	3379	3437	3495	3553	3611	3669	3727	3785	3844
48	3902	3960	4018	4076	4134	4192	4250	4308	4366	4424
49	4482	4540	4598	4656	4714	4772	4830	4888	4945	5003
750	87 5061	5119	5177	5235	5293	5351	5409	5466	5524	5582

N	0	1	2	3	4	5	6	7	8	9

SIX-PLACE MANTISSAS FOR COMMON LOGARITHMS (Continued)

N	0	1	2	3	4	5	6	7	8	9
750	87 5061	5119	5177	5235	5293	5351	5409	5466	5524	5582
51	5640	5698	5756	5813	5871	5929	5987	6045	6102	6160
52	6218	6276	6333	6391	6449	6507	6564	6622	6680	6737
53	6795	6853	6910	6968	7026	7083	7141	7199	7256	7314
54	7371	7429	7487	7544	7602	7659	7717	7774	7832	7889
55	7947	8004	8062	8119	8177	8234	8292	8349	8407	8464
56	8522	8579	8637	8694	8752	8809	8866	8924	8981	9039
57	9096	9153	9211	9268	9325	9383	9440	9497	9555	9612
58	87 9669	9726	9784	9841	9898	9956	*0013	*0070	*0127	*0185
59	88 0242	0299	0356	0413	0417	0528	0585	0642	0699	0756
760	0814	0871	0928	0985	1042	1099	1156	1213	1271	1328
61	1385	1442	1499	1556	1613	1670	1727	1784	1841	1898
62	1955	2012	2069	2126	2183	2240	2297	2354	2411	2468
63	2525	2581	2638	2695	2752	2809	2866	2923	2980	3037
64	3093	3150	3207	3264	3321	3377	3434	3491	3548	3605
65	3661	3718	3775	3832	3888	3945	4002	4059	4115	4172
66	4229	4285	4342	4399	4455	4512	4569	4625	4682	4739
67	4795	4852	4909	4965	5022	5078	5135	5192	5248	5305
68	5361	5418	5474	5531	5587	5644	5700	5757	5813	5870
69	5926	5983	6039	6096	6152	6209	6265	6321	6378	6434
770	6491	6547	6604	6660	6716	6773	6829	6885	6942	6998
71	7054	7111	7167	7223	7280	7336	7392	7449	7505	7561
72	7617	7674	7730	7786	7842	7898	7955	8011	8067	8123
73	8179	8236	8292	8348	8404	8460	8516	8573	8629	8685
74	8741	8797	8853	8909	8965	9021	9077	9134	9190	9246
75	9302	9358	9414	9470	9526	9582	9638	9694	9750	9806
76	88 9862	9918	9974	*0030	*0086	*0141	*0197	*0253	*0309	*0365
77	89 0421	0477	0533	0589	0645	0700	0756	0812	0868	0924
78	0980	1035	1091	1147	1203	1259	1314	1370	1426	1482
79	1537	1593	1649	1705	1760	1816	1872	1928	1983	2039
780	2095	2150	2206	2262	2317	2373	2429	2484	2540	2595
81	2651	2707	2762	2818	2873	2929	2985	3040	3096	3151
82	3207	3262	3318	3373	3429	3484	3540	3595	3651	3706
83	3762	3817	3873	3928	3984	4039	4094	4150	4205	4261
84	4316	4371	4427	4482	4538	4593	4648	4704	4759	4814
85	4870	4925	4980	5036	5091	5146	5201	5257	5312	5367
86	5423	5478	5533	5588	5644	5699	5754	5809	5864	5920
87	5975	6030	6085	6140	6195	6251	6306	6361	6416	6471
88	6526	6581	6636	6692	6747	6802	6857	6912	6967	7022
89	7077	7132	7187	7242	7297	7352	7407	7462	7517	7572
790	7627	7682	7737	7792	7847	7902	7957	8012	8067	8122
91	8176	8231	8286	8341	8396	8451	8506	8561	8615	8670
92	8725	8780	8835	8890	8944	8999	9054	9109	9164	9218
93	9273	9328	9383	9437	9492	9547	9602	9656	9711	9766
94	89 9821	9875	9930	9985	*0039	*0094	*0149	*0203	*0258	*0312
95	90 0367	0422	0476	0531	0586	0640	0695	0749	0804	0859
96	0913	0968	1022	1077	1131	1186	1240	1295	1349	1404
97	1458	1513	1567	1622	1676	1731	1785	1840	1894	1948
98	2003	2057	2112	2166	2221	2275	2329	2384	2438	2492
99	2547	2601	2655	2710	2764	2818	2873	2927	2981	3036
800	90 3090	3144	3199	3253	3307	3361	3416	3470	3524	3578

N	0	1	2	3	4	5	6	7	8	9

SIX-PLACE MANTISSAS FOR COMMON LOGARITHMS (Continued)

N	0	1	2	3	4	5	6	7	8	9
800	90 3090	3144	3199	3253	3307	3361	3416	3470	3524	3578
01	3633	3687	3741	3795	3849	3904	3958	4012	4066	4120
02	4174	4229	4283	4337	4391	4445	4499	4553	4607	4661
03	4716	4770	4824	4878	4932	4986	5040	5094	5148	5202
04	5256	5310	5364	5418	5472	5526	5580	5634	5688	5742
05	5796	5850	5904	5958	6012	6066	6119	6173	6227	6281
06	6335	6389	6443	6497	6551	6604	6658	6712	6766	6820
07	6874	6927	6981	7035	7089	7143	7196	7250	7304	7358
08	7411	7465	7519	7573	7626	7680	7734	7787	7841	7895
09	7949	8002	8056	8110	8163	8217	8270	8324	8378	8431
810	8485	8539	8592	8646	8699	8753	8807	8860	8914	8967
11	9021	9074	9128	9181	9235	9289	9342	9396	9449	9503
12	90 9556	9610	9663	9716	9770	9823	9877	9930	9984	*0037
13	91 0091	0144	0197	0251	0304	0358	0411	0464	0518	0571
14	0624	0678	0731	0784	0838	0891	0944	0998	1051	1104
15	1158	1211	1264	1317	1371	1424	1477	1530	1584	1637
16	1690	1743	1797	1850	1903	1956	2009	2063	2116	2169
17	2222	2275	2328	2381	2435	2488	2541	2594	2647	2700
18	2753	2806	2859	2913	2966	3019	3072	3125	3178	3231
19	3284	3337	3390	3443	3496	3549	3602	3655	3708	3761
820	3814	3867	3920	3973	4026	4079	4132	4184	4237	4290
21	4343	4396	4449	4502	4555	4608	4660	4713	4766	4819
22	4872	4925	4977	5030	5083	5136	5189	5241	5294	5347
23	5400	5453	5505	5558	5611	5664	5716	5769	5822	5875
24	5927	5980	6033	6085	6138	6191	6243	6296	6349	6401
25	6454	6507	6559	6612	6664	6717	6770	6822	6875	6927
26	6980	7033	7085	7138	7190	7243	7295	7348	7400	7453
27	7506	7558	7611	7663	7716	7768	7820	7873	7925	7978
28	8030	8083	8135	8188	8240	8293	8345	8397	8450	8502
29	8555	8607	8659	8712	8764	8816	8869	8921	8973	9026
830	9078	9130	9183	9235	9287	9340	9392	9444	9496	9549
31	91 9601	9653	9706	9758	9810	9862	9914	9967	*0019	*0071
32	92 0123	0176	0228	0280	0332	0384	0436	0489	0541	0593
33	0645	0697	0749	0801	0853	0906	0958	1010	1062	1114
34	1166	1218	1270	1322	1374	1426	1478	1530	1582	1634
35	1686	1738	1790	1842	1894	1946	1998	2050	2102	2154
36	2206	2258	2310	2362	2414	2466	2518	2570	2622	2674
37	2725	2777	2829	2881	2933	2985	3037	3089	3140	3192
38	3244	3296	3348	3399	3451	3503	3555	3607	3658	3710
39	3762	3814	3865	3917	3969	4021	4072	4124	4176	4228
840	4279	4331	4383	4434	4486	4538	4589	4641	4693	4744
41	4796	4848	4899	4951	5003	5054	5106	5157	5209	5261
42	5312	5364	5415	5467	5518	5570	5621	5673	5725	5776
43	5828	5879	5931	5982	6034	6085	6137	6188	6240	6291
44	6342	6394	6445	6497	6548	6600	6651	6702	6754	6805
45	6857	6908	6959	7011	7062	7114	7165	7216	7268	7319
46	7370	7422	7473	7524	7576	7627	7678	7730	7781	7832
47	7883	7935	7986	8037	8088	8140	8191	8242	8293	8345
48	8396	8447	8498	8549	8601	8652	8703	8754	8805	8857
49	8908	8959	9010	9061	9112	9163	9215	9266	9317	9368
850	92 9419	9470	9521	9572	9623	9674	9725	9776	9827	9879
N	0	1	2	3	4	5	6	7	8	9

SIX-PLACE MANTISSAS FOR COMMON LOGARITHMS (Continued)

N	0	1	2	3	4	5	6	7	8	9
850	92 9419	9470	9521	9572	9623	9674	9725	9776	9827	9879
51	92 9930	9981	*0032	*0083	*0134	*0185	*0236	*0287	*0338	*0389
52	93 0440	0491	0542	0592	0643	0694	0745	0796	0847	0898
53	0949	1000	1051	1102	1153	1204	1254	1305	1356	1407
54	1458	1509	1560	1610	1661	1712	1763	1814	1865	1915
55	1966	2017	2068	2118	2169	2220	2271	2322	2372	2423
56	2474	2524	2575	2626	2677	2727	2778	2829	2879	2930
57	2981	3031	3082	3133	3183	3234	3285	3335	3386	3437
58	3487	3538	3589	3639	3690	3740	3791	3841	3892	3943
59	3993	4044	4094	4145	4195	4246	4296	4347	4397	4448
860	4498	4549	4599	4650	4700	4751	4801	4852	4902	4953
61	5003	5054	5104	5154	5205	5255	5306	5356	5406	5457
62	5507	5558	5608	5658	5709	5759	5809	5860	5910	5960
63	6011	6061	6111	6162	6212	6262	6313	6363	6413	6463
64	6514	6564	6614	6665	6715	6765	6815	6865	6916	6966
65	7016	7066	7166	7167	7217	7267	7317	7367	7418	7468
66	7518	7568	7618	7668	7718	7769	7819	7869	7919	7969
67	8019	8069	8119	8169	8219	8269	8320	8370	8420	8470
68	8520	8570	8620	8670	8720	8770	8820	8870	8920	8970
69	9020	9070	9120	9170	9220	9270	9320	9369	9419	9469
870	93 9519	9569	9619	9669	9719	9769	9819	9869	9918	9968
71	94 0018	0068	0118	0168	0218	0267	0317	0367	0417	0467
72	0516	0566	0616	0666	0716	0765	0815	0865	0915	0964
73	1014	1064	1114	1163	1213	1263	1313	1362	1412	1462
74	1511	1561	1611	1660	1710	1760	1809	1859	1909	1958
75	2008	2058	2107	2157	2207	2256	2306	2355	2405	2455
76	2504	2554	2603	2653	2702	2752	2801	2851	2901	2950
77	3000	3049	3099	3148	3198	3247	3297	3346	3396	3445
78	3495	3544	3593	3643	3692	3742	3791	3841	3890	3939
79	3989	4038	4088	4137	4186	4236	4285	4335	4384	4433
880	4483	4532	4581	4631	4680	4729	4779	4828	4877	4927
81	4976	5025	5074	5124	5173	5222	5272	5321	5370	5419
82	5469	5518	5567	5616	5665	5715	5764	5813	5862	5912
83	5961	6010	6059	6108	6157	6207	6256	6305	6354	6403
84	6452	6501	6551	6600	6649	6698	6747	6796	6845	6894
85	6943	6992	7041	7090	7139	7189	7238	7287	7336	7385
86	7434	7483	7532	7581	7630	7679	7728	7777	7826	7875
87	7924	7973	8022	8070	8119	8168	8217	8266	8315	8364
88	8413	8462	8511	8560	8608	8657	8706	8755	8804	8853
89	8902	8951	8999	9048	9097	9146	9195	9244	9292	9341
890	9390	9439	9488	9536	9585	9634	9683	9731	9780	9829
91	94 9878	9926	9975	*0024	*0073	*0121	*0170	*0219	*0267	*0316
92	95 0365	0414	0462	0511	0560	0608	0657	0706	0754	0803
93	0851	0900	0949	0997	1046	1095	1143	1192	1240	1289
94	1338	1386	1435	1483	1532	1580	1629	1677	1726	1775
95	1823	1872	1920	1969	2017	2066	2114	2163	2211	2260
96	2308	2356	2405	2453	2502	2550	2599	2647	2696	2744
97	2792	2841	2889	2938	2986	3034	3083	3131	3180	3228
98	3276	3325	3373	3421	3470	3518	3566	3615	3663	3711
99	3760	3808	3856	3905	3953	4001	4049	4098	4146	4194
900	95 4243	4291	4339	4387	4435	4484	4532	4580	4628	4677
N	0	1	2	3	4	5	6	7	8	9

SIX-PLACE MANTISSAS FOR COMMON LOGARITHMS (Continued)

N	0	1	2	3	4	5	6	7	8	9
900	95 4243	4291	4339	4387	4435	4484	4532	4580	4628	4677
01	4725	4773	4821	4869	4918	4966	5014	5062	5110	5158
02	5207	5255	5303	5351	5399	5447	5495	5543	5592	5640
03	5688	5736	5784	5832	5880	5928	5976	6024	6072	6120
04	6168	6216	6265	6313	6361	6409	6457	6505	6553	6601
05	6649	6697	6745	6793	6840	6888	6936	6984	7032	7080
06	7128	7176	7224	7272	7320	7368	7416	7464	7512	7559
07	7607	7655	7703	7751	7799	7847	7894	7942	7990	8038
08	8086	8134	8181	8229	8277	8325	8373	8421	8468	8516
09	8564	8612	8659	8707	8755	8803	8850	8898	8946	8994
910	9041	9089	9137	9185	9232	9280	9328	9375	9423	9471
11	9518	9566	9614	9661	9709	9757	9804	9852	9900	9947
12	95 9995	*0042	*0090	*0138	*0185	*0233	*0280	*0328	*0376	*0423
13	96 0471	0518	0566	0613	0661	0709	0756	0804	0851	0899
14	0946	0994	1041	1089	1136	1184	1231	1279	1326	1374
15	1421	1469	1516	1563	1611	1658	1706	1753	1801	1848
16	1895	1943	1990	2038	2085	2132	2180	2227	2275	2322
17	2369	2417	2464	2511	2559	2606	2653	2701	2748	2795
18	2843	2890	2937	2985	3032	3079	3126	3174	3221	3268
19	3316	3363	3410	3457	3504	3552	3599	3646	3693	3741
920	3788	3835	3882	3929	3977	4024	4071	4118	4165	4212
21	4260	4307	4354	4401	4448	4495	4542	4590	4637	4684
22	4731	4778	4825	4872	4919	4966	5013	5061	5108	5155
23	5202	5249	5296	5343	5390	5437	5484	5531	5578	5625
24	5672	5719	5766	5813	5860	5907	5954	6001	6048	6095
25	6142	6189	6236	6283	6329	6376	6423	6470	6517	6564
26	6611	6658	6705	6752	6799	6845	6892	6939	6986	7033
27	7080	7127	7173	7220	7267	7314	7361	7408	7454	7501
28	7548	7595	7642	7688	7735	7782	7829	7875	7922	7969
29	8016	8062	8109	8156	8203	8249	8296	8343	8390	8436
930	8483	8530	8576	8623	8670	8716	8763	8810	8856	8903
31	8950	8996	9043	9090	9136	9183	9229	9276	9323	9369
32	9416	9463	9509	9556	9602	9649	9695	9742	9789	9835
33	96 9882	9928	9975	*0021	*0068	*0114	*0161	*0207	*0254	*0300
34	97 0347	0393	0440	0486	0533	0579	0626	0672	0719	0765
35	0812	0858	0904	0951	0997	1044	1090	1137	1183	1229
36	1276	1322	1369	1415	1461	1508	1554	1601	1647	1693
37	1740	1786	1832	1879	1925	1971	2018	2064	2110	2157
38	2203	2249	2295	2342	2388	2434	2481	2527	2573	2619
39	2666	2712	2758	2804	2851	2897	2943	2989	3035	3082
940	3128	3174	3220	3266	3313	3359	3405	3451	3497	3543
41	3590	3636	3682	3728	3774	3820	3866	3913	3959	4005
42	4051	4097	4143	4189	4235	4281	4327	4374	4420	4466
43	4512	4558	4604	4650	4696	4742	4788	4834	4880	4926
44	4972	5018	5064	5110	5156	5202	5248	5294	5340	5386
45	5432	5478	5524	5570	5616	5662	5707	5753	5799	5845
46	5891	5937	5983	6029	6075	6121	6167	6212	6258	6304
47	6350	6396	6442	6488	6533	6579	6625	6671	6717	6763
48	6808	6854	6900	6946	6992	7037	7083	7129	7175	7220
49	7266	7312	7358	7403	7449	7495	7541	7586	7632	7678
950	97 7724	7769	7815	7861	7906	7952	7998	8043	8089	8135
N	0	1	2	3	4	5	6	7	8	9

SIX-PLACE MANTISSAS FOR COMMON LOGARITHMS (Continued)

N	0	1	2	3	4	5	6	7	8	9
950	97 7724	7769	7815	7861	7906	7952	7998	8043	8089	8135
51	8181	8226	8272	8317	8363	8409	8454	8500	8546	8591
52	8637	8683	8728	8774	8819	8865	8911	8956	9002	9047
53	9093	9138	9184	9230	9275	9321	9366	9412	9457	9503
54	97 9548	9594	9639	9685	9730	9776	9821	9867	9912	9958
55	98 0003	0049	0094	0140	0185	0231	0276	0322	0367	0412
56	0458	0503	0549	0594	0640	0685	0730	0776	0821	0867
57	0912	0957	1003	1048	1093	1139	1184	1229	1275	1320
58	1366	1411	1456	1501	1547	1592	1637	1683	1728	1773
59	1819	1864	1909	1954	2000	2045	2090	2135	2181	2226
960	2271	2316	2362	2407	2452	2497	2543	2588	2633	2678
61	2723	2769	2814	2859	2904	2949	2994	3040	3085	3130
62	3175	3220	3265	3310	3356	3401	3446	3491	3536	3581
63	3626	3671	3716	3762	3807	3852	3897	3942	3987	4032
64	4077	4122	4167	4212	4257	4302	4347	4392	4437	4482
65	4527	4572	4617	4662	4707	4752	4797	4842	4887	4932
66	4977	5022	5067	5112	5157	5202	5247	5292	5337	5382
67	5426	5471	5516	5561	5606	5651	5696	5741	5786	5830
68	5875	5920	5965	6010	6055	6100	6144	6189	6234	6279
69	6324	6369	6413	6458	6503	6548	6593	6637	6682	6727
970	6772	6817	6861	6906	6951	6996	7040	7085	7130	7175
71	7219	7264	7309	7353	7398	7443	7488	7532	7577	7622
72	7666	7711	7756	7800	7845	7890	7934	7979	8024	8068
73	8113	8157	8202	8247	8291	8336	8381	8425	8470	8514
74	8559	8604	8648	8693	8737	8782	8826	8871	8916	8960
75	9005	9049	9094	9138	9183	9227	9272	9316	9361	9405
76	9450	9494	9539	9583	9628	9672	9717	9761	9806	9850
77	98 9895	9939	9983	*0028	*0072	*0117	*0161	*0206	*0250	*0294
78	99 0339	0383	0428	0472	0516	0561	0605	0650	0694	0738
79	0783	0827	0871	0916	0960	1004	1049	1093	1137	1182
980	1226	1270	1315	1359	1403	1448	1492	1536	1580	1625
81	1669	1713	1758	1802	1846	1890	1935	1979	2023	2067
82	2111	2156	2200	2244	2288	2333	2377	2421	2465	2509
83	2554	2598	2642	2686	2730	2774	2819	2863	2907	2951
84	2995	3039	3083	3127	3172	3216	3260	3304	3348	3392
85	3436	3480	3524	3568	3613	3657	3701	3745	3789	3833
86	3877	3921	3965	4009	4053	4097	4141	4185	4229	4273
87	4317	4361	4405	4449	4493	4537	4581	4625	4669	4713
88	4757	4801	4845	4889	4933	4977	5021	5065	5108	5152
89	5196	5240	5284	5328	5372	5416	5460	5504	5547	5591
990	5635	5679	5723	5767	5811	5854	5898	5942	5986	6030
91	6074	6117	6161	6205	6249	6293	6337	6380	6424	6468
92	6512	6555	6599	6643	6687	6731	6774	6818	6862	6906
93	6949	6993	7037	7080	7124	7168	7212	7255	7299	7343
94	7386	7430	7474	7517	7561	7605	7648	7692	7736	7779
95	7823	7867	7910	7954	7998	8041	8085	8129	8172	8216
96	8259	8303	8347	8390	8434	8477	8521	8564	8608	8652
97	8695	8739	8782	8826	8869	8913	8956	9000	9043	9087
98	9131	9174	9218	9261	9305	9348	9392	9435	9479	9522
99	99 9565	9609	9652	9696	9739	9783	9826	9870	9913	9957
1000	00 0000	0043	0087	0130	0174	0217	0260	0304	0347	0391
N	0	1	2	3	4	5	6	7	8	9

NATURAL OR NAPERIAN LOGARITHMS
0.000–0.499

N	0	1	2	3	4	5	6	7	8	9
0.00	$-\infty$	-6‡ .90776	-6 .21461	-5 .80914	-5 .52146	-5 .29832	-5 .11600	-4 .96185	-4 .82831	-4 .71053
.01	-4.60517	.50986	.42285	.34281	.26870	.19971	.13517	.07454	.01738	*.96332
.02	-3.91202	.86323	.81671	.77226	.72970	.68888	.64966	.61192	.57555	.54046
.03	.50656	.47377	.44202	.41125	.38139	.35241	.32424	.29684	.27017	.24419
.04	.21888	.19418	.17009	.14656	.12357	.10109	.07911	.05761	.03655	.01593
.05	-2.99573	.97593	.95651	.93746	.91877	.90042	.88240	.86470	.84731	.83022
.06	.81341	.79688	.78062	.76462	.74887	.73337	.71810	.70306	.68825	.67365
.07	.65926	.64508	.63109	.61730	.60369	.59027	.57702	.56395	.55105	.53831
.08	.52573	.51331	.50104	.48891	.47694	.46510	.45341	.44185	.43042	.41912
.09	.40795	.39690	.38597	.37516	.36446	.35388	.34341	.33304	.32279	.31264
0.10	-2.30259	.29263	.28278	.27303	.26336	.25379	.24432	.23493	.22562	.21641
.11	.20727	.19823	.18926	.18037	.17156	.16282	.15417	.14558	.13707	.12863
.12	.12026	.11196	.10373	.09557	.08747	.07944	.07147	.06357	.05573	.04794
.13	.04022	.03256	.02495	.01741	.00992	.00248	*.99510	*.98777	*.98050	*.97328
.14	-1.96611	.95900	.95193	.94491	.93794	.93102	.92415	.91732	.91054	.90381
.15	.89712	.89048	.88387	.87732	.87080	.86433	.85790	.85151	.84516	.83885
.16	.83258	.82635	.82016	.81401	.80789	.80181	.79577	.78976	.78379	.77786
.17	.77196	.76609	.76026	.75446	.74870	.74297	.73727	.73161	.72597	.72037
.18	.71480	.70926	.70375	.69827	.69282	.68740	.68201	.67665	.67131	.66601
.19	.66073	.65548	.65026	.64507	.63990	.63476	.62964	.62455	.61949	.61445
0.20	-1.60944	.60445	.59949	.59455	.58964	.58475	.57988	.57504	.57022	.56542
.21	.56065	.55590	.55117	.54646	.54178	.53712	.53248	.52786	.52326	.51868
.22	.51413	.50959	.50508	.50058	.49611	.49165	.48722	.48281	.47841	.47403
.23	.46968	.46534	.46102	.45672	.45243	.44817	.44392	.43970	.43548	.43129
.24	.42712	.42296	.41882	.41469	.41059	.40650	.40242	.39837	.39433	.39030
.25	.38629	.38230	.37833	.37437	.37042	.36649	.36258	.35868	.35480	.35093
.26	.34707	.34323	.33941	.33560	.33181	.32803	.32426	.32051	.31677	.31304
.27	.30933	.30564	.30195	.29828	.29463	.29098	.28735	.28374	.28013	.27654
.28	.27297	.26940	.26585	.26231	.25878	.25527	.25176	.24827	.24479	.24133
.29	.23787	.23443	.23100	.22758	.22418	.22078	.21740	.21402	.21066	.20731
0.30	-1.20397	.20065	.19733	.19402	.19073	.18744	.18417	.18091	.17766	.17441
.31	.17118	.16796	.16475	.16155	.15836	.15518	.15201	.14885	.14570	.14256
.32	.13943	.13631	.13320	.13010	.12701	.12393	.12086	.11780	.11474	.11170
.33	.10866	.10564	.10262	.09961	.09661	.09362	.09064	.08767	.08471	.08176
.34	.07881	.07587	.07294	.07002	.06711	.06421	.06132	.05843	.05555	.05268
.35	-1.04982	.04697	.04412	.04129	.03846	.03564	.03282	.03002	.02722	.02443
.36	.02165	.01888	.01611	.01335	.01060	.00786	.00512	.00239	*.99967	*.99696
.37	-0.99425	.99155	.98886	.98618	.98350	.98083	.97817	.97551	.97286	.97022
.38	.96758	.96496	.96233	.95972	.95711	.95451	.95192	.94933	.94675	.94418
.39	.94161	.93905	.93649	.93395	.93140	.92887	.92634	.92382	.92130	.91879
0.40	-0.91629	.91379	.91130	.90882	.90634	.90387	.90140	.89894	.89649	.89404
.41	.89160	.88916	.88673	.88431	.88189	.87948	.87707	.87467	.87227	.86988
.42	.86750	.86512	.86275	.86038	.85802	.85567	.85332	.85097	.84863	.84630
.43	.84397	.84165	.83933	.83702	.83471	.83241	.83011	.82782	.82554	.82326
.44	.82098	.81871	.81645	.81419	.81193	.80968	.80744	.80520	.80296	.80073
.45	.79851	.79629	.79407	.79186	.78966	.78746	.78526	.78307	.78089	.77871
.46	.77653	.77436	.77219	.77003	.76787	.76572	.76357	.76143	.75929	.75715
.47	.75502	.75290	.75078	.74866	.74655	.74444	.74234	.74024	.73814	.73605
.48	.73397	.73189	.72981	.72774	.72567	.72361	.72155	.71949	.71744	.71539
.49	.71335	.71131	.70928	.70725	.70522	.70320	.70118	.69917	.69716	.69515

‡ Note that the whole number values are given above the decimal values for the first line. In the second and following lines they are given at the left. All decimal values are negative on this page.

NATURAL OR NAPERIAN LOGARITHMS (Continued)
0.500–0.999

N	0	1	2	3	4	5	6	7	8	9
0.50	−0.69315	.69115	.68916	.68717	.68518	.68320	.68122	.67924	.67727	.67531
.51	.67334	.67139	.66943	.66748	.66553	.66359	.66165	.65971	.65778	.65585
.52	.65393	.65201	.65009	.64817	.64626	.64436	.64245	.64055	.63866	.63677
.53	.63488	.63299	.63111	.62923	.62736	.62549	.62362	.62176	.61990	.61804
.54	.61619	.61434	.61249	.61065	.60881	.60697	.60514	.60331	.60148	.59966
.55	.59784	.59602	.59421	.59240	.59059	.58879	.58699	.58519	.58340	.58161
.56	.57982	.57803	.57625	.57448	.57270	.57093	.56916	.56740	.56563	.56387
.57	.56212	.56037	.55862	.55687	.55513	.55339	.55165	.54991	.54818	.54645
.58	.54473	.54300	.54128	.53957	.53785	.53614	.53444	.53273	.53103	.52933
.59	.52763	.52594	.52425	.52256	.52088	.51919	.51751	.51584	.51416	.51249
0.60	−0.51083	.50916	.50750	.50584	.50418	.50253	.50088	.49923	.49758	.49594
.61	.49430	.49266	.49102	.48939	.48776	.48613	.48451	.48289	.48127	.47965
.62	.47804	.47642	.47482	.47321	.47160	.47000	.46840	.46681	.46522	.46362
.63	.46204	.46045	.45887	.45728	.45571	.45413	.45256	.45099	.44942	.44785
.64	.44629	.44473	.44317	.44161	.44006	.43850	.43696	.43541	.43386	.43232
.65	.43078	.42925	.42771	.42618	.42465	.42312	.42159	.42007	.41855	.41703
.66	.41552	.41400	.41249	.41098	.40947	.40797	.40647	.40497	.40347	.40197
.67	.40048	.39899	.39750	.39601	.39453	.39304	.39156	.39008	.38861	.38713
.68	.38566	.38419	.38273	.38126	.37980	.37834	.37688	.37542	.37397	.37251
.69	.37106	.36962	.36817	.36673	.36528	.36384	.36241	.36097	.35954	.35810
0.70	−0.35667	.35525	.35382	.35240	.35098	.34956	.34814	.34672	.34531	.34390
.71	.34249	.34108	.33968	.33827	.33687	.33547	.33408	.33268	.33129	.32989
.72	.32850	.32712	.32573	.32435	.32296	.32158	.32021	.31883	.31745	.31608
.73	.31471	.31334	.31197	.31061	.30925	.30788	.30653	.30517	.30381	.30246
.74	.30111	.29975	.29841	.29706	.29571	.29437	.29303	.29169	.29035	.28902
.75	.28768	.28635	.28502	.28369	.28236	.28104	.27971	.27839	.27707	.27575
.76	.27444	.27312	.27181	.27050	.26919	.26788	.26657	.26527	.26397	.26266
.77	.26136	.26007	.25877	.25748	.25618	.25489	.25360	.25231	.25103	.24974
.78	.24846	.24718	.24590	.24462	.24335	.24207	.24080	.23953	.23826	.23699
.79	.23572	.23446	.23319	.23193	.23067	.22941	.22816	.22690	.22565	.22439
0.80	−0.22314	.22189	.22065	.21940	.21816	.21691	.21567	.21433	.21319	.21196
.81	.21072	.20949	.20825	.20702	.20579	.20457	.20334	.20212	.20089	.19967
.82	.19845	.19723	.19601	.19480	.19358	.19237	.19116	.18995	.18874	.18754
.83	.18633	.18513	.18392	.18272	.18152	.18032	.17913	.17793	.17674	.17554
.84	.17435	.17316	.17198	.17079	.16960	.16842	.16724	.16605	.16487	.16370
.85	−0.16252	.16134	.16017	.15900	.15782	.15665	.15548	.15432	.15315	.15199
.86	.15082	.14966	.14850	.14734	.14618	.14503	.14387	.14272	.14156	.14041
.87	.13926	.13811	.13697	.13582	.13467	.13353	.13239	.13125	.13011	.12897
.88	.12783	.12670	.12556	.12443	.12330	.12217	.12104	.11991	.11878	.11766
.89	.11653	.11541	.11429	.11317	.11205	.11093	.10981	.10870	.10759	.10647
0.90	−0.10536	.10425	.10314	.10203	.10093	.09982	.09872	.09761	.09651	.09541
.91	.09431	.09321	.09212	.09102	.08992	.08883	.08774	.08665	.08556	.08447
.92	.08338	.08230	.08121	.08013	.07904	.07796	.07688	.07580	.07472	.07365
.93	.07257	.07150	.07042	.06935	.06828	.06721	.06614	.06507	.06401	.06294
.94	.06188	.06081	.05975	.05869	.05763	.05657	.05551	.05446	.05340	.05235
.95	.05129	.05024	.04919	.04814	.04709	.04604	.04500	.04395	.04291	.04186
.96	.04082	.03978	.03874	.03770	.03666	.03563	.03459	.03356	.03252	.03149
.97	.03046	.02943	.02840	.02737	.02634	.02532	.02429	.02327	.02225	.02122
.98	.02020	.01918	.01816	.01715	.01613	.01511	.01410	.01309	.01207	.01106
.99	.01005	.00904	.00803	.00702	.00602	.00501	.00401	.00300	.00200	.00100

NATURAL OR NAPERIAN LOGARITHMS (Continued)

To find the natural logarithm of a number which is $\frac{1}{10}$, $\frac{1}{100}$, $\frac{1}{1000}$, etc. of a number whose logarithm is given, subtract from the given logarithm $\log_e 10$, $2 \log_e 10$, $3 \log_e 10$, etc.

To find the natural logarithm of a number which is 10, 100, 1000, etc. times a number whose logarithm is given, add to the given logarithm $\log_e 10$, $2 \log_e 10$, $3 \log_e 10$, etc.

$\log_e 10 = 2.30258\ 50930$	$6 \log_e 10 = 13.81551\ 05580$
$2 \log_e 10 = 4.60517\ 01860$	$7 \log_e 10 = 16.11809\ 56510$
$3 \log_e 10 = 6.90775\ 52790$	$8 \log_e 10 = 18.42068\ 07440$
$4 \log_e 10 = 9.21034\ 03720$	$9 \log_e 10 = 20.72326\ 58369$
$5 \log_e 10 = 11.51292\ 54650$	$10 \log_e 10 = 23.02585\ 09299$

See preceding table for logarithms for numbers between 0.000 and 0.999.

1.00–4.99

N	0	1	2	3	4	5	6	7	8	9
1.0	0.00000	.00995	.01980	.02956	.03922	.04879	.05827	.06766	.07696	.08618
.1	.09531	.10436	.11333	.12222	.13103	.13976	.14842	.15700	.16551	.17395
.2	.18232	.19062	.19885	.20701	.21511	.22314	.23111	.23902	.24686	.25464
.3	.26236	.27003	.27763	.28518	.29267	.30010	.30748	.31481	.32208	.32930
.4	.33647	.34359	.35066	.35767	.36464	.37156	.37844	.38526	.39204	.39878
.5	.40547	.41211	.41871	.42527	.43178	.43825	.44469	.45108	.45742	.46373
.6	.47000	.47623	.48243	.48858	.49470	.50078	.50682	.51282	.51879	.52473
.7	.53063	.53649	.54232	.54812	.55389	.55962	.56531	.57098	.57661	.58222
.8	.58779	.59333	.59884	.60432	.60977	.61519	.62058	.62594	.63127	.63658
.9	.64185	.64710	.65233	.65752	.66269	.66783	.67294	.67803	.68310	.68813
2.0	0.69315	.69813	.70310	.70804	.71295	.71784	.72271	.72755	.73237	.73716
.1	.74194	.74669	.75142	.75612	.76081	.76547	.77011	.77473	.77932	.78390
.2	.78846	.79299	.79751	.80200	.80648	.81093	.81536	.81978	.82418	.82855
.3	.83291	.83725	.84157	.84587	.85015	.85442	.85866	.86289	.86710	.87129
.4	.87547	.87963	.88377	.88789	.89200	.89609	.90016	.90422	.90826	.91228
.5	.91629	.92028	.92426	.92822	.93216	.93609	.94001	.94391	.94779	.95166
.6	.95551	.95935	.96317	.96698	.97078	.97456	.97833	.98208	.98582	.98954
.7	.99325	.99695	*.00063	*.00430	*.00796	*.01160	*.01523	*.01885	*.02245	*.02604
.8	1.02962	.03318	.03674	.04028	.04380	.04732	.05082	.05431	.05779	.06126
.9	.06471	.06815	.07158	.07500	.07841	.08181	.08519	.08856	.09192	.09527
3.0	1.09861	.10194	.10526	.10856	.11186	.11514	.11841	.12168	.12493	.12817
.1	.13140	.13462	.13783	.14103	.14422	.14740	.15057	.15373	.15688	.16002
.2	.16315	.16627	.16938	.17248	.17557	.17865	.18173	.18479	.18784	.19089
.3	.19392	.19695	.19996	.20297	.20597	.20896	.21194	.21491	.21788	.22083
.4	.22378	.22671	.22964	.23256	.23547	.23837	.24127	.24415	.24703	.24990
.5	.25276	.25562	.25846	.26130	.26413	.26695	.26976	.27257	.27536	.27815
.6	.28093	.28371	.28647	.28923	.29198	.29473	.29746	.30019	.30291	.30563
.7	.30833	.31103	.31372	.31641	.31909	.32176	.32442	.32708	.32972	.33237
.8	.33500	.33763	.34025	.34286	.34547	.34807	.35067	.35325	.35584	.35841
.9	.36098	.36354	.36609	.36864	.37118	.37372	.37624	.37877	.38128	.38379
4.0	1.38629	.38879	.39128	.39377	.39624	.39872	.40118	.40364	.40610	.40854
.1	.41099	.41342	.41585	.41828	.42070	.42311	.42552	.42792	.43031	.43270
.2	.43508	.43746	.43984	.44220	.44456	.44692	.44927	.45161	.45395	.45629
.3	.45862	.46094	.46326	.46557	.46787	.47018	.47247	.47476	.47705	.47933
.4	.48160	.48387	.48614	.48840	.49065	.49290	.49515	.49739	.49962	.50185
.5	.50408	.50630	.50851	.51072	.51293	.51513	.51732	.51951	.52170	.52388
.6	.52606	.52823	.53039	.53256	.53471	.53687	.53902	.54116	.54330	.54543
.7	.54756	.54969	.55181	.55393	.55604	.55814	.56025	.56235	.56444	.56653
.8	.56862	.57070	.57277	.57485	.57691	.57898	.58104	.58309	.58515	.58719
.9	.58924	.59127	.59331	.59534	.59737	.59939	.60141	.60342	.60543	.60744

NATURAL OR NAPERIAN LOGARITHMS (Continued)
5.00–9.99

N	0	1	2	3	4	5	6	7	8	9
5.0	1.60944	.61144	.61343	.61542	.61741	.61939	.62137	.62334	.62531	.62728
.1	.62924	.63120	.63315	.63511	.63705	.63900	.64094	.64287	.64481	.64673
.2	.64866	.65058	.65250	.65441	.65632	.65823	.66013	.66203	.66393	.66582
.3	.66771	.66959	.67147	.67335	.67523	.67710	.67896	.68083	.68269	.68455
.4	.68640	.68825	.69010	.69194	.69378	.69562	.69745	.69928	.70111	.70293
.5	.70475	.70656	.70838	.71019	.71199	.71380	.71560	.71740	.71919	.72098
.6	.72277	.72455	.72633	.72811	.72988	.73166	.73342	.73519	.73695	.73871
.7	.74047	.74222	.74397	.74572	.74746	.74920	.75094	.75267	.75440	.75613
.8	.75786	.75958	.76130	.76302	.76473	.76644	.76815	.76985	.77156	.77326
.9	.77495	.77665	.77834	.78002	.78171	.78339	.78507	.78675	.78842	.79009
6.0	1.79176	.79342	.79509	.79675	.79840	.80006	.80171	.80336	.80500	.80665
.1	.80829	.80993	.81156	.81319	.81482	.81645	.81808	.81970	.82132	.82294
.2	.82455	.82616	.82777	.82938	.83098	.83258	.83418	.83578	.83737	.83896
.3	.84055	.84214	.84372	.84530	.84688	.84845	.85003	.85160	.85317	.85473
.4	.85630	.85786	.85942	.86097	.86253	.86408	.86563	.86718	.86872	.87026
.5	.87180	.87334	.87487	.87641	.87794	.87947	.88099	.88251	.88403	.88555
.6	.88707	.88858	.89010	.89160	.89311	.89462	.89612	.89762	.89912	.90061
.7	.90211	.90360	.90509	.90658	.90806	.90954	.91102	.91250	.91398	.91545
.8	.91692	.91839	.91986	.92132	.92279	.92425	.92571	.92716	.92862	.93007
.9	.93152	.93297	.93442	.93586	.93730	.93874	.94018	.94162	.94305	.94448
7.0	1.94591	.94734	.94876	.95019	.95161	.95303	.95445	.95586	.95727	.95869
.1	.96009	.96150	.96291	.96431	.96571	.96711	.96851	.96991	.97130	.97269
.2	.97408	.97547	.97685	.97824	.97962	.98100	.98238	.98376	.98513	.98650
.3	.98787	.98924	.99061	.99198	.99334	.99470	.99606	.99742	.99877	*.00013
.4	2.00148	.00283	.00418	.00553	.00687	.00821	.00956	.01089	.01223	.01357
.5	.01490	.01624	.01757	.01890	.02022	.02155	.02287	.02419	.02551	.02683
.6	.02815	.02946	.03078	.03209	.03340	.03471	.03601	.03732	.03862	.03992
.7	.04122	.04252	.04381	.04511	.04640	.04769	.04898	.05027	.05156	.05284
.8	.05412	.05540	.05668	.05796	.05924	.06051	.06179	.06306	.06433	.06560
.9	.06686	.06813	.06939	.07065	.07191	.07317	.07443	.07568	.07694	.07819
8.0	2.07944	.08069	.08194	.08318	.08443	.08567	.08691	.08815	.08939	.09063
.1	.09186	.09310	.09433	.09556	.09679	.09802	.09924	.10047	.10169	.10291
.2	.10413	.10535	.10657	.10779	.10900	.11021	.11142	.11263	.11384	.11505
.3	.11626	.11746	.11866	.11986	.12106	.12226	.12346	.12465	.12585	.12704
.4	.12823	.12942	.13061	.13180	.13298	.13417	.13535	.13653	.13771	.13889
.5	.14007	.14124	.14242	.14359	.14476	.14593	.14710	.14827	.14943	.15060
.6	.15176	.15292	.15409	.15524	.15640	.15756	.15871	.15987	.16102	.16217
.7	.16332	.16447	.16562	.16677	.16791	.16905	.17020	.17134	.17248	.17361
.8	.17475	.17589	.17702	.17816	.17929	.18042	.18155	.18267	.18380	.18493
.9	.18605	.18717	.18830	.18942	.19054	.19165	.19277	.19389	.19500	.19611
9.0	2.19722	.19834	.19944	.20055	.20166	.20276	.20387	.20497	.20607	.20717
.1	.20827	.20937	.21047	.21157	.21266	.21375	.21485	.21594	.21703	.21812
.2	.21920	.22029	.22138	.22246	.22354	.22462	.22570	.22678	.22786	.22894
.3	.23001	.23109	.23216	.23324	.23431	.23538	.23645	.23751	.23858	.23965
.4	.24071	.24177	.24284	.24390	.24496	.24601	.24707	.24813	.24918	.25024
.5	.25129	.25234	.25339	.25444	.25549	.25654	.25759	.25863	.25968	.26072
.6	.26176	.26280	.26384	.26488	.26592	.26696	.26799	.26903	.27006	.27109
.7	.27213	.27316	.27419	.27521	.27624	.27727	.27829	.27932	.28034	.28136
.8	.28238	.28340	.28442	.28544	.28646	.28747	.28849	.28950	.29051	.29152
.9	.29253	.29354	.29455	.29556	.29657	.29757	.29858	.29958	.30058	.30158

NATURAL OR NAPERIAN LOGARITHMS (Continued)

Constants

$\log_e 10 =$	2.30258 50930	$6 \log_e 10 =$	13.81551 05580
$2 \log_e 10 =$	4.60517 01860	$7 \log_e 10 =$	16.11809 56510
$3 \log_e 10 =$	6.90775 52790	$8 \log_e 10 =$	18.42068 07440
$4 \log_e 10 =$	9.21034 03720	$9 \log_e 10 =$	20.72326 58369
$5 \log_e 10 =$	11.51292 54650	$10 \log_e 10 =$	23.02585 09299

10.0–49.9

N	0	1	2	3	4	5	6	7	8	9
10.	2.30259	.31254	.32239	.33214	.34181	.35138	.36085	.37024	.37955	.38876
11.	.39790	.40695	.41591	.42480	.43361	.44235	.45101	.45959	.46810	.47654
12.	.48491	.49321	.50144	.50960	.51770	.52573	.53370	.54160	.54945	.55723
13.	.56495	.57261	.58022	.58776	.59525	.60269	.61007	.61740	.62467	.63189
14.	.63906	.64617	.65324	.66026	.66723	.67415	.68102	.68785	.69463	.70136
15.	.70805	.71469	.72130	.72785	.73437	.74084	.74727	.75366	.76001	.76632
16.	.77259	.77882	.78501	.79117	.79728	.80336	.80940	.81541	.82138	.82731
17.	.83321	.83908	.84491	.85071	.85647	.86220	.86790	.87356	.87920	.88480
18.	.89037	.89591	.90142	.90690	.91235	.91777	.92316	.92852	.93386	.93916
19.	.94444	.94969	.95491	.96011	.96527	.97041	.97553	.98062	.98568	.99072
20.	2.99573	*.00072	*.00568	*.01062	*.01553	*.02042	*.02529	*.03013	*.03495	*.03975
21.	3.04452	.04927	.05400	.05871	.06339	.06805	.07269	.07731	.08191	.08649
22.	.09104	.09558	.10009	.10459	.10906	.11352	.11795	.12236	.12676	.13114
23.	.13549	.13983	.14415	.14845	.15274	.15700	.16125	.16548	.16969	.17388
24.	.17805	.18221	.18635	.19048	.19458	.19867	.20275	.20680	.21084	.21487
25.	.21888	.22287	.22684	.23080	.23475	.23868	.24259	.24649	.25037	.25424
26.	.25810	.26194	.26576	.26957	.27336	.27714	.28091	.28466	.28840	.29213
27.	.29584	.29953	.30322	.30689	.31054	.31419	.31782	.32143	.32504	.32863
28.	.33220	.33577	.33932	.34286	.34639	.34990	.35341	.35690	.36038	.36384
29.	.36730	.37074	.37417	.37759	.38099	.38439	.38777	.39115	.39451	.39786
30.	3.40120	.40453	.40784	.41115	.41444	.41773	.42100	.42426	.42751	.43076
31.	.43399	.43721	.44042	.44362	.44681	.44999	.45316	.45632	.45947	.46261
32.	.46574	.46886	.47197	.47507	.47816	.48124	.48431	.48738	.49043	.49347
33.	.49651	.49953	.50255	.50556	.50856	.51155	.51453	.51750	.52046	.52342
34.	.52636	.52930	.53223	.53515	.53806	.54096	.54385	.54674	.54962	.55249
35.	.55535	.55820	.56105	.56388	.56671	.56953	.57235	.57515	.57795	.58074
36.	.58352	.58629	.58906	.59182	.59457	.59731	.60005	.60278	.60550	.60821
37.	.61092	.61362	.61631	.61899	.62167	.62434	.62700	.62966	.63231	.63495
38.	.63759	.64021	.64284	.64545	.64806	.65066	.65325	.65584	.65842	.66099
39.	.66356	.66612	.66868	.67122	.67377	.67630	.67883	.68135	.68387	.68638
40.	3.68888	.69138	.69387	.69635	.69883	.70130	.70377	.70623	.70868	.71113
41.	.71357	.71601	.71844	.72086	.72328	.72569	.72810	.73050	.73290	.73529
42.	.73767	.74005	.74242	.74479	.74715	.74950	.75185	.75420	.75654	.75887
43.	.76120	.76352	.76584	.76815	.77046	.77276	.77506	.77735	.77963	.78191
44.	.78419	.78646	.78872	.79098	.79324	.79549	.79773	.79997	.80221	.80444
45.	.80666	.80888	.81110	.81331	.81551	.81771	.81991	.82210	.82428	.82647
46.	.82864	.83081	.83298	.83514	.83730	.83945	.84160	.84374	.84588	.84802
47.	.85015	.85227	.85439	.85651	.85862	.86073	.86283	.86493	.86703	.86912
48.	.87120	.87328	.87536	.87743	.87950	.88156	.88362	.88568	.88773	.88978
49.	.89182	.89386	.89589	.89792	.89995	.90197	.90399	.90600	.90801	.91002

NATURAL OR NAPERIAN LOGARITHMS (Continued)
50.0–99.9

N	0	1	2	3	4	5	6	7	8	9
50.	3.91202	.91402	.91602	.91801	.91999	.92197	.92395	.92593	.92790	.92986
51.	.93183	.93378	.93574	.93769	.93964	.94158	.94352	.94546	.94739	.94932
52.	.95124	.95316	.95508	.95700	.95891	.96081	.96272	.96462	.96651	.96840
53.	.97029	.97218	.97406	.97594	.97781	.97968	.98155	.98341	.98527	.98713
54.	.98898	.99083	.99268	.99452	.99636	.99820	*.00003	*.00186	*.00369	*.00551
55.	4.00733	.00915	.01096	.01277	.01458	.01638	.01818	.01998	.02177	.02356
56.	.02535	.02714	.02892	.03069	.03247	.03424	.03601	.03777	.03954	.04130
57.	.04305	.04480	.04655	.04830	.05004	.05178	.05352	.05526	.05699	.05872
58.	.06044	.06217	.06389	.06560	.06732	.06903	.07073	.07244	.07414	.07584
59.	.07754	.07923	.08092	.08261	.08429	.08598	.08766	.08933	.09101	.09268
60.	4.09434	.09601	.09767	.09933	.10099	.10264	.10429	.10594	.10759	.10923
61.	.11087	.11251	.11415	.11578	.11741	.11904	.12066	.12228	.12390	.12552
62.	.12713	.12875	.13036	.13196	.13357	.13517	.13677	.13836	.13996	.14155
63.	.14313	.14472	.14630	.14789	.14946	.15104	.15261	.15418	.15575	.15732
64.	.15888	.16044	.16200	.16356	.16511	.16667	.16821	.16976	.17131	.17285
65.	.17439	.17592	.17746	.17899	.18052	.18205	.18358	.18510	.18662	.18814
66.	.18965	.19117	.19268	.19419	.19570	.19720	.19870	.20020	.20170	.20320
67.	.20469	.20618	.20767	.20916	.21065	.21213	.21361	.21509	.21656	.21804
68.	.21951	.22098	.22244	.22391	.22537	.22683	.22829	.22975	.23120	.23266
69.	.23411	.23555	.23700	.23844	.23989	.24133	.24276	.24420	.24563	.24707
70.	4.24850	.24992	.25135	.25277	.25419	.25561	.25703	.25845	.25986	.26127
71.	.26268	.26409	.26549	.26690	.26830	.26970	.27110	.27249	.27388	.27528
72.	.27667	.27805	.27944	.28082	.28221	.28359	.28496	.28634	.28772	.28909
73.	.29046	.29183	.29320	.29456	.29592	.29729	.29865	.30000	.30136	.30271
74.	.30407	.30542	.30676	.30811	.30946	.31080	.31214	.31348	.31482	.31615
75.	.31749	.31882	.32015	.32149	.32281	.32413	.32546	.32678	.32810	.32942
76.	.33073	.33205	.33336	.33467	.33598	.33729	.33860	.33990	.34120	.34251
77.	.34381	.34510	.34640	.34769	.34899	.35028	.35157	.35286	.35414	.35543
78.	.35671	.35800	.35927	.36055	.36182	.36310	.36437	.36564	.36691	.36818
79.	.36945	.37071	.37198	.37324	.37450	.37576	.37701	.37827	.37952	.38078
80.	4.38203	.38328	.38452	.38577	.38701	.38826	.38950	.39074	.39198	.39321
81.	.39445	.39568	.39692	.39815	.39938	.40060	.40183	.40305	.40428	.40550
82.	.40672	.40794	.40916	.41037	.41159	.41280	.41401	.41522	.41643	.41764
83.	.41884	.42004	.42125	.42245	.42365	.42485	.42604	.42724	.42843	.42963
84.	.43082	.43201	.43319	.43438	.43557	.43675	.43793	.43912	.44030	.44147
85.	.44265	.44383	.44500	.44617	.44735	.44852	.44969	.45085	.45202	.45318
86.	.45435	.45551	.45667	.45783	.45899	.46014	.46130	.46245	.46361	.46476
87.	.46591	.46706	.46820	.46935	.47050	.47164	.47278	.47392	.47506	.47620
88.	.47734	.47847	.47961	.48074	.48187	.48300	.48413	.48526	.48639	.48751
89.	.48864	.48976	.49088	.49200	.49312	.49424	.49536	.49647	.49758	.49870
90.	4.49981	.50092	.50203	.50314	.50424	.50535	.50645	.50756	.50866	.50976
91.	.51086	.51196	.51305	.51415	.51525	.51634	.51743	.51852	.51961	.52070
92.	.52179	.52287	.52396	.52504	.52613	.52721	.52829	.52937	.53045	.53152
93.	.53260	.53367	.53475	.53582	.53689	.53796	.53903	.54010	.54116	.54223
94.	.54329	.54436	.54542	.54648	.54754	.54860	.54966	.55071	.55177	.55282
95.	.55388	.55493	.55598	.55703	.55808	.55913	.56017	.56122	.56226	.56331
96.	.56435	.56539	.56643	.56747	.56851	.56954	.57058	.57161	.57265	.57368
97.	.57471	.57574	.57677	.57780	.57883	.57985	.58088	.58190	.58292	.58395
98.	.58497	.58599	.58701	.58802	.58904	.59006	.59107	.59208	.59310	.59411
99.	.59512	.59613	.59714	.59815	.59915	.60016	.60116	.60217	.60317	.60417

NATURAL OR NAPERIAN LOGARITHMS (Continued)
0–499

N	0	1	2	3	4	5	6	7	8	9
0	− ∞	0.00000	0.69315	1.09861	.38629	.60944	.79176	.94591	*.07944	*.19722
1	2.30259	.39790	.48491	.56495	.63906	.70805	.77259	.83321	.89037	.94444
2	.99573	*.04452	*.09104	*.13549	*.17805	*.21888	*.25810	*.29584	*.33220	*.36730
3	3.40120	.43399	.46574	.49651	.52636	.55535	.58352	.61092	.63759	.66356
4	.68888	.71357	.73767	.76120	.78419	.80666	.82864	.85015	.87120	.89182
5	.91202	.93183	.95124	.97029	.98898	*.00733	*02535	*.04305	*.06044	*.07754
6	4.09434	.11087	.12713	.14313	.15888	.17439	.18965	.20469	.21951	.23411
7	.24850	.26268	.27667	.29046	.30407	.31749	.33073	.34381	.35671	.36945
8	.38203	.39445	.40672	.41884	.43082	.44265	.45435	.46591	.47734	.48864
9	.49981	.51086	.52179	.53260	.54329	.55388	.56435	.57471	.58497	.59512
10	4.60517	.61512	.62497	.63473	.64439	.65396	.66344	.67283	.68213	.69135
11	.70048	.70953	.71850	.72739	.73620	.74493	.75359	.76217	.77068	.77912
12	.78749	.79579	.80402	.81218	.82028	.82831	.83628	.84419	.85203	.85981
13	.86753	.87520	.88280	.89035	.89784	.90527	.91265	.91998	.92725	.93447
14	.94164	.94876	.95583	.96284	.96981	.97673	.98361	.99043	.99721	* 00395
15	5.01064	.01728	.02388	.03044	.03695	.04343	.04986	.05625	.06260	.06890
16	.07517	.08140	.08760	.09375	.09987	.10595	.11199	.11799	.12396	.12990
17	.13580	.14166	.14749	.15329	.15906	.16479	.17048	.17615	.18178	.18739
18	.19296	.19850	.20401	.20949	.21494	.22036	.22575	.23111	.23644	.24175
19	.24702	.25227	.25750	.26269	.26786	.27300	.27811	.28320	.28827	.29330
20	5.29832	.30330	.30827	.31321	.31812	.32301	.32788	.33272	.33754	.34233
21	.34711	.35186	.35659	.36129	.36598	.37064	.37528	.37990	.38450.	.38907
22	.39363	.39816	.40268	.40717	.41165	.41610	.42053	.42495	.42935	.43372
23	.43808	.44242	.44674	.45104	.45532	.45959	.46383	.46806	.47227	.47646
24	.48064	.48480	.48894	.49306	.49717	.50126	.50533	.50939	.51343	.51745
25	.52146	.52545	.52943	.53339	.53733	.54126	.54518	.54908	.55296	.55683
26	.56068	.56452	.56834	.57215	.57595	.57973	.58350	.58725	.59099	.59471
27	.59842	.60212	.60580	.60947	.61313	.61677	.62040	.62402	.62762	.63121
28	.63479	.63835	.64191	.64545	.64897	.65249	.65599	.65948	.66296	.66643
29	.66988	.67332	.67675	.68017	.68358	.68698	.69036	.69373	.69709	.70044
30	5.70378	.70711	.71043	.71373	.71703	.72031	.72359	.72685	.73010	.73334
31	.73657	.73979	.74300	.74620	.74939	.75257	.75574	.75890	.76205	.76519
32	.76832	.77144	.77455	.77765	.78074	.78383	.78690	.78996	.79301	.79606
33	.79909	.80212	.80513	.80814	.81114	.81413	.81711	.82008	.82305	.82600
34	.82895	.83188	.83481	.83773	.84064	.84354	.84644	.84932	.85220	.85507
35	.85793	.86079	.86363	.86647	.86930	.87212	.87493	.87774	.88053	.88332
36	.88610	.88888	.89164	.89440	.89715	.89990	.90263	.90536	.90808	.91080
37	.91350	.91620	.91889	.92158	.92426	.92693	.92959	.93225	.93489	.93754
38	.94017	.94280	.94542	.94803	.95064	.95324	.95584	.95842	.96101	.96358
39	.96615	.96871	.97126	.97381	.97635	.97889	.98141	.98394	.98645	.98896
40	5.99146	.99396	.99645	.99894	*.00141	*.00389	*.00635	*.00881	*.01127	*.01372
41	6.01616	.01859	.02102	.02345	.02587	.02828	.03069	.03309	.03548	.03787
42	.04025	.04263	.04501	.04737	.04973	.05209	.05444	.05678	.05912	.06146
43	.06379	.06611	.06843	.07074	.07304	.07535	.07764	.07993	.08222	.08450
44	.08677	.08904	.09131	.09357	.09582	.09807	.10032	.10256	.10479	.10702
45	.10925	.11147	.11368	.11589	.11810	.12030	.12249	.12468	.12687	.12905
46	.13123	.13340	.13556	.13773	.13988	.14204	.14419	.14633	.14847	.15060
47	.15273	.15486	.15698	.15910	.16121	.16331	.16542	.16752	.16961	.17170
48	.17379	.17587	.17794	.18002	.18208	.18415	.18621	.18826	.19032	.19236
49	.19441	.19644	.19848	.20051	.20254	.20456	.20658	.20859	.21060	.21261

NATURAL OR NAPERIAN LOGARITHMS (Continued)

500–999

N	0	1	2	3	4	5	6	7	8	9
50	6.21461	.21661	.21860	.22059	.22258	.22456	.22654	.22851	.23048	.23245
51	.23441	.23637	.23832	.24028	.24222	.24417	.24611	.24804	.24998	.25190
52	.25383	.25575	.25767	.25958	.26149	.26340	.26530	.26720	.26910	.27099
53	.27288	.27476	.27664	.27852	.28040	.28227	.28413	.28600	.28786	.28972
54	.29157	.29342	.29527	.29711	.29895	.30079	.30262	.30445	.30628	.30810
55	.30992	.31173	.31355	.31536	.31716	.31897	.32077	.32257	.32436	.32615
56	.32794	.32972	.33150	.33328	.33505	.33683	.33859	.34036	.34212	.34388
57	.34564	.34739	.34914	.35089	.35263	.35437	.35611	.35784	.35957	.36130
58	.36303	.36475	.36647	.36819	.36990	.37161	.37332	.37502	.37673	.37843
59	.38012	.38182	.38351	.38519	.38688	.38856	.39024	.39192	.39359	.39526
60	6.39693	.39859	.40026	.40192	.40357	.40523	.40688	.40853	.41017	.41182
61	.41346	.41510	.41673	.41836	.41999	.42162	.42325	.42487	.42649	.42811
62	.42972	.43133	.43294	.43455	.43615	.43775	.43935	.44095	.44254	.44413
63	.44572	.44731	.44889	.45047	.45205	.45362	.45520	.45677	.45834	.45990
64	.46147	.46303	.46459	.46614	.46770	.46925	.47080	.47235	.47389	.47543
65	.47697	.47851	.48004	.48158	.48311	.48464	.48616	.48768	.48920	.49072
66	.49224	.49375	.49527	.49677	.49828	.49979	.50129	.50279	.50429	.50578
67	.50728	.50877	.51026	.51175	.51323	.51471	.51619	.51767	.51915	.52062
68	.52209	.52356	.52503	.52649	.52796	.52942	.53088	.53233	.53379	.53524
69	.53669	.53814	.53959	.54103	.54247	.54391	.54535	.54679	.54822	.54965
70	6.55108	.55251	.55393	.55536	.55678	.55820	.55962	.56103	.56244	.56386
71	.56526	.56667	.56808	.56948	.57088	.57228	.57368	.57508	.57647	.57786
72	.57925	.58064	.58203	.58341	.58479	.58617	.58755	.58893	.59030	.59167
73	.59304	.59441	.59578	.59715	.59851	.59987	.60123	.60259	.60394	.60530
74	.60665	.60800	.60935	.61070	.61204	.61338	.61473	.61607	.61740	.61874
75	.62007	.62141	.62274	.62407	.62539	.62672	.62804	.62936	.63068	.63200
76	.63332	.63463	.63595	.63726	.63857	.63988	.64118	.64249	.64379	.64509
77	.64639	.64769	.64898	.65028	.65157	.65286	.65415	.65544	.65673	.65801
78	.65929	.66058	.66185	.66313	.66441	.66568	.66696	.66823	.66950	.67077
79	.67203	.67330	.67456	.67582	.67708	.67834	.67960	.68085	.68211	.68336
80	6.68461	.68586	.68711	.68835	.68960	.69084	.69208	.69332	.69456	.69580
81	.69703	.69827	.69950	.70073	.70196	.70319	.70441	.70564	.70686	.70808
82	.70930	.71052	.71174	.71296	.71417	.71538	.71659	.71780	.71901	.72022
83	.72143	.72263	.72383	.72503	.72623	.72743	.72863	.72982	.73102	.73221
84	.73340	.73459	.73578	.73697	.73815	.73934	.74052	.74170	.74288	.74406
85	.74524	.74641	.74759	.74876	.74993	.75110	.75227	.75344	.75460	.75577
86	.75693	.75809	.75926	.76041	.76157	.76273	.76388	.76504	.76619	.76734
87	.76849	.76964	.77079	.77194	.77308	.77422	.77537	.77651	.77765	.77878
88	.77992	.78106	.78219	.78333	.78446	.78559	.78672	.78784	.78897	.79010
89	.79122	.79234	.79347	.79459	.79571	.79682	.79794	.79906	.80017	.80128
90	6.80239	.80351	.80461	.80572	.80683	.80793	.80904	.81014	.81124	.81235
91	.81344	.81454	.81564	.81674	.81783	.81892	.82002	.82111	.82220	.82329
92	.82437	.82546	.82655	.82763	.82871	.82979	.83087	.83195	.83303	.83411
93	.83518	.83626	.83733	.83841	.83948	.84055	.84162	.84268	.84375	.84482
94	.84588	.84694	.84801	.84907	.85013	.85118	.85224	.85330	.85435	.85541
95	.85646	.85751	.85857	.85961	.86066	.86171	.86276	.86380	.86485	.86589
96	.86693	.86797	.86901	.87005	.87109	.87213	.87316	.87420	.87523	.87626
97	.87730	.87833	.87936	.88038	.88141	.88244	.88346	.88449	.88551	.88653
98	.88755	.88857	.88959	.89061	.89163	.89264	.89366	.89467	.89568	.89669
99	.89770	.89871	.89972	.90073	.90174	.90274	.90375	.90475	.90575	.90675

RADIX TABLE OF NATURAL LOGARITHMS

x	n	$\log[1 + x(10^{-n})]$	$-\log[1 - x(10^{-n})]$
1	10	0.00000 00000 99999 99999 50000	0.00000 00001 00000 00000 50000
2	10	0.00000 00001 99999 99998 00000	0.00000 00002 00000 00002 00000
3	10	0.00000 00002 99999 99995 50000	0.00000 00003 00000 00004 50000
4	10	0.00000 00003 99999 99992 00000	0.00000 00004 00000 00008 00000
5	10	0.00000 00004 99999 99987 50000	0.00000 00005 00000 00012 50000
6	10	0.00000 00005 99999 99982 00000	0.00000 00006 00000 00018 00000
7	10	0.00000 00006 99999 99975 50000	0.00000 00007 00000 00024 50000
8	10	0.00000 00007 99999 99968 00000	0.00000 00008 00000 00032 00000
9	10	0.00000 00008 99999 99959 50000	0.00000 00009 00000 00040 50000
1	9	0.00000 00009 99999 99950 00000	0.00000 00010 00000 00050 00000
2	9	0.00000 00019 99999 99800 00000	0.00000 00020 00000 00200 00000
3	9	0.00000 00029 99999 99550 00000	0.00000 00030 00000 00450 00000
4	9	0.00000 00039 99999 99200 00000	0.00000 00040 00000 00800 00000
5	9	0.00000 00049 99999 98750 00000	0.00000 00050 00000 01250 00000
6	9	0.00000 00059 99999 98200 00001	0.00000 00060 00000 01800 00001
7	9	0.00000 00069 99999 97550 00001	0.00000 00070 00000 02450 00001
8	9	0.00000 00079 99999 96800 00002	0.00000 00080 00000 03200 00002
9	9	0.00000 00089 99999 95950 00002	0.00000 00090 00000 04050 00002
1	8	0.00000 00099 99999 95000 00003	0.00000 00100 00000 05000 00003
2	8	0.00000 00199 99999 80000 00027	0.00000 00200 00000 20000 00027
3	8	0.00000 00299 99999 55000 00090	0.00000 00300 00000 45000 00090
4	8	0.00000 00399 99999 20000 00213	0.00000 00400 00000 80000 00213
5	8	0.00000 00499 99998 75000 00417	0.00000 00500 00001 25000 00417
6	8	0.00000 00599 99998 20000 00720	0.00000 00600 00001 80000 00720
7	8	0.00000 00699 99997 55000 01143	0.00000 00700 00002 45000 01143
8	8	0.00000 00799 99996 80000 01707	0.00000 00800 00003 20000 01707
9	8	0.00000 00899 99995 95000 02430	0.00000 00900 00004 05000 02430
1	7	0.00000 00999 99995 00000 03333	0.00000 01000 00005 00000 03333
2	7	0.00000 01999 99980 00000 26667	0.00000 02000 00020 00000 26667
3	7	0.00000 02999 99955 00000 90000	0.00000 03000 00045 00000 90000
4	7	0.00000 03999 99920 00002 13333	0.00000 04000 00080 00002 13333
5	7	0.00000 04999 99875 00004 16667	0.00000 05000 00125 00004 16667
6	7	0.00000 05999 99820 00007 20000	0.00000 06000 00180 00007 20000
7	7	0.00000 06999 99755 00011 43333	0.00000 07000 00245 00011 43334
8	7	0.00000 07999 99680 00017 06666	0.00000 08000 00320 00017 06668
9	7	0.00000 08999 99595 00024 29998	0.00000 09000 00405 00024 30002
1	6	0.00000 09999 99500 00033 33331	0.00000 10000 00500 00033 33336
2	6	0.00000 19999 98000 00266 66627	0.00000 20000 02000 00266 66707
3	6	0.00000 29999 95500 00899 99798	0.00000 30000 04500 00900 00203
4	6	0.00000 39999 92000 02133 32693	0.00000 40000 08000 02133 33973
5	6	0.00000 49999 87500 04166 65104	0.00000 50000 12500 04166 68229
6	6	0.00000 59999 82000 07199 96760	0.00000 60000 18000 07200 03240
7	6	0.00000 69999 75500 11433 27331	0.00000 70000 24500 11433 39336
8	6	0.00000 79999 68000 17066 56427	0.00000 80000 32000 17066 76907
9	6	0.00000 89999 59500 24299 83598	0.00000 90000 40500 24300 16403

For $n > 10$, $\log[1 \pm x(10^{-n})] = \pm x(10^{-n}) - \frac{1}{2}x^2(10^{-2n})$ to 25 decimals.

RADIX TABLE OF NATURAL LOGARITHMS (Continued)

x	n	$\log[1 + x(10^{-n})]$	$-\log[1 - x)10^{-n})]$
1	5	0.00000 99999 50000 33333 08334	0.00001 00000 50000 33333 58334
2	5	0.00001 99998 00002 66662 66673	0.00002 00002 00002 66670 66673
3	5	0.00002 99995 50008 99979 75049	0.00003 00004 50009 00020 25049
4	5	0.00003 99992 00021 33269 33538	0.00004 00008 00021 33397 33538
5	5	0.00004 99987 50041 66510 42292	0.00005 00012 50041 66822 92292
6	5	0.00005 99982 00071 99676 01555	0.00006 00018 00072 00324 01555
7	5	0.00006 99975 50114 32733 11695	0.00007 00024 50114 33933 61695
8	5	0.00007 99968 00170 65642 73220	0.00008 00032 00170 67690 73221
9	5	0.00008 99959 50242 98359 86809	0.00009 00040 50243 01640 36811
1	4	0.00009 99950 00333 30833 53332	0.00010 00050 00333 35833 53335
2	4	0.00019 99800 02666 26673 06560	0.00020 00200 02667 06673 06773
3	4	0.00029 99550 08997 97548 58785	0.00030 00450 09002 02548 61215
4	4	0.00039 99200 21326 93538 06509	0.00040 00800 21339 73538 20162
5	4	0.00049 98750 41651 04791 40636	0.00050 01250 41682 29791 92719
6	4	0.00059 98200 71967 61554 42280	0.00060 01800 72032 41555 97800
7	4	0.00069 97551 14273 34192 77369	0.00070 02451 14393 39196 69533
8	4	0.00079 96801 70564 33215 90059	0.00080 03201 70769 13224 63873
9	4	0.00089 95952 42836 09300 94948	0.00090 04052 43164 14318 66419
1	3	0.00099 95003 33083 53316 68094	0.00100 05003 33583 53350 01430
2	3	0.00199 80026 62673 05601 82538	0.00200 20026 70673 07735 16511
3	3	0.00299 55089 79798 47881 16106	0.00300 45090 20298 72181 32509
4	3	0.00399 20212 69537 45299 90751	0.00400 80213 97538 81834 87927
5	3	0.00498 75415 11039 07361 21022	0.00501 25418 23544 28204 30937
6	3	0.00598 20716 77547 46378 20189	0.00601 80723 25563 01620 19350
7	3	0.00697 56137 36425 24209 95222	0.00702 46149 36964 45987 41123
8	3	0.00796 81696 49176 87351 07973	0.00803 21716 97264 25903 86494
9	3	0.00895 97413 71471 90444 31465	0.00904 07446 52149 06220 55241
1	2	0.00995 03308 53168 08284 82154	0.01005 03358 53501 44118 35489
2	2	0.01980 26272 96179 71302 60291	0.02020 27073 17519 44840 80453
3	2	0.02955 88022 41544 40273 26194	0.03045 92074 84708 54591 92613
4	2	0.03922 07131 53281 29626 92009	0.04082 19945 20255 12955 45771
5	2	0.04879 01641 69432 00306 53744	0.05129 32943 87550 53342 61961
6	2	0.05826 89081 23975 77552 57184	0.06187 54037 18087 47179 78001
7	2	0.06765 86484 73814 80526 84159	0.07257 06928 34835 43071 15733
8	2	0.07696 10411 36128 32498 42170	0.08338 16089 39051 05839 47658
9	2	0.08617 76962 41052 33234 13335	0.09431 06794 71241 32687 71427
1	1	0.09531 01798 04324 86004 39521	0.10536 05156 57826 30122 75010
2	1	0.18232 15567 93954 62621 17180	0.22314 35513 14209 75576 62951
3	1	0.26236 42644 67491 05203 54960	0.35667 49439 38732 37891 26387
4	1	0.33647 22366 21212 93050 45934	0.51082 56237 65990 68320 55141
5	1	0.40546 51081 08164 38197 80131	0.69314 71805 59945 30941 72321
6	1	0.47000 36292 45735 55365 09370	0.91629 07318 74155 06518 35272
7	1	0.53062 82510 62170 39623 15432	1.20397 28043 25935 99262 27462
8	1	0.58778 66649 02119 00818 97311	1.60943 79124 34100 37460 07593
9	1	0.64185 38861 72394 77599 10360	2.30258 50929 94045 68401 79915
1	0	0.69314 71805 59945 30941 72321	∞

For $n > 10$, $\log[1 \pm x(10^{-n})] = \pm x(10^{-n}) - \frac{1}{2} x^2 (10^{-2n})$ to 25 decimals.

EXPONENTIAL FUNCTIONS

Values of e^x, $\log e^x$ and e^{-x} where e is the base of the natural system of logarithms $2.71828\ldots$ and x has values from 0 to 10. Facilitating the solution of exponential equations, these tables also serve as a table of natural or Naperian antilogarithms. For instance, if the logarithm or exponent $x = 3.26$, the corresponding number or value of e^x is 26.050. Its reciprocal e^{-x} is .038388.

x	e^x	$\mathrm{Log}_{10}(e^x)$	e^{-x}	x	e^x	$\mathrm{Log}_{10}(e^x)$	e^{-x}
0.00	1.0000	0.00000	1.000000	**0.50**	1.6487	0.21715	0.606531
0.01	1.0101	.00434	0.990050	0.51	1.6653	.22149	.600496
0.02	1.0202	.00869	.980199	0.52	1.6820	.22583	.594521
0.03	1.0305	.01303	.970446	0.53	1.6989	.23018	.588605
0.04	1.0408	.01737	.960789	0.54	1.7160	.23452	.582748
0.05	1.0513	0.02171	0.951229	**0.55**	1.7333	0.23886	0.576950
0.06	1.0618	.02606	.941765	0.56	1.7507	.24320	.571209
0.07	1.0725	.03040	.932394	0.57	1.7683	.24755	.565525
0.08	1.0833	.03474	.923116	0.58	1.7860	.25189	.559898
0.09	1.0942	.03909	.913931	0.59	1.8040	.25623	.554327
0.10	1.1052	0.04343	0.904837	**0.60**	1.8221	0.26058	0.548812
0.11	1.1163	.04777	.895834	0.61	1.8404	.26492	.543351
0.12	1.1275	.05212	.886920	0.62	1.8589	.26926	.537944
0.13	1.1388	.05646	.878095	0.63	1.8776	.27361	.532592
0.14	1.1503	.06080	.869358	0.64	1.8965	.27795	.527292
0.15	1.1618	0.06514	0.860708	**0.65**	1.9155	0.28229	0.522046
0.16	1.1735	.06949	.852144	0.66	1.9348	.28663	.516851
0.17	1.1853	.07383	.843665	0.67	1.9542	.29098	.511709
0.18	1.1972	.07817	.835270	0.68	1.9739	.29532	.506617
0.19	1.2092	.08252	.826959	0.69	1.9937	.29966	.501576
0.20	1.2214	0.08686	0.818731	**0.70**	2.0138	0.30401	0.496585
0.21	1.2337	.09120	.810584	0.71	2.0340	.30835	.491644
0.22	1.2461	.09554	.802519	0.72	2.0544	.31269	.486752
0.23	1.2586	.09989	.794534	0.73	2.0751	.31703	.481909
0.24	1.2712	.10423	.786628	0.74	2.0959	.32138	.477114
0.25	1.2840	0.10857	0.778801	**0.75**	2.1170	0.32572	0.472367
0.26	1.2969	.11292	.771052	0.76	2.1383	.33006	.467666
0.27	1.3100	.11726	.763379	0.77	2.1598	.33441	.463013
0.28	1.3231	.12160	.755784	0.78	2.1815	.33875	.458406
0.29	1.3364	.12595	.748264	0.79	2.2034	.34309	.453845
0.30	1.3499	0.13029	0.740818	**0.80**	2.2255	0.34744	0.449329
0.31	1.3634	.13463	.733447	0.81	2.2479	.35178	.444858
0.32	1.3771	.13897	.726149	0.82	2.2705	.35612	.440432
0.33	1.3910	.14332	.718924	0.83	2.2933	.36046	.436049
0.34	1.4049	.14766	.711770	0.84	2.3164	.36481	.431711
0.35	1.4191	0.15200	0.704688	**0.85**	2.3396	0.36915	0.427415
0.36	1.4333	.15635	.697676	0.86	2.3632	.37349	.423162
0.37	1.4477	.16069	.690734	0.87	2.3869	.37784	.418952
0.38	1.4623	.16503	.683861	0.88	2.4109	.38218	.414783
0.39	1.4770	.16937	.677057	0.89	2.4351	.38652	.410656
0.40	1.4918	0.17372	0.670320	**0.90**	2.4596	0.39087	0.406570
0.41	1.5068	.17806	.663650	0.91	2.4843	.39521	.402524
0.42	1.5220	.18240	.657047	0.92	2.5093	.39955	.398519
0.43	1.5373	.18675	.650509	0.93	2.5345	.40389	.394554
0.44	1.5527	.19109	.644036	0.94	2.5600	.40824	.390628
0.45	1.5683	0.19543	0.637628	**0.95**	2.5857	0.41258	0.386741
0.46	1.5841	.19978	.631284	0.96	2.6117	.41692	.382893
0.47	1.6000	.20412	.625002	0.97	2.6379	.42127	.379083
0.48	1.6161	.20846	.618783	0.98	2.6645	.42561	.375311
0.49	1.6323	.21280	.612626	0.99	2.6912	.42995	.371577
0.50	1.6487	0.21715	0.606531	**1.00**	2.7183	0.43429	0.367879

EXPONENTIAL FUNCTIONS (Continued)

x	e^x	$\text{Log}_{10}(e^x)$	e^{-x}	x	e^x	$\text{Log}_{10}(e^x)$	e^{-x}
1.00	2.7183	0.43429	0.367879	**1.50**	4.4817	0.65144	0.223130
1.01	2.7456	.43864	.364219	1.51	4.5267	.65578	.220910
1.02	2.7732	.44298	.360595	1.52	4.5722	.66013	.218712
1.03	2.8011	.44732	.357007	1.53	4.6182	.66447	.216536
1.04	2.8292	.45167	.353455	1.54	4.6646	.66881	.214381
1.05	2.8577	0.45601	0.349938	**1.55**	4.7115	0.67316	0.212248
1.06	2.8864	.46035	.346456	1.56	4.7588	.67750	.210136
1.07	2.9154	.46470	.343009	1.57	4.8066	.68184	.208045
1.08	2.9447	.46904	.339596	1.58	4.8550	.68619	.205975
1.09	2.9743	.47338	.336216	1.59	4.9037	.69053	.203926
1.10	3.0042	0.47772	0.332871	**1.60**	4.9530	0.69487	0.201897
1.11	3.0344	.48207	.329559	1.61	5.0028	.69921	.199888
1.12	3.0649	.48641	.326280	1.62	5.0531	.70356	.197899
1.13	3.0957	.49075	.323033	1.63	5.1039	.70790	.195930
1.14	3.1268	.49510	.319819	1.64	5.1552	.71224	.193980
1.15	3.1582	0.49944	0.316637	**1.65**	5.2070	0.71659	0.192050
1.16	3.1899	.50378	.313486	1.66	5.2593	.72093	.190139
1.17	3.2220	.50812	.310367	1.67	5.3122	.72527	.188247
1.18	3.2544	.51247	.307279	1.68	5.3656	.72961	.186374
1.19	3.2871	.51681	.304221	1.69	5.4195	.73396	.184520
1.20	3.3201	0.52115	0.301194	**1.70**	5.4739	0.73830	0.182684
1.21	3.3535	.52550	.298197	1.71	5.5290	.74264	.180866
1.22	3.3872	.52984	.295230	1.72	5.5845	.74699	.179066
1.23	3.4212	.53418	.292293	1.73	5.6407	.75133	.177284
1.24	3.4556	.53853	.289384	1.74	5.6973	.75567	.175520
1.25	3.4903	0.54287	0.286505	**1.75**	5.7546	0.76002	0.173774
1.26	3.5254	.54721	.283654	1.76	5.8124	.76436	.172045
1.27	3.5609	.55155	.280832	1.77	5.8709	.76870	.170333
1.28	3.5966	.55590	.278037	1.78	5.9299	.77304	.168638
1.29	3.6328	.56024	.275271	1.79	5.9895	.77739	.166960
1.30	3.6693	0.56458	0.272532	**1.80**	6.0496	0.78173	0.165299
1.31	3.7062	.56893	.269820	1.81	6.1104	.78607	.163654
1.32	3.7434	.57327	.267135	1.82	6.1719	.79042	.162026
1.33	3.7810	.57761	.264477	1.83	6.2339	.79476	.160414
1.34	3.8190	.58195	.261846	1.84	6.2965	.79910	.158817
1.35	3.8574	0.58630	0.259240	**1.85**	6.3598	0.80344	0.157237
1.36	3.8962	.59064	.256661	1.86	6.4237	.80779	.155673
1.37	3.9354	.59498	.254107	1.87	6.4883	.81213	.154124
1.38	3.9749	.59933	.251579	1.88	6.5535	.81647	.152590
1.39	4.0149	.60367	.249075	1.89	6.6194	.82082	.151072
1.40	4.0552	0.60801	0.246597	**1.90**	6.6859	0.82516	0.149569
1.41	4.0960	.61236	.244143	1.91	6.7531	.82950	.148080
1.42	4.1371	.61670	.241714	1.92	6.8210	.83385	.146607
1.43	4.1787	.62104	.239309	1.93	6.8895	.83819	.145148
1.44	4.2207	.62538	.236928	1.94	6.9588	.84253	.143704
1.45	4.2631	0.62973	0.234570	**1.95**	7.0287	0.84687	0.142274
1.46	4.3060	.63407	.232236	1.96	7.0993	.85122	.140858
1.47	4.3492	.63841	.229925	1.97	7.1707	.85556	.139457
1.48	4.3929	.64276	.227638	1.98	7.2427	.85990	.138069
1.49	4.4371	.64710	.225373	1.99	7.3155	.86425	.136695
1.50	4.4817	0.65144	0.223130	**2.00**	7.3891	0.86859	0.135335

EXPONENTIAL FUNCTIONS (Continued)

x	e^x	$\text{Log}_{10}(e^x)$	e^{-x}	x	e^x	$\text{Log}_{10}(e^x)$	e^{-x}
2.00	7.3891	0.86859	0.135335	**2.50**	12.182	1.08574	0.082085
2.01	7.4633	.87293	.133989	2.51	12.305	1.09008	.081268
2.02	7.5383	.87727	.132655	2.52	12.429	1.09442	.080460
2.03	7.6141	.88162	.131336	2.53	12.554	1.09877	.079659
2.04	7.6906	.88596	.130029	2.54	12.680	1.10311	.078866
2.05	7.7679	0.89030	0.128735	**2.55**	12.807	1.10745	0.078082
2.06	7.8460	.89465	.127454	2.56	12.936	1.11179	.077305
2.07	7.9248	.89899	.126186	2.57	13.066	1.11614	.076536
2.08	8.0045	.90333	.124930	2.58	13.197	1.12048	.075774
2.09	8.0849	.90768	.123687	2.59	13.330	1.12482	.075020
2.10	8.1662	0.91202	0.122456	**2.60**	13.464	1.12917	0.074274
2.11	8.2482	.91636	.121238	2.61	13.599	1.13351	.073535
2.12	8.3311	.92070	.120032	2.62	13.736	1.13785	.072803
2.13	8.4149	.92505	.118837	2.63	13.874	1.14219	.072078
2.14	8.4994	.92939	.117655	2.64	14.013	1.14654	.071361
2.15	8.5849	0.93373	0.116484	**2.65**	14.154	1.15088	0.070651
2.16	8.6711	.93808	.115325	2.66	14.296	1.15522	.069948
2.17	8.7583	.94242	.114178	2.67	14.440	1.15957	.069252
2.18	8.8463	.94676	.113042	2.68	14.585	1.16391	.068563
2.19	8.9352	.95110	.111917	2.69	14.732	1.16825	.067881
2.20	9.0250	0.95545	0.110803	**2.70**	14.880	1.17260	0.067206
2.21	9.1157	.95979	.109701	2.71	15.029	1.17694	.066537
2.22	9.2073	.96413	.108609	2.72	15.180	1.18128	.065875
2.23	9.2999	.96848	.107528	2.73	15.333	1.18562	.065219
2.24	9.3933	.97282	.106459	2.74	15.487	1.18997	.064570
2.25	9.4877	0.97716	0.105399	**2.75**	15.643	1.19431	0.063928
2.26	9.5831	.98151	.104350	2.76	15.800	1.19865	.063292
2.27	9.6794	.98585	.103312	2.77	15.959	1.20300	.062662
2.28	9.7767	.99019	.102284	2.78	16.119	1.20734	.062039
2.29	9.8749	.99453	.101266	2.79	16.281	1.21168	.061421
2.30	9.9742	0.99888	0.100259	**2.80**	16.445	1.21602	0.060810
2.31	10.074	1.00322	.099261	2.81	16.610	1.22037	.060205
2.32	10.176	1.00756	.098274	2.82	16.777	1.22471	.059606
2.33	10.278	1.01191	.097296	2.83	16.945	1.22905	.059013
2.34	10.381	1.01625	.096328	2.84	17.116	1.23340	.058426
2.35	10.486	1.02059	0.095369	**2.85**	17.288	1.23774	0.057844
2.36	10.591	1.02493	.094420	2.86	17.462	1.24208	.057269
2.37	10.697	1.02928	.093481	2.87	17.637	1.24643	.056699
2.38	10.805	1.03362	.092551	2.88	17.814	1.25077	.056135
2.39	10.913	1.03796	.091630	2.89	17.993	1.25511	.055576
2.40	11.023	1.04231	0.090718	**2.90**	18.174	1.25945	0.055023
2.41	11.134	1.04665	.089815	2.91	18.357	1.26380	.054476
2.42	11.246	1.05099	.088922	2.92	18.541	1.26814	.053934
2.43	11.359	1.05534	.088037	2.93	18.728	1.27248	.053397
2.44	11.473	1.05968	.087161	2.94	18.916	1.27683	.052866
2.45	11.588	1.06402	0.086294	**2.95**	19.106	1.28117	0.052340
2.46	11.705	1.06836	.085435	2.96	19.298	1.28551	.051819
2.47	11.822	1.07271	.084585	2.97	19.492	1.28985	.051303
2.48	11.941	1.07705	.083743	2.98	19.688	1.29420	.050793
2.49	12.061	1.08139	.082910	2.99	19.886	1.29854	.050287
2.50	12.182	1.08574	0.082085	**3.00**	20.086	1.30288	0.049787

EXPONENTIAL FUNCTIONS (Continued)

x	e^x	$Log_{10}(e^x)$	e^{-x}	x	e^x	$Log_{10}(e^x)$	e^{-x}
3.00	20.086	1.30288	0.049787	**3.50**	33.115	1.52003	0.030197
3.01	20.287	1.30723	.049292	3.51	33.448	1.52437	.029897
3.02	20.491	1.31157	.048801	3.52	33.784	1.52872	.029599
3.03	20.697	1.31591	.048316	3.53	34.124	1.53306	.029305
3.04	20.905	1.32026	.047835	3.54	34.467	1.53740	.029013
3.05	21.115	1.32460	0.047359	**3.55**	34.813	1.54175	0.028725
3.06	21.328	1.32894	.046888	3.56	35.163	1.54609	.028439
3.07	21.542	1.33328	.046421	3.57	35.517	1.55043	.028156
3.08	21.758	1.33763	.045959	3.58	35.874	1.55477	.027876
3.09	21.977	1.34197	.045502	3.59	36.234	1.55912	.027598
3.10	22.198	1.34631	0.045049	**3.60**	36.598	1.56346	0.027324
3.11	22.421	1.35066	.044601	3.61	36.966	1.56780	.027052
3.12	22.646	1.35500	.044157	3.62	37.338	1.57215	.026783
3.13	22.874	1.35934	.043718	3.63	37.713	1.57649	.026516
3.14	23.104	1.36368	.043283	3.64	38.092	1.58083	.026252
3.15	23.336	1.36803	0.042852	**3.65**	38.475	1.58517	0.025991
3.16	23.571	1.37237	.042426	3.66	38.861	1.58952	.025733
3.17	23.807	1.37671	.042004	3.67	39.252	1.59386	.025476
3.18	24.047	1.38106	.041586	3.68	39.646	1.59820	.025223
3.19	24.288	1.38540	.041172	3.69	40.045	1.60255	.024972
3.20	24.533	1.38974	0.040762	**3.70**	40.447	1.60689	0.024724
3.21	24.779	1.39409	.040357	3.71	40.854	1.61123	.024478
3.22	25.028	1.39843	.039955	3.72	41.264	1.61558	.024234
3.23	25.280	1.40277	.039557	3.73	41.679	1.61992	.023993
3.24	25.534	1.40711	.039164	3.74	42.098	1.62426	.023754
3.25	25.790	1.41146	0.038774	**3.75**	42.521	1.62860	0.023518
3.26	26.050	1.41580	.038388	3.76	42.948	1.63295	.023284
3.27	26.311	1.42014	.038006	3.77	43.380	1.63729	.023052
3.28	26.576	1.42449	.037628	3.78	43.816	1.64163	.022823
3.29	26.843	1.42883	.037254	3.79	44.256	1.64598	.022596
3.30	27.113	1.43317	0.036883	**3.80**	44.701	1.65032	0.022371
3.31	27.385	1.43751	.036516	3.81	45.150	1.65466	.022148
3.32	27.660	1.44186	.036153	3.82	45.604	1.65900	.021928
3.33	27.938	1.44620	.035793	3.83	46.063	1.66335	.021710
3.34	28.219	1.45054	.035437	3.84	46.525	1.66769	.021494
3.35	28.503	1.45489	0.035084	**3.85**	46.993	1.67203	0.021280
3.36	28.789	1.45923	.034735	3.86	47.465	1.67638	.021068
3.37	29.079	1.46357	.034390	3.87	47.942	1.68072	.020858
3.38	29.371	1.46792	.034047	3.88	48.424	1.68506	.020651
3.39	29.666	1.47226	.033709	3.89	48.911	1.68941	.020445
3.40	29.964	1.47660	0.033373	**3.90**	49.402	1.69375	0.020242
3.41	30.265	1.48094	.033041	3.91	49.899	1.69809	.020041
3.42	30.569	1.48529	.032712	3.92	50.400	1.70243	.019841
3.43	30.877	1.48963	.032387	3.93	50.907	1.70678	.019644
3.44	31.187	1.49397	.032065	3.94	51.419	1.71112	.019448
3.45	31.500	1.49832	0.031746	**3.95**	51.935	1.71546	0.019255
3.46	31.817	1.50266	.031430	3.96	52.457	1.71981	.019063
3.47	32.137	1.50700	.031117	3.97	52.985	1.72415	.018873
3.48	32.460	1.51134	.030807	3.98	53.517	1.72849	.018686
3.49	32.786	1.51569	.030501	3.99	54.055	1.73283	.018500
3.50	33.115	1.52003	0.030197	**4.00**	54.598	1.73718	0.018316

EXPONENTIAL FUNCTIONS (Continued)

x	e^x	$\text{Log}_{10}(e^x)$	e^{-x}	x	e^x	$\text{Log}_{10}(e^x)$	e^{-x}
4.00	54.598	1.73718	0.018316	**4.50**	90.017	1.95433	0.011109
4.01	55.147	1.74152	.018133	4.51	90.922	1.95867	.010998
4.02	55.701	1.74586	.017953	4.52	91.836	1.96301	.010889
4.03	56.261	1.75021	.017774	4.53	92.759	1.96735	.010781
4.04	56.826	1.75455	.017597	4.54	93.691	1.97170	.010673
4.05	57.397	1.75889	0.017422	**4.55**	94.632	1.97604	0.010567
4.06	57.974	1.76324	.017249	4.56	95.583	1.98038	.010462
4.07	58.557	1.76758	.017077	4.57	96.544	1.98473	.010358
4.08	59.145	1.77192	.016907	4.58	97.514	1.98907	.010255
4.09	59.740	1.77626	.016739	4.59	98.494	1.99341	.010153
4.10	60.340	1.78061	0.016573	**4.60**	99.484	1.99775	0.010052
4.11	60.947	1.78495	.016408	4.61	100.48	2.00210	.009952
4.12	61.559	1.78929	.016245	4.62	101.49	2.00644	.009853
4.13	62.178	1.79364	.016083	4.63	102.51	2.01078	.009755
4.14	62.803	1.79798	.015923	4.64	103.54	2.01513	.009658
4.15	63.434	1.80232	0.015764	**4.65**	104.58	2.01947	0.009562
4.16	64.072	1.80667	.015608	4.66	105.64	2.02381	.009466
4.17	64.715	1.81101	.015452	4.67	106.70	2.02816	.009372
4.18	65.366	1.81535	.015299	4.68	107.77	2.03250	.009279
4.19	66.023	1.81969	.015146	4.69	108.85	2.03684	.009187
4.20	66.686	1.82404	0.014996	**4.70**	109.95	2.04118	0.009095
4.21	67.357	1.82838	.014846	4.71	111.05	2.04553	.009005
4.22	68.033	1.83272	.014699	4.72	112.17	2.04987	.008915
4.23	68.717	1.83707	.014552	4.73	113.30	2.05421	.008826
4.24	69.408	1.84141	.014408	4.74	114.43	2.05856	.008739
4.25	70.105	1.84575	0.014264	**4.75**	115.58	2.06290	0.008652
4.26	70.810	1.85009	.014122	4.76	116.75	2.06724	.008566
4.27	71.522	1.85444	.013982	4.77	117.92	2.07158	.008480
4.28	72.240	1.85878	.013843	4.78	119.10	2.07593	.008396
4.29	72.966	1.86312	.013705	4.79	120.30	2.08027	.008312
4.30	73.700	1.86747	0.013569	**4.80**	121.51	2.08461	0.008230
4.31	74.440	1.87181	.013434	4.81	122.73	2.08896	.008148
4.32	75.189	1.87615	.013300	4.82	123.97	2.09330	.008067
4.33	75.944	1.88050	.013168	4.83	125.21	2.09764	.007987
4.34	76.708	1.88484	.013037	4.84	126.47	2.10199	.007907
4.35	77.478	1.88918	0.012907	**4.85**	127.74	2.10633	0.007828
4.36	78.257	1.89352	.012778	4.86	129.02	2.11067	.007750
4.37	79.044	1.89787	.012651	4.87	130.32	2.11501	.007673
4.38	79.838	1.90221	.012525	4.88	131.63	2.11936	.007597
4.39	80.640	1.90655	.012401	4.89	132.95	2.12370	.007521
4.40	81.451	1.91090	0.012277	**4.90**	134.29	2.12804	0.007447
4.41	82.269	1.91524	.012155	4.91	135.64	2.13239	.007372
4.42	83.096	1.91958	.012034	4.92	137.00	2.13673	.007299
4.43	83.931	1.92392	.011914	4.93	138.38	2.14107	.007227
4.44	84.775	1.92827	.011796	4.94	139.77	2.14541	.007155
4.45	85.627	1.93261	0.011679	**4.95**	141.17	2.14976	0.007083
4.46	86.488	1.93695	.011562	4.96	142.59	2.15410	.007013
4.47	87.357	1.94130	.011447	4.97	144.03	2.15844	.006943
4.48	88.235	1.94564	.011333	4.98	145.47	2.16279	.006874
4.49	89.121	1.94998	.011221	4.99	146.94	2.16713	.006806
4.50	90.017	1.95433	0.011109	**5.00**	148.41	2.17147	0.006738

EXPONENTIAL FUNCTIONS (Continued)

x	e^x	$\text{Log}_{10}(e^x)$	e^{-x}	x	e^x	$\text{Log}_{10}(e^x)$	e^{-x}
5.00	148.41	2.17147	0.006738	**5.50**	244.69	2.38862	0.0040868
5.01	149.90	2.17582	.006671	5.55	257.24	2.41033	.0038875
5.02	151.41	2.18016	.006605	5.60	270.43	2.43205	.0036979
5.03	152.93	2.18450	.006539	5.65	284.29	2.45376	.0035175
5.04	154.47	2.18884	.006474	5.70	298.87	2.47548	.0033460
5.05	156.02	2.19319	0.006409	**5.75**	314.19	2.49719	0.0031828
5.06	157.59	2.19753	.006346	5.80	330.30	2.51891	.0030276
5.07	159.17	2.20187	.006282	5.85	347.23	2.54062	.0028799
5.08	160.77	2.20622	.006220	5.90	365.04	2.56234	.0027394
5.09	162.39	2.21056	.006158	5.95	383.75	2.58405	.0026058
5.10	164.02	2.21490	0.006097	**6.00**	403.43	2.60577	0.0024788
5.11	165.67	2.21924	.006036	6.05	424.11	2.62748	.0023579
5.12	167.34	2.22359	.005976	6.10	445.86	2.64920	.0022429
5.13	169.02	2.22793	.005917	6.15	468.72	2.67091	.0021335
5.14	170.72	2.23227	.005858	6.20	492.75	2.69263	.0020294
5.15	172.43	2.23662	0.005799	**6.25**	518.01	2.71434	0.0019305
5.16	174.16	2.24096	.005742	6.30	544.57	2.73606	.0018363
5.17	175.91	2.24530	.005685	6.35	572.49	2.75777	.0017467
5.18	177.68	2.24965	.005628	6.40	601.85	2.77948	.0016616
5.19	179.47	2.25399	.005572	6.45	632.70	2.80120	.0015805
5.20	181.27	2.25833	0.005517	**6.50**	665.14	2.82291	0.0015034
5.21	183.09	2.26267	.005462	6.55	699.24	2.84463	.0014301
5.22	184.93	2.26702	.005407	6.60	735.10	2.86634	.0013604
5.23	186.79	2.27136	.005354	6.65	772.78	2.88806	.0012940
5.24	188.67	2.27570	.005300	6.70	812.41	2.90977	.0012309
5.25	190.57	2.28005	0.005248	**6.75**	854.06	2.93149	0.0011709
5.26	192.48	2.28439	.005195	6.80	897.85	2.95320	.0011138
5.27	194.42	2.28873	.005144	6.85	943.88	2.97492	.0010595
5.28	196.37	2.29307	.005092	6.90	992.27	2.99663	.0010078
5.29	198.34	2.29742	.005042	6.95	1043.1	3.01835	.0009586
5.30	200.34	2.30176	0.004992	**7.00**	1096.6	3.04006	0.0009119
5.31	202.35	2.30610	.004942	7.05	1152.9	3.06178	.0008674
5.32	204.38	2.31045	.004893	7.10	1212.0	3.08349	.0008251
5.33	206.44	2.31479	.004844	7.15	1274.1	3.10521	.0007849
5.34	208.51	2.31913	.004796	7.20	1339.4	3.12692	.0007466
5.35	210.61	2.32348	0.004748	**7.25**	1408.1	3.14863	0.0007102
5.36	212.72	2.32782	.004701	7.30	1480.3	3.17035	.0006755
5.37	214.86	2.33216	.004654	7.35	1556.2	3.19206	.0006426
5.38	217.02	2.33650	.004608	7.40	1636.0	3.21378	.0006113
5.39	219.20	2.34085	.004562	7.45	1719.9	3.23549	.0005814
5.40	221.41	2.34519	0.004517	**7.50**	1808.0	3.25721	0.0005531
5.41	223.63	2.34953	.004472	7.55	1900.7	3.27892	.0005261
5.42	225.88	2.35388	.004427	7.60	1998.2	3.30064	.0005005
5.43	228.15	2.35822	.004383	7.65	2100.6	3.32235	.0004760
5.44	230.44	2.36256	.004339	7.70	2208.3	3.34407	.0004528
5.45	232.76	2.36690	0.004296	**7.75**	2321.6	3.36578	0.0004307
5.46	235.10	2.37125	.004254	7.80	2440.6	3.38750	.0004097
5.47	237.46	2.37559	.004211	7.85	2565.7	3.40921	.0003898
5.48	239.85	2.37993	.004169	7.90	2697.3	3.43093	.0003707
5.49	242.26	2.38428	.004128	7.95	2835.6	3.45264	.0003527
5.50	244.69	2.38862	0.004087	**8.00**	2981.0	3.47436	0.0003355

EXPONENTIAL FUNCTIONS (Continued)

x	e^x	$\text{Log}_{10}(e^x)$	e^{-x}
8.00	2981.0	3.47436	0.0003355
8.05	3133.8	3.49607	.0003191
8.10	3294.5	3.51779	.0003035
8.15	3463.4	3.53950	.0002887
8.20	3641.0	3.56121	.0002747
8.25	3827.6	3.58293	0.0002613
8.30	4023.9	3.60464	.0002485
8.35	4230.2	3.62636	.0002364
8.40	4447.1	3.64807	.0002249
8.45	4675.1	3.66979	.0002139
8.50	4914.8	3.69150	0.0002035
8.55	5166.8	3.71322	.0001935
8.60	5431.7	3.73493	.0001841
8.65	5710.1	3.75665	.0001751
8.70	6002.9	3.77836	.0001666
8.75	6310.7	3.80008	0.0001585
8.80	6634.2	3.82179	.0001507
8.85	6974.4	3.84351	.0001434
8.90	7332.0	3.86522	.0001364
8.95	7707.9	3.88694	.0001297
9.00	8103.1	3.90865	0.0001234
9.05	8518.5	3.93037	.0001174
9.10	8955.3	3.95208	.0001117
9.15	9414.4	3.97379	.0001062
9.20	9897.1	3.99551	.0001010
9.25	10405	4.01722	0.0000961
9.30	10938	4.03894	.0000914
9.35	11499	4.06065	.0000870
9.40	12088	4.08237	.0000827
9.45	12708	4.10408	.0000787
9.50	13360	4.12580	0.0000749
9.55	14045	4.14751	.0000712
9.60	14765	4.16923	.0000677
9.65	15522	4.19094	.0000644
9.70	16318	4.21266	.0000613
9.75	17154	4.23437	0.0000583
9.80	18034	4.25609	.0000555
9.85	18958	4.27780	.0000527
9.90	19930	4.29952	.0000502
9.95	20952	4.32123	0.0000477
10.00	22026	4.34294	0.0000454

RADIX TABLE OF THE EXPONENTIAL FUNCTION

x	n	$e^{[x(10^{-n})]}$	$e^{-[x(10^{-n})]}$
1	10	1.00000 00001 00000 00000 50000	0.99999 99999 00000 00000 50000
2	10	1.00000 00002 00000 00002 00000	0.99999 99998 00000 00002 00000
3	10	1.00000 00003 00000 00004 50000	0.99999 99997 00000 00004 50000
4	10	1.00000 00004 00000 00008 00000	0.99999 99996 00000 00008 00000
5	10	1.00000 00005 00000 00012 50000	0.99999 99995 00000 00012 50000
6	10	1.00000 00006 00000 00018 00000	0.99999 99994 00000 00018 00000
7	10	1.00000 00007 00000 00024 50000	0.99999 99993 00000 00024 50000
8	10	1.00000 00008 00000 00032 00000	0.99999 99992 00000 00032 00000
9	10	1.00000 00009 00000 00040 50000	0.99999 99991 00000 00040 50000
1	9	1.00000 00010 00000 00050 00000	0.99999 99990 00000 00050 00000
2	9	1.00000 00020 00000 00200 00000	0.99999 99980 00000 00200 00000
3	9	1.00000 00030 00000 00450 00000	0.99999 99970 00000 00450 00000
4	9	1.00000 00040 00000 00800 00000	0.99999 99960 00000 00800 00000
5	9	1.00000 00050 00000 01250 00000	0.99999 99950 00000 01250 00000
6	9	1.00000 00060 00000 01800 00000	0.99999 99940 00000 01800 00000
7	9	1.00000 00070 00000 02450 00001	0.99999 99930 00000 02449 99999
8	9	1.00000 00080 00000 03200 00001	0.99999 99920 00000 03199 99999
9	9	1.00000 00090 00000 04050 00001	0.99999 99910 00000 04049 99999
1	8	1.00000 00100 00000 05000 00002	0.99999 99900 00000 04999 99998
2	8	1.00000 00200 00000 20000 00013	0.99999 99800 00000 19999 99987
3	8	1.00000 00300 00000 45000 00045	0.99999 99700 00000 44999 99955
4	8	1.00000 00400 00000 80000 00107	0.99999 99600 00000 79999 99893
5	8	1.00000 00500 00001 25000 00208	0.99999 99500 00001 24999 99792
6	8	1.00000 00600 00001 80000 00360	0.99999 99400 00001 79999 99640
7	8	1.00000 00700 00002 45000 00572	0.99999 99300 00002 44999 99428
8	8	1.00000 00800 00003 20000 00853	0.99999 99200 00003 19999 99147
9	8	1.00000 00900 00004 05000 01215	0.99999 99100 00004 04999 98785
1	7	1.00000 01000 00005 00000 01667	0.99999 99000 00004 99999 98333
2	7	1.00000 02000 00020 00000 13333	0.99999 98000 00019 99999 86667
3	7	1.00000 03000 00045 00000 45000	0.99999 97000 00044 99999 55000
4	7	1.00000 04000 00080 00001 06667	0.99999 96000 00079 99998 93333
5	7	1.00000 05000 00125 00002 08333	0.99999 95000 00124 99997 91667
6	7	1.00000 06000 00180 00003 60000	0.99999 94000 00179 99996 40000
7	7	1.00000 07000 00245 00005 71667	0.99999 93000 00244 99994 28333
8	7	1.00000 08000 00320 00008 53334	0.99999 92000 00319 99991 46667
9	7	1.00000 09000 00405 00012 15000	0.99999 91000 00404 99987 85000
1	6	1.00000 10000 00500 00016 66667	0.99999 90000 00499 99983 33334
2	6	1.00000 20000 02000 00133 33340	0.99999 80000 01999 99866 66673
3	6	1.00000 30000 04500 00450 00034	0.99999 70000 04499 99550 00034
4	6	1.00000 40000 08000 01066 66773	0.99999 60000 07999 98933 33440
5	6	1.00000 50000 12500 02083 33594	0.99999 50000 12499 97916 66927
6	6	1.00000 60000 18000 03600 00540	0.99999 40000 17999 96400 00540
7	6	1.00000 70000 24500 05716 67667	0.99999 30000 24499 94283 34334
8	6	1.00000 80000 32000 08533 35040	0.99999 20000 31999 91466 68373
9	6	1.00000 90000 40500 12150 02734	0.99999 10000 40499 87850 02734

For $n > 10$, $e^{\pm[x(10^{-n})]} = 1 \pm x(10^{-n}) + \frac{1}{2} x^2 (10^{-2n})$ to 25 decimals.

RADIX TABLE OF THE EXPONENTIAL FUNCTION

x	n	$e^{[x(10^{-n})]}$	$e^{-[x(10^{-n})]}$
1	5	1.00001 00000 50000 16666 70833	0.99999 00000 49999 83333 37500
2	5	1.00002 00002 00001 33334 00000	0.99998 00001 99998 66667 33333
3	5	1.00003 00004 50004 50003 37502	0.99997 00004 49995 50003 37498
4	5	1.00004 00008 00010 66677 33342	0.99996 00007 99989 33343 99991
5	5	1.00005 00012 50020 83359 37526	0.99995 00012 49979 16692 70807
6	5	1.00006 00018 00036 00054 00065	0.99994 00017 99964 00053 99935
7	5	1.00007 00024 50057 16766 70973	0.99993 00024 49942 83433 37360
8	5	1.00008 00032 00085 33504 00273	0.99992 00031 99914 66837 33060
9	5	1.00009 00040 50121 50273 37992	0.99991 00040 49878 50273 37008
1	4	1.00010 00050 00166 67083 34167	0.99990 00049 99833 33749 99167
2	4	1.00020 00200 01333 40000 26668	0.99980 00199 98666 73333 06668
3	4	1.00030 00450 04500 33752 02510	0.99970 00449 95500 33747 97510
4	4	1.00040 00800 10667 73341 86724	0.99960 00799 89334 39991 46724
5	4	1.00050 01250 20835 93776 04384	0.99950 01249 79169 27057 29384
6	4	1.00060 01800 36005 40064 80648	0.99940 01799 64005 39935 20648
7	4	1.00070 02450 57176 67223 40801	0.99930 02449 42843 33609 95801
8	4	1.00080 03200 85350 40273 10308	0.99920 03199 14683 73060 30307
9	4	1.00090 04051 21527 34242 14882	0.99910 04048 78527 33257 99880
1	3	1.00100 05001 66708 34166 80558	0.99900 04998 33374 99166 80554
2	3	1.00200 20013 34000 26675 55810	0.99800 19986 67333 06675 55302
3	3	1.00300 45045 03377 02601 29341	0.99700 44955 03372 97601 20662
4	3	1.00400 80106 77341 87235 88080	0.99600 79893 43991 47235 23064
5	3	1.00501 25208 59401 06338 35662	0.99501 24791 92682 31335 25642
6	3	1.00601 80360 54064 86485 55845	0.99401 79640 53935 26474 44988
7	3	1.00702 45572 66848 55523 16000	0.99302 44429 33235 10490 47970
8	3	1.00803 20855 04273 43117 20736	0.99203 19148 37060 63033 98697
9	3	1.00904 06217 73867 81406 25705	0.99104 03787 72883 66216 45648
1	2	1.01005 01670 84168 05754 21655	0.99004 98337 49168 05357 39060
2	2	1.02020 13400 26755 81016 01439	0.98019 86733 06755 30222 08141
3	2	1.03045 45339 53516 85561 24400	0.97044 55335 48508 17693 25284
4	2	1.04081 07741 92388 22675 70448	0.96078 94391 52323 20943 92107
5	2	1.05127 10963 76024 03969 75176	0.95122 94245 00714 00909 14253
6	2	1.06183 65465 45359 62222 46849	0.94176 45335 84248 70953 71528
7	2	1.07250 81812 54216 47905 31039	0.93239 38199 05948 22885 79726
8	2	1.08328 70676 74958 55443 59878	0.92311 63463 86635 78291 07598
9	2	1.09417 42837 05210 35787 28976	0.91393 11852 71228 18674 73535
1	1	1.10517 09180 75647 62481 17078	0.90483 74180 35959 57316 42491
2	1	1.22140 27581 60169 83392 10720	0.81873 07530 77981 85866 99355
3	1	1.34985 88075 76003 10398 37443	0.74081 82206 81717 86606 68738
4	1	1.49182 46976 41270 31782 48530	0.67032 00460 35639 30074 44329
5	1	1.64872 12707 00128 14684 86508	0.60653 06597 12633 42360 37995
6	1	1.82211 88003 90508 97487 53677	0.54881 16360 94026 43262 84589
7	1	2.01375 27074 70476 52162 45494	0.49658 53037 91409 51470 48001
8	1	2.22554 09284 92467 60457 95375	0.44932 89641 17221 59143 01024
9	1	2.45960 31111 56949 66380 01266	0.40656 96597 40599 11188 34542
1	0	2.71828 18284 59045 23536 02875	0.36787 94411 71442 32159 55238

For $n > 10$, $e^{\pm[x(10^{-n})]} = 1 \pm x(10^{-n}) + \frac{1}{2}x^2(10^{-2n})$ to 25 decimals.

HYPERBOLIC AND RELATED FUNCTIONS

Dr. Madhu S. Gupta

HYPERBOLIC FUNCTIONS

Geometrical Definition

Let O be the center, A the vertex, and P any point with coordinates (x,y) on the branch B'AB of the rectangular hyperbola $X^2 - Y^2 = a^2$. Set OM = x, MP = y and OA = a. The shaded area shown in the figure is given by

$$\text{Area OPAP}' = a^2 \log_e \frac{(x + y)}{a}$$

If the angle POP' in hyperbolic radians is denoted by u,

$$u = \frac{\text{area OPAP}'}{a^2} \text{ hyperbolic radians.}$$

The hyperbolic functions are defined by

hyperbolic sine of u = sinh u = y/a
hyperbolic cosine of u = cosh u - x/a

The approximate length of the hyperbolic curve is given by

$$\text{arc AP} = \frac{3}{2} y - \frac{1}{2} \tan^{-1} y$$

while the straight line distance is

$$\text{line AP} = \sqrt{\sinh^2 u + (\cosh u - 1)^2}$$

Exponential Definition

hyperbolic sine of $u = \sinh u = \frac{1}{2} (e^u - e^{-u})$ $\operatorname{csch} u = \frac{1}{\sinh u},$

hyperbolic cosine of $u = \cosh u = \frac{1}{2} (e^u + e^{-u})$ $\operatorname{sech} u = \frac{1}{\cosh u},$

hyperbolic tangent of $u = \tanh u = \frac{\sinh u}{\cosh u} = \frac{e^u - e^{-u}}{e^u + e^{-u}}$ $\coth u = \frac{1}{\tanh u},$

Domain and Range for Real Argument

Function	Domain (interval of u)	Range (interval of function)	Remarks
sinh u	$(-\infty, +\infty)$	$(-\infty, +\infty)$	
cosh u	$(-\infty, +\infty)$	$[1, +\infty)$	
tanh u	$(-\infty, +\infty)$	$(-1, +1)$	
cosech u	$(-\infty, 0)$	$(0, -\infty)$	Two branches, pole
	$(0, +\infty)$	$(+\infty, 0)$	at $u = 0$.
sech u	$(-\infty, +\infty)$	$(0, 1]$	
coth u	$(-\infty, 0)$	$(-1, -\infty)$	Two branches, pole
	$(0, +\infty)$	$(+\infty, 1)$	at $u = 0$

Hyperbolic Functions In Terms of One Another

Function	$\sinh x$	$\cosh x$	$\tanh x$
$\sinh x =$	$\sinh x$	$\pm \sqrt{\cosh^2 x - 1}$	$\dfrac{\tanh x}{\sqrt{1 - \tanh^2 x}}$
$\cosh x =$	$\sqrt{1 + \sinh^2 x}$	$\cosh x$	$\dfrac{1}{\sqrt{1 - \tanh^2 x}}$
$\tanh x =$	$\dfrac{\sinh x}{\sqrt{1 + \sinh^2 x}}$	$\pm \dfrac{\sqrt{\cosh^2 x - 1}}{\cosh x}$	$\tanh x$
$\operatorname{cosech} x =$	$\dfrac{1}{\sinh x}$	$\pm \dfrac{1}{\sqrt{\cosh^2 x - 1}}$	$\dfrac{\sqrt{1 - \tanh^2 x}}{\tanh x}$
$\operatorname{sech} x =$	$\dfrac{1}{\sqrt{1 + \sinh^2 x}}$	$\dfrac{1}{\cosh x}$	$\sqrt{1 - \tanh^2 x}$
$\coth x =$	$\dfrac{\sqrt{1 + \sinh^2 x}}{\sinh x}$	$\pm \dfrac{\cosh x}{\sqrt{\cosh^2 x - 1}}$	$\dfrac{1}{\tanh x}$

Function	$\operatorname{cosech} x$	$\operatorname{sech} x$	$\coth x$
$\sinh x =$	$\dfrac{1}{\operatorname{cosech} x}$	$\pm \dfrac{\sqrt{1 - \operatorname{sech}^2 x}}{\operatorname{sech} x}$	$\dfrac{\pm 1}{\sqrt{\coth^2 x - 1}}$
$\cosh x =$	$\pm \dfrac{\sqrt{\operatorname{cosech}^2 x + 1}}{\operatorname{cosech} x}$	$\dfrac{1}{\operatorname{sech} x}$	$\pm \dfrac{\coth x}{\sqrt{\coth^2 x - 1}}$
$\tanh x =$	$\dfrac{1}{\sqrt{\operatorname{cosech}^2 x + 1}}$	$\pm \sqrt{1 - \operatorname{sech}^2 x}$	$\dfrac{1}{\coth x}$
$\operatorname{cosech} x =$	$\operatorname{cosech} x$	$\pm \dfrac{\operatorname{sech} x}{\sqrt{1 - \operatorname{sech}^2 x}}$	$\pm \dfrac{\sqrt{\coth^2 x - 1}}{1}$
$\operatorname{sech} x =$	$\pm \dfrac{\operatorname{cosec} x}{\sqrt{\operatorname{cosech}^2 x + 1}}$	$\operatorname{sech} x$	$\pm \dfrac{\sqrt{\coth^2 x - 1}}{\coth x}$
$\coth x =$	$\sqrt{\operatorname{cosech}^2 x + 1}$	$\pm \dfrac{1}{\sqrt{1 - \operatorname{sech}^2 x}}$	$\coth x$

Whenever two signs are shown, choose $+$ sign if x is positive, $-$ sign if x is negative.

Special Values of Hyperbolic Functions

x	0	$\dfrac{\pi}{2} i$	πi	$\dfrac{3\pi}{2} i$	∞
$\sinh x$	0	i	0	$-i$	∞
$\cosh x$	1	0	-1	0	∞
$\tanh x$	0	∞i	0	$-\infty i$	1
$\operatorname{csch} x$	∞	$-i$	∞	i	0
$\operatorname{sech} x$	1	∞	-1	∞	0
$\coth x$	∞	0	∞	0	1

Symmetry and Periodicity

$$\sinh(-u) = -\sinh u, \qquad \operatorname{csch}(-u) = -\operatorname{csch} u$$
$$\cosh(-u) = \cosh u, \qquad \operatorname{sech}(-u) = \operatorname{sech} u$$
$$\tanh(-u) = -\tanh u, \qquad \coth(-u) = -\coth u$$

$\sinh u$, $\cosh u$, $\operatorname{cosech} u$ and $\operatorname{sech} u$ are periodic with a period $2\pi i$; $\tanh u$ and $\coth u$ are periodic with a period πi.

Fundamental Identities

Reciprocal Relations

$$\text{csch } u = \frac{1}{\sinh u}, \qquad \text{sech } u = \frac{1}{\cosh u}, \qquad \coth u = \frac{1}{\tanh u}$$

Product Relations

$$\sinh u = \tanh u \cosh u \qquad \cosh u = \coth u \sinh u$$
$$\tanh u = \sinh u \text{ sech } u \qquad \coth u = \cosh u \text{ cosech } u$$
$$\text{sech } u = \text{cosech } u \tanh u \qquad \text{cosech } u = \text{sech } u \coth u$$

Quotient Relations

$$\sinh u = \frac{\tanh u}{\text{sech } u} \qquad \cosh u = \frac{\coth u}{\text{cosech } u} \qquad \tanh u = \frac{\sinh u}{\cosh u}$$

$$\text{cosech } u = \frac{\text{sech } u}{\tanh u} \qquad \text{sech } u = \frac{\text{cosech } u}{\coth u} \qquad \coth u = \frac{\cosh u}{\sinh u}$$

Relations Between Squares of Functions

$$\cosh^2 u - \sinh^2 u = 1, \qquad \tanh^2 u + \text{sech}^2 u = 1$$
$$\coth^2 u - \text{csch}^2 u = 1, \qquad \text{csch}^2 u - \text{sech}^2 u = \text{csch}^2 u \text{ sech}^2 u$$

Angle-Sum and Angle-Difference Relations

$$\sinh (u + v) = \sinh u \cosh v + \cosh u \sinh v$$
$$\sinh (u - v) = \sinh u \cosh v - \cosh u \sinh v$$
$$\cosh (u + v) = \cosh u \cosh v + \sinh u \sinh v$$
$$\cosh (u - v) = \cosh u \cosh v - \sinh u \sinh v$$

$$\tanh (u + v) = \frac{\tanh u + \tanh v}{1 + \tanh u \tanh v} = \frac{\sinh 2u + \sinh 2v}{\cosh 2u + \cosh 2v}$$

$$\tanh (u - v) = \frac{\tanh u - \tanh v}{1 - \tanh u \tanh v} = \frac{\sinh 2u - \sinh 2v}{\cosh 2u - \cosh 2v}$$

$$\coth (u + v) = \frac{1 + \coth u \coth v}{\coth u + \coth v} = \frac{\sinh 2u - \sinh 2v}{\cosh 2u - \cosh 2v}$$

$$\coth (u - v) = \frac{1 - \coth u \coth v}{\coth u - \coth v} = \frac{\sinh 2u + \sinh 2v}{\cosh 2u - \cosh 2v}$$

Multiple Angle Relations

$$\sinh 2u = 2 \sinh u \cosh u = \frac{2 \tanh u}{1 - \tanh^2 u}$$

$$\cosh 2u = \cosh^2 u + \sinh^2 u = 2 \cosh^2 u - 1 = 1 + 2 \sinh^2 u = \frac{1 + \tanh^2 u}{1 - \tanh^2 u}$$

$$\tanh 2u = \frac{2 \tanh u}{1 + \tanh^2 u}$$

$$\coth 2u = \frac{\coth^2 u + 1}{2 \coth u}$$

$$\sinh 3u = 3 \sinh u + 4 \sinh^3 u = \sinh u \, (4 \cosh^2 u - 1)$$
$$\cosh 3u = 4 \cosh^3 u - 3 \cosh u = \cosh u \, (1 + 4 \sinh^2 u)$$

$$\tanh 3u = \frac{3 \tanh u + \tanh^3 u}{1 + 3 \tanh^2 u}$$

$$\coth 3u = \frac{3 \coth u + \coth^3 u}{1 + 3 \coth^2 u}$$

$$\sinh 4u = 4 \sinh u \cosh u(2 \cosh^2 u - 1)$$
$$= 4 \sinh u \cosh u(1 + 2 \sinh^2 u)$$
$$= 4 \sinh u \cosh u(\cosh^2 u + \sinh^2 u)$$

$$\cosh 4u = 1 + 8 \cosh^2 u(\cosh^2 u - 1)$$
$$= 1 + 8 \sinh^2 u(\sinh^2 u + 1)$$
$$= \cosh^4 u + 6 \sinh^2 u \cosh^2 u + \sinh^4 u$$

$$\tanh 4u = \frac{4 \tanh u(1 + \tanh^2 u)}{1 + 6 \tanh^2 u + \tanh^4 u}$$

$$\coth 4u = \frac{\coth^4 u + 6 \coth^2 u + 1}{4 \coth u(\coth^2 u + 1)}$$

$$\sinh 5u = \sinh u(16 \sinh^4 u + 20 \sinh^2 u + 5)$$
$$= \sinh u(16 \cosh^4 u - 12 \cosh^2 u + 1)$$

$$\cosh 5u = \cosh u(16 \cosh^4 u - 20 \cosh^2 u + 5)$$
$$= \cosh u(16 \sinh^4 u + 12 \sinh^2 u + 1)$$

$$\sinh 6u = 2 \sinh u \cosh u(16 \cosh^4 u - 16 \cosh^2 u + 3)$$
$$= 2 \sinh u \cosh u(16 \sinh^4 u + 16 \sinh^2 u + 3)$$

$$\cosh 6u = 32 \cosh^6 u - 48 \cosh^4 u + 18 \cosh^2 u - 1$$
$$= 32 \sinh^6 u + 48 \sinh^4 u + 18 \sinh^2 u + 1$$

$$\sinh nu = \sinh u \left[(2 \cosh u)^{n-1} - \frac{(n-2)}{1!} \cdot (2 \cosh u)^{n-3} + \frac{(n-3)(n-4)}{2!} \right.$$
$$\left. \cdot (2 \cosh u)^{n-5} - \frac{(n-4)(n-5)(n-6)}{3!} (2 \cosh u)^{n-7} + \cdots \right].$$

$$\cosh nu = \frac{1}{2} \left[(2 \cosh u)^n - \frac{n}{1!} (2 \cosh u)^{n-2} + \frac{n(n-3)}{2!} (2 \cosh u)^{n-4} \right.$$
$$\left. - \frac{n(n-4)(n-5)}{3!} (2 \cosh u)^{n-6} + \cdots \right].$$

Half Angle Relations

$$\sinh \tfrac{1}{2}u = \pm \sqrt{\tfrac{1}{2}(\cosh u - 1)}$$
$$\cosh \tfrac{1}{2}u = \sqrt{\tfrac{1}{2}(\cosh u + 1)}$$

$$\tanh \frac{u}{2} = \frac{\sinh u}{1 + \cosh u} = \frac{\cosh u - 1}{\sinh u} = \pm \sqrt{\frac{\cosh u - 1}{\cosh u + 1}}$$

$$\coth \frac{u}{2} = \frac{1 + \cosh u}{\sinh u} = \frac{\sinh u}{\cosh u - 1} = \pm \sqrt{\frac{\cosh u + 1}{\cosh u - 1}}$$

Choose $+$ sign if u is positive, otherwise choose the $-$ sign.

Function Sum and Function Difference Relations

$$\sinh u + \sinh v = 2 \sinh \tfrac{1}{2}(u + v) \cosh \tfrac{1}{2}(u - v)$$
$$\sinh u - \sinh v = 2 \cosh \tfrac{1}{2}(u + v) \sinh \tfrac{1}{2}(u - v)$$
$$\cosh u + \cosh v = 2 \cosh \tfrac{1}{2}(u + v) \cosh \tfrac{1}{2}(u - v)$$
$$\cosh u - \cosh v = 2 \sinh \tfrac{1}{2}(u + v) \sinh \tfrac{1}{2}(u - v)$$

$$\tanh u + \tanh v = (1 + \tanh u \tanh v) \tanh (u + v) = \frac{\sinh (u + v)}{\cosh u \cosh v}$$

$$\tanh u - \tanh v = (1 - \tanh u \tanh v) \tanh (u - v) = \frac{\sinh (u - v)}{\cosh u \cosh v}$$

$$\coth u + \coth v = \frac{1 + \coth u \coth v}{\coth (u + v)} = \frac{\sinh (u + v)}{\sinh u \sinh v}$$

$$\coth u - \coth v = \frac{1 - \coth u \coth v}{\coth (u - v)} = \frac{\sinh (u - v)}{\sinh u \sinh v}$$

$$\sinh u + \cosh u = \frac{1 + \tanh \frac{1}{2}u}{1 - \tanh \frac{1}{2}u} = e^u \qquad \cosh u - \sinh u = \frac{1 - \tanh \frac{1}{2}u}{1 + \tanh \frac{1}{2}u} = e^{-u}$$

Function Product Relations

$$\sinh u \cosh v = \tfrac{1}{2} \sinh (u + v) + \tfrac{1}{2} \sinh (u - v)$$
$$\cosh u \sinh v = \tfrac{1}{2} \sinh (u + v) - \tfrac{1}{2} \sinh (u - v)$$
$$\cosh u \cosh v = \tfrac{1}{2} \cosh (u + v) + \tfrac{1}{2} \cosh (u - v)$$
$$\sinh u \sinh v = \tfrac{1}{2} \cosh (u + v) - \tfrac{1}{2} \cosh (u - v)$$
$$\sinh (u + v) \sinh (u - v) = \sinh^2 u - \sinh^2 v = \cosh^2 u - \cosh^2 v$$
$$\cosh (u + v) \cosh (u - v) = \sinh^2 u + \cosh^2 v = \cosh^2 u + \sinh^2 v$$

Power Relations

$$\sinh^2 u = \tfrac{1}{2}(\cosh 2u - 1)$$
$$\cosh^2 u = \tfrac{1}{2}(\cosh 2u + 1)$$
$$\sinh^3 u = \tfrac{1}{4}(-3 \sinh u + \sinh 3u)$$
$$\cosh^3 u = \tfrac{1}{4}(3 \cosh u + \cosh 3u)$$
$$\sinh^4 u = \tfrac{1}{8}(3 - 4 \cosh 2u + \cosh 4u)$$
$$\cosh^4 u = \tfrac{1}{8}(3 + 4 \cosh 2u + \cosh 4u)$$
$$\sinh^5 u = \tfrac{1}{16}(10 \sinh u - 5 \sinh 3u + \sinh 5u)$$
$$\cosh^5 u = \tfrac{1}{16}(10 \cosh u + 5 \cosh 3u + \cosh 5u)$$
$$\sinh^6 u = \tfrac{1}{32}(-10 + 15 \cosh 2u - 6 \cosh 4u + \cosh 6u)$$
$$\cosh^6 u = \tfrac{1}{32}(10 + 15 \cosh 2u + 6 \cosh 4u + \cosh 6u)$$
$$(\cosh u \pm \sinh u)^n = \cosh nu \pm \sinh nu$$

Relations with Circular Functions

$$\begin{aligned} \sinh iu &= i \sin u, & \sinh u &= -i \sin iu \\ \cosh iu &= \cos u, & \cosh u &= \cos iu \\ \tanh iu &= i \tan u, & \tanh u &= -i \tan iu \\ \operatorname{cosech} iu &= -i \operatorname{cosec} u & \operatorname{cosech} u &= i \operatorname{cosec} iu \\ \operatorname{sech} iu &= \sec u & \operatorname{sech} u &= \sec iu \\ \coth iu &= -i \cot u & \coth u &= i \coth iu \end{aligned}$$

Hyperbolic Functions of Complex Argument

$$\sinh (u + iv) = \sinh u \cos v + i \cosh u \sin v$$
$$\sinh (u - iv) = \sinh u \cos v - i \cosh u \sin v$$
$$\cosh (u + iv) = \cosh u \cos v + i \sinh u \sin v$$
$$\cosh (u - iv) = \cosh u \cos v - i \sinh u \sin v$$

$$\tanh (u + iv) = \frac{\sinh 2u + i \sin 2v}{\cosh 2u + \cos 2v}$$

$$\tanh (u - iv) = \frac{\sinh 2u - i \sin 2v}{\cosh 2u + \cos 2v}$$

$$\coth (u + iv) = \frac{\sinh 2u - i \sin 2v}{\cosh 2u - \cos 2v}$$

$$\coth (u - iv) = \frac{\sinh 2u + i \sin 2v}{\cosh 2u - \cos 2v}$$

$$\sinh\left(u + \tfrac{1}{2}\pi i\right) = i\cosh u, \qquad \cosh\left(u + \tfrac{1}{2}\pi i\right) = i\sinh u$$
$$\sinh\left(u + \pi i\right) = -\sinh u, \qquad \cosh\left(u + \pi i\right) = -\cosh u$$
$$\sinh\left(u + 2\pi i\right) = \sinh u, \qquad \cosh\left(u + 2\pi i\right) = \cosh u$$

Series for Hyperbolic Functions

(see series expansions for sinh nu and cosh nu under multiple angle relations).

$$\sinh x = x + \frac{x^3}{3!} + \frac{x^5}{5!} + \frac{x^7}{7!} + \cdots + \frac{x^{2n+1}}{(2n+1)!} + \cdots \qquad |x| < \infty$$

$$\sinh ax = \frac{2}{\pi}\sinh \pi a \left[\frac{\sin x}{a^2 + 1^2} - \frac{2\sin 2x}{a^2 + 2^2} + \frac{3\sin 3x}{a^2 + 3^2} - + \cdots \right]$$

$$= \frac{2}{\pi}\sinh \pi a \sum_{n=1}^{\infty} (-1)^{n+1} \frac{n \sin nx}{n^2 + a^2}, \qquad |x| < \pi$$

$$\cosh x = 1 + \frac{x^2}{2!} + \frac{x^4}{4!} + \frac{x^6}{6!} + \cdots + \frac{x^{2n}}{(2n)!} + \cdots \qquad |x| < \infty$$

$$\cosh ax = \frac{2a}{\pi}\sinh \pi a \left[\frac{1}{2a^2} - \frac{\cos x}{a^2 + 1^2} + \frac{\cos 2x}{a^2 + 2^2} - \frac{\cos 3x}{a^2 + 3^2} + - \cdots \right]$$

$$= \frac{\sinh \pi a}{a\pi} + \frac{2a}{\pi}\sinh \pi a \sum_{n=1}^{\infty} (-1)^n \frac{\cos nx}{n^2 + a^2}, \qquad |x| < \pi$$

$$\tanh x = x - \frac{1}{3}x^3 + \frac{2}{15}x^5 - \frac{17}{315}x^7 + \frac{62}{2835}x^9 - \cdots$$

$$+ \frac{2^{2n}(2^{2n} - 1)B_{2n}x^{2n-1}}{(2n)!} \pm \cdots \quad (1) \qquad |x| < \frac{\pi}{2}$$

$$\tanh x = 1 - 2e^{-2x} + 2e^{-4x} - 2e^{-6x} + - \cdots$$

$$= 1 + 2\sum_{n=1}^{\infty} (-1)^n e^{-2nx}, \qquad \text{Re}(x) > 0$$

$$\tanh x = 2x \left[\frac{1}{\left(\frac{\pi}{2}\right)^2 + x^2} + \frac{1}{\left(\frac{3\pi}{2}\right)^2 + x^2} + \frac{1}{\left(\frac{5\pi}{2}\right)^2 + x^2} + \cdots \right]$$

$$= 2x \sum_{n=0}^{\infty} \frac{1}{\left(n + \frac{1}{2}\right)^2 \pi^2 + x^2}$$

$$\coth x = \frac{1}{x} + \frac{x}{3} - \frac{x^3}{45} + \frac{2x^5}{945} - \frac{x^7}{4725} + \cdots + \frac{2^{2n}}{(2n)!} B_{2n}x^{2n-1} \pm \cdots \quad (1)$$
$$0 < |x| < \pi$$

$$\coth x = 1 + 2e^{-2x} + 2e^{-4x} + 2e^{-6x} + \cdots$$

$$= 1 + 2\sum_{n=1}^{\infty} e^{-2nx} \qquad \text{Re}(x) > 0$$

$$\coth x = \frac{1}{x} + 2x \left[\frac{1}{\pi^2 + x^2} + \frac{1}{(2\pi)^2 + x^2} + \frac{1}{(3\pi)^2 + x^2} + \cdots \right]$$

$$= \frac{1}{x} + 2x \sum_{n=1}^{\infty} \frac{1}{(n\pi)^2 + x^2}$$

(1) B_{2n} denotes Bernoulli numbers.

$$\text{sech } x = 1 - \frac{1}{2!} x^2 + \frac{5}{4!} x^4 - \frac{61}{6!} x^6 + \frac{1385}{8!} x^8 - \cdots + \frac{E_{2n} x^{2n}}{(2n)!} \pm \cdots \quad (2)$$

$$|x| < \frac{\pi}{2}$$

$$\text{sech } x = 2e^{-x} - 2e^{-3x} + 2e^{-5x} - 2e^{-7x} + - \cdots$$

$$= 2 \sum_{n=0}^{\infty} (-1)^n e^{-(2n+1)x}, \text{ Re } (x) > 0$$

$$\text{sech } x = 4\pi \left[\frac{1}{\pi^2 + 4x^2} - \frac{3}{(3\pi)^2 + 4x^2} + \frac{5}{(5\pi)^2 + 4x^2} - + \cdots \right]$$

$$= 4\pi \sum_{n=0}^{\infty} \frac{(-1)^n (2n+1)}{(2n+1)^2 \pi^2 + 4x^2}$$

$$\text{cosech } x = \frac{1}{x} - \frac{x}{6} + \frac{7x^3}{360} - \frac{31x^5}{15,120} + \cdots - \frac{2(2^{2n-1} - 1)}{(2n)!} B_{2n} x^{2n-1} + \cdots \quad (1)$$

$$0 < |x| < \pi$$

$$\text{cosech } x = 2e^{-x} + 2e^{-3x} + 2e^{-5x} + \cdots$$

$$= 2 \sum_{n=0}^{\infty} e^{-(2n+1)x}, \text{ Re } (x) > 0$$

$$\text{cosech } x = \frac{1}{x} - \frac{2x}{\pi^2 + x^2} + \frac{2x}{(2\pi)^2 + x^2} - \frac{2x}{(3\pi)^2 + x^2} + - \cdots$$

$$= \frac{1}{x} + 2x \sum_{n=1}^{\infty} \frac{(-1)^n}{(n\pi)^2 + x^2}$$

[2] E_{2n} denotes Euler numbers.

INVERSE HYPERBOLIC FUNCTIONS

Definitions

If $x = \sinh y$, then $y = \sinh^{-1} x$.   Other inverse functions are denned similarly.

Domain and Range

Function	Domain	Range	Remarks
$\sinh^{-1} x$	$(-\infty, +\infty)$	$(-\infty, +\infty)$	odd function
$\cosh^{-1} x$	$[1, +\infty)$	$(-\infty, +\infty)$	even function double valued
$\tanh^{-1} x$	$(-1, 1)$	$(-\infty, +\infty)$	odd function
$\operatorname{cosech}^{-1} x$	$(-\infty, 0), (0, \infty)$	$(0, -\infty), (\infty, 0)$	odd function two branches, pole at $x = 0$
$\operatorname{sech}^{-1} x$	$(0, 1]$	$(-\infty, +\infty)$	double valued
$\coth^{-1} x$	$(-\infty, -1), (1, \infty)$	$(0, -\infty), (\infty, 0)$	odd function two branches

Graph of the Inverse Functions

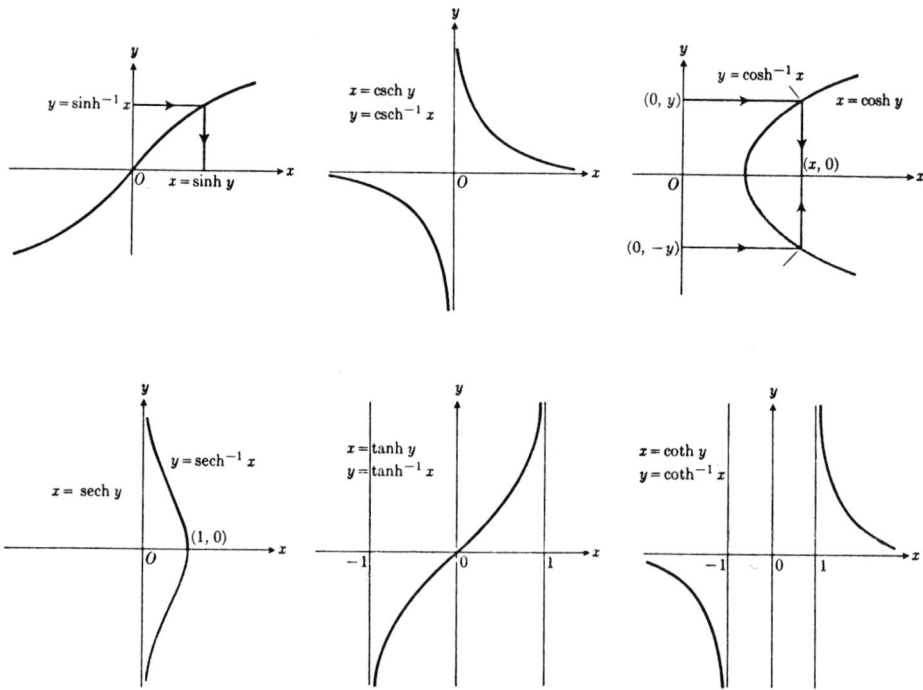

Inverse Hyperbolic Functions In Terms of One Another

Function	$\sinh^{-1} x$	$\cosh^{-1} x$ $+$ if $x > 0$ $-$ if $x < 0$	$\tanh^{-1} x$
$\sinh^{-1} x =$	$\sinh^{-1} x$	$\pm \cosh^{-1} \sqrt{x^2 + 1}$	$\tanh^{-1} \dfrac{x}{\sqrt{1 + x^2}}$
$\cosh^{-1} x =$	$\pm \sinh^{-1} \sqrt{x^2 - 1}$	$\cosh^{-1} x$	$\pm \tanh^{-1} \dfrac{\sqrt{x^2 - 1}}{x}$
$\tanh^{-1} x =$	$\sinh^{-1} \dfrac{x}{\sqrt{1 - x^2}}$	$\pm \cosh^{-1} \dfrac{1}{\sqrt{1 - x^2}}$	$\tanh^{-1} x$
$\operatorname{cosech}^{-1} x =$	$\sinh^{-1} \dfrac{1}{x}$	$\pm \cosh^{-1} \dfrac{\sqrt{x^2 + 1}}{x}$	$\tanh^{-1} \dfrac{1}{\sqrt{1 + x^2}}$
$\operatorname{sech}^{-1} x =$	$\pm \sinh^{-1} \dfrac{\sqrt{1 - x^2}}{x}$	$\cosh^{-1} \dfrac{1}{x}$	$\pm \tanh^{-1} \sqrt{1 - x^2}$
$\coth^{-1} x =$	$\sinh^{-1} \dfrac{1}{\sqrt{x^2 - 1}}$	$\pm \cosh^{-1} \dfrac{x}{\sqrt{x^2 - 1}}$	$\tanh^{-1} \dfrac{1}{x}$

Function	$\operatorname{cosech}^{-1} x$	$\operatorname{sech}^{-1} x$ $+$ if $x > 0$ $-$ if $x < 0$	$\coth^{-1} x$
$\sinh^{-1} x =$	$\operatorname{cosech}^{-1} \dfrac{1}{x}$	$\pm \operatorname{sech}^{-1} \dfrac{1}{\sqrt{1 + x^2}}$	$\coth^{-1} \dfrac{\sqrt{1 + x^2}}{x}$
$\cosh^{-1} x =$	$\pm \operatorname{cosech}^{-1} \dfrac{1}{\sqrt{x^2 - 1}}$	$\operatorname{sech}^{-1} \dfrac{1}{x}$	$\pm \coth^{-1} \dfrac{x}{\sqrt{x^2 - 1}}$
$\tanh^{-1} x =$	$\operatorname{cosech}^{-1} \dfrac{\sqrt{1 - x^2}}{x}$	$\pm \operatorname{sech}^{-1} \sqrt{1 - x^2}$	$\coth^{-1} \dfrac{1}{x}$
$\operatorname{cosech}^{-1} x =$	$\operatorname{cosech}^{-1} x$	$\pm \operatorname{sech}^{-1} \dfrac{x}{\sqrt{x^2 + 1}}$	$\coth^{-1} \sqrt{1 + x^2}$
$\operatorname{sech}^{-1} x =$	$\pm \operatorname{cosech}^{-1} \dfrac{x}{\sqrt{1 - x^2}}$	$\operatorname{sech}^{-1} x$	$\pm \coth^{-1} \dfrac{1}{\sqrt{1 - x^2}}$
$\coth^{-1} x =$	$\operatorname{cosech}^{-1} \sqrt{x^2 - 1}$	$\operatorname{sech}^{-1} \dfrac{\sqrt{x^2 - 1}}{x}$	$\coth^{-1} x$

Fundamental Identities

Relations with Logarithmic Functions

$$\sinh^{-1} x = \log_e (x + \sqrt{x^2 + 1})$$

$$\cosh^{-1} x = \log_e (x \pm \sqrt{x^2 - 1}), \quad x \geq 1. \quad \text{The plus sign is used for the principal value.}$$

$$\tanh^{-1} x = \tfrac{1}{2} \log_e \left(\frac{1 + x}{1 - x}\right), \quad x^2 < 1$$

$$\operatorname{csch}^{-1} x = \log_e \left(\frac{1 \pm \sqrt{1 + x^2}}{x}\right). \quad \text{The plus sign is used if } x > 0, \text{ the minus sign if } x < 0.$$

$$\operatorname{sech}^{-1} x = \log_e \left(\frac{1 \pm \sqrt{1 - x^2}}{x}\right), \quad 0 < x \leq 1. \quad \text{The plus sign is used for the principal values.}$$

$$\coth^{-1} x = \tfrac{1}{2} \log_e \left(\frac{x + 1}{x - 1}\right), \quad x^2 > 1$$

Relations with Circular Functions

$$\sinh^{-1} x = -i \sin^{-1} (ix) \qquad \sinh^{-1} (ix) = i \sin^{-1} x$$
$$\cosh^{-1} x = \pm i \cos^{-1} x \qquad \cosh^{-1} (ix) = \pm i \cos^{-1} (ix)$$
$$\tanh^{-1} x = -i \tan^{-1} (ix) \qquad \tanh^{-1} (ix) = i \tan^{-1} x$$
$$\operatorname{cosech}^{-1} x = i \operatorname{cosec}^{-1} (ix) \qquad \operatorname{cosech}^{-1} (ix) = -i \operatorname{cosec}^{-1} x$$
$$\operatorname{sech}^{-1} x = \pm i \sec^{-1} x \qquad \operatorname{sech}^{-1} (ix) = \pm i \sec^{-1} (ix)$$
$$\coth^{-1} x = i \coth^{-1} (ix) \qquad \coth^{-1} (ix) = -i \cot^{-1} (x)$$

Function Sum and Function Difference Relations

$$\sinh^{-1} x + \sinh^{-1} y = \sinh^{-1} (x \sqrt{1 + y^2} + y \sqrt{1 + x^2})$$
$$\sinh^{-1} x - \sinh^{-1} y = \sinh^{-1} (x \sqrt{1 + y^2} - y \sqrt{1 + x^2})$$
$$\cosh^{-1} x + \cosh^{-1} y = \cosh^{-1} (xy + \sqrt{(x^2 - 1)(y^2 - 1)})$$
$$\cosh^{-1} x - \cosh^{-1} y = \cosh^{-1} (xy - \sqrt{(x^2 - 1)(y^2 - 1)})$$
$$\tanh^{-1} x + \tanh^{-1} y = \tanh^{-1} \left(\frac{x + y}{1 + xy}\right)$$
$$\tanh^{-1} x - \tanh^{-1} y = \tanh^{-1} \left(\frac{x - y}{1 - xy}\right)$$
$$\sinh^{-1} x + \cosh^{-1} y = \sinh^{-1} (xy + \sqrt{(1 + x^2)(y^2 - 1)})$$
$$= \cosh^{-1} (y \sqrt{1 + x^2} + x \sqrt{y^2 - 1})$$
$$\sinh^{-1} x - \cosh^{-1} y = \sinh^{-1} (xy - \sqrt{(1 + x^2)(y^2 - 1)})$$
$$= \cosh^{-1} (y \sqrt{1 + x^2} - x \sqrt{y^2 - 1})$$
$$\tanh^{-1} x + \coth^{-1} y = \tanh^{-1} \left(\frac{xy + 1}{y + x}\right)$$
$$= \coth^{-1} \left(\frac{y + x}{xy + 1}\right)$$
$$\tanh^{-1} x - \coth^{-1} y = \tanh^{-1} \left(\frac{xy - 1}{y - x}\right)$$
$$= \coth^{-1} \left(\frac{y - x}{xy - 1}\right)$$

Series Expansions

$$\sinh^{-1} x = x - \frac{1}{2 \cdot 3} x^3 + \frac{1 \cdot 3}{2 \cdot 4 \cdot 5} x^5 - \frac{1 \cdot 3 \cdot 5}{2 \cdot 4 \cdot 6 \cdot 7} x^7 + \cdots$$

$$+ (-1)^n \cdot \frac{1 \cdot 3 \cdot 5 \ldots (2n-1)}{2 \cdot 4 \cdot 6 \ldots 2n(2n+1)} x^{2n+1} \pm \cdots \qquad |x| < 1$$

$$\sinh^{-1} x = \ln(2x) + \frac{1}{2} \cdot \frac{1}{2x^2} - \frac{1 \cdot 3}{2 \cdot 4} \cdot \frac{1}{4x^4} + \frac{1 \cdot 3 \cdot 5}{2 \cdot 4 \cdot 6} \cdot \frac{1}{6x^6} - \cdots$$

$$= \ln(2x) + \sum_{n=1}^{\infty} (-1)^{n+1} \frac{(2n)! x^{-2n}}{2^{2n}(n!)^2 2n}, \qquad |x| > 1$$

$$\cosh^{-1} x = \pm \left[\ln(2x) - \frac{1}{2 \cdot 2x^2} - \frac{1 \cdot 3}{2 \cdot 4 \cdot 4x^4} - \frac{1 \cdot 3 \cdot 5}{2 \cdot 4 \cdot 6 \cdot 6x^6} - \cdots \right] \qquad x > 1$$

$$\operatorname{cosech}^{-1} x = \frac{1}{x} - \frac{1}{2} \cdot \frac{1}{3x^3} + \frac{1 \cdot 3}{2 \cdot 4} \cdot \frac{1}{5x^5} - \frac{1 \cdot 3 \cdot 5}{2 \cdot 4 \cdot 6} \cdot \frac{1}{7x^7} + - \cdots$$

$$= \sum_{n=0}^{\infty} (-1)^n \frac{(2n)! x^{-2n-1}}{2^{2n}(n!)^2(2n+1)}, \qquad |x| > 1$$

$$\operatorname{cosech}^{-1} x = \ln \frac{2}{x} + \frac{1}{2} \cdot \frac{x^2}{2} - \frac{1 \cdot 3}{2 \cdot 4} \cdot \frac{x^4}{4} + \frac{1 \cdot 3 \cdot 5}{2 \cdot 4 \cdot 6} \cdot \frac{x^6}{6} - + \cdots$$

$$= \ln \frac{2}{x} + \sum_{n=1}^{\infty} \frac{(-1)^{n+1}(2n)! x^{2n}}{2^{2n}(n!)^2 2n}, \qquad 0 < x < 1$$

$$\operatorname{sech}^{-1} x = \ln \frac{2}{x} - \frac{1}{2} \frac{x^2}{2} - \frac{1 \cdot 3}{2 \cdot 4} \cdot \frac{x^4}{4} - \frac{1 \cdot 3 \cdot 5}{2 \cdot 4 \cdot 6} \cdot \frac{x^6}{6} - - \cdots$$

$$= \ln \frac{2}{x} - \sum_{n=1}^{\infty} \frac{(2n)! x^{2n}}{2^{2n}(n!)^2 2n}, \qquad 0 < x < 1$$

$$* \tanh^{-1} x = x + \frac{x^3}{3} + \frac{x^5}{5} + \frac{x^7}{7} + \cdots + \frac{x^{2n+1}}{2n+1} + \cdots \qquad |x| < 1$$

$$* \coth^{-1} x = \frac{1}{x} + \frac{1}{3x^3} + \frac{1}{5x^5} + \frac{1}{7x^7} + \cdots + \frac{1}{(2n+1)x^{2n+1}} + \cdots \qquad |x| > 1$$

GUDERMANNIAN FUNCTION

This function is useful because it relates circular and hyperbolic functions without the use of functions of imaginary argument.

Definition

$$\gamma = \text{the gudermannian of } x, \text{ written as } \mathbf{gd}\ x$$

$$= 2 \tan^{-1} e^x - \frac{\pi}{2}$$

$$x = \text{gd}^{-1} \gamma$$

$$= \ln \tan \left(\frac{\pi}{4} + \frac{\gamma}{2} \right)$$

$$= \ln (\sec \gamma + \tan \gamma)$$

* Can also be written as arg tanh x and arg coth x respectively.

Special Values of Gudermannian Function

x	0	∞	$-\infty$
gd x	0	$\frac{1}{2}\pi$	$-\frac{1}{2}\pi$

Relations with Hyperbolic and Circular Functions

$$\sinh x = \tan (\text{gd } x) \qquad \text{cosech } x = \cot (\text{gd } x)$$
$$\cosh x = \sec (\text{gd } x) \qquad \text{sech } (x) = \cos (\text{gd } x)$$
$$\tanh x = \sin (\text{gd } x) \qquad \coth (x) = \text{cosec } (\text{gd } x)$$

Derivatives

$$\frac{d}{dx} (\text{gd } x) = \text{sech } x$$

$$\frac{d}{dx} (\text{gd}^{-1} \gamma) = \sec \gamma$$

Fundamental Identities

$$\tanh (\tfrac{1}{2}x) = \tan (\tfrac{1}{2}\text{gd } x)$$
$$e^x = \cosh x + \sinh x = \sec (\text{gd } x) + \tan (\text{gd } x)$$
$$= \tan \left(\frac{\pi}{4} + \frac{1}{2} \text{gd } x\right) = \frac{1 + \sin (\text{gd } x)}{\cos (\text{gd } x)} = \frac{1 + \tan (\tfrac{1}{2}\text{gd } x)}{1 - \tan (\tfrac{1}{2}\text{gd } x)}$$
$$\text{gd } x = 2 \tan^{-1} \left(\tanh \frac{1}{2} x\right) = \int_0^x \frac{dt}{\cosh t}$$
$$\text{gd}^{-1} \gamma = \int_0^\gamma \frac{dt}{\cos t}$$
$$i \, \text{gd}^{-1} \gamma = \text{gd } i\gamma, \text{ where } i = \sqrt{-1}.$$

If

$$\alpha + i\beta = \text{gd}(x + iy)$$

then

$$\tan \alpha = \frac{\sinh x}{\cos y} \qquad \tanh \beta = \frac{\sin y}{\cosh x}$$

$$\tanh x = \frac{\sin \alpha}{\cosh \beta} \qquad \tan y = \frac{\sinh \beta}{\cosh \alpha}$$

Series Expansions

$$\text{gd } x = x - \frac{1}{6} x^3 + \frac{1}{24} x^5 - \frac{61}{5040} x^7 + - \cdots$$

$$= \sum_{n=0}^{\infty} \frac{E_{2n}}{(2n + 1)!} x^{2n+1}, \quad |x| < 1 *$$

$$\text{gd } x = \frac{\pi}{2} - \text{sech } x - \frac{1}{2} \frac{\text{sech}^3 x}{3} - \frac{1 \cdot 3}{2 \cdot 4} \frac{\text{sech}^5 x}{5} + - \cdots$$

$$= \frac{\pi}{2} - \sum_{n=0}^{\infty} \frac{(2n)!}{2^{2n}(n!)^2} \frac{\text{sech}^{2n+1} x}{(2n + 1)} \qquad x \text{ large}$$

*E_n denotes Euler numbers.

$$\text{gd } x = \frac{2}{1} \tanh \frac{x}{2} - \frac{2}{3} \tanh^3 \frac{x}{2} + \frac{2}{5} \tanh^5 \frac{x}{2} - \frac{2}{7} \tanh^7 \frac{x}{2} + - \cdots$$

$$= 2 \sum_{n=0}^{\infty} \frac{(-1)^n}{2n+1} \tanh^{2n+1} \frac{x}{2}$$

$$\text{gd}^{-1} \gamma = \gamma + \frac{1}{6} \gamma^3 + \frac{1}{24} \gamma^5 + \frac{61}{5040} \gamma^7 + \cdots$$

$$= \sum_{n=0}^{\infty} \frac{(-1)^n E_{2n} \gamma^{2n+1}}{(2n+1)!}, \qquad |\gamma| < \frac{\pi}{2} \ *$$

$$\text{gd}^{-1} \gamma = \frac{2}{1} \tan \frac{\gamma}{2} + \frac{2}{3} \tan^3 \frac{\gamma}{2} + \frac{2}{5} \tan^5 \frac{\gamma}{2} + \cdots$$

$$= 2 \sum_{n=0}^{\infty} \frac{1}{2n+1} \tan^{2n+1} \frac{\gamma}{2}$$

*E_n are Euler's numbers.

References

1. For extensive tables of inverse hyperbolic functions: Tables of Inverse Hyperbolic Functions, Harvard University Computation Laboratory (Cambridge, Harvard University Press, 1949).
2. For tables of hyperbolic functions with complex argument: Tables of Complex Hyperbolic and Circular Functions, A. E. Kennelly (Cambridge, Harvard University Press, 1914).

HYPERBOLIC FUNCTIONS AND THEIR COMMON LOGARITHMS

The logarithms given below show the mantissa only. The proper characteristic must be added.

x	Sinh x Value	Sinh x $\log_{10}$	Cosh x Value	Cosh x $\log_{10}$	Tanh x Value	Tanh x $\log_{10}$	Coth x Value	Coth x $\log_{10}$
0.00	0.00000	$-\infty$	1.00000	.00000	0.00000	$-\infty$	∞	∞
0.01	.01000	.00001	1.00005	.00002	.01000	.99999	100.003	.00001
0.02	.02000	.30106	1.00020	.00009	.02000	.30097	50.007	.69903
0.03	.03000	.47719	1.00045	.00020	.02999	.47699	33.343	.52301
0.04	.04001	.60218	1.00080	.00035	.03998	.60183	25.013	.39817
0.05	0.05002	.69915	1.00125	.00054	0.04996	.69861	20.017	.30139
0.06	.06004	.77841	1.00180	.00078	.05993	.77763	16.687	.22237
0.07	.07006	.84545	1.00245	.00106	.06989	.84439	14.309	.15561
0.08	.08009	.90355	1.00320	.00139	.07983	.90216	12.527	.09784
0.09	.09012	.95483	1.00405	.00176	.08976	.95307	11.141	.04693
0.10	0.10017	.00072	1.00500	.00217	0.09967	.99856	10.0333	.00144
0.11	.11022	.04227	1.00606	.00262	.10956	.03965	9.1275	.96035
0.12	.12029	.08022	1.00721	.00312	.11943	.07710	8.3733	.92290
0.13	.13037	.11517	1.00846	.00366	.12927	.11151	7.7356	.88849
0.14	.14046	.14755	1.00982	.00424	.13909	.14330	7.1895	.85670
0.15	0.15056	.17772	1.01127	.00487	0.14889	.17285	6.7166	.82715
0.16	.16068	.20597	1.01283	.00554	.15865	.20044	6.3032	.79956
0.17	.17082	.23254	1.01448	.00625	.16838	.22629	5.9389	.77371
0.18	.18097	.25762	1.01624	.00700	.17808	.25062	5.6154	.74938
0.19	.19115	.28136	1.01810	.00779	.18775	.27357	5.3263	.72643
0.20	0.20134	.30392	1.02007	.00863	0.19738	.29529	5.0665	.70471
0.21	.21155	.32541	1.02213	.00951	.20697	.31590	4.8317	.68410
0.22	.22178	.34592	1.02430	.01043	.21652	.33549	4.6186	.66451
0.23	.23203	.36555	1.02657	.01139	.22603	.35416	4.4242	.64584
0.24	.24231	.38437	1.02894	.01239	.23550	.37198	4.2464	.62802
0.25	0.25261	.40245	1.03141	.01343	0.24492	.38902	4.0830	.61098
0.26	.26294	.41986	1.03399	.01452	.25430	.40534	3.9324	.59466
0.27	.27329	.43663	1.03667	.01564	.26362	.42099	3.7933	.57901
0.28	.28367	.45282	1.03946	.01681	.27291	.43601	3.6643	.56399
0.29	.29408	.46847	1.04235	.01801	.28213	.45046	3.5444	.54954
0.30	0.30452	.48362	1.04534	.01926	0.29131	.46436	3.4327	.53564
0.31	.31499	.49830	1.04844	.02054	.30044	.47775	3.3285	.52225
0.32	.32549	.51254	1.05164	.02187	.30951	.49067	3.2309	.50933
0.33	.33602	.52637	1.05495	.02323	.31852	.50314	3.1395	.49686
0.34	.34659	.53981	1.05836	.02463	.32748	.51518	3.0536	.48482
0.35	0.35719	.55290	1.06188	.02607	0.33638	.52682	2.9729	.47318
0.36	.36783	.56564	1.06550	.02755	.34521	.53809	2.8968	.46191
0.37	.37850	.57807	1.06923	.02907	.35399	.54899	2.8249	.45101
0.38	.38921	.59019	1.07307	.03063	.36271	.55956	2.7570	.44044
0.39	.39996	.60202	1.07702	.03222	.37136	.56980	2.6928	.43020
0.40	0.41075	.61358	1.08107	.03385	0.37995	.57973	2.6319	.42027
0.41	.42158	.62488	1.08523	.03552	.38847	.58936	2.5742	.41064
0.42	.43246	.63594	1.08950	.03723	.39693	.59871	2.5193	.40129
0.43	.44337	.64677	1.09388	.03897	.40532	.60780	2.4672	.39220
0.44	.45434	.65738	1.09837	.04075	.41364	.61663	2.4175	.38337
0.45	0.46534	.66777	1.10297	.04256	0.42190	.62521	2.3702	.37479
0.46	.47640	.67797	1.10768	.04441	.43008	.63355	2.3251	.36645
0.47	.48750	.68797	1.11250	.04630	.43820	.64167	2.2821	.35833
0.48	.49865	.69779	1.11743	.04822	.44624	.64957	2.2409	.35043
0.49	.50984	.70744	1.12247	.05018	.45422	.65726	2.2016	.34274

HYPERBOLIC FUNCTIONS AND THEIR COMMON LOGARITHMS (Continued)

x	Sinh x Value	Sinh x $\log_{10}$	Cosh x Value	Cosh x $\log_{10}$	Tanh x Value	Tanh x $\log_{10}$	Coth x Value	Coth x $\log_{10}$
0.50	0.52110	.71692	1.12763	.05217	0.46212	.66475	2.1640	.33525
0.51	.53240	.72624	1.13289	.05419	.46995	.67205	2.1279	.32795
0.52	.54375	.73540	1.13827	.05625	.47770	.67916	2.0934	.32084
0.53	.55516	.74442	1.14377	.05834	.48538	.68608	2.0602	.31392
0.54	.56663	.75330	1.14938	.06046	.49299	.69284	2.0284	.30716
0.55	0.57815	.76204	1.15510	.06262	0.50052	.69942	1.9979	.30058
0.56	.58973	.77065	1.16094	.06481	.50798	.70584	1.9686	.29416
0.57	.60137	.77914	1.16690	.06703	.51536	.71211	1.9404	.28789
0.58	.61307	.78751	1.17297	.06929	.52267	.71822	1.9133	.28178
0.59	.62483	.79576	1.17916	.07157	.52990	.72419	1.8872	.27581
0.60	0.63665	.80390	1.18547	.07389	0.53705	.73001	1.8620	.26999
0.61	.64854	.81194	1.19189	.07624	.54413	.73570	1.8378	.26430
0.62	.66049	.81987	1.19844	.07861	.55113	.74125	1.8145	.25875
0.63	.67251	.82770	1.20510	.08102	.55805	.74667	1.7919	.25333
0.64	.68459	.83543	1.21189	.08346	.56490	.75197	1.7702	.24803
0.65	0.69675	.84308	1.21879	.08593	0.57167	.75715	1.7493	.24285
0.66	.70897	.85063	1.22582	.08843	.57836	.76220	1.7290	.23780
0.67	.72126	.85809	1.23297	.09095	.58498	.76714	1.7095	.23286
0.68	.73363	.86548	1.24025	.09351	.59152	.77197	1.6906	.22803
0.69	.74607	.87278	1.24765	.09609	.59798	.77669	1.6723	.22331
0.70	0.75858	.88000	1.25517	.09870	0.60437	.78130	1.6546	.21870
0.71	.77117	.88715	1.26282	.10134	.61068	.78581	1.6375	.21419
0.72	.78384	.89423	1.27059	.10401	.61691	.79022	1.6210	.20978
0.73	.79659	.90123	1.27849	.10670	.62307	.79453	1.6050	.20547
0.74	.80941	.90817	1.28652	.10942	.62915	.79875	1.5895	.20125
0.75	0.82232	.91504	1.29468	.11216	0.63515	.80288	1.5744	.19712
0.76	.83530	.92185	1.30297	.11493	.64108	.80691	1.5599	.19309
0.77	.84838	.92859	1.31139	.11773	.64693	.81086	1.5458	.18914
0.78	.86153	.93527	1.31994	.12055	.65271	.81472	1.5321	.18528
0.79	.87478	.94190	1.32862	.12340	.65841	.81850	1.5188	.18150
0.80	0.88811	.94846	1.33743	.12627	0.66404	.82219	1.5059	.17781
0.81	.90152	.95498	1.34638	.12917	.66959	.82581	1.4935	.17419
0.82	.91503	.96144	1.35547	.13209	.67507	.82935	1.4813	.17065
0.83	.92863	.96784	1.36468	.13503	.68048	.83281	1.4696	.16719
0.84	.94233	.97420	1.37404	.13800	.68581	.83620	1.4581	.16380
0.85	0.95612	.98051	1.38353	.14099	0.69107	.83952	1.4470	.16048
0.86	.97000	.98677	1.39316	.14400	.69626	.84277	1.4362	.15723
0.87	.98398	.99299	1.40293	.14704	.70137	.84595	1.4258	.15405
0.88	.99806	.99916	1.41284	.15009	.70642	.84906	1.4156	.15094
0.89	1.01224	.00528	1.42289	.15317	.71139	.85211	1.4057	.14789
0.90	1.02652	.01137	1.43309	.15627	0.71630	.85509	1.3961	.14491
0.91	1.04090	.01741	1.44342	.15939	.72113	.85801	1.3867	.14199
0.92	1.05539	.02341	1.45390	.16254	.72590	.86088	1.3776	.13912
0.93	1.06998	.02937	1.46453	.16570	.73059	.86368	1.3687	.13632
0.94	1.08468	.03530	1.47530	.16888	.73522	.86642	1.3601	.13358
0.95	1.09948	.04119	1.48623	.17208	0.73978	.86910	1.3517	.13090
0.96	1.11440	.04704	1.49729	.17531	.74428	.87173	1.3436	.12827
0.97	1.12943	.05286	1.50851	.17855	.74870	.87431	1.3356	.12569
0.98	1.14457	.05864	1.51988	.18181	.75307	.87683	1.3279	.12317
0.99	1.15983	.06439	1.53141	.18509	.75736	.87930	1.3204	.12070

HYPERBOLIC FUNCTIONS AND THEIR COMMON LOGARITHMS (Continued)

x	Sinh x Value	Sinh x $\log_{10}$	Cosh x Value	Cosh x $\log_{10}$	Tanh x Value	Tanh x $\log_{10}$	Coth x Value	Coth x $\log_{10}$
1.00	1.17520	.07011	1.54308	.18839	0.76159	.88172	1.3130	.11828
1.01	1.19069	.07580	1.55491	.19171	.76576	.88409	1.3059	.11591
1.02	1.20630	.08146	1.56689	.19504	.76987	.88642	1.2989	.11358
1.03	1.22203	.08708	1.57904	.19839	.77391	.88869	1.2921	.11131
1.04	1.23788	.09268	1.59134	.20176	.77789	.89092	1.2855	.10908
1.05	1.25386	.09825	1.60379	.20515	0.78181	.89310	1.2791	.10690
1.06	1.26996	.10379	1.61641	.20855	.78566	.89524	1.2728	.10476
1.07	1.28619	.10930	1.62919	.21197	.78946	.89733	1.2667	.10267
1.08	1.30254	.11479	1.64214	.21541	.79320	.89938	1.2607	.10062
1.09	1.31903	.12025	1.65525	.21886	.79688	.90139	1.2549	.09861
1.10	1.33565	.12569	1.66852	.22233	0.80050	.90336	1.2492	.09664
1.11	1.35240	.13111	1.68196	.22582	.80406	.90529	1.2437	.09471
1.12	1.36929	.13649	1.69557	.22931	.80757	.90718	1.2383	.09282
1.13	1.38631	.14186	1.70934	.23283	.81102	.90903	1.2330	.09097
1.14	1.40347	.14720	1.72329	.23636	.81441	.91085	1.2279	.08915
1.15	1.42078	.15253	1.73741	.23990	0.81775	.91262	1.2229	.08738
1.16	1.43822	.15783	1.75171	.24346	.82104	.91436	1.2180	.08564
1.17	1.45581	.16311	1.76618	.24703	.82427	.91607	1.2132	.08393
1.18	1.47355	.16836	1.78083	.25062	.82745	.91774	1.2085	.08226
1.19	1.49143	.17360	1.79565	.25422	.83058	.91938	1.2040	.08062
1.20	1.50946	.17882	1.81066	.25784	0.83365	.92099	1.1995	.07901
1.21	1.52764	.18402	1.82584	.26146	.83668	.92256	1.1952	.07744
1.22	1.54598	.18920	1.84121	.26510	.83965	.92410	1.1910	.07590
1.23	1.56447	.19437	1.85676	.26876	.84258	.92561	1.1868	.07439
1.24	1.58311	.19951	1.87250	.27242	.84546	.92709	1.1828	.07291
1.25	1.60192	.20464	1.88842	.27610	0.84828	.92854	1.1789	.07146
1.26	1.62088	.20975	1.90454	.27979	.85106	.92996	1.1750	.07004
1.27	1.64001	.21485	1.92084	.28349	.85380	.93135	1.1712	.06865
1.28	1.65930	.21993	1.93734	.28721	.85648	.93272	1.1676	.06728
1.29	1.67876	.22499	1.95403	.29093	.85913	.93406	1.1640	.06594
1.30	1.69838	.23004	1.97091	.29467	0.86172	.93537	1.1605	.06463
1.31	1.71818	.23507	1.98800	.29842	.86428	.93665	1.1570	.06335
1.32	1.73814	.24009	2.00528	.30217	.86678	.93791	1.1537	.06209
1.33	1.75828	.24509	2.02276	.30594	.86925	.93914	1.1504	.06086
1.34	1.77860	.25008	2.04044	.30972	.87167	.94035	1.1472	.05965
1.35	1.79909	.25505	2.05833	.31352	0.87405	.94154	1.1441	.05846
1.36	1.81977	.26002	2.07643	.31732	.87639	.94270	1.1410	.05730
1.37	1.84062	.26496	2.09473	.32113	.87869	.94384	1.1381	.05616
1.38	1.86166	.26990	2.11324	.32495	.88095	.94495	1.1351	.05505
1.39	1.88289	.27482	2.13196	.32878	.88317	.94604	1.1323	.05396
1.40	1.90430	.27974	2.15090	.33262	0.88535	.94712	1.1295	.05288
1.41	1.92591	.28464	2.17005	.33647	.88749	.94817	1.1268	.05183
1.42	1.94770	.28952	2.18942	.34033	.88960	.94919	1.1241	.05081
1.43	1.96970	.29440	2.20900	.34420	.89167	.95020	1.1215	.04980
1.44	1.99188	.29926	2.22881	.34807	.89370	.95119	1.1189	.04881
1.45	2.01427	.30412	2.24884	.35196	0.89569	.95216	1.1165	.04784
1.46	2.03686	.30896	2.26910	.35585	.89765	.95311	1.1140	.04689
1.47	2.05965	.31379	2.28958	.35976	.89958	.95404	1.1116	.04596
1.48	2.08265	.31862	2.31029	.36367	.90147	.95495	1.1093	.04505
1.49	2.10586	.32343	2.33123	.36759	.90332	.95584	1.1070	.04416

HYPERBOLIC FUNCTIONS AND THEIR COMMON LOGARITHMS (Continued)

x	Sinh x Value	$\log_{10}$	Cosh x Value	$\log_{10}$	Tanh x Value	$\log_{10}$	Coth x Value	$\log_{10}$
1.50	2.12928	.32823	2.35241	.37151	0.90515	.95672	1.1048	.04328
1.51	2.15291	.33303	2.37382	.37545	.90694	.95758	1.1026	.04242
1.52	2.17676	.33781	2.39547	.37939	.90870	.95842	1.1005	.04158
1.53	2.20082	.34258	2.41736	.38334	.91042	.95924	1.0984	.04076
1.54	2.22510	.34735	2.43949	.38730	.91212	.96005	1.0963	.03995
1.55	2.24961	.35211	2.46186	.39126	0.91379	.96084	1.0943	.03916
1.56	2.27434	.35686	2.48448	.39524	.91542	.96162	1.0924	.03838
1.57	2.29930	.36160	2.50735	.39921	.91703	.96238	1.0905	.03762
1.58	2.32449	.36633	2.53047	.40320	.91860	.96313	1.0886	.03687
1.59	2.34991	.37105	2.55384	.40719	.92015	.96386	1.0868	.03614
1.60	2.37557	.37577	2.57746	.41119	0.92167	.96457	1.0850	.03543
1.61	2.40146	.38048	2.60135	.41520	.92316	.96528	1.0832	.03472
1.62	2.42760	.38518	2.62549	.41921	.92462	.96597	1.0815	.03403
1.63	2.45397	.38987	2.64990	.42323	.92606	.96664	1.0798	.03336
1.64	2.48059	.39456	2.67457	.42725	.92747	.96730	1.0782	.03270
1.65	2.50746	.39923	2.69951	.43129	0.92886	.96795	1.0766	.03205
1.66	2.53459	.40391	2.72472	.43532	.93022	.96858	1.0750	.03142
1.67	2.56196	.40857	2.75021	.43937	.93155	.96921	1.0735	.03079
1.68	2.58959	.41323	2.77596	.44341	.93286	.96982	1.0720	.03018
1.69	2.61748	.41788	2.80200	.44747	.93415	.97042	1.0705	.02958
1.70	2.64563	.42253	2.82832	.45153	.93541	.97100	1.0691	.02900
1.71	2.67405	.42717	2.85491	.45559	.93665	.97158	1.0676	.02842
1.72	2.70273	.43180	2.88180	.45966	.93786	.97214	1.0663	.02786
1.73	2.73168	.43643	2.90897	.46374	.93906	.97269	1.0649	.02731
1.74	2.76091	.44105	2.93643	.46782	.94023	.97323	1.0636	.02677
1.75	2.79041	.44567	2.96419	.47191	0.94138	.97376	1.0623	.02624
1.76	2.82020	.45028	2.99224	.47600	.94250	.97428	1.0610	.02572
1.77	2.85026	.45488	3.02059	.48009	.94361	.97479	1.0598	.02521
1.78	2.88061	.45948	3.04925	.48419	.94470	.97529	1.0585	.02471
1.79	2.91125	.46408	3.07821	.48830	.94576	.97578	1.0574	.02422
1.80	2.94217	.46867	3.10747	.49241	0.94681	.97626	1.0562	.02374
1.81	2.97340	.47325	3.13705	.49652	.94783	.97673	1.0550	.02327
1.82	3.00492	.47783	3.16694	.50064	.94884	.97719	1.0539	.02281
1.83	3.03674	.48241	3.19715	.50476	.94983	.97764	1.0528	.02236
1.84	3.06886	.48698	3.22768	.50889	.95080	.97809	1.0518	.02191
1.85	3.10129	.49154	3.25853	.51302	0.95175	.97852	1.0507	.02148
1.86	3.13403	.49610	3.28970	.51716	.95268	.97895	1.0497	.02105
1.87	3.16709	.50066	3.32121	.52130	.95359	.97936	1.0487	.02064
1.88	3.20046	.50521	3.35305	.52544	.95449	.97977	1.0477	.02023
1.89	3.23415	.50976	3.38522	.52959	.95537	.98017	1.0467	.01983
1.90	3.26816	.51430	3.41773	.53374	0.95624	.98057	1.0458	.01943
1.91	3.30250	.51884	3.45058	.53789	.95709	.98095	1.0448	.01905
1.92	3.33718	.52338	3.48378	.54205	.95792	.98133	1.0439	.01867
1.93	3.37218	.52791	3.51733	.54621	.95873	.98170	1.0430	.01830
1.94	3.40752	.53244	3.55123	.55038	.95953	.98206	1.0422	.01794
1.95	3.44321	.53696	3.58548	.55455	0.96032	.98242	1.0413	.01758
1.96	3.47923	.54148	3.62009	.55872	.96109	.98276	1.0405	.01724
1.97	3.51561	.54600	3.65507	.56290	.96185	.98311	1.0397	.01689
1.98	3.55234	.55051	3.69041	.56707	.96259	.98344	1.0389	.01656
1.99	3.58942	.55502	3.72611	.57126	.96331	.98377	1.0381	.01623

HYPERBOLIC FUNCTIONS AND THEIR COMMON LOGARITHMS (Continued)

x	Sinh x Value	Sinh x log₁₀	Cosh x Value	Cosh x log₁₀	Tanh x Value	Tanh x log₁₀	Coth x Value	Coth x log₁₀
2.00	3.62686	.55953	3.76220	.57544	0.96403	.98409	1.0373	.01591
2.01	3.66466	.56403	3.79865	.57963	.96473	.98440	1.0366	.01560
2.02	3.70283	.56853	3.83549	.58382	.96541	.98471	1.0358	.01529
2.03	3.74138	.57303	3.87271	.58802	.96609	.98502	1.0351	.01498
2.04	3.78029	.57753	3.91032	.59221	.96675	.98531	1.0344	.01469
2.05	3.81958	.58202	3.94832	.59641	0.96740	.98560	1.0337	.01440
2.06	3.85926	.58650	3.98671	.60061	.96803	.98589	1.0330	.01411
2.07	3.89932	.59099	4.02550	.60482	.96865	.98617	1.0324	.01383
2.08	3.93977	.59547	4.06470	.60903	.96926	.98644	1.0317	.01356
2.09	3.98061	.59995	4.10430	.61324	.96986	.98671	1.0311	.01329
2.10	4.02186	.60443	4.14431	.61745	0.97045	.98697	1.0304	.01303
2.11	4.06350	.60890	4.18474	.62167	.97103	.98723	1.0298	.01277
2.12	4.10555	.61337	4.22558	.62589	.97159	.98748	1.0292	.01252
2.13	4.14801	.61784	4.26685	.63011	.97215	.98773	1.0286	.01227
2.14	4.19089	.62231	4.30855	.63433	.97269	.98798	1.0281	.01202
2.15	4.23419	.62677	4.35067	.63856	0.97323	.98821	1.0275	.01179
2.16	4.27791	.63123	4.39323	.64278	.97375	.98845	1.0270	.01155
2.17	4.32205	.63569	4.43623	.64701	.97426	.98868	1.0264	.01132
2.18	4.36663	.64015	4.47967	.65125	.97477	.98890	1.0259	.01110
2.19	4.41165	.64460	4.52356	.65548	.97526	.98912	1.0254	.01088
2.20	4.45711	.64905	4.56791	.65972	0.97574	.98934	1.0249	.01066
2.21	4.50301	.65350	4.61271	.66396	.97622	.98955	1.0244	.01045
2.22	4.54936	.65795	4.65797	.66820	.97668	.98975	1.0239	.01025
2.23	4.59617	.66240	4.70370	.67244	.97714	.98996	1.0234	.01004
2.24	4.64344	.66684	4.74989	.67668	.97759	.99016	1.0229	.00984
2.25	4.69117	.67128	4.79657	.68093	0.97803	.99035	1.0225	.00965
2.26	4.73937	.67572	4.84372	.68518	.97846	.99054	1.0220	.00946
2.27	4.78804	.68016	4.89136	.68943	.97888	.99073	1.0216	.00927
2.28	4.83720	.68459	4.93948	.69368	.97929	.99091	1.0211	.00909
2.29	4.88684	.68903	4.98810	.69794	.97970	.99109	1.0207	.00891
2.30	4.93696	.69346	5.03722	.70219	0.98010	.99127	1.0203	.00873
2.31	4.98758	.69789	5.08684	.70645	.98049	.99144	1.0199	.00856
2.32	5.03870	.70232	5.13697	.71071	.98087	.99161	1.0195	00839
2.33	5.09032	.70675	5.18762	.71497	.98124	.99178	1.0191	.00822
2.34	5.14245	.71117	5.23878	.71923	.98161	.99194	1.0187	.00806
2.35	5.19510	.71559	5.29047	.72349	0.98197	.99210	1.0184	.00790
2.36	5.24827	.72002	5.34269	.72776	.98233	.99226	1.0180	.00774
2.37	5.30196	.72444	5.39544	.73203	.98267	.99241	1.0176	.00759
2.38	5.35618	.72885	5.44873	.73630	.98301	.99256	1.0173	.00744
2.39	5.41093	.73327	5.50256	.74056	.98335	.99271	1.0169	.00729
2.40	5.46623	.73769	5.55695	.74484	0.98367	.99285	1.0166	.00715
2.41	5.52207	.74210	5.61189	.74911	.98400	.99299	1.0163	.00701
2.42	5.57847	.74652	5.66739	.75338	.98431	.99313	1.0159	.00687
2.43	5.63542	.75093	5.72346	.75766	.98462	.99327	1.0156	.00673
2.44	5.69294	.75534	5.78010	.76194	.98492	.99340	1.0153	.00660
2.45	5.75103	.75975	5.83732	.76621	0.98522	.99353	1.0150	.00647
2.46	5.80969	.75415	5.89512	.77049	.98551	.99366	1.0147	.00634
2.47	5.86893	.76856	5.95352	.77477	.98579	.99379	1.0144	.00621
2.48	5.92876	.77296	6.01250	.77906	.98607	.99391	1.0141	.00609
2.49	5.98918	.77737	6.07209	.78334	.98635	.99403	1.0138	.00597

HYPERBOLIC FUNCTIONS AND THEIR COMMON LOGARITHMS (Continued)

x	Sinh x Value	Sinh x log$_{10}$	Cosh x Value	Cosh x log$_{10}$	Tanh x Value	Tanh x log$_{10}$	Coth x Value	Coth x log$_{10}$
2.50	6.05020	.78177	6.13229	.78762	0.98661	.99415	1.0136	.00585
2.51	6.11183	.78617	6.19310	.79191	.98688	.99426	1.0133	.00574
2.52	6.17407	.79057	6.25453	.79619	.98714	.99438	1.0130	.00562
2.53	6.23692	.79497	6.31658	.80048	.98739	.99449	1.0128	.00551
2.54	6.30040	.79937	6.37927	.80477	.98764	.99460	1.0125	.00540
2.55	6.36451	.80377	6.44259	.80906	0.98788	.99470	1.0123	.00530
2.56	6.42926	.80816	6.50656	.81335	.98812	.99481	1.0120	.00519
2.57	6.49464	.81256	6.57118	.81764	.98835	.99491	1.0118	.00509
2.58	6.56068	.81695	6.63646	.82194	.98858	.99501	1.0115	.00499
2.59	6.62738	.82134	6.70240	.82623	.98881	.99511	1.0113	.00489
2.60	6.69473	.82573	6.76901	.83052	0.98903	.99521	1.0111	.00479
2.61	6.76276	.83012	6.83629	.83482	.98924	.99530	1.0109	.00470
2.62	6.83146	.83451	6.90426	.83912	.98946	.99540	1.0107	.00460
2.63	6.90085	.83890	6.97292	.84341	.98966	.99549	1.0104	.00451
2.64	6.97092	.84329	7.04228	.84771	.98987	.99558	1.0102	.00442
2.65	7.04169	.84768	7.11234	.85201	0.99007	.99566	1.0100	.00434
2.66	7.11317	.85206	7.18312	.85631	.99026	.99575	1.0098	.00425
2.67	7.18536	.85645	7.25461	.86061	.99045	.99583	1.0096	.00417
2.68	7.25827	.86083	7.32683	.86492	.99064	.99592	1.0094	.00408
2.69	7.33190	.86522	7.39978	.86922	.99083	.99600	1.0093	.00400
2.70	7.40626	.86960	7.47347	.87352	0.99101	.99608	1.0091	.00392
2.71	7.48137	.87398	7.54791	.87783	.99118	.99615	1.0089	.00385
2.72	7.55722	.87836	7.62310	.88213	.99136	.99623	1.0087	.00377
2.73	7.63383	.88274	7.69905	.88644	.99153	.99631	1.0085	.00369
2.74	7.71121	.88712	7.77578	.89074	.99170	.99638	1.0084	.00362
2.75	7.78935	.89150	7.85328	.89505	0.99186	.99645	1.0082	.00355
2.76	7.86828	.89588	7.93157	.89936	.99202	.99652	1.0080	.00348
2.77	7.94799	.90026	8.01065	.90367	.99218	.99659	1.0079	.00341
2.78	8.02849	.90463	8.09053	.90798	.99233	.99666	1.0077	.00334
2.79	8.10980	.90901	8.17122	.91229	.99248	.99672	1.0076	.00328
2.80	8.19192	.91339	8.25273	.91660	0.99263	.99679	1.0074	.00321
2.81	8.27486	.91776	8.33506	.92091	.99278	.99685	1.0073	.00315
2.82	8.35862	.92213	8.41823	.92522	.99292	.99691	1.0071	.00309
2.83	8.44322	.92651	8.50224	.92953	.99306	.99698	1.0070	.00302
2.84	8.52867	.93088	8.58710	.93385	.99320	.99704	1.0069	.00296
2.85	8.61497	.93525	8.67281	.93816	0.99333	.99709	1.0067	.00291
2.86	8.70213	.93963	8.75940	.94247	.99346	.99715	1.0066	.00285
2.87	8.79016	.94400	8.84686	.94679	.99359	.99721	1.0065	.00279
2.88	8.87907	.94837	8.93520	.95110	.99372	.99726	1.0063	.00274
2.89	8.96887	.95274	9.02444	.95542	.99384	.99732	1.0062	.00268
2.90	9.05956	.95711	9.11458	.95974	0.99396	.99737	1.0061	.00263
2.91	9.15116	.96148	9.20564	.96405	.99408	.99742	1.0060	.00258
2.92	9.24368	.96584	9.29761	.96837	.99420	.99747	1.0058	.00253
2.93	9.33712	.97021	9.39051	.97269	.99431	.99752	1.0057	.00248
2.94	9.43149	.97458	9.48436	.97701	.99443	.99757	1.0056	.00243
2.95	9.52681	.97895	9.57915	.98133	0.99454	.99762	1.0055	.00238
2.96	9.62308	.98331	9.67490	.98565	.99464	.99767	1.0054	.00233
2.97	9.72031	.98768	9.77161	.98997	.99475	.99771	1.0053	.00229
2.98	9.81851	.99205	9.86930	.99429	.99485	.99776	1.0052	.00224
2.99	9.91770	.99641	9.96798	.99861	.99496	.99780	1.0051	.00220

HYPERBOLIC FUNCTIONS AND THEIR COMMON LOGARITHMS (Continued)

x	Sinh x Value	Sinh x $\log_{10}$	Cosh x Value	Cosh x $\log_{10}$	Tanh x Value	Tanh x $\log_{10}$	Coth x Value	Coth x $\log_{10}$
3.0	10.0179	.00078	10.0677	.00293	0.99505	.99785	1.0050	.00215
3.1	11.0765	.04440	11.1215	.04616	.99595	.99824	1.0041	.00176
3.2	12.2459	.08799	12.2866	.08943	.99668	.99856	1.0033	.00144
3.3	13.5379	.13155	13.5748	.13273	.99728	.99882	1.0027	.00118
3.4	14.9654	.17509	14.9987	.17605	.99777	.99903	1.0022	.00097
3.5	16.5426	.21860	16.5728	.21940	0.99818	.99921	1.0018	.00079
3.6	18.2855	.26211	18.3128	.26275	.99851	.99935	1.0015	.00065
3.7	20.2113	.30559	20.2360	.30612	.99878	.99947	1.0012	.00053
3.8	22.3394	.34907	22.3618	.34951	.99900	.99957	1.0010	.00043
3.9	24.6911	.39254	24.7113	.39290	.99918	.99964	1.0008	.00036
4.0	27.2899	.43600	27.3082	.43629	0.99933	.99971	1.0007	.00029
4.1	30.1619	.47946	30.1784	.47970	.99945	.99976	1.0005	.00024
4.2	33.3357	.52291	33.3507	.52310	.99955	.99980	1.0004	.00020
4.3	36.8431	.56636	36.8567	.56652	.99963	.99984	1.0004	.00016
4.4	40.7193	.60980	40.7316	.60993	.99970	.99987	1.0003	.00013
4.5	45.0030	.65324	45.0141	.65335	0.99975	.99989	1.0002	.00011
4.6	49.7371	.69668	49.7472	.69677	.99980	.99991	1.0002	.00009
4.7	54.9690	.74012	54.9781	.74019	.99983	.99993	1.0002	.00007
4.8	60.7511	.78355	60.7593	.78361	.99986	.99994	1.0001	.00006
4.9	67.1412	.82699	67.1486	.82704	.99989	.99995	1.0001	.00005
5.0	74.2032	.87042	74.2099	.87046	0.99991	.99996	1.0001	.00004
5.1	82.008	.91386	82.014	.91389	.99993	.99997	1.0001	.00003
5.2	90.633	.95729	90.639	.95731	.99994	.99997	1.0001	.00003
5.3	100.17	.00072	100.17	.00074	.99995	.99998	1.0000	.00002
5.4	110.70	.04415	110.71	.04417	.99996	.99998	1.0000	.00002
5.5	122.34	.08758	122.35	.08760	0.99997	.99999	1.0000	.00001
5.6	135.21	.13101	135.22	.13103	.99997	.99999	1.0000	.00001
5.7	149.43	.17444	149.44	.17445	.99998	.99999	1.0000	.00001
5.8	165.15	.21787	165.15	.21788	.99998	.99999	1.0000	.00001
5.9	182.52	.26130	182.52	.26131	.99998	.99999	1.0000	.00001
6.0	201.71	.30473	201.72	.30474	0.99999	.00000	1.0000	.00000
6.1	222.93	.34817	222.93	.34817	.99999	.00000	1.0000	.00000
6.2	246.37	.39159	246.38	.39161	.99999	.00000	1.0000	.00000
6.3	272.29	.43503	272.29	.43503	.99999	.00000	1.0000	.00000
6.4	300.92	.47845	300.92	.47845	.99999	.00000	1.0000	.00000
6.5	332.57	.52188	332.57	.52188	1.0000	.00000	1.0000	.00000
6.6	367.55	.56532	367.55	.56532	1.0000	.00000	1.0000	.00000
6.7	406.20	.60874	406.20	.60874	1.0000	.00000	1.0000	.00000
6.8	448.92	.65217	448.92	.65217	1.0000	.00000	1.0000	.00000
6.9	496.14	.69560	496.14	.69560	1.0000	.00000	1.0000	.00000
7.0	548.32	.73903	548.32	.73903	1.0000	.00000	1.0000	.00000
7.1	605.98	.78246	605.98	.78246	1.0000	.00000	1.0000	.00000
7.2	669.72	.82589	669.72	.82589	1.0000	.00000	1.0000	.00000
7.3	740.15	.86932	740.15	.86932	1.0000	.00000	1.0000	.00000
7.4	817.99	.91275	817.99	.91275	1.0000	.00000	1.0000	.00000
7.5	904.02	.95618	904.02	.95618	1.0000	.00000	1.0000	.00000
7.6	999.10	.99961	999.10	.99961	1.0000	.00000	1.0000	.00000
7.7	1104.2	.04305	1104.2	.04305	1.0000	.00000	1.0000	.00000
7.8	1220.3	.08647	1220.3	.08647	1.0000	.00000	1.0000	.00000
7.9	1348.6	.12988	1348.6	.12988	1.0000	.00000	1.0000	.00000

HYPERBOLIC FUNCTIONS AND THEIR COMMON LOGARITHMS (Continued)

x	Sinh x		Cosh x		Tanh x		Coth x	
	Value	$\log_{10}$	Value	$\log_{10}$	Value	$\log_{10}$	Value	$\log_{10}$
8.0	1490.5	.17333	1490.5	.17333	1.0000	.00000	1.0000	.00000
8.1	1647.2	.21675	1647.2	.21675	1.0000	.00000	1.0000	.00000
8.2	1820.5	.26019	1820.5	.26019	1.0000	.00000	1.0000	.00000
8.3	2011.9	.30360	2011.9	.30360	1.0000	.00000	1.0000	.00000
8.4	2223.5	.34704	2223.5	.34704	1.0000	.00000	1.0000	.00000
8.5	2457.4	.39048	2457.4	.39048	1.0000	.00000	1.0000	.00000
8.6	2715.8	.43390	2715.8	.43390	1.0000	.00000	1.0000	.00000
8.7	3001.5	.47734	3001.5	.47734	1.0000	.00000	1.0000	.00000
8.8	3317.1	.52076	3317.1	.52076	1.0000	.00000	1.0000	.00000
8.9	3666.0	.56419	3666.0	.56419	1.0000	.00000	1.0000	.00000
9.0	4051.5	.60762	4051.5	.60762	1.0000	.00000	1.0000	.00000
9.1	4477.6	.65105	4477.6	.65105	1.0000	.00000	1.0000	.00000
9.2	4948.6	.69448	4948.6	.69448	1.0000	.00000	1.0000	.00000
9.3	5469.0	.73791	5469.0	.73791	1.0000	.00000	1.0000	.00000
9.4	6044.2	.78134	6044.2	.78134	1.0000	.00000	1.0000	.00000
9.5	6679.9	.82477	6679.9	.82477	1.0000	.00000	1.0000	.00000
9.6	7382.4	.86820	7382.4	.86820	1.0000	.00000	1.0000	.00000
9.7	8158.8	.91163	8158.8	.91163	1.0000	.00000	1.0000	.00000
9.8	9016.9	.95506	9016.9	.95506	1.0000	.00000	1.0000	.00000
9.9	9965.2	.99849	9965.2	.99849	1.0000	.00000	1.0000	.00000
10.0	11013.2	.04191	11013.2	.04191	1.0000	.00000	1.0000	.00000

EXPONENTIAL AND HYPERBOLIC FUNCTIONS FOR πx

x	$e^{\pi x}$	$e^{-\pi x}$	$\sinh \pi x$	$\cosh \pi x$	$\tanh \pi x$
0.00	1.00000	1.00000	0.00000	1.00000	0.00000
0.01	1.03191	0.96907	0.03142	1.00049	0.03141
0.02	1.06485	0.93910	0.06287	1.00197	0.06275
0.03	1.09883	0.91006	0.09439	1.00444	0.09397
0.04	1.13390	0.88191	0.12599	1.00791	0.12501
0.05	1.17009	0.85464	0.15773	1.01236	0.15580
0.06	1.20743	0.82820	0.18961	1.01782	0.18629
0.07	1.24597	0.80259	0.22169	1.02428	0.21643
0.08	1.28573	0.77777	0.25398	1.03175	0.24617
0.09	1.32676	0.75371	0.28653	1.04024	0.27544
0.10	1.36911	0.73040	0.31935	1.04976	0.30422
0.11	1.41280	0.70781	0.35249	1.06031	0.33245
0.12	1.45789	0.68592	0.38598	1.07191	0.36009
0.13	1.50442	0.66471	0.41986	1.08456	0.38712
0.14	1.55243	0.64415	0.45414	1.09829	0.41350
0.15	1.60198	0.62423	0.48887	1.11310	0.43920
0.16	1.65310	0.60492	0.52409	1.12901	0.46420
0.17	1.70586	0.58621	0.55982	1.14604	0.48849
0.18	1.76030	0.56808	0.59611	1.16419	0.51204
0.19	1.81648	0.55051	0.63298	1.18350	0.53484
0.20	1.87446	0.53349	0.67048	1.20397	0.55689
0.21	1.93428	0.51699	0.70865	1.22563	0.57819
0.22	1.99601	0.50100	0.74751	1.24850	0.59872
0.23	2.05971	0.48550	0.78710	1.27261	0.61850
0.24	2.12545	0.47049	0.82748	1.29797	0.63752
0.25	2.19328	0.45594	0.86867	1.32461	0.65579
0.26	2.26328	0.44184	0.91072	1.35256	0.67333
0.27	2.33551	0.42817	0.95367	1.38184	0.69014
0.28	2.41005	0.41493	0.99756	1.41249	0.70624
0.29	2.48696	0.40210	1.04243	1.44453	0.72164
0.30	2.56633	0.38966	1.08834	1.47800	0.73636
0.31	2.64824	0.37761	1.13531	1.51292	0.75041
0.32	2.73275	0.36593	1.18341	1.54934	0.76382
0.33	2.81997	0.35461	1.23268	1.58729	0.77659
0.34	2.90997	0.34365	1.28316	1.62681	0.78876
0.35	3.00284	0.33302	1.33491	1.66793	0.80034
0.36	3.09867	0.32272	1.38798	1.71070	0.81135
0.37	3.19756	0.31274	1.44241	1.75515	0.82182
0.38	3.29961	0.30307	1.49827	1.80134	0.83176
0.39	3.40492	0.29369	1.55561	1.84931	0.84119
0.40	3.51359	0.28461	1.61449	1.89910	0.85013
0.41	3.62572	0.27581	1.67496	1.95076	0.85862
0.42	3.74143	0.26728	1.73708	2.00436	0.86665
0.43	3.86084	0.25901	1.80091	2.05993	0.87426
0.44	3.98406	0.25100	1.86653	2.11753	0.88147
0.45	4.11121	0.24324	1.93398	2.17722	0.88828
0.46	4.24241	0.23571	2.00335	2.23906	0.89473
0.47	4.37781	0.22842	2.07469	2.30312	0.90082
0.48	4.51753	0.22136	2.14808	2.36944	0.90658
0.49	4.66170	0.21451	2.22359	2.43811	0.91202
0.50	4.81048	0.20788	2.30130	2.50918	0.91715
0.51	4.96400	0.20145	2.38128	2.58273	0.92200
0.52	5.12243	0.19522	2.46360	2.65882	0.92658
0.53	5.28591	0.18918	2.54836	2.73754	0.93089
0.54	5.45460	0.18333	2.63564	2.81897	0.93497

EXPONENTIAL, HYPERBOLIC FUNCTIONS FOR πx (Continued)

x	$e^{\pi x}$	$e^{-\pi x}$	πx	$\cosh \pi x$	$\tanh \pi x$
0.55	5.62869	0.17766	2.72551	2.90317	0.93880
0.56	5.80832	0.17217	2.81808	2.99024	0.94242
0.57	5.99369	0.16684	2.91343	3.08027	0.94584
0.58	6.18498	0.16168	3.01165	3.17333	0.94905
0.59	6.38237	0.15668	3.11284	3.26953	0.95208
0.60	6.58606	0.15184	3.21711	3.36895	0.95493
0.61	6.79625	0.14714	3.32456	3.47170	0.95762
0.62	7.01315	0.14259	3.43528	3.57787	0.96015
0.63	7.23698	0.13818	3.54940	3.68758	0.96253
0.64	7.46794	0.13391	3.66702	3.80092	0.96477
0.65	7.70628	0.12976	3.78826	3.91802	0.96688
0.66	7.95222	0.12575	3.91323	4.03899	0.96887
0.67	8.20601	0.12186	4.04208	4.16394	0.97073
0.68	8.46790	0.11809	4.17491	4.29300	0.97249
0.69	8.73815	0.11444	4.31186	4.42630	0.97415
0.70	9.01703	0.11090	4.45306	4.56396	0.97570
0.71	9.30480	0.10747	4.59867	4.70614	0.97716
0.72	9.60176	0.10415	4.74881	4.85296	0.97854
0.73	9.90820	0.10093	4.90364	5.00456	0.97983
0.74	10.22442	0.09781	5.06331	5.16111	0.98105
0.75	10.55072	0.09478	5.22797	5.32275	0.98219
0.76	10.88745	0.09185	5.39780	5.48965	0.98327
0.77	11.23492	0.08901	5.57295	5.66196	0.98428
0.78	11.59347	0.08626	5.75361	5.83986	0.98523
0.79	11.96347	0.08359	5.93994	6.02353	0.98612
0.80	12.34528	0.08100	6.13214	6.21314	0.98696
0.81	12.73928	0.07850	6.33039	6.40889	0.98775
0.82	13.14585	0.07607	6.53489	6.61096	0.98849
0.83	13.56539	0.07372	6.74584	6.81955	0.98919
0.84	13.99833	0.07144	6.96344	7.03488	0.98985
0.85	14.44508	0.06923	7.18793	7.25715	0.99046
0.86	14.90609	0.06709	7.41950	7.48659	0.99104
0.87	15.38181	0.06501	7.65840	7.72341	0.99158
0.88	15.87271	0.06300	7.90486	7.96786	0.99209
0.89	16.37929	0.06105	8.15912	8.22017	0.99257
0.90	16.90202	0.05916	8.41243	8.48059	0.99302
0.91	17.44145	0.05733	8.69206	8.74939	0.99345
0.92	17.99808	0.05556	8.97126	9.02682	0.99384
0.93	18.57248	0.05384	9.25932	9.31316	0.99422
0.94	19.16522	0.05218	9.55652	9.60870	0.99457
0.95	19.77687	0.05056	9.86315	9.91372	0.99490
0.96	20.40804	0.04900	10.17952	10.22852	0.99521
0.97	21.05935	0.04748	10.50594	10.55342	0.99550
0.98	21.73146	0.04602	10.84272	10.88874	0.99577
0.99	22.42501	0.04459	11.19021	11.23480	0.99603
1.00	23.14069	0.04321	11.54874	11.59195	0.99627

INVERSE HYPERBOLIC FUNCTIONS

x	$\sinh^{-1} x$	$\tanh^{-1} x$	$\operatorname{cosech}^{-1} x$	$\operatorname{sech}^{-1} x$
0.0	0.00000	0.00000	∞	∞
0.01	0.01000	0.01000	5.29834	5.29829
0.02	0.02000	0.02000	4.60527	4.60507
0.03	0.03000	0.03001	4.19993	4.19948
0.04	0.03999	0.04002	3.91242	3.91162
0.05	0.04998	0.05004	3.68950	3.68825
0.06	0.05996	0.06007	3.50746	3.50566
0.07	0.06994	0.07011	3.35363	3.35118
0.08	0.07991	0.08017	3.22047	3.21727
0.09	0.08988	0.09024	3.10311	3.09906
0.10	0.09983	0.10034	2.99822	2.99322
0.11	0.10978	0.11045	2.90343	2.89738
0.12	0.11971	0.12058	2.81699	2.80979
0.13	0.12964	0.13074	2.73757	2.72912
0.14	0.13955	0.14093	2.66412	2.65432
0.15	0.14944	0.15114	2.59585	2.58459
0.16	0.15933	0.16139	2.53207	2.51927
0.17	0.16919	0.17167	2.47225	2.45780
0.18	0.17904	0.18198	2.41595	2.39975
0.19	0.18888	0.19234	2.36278	2.34473
0.20	0.19869	0.20273	2.31244	2.29243
0.21	0.20849	0.21317	2.26464	2.24258
0.22	0.21826	0.22366	2.21916	2.19495
0.23	0.22802	0.23419	2.17579	2.14933
0.24	0.23775	0.24477	2.13436	2.10554
0.25	0.24747	0.25541	2.09471	2.06344
0.26	0.25716	0.26611	2.05671	2.02288
0.27	0.26682	0.27686	2.02023	1.98374
0.28	0.27646	0.28768	1.98516	1.94591
0.29	0.28608	0.29857	1.95141	1.90930
0.30	0.29567	0.30952	1.91890	1.87382
0.31	0.30524	0.32055	1.88753	1.83939
0.32	0.31478	0.33165	1.85725	1.80594
0.33	0.32429	0.34283	1.82799	1.77340
0.34	0.33377	0.35409	1.79968	1.74172
0.35	0.34322	0.36544	1.77228	1.71083
0.36	0.35265	0.37689	1.74573	1.68070
0.37	0.36204	0.38842	1.71999	1.65127
0.38	0.37140	0.40006	1.69502	1.62250
0.39	0.38073	0.41180	1.67078	1.59436
0.40	0.39004	0.42365	1.64723	1.56680
0.41	0.39930	0.43561	1.62434	1.53979
0.42	0.40854	0.44769	1.60209	1.51331
0.43	0.41774	0.45990	1.58043	1.48731
0.44	0.42691	0.47223	1.55935	1.46178
0.45	0.43605	0.48470	1.53882	1.43669
0.46	0.44515	0.49731	1.51881	1.41200
0.47	0.45422	0.51007	1.49931	1.38771
0.48	0.46325	0.52298	1.48029	1.36379
0.49	0.47225	0.53606	1.46174	1.34021
0.50	0.48121	0.54931	1.44364	1.31696

INVERSE HYPERBOLIC FUNCTIONS (Continued)

x	$\sinh^{-1} x$	$\tanh^{-1} x$	$\text{cosech}^{-1} x$	$\text{sech}^{-1} x$
0.50	0.48121	0.54931	1.44364	1.31696
0.51	0.49014	0.56273	1.42596	1.29401
0.52	0.49903	0.57634	1.40870	1.27136
0.53	0.50788	0.59015	1.39183	1.24898
0.54	0.51670	0.60416	1.37535	1.22686
0.55	0.52548	0.61838	1.35924	1.20497
0.56	0.53422	0.63283	1.34348	1.18331
0.57	0.54293	0.64752	1.32807	1.16186
0.58	0.55160	0.66246	1.31299	1.14060
0.59	0.56023	0.67767	1.29824	1.11952
0.60	0.56882	0.69315	1.28380	1.09861
0.61	0.57738	0.70892	1.26965	1.07785
0.62	0.58590	0.72501	1.25580	1.05723
0.63	0.59438	0.74142	1.24223	1.03673
0.64	0.60282	0.75817	1.22894	1.01635
0.65	0.61122	0.77530	1.21591	0.99606
0.66	0.61959	0.79281	1.20314	0.97585
0.67	0.62792	0.81074	1.19062	0.95572
0.68	0.63620	0.82911	1.17834	0.93564
0.69	0.64446	0.84796	1.16629	0.91560
0.70	0.65267	0.86730	1.15448	0.89559
0.71	0.66084	0.88718	1.14288	0.87559
0.72	0.66897	0.90764	1.13151	0.85558
0.73	0.67707	0.92873	1.12034	0.83555
0.74	0.68513	0.95048	1.10938	0.81549
0.75	0.69315	0.97296	1.09861	0.79537
0.76	0.70113	0.99622	1.08804	0.77517
0.77	0.70907	1.02033	1.07766	0.75487
0.78	0.71697	1.04537	1.06746	0.73445
0.79	0.72484	1.07143	1.05744	0.71388
0.80	0.73267	1.09861	1.04759	0.69315
0.81	0.74046	1.12703	1.03792	0.67221
0.82	0.74821	1.15682	1.02840	0.65103
0.83	0.75592	1.18814	1.01905	0.62958
0.84	0.76360	1.22117	1.00986	0.60781
0.85	0.77124	1.25615	1.00082	0.58568
0.86	0.77884	1.29334	0.99193	0.56313
0.87	0.78640	1.33308	0.98319	0.54008
0.88	0.79393	1.37577	0.97459	0.51647
0.89	0.80142	1.42193	0.96613	0.49220
0.90	0.80887	1.47222	0.95780	0.46715
0.91	0.81628	1.52752	0.94961	0.44116
0.92	0.82366	1.58903	0.94154	0.41406
0.93	0.83100	1.65839	0.93361	0.38560
0.94	0.83830	1.73805	0.92580	0.35542
0.95	0.84557	1.83178	0.91810	0.32304
0.96	0.85280	1.94591	0.91053	0.28768
0.97	0.86000	2.09230	0.90307	0.24807
0.98	0.86716	2.29756	0.89573	0.20169
0.99	0.87428	2.64665	0.88850	0.14201
1.00	0.88137	∞	0.88137	0.00000

INVERSE HYPERBOLIC FUNCTIONS (Continued)

x	$\sinh^{-1} x$	$\cosh^{-1} x$	$\operatorname{cosech}^{-1} x$	$\coth^{-1} x$
1.00	0.88137	0.00000	0.88137	∞
1.01	0.88843	0.14130	0.87436	2.65165
1.02	0.89545	0.19967	0.86744	2.30756
1.03	0.90243	0.24434	0.86063	2.10730
1.04	0.90938	0.28191	0.85391	1.96591
1.05	0.91629	0.31492	0.84730	1.85679
1.06	0.92317	0.34470	0.84078	1.76806
1.07	0.93002	0.37202	0.83435	1.69340
1.08	0.93683	0.39738	0.82801	1.62905
1.09	0.94360	0.42114	0.82177	1.57255
1.10	0.95035	0.44357	0.81561	1.52226
1.11	0.95706	0.46485	0.80954	1.47698
1.12	0.96373	0.48513	0.80355	1.43584
1.13	0.97038	0.50453	0.79764	1.39817
1.14	0.97699	0.52316	0.79182	1.36346
1.15	0.98357	0.54110	0.78607	1.33129
1.16	0.99011	0.55840	0.78041	1.30134
1.17	0.99663	0.57514	0.77482	1.27334
1.18	1.00311	0.59135	0.76930	1.24706
1.19	1.00956	0.60708	0.76386	1.22232
1.20	1.01597	0.62236	0.75849	1.19895
1.21	1.02236	0.63724	0.75319	1.17682
1.22	1.02871	0.65173	0.74796	1.15582
1.23	1.03504	0.66586	0.74279	1.13584
1.24	1.04133	0.67966	0.73770	1.11680
1.25	1.04759	0.69315	0.73267	1.09861
1.26	1.05382	0.70634	0.72770	1.08122
1.27	1.06003	0.71924	0.72280	1.06456
1.28	1.06620	0.73189	0.71796	1.04857
1.29	1.07234	0.74428	0.71318	1.03321
1.30	1.07845	0.75643	0.70846	1.01844
1.31	1.08453	0.76836	0.70380	1.00422
1.32	1.09059	0.78007	0.69920	0.99050
1.33	1.09661	0.79157	0.69465	0.97727
1.34	1.10261	0.80288	0.69016	0.96448
1.35	1.10857	0.81400	0.68572	0.95212
1.36	1.11451	0.82494	0.68134	0.94016
1.37	1.12042	0.83570	0.67701	0.92857
1.38	1.12630	0.84630	0.67273	0.91734
1.39	1.13216	0.85673	0.66851	0.90645
1.40	1.13798	0.86701	0.66433	0.89588
1.41	1.14378	0.87715	0.66020	0.88561
1.42	1.14955	0.88714	0.65612	0.87563
1.43	1.15530	0.89699	0.65209	0.86593
1.44	1.16101	0.90670	0.64811	0.85649
1.45	1.16670	0.91629	0.64417	0.84730
1.46	1.17237	0.92575	0.64028	0.83835
1.47	1.17801	0.93509	0.63643	0.82962
1.48	1.18362	0.94432	0.63263	0.82111
1.49	1.18920	0.95343	0.62886	0.81282
1.50	1.19476	0.96242	0.62515	0.80472

INVERSE HYPERBOLIC FUNCTIONS (Continued)

x	$\sinh^{-1} x$	$\cosh^{-1} x$	$\operatorname{cosech}^{-1} x$	$\coth^{-1} x$
1.50	1.19476	0.96242	0.62515	0.80472
1.51	1.20030	0.97131	0.62147	0.79681
1.52	1.20581	0.98010	0.61783	0.78909
1.53	1.21129	0.98879	0.61424	0.78155
1.54	1.21675	0.99737	0.61068	0.77418
1.55	1.22218	1.00587	0.60716	0.76697
1.56	1.22759	1.01426	0.60368	0.75991
1.57	1.23298	1.02257	0.60024	0.75301
1.58	1.23834	1.03079	0.59684	0.74626
1.59	1.24367	1.03892	0.59347	0.73965
1.60	1.24898	1.04697	0.59014	0.73317
1.61	1.25427	1.05493	0.58685	0.72682
1.62	1.25954	1.06282	0.58359	0.72061
1.63	1.26478	1.07063	0.58036	0.71451
1.64	1.26999	1.07836	0.57717	0.70853
1.65	1.27519	1.08601	0.57401	0.70267
1.66	1.28036	1.09360	0.57089	0.69692
1.67	1.28551	1.10111	0.56780	0.69128
1.68	1.29064	1.10855	0.56474	0.68574
1.69	1.29574	1.11592	0.56171	0.68030
1.70	1.30082	1.12323	0.55871	0.67496
1.71	1.30588	1.13047	0.55574	0.66972
1.72	1.31092	1.13765	0.55281	0.66457
1.73	1.31593	1.14476	0.54990	0.65951
1.74	1.32093	1.15182	0.54702	0.65453
1.75	1.32590	1.15881	0.54417	0.64964
1.76	1.33085	1.16574	0.54135	0.64483
1.77	1.33578	1.17262	0.53856	0.64011
1.78	1.34069	1.17944	0.53579	0.63546
1.79	1.34557	1.18620	0.53305	0.63088
1.80	1.35044	1.19291	0.53034	0.62638
1.81	1.35529	1.19957	0.52766	0.62195
1.82	1.36011	1.20617	0.52500	0.61759
1.83	1.36492	1.21272	0.52237	0.61330
1.84	1.36970	1.21922	0.51976	0.60908
1.85	1.37447	1.22567	0.51718	0.60492
1.86	1.37921	1.23207	0.51462	0.60082
1.87	1.38394	1.23842	0.51208	0.59679
1.88	1.38864	1.24473	0.50957	0.59281
1.89	1.39333	1.25098	0.50709	0.58890
1.90	1.39800	1.25720	0.50462	0.58504
1.91	1.40265	1.26336	0.50218	0.58123
1.92	1.40728	1.26949	0.49977	0.57748
1.93	1.41188	1.27557	0.49737	0.57379
1.94	1.41648	1.28160	0.49500	0.57014
1.95	1.42105	1.28760	0.49265	0.56655
1.96	1.42560	1.29355	0.49032	0.56301
1.97	1.43014	1.29946	0.48801	0.55951
1.98	1.43466	1.30533	0.48572	0.55606
1.99	1.43915	1.31117	0.48346	0.55266
2.00	1.44364	1.31696	0.48121	0.54931

INVERSE HYPERBOLIC FUNCTIONS (Continued)

x	$\sinh^{-1} x$	$\cosh^{-1} x$	$\operatorname{cosech}^{-1} x$	$\coth^{-1} x$
2.00	1.44364	1.31696	0.48121	0.54931
2.10	1.48748	1.37286	0.45982	0.51805
2.20	1.52966	1.42542	0.44019	0.49041
2.30	1.57028	1.47504	0.42213	0.46578
2.40	1.60944	1.52208	0.40547	0.44365
2.50	1.64723	1.56680	0.39004	0.42365
2.60	1.68374	1.60944	0.37571	0.40547
2.70	1.71905	1.65019	0.36239	0.38885
2.80	1.75323	1.68924	0.34996	0.37361
2.90	1.78634	1.72671	0.33834	0.35956
3.00	1.81845	1.76275	0.32745	0.34657
3.10	1.84960	1.79746	0.31723	0.33452
3.20	1.87986	1.83094	0.30763	0.32331
3.30	1.90927	1.86328	0.29857	0.31285
3.40	1.93788	1.89456	0.29003	0.30307
3.50	1.96572	1.92485	0.28196	0.29389
3.60	1.99284	1.95421	0.27432	0.28527
3.70	2.01926	1.98270	0.26708	0.27716
3.80	2.04503	2.01037	0.26021	0.26950
3.90	2.07017	2.03727	0.25368	0.26226
4.00	2.09471	2.06344	0.24747	0.25541
4.10	2.11869	2.08892	0.24155	0.24892
4.20	2.14211	2.11375	0.23590	0.24275
4.30	2.16502	2.13796	0.23051	0.23689
4.40	2.18742	2.16158	0.22536	0.23131
4.50	2.20935	2.18464	0.22043	0.22599
4.60	2.23081	2.20717	0.21571	0.22092
4.70	2.25184	2.22920	0.21119	0.21607
4.80	2.27244	2.25073	0.20685	0.21143
4.90	2.29264	2.27180	0.20269	0.20699
5.00	2.31244	2.29243	0.19869	0.20273
5.10	2.33186	2.31263	0.19484	0.19865
5.20	2.35093	2.33243	0.19114	0.19473
5.30	2.36964	2.35183	0.18758	0.19097
5.40	2.38801	2.37086	0.18414	0.18735
5.50	2.40606	2.38953	0.18083	0.18386
5.60	2.42379	2.40784	0.17764	0.18051
5.70	2.44122	2.42583	0.17455	0.17727
5.80	2.45836	2.44349	0.17157	0.17415
5.90	2.47521	2.46084	0.16869	0.17114
6.00	2.49178	2.47789	0.16590	0.16824
6.10	2.50809	2.49465	0.16321	0.16543
6.20	2.52414	2.51113	0.16060	0.16271
6.30	2.53994	2.52734	0.15807	0.16008
6.40	2.55549	2.54329	0.15562	0.15754
6.50	2.57081	2.55898	0.15325	0.15508
6.60	2.58591	2.57443	0.15094	0.15269
6.70	2.60078	2.58964	0.14871	0.15038
6.80	2.61543	2.60462	0.14653	0.14813
6.90	2.62988	2.61938	0.14442	0.14596
7.00	2.64412	2.63392	0.14238	0.14384

GUDERMANNIAN FUNCTION

x	0	1	2	3	4	5	6	7	8	9
0.0	0.00000	0.01000	0.02000	0.03000	0.03999	0.04998	0.05996	0.06994	0.07991	0.08988
0.1	0.09983	0.10978	0.11971	0.12964	0.13954	0.14944	0.15932	0.16919	0.17904	0.18887
0.2	0.19868	0.20847	0.21825	0.22800	0.23773	0.24744	0.25712	0.26678	0.27641	0.28602
0.3	0.29560	0.30515	0.31467	0.32417	0.33363	0.34307	0.35247	0.36184	0.37117	0.38047
0.4	0.38974	0.39897	0.40817	0.41733	0.42645	0.43554	0.44459	0.45359	0.46256	0.47149
0.5	0.48038	0.48923	0.49803	0.50680	0.51552	0.52420	0.53284	0.54143	0.54997	0.55848
0.6	0.56694	0.57535	0.58372	0.59204	0.60031	0.60854	0.61672	0.62486	0.63294	0.64098
0.7	0.64897	0.65692	0.66481	0.67266	0.68045	0.68820	0.69590	0.70355	0.71115	0.71870
0.8	0.72620	0.73366	0.74106	0.74841	0.75571	0.76297	0.77017	0.77732	0.78443	0.79148
0.9	0.79848	0.80544	0.81234	0.81919	0.82599	0.83275	0.83945	0.84611	0.85271	0.85926
1.0	0.86577	0.87223	0.87863	0.88499	0.89130	0.89756	0.90377	0.90993	0.91604	0.92211
1.1	0.92813	0.93410	0.94002	0.94589	0.95172	0.95750	0.96323	0.96892	0.97455	0.98015
1.2	0.98569	0.99119	0.99665	1.00205	1.00742	1.01274	1.01801	1.02324	1.02842	1.03356
1.3	1.03866	1.04371	1.04872	1.05368	1.05860	1.06348	1.06832	1.07312	1.07787	1.08258
1.4	1.08725	1.09188	1.09647	1.10101	1.10552	1.10999	1.11441	1.11880	1.12315	1.12746
1.5	1.13173	1.13596	1.14015	1.14431	1.14843	1.15251	1.15655	1.16056	1.16453	1.16846
1.6	1.17236	1.17622	1.18005	1.18384	1.18760	1.19132	1.19500	1.19866	1.20228	1.20586
1.7	1.20941	1.21293	1.21642	1.21987	1.22330	1.22668	1.23004	1.23337	1.23666	1.23993
1.8	1.24316	1.24636	1.24954	1.25268	1.25579	1.25888	1.26193	1.26496	1.26795	1.27092
1.9	1.27386	1.27677	1.27966	1.28251	1.28534	1.28815	1.29092	1.29367	1.29639	1.29909
2.0	1.30176	1.30441	1.30703	1.30962	1.31219	1.31473	1.31726	1.31975	1.32222	1.32467
2.1	1.32710	1.32950	1.33188	1.33423	1.33656	1.33887	1.34116	1.34343	1.34567	1.34789
2.2	1.35009	1.35227	1.35443	1.35656	1.35868	1.36077	1.36285	1.36490	1.36694	1.36895
2.3	1.37095	1.37292	1.37488	1.37682	1.37873	1.38063	1.38251	1.38438	1.38622	1.38805
2.4	1.38986	1.39165	1.39342	1.39518	1.39691	1.39864	1.40034	1.40203	1.40370	1.40535
2.5	1.40699	1.40862	1.41022	1.41181	1.41339	1.41495	1.41649	1.41802	1.41954	1.42104
2.6	1.42252	1.42399	1.42545	1.42689	1.42832	1.42973	1.43113	1.43251	1.43388	1.43524
2.7	1.43659	1.43792	1.43924	1.44054	1.44183	1.44311	1.44438	1.44564	1.44688	1.44811
2.8	1.44933	1.45053	1.45173	1.45291	1.45408	1.45524	1.45638	1.45752	1.45864	1.45976
2.9	1.46086	1.46195	1.46303	1.46410	1.46516	1.46621	1.46725	1.46828	1.46930	1.47031
3.0	1.47130	1.47229	1.47327	1.47424	1.47520	1.47615	1.47709	1.47802	1.47894	1.47986
3.1	1.48076	1.48165	1.48254	1.48342	1.48428	1.48514	1.48600	1.48684	1.48767	1.48850
3.2	1.48932	1.49013	1.49093	1.49172	1.49251	1.49329	1.49406	1.49482	1.49558	1.49632
3.3	1.49706	1.49780	1.49852	1.49924	1.49995	1.50066	1.50135	1.50204	1.50273	1.50340
3.4	1.50407	1.50474	1.50539	1.50605	1.50669	1.50733	1.50796	1.50858	1.50920	1.50981
3.5	1.51042	1.51102	1.51161	1.51220	1.51279	1.51336	1.51393	1.51450	1.51506	1.51561
3.6	1.51616	1.51671	1.51724	1.51778	1.51830	1.51883	1.51934	1.51985	1.52036	1.52086
3.7	1.52136	1.52185	1.52234	1.52282	1.52330	1.52377	1.52424	1.52470	1.52516	1.52561
3.8	1.52606	1.52651	1.52695	1.52738	1.52782	1.52824	1.52867	1.52909	1.52950	1.52991
3.9	1.53032	1.53072	1.53112	1.53151	1.53190	1.53229	1.53267	1.53305	1.53343	1.53380
4.0	1.53417	1.53453	1.53489	1.53525	1.53561	1.53596	1.53630	1.53664	1.53698	1.53732
4.1	1.53765	1.53798	1.53831	1.53863	1.53895	1.53927	1.53958	1.53989	1.54020	1.54051
4.2	1.54081	1.54111	1.54140	1.54169	1.54198	1.54227	1.54255	1.54283	1.54311	1.54339
4.3	1.54366	1.54393	1.54420	1.54446	1.54472	1.54498	1.54524	1.54550	1.54575	1.54600
4.4	1.54624	1.54649	1.54673	1.54697	1.54721	1.54744	1.54767	1.54790	1.54813	1.54836
4.5	1.54858	1.54880	1.54902	1.54924	1.54945	1.54966	1.54987	1.55008	1.55029	1.55049
4.6	1.55069	1.55089	1.55109	1.55129	1.55148	1.55167	1.55186	1.55205	1.55224	1.55242
4.7	1.55261	1.55279	1.55297	1.55314	1.55332	1.55349	1.55367	1.55384	1.55400	1.55417
4.8	1.55434	1.55450	1.55466	1.55482	1.55498	1.55514	1.55530	1.55545	1.55560	1.55575
4.9	1.55590	1.55605	1.55620	1.55634	1.55649	1.55663	1.55677	1.55691	1.55705	1.55719

GUDERMANNIAN FUNCTION (Continued)

x	0	1	2	3	4	5	6	7	8	9
5.0	1.55732	1.55745	1.55759	1.55772	1.55785	1.55798	1.55811	1.55823	1.55836	1.55848
5.1	1.55860	1.55872	1.55884	1.55896	1.55908	1.55920	1.55931	1.55943	1.55954	1.55965
5.2	1.55976	1.55987	1.55998	1.56009	1.56020	1.56030	1.56041	1.56051	1.56061	1.56071
5.3	1.56081	1.56091	1.56101	1.56111	1.56120	1.56130	1.56139	1.56149	1.56158	1.56167
5.4	1.56176	1.56185	1.56194	1.56203	1.56212	1.56220	1.56229	1.56237	1.56246	1.56254
5.5	1.56262	1.56270	1.56278	1.56286	1.56294	1.56302	1.56310	1.56318	1.56325	1.56333
5.6	1.56340	1.56347	1.56355	1.56362	1.56369	1.56376	1.56383	1.56390	1.56397	1.56404
5.7	1.56410	1.56417	1.56424	1.56430	1.56437	1.56443	1.56449	1.56456	1.56462	1.56468
5.8	1.56474	1.56480	1.56486	1.56492	1.56498	1.56504	1.56509	1.56515	1.56521	1.56526
5.9	1.56532	1.56537	1.56543	1.56548	1.56553	1.56558	1.56564	1.56569	1.56574	1.56579
6.0	1.56584	1.56589	1.56594	1.56599	1.56603	1.56608	1.56613	1.56617	1.56622	1.56627
6.1	1.56631	1.56636	1.56640	1.56644	1.56649	1.56653	1.56657	1.56661	1.56666	1.56670
6.2	1.56674	1.56678	1.56682	1.56686	1.56690	1.56694	1.56697	1.56701	1.56705	1.56709
6.3	1.56712	1.56716	1.56720	1.56723	1.56727	1.56730	1.56734	1.56737	1.56741	1.56744
6.4	1.56747	1.56751	1.56754	1.56757	1.56760	1.56764	1.56767	1.56770	1.56773	1.56776
6.5	1.56779	1.56782	1.56785	1.56788	1.56791	1.56794	1.56796	1.56799	1.56802	1.56805
6.6	1.56808	1.56810	1.56813	1.56816	1.56818	1.56821	1.56823	1.56826	1.56828	1.56831
6.7	1.56833	1.56836	1.56838	1.56841	1.56843	1.56845	1.56848	1.56850	1.56852	1.56855
6.8	1.56857	1.56859	1.56861	1.56863	1.56866	1.56868	1.56870	1.56872	1.56874	1.56876
6.9	1.56878	1.56880	1.56882	1.56884	1.56886	1.56888	1.56890	1.56892	1.56894	1.56895
7.0	1.56897	1.56899	1.56901	1.56903	1.56904	1.56906	1.56908	1.56910	1.56911	1.56913
7.1	1.56915	1.56916	1.56918	1.56919	1.56921	1.56923	1.56924	1.56926	1.56927	1.56929
7.2	1.56930	1.56932	1.56933	1.56935	1.56936	1.56938	1.56939	1.56940	1.56942	1.56943
7.3	1.56945	1.56946	1.56947	1.56949	1.56950	1.56951	1.56952	1.56954	1.56955	1.56956
7.4	1.56957	1.56959	1.56960	1.56961	1.56962	1.56963	1.56965	1.56966	1.56967	1.56968
7.5	1.56969	1.56970	1.56971	1.56972	1.56973	1.56974	1.56975	1.56976	1.56978	1.56979
7.6	1.56980	1.56981	1.56982	1.56983	1.56983	1.56984	1.56985	1.56986	1.56987	1.56988
7.7	1.56989	1.56990	1.56991	1.56992	1.56993	1.56993	1.56994	1.56995	1.56996	1.56997
7.8	1.56998	1.56999	1.56999	1.57000	1.57001	1.57002	1.57002	1.57003	1.57004	1.57005
7.9	1.57005	1.57006	1.57007	1.57008	1.57008	1.57008	1.57010	1.57010	1.57011	1.57012
8.0	1.57013	1.57013	1.57014	1.57015	1.57015	1.57016	1.57016	1.57017	1.57018	1.57018
8.1	1.57019	1.57020	1.57020	1.57021	1.57021	1.57022	1.57022	1.57023	1.57024	1.57024
8.2	1.57025	1.57025	1.57026	1.57026	1.57027	1.57027	1.57028	1.57028	1.57029	1.57029
8.3	1.57030	1.57030	1.57031	1.57031	1.57032	1.57032	1.57033	1.57033	1.57034	1.57034
8.4	1.57035	1.57035	1.57036	1.57036	1.57036	1.57037	1.57037	1.57038	1.57038	1.57039
8.5	1.57039	1.57039	1.57040	1.57040	1.57041	1.57041	1.57041	1.57042	1.57042	1.57042
8.6	1.57043	1.57043	1.57044	1.57044	1.57044	1.57045	1.57045	1.57045	1.57046	1.57046
8.7	1.57046	1.57047	1.57047	1.57047	1.57048	1.57048	1.57048	1.57049	1.57049	1.57049
8.8	1.57049	1.57050	1.57050	1.57050	1.57051	1.57051	1.57051	1.57052	1.57052	1.57052
8.9	1.57052	1.57053	1.57053	1.57053	1.57053	1.57054	1.57054	1.57054	1.57054	1.57055
9.0	1.57055	1.57055	1.57055	1.57056	1.57056	1.57056	1.57056	1.57057	1.57057	1.57057
9.1	1.57057	1.57058	1.57058	1.57058	1.57058	1.57058	1.57059	1.57059	1.57059	1.57059
9.2	1.57059	1.57060	1.57060	1.57060	1.57060	1.57060	1.57061	1.57061	1.57061	1.57061
9.3	1.57061	1.57062	1.57062	1.57062	1.57062	1.57062	1.57062	1.57063	1.57063	1.57063
9.4	1.57063	1.57063	1.57063	1.57064	1.57064	1.57064	1.57064	1.57064	1.57064	1.57065
9.5	1.57065	1.57065	1.57065	1.57065	1.57065	1.57065	1.57066	1.57066	1.57066	1.57066
9.6	1.57066	1.57066	1.57066	1.57066	1.57067	1.57067	1.57067	1.57067	1.57067	1.57067
9.7	1.57067	1.57067	1.57068	1.57068	1.57068	1.57068	1.57068	1.57068	1.57068	1.57068
9.8	1.57069	1.57069	1.57069	1.57069	1.57069	1.57069	1.57069	1.57069	1.57069	1.57069
9.9	1.57070	1.57070	1.57070	1.57070	1.57070	1.57070	1.57070	1.57070	1.57070	1.57070

INVERSE GUDERMANNIAN FUNCTION

x	0	1	2	3	4	5	6	7	8	9
0.0	0.00000	0.01000	0.02000	0.03000	0.04001	0.05002	0.06004	0.07006	0.08009	0.09012
0.1	0.10017	0.11022	0.12029	0.13037	0.14046	0.15057	0.16069	0.17082	0.18098	0.19115
0.2	0.20135	0.21156	0.22180	0.23206	0.24234	0.25265	0.26298	0.27334	0.28373	0.29415
0.3	0.30460	0.31509	0.32561	0.33616	0.34675	0.35737	0.36804	0.37874	0.38949	0.40028
0.4	0.41111	0.42199	0.43292	0.44390	0.45493	0.46600	0.47714	0.48833	0.49957	0.51087
0.5	0.52224	0.53366	0.54515	0.55671	0.56834	0.58003	0.59180	0.60364	0.61555	0.62755
0.6	0.63962	0.65178	0.66402	0.67636	0.68878	0.70129	0.71390	0.72661	0.73942	0.75233
0.7	0.76535	0.77848	0.79172	0.80508	0.81856	0.83217	0.84590	0.85976	0.87376	0.88790
0.8	0.90218	0.91660	0.93118	0.94592	0.96082	0.97589	0.99113	1.00654	1.02215	1.03794
0.9	1.05392	1.07011	1.08651	1.10313	1.11997	1.13704	1.15435	1.17192	1.18974	1.20783
1.0	1.22619	1.24485	1.26380	1.28306	1.30265	1.32258	1.34285	1.36349	1.38451	1.40593
1.1	1.42776	1.45003	1.47275	1.49594	1.51963	1.54384	1.56860	1.59394	1.61987	1.64645
1.2	1.67370	1.70166	1.73037	1.75987	1.79022	1.82147	1.85367	1.88689	1.92120	1.95667
1.3	1.99340	2.03147	2.07100	2.11210	2.15491	2.19959	2.24630	2.29524	2.34666	2.40080
1.4	2.45800	2.51861	2.58307	2.65193	2.72583	2.80558	2.89219	2.98695	3.09160	3.20843
1.5	3.34068	3.49307	3.67286	3.89217	4.17343	4.56609	5.22169	7.82865		

VII. ANALYTIC GEOMETRY

ANALYTIC GEOMETRY

Dr. Howard Eves

RECTANGULAR COORDINATES IN A PLANE

Rectangular (Cartesian) Coordinates

Let $X'X$ (called the *x-axis*) and $Y'Y$ (called the *y-axis*) be two perpendicular lines (here taken horizontally and vertically, respectively) intersecting in point O (called the *origin*). Then any point P in the plane of the axes is located by the distance x (called the *abscissa*) and the distance y (called the *ordinate*) from $Y'Y$ and $X'X$, respectively, to P, where x is taken as positive to the right and negative to the left of $Y'Y$, and y is taken as positive above and negative below $X'X$. The ordered pair of numbers, (x,y), are called *rectangular coordinates* of the point P.

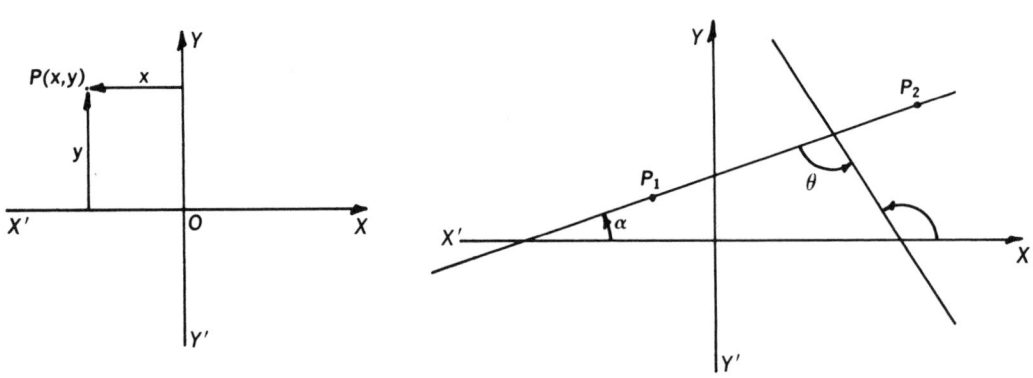

Points, Slopes, Angles

Let $P_1(x_1,y_1)$ and $P_2(x_2,y_2)$ be any two points and let α be the angle measured counterclockwise from $X'X$ to P_1P_2.

Distance between P_1 and P_2:
$$\sqrt{(x_2 - x_1)^2 + (y_2 - y_1)^2}$$

Point dividing P_1P_2 in ratio $\dfrac{r}{s}$:
$$\left(\frac{rx_2 + sx_1}{r + s}, \frac{ry_2 + sy_1}{r + s}\right)$$

Midpoint of P_1P_2:
$$\left(\frac{x_1 + x_2}{2}, \frac{y_1 + y_2}{2}\right)$$

Slope m of P_1P_2:
$$m = \tan\alpha = \frac{y_2 - y_1}{x_2 - x_1}$$

Angle θ between two lines of slopes m_1 and m_2:
$$\tan\theta = \frac{m_2 - m_1}{1 + m_1 m_2}$$

For parallel lines:
$$m_1 = m_2$$

For perpendicular lines:
$$m_1 m_2 = -1$$

Points P_1, P_2, P_3 are collinear if and only if
$$\begin{vmatrix} x_1 & y_1 & 1 \\ x_2 & y_2 & 1 \\ x_3 & y_3 & 1 \end{vmatrix} = 0.$$

Polygonal Areas

Area of triangle $P_1 P_2 P_3$:

$$\frac{1}{2}\begin{vmatrix} x_1 & y_1 & 1 \\ x_2 & y_2 & 1 \\ x_3 & y_3 & 1 \end{vmatrix} = \tfrac{1}{2}(x_1 y_2 + x_2 y_3 + x_3 y_1 - y_1 x_2 - y_2 x_3 - y_3 x_1)$$

Area of polygon $P_1 P_2 \cdots P_n$:

$$\tfrac{1}{2}(x_1 y_2 + x_2 y_3 + \cdots + x_{n-1} y_n + x_n y_1 - y_1 x_2 - y_2 x_3 - \cdots - y_{n-1} x_n - y_n x_1)$$

Note. The parenthesis in the last formula is remembered by the device

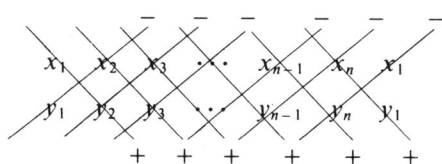

Here one adds the products of coordinates on the lines slanting downward to the right and subtracts the products of coordinates on the lines slanting upward to the right. The area is positive or negative according as $P_1 P_2 \cdots P_n$ is a counterclockwise or clockwise polygon.

Straight Lines

Line parallel to y-axis: $x = a$

Line parallel to x-axis: $y = b$

Slope y-intercept form: $y = mx + b$

Intercept form: $\dfrac{x}{a} + \dfrac{y}{b} = 1$

Point-slope form: $y - y_1 = m(x - x_1)$

Two-point form: $\dfrac{y - y_1}{x - x_1} = \dfrac{y_2 - y_1}{x_2 - x_1}$

or

$$\begin{vmatrix} x & y & 1 \\ x_1 & y_1 & 1 \\ x_2 & y_2 & 1 \end{vmatrix} = 0$$

Normal form: $x \cos \omega + y \sin \omega = p$

General form: $Ax + By + C = 0$

Slope: $m = -\dfrac{A}{B}$

Intercepts: $a = -\dfrac{C}{A}, \quad b = -\dfrac{C}{B}$

To reduce $Ax + By + C = 0$ to normal form, divide by $\pm \sqrt{A^2 + B^2}$, where the sign of the radical is chosen opposite to the sign of C when $C \neq 0$ and the same as the sign of B when $C = 0$.

Distance from $Ax + By + C = 0$ to P_1: $\dfrac{Ax_1 + By_1 + C}{\pm \sqrt{A^2 + B^2}}$

Formulas for Use in Analytic Geometry

Angle θ between lines $A_1x + B_1y + C_1 = 0$
and $A_2x + B_2y + C_2 = 0$

$$\tan \theta = \frac{A_1B_2 - A_2B_1}{A_1A_2 + B_1B_2}$$

Lines parallel: $A_1B_2 = A_2B_1$

Lines perpendicular: $A_1A_2 = -B_1B_2$

Lines $A_1x + B_1y + C_1 = 0$, $A_2x + B_2y + C_2 = 0$, $A_3x + B_3y + C_3 = 0$ are concurrent if and only if

$$\begin{vmatrix} A_1 & B_1 & C_1 \\ A_2 & B_2 & C_2 \\ A_3 & B_3 & C_3 \end{vmatrix} = 0.$$

Line of Best Fit

In seeking the straight line which best fits a given set of n points $P_1(x_1, y_1)$, $P_2(x_2, y_2)$, $\cdots$, $P_n(x_n, y_n)$, calculate

$$\overline{x} = \frac{x_1 + x_2 + \cdots + x_n}{n}, \quad \overline{y} = \frac{y_1 + y_2 + \cdots + y_n}{n},$$

$$m = \frac{(x_1y_1 + x_2y_2 + \cdots + x_ny_n) - n\overline{x}\overline{y}}{(x_1^2 + x_2^2 + \cdots + x_n^2) - n\overline{x}^2}.$$

Then the sought line is given by

$$y - \overline{y} = m(x - \overline{x}).$$

Circles

Center at origin, radius r: $x^2 + y^2 = r^2$

Center at (h, k), radius r: $(x - h)^2 + (y - k)^2 = r^2$

General form: $\begin{cases} Ax^2 + Ay^2 + Dx + Ey + F = 0, A \neq 0 \\ x^2 + y^2 + 2dx + 2ey + f = 0 \end{cases}$

    Center: $(-d, -e)$

    Radius: $r = \sqrt{d^2 + e^2 - f}$

Circle on P_1P_2 as diameter: $(x - x_1)(x - x_2) + (y - y_1)(y - y_2) = 0$

Three-point form: $\begin{vmatrix} x^2 + y^2 & x & y & 1 \\ x_1^2 + y_1^2 & x_1 & y_1 & 1 \\ x_2^2 + y_2^2 & x_2 & y_2 & 1 \\ x_3^2 + y_3^2 & x_3 & y_3 & 1 \end{vmatrix} = 0$

Conic Sections

A *conic section* is the locus of a point P that moves in the plane of a fixed point F (called a *focus*) and a fixed line d (called a *directrix*), F not on d, such that the ratio of the distance of P from F to its distance from d is a constant e (called the *eccentricity*).

If $e = 1$, the conic is a *parabola*; if $e < 1$, an *ellipse*; if $e > 1$, a *hyperbola*.

Focus, $(0,0)$; directrix, $x = -a$: $x^2 + y^2 = e^2(x + a)^2$

Parabolas (e = 1)

Let p = distance from the vertex to the focus, e = eccentricity.

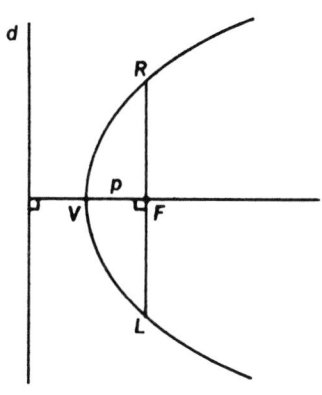

V: vertex
F: focus
d: directrix
LR: latus rectum
line VF: axis

Latus rectum:	$4p$
Distance from vertex to directrix:	p
Vertex at origin, focus at $(p,0)$:	$y^2 = 4px$
Vertex at origin, focus at $(-p,0)$:	$y^2 = -4px$
Vertex at origin, focus at $(0,p)$:	$x^2 = 4py$
Vertex at origin, focus at $(0,-p)$:	$x^2 = -4py$
Vertex, (h,k); focus, $(h + p,k)$:	$(y - k)^2 = 4p(x - h)$
Vertex, (h,k); focus, $(h - p,k)$:	$(y - k)^2 = -4p(x - h)$
Vertex, (h,k); focus, $(h,k + p)$:	$(x - h)^2 = 4p(y - k)$
Vertex, (h,k); focus, $(h,k - p)$:	$(x - h)^2 = -4p(y - k)$
General form, axis parallel to $X'X$:	$Cy^2 + Dx + Ey + F = 0$
General form, axis parallel to $Y'Y$:	$\begin{cases} Ax^2 + Dx + Ey + F = 0 \\ y = ax^2 + bx + c \end{cases}$
General form, axis oblique to coordinate axes:	$Ax^2 + Bxy + Cy^2 + Dx + Ey + F = 0$, $B^2 - 4AC = 0$

Ellipses (e < 1)

Let $2a$ = major axis, $2b$ = minor axis, e = eccentricity.

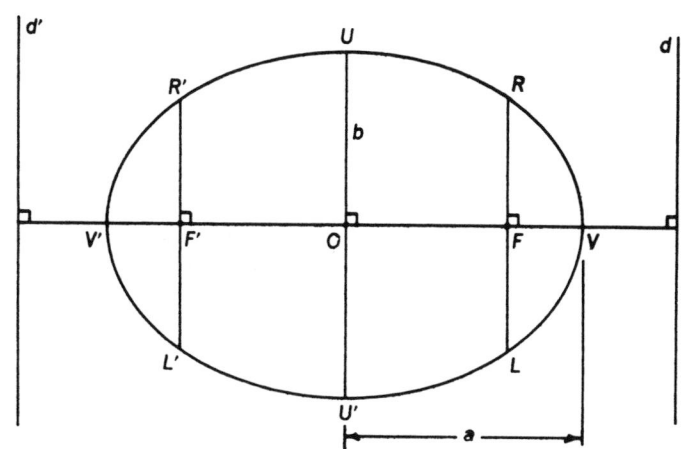

O: center
V, V': vertices
$V'V$: major axis = $2a$
$U'U$: minor axis = $2b$
F, F': foci
d, d': directrices
$LR, L'R'$: latera recta

Formulas for Use in Analytic Geometry

Eccentricity: $e = \dfrac{\sqrt{a^2 - b^2}}{a}$

Latus rectum: $\dfrac{2b^2}{a}$

Distance from center to either focus: $\sqrt{a^2 - b^2}$

Distance from center to either directrix: $\dfrac{a}{e}$

Sum of distances from any point on ellipse to the foci: $2a$

Center at origin, foci on $X'X$: $\dfrac{x^2}{a^2} + \dfrac{y^2}{b^2} = 1$

Center at origin, foci on $Y'Y$: $\dfrac{x^2}{b^2} + \dfrac{y^2}{a^2} = 1$

Center at (h,k), major axis parallel to $X'X$: $\dfrac{(x - h)^2}{a^2} + \dfrac{(y - k)^2}{b^2} = 1$

Center at (h,k), major axis parallel to $Y'Y$: $\dfrac{(x - h)^2}{b^2} + \dfrac{(y - k)^2}{a^2} = 1$

General form, axes parallel to coordinate axes: $Ax^2 + Cy^2 + Dx + Ey + F = 0, AC > 0$

General form, axes oblique to coordinate axes: $Ax^2 + Bxy + Cy^2 + Dx + Ey + F = 0,$
                                            $B^2 - 4AC < 0$

For a *circle*: $a = b$, $e = 0$, foci coincide at the center of the circle, directrices are at infinity.

Hyperbolas (e > 1)

Let $2a$ = transverse axis, $2b$ = conjugate axis, e = eccentricity.

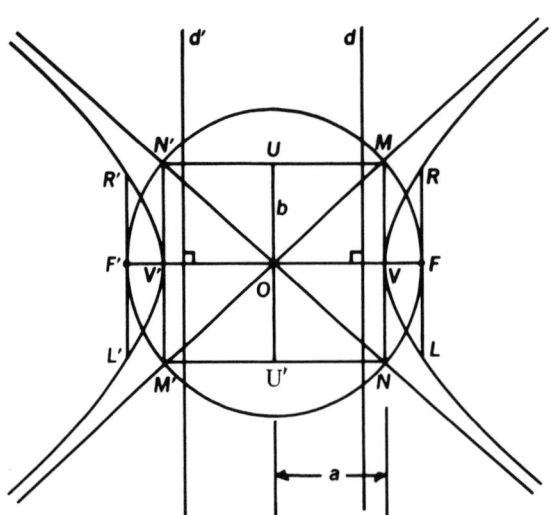

O: center
V, V': vertices
$V'V$: transverse axis = $2a$
$U'U$: conjugate axis = $2b$
F, F': foci
d, d': directrices
$LR, L'R'$: latera recta
lines $M'M$ and $N'N$: asymptotes

Formulas for Use in Analytic Geometry

Eccentricity:	$e = \dfrac{\sqrt{a^2 + b^2}}{a}$
Latus rectum:	$\dfrac{2b^2}{a}$
Distance from center to either focus:	$\sqrt{a^2 + b^2}$
Distance from center to either directrix:	$\dfrac{a}{e}$
Difference of distances of any point on hyperbola from foci:	$2a$
Center at origin, foci on $X'X$:	$\dfrac{x^2}{a^2} - \dfrac{y^2}{b^2} = 1$
Slopes of asymptotes:	$\pm \dfrac{b}{a}$
Center at origin, foci on $Y'Y$:	$\dfrac{y^2}{a^2} - \dfrac{x^2}{b^2} = 1$
Slopes of asymptotes:	$\pm \dfrac{a}{b}$
Center at (h,k), transverse axis parallel to $X'X$:	$\dfrac{(x - h)^2}{a^2} - \dfrac{(y - k)^2}{b^2} = 1$
Slopes of asymptotes:	$\pm \dfrac{b}{a}$
Center at (h, k), transverse axis parallel to $Y'Y$:	$\dfrac{(y - k)^2}{a^2} - \dfrac{(x - h)^2}{b^2} = 1$
Slopes of asymptotes:	$\pm \dfrac{a}{b}$
Center at origin, $X'X$ and $Y'Y$ for asymptotes:	$xy = c$
Center at (h,k), asymptotes parallel to $X'X$ and $Y'Y$:	$(x - h)(y - k) = c$
General form, axes parallel to coordinate axes:	$Ax^2 + Cy^2 + Dx + Ey + F = 0,\ AC < 0$
General form, axes oblique to coordinate axes:	$Ax^2 + Bxy + Cy^2 + Dx + Ey + F = 0,$ $B^2 - 4AC > 0$

For a *rectangular hyperbola*: $a = b$, $e = \sqrt{2}$, asymptotes are perpendicular.

General Equation of Second Degree

The nature of the graph of the general quadratic equation in x and y,

$$ax^2 + 2hxy + by^2 + 2gx + 2fy + c = 0,$$

is described in the following table in terms of the values of

$$\Delta = \begin{vmatrix} a & h & g \\ h & b & f \\ g & f & c \end{vmatrix}, \quad J = \begin{vmatrix} a & h \\ h & b \end{vmatrix},$$

$$I = a + b, \quad K = \begin{vmatrix} a & g \\ g & c \end{vmatrix} + \begin{vmatrix} b & f \\ f & c \end{vmatrix}.$$

Formulas for Use in Analytic Geometry

Case	$\triangle$	J	$\triangle/I$	K	Conic
1	$\neq 0$	> 0	< 0		real ellipse
2	$\neq 0$	> 0	> 0		imaginary ellipse
3	$\neq 0$	< 0			hyperbola
4	$\neq 0$	0			parabola
5	0	< 0			real intersecting lines
6	0	> 0			conjugate complex intersecting lines
7	0	0		< 0	real distinct parallel lines
8	0	0		> 0	conjugate complex parallel lines
9	0	0		0	coincident lines

In cases 1, 2, and 3, the center (x_0, y_0) of the conic is given by the simultaneous solution of the equations

$$ax + hy + g = 0, \quad hx + by + f = 0.$$

The equations of the axes of the conic are

$$y - y_0 = m(x - x_0), \quad y - y_0 = -\frac{1}{m}(x - x_0),$$

where m is the positive root of

$$hm^2 + (a - b)m - h = 0.$$

Transformation of Coordinates

To transform an equation of a curve from an old system of rectangular coordinates (x, y) to a new system of rectangular coordinates (x', y'), substitute for each old variable in the equation of the curve its expression in terms of the new variables.

Translation:
$$\begin{cases} x = x' + h \\ y = y' + k \end{cases}$$
The new axes are parallel to the old axes and the coordinates of the new origin in terms of the old system are (h, k).

Rotation:
$$\begin{cases} x = x' \cos\theta - y' \sin\theta \\ y = x' \sin\theta + y' \cos\theta \end{cases}$$
The new origin is coincident with the old origin and the new axes make an angle θ with the old axes.

To remove the xy-term from the equation

$$ax^2 + 2hxy + by^2 + 2gx + 2fy + c = 0,$$

rotate the coordinate axes about the origin through the acute angle $\theta = \arctan m$, where m is the positive root of

$$hm^2 + (a - b)m - h = 0.$$

OBLIQUE COORDINATES IN A PLANE

Oblique (Cartesian) Coordinates

Let $X'X$ (called the *x-axis*, here taken horizontally) and $Y'Y$ (called the *y-axis*) be two lines intersecting in point O (called the *origin*), and denote by ω the counterclockwise angle from $X'X$ to $Y'Y$. Then any point P in the plane of the axes is located by the distance x (called the *abscissa*) measured parallel to the x-axis and the distance y (called

Formulas for Use in Analytic Geometry

the *ordinate*) measured parallel to the *y*-axis from $Y'Y$ and $X'X$, respectively, to P, **where** x is taken as positive to the right and negative to the left of $Y'Y$, and y is taken as positive above and negative below $X'X$. The ordered pair of numbers, (x,y), are called *oblique coordinates* of the point P. If $\omega = 90°$, this coordinate system becomes a rectangular (Cartesian) coordinate system.

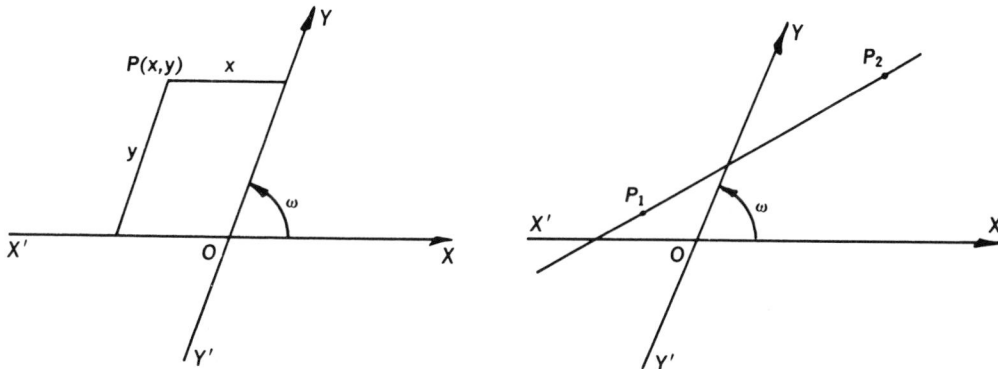

Points

Let $P_1(x_1,y_1)$ and $P_2(x_2,y_2)$ be any two points.
Distance between P_1 and P_2:

$$\sqrt{(x_2 - x_1)^2 + (y_2 - y_1)^2 + 2(x_2 - x_1)(y_2 - y_1)\cos \omega}$$

Point dividing $P_1 P_2$ in ratio $\dfrac{r}{s}$:
$$\left(\frac{rx_2 + sx_1}{r + s}, \frac{ry_2 + sy_1}{r + s}\right)$$

Midpoint of $P_1 P_2$:
$$\left(\frac{x_1 + x_2}{2}, \frac{y_1 + y_2}{2}\right)$$

Points P_1, P_2, P_3 are collinear if and only if
$$\begin{vmatrix} x_1 & y_1 & 1 \\ x_2 & y_2 & 1 \\ x_3 & y_3 & 1 \end{vmatrix} = 0.$$

Polygonal Areas

Area of triangle $P_1 P_2 P_3$:

$$\sin \omega \begin{vmatrix} x_1 & y_1 & 1 \\ x_2 & y_2 & 1 \\ x_3 & y_3 & 1 \end{vmatrix} = \tfrac{1}{2}(\sin \omega)(x_1 y_2 + x_2 y_3 + x_3 y_1 - y_1 x_2 - y_2 x_3 - y_3 x_1)$$

Area of polygon $P_1 P_2 \cdots P_n$:

$$\tfrac{1}{2}(\sin \omega)(x_1 y_2 + x_2 y_3 + \cdots + x_{n-1} y_n + x_n y_1 - y_1 x_2 - y_2 x_3 - \cdots - y_{n-1} x_n - y_n x_1)$$

The area is positive or negative according as $P_1 P_2 \cdots P_n$ is a counterclockwise or clockwise polygon.

Straight Lines

Line parallel to y-axis: $x = a$

Line parallel to x-axis: $y = b$

ANALYTIC GEOMETRY

Formulas for Use in Analytic Geometry

Intercept form: $\dfrac{x}{a} + \dfrac{y}{b} = 1$

Two-point form: $\dfrac{y - y_1}{x - x_1} = \dfrac{y_2 - y_1}{x_2 - x_1}$, or $\begin{vmatrix} x & y & 1 \\ x_1 & y_1 & 1 \\ x_2 & y_2 & 1 \end{vmatrix} = 0$

General form: $Ax + By + C = 0$

Intercepts: $a = -\dfrac{C}{A}, \quad b = -\dfrac{C}{B}$

Distance from $Ax + By + C = 0$ to P_1: $\dfrac{(Ax_1 + By_1 + C) \sin \omega}{\pm \sqrt{A^2 + B^2 - 2AB \cos \omega}}$

Angle θ between lines $A_1x + B_1y + C_1 = 0$
and $A_2x + B_2y + C_2 = 0$:

$$\tan \theta = \frac{(A_1B_2 - A_2B_1) \sin \omega}{A_1A_2 + B_1B_2 - (A_1B_2 + A_2B_1) \cos \omega}$$

Lines parallel: $A_1B_2 = A_2B_1$

Lines perpendicular: $A_1A_2 + B_1B_2 = (A_1B_2 + A_2B_1) \cos \omega$

Lines $A_1x + B_1y + C_1 = 0$, $A_2x + B_2y + C_2 = 0$, $A_3x + B_3y + C_3 = 0$ are concurrent if and only if

$$\begin{vmatrix} A_1 & B_1 & C_1 \\ A_2 & B_2 & C_2 \\ A_3 & B_3 & C_3 \end{vmatrix} = 0.$$

Circles

Center at (h, k), radius r: $(x - h)^2 + (y - k)^2 + 2(x - h)(y - k) \cos \omega = r^2$

Transformation of Coordinates

Translation: $\begin{cases} x = x' + h \\ y = y' + k \end{cases}$ The new axes are parallel to the old axes and the coordinates of the new origin in terms of the old system are (h, k).

From one oblique system to another, origin fixed: $\begin{cases} x = \dfrac{x' \sin (\omega - \theta) + y' \sin (\omega - \omega' - \theta)}{\sin \omega} \\ y = \dfrac{x' \sin \theta + y' \sin (\omega' + \theta)}{\sin \omega} \end{cases}$

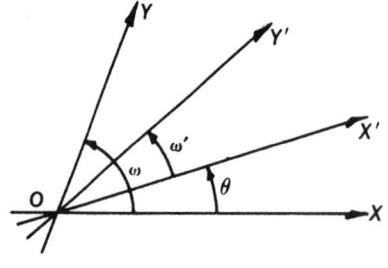

The old and new origins coincide; the old axes intersect at angle ω; the new axes intersect at angle ω'; the counterclockwise angle from x-axis to x'-axis is θ.

Formulas for Use in Analytic Geometry

POLAR COORDINATES IN A PLANE

Polar Coordinates

In a plane, let OX (called the *initial line*) be a fixed ray radiating from point O (called the *pole* or *origin*). Then any point P, other than O, in the plane is located by angle θ (called the *vectorial angle*) measured from OX to the line determined by O and P and the distance r (called the *radius vector*) from O to P, where θ is taken as positive if measured counterclockwise and negative if measured clockwise, and r is taken as positive if measured along the terminal side of angle θ and negative if measured along the terminal side of θ produced through the pole. Such an ordered pair of numbers, (r, θ), are called *polar coordinates* of the point P. The polar coordinates of the pole O are taken as $(0, \theta)$, where θ is arbitrary. It follows that, for a given initial line and pole, each point of the plane has infinitely many polar coordinates, but each pair of co-ordinates corresponds to only one point.

Example

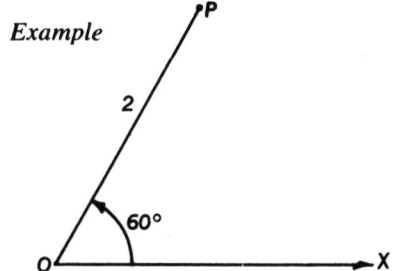

Some polar coordinates of P are: $(2, 60°)$, $(2, 420°)$, $(2, -300°)$, $(-2, 240°)$, $(-2, -120°)$.

Points

Distance between P_1 and P_2: $\quad \sqrt{r_1^2 + r_2^2 - 2r_1 r_2 \cos(\theta_1 - \theta_2)}$

Points P_1, P_2, P_3 are collinear if and only if

$$r_2 r_3 \sin(\theta_3 - \theta_2) + r_3 r_1 \sin(\theta_1 - \theta_3) + r_1 r_2 \sin(\theta_2 - \theta_1) = 0.$$

Polygonal Areas

Area of triangle $P_1 P_2 P_3$:

$$\tfrac{1}{2}[r_1 r_2 \sin(\theta_2 - \theta_1) + r_2 r_3 \sin(\theta_3 - \theta_2) + r_3 r_1 \sin(\theta_1 - \theta_3)]$$

Area of polygon $P_1 P_2 \cdots P_n$:

$$\tfrac{1}{2}[r_1 r_2 \sin(\theta_2 - \theta_1) + r_2 r_3 \sin(\theta_3 - \theta_2) + \cdots + r_{n-1} r_n \sin(\theta_n - \theta_{n-1}) + r_n r_1 \sin(\theta_1 - \theta_n)]$$

The area is positive or negative according as $P_1 P_2 \cdots P_n$ is a counterclockwise or clockwise polygon.

Straight Lines

Let p = distance of line from O, ω = counterclockwise angle from OX to the perpendicular through O to the line.

Normal form: $\quad r \cos(\theta - \omega) = p$

Two-point form: $\quad r[r_1 \sin(\theta - \theta_1) - r_2 \sin(\theta - \theta_2)] = r_1 r_2 \sin(\theta_2 - \theta_1)$

Circles

Center at pole, radius a: $\quad r = a$
Center at $(a, 0)$ and passing
  through the pole: $\quad r = 2a \cos \theta$

Center at $\left(a, \dfrac{\pi}{2}\right)$ and passing

through the pole: $\qquad\qquad\qquad$ $r = 2a \sin \theta$

Center (h, α), radius a: $\qquad\qquad$ $r^2 - 2hr \cos (\theta - \alpha) + h^2 - a^2 = 0$

Conics

Let $2p$ = distance from directrix to focus, e = eccentricity.

Focus at pole, directrix to left of pole: $\qquad$ $r = \dfrac{2ep}{1 - e \cos \theta}$

Focus at pole, directrix to right of pole: $\qquad$ $r = \dfrac{2ep}{1 + e \cos \theta}$

Focus at pole, directrix below pole: $\qquad$ $r = \dfrac{2ep}{1 - e \sin \theta}$

Focus at pole, directrix above pole: $\qquad$ $r = \dfrac{2ep}{1 + e \sin \theta}$

Parabola with vertex at pole,
   directrix to left of pole: $\qquad$ $r = \dfrac{4p \cos \theta}{\sin^2 \theta}$

Ellipse with center at pole, semiaxes a and
   b horizontal and vertical, respectively: $\quad$ $r^2 = \dfrac{a^2 b^2}{a^2 \sin^2 \theta + b^2 \cos^2 \theta}$

Hyperbola with center at pole, semiaxes a
   and b horizontal and vertical, respec-
   tively: $\qquad$ $r^2 = \dfrac{a^2 b^2}{a^2 \sin^2 \theta - b^2 \cos^2 \theta}$

Relations Between Rectangular and Polar Coordinates

Let the positive x-axis coincide with the initial line and let r be nonnegative.

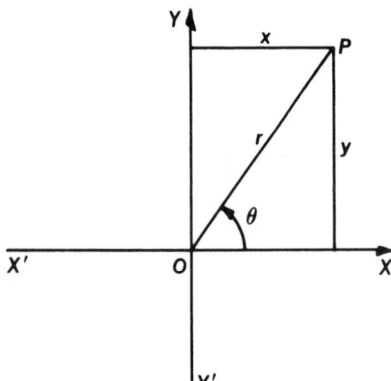

$$x = r \cos \theta, \quad y = r \sin \theta,$$

$$r = \sqrt{x^2 + y^2}, \quad \theta = \arctan \frac{y}{x},$$

$$\sin \theta = \frac{y}{\sqrt{x^2 + y^2}}, \quad \cos \theta = \frac{x}{\sqrt{x^2 + y^2}}$$

RECTANGULAR COORDINATES IN SPACE

Rectangular (Cartesian) Coordinates

Let $X'X$, $Y'Y$, $Z'Z$ (called the *x-axis*, the *y-axis*, and the *z-axis*, respectively) be three mutually perpendicular lines in space intersecting in a point O (called the *origin*), forming in this way three mutually perpendicular planes XOY, XOZ, YOZ (called the *xy-*

plane, the *xz-plane*, and the *yz-plane*, respectively). Then any point *P* of space is located by its signed distances *x*, *y*, *z* from the *yz*-plane, the *xz*-plane, and the *xy*-plane, respectively, where *x* and *y* are the rectangular coordinates with respect to the axes *X'X* and *Y'Y* of the orthogonal projection *P'* of *P* on the *xy*-plane (here taken horizontally) and *z* is taken as positive above and negative below the *xy*-plane. The ordered triple of numbers, (x, y, z), are called *rectangular coordinates* of the point *P*.

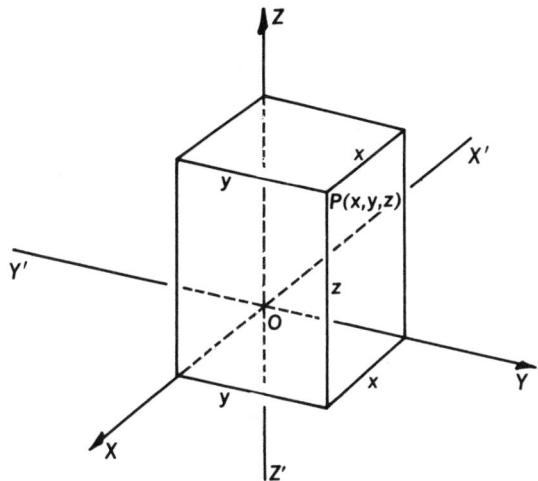

Points

Let $P_1(x_1, y_1, z_1)$ and $P_2(x_2, y_2, z_2)$ be any two points.

Distance between P_1 and P_2:
$$\sqrt{(x_2 - x_1)^2 + (y_2 - y_1)^2 + (z_2 - z_1)^2}$$

Point dividing $P_1 P_2$ in ratio $\dfrac{r}{s}$:
$$\left(\frac{rx_2 + sx_1}{r + s}, \quad \frac{ry_2 + sy_1}{r + s}, \quad \frac{rz_2 + sz_1}{r + s} \right)$$

Midpoint of $P_1 P_2$:
$$\left(\frac{x_1 + x_2}{2}, \quad \frac{y_1 + y_2}{2} \quad \frac{z_1 + z_2}{2} \right)$$

Points P_1, P_2, P_3 are collinear if and only if
$$x_2 - x_1 : y_2 - y_1 : z_2 - z_1 = x_3 - x_1 : y_3 - y_1 : z_3 - z_1.$$

Points P_1, P_2, P_3, P_4 are coplanar if and only if
$$\begin{vmatrix} x_1 & y_1 & z_1 & 1 \\ x_2 & y_2 & z_2 & 1 \\ x_3 & y_3 & z_3 & 1 \\ x_4 & y_4 & z_4 & 1 \end{vmatrix} = 0.$$

Area of triangle $P_1 P_2 P_3$:
$$\frac{1}{2} \sqrt{ \begin{vmatrix} y_1 & z_1 & 1 \\ y_2 & z_2 & 1 \\ y_3 & z_3 & 1 \end{vmatrix}^2 + \begin{vmatrix} z_1 & x_1 & 1 \\ z_2 & x_2 & 1 \\ z_3 & x_3 & 1 \end{vmatrix}^2 + \begin{vmatrix} x_1 & y_1 & 1 \\ x_2 & y_2 & 1 \\ x_3 & y_3 & 1 \end{vmatrix}^2 }$$

ANALYTIC GEOMETRY

Formulas for Use in Analytic Geometry

Volume of tetrahedron $P_1 P_2 P_3 P_4$: $\frac{1}{6} \begin{vmatrix} x_1 & y_1 & z_1 & 1 \\ x_2 & y_2 & z_2 & 1 \\ x_3 & y_3 & z_3 & 1 \\ x_4 & y_4 & z_4 & 1 \end{vmatrix}$

Direction Numbers and Direction Cosines

Let α, β, γ (called *direction angles*) be the angles that $P_1 P_2$, or any line parallel to $P_1 P_2$, makes with the x-, y-, and z-axis, respectively. Let $d =$ distance between P_1 and P_2.
Direction cosines of $P_1 P_2$:

$$\cos \alpha = \frac{x_2 - x_1}{d}, \quad \cos \beta = \frac{y_2 - y_1}{d}, \quad \cos \gamma = \frac{z_2 - z_1}{d}$$

$$\cos^2 \alpha + \cos^2 \beta + \cos^2 \gamma = 1$$

If a, b, c are direction numbers of $P_1 P_2$, then:

$$a : b : c = x_2 - x_1 : y_2 - y_1 : z_2 - z_1$$
$$= \cos \alpha : \cos \beta : \cos \gamma$$

$$\cos \alpha = \frac{a}{\pm \sqrt{a^2 + b^2 + c^2}}, \quad \cos \beta = \frac{b}{\pm \sqrt{a^2 + b^2 + c^2}},$$

$$\cos \gamma = \frac{c}{\pm \sqrt{a^2 + b^2 + c^2}}$$

Angle between two lines with direction angles $\alpha_1, \beta_1, \gamma_1$ and $\alpha_2, \beta_2, \gamma_2$:

$$\cos \theta = \cos \alpha_1 \cos \alpha_2 + \cos \beta_1 \cos \beta_2 + \cos \gamma_1 \cos \gamma_2$$

For parallel lines: $\alpha_1 = \alpha_2, \ \beta_1 = \beta_2, \ \gamma_1 = \gamma_2$
For perpendicular lines:

$$\cos \alpha_1 \cos \alpha_2 + \cos \beta_1 \cos \beta_2 + \cos \gamma_1 \cos \gamma_2 = 0$$

Angle between two lines with directions (a_1, b_1, c_1) and (a_2, b_2, c_2):

$$\cos \theta = \frac{a_1 a_2 + b_1 b_2 + c_1 c_2}{\sqrt{a_1^2 + b_1^2 + c_1^2} \ \sqrt{a_2^2 + b_2^2 + c_2^2}}$$

$$\sin \theta = \frac{\sqrt{(b_1 c_2 - c_1 b_2)^2 + (c_1 a_2 - a_1 c_2)^2 + (a_1 b_2 - b_1 a_2)^2}}{\sqrt{a_1^2 + b_1^2 + c_1^2} \ \sqrt{a_2^2 + b_2^2 + c_2^2}}$$

For parallel lines: $a_1 : b_1 : c_1 = a_2 : b_2 : c_2$
For perpendicular lines: $a_1 a_2 + b_1 b_2 + c_1 c_2 = 0$

The direction

$$(b_1 c_2 - c_1 b_2, c_1 a_2 - a_1 c_2, a_1 b_2 - b_1 a_2)$$

is perpendicular to both directions (a_1, b_1, c_1) and (a_2, b_2, c_2).
The directions (a_1, b_1, c_1), (a_2, b_2, c_2), (a_3, b_3, c_3) are parallel to a common plane if and only if

$$\begin{vmatrix} a_1 & b_1 & c_1 \\ a_2 & b_2 & c_2 \\ a_3 & b_3 & c_3 \end{vmatrix} = 0.$$

Formulas for Use in Analytic Geometry

Straight Lines

Point-direction form:
$$\frac{x - x_1}{a} = \frac{y - y_1}{b} = \frac{z - z_1}{c}$$

Two-point form:
$$\frac{x - x_1}{x_2 - x_1} = \frac{y - y_1}{y_2 - y_1} = \frac{z - z_1}{z_2 - z_1}$$

Parametric form: $x = x_1 + ta, \ y = y_1 + tb, \ z = z_1 + tc$

General form:
$$\begin{cases} A_1 x + B_1 y + C_1 z + D_1 = 0 \\ A_2 x + B_2 y + C_2 z + D_2 = 0 \end{cases}$$

Direction of line: $(B_1 C_2 - C_1 B_2, C_1 A_2 - A_1 C_2, A_1 B_2 - B_1 A_2)$

Projection of segment $P_1 P_2$ on any line having the direction (a, b, c):

$$\frac{(x_2 - x_1)a + (y_2 - y_1)b + (z_2 - z_1)c}{\sqrt{a^2 + b^2 + c^2}}$$

Distance from point P_0 to line through P_1 in direction (a, b, c):

$$\sqrt{\frac{\begin{vmatrix} y_0 - y_1 & z_0 - z_1 \\ b & c \end{vmatrix}^2 + \begin{vmatrix} z_0 - z_1 & x_0 - x_1 \\ c & a \end{vmatrix}^2 + \begin{vmatrix} x_0 - x_1 & y_0 - y_1 \\ a & b \end{vmatrix}^2}{a^2 + b^2 + c^2}}$$

Distance between line through P_1 in direction (a_1, b_1, c_1) and line through P_2 in direction (a_2, b_2, c_2):

$$\pm \frac{\begin{vmatrix} x_2 - x_1 & y_2 - y_1 & z_2 - z_1 \\ a_1 & b_1 & c_1 \\ a_2 & b_2 & c_2 \end{vmatrix}}{\sqrt{\begin{vmatrix} b_1 & c_1 \\ b_2 & c_2 \end{vmatrix}^2 + \begin{vmatrix} c_1 & a_1 \\ c_2 & a_2 \end{vmatrix}^2 + \begin{vmatrix} a_1 & b_1 \\ a_2 & b_2 \end{vmatrix}^2}}$$

The line through P_1 in direction (a_1, b_1, c_1) and the line through P_2 in direction (a_2, b_2, c_2) intersect if and only if

$$\begin{vmatrix} x_2 - x_1 & y_2 - y_1 & z_2 - z_1 \\ a_1 & b_1 & c_1 \\ a_2 & b_2 & c_2 \end{vmatrix} = 0.$$

Planes

General form: $Ax + By + Cz + D = 0$

Direction of normal: (A, B, C)

Perpendicular to yz-plane: $By + Cz + D = 0$

Perpendicular to xz-plane: $Ax + Cz + D = 0$

Perpendicular to xy-plane: $Ax + By + D = 0$

Perpendicular to x-axis: $Ax + D = 0$

Perpendicular to y-axis: $By + D = 0$

Perpendicular to z-axis: $Cz + D = 0$

Intercept form:
$$\frac{x}{a} + \frac{y}{b} + \frac{z}{c} = 1$$

Plane through point P_1 and perpendicular to direction (a, b, c):

$$a(x - x_1) + b(y - y_1) + c(z - z_1) = 0$$

Formulas for Use in Analytic Geometry

Plane through point P_1 **and parallel to directions** (a_1,b_1,c_1) **and** (a_2,b_2,c_2):

$$\begin{vmatrix} x - x_1 & y - y_1 & z - z_1 \\ a_1 & b_1 & c_1 \\ a_2 & b_2 & c_2 \end{vmatrix} = 0$$

Plane through points P_1 **and** P_2 **parallel to direction** (a,b,c):

$$\begin{vmatrix} x - x_1 & y - y_1 & z - z_1 \\ x_2 - x_1 & y_2 - y_1 & z_2 - z_1 \\ a & b & c \end{vmatrix} = 0$$

Three-point form:

$$\begin{vmatrix} x & y & z & 1 \\ x_1 & y_1 & z_1 & 1 \\ x_2 & y_2 & z_2 & 1 \\ x_3 & y_3 & z_3 & 1 \end{vmatrix} = 0 \quad \text{or} \quad \begin{vmatrix} x - x_1 & y - y_1 & z - z_1 \\ x_2 - x_1 & y_2 - y_1 & z_2 - z_1 \\ x_3 - x_1 & y_3 - y_1 & z_3 - z_1 \end{vmatrix} = 0$$

Normal form (p = distance from origin to plane; α, β, γ are direction angles of perpendicular to plane from origin):

$$x \cos \alpha + y \cos \beta + z \cos \gamma = p$$

To reduce $Ax + By + Cz + D = 0$ to normal form, divide by $\pm \sqrt{A^2 + B^2 + C^2}$, where the sign of the radical is chosen opposite to the sign of D when $D \neq 0$, the same as the sign of C when $D = 0$ and $C \neq 0$, the same as the sign of B when $C = D = 0$.

Distance from point P_1 to plane $Ax + By + Cz + D = 0$:

$$\frac{Ax_1 + By_1 + Cz_1 + D}{\pm \sqrt{A^2 + B^2 + C^2}}$$

Angle θ **between planes** $A_1 x + B_1 y + C_1 z + D_1 = 0$ **and** $A_2 x + B_2 y + C_2 z + D_2 = 0$:

$$\cos \theta = \frac{A_1 A_2 + B_1 B_2 + C_1 C_2}{\sqrt{A_1^2 + B_1^2 + C_1^2} \sqrt{A_2^2 + B_2^2 + C_2^2}}$$

Planes parallel: $\quad A_1 : B_1 : C_1 = A_2 : B_2 : C_2$

Planes perpendicular: $\quad A_1 A_2 + B_1 B_2 + C_1 C_2 = 0$

Spheres

Center at origin, radius r: $\quad x^2 + y^2 + z^2 = r^2$

Center at (g,h,k), radius r: $\quad (x - g)^2 + (y - h)^2 + (z - k)^2 = r^2$

General form: $\quad \begin{cases} Ax^2 + Ay^2 + Az^2 + Dx + Ey + Fz + M = 0, & A \neq 0 \\ x^2 + y^2 + z^2 + 2dx + 2ey + 2fz + m = 0 \end{cases}$

Center: $\quad (-d, -e, -f)$

Radius: $\quad r = \sqrt{d^2 + e^2 + f^2 - m}$

Sphere on $P_1 P_2$ as diameter:

$$(x - x_1)(x - x_2) + (y - y_1)(y - y_2) + (z - z_1)(z - z_2) = 0$$

Four-point form:

$$\begin{vmatrix} x^2 + y^2 + z^2 & x & y & z & 1 \\ x_1^2 + y_1^2 + z_1^2 & x_1 & y_1 & z_1 & 1 \\ x_2^2 + y_2^2 + z_2^2 & x_2 & y_2 & z_2 & 1 \\ x_3^2 + y_3^2 + z_3^2 & x_3 & y_3 & z_3 & 1 \\ x_4^2 + y_4^2 + z_4^2 & x_4 & y_4 & z_4 & 1 \end{vmatrix} = 0$$

The Seventeen Quadric Surfaces in Standard Form

1. Real ellipsoid: $x^2/a^2 + y^2/b^2 + z^2/c^2 = 1$
2. Imaginary ellipsoid: $x^2/a^2 + y^2/b^2 + z^2/c^2 = -1$
3. Hyperboloid of one sheet: $x^2/a^2 + y^2/b^2 - z^2/c^2 = 1$
4. Hyperboloid of two sheets: $x^2/a^2 + y^2/b^2 - z^2/c^2 = -1$
5. Real quadric cone: $x^2/a^2 + y^2/b^2 - z^2/c^2 = 0$
6. Imaginary quadric cone: $x^2/a^2 + y^2/b^2 + z^2/c^2 = 0$
7. Elliptic paraboloid: $x^2/a^2 + y^2/b^2 + 2z = 0$
8. Hyperbolic paraboloid: $x^2/a^2 - y^2/b^2 + 2z = 0$
9. Real elliptic cylinder: $x^2/a^2 + y^2/b^2 = 1$
10. Imaginary elliptic cylinder: $x^2/a^2 + y^2/b^2 = -1$
11. Hyperbolic cylinder: $x^2/a^2 - y^2/b^2 = -1$
12. Real intersecting planes: $x^2/a^2 - y^2/b^2 = 0$
13. Imaginary intersecting planes: $x^2/a^2 + y^2/b^2 = 0$
14. Parabolic cylinder: $x^2 + 2rz = 0$
15. Real parallel planes: $x^2 = a^2$
16. Imaginary parallel planes: $x^2 = -a^2$
17. Coincident planes: $x^2 = 0$

General Equation of Second Degree

The nature of the graph of the general quadratic equation in x, y, z,

$$ax^2 + by^2 + cz^2 + 2fyz + 2gzx + 2hxy + 2px + 2qy + 2rz + d = 0,$$

is described in the following table in terms of $\rho_3, \rho_4, \Delta, k_1, k_2, k_3$, where

$$e = \begin{bmatrix} a & h & g \\ h & b & f \\ g & f & c \end{bmatrix}, \quad E = \begin{bmatrix} a & h & g & p \\ h & b & f & q \\ g & f & c & r \\ p & q & r & d \end{bmatrix},$$

$$\rho_3 = \text{rank } e, \quad \rho_4 = \text{rank } E,$$
$$\Delta = \text{determinant of } E,$$

k_1, k_2, k_3 are the roots of $\begin{vmatrix} a - x & h & g \\ h & b - x & f \\ g & f & c - x \end{vmatrix} = 0.$

Formulas for Use in Analytic Geometry

Case	ρ_3	ρ_4	Sign of Δ	Nonzero k's same sign?	Quadric Surface
1	3	4	−	yes	Real ellipsoid
2	3	4	+	yes	Imaginary ellipsoid
3	3	4	+	no	Hyperboloid of one sheet
4	3	4	−	no	Hyperboloid of two sheets
5	3	3		no	Real quadric cone
6	3	3		yes	Imaginary quadric cone
7	2	4	−	yes	Elliptic paraboloid
8	2	4	+	no	Hyperbolic paraboloid
9	2	3		yes	Real elliptic cylinder
10	2	3		yes	Imaginary elliptic cylinder
11	2	3		no	Hyperbolic cylinder
12	2	2		no	Real intersecting planes
13	2	2		yes	Imaginary intersecting planes
14	1	3			Parabolic cylinder
15	1	2			Real parallel planes
16	1	2			Imaginary parallel planes
17	1	1			Coincident planes

Cylindrical and Conical Surfaces

Any equation in just two of the variables x, y, z represents a *cylindrical surface* whose elements are parallel to the axis of the missing variable.

Any equation homogeneous in the variables x, y, z represents a *conical surface* whose vertex is at the origin.

Transformation of Coordinates

To transform an equation of a surface from an old system of rectangular coordinates (x, y, z) to a new system of rectangular coordinates (x', y', z'), substitute for each old variable in the equation of the surface its expression in terms of the new variables.

Translation:

$x = x' + h$ The new axes are parallel to the old axes and the coordinates of
$y = y' + k$ the new origin in terms of the old system are (h, k, l).
$z = z' + l$

Rotation about the origin:

$x = \lambda_1 x' + \lambda_2 y' + \lambda_3 z'$ The new origin is coincident with the old origin and
$y = \mu_1 x' + \mu_2 y' + \mu_3 z'$ the x'-axis, y'-axis, z'-axis have direction cosines
$z = \nu_1 x' + \nu_2 y' + \nu_3 z'$ $(\lambda_1, \mu_1, \nu_1), (\lambda_2, \mu_2, \nu_2), (\lambda_3, \mu_3, \nu_3)$, respectively, with respect to the old system of axes.

$x' = \lambda_1 x + \mu_1 y + \nu_1 z$
$y' = \lambda_2 x + \mu_2 y + \nu_2 z$
$z' = \lambda_3 x + \mu_3 y + \nu_3 z$

Cylindrical Coordinates

If (r, θ, z) are the cylindrical coordinates and (x, y, z) the rectangular coordinates of a point P, then

$$x = r \cos \theta, \quad r = \sqrt{x^2 + y^2},$$

$$y = r \sin \theta, \quad \theta = \arctan \frac{y}{x},$$

$$z = z, \qquad z = z.$$

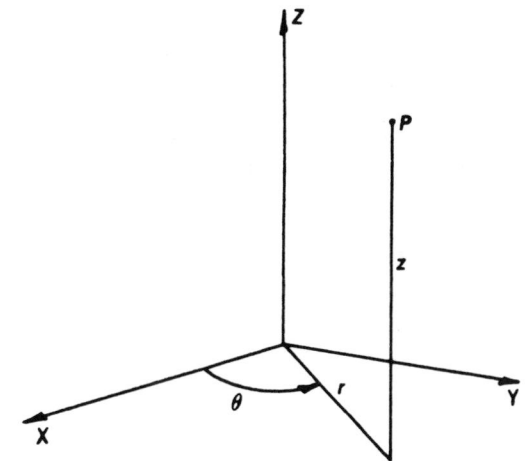

Spherical Coordinates

If (ρ, θ, ϕ) are the spherical coordinates and (x, y, z) the rectangular coordinates of a point P, then

$$x = \rho \cos \theta \sin \phi$$

$$y = \rho \sin \theta \sin \phi$$

$$z = \rho \cos \phi$$

$$\phi = \arccos \frac{z}{\sqrt{x^2 + y^2 + z^2}},$$

$$\theta = \arctan \frac{y}{x}.$$

$$p^2 = x^2 + y^2 + z^2$$

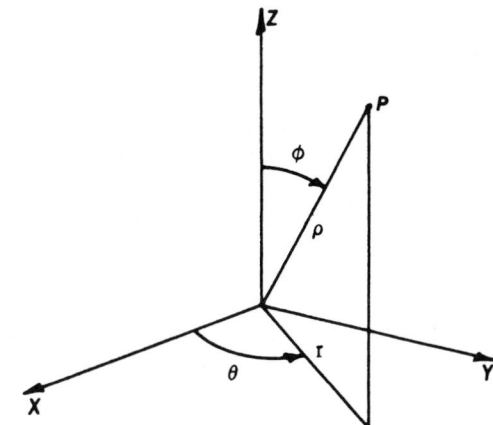

ANALYTIC GEOMETRY

CURVES AND SURFACES

Dr. Howard Eves

The curves and surfaces collected here for reference appear frequently in mathematical literature. The equations most generally associated with each figure are given. The equation of a plane curve when placed otherwise on the coordinate frame of reference may often be found from the given equation by the following rules.

RECTANGULAR COORDINATES

1. If a given curve is reflected in the x-axis, the new equation is obtained from the old by replacing y by $-y$.

2. If a given curve is reflected in the y-axis, the new equation is obtained from the old by replacing x by $-x$.

3. If a given curve is reflected in the origin, the new equation is obtained from the old by replacing x by $-x$ and y by $-y$.

4. If a given curve is reflected in the line $y = x$, the new equation is obtained from the old by interchanging x and y.

5. If a given curve is rotated about the origin through 90°, the new equation is obtained from the old by replacing x by y and y by $-x$.

6. If a given curve is rotated about the origin through $-90°$, the new equation is obtained from the old by replacing x by $-y$ and y by x.

7. If a given curve is translated a distance h in the x-direction, the new equation is obtained from the old by replacing x by $x - h$.

8. If a given curve is translated a distance k in the y-direction, the new equation is obtained from the old by replacing y by $y - k$.

9. If a given curve is altered by multiplying all the abscissas by a, the new equation is obtained from the old by replacing x by x/a.

10. If a given curve is altered by multiplying all the ordinates by b, the new equation is obtained from the old by replacing y by y/b.

POLAR COORDINATES

1. If a given curve is reflected in the polar axis, the new equation is obtained from the old by replacing θ by $-\theta$, or by replacing r by $-r$ and θ by $\pi - \theta$.

2. If a given curve is reflected in the 90° axis, the new equation is obtained from the old by replacing θ by $\pi - \theta$, or by replacing r by $-r$ and θ by $-\theta$.

3. If a given curve is reflected in the pole, the new equation is obtained from the old by replacing θ by $\pi + \theta$, or by replacing r by $-r$.

4. If a given curve is rotated about the pole through an angle α, the new equation is obtained from the old by replacing θ by $\theta - \alpha$.

PLANE CURVES

Archimedean spiral
  See: Spiral of Archimedes

Astroid
  See: Hypocycloid of four cusps

Bifolium

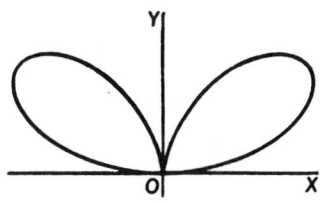

$$(x^2 + y^2)^2 = ax^2 y$$
$$r = a \sin \theta \cos^2 \theta$$

Cardioid

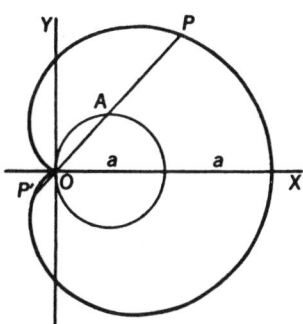

$$(x^2 + y^2 - ax)^2 = a^2(x^2 + y^2)$$
$$r = a(\cos \theta + 1)$$
$$\text{or}$$
$$r = a(\cos \theta - 1)$$
$$[P'A = AP = a]$$

Cassinian curves

See: Ovals of Cassini

Catenary, Hyperbolic cosine

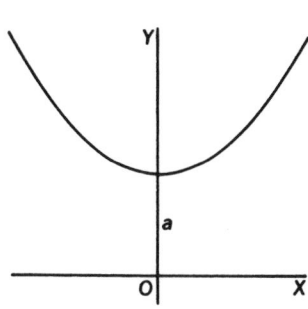

$$y = \frac{a}{2}(e^{x/a} + e^{-x/a}) = a \cosh \frac{x}{a}$$

Circle
(a)

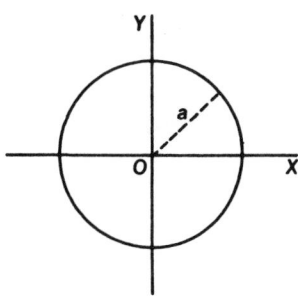

$$x^2 + y^2 = a^2$$
$$r = a$$

(b)

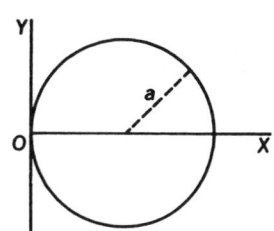

$$x^2 + y^2 = 2ax$$
$$r = 2a \cos \theta$$

(c)

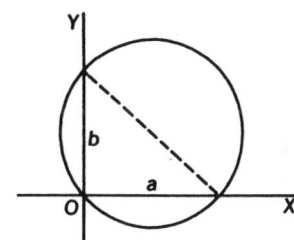

$$x^2 + y^2 = ax + by$$
$$r = a \cos \theta + b \sin \theta$$

Cissoid of Diocles

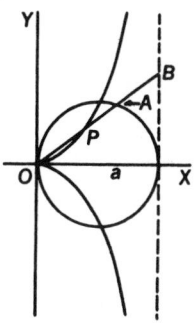

$$y^2(a - x) = x^3$$
$$r = a \sin \theta \tan \theta$$
$$[OP = AB]$$

Cochleoid, Oui-ja board curve

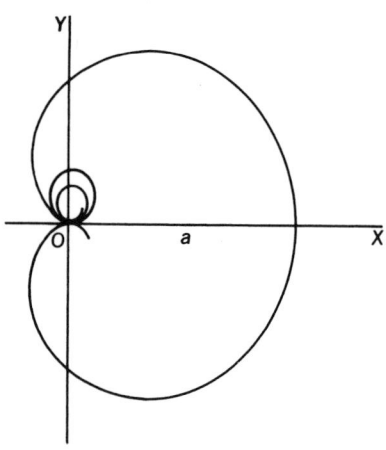

$$(x^2 + y^2) \tan^{-1}(y/x) = ay$$
$$r\theta = a \sin \theta$$

Companion to the cycloid

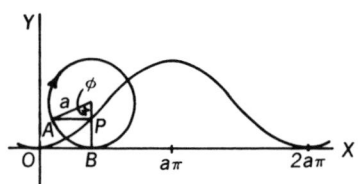

$$\begin{cases} x = a\phi \\ y = a(1 - \cos \phi) \end{cases}$$
$$[OB = \widehat{AB}]$$
(This is a sinusoid)

Conchoid of Nicomedes
(a) $a < b$

(b) $a > b$

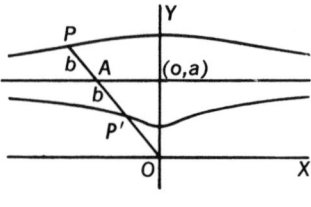

$$(y - a)^2(x^2 + y^2) = b^2 y^2$$
$$r = a \csc \theta \pm b$$
$$[P'A = AP = b]$$

Conic sections
See: Circle; Ellipse; Hyperbola; Parabola

Cosecant curve

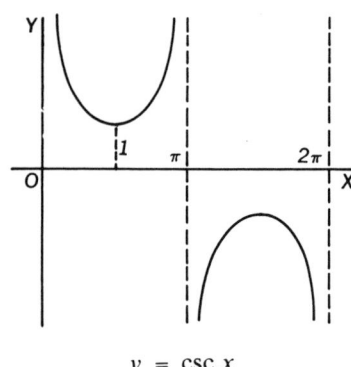

$$y = \csc x$$

Cosine curve

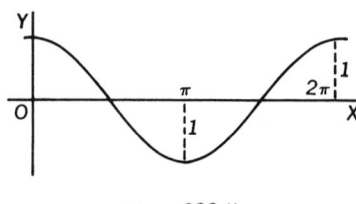

$$y = \cos x$$

Cotangent curve

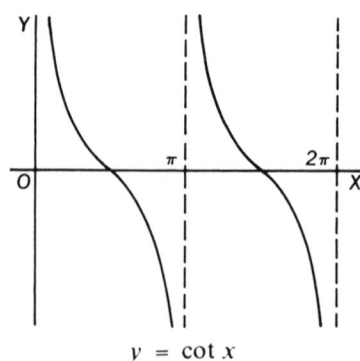

$$y = \cot x$$

Cubical parabola (special)

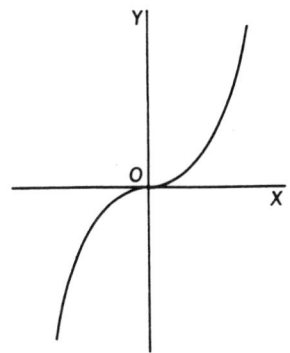

$$y = ax^3, \quad a > 0$$

$$r^2 = \frac{1}{a} \sec^2 \theta \tan \theta, \quad a > 0$$

Cubical parabola (general)

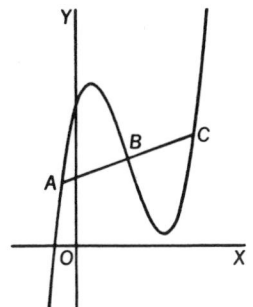

$$y = ax^3 + bx^2 + cx + d, \quad a > 0$$
$$[AB = BC]$$
$$\text{(abscissa of } B = -b/3a)$$

Curtate cycloid, Trochoids
  See: Cycloid, curtate

Cycloid (cusp at origin)

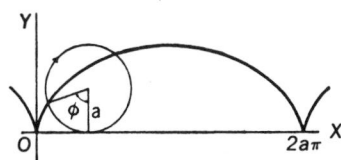

$$x = a \arccos \frac{a - y}{a} \mp \sqrt{2ay - y^2}$$

$$\begin{cases} x = a(\phi - \sin \phi) \\ y = a(1 - \cos \phi) \end{cases}$$

(For one arch: arc length = $8a$;
area = $3\pi a^2$)

Cycloid (vertex at origin)

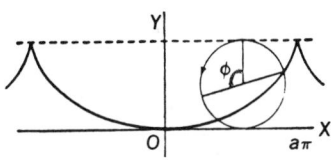

$$x = 2a \arcsin \sqrt{y/2a} + \sqrt{2ay - y^2}$$

$$\begin{cases} x = a(\phi + \sin \phi) \\ y = a(1 - \cos \phi) \end{cases}$$

Cycloid, curtate

$$\begin{cases} x = a\phi - b \sin \phi \\ y = a - b \cos \phi \end{cases}$$
$$a > b$$

Cycloid, prolate

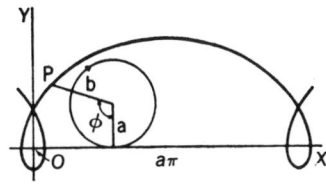

$$\begin{cases} x = a\phi - b \sin \phi \\ y = a - b \cos \phi \end{cases}$$
$$a < b$$

Deltoid
  See: Hypocycloid of three cusps

Ellipse

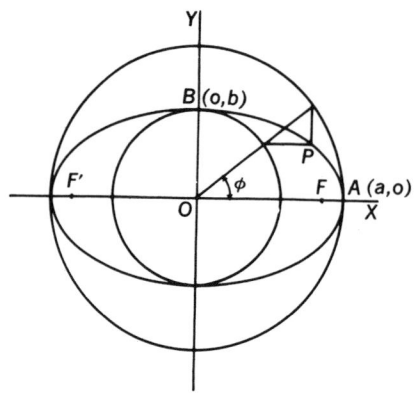

$$x^2/a^2 + y^2/b^2 = 1$$

$$\begin{cases} x = a \cos \phi \\ y = b \sin \phi \end{cases}$$

$$[BF' = BF = a, \quad PF' + PF = 2a]$$

Epicycloid

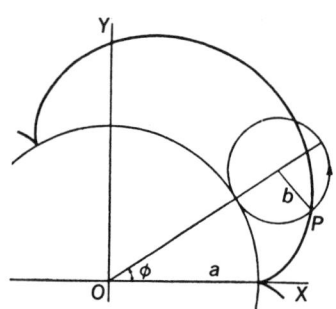

$$\begin{cases} x = (a + b) \cos \phi - b \cos\left(\dfrac{a + b}{b} \phi\right) \\ y = (a + b) \sin \phi - b \sin\left(\dfrac{a + b}{b} \phi\right) \end{cases}$$

Equiangular spiral

See: Spiral, logarithmic or equiangular

Equilateral hyperbola

See: Hyperbola, equilateral or rectangular

Evolute of ellipse

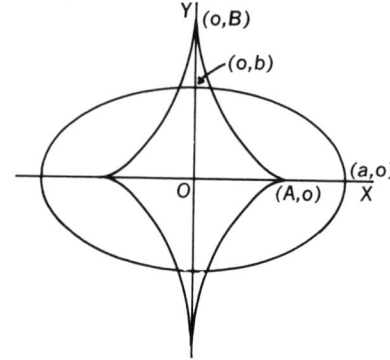

$$(ax)^{2/3} + (by)^{2/3} = (a^2 - b^2)^{2/3}$$

$$\begin{cases} x = A \cos^3 \phi \\ y = B \sin^3 \phi \end{cases}$$

$$[A = (a^2 - b^2)/a, \quad B = (a^2 - b^2)/b]$$

Exponential curve

(1) $a > 0$

(2) $a < 0$

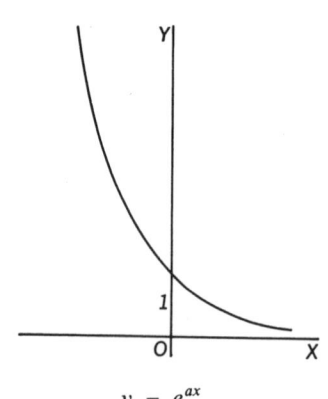

$$y = e^{ax}$$

Curves and Surfaces

Folium of Descartes

Hyperbola

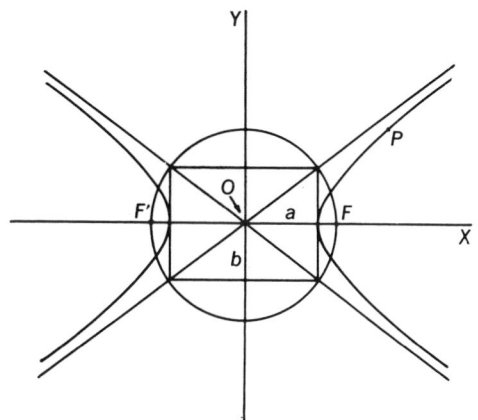

$$x^3 + y^3 - 3axy = 0$$

$$\begin{cases} x = 3a\phi/(1 + \phi^3) \\ y = 3a\phi^2/(1 + \phi^3) \end{cases}$$

$$r = \frac{3a \sin \theta \cos \theta}{\sin^3\theta + \cos^3\theta}$$

[asymptote: $x + y + a = 0$]

$$x^2/a^2 - y^2/b^2 = 1$$
$$[F'P - FP = 2a]$$

Hyperbola, equilateral or rectangular
(1)

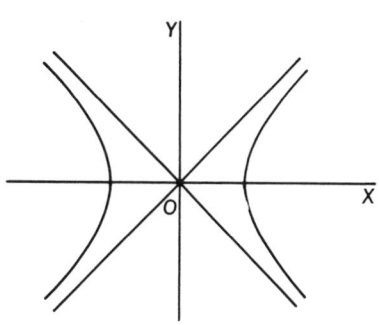

$$x^2 - y^2 = a^2$$

Gamma function

(2)

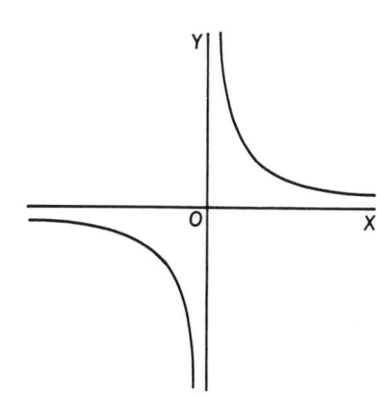

$$\Gamma(n) = \int_0^\infty x^{n-1}e^{-x}dx \quad (n > 0)$$

$$\Gamma(n) = \frac{\Gamma(n + 1)}{n} \quad (0 > n \neq -1, -2, -3, \ldots)$$

$$xy = k, \quad k > 0$$

Curves and Surfaces

(3)

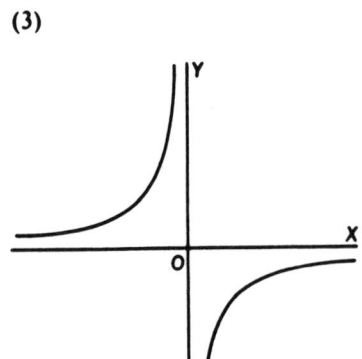

$$xy = k, \quad k < 0$$

Hypocycloid of three cusps, Deltoid

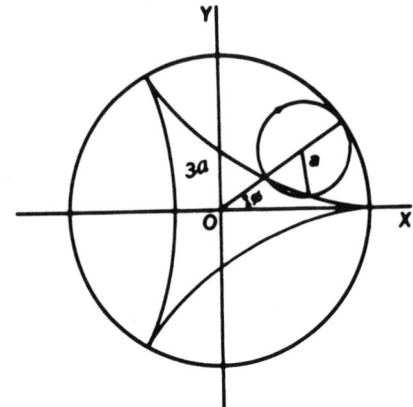

$$\begin{cases} x = 2a \cos \phi + a \cos 2\phi \\ y = 2a \sin \phi - a \sin 2\phi \end{cases}$$

Hyperbolic functions*

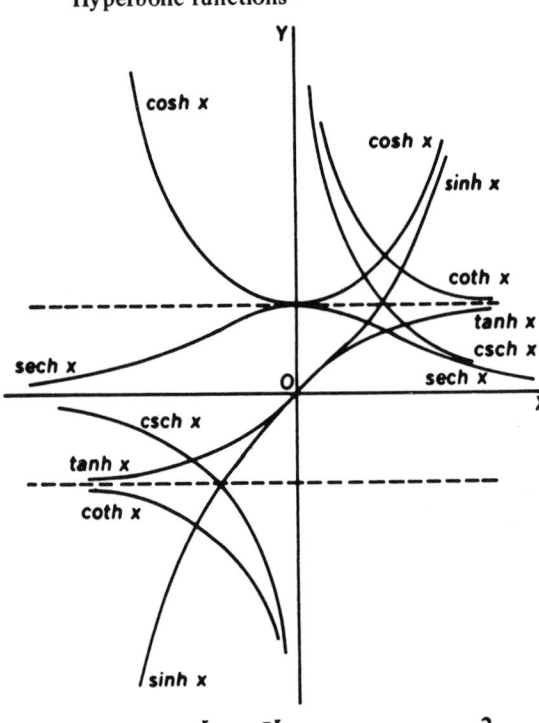

$$\sinh x = \frac{e^x - e^{-x}}{2} \qquad \operatorname{csch} x = \frac{2}{e^x - e^{-x}}$$

$$\cosh x = \frac{e^x + e^{-x}}{2} \qquad \operatorname{sech} x = \frac{2}{e^x + e^{-x}}$$

$$\tanh x = \frac{e^x - e^{-x}}{e^x + e^{-x}} \qquad \coth x = \frac{e^x + e^{-x}}{e^x - e^{-x}}$$

Hyperbolic spiral
See: Spiral, hyperbolic or reciprocal

Hypocycloid of four cusps, Astroid

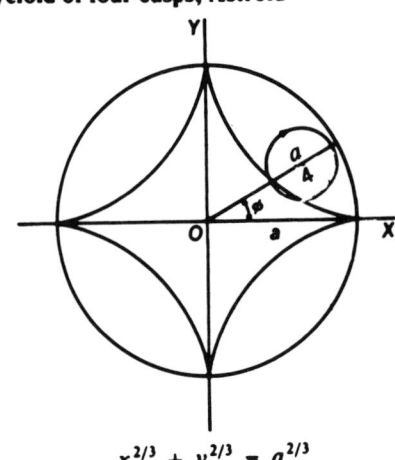

$$x^{2/3} + y^{2/3} = a^{2/3}$$
$$\begin{cases} x = a \cos^3 \phi \\ y = a \sin^3 \phi \end{cases}$$

Inverse cosine curve

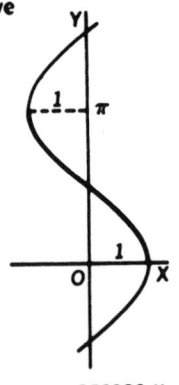

$$y = \arccos x$$

Inverse sine curve

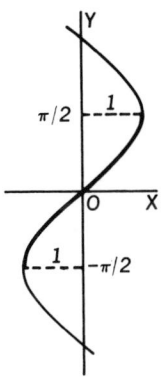

$$y = \arcsin x$$

Inverse tangent curve

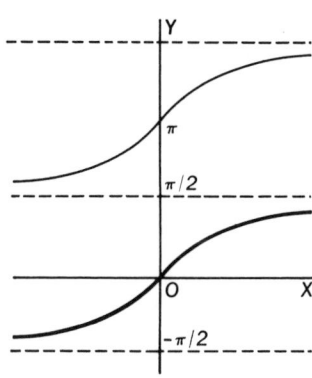

$$y = \arctan x$$

Involute of circle

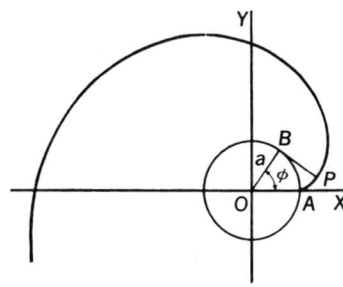

$$\begin{cases} x = a\cos\phi + a\phi\sin\phi \\ y = a\sin\phi - a\phi\cos\phi \end{cases}$$

$$[BP = \widehat{BA}]$$

Lemniscate of Bernoulli, Two-leaved rose

(a)

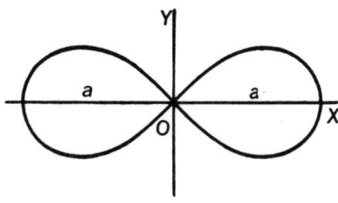

$$(x^2 + y^2)^2 = a^2(x^2 - y^2)$$
$$r^2 = a^2 \cos 2\theta$$

(b)

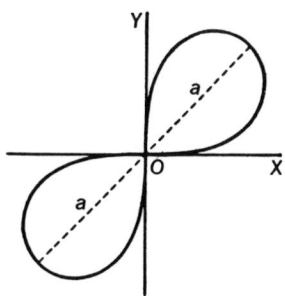

$$(x^2 + y^2)^2 = 2a^2xy$$
$$r^2 = a^2 \sin 2\theta$$

Limacon of Pascal

(1) $a > b$

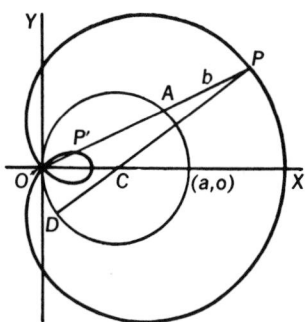

[If $a = 2b$, the curve is called the *trisectrix*, since then $\sphericalangle OPD = \frac{1}{3}\sphericalangle OCD$.]

(2) $a = b$

See: Cardioid

ANALYTIC GEOMETRY
Curves and Surfaces

(3) $a < b$

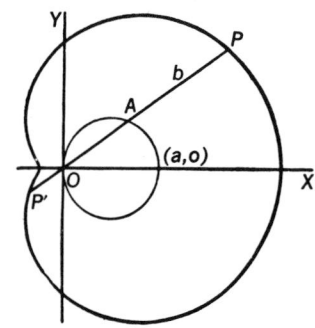

$$(x^2 + y^2 - ax)^2 = b^2(x^2 + y^2)$$
$$r = b + a \cos \theta$$
$$[P'A = AP = b]$$

Lituus

$$r^2\theta = a^2$$

Logarithmic curve
(1) $a > 1$

(2) $0 < a < 1$

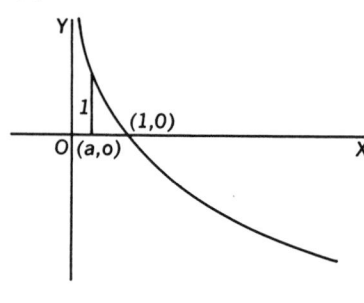

$$y = \log_a x$$

Logarithmic spiral
See: Spiral, logarithmic or equiangular

Nephroid

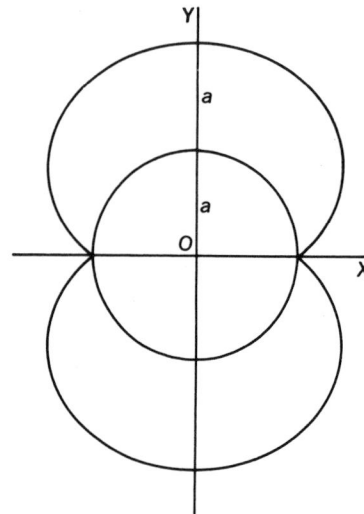

$$\begin{cases} x = \tfrac{1}{2}a(3 \cos \phi - \cos 3\phi) \\ y = \tfrac{1}{2}a(3 \sin \phi - \sin 3\phi) \end{cases}$$

[The nephroid is a 2-cusped epicycloid.]

Oui-ja board curve
See: Cochleoid

Ovals of Cassini
(1) $b > k$

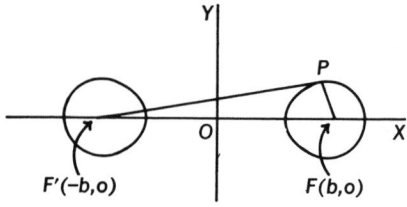

(2) $b = k$
   See: Lemniscate of Bernoulli

(3) $b < k$

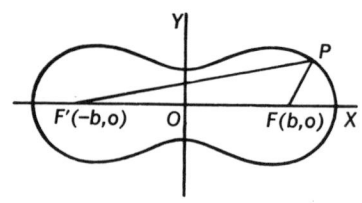

$$(x^2 + y^2 + b^2)^2 - 4b^2x^2 = k^4$$
$$r^4 + b^4 - 2r^2b^2 \cos 2\theta = k^4$$
$$[F'P \cdot FP = k^2]$$

[These curves are sections of a torus on planes parallel to the axis of the torus.]

Parabola

(1)

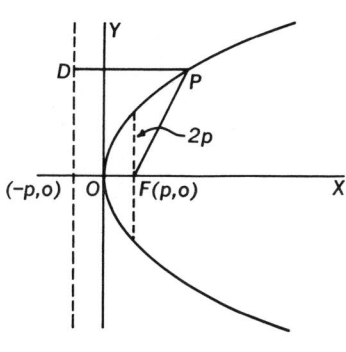

$$y^2 = 4px$$
$$[DP = FP]$$

(2)

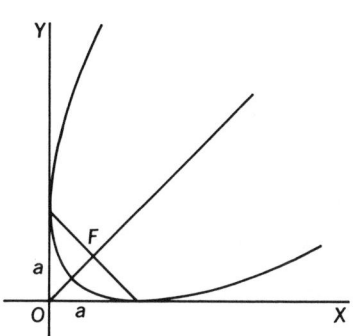

$$\pm x^{1/2} \pm y^{1/2} = a^{1/2}$$
$$(x - y)^2 - 2a(x + y) + a^2 = 0$$

(3)

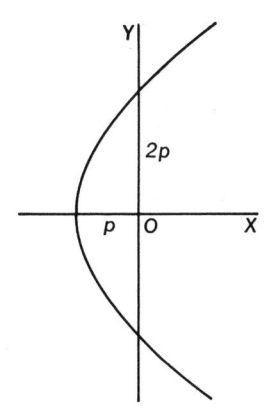

$$r = 2p/(1 - \cos\theta)$$

(4)

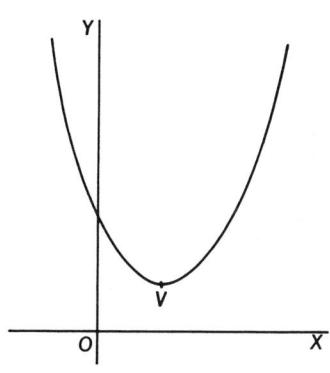

$$y = ax^2 + bx + c, \quad a > 0$$
$$[\text{abscissa of vertex} = -b/2a]$$

Parabolic spiral

See: Spiral, parabolic

Power functions

(1)

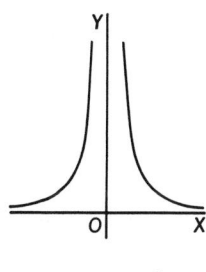

$$y = x^{-2}$$

(2) Equilateral hyperbola

$$y = x^{-1}$$

(3)

$$y = x^{-1/2}$$

(4) Cubical parabola

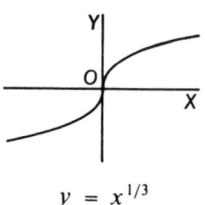

$$y = x^{1/3}$$

(5) Half of a parabola

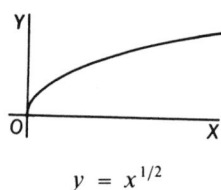

$$y = x^{1/2}$$

(6) Semicubical parabola

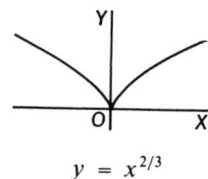

$$y = x^{2/3}$$

(7) Half of semicubical parabola

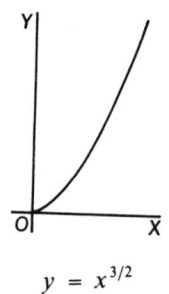

$$y = x^{3/2}$$

(8) Parabola

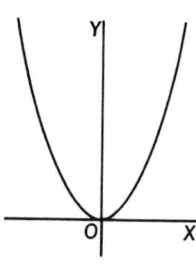

$$y = x^2$$

(9) Cubical parabola

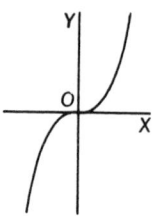

$$y = x^3$$

Probability curve

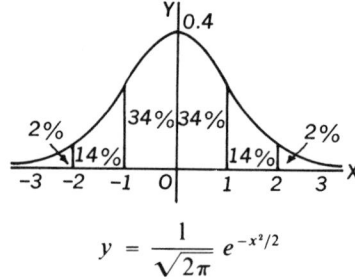

$$y = \frac{1}{\sqrt{2\pi}} e^{-x^2/2}$$

Prolate cycloid
  See: Cycloid, prolate

Pursuit curve
  See: Tractrix

Quadratrix of Hippias

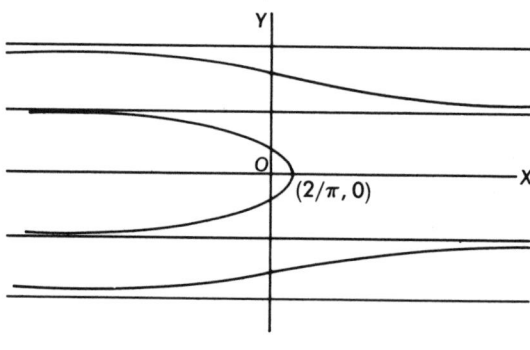

$$y = x \tan (\pi y/2)$$

Reciprocal spiral
  See: Spiral, hyperbolic or reciprocal

Rectangular hyperbola
  See: Hyperbola, equilateral or rectangular

Rose curves
  (1) Two-leaved
    See: Lemniscate of Bernoulli, Two-
    leaved rose

(2) Three-leaved

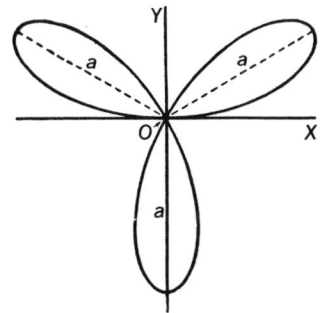

$$r = a \sin 3\theta$$

(3) Three-leaved

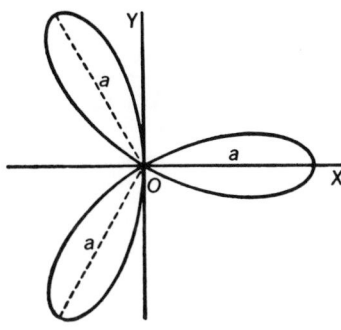

$$r = a \cos 3\theta$$

(4) Four-leaved

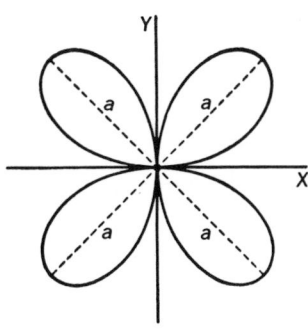

$$r = a \sin 2\theta$$

(5) Four-leaved

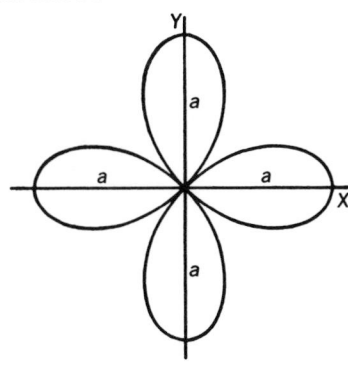

$$r = a \cos 2\theta$$

(6) *n*-leaved

The roses $r = a \sin n\theta$ and $r = a \cos n\theta$, have, for n an even integer, $2n$ leaves; for n an odd integer, n leaves. The roses $r^2 = a \sin n\theta$ and $r^2 = a \cos n\theta$, have, for n an even integer, n leaves; for n an odd integer, $2n$ leaves.

Secant curve

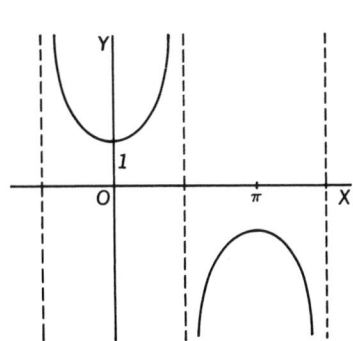

$$y = \sec x$$

Semicubical parabola

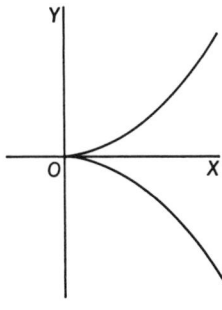

$$y^2 = ax^3$$

$$r = \frac{1}{a} \tan^2 \theta \sec \theta$$

Curves and Surfaces

Serpentine curve

$$(a^2 + x^2)y = abx$$

$$\begin{cases} x = a \cot \phi \\ y = b \sin \phi \cos \phi \end{cases}$$

Sine curve

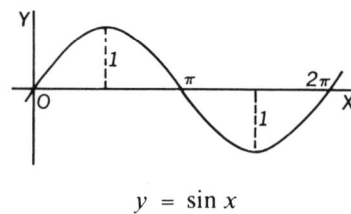

$$y = \sin x$$

Sinusoid

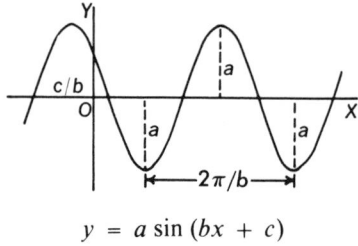

$$y = a \sin (bx + c)$$

Spiral of Archimedes

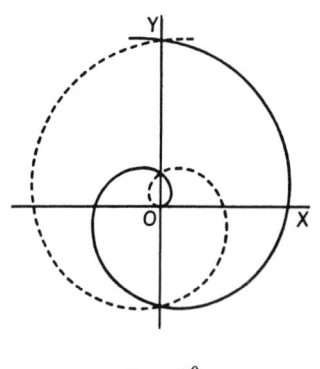

$$r = a\theta$$

Spiral, hyperbolic or reciprocal

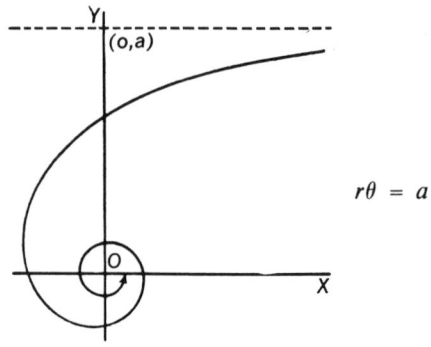

$$r\theta = a$$

Spiral, logarithmic or equiangular

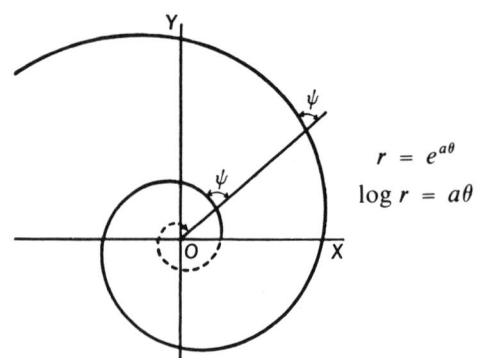

$$r = e^{a\theta}$$

$$\log r = a\theta$$

Spiral, parabolic

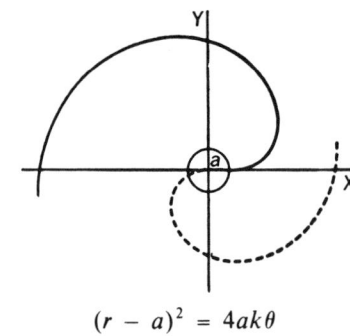

$$(r - a)^2 = 4ak\theta$$

Strophoid

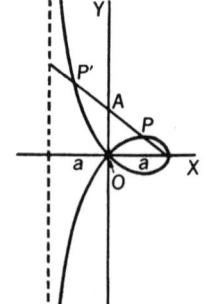

$$y^2 = x^2 \frac{a - x}{a + x}$$

$$r = a \cos 2\theta \sec \theta$$

$$[P'A = AP = OA]$$

Curves and Surfaces

Tangent curve

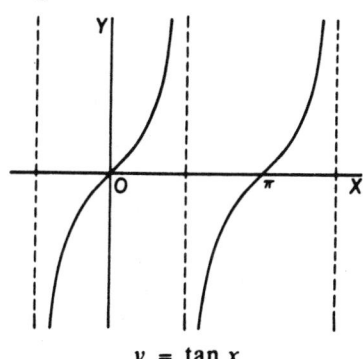

$$y = \tan x$$

Tractrix, Pursuit curve

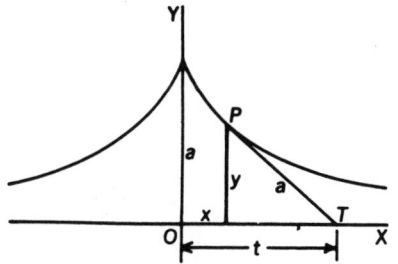

$$x = a \operatorname{sech}^{-1}(y/a) - \sqrt{a^2 - y^2}$$

$$\begin{cases} x = t - a \tanh(t/a) \\ y = a \operatorname{sech}(t/a) \end{cases}$$

$$[PT = a]$$

Trajectory (a parabola)

$$y = x \tan \alpha - gx^2/(2v_0^2 \cos^2 \alpha)$$

$$x = (v_0 \cos \alpha)t$$

$$y = (v_0 \sin \alpha)t - gt^2/2$$

Trigonometric functions

See: Cosecant curve; Cosine curve; Cotangent curve; Secant curve Sine curve; Tangent curve

Trisectrix

See: Limaçon of Pascal (1)

Witch of Agnesi

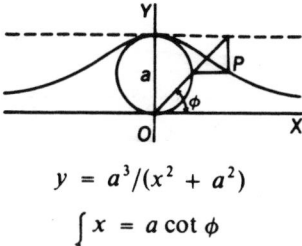

$$y = a^3/(x^2 + a^2)$$

$$\begin{cases} x = a \cot \phi \\ y = a \sin^2 \phi \end{cases}$$

QUADRIC SURFACES*

Ellipsoid

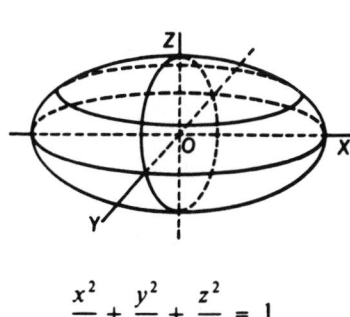

$$\frac{x^2}{a^2} + \frac{y^2}{b^2} + \frac{z^2}{c^2} = 1$$

Elliptic cone

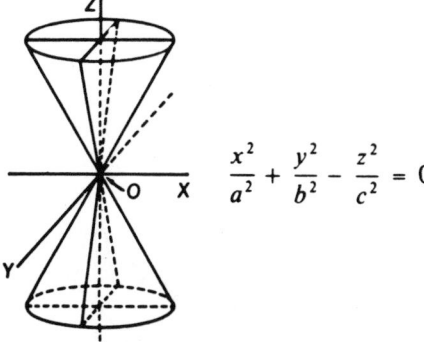

$$\frac{x^2}{a^2} + \frac{y^2}{b^2} - \frac{z^2}{c^2} = 0$$

*Each of the equations is given for the case where the origin is located at $(0, 0, 0)$, the center of the quadric surface. If, however, the center of the surface is at (h, k, l), replace x by $x - h$, y by $y - k$, and z by $z - l$, and the particular standardized form will be that of the surface with center at (h, k, l). For example, the elliptic paraboloid would be

$$\frac{(x - h)^2}{a^2} + \frac{(y - k)^2}{b^2} = c(z - l).$$

Elliptic cylinder

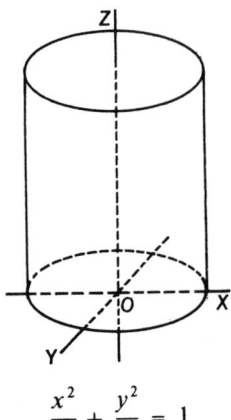

$$\frac{x^2}{a^2} + \frac{y^2}{b^2} = 1$$

Hyperboloid of one sheet

$$\frac{x^2}{a^2} + \frac{y^2}{b^2} - \frac{z^2}{c^2} = 1$$

Elliptic paraboloid

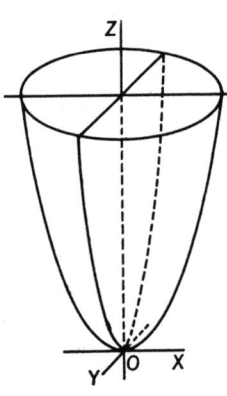

$$\frac{x^2}{a^2} + \frac{y^2}{b^2} = cz$$

Hyperboloid of two sheets

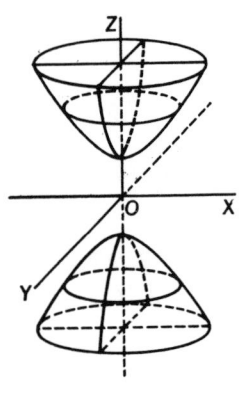

$$\frac{z^2}{c^2} - \frac{x^2}{a^2} - \frac{y^2}{b^2} = 1$$

Hyperbolic paraboloid

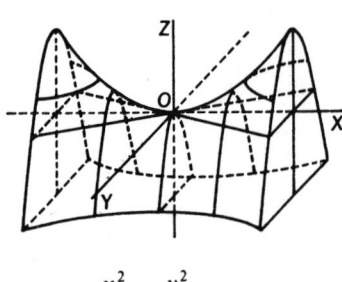

$$\frac{x^2}{a^2} - \frac{y^2}{b^2} = cz$$

Sphere

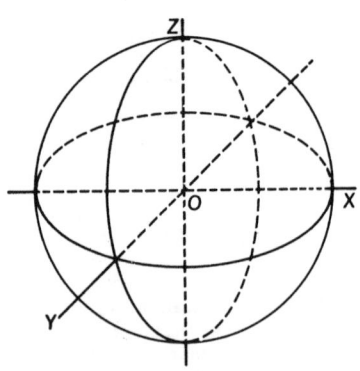

$$x^2 + y^2 + z^2 = a^2$$

PATTERNS OF REGULAR POLYHEDRA

Tetrahedron

Octahedron

Hexahedron, or **Cube**

Icosahedron

Dodecahedron

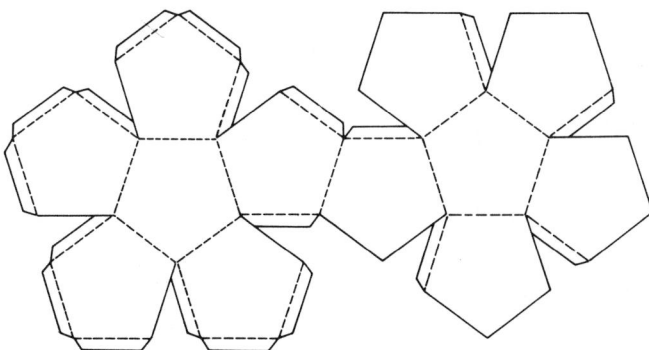

VIII. CALCULUS

Derivatives *

In the following formulas u, v, w represent functions of x, while a, c, n represent fixed real numbers. All arguments in the trigonometric functions are measured in radians, and all inverse trigonometric and hyperbolic functions represent principal values.

1. $\dfrac{d}{dx}(a) = 0$

2. $\dfrac{d}{dx}(x) = 1$

3. $\dfrac{d}{dx}(au) = a\dfrac{du}{dx}$

4. $\dfrac{d}{dx}(u + v - w) = \dfrac{du}{dx} + \dfrac{dv}{dx} - \dfrac{dw}{dx}$

5. $\dfrac{d}{dx}(uv) = u\dfrac{dv}{dx} + v\dfrac{du}{dx}$

6. $\dfrac{d}{dx}(uvw) = uv\dfrac{dw}{dx} + vw\dfrac{du}{dx} + uw\dfrac{dv}{dx}$ and so on to n factors

7. $\dfrac{d}{dx}\left(\dfrac{u}{v}\right) = \dfrac{v\dfrac{du}{dx} - u\dfrac{dv}{dx}}{v^2} = \dfrac{1}{v}\dfrac{du}{dx} - \dfrac{u}{v^2}\dfrac{dv}{dx}$

8. $\dfrac{d}{dx}(u^n) = nu^{n-1}\dfrac{du}{dx}$

9. $\dfrac{d}{dx}(\sqrt{u}) = \dfrac{1}{2\sqrt{u}}\dfrac{du}{dx}$

10. $\dfrac{d}{dx}\left(\dfrac{1}{u}\right) = -\dfrac{1}{u^2}\dfrac{du}{dx}$

11. $\dfrac{d}{dx}\left(\dfrac{1}{u^n}\right) = -\dfrac{n}{u^{n+1}}\dfrac{du}{dx}$

12. $\dfrac{d}{dx}\left(\dfrac{u^n}{v^m}\right) = \dfrac{u^{n-1}}{v^{m+1}}\left(nv\dfrac{du}{dx} - mu\dfrac{dv}{dx}\right)$

13. $\dfrac{d}{dx}(u^n v^m) = u^{n-1}v^{m-1}\left(nv\dfrac{du}{dx} + mu\dfrac{dv}{dx}\right)$

14. $\dfrac{d}{dx}[f(u)] = \dfrac{d}{du}[f(u)] \cdot \dfrac{du}{dx}$

*Let $y = f(x)$ and $\dfrac{dy}{dx} = \dfrac{d[f(x)]}{dx} = f'(x)$ define respectively a function and its derivative for any value x in their common domain. The differential for the function at such a value x is accordingly defined as

$$dy = d[f(x)] = \dfrac{dy}{dx}\,dx = \dfrac{d[f(x)]}{dx}\,dx = f'(x)dx$$

Each derivative formula has an associated differential formula. For example, formula 6 above has the differential formula

$$d(uvw) = uv\,dw + vw\,du + uw\,dv$$

DERIVATIVES (Continued)

15. $\dfrac{d^2}{dx^2}[f(u)] = \dfrac{df(u)}{du} \cdot \dfrac{d^2u}{dx^2} + \dfrac{d^2f(u)}{du^2} \cdot \left(\dfrac{du}{dx}\right)^2$

16. $\dfrac{d^n}{dx^n}[uv] = \dbinom{n}{0} v \dfrac{d^n u}{dx^n} + \dbinom{n}{1} \dfrac{dv}{dx} \dfrac{d^{n-1}u}{dx^{n-1}} + \dbinom{n}{2} \dfrac{d^2v}{dx^2} \dfrac{d^{n-2}u}{dx^{n-2}}$

$$+ \cdots + \dbinom{n}{k} \dfrac{d^k v}{dx^k} \dfrac{d^{n-k}u}{dx^{n-k}} + \cdots + \dbinom{n}{n} u \dfrac{d^n v}{dx^n}$$

where $\dbinom{n}{r} = \dfrac{n!}{r!(n-r)!}$ the binomial coefficient, n non-negative integer and $\dbinom{n}{0} = 1$.

17. $\dfrac{du}{dx} = \dfrac{1}{\dfrac{dx}{du}}$ if $\dfrac{dx}{du} \neq 0$

18. $\dfrac{d}{dx}(\log_a u) = (\log_a e)\dfrac{1}{u}\dfrac{du}{dx}$

19. $\dfrac{d}{dx}(\log_e u) = \dfrac{1}{u}\dfrac{du}{dx}$

20. $\dfrac{d}{dx}(a^u) = a^u(\log_e a)\dfrac{du}{dx}$

21. $\dfrac{d}{dx}(e^u) = e^u\dfrac{du}{dx}$

22. $\dfrac{d}{dx}(u^v) = vu^{v-1}\dfrac{du}{dx} + (\log_e u)u^v\dfrac{dv}{dx}$

23. $\dfrac{d}{dx}(\sin u) = \dfrac{du}{dx}(\cos u)$

24. $\dfrac{d}{dx}(\cos u) = -\dfrac{du}{dx}(\sin u)$

25. $\dfrac{d}{dx}(\tan u) = \dfrac{du}{dx}(\sec^2 u)$

26. $\dfrac{d}{dx}(\cot u) = -\dfrac{du}{dx}(\csc^2 u)$

27. $\dfrac{d}{dx}(\sec u) = \dfrac{du}{dx}\sec u \cdot \tan u$

28. $\dfrac{d}{dx}(\csc u) = -\dfrac{du}{dx}\csc u \cdot \cot u$

29. $\dfrac{d}{dx}(\text{vers } u) = \dfrac{du}{dx}\sin u$

30. $\dfrac{d}{dx}(\arcsin u) = \dfrac{1}{\sqrt{1-u^2}}\dfrac{du}{dx}, \qquad \left(-\dfrac{\pi}{2} \leq \arcsin u \leq \dfrac{\pi}{2}\right)$

DERIVATIVES (Continued)

31. $\dfrac{d}{dx}(\text{arc cos } u) = -\dfrac{1}{\sqrt{1-u^2}}\dfrac{du}{dx}$, $(0 \leq \text{arc cos } u \leq \pi)$

32. $\dfrac{d}{dx}(\text{arc tan } u) = \dfrac{1}{1+u^2}\dfrac{du}{dx}$, $\left(-\dfrac{\pi}{2} < \text{arc tan } u < \dfrac{\pi}{2}\right)$

33. $\dfrac{d}{dx}(\text{arc cot } u) = -\dfrac{1}{1+u^2}\dfrac{du}{dx}$, $(0 \leq \text{arc cot } u \leq \pi)$

34. $\dfrac{d}{dx}(\text{arc sec } u) = \dfrac{1}{u\sqrt{u^2-1}}\dfrac{du}{dx}$, $\left(0 \leq \text{arc sec } u < \dfrac{\pi}{2}, -\pi \leq \text{arc sec } u < -\dfrac{\pi}{2}\right)$

35. $\dfrac{d}{dx}(\text{arc csc } u) = -\dfrac{1}{u\sqrt{u^2-1}}\dfrac{du}{dx}$, $\left(0 < \text{arc csc } u \leq \dfrac{\pi}{2}, -\pi < \text{arc csc } u \leq -\dfrac{\pi}{2}\right)$

36. $\dfrac{d}{dx}(\text{arc vers } u) = \dfrac{1}{\sqrt{2u-u^2}}\dfrac{du}{dx}$, $(0 \leq \text{arc vers } u \leq \pi)$

37. $\dfrac{d}{dx}(\sinh u) = \dfrac{du}{dx}(\cosh u)$

38. $\dfrac{d}{dx}(\cosh u) = \dfrac{du}{dx}(\sinh u)$

39. $\dfrac{d}{dx}(\tanh u) = \dfrac{du}{dx}(\text{sech}^2 u)$

40. $\dfrac{d}{dx}(\coth u) = -\dfrac{du}{dx}(\text{csch}^2 u)$

41. $\dfrac{d}{dx}(\text{sech } u) = -\dfrac{du}{dx}(\text{sech } u \cdot \tanh u)$

42. $\dfrac{d}{dx}(\text{csch } u) = -\dfrac{du}{dx}(\text{csch } u \cdot \coth u)$

43. $\dfrac{d}{dx}(\sinh^{-1} u) = \dfrac{d}{dx}[\log(u + \sqrt{u^2+1})] = \dfrac{1}{\sqrt{u^2+1}}\dfrac{du}{dx}$

44. $\dfrac{d}{dx}(\cosh^{-1} u) = \dfrac{d}{dx}[\log(u + \sqrt{u^2-1})] = \dfrac{1}{\sqrt{u^2-1}}\dfrac{du}{dx}$, $(u > 1, \cosh^{-1} u > 0)$

45. $\dfrac{d}{dx}(\tanh^{-1} u) = \dfrac{d}{dx}\left[\dfrac{1}{2}\log\dfrac{1+u}{1-u}\right] = \dfrac{1}{1-u^2}\dfrac{du}{dx}$, $(u^2 < 1)$

46. $\dfrac{d}{dx}(\coth^{-1} u) = \dfrac{d}{dx}\left[\dfrac{1}{2}\log\dfrac{u+1}{u-1}\right] = \dfrac{1}{1-u^2}\dfrac{du}{dx}$, $(u^2 > 1)$

47. $\dfrac{d}{dx}(\text{sech}^{-1} u) = \dfrac{d}{dx}\left[\log\dfrac{1+\sqrt{1-u^2}}{u}\right] = -\dfrac{1}{u\sqrt{1-u^2}}\dfrac{du}{dx}$, $(0 < u < 1, \text{sech}^{-1} u > 0)$

48. $\dfrac{d}{dx}(\text{csch}^{-1} u) = \dfrac{d}{dx}\left[\log\dfrac{1+\sqrt{1+u^2}}{u}\right] = -\dfrac{1}{|u|\sqrt{1+u^2}}\dfrac{du}{dx}$

49. $\dfrac{d}{dq} \displaystyle\int_p^q f(x)\, dx = f(q),$ [p constant]

50. $\dfrac{d}{dp} \displaystyle\int_p^q f(x)\, dx = -f(p),$ [q constant]

51. $\dfrac{d}{da} \displaystyle\int_p^q f(x, a)\, dx = \displaystyle\int_p^q \dfrac{\partial}{\partial a}[f(x, a)]\, dx + f(q, a)\dfrac{dq}{da} - f(p, a)\dfrac{dp}{da}$

CALCULUS

INTEGRATION

The following is a brief discussion of some integration techniques. A more complete discussion can be found in a number of good text books. However, the purpose of this introduction is simply to discuss a few of the important techniques which may be used, in conjunction with the integral table which follows, to integrate particular functions.

No matter how extensive the integral table, it is a fairly uncommon occurrence to find in the table the exact integral desired. Usually some form of transformation will have to be made. The simplest type of transformation, and yet the most general, is substitution. Simple forms of substitution, such as $y = ax$, are employed almost unconsciously by experienced users of integral tables. Other substitutions may require more thought. In some sections of the tables, appropriate substitutions are suggested for integrals which are similar to, but not exactly like, integrals in the table. Finding the right substitution is largely a matter of intuition and experience.

Several precautions must be observed when using substitutions:

1. Be sure to make the substitution in the dx term, as well as everywhere else in the integral.
2. Be sure that the function substituted is one-to-one and continuous. If this is not the case, the integral must be restricted in such a way as to make it true. See the example following.
3. With definite integrals, the limits should also be expressed in terms of the new dependent variable. With indefinite integrals, it is necessary to perform the reverse substitution to obtain the answer in terms of the original independent variable. This may also be done for definite integrals, but it is usually easier to change the limits.

Example:

$$\int \frac{x^4}{\sqrt{a^2 - x^2}} \, dx$$

Here we make the substitution $x = |a| \sin \theta$. Then $dx = |a| \cos \theta \, d\theta$, and

$$\sqrt{a^2 - x^2} = \sqrt{a^2 - a^2 \sin^2 \theta} = |a|\sqrt{1 - \sin^2 \theta} = |a \cos \theta|$$

Notice the absolute value signs. It is very important to keep in mind that a square root radical always denotes the positive square root, and to assure the sign is always kept positive. Thus $\sqrt{x^2} = |x|$. Failure to observe this is a common cause of errors in integration.

Notice also that the indicated substitution is not a one-to-one function, that is, it does not have a unique inverse. Thus we must restrict the range of θ in such a way as to make the function one-to-one. Fortunately, this is easily done by solving for θ

$$\theta = \sin^{-1} \frac{x}{|a|}$$

and restricting the inverse sine to the principal values, $-\frac{\pi}{2} \leq \theta \leq \frac{\pi}{2}$.

Thus the integral becomes

$$\int \frac{a^4 \sin^4 \theta |a| \cos \theta \, d\theta}{|a| |\cos \theta|}$$

Now, however, in the range of values chosen for θ, $\cos \theta$ is always positive. Thus we may remove the absolute value signs from $\cos \theta$ in the denominator. (This is one of the reasons that the principal values of the inverse trigonometric functions are defined as they are.)

Then the $\cos \theta$ terms cancel, and the integral becomes

$$a^4 \int \sin^4 \theta \, d\theta$$

By application of integral formulas 299 and 296, we integrate this to

$$-a^4 \frac{\sin^3 \theta \cos \theta}{4} - \frac{3a^4}{8} \cos \theta \sin \theta + \frac{3a^4}{8} \theta + C$$

We now must perform the inverse substitution to get the result in terms of x. We have

$$\theta = \sin^{-1} \frac{x}{|a|}$$

$$\sin \theta = \frac{x}{|a|}$$

Then

$$\cos \theta = \pm \sqrt{1 - \sin^2 \theta} = \pm \sqrt{1 - \frac{x^2}{a^2}} = \pm \frac{\sqrt{a^2 - x^2}}{|a|}.$$

Because of the previously mentioned fact that $\cos \theta$ is positive, we may omit the $\pm$ sign. The reverse substitution then produces the final answer

$$\int \frac{x^4}{\sqrt{a^2 - x^2}} dx = -\tfrac{1}{4} x^3 \sqrt{a^2 - x^2} - \tfrac{3}{8} a^2 x \sqrt{a^2 - x^2} + \frac{3a^4}{8} \sin^{-1} \frac{x}{|a|} + C.$$

Any rational function of x may be integrated, if the denominator is factored into linear and irreducible quadratic factors. The function may then be broken into partial fractions, and the individual partial fractions integrated by use of the appropriate formula from the integral table. See the section on partial fractions for further information.

Many integrals may be reduced to rational functions by proper substitutions. For example,

$$z = \tan \frac{x}{2}$$

will reduce any rational function of the six trigonometric functions of x to a rational function of z. (Frequently there are other substitutions which are simpler to use, but this one will always work. See integral formula number 484.)

Any rational function of x and $\sqrt{ax + b}$ may be reduced to a rational function of z by making the substitution

$$z = \sqrt{ax + b}.$$

Other likely substitutions will be suggested by looking at the form of the integrand.

The other main method of transforming integrals is integration by parts. This involves applying formula number 5 or 6 in the accompanying integral table. The critical factor in this method is the choice of the functions u and v. In order for the method to be successful, $v = \int dv$ and $\int v \, du$ must be easier to integrate than the original integral. Again, this choice is largely a matter of intuition and experience.

Example:

$$\int x \sin x \, dx$$

Two obvious choices are $u = x$, $dv = \sin x \, dx$, or $u = \sin x$, $dv = x \, dx$. Since a preliminary mental calculation indicates that $\int v \, du$ in the second choice would be more, rather than less, complicated than the original integral (it would contain x^2), we use the first choice.

$$u = x \qquad\qquad du = dx$$

$$dv = \sin x \, dx \qquad\qquad v = -\cos x$$

$$\int x \sin x \, dx = \int u \, dv = uv - \int v \, du = -x \cos x + \int \cos x \, dx$$

$$= \sin x - x \cos x$$

Of course, this result could have been obtained directly from the integral table, but it provides a simple example of the method. In more complicated examples the choice of u and v may not be so obvious, and several different choices may have to be tried. Of course, there is no guarantee that any of them will work.

Integration by parts may be applied more than once, or combined with substitution. A fairly common case is illustrated by the following example.

Example:

$$\int e^x \sin x \, dx$$

Let

$$u = e^x \qquad \text{Then} \quad du = e^x \, dx$$

$$dv = \sin x \, dx \qquad\qquad v = -\cos x$$

$$\int e^x \sin x \, dx = \int u \, dv = uv - \int v \, du = -e^x \cos x + \int e^x \cos x \, dx$$

In this latter integral,

$$\text{let} \quad u = e^x \qquad\qquad \text{Then} \quad du = e^x \, dx$$

$$dv = \cos x \, dx \qquad\qquad v = \sin x$$

$$\int e^x \sin x \, dx = -e^x \cos x + \int e^x \cos x \, dx = -e^x \cos x + \int u \, dv$$

$$= -e^x \cos x + uv - \int v \, du$$

$$= -e^x \cos x + e^x \sin x - \int e^x \sin x \, dx$$

This looks as if a circular transformation has taken place, since we are back at the same integral we started from. However, the above equation can be solved algebraically for the required integral:

$$\int e^x \sin x \, dx = \tfrac{1}{2}(e^x \sin x - e^x \cos x)$$

In the second integration by parts, if the parts had been chosen as $u = \cos x$, $dv = e^x \, dx$, we would indeed have made a circular transformation, and returned to the starting place. In general, when doing repeated integration by parts, one should never choose the function u at any stage to be the same as the function v at the previous stage, or a constant times the previous v.

The following rule is called the extended rule for integration by parts. It is the result of $n + 1$ successive applications of integration by parts.

If

$$g_1(x) = \int g(x)\, dx, \qquad g_2(x) = \int g_1(x)\, dx,$$

$$g_3(x) = \int g_2(x)\, dx, \ldots, g_m(x) = \int g_{m-1}(x)\, dx, \ldots,$$

then

$$\int f(x) \cdot g(x)\, dx = f(x) \cdot g_1(x) - f'(x) \cdot g_2(x) + f''(x) \cdot g_3(x) - + \cdots$$

$$+ (-1)^n f^{(n)}(x) g_{n+1}(x) + (-1)^{n+1} \int f^{(n+1)}(x) g_{n+1}(x)\, dx.$$

A useful special case of the above rule is when $f(x)$ is a polynomial of degree n. Then $f^{(n+1)}(x) = 0$, and

$$\int f(x) \cdot g(x)\, dx = f(x) \cdot g_1(x) - f'(x) \cdot g_2(x) + f''(x) \cdot g_3(x) - + \cdots + (-1)^n f^{(n)}(x) g_{n+1}(x) + C$$

Example:
If $f(x) = x^2, g(x) = \sin x$

$$\int x^2 \sin x\, dx = -x^2 \cos x + 2x \sin x + 2 \cos x + C$$

Another application of this formula occurs if

$$f''(x) = af(x) \quad \text{and} \quad g''(x) = bg(x),$$

where a and b are unequal constants. In this case, by a process similar to that used in the above example for $\int e^x \sin x\, dx$, we get the formula

$$\int f(x)g(x)\, dx = \frac{f(x) \cdot g'(x) - f'(x) \cdot g(x)}{b - a} + C$$

This formula could have been used in the example mentioned. Here is another example.

Example:
If $f(x) = e^{2x}, g(x) = \sin 3x$, then $a = 4, b = -9$, and

$$\int e^{2x} \sin 3x\, dx = \frac{3 e^{2x} \cos 3x - 2 e^{2x} \sin 3x}{-9 - 4} + C = \frac{e^{2x}}{13}(2 \sin 3x - 3 \cos 3x) + C$$

The following additional points should be observed when using this table.

1. A constant of integration is to be supplied with the answers for indefinite integrals.
2. Logarithmic expressions are to base $e = 2.71828\ldots$, unless otherwise specified, and are to be evaluated for the absolute value of the arguments involved therein.
3. All angles are measured in radians, and inverse trigonometric and hyperbolic functions represent principal values, unless otherwise indicated.
4. If the application of a formula produces either a zero denominator or the square root of a negative number in the result, there is usually available another form of the answer which avoids this difficulty. In many of the results, the excluded values are specified, but when such are omitted it is presumed that one can tell what these should be, especially when difficulties of the type herein mentioned are obtained.
5. When inverse trigonometric functions occur in the integrals, be sure that any replacements made for them are strictly in accordance with the rules for such functions. This causes

little difficulty when the argument of the inverse trigonometric function is positive, since then all angles involved are in the first quadrant. However, if the argument is negative, special care must be used. Thus if $u > 0$,

$$\sin^{-1} u = \cos^{-1}\sqrt{1 - u^2} = \csc^{-1}\frac{1}{u}, \text{ etc.}$$

However, if $u < 0$,

$$\sin^{-1} u = -\cos^{-1}\sqrt{1 - u^2} = -\pi - \csc^{-1}\frac{1}{u}, \text{ etc.}$$

See the section on inverse trigonometric functions for a full treatment of the allowable substitutions.

6. In integrals 340–345 and some others, the right side includes expressions of the form

$$A \tan^{-1}[B + C \tan f(x)].$$

In these formulas, the $\tan^{-1}$ does not necessarily represent the principal value. Instead of always employing the principal branch of the inverse tangent function, one must instead use that branch of the inverse tangent function upon which $f(x)$ lies for any particular choice of x.

Example:

$$\int_0^{4\pi} \frac{dx}{2 + \sin x} = \frac{2}{\sqrt{3}}\tan^{-1}\frac{2\tan\frac{x}{2} + 1}{\sqrt{3}}\Bigg]_0^{4\pi}$$

$$= \frac{2}{\sqrt{3}}\left[\tan^{-1}\frac{2\tan 2\pi + 1}{\sqrt{3}} - \tan^{-1}\frac{2\tan 0 + 1}{\sqrt{3}}\right]$$

$$= \frac{2}{\sqrt{3}}\left[\frac{13\pi}{6} - \frac{\pi}{6}\right] = \frac{4\pi}{\sqrt{3}} = \frac{4\sqrt{3}\pi}{3}$$

Here

$$\tan^{-1}\frac{2\tan 2\pi + 1}{\sqrt{3}} = \tan^{-1}\frac{1}{\sqrt{3}} = \frac{13\pi}{6},$$

since $f(x) = 2\pi$; and

$$\tan^{-1}\frac{2\tan 0 + 1}{\sqrt{3}} = \tan^{-1}\frac{1}{\sqrt{3}} = \frac{\pi}{6},$$

since $f(x) = 0$.

7. B_n and E_n where used in Integrals represents the Bernoulli and Euler numbers as defined in the tables contained from pages 577–583.

ELEMENTARY FORMS

1. $\int a\,dx = ax$

2. $\int a \cdot f(x)\,dx = a \int f(x)\,dx$

3. $\int \phi(y)\,dx = \int \frac{\phi(y)}{y'}\,dy,$ where $y' = \dfrac{dy}{dx}$

4. $\int (u + v)\,dx = \int u\,dx + \int v\,dx,$ where u and v are any functions of x

5. $\int u\,dv = u \int dv - \int v\,du = uv - \int v\,du$

6. $\int u \dfrac{dv}{dx}\,dx = uv - \int v \dfrac{du}{dx}\,dx$

7. $\int x^n\,dx = \dfrac{x^{n+1}}{n+1},$ except $n = -1$

8. $\int \dfrac{f'(x)\,dx}{f(x)} = \log f(x),$ $(df(x) = f'(x)\,dx)$

9. $\int \dfrac{dx}{x} = \log x$

10. $\int \dfrac{f'(x)\,dx}{2\sqrt{f(x)}} = \sqrt{f(x)},$ $(df(x) = f'(x)\,dx)$

11. $\int e^x\,dx = e^x$

12. $\int e^{ax}\,dx = e^{ax}/a$

13. $\int b^{ax}\,dx = \dfrac{b^{ax}}{a \log b},$ $(b > 0)$

14. $\int \log x\,dx = x \log x - x$

15. $\int a^x \log a\,dx = a^x,$ $(a > 0)$

16. $\int \dfrac{dx}{a^2 + x^2} = \dfrac{1}{a}\tan^{-1}\dfrac{x}{a}$

INTEGRALS (Continued)

17. $\displaystyle\int \frac{dx}{a^2 - x^2} = \begin{cases} \dfrac{1}{a}\tanh^{-1}\dfrac{x}{a} \\ \text{or} \\ \dfrac{1}{2a}\log\dfrac{a + x}{a - x}, \end{cases} \quad (a^2 > x^2)$

18. $\displaystyle\int \frac{dx}{x^2 - a^2} = \begin{cases} -\dfrac{1}{a}\coth^{-1}\dfrac{x}{a} \\ \text{or} \\ \dfrac{1}{2a}\log\dfrac{x - a}{x + a}, \end{cases} \quad (x^2 > a^2)$

19. $\displaystyle\int \frac{dx}{\sqrt{a^2 - x^2}} = \begin{cases} \sin^{-1}\dfrac{x}{|a|} \\ \text{or} \\ -\cos^{-1}\dfrac{x}{|a|}, \end{cases} \quad (a^2 > x^2)$

20. $\displaystyle\int \frac{dx}{\sqrt{x^2 \pm a^2}} = \log\left(x + \sqrt{x^2 \pm a^2}\right)$

21. $\displaystyle\int \frac{dx}{x\sqrt{x^2 - a^2}} = \frac{1}{|a|}\sec^{-1}\frac{x}{a}$

22. $\displaystyle\int \frac{dx}{x\sqrt{a^2 \pm x^2}} = -\frac{1}{a}\log\left(\frac{a + \sqrt{a^2 \pm x^2}}{x}\right)$

FORMS CONTAINING $(a + bx)$

For forms containing $a + bx$, but not listed in the table, the substitution $u = \dfrac{a + bx}{x}$ may prove helpful.

23. $\displaystyle\int (a + bx)^n \, dx = \frac{(a + bx)^{n+1}}{(n + 1)b}, \quad (n \neq -1)$

24. $\displaystyle\int x(a + bx)^n \, dx$

$$= \frac{1}{b^2(n + 2)}(a + bx)^{n+2} - \frac{a}{b^2(n + 1)}(a + bx)^{n+1}, \quad (n \neq -1, -2)$$

25. $\displaystyle\int x^2(a + bx)^n \, dx = \frac{1}{b^3}\left[\frac{(a + bx)^{n+3}}{n + 3} - 2a\frac{(a + bx)^{n+2}}{n + 2} + a^2\frac{(a + bx)^{n+1}}{n + 1}\right]$

INTEGRALS (Continued)

26. $\displaystyle\int x^m(a+bx)^n\,dx = \begin{cases} \dfrac{x^{m+1}(a+bx)^n}{m+n+1} + \dfrac{an}{m+n+1}\displaystyle\int x^m(a+bx)^{n-1}\,dx \\[2em] \text{or} \\[1em] \dfrac{1}{a(n+1)}\left[-x^{m+1}(a+bx)^{n+1} \right. \\[2em] \qquad\qquad \left. + (m+n+2)\displaystyle\int x^m(a+bx)^{n+1}\,dx\right] \\[2em] \text{or} \\[1em] \dfrac{1}{b(m+n+1)}\left[x^m(a+bx)^{n+1} - ma\displaystyle\int x^{m-1}(a+bx)^n\,dx\right] \end{cases}$

27. $\displaystyle\int \frac{dx}{a+bx} = \frac{1}{b}\log(a+bx)$

28. $\displaystyle\int \frac{dx}{(a+bx)^2} = -\frac{1}{b(a+bx)}$

29. $\displaystyle\int \frac{dx}{(a+bx)^3} = -\frac{1}{2b(a+bx)^2}$

30. $\displaystyle\int \frac{x\,dx}{a+bx} = \begin{cases} \dfrac{1}{b^2}[a+bx-a\log(a+bx)] \\[1.5em] \qquad\text{or} \\[1em] \dfrac{x}{b} - \dfrac{a}{b^2}\log(a+bx) \end{cases}$

31. $\displaystyle\int \frac{x\,dx}{(a+bx)^2} = \frac{1}{b^2}\left[\log(a+bx) + \frac{a}{a+bx}\right]$

32. $\displaystyle\int \frac{x\,dx}{(a+bx)^n} = \frac{1}{b^2}\left[\frac{-1}{(n-2)(a+bx)^{n-2}} + \frac{a}{(n-1)(a+bx)^{n-1}}\right], \qquad n \neq 1, 2$

33. $\displaystyle\int \frac{x^2\,dx}{a+bx} = \frac{1}{b^3}\left[\frac{1}{2}(a+bx)^2 - 2a(a+bx) + a^2\log(a+bx)\right]$

34. $\displaystyle\int \frac{x^2\,dx}{(a+bx)^2} = \frac{1}{b^3}\left[a+bx - 2a\log(a+bx) - \frac{a^2}{a+bx}\right]$

35. $\displaystyle\int \frac{x^2\,dx}{(a+bx)^3} = \frac{1}{b^3}\left[\log(a+bx) + \frac{2a}{a+bx} - \frac{a^2}{2(a+bx)^2}\right]$

36. $\displaystyle\int \frac{x^2\,dx}{(a+bx)^n} = \frac{1}{b^3}\left[\frac{-1}{(n-3)(a+bx)^{n-3}} \right.$
$\left. + \frac{2a}{(n-2)(a+bx)^{n-2}} - \frac{a^2}{(n-1)(a+bx)^{n-1}}\right], \qquad n \neq 1, 2, 3$

INTEGRALS (Continued)

37. $\displaystyle\int \frac{dx}{x(a + bx)} = -\frac{1}{a}\log\frac{a + bx}{x}$

38. $\displaystyle\int \frac{dx}{x(a + bx)^2} = \frac{1}{a(a + bx)} - \frac{1}{a^2}\log\frac{a + bx}{x}$

39. $\displaystyle\int \frac{dx}{x(a + bx)^3} = \frac{1}{a^3}\left[\frac{1}{2}\left(\frac{2a + bx}{a + bx}\right)^2 + \log\frac{x}{a + bx}\right]$

40. $\displaystyle\int \frac{dx}{x^2(a + bx)} = -\frac{1}{ax} + \frac{b}{a^2}\log\frac{a + bx}{x}$

41. $\displaystyle\int \frac{dx}{x^3(a + bx)} = \frac{2bx - a}{2a^2x^2} + \frac{b^2}{a^3}\log\frac{x}{a + bx}$

42. $\displaystyle\int \frac{dx}{x^2(a + bx)^2} = -\frac{a + 2bx}{a^2x(a + bx)} + \frac{2b}{a^3}\log\frac{a + bx}{x}$

FORMS CONTAINING $c^2 \pm x^2$, $x^2 - c^2$

43. $\displaystyle\int \frac{dx}{c^2 + x^2} = \frac{1}{c}\tan^{-1}\frac{x}{c}$

44. $\displaystyle\int \frac{dx}{c^2 - x^2} = \frac{1}{2c}\log\frac{c + x}{c - x}, \qquad (c^2 > x^2)$

45. $\displaystyle\int \frac{dx}{x^2 - c^2} = \frac{1}{2c}\log\frac{x - c}{x + c}, \qquad (x^2 > c^2)$

46. $\displaystyle\int \frac{x\,dx}{c^2 \pm x^2} = \pm\frac{1}{2}\log(c^2 \pm x^2)$

47. $\displaystyle\int \frac{x\,dx}{(c^2 \pm x^2)^{n+1}} = \mp\frac{1}{2n(c^2 \pm x^2)^n}$

48. $\displaystyle\int \frac{dx}{(c^2 \pm x^2)^n} = \frac{1}{2c^2(n - 1)}\left[\frac{x}{(c^2 \pm x^2)^{n-1}} + (2n - 3)\int \frac{dx}{(c^2 \pm x^2)^{n-1}}\right]$

49. $\displaystyle\int \frac{dx}{(x^2 - c^2)^n} = \frac{1}{2c^2(n - 1)}\left[-\frac{x}{(x^2 - c^2)^{n-1}} - (2n - 3)\int \frac{dx}{(x^2 - c^2)^{n-1}}\right]$

50. $\displaystyle\int \frac{x\,dx}{x^2 - c^2} = \frac{1}{2}\log(x^2 - c^2)$

51. $\displaystyle\int \frac{x\,dx}{(x^2 - c^2)^{n+1}} = -\frac{1}{2n(x^2 - c^2)^n}$

INTEGRALS (Continued)

FORMS CONTAINING $a + bx$ and $c + dx$

$$u = a + bx, \qquad v = c + dx, \qquad k = ad - bc$$

If $k = 0$, then $v = \dfrac{c}{a}u$

52. $\displaystyle\int \frac{dx}{u \cdot v} = \frac{1}{k} \cdot \log\left(\frac{v}{u}\right)$

53. $\displaystyle\int \frac{x\, dx}{u \cdot v} = \frac{1}{k}\left[\frac{a}{b}\log(u) - \frac{c}{d}\log(v)\right]$

54. $\displaystyle\int \frac{dx}{u^2 \cdot v} = \frac{1}{k}\left(\frac{1}{u} + \frac{d}{k}\log\frac{v}{u}\right)$

55. $\displaystyle\int \frac{x\, dx}{u^2 \cdot v} = \frac{-a}{bku} - \frac{c}{k^2}\log\frac{v}{u}$

56. $\displaystyle\int \frac{x^2\, dx}{u^2 \cdot v} = \frac{a^2}{b^2 ku} + \frac{1}{k^2}\left[\frac{c^2}{d}\log(v) + \frac{a(k - bc)}{b^2}\log(u)\right]$

57. $\displaystyle\int \frac{dx}{u^n \cdot v^m} = \frac{1}{k(m-1)}\left[\frac{-1}{u^{n-1} \cdot v^{m-1}} - (m + n - 2)b\int \frac{dx}{u^n \cdot v^{m-1}}\right]$

58. $\displaystyle\int \frac{u}{v}\,dx = \frac{bx}{d} + \frac{k}{d^2}\log(v)$

59. $\displaystyle\int \frac{u^m\, dx}{v^n} = \begin{cases} \dfrac{-1}{k(n-1)}\left[\dfrac{u^{m+1}}{v^{n-1}} + b(n - m - 2)\displaystyle\int \dfrac{u^m}{v^{n-1}}\,dx\right] \\[4pt] \text{or} \\[4pt] \dfrac{-1}{d(n-m-1)}\left[\dfrac{u^m}{v^{n-1}} + mk\displaystyle\int \dfrac{u^{m-1}}{v^n}\,dx\right] \\[4pt] \text{or} \\[4pt] \dfrac{-1}{d(n-1)}\left[\dfrac{u^m}{v^{n-1}} - mb\displaystyle\int \dfrac{u^{m-1}}{v^{n-1}}\,dx\right] \end{cases}$

FORMS CONTAINING $(a + bx^n)$

60. $\displaystyle\int \frac{dx}{a + bx^2} = \frac{1}{\sqrt{ab}}\tan^{-1}\frac{x\sqrt{ab}}{a}, \qquad (ab > 0)$

61. $\displaystyle\int \frac{dx}{a + bx^2} = \begin{cases} \dfrac{1}{2\sqrt{-ab}}\log\dfrac{a + x\sqrt{-ab}}{a - x\sqrt{-ab}}, \qquad (ab < 0) \\[4pt] \text{or} \\[4pt] \dfrac{1}{\sqrt{-ab}}\tanh^{-1}\dfrac{x\sqrt{-ab}}{a}, \qquad (ab < 0) \end{cases}$

INTEGRALS (Continued)

62. $\displaystyle\int \frac{dx}{a^2 + b^2x^2} = \frac{1}{ab}\tan^{-1}\frac{bx}{a}$

63. $\displaystyle\int \frac{x\,dx}{a + bx^2} = \frac{1}{2b}\log(a + bx^2)$

64. $\displaystyle\int \frac{x^2\,dx}{a + bx^2} = \frac{x}{b} - \frac{a}{b}\int \frac{dx}{a + bx^2}$

65. $\displaystyle\int \frac{dx}{(a + bx^2)^2} = \frac{x}{2a(a + bx^2)} + \frac{1}{2a}\int \frac{dx}{a + bx^2}$

66. $\displaystyle\int \frac{dx}{a^2 - b^2x^2} = \frac{1}{2ab}\log\frac{a + bx}{a - bx}$

67. $\displaystyle\int \frac{dx}{(a + bx^2)^{m+1}} = \begin{cases} \dfrac{1}{2ma}\dfrac{x}{(a + bx^2)^m} + \dfrac{2m-1}{2ma}\displaystyle\int \dfrac{dx}{(a + bx^2)^m} \\[2mm] \qquad\qquad\text{or} \\[2mm] \dfrac{(2m)!}{(m!)^2}\left[\dfrac{x}{2a}\displaystyle\sum_{r=1}^{m}\dfrac{r!(r-1)!}{(4a)^{m-r}(2r)!(a + bx^2)^r} + \dfrac{1}{(4a)^m}\displaystyle\int \dfrac{dx}{a + bx^2}\right]\end{cases}$

68. $\displaystyle\int \frac{x\,dx}{(a + bx^2)^{m+1}} = -\frac{1}{2bm(a + bx^2)^m}$

69. $\displaystyle\int \frac{x^2\,dx}{(a + bx^2)^{m+1}} = \frac{-x}{2mb(a + bx^2)^m} + \frac{1}{2mb}\int \frac{dx}{(a + bx^2)^m}$

70. $\displaystyle\int \frac{dx}{x(a + bx^2)} = \frac{1}{2a}\log\frac{x^2}{a + bx^2}$

71. $\displaystyle\int \frac{dx}{x^2(a + bx^2)} = -\frac{1}{ax} - \frac{b}{a}\int \frac{dx}{a + bx^2}$

72. $\displaystyle\int \frac{dx}{x(a + bx^2)^{m+1}} = \begin{cases} \dfrac{1}{2am(a + bx^2)^m} + \dfrac{1}{a}\displaystyle\int \dfrac{dx}{x(a + bx^2)^m} \\[2mm] \qquad\qquad\text{or} \\[2mm] \dfrac{1}{2a^{m+1}}\left[\displaystyle\sum_{r=1}^{m}\dfrac{a^r}{r(a + bx^2)^r} + \log\dfrac{x^2}{a + bx^2}\right]\end{cases}$

73. $\displaystyle\int \frac{dx}{x^2(a + bx^2)^{m+1}} = \frac{1}{a}\int \frac{dx}{x^2(a + bx^2)^m} - \frac{b}{a}\int \frac{dx}{(a + bx^2)^{m+1}}$

74. $\displaystyle\int \frac{dx}{a + bx^3} = \frac{k}{3a}\left[\frac{1}{2}\log\frac{(k + x)^3}{a + bx^3} + \sqrt{3}\tan^{-1}\frac{2x - k}{k\sqrt{3}}\right], \qquad \left(k = \sqrt[3]{\frac{a}{b}}\right)$

75. $\displaystyle\int \frac{x\,dx}{a + bx^3} = \frac{1}{3bk}\left[\frac{1}{2}\log\frac{a + bx^3}{(k + x)^3} + \sqrt{3}\tan^{-1}\frac{2x - k}{k\sqrt{3}}\right], \qquad \left(k = \sqrt[3]{\frac{a}{b}}\right)$

INTEGRALS (Continued)

76. $\displaystyle\int \frac{x^2\,dx}{a + bx^3} = \frac{1}{3b}\log(a + bx^3)$

77. $\displaystyle\int \frac{dx}{a + bx^4} = \frac{k}{2a}\left[\frac{1}{2}\log\frac{x^2 + 2kx + 2k^2}{x^2 - 2kx + 2k^2} + \tan^{-1}\frac{2kx}{2k^2 - x^2}\right],$

$$\left(ab > 0, k = \sqrt[4]{\frac{a}{4b}}\right)$$

78. $\displaystyle\int \frac{dx}{a + bx^4} = \frac{k}{2a}\left[\frac{1}{2}\log\frac{x + k}{x - k} + \tan^{-1}\frac{x}{k}\right], \qquad \left(ab < 0, k = \sqrt[4]{-\frac{a}{b}}\right)$

79. $\displaystyle\int \frac{x\,dx}{a + bx^4} = \frac{1}{2bk}\tan^{-1}\frac{x^2}{k}, \qquad \left(ab > 0, k = \sqrt{\frac{a}{b}}\right)$

80. $\displaystyle\int \frac{x\,dx}{a + bx^4} = \frac{1}{4bk}\log\frac{x^2 - k}{x^2 + k}, \qquad \left(ab < 0, k = \sqrt{-\frac{a}{b}}\right)$

81. $\displaystyle\int \frac{x^2\,dx}{a + bx^4} = \frac{1}{4bk}\left[\frac{1}{2}\log\frac{x^2 - 2kx + 2k^2}{x^2 + 2kx + 2k^2} + \tan^{-1}\frac{2kx}{2k^2 - x^2}\right],$

$$\left(ab > 0, k = \sqrt[4]{\frac{a}{4b}}\right)$$

82. $\displaystyle\int \frac{x^2\,dx}{a + bx^4} = \frac{1}{4bk}\left[\log\frac{x - k}{x + k} + 2\tan^{-1}\frac{x}{k}\right], \qquad \left(ab < 0, k = \sqrt[4]{-\frac{a}{b}}\right)$

83. $\displaystyle\int \frac{x^3\,dx}{a + bx^4} = \frac{1}{4b}\log(a + bx^4)$

84. $\displaystyle\int \frac{dx}{x(a + bx^n)} = \frac{1}{an}\log\frac{x^n}{a + bx^n}$

85. $\displaystyle\int \frac{dx}{(a + bx^n)^{m+1}} = \frac{1}{a}\int \frac{dx}{(a + bx^n)^m} - \frac{b}{a}\int \frac{x^n\,dx}{(a + bx^n)^{m+1}}$

86. $\displaystyle\int \frac{x^m\,dx}{(a + bx^n)^{p+1}} = \frac{1}{b}\int \frac{x^{m-n}\,dx}{(a + bx^n)^p} - \frac{a}{b}\int \frac{x^{m-n}\,dx}{(a + bx^n)^{p+1}}$

87. $\displaystyle\int \frac{dx}{x^m(a + bx^n)^{p+1}} = \frac{1}{a}\int \frac{dx}{x^m(a + bx^n)^p} - \frac{b}{a}\int \frac{dx}{x^{m-n}(a + bx^n)^{p+1}}$

INTEGRALS (Continued)

88. $\displaystyle\int x^m(a + bx^n)^p\, dx = \begin{cases} \end{cases}$

$$\frac{1}{b(np + m + 1)}\left[x^{m-n+1}(a + bx^n)^{p+1} \right.$$

$$\left. - a(m - n + 1)\int x^{m-n}(a + bx^n)^p\, dx \right]$$

or

$$\frac{1}{np + m + 1}\left[x^{m+1}(a + bx^n)^p \right.$$

$$\left. + anp\int x^m(a + bx^n)^{p-1}\, dx \right]$$

or

$$\frac{1}{a(m + 1)}\left[x^{m+1}(a + bx^n)^{p+1} \right.$$

$$\left. - (m + 1 + np + n)b\int x^{m+n}(a + bx^n)^p\, dx \right]$$

or

$$\frac{1}{an(p + 1)}\left[-x^{m+1}(a + bx^n)^{p+1} \right.$$

$$\left. + (m + 1 + np + n)\int x^m(a + bx^n)^{p+1}\, dx \right]$$

FORMS CONTAINING $c^3 \pm x^3$

89. $\displaystyle\int \frac{dx}{c^3 \pm x^3} = \pm\frac{1}{6c^2}\log\frac{(c \pm x)^3}{c^3 \pm x^3} + \frac{1}{c^2\sqrt{3}}\tan^{-1}\frac{2x \mp c}{c\sqrt{3}}$

90. $\displaystyle\int \frac{dx}{(c^3 \pm x^3)^2} = \frac{x}{3c^3(c^3 \pm x^3)} + \frac{2}{3c^3}\int\frac{dx}{c^3 \pm x^3}$

91. $\displaystyle\int \frac{dx}{(c^3 \pm x^3)^{n+1}} = \frac{1}{3nc^3}\left[\frac{x}{(c^3 \pm x^3)^n} + (3n - 1)\int\frac{dx}{(c^3 \pm x^3)^n} \right]$

92. $\displaystyle\int \frac{x\, dx}{c^3 \pm x^3} = \frac{1}{6c}\log\frac{c^3 \pm x^3}{(c \pm x)^3} \pm \frac{1}{c\sqrt{3}}\tan^{-1}\frac{2x \mp c}{c\sqrt{3}}$

93. $\displaystyle\int \frac{x\, dx}{(c^3 \pm x^3)^2} = \frac{x^2}{3c^3(c^3 \pm x^3)} + \frac{1}{3c^3}\int\frac{x\, dx}{c^3 \pm x^3}$

94. $\displaystyle\int \frac{x\, dx}{(c^3 \pm x^3)^{n+1}} = \frac{1}{3nc^3}\left[\frac{x^2}{(c^3 \pm x^3)^n} + (3n - 2)\int\frac{x\, dx}{(c^3 \pm x^3)^n} \right]$

95. $\displaystyle\int \frac{x^2\, dx}{c^3 \pm x^3} = \pm\frac{1}{3}\log(c^3 \pm x^3)$

INTEGRALS (Continued)

96. $\int \dfrac{x^2\,dx}{(c^3 \pm x^3)^{n+1}} = \mp \dfrac{1}{3n(c^3 \pm x^3)^n}$

97. $\int \dfrac{dx}{x(c^3 \pm x^3)} = \dfrac{1}{3c^3} \log \dfrac{x^3}{c^3 \pm x^3}$

98. $\int \dfrac{dx}{x(c^3 \pm x^3)^2} = \dfrac{1}{3c^3(c^3 \pm x^3)} + \dfrac{1}{3c^6} \log \dfrac{x^3}{c^3 \pm x^3}$

99. $\int \dfrac{dx}{x(c^3 \pm x^3)^{n+1}} = \dfrac{1}{3nc^3(c^3 \pm x^3)^n} + \dfrac{1}{c^3} \int \dfrac{dx}{x(c^3 \pm x^3)^n}$

100. $\int \dfrac{dx}{x^2(c^3 \pm x^3)} = -\dfrac{1}{c^3 x} \mp \dfrac{1}{c^3} \int \dfrac{x\,dx}{c^3 \pm x^3}$

101. $\int \dfrac{dx}{x^2(c^3 \pm x^3)^{n+1}} = \dfrac{1}{c^3} \int \dfrac{dx}{x^2(c^3 \pm x^3)^n} \mp \dfrac{1}{c^3} \int \dfrac{x\,dx}{(c^3 \pm x^3)^{n+1}}$

FORMS CONTAINING $c^4 \pm x^4$

102. $\int \dfrac{dx}{c^4 + x^4} = \dfrac{1}{2c^3\sqrt{2}} \left[\dfrac{1}{2} \log \dfrac{x^2 + cx\sqrt{2} + c^2}{x^2 - cx\sqrt{2} + c^2} + \tan^{-1} \dfrac{cx\sqrt{2}}{c^2 - x^2} \right]$

103. $\int \dfrac{dx}{c^4 - x^4} = \dfrac{1}{2c^3} \left[\dfrac{1}{2} \log \dfrac{c + x}{c - x} + \tan^{-1} \dfrac{x}{c} \right]$

104. $\int \dfrac{x\,dx}{c^4 + x^4} = \dfrac{1}{2c^2} \tan^{-1} \dfrac{x^2}{c^2}$

105. $\int \dfrac{x\,dx}{c^4 - x^4} = \dfrac{1}{4c^2} \log \dfrac{c^2 + x^2}{c^2 - x^2}$

106. $\int \dfrac{x^2\,dx}{c^4 + x^4} = \dfrac{1}{2c\sqrt{2}} \left[\dfrac{1}{2} \log \dfrac{x^2 - cx\sqrt{2} + c^2}{x^2 + cx\sqrt{2} + c^2} + \tan^{-1} \dfrac{cx\sqrt{2}}{c^2 - x^2} \right]$

107. $\int \dfrac{x^2\,dx}{c^4 - x^4} = \dfrac{1}{2c} \left[\dfrac{1}{2} \log \dfrac{c + x}{c - x} - \tan^{-1} \dfrac{x}{c} \right]$

108. $\int \dfrac{x^3\,dx}{c^4 \pm x^4} = \pm \dfrac{1}{4} \log (c^4 \pm x^4)$

FORMS CONTAINING $(a + bx + cx^2)$

$$X = a + bx + cx^2 \text{ and } q = 4ac - b^2$$

If $q = 0$, then $X = c\left(x + \dfrac{b}{2c}\right)^2$, and formulas starting with 23 should be used in place of these.

109. $\int \dfrac{dx}{X} = \dfrac{2}{\sqrt{q}} \tan^{-1} \dfrac{2cx + b}{\sqrt{q}}, \qquad (q > 0)$

INTEGRALS (Continued)

110. $\displaystyle\int \frac{dx}{X} = \begin{cases} \dfrac{-2}{\sqrt{-q}} \tanh^{-1} \dfrac{2cx+b}{\sqrt{-q}} \\[3mm] \qquad\qquad \text{or} \\[3mm] \dfrac{1}{\sqrt{-q}} \log \dfrac{2cx+b-\sqrt{-q}}{2cx+b+\sqrt{-q}}, \qquad (q<0) \end{cases}$

111. $\displaystyle\int \frac{dx}{X^2} = \frac{2cx+b}{qX} + \frac{2c}{q}\int \frac{dx}{X}$

112. $\displaystyle\int \frac{dx}{X^3} = \frac{2cx+b}{q}\left(\frac{1}{2X^2} + \frac{3c}{qX}\right) + \frac{6c^2}{q^2}\int \frac{dx}{X}$

113. $\displaystyle\int \frac{dx}{X^{n+1}} = \begin{cases} \dfrac{2cx+b}{nqX^n} + \dfrac{2(2n-1)c}{qn}\int \dfrac{dx}{X^n} \\[3mm] \qquad\qquad \text{or} \\[3mm] \dfrac{(2n)!}{(n!)^2}\left(\dfrac{c}{q}\right)^n\left[\dfrac{2cx+b}{q}\sum_{r=1}^{n}\left(\dfrac{q}{cX}\right)^r\left(\dfrac{(r-1)!r!}{(2r)!}\right) + \int\dfrac{dx}{X}\right] \end{cases}$

114. $\displaystyle\int \frac{x\,dx}{X} = \frac{1}{2c}\log X - \frac{b}{2c}\int \frac{dx}{X}$

115. $\displaystyle\int \frac{x\,dx}{X^2} = -\frac{bx+2a}{qX} - \frac{b}{q}\int \frac{dx}{X}$

116. $\displaystyle\int \frac{x\,dx}{X^{n+1}} = -\frac{2a+bx}{nqX^n} - \frac{b(2n-1)}{nq}\int \frac{dx}{X^n}$

117. $\displaystyle\int \frac{x^2}{X}\,dx = \frac{x}{c} - \frac{b}{2c^2}\log X + \frac{b^2-2ac}{2c^2}\int \frac{dx}{X}$

118. $\displaystyle\int \frac{x^2}{X^2}\,dx = \frac{(b^2-2ac)x+ab}{cqX} + \frac{2a}{q}\int \frac{dx}{X}$

119. $\displaystyle\int \frac{x^m\,dx}{X^{n+1}} = -\frac{x^{m-1}}{(2n-m+1)cX^n} - \frac{n-m+1}{2n-m+1}\cdot\frac{b}{c}\int \frac{x^{m-1}\,dx}{X^{n+1}}$
$$+ \frac{m-1}{2n-m+1}\cdot\frac{a}{c}\int \frac{x^{m-2}\,dx}{X^{n+1}}$$

120. $\displaystyle\int \frac{dx}{xX} = \frac{1}{2a}\log \frac{x^2}{X} - \frac{b}{2a}\int \frac{dx}{X}$

121. $\displaystyle\int \frac{dx}{x^2X} = \frac{b}{2a^2}\log \frac{X}{x^2} - \frac{1}{ax} + \left(\frac{b^2}{2a^2} - \frac{c}{a}\right)\int \frac{dx}{X}$

122. $\displaystyle\int \frac{dx}{xX^n} = \frac{1}{2a(n-1)X^{n-1}} - \frac{b}{2a}\int \frac{dx}{X^n} + \frac{1}{a}\int \frac{dx}{xX^{n-1}}$

INTEGRALS (Continued)

123. $\int \dfrac{dx}{x^m X^{n+1}} = -\dfrac{1}{(m-1)ax^{m-1}X^n} - \dfrac{n+m-1}{m-1}\cdot\dfrac{b}{a}\int \dfrac{dx}{x^{m-1}X^{n+1}}$

$$-\dfrac{2n+m-1}{m-1}\cdot\dfrac{c}{a}\int \dfrac{dx}{x^{m-2}X^{n+1}}$$

FORMS CONTAINING $\sqrt{a+bx}$

124. $\int \sqrt{a+bx}\,dx = \dfrac{2}{3b}\sqrt{(a+bx)^3}$

125. $\int x\sqrt{a+bx}\,dx = -\dfrac{2(2a-3bx)\sqrt{(a+bx)^3}}{15b^2}$

126. $\int x^2\sqrt{a+bx}\,dx = \dfrac{2(8a^2 - 12abx + 15b^2x^2)\sqrt{(a+bx)^3}}{105b^3}$

127. $\int x^m\sqrt{a+bx}\,dx = \begin{cases} \dfrac{2}{b(2m+3)}\left[x^m\sqrt{(a+bx)^3} - ma\int x^{m-1}\sqrt{a+bx}\,dx \right] \\ \text{or} \\ \dfrac{2}{b^{m+1}}\sqrt{a+bx}\displaystyle\sum_{r=0}^{m}\dfrac{m!(-a)^{m-r}}{r!(m-r)!(2r+3)}(a+bx)^{r+1} \end{cases}$

128. $\int \dfrac{\sqrt{a+bx}}{x}dx = 2\sqrt{a+bx} + a\int \dfrac{dx}{x\sqrt{a+bx}}$

129. $\int \dfrac{\sqrt{a+bx}}{x^2}dx = -\dfrac{\sqrt{a+bx}}{x} + \dfrac{b}{2}\int \dfrac{dx}{x\sqrt{a+bx}}$

130. $\int \dfrac{\sqrt{a+bx}}{x^m}dx = -\dfrac{1}{(m-1)a}\left[\dfrac{\sqrt{(a+bx)^3}}{x^{m-1}} + \dfrac{(2m-5)b}{2}\int \dfrac{\sqrt{a+bx}}{x^{m-1}}dx \right]$

131. $\int \dfrac{dx}{\sqrt{a+bx}} = \dfrac{2\sqrt{a+bx}}{b}$

132. $\int \dfrac{x\,dx}{\sqrt{a+bx}} = -\dfrac{2(2a-bx)}{3b^2}\sqrt{a+bx}$

133. $\int \dfrac{x^2\,dx}{\sqrt{a+bx}} = \dfrac{2(8a^2 - 4abx + 3b^2x^2)}{15b^3}\sqrt{a+bx}$

INTEGRALS (Continued)

134. $\displaystyle\int \frac{x^m\, dx}{\sqrt{a + bx}} = \begin{cases} \dfrac{2}{(2m + 1)b}\left[x^m\sqrt{a + bx} - ma\displaystyle\int \dfrac{x^{m-1}\, dx}{\sqrt{a + bx}}\right] \\[6pt] \text{or} \\[6pt] \dfrac{2(-a)^m\sqrt{a + bx}}{b^{m+1}}\displaystyle\sum_{r=0}^{m}\dfrac{(-1)^r m!(a + bx)^r}{(2r + 1)r!(m - r)!a^r} \end{cases}$

135. $\displaystyle\int \frac{dx}{x\sqrt{a + bx}} = \frac{1}{\sqrt{a}}\log\left(\frac{\sqrt{a + bx} - \sqrt{a}}{\sqrt{a + bx} + \sqrt{a}}\right), \qquad (a > 0)$

136. $\displaystyle\int \frac{dx}{x\sqrt{a + bx}} = \frac{2}{\sqrt{-a}}\tan^{-1}\sqrt{\frac{a + bx}{-a}}, \qquad (a < 0)$

137. $\displaystyle\int \frac{dx}{x^2\sqrt{a + bx}} = -\frac{\sqrt{a + bx}}{ax} - \frac{b}{2a}\int \frac{dx}{x\sqrt{a + bx}}$

138. $\displaystyle\int \frac{dx}{x^n\sqrt{a + bx}} = \begin{cases} -\dfrac{\sqrt{a + bx}}{(n - 1)ax^{n-1}} - \dfrac{(2n - 3)b}{(2n - 2)a}\displaystyle\int \dfrac{dx}{x^{n-1}\sqrt{a + bx}} \\[6pt] \text{or} \\[6pt] \dfrac{(2n - 2)!}{[(n - 1)!]^2}\left[-\dfrac{\sqrt{a + bx}}{a}\displaystyle\sum_{r=1}^{n-1}\dfrac{r!(r - 1)!}{x^r(2r)!}\left(-\dfrac{b}{4a}\right)^{n-r-1}\right. \\[6pt] \left. + \left(-\dfrac{b}{4a}\right)^{n-1}\displaystyle\int \dfrac{dx}{x\sqrt{a + bx}}\right] \end{cases}$

139. $\displaystyle\int (a + bx)^{\pm\frac{n}{2}}\, dx = \frac{2(a + bx)^{\frac{2\pm n}{2}}}{b(2 \pm n)}$

140. $\displaystyle\int x(a + bx)^{\pm\frac{n}{2}}\, dx = \frac{2}{b^2}\left[\frac{(a + bx)^{\frac{4\pm n}{2}}}{4 \pm n} - \frac{a(a + bx)^{\frac{2\pm n}{2}}}{2 \pm n}\right]$

141. $\displaystyle\int \frac{dx}{x(a + bx)^{\frac{m}{2}}} = \frac{1}{a}\int \frac{dx}{x(a + bx)^{\frac{m-2}{2}}} - \frac{b}{a}\int \frac{dx}{(a + bx)^{\frac{m}{2}}}$

142. $\displaystyle\int \frac{(a + bx)^{\frac{n}{2}}\, dx}{x} = b\int (a + bx)^{\frac{n-2}{2}}\, dx + a\int \frac{(a + bx)^{\frac{n-2}{2}}}{x}\, dx$

143. $\displaystyle\int f(x, \sqrt{a + bx})\, dx = \frac{2}{b}\int f\left(\frac{z^2 - a}{b}, z\right)z\, dz, \qquad (z = \sqrt{a + bx})$

FORMS CONTAINING $\sqrt{a + bx}$ and $\sqrt{c + dx}$

$$u = a + bx \qquad v = c + dx \qquad k = ad - bc$$

If $k = 0$, then $v = \dfrac{c}{a}u$, and formulas starting with 124 should be used in place of these.

144. $\displaystyle\int \frac{dx}{\sqrt{uv}} = \begin{cases} \dfrac{2}{\sqrt{bd}} \tanh^{-1} \dfrac{\sqrt{bduv}}{bv}, & bd > o, \ k < o \\[2ex] \text{or} \\[1ex] \dfrac{2}{\sqrt{bd}} \tanh^{-1} \dfrac{\sqrt{bduv}}{du}, & bd > o, \ k > o. \\[2ex] \text{or} \\[1ex] \dfrac{1}{\sqrt{bd}} \log \dfrac{(bv + \sqrt{bduv})^2}{v}, & (bd > 0) \end{cases}$

145. $\displaystyle\int \frac{dx}{\sqrt{uv}} = \begin{cases} \dfrac{2}{\sqrt{-bd}} \tan^{-1} \dfrac{\sqrt{-bduv}}{bv} \\[2ex] \text{or} \\[1ex] -\dfrac{1}{\sqrt{-bd}} \sin^{-1} \left(\dfrac{2bdx + ad + bc}{|k|} \right), & (bd < 0) \end{cases}$

146. $\displaystyle\int \sqrt{uv}\, dx = \frac{k + 2bv}{4bd} \sqrt{uv} - \frac{k^2}{8bd} \int \frac{dx}{\sqrt{uv}}$

147. $\displaystyle\int \frac{dx}{v\sqrt{u}} = \begin{cases} \dfrac{1}{\sqrt{kd}} \log \dfrac{d\sqrt{u} - \sqrt{kd}}{d\sqrt{u} + \sqrt{kd}} \\[2ex] \text{or} \\[1ex] \dfrac{1}{\sqrt{kd}} \log \dfrac{(d\sqrt{u} - \sqrt{kd})^2}{v}, & (kd > 0) \end{cases}$

148. $\displaystyle\int \frac{dx}{v\sqrt{u}} = \frac{2}{\sqrt{-kd}} \tan^{-1} \frac{d\sqrt{u}}{\sqrt{-kd}}, \qquad (kd < 0)$

149. $\displaystyle\int \frac{x\, dx}{\sqrt{uv}} = \frac{\sqrt{uv}}{bd} - \frac{ad + bc}{2bd} \int \frac{dx}{\sqrt{uv}}$

150. $\displaystyle\int \frac{dx}{v\sqrt{uv}} = \frac{-2\sqrt{uv}}{kv}$

INTEGRALS (Continued)

151. $\displaystyle\int \frac{v\,dx}{\sqrt{uv}} = \frac{\sqrt{uv}}{b} - \frac{k}{2b}\int \frac{dx}{\sqrt{uv}}$

152. $\displaystyle\int \sqrt{\frac{v}{u}}\,dx = \frac{v}{|v|}\int \frac{v\,dx}{\sqrt{uv}}$

153. $\displaystyle\int v^m\sqrt{u}\,dx = \frac{1}{(2m+3)d}\left(2v^{m+1}\sqrt{u} + k\int \frac{v^m\,dx}{\sqrt{u}}\right)$

154. $\displaystyle\int \frac{dx}{v^m\sqrt{u}} = -\frac{1}{(m-1)k}\left(\frac{\sqrt{u}}{v^{m-1}} + \left(m-\frac{3}{2}\right)b\int \frac{dx}{v^{m-1}\sqrt{u}}\right)$

155. $\displaystyle\int \frac{v^m\,dx}{\sqrt{u}} = \begin{cases} \dfrac{2}{b(2m+1)}\left[v^m\sqrt{u} - mk\displaystyle\int \frac{v^{m-1}}{\sqrt{u}}\,dx\right] \\[6pt] \qquad\text{or} \\[6pt] \dfrac{2(m!)^2\sqrt{u}}{b(2m+1)!}\displaystyle\sum_{r=0}^{m}\left(-\frac{4k}{b}\right)^{m-r}\frac{(2r)!}{(r!)^2}v^r \end{cases}$

FORMS CONTAINING $\sqrt{x^2 \pm a^2}$

156. $\displaystyle\int \sqrt{x^2 \pm a^2}\,dx = \tfrac{1}{2}[x\sqrt{x^2 \pm a^2} \pm a^2\log(x + \sqrt{x^2 \pm a^2})]$

157. $\displaystyle\int \frac{dx}{\sqrt{x^2 \pm a^2}} = \log(x + \sqrt{x^2 \pm a^2})$

158. $\displaystyle\int \frac{dx}{x\sqrt{x^2 - a^2}} = \frac{1}{|a|}\sec^{-1}\frac{x}{a}$

159. $\displaystyle\int \frac{dx}{x\sqrt{x^2 + a^2}} = -\frac{1}{a}\log\left(\frac{a + \sqrt{x^2 + a^2}}{x}\right)$

160. $\displaystyle\int \frac{\sqrt{x^2 + a^2}}{x}\,dx = \sqrt{x^2 + a^2} - a\log\left(\frac{a + \sqrt{x^2 + a^2}}{x}\right)$

161. $\displaystyle\int \frac{\sqrt{x^2 - a^2}}{x}\,dx = \sqrt{x^2 - a^2} - |a|\sec^{-1}\frac{x}{a}$

162. $\displaystyle\int \frac{x\,dx}{\sqrt{x^2 \pm a^2}} = \sqrt{x^2 \pm a^2}$

163. $\displaystyle\int x\sqrt{x^2 \pm a^2}\,dx = \tfrac{1}{3}\sqrt{(x^2 \pm a^2)^3}$

INTEGRALS (Continued)

164. $\int \sqrt{(x^2 \pm a^2)^3}\, dx = \dfrac{1}{4}\bigg[x\sqrt{(x^2 \pm a^2)^3} \pm \dfrac{3a^2 x}{2}\sqrt{x^2 \pm a^2}$

$$+ \dfrac{3a^4}{2} \log (x + \sqrt{x^2 \pm a^2}) \bigg]$$

165. $\int \dfrac{dx}{\sqrt{(x^2 \pm a^2)^3}} = \dfrac{\pm x}{a^2 \sqrt{x^2 \pm a^2}}$

166. $\int \dfrac{x\, dx}{\sqrt{(x^2 \pm a^2)^3}} = \dfrac{-1}{\sqrt{x^2 \pm a^2}}$

167. $\int x\sqrt{(x^2 \pm a^2)^3}\, dx = \tfrac{1}{5}\sqrt{(x^2 \pm a^2)^5}$

168. $\int x^2\sqrt{x^2 \pm a^2}\, dx = \dfrac{x}{4}\sqrt{(x^2 \pm a^2)^3} \mp \dfrac{a^2}{8}x\sqrt{x^2 \pm a^2} - \dfrac{a^4}{8}\log (x + \sqrt{x^2 \pm a^2})$

169. $\int x^3\sqrt{x^2 + a^2}\, dx = (\tfrac{1}{5}x^2 - \tfrac{2}{15}a^2)\sqrt{(a^2 + x^2)^3}$

170. $\int x^3\sqrt{x^2 - a^2}\, dx = \dfrac{1}{5}\sqrt{(x^2 - a^2)^5} + \dfrac{a^2}{3}\sqrt{(x^2 - a^2)^3}$

171. $\int \dfrac{x^2\, dx}{\sqrt{x^2 \pm a^2}} = \dfrac{x}{2}\sqrt{x^2 \pm a^2} \mp \dfrac{a^2}{2}\log (x + \sqrt{x^2 \pm a^2})$

172. $\int \dfrac{x^3\, dx}{\sqrt{x^2 \pm a^2}} = \dfrac{1}{3}\sqrt{(x^2 \pm a^2)^3} \mp a^2\sqrt{x^2 \pm a^2}$

173. $\int \dfrac{dx}{x^2\sqrt{x^2 \pm a^2}} = \mp\dfrac{\sqrt{x^2 \pm a^2}}{a^2 x}$

174. $\int \dfrac{dx}{x^3\sqrt{x^2 + a^2}} = -\dfrac{\sqrt{x^2 + a^2}}{2a^2 x^2} + \dfrac{1}{2a^3}\log\dfrac{a + \sqrt{x^2 + a^2}}{x}$

175. $\int \dfrac{dx}{x^3\sqrt{x^2 - a^2}} = \dfrac{\sqrt{x^2 - a^2}}{2a^2 x^2} + \dfrac{1}{2|a^3|}\sec^{-1}\dfrac{x}{a}$

176. $\int x^2\sqrt{(x^2 \pm a^2)^3}\, dx = \dfrac{x}{6}\sqrt{(x^2 \pm a^2)^5} \mp \dfrac{a^2 x}{24}\sqrt{(x^2 \pm a^2)^3} - \dfrac{a^4 x}{16}\sqrt{x^2 \pm a^2}$

$$\mp \dfrac{a^6}{16}\log (x + \sqrt{x^2 \pm a^2})$$

177. $\int x^3\sqrt{(x^2 \pm a^2)^3}\, dx = \dfrac{1}{7}\sqrt{(x^2 \pm a^2)^7} \mp \dfrac{a^2}{5}\sqrt{(x^2 \pm a^2)^5}$

INTEGRALS (Continued)

178. $\displaystyle\int \frac{\sqrt{x^2 \pm a^2}\, dx}{x^2} = -\frac{\sqrt{x^2 \pm a^2}}{x} + \log\left(x + \sqrt{x^2 \pm a^2}\right)$

179. $\displaystyle\int \frac{\sqrt{x^2 + a^2}}{x^3}\, dx = -\frac{\sqrt{x^2 + a^2}}{2x^2} - \frac{1}{2a} \log \frac{a + \sqrt{x^2 + a^2}}{x}$

180. $\displaystyle\int \frac{\sqrt{x^2 - a^2}}{x^3}\, dx = -\frac{\sqrt{x^2 - a^2}}{2x^2} + \frac{1}{2|a|} \sec^{-1} \frac{x}{a}$

181. $\displaystyle\int \frac{\sqrt{x^2 \pm a^2}}{x^4}\, dx = \mp \frac{\sqrt{(x^2 \pm a^2)^3}}{3a^2 x^3}$

182. $\displaystyle\int \frac{x^2\, dx}{\sqrt{(x^2 \pm a^2)^3}} = \frac{-x}{\sqrt{x^2 \pm a^2}} + \log\left(x + \sqrt{x^2 \pm a^2}\right)$

183. $\displaystyle\int \frac{x^3\, dx}{\sqrt{(x^2 \pm a^2)^3}} = \sqrt{x^2 \pm a^2} \pm \frac{a^2}{\sqrt{x^2 \pm a^2}}$

184. $\displaystyle\int \frac{dx}{x\sqrt{(x^2 + a^2)^3}} = \frac{1}{a^2\sqrt{x^2 + a^2}} - \frac{1}{a^3} \log \frac{a + \sqrt{x^2 + a^2}}{x}$

185. $\displaystyle\int \frac{dx}{x\sqrt{(x^2 - a^2)^3}} = -\frac{1}{a^2\sqrt{x^2 - a^2}} - \frac{1}{|a^3|} \sec^{-1} \frac{x}{a}$

186. $\displaystyle\int \frac{dx}{x^2\sqrt{(x^2 \pm a^2)^3}} = -\frac{1}{a^4}\left[\frac{\sqrt{x^2 \pm a^2}}{x} + \frac{x}{\sqrt{x^2 \pm a^2}}\right]$

187. $\displaystyle\int \frac{dx}{x^3\sqrt{(x^2 + a^2)^3}} = -\frac{1}{2a^2 x^2\sqrt{x^2 + a^2}} - \frac{3}{2a^4\sqrt{x^2 + a^2}}$

$$+ \frac{3}{2a^5} \log \frac{a + \sqrt{x^2 + a^2}}{x}$$

188. $\displaystyle\int \frac{dx}{x^3\sqrt{(x^2 - a^2)^3}} = \frac{1}{2a^2 x^2\sqrt{x^2 - a^2}} - \frac{3}{2a^4\sqrt{x^2 - a^2}} - \frac{3}{2|a^5|} \sec^{-1} \frac{x}{a}$

189. $\displaystyle\int \frac{x^m}{\sqrt{x^2 \pm a^2}}\, dx = \frac{1}{m} x^{m-1}\sqrt{x^2 \pm a^2} \mp \frac{m-1}{m} a^2 \int \frac{x^{m-2}}{\sqrt{x^2 \pm a^2}}\, dx$

190. $\displaystyle\int \frac{x^{2m}}{\sqrt{x^2 \pm a^2}}\, dx = \frac{(2m)!}{2^{2m}(m!)^2}\left[\sqrt{x^2 \pm a^2} \sum_{r=1}^{m} \frac{r!(r-1)!}{(2r)!}(\mp a^2)^{m-r}(2x)^{2r-1}\right.$

$$\left. + (\mp a^2)^m \log\left(x + \sqrt{x^2 \pm a^2}\right)\right]$$

191. $\displaystyle\int \frac{x^{2m+1}}{\sqrt{x^2 \pm a^2}}\, dx = \sqrt{x^2 \pm a^2} \sum_{r=0}^{m} \frac{(2r)!(m!)^2}{(2m+1)!(r!)^2}(\mp 4a^2)^{m-r} x^{2r}$

INTEGRALS (Continued)

192. $\int \dfrac{dx}{x^m \sqrt{x^2 \pm a^2}} = \mp \dfrac{\sqrt{x^2 \pm a^2}}{(m-1)a^2 x^{m-1}} \mp \dfrac{(m-2)}{(m-1)a^2} \int \dfrac{dx}{x^{m-2}\sqrt{x^2 \pm a^2}}$

193. $\int \dfrac{dx}{x^{2m}\sqrt{x^2 \pm a^2}} = \sqrt{x^2 \pm a^2} \sum_{r=0}^{m-1} \dfrac{(m-1)!\,m!\,(2r)!\,2^{2m-2r-1}}{(r!)^2 (2m)!\,(\mp a^2)^{m-r} x^{2r+1}}$

194. $\int \dfrac{dx}{x^{2m+1}\sqrt{x^2 + a^2}} = \dfrac{(2m)!}{(m!)^2}\left[\dfrac{\sqrt{x^2 + a^2}}{a^2} \sum_{r=1}^{m} (-1)^{m-r+1} \dfrac{r!\,(r-1)!}{2(2r)!\,(4a^2)^{m-r}x^{2r}} \right.$

$\left. + \dfrac{(-1)^{m+1}}{2^{2m}a^{2m+1}} \log \dfrac{\sqrt{x^2 + a^2} + a}{x} \right]$

195. $\int \dfrac{dx}{x^{2m+1}\sqrt{x^2 - a^2}} = \dfrac{(2m)!}{(m!)^2}\left[\dfrac{\sqrt{x^2 - a^2}}{a^2} \sum_{r=1}^{m} \dfrac{r!\,(r-1)!}{2(2r)!\,(4a^2)^{m-r}x^{2r}} \right.$

$\left. + \dfrac{1}{2^{2m}|a|^{2m+1}} \sec^{-1}\dfrac{x}{a} \right]$

196. $\int \dfrac{dx}{(x-a)\sqrt{x^2 - a^2}} = -\dfrac{\sqrt{x^2 - a^2}}{a(x-a)}$

197. $\int \dfrac{dx}{(x+a)\sqrt{x^2 - a^2}} = \dfrac{\sqrt{x^2 - a^2}}{a(x+a)}$

198. $\int f(x, \sqrt{x^2 + a^2})\,dx = a \int f(a \tan u, a \sec u) \sec^2 u\,du, \qquad \left(u = \tan^{-1}\dfrac{x}{a},\, a > 0 \right)$

199. $\int f(x, \sqrt{x^2 - a^2})\,dx = a \int f(a \sec u, a \tan u) \sec u \tan u\,du, \qquad \left(u = \sec^{-1}\dfrac{x}{a}, \right.$

$\left. a > 0 \right)$

FORMS CONTAINING $\sqrt{a^2 - x^2}$

200. $\int \sqrt{a^2 - x^2}\,dx = \dfrac{1}{2}\left[x\sqrt{a^2 - x^2} + a^2 \sin^{-1}\dfrac{x}{|a|} \right]$

201. $\int \dfrac{dx}{\sqrt{a^2 - x^2}} = \begin{cases} \sin^{-1}\dfrac{x}{|a|} \\ \text{or} \\ -\cos^{-1}\dfrac{x}{|a|} \end{cases}$

202. $\int \dfrac{dx}{x\sqrt{a^2 - x^2}} = -\dfrac{1}{a}\log\left(\dfrac{a + \sqrt{a^2 - x^2}}{x} \right)$

INTEGRALS (Continued)

203. $\displaystyle\int \frac{\sqrt{a^2 - x^2}}{x}\, dx = \sqrt{a^2 - x^2} - a \log\left(\frac{a + \sqrt{a^2 - x^2}}{x}\right)$

204. $\displaystyle\int \frac{x\, dx}{\sqrt{a^2 - x^2}} = -\sqrt{a^2 - x^2}$

205. $\displaystyle\int x\sqrt{a^2 - x^2}\, dx = -\tfrac{1}{3}\sqrt{(a^2 - x^2)^3}$

206. $\displaystyle\int \sqrt{(a^2 - x^2)^3}\, dx = \frac{1}{4}\left[x\sqrt{(a^2 - x^2)^3} + \frac{3a^2 x}{2}\sqrt{a^2 - x^2} + \frac{3a^4}{2}\sin^{-1}\frac{x}{|a|}\right]$

207. $\displaystyle\int \frac{dx}{\sqrt{(a^2 - x^2)^3}} = \frac{x}{a^2\sqrt{a^2 - x^2}}$

208. $\displaystyle\int \frac{x\, dx}{\sqrt{(a^2 - x^2)^3}} = \frac{1}{\sqrt{a^2 - x^2}}$

209. $\displaystyle\int x\sqrt{(a^2 - x^2)^3}\, dx = -\tfrac{1}{5}\sqrt{(a^2 - x^2)^5}$

210. $\displaystyle\int x^2\sqrt{a^2 - x^2}\, dx = -\frac{x}{4}\sqrt{(a^2 - x^2)^3} + \frac{a^2}{8}\left(x\sqrt{a^2 - x^2} + a^2\sin^{-1}\frac{x}{|a|}\right)$

211. $\displaystyle\int x^3\sqrt{a^2 - x^2}\, dx = \left(-\tfrac{1}{5}x^2 - \tfrac{2}{15}a^2\right)\sqrt{(a^2 - x^2)^3}$

212. $\displaystyle\int x^2\sqrt{(a^2 - x^2)^3}\, dx = -\frac{1}{6}x\sqrt{(a^2 - x^2)^5} + \frac{a^2 x}{24}\sqrt{(a^2 - x^2)^3}$

$$+ \frac{a^4 x}{16}\sqrt{a^2 - x^2} + \frac{a^6}{16}\sin^{-1}\frac{x}{|a|}$$

213. $\displaystyle\int x^3\sqrt{(a^2 - x^2)^3}\, dx = \frac{1}{7}\sqrt{(a^2 - x^2)^7} - \frac{a^2}{5}\sqrt{(a^2 - x^2)^5}$

214. $\displaystyle\int \frac{x^2\, dx}{\sqrt{a^2 - x^2}} = -\frac{x}{2}\sqrt{a^2 - x^2} + \frac{a^2}{2}\sin^{-1}\frac{x}{|a|}$

215. $\displaystyle\int \frac{dx}{x^2\sqrt{a^2 - x^2}} = -\frac{\sqrt{a^2 - x^2}}{a^2 x}$

216. $\displaystyle\int \frac{\sqrt{a^2 - x^2}}{x^2}\, dx = -\frac{\sqrt{a^2 - x^2}}{x} - \sin^{-1}\frac{x}{|a|}$

217. $\displaystyle\int \frac{\sqrt{a^2 - x^2}}{x^3}\, dx = -\frac{\sqrt{a^2 - x^2}}{2x^2} + \frac{1}{2a}\log\frac{a + \sqrt{a^2 - x^2}}{x}$

218. $\displaystyle\int \frac{\sqrt{a^2 - x^2}}{x^4}\, dx = -\frac{\sqrt{(a^2 - x^2)^3}}{3a^2 x^3}$

INTEGRALS (Continued)

219. $\displaystyle\int \frac{x^2\,dx}{\sqrt{(a^2-x^2)^3}} = \frac{x}{\sqrt{a^2-x^2}} - \sin^{-1}\frac{x}{|a|}$

220. $\displaystyle\int \frac{x^3\,dx}{\sqrt{a^2-x^2}} = -\frac{2}{3}(a^2-x^2)^{\frac{1}{2}} - x^2(a^2-x^2)^{\frac{1}{2}} = -\frac{1}{3}\sqrt{a^2-x^2}\,(x^2+2a^2)$

221. $\displaystyle\int \frac{x^3\,dx}{\sqrt{(a^2-x^2)^3}} = 2(a^2-x^2)^{\frac{1}{2}} + \frac{x^2}{(a^2-x^2)^{\frac{1}{2}}} = \frac{a^2}{\sqrt{a^2-x^2}} + \sqrt{a^2-x^2}$

222. $\displaystyle\int \frac{dx}{x^3\sqrt{a^2-x^2}} = -\frac{\sqrt{a^2-x^2}}{2a^2x^2} - \frac{1}{2a^3}\log\frac{a+\sqrt{a^2-x^2}}{x}$

223. $\displaystyle\int \frac{dx}{x\sqrt{(a^2-x^2)^3}} = \frac{1}{a^2\sqrt{a^2-x^2}} - \frac{1}{a^3}\log\frac{a+\sqrt{a^2-x^2}}{x}$

224. $\displaystyle\int \frac{dx}{x^2\sqrt{(a^2-x^2)^3}} = \frac{1}{a^4}\left[-\frac{\sqrt{a^2-x^2}}{x} + \frac{x}{\sqrt{a^2-x^2}}\right]$

225. $\displaystyle\int \frac{dx}{x^3\sqrt{(a^2-x^2)^3}} = -\frac{1}{2a^2x^2\sqrt{a^2-x^2}} + \frac{3}{2a^4\sqrt{a^2-x^2}}$

$$-\frac{3}{2a^5}\log\frac{a+\sqrt{a^2-x^2}}{x}$$

226. $\displaystyle\int \frac{x^m}{\sqrt{a^2-x^2}}\,dx = -\frac{x^{m-1}\sqrt{a^2-x^2}}{m} + \frac{(m-1)a^2}{m}\int \frac{x^{m-2}}{\sqrt{a^2-x^2}}\,dx$

227. $\displaystyle\int \frac{x^{2m}}{\sqrt{a^2-x^2}}\,dx = \frac{(2m)!}{(m!)^2}\left[-\sqrt{a^2-x^2}\sum_{r=1}^{m}\frac{r!(r-1)!}{2^{2m-2r+1}(2r)!}a^{2m-2r}x^{2r-1}\right.$

$$\left. + \frac{a^{2m}}{2^{2m}}\sin^{-1}\frac{x}{|a|}\right]$$

228. $\displaystyle\int \frac{x^{2m+1}}{\sqrt{a^2-x^2}}\,dx = -\sqrt{a^2-x^2}\sum_{r=0}^{m}\frac{(2r)!(m!)^2}{(2m+1)!(r!)^2}(4a^2)^{m-r}x^{2r}$

229. $\displaystyle\int \frac{dx}{x^m\sqrt{a^2-x^2}} = -\frac{\sqrt{a^2-x^2}}{(m-1)a^2x^{m-1}} + \frac{m-2}{(m-1)a^2}\int \frac{dx}{x^{m-2}\sqrt{a^2-x^2}}$

230. $\displaystyle\int \frac{ax}{x^{2m}\sqrt{a^2-x^2}} = -\sqrt{a^2-x^2}\sum_{r=0}^{m-1}\frac{(m-1)!m!(2r)!2^{2m-2r-1}}{(r!)^2(2m)!a^{2m-2r}x^{2r+1}}$

231. $\displaystyle\int \frac{dx}{x^{2m+1}\sqrt{a^2-x^2}} = \frac{(2m)!}{(m!)^2}\left[-\frac{\sqrt{a^2-x^2}}{a^2}\sum_{r=1}^{m}\frac{r!(r-1)!}{2(2r)!(4a^2)^{m-r}x^{2r}}\right.$

$$\left. + \frac{1}{2^{2m}a^{2m+1}}\log\frac{a-\sqrt{a^2-x^2}}{x}\right]$$

INTEGRALS (Continued)

232. $\displaystyle\int \frac{dx}{(b^2 - x^2)\sqrt{a^2 - x^2}} = \frac{1}{2b\sqrt{a^2 - b^2}} \log \frac{(b\sqrt{a^2 - x^2} + x\sqrt{a^2 - b^2})^2}{b^2 - x^2},$

$$(a^2 > b^2)$$

233. $\displaystyle\int \frac{dx}{(b^2 - x^2)\sqrt{a^2 - x^2}} = \frac{1}{b\sqrt{b^2 - a^2}} \tan^{-1} \frac{x\sqrt{b^2 - a^2}}{b\sqrt{a^2 - x^2}}, \qquad (b^2 > a^2)$

234. $\displaystyle\int \frac{dx}{(b^2 + x^2)\sqrt{a^2 - x^2}} = \frac{1}{b\sqrt{a^2 + b^2}} \tan^{-1} \frac{x\sqrt{a^2 + b^2}}{b\sqrt{a^2 - x^2}}$

235. $\displaystyle\int \frac{\sqrt{a^2 - x^2}}{b^2 + x^2} dx = \frac{\sqrt{a^2 + b^2}}{|b|} \sin^{-1} \frac{x\sqrt{a^2 + b^2}}{|a|\sqrt{x^2 + b^2}} - \sin^{-1} \frac{x}{|a|}$

236. $\displaystyle\int f(x, \sqrt{a^2 - x^2})\, dx = a \int f(a \sin u, a \cos u) \cos u\, du, \qquad \left(u = \sin^{-1} \frac{x}{a},\, a > 0 \right)$

FORMS CONTAINING $\sqrt{a + bx + cx^2}$

$$X = a + bx + cx^2,\, q = 4ac - b^2,\, \text{and } k = \frac{4c}{q}$$

If $q = 0$, then $\sqrt{X} = \sqrt{c}\, \left| x + \dfrac{b}{2c} \right|$

237. $\displaystyle\int \frac{dx}{\sqrt{X}} = \begin{cases} \dfrac{1}{\sqrt{c}} \log\left(2\sqrt{cX} + 2cx + b\right) \\[2mm] \text{or} \\[2mm] \dfrac{1}{\sqrt{c}} \sinh^{-1} \dfrac{2cx + b}{\sqrt{q}}, \qquad (c > 0) \end{cases}$

238. $\displaystyle\int \frac{dx}{\sqrt{X}} = -\frac{1}{\sqrt{-c}} \sin^{-1} \frac{2cx + b}{\sqrt{-q}}, \qquad (c < 0)$

239. $\displaystyle\int \frac{dx}{X\sqrt{X}} = \frac{2(2cx + b)}{q\sqrt{X}}$

240. $\displaystyle\int \frac{dx}{X^2\sqrt{X}} = \frac{2(2cx + b)}{3q\sqrt{X}}\left(\frac{1}{X} + 2k \right)$

241. $\displaystyle\int \frac{dx}{X^n\sqrt{X}} = \begin{cases} \dfrac{2(2cx + b)\sqrt{X}}{(2n - 1)qX^n} + \dfrac{2k(n - 1)}{2n - 1} \displaystyle\int \frac{dx}{X^{n-1}\sqrt{X}} \\[3mm] \text{or} \\[3mm] \dfrac{(2cx + b)(n!)(n - 1)!4^n k^{n-1}}{q[(2n)!]\sqrt{X}} \displaystyle\sum_{r=0}^{n-1} \frac{(2r)!}{(4kX)^r(r!)^2} \end{cases}$

INTEGRALS (Continued)

242. $\displaystyle\int \sqrt{X}\, dx = \frac{(2cx + b)\sqrt{X}}{4c} + \frac{1}{2k}\int \frac{dx}{\sqrt{X}}$

243. $\displaystyle\int X\sqrt{X}\, dx = \frac{(2cx + b)\sqrt{X}}{8c}\left(X + \frac{3}{2k}\right) + \frac{3}{8k^2}\int \frac{dx}{\sqrt{X}}$

244. $\displaystyle\int X^2\sqrt{X}\, dx = \frac{(2cx + b)\sqrt{X}}{12c}\left(X^2 + \frac{5X}{4k} + \frac{15}{8k^2}\right) + \frac{5}{16k^3}\int \frac{dx}{\sqrt{X}}$

245. $\displaystyle\int X^n\sqrt{X}\, dx = \begin{cases} \dfrac{(2cx + b)X^n\sqrt{X}}{4(n + 1)c} + \dfrac{2n + 1}{2(n + 1)k}\displaystyle\int X^{n-1}\sqrt{X}\, dx \\[2mm] \qquad\qquad\text{or} \\[2mm] \dfrac{(2n + 2)!}{[(n + 1)!]^2(4k)^{n+1}}\left[\dfrac{k(2cx + b)\sqrt{X}}{c}\displaystyle\sum_{r=0}^{n}\dfrac{r!(r + 1)!(4kX)^r}{(2r + 2)!}\right. \\[4mm] \qquad\qquad\qquad\qquad\qquad\qquad\qquad \left. + \displaystyle\int \dfrac{dx}{\sqrt{X}}\right] \end{cases}$

246. $\displaystyle\int \frac{x\, dx}{\sqrt{X}} = \frac{\sqrt{X}}{c} - \frac{b}{2c}\int \frac{dx}{\sqrt{X}}$

247. $\displaystyle\int \frac{x\, dx}{X\sqrt{X}} = -\frac{2(bx + 2a)}{q\sqrt{X}}$

248. $\displaystyle\int \frac{x\, dx}{X^n\sqrt{X}} = -\frac{\sqrt{X}}{(2n - 1)cX^n} - \frac{b}{2c}\int \frac{dx}{X^n\sqrt{X}}$

249. $\displaystyle\int \frac{x^2\, dx}{\sqrt{X}} = \left(\frac{x}{2c} - \frac{3b}{4c^2}\right)\sqrt{X} + \frac{3b^2 - 4ac}{8c^2}\int \frac{dx}{\sqrt{X}}$

250. $\displaystyle\int \frac{x^2\, dx}{X\sqrt{X}} = \frac{(2b^2 - 4ac)x + 2ab}{cq\sqrt{X}} + \frac{1}{c}\int \frac{dx}{\sqrt{X}}$

251. $\displaystyle\int \frac{x^2\, dx}{X^n\sqrt{X}} = \frac{(2b^2 - 4ac)x + 2ab}{(2n - 1)cqX^{n-1}\sqrt{X}} + \frac{4ac + (2n - 3)b^2}{(2n - 1)cq}\int \frac{dx}{X^{n-1}\sqrt{X}}$

252. $\displaystyle\int \frac{x^3\, dx}{\sqrt{X}} = \left(\frac{x^2}{3c} - \frac{5bx}{12c^2} + \frac{5b^2}{8c^3} - \frac{2a}{3c^2}\right)\sqrt{X} + \left(\frac{3ab}{4c^2} - \frac{5b^3}{16c^3}\right)\int \frac{dx}{\sqrt{X}}$

253. $\displaystyle\int \frac{x^n\, dx}{\sqrt{X}} = \frac{1}{nc}x^{n-1}\sqrt{X} - \frac{(2n - 1)b}{2nc}\int \frac{x^{n-1}\, dx}{\sqrt{X}} - \frac{(n - 1)a}{nc}\int \frac{x^{n-2}\, dx}{\sqrt{X}}$

INTEGRALS (Continued)

254. $\displaystyle\int x\sqrt{X}\,dx = \frac{X\sqrt{X}}{3c} - \frac{b(2cx+b)}{8c^2}\sqrt{X} - \frac{b}{4ck}\int\frac{dx}{\sqrt{X}}$

255. $\displaystyle\int xX\sqrt{X}\,dx = \frac{X^2\sqrt{X}}{5c} - \frac{b}{2c}\int X\sqrt{X}\,dx$

256. $\displaystyle\int xX^n\sqrt{X}\,dx = \frac{X^{n+1}\sqrt{X}}{(2n+3)c} - \frac{b}{2c}\int X^n\sqrt{X}\,dx$

257. $\displaystyle\int x^2\sqrt{X}\,dx = \left(x - \frac{5b}{6c}\right)\frac{X\sqrt{X}}{4c} + \frac{5b^2-4ac}{16c^2}\int\sqrt{X}\,dx$

258. $\displaystyle\int\frac{dx}{x\sqrt{X}} = -\frac{1}{\sqrt{a}}\log\frac{2\sqrt{aX}+bx+2a}{x}, \qquad (a>0)$

259. $\displaystyle\int\frac{dx}{x\sqrt{X}} = \frac{1}{\sqrt{-a}}\sin^{-1}\left(\frac{bx+2a}{|x|\sqrt{-q}}\right), \qquad (a<0)$

260. $\displaystyle\int\frac{dx}{x\sqrt{X}} = -\frac{2\sqrt{X}}{bx}, \qquad (a=0)$

261. $\displaystyle\int\frac{dx}{x^2\sqrt{X}} = -\frac{\sqrt{X}}{ax} - \frac{b}{2a}\int\frac{dx}{x\sqrt{X}}$

262. $\displaystyle\int\frac{\sqrt{X}\,dx}{x} = \sqrt{X} + \frac{b}{2}\int\frac{dx}{\sqrt{X}} + a\int\frac{dx}{x\sqrt{X}}$

263. $\displaystyle\int\frac{\sqrt{X}\,dx}{x^2} = -\frac{\sqrt{X}}{x} + \frac{b}{2}\int\frac{dx}{x\sqrt{X}} + c\int\frac{dx}{\sqrt{X}}$

FORMS INVOLVING $\sqrt{2ax-x^2}$

264. $\displaystyle\int\sqrt{2ax-x^2}\,dx = \frac{1}{2}\left[(x-a)\sqrt{2ax-x^2} + a^2\sin^{-1}\frac{x-a}{|a|}\right]$

265. $\displaystyle\int\frac{dx}{\sqrt{2ax-x^2}} = \begin{cases} \cos^{-1}\dfrac{a-x}{|a|} \\ \quad\text{or} \\ \sin^{-1}\dfrac{x-a}{|a|} \end{cases}$

INTEGRALS (Continued)

266. $\int x^n \sqrt{2ax - x^2}\, dx = \begin{cases} -\dfrac{x^{n-1}(2ax - x^2)^{\frac{3}{2}}}{n+2} + \dfrac{(2n+1)a}{n+2} \int x^{n-1}\sqrt{2ax - x^2}\, dx \\[1em] \text{or} \\[1em] \sqrt{2ax - x^2}\left[\dfrac{x^{n+1}}{n+2} - \sum\limits_{r=0}^{n} \dfrac{(2n+1)!(r!)^2 a^{n-r+1}}{2^{n-r}(2r+1)!(n+2)!n!} x^r \right] \\[1em] \qquad\qquad + \dfrac{(2n+1)!a^{n+2}}{2^n n!(n+2)!} \sin^{-1} \dfrac{x-a}{|a|} \end{cases}$

267. $\int \dfrac{\sqrt{2ax - x^2}}{x^n}\, dx = \dfrac{(2ax - x^2)^{\frac{3}{2}}}{(3 - 2n)ax^n} + \dfrac{n-3}{(2n-3)a} \int \dfrac{\sqrt{2ax - x^2}}{x^{n-1}}\, dx$

268. $\int \dfrac{x^n\, dx}{\sqrt{2ax - x^2}} = \begin{cases} \dfrac{-x^{n-1}\sqrt{2ax - x^2}}{n} + \dfrac{a(2n-1)}{n} \int \dfrac{x^{n-1}}{\sqrt{2ax - x^2}}\, dx \\[1em] \text{or} \\[1em] -\sqrt{2ax - x^2} \sum\limits_{r=1}^{n} \dfrac{(2n)!r!(r-1)!a^{n-r}}{2^{n-r}(2r)!(n!)^2} x^{r-1} \\[1em] \qquad\qquad + \dfrac{(2n)!a^n}{2^n(n!)^2} \sin^{-1} \dfrac{x-a}{|a|} \end{cases}$

269. $\int \dfrac{dx}{x^n\sqrt{2ax - x^2}} = \begin{cases} \dfrac{\sqrt{2ax - x^2}}{a(1 - 2n)x^n} + \dfrac{n-1}{(2n-1)a} \int \dfrac{dx}{x^{n-1}\sqrt{2ax - x^2}} \\[1em] \text{or} \\[1em] -\sqrt{2ax - x^2} \sum\limits_{r=0}^{n-1} \dfrac{2^{n-r}(n-1)!n!(2r)!}{(2n)!(r!)^2 a^{n-r}x^{r+1}} \end{cases}$

270. $\int \dfrac{dx}{(2ax - x^2)^{\frac{3}{2}}} = \dfrac{x-a}{a^2\sqrt{2ax - x^2}}$

271. $\int \dfrac{x\, dx}{(2ax - x^2)^{\frac{3}{2}}} = \dfrac{x}{a\sqrt{2ax - x^2}}$

MISCELLANEOUS ALGEBRAIC FORMS

272. $\int \dfrac{dx}{\sqrt{2ax + x^2}} = \log\left(x + a + \sqrt{2ax + x^2}\right)$

273. $\int \sqrt{ax^2 + c}\, dx = \dfrac{x}{2}\sqrt{ax^2 + c} + \dfrac{c}{2\sqrt{a}} \log\left(x\sqrt{a} + \sqrt{ax^2 + c}\right), \qquad (a > 0)$

274. $\int \sqrt{ax^2 + c}\, dx = \dfrac{x}{2}\sqrt{ax^2 + c} + \dfrac{c}{2\sqrt{-a}} \sin^{-1}\left(x\sqrt{-\dfrac{a}{c}}\right), \qquad (a < 0)$

INTEGRALS (Continued)

275. $\displaystyle\int \sqrt{\frac{1+x}{1-x}}\,dx = \sin^{-1} x - \sqrt{1-x^2}$

276. $\displaystyle\int \frac{dx}{x\sqrt{ax^n + c}} = \begin{cases} \dfrac{1}{n\sqrt{c}} \log \dfrac{\sqrt{ax^n + c} - \sqrt{c}}{\sqrt{ax^n + c} + \sqrt{c}} \\[6pt] \text{or} \\[6pt] \dfrac{2}{n\sqrt{c}} \log \dfrac{\sqrt{ax^n + c} - \sqrt{c}}{\sqrt{x^n}}, \quad (c > 0) \end{cases}$

277. $\displaystyle\int \frac{dx}{x\sqrt{ax^n + c}} = \frac{2}{n\sqrt{-c}} \sec^{-1} \sqrt{-\frac{ax^n}{c}}, \quad (c < 0)$

278. $\displaystyle\int \frac{dx}{\sqrt{ax^2 + c}} = \frac{1}{\sqrt{a}} \log (x\sqrt{a} + \sqrt{ax^2 + c}), \quad (a > 0)$

279. $\displaystyle\int \frac{dx}{\sqrt{ax^2 + c}} = \frac{1}{\sqrt{-a}} \sin^{-1}\left(x\sqrt{-\frac{a}{c}}\right), \quad (a < 0)$

280. $\displaystyle\int (ax^2 + c)^{m + \frac{1}{2}}\,dx = \begin{cases} \dfrac{x(ax^2 + c)^{m + \frac{1}{2}}}{2(m+1)} + \dfrac{(2m+1)c}{2(m+1)} \displaystyle\int (ax^2 + c)^{m - \frac{1}{2}}\,dx \\[8pt] \text{or} \\[8pt] x\sqrt{ax^2 + c} \displaystyle\sum_{r=0}^{m} \dfrac{(2m+1)!(r!)^2 c^{m-r}}{2^{2m-2r+1} m!(m+1)!(2r+1)!}(ax^2 + c)^r \\[8pt] + \dfrac{(2m+1)! c^{m+1}}{2^{2m+1} m!(m+1)!} \displaystyle\int \dfrac{dx}{\sqrt{ax^2 + c}} \end{cases}$

281. $\displaystyle\int x(ax^2 + c)^{m + \frac{1}{2}}\,dx = \frac{(ax^2 + c)^{m + \frac{3}{2}}}{(2m+3)a}$

282. $\displaystyle\int \frac{(ax^2 + c)^{m + \frac{1}{2}}}{x}\,dx = \begin{cases} \dfrac{(ax^2 + c)^{m + \frac{1}{2}}}{2m+1} + c \displaystyle\int \dfrac{(ax^2 + c)^{m - \frac{1}{2}}}{x}\,dx \\[8pt] \text{or} \\[8pt] \sqrt{ax^2 + c} \displaystyle\sum_{r=0}^{m} \dfrac{c^{m-r}(ax^2 + c)^r}{2r+1} + c^{m+1} \displaystyle\int \dfrac{dx}{x\sqrt{ax^2 + c}} \end{cases}$

283. $\displaystyle\int \frac{dx}{(ax^2 + c)^{m + \frac{1}{2}}} = \begin{cases} \dfrac{x}{(2m-1)c(ax^2 + c)^{m - \frac{1}{2}}} + \dfrac{2m-2}{(2m-1)c} \displaystyle\int \dfrac{dx}{(ax^2 + c)^{m - \frac{1}{2}}} \\[8pt] \text{or} \\[8pt] \dfrac{x}{\sqrt{ax^2 + c}} \displaystyle\sum_{r=0}^{m-1} \dfrac{2^{2m-2r-1}(m-1)!m!(2r)!}{(2m)!(r!)^2 c^{m-r}(ax^2 + c)^r} \end{cases}$

INTEGRALS (Continued)

284. $\displaystyle\int \frac{dx}{x^m \sqrt{ax^2 + c}} = -\frac{\sqrt{ax^2 + c}}{(m-1)cx^{m-1}} - \frac{(m-2)a}{(m-1)c} \int \frac{dx}{x^{m-2}\sqrt{ax^2 + c}}$

285. $\displaystyle\int \frac{1 + x^2}{(1 - x^2)\sqrt{1 + x^4}}\, dx = \frac{1}{\sqrt{2}} \log \frac{x\sqrt{2} + \sqrt{1 + x^4}}{1 - x^2}$

286. $\displaystyle\int \frac{1 - x^2}{(1 + x^2)\sqrt{1 + x^4}}\, dx = \frac{1}{\sqrt{2}} \tan^{-1} \frac{x\sqrt{2}}{\sqrt{1 + x^4}}$

287. $\displaystyle\int \frac{dx}{x\sqrt{x^n + a^2}} = -\frac{2}{na} \log \frac{a + \sqrt{x^n + a^2}}{\sqrt{x^n}}$

288. $\displaystyle\int \frac{dx}{x\sqrt{x^n - a^2}} = -\frac{2}{na} \sin^{-1} \frac{a}{\sqrt{x^n}}$

289. $\displaystyle\int \sqrt{\frac{x}{a^3 - x^3}}\, dx = \frac{2}{3} \sin^{-1} \left(\frac{x}{a}\right)^{\frac{3}{2}}$

FORMS INVOLVING TRIGONOMETRIC FUNCTIONS

290. $\displaystyle\int (\sin ax)\, dx = -\frac{1}{a} \cos ax$

291. $\displaystyle\int (\cos ax)\, dx = \frac{1}{a} \sin ax$

292. $\displaystyle\int (\tan ax)\, dx = -\frac{1}{a} \log \cos ax = \frac{1}{a} \log \sec ax$

293. $\displaystyle\int (\cot ax)\, dx = \frac{1}{a} \log \sin ax = -\frac{1}{a} \log \csc ax$

294. $\displaystyle\int (\sec ax)\, dx = \frac{1}{a} \log (\sec ax + \tan ax) = \frac{1}{a} \log \tan \left(\frac{\pi}{4} + \frac{ax}{2}\right)$

295. $\displaystyle\int (\csc ax)\, dx = \frac{1}{a} \log (\csc ax - \cot ax) = \frac{1}{a} \log \tan \frac{ax}{2}$

296. $\displaystyle\int (\sin^2 ax)\, dx = -\frac{1}{2a} \cos ax \sin ax + \frac{1}{2}x = \frac{1}{2}x - \frac{1}{4a} \sin 2ax$

297. $\displaystyle\int (\sin^3 ax)\, dx = -\frac{1}{3a}(\cos ax)(\sin^2 ax + 2)$

298. $\displaystyle\int (\sin^4 ax)\, dx = \frac{3x}{8} - \frac{\sin 2ax}{4a} + \frac{\sin 4ax}{32a}$

299. $\displaystyle\int (\sin^n ax)\, dx = -\frac{\sin^{n-1} ax \cos ax}{na} + \frac{n-1}{n} \int (\sin^{n-2} ax)\, dx$

INTEGRALS (Continued)

300. $\displaystyle\int (\sin^{2m} ax)\, dx = -\frac{\cos ax}{a} \sum_{r=0}^{m-1} \frac{(2m)!\,(r!)^2}{2^{2m-2r}(2r+1)!(m!)^2} \sin^{2r+1} ax + \frac{(2m)!}{2^{2m}(m!)^2} x$

301. $\displaystyle\int (\sin^{2m+1} ax)\, dx = -\frac{\cos ax}{a} \sum_{r=0}^{m} \frac{2^{2m-2r}(m!)^2(2r)!}{(2m+1)!(r!)^2} \sin^{2r} ax$

302. $\displaystyle\int (\cos^2 ax)\, dx = \frac{1}{2a} \sin ax \cos ax + \frac{1}{2}x = \frac{1}{2}x + \frac{1}{4a} \sin 2ax$

303. $\displaystyle\int (\cos^3 ax)\, dx = \frac{1}{3a}(\sin ax)(\cos^2 ax + 2)$

304. $\displaystyle\int (\cos^4 ax)\, dx = \frac{3x}{8} + \frac{\sin 2ax}{4a} + \frac{\sin 4ax}{32a}$

305. $\displaystyle\int (\cos^n ax)\, dx = \frac{1}{na} \cos^{n-1} ax \sin ax + \frac{n-1}{n} \int (\cos^{n-2} ax)\, dx$

306. $\displaystyle\int (\cos^{2m} ax)\, dx = \frac{\sin ax}{a} \sum_{r=0}^{m-1} \frac{(2m)!\,(r!)^2}{2^{2m-2r}(2r+1)!(m!)^2} \cos^{2r+1} ax + \frac{(2m)!}{2^{2m}(m!)^2} x$

307. $\displaystyle\int (\cos^{2m+1} ax)\, dx = \frac{\sin ax}{a} \sum_{r=0}^{m} \frac{2^{2m-2r}(m!)^2(2r)!}{(2m+1)!(r!)^2} \cos^{2r} ax$

308. $\displaystyle\int \frac{dx}{\sin^2 ax} = \int (\csc^2 ax)\, dx = -\frac{1}{a} \cot ax$

309. $\displaystyle\int \frac{dx}{\sin^m ax} = \int (\csc^m ax)\, dx = -\frac{1}{(m-1)a} \cdot \frac{\cos ax}{\sin^{m-1} ax} + \frac{m-2}{m-1} \int \frac{dx}{\sin^{m-2} ax}$

310. $\displaystyle\int \frac{dx}{\sin^{2m} ax} = \int (\csc^{2m} ax)\, dx = -\frac{1}{a} \cos ax \sum_{r=0}^{m-1} \frac{2^{2m-2r-1}(m-1)!\,m!(2r)!}{(2m)!\,(r!)^2 \sin^{2r+1} ax}$

311. $\displaystyle\int \frac{dx}{\sin^{2m+1} ax} = \int (\csc^{2m+1} ax)\, dx =$

$\displaystyle -\frac{1}{a} \cos ax \sum_{r=0}^{m-1} \frac{(2m)!\,(r!)^2}{2^{2m-2r}(m!)^2(2r+1)! \sin^{2r+2} ax} + \frac{1}{a} \cdot \frac{(2m)!}{2^{2m}(m!)^2} \log \tan \frac{ax}{2}$

312. $\displaystyle\int \frac{dx}{\cos^2 ax} = \int (\sec^2 ax)\, dx = \frac{1}{a} \tan ax$

313. $\displaystyle\int \frac{dx}{\cos^n ax} = \int (\sec^n ax)\, dx = \frac{1}{(n-1)a} \cdot \frac{\sin ax}{\cos^{n-1} ax} + \frac{n-2}{n-1} \int \frac{dx}{\cos^{n-2} ax}$

314. $\displaystyle\int \frac{dx}{\cos^{2m} ax} = \int (\sec^{2m} ax)\, dx = \frac{1}{a} \sin ax \sum_{r=0}^{m-1} \frac{2^{2m-2r-1}(m-1)!\,m!(2r)!}{(2m)!\,(r!)^2 \cos^{2r+1} ax}$

INTEGRALS (Continued)

315. $\displaystyle\int \frac{dx}{\cos^{2m+1} ax} = \int (\sec^{2m+1} ax)\, dx =$

$$\frac{1}{a} \sin ax \sum_{r=0}^{m-1} \frac{(2m)!\,(r!)^2}{2^{2m-2r}(m!)^2(2r+1)!\cos^{2r+2} ax}$$

$$+ \frac{1}{a} \cdot \frac{(2m)!}{2^{2m}(m!)^2} \log\,(\sec ax + \tan ax)$$

316. $\displaystyle\int (\sin mx)(\sin nx)\, dx = \frac{\sin(m-n)x}{2(m-n)} - \frac{\sin(m+n)x}{2(m+n)}, \qquad (m^2 \neq n^2)$

317. $\displaystyle\int (\cos mx)(\cos nx)\, dx = \frac{\sin(m-n)x}{2(m-n)} + \frac{\sin(m+n)x}{2(m+n)}, \qquad (m^2 \neq n^2)$

318. $\displaystyle\int (\sin ax)(\cos ax)\, dx = \frac{1}{2a} \sin^2 ax$

319. $\displaystyle\int (\sin mx)(\cos nx)\, dx = -\frac{\cos(m-n)x}{2(m-n)} - \frac{\cos(m+n)x}{2(m+n)}, \qquad (m^2 \neq n^2)$

320. $\displaystyle\int (\sin^2 ax)(\cos^2 ax)\, dx = -\frac{1}{32a} \sin 4ax + \frac{x}{8}$

321. $\displaystyle\int (\sin ax)(\cos^m ax)\, dx = -\frac{\cos^{m+1} ax}{(m+1)a}$

322. $\displaystyle\int (\sin^m ax)(\cos ax)\, dx = \frac{\sin^{m+1} ax}{(m+1)a}$

323. $\displaystyle\int (\cos^m ax)(\sin^n ax)\, dx = \begin{cases} \dfrac{\cos^{m-1} ax\, \sin^{n+1} ax}{(m+n)a} \\[2ex] \qquad + \dfrac{m-1}{m+n}\displaystyle\int (\cos^{m-2} ax)(\sin^n ax)\, dx \\[2ex] \text{or} \\[2ex] -\dfrac{\sin^{n-1} ax\, \cos^{m+1} ax}{(m+n)a} \\[2ex] \qquad + \dfrac{n-1}{m+n}\displaystyle\int (\cos^m ax)(\sin^{n-2} ax)\, dx \end{cases}$

324. $\displaystyle\int \frac{\cos^m ax}{\sin^n ax}\, dx = \begin{cases} -\dfrac{\cos^{m+1} ax}{(n-1)a\,\sin^{n-1} ax} - \dfrac{m-n+2}{n-1}\displaystyle\int \dfrac{\cos^m ax}{\sin^{n-2} ax}\, dx \\[2ex] \text{or} \\[2ex] \dfrac{\cos^{m-1} ax}{a(m-n)\,\sin^{n-1} ax} + \dfrac{m-1}{m-n}\displaystyle\int \dfrac{\cos^{m-2} ax}{\sin^n ax}\, dx \end{cases}$

INTEGRALS (Continued)

325. $\displaystyle\int \frac{\sin^m ax}{\cos^n ax}\,dx =$
$\begin{cases}
\dfrac{\sin^{m+1} ax}{a(n-1)\cos^{n-1} ax} - \dfrac{m-n+2}{n-1}\displaystyle\int \dfrac{\sin^m ax}{\cos^{n-2} ax}\,dx \\[4pt]
\qquad\qquad\text{or} \\[4pt]
-\dfrac{\sin^{m-1} ax}{a(m-n)\cos^{n-1} ax} + \dfrac{m-1}{m-n}\displaystyle\int \dfrac{\sin^{m-2} ax}{\cos^n ax}\,dx
\end{cases}$

326. $\displaystyle\int \frac{\sin ax}{\cos^2 ax}\,dx = \frac{1}{a\cos ax} = \frac{\sec ax}{a}$

327. $\displaystyle\int \frac{\sin^2 ax}{\cos ax}\,dx = -\frac{1}{a}\sin ax + \frac{1}{a}\log\tan\left(\frac{\pi}{4} + \frac{ax}{2}\right)$

328. $\displaystyle\int \frac{\cos ax}{\sin^2 ax}\,dx = -\frac{1}{a\sin ax} = -\frac{\csc ax}{a}$

329. $\displaystyle\int \frac{dx}{(\sin ax)(\cos ax)} = \frac{1}{a}\log\tan ax$

330. $\displaystyle\int \frac{dx}{(\sin ax)(\cos^2 ax)} = \frac{1}{a}\left(\sec ax + \log\tan\frac{ax}{2}\right)$

331. $\displaystyle\int \frac{dx}{(\sin ax)(\cos^n ax)} = \frac{1}{a(n-1)\cos^{n-1} ax} + \int \frac{dx}{(\sin ax)(\cos^{n-2} ax)}$

332. $\displaystyle\int \frac{dx}{(\sin^2 ax)(\cos ax)} = -\frac{1}{a}\csc ax + \frac{1}{a}\log\tan\left(\frac{\pi}{4} + \frac{ax}{2}\right)$

333. $\displaystyle\int \frac{dx}{(\sin^2 ax)(\cos^2 ax)} = -\frac{2}{a}\cot 2ax$

334. $\displaystyle\int \frac{dx}{\sin^m ax \cos^n ax} =$
$\begin{cases}
-\dfrac{1}{a(m-1)(\sin^{m-1} ax)(\cos^{n-1} ax)} \\[4pt]
\qquad\qquad + \dfrac{m+n-2}{m-1}\displaystyle\int \dfrac{dx}{(\sin^{m-2} ax)(\cos^n ax)} \\[4pt]
\qquad\qquad\text{or} \\[4pt]
\dfrac{1}{a(n-1)\sin^{m-1} ax \cos^{n-1} ax} \\[4pt]
\qquad\qquad - \dfrac{m+n-2}{n-1}\displaystyle\int \dfrac{dx}{\sin^m ax \cos^{n-2} ax}
\end{cases}$

335. $\displaystyle\int \sin(a+bx)\,dx = -\frac{1}{b}\cos(a+bx)$

336. $\displaystyle\int \cos(a+bx)\,dx = \frac{1}{b}\sin(a+bx)$

337. $\displaystyle\int \frac{dx}{1 \pm \sin ax} = \mp\frac{1}{a}\tan\left(\frac{\pi}{4} \mp \frac{ax}{2}\right)$

INTEGRALS (Continued)

338. $\int \dfrac{dx}{1 + \cos ax} = \dfrac{1}{a} \tan \dfrac{ax}{2}$

339. $\int \dfrac{dx}{1 - \cos ax} = -\dfrac{1}{a} \cot \dfrac{ax}{2}$

*340. $\int \dfrac{dx}{a + b \sin x} = \begin{cases} \dfrac{2}{\sqrt{a^2 - b^2}} \tan^{-1} \dfrac{a \tan \dfrac{x}{2} + b}{\sqrt{a^2 - b^2}} \\[2mm] \text{or} \\[2mm] \dfrac{1}{\sqrt{b^2 - a^2}} \log \dfrac{a \tan \dfrac{x}{2} + b - \sqrt{b^2 - a^2}}{a \tan \dfrac{x}{2} + b + \sqrt{b^2 - a^2}} \end{cases}$

*341. $\int \dfrac{dx}{a + b \cos x} = \begin{cases} \dfrac{2}{\sqrt{a^2 - b^2}} \tan^{-1} \dfrac{\sqrt{a^2 - b^2} \tan \dfrac{x}{2}}{a + b} \\[2mm] \text{or} \\[2mm] \dfrac{1}{\sqrt{b^2 - a^2}} \log \left(-\dfrac{\sqrt{b^2 - a^2} \tan \dfrac{x}{2} + a + b}{\sqrt{b^2 - a^2} \tan \dfrac{x}{2} - a - b} \right) \end{cases}$

*342. $\int \dfrac{dx}{a + b \sin x + c \cos x}$

$= \begin{cases} \dfrac{1}{\sqrt{b^2 + c^2 - a^2}} \log \dfrac{b - \sqrt{b^2 + c^2 - a^2} + (a - c) \tan \dfrac{x}{2}}{b + \sqrt{b^2 + c^2 - a^2} + (a - c) \tan \dfrac{x}{2}}, & \text{if } a^2 < b^2 + c^2, a \neq c \\[4mm] \text{or} \\[2mm] \dfrac{2}{\sqrt{a^2 - b^2 - c^2}} \tan^{-1} \dfrac{b + (a - c) \tan \dfrac{x}{2}}{\sqrt{a^2 - b^2 - c^2}}, & \text{if } a^2 > b^2 + c^2 \\[4mm] \text{or} \\[2mm] \dfrac{1}{a} \left[\dfrac{a - (b + c) \cos x - (b - c) \sin x}{a - (b - c) \cos x + (b + c) \sin x} \right], & \text{if } a^2 = b^2 + c^2, a \neq c. \end{cases}$

*343. $\int \dfrac{\sin^2 x \, dx}{a + b \cos^2 x} = \dfrac{1}{b} \sqrt{\dfrac{a + b}{a}} \tan^{-1} \left(\sqrt{\dfrac{a}{a + b}} \tan x \right) - \dfrac{x}{b}, \qquad (ab > 0, \text{ or } |a| > |b|)$

*See note 6 – page 386.

INTEGRALS (Continued)

*344. $\displaystyle\int \frac{dx}{a^2 \cos^2 x + b^2 \sin^2 x} = \frac{1}{ab} \tan^{-1}\left(\frac{b \tan x}{a}\right)$

*345. $\displaystyle\int \frac{\cos^2 cx}{a^2 + b^2 \sin^2 cx}\, dx = \frac{\sqrt{a^2 + b^2}}{ab^2 c} \tan^{-1} \frac{\sqrt{a^2 + b^2}\, \tan cx}{a} - \frac{x}{b^2}$

346. $\displaystyle\int \frac{\sin cx \cos cx}{a \cos^2 cx + b \sin^2 cx}\, dx = \frac{1}{2c(b - a)} \log\,(a \cos^2 cx + b \sin^2 cx)$

347. $\displaystyle\int \frac{\cos cx}{a \cos cx + b \sin cx}\, dx = \int \frac{dx}{a + b \tan cx} =$

$$\frac{1}{c(a^2 + b^2)}[acx + b \log\,(a \cos cx + b \,\mathrm{si}$$

348. $\displaystyle\int \frac{\sin cx}{a \sin cx + b \cos cx}\, dx = \int \frac{dx}{a + b \cot cx} =$

$$\frac{1}{c(a^2 + b^2)}[acx - b \log\,(a \sin cx + b \,\mathrm{cc}$$

*349. $\displaystyle\int \frac{dx}{a \cos^2 x + 2b \cos x \sin x + c \sin^2 x} = \begin{cases} \dfrac{1}{2\sqrt{b^2 - ac}} \log \dfrac{c \tan x + b - \sqrt{b^2}}{c \tan x + b + \sqrt{b^2}} \\[4pt] \qquad\qquad\qquad\qquad (b^2 \\[6pt] \text{or} \\[6pt] \dfrac{1}{\sqrt{ac - b^2}} \tan^{-1} \dfrac{c \tan x + b}{\sqrt{ac - b^2}}, \quad (b^2 \\[6pt] \text{or} \\[6pt] -\dfrac{1}{c \tan x + b}, \qquad (b^2 = ac) \end{cases}$

350. $\displaystyle\int \frac{\sin ax}{1 \pm \sin ax}\, dx = \pm x + \frac{1}{a} \tan\left(\frac{\pi}{4} \mp \frac{ax}{2}\right)$

351. $\displaystyle\int \frac{dx}{(\sin ax)(1 \pm \sin ax)} = \frac{1}{a} \tan\left(\frac{\pi}{4} \mp \frac{ax}{2}\right) + \frac{1}{a} \log \tan \frac{ax}{2}$

352. $\displaystyle\int \frac{dx}{(1 + \sin ax)^2} = -\frac{1}{2a} \tan\left(\frac{\pi}{4} - \frac{ax}{2}\right) - \frac{1}{6a} \tan^3\left(\frac{\pi}{4} - \frac{ax}{2}\right)$

353. $\displaystyle\int \frac{dx}{(1 - \sin ax)^2} = \frac{1}{2a} \cot\left(\frac{\pi}{4} - \frac{ax}{2}\right) + \frac{1}{6a} \cot^3\left(\frac{\pi}{4} - \frac{ax}{2}\right)$

354. $\displaystyle\int \frac{\sin ax}{(1 + \sin ax)^2}\, dx = -\frac{1}{2a} \tan\left(\frac{\pi}{4} - \frac{ax}{2}\right) + \frac{1}{6a} \tan^3\left(\frac{\pi}{4} - \frac{ax}{2}\right)$

*See note 6 – page 386.

INTEGRALS (Continued)

355. $\displaystyle\int \frac{\sin ax}{(1 - \sin ax)^2}\,dx = -\frac{1}{2a}\cot\left(\frac{\pi}{4} - \frac{ax}{2}\right) + \frac{1}{6a}\cot^3\left(\frac{\pi}{4} - \frac{ax}{2}\right)$

356. $\displaystyle\int \frac{\sin x\,dx}{a + b\sin x} = \frac{x}{b} - \frac{a}{b}\int \frac{dx}{a + b\sin x}$

357. $\displaystyle\int \frac{dx}{(\sin x)(a + b\sin x)} = \frac{1}{a}\log\tan\frac{x}{2} - \frac{b}{a}\int \frac{dx}{a + b\sin x}$

358. $\displaystyle\int \frac{dx}{(a + b\sin x)^2} = \frac{b\cos x}{(a^2 - b^2)(a + b\sin x)} + \frac{a}{a^2 - b^2}\int \frac{dx}{a + b\sin x}$

359. $\displaystyle\int \frac{\sin x\,dx}{(a + b\sin x)^2} = \frac{a\cos x}{(b^2 - a^2)(a + b\sin x)} + \frac{b}{b^2 - a^2}\int \frac{dx}{a + b\sin x}$

*360. $\displaystyle\int \frac{dx}{a^2 + b^2\sin^2 cx} = \frac{1}{ac\sqrt{a^2 + b^2}}\tan^{-1}\frac{\sqrt{a^2 + b^2}\,\tan cx}{a}$

*361. $\displaystyle\int \frac{dx}{a^2 - b^2\sin^2 cx} = \begin{cases} \dfrac{1}{ac\sqrt{a^2 - b^2}}\tan^{-1}\dfrac{\sqrt{a^2 - b^2}\,\tan cx}{a}, & (a^2 > b^2) \\[2mm] \text{or} \\[2mm] \dfrac{1}{2ac\sqrt{b^2 - a^2}}\log\dfrac{\sqrt{b^2 - a^2}\,\tan cx + a}{\sqrt{b^2 - a^2}\,\tan cx - a}, & (a^2 < b^2) \end{cases}$

362. $\displaystyle\int \frac{\cos ax}{1 + \cos ax}\,dx = x - \frac{1}{a}\tan\frac{ax}{2}$

363. $\displaystyle\int \frac{\cos ax}{1 - \cos ax}\,dx = -x - \frac{1}{a}\cot\frac{ax}{2}$

364. $\displaystyle\int \frac{dx}{(\cos ax)(1 + \cos ax)} = \frac{1}{a}\log\tan\left(\frac{\pi}{4} + \frac{ax}{2}\right) - \frac{1}{a}\tan\frac{ax}{2}$

365. $\displaystyle\int \frac{dx}{(\cos ax)(1 - \cos ax)} = \frac{1}{a}\log\tan\left(\frac{\pi}{4} + \frac{ax}{2}\right) - \frac{1}{a}\cot\frac{ax}{2}$

366. $\displaystyle\int \frac{dx}{(1 + \cos ax)^2} = \frac{1}{2a}\tan\frac{ax}{2} + \frac{1}{6a}\tan^3\frac{ax}{2}$

367. $\displaystyle\int \frac{dx}{(1 - \cos ax)^2} = -\frac{1}{2a}\cot\frac{ax}{2} - \frac{1}{6a}\cot^3\frac{ax}{2}$

368. $\displaystyle\int \frac{\cos ax}{(1 + \cos ax)^2}\,dx = \frac{1}{2a}\tan\frac{ax}{2} - \frac{1}{6a}\tan^3\frac{ax}{2}$

369. $\displaystyle\int \frac{\cos ax}{(1 - \cos ax)^2}\,dx = \frac{1}{2a}\cot\frac{ax}{2} - \frac{1}{6a}\cot^3\frac{ax}{2}$

*See note 6–page 386.

INTEGRALS (Continued)

370. $\displaystyle \int \frac{\cos x \, dx}{a + b \cos x} = \frac{x}{b} - \frac{a}{b} \int \frac{dx}{a + b \cos x}$

371. $\displaystyle \int \frac{dx}{(\cos x)(a + b \cos x)} = \frac{1}{a} \log \tan \left(\frac{x}{2} + \frac{\pi}{4} \right) - \frac{b}{a} \int \frac{dx}{a + b \cos x}$

372. $\displaystyle \int \frac{dx}{(a + b \cos x)^2} = \frac{b \sin x}{(b^2 - a^2)(a + b \cos x)} - \frac{a}{b^2 - a^2} \int \frac{dx}{a + b \cos x}$

373. $\displaystyle \int \frac{\cos x}{(a + b \cos x)^2} \, dx = \frac{a \sin x}{(a^2 - b^2)(a + b \cos x)} - \frac{b}{a^2 - b^2} \int \frac{dx}{a + b \cos x}$

*374. $\displaystyle \int \frac{dx}{a^2 + b^2 - 2ab \cos cx} = \frac{2}{c(a^2 - b^2)} \tan^{-1} \left(\frac{a + b}{a - b} \tan \frac{cx}{2} \right)$

*375. $\displaystyle \int \frac{dx}{a^2 + b^2 \cos^2 cx} = \frac{1}{ac\sqrt{a^2 + b^2}} \tan^{-1} \frac{a \tan cx}{\sqrt{a^2 + b^2}}$

*376. $\displaystyle \int \frac{dx}{a^2 - b^2 \cos^2 cx} = \begin{cases} \dfrac{1}{ac\sqrt{a^2 - b^2}} \tan^{-1} \dfrac{a \tan cx}{\sqrt{a^2 - b^2}}, & (a^2 > b^2) \\[2ex] \text{or} \\[2ex] \dfrac{1}{2ac\sqrt{b^2 - a^2}} \log \dfrac{a \tan cx - \sqrt{b^2 - a^2}}{a \tan cx + \sqrt{b^2 - a^2}}, & (b^2 > a^2) \end{cases}$

377. $\displaystyle \int \frac{\sin ax}{1 \pm \cos ax} \, dx = \mp \frac{1}{a} \log (1 \pm \cos ax)$

378. $\displaystyle \int \frac{\cos ax}{1 \pm \sin ax} \, dx = \pm \frac{1}{a} \log (1 \pm \sin ax)$

379. $\displaystyle \int \frac{dx}{(\sin ax)(1 \pm \cos ax)} = \pm \frac{1}{2a(1 \pm \cos ax)} + \frac{1}{2a} \log \tan \frac{ax}{2}$

380. $\displaystyle \int \frac{dx}{(\cos ax)(1 \pm \sin ax)} = \mp \frac{1}{2a(1 \pm \sin ax)} + \frac{1}{2a} \log \tan \left(\frac{\pi}{4} + \frac{ax}{2} \right)$

381. $\displaystyle \int \frac{\sin ax}{(\cos ax)(1 \pm \cos ax)} \, dx = \frac{1}{a} \log (\sec ax \pm 1)$

382. $\displaystyle \int \frac{\cos ax}{(\sin ax)(1 \pm \sin ax)} \, dx = -\frac{1}{a} \log (\csc ax \pm 1)$

383. $\displaystyle \int \frac{\sin ax}{(\cos ax)(1 \pm \sin ax)} \, dx = \frac{1}{2a(1 \pm \sin ax)} \pm \frac{1}{2a} \log \tan \left(\frac{\pi}{4} + \frac{ax}{2} \right)$

384. $\displaystyle \int \frac{\cos ax}{(\sin ax)(1 \pm \cos ax)} \, dx = -\frac{1}{2a(1 \pm \cos ax)} \pm \frac{1}{2a} \log \tan \frac{ax}{2}$

*See note 6 – page 386.

INTEGRALS (Continued)

385. $\int \dfrac{dx}{\sin ax \pm \cos ax} = \dfrac{1}{a\sqrt{2}} \log \tan\left(\dfrac{ax}{2} \pm \dfrac{\pi}{8}\right)$

386. $\int \dfrac{dx}{(\sin ax \pm \cos ax)^2} = \dfrac{1}{2a} \tan\left(ax \mp \dfrac{\pi}{4}\right)$

387. $\int \dfrac{dx}{1 + \cos ax \pm \sin ax} = \pm \dfrac{1}{a} \log\left(1 \pm \tan \dfrac{ax}{2}\right)$

388. $\int \dfrac{dx}{a^2 \cos^2 cx - b^2 \sin^2 cx} = \dfrac{1}{2abc} \log \dfrac{b \tan cx + a}{b \tan cx - a}$

389. $\int x(\sin ax)\,dx = \dfrac{1}{a^2} \sin ax - \dfrac{x}{a} \cos ax$

390. $\int x^2(\sin ax)\,dx = \dfrac{2x}{a^2} \sin ax - \dfrac{a^2x^2 - 2}{a^3} \cos ax$

391. $\int x^3(\sin ax)\,dx = \dfrac{3a^2x^2 - 6}{a^4} \sin ax - \dfrac{a^2x^3 - 6x}{a^3} \cos ax$

392. $\int x^m \sin ax\,dx = \begin{cases} -\dfrac{1}{a} x^m \cos ax + \dfrac{m}{a} \displaystyle\int x^{m-1} \cos ax\,dx \\[2mm] \qquad\qquad \text{or} \\[2mm] \cos ax \displaystyle\sum_{r=0}^{\left[\frac{m}{2}\right]} (-1)^{r+1} \dfrac{m!}{(m-2r)!} \cdot \dfrac{x^{m-2r}}{a^{2r+1}} \\[4mm] + \sin ax \displaystyle\sum_{r=0}^{\left[\frac{m-1}{2}\right]} (-1)^r \dfrac{m!}{(m-2r-1)!} \cdot \dfrac{x^{m-2r-1}}{a^{2r+2}} \end{cases}$

Note: $[s]$ means greatest integer $\leq s$; $[3\frac{1}{2}] = 3$, $[\frac{1}{2}] = 0$, etc.

393. $\int x(\cos ax)\,dx = \dfrac{1}{a^2} \cos ax + \dfrac{x}{a} \sin ax$

394. $\int x^2(\cos ax)\,dx = \dfrac{2x \cos ax}{a^2} + \dfrac{a^2x^2 - 2}{a^3} \sin ax$

395. $\int x^3(\cos ax)\,dx = \dfrac{3a^2x^2 - 6}{a^4} \cos ax + \dfrac{a^2x^3 - 6x}{a^3} \sin ax$

396. $\int x^m(\cos ax)\,dx = \begin{cases} \dfrac{x^m \sin ax}{a} - \dfrac{m}{a} \displaystyle\int x^{m-1} \sin ax\,dx \\[2mm] \qquad\qquad \text{or} \\[2mm] \sin ax \displaystyle\sum_{r=0}^{\left[\frac{m}{2}\right]} (-1)^r \dfrac{m!}{(m-2r)!} \cdot \dfrac{x^{m-2r}}{a^{2r+1}} \\[4mm] + \cos ax \displaystyle\sum_{r=0}^{\left[\frac{m-1}{2}\right]} (-1)^r \dfrac{m!}{(m-2r-1)!} \cdot \dfrac{x^{m-2r-1}}{a^{2r+2}} \end{cases}$

See note integral 392.

INTEGRALS (Continued)

397. $\displaystyle\int \frac{\sin ax}{x}\,dx = \sum_{n=0}^{\infty} (-1)^n \frac{(ax)^{2n+1}}{(2n+1)(2n+1)!}$

398. $\displaystyle\int \frac{\cos ax}{x}\,dx = \log x + \sum_{n=1}^{\infty} (-1)^n \frac{(ax)^{2n}}{2n(2n)!}$

399. $\displaystyle\int x(\sin^2 ax)\,dx = \frac{x^2}{4} - \frac{x \sin 2ax}{4a} - \frac{\cos 2ax}{8a^2}$

400. $\displaystyle\int x^2(\sin^2 ax)\,dx = \frac{x^3}{6} - \left(\frac{x^2}{4a} - \frac{1}{8a^3}\right)\sin 2ax - \frac{x \cos 2ax}{4a^2}$

401. $\displaystyle\int x(\sin^3 ax)\,dx = \frac{x \cos 3ax}{12a} - \frac{\sin 3ax}{36a^2} - \frac{3x \cos ax}{4a} + \frac{3 \sin ax}{4a^2}$

402. $\displaystyle\int x(\cos^2 ax)\,dx = \frac{x^2}{4} + \frac{x \sin 2ax}{4a} + \frac{\cos 2ax}{8a^2}$

403. $\displaystyle\int x^2(\cos^2 ax)\,dx = \frac{x^3}{6} + \left(\frac{x^2}{4a} - \frac{1}{8a^3}\right)\sin 2ax + \frac{x \cos 2ax}{4a^2}$

404. $\displaystyle\int x(\cos^3 ax)\,dx = \frac{x \sin 3ax}{12a} + \frac{\cos 3ax}{36a^2} + \frac{3x \sin ax}{4a} + \frac{3 \cos ax}{4a^2}$

405. $\displaystyle\int \frac{\sin ax}{x^m}\,dx = -\frac{\sin ax}{(m-1)x^{m-1}} + \frac{a}{m-1}\int \frac{\cos ax}{x^{m-1}}\,dx$

406. $\displaystyle\int \frac{\cos ax}{x^m}\,dx = -\frac{\cos ax}{(m-1)x^{m-1}} - \frac{a}{m-1}\int \frac{\sin ax}{x^{m-1}}\,dx$

407. $\displaystyle\int \frac{x}{1 \pm \sin ax}\,dx = \mp \frac{x \cos ax}{a(1 \pm \sin ax)} + \frac{1}{a^2}\log(1 \pm \sin ax)$

408. $\displaystyle\int \frac{x}{1 + \cos ax}\,dx = \frac{x}{a}\tan\frac{ax}{2} + \frac{2}{a^2}\log\cos\frac{ax}{2}$

409. $\displaystyle\int \frac{x}{1 - \cos ax}\,dx = -\frac{x}{a}\cot\frac{ax}{2} + \frac{2}{a^2}\log\sin\frac{ax}{2}$

410. $\displaystyle\int \frac{x + \sin x}{1 + \cos x}\,dx = x \tan\frac{x}{2}$

411. $\displaystyle\int \frac{x - \sin x}{1 - \cos x}\,dx = -x \cot\frac{x}{2}$

412. $\displaystyle\int \sqrt{1 - \cos ax}\,dx = -\frac{2 \sin ax}{a\sqrt{1 - \cos ax}} = -\frac{2\sqrt{2}}{a}\cos\left(\frac{ax}{2}\right)$

413. $\displaystyle\int \sqrt{1 + \cos ax}\,dx = \frac{2 \sin ax}{a\sqrt{1 + \cos ax}} = \frac{2\sqrt{2}}{a}\sin\left(\frac{ax}{2}\right)$

INTEGRALS (Continued)

414. $\int \sqrt{1 + \sin x}\, dx = \pm 2 \left(\sin \dfrac{x}{2} - \cos \dfrac{x}{2} \right),$

[use + if $(8k - 1)\dfrac{\pi}{2} < x \le (8k + 3)\dfrac{\pi}{2}$, otherwise $-$; k an integer]

415. $\int \sqrt{1 - \sin x}\, dx = \pm 2 \left(\sin \dfrac{x}{2} + \cos \dfrac{x}{2} \right),$

[use + if $(8k - 3)\dfrac{\pi}{2} < x \le (8k + 1)\dfrac{\pi}{2}$, otherwise $-$; k an integer]

416. $\int \dfrac{dx}{\sqrt{1 - \cos x}} = \pm \sqrt{2} \log \tan \dfrac{x}{4},$

[use + if $4k\pi < x < (4k + 2)\pi$, otherwise $-$; k an integer]

417. $\int \dfrac{dx}{\sqrt{1 + \cos x}} = \pm \sqrt{2} \log \tan \left(\dfrac{x + \pi}{4} \right),$

[use + if $(4k - 1)\pi < x < (4k + 1)\pi$, otherwise $-$; k an integer]

418. $\int \dfrac{dx}{\sqrt{1 - \sin x}} = \pm \sqrt{2} \log \tan \left(\dfrac{x}{4} - \dfrac{\pi}{8} \right),$

[use + if $(8k + 1)\dfrac{\pi}{2} < x < (8k + 5)\dfrac{\pi}{2}$, otherwise $-$; k an integer]

419. $\int \dfrac{dx}{\sqrt{1 + \sin x}} = \pm \sqrt{2} \log \tan \left(\dfrac{x}{4} + \dfrac{\pi}{8} \right),$

[use + if $(8k - 1)\dfrac{\pi}{2} < x < (8k + 3)\dfrac{\pi}{2}$, otherwise $-$; k an integer]

420. $\int (\tan^2 ax)\, dx = \dfrac{1}{a} \tan ax - x$

421. $\int (\tan^3 ax)\, dx = \dfrac{1}{2a} \tan^2 ax + \dfrac{1}{a} \log \cos ax$

422. $\int (\tan^4 ax)\, dx = \dfrac{\tan^3 ax}{3a} - \dfrac{1}{a} \tan x + x$

423. $\int (\tan^n ax)\, dx = \dfrac{\tan^{n-1} ax}{a(n - 1)} - \int (\tan^{n-2} ax)\, dx$

424. $\int (\cot^2 ax)\, dx = -\dfrac{1}{a} \cot ax - x$

425. $\int (\cot^3 ax)\, dx = -\dfrac{1}{2a} \cot^2 ax - \dfrac{1}{a} \log \sin ax$

426. $\int (\cot^4 ax)\, dx = -\dfrac{1}{3a} \cot^3 ax + \dfrac{1}{a} \cot ax + x$

INTEGRALS (Continued)

427. $\displaystyle \int (\cot^n ax)\, dx = -\frac{\cot^{n-1} ax}{a(n-1)} - \int (\cot^{n-2} ax)\, dx$

428. $\displaystyle \int \frac{x}{\sin^2 ax}\, dx = \int x(\csc^2 ax)\, dx = -\frac{x \cot ax}{a} + \frac{1}{a^2}\log \sin ax$

429. $\displaystyle \int \frac{x}{\sin^n ax}\, dx = \int x(\csc^n ax)\, dx = -\frac{x \cos ax}{a(n-1)\sin^{n-1} ax}$

$$-\frac{1}{a^2(n-1)(n-2)\sin^{n-2} ax} + \frac{(n-2)}{(n-1)}\int \frac{x}{\sin^{n-2} ax}\, dx$$

430. $\displaystyle \int \frac{x}{\cos^2 ax}\, dx = \int x(\sec^2 ax)\, dx = \frac{1}{a}x \tan ax + \frac{1}{a^2}\log \cos ax$

431. $\displaystyle \int \frac{x}{\cos^n ax}\, dx = \int x(\sec^n ax)\, dx = \frac{x \sin ax}{a(n-1)\cos^{n-1} ax}$

$$-\frac{1}{a^2(n-1)(n-2)\cos^{n-2} ax} + \frac{n-2}{n-1}\int \frac{x}{\cos^{n-2} ax}\, dx$$

432. $\displaystyle \int \frac{\sin ax}{\sqrt{1 + b^2 \sin^2 ax}}\, dx = -\frac{1}{ab}\sin^{-1}\frac{b \cos ax}{\sqrt{1 + b^2}}$

433. $\displaystyle \int \frac{\sin ax}{\sqrt{1 - b^2 \sin^2 ax}}\, dx = -\frac{1}{ab}\log (b \cos ax + \sqrt{1 - b^2 \sin^2 ax})$

434. $\displaystyle \int (\sin ax)\sqrt{1 + b^2 \sin^2 ax}\, dx = -\frac{\cos ax}{2a}\sqrt{1 + b^2 \sin^2 ax}$

$$-\frac{1 + b^2}{2ab}\sin^{-1}\frac{b \cos ax}{\sqrt{1 + b^2}}$$

435. $\displaystyle \int (\sin ax)\sqrt{1 - b^2 \sin^2 ax}\, dx = -\frac{\cos ax}{2a}\sqrt{1 - b^2 \sin^2 ax}$

$$-\frac{1 - b^2}{2ab}\log (b \cos ax + \sqrt{1 - b^2 \sin^2 ax})$$

436. $\displaystyle \int \frac{\cos ax}{\sqrt{1 + b^2 \sin^2 ax}}\, dx = \frac{1}{ab}\log (b \sin ax + \sqrt{1 + b^2 \sin^2 ax})$

437. $\displaystyle \int \frac{\cos ax}{\sqrt{1 - b^2 \sin^2 ax}}\, dx = \frac{1}{ab}\sin^{-1}(b \sin ax)$

438. $\displaystyle \int (\cos ax)\sqrt{1 + b^2 \sin^2 ax}\, dx = \frac{\sin ax}{2a}\sqrt{1 + b^2 \sin^2 ax}$

$$+\frac{1}{2ab}\log (b \sin ax + \sqrt{1 + b^2 \sin^2 ax})$$

INTEGRALS (Continued)

439. $\int (\cos ax) \sqrt{1 - b^2 \sin^2 ax}\, dx = \dfrac{\sin ax}{2a} \sqrt{1 - b^2 \sin^2 ax} + \dfrac{1}{2ab} \sin^{-1} (b \sin ax)$

440. $\int \dfrac{dx}{\sqrt{a + b \tan^2 cx}} = \dfrac{\pm 1}{c\sqrt{a - b}} \sin^{-1}\left(\sqrt{\dfrac{a - b}{a}} \sin cx \right), \qquad (a > |b|)$

[use $+$ if $(2k - 1)\dfrac{\pi}{2} < x \le (2k + 1)\dfrac{\pi}{2}$, otherwise $-$; k an integer]

FORMS INVOLVING INVERSE TRIGONOMETRIC FUNCTIONS

441. $\int (\sin^{-1} ax)\, dx = x \sin^{-1} ax + \dfrac{\sqrt{1 - a^2 x^2}}{a}$

442. $\int (\cos^{-1} ax)\, dx = x \cos^{-1} ax - \dfrac{\sqrt{1 - a^2 x^2}}{a}$

443. $\int (\tan^{-1} ax)\, dx = x \tan^{-1} ax - \dfrac{1}{2a} \log (1 + a^2 x^2)$

444. $\int (\cot^{-1} ax)\, dx = x \cot^{-1} ax + \dfrac{1}{2a} \log (1 + a^2 x^2)$

445. $\int (\sec^{-1} ax)\, dx = x \sec^{-1} ax - \dfrac{1}{a} \log (ax + \sqrt{a^2 x^2 - 1})$

446. $\int (\csc^{-1} ax)\, dx = x \csc^{-1} ax + \dfrac{1}{a} \log (ax + \sqrt{a^2 x^2 - 1})$

447. $\int \left(\sin^{-1} \dfrac{x}{a} \right) dx = x \sin^{-1} \dfrac{x}{a} + \sqrt{a^2 - x^2}, \qquad (a > 0)$

448. $\int \left(\cos^{-1} \dfrac{x}{a} \right) dx = x \cos^{-1} \dfrac{x}{a} - \sqrt{a^2 - x^2}, \qquad (a > 0)$

449. $\int \left(\tan^{-1} \dfrac{x}{a} \right) dx = x \tan^{-1} \dfrac{x}{a} - \dfrac{a}{2} \log (a^2 + x^2)$

450. $\int \left(\cot^{-1} \dfrac{x}{a} \right) dx = x \cot^{-1} \dfrac{x}{a} + \dfrac{a}{2} \log (a^2 + x^2)$

451. $\int x[\sin^{-1}(ax)]\, dx = \dfrac{1}{4a^2}[(2a^2 x^2 - 1)\sin^{-1}(ax) + ax\sqrt{1 - a^2 x^2}]$

452. $\int x[\cos^{-1}(ax)]\, dx = \dfrac{1}{4a^2}[(2a^2 x^2 - 1)\cos^{-1}(ax) - ax\sqrt{1 - a^2 x^2}]$

INTEGRALS (Continued)

453. $\displaystyle\int x^n[\sin^{-1}(ax)]\,dx = \frac{x^{n+1}}{n+1}\sin^{-1}(ax) - \frac{a}{n+1}\int \frac{x^{n+1}\,dx}{\sqrt{1-a^2x^2}}, \qquad (n \neq -1)$

454. $\displaystyle\int x^n[\cos^{-1}(ax)]\,dx = \frac{x^{n+1}}{n+1}\cos^{-1}(ax) + \frac{a}{n+1}\int \frac{x^{n+1}\,dx}{\sqrt{1-a^2x^2}}, \qquad (n \neq -1)$

455. $\displaystyle\int x(\tan^{-1}ax)\,dx = \frac{1+a^2x^2}{2a^2}\tan^{-1}ax - \frac{x}{2a}$

456. $\displaystyle\int x^n(\tan^{-1}ax)\,dx = \frac{x^{n+1}}{n+1}\tan^{-1}ax - \frac{a}{n+1}\int \frac{x^{n+1}}{1+a^2x^2}\,dx$

457. $\displaystyle\int x(\cot^{-1}ax)\,dx = \frac{1+a^2x^2}{2a^2}\cot^{-1}ax + \frac{x}{2a}$

458. $\displaystyle\int x^n(\cot^{-1}ax)\,dx = \frac{x^{n+1}}{n+1}\cot^{-1}ax + \frac{a}{n+1}\int \frac{x^{n+1}}{1+a^2x^2}\,dx$

459. $\displaystyle\int \frac{\sin^{-1}(ax)}{x^2}\,dx = a\log\left(\frac{1-\sqrt{1-a^2x^2}}{x}\right) - \frac{\sin^{-1}(ax)}{x}$

460. $\displaystyle\int \frac{\cos^{-1}(ax)\,dx}{x^2} = -\frac{1}{x}\cos^{-1}(ax) + a\log\frac{1+\sqrt{1-a^2x^2}}{x}$

461. $\displaystyle\int \frac{\tan^{-1}(ax)\,dx}{x^2} = -\frac{1}{x}\tan^{-1}(ax) - \frac{a}{2}\log\frac{1+a^2x^2}{x^2}$

462. $\displaystyle\int \frac{\cot^{-1}ax}{x^2}\,dx = -\frac{1}{x}\cot^{-1}ax - \frac{a}{2}\log\frac{x^2}{a^2x^2+1}$

463. $\displaystyle\int (\sin^{-1}ax)^2\,dx = x(\sin^{-1}ax)^2 - 2x + \frac{2\sqrt{1-a^2x^2}}{a}\sin^{-1}ax$

464. $\displaystyle\int (\cos^{-1}ax)^2\,dx = x(\cos^{-1}ax)^2 - 2x - \frac{2\sqrt{1-a^2x^2}}{a}\cos^{-1}ax$

465. $\displaystyle\int (\sin^{-1}ax)^n\,dx = \begin{cases} x(\sin^{-1}ax)^n + \dfrac{n\sqrt{1-a^2x^2}}{a}(\sin^{-1}ax)^{n-1} \\ \qquad\qquad\qquad\qquad - n(n-1)\displaystyle\int (\sin^{-1}ax)^{n-2}\,dx \\[4pt] \qquad\qquad\text{or} \\ \displaystyle\sum_{r=0}^{\left[\frac{n}{2}\right]} (-1)^r \frac{n!}{(n-2r)!}x(\sin^{-1}ax)^{n-2r} \\[4pt] \qquad + \displaystyle\sum_{r=0}^{\left[\frac{n-1}{2}\right]} (-1)^r \frac{n!\sqrt{1-a^2x^2}}{(n-2r-1)!a}(\sin^{-1}ax)^{n-2r-1} \end{cases}$

Note: $[s]$ means greatest integer $\leq s$. Thus $[3.5]$ means 3; $[5] = 5$, $[\frac{1}{2}] = 0$.

INTEGRALS (Continued)

466. $\displaystyle\int (\cos^{-1} ax)^n \, dx = \begin{cases} x(\cos^{-1} ax)^n - \dfrac{n\sqrt{1 - a^2x^2}}{a}(\cos^{-1} ax)^{n-1} \\[2mm] \qquad\qquad\qquad\qquad -n(n-1)\displaystyle\int (\cos^{-1} ax)^{n-2}\, dx \\[2mm] \qquad\qquad\text{or} \\[2mm] \displaystyle\sum_{r=0}^{\left[\frac{n}{2}\right]} (-1)^r \dfrac{n!}{(n-2r)!}\, x(\cos^{-1} ax)^{n-2r} \\[2mm] \qquad - \displaystyle\sum_{r=0}^{\left[\frac{n-1}{2}\right]} (-1)^r \dfrac{n!\sqrt{1 - a^2x^2}}{(n-2r-1)!a}(\cos^{-1} ax)^{n-2r-1} \end{cases}$

467. $\displaystyle\int \frac{1}{\sqrt{1 - a^2x^2}}(\sin^{-1} ax)\, dx = \frac{1}{2a}(\sin^{-1} ax)^2$

468. $\displaystyle\int \frac{x^n}{\sqrt{1 - a^2x^2}}(\sin^{-1} ax)\, dx = -\frac{x^{n-1}}{na^2}\sqrt{1 - a^2x^2}\,\sin^{-1} ax + \frac{x^n}{n^2 a}$

$$+ \frac{n-1}{na^2}\int \frac{x^{n-2}}{\sqrt{1 - a^2x^2}}\sin^{-1} ax\, dx$$

469. $\displaystyle\int \frac{1}{\sqrt{1 - a^2x^2}}(\cos^{-1} ax)\, dx = -\frac{1}{2a}(\cos^{-1} ax)^2$

470. $\displaystyle\int \frac{x^n}{\sqrt{1 - a^2x^2}}(\cos^{-1} ax)\, dx = -\frac{x^{n-1}}{na^2}\sqrt{1 - a^2x^2}\,\cos^{-1} ax - \frac{x^n}{n^2 a}$

$$+ \frac{n-1}{na^2}\int \frac{x^{n-2}}{\sqrt{1 - a^2x^2}}\cos^{-1} ax\, dx$$

471. $\displaystyle\int \frac{\tan^{-1} ax}{a^2x^2 + 1}\, dx = \frac{1}{2a}(\tan^{-1} ax)^2$

472. $\displaystyle\int \frac{\cot^{-1} ax}{a^2x^2 + 1}\, dx = -\frac{1}{2a}(\cot^{-1} ax)^2$

473. $\displaystyle\int x \sec^{-1} ax\, dx = \frac{x^2}{2}\sec^{-1} ax - \frac{1}{2a^2}\sqrt{a^2x^2 - 1}$

474. $\displaystyle\int x^n \sec^{-1} ax\, dx = \frac{x^{n+1}}{n+1}\sec^{-1} ax - \frac{1}{n+1}\int \frac{x^n\, dx}{\sqrt{a^2x^2 - 1}}$

475. $\displaystyle\int \frac{\sec^{-1} ax}{x^2}\, dx = -\frac{\sec^{-1} ax}{x} + \frac{\sqrt{a^2x^2 - 1}}{x}$

476. $\displaystyle\int x \csc^{-1} ax\, dx = \frac{x^2}{2}\csc^{-1} ax + \frac{1}{2a^2}\sqrt{a^2x^2 - 1}$

477. $\displaystyle\int x^n \csc^{-1} ax\, dx = \frac{x^{n+1}}{n+1}\csc^{-1} ax + \frac{1}{n+1}\int \frac{x^n\, dx}{\sqrt{a^2x^2 - 1}}$

INTEGRALS (Continued)

478. $\int \dfrac{\csc^{-1} ax}{x^2}\, dx = -\dfrac{\csc^{-1} ax}{x} - \dfrac{\sqrt{a^2 x^2 - 1}}{x}$

FORMS INVOLVING TRIGONOMETRIC SUBSTITUTIONS

479. $\int f(\sin x)\, dx = 2 \int f\left(\dfrac{2z}{1 + z^2}\right) \dfrac{dz}{1 + z^2}, \qquad \left(z = \tan \dfrac{x}{2}\right)$

480. $\int f(\cos x)\, dx = 2 \int f\left(\dfrac{1 - z^2}{1 + z^2}\right) \dfrac{dz}{1 + z^2}, \qquad \left(z = \tan \dfrac{x}{2}\right)$

*481. $\int f(\sin x)\, dx = \int f(u)\dfrac{du}{\sqrt{1 - u^2}}, \qquad (u = \sin x)$

*482. $\int f(\cos x)\, dx = -\int f(u)\dfrac{du}{\sqrt{1 - u^2}}, \qquad (u = \cos x)$

*483. $\int f(\sin x, \cos x)\, dx = \int f(u, \sqrt{1 - u^2})\dfrac{du}{\sqrt{1 - u^2}}, \qquad (u = \sin x)$

484. $\int f(\sin x, \cos x)\, dx = 2 \int f\left(\dfrac{2z}{1 + z^2}, \dfrac{1 - z^2}{1 + z^2}\right) \dfrac{dz}{1 + z^2}, \qquad \left(z = \tan \dfrac{x}{2}\right)$

LOGARITHMIC FORMS

485. $\int (\log x)\, dx = x \log x - x$

486. $\int x(\log x)\, dx = \dfrac{x^2}{2} \log x - \dfrac{x^2}{4}$

487. $\int x^2(\log x)\, dx = \dfrac{x^3}{3} \log x - \dfrac{x^3}{9}$

488. $\int x^n(\log ax)\, dx = \dfrac{x^{n+1}}{n + 1} \log ax - \dfrac{x^{n+1}}{(n + 1)^2}$

489. $\int (\log x)^2\, dx = x(\log x)^2 - 2x \log x + 2x$

490. $\int (\log x)^n\, dx = \begin{cases} x(\log x)^n - n \int (\log x)^{n-1}\, dx, & (n \neq -1) \\ \text{or} \\ (-1)^n n!\, x \displaystyle\sum_{r=0}^{n} \dfrac{(-\log x)^r}{r!} \end{cases}$

---

*The square roots appearing in these formulas may be plus or minus, depending on the quadrant of x. Care must be used to give them the proper sign.

INTEGRALS (Continued)

491. $\displaystyle\int \frac{(\log x)^n}{x}\, dx = \frac{1}{n+1}(\log x)^{n+1}$

492. $\displaystyle\int \frac{dx}{\log x} = \log(\log x) + \log x + \frac{(\log x)^2}{2 \cdot 2!} + \frac{(\log x)^3}{3 \cdot 3!} + \cdots$

493. $\displaystyle\int \frac{dx}{x \log x} = \log(\log x)$

494. $\displaystyle\int \frac{dx}{x(\log x)^n} = -\frac{1}{(n-1)(\log x)^{n-1}}$

495. $\displaystyle\int \frac{x^m\, dx}{(\log x)^n} = -\frac{x^{m+1}}{(n-1)(\log x)^{n-1}} + \frac{m+1}{n-1}\int \frac{x^m\, dx}{(\log x)^{n-1}}$

496. $\displaystyle\int x^m(\log x)^n\, dx = \begin{cases} \dfrac{x^{m+1}(\log x)^n}{m+1} - \dfrac{n}{m+1}\displaystyle\int x^m(\log x)^{n-1}\, dx \\[2mm] \text{or} \\[2mm] (-1)^n \dfrac{n!}{m+1} x^{m+1} \displaystyle\sum_{r=0}^{n} \dfrac{(-\log x)^r}{r!(m+1)^{n-r}} \end{cases}$

497. $\displaystyle\int x^p \cos(b \ln x)\, dx = \frac{x^{p+1}}{(p+1)^2 + b^2} \cdot \left[b \sin(b \ln x) + (p+1)\cos(b \ln x) \right] + c$

498. $\displaystyle\int x^p \sin(b \ln x)\, dx = \frac{x^{p+1}}{(p+1)^2 + b^2} \cdot \left[(p+1)\sin(b \ln x) - b \cos(b \ln x) \right] + c$

499. $\displaystyle\int [\log(ax+b)]\, dx = \frac{ax+b}{a}\log(ax+b) - x$

500. $\displaystyle\int \frac{\log(ax+b)}{x^2}\, dx = \frac{a}{b}\log x - \frac{ax+b}{bx}\log(ax+b)$

501. $\displaystyle\int x^m[\log(ax+b)]\, dx = \frac{1}{m+1}\left[x^{m+1} - \left(-\frac{b}{a}\right)^{m+1}\right]\log(ax+b)$

$$-\frac{1}{m+1}\left(-\frac{b}{a}\right)^{m+1}\sum_{r=1}^{m+1}\frac{1}{r}\left(-\frac{ax}{b}\right)^r$$

502. $\displaystyle\int \frac{\log(ax+b)}{x^m}\, dx = -\frac{1}{m-1}\frac{\log(ax+b)}{x^{m-1}} + \frac{1}{m-1}\left(-\frac{a}{b}\right)^{m-1}\log\frac{ax+b}{x}$

$$+\frac{1}{m-1}\left(-\frac{a}{b}\right)^{m-1}\sum_{r=1}^{m-2}\frac{1}{r}\left(-\frac{b}{ax}\right)^r, (m>2)$$

503. $\displaystyle\int \left[\log\frac{x+a}{x-a}\right]dx = (x+a)\log(x+a) - (x-a)\log(x-a)$

504. $\displaystyle\int x^m\left[\log\frac{x+a}{x-a}\right]dx = \frac{x^{m+1}-(-a)^{m+1}}{m+1}\log(x+a) - \frac{x^{m+1}-a^{m+1}}{m+1}\log(x-a)$

$$+\frac{2a^{m+1}}{m+1}\sum_{r=1}^{\left[\frac{m+1}{2}\right]}\frac{1}{m-2r+2}\left(\frac{x}{a}\right)^{m-2r+2}$$

See note integral 392.

INTEGRALS (Continued)

505. $\displaystyle\int \frac{1}{x^2}\left[\log\frac{x+a}{x-a}\right]dx = \frac{1}{x}\log\frac{x-a}{x+a} - \frac{1}{a}\log\frac{x^2-a^2}{x^2}$

506. $\displaystyle\int (\log X)\, dx = \begin{cases}\left(x+\dfrac{b}{2c}\right)\log X - 2x + \dfrac{\sqrt{4ac-b^2}}{c}\tan^{-1}\dfrac{2cx+b}{\sqrt{4ac-b^2}}, \\ \hspace{8cm}(b^2-4ac<0) \\[0.3cm] \text{or} \\[0.3cm] \left(x+\dfrac{b}{2c}\right)\log X - 2x + \dfrac{\sqrt{b^2-4ac}}{c}\tanh^{-1}\dfrac{2cx+b}{\sqrt{b^2-4ac}}, \\ \hspace{8cm}(b^2-4ac>0) \\[0.3cm] \text{where} \\[0.3cm] X = a+bx+cx^2 \end{cases}$

507. $\displaystyle\int x^n(\log X)\, dx = \frac{x^{n+1}}{n+1}\log X - \frac{2c}{n+1}\int\frac{x^{n+2}}{X}\,dx - \frac{b}{n+1}\int\frac{x^{n+1}}{X}\,dx$

$$\text{where } X = a+bx+cx^2$$

508. $\displaystyle\int [\log(x^2+a^2)]\, dx = x\log(x^2+a^2) - 2x + 2a\tan^{-1}\frac{x}{a}$

509. $\displaystyle\int [\log(x^2-a^2)]\, dx = x\log(x^2-a^2) - 2x + a\log\frac{x+a}{x-a}$

510. $\displaystyle\int x[\log(x^2\pm a^2)]\, dx = \tfrac{1}{2}(x^2\pm a^2)\log(x^2\pm a^2) - \tfrac{1}{2}x^2$

511. $\displaystyle\int [\log(x+\sqrt{x^2\pm a^2})]\, dx = x\log(x+\sqrt{x^2\pm a^2}) - \sqrt{x^2\pm a^2}$

512. $\displaystyle\int x[\log(x+\sqrt{x^2\pm a^2})]\, dx = \left(\frac{x^2}{2}\pm\frac{a^2}{4}\right)\log(x+\sqrt{x^2\pm a^2}) - \frac{x\sqrt{x^2\pm a^2}}{4}$

513. $\displaystyle\int x^m[\log(x+\sqrt{x^2\pm a^2})]\, dx = \frac{x^{m+1}}{m+1}\log(x+\sqrt{x^2\pm a^2})$

$$-\frac{1}{m+1}\int\frac{x^{m+1}}{\sqrt{x^2\pm a^2}}\,dx$$

514. $\displaystyle\int \frac{\log(x+\sqrt{x^2+a^2})}{x^2}\, dx = -\frac{\log(x+\sqrt{x^2+a^2})}{x} - \frac{1}{a}\log\frac{a+\sqrt{x^2+a^2}}{x}$

515. $\displaystyle\int \frac{\log(x+\sqrt{x^2-a^2})}{x^2}\, dx = -\frac{\log(x+\sqrt{x^2-a^2})}{x} + \frac{1}{|a|}\sec^{-1}\frac{x}{a}$

INTEGRALS (Continued)

516. $\displaystyle\int x^n \log(x^2 - a^2)\,dx = \frac{1}{n+1}\left[x^{n+1}\log(x^2 - a^2) - a^{n+1}\log(x - a)\right.$

See note integral 392. $\qquad\qquad\left. -(-a)^{n+1}\log(x+a) - 2\sum_{r=0}^{\left[\frac{n}{2}\right]}\frac{a^{2r}x^{n-2r+1}}{n-2r+1}\right]$

EXPONENTIAL FORMS

517. $\displaystyle\int e^x\,dx = e^x$

518. $\displaystyle\int e^{-x}\,dx = -e^{-x}$

519. $\displaystyle\int e^{ax}\,dx = \frac{e^{ax}}{a}$

520. $\displaystyle\int x\,e^{ax}\,dx = \frac{e^{ax}}{a^2}(ax - 1)$

521. $\displaystyle\int x^m e^{ax}\,dx = \begin{cases}\dfrac{x^m e^{ax}}{a} - \dfrac{m}{a}\displaystyle\int x^{m-1}e^{ax}\,dx \\[2mm] \qquad\quad\text{or} \\[2mm] e^{ax}\displaystyle\sum_{r=0}^{m}(-1)^r\dfrac{m!\,x^{m-r}}{(m-r)!\,a^{r+1}}\end{cases}$

522. $\displaystyle\int \frac{e^{ax}\,dx}{x} = \log x + \frac{ax}{1!} + \frac{a^2x^2}{2\cdot 2!} + \frac{a^3x^3}{3\cdot 3!} + \cdots$

523. $\displaystyle\int \frac{e^{ax}}{x^m}\,dx = -\frac{1}{m-1}\frac{e^{ax}}{x^{m-1}} + \frac{a}{m-1}\int\frac{e^{ax}}{x^{m-1}}\,dx$

524. $\displaystyle\int e^{ax}\log x\,dx = \frac{e^{ax}\log x}{a} - \frac{1}{a}\int\frac{e^{ax}}{x}\,dx$

525. $\displaystyle\int \frac{dx}{1 + e^x} = x - \log(1 + e^x) = \log\frac{e^x}{1 + e^x}$

526. $\displaystyle\int \frac{dx}{a + be^{px}} = \frac{x}{a} - \frac{1}{ap}\log(a + be^{px})$

527. $\displaystyle\int \frac{dx}{ae^{mx} + be^{-mx}} = \frac{1}{m\sqrt{ab}}\tan^{-1}\left(e^{mx}\sqrt{\frac{a}{b}}\right), \qquad (a > 0, b > 0)$

528. $\displaystyle\int \frac{dx}{ae^{mx} - be^{-mx}} = \begin{cases}\dfrac{1}{2m\sqrt{ab}}\log\dfrac{\sqrt{a}\,e^{mx} - \sqrt{b}}{\sqrt{a}\,e^{mx} + \sqrt{b}} \\[2mm] \qquad\quad\text{or} \\[2mm] \dfrac{-1}{m\sqrt{ab}}\tanh^{-1}\left(\sqrt{\dfrac{a}{b}}\,e^{mx}\right), \qquad (a > 0, b > 0)\end{cases}$

INTEGRALS (Continued)

529. $\displaystyle\int (a^x - a^{-x})\,dx = \frac{a^x + a^{-x}}{\log a}$

530. $\displaystyle\int \frac{e^{ax}}{b + ce^{ax}}\,dx = \frac{1}{ac}\log(b + ce^{ax})$

531. $\displaystyle\int \frac{x\,e^{ax}}{(1 + ax)^2}\,dx = \frac{e^{ax}}{a^2(1 + ax)}$

532. $\displaystyle\int x\,e^{-x^2}\,dx = -\tfrac{1}{2}e^{-x^2}$

533. $\displaystyle\int e^{ax}[\sin(bx)]\,dx = \frac{e^{ax}[a\sin(bx) - b\cos(bx)]}{a^2 + b^2}$

534. $\displaystyle\int e^{ax}[\sin(bx)][\sin(cx)]\,dx = \frac{e^{ax}[(b - c)\sin(b - c)x + a\cos(b - c)x]}{2[a^2 + (b - c)^2]}$

$$-\frac{e^{ax}[(b + c)\sin(b + c)x + a\cos(b + c)x]}{2[a^2 + (b + c)^2]}$$

535. $\displaystyle\int e^{ax}[\sin(bx)][\cos(cx)]\,dx = \begin{cases} \dfrac{e^{ax}[a\sin(b - c)x - (b - c)\cos(b - c)x]}{2[a^2 + (b - c)^2]} \\[2ex] \quad + \dfrac{e^{ax}[a\sin(b + c)x - (b + c)\cos(b + c)x]}{2[a^2 + (b + c)^2]} \\[2ex] \qquad\qquad\qquad \text{or} \\[1ex] \dfrac{e^{ax}}{\rho}[(a\sin bx - b\cos bx)[\cos(cx - \alpha)] \\[1ex] \qquad\qquad\qquad -c(\sin bx)\sin(cx - \alpha)] \\[1ex] \text{where} \\[1ex] \rho = \sqrt{(a^2 + b^2 - c^2)^2 + 4a^2c^2}, \\[1ex] \rho\cos\alpha = a^2 + b^2 - c^2, \qquad \rho\sin\alpha = 2ac \end{cases}$

536. $\displaystyle\int e^{ax}[\sin(bx)][\sin(bx + c)]\,dx$

$$= \frac{e^{ax}\cos c}{2a} - \frac{e^{ax}[a\cos(2bx + c) + 2b\sin(2bx + c)]}{2(a^2 + 4b^2)}$$

537. $\displaystyle\int e^{ax}[\sin(bx)][\cos(bx + c)]\,dx$

$$= \frac{-e^{ax}\sin c}{2a} + \frac{e^{ax}[a\sin(2bx + c) - 2b\cos(2bx + c)]}{2(a^2 + 4b^2)}$$

538. $\displaystyle\int e^{ax}[\cos(bx)]\,dx = \frac{e^{ax}}{a^2 + b^2}[a\cos(bx) + b\sin(bx)]$

INTEGRALS (Continued)

539. $\int e^{ax}[\cos(bx)][\cos(cx)]\,dx = \dfrac{e^{ax}[(b-c)\sin(b-c)x + a\cos(b-c)x]}{2[a^2+(b-c)^2]}$

$$+\dfrac{e^{ax}[(b+c)\sin(b+c)x + a\cos(b+c)x]}{2[a^2+(b+c)^2]}$$

540. $\int e^{ax}[\cos(bx)][\cos(bx+c)]\,dx$

$$= \dfrac{e^{ax}\cos c}{2a} + \dfrac{e^{ax}[a\cos(2bx+c) + 2b\sin(2bx+c)]}{2(a^2+4b^2)}$$

541. $\int e^{ax}[\cos(bx)][\sin(bx+c)]\,dx$

$$= \dfrac{e^{ax}\sin c}{2a} + \dfrac{e^{ax}[a\sin(2bx+c) - 2b\cos(2bx+c)]}{2(a^2+4b^2)}$$

542. $\int e^{ax}[\sin^n bx]\,dx = \dfrac{1}{a^2+n^2b^2}\bigg[(a\sin bx - nb\cos bx)\,e^{ax}\sin^{n-1}bx$

$$+ n(n-1)b^2 \int e^{ax}[\sin^{n-2}bx]\,dx\bigg]$$

543. $\int e^{ax}[\cos^n bx]\,dx = \dfrac{1}{a^2+n^2b^2}\bigg[(a\cos bx + nb\sin bx)\,e^{ax}\cos^{n-1}bx$

$$+ n(n-1)b^2 \int e^{ax}[\cos^{n-2}bx]\,dx\bigg]$$

544. $\int x^m e^x \sin x\,dx = \dfrac{1}{2}x^m e^x(\sin x - \cos x) - \dfrac{m}{2}\int x^{m-1} e^x \sin x\,dx$

$$+\dfrac{m}{2}\int x^{m-1} e^x \cos x\,dx$$

545. $\int x^m e^{ax}[\sin bx]\,dx = \begin{cases} x^m e^{ax}\dfrac{a\sin bx - b\cos bx}{a^2+b^2} \\[2mm] \qquad -\dfrac{m}{a^2+b^2}\displaystyle\int x^{m-1} e^{ax}(a\sin bx - b\cos bx)\,dx \\[2mm] \qquad\qquad \text{or} \\[2mm] e^{ax}\displaystyle\sum_{r=0}^{m}\dfrac{(-1)^r m!\,x^{m-r}}{\rho^{r+1}(m-r)!}\sin[bx - (r+1)\alpha] \\[2mm] \qquad\qquad \text{where} \\[2mm] \rho = \sqrt{a^2+b^2}, \qquad \rho\cos\alpha = a, \qquad \rho\sin\alpha = b \end{cases}$

546. $\int x^m e^x \cos x\,dx = \dfrac{1}{2}x^m e^x(\sin x + \cos x)$

$$-\dfrac{m}{2}\int x^{m-1} e^x \sin x\,dx - \dfrac{m}{2}\int x^{m-1} e^x \cos x\,dx$$

INTEGRALS (Continued)

547. $\displaystyle\int x^m e^{ax} \cos bx \, dx =$

$$
\begin{cases}
x^m e^{ax} \dfrac{a \cos bx + b \sin bx}{a^2 + b^2} \\[2ex]
\qquad - \dfrac{m}{a^2 + b^2} \displaystyle\int x^{m-1} e^{ax}(a \cos bx + b \sin bx) \, dx \\[2ex]
\text{or} \\[1ex]
e^{ax} \displaystyle\sum_{r=0}^{m} \dfrac{(-1)^r m! x^{m-r}}{\rho^{r+1}(m-r)!} \cos\left[bx - (r+1)\alpha\right] \\[2ex]
\text{where} \\[1ex]
\rho = \sqrt{a^2 + b^2}, \qquad \rho \cos \alpha = a, \qquad \rho \sin \alpha = b
\end{cases}
$$

548. $\displaystyle\int e^{ax}(\cos^m x)(\sin^n x) \, dx =$

$$
\begin{cases}
\dfrac{e^{ax} \cos^{m-1} x \sin^n x [a \cos x + (m+n) \sin x]}{(m+n)^2 + a^2} \\[2ex]
\qquad - \dfrac{na}{(m+n)^2 + a^2} \displaystyle\int e^{ax}(\cos^{m-1} x)(\sin^{n-1} x) \, dx \\[2ex]
\qquad + \dfrac{(m-1)(m+n)}{(m+n)^2 + a^2} \displaystyle\int e^{ax}(\cos^{m-2} x)(\sin^n x) \, dx \\[2ex]
\text{or} \\[1ex]
\dfrac{e^{ax} \cos^m x \sin^{n-1} x [a \sin x - (m+n) \cos x]}{(m+n)^2 + a^2} \\[2ex]
\qquad + \dfrac{ma}{(m+n)^2 + a^2} \displaystyle\int e^{ax}(\cos^{m-1} x)(\sin^{n-1} x) \, dx \\[2ex]
\qquad + \dfrac{(n-1)(m+n)}{(m+n)^2 + a^2} \displaystyle\int e^{ax}(\cos^m x)(\sin^{n-2} x) \, dx \\[2ex]
\text{or} \\[1ex]
\dfrac{e^{ax}(\cos^{m-1} x)(\sin^{n-1} x)(a \sin x \cos x + m \sin^2 x - n \cos^2)}{(m+n)^2 + a^2} \\[2ex]
\qquad + \dfrac{m(m-1)}{(m+n)^2 + a^2} \displaystyle\int e^{ax}(\cos^{m-2} x)(\sin^n x) \, dx \\[2ex]
\qquad + \dfrac{n(n-1)}{(m+n)^2 + a^2} \displaystyle\int e^{ax}(\cos^m x)(\sin^{n-2} x) \, dx \\[2ex]
\text{or} \\[1ex]
\dfrac{e^{ax}(\cos^{m-1} x)(\sin^{n-1} x)(a \cos x \sin x + m \sin^2 x - n \cos^2 x)}{(m+n)^2 + a^2} \\[2ex]
\qquad + \dfrac{m(m-1)}{(m+n)^2 + a^2} \displaystyle\int e^{ax}(\cos^{m-2} x)(\sin^{n-2} x) \, dx \\[2ex]
\qquad + \dfrac{(n-m)(n+m-1)}{(m+n)^2 + a^2} \displaystyle\int e^{ax}(\cos^m x)(\sin^{n-2} x) \, dx
\end{cases}
$$

INTEGRALS (Continued)

549. $\int x\,e^{ax}(\sin bx)\,dx = \dfrac{x\,e^{ax}}{a^2 + b^2}(a\sin bx - b\cos bx)$

$$-\dfrac{e^{ax}}{(a^2 + b^2)^2}[(a^2 - b^2)\sin bx - 2ab\cos bx]$$

550. $\int x\,e^{ax}(\cos bx)\,dx = \dfrac{x\,e^{ax}}{a^2 + b^2}(a\cos bx + b\sin bx)$

$$-\dfrac{e^{ax}}{(a^2 + b^2)^2}[(a^2 - b^2)\cos bx + 2ab\sin bx]$$

551. $\int \dfrac{e^{ax}}{\sin^n x}\,dx = -\dfrac{e^{ax}[a\sin x + (n-2)\cos x]}{(n-1)(n-2)\sin^{n-1} x} + \dfrac{a^2 + (n-2)^2}{(n-1)(n-2)}\int \dfrac{e^{ax}}{\sin^{n-2} x}\,dx$

552. $\int \dfrac{e^{ax}}{\cos^n x}\,dx = -\dfrac{e^{ax}[a\cos x - (n-2)\sin x]}{(n-1)(n-2)\cos^{n-1} x} + \dfrac{a^2 + (n-2)^2}{(n-1)(n-2)}\int \dfrac{e^{ax}}{\cos^{n-2} x}\,dx$

553. $\int e^{ax}\tan^n x\,dx = e^{ax}\dfrac{\tan^{n-1} x}{n-1} - \dfrac{a}{n-1}\int e^{ax}\tan^{n-1} x\,dx - \int e^{ax}\tan^{n-2} x\,dx$

HYPERBOLIC FORMS

554. $\int (\sinh x)\,dx = \cosh x$

555. $\int (\cosh x)\,dx = \sinh x$

556. $\int (\tanh x)\,dx = \log\cosh x$

557. $\int (\coth x)\,dx = \log\sinh x$

558. $\int (\operatorname{sech} x)\,dx = \tan^{-1}(\sinh x)$

559. $\int \operatorname{csch} x\,dx = \log\tanh\left(\dfrac{x}{2}\right)$

560. $\int x(\sinh x)\,dx = x\cosh x - \sinh x$

561. $\int x^n(\sinh x)\,dx = x^n\cosh x - n\int x^{n-1}(\cosh x)\,dx$

562. $\int x(\cosh x)\,dx = x\sinh x - \cosh x$

563. $\int x^n(\cosh x)\,dx = x^n\sinh x - n\int x^{n-1}(\sinh x)\,dx$

CALCULUS

INTEGRALS (Continued)

564. $\displaystyle\int (\text{sech } x)(\tanh x)\, dx = -\text{sech } x$

565. $\displaystyle\int (\text{csch } x)(\coth x)\, dx = -\text{csch } x$

566. $\displaystyle\int (\sinh^2 x)\, dx = \dfrac{\sinh 2x}{4} - \dfrac{x}{2}$

567. $\displaystyle\int (\sinh^m x)(\cosh^n x)\, dx =$
$$
\begin{cases}
\dfrac{1}{m+n}(\sinh^{m+1} x)(\cosh^{n-1} x) \\[2mm]
\qquad + \dfrac{n-1}{m+n}\displaystyle\int (\sinh^m x)(\cosh^{n-2} x)\, dx \\[2mm]
\qquad\qquad \text{or} \\[2mm]
\dfrac{1}{m+n}\sinh^{m-1} x \cosh^{n+1} x \\[2mm]
\qquad - \dfrac{m-1}{m+n}\displaystyle\int (\sinh^{m-2} x)(\cosh^n x)\, dx, \qquad (m+n \neq 0)
\end{cases}
$$

568. $\displaystyle\int \dfrac{dx}{(\sinh^m x)(\cosh^n x)} =$
$$
\begin{cases}
-\dfrac{1}{(m-1)(\sinh^{m-1} x)(\cosh^{n-1} x)} \\[2mm]
\qquad - \dfrac{m+n-2}{m-1}\displaystyle\int \dfrac{dx}{(\sinh^{m-2} x)(\cosh^n x)}, \qquad (m \neq 1) \\[2mm]
\qquad\qquad \text{or} \\[2mm]
\dfrac{1}{(n-1)\sinh^{m-1} x \cosh^{n-1} x} \\[2mm]
\qquad + \dfrac{m+n-2}{n-1}\displaystyle\int \dfrac{dx}{(\sinh^m x)(\cosh^{n-2} x)}, \qquad (n \neq 1)
\end{cases}
$$

569. $\displaystyle\int (\tanh^2 x)\, dx = x - \tanh x$

570. $\displaystyle\int (\tanh^n x)\, dx = -\dfrac{\tanh^{n-1} x}{n-1} + \int (\tanh^{n-2} x)\, dx, \qquad (n \neq 1)$

571. $\displaystyle\int (\text{sech}^2 x)\, dx = \tanh x$

572. $\displaystyle\int (\cosh^2 x)\, dx = \dfrac{\sinh 2x}{4} + \dfrac{x}{2}$

573. $\displaystyle\int (\coth^2 x)\, dx = x - \coth x$

574. $\displaystyle\int (\coth^n x)\, dx = -\dfrac{\coth^{n-1} x}{n-1} + \int \coth^{n-2} x\, dx, \qquad (n \neq 1)$

INTEGRALS (Continued)

575. $\int (\text{csch}^2\, x)\, dx = -\text{ctnh}\, x$

576. $\int (\sinh mx)(\sinh nx)\, dx = \dfrac{\sinh (m+n)x}{2(m+n)} - \dfrac{\sinh (m-n)x}{2(m-n)}, \qquad (m^2 \neq n^2)$

577. $\int (\cosh mx)(\cosh nx)\, dx = \dfrac{\sinh (m+n)x}{2(m+n)} + \dfrac{\sinh (m-n)x}{2(m-n)}, \qquad (m^2 \neq n^2)$

578. $\int (\sinh mx)(\cosh nx)\, dx = \dfrac{\cosh (m+n)x}{2(m+n)} + \dfrac{\cosh (m-n)x}{2(m-n)}, \qquad (m^2 \neq n^2)$

579. $\int \left(\sinh^{-1} \dfrac{x}{a}\right) dx = x \sinh^{-1} \dfrac{x}{a} - \sqrt{x^2 + a^2}, \qquad (a > 0)$

580. $\int x \left(\sinh^{-1} \dfrac{x}{a}\right) dx = \left(\dfrac{x^2}{2} + \dfrac{a^2}{4}\right) \sinh^{-1} \dfrac{x}{a} - \dfrac{x}{4}\sqrt{x^2 + a^2}, \qquad (a > 0)$

581. $\int x^n (\sinh^{-1} x)\, dx = \dfrac{x^{n+1}}{n+1} \sinh^{-1} x - \dfrac{1}{n+1}\int \dfrac{x^{n+1}}{(1+x^2)^{\frac{1}{2}}}\, dx, \qquad (n \neq -1)$

582. $\int \left(\cosh^{-1} \dfrac{x}{a}\right) dx = \begin{cases} x \cosh^{-1} \dfrac{x}{a} - \sqrt{x^2 - a^2}, & \left(\cosh^{-1} \dfrac{x}{a} > 0\right) \\[2mm] \qquad\qquad \text{or} \\[2mm] x \cosh^{-1} \dfrac{x}{a} + \sqrt{x^2 - a^2}, & \left(\cosh^{-1} \dfrac{x}{a} < 0\right), \qquad (a > 0) \end{cases}$

583. $\int x \left(\cosh^{-1} \dfrac{x}{a}\right) dx = \dfrac{2x^2 - a^2}{4} \cosh^{-1} \dfrac{x}{a} - \dfrac{x}{4}(x^2 - a^2)^{\frac{1}{2}}$

584. $\int x^n (\cosh^{-1} x)\, dx = \dfrac{x^{n+1}}{n+1} \cosh^{-1} x - \dfrac{1}{n+1}\int \dfrac{x^{n+1}}{(x^2 - 1)^{\frac{1}{2}}}\, dx, \qquad (n \neq -1)$

585. $\int \left(\tanh^{-1} \dfrac{x}{a}\right) dx = x \tanh^{-1} \dfrac{x}{a} + \dfrac{a}{2} \log (a^2 - x^2), \qquad \left(\left|\dfrac{x}{a}\right| < 1\right)$

586. $\int \left(\coth^{-1} \dfrac{x}{a}\right) dx = x \coth^{-1} \dfrac{x}{a} + \dfrac{a}{2} \log (x^2 - a^2), \qquad \left(\left|\dfrac{x}{a}\right| > 1\right)$

587. $\int x \left(\tanh^{-1} \dfrac{x}{a}\right) dx = \dfrac{x^2 - a^2}{2} \tanh^{-1} \dfrac{x}{a} + \dfrac{ax}{2}, \qquad \left(\left|\dfrac{x}{a}\right| < 1\right)$

588. $\int x^n \left(\tanh^{-1} x\right) dx = \dfrac{x^{n+1}}{n+1} \tanh^{-1} x - \dfrac{1}{n+1}\int \dfrac{x^{n+1}}{1 - x^2}\, dx, \qquad (n \neq -1)$

589. $\int x \left(\coth^{-1} \dfrac{x}{a}\right) dx = \dfrac{x^2 - a^2}{2} \coth^{-1} \dfrac{x}{a} + \dfrac{ax}{2}, \qquad \left(\left|\dfrac{x}{a}\right| > 1\right)$

590. $\int x^n (\coth^{-1} x)\, dx = \dfrac{x^{n+1}}{n+1} \coth^{-1} x + \dfrac{1}{n+1}\int \dfrac{x^{n+1}}{x^2 - 1}\, dx, \qquad (n \neq -1)$

INTEGRALS (Continued)

591. $\displaystyle\int (\mathrm{sech}^{-1}\, x)\, dx = x\, \mathrm{sech}^{-1}\, x + \sin^{-1}\, x$

592. $\displaystyle\int x\, \mathrm{sech}^{-1}\, x\, dx = \frac{x^2}{2}\, \mathrm{sech}^{-1}\, x - \frac{1}{2}\sqrt{1 - x^2}$

593. $\displaystyle\int x^n\, \mathrm{sech}^{-1}\, x\, dx = \frac{x^{n+1}}{n+1}\, \mathrm{sech}^{-1}\, x + \frac{1}{n+1}\int \frac{x^n}{(1 - x^2)^{\frac{1}{2}}}\, dx, \qquad (n \neq -1)$

594. $\displaystyle\int \mathrm{csch}^{-1}\, x\, dx = x\, \mathrm{csch}^{-1}\, x + \frac{x}{|x|}\, \sinh^{-1}\, x$

595. $\displaystyle\int x\, \mathrm{csch}^{-1}\, x\, dx = \frac{x^2}{2}\, \mathrm{csch}^{-1}\, x + \frac{1}{2}\frac{x}{|x|}\sqrt{1 + x^2}$

596. $\displaystyle\int x^n\, \mathrm{csch}^{-1}\, x\, dx = \frac{x^{n+1}}{n+1}\, \mathrm{csch}^{-1}\, x + \frac{1}{n+1}\frac{x}{|x|}\int \frac{x^n}{(x^2 + 1)^{\frac{1}{2}}}\, dx, \qquad (n \neq -1)$

DEFINITE INTEGRALS

597. $\displaystyle\int_0^\infty x^{n-1}\, e^{-x}\, dx = \int_0^1 \left(\log\frac{1}{x}\right)^{n-1}\, dx = \frac{1}{n}\prod_{m=1}^\infty \frac{\left(1 + \dfrac{1}{m}\right)^n}{1 + \dfrac{n}{m}}$

$$= \Gamma(n),\ n \neq 0,\ -1,\ -2,\ -3,\ldots \qquad \text{(Gamma Function)}$$

598. $\displaystyle\int_0^\infty t^n p^{-t}\, dt = \frac{n!}{(\log p)^{n+1}}, \qquad (n = 0, 1, 2, 3,\ldots \text{ and } p > 0)$

599. $\displaystyle\int_0^\infty t^{n-1}\, e^{-(a+1)t}\, dt = \frac{\Gamma(n)}{(a + 1)^n}, \qquad (n > 0,\ a > -1)$

600. $\displaystyle\int_0^1 x^m \left(\log\frac{1}{x}\right)^n dx = \frac{\Gamma(n + 1)}{(m + 1)^{n+1}}, \qquad (m > -1,\ n > -1)$

601. $\Gamma(n)$ is finite if $n > 0,\ \Gamma(n + 1) = n\Gamma(n)$

602. $\Gamma(n)\cdot\Gamma(1 - n) = \dfrac{\pi}{\sin n\pi}$

603. $\Gamma(n) = (n - 1)!$ if $n = $ integer > 0

604. $\Gamma(\frac{1}{2}) = 2\displaystyle\int_0^\infty e^{-t^2}\, dt = \sqrt{\pi} = 1.7724538509\cdots = (-\frac{1}{2})!$

605. $\Gamma(n + \frac{1}{2}) = \dfrac{1\cdot 3\cdot 5\ldots(2n - 1)}{2^n}\sqrt{\pi} \qquad n = 1, 2, 3,\ldots$

606. $\Gamma(-n + \frac{1}{2}) = \dfrac{(-1)^n 2^n\sqrt{\pi}}{1\cdot 3\cdot 5\ldots(2n - 1)} \qquad n = 1, 2, 3,\ldots$

DEFINITE INTEGRALS (Continued)

607. $\displaystyle\int_0^1 x^{m-1}(1-x)^{n-1}\,dx = \int_0^\infty \frac{x^{m-1}}{(1+x)^{m+n}}\,dx = \frac{\Gamma(m)\Gamma(n)}{\Gamma(m+n)} = B(m,n)$

(Beta function)

608. $B(m,n) = B(n,m) = \dfrac{\Gamma(m)\Gamma(n)}{\Gamma(m+n)}$, where m and n are any positive real numbers.

609. $\displaystyle\int_a^b (x-a)^m(b-x)^n\,dx = (b-a)^{m+n+1}\,\frac{\Gamma(m+1)\cdot\Gamma(n+1)}{\Gamma(m+n+2)}$,

$(m>-1, n>-1, b>a)$

610. $\displaystyle\int_1^\infty \frac{dx}{x^m} = \frac{1}{m-1}$, $\qquad [m>1]$

611. $\displaystyle\int_0^\infty \frac{dx}{(1+x)x^p} = \pi\csc p\pi$, $\qquad [p<1]$

612. $\displaystyle\int_0^\infty \frac{dx}{(1-x)x^p} = -\pi\cot p\pi$, $\qquad [p<1]$

613. $\displaystyle\int_0^\infty \frac{x^{p-1}\,dx}{1+x} = \frac{\pi}{\sin p\pi}$

$\qquad\qquad = B(p,1-p) = \Gamma(p)\Gamma(1-p)$, $\qquad [0<p<1]$

614. $\displaystyle\int_0^\infty \frac{x^{m-1}\,dx}{1+x^n} = \frac{\pi}{n\sin\dfrac{m\pi}{n}}$, $\qquad [0<m<n]$

615. $\displaystyle\int_0^\infty \frac{x^a\,dx}{(m+x^b)^c} = m^{\frac{a+1-bc}{b}}\frac{\left[\Gamma\!\left(\dfrac{a+1}{b}\right)\Gamma\!\left(c-\dfrac{a+1}{b}\right)\right]}{b\,\Gamma(c)}$

$\left(a>-1, b>0, m>0, c>\dfrac{a+1}{b}\right)$

616. $\displaystyle\int_0^\infty \frac{dx}{(1+x)\sqrt{x}} = \pi$

617. $\displaystyle\int_0^\infty \frac{a\,dx}{a^2+x^2} = \frac{\pi}{2}$, if $a>0$; 0, if $a=0$; $-\dfrac{\pi}{2}$, if $a<0$

618. $\displaystyle\int_0^a (a^2-x^2)^{\frac{n}{2}}\,dx = \frac{1}{2}\int_{-a}^a (a^2-x^2)^{\frac{n}{2}}\,dx = \frac{1\cdot 3\cdot 5\ldots n}{2\cdot 4\cdot 6\ldots(n+1)}\cdot\frac{\pi}{2}\cdot a^{n+1}$ $\qquad$ (n odd)

619. $\displaystyle\int_0^a x^m(a^2-x^2)^{\frac{n}{2}}\,dx = \begin{cases}\dfrac{1}{2}a^{m+n+1}B\!\left(\dfrac{m+1}{2},\dfrac{n+2}{2}\right)\\[2mm] \text{or}\\[2mm] \dfrac{1}{2}a^{m+n+1}\dfrac{\Gamma\!\left(\dfrac{m+1}{2}\right)\Gamma\!\left(\dfrac{n+2}{2}\right)}{\Gamma\!\left(\dfrac{m+n+3}{2}\right)}\end{cases}$

DEFINITE INTEGRALS (Continued)

620. $\displaystyle\int_0^{\pi/2} (\sin^n x)\, dx = \begin{cases} \displaystyle\int_0^{\pi/2} (\cos^n x)\, dx \\[2ex] \text{or} \\[1ex] \dfrac{1 \cdot 3 \cdot 5 \cdot 7 \ldots (n-1)}{2 \cdot 4 \cdot 6 \cdot 8 \ldots (n)} \dfrac{\pi}{2}, \quad (n \text{ an even integer}, n \neq 0) \\[2ex] \text{or} \\[1ex] \dfrac{2 \cdot 4 \cdot 6 \cdot 8 \ldots (n-1)}{1 \cdot 3 \cdot 5 \cdot 7 \ldots (n)}, \quad (n \text{ an odd integer}, n \neq 1) \\[2ex] \text{or} \\[1ex] \dfrac{\sqrt{\pi}}{2} \dfrac{\Gamma\left(\dfrac{n+1}{2}\right)}{\Gamma\left(\dfrac{n}{2}+1\right)}, \quad (n > -1) \end{cases}$

621. $\displaystyle\int_0^\infty \frac{\sin mx\, dx}{x} = \frac{\pi}{2},$ if $m > 0$; 0, if $m = 0$; $-\dfrac{\pi}{2}$, if $m < 0$

622. $\displaystyle\int_0^\infty \frac{\cos x\, dx}{x} = \infty$

623. $\displaystyle\int_0^\infty \frac{\tan x\, dx}{x} = \frac{\pi}{2}$

624. $\displaystyle\int_0^\pi \sin ax \cdot \sin bx\, dx = \int_0^\pi \cos ax \cdot \cos bx\, dx = 0, \qquad (a \neq b; a, b \text{ integers})$

625. $\displaystyle\int_0^{\pi/a} [\sin (ax)][\cos (ax)]\, dx = \int_0^\pi [\sin (ax)][\cos (ax)]\, dx = 0$

626. $\displaystyle\int_0^\pi [\sin (ax)][\cos (bx)]\, dx = \frac{2a}{a^2 - b^2},$ if $a - b$ is odd, or 0 if $a - b$ is even

627. $\displaystyle\int_0^\infty \frac{\sin x \cos mx\, dx}{x}$

$$= 0, \text{ if } m < -1 \text{ or } m > 1; \frac{\pi}{4}, \text{ if } m = \pm 1; \frac{\pi}{2}, \text{ if } m^2 < 1$$

628. $\displaystyle\int_0^\infty \frac{\sin ax \sin bx}{x^2}\, dx = \frac{\pi a}{2}, \qquad (a \leq b)$

629. $\displaystyle\int_0^\pi \sin^2 mx\, dx = \int_0^\pi \cos^2 mx\, dx = \frac{\pi}{2}$

630. $\displaystyle\int_0^\infty \frac{\sin^2 (px)}{x^2}\, dx = \frac{\pi p}{2}$

DEFINITE INTEGRALS (Continued)

631. $\displaystyle\int_0^\infty \frac{\sin x}{x^p}\,dx = \frac{\pi}{2\Gamma(p)\sin(p\pi/2)}, \qquad 0 < p < 1$

632. $\displaystyle\int_0^\infty \frac{\cos x}{x^p}\,dx = \frac{\pi}{2\Gamma(p)\cos(p\pi/2)}, \qquad 0 < p < 1$

633. $\displaystyle\int_0^\infty \frac{1 - \cos px}{x^2}\,dx = \frac{\pi p}{2}$

634. $\displaystyle\int_0^\infty \frac{\sin px \cos qx}{x}\,dx = \left\{ 0,\quad q > p > 0;\quad \frac{\pi}{2},\ p > q > 0;\quad \frac{\pi}{4},\ p = q > 0 \right\}$

635. $\displaystyle\int_0^\infty \frac{\cos(mx)}{x^2 + a^2}\,dx = \frac{\pi}{2|a|}\,e^{-|ma|}$

636. $\displaystyle\int_0^\infty \cos(x^2)\,dx = \int_0^\infty \sin(x^2)\,dx = \frac{1}{2}\sqrt{\frac{\pi}{2}}$

637. $\displaystyle\int_0^\infty \sin ax^n\,dx = \frac{1}{na^{1/n}}\,\Gamma(1/n)\sin\frac{\pi}{2n}, \qquad n > 1$

638. $\displaystyle\int_0^\infty \cos ax^n\,dx = \frac{1}{na^{1/n}}\,\Gamma(1/n)\cos\frac{\pi}{2n}, \qquad n > 1$

639. $\displaystyle\int_0^\infty \frac{\sin x}{\sqrt{x}}\,dx = \int_0^\infty \frac{\cos x}{\sqrt{x}}\,dx = \sqrt{\frac{\pi}{2}}$

640. (a) $\displaystyle\int_0^\infty \frac{\sin^3 x}{x}\,dx = \frac{\pi}{4}$ (b) $\displaystyle\int_0^\infty \frac{\sin^3 x}{x^2}\,dx\ \frac{3}{4}\log 3$

641. $\displaystyle\int_0^\infty \frac{\sin^3 x}{x^3}\,dx = \frac{3\pi}{8}$

642. $\displaystyle\int_0^\infty \frac{\sin^4 x}{x^4}\,dx = \frac{\pi}{3}$

643. $\displaystyle\int_0^{\pi/2} \frac{dx}{1 + a\cos x} = \frac{\cos^{-1} a}{\sqrt{1 - a^2}}, \qquad (a < 1)$

644. $\displaystyle\int_0^\pi \frac{dx}{a + b\cos x} = \frac{\pi}{\sqrt{a^2 - b^2}}, \qquad (a > b \geq 0)$

645. $\displaystyle\int_0^{2\pi} \frac{dx}{1 + a\cos x} = \frac{2\pi}{\sqrt{1 - a^2}}, \qquad (a^2 < 1)$

646. $\displaystyle\int_0^\infty \frac{\cos ax - \cos bx}{x}\,dx = \log\frac{b}{a}$

647. $\displaystyle\int_0^{\pi/2} \frac{dx}{a^2\sin^2 x + b^2\cos^2 x} = \frac{\pi}{2ab}$

DEFINITE INTEGRALS (Continued)

648. $\displaystyle\int_0^{\pi/2} \frac{dx}{(a^2 \sin^2 x + b^2 \cos^2 x)^2} = \frac{\pi(a^2 + b^2)}{4a^3 b^3}$, $(a, b > 0)$

649. $\displaystyle\int_0^{\pi/2} \sin^{n-1} x \cos^{m-1} x \, dx = \frac{1}{2} B\left(\frac{n}{2}, \frac{m}{2}\right)$, *m* and *n* positive integers

650. $\displaystyle\int_0^{\pi/2} (\sin^{2n+1} \theta) \, d\theta = \frac{2 \cdot 4 \cdot 6 \ldots (2n)}{1 \cdot 3 \cdot 5 \ldots (2n+1)}$, $(n = 1, 2, 3 \ldots)$

651. $\displaystyle\int_0^{\pi/2} (\sin^{2n} \theta) \, d\theta = \frac{1 \cdot 3 \cdot 5 \ldots (2n-1)}{2 \cdot 4 \ldots (2n)}\left(\frac{\pi}{2}\right)$, $(n = 1, 2, 3 \ldots)$

652. $\displaystyle\int_0^{\pi/2} \frac{x}{\sin x} \, dx = 2\left\{\frac{1}{1^2} - \frac{1}{3^2} + \frac{1}{5^2} - \frac{1}{7^2} + \cdots\right\}$

653. $\displaystyle\int_0^{\pi/2} \frac{dx}{1 + \tan^m x} = \frac{\pi}{4}$

654. $\displaystyle\int_0^{\pi/2} \sqrt{\cos \theta} \, d\theta = \frac{(2\pi)^{\frac{3}{2}}}{[\Gamma(\frac{1}{4})]^2}$

655. $\displaystyle\int_0^{\pi/2} (\tan^h \theta) \, d\theta = \frac{\pi}{2 \cos\left(\dfrac{h\pi}{2}\right)}$, $(0 < h < 1)$

656. $\displaystyle\int_0^{\infty} \frac{\tan^{-1}(ax) - \tan^{-1}(bx)}{x} \, dx = \frac{\pi}{2} \log \frac{a}{b}$, $(a, b > 0)$

657. The area enclosed by a curve defined through the equation $x^{\frac{b}{c}} + y^{\frac{b}{c}} = a^{\frac{b}{c}}$ where $a > 0$, *c* a positive odd integer and *b* a positive even integer is given by

$$\frac{\left[\Gamma\left(\dfrac{c}{b}\right)\right]^2}{\Gamma\left(\dfrac{2c}{b}\right)} \left(\frac{2ca^2}{b}\right)$$

658. $I = \displaystyle\iiint_R x^{h-1} y^{m-1} z^{n-1} \, dv$, where *R* denotes the region of space bounded by

the co-ordinate planes and that portion of the surface $\left(\dfrac{x}{a}\right)^p + \left(\dfrac{y}{b}\right)^q + \left(\dfrac{z}{c}\right)^k = 1$,

which lies in the first octant and where *h, m, n, p, q, k, a, b, c*, denote positive real numbers is given by

$$\int_0^a x^{h-1} \, dx \int_0^{b\left[1-\left(\frac{x}{a}\right)^p\right]^{\frac{1}{q}}} y^m \, dy \int_0^{c\left[1-\left(\frac{x}{a}\right)^p-\left(\frac{y}{b}\right)^q\right]^{\frac{1}{k}}} z^{n-1} \, dz$$

$$= \frac{a^h b^m c^n}{pqk} \frac{\Gamma\left(\dfrac{h}{p}\right)\Gamma\left(\dfrac{m}{q}\right)\Gamma\left(\dfrac{n}{k}\right)}{\Gamma\left(\dfrac{h}{p} + \dfrac{m}{q} + \dfrac{n}{k} + 1\right)}$$

DEFINITE INTEGRALS (Continued)

659. $\displaystyle\int_0^\infty e^{-ax}\,dx = \frac{1}{a}, \qquad (a > 0)$

660. $\displaystyle\int_0^\infty \frac{e^{-ax} - e^{-bx}}{x}\,dx = \log\frac{b}{a}, \qquad (a, b > 0)$

661. $\displaystyle\int_0^\infty x^n e^{-ax}\,dx = \begin{cases} \dfrac{\Gamma(n+1)}{a^{n+1}}, & (n > -1, a > 0) \\[2mm] \qquad\text{or} \\[2mm] \dfrac{n!}{a^{n+1}}, & (a > 0, n \text{ positive integer}) \end{cases}$

662. $\displaystyle\int_0^\infty x^n \exp(-ax^p)\,dx = \frac{\Gamma(k)}{pa^k}, \qquad \left(n > -1, p > 0, a > 0, k = \frac{n+1}{p}\right)$

663. $\displaystyle\int_0^\infty e^{-a^2x^2}\,dx = \frac{1}{2a}\sqrt{\pi} = \frac{1}{2a}\Gamma\left(\frac{1}{2}\right), \qquad (a > 0)$

664. $\displaystyle\int_0^\infty x e^{-x^2}\,dx = \tfrac{1}{2}$

665. $\displaystyle\int_0^\infty x^2 e^{-x^2}\,dx = \frac{\sqrt{\pi}}{4}$

666. $\displaystyle\int_0^\infty x^{2n} e^{-ax^2}\,dx = \frac{1 \cdot 3 \cdot 5 \ldots (2n-1)}{2^{n+1}a^n}\sqrt{\frac{\pi}{a}}$

667. $\displaystyle\int_0^\infty x^{2n+1} e^{-ax^2}\,dx = \frac{n!}{2a^{n+1}}, \qquad (a > 0)$

668. $\displaystyle\int_0^1 x^m e^{-ax}\,dx = \frac{m!}{a^{m+1}}\left[1 - e^{-a}\sum_{r=0}^{m}\frac{a^r}{r!}\right]$

669. $\displaystyle\int_0^\infty e^{\left(-x^2 - \frac{a^2}{x^2}\right)}\,dx = \frac{e^{-2a}\sqrt{\pi}}{2}, \qquad (a \geq 0)$

670. $\displaystyle\int_0^\infty e^{-nx}\sqrt{x}\,dx = \frac{1}{2n}\sqrt{\frac{\pi}{n}}$

671. $\displaystyle\int_0^\infty \frac{e^{-nx}}{\sqrt{x}}\,dx = \sqrt{\frac{\pi}{n}}$

672. $\displaystyle\int_0^\infty e^{-ax}(\cos mx)\,dx = \frac{a}{a^2 + m^2}, \qquad (a > 0)$

673. $\displaystyle\int_0^\infty e^{-ax}(\sin mx)\,dx = \frac{m}{a^2 + m^2}, \qquad (a > 0)$

DEFINITE INTEGRALS (Continued)

674. $\displaystyle\int_0^\infty x\,e^{-ax}[\sin(bx)]\,dx = \frac{2ab}{(a^2+b^2)^2}, \qquad (a > 0)$

675. $\displaystyle\int_0^\infty x\,e^{-ax}[\cos(bx)]\,dx = \frac{a^2-b^2}{(a^2+b^2)^2}, \qquad (a > 0)$

676. $\displaystyle\int_0^\infty x^n\,e^{-ax}[\sin(bx)]\,dx = \frac{n![(a+ib)^{n+1} - (a-ib)^{n+1}]}{2i(a^2+b^2)^{n+1}}, \qquad (i^2 = -1, a > 0)$

677. $\displaystyle\int_0^\infty x^n\,e^{-ax}[\cos(bx)]\,dx = \frac{n![(a-ib)^{n+1} + (a+ib)^{n+1}]}{2(a^2+b^2)^{n+1}}, \qquad (i^2 = -1, a > 0)$

678. $\displaystyle\int_0^\infty \frac{e^{-ax}\sin x}{x}\,dx = \cot^{-1} a, \qquad (a > 0)$

679. $\displaystyle\int_0^\infty e^{-a^2x^2}\cos bx\,dx = \frac{\sqrt{\pi}}{2a}\exp\left(-\frac{b^2}{4a^2}\right), \qquad (ab \neq 0)$

680. $\displaystyle\int_0^\infty e^{-t\cos\phi}\,t^{b-1}\sin(t\sin\phi)\,dt = [\Gamma(b)]\sin(b\phi), \qquad \left(b > 0, -\frac{\pi}{2} < \phi < \frac{\pi}{2}\right)$

681. $\displaystyle\int_0^\infty e^{-t\cos\phi}\,t^{b-1}[\cos(t\sin\phi)]\,dt = [\Gamma(b)]\cos(b\phi), \qquad \left(b > 0, -\frac{\pi}{2} < \phi < \frac{\pi}{2}\right)$

682. $\displaystyle\int_0^\infty t^{b-1}\cos t\,dt = [\Gamma(b)]\cos\left(\frac{b\pi}{2}\right), \qquad (0 < b < 1)$

683. $\displaystyle\int_0^\infty t^{b-1}(\sin t)\,dt = [\Gamma(b)]\sin\left(\frac{b\pi}{2}\right), \qquad (0 < b < 1)$

684. $\displaystyle\int_0^1 (\log x)^n\,dx = (-1)^n \cdot n!$

685. $\displaystyle\int_0^1 \left(\log\frac{1}{x}\right)^{\frac{1}{2}}\,dx = \frac{\sqrt{\pi}}{2}$

686. $\displaystyle\int_0^1 \left(\log\frac{1}{x}\right)^{-\frac{1}{2}}\,dx = \sqrt{\pi}$

687. $\displaystyle\int_0^1 \left(\log\frac{1}{x}\right)^n\,dx = n!$

688. $\displaystyle\int_0^1 x\log(1-x)\,dx = -\tfrac{3}{4}$

689. $\displaystyle\int_0^1 x\log(1+x)\,dx = \tfrac{1}{4}$

690. $\displaystyle\int_0^1 x^m(\log x)^n\,dx = \frac{(-1)^n n!}{(m+1)^{n+1}}, \qquad m > -1, n = 0, 1, 2, \ldots$

If $n \neq 0, 1, 2, \ldots$ replace $n!$ by $\Gamma(n+1)$.

DEFINITE INTEGRALS (Continued)

691. $\displaystyle\int_0^1 \frac{\log x}{1 + x}\,dx = -\frac{\pi^2}{12}$

692. $\displaystyle\int_0^1 \frac{\log x}{1 - x}\,dx = -\frac{\pi^2}{6}$

693. $\displaystyle\int_0^1 \frac{\log (1 + x)}{x}\,dx = \frac{\pi^2}{12}$

694. $\displaystyle\int_0^1 \frac{\log (1 - x)}{x}\,dx = -\frac{\pi^2}{6}$

695. $\displaystyle\int_0^1 (\log x)[\log (1 + x)]\,dx = 2 - 2\log 2 - \frac{\pi^2}{12}$

696. $\displaystyle\int_0^1 (\log x)[\log (1 - x)]\,dx = 2 - \frac{\pi^2}{6}$

697. $\displaystyle\int_0^1 \frac{\log x}{1 - x^2}\,dx = -\frac{\pi^2}{8}$

698. $\displaystyle\int_0^1 \log \left(\frac{1 + x}{1 - x}\right) \cdot \frac{dx}{x} = \frac{\pi^2}{4}$

699. $\displaystyle\int_0^1 \frac{\log x\,dx}{\sqrt{1 - x^2}} = -\frac{\pi}{2}\log 2$

700. $\displaystyle\int_0^1 x^m \left[\log \left(\frac{1}{x}\right)\right]^n dx = \frac{\Gamma(n + 1)}{(m + 1)^{n+1}}, \qquad \text{if } m + 1 > 0, n + 1 > 0$

701. $\displaystyle\int_0^1 \frac{(x^p - x^q)\,dx}{\log x} = \log \left(\frac{p + 1}{q + 1}\right), \qquad (p + 1 > 0, q + 1 > 0)$

702. $\displaystyle\int_0^1 \frac{dx}{\sqrt{\log \left(\dfrac{1}{x}\right)}} = \sqrt{\pi}\,,\ (\text{same as integral 686})$

703. $\displaystyle\int_0^\infty \log \left(\frac{e^x + 1}{e^x - 1}\right) dx = \frac{\pi^2}{4}$

704. $\displaystyle\int_0^{\pi/2} (\log \sin x)\,dx = \int_0^{\pi/2} \log \cos x\,dx = -\frac{\pi}{2}\log 2$

705. $\displaystyle\int_0^{\pi/2} (\log \sec x)\,dx = \int_0^{\pi/2} \log \csc x\,dx = \frac{\pi}{2}\log 2$

706. $\displaystyle\int_0^\pi x(\log \sin x)\,dx = -\frac{\pi^2}{2}\log 2$

707. $\displaystyle\int_0^{\pi/2} (\sin x)(\log \sin x)\,dx = \log 2 - 1$

DEFINITE INTEGRALS (Continued)

708. $\displaystyle\int_0^{\pi/2} (\log \tan x)\, dx = 0$

709. $\displaystyle\int_0^{\pi} \log(a \pm b \cos x)\, dx = \pi \log\left(\frac{a + \sqrt{a^2 - b^2}}{2}\right), \qquad (a \geq b)$

710. $\displaystyle\int_0^{\pi} \log(a^2 - 2ab \cos x + b^2)\, dx = \begin{cases} 2\pi \log a, & a \geq b > 0 \\ 2\pi \log b, & b \geq a > 0 \end{cases}$

711. $\displaystyle\int_0^{\infty} \frac{\sin ax}{\sinh bx}\, dx = \frac{\pi}{2b} \tanh \frac{a\pi}{2b}$

712. $\displaystyle\int_0^{\infty} \frac{\cos ax}{\cosh bx}\, dx = \frac{\pi}{2b} \operatorname{sech} \frac{a\pi}{2b}$

713. $\displaystyle\int_0^{\infty} \frac{dx}{\cosh ax} = \frac{\pi}{2a}$

714. $\displaystyle\int_0^{\infty} \frac{x\, dx}{\sinh ax} = \frac{\pi^2}{4a^2}$

715. $\displaystyle\int_0^{\infty} e^{-ax}(\cosh bx)\, dx = \frac{a}{a^2 - b^2}, \qquad (0 \leq |b| < a)$

716. $\displaystyle\int_0^{\infty} e^{-ax}(\sinh bx)\, dx = \frac{b}{a^2 - b^2}, \qquad (0 \leq |b| < a)$

717. $\displaystyle\int_0^{\infty} \frac{\sinh ax}{e^{bx} + 1}\, dx = \frac{\pi}{2b} \csc \frac{a\pi}{b} - \frac{1}{2a}$

718. $\displaystyle\int_0^{\infty} \frac{\sinh ax}{e^{bx} - 1}\, dx = \frac{1}{2a} - \frac{\pi}{2b} \cot \frac{a\pi}{b}$

719. $\displaystyle\int_0^{\pi/2} \frac{dx}{\sqrt{1 - k^2 \sin^2 x}} = \frac{\pi}{2}\left[1 + \left(\frac{1}{2}\right)^2 k^2 + \left(\frac{1 \cdot 3}{2 \cdot 4}\right)^2 k^4 \right.$

$$\left. + \left(\frac{1 \cdot 3 \cdot 5}{2 \cdot 4 \cdot 6}\right)^2 k^6 + \cdots\right], \text{ if } k^2 < 1$$

720. $\displaystyle\int_0^{\pi/2} \sqrt{1 - k^2 \sin^2 x}\, dx = \frac{\pi}{2}\left[1 - \left(\frac{1}{2}\right)^2 k^2 - \left(\frac{1 \cdot 3}{2 \cdot 4}\right)^2 \frac{k^4}{3}\right.$

$$\left. - \left(\frac{1 \cdot 3 \cdot 5}{2 \cdot 4 \cdot 6}\right)^2 \frac{k^6}{5} - \cdots\right], \text{ if } k^2 < 1$$

721. $\displaystyle\int_0^{\infty} e^{-x} \log x\, dx = -\gamma = -0.5772157\ldots$

722. $\displaystyle\int_0^{\infty} e^{-x^2} \log x\, dx = -\frac{\sqrt{\pi}}{4}(\gamma + 2 \log 2)$

DEFINITE INTEGRALS (Continued)

723. $\int_0^\infty \left(\dfrac{1}{1 - e^{-x}} - \dfrac{1}{x} \right) e^{-x}\, dx = \gamma = 0.5772157\ldots$ [Euler's Constant]

724. $\int_0^\infty \dfrac{1}{x} \left(\dfrac{1}{1 + x} - e^{-x} \right) dx = \gamma = 0.5772157\ldots$

For n even:

725. $\int \cos^n x\, dx \;=\; \dfrac{1}{2}n^{-1} \displaystyle\sum_{k=0}^{\frac{n}{2}-1} \binom{n}{k} \dfrac{\sin\,(n-2k)\,x}{(n-2k)} \;+\; \dfrac{1}{2^n}\binom{n}{\frac{n}{2}} x$

726. $\int \sin^n x\, dx \;=\; \dfrac{1}{2^{n-1}} \displaystyle\sum_{k=0}^{\frac{n}{2}-1} \binom{n}{k} \dfrac{\sin\,[(n-2k)\,(\frac{\pi}{2}-x)]}{2k-n} + \dfrac{1}{2^n}\binom{n}{\frac{n}{2}} x$

For n odd:

727. $\int \cos^n x\, dx \;=\; \dfrac{1}{2^{n-1}} \displaystyle\sum_{k=0}^{\frac{n-1}{2}} \binom{n}{k} \dfrac{\sin\,(n-2k)\,x}{(n-2k)}$

728. $\int \sin^n x\, dx \;=\; \dfrac{1}{2^{n-1}} \displaystyle\sum_{k=0}^{\frac{n-1}{2}} \binom{n}{k} \dfrac{\sin\,[n-2k)\,(\frac{\pi}{2}-x)]}{2k-n}$

SERIES EXPANSION

The expression in parentheses following certain of the series indicates the region of convergence. If not otherwise indicated it is to be understood that the series converges for all finite values of x.

BINOMIAL

$$(x + y)^n = x^n + nx^{n-1}y + \frac{n(n-1)}{2!} x^{n-2}y^2$$
$$+ \frac{n(n-1)(n-2)}{3!} x^{n-3}y^3 + \cdots (y^2 < x^2)$$

$$(1 \pm x)^n = 1 \pm nx + \frac{n(n-1)x^2}{2!} \pm \frac{n(n-1)(n-2)x^3}{3!} + \cdots \text{ etc.} \quad (x^2 < 1)$$

$$(1 \pm x)^{-n} = 1 \mp nx + \frac{n(n+1)x^2}{2!} \mp \frac{n(n+1)(n+2)x^3}{3!} + \cdots \text{ etc.} \quad (x^2 < 1)$$

$$(1 \pm x)^{-1} = 1 \mp x + x^2 \mp x^3 + x^4 \mp x^5 + \cdots \qquad (x^2 < 1)$$
$$(1 \pm x)^{-2} = 1 \mp 2x + 3x^2 \mp 4x^3 + 5x^4 \mp 6x^5 + \cdots \qquad (x^2 < 1)$$

REVERSION OF SERIES

Let a series be represented by

$$y = a_1 x + a_2 x^2 + a_3 x^3 + a_4 x^4 + a_5 x^5 + a_6 x^6 + \cdots \quad (a_1 \neq 0)$$

to find the coefficients of the series

$$x = A_1 y + A_2 y^2 + A_3 y^3 + A_4 y^4 + \cdots$$

$$A_1 = \frac{1}{a_1} \qquad A_2 = -\frac{a_2}{a_1^3} \qquad A_3 = \frac{1}{a_1^5} (2a_2^2 - a_1 a_3)$$

$$A_4 = \frac{1}{a_1^7} (5a_1 a_2 a_3 - a_1^2 a_4 - 5a_2^3)$$

$$A_5 = \frac{1}{a_1^9} (6a_1^2 a_2 a_4 + 3a_1^2 a_3^2 + 14a_2^4 - a_1^3 a_5 - 21a_1 a_2^2 a_3)$$

$$A_6 = \frac{1}{a_1^{11}} (7a_1^3 a_2 a_5 + 7a_1^3 a_3 a_4 + 84a_1 a_2^3 a_3 - a_1^4 a_6 - 28a_1^2 a_2^2 a_4 - 28a_1^2 a_2 a_3^2 - 42a_2^5)$$

$$A_7 = \frac{1}{a_1^{13}} (8a_1^4 a_2 a_6 + 8a_1^4 a_3 a_5 + 4a_1^4 a_4^2 + 120a_1^2 a_2^3 a_4$$
$$+ 180a_1^2 a_2^2 a_3^2 + 132a_2^6 - a_1^5 a_7$$
$$- 36a_1^3 a_2^2 a_5 - 72a_1^3 a_2 a_3 a_4 - 12a_1^3 a_3^3 - 330a_1 a_2^4 a_3)$$

TAYLOR

1. $f(x) = f(a) + (x - a)f'(a) + \dfrac{(x - a)^2}{2!} f''(a) + \dfrac{(x - a)^3}{3!} f'''(a)$
$$+ \cdots + \frac{(x - a)^n}{n!} f^{(n)}(a) + \cdots \text{ (Taylor's Series)}$$

Series

(Increment form)

2. $f(x + h) = f(x) + hf'(x) + \dfrac{h^2}{2!} f''(x) + \dfrac{h^3}{3!} f'''(x) + \cdots$

$$= f(h) + xf'(h) + \frac{x^2}{2!} f''(h) + \frac{x^3}{3!} f'''(h) + \cdots$$

3. If $f(x)$ is a function possessing derivatives of all orders throughout the interval $a \leqq x \leqq b$, then there is a value X, with $a < X < b$, such that

$$f(b) = f(a) + (b - a)f'(a) + \frac{(b - a)^2}{2!} f''(a) + \cdots$$

$$+ \frac{(b - a)^{n-1}}{(n - 1)!} f^{(n-1)}(a) + \frac{(b - a)^n}{n!} f^{(n)}(X)$$

$$f(a + h) = f(a) + hf'(a) + \frac{h^2}{2!} f''(a) + \cdots + \frac{h^{n-1}}{(n - 1)!} f^{(n-1)}(a)$$

$$+ \frac{h^n}{n!} f^{(n)}(a + \theta h), \quad b = a + h, \, 0 < \theta < 1.$$

or

$$f(x) = f(a) + (x - a)f'(a) + \frac{(x - a)^2}{2!} f''(a) + \cdots + (x - a)^{n-1} \frac{f^{(n-1)}(a)}{(n - 1)!} + R_n,$$

where

$$R_n = \frac{f^{(n)}[a + \theta \cdot (x - a)]}{n!} (x - a)^n, \quad 0 < \theta < 1.$$

The above forms are known as Taylor's series with the remainder term.

4. *Taylor's series for a function of two variables*

If $\left(h \dfrac{\partial}{\partial x} + k \dfrac{\partial}{\partial y} \right) f(x, y) = h \dfrac{\partial f(x, y)}{\partial x} + k \dfrac{\partial f(x, y)}{\partial y}$;

$$\left(h \frac{\partial}{\partial x} + k \frac{\partial}{\partial y} \right)^2 f(x, y) = h^2 \frac{\partial^2 f(x, y)}{\partial x^2} + 2hk \frac{\partial^2 f(x, y)}{\partial x \, \partial y} + k^2 \frac{\partial^2 f(x, y)}{\partial y^2}$$

etc., and if $\left(h \dfrac{\partial}{\partial x} + k \dfrac{\partial}{\partial y} \right)^n f(x, y) \Big|_{\substack{x = a \\ y = b}}$ with the bar and subscripts means that after differentiation we are to replace x by a and y by b,

$$f(a + h, b + k) = f(a, b) + \left(h \frac{\partial}{\partial x} + k \frac{\partial}{\partial y} \right) f(x, y) \Big|_{\substack{x = a \\ y = b}} + \cdots$$

$$+ \frac{1}{n!} \left(h \frac{\partial}{\partial x} + k \frac{\partial}{\partial y} \right)^n f(x, y) \Big|_{\substack{x = a \\ y = b}} + \cdots$$

MACLAURIN

$$f(x) = f(0) + xf'(0) + \frac{x^2}{2!} f''(0) + \frac{x^3}{3!} f'''(0) + \cdots + x^{n-1} \frac{f^{(n-1)}(0)}{(n - 1)!} + R_n,$$

where

$$R_n = \frac{x^n f^{(n)}(\theta x)}{n!}, \quad 0 < \theta < 1.$$

CALCULUS
Series

EXPONENTIAL

$$e = 1 + \frac{1}{1!} + \frac{1}{2!} + \frac{1}{3!} + \frac{1}{4!} + \cdots$$

$$e^x = 1 + x + \frac{x^2}{2!} + \frac{x^3}{3!} + \frac{x^4}{4!} + \cdots \qquad \text{(all real values of } x\text{)}$$

$$a^x = 1 + x \log_e a + \frac{(x \log_e a)^2}{2!} + \frac{(x \log_e a)^3}{3!} + \cdots$$

$$e^x = e^a \left[1 + (x - a) + \frac{(x - a)^2}{2!} + \frac{(x - a)^3}{3!} + \cdots \right]$$

LOGARITHMIC

$$\log_e x = \frac{x - 1}{x} + \frac{1}{2}\left(\frac{x - 1}{x}\right)^2 + \frac{1}{3}\left(\frac{x - 1}{x}\right)^3 + \cdots \qquad (x > \tfrac{1}{2})$$

$$\log_e x = (x - 1) - \tfrac{1}{2}(x - 1)^2 + \tfrac{1}{3}(x - 1)^3 - \cdots \qquad (2 \geq x > 0)$$

$$\log_e x = 2\left[\frac{x - 1}{x + 1} + \frac{1}{3}\left(\frac{x - 1}{x + 1}\right)^3 + \frac{1}{5}\left(\frac{x - 1}{x + 1}\right)^5 + \cdots \right] \qquad (x > 0)$$

$$\log_e(1 + x) = x - \tfrac{1}{2}x^2 + \tfrac{1}{3}x^3 - \tfrac{1}{4}x^4 + \cdots \qquad (-1 < x \leq 1)$$

$$\log_e(n + 1) - \log_e(n - 1) = 2\left[\frac{1}{n} + \frac{1}{3n^3} + \frac{1}{5n^5} + \cdots \right]$$

$$\log_e(a + x) = \log_e a + 2\left[\frac{x}{2a + x} + \frac{1}{3}\left(\frac{x}{2a + x}\right)^3 + \frac{1}{5}\left(\frac{x}{2a + x}\right)^5 + \cdots \right]$$

$$(a > 0, \ -a < x < +\infty)$$

$$\log_e \frac{1 + x}{1 - x} = 2\left[x + \frac{x^3}{3} + \frac{x^5}{5} + \cdots + \frac{x^{2n-1}}{2n - 1} + \cdots \right], \qquad -1 < x < 1$$

$$\log_e x = \log_e a + \frac{(x - a)}{a} - \frac{(x - a)^2}{2a^2} + \frac{(x - a)^3}{3a^3} - + \cdots, \qquad 0 < x \leq 2a$$

TRIGONOMETRIC

$$\sin x = x - \frac{x^3}{3!} + \frac{x^5}{5!} - \frac{x^7}{7!} + \cdots \qquad \text{(all real values of } x\text{)}$$

$$\cos x = 1 - \frac{x^2}{2!} + \frac{x^4}{4!} - \frac{x^6}{6!} + \cdots \qquad \text{(all real values of } x\text{)}$$

$$\tan x = x + \frac{x^3}{3} + \frac{2x^5}{15} + \frac{17x^7}{315} + \frac{62x^9}{2835} + \cdots + \frac{(-1)^{n-1} 2^{2n}(2^{2n} - 1) B_{2n}}{(2n)!} x^{2n-1} + \cdots,$$

$$\left[x^2 < \frac{\pi^2}{4}, \text{ and } B_n \text{ represents the } n\text{'th Bernoulli number.} \right]$$

$$\cot x = \frac{1}{x} - \frac{x}{3} - \frac{x^3}{45} - \frac{2x^5}{945} - \frac{x^7}{4725} - \cdots - \frac{(-1)^{n+1}2^{2n}}{(2n)!} B_{2n}x^{2n-1} - \cdots,$$

$$[x^2 < \pi^2, \text{ and } B_n \text{ represents the } n\text{'th Bernoulli number.}]$$

Series

$$\sec x = 1 + \frac{x^2}{2} + \frac{5}{24} x^4 + \frac{61}{720} x^6 + \frac{277}{8064} x^8 + \cdots + \frac{(-1)^n}{(2n)!} E_{2n} x^{2n} + \cdots ,$$

$$\left[x^2 < \frac{\pi^2}{4} , \text{ and } E_n \text{ represents the } n\text{'th Euler number.} \right]$$

$$\csc x = \frac{1}{x} + \frac{x}{6} + \frac{7}{360} x^3 + \frac{31}{15,120} x^5 + \frac{127}{604,800} x^7 + \cdots$$

$$+ \frac{(-1)^{n+1} 2 (2^{2n-1} - 1)}{(2n)!} B_{2n} x^{2n-1} + \cdots ,$$

$$[x^2 < \pi^2, \text{ and } B_n \text{ represents } n\text{'th Bernoulli number.}]$$

$$\sin x = x \left(1 - \frac{x^2}{\pi^2}\right)\left(1 - \frac{x^2}{2^2 \pi^2}\right)\left(1 - \frac{x^2}{3^2 \pi^2}\right) \cdots \qquad (x^2 < \infty)$$

$$\cos x = \left(1 - \frac{4x^2}{\pi^2}\right)\left(1 - \frac{4x^2}{3^2 \pi^2}\right)\left(1 - \frac{4x^2}{5^2 \pi^2}\right) \cdots \qquad (x^2 < \infty)$$

$$\sin^{-1} x = x + \frac{x^3}{2 \cdot 3} + \frac{1 \cdot 3}{2 \cdot 4 \cdot 5} x^5 + \frac{1 \cdot 3 \cdot 5}{2 \cdot 4 \cdot 6 \cdot 7} x^7 + \cdots \qquad \left(x^2 < 1, -\frac{\pi}{2} < \sin^{-1} x < \frac{\pi}{2}\right)$$

$$\cos^{-1} x = \frac{\pi}{2} - \left(x + \frac{x^3}{2 \cdot 3} + \frac{1 \cdot 3}{2 \cdot 4 \cdot 5} x^5 + \frac{1 \cdot 3 \cdot 5 x^7}{2 \cdot 4 \cdot 6 \cdot 7} + \cdots \right) \qquad (x^2 < 1, 0 < \cos^{-1} x < \pi)$$

$$\tan^{-1} x = x - \frac{x^3}{3} + \frac{x^5}{5} - \frac{x^7}{7} + \cdots \qquad (x^2 < 1)$$

$$\tan^{-1} x = \frac{\pi}{2} - \frac{1}{x} + \frac{1}{3x^3} - \frac{1}{5x^5} + \frac{1}{7x^7} - \cdots \qquad (x > 1)$$

$$\tan^{-1} x = -\frac{\pi}{2} - \frac{1}{x} + \frac{1}{3x^3} - \frac{1}{5x^5} + \frac{1}{7x^7} - \cdots \qquad (x < -1)$$

$$\cot^{-1} x = \frac{\pi}{2} - x + \frac{x^3}{3} - \frac{x^5}{5} + \frac{x^7}{7} - \cdots \qquad (x^2 < 1)$$

$$\log_e \sin x = \log_e x - \frac{x^2}{6} - \frac{x^4}{180} - \frac{x^6}{2835} - \cdots \qquad (x^2 < \pi^2)$$

$$\log_e \cos x = -\frac{x^2}{2} - \frac{x^4}{12} - \frac{x^6}{45} - \frac{17x^8}{2520} - \cdots \qquad \left(x^2 < \frac{\pi^2}{4}\right)$$

$$\log_e \tan x = \log_e x + \frac{x^2}{3} + \frac{7x^4}{90} + \frac{62x^6}{2835} + \cdots \qquad \left(x^2 < \frac{\pi^2}{4}\right)$$

$$e^{\sin x} = 1 + x + \frac{x^2}{2!} - \frac{3x^4}{4!} - \frac{8x^5}{5!} - \frac{3x^6}{6!} + \frac{56x^7}{7!} + \cdots$$

$$e^{\cos x} = e \left(1 - \frac{x^2}{2!} + \frac{4x^4}{4!} - \frac{31x^6}{6!} + \cdots \right)$$

$$e^{\tan x} = 1 + x + \frac{x^2}{2!} + \frac{3x^3}{3!} + \frac{9x^4}{4!} + \frac{37x^5}{5!} + \cdots \qquad \left(x^2 < \frac{\pi^2}{4}\right)$$

$$\sin x = \sin a + (x - a) \cos a - \frac{(x - a)^2}{2!} \sin a$$

$$- \frac{(x - a)^3}{3!} \cos a + \frac{(x - a)^4}{4!} \sin a + \cdots$$

VECTOR ANALYSIS

Definitions

Any quantity which is completely determined by its magnitude is called a *scalar*. Examples of such are mass, density, temperature, etc. Any quantity which is completely determined by its magnitude and direction is called a *vector*. Examples of such are velocity, acceleration, force, etc. A vector quantity is represented by a directed line segment, the length of which represents the magnitude of the vector. A vector quantity is usually represented by a boldfaced letter such as $\mathbf{V}$. Two vectors $\mathbf{V}_1$ and $\mathbf{V}_2$ are equal to one another if they have equal magnitudes and are acting in the same directions. A negative vector, written as $-\mathbf{V}$, is one which acts in the opposite direction to $\mathbf{V}$, but is of equal magnitude to it. If we represent the magnitude of $\mathbf{V}$ by v, we write $|\mathbf{V}| = v$. A vector parallel to $\mathbf{V}$, but equal to the reciprocal of its magnitude is written as $\mathbf{V}^{-1}$ or as $\dfrac{1}{\mathbf{V}}$.

The *unit vector* $\dfrac{\mathbf{V}}{v}$ $(v \neq 0)$ is that vector which has the same direction as $\mathbf{V}$, but has a magnitude of unity (sometimes represented as $\mathbf{V}_0$ or $\hat{\mathbf{v}}$).

Vector Algebra

The vector sum of $\mathbf{V}_1$ and $\mathbf{V}_2$ is represented by $\mathbf{V}_1 + \mathbf{V}_2$. The vector sum of $\mathbf{V}_1$ and $-\mathbf{V}_2$, or the difference of the vector $\mathbf{V}_2$ from $\mathbf{V}_1$ is represented by $\mathbf{V}_1 - \mathbf{V}_2$.

If r is a scalar, then $r\mathbf{V} = \mathbf{V}r$, and represents a vector r times the magnitude of $\mathbf{V}$, in the same direction as $\mathbf{V}$ if r is positive, and in the opposite direction if r is negative. If r and s are scalars, $\mathbf{V}_1$, $\mathbf{V}_2$, $\mathbf{V}_3$, vectors, then the following rules of scalars and vectors hold:

$$\mathbf{V}_1 + \mathbf{V}_2 = \mathbf{V}_2 + \mathbf{V}_1$$

$$(r + s)\mathbf{V}_1 = r\mathbf{V}_1 + s\mathbf{V}_1; \qquad r(\mathbf{V}_1 + \mathbf{V}_2) = r\mathbf{V}_1 + r\mathbf{V}_2$$

$$\mathbf{V}_1 + (\mathbf{V}_2 + \mathbf{V}_3) = (\mathbf{V}_1 + \mathbf{V}_2) + \mathbf{V}_3 = \mathbf{V}_1 + \mathbf{V}_2 + \mathbf{V}_3$$

Vectors in Space

A plane is described by two distinct vectors $\mathbf{V}_1$ and $\mathbf{V}_2$. Should these vectors not intersect each other, then one is displaced parallel to itself until they do (fig. 1.) Any other vector $\mathbf{V}$ lying in this plane is given by

$$\mathbf{V} = r\mathbf{V}_1 + s\mathbf{V}_2$$

VECTOR ANALYSIS (Continued)

A *position vector* specifies the position in space of a point relative to a fixed origin. If therefore $\mathbf{V}_1$ and $\mathbf{V}_2$ are the position vectors of the points A and B, relative to the origin O, then any point P on the line AB has a position vector $\mathbf{V}$ given by

$$\mathbf{V} = r\mathbf{V}_1 + (1 - r)\mathbf{V}_2$$

The scalar "r" can be taken as the parametric representation of P since $r = 0$ implies $P = B$ and $r = 1$ implies $P = A$. (fig. 2). If P divides the line AB in the ratio $r:s$ then

$$\mathbf{V} = \left(\frac{r}{r + s}\right)\mathbf{V}_1 + \left(\frac{s}{r + s}\right)\mathbf{V}_2$$

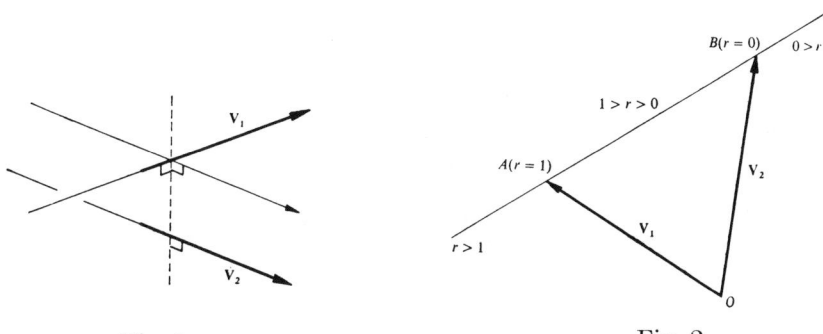

Fig. 1.   Fig. 2.

The vectors $\mathbf{V}_1$, $\mathbf{V}_2$, $\mathbf{V}_3$, . . . , $\mathbf{V}_n$ are said to be *linearly dependent* if there exist scalars r_1, r_2, r_3, . . . , r_n, not all zero, such that

$$r_1\mathbf{V}_1 + r_2\mathbf{V}_2 + \cdots + r_n\mathbf{V}_n = 0$$

A vector $\mathbf{V}$ is linearly dependent upon the set of vectors $\mathbf{V}_1$, $\mathbf{V}_2$, $\mathbf{V}_3$, . . . , $\mathbf{V}_n$ if

$$\mathbf{V} = r_1\mathbf{V}_1 + r_2\mathbf{V}_2 + r_3\mathbf{V}_3 + \cdots + r_n\mathbf{V}_n$$

Three vectors are linearly dependent if and only if they are co-planar.

All points in space can be uniquely determined by linear dependence upon three *base vectors* i.e. three vectors any one of which is linearly independent of the other two. The simplest set of base vectors are the unit vectors along the coordinate Ox, Oy and Oz axes. These are usually designated by $\mathbf{i}$, $\mathbf{j}$ and $\mathbf{k}$ respectively.

If $\mathbf{V}$ is a vector in space, and a, b and c are the respective magnitudes of the projections of the vector along the axes then

$$\mathbf{V} = a\mathbf{i} + b\mathbf{j} + c\mathbf{k}$$

and

$$v = \sqrt{a^2 + b^2 + c^2}$$

and the direction cosines of $\mathbf{V}$ are

$$\cos \alpha = a/v, \quad \cos \beta = b/v, \quad \cos \gamma = c/v.$$

The law of addition yields

$$\mathbf{V}_1 + \mathbf{V}_2 = (a_1 + a_2)\mathbf{i} + (b_1 + b_2)\mathbf{j} + (c_1 + c_2)\mathbf{k}$$

The Scalar, Dot, or Inner Product of Two Vectors V_1 and V_2

This product is represented as $V_1 \cdot V_2$ and is defined to be equal to $v_1 v_2 \cos \theta$, where θ is the angle from V_1 to V_2, i.e.,

$$V_1 \cdot V_2 = v_1 v_2 \cos \theta$$

The following rules apply for this product:

$$V_1 \cdot V_2 = a_1 a_2 + b_1 b_2 + c_1 c_2 = V_2 \cdot V_1$$

It should be noted that this verifies that scalar multiplication is commutative.

$$(V_1 + V_2) \cdot V_3 = V_1 \cdot V_3 + V_2 \cdot V_3$$
$$V_1 \cdot (V_2 + V_3) = V_1 \cdot V_2 + V_1 \cdot V_3$$

If V_1 is perpendicular to V_2 then $V_1 \cdot V_2 = 0$, and if V_1 is parallel to V_2 then $V_1 \cdot V_2 = v_1 v_2 = r w_1{}^2$

In particular

and
$$i \cdot i = j \cdot j = k \cdot k = 1,$$
$$i \cdot j = j \cdot k = k \cdot i = 0$$

The Vector or Cross Product of Vectors V_1 and V_2

This product is represented as $V_1 \times V_2$ and is defined to be equal to $v_1 v_2 (\sin \theta) 1$, where θ is the angle from V_1 to V_2 and 1 is a unit vector perpendicular to the plane of V_1 and V_2 and so directed that a right-handed screw driven in the direction of 1 would carry V_1 into V_2, i.e.,

$$V_1 \times V_2 = v_1 v_2 (\sin \theta) 1$$

and
$$\tan \theta = \frac{|V_1 \times V_2|}{V_1 \cdot V_2}$$

The following rules apply for vector products:

$$V_1 \times V_2 = -V_2 \times V_1$$
$$V_1 \times (V_2 + V_3) = V_1 \times V_2 + V_1 \times V_3$$
$$(V_1 + V_2) \times V_3 = V_1 \times V_3 + V_2 \times V_3$$
$$V_1 \times (V_2 \times V_3) = V_2 (V_3 \cdot V_1 - V_3 (V_1 \cdot V_2)$$
$$i \times i = j \times j = k \times k = 0.1 \text{ (zero vector)}$$
$$= 0$$

$$i \times j = k, \qquad j \times k = i, \qquad k \times i = j$$

If $V_1 = a_1 i + b_1 j + c_1 k$, $\qquad V_2 = a_2 i + b_2 j + c_2 k$, $\qquad V_3 = a_3 i + b_3 j + c_3 k$,

then

$$V_1 \times V_2 = \begin{vmatrix} i & j & k \\ a_1 & b_1 & c_1 \\ a_2 & b_2 & c_2 \end{vmatrix} = (b_1 c_2 - b_2 c_1) i + (c_1 a_2 - c_2 a_1) j + (a_1 b_2 - a_2 b_1) k$$

It should be noted that, since $V_1 \times V_2 = -V_2 \times V_1$, the vector product is not commutative.

Scalar Triple Product

There is only one possible interpretation of the expression $\mathbf{V}_1 \cdot \mathbf{V}_2 \times \mathbf{V}_3$ and that is $\mathbf{V}_1 \cdot (\mathbf{V}_2 \times \mathbf{V}_3)$ which is obviously a scalar.

Further $\mathbf{V}_1 \cdot (\mathbf{V}_2 \times \mathbf{V}_3) = (\mathbf{V}_1 \times \mathbf{V}_2) \cdot \mathbf{V}_3 = \mathbf{V}_2 \cdot (\mathbf{V}_3 \times \mathbf{V}_1)$

$$= \begin{vmatrix} a_1 & b_1 & c_1 \\ a_2 & b_2 & c_2 \\ a_3 & b_3 & c_3 \end{vmatrix}$$

$$= v_1 v_2 v_3 \cos \phi \sin \theta,$$

Where θ is the angle between $\mathbf{V}_2$ and $\mathbf{V}_3$ and ϕ is the angle between $\mathbf{V}_1$ and the normal to the plane of $\mathbf{V}_2$ and $\mathbf{V}_3$.

This product is called the *scalar triple product* and is written as $[\mathbf{V}_1\mathbf{V}_2\mathbf{V}_3]$.

The determinant indicates that it can be considered as the volume of the parallelepiped whose three determining edges are $\mathbf{V}_1$, $\mathbf{V}_2$ and $\mathbf{V}_3$.

It also follows that cyclic permutation of the subscripts does not change the value of the scalar triple product so that

$$[\mathbf{V}_1\mathbf{V}_2\mathbf{V}_3] = [\mathbf{V}_2\mathbf{V}_3\mathbf{V}_1] = [\mathbf{V}_3\mathbf{V}_1\mathbf{V}_2]$$

but $\quad [\mathbf{V}_1\mathbf{V}_2\mathbf{V}_3] = -[\mathbf{V}_2\mathbf{V}_1\mathbf{V}_3] \quad$ etc. $\qquad$ and $\quad [\mathbf{V}_1\mathbf{V}_1\mathbf{V}_2] \equiv 0$ etc.

Given three non-coplanar reference vectors $\mathbf{V}_1$, $\mathbf{V}_2$ and $\mathbf{V}_3$, the *reciprocal system is* given by $\mathbf{V}_1^*$, $\mathbf{V}_2^*$ and $\mathbf{V}_3^*$, where

$$1 = v_1 v_1^* = v_2 v_2^* = v_3 v_3^*$$

$$0 = v_1 v_2^* = v_1 v_3^* = v_2 v_1^* \quad \text{etc.}$$

$$\mathbf{V}_1^* = \frac{\mathbf{V}_2 \times \mathbf{V}_3}{[\mathbf{V}_1\mathbf{V}_2\mathbf{V}_3]}, \qquad \mathbf{V}_2^* = \frac{\mathbf{V}_3 \times \mathbf{V}_1}{[\mathbf{V}_1\mathbf{V}_2\mathbf{V}_3]}, \qquad \mathbf{V}_3^* = \frac{\mathbf{V}_1 \times \mathbf{V}_2}{[\mathbf{V}_1\mathbf{V}_2\mathbf{V}_3]}$$

The system $\mathbf{i}, \mathbf{j}, \mathbf{k}$ is its own reciprocal.

Vector Triple Product

The product $\mathbf{V}_1 \times (\mathbf{V}_2 \times \mathbf{V}_3)$ defines the *vector triple product*. Obviously, in this case, the brackets are vital to the definition.

$$\mathbf{V}_1 \times (\mathbf{V}_2 \times \mathbf{V}_3) = (\mathbf{V}_1 \cdot \mathbf{V}_3)\mathbf{V}_2 - (\mathbf{V}_1 \cdot \mathbf{V}_2)\mathbf{V}_3$$

$$= \begin{vmatrix} \mathbf{i} & \mathbf{j} & \mathbf{k} \\ a_1 & b_1 & c_1 \\ \begin{vmatrix} b_2 & c_2 \\ b_3 & c_3 \end{vmatrix} & \begin{vmatrix} c_2 & a_2 \\ c_3 & a_3 \end{vmatrix} & \begin{vmatrix} a_2 & b_2 \\ a_3 & b_3 \end{vmatrix} \end{vmatrix}$$

i.e. it is a vector, perpendicular to $\mathbf{V}_1$, lying in the plane of $\mathbf{V}_2$, $\mathbf{V}_3$.

Similarly $\qquad (\mathbf{V}_1 \times \mathbf{V}_2) \times \mathbf{V}_3 = \begin{vmatrix} \mathbf{i} & \mathbf{j} & \mathbf{k} \\ \begin{vmatrix} b_1 & c_1 \\ b_2 & c_2 \end{vmatrix} & \begin{vmatrix} c_1 & a_1 \\ c_2 & a_2 \end{vmatrix} & \begin{vmatrix} a_1 & b_1 \\ a_2 & b_2 \end{vmatrix} \\ a_3 & b_3 & c_3 \end{vmatrix}$

$$\mathbf{V}_1 \times (\mathbf{V}_2 \times \mathbf{V}_3) + \mathbf{V}_2 \times (\mathbf{V}_3 \times \mathbf{V}_1) + \mathbf{V}_3 \times (\mathbf{V}_1 + \mathbf{V}_2) \equiv 0$$

If $\mathbf{V}_1 \times (\mathbf{V}_2 \times \mathbf{V}_3) = (\mathbf{V}_1 \times \mathbf{V}_2) \times \mathbf{V}_3$ then $\mathbf{V}_1, \mathbf{V}_2, \mathbf{V}_3$ form an *orthogonal set*. Thus $\mathbf{i}, \mathbf{j}, \mathbf{k}$ form an orthogonal set.

Geometry of the Plane, Straight Line and Sphere

The position vectors of the fixed points A, B, C, D relative to O are $\mathbf{V}_1, \mathbf{V}_2, \mathbf{V}_3, \mathbf{V}_4$ and the position vector of the variable point P is $\mathbf{V}$.

The vector form of the equation of the straight line through A parallel to $\mathbf{V}_2$ is

$$\mathbf{V} = \mathbf{V}_1 + r\mathbf{V}_2$$

or $\quad (\mathbf{V} - \mathbf{V}_1) = r\mathbf{V}_2$

or $\quad (\mathbf{V} - \mathbf{V}_1) \times \mathbf{V}_2 = 0$

while that of the plane through A perpendicular to $\mathbf{V}_2$ is

$$(\mathbf{V} - \mathbf{V}_1) \cdot \mathbf{V}_2 = 0$$

The equation of the line AB is

$$\mathbf{V} = r\mathbf{V}_1 + (1 - r)\mathbf{V}_2$$

and those of the bisectors of the angles between $\mathbf{V}_1$ and $\mathbf{V}_2$ are

$$\mathbf{V} = r\left(\frac{\mathbf{V}_1}{v} \pm \frac{\mathbf{V}_2}{v_2}\right)$$

or $\quad \mathbf{V} = r(\hat{\mathbf{v}}_1 \pm \hat{\mathbf{v}}_2)$

The perpendicular from C to the line through A parallel to $\mathbf{V}_2$ has as its equation

$$\mathbf{V} = \mathbf{V}_1 - \mathbf{V}_3 - \hat{\mathbf{v}}_2 \cdot (\mathbf{V}_1 - \mathbf{V}_3)\hat{\mathbf{v}}_2.$$

The condition for the intersection of the two lines,

$$\mathbf{V} = \mathbf{V}_1 + r\mathbf{V}_3$$

and $\quad \mathbf{V} = \mathbf{V}_2 + s\mathbf{V}_4$

is $\quad [(\mathbf{V}_1 - \mathbf{V}_2)\mathbf{V}_3\mathbf{V}_4] = 0.$

The common perpendicular to the above two lines is the line of intersection of the two planes

$$[(\mathbf{V} - \mathbf{V}_1)\mathbf{V}_3(\mathbf{V}_3 \times \mathbf{V}_4)] = 0$$

and $\quad [(\mathbf{V} - \mathbf{V}_2)\mathbf{V}_4(\mathbf{V}_3 \times \mathbf{V}_4)] = 0$

and the length of this perpendicular is

$$\frac{[(\mathbf{V}_1 - \mathbf{V}_2)\mathbf{V}_3\mathbf{V}_4]}{|\mathbf{V}_3 \times \mathbf{V}_4|}.$$

The equation of the line perpendicular to the plane ABC is

$$\mathbf{V} = \mathbf{V}_1 \times \mathbf{V}_2 + \mathbf{V}_2 \times \mathbf{V}_3 + \mathbf{V}_3 \times \mathbf{V}_1$$

and the distance of the plane from the origin is

$$\frac{[\mathbf{V}_1\mathbf{V}_2\mathbf{V}_3]}{|(\mathbf{V}_2 - \mathbf{V}_1) \times (\mathbf{V}_3 - \mathbf{V}_1)|}.$$

In general the vector equation

$$\mathbf{V} \cdot \mathbf{V}_2 = r$$

defines the plane which is perpendicular to $\mathbf{V}_2$, and the perpendicular distance from A to this plane is

$$\frac{r - \mathbf{V}_1 \cdot \mathbf{V}_2}{v_2}.$$

The distance from A, measured along a line parallel to $\mathbf{V}_3$, is

$$\frac{r - \mathbf{V}_1 \cdot \mathbf{V}_2}{\mathbf{V}_2 \cdot \hat{\mathbf{v}}_3} \quad \text{or} \quad \frac{r - \mathbf{V}_1 \cdot \mathbf{V}_2}{v_2 \cos \theta}$$

where θ is the angle beween $\mathbf{V}_2$ and $\mathbf{V}_3$.
(If this plane contains the point C then $r = \mathbf{V}_3 \cdot \mathbf{V}_2$ and if it passes through the origin then $r = 0$.)

Given two planes

$$\mathbf{V} \cdot \mathbf{V}_1 = r$$

$$\mathbf{V} \cdot \mathbf{V}_2 = s$$

then any plane through the line of intersection of these two planes is given by

$$\mathbf{V} \cdot (\mathbf{V}_1 + \lambda \mathbf{V}_2) = r + \lambda s$$

where λ is a scalar parameter. In particular $\lambda = \pm v_1/v_2$ yields the equation of the two planes bisecting the angle between the given planes.

The plane through A parallel to the plane of $\mathbf{V}_2$, $\mathbf{V}_3$ is

$$\mathbf{V} = \mathbf{V}_1 + r\mathbf{V}_2 + s\mathbf{V}_3$$

$$\text{or} \quad (\mathbf{V} - \mathbf{V}_1) \cdot \mathbf{V}_2 \times \mathbf{V}_3 = 0$$

$$\text{or} \quad [\mathbf{V}\mathbf{V}_2\mathbf{V}_3] - [\mathbf{V}_1\mathbf{V}_2\mathbf{V}_3] = 0$$

so that the expansion in rectangular Cartesian coordinates yields

$$\begin{vmatrix} (x - a_1) & (y - b_1) & (z - c_1) \\ a_2 & b_2 & c_2 \\ a_3 & b_3 & c_3 \end{vmatrix} = 0 \qquad (\mathbf{V} \equiv x\mathbf{i} + y\mathbf{j} + z\mathbf{k})$$

which is obviously the usual linear equation in x, y and z.

The plane through AB parallel to $\mathbf{V}_3$ is given by

$$[(\mathbf{V} - \mathbf{V}_1)(\mathbf{V}_1 - \mathbf{V}_2)\mathbf{V}_3] = 0$$

$$\text{or} \quad [\mathbf{V}\mathbf{V}_2\mathbf{V}_3] - [\mathbf{V}\mathbf{V}_1\mathbf{V}_3] - [\mathbf{V}_1\mathbf{V}_2\mathbf{V}_3] = 0$$

The plane through the three points A, B and C is

$$\mathbf{V} = \mathbf{V}_1 + s(\mathbf{V}_2 - \mathbf{V}_1) + t(\mathbf{V}_3 - \mathbf{V}_1)$$

$$\text{or} \quad \mathbf{V} = r\mathbf{V}_1 + s\mathbf{V}_2 + t\mathbf{V}_3 \qquad (r + s + t \equiv 1)$$

$$\text{or} \quad [(\mathbf{V} - \mathbf{V}_1)(\mathbf{V}_1 - \mathbf{V}_2)(\mathbf{V}_2 - \mathbf{V}_3)] = 0$$

$$\text{or} \quad [\mathbf{V}\mathbf{V}_1\mathbf{V}_2] + [\mathbf{V}\mathbf{V}_2\mathbf{V}_3] + [\mathbf{V}\mathbf{V}_3\mathbf{V}_1] - [\mathbf{V}_1\mathbf{V}_2\mathbf{V}_3] = 0$$

For four points A, B, C, D to be coplanar, then

$$r\mathbf{Y}_1 + s\mathbf{V}_2 + t\mathbf{V}_3 + u\mathbf{V}_4 \equiv 0 \equiv r + s + t + u$$

The following formulae relate to a sphere when the vectors are taken to lie in three dimensional space and to a circle when the space is two dimensional. For a circle in three dimensions take the intersection of the sphere with a plane.

The equation of a sphere with center O and radius OA is

$$\mathbf{V} \cdot \mathbf{V} = v_1^2 \qquad (\text{not } \mathbf{V} = \mathbf{V}_1)$$

$$\text{or} \qquad (\mathbf{V} - \mathbf{V}_1) \cdot (\mathbf{V} + \mathbf{V}_1) = 0$$

while that of a sphere with center B radius v_1 is

$$(\mathbf{V} - \mathbf{V}_2) \cdot (\mathbf{V} - \mathbf{V}_2) = v_1^2$$

$$\text{or} \qquad \mathbf{V} \cdot (\mathbf{V} - 2\mathbf{V}_2) = v_1^2 - v_2^2$$

If the above sphere passes through the origin then

$$\mathbf{V} \cdot (\mathbf{V} - 2\mathbf{V}_2) = 0$$

(note that in two dimensional polar coordinates this is simply)

$$r = 2a \cdot \cos \theta$$

while in three dimensional Cartesian coordinates it is

$$x^2 + y^2 + z^2 - 2(a_2 x + b_2 y + c_2 x) = 0.$$

The equation of a sphere having the points A and B as the extremities of a diameter is

$$(\mathbf{V} - \mathbf{V}_1) \cdot (\mathbf{V} - \mathbf{V}_2) = 0.$$

The square of the length of the tangent from C to the sphere with center B and radius v_1 is given by

$$(\mathbf{V}_3 - \mathbf{V}_2) \cdot (\mathbf{V}_3 - \mathbf{V}_2) = v_1^2$$

The condition that the plane $\mathbf{V} \cdot \mathbf{V}_3 = s$ is tangential to the sphere $(\mathbf{V} - \mathbf{V}_2) \cdot (\mathbf{V} - \mathbf{V}_2) = v_1^2$ is

$$(s - \mathbf{V}_3 \cdot \mathbf{V}_2) \cdot (s - \mathbf{V}_3 \cdot \mathbf{V}_2) = v_1^2 v_3^2.$$

The equation of the tangent plane at D, on the surface of sphere $(\mathbf{V} - \mathbf{V}_2) \cdot (\mathbf{V} - \mathbf{V}_2) = v_1^2$, is

$$(\mathbf{V} - \mathbf{V}_4) \cdot (\mathbf{V}_4 - \mathbf{V}_2) = 0$$

$$\text{or} \qquad \mathbf{V} \cdot \mathbf{V}_4 - \mathbf{V}_2 \cdot (\mathbf{V} + \mathbf{V}_4) = v_1^2 - v_2^2$$

The condition that the two circles $(\mathbf{V} - \mathbf{V}_2) \cdot (\mathbf{V} - \mathbf{V}_2) = v_1^2$ and $(\mathbf{V} - \mathbf{V}_4) \cdot (\mathbf{V} - \mathbf{V}_4) = v_3^2$ intersect orthogonally is clearly

$$(\mathbf{V}_2 - \mathbf{V}_4) \cdot (\mathbf{V}_2 - \mathbf{V}_4) = v_1^2 + v_3^2$$

The polar plane of D with respect to the circle

$$(\mathbf{V} - \mathbf{V}_2) \cdot (\mathbf{V} - \mathbf{V}_2) = v_1^2 \quad \text{is}$$

$$\mathbf{V} \cdot \mathbf{V}_4 - \mathbf{V}_2 \cdot (\mathbf{V} + \mathbf{V}_4) = v_1^2 - v_2^2$$

Any sphere through the intersection of the two spheres $(\mathbf{V} - \mathbf{V}_2) \cdot (\mathbf{V} - \mathbf{V}_2) = v_1^2$ and $(\mathbf{V} - \mathbf{V}_4) \cdot (\mathbf{V} - \mathbf{V}_4) = v_3^2$ is given by

$$(\mathbf{V} - \mathbf{V}_2) \cdot (\mathbf{V} - \mathbf{V}_2) + \lambda(\mathbf{V} - \mathbf{V}_4) \cdot (\mathbf{V} - \mathbf{V}_4) = v_1^2 + \lambda v_3^2$$

while the radical plane of two such spheres is

$$\mathbf{V} \cdot (\mathbf{V}_2 - \mathbf{V}_4) = -\tfrac{1}{2}(v_1^2 - v_2^2 - v_3^2 + v_4^2)$$

Differentiation of Vectors

If $\mathbf{V}_1 = a_1\mathbf{i} + b_1\mathbf{j} + c_1\mathbf{k}$, and $\mathbf{V}_2 = a_2\mathbf{i} + b_2\mathbf{j} + c_2\mathbf{k}$, and if $\mathbf{V}_1$ and $\mathbf{V}_2$ are functions of the scalar t, then

$$\frac{d}{dt}(\mathbf{V}_1 + \mathbf{V}_2 + \cdots) = \frac{d\mathbf{V}_1}{dt} + \frac{d\mathbf{V}_2}{dt} + \cdots,$$

$$\text{where} \quad \frac{d\mathbf{V}_1}{dt} = \frac{da_1}{dt}\mathbf{i} + \frac{db_1}{dt}\mathbf{j} + \frac{dc_1}{dt}\mathbf{k}, \text{ etc.}$$

$$\frac{d}{dt}(\mathbf{V}_1 \cdot \mathbf{V}_2) = \frac{d\mathbf{V}_1}{dt} \cdot \mathbf{V}_2 + \mathbf{V}_1 \cdot \frac{d\mathbf{V}_2}{dt}$$

$$\frac{d}{dt}(\mathbf{V}_1 \times \mathbf{V}_2) = \frac{d\mathbf{V}_1}{dt} \times \mathbf{V}_2 + \mathbf{V}_1 \times \frac{d\mathbf{V}_2}{dt}$$

$$\mathbf{V} \cdot \frac{d\mathbf{V}}{dt} = v \cdot \frac{dv}{dt}$$

In particular, if $\mathbf{V}$ is a vector of constant length then the right hand side of the last equation is identically zero showing that $\mathbf{V}$ is perpendicular to its derivative.

The derivatives of the triple products are

$$\frac{d}{dt}[\mathbf{V}_1\mathbf{V}_2\mathbf{V}_3] = \left[\left(\frac{d\mathbf{V}_1}{dt}\right)\mathbf{V}_2\mathbf{V}_3\right] + \left[\mathbf{V}_1\left(\frac{d\mathbf{V}_2}{dt}\right)\mathbf{V}_3\right] + \left[\mathbf{V}_1\mathbf{V}_2\left(\frac{d\mathbf{V}_3}{dt}\right)\right]$$

$$\text{and} \quad \frac{d}{dt}\left\{\mathbf{V}_1 \times (\mathbf{V}_2 \times \mathbf{V}_3)\right\} = \left(\frac{d\mathbf{V}_1}{dt}\right) \times (\mathbf{V}_2 \times \mathbf{V}_3) + \mathbf{V}_1$$
$$\times \left(\left(\frac{d\mathbf{V}_2}{dt}\right) \times \mathbf{V}_3\right) + \mathbf{V}_1 \times \left(\mathbf{V}_2 \times \left(\frac{d\mathbf{V}_3}{dt}\right)\right)$$

Geometry of Curves in Space

s = the *length of arc*, measured from some fixed point on the curve (fig. 3).

$\mathbf{V}_1$ = the position vector of the point A on the curve

$\mathbf{V}_1 + \delta\mathbf{V}_1$ = the position vector of the point P in the neighborhood of A

$\hat{\mathbf{t}}$ = the *unit tangent* to the curve at the point A, measured in the direction of s increasing.

The *normal plane* is that plane which is perpendicular to the unit tangent. The principal normal is defined as the intersection of the normal plane with the plane defined by $\mathbf{V}_1$ and $\mathbf{V}_1 + \delta\mathbf{V}_1$ in the limit as $\delta\mathbf{V}_1 - 0$.

$\hat{\mathbf{n}}$ = the *unit normal* (principal) at the point A. The plane defined by $\hat{\mathbf{t}}$ and $\hat{\mathbf{n}}$ is called the *osculating plane* (alternatively plane of curvature or local plane).

ρ = the radius of curvature at A

$\delta\theta$ = the angle subtended at the origin by $\delta\mathbf{V}_1$.

$$\kappa = \frac{d\theta}{ds} = \frac{1}{\rho}$$

$\hat{\mathbf{b}}$ = the *unit binormal* i.e. the unit vector which is parallel to $\hat{\mathbf{t}} \times \hat{\mathbf{n}}$ at the point A :
λ = the *torsion* of the curve at A

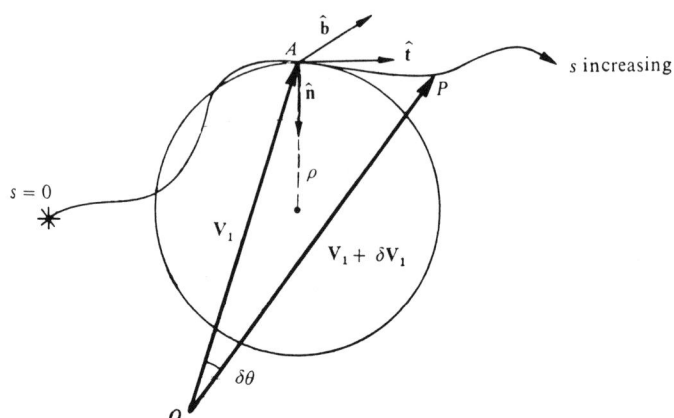

Figure 3.

Frenet's Formulae:

$$\frac{d\hat{\mathbf{t}}}{ds} = \kappa\hat{\mathbf{n}}$$

$$\frac{d\hat{\mathbf{n}}}{ds} = -\kappa\hat{\mathbf{t}} + \lambda\hat{\mathbf{b}}$$

$$\frac{d\hat{\mathbf{b}}}{ds} = -\lambda\hat{\mathbf{n}}$$

The following formulae are also applicable:

Unit tangent $\qquad\qquad\qquad \hat{\mathbf{t}} = \dfrac{d\mathbf{V}_1}{ds}$

Equation of the tangent $\qquad (\mathbf{V} - \mathbf{V}_1) \times \hat{\mathbf{t}} = 0$

$\qquad\qquad\qquad$ or $\qquad \mathbf{V} = \mathbf{V}_1 + q\hat{\mathbf{t}}$

Unit normal $\qquad\qquad\qquad \hat{\mathbf{n}} = \dfrac{1}{\kappa}\dfrac{d^2\mathbf{V}_1}{ds^2}$

Equation of the normal plane $\qquad (\mathbf{V} - \mathbf{V}_1) \cdot \hat{\mathbf{t}} = 0$

Equation of the normal $\qquad (\mathbf{V} - \mathbf{V}_1) \times \hat{\mathbf{n}} = 0$

$\qquad\qquad\qquad$ or $\qquad \mathbf{V} = \mathbf{V}_1 + r\hat{\mathbf{n}}$

Unit binormal $\qquad \hat{\mathbf{b}} = \hat{\mathbf{t}} \times \hat{\mathbf{n}}$

Equation of the binormal $\qquad (\mathbf{V} - \mathbf{V}_1) \times \hat{\mathbf{b}} = 0$

$\qquad\qquad\qquad$ or $\qquad \mathbf{V} = \mathbf{V}_1 + u\hat{\mathbf{b}}$

$\qquad\qquad\qquad$ or $\qquad \mathbf{V} = \mathbf{V}_1 + w\dfrac{d\mathbf{V}_1}{ds} \times \dfrac{d^2\mathbf{V}_1}{ds^2}$

Equation of the osculating plane:

$$[(\mathbf{V} - \mathbf{V}_1)\hat{\mathbf{t}}\hat{\mathbf{n}}] = 0$$

$$\text{or} \qquad \left[(\mathbf{V} - \mathbf{V}_1)\left(\frac{d\mathbf{V}_1}{ds}\right)\left(\frac{d^2\mathbf{V}_1}{ds^2}\right) \right] = 0$$

A *geodetic line* on a surface is a curve, the osculating plane of which is everywhere normal to the surface.

The differential equation of the geodetic is

$$[\hat{n}\,dV_1\,d^2V_1] = 0$$

Differential Operators—Rectangular Coordinates

$$dS = \frac{\partial S}{\partial x} \cdot dx + \frac{\partial S}{\partial y} \cdot dy + \frac{\partial S}{\partial z} \cdot dz$$

By definition

$$\nabla \equiv \text{del} \equiv \mathbf{i}\frac{\partial}{\partial x} + \mathbf{j}\frac{\partial}{\partial y} + \mathbf{k}\frac{\partial}{\partial z}$$

$$\nabla^2 \equiv \text{Laplacian} \equiv \frac{\partial^2}{\partial x^2} + \frac{\partial^2}{\partial y^2} + \frac{\partial^2}{\partial z^2}$$

If S is a scalar function, then

$$\nabla S \equiv \text{grad } S \equiv \frac{\partial S}{\partial x}\mathbf{i} + \frac{\partial S}{\partial y}\mathbf{j} + \frac{\partial S}{\partial z}\mathbf{k}$$

Grad S defines both the direction and magnitude of the maximum rate of increase of S at any point. Hence the name *gradient* and also its vectorial nature. ∇S is independent of the choice of rectangular coordinates.

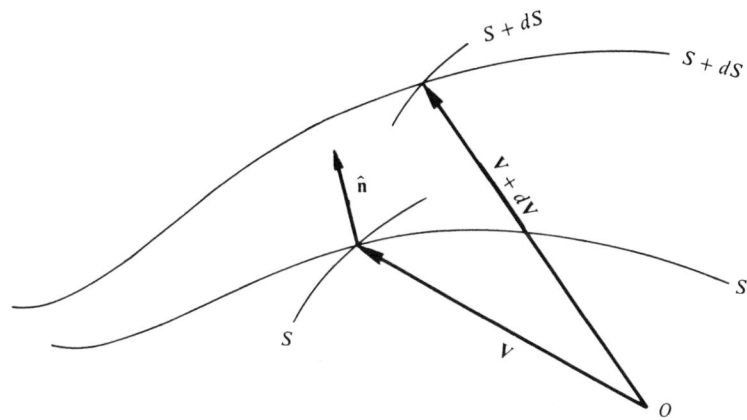

Figure 4

$$\nabla S = \frac{\partial S}{\partial n}\hat{n}$$

where $\hat{n}$ is the unit normal to the surface $S = $ constant, in the direction of S increasing. The total derivative of S at a point having the position vector V is given by (fig. 4)

$$dS = \frac{\partial S}{\partial n}\hat{n} \cdot dV$$

$$= dV \cdot \nabla S$$

and the directional derivative of S in the direction of U is

$$U \cdot \nabla S = U \cdot (\nabla S) = (U \cdot \nabla)S$$

Similarly the directional derivative of the vector V in the direction of U is

$$(U \cdot \nabla)V$$

The *distributive* law holds for finding a gradient. Thus if S and T are scalar functions

$$\nabla(S + T) = \nabla S + \nabla T$$

The *associative* law becomes the rule for differentiating a product:

$$\nabla(ST) = S\nabla T + T\nabla S$$

If $\mathbf{V}$ is a vector function with the magnitudes of the components parallel to the three coordinate axes V_x, V_y, V_z, then

$$\nabla \cdot \mathbf{V} \equiv \text{div } \mathbf{V} \equiv \frac{\partial V_x}{\partial x} + \frac{\partial V_y}{\partial y} + \frac{\partial V_z}{\partial z}$$

The divergence obeys the distributive law. Thus, if $\mathbf{V}$ and $\mathbf{U}$ are vectors functions, then

$$\nabla \cdot (\mathbf{V} + \mathbf{U}) = \nabla \cdot \mathbf{V} + \nabla \cdot \mathbf{U}$$
$$\nabla \cdot (S\mathbf{V}) = (\nabla S) \cdot \mathbf{V} + S(\nabla \cdot \mathbf{V})$$
$$\nabla \cdot (\mathbf{U} \times \mathbf{V}) = \mathbf{V} \cdot (\nabla \times \mathbf{U}) - \mathbf{U} \cdot (\nabla \times \mathbf{V})$$

As with the gradient of a scalar, the divergence of a vector is invariant under a transformation from one set of rectangular coordinates to another.

$$\nabla \times \mathbf{V} \equiv \text{curl } \mathbf{V} \quad (\text{sometimes } \nabla \wedge \mathbf{V} \text{ or rot } \mathbf{V})$$

$$\equiv \left(\frac{\partial \mathbf{V}_z}{\partial y} - \frac{\partial \mathbf{V}_y}{\partial z}\right)\mathbf{i} + \left(\frac{\partial \mathbf{V}_x}{\partial z} - \frac{\partial \mathbf{V}_z}{\partial x}\right)\mathbf{j} + \left(\frac{\partial \mathbf{V}_y}{\partial x} - \frac{\partial \mathbf{V}_x}{\partial y}\right)\mathbf{k}$$

$$= \begin{vmatrix} \mathbf{i} & \mathbf{j} & \mathbf{k} \\ \dfrac{\partial}{\partial x} & \dfrac{\partial}{\partial y} & \dfrac{\partial}{\partial z} \\ V_x & V_y & V_z \end{vmatrix}$$

The *curl* (or *rotation*) of a vector is a vector which is invariant under a transformation from one set of rectangular coordinates to another.

$$\nabla \times (\mathbf{U} + \mathbf{V}) = \nabla \times \mathbf{U} + \nabla \times \mathbf{V}$$
$$\nabla \times (S\mathbf{V}) = (\nabla S) \times \mathbf{V} + S(\nabla \times \mathbf{V})$$
$$\nabla \times (\mathbf{U} \times \mathbf{V}) = (\mathbf{V} \cdot \nabla)\mathbf{U} - (\mathbf{U} \cdot \nabla)\mathbf{V} + \mathbf{U}(\nabla \cdot \mathbf{V}) - \mathbf{V}(\nabla \cdot \mathbf{U})$$

$$\text{grad } (\mathbf{U} \cdot \mathbf{V}) = \nabla(\mathbf{U} \cdot \mathbf{V})$$
$$= (\mathbf{V} \cdot \nabla)\mathbf{U} + (\mathbf{U} \cdot \nabla)\mathbf{V} + \mathbf{V} \times (\nabla \times \mathbf{U}) + \mathbf{U} \times (\nabla \times \mathbf{V})$$

If
$$\mathbf{V} = V_x\mathbf{i} + V_y\mathbf{j} + V_z\mathbf{k}$$
$$\nabla \cdot \mathbf{V} = \nabla V_x \cdot \mathbf{i} + \nabla V_y \cdot \mathbf{j} + \nabla V_z \cdot \mathbf{k}$$
and
$$\nabla \times \mathbf{V} = \nabla V_x \times \mathbf{i} + \nabla V_y \times \mathbf{j} + \nabla V_z \times \mathbf{k}$$

The operator ∇ can be used more than once. The number of possibilities where ∇ is used twice are

$$\nabla \cdot (\nabla\theta) \equiv \text{div grad } \theta$$
$$\nabla \times (\nabla\theta) \equiv \text{curl grad } \theta$$
$$\nabla(\nabla \cdot \mathbf{V}) \equiv \text{grad div } \mathbf{V}$$
$$\nabla \cdot (\nabla \times \mathbf{V}) \equiv \text{div curl } \mathbf{V}$$
$$\nabla \times (\nabla \times \mathbf{V}) \equiv \text{curl curl } \mathbf{V}$$

Thus: div grad $S \equiv \nabla \cdot (\nabla S) \equiv$ Laplacian $S \equiv \nabla^2 S$

$$\equiv \frac{\partial^2 S}{\partial x^2} + \frac{\partial^2 S}{\partial y^2} + \frac{\partial^2 S}{\partial z^2}$$

curl grad $S \equiv 0$; curl curl $\mathbf{V} \equiv$ grad div $\mathbf{V} - \nabla^2 \mathbf{V}$;

div curl $\mathbf{V} \equiv$ 0

Taylor's expansion in three dimensions can be written

$$f(\mathbf{V} + \boldsymbol{\varepsilon}) = e^{\boldsymbol{\varepsilon} \cdot \nabla} f(\mathbf{V})$$

where $\mathbf{V} = x\mathbf{i} + y\mathbf{j} + z\mathbf{k}$

and $\boldsymbol{\varepsilon} = h\mathbf{i} + l\mathbf{j} + m\mathbf{k}$

(note the analogy with $f_p = e^{phD} f_0$ in finite difference methods).

Orthogonal Curvilinear Coordinates

If at a point P there exist three uniform point functions u, v and w so that the surfaces $u =$ const., $v =$ const., and $w =$ const., intersect in three distinct curves through P then the surfaces are called the *coordinate surfaces* through P. The three lines of intersection are referred to as the *coordinate lines* and their tangents a, b, and c as the *coordinate axes*. When the coordinate axes form an orthogonal set the system is said to define *orthogonal curvilinear coordinates* at P.

Consider an infinitesimal volume enclosed by the surfaces u, v, w, $u + du$, $v + dv$, and $w + dw$ (fig. 5).

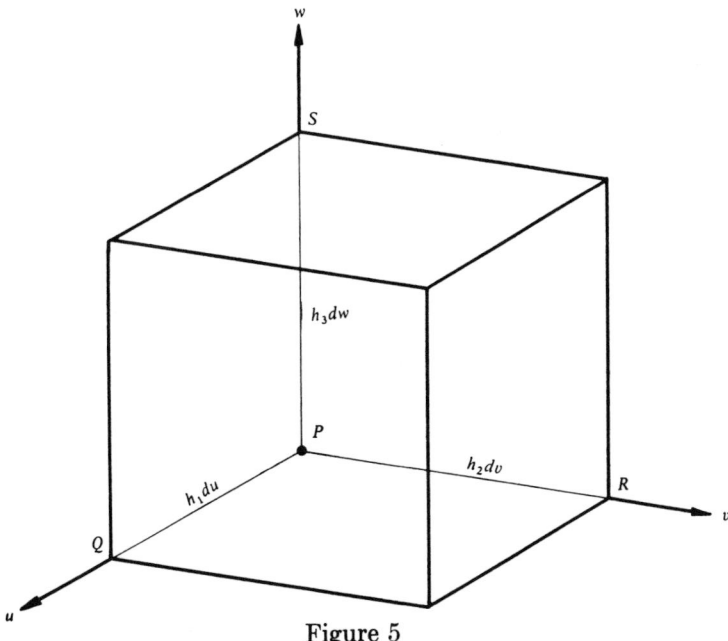

Figure 5

The surface $PRS \equiv u = $ const., and the face of the curvilinear figure immediately opposite this is $u + du = $ const. etc.

In terms of these surface constants

$$
\begin{aligned}
P &= P(u,v,w) \\
Q &= Q(u + du,v,w) \qquad \text{and} \qquad PQ = h_1 du \\
R &= R(u,v + dv,w) \qquad\qquad\qquad PR = h_2 dv \\
S &= S(u,v,w + dw) \qquad\qquad\qquad PS = h_3 dw
\end{aligned}
$$

where h_1, h_2, and h_3 are functions of u, v, and w.

In rectangular Cartesians $\mathbf{i}$, $\mathbf{j}$, $\mathbf{k}$

$$
h_1 = 1, \qquad h_2 = 1, \qquad h_3 = 1.
$$

$$
\frac{\hat{\mathbf{a}}}{h_1} \frac{\partial}{\partial u} = \mathbf{i}\frac{\partial}{\partial x}, \qquad \frac{\hat{\mathbf{b}}}{h_2} \frac{\partial}{\partial v} = \mathbf{j}\frac{\partial}{\partial y}, \qquad \frac{\hat{\mathbf{c}}}{h_3} \frac{\partial}{\partial w} = \mathbf{k}\frac{\partial}{\partial z}.
$$

In cylindrical coordinates $\hat{\mathbf{r}}$, $\hat{\boldsymbol{\phi}}$, $\hat{\mathbf{k}}$

$$
h_1 = 1, \qquad h_2 = r \qquad h_3 = 1.
$$

$$
\frac{\hat{\mathbf{a}}}{h_1} \frac{\partial}{\partial u} = \hat{\mathbf{r}}\frac{\partial}{\partial r}, \qquad \frac{\hat{\mathbf{b}}}{h_2} \frac{\partial}{\partial v} = \frac{\hat{\boldsymbol{\phi}}}{r}\frac{\partial}{\partial \phi}, \qquad \frac{\hat{\mathbf{c}}}{h_3} \frac{\partial}{\partial w} = \hat{\mathbf{k}}\frac{\partial}{\partial z}
$$

In spherical coordinates $\hat{\mathbf{r}}$, $\hat{\boldsymbol{\theta}}$, $\hat{\boldsymbol{\phi}}$

$$
h_1 = 1, \qquad h_2 = r, \qquad h_3 = r\sin\theta
$$

$$
\frac{\hat{\mathbf{a}}}{h_1} \frac{\partial}{\partial u} = \hat{\mathbf{r}}\frac{\partial}{\partial r}, \qquad \frac{\mathbf{b}}{h_2} \frac{\partial}{\partial v} = \frac{\hat{\boldsymbol{\phi}}}{r}\frac{\partial}{\partial \theta}, \qquad \frac{\hat{\mathbf{c}}}{h_3} \frac{\partial}{\partial w} = \frac{\hat{\boldsymbol{\phi}}}{r\sin\theta}\frac{\partial}{\partial \phi}
$$

The general expressions for grad, div and curl together with those for ∇^2 and the directional derivative are, in orthogonal curvilinear coordinates, given by

$$
\nabla S = \frac{\hat{\mathbf{a}}}{h_1}\frac{\partial S}{\partial u} + \frac{\hat{\mathbf{b}}}{h_2}\frac{\partial S}{\partial v} + \frac{\hat{\mathbf{c}}}{h_3}\frac{\partial S}{\partial w}
$$

$$
(\mathbf{V} \cdot \nabla)S = \frac{V_1}{h_1}\frac{\partial S}{\partial u} + \frac{V_2}{h_2}\frac{\partial S}{\partial v} + \frac{V_3}{h_3}\frac{\partial S}{\partial w}
$$

$$
\nabla \cdot \mathbf{V} = \frac{1}{h_1 h_2 h_3}\left\{\frac{\partial}{\partial u}(h_2 h_3 V_1) + \frac{\partial}{\partial v}(h_3 h_1 V_2) + \frac{\partial}{\partial w}(h_1 h_2 V_3)\right\}
$$

$$
\nabla \times \mathbf{V} = \frac{\hat{\mathbf{a}}}{h_2 h_3}\left\{\frac{\partial}{\partial v}(h_3 V_3) - \frac{\partial}{\partial w}(h_2 V_2)\right\} + \frac{\hat{\mathbf{b}}}{h_3 h_1}\left\{\frac{\partial}{\partial w}(h_1 V_1) - \frac{\partial}{\partial u}(h_3 V_3)\right\}
$$

$$
+ \frac{\hat{\mathbf{c}}}{h_1 h_2}\left\{\frac{\partial}{\partial u}(h_2 V_2) - \frac{\partial}{\partial v}(h_1 V_1)\right\}
$$

$$
\nabla^2 S = \frac{1}{h_1 h_2 h_3}\left\{\frac{\partial}{\partial u}\left(\frac{h_2 h_3}{h_1}\frac{\partial S}{\partial u}\right) + \frac{\partial}{\partial v}\left(\frac{h_3 h_1}{h_2}\frac{\partial S}{\partial v}\right) + \frac{\partial}{\partial w}\left(\frac{h_1 h_2}{h_3}\frac{\partial S}{\partial w}\right)\right\}
$$

FORMULAS OF VECTOR ANALYSIS

	Rectangular coordinates	Cylindrical coordinates	Spherical coordinates
Conversion to rectangular coordinates		$x = r\cos\varphi \quad y = r\sin\varphi \quad z = z$	$x = r\cos\varphi\sin\theta \quad y = r\sin\varphi\sin\theta$ $z = r\cos\theta$
Gradient	$\nabla\phi = \dfrac{\partial\phi}{\partial x}\mathbf{i} + \dfrac{\partial\phi}{\partial y}\mathbf{j} + \dfrac{\partial\phi}{\partial z}\mathbf{k}$	$\nabla\phi = \dfrac{\partial\phi}{\partial r}\mathbf{r} + \dfrac{1}{r}\dfrac{\partial\phi}{\partial\varphi}\boldsymbol{\phi} + \dfrac{\partial\phi}{\partial z}\mathbf{k}$	$\nabla\phi = \dfrac{\partial\phi}{\partial r}\mathbf{r} + \dfrac{1}{r}\dfrac{\partial\phi}{\partial\theta}\boldsymbol{\theta} + \dfrac{1}{r\sin\theta}\dfrac{\partial\phi}{\partial\varphi}\boldsymbol{\phi}$
Divergence	$\nabla\cdot\mathbf{A} = \dfrac{\partial A_x}{\partial x} + \dfrac{\partial A_y}{\partial y} + \dfrac{\partial A_z}{\partial z}$	$\nabla\cdot\mathbf{A} = \dfrac{1}{r}\dfrac{\partial(rA_r)}{\partial r} + \dfrac{1}{r}\dfrac{\partial A_\varphi}{\partial\varphi} + \dfrac{\partial A_z}{\partial z}$	$\nabla\cdot\mathbf{A} = \dfrac{1}{r^2}\dfrac{\partial(r^2 A_r)}{\partial r} + \dfrac{1}{r\sin\theta}\dfrac{\partial(A_\theta\sin\theta)}{\partial\theta} + \dfrac{1}{r\sin\theta}\dfrac{\partial A_\varphi}{\partial\varphi}$
Curl	$\nabla\times\mathbf{A} = \begin{vmatrix} \mathbf{i} & \mathbf{j} & \mathbf{k} \\ \dfrac{\partial}{\partial x} & \dfrac{\partial}{\partial y} & \dfrac{\partial}{\partial z} \\ A_x & A_y & A_z \end{vmatrix}$	$\nabla\times\mathbf{A} = \begin{vmatrix} \dfrac{1}{r}\mathbf{r} & \boldsymbol{\phi} & \dfrac{1}{r}\mathbf{k} \\ \dfrac{\partial}{\partial r} & \dfrac{\partial}{\partial\varphi} & \dfrac{\partial}{\partial z} \\ A_r & rA_\varphi & A_z \end{vmatrix}$	$\nabla\times\mathbf{A} = \begin{vmatrix} \dfrac{\mathbf{r}}{r^2\sin\theta} & \dfrac{\boldsymbol{\theta}}{r\sin\theta} & \dfrac{\boldsymbol{\phi}}{r} \\ \dfrac{\partial}{\partial r} & \dfrac{\partial}{\partial\theta} & \dfrac{\partial}{\partial\varphi} \\ A_r & rA_\theta & rA_\varphi\sin\theta \end{vmatrix}$
Laplacian	$\nabla^2\phi = \dfrac{\partial^2\phi}{\partial x^2} + \dfrac{\partial^2\phi}{\partial y^2} + \dfrac{\partial^2\phi}{\partial z^2}$	$\nabla^2\phi = \dfrac{1}{r}\dfrac{\partial}{\partial r}\left(r\dfrac{\partial\phi}{\partial r}\right) + \dfrac{1}{r^2}\dfrac{\partial^2\phi}{\partial\varphi^2} + \dfrac{\partial^2\phi}{\partial z^2}$	$\nabla^2\phi = \dfrac{1}{r^2}\dfrac{\partial}{\partial r}\left(r^2\dfrac{\partial\phi}{\partial r}\right) + \dfrac{1}{r^2\sin\theta}\dfrac{\partial}{\partial\theta}\left(\sin\theta\dfrac{\partial\phi}{\partial\theta}\right) + \dfrac{1}{r^2\sin^2\theta}\dfrac{\partial^2\phi}{\partial\varphi^2}$

Transformation of Integrals

s = the distance along some curve "C" in space and is measured from some fixed point.

S = a surface area

V = a volume contained by a specified surface

$\hat{\mathbf{t}}$ = the unit tangent to C at the point P

$\hat{\mathbf{n}}$ = the unit outward pointing normal

F = some vector function

ds = the vector element of curve ($= \hat{\mathbf{t}}\, ds$)

dS = the vector element of surface ($= \hat{\mathbf{n}}\, dS$)

Then
$$\int_{(c)} \mathbf{F} \cdot \hat{\mathbf{t}}\, ds = \int_{(c)} \mathbf{F} \cdot d\mathbf{s}$$

and when
$$\mathbf{F} = \nabla\phi$$

$$\int_{(c)} (\nabla\phi) \cdot \hat{\mathbf{t}}\, ds = \int_{(c)} d\phi$$

Gauss' Theorem (Green's Theorem)

When S defines a closed region having a volume V

$$\iiint_{(v)} (\nabla \cdot \mathbf{F})\, dV = \iint_{(s)} (\mathbf{F} \cdot \hat{\mathbf{n}})\, dS = \iint_{(s)} \mathbf{F} \cdot dS$$

also
$$\iiint_{(v)} (\nabla\phi)\, dV = \iint_{(s)} \phi\hat{\mathbf{n}}\, dS$$

and
$$\iiint_{(v)} (\nabla \times \mathbf{F})\, dV = \iint_{(s)} (\hat{\mathbf{n}} \times \mathbf{F})\, dS$$

Stokes' Theorem

When C is closed and bounds the open surface S.

$$\iint_{(s)} \hat{\mathbf{n}} \cdot (\nabla \times \mathbf{F})\, dS = \int_{(c)} \mathbf{F} \cdot d\mathbf{s}$$

also
$$\iint_{(s)} (\hat{\mathbf{n}} \times \nabla\phi)\, dS = \int_{(c)} \phi\, d\mathbf{s}$$

Green's Theorem

$$\iint_{(s)} (\nabla\phi \cdot \nabla\theta)\, dS = \iint_{(s)} \phi\hat{\mathbf{n}} \cdot (\nabla\theta)\, dS = \iiint_{(v)} \phi(\nabla^2\theta)\, dV$$

$$= \iint_{(s)} \theta \cdot \hat{\mathbf{n}}(\nabla\phi)\, dS = \iiint_{(v)} \theta(\nabla^2\phi)\, dV$$

MOMENT OF INERTIA FOR VARIOUS BODIES OF MASS

The mass of the body is indicated by m.

Body	Axis	Moment of inertia
Uniform thin rod	Normal to the length, at one end	$m\dfrac{l^2}{3}$
Uniform thin rod	Normal to the length, at the center	$m\dfrac{l^2}{12}$
Thin rectangular sheet, sides a and b	Through the center parallel to b	$m\dfrac{a^2}{12}$
Thin rectangular sheet, sides a and b	Through the center perpendicular to the sheet	$m\dfrac{a^2 + b^2}{12}$
Thin circular sheet of radius r	Normal to the plate through the center	$m\dfrac{r^2}{2}$
Thin circular sheet of radius r	Along any diameter	$m\dfrac{r^2}{4}$
Thin circular ring. Radii r_1 and r_2	Through center normal to plane of ring	$m\dfrac{r_1^2 + r_2^2}{2}$
Thin circular ring. Radii r_1 and r_2	Any diameter	$m\dfrac{r_1^2 + r_2^2}{4}$
Rectangular parallelopiped, edges a, b, and c	Through center perpendicular to face ab, (parallel to edge c)	$m\dfrac{a^2 + b^2}{12}$
Sphere, radius r	Any diameter	$m\dfrac{2}{5}r^2$
Spherical shell, external radius, r_1, internal radius r_2	Any diameter	$m\dfrac{2}{5}\dfrac{(r_1^5 - r_2^5)}{(r_1^3 - r_2^3)}$
Spherical shell, very thin, mean radius, r	Any diameter	$m\dfrac{2}{3}r^2$
Right circular cylinder of radius r, length l	The longitudinal axis of the solid	$m\dfrac{r^2}{2}$
Right circular cylinder of radius r, length l	Transverse diameter	$m\left(\dfrac{r^2}{4} + \dfrac{l^2}{12}\right)$
Hollow circular cylinder, length l, radii r_1 and r_2	The longitudinal axis of the figure	$m\dfrac{(r_1^2 + r_2^2)}{2}$
Thin cylindrical shell, length l, mean radius, r	The longitudinal axis of the figure	mr^2
Hollow circular cylinder, length l, radii r_1 and r_2	Transverse diameter	$m\left[\dfrac{r_1^2 + r_2^2}{4} + \dfrac{l^2}{12}\right]$
Hollow circular cylinder, length l, very thin, mean radius	Transverse diameter	$m\left(\dfrac{r^2}{2} + \dfrac{l^2}{12}\right)$
Elliptic cylinder, length l, transverse semiaxes a and b	Longitudinal axis	$m\left(\dfrac{a^2 + b^2}{4}\right)$
Right cone, altitude h, radius of base r	Axis of the figure	$m\dfrac{3}{10}r^2$
Spheroid of revolution, equatorial radius r	Polar axis	$m\dfrac{2r^2}{5}$
Ellipsoid, axes $2a$, $2b$, $2c$	Axis $2a$	$m\dfrac{(b^2 + c^2)}{5}$

Differential equation	Method of solution
Separation of variables $f_1(x) g_1(y) dx + f_2(x) g_2(y) dy = 0$	$$\int \frac{f_1(x)}{f_2(x)} dx + \int \frac{g_2(y)}{g_1(y)} dy = c$$
Exact equation $M(x,y)dx + N(x,y)dy = 0$ where $\partial M/\partial y = \partial N/\partial x$	$$\int M \partial x + \int \left(N - \frac{\partial}{\partial y} \int M \partial x \right) dy = c$$ where ∂x indicates that the integration is to be performed with respect to x keeping y constant.
Linear first order equation $\frac{dy}{dx} + P(x)y = Q(x)$	$$ye^{\int Pdx} = \int Qe^{\int Pdx} dx + c$$
Bernoulli's equation $\frac{dy}{dx} + P(x)y = Q(x)y^n$	$$ve^{(1-n)\int Pdx} = (1-n)\int Qe^{(1-n)\int Pdx} dx + c$$ where $v = y^{1-n}$. If $n = 1$, the solution is $$\ln y = \int (Q - P) dx + c$$
Homogeneous equation $\frac{dy}{dx} = F\left(\frac{y}{x}\right)$	$$\ln x = \int \frac{dv}{F(v) - v} + c$$ where $v = y/x$. If $F(v) = v$, the solution is $y = cx$
Reducible to homogeneous $(a_1 x + b_1 y + c_1) dx + (a_2 x + b_2 y + c_2) dy = 0$ $\frac{a_1}{a_2} \neq \frac{b_1}{b_2}$	Set $u = a_1 x + b_1 y + c_1$, $v = a_2 x + b_2 y + c_2$ Eliminate x and y and the equation becomes homogenous
Reducible to separable $(a_1 x + b_1 y + c_1) dx + (a_2 x + b_2 y + c_2) dy = 0$ $\frac{a_1}{a_2} = \frac{b_1}{b_2}$	Set $u = a_1 x + b_1 y$ Eliminate x or y and equation becomes separable

$F(xy)\,dx + x\,G(xy)dy = 0$	$\ln x = \displaystyle\int \frac{G(v)\,dv}{v\{G(v) - F(v)\}} + c$ where $v = xy$. If $G(v) = F(v)$, the solution is $xy = c$.

Linear, homogeneous second order equation

$$\frac{d^2 y}{dx^2} + b\,\frac{dy}{dx} + cy = 0$$

b, c are real constants

Let m_1, m_2 be the roots of $m^2 + bm + c = 0$. Then there are 3 cases:

Case 1. m_1, m_2 real and distinct:
$$y = c_1 e^{m_1 x} + c_2 e^{m_2 x}$$

Case 2. m_1, m_2 real and equal:
$$y = c_1 e^{m_1 x} + c_2 x e^{m_1 x}$$

Case 3. $m_1 = p + qi,\ m_2 = p - qi$:
$$y = e^{px}(c_1 \cos qx + c_2 \sin qx)$$

where $p = -b/2,\ q = \sqrt{4c - b^2}/2$

Linear, nonhomogeneous second order equation

$$\frac{d^2 y}{dx^2} + b\,\frac{dy}{dx} + cy = R(x)$$

b, c are real constants

There are 3 cases corresponding to those immediately above:

Case 1.
$$y = c_1 e^{m_1 x} + c_2 e^{m_2 x}$$
$$+ \frac{e^{m_1 x}}{m_1 - m_2}\int e^{-m_1 x}\,R(x)\,dx$$
$$+ \frac{e^{m_2 x}}{m_2 - m_1}\int e^{-m_2 x}\,R(x)\,dx$$

Case 2.
$$y = c_1 e^{m_1 x} + c_2 x e^{m_1 x}$$
$$+ x e^{m_1 x}\int e^{-m_1 x}\,R(x)\,dx$$
$$- e^{m_1 x}\int x e^{-m_1 x}\,R(x)\,dx$$

Case 3.
$$y = e^{px}(c_1 \cos qx + c_2 \sin qx)$$
$$+ \frac{e^{px}\sin qx}{q}\int e^{-px}\,R(x)\cos qx\,dx$$
$$- \frac{e^{px}\cos qx}{q}\int e^{-px}\,R(x)\sin qx\,dx$$

Euler or Cauchy equation	Putting $x = e^t$, the equation becomes
$x^2 \dfrac{d^2 y}{dx^2} + bx \dfrac{dy}{dx} + cy = S(x)$	$\dfrac{d^2 y}{dt^2} + (b - 1) \dfrac{dy}{dt} + cy = S(e^t)$ and can then be solved as a linear second ord equation.
Bessel's equation $x^2 \dfrac{d^2 y}{dx^2} + x \dfrac{dy}{dx} + (\lambda^2 x^2 - n^2) y = 0$	$y = c_1 J_n(\lambda x) + c_2 Y_n(\lambda x)$ See pages 500–534.
Transformed Bessel's equation $x^2 \dfrac{d^2 y}{dx^2} + (2p + 1)x \dfrac{dy}{dx} + (\alpha^2 x^{2r} + \beta^2)y = 0$	$y = x^{-p} \left\{ c_1 J_{q/r}\left(\dfrac{\alpha}{r} x^r\right) + c_2 Y_{q/r}\left(\dfrac{\alpha}{r} x^r\right) \right.$ where $q = \sqrt{p^2 - \beta^2}$.
Legendre's equation $(1 - x^2) \dfrac{d^2 y}{dx^2} - 2x \dfrac{dy}{dx} + n(n + 1)y = 0$	$y = c_1 P_n(x) + c_2 Q_n(x)$ See pages 557, 561, 564–576.

SPECIAL FORMULAS

Certain types of differential equations occur sufficiently often to justify the use of formulas for the corresponding particular solutions. The following set of tables I to XIV covers all first, second and nth order ordinary linear differential equations with constant coefficients for which the right members are of the form $P(x)e^{rx}\sin sx$ or $P(x)e^{rx}\cos sx$, where r and s are constants and $P(x)$ is a polynomial of degree n.

When the right member of a reducible linear partial differential equation with constant coefficients is not zero, particular solutions for certain types of right members are contained in tables XV to XXI. In these tables both F and P are used to denote polynomials, and it is assumed that no denominator is zero. In any formula the roles of x and y may be reversed throughout, changing a formula in which x dominates to one in which y dominates. Tables XIX, XX, XXI are applicable whether the equations are reducible or not. The symbol $\binom{m}{n}$ stands for $\dfrac{m!}{(m-n)!n!}$ and is the $n+1$ st coefficient in the expansion of $(a+b)^m$. Also $0!=1$ by definition.

The tables as herewith given are those contained in the text *Differential Equations* by Ginn and Company (1955) and are published with their kind permission and that of the author, Professor Frederick H. Steen.

Solution of Linear Differential Equations with Constant Coefficients

Any linear differential equation with constant coefficients may be written in the form

$$p(D)y = R(x),$$

where D is the differential operator

$$Dy = \frac{dy}{dx},$$

$p(D)$ is a polynomial in D,
y is the dependent variable,
x is the independent variable,
$R(x)$ is an arbitrary function of x.

A power of D represents repeated differentiation, that is

$$D^n y = \frac{d^n y}{dx^n}.$$

For such an equation, the general solution may be written in the form

$$y = y_c + y_p,$$

where y_p is any particular solution, and y_c is called the *complementary function*. This complementary function is defined as the general solution of the *homogeneous equation*, which is the original differential equation with the right side replaced by zero, i.e.

$$p(D)y = 0$$

The complementary function y_c may be determined as follows:

1. Factor the polynomial $p(D)$ into real and complex linear factors, just as if D were a variable instead of an operator.

2. For each non-repeated linear factor of the form $(D - a)$, where a is real, write down a term of the form

$$ce^{ax},$$

where c is an arbitrary constant.

3. For each repeated real linear factor of the form $(D - a)^n$, write down n terms of the form

$$c_1e^{ax} + c_2xe^{ax} + c_3x^2e^{ax} + \cdots + c_nx^{n-1}e^{ax},$$

where the c_i's are arbitrary constants.

4. For each non-repeated conjugate complex pair of factors of the form $(D - a + ib)(D - a - ib)$, write down 2 terms of the form

$$c_1e^{ax} \cos bx + c_2e^{ax} \sin bx$$

5. For each repeated conjugate complex pair of factors of the form $(D - a + ib)^n(D - a - ib)^n$, write down $2n$ terms of the form

$$c_1e^{ax} \cos bx + c_2e^{ax} \sin bx + c_3xe^{ax} \cos bx + c_4xe^{ax} \sin bx + \cdots$$
$$+ c_{2n-1}x^{n-1}e^{ax} \cos bx + c_{2n}x^{n-1}e^{ax} \sin bx$$

6. The sum of all the terms thus written down is the complementary function y_c.

To find the particular solution y_p, use the following tables, as shown in the examples. For cases not shown in the tables, there are various methods of finding y_p. The most general method is called *variation of parameters*. The following example illustrates the method:

Find y_p for $(D^2 - 4)y = e^x$.

This example can be solved most easily by use of equation 63 in the tables following. However it is given here as an example of the method of variation of parameters.

The complementary function is

$$y_c = c_1e^{2x} + c_2e^{-2x}$$

To find y_p, replace the constants in the complementary function with unknown functions,

$$y_p = ue^{2x} + ve^{-2x}.$$

We now prepare to substitute this assumed solution into the original equation. We begin by taking all the necessary derivatives:

$$y_p = ue^{2x} + ve^{-2x}$$
$$y_p' = 2ue^{2x} - 2ve^{-2x} + u'e^{2x} + v'e^{-2x}$$

For each derivative of y_p except the highest, we set the sum of all the terms containing u' and v' to 0. Thus the above equation becomes

$$u'e^{2x} + v'e^{-2x} = 0 \quad \text{and} \quad y_p' = 2ue^{2x} - 2ve^{-2x}$$

Continuing to differentiate, we have

$$y_p'' = 4ue^{2x} + 4ve^{-2x} + 2u'e^{2x} - 2v'e^{-2x}$$

When we substitute into the original equation, all the terms not containing u' or v' cancel out. This is a consequence of the method by which y_p was set up.

Thus all that is necessary is to write down the terms containing u' or v' in the highest order derivative of y_p, multiply by the constant coefficient of the highest power of D in $p(D)$, and set it equal to $R(x)$. Together with the previous terms in u' and v' which were set equal to 0, this gives us as many linear equations in the first derivatives of the unknown functions as there are unknown functions. The first derivatives may then be solved for by algebra, and the unknown functions found by integration. In the present example, this becomes

$$u'e^{2x} + v'e^{-2x} = 0$$
$$2u'e^{2x} - 2v'e^{-2x} = e^x.$$

We eliminate v' and u' separately, getting

$$4u'e^{2x} = e^x$$
$$4v'e^{-2x} = -e^x.$$

Thus

$$u' = \tfrac{1}{4}e^{-x}$$
$$v' = -\tfrac{1}{4}e^{3x}.$$

Therefore, by integrating

$$u = -\tfrac{1}{4}e^{-x}$$
$$v = -\tfrac{1}{12}e^{3x}.$$

A constant of integration is not needed, since we need only one particular solution. Thus

$$y_p = ue^{2x} + ve^{-2x} = -\tfrac{1}{4}e^{-x}e^{2x} - \tfrac{1}{12}e^{3x}e^{-2x}$$
$$= -\tfrac{1}{4}e^x - \tfrac{1}{12}e^x = -\tfrac{1}{3}e^x,$$

and the general solution is

$$y = y_c + y_p = c_1e^{2x} + c_2e^{-2x} - \tfrac{1}{3}e^x.$$

The following examples illustrate the use of the tables.

Example 1. Solve $(D^2 - 4)y = \sin 3x$.

Substitution of $q = -4, s = 3$ in formula 24 gives

$$y_p = \frac{\sin 3x}{-9 - 4},$$

wherefore the general solution is

$$y = c_1e^{2x} + c_2e^{-2x} - \frac{\sin 3x}{13}.$$

Example 2. Obtain a particular solution of $(D^2 - 4D + 5)y = x^2e^{3x}\sin x$.

Applying formula 40 with $a = 2, b = 1, r = 3, s = 1, P(x) = x^2, s + b = 2, s - b = 0,$
$a - r = -1, (a - r)^2 + (s + b)^2 = 5, (a - r)^2 + (s - b)^2 = 1$, we have

$$y_p = \frac{e^{3x}\sin x}{2}\left[\left(\frac{2}{5} - \frac{0}{1}\right)x^2 + \left(\frac{2(-1)2}{25} - \frac{2(-1)0}{1}\right)2x\right.$$

$$\left. + \left(\frac{3\cdot 1\cdot 2 - 2^3}{125} - \frac{3\cdot 1\cdot 0 - 0}{1}\right)2\right]$$

$$- \frac{e^{3x}\cos x}{2}\left[\left(\frac{-1}{5} - \frac{-1}{1}\right)x^2 + \left(\frac{1 - 4}{25} - \frac{1 - 0}{1}\right)2x\right.$$

$$\left. + \left(\frac{-1 - 3(-1)4}{125} - \frac{-1 - 3(-1)0}{1}\right)2\right]$$

$$= (\tfrac{1}{5}x^2 - \tfrac{4}{25}x - \tfrac{2}{125})e^{3x}\sin x + (-\tfrac{2}{5}x^2 + \tfrac{28}{25}x - \tfrac{136}{125})e^{3x}\cos x.$$

The special formulas effect a very considerable saving of time in problems of this type.

Example 3.   Obtain a particular solution of $(D^2 - 4D + 5)y = x^2e^{2x} \cos x$.   (Compare with Example 2.)

Formula 40 is not applicable here since for this equation $r = a$, $s = b$, wherefore the denominator $(a - r)^2 + (s - b)^2 = 0$.   We turn instead to formula 44.   Substituting $a = 2$, $b = 1$, $P(x) = x^2$ and replacing sin by cos, cos by $-\sin$, we obtain

$$y_p = \frac{e^{2x}\cos x}{4}\left(x^2 - \tfrac{2}{4}\right) + \frac{e^{2x}\sin x}{2}\int \left(x^2 - \tfrac{1}{2}\right)dx$$

$$= \left(\frac{x^2}{4} - \frac{1}{8}\right)e^{2x}\cos x + \left(\frac{x^3}{6} - \frac{x}{4}\right)e^{2x}\sin x,$$

which is the required solution.

Example 4.   Find z_p for $(D_x - 3D_y)z = \ln(y + 3x)$.

Referring to Table XV we note that formula 69 (not 68) is applicable.   This gives

$$z_p = x \ln(y + 3x).$$

It is easily seen that $-\dfrac{y}{3}\ln(y + 3x)$ would serve equally well.

Example 5.   Solve $(D_x + 2D_y - 4)z = y \cos(y - 2x)$.

Since R in formula 76 contains a polynomial in x, not y, we rewrite the given equation in the form

$$(D_y + \tfrac{1}{2}D_x - 2)z = \tfrac{1}{2}y \cos(y - 2x).$$

Then

$$z_c = e^{2y}F(x - \tfrac{1}{2}y) = e^{2y}f(2x - y),$$

and by the formula

$$z_p = -\tfrac{1}{2}\cos(y - 2x)\cdot\left(\frac{y}{2} + \frac{\frac{1}{2}}{2}\right)$$

$$= -\tfrac{1}{8}(2y + 1)\cos(y - 2x).$$

Example 6.   Find z_p for $(D_x + 4D_y)^3z = (2x - y)^2$.

Using formula 79, we obtain

$$z_p = \frac{\int\int\int u^2\,du^3}{[2 + 4(-1)]^3} = \frac{u^5}{5\cdot4\cdot3\cdot(-8)} = -\frac{(2x - y)^5}{480}.$$

Example 7.   Find z_p for $(D_x^3 + 5D_x^2D_y - 7D_x + 4)z = e^{2x+3y}$.

By formula 87

$$z_p = \frac{e^{2x+3y}}{2^3 + 5\cdot2^2\cdot3 - 7\cdot2 + 4} = \frac{e^{2x+3y}}{58}.$$

Example 8.   Find z_p for

$$(D_x^4 + 6D_x^3D_y + D_xD_y + D_y^2 + 9)z = \sin(3x + 4y).$$

Since every term in the left member is of *even* degree in the two operators D_x and D_y, formula 90 is applicable.

It gives

$$z_p = \frac{\sin(3x + 4y)}{(-9)^2 + 6(-9)(-12) + (-12) + (-16) + 9}$$

$$= \frac{\sin(3x + 4y)}{710}$$

DIFFERENTIAL EQUATIONS

TABLE I: $(D - a)y = R$

R	y_p
1. e^{rx}	$\dfrac{e^{rx}}{r-a}$
2. $\sin sx$*	$-\dfrac{a\sin sx + s\cos sx}{a^2+s^2} = -\dfrac{1}{\sqrt{a^2+s^2}}\sin\left(sx + \tan^{-1}\dfrac{s}{a}\right)$
3. $P(x)$	$-\dfrac{1}{a}\left[P(x) + \dfrac{P'(x)}{a} + \dfrac{P''(x)}{a^2} + \cdots + \dfrac{P^{(n)}(x)}{a^n}\right]$
4. $e^{rx}\sin sx$*	Replace a by $a - r$ in formula 2 and multiply by e^{rx}.
5. $P(x)e^{rx}$	Replace a by $a - r$ in formula 3 and multiply by e^{rx}.
6. $P(x)\sin sx$*	$-\sin sx\left[\dfrac{a}{a^2+s^2}P(x) + \dfrac{a^2-s^2}{(a^2+s^2)^2}P'(x) + \dfrac{a^3-3as^2}{(a^2+s^2)^3}P''(x) + \cdots\right.$ $\left. + \dfrac{a^k - \binom{k}{2}a^{k-2}s^2 + \binom{k}{4}a^{k-4}s^4 - \cdots}{(a^2+s^2)^k}P^{(k-1)}(x) + \cdots\right]$ $-\cos sx\left[\dfrac{s}{a^2+s^2}P(x) + \dfrac{2as}{(a^2+s^2)^2}P'(x) + \dfrac{3a^2s - s^3}{(a^2+s^2)^3}P''(x) + \cdots\right.$ $\left. + \dfrac{\binom{k}{1}a^{k-1}s - \binom{k}{3}a^{k-3}s^3 + \cdots}{(a^2+s^2)^k}P^{(k-1)}(x) + \cdots\right]$
7. $P(x)e^{rx}\sin sx$*	Replace a by $a - r$ in formula 6 and multiply by e^{rx}.
8. e^{ax}	xe^{ax}
9. $e^{ax}\sin sx$*	$-\dfrac{e^{ax}\cos sx}{s}$
10. $P(x)e^{ax}$	$e^{ax}\displaystyle\int P(x)\,dx$
11. $P(x)e^{ax}\sin sx$*	$\dfrac{e^{ax}\sin sx}{s}\left[\dfrac{P'(x)}{s^3} - \dfrac{P'''(x)}{s^3} + \dfrac{P^{v}(x)}{s^5} - \cdots\right] - \dfrac{e^{ax}\cos sx}{s}\left[P(x) - \dfrac{P''(x)}{s^2} + \dfrac{P^{iv}(x)}{s^4} - \cdots\right]$

* For $\cos sx$ in R replace "sin" by "cos" and "cos" by "$-\sin$" in y_p.

$$D^n = \dfrac{d^n}{dx^n} \qquad \binom{m}{n} = \dfrac{m!}{(m-n)!\,n!} \qquad 0! = 1$$

DIFFERENTIAL EQUATIONS (Continued)

TABLE II: $(D - a)^2 y = R$

R	y_p
12. e^{rx}	$\dfrac{e^{rx}}{(r-a)^2}$
13. $\sin sx$*	$\dfrac{1}{(a^2+s^2)^2}[(a^2-s^2)\sin sx + 2as\cos sx] = \dfrac{1}{a^2+s^2}\sin\left(sx+\tan^{-1}\dfrac{2as}{a^2-s^2}\right)$
14. $P(x)$	$\dfrac{1}{a^2}\left[P(x) + \dfrac{2P'(x)}{a} + \dfrac{3P''(x)}{a^2} + \cdots + \dfrac{(n+1)P^{(n)}(x)}{a^n}\right]$
15. $e^{rx}\sin sx$*	Replace a by $a-r$ in formula 13 and multiply by e^{rx}.
16. $P(x)e^{rx}$	Replace a by $a-r$ in formula 14 and multiply by e^{rx}.
17. $P(x)\sin sx$*	$\sin sx\left[\dfrac{a^2-s^2}{(a^2+s^2)^2}P(x) + 2\dfrac{a^3-3as^2}{(a^2+s^2)^3}P'(x) + 3\dfrac{a^4-6a^2s^2+s^4}{(a^2+s^2)^4}P''(x) + \cdots \right.$

$$+ (k-1)\frac{a^k - \binom{k}{2}a^{k-2}s^2 + \binom{k}{4}a^{k-4}s^4 - \cdots}{(a^2+s^2)^k}P^{(k-2)}(x) + \cdots\Bigg]$$

$$+ \cos sx\left[\frac{2as}{(a^2+s^2)^2}P(x) + 2\frac{3a^2s-s^3}{(a^2+s^2)^3}P'(x) + 3\frac{4a^3s-4as^3}{(a^2+s^2)^4}P''(x) + \cdots \right.$$

$$+ (k-1)\frac{\binom{k}{1}a^{k-1}s - \binom{k}{3}a^{k-3}s^3 + \cdots}{(a^2+s^2)^k}P^{(k-2)}(x) + \cdots\Bigg]$$

R	y_p
18. $P(x)e^{rx}\sin sx$*	Replace a by $a-r$ in formula 17 and multiply by e^{rx}.
19. e^{az}	$\tfrac{1}{2}x^2 e^{az}$
20. $e^{az}\sin sx$*	$-\dfrac{e^{az}\sin sx}{s^2}$
21. $P(x)e^{az}$	$e^{az}\displaystyle\iint P(x)\,dx\,dx$
22. $P(x)e^{az}\sin sx$*	$-\dfrac{e^{az}\sin sx}{s^2}\left[P(x) - \dfrac{3P''(x)}{s^2} + \dfrac{5P^{iv}(x)}{s^4} - \dfrac{7P^{vi}(x)}{s^6} + \cdots \right.$

$$- \frac{e^{az}\cos sx}{s^2}\left[\frac{2P'(\cdot)}{s} - \frac{4P'''(x)}{s^3} + \frac{6P^{v}(x)}{s^5} - \cdots\right]$$

* For $\cos sx$ in R replace "sin" by "cos" and "cos" by "− sin" in y_p.

DIFFERENTIAL EQUATIONS (Continued)

TABLE III: $(D^2 + q)y = R$

R	y_p
23. e^{rx}	$\dfrac{e^{rx}}{r^2+q}$
24. $\sin sx$*	$\dfrac{\sin sx}{-s^2+q}$
25. $P(x)$	$\dfrac{1}{q}\left[P(x) - \dfrac{P''(x)}{q} + \dfrac{P^{iv}(x)}{q^2} - \cdots + (-1)^k\,\dfrac{P^{(2k)}(x)}{q^k}\cdots\right]$
26. $e^{rx}\sin sx$*	$\dfrac{(r^2-s^2+q)e^{rx}\sin sx - 2\,rse^{rx}\cos sx}{(r^2-s^2+q)^2+(2rs)^2} = \dfrac{e^{rx}}{\sqrt{(r^2-s^2+q)^2+(2rs)^2}}\sin\left[sx - \tan^{-1}\dfrac{2rs}{r^2-s^2+q}\right]$
27. $P(x)e^{rx}$	$\dfrac{e^{rx}}{r^2+q}\left[P(x) - \dfrac{2r}{r^2+q}P'(x) + \dfrac{3r^2-q}{(r^2+q)^2}P''(x) - \dfrac{4r^3-4qr}{(r^2+q)^3}P'''(x)\right.$ $+ \cdots + (-1)^{k-1}\dfrac{\binom{k}{1}r^{k-1} - \binom{k}{3}r^{k-3}q + \binom{k}{5}r^{k-5}q^2 - \cdots}{(r^2+q)^{k-1}}P^{(k-1)}(x) + \cdots\Big]$
28. $P(x)\sin sx$*	$\dfrac{\sin sx}{(-s^2+q)}\left[P(x) - \dfrac{3s^2+q}{(-s^2+q)^2}P''(x) + \dfrac{5s^4+10s^2q+q^2}{(-s^2+q)^4}P^{iv}(x) + \cdots\right.$ $+ (-1)^k\,\dfrac{\binom{2k+1}{1}s^{2k} + \binom{2k+1}{3}s^{2k-2}q + \binom{2k+1}{5}s^{2k-4}q^2 + \cdots}{(-s^2+q)^{2k}}P^{(2k)}(x) + \cdots\Big]$ $- \dfrac{s\cos sx}{(-s^2+q)}\left[\dfrac{2P'(x)}{(-s^2+q)} - \dfrac{4s^2+4q}{(-s^2+q)^3}P'''(x) + \cdots\right.$ $+ (-1)^{k+1}\dfrac{\binom{2k}{1}s^{2k-2} + \binom{2k}{3}s^{2k-4}q + \cdots}{(-s^2+q)^{2k-1}}P^{(2k-1)}(x) + \cdots\Big]$

TABLE IV: $(D^2 + b^2)y = R$

R	y_p
29. $\sin bx$*	$-\dfrac{x\cos bx}{2b}$
30. $P(x)\sin bx$*	$-\dfrac{x\cos bx}{2b}\left[P(x) - \dfrac{P''(x)}{(2b)^2} + \dfrac{P^{iv}(x)}{(2b)^4} - \cdots\right] - \dfrac{\sin bx}{(2b)^2}\left[P(x) - \dfrac{P''(x)}{(2b)^2} + \cdots\right] - \dfrac{\cos bx}{2b}\displaystyle\int\left[P(x) - \dfrac{P''(x)}{(2b)^2} + \cdots\right]dx$

* For cos sx in R replace "sin" by "cos" and "cos" by " $-$ sin" in y_p.

DIFFERENTIAL EQUATIONS (Continued)

TABLE V: $(D^2 + pD + q)y = R$

R	y_p
31. e^{rx}	$\dfrac{e^{rx}}{r^2 + pr + q}$
32. $\sin sx$*	$\dfrac{(q - s^2)\sin sx - ps\cos sx}{(q - s^2)^2 + (ps)^2} = \dfrac{1}{\sqrt{(q - s^2)^2 + (ps)^2}}\sin\left(sx - \tan^{-1}\dfrac{ps}{q - s^2}\right)$
33. $P(x)$	$\dfrac{1}{q}\Big[P(x) - \dfrac{p}{q}P'(x) + \dfrac{p^2 - q}{q^2}P''(x) - \dfrac{p^3 - 2pq}{q^3}P'''(x) + \cdots$ $+ (-1)^n\dfrac{p^n - \binom{n-1}{1}p^{n-2}q + \binom{n-2}{2}p^{n-4}q^2 - \cdots}{q^n}P^{(n)}(x)\Big]$
34. $e^{rx}\sin sx$*	Replace p by $p + 2r$, q by $q + pr + r^2$ in formula 32 and multiply by e^{rx}.
35. $P(x)e^{rx}$	Replace p by $p + 2r$, q by $q + pr + r^2$ in formula 33 and multiply by e^{rx}.

TABLE VI: $(D - b)(D - a)y = R$

R	y_p
36. $P(x)\sin sx$*	$\dfrac{\sin sx}{b - a}\Big[\left(\dfrac{a}{a^2 + s^2} - \dfrac{b}{b^2 + s^2}\right)P(x) + \left(\dfrac{a^2 - s^2}{(a^2 + s^2)^2} - \dfrac{b^2 - s^2}{(b^2 + s^2)^2}\right)P'(x)$ $+ \left(\dfrac{a^3 - 3as^2}{(a^2 + s^2)^3} - \dfrac{b^3 - 3bs^2}{(b^2 + s^2)^3}\right)P''(x) + \cdots\Big]$ $+ \dfrac{\cos sx}{b - a}\Big[\left(\dfrac{s}{a^2 + s^2} - \dfrac{s}{b^2 + s^2}\right)P(x) + \left(\dfrac{2as}{(a^2 + s^2)^2} - \dfrac{2bs}{(b^2 + s^2)^2}\right)P'(x)$ $+ \left(\dfrac{3a^2s - s^3}{(a^2 + s^2)^3} - \dfrac{3b^2s - s^3}{(b^2 + s^2)^3}\right)P''(x) + \cdots\Big]$†
37. $P(x)e^{rx}\sin sx$*	Replace a by $a - r$, b by $b - r$ in formula 36 and multiply by e^{rx}.
38. $P(x)e^{ax}$	$\dfrac{e^{ax}}{a - b}\Big[\displaystyle\int P(x)dx + \dfrac{P(x)}{(b - a)} + \dfrac{P'(x)}{(b - a)^2} + \dfrac{P''(x)}{(b - a)^3} + \cdots + \dfrac{P^{(n)}(x)}{(b - a)^{n+1}}\Big]$

* For cos sx in R replace "sin" by "cos" and "cos" by "− sin" in y_p.

† For additional terms, compare with formula 6.

DIFFERENTIAL EQUATIONS (Continued)

TABLE VII: $(D^2 - 2aD + a^2 + b^2)y = R$

R	y_p

39. $P(x)\sin sx$*

$$\frac{\sin sx}{2b}\left[\left(\frac{s+b}{a^2+(s+b)^2} - \frac{s-b}{a^2+(s-b)^2}\right)P(x) + \left(\frac{2a(s+b)}{[a^2+(s+b)^2]^2} - \frac{2a(s-b)}{[a^2+(s-b)^2]^2}\right)P'(x)\right.$$

$$+ \left(\frac{3a^2(s+b)-(s+b)^3}{[a^2+(s+b)^2]^3} - \frac{3a^2(s-b)-(s-b)^3}{[a^2+(s-b)^2]^3}\right)P''(x) + \cdots\right]$$

$$- \frac{\cos sx}{2b}\left[\left(\frac{a}{a^2+(s+b)^2} - \frac{a}{a^2+(s-b)^2}\right)P(x) + \left(\frac{a^2-(s+b)^2}{[a^2+(s+b)^2]^2} - \frac{a^2-(s-b)^2}{[a^2+(s-b)^2]^2}\right)P'(x)\right.$$

$$+ \left(\frac{a^3-3a(s+b)^2}{[a^2+(s+b)^2]^3} - \frac{a^3-3a(s-b)^2}{[a^2+(s-b)^2]^3}\right)P''(x) + \cdots\right]^\dagger$$

40. $P(x)e^{rx}\sin sx$* Replace a by $a-r$ in formula 39 and multiply by e^{rx}.

41. $P(x)e^{ax}$

$$\frac{e^{ax}}{b^2}\left[P(x) - \frac{P''(x)}{b^2} + \frac{P^{iv}(x)}{b^4} - \cdots\right]$$

42. $e^{ax}\sin sx$*

$$\frac{e^{ax}\sin sx}{-s^2+b^2}$$

43. $e^{ax}\sin bx$*

$$-\frac{xe^{ax}\cos bx}{2b}$$

44. $P(x)e^{ax}\sin bx$*

$$\frac{e^{ax}\sin bx}{(2b)^2}\left[P(x) - \frac{P''(x)}{(2b)^2} + \frac{P^{iv}(x)}{(2b)^4} - \cdots\right] - \frac{e^{ax}\cos bx}{2b}\int\left[P(x) - \frac{P''(x)}{(2b)^2} + \frac{P^{iv}(x)}{(2b)^4} - \cdots\right]dx$$

* For cos sx in R replace "sin" by "cos" and "cos" by "− sin" in y_p.

† For additional terms, compare with formula 6.

DIFFERENTIAL EQUATIONS (Continued)

TABLE VIII: $f(D)y = [D^n + a_{n-1}D^{n-1} + \cdots + a_1 D + a_0]y = R$

R	y_p
45. e^{rx}	$\dfrac{e^{rx}}{f(r)}$
46. $\sin sx\,*$	$\dfrac{[a_0 - a_2 s^2 + a_4 s^4 - \cdots]\sin sx - [a_1 s - a_3 s^3 + a_5 s^5 + \cdots]\cos sx}{[a_0 - a_2 s^2 + a_4 s^4 - \cdots]^2 + [a_1 s - a_3 s^3 + a_5 s^5 - \cdots]^2}$

TABLE IX: $f(D^2)y = R$

47. $\sin sx\,*$	$\dfrac{\sin sx}{f(-s^2)} = \dfrac{\sin sx}{a_0 - a_2 s^2 + \cdots \pm s^{2n}}$

TABLE X: $(D - a)^n y = R$

48. e^{rx}	$\dfrac{e^{rx}}{(r - a)^n}$
49. $\sin sx\,*$	$\dfrac{(-1)^n}{(a^2 + s^2)^n}\left\{\left[a^n - \binom{n}{2}a^{n-2}s^2 + \binom{n}{4}a^{n-4}s^4 - \cdots\right]\sin sx + \left[\binom{n}{1}a^{n-1}s - \binom{n}{3}a^{n-3}s^3 + \cdots\right]\cos sx\right\}$
50. $P(x)$	$\dfrac{(-1)^n}{a^n}\left[P(x) + \binom{n}{1}\dfrac{P'(x)}{a} + \binom{n+1}{2}\dfrac{P''(x)}{a^2} + \binom{n+2}{3}\dfrac{P'''(x)}{a^3} + \cdots\right]$
51. $e^{rx}\sin sx\,*$	Replace a by $a - r$ in formula 49 and multiply by e^{rx}.
52. $e^{rx}P(x)$	Replace a by $a - r$ in formula 50 and multiply by e^{rx}.

* For $\cos sx$ in R replace "sin" by "cos" and "cos" by "$-$ sin" in y_p.

DIFFERENTIAL EQUATIONS (Continued)

53. $P(x)\sin sx$*

$(-1)^n \sin sx[A_n P(x) + \binom{n}{1}A_{n+1}P'(x) + \binom{n+1}{2}A_{n+2}P''(x) + \binom{n+2}{3}A_{n+3}P'''(x) + \cdots]$
$+ (-1)^n \cos sx[B_n P(x) + \binom{n}{1}B_{n+1}P'(x) + \binom{n+1}{2}B_{n+2}P''(x) + \binom{n+2}{3}B_{n+3}P'''(x) + \cdots]$

$A_1 = \dfrac{a}{a^2+s^2}$, $A_2 = \dfrac{a^2-s^2}{(a^2+s^2)^2}$, $\cdots$, $A_k = \dfrac{a^k - \binom{k}{2}a^{k-2}s^2 + \binom{k}{4}a^{k-4}s^4 - \cdots}{(a^2+s^2)^k}$

$B_1 = \dfrac{s}{a^2+s^2}$, $B_2 = \dfrac{2as}{(a^2+s^2)^2}$, $\cdots$, $B_k = \dfrac{\binom{k}{1}a^{k-1}s - \binom{k}{3}a^{k-3}s^3 + \cdots}{(a^2+s^2)^k}$

54. $P(x)e^{rx}\sin sx$* Replace a by $a - r$ in formula 53 and multiply by e^{rx}.

55. $e^{ax}P(x)$ $\quad e^{ax}\displaystyle\iint\cdots\int P(x)\,dx^n$

56. $P(x)e^{ax}\sin sx$*

$(-1)^{\frac{n-1}{2}}\dfrac{e^{ax}\sin sx}{s^n}\left[\binom{n}{n-1}\dfrac{P'(x)}{s} - \binom{n+2}{n-1}\dfrac{P'''(x)}{s^3} + \binom{n+4}{n-1}\dfrac{P^{\mathrm{v}}(x)}{s^5} - \cdots\right]$
$+ (-1)^{\frac{n+1}{2}}\dfrac{e^{ax}\cos sx}{s^n}\left[\binom{n-1}{n-1}P(x) - \binom{n+1}{n-1}\dfrac{P''(x)}{s^2} + \binom{n+3}{n-1}\dfrac{P^{\mathrm{iv}}(x)}{s^4} - \cdots\right]$ (n odd)

$(-1)^{\frac{n}{2}}\dfrac{e^{ax}\sin sx}{s^n}\left[\binom{n-1}{n-1}P(x) - \binom{n+1}{n-1}\dfrac{P''(x)}{s^2} + \binom{n+3}{n-1}\dfrac{P^{\mathrm{iv}}(x)}{s^4} - \cdots\right]$
$+ (-1)^{\frac{n}{2}}\dfrac{e^{ax}\cos sx}{s^n}\left[\binom{n}{n-1}\dfrac{P'(x)}{s} - \binom{n+2}{n-1}\dfrac{P'''(x)}{s^3} + \binom{n+4}{n-1}\dfrac{P^{\mathrm{v}}(x)}{s^5} - \cdots\right]$ (n even)

TABLE XI: $(D - a)^n f(D)y = R$

57. e^{ax} $\quad \dfrac{x^n}{n!}\cdot\dfrac{e^{ax}}{f(a)}$

* For cos sx in R replace "sin" by "cos" and "cos" by "$-$ sin" in y_p.

DIFFERENTIAL EQUATIONS (Continued)

TABLE XII: $(D^2 + q)^n y = R$

R	y_p
58. e^{rx}	$e^{rx}/(r^2+q)^n$
59. $\sin sx$*	$\sin sx/(q-s^2)^n$
60. $P(x)$	$\dfrac{1}{q^n}\left[P(x) - \binom{n}{1}\dfrac{P''(x)}{q} + \binom{n+1}{2}\dfrac{P^{iv}(x)}{q^2} - \binom{n+2}{3}\dfrac{P^{vi}(x)}{q^3} + \cdots\right]$
61. $e^{rx}\sin sx$*	$\dfrac{e^{rx}}{(A^2+B^2)^n}\left\{[A^n - \binom{n}{2}A^{n-2}B^2 + \binom{n}{4}A^{n-4}B^4 - \cdots]\sin sx - [\binom{n}{1}A^{n-1}B - \binom{n}{3}A^{n-3}B^3 + \cdots]\cos sx\right\}$

$$A = r^2 - s^2 + q, \qquad B = 2rs$$

TABLE XIII: $(D^2 + b^2)^n y = R$

R	y_p
62. $\sin bx$*	$(-1)^{\frac{n+1}{2}}\dfrac{x^n\cos bx}{n!(2b)^n}$ (n odd), $\qquad (-1)^{\frac{n}{2}}\dfrac{x^n\sin bx}{n!(2b)^n}$ (n even)

TABLE XIV: $(D^n - q)y = R$

R	y_p
63. e^{rx}	$e^{rx}/(r^n - q)$
64. $P(x)$	$-\dfrac{1}{q}\left[P(x)\,\dfrac{P^{(n)}(x)}{q} + \dfrac{P^{(2n)}(x)}{q^2} + \cdots\right]$
65. $\sin sx$*	$-\dfrac{q\sin sx + (-1)^{\frac{n-1}{2}}s^n\cos sx}{q^2+s^{2n}}$ (n odd), $\qquad \dfrac{\sin sx}{(-s^2)^{n/2}-q}$ (n even)
66. $e^{rx}\sin sx$*	$\dfrac{Ae^{rx}\sin sr - Be^{rx}\cos sx}{A^2+B^2} = \dfrac{e^{rx}}{\sqrt{A^2+B^2}}\sin\left(sx - \tan^{-1}\dfrac{B}{A}\right)$

$$A = [r^n - \binom{n}{2}r^{n-2}s^2 + \binom{n}{4}r^{n-4}s^4 - \cdots] - q, \qquad B = [\binom{n}{1}r^{n-1}s - \binom{n}{3}r^{n-3}s^3 + \cdots]$$

*For cos sx in R replace "sin" by "cos" and "cos" by " $-$ sin" in y_p.

DIFFERENTIAL EQUATIONS (Continued)

TABLE XV: $(D_x + mD_y)z = R$

R	z_p
67. e^{ax+by}	$\dfrac{e^{ax+by}}{a+mb}$
68. $f(ax+by)$	$\dfrac{\int f(u)du}{a+mb},\ u=ax+by$
69. $f(y-mx)$	$xf(y-mx)$
70. $\phi(x,y)f(y-mx)$	$f(y-mx)\int \phi(x,\,a+mx)dx \quad (a=y-mx \text{ after integration})$

TABLE XVI: $(D_x + mD_y - k)z = R$

71. e^{ax+by}	$\dfrac{e^{ax+by}}{a+mb-k}$
72. $\sin(ax+by)$*	$-\dfrac{(a+bm)\cos(ax+by)+k\sin(ax+by)}{(a+bm)^2+k^2}$
73. $e^{\alpha x+\beta y}\sin(ax+by)$	Replace k in 72 by $k-\alpha-m\beta$ and multiply by $e^{\alpha x+\beta y}$
74. $e^{zk}f(ax+by)$	$\dfrac{e^{kx}\int f(u)du}{a+mb},\ u=ax+by$
75. $f(y-mx)$	$-\dfrac{f(y-mx)}{k}$
76. $P(x)f(y-mx)$	$-\dfrac{1}{k}f(y-mx)\left[P(x)+\dfrac{P'(x)}{k}+\dfrac{P''(x)}{k^2}+\cdots+\dfrac{P^{(n)}(x)}{k^n}\right]$
77. $e^{kx}f(y-mx)$	$xe^{kx}f(y-mx)$

* For $\cos(ax+by)$ replace "sin" by "cos," and "cos" by "$-\sin$" in z_p.

$$D_x=\frac{\partial}{\partial x}; \qquad D_y=\frac{\partial}{\partial y}; \qquad D_x^kD_y^r=\frac{\partial^{k+r}}{\partial_x^k\partial_y^r}$$

DIFFERENTIAL EQUATIONS (Continued)

TABLE XVII: $(D_z + mD_y)^n z = R$

R	z_p
78. e^{ax+by}	$\dfrac{e^{ax+by}}{(a+mb)^n}$
79. $f(ax + by)$	$\dfrac{\int\int\cdots\int f(u)du^n}{(a+mb)^n}$, $u = ax + by$
80. $f(y - mx)$	$\dfrac{x^n}{n!}f(y-mx)$
81. $\phi(x,y)f(y+mx)$	$f(y-mx)\int\int\cdots\int\phi(x, a+mx)dx^n$ $(a = y - mx$ after integration$)$

TABLE XVIII: $(D_z + mD_y - k)^n z = R$

R	z_p
82. e^{ax+by}	$\dfrac{e^{ax+by}}{(a+mb-k)^n}$
83. $f(y - mx)$	$\dfrac{(-1)^n f(y-mx)}{k^n}$
84. $P(x)f(y-mx)$	$\dfrac{(-1)^n}{k^n}f(y-mx)\left[P(x) + \binom{n}{1}\dfrac{P'(x)}{k} + \binom{n+1}{2}\dfrac{P''(x)}{k^2} + \binom{n+2}{3}\dfrac{P'''(x)}{k^3} + \cdots\right]$
85. $e^{kx}f(ax + by)$	$\dfrac{e^{kx}\int\int\cdots\int f(u)du^n}{(a+mb)^n}$, $u = ax + by$
86. $e^{kx}f(y - mx)$	$\dfrac{x^n}{n!}e^{kx}f(y-mx)$

DIFFERENTIAL EQUATIONS (Continued)

TABLE XIX: $[D_x{}^n + a_1 D_x{}^{n-1} D_y + a_2 D_x{}^{n-2} D_y{}^2 + \cdots + a^n D_y{}^n] z = R$

87. e^{ax+by}
$$\frac{e^{ax+by}}{a + a_1 a^{n-1} b + a_2 a^{n-2} b^2 + \cdots + a_n b^n}$$

88. $f(ax + by)$
$$\frac{\int\int \cdots \int f(u) du^n}{a^n + a_1 a^{n-1} b + a_2 a^{n-2} b^2 + \cdots + a^n b^n}, \quad (u = ax + by)$$

TABLE XX: $F(D_x, D_y) z = R$

89. e^{ax+by}
$$\frac{e^{ax+by}}{F(a, b)}$$

TABLE XXI: $F(D_x{}^2, D_x D_y, D_y{}^2) z = R$

90. $\sin(ax + by)^*$
$$\frac{\sin(ax + by)}{F(-a^2, -ab, -b^2)}$$

* For $\cos(ax + by)$ replace "sin" by "cos", and "cos" by "$-\sin$" in z_p.

The Gamma Function

Definition: $\Gamma(n) = \int_{0}^{\infty} t^{n-1} e^{-t} dt \quad n > 0$

Recursion Formula: $\Gamma(n + 1) = n\Gamma(n)$

$\Gamma(n + 1) = n!$ if $n = 0,1,2, \ldots$ where $0! = 1$

For $n < 0$ the gamma function can be defined by using

$$\Gamma(n) = \frac{\Gamma(n + 1)}{n}$$

Graph:

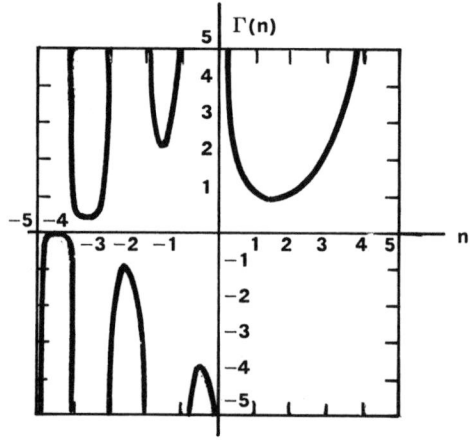

Special Values: $\Gamma(\tfrac{1}{2}) = \sqrt{\pi}$

$$\Gamma(m + \tfrac{1}{2}) = \frac{1 \cdot 3 \cdot 5 \cdots (2m - 1)}{2^{m}} \sqrt{\pi} \qquad m = 1,2,3,\ldots$$

$$\Gamma(-m + \tfrac{1}{2}) = \frac{(-1)^{m} 2^{m} \sqrt{\pi}}{1 \cdot 3 \cdot 5 \cdots (2m - 1)} \qquad m = 1,2,3,\ldots$$

Definition: $\Gamma(x + 1) = \lim\limits_{k \to \infty} \dfrac{1 \cdot 2 \cdot 3 \cdots k}{(x + 1)(x + 2) \cdots (x + k)} k^{x}$

$$\frac{1}{\Gamma(x)} = xe^{\gamma x} \prod_{m=1}^{\infty} \left\{ \left(1 + \frac{x}{m}\right) e^{-x/m} \right\}$$

This is an infinite product representation for the gamma function where γ is Euler's constant.

Properties:

$$\Gamma'(1) = \int_0^\infty e^{-x} \ln x \, dx = -\gamma$$

$$\frac{\Gamma'(x)}{\Gamma(x)} = -\gamma + \left(\frac{1}{1} - \frac{1}{x}\right) + \left(\frac{1}{2} - \frac{1}{x+1}\right) + \dots + \left(\frac{1}{n} - \frac{1}{x+n-1}\right) + \dots$$

$$\Gamma(x+1) = \sqrt{2\pi x} \; x^x e^{-x} \left\{ 1 + \frac{1}{12x} + \frac{1}{288x^2} - \frac{139}{51,840x^3} + \dots \right\}$$

This is called *Stirling's asymptotic series.*

If we let $x = n$ a positive integer, then a useful approximation for $n!$ where n is large [e.g. $n > 10$] is given by *Stirling's formula*

$$n! \approx \sqrt{2\pi n} \; n^n e^{-n}$$

GAMMA FUNCTION*

Values of $\Gamma(n) = \int_0^\infty e^{-x} x^{n-1} \, dx; \; \Gamma(n+1) = n\Gamma(n)$

n	$\Gamma(n)$	n	$\Gamma(n)$	n	$\Gamma(n)$	n	$\Gamma(n)$
1.00	1.00000	1.25	.90640	1.50	.88623	1.75	.91906
1.01	.99433	1.26	.90440	1.51	.88659	1.76	.92137
1.02	.98884	1.27	.90250	1.52	.88704	1.77	.92376
1.03	.98355	1.28	.90072	1.53	.88757	1.78	.92623
1.04	.97844	1.29	.89904	1.54	.88818	1.79	.92877
1.05	.97350	1.30	.89747	1.55	.88887	1.80	.93138
1.06	.96874	1.31	.89600	1.56	.88964	1.81	.93408
1.07	.96415	1.32	.89464	1.57	.89049	1.82	.93685
1.08	.95973	1.33	.89338	1.58	.89142	1.83	.93969
1.09	.95546	1.34	.89222	1.59	.89243	1.84	.94261
1.10	.95135	1.35	.89115	1.60	.89352	1.85	.94561
1.11	.94740	1.36	.89018	1.61	.89468	1.86	.94869
1.12	.94359	1.37	.88931	1.62	.89592	1.87	.95184
1.13	.93993	1.38	.88854	1.63	.89724	1.88	.95507
1.14	.93642	1.39	.88785	1.64	.89864	1.89	.95838
1.15	.93304	1.40	.88726	1.65	.90012	1.90	.96177
1.16	.92980	1.41	.88676	1.66	.90167	1.91	.96523
1.17	.92670	1.42	.88636	1.67	.90330	1.92	.96877
1.18	.92373	1.43	.88604	1.68	.90500	1.93	.97240
1.19	.92089	1.44	.88581	1.69	.90678	1.94	.97610
1.20	.91817	1.45	.88566	1.70	.90864	1.95	.97988
1.21	.91558	1.46	.88560	1.71	.91057	1.96	.98374
1.22	.91311	1.47	.88563	1.72	.91258	1.97	.98768
1.23	.91075	1.48	.88575	1.73	.91466	1.98	.99171
1.24	.90852	1.49	.88595	1.74	.91683	1.99	.99581
						2.00	1.00000

* For large positive values of z, $\Gamma(z)$ approximates Stirling's asymptotic series

$$z^z e^{-z} \sqrt{\frac{2\pi}{z}} \left[1 + \frac{1}{12z} + \frac{1}{288z^2} - \frac{139}{51840z^3} - \frac{571}{2488320z^4} + \dots \right].$$

GAMMA FUNCTION AND ITS NATURAL LOGARITHM

n	$\Gamma(n)$	$\log_e \Gamma(n)$		n	$\Gamma(n)$	$\log_e \Gamma(n)$	
1.000	1.00000 00	0.00000 00	0.000	1.250	0.90640 25	−0.09827 18	0.250
1.005	0.99713 85	−0.00286 56	0.005	1.255	0.90538 58	−0.09939 42	0.255
1.010	0.99432 59	−0.00569 03	0.010	1.260	0.90439 71	−0.10048 67	0.260
1.015	0.99156 13	−0.00847 45	0.015	1.265	0.90343 63	−0.10154 97	0.265
1.020	0.98884 42	−0.01121 85	0.020	1.270	0.90250 31	−0.10258 32	0.270
1.025	0.98617 40	−0.01392 25	0.025	1.275	0.90159 72	−0.10358 74	0.275
1.030	0.98355 00	−0.01658 69	0.030	1.280	0.90071 85	−0.10456 25	0.280
1.035	0.98097 16	−0.01921 18	0.035	1.285	0.89986 67	−0.10550 87	0.285
1.040	0.97843 82	−0.02179 77	0.040	1.290	0.89904 16	−0.10642 60	0.290
1.045	0.97594 93	−0.02434 46	0.045	1.295	0.89824 30	−0.10731 47	0.295
1.050	0.97350 43	−0.02685 31	0.050	1.300	0.89747 07	−0.10817 48	0.300
1.055	0.97110 26	−0.02932 32	0.055	1.305	0.89672 45	−0.10900 66	0.305
1.060	0.96874 36	−0.03175 53	0.060	1.310	0.89600 42	−0.10981 02	0.310
1.065	0.96642 70	−0.03414 95	0.065	1.315	0.89530 96	−0.11058 57	0.315
1.070	0.96415 20	−0.03650 63	0.070	1.320	0.89464 05	−0.11133 34	0.320
1.075	0.96191 83	−0.03882 57	0.075	1.325	0.89399 67	−0.11205 32	0.325
1.080	0.95972 53	−0.04110 82	0.080	1.330	0.89337 81	−0.11274 54	0.330
1.085	0.95757 25	−0.04335 38	0.085	1.335	0.89278 44	−0.11341 02	0.335
1.090	0.95545 95	−0.04556 29	0.090	1.340	0.89221 55	−0.11404 76	0.340
1.095	0.95338 57	−0.04773 57	0.095	1.345	0.89167 12	−0.11465 78	0.345
1.100	0.95135 08	−0.04987 24	0.100	1.350	0.89115 14	−0.11524 09	0.350
1.105	0.94935 42	−0.05197 33	0.105	1.355	0.89065 59	−0.11579 71	0.355
1.110	0.94739 55	−0.05403 86	0.110	1.360	0.89018 45	−0.11632 65	0.360
1.115	0.94547 43	−0.05606 86	0.115	1.365	0.88973 71	−0.11682 92	0.365
1.120	0.94359 02	−0.05806 33	0.120	1.370	0.88931 35	−0.11730 55	0.370
1.125	0.94174 27	−0.06002 32	0.125	1.375	0.88891 36	−0.11775 53	0.375
1.130	0.93993 14	−0.06194 83	0.130	1.380	0.88853 71	−0.11817 88	0.380
1.135	0.93815 60	−0.06383 90	0.135	1.385	0.88818 41	−0.11857 62	0.385
1.140	0.93641 61	−0.06569 54	0.140	1.390	0.88785 43	−0.11894 76	0.390
1.145	0.93471 12	−0.06751 77	0.145	1.395	0.88754 76	−0.11929 32	0.395
1.150	0.93304 09	−0.06930 62	0.150	1.400	0.88726 38	−0.11961 29	0.400
1.155	0.93140 50	−0.07106 11	0.155	1.405	0.88700 29	−0.11990 70	0.405
1.160	0.92980 31	−0.07278 25	0.160	1.410	0.88676 47	−0.12017 57	0.410
1.165	0.92823 47	−0.07447 07	0.165	1.415	0.88654 90	−0.12041 89	0.415
1.170	0.92669 96	−0.07612 58	0.170	1.420	0.88635 58	−0.12063 68	0 420
1.175	0.92519 74	−0.07774 81	0.175	1.425	0.88618 49	−0.12082 97	0.425
1.180	0.92372 78	−0.07933 78	0.180	1.430	0.88603 62	−0.12099 74	0.430
1.185	0.92229 05	−0.08089 51	0.185	1.435	0.88590 97	−0.12114 03	0.435
1.190	0.92088 50	−0.08242 01	0.190	1.440	0.88580 51	−0.12125 84	0.440
1.195	0.91951 12	−0.08391 30	0.195	1.445	0.88572 23	−0.12135 18	0.445
1.200	0.91816 87	−0.08537 41	0.200	1.450	0.88566 14	−0.12142 06	0.450
1.205	0.91685 73	−0.08680 35	0.205	1.455	0.88562 21	−0.12146 50	0.455
1.210	0.91557 65	−0.08820 14	0.210	1.460	0.88560 43	−0.12148 50	0.460
1.215	0.91432 62	−0.08956 79	0.215	1.465	0.88560 80	−0.12148 08	0.465
1.220	0.91310 59	−0.09090 34	0.220	1.470	0.88563 31	−0.12145 25	0.470
1.225	0.91191 56	−0.09220 78	0.225	1.475	0.88567 95	−0.12140 02	0.475
1.230	0.91075 49	−0.09348 15	0.230	1.480	0.88574 70	−0.12132 40	0.480
1.235	0.90962 34	−0.09472 46	0.235	1.485	0.88583 56	−0.12122 40	0.485
1.240	0.90852 11	−0.09593 72	0.240	1.490	0.88594 51	−0.12110 03	0.490
1.245	0.90744 75	−0.09711 96	0.245	1.495	0.88607 56	−0.12095 30	0.495
	$y!$	$\log_e y!$	y		$y!$	$\log_e y!$	y

GAMMA FUNCTION AND ITS NATURAL LOGARITHM (Continued)

n	$\Gamma(n)$	$\log_e \Gamma(n)$		n	$\Gamma(n)$	$\log_e \Gamma(n)$	
1.500	0.88622 69	−0.12078 22	0.500	1.750	0.91906 25	−0.08440 11	0.750
1.505	0.88639 90	−0.12058 81	0.505	1.755	0.92020 92	−0.08315 42	0.755
1.510	0.88659 17	−0.12037 07	0.510	1.760	0.92137 49	−0.08188 83	0.760
1.515	0.88680 50	−0.12013 02	0.515	1.765	0.92255 95	−0.08060 34	0.765
1.520	0.88703 88	−0.11986 66	0.520	1.770	0.92376 31	−0.07929 96	0.770
1.525	0.88729 30	−0.11958 00	0.525	1.775	0.92498 57	−0.07797 70	0.775
1.530	0.88756 76	−0.11927 06	0.530	1.780	0.92622 73	−0.07663 56	0.780
1.535	0.88786 25	−0.11893 84	0.535	1.785	0.92748 79	−0.07527 55	0.785
1.540	0.88817 77	−0.11858 35	0.540	1.790	0.92876 75	−0.07389 69	0.790
1.545	0.88851 30	−0.11820 61	0.545	1.795	0.93006 61	−0.07249 96	0.795
1.550	0.88886 83	−0.11780 61	0.550	1.800	0.93138 38	−0.07108 39	0.800
1.555	0.88924 38	−0.11738 39	0.555	1.805	0.93272 05	−0.06964 97	0.805
1.560	0.88963 92	−0.11693 93	0.560	1.810	0.93407 63	−0.06819 72	0.810
1.565	0.89005 45	−0.11647 25	0.565	1.815	0.93545 11	−0.06672 64	0.815
1.570	0.89048 97	−0.11598 37	0.570	1.820	0.93684 51	−0.06523 73	0.820
1.575	0.89094 48	−0.11547 28	0.575	1.825	0.93825 82	−0.06373 01	0.825
1.580	0.89141 96	−0.11494 01	0.580	1.830	0.93969 04	−0.06220 48	0.830
1.585	0.89191 41	−0.11438 55	0.585	1.835	0.94114 18	−0.06066 15	0.835
1.590	0.89242 82	−0.11380 92	0.590	1.840	0.94261 24	−0.05910 01	0.840
1.595	0.89296 20	−0.11321 13	0.595	1.845	0.94410 22	−0.05752 09	0.845
1.600	0.89351 53	−0.11259 18	0.600	1.850	0.94561 12	−0.05592 38	0.850
1.605	0.89408 82	−0.11195 08	0.605	1.855	0.94713 95	−0.05430 89	0.855
1.610	0.89468 06	−0.11128 85	0.610	1.860	0.94868 70	−0.05267 63	0.860
1.615	0.89529 24	−0.11060 49	0.615	1.865	0.95025 39	−0.05102 60	0.865
1.620	0.89592 37	−0.10990 01	0.620	1.870	0.95184 02	−0.04935 81	0.870
1.625	0.89657 43	−0.10917 41	0.625	1.875	0.95344 58	−0.04767 27	0.875
1.630	0.89724 42	−0.10842 72	0.630	1.880	0.95507 09	−0.04596 97	0.880
1.635	0.89793 35	−0.10765 93	0.635	1.885	0.95671 53	−0.04424 94	0.885
1.640	0.89864 20	−0.10687 05	0.640	1.890	0.95837 93	−0.04251 16	0.890
1.645	0.89936 98	−0.10606 10	0.645	1.895	0.96006 28	−0.04075 66	0.895
1.650	0.90011 68	−0.10523 07	0.650	1.900	0.96176 58	−0.03898 43	0.900
1.655	0.90088 30	−0.10437 99	0.655	1.905	0.96348 85	−0.03719 48	0.905
1.660	0.90166 84	−0.10350 85	0.660	1.910	0.96523 07	−0.03538 81	0.910
1.665	0.90247 29	−0.10261 66	0.665	1.915	0.96699 27	−0.03356 44	0.915
1.670	0.90329 65	−0.10170 44	0.670	1.920	0.96877 43	−0.03172 36	0.920
1.675	0.90413 92	−0.10077 19	0.675	1.925	0.97057 57	−0.02986 59	0.925
1.680	0.90500 10	−0.09981 92	0.680	1.930	0.97239 69	−0.02799 12	0.930
1.685	0.90588 19	−0.09884 63	0.685	1.935	0.97423 80	−0.02609 97	0.935
1.690	0.90678 18	−0.09785 34	0.690	1.940	0.97609 89	−0.02419 14	0.940
1.695	0.90770 08	−0.09684 05	0.695	1.945	0.97797 98	−0.02226 63	0.945
1.700	0.90863 87	−0.09580 77	0.700	1.950	0.97988 07	−0.02032 45	0.950
1.705	0.90959 57	−0.09475 51	0.705	1.955	0.98180 16	−0.01836 61	0.955
1.710	0.91057 17	−0.09368 27	0.710	1.960	0.98374 25	−0.01639 11	0.960
1.715	0.91156 66	−0.09259 06	0.715	1.965	0.98570 37	−0.01439 95	0.965
1.720	0.91258 06	−0.09147 89	0.720	1.970	0.98768 50	−0.01239 15	0.970
1.725	0.91361 35	−0.09034 77	0.725	1.975	0.98968 65	−0.01036 70	0.975
1.730	0.91466 54	−0.08919 70	0.730	1.980	0.99170 84	−0.00832 62	0.980
1.735	0.91573 62	−0.08802 69	0.735	1.985	0.99375 06	−0.00626 90	0.985
1.740	0.91682 60	−0.08683 75	0.740	1.990	0.99581 33	−0.00419 55	0.990
1.745	0.91793 48	−0.08562 89	0.745	1.995	0.99789 64	−0.00210 59	0.995
				2.000	1.00000 00	0.00000 00	1.000
	$y!$	$\log_e y!$	y		$y!$	$\log_e y!$	y

GAMMA FUNCTION FOR COMPLEX ARGUMENTS
$x = 1.0$

y	$\Re \ln \Gamma(z) = \log_e |\Gamma(z)|$	$\Im \ln \Gamma(z)$	y	$\Re \ln \Gamma(z) = \log_e |\Gamma(z)|$	$\Im \ln \Gamma(z)$
0.0	0.00000	0.00000	5.0	− 6.13032	3.81590
0.1	− 0.00820	− 0.05732	5.1	− 6.27750	3.97816
0.2	− 0.03248	− 0.11230	5.2	− 6.42487	4.14238
0.3	− 0.07195	− 0.16282	5.3	− 6.57243	4.30850
0.4	− 0.12529	− 0.20716	5.4	− 6.72016	4.47650
0.5	− 0.19095	− 0.24406	5.5	− 6.86807	4.64634
0.6	− 0.26729	− 0.27274	5.6	− 7.01614	4.81799
0.7	− 0.35277	− 0.29283	5.7	− 7.16437	4.99142
0.8	− 0.44598	− 0.30423	5.8	− 7.31275	5.16659
0.9	− 0.54571	− 0.30707	5.9	− 7.46128	5.34348
1.0	− 0.65092	− 0.30164	6.0	− 7.60996	5.52205
1.1	− 0.76078	− 0.28827	6.1	− 7.75877	5.70229
1.2	− 0.87459	− 0.26733	6.2	− 7.90772	5.88415
1.3	− 0.99177	− 0.23922	6.3	− 8.05680	6.06762
1.4	− 1.11186	− 0.20430	6.4	− 8.20601	6.25267
1.5	− 1.23448	− 0.16294	6.5	− 8.35534	6.43928
1.6	− 1.35931	− 0.11547	6.6	− 8.50478	6.62742
1.7	− 1.48609	− 0.06220	6.7	− 8.65434	6.81707
1.8	− 1.61460	− 0.00342	6.8	− 8.80402	7.00821
1.9	− 1.74464	+0.06061	6.9	− 8.95380	7.20081
2.0	− 1.87608	0.12965	7.0	− 9.10368	7.39486
2.1	− 2.00876	0.20346	7.1	− 9.25367	7.59033
2.2	− 2.14258	0.28185	7.2	− 9.40375	7.78720
2.3	− 2.27744	0.36461	7.3	− 9.55394	7.98546
2.4	− 2.41324	0.45159	7.4	− 9.70421	8.18508
2.5	− 2.54991	0.54260	7.5	− 9.85458	8.38605
2.6	− 2.68738	0.63751	7.6	− 10.00504	8.58835
2.7	− 2.82259	0.73617	7.7	− 10.15558	8.79197
2.8	− 2.96448	0.83844	7.8	− 10.30621	8.99687
2.9	− 3.10402	0.94421	7.9	− 10.45692	9.20306
3.0	− 3.24414	1.05335	8.0	− 10.60771	9.41051
3.1	− 3.38483	1.16577	8.1	− 10.75858	9.61920
3.2	− 3.52603	1.28135	8.2	− 10.90952	9.82913
3.3	− 3.66773	1.40001	8.3	− 11.06054	10.04027
3.4	− 3.80988	1.52165	8.4	− 11.21163	10.25262
3.5	− 3.95247	1.64619	8.5	− 11.36280	10.46615
3.6	− 4.09546	1.77355	8.6	− 11.51403	10.68086
3.7	− 4.23884	1.90365	8.7	− 11.66533	10.89673
3.8	− 4.38259	2.03642	8.8	− 11.81669	11.11374
3.9	− 4.52668	2.17179	8.9	− 11.96812	11.33189
4.0	− 4.67110	2.30970	9.0	− 12.11962	11.55116
4.1	− 4.81583	2.45008	9.1	− 12.27117	11.77153
4.2	− 4.96086	2.59287	9.2	− 12.42279	11.99301
4.3	− 5.10618	2.73803	9.3	− 12.57446	12.21557
4.4	− 5.25176	2.88549	9.4	− 12.72619	12.43920
4.5	− 5.39761	3.03520	9.5	− 12.87798	12.66390
4.6	− 5.54370	3.18711	9.6	− 13.02982	12.88964
4.7	− 5.69002	3.34118	9.7	− 13.18172	13.11643
4.8	− 5.83658	3.49737	9.8	− 13.33367	13.34424
4.9	− 5.98335	3.65562	9.9	− 13.48568	13.57307
5.0	− 6.13032	3.81590	10.0	− 13.63773	13.80291

Linear interpolation will yield about three figures; eight-point interpolation will yield about eight figures.

$\Re \ln \Gamma(z) = \log_e |\Gamma(z)|$ $\Im \ln \Gamma(z) = \arg \Gamma(z)$

GAMMA FUNCTION FOR COMPLEX ARGUMENTS
$$x = 1.1$$

y	$\Re \ln \Gamma(z) = \log_e |\Gamma(z)|$	$\Im \ln \Gamma(z)$	y	$\Re \ln \Gamma(z) = 1_e |\Gamma(z)|$	$\Im \ln \Gamma(z)$
0.0	−0.04987	0.00000	5.0	− 5.96894	3.96199
0.1	−0.05702	−0.04207	5.1	− 6.11415	4.12447
0.2	−0.07824	−0.08231	5.2	− 6.25960	4.28889
0.3	−0.11291	−0.11905	5.3	− 6.40527	4.45521
0.4	−0.16008	−0.15087	5.4	− 6.55114	4.62340
0.5	−0.21859	−0.17666	5.5	− 6.69723	4.79343
0.6	−0.28719	−0.19566	5.6	− 6.84351	4.96526
0.7	−0.36464	−0.20740	5.7	− 6.98998	5.13886
0.8	−0.44979	−0.21167	5.8	− 7.13664	5.31419
0.9	−0.54158	−0.20844	5.9	− 7.28347	5.49124
1.0	−0.63909	−0.19782	6.0	− 7.43048	5.66997
1.1	−0.74154	−0.18001	6.1	− 7.57765	5.85035
1.2	−0.84826	−0.15525	6.2	− 7.72498	6.03236
1.3	−0.95869	−0.12384	6.3	− 7.87247	6.25198
1.4	−1.07235	−0.08605	6.4	− 8.02011	6.40116
1.5	−1.18886	−0.04217	6.5	− 8.16790	6.58790
1.6	−1.30787	+0.00752	6.6	− 8.31582	6.77617
1.7	−1.42911	0.06276	6.7	− 8.46389	6.96595
1.8	−1.55234	0.12330	6.8	− 8.61208	7.15720
1.9	−1.67734	0.18890	6.9	− 8.76041	7.34992
2.0	−1.80396	0.25936	7.0	− 8.90886	7.54408
2.1	−1.93203	0.33446	7.1	− 9.05744	7.73966
2.2	−2.06143	0.41402	7.2	− 9.20613	7.93664
2.3	−2.19204	0.49787	7.3	− 9.35494	8.13501
2.4	−2.32376	0.58583	7.4	− 9.50387	8.33473
2.5	−2.45650	0.67775	7.5	− 9.65290	8.53580
2.6	−2.59018	0.77350	7.6	− 9.80203	8.73820
2.7	−2.72474	0.87293	7.7	− 9.95128	8.94191
2.8	−2.86010	0.97592	7.8	−10.10062	9.14690
2.9	−2.99623	1.08236	7.9	−10.25006	9.35318
3.0	−3.13305	1.19214	8.0	−10.39960	9.56071
3.1	−3.27054	1.30514	8.1	−10.54923	9.76950
3.2	−3.40864	1.42128	8.2	−10.69895	9.97950
3.3	−3.54732	1.54045	8.3	−10.84876	10.19073
3.4	−3.68655	1.66258	8.4	−10.99866	10.40315
3.5	−3.82629	1.78758	8.5	−11.14864	10.61676
3.6	−3.96651	1.91537	8.6	−11.29870	10.83154
3.7	−4.10720	2.04589	8.7	−11.44885	11.04749
3.8	−4.24832	2.17905	8.8	−11.59908	11.26457
3.9	−4.38985	2.31479	8.9	−11.74938	11.48279
4.0	−4.53178	2.45304	9.0	−11.89976	11.70213
4.1	−4.67408	2.59376	9.1	−12.05021	11.92257
4.2	−4.81673	2.73687	9.2	−12.20074	12.14411
4.3	−4.95972	2.88233	9.3	−12.35133	12.36673
4.4	−5.10303	3.03008	9.4	−12.50200	12.59043
4.5	−5.24665	3.18007	9.5	−12.65273	12.81519
4.6	−5.39057	3.33225	9.6	−12.80353	13.04099
4.7	−5.53477	3.48657	9.7	−12.95439	13.26784
4.8	−5.67924	3.64300	9.8	−13.10532	13.49571
4.9	−5.82396	3.80148	9.9	−13.25631	13.72460
5.0	−5.96894	3.96199	10.0	−13.40736	13.95449

Linear interpolation will yield about three figures; eight-point interpolation will yield about eight figures.

$$\Re \ln \Gamma(z) = \log_e |\Gamma(z)| \qquad\qquad \Im \ln \Gamma(z) = \arg \Gamma(z)$$

GAMMA FUNCTION FOR COMPLEX ARGUMENTS
$x = 1.2$

y	$\Re \ln \Gamma(z) = \log_e \lvert \Gamma(z) \rvert$	$\Im \ln \Gamma(z)$	y	$\Re \ln \Gamma(z) = \log_e \lvert \Gamma(z) \rvert$	$\Im \ln \Gamma(z)$
0.0	−0.08537	0.00000	5.0	− 5.80732	4.10610
0.1	−0.09170	−0.02866	5.1	− 5.95058	4.26883
0.2	−0.11051	−0.05586	5.2	− 6.09410	4.43349
0.3	−0.14135	−0.08026	5.3	− 6.23789	4.60005
0.4	−0.18352	−0.10066	5.4	− 6.38192	4.76847
0.5	−0.23614	−0.11611	5.5	− 6.52619	4.93871
0.6	−0.29825	−0.12588	5.6	− 6.67069	5.11075
0.7	−0.36885	−0.12949	5.7	− 6.81541	5.28455
0.8	−0.44698	−0.12664	5.8	− 6.96035	5.46009
0.9	−0.53174	−0.11721	5.9	− 7.10549	5.63732
1.0	−0.62233	−0.10119	6.0	− 7.25083	5.81623
1.1	−0.71804	−0.07869	6.1	− 7.39636	5.99679
1.2	−0.81823	−0.04984	6.2	− 7.54209	6.17898
1.3	−0.92238	−0.01484	6.3	− 7.68799	6.36275
1.4	−1.03001	+0.02611	6.4	− 7.83407	6.54810
1.5	−1.14074	0.07278	6.5	− 7.98031	6.73500
1.6	−1.25421	0.12496	6.6	− 8.12673	6.92342
1.7	−1.37015	0.18241	6.7	− 8.27330	7.11334
1.8	−1.48830	0.24494	6.8	− 8.42002	7.30474
1.9	−1.60844	0.31234	6.9	− 8.56690	7.49759
2.0	−1.73039	0.38443	7.0	− 8.71393	7.69189
2.1	−1.85398	0.46101	7.1	− 8.86109	7.88760
2.2	−1.97907	0.54192	7.2	− 9.00840	8.08471
2.3	−2.10553	0.62700	7.3	− 9.15584	8.28319
2.4	−2.23326	0.71610	7.4	− 9.30341	8.48304
2.5	−2.36215	0.80908	7.5	− 9.45110	8.68422
2.6	−2.49211	0.90579	7.6	− 9.59892	8.88673
2.7	−2.62308	1.00613	7.7	− 9.74687	9.09055
2.8	−2.75497	1.10996	7.8	− 9.89493	9.29566
2.9	−2.88773	1.21718	7.9	−10.04310	9.50204
3.0	−3.02130	1.32769	8.0	−10.19139	9.70968
3.1	−3.15563	1.44138	8.1	−10.33978	9.91856
3.2	−3.29066	1.55816	8.2	−10.48828	10.12866
3.3	−3.42637	1.67794	8.3	−10.63689	10.33998
3.4	−3.56270	1.80064	8.4	−10.78559	10.55250
3.5	−3.69962	1.92618	8.5	−10.93440	10.76620
3.6	−3.83711	2.05448	8.6	−11.08330	10.98107
3.7	−3.97513	2.18547	8.7	−11.23229	11.19710
3.8	−4.11364	2.31909	8.8	−11.38138	11.41427
3.9	−4.25264	2.45526	8.9	−11.53056	11.63257
4.0	−4.39209	2.59393	9.0	−11.67983	11.85199
4.1	−4.53197	2.73504	9.1	−11.82918	12.07251
4.2	−4.67226	2.87853	9.2	−11.97861	12.29413
4.3	−4.81294	3.02434	9.3	−12.12813	12.51683
4.4	−4.95399	3.17243	9.4	−12.27773	12.74060
4.5	−5.09541	3.32274	9.5	−12.42741	12.96543
4.6	−5.23716	3.47523	9.6	−12.57717	13.19130
4.7	−5.37924	3.62986	9.7	−12.72700	13.41822
4.8	−5.52164	3.78657	9.8	−12.87691	13.64616
4.9	−5.66433	3.94533	9.9	−13.02689	13.87511
5.0	−5.80732	4.10610	10.0	−13.17694	14.10508

Linear interpolation will yield about three figures; eight-point interpolation will yield about eight figures.

$\Re \ln \Gamma(z) = \log_e \lvert \Gamma(z) \rvert$ $\qquad\qquad$ $\Im \ln \Gamma(z) = \arg \Gamma(z)$

GAMMA FUNCTION FOR COMPLEX ARGUMENTS
$$x = 1.3$$

y	$\Re \ln \Gamma(z) = \log_e \lvert \Gamma(z) \rvert$	$\mathscr{I} \ln \Gamma(z)$	y	$\Re \ln \Gamma(z) = \log_e \lvert \Gamma(z) \rvert$	$\mathscr{I} \ln \Gamma(z)$
0.0	−0.10817	−0.00000	5.0	− 5.64541	4.24824
0.1	−0.11384	−0.01672	5.1	− 5.78673	4.41126
0.2	−0.13070	−0.03226	5.2	− 5.92835	4.57621
0.3	−0.15843	−0.04550	5.3	− 6.07027	4.74303
0.4	−0.19649	−0.05545	5.4	− 6.21246	4.91171
0.5	−0.24421	−0.06127	5.5	− 6.35492	5.08220
0.6	−0.30082	−0.06230	5.6	− 6.49765	5.25448
0.7	−0.36553	−0.05805	5.7	− 6.64063	5.42852
0.8	−0.43755	−0.04821	5.8	− 6.78385	5.60428
0.9	−0.15610	−0.03257	5.9	− 6.92730	5.78173
1.0	−0.60048	−0.01108	6.0	− 7.07099	5.96085
1.1	−0.69007	+0.01628	6.1	− 7.21489	6.14161
1.2	−0.78427	0.04942	6.2	− 7.35901	6.32399
1.3	−0.88259	0.08822	6.3	− 7.50333	6.50796
1.4	−0.98459	0.13255	6.4	− 7.64785	6.69349
1.5	−1.08987	0.18224	6.5	− 7.79257	6.88057
1.6	−1.19810	0.23711	6.6	− 7.93747	7.06916
1.7	−1.30899	0.29700	6.7	− 8.08255	7.25925
1.8	−1.42227	0.36172	6.8	− 8.22781	7.45081
1.9	−1.53773	0.43111	6.9	− 8.37325	7.64383
2.0	−1.65518	0.50500	7.0	− 8.51885	7.83828
2.1	−1.77443	0.58323	7.1	− 8.66461	8.03414
2.2	−1.89533	0.66565	7.2	− 8.81053	8.23139
2.3	−2.01776	0.75212	7.3	− 8.95660	8.43002
2.4	−2.14159	0.84250	7.4	− 9.10282	8.63000
2.5	−2.26672	0.93666	7.5	− 9.24919	8.83132
2.6	−2.39305	1.03448	7.6	− 9.39569	9.03396
2.7	−2.52049	1.13583	7.7	− 9.54234	9.23791
2.8	−2.64898	1.24062	7.8	− 9.68912	9.44314
2.9	−2.77843	1.34873	7.9	− 9.83603	9.64964
3.0	−2.90879	1.46006	8.0	− 9.98307	9.85740
3.1	−3.04001	1.57453	8.1	−10.13023	10.06639
3.2	−3.17202	1.69204	8.2	−10.27751	10.27661
3.3	−3.30478	1.81251	8.3	−10.42491	10.48804
3.4	−3.43826	1.93586	8.4	−10.57243	10.70067
3.5	−3.57240	2.06201	8.5	−10.72006	10.91447
3.6	−3.70717	2.19090	8.6	−10.86780	11.12944
3.7	−3.84255	2.32244	8.7	−11.01564	11.34557
3.8	−3.97849	2.45658	8.8	−11.16360	11.56284
3.9	−4.11497	2.59324	8.9	−11.31165	11.78123
4.0	−4.25196	2.73239	9.0	−11.45981	12.00075
4.1	−4.38945	2.87394	9.1	−11.60806	12.22136
4.2	−4.52739	3.01786	9.2	−11.75641	12.44307
4.3	−4.66578	3.16408	9.3	−11.90485	12.66585
4.4	−4.80460	3.31256	9.4	−12.05339	12.88971
4.5	−4.94382	3.46324	9.5	−12.20202	13.11462
4.6	−5.08342	3.61609	9.6	−12.35073	13.34058
4.7	−5.22340	3.77106	9.7	−12.49953	13.56757
4.8	−5.36374	3.92810	9.8	−12.64842	13.79559
4.9	−5.50441	4.08717	9.9	−12.79739	14.02463
5.0	−5.64541	4.24824	10.0	−12.94644	14.25466

Linear interpolation will yield about three figures; eight-point interpolation will yield about eight figures.

$$\Re \ln \Gamma(z) = \log_e \lvert \Gamma(z) \rvert \qquad\qquad \mathscr{I} \ln \Gamma(z) = \arg \Gamma(z)$$

GAMMA FUNCTION FOR COMPLEX ARGUMENTS
$x = 1.4$

y	$\Re \ln \Gamma(z) = \log_e |\Gamma(z)|$	$\Im \ln \Gamma(z)$	y	$\Re \ln \Gamma(z) = \log_e |\Gamma(z)|$	$\Im \ln \Gamma(z)$
0.0	−0.11961	0.00000	5.0	−5.48320	4.38843
0.1	−0.12473	−0.00597	5.1	−5.62259	4.55178
0.2	−0.14000	−0.01097	5.2	−5.76231	4.71704
0.3	−0.16516	−0.01406	5.3	−5.90236	4.88417
0.4	−0.19979	−0.01439	5.4	−6.04273	5.05314
0.5	−0.24337	−0.01125	5.5	−6.18340	5.22391
0.6	−0.29530	−0.00402	5.6	−6.32436	5.39646
0.7	−0.35492	+0.00776	5.7	−6.46560	5.57076
0.8	−0.42158	0.02442	5.8	−6.60712	5.74677
0.9	−0.49463	0.04618	5.9	−6.74889	5.92447
1.0	−0.57345	0.07318	6.0	−6.89093	6.10383
1.1	−0.65748	0.10546	6.1	−7.03321	6.28482
1.2	−0.74620	0.14300	6.2	−7.17572	6.46742
1.3	−0.83914	0.18576	6.3	−7.31847	6.65160
1.4	−0.93588	0.23363	6.4	−7.46144	6.83734
1.5	−1.03606	0.28650	6.5	−7.60463	7.02462
1.6	−1.13934	0.34426	6.6	−7.74803	7.21341
1.7	−1.24543	0.40674	6.7	−7.89163	7.40369
1.8	−1.35407	0.47383	6.8	−8.03543	7.59543
1.9	−1.46505	0.54537	6.9	−8.17943	7.78863
2.0	−1.57816	0.62123	7.0	−8.32360	7.98325
2.1	−1.69322	0.70126	7.1	−8.46797	8.17928
2.2	−1.81008	0.78534	7.2	−8.61250	8.37670
2.3	−1.92859	0.87334	7.3	−8.75721	8.57549
2.4	−2.04863	0.96513	7.4	−8.90209	8.77563
2.5	−2.17009	1.06059	7.5	−9.04713	8.97710
2.6	−2.29287	1.15962	7.6	−9.19233	9.17989
2.7	−2.41687	1.26211	7.7	−9.33768	9.38398
2.8	−2.54201	1.36795	7.8	−9.48318	9.58935
2.9	−2.66822	1.47704	7.9	−9.62883	9.79599
3.0	−2.79544	1.58930	8.0	−9.77462	10.00388
3.1	−2.92359	1.70464	8.1	−9.92056	10.21300
3.2	−3.05262	1.82297	8.2	−10.06662	10.42335
3.3	−3.18249	1.94421	8.3	−10.21282	10.63490
3.4	−3.31315	2.06828	8.4	−10.35915	10.84765
3.5	−3.44454	2.19512	8.5	−10.50561	11.06157
3.6	−3.57664	2.32465	8.6	−10.65219	11.27666
3.7	−3.70940	2.45681	8.7	−10.79889	11.49290
3.8	−3.84280	2.59153	8.8	−10.94571	11.71028
3.9	−3.97679	2.72876	8.9	−11.09264	11.92878
4.0	−4.11135	2.86842	9.0	−11.23969	12.14840
4.1	−4.24646	3.01048	9.1	−11.38685	12.36912
4.2	−4.38209	3.15488	9.2	−11.53411	12.59093
4.3	−4.51821	3.30156	9.3	−11.68148	12.81381
4.4	−4.65480	3.45047	9.4	−11.82896	13.03776
4.5	−4.79184	3.60158	9.5	−11.97653	13.26277
4.6	−4.92932	3.75483	9.6	−12.12421	13.48882
4.7	−5.06721	3.91018	9.7	−12.27198	13.71591
4.8	−5.20549	4.06759	9.8	−12.41985	13.94401
4.9	−5.34416	4.22702	9.9	−12.56781	14.17313
5.0	−5.48320	4.38843	10.0	−12.71586	14.40326

Linear interpolation will yield about three figures; eight-point interpolation will yield about eight figures.

$$\Re \ln \Gamma(z) = \log_e |\Gamma(z)| \qquad\qquad \Im \ln \Gamma(z) = \arg \Gamma(z)$$

GAMMA FUNCTION FOR COMPLEX ARGUMENTS
$x = 1.5$

y	$\Re \ln \Gamma(z) = \log_e |\Gamma(z)|$	$\Im \ln \Gamma(z)$	y	$\Re \ln \Gamma(z) = \log_e |\Gamma(z)|$	$\Im \ln \Gamma(z)$
0.0	−0.12078	0.00000	5.0	−5.32063	4.52667
0.1	−0.12545	0.00379	5.1	−5.45810	4.69038
0.2	−0.13939	0.00839	5.2	−5.59594	4.85599
0.3	−0.16238	0.01461	5.3	−5.73414	5.02346
0.4	−0.19412	0.02315	5.4	−5.87269	5.19275
0.5	−0.23419	0.03467	5.5	−6.01158	5.36384
0.6	−0.28208	0.04969	5.6	−6.15078	5.53669
0.7	−0.33728	0.06867	5.7	−6.29030	5.71128
0.8	−0.39924	0.09192	5.8	−6.43012	5.88757
0.9	−0.46739	0.11969	5.9	−6.57023	6.06555
1.0	−0.54122	0.15214	6.0	−6.71062	6.24517
1.1	−0.62022	0.18936	6.1	−6.85128	6.42641
1.2	−0.70392	0.23137	6.2	−6.99221	6.60926
1.3	−0.79189	0.27817	6.3	−7.13339	6.79368
1.4	−0.88376	0.32970	6.4	−7.27482	6.97966
1.5	−0.97915	0.38589	6.5	−7.41649	7.16716
1.6	−1.07776	0.44666	6.6	−7.55839	7.35616
1.7	−1.17932	0.51190	6.7	−7.70051	7.54666
1.8	−1.28355	0.58149	6.8	−7.84286	7.73861
1.9	−1.39024	0.65532	6.9	−7.98542	7.93200
2.0	−1.49920	0.73328	7.0	−8.12818	8.12682
2.1	−1.61023	0.81525	7.1	−8.27115	8.32304
2.2	−1.72317	0.90111	7.2	−8.41431	8.52064
2.3	−1.83790	0.99076	7.3	−8.55766	8.71961
2.4	−1.95426	1.08407	7.4	−8.70120	8.91992
2.5	−2.07215	1.18096	7.5	−8.84491	9.12156
2.6	−2.19146	1.28131	7.6	−8.98881	9.32452
2.7	−2.31210	1.38503	7.7	−9.13287	9.52877
2.8	−2.43398	1.49202	7.8	−9.27710	9.73429
2.9	−2.55701	1.60219	7.9	−9.42149	9.94108
3.0	−2.68114	1.71547	8.0	−9.56604	10.14912
3.1	−2.80629	1.83176	8.1	−9.71075	10.35839
3.2	−2.93240	1.95098	8.2	−9.85560	10.56888
3.3	−3.05942	2.07307	8.3	−10.00060	10.78057
3.4	−3.18730	2.19794	8.4	−10.14575	10.99345
3.5	−3.31598	2.32553	8.5	−10.29104	11.20751
3.6	−3.44544	2.45578	8.6	−10.43646	11.42273
3.7	−3.57563	2.58862	8.7	−10.58202	11.63909
3.8	−3.70650	2.72398	8.8	−10.72771	11.85659
3.9	−3.83804	2.86182	8.9	−10.87352	12.07522
4.0	−3.97020	3.00207	9.0	−11.01946	12.29495
4.1	−4.10296	3.14469	9.1	−11.16553	12.51579
4.2	−4.23629	3.28962	9.2	−11.31171	12.73771
4.3	−4.37016	3.43680	9.3	−11.45801	12.96070
4.4	−4.50455	3.58620	9.4	−11.60442	13.18476
4.5	−4.63943	3.73777	9.5	−11.75095	13.40987
4.6	−4.77480	3.89147	9.6	−11.89759	13.63603
4.7	−4.91061	4.04724	9.7	−12.04433	13.86321
4.8	−5.04687	4.20506	9.8	−12.19118	14.09142
4.9	−5.18355	4.36488	9.9	−12.33814	14.32064
5.0	−5.32063	4.52667	10.0	−12.48519	14.55086

Linear interpolation will yield about three figures; eight-point interpolation will yield about eight figures.

$$\Re \ln \Gamma(z) = \log_e |\Gamma(z)| \qquad \qquad \Im \ln \Gamma(z) = \arg \Gamma(z)$$

SPECIAL FUNCTIONS

GAMMA FUNCTION FOR COMPLEX ARGUMENTS
$x = 1.6$

y	$\Re \ln \Gamma(z) = \log_e \lvert \Gamma(z) \rvert$	$\Im \ln \Gamma(z)$	y	$\Re \ln \Gamma(z) = \log_e \lvert \Gamma(z) \rvert$	$\Im \ln \Gamma(z)$
0.0	−0.11259	0.00000	5.0	−5.15767	4.66299
0.1	−0.11688	0.01272	5.1	−5.29324	4.82710
0.2	−0.12969	0.02614	5.2	−5.42921	4.99309
0.3	−0.15085	0.04093	5.3	−5.56558	5.16093
0.4	−0.18012	0.05771	5.4	−5.70233	5.33058
0.5	−0.21716	0.07706	5.5	−5.83944	5.50201
0.6	−0.26156	0.09944	5.6	−5.97690	5.67519
0.7	−0.31289	0.12528	5.7	−6.11470	5.85010
0.8	−0.37069	0.15489	5.8	−6.25283	6.02670
0.9	−0.43449	0.18851	5.9	−6.39128	6.20497
1.0	−0.50382	0.22633	6.0	−6.53004	6.38488
1.1	−0.57826	0.26845	6.1	−6.66910	6.56641
1.2	−0.65737	0.31495	6.2	−6.80844	6.74953
1.3	−0.74077	0.36584	6.3	−6.94806	6.93422
1.4	−0.82810	0.42111	6.4	−7.08795	7.12044
1.5	−0.91903	0.48071	6.5	−7.22811	7.30819
1.6	−1.01326	0.54460	6.6	−7.36852	7.49744
1.7	−1.11052	0.61269	6.7	−7.50917	7.68816
1.8	−1.21057	0.68490	6.8	−7.65007	7.88034
1.9	−1.31318	0.76114	6.9	−7.79120	8.07396
2.0	−1.41816	0.84132	7.0	−7.93256	8.26899
2.1	−1.52532	0.92534	7.1	−8.07413	8.46541
2.2	−1.63450	1.01310	7.2	−8.21592	8.66322
2.3	−1.74556	1.10450	7.3	−8.35792	8.86238
2.4	−1.85836	1.19946	7.4	−8.50012	9.06288
2.5	−1.97279	1.29786	7.5	−8.64252	9.26471
2.6	−2.08874	1.39963	7.6	−8.78511	9.46785
2.7	−2.20610	1.50467	7.7	−8.92789	9.67227
2.8	−2.32478	1.61291	7.8	−9.07085	9.87797
2.9	−2.44472	1.72425	7.9	−9.21399	10.08493
3.0	−2.56582	1.83862	8.0	−9.35730	10.29314
3.1	−2.68802	1.95594	8.1	−9.50079	10.50257
3.2	−2.81127	2.07613	8.2	−9.64443	10.71321
3.3	−2.93549	2.19914	8.3	−9.78824	10.92505
3.4	−3.06063	2.32488	8.4	−9.93221	11.13808
3.5	−3.18666	2.45329	8.5	−10.07633	11.35228
3.6	−3.31351	2.58432	8.6	−10.22060	11.56764
3.7	−3.44116	2.71790	8.7	−10.36501	11.78415
3.8	−3.56955	2.85396	8.8	−10.50958	12.00178
3.9	−3.69866	2.99247	8.9	−10.65428	12.22054
4.0	−3.82845	3.13336	9.0	−10.79911	12.44041
4.1	−3.95889	3.27659	9.1	−10.94409	12.66137
4.2	−4.08994	3.42209	9.2	−11.08919	12.88341
4.3	−4.22159	3.56983	9.3	−11.23442	13.10653
4.4	−4.35380	3.71977	9.4	−11.37978	13.33071
4.5	−4.48655	3.87184	9.5	−11.52526	13.55594
4.6	−4.61982	4.02602	9.6	−11.67086	13.78220
4.7	−4.75359	4.18227	9.7	−11.81658	14.00950
4.8	−4.88783	4.34053	9.8	−11.96242	14.23782
4.9	−5.02253	4.50079	9.9	−12.10836	14.46714
5.0	−5.15767	4.66299	10.0	−12.25442	14.69747

Linear interpolation will yield about three figures; eight-point interpolation will yield about eight figures

$\Re \ln \Gamma(z) = \log_e \lvert \Gamma(z) \rvert$ $\qquad$ $\Im \ln \Gamma(z) = \arg \Gamma(z)$

GAMMA FUNCTION FOR COMPLEX ARGUMENTS
x = 1.7

y	$\Re \ln \Gamma(z) = \log_e |\Gamma(z)|$	$\Im \ln \Gamma(z)$	y	$\Re \ln \Gamma(z) = \log_e |\Gamma(z)|$	$\Im \ln \Gamma(z)$
0.0	−0.09581	0.00000	5.0	−4.99429	4.79739
0.1	−0.09977	0.02096	5.1	−5.12797	4.96193
0.2	−0.11161	0.04251	5.2	−5.26209	5.12834
0.3	−0.13121	0.06524	5.3	−5.39664	5.29658
0.4	−0.15835	0.08971	5.4	−5.53159	5.46662
0.5	−0.19275	0.11639	5.5	−5.66694	5.63842
0.6	−0.23410	0.14573	5.6	−5.80267	5.81197
0.7	−0.28203	0.17811	5.7	−5.93877	5.98722
0.8	−0.33614	0.21382	5.8	−6.07523	6.16416
0.9	−0.39604	0.25313	5.9	−6.21203	6.34276
1.0	−0.46133	0.29620	6.0	−6.34916	6.52299
1.1	−0.53162	0.34317	6.1	−6.48662	6.70482
1.2	−0.60653	0.39413	6.2	−6.62439	6.88823
1.3	−0.68572	0.44913	6.3	−6.76246	7.07320
1.4	−0.76885	0.50817	6.4	−6.90083	7.25971
1.5	−0.85561	0.57125	6.5	−7.03948	7.44773
1.6	−0.94574	0.63833	6.6	−7.17840	7.63724
1.7	−1.03895	0.70936	6.7	−7.31760	7.82821
1.8	−1.13503	0.78428	6.8	−7.45705	8.02064
1.9	−1.23376	0.86303	6.9	−7.59676	8.21449
2.0	−1.33493	0.94553	7.0	−7.73671	8.40976
2.1	−1.43838	1.03169	7.1	−7.87690	8.60641
2.2	−1.54395	1.12145	7.2	−8.01733	8.80443
2.3	−1.65148	1.21470	7.3	−8.15798	9.00381
2.4	−1.76084	1.31138	7.4	−8.29885	9.20452
2.5	−1.87192	1.41140	7.5	−8.43994	9.40656
2.6	−1.98459	1.51468	7.6	−8.58123	9.60989
2.7	−2.09877	1.62113	7.7	−8.72273	9.81451
2.8	−2.21435	1.73069	7.8	−8.86443	10.02040
2.9	−2.33125	1.84328	7.9	−9.00632	10.22754
3.0	−2.44940	1.95882	8.0	−9.14840	10.43592
3.1	−2.56872	2.07724	8.1	−9.29066	10.64553
3.2	−2.68915	2.19848	8.2	−9.43310	10.85634
3.3	−2.81063	2.32247	8.3	−9.57572	11.06835
3.4	−2.93310	2.44914	8.4	−9.71851	11.28154
3.5	−3.05650	2.57844	8.5	−9.86147	11.49590
3.6	−3.18080	2.71031	8.6	−10.00459	11.71142
3.7	−3.30594	2.84468	8.7	−10.14787	11.92807
3.8	−3.43189	2.98151	8.8	−10.29130	12.14586
3.9	−3.55861	3.12074	8.9	−10.43489	12.36476
4.0	−3.68605	3.26232	9.0	−10.57863	12.58476
4.1	−3.81420	3.40620	9.1	−10.72251	12.80586
4.2	−3.94301	3.55233	9.2	−10.86654	13.02804
4.3	−4.07245	3.70068	9.3	−11.01071	13.25129
4.4	−4.20251	3.85118	9.4	−11.15501	13.47560
4.5	−4.33315	4.00381	9.5	−11.29945	13.70096
4.6	−4.46434	4.15852	9.6	−11.44402	13.92735
4.7	−4.59608	4.31527	9.7	−11.58871	14.15477
4.8	−4.72833	4.47402	9.8	−11.73354	14.38321
4.9	−4.86107	4.63474	9.9	−11.87848	14.61265
5.0	−4.99429	4.79739	10.0	−12.02355	14.84309

Linear interpolation will yield about three figures; eight-point interpolation will yield about eight figures.

$$\Re \ln \Gamma(z) = \log_e |\Gamma(z)| \qquad\qquad \Im \ln \Gamma(z) = \arg \Gamma(z)$$

GAMMA FUNCTION FOR COMPLEX ARGUMENTS
$x = 1.8$

y	$\Re \ln \Gamma(z) = \log_e |\Gamma(z)|$	$\Im \ln \Gamma(z)$	y	$\Re \ln \Gamma(z) = \log_e |\Gamma(z)|$	$\Im \ln \Gamma(z)$
0.0	-0.07108	0.00000	5.0	-4.83046	4.92990
0.1	-0.07477	0.02859	5.1	-4.96227	5.09491
0.2	-0.08578	0.05769	5.2	-5.09455	5.26177
0.3	-0.10401	0.08783	5.3	-5.22729	5.43044
0.4	-0.12929	0.11946	5.4	-5.36046	5.60089
0.5	-0.16140	0.15305	5.5	-5.49407	5.77310
0.6	-0.20007	0.18897	5.6	-5.62808	5.94703
0.7	-0.24498	0.22758	5.7	-5.76249	6.12266
0.8	-0.29581	0.26917	5.8	-5.89728	6.29997
0.9	-0.35222	0.31396	5.9	-6.03244	6.47891
1.0	-0.41385	0.36216	6.0	-6.16796	6.65948
1.1	-0.48036	0.41390	6.1	-6.30383	6.84164
1.2	-0.55143	0.46928	6.2	-6.44004	7.02538
1.3	-0.62673	0.52837	6.3	-6.57657	7.21066
1.4	-0.70597	0.59120	6.4	-6.71341	7.39746
1.5	-0.78885	0.65778	6.5	-6.85057	7.58577
1.6	-0.87511	0.72810	6.6	-6.98802	7.77556
1.7	-0.96452	0.80213	6.7	-7.12576	7.96682
1.8	-1.05685	0.87984	6.8	-7.26378	8.15951
1.9	-1.15188	0.96117	6.9	-7.40207	8.35362
2.0	-1.24944	1.04606	7.0	-7.54063	8.54914
2.1	-1.34934	1.13446	7.1	-7.67944	8.74603
2.2	-1.45143	1.22629	7.2	-7.81851	8.94430
2.3	-1.55557	1.32148	7.3	-7.95782	9.14391
2.4	-1.66161	1.41997	7.4	-8.09737	9.34485
2.5	-1.76944	1.52168	7.5	-8.23715	9.54710
2.6	-1.87895	1.62655	7.6	-8.37715	9.75064
2.7	-1.99003	1.73449	7.7	-8.51737	9.95547
2.8	-1.10259	1.84545	7.8	-8.65781	10.16156
2.9	-2.21654	1.95935	7.9	-8.79846	10.36891
3.0	-2.33181	2.07613	8.0	-8.93931	10.57748
3.1	-2.44832	2.19573	8.1	-9.08036	10.78728
3.2	-2.56599	2.31808	8.2	-9.22160	10.99827
3.3	-2.68478	2.44311	8.3	-9.36303	11.21046
3.4	-2.80462	2.57078	8.4	-9.50465	11.42383
3.5	-2.92546	2.70103	8.5	-9.64645	11.63836
3.6	-3.04724	2.83379	8.6	-9.78842	11.85405
3.7	-3.16992	2.96901	8.7	-9.93057	12.07087
3.8	-3.29346	3.10665	8.8	-10.07288	12.28881
3.9	-3.41782	3.24666	8.9	-10.21536	12.50787
4.0	-3.54296	3.38897	9.0	-10.35800	12.72803
4.1	-3.66884	3.53356	9.1	-10.50080	12.94928
4.2	-3.79543	3.68037	9.2	-10.64375	13.17161
4.3	-3.92271	3.82935	9.3	-10.78686	13.39500
4.4	-4.05063	3.98048	9.4	-10.93011	13.61945
4.5	-4.17918	4.13370	9.5	-11.07350	13.84494
4.6	-4.30833	4.28897	9.6	-11.21704	14.07147
4.7	-4.43806	4.44627	9.7	-11.36072	14.29902
4.8	-4.56833	4.60554	9.8	-11.50453	14.52759
4.9	-4.66914	4.76676	9.9	-11.64848	14.75716
5.0	-4.83046	4.92990	10.0	-11.79255	14.98772

Linear interpolation will yield about three figures; eight-point interpolation will yield about eight figures.

$$\Re \ln \Gamma(z) = \log_e |\Gamma(z)| \qquad\qquad \Im \ln \Gamma(z) = \arg \Gamma(z)$$

GAMMA FUNCTION FOR COMPLETE ARGUMENTS
$x = 1.9$

y	$\Re \ln \Gamma(z) = \log_e |\Gamma(z)|$	$\Im \ln \Gamma(z)$	y	$\Re \ln \Gamma(z) = \log_e |\Gamma(z)|$	$\Im \ln \Gamma(z)$
0.0	−0.03898	0.00000	5.0	− 4.66613	5.06053
0.1	−0.04242	0.03569	5.1	− 4.79608	5.22604
0.2	−0.05270	0.07184	5.2	− 4.92655	5.39337
0.3	−0.06975	0.10890	5.3	− 5.05749	5.56251
0.4	−0.09340	0.14727	5.4	− 5.18891	5.73341
0.5	−0.12349	0.18736	5.5	− 5.32078	5.90605
0.6	−0.15978	0.22952	5.6	− 5.45309	6.08040
0.7	−0.20201	0.27408	5.7	− 5.58582	6.25643
0.8	−0.24990	0.32129	5.8	− 5.71896	6.43413
0.9	−0.30316	0.37139	5.9	− 5.85250	6.61345
1.0	−0.36148	0.42457	6.0	− 5.98642	6.79438
1.1	−0.42456	0.48098	6.1	− 6.12071	6.97690
1.2	−0.49210	0.54071	6.2	− 6.25536	7.16097
1.3	−0.56382	0.60386	6.3	− 6.39036	7.34659
1.4	−0.63944	0.67047	6.4	− 6.52570	7.53372
1.5	−0.71870	0.74056	6.5	− 6.66136	7.72234
1.6	−0.80136	0.81416	6.6	− 6.79735	7.92143
1.7	−0.88718	0.89124	6.7	− 6.93364	8.10398
1.8	−0.97596	0.97178	6.8	− 7.07023	8.29696
1.9	−1.06749	1.05574	6.9	− 7.20712	8.49135
2.0	−1.16160	1.14310	7.0	− 7.34429	8.68713
2.1	−1.25812	1.23379	7.1	− 7.48173	8.88429
2.2	−1.35688	1.32777	7.2	− 7.61945	9.08281
2.3	−1.45775	1.42497	7.3	− 7.75742	9.28267
2.4	−1.56060	1.52534	7.4	− 7.89565	9.48385
2.5	−1.66529	1.62881	7.5	− 8.03413	9.68634
2.6	−1.77174	1.73533	7.6	− 8.17285	9.89012
2.7	−1.87982	1.84483	7.7	− 8.31180	10.09517
2.8	−1.98944	1.95726	7.8	− 8.45099	10.30148
2.9	−2.10052	2.07255	7.9	− 8.59039	10.50904
3.0	−2.21298	2.19064	8.0	− 8.73002	10.71782
3.1	−2.32674	2.31147	8.1	− 8.86986	10.92782
3.2	−2.44173	2.43498	8.2	− 9.00991	11.13902
3.3	−2.55788	2.56113	8.3	− 9.15016	11.35140
3.4	−2.67515	2.68985	8.4	− 9.29060	11.56496
3.5	−2.79346	2.82109	8.5	− 9.43125	11.77967
3.6	−2.91278	2.95480	8.6	− 9.57208	11.99554
3.7	−3.03304	3.09093	8.7	− 9.71309	12.21253
3.8	−3.15422	3.22944	8.8	− 9.85429	12.43065
3.9	−3.27626	3.37026	8.9	− 9.99567	12.64988
4.0	−3.39912	3.51336	9.0	−10.13721	12.87021
4.1	−3.52277	3.65870	9.1	−10.27893	13.09162
4.2	−3.64718	3.80622	9.2	−10.42081	13.31410
4.3	−3.77231	3.95589	9.3	−10.56286	13.53765
4.4	−3.89814	4.10768	9.4	−10.70506	13.76225
4.5	−4.02462	4.26153	9.5	−10.84742	13.98789
4.6	−4.15175	4.41741	9.6	−10.98993	14.21457
4.7	−4.27948	4.57528	9.7	−11.13259	14.44226
4.8	−4.40781	4.73512	9.8	−11.27539	14.67097
4.9	−4.53670	4.89688	9.9	−11.41834	14.90067
5.0	−4.66613	5.06053	10.0	−11.56143	15.13137

Linear interpolation will yield about three figures; eight-point interpolation will yield about eight figures.

$$\Re \ln \Gamma(z) = \log_e |\Gamma(z)| \qquad\qquad \Im \ln \Gamma(z) = \arg \Gamma(z)$$

GAMMA FUNCTION FOR COMPLEX ARGUMENTS
$x = 2.0$

y	$\Re \ln \Gamma(z) = \log_e |\Gamma(z)|$	$\Im \ln \Gamma(z)$	y	$\Re \ln \Gamma(z) = \log_e |\Gamma(z)|$	$\Im \ln \Gamma(z)$
0.0	−0.00000	0.00000	5.0	− 4.50128	5.18930
0.1	−0.00322	0.04235	5.1	− 4.62940	5.35534
0.2	−0.01287	0.08509	5.2	− 4.75806	5.52319
0.3	−0.02886	0.12864	5.3	− 4.88723	5.69281
0.4	−0.05108	0.17335	5.4	− 5.01690	5.86419
0.5	−0.07937	0.21959	5.5	− 5.14706	6.03729
0.6	−0.11355	0.26768	5.6	− 5.27768	6.21208
0.7	−0.15338	0.31790	5.7	− 5.40874	6.38855
0.8	−0.19863	0.37052	5.8	− 5.54025	6.56665
0.9	−0.24904	0.42574	5.9	− 5.67217	6.74638
1.0	−0.30435	0.48376	6.0	− 5.80450	6.92770
1.1	−0.36429	0.54471	6.1	− 5.93723	7.11059
1.2	−0.42859	0.60873	6.2	− 6.07033	7.29503
1.3	−0.49700	0.67588	6.3	− 6.20381	7.48100
1.4	−0.56927	0.74625	6.4	− 6.33765	7.66847
1.5	−0.64516	0.81985	6.5	− 6.47184	7.85743
1.6	−0.72443	0.89673	6.6	− 6.60636	8.04785
1.7	−0.80689	0.97687	6.7	− 6.74122	8.23971
1.8	−0.89231	1.06028	6.8	− 6.87639	8.43299
1.9	−0.98053	1.14693	6.9	− 7.01188	8.62768
2.0	−1.07136	1.23680	7.0	− 7.14767	8.82376
2.1	−1.16464	1.32984	7.1	− 7.28375	9.02120
2.2	−1.26022	1.42601	7.2	− 7.42012	9.21999
2.3	−1.35796	1.52528	7.3	− 7.55677	9.42012
2.4	−1.45773	1.62759	7.4	− 7.69369	9.62156
2.5	−1.55941	1.73289	7.5	− 7.83087	9.82430
2.6	−1.66288	1.84113	7.6	− 7.96831	10.02832
2.7	−1.76806	1.95226	7.7	− 8.10600	10.23362
2.8	−1.87484	2.06621	7.8	− 8.24394	10.44016
2.9	−1.98313	2.18294	7.9	− 8.38211	10.64794
3.0	−2.09285	2.30240	8.0	− 8.52052	10.85695
3.1	−2.20393	2.42452	8.1	− 8.65915	11.06716
3.2	−2.31629	2.54926	8.2	− 8.79801	11.27857
3.3	−2.42988	2.67657	8.3	− 8.93708	11.49117
3.4	−2.54462	2.80640	8.4	− 9.07637	11.70493
3.5	−2.66047	2.93869	8.5	− 9.21586	11.91984
3.6	−2.77736	3.07340	8.6	− 9.35555	12.13590
3.7	−2.89526	3.21048	8.7	− 9.49544	12.35308
3.8	−3.01411	3.34989	8.8	− 9.63553	12.57138
3.9	−3.13386	3.49159	8.9	− 9.77580	12.79079
4.0	−3.25449	3.63552	9.0	− 9.91626	13.01130
4.1	−3.37595	3.78164	9.1	−10.05689	13.23288
4.2	−3.49821	3.92993	9.2	−10.19771	13.45553
4.3	−3.62123	4.08033	9.3	−10.33870	13.67925
4.4	−3.74498	4.23281	9.4	−10.47986	13.90401
4.5	−3.86943	4.38732	9.5	−10.62118	14.12981
4.6	−3.99455	4.54385	9.6	−10.76267	14.35664
4.7	−4.12032	4.70234	9.7	−10.90431	14.58449
4.8	−4.24672	4.86277	9.8	−11.04611	14.81335
4.9	−4.37371	5.02510	9.9	−11.18807	15.04320
5.0	−4.50128	5.18930	10.0	−11.33017	15.27404

Linear interpolation will yield about three figures; eight-point interpolation will yield about eight figures.

$$\Re \ln \Gamma(z) = \log_e |\Gamma(z)| \qquad\qquad \Im \ln \Gamma(z) = \arg \Gamma(z)$$

The Beta Function

Definition: $B(m,n) = \displaystyle\int_0^1 t^{m-1}(1-t)^{m-1}\, dt \quad m > 0, n > 0$

Relationship with
Gamma Function $\qquad B(m,n) = \dfrac{\Gamma(m)\Gamma(n)}{\Gamma(m+n)}$

Properties:

$$B(m,n) = B(n,m)$$

$$B(m,n) = 2\int_0^{\pi/2} \sin^{2m-1}\theta \, \cos^{2n-1}\theta \, d\theta$$

$$B(m,n) = \int_0^\infty \frac{t^{m-1}}{(1+t)^{m+n}}\, dt$$

$$B(m,n) = r^n(r+1)^m \int_0^1 \frac{t^{m-1}(1-t)^{n-1}}{(r+t)^{m+n}}\, dt$$

The Error Function

Definition: $erf\, x = \dfrac{2}{\sqrt{\pi}}\displaystyle\int_0^x e^{-t^2}\, dt$

Series: $erf\, x = \dfrac{2}{\sqrt{\pi}}\left(x - \dfrac{x^3}{3} + \dfrac{1}{2!}\dfrac{x^5}{5} - \dfrac{1}{3!}\dfrac{x^7}{7} + \ldots\right)$

Property: $erf\, x = -erf\,(-x)$

Relationship with Normal Probability Function $f(t)$: $\displaystyle\int_0^x f(t)\, dt = \frac{1}{2} erf\left(\frac{x}{\sqrt{2}}\right)$

To evaluate $erf\,(2.3)$, one proceeds as follows: Since $\dfrac{x}{\sqrt{2}} = 2.3$, one finds $x = (2.3)(\sqrt{2}) = 3.25$. In the normal probability function table (page 753), one finds the entry 0.4994 opposite the value 3.25. Thus $erf\,(2.3) = 2(0.4994) = 0.9988$.

$$erfc\, z = 1 - erf\, z = \frac{2}{\sqrt{\pi}}\int_z^\infty e^{-t^2}\, dt$$

is known as the complimentary error function.

BESSEL FUNCTIONS

1. **Bessel's differential equation for a real variable x is**

$$x^2 \frac{d^2 y}{dx^2} + x \frac{dy}{dx} + (x^2 - n^2) y = 0$$

2. **When n is not an integer, two independent solutions of the equation are $J_n(x)$ and $J_{-n}(x)$, where**

$$J_n(x) = \sum_{k=0}^{\infty} \frac{(-1)^k}{k! \, \Gamma(n + k + 1)} \left(\frac{x}{2}\right)^{n+2k}$$

3. **If n is an integer $J_{-n}(x) = (-1)^n J_n(x)$, where**

$$J_n(x) = \frac{x^n}{2^n n!} \left\{ 1 - \frac{x^2}{2^2 \cdot 1!(n + 1)} + \frac{x^4}{2^4 \cdot 2!(n + 1)(n + 2)} \right.$$
$$\left. - \frac{x^6}{2^6 \cdot 3!(n + 1)(n + 2)(n + 3)} + \cdots \right\}$$

4. **For $n = 0$ and $n = 1$, this formula becomes**

$$J_0(x) = 1 - \frac{x^2}{2^2 (1!)^2} + \frac{x^4}{2^4 (2!)^2} - \frac{x^6}{2^6 (3!)^2} + \frac{x^8}{2^8 (4!)^2} - \cdots$$

$$J_1(x) = \frac{x}{2} - \frac{x^3}{2^3 \cdot 1! 2!} + \frac{x^5}{2^5 \cdot 2! 3!} - \frac{x^7}{2^7 \cdot 3! 4!} + \frac{x^9}{2^9 \cdot 4! 5!} - \cdots$$

5. **When x is large and positive, the following asymptotic series may be used**

$$J_0(x) = \left(\frac{2}{\pi x}\right)^{\frac{1}{2}} \left\{ P_0(x) \cos\left(x - \frac{\pi}{4}\right) - Q_0(x) \sin\left(x - \frac{\pi}{4}\right) \right\}$$

$$J_1(x) = \left(\frac{2}{\pi x}\right)^{\frac{1}{2}} \left\{ P_1(x) \cos\left(x - \frac{3\pi}{4}\right) - Q_1(x) \sin\left(x - \frac{3\pi}{4}\right) \right\},$$

where

$$P_0(x) \sim 1 - \frac{1^2 \cdot 3^2}{2!(8x)^2} + \frac{1^2 \cdot 3^2 \cdot 5^2 \cdot 7^2}{4!(8x)^4} - \frac{1^2 \cdot 3^2 \cdot 5^2 \cdot 7^2 \cdot 9^2 \cdot 11^2}{6!(8x)^6} + \cdots$$

$$Q_0(x) \sim - \frac{1^2}{1!8x} + \frac{1^2 \cdot 3^2 \cdot 5^2}{3!(8x)^3} - \frac{1^2 \cdot 3^2 \cdot 5^2 \cdot 7^2 \cdot 9^2}{5!(8x)^5} + - \cdots$$

$$P_1(x) \sim 1 + \frac{1^2 \cdot 3 \cdot 5}{2!(8x)^2} - \frac{1^2 \cdot 3^2 \cdot 5^2 \cdot 7 \cdot 9}{4!(8x)^4} + \frac{1^2 \cdot 3^2 \cdot 5^2 \cdot 7^2 \cdot 9^2 \cdot 11 \cdot 13}{6!(8x)^6} - + \cdots$$

$$Q_1(x) \sim \frac{1 \cdot 3}{1!8x} - \frac{1^2 \cdot 3^2 \cdot 5 \cdot 7}{3!(8x)^3} + \frac{1^2 \cdot 3^2 \cdot 5^2 \cdot 7^2 \cdot 9 \cdot 11}{5!(8x)^5} - \cdots$$

[In $P_1(x)$ the signs alternate from + to − after the first term]

6. If $x > 25$, it is convenient to use the formulas

$$J_0(x) = A_0(x) \sin x + B_0(x) \cos x$$
$$J_1(x) = B_1(x) \sin x - A_1(x) \cos x,$$

where

$$A_0(x) = \frac{P_0(x) - Q_0(x)}{(\pi x)^{\frac{1}{2}}} \quad \text{and} \quad A_1(x) = \frac{P_1(x) - Q_1(x)}{(\pi x)^{\frac{1}{2}}}$$

$$B_0(x) = \frac{P_0(x) + Q_0(x)}{(\pi x)^{\frac{1}{2}}} \quad \text{and} \quad B_1(x) = \frac{P_1(x) + Q_1(x)}{(\pi x)^{\frac{1}{2}}}$$

7. The zeros of $J_0(x)$ and $J_1(x)$

If $j_{0,s}$ and $j_{1,s}$ are the s'th zeros of $J_0(x)$ and $J_1(x)$ respectively, and if $a = 4s - 1$, $b = 4s + 1$

$$j_{0,s} \sim \frac{1}{4}\pi a\left\{1 + \frac{2}{\pi^2 a^2} - \frac{62}{3\pi^4 a^4} + \frac{15,116}{15\pi^6 a^6} - \frac{12,554,474}{105\pi^8 a^8} + \frac{8,368,654,292}{315\pi^{10} a^{10}} - + \cdots\right\}$$

$$j_{1,s} \sim \frac{1}{4}\pi b\left\{1 - \frac{6}{\pi^2 b^2} + \frac{6}{\pi^4 b^4} - \frac{4716}{5\pi^6 b^6} + \frac{3,902,418}{35\pi^8 b^8} - \frac{895,167,324}{35\pi^{10} b^{10}} + \cdots\right\}$$

$$J_1(j_{0,s}) \sim \frac{(-1)^{s+1} 2^{\frac{1}{2}}}{\pi a^{\frac{1}{2}}}\left\{1 - \frac{56}{3\pi^4 a^4} + \frac{9664}{5\pi^6 a^6} - \frac{7,381,280}{21\pi^8 a^8} + \cdots\right\}$$

$$J_0(j_{1,s}) \sim \frac{(-1)^s 2^{\frac{1}{2}}}{\pi b^{\frac{1}{2}}}\left\{1 + \frac{24}{\pi^4 b^4} - \frac{19,584}{10\pi^6 b^6} + \frac{2,466,720}{7\pi^8 b^8} - \cdots\right\}$$

8. Table of zeros for $J_0(x)$ and $J_1(x)$

$$J_1(\alpha_n) = 0 \qquad J_0(\beta_n) = 0$$

Roots α_n	$J_1(\alpha_n)$	Roots β_n	$J_0(\beta_n)$
2.4048	0.5191	0.0000	1.0000
5.5201	−0.3403	3.8317	−0.4028
8.6537	0.2715	7.0156	0.3001
11.7915	−0.2325	10.1735	−0.2497
14.9309	0.2065	13.3237	0.2184
18.0711	−0.1877	16.4706	−0.1965
21.2116	0.1733	19.6159	0.1801

9. Recurrence formulas

$$J_{n-1}(x) + J_{n+1}(x) = \frac{2n}{x} J_n(x) \qquad\qquad n J_n(x) + x J_n'(x) = x J_{n-1}(x)$$

$$J_{n-1}(x) - J_{n+1}(x) = 2 J_n'(x) \qquad\qquad n J_n(x) - x J_n'(x) = x J_{n+1}(x)$$

10. If J_n is written for $J_n(x)$ and $J_n^{(k)}$ is written for $\dfrac{d^k}{dx^k}\{J_n(x)\}$, then the following derivative relationships are important

$$J_0^{(r)} = -J_1^{(r-1)}$$

$$J_0^{(2)} = -J_0 + \frac{1}{x} J_1 = \frac{1}{2}(J_2 - J_0)$$

$$J_0^{(3)} = \frac{1}{x} J_0 + \left(1 - \frac{2}{x^2}\right) J_1 = \frac{1}{4}(-J_3 + 3J_1)$$

$$J_0^{(4)} = \left(1 - \frac{3}{x^2}\right) J_0 - \left(\frac{2}{x} - \frac{6}{x^3}\right) J_1 = \frac{1}{8}(J_4 - 4J_2 + 3J_0), \text{ etc.}$$

11. Half order Bessel functions

$$J_{\frac{1}{2}}(x) = \sqrt{\frac{2}{\pi x}} \sin x$$

$$J_{-\frac{1}{2}}(x) = \sqrt{\frac{2}{\pi x}} \cos x$$

$$J_{n+\frac{3}{2}}(x) = -x^{n+\frac{1}{2}} \frac{d}{dx}\{x^{-(n+\frac{1}{2})} J_{n+\frac{1}{2}}(x)\}$$

$$J_{n-\frac{1}{2}}(x) = x^{-(n+\frac{1}{2})} \frac{d}{dx}\{x^{n+\frac{1}{2}} J_{n+\frac{1}{2}}(x)\}$$

n	$\left(\dfrac{\pi x}{2}\right)^{\frac{1}{2}} J_{n+\frac{1}{2}}(x)$	$\left(\dfrac{\pi x}{2}\right)^{\frac{1}{2}} J_{-(n+\frac{1}{2})}(x)$
0	$\sin x$	$\cos x$
1	$\dfrac{\sin x}{x} - \cos x$	$-\dfrac{\cos x}{x} - \sin x$
2	$\left(\dfrac{3}{x^2} - 1\right)\sin x - \dfrac{3}{x}\cos x$	$\left(\dfrac{3}{x^2} - 1\right)\cos x + \dfrac{3}{x}\sin x$
3	$\left(\dfrac{15}{x^3} - \dfrac{6}{x}\right)\sin x - \left(\dfrac{15}{x^2} - 1\right)\cos x$	$-\left(\dfrac{15}{x^3} - \dfrac{6}{x}\right)\cos x - \left(\dfrac{15}{x^2} - 1\right)\sin x$
	etc.	

12. Additional solutions to Bessel's equation are

$Y_n(x)$ (also called Weber's function, and sometimes denoted by $N_n(x)$)
$H_n^{(1)}(x)$ and $H_n^{(2)}(x)$ (also called Hankel functions)

These solutions are defined as follows

$$Y_n(x) = \begin{cases} \dfrac{J_n(x)\cos(n\pi) - J_{-n}(x)}{\sin(n\pi)} & n \text{ not an integer} \\[3mm] \lim_{\nu \to n} \dfrac{J_\nu(x)\cos(\nu\pi) - J_{-\nu}(x)}{\sin(\nu\pi)} & n \text{ an integer} \end{cases}$$

$$H_n^{(1)}(x) = J_n(x) + iY_n(x)$$
$$H_n^{(2)}(x) = J_n(x) - iY_n(x)$$

The additional properties of these functions may all be derived from the above relations and the known properties of $J_n(x)$.

13. Complete solutions to Bessel's equation may be written as

$$c_1 J_n(x) + c_2 J_{-n}(x) \qquad \text{if } n \text{ is not an integer,}$$

or

$$c_1 J_n(x) + c_2 Y_n(x)$$

or

$$\left. c_1 H_n^{(1)}(x) + c_2 H_n^{(2)}(x) \right\} \text{ for any value of } n$$

14. The modified (or hyperbolic) Bessel's differential equation is

$$x^2 \frac{d^2 y}{dx^2} + x \frac{dy}{dx} - (x^2 + n^2) y = 0$$

15. When n is not an integer, two independent solutions of the equation are $I_n(x)$ and $I_{-n}(x)$, where

$$I_n(x) = \sum_{k=0}^{\infty} \frac{1}{k! \Gamma(n + k + 1)} \left(\frac{x}{2}\right)^{n+2k}$$

16. If n is an integer,

$$I_n(x) = I_{-n}(x) = \frac{x^n}{2^n n!} \left\{ 1 + \frac{x^2}{2^2 \cdot 1!(n + 1)} + \frac{x^4}{2^4 \cdot 2!(n + 1)(n + 2)} \right.$$
$$\left. + \frac{x^6}{2^6 \cdot 3!(n + 1)(n + 2)(n + 3)} + \cdots \right\}$$

17. For $n = 0$ and $n = 1$, this formula becomes

$$I_0(x) = 1 + \frac{x^2}{2^2 (1!)^2} + \frac{x^4}{2^4 (2!)^2} + \frac{x^6}{2^6 (3!)^2} + \frac{x^8}{2^8 (4!)^2} + \cdots$$

$$I_1(x) = \frac{x}{2} + \frac{x^3}{2^3 \cdot 1! 2!} + \frac{x^5}{2^5 \cdot 2! 3!} + \frac{x^7}{2^7 \cdot 3! 4!} + \frac{x^9}{2^9 \cdot 4! 5!} + \cdots$$

18. Another solution to the modified Bessel's equation is

$$K_n(x) = \begin{cases} \dfrac{1}{2} \pi \dfrac{I_{-n}(x) - I_n(x)}{\sin(n\pi)} & n \text{ not an integer} \\[2ex] \lim_{v \to n} \dfrac{1}{2} \pi \dfrac{I_{-v}(x) - I_v(x)}{\sin(v\pi)} & n \text{ an integer} \end{cases}$$

This function is linearly independent of $I_n(x)$ for all values of n. Thus the complete solution to the modified Bessel's equation may be written as

$$c_1 I_n(x) + c_2 I_{-n}(x) \qquad n \text{ not an integer}$$

or

$$c_1 I_n(x) + c_2 K_n(x) \qquad \text{any } n$$

19. The following relations hold among the various Bessel functions:

$$I_n(z) = i^{-m} J_m(iz)$$

$$Y_n(iz) = (i)^{n+1} I_n(z) - \frac{2}{\pi} i^{-n} K_n(z)$$

Most of the properties of the modified Bessel function may be deduced from the known properties of $J_n(x)$ by use of these relations and those previously given.

20. Recurrence formulas

$$I_{n-1}(x) - I_{n+1}(x) = \frac{2n}{x} I_n(x) \qquad I_{n-1}(x) + I_{n+1}(x) = 2 I_n'(x)$$

$$I_{n-1}(x) - \frac{n}{x} I_n(x) = I_n'(x) \qquad I_n'(x) = I_{n+1}(x) + \frac{n}{x} I_n(z)$$

BESSEL FUNCTIONS FOR SPHERICAL COORDINATES

$$j_n(x) = \sqrt{\frac{\pi}{2x}}\, J_{(n+\frac{1}{2})}(x), \quad y_n(x) = \sqrt{\frac{\pi}{2x}}\, Y_{(n+\frac{1}{2})}(x) = (-1)^{n+1} \sqrt{\frac{\pi}{2x}}\, J_{-(n+\frac{1}{2})}(x)$$

x	$j_0(x)$	$y_0(x)$	$j_1(x)$	$y_1(x)$	$j_2(x)$	$y_2(x)$
0.0	1.0000	$-\infty$	0.0000	$-\infty$	0.0000	$-\infty$
0.1	0.9983	-9.9500	0.0333	-100.50	0.0007	-3005.0
0.2	0.9933	-4.9003	0.0664	-25.495	0.0027	-377.52
0.4	0.9735	-2.3027	0.1312	-6.7302	0.0105	-48.174
0.6	0.9411	-1.3756	0.1929	-3.2337	0.0234	-14.793
0.8	0.8967	-0.8709	0.2500	-1.9853	0.0408	-6.5740
1.0	0.8415	-0.5403	0.3012	-1.3818	0.0620	-3.6050
1.2	0.7767	-0.3020	0.3453	-1.0283	0.0865	-2.2689
1.4	0.7039	-0.1214	0.3814	-0.7906	0.1133	-1.5728
1.6	0.6247	$+0.0182$	0.4087	-0.6133	0.1416	-1.1682
1.8	0.5410	0.1262	0.4268	-0.4709	0.1703	-0.9111
2.0	0.4546	0.2081	0.4354	-0.3506	0.1984	-0.7340
2.2	0.3675	0.2675	0.4345	-0.2459	0.2251	-0.6028
2.4	0.2814	0.3072	0.4245	-0.1534	0.2492	-0.4990
2.6	0.1983	0.3296	0.4058	-0.0715	0.2700	-0.4121
2.8	0.1196	0.3365	0.3792	$+0.0005$	0.2867	-0.3359
3.0	$+0.0470$	0.3300	0.3457	0.0630	0.2986	-0.2670
3.2	-0.0182	0.3120	0.3063	0.1157	0.3054	-0.2035
3.4	-0.0752	0.2844	0.2622	0.1588	0.3066	-0.1442
3.6	-0.1229	0.2491	0.2150	0.1921	0.3021	-0.0890
3.8	-0.1610	0.2082	0.1658	0.2158	0.2919	-0.0378
4.0	-0.1892	0.1634	0.1161	0.2301	0.2763	$+0.0091$
4.2	-0.2075	0.1167	0.0673	0.2353	0.2556	0.0514
4.4	-0.2163	0.0698	$+0.0207$	0.2321	0.2304	0.0884
4.6	-0.2160	$+0.0244$	-0.0226	0.2213	0.2013	0.1200
4.8	-0.2075	-0.0182	-0.0615	0.2037	0.1691	0.1456
5.0	-0.1918	-0.0567	-0.0951	0.1804	0.1347	0.1650
5.2	-0.1699	-0.0901	-0.1228	0.1526	0.0991	0.1781
5.4	-0.1431	-0.1175	-0.1440	0.1213	0.0631	0.1850
5.6	-0.1127	-0.1385	-0.1586	0.0880	$+0.0277$	0.1856
5.8	-0.0801	-0.1527	-0.1665	0.0538	-0.0060	0.1805
6.0	-0.0466	-0.1600	-0.1678	$+0.0199$	-0.0373	0.1700
6.2	-0.0134	-0.1607	-0.1629	-0.0125	-0.0654	0.1547
6.4	$+0.0182$	-0.1552	-0.1523	-0.0425	-0.0896	0.1353
6.6	0.0472	-0.1440	-0.1368	-0.0690	-0.1094	0.1126
6.8	0.0727	-0.1278	-0.1172	-0.0915	-0.1243	0.0875
7.0	0.0939	-0.1077	-0.0943	-0.1092	-0.1343	0.0609
7.2	0.1102	-0.0845	-0.0692	-0.1220	-0.1391	0.0337
7.4	0.1215	-0.0593	-0.0429	-0.1295	-0.1388	$+0.0068$
7.6	0.1274	-0.0331	-0.0163	-0.1317	-0.1338	-0.0189
7.8	0.1280	-0.0069	$+0.0095$	-0.1289	-0.1244	-0.0427
8.0	0.1237	$+0.0182$	0.0336	-0.1214	-0.1111	-0.0637

Taken from Vibration and Sound with the permission of Philip Morse, author, and McGraw-Hill Book Company, Inc., publisher.

BESSEL FUNCTIONS $J_0(x)$ AND $J_1(x)$

x	$J_0(x)$	$J_1(x)$	x	$J_0(x)$	$J_1(x)$	x	$J_0(x)$	$J_1(x)$
0.0	1.0000	.0000	**5.0**	−.1776	−.3276	**10.0**	−.2459	.0435
0.1	.9975	.0499	5.1	−.1443	−.3371	10.1	−.2490	.0184
0.2	.9900	.0995	5.2	−.1103	−.3432	10.2	−.2496	−.0066
0.3	.9776	.1483	5.3	−.0758	−.3460	10.3	−.2477	−.0313
0.4	.9604	.1960	5.4	−.0412	−.3453	10.4	−.2434	−.0555
0.5	.9385	.2423	**5.5**	−.0068	−.3414	**10.5**	−.2366	−.0789
0.6	.9120	.2867	5.6	.0270	−.3343	10.6	−.2276	−.1012
0.7	.8812	.3290	5.7	.0599	−.3241	10.7	−.2164	−.1224
0.8	.8463	.3688	5.8	.0917	−.3110	10.8	−.2032	−.1422
0.9	.8075	.4059	5.9	.1220	−.2951	10.9	−.1881	−.1603
1.0	.7652	.4401	**6.0**	.1506	−.2767	**11.0**	−.1712	−.1768
1.1	.7196	.4709	6.1	.1773	−.2559	11.1	−.1528	−.1913
1.2	.6711	.4983	6.2	.2017	−.2329	11.2	−.1330	−.2039
1.3	.6201	.5220	6.3	.2238	−.2081	11.3	−.1121	−.2143
1.4	.5669	.5419	6.4	.2433	−.1816	11.4	−.0902	−.2225
1.5	.5118	.5579	**6.5**	.2601	−.1538	**11.5**	−.0677	−.2284
1.6	.4554	.5699	6.6	.2740	−.1250	11.6	−.0446	−.2320
1.7	.3980	.5778	6.7	.2851	−.0953	11.7	−.0213	−.2333
1.8	.3400	.5815	6.8	.2931	−.0652	11.8	.0020	−.2323
1.9	.2818	.5812	6.9	.2981	−.0349	11.9	.0250	−.2290
2.0	.2239	.5767	**7.0**	.3001	−.0047	**12.0**	.0477	−.2234
2.1	.1666	.5683	7.1	.2991	.0252	12.1	.0697	−.2157
2.2	.1104	.5560	7.2	.2951	.0543	12.2	.0908	−.2060
2.3	.0555	.5399	7.3	.2882	.0826	12.3	.1108	−.1943
2.4	.0025	.5202	7.4	.2786	.1096	12.4	.1296	−.1807
2.5	−.0484	.4971	**7.5**	.2663	.1352	**12.5**	.1469	−.1655
2.6	−.0968	.4708	7.6	.2516	.1592	12.6	.1626	−.1487
2.7	−.1424	.4416	7.7	.2346	.1813	12.7	.1766	−.1307
2.8	−.1850	.4097	7.8	.2154	.2014	12.8	.1887	−.1114
2.9	−.2243	.3754	7.9	.1944	.2192	12.9	.1988	−.0912
3.0	−.2601	.3391	**8.0**	.1717	.2346	**13.0**	.2069	−.0703
3.1	−.2921	.3009	8.1	.1475	.2476	13.1	.2129	−.0489
3.2	−.3202	.2613	8.2	.1222	.2580	13.2	.2167	−.0271
3.3	−.3443	.2207	8.3	.0960	.2657	13.3	.2183	−.0052
3.4	−.3643	.1792	8.4	.0692	.2708	13.4	.2177	.0166
3.5	−.3801	.1374	**8.5**	.0419	.2731	**13.5**	.2150	.0380
3.6	−.3918	.0955	8.6	.0146	.2728	13.6	.2101	.0590
3.7	−.3992	.0538	8.7	−.0125	.2697	13.7	.2032	.0791
3.8	−.4026	.0128	8.8	−.0392	.2641	13.8	.1943	.0984
3.9	−.4018	−.0272	8.9	−.0653	.2559	13.9	.1836	.1165
4.0	−.3971	−.0660	**9.0**	−.0903	.2453	**14.0**	.1711	.1334
4.1	−.3887	−.1033	9.1	−.1142	.2324	14.1	.1570	.1488
4.2	−.3766	−.1386	9.2	−.1367	.2174	14.2	.1414	.1626
4.3	−.3610	−.1719	9.3	−.1577	.2004	14.3	.1245	.1747
4.4	−.3423	−.2028	9.4	−.1768	.1816	14.4	.1065	.1850
4.5	−.3205	−.2311	**9.5**	−.1939	.1613	**14.5**	.0875	.1934
4.6	−.2961	−.2566	9.6	−.2090	.1395	14.6	.0679	.1999
4.7	−.2693	−.2791	9.7	−.2218	.1166	14.7	.0476	.2043
4.8	−.2404	−.2985	9.8	−.2323	.0928	14.8	.0271	.2066
4.9	−.2097	−.3147	9.9	−.2403	.0684	14.9	.0064	.2069

BESSEL FUNCTION J_0

T	.00	.01	.02	.03	.04
0.0	1.0000000	.9999750	.9999000	.9997750	.9996000
.1	.9975016	.9969773	.9964032	.9957795	.9951060
.2	.9900250	.9890054	.9879366	.9868187	.9856518
.3	.9776262	.9761189	.9745634	.9729597	.9713081
.4	.9603982	.9584145	.9563838	.9543065	.9521825
.5	.9384698	.9360245	.9335339	.9309983	.9284179
.6	.9120049	.9091162	.9061843	.9032094	.9001918
.7	.8812009	.8778904	.8745391	.8711471	.8677147
.8	.8462874	.8425797	.8388338	.8350500	.8312284
.9	.8075238	.8034465	.7993339	.7951863	.7910039
1.0	.7651977	.7607810	.7563321	.7518513	.7473390
1.1	.7196220	.7148985	.7101461	.7053653	.7005564
1.2	.6711327	.6661371	.6611163	.6560706	.6510004
1.3	.6200860	.6148549	.6096023	.6043287	.5990343
1.4	.5668551	.5614267	.5559807	.5505176	.5450376
1.5	.5118277	.5062414	.5006415	.4950285	.4894026
1.6	.4554022	.4496983	.4439850	.4382625	.4325313
1.7	.3979849	.3922044	.3864185	.3806276	.3748321
1.8	.3399864	.3341705	.3283532	.3225351	.3167166
1.9	.2818186	.2760083	.2702008	.2643965	.2585959
2.0	.2238908	.2181268	.2123697	.2066198	.2008776
2.1	.1666070	.1609293	.1552625	.1496068	.1439626
2.2	.1103623	.1048098	.0992720	.0937491	.0882416
2.3	.0555398	.0501501	.0447787	.0394259	.0340921
2.4	.0025077	−.0026834	−.0078527	−.0129999	−.0181247
2.5	−.0483838	−.0533423	−.0582758	−.0631839	−.0680664
2.6	−.0968050	−.1014992	−.1061654	−.1108031	−.1154123
2.7	−.1424494	−.1468500	−.1512198	−.1555585	−.1598658
2.8	−.1850360	−.1891165	−.1931636	−.1971771	−.2011568
2.9	−.2243115	−.2280481	−.2317491	−.2354142	−.2390434
3.0	−.2600520	−.2634239	−.2667583	−.2700551	−.2733140
3.1	−.2920643	−.2950541	−.2980048	−.3009162	−.3037884
3.2	−.3201882	−.3227815	−.3253345	−.3278471	−.3303193
3.3	−.3442963	−.3464823	−.3486272	−.3507308	−.3527931
3.4	−.3642956	−.3660670	−.3677967	−.3694845	−.3711306
3.5	−.3801277	−.3814805	−.3827914	−.3840603	−.3852873
3.6	−.3917690	−.3927027	−.3935947	−.3944449	−.3952533
3.7	−.3992302	−.3997479	−.4002242	−.4006593	−.4010532
3.8	−.4025564	−.4026643	−.4027318	−.4027588	−.4027456
3.9	−.4018260	−.4015339	−.4012023	−.4008316	−.4004218
4.0	−.3971498	−.3964704	−.3957530	−.3949979	−.3942053
4.1	−.3886697	−.3876188	−.3865318	−.3854088	−.3842500
4.2	−.3765571	−.3751534	−.3737157	−.3722440	−.3707386
4.3	−.3610111	−.3592761	−.3575093	−.3557108	−.3538810
4.4	−.3422568	−.3402143	−.3381424	−.3360414	−.3339116
4.5	−.3205425	−.3182185	−.3158678	−.3134908	−.3110877
4.6	−.2961378	−.2935603	−.2909591	−.2883344	−.2856866
4.7	−.2693308	−.2665295	−.2637076	−.2608653	−.2580029
4.8	−.2404253	−.2374315	−.2344201	−.2313916	−.2283462
4.9	−.2097383	−.2065842	−.2034158	−.2002335	−.1970377

BESSEL FUNCTION J_0

T	.05	.06	.07	.08	.09
0.0	.9993751	.9991002	.9987754	.9984006	.9979760
.1	.9943829	.9936102	.9927880	.9919164	.9909953
.2	.9844359	.9831713	.9818579	.9804958	.9790853
.3	.9696087	.9678615	.9660667	.9642245	.9623350
.4	.9500121	.9477955	.9455328	.9432242	.9408698
.5	.9257928	.9231233	.9204096	.9176518	.9148501
.6	.8971316	.8940292	.8908846	.8876982	.8844702
.7	.8642423	.8607300	.8571780	.8535868	.8499565
.8	.8273695	.8234734	.8195405	.8155711	.8115654
.9	.7867871	.7825361	.7782514	.7739332	.7695819
1.0	.7427956	.7382212	.7336163	.7289813	.7243164
1.1	.6957198	.6908557	.6859646	.6810469	.6761028
1.2	.6459061	.6407880	.6356466	.6304822	.6252952
1.3	.5937196	.5883850	.5830309	.5776576	.5722655
1.4	.5395413	.5340289	.5285010	.5229579	.5174000
1.5	.4837644	.4781143	.4724526	.4667797	.4610961
1.6	.4267919	.4210446	.4152898	.4095280	.4037595
1.7	.3690325	.3632292	.3574225	.3516128	.3458007
1.8	.3108980	.3050797	.2992623	.2934460	.2876313
1.9	.2527992	.2470071	.2412197	.2354376	.2296612
2.0	.1951434	.1894177	.1837008	.1779931	.1722950
2.1	.1383305	.1327106	.1271035	.1215095	.1159290
2.2	.0827499	.0772742	.0718150	.0663726	.0609474
2.3	.0287776	.0234828	.0182081	.0129538	.0077202
2.4	−.0232267	−.0283057	−.0333611	−.0383929	−.0434005
2.5	−.0729229	−.0777531	−.0825567	−.0873334	−.0920829
2.6	−.1199924	−.1245434	−.1290648	−.1335565	−.1380181
2.7	−.1641414	−.1683852	−.1725967	−.1767759	−.1809224
2.8	−.2051024	−.2090137	−.2128905	−.2167325	−.2205396
2.9	−.2426364	−.2461931	−.2497131	−.2531964	−.2566427
3.0	−.2765350	−.2797178	−.2828623	−.2859683	−.2890357
3.1	−.3066211	−.3094142	−.3121675	−.3148811	−.3175547
3.2	−.3327508	−.3351416	−.3374917	−.3398009	−.3420691
3.3	−.3548140	−.3567934	−.3587314	−.3606277	−.3624825
3.4	−.3727349	−.3742972	−.3758177	−.3772963	−.3787330
3.5	−.3864724	−.3876155	−.3887167	−.3897760	−.3907934
3.6	−.3960201	−.3967452	−.3974287	−.3980707	−.3986712
3.7	−.4014061	−.4017178	−.4019887	−.4022187	−.4024079
3.8	−.4026921	−.4025986	−.4024651	−.4022918	−.4020787
3.9	−.3999730	−.3994854	−.3989591	−.3983943	−.3977912
4.0	−.3933752	−.3925079	−.3916035	−.3906622	−.3896842
4.1	−.3830556	−.3818259	−.3805609	−.3792610	−.3779263
4.2	−.3691998	−.3676276	−.3660225	−.3643845	−.3627140
4.3	−.3520200	−.3501281	−.3482056	−.3462527	−.3442697
4.4	−.3317533	−.3295666	−.3273519	−.3251095	−.3228396
4.5	−.3086589	−.3062045	−.3037249	−.3012204	−.2986913
4.6	−.2830159	−.2803228	−.2776073	−.2748700	−.2721110
4.7	−.2551208	−.2522193	−.2492987	−.2463592	−.2434014
4.8	−.2252843	−.2222062	−.2191122	−.2160027	−.2128779
4.9	−.1938286	−.1906067	−.1873722	−.1841255	−.1808669

SPECIAL FUNCTIONS

BESSEL FUNCTION J_0

T	.00	.01	.02	.03	.04
5.0	−.1775968	−.1743154	−.1710232	−.1677205	−.1644075
5.1	−.1443347	−.1409599	−.1375776	−.1341882	−.1307919
5.2	−.1102904	−.1068561	−.1034176	−.0999753	−.0965297
5.3	−.0758031	−.0723430	−.0688822	−.0654211	−.0619598
5.4	−.0412101	−.0377578	−.0343082	−.0308615	−.0274180
5.5	−.0068439	−.0034323	−.0000266	.0033730	.0067661
5.6	.0269709	.0303098	.0336398	.0369605	.0402716
5.7	.0599200	.0631556	.0663792	.0695906	.0727894
5.8	.0917026	.0948055	.0978937	.1009668	.1040245
5.9	.1220334	.1249761	.1279015	.1308091	.1336987
6.0	.1506453	.1534022	.1561393	.1588562	.1615527
6.1	.1772914	.1798391	.1823646	.1848678	.1873484
6.2	.2017472	.2040644	.2063574	.2086262	.2108705
6.3	.2238120	.2258800	.2279222	.2299383	.2319283
6.4	.2433106	.2451134	.2468888	.2486369	.2503573
6.5	.2600946	.2616188	.2631145	.2645817	.2660201
6.6	.2740434	.2752785	.2764843	.2776606	.2788074
6.7	.2850647	.2860032	.2869117	.2877901	.2886385
6.8	.2930956	.2937327	.2943394	.2949159	.2954620
6.9	.2981020	.2984359	.2987395	.2990127	.2992557
7.0	.3000793	.3001111	.3001128	.3000846	.3000264
7.1	.2990514	.2987851	.2984893	.2981641	.2978096
7.2	.2950707	.2945131	.2939268	.2933119	.2926686
7.3	.2882169	.2873774	.2865103	.2856158	.2846939
7.4	.2785962	.2774868	.2763512	.2751894	.2740018
7.5	.2663397	.2649748	.2635853	.2621712	.2607329
7.6	.2516018	.2499982	.2483717	.2467225	.2450508
7.7	.2345591	.2327355	.2308910	.2290257	.2271400
7.8	.2154078	.2133848	.2113430	.2092828	.2072042
7.9	.1943618	.1921618	.1899452	.1877126	.1854639
8.0	.1716508	.1692974	.1669299	.1645488	.1621542
8.1	.1475175	.1450356	.1425423	.1400378	.1375223
8.2	.1222153	.1196308	.1170375	.1144357	.1118256
8.3	.0960061	.0933456	.0906789	.0880063	.0853282
8.4	.0691573	.0664476	.0637345	.0610183	.0582992
8.5	.0419393	.0392076	.0364752	.0337424	.0310094
8.6	.0146230	.0118963	.0091717	.0064492	.0037293
8.7	−.0125227	−.0152177	−.0179081	−.0205935	−.0232739
8.8	−.0392338	−.0418710	−.0445011	−.0471237	−.0497387
8.9	−.0652532	−.0678075	−.0703522	−.0728869	−.0754116
9.0	−.0903336	−.0927808	−.0952160	−.0976390	−.1000496
9.1	−.1142392	−.1165565	−.1188596	−.1211483	−.1234224
9.2	−.1367484	−.1389144	−.1410642	−.1431976	−.1453143
9.3	−.1576552	−.1596503	−.1616274	−.1635862	−.1655265
9.4	−.1767716	−.1785781	−.1803648	−.1821316	−.1838783
9.5	−.1939287	−.1955308	−.1971117	−.1986712	−.2002092
9.6	−.2089787	−.2103628	−.2117244	−.2130634	−.2143797
9.7	−.2217955	−.2229502	−.2240814	−.2251890	−.2262730
9.8	−.2322760	−.2331923	−.2340844	−.2349521	−.2357955
9.9	−.2403411	−.2410124	−.2416590	−.2422808	−.2428777

BESSEL FUNCTION J_0

T	.05	.06	.07	.08	.09
5.0	−.1610847	−.1577524	−.1544109	−.1510606	−.1477018
5.1	−.1273892	−.1239803	−.1205657	−.1171456	−.1137204
5.2	−.0930810	−.0896295	−.0861757	−.0827198	−.0792621
5.3	−.0584989	−.0550386	−.0515792	−.0481211	−.0446646
5.4	−.0239781	−.0205422	−.0171104	−.0136833	−.0102610
5.5	.0101524	.0135315	.0169033	.0202673	.0236233
5.6	.0435728	.0468638	.0501444	.0534141	.0566727
5.7	.0759753	.0791482	.0823076	.0854533	.0885851
5.8	.1070666	.1100928	.1131028	.1160964	.1190734
5.9	.1365701	.1394230	.1422573	.1450725	.1478686
6.0	.1642286	.1668837	.1695178	.1721306	.1747218
6.1	.1898062	.1922411	.1946529	.1970413	.1994061
6.2	.2130901	.2152848	.2174546	.2195991	.2217183
6.3	.2338920	.2358292	.2377398	.2396237	.2414807
6.4	.2520501	.2537151	.2553522	.2569612	.2585420
6.5	.2674298	.2688106	.2701625	.2714853	.2727789
6.6	.2799246	.2810122	.2820700	.2830981	.2840964
6.7	.2894568	.2902449	.2910029	.2917307	.2924283
6.8	.2959779	.2964633	.2969185	.2973434	.2977379
6.9	.2994685	.2996510	.2998033	.2999254	.3000174
7.0	.2999383	.2998204	.2996727	.2994953	.2992881
7.1	.2974258	.2970128	.2965707	.2960996	.2955996
7.2	.2919969	.2912970	.2905689	.2898128	.2890288
7.3	.2837448	.2827687	.2817656	.2807358	.2796793
7.4	.2727883	.2715492	.2702846	.2689947	.2676797
7.5	.2592704	.2577839	.2562736	.2547397	.2531824
7.6	.2433568	.2416407	.2399026	.2381429	.2363617
7.7	.2252341	.2233081	.2213622	.2193967	.2174119
7.8	.2051076	.2029932	.2008612	.1987118	.1965453
7.9	.1831996	.1809198	.1786247	.1763147	.1739900
8.0	.1597463	.1573255	.1548919	.1524459	.1499876
8.1	.1349963	.1324598	.1299132	.1273568	.1247907
8.2	.1092075	.1065816	.1039483	.1013077	.0986602
8.3	.0826448	.0799563	.0772630	.0745652	.0718632
8.4	.0555775	.0528534	.0501273	.0473994	.0446699
8.5	.0282765	.0255440	.0228121	.0200812	.0173513
8.6	.0010122	−.0017019	−.0044128	−.0071200	−.0098234
8.7	−.0259489	−.0286182	−.0312816	−.0339388	−.0365896
8.8	−.0523457	−.0549445	−.0575350	−.0601167	−.0626896
8.9	−.0779258	−.0804295	−.0829224	−.0854042	−.0878747
9.0	−.1024475	−.1048325	−.1072044	−.1095629	−.1119080
9.1	−.1256816	−.1279258	−.1301548	−.1323684	−.1345663
9.2	−.1474143	−.1494972	−.1515629	−.1536113	−.1556421
9.3	−.1674482	−.1693511	−.1712351	−.1730999	−.1749455
9.4	−.1856048	−.1873109	−.1889965	−.1906615	−.1923056
9.5	−.2017255	−.2032202	−.2046929	−.2061437	−.2075723
9.6	−.2156732	−.2169439	−.2181915	−.2194161	−.2206174
9.7	−.2273333	−.2283698	−.2293823	−.2303710	−.2313356
9.8	−.2366145	−.2374090	−.2381789	−.2389243	−.2396451
9.9	−.2434497	−.2439968	−.2445190	−.2450163	−.2454885

BESSEL FUNCTION J_0

T	.00	.01	.02	.03	.04
10.0	− .2459358	− .2463580	− .2467551	− .2471272	− .2474743
10.1	− .2490297	− .2492011	− .2493474	− .2494687	− .2495649
10.2	− .2496171	− .2495385	− .2494350	− .2493067	− .2491536
10.3	− .2477168	− .2473914	− .2470416	− .2466674	− .2462690
10.4	− .2433718	− .2428051	− .2422148	− .2416008	− .2409633
10.5	− .2366482	− .2358483	− .2350255	− .2341800	− .2333120
10.6	− .2276350	− .2266119	− .2255670	− .2245006	− .2234127
10.7	− .2164427	− .2152085	− .2139539	− .2126791	− .2113843
10.8	− .2032020	− .2017708	− .2003208	− .1988522	− .1973650
10.9	− .1880622	− .1864501	− .1848208	− .1831745	− .1815115
11.0	− .1711903	− .1694147	− .1676238	− .1658178	− .1639968
11.1	− .1527683	− .1508483	− .1489149	− .1469684	− .1450089
11.2	− .1329919	− .1309477	− .1288922	− .1268256	− .1247483
11.3	− .1120685	− .1099213	− .1077650	− .1055999	− .1034261
11.4	− .0902145	− .0879865	− .0857517	− .0835102	− .0812623
11.5	− .0676539	− .0653678	− .0630771	− .0607821	− .0584830
11.6	− .0446157	− .0422945	− .0399711	− .0376456	− .0353184
11.7	− .0213313	− .0189982	− .0166653	− .0143327	− .0120006
11.8	.0019672	.0042889	.0066082	.0089249	.0112388
11.9	.0250494	.0273370	.0296200	.0318980	.0341710
12.0	.0476893	.0499204	.0521447	.0543619	.0565718
12.1	.0696668	.0718199	.0739640	.0760989	.0782245
12.2	.0907701	.0928245	.0948680	.0969003	.0989212
12.3	.1107980	.1127342	.1146576	.1165679	.1184651
12.4	.1295610	.1313609	.1331462	.1349167	.1366724
12.5	.1468841	.1485309	.1501615	.1517758	.1533737
12.6	.1626073	.1640860	.1655471	.1669905	.1684160
12.7	.1765879	.1778851	.1791636	.1804231	.1816637
12.8	.1887014	.1898058	.1908904	.1919550	.1929997
12.9	.1988424	.1997446	.2006261	.2014869	.2023269
13.0	.2069261	.2076187	.2082899	.2089399	.2095684
13.1	.2128882	.2133659	.2138219	.2142562	.2146687
13.2	.2166859	.2169457	.2171835	.2173995	.2175935
13.3	.2182981	.2183389	.2183579	.2183551	.2183304
13.4	.2177252	.2175484	.2173499	.2171299	.2168884
13.5	.2149892	.2145981	.2141858	.2137525	.2132981
13.6	.2101332	.2095332	.2089128	.2082720	.2076107
13.7	.2032208	.2024195	.2015986	.2007581	.1998982
13.8	.1943356	.1933424	.1923305	.1913002	.1902515
13.9	.1835799	.1824059	.1812145	.1800059	.1787801
14.0	.1710735	.1697317	.1683739	.1670002	.1656108
14.1	.1569529	.1554577	.1539481	.1524242	.1508861
14.2	.1413694	.1397368	.1380914	.1364334	.1347629
14.3	.1244877	.1227348	.1209709	.1191961	.1174107
14.4	.1064841	.1046292	.1027650	.1008919	.0990100
14.5	.0875449	.0856069	.0836617	.0817095	.0797504
14.6	.0678641	.0658629	.0638565	.0618450	.0598288
14.7	.0476418	.0455977	.0435503	.0415000	.0394470
14.8	.0270823	.0250157	.0229481	.0208795	.0188102
14.9	.0063915	.0043232	.0022558	.0001896	− .0018753

BESSELL FUNCTION J_0

T	.05	.06	.07	.08	.09
10.0	−.2477962	−.2480931	−.2483649	−.2486116	−.2488332
10.1	−.2496361	−.2496822	−.2497034	−.2496996	−.2496708
10.2	−.2489758	−.2487732	−.2485460	−.2482942	−.2480177
10.3	−.2458463	−.2453994	−.2449285	−.2444335	−.2439146
10.4	−.2403022	−.2396178	−.2389101	−.2381792	−.2374252
10.5	−.2324214	−.2315085	−.2305732	−.2296158	−.2286364
10.6	−.2223036	−.2211732	−.2200218	−.2188495	−.2176565
10.7	−.2100695	−.2087349	−.2073807	−.2060071	−.2046141
10.8	−.1958594	−.1943357	−.1927939	−.1912343	−.1896570
10.9	−.1798318	−.1781356	−.1764232	−.1746947	−.1729504
11.0	−.1621611	−.1603109	−.1584463	−.1565675	−.1546748
11.1	−.1430367	−.1410520	−.1390549	−.1370458	−.1350247
11.2	−.1226602	−.1205618	−.1184532	−.1163346	−.1142063
11.3	−.1012439	−.0990535	−.0968552	−.0946491	−.0924354
11.4	−.0790083	−.0767484	−.0744828	−.0722117	−.0699353
11.5	−.0561801	−.0538735	−.0515636	−.0492505	−.0469344
11.6	−.0329897	−.0306597	−.0283286	−.0259967	−.0236642
11.7	−.0096694	−.0073391	−.0050101	−.0026825	−.0003567
11.8	.0135496	.0158571	.0181610	.0204612	.0227574
11.9	.0364386	.0387007	.0409570	.0432074	.0454516
12.0	.0587743	.0609690	.0631559	.0653346	.0675049
12.1	.0803406	.0824468	.0845431	.0866292	.0887050
12.2	.1009306	.1029283	.1049140	.1068877	.1088491
12.3	.1203489	.1222191	.1240756	.1259182	.1277467
12.4	.1384129	.1401382	.1418482	.1435426	.1452212
12.5	.1549550	.1565195	.1580671	.1595977	.1611111
12.6	.1698236	.1712131	.1725845	.1739374	.1752719
12.7	.1828851	.1840872	.1852700	.1864334	.1875772
12.8	.1940242	.1950286	.1960127	.1969764	.1979197
12.9	.2031460	.2039441	.2047213	.2054773	.2062123
13.0	.2101755	.2107612	.2113253	.2118679	.2123888
13.1	.2150594	.2154284	.2157755	.2161009	.2164043
13.2	.2177657	.2179159	.2180443	.2181508	.2182354
13.3	.2182839	.2182156	.2181256	.2180138	.2178803
13.4	.2166254	.2163409	.2160349	.2157076	.2153590
13.5	.2128227	.2123263	.2118092	.2112712	.2107125
13.6	.2069293	.2062276	.2055059	.2047641	.2040024
13.7	.1990189	.1981203	.1972026	.1962659	.1953102
13.8	.1891845	.1880993	.1869962	.1858751	.1847363
13.9	.1775373	.1762777	.1750014	.1737085	.1723991
14.0	.1642058	.1627855	.1613498	.1598991	.1584334
14.1	.1493340	.1477681	.1461885	.1445954	.1429890
14.2	.1330800	.1313851	.1296782	.1279596	.1262293
14.3	.1156147	.1138085	.1119921	.1101658	.1083297
14.4	.0971195	.0952206	.0933135	.0913984	.0894754
14.5	.0777848	.0758127	.0738344	.0718500	.0698599
14.6	.0578079	.0557827	.0537533	.0517198	.0496826
14.7	.0373914	.0353334	.0332733	.0312113	.0291476
14.8	.0167404	.0146704	.0126003	.0105303	.0084606
14.9	−.0039386	−.0060002	−.0080597	−.0101171	−.0121721

BESSEL FUNCTION J_0

T	.00	.01	.02	.03	.04
15.0	− .0142245	− .0162741	− .0183207	− .0203641	− .0224042
15.1	− .0345619	− .0365725	− .0385782	− .0405787	− .0425738
15.2	− .0544208	− .0563729	− .0583180	− .0602560	− .0621868
15.3	− .0736075	− .0754820	− .0773477	− .0792045	− .0810521
15.4	− .0919362	− .0937150	− .0954833	− .0972409	− .0989876
15.5	− .1092307	− .1108968	− .1125507	− .1141923	− .1158215
15.6	− .1253260	− .1268636	− .1283875	− .1298977	− .1313938
15.7	− .1400702	− .1414649	− .1428446	− .1442091	− .1455583
15.8	− .1533257	− .1545646	− .1557872	− .1569934	− .1581832
15.9	− .1649705	− .1660422	− .1670966	− .1681336	− .1691532
16.0	− .1748991	− .1757940	− .1766708	− .1775294	− .1783697
16.1	− .1830237	− .1837341	− .1844257	− .1850984	− .1857523
16.2	− .1892749	− .1897949	− .1902956	− .1907770	− .1912390
16.3	− .1936024	− .1939279	− .1942339	− .1945203	− .1947870
16.4	− .1959748	− .1961039	− .1962134	− .1963031	− .1963732
16.5	− .1963807	− .1963133	− .1962262	− .1961196	− .1959935
16.6	− .1948279	− .1945657	− .1942843	− .1939836	− .1936637
16.7	− .1913435	− .1908905	− .1904186	− .1899280	− .1894187
16.8	− .1859739	− .1853355	− .1846791	− .1840045	− .1833120
16.9	− .1787834	− .1779672	− .1771337	− .1762830	− .1754152
17.0	− .1698543	− .1688694	− .1678682	− .1668508	− .1658174
17.1	− .1592853	− .1581425	− .1569846	− .1558116	− .1546238
17.2	− .1471911	− .1459027	− .1446004	− .1432844	− .1419548
17.3	− .1337006	− .1322802	− .1308473	− .1294021	− .1279449
17.4	− .1189559	− .1174182	− .1158697	− .1143105	− .1127408
17.5	− .1031104	− .1014715	− .0998235	− .0981664	− .0965004
17.6	− .0863279	− .0846047	− .0828740	− .0811360	− .0793908
17.7	− .0687804	− .0669904	− .0651947	− .0633935	− .0615870
17.8	− .0506464	− .0488078	− .0469654	− .0451192	− .0432696
17.9	− .0321095	− .0302408	− .0283701	− .0264976	− .0246235
18.0	− .0133558	− .0114757	− .0095956	− .0077155	− .0058357
18.1	.0054270	.0072997	.0091706	.0110396	.0129064
18.2	.0240523	.0258990	.0277422	.0295815	.0314169
18.3	.0423358	.0441384	.0459356	.0477272	.0495131
18.4	.0600979	.0618387	.0635723	.0652987	.0670175
18.5	.0771648	.0788268	.0804800	.0821243	.0837595
18.6	.0933708	.0949380	.0964948	.0980411	.0995768
18.7	.1085595	.1100167	.1114621	.1128956	.1143171
18.8	.1225853	.1239187	.1252390	.1265461	.1278398
18.9	.1353152	.1365122	.1376949	.1388632	.1400170
19.0	.1466294	.1476788	.1487129	.1497316	.1507347
19.1	.1564231	.1573152	.1581912	.1590508	.1598942
19.2	.1646067	.1653335	.1660435	.1667364	.1674124
19.3	.1711073	.1716625	.1722003	.1727206	.1732233
19.4	.1758692	.1762481	.1766092	.1769525	.1772779
19.5	.1788538	.1790536	.1792354	.1793991	.1795449
19.6	.1800407	.1800603	.1800618	.1800454	.1800109
19.7	.1794272	.1792673	.1790895	.1788939	.1786806
19.8	.1770286	.1766917	.1763373	.1759654	.1755761
19.9	.1728777	.1723681	.1718414	.1712978	.1707374

BESSEL FUNCTION J_0

T	.05	.06	.07	.08	.09
15.0	− .0244406	− .0264732	− .0285019	− .0305263	− .0325464
15.1	− .0445634	− .0465472	− .0485250	− .0504967	− .0524620
15.2	− .0641100	− .0660256	− .0679333	− .0698330	− .0717245
15.3	− .0828904	− .0847192	− .0865384	− .0883477	− .0901471
15.4	− .1007233	− .1024478	− .1041610	− .1058626	− .1075525
15.5	− .1174380	− .1190418	− .1206326	− .1222103	− .1237748
15.6	− .1328759	− .1343438	− .1357973	− .1372363	− .1386606
15.7	− .1468921	− .1482104	− .1495130	− .1507998	− .1520708
15.8	− .1593565	− .1605130	− .1616528	− .1627757	− .1638816
15.9	− .1701552	− .1711396	− .1721063	− .1730551	− .1739861
16.0	− .1791917	− .1799952	− .1807802	− .1815467	− .1822945
16.1	− .1863871	− .1870029	− .1875996	− .1881773	− .1887357
16.2	− .1916815	− .1921047	− .1925084	− .1928926	− .1932572
16.3	− .1950342	− .1952616	− .1954694	− .1956576	− .1958260
16.4	− .1964235	− .1964543	− .1964653	− .1964567	− .1964285
16.5	− .1958479	− .1956827	− .1954981	− .1952941	− .1950707
16.6	− .1933247	− .1929665	− .1925892	− .1921930	− .1917777
16.7	− .1888908	− .1883442	− .1877792	− .1871958	− .1865940
16.8	− .1826015	− .1818732	− .1811272	− .1803635	− .1795822
16.9	− .1745303	− .1736286	− .1727100	− .1717747	− .1708227
17.0	− .1647680	− .1637027	− .1626217	− .1615250	− .1604129
17.1	− .1534212	− .1522039	− .1509721	− .1497260	− .1484656
17.2	− .1406118	− .1392556	− .1378862	− .1365038	− .1351086
17.3	− .1264757	− .1249947	− .1235021	− .1219979	− .1204825
17.4	− .1111607	− .1095704	− .1079700	− .1063598	− .1047399
17.5	− .0948257	− .0931425	− .0914510	− .0897512	− .0880435
17.6	− .0776387	− .0758799	− .0741145	− .0723426	− .0705645
17.7	− .0597754	− .0579587	− .0561374	− .0543114	− .0524810
17.8	− .0414167	− .0395607	− .0377018	− .0358402	− .0339760
17.9	− .0227480	− .0208713	− .0189935	− .0171149	− .0152356
18.0	− .0039563	− .0020776	− .0001997	.0016771	.0035528
18.1	.0147709	.0166330	.0184923	.0203487	.0222021
18.2	.0332481	.0350750	.0368974	.0387152	.0405280
18.3	.0512931	.0530669	.0548345	.0565956	.0583501
18.4	.0687288	.0704323	.0721278	.0738151	.0754942
18.5	.0853855	.0870020	.0886089	.0902061	.0917935
18.6	.1011017	.1026157	.1041186	.1056103	.1070906
18.7	.1157264	.1171234	.1185079	.1198798	.1212390
18.8	.1291201	.1303868	.1316397	.1328789	.1341041
18.9	.1411562	.1422807	.1433904	.1444851	.1455648
19.0	.1517223	.1526942	.1536503	.1545905	.1555148
19.1	.1607211	.1615315	.1623253	.1631025	.1638630
19.2	.1680713	.1687130	.1693375	.1699448	.1705347
19.3	.1737084	.1741760	.1746258	.1750580	.1754725
19.4	.1775854	.1778749	.1781466	.1784003	.1786361
19.5	.1796726	.1797823	.1798739	.1799475	.1800031
19.6	.1799585	.1798881	.1797998	.1796935	.1795693
19.7	.1784494	.1782006	.1779340	.1776498	.1773480
19.8	.1751695	.1747456	.1743044	.1738459	.1733704
19.9	.1701602	.1695663	.1689557	.1683285	.1676848

BESSEL FUNCTION J_0

T	.00	.01	.02	.03	.04
20.0	.1670247	.1663482	.1656554	.1649464	.1642212
20.1	.1595361	.1587003	.1578491	.1569825	.1561007
20.2	.1504946	.1495086	.1485082	.1474935	.1464645
20.3	.1399977	.1388722	.1377333	.1365812	.1354160
20.4	.1281571	.1269038	.1256384	.1243611	.1230720
20.5	.1150970	.1137290	.1123504	.1109612	.1095615
20.6	.1009532	.0994848	.0980071	.0965203	.0950246
20.7	.0858717	.0843178	.0827563	.0811872	.0796108
20.8	.0700069	.0683835	.0667540	.0651187	.0634776
20.9	.0535204	.0518439	.0501631	.0484780	.0467889
21.0	.0365791	.0348665	.0331512	.0314334	.0297133
21.1	.0193536	.0176221	.0158896	.0141564	.0124226
21.2	.0020167	.0002836	−.0014488	−.0031802	−.0049105
21.3	−.0152587	−.0169762	−.0186913	−.0204036	−.0221131
21.4	−.0323011	−.0339860	−.0356667	−.0373431	−.0390149
21.5	−.0489420	−.0505777	−.0522076	−.0538314	−.0554492
21.6	−.0650179	−.0665883	−.0681513	−.0697068	−.0712545
21.7	−.0803714	−.0818612	−.0833421	−.0848140	−.0862767
21.8	−.0948530	−.0962478	−.0976323	−.0990063	−.1003699
21.9	−.1083229	−.1096091	−.1108838	−.1121469	−.1133981
22.0	−.1206515	−.1218169	−.1229697	−.1241096	−.1252366
22.1	−.1317214	−.1327550	−.1337749	−.1347809	−.1357731
22.2	−.1414282	−.1423203	−.1431977	−.1440605	−.1449085
22.3	−.1496814	−.1504237	−.1511507	−.1518622	−.1525582
22.4	−.1564055	−.1569913	−.1575612	−.1581151	−.1586529
22.5	−.1615403	−.1619646	−.1623724	−.1627639	−.1631389
22.6	−.1650419	−.1653010	−.1655435	−.1657694	−.1659785
22.7	−.1668827	−.1669748	−.1670502	−.1671089	−.1671509
22.8	−.1670515	−.1669765	−.1668849	−.1667766	−.1666517
22.9	−.1655542	−.1653135	−.1650564	−.1647829	−.1644931
23.0	−.1624128	−.1620096	−.1615903	−.1611551	−.1607040
23.1	−.1576658	−.1571047	−.1565282	−.1559363	−.1553290
23.2	−.1513673	−.1506547	−.1499273	−.1491852	−.1484286
23.3	−.1435868	−.1427303	−.1418600	−.1409758	−.1400779
23.4	−.1344080	−.1334168	−.1324128	−.1313959	−.1303663
23.5	−.1239282	−.1228128	−.1216856	−.1205467	−.1193963
23.6	−.1122573	−.1110293	−.1097907	−.1085417	−.1072823
23.7	−.0995165	−.0981886	−.0968514	−.0955051	−.0941498
23.8	−.0858371	−.0844229	−.0830008	−.0815710	−.0801337
23.9	−.0713592	−.0698732	−.0683807	−.0668820	−.0653773
24.0	−.0562303	−.0546874	−.0531398	−.0515874	−.0500306
24.1	−.0406036	−.0390195	−.0374323	−.0358420	−.0342487
24.2	−.0246367	−.0230274	−.0214166	−.0198042	−.0181905
24.3	−.0084900	−.0068717	−.0052533	−.0036351	−.0020171
24.4	.0076750	.0092863	.0108961	.0125040	.0141101
24.5	.0236974	.0252857	.0268708	.0284525	.0300307
24.6	.0394183	.0409677	.0425125	.0440524	.0455872
24.7	.0546823	.0561777	.0576669	.0591498	.0606261
24.8	.0693393	.0707661	.0721851	.0735964	.0749998
24.9	.0832460	.0845901	.0859252	.0872512	.0885679

BESSEL FUNCTION J_0

T	.05	.06	.07	.08	.09
20.0	.1634800	.1627228	.1619498	.1611609	.1603563
20.1	.1552037	.1542916	.1533645	.1524226	.1514659
20.2	.1454214	.1443643	.1432932	.1422083	.1411098
20.3	.1342379	.1330469	.1318432	.1306269	.1293982
20.4	.1217712	.1204589	.1191352	.1178002	.1164541
20.5	.1081516	.1067316	.1053016	.1038618	.1024123
20.6	.0935202	.0920071	.0904855	.0889557	.0874177
20.7	.0780272	.0764366	.0748391	.0732348	.0716240
20.8	.0618310	.0601790	.0585217	.0568595	.0551923
20.9	.0450960	.0433993	.0416991	.0399956	.0382888
21.0	.0279911	.0262669	.0245408	.0228132	.0210841
21.1	.0106883	.0089538	.0072192	.0054847	.0037505
21.2	−.0066394	−.0083669	−.0100928	−.0118168	−.0135388
21.3	−.0238196	−.0255230	−.0272229	−.0289194	−.0306122
21.4	−.0406821	−.0423444	−.0440018	−.0456539	−.0473007
21.5	−.0570606	−.0586656	−.0602640	−.0618556	−.0634403
21.6	−.0727945	−.0743264	−.0758502	−.0773658	−.0788729
21.7	−.0877302	−.0891742	−.0906086	−.0920333	−.0934482
21.8	−.1017228	−.1030649	−.1043961	−.1057162	−.1070252
21.9	−.1146375	−.1158648	−.1170800	−.1182829	−.1194734
22.0	−.1263506	−.1274514	−.1285390	−.1296133	−.1306741
22.1	−.1367512	−.1377151	−.1386649	−.1396004	−.1405215
22.2	−.1457416	−.1465597	−.1473628	−.1481509	−.1489238
22.3	−.1532387	−.1539035	−.1545527	−.1551861	−.1558037
22.4	−.1591747	−.1596803	−.1601697	−.1606428	−.1610997
22.5	−.1634974	−.1638394	−.1641649	−.1644738	−.1647662
22.6	−.1661710	−.1663467	−.1665058	−.1666481	−.1667738
22.7	−.1671761	−.1671846	−.1671764	−.1671515	−.1671098
22.8	−.1665101	−.1663520	−.1661773	−.1659861	−.1657784
22.9	−.1641870	−.1638645	−.1635258	−.1631710	−.1627999
23.0	−.1602370	−.1597541	−.1592555	−.1587412	−.1582113
23.1	−.1547065	−.1540688	−.1534159	−.1527480	−.1520651
23.2	−.1476574	−.1468718	−.1460719	−.1452576	−.1444293
23.3	−.1391664	−.1382414	−.1373029	−.1363511	−.1353861
23.4	−.1293241	−.1282695	−.1272024	−.1261232	−.1250317
23.5	−.1182343	−.1170611	−.1158767	−.1146811	−.1134747
23.6	−.1060127	−.1047331	−.1034435	−.1021441	−.1008351
23.7	−.0927856	−.0914128	−.0900313	−.0886415	−.0872434
23.8	−.0786889	−.0772369	−.0757778	−.0743117	−.0728388
23.9	−.0638667	−.0623503	−.0608283	−.0593009	−.0577681
24.0	−.0484694	−.0469040	−.0453345	−.0437612	−.0421842
24.1	−.0326527	−.0310540	−.0294530	−.0278496	−.0262441
24.2	−.0165757	−.0149599	−.0133433	−.0117260	−.0101082
24.3	−.0003997	.0012172	.0028332	.0044483	.0060623
24.4	.0157141	.0173158	.0189152	.0205120	.0221062
24.5	.0316054	.0331762	.0347430	.0363057	.0378642
24.6	.0471169	.0486412	.0501601	.0516733	.0531807
24.7	.0620958	.0635587	.0650146	.0664635	.0679051
24.8	.0763951	.0777822	.0791610	.0805313	.0818930
24.9	.0898752	.0911731	.0924613	.0937397	.0950082

BESSEL FUNCTION J_0

T	.00	.01	.02	.03	.04
25.0	.0962668	.0975152	.0987534	.0999812	.1011985
25.1	.1082757	.1094164	.1105457	.1116634	.1127696
25.2	.1191571	.1201791	.1211887	.1221858	.1231703
25.3	.1288072	.1297009	.1305812	.1314482	.1323016
25.4	.1371348	.1378917	.1386345	.1393632	.1400777
25.5	.1440622	.1446753	.1452738	.1458574	.1464263
25.6	.1495258	.1499896	.1504383	.1508718	.1512900
25.7	.1534770	.1537875	.1540825	.1543621	.1546260
25.8	.1558824	.1560371	.1561761	.1562995	.1564071
25.9	.1567239	.1567219	.1567041	.1566707	.1566216
26.0	.1559993	.1558411	.1556673	.1554781	.1552734
26.1	.1537218	.1534096	.1530822	.1527396	.1523819
26.2	.1499200	.1494575	.1489803	.1484883	.1479817
26.3	.1446375	.1440300	.1434082	.1427724	.1421225
26.4	.1379327	.1371866	.1364271	.1356543	.1348682
26.5	.1298776	.1290010	.1281119	.1272102	.1262962
26.6	.1205577	.1195597	.1185503	.1175293	.1164970
26.7	.1100704	.1089615	.1078422	.1067125	.1055726
26.8	.0985245	.0973162	.0960986	.0948719	.0936361
26.9	.0860391	.0847437	.0834404	.0821291	.0808102
27.0	.0727419	.0713727	.0699969	.0686145	.0672259
27.1	.0587684	.0573393	.0559049	.0544655	.0530212
27.2	.0442603	.0427857	.0413073	.0398254	.0383400
27.3	.0293640	.0278587	.0263513	.0248417	.0233302
27.4	.0142293	.0127085	.0111870	.0096650	.0081426
27.5	−.0009922	−.0025133	−.0040336	−.0055529	−.0070711
27.6	−.0161486	−.0176548	−.0191587	−.0206602	−.0221590
27.7	−.0310890	−.0325655	−.0340381	−.0355069	−.0369715
27.8	−.0456656	−.0470977	−.0485245	−.0499460	−.0513619
27.9	−.0597344	−.0611079	−.0624749	−.0638351	−.0651885
28.0	−.0731570	−.0744586	−.0757523	−.0770380	−.0783155
28.1	−.0858021	−.0870191	−.0882269	−.0894254	−.0906146
28.2	−.0975466	−.0986670	−.0997772	−.1008770	−.1019663
28.3	−.1082765	−.1092896	−.1102915	−.1112819	−.1122609
28.4	−.1178886	−.1187847	−.1196686	−.1205403	−.1213995
28.5	−.1262911	−.1270617	−.1278193	−.1285638	−.1292952
28.6	−.1334046	−.1340423	−.1346665	−.1352769	−.1358737
28.7	−.1391625	−.1396616	−.1401466	−.1406174	−.1410739
28.8	−.1435124	−.1438684	−.1442098	−.1445367	−.1448490
28.9	−.1464158	−.1466256	−.1468206	−.1470008	−.1471663
29.0	−.1478488	−.1479107	−.1479578	−.1479901	−.1480077
29.1	−.1478020	−.1477161	−.1476154	−.1475000	−.1473698
29.2	−.1462813	−.1460487	−.1458017	−.1455402	−.1452642
29.3	−.1433065	−.1429303	−.1425399	−.1421354	−.1417168
29.4	−.1389125	−.1383968	−.1378675	−.1373245	−.1367680
29.5	−.1331479	−.1324983	−.1318357	−.1311601	−.1304717
29.6	−.1260746	−.1252980	−.1245092	−.1237083	−.1228952
29.7	−.1177675	−.1168722	−.1159655	−.1150475	−.1141184
29.8	−.1083137	−.1073089	−.1062938	−.1052683	−.1042327
29.9	−.0978112	−.0967073	−.0955941	−.0944718	−.0933404

BESSEL FUNCTION J_0

T	.05	.06	.07	.08	.09
25.0	.1024052	.1036012	.1047863	.1059606	.1071237
25.1	.1138641	.1149467	.1160175	.1170762	.1181228
25.2	.1241421	.1251011	.1260472	.1269803	.1279003
25.3	.1331415	.1339678	.1347803	.1355790	.1363639
25.4	.1407778	.1414636	.1421350	.1427920	.1434344
25.5	.1469803	.1475194	.1480436	.1485527	.1490468
25.6	.1516929	.1520805	.1524527	.1528096	.1531510
25.7	.1548744	.1551072	.1553244	.1555261	.1557120
25.8	.1564991	.1565755	.1566361	.1566811	.1567103
25.9	.1565569	.1564766	.1563807	.1562691	.1561420
26.0	.1550532	.1548177	.1545667	.1543004	.1540187
26.1	.1520090	.1516211	.1512182	.1508004	.1503676
26.2	.1474605	.1469248	.1463745	.1458099	.1452308
26.3	.1414587	.1407810	.1400895	.1393842	.1386652
26.4	.1340689	.1332565	.1324311	.1315928	.1307416
26.5	.1253699	.1244315	.1234809	.1225183	.1215439
26.6	.1154534	.1143986	.1133328	.1122561	.1111686
26.7	.1044225	.1032625	.1020925	.1009128	.0997234
26.8	.0923915	.0911380	.0898759	.0886053	.0873263
26.9	.0794837	.0781497	.0768084	.0754599	.0741044
27.0	.0658310	.0644300	.0630232	.0616105	.0601922
27.1	.0515721	.0501184	.0486602	.0471977	.0457310
27.2	.0368513	.0353596	.0338648	.0323671	.0308668
27.3	.0218170	.0203021	.0187857	.0172680	.0157491
27.4	.0066199	.0050970	.0035743	.0020517	.0005295
27.5	−.0085880	−.0101035	−.0116175	−.0131298	−.0146402
27.6	−.0236551	−.0251483	−.0266384	−.0281254	−.0296090
27.7	−.0384319	−.0398880	−.0413395	−.0427864	−.0442285
27.8	−.0527722	−.0541768	−.0555754	−.0569680	−.0583543
27.9	−.0665348	−.0678741	−.0692060	−.0705306	−.0718476
28.0	−.0795847	−.0808455	−.0820977	−.0833414	−.0845762
28.1	−.0917943	−.0929644	−.0941248	−.0952754	−.0964160
28.2	−.1030451	−.1041131	−.1051704	−.1062168	−.1072522
28.3	−.1132283	−.1141841	−.1151281	−.1160602	−.1169804
28.4	−.1222464	−.1230807	−.1239024	−.1247114	−.1255077
28.5	−.1300134	−.1307184	−.1314101	−.1320884	−.1327532
28.6	−.1364566	−.1370257	−.1375809	−.1381221	−.1386494
28.7	−.1415162	−.1419442	−.1423579	−.1427572	−.1431420
28.8	−.1451468	−.1454299	−.1456984	−.1459522	−.1461914
28.9	−.1473170	−.1474530	−.1475741	−.1476805	−.1477720
29.0	−.1480104	−.1479983	−.1479714	−.1479297	−.1478733
29.1	−.1472250	−.1470655	−.1468913	−.1467026	−.1464992
29.2	−.1449738	−.1446690	−.1443498	−.1440163	−.1436686
29.3	−.1412842	−.1408377	−.1403771	−.1399028	−.1394145
29.4	−.1361980	−.1356145	−.1350177	−.1344077	−.1337843
29.5	−.1297704	−.1290564	−.1283297	−.1275905	−.1268387
29.6	−.1220701	−.1212331	−.1203842	−.1195236	−.1186514
29.7	−.1131781	−.1122268	−.1112647	−.1102917	−.1093080
29.8	−.1031870	−.1021313	−.1010658	−.0999905	−.0989056
29.9	−.0922000	−.0910508	−.0898929	−.0887264	−.0875514

BESSEL FUNCTION J_0

T	.00	.01	.02	.03	.04
30.0	− .0863680	− .0851764	− .0839766	− .0827689	−.0815533
30.1	− .0741014	− .0728342	− .0715601	− .0702793	− .0689919
30.2	− .0611363	− .0598064	− .0584709	− .0571301	− .0557839
30.3	− .0476042	− .0462250	− .0448417	− .0434543	− .0420631
30.4	− .0336418	− .0322273	− .0308101	− .0293902	− .0279678
30.5	− .0193897	− .0179541	− .0165171	− .0150790	− .0136398
30.6	− .0049909	− .0035485	− .0021062	− .0006641	.0007775
30.7	.0094108	.0108456	.0122788	.0137103	.0151400
30.8	.0236718	.0250846	.0264945	.0279013	.0293049
30.9	.0376503	.0390273	.0403999	.0417680	.0431315
31.0	.0512082	.0525356	.0538574	.0551733	.0564834
31.1	.0642115	.0654763	.0667343	.0679851	.0692287
31.2	.0765325	.0777224	.0789042	.0800776	.0812426
31.3	.0880507	.0891540	.0902480	.0913326	.0924077
31.4	.0986537	.0996597	.1006553	.1016406	.1026154

BESSEL FUNCTION J_0

T	.05	.06	.07	.08	.09
30.0	− .0803300	− .0790990	− .0778605	− .0766147	− .0753616
30.1	− .0676981	− .0663979	− .0650914	− .0637790	− .0624605
30.2	− .0544327	− .0530764	− .0517153	− .0503495	− .0489791
30.3	− .0406681	− .0392695	− .0378674	− .0364620	− .0350535
30.4	− .0265431	− .0251162	− .0236873	− .0222565	− .0208239
30.5	− .0121997	− .0107588	− .0093174	− .0078755	− .0064332
30.6	.0022186	.0036590	.0050986	.0065371	.0079746
30.7	.0165677	.0179934	.0194167	.0208376	.0222560
30.8	.0307051	.0321017	.0334947	.0348839	.0362691
30.9	.0444903	.0458442	.0471930	.0485367	.0498752
31.0	.0577873	.0590850	.0603764	.0616614	.0629398
31.1	.0704650	.0716939	.0729152	.0741288	.0753347
31.2	.0823992	.0835472	.0846864	.0858168	.0869383
31.3	.0934732	.0945292	.0955752	.0966114	.0976377
31.4	.1035796	.1045332	.1054759	.1064079	.1073289

SPECIAL FUNCTIONS

BESSEL FUNCTION J_1

T	.00	.01	.02	.03	.04
0.0	0.0000000	.0049999	.0099995	.0149983	.0199960
.1	.0499375	.0549169	.0598921	.0648628	.0698286
.2	.0995008	.1044223	.1093358	.1142412	.1191381
.3	.1483188	.1531455	.1579607	.1627641	.1675553
.4	.1960266	.2007225	.2054034	.2100689	.2147188
.5	.2422685	.2467987	.2513105	.2558035	.2602774
.6	.2867010	.2910319	.2953412	.2996284	.3038932
.7	.3289957	.3330955	.3371705	.3412203	.3452448
.8	.3688420	.3726806	.3764916	.3802745	.3840292
.9	.4059495	.4094991	.4130184	.4165071	.4199649
1.0	.4400506	.4432858	.4464882	.4496577	.4527939
1.1	.4709024	.4738003	.4766634	.4794913	.4822840
1.2	.4982891	.5008297	.5033336	.5058006	.5082305
1.3	.5220232	.5241895	.5263174	.5284070	.5304580
1.4	.5419477	.5437255	.5454638	.5471625	.5488215
1.5	.5579365	.5593150	.5606532	.5619508	.5632079
1.6	.5698959	.5708676	.5717984	.5726881	.5735368
1.7	.5777652	.5783259	.5788453	.5793235	.5797604
1.8	.5815170	.5816656	.5817731	.5818396	.5818649
1.9	.5811571	.5808962	.5805946	.5802523	.5798695
2.0	.5767248	.5760601	.5753554	.5746109	.5738267
2.1	.5682921	.5672326	.5661342	.5649970	.5638212
2.2	.5559630	.5545208	.5530410	.5515239	.5499696
2.3	.5398725	.5380627	.5362170	.5343358	.5324190
2.4	.5201853	.5180259	.5158327	.5136058	.5113456
2.5	.4970941	.4946060	.4920863	.4895351	.4869528
2.6	.4708183	.4680247	.4652020	.4623503	.4594700
2.7	.4416014	.4385280	.4354281	.4323020	.4291500
2.8	.4097092	.4063837	.4030346	.3996622	.3962667
2.9	.3754275	.3718794	.3683108	.3647218	.3611130
3.0	.3390590	.3353194	.3315626	.3277886	.3239979
3.1	.3009211	.2970226	.2931100	.2891837	.2852440
3.2	.2613432	.2573192	.2532845	.2492394	.2451844
3.3	.2206635	.2165481	.2124255	.2082960	.2041599
3.4	.1792259	.1750538	.1708779	.1666987	.1625163
3.5	.1373775	.1331835	.1289892	.1247949	.1206010
3.6	.0954655	.0912841	.0871059	.0829311	.0787602
3.7	.0538340	.0496993	.0455712	.0414500	.0373359
3.8	.0128210	.0087665	.0047218	.0006872	−.0033369
3.9	−.0272440	−.0311861	−.0351151	−.0390308	−.0429330
4.0	−.0660433	−.0698418	−.0736243	−.0773905	−.0811401
4.1	−.1032733	−.1068987	−.1105054	−.1140928	−.1176609
4.2	−.1386469	−.1420717	−.1454750	−.1488565	−.1522160
4.3	−.1718966	−.1750950	−.1782695	−.1814198	−.1845457
4.4	−.2027755	−.2057242	−.2086467	−.2115429	−.2144125
4.5	−.2310604	−.2337384	−.2363882	−.2390097	−.2416027
4.6	−.2565528	−.2589416	−.2613006	−.2636296	−.2659284
4.7	−.2790807	−.2811647	−.2832174	−.2852387	−.2872286
4.8	−.2984999	−.3002661	−.3019999	−.3037013	−.3053702
4.9	−.3146947	−.3161332	−.3175386	−.3189107	−.3202495

BESSEL FUNCTION J_1

T	.05	.06	.07	.08	.09
0.0	.0249922	.0299865	.0349786	.0399680	.0449545
.1	.0747893	.0797443	.0846933	.0896360	.0945720
.2	.1240260	.1289046	.1337735	.1386325	.1434810
.3	.1723340	.1770997	.1818522	.1865911	.1913160
.4	.2193525	.2239699	.2285705	.2331540	.2377201
.5	.2647318	.2691665	.2735811	.2779752	.2823486
.6	.3081355	.3123547	.3165506	.3207230	.3248715
.7	.3492436	.3532164	.3571629	.3610829	.3649760
.8	.3877554	.3914529	.3951213	.3987603	.4023699
.9	.4233917	.4267871	.4301509	.4334829	.4367829
1.0	.4558968	.4589660	.4620014	.4650027	.4679698
1.1	.4850413	.4877629	.4904486	.4930984	.4957119
1.2	.5106233	.5129786	.5152965	.5175766	.5198189
1.3	.5324703	.5344439	.5363785	.5382741	.5401305
1.4	.5504407	.5520200	.5535593	.5550586	.5565177
1.5	.5644245	.5656003	.5667354	.5678298	.5688833
1.6	.5743443	.5751108	.5758362	.5765204	.5771634
1.7	.5801562	.5805107	.5808241	.5810962	.5813272
1.8	.5818493	.5817926	.5816951	.5815566	.5813772
1.9	.5794463	.5789825	.5784784	.5779341	.5773495
2.0	.5730028	.5721393	.5712364	.5702942	.5693127
2.1	.5626069	.5613543	.5600635	.5587345	.5573677
2.2	.5483784	.5467502	.5450854	.5433841	.5416464
2.3	.5304671	.5284801	.5264582	.5244016	.5223106
2.4	.5090521	.5067256	.5043663	.5019745	.4995503
2.5	.4843396	.4816957	.4790214	.4763168	.4735824
2.6	.4565613	.4536245	.4506598	.4476676	.4446480
2.7	.4259723	.4227693	.4195412	.4162882	.4130109
2.8	.3928485	.3894079	.3859452	.3824607	.3789547
2.9	.3574845	.3538368	.3501700	.3464846	.3427808
3.0	.3201909	.3163677	.3125289	.3086746	.3048052
3.1	.2812912	.2773257	.2733478	.2693579	.2653563
3.2	.2411197	.2370457	.2329627	.2288711	.2247712
3.3	.2000177	.1958696	.1917161	.1875574	.1833938
3.4	.1583313	.1541439	.1499545	.1457634	.1415709
3.5	.1164079	.1122159	.1080253	.1038365	.0996498
3.6	.0745934	.0704312	.0662737	.0621215	.0579748
3.7	.0332293	.0291307	.0250402	.0209582	.0168850
3.8	− .0073502	− .0113524	− .0153432	− .0193223	− .0232894
3.9	− .0468212	− .0506953	− .0545548	− .0583995	− .0622291
4.0	− .0848728	− .0885884	− .0922865	− .0959669	− .0996292
4.1	− .1212093	− .1247378	− .1282461	− .1317339	− .1352009
4.2	− .1555532	− .1588679	− .1621598	− .1654287	− .1686744
4.3	− .1876469	− .1907233	− .1937745	− .1968005	− .1998009
4.4	− .2172552	− .2200710	− .2228596	− .2256209	− .2283545
4.5	− .2441671	− .2467026	− .2492091	− .2516864	− .2541344
4.6	− .2681970	− .2704352	− .2726428	− .2748196	− .2769657
4.7	− .2891868	− .2911133	− .2930080	− .2948707	− .2967014
4.8	− .3070064	− .3086098	− .3101805	− .3117182	− .3132230
4.9	− .3215549	− .3228269	− .3240653	− .3252702	− .3264415

BESSEL FUNCTION J_1

T	.00	.01	.02	.03	.04
5.0	− .3275791	− .3286831	− .3297533	− .3307898	− .3317925
5.1	− .3370972	− .3378626	− .3385940	− .3392915	− .3399550
5.2	− .3432230	− .3436489	− .3440409	− .3443991	− .3447234
5.3	− .3459608	− .3460493	− .3461043	− .3461259	− .3461140
5.4	− .3453448	− .3451009	− .3448242	− .3445147	− .3441725
5.5	− .3414382	− .3408699	− .3402696	− .3396376	− .3389739
5.6	− .3343328	− .3334507	− .3325379	− .3315946	− .3306208
5.7	− .3241477	− .3229651	− .3217534	− .3205126	− .3192429
5.8	− .3110277	− .3095607	− .3080661	− .3065442	− .3049952
5.9	− .2951424	− .2934090	− .2916501	− .2898658	− .2880563
6.0	− .2766839	− .2747045	− .2727017	− .2706758	− .2686269
6.1	− .2558648	− .2536618	− .2514378	− .2491929	− .2469275
6.2	− .2329166	− .2305141	− .2280930	− .2256536	− .2231961
6.3	− .2080869	− .2055105	− .2029180	− .2003100	− .1976865
6.4	− .1816375	− .1789139	− .1761771	− .1734274	− .1706650
6.5	− .1538413	− .1509984	− .1481451	− .1452818	− .1424086
6.6	− .1249802	− .1220465	− .1191054	− .1161571	− .1132019
6.7	− .0953421	− .0923468	− .0893469	− .0863427	− .0833346
6.8	− .0652187	− .0621909	− .0591615	− .0561307	− .0530989
6.9	− .0349021	− .0318710	− .0288412	− .0258130	− .0227866
7.0	− .0046828	− .0016773	.0013241	.0043211	.0073134
7.1	.0251533	.0281050	.0310498	.0339875	.0369177
7.2	.0543274	.0571980	.0600589	.0629100	.0657511
7.3	.0825704	.0853335	.0880844	.0908230	.0935488
7.4	.1096251	.1122557	.1148718	.1174730	.1200593
7.5	.1352484	.1377232	.1401811	.1426220	.1450456
7.6	.1592138	.1615109	.1637892	.1660484	.1682883
7.7	.1813127	.1834125	.1854916	.1875497	.1895868
7.8	.2013569	.2032417	.2051041	.2069439	.2087611
7.9	.2191794	.2208337	.2224642	.2240708	.2256533
8.0	.2346363	.2360471	.2374329	.2387936	.2401291
8.1	.2476078	.2487643	.2498950	.2509996	.2520782
8.2	.2579986	.2588928	.2597605	.2606016	.2614159
8.3	.2657393	.2663657	.2669651	.2675375	.2680829
8.4	.2707863	.2711419	.2714704	.2717718	.2720460
8.5	.2731220	.2732065	.2732640	.2732946	.2732981
8.6	.2727548	.2725706	.2723596	.2721221	.2718580
8.7	.2697190	.2692707	.2687964	.2682961	.2677699
8.8	.2640737	.2633687	.2626384	.2618831	.2611028
8.9	.2559024	.2549502	.2539740	.2529738	.2519497
9.0	.2453118	.2441244	.2429143	.2416816	.2404263
9.1	.2324307	.2310222	.2295925	.2281416	.2266698
9.2	.2174087	.2157950	.2141618	.2125092	.2108375
9.3	.2004139	.1986130	.1967943	.1949582	.1931047
9.4	.1816322	.1796634	.1776789	.1756789	.1736637
9.5	.1612644	.1591486	.1570192	.1548765	.1527208
9.6	.1395248	.1372840	.1350319	.1327688	.1304950
9.7	.1166386	.1142959	.1119443	.1095840	.1072154
9.8	.0928401	.0904193	.0879920	.0855585	.0831189
9.9	.0683698	.0658953	.0634167	.0609343	.0584484

BESSEL FUNCTION J_1

T	.05	.06	.07	.08	.09
5.0	−.3327613	−.3336963	−.3345974	−.3354646	−.3362979
5.1	−.3405846	−.3411802	−.3417418	−.3422695	−.3427632
5.2	−.3450140	−.3452707	−.3454938	−.3456831	−.3458388
5.3	−.3460688	−.3459903	−.3458785	−.3457337	−.3455557
5.4	−.3437977	−.3433905	−.3429508	−.3424788	−.3419746
5.5	−.3382786	−.3375518	−.3367938	−.3360045	−.3351841
5.6	−.3296168	−.3285826	−.3275185	−.3264245	−.3253009
5.7	−.3179445	−.3166176	−.3152623	−.3138787	−.3124672
5.8	−.3034193	−.3018166	−.3001874	−.2985318	−.2968501
5.9	−.2862220	−.2843629	−.2824793	−.2805715	−.2786396
6.0	−.2665553	−.2644612	−.2623449	−.2602066	−.2580464
6.1	−.2446417	−.2423358	−.2400101	−.2376649	−.2353003
6.2	−.2207209	−.2182281	−.2157181	−.2131910	−.2106472
6.3	−.1950479	−.1923944	−.1897264	−.1870440	−.1843476
6.4	−.1678903	−.1651035	−.1623049	−.1594949	−.1566736
6.5	−.1395260	−.1366341	−.1337333	−.1308238	−.1279060
6.6	−.1102401	−.1072720	−.1042978	−.1013179	−.0983326
6.7	−.0803228	−.0773076	−.0742893	−.0712681	−.0682445
6.8	−.0500663	−.0470332	−.0440000	−.0409669	−.0379341
6.9	−.0197623	−.0167404	−.0137213	−.0107051	−.0076922
7.0	.0103007	.0132828	.0162594	.0192302	.0221949
7.1	.0398402	.0427547	.0456609	.0485586	.0514476
7.2	.0685817	.0714017	.0742109	.0770089	.0797955
7.3	.0962619	.0989617	.1016482	.1043211	.1069802
7.4	.1226303	.1251857	.1277255	.1302494	.1327571
7.5	.1474518	.1498404	.1522110	.1545636	.1568979
7.6	.1705088	.1727096	.1748906	.1770516	.1791923
7.7	.1916026	.1935970	.1955697	.1975208	.1994499
7.8	.2105554	.2123267	.2140749	.2157999	.2175014
7.9	.2272116	.2287457	.2302553	.2317403	.2332007
8.0	.2414393	.2427241	.2439835	.2452173	.2464254
8.1	.2531307	.2541570	.2551569	.2561306	.2570778
8.2	.2622036	.2629644	.2636985	.2644056	.2650859
8.3	.2686012	.2690924	.2695566	.2699936	.2704035
8.4	.2722931	.2725131	.2727059	.2728717	.2730104
8.5	.2732747	.2732244	.2731472	.2730432	.2729124
8.6	.2715674	.2712504	.2709069	.2705372	.2701412
8.7	.2672179	.2666402	.2660368	.2654079	.2647535
8.8	.2602976	.2594677	.2586131	.2577339	.2568303
8.9	.2509019	.2498306	.2487357	.2476176	.2464762
9.0	.2391487	.2378489	.2365270	.2351833	.2338178
9.1	.2251772	.2236640	.2221304	.2205765	.2190026
9.2	.2091467	.2074370	.2057087	.2039620	.2021970
9.3	.1912342	.1893468	.1874427	.1855221	.1835852
9.4	.1716335	.1695884	.1675288	.1654548	.1633666
9.5	.1505523	.1483711	.1461775	.1439718	.1417542
9.6	.1282106	.1259159	.1236111	.1212965	.1189722
9.7	.1048385	.1024537	.1000612	.0976613	.0952542
9.8	.0806737	.0782229	.0757669	.0733059	.0708401
9.9	.0559592	.0534670	.0509720	.0484745	.0459746

BESSEL FUNCTION J_1

T	.00	.01	.02	.03	.04
10.0	.0434727	.0409691	.0384638	.0359573	.0334497
10.1	.0183955	.0158874	.0133801	.0108741	.0083694
10.2	−.0066157	−.0091038	−.0115886	−.0140698	−.0165471
10.3	−.0313178	−.0337618	−.0362001	−.0386324	−.0410586
10.4	−.0554728	−.0578492	−.0602176	−.0625779	−.0649296
10.5	−.0788500	−.0811364	−.0834125	−.0856782	−.0879333
10.6	−.1012287	−.1034034	−.1055659	−.1077159	−.1098532
10.7	−.1223994	−.1244424	−.1264711	−.1284855	−.1304852
10.8	−.1421666	−.1440590	−.1459354	−.1477956	−.1496394
10.9	−.1603497	−.1620744	−.1637815	−.1654708	−.1671422
11.0	−.1767853	−.1783270	−.1798496	−.1813530	−.1828371
11.1	−.1913283	−.1926735	−.1939984	−.1953028	−.1965868
11.2	−.2038531	−.2049904	−.2061063	−.2072008	−.2082738
11.3	−.2142550	−.2151751	−.2160729	−.2169486	−.2178019
11.4	−.2224506	−.2231462	−.2238192	−.2244693	−.2250966
11.5	−.2283786	−.2288450	−.2292883	−.2297085	−.2301055
11.6	−.2320005	−.2322350	−.2324463	−.2326344	−.2327992
11.7	−.2333002	−.2333026	−.2332817	−.2332378	−.2331707
11.8	−.2322847	−.2320568	−.2318060	−.2315324	−.2312361
11.9	−.2289832	−.2285292	−.2280528	−.2275541	−.2270334
12.0	−.2234471	−.2227732	−.2220777	−.2213608	−.2206225
12.1	−.2157490	−.2148637	−.2139578	−.2130314	−.2120846
12.2	−.2059820	−.2048957	−.2037900	−.2026649	−.2015206
12.3	−.1942588	−.1929838	−.1916907	−.1903795	−.1890506
12.4	−.1807102	−.1792605	−.1777942	−.1763114	−.1748122
12.5	−.1654838	−.1638750	−.1622513	−.1606127	−.1589594
12.6	−.1487423	−.1469916	−.1452276	−.1434505	−.1416606
12.7	−.1306622	−.1287877	−.1269019	−.1250050	−.1230971
12.8	−.1114316	−.1094528	−.1074646	−.1054674	−.1034612
12.9	−.0912483	−.0891854	−.0871153	−.0850381	−.0829541
13.0	−.0703181	−.0681921	−.0660609	−.0639249	−.0617841
13.1	−.0488525	−.0466847	−.0445140	−.0423405	−.0401645
13.2	−.0270667	−.0248789	−.0226902	−.0205009	−.0183113
13.3	−.0051775	−.0029912	−.0008063	.0013771	.0035587
13.4	.0165990	.0187622	.0209219	.0230780	.0252301
13.5	.0380493	.0401683	.0422817	.0443894	.0464911
13.6	.0589646	.0610188	.0630655	.0651044	.0671353
13.7	.0791428	.0811125	.0830728	.0850233	.0869640
13.8	.0983905	.1002570	.1021121	.1039558	.1057877
13.9	.1165249	.1182704	.1200029	.1217222	.1234282
14.0	.1333752	.1349834	.1365770	.1381560	.1397201
14.1	.1487844	.1502404	.1516805	.1531045	.1545122
14.2	.1626107	.1639013	.1651747	.1664308	.1676695
14.3	.1747291	.1758426	.1769380	.1780149	.1790734
14.4	.1850317	.1859585	.1868661	.1877546	.1886237
14.5	.1934295	.1941616	.1948740	.1955664	.1962389
14.6	.1998527	.2003843	.2008956	.2013866	.2018572
14.7	.2042513	.2045785	.2048851	.2051711	.2054365
14.8	.2065956	.2067165	.2068167	.2068963	.2069553
14.9	.2068762	.2067910	.2066853	.2065590	.2064124

BESSEL FUNCTION J_1

T	.05	.06	.07	.08	.09
10.0	.0309412	.0284322	.0259229	.0234135	.0209043
10.1	.0058663	.0033652	.0008662	−.0016305	−.0041246
10.2	−.0190205	−.0214895	−.0239540	−.0264137	−.0288684
10.3	−.0434783	−.0458914	−.0482976	−.0506967	−.0530885
10.4	−.0672727	−.0696068	−.0719318	−.0742475	−.0765537
10.5	−.0901775	−.0924107	−.0946326	−.0968431	−.0990418
10.6	−.1119776	−.1140889	−.1161870	−.1182715	−.1203424
10.7	−.1324701	−.1344401	−.1363949	−.1383343	−.1402583
10.8	−.1514668	−.1532774	−.1550711	−.1568479	−.1586075
10.9	−.1687954	−.1704305	−.1720471	−.1736452	−.1752247
11.0	−.1843017	−.1857467	−.1871720	−.1885774	−.1899629
11.1	−.1978500	−.1990926	−.2003142	−.2015150	−.2026946
11.2	−.2093252	−.2103549	−.2113628	−.2123488	−.2133129
11.3	−.2186329	−.2194415	−.2202277	−.2209912	−.2217322
11.4	−.2257010	−.2262825	−.2268410	−.2273766	−.2278891
11.5	−.2304793	−.2308300	−.2311575	−.2314617	−.2317427
11.6	−.2329407	−.2330591	−.2331542	−.2332261	−.2332747
11.7	−.2330806	−.2329674	−.2328312	−.2326720	−.2324898
11.8	−.2309170	−.2305754	−.2302111	−.2298243	−.2294150
11.9	−.2264905	−.2259255	−.2253387	−.2247299	−.2240994
12.0	−.2198629	−.2190821	−.2182803	−.2174574	−.2166136
12.1	−.2111175	−.2101303	−.2091230	−.2080958	−.2070488
12.2	−.2003572	−.1991749	−.1979738	−.1967540	−.1955156
12.3	−.1877039	−.1863397	−.1849580	−.1835591	−.1821432
12.4	−.1732969	−.1717656	−.1702185	−.1686557	−.1670774
12.5	−.1572917	−.1556097	−.1539136	−.1522036	−.1504797
12.6	−.1398581	−.1380431	−.1362158	−.1343765	−.1325252
12.7	−.1211786	−.1192494	−.1173100	−.1153604	−.1134008
12.8	−.1014463	−.0994229	−.0973912	−.0953513	−.0933036
12.9	−.0808634	−.0787663	−.0766630	−.0745538	−.0724387
13.0	−.0596388	−.0574892	−.0553356	−.0531781	−.0510170
13.1	−.0379861	−.0358056	−.0336232	−.0314391	−.0292535
13.2	−.0161215	−.0139317	−.0117422	−.0095532	−.0073649
13.3	.0057383	.0079157	.0100907	.0122630	.0144326
13.4	.0273781	.0295218	.0316610	.0337954	.0359249
13.5	.0485866	.0506758	.0527583	.0548341	.0569029
13.6	.0691581	.0711725	.0731784	.0751755	.0771637
13.7	.0888946	.0908150	.0927250	.0946243	.0965129
13.8	.1076079	.1094160	.1112119	.1129955	.1147665
13.9	.1251207	.1267995	.1284645	.1301156	.1317525
14.0	.1412691	.1428030	.1443216	.1458248	.1473124
14.1	.1559036	.1572785	.1586368	.1599783	.1613030
14.2	.1688906	.1700940	.1712797	.1724475	.1735973
14.3	.1801133	.1811346	.1821372	.1831209	.1840858
14.4	.1894735	.1903038	.1911147	.1919059	.1926775
14.5	.1968915	.1975240	.1981364	.1987287	.1993008
14.6	.2023074	.2027371	.2031464	.2035352	.2039035
14.7	.2056813	.2059054	.2061089	.2062918	.2064540
14.8	.2069936	.2070113	.2070084	.2069849	.2069408
14.9	.2062452	.2060577	.2058498	.2056215	.2053729

BESSEL FUNCTION J_1

T	.00	.01	.02	.03	.04
15.0	.2051040	.2048149	.2045057	.2041762	.2038267
15.1	.2013102	.2008214	.2003130	.1997849	.1992373
15.2	.1955454	.1948631	.1941618	.1934416	.1927027
15.3	.1878794	.1870115	.1861255	.1852216	.1842998
15.4	1784003	.1773565	.1762958	.1752183	.1741239
15.5	.1672132	.1660051	.1647812	.1635418	.1622868
15.6	.1544396	.1530801	.1517062	.1503181	.1489160
15.7	.1402157	.1387193	.1372099	.1356878	.1341533
15.8	.1246913	.1230735	.1214444	.1198043	.1181532
15.9	.1080279	.1063054	.1045735	.1028322	.1010818
16.0	.0903972	.0885878	.0867707	.0849461	.0831142
16.1	.0719794	.0701015	.0682178	.0663284	.0644336
16.2	.0529615	.0510340	.0491027	.0471677	.0452291
16.3	.0335351	.0315774	.0296179	.0276565	.0256936
16.4	.0138947	.0119264	.0099581	.0079901	.0060224
16.5	−.0057642	−.0077236	−.0096811	−.0116364	−.0135893
16.6	−.0252471	−.0271783	−.0291056	−.0310289	−.0329479
16.7	−.0443624	−.0462465	−.0481248	−.0499972	−.0518635
16.8	−.0629232	−.0647418	−.0665528	−.0683562	−.0701516
16.9	−.0807493	−.0824847	−.0842110	−.0859278	−.0876351
17.0	−.0976685	−.0993042	−.1009291	−.1025429	−.1041456
17.1	−.1135188	−.1150392	−.1165472	−.1180427	−.1195255
17.2	−.1281497	−.1295403	−.1309172	−.1322802	−.1336293
17.3	−.1414233	−.1426712	−.1439041	−.1451219	−.1463246
17.4	−.1532162	−.1543097	−.1553872	−.1564487	−.1574939
17.5	−.1634200	−.1643493	−.1652617	−.1661571	−.1670354
17.6	−.1719427	−.1726995	−.1734387	−.1741601	−.1748638
17.7	−.1787096	−.1792874	−.1798469	−.1803883	−.1809113
17.8	−.1836635	−.1840575	−.1844329	−.1847898	−.1851280
17.9	−.1867654	−.1869728	−.1871614	−.1873313	−.1874824
18.0	−.1879949	−.1880146	−.1880156	−.1879979	−.1879614
18.1	−.1873502	−.1871831	−.1869975	−.1867933	−.1865706
18.2	−.1848479	−.1844967	−.1841273	−.1837398	−.1833341
18.3	−.1805231	−.1799922	−.1794437	−.1788776	−.1782940
18.4	−.1744283	−.1737241	−.1730029	−.1722648	−.1715100
18.5	−.1666336	−.1657639	−.1648780	−.1639762	−.1630586
18.6	−.1572254	−.1561996	−.1551588	−.1541031	−.1530325
18.7	−.1463053	−.1451345	−.1439499	−.1427515	−.1415396
18.8	−.1339897	−.1326863	−.1313703	−.1300419	−.1287013
18.9	−.1204080	−.1189855	−.1175520	−.1161074	−.1146521
19.0	−.1057014	−.1041747	−.1026383	−.1010925	−.0995375
19.1	−.0900216	−.0884062	−.0867828	−.0851517	−.0835128
19.2	−.0735290	−.0718414	−.0701476	−.0684476	−.0667417
19.3	−.0563913	−.0546486	−.0529015	−.0511499	−.0493942
19.4	−.0387816	−.0370015	−.0352186	−.0334331	−.0316452
19.5	−.0208771	−.0190773	−.0172765	−.0154749	−.0136727
19.6	−.0028566	−.0010551	.0007456	.0025454	.0043439
19.7	.0151006	.0168860	.0186688	.0204488	.0222259
19.8	.0328168	.0345684	.0363156	.0380584	.0397965
19.9	.0501174	.0518181	.0535127	.0552011	.0568832

BESSEL FUNCTION J_1

T	.05	.06	.07	.08	.09
15.0	.2034571	.2030675	.2026580	.2022286	.2017793
15.1	.1986703	.1980838	.1974780	.1968530	.1962088
15.2	.1919450	.1911688	.1903740	.1895608	.1887292
15.3	.1833603	.1824032	.1814285	.1804363	.1794269
15.4	.1730130	.1718855	.1707417	.1695816	.1684054
15.5	.1610165	.1597310	.1584304	.1571149	.1557846
15.6	.1474999	.1460700	.1446265	.1431695	.1416992
15.7	.1326063	.1310471	.1294758	.1278927	.1262978
15.8	.1164915	.1148192	.1131365	.1114436	.1097407
15.9	.0993224	.0975542	.0957774	.0939922	.0921987
16.0	.0812751	.0794291	.0775764	.0757170	.0738513
16.1	.0625336	.0606285	.0587186	.0568040	.0548849
16.2	.0432872	.0413423	.0393944	.0374437	.0354906
16.3	.0237294	.0217640	.0197976	.0178305	.0158628
16.4	.0040553	.0020891	.0001238	−.0018403	−.0038031
16.5	−.0155397	−.0174874	−.0194322	−.0213739	−.0233122
16.6	−.0348625	−.0367725	−.0386776	−.0405778	−.0424728
16.7	−.0537236	−.0555771	−.0574241	−.0592642	−.0610973
16.8	−.0719390	−.0737182	−.0754890	−.0772512	−.0790047
16.9	−.0893326	−.0910202	−.0926978	−.0943651	−.0960221
17.0	−.1057370	−.1073169	−.1088852	−.1104417	−.1119863
17.1	−.1209956	−.1224528	−.1238970	−.1253279	−.1267455
17.2	−.1349642	−.1362850	−.1375914	−.1388833	−.1401607
17.3	−.1475120	−.1486840	−.1498406	−.1509815	−.1521067
17.4	−.1585228	−.1595354	−.1605315	−.1615110	−.1624738
17.5	−.1678966	−.1687405	−.1695672	−.1703765	−.1711684
17.6	−.1755497	−.1762176	−.1768677	−.1774997	−.1781137
17.7	−.1814160	−.1819024	−.1823704	−.1828199	−.1832509
17.8	−.1854476	−.1857486	−.1860308	−.1862944	−.1865392
17.9	−.1876147	−.1877283	−.1878231	−.1878991	−.1879564
18.0	−.1879062	−.1878323	−.1877397	−.1876285	−.1874987
18.1	−.1863295	−.1860699	−.1857919	−.1854956	−.1851809
18.2	−.1829104	−.1824688	−.1820091	−.1815316	−.1810362
18.3	−.1776930	−.1770745	−.1764388	−.1757858	−.1751156
18.4	−.1707385	−.1699503	−.1691457	−.1683247	−.1674873
18.5	−.1621252	−.1611761	−.1602115	−.1592314	−.1582360
18.6	−.1519474	−.1508476	−.1497334	−.1486049	−.1474621
18.7	−.1403142	−.1390754	−.1378235	−.1365584	−.1352805
18.8	−.1273486	−.1259838	−.1246073	−.1232190	−.1218192
18.9	−.1131861	−.1117096	−.1102227	−.1087256	−.1072185
19.0	−.0979733	−.0964002	−.0948183	−.0932278	−.0916289
19.1	−.0818666	−.0802130	−.0785523	−.0768846	−.0752101
19.2	−.0650301	−.0633128	−.0615901	−.0598622	−.0581292
19.3	−.0476344	−.0458709	−.0441036	−.0423329	−.0405588
19.4	−.0298551	−.0280629	−.0262688	−.0244730	−.0226757
19.5	−.0118701	−.0100672	−.0082642	−.0064613	−.0046587
19.6	.0061411	.0079368	.0097307	.0115228	.0133128
19.7	.0239998	.0257705	.0275377	.0293012	.0310610
19.8	.0415298	.0432580	.0449810	.0466988	.0484109
19.9	.0585587	.0602276	.0618897	.0635447	.0651926

BESSEL FUNCTION J_1

T	.00	.01	.02	.03	.04
20.0	.0668331	.0684662	.0700916	.0717092	.0733189
20.1	.0828010	.0843506	.0858911	.0874222	.0889438
20.2	.0978664	.0993176	.1007583	.1021881	.1036071
20.3	.1118844	.1132233	.1145503	.1158652	.1171679
20.4	.1247210	.1259349	.1271356	.1283231	.1294972
20.5	.1362547	.1373321	.1383953	.1394442	.1404787
20.6	.1463774	.1473083	.1482241	.1491247	.1500099
20.7	.1549955	.1557714	.1565314	.1572754	.1580034
20.8	.1620307	.1626447	.1632421	.1638229	.1643871
20.9	.1674209	.1678675	.1682972	.1687099	.1691055
21.0	.1711203	.1713960	.1716544	.1718957	.1721196
21.1	.1731003	.1732031	.1732886	.1733568	.1734076
21.2	.1733493	.1732790	.1731915	.1730868	.1729649
21.3	.1718730	.1716312	.1713724	.1710966	.1708039
21.4	.1686941	.1682839	.1678572	.1674139	.1669541
21.5	.1638521	.1632784	.1626887	.1620831	.1614616
21.6	.1574027	.1566720	.1559260	.1551648	.1543884
21.7	.1494174	.1485376	.1476434	.1467348	.1458121
21.8	.1399825	.1389630	.1379301	.1368840	.1358246
21.9	.1291982	.1280498	.1268892	.1257164	.1245316
22.0	.1171778	.1159125	.1146362	.1133490	.1120511
22.1	.1040461	.1026770	.1012982	.0999099	.0985123
22.2	.0899387	.0884797	.0870126	.0855375	.0840545
22.3	.0749998	.0734659	.0719255	.0703785	.0688253
22.4	.0593815	.0577884	.0561902	.0545871	.0529793
22.5	.0432420	.0416056	.0399658	.0383228	.0366766
22.6	.0267439	.0250807	.0234157	.0217492	.0200812
22.7	.0100524	.0083791	.0067056	.0050322	.0033591
22.8	−.0066657	−.0083325	−.0099978	−.0116614	−.0133231
22.9	−.0232443	−.0248881	−.0265288	−.0281660	−.0297998
23.0	−.0395193	−.0411239	−.0427237	−.0443186	−.0459083
23.1	−.0553305	−.0568801	−.0584233	−.0599601	−.0614902
23.2	−.0705228	−.0720022	−.0734738	−.0749374	−.0763929
23.3	−.0849479	−.0863427	−.0877284	−.0891046	−.0904714
23.4	−.0984658	−.0997626	−.1010489	−.1023245	−.1035894
23.5	−.1109461	−.1121324	−.1133070	−.1144697	−.1156206
23.6	−.1222693	−.1233337	−.1243854	−.1254242	−.1264500
23.7	−.1323277	−.1332602	−.1341790	−.1350840	−.1359752
23.8	−.1410266	−.1418185	−.1425959	−.1433588	−.1441070
23.9	−.1482855	−.1489295	−.1495583	−.1501720	−.1507705
24.0	−.1540381	−.1545284	−.1550031	−.1554621	−.1559054
24.1	−.1582335	−.1585659	−.1588823	−.1591828	−.1594672
24.2	−.1608365	−.1610084	−.1611641	−.1613036	−.1614270
24.3	−.1618278	−.1618381	−.1618321	−.1618101	−.1617718
24.4	−.1612042	−.1610534	−.1608865	−.1607037	−.1605049
24.5	−.1589784	−.1586687	−.1583432	−.1580021	−.1576454
24.6	−.1551791	−.1547142	−.1542340	−.1537387	−.1532282
24.7	−.1498504	−.1492356	−.1486061	−.1479620	−.1473034
24.8	−.1430514	−.1422934	−.1415214	−.1407357	−.1399362
24.9	− .1348557	−.1339625	−.1330564	−.1321373	−.1312054

BESSEL FUNCTION J_1

T	.05	.06	.07	.08	.09
20.0	.0749204	.0765137	.0780985	.0796748	.0812423
20.1	.0904558	.0919581	.0934504	.0949326	.0964047
20.2	.1050150	.1064117	.1077972	.1091712	.1105336
20.3	.1184583	.1197362	.1210015	.1222542	.1234941
20.4	.1306578	.1318048	.1329381	.1340576	.1351631
20.5	.1414986	.1425040	.1434946	.1444704	.1454314
20.6	.1508798	.1517342	.1525730	.1533962	.1542037
20.7	.1587152	.1594109	.1600904	.1607535	.1614003
20.8	.1649347	.1654655	.1659796	.1664769	.1669573
20.9	.1694841	.1698456	.1701900	.1705173	.1708274
21.0	.1723263	.1725157	.1726878	.1728426	.1729801
21.1	.1734412	.1734574	.1734563	.1734379	.1734022
21.2	.1728258	.1726695	.1724960	.1723054	.1720977
21.3	.1704943	.1701678	.1698245	.1694644	.1690876
21.4	.1664779	.1659852	.1654763	.1649511	.1644097
21.5	.1608242	.1601711	.1595023	.1588180	.1581181
21.6	.1535970	.1527906	.1519694	.1511334	.1502827
21.7	.1448752	.1439243	.1429595	.1419808	.1409885
21.8	.1347522	.1336669	.1325687	.1314578	.1303342
21.9	.1233350	.1221266	.1209065	.1196749	.1184320
22.0	.1107426	.1094237	.1080944	.1067550	.1054055
22.1	.0971055	.0956897	.0942649	.0928314	.0913893
22.2	.0825638	.0810655	.0795598	.0780469	.0765268
22.3	.0672658	.0657003	.0641290	.0625520	.0609695
22.4	.0513669	.0497501	.0481290	.0465039	.0448748
22.5	.0350275	.0333756	.0317212	.0300643	.0284051
22.6	.0184119	.0167415	.0150702	.0133982	.0117255
22.7	.0016863	.0000141	−.0016574	−.0033279	−.0049974
22.8	−.0149827	−.0166401	−.0182951	−.0199476	−.0215974
22.9	−.0314299	−.0330561	−.0346783	−.0362964	−.0379101
23.0	−.0474927	−.0490718	−.0506452	−.0522129	−.0537747
23.1	−.0630134	−.0645298	−.0660391	−.0675411	−.0690357
23.2	−.0778402	−.0792791	−.0807094	−.0821311	−.0835440
23.3	−.0918286	−.0931761	−.0945136	−.0958412	−.0971586
23.4	−.1048434	−.1060864	−.1073183	−.1085390	−.1097483
23.5	−.1167594	−.1178861	−.1190005	−.1201026	−.1211922
23.6	−.1274628	−.1284624	−.1294488	−.1304219	−.1313815
23.7	−.1368525	−.1377157	−.1385648	−.1393997	−.1402203
23.8	−.1448406	−.1455593	−.1462633	−.1469523	−.1476264
23.9	−.1513536	−.1519214	−.1524738	−.1530107	−.1535322
24.0	−.1563330	−.1567448	−.1571408	−.1575209	−.1578852
24.1	−.1597356	−.1599880	−.1602243	−.1604445	−.1606486
24.2	−.1615342	−.1616253	−.1617002	−.1617589	−.1618015
24.3	−.1617175	−.1616470	−.1615604	−.1614577	−.1613390
24.4	−.1602902	−.1600595	−.1598130	−.1595506	−.1592724
24.5	−.1572730	−.1568852	−.1564818	−.1560629	−.1556287
24.6	−.1527026	−.1521619	−.1516064	−.1510359	−.1504505
24.7	−.1466304	−.1459431	−.1452414	−.1445255	−.1437955
24.8	−.1391230	−.1382963	−.1374562	−.1366026	−.1357357
24.9	−.1302607	−.1293035	−.1283337	−.1273515	−.1263570

BESSEL FUNCTION J_1

T	.00	.01	.02	.03	.04
25.0	−.1253502	−.1243314	−.1233006	−.1222578	−.1212033
25.1	−.1146348	−.1135009	−.1123561	−.1112005	−.1100344
25.2	−.1028206	−.1015834	−.1003365	−.0990801	−.0978143
25.3	−.0900295	−.0887017	−.0873655	−.0860211	−.0846686
25.4	−.0763926	−.0749876	−.0735757	−.0721571	−.0707318
25.5	−.0620485	−.0605808	−.0591076	−.0576290	−.0561453
25.6	−.0471429	−.0456272	−.0441075	−.0425840	−.0410569
25.7	−.0318259	−.0302775	−.0287266	−.0271735	−.0256183
25.8	−.0162515	−.0146859	−.0131194	−.0115523	−.0099846
25.9	−.0005755	.0009916	.0025581	.0041237	.0056883
26.0	.0150457	.0165989	.0181497	.0196982	.0212441
26.1	.0304572	.0319809	.0335009	.0350169	.0365288
26.2	.0455065	.0469857	.0484597	.0499283	.0513914
26.3	.0600453	.0614655	.0628791	.0642858	.0656857
26.4	.0739309	.0752783	.0766176	.0779488	.0792716
26.5	.0870278	.0882891	.0895412	.0907838	.0920169
26.6	.0992087	.1003718	.1015244	.1026665	.1037979
26.7	.1103559	.1114095	.1124517	.1134822	.1145010
26.8	.1203624	.1212965	.1222182	.1231273	.1240238
26.9	.1291329	.1299386	.1307311	.1315103	.1322760
27.0	.1365847	.1372546	.1379105	.1385524	.1391803
27.1	.1426487	.1431765	.1436899	.1441887	.1446729
27.2	.1472696	.1476507	.1480168	.1483681	.1487043
27.3	.1504068	.1506378	.1508537	.1510544	.1512400
27.4	.1520345	.1521137	.1521776	.1522264	.1522600
27.5	1521419	.1520691	.1519811	.1518779	.1517597
27.6	.1507335	.1505100	.1502714	.1500180	.1497496
27.7	.1478289	.1474573	.1470712	.1466705	.1462553
27.8	.1434622	.1429469	.1424175	.1418741	.1413166
27.9	.1376822	.1370288	.1363619	.1356817	.1349881
28.0	.1305515	.1297669	.1289697	.1281599	.1273375
28.1	.1221457	.1212383	.1203191	.1193882	.1184457
28.2	.1125531	.1115323	.1105007	.1094584	.1084056
28.3	.1018732	.1007495	.0996162	.0984734	.0973211
28.4	.0902161	.0890012	.0877778	.0865461	.0853062
28.5	.0777014	.0764076	.0751066	.0737985	.0724836
28.6	.0644564	.0630968	.0617315	.0603604	.0589838
28.7	.0506155	.0492040	.0477880	.0463678	.0449434
28.8	.0363185	.0348692	.0334170	.0319619	.0305041
28.9	.0217093	.0202368	.0187628	.0172874	.0158109
29.0	.0069342	.0054533	.0039723	.0024914	.0010108
29.1	−.0078591	−.0093337	−.0108069	−.0122786	−.0137485
29.2	−.0225233	−.0239770	−.0254278	−.0268756	−.0283202
29.3	−.0369130	−.0383314	−.0397454	−.0411550	−.0425600
29.4	−.0508859	−.0522549	−.0536183	−.0549758	−.0563273
29.5	−.0643044	−.0656106	−.0669098	−.0682019	−.0694868
29.6	−.0770368	−.0782674	−.0794898	−.0807039	−.0819095
29.7	−.0889586	−.0901017	−.0912354	−.0923596	−.0934742
29.8	−.0999541	−.1009985	−.1020325	−.1030559	−.1040687
29.9	−.1099168	−.1108525	−.1117768	−.1126896	−.1135909

BESSEL FUNCTION J_1

T	.05	.06	.07	.08	.09
25.0	−.1201371	−.1190593	−.1179701.	−.1168695	−.1157577
25.1	−.1088577	−.1076706	−.1064732	−.1052656	−.1040481
25.2	−.0965392	−.0952550	−.0939618	−.0926597	−.0913489
25.3	−.0833083	−.0819401	−.0805643	−.0791811	−.0777904
25.4	−.0693000	−.0678618	−.0664174	−.0649670	−.0635107
25.5	−.0546566	−.0531630	−.0516647	−.0501618	−.0486544
25.6	−.0395262	−.0379922	−.0364551	−.0349148	−.0333717
25.7	−.0240612	−.0225022	−.0209416	−.0193795	−.0178161
25.8	−.0084164	−.0068481	−.0052797	−.0037114	−.0021433
25.9	.0072517	.0088138	.0103744	.0119333	.0134905
26.0	.0227873	.0243276	.0258649	.0273991	.0289299
26.1	.0380365	.0395398	.0410387	.0425328	.0440221
26.2	.0528487	.0543003	.0557458	.0571853	.0586185
26.3	.0670784	.0684639	.0698420	.0712126	.0725757
26.4	.0805861	.0818920	.0831893	.0844778	.0857573
26.5	.0932404	.0944540	.0956578	.0968516	.0980353
26.6	.1049185	.1060282	.1071269	.1082144	.1092908
26.7	.1155080	.1165030	.1174861	.1184571	.1194159
26.8	.1249076	.1257786	.1266367	.1274818	.1283139
26.9	.1330283	.1337670	.1344920	.1352034	.1359010
27.0	.1397940	.1403935	.1409788	.1415498	.1421065
27.1	.1451425	.1455974	.1460376	.1464631	.1468738
27.2	.1490257	.1493320	.1496233	.1498995	.1501607
27.3	.1514104	.1515656	.1517056	.1518304	.1519401
27.4	.1522783	.1522814	.1522693	.1522420	.1521996
27.5	.1516263	.1514779	.1513143	.1511358	.1509421
27.6	.1494665	.1491684	.1488556	.1485281	.1481858
27.7	.1458256	.1453815	.1449231	.1444504	.1439634
27.8	.1407453	.1401601	.1395612	.1389485	.1383222
27.9	.1342813	.1335613	.1328283	.1320822	.1313233
28.0	.1265027	.1256556	.1247963	.1239248	.1230412
28.1	.1174918	.1165264	.1155498	.1145619	.1135630
28.2	.1073424	.1062688	.1051849	.1040910	.1029870
28.3	.0961595	.0949888	.0938089	.0926201	.0914225
28.4	.0840582	.0828022	.0815384	.0802669	.0789879
28.5	.0711619	.0698335	.0684987	.0671574	.0658099
28.6	.0576018	.0562145	.0548221	.0534247	.0520224
28.7	.0435151	.0420829	.0406470	.0392075	.0377646
28.8	.0290438	.0275811	.0261161	.0246491	.0231801
28.9	.0143332	.0128547	.0113754	.0098954	.0084150
29.0	−.0004694	−.0019490	−.0034280	−.0049060	−.0063831
29.1	−.0152165	−.0166825	−.0181463	−.0196078	−.0210669
29.2	−.0297615	−.0311993	−.0326335	−.0340639	−.0354905
29.3	−.0439603	−.0453557	−.0467461	−.0481314	−.0485113
29.4	−.0576728	−.0590121	−.0603450	−.0616715	−.0629913
29.5	−.0707643	−.0720343	−.0732966	−.0745513	−.0757980
29.6	−.0831065	−.0842948	−.0854742	−.0866448	−.0878063
29.7	−.0945791	−.0956741	−.0967593	−.0978344	−.0988994
29.8	−.1050708	−.1060620	−.1070423	−.1080116	−.1089698
29.9	−.1144805	−.1153584	−.1162245	−.1170787	−.1179209

BESSEL FUNCTION J_1

T	.00	.01	.02	.03	.04
30.0	−.1187511	−.1195691	−.1203749	−.1211684	−.1219495
30.1	−.1263727	−.1270653	−.1277450	−.1284116	−.1290653
30.2	−.1327098	−.1332705	−.1338177	−.1343514	−.1348714
30.3	−.1377037	−.1381273	−.1385370	−.1389328	−.1393145
30.4	−.1413090	−.1415918	−.1418604	−.1421147	−.1423547
30.5	−.1434943	−.1436339	−.1437592	−.1438701	−.1439666
30.6	−.1442426	−.1442382	−.1442194	−.1441861	−.1441385
30.7	−.1435512	−.1434032	−.1432409	−.1430644	−.1428736
30.8	−.1414315	−.1411419	−.1408382	−.1405206	−.1401891
30.9	−.1379094	−.1374814	−.1370399	−.1365848	−.1361162
31.0	−.1330243	−.1324628	−.1318882	−.1313006	−.1307001
31.1	−.1268294	−.1261403	−.1254388	−.1247250	−.1239990
31.2	−.1193904	−.1185810	−.1177600	−.1169275	−.1160836
31.3	−.1107855	−.1098642	−.1089323	−.1079897	−.1070368
31.4	−.1011040	−.1000804	−.0990471	−.0980043	−.0969520

BESSEL FUNCTION J_1

T	.05	.06	.07	.08	.09
30.0	−.1227182	−.1234744	−.1242180	−.1249490	−.1256672
30.1	−.1297058	−.1303332	−.1309473	−.1315482	−.1321357
30.2	−.1353778	−.1358705	−.1363495	−.1368148	−.1372661
30.3	−.1396822	−.1400358	−.1403753	−.1407007	−.1410119
30.4	−.1425805	−.1427920	−.1429891	−.1431719	−.1433403
30.5	−.1440486	−.1441162	−.1441695	−.1442083	−.1442327
30.6	−.1440765	−.1440001	−.1439094	−.1438043	−.1436849
30.7	−.1426686	−.1424495	−.1422161	−.1419687	−.1417071
30.8	−.1398436	−.1394843	−.1391112	−.1387243	−.1383237
30.9	−.1356342	−.1351388	−.1346300	−.1341080	−.1335727
31.0	−.1300868	−.1294606	−.1288217	−.1281702	−.1275060
31.1	−.1232608	−.1225106	−.1217483	−.1209742	−.1201882
31.2	−.1152284	−.1143619	−.1134843	−.1125956	−.1116960
31.3	−.1060733	−.1050996	−.1041158	−.1031218	−.1021178
31.4	−.0958903	−.0948194	−.0937394	−.0926504	−.0915524

HYPERBOLIC BESSEL FUNCTIONS

$$I_m(x) = i^{-m}J_m(ix)$$

x	$I_0(x)$	$I_1(x)$	$I_2(x)$
0.0	1.0000	0.0000	0.0000
0.1	1.0025	0.0501	0.0012
0.2	1.0100	0.1005	0.0050
0.4	1.0404	0.2040	0.0203
0.6	1.0920	0.3137	0.0464
0.8	1.1665	0.4329	0.0844
1.0	1.2661	0.5652	0.1357
1.2	1.3937	0.7147	0.2026
1.4	1.5534	0.8861	0.2875
1.6	1.7500	1.0848	0.3940
1.8	1.9896	1.3172	0.5260
2.0	2.2796	1.5906	0.6889
2.2	2.6291	1.9141	0.8891
2.4	3.0493	2.2981	1.1342
2.6	3.5533	2.7554	1.4337
2.8	4.1573	3.3011	1.7994
3.0	4.8808	3.9534	2.2452
3.2	5.7472	4.7343	2.7883
3.4	6.7848	5.6701	3.4495
3.6	8.0277	6.7927	4.2540
3.8	9.5169	8.1404	5.2325
4.0	11.302	9.7595	6.4222
4.2	13.442	11.706	7.8684
4.4	16.010	14.046	9.6258
4.6	19.093	16.863	11.761
4.8	22.794	20.253	14.355
5.0	27.240	24.336	17.506
5.2	32.584	29.254	21.332
5.4	39.009	35.182	25.978
5.6	46.738	42.328	31.620
5.8	56.038	50.946	38.470
6.0	67.234	61.342	46.787
6.2	80.718	73.886	56.884
6.4	96.962	89.026	69.141
6.6	116.54	107.30	84.021
6.8	140.14	129.38	102.08
7.0	168.59	156.04	124.01
7.2	202.92	188.25	150.63
7.4	244.34	227.17	182.94
7.6	294.33	274.22	222.17
7.8	354.68	331.10	269.79
8.0	427.56	399.87	327.60

Taken from *Vibration and Sound* with the permission of Philip Morse, author, and McGraw-Hill Book Company, Inc., publisher.

ELLIPTIC INTEGRALS OF THE FIRST, SECOND AND THIRD KIND

An elliptic integral has the form $\int R(x, \sqrt{f(x)})dx$, where R represents a rational function and $f(x) = a + bx + cx^2 + dx^3 + ex^4$, an algebraic function of the third or fourth degree.

1. Elliptic integrals of the *first kind* are represented by

$$F(k, \phi) = \int_0^\phi \frac{d\Phi}{\sqrt{1 - k^2 \sin^2 \Phi}}$$

$$= \int_0^x \frac{d\xi}{\sqrt{(1 - \xi^2)(1 - k^2\xi^2)}}, \quad x = \sin \phi, \, k^2 < 1.$$

2. Elliptic integrals of the second kind are represented by

$$E(k, \phi) = \int_0^\phi \sqrt{1 - k^2 \sin^2 \Phi} \, d\Phi$$

$$= \int_0^x \frac{\sqrt{1 - k^2\xi^2}}{\sqrt{1 - \xi^2}} \, d\xi, \quad x = \sin \phi, \, k^2 < 1.$$

3. Elliptic integrals of the third kind are represented as

$$\pi(k, n, \phi) = \int_0^\phi \frac{d\Phi}{(1 + n \sin^2 \Phi) \sqrt{1 - k^2 \sin^2 \Phi}},$$

$$k^2 < 1, \, n \text{ an integer.}$$

Elliptic integrals of the third kind are also presented as

$$\pi_1(k, n, x) = \int_0^x \frac{d\xi}{(1 + n\xi^2) \sqrt{(1 - \xi^2)(1 - k^2\xi^2)}},$$

$$x = \sin \phi, \, k^2 < 1, \, n \text{ an integer.}$$

4. The complete integrals are

$$K = F\left(k, \frac{\pi}{2}\right) = \frac{\pi}{2}\left[1 + \left(\frac{1}{2}\right)^2 k^2 + \left(\frac{3}{2 \cdot 4}\right)^2 k^4 \right.$$

$$\left. + \left(\frac{3 \cdot 5}{2 \cdot 4 \cdot 6}\right)^2 k^6 + \cdots\right]$$

$$E = E\left(k, \frac{\pi}{2}\right) = \frac{\pi}{2}\left[1 - \left(\frac{1}{2^2}\right) k^2 - \left(\frac{3^2}{2^2 \cdot 4^2}\right) \frac{k^4}{3}\right.$$

$$\left. - \left(\frac{3^2 \cdot 5^2}{2^2 \cdot 4^2 \cdot 6^2}\right) \frac{k^6}{5} - \left(\frac{3^2 \cdot 5^2 \cdot 7^2}{2^2 \cdot 4^2 \cdot 6^2 \cdot 8^2}\right) \frac{k^8}{7} - \cdots\right].$$

$$K' = F\left(\sqrt{1 - k^2}, \frac{\pi}{2}\right), \, E' = E\left(\sqrt{1 - k^2}, \frac{\pi}{2}\right)$$

5. The following relation holds between K, K', E, E', namely

$$KE' + EK' - KK' = \frac{\pi}{2} \quad \text{Legendre's relation}$$

E: see 2 above. $E' = \int_0^{\pi/2} (1 - k'^2 \sin^2 \phi)^{\frac{1}{2}}d\phi. \quad k' = \sqrt{(1 - k^2)}$

$$K = \int_0^{\pi/2} (1 - k^2 \sin^2 \phi)^{-\frac{1}{2}}d\phi \qquad K' = \int_0^{\pi/2} (1 - k'^2 \sin^2 \phi)^{-\frac{1}{2}}d\phi$$

6. To evaluate elliptic integrals for values outside the range contained in the following tables, these relations are useful

$$F(k, \pi) = 2K; E(k, \pi) = 2E$$

$$F(k, \phi + m\pi) = mF(k, \pi) + F(k, \phi) = 2mK + F(k, \phi)$$
$$m = 0, 1, 2, 3, \ldots$$

$$E(k, \phi + m\pi) = mE(k, \pi) + E(k, \phi) = 2mE + E(k, \phi)$$
$$m = 0, 1, 2, 3, \ldots$$

7. If $u = F(k, \phi) = \displaystyle\int_0^\phi \frac{d\Phi}{\sqrt{1 - k^2 \sin^2 \Phi}}$ $(k^2 < 1)$,

$$= \text{elliptic integral of the first kind.}$$

$$u = \int_0^x \frac{dx}{\sqrt{(1 - \xi^2)(1 - k^2\xi^2)}}, \text{ where } x = \sin \phi.$$

ϕ is called the amplitude of u or am u.
k is called the modulus.

$$k' = \sqrt{1 - k^2} = \text{the complementary modulus.}$$

$\sin \phi = \text{sn } u = x$ $\tan \phi = \text{tn } u = \dfrac{x}{\sqrt{1 - x^2}}.$

$\cos \phi = \text{cn } u = \sqrt{1 - x^2}.$ $\Delta\phi = \text{dn } u = \sqrt{1 - k^2 x^2}.$

am $0 = 0.$ sn $0 = 0.$

cn $0 = 1.$ dn $0 = 1.$

am $(-u) = -\text{am } u.$ sn $(-u) = -\text{sn } u.$

cn $(-u) = \text{cn } u.$ dn $(-u) = \text{dn } u.$

tn $(-u) = -\text{tn } u.$
sn$^2 u + \text{cn}^2 u = 1.$
dn$^2 u + k^2 \text{sn}^2 u = 1.$
dn$^2 u - k^2 \text{cn}^2 u = 1 - k^2 = k'^2.$

$$\text{sn } u = u - (1 + k^2) \frac{u^3}{3!} + (1 + 14k^2 + k^4) \frac{u^5}{5!}$$

$$- (1 + 135k^2 + 135k^4 + k^6) \frac{u^7}{7!} + \cdots$$

Periods: $4k$ and $2ik'$

$$\text{cn } u = 1 - \frac{u^2}{2!} + (1 + 4k^2) \frac{u^4}{4!} - (1 + 44k^2 + 16k^4) \frac{u^6}{6!} + \cdots$$

Periods: $4k$ and $2k + 2ik'$

$$\text{dn } u = 1 - k^2 \frac{u^2}{2!} + k^2(4 + k^2) \frac{u^4}{4!} - k^2(16 + 44k^2 + k^4) \frac{u^6}{6!} + \cdots$$

Periods: $2k$ and $4ik'$

ELLIPTIC INTEGRALS OF THE FIRST KIND: $F(k, \phi)^*$

$$F(k, \phi) = \int_0^\phi \frac{d\Phi}{\sqrt{1 - k^2 \sin^2 \Phi}}, \qquad \theta = \sin^{-1} k$$

θ / ϕ	5°	10°	15°	20°	25°	30°	35°	40°	45°
1°	0.0175	0.0175	0.0175	0.0175	0.0175	0.0175	0.0175	0.0175	0.0175
2°	0.0349	0.0349	0.0349	0.0349	0.0349	0.0349	0.0349	0.0349	0.0349
3°	0.0524	0.0524	0.0524	0.0524	0.0524	0.0524	0.0524	0.0524	0.0524
4°	0.0698	0.0698	0.0698	0.0698	0.0698	0.0698	0.0698	0.0698	0.0698
5°	0.0873	0.0873	0.0873	0.0873	0.0873	0.0873	0.0873	0.0873	0.0873
6°	0.1047	0.1047	0.1047	0.1047	0.1048	0.1048	0.1048	0.1048	0.1048
7°	0.1222	0.1222	0.1222	0.1222	0.1222	0.1222	0.1223	0.1223	0.1223
8°	0.1396	0.1396	0.1397	0.1397	0.1397	0.1397	0.1398	0.1398	0.1399
9°	0.1571	0.1571	0.1571	0.1572	0.1572	0.1572	0.1573	0.1573	0.1574
10°	0.1745	0.1746	0.1746	0.1746	0.1747	0.1748	0.1748	0.1749	0.1750
11°	0.1920	0.1920	0.1921	0.1921	0.1922	0.1923	0.1924	0.1925	0.1926
12°	0.2095	0.2095	0.2095	0.2096	0.2097	0.2098	0.2099	0.2101	0.2102
13°	0.2269	0.2270	0.2270	0.2271	0.2272	0.2274	0.2275	0.2277	0.2279
14°	0.2444	0.2444	0.2445	0.2446	0.2448	0.2450	0.2451	0.2453	0.2456
15°	0.2618	0.2619	0.2620	0.2621	0.2623	0.2625	0.2628	0.2630	0.2633
16°	0.2793	0.2794	0.2795	0.2797	0.2799	0.2802	0.2804	0.2808	0.2811
17°	0.2967	0.2968	0.2970	0.2972	0.2975	0.2978	0.2981	0.2985	0.2989
18°	0.3142	0.3143	0.3145	0.3148	0.3151	0.3154	0.3159	0.3163	0.3167
19°	0.3317	0.3318	0.3320	0.3323	0.3327	0.3331	0.3336	0.3341	0.3347
20°	0.3491	0.3493	0.3495	0.3499	0.3503	0.3508	0.3514	0.3520	0.3526
21°	0.3666	0.3668	0.3671	0.3675	0.3680	0.3685	0.3692	0.3699	0.3706
22°	0.3840	0.3842	0.3846	0.3851	0.3856	0.3863	0.3871	0.3879	0.3887
23°	0.4015	0.4017	0.4021	0.4027	0.4033	0.4041	0.4049	0.4059	0.4068
24°	0.4190	0.4192	0.4197	0.4203	0.4210	0.4219	0.4229	0.4239	0.4250
25°	0.4364	0.4367	0.4372	0.4379	0.4387	0.4397	0.4408	0.4420	0.4433
26°	0.4539	0.4542	0.4548	0.4556	0.4565	0.4576	0.4588	0.4602	0.4616
27°	0.4714	0.4717	0.4724	0.4732	0.4743	0.4755	0.4769	0.4784	0.4800
28°	0.4888	0.4893	0.4899	0.4909	0.4921	0.4934	0.4950	0.4967	0.4985
29°	0.5063	0.5068	0.5075	0.5086	0.5099	0.5114	0.5132	0.5150	0.5170
30°	0.5238	0.5243	0.5251	0.5263	0.5277	0.5294	0.5313	0.5334	0.5356
31°	0.5412	0.5418	0.5427	0.5440	0.5456	0.5475	0.5496	0.5519	0.5543
32°	0.5587	0.5593	0.5603	0.5617	0.5635	0.5656	0.5679	0.5704	0.5731
33°	0.5762	0.5769	0.5780	0.5795	0.5814	0.5837	0.5862	0.5890	0.5920
34°	0.5937	0.5944	0.5956	0.5973	0.5994	0.6018	0.6046	0.6077	0.6109
35°	0.6111	0.6119	0.6133	0.6151	0.6173	0.6200	0.6231	0.6264	0.6300
36°	0.6286	0.6295	0.6309	0.6329	0.6353	0.6383	0.6416	0.6452	0.6491
37°	0.6461	0.6470	0.6486	0.6507	0.6534	0.6565	0.6602	0.6641	0.6684
38°	0.6636	0.6646	0.6662	0.6685	0.6714	0.6749	0.6788	0.6831	0.6877
39°	0.6810	0.6821	0.6839	0.6864	0.6895	0.6932	0.6975	0.7021	0.7071
40°	0.6985	0.6997	0.7016	0.7043	0.7076	0.7116	0.7162	0.7213	0.7267
41°	0.7160	0.7173	0.7193	0.7222	0.7258	0.7301	0.7350	0.7405	0.7463
42°	0.7335	0.7348	0.7370	0.7401	0.7440	0.7486	0.7539	0.7598	0.7661
43°	0.7510	0.7524	0.7548	0.7580	0.7622	0.7671	0.7728	0.7791	0.7859
44°	0.7685	0.7700	0.7725	0.7760	0.7804	0.7857	0.7918	0.7986	0.8059
45°	0.7859	0.7876	0.7903	0.7940	0.7987	0.8044	0.8109	0.8181	0.8260

* For useful information about these tables see preceding page.

ELLIPTIC INTEGRALS OF THE FIRST KIND: $F(k, \phi)$ (Continued)

$$F(k, \phi) = \int_0^\phi \frac{d\Phi}{\sqrt{1 - k^2 \sin^2 \Phi}}, \qquad \theta = \sin^{-1} k$$

θ / ϕ	50°	55°	60°	65°	70°	75°	80°	85°	90°
1°	0.0175	0.0175	0.0175	0.0175	0.0175	0.0175	0.0175	0.0175	0.0175
2°	0.0349	0.0349	0.0349	0.0349	0.0349	0.0349	0.0349	0.0349	0.0349
3°	0.0524	0.0524	0.0524	0.0524	0.0524	0.0524	0.0524	0.0524	0.0524
4°	0.0698	0.0699	0.0699	0.0699	0.0699	0.0699	0.0699	0.0699	0.0699
5°	0.0873	0.0873	0.0873	0.0874	0.0874	0.0874	0.0874	0.0874	0.0874
6°	0.1048	0.1048	0.1049	0.1049	0.1049	0.1049	0.1049	0.1049	0.1049
7°	0.1224	0.1224	0.1224	0.1224	0.1224	0.1225	0.1225	0.1225	0.1225
8°	0.1399	0.1399	0.1400	0.1400	0.1400	0.1401	0.1401	0.1401	0.1401
9°	0.1575	0.1575	0.1576	0.1576	0.1577	0.1577	0.1577	0.1577	0.1577
10°	0.1751	0.1751	0.1752	0.1753	0.1753	0.1754	0.1754	0.1754	0.1754
11°	0.1927	0.1928	0.1929	0.1930	0.1930	0.1931	0.1931	0.1932	0.1932
12°	0.2103	0.2105	0.2106	0.2107	0.2108	0.2109	0.2109	0.2110	0.2110
13°	0.2280	0.2282	0.2284	0.2285	0.2286	0.2287	0.2288	0.2288	0.2289
14°	0.2458	0.2460	0.2462	0.2464	0.2465	0.2466	0.2467	0.2468	0.2468
15°	0.2636	0.2638	0.2641	0.2643	0.2645	0.2646	0.2647	0.2648	0.2648
16°	0.2814	0.2817	0.2820	0.2823	0.2825	0.2827	0.2828	0.2829	0.2830
17°	0.2993	0.2997	0.3000	0.3003	0.3006	0.3008	0.3010	0.3011	0.3012
18°	0.3172	0.3177	0.3181	0.3185	0.3188	0.3191	0.3193	0.3194	0.3195
19°	0.3352	0.3357	0.3362	0.3367	0.3371	0.3374	0.3377	0.3378	0.3379
20°	0.3533	0.3539	0.3545	0.3550	0.3555	0.3559	0.3561	0.3563	0.3564
21°	0.3714	0.3721	0.3728	0.3734	0.3740	0.3744	0.3747	0.3749	0.3750
22°	0.3896	0.3904	0.3912	0.3919	0.3926	0.3931	0.3935	0.3937	0.3938
23°	0.4078	0.4088	0.4097	0.4105	0.4113	0.4119	0.4123	0.4126	0.4127
24°	0.4261	0.4272	0.4283	0.4292	0.4301	0.4308	0.4313	0.4316	0.4317
25°	0.4446	0.4458	0.4470	0.4481	0.4490	0.4498	0.4504	0.4508	0.4509
26°	0.4630	0.4645	0.4658	0.4670	0.4681	0.4690	0.4697	0.4701	0.4702
27°	0.4816	0.4832	0.4847	0.4861	0.4873	0.4884	0.4891	0.4896	0.4897
28°	0.5003	0.5021	0.5038	0.5053	0.5067	0.5079	0.5087	0.5092	0.5094
29°	0.5190	0.5210	0.5229	0.5247	0.5262	0.5275	0.5285	0.5291	0.5293
30°	0.5379	0.5401	0.5422	0.5442	0.5459	0.5474	0.5484	0.5491	0.5493
31°	0.5568	0.5593	0.5617	0.5639	0.5658	0.5674	0.5686	0.5693	0.5696
32°	0.5759	0.5786	0.5812	0.5837	0.5858	0.5876	0.5889	0.5898	0.5900
33°	0.5950	0.5980	0.6010	0.6037	0.6060	0.6080	0.6095	0.6104	0.6107
34°	0.6143	0.6176	0.6208	0.6238	0.6265	0.6287	0.6303	0.6313	0.6317
35°	0.6336	0.6373	0.6408	0.6441	0.6471	0.6495	0.6513	0.6525	0.6528
36°	0.6531	0.6571	0.6610	0.6647	0.6679	0.6706	0.6726	0.6739	0.6743
37°	0.6727	0.6771	0.6814	0.6854	0.6890	0.6919	0.6941	0.6955	0.6960
38°	0.6925	0.6973	0.7019	0.7063	0.7102	0.7135	0.7159	0.7175	0.7180
39°	0.7123	0.7176	0.7227	0.7275	0.7318	0.7353	0.7380	0.7397	0.7403
40°	0.7323	0.7380	0.7436	0.7488	0.7535	0.7575	0.7604	0.7623	0.7629
41°	0.7524	0.7586	0.7647	0.7704	0.7756	0.7799	0.7831	0.7852	0.7859
42°	0.7727	0.7794	0.7860	0.7922	0.7979	0.8026	0.8062	0.8084	0.8092
43°	0.7931	0.8004	0.8075	0.8143	0.8204	0.8256	0.8295	0.8320	0.8328
44°	0.8136	0.8215	0.8293	0.8367	0.8433	0.8490	0.8533	0.8560	0.8569
45°	0.8343	0.8428	0.8512	0.8592	0.8665	0.8727	0.8774	0.8804	0.8814

ELLIPTIC INTEGRALS OF THE FIRST KIND: $F(k, \phi)$ (Continued)

$$F(k, \phi) = \int_0^\phi \frac{d\Phi}{\sqrt{1 - k^2 \sin^2 \Phi}}, \qquad \theta = \sin^{-1} k$$

ϕ \ θ	5°	10°	15°	20°	25°	30°	35°	40°	45°
46°	0.8034	0.8052	0.8080	0.8120	0.8170	0.8230	0.8300	0.8378	0.8462
47°	0.8209	0.8227	0.8258	0.8300	0.8353	0.8418	0.8492	0.8575	0.8666
48°	0.8384	0.8403	0.8436	0.8480	0.8537	0.8606	0.8685	0.8773	0.8870
49°	0.8559	0.8579	0.8614	0.8661	0.8721	0.8794	0.8878	0.8972	0.9076
50°	0.8734	0.8756	0.8792	0.8842	0.8905	0.8982	0.9072	0.9173	0.9283
51°	0.8909	0.8932	0.8970	0.9023	0.9090	0.9172	0.9267	0.9374	0.9491
52°	0.9084	0.9108	0.9148	0.9204	0.9275	0.9361	0.9462	0.9575	0.9701
53°	0.9259	0.9284	0.9326	0.9385	0.9460	0.9551	0.9658	0.9778	0.9912
54°	0.9434	0.9460	0.9505	0.9567	0.9646	0.9742	0.9855	0.9982	1.0124
55°	0.9609	0.9637	0.9683	0.9748	0.9832	0.9933	1.0052	1.0187	1.0337
56°	0.9784	0.9813	0.9862	0.9930	1.0018	1.0125	1.0250	1.0393	1.0552
57°	0.9959	0.9989	1.0041	1.0112	1.0204	1.0317	1.0449	1.0600	1.0768
58°	1.0134	1.0166	1.0219	1.0295	1.0391	1.0509	1.0648	1.0807	1.0985
59°	1.0309	1.0342	1.0398	1.0477	1.0578	1.0702	1.0848	1.1016	1.1204
60°	1.0484	1.0519	1.0577	1.0660	1.0766	1.0896	1.1049	1.1226	1.1424
61°	1.0659	1.0695	1.0757	1.0843	1.0953	1.1089	1.1250	1.1436	1.1646
62°	1.0834	1.0872	1.0936	1.1026	1.1141	1.1284	1.1452	1.1648	1.1868
63°	1.1009	1.1049	1.1115	1.1209	1.1330	1.1478	1.1655	1.1860	1.2093
64°	1.1184	1.1225	1.1295	1.1392	1.1518	1.1674	1.1859	1.2073	1.2318
65°	1.1359	1.1402	1.1474	1.1575	1.1707	1.1869	1.2063	1.2288	1.2545
66°	1.1534	1.1579	1.1654	1.1759	1.1896	1.2065	1.2267	1.2503	1.2773
67°	1.1709	1.1756	1.1833	1.1943	1.2085	1.2262	1.2472	1.2719	1.3002
68°	1.1884	1.1932	1.2013	1.2127	1.2275	1.2458	1.2678	1.2936	1.3232
69°	1.2059	1.2109	1.2193	1.2311	1.2465	1.2655	1.2885	1.3154	1.3464
70°	1.2234	1.2286	1.2373	1.2495	1.2655	1.2853	1.3092	1.3372	1.3697
71°	1.2410	1.2463	1.2553	1.2680	1.2845	1.3051	1.3299	1.3592	1.3931
72°	1.2585	1.2640	1.2733	1.2864	1.3036	1.3249	1.3507	1.3812	1.4167
73°	1.2760	1.2817	1.2913	1.3049	1.3226	1.3448	1.3715	1.4033	1.4403
74°	1.2935	1.2994	1.3093	1.3234	1.3417	1.3647	1.3924	1.4254	1.4640
75°	1.3110	1.3171	1.3273	1.3418	1.3608	1.3846	1.4134	1.4477	1.4879
76°	1.3285	1.3348	1.3454	1.3603	1.3800	1.4045	1.4344	1.4700	1.5118
77°	1.3460	1.3525	1.3634	1.3788	1.3991	1.4245	1.4554	1.4923	1.5359
78°	1.3636	1.3702	1.3814	1.3974	1.4183	1.4445	1.4765	1.5147	1.5600
79°	1.3811	1.3879	1.3995	1.4159	1.4374	1.4645	1.4976	1.5372	1.5842
80°	1.3986	1.4056	1.4175	1.4344	1.4566	1.4846	1.5187	1.5597	1.6085
81°	1.4161	1.4234	1.4356	1.4530	1.4758	1.5046	1.5399	1.5823	1.6328
82°	1.4336	1.4411	1.4536	1.4715	1.4950	1.5247	1.5611	1.6049	1.6572
83°	1.4512	1.4588	1.4717	1.4901	1.5143	1.5448	1.5823	1.6276	1.6817
84°	1.4687	1.4765	1.4897	1.5086	1.5335	1.5649	1.6035	1.6502	1.7062
85°	1.4862	1.4942	1.5078	1.5272	1.5527	1.5850	1.6248	1.6730	1.7308
86°	1.5037	1.5120	1.5259	1.5457	1.5720	1.6052	1.6461	1.6957	1.7554
87°	1.5212	1.5297	1.5439	1.5643	1.5912	1.6253	1.6673	1.7184	1.7801
88°	1.5388	1.5474	1.5620	1.5829	1.6105	1.6454	1.6886	1.7412	1.8047
89°	1.5563	1.5651	1.5801	1.6015	1.6297	1.6656	1.7099	1.7640	1.8294
90°	1.5738	1.5828	1.5981	1.6200	1.6490	1.6858	1.7312	1.7863	1.8541

ELLIPTIC INTEGRALS OF THE FIRST KIND: $F(k, \phi)$ (Continued)

$$F(k, \phi) = \int_0^\phi \frac{d\Phi}{\sqrt{1 - k^2 \sin^2 \Phi}}, \qquad \theta = \sin^{-1} k$$

θ / ϕ	50°	55°	60°	65°	70°	75°	80°	85°	90°
46°	0.8552	0.8643	0.8734	0.8821	0.8900	0.8968	0.9019	0.9052	0.9063
47°	0.8761	0.8860	0.8958	0.9053	0.9139	0.9212	0.9269	0.9304	0.9316
48°	0.8973	0.9079	0.9185	0.9287	0.9381	0.9461	0.9523	0.9561	0.9575
49°	0.9186	0.9300	0.9415	0.9525	0.9627	0.9714	0.9781	0.9824	0.9838
50°	0.9401	0.9523	0.9647	0.9766	0.9876	0.9971	1.0044	1.0091	1.0107
51°	0.9617	0.9748	0.9881	1.0010	1.0130	1.0233	1.0313	1.0364	1.0381
52°	0.9835	0.9976	1.0118	1.0258	1.0387	1.0499	1.0587	1.0642	1.0662
53°	1.0055	1.0205	1.0359	1.0509	1.0649	1.0771	1.0866	1.0927	1.0948
54°	1.0277	1.0437	1.0602	1.0764	1.0915	1.1048	1.1152	1.1219	1.1242
55°	1.0500	1.0672	1.0848	1.1022	1.1186	1.1331	1.1444	1.1517	1.1542
56°	1.0725	1.0908	1.1097	1.1285	1.1462	1.1619	1.1743	1.1823	1.1851
57°	1.0952	1.1147	1.1349	1.1551	1.1743	1.1914	1.2049	1.2136	1.2167
58°	1.1180	1.1389	1.1605	1.1822	1.2030	1.2215	1.2362	1.2458	1.2492
59°	1.1411	1.1632	1.1864	1.2097	1.2321	1.2522	1.2684	1.2789	1.2826
60°	1.1643	1.1879	1.2125	1.2376	1.2619	1.2837	1.3014	1.3129	1.3170
61°	1.1877	1.2128	1.2392	1.2660	1.2922	1.3159	1.3352	1.3480	1.3524
62°	1.2113	1.2379	1.2661	1.2949	1.3231	1.3490	1.3701	1.3841	1.3890
63°	1.2351	1.2633	1.2933	1.3242	1.3547	1.3828	1.4059	1.4214	1.4268
64°	1.2591	1.2890	1.3209	1.3541	1.3870	1.4175	1.4429	1.4599	1.4659
65°	1.2833	1.3149	1.3489	1.3844	1.4199	1.4532	1.4810	1.4998	1.5065
66°	1.3076	1.3411	1.3773	1.4153	1.4536	1.4898	1.5203	1.5411	1.5485
67°	1.3321	1.3675	1.4060	1.4467	1.4880	1.5274	1.5610	1.5840	1.5923
68°	1.3568	1.3942	1.4351	1.4786	1.5232	1.5661	1.6030	1.6287	1.6379
69°	1.3817	1.4212	1.4646	1.5111	1.5591	1.6059	1.6466	1.6752	1.6856
70°	1.4068	1.4484	1.4944	1.5441	1.5959	1.6468	1.6918	1.7237	1.7354
71°	1.4320	1.4759	1.5246	1.5777	1.6335	1.6891	1.7388	1.7745	1.7877
72°	1.4574	1.5036	1.5552	1.6118	1.6720	1.7326	1.7876	1.8277	1.8427
73°	1.4830	1.5315	1.5862	1.6465	1.7113	1.7774	1.8384	1.8837	1.9008
74°	1.5087	1.5597	1.6175	1.6818	1.7516	1.8237	1.8915	1.9427	1.9623
75°	1.5345	1.5882	1.6492	1.7176	1.7927	1.8715	1.9468	2.0050	2.0276
76°	1.5606	1.6168	1.6812	1.7540	1.8347	1.9207	2.0047	2.0711	2.0973
77°	1.5867	1.6457	1.7136	1.7909	1.8777	1.9716	2.0653	2.1414	2.1721
78°	1.6130	1.6748	1.7462	1.8284	1.9215	2.0240	2.1288	2.2164	2.2528
79°	1.6394	1.7040	1.7792	1.8664	1.9663	2.0781	2.1954	2.2969	2.3404
80°	1.6660	1.7335	1.8125	1.9048	2.0119	2.1339	2.2653	2.3836	2.4362
81°	1.6926	1.7631	1.8461	1.9438	2.0584	2.1913	2.3387	2.4775	2.5421
82°	1.7193	1.7929	1.8799	1.9831	2.1057	2.2504	2.4157	2.5795	2.6603
83°	1.7462	1.8228	1.9140	2.0229	2.1537	2.3110	2.4965	2.6911	2.7942
84°	1.7731	1.8528	1.9482	2.0630	2.2024	2.3731	2.5811	2.8136	2.9487
85°	1.8001	1.8830	1.9826	2.1035	2.2518	2.4366	2.6694	2.9487	3.1313
86°	1.8271	1.9132	2.0172	2.1442	2.3017	2.5013	2.7612	3.0978	3.3547
87°	1.8542	1.9435	2,0519	2.1852	2.3520	2.5670	2.8561	3.2620	3.6425
88°	1.8813	1.9739	2.0867	2.2263	2.4026	2.6336	2.9537	3.4412	4.0481
89°	1.9084	2.0043	2.1216	2.2675	2.4535	2.7007	3.0530	3.6328	4.7413
90°	1.9356	2.0347	2.1565	2.3088	2.5046	2.7681	3.1534	3.8317	———

ELLIPTIC INTEGRALS OF THE SECOND KIND: $E(k, \phi)$

$$E(k, \phi) = \int_0^\phi \sqrt{(1 - k^2 \sin^2 \Phi)} d\Phi, \quad \theta = \sin^{-1} k$$

θ / ϕ	5°	10°	15°	20°	25°	30°	35°	40°	45°
1°	0.0175	0.0175	0.0175	0.0175	0.0175	0.0175	0.0175	0.0175	0.0175
2°	0.0349	0.0349	0.0349	0.0349	0.0349	0.0349	0.0349	0.0349	0.0349
3°	0.0524	0.0524	0.0524	0.0524	0.0524	0.0524	0.0524	0.0523	0.0523
4°	0.0698	0.0698	0.0698	0.0698	0.0698	0.0698	0.0698	0.0698	0.0698
5°	0.0873	0.0873	0.0873	0.0873	0.0872	0.0872	0.0872	0.0872	0.0872
6°	0.1047	0.1047	0.1047	0.1047	0.1047	0.1047	0.1047	0.1046	0.1046
7°	0.1222	0.1222	0.1222	0.1221	0.1221	0.1221	0.1221	0.1220	0.1220
8°	0.1396	0.1396	0.1396	0.1396	0.1395	0.1395	0.1395	0.1394	0.1394
9°	0.1571	0.1571	0.1570	0.1570	0.1570	0.1569	0.1569	0.1568	0.1568
10°	0.1745	0.1745	0.1745	0.1744	0.1744	0.1743	0.1742	0.1742	0.1741
11°	0.1920	0.1920	0.1919	0.1918	0.1918	0.1917	0.1916	0.1915	0.1914
12°	0.2094	0.2094	0.2093	0.2093	0.2092	0.2091	0.2089	0.2088	0.2087
13°	0.2269	0.2268	0.2268	0.2267	0.2265	0.2264	0.2263	0.2261	0.2259
14°	0.2443	0.2443	0.2442	0.2441	0.2439	0.2437	0.2436	0.2433	0.2431
15°	0.2618	0.2617	0.2616	0.2615	0.2613	0.2611	0.2608	0.2606	0.2603
16°	0.2792	0.2791	0.2790	0.2788	0.2786	0.2784	0.2781	0.2778	0.2775
17°	0.2967	0.2966	0.2964	0.2962	0.2959	0.2956	0.2953	0.2949	0.2946
18°	0.3141	0.3140	0.3138	0.3136	0.3133	0.3129	0.3125	0.3121	0.3116
19°	0.3316	0.3314	0.3312	0.3309	0.3305	0.3301	0.3296	0.3291	0.3286
20°	0.3490	0.3489	0.3486	0.3483	0.3478	0.3473	0.3468	0.3462	0.3456
21°	0.3665	0.3663	0.3660	0.3656	0.3651	0.3645	0.3639	0.3632	0.3625
22°	0.3839	0.3837	0.3834	0.3829	0.3823	0.3817	0.3809	0.3802	0.3793
23°	0.4013	0.4011	0.4007	0.4002	0.3996	0.3988	0.3980	0.3971	0.3961
24°	0.4188	0.4185	0.4181	0.4175	0.4168	0.4159	0.4150	0.4139	0.4129
25°	0.4362	0.4359	0.4354	0.4348	0.4339	0.4330	0.4319	0.4308	0.4296
26°	0.4537	0.4533	0.4528	0.4520	0.4511	0.4500	0.4488	0.4475	0.4462
27°	0.4711	0.4707	0.4701	0.4693	0.4682	0.4670	0.4657	0.4643	0.4628
28°	0.4886	0.4881	0.4874	0.4865	0.4854	0.4840	0.4825	0.4809	0.4793
29°	0.5060	0.5055	0.5048	0.5037	0.5025	0.5010	0.4993	0.4975	0.4957
30°	0.5234	0.5229	0.5221	0.5209	0.5195	0.5179	0.5161	0.5141	0.5120
31°	0.5409	0.5403	0.5394	0.5381	0.5366	0.5348	0.5327	0.5306	0.5283
32°	0.5583	0.5577	0.5567	0.5553	0.5536	0.5516	0.5494	0.5470	0.5446
33°	0.5757	0.5751	0.5740	0.5725	0.5706	0.5684	0.5660	0.5634	0.5607
34°	0.5932	0.5924	0.5912	0.5896	0.5876	0.5852	0.5826	0.5797	0.5768
35°	0.6106	0.6098	0.6085	0.6067	0.6045	0.6019	0.5991	0.5960	0.5928
36°	0.6280	0.6272	0.6258	0.6238	0.6214	0.6186	0.6155	0.6122	0.6087
37°	0.6455	0.6445	0.6430	0.6409	0.6383	0.6353	0.6319	0.6283	0.6245
38°	0.6629	0.6619	0.6602	0.6580	0.6552	0.6519	0.6483	0.6444	0.6403
39°	0.6803	0.6792	0.6775	0.6750	0.6720	0.6685	0.6646	0.6604	0.6559
40°	0.6977	0.6966	0.6947	0.6921	0.6888	0.6851	0.6808	0.6763	0.6715
41°	0.7152	0.7139	0.7119	0.7091	0.7056	0.7016	0.6970	0.6921	0.6870
42°	0.7326	0.7313	0.7291	0.7261	0.7224	0.7180	0.7132	0.7079	0.7024
43°	0.7500	0.7486	0.7463	0.7431	0.7391	0.7345	0.7293	0.7237	0.7178
44°	0.7674	0.7659	0.7634	0.7600	0.7558	0.7508	0.7453	0.7393	0.7330
45°	0.7849	0.7832	0.7806	0.7770	0.7725	0.7672	0.7613	0.7549	0.7482

ELLIPTIC INTEGRALS OF THE SECOND KIND: $E(k, \phi)$ (Continued)

$$E(k, \phi) = \int_0^\phi \sqrt{(1 - k^2 \sin^2 \Phi)}d\Phi, \quad \theta = \sin^{-1} k$$

θ / ϕ	50°	55°	60°	65°	70°	75°	80°	85°	90°
1°	0.0175	0.0175	0.0175	0.0175	0.0175	0.0175	0.0175	0.0175	0.0175
2°	0.0349	0.0349	0.0349	0.0349	0.0349	0.0349	0.0349	0.0349	0.0349
3°	0.0523	0.0523	0.0523	0.0523	0.0523	0.0523	0.0523	0.0523	0.0523
4°	0.0698	0.0698	0.0698	0.0698	0.0698	0.0698	0.0698	0.0698	0.0698
5°	0.0872	0.0872	0.0872	0.0872	0.0872	0.0872	0.0872	0.0872	0.0872
6°	0.1046	0.1046	0.1046	0.1046	0.1046	0.1045	0.1045	0.1045	0.1045
7°	0.1220	0.1220	0.1219	0.1219	0.1219	0.1219	0.1219	0.1219	0.1219
8°	0.1394	0.1393	0.1393	0.1393	0.1392	0.1392	0.1392	0.1392	0.1392
9°	0.1567	0.1566	0.1566	0.1566	0.1565	0.1565	0.1565	0.1564	0.1564
10°	0.1740	0.1739	0.1739	0.1738	0.1738	0.1737	0.1737	0.1737	0.1736
11°	0.1913	0.1912	0.1911	0.1910	0.1909	0.1909	0.1908	0.1908	0.1908
12°	0.2085	0.2084	0.2083	0.2082	0.2081	0.2080	0.2080	0.2079	0.2079
13°	0.2258	0.2256	0.2254	0.2253	0.2252	0.2251	0.2250	0.2250	0.2250
14°	0.2429	0.2427	0.2425	0.2424	0.2422	0.2421	0.2420	0.2419	0.2419
15°	0.2601	0.2598	0.2596	0.2594	0.2592	0.2590	0.2589	0.2588	0.2588
16°	0.2771	0.2768	0.2765	0.2763	0.2761	0.2759	0.2757	0.2757	0.2756
17°	0.2942	0.2938	0.2935	0.2932	0.2929	0.2927	0.2925	0.2924	0.2924
18°	0.3112	0.3107	0.3103	0.3099	0.3096	0.3094	0.3092	0.3091	0.3090
19°	0.3281	0.3276	0.3271	0.3267	0.3263	0.3260	0.3258	0.3256	0.3256
20°	0.3450	0.3444	0.3438	0.3433	0.3429	0.3425	0.3422	0.3421	0.3420
21°	0.3618	0.3611	0.3604	0.3598	0.3593	0.3589	0.3586	0.3584	0.3584
22°	0.3785	0.3777	0.3770	0.3763	0.3757	0.3752	0.3749	0.3747	0.3746
23°	0.3952	0.3943	0.3935	0.3927	0.3920	0.3915	0.3911	0.3908	0.3907
24°	0.4118	0.4108	0.4098	0.4090	0.4082	0.4076	0.4071	0.4068	0.4067
25°	0.4284	0.4272	0.4261	0.4251	0.4243	0.4236	0.4230	0.4227	0.4226
26°	0.4449	0.4436	0.4423	0.4412	0.4402	0.4394	0.4389	0.4385	0.4384
27°	0.4613	0.4598	0.4584	0.4572	0.4561	0.4552	0.4545	0.4541	0.4540
28°	0.4776	0.4760	0.4744	0.4730	0.4718	0.4708	0.4701	0.4696	0.4695
29°	0.4938	0.4920	0.4903	0.4887	0.4874	0.4863	0.4855	0.4850	0.4848
30°	0.5100	0.5080	0.5061	0.5044	0.5029	0.5016	0.5007	0.5002	0.5000
31°	0.5261	0.5239	0.5218	0.5199	0.5182	0.5169	0.5159	0.5152	0.5150
32°	0.5421	0.5396	0.5373	0.5352	0.5334	0.5319	0.5308	0.5301	0.5299
33°	0.5580	0.5553	0.5528	0.5505	0.5485	0.5468	0.5456	0.5449	0.5446
34°	0.5738	0.5709	0.5681	0.5656	0.5634	0.5616	0.5603	0.5595	0.5592
35°	0.5895	0.5863	0.5833	0.5806	0.5782	0.5762	0.5748	0.5739	0.5736
36°	0.6051	0.6017	0.5984	0.5954	0.5928	0.5907	0.5891	0.5881	0.5878
37°	0.6207	0.6169	0.6134	0.6101	0.6073	0.6050	0.6032	0.6022	0.6018
38°	0.6361	0.6321	0.6282	0.6247	0.6216	0.6191	0.6172	0.6160	0.6157
39°	0.6515	0.6471	0.6429	0.6391	0.6357	0.6330	0.6310	0.6297	0.6293
40°	0.6667	0.6620	0.6575	0.6533	0.6497	0.6468	0.6446	0.6432	0.6428
41°	0.6818	0.6767	0.6719	0.6674	0.6636	0.6604	0.6580	0.6566	0.6561
42°	0.6969	0.6914	0.6862	0.6814	0.6772	0.6738	0.6712	0.6697	0.6691
43°	0.7118	0.7059	0.7003	0.6952	0.6907	0.6870	0.6843	0.6826	0.6820
44°	0.7266	0.7204	0.7144	0.7088	0.7040	0.7000	0.6971	0.6953	0.6947
45°	0.7414	0.7346	0.7282	0.7223	0.7171	0.7129	0.7097	0.7078	0.7071

ELLIPTIC INTEGRALS OF THE SECOND KIND: $E(k, \phi)$ (Continued)

$$E(k, \phi) = \int_0^\phi \sqrt{(1 - k^2 \sin^2 \Phi)}\,d\Phi, \quad \theta = \sin^{-1} k$$

$\phi \backslash \theta$	5°	10°	15°	20°	25°	30°	35°	40°	45°
46°	0.8023	0.8006	0.7977	0.7939	0.7891	0.7835	0.7772	0.7704	0.7633
47°	0.8197	0.8179	0.8149	0.8108	0.8057	0.7998	0.7931	0.7858	0.7782
48°	0.8371	0.8352	0.8320	0.8277	0.8223	0.8160	0.8089	0.8012	0.7931
49°	0.8545	0.8525	0.8491	0.8446	0.8389	0.8322	0.8247	0.8165	0.8079
50°	0.8719	0.8698	0.8663	0.8614	0.8554	0.8483	0.8404	0.8317	0.8227
51°	0.8894	0.8871	0.8834	0.8783	0.8719	0.8644	0.8560	0.8469	0.8373
52°	0.9068	0.9044	0.9004	0.8951	0.8884	0.8805	0.8716	0.8620	0.8518
53°	0.9242	0.9217	0.9175	0.9119	0.9048	0.8965	0.8872	0.8770	0.8663
54°	0.9416	0.9389	0.9345	0.9287	0.9212	0.9125	0.9026	0.8919	0.8806
55°	0.9590	0.9562	0.9517	0.9454	0.9376	0.9284	0.9181	0.9068	0.8949
56°	0.9764	0.9735	0.9687	0.9622	0.9540	0.9443	0.9335	0.9216	0.9091
57°	0.9938	0.9908	0.9858	0.9789	0.9703	0.9602	0.9488	0.9363	0.9232
58°	1.0112	1.0080	1.0028	0.9956	0.9866	0.9760	0.9641	0.9510	0.9372
59°	1.0286	1.0253	1.0198	1.0123	1.0029	1.9918	0.9793	0.9656	0.9511
60°	1.0460	1.0426	1.0368	1.0290	1.0191	1.0076	0.9945	0.9801	0.9650
61°	1.0634	1.0598	1.0538	1.0456	1.0354	1.0233	1.0096	0.9946	0.9787
62°	1.0808	1.0771	1.0708	1.0623	1.0516	1.0389	1.0246	1 0090	0.9924
63°	1.0982	1.0943	1.0878	1.0789	1.0678	1.0546	1.0397	1.0233	1.0060
64°	1.1156	1.1115	1.1048	1.0955	1.0839	1.0702	1.0547	1.0376	1.0195
65°	1.1330	1.1288	1.1218	1.1121	1.1001	1.0858	1.0696	1.0518	1.0329
66°	1.1504	1.1460	1.1387	1.1287	1.1162	1.1013	1.0845	1.0660	1.0463
67°	1.1678	1.1632	1.1557	1.1453	1.1323	1.1168	1.0993	1.0801	1.0596
68°	1.1852	1.1805	1.1726	1.1618	1.1483	1.1323	1.1141	1.0941	1.0728
69°	1.2026	1.1977	1.1896	1.1784	1.1644	1.1478	1.1289	1.1081	1.0859
70°	1.2200	1.2149	1.2065	1.1949	1.1804	1.1632	1.1436	1.1221	1.0990
71°	1.2374	1.2321	1.2234	1.2114	1.1964	1.1786	1.1583	1.1359	1.1120
72°	1.2548	1.2493	1.2403	1.2280	1.2124	1.1939	1.1729	1.1498	1.1250
73°	1.2722	1.2666	1.2573	1.2445	1.2284	1.2093	1.1875	1.1636	1.1379
74°	1.2896	1.2838	1.2742	1.2609	1.2443	1.2246	1.2021	1.1773	1.1507
75°	1.3070	1.3010	1.2911	1.2774	1.2603	1.2399	1.2167	1.1910	1.1635
76°	1.3244	1.3182	1.3080	1.2939	1.2762	1.2552	1.2312	1.2047	1.1762
77°	1.3418	1.3354	1.3249	1.3104	1.2921	1.2704	1.2457	1.2183	1.1889
78°	1.3592	1.3526	1.3417	1.3268	1.3080	1.2856	1.2601	1.2319	1.2015
79°	1.3765	1.3698	1.3586	1.3432	1.3239	1.3009	1.2746	1.2454	1.2141
80°	1.3939	1.3870	1.3755	1.3597	1.3398	1.3161	1.2890	1.2590	1.2266
81°	1.4113	1.4042	1.3924	1.3761	1.3556	1.3312	1.3034	1.2725	1.2391
82°	1.4287	1.4214	1.4093	1.3925	1.3715	1.3464	1.3177	1.2859	1.2516
83°	1.4461	1.4386	1.4261	1.4090	1.3873	1.3616	1.3321	1.2994	1.2640
84°	1.4635	1.4558	1.4430	1.4254	1.4032	1.3767	1.3464	1.3128	1.2765
85°	1.4809	1.4729	1.4598	1.4418	1.4190	1.3919	1.3608	1.3262	1.2889
86°	1.4983	1.4901	1.4767	1.4582	1.4348	1.4070	1.3751	1.3396	1.3012
87°	1.5156	1.5073	1.4936	1.4746	1.4507	1.4221	1.3894	1.3530	1.3136
88°	1.5330	1.5245	1.5104	1.4910	1.4665	1.4372	1.4037	1.3664	1.3260
89°	1.5504	1.5417	1.5273	1.5074	1.4823	1.4523	1.4180	1.3798	1.3383
90°	1.5678	1.5589	1.5442	1.5238	1.4981	1.4675	1.4323	1.3931	1.3506

ELLIPTIC INTEGRALS OF THE SECOND KIND: $E(k, \phi)$ (Continued)

$$E(k, \phi) = \int_0^\phi \sqrt{(1 - k^2 \sin^2 \Phi)}\,d\Phi, \quad \theta = \sin^{-1} k$$

θ / ϕ	50°	55°	60°	65°	70°	75°	80°	85°	90°
46°	0.7560	0.7488	0.7419	0.7356	0.7301	0.7255	0.7221	0.7200	0.7193
47°	0.7705	0.7628	0.7555	0.7488	0.7429	0.7380	0.7344	0.7321	0.7314
48°	0.7849	0.7768	0.7690	0.7618	0.7555	0.7502	0.7464	0.7440	0.7431
49°	0.7992	0.7905	0.7822	0.7746	0.7679	0.7623	0.7581	0.7556	0.7547
50°	0.8134	0.8042	0.7954	0.7872	0.7801	0.7741	0.7697	0.7670	0.7660
51°	0.8275	0.8177	0.8084	0.7997	0.7921	0.7858	0.7811	0.7781	0.7771
52°	0.8414	0.8311	0.8212	0.8120	0.8039	0.7972	0.7922	0.7891	0.7880
53°	0.8553	0.8444	0.8339	0.8241	0.8155	0.8084	0.8031	0.7998	0.7986
54°	0.8690	0.8575	0.8464	0.8361	0.8270	0.8194	0.8137	0.8102	0.8090
55°	0.8827	0.8705	0.8588	0.8479	0.8382	0.8302	0.8242	0.8204	0.8192
56°	0.8962	0.8834	0.8710	0.8595	0.8493	0.8408	0.8344	0.8304	0.8290
57°	0.9096	0.8961	0.8831	0.8709	0.8601	0.8511	0.8443	0.8401	0.8387
58°	0.9230	0.9088	0.8950	0.8822	0.8707	0.8612	0.8540	0.8496	0.8480
59°	0.9362	0.9213	0.9068	0.8932	0.8812	0.8711	0.8635	0.8588	0.8572
60°	0.9493	0.9336	0.9184	0.9042	0.8914	0.8808	0.8728	0.8677	0.8660
61°	0.9623	0.9459	0.9299	0.9149	0.9015	0.8903	0.8817	0.8764	0.8746
62°	0.9752	0.9580	0.9412	0.9254	0.9113	0.8995	0.8905	0.8849	0.8829
63°	0.9880	0.9700	0.9524	0.9358	0.9210	0.9085	0.8990	0.8930	0.8910
64°	1.0007	0.9818	0.9634	0.9460	0.9304	0.9173	0.9072	0.9009	0.8988
65°	1.0133	0.9936	0.9743	0.9561	0.9397	0.9258	0.9152	0.9086	0.9063
66°	1.0258	1.0052	0.9850	0.9659	0.9487	0.9341	0.9230	0.9159	0.9135
67°	1.0383	1.0167	0.9956	0.9756	0.9576	0.9422	0.9305	0.9230	0.9205
68°	1.0506	1.0281	1.0061	0.9852	0.9662	0.9501	0.9377	0.9299	0.9272
69°	1.0628	1.0394	1.0164	0.9946	0.9747	0.9578	0.9447	0.9364	0.9336
70°	1.0750	1.0506	1.0266	1.0038	0.9830	0.9652	0.9514	0.9427	0.9397
71°	1.0871	1.0617	1.0367	1.0129	0.9911	0.9724	0.9579	0.9487	0.9455
72°	1,0991	1.0727	1.0467	1.0218	0.9990	0.9794	0.9642	0.9544	0.9511
73°	1.1110	1.0836	1.0565	1.0306	1.0067	0.9862	0.9702	0.9599	0.9563
74°	1.1228	1.0944	1.0662	1.0392	1.0143	0.9928	0.9759	0.9650	0.9613
75°	1.1346	1.1051	1.0759	1.0477	1.0217	0.9992	0.9814	0.9699	0.9659
76°	1.1463	1.1158	1.0854	1.0561	1.0290	1.0053	0.9867	0.9745	0.9703
77°	1.1580	1.1263	1.0948	1.0643	1.0361	1.0113	0.9917	0.9789	0.9744
78°	1.1695	1.1368	1.1041	1.0724	1.0430	1.0171	0.9965	0.9829	0.9781
79°	1.1811	1.1472	1.1133	1.0805	1.0498	1.0228	1.0011	0.9867	0.9816
80°	1.1926	1.1576	1.1225	1.0884	1.0565	1.0282	1.0054	0.9902	0.9848
81°	1.2040	1.1678	1.1316	1.0962	1.0630	1.0335	1.0096	0.9935	0.9877
82°	1.2154	1.1781	1.1406	1.1040	1.0695	1.0387	1.0135	0.9965	0.9903
83°	1.2267	1.1883	1.1495	1.1116	1.0758	1.0437	1.0173	0.9992	0.9925
84°	1.2381	1.1984	1.1584	1.1192	1.0821	1.0486	1.0209	1.0017	0.9945
85°	1.2493	1.2085	1.1673	1.1267	1.0882	1.0534	1.0244	1.0039	0.9962
86°	1.2606	1.2186	1.1761	1.1342	1.0944	1.0581	1.0277	1.0060	0.9976
87°	1.2719	1.2286	1.1848	1.1417	1.1004	1.0628	1.0309	1.0078	0.9986
88°	1.2831	1.2386	1.1936	1.1491	1.1064	1.0673	1.0340	1.0095	0.9994
89°	1.2943	1.2487	1.2023	1.1565	1.1124	1.0719	1.0371	1.0111	0.9998
90°	1.3055	1.2587	1.2111	1.1638	1.1184	1.0764	1.0401	1.0127	1.0000

COMPLETE ELLIPTIC INTEGRALS

$$K = \int_0^{\pi/2} \frac{d\Phi}{\sqrt{1 - k^2 \sin^2 \Phi}} = F\left(k, \frac{\pi}{2}\right)$$

$\sin^{-1} k$	K	$\log K$	$\sin^{-1} k$	K	$\log K$
0°	1.5708	0.196120	**40°**	1.7868	0.252068
1	1.5709	0.196153	41	1.7992	0.255085
2	1.5713	0.196252	42	1.8122	0.258197
3	1.5719	0.196418	43	1.8256	0.261406
4	1.5727	0.196649	44	1.8396	0.264716
5	1.5738	0.196947	**45**	1.8541	0.268127
6	1.5751	0.197312	46	1.8691	0.271644
7	1.5767	0.197743	47	1.8848	0.275267
8	1.5785	0.198241	48	1.9011	0.279001
9	1.5805	0.198806	49	1.9180	0.282848
10	1.5828	0.199438	**50**	1.9356	0.286811
11	1.5854	0.200137	51	1.9539	0.290895
12	1.5882	0.200904	52	1.9729	0.295101
13	1.5913	0.201740	53	1.9927	0.299435
14	1.5946	0.202643	54	2.0133	0.303901
15	1.5981	0.203615	**55**	2.0347	0.308504
16	1.6020	0.204657	56	2.0571	0.313247
17	1.6061	0.205768	57	2.0804	0.318138
18	1.6105	0.206948	58	2.1047	0.323182
19	1.6151	0.208200	59	2.1300	0.328384
20	1.6200	0.209522	**60**	2.1565	0.333753
21	1.6252	0.210916	61	2.1842	0.339295
22	1.6307	0.212382	62	2.2132	0.345020
23	1.6365	0.213921	63	2.2435	0.350936
24	1.6426	0.215533	64	2.2754	0.357053
25	1.6490	0.217219	**65**	2.3088	0.363384
26	1.6557	0.218981	66	2.3439	0.369940
27	1.6627	0.220818	67	2.3809	0.376736
28	1.6701	0.222732	68	2.4198	0.383787
29	1.6777	0.224723	69	2.4610	0.391112
30	1.6858	0.226793	**70**	2.5046	0.398730
31	1.6941	0.228943	71	2.5507	0.406665
32	1.7028	0.231173	72	2.5998	0.414943
33	1.7119	0.233485	73	2.6521	0.423596
34	1.7214	0.235880	74	2.7081	0.432660
35	1.7312	0.238359	**75**	2.7681	0.442176
36	1.7415	0.240923	76	2.8327	0.452196
37	1.7522	0.243575	77	2.9026	0.462782
38	1.7633	0.246315	78	2.9786	0.474008
39	1.7748	0.249146	79	3.0617	0.485967
40	1.7868	0.252068	**80**	3.1534	0.498777

COMPLETE ELLIPTIC INTEGRALS (Continued)

$$K = \int_0^{\pi/2} \frac{d\Phi}{\sqrt{1 - k^2 \sin^2 \Phi}} = F\left(k, \frac{\pi}{2}\right)$$

$\sin^{-1} k$	K	$\log K$	$\sin^{-1} k$	K	$\log K$
80°	3.1534	0.498777	**85°**	3.8317	0.583396
81	3.2553	0.512591	86	4.0528	0.607751
82	3.3699	0.527613	87	4.3387	0.637355
83	3.5004	0.544120	88	4.7427	0.676027
84	3.6519	0.562514	89	5.4349	0.735192
85	3.8317	0.583396	**90**	∞	∞

Values of K for $\sin^{-1} k = 85°$ to $89°$ by $0.1°$ and $89°$ to $90°$ by minutes

$\sin^{-1} k$	K	$\log K$	$\sin^{-1} k$		K	$\log K$
85.0°	3.832	0.58343	**89°**	**0′**	5.435	0.73520
85.1	3.852	0.58569	89	2	5.469	0.73791
85.2	3.872	0.58794	89	4	5.504	0.74068
85.3	3.893	0.59028	89	6	5.540	0.74351
85.4	3.914	0.59262	89	8	5.578	0.74648
85.5	3.936	0.59506	**89**	**10**	5.617	0.74950
85.6	3.958	0.59748	89	12	5.658	0.75266
85.7	3.981	0.59999	89	14	5.700	0.75587
85.8	4.004	0.60249	89	16	5.745	0.75929
85.9	4.028	0.60509	89	18	5.791	0.76275
86.0	4.053	0.60778	**89**	**20**	5.840	0.76641
86.1	4.078	0.61045	89	22	5.891	0.77019
86.2	4.104	0.61321	89	24	5.946	0.77422
86.3	4.130	0.61595	89	26	6.003	0.77837
86.4	4.157	0.61878	89	28	6.063	0.78269
86.5	4.185	0.62170	**89**	**30**	6.128	0.78732
86.6	4.214	0.62469	89	32	6.197	0.79218
86.7	4.244	0.62778	89	34	6.271	0.79734
86.8	4.274	0.63083	89	36	6.351	0.80284
86.9	4.306	0.63407	89	38	6.438	0.80875
87.0	4.339	0.63739	**89**	**40**	6.533	0.81511
87.1	4.372	0.64068	89	41	6.584	0.81849
87.2	4.407	0.64414	89	42	6.639	0.82210
87.3	4.444	0.64777	89	43	6.696	0.82582
87.4	4.481	0.65137	89	44	6.756	0.82969
87.5	4.520	0.65514	**89**	**45**	6.821	0.83385
87.6	4.561	0.65916	89	46	6.890	0.83822
87.7	4.603	0.66304	89	47	6.964	0.84286
87.8	4.648	0.66727	89	48	7.044	0.84782
87.9	4.694	0.67154	89	49	7.131	0.85315
88.0	4.743	0.67605	**89**	**50**	7.226	0.85890
88.1	4.794	0.68070	89	51	7.332	0.86522
88.2	4.848	0.68556	89	52	7.449	0.87210
88.3	4.905	0.69064	89	53	7.583	0.87984
88.4	4.965	0.69592	89	54	7.737	0.88857
88.5	5.030	0.70157	**89**	**55**	7.919	0.89867
88.6	5.099	0.70749	89	56	8.143	0.91078
88.7	5.173	0.71374	89	57	8.430	0.92583
88.8	5.253	0.72041	89	58	8.836	0.94626
88.9	5.340	0.72754	89	59	9.529	0.97905
89.0	5.435	0.73520	**90**	**0**	∞	∞

COMPLETE ELLIPTIC INTEGRALS (Continued)

$$E = \int_0^{\pi/2} \sqrt{1 - k^2 \sin^2 \Phi} \cdot d\Phi = E\left(k, \frac{\pi}{2}\right)$$

$\sin^{-1} k$	E	$\log E$	$\sin^{-1} k$	E	$\log E$
0°	1.5708	0.196120	45°	1.3506	0.130541
1	1.5707	0.196087	46	1.3418	0.127690
2	1.5703	0.195988	47	1.3329	0.124788
3	1.5697	0.195822	48	1.3238	0.121836
4	1.5689	0.195591	49	1.3147	0.118836
5	1.5678	0.195293	50	1.3055	0.115790
6	1.5665	0.194930	51	1.2963	0.112698
7	1.5649	0.194500	52	1.2870	0.109563
8	1.5632	0.194004	53	1.2776	0.106386
9	1.5611	0.193442	54	1.2681	0.103169
10	1.5589	0.192815	55	1.2587	0.099915
11	1.5564	0.192121	56	1.2492	0.096626
12	1.5537	0.191362	57	1.2397	0.093303
13	1.5507	0.190537	58	1.2301	0.089950
14	1.5476	0.189646	59	1.2206	0.086569
15	1.5442	0.188690	60	1.2111	0.083164
16	1.5405	0.187668	61	1.2015	0.079738
17	1.5367	0.186581	62	1.1920	0.076293
18	1.5326	0.185428	63	1.1826	0.072834
19	1.5283	0.184210	64	1.1732	0.069364
20	1.5238	0.182928	65	1.1638	0.065889
21	1.5191	0.181580	66	1.1545	0.062412
22	1.5141	0.180168	67	1.1453	0.058937
23	1.5090	0.178691	68	1.1362	0.055472
24	1.5037	0.177150	69	1.1272	0.052020
25	1.4981	0.175545	70	1.1184	0.048589
26	1.4924	0.173876	71	1.1096	0.045183
27	1.4864	0.172144	72	1.1011	0.041812
28	1.4803	0.170348	73	1.0927	0.038481
29	1.4740	0.168489	74	1.0844	0.035200
30	1.4675	0.166567	75	1.0764	0.031976
31	1.4608	0.164583	76	1.0686	0.028819
32	1.4539	0.162537	77	1.0611	0.025740
33	1.4469	0.160429	78	1.0538	0.022749
34	1.4397	0.158261	79	1.0468	0.019858
35	1.4323	0.156031	80	1.0401	0.017081
36	1.4248	0.153742	81	1.0338	0.014432
37	1.4171	0.151393	82	1.0278	0.011927
38	1.4092	0.148985	83	1.0223	0.009584
39	1.4013	0.146519	84	1.0172	0.007422
40°	1.3931	0.143995	85	1.0127	0.005465
41	1.3849	0.141414	86	1.0086	0.003740
42	1.3765	0.138778	87	1.0053	0.002278
43	1.3680	0.136086	88	1.0026	0.001121
44	1.3594	0.133340	89	1.0008	0.000326
45	1.3506	0.130541	90	1.0000	0.000000

SINE, COSINE, AND EXPONENTIAL INTEGRALS

$$Si(x) = \int_0^x \frac{\sin v}{v}\,dv; \qquad Ci(x) = \int_\infty^x \frac{\cos v}{v}\,dv;$$

$$Ei(x) = \int_{-\infty}^x \frac{e^v}{v}\,dv; \qquad E_1(x) = -Ei(-x) = \int_x^\infty \frac{e^{-v}}{v}\,dv$$

Interpolation can be by iterative linear interpolation or by means of Everett's Formula using throwback to second differences. With this in view the modified second differences have been tabulated where relevant.

Everett's Formula.

$$f_p = (1 - p)f_0 + pf_1 + E_2\delta_{m0}^2 + F_2\delta_{m1}^2$$

SINE, COSINE, AND EXPONENTIAL INTEGRALS

x	$Si(x)$	δ_m^2	$Ci(x)$	δ_m^2	$Ei(x)$	δ_m^2	$E_1(x) = -Ei(-x)$	δ_m^2
.00	.00000		$-\infty$		$-\infty$		$+\infty$	
.01	.01000	0	−4.02798		−4.01790		4.03790	
.02	.02000	0	−3.33482		−3.31476		3.35476	
.03	.03000	0	−2.92957		−2.89912		2.95912	
.04	.04000	−2	−2.64206		−2.60126		2.68126	
.05	.04999	2	−2.41914		−2.36788		2.46790	
.06	.05999	−2	−2.23709		−2.17528		2.29531	
.07	.06998	0	−2.08327		−2.01080		2.15084	
.08	.07997	0	−1.95011		−1.86688		2.02694	
.09	.08996	−2	−1.83275		−1.73866		1.91874	
.10	.09994	2	−1.72787	−997	−1.62281	−989	1.82292	990
.11	.10993	−3	−1.63308	−829	−1.51696	−816	1.73711	816
.12	.11990	2	−1.54665	−695	−1.41935	−687	1.65954	688
.13	.12988	−1	−1.46723	−594	−1.32866	−582	1.58890	585
.14	.13985	−1	−1.39379	−514	−1.24384	−505	1.52415	503
.15	.14981	0	−1.32552	−449	−1.16409	−436	1.46446	441
.16	.15977	0	−1.26176	−394	−1.08873	−384	1.40919	384
.17	.16973	−1	−1.20196	−349	−1.01723	−341	1.35778	342
.18	.17968	−1	−1.14567	−314	−.94915	−302	1.30980	303
.19	.18962	0	−1.09253	−281	−.88410	−270	1.26486	272
.20	.19956	−1	−1.04221	−254	−.82176	−244	1.22265	245
.21	.20949	−1	−.99444	−231	−.76187	−222	1.18290	223
.22	.21941	1	−.94899	−212	−.70420	−199	1.14538	201
.23	.22933	−3	−.90566	−194	−.64853	−184	1.10988	186
.24	.23923	0	−.86427	−177	−.59470	−166	1.07624	167
.25	.24913	0	−.82466	−166	−.54254	−155	1.04428	158
.26	.25903	−3	−.78671	−153	−.49193	−142	1.01389	142
.27	.26891	−1	−.75029	−142	−.44274	−131	.98493	134
.28	.27878	1	−.71529	−132	−.39486	−122	.95731	122
.29	.28865	−3	−.68161	−124	−.34820	−113	.93092	115
.30	.29850	1	−.64917	−117	−.30267	−105	.90568	107
.31	.30835	−1	−.61790	−107	−.25819	−96	.88151	100
.32	.31819	−2	−.58771	−103	−.21468	−94	.85834	92
.33	.32801	−1	−.55855	−97	−.17210	−83	.83610	90
.34	.33782	1	−.53036	−91	−.13036	−81	.81475	82
.35	.34763	−3	−.50308	−86	−.08943	−76	.79422	77
.36	.35742	−1	−.47666	−84	−.04926	−69	.77446	74
.37	.36720	−3	−.45107	−76	−.00979	−67	.75544	69
.38	.37696	1	−.42625	−76	.02901	−63	.73711	66
.39	.38672	−3	−.40218	−70	.06718	−57	.71944	60
.40	.39646	−1	−.37881	−67	.10477	−58	.70238	59
.41	.40619	−1	−.35611	−65	.14179	−53	.68591	56
.42	.41591	−2	−.33406	−60	.17828	−50	.67000	51
.43	.42561	−2	−.31262	−61	.21427	−47	.65461	51
.44	.43529	1	−.29178	−54	.24979	−45	.63973	48
.45	.44497	−2	−.27149	−56	.28486	−43	.62533	46
.46	.45463	−2	−.25175	−52	.31950	−40	.61139	43
.47	.46427	−1	−.23253	−48	.35374	−39	.59788	41
.48	.47390	−2	−.21380	−50	.38759	−36	.58478	42
.49	.48351	−1	.19556	−46	.42108	−35	.57209	36
.50	.49311	−2	−.17778	−45	.45422	−33	.55977	37

SINE, COSINE, AND EXPONENTIAL INTEGRALS (Continued)

x	$Si(x)$	δ_m^2	$Ci(x)$	δ_m^2	$Ei(x)$	δ_m^2	$E_1(x) = -Ei(-x)$	δ_m^2
.50	.49311	−2	−.17778	−45	.45422	−33	.55977	37
.51	.50269	−2	−.16045	−43	.48703	−31	.54782	35
.52	.51225	−1	−.14355	−42	.51953	−30	.53622	33
.53	.52180	−2	−.12707	−40	.55173	−28	.52495	32
.54	.53133	−2	−.11099	−39	.58365	−29	.51400	31
.55	.54084	−2	−.09530	−38	.61529	−24	.50336	30
.56	.55033	−1	−.07999	−36	.64668	−25	.49302	28
.57	.55981	−2	−.06504	−35	.67782	−23	.48296	27
.58	.56927	−2	−.05044	−35	.70873	−23	.47317	27
.59	.57871	−2	−.03619	−33	.73941	−21	.46365	25
.60	.58813	−2	−.02227	−34	.76988	−20	.45438	24
.61	.59753	−2	−.00868	−29	.80015	−19	.44535	24
.62	.60691	−2	.00461	−33	.83023	−19	.43656	23
.63	.61627	−2	.01758	−28	.86012	−17	.42800	20
.64	.62561	0	.03026	−29	.88984	−17	.41965	23
.65	.63494	−3	.04265	−28	.91939	−16	.41152	20
.66	.64424	−3	.05476	−28	.94878	−15	.40359	19
.67	.65351	0	.06659	−25	.97802	−14	.39585	21
.68	.66277	−2	.07816	−28	1.00712	−14	.38831	18
.69	.67201	−3	.08946	−25	1.03608	−13	.38095	18
.70	.68122	−2	.10051	−24	1.06491	−13	.37377	17
.71	.69041	−2	.11132	−25	1.09361	−11	.36676	17
.72	.69958	−2	.12188	−24	1.12220	−11	.35992	16
.73	.70873	−3	.13220	−21	1.15068	−10	.35324	15
.74	.71785	−2	.14230	−25	1.17906	−12	.34671	16
.75	.72695	−2	.15216	−20	1.20733	−9	.34034	15
.76	.73603	−3	.16181	−22	1.23551	−9	.33412	12
.77	.74508	−2	.17124	−21	1.26360	−8	.32803	16
.78	.75411	−2	.18046	−21	1.29161	−8	.32209	13
.79	.76312	−3	.18947	−20	1.31954	−7	.31628	13
.80	.77210	−3	.19828	−20	1.34740	−9	.31060	12
.81	.78105	−2	.20689	−20	1.37518	−6	.30504	13
.82	.78998	−3	.21530	−17	1.40290	−6	.29961	12
.83	.79888	−2	.22353	−19	1.43056	−6	.29430	11
.84	.80776	−3	.23157	−19	1.45816	−5	.28910	12
.85	.81661	−2	.23942	−16	1.48571	−3	.28402	11
.86	.82544	−3	.24710	−18	1.51322	−7	.27905	10
.87	.83424	−3	.25460	−18	1.54067	−2	.27418	10
.88	.84301	−3	.26192	−15	1.56809	−4	.26941	12
.89	.85175	−2	.26908	−17	1.59547	−4	.26475	8
.90	.86047	−3	.27607	−17	1.62281	−1	.26018	10
.91	.86916	−3	.28289	−14	1.65013	−5	.25571	10
.92	.87782	−1	.28956	−18	1.67741	0	.25134	7
.93	.88646	−5	.29606	−13	1.70468	−4	.24705	9
.94	.89506	−1	.30242	−18	1.73192	0	.24285	9
.95	.90364	−3	.30861	−13	1.75915	−2	.23874	8
.96	.91219	−5	.31466	−15	1.78636	−1	.23471	8
.97	.92070	−1	.32056	−14	1.81356	−1	.23076	8
.98	.92919	−3	.32632	−15	1.84075	−1	.22689	8
.99	.93765	−3	.33193	−14	1.86793	2	.22310	7
1.00	.94608	−3	.33740	−13	1.89512	−2	.21938	8

SINE, COSINE, AND EXPONENTIAL INTEGRALS (Continued)

x	$Si(x)$	δ_m^2	$Ci(x)$	δ_m^2	$Ei(x)$	$E_1(x) = -Ei(-x)$
1.0	.94608	-301	.33740	-1376	1.89512	.21938
1.1	1.02869	-324	.38487	-1181	2.16738	.18599
1.2	1.10805	-345	.42046	-1025	2.44209	.15841
1.3	1.18396	-365	.44574	-897	2.72140	.13545
1.4	1.25623	-382	.46201	-789	3.00721	.11622
1.5	1.32468	-396	.47036	-695	3.30129	.10002
1.6	1.38918	-409	.47173	-612	3.60532	.08631
1.7	1.44959	-419	.46697	-538	3.92096	.07465
1.8	1.50582	-427	.45681	-470	4.24987	.06471
1.9	1.55778	-433	.44194	-408	4.59371	.05620
2.0	1.60541	-436	.42298	-350	4.95423	.04890
2.1	1.64870	-436	.40051	-296	5.33324	.04261
2.2	1.68762	-435	.37507	-246	5.73261	.03719
2.3	1.72221	-431	.34718	-198	6.15438	.03250
2.4	1.75249	-425	.31729	-153	6.60067	.02844
2.5	1.77852	-416	.28587	-111	7.07377	.02491
2.6	1.80039	-406	.25334	-71	7.57611	.02185
2.7	1.81821	-394	.22008	-34	8.11035	.01918
2.8	1.83210	-379	.18649	1	8.67930	.01686
2.9	1.84220	-363	.15290	33	9.28602	.01482
3.0	1.84865	-346	.11963	63	9.93383	.01305
3.1	1.85166	-327	.08699	91	10.6263	.01149
3.2	1.85140	-306	.05526	116	11.3673	.01013
3.3	1.84808	-285	.02468	139	12.1610	.00894
3.4	1.84191	-262	$-.00452$	159	13.0121	.00789
3.5	1.83313	-239	$-.03213$	177	13.9254	.00697
3.6	1.82195	-215	$-.05797$	192	14.9063	.00616
3.7	1.80862	-191	$-.08190$	205	15.9606	.00545
3.8	1.79339	-166	$-.10378$	216	17.0948	.00482
3.9	1.77650	-141	$-.12350$	224	18.3157	.00427
4.0	1.75820	-116	$-.14098$	230	19.6309	.00378
4.1	1.73874	-91	$-.15617$	234	21.0485	.00335
4.2	1.71837	-67	$-.16901$	236	22.5774	.00297
4.3	1.69732	-44	$-.17951$	235	24.2274	.00263
4.4	1.67583	-21	$-.18766$	232	26.0090	.00234
4.5	1.65414	2	$-.19349$	228	27.9337	.00207
4.6	1.63246	23	$-.19705$	221	30.0141	.00184
4.7	1.61101	43	$-.19839$	213	32.2639	.00164
4.8	1.58998	62	$-.19760$	204	34.6979	.00145
4.9	1.56956	79	$-.19478$	193	37.3325	.00129
5.0	1.54993	95	$-.19003$	181	40.1853	.00115
5.1	1.53125	110	$-.18348$	167	43.2757	.00102
5.2	1.51367	123	$-.17525$	153	46.6249	.00091
5.3	1.49732	134	$-.16551$	137	50.2557	.00081
5.4	1.48230	144	$-.15439$	121	54.1935	.00072
5.5	1.46872	152	$-.14205$	105	58.4655	.00064
5.6	1.45667	159	$-.12867$	88	63.1018	.00057
5.7	1.44620	164	$-.11441$	71	68.1350	.00051
5.8	1.43736	167	$-.09944$	54	73.6008	.00045
5.9	1.43018	168	$-.08393$	37	79.5382	.00040

SINE, COSINE, AND EXPONENTIAL INTEGRALS (Continued)

x	$Si(x)$	δ_m^2	$Ci(x)$	δ_m^2	$Ei(x)$	$E_1(x) = -Ei(-x)$
6.0	1.42469	168	−.06806	20	85.9898	.00036
6.1	1.42087	166	−.05198	3	93.0020	.00032
6.2	1.41871	163	−.03587	−13	100.626	.00029
6.3	1.41817	158	−.01989	−28	108.916	.00026
6.4	1.41922	152	−.00418	−43	117.935	.00023
6.5	1.42179	145	.01110	−56	127.747	.00020
6.6	1.42582	137	.02582	−69	138.426	.00018
6.7	1.43121	128	.03986	−81	150.050	.00016
6.8	1.43787	117	.05308	−92	162.707	.00014
6.9	1.44570	106	.06539	−101	176.491	.00013
7.0	1.45460	94	.07670	−109	191.505	.00012
7.1	1.46443	82	.08691	−116	207.863	.00010
7.2	1.47509	69	.09596	−122	225.688	.00009
7.3	1.48644	56	.10379	−127	245.116	.00008
7.4	1.49834	43	.11036	−130	266.296	.00007
7.5	1.51068	30	.11563	−131	289.388	.00007
7.6	1.52331	16	.11960	−132	314.572	.00006
7.7	1.53611	3	.12225	−131	342.040	.00005
7.8	1.54894	−10	.12359	−129	372.006	.00005
7.9	1.56167	−22	.12364	−126	404.701	.00004
8.0	1.57419	−34	.12.	−122	440.380	.00004
8.1	1.58637	−45	.12002	−116	479.322	.00003
8.2	1.59810	−55	.11644	−110	521.831	.00003
8.3	1.60928	−65	.11177	−103	568.242	.00003
8.4	1.61981	−74	.10607	−94	618.919	.00002
8.5	1.62960	−82	.09943	−86	674.264	.00002
8.6	1.63857	−89	.09194	−76	734.714	.00002
8.7	1.64665	−95	.08368	−66	800.749	.00002
8.8	1.65379	−100	.07476	−56	872.895	.00002
8.9	1.65993	−104	.06528	−45	951.728	.00001
9.0	1.66504	−106	.05535	−35	1037.88	.00001
9.1	1.66908	−108	.04507	−24	1132.04	.00001
9.2	1.67205	−109	.03455	−13	1234.96	.00001
9.3	1.67393	−108	.02391	−2	1347.48	.00001
9.4	1.67473	−107	.01325	9	1470.51	.00001
9.5	1.67446	−104	.00268	19	1605.03	.00001
9.6	1.67316	−101	−.00771	29	1752.14	.00001
9.7	1.67084	−96	−.01780	38	1913.05	.00001
9.8	1.66757	−91	−.02752	47	2089.05	.00001
9.9	1.66338	−85	−.03676	55	2281.58	.00000
10.0	1.65835	−78	−.04546	63	2492.23	.00000

SINE, COSINE, AND EXPONENTIAL INTEGRALS (Continued)

x	$Si(x)$	δ_m^2	$Ci(x)$	δ_m^2
10.0	1.65835	-2001	$-.04546$	1616
10.5	1.62294	-944	$-.07828$	2255
11.0	1.57831	229	$-.08956$	2323
11.5	1.53571	1252	$-.07857$	1849
12.0	1.50497	1898	$-.04978$	987
12.5	1.49234	2051	$-.01141$	-35
13.0	1.49936	1720	.02676	-968
13.5	1.52291	1007	.05576	-1610
14.0	1.55621	116	.06940	-1828
14.5	1.59072	-745	.06554	-1604
15.0	1.61819	-1371	.04628	-1019
15.5	1.63258	-1638	.01719	-231
16.0	1.63130	-1500	$-.01420$	559
16.5	1.61563	-1020	$-.04031$	1173
17.0	1.59014	-326	$-.05524$	1471
17.5	1.56146	407	$-.05610$	1406
18.0	1.53661	999	$-.04348$	1014
18.5	1.52128	1327	$-.02111$	400
19.0	1.51863	1320	.00515	-276
19.5	1.52863	1000	.02883	-849
20.0	1.54824	462	.04442	-1195
20.5	1.57232	-163	.04859	-1240
21.0	1.59489	-717	.04089	-985
21.5	1.61063	-1077	.02373	-511
22.0	1.61608	-1161	.00164	67
22.5	1.61041	-967	$-.01986$	599
23.0	1.59546	-550	$-.03566$	969
23.5	1.57521	-19	$-.04221$	1090
24.0	1.55474	493	$-.03833$	946
24.5	1.53896	870	$-.02538$	579
25.0	1.53148	1020	$-.00685$	96
25.5	1.53376	921	.01262	-399
26.0	1.54487	605	.02830	-776
26.5	1.56180	161	.03657	-954
27.0	1.58029	-314	.03572	-894
27.5	1.59581	-700	.02630	-626
28.0	1.60475	-781	.01087	-214
28.5	1.60581	-1062	$-.00664$	232
29.0	1.59731	-530	$-.02195$	610
29.5	1.58331	-275	$-.03144$	826
30.0	1.56676	160	$-.03303$	837
30.5	1.55172	534	$-.02660$	649
31.0	1.54177	765	$-.01395$	307
31.5	1.53914	808	.00166	-94
32.0	1.54424	653	.01639	-464
32.5	1.55560	345	.02670	-705
33.0	1.57028	-33	.03026	-777
33.5	1.58466	-397	.02639	-653
34.0	1.59526	-651	.01626	-377
34.5	1.59964	-742	.00250	-22

SINE, COSINE, AND EXPONENTIAL INTEGRALS (Continued)

x	$Si(x)$	δ_m^2	$Ci(x)$	δ_m^2
35.0	1.59692	−650	−.01148	335
35.5	1.58797	−408	−.02228	592
36.0	1.57511	−70	−.02741	709
36.5	1.56156	273	−.02576	646
37.0	1.55061	541	−.01792	429
37.5	1.54483	673	−.00596	117
38.0	1.54549	638	.00713	−216
38.5	1.55226	449	.01816	−490
39.0	1.56334	157	.02451	−638
39.5	1.57594	−164	.02476	−625
40.0	1.58698	−437	.01902	−467
40.5	1.59384	−603	.00881	−195
41.0	1.59494	−611	−.00328	114
41.5	1.59018	−479	−.01429	391
42.0	1.58083	−230	−.02157	563
42.5	1.56927	68	−.02346	599
43.0	1.55835	343	−.01962	486
43.5	1.55070	527	−.01112	262
44.0	1.54809	581	−.00011	−26
44.5	1.55104	494	.01067	−295
45.0	1.55872	286	.01863	−491
45.5	1.56915	18	.02190	−562
46.0	1.57976	−254	.01979	−496
46.5	1.58796	−451	.01293	−313
47.0	1.59184	−544	.00307	−52
47.5	1.59052	−496	−.00731	207
48.0	1.58445	−331	−.01571	416
48.5	1.57520	−93	−.02013	521
49.0	1.56506	168	−.01957	494
49.5	1.55652	381	−.01428	351
50.0	1.55162	495	−.00563	125
50.5	1.55146	491	.00422	−128
51.0	1.55600	365	.01285	−345
51.5	1.56404	154	.01819	−471
52.0	1.57356	−88	.01902	−484
52.5	1.58224	−310	.01522	−379
53.0	1.58797	−446	.00779	−182
53.5	1.58943	−477	−.00139	54
54.0	1.58633	−385	−.01006	272
54.5	1.57953	−210	−.01613	422
55.0	1.57072	21	−.01817	463
55.5	1.56210	236	−.01577	396
56.0	1.55574	393	−.00958	232
56.5	1.55314	454	−.00117	12
57.0	1.55488	401	.00737	−202
57.5	1.56046	251	.01398	−369
58.0	1.56845	44	.01707	−437
58.5	1.57687	−168	.01597	−403
59.0	1.58368	−340	.01101	−272
59.5	1.58724	−423	.00345	−72

SINE, COSINE, AND EXPONENTIAL INTEGRALS (Continued)

x	$Si(x)$	δ_m^2	$Ci(x)$	δ_m^2
60.0	1.58675	−404	−.00481	136
60.5	1.58239	−287	−.01177	311
61.0	1.57528	−99	−.01576	408
61.5	1.56721	103	−.01585	402
62.0	1.56013	284	−.01209	301
62.5	1.55576	389	−.00545	127
63.0	1.55511	401	.00241	−75
63.5	1.55829	311	.00956	−256
64.0	1.56445	151	.01427	−368
64.5	1.57206	−44	.01545	−395
65.0	1.57925	−227	.01285	−321
65.5	1.58427	−350	.00717	−173
66.0	1.58594	−388	−.00017	16
66.5	1.58390	−329	−.00736	199
67.0	1.57871	−193	−.01265	331
67.5	1.57167	−11	−.01478	378
68.0	1.56452	171	−.01329	335
68.5	1.55900	309	−.00859	211
69.0	1.55643	369	−.00187	37
69.5	1.55739	338	.00521	−144
70.0	1.56159	229	.01092	−285
70.5	1.56798	61	.01390	−359
71.0	1.57496	−116	.01345	−340
71.5	1.58083	−263	.00974	−242
72.0	1.58418	−346	.00371	−85
72.5	1.58422	−340	−.00314	90
73.0	1.58100	−253	−.00913	240
73.5	1.57535	−109	−.01282	332
74.0	1.56866	64	−.01334	339
74.5	1.56258	218	−.01061	267
75.0	1.55858	317	−.00533	127
75.5	1.55761	336	.00117	−39
76.0	1.55986	275	.00730	−193
76.5	1.56474	147	.01158	−302
77.0	1.57103	−15	.01298	−331
77.5	1.57718	−169	.01121	−283
78.0	1.58171	−287	.00673	−165
78.5	1.58351	−323	.00067	−9
79.0	1.58221	−290	−.00548	149
79.5	1.57814	−182	−.01021	265
80.0	1.57233	−31	−.01240	317
80.5	1.56622	126	−.01155	294
81.0	1.56131	246	−.00789	195
81.5	1.55876	309	−.00236	53
82.0	1.55917	296	.00368	−102
82.5	1.56241	209	.00875	−229
83.0	1.56765	73	.01163	−300
83.5	1.57359	−77	.01164	−296
84.0	1.57879	−212	.00882	−220
84.5	1.58197	−287	.00389	−93

SINE, COSINE, AND EXPONENTIAL INTEGRALS (Continued)

x	$Si(x)$	δ_m^2	$Ci(x)$	δ_m^2
85.0	1.58240	−296	−.00193	55
85.5	1.58000	−232	−.00722	192
86.0	1.57538	−110	−.01068	274
86.5	1.56970	36	−.01151	295
87.0	1.56436	169	−.00952	239
87.5	1.56064	264	−.00524	129
88.0	1.55944	291	.00027	−14
88.5	1.56102	246	.00565	−149
89.0	1.56496	144	.00960	−250
89.5	1.57028	5	.01116	−285
90.0	1.57566	−128	.00999	−254
90.5	1.57981	−236	.00639	−157
91.0	1.58171	−280	.00128	−26
91.5	1.58093	−255	−.00408	108
92.0	1.57770	−174	−.00840	220
92.5	1.57281	−44	−.01062	273
93.0	1.56749	90	−.01023	259
93.5	1.56303	203	−.00736	185
94.0	1.56051	264	−.00272	63
94.5	1.56052	263	.00253	−70
95.0	1.56304	192	.00711	−186
95.5	1.56741	83	.00991	−256
96.0	1.57257	−52	.01026	−261
96.5	1.57724	−170	.00811	−203
97.0	1.58029	−244	.00401	−98
97.5	1.58100	−262	−.00103	33
98.0	1.57921	−210	−.00576	150
98.5	1.57540	−114	−.00905	234
99.0	1.57050	13	−.01010	260
99.5	1.56572	135	−.00867	218
100.0	1.56223	222	−.00515	127

ORTHOGONAL POLYNOMIALS

I

Name: Legendre   *Symbol*: $P_n(x)$ *Interval*: $[-1, 1]$

Differential Equation: $(1 - x^2)y'' - 2xy' + n(n + 1)y = 0$
$$y = P_n(x)$$

Explicit Expression: $P_n(x) = \dfrac{1}{2^n} \displaystyle\sum_{m=0}^{[n/2]} (-1)^m \binom{n}{m}\binom{2n - 2m}{n} x^{n-2m}$

Recurrence Relation: $(n + 1)P_{n+1}(x) = (2n + 1)xP_n(x) - nP_{n-1}(x)$

Weight: 1   *Standardization*: $P_n(1) = 1$

Norm: $\displaystyle\int_{-1}^{+1} [P_n(x)]^2 dx = \dfrac{2}{2n + 1}$

Rodrigues' Formula: $P_n(x) = \dfrac{(-1)^n}{2^n n!} \dfrac{d^n}{dx^n} \{(1 - x^2)^n\}$

Generating Function: $R^{-1} = \displaystyle\sum_{n=0}^{\infty} P_n(x)z^n; \quad -1 < x < 1, \quad |z| < 1,$
$$R = \sqrt{1 - 2xz + z^2}.$$

Inequality: $|P_n(x)| \le 1, \quad -1 \le x \le 1.$

II

Name: Tschebysheff, First Kind   *Symbol*: $T_n(x)$ *Interval*: $[-1, 1]$

Differential Equation: $(1 - x^2)y'' - xy' + n^2 y = 0$
$$y = T_n(x)$$

Explicit Expression: $\dfrac{n}{2} \displaystyle\sum_{m=0}^{[n/2]} (-1)^m \dfrac{(n - m - 1)!}{m!(n - 2m)!} (2x)^{n-2m} = \cos(n \arccos x) = T_n(x)$

Recurrence Relation: $T_{n+1}(x) = 2xT_n(x) - T_{n-1}(x)$

Weight: $(1 - x^2)^{-1/2}$ *Standardization*: $T_n(1) = 1$

Norm: $\displaystyle\int_{-1}^{+1} (1 - x^2)^{-1/2}[T_n(x)]^2 dx = \begin{cases} \pi/2, & n \ne 0 \\ \pi, & n = 0 \end{cases}$

Rodrigues' Formula: $\dfrac{(-1)^n(1 - x^2)^{1/2}\sqrt{\pi}}{2^{n+1}\Gamma(n + \frac{1}{2})} \dfrac{d^n}{dx^n} \{(1 - x^2)^{n-(1/2)}\} = T_n(x)$

Generating Function: $\dfrac{1 - xz}{1 - 2xz + z^2} = \displaystyle\sum_{n=0}^{\infty} T_n(x)z^n, \quad -1 < x < 1, \quad |z| < 1.$

Inequality: $|T_n(x)| \le 1, \quad -1 \le x \le 1.$

III

Name: Tschebysheff, Second Kind   *Symbol*: $U_n(x)$ *Interval*: $[-1, 1]$

Differential Equation: $(1 - x^2)y'' - 3xy' + n(n + 2)y = 0$

$$y = U_n(x)$$

Explicit Expression: $U_n(x) = \sum_{m=0}^{[n/2]} (-1)^m \frac{(m - n)!}{m!(n - 2m)!} (2x)^{n-2m}$

$$U_n(\cos \theta) = \frac{\sin[(n + 1)\theta]}{\sin \theta}$$

Recurrence Relation: $U_{n+1}(x) = 2xU_n(x) - U_{n-1}(x)$

Weight: $(1 - x^2)^{1/2}$ *Standardization*: $U_n(1) = n + 1$

Norm: $\displaystyle\int_{-1}^{+1} (1 - x^2)^{1/2}[U_n(x)]^2 \, dx = \frac{\pi}{2}$

Rodrigues' Formula: $U_n(x) = \dfrac{(-1)^n(n + 1)\sqrt{\pi}}{(1 - x^2)^{1/2}2^{n+1}\Gamma(n + \frac{3}{2})} \dfrac{d^n}{dx^n} \{(1 - x^2)^{n+(1/2)}\}$

Generating Function: $\dfrac{1}{1 - 2xz + z^2} = \displaystyle\sum_{n=0}^{\infty} U_n(x)z^n, \; -1 < x < 1, \; |z| < 1.$

Inequality: $|U_n(x)| \le n + 1, \; -1 \le x \le 1.$

IV

Name: Jacobi   *Symbol*: $P_n^{(\alpha,\beta)}(x)$ *Interval*: $[-1, 1]$

Differential Equation:

$$(1 - x^2)y'' + [\beta - \alpha - (\alpha + \beta + 2)x]y' + n(n + \alpha + \beta + 1)y = 0$$
$$y = P_n^{(\alpha,\beta)}(x)$$

Explicit Expression: $P_n^{(\alpha,\beta)}(x) = \dfrac{1}{2^n} \displaystyle\sum_{m=0}^{n} \binom{n + \alpha}{m}\binom{n + \beta}{n - m}(x - 1)^{n-m}(x + 1)^m$

Recurrence Relation: $2(n + 1)(n + \alpha + \beta + 1)(2n + \alpha + \beta)P_{n+1}^{(\alpha,\beta)}(x)$

$$= (2n + \alpha + \beta + 1)[(\alpha^2 - \beta^2) + (2n + \alpha + \beta + 2)$$
$$\times (2n + \alpha + \beta)x]P_n^{(\alpha,\beta)}(x)$$
$$- 2(n + \alpha)(n + \beta)(2n + \alpha + \beta + 2)P_{n-1}^{(\alpha,\beta)}(x)$$

Weight: $(1 - x)^\alpha(1 + x)^\beta; \; \alpha, \beta > 1$ *Standardization*: $P_n^{(\alpha,\beta)}(x) = \binom{n + \alpha}{n}$

Norm: $\displaystyle\int_{-1}^{+1} (1 - x)^\alpha(1 + x)^\beta[P_n^{(\alpha,\beta)}(x)]^2 \, dx = \dfrac{2^{\alpha+\beta+1}\Gamma(n + \alpha + 1)\Gamma(n + \beta + 1)}{(2n + \alpha + \beta + 1)n!\Gamma(n + \alpha + \beta + 1)}$

Rodrigues' Formula: $P_n^{(\alpha,\beta)}(x) = \dfrac{(-1)^n}{2^n n!(1 - x)^\alpha(1 + x)^\beta} \dfrac{d^n}{dx^n} \{(1 - x)^{n+\alpha}(1 + x)^{n+\beta}\}$

IV (Continued)

Generating Function: $R^{-1}(1 - z + R)^{-\alpha}(1 + z + R)^{-\beta} = \sum_{n=0}^{\infty} 2^{-\alpha-\beta} P_n^{(\alpha,\beta)}(x) z^n,$

$$R = \sqrt{1 - 2xz + z^2}, \; |z| < 1$$

Inequality: $\max\limits_{-1 \le x \le 1} |P_n^{(\alpha,\beta)}(x)| = \begin{cases} \binom{n+q}{n} \sim n^q \text{ if } q = \max(\alpha, \beta) \ge -\frac{1}{2} \\ |P_n^{(\alpha,\beta)}(x')| \sim n^{-1/2} \text{ if } q < -\frac{1}{2} \\ x' \text{ is one of the two maximum points nearest} \\ \dfrac{\beta - \alpha}{\alpha + \beta + 1} \end{cases}$

V

Name: Generalized Laguerre   *Symbol*: $L_n^{(\alpha)}(x)$ *Interval*: $[0, \infty]$

Differential Equation: $xy'' + (\alpha + 1 - x)y' + ny = 0$

$$y = L_n^{(\alpha)}(x)$$

Explicit Expression: $L_n^{(\alpha)}(x) = \sum_{m=0}^{n} (-1)^m \binom{n+\alpha}{n-m} \frac{1}{m!} x^m$

Recurrence Relation: $(n+1) L_{n+1}^{(\alpha)}(x) = [(2n + \alpha + 1) - x] L_n^{(\alpha)}(x) - (n+\alpha) L_{n-1}^{(\alpha)}(x)$

Weight: $x^\alpha e^{-x}, \; \alpha > -1$ *Standardization*: $L_n^{(\alpha)}(x) = \dfrac{(-1)^n}{n!} x^n + \cdots$

Norm: $\displaystyle\int_0^\infty x^\alpha e^{-x} [L_n^{(\alpha)}(x)]^2 dx = \dfrac{\Gamma(n + \alpha + 1)}{n!}$

Rodrigues' Formula: $L_n^{(\alpha)}(x) = \dfrac{1}{n! x^\alpha e^{-x}} \dfrac{d^n}{dx^n} \{x^{n+\alpha} e^{-x}\}$

Generating Function: $(1 - z)^{-\alpha-1} \exp\left(\dfrac{xz}{z-1}\right) = \sum_{n=0}^{\infty} L_n^{(\alpha)}(x) z^n$

Inequality: $|L_n^{(\alpha)}(x)| \le \dfrac{\Gamma(n + \alpha + 1)}{n! \Gamma(\alpha + 1)} e^{x/2}; \quad \begin{matrix} x \ge 0 \\ \alpha > 0 \end{matrix}$

$$|L_n^{(\alpha)}(x)| \le \left[2 - \dfrac{\Gamma(\alpha + n + 1)}{n! \Gamma(\alpha + 1)}\right] e^{x/2}; \quad \begin{matrix} x \ge 0 \\ -1 < \alpha < 0 \end{matrix}$$

Orthogonal Polynomials

Name: Hermite *Symbol:* $H_n(x)$ *Interval:* $[-\infty, \infty]$

Differential Equation: $y'' - 2xy' + 2ny = 0$

Explicit Expression: $H_n(x) = \displaystyle\sum_{m=0}^{[n/2]} \frac{(-1)^m \, n! \, (2x)^{n-2m}}{m! \, (n-2m)!}$

Recurrence Relation: $H_{n+1}(x) = 2x \, H_n(x) - 2nH_{n-1}(x)$

Weight: e^{-x^2} *Standardization:* $H_n(1) = 2^n x^n + \ldots$

Norm: $\displaystyle\int_{-\infty}^{\infty} e^{-x^2} \, [H_n(x)]^2 \, dx = 2^n \, n! \, \sqrt{\pi}$

Rodriques' Formula: $H_n(x) = (-1)^n \, e^{x^2} \, \dfrac{d^n}{dx^n} \, (e^{-x^2})$

Generating Function: $e^{-z^2 + 2zx} = \displaystyle\sum_{n=0}^{\infty} H_n(x) \, \frac{z^n}{n!}$

Inequality: $|H_n(x)| < e^{\frac{x^2}{2}} \, k \, 2^{n/2} \, \sqrt{n!}$ $k \approx 1.086435$

Coefficients for Orthogonal Polynomials, and for x^n in Terms of Orthogonal Polynomials[a]

I. Legendre Polynomials: $P_n(x) = a_n^{-1} \sum_{m=0}^{n} c_m x^m \qquad x^n = b_n^{-1} \sum_{m=0}^{n} d_m P_m(x)$

	a_n	x^0	x^1	x^2	x^3	x^4	x^5	x^6	x^7
b_n		1	1	3	5	35	63	231	429
P_0	1	1 1		1		7		33	
P_1	1		1 1		3		27		143
P_2	2	−1		3 2		20		110	
P_3	2		−3		5 2		28		182
P_4	8	3		−30		35 8		72	
P_5	8		15		−70		63 8		88
P_6	16	−5		105		−315		231 16	
P_7	16		−35		315		−693		429 16

$$P_6(x) = \frac{1}{16}[231x^6 - 315x^4 + 105x^2 - 5] \qquad x^6 = \frac{1}{231}[33P_0 + 110P_2 + 72P_4 + 16P_6]$$

II. Tschebysheff Polynomials: $T_n(x) = \sum_{m=0}^{n} c_m x^m \qquad x^n = b_n^{-1} \sum_{m=0}^{n} d_m T_m(x)$

	x^0	x^1	x^2	x^3	x^4	x^5	x^6	x^7
b_n	1	1	2	4	8	16	32	64
T_0	1 1		1		3		10	
T_1		1 1		3		10		35
T_2	−1		2 1		4		15	
T_3		−3		4 1		5		21
T_4	1		−8		8 1		6	
T_5		5		−20		16 1		7
T_6	−1		18		−48		32 1	
T_7		−7		56		−112		64 1

$$T_6(x) = 32x^6 - 48x^4 + 18x^2 - 1 \qquad x^6 = \frac{1}{32}[10T_0 + 15T_2 + 6T_4 + T_6]$$

III. Tschebysheff Polynomials: $U_n(x) = \sum_{m=0}^{n} c_m x^m \qquad x^n = b_n^{-1} \sum_{m=0}^{n} d_m U_m(x)$

	x^0	x^1	x^2	x^3	x^4	x^5	x^6	x^7
b_n	1	2	4	8	16	32	64	128
U_0	1 1		1		2		5	
U_1		2 1		2		5		14
U_2	−1		4 1		3		9	
U_3		−4		8 1		4		14
U_4	1		−12		16 1		5	
U_5		6		−32		32 1		6
U_6	−1		24		−80		64 1	
U_7		−8		80		−192		128 1

$$U_6(x) = 64x^6 - 80x^4 + 24x^3 - 1 \qquad x^6 = \frac{1}{64}[5U_0 + 9U_2 + 5U_4 + U_6]$$

Coefficients for Orthogonal Polynomials, and for x^n in Terms of Orthogonal Polynomials* (continued)

IV. Jacobi Polynomials $P_n^{(\alpha,\beta)}(x) = a_n^{-1} \displaystyle\sum_{m=0}^{n} c_m (x-1)^m$

	α_n	$(x-1)^0$	$(x-1)^1$	$(x-1)^2$	$(x-1)^3$	$(x-1)^4$	$(x-1)^5$	$(x-1)^6$
$P_0^{(\alpha,\beta)}$	1	1						
$P_1^{(\alpha,\beta)}$	2	$2(\alpha+1)$	$\alpha+\beta+2$					
$P_2^{(\alpha,\beta)}$	8	$4(\alpha+1)_2$	$4(\alpha+\beta+3)(\alpha+2)$	$(\alpha+\beta+3)_2$				
$P_3^{(\alpha,\beta)}$	48	$8(\alpha+1)_3$	$12(\alpha+\beta+4)(\alpha+2)_2$	$6(\alpha+\beta+4)_2(\alpha+3)$	$(\alpha+\beta+4)_3$			
$P_4^{(\alpha,\beta)}$	384	$16(\alpha+1)_4$	$32(\alpha+\beta+5)(\alpha+2)_3$	$24(\alpha+\beta+5)_2(\alpha+3)_2$	$8(\alpha+\beta+5)_3(\alpha+4)$	$(\alpha+\beta+5)_4$		
$P_5^{(\alpha,\beta)}$	3840	$32(\alpha+1)_5$	$80(\alpha+\beta+6)(\alpha+2)_4$	$80(\alpha+\beta+6)_2(\alpha+3)_3$	$40(\alpha+\beta+6)_3(\alpha+4)_2$	$10(\alpha+\beta+6)_4(\alpha+5)$	$(\alpha+\beta+6)_5$	
$P_6^{(\alpha,\beta)}$	46080	$64(\alpha+1)_6$	$192(\alpha+\beta+7)(\alpha+2)_5$	$240(\alpha+\beta+7)_2(\alpha+3)_4$	$160(\alpha+\beta+7)_3(\alpha+4)_3$	$60(\alpha+\beta+7)_4(\alpha+5)_2$	$12(\alpha+\beta+7)_5(\alpha+6)$	$(\alpha+\beta+7)_6$

$$(m)_n = m(m+1)(m+2)\cdots(m+n-1)$$

$$P_5^{(1,1)}(x) = \frac{1}{3840}\left[(8)_5(x-1)^5+10(8)_4(6)(x-1)^4+40(8)_2(5)_2(x-1)^3+80(8)_2(4)_3(x-1)^2+80(8)(3)_4(x-1)+32(2)_5\right]$$

$$P_5^{(1,1)}(x) = \frac{1}{3840}\left[95040(x-1)^5+475200(x-1)^4+864000(x-1)^3+691200(x-1)^2+230400(x-1)+23040\right]$$

Coefficients for Orthogonal Polynomials, and for x^n in Terms of Orthogonal Polynomials* (continued)

V. Laguerre Polynomials: $L_n(x) = \sum_{m=0}^{n} c_m x^m \qquad x^n = b_n^{-1} \sum_{m=0}^{n} d_m L_m(x)$

	x^0	x^1	x^2	x^3	x^4	x^5	x^6	x^7
b_m	1	1	2	6	24	120	720	5040
L_0	1 1	1	2	6	24	120	720	5040
L_1	1	-1 -1	-4	-18	-96	-600	-4320	-35280
L_2	2	-4	1 2	18	144	1200	10800	105840
L_3	6	-18	9	-1 -6	-96	-1200	-14400	-176400
L_4	24	-96	72	-16	1 24	600	10800	17640
L_5	120	-600	600	-200	25	-1 -120	-4320	-105840
L_6	720	-4320	5400	-2400	450	-36	1 720	35280
L_7	5040	-35280	52920	-29400	7350	-882	49	-1 -5040

$$L_6(x) = x^6 - 36x^5 + 450x^4 - 2400x^3 + 5400x^2 - 4320x + 720$$

$$x^6 = \frac{1}{720}\left[720L_0 - 4320L_1 + 10800L_2 - 14400L_3 + 10800L_4 - 4320L_5 + 720L_6\right]$$

VI. Hermite polynomials: $H_n(x) = \sum_{m=0}^{n} c_m x^m \qquad x^n = b_n^{-1} \sum_{m=0}^{n} d_m H_m(x)$

	x^0	x^1	x^2	x^3	x^4	x^5	x^6	x^7
b_n	1	2	4	8	16	32	64	128
H_0	1 1		2		12		120	
H_1		2 1		6		60		840
H_2	-2		4 1		12		180	
H_3		-12		8 1		20		420
H_4	12		-48		16 1		30	
H_5		120		-160		32 1		42
H_6	-120		720		-480		64 1	
H_7		-1680		3360		-1344		128 1

$$H_6(x) = 64x^6 - 480x^4 + 720x^2 - 120 \qquad x^6 = \frac{1}{64}\left[120\,H_0 + 180\,H_2 + 30H_4 + H_6\right]$$

Abridged from Abramowitz, M. and Stegun, I. A., Eds., *Handbook of Mathematical Functions*, National Bureau of Standards, Washington, D. C., 1964.

LEGENDRE FUNCTIONS

In the following, m and n are positive integers.

1. The differential equation $(1 - z^2) \dfrac{d^2w}{dz^2} - 2z \dfrac{dw}{dz} + n(n + 1)z = 0$ is known as Legendre's differential equation. The Legendre polynomials $P_0(z)$, $P_1(z)$, $P_2(z)$, . . . are solutions of this equation, and are referred to as Surface Zonal Harmonics, for which tables are herewith given.

2. The solution of Legendre's equation can be stated as

$$w = AP_n(z) + BQ_n(z) \qquad |z| < 1$$
$$\text{or}$$
$$w = AP_n(z) + B\mathfrak{Q}_n(z) \qquad |z| > 1,$$

where A and B are arbitrary constants, $P_n(z)$ the Legendre polynomials, $Q_n(z)$ and $\mathfrak{Q}_n(z)$ Legendre functions of the second kind.

3. The differential equation $(1 - z^2) \dfrac{d^2u}{dz^2} - 2z \dfrac{du}{dz} + \left[n(n + 1) - \dfrac{m^2}{1 - z^2} \right] u = 0$ which is obtained from the Legendre equation in 1. after it has been differentiated m times and u replaced by $(1 - z^2)^{m/2} \left(\dfrac{d^m w}{dz^m} \right)$ is referred to as the "associated Legendre differential equation."

4. The solution for the "associated Legendre differential equation" is given by

$$u = AP_n^m(z) + BQ_n^m(z),$$

where A and B are arbitrary constants and $P_n^m(z)$, $Q_n^m(z)$ are called associated Legendre functions.

5. $P_n(z) = \displaystyle\sum_{1=0}^{m} (-1)^r \frac{(2n - 2r)!}{2^n(r!)(n - r_r)!(n - 2r)!} z^{n-2r} \quad m = \tfrac{1}{2}n,\ n$ even

$$m = \tfrac{1}{2}(n - 1),\ n \text{ odd}$$

$$Q_n(z) = \tfrac{1}{2}P_n(z) \log_e \frac{1 + z}{1 - z} - \sum_{r=1}^{n} \frac{1}{r} P_{r-1}(z) P_{n-r}(z)$$

$$= P_n(z)Q_0(z) - \sum_{r=1}^{n} \frac{1}{r} P_{r-1}(z) P_{n-r}(z)$$

$$Q_0(z) = \tfrac{1}{2} \log_e \frac{1 + z}{1 - z} = \tanh^{-1} z$$

$$\mathfrak{Q}_n(z) = \tfrac{1}{2}P_n(z) \log_e \frac{z + 1}{z - 1} - \sum_{r=1}^{n} \frac{1}{r} P_{r-1}(z)\, P_{n-r}(z)$$

$$= P_n(z)\mathfrak{Q}_0(z) - \sum_{r=1}^{n} \frac{1}{r} P_{r-1}(z) P_{n-r}(z)$$

$$\mathfrak{Q}_0(z) = \tfrac{1}{2} \log_e \frac{z + 1}{z - 1} = \operatorname{ctnh}^{-1} z$$

LEGENDRE FUNCTIONS (Continued)

6.

n	$P_n(z)$	$Q_n(z)$
0	1	$\dfrac{\log_e}{2}\dfrac{(1+z)}{(1-z)}$
1	z	$zQ_0(z) - 1$
2	$\dfrac{1}{2}(3z^2 - 1)$	$\dfrac{1}{2}(3z^2 - 1)Q_0(z) - \dfrac{3}{2}z$
3	$\dfrac{1}{2}(5z^3 - 3z)$	$\dfrac{1}{2}(5z^3 - 3z)Q_0(z) - \dfrac{5}{2}z^2 + \dfrac{2}{3}$
4	$\dfrac{1}{8}(35z^4 - 30z^2 + 3)$	$\dfrac{1}{8}(35z^4 - 30z^2 + 3)Q_0(z) - \dfrac{35}{8}z^3 + \dfrac{55}{24}z$
5	$\dfrac{1}{8}(63z^5 - 70z^3 + 15z)$	$\dfrac{1}{8}(63z^5 - 70z^3 + 15z)Q_0(z) - \dfrac{63}{8}z^4 + \dfrac{49}{8}z^2 - \dfrac{8}{15}$

7. $\dfrac{1}{(1 - 2xZ + Z^2)^{1/2}} = \sum P_n(x)Z^n$

If $x = \cos\theta = \tfrac{1}{2}(e^{i\theta} + e^{-i\theta})$, $i = \sqrt{-1}$, then

$$[1 - Z(e^{i\theta} + e^{-i\theta}) + Z^2]^{-1/2} = \sum_{n=0}^{\infty} P_n(\cos\theta)Z^n$$

$P_0(\cos\theta) = 1$

$P_1(\cos\theta) = \cos\theta$

$P_2(\cos\theta) = \dfrac{1}{4}(3\cos 2\theta + 1)$

$P_3(\cos\theta) = \dfrac{1}{8}(5\cos 3\theta + 3\cos\theta)$

$P_4(\cos\theta) = \dfrac{1}{64}(35\cos 4\theta + 20\cos 2\theta + 9)$

$$P_n(\cos\theta) = \frac{(2n)!}{2^{2n}(n!)^2}\left[\cos n\theta + \frac{1}{1}\frac{n}{2n-1}\cos(n-2)\theta \right.$$
$$+ \frac{1\cdot 3}{1\cdot 2}\frac{n(n-1)}{(2n-1)(2n-3)}\cos(n-4)\theta$$
$$\left. + \frac{1\cdot 3\cdot 5}{1\cdot 2\cdot 3}\frac{n(n-1)(n-2)}{(2n-1)(2n-3)(2n-5)}\cos(n-6)\theta + \cdots\right]$$

LEGENDRE FUNCTIONS (Continued)

8. $P_{2n+1}(0) = 0$

$$P_{2n}(0) = (-1)^n \frac{1 \cdot 3 \cdot 5 \cdots (2n-1)}{2 \cdot 4 \cdot 6 \cdot 8 \cdots (2n)}$$

$$P_n(1) = 1$$

$$P_n(-1) = (-1)^n$$

$$P_n(z) = \frac{1}{2^n n!} \frac{d^n}{dz^n} (z^2 - 1)^n \quad \text{(Rodrigues' formula)}$$

$$P_n^m(z) = (1 - z^2)^{m/2} \frac{d^m[P_n(z)]}{dz^m}$$

$$Q_n^m(z) = (1 - z^2)^{m/2} \frac{d^m[Q_n(z)]}{dz^m}$$

9. Important recurrence and orthogonality relations (note that w_n stands for either P_n or Q_n in the following)

$$(n+1)[w_{n+1}(z)] - (2n+1)z[w_n(z)] + n[w_{n-1}(z)] = 0$$

$$z \frac{d[w_n(z)]}{dz} - z \frac{d[w_{n-1}(z)]}{dz} = n[w_n(z)]$$

$$\frac{d[w_{n+1}(z)]}{dz} - z \frac{d[w_n(z)]}{dz} = (n+1)[w_n(z)]$$

$$\frac{d[w_{n+1}(z)]}{dz} - \frac{d}{dz}[w_{n-1}(z)] = (2n+1)[w_n(z)]$$

$$(z^2 - 1) \frac{d}{dz}[w_n(z)] = nz[w_n(z)] - n[w_{n-1}(z)]$$

$$\int_{-1}^{1} [P_m(z)][P_n(z)]dz \begin{cases} = 0 & m \neq n \\ = \dfrac{2}{2n+1} & m = n \end{cases}$$

$$\int_{-1}^{1} [P_n^m(z)][P_r^m(z)]dz \begin{cases} = 0 & r \neq n \\ = \dfrac{2}{2n+1} \dfrac{(n+m)!}{(n-m)!} & r = n > m. \end{cases}$$

SURFACE ZONAL HARMONICS

$$P_n(x) = \frac{1}{2^n n!} \frac{d^n}{dx^n} (x^2 - 1)^n$$

x	$P_1(x)$	$P_2(x)$	$P_3(x)$	$P_4(x)$	$P_5(x)$
0	0	$-.5$	0	.375	0
.01	.01	$-.49985$	$-.0149975$	.37463	.018741
.02	.02	$-.4994$	$-.02998$	.37350	.037430
.03	.03	$-.49865$	$-.0449325$	.37163	.056014
.04	.04	$-.4976$	$-.05984$	.36901	.074441
.05	.05	$-.49625$	$-.0746875$	.36565	.092659
.06	.06	$-.4946$	$-.08946$	.36156	.11062
.07	.07	$-.49265$	$-.10414$	.35673	.12826
.08	.08	$-.4904$	$-.11872$	.35118	.14555
.09	.09	$-.48785$	$-.13318$	.34491	.16242
.10	.10	$-.485$	$-.1475$	.33794	.17883
.11	.11	$-.48185$	$-.16167$	.33027	.19473
.12	.12	$-.4784$	$-.17568$	.32191	.21008
.13	.13	$-.47465$	$-.18951$	.31287	.22482
.14	.14	$-.4706$	$-.20314$	.30318	.23891
.15	.15	$-.46625$	$-.21656$	.29284	.25232
.16	.16	$-.4616$	$-.22976$	.28187	.26499
.17	.17	$-.45665$	$-.24272$	.27028	.27688
.18	.18	$-.4514$	$-.25542$	.25809	.28796
.19	.19	$-.44585$	$-.26785$	.24533	.29818
.20	.20	$-.44$	$-.28$	.232	.30752
.21	.21	$-.43385$	$-.29185$	.21813	.31593
.22	.22	$-.4274$	$-.30338$	.20375	.32339
.23	.23	$-.42065$	$-.31458$	.18887	.32986
.24	.24	$-.4136$	$-.32544$	.17352	.33531
.25	.25	$-.40625$	$-.33594$	.15771	.33972
.26	.26	$-.3986$	$-.34606$	.14149	.34307
.27	.27	$-.39065$	$-.35579$	.12488	.34532
.28	.28	$-.3824$	$-.36512$	.10789	.34647
.29	.29	$-.37385$	$-.37403$	.09057	.34650
.30	.30	$-.365$	$-.3825$	.07294	.34539
.31	.31	$-.35585$	$-.39052$	.05503	.34312
.32	.32	$-.3464$	$-.39808$	.03688	.33970
.33	.33	$-.33665$	$-.40516$	.01851	.33512
.34	.34	$-.3266$	$-.41174$	$-.00004$	.32937
.35	.35	$-.31625$	$-.41781$	$-.01872$	.32245
.36	.36	$-.3056$	$-.42336$	$-.03752$	.31438
.37	.37	$-.29465$	$-.42837$	$-.05638$	.30514
.38	.38	$-.2834$	$-.43282$	$-.07528$	.29477
.39	.39	$-.27185$	$-.43670$	$-.09416$	.28326
.40	.40	$-.26$	$-.44$	$-.113$	.27064
.41	.41	$-.24785$	$-.44270$	$-.13175$	.25693
.42	.42	$-.2354$	$-.44478$	$-.15036$	.24215
.43	.43	$-.22265$	$-.44623$	$-.16880$	.22633
.44	.44	$-.2096$	$-.44704$	$-.18702$	.20951
.45	.45	$-.19625$	$-.44719$	$-.20497$	.19172
.46	.46	$-.1826$	$-.44666$	$-.22261$	.17301
.47	.47	$-.16865$	$-.44544$	$-.23989$	.15341
.48	.48	$-.1544$	$-.44352$	$-.25676$	.13298
.49	.49	$-.13985$	$-.44088$	$-.27316$	.11177

SURFACE ZONAL HARMONICS (Continued)

x	$P_6(x)$	$P_7(x)$	$P_8(x)$	$P_9(x)$	$P_{10}(x)$
0	− .3125	− 0	.2734	0	− .2461
.01	− .31184	− .021855	.2725	.0246	− .2447
.02	− .30988	− .043593	.2695	.0489	− .2407
.03	− .30661	− .065094	.2646	.0729	− .2340
.04	− .30205	− .086244	.2578	.0961	− .2247
.05	− .29622	− .10693	.2492	.1186	− .2130
.06	− .28913	− .12703	.2387	.1400	− .1989
.07	− .28081	− .14644	.2265	.1601	− .1826
.08	− .27130	− .16506	.2126	.1789	− .1642
.09	− .26063	− .18278	.1972	.1960	− .1440
.10	− .24883	− .19949	.1803	.2114	− .1221
.11	− .23595	− .21511	.1621	.2249	− .0989
.12	− .22204	− .22955	.1426	.2364	− .0745
.13	− .20715	− .24271	.1221	.2457	− .0492
.14	− .19133	− .25453	.1006	.2529	− .0233
.15	− .17465	− .26492	.0783	.2577	.0020
.16	− .15716	− .27383	.0554	.2601	.0293
.17	− .13894	− .28119	.0319	.2602	.0553
18	− .12005	− .28695	.0082	.2579	.0808
.19	− .10057	− .29107	− .0157	.2531	.1055
.20	− .080576	− .29352	− .0396	.2460	.1291
.21	− .060144	− .29426	− 0632	.2365	.1513
.22	− .039357	− .29327	− .0865	.2247	.1718
.23	− .018300	− .29055	− .1093	.2108	.1905
.24	.002941	− .28610	− .1313	.1948	.2070
.25	.024277	− .27992	− .1525	.1768	.2212
.26	.045618	− .27203	− .1725	.1571	.2329
.27	.066872	− .26246	− .1914	.1357	.2419
.28	.087947	− .25124	− .2089	.1129	.2480
.29	.10875	− .23843	− .2248	.0888	.2513
.30	.12918	− .22407	− .2391	.0637	.2515
.31	.14915	− .20824	− .2515	.0378	.2487
.32	.16856	− .19100	− .2621	.0114	.2428
.33	.18732	− .17244	− .2706	− .0154	.2339
.34	.20534	− .15266	− .2770	− .0422	.2220
.35	.22251	− .13176	− .2812	− .0688	.2073
.36	.23875	− .10984	− .2831	− .0948	.1899
.37	.25397	− .087036	− .2826	− .1201	.1699
.38	.26808	− .063467	− .2798	− .1444	.1476
.39	.28100	− .039271	− .2746	− .1674	.1231
.40	.29264	− .014590	− .2670	− .1888	.0968
.41	.30291	.010424	− .2570	− .2083	.0690
.42	.31176	.035614	− .2447	− .2258	.0401
.43	.31909	.060820	− .2302	− .2410	.0103
.44	32486	.085873	− .2134	− .2537	− .0200
.45	.32898	.11060	− .1945	− .2637	− .0503
.46	.33141	.13483	− .1737	− .2708	− .0803
.47	.33209	.15838	− .1510	− .2749	− .1095
.48	.33098	.18107	− .1267	− .2758	− .1375
.49	.32804	.20272	− .1008	− .2735	− .1639

SURFACE ZONAL HARMONICS (Continued)

x	$P_1(x)$	$P_2(x)$	$P_3(x)$	$P_4(x)$	$P_5(x)$
0.50	0.50	−0.125	−0.4375	−0.28906	0.08984
.51	.51	−.10985	−.43337	−.30440	.06726
.52	.52	−.0944	−.42848	−.31912	.04409
.53	53	−.07865	−.42281	−.33317	.02041
.54	.54	−.0626	−.41634	−.34649	−.00372
55	.55	−.04625	−.40906	−.35904	−.02819
.56	.56	−.0296	−.40096	−.37074	−.05294
.57	.57	−.01265	−.39202	−.38155	−.07786
.58	.58	.0046	−.38222	−.39140	−.10285
.59	.59	.02215	−.37155	−.40024	−.12781
.60	.60	.04	−.36	−.408	−.15264
.61	.61	.05815	−.34755	−.41462	−.17721
.62	.62	.0766	−.33418	−.42004	−.20142
.63	.63	.09535	−.31988	−.42418	−.22512
.64	.64	.1144	−.30464	−.42700	−.24819
.65	.65	.13375	−.28844	−.42841	−.27049
.66	.66	.1534	−.27126	−.42836	−.29188
.67	.67	.17335	−.25309	−.42676	−.31220
.68	.68	.1936	−.23392	−.42356	−.33131
.69	.69	.21415	−.21373	−.41869	−.34903
.70	.70	.235	−.1925	−.41206	−.36520
.71	.71	.25615	−.17022	−.40361	−.37964
.72	.72	.2776	−.14688	−.39327	−.39217
.73	.73	.29935	−.12246	−.38095	−.40260
.74	.74	.3214	−.09694	−.36659	−.41074
.75	.75	.34375	−.07031	−.35010	−.41638
.76	.76	.3664	−.04256	−.33140	−.41931
.77	.77	.38935	−.01367	−.31043	−.41932
.78	.78	.4126	.01638	−.28709	−.41618
.79	.79	.43615	.04760	−.26131	−.40966
.80	.80	.46	.08	−.233	−.39952
.81	.81	.48415	.11360	−.20208	−.38552
.82	.82	.5086	.14842	−.16847	−.36739
.83	.83	.53335	.18447	−.13207	−.34489
.84	.84	.5584	.22176	−.09281	−.31774
.85	.85	.58375	.26031	−.05060	−.28566
.86	.86	.6094	.30014	−.00534	−.24838
.87	.87	.63535	.34126	.04305	−.20559
.88	.88	.6616	.38368	.09467	−.15699
.89	.89	.68815	.42742	.14960	−.10228
.90	.90	.715	.4725	.20794	−.04114
.91	.91	.74215	.51893	.26978	0.02676
.92	.92	.7696	.56672	.33522	.10175
.93	.93	.79735	.61589	.40435	.18417
.94	.94	.8254	.66646	.47728	.27438
.95	.95	.85373	.71844	.55409	.37274
.96	.96	.8824	.77184	.63489	.47962
.97	.97	.91135	.82668	.71978	.59539
.98	.98	.9406	.88298	.80886	.72045
.99	.99	.97015	.94075	.90223	.85518
100	1	1	1	1	1,

SURFACE ZONAL HARMONICS (Continued)

x	$P_6(x)$	$P_7(x)$	$P_8(x)$	$P_9(x)$	$P_{10}(x)$
.50	0.32324	0.22314	−0.0736	−0.2679	−0.1882
.51	.31655	.24217	−.0454	−.2590	−.2101
.52	.30796	.25961	−.0163	−.2468	−.2291
.53	.29747	.27530	.0133	−.2314	−.2450
.54	.28506	.28906	.0432	−.2128	−.2573
.55	.27077	.30074	.0732	−.1913	−.2658
.56	.25460	.31016	.1029	−.1669	−.2701
.57	.23660	.31719	.1320	−.1399	−.2702
.58	.21681	.32169	.1601	−.1105	−.2659
.59	.19528	.32353	.1870	−.0791	−.2570
.60	.17210	.32260	.2133	−.0450	−.2433
.61	.14733	.31880	.2357	−.0118	−.2258
.63	.12109	.31207	.2568	.0234	−.2036
.63	.093475	.30232	.2753	.0589	−.1773
.64	.064623	.28954	.2909	.0943	−.1471
.65	.034675	.27371	.3032	.1290	−.1136
.66	.003790	.25483	.3120	.1625	−.0771
.67	−.027853	.23295	.3170	.1941	−.0382
.68	−.060059	.20813	.3179	.2233	.0024
.69	−.092615	.18049	.3145	.2495	.0440
.70	−.12529	.15016	.3067	.2721	.0858
.71	−.15782	.11731	.2943	.2904	.1269
.72	−.18994	.082166	.2771	.3039	.1663
.73	−.22136	.044990	.2553	.3120	.2030
.74	−.25175	.006087	.2287	.3143	.2360
.75	−.28078	−.034184	.1976	.3103	.2644
.76	−.30807	−.075411	.1621	.2997	.2869
.77	−.33325	−.11713	.1225	.2823	.3027
.78	−.35589	−.15881	.0791	.2578	.3108
.79	−.37557	−.19987	.0326	.2263	.3103
.80	−.39180	−.23965	−.0167	.1879	.3005
.81	−.40409	−.27743	−.0678	.1429	.2810
.82	−.41193	−.31240	−.1199	.0920	.2513
.83	−.41475	−.34368	−.1720	.0359	.1942
.84	−.41198	−.37033	−.2228	−.0243	.1617
.85	−.40300	−.39130	−.2710	−.0873	.1029
.86	−.38716	−.40545	−.3150	−.1513	.0362
.87	−.36379	−.41156	−.3530	−.2143	−.0366
.88	−.33217	−.40829	−.3830	−.2738	−.1130
.89	−.29156	−.39423	−.4028	−.3267	−.1899
.90	−.24116	−.36782	−.4097	−.3695	−.2631
.91	−.18018	−.32743	−.4010	−.3983	−.3277
.92	−.10774	−.27129	−.3737	−.4083	−.3773
.93	−.02295	−.19749	−.3243	−.3941	−.4046
.94	.07512	−.10404	−.2491	−.3498	−.4006
.95	.18745	.01123	−.1440	−.2684	−.3549
.96	.31506	.15060	−.0046	−.1422	−.2552
.97	.45899	.31650	.1740	.0375	−.0875
.98	.62035	.51151	.3971	.2804	.1647
.99	.80029	.73838	.6704	.5973	.5201
1.00	1	1	1	1	1

SURFACE ZONAL HARMONICS (Continued)

θ deg.	$P_1(\cos \theta)$	$P_2(\cos \theta)$	$P_3(\cos \theta)$	$P_4(\cos \theta)$	$P_5(\cos \theta)$
0	1	1	1	1	1
1	0.99985	0.99954	0.99909	0.99848	0.99772
2	.99939	.99817	.99635	.99392	.99088
3	.99863	.99589	.99179	.98634	.97954
4	.99756	.99270	.98543	.97577	.96377
5	.99619	.98861	.97728	.96227	.94368
6	.99452	.98361	.96736	.94589	.91939
7	.99255	.97772	.95569	.92670	.89108
8	.99027	.97095	.94232	.90480	.85893
9	.98769	.96329	.92726	.88026	.82315
10	.98481	.95477	.91057	.85321	.78399
11	.98163	.94539	.89228	.82376	.74170
12	.97815	.93516	.87244	.79204	.69656
13	.97437	.92410	.85111	.75819	.64888
14	.97030	.91221	.82833	.72235	.59895
15	.96593	.89952	.80416	.68470	.54713
16	.96126	.88604	.77868	.64537	.49373
17	.95630	.87178	.75194	.60456	.43911
18	.95106	.85676	.72401	.56244	.38363
19	.94552	.84101	.69497	.51918	.32763
20	.93969	.82453	.66488	.47498	.27149
21	.93358	.80736	.63384	.43002	.21556
22	.92718	.78950	.60190	.38450	.16019
23	.92050	.77099	.56917	.33862	.10573
24	.91355	.75185	.53572	.29256	.05252
25	.90631	.73209	.50163	.24653	.00088
26	.89879	.71175	.46699	.20072	− .04887
27	.89101	.69084	.43190	.15531	− .09642
28	.88295	.66939	.39644	.11051	− .14151
29	.87462	,64744	.36069	.06649	− .18388
30	.86603	.62500	.32476	.02344	− .22327
31	.85717	.60210	.28873	− .01847	− .25949
32	.84805	.57878	.25269	− .05907	− .29233
33	.83867	.55505	.21673	− .09820	− .32163
34	.82904	.53095	.18094	− .13570	− .34726
35	.81915	.50652	.14542	− .17142	− .36910
36	.80902	.48176	.11025	− .20524	− .38707
37	.79864	.45673	.07551	− .23701	− .40113
38	.78801	.43144	.04129	− .26664	− .41124
39	.77715	.40593	.00769	− .29400	− .41741
40	.76604	.38024	− .02523	− .31900	− .41968
41	.75471	.35438	− .05738	− .34157	− .41811
42	.74314	.32840	− .08869	− .36163	− .41279
43	.73135	.30232	− .11907	− .37913	− .40385
44	.71934	.27617	− .14845	− .39401	− .39141
45	.70711	.25000	− .17678	− .40625	− .37565
46	.69466	.22383	− .20397	− .41582	− .35677
47	.68200	.19768	− .22997	− .42273	− .33496
48	.66913	.17160	− .25471	− .42696	− .31048
49	.65606	.14562	− .27815	− .42856	− .28357

For $P_n(\cos \theta)$, use the definition of $P_n(x)$ given on the first page of this table, and put $x = \cos \theta$.

SURFACE ZONAL HARMONICS (Continued)

$\theta°$	$P_6(\cos\theta)$	$P_7(\cos\theta)$	$P_8(\cos\theta)$	$P_9(\cos\theta)$	$P_{10}(\cos\theta)$
0	1	1	1	1	1
1	0.99680	0.99574	0.9945	0.9932	0.9916
2	.98725	.98301	.9782	.9728	.9668
3	.97142	.96198	.9513	.9393	.9260
4	.94947	.93291	.9142	.8933	.8704
5	.92160	.89616	.8675	.8358	.8012
6	.88808	.85220	.8121	.7680	.7203
7	.84922	.80158	.7487	.6911	.6296
8	.80538	.74493	.6784	.6069	.5312
9	.75698	.68296	.6024	.5168	.4277
10	.70447	.61644	.5218	.4228	.3214
11	.64833	.54619	.4380	.3266	.2150
12	.58909	.47307	.3522	.2302	.1108
13	.52729	.39798	.2657	.1353	.0113
14	.46350	.32183	.1799	.0437	−.0813
15	.39831	.24554	.0962	−.0428	−.1651
16	.33229	.17001	.0157	−.1227	−.2381
17	.26606	.09614	−.0604	−.1946	−.2992
18	.20020	.02477	−.1310	−.2573	−.3471
19	.13529	−.04327	−.1951	−.3100	−.3813
20	.07190	−.10723	−.2518	−.3517	−.4013
21	.01059	−.16640	−.3005	−.3821	−.4073
22	−.04813	−.22217	−.3407	−.4009	−.3997
23	−.10376	−.26800	−.3718	−.4082	−.3793
24	−.15585	−.30942	−.3936	−.4042	−.3473
25	−.20398	−.34408	−.4062	−.3896	−.3052
26	−.24779	−.37172	−.4096	−.3650	−.2547
27	−.28694	−.39216	−.4041	−.3515	−.1975
28	−.32117	−.40534	−.3900	−.2902	−.1358
29	−.35025	−.41130	−.3680	−.2424	−.0716
30	−.37402	−.41018	−.3388	−.1896	−.0070
31	−.39238	−.40221	−.3031	−.1332	.0559
32	−.40527	−.38771	−.2619	−.0749	.1150
33	−.41269	−.36710	−.2162	−.0161	.1689
34	−.41471	−.34086	−.1670	.0415	.2157
35	−.41145	−.30956	−.1154	.0966	.2542
36	−.40307	−.27382	−.0627	.1476	.2833
37	−.38980	−.23432	−.0098	.1935	.3024
38	−.37191	−.19178	.0421	.2331	.3111
39	−.34972	−.14695	.0919	.2655	.3093
40	−.32357	−.10060	.1386	.2900	.2973
41	−.29387	−.05351	.1814	.3062	.2758
42	−.26104	−.00645	.2194	.3137	.2455
43	−.22554	.03982	.2519	.3127	.2077
44	−.18784	.08455	.2784	.3031	.1637
45	−.14844	.12706	.2983	.2855	.1151
46	−.10783	.16668	.3115	.2605	.0635
47	−.06654	.20283	.3176	.2288	.0107
48	−.02508	.23497	.3167	.1915	−.0416
49	.01606	.26263	.3090	.1495	−.0918

SURFACE ZONAL HARMONICS (Continued)

$\theta°$	$P_1(\cos\theta)$	$P_2(\cos\theta)$	$P_3(\cos\theta)$	$P_4(\cos\theta)$	$P_5(\cos\theta)$
50	0.64279	0.11976	−0.30022	−0.42753	−0.25449
51	.62932	.09407	−.32088	−.42394	−.22353
52	.61566	.06856	−.34009	−.41784	−.19097
53	.60182	.04327	−.35781	−.40929	−.15712
54	.58779	.01824	−.37399	−.39837	−.12229
55	.57358	−.00652	−.38861	−.38519	−.08679
56	.55919	−.03095	−.40164	−.36983	−.05093
57	.54464	−.05505	−.41307	−.35241	−.01503
58	.52992	−.07878	−.42286	−.33306	.02060
59	.51504	−.10210	−.43100	−.31189	.05566
60	.50000	−.12500	−.43750	−.28906	.08984
61	.48481	−.14744	−.44234	−.26471	.12287
62	.46947	−.16939	−.44552	−.23899	.15446
63	.45399	−.19084	−.44706	−.21205	.18436
64	.43837	−.21175	−.44695	−.18407	.21232
65	.42262	−.23209	−.44522	−.15521	.23811
66	.40674	−.25185	−.44188	−.12564	.26152
67	.39073	−.27099	−.43696	−.09554	.28238
68	.37461	−.28950	−.43049	−.06508	.30051
69	.35837	−.30736	−.42249	−.03444	.31577
70	.34202	−.32453	−.41301	−.00380	.32807
71	.32557	−.34101	−.40208	.02667	.33730
72	.30902	−.35676	−.38975	.05680	.34340
73	.29237	−.37178	−.37608	.08641	.34634
74	.27564	−.38604	−.36110	.11534	.34611
75	.25882	−.39952	−.34488	.14343	.34273
76	.24192	−.41221	−.32749	.17051	.33624
77	.22495	−.42410	−.30897	.19644	.32672
78	.20791	−.43516	−.28940	.22107	.31425
79	.19081	−.44539	−.26885	.24427	.29897
80	.17365	−.45477	−.24738	.26590	.28102
81	.15643	−.46329	−.22508	.28585	.26056
82	.13917	−.47095	−.20202	.30401	.23777
83	.12187	−.47772	−.17828	.32027	.21288
84	.10453	−.48361	−.15394	.33455	.18610
85	.08716	−.48861	−.12908	.34677	.15766
86	.06976	−.49270	−.10379	.35686	.12784
87	.05234	−.49589	−.07815	.36476	09688
88	.03490	−.49817	−.05224	.37044	.06507
89	.01745	−.49954	−.02617	.37386	.03268
90	0	−.50000	0	.37500	0

SURFACE ZONAL HARMONICS (Continued)

$\theta°$	$P_6(\cos\theta)$	$P_7(\cos\theta)$	$P_8(\cos\theta)$	$P_9(\cos\theta)$	$P_{10}(\cos\theta)$
50	0.05638	0.28543	0.2947	0.1041	−0.1381
51	.09539	.30308	.2742	.0565	−.1792
52	.13265	.31535	.2480	.0080	−.2137
53	.16772	.32213	.2167	−.0400	−.2407
54	.20020	.32336	.1812	−.0863	−.2594
55	.22972	.31910	.1422	−.1296	−.2692
56	.25597	.30949	.1005	−.1689	−.2700
57	.27866	.29475	.0572	−.2032	−.2617
58	.29756	.27518	.0131	−.2315	−.2449
59	.31246	.25117	−.0309	−.2533	−.2201
60	.32324	.22314	−.0736	−.2679	−.1882
61	.32980	.19162	−.1144	−.2751	−.1504
62	.33210	.15715	−.1523	−.2747	−.1080
63	.33016	.12034	−.1865	−.2669	−.0624
64	.32403	.08181	−.2163	−.2518	−.0151
65	.31383	.04222	−.2411	−.2300	.0323
66	.29971	.00223	−.2605	−.2022	.0783
67	.28189	−.03748	−.2741	−.1690	.1213
68	.26062	−.07627	−.2816	−.1315	.1599
69	.23617	−.11348	−.2829	−.0906	.1929
70	.20888	−.14853	−.2780	−.0476	.2193
71	.17910	−.18082	−.2671	−.0035	.2382
72	.14721	−.20986	−.2504	.0404	.2491
73	.11363	−.23516	−.2283	.0829	.2516
74	.07878	−.25634	−.2014	.1230	.2457
75	.04310	−.27305	−.1702	.1595	.2316
76	.00704	−.28504	−.1355	.1915	.2099
77	−.02896	−.29214	−.0979	.2181	.1813
78	−.06444	−.29424	−.0583	.2387	.1468
79	−.09897	−.29133	−.0176	.2526	.1074
80	−.13212	−.28348	.0233	.2596	.0647
81	−.16348	−.27083	.0636	.2595	.0199
82	−.19267	−.25360	.1024	.2523	−.0254
83	−.21933	−.23211	.1389	.2383	−.0698
84	−.24313	−.20671	.1722	.2177	−.1118
85	−.26378	−.17784	.2017	.1913	−.1499
86	−.28103	−.14598	.2268	.1597	−.1830
87	−.29467	−.11168	.2469	.1237	−.2099
88	−.30454	−.07551	.2615	.0844	−.2298
89	−.31050	−.03807	.2704	.0428	−.2420
90	−.31250	0	.2734	0	−.2461

For larger tables, see "Report of the British Association for the Advancement of Science," 1879, pp. 54–57, Philosophical Magazine, Dec., 1891, "Tafeln der Besselschen, Theta-, Kugel- und anderer Funktionen" by K. Hayashi and "Fünfstellige Funktionentafeln" by K. Hayashi.

SURFACE ZONAL HARMONICS—FIRST DERIVATIVES

$$\frac{d}{d\theta} P_n(\cos\theta)$$

$\theta°$	$\frac{d}{d\theta} P_1$	$\frac{d}{d\theta} P_2$	$\frac{d}{d\theta} P_3$	$\frac{d}{d\theta} P_4$	$\frac{d}{d\theta} P_5$	$\frac{d}{d\theta} P_6$	$\frac{d}{d\theta} P_7$
0	0	0	0	0	0	0	0
1	−0.0175	−0.0523	−0.1047	−0.1744	−0 2615	−0.3659	−0.488
2	−.0349	−.1046	−.2091	−.3480	−.5213	−.7284	−.969
3	−.0523	−.1568	−.3129	−.5201	−.7775	−1.0841	−1.438
4	−.0698	−.2088	−.4160	−.6901	−1.0286	−1.4295	−1.890
5	−.0872	−.2605	−.5180	−.8570	−1.2728	−1.7614	−2.317
6	−.1045	−.3119	−.6186	−1.0197	−1.5085	−2.0768	−2.715
7	−.1219	−.3629	−.7176	−1.1781	−1.7341	−2.3727	−3.080
8	−.1392	−.4135	−.8148	−1.3315	−1.9481	−2.6465	−3.405
9	−.1564	−.4635	−.9099	−1.4789	−2.1492	−2.8954	−3.689
10	−.1736	−.5130	−1.0026	−1.6199	−2.3360	−3.1174	−3.926
11	−.1908	−.5619	−1.0928	−1.7537	−2.5074	−3.3104	−4.116
12	−.2079	−.6101	−1.1801	−1.8799	−2.6621	−3.4729	−4.254
13	−.2250	−.6576	−1.2643	−1.9978	−2.7993	−3.6034	−4.341
14	−.2419	−.7042	−1.3453	−2.1069	−2.9181	−3.7008	−4.376
15	−.2588	−.7500	−1.4229	−2.2069	−3.0178	−3.7646	−4.358
16	−.2756	−.7949	−1.4968	−2.2973	−3.0978	−3.7943	−4.288
17	−.2924	−.8388	−1.5668	−2.3777	−3.1576	−3.7899	−4.169
18	−.3090	−.8817	−1.6328	−2.4478	−3.1970	−3.7518	−4.001
19	−.3256	−.9235	−1.6946	−2.5073	−3.2158	−3.6806	−3.788
20	−.3420	−.9642	−1.7520	−2.5560	−3.2141	−3.5774	−3.534
21	−.3584	−1.0037	−1.8050	−2 5937	−3.1920	−3.4435	−3.241
22	−.3746	−1.0420	−1.8534	−2.6203	−3.1497	−3.2804	−2.915
23	−.3907	−1.0790	−1.8970	−2.6357	−3.0877	−3.0917	−2.561
24	−.4067	−1.1147	−1.9357	−2.6400	−3.0067	−2.8749	−2.183
25	−.4226	−1.1491	−1.9696	−2.6330	−2.9073	−2.6371	−1.787
26	−.4384	−1.1820	−1.9984	−2.6150	−2.7903	−2.3794	−1.378
27	−.4540	−1.2135	−2.0222	−2.5861	−2.6568	−2.1046	−.963
28	−.4695	−1.2436	−2.0408	−2.5464	−2.5077	−1.8156	−.548
29	−.4848	−1.2721	−2.0542	−2.4961	−2.3443	−1.5155	−.136
30	−.5000	−1.2990	−2.0625	−2.4357	−2.1680	−1.2077	.263
31	−.5150	−1.3244	−2.0654	−2.3654	−1.9799	−.8953	.647
32	−.5299	−1.3482	−2.0635	−2.2855	−1.7817	−.5815	1.010
33	−.5446	−1.3703	−2.0562	−2.1966	−1.5748	−.2697	1.347
34	−.5592	−1.3908	−2.0437	−2.0991	−1.3608	.0370	1.654
35	−.5736	−1.4095	−2.0262	−1.9934	−1.1413	.3354	1.927
36	−.5878	−1.4266	−2.0036	−1.8802	−.9179	.6225	2.162
37	−.6018	−1.4419	−1.9761	−1.7600	−.6924	.8955	2.357
38	−.6157	−1.4554	−1.9438	−1.6334	−.4664	1.1516	2.510
39	−.6293	−1.4672	−1.9066	−1.5011	−.2415	1.3885	2.620
40	−.6428	−1.4772	−1.8648	−1.3637	−.0194	1.6038	2.684
41	−.6561	−1.4854	−1.8185	−1.2219	.1983	1.7955	2.705
43	−.6691	−1.4918	−1.7678	−1.0764	.4100	1.9620	2.681
43	−.6820	−1.4963	−1.7129	−.9279	.6142	2.1017	2.614
44	−.6947	−1.4991	−1.6539	−.7772	.8095	2.2136	2.506
45	−.7071	−1.5000	−1.5910	−.6250	.9943	2.2969	2.359
46	−.7193	−1.4991	−1.5244	−.4720	1.1677	2.3510	2.176
47	−.7314	−1.4963	−1.4542	−.3190	1.3282	2.3757	1.961
48	−.7431	−1.4918	−1.3808	−.1668	1.4749	2.3715	1.717
49	−.7547	−1.4854	−1.3042	−.0160	1.6067	2.3382	1.449

SURFACE ZONAL HARMONICS—FIRST DERIVATIVES (Continued)

$$\frac{d}{d\theta} P_n(\cos \theta)$$

$\theta°$	$\frac{d}{d\theta} P_1$	$\frac{d}{d\theta} P_2$	$\frac{d}{d\theta} P_3$	$\frac{d}{d\theta} P_4$	$\frac{d}{d\theta} P_5$	$\frac{d}{d\theta} P_6$	$\frac{d}{d\theta} P_7$
50	−0.7660	−1.4772	−1.2248	0.1327	1.7229	2.2772	1.161
51	−.7771	−1.4672	−1.1427	.2784	1.8225	2.1892	.859
52	−.7880	−1.4554	−1.0581	.4205	1.9053	2.0760	.546
53	−.7986	−1.4419	−.9714	.5584	1.9704	1.9387	.230
54	−.8090	−1.4266	−.8828	.6914	2.0173	1.7797	−.088
55	−.8192	−1.4095	−.7925	.8188	2.0474	1.6009	−.399
56	−.8290	−1.3908	−.7007	.9401	2.0587	1.4046	−.700
57	−.8387	−1.3703	−.6078	1.0546	2.0521	1.1936	−.986
58	−.8480	−1.3482	−.5140	1.1620	2.0281	.9699	−1.252
59	−.8572	−1.3244	−.4196	1.2617	1.9866	.7369	−1.495
60	−.8660	−1.2990	−.3248	1.3532	1.9283	.4973	−1.711
61	−.8746	−1.2721	−.2299	1.4361	1.8538	.2540	−1.896
62	−.8829	−1.2436	−.1351	1.5101	1.7640	.0099	−2.048
63	−.8910	−1.2135	−.0409	1.5748	1.6596	−.2321	−2.165
64	−.8988	−1.1820	.0527	1.6306	1.5420	−.4691	−2.244
65	−.9063	−1.1491	.1454	1.6755	1.4114	−.6983	−2.286
66	−.9135	−1.1147	.2368	1.7111	1.2698	−.9170	−2.290
67	−.9205	−1.0790	.3268	1.7366	1.1187	−1.1226	−2.255
68	−.9272	−1.0420	.4149	1.7520	.9580	−1.3129	−2.183
69	−.9336	−1.0037	.5011	1.7574	.7906	−1.4855	−2.076
70	−.9397	−.9642	.5851	1.7525	.6173	−1.6386	−1.984
71	−.9455	−.9235	.6666	1.7376	.4397	−1.7704	−1.762
72	−.9511	−.8817	.7455	1.7131	.2594	−1.8794	−1.561
73	−.9563	−.8388	.8214	1.6787	.0776	−1.9646	−1.334
74	−.9613	−.7949	.8941	1.6349	−.1037	−2.0248	−1.088
75	−.9659	−.7500	.9636	1.5819	−.2833	−2.0596	−.824
76	−.9703	−.7042	1.0295	1.5200	−.4595	−2.0687	−.548
77	−.9744	−.6576	1.0918	1.4498	−.6309	−2.0520	−.264
78	−.9781	−.6101	1.1501	1.3714	−.7961	−2.0098	.023
79	−.9816	−.5619	1.2044	1.2854	−.9537	−1.9428	.309
80	−.9848	−.5130	1.2545	1.1923	−1.1023	−1.8519	.589
81	−.9877	−.4635	1.3003	1.0296	−1.2407	−1.7382	.858
82	−.9903	−.4135	1.3416	.9870	−1.3679	−1.6032	1.112
83	−.9925	−.3629	1.3783	.8758	−1.4831	−1.4487	1.348
84	−.9945	−.3119	1.4103	.7598	−1.5841	−1.2760	1.559
85	−.9962	−.2605	1.4376	.6396	−1.6715	−1.0881	1.745
86	−.9976	−.2088	1.4599	.5160	−1.7440	−.8868	1.901
87	−.9986	−.1568	1.4774	.3895	−1.8009	−.6747	2.024
88	−.9994	−.1046	1.4899	.2608	−1.8420	−.4544	2.115
89	−.9998	−.0523	1.4975	.1308	−1.8667	−.2286	2.169
90	−1.0000	0	1.5000	0	−1.8750	0	2.187

Note that

$$\frac{d}{dx} P_n(x) = -\frac{1}{\sin \theta} \frac{d}{d\theta} P_n(\cos \theta)$$

where

$$x = \cos \theta$$

BERNOULLI AND EULER NUMBERS—POLYNOMIALS

There are numerous sets of defined numbers and polynomials, among which the more important ones are those classified under the names of Bernoulli and Euler.

The *Bernoulli Polynomials* are generated by the defining condition

$$\frac{te^{tx}}{e^t - 1} = B_0(x) + B_1(x)t + B_2(x)\frac{t^2}{2!} + B_3(x)\frac{t^3}{3!} + \cdots$$

$$B_0(x) = 1, \quad B_1(x) = x - \tfrac{1}{2}, \quad B_2(x) = x^2 - x + \tfrac{1}{6}$$

$$B_3(x) = x^3 - \frac{3}{2}x^2 + \frac{x}{2}, \quad B_4(x) = x^4 - 2x^3 + x^2 - \tfrac{1}{30}, \dots$$

The following useful relations should be noted

$$B_n'(x) = nB_{n-1}(x), \quad \int_a^x B_n(x)\,dx = \frac{1}{n+1}[B_{n+1}(x) - B_{n+1}(a)]$$

The Bernoulli numbers $B_0, B_1, B_2, \dots$, can be obtained by putting $x = 0$ in the respective polynomials. A simpler method is to use the generating function

$$\frac{x}{e^x - 1} = \sum_{n=0}^{\infty} \frac{B_n x^n}{n!}$$

and read the coefficients from the expansion. Here,

$$B_0 = 1, \quad B_1 = -\tfrac{1}{2}, \quad B_2 = \tfrac{1}{6}, \quad B_4 = -\tfrac{1}{30},$$

$$B_6 = \tfrac{1}{42}, \quad B_8 = -\tfrac{1}{30}, \dots B_{2n+1} = 0 \quad (n \geq 1)$$

An important application for the Bernoulli coefficients is in its use involved for the Euler-Maclaurin Sum Formula:

$$\sum_{x=1}^{n-1} f(x) = \int_1^n f(x)\,dx + \left[\sum_{i=1}^{\infty} \frac{B_i}{i!} f^{(i-1)}(x)\right]_{x=1}^{x=n}$$

$$= \left[\int f(x)\,dx - \frac{1}{2}f(x) + \frac{1}{12}f'(x) - \frac{1}{720}f'''(x)\right.$$

$$\left. + \frac{1}{30,240}f^{(V)}(x) - \frac{1}{1,209,600}f^{(VII)}(x)\right]_{x=1}^{x=n}$$

Examples:

$$\sum_{x=1}^{n-1} \sqrt{x} = \sqrt{n}\left\{\frac{2}{3}n - \frac{1}{2} + \frac{1}{24n} - \frac{1}{1,920n^3}\right.$$

$$\left. + \frac{1}{9,216n^5} - \frac{11}{163,840n^7}\right\} - 0.207,886,224,977,355$$

correct to 12 places for $n \geq 10$.

$\log_e(x!) = \log_e \Gamma(x+1)$

$$= \left(x + \frac{1}{2}\right)\log_e x - x + \frac{1}{12x} - \frac{1}{360x^3} + \frac{1}{1,260x^5} - \frac{1}{1,680x^7}$$

$$+ 0.918,938,533,205$$

accurate to 12 places for $x \geq 10$.

$$f(x)\,(\text{digamma function}) = \frac{d\log\Gamma(x)}{dx}$$

$$= 1 + \frac{1}{2} + \frac{1}{3} + \cdots + \frac{1}{x-1} - \gamma$$

(Euler Constant) for x integer.

By Euler-Maclaurin

$$f(x) = \log_e x - \frac{1}{2x} - \frac{1}{12x^2} + \frac{1}{120x^4} - \frac{1}{252x^6} + \frac{1}{240x^8} - \frac{5}{660x^{10}} + \frac{691}{32{,}760x^{12}}$$

correct to 12 places for $x \geq 10$.

The Euler numbers together with their respective polynomials can be generated from

$$\frac{2e^{tx}}{e^t + 1} = \sum_{i=0}^{\infty} E_i(x)\frac{t^i}{i!}$$

and the relation

$$x^n = \frac{1}{2}\left[E_n(x+1) + E_n(x)\right]$$

The Euler polynomials are

$$E_0(x) = 1, \quad E_1(x) = x - \frac{1}{2}, \quad E_2(x) = x^2 - x$$

$$E_3(x) = x^3 - \frac{3}{2}x^2 + \frac{1}{4}, \quad E_4(x) = x^4 - 2x^3 + x$$

$$E_5(x) = x^5 - \frac{5}{2}x^4 + \frac{5}{2}x^2 - \frac{1}{2}$$

Tables which follow record the first fifteen polynomials of $B_k(x)$ and $E_k(x)$. The first sixty Bernoulli and Euler numbers are given in a separate table. The value of $x^n/n!$ is also important and this is given in a succeeding table for values of x from 1 to 9 and n from 1 to 50.

COEFFICIENTS b_k OF THE BERNOULLI POLYNOMIALS $B_n(x) = \sum_{k=0}^{n} b_k x^k$

$n\backslash k$	0	1	2	3	4	5	6	7	8	9	10	11	12	13	14	15
0	1															
1	$-\frac{1}{2}$	1														
2	$\frac{1}{6}$	-1	1													
3	0	$\frac{1}{2}$	$-\frac{3}{2}$	1												
4	$-\frac{1}{30}$	0	1	-2	1											
5	0	$-\frac{1}{6}$	0	$\frac{5}{3}$	$-\frac{5}{2}$	1										
6	$\frac{1}{42}$	0	$-\frac{1}{2}$	0	$\frac{5}{2}$	-3	1									
7	0	$\frac{1}{6}$	0	$-\frac{7}{6}$	0	$\frac{7}{2}$	$-\frac{7}{2}$	1								
8	$-\frac{1}{30}$	0	$\frac{2}{3}$	0	$-\frac{7}{3}$	0	$\frac{14}{3}$	-4	1							
9	0	$-\frac{3}{10}$	0	2	0	$-\frac{21}{5}$	0	6	$-\frac{9}{2}$	1						
10	$\frac{5}{66}$	0	$-\frac{3}{2}$	0	5	0	-7	0	$\frac{15}{2}$	-5	1					
11	0	$\frac{5}{6}$	0	$-\frac{11}{2}$	0	11	0	-11	0	$\frac{55}{6}$	$-\frac{11}{2}$	1				
12	$-\frac{691}{2730}$	0	5	0	$-\frac{33}{2}$	0	22	0	$-\frac{33}{2}$	0	11	-6	1			
13	0	$-\frac{691}{210}$	0	$\frac{65}{3}$	0	$-\frac{429}{10}$	0	$\frac{286}{7}$	0	$-\frac{143}{6}$	0	13	$-\frac{13}{2}$	1		
14	$\frac{7}{6}$	0	$-\frac{691}{30}$	0	$\frac{455}{6}$	0	$-\frac{1001}{10}$	0	$\frac{143}{2}$	0	$-\frac{1001}{30}$	0	$\frac{91}{6}$	-7	1	
15	0	$\frac{35}{2}$	0	$-\frac{691}{6}$	0	$\frac{455}{2}$	0	$-\frac{429}{2}$	0	$\frac{715}{6}$	0	$-\frac{91}{2}$	0	$\frac{35}{2}$	$-\frac{15}{2}$	1

COEFFICIENTS e_k OF THE EULER POLYNOMIALS $E_n(x) = \sum_{k=0}^{n} e_k x^k$

$n\backslash k$	0	1	2	3	4	5	6	7	8	9	10	11	12	13	14	15
0	1															
1	$-\frac{1}{2}$	1														
2	0	-1	1													
3	$\frac{1}{4}$	0	$-\frac{3}{2}$	1												
4	0	1	0	-2	1											
5	$-\frac{1}{2}$	0	$\frac{5}{2}$	0	$-\frac{5}{2}$	1										
6	0	-3	0	5	0	-3	1									
7	$\frac{17}{8}$	0	$-\frac{21}{2}$	0	$\frac{35}{4}$	0	$-\frac{7}{2}$	1								
8	0	17	0	-28	0	14	0	-4	1							
9	$-\frac{31}{2}$	0	$\frac{153}{2}$	0	-63	0	21	0	$-\frac{9}{2}$	1						
10	0	-155	0	255	0	-126	0	30	0	-5	1					
11	$\frac{691}{4}$	0	$-\frac{1705}{2}$	0	$\frac{2805}{4}$	0	-231	0	$\frac{165}{4}$	0	$-\frac{11}{2}$	1				
12	0	2073	0	-3410	0	1683	0	-396	0	55	0	-6	1			
13	$-\frac{5461}{2}$	0	$\frac{26949}{2}$	0	$-\frac{22165}{2}$	0	$\frac{7293}{2}$	0	$-\frac{1287}{2}$	0	$\frac{143}{2}$	0	$-\frac{13}{2}$	1		
14	0	-38227	0	62881	0	-31031	0	7293	0	-1001	0	91	0	-7	1	
15	$\frac{929569}{16}$	0	$-\frac{573405}{2}$	0	$\frac{943215}{4}$	0	$-\frac{155155}{2}$	0	$\frac{109395}{8}$	0	$-\frac{3003}{2}$	0	$\frac{455}{4}$	0	$-\frac{15}{2}$	1

BERNOULLI NUMBERS
$$B_n = N/D$$

n	N	D	B_n
0	1	1	(0) 1.0000 00000
1	− 1	2	(−1) − 5.0000 00000*
2	1	6	(−1) 1.6666 66667
4	− 1	30	(−2) − 3.3333 33333
6	1	42	(−2) 2.3809 52381
8	− 1	30	(−2) − 3.3333 33333
10	5	66	(−2) 7.5757 57576
12	− 691	2730	(−1) − 2.5311 35531
14	7	6	(0) 1.1666 66667
16	− 3617	510	(0) − 7.0921 56863
18	43867	798	(1) 5.4971 17794
20	− 1 74611	330	(2) − 5.2912 42424
22	8 54513	138	(3) 6.1921 23188
24	− 2363 64091	2730	(4) − 8.6580 25311
26	85 53103	6	(6) 1.4255 17167
28	− 2 37494 61029	870	(7) − 2.7298 23107
30	861 58412 76005	14322	(8) 6.0158 08739
32	− 770 93210 41217	510	(10) − 1.5116 31577
34	257 76878 58367	6	(11) 4.2961 46431
36	− 26315 27155 30534 77373	19 19190	(13) − 1.3711 65521
38	2 92999 39138 41559	6	(14) 4.8833 23190
40	− 2 61082 71849 64491 22051	13530	(16) − 1.9296 57934
42	15 20097 64391 80708 02691	1806	(17) 8.4169 30476
44	− 278 33269 57930 10242 35023	690	(19) − 4.0338 07185
46	5964 51111 59391 21632 77961	282	(21) 2.1150 74864
48	− 560 94033 68997 81768 62491 27547	46410	(23) − 1.2086 62652
50	49 50572 05241 07964 82124 77525	66	(24) 7.5008 66746
52	− 80116 57181 35489 95734 79249 91853	1590	(26) − 5.0387 78101
54	29 14996 36348 84862 42141 81238 12691	798	(28) 3.6528 77648
56	− 2479 39292 93132 26753 68541 57396 63229	870	(30) − 2.8498 76930
58	84483 61334 88800 41862 04677 59940 36021	354	(32) 2.3865 42750
60	− 121 52331 40483 75557 20403 04994 07982 02460 41491	567 86730	(34) − 2.1399 94926

*The floating decimal point notation is used here. For example for $n = 1$, $B_1 = -\frac{1}{2} = -.500000 = (-5.00000)(10^{-1}) = (-1) - 5.0000,0000$.

EULER NUMBERS

n	En
0	1
2	−1
4	5
6	−61
8	1385
10	−50521
12	27 02765
14	−1993 60981
16	1 93915 12145
18	−240 48796 75441
20	37037 11882 37525
22	−69 34887 43931 37901
24	15514 53416 35570 86905
26	−40 87072 50929 31238 92361
28	12522 59641 40362 98654 68285
30	−44 15438 93249 02310 45536 82821
32	17751 93915 79539 28943 66647 89665
34	−80 72329 92358 87898 06216 82474 53281
36	41222 06033 95177 02122 34707 96712 59045
38	−234 89580 52704 31082 52017 82857 61989 47741
40	1 48511 50718 11498 00178 77156 78140 58266 84425
42	−1036 46227 33519 61211 93979 57304 74518 59763 10201
44	7 94757 94225 97592 70360 80405 10088 07061 95192 73805
46	−6667 53751 66855 44977 43502 84747 73748 19752 41076 84661
48	60 96278 64556 85421 58691 68574 28768 43153 97653 90444 35185
50	−60532 85248 18862 18963 14383 78511 16490 88103 49822 51468 15121
52	650 61624 86684 60884 77158 70634 08082 29834 83644 23676 53855 76565
54	−7 54665 99390 08739 09806 14325 65889 73674 42122 40024 71169 98586 45581
56	9420 32189 64202 41204 20228 62376 90583 22720 93888 52599 64600 93949 05945
58	−126 22019 25180 62187 19903 40923 72874 89255 48234 10611 91825 59406 99649 20041
60	181089 11496 57923 04965 45807 74165 21586 88733 48734 92363 14106 00809 54542 31325

SPECIAL FUNCTIONS

BERNOULLI AND EULER POLYNOMIALS, REIMANN ZETA FUNCTION

$$x^n/n!$$

$n\backslash x$	2		3		4		5	
1	(0) 2.0000	00000	(0) 3.0000	00000	(0) 4.0000	00000	(0) 5.0000	00000
2	(0) 2.0000	00000	(0) 4.5000	00000	(0) 8.0000	00000	(1) 1.2500	00000
3	(0) 1.3333	33333	(0) 4.5000	00000	(1) 1.0666	66667	(1) 2.0833	33333
4	(− 1) 6.6666	66667	(0) 3.3750	00000	(1) 1.0666	66667	(1) 2.6041	66667
5	(− 1) 2.6666	66667	(0) 2.0250	00000	(0) 8.5333	33333	(1) 2.6041	66667
6	(− 2) 8.8888	88889	(0) 1.0125	00000	(0) 5.6888	88889	(1) 2.1701	38889
7	(− 2) 2.5396	82540	(− 1) 4.3392	85714	(0) 3.2507	93651	(1) 1.5500	99206
8	(− 3) 6.3492	06349	(− 1) 1.6272	32143	(0) 1.6253	96825	(0) 9.6881	20040
9	(− 3) 1.4109	34744	(− 2) 5.4241	07143	(− 1) 7.2239	85891	(0) 5.3822	88911
10	(− 4) 2.8218	69489	(− 2) 1.6272	32144	(− 1) 2.8895	94356	(0) 2.6911	44455
11	(− 5) 5.1306	71797	(− 3) 4.4379	05844	(− 1) 1.0507	61584	(0) 1.2232	47480
12	(− 6) 8.5511	19662	(− 3) 1.1094	76461	(− 2) 3.5025	38614	(− 1) 5.0968	64499
13	(− 6) 1.3155	56871	(− 4) 2.5603	30295	(− 2) 1.0777	04189	(− 1) 1.9603	32500
14	(− 7) 1.8793	66959	(− 5) 5.4864	22060	(− 3) 3.0791	54825	(− 2) 7.0011	87499
15	(− 8) 2.5058	22612	(− 5) 1.0972	84412	(− 4) 8.2110	79534	(− 2) 2.3337	29166
16	(− 9) 3.1322	78264	(− 6) 2.0574	08272	(− 4) 2.0527	69883	(− 3) 7.2929	03644
17	(−10) 3.6850	33252	(− 7) 3.6307	20481	(− 5) 4.8300	46785	(− 3) 2.1449	71660
18	(−11) 4.0944	81391	(− 8) 6.0512	00801	(− 5) 1.0733	43730	(− 4) 5.9582	54611
19	(−12) 4.3099	80412	(− 9) 9.5545	27582	(− 6) 2.2596	71011	(− 4) 1.5679	61740
20	(−13) 4.3099	80413	(− 9) 1.4331	79137	(− 7) 4.5193	42021	(− 5) 3.9199	04350
21	(−14) 4.1047	43250	(−10) 2.0473	98768	(− 8) 8.6082	70516	(− 6) 9.3331	05595
22	(−15) 3.7315	84772	(−11) 2.7919	07410	(− 8) 1.5651	40093	(− 6) 2.1211	60362
23	(−16) 3.2448	56324	(−12) 3.6416	18361	(− 9) 2.7219	82772	(− 7) 4.6112	18179
24	(−17) 2.7040	46937	(−13) 4.5520	22952	(−10) 4.5366	37953	(− 8) 9.6067	04540
25	(−18) 2.1632	37550	(−14) 5.4624	27543	(−11) 7.2586	20726	(− 8) 1.9213	40908
26	(−19) 1.6640	28884	(−15) 6.3028	01010	(−11) 1.1167	10881	(− 9) 3.6948	86362
27	(−20) 1.2326	13988	(−16) 7.0031	12233	(−12) 1.6543	86490	(−10) 6.8423	82151
28	(−22) 8.8043	85630	(−17) 7.5033	34535	(−13) 2.3634	09271	(−10) 1.2218	53956
29	(−23) 6.0719	90089	(−18) 7.7620	70209	(−14) 3.2598	74857	(−11) 2.1066	44751
30	(−24) 4.0479	93393	(−19) 7.7620	70209	(−15) 4.3464	99810	(−12) 3.5110	74585
31	(−25) 2.6116	08641	(−20) 7.5116	80847	(−16) 5.6083	86851	(−13) 5.6630	23524
32	(−26) 1.6322	55401	(−21) 7.0422	00795	(−17) 7.0104	83564	(−14) 8.8484	74257
33	(−28) 9.8924	56972	(−22) 6.4020	00722	(−18) 8.4975	55834	(−14) 1.3406	77918
34	(−29) 5.8190	92337	(−23) 5.6488	24167	(−19) 9.9971	24511	(−15) 1.9715	85173
35	(−30) 3.3251	95620	(−24) 4.8418	49286	(−19) 1.1425	28515	(−16) 2.8165	50246
36	(−31) 1.8473	30900	(−25) 4.0348	74405	(−20) 1.2694	76128	(−17) 3.9118	75343
37	(−33) 9.9855	72436	(−26) 3.2715	19788	(−21) 1.3724	06625	(−18) 5.2863	18032
38	(−34) 5.2555	64439	(−27) 2.5827	78779	(−22) 1.4446	38552	(−19) 6.9556	81619
39	(−35) 2.6951	61251	(−28) 1.9867	52908	(−23) 1.4816	80567	(−20) 8.9175	40539
40	(−36) 1.3475	80626	(−29) 1.4900	64681	(−24) 1.4816	80567	(−20) 1.1146	92567
41	(−38) 6.5735	64028	(−30) 1.0902	91230	(−25) 1.4455	42017	(−21) 1.3593	81180
42	(−39) 3.1302	68584	(−32) 7.7877	94498	(−26) 1.3767	06682	(−22) 1.6183	10928
43	(−40) 1.4559	38876	(−33) 5.4333	44999	(−27) 1.2806	57379	(−23) 1.8817	56893
44	(−42) 6.6179	03983	(−34) 3.7045	53408	(−28) 1.1642	33981	(−24) 2.1383	60106
45	(−43) 2.9412	90659	(−35) 2.4697	02271	(−29) 1.0348	74650	(−25) 2.3759	55673
46	(−44) 1.2788	22026	(−36) 1.6106	75395	(−31) 8.9989	09998	(−26) 2.5825	60514
47	(−46) 5.4417	95855	(−37) 1.0280	90677	(−32) 7.6586	46807	(−27) 2.7474	04803
48	(−47) 2.2674	14940	(−39) 6.4255	66736	(−33) 6.3822	05674	(−28) 2.8618	80003
49	(−49) 9.2547	54855	(−40) 3.9340	20450	(−34) 5.2099	63815	(−29) 2.9202	85717
50	(−50) 3.7019	10942	(−41) 2.3604	12270	(−35) 4.1679	71052	(−30) 2.9202	85717

BERNOULLI AND EULER POLYNOMIALS, REIMANN ZETA FUNCTION

$$x^n/n!$$

$n \backslash x$	6		7		8		9	
1	(0) 6.0000	00000	(0) 7.0000	00000	(0) 8.0000	00000	(0) 9.0000	00000
2*	(1) 1.8000	00000	(1) 2.4500	00000	(1) 3.2000	00000	(1) 4.0500	00000
3	(1) 3.6000	00000	(1) 5.7166	66667	(1) 8.5333	33333	(2) 1.2150	00000
4	(1) 5.4000	00000	(2) 1.0004	16667	(2) 1.7066	66667	(2) 2.7337	50000
5	(1) 6.4800	00000	(2) 1.4005	83333	(2) 2.7306	66667	(2) 4.9207	50000
6	(1) 6.4800	00000	(2) 1.6340	13889	(2) 3.6408	88889	(2) 7.3811	25000
7	(1) 5.5542	85714	(2) 1.6340	13889	(2) 4.1610	15873	(2) 9.4900	17857
8	(1) 4.1657	14286	(2) 1.4297	62153	(2) 4.1610	15873	(3) 1.0676	27009
9	(1) 2.7771	42857	(2) 1.1120	37230	(2) 3.6986	80776	(3) 1.0676	27009
10	(1) 1.6662	85714	(1) 7.7842	60610	(2) 2.9589	44621	(2) 9.6086	43080
11	(0) 9.0888	31169	(1) 4.9536	20388	(2) 2.1519	59724	(2) 7.8616	17066
12	(0) 4.5444	15584	(1) 2.8896	11893	(2) 1.4346	39816	(2) 5.8962	12799
13	(0) 2.0974	22577	(1) 1.5559	44865	(1) 8.8285	52715	(2) 4.0819	93476
14	(− 1) 8.9889	53903	(0) 7.7797	24327	(1) 5.0448	87266	(2) 2.6241	38663
15	(− 1) 3.5955	81561	(0) 3.6305	38019	(1) 2.6906	06542	(2) 1.5744	83198
16	(− 1) 1.3483	43085	(0) 1.5883	60383	(1) 1.3453	03271	(1) 8.8564	67988
17	(− 2) 4.7588	57949	(− 1) 6.5403	07461	(0) 6.3308	38921	(1) 4.6887	18347
18	(− 2) 1.5862	85983	(− 1) 2.5434	52902	(0) 2.8137	06187	(1) 2.3443	59173
19	(− 3) 5.0093	24157	(− 2) 9.3706	15954	(0) 1.1847	18395	(1) 1.1104	85924
20	(− 3) 1.5027	97247	(− 2) 3.2797	15584	(− 1) 4.7388	73579	(0) 4.9971	86660
21	(− 4) 4.2937	06421	(− 2) 1.0932	38528	(− 1) 1.8052	85173	(0) 2.1416	51426
22	(− 4) 1.1710	10841	(− 3) 3.4784	86224	(− 2) 6.5646	73356	(− 1) 8.7613	01286
23	(− 5) 3.0548	10892	(− 3) 1.0586	69721	(− 2) 2.2833	64645	(− 1) 3.4283	35286
24	(− 6) 7.6370	27230	(− 4) 3.0877	86685	(− 3) 7.6112	15485	(− 1) 1.2856	25732
25	(− 6) 1.8328	86535	(− 5) 8.6458	02719	(− 3) 2.4355	88956	(− 2) 4.6282	52637
26	(− 7) 4.2297	38158	(− 5) 2.3277	16117	(− 4) 7.4941	19863	(− 2) 1.6020	87451
27	(− 8) 9.3994	18129	(− 6) 6.0348	19562	(− 4) 2.2204	79959	(− 3) 5.3402	91503
28	(− 8) 2.0141	61028	(− 6) 1.5087	04890	(− 5) 6.3442	28454	(− 3) 1.7165	22269
29	(− 9) 4.1672	29712	(− 7) 3.6417	01460	(− 5) 1.7501	31987	(− 4) 5.3271	38075
30	(−10) 8.3344	59424	(− 8) 8.4973	03406	(− 6) 4.6670	18634	(− 4) 1.5981	41423
31	(−10) 1.6131	21179	(− 8) 1.9187	45930	(− 6) 1.2043	91905	(− 5) 4.6397	65421
32	(−11) 3.0246	02211	(− 9) 4.1972	56723	(− 7) 3.0109	79764	(− 5) 1.3049	34025
33	(−12) 5.4992	76746	(−10) 8.9032	71836	(− 8) 7.2993	44881	(− 6) 3.5589	10976
34	(−13) 9.7046	06022	(−10) 1.8330	26555	(− 8) 1.7174	92913	(− 7) 9.4206	46701
35	(−13) 1.6636	46746	(−11) 3.6660	53108	(− 9) 3.9256	98086	(− 7) 2.4224	52008
36	(−14) 2.7727	44578	(−12) 7.1284	36600	(−10) 8.7237	73527	(− 8) 6.0561	30022
37	(−15) 4.4963	42559	(−12) 1.3486	23141	(−10) 1.8862	21303	(− 8) 1.4731	12708
38	(−16) 7.0994	88250	(−13) 2.4843	05785	(−11) 3.9709	92217	(− 9) 3.4889	51151
39	(−16) 1.0922	28962	(−14) 4.4590	10384	(−12) 8.1456	25061	(−10) 8.0514	25733
40	(−17) 1.6383	43443	(−15) 7.8032	68172	(−12) 1.6291	25012	(−10) 1.8115	70790
41	(−18) 2.3975	75770	(−15) 1.3322	65298	(−13) 3.1787	80512	(−11) 3.9766	18807
42	(−19) 3.4251	08241	(−16) 2.2204	42162	(−14) 6.0548	20021	(−12) 8.5213	26014
43	(−20) 4.7792	20803	(−17) 3.6146	73288	(−14) 1.1264	78144	(−12) 1.7835	33352
44	(−21) 6.5171	19276	(−18) 5.7506	16594	(−15) 2.0481	42079	(−13) 3.6481	36401
45	(−22) 8.6894	92369	(−19) 8.9454	03592	(−16) 3.6411	41473	(−14) 7.2962	72804
46	(−22) 1.1334	12048	(−19) 1.3612	57068	(−17) 6.3324	19955	(−14) 1.4275	31635
47	(−23) 1.4469	08998	(−20) 2.0274	04144	(−17) 1.0778	58716	(−15) 2.7335	71217
48	(−24) 1.8086	36247	(−21) 2.9566	31045	(−18) 1.7964	31193	(−16) 5.1254	46033
49	(−25) 2.2146	56629	(−22) 4.2237	58634	(−19) 2.9329	48887	(−17) 9.4140	84548
50	(−26) 2.6575	87955	(−23) 5.9132	62088	(−20) 4.6927	18219	(−17) 1 6945	35219

*The floating decimal point notation is used here. For example (1) 1.8000,000 = (1.8000,000) 10.

STIRLING NUMBERS

Stirling numbers

The Stirling numbers are used for reducing factorials such as $x^{(n)}$ to polynomials in x and vice versa.

Stirling numbers of the first kind

The factorial polynomial $x^{(n)}$ is defined and represented by

$$x^{(n)} = x(x - 1)(x - 2)\cdots(x - n + 1)$$

where $x^{(0)}$ is 1 by definition.

If n is a non-negative integer, then

$$x^{(n)} = s_{n1}x + s_{n2}x^2 + \cdots + s_{nn}x^n.$$

Here the numbers $s_{n1}, s_{n2}, s_{n3}, \ldots$, are Stirling numbers of the first kind. A table listing these numbers with an example using same follows.

STIRLING NUMBERS OF THE FIRST KIND

n	s_{n1}	s_{n2}	s_{n3}	s_{n4}	s_{n5}	s_{n6}	s_{n7}	s_{n8}
1	1	0	0	0	0	0	0	0
2	−1	1	0	0	0	0	0	0
3	2	−3	1	0	0	0	0	0
4	−6	11	−6	1	0	0	0	0
5	24	−50	35	−10	1	0	0	0
6	−120	274	−225	85	−15	1	0	0
7	720	−1 764	1 624	−735	175	−21	1	0
8	−5 040	13 068	−13 132	6 769	−1 960	322	−28	1

The table may be continued by using the recurrence formula

$$s_{ni} = s_{n-1,i-1} - (n - 1)s_{n-1,i}, \quad i = 1, 2, \ldots, n$$

where $s_{n0} = 0$ for all n.

Example

Express $3x^{(3)} + 2x^{(1)}$ using Stirling's numbers of the first kind

$$3x^{(3)} = 3(2x - 3x^2 + x^3)$$
$$= 6x - 9x^2 + 3x^3$$
$$2x^{(1)} = 2x$$
$$\therefore 3x^{(3)} + 2x^{(1)} = 8x - 9x^2 + 3x^3$$

This may be verified by carrying out the indicated operations as follows

$$3x^{(3)} + 2x^{(1)} = 3(x)(x - 1)(x - 2) + 2x$$
$$= 3x^3 - 9x^2 + 6x + 2x$$
$$= 8x - 9x^2 + 3x^3$$

Stirling numbers of the second kind

For every non-negative integer n the function defined by x^n can be expressed as a linear combination of factorial powers of x not higher than the n'th. In other words

$$x^n = t_{n1}x^{(1)} + t_{n2}x^{(2)} + \cdots + t_{nn}x^{(n)}.$$

The numbers $t_{n1}, t_{n2}, \ldots, t_{nn}$ are called Stirling's numbers of the second kind.

A table listing these numbers with an example using same follows.

STIRLING NUMBERS OF THE SECOND KIND

n	t_{n1}	t_{n2}	t_{n3}	t_{n4}	t_{n5}	t_{n6}	t_{n7}	t_{n8}
1	1	0	0	0	0	0	0	0
2	1	1	0	0	0	0	0	0
3	1	3	1	0	0	0	0	0
4	1	7	6	1	0	0	0	0
5	1	15	25	10	1	0	0	0
6	1	31	90	65	15	1	0	0
7	1	63	301	350	140	21	1	0
8	1	127	966	1 701	1 050	266	28	1

This table may be continued by using the recurrence formula

$$t_{ni} = i t_{n-1,i} + t_{n-1,i-1}, \quad i = 1, 2, \dots, n$$

where $t_{n0} = 0$ for all n.

Example

Express $2x^3 - 3x^2 + x + 2$ by use of factorial powers

$$2x^3 = 2[x^{(1)} + 3x^{(2)} + x^{(3)}] = 2x^{(1)} + 6x^{(2)} + 2x^{(3)}$$
$$-3x^2 = -3[x^{(1)} + x^{(2)}] \qquad = -3x^{(1)} - 3x^{(2)}$$
$$x = x^{(1)} \qquad\qquad = x^{(1)}$$
$$+2 = +2x^{(0)} \qquad\qquad = 2x^{(0)}$$

$$\therefore 2x^3 - 3x^2 + x + 2 = 2 + 3x^{(2)} + 2x^{(3)}$$

FOURIER SERIES

(Also see Index for Cosine and Sine Transforms)

1. If $f(x)$ is a bounded periodic function of period $2L$ (i.e. $f(x + 2L) = f(x)$), and satisfies the *Dirichlet conditions*:

  a) In any period $f(x)$ is continuous, except possibly for a finite number of jump discontinuities

  b) In any period $f(x)$ has only a finite number of maxima and minima.

Then $f(x)$ may be represented by the *Fourier series*

$$\frac{a_0}{2} + \sum_{n=1}^{\infty} \left(a_n \cos \frac{n\pi x}{L} + b_n \sin \frac{n\pi x}{L} \right),$$

where a_n and b_n are as determined below. This series will converge to $f(x)$ at every point where $f(x)$ is continuous, and to

$$\frac{f(x^+) + f(x^-)}{2}$$

(i.e. the average of the left-hand and right-hand limits) at every point where $f(x)$ has a jump discontinuity.

$$a_n = \frac{1}{L} \int_{-L}^{L} f(x) \cos \frac{n\pi x}{L} \, dx, \quad n = 0, 1, 2, 3, \ldots;$$

$$b_n = \frac{1}{L} \int_{-L}^{L} f(x) \sin \frac{n\pi x}{L} \, dx, \quad n = 1, 2, 3, \ldots$$

We may also write

$$a_n = \frac{1}{L} \int_{\alpha}^{\alpha+2L} f(x) \cos \frac{n\pi x}{L} \, dx \text{ and } b_n = \frac{1}{L} \int_{\alpha}^{\alpha+2L} f(x) \sin \frac{n\pi x}{L} \, dx,$$

where α is any real number. Thus if $\alpha = 0$,

$$a_n = \frac{1}{L} \int_{0}^{2L} f(x) \cos \frac{n\pi x}{L} \, dx, \quad n = 0, 1, 2, 3, \ldots;$$

$$b_n = \frac{1}{L} \int_{0}^{2L} f(x) \sin \frac{n\pi x}{L} \, dx, \quad n = 1, 2, 3, \ldots$$

2. If in addition to the above restrictions, $f(x)$ is even (i.e. $f(-x) = f(x)$), the Fourier series reduces to

$$\frac{a_0}{2} + \sum_{n=1}^{\infty} a_n \cos \frac{n\pi x}{L}.$$

That is, $b_n = 0$. In this case, a simpler formula for a_n is

$$a_n = \frac{2}{L} \int_0^L f(x) \cos \frac{n\pi x}{L} \, dx, \quad n = 0, 1, 2, 3, \ldots$$

3. If in addition to the restrictions in (1), $f(x)$ is an odd function (i.e. $f(-x) = -f(x)$), then the Fourier series reduces to

$$\sum_{n=1}^{\infty} b_n \sin \frac{n\pi x}{L}.$$

That is, $a_n = 0$. In this case, a simpler formula for the b_n is

$$b_n = \frac{2}{L} \int_0^L f(x) \sin \frac{n\pi x}{L} \, dx, \quad n = 1, 2, 3, \ldots$$

4. If in addition to the restrictions in (2) above, $f(x) = -f(L - x)$, then a_n will be 0 for all even values of n, including $n = 0$. Thus in this case, the expansion reduces to

$$\sum_{m=1}^{\infty} a_{2m-1} \cos \frac{(2m - 1)\pi x}{L}.$$

5. If in addition to the restrictions in (3) above, $f(x) = f(L - x)$, then b_n will be 0 for all even values of n. Thus in this case, the expansion reduces to

$$\sum_{m=1}^{\infty} b_{2m-1} \sin \frac{(2m - 1)\pi x}{L}.$$

(The series in (4) and (5) are known as *odd-harmonic series*, since only the odd harmonics appear. Similar rules may be stated for even-harmonic series, but when a series appears in the even-harmonic form, it means that $2L$ has not been taken as the smallest period of $f(x)$. Since any integral multiple of a period is also a period, series obtained in this way will also work, but in general computation is simplified if $2L$ is taken to be the smallest period.)

6. If we write the Euler definitions for $\cos \theta$ and $\sin \theta$, we obtain the complex form of the Fourier Series known either as the "Complex Fourier Series" or the "Exponential Fourier Series" of $f(x)$. It is represented as

$$f(x) = \frac{1}{2} \sum_{n=-\infty}^{n=+\infty} c_n e^{i\omega_n x},$$

where

$$c_n = \frac{1}{L} \int_{-L}^{L} f(x) e^{-i\omega_n x} dx, \quad n = 0, \pm 1, \pm 2, \pm 3, \ldots$$

with $\omega_n = \frac{n\pi}{L}$, $n = 0, \pm 1, \pm 2, \ldots$

The set of coefficients $\{c_n\}$ is often referred to as the Fourier spectrum.

7. If both sine and cosine terms are present and if $f(x)$ is of period $2L$ and expandable by a Fourier series, it can be represented as

$$f(x) = \frac{a_0}{2} + \sum_{n=1}^{\infty} c_n \cos\left(\frac{n\pi x}{L} + \phi_n\right),$$

where $a_n = c_n \cos\phi_n,$ $b_n = c_n \cos\phi_n, \quad c_n = \sqrt{a_n^2 + b_n^2}, \quad \phi_n = \arctan\left(\frac{a_n}{b_n}\right)$

It can also be represented as

$$f(x) = \frac{a_0}{2} + \sum_{n=1}^{\infty} c_n \sin\left(\frac{n\pi x}{L} + \phi_n\right),$$

where $a_n = c_n \sin\phi_n,$ $b_n = -c_n \sin\phi_n, \quad c_n = \sqrt{a_n^2 + b_n^2}, \quad \phi_n = \arctan\left(-\frac{b_n}{a_n}\right)$

where the quadrant of ϕ_n is chosen so as to make the formulas for $a_n, b_n,$ and c_n hold.

8. The following table of trigonometric identities should be helpful for developing Fourier Series.

	n **	n even	n odd	$n/2$ odd	$n/2$ even
$\sin n\pi$	0	0	0	0	0
$\cos n\pi$	$(-1)^n$	$+1$	-1	$+1$	$+1$
$\sin \frac{n\pi}{2}$ *		0	$(-1)^{(n-1)/2}$	0	0
$\cos \frac{n\pi}{2}$ *		$(-1)^{n/2}$	0	-1	$+1$
$\sin \frac{n\pi}{4}$			$\frac{\sqrt{2}}{2}(-1)^{(n^2+4n+11)/8}$	$(-1)^{(n-2)/4}$	0

*A useful formula for $\sin \frac{n\pi}{2}$ and $\cos \frac{n\pi}{2}$ is given by

$$\sin \frac{n\pi}{2} = \frac{(i)^{n+1}}{2}[(-1)^n - 1] \text{ and } \cos \frac{n\pi}{2} = \frac{(i)^n}{2}[(-1)^n + 1], \text{ where } i^2 = -1.$$

** n any integer.

AUXILIARY FORMULAS FOR FOURIER SERIES

$$1 = \frac{4}{\pi}\left[\sin\frac{\pi x}{k} + \frac{1}{3}\sin\frac{3\pi x}{k} + \frac{1}{5}\sin\frac{5\pi x}{k} + \cdots\right] \qquad [0 < x < k]$$

$$x = \frac{2k}{\pi}\left[\sin\frac{\pi x}{k} - \frac{1}{2}\sin\frac{2\pi x}{k} + \frac{1}{3}\sin\frac{3\pi x}{k} - \cdots\right] \qquad [-k < x < k]$$

$$x = \frac{k}{2} - \frac{4k}{\pi^2}\left[\cos\frac{\pi x}{k} + \frac{1}{3^2}\cos\frac{3\pi x}{k} + \frac{1}{5^2}\cos\frac{5\pi x}{k} + \cdots\right] \qquad [0 < x < k]$$

$$x^2 = \frac{2k^2}{\pi^3}\left[\left(\frac{\pi^2}{1} - \frac{4}{1}\right)\sin\frac{\pi x}{k} - \frac{\pi^2}{2}\sin\frac{2\pi x}{k} + \left(\frac{\pi^2}{3} - \frac{4}{3^3}\right)\sin\frac{3\pi x}{k}\right.$$
$$\left. - \frac{\pi^2}{4}\sin\frac{4\pi x}{k} + \left(\frac{\pi^2}{5} - \frac{4}{5^3}\right)\sin\frac{5\pi x}{k} + \cdots\right] \qquad [0 < x < k]$$

$$x^2 = \frac{k^2}{3} - \frac{4k^2}{\pi^2}\left[\cos\frac{\pi x}{k} - \frac{1}{2^2}\cos\frac{2\pi x}{k} + \frac{1}{3^2}\cos\frac{3\pi x}{k} - \frac{1}{4^2}\cos\frac{4\pi x}{k} + \cdots\right]$$
$$[-k < x < k]$$

$$1 - \frac{1}{3} + \frac{1}{5} - \frac{1}{7} + \cdots = \frac{\pi}{4}$$

$$1 + \frac{1}{2^2} + \frac{1}{3^2} + \frac{1}{4^2} + \cdots = \frac{\pi^2}{6}$$

$$1 - \frac{1}{2^2} + \frac{1}{3^2} - \frac{1}{4^2} + \cdots = \frac{\pi^2}{12}$$

$$1 + \frac{1}{3^2} + \frac{1}{5^2} + \frac{1}{7^2} + \cdots = \frac{\pi^2}{8}$$

$$\frac{1}{2^2} + \frac{1}{4^2} + \frac{1}{6^2} + \frac{1}{8^2} + \cdots = \frac{\pi^2}{24}$$

FOURIER EXPANSIONS FOR BASIC PERIODIC FUNCTIONS

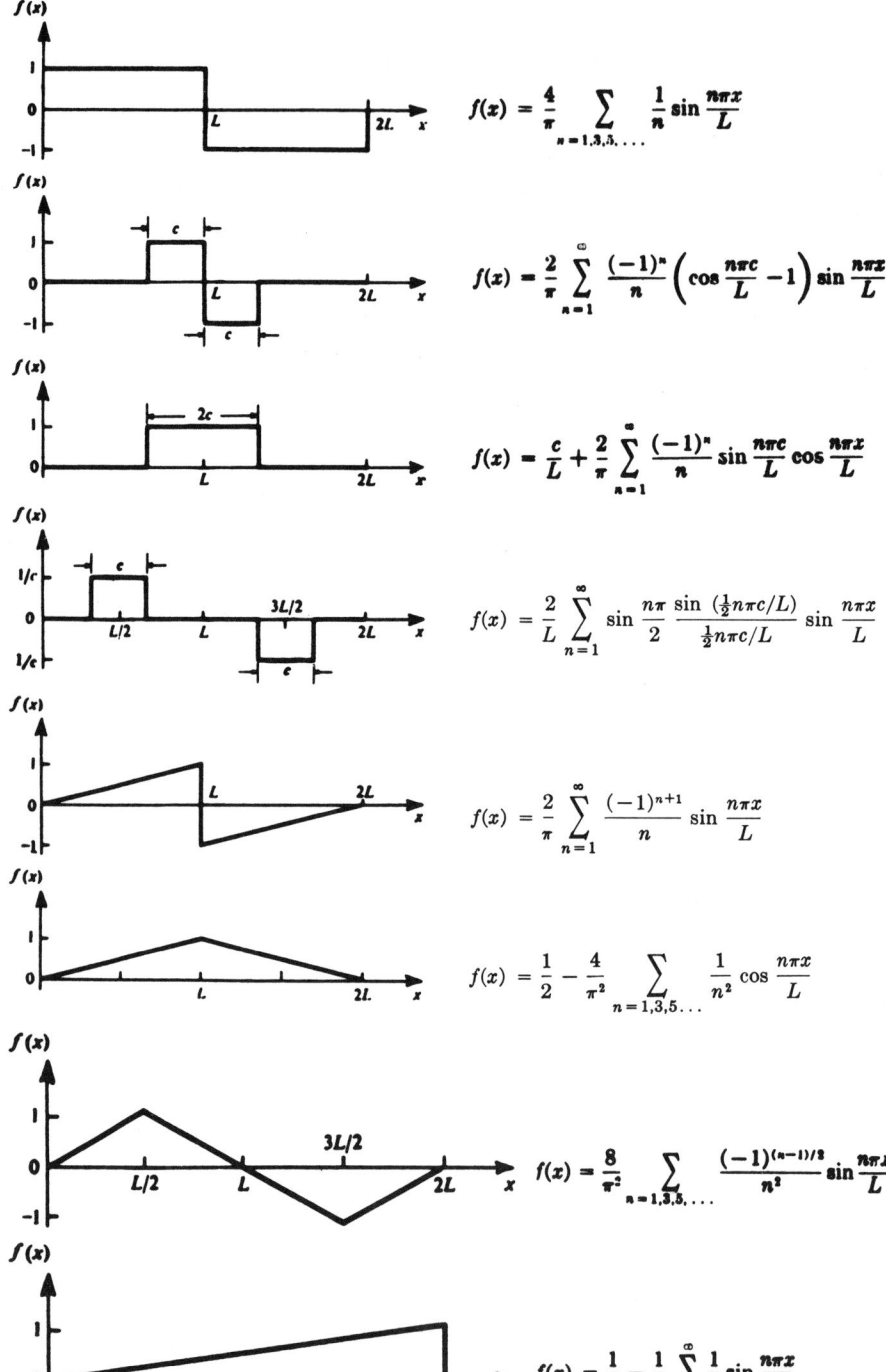

$$f(x) = \frac{4}{\pi} \sum_{n=1,3,5,\ldots} \frac{1}{n} \sin \frac{n\pi x}{L}$$

$$f(x) = \frac{2}{\pi} \sum_{n=1}^{\infty} \frac{(-1)^n}{n} \left(\cos \frac{n\pi c}{L} - 1 \right) \sin \frac{n\pi x}{L}$$

$$f(x) = \frac{c}{L} + \frac{2}{\pi} \sum_{n=1}^{\infty} \frac{(-1)^n}{n} \sin \frac{n\pi c}{L} \cos \frac{n\pi x}{L}$$

$$f(x) = \frac{2}{L} \sum_{n=1}^{\infty} \sin \frac{n\pi}{2} \frac{\sin \left(\frac{1}{2} n\pi c/L \right)}{\frac{1}{2} n\pi c/L} \sin \frac{n\pi x}{L}$$

$$f(x) = \frac{2}{\pi} \sum_{n=1}^{\infty} \frac{(-1)^{n+1}}{n} \sin \frac{n\pi x}{L}$$

$$f(x) = \frac{1}{2} - \frac{4}{\pi^2} \sum_{n=1,3,5,\ldots} \frac{1}{n^2} \cos \frac{n\pi x}{L}$$

$$f(x) = \frac{8}{\pi^2} \sum_{n=1,3,5,\ldots} \frac{(-1)^{(n-1)/2}}{n^2} \sin \frac{n\pi x}{L}$$

$$f(x) = \frac{1}{2} - \frac{1}{\pi} \sum_{n=1}^{\infty} \frac{1}{n} \sin \frac{n\pi x}{L}$$

FOURIER EXPANSIONS FOR BASIC PERIODIC FUNCTIONS (Continued)

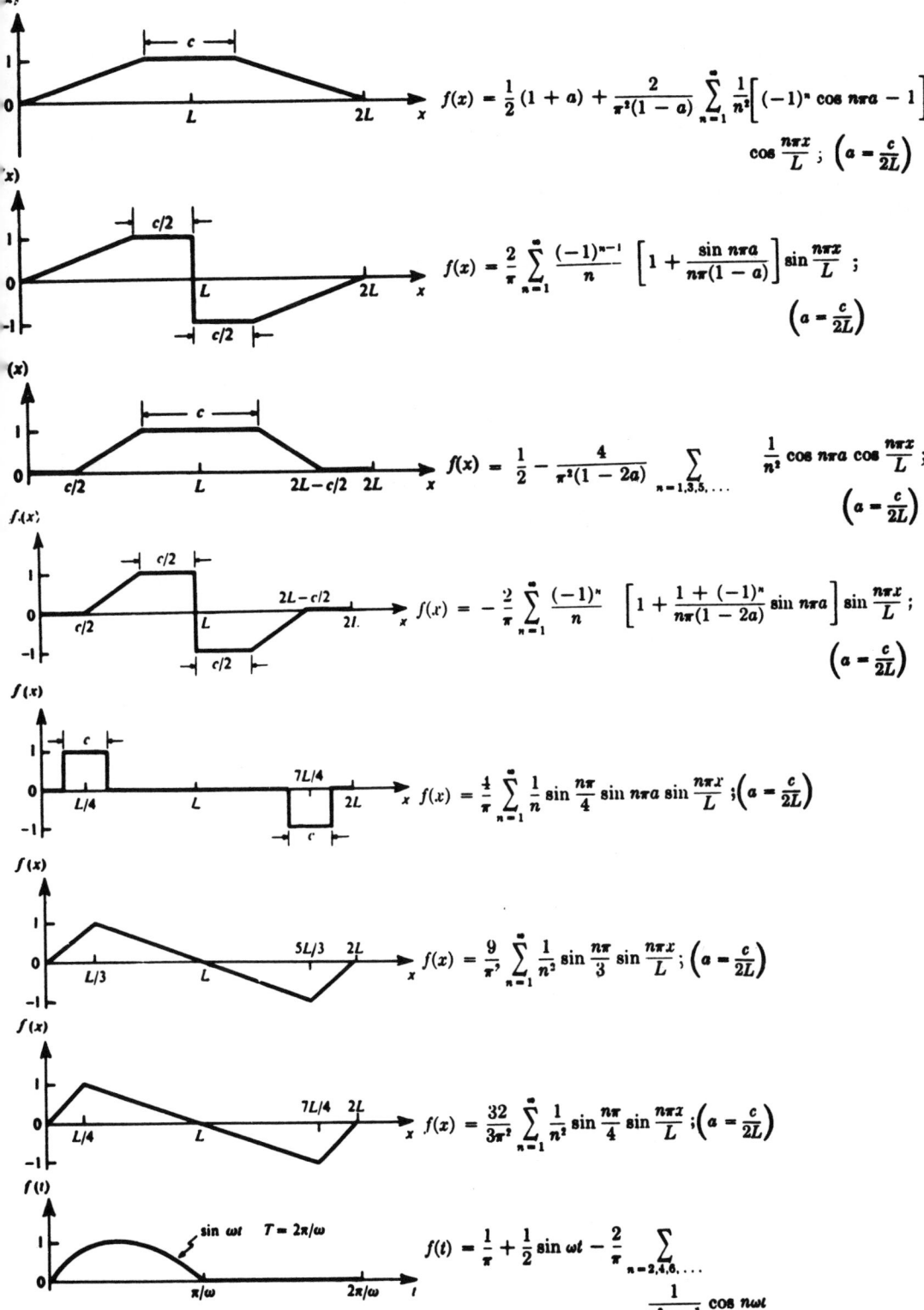

$$f(x) = \frac{1}{2}(1 + a) + \frac{2}{\pi^2(1-a)} \sum_{n=1}^{\infty} \frac{1}{n^2}\left[(-1)^n \cos n\pi a - 1\right] \cos \frac{n\pi x}{L} \; ; \; \left(a = \frac{c}{2L}\right)$$

$$f(x) = \frac{2}{\pi} \sum_{n=1}^{\infty} \frac{(-1)^{n-1}}{n}\left[1 + \frac{\sin n\pi a}{n\pi(1-a)}\right]\sin \frac{n\pi x}{L} \; ; \; \left(a = \frac{c}{2L}\right)$$

$$f(x) = \frac{1}{2} - \frac{4}{\pi^2(1-2a)} \sum_{n=1,3,5,\ldots} \frac{1}{n^2}\cos n\pi a \cos \frac{n\pi x}{L} \; ; \; \left(a = \frac{c}{2L}\right)$$

$$f(x) = -\frac{2}{\pi} \sum_{n=1}^{\infty} \frac{(-1)^n}{n}\left[1 + \frac{1+(-1)^n}{n\pi(1-2a)}\sin n\pi a\right]\sin \frac{n\pi x}{L} \; ; \; \left(a = \frac{c}{2L}\right)$$

$$f(x) = \frac{4}{\pi} \sum_{n=1}^{\infty} \frac{1}{n}\sin \frac{n\pi}{4}\sin n\pi a \sin \frac{n\pi x}{L} \; ; \left(a = \frac{c}{2L}\right)$$

$$f(x) = \frac{9}{\pi^2} \sum_{n=1}^{\infty} \frac{1}{n^2}\sin \frac{n\pi}{3}\sin \frac{n\pi x}{L} \; ; \left(a = \frac{c}{2L}\right)$$

$$f(x) = \frac{32}{3\pi^2} \sum_{n=1}^{\infty} \frac{1}{n^2}\sin \frac{n\pi}{4}\sin \frac{n\pi x}{L} \; ; \left(a = \frac{c}{2L}\right)$$

$$f(t) = \frac{1}{\pi} + \frac{1}{2}\sin \omega t - \frac{2}{\pi} \sum_{n=2,4,6,\ldots} \frac{1}{n^2-1}\cos n\omega t$$

Extracted from graphs and formulas, pages 372, 373, Differential Equations in Engineering Problems, Salvadori and Schwarz, published by Prentice-Hall, Inc., 1954.

THE FOURIER TRANSFORMS

Dr. R. E. Gaskell

For a piecewise continuous function $F(x)$ over a finite interval $0 \leq x \leq \pi$, the *finite Fourier cosine transform* of $F(x)$ is

$$f_c(n) = \int_0^\pi F(x) \cos nx \, dx \quad (n = 0, 1, 2, \ldots). \tag{4}$$

If x ranges over the interval $0 \leq x \leq L$, the substitution $x' = \pi x / L$ allows the use of this definition, also. The inverse transform is written

$$\overline{F}(x) = \frac{1}{\pi} f_c(0) - \frac{2}{\pi} \sum_{n=1}^{\infty} f_c(n) \cos nx \quad (0 < x < \pi) \tag{5}$$

where $\overline{F}(x) = \dfrac{[F(x + 0) + F(x - 0)]}{2}$. We observe that $\overline{F}(x) = F(x)$ at points of continuity. The formula

$$
\begin{aligned}
f_c^{(2)}(n) &= \int_0^\pi F''(x) \cos nx \, dx \\
&= -n^2 f_c(n) - F'(0) + (-1)^n F'(\pi)
\end{aligned}
\tag{6}
$$

makes the finite Fourier cosine transform useful in certain boundary value problems.

Analogously, the *finite Fourier sine transform* of $F(x)$ is

$$f_s(n) = \int_0^\pi F(x) \sin nx \, dx \quad (n = 1, 2, 3, \ldots) \tag{7}$$

and

$$\overline{F}(x) = \frac{2}{\pi} \sum_{n=1}^{\infty} f_s(n) \sin nx \quad (0 < x < \pi) \tag{8}$$

Corresponding to (6) we have

$$
\begin{aligned}
f_s^{(2)}(n) &= \int_0^\pi F''(x) \sin nx \, dx \\
&= -n^2 f_s(n) - nF(0) - n(-1)^n F(\pi).
\end{aligned}
\tag{9}
$$

FOURIER TRANSFORMS

If $F(x)$ is defined for $x \geq 0$ and is piecewise continuous over any finite interval, and if

$$\int_0^\infty F(x) \, dx$$

is absolutely convergent, then

$$f_c(\alpha) = \sqrt{\frac{2}{\pi}} \int_0^\infty F(x) \cos(\alpha x) \, dx \tag{10}$$

is the *Fourier cosine transform* of $F(x)$. Furthermore,

$$\overline{F}(x) = \sqrt{\frac{2}{\pi}} \int_0^\infty f_c(\alpha) \cos(\alpha x) \, d\alpha. \tag{11}$$

The Fourier Transforms

If $\lim\limits_{x \to \infty} \dfrac{d^n F}{dx^n} = 0$, an important property of the Fourier cosine transform

$$f_c^{(2r)}(\alpha) = \sqrt{\frac{2}{\pi}} \int_0^\infty \left(\frac{d^{2r} F}{dx^{2r}}\right) \cos(\alpha x)\, dx$$

$$= -\sqrt{\frac{2}{\pi}} \sum_{n=0}^{r-1} (-1)^n a_{2r-2n-1} \alpha^{2n} + (-1)^r \alpha^{2r} f_c(\alpha) \tag{12}$$

where $\lim\limits_{x \to 0} \dfrac{d^r F}{dx^r} = a_r$, makes it useful in the solution of many problems.

Under the same conditions,

$$f_s(\alpha) = \sqrt{\frac{2}{\pi}} \int_0^\infty F(x) \sin(\alpha x)\, dx \tag{13}$$

defines the *Fourier sine transform* of $F(x)$, and

$$\bar{F}(x) = \sqrt{\frac{2}{\pi}} \int_0^\infty f_s(\alpha) \sin(\alpha x)\, d\alpha. \tag{14}$$

Corresponding to (12) we have

$$f_s^{(2r)}(\alpha) = \sqrt{\frac{2}{\pi}} \int_0^\infty \frac{d^{2r} F}{dx^{2r}} \sin(\alpha x)\, dx$$

$$= -\sqrt{\frac{2}{\pi}} \sum_{n=1}^{r} (-1)^n \alpha^{2n-1} a_{2r-2n} + (-1)^{r-1} \alpha^{2r} f_s(\alpha). \tag{15}$$

Similarly, if $F(x)$ is defined for $-\infty < x < \infty$, and if $\int_{-\infty}^\infty F(x)\, dx$ is absolutely convergent, then

$$f(\alpha) = \frac{1}{\sqrt{2\pi}} \int_{-\infty}^\infty F(x) e^{i\alpha x}\, dx \tag{16}$$

is the *Fourier transform* of $F(x)$, and

$$\bar{F}(x) = \frac{1}{\sqrt{2\pi}} \int_{-\infty}^\infty f(\alpha) e^{-i\alpha x}\, d\alpha. \tag{17}$$

Also, if

$$\lim\limits_{|x| \to \infty} \left| \frac{d^n F}{dx^n} \right| = 0 \quad (n = 1, 2, \ldots, r-1),$$

then

$$f^{(r)}(\alpha) = \frac{1}{\sqrt{2\pi}} \int_{-\infty}^\infty F^{(r)}(x) e^{i\alpha x}\, dx = (-i\alpha)^r f(\alpha). \tag{18}$$

SPECIAL FUNCTIONS
The Fourier Transforms

FINITE SINE TRANSFORMS

	$f_s(n)$	$F(x)$
1	$f_s(n) = \int_0^\pi F(x) \sin nx \, dx \ (n = 1, 2, \cdots)$	$F(x)$
2	$(-1)^{n+1} f_s(n)$	$F(\pi - x)$
3	$\dfrac{1}{n}$	$\dfrac{\pi - x}{\pi}$
4	$\dfrac{(-1)^{n+1}}{n}$	$\dfrac{x}{\pi}$
5	$\dfrac{1 - (-1)^n}{n}$	1
6	$\dfrac{2}{n^2} \sin \dfrac{n\pi}{2}$	$\begin{cases} x & \text{when } 0 < x < \pi/2 \\ \pi - x & \text{when } \pi/2 < x < \pi \end{cases}$
7	$\dfrac{(-1)^{n+1}}{n^3}$	$\dfrac{x(\pi^2 - x^2)}{6\pi}$
8	$\dfrac{1 - (-1)^n}{n^3}$	$\dfrac{x(\pi - x)}{2}$
9	$\dfrac{\pi^2(-1)^{n-1}}{n} - \dfrac{2[1 - (-1)^n]}{n^3}$	x^2
10	$\pi(-1)^n \left(\dfrac{6}{n^3} - \dfrac{\pi^2}{n} \right)$	x^3
11	$\dfrac{n}{n^2 + c^2} [1 - (-1)^n e^{c\pi}]$	e^{cx}
12	$\dfrac{n}{n^2 + c^2}$	$\dfrac{\sinh c(\pi - x)}{\sinh c\pi}$
13	$\dfrac{n}{n^2 - k^2} \ (k \neq 0, 1, 2, \cdots)$	$\dfrac{\sin k(\pi - x)}{\sin k\pi}$
14	$\begin{cases} \dfrac{\pi}{2} & \text{when } n = m \\ 0 & \text{when } n \neq m \end{cases} \ (m = 1, 2, \cdots)$	$\sin mx$
15	$\dfrac{n}{n^2 - k^2} [1 - (-1)^n \cos k\pi]$ $(k \neq 1, 2, \cdots)$	$\cos kx$
16	$\begin{cases} \dfrac{n}{n^2 - m^2} [1 - (-1)^{n+m}] & \\ \qquad \text{when } n \neq m = 1, 2, \cdots \\ 0 \qquad \text{when } n = m \end{cases}$	$\cos mx$
17	$\dfrac{n}{(n^2 - k^2)^2} \ (k \neq 0, 1, 2, \cdots)$	$\dfrac{\pi \sin kx}{2k \sin^2 k\pi} - \dfrac{x \cos k(\pi - x)}{2k \sin k\pi}$
18	$\dfrac{b^n}{n} \ (|b| \leq 1)$	$\dfrac{2}{\pi} \arctan \dfrac{b \sin x}{1 - b \cos x}$
19	$\dfrac{1 - (-1)^n}{n} b^n \ (|b| \leq 1)$	$\dfrac{2}{\pi} \arctan \dfrac{2b \sin x}{1 - b^2}$

FINITE COSINE TRANSFORMS

$f_c(n)$	$F(x)$
1 $f_c(n) = \displaystyle\int_0^\pi F(x)\cos nx\,dx \quad (n = 0, 1, 2, \cdots)$	$F(x)$
2 $(-1)^n f_c(n)$	$F(\pi - x)$
3 0 when $n = 1, 2, \cdots$; $f_c(0) = \pi$	1
4 $\dfrac{2}{n}\sin\dfrac{n\pi}{2}$; $f_c(0) = 0$	$\begin{cases} 1 \text{ when } 0 < x < \pi/2 \\ -1 \text{ when } \pi/2 < x < \pi \end{cases}$
5 $-\dfrac{1-(-1)^n}{n^2}$; $f_c(0) = \dfrac{\pi^2}{2}$	x
6 $\dfrac{(-1)^n}{n^2}$; $f_c(0) = \dfrac{\pi^2}{6}$	$\dfrac{x^2}{2\pi}$
7 $\dfrac{1}{n^2}$; $f_c(0) = 0$	$\dfrac{(\pi-x)^2}{2\pi} - \dfrac{\pi}{6}$
8 $3\pi^2\dfrac{(-1)^n}{n^2} - 6\dfrac{1-(-1)^n}{n^4}$; $f_c(0) = \dfrac{\pi^4}{4}$	x^3
9 $\dfrac{(-1)^n e^c \pi - 1}{n^2 + c^2}$	$\dfrac{1}{c}e^{cx}$
10 $\dfrac{1}{n^2 + c^2}$	$\dfrac{\cosh c(\pi - x)}{c\sinh c\pi}$
11 $\dfrac{k}{n^2 - k^2}[(-1)^n\cos\pi k - 1]$ $\quad (k \neq 0, 1, 2, \cdots)$	$\sin kx$
12 $\dfrac{(-1)^{n+m} - 1}{n^2 - m^2}$; $f_c(m) = 0 \quad (m = 1, 2, \cdots)$	$\dfrac{1}{m}\sin mx$
13 $\dfrac{1}{n^2 - k^2} \quad (k \neq 0, 1, 2, \cdots)$	$-\dfrac{\cos k(\pi - x)}{k\sin k\pi}$
14 0 when $n = 1, 2, \cdots$; $\quad f_c(m) = \dfrac{\pi}{2} \quad (m = 1, 2, \cdots)$	$\cos mx$

SPECIAL FUNCTIONS
The Fourier Transforms

FOURIER SINE TRANSFORMS**

$F(x)$	$f_s(\alpha)$
1 $\begin{cases} 1 & (0 < x < a) \\ 0 & (x > a) \end{cases}$	$\sqrt{\dfrac{2}{\pi}} \left[\dfrac{1 - \cos\alpha}{\alpha} \right]$
2 $\quad x^{p-1} \ (0 < p < 1)$	$\sqrt{\dfrac{2}{\pi}} \dfrac{\Gamma(p)}{\alpha^p} \sin\dfrac{p\pi}{2}$
3 $\begin{cases} \sin x & (0 < x < a) \\ 0 & (x > a) \end{cases}$	$\dfrac{1}{\sqrt{2\pi}} \left[\dfrac{\sin[a(1-\alpha)]}{1-\alpha} - \dfrac{\sin[a(1+\alpha)]}{1+\alpha} \right]$
4 $\quad e^{-x}$	$\sqrt{\dfrac{2}{\pi}} \left[\dfrac{\alpha}{1+\alpha^2} \right]$
5 $\quad xe^{-x^2/2}$	$\alpha e^{-\alpha^2/2}$
6 $\quad \cos\dfrac{x^2}{2}$	$\sqrt{2} \left[\sin\dfrac{\alpha^2}{2} C\!\left(\dfrac{\alpha^2}{2}\right) - \cos\dfrac{\alpha^2}{2} S\!\left(\dfrac{\alpha^2}{2}\right) \right]^*$
7 $\quad \sin\dfrac{x^2}{2}$	$\sqrt{2} \left[\cos\dfrac{\alpha^2}{2} C\!\left(\dfrac{\alpha^2}{2}\right) + \sin\dfrac{\alpha^2}{2} S\!\left(\dfrac{\alpha^2}{2}\right) \right]^*$

*$C(y)$ and $S(y)$ are the Fresnel integrals

$$C(y) = \frac{1}{\sqrt{2\pi}} \int_0^y \frac{1}{\sqrt{t}} \cos t \, dt,$$

$$S(y) = \frac{1}{\sqrt{2\pi}} \int_0^y \frac{1}{\sqrt{t}} \sin t \, dt.$$

**More extensive tables of the Fourier sine and cosine transforms can be found in Fritz Oberhettinger, "Tabellen zur-Fourier Transformation," Springer (1957).

FOURIER COSINE TRANSFORMS

$F(x)$	$f_c(\alpha)$
1 $\begin{cases} 1 & (0 < x < a) \\ 0 & (x > a) \end{cases}$	$\sqrt{\dfrac{2}{\pi}} \dfrac{\sin a\alpha}{\alpha}$
2 $\quad x^{p-1} \ \ (0 < p < 1)$	$\sqrt{\dfrac{2}{\pi}} \dfrac{\Gamma(p)}{\alpha^p} \cos\dfrac{p\pi}{2}$
3 $\begin{cases} \cos x & (0 < x < a) \\ 0 & (x > a) \end{cases}$	$\dfrac{1}{\sqrt{2\pi}} \left[\dfrac{\sin[a(1-\alpha)]}{1-\alpha} + \dfrac{\sin[a(1+\alpha)]}{1+\alpha} \right]$
4 $\quad e^{-x}$	$\sqrt{\dfrac{2}{\pi}} \left(\dfrac{1}{1+\alpha^2} \right)$
5 $\quad e^{-x^2/2}$	$e^{-\alpha^2/2}$
6 $\quad \cos\dfrac{x^2}{2}$	$\cos\left(\dfrac{\alpha^2}{2} - \dfrac{\pi}{4} \right)$
7 $\quad \sin\dfrac{x^2}{2}$	$\cos\left(\dfrac{\alpha^2}{2} + \dfrac{\pi}{4} \right)$

FOURIER TRANSFORMS*

$F(x)$	$f(\alpha)$
1 $\dfrac{\sin ax}{x}$	$\begin{cases} \sqrt{\dfrac{\pi}{2}} & \lvert \alpha \rvert < a \\ 0 & \lvert \alpha \rvert > a \end{cases}$
2 $\begin{cases} e^{iwx} & (p < x < q) \\ 0 & (x < p,\ x > q) \end{cases}$	$\dfrac{i}{\sqrt{2\pi}} \dfrac{e^{ip(w+\alpha)} - e^{iq(w+\alpha)}}{(w+\alpha)}$
3 $\begin{cases} e^{-cx+iwx} & (x > 0) \\ 0 & (x < 0) \end{cases} \quad (c > 0)$	$\dfrac{i}{\sqrt{2\pi}(w+\alpha+ic)}$
4 $e^{-px^2} \quad R(p) > 0$	$\dfrac{1}{\sqrt{2p}} e^{-\alpha^2/4p}$
5 $\cos px^2$	$\dfrac{1}{\sqrt{2p}} \cos\left[\dfrac{\alpha^2}{4p} - \dfrac{\pi}{4}\right]$
6 $\sin px^2$	$\dfrac{1}{\sqrt{2p}} \cos\left[\dfrac{\alpha^2}{4p} + \dfrac{\pi}{4}\right]$
7 $\lvert x \rvert^{-p} \quad (0 < p < 1)$	$\sqrt{\dfrac{2}{\pi}} \dfrac{\Gamma(1-p)\sin\dfrac{p\pi}{2}}{\lvert \alpha \rvert^{(1-p)}}$
8 $\dfrac{e^{-a\lvert x \rvert}}{\sqrt{\lvert x \rvert}}$	$\dfrac{\sqrt{\sqrt{(a^2+\alpha^2)}+a}}{\sqrt{a^2+\alpha^2}}$
9 $\dfrac{\cosh ax}{\cosh \pi x} \quad (-\pi < a < \pi)$	$\sqrt{\dfrac{2}{\pi}} \dfrac{\cos\dfrac{a}{2}\cosh\dfrac{\alpha}{2}}{\cosh \alpha + \cos a}$
10 $\dfrac{\sinh ax}{\sinh \pi x} \quad (-\pi < a < \pi)$	$\dfrac{1}{\sqrt{2\pi}} \dfrac{\sin a}{\cosh \alpha + \cos a}$
11 $\begin{cases} \dfrac{1}{\sqrt{a^2-x^2}} & (\lvert x \rvert < a) \\ 0 & (\lvert x \rvert > a) \end{cases}$	$\sqrt{\dfrac{\pi}{2}} J_0(a\alpha)$
12 $\dfrac{\sin[b\sqrt{a^2+x^2}]}{\sqrt{a^2+x^2}}$	$\begin{cases} 0 & (\lvert \alpha \rvert > b) \\ \sqrt{\dfrac{\pi}{2}} J_0(a\sqrt{b^2-\alpha^2}) & (\lvert \alpha \rvert < b) \end{cases}$
13 $\begin{cases} P_n(x) & (\lvert x \rvert < 1) \\ 0 & (\lvert x \rvert > 1) \end{cases}$	$\dfrac{i^n}{\sqrt{\alpha}} J_{n+\frac{1}{2}}(\alpha)$
14 $\begin{cases} \dfrac{\cos[b\sqrt{a^2-x^2}]}{\sqrt{a^2-x^2}} & (\lvert x \rvert < a) \\ 0 & (\lvert x \rvert > a) \end{cases}$	$\sqrt{\dfrac{\pi}{2}} J_0(a\sqrt{a^2+b^2})$
15 $\begin{cases} \dfrac{\cosh[b\sqrt{a^2-x^2}]}{\sqrt{a^2-x^2}} & (\lvert x \rvert < a) \\ 0 & (\lvert x \rvert > a) \end{cases}$	$\sqrt{\dfrac{\pi}{2}} J_0(a\sqrt{\alpha^2-b^2})$

*More extensive tables of Fourier transforms can be found in W. Magnus and F. Oberhettinger, "Formulas and Theorems of the Special Functions of Mathematical Physics," pp. 116–120. Chelsea (1949).

SPECIAL FUNCTIONS
The Fourier Transforms

The following functions appear among the entries of the tables on transforms.

Function	Definition	Name
$Ei(x)$	$\displaystyle\int_{-x}^{x} \frac{e^v}{v}\, dv$; or sometimes defined as $$-Ei(-x) = \int_{x}^{\infty} \frac{e^{-v}}{v}\, dv$$	Sine, Cosine, and Exponential Integral tables pages 548–556
$Si(x)$	$\displaystyle\int_{0}^{x} \frac{\sin v}{v}\, dv$	Sine, Cosine, and Exponential Integral tables pages 548–556
$Ci(x)$	$\displaystyle\int_{x}^{x} \frac{\cos v}{v}\, dv$; or sometimes defined as negative of this integral	Sine, Cosine, and Exponential Integral tables pages 548–546
$erf(x)$	$\displaystyle\frac{2}{\sqrt{\pi}} \int_{0}^{x} e^{-v^2}\, dv$	Error function
$erfc(x)$	$\displaystyle 1 - erf(x) = \frac{2}{\sqrt{\pi}} \int_{x}^{\infty} e^{-v^2}\, dv$	Complementary function to error function
$L_n(x)$	$\displaystyle\frac{e^x}{n!} \frac{d^n}{dx^n} (x^n e^{-x}),\ \ n = 0, 1, \cdots$	Laguerre polynomial of degree n

THE LAPLACE TRANSFORM

Dr. R. E. Gaskell

If $F(t)$ is a piecewise continuous real-valued function of the real variable $t(0 \leq t < \infty)$, and if $F(t)$ is of exponential order, that is if $|F(t)| < Me^{at}(t > T; M, a, T$ positive constants) then the *Laplace transform* of $F(t)$,

$$L\{F(t)\} = f(s) = \int_0^\infty e^{-st}F(t)\,dt, \tag{1}$$

exists in the half-plane of the complex variable s for which the real part of s is greater than some fixed value s_0, i.e., $R(s) \geq s_0$. Furthermore

$$F(t) = \frac{1}{2\pi i}\int_{a-i\infty}^{a+i\infty} e^{st}f(s)\,ds, \tag{2}$$

where $a > s_0$. The important property

$$L\{F^{(r)}(t)\} = \int_0^\infty e^{-st}\left(\frac{d^r F}{dt^r}\right)dt$$

$$= s^r f(s) - \sum_{n=0}^{r-1} s^{r-1-n}F^{(n)}(+0) \tag{3}$$

makes the Laplace transform very useful for solving linear differential equations with constant coefficients, and many boundary value problems.

LAPLACE OPERATIONS*

	$F(t)$	$f(s)$
1	$F(t)$	$\int_0^\infty e^{-st} F(t)\, dt$
2	$AF(t) + BG(t)$	$Af(s) + Bg(s)$
3	$F'(t)$	$sf(s) - F(+0)$
4	$F^{(n)}(t)$	$s^n f(s) - s^{n-1} F(+0) - s^{n-2} F'(+0) - \cdots \\ \qquad\qquad - F^{(n-1)}(+0)$
5	$\int_0^t F(\tau)\, d\tau$	$\dfrac{1}{s} f(s)$
6	$\int_0^t \int_0^\tau F(\lambda)\, d\lambda\, d\tau$	$\dfrac{1}{s^2} f(s)$
7	$\int_0^t F_1(t - \tau) F_2(\tau)\, d\tau = F_1 * F_2$	$f_1(s) f_2(s)$
8	$tF(t)$	$-f'(s)$
9	$t^n F(t)$	$(-1)^n f^{(n)}(s)$
10	$\dfrac{1}{t} F(t)$	$\int_s^\infty f(x)\, dx$
11	$e^{at} F(t)$	$f(s - a)$
12	$F(t - b)$, where $F(t) = 0$ when $t < 0$	$e^{-bs} f(s)$
13	$\dfrac{1}{c} F\left(\dfrac{t}{c}\right)$	$f(cs)$
14	$\dfrac{1}{c} e^{(bt)/c} F\left(\dfrac{t}{c}\right)$	$f(cs - b)$
15	$F(t + a) = F(t)$	$\dfrac{\displaystyle\int_0^a e^{-st} F(t)\, dt}{1 - e^{-as}}$
16	$F(t + a) = -F(t)$	$\dfrac{\displaystyle\int_0^a e^{-st} F(t)\, dt}{1 + e^{-as}}$
17	$F_1(t)$, the half-wave rectification of $F(t)$ in No. 16	$\dfrac{f(s)}{1 - e^{-as}}$
18	$F_2(t)$, the full-wave rectification of $F(t)$ in No. 16	$f(s) \coth \dfrac{as}{2}$
19	$\displaystyle\sum_1^m \dfrac{p(a_n)}{q'(a_n)} e^{a_n t}$	$\dfrac{p(s)}{q(s)}$, $q(s) = (s - a_1)(s - a_2) \cdots (s - a_m)$
20	$e^{at} \displaystyle\sum_{n=1}^r \dfrac{\phi^{(r-n)}(a)}{(r - n)!} \dfrac{t^{n-1}}{(n - 1)!} + \cdots$	$\dfrac{p(s)}{q(s)} = \dfrac{\phi(s)}{(s - a)^r}$

*These tables of Laplace Operations, Laplace Transforms, and Finite Fourier sine and cosine transforms were taken from "Modern Operational Mathematics in Engineering", by permission of the author, R. V. Churchill, and the publisher, McGraw-Hill Book Company, Inc.

LAPLACE TRANSFORMS

	$f(s)$	$F(t)$
1	$\dfrac{1}{s}$	$\mu(t)$, unit step function
2	$\dfrac{1}{s^2}$	t
3	$\dfrac{1}{s^n}$ $(n = 1, 2, \ldots)$	$\dfrac{t^{n-1}}{(n-1)!}$
4	$\dfrac{1}{\sqrt{s}}$	$\dfrac{1}{\sqrt{\pi t}}$
5	$s^{-3/2}$	$2\sqrt{\dfrac{t}{\pi}}$
6	$s^{-[n+(1/2)]}$ $(n = 1, 2, \ldots)$	$\dfrac{2^n t^{n-(1/2)}}{1 \cdot 3 \cdot 5 \cdots (2n-1)\sqrt{\pi}}$
7	$\dfrac{\Gamma(k)}{s^k}$ $(k > 0)$	t^{k-1}
8	$\dfrac{1}{s-a}$	e^{at}
9	$\dfrac{1}{(s-a)^2}$	te^{at}
10	$\dfrac{1}{(s-a)^n}$ $(n = 1, 2, \ldots)$	$\dfrac{1}{(n-1)!}\, t^{n-1} e^{at}$
11	$\dfrac{\Gamma(k)}{(s-a)^k}$ $(k > 0)$	$t^{k-1} e^{at}$
12*	$\dfrac{1}{(s-a)(s-b)}$	$\dfrac{1}{a-b}(e^{at} - e^{bt})$
13*	$\dfrac{s}{(s-a)(s-b)}$	$\dfrac{1}{a-b}(ae^{at} - be^{bt})$
14*	$\dfrac{1}{(s-a)(s-b)(s-c)}$	$-\dfrac{(b-c)e^{at} + (c-a)e^{bt} + (a-b)e^{ct}}{(a-b)(b-c)(c-a)}$
15	$\dfrac{1}{s^2 + a^2}$	$\dfrac{1}{a}\sin at$
16	$\dfrac{s}{s^2 + a^2}$	$\cos at$
17	$\dfrac{1}{s^2 - a^2}$	$\dfrac{1}{a}\sinh at$
18	$\dfrac{s}{s^2 - a^2}$	$\cosh at$

*Here a, b, and (in 14) c represent distinct constants.

LAPLACE TRANSFORMS (Continued)

	$f(s)$	$F(t)$
19	$\dfrac{1}{s(s^2 + a^2)}$	$\dfrac{1}{a^2}(1 - \cos at)$
20	$\dfrac{1}{s^2(s^2 + a^2)}$	$\dfrac{1}{a^3}(at - \sin at)$
21	$\dfrac{1}{(s^2 + a^2)^2}$	$\dfrac{1}{2a^3}(\sin at - at \cos at)$
22	$\dfrac{s}{(s^2 + a^2)^2}$	$\dfrac{t}{2a}\sin at$
23	$\dfrac{s^2}{(s^2 + a^2)^2}$	$\dfrac{1}{2a}(\sin at + at \cos at)$
24	$\dfrac{s^2 - a^2}{(s^2 + a^2)^2}$	$t \cos at$
25	$\dfrac{s}{(s^2 + a^2)(s^2 + b^2)}\ (a^2 \neq b^2)$	$\dfrac{\cos at - \cos bt}{b^2 - a^2}$
26	$\dfrac{1}{(s - a)^2 + b^2}$	$\dfrac{1}{b}e^{at}\sin bt$
27	$\dfrac{s - a}{(s - a)^2 + b^2}$	$e^{at}\cos bt$
27.1	$\dfrac{1}{[(s + a)^2 + b^2]^n}$	$\dfrac{-e^{-at}}{4^{n-1}b^{2n}}\displaystyle\sum_{r=1}^{n}\binom{2n - r - 1}{n - 1}(-2t)^{r-1}\dfrac{d^r}{dt^r}[\cos(bt)]$
27.2	$\dfrac{s}{[(s + a)^2 + b^2]^n}$	$\dfrac{e^{-at}}{4^{n-1}b^{2n}}\left\{\displaystyle\sum_{r=1}^{n}\binom{2n - r - 1}{n - 1}\dfrac{1}{(r-1)!}\right.$ $(-2t)^{r-1}\dfrac{d^r}{dt^r}[a\cos(bt) + b\sin(bt)]$ $-2b\displaystyle\sum_{r=1}^{n-1}\dfrac{1}{(r-1)!}\binom{2n - r - 2}{n - 1}$ $\left.(-2t)^{r-1}\dfrac{d^r}{dt^r}[\sin bt]\right\}$
28	$\dfrac{3a^2}{s^3 + a^3}$	$e^{-at} - e^{(at)/2}\left(\cos\dfrac{at\sqrt{3}}{2} - \sqrt{3}\sin\dfrac{at\sqrt{3}}{2}\right)$
29	$\dfrac{4a^3}{s^4 + 4a^4}$	$\sin at \cosh at - \cos at \sinh at$
30	$\dfrac{s}{s^4 + 4a^4}$	$\dfrac{1}{2a^2}\sin at \sinh at$

LAPLACE TRANSFORMS (Continued)

	$f(s)$	$F(t)$
31	$\dfrac{1}{s^4 - a^4}$	$\dfrac{1}{2a^3}\,(\sinh at - \sin at)$
32	$\dfrac{s}{s^4 - a^4}$	$\dfrac{1}{2a^2}\,(\cosh at - \cos at)$
33	$\dfrac{8a^3 s^2}{(s^2 + a^2)^3}$	$(1 + a^2 t^2)\sin at - \cos at$
34*	$\dfrac{1}{s}\left(\dfrac{s-1}{s}\right)^n$	$L_n(t) = \dfrac{e^t}{n!}\dfrac{d^n}{dt^n}\,(t^n e^{-t})$
35	$\dfrac{s}{(s-a)^{3/2}}$	$\dfrac{1}{\sqrt{\pi t}}\,e^{at}(1 + 2at)$
36	$\sqrt{s-a} - \sqrt{s-b}$	$\dfrac{1}{2\sqrt{\pi t^3}}\,(e^{bt} - e^{at})$
37	$\dfrac{1}{\sqrt{s}+a}$	$\dfrac{1}{\sqrt{\pi t}} - ae^{a^2 t}\,\mathrm{erfc}\,(a\sqrt{t})$
38	$\dfrac{\sqrt{s}}{s - a^2}$	$\dfrac{1}{\sqrt{\pi t}} + ae^{a^2 t}\,\mathrm{erf}\,(a\sqrt{t})$
39	$\dfrac{\sqrt{s}}{s + a^2}$	$\dfrac{1}{\sqrt{\pi t}} - \dfrac{2a}{\sqrt{\pi}}\,e^{-a^2 t}\displaystyle\int_0^{a\sqrt{t}} e^{\lambda^2}\,d\lambda$
40	$\dfrac{1}{\sqrt{s}(s - a^2)}$	$\dfrac{1}{a}\,e^{a^2 t}\,\mathrm{erf}\,(a\sqrt{t})$
41	$\dfrac{1}{\sqrt{s}(s + a^2)}$	$\dfrac{2}{a\sqrt{\pi}}\,e^{-a^2 t}\displaystyle\int_0^{a\sqrt{t}} e^{\lambda^2}\,d\lambda$
42	$\dfrac{b^2 - a^2}{(s - a^2)(b + \sqrt{s})}$	$e^{a^2 t}[b - a\,\mathrm{erf}\,(a\sqrt{t})] - be^{b^2 t}\,\mathrm{erfc}\,(b\sqrt{t})$
43	$\dfrac{1}{\sqrt{s}(\sqrt{s} + a)}$	$e^{a^2 t}\,\mathrm{erfc}\,(a\sqrt{t})$
44	$\dfrac{1}{(s + a)\sqrt{s + b}}$	$\dfrac{1}{\sqrt{b-a}}\,e^{-at}\,\mathrm{erf}\,(\sqrt{b-a}\,\sqrt{t})$
45	$\dfrac{b^2 - a^2}{\sqrt{s}(s - a^2)(\sqrt{s} + b)}$	$e^{a^2 t}\left[\dfrac{b}{a}\,\mathrm{erf}\,(a\sqrt{t}) - 1\right] + e^{b^2 t}\,\mathrm{erfc}\,(b\sqrt{t})$
46†	$\dfrac{(1 - s)^n}{s^{n+(1/2)}}$	$\dfrac{n!}{(2n)!\,\sqrt{\pi t}}\,H_{2n}(\sqrt{t})$
47	$\dfrac{(1 - s)^n}{s^{n+(3/2)}}$	$-\dfrac{n!}{\sqrt{\pi}(2n + 1)!}\,H_{2n+1}(\sqrt{t})$

*$L_n(t)$ is the Laguerre polynomial of degree n.

†$H_n(x)$ is the Hermite polynomial, $H_n(x) = e^{x^2}\dfrac{d^n}{dx^n}\,(e^{-x^2})$.

LAPLACE TRANSFORMS (Continued)

	$f(s)$	$F(t)$
48*	$\dfrac{\sqrt{s+2a}}{\sqrt{s}}-1$	$ae^{-at}[I_1(at)+I_0(at)]$
49	$\dfrac{1}{\sqrt{s+a}\,\sqrt{s+b}}$	$e^{-(1/2)(a+b)t}I_0\left(\dfrac{a-b}{2}\,t\right)$
50	$\dfrac{\Gamma(k)}{(s+a)^k(s+b)^k}\ (k\ge 0)$	$\sqrt{\pi}\left(\dfrac{t}{a-b}\right)^{k-(1/2)}e^{-(1/2)(a+b)t}I_{k-(1/2)}\left(\dfrac{a-b}{2}\,t\right)$
51	$\dfrac{1}{(s+a)^{1/2}(s+b)^{3/2}}$	$te^{-(1/2)(a+b)t}\left[I_0\left(\dfrac{a-b}{2}\,t\right)+I_1\left(\dfrac{a-b}{2}\,t\right)\right]$
52	$\dfrac{\sqrt{s+2a}-\sqrt{s}}{\sqrt{s+2a}+\sqrt{s}}$	$\dfrac{1}{t}\,e^{-at}I_1(at)$
53	$\dfrac{(a-b)^k}{(\sqrt{s+a}+\sqrt{s+b})^{2k}}\ (k>0)$	$\dfrac{k}{t}\,e^{-(1/2)(a+b)t}I_k\left(\dfrac{a-b}{2}\,t\right)$
54	$\dfrac{(\sqrt{s+a}+\sqrt{s})^{-2\nu}}{\sqrt{s}\,\sqrt{s+a}}\ (\nu>-1)$	$\dfrac{1}{a^\nu}\,e^{-(1/2)(at)}I_\nu\left(\dfrac{1}{2}\,at\right)$
55	$\dfrac{1}{\sqrt{s^2+a^2}}$	$J_0(at)$
56	$\dfrac{(\sqrt{s^2+a^2}-s)^\nu}{\sqrt{s^2+a^2}}\ (\nu>-1)$	$a^\nu J_\nu(at)$
57	$\dfrac{1}{(s^2+a^2)^k}\ (k>0)$	$\dfrac{\sqrt{\pi}}{\Gamma(k)}\left(\dfrac{t}{2a}\right)^{k-(1/2)}J_{k-(1/2)}(at)$
58	$(\sqrt{s^2+a^2}-s)^k\ (k>0)$	$\dfrac{ka^k}{t}\,J_k(at)$
59	$\dfrac{(s-\sqrt{s^2-a^2})^\nu}{\sqrt{s^2-a^2}}\ (\nu>-1)$	$a^\nu I_\nu(at)$
60	$\dfrac{1}{(s^2-a^2)^k}\ (k>0)$	$\dfrac{\sqrt{\pi}}{\Gamma(k)}\left(\dfrac{t}{2a}\right)^{k-(1/2)}I_{k-(1/2)}(at)$
61	$\dfrac{e^{-ks}}{s}$	$S_k(t)=\begin{cases}0\text{ when }0<t<k\\1\text{ when }t>k\end{cases}$
62	$\dfrac{e^{-ks}}{s^2}$	$\begin{cases}0\text{ when }0<t<k\\t-k\text{ when }t>k\end{cases}$
63	$\dfrac{e^{-ks}}{s^\mu}\ (\mu>0)$	$\begin{cases}0\qquad\qquad\text{ when }0<t<k\\\dfrac{(t-k)^{\mu-1}}{\Gamma(\mu)}\ \text{ when }t>k\end{cases}$
64	$\dfrac{1-e^{-ks}}{s}$	$\begin{cases}1\text{ when }0<t<k\\0\text{ when }t>k\end{cases}$

*$I_n(x)=i^{-n}J_n(ix)$, where J_n is Bessel's function of the first kind.

LAPLACE TRANSFORMS (Continued)

	$f(s)$	$F(t)$
65	$\dfrac{1}{s(1 - e^{-ks})} = \dfrac{1 + \coth \frac{1}{2}ks}{2s}$	$S(k, t) = n$ when $\qquad (n - 1)k < t < nk\,(n = 1, 2, \ldots)$
66	$\dfrac{1}{s(e^{ks} - a)}$	$\begin{cases} 0 \text{ when } 0 < t < k \\ 1 + a + a^2 + \cdots + a^{n-1} \\ \quad \text{ when } nk < t < (n + 1)k\,(n = 1, 2, \ldots) \end{cases}$
67	$\dfrac{1}{s} \tanh ks$	$M(2k, t) = (-1)^{n-1}$ $\quad$ when $2k(n - 1) < t < 2kn$ $\qquad\qquad\qquad\qquad (n = 1, 2, \ldots)$
68	$\dfrac{1}{s(1 + e^{-ks})}$	$\dfrac{1}{2}\, M(k, t) + \dfrac{1}{2} = \dfrac{1 - (-1)^n}{2}$ $\qquad$ when $(n - 1)k < t < nk$
69*	$\dfrac{1}{s^2} \tanh ks$	$H(2k, t)$
70	$\dfrac{1}{s \sinh ks}$	$2S(2k, t + k) - 2 = 2(n - 1)$ $\quad$ when $(2n - 3)k < t < (2n - 1)k \;\; (t > 0)$
71	$\dfrac{1}{s \cosh ks}$	$M(2k, t + 3k) + 1 = 1 + (-1)^n$ $\quad$ when $(2n - 3)k < t < (2n - 1)k \;\; (t > 0)$
72	$\dfrac{1}{s} \coth ks$	$2S(2k, t) - 1 = 2n - 1$ $\qquad$ when $2k(n - 1) < t < 2kn$
73	$\dfrac{k}{s^2 + k^2} \coth \dfrac{\pi s}{2k}$	$\lvert \sin kt \rvert$
74	$\dfrac{1}{(s^2 + 1)(1 - e^{-\pi s})}$	$\begin{cases} \sin t \text{ when } (2n - 2)\pi < t < (2n - 1)\pi \\ 0 \quad \text{ when } (2n - 1)\pi < t < 2n\pi \end{cases}$
75	$\dfrac{1}{s}\, e^{-k/s}$	$J_0(2 \sqrt{kt})$
76	$\dfrac{1}{\sqrt{s}}\, e^{-k/s}$	$\dfrac{1}{\sqrt{\pi t}} \cos 2 \sqrt{kt}$
77	$\dfrac{1}{\sqrt{s}}\, e^{k/s}$	$\dfrac{1}{\sqrt{\pi t}} \cosh 2 \sqrt{kt}$
78	$\dfrac{1}{s^{3/2}}\, e^{-k/s}$	$\dfrac{1}{\sqrt{\pi k}} \sin 2 \sqrt{kt}$
79	$\dfrac{1}{s^{3/2}}\, e^{k/s}$	$\dfrac{1}{\sqrt{\pi k}} \sinh 2 \sqrt{kt}$
80	$\dfrac{1}{s^{\mu}}\, e^{-k/s}(\mu > 0)$	$\left(\dfrac{t}{k}\right)^{(\mu - 1)/2} J_{\mu-1}(2 \sqrt{kt})$

*$H(2k, t) = k + (r - k)(-1)^n$ where $t = 2kn + r; 0 \le r < 2k; n = 0, 1, 2, \ldots$.

LAPLACE TRANSFORMS (Continued)

	$f(s)$	$F(t)$
81	$\dfrac{1}{s^\mu} e^{k/s} (\mu > 0)$	$\left(\dfrac{t}{k}\right)^{(\mu-1)/2} I_{\mu-1}(2\sqrt{kt})$
82	$e^{-k\sqrt{s}} (k > 0)$	$\dfrac{k}{2\sqrt{\pi t^3}} \exp\left(-\dfrac{k^2}{4t}\right)$
83	$\dfrac{1}{s} e^{-k\sqrt{s}} (k \geqq 0)$	$\operatorname{erfc}\left(\dfrac{k}{2\sqrt{t}}\right)$
84	$\dfrac{1}{\sqrt{s}} e^{-k\sqrt{s}} (k \geqq 0)$	$\dfrac{1}{\sqrt{\pi t}} \exp\left(-\dfrac{k^2}{4t}\right)$
85	$s^{-3/2} e^{-k\sqrt{s}} (k \geqq 0)$	$2\sqrt{\dfrac{t}{\pi}} \exp\left(-\dfrac{k^2}{4t}\right) - k\operatorname{erfc}\left(\dfrac{k}{2\sqrt{t}}\right)$
86	$\dfrac{ae^{-k\sqrt{s}}}{s(a+\sqrt{s})} (k \geqq 0)$	$-e^{ak}e^{a^2 t}\operatorname{erfc}\left(a\sqrt{t}+\dfrac{k}{2\sqrt{t}}\right) + \operatorname{erfc}\left(\dfrac{k}{2\sqrt{t}}\right)$
87	$\dfrac{e^{-k\sqrt{s}}}{\sqrt{s}(a+\sqrt{s})} (k \geqq 0)$	$e^{ak}e^{a^2 t}\operatorname{erfc}\left(a\sqrt{t}+\dfrac{k}{2\sqrt{t}}\right)$
88	$\dfrac{e^{-k\sqrt{s(s+a)}}}{\sqrt{s(s+a)}}$	$\begin{cases} 0 & \text{when } 0 < t < k \\ e^{-(1/2)(at)} I_0(\frac{1}{2}a\sqrt{t^2-k^2}) & \text{when } t > k \end{cases}$
89	$\dfrac{e^{-k\sqrt{s^2+a^2}}}{\sqrt{s^2+a^2}}$	$\begin{cases} 0 & \text{when } 0 < t < k \\ J_0(a\sqrt{t^2-k^2}) & \text{when } t > k \end{cases}$
90	$\dfrac{e^{-k\sqrt{s^2-a^2}}}{\sqrt{s^2-a^2}}$	$\begin{cases} 0 & \text{when } 0 < t < k \\ I_0(a\sqrt{t^2-k^2}) & \text{when } t > k \end{cases}$
91	$\dfrac{e^{-k(\sqrt{s^2+a^2}-s)}}{\sqrt{s^2+a^2}} (k \geqq 0)$	$J_0(a\sqrt{t^2+2kt})$
92	$e^{-ks} - e^{-k\sqrt{s^2+a^2}}$	$\begin{cases} 0 & \text{when } 0 < t < k \\ \dfrac{ak}{\sqrt{t^2-k^2}} J_1(a\sqrt{t^2-k^2}) & \text{when } t > k \end{cases}$
93	$e^{-k\sqrt{s^2+a^2}} - e^{-ks}$	$\begin{cases} 0 & \text{when } 0 < t < k \\ \dfrac{ak}{\sqrt{t^2-k^2}} I_1(a\sqrt{t^2-k^2}) & \text{when } t > k \end{cases}$
94	$\dfrac{a^\nu e^{-k\sqrt{s^2-a^2}}}{\sqrt{s^2+a^2}(\sqrt{s^2+a^2}+s)^\nu}$ $(\nu > -1)$	$\begin{cases} 0 & \text{when } 0 < t < k \\ \left(\dfrac{t-k}{t+k}\right)^{(1/2)\nu} J_\nu(a\sqrt{t^2-k^2}) & \text{when } t > k \end{cases}$
95	$\dfrac{1}{s} \log s$	$\Gamma'(1) - \log t \, [\Gamma'(1) = -0.5772]$
96	$\dfrac{1}{s^k} \log s \, (k > 0)$	$t^{k-1}\left\{\dfrac{\Gamma'(k)}{[\Gamma(k)]^2} - \dfrac{\log t}{\Gamma(k)}\right\}$
97	$\dfrac{\log s}{s-a} \, (a > 0)$	$e^{at}[\log a - \operatorname{Ei}(-at)]$

LAPLACE TRANSFORMS (Continued)

	$f(s)$	$F(t)$
98	$\dfrac{\log s}{s^2 + 1}$	$\cos t\, Si(t) - \sin t\, Ci(t)$
99	$\dfrac{s \log s}{s^2 + 1}$	$-\sin t\, Si(t) - \cos t\, Ci(t)$
100	$\dfrac{1}{s} \log (1 + ks)\,(k > 0)$	$-\operatorname{Ei}\left(-\dfrac{t}{k}\right)$
101	$\log \dfrac{s - a}{s - b}$	$\dfrac{1}{t}\,(e^{bt} - e^{at})$
102	$\dfrac{1}{s} \log (1 + k^2 s^2)$	$-2Ci\left(\dfrac{t}{k}\right)$
103	$\dfrac{1}{s} \log (s^2 + a^2)\quad (a > 0)$	$2 \log a - 2Ci(at)$
104	$\dfrac{1}{s^2} \log (s^2 + a^2)\quad (a > 0)$	$\dfrac{2}{a}\,[at \log a + \sin at - at\, Ci(at)]$
105	$\log \dfrac{s^2 + a^2}{s^2}$	$\dfrac{2}{t}\,(1 - \cos at)$
106	$\log \dfrac{s^2 - a^2}{s^2}$	$\dfrac{2}{t}\,(1 - \cosh at)$
107	$\arctan \dfrac{k}{s}$	$\dfrac{1}{t} \sin kt$
108	$\dfrac{1}{s} \arctan \dfrac{k}{s}$	$Si(kt)$
109	$e^{k^2 s^2} \operatorname{erfc}(ks)\quad (k > 0)$	$\dfrac{1}{k \sqrt{\pi}} \exp\left(-\dfrac{t^2}{4k^2}\right)$
110	$\dfrac{1}{s} e^{k^2 s^2} \operatorname{erfc}(ks)\quad (k > 0)$	$\operatorname{erf}\left(\dfrac{t}{2k}\right)$
111	$e^{ks} \operatorname{erfc}(\sqrt{ks})\quad (k > 0)$	$\dfrac{\sqrt{k}}{\pi \sqrt{t}(t + k)}$
112	$\dfrac{1}{\sqrt{s}} \operatorname{erfc}(\sqrt{ks})$	$\begin{cases} 0 & \text{when } 0 < t < k \\ (\pi t)^{-1/2} & \text{when } t > k \end{cases}$
113	$\dfrac{1}{\sqrt{s}} e^{ks} \operatorname{erfc}(\sqrt{ks})\,(k > 0)$	$\dfrac{1}{\sqrt{\pi(t + k)}}$
114	$\operatorname{erf}\left(\dfrac{k}{\sqrt{s}}\right)$	$\dfrac{1}{\pi t} \sin (2k \sqrt{t})$
115	$\dfrac{1}{\sqrt{s}} e^{k^2/s} \operatorname{erfc}\left(\dfrac{k}{\sqrt{s}}\right)$	$\dfrac{1}{\sqrt{\pi t}} e^{-2k \sqrt{t}}$

LAPLACE TRANSFORMS (Continued)

	$f(s)$	$F(t)$
115.1	$-e^{as}\,\text{Ei}(-as)$	$\dfrac{1}{t+a}\,;\,(a>0)$
115.2	$\dfrac{1}{a}+se^{as}\,\text{Ei}(-as)$	$\dfrac{1}{(t+a)^2}\,;\,(a>0)$
115.3	$\left[\dfrac{\pi}{2}-\text{Si}(s)\right]\cos s+\text{Ci}(s)\sin s$	$\dfrac{1}{t^2+1}$
116*	$K_0(ks)$	$\begin{cases}0 & \text{when } 0<t<k \\ (t^2-k^2)^{-1/2} & \text{when } t>k\end{cases}$
117	$K_0(k\sqrt{s})$	$\dfrac{1}{2t}\exp\left(-\dfrac{k^2}{4t}\right)$
118	$\dfrac{1}{s}\,e^{ks}K_1(ks)$	$\dfrac{1}{k}\sqrt{t(t+2k)}$
119	$\dfrac{1}{\sqrt{s}}\,K_1(k\sqrt{s})$	$\dfrac{1}{k}\exp\left(-\dfrac{k^2}{4t}\right)$
120	$\dfrac{1}{\sqrt{s}}\,e^{k/s}K_0\left(\dfrac{k}{s}\right)$	$\dfrac{2}{\sqrt{\pi t}}\,K_0(2\sqrt{2kt})$
121	$\pi e^{-ks}I_0(ks)$	$\begin{cases}[t(2k-t)]^{-1/2} & \text{when } 0<t<2k \\ 0 & \text{when } t>2k\end{cases}$
122**	$e^{-ks}I_1(ks)$	$\begin{cases}\dfrac{k-t}{\pi k\sqrt{t(2k-t)}} & \text{when } 0<t<2k \\ 0 & \text{when } t>2k\end{cases}$

*$K_n(x)$ is Bessel's function of the second kind for the imaginary argument.
**Several additional transforms, especially those involving other Bessel functions, can be found in the tables by G. A. Campbell and R. M. Foster, "Fourier Integrals for Practical Applications", or "Vol. 1, Bateman Manuscript Project, Transform Tables, McGraw-Hill, 1955", or N. W. McLachlan and P. Humbert, "Formulaire pour le calcul symbolique". In the tables by Campbell and Foster, only those entries containing the condition $0<g$ or $k<g$, where g is our t, are Laplace transforms.

THE Z TRANSFORM
B. Girling

When $F(t)$, a continuous function of time, is sampled at regular intervals of period T the usual Laplace transform techniques are modified. The diagramatic form of a simple sampler together with its associated input-output waveforms is shown below

$$\frac{1}{T} \equiv F_s \qquad \text{the sampling frequency}$$

Defining the set of impulse functions $\delta_T(t)$ by

$$\delta_T(t) \equiv \sum_{n=0}^{\infty} \delta(t - nT)$$

the input-output relationship of the sampler becomes

$$F^*(t) = F(t) \cdot \delta_T(t)$$
$$= \sum_{n=0}^{\infty} F(nT) \cdot \delta(t - nT).$$

While for a given $F(t)$ and T the $F^*(t)$ is unique, the converse is not true.

The Laplace transform can be used to define $F^*(s)$ as follows

$$L\{F^*(t)\} \equiv f^*(s)$$
$$= \sum_{n=0}^{\infty} F(nT) \cdot e^{-nTs}.$$

The variable 'z' is introduced by means of the transformation

$$z = e^{Ts}$$

and since any function of s can now be replaced by a corresponding function of z we have

$$f(z) = \sum_{n=0}^{\infty} F(nT) \cdot z^{-n}$$

where
$$f^*(s) \equiv f(z)$$

and
$$s = \frac{1}{T} \ln z$$

The Z operator can now be defined in terms of the Laplace operator by the relationship

$$Z\{F(t)\} \equiv L\{F^*(t)\}$$

THE Z TRANSFORM (Continued)

An alternative definition (quoted without proof) is

$$Z\{F(t)\} = \sum \text{ residues of } \left[\left(\frac{1}{1 - e^{Tz}z^{-1}} \right) \cdot f(z) \right]$$

The inverse z transform

$$Z^{-1}\{f(z)\} \equiv F^*(t)$$
$$= \frac{1}{2\pi j} \oint f(z) \cdot z^{n-1} \, dz$$

where the contour of integration encloses all the singularities of the integrand. In the following table Greek letters denote constants.

$F(t)$	$f(z) = Z\{F(t)\}$
$\alpha F(t)$	$\alpha f(z)$
$F(t) + G(t)$	$f(z) + g(z)$
$F(t + T)$	$zf(z) - zF(0)$
$F(t + 2T)$	$z^2 f(z) - z^2 F(0) - zF(T)$
$F(t + mT)$	$z^m f(z) - \displaystyle\sum_{r=0}^{m-1} z^{m-r} F(rT)$ $= z^m f(z)$ when $F(rT) = 0, 0 \leq r \leq m - 1$
$F(t - mT)$	$z^{-m} f(z)$
$e^{\alpha t} F(t)$	$f(e^{-\alpha T} z)$
$e^{-\alpha t} F(t)$	$f(e^{\alpha T} z)$
$t \cdot F(t)$	$-Tz \dfrac{d}{dz} f(z)$
$t^{-1} F(t)$	$-\dfrac{1}{T} \displaystyle\int_0^z \frac{f(z)}{z} \, dz$
$\displaystyle\sum_{m=0}^{T/t} F(mT)$	$\left(\dfrac{z}{z - 1} \right) f(z)$

The following limits are also valid

$$\lim_{t \to 0} F(t) = \lim_{z \to \infty} f(z)$$
$$\lim_{t \to \infty} F^*(t) = \lim_{z \to 1} \left[\left(\frac{z - 1}{z} \right) f(z) \right]$$

In the table which follows, the Heavyside unit step function is defined by

$$H(t - nT) \equiv \begin{cases} 1; \, t \geq nT \\ 0; \, t < nT. \end{cases}$$

THE Z TRANSFORM (Continued)

$F(t)$	$f(z)$
$\delta(t)$	1
$\delta(t - mT)$	$\dfrac{1}{z^m}$
$H(t)$	$\dfrac{z}{z - 1}$
$H(t - T)$	$\dfrac{1}{z - 1}$
$H(t - mT)$	$\dfrac{z}{z^m \cdot (z - 1)}$
$H(t) - H(t - T)$	1
$H(t) - H(t - 2T)$	$1 + \dfrac{1}{z}$
$H(t - mT) - H(t - \overline{m + 1}T)$	$\dfrac{1}{z}\, m$
$\dfrac{T}{t} H(t - T)$	$\ln\left(\dfrac{z}{z - 1}\right)$
t	$\dfrac{Tz}{(z - 1)^2}$
t^2	$\dfrac{T^2 z(z + 1)}{(z - 1)^3}$
t^3	$\dfrac{T^3 z(z^2 + 4z + 1)}{(z - 1)^4}$
t^n	$(-1)^n \lim\limits_{\chi \to 0} \dfrac{\partial^n}{\partial \chi^n}\left(\dfrac{z}{z - e^{-\chi T}}\right)$
$1 - a^{\omega t}$	$\dfrac{z(1 - a^{\omega T})}{(z - 1)(z - a^{\omega T})}$
$a^{\omega t}$	$\dfrac{z}{(z - a^{\omega T})}$
$t a^{\omega t}$	$\dfrac{Tz a^{\omega T}}{(z - a^{\omega T})^2}$
$t^2 a^{\omega t}$	$\dfrac{T^2 a^{\omega T} z(z + a^{\omega T})}{(z - a^{\omega T})^3}$
$\sin \omega t$	$\dfrac{z \sin \omega T}{z^2 - 2z \cos \omega T + 1}$
$\cos \omega t$	$\dfrac{z(z - \cos \omega T)}{z^2 - 2z \cos \omega T + 1}$
$\sinh \omega t$	$\dfrac{z \sinh \omega T}{z^2 - 2z \cosh \omega T + 1}$
$\cosh \omega t$	$\dfrac{z(z - \cosh \omega T)}{z^2 - 2z \cosh \omega T + 1}$
$e^{-\alpha t} \sin \omega t$	$\dfrac{z e^{-\alpha T} \sin \omega T}{z^2 - 2z e^{-T} \cos \omega T + e^{-2\alpha T}}$
$e^{-\alpha t} \cos \omega t$	$\dfrac{z(z - e^{-\alpha T} \cos \omega T)}{z^2 - 2z e^{-T} \cos \omega T + e^{-2\alpha T}}$
$e^{-\alpha t} \sinh \omega t$	$\dfrac{z e^{-\alpha T} \sinh \omega T}{z^2 - 2z e^{-\alpha T} \cosh \omega T + e^{-2\alpha T}}$
$e^{-\alpha t} \cosh \omega t$	$\dfrac{z(z - e^{-\alpha T} \cosh \omega T)}{z^2 - 2z e^{-\alpha T} \cosh \omega T + e^{-2\alpha T}}$

THE Z TRANSFORM (Continued)

$F(t)$	$f(z)$
$-\dfrac{1}{a}\left[\delta(t) - a^{t/T}\right]$	$\dfrac{1}{z - a}$
$\dfrac{1}{(a-b)}\left[a^{\left(\frac{t}{T}-1\right)} - b^{\left(\frac{t}{T}-1\right)}\right]$	$\dfrac{1}{(z-a)(z-b)}$
$\dfrac{1}{(a-b)}\left[a^{\frac{t}{T}} - b^{\frac{t}{T}}\right]$	$\dfrac{z}{(z-a)(z-b)}$
$\dfrac{1}{(a-b)}\left[(a-c)a^{\left(\frac{t}{T}-1\right)} - (b-c)b^{\left(\frac{t}{T}-1\right)}\right]$	$\dfrac{z-c}{(z-a)(z-b)}$
$\dfrac{1}{(a-b)}\left[a^{\left(\frac{t}{T}+1\right)} - b^{\left(\frac{T}{t}+1\right)}\right]$	$\dfrac{z^2}{(z-a)(z-b)}$
$\dfrac{1}{\left(\frac{t}{T}\right)!}$	$e^{1/z}$
$\dfrac{1}{\left(\frac{2t}{T}\right)!}$	$\cosh(z^{-\frac{1}{2}})$

Methods of evaluating inverse z transforms.

(1) Cauchy's residue theorem.

For $t = nT$,

$$G(nT) = \sum_{\text{all } z_k} [\text{residues of } g(z)z^{n-1} \text{ at } z_k]$$

where the z_k define all the poles of $g(z)z^{n-1}$.

(2) Partial fractions.

Expand $g(z)/z$ into partial fractions. The product of z with each of the partial fractions will then be recognizable from the standard forms in the table of z transforms. Note however that the continuous functions obtained are only valid at the sampling instants.

(3) Power series expansion by long division using detached coefficients.

$g(z)$ is expanded into a power series in z^{-1} and the coefficient of the term in z^{-n} is the value of $g(nT)$ i.e. the value of $G(t)$ at the nth sampling instant.

The z transform as a means of determining approximately the inverse Laplace transform.

Since
$$z \equiv e^{Ts}$$

$$s^{-1} = \frac{T}{2}\left[\frac{1}{v} - \frac{v}{3} - \frac{4v^3}{45} - \frac{44v^5}{945} - \cdots \right]$$

where
$$v \equiv \frac{1 - z^{-1}}{1 + z^{-1}},$$

the series being very rapid in its convergence. Given $g(s)$, to find its inverse Laplace transform the following operations are carried out:-

(i) Divide the numerator and denominator of $g(s)$ by the highest power of s yielding as an alternative form for $g(s)$ the quotient of two polynomials in s^{-1}.

(ii) Chose as a numerical value of T, that which makes $2\pi/T$ much larger than the imaginary part of the poles of $G(s)$.

(iii) Substitute into the alternative form for $g(s)$ obtained in (i) above the expansion for s^{-n} determined from the following short table of approximations.

THE Z TRANSFORM (Continued)

Do not at this stage insert the numerical value for T as tabulations with different intervals may be required.

(iv) Divide by T.

(v) Insert the chosen value for T and divide the numerator by the denominator.

(vi) The coefficient of z^{-n} is the required value of the function at $t = nT$.

s^{-n}	z transform (approximate)
s^{-1}	$\dfrac{T}{2}\left[\dfrac{1 + z^{-1}}{1 - z^{-1}}\right]$
s^{-2}	$\dfrac{T^2}{12}\left[\dfrac{1 + 10z^{-1} + z^{-2}}{(1 - z^{-1})^2}\right]$
s^{-3}	$\dfrac{T^3}{3}\left[\dfrac{z^{-1} + z^{-2}}{(1 - z^{-1})^3}\right]$
s^{-4}	$\dfrac{T^4}{144}\left[\dfrac{1 + 20z^{-1} + 102z^{-2} + 20z^{-3} + z^{-4}}{(1 - z^{-1})^4}\right]$
s^{-5}	$\dfrac{T^5}{24}\left[\dfrac{z^{-1} + 11z^{-2} + 11z^{-3} + z^{-4}}{(1 - z^{-1})^5}\right]$
s^{-6}	$\dfrac{T^6}{4}\left[\dfrac{z^{-2} + 2z^{-3} + z^{-4}}{(1 - z^{-1})^6}\right]$
s^{-7}	$\dfrac{T^7}{8}\left[\dfrac{z^{-2} + 3z^{-3} + 3z^{-4} + z^{-5}}{(1 - z^{-1})^7}\right]$

Additional material on Z-transforms can be found in the papers by Boxer, R. and Thaler, S., A simplified method of solving linear and nonlinear systems. *Proc. IEE,* 1956, 89–101, and Boxer, R., A note on numerical transform calculus, *Proc. IEE,* 1957, 1401–1406.

COMPLEX VARIABLES

Complex Numbers

Cartesian Form

The cartesian form of a complex number is $z = x + iy$, where x and y are real numbers and i, called the imaginary unit, has the property that $i^2 = -1$. The real numbers x and y are called the real and imaginary parts of $x + iy$, respectively.

Polar Form

$z = re^{i\theta} = r(\cos\theta + i\sin\theta)$

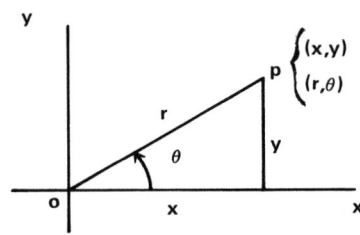

Modulus

$$r = |z| = (x^2 + y^2)^{1/2}$$

Argument

$$\theta = \arg z = \arctan\frac{y}{x}$$

Complex Conjugate

$$\bar{z} = x - iy, \quad |\bar{z}| = |z|, \quad \arg\bar{z} = -\arg z$$

Addition and Subtraction

$$z_1 \pm z_2 = (x_1 + iy_1) \pm (x_2 + iy_2) = (x_1 \pm x_2) + (y_1 \pm y_2)$$

Multiplication

$$z_1 z_2 = (x_1 + iy_1)(x_2 + iy_2) = (x_1 x_2 - y_1 y_2) + i(x_1 y_2 + x_2 y_1)$$

$$|z_1 z_2| = |z_1|\,|z_2|, \quad \arg(z_1 z_2) = \arg z_1 + \arg z_2$$

Division

$$\frac{z_1}{z_2} = \frac{z_1 \bar{z}_2}{z_2 \bar{z}_2} = \frac{(x_1 x_2 + y_1 y_2) + i(x_2 y_1 - x_1 y_2)}{x_2^2 + y_2^2}$$

$$\left|\frac{z_1}{z_2}\right| = \frac{|z_1|}{|z_2|}, \quad \arg\left(\frac{z_1}{z_2}\right) = \arg z_1 - \arg z_2$$

Powers

$$z^n = r^n e^{in\theta} = r^n(\cos n\theta + i\sin n\theta) \quad \text{(DeMoivre's Theorem)}$$

Roots

$$z^{\frac{1}{n}} = r^{\frac{1}{n}} e^{i\theta/n} = r^{\frac{1}{n}} \left[\cos \frac{\theta + 2k\pi}{n} + i \sin \frac{\theta + 2k\pi}{n} , k = 1, 2, \ldots, n-1 \right]$$

(Principal root if $-\pi < \theta < \pi$)

Functions of a Complex Variable

A complex function

$$w = f(z) = u(x, y) + iv(x, y) = |w| e^{i\phi}$$

$$(z = x + iy = |z| e^{i\theta})$$

associates one or more values of the complex dependent variable w with each value of the complex independent variable z in a given domain of definition.

Cauchy-Riemann Equations

$$\frac{\partial u}{\partial x} = \frac{\partial v}{\partial y}, \quad \frac{\partial u}{\partial y} = -\frac{\partial v}{\partial x}$$

A function $w = f(z)$ differentiable at each point of a certain neighborhood of a point z_0 (i.e., at each point of a circle with center z_0 and an arbitrary small radius) is said to be analytic at the point z_0. A function is called analytic in a connected domain if it is analytic at each point in the domain.

A necessary and sufficient condition that the function $f(z) = u(x,y) + iv(x,y)$ is analytic is that it satisfy the Cauchy-Riemann conditions.

Cauchy-Goursat Theorem

If a function $f(z)$ is analytic at all points within and on a simple closed curve C, then

$$\int_c f(z) \, dz = 0$$

Cauchy's Integral Formula

If $f(z)$ is analytic inside and on a simple closed curve C and if z_0 is interior to C, then

$$f(z) = \frac{1}{2\pi i} \int_c \frac{f(z)}{z - z_0} \, dz$$

Also, the derivatives $f'(z)$, $f''(z)$, ... of all orders exist, and

$$f^n(z) = \frac{n!}{2\pi i} \int_c \frac{f(z)}{(z - z_0)^{n+1}} \, dz$$

Taylor-Series Expansion

If $f(z)$ is analytic inside and on a circle C of radius r about $z = z_0$, then there exists a unique and uniformly convergent series expansion in powers of $z - z_0$,

$$f(z) = \sum_{n=0}^{\infty} a_n (z - z_0)^n, \quad (|z - z_0| \leq r, z_0 \neq \infty)$$

where

$$a_n = \frac{1}{n!} f^n(z_0) = \frac{1}{2\pi i} \int_C \frac{f(s)}{(s-z_0)^{n+1}} ds$$

If $M(r)$ is an upper bound on $|f(z)|$ on C, then

$$|a_n| = \frac{1}{n!} |f^{(n)}(z_0)| \leqslant \frac{M(r)}{r^n} \qquad \text{(Cauchy's Inequality)}$$

If Taylor's series is terminated with the term $a_{n-1} (z - z_0)^{n-1}$, the remainder $R_n(z)$ is given by

$$R_n(z) = \frac{(z-z_0)^n}{2\pi i} \int_C \frac{f(s)\, ds}{(s-z_0)^n (s-z)}$$

$$|R_n(z)| \leqslant \left(\frac{|z-z_0|}{r} \right)^n \frac{M(r)\, r}{r - |z-z_0|}$$

Laurent-Series Expansion

If $f(z)$ is analytic throughout the annular region between and on the concentric circles C_1 and C_2 centered at $z = z_0$ and radii r_1 and $r_2 < r_1$, respectively, there exists a unique series expansion in terms of positive and negative powers of $z - z_0$

$$f(z) = \sum_{n=0}^{\infty} a_n (z - z_0)^n + \sum_{n=1}^{\infty} b_n (z - z_0)^{-n}$$

where

$$a_n = \frac{1}{2\pi i} \int_C \frac{f(s)}{(s-z_0)^{n+1}} ds, \qquad b_n = \frac{1}{2\pi i} \int_C \frac{f(s)}{(s-z_0)^{-n+1}} ds$$

$$(n = 0, 1, 2, \dots) \qquad\qquad (n = 1, 2, \dots)$$

Zeros and Isolated Singularities

Zeros

The points z for which $f(z) = 0$ are called the zeros of $f(z)$. A function $f(z)$ analytic at $z = z_0$ has a zero of order m, where m is a positive integer at $z = z_0$ if and only if the first m coefficients $a_0, a_1, \dots, a_{m-1}$ in the Taylor-series expansion about $z = z_0$ vanish.

Singularities

A singular point or singularity of the function $f(z)$ is any point where $f(z)$ is not analytic. An isolated singularity of $f(z)$ at $z = z_0$ is

1. A removable singularity if and only if all coefficients b_n in the Laurent-series expansion of $f(z)$ about $z = z_0$ vanish.
2. A pole of order m (m = 1,2,...) if and only if $(z - z_0)^m f(z)$, but not $(z - z_0)^{m-1} f(z)$ is analytic at $z = z_0$, i.e., if and only if $b_m \neq 0$, $b_{m+1} = b_{m+2} = \dots = 0$ in the Laurent-series expansion of $f(z)$ about $z = z_0$, or if $\frac{1}{f(z)}$ is analytic and has a zero of order m at $z = z_0$.
3. An isolated essential singularity if and only if the Laurent-series expansion of $f(z)$ about $z = z_0$ has an infinite number of terms involving negative powers of $z - z_0$.

Residues

Given a point $z = z_0$, where $f(z)$ is either analytic or has an isolated singularity, the residue of $f(z)$ at $z = z_0$ is the coefficient of $(z - z_0)^{-1}$ in the Laurent-series expansion of $f(z)$ about $z = z_0$, or

$$R_k = b_1 = \frac{1}{2\pi i} \int_c f(z)\, dz$$

If $f(z)$ is either analytic or has a removable singularity at $z = z_0$, then $b_1 = 0$. If $z = z_0$ is a pole of order m, then

$$b_1 = \frac{1}{(m-1)!} \frac{d^{m-1}}{dz^{m-1}} [(z - z_0)^m f(z)]_{z=z_0}$$

For every simple closed contour C enclosing at most a finite number of singularities $z_1, z_2, \ldots, z_n$ of a single-valued function $f(z)$ continuous on C,

$$\frac{1}{2\pi i} \int_c f(z)\, dz = \sum_{k=1}^{n} R_k$$

where the R_k are the residues of $f(z)$ at the singularities.

Mappings or Transformations

A function $w = f(z)$ maps points of the z-plane into corresponding points of the w-plane. At every point z such that $f(z)$ is analytic and $f'(z) \neq 0$, the mapping is conformal, i.e., the angle between two curves through such a point is reproduced in magnitude and sense by the angle between the corresponding curves in the w-plane.

A table giving real and imaginary parts, zeros, and singularities for frequently used functions of a complex variable and a table illustrating a number of special transformations of interest in various applications are provided.

Real and Imaginary Parts, Zeros, and Singularities for a Number of Frequently Used Functions

$$f(z) = u(x,y) + iv(x,y) \quad \text{of a Complex Variable } z = x + iy$$

Note: $|f(z)| = \sqrt{u^2 + v^2}$ $\quad \arg f(z) = \arctan \dfrac{v}{u}$

Function $f(z)$	$u(x,y)$	$v(x,y)$	Zeros (order m)	Isolated singularities
z	x	y	$z=0$ $\quad m=1$	Pole ($m=1$) at $z=\infty$
z^2	$x^2 - y^2$	$2xy$	$z=0$ $\quad m=2$	Pole ($m=2$) at $z=\infty$
$\dfrac{1}{z}$	$\dfrac{x}{x^2+y^2}$	$-\dfrac{y}{x^2+y^2}$	$z=\infty$ $\quad m=1$	Pole ($m=1$) at $z=0$
$\dfrac{1}{z^2}$	$\dfrac{x^2-y^2}{(x^2+y^2)^2}$	$\dfrac{-2xy}{(x^2+y^2)^2}$	$z=\infty$ $\quad m=2$	Pole ($m=2$) at $z=0$
$\dfrac{1}{z-(a+ib)}$ (a, b real)	$\dfrac{(x-a)}{(x-a)^2+(y-b)^2}$	$-\dfrac{(y-b)}{(x-a)^2+(y-b)^2}$	$z=\infty$ $\quad m=1$	Pole ($m=1$) at $z=a+ib$
$\sqrt{z}$	$\pm\left(\dfrac{x+\sqrt{x^2+y^2}}{2}\right)^{1/2}$	$\pm\left(\dfrac{-x+\sqrt{x^2+y^2}}{2}\right)^{1/2}$	Zero of order 1 at $z=0$ (branch point)	Branch point ($m=1$) at $z=0$ Branch point ($m=1$) at $z=\infty$
e^z	$e^x\cos y$	$e^x \sin y$	$\cdots\cdots\cdots\cdots$	Essential singularity at $z=\infty$
$\sin z$	$\sin x \cosh y$	$\cos x \sinh y$	$z=k\pi$ $\quad m=1$ ($k=0,\pm1,\pm2,\pm\dots$)	Essential singularity at $z=\infty$
$\cos z$	$\cos x \cosh y$	$-\sin x \sinh y$	$z=(k+\tfrac{1}{2})\pi$ $\quad m=1$ ($k=0,\pm1,\pm2,\pm\dots$)	Essential singularity at $z=\infty$
$\sinh z$	$\sinh x \cos y$	$\cosh x \sin y$	$z=k\pi i$ $\quad m=1$ ($k=0,\pm1,\pm2,\pm\dots$)	Essential singularity at $z=\infty$
$\cosh z$	$\cosh x \cos y$	$\sinh x \sin y$	$z=(k+\tfrac{1}{2})\pi i$ $\quad m=1$ ($k=0,\pm1,\pm2,\pm\dots$)	Essential singularity at $z=\infty$

Real and Imaginary Parts, Zeros, and Singularities for a Number of Frequently Used Functions

$$f(z) = u\,(x,y) + iv\,(x,y) \text{ of a Complex Variable } z = x + iy$$

Function $f(z)$	$u(x,y)$	$v(x,y)$	Zeros (order m)	Isolated singularities
$\tan z$	$\dfrac{\sin 2x}{\cos 2x + \cosh 2y}$	$\dfrac{\sinh 2y}{\cos 2x + \cosh 2y}$	$z = k\pi \qquad m = 1$ $(k = 0, \pm1, \pm2, \pm \ldots)$	Essential singularity at $z = \infty$ Poles ($m = 1$) at $z = (k + \tfrac{1}{2})\pi$ $(k = 0, \pm1, \pm2, \pm \ldots)$
$\tanh z$	$\dfrac{\sinh 2x}{\cosh 2x + \cos 2y}$	$\dfrac{\sin 2y}{\cosh 2x + \cos 2y}$	$z = k\pi i \qquad m = 1$ $(k = 0, \pm1, \pm2, \pm \ldots)$	Essential singularity at $z = \infty$ Poles ($m = 1$) at $z = (k+\tfrac{1}{2})\pi i$ $(k = 0, \pm1, \pm2, \pm \ldots)$
$\log_e z$	$\tfrac{1}{2}\log_e (x^2 + y^2)$	$\arctan \dfrac{y}{x} + 2k\pi$ $(k = 0, \pm1, \pm2, + \ldots)$	$z = 1 \qquad m = 1$ (branch corresponding to $k=0$ only)	Branch points of infinite order at $z = 0$, $z = \infty$; both are essential singularities

From Korn, G. A. and Korn, T. M., *Mathematical Handbook for Scientists & Engineers*, 2nd ed., McGraw-Hill, New York, 1968, 189. With permission.

Table of Transformations of Regions

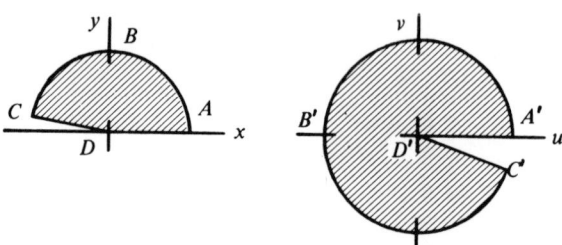

FIGURE 1. $\omega = z^2$.

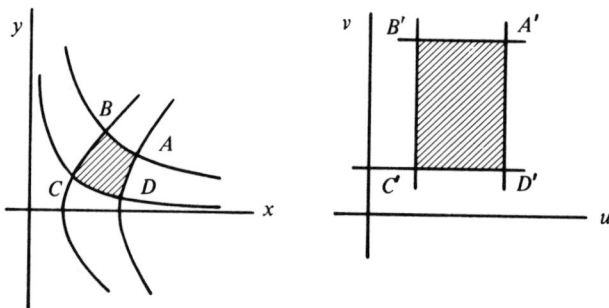

FIGURE 2. $\omega = z^2$.

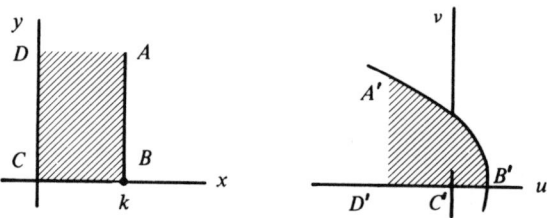

FIGURE 3. $\omega = z^2$; A′ B′ on parabola $\rho = \dfrac{2k^2}{1 + \cos \phi}$

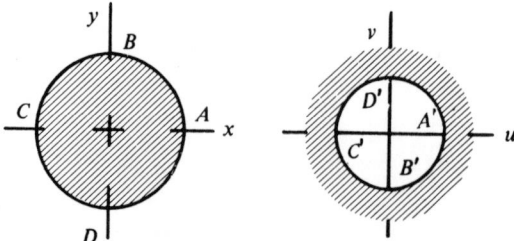

FIGURE 4. $\omega = 1/z$.

(From Churchill, R. V., Brown, J. W., and Verhey, R. F., *Complex Variables and Applications*, 34d ed., McGraw-Hill, New York, 1974, 314 – 324. With permission.)

Table of Transformations of Regions (continued)

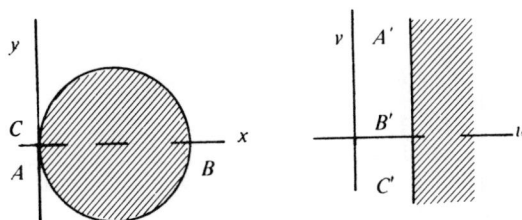

FIGURE 5. $\omega = 1/z$.

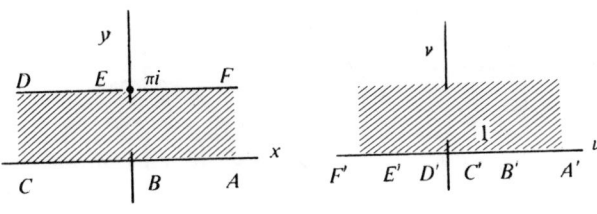

FIGURE 6. $\omega = e^z$.

FIGURE 7. $\omega = e^z$.

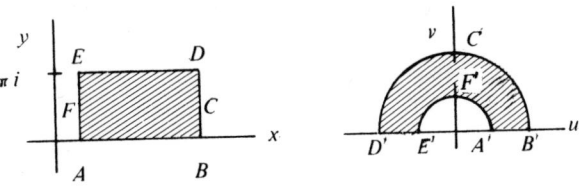

FIGURE 8. $\omega = e^z$.

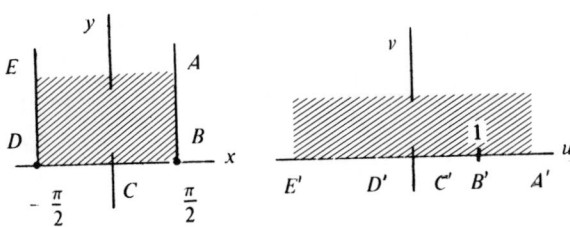

FIGURE 9. $\omega = \sin z$.

Table of Transformations of Regions (continued)

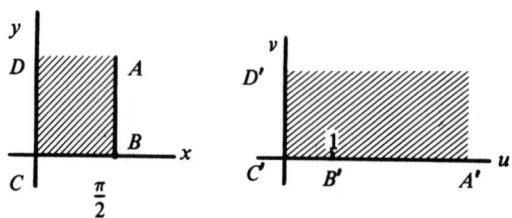

FIGURE 10. $\omega = \sin z$.

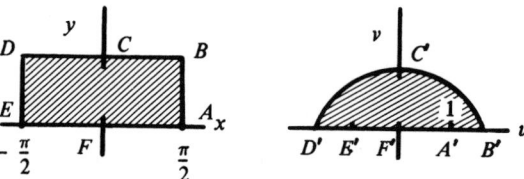

FIGURE 11. $\omega = \sin z$; BCD: $y = k$, $B'\,C'\,D'$ is on ellipse $\left(\dfrac{u}{\cosh k}\right)^2 + \left(\dfrac{v}{\sinh k}\right)^2 = 1$.

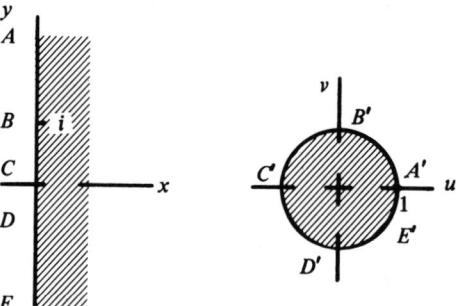

FIGURE 12. $\omega = \dfrac{z-1}{z+1}$.

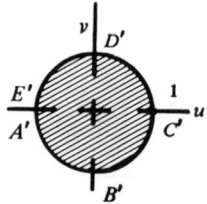

FIGURE 13. $\omega = \dfrac{i-z}{i+z}$.

Table of Transformations of Regions (continued)

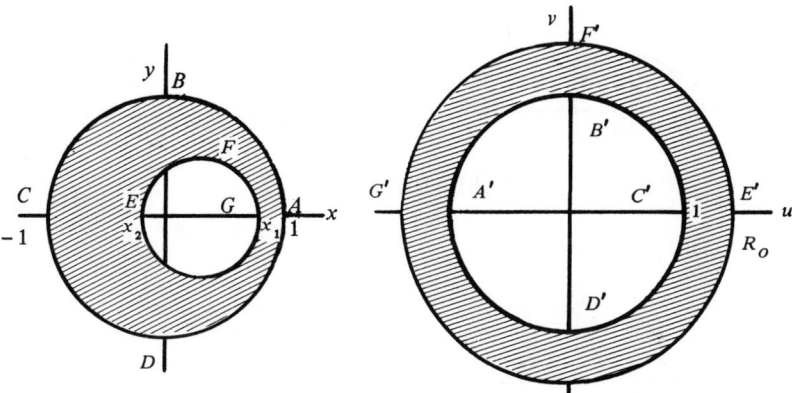

FIGURE 14. $\omega = \dfrac{z-a}{az-1}$; $a = \dfrac{1 + x_1 x_2 + \sqrt{(1-x_1{}^2)(1-x_2{}^2)}}{x_1 + x_2}$;

$R_0 = \dfrac{1 - x_1 x_2 + \sqrt{(1-x_1{}^2)(1-x_2{}^2)}}{x_1 - x_2}$ $(a > 1$ and $R_0 > 1$ when $-1 < x_2 < x_1 < 1)$.

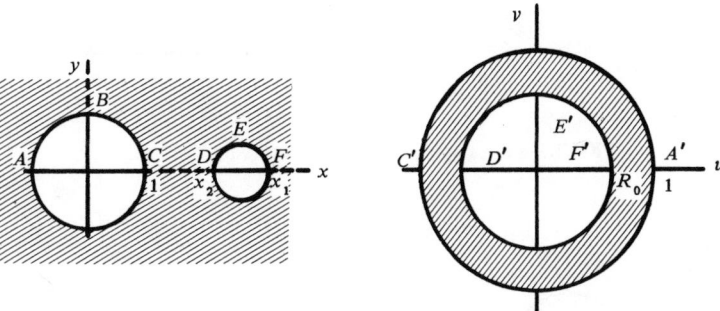

FIGURE 15. $\omega = \dfrac{z-a}{az-1}$; $a = \dfrac{1 + x_1 x_2 + \sqrt{(x_1{}^2-1)(x_2{}^2-1)}}{x_1 + x_2}$;

$R_0 = \dfrac{x_1 x_2 - 1 - \sqrt{(x_1{}^2-1)(x_2{}^2-1)}}{x_1 - x_2}$ $(x_2 < a < x_1$ and $0 < R_0 < 1$ when $1 < x_2 < x_1)$.

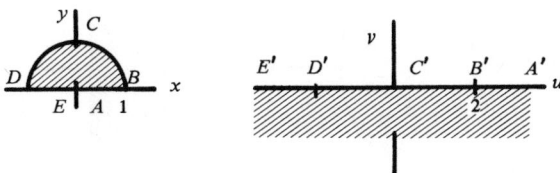

FIGURE 16. $\omega = z + 1/z$.

Table of Transformations of Regions (continued)

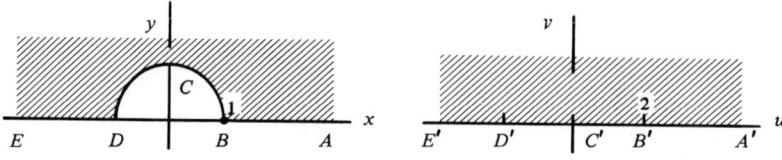

FIGURE 17. $\omega = z + 1/z$.

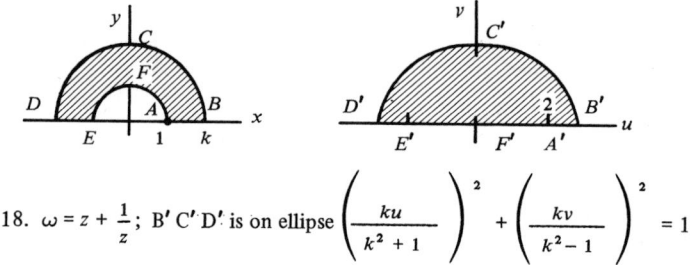

FIGURE 18. $\omega = z + \dfrac{1}{z}$; B' C' D' is on ellipse $\left(\dfrac{ku}{k^2+1}\right)^2 + \left(\dfrac{kv}{k^2-1}\right)^2 = 1$.

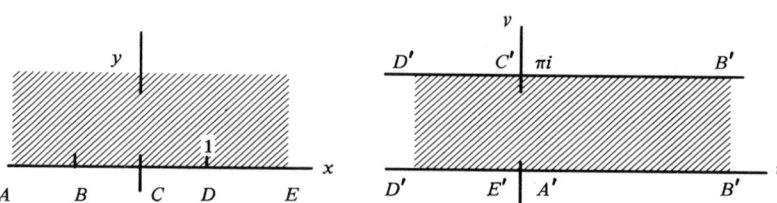

FIGURE 19. $\omega = \log_e \dfrac{z-1}{z+1}$; $z = -\coth \dfrac{\omega}{2}$.

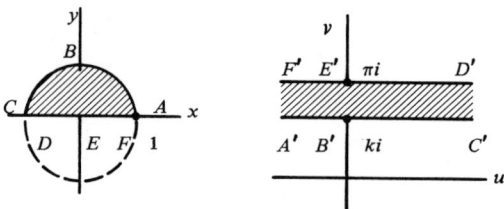

FIGURE 20. $\omega = \log_e \dfrac{z-1}{z+1}$; ABC is on circle $x^2 + y^2 - 2y \cot k = 1$.

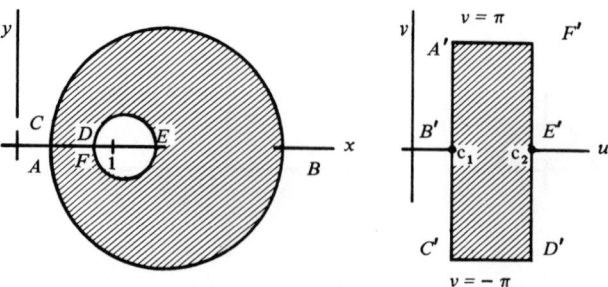

FIGURE 21. $\omega = \log_e \dfrac{z+1}{z-1}$; centers of circles at $z = \coth c_n$, radii: $\operatorname{csch} c_n$ ($n = 1, 2$).

Table of Transformations of Regions (continued)

FIGURE 22. $\omega = k \log_e \dfrac{k}{1-k} + \log_e 2 (1-k) + i\pi - k \log_e(z+1)$

$- (1-k) \log_e(z-1); \; x_1 = 2k - 1.$

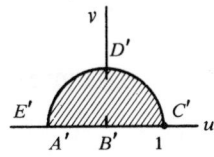

FIGURE 23. $\omega = \tan^2 \dfrac{z}{2} = \dfrac{1 - \cos z}{1 + \cos z}$

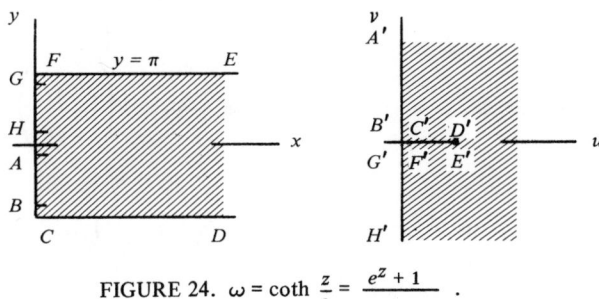

FIGURE 24. $\omega = \coth \dfrac{z}{2} = \dfrac{e^z + 1}{e^z - 1}$.

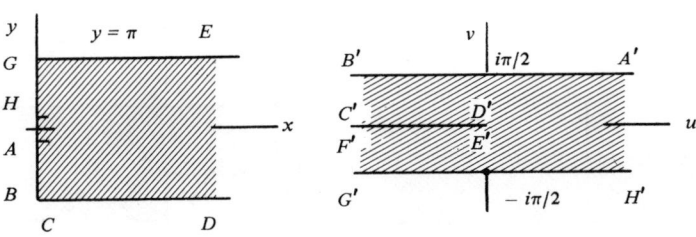

FIGURE 25. $\omega = \log_e \coth \dfrac{z}{2}$.

Table of Transformations of Regions (continued)

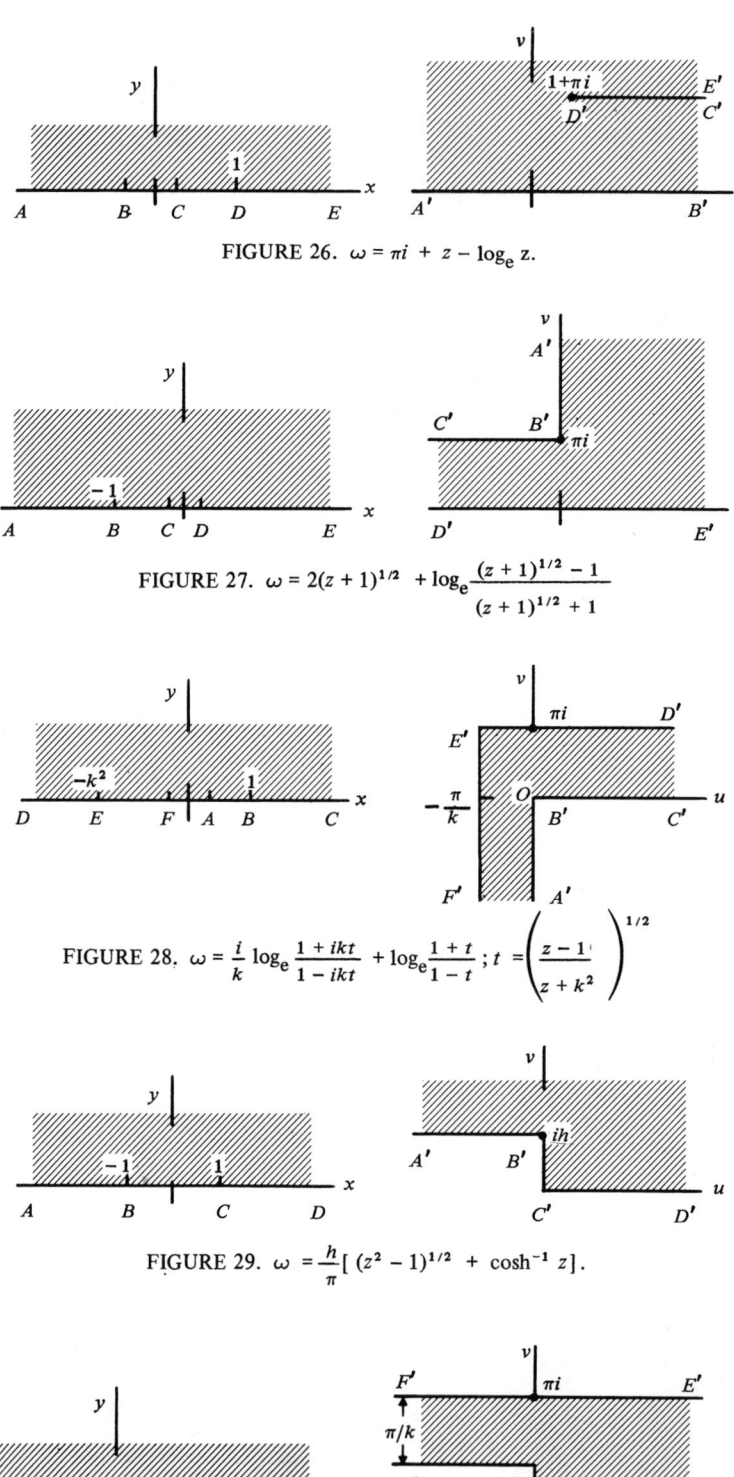

FIGURE 26. $\omega = \pi i + z - \log_e z$.

FIGURE 27. $\omega = 2(z + 1)^{1/2} + \log_e \dfrac{(z + 1)^{1/2} - 1}{(z + 1)^{1/2} + 1}$

FIGURE 28. $\omega = \dfrac{i}{k} \log_e \dfrac{1 + ikt}{1 - ikt} + \log_e \dfrac{1 + t}{1 - t}$; $t = \left(\dfrac{z - 1}{z + k^2} \right)^{1/2}$

FIGURE 29. $\omega = \dfrac{h}{\pi} [\, (z^2 - 1)^{1/2} + \cosh^{-1} z \,]$.

FIGURE 30. $\omega = \cosh^{-1} \left(\dfrac{2z - k - 1}{k - 1} \right) - \dfrac{1}{k} \cosh^{-1} \left[\dfrac{(k + 1)z - 2k}{(k - 1)z} \right]$.

FINITE DIFFERENCES

Uniform interval h.

If a function $f(x)$ is tabulated at a uniform interval h, that is, for arguments given by $x_n = x_0 + nh$, where n is an integer, then the function $f(x)$ may be denoted by f_n.

This can be generalized so that for all values of p, and in particular for $0 \leqq p \leqq 1$,

$$f(x_0 + ph) = f(x_p) = f_p ,$$

where the argument designated x_0 can be chosen quite arbitrarily.

The notation $x = a(h)b(H)C$ means that the arguments run from a to b inclusive at the uniform interval h and thereafter continue to C at the uniform interval H.

The statement $f(x)$ 4D means that the function $f(x)$ is to be tabulated and the answer rounded off to four places of decimals.

The statement $f(x)$ 5S means that the function $f(x)$ is to be tabulated with the answer being rounded off to five significant figures.

The following table lists and defines the standard operators used in numerical analysis.

Symbol	Function	Definition
E	Displacement	$Ef_p = f_{p+1}$
Δ	Forward difference	$\Delta f_p = f_{p+1} - f_p$
∇	Backward difference	$\nabla f_p = f_p - f_{p-1}$
$\wedge$	Divided difference	See page 637
δ	Central difference	$\delta f_p = f_{p+\frac{1}{2}} - f_{p-\frac{1}{2}}$
μ	Average	$\mu f_p = \frac{1}{2}(f_{p+\frac{1}{2}} + f_{p-\frac{1}{2}})$
Δ^{-1}	Backward sum	$\Delta^{-1}f_p = \Delta^{-1}f_{p-1} + f_{p-1}$
∇^{-1}	Forward sum	$\nabla^{-1}f_p = \nabla^{-1}f_{p-1} + f_p$
δ^{-1}	Central sum	$\delta^{-1}f_p = \delta^{-1}f_{p-1} + f_{p-\frac{1}{2}}$
D	Differentiation	$Df_p = \frac{d}{dx}f(x) = \frac{1}{h} \cdot \frac{d}{dp}f_p$
$I(=D^{-1})$	Integration	$If_p = \int^x f(x)dx = h \int^p f_p dp$
$J(=\Delta D^{-1})$	Definite integration	$Jf_p = h \int_p^{p+1} f_p dp$

I, Δ^{-1}, ∇^{-1} and δ^{-1} all imply the existence of an arbitrary constant which is determined by the initial conditions of the problem.

Where no confusion can arise the f can be omitted as, for example in writing Δ_p for Δf_p.

Higher differences are formed by successive operations, e.g.,

$$\begin{aligned}
\Delta^2 f_p &= \Delta_p^2 \\
&= \Delta \cdot \Delta_p \\
&= \Delta(f_{p+1} - f_p) \\
&= \Delta_{p+1} - \Delta_p \\
&= f_{p+2} - f_{p+1} - f_{p+1} + f_p .
\end{aligned}$$

Thus $\Delta_p^2 = f_{p+2} - 2f_{p+1} + f_p$.

Note that $f_p \equiv \Delta_p^0 \equiv \nabla_p^0 \equiv \delta_p^0$.

The disposition of the differences and sums relative to the function values is as shown (the arguments are omitted in these cases in the interests of clarity). In manuscript working double spacing is recommended.

Calculus of Finite Differences

Forward difference scheme

$$\Delta_{-1}^{-2} \quad f_{-2} \quad \Delta_{-3}^{2}$$
$$\Delta_{-1}^{-1} \quad \Delta_{-2} \quad \Delta_{-3}^{3}$$
$$\Delta_{0}^{-2} \quad f_{-1} \quad \Delta_{-2}^{2}$$
$$\Delta_{0}^{-1} \quad \Delta_{-1} \quad \Delta_{-2}^{3}$$
$$\Delta_{1}^{-2} \quad f_{0} \quad \Delta_{-1}^{2}$$
$$\Delta_{1}^{-1} \quad \Delta_{0} \quad \Delta_{-1}^{3}$$
$$\Delta_{2}^{-2} \quad f_{1} \quad \Delta_{0}^{2}$$
$$\Delta_{2}^{-1} \quad \Delta_{1} \quad \Delta_{0}^{3}$$
$$\Delta_{3}^{-2} \quad f_{2} \quad \Delta_{1}^{2}$$

Backward difference scheme

$$\nabla_{-3}^{-2} \quad f_{-2} \quad \nabla_{-1}^{2}$$
$$\nabla_{-2}^{-1} \quad \nabla_{-1} \quad \nabla_{0}^{3}$$
$$\nabla_{-2}^{-2} \quad f_{-1} \quad \nabla_{0}^{2}$$
$$\nabla_{-1}^{-1} \quad \nabla_{0} \quad \nabla_{1}^{3}$$
$$\nabla_{-1}^{-2} \quad f_{0} \quad \nabla_{1}^{2}$$
$$\nabla_{0}^{-1} \quad \nabla_{1} \quad \nabla_{2}^{3}$$
$$\nabla_{0}^{-2} \quad f_{1} \quad \nabla_{2}^{2}$$
$$\nabla_{1}^{-1} \quad \nabla_{2} \quad \nabla_{3}^{3}$$
$$\nabla_{1}^{-2} \quad f_{2} \quad \nabla_{3}^{2}$$

Central difference scheme

$$\delta_{-2}^{-2} \quad f_{-2} \quad \delta_{-2}^{2} \quad \delta_{-2}^{4}$$
$$\delta_{-1\frac{1}{2}}^{-1} \quad \delta_{-1\frac{1}{2}} \quad \delta_{-1\frac{1}{2}}^{3}$$
$$\delta_{-1}^{-2} \quad f_{-1} \quad \delta_{-1}^{2} \quad \delta_{-1}^{4}$$
$$\delta_{-\frac{1}{2}}^{-1} \quad \delta_{-\frac{1}{2}} \quad \delta_{-\frac{1}{2}}^{3}$$
$$\delta_{0}^{-2} \quad f_{0} \quad \delta_{0}^{2} \quad \delta_{0}^{4}$$
$$\delta_{\frac{1}{2}}^{-1} \quad \delta_{\frac{1}{2}} \quad \delta_{\frac{1}{2}}^{3}$$
$$\delta_{1}^{-2} \quad f_{1} \quad \delta_{1}^{2} \quad \delta_{1}^{4}$$
$$\delta_{1\frac{1}{2}}^{-1} \quad \delta_{1\frac{1}{2}} \quad \delta_{1\frac{1}{2}}^{3}$$
$$\delta_{2}^{-2} \quad f_{2}' \quad \delta_{2}^{2} \quad \delta_{2}^{4}$$

In the forward difference scheme the subscripts are seen to move forward into the difference table and no fractional subscripts occur. In the backward difference scheme the subscripts lie on diagonals slanting backwards into the table while in the central difference scheme the subscripts maintain their position and the odd order subscripts are fractional.

All three however are merely alternative ways of labeling the same numerical quantities as any difference is the result of subtracting the number diagonally above it in the preceding column from that diagonally below it in the preceding column or, alternatively, it is the sum of the number diagonally above it in the subsequent column with that immediately above it in its own column.

In general $\Delta_{p-\frac{1}{2}n}^{n} \equiv \delta_{p}^{n} \equiv \nabla_{p+\frac{1}{2}n}^{n}$.

If a polynomial of degree r is tabulated exactly i.e., without any round-off errors, then the rth differences are constant.

Tabulate $f(x)3D$ for $x = -.4 \ (.2) \ .8$ where $f(x) = x^3 - .3x^2 + .07x - .123$.

x	f	δ	δ^2	δ^3	δ^4
$-.4$	$-.263$				
		106			
$-.2$	$-.157$		-72		
		34		48	
$+0$	$-.123$		-24		0
		10		48	
$.2$	$-.113$		$+24$		0
		34		48	
$.4$	$-.079$		72		0
		106		48	
$.6$	$+.027$		120		
		226			
$.8$	$.253$				

Had the function been rounded off to two places of decimals then the third differences would not have been constant. The differences are conventionally expressed in units of the least significant decimal as shown. This obviates the need to write down non-significant zeros. In any well tabulated function the differences decrease in magnitude.

The effect of an error term e in any function value is superimposed upon the difference table in a manner shown in the following table:

f	δ	δ^2	δ^3	δ^4	δ^5
0		0		0	
	0		0		$+1e$
0		0		$+1e$	
	0		$+1e$		$-5e$
0		$+1e$		$-4e$	
	$+1e$		$-3e$		$+10e$
$+e$		$-2e$		$+6e$	
	$-1e$		$+3e$		$-10e$
0		$+1e$		$-4e$	
	0		$-1e$		$+5e$
0		0		$+1e$	
	0		0		$-1e$
0		0		0	

In particular since round-off can contribute an error of half a unit (of the least significant decimal) in the function values, reference to the table of binomial coefficients will show that the maximum effect of this upon the twelfth differences (say) is $924(\frac{1}{2}) = 462$. This could give trouble if the problem does not require this to be multiplied by a small constant and is in fact one of the reasons why numerical differentiation is unreliable.

The following table enables the simpler operators to be expressed in terms of the others:

	E	Δ	δ, μ	∇
E	—	$1 + \Delta$	$1 + \mu\delta + \frac{1}{2}\delta^2$	$(1 - \nabla)^{-1}$
Δ	$E - 1$	—	$\mu\delta + \frac{1}{2}\delta^2$	$\nabla(1 - \nabla)^{-1}$
δ	$E^{\frac{1}{2}} - E^{-\frac{1}{2}}$	$\Delta(1 + \Delta)^{-\frac{1}{2}}$	$2(\mu^2 - 1)^{\frac{1}{2}}$	$\nabla(1 - \nabla)^{-\frac{1}{2}}$
∇	$-E^{-1}$	$\Delta(1 + \Delta)^{-1}$	$\mu\delta - \frac{1}{2}\delta^2$	—
μ	$\frac{1}{2}(E^{\frac{1}{2}} + E^{-\frac{1}{2}})$	$\frac{1}{2}(2 + \Delta)(1 + \Delta)^{-\frac{1}{2}}$	$(1 + \frac{1}{4}\delta^2)^{\frac{1}{2}}$	$\frac{1}{2}(2 - \nabla)(1 - \nabla)^{-\frac{1}{2}}$

In addition to the above there are other identities by means of which the above table can be extended, viz.,

$$E = e^{hD} = \Delta\nabla^{-1}$$

$$\mu = E^{-\frac{1}{2}} + \frac{1}{2}\delta = E^{\frac{1}{2}} - \frac{1}{2}\delta = \cosh\left(\frac{1}{2}hD\right)$$

$$\delta = E^{-\frac{1}{2}}\Delta = E^{\frac{1}{2}}\nabla = (\Delta\nabla)^{\frac{1}{2}} = 2\sinh\left(\frac{1}{2}hD\right).$$

Note the emergence of Taylor's series from

$$f_p = E^p f_0$$

$$= e^{phD} f_0$$

$$= f_0 + phD f_0 + \frac{1}{2!} p^2 h^2 D^2 f_0 + \cdots.$$

NUMERICAL METHODS

Calculus of Finite Differences

FUNCTION BUILD-UP FROM DIFFERENCES

Backward differences will be used here since the notation is simpler in this case.

If a function is tabulated as far as f_0 say, then the difference table can be built up. Assuming the differences up to and including ∇_0'' have been formed, if ∇_1'' is known it follows from the definition of backward differences that f_1 can be found from

$$f_1 = f_0 + \nabla_0 + \nabla_0^2 + \nabla_0^3 + \nabla_0^4 + \cdots + \nabla_0^{n-1} + \nabla_1^n .$$

For example, in the cubic tabulated earlier if we take $x_0 = .8$ then $f_0 = .253$ and f_1 can be built-up using the above scheme as follows:

$$f_1 = .253 + (226 + 120 + 48)(10^{-3})$$
$$= .647$$

INTERPOLATION

Finite difference interpolation entails taking a given set of points and fitting a function to them. This function is usualy a polynomial, although it is rarely found explicitly as such. Central differences formulae are in general to be preferred to those involving either forward or backward differences, although the latter may be essential at the extremities of a table where the central differences may not extend far enough.

The most useful of the central differences formulae are those of *Bessel* and *Everett*, the latter particularly so since it only utilizes even order differences. Nevertheless all central difference formulae stopping at the same difference are equivalent.

Notation used:

$$\Delta_{-m_r}^r \equiv \delta_{(r/2)-m_r}^r \equiv \nabla_{r-m_r}^r$$
$$p = \frac{x - x_0}{h} = 1 - q \quad (\text{usually } 0 \leqq p \leqq 1) .$$

Any number of finite difference interpolation formulae can be obtained from the following schematic (shown for central differences only, but easily extensible by the above identities):

$$y_p = \sum_{r=0}^{} \binom{p + m_{r-1}}{r} \cdot \delta_{(r/2)-m_r}^r$$
$$= f_{-m_0} + \binom{p + m_0}{1} \delta_{\frac{1}{2}-m_1} + \binom{p + m_1}{2} \delta_{1-m_2}^2 + \binom{p + m_2}{3} \delta_{1\frac{1}{2}-m_3}^3 \cdots ,$$

where the m_r are integers so chosen that the binomial coefficient term $\binom{p + m_{r-1}}{r}$ contains all the linear factors occurring in the preceding term $\binom{p + m_{r-2}}{r - 1}$. Obviously $m_{r+1} = m_r$ or $1 + m_r$.

Further formulae are obtained by taking linear combinations of the formulae obtained from the above schematic, or by using the standard identity transformations upon chosen terms of one of the formulae.

Another way of obtaining interpolation formulae is to apply the standard identity transformations to the operator E in the operational form of the interpolation formula, viz., $f_p = E^p f_0,$

Newton's forward formula

$$f_p = f_0 + p\Delta_0 + \frac{1}{2!} p(p - 1)\Delta_0^2 + \frac{1}{3!} p(p - 1)(p - 2)\Delta_0^3 \cdots \quad 0 \leqq p \leqq 1$$

Calculus of Finite Differences

Newton's backward formula

$$f_p = f_0 + p\nabla_0 + \frac{1}{2!}p(p+1)\nabla_0^2 + \frac{1}{3!}p(p+1)(p+2)\nabla_0^3 \cdots \quad 0 \leqq p \leqq 1$$

Gauss' forward formula

$$f_p = f_0 + p\delta_{\frac{1}{2}} + G_2\delta_0^2 + G_3\delta_{\frac{1}{2}}^3 + G_4\delta_0^4 + G_5\delta_{\frac{1}{2}}^5 \cdots \qquad 0 \leqq p \leqq 1$$

Gauss' backward formula

$$f_p = f_0 + p\delta_{-\frac{1}{2}} + G_2^*\delta_0^2 + G_3\delta_{-\frac{1}{2}}^3 + G_4^*\delta_0^4 + G_5\delta_{-\frac{1}{2}}^5 \cdots \qquad 0 \leqq p \leqq 1$$

In the above $G_{2n} = \begin{pmatrix} p+n-1 \\ 2n \end{pmatrix}$

$$G_{2n}^* = \begin{pmatrix} p+n \\ 2n \end{pmatrix}$$

$$G_{2n+1} = \begin{pmatrix} p+n \\ 2n+1 \end{pmatrix}$$

Stirling's formula

$$f_p = f_0 + \tfrac{1}{2}p(\delta_{\frac{1}{2}} + \delta_{-\frac{1}{2}}) + \tfrac{1}{2}p^2\delta_0^2 + S_3(\delta_{\frac{1}{2}}^3 + \delta_{-\frac{1}{2}}^3) + S_4\delta_0^4 + \cdots \qquad -\tfrac{1}{2} \leqq p \leqq \tfrac{1}{2}$$

Steffenson's formula

$$f_p = f_0 + \tfrac{1}{2}p(p+1)\delta_{\frac{1}{2}} - \tfrac{1}{2}(p-1)p\delta_{-\frac{1}{2}} + (S_3 + S_4)\delta_{\frac{1}{2}}^3 + (S_3 - S_4)\delta_{-\frac{1}{2}}^3 \cdots -\tfrac{1}{2} \leqq p \leqq \tfrac{1}{2}.$$

In the above $S_{2n+1} = \dfrac{1}{2}\begin{pmatrix} p+n \\ 2n+1 \end{pmatrix}$

$$S_{2n+2} = \frac{p}{2n+2}\begin{pmatrix} p+n \\ 2n+1 \end{pmatrix}$$

$$S_{2n+1} + S_{2n+2} = \begin{pmatrix} p+n+1 \\ 2n+2 \end{pmatrix}$$

$$S_{2n+1} - S_{2n+2} = -\begin{pmatrix} p+n \\ 2n+2 \end{pmatrix}$$

Bessel's formula

$$f_p = f_0 + p\delta_{\frac{1}{2}} + B_2(\delta_0^2 + \delta_1^2) + B_3\delta_{\frac{1}{2}}^3 + B_4(\delta_0^4 + \delta_1^4) + B_5\delta_{\frac{1}{2}}^5 + \cdots \qquad 0 \leqq p \leqq 1$$

Everett's formula

$$f_p = (1-p)f_0 + pf_1 + E_2\delta_0^2 + F_2\delta_1^2 + E_4\delta_0^4 + F_4\delta_1^4 + E_6\delta_0^6 + F_6\delta_1^6 + \cdots \quad 0 \leqq p \leqq 1$$

The coefficients in the above two formulae are related to each other and to the coefficients in the Gaussian formulae by the identities

$$\begin{aligned}
B_{2n} &\equiv \tfrac{1}{2}G_{2n} \equiv \tfrac{1}{2}(E_{2n} + F_{2n}) \\
B_{2n+1} &\equiv G_{2n+1} - \tfrac{1}{2}G_{2n} \equiv \tfrac{1}{2}(F_{2n} - E_{2n}) \\
E_{2n} &\equiv G_{2n} - G_{2n+1} \equiv B_{2n} - B_{2n+1} \\
F_{2n} &\equiv G_{2n+1} \equiv B_{2n} + B_{2n+1}
\end{aligned}$$

Also for $q \equiv 1 - p$ the following symmetrical relationships hold:

$$\begin{aligned}
B_{2n}(p) &\equiv B_{2n}(q) \\
B_{2n+1}(p) &\equiv -B_{2n+1}(q) \\
E_{2n}(p) &\equiv F_{2n}(q) \\
F_{2n}(p) &\equiv E_{2n}(q)
\end{aligned}$$

as can be seen from the tables of these coefficients.

p	B_2	B_3	B_4	B_5	B_6	B_7	$(1 - p)$
0.00	-0.000000	0.0000000	0.000000	-0.000000	-0.00000	0.00000	1.00
0.01	2475	8085	415	81	8	1	0.99
0.02	4900	15680	825	158	17	2	0.98
0.03	7275	22795	1230	231	25	3	0.97
0.04	9600	29440	1631	300	33	4	0.96
0.05	-0.011875	0.0035625	0.002026	-0.000365	-0.00041	0.00005	0.95
0.06	14100	41360	2416	425	49	6	0.94
0.07	16275	46655	2801	482	57	7	0.93
0.08	18400	51520	3180	534	64	8	0.92
0.09	20475	55965	3552	583	72	8	0.91
0.10	-0.022500	0.0060000	0.003919	-0.000627	-0.00080	0.00009	0.90
0.11	24475	63635	4279	667	87	10	0.89
0.12	26400	66880	4632	704	94	10	0.88
0.13	28275	69745	4979	737	101	11	0.87
0.14	30100	72240	5319	766	109	11	0.86
0.15	-0.031875	0.0074375	0.005651	-0.000791	-0.00115	0.00012	0.85
0.16	33600	76160	5976	813	122	12	0.84
0.17	35275	77605	6294	831	129	12	0.83
0.18	36900	78720	6604	845	135	12	0.82
0.19	38475	79515	6906	856	142	13	0.81
0.20	-0.040000	0.0080000	0.007200	-0.000864	-0.00148	0.00013	0.80
0.21	41475	80185	7486	868	154	13	0.79
0.22	42900	80080	7763	870	160	13	0.78
0.23	44275	79695	8033	868	165	13	0.77
0.24	45600	79040	8293	862	171	13	0.76
0.25	-0.046875	0.0078125	0.008545	-0.000554	-0.00176	0.00013	0.75
0.26	48100	76960	8788	844	181	12	0.74
0.27	49275	75555	9022	830	186	12	0.73
0.28	50400	73920	9247	814	191	12	0.72
0.29	51475	72065	9462	795	196	12	0.71
0.30	-0.052500	0.0070000	0.009669	-0.000773	-0.00200	0.00011	0.70
0.31	53475	67735	9866	750	204	11	0.69
0.32	54400	65280	10053	724	208	11	0.68
0.33	55275	62645	10231	696	212	10	0.67
0.34	56100	59840	10399	666	216	10	0.66
0.35	-0.056875	0.0056875	0.010557	-0.000633	-0.00219	0.00009	0.65
0.36	57600	53760	10706	600	222	9	0.64
0.37	58275	50505	10844	564	225	8	0.63
0.38	58900	47120	10973	527	228	8	0.62
0.39	59475	43615	11092	488	231	7	0.61
0.40	-0.060000	0.0040000	0.011200	-0.000448	-0.00233	0.00007	0.60
0.41	60475	36285	11298	407	235	6	0.59
0.42	60900	32480	11386	364	237	5	0.58
0.43	61275	28595	11464	321	239	5	0.57
0.44	61600	24640	11532	277	240	4	0.56
0.45	-0.061875	0.0020625	0.011589	-0.000232	-0.00241	0.00003	0.55
0.46	62100	16560	11635	186	242	3	0.54
0.47	62275	12455	11672	140	243	2	0.53
0.48	62400	8320	11698	94	244	1	0.52
0.49	62475	4165	11714	47	244	1	0.51
0.50	-0.062500	0.0000000	0.011719	-0.000000	-0.00244	0.00000	0.50
$(1 - p)$	B_2	$-B_3$	B_4	$-B_5$	B_6	$-B_7$	p

Bessel's formula (unmodified)

(a) $f_p = f_0 + p\delta_{\frac{1}{2}} + B_2(\delta_0^2 + \delta_1^2) + B_3\delta_{\frac{1}{2}}^3 + B_4(\delta_0^4 + \delta_1^4)$
$$+ B_5\delta_{\frac{1}{2}}^5 + B_6(\delta_0^6 + \delta_1^6) + B_7\delta_{\frac{1}{2}}^7 + \cdots.$$

The end terms can be neglected, i.e., they contribute less than half a unit in the last place of decimals, if the differences are less than the values shown in the following list:

$$
\begin{array}{ll}
\text{Neglect} \quad B_7\delta_{\frac{1}{2}}^7 \text{ if } & \delta^7 < 3500 \\
B_6(\delta_0 + \delta_1) & \delta^6 < 100 \\
B_5\delta_{\frac{1}{2}}^5 & \delta^5 < 500 \\
B_4(\delta_0^4 + \delta_1^4) & \delta^4 < 20 \\
B_3\delta_{\frac{1}{2}}^3 & \delta^3 < 60 \\
B_2(\delta_0^2 + \delta_1^2) & \delta^2 < 4
\end{array}
$$

A powerful simplification is that of throwback. If the higher differences are less than a specified value they can be combined with the lower order ones as follows:

If $\quad \delta^6 < 10{,}000 \quad$ use $\quad \delta_m^4 \equiv \delta^4 - 0.20697\delta^6$

and if $\delta^6 < 1{,}000^* \quad$ use $\quad \delta_m^4 \equiv \delta^4 - 0.2\delta^6$
in the modified form of Bessel's formula

(b) $f_p = f_0 + p\delta_{\frac{1}{2}} + B_2(\delta_0^2 + \delta_1^2) + B_3\delta_{\frac{1}{2}}^3 + B_4(\delta_{m0}^4 + \delta_{m1}^4) + B_5\delta_{\frac{1}{2}}^5$.

If $\delta^4 < 1{,}000$ and $\delta^6 < 1{,}000^*$ use $\delta_m^2 \equiv \delta^2 - 0.18393\delta^4 + 0.03808\delta^6$
and if $\delta^4 < 1{,}000^*$ use $\delta_m^2 \equiv \delta^2 - 0.18393\delta^4$
in the modified form of Bessel's formula

(c) $f_p = f_0 + p\delta_{\frac{1}{2}} + B_2(\delta_{m0}^2 + \delta_{m1}^2) + B_3\delta_{\frac{1}{2}}^3$.

---

* Higher even order differences are negligible. Throwback involving odd order differences is of little practical use.

p	E_2	F_2	E_4	F_4	E_6	F_6	$(1-p)$
0.00	-0.000000	-0.0000000	0.000000	0.000000	-0.00000	-0.00000	1.00
0.01	32835	16665	496	33	9	7	0.99
0.02	64680	33320	983	67	19	14	0.98
0.03	95545	49955	1461	100	28	21	0.97
0.04	125440	66560	1931	133	37	29	0.96
0.05	-0.0154375	-0.0083125	0.002391	0.001661	-0.00046	-0.00036	0.95
0.06	182360	99640	2842	199	55	43	0.94
0.07	209405	116095	3283	232	64	50	0.93
0.08	235520	132480	3714	264	72	57	0.92
0.09	260715	148785	4135	297	80	64	0.91
0.10	-0.0285000	-0.0165000	0.004546	0.003292	-0.00089	-0.00070	0.90
0.11	308385	181115	4946	361	97	77	0.89
0.12	330880	197120	5336	393	105	84	0.88
0.13	352495	213005	5716	424	112	91	0.87
0.14	373240	228760	6085	455	120	97	0.86
0.15	-0.0393125	-0.0244375	0.006442	0.004860	-0.00127	-0.00104	0.85
0.16	412160	259840	6789	516	134	110	0.84
0.17	430355	275145	7125	546	141	117	0.83
0.18	447720	290280	7449	576	148	123	0.82
0.19	464265	305235	7762	605	154	129	0.81
0.20	-0.0480000	-0.0320000	0.008064	0.006336	-0.00161	-0.00135	0.80
0.21	494935	334565	8354	662	167	141	0.79
0.22	509080	348920	8633	689	172	147	0.78
0.23	522445	363055	8900	716	178	153	0.77
0.24	535040	376960	9156	743	184	158	0.76
0.25	-0.0546875	-0.0390625	0.009399	0.007690	-0.00189	-0.00164	0.75
0.26	557960	404040	9632	794	194	169	0.74
0.27	568305	417195	9852	819	199	174	0.73
0.28	577920	430080	10060	843	203	179	0.72
0.29	586815	442685	10257	867	207	184	0.71
0.30	-0.0595000	-0.0455000	0.010442	0.008895	-0.00212	-0.00189	0.70
0.31	602485	467015	10615	912	215	193	0.69
0.32	609280	478720	10777	933	219	198	0.68
0.33	615395	490105	10927	954	222	202	0.67
0.34	620840	501160	11065	973	226	206	0.66
0.35	-0.0625625	-0.0511875	0.011191	0.009924	-0.00229	-0.00210	0.65
0.36	629760	522240	11305	1011	231	213	0.64
0.37	633255	532245	11408	1028	234	217	0.63
0.38	636120	541880	11500	1045	236	220	0.62
0.39	638365	551135	11580	1060	238	223	0.61
0.40	-0.0640000	-0.0560000	0.011648	0.010752	$-.00240$	-0.00226	0.60
0.41	641035	568465	11705	1089	241	229	0.59
0.42	641480	576520	11751	1102	242	232	0.58
0.43	641345	584155	11785	1114	243	234	0.57
0.44	640640	591360	11808	1125	244	236	0.56
0.45	-0.0639375	-0.0598125	0.011820	0.011357	-0.00245	-0.00238	0.55
0.46	637560	604440	11822	1145	245	240	0.54
0.47	635205	610295	11812	1153	245	241	0.53
0.48	632320	615680	11792	1160	245	242	0.52
0.49	628915	620585	11760	1167	245	243	0.51
0.50	-0.0625000	-0.0625000	0.011719	0.011719	-0.00244	-0.00244	0.50
$(1-p)$	F_2	E_2	F_4	E_4	F_6	E_6	p

Everett's formula (unmodified)

(a) $f_p = (1 - p)f_0 + pf_1 + E_2\delta_0^2 + F_2\delta_1^2 + E_4\delta_0^4 + F_4\delta_1^4 + E_6\delta_0^6 + F_6\delta_1^6 + \cdots$

As with Bessel's formula, end terms can be neglected as follows:

$$\text{Neglect} \quad E_6\delta_0^6 + F_6\delta_1^6 \quad \text{if} \quad \delta^6 < 100$$
$$E_4\delta_0^4 + F_4\delta_1^4 \qquad \delta^4 < 20$$
$$E_2\delta_0^2 + F_2\delta_1^2 \qquad \delta^2 < 4$$

The corresponding throwback formulae are

(b) $\quad f_p = (1 - p)f_0 + pf_1 + E_2\delta_0^2 + F_2\delta_1^2 + E_4\delta_{m0}^4 + F_4\delta_{m1}^4,$

where $\delta_m^4 \equiv \delta^4 - 0.20697\delta^6 \quad$ providing $\delta^6 < 10,000*$

or $\quad \delta_m^4 \equiv \delta^4 - 0.2\delta^6 \qquad$ providing $\delta^6 < 1,000*;$

(c) $\quad f_p = (1 - p)f_0 + pf_1 + E_2\delta_{m0}^4 + F_2\delta_{m1}^2$

where $\delta_m^2 \equiv \delta^2 - 0.18393\delta^4 + 0.03808\delta^6 \quad$ if $\quad \delta^4, \delta^6 < 1,000*.$

Generalized Throwback

Using 0.184 instead of the more precise value of 0.18393 we obtain a very simple but nevertheless accurate interpolation formulae

$$f \equiv (1 - p)f_0 + pf_1 + E_2\delta_{m0}^2 + F_2\delta_{m1}^2 + P_4\theta_0^4 + Q_4\theta_1^4,$$

where $\quad \delta_m^2 \equiv \delta^2 - 0.184\delta^4 + 0.03882\delta^6 - 0.0083\delta^8 + 0.0019\delta^{10}$

and $\quad 100\theta^4 \equiv \delta^4 - 0.2783\delta^6 + 0.0685\delta^8 - 0.0168\delta^{10}$

and $\quad P_4 \equiv 100(E_4 + 0.184E_2); \quad Q_4 \equiv 100(F_4 + 0.184F_2).$

Symmetric formulae for interpolation to halves (sub-tabulation to halves)

When $p = \frac{1}{2}$ is substituted into Bessel's interpolation formula the odd coefficients B_{2n+1} all become zero and the resulting formula is

$$f_{\frac{1}{2}} = \left(1 - \frac{1}{8}\delta^2 + \frac{3}{128}\delta^4 - \frac{5}{1024}\delta^6 + \frac{35}{32768}\delta^8 - \cdots\right)\mu f_{\frac{1}{2}}.$$

If this is truncated after one, two, three terms etc. the following formulae and error terms are obtained:

Error

$f_{\frac{1}{2}} = \frac{1}{2}(f_0 + f_1)$ $\qquad\qquad\qquad\qquad\qquad\qquad -\dfrac{1}{8}\mu\delta_{\frac{1}{2}}^2$

$f_{\frac{1}{2}} = (-f_{-1} + 9f_0 + 9f_1 - f_2)/16$ $\qquad\qquad +\dfrac{3}{128}\mu\delta_{\frac{1}{2}}^4$

$f_{\frac{1}{2}} = (3f_{-2} - 25f_{-1} + 150f_0 + 150f_1 - 25f_2 + 3f_3)/256$ $\qquad -\dfrac{5}{1024}\mu\delta_{\frac{1}{2}}^6$

$f_{\frac{1}{2}} = (-5f_{-3} + 49f_{-2} - 245f_{-1} + 1225f_0 + 1225f_1 - 245f_2 + 49f_3 - 5f_4)/2048$ $\qquad +\dfrac{35}{32768}\mu\delta_{\frac{1}{2}}^8$

---

* Higher order differences are negligible.

Similarly, unsymmetric formulae for subtabulation to halves can be obtained from Newton's formula by substituting $p = \frac{1}{2}$ and truncating, e.g.,

Error

$$f_{\frac{1}{2}} = \left(1 + \frac{1}{2}\Delta - \frac{1}{8}\Delta^2 + \frac{1}{16}\Delta^3 - \frac{5}{128}\Delta^4 + \frac{7}{256}\Delta^5 \cdots\right)f_0$$

$$f_{\frac{1}{2}} = (3f_0 + 6f_1 - f_2)/8 \qquad\qquad\qquad \frac{+1}{16}\Delta_0^3$$

$$f_{\frac{1}{2}} = (5f_0 + 15f_1 - 5f_2 + f_3)/16 \qquad\qquad \frac{-5}{128}\Delta_0^4$$

$$f_{\frac{1}{2}} = (35f_0 + 140f_1 - 70f_2 + 28f_3 - 5f_4)/128 \qquad \frac{+7}{256}\Delta_0^5$$

The formula obtained by considering the first two terms only of the series is identical with the first one derived from Bessel's formula.

Interpolation techniques which do not require the function to be tabulated for equal interval of the argument

a) Lagrangian Polynomials

The interpolated value is obtained from a set of points which bridge the required point. The nearer the argument of the required value is to the center of the range of arguments of the function values used the better.

For an odd number of points

$$f(x) = \sum_{r=-n}^{n} L_r f_r \, .$$

For an even number of points

$$f(x) = \sum_{r=-n}^{n+1} L_r f_r \, .$$

The interpolating polynomial is of degree $2n$ in the first case and $2n + 1$ in the second. Further, it must pass through the given points $f_{-n}, f_{1-n}, f_{2-n}, \cdots, f_n$ or f_{1+n} as the case may be.

The coefficient L_r associated with the function value f_r is given by

$$L_r = \frac{(x - x_{-n})(x - x_{1-n}) \cdots (x - x_{r-1})(x - x_{r+1}) \cdots (x - x_{n-1})(x - x_n)}{(x_r - x_{-n})(x_r - x_{1-n}) \cdots (x_r - x_{r-1})(x_r - x_{r+1}) \cdots (x_r - x_{n-1})(x_r - x_n)}$$

for the first case with an additional factor $(x - x_{1+n})/(x_r - x_{1+n})$ in the second.

The error involved is equal to the $(2n + 2)$th. derivative, at some point in the range, multiplied by

$$(x - x_{-n})(x - x_{1-n}) \cdots (x - x_{1-n})/(2n + 2)!$$

in the case of the even number of points, and the $(2n + 1)$th. derivative, again at some point in the range, multiplied by

$$(x - x_{-n})(x - x_{1-n}) \cdots (x - x_n)/(2n + 1)!$$

in the other case.

In both cases the multipliers are functions which oscillate with an amplitude which increases substantially as the argument of the required point departs from the center of the range. When the arguments are spaced at equal intervals h and the point x is nearer to x_0 than to the other points, then $L_r(p)$ can be tabulated for $p = (x - x_0)/h$.

If the degree of the approximating polynomial is known the method is very powerful, otherwise it is best avoided.

b) Divided differences

The layout of a divided difference table is similar to that of an ordinary finite difference table.

x_{-1}	f_{-1}		Δ^2_{-1}		Δ^4_{-1}
		$\Delta_{-\frac{1}{2}}$		$\Delta_{-\frac{1}{2}}$	
x_0	f_0		Δ^2_0		Δ^4_0
		$\Delta_{\frac{1}{2}}$		$\Delta^3_{\frac{1}{2}}$	
x_1	f_1		Δ^2_1		Δ^4_1

where the $\triangle$'s are defined as follows:

$$\triangle_r^0 \equiv f_r, \qquad \triangle_{r+\frac{1}{2}} \equiv (f_{r+1} - f_r)/(x_{r+1} - x_r),$$

and in general

$$\triangle_r^{2n} \equiv (\triangle_{r+\frac{1}{2}}^{2n-1} - \triangle_{r-\frac{1}{2}}^{2n-1})/(x_{r+n} - x_{r-n})$$

and

$$\triangle_{r+\frac{1}{2}}^{2n+1} \equiv (\triangle_{r+1}^{2n} - \triangle_r^{2n})/(x_{r+1+n} - x_{r-n}).$$

Divided differences can with advantage be replaced by adjusted divided differences.

c) Adjusted divided differences

These differences are a modified form of the above and, when the interval of tabulation becomes constant, they reduce to ordinary central differences. Formulae analogous to all the existing formulae involving forward, central and backward differences can be obtained by means of Sheppard's rules which are stated below.

x_{-1}	p_{-1}	f_{-1}		δ_{-1}^2		δ_{-1}^4
			$\delta_{-\frac{1}{2}}$		$\delta_{-\frac{1}{2}}^3$	
x_0	p_0	f_0		δ_0^2		δ_0^4
			$\delta_{\frac{1}{2}}$		$\delta_{\frac{1}{2}}^3$	
x_1	p_1	f_1		δ_1^2		δ_1^4
			$\delta_{1\frac{1}{2}}$		$\delta_{1\frac{1}{2}}^3$	
x_2	p_2	f_2		δ_2^2		δ_2^4

where h is the total range of arguments divided by the number of intervals in that range, the result being rounded to a suitable figure and $x_k \cong p_k \cdot h$ or $(x/h)_k = p_k + w_k$ where the w's are used to shift the origin, if necessary, and to round-off the p's.

Define

$$\delta_r \equiv \frac{1}{(p_{r+\frac{1}{2}} - p_{r-\frac{1}{2}})} (f_{r+\frac{1}{2}} - f_{r-\frac{1}{2}})$$

and

$$\delta_r^2 \equiv \frac{2}{(p_{r+1} - p_{r-1})} (\delta_{r+\frac{1}{2}} - \delta_{r-\frac{1}{2}}).$$

In general

$$\delta_r^{2n+1} \equiv \frac{2n + 1}{(p_{r+\frac{1}{2}+n} - p_{r-\frac{1}{2}-n})} (\delta_{r+\frac{1}{2}}^{2n} - \delta_{r-\frac{1}{2}}^{2n}),$$

$$\delta_r^{2n} \equiv \frac{2n}{(p_{r+n} - p_{r-n})} (\delta_{r+\frac{1}{2}}^{2n-1} - \delta_{r+\frac{1}{2}}^{2n-1}).$$

The formula will be in the form

$$f(x) = f_0 + \sum_{r=1}^{N} \left\{ \prod (p - p_j \cdot) \frac{\delta_s^r}{r!} \right\},$$

where the product part of each term of the formula consists of r factors and the p_j's and s are chosen as follows:

   a) When $r = 1$, $j = 0$ and $s = +\frac{1}{2}$, or $-\frac{1}{2}$, thereafter:—

b) r is increased by unity and s is either increased or decreased by $\frac{1}{2}$. Thus the p's, involved in the new divided difference of the series, are all those which are necessary for the computation of the divided difference used in the *preceding term* plus one more added either to the beginning or to the end of the set.

c) The product part of the term consists of factors $(p - p_j)$ such that all the p's necessary for the evaluation of the *previous* divided difference are involved. For example, Gauss' forward difference interpolation formula in terms of adjusted divided differences is obtained by following the path shown below

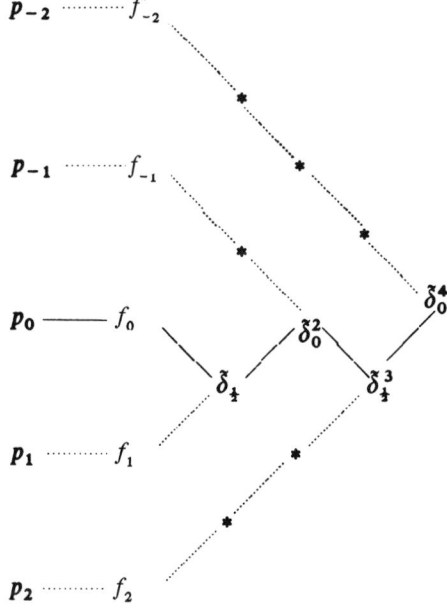

The solid line indicates the path chosen through the difference table.

$$f(x) = f_0 + (p - p_0)\delta_{\frac{1}{2}} + \frac{1}{2!} \cdot (p - p_0)(p - p_1)\delta_0^2 + \frac{1}{3!} \cdot (p - p_0)(p - p_1)(p - p_{-1})\delta_{\frac{1}{2}}^3$$

$$+ \frac{1}{4!} \cdot (p - p_0)(p - p_1)(p - p_{-1})(p - p_2)\delta_0^4 \cdots$$

Similarly Gauss' backward difference interpolation formula is

$$f(x) = f_0 + (p - p_0)\delta_{-\frac{1}{2}} + \frac{1}{2!} \cdot (p - p_0)(p - p_{-1})\delta_0^2 + \frac{1}{3!} \cdot (p - p_0)(p - p_{-1})(p - p_1)\delta_{-\frac{1}{2}}^3$$

$$+ \frac{1}{4!} \cdot (p - p_0)(p - p_{-1})(p - p_1)(p - p_{-2})\delta_0^4 \cdots ,$$

and Stirling's formula is

$$f(x) = f_0 + \frac{(p - p_0)}{2}[\delta_{\frac{1}{2}} + \delta_{-\frac{1}{2}}] + \frac{1}{2!} \cdot \frac{(p - p_0)}{2}[(p - p_{-1}) + (p - p_1)]\delta_0^2$$

$$+ \frac{1}{3!} \cdot \frac{(p - p_1)(p - p_0)(p - p_{-1})}{2}[\delta_{\frac{1}{2}}^3 + \delta_{-\frac{1}{2}}^3]$$

$$+ \frac{1}{4!} \cdot \frac{(p - p_1)(p - p_0)(p - p_{-1})}{2}[(p - p_{-2}) + (p - p_2)]\delta_0^4 \cdots$$

Replacing the odd order differences, in Gauss' forward formula, by combinations of the previous even order differences the formula analogous to Everett's is obtained, i.e.,

$$f(x) = \left[1 - \frac{(p - p_0)}{(p_1 - p_0)} \right] f_0 + \frac{!(p - p_0)}{(p_1 - p_0)} f_1 - \frac{1}{2!} \frac{(p - p_0)(p - p_1)(p - p_2)}{(p_2 - p_{-1})} \delta_0^2$$

$$+ \frac{1}{2!} \frac{(p - p_0)(p - p_1)(p - p_{-1})}{(p_2 - p_{-1})} \delta_1^2 - \cdots .$$

d) Iterative linear interpolation

Neville's modification of Aiken's method of iterative linear interpolation is one of the most powerful methods of interpolation when the arguments are unevenly spaced as no prior knowledge of the order of the approximating polynomial is necessary nor is a difference table required.

The values obtained are successive approximations to the required result and the process terminates when there is no appreciable change. These values are of course useless if a new interpolation is required when the procedure must be started afresh.

Defining
$$f_{r,s} \equiv \frac{(x_s - x)f_r - (x_r - x)f_s}{(x_s - x_r)}$$

$$f_{r,s,t} \equiv \frac{(x_t - x)f_{r,s} - (x_r - x)f_{s,t}}{(x_t - x_r)}$$

$$f_{r,s,t,u} \equiv \frac{(x_u - x)f_{r,s,t} - (x_r - x)f_{s,t,u}}{(x_u - x_r)} ,$$

the computation is laid out as follows:

x_{-1}	$(x_{-1} - x)$	f_{-1}			
			$f_{-1,0}$		
x_0	$(x_0 - x)$	f_0		$f_{-1\,0,1}$	
			$f_{0,1}$		$f_{-1\,0\,1,2}$
x_1	$(x_1 - x)$	f_1		$f_{0,1,2}$	
			$f_{1,2}$		
x_2	$(x_2 - x)$	f_2			

As the iterates tend to their limit the common leading figures can be omitted.

e) Gauss' trigonometric interpolation formula

This is of greatest value when the function is periodic, i.e., a Fourier series expansion is possible.

$$f(x) = \sum_{r=0}^{n} C_r f_r ,$$

where $C_r = N_r(x)/N_r(x_r)$ and

$$N_r(x) = \left[\sin \frac{(x - x_0)}{2} \right] \left[\sin \frac{(x - x_1)}{2} \right] \cdots \left[\sin \frac{(x - x_{r-1})}{2} \right]$$

$$\left[\sin \frac{(x - x_{r+1})}{2} \right] \cdots \left[\sin \frac{(x - x_n)}{2} \right] .$$

This is similar to the Lagrangian formula.

f) Reciprocal differences

These are used when the quotient of two polynomials will give a better representation of the interpolating function than a simple polynomial expression.

A convenient layout is as shown below:

$$
\begin{array}{llll}
x_{-1} & f_{-1} \\
 & & \rho_{-\frac{1}{2}} \\
x_0 & f_0 & & \rho_0^2 \\
 & & \rho_{\frac{1}{2}} & & \rho_{\frac{1}{2}}^3 \\
x_1 & f_1 & & \rho_1^2 & & \rho_1^4 \\
 & & \rho_{1\frac{1}{2}} & & \rho_{1\frac{1}{2}}^3 \\
x_2 & f_2 & & \rho_2^2 \\
 & & \rho_{2\frac{1}{2}} \\
x_3 & f_3
\end{array}
$$

where

$$\rho_{r+\frac{1}{2}} \equiv \frac{x_{r+1} - x_r}{f_{r+1} - f_r}$$

and

$$\rho_r^2 \equiv \frac{x_{r+1} - x_{r-1}}{f_{r+\frac{1}{2}} - f_{r-\frac{1}{2}}} + f_r$$

In general

$$\rho_{r+\frac{1}{2}}^{2n+1} \equiv \frac{x_{r+n+1} - x_{r-n}}{\rho_{r+1}^{2n} - \rho_r^{2n}} + \rho_{r+\frac{1}{2}}^{2n-1}$$

$$\rho_r^{2n} \equiv \frac{x_{r+n} - x_{r-n}}{\rho_{r+\frac{1}{2}}^{2n-1} - \rho_{r-\frac{1}{2}}^{2n-1}} + \rho_r^{2n-2}$$

The interpolation formula is expressed in the form of a continued fraction expansion.

The expansion corresponding to Newton's forward difference interpolation formula, in the sense of the differences involved, is

$$f(x) = f_0 + \cfrac{(x - x_0)}{\rho_{\frac{1}{2}} + \cfrac{(x_2 - x_1)}{\rho_1 - f_0 + \cfrac{(x - x_2)}{\rho_{1\frac{1}{2}}^3 - \rho_{\frac{1}{2}} + \cfrac{(x_4 - x_3)}{\rho_2^4 - \rho_1^2 + \cfrac{(x - x_4)}{\text{etc.}}}}}}$$

while that corresponding to Gauss' forward formula is

$$f(x) = f_0 + \cfrac{(x - x_0)}{\rho_{\frac{1}{2}} + \cfrac{(x_2 - x_1)}{\rho_0^2 - f_0 + \cfrac{(x_3 - x_{-1})}{\rho_{\frac{1}{2}}^3 - \rho_{\frac{1}{2}} + \cfrac{(x_4 - x_2)}{\rho_0^4 - \rho_0^2 + \cfrac{(x - x_{-2})}{\text{etc.}}}}}}$$

Inverse interpolation

Any method of interpolation which does not require the arguments to be evenly spaced will be satisfactory, by simply interchanging the roles of the arguments and the function values.

Alternative (i) Sub-tabulate the function until linear interpolation is adequate and simple ratio and proportion will yield the result.

Alternative (ii) Find an approximate value for p from

$$p \cong (f_p - f_0)/(f_1 - f_0)$$

and then iterate using *any* of the standard interpolation formulae;
e.g., Bessel

$$p = [f_p - f_0 - B_2(\delta_0^2 + \delta_1^2) - B_3\delta_{\frac{1}{2}}^3 - \cdots \text{ etc.}]/\delta_{\frac{1}{2}}$$

where the Bessel's coefficients on the right hand side are evaluated for the approximate p.
Everrett

$$p = [f_p - f_0 - E_2\delta_0^2 - F_2\delta_1^2 - E_4\delta^4 - F_4\delta_0^4 \cdots]/\delta_{\frac{1}{2}}$$

Newton forward

$$p = [f_p - f_0 - \frac{1}{2!}p(p-1)\Delta_0^2 - \frac{1}{3!}p(p-1)(p-2)\Delta_0^3 \cdots]/\Delta_0$$

Newton backward

$$p = [f_p - f_0 - \frac{1}{2!}p(p+1)\nabla_0^2 - \frac{1}{3!}p(p+1)(p+2)\nabla_0^3 \cdots]/\nabla_0.$$

Note that the divisors are in fact identical.

Lozenge Diagram — Interpolation

The following figure shows a scheme for writing down any of the standard interpolation formulas by associating it with a prescribed path through the diagram, called a lozenge diagram.

y_{-4}	$(u+4)_1$	$\Delta^2 y_{-5}$	$(u+5)_3$	$\Delta^4 y_{-6}$	$(u+6)_5$	$\Delta^6 y_{-7}$	$(u+7)_7$
1	Δy_{-4}	$(u+4)_2$	$\Delta^3 y_{-5}$	$(u+5)_4$	$\Delta^5 y_{-6}$	$(u+6)_6$	$\Delta^7 y_{-7}$
y_{-3}	$(u+3)_1$	$\Delta^2 y_{-4}$	$(u+4)_3$	$\Delta^4 y_{-5}$	$(u+5)_5$	$\Delta^6 y_{-6}$	$(u+6)_7$
1	Δy_{-3}	$(u+3)_2$	$\Delta^3 y_{-4}$	$(u+4)_4$	$\Delta^5 y_{-5}$	$(u+5)_6$	$\Delta^7 y_{-6}$
y_{-2}	$(u+2)_1$	$\Delta^2 y_{-3}$	$(u+3)_3$	$\Delta^4 y_{-4}$	$(u+4)_5$	$\Delta^6 y_{-5}$	$(u+5)_7$
1	Δy_{-2}	$(u+2)_2$	$\Delta^3 y_{-3}$	$(u+3)_4$	$\Delta^5 y_{-4}$	$(u+4)_6$	$\Delta^7 y_{-5}$
y_{-1}	$(u+1)_1$	$\Delta^2 y_{-2}$	$(u+2)_3$	$\Delta^4 y_{-3}$	$(u+3)_5$	$\Delta^6 y_{-4}$	$(u+4)_7$
1	Δy_{-1}	$(u+1)_2$	$\Delta^3 y_{-2}$	$(u+2)_4$	$\Delta^5 y_{-3}$	$(u+3)_6$	$\Delta^7 y_{-4}$
y_0	$(u)_1$	$\Delta^2 y_{-1}$	$(u+1)_3$	$\Delta^4 y_{-2}$	$(u+2)_5$	$\Delta^6 y_{-3}$	$(u+3)_7$
1	Δy_0	$(u)_2$	$\Delta^3 y_{-1}$	$(u+1)_4$	$\Delta^5 y_{-2}$	$(u+2)_6$	$\Delta^7 y_{-3}$
y_1	$(u-1)_1$	$\Delta^2 y_0$	$(u)_3$	$\Delta^4 y_{-1}$	$(u+1)_5$	$\Delta^6 y_{-2}$	$(u+2)_7$
1	Δy_1	$(u-1)_2$	$\Delta^3 y_0$	$(u)_4$	$\Delta^5 y_{-1}$	$(u+1)_6$	$\Delta^7 y_{-2}$
y_2	$(u-2)_1$	$\Delta^2 y_1$	$(u-1)_3$	$\Delta^4 y_0$	$(u)_5$	$\Delta^6 y_{-1}$	$(u+1)_7$
1	Δy_2	$(u-2)_2$	$\Delta^3 y_1$	$(u-1)_4$	$\Delta^5 y_0$	$(u)_6$	$\Delta^7 y_{-1}$
y_3	$(u-3)_1$	$\Delta^2 y_2$	$(u-2)_3$	$\Delta^4 y_1$	$(u-1)_5$	$\Delta^6 y_0$	$(u)_7$
1	Δy_3	$(u-3)_2$	$\Delta^3 y_2$	$(u-2)_4$	$\Delta^5 y_1$	$(u-1)_6$	$\Delta^7 y_0$
y_4	$(u-4)_1$	$\Delta^2 y_3$	$(u-3)_3$	$\Delta^4 y_2$	$(u-2)_5$	$\Delta^6 y_1$	$(u-1)_7$

→ **Gregory-Newton (Forward)**   →→ **Stirling**

→→ **Gregory-Newton (Backward)**   ...→.... **Bessel**

~~~ **Gauss (I)**

$$(u+k)_s \equiv \frac{1}{s!}(u+k)^{[s]}$$

Lozenge diagram showing paths for some of the standard interpolation formulas. (From Kunz, K. S., *Numerical Analysis*, McGraw-Hill, New York, 1957, 75–77, 80, 81. With permission.)

To convert a path through the lozenge to an interpolation formula the following rules are formulated:

1. Each time a difference column is crossed from left to right a term is added.
2. If a path enters a difference column (from the left) at a positive slope, the term added is the product of the difference, say $\Delta^k y_{-p}$, at which the column is crossed and the factorial $(u + p - 1)_k$ lying just below that difference.
3. If a path enters a difference column (from the left) at a positive slope, the term added is the product of the difference, say $\Delta^k y_{-p}$, at which the column is crossed and the factorial $(u + p)_k$ lying just above that difference.
4. If a path enters a difference column horizontally (from the left), the term added is the product of the difference, say $\Delta^k y_{-p}$, at which the column is crossed and the average of the two factorials $(u + p)_k$ and $(u + p-1)_k$ lying, respectively, just above and just below that difference.

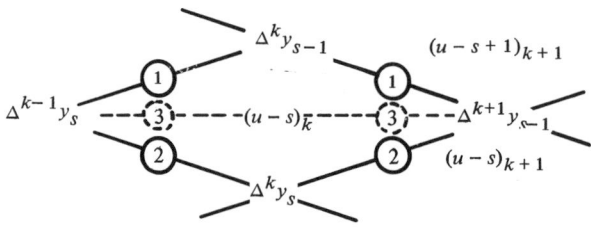

5. If a path crosses a difference column (from left to right) between two differences, say $\Delta^k y_{-(p+1)}$ and $\Delta^k y_{-p}$, then the added term is the product of the average of these two differences and the factorial $(u + p)_k$ at which the column is crossed.
6. Any portion of a path traversed from right to left gives rise to the same terms as would arise from going along this portion from left to right except that the sign of each term is changed.
7. The zero-difference column corresponding to the tabulated values may be treated by the same rules as any other difference columns provided one thinks of the lozenge as being entered just to the left of this column. Thus this column can be crossed by a path making a positive, negative, or zero slope, just as is true of the other columns.

Examples

Write down the interpolation formulas whose paths are shown on the lozenge diagram.

It is clear that, since the lozenge employs descending differences, all formulas will be in terms of descending differences. If one wishes the central-difference formulas to appear as they have been written in the earlier sections of the chapter, one should use central-difference notation for the differences.

Gregory-Newton (Forward) — Applying Rules 1, 3, and 7 to the diagonal path that slopes downward from y_0, one obtains the formula

$$y = y_0 + (u)_1 \Delta y_0 + (u)_2 \Delta^2 y_0 + (u)_3 \Delta^3 y_0 + \ldots + (u)_m \Delta^m y_0$$

Note: $(u)_r = u^{[r]}/r!$

Gregory-Newton (Backward) — Employing Rules 1, 2, and 7 to the diagonal path that slopes upward from y_0, one obtains the formula

$$y = y_0 + (u)_1 \Delta y_{-1} + (u + 1)_2 \Delta^2 y_{-2} + (u + 2)_3 \Delta^3 y_{-3} + \ldots$$

$$+ (u + m - 1)_m \Delta^m y_{-m}$$

Gauss (I) — Employing Rules 1, 2, 3, and 7 to the zigzag path shown, one has

$$y = y_0 + (u)_1 \, \Delta y_0 + (u)_2 \, \Delta^2 y_{-1} + (u+1)_3 \, \Delta^3 y_{-1} + (u+1)_4 \, \Delta^4 y_{-2} + \dots$$

$$+ (u+k-1)_{2k-1} \, \Delta^{2k-1} y_{-k+1} + (u+k-1)_{2k} \, \Delta^{2k} y_{-k} + \dots$$

where, as before, the series is terminated at any desired difference.

Stirling's — Employing Rules 1, 4, 5, and 7 to the horizontal path through y_0,

$$y = y_0 + (u)_1 \, \frac{\Delta y_{-1} + \Delta y_0}{2} + \frac{(u)_2 + (u+1)_2}{2} \, \Delta^2 y_{-1}$$

$$+ (u+1)_3 \, \frac{\Delta^2 y_{-2} + \Delta^3 y_{-1}}{2} + \dots$$

$$+ (u+k-1)_{2k-1} \, \frac{\Delta^{2k-1} y_{-k} + \Delta^{2k-1} y_{-k+1}}{2}$$

$$+ \frac{(u+k-1)_{2k} + (u+k)_{2k}}{2} \, \Delta^{2k} y_{-k} + \dots$$

Now

$$(u+k-1)_{2k-1} = \frac{1}{(2k-1)!} \, u(u^2-1)(u^2-4) \dots [u^2-(k-1)^2]$$

and

$$\frac{(u+k-1)_{2k} + (u+k)_{2k}}{2} = \frac{1}{2k!} \, u^2(u^2-1)(u^2-4) \dots [u^2-(k-1)^2]$$

Therefore, one may write

$$y = y_0 + u \, \frac{\Delta y_{-1} + \Delta y_0}{2} + \frac{1}{2!} \, u^2 \, \Delta^2 y_{-1} + \frac{1}{3!} \, u \, (u^2-1) \, \frac{\Delta^3 y_{-2} + \Delta^3 y_{-1}}{2}$$

$$+ \frac{1}{4!} \, u^2(u^2-1) \, \Delta^4 y_{-2} + \dots$$

$$+ \frac{1}{(2k-1)!} \, u(u^2-1)(u^2-4) \dots [u^2-(k-1)^2] \, \frac{\Delta^{2k-1} y_{-k} + \Delta^{2k-1} y_{-k+1}}{2}$$

$$+ \frac{1}{(2k)!} \, u^2(u^2-1)(u^2-4) \dots [u^2-(k-1)^2] \, \Delta^{2k} y_{-k} + \dots$$

This is the expression of Stirling's formula when descending differences are employed.

Bessel's — Employing the rules above to the horizontal path through Δy_0, one has

$$y = \frac{y_0 + y_1}{2} + \frac{(u)_1 + (u-1)_1}{2} \, \Delta y_0 + (u)_2 \, \frac{\Delta^2 y_{-1} + \Delta^2 y_0}{2}$$

$$+ \frac{(u+1)_3 + (u)_3}{2} \, \Delta^3 y_{-1} + \dots$$

$$+ \frac{(u+k-1)_{2k-1} + (u+k-2)_{2k-1}}{2} \, \Delta^{2k-1} y_{-k+1}$$

$$+ (u+k-1)_{2k} \, \frac{\Delta^{2k} y_{-k} + \Delta^{2k} y_{-k+1}}{2}$$

or

$$y = \frac{y_0 + y_1}{2} + (u - \tfrac{1}{2}) \, \Delta y_0 + \frac{1}{2!} \, u^{[2]} \, \frac{\Delta^2 y_{-1} + \Delta^2 y_0}{2}$$

$$+ \frac{1}{3!} \, (u - \tfrac{1}{2}) \, u^{[2]} \, \Delta^3 y_{-1} + \frac{1}{4!} \, (u + 1)^{[4]} \, \frac{\Delta^4 y_{-2} + \Delta^4 y_{-1}}{2} + \ldots$$

$$+ \frac{1}{(2k)!} \, (u + k - 1)^{[2k]} \, \frac{\Delta^{2k} y_{-k} + \Delta^{2k} y_{-k+1}}{2}$$

$$+ \frac{1}{(2k+1)!} \, (u - \tfrac{1}{2}) \, (u + k - 1)^{[2k]} \, \Delta^{2k+1} y_{-k} + \ldots$$

Remainder Term

The remainder term for a series terminated on a single difference, say the mth difference, is just the (m + 1)th term of the series if the series were extended, with, however, $h^{m+1} f^{m+1} (\xi)$ replacing the (m + 1)th difference (or mean difference). For a formula terminated on the mean of two differences, one must average the error terms for those formulas ending on each of the two differences.

NUMERICAL DIFFERENTIATION FORMULAS

The notation used is defined as follows:

$$h^n \frac{d^n}{dx^n} f(x_0 + ph) \equiv h^n \frac{d^n}{dx^n} f_p \equiv \frac{d^n}{dp^n} f_p$$

Derivatives at tabular points.

$$
\begin{aligned}
h f_0^{(1)} &= \left(\Delta - \frac{\Delta^2}{2} + \frac{\Delta^3}{3} - \frac{\Delta^4}{4} + \frac{\Delta^5}{5} - \frac{\Delta^6}{6} \cdots \right) f_0 \\
&= \left(\mu\delta - \tfrac{1}{6}\mu\delta^3 + \tfrac{1}{30}\mu\delta^5 - \tfrac{1}{140}\mu\delta^7 \cdots \right) f_0 \\
&= \left(\nabla + \frac{\nabla^2}{2} + \frac{\nabla^3}{3} + \frac{\nabla^4}{4} + \frac{\nabla^5}{5} + \frac{\nabla^6}{6} \cdots \right) f_0
\end{aligned}
$$

$$
\begin{aligned}
h^2 f_0^{(2)} &= \left(\Delta^2 - \Delta^3 + \tfrac{11}{12}\Delta^4 - \tfrac{5}{6}\Delta^5 + \tfrac{137}{180}\Delta^6 - \tfrac{7}{10}\Delta^7 \cdots \right) f_0 \\
&= \left(\delta^2 - \tfrac{1}{12}\delta^4 + \tfrac{1}{90}\delta^6 - \tfrac{1}{560}\delta^8 \cdots \right) f_0 \\
&= \left(\nabla^2 + \nabla^3 + \tfrac{11}{12}\nabla^4 + \tfrac{5}{6}\nabla^5 + \tfrac{137}{180}\nabla^6 + \tfrac{7}{10}\nabla^7 \cdots \right) f_0
\end{aligned}
$$

$$
\begin{aligned}
h^3 f_0^{(3)} &= \left(\Delta^3 - \tfrac{3}{2}\Delta^4 + \tfrac{21}{12}\Delta^5 - \tfrac{45}{24}\Delta^6 + \tfrac{348}{180}\Delta^7 - \tfrac{79}{40}\Delta^8 \cdots \right) f_0 \\
&= \left(\mu\delta^3 - \tfrac{1}{4}\mu\delta^5 + \tfrac{7}{120}\mu\delta^7 - \tfrac{41}{3024}\mu\delta^9 \cdots \right) f_0 \\
&= \left(\nabla^3 + \tfrac{3}{2}\nabla^4 + \tfrac{21}{12}\nabla^5 + \tfrac{45}{24}\nabla^6 + \tfrac{348}{180}\nabla^7 + \tfrac{79}{40}\nabla^8 \cdots \right) f_0
\end{aligned}
$$

Higher derivatives can be found by direct multiplication of the above formulae e.g.

$$h^5 f_0^{(5)} = h^3 \frac{d^3}{dp^3} \left(h^2 \frac{d^2}{dp^2} f_0 \right)$$

$$
\begin{aligned}
\therefore h^5 f_0^{(5)} &= \left(\mu\delta^3 - \tfrac{1}{4}\mu\delta^5 + \tfrac{7}{120}\mu\delta^7 \cdots \right)\left(\delta^2 - \tfrac{1}{12}\delta^4 + \tfrac{1}{90}\delta^6 - \tfrac{1}{560}\delta^8 \cdots \right) f_0 \\
&= \left(\mu\delta^5 - \tfrac{1}{3}\mu\delta^7 + \tfrac{13}{144}\mu\delta^9 \cdots \right) f_0
\end{aligned}
$$

The identity $\mu^2 \equiv 1 + \tfrac{1}{4}\delta^2$ is used to ensure that no powers of 'μ,' other than the first, appear in any formula.

$$
\begin{aligned}
h^4 f_0^{(4)} &= \left(\delta^4 - \tfrac{1}{6}\delta^6 + \tfrac{7}{240}\delta^8 - \tfrac{41}{7560}\delta^{10} \cdots \right) f_0 \\
h^6 f_0^{(6)} &= \left(\delta^6 - \tfrac{1}{4}\delta^8 + \tfrac{13}{240}\delta^{10} \cdots \right) f_0 \\
h^7 f_0^{(7)} &= \left(\mu\delta^7 - \tfrac{5}{12}\mu\delta^9 + \tfrac{31}{240}\mu\delta^{11} \cdots \right) f_0
\end{aligned}
$$

The preceding formulae can be truncated, as in the examples, and the differences expressed in terms of the function values. The resulting formulae are of the type

$$h^n f_0^{(n)} = \sum_{r=1}^{k} a_r \cdot f_r + \epsilon$$

where

$$\sum_{r=1}^{k} a_r = 0$$

and the principal part of the error 'ϵ' is the first neglected difference. It is still necessary for the differences to be converging.

In the following formulae only the order of the differences constituting the error term are indicated.

$$hf_0^{(1)} \simeq (f_1 - f_0) - \tfrac{1}{2}\Delta^2$$
$$\simeq \tfrac{1}{2}(-f_2 + 4f_1 - 3f_0) + \tfrac{1}{3}\Delta^3$$
$$\simeq \tfrac{1}{6}(2f_3 - 9f_2 + 18f_1 - 11f_0) - \tfrac{1}{4}\Delta^4$$
$$\simeq \tfrac{1}{2}(f_1 - f_{-1}) - \tfrac{1}{6}\mu\delta^3$$
$$\simeq \tfrac{1}{12}(-f_2 + 8f_1 - 8f_{-1} + f_2) + \tfrac{1}{30}\mu\delta^5$$
$$\simeq \tfrac{1}{60}(f_3 - 9f_2 + 45f_1 - 45f_{-1} + 9f_{-2} - f_{-3}) - \tfrac{1}{140}\mu\delta^7$$
$$\simeq (f_0 - f_{-1}) + \tfrac{1}{2}\nabla^2$$
$$\simeq \tfrac{1}{2}(3f_0 - 4f_{-1} + f_{-2}) + \tfrac{1}{3}\nabla^3$$
$$\simeq \tfrac{1}{6}(11f_0 - 18f_{-1} + 9f_{-2} - 2f_{-3}) + \tfrac{1}{4}\nabla^4$$

$$h^2 f_0^{(2)} \simeq (f_2 - 2f_1 + f_0) - \Delta^3$$
$$\simeq (-f_3 + 4f_2 - 5f_1 + 2f_0) + \tfrac{11}{12}\Delta^4$$
$$\simeq (11f_4 - 56f_3 + 114f_2 - 104f_1 + 35f_0) - \tfrac{5}{6}\Delta^5$$
$$\simeq (f_1 - 2f_0 + f_{-1}) - \tfrac{1}{12}\delta^4$$
$$\simeq \tfrac{1}{12}(-f_2 + 16f_1 - 30f_0 + 16f_{-1} - f_{-2}) + \tfrac{1}{90}\delta^6$$
$$\simeq \tfrac{1}{180}(2f_3 - 27f_2 + 270f_1 - 490f_0 + 270f_{-1} - 27f_{-2} + 2f_{-3}) - \tfrac{1}{560}\delta^8$$
$$\simeq (f_0 - 2f_{-1} + f_{-2}) + \nabla^3$$
$$\simeq (2f_0 - 5f_{-1} + 4f_{-2} - f_{-3}) + \tfrac{11}{12}\nabla^4$$
$$\simeq (35f_0 - 104f_{-1} + 114f_{-2} - 56f_{-3} + 11f_{-4}) + \tfrac{5}{6}\nabla^5$$

$$h^3 f_0^{(3)} \simeq (f_3 - 3f_2 + 3f_1 - f_0) - \tfrac{3}{2}\Delta^4$$
$$\simeq \tfrac{1}{2}(-3f_4 + 14f_3 - 24f_2 + 18f_1 - 5f_0) + \tfrac{21}{12}\Delta^5$$
$$\simeq \tfrac{1}{2}(f_2 - 2f_1 + 2f_{-1} - f_{-2}) - \tfrac{1}{4}\mu\delta^5$$
$$\simeq \tfrac{1}{8}(-f_3 + 8f_2 - 13f_1 + 13f_{-1} - 8f_{-2} + f_{-3}) + \tfrac{7}{120}\mu\delta^7$$
$$\simeq (f_0 - 3f_{-1} + 3f_{-2} - f_{-3}) + \tfrac{3}{2}\nabla^4$$
$$\simeq \tfrac{1}{2}(5f_0 - 18f_{-1} + 24f_{-2} - 14f_{-3} + 3f_{-4}) + \tfrac{21}{12}\nabla^5$$

For derivatives at half-way points there exist analagous formulae. The operators act upon f_0 and f_1, in the case of the forward and backward differences, and upon $f_{1/2}$ in the case of the central differences δ_0^{2n+1} being meaningless.

$$hf_{1/2}^{(1)} = (\Delta - \tfrac{1}{24}\Delta^3 + \tfrac{1}{24}\Delta^4 - \tfrac{71}{1920}\Delta^5 \cdots)f_0$$
$$= (\delta - \tfrac{1}{24}\delta^3 + \tfrac{3}{640}\delta^5 - \tfrac{5}{7168}\delta^7 \cdots)f_{1/2}$$
$$= (\nabla - \nabla^2 + \tfrac{23}{24}\nabla^3 + \tfrac{11}{12}\nabla^4 + \tfrac{563}{640}\nabla^5 \cdots)f_0$$
$$= (\nabla - \tfrac{1}{24}\nabla^3 - \tfrac{1}{24}\nabla^4 - \tfrac{71}{1920}\nabla^5 \cdots)f_1$$

$$h^2 f_{1/2}^{(2)} = (\Delta^2 - \tfrac{1}{12}\Delta^4 + \tfrac{1}{12}\Delta^5 - \tfrac{13}{180}\Delta^6 \cdots)f_0$$
$$= (\mu\delta^2 - \tfrac{5}{24}\mu\delta^4 + \tfrac{259}{5760}\mu\delta^6 - \tfrac{3229}{322560}\mu\delta^8 \cdots)f_{1/2}$$
$$= (\nabla^2 - \tfrac{1}{12}\nabla^4 - \tfrac{1}{12}\nabla^5 - \tfrac{13}{180}\nabla^6 \cdots)f_1$$

$$h^3 f_{1/2}^{(3)} = (\Delta^3 - \tfrac{1}{8}\Delta^5 + \tfrac{1}{8}\Delta^6 - \tfrac{203}{1920}\Delta^7 \cdots)f_0$$
$$= (\delta^3 - \tfrac{1}{8}\delta^5 + \tfrac{37}{1920}\delta^7 - \tfrac{2229}{967680}\delta^9 \cdots)f_{1/2}$$
$$= (\nabla^3 - \tfrac{1}{8}\nabla^5 - \tfrac{1}{8}\nabla^6 - \tfrac{203}{1920}\nabla^7 \cdots)f_1$$

As for tabular values, these formulae can be used to yield higher derivatives by multiplication of the operator series. Derivative formulae involving function values can also be obtained by truncation of the above series.

$$hf_{1/2}^{(1)} \simeq \tfrac{1}{24}(-f_3 + 3f_2 + 21f_1 - 23f_0) - \tfrac{1}{24}\Delta^4$$
$$\simeq \tfrac{1}{24}(f_4 - 5f_3 + 9f_2 + 13f_1 - 22f_0) - \tfrac{71}{1920}\Delta^5$$
$$\simeq (f_1 - f_0) - \tfrac{1}{24}\delta^3$$
$$\simeq \tfrac{1}{24}(-f_2 + 27f_1 - 27f_0 + f_{-1}) + \tfrac{3}{640}\delta^5$$
$$\simeq \tfrac{1}{1920}(3f_3 - 95f_2 + 2190f_1 - 2190f_0 + 95f_{-1} - 3f_{-2}) - \tfrac{5}{7168}\delta^7$$
$$\simeq (f_0 - f_{-1}) + \nabla^2$$
$$\simeq \tfrac{1}{24}(23f_1 - 21f_0 - 3f_{-1} + f_{-2}) - \tfrac{1}{24}\nabla^4$$
$$\simeq \tfrac{1}{24}(22f_1 - 17f_0 - 9f_{-1} + 5f_{-2} - f_{-3}) - \tfrac{71}{1920}\nabla^5$$

$$h^2 f_{1/2}^{(2)} \simeq (f_2 - 2f_1 + f_0) - \tfrac{1}{12}\Delta^4$$
$$\simeq \tfrac{1}{12}(-f_4 + 4f_3 + 6f_2 - 20f_1 + 11f_0) + \tfrac{1}{12}\Delta^5$$
$$\simeq \tfrac{1}{2}(f_2 - f_1 - f_0 + f_{-1}) - \tfrac{5}{24}\mu\delta^4$$
$$\simeq \tfrac{1}{48}(5f_3 + 33f_2 - 38f_1 - 38f_0 + 33f_{-1} + 5f_{-2}) + \tfrac{259}{5760}\mu\delta^6$$
$$\simeq (f_1 - 2f_0 + f_{-1}) - \tfrac{1}{12}\nabla^4$$
$$\simeq \tfrac{1}{12}(11f_1 - 20f_0 + 6f_{-1} + 4f_{-2} - f_{-3}) - \tfrac{1}{12}\nabla^5$$

$$h^3 f_{1/2}^{(3)} \simeq (f_3 - 3f_2 + 3f_1 - f_0) - \tfrac{1}{8}\Delta^5$$
$$\simeq (f_2 - 3f_1 + 3f_0 - f_{-1}) - \tfrac{1}{8}\delta^5$$
$$\simeq \tfrac{1}{8}(-f_3 + 13f_2 - 34f_1 + 34f_0 - 13f_{-1} + f_{-2}) + \tfrac{37}{1920}\delta^7$$
$$\simeq (f_1 - 3f_0 + 3f_{-1} - f_{-2}) - \tfrac{1}{8}\nabla^5$$

To calculate the derivative at an intermediate point 'p' the values of the derivative at tabular and half-way points can be evaluated and then interpolated, or the following formulae which involve the derivatives of Bessel's coefficients can be used. B_r' denotes the first derivative and B_r'' the second etc. Note that the formula for the fourth derivative involves $B_4'' - \tfrac{1}{24}$ which is the same as B_6^{IV}

$$hf_p' = \delta_{1/2} + \tfrac{1}{2}(p - \tfrac{1}{2})(\delta_0^2 + \delta_1^2) + B_3'\delta_{1/2}^3 + B_4'(\delta_0^4 + \delta_1^4) + B_5'\delta_{1/2}^5$$
$$+ B_6'(\delta_0^6 + \delta_1^6) + B_7'\delta_{1/2}^7 + \cdots$$
$$h^2 f_p'' = \delta_0^2 + p\delta_{1/2}^3 + B_4''(\delta_0^4 + \delta_1^4) + B_5''\delta_{1/2}^5 + B_6''(\delta_0^6 + \delta_1^6) + B_7''\delta_{1/2}^7 + \cdots$$
$$h^3 f_p'' = \delta_{1/2}^3 + \tfrac{1}{2}(p - \tfrac{1}{2})(\delta_0^4 + \delta_1^4) + B_5'''\delta_{1/2}^5 + B_6'''(\delta_0^6 + \delta_1^6) + B_7'''\delta_{1/2}^7 + \cdots$$
$$h^4 f_p = \delta_0^4 + p\delta_{1/2}^5 + (B_4'' - 0.417)(\delta_0^6 + \delta_1^6) + \cdots$$

To find the value of p at which a derivative has a given value a technique of successive approximation using these tables can be employed as an alternative to inverse interpolation in a table of the appropriate derivative.

Starting values for this procedure are given by

$$p \simeq \tfrac{1}{2} + 2(h^n f_p^{(n)} - \delta_{1/2}^n)/(\delta_0^{n+1} + \delta_1^{n+1}) \quad \text{when } n \text{ is odd}$$

and

$$p \simeq (h^n f_p^{(n)} - \delta_0^n)/\delta_{1/2}^{n+1} \quad \text{when } n \text{ is even}$$

DIFFERENTIATION TABLES FOR NON-TABULAR POINTS

p	B_3'	B_4'	B_5'	B_6'	B_7'	$(1 - p)$
.00	+.083333	+.041667	−.00833	−.0083	+.0012	1.00
.01	78383	41238	792	83	11	.99
.02	73533	40784	750	82	11	.98
.03	68783	40306	709	81	10	.97
.04	64133	39805	667	81	10	.96
.05	+.059583	+.039281	−.00626	−.0080	+.0009	.95
.06	55133	38735	585	79	9	.94
.07	50783	38166	544	78	8	.93
.08	46533	37576	504	77	7	.92
.09	42383	36965	464	76	7	.91
.10	+.038333	+.036333	−.00425	−.0075	+.0006	.90
.11	34383	35682	385	74	6	.89
.12	30533	35011	347	72	5	.88
.13	26783	34321	309	71	5	.87
.14	23133	33612	271	70	4	.86
.15	+.019583	+.032885	−.00234	−.0068	+.0004	.85
.16	16133	32141	198	67	3	.84
.17	12783	31380	162	66	3	.83
.18	9533	30603	128	64	2	.82
.19	6383	29809	93	63	1	.81
.20	+.003333	+.029000	−.00060	−.0061	+.0001	.80
.21	+ 383	28176	− 27	59	+ 1	.79
.22	− 2467	27337	+ 4	58	− 0	.78
.23	5217	26485	35	56	0	.77
.24	7867	25619	65	54	1	.76
.25	−.010417	+.024740	+.00094	−.0052	−.0001	.75
.26	12867	23848	123	51	2	.74
.27	15217	22944	150	49	2	.73
.28	17467	22029	176	47	3	.72
.29	19617	21103	201	45	3	.71
.30	−.021667	+.020167	+.00225	−.0043	−.0003	.70
.31	23617	19220	249	41	4	.69
.32	25467	18264	271	39	4	.68
.33	27217	17299	292	37	4	.67
.34	28867	16325	311	35	5	.66
.35	−.030417	+.015344	+.00330	−.0033	−.0005	.65
.36	31867	14355	348	31	5	.64
.37	33217	13359	364	29	5	.63
.38	34467	12356	380	27	6	.62
.39	35617	11347	394	24	6	.61
.40	−.036667	+.010333	+.00407	−.0022	−.0006	.60
.41	37617	9314	418	20	6	.59
.42	38467	8291	429	18	6	.58
.43	39217	7263	438	16	7	.57
.44	39867	6232	446	13	7	.56
.45	−.040417	+.005198	+.00453	−.0011	−.0007	.55
.46	40867	4161	459	9	7	.54
.47	41217	3123	463	7	7	.53
.48	41467	2083	466	4	7	.52
.49	41617	1042	468	2	7	.51
.50	−.041667	+.000000	+.00469	−.0000	−.0007	.50
$(1 - p)$	B_3'	$-B_4'$	B_5'	$-B_6'$	B_7'	p

DIFFERENTIATION TABLES FOR NON-TABULAR POINTS

p	B_4''	B_5''	B_6''	B_7''	$(1 - p)$
.00	− .041667	+ .04167	+ .0056	− .0056	1.00
.01	44142	4164	62	56	.99
.02	46567	4157	68	56	.98
.03	48942	4145	74	56	.97
.04	51267	4128	80	57	.96
.05	− .053542	+ .04106	+ .0086	− .0057	.95
.06	55767	4080	91	57	.94
.07	57942	4050	97	56	.93
.08	60067	4015	103	56	.92
.09	62142	3976	108	56	.91
.10	− .064167	+ .03933	+ .0113	− .0056	.90
.11	66142	3886	119	55	.89
.12	68067	3835	124	55	.88
.13	69942	3781	129	54	.87
.14	71767	3722	134	54	.86
.15	− .073542	+ .03660	+ .0139	− .0053	.85
.16	75267	3595	143	52	.84
.17	76942	3526	148	51	.83
.18	78567	3454	152	51	.82
.19	80142	3378	157	50	.81
.20	− .081667	+ .03300	+ .0161	− .0049	.80
.21	83142	3219	165	48	.79
.22	84567	3134	169	46	.78
.23	85942	3047	173	45	.77
.24	87267	2957	176	44	.76
.25	− .088542	+ .02865	+ .0180	− .0043	.75
.26	89767	2770	184	42	.74
.27	90942	2672	187	40	.73
.28	92067	2573	190	39	.72
.29	93142	2471	193	37	.71
.30	− .094167	+ .02367	+ .0196	− .0036	.70
.31	95142	2261	199	34	.69
.32	96067	2153	201	33	.68
.33	96942	2043	204	31	.67
.34	97767	1932	206	29	.66
.35	− .098542	+ .01819	+ .0209	− .0028	.65
.36	99267	1704	211	26	.64
.37	99942	1588	213	24	.63
.38	100567	1471	214	23	.62
.39	101142	1353	216	21	.61
.40	− .101667	+ .01233	+ .0218	− .0019	.60
.41	102142	1113	219	17	.59
.42	102567	991	220	15	.58
.43	102942	869	221	13	.57
.44	103267	746	222	11	.56
.45	− .103542	+ .00623	+ .0223	− .0010	.55
.46	103767	499	224	8	.54
.47	103942	375	224	6	.53
.48	104067	250	225	4	.52
.49	104142	125	225	2	.51
.50	− .104167	+ .00000	+ .0225	− .0000	.50
$(1 - p)$	B_4''	$-B_5''$	B_6''	$-B_7''$	p

DIFFERENTIATION TABLES FOR NON-TABULAR POINTS

p	B_5'''	B_6'''	B_7'''	$(1 - p)$
.00	− .00000	+.0625	− .0042	1.00
.01	495	617	33	.99
.02	980	608	25	.98
.03	1455	599	17	.97
.04	1920	590	9	.96
.05	− .02375	+.0580	− .0001	.95
.06	2820	571	+ 7	.94
.07	3255	561	14	.93
.08	3680	551	22	.92
.09	4095	540	29	.91
.10	− .04500	+.0530	+.0037	.90
.11	4895	519	44	.89
.12	5280	508	51	.88
.13	5655	497	58	.87
.14	6020	486	65	.86
.15	− .06375	+.0475	+.0071	.85
.16	6720	463	78	.84
.17	7055	451	84	.83
.18	7380	439	90	.82
.19	7695	427	96	.81
.20	− .08000	+.0415	+.0102	.80
.21	8295	403	108	.79
.22	8580	390	114	.78
.23	8855	377	119	.77
.24	9120	365	124	.76
.25	− .09375	+.0352	+.0129	.75
.26	9620	338	134	.74
.27	9855	325	139	.73
.28	10080	312	143	.72
.29	10295	299	148	.71
.30	− .10500	+.0285	+.0152	.70
.31	10695	271	156	.69
.32	10880	258	159	.68
.33	11055	244	163	.67
.34	11220	230	166	.66
.35	− .11375	+.0216	.0169	.65
.36	11520	202	172	.64
.37	11655	188	175	.63
.38	11780	174	178	.62
.39	11895	159	180	.61
.40	− .12000	+.0145	+.0182	.60
.41	12095	131	184	.59
.42	12180	116	186	.58
.43	12255	102	188	.57
.44	12320	87	189	.56
.45	− .12375	+.0073	+.0190	.55
.46	12420	58	191	.54
.47	12455	44	192	.53
.48	12480	29	192	.52
.49	12495	15	193	.51
.50	− .12500	+.0000	+.0193	.50
$(1 - p)$	B_5'''	B_6'''	B_7'''	p

Caution

Numerical differentiation is error magnifying and many guarding figures are usually necessary. This is due to two factors namely:

a) the interval h enters each formula in the form $1/h^n$

b) each formula starts with the nth order difference.

Both of these combine to make numerical differentiation unreliable. e.g. Suppose the formula $f^{(2)} = (\Delta^2 - \Delta^3 + \frac{11}{12}\Delta^4)/h^2$ is used with $h = 0.1$ and an error of 5×10^{-4} can be tolerated in the derivative. For an error of e in each of the tabulated values

$$5 \times 10^{-4} = \frac{1}{0.01}(2e + 3e + \frac{11}{12}6e)$$
$$= 100(\frac{21}{2}e)$$
$$= 1050e$$

and therefore $e \simeq 5 \times 10^{-7}$ i.e. the function must be tabulated to *six* places of decimals before the second derivative can be correct to *three*.

If, on the other hand, h had been unity in magnitude then

$$5 \times 10^{-4} = 10.5e$$

i.e. $e \simeq 5 \times 10^{-5}$ and the function would need only one guarding figure to produce the required degree of accuracy in the second derivative.

Obviously this effect is magnified for higher derivatives. In any case, the largest value of h, which permits the function to be well represented by a converging table of differences, should be used.

INTEGRATION FORMULAS

Integration is a smoothing procedure and as such errors in tabulated values tend to be cancelled out.

Notation used:

$$\int_{x_0}^{x_n} f(x) \cdot dx = h \int_0^n f_p \cdot dp$$

where

$$f_p \equiv f(x_0 + ph) \equiv f(x)$$

$$\int_0^n f_p \cdot dp = \tfrac{1}{2} f_0 + f_1 + f_2 + \cdots + f_{n-1} + \tfrac{1}{2} f_n + \tfrac{1}{12}(\Delta_0 - \nabla_n) - \tfrac{1}{24}(\Delta_0^2 + \nabla_n^2)$$
$$+ \tfrac{19}{720}(\Delta_0^3 - \nabla_n^3) - \tfrac{3}{160}(\Delta_0^4 + \nabla_n^4) \cdots$$
$$= \tfrac{1}{2} f_0 + f_1 + f_2 + \cdots + f_{n-1} + \tfrac{1}{2} f_n + \tfrac{1}{12}(\mu\delta_0 - \mu\delta_n)$$
$$- \tfrac{11}{720}(\mu\delta_0^3 - \mu\delta_n^3) + \tfrac{191}{60480}(\mu\delta_0^5 - \mu\delta_n^5) - \cdots$$

In particular

$$\int_0^1 f_p \cdot dp = (1 + \tfrac{1}{2}\Delta - \tfrac{1}{12}\Delta^2 + \tfrac{1}{24}\Delta^3 - \tfrac{19}{720}\Delta^4 + \tfrac{3}{160}\Delta^5 - \tfrac{863}{60480}\Delta^6 + \cdots) f_0$$
$$= (1 + \tfrac{1}{2}\nabla + \tfrac{5}{12}\nabla^2 + \tfrac{3}{8}\nabla^3 + \tfrac{251}{720}\nabla^4 + \tfrac{95}{288}\nabla^5 + \tfrac{19087}{60480}\nabla^6 \cdots) f_0$$
$$= (1 - \tfrac{1}{2}\nabla - \tfrac{1}{12}\nabla^2 - \tfrac{1}{24}\nabla^3 - \tfrac{19}{720}\nabla^4 - \tfrac{3}{160}\nabla^5 - \tfrac{863}{60480}\nabla^6 \cdots) f_1$$
$$= (\mu - \tfrac{1}{12}\mu\delta^2 + \tfrac{11}{720}\mu\delta^4 - \tfrac{191}{60480}\mu\delta^6 + \cdots) f_{1/2}$$

$$\int_0^{n+(1/2)} f_p \cdot dp = \tfrac{1}{2} f_0 + f_1 + f_2 \cdots + f_n + (\tfrac{1}{12}\mu\delta - \tfrac{11}{720}\mu\delta^3 + \tfrac{191}{60480}\mu\delta^5 \cdots) f_0$$
$$+ (\tfrac{1}{24}\delta - \tfrac{17}{5760}\delta^3 + \tfrac{367}{967680}\delta^5 \cdots) f_{n+(1/2)}$$

In particular

$$\int_0^{1/2} f_p \cdot dp = \tfrac{1}{2} f_0 + (\tfrac{1}{8}\delta - \tfrac{1}{24}\mu\delta^2 + \tfrac{1}{384}\delta^3 + \tfrac{11}{1440}\mu\delta^4 - \tfrac{13}{46080}\delta^5 \cdots) f_{1/2}$$

Symmetric range integrals

$$\int_{-1/2}^{1/2} f_p \cdot dp = (1 + \tfrac{1}{24}\delta^2 - \tfrac{17}{5760}\delta^4 + \tfrac{367}{967680}\delta^6 - \tfrac{27859}{464486400}\delta^8 \cdots) f_0$$

$$\int_{-1}^{1} f_p \cdot dp = 2(1 + \tfrac{1}{6}\delta^2 - \tfrac{1}{180}\delta^4 + \tfrac{1}{1512}\delta^6 - \tfrac{23}{226800}\delta^8 + \cdots) f_0$$

$$\int_{-2}^{2} f_p \cdot dp = 4(1 + \tfrac{2}{3}\delta^2 + \tfrac{7}{90}\delta^4 - \tfrac{2}{945}\delta^6 + \tfrac{13}{56700}\delta^8 - \cdots) f_0$$

$$\int_{-3}^{3} f_p \cdot dp = 6(1 + \tfrac{3}{2}\delta^2 + \tfrac{11}{20}\delta^4 + \tfrac{41}{840}\delta^6 - \tfrac{3}{2800}\delta^8 + \cdots) f_0$$

$$\int_{-4}^{4} f_p \cdot dp = 8(1 + \tfrac{8}{3}\delta^2 + \tfrac{217}{90}\delta^4 + \tfrac{92}{189}\delta^6 + \tfrac{989}{28350}\delta^8 + \cdots) f_0$$

The differences in the above formulae can be replaced by their function values, after truncation of the series, if extensive differencing is to be avoided.

When this is done, the formulae take on the forms

$$\sum_m A_m \cdot f_m$$

Some typical formulae of this type, used in the iterative starting of the solution of ordinary differential equations, can be found on pages 680. These are essentially quadrature formulae as are the predictor corrector formulae of pages 687.

When the limits involved in the integrals are not tabular or half-way points, formulae analogous to Bessel's interpolation formula can be used, the corresponding coefficients being designated by B^* etc. Single integration.

$$\int_0^p f_p \cdot dp = \tfrac{1}{2}p(f_0 + f_1)' + B_1^* \delta_{1/2} + B_2^*(\delta_0^2 + \delta_1^2) + B_3^* \delta_{1/2}^3$$

$$+ B_4^*(\delta_0^4 + \delta_1^4) + B_5^* \delta_{1/2}^5 + B_6^*(\delta_0^6 + \delta_1^6)$$

$$\iint_0^p f_p \cdot d^2 p = B_0^{**}(f_0 + f_1) + B_1^{**} \delta_{1/2} + B_2^{**}(\delta_0 + \delta_1) + B_3^{**} \delta_{1/2}$$

$$+ B_4^{**}(\delta_0 + \delta_1) + B_5^{**} \delta_{1/2}$$

INTEGRATION TABLES FOR NON-TABULAR POINTS

p	B_1^*	B_2^*	B_3^*	B_4^*	B_5^*	B_6^*
.00	− .000000	− .000000	+ .000000	+ .00000	− .00000	− .0000
.01	4950	12	4	0	0	0
.02	9800	49	16	1	0	0
.03	14550	110	35	2	0	0
.04	19200	195	61	3	1	0
.05	− .023750	− .000302	+ .000094	+ .00005	− .00001	− .0000
.06	28200	432	133	7	1	0
.07	32550	584	177	10	2	0
.08	36800	757	226	13	2	0
.09	40950	952	279	16	3	0
.10	− .045000	− .001167	+ .000338	+ .00020	− .00003	− .0000
.11	48950	1402	399	24	4	0
.12	52800	1656	465	29	5	1
.13	56550	1929	533	33	6	1
.14	60200	2221	604	39	6	1
.15	− .063750	− .002531	+ .000677	+ .00044	− .00007	− .0001
.16	67200	2859	753	50	8	1
.17	70550	3203	830	56	9	1
.18	73800	3564	908	62	10	1
.19	76950	3941	987	69	10	1
.20	− .080000	− .004333	+ .001067	+ .00076	− .00011	− .0002
.21	82950	4741	1147	84	12	2
.22	85800	5163	1227	91	13	2
.23	88550	5599	1307	99	14	2
.24	91200	6048	1386	107	15	2
.25	− .093750	− .006510	+ .001465	+ .00116	− .00016	− .0002
.26	96200	6985	1542	124	16	3
.27	98550	7472	1619	133	17	3
.28	100800	7971	1693	142	18	3
.29	102950	8480	1766	152	19	3
.30	− .105000	− .009000	+ .001838	+ .00161	− .00020	− .0003
.31	106950	9530	1906	171	20	4
.32	108800	10069	1973	181	21	4
.33	110550	10618	2037	191	22	4
.34	112200	11175	2098	202	23	4
.35	− .113750	− .011740	+ .002157	+ .00212	− .00023	− .0004
.36	115200	12312	2212	223	24	5
.37	116550	12891	2264	233	24	5
.38	117800	13477	2313	244	25	5
.39	118950	14069	2358	255	25	5
.40	− .120000	− .014667	+ .002400	+ .00266	− .00026	− .0005
.41	120950	15269	2438	278	26	6
.42	121800	15876	2473	289	27	6
.43	122550	16487	2503	301	27	6
.44	123200	17101	2530	312	27	6
.45	− .123750	− .017719	+ .002552	+ .00324	− .00028	− .0007
.46	124200	18339	2571	335	28	7
.47	124550	18961	2585	347	28	7
.48	124800	19584	2596	359	28	7
.49	124950	20208	2602	370	28	8
.50	− .125000	− .020833	+ .002604	+ .00382	− .00028	− .0008

INTEGRATION TABLES FOR NON-TABULAR POINTS (Continued)

p	B_1^*	B_2^*	B_3^*	B_4^*	B_5^*	B_6^*
.50	$-.125000$	$-.020833$	$+.002604$	$+.00382$	$-.00028$	$-.0008$
.51	124950	21458	2602	394	28	8
.52	124800	22083	2596	405	28	8
.53	124550	22706	2585	417	28	9
.54	124200	23328	2571	429	28	9
.55	$-.123750$	$-.023948$	$+.002552$	$+.00440$	$-.00028$	$-.0009$
.56	123200	24565	2530	452	27	9
.57	122550	25180	2503	463	27	10
.58	121800	25791	2473	475	27	10
.59	120950	26398	2438	486	26	10
.60	$-.120000$	$-.027000$	$+.002400$	$+.00497$	$-.00026$	$-.0010$
.61	118950	27597	2358	509	25	11
.62	117800	28189	2313	520	25	11
.63	116550	28775	2264	530	24	11
.64	115200	29355	2212	541	24	11
.65	$-.113750$	$-.029927$	$+.002157$	$+.00552$	$-.00023$	$-.0011$
.66	112200	30492	2098	562	23	12
.67	110550	31049	2037	573	22	12
.68	108800	31597	1973	583	21	12
.69	106950	32137	1906	593	20	12
.70	$-.105000$	$-.032667$	$+.001838$	$+.00603$	$-.00020$	$-.0012$
.71	102950	33187	1766	612	19	13
.72	100800	33696	1693	621	18	13
.73	98550	34194	1619	631	17	13
.74	96200	34681	1542	640	16	13
.75	$-.093750$	$-.035156$	$+.001465$	$+.00648$	$-.00016$	$-.0013$
.76	91200	35619	1386	657	15	14
.77	88550	36068	1307	665	14	14
.78	85800	36504	1227	673	13	14
.79	82950	36926	1147	680	12	14
.80	$-.080000$	$-.037333$	$+.001067$	$+.00688$	$-.00011$	$-.0014$
.81	76950	37726	987	695	10	14
.82	73800	38103	908	701	10	15
.83	70550	38464	830	708	9	15
.84	67200	38808	753	714	8	15
.85	$-.063750$	$-.039135$	$+.000677$	$+.00720$	$-.00007$	$-.0015$
.86	60200	39445	604	725	6	15
.87	56550	39737	533	730	6	15
.88	52800	40011	465	735	5	15
.89	48950	40265	399	740	4	15
.90	$-.045000$	$-.040500$	$+.000337$	$+.00744$	$-.00003$	$-.0015$
.91	40950	40715	279	748	3	15
.92	36800	40909	226	751	2	16
.93	32550	41083	177	754	2	16
.94	28200	41235	133	757	1	16
.95	$-.023750$	$-.041365$	$+.000094$	$+.00759$	$-.00001$	$-.0016$
.96	19200	41472	61	761	1	16
.97	14550	41556	35	762	0	16
.98	9800	41617	16	763	0	16
.99	4950	41654	4	764	0	16
1.00	$-.000000$	$-.041667$	$+.000000$	$+.00764$	$-.00000$	$-.0016$

INTEGRATION TABLES FOR NON-TABULAR POINTS

p	B_0^{**}	B_1^{**}	B_2^{**}	B_3^{**}	B_4^{**}	B_5^{**}
.00	+.000000	−.000000	−.000000	+.00000	+.00000	−.0000
.01	25	25	0	0	0	0
.02	100	99	0	0	0	0
.03	225	220	1	0	0	0
.04	400	389	3	0	0	0
.05	+.000625	−.000604	−.000005	+.00000	+.00000	−.0000
.06	900	864	9	0	0	0
.07	1225	1168	14	0	0	0
.08	1600	1515	20	1	0	0
.09	2025	1904	29	1	0	0
.10	+.002500	−.002333	−.000040	+.00001	+.00001	−.0000
.11	3025	2803	52	2	1	0
.12	3600	3312	68	2	1	0
.13	4225	3859	86	2	1	0
.14	4900	4443	106	3	2	0
.15	+.005625	−.005063	−.000130	+.00004	+.00002	−.0000
.16	6400	5717	157	4	3	0
.17	7225	6406	187	5	3	0
.18	8100	7128	221	6	4	0
.19	9025	7882	259	7	4	0
.20	+.010000	−.008667	−.000300	+.00008	+.00005	−.0000
.21	11025	9481	345	9	6	0
.22	12100	10325	395	10	7	0
.23	13225	11197	449	12	8	0
.24	14400	12096	507	13	9	0
.25	+.015625	−.013021	−.000570	+.00014	+.00010	−.0000
.26	16900	13971	637	16	11	0
.27	18225	14945	709	17	12	0
.28	19600	15941	787	19	14	0
.29	21025	16960	869	21	15	0
.30	+.022500	−.018000	−.000956	+.00023	+.00017	−.0000
.31	24025	19060	1049	25	19	0
.32	25600	20139	1147	26	20	0
.33	27225	21235	1250	28	22	0
.34	28900	22349	1359	31	24	0
.35	+.030625	−.023479	−.001474	+.00033	+.00026	−.0000
.36	32400	24624	1594	35	28	0
.37	34225	25783	1720	37	31	0
.38	36100	26955	1852	39	33	0
.39	38025	28138	1990	42	36	0
.40	+.040000	−.029333	−.002133	+.00044	+.00038	−.0000
.41	42025	30538	2283	47	41	0
.42	44100	31752	2439	49	44	1
.43	46225	32974	2601	51	47	1
.44	48400	34203	2768	54	50	1
.45	+.050625	−.035438	−.002943	+.00057	+.00053	−.0001
.46	52900	36677	3123	59	56	1
.47	55225	37921	3309	62	60	1
.48	57600	39168	3502	64	63	1
.49	60025	40417	3701	67	67	1
.50	+.062500	−.041667	−.003906	+.00069	+.00071	−.0001

INTEGRATION TABLES FOR NON-TABULAR POINTS (Continued)

p	B_0^{**}	B_1^{**}	B_2^{**}	B_3^{**}	B_4^{**}	B_5^{**}
.50	+.062500	−.041667	−.003906	+.00069	+.00071	−.0001
.51	65025	42916	4118	72	74	1
.52	67600	44165	4335	75	78	1
.53	70225	45412	4559	77	83	1
.54	72900	46656	4790	80	87	1
.55	+.075625	−.047896	−.005026	+.00082	+.00091	−.0001
.56	78400	49131	5268	85	96	1
.57	81225	50359	5517	87	100	1
.58	84100	51581	5772	90	105	1
.59	87025	52795	6033	92	110	1
.60	+.090000	−.054000	−.006300	+.00095	+.00115	−.0001
.61	93025	55195	6573	97	120	1
.62	96100	56379	6852	100	125	1
.63	99225	57550	7137	102	130	1
.64	102400	58709	7427	104	135	1
.65	+.105625	−.059854	−.007724	+.00106	+.00141	−.0001
.66	108900	60984	8026	108	146	1
.67	112225	62098	8334	110	152	1
.68	115600	63195	8647	112	158	1
.69	119025	64274	8966	114	164	1
.70	+.122500	−.065333	−.009290	+.00116	+.00170	−.0001
.71	126025	66373	9619	118	176	1
.72	129600	67392	9953	120	182	1
.73	133225	68389	10293	121	188	1
.74	136900	69363	10637	123	195	1
.75	+.140625	−.070313	−.010986	+.00125	+.00201	−.0001
.76	144400	71237	11340	126	207	1
.77	148225	72136	11699	127	214	1
.78	152100	73008	12062	129	221	1
.79	156025	73852	12429	130	228	1
.80	+.160000	−.074667	−.012800	+.00131	+.00234	−.0001
.81	164025	75451	13175	132	241	1
.82	168100	76205	13554	133	248	1
.83	172225	76927	13937	134	255	1
.84	176400	77616	14324	134	262	1
.85	+.180625	−.078271	−.014713	+.00135	+.00270	−.0001
.86	184900	78891	15106	136	277	1
.87	189225	79474	15502	136	284	1
.88	193600	80021	15901	137	291	1
.89	198025	80530	16302	137	299	1
.90	+.202500	−.081000	−.016706	+.00138	+.00306	−.0001
.91	207025	81430	17112	138	314	1
.92	211600	81819	17520	138	321	1
.93	216225	82165	17930	138	329	1
.94	220900	82469	18342	139	336	1
.95	+.225625	−.082729	−.018755	+.00139	+.00344	−.0001
.96	230400	82944	19169	139	351	1
.97	235225	83113	19584	139	359	1
.98	240100	83235	20000	139	367	1
.99	245025	83308	20417	139	374	1
1.00	+.250000	−.083333	−.020833	+.00139	+.00382	−.0001

GAUSS-TYPE WEIGHTS ABSCISSAE

Quadrature formulae using unevenly spaced ordinates. Some high accuracy formulae involve the use of abscissae which are unevenly spaced throughout the interval. The interval itself is usually subject to a transformation and various 'weighting functions' are involved.

To change the interval (a, b) in x to that of (θ, ϕ) in t the transformation

$$t = \frac{(a\theta - b\phi)}{(a - b)} + \frac{(\theta - \phi)x}{(a - b)}$$

is used.

Some of the more popular weighting functions and their associated intervals are given below. The general formulae are of two main types derived from

$$\int_a^b W(x) \cdot F(x) \cdot dx = \int_\theta^\phi \omega(t) \cdot f(t) \cdot dt$$

namely

$$\int_\theta^\phi \omega(t) \cdot f(t) \cdot dt = \sum_t \{H_t \cdot f(x_t)\}$$

and

$$\int_\theta^\phi \omega(t) \cdot f(t) \cdot dt = H \sum_t \{f(x_t) \pm f(-x_t)\}$$

$\omega(t)$	(θ, ϕ)	x_t are the zeros of:
1	$(-1, 1)$	$P_n(x)$
$t^{1/2}$	$(0, 1)$	$x^{-1/2} \cdot P_{2n+1}(\sqrt{x})$
$t^{-1/2}$	$(0, 1)$	$P_n(\sqrt{x})$
$(1 - t^2)^{1/2}$	$(-1, 1)$	$S_n(x)$
$(1 - t^2)^{-1/2}$	$(-1, 1)$	$T_n(x)$
e^{-t}	$(0, \infty)$	$L_n(x)$
e^{-t^2}	$(-\infty, \infty)$	$H_n(x)$

Some useful tables of abscissae x_t and their corresponding H_t are as follows.

Gaussian Quadrature.

$$\int_{-1}^{1} f(x) \cdot dx = \sum_{1}^{n} \{H_t \cdot f(x_t)\}$$

The x_t occur in pairs symmetrically placed with respect to the origin.

$\pm x_t$	H_t
n = 2	
0.5773503	1.0000000
n = 3	
0.7745967	0.5555556
0.0000000	0.8888889
n = 4	
0.8611363	0.3478548
0.3399810	0.6521452
n = 5	
0.9061798	0.2369269
0.5384693	0.4786287
0.0000000	0.5688889
n = 6	
0.9324695	0.1713245
0.6612094	0.3607616
0.2386192	0.4679139
n = 7	
0.9491079	0.1294850
0.7415312	0.2797054
0.4058452	0.3818301
0.0000000	0.4179592
n = 8	
0.9602899	0.1012285
0.7966665	0.2223810
0.5255324	0.3137066
0.1834346	0.3626838
n = 9	
0.9681602	0.0812744
0.8360311	0.1806482
0.6133714	0.2606107
0.3242534	0.3123471
0.0000000	0.3302394
n = 10	
0.9739065	0.0666713
0.8650634	0.1494513
0.6794096	0.2190864
0.4333954	0.2692602
0.1488743	0.2955242

$\pm x_i$	H_i
$n = 11$	
0.9782287	0.0556686
0.8870626	0.1255804
0.7301520	0.1862902
0.5190961	0.2331938
0.2695432	0.2628045
0.0000000	0.2729251
$n = 12$	
0.9815606	0.0471753
0.9041173	0.1069393
0.7699027	0.1600783
0.5873180	0.2031674
0.3678315	0.2334925
0.1253334	0.2491470
$n = 13$	
0.9841831	0.0404840
0.9175984	0.0921215
0.8015781	0.1388735
0.6423493	0.1781460
0.4484928	0.2078160
0.2304583	0.2262832
0.0000000	0.2325516
$n = 14$	
0.9862838	0.0351195
0.9284349	0.0801581
0.8272013	0.1215186
0.6872929	0.1572032
0.5152486	0.1855384
0.3191124	0.2051985
0.1080549	0.2152639
$n = 15$	
0.9879925	0.0307532
0.9372734	0.0703660
0.8482066	0.1071592
0.7244177	0.1395707
0.5709722	0.1662692
0.3941513	0.1861610
0.2011941	0.1984315
0.0000000	0.2025782
$n = 16$	
0.9894009	0.0271525
0.9445750	0.0622535
0.8656312	0.0951585
0.7554044	0.1246290
0.6178762	0.1495960
0.4580168	0.1691565
0.2816036	0.1826034
0.0950125	0.1894506

Laguerre Quadrature.

$$\int_0^\infty e^{-x} \cdot f(x) \cdot dx = \sum_1^n \{H_t \cdot f(x_t)\}$$

x_t	H_t
n = 2	
0.5857864	0.8535534
3.4142136	0.1464466
n = 3	
0.4157746	0.7110930
2.2942804	0.2785177
6.2899451	0.0103893
n = 4	
0.3225477	0.6031541
1.7457611	0.3574187
4.5366203	0.0388879
9.3950709	0.0005393
n = 5	
0.2635603	0.5217556
1.4134031	0.3986668
3.5964258	0.0759424
7.0858100	0.0036118
12.6408008	0.0000234
n = 6	
0.2228466	0.4589647
1.1889321	0.4170008
2.9927363	0.1133734
5.7751436	0.0103992
9.8374674	0.0002610
15.9828740	0.0000009

Hermitian Quadrature.

$$e^{-x^2} \cdot f(x) \cdot dx = H_t \cdot f(x_t)$$

The abscissae are symmetrically placed with respect to the origin.

$\pm x_t$	H_t
	$n = 2$	
0.7071068	0.8862269
	$n = 3$	
0.0000000	1.1816359
1.2247449	0.2954090
	$n = 4$	
0.5246476	0.8049141
1.6506801	0.0813128
	$n = 5$	
0.0000000	0.9453087
0.9585725	0.3936193
2.0201829	0.0199532
	$n = 6$	
0.4360774	0.7246296
1.3358491	0.1570673
2.3506050	0.0045300
	$n = 7$	
0.0000000	0.8102646
0.8162879	0.4256073
1.6735516	0.0545156
2.6519614	0.0009718
	$n = 8$	
0.3811870	0.6611470
1.1571937	0.2078023
1.9816568	0.0170780
2.9306374	0.0001996
	$n = 9$	
0.0000000	0.7202352
0.7235510	0.4326516
1.4685533	0.0884745
2.2665806	0.0049436
3.1909932	0.0000396
	$n = 10$	
0.3429013	0.6108626
1.0366108	0.2401386
1.7566836	0.0338744
2.5327317	0.0013436
3.4361591	0.0000076

$\pm x_t$	H_t
	$n = 11$
0.0000000	0.6547593
0.6568096	0.4293598
1.3265571	0.1172279
2.0259480	0.0119114
2.7832901	0.0003468
3.6684708	0.0000014
	$n = 12$
0.3142404	0.5701352
0.9477884	0.2604923
1.5976826	0.0516080
2.2795071	0.0039054
3.0206370	0.0000857
3.8897249	0.0000003

Radau Quadrature.

$$\int_{-1}^{1} f(x) \cdot dx = H_1 \cdot f(-1) + H_n \cdot f(1) + \sum_{2}^{n-1} \{H_t \cdot f(x_t)\}$$

$\pm x_t$	H_t
$n = 2$	
1.0000000	1.0000000
$n = 3$	
1.0000000	0.3333333
0.0000000	1.3333333
$n = 4$	
1.0000000	0.1666667
0.4472136	0.8333333
$n = 5$	
1.0000000	0.1000000
0.6546537	0.5444444
0.0000000	0.7111111
$n = 6$	
1.0000000	0.0666667
0.7650553	0.3784750
0.2852315	0.5548584
$n = 7$	
1.0000000	0.0476190
0.8302239	0.2768260
0.4688488	0.4317454
0.0000000	0.4876190
$n = 8$	
1.0000000	0.0357143
0.8717402	0.2107042
0.5917002	0.3411227
0.2092992	0.4124588
$n = 9$	
1.0000000	0.0277778
0.8997580	0.1654954
0.6771863	0.2745387
0.3631175	0.3464285
0.0000000	0.3715193
$n = 10$	
1.0000000	0.0222222
0.9195339	0.1333060
0.7387739	0.2248893
0.4779249	0.2920427
0.1652790	0.3275398

$\pm x_t$	H_t
	$n = 11$
1.0000000	0.0181818
0.9340014	0.1096123
0.7844835	0.1871699
0.5652353	0.2480481
0.2957581	0.2868791
0.0000000	0.3002176

Chebyshev-Radau Quadrature.

$$\int_{-1}^{1} x \cdot f(x) \cdot dx = H \cdot \sum_{1}^{n} \{f(x_t) - f(-x_t)\}$$

x_t	H
$n = 1$	
0.7745967	0.4303315
$n = 2$	
0.5002990	0.2393715
0.8922365	
$n = 3$	
0.4429861	
0.7121545	0.1599145
0.9293066	
$n = 4$	
0.3549416	
0.6433097	0.1223363
0.7783202	
0.9481574	

Chebyshev Quadrature.

$$\int_{-1}^{1} f(x) \cdot dx = \frac{2}{n} \cdot \sum_{1}^{n} f(x_t)$$

The abscissae are skew symmetric with respect to the origin.

x_t	x_t
$n = 2$	$n = 6$
−0.5773503	−0.8662468
+0.5773503	−0.4225187
$n = 3$	−0.2666354
−0.7071068	+0.2666354
0.0000000	+0.4225187
+0.7071068	+0.8662468
$n = 4$	$n = 7$
−0.7946545	−0.8838617
−0.1875925	−0.5296568
+0.1875925	−0.3239118
+0.7946545	0.0000000
$n = 5$	+0.3239118
−0.8324975	+0.5296568
−0.3745414	+0.8838617
0.0000000	
+0.3745414	
+0.8324975	

THE NUMERICAL SOLUTION OF DIFFERENTIAL EQUATIONS

Introduction

The aim is to produce a numerical approximation to the solution of the differential equation, correct to a specified number of decimals.
The principal factors affecting accuracy are
  a) the form of the equation,
  b) the interval of tabulation,
  c) the formula chosen to effect the integration.
The main types of equation considered here are classified as follows

TABLE I

I.V.* = Initial value problems, sometimes referred to as Marching problems.
B.V.' = Boundary value problems, sometimes referred to as Jury problems.

Ordinary differential equations

With initial value problems, all the conditions required to determine uniquely the constants arising from the integration procedure are given at one point. With boundary value problems these conditions are given at two or more points.

For ordinary boundary value problems the solution can usually be based upon initial value techniques as follows. One of the boundary points is chosen as the principal point and the variables which are given at the other boundary point(s) are estimated at this point. This is repeated for a number of different estimates and a combination of the resulting solutions is chosen so that the numerical values satisfy both the differential equation and also all the original boundary conditions.

The principal methods of solving ordinary initial value differential equations to be considered are classified as follows. Purely analytical techniques will not be dealt with.

In the direct methods the value at any point is obtained from the value at the preceeding point without any iteration. In the case of the Taylor's series approach it is a simple matter to include a running check on previously computed values. With the Runge-Kutta and Chebyshev techniques checking is more difficult. For linear differential equations, or any for which repeated differentiation is practical, the Taylors series method can be used with a

THE NUMERICAL SOLUTION OF DIFFERENTIAL EQUATIONS (Continued)

TABLE II

Ordinary Initial value differential equations

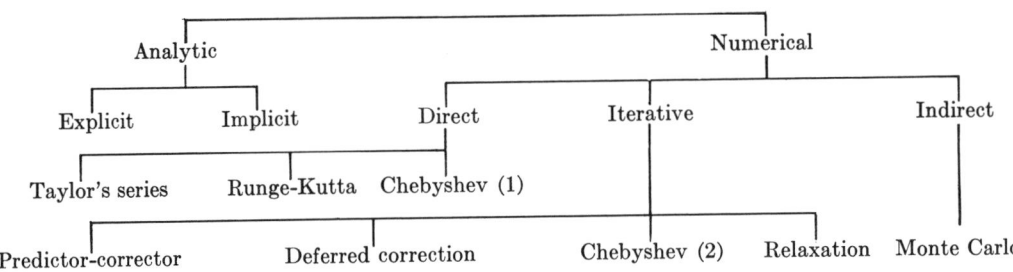

large step length. The basic disadvantages of direct methods are that the amount of calculation can be heavy and previously computed values are ignored. In addition a prior knowledge of the order of the approximation is necessary for the most efficient use of the basic Runga-Kutta approach and the direct Chebyshev method requires normalization of the range of the argument to either $(-1, +1)$ or $(0, +1)$.

With the iterative methods to be described, initial approximations are made and these are then refined until successive approximations agree to the required number of decimals. This is carried out either a point at a time or simultaneously over the whole range. They have the advantage of being self correcting in the sense that small computational errors are eliminated in subsequent iterations.

In this group of methods the predictor-corrector methods are particularly suitable for desk machine operation, especially with the more complicated non-linear differential equation. Their accuracy is controlled by the corrector formula which has associated with it an indication of the maximum interval to ensure convergence. These formulae are expressed either in terms of ordinates or backward and or central differences.

The deferred corrector methods are particularly suitable for desk machine work and are highly recommended. Relaxation methods are seldom used for initial value problems but they are naturally applicable to boundary value problems and in fact an initial value problem has to be converted to a boundary value one if relaxation is to be used.

Some predictor-corrector methods can be modified to be non-iterative but all will require special starting techniques to get under way.

General observations applicable to all methods

There will always be an optimum interval "h" of the argument (independent variable) and the method chosen should be able to take into account the need for changing this as the solution proceeds.

Build-up error due to rounding-off of differences can cause trouble. Two or three guarding figures should be held and there should always be running and terminal checks incorporated in any solution.

The stability of the method i.e. the convergence to the wanted solution, depends upon the differential equation as well as the method chosen. Starting with the last computed value and integrating in the reverse direction back to the original origin will check this.

The truncation error due to using a finite approximation to an infinite series will reduce the number of significant decimals obtained. However, this can be corrected at a later stage.

THE NUMERICAL SOLUTION OF DIFFERENTIAL EQUATIONS (Continued)

Any order differential equation can be reduced to a number of simultaneous differential equations of the first order and so the solution of first order differential equations is considered in detail. In some cases there will however be a loss of convenience if such a reduction is employed.

e.g.   Given $y'' = xy - \sin x$ with $y(0) = 1, \quad y'(0) = 0.$
This reduces to $y' = w$ with $y(0) = 1$
$z' = v$ $z(0) = 0$
$v' = -z$ $v(0) = 1$
$w' = xy - z$ $w(0) = 0$

DIRECT METHODS

Taylor's series

Applicable to all linear equations and those non-linear equations whose higher derivatives can be easily found.

e.g. $y' = f(x,y)$ i.e. $y^{(1)} = f(x,y^{(0)})$

then $y^{(n+1)} = \dfrac{\partial y^{(n)}}{\partial x} + y^{(1)} \dfrac{\partial y^{(n)}}{\partial y}$

(since $y^{(n)}$ can be reduced to a function of x and y only.)

Finally $x_1 = x_0 + h$

and $y_1 = y_0 + \dfrac{h y_0^{(1)}}{1!} + \dfrac{h^2 y_0^{(2)}}{2!} + \dfrac{h^3 y_0^{(3)}}{3!} + \dfrac{h^4 y_0^{(4)}}{4!} + \cdots$

In practice the computational procedure is simplified by introducing the reduced derivatives defined by

$$\tau^{(n)} \equiv \frac{h^n y^{(n)}}{n!} \qquad\qquad (\tau^{(0)} \equiv y)$$

from which it follows that $\dfrac{d\tau^{(n)}}{dx} = \dfrac{(n+1)\tau^{(n+1)}}{h}$

For linear equations a recurrence relationship is obtained by means of Liebnitz's theorem to generate any particular $\tau^{(n)}$ from the preceeding τ's. Thus, given the differential equation and the initial conditions, the sequence $\tau^{(0)}, \tau^{(1)} \tau^{(2)}, \tau^{(3)}, \ldots, \tau^{(n)}$ is computed until the terms cease to have any significance with regard to the number of places of decimals required.

If the Taylor's series is re-arranged then not only can the new function value be computed but a running check on the previously computed value be obtained with a minimum of effort. This can also be applied to as many of the derivatives as are desired.

$$y_1 = (\tau_0^{(0)} + \tau_0^{(2)} + \tau_0^{(4)} + \tau_0^{(6)} \cdots) + (\tau_0^{(1)} + \tau_0^{(3)} + \tau_0^{(5)} + \cdots)$$
$$\tau_1^{(1)} = (2\tau_0^{(2)} + 4\tau_0^{(4)} + 6\tau_0^{(6)} + \cdots) + (\tau_0^{(1)} + 3\tau_0^{(3)} + 5\tau_0^{(5)} + \cdots)$$

The checking formulae corresponding to the above pair are

$$y_{-1} = (\tau_0^{(0)} + \tau_0^{(2)} + \tau_0^{(4)} + \tau_0^{(6)} \cdots) - (\tau_0^{(1)} + \tau_0^{(3)} + \tau_0^{(5)} \cdots)$$
$$\tau_{-1}^{(1)} = (2\tau_0^{(2)} + 4\tau_0^{(4)} + 6\tau_0^{(6)} + \cdots) - (\tau_0^{(1)} + 3\tau_0^{(3)} + 5\tau_0^{(5)} + \cdots)$$

THE NUMERICAL SOLUTION OF DIFFERENTIAL EQUATIONS (Continued)

It will be seen that the sums inside the brackets which are used to evaluate the y_1 and the $\tau_1^{(1)}$ are also used to evaluate the y_{-1} and the $\tau_{-1}^{(1)}$. A shift of origin from (x_0,y_0) to (x_1,y_1) is then made, in accordance with the usual procedure for advancing the solution of a differential equation, and the process repeated. If too many terms are necessary, before the τ's assume negligible proportions, then the interval of tabulation "h" should be reduced. Conversely, if only a few terms have significance, then "h" should be increased.

Computational layout for one such stage

x_0			y_0	
	$\tau_0^{(0)}$	$\tau_0^{(1)}$		
	$\tau_0^{(2)}$	$\tau_0^{(3)}$		
	$\tau_0^{(4)}$	$\tau_0^{(5)}$		
	$\cdot\;\cdot\;\cdot$	$\cdot\;\cdot\;\cdot\;\cdot$		
	$\tau_0^{(2n)}$	$\tau_0^{(2n+1)}$		
x_1	$\displaystyle\sum_{r=0}^{n} \tau_0^{(2n)}$	$\displaystyle\sum_{r=0}^{n} \tau_0^{(2n+1)}$	y_1	y_{-1}
	$\displaystyle\sum_{r=0}^{n} 2r\tau_0^{(2r)}$	$\displaystyle\sum_{r=0}^{n} (2r+1)\tau_0^{(2r+1)}$	$\tau_1^{(1)}$	$\tau_{-1}^{(1)}$

Method of Runge-Kutta

An nth order Runge-Kutta process has an error of $0(h^{n+1})$. If $y' = f(x,y)$ then $y_1 = y_0 + K$, where K is the weighted mean of "n" evaluations of $h \cdot y'$ taken at specified points. There are an infinity of such formulae and the weights, and the constants necessary to determine the specified points, are tabulated for some simple cases only.

At any stage of the numerical solution, only the function value at the beginning of the stage need be known. This means that no special starting technique is necessary, but against this must be set the fact that the function must be evaluated "n" times per step. Further, previously computed values are not used to check the computation. Error analysis is not easy and the usual check is simply one of repeating the calculations at a different interval (one simple formula involving an error check is given at the end). Alternatively a finite difference check can be used.

If the functions are not smooth or if a frequent change in step length, particularly when such a change is expected to be a decrease, is envisaged then this process is of particular importance.

Second order systems   Error $= 0(h^3)$

Given $y' = f(x,y)$ and y_0
Then $x_1 = x_0 + h$ and $y_1 = y_0 + K$
where $K = \omega_1 k_1 + \omega_2 k_2$ $(\omega_1 + \omega_2 = 1)$
and $k_r = h \cdot f(x_0 + a_r h, y_0 + b_r k_1)$

THE NUMERICAL SOLUTION OF DIFFERENTIAL EQUATIONS (Continued)

Six typical systems are listed

(i)

r	a_r	b_r	ω_r
1	0	0	-1
2	$\frac{1}{4}$	$\frac{1}{4}$	2

(ii)

r	a_r	b_r	ω_r
1	0	0	0
2	$\frac{1}{2}$	$\frac{1}{2}$	1

(iii)

r	a_r	b_r	ω_r
1	0	0	$\frac{2}{3}$
2	$\frac{3}{4}$	$\frac{3}{4}$	$\frac{1}{3}$

(iv)

r	a_r	b_r	ω_r
1	0	0	$\frac{1}{2}$
2	1	1	$\frac{1}{2}$

(v)

r	a_r	b_r	ω_r
1	0	0	$\frac{1}{4}$
2	$\frac{2}{3}$	$\frac{2}{3}$	$\frac{3}{4}$

(vi)

r	a_r	b_r	ω_r
1	0	0	$-\frac{1}{2}$
2	$\frac{1}{3}$	$\frac{1}{3}$	$1\frac{1}{2}$

Third order systems   Error $= 0(h^4)$

Given $y' = f(x,y)$ and y_0
Then $x_1 = x_0 + h$ and $y_1 = y_0 + K$
where $K = \omega_1 k_1 + \omega_2 k_2 + \omega_3 k_3$ $(\omega_1 + \omega_2 + \omega_3 = 1)$
and $k_r = h \cdot f(x_0 + a_r h, y_0 + b_r k_1 + c_r k_2)$
Four typical systems are listed

(i)

r	a_r	b_r	c_r	ω_r
1	0	0	0	$\frac{2}{3}$
2	$\frac{1}{4}$	$\frac{1}{4}$	0	$-\frac{4}{3}$
3	$\frac{1}{2}$	$\frac{1}{10}$	$\frac{2}{5}$	$\frac{5}{3}$

(ii)

r	a_r	b_r	c_r	ω_r
1	0	0	0	$\frac{1}{4}$
2	$\frac{1}{3}$	$\frac{1}{3}$	0	0
3	$\frac{2}{3}$	0	$\frac{2}{3}$	$\frac{3}{4}$

(iii)

r	a_r	b_r	c_r	ω_r
1	0	0	0	$\frac{1}{6}$
2	$\frac{1}{2}$	$\frac{1}{2}$	0	$\frac{2}{3}$
3	1	-1	2	$\frac{1}{6}$

(iv)

r	a_r	b_r	c_r	ω_r
1	0	0	0	$\frac{1}{4}$
2	$\frac{2}{3}$	$\frac{2}{3}$	0	$\frac{1}{2}$
3	$\frac{2}{3}$	$-\frac{1}{3}$	1	$\frac{1}{4}$

Fourth order systems   Error $= (h^5)$

Given $y' = f(x,y)$ and y_0
Then $x_1 = x_0 + h$ and $y_1 = y_0 + K$
where $K = \omega_1 k_1 + \omega_2 k_2 + \omega_3 k_3 + \omega_4 k_4$ $(\omega_1 + \omega_2 + \omega_3 + \omega_4 = 1)$
and $k_r = h \cdot f(x_0 + a_r, y_0 + b_r k_1 + c_r k_2 + d_r k_3)$

THE NUMERICAL SOLUTION OF DIFFERENTIAL EQUATIONS (Continued)

Four typical systems are listed. The third is of particular importance both from the point of view of simplicity of numerical constants and of and the sequential relationships between the various k's.

(i)

r	a_r	b_r	c_r	d_r	ω_r
1	0	0	0	0	$\frac{1}{8}$
2	$\frac{1}{3}$	$\frac{1}{3}$	0	0	$\frac{3}{8}$
3	$\frac{2}{3}$	$-\frac{1}{3}$	1	0	$\frac{3}{8}$
4	1	1	-1	1	$\frac{1}{8}$

(ii)

r	a_r	b_r	c_r	d_r	ω_r
1	0	0	0	0	$\frac{1}{6}$
2	1	1	0	0	0
3	$\frac{1}{2}$	$\frac{3}{8}$	$\frac{1}{8}$	0	$\frac{2}{3}$
4	1	$-\frac{1}{2}$	$-\frac{1}{2}$	2	$\frac{1}{6}$

(iii)

r	a_r	b_r	c_r	d_r	ω_r
1	0	0	0	0	$\frac{1}{6}$
2	$\frac{1}{2}$	$\frac{1}{2}$	0	0	$\frac{1}{3}$
3	$\frac{1}{2}$	0	$\frac{1}{2}$	0	$\frac{1}{3}$
4	1	0	0	1	$\frac{1}{6}$

(iv)

r	a_r	b_r	c_r	d_r	ω_r
1	0	0	0	0	0
2	$\frac{1}{2}$	$\frac{1}{2}$	0	0	$\frac{2}{3}$
3	0	$-\frac{1}{2}$	$\frac{1}{2}$	0	$\frac{1}{6}$
4	1	$-\frac{1}{2}$	$1\frac{1}{2}$	1	$\frac{1}{6}$

Fifth order systems   Error $= 0(h^6)$

The number of terms required to form the weighted mean "K" increases, for orders greater than the fourth and, in addition, the coefficients are much less easy to handle.

The following system requires one additional term.

Given $y' = f(x,y)$ and y_0

Then $x_1 = x_0 + h$, and $y_1 = y_0 + K$

where $K = \omega_1 k_1 + \omega_2 k_2 + \omega_3 k_3 + \omega_4 k_4 + \omega_5 k_5 + \omega_6 k_6$

$$(\omega_1 + \omega_2 + \omega_3 + \omega_4 + \omega_5 + \omega_6 = 1)$$

and $k_r = h \cdot f(x_0 + a_r h, y_0 + b_r k_1 + c_r k_2 + d_r k_3 + e_r k_4 + f_r k_5)$

r	a_r	b_r	c_r	d_r	e_r	f_r	ω_r
1	0	0	0	0	0	0	$23/192$
2	$\frac{1}{3}$	$\frac{1}{3}$	0	0	0	0	0
3	$\frac{2}{5}$	$\frac{4}{25}$	$\frac{16}{25}$	0	0	0	$125/192$
4	1	$\frac{1}{4}$	-3	$\frac{15}{4}$	0	0	0
5	$\frac{2}{3}$	$\frac{2}{27}$	$\frac{10}{9}$	$\frac{50}{81}$	$\frac{8}{81}$	0	$-27/64$
6	$\frac{4}{5}$	$\frac{2}{25}$	$\frac{12}{25}$	$\frac{2}{15}$	$\frac{8}{75}$	0	$125/192$

THE NUMERICAL SOLUTION OF DIFFERENTIAL EQUATIONS (Continued)

An example of computational layout

Consider formula (iii) of the fourth order systems. On substituting the values from the table the resulting formulae are as follows

$$y' = f(x,y)$$
$$x_1 = x_0 + h$$
$$k_1 = h \cdot f(x_0, y_0)$$
$$k_2 = h \cdot f(x_0 + \tfrac{1}{2}h, \; y_0 + \tfrac{1}{2}k_1)$$
$$k_3 = h \cdot f(x_0 + \tfrac{1}{2}h, \; y_0 + \tfrac{1}{2}k_2)$$
$$k_4 = h \cdot f(x_0 + h, \; y_0 + k_3)$$
$$y_1 = y_0 + \tfrac{1}{6}(k_1 + 2k_2 + 2k_3 + k_4)$$

and the layout of one state of the calculation is

x	y	$k_r = hy'$	K
$\boldsymbol{x_0}$	$\boldsymbol{y_0}$	k_1	
$x_0 + \tfrac{1}{2}h$	$y_0 + \tfrac{1}{2}k_1$	k_2	
$x_0 + \tfrac{1}{2}h$	$y_0 + \tfrac{1}{2}k_2$	k_3	
$x_0 + h$	$y_0 + k_3$	k_4	
			$(k_1 + 2k_2 + 2k_3 + k_4)$
$x_1 = x_0 + h$	$y_1 = y_0 + K$		

The starting values for this stage are underlined.

Extension of the Runge-Kutta approach to simultaneous differential equations

Consider again table (iii) of the fourth order systems. It can be extended to cover any number of simultaneous D.E's. The extension to two is shown in detail and the general case can be easily deduced from it.

$$\text{Given} \quad y' = f(x,y,z)$$
$$\text{and} \quad z' = g(x,y,z)$$
$$x_1 = x_0 + h$$
$$\text{we obtain} \quad y_1 = y_0 + K$$
$$\text{and} \quad z_1 = z_0 + M$$
$$\text{where} \quad K = \omega_1 k_1 + \omega_2 k_2 + \omega_3 k_3 + \omega_4 k_4$$
$$M = \omega_1 m_1 + \omega_2 m_2 + \omega_3 m_3 + \omega_4 m_4$$
$$\text{and} \quad k_1 = h \cdot f(x_0, y_0, z_0)$$
$$k_2 = h \cdot f(x_0 + \tfrac{1}{2}h, \; y_0 + \tfrac{1}{2}k_1, \; z_0 + \tfrac{1}{2}m_1)$$
$$k_3 = h \cdot f(x_0 + \tfrac{1}{2}h, \; y_0 + \tfrac{1}{2}k_2, \; z_0 + \tfrac{1}{2}m_2)$$
$$k_4 = h \cdot f(x_0 + h, \; y_0 + k_3, \; z_0 + m_3)$$

THE NUMERICAL SOLUTION OF DIFFERENTIAL EQUATIONS (Continued)

$$\text{and} \quad m_1 = h \cdot g(x_0, y_0, z_0)$$

$$m_2 = h \cdot g(x_0 + \tfrac{1}{2}h, y_0 + \tfrac{1}{2}k_1, z_0 + \tfrac{1}{2}m_1)$$

$$m_3 = h \cdot g(x_0 + \tfrac{1}{2}h, y_0 + \tfrac{1}{2}k_2, z_0 + \tfrac{1}{2}m_2)$$

$$m_4 = h \cdot g(x_0 + h, y_0 + k_3, z_0 + m_3)$$

and the computational layout will be similar to the previous one

x	y	z	$k_r = hf$ $K = \Sigma \omega_r k_r$	$m_r = hg$ $M = \Sigma \omega_r m_r$
x_0	y_0	z_0	k_1	m_1
$x_0 + \tfrac{1}{2}h$	$y_0 + \tfrac{1}{2}k_1$	$z_0 + \tfrac{1}{2}m_1$	k_2	m_2
$x_0 + \tfrac{1}{2}h$	$y_0 + \tfrac{1}{2}k_2$	$z_0 + \tfrac{1}{2}m_2$	k_3	m_3
$x_0 + h$	$y_0 + k_3$	$z_0 + m_3$	k_4	m_4
			"K"	"M"
$x_1 = x_0 + h$	$y_1 = y_0 + K$	$z_1 = z_0 + M$		

The use of Runge-Kutta techniques for higher order differential equations

A schematic for the general second order differential equation is shown.

Given $y'' = f(x, y, y')$ and y_0, y_0' the reduced derivatives can be used i.e.

$$\tau^{(n)} \equiv \frac{h^n}{n!} \cdot y^{(n)}$$

Then $\quad y'' = f\left(x, y, \dfrac{\tau^{(1)}}{h}\right)$

and $\quad x_1 = x_0 + h$

$\qquad y_1 = y_0 + \tau_0^{(1)} + K$

$\qquad \tau_1^{(1)} = \tau_0^{(1)} + K'$

where $\quad K = \displaystyle\sum_{r=1}^{4} \omega_r k_r \qquad\qquad \left(1 = \displaystyle\sum_{r=1}^{4} \omega_r\right)$

and $\quad K' = \displaystyle\sum_{r=1}^{4} \omega_r' k_r \qquad\qquad \left(1 = \displaystyle\sum_{r=1}^{4} \omega_r'\right)$

$$k_r = \frac{h^2}{2} \cdot f(x_0 + a_r h, y_0 + b_r \tau_0^{(1)} + c_r k_1 + d_r k_2 + e_r k_3, \{\tau_0^{(1)} + g_r k_{r-1}\}/h)$$

THE NUMERICAL SOLUTION OF DIFFERENTIAL EQUATIONS (Continued)

r	a_r	b_r	c_r	d_r	e_r	g_r	ω_r	ω_r'
1	0	0	0	0	0	0	0	$\frac{1}{3}$
2	$\frac{1}{2}$	$\frac{1}{2}$	$\frac{1}{4}$	0	0	1	$\frac{1}{3}$	$\frac{2}{3}$
3	$\frac{1}{2}$	$\frac{1}{2}$	$\frac{1}{4}$	0	0	1	$\frac{1}{3}$	$\frac{3}{2}$
4	1	1	0	0	1	2	$\frac{1}{3}$	$\frac{1}{3}$

The computational layout being as follows

x	y	τ	k, K, K'
x_0	y_0	$\tau_0^{(1)}$	k_1
$x_0 + \frac{1}{2}h$	$y_0 + \frac{1}{2}\tau_0^{(1)} + \frac{1}{4}k_1$	$\tau_0^{(1)} + k_1$	k_2
$x_0 + \frac{1}{2}h$	$y_0 + \frac{1}{2}\tau_0^{(1)} + \frac{1}{4}k_1$	$\tau_0^{(1)} + k_2$	k_3
$x_0 + h$	$y_0 + \tau_0^{(1)} + k_3$	$\tau_0^{(1)} + 2k_3$	k_4
			K
			K'

$$x_1 = x_0 + h \qquad y_1 = y_0 + \tau_0^{(1)} + K \tau_1^{(1)} = \tau_0^{(1)} + K'$$

where
$$K = \omega_1 k_1 + \omega_2 k_2 + \omega_3 k_3 + \omega_4 k_4$$
$$K' = \omega_1' k_1 + \omega_2' k_2 + \omega_3' k_3 + \omega_4' k_4$$

Chebyshev Polynomials (1)

The Chebyshev polynomial of degree r in x where $-1 \leq x \leq 1$ is denoted by $T_r \equiv T_r(x)$.

$$T_r(x) \equiv \cos(r \cdot \cos^{-1} x)$$
$$\text{and} \quad 2x \cdot T_r = T_{r+1} + T_{r-1}$$

The shifted Chebyshev polynomials of degree r in x where $0 \leq x \leq 1$ are denoted by $T_r^* \equiv T_r^*(x)$.

$$T_r^*(x) \equiv \cos(r \cdot \cos^{-1}(2x - 1))$$
$$\text{and} \quad 2(2x - 1) \cdot T_r^* = T_{r+1}^* + T_{r-1}^*$$

N.B. $T_r^*(x^2) = T_{2r}(x)$

Both types of polynomials can be used for linear differential equations over a finite interval. The equation is assumed to have polynomial coefficients—if not then suitable polynomial approximations should be inserted. The finite range must first be normalized to either $(-1,1)$ or $(0,1)$.

a) Chebyshev polynomials

$$T_0 = 1$$
$$T_r(1) = 1$$
$$T_r(-1) = (-1)^r$$
$$T_{2r}(0) = (-1)^r$$
$$T_{2r+1}(0) = 0$$

THE NUMERICAL SOLUTION OF DIFFERENTIAL EQUATIONS (Continued)

The solution of the equation $y^{(1)} = f(x,y)$ is assumed to have the form

$$y = \tfrac{1}{2}a_0 + a_1 T_1 + a_2 T_2 + a_3 T_3 + a_4 T_4 + \cdots$$

where $a_r = 0$ for all $r > N$

i.e.
$$y = \tfrac{1}{2}a_0 + a_1 T_1 + a_2 T_2 + \cdots + a_N T_N.$$

similarly
$$y^{(1)} = \tfrac{1}{2}a_0^{(1)} + \sum_{r=1}^{N} a_r^{(1)} T_r \text{ etc.}$$

Writing $C_r(y^{(s)}) \equiv$ the coefficient of T_r in the expansion of $y^{(s)}$ (the s th derivative of y with respect to x)

$$C_r(y^{(s)}) = a_r^{(s)} \tag{1}$$

Further
$$C_r(xy) = \tfrac{1}{2}(a_{r+1} + a_{r-1})$$

and
$$C_r(x^2 y) = \tfrac{1}{4}(a_{r+2} + 2a_r + a_{r-2})$$

in general
$$C_r(x^p y^{(s)}) = 2^{-p} \sum_{i=0}^{p} \binom{p}{i} a_{|r-p+2i|}^{(s)} \qquad \left(\begin{matrix} r = 0,1,2 \cdots \\ s = 1,2, \ldots \end{matrix}\right) \tag{2}$$

In addition the Chebyshev recurrence relationship itself yields

$$a_{r-1}^{(s)} = 2r \cdot a_r^{(s-1)} + a_{r+1}^{(s)} \tag{3}$$

Method of solution

(i) Obtain a relationship between the a's and the $a^{(1)}$'s from $C_r\{y^{(1)} - f(x,y)\} = 0$, e.g. If $(x^2 + 1)y^{(1)} - 4xy = 0$.

Then
$$a_{r-2}^{(1)} + 6a_r^{(1)} + a_{r+2}^{(1)} - 8a_{r-1} - 8a_{r+1} = 0 \tag{4}$$

since
$$C_r\{x^2 y^{(1)}\} + C_r\{y^{(1)}\} - 4C_r\{xy\} = 0$$

(ii) From (3) with $s = 1$.

$$a_{r-1}^{(1)} = 2ra_r + a_{r+1}^{(1)} \tag{5}$$

(iii) Substitute (5) into (4) in such a manner that the suffix of one of the a's is *less* than all the other suffices. The above example yields

$$2(r - 5)a_{r-1} = 8a_{r+1} - 7a_r^{(1)} - a_{r+2}^{(1)} \tag{4a}$$

(iv) Equations (4a) and (5) are then used to generate the a's and $a^{(1)}$'s by recurrence *backwards* from some arbitrarily chosen values of a_N and $a_N^{(1)}$.

e.g.   Set $a_N = 1$, $a_N^{(1)} = 1$ and $a_r = a_r^{(1)} = 0$, all $r > N$

The values found will however be far too large, in general, so a scale factor has to be determined.

(v) The initial conditions will be given either at the origin or at the extremities of the range.

THE NUMERICAL SOLUTION OF DIFFERENTIAL EQUATIONS (Continued)

Noting that

$$y(0) \quad = \tfrac{1}{2}a_0 - a_2 + a_4 - a_6 + a_8 \cdots$$

$$y(1) \quad = \tfrac{1}{2}a_0 + a_1 + a_2 + a_3 + a_4 \cdots$$

$$y(-1) = \tfrac{1}{2}a_0 - a_1 + a_2 - a_3 + a_4 \cdots$$

If $y(0)$ is given then the scale factor is

$$K = y(0)/(\tfrac{1}{2}a_0 - a_1 + a_2 - a_3 + a_4 \cdots)$$

where the values inside the brackets are the values just computed.

(vi) The values for $a_r^{(1)}$ just computed, when multiplied by K, should satisfy the given equation at the origin

$$\text{i.e.} \qquad y^{(1)} = f(x,y) \qquad \text{at } x = 0, \quad y = y(0),$$

$$\text{or} \qquad y^{(1)}(0) = K(\tfrac{1}{2}a_0^{(1)} - a_2^{(1)} + a_4^{(1)} - a_6^{(1)} + \cdots)$$

This in general will not be the case and so the computation is repeated with different starting values for the a_N and the $a_N^{(1)}$. A linear combination of the two sets is then chosen so that both the a's *and* the $a^{(1)}$'s satisfy the given conditions.

The method can be extended to equations of higher degree if the necessary $a_r^{(s)}$ are tabulated. This will, of course, necessitate a linear combination of $s + 1$ sets of results.

(b) Shifted Chebyshev polynomials
Fundamental values

$$T_0^* = 1$$

$$T_r^*(1) = 1$$

$$T_{2r}^*(\tfrac{1}{2}) = (-1)^r$$

$$T_{2r+1}^*(\tfrac{1}{2}) = 0$$

$$T_{2r}^*(0) = 1$$

$$T_{2r+1}^*(0) = -1$$

And correspondingly

$$y = \tfrac{1}{2}a_0 + a_1 T_1^* + a_2 T_2^* + \cdots + a_N T_N^*$$

$$C_r^*(y^{(s)}) = a_r^{(s)}$$

$$C_r^*(x^p y^{(s)}) = 2^{-2p} \sum_{i=0}^{2p} \binom{2p}{i} a_{|r-p+i|}^{(s)} \qquad\qquad \left(\begin{matrix} r = 0,1,2 \cdots \\ s = 1,2, \cdots \end{matrix}\right)$$

also

$$a_{r-1}^{(s)} = 4r \ a_r^{(s-1)} + a_{r+1}^{(s)}$$

In addition the initial values yield

$$y(0) = \tfrac{1}{2}a_0 - a_1 + a_2 - a_3 + \cdots$$

$$y(\tfrac{1}{2}) = \tfrac{1}{2}a_0 - a_2 + a_4 - a_6 + \cdots$$

$$y(1) = \tfrac{1}{2}a_0 + a_1 + a_2 + a_3 + \cdots$$

The computational procedure being identical with that of the preceding section.

THE NUMERICAL SOLUTION OF DIFFERENTIAL EQUATIONS (Continued)

ITERATIVE METHODS

With the iterative methods of solution of differential equations, two fundamental approaches exist

a) Point iteration.

b) Block iteration.

In the former, the solution at each point is refined as far as is necessary before the next point is considered. The latter, on the other hand, involves successive sweeps over the whole range of integration until no further improvement is detected.

With either group of methods the number of iterations should be small, i.e. if more than three or four applications of the iterative formula in question are necessary then the interval of tabulation should be reduced—in practice this is usually taken to mean halved.

The restriction on the number of iterations does not apply to the Chebyshev method since here the coefficients of an approximating polynomial are being determined and thus the iterations are continued until the required number of significant places is obtained. The solution of the differential equation is then obtained by direct substitution into the polynomial.

When only one starting value is given, as is usual at the beginning of the tabulation of a first order equation, then special starting techniques are necessary for the point iteration approach as a knowledge of the function at several consecutive points is necessary before it can be evaluated at the next point. Either one of the direct methods previously tabulated can be invoked or an iterative starting formula used.

With the iterative predictor-corrector methods, the starting formulae are of the same type.

Doubling the interval of tabulation does not give any trouble with the point iteration schemes whereas halving the interval requires the use of an interpolation routine.

The block iteration schemes require a fresh start to be made if the interval is to be changed.

Iterative Starting Formulae

Notation used: $x_r \equiv x_0 + rh$

$y_r \equiv y(x_r)$

$f_r \equiv f(x_r, y_r) \equiv hy'_r$

$E_r \equiv$ The truncation error in the expression for y_r.

The superscript (ν) denotes the νth iterate.

Since the iterative starting formulae require initial values to be inserted the first iterative values are obtained from

$$y_r^{(1)} = y_0 + rf_0 \qquad r = 1(1)n - 1$$

This enables "n" starting values to be determined, including the given value y_0, for use with the following groups of formulae.

It will be seen that the values of y_0 and f_0 are unaltered as they will be the given values; f_0 being simply a function of h, x_0 and y_0 determined by the differential equation in question. Further, as each of the other values are refined, they are used in the succeeding equations.

E.g., anticipating the table associated with $n = 3$ in group 1, we obtain, on writing out the formulae in full

ITERATIVE STARTING FORMULAE (Continued)

$$y_1^{(\nu+1)} = \left(y_0 + \frac{5}{12}f_0\right) + \frac{(8f_1^{(\nu)} - f_2^{(\nu)})}{12} + \frac{\delta^3}{24}$$

$$y_2^{(\nu+1)} = \left(y_0 + \frac{1}{3}f_0\right) + \frac{4}{3}f_1^{(\nu+1)} + \frac{1}{3}f_2^{(\nu)} - \frac{\delta^4}{90}$$

The worst error term in the above is $\delta^3/24$ and thus for the contribution from this source to be less than 1/2 unit in the last significant figure $\delta^3/24 < 1/2$ i.e. $\delta^3 < 12$. If this is not so then the interval h must be reduced.

The coefficients A_{rs} (and A_{rs}^*) can be expressed as rational fractions in the form $A_{rs} =$ Numerator of $A_{rs}/D_r \equiv$ Num. A_{rs}/D_r. The tabulation will therefore be of

Num. A_{rs}	D_r	E_r
$s = 0(1)n - 1$ $r = 1(1)n - 1$	$r = 1(1)n - 1$	$r = 1(1)n - 1$

where E_r indicates the principal error term associated with f_r.

Group 1

$$y_1^{(\nu+1)} = y_0 + A_{10}f_0 + \sum_{s=1}^{n-1} A_{1s}f_s^{(\nu)} + E_1$$

$$y_r^{(\nu+1)} = y_0 + A_{r0}f_0 + \sum_{s=1}^{r-1} A_{rs}f_s^{(\nu+1)} + \sum_{s=r}^{n-1} A_{rs}f_s^{(\nu)} + E_r, \quad r = 2(1)n - 1$$

$n = 2$

r \ s	Num. A_{rs} 0	1	D_r	E_r
1	1	1	2	$-\frac{1}{12}\delta^2$

Requires $\delta^2 < 6$

$n = 3$

r \ s	Num. A_{rs} 0	1	2	D_r	E_r
1	5	8	-1	12	$\frac{1}{24}\delta^3$
2	1	4	1	3	$-\frac{1}{90}\delta^4$

Requires $\delta^3 < 12$

$n = 4$

r \ s	Num. A_{rs} 0	1	2	3	D_r	E_r
1	9	19	-5	1	24	$-\frac{19}{720}\delta_4$
2	1	4	1	0	3	$-\frac{1}{90}\delta^4$
3	3	9	9	3	8	$-\frac{3}{80}\delta^4$

Requires $\delta^4 < 13$

ITERATIVE STARTING FORMULAE (Continued)

$n = 5$

s r	Num. A_{rs} 0	1	2	3	4	D_r	E_r
1	251	646	−264	106	−19	720	$\dfrac{3}{160}\delta^5$
2	29	124	24	4	−1	90	$\dfrac{1}{90}\delta^5$
3	27	102	72	42	−3	80	$\dfrac{3}{160}\delta^5$
4	14	64	24	64	14	45	$-\dfrac{1}{105}\delta^6$

Requires $\delta^5 < 27$

$n = 6$

s r	Num. A_{rs} 0	1	2	3	4	5	D_r	E_r
1	493	1337	−618	302	−83	9	1440	$-\dfrac{14}{695}\delta^6$
2	28	129	14	14	−6	1	90	$-\dfrac{1}{105}\delta^6$
3	51	219	114	114	−21	3	160	$-\dfrac{3}{224}\delta^6$
4	28	128	48	128	28	0	90	$-\dfrac{1}{105}\delta^6$
5	95	375	250	250	375	95	288	$-\dfrac{1}{42}\delta^6$

Requires $\delta^6 < 21$

Group 2

The formulae of this group involve the function values as well as the derivatives and consequently tend to have smaller truncation errors.

$$y_r^{(\nu+1)} = \sum_{s=0}^{r-1} A_{rs}^{*} y_s^{(\nu+1)} + \sum_{s=0}^{r-1} A_{rs} f_s^{(\nu+1)} + \sum_{s=r}^{n-1} A_{rs} f_s^{(\nu)} + E_r, \qquad r = 1(1)n - 1$$

$n = 4$

s r	Num. A_{rs} 0	1	2	Num. A_{rs} 0	1	2	3	D_r	E_r
1	24	0	0	9	19	−5	1	24	$-\dfrac{19}{720}\delta^4$
2	33	24	0	10	57	24	−1	57	$\dfrac{1}{342}\delta^5$
3	11	27	−27	3	27	27	3	11	$-\dfrac{1}{513}\delta^6$

Requires $\delta^4 < 18$

ITERATIVE STARTING FORMULAE (Continued)

$n = 5$	Num. A_{rs}^*				Num. A_{rs}					D_r	E_r
s r	0	1	2	3	0	1	2	3	4		
1	720	0	0	0	251	646	-264	106	-19	720	$\dfrac{3}{160}\,\delta^5$
2	990	1440	0	0	281	2056	1176	-104	11	2430	$-\dfrac{1}{729}\,\delta^6$
3	550	2160	-1350	0	141	1656	2376	456	-9	1360	$\dfrac{1}{2539}\,\delta^7$
4	25	160	0	-160	6	96	216	96	6	25	$-\dfrac{1}{2625}\,\delta^8$

Requires $\delta^5 < 27$

$n = 6$	Num. A_{rs}^*				
s r	0	1	2	3	4
1	1440	0	0	0	0
2	24390	53280	0	0	0
3	9550	51570	-17550	0	0
4	3425	29560	14040	-35960	0
5	137	1625	2000	-2000	-1625

	Num. A_{rs}						D_r	E_r
s r	0	1	2	3	4	5		
1	475	1427	-798	482	-173	27	1440	$-\dfrac{1}{70}\,\delta^6$
2	6589	58528	41608	-5752	1223	-136	77670	$\dfrac{31}{290}\,\delta^7$
3	2337	33687	62352	16512	-693	45	43570	$-\dfrac{1}{9072}\,\delta^8$
4	786	15540	45720	29280	3210	-36	11065	$\dfrac{1}{16800}\,\delta^9$
5	30	750	3000	3000	750	30	137	$-\dfrac{1}{12659}\,\delta^{10}$

Requires $\delta^6 < 35$

Group 3

In this group neither y_r nor f_r appears on the right hand side i.e. $A_{ss}^* \equiv A_{ss} \equiv 0$.

$$y_r^{(\nu+1)} = \sum_{s=0}^{r-1} A_{rs}^* y_s^{(\nu+1)} + \sum_{s=r+1}^{n-1} A_{rs}^* y^{(\nu)} + \sum_{s=0}^{r-1} A_{rs} f^{(\nu+1)} + \sum_{s=r+1}^{n-1} A_{rs} f^{(\nu)} + E_r$$

ITERATIVE STARTING FORMULAE (Continued)

$n = 3$

r \ s	Num. A_{rs}^* 0	1	2	Num. A_{rs} 0	1	2	D_r	E_r
1	2	0	2	1	0	-1	4	$\frac{1}{24}\delta^3$
2	5	-4	0	2	4	0	1	$\frac{1}{12}\delta^3$

Requires $\delta^3 < 6$

$n = 4$

r \ s	Num. A_{rs}^* 0	1	2	3	Num. A_{rs} 0	1	2	3	D_r	E_r
1	8	0	0	19	3	0	-27	-6	27	$\frac{1}{180}\delta^5$
2	19	0	0	8	6	27	0	-3	27	$\frac{1}{180}\delta^5$
3	10	9	-18	0	3	18	9	0	1	$\frac{1}{20}\delta^5$

Requires $\delta^5 < 10$

$n = 5$

r \ s	Num. A_{rs}^* 0	1	2	3	4	Num. A_{rs} 0	1	2	3	4	D_r	E_r
1	19	0	-216	224	69	6	0	-216	-192	-18	96	$\frac{1}{1120}\delta^7$
2	11	16	0	16	11	3	24	0	-24	-3	54	$\frac{1}{2520}\delta^7$
3	69	224	-216	0	19	18	192	216	0	-6	96	$\frac{1}{805}\delta^7$
4	47	192	-108	-128	0	12	144	216	48	0	3	$\frac{1}{70}\delta^7$

Requires $\delta^7 < 35$

Group 4

In this group the starting values are symmetrically placed with respect to the origin. These formulae usually have a better truncation error and their coefficients exhibit a certain degree of skew symmetry.

Assuming that y_r, and hence f_r, are found before y_{-r} and f_{-r} the formulae used are, for $N \equiv (n-1)/2$ where n denotes the odd number of points involved, as follows

$$y_r^{(\nu+1)} = y_0 + \sum_{s=-N}^{-r} A_{rs}f_s^{(\nu)} + \sum_{s=-r+1}^{r-1} A_{rs}f_s^{(\nu+1)} + \sum_{s=r}^{N} A_{rs}f_s^{(\nu)} + E_r$$

which is followed immediately by

$$y_{-r}^{(\nu+1)} = y_0 + \sum_{s=-N}^{-r} A_{rs}f_s^{(\nu)} + \sum_{s=-r+1}^{r} A_{rs}f_s^{(\nu+1)} + \sum_{s=r+1}^{N} A_{rs}f_s^{(r)} + E_r$$

ITERATIVE STARTING FORMULAE (Continued)

The formulae are tabulated in the order in which they are to be used i.e. $r = 1, -1, 2, -2, 3, -3$.

$n = 3$

s	Num. A_{rs}			D_r	E_r
r	-1	0	1		
1	-1	8	5	12	$-\dfrac{1}{24}\delta^3$
-1	-5	-8	1	12	$-\dfrac{1}{24}\delta^3$

Requires $\delta^3 < 12$

$n = 5$

s	Num. A_{rs}					D_r	E_r
r	-2	-1	0	1	2		
1	11	-74	456	346	-19	720	$\dfrac{1}{144}\delta^5$
-1	19	-346	-456	74	-11	720	$\dfrac{1}{144}\delta^5$
2	-1	4	24	124	29	90	$-\dfrac{1}{90}\delta^5$
-2	-29	-124	-24	-4	1	90	$-\dfrac{1}{90}\delta^5$

Requires $\delta^5 < 45$

$n = 7$

s	Num. A_{rs}							D_r	E_r
r	-3	-2	-1	0	1	2	3		
1	-191	1608	-6771	37504	30819	-2760	271	60480	$\dfrac{1}{633}\delta^7$
-1	-271	2760	-30819	-37504	6771	-1608	191	60480	$\dfrac{1}{633}\delta^7$
2	5	-30	33	1328	4863	1398	-37	3780	$\dfrac{1}{8172}\delta^7$
-2	37	-1398	-4863	-1328	-33	30	-5	3780	$\dfrac{1}{8172}\delta^7$
3	-29	216	-729	2176	1161	3240	685	2240	$\dfrac{9}{896}\delta^7$
-3	-685	-3240	-1161	-2176	729	-216	29	2240	$\dfrac{9}{896}\delta^7$

Requires $\delta^7 < 50$

Group 5

As group 4, with the addition of function values. The same observations apply. y_0 and f_0 do not alter from cycle to cycle. Defining N the same as for group 4, the formulae used are:

ITERATIVE STARTING FORMULAE (Continued)

$$y_r^{(\nu+1)} = \sum_{s=-N}^{-r} A_{rs}^* y_s^{(\nu)} + \sum_{s=-r+1}^{r-1} A_{rs}^* y_s^{(\nu+1)} + \sum_{s=r}^{N} A_{rs}^* y_s^{(\nu)}$$

$$+ \sum_{s=-N}^{-r} A_{rs} f_s^{(\nu)} + \sum_{s=-r+1}^{r-1} A_{rs} f_s^{(\nu+1)} + \sum_{s=r}^{N} A_{rs} f_s^{(\nu)} + E_r$$

$n = 5$ Num. A_{rs}^*

r \ s	-2	-1	0	1	2
1	-85	0	540	0	-135
-1	-135	0	540	0	-85
2	0	1360	1350	-2160	0
-2	0	-2160	1350	1360	0

r \ s	-2	-1	0	1	2	D_r	E_r
		Num. A_{rs}					
1	-24	-144	216	336	36	320	$-\dfrac{1}{1643}\delta^7$
-1	-36	-336	-216	144	24	320	$-\dfrac{1}{1643}\delta^7$
2	-9	456	2376	1656	141	550	$-\dfrac{1}{1067}\delta^7$
-2	-141	-1656	-2376	-456	9	550	$-\dfrac{1}{1067}\delta^7$

Requires $\delta^7 < 533$

The coefficients become unwieldy for higher values of n.

Continuing the solution

Two formulae are used to continue the solution once sufficient starting values have been obtained. The first, the "predictor," is used to obtain an estimate of the next value. It is used once only and can be appreciably less accurate than the second, the "corrector," which determines the precision.

The corrector is used iteratively until sufficient significant figures are obtained.

Predictors and correctors can involve either backward differences, central differences or function values.

Predictor-corrector formulae involving backward differences

A typical predictor formula is

$$y_1 = y_0 + \left(1 + \frac{1}{2}\nabla + \frac{5}{12}\nabla^2 + \frac{3}{8}\nabla^3 + \frac{251}{720}\nabla^4 + \frac{95}{288}\nabla^5 + \frac{19087}{60480}\nabla^6 + \cdots\right)f_0$$

this is followed by

$$f_1 = h \cdot y_1',$$

where y' is defined as a function of x and y.

PREDICTOR-CORRECTOR METHODS

This predicted value of f_1 is used to generate all the backward differences ∇_1^r for $r = 1(1)6$.

These are then used with a corrector formula such as

$$y_1 = y_0 + \left(1 - \frac{1}{2}\nabla - \frac{1}{12}\nabla^2 - \frac{1}{24}\nabla^3 - \frac{19}{720}\nabla^4 - \frac{3}{160}\nabla^5 - \frac{863}{60480}\nabla^6 - \cdots\right)f_1$$

to recompute y_1 and thus f_1. Note that all the backward differences ∇_1^r must then be recomputed before the corrector is applied once more.

The numerical coefficients tend to be rather high and round-off errors can become troublesome if differences beyond ∇^6 are significant.

An alternative method of *prediction* when one particular column of differences is nearly constant (say for example $\nabla^6 \sim k$) is to use the recurrence formula

$$\nabla_1^{r-1} = \nabla_1^r + \nabla_0^{r-1}$$

to generate the required differences. The overall effect is as if

$$f_1 = (1 + \nabla + \nabla^2 + \nabla^3 + \nabla^4 + \nabla^5]f_0 + k$$

had been used as a predictor.

Even when ∇^6 is not constant it can usually be estimated with sufficient accuracy from the preceding entries in the column, i.e., it is extrapolated from a knowledge of the previous differences, and is then used in the predictor

$$f_1 = (1 + \nabla + \nabla^2 + \nabla^3 + \nabla^4 + \nabla^5)f_0 + \nabla^6 f_1$$

The corrector quoted in the example is the first of a group of such formulae having the general form

$$y_1 = y_r + \sum_{s=0} A_{rs}\nabla_s f_1 \qquad r < 0.$$

Truncating the infinite series at $s = 6$, we have

	s	0	1	2	A_{rs} 3	4	5	6
r								
0	1		$-\frac{1}{2}$	$-\frac{1}{12}$	$-\frac{1}{24}$	$-\frac{19}{720}$	$-\frac{3}{160}$	$-\frac{863}{60480}$
-1	2	-2		$\frac{1}{3}$	0	$\frac{-1}{90}$	$\frac{-1}{90}$	$\frac{-37}{3780}$
-2	3		$\frac{-9}{2}$	$\frac{9}{4}$	$\frac{-3}{8}$	$\frac{-3}{80}$	$\frac{-3}{160}$	$\frac{-29}{2240}$
-3	4	-8		$\frac{20}{3}$	$\frac{-8}{3}$	$\frac{14}{45}$	0	$\frac{-8}{945}$
-4	5		$\frac{-25}{2}$	$\frac{175}{12}$	$\frac{-225}{24}$	$\frac{425}{144}$	$\frac{-95}{288}$	$\frac{-275}{12096}$
-5	6	-18		27	-24	$\frac{123}{10}$	$\frac{-33}{10}$	$\frac{41}{140}$

PREDICTOR-CORRECTOR METHODS (Continued)

Predictor-corrector formulae involving central differences

In these formulae, the predictors and the correctors have the same form. In fact the corrector has the same coefficients as the predictor on the previous line of the table with the addition of one more term, together with an estimate of the error.

The formulae involved are

$$\text{Predictor} \qquad y_1 = y_{1-2r} + \sum_{s=0}^{r-1} A_{rs} \delta^{2s} f_{1-r}$$

$$\text{Corrector} \qquad y_1 = y_{3-2r} + \sum_{s=0}^{r-1} B_{rs} \delta^{2s} f_{2-r} + \text{Error} \; (\equiv B_{rr} \delta^{2r})$$

$$A_{rs}$$

r \ s	0	1	2	3	4
2	4	$\dfrac{8}{3}$			
3	6	9	$\dfrac{33}{10}$		
4	8	$\dfrac{64}{3}$	$\dfrac{868}{45}$	$\dfrac{736}{189}$	
5	10	$\dfrac{125}{3}$	$\dfrac{875}{18}$	$\dfrac{17225}{756}$	$\dfrac{20225}{4536}$

$$B_{rs}$$

r \ s	0	1	2	3	4	5
2	2	$\dfrac{1}{3}$	$\dfrac{-1}{90}$			
3	4	$\dfrac{8}{3}$	$\dfrac{14}{45}$	$\dfrac{-8}{945}$		
4	6	9	$\dfrac{33}{10}$	$\dfrac{41}{140}$	$\dfrac{-9}{1400}$	
5	8	$\dfrac{64}{3}$	$\dfrac{868}{45}$	$\dfrac{736}{189}$	$\dfrac{3956}{14175}$	$\dfrac{-2368}{467775}$

e.g. Suppose that enough starting values have been obtained to indicate that the sixth differences are of the order of 50 (say).

The corrector corresponding to $r = 3$ has an error term of magnitude $8\delta^6/945$ which is less than $\frac{1}{2}$ when $\delta^6 = 50$.

Therefore label the last computed value y_0 and use the predictor

$$y_1 = y_{-5} + 6f_{-2} + 9\delta^2_{-2} + \frac{33}{10}\delta^4_{-2} \quad (r = 3 \text{ in the above table}).$$

From this value of y_1, generate $f_1 \; (= hy'_1)$ and carry the differences back to the sixth differences column.

PREDICTOR-CORRECTOR METHODS (Continued)

The corrector to use is then

$$y_1 = y_{-3} + 4f_{-1} + \frac{8}{3}\delta_{-1}^2 + \frac{14}{45}\delta_{-1}^4 \qquad (r = 3 \text{ above}).$$

Note that the error term should strictly be expressed in terms of δ_{-1}^6 and so an adequate check cannot be carried out until the next term has been computed.

Note also that, in common with all predictor-corrector methods, any form of predictor can be used, as the refinement depends only upon the corrector.

Predictor-corrector formulae involving function values

The general form of the simplest type of predictor is

$$y_1 = y_r + \sum_{s=r}^{0} A_{rs}f_s + E_r \qquad < 0$$

			A_{rs}				E_r
s $\backslash$ r	0	-1	-2	-3	-4	-5	
0	1						$\frac{1}{2}\delta$
-1	2	0					$\frac{1}{3}\delta^2$
-2	$\frac{9}{4}$	0	$\frac{3}{4}$				$\frac{3}{8}\delta^3$
-3	$\frac{8}{3}$	$-\frac{4}{3}$	$\frac{8}{3}$	0			$\frac{14}{45}\delta^4$
-4	$\frac{55}{24}$	$\frac{5}{24}$	$\frac{5}{24}$	$\frac{55}{24}$	0		$\frac{95}{144}\delta^5$
-5	$\frac{33}{10}$	$-\frac{42}{10}$	$\frac{78}{10}$	$-\frac{42}{10}$	$\frac{33}{10}$	0	$\frac{41}{140}\delta^6$

An alternative group of predictor formulae have the form

$$y_1 = y_0 + \sum_{s=r}^{0} A_{rs}f_s + E_r \qquad (r < 0)$$

			A_{rs}			E_r
s $\backslash$ r	0	-1	-2	-3	-4	
-1	$\frac{3}{2}$	$-\frac{1}{2}$				$\frac{5}{12}\delta^2$
-2	$\frac{23}{12}$	$-\frac{4}{3}$	$\frac{5}{12}$			$\frac{3}{8}\delta^3$
-3	$\frac{55}{24}$	$-\frac{59}{24}$	$\frac{37}{24}$	$-\frac{3}{8}$		$\frac{25}{72}\delta^4$
-4	$\frac{1901}{720}$	$-\frac{1387}{360}$	$\frac{327}{90}$	$-\frac{637}{360}$	$\frac{251}{720}$	$\frac{95}{288}\delta^5$

The correctors fall roughly into main groups. The first group is similar to the predictors tabulated above in that the emphasis is upon a weighted mean of the derivatives rather than the function values.

PREDICTOR-CORRECTOR METHODS (Continued)

Group 1

$$y_1 = y_r + \sum_{s=r}^{0} A_{rs}f_s + E_r \qquad (r < 0)$$

r \ s	1	0	−1	−2	−3	−4	−5	E_r
0	$\frac{1}{2}$	$\frac{1}{2}$						$\frac{-1}{12}\delta^2$
−1	$\frac{1}{3}$	$\frac{4}{3}$	$\frac{1}{3}$					$\frac{-1}{90}\delta^4$
−2	$\frac{3}{8}$	$\frac{9}{8}$	$\frac{9}{8}$	$\frac{3}{8}$				$\frac{-3}{80}\delta^4$
−3	$\frac{14}{45}$	$\frac{64}{45}$	$\frac{24}{45}$	$\frac{64}{45}$	$\frac{14}{45}$			$\frac{-1}{105}\delta^6$
−4	$\frac{95}{288}$	$\frac{375}{288}$	$\frac{125}{144}$	$\frac{125}{144}$	$\frac{375}{288}$	$\frac{95}{288}$		$\frac{-1}{44}\delta^6$
−5	$\frac{41}{140}$	$\frac{54}{35}$	$\frac{27}{140}$	$\frac{68}{35}$	$\frac{27}{140}$	$\frac{54}{35}$	$\frac{41}{140}$	$\frac{-1}{140}\delta^8$
−6	$\frac{3}{10}$	$\frac{3}{2}$	$\frac{3}{10}$	$\frac{9}{5}$	$\frac{3}{10}$	$\frac{3}{2}$	$\frac{3}{10}$	$\frac{-1}{140}\delta^6$

The second group involves the computation of a weighted mean of the function value as well as the derivatives.

Group 2

$$y_1 = \sum_{s=-4}^{0} A^*_{rs}y_s + \sum_{s=-4}^{1} A_{rs}f_s + E_r$$

r \ s	−4	−3	−2	−1	0
1	0	0	0	−1	2
2	0	0	1	$\frac{27}{11}$	$\frac{-27}{11}$
3	0	1	$\frac{32}{5}$	0	$\frac{-32}{5}$
4	1	$\frac{1625}{137}$	$\frac{2000}{137}$	$\frac{-2000}{137}$	$\frac{-1625}{137}$
5	0	0	0	$\frac{1}{5}$	$\frac{4}{5}$
6	0	0	0	$\frac{-19}{13}$	$\frac{32}{13}$
7	0	0	$\frac{32}{5}$	$\frac{-27}{5}$	0
8	0	0	$\frac{136}{55}$	$\frac{27}{11}$	$\frac{-216}{55}$

PREDICTOR-CORRECTOR METHODS (Continued)

s \ r	-4	-3	-2	-1	0	1	E_r
1	0	0	0	$\frac{1}{2}$	0	$-\frac{1}{2}$	$\frac{-1}{12}\delta^3$
2	0	0	$\frac{3}{11}$	$\frac{27}{11}$	$\frac{27}{11}$	$\frac{3}{11}$	$\frac{-1}{513}\delta^6$
3	0	$\frac{6}{25}$	$\frac{96}{25}$	$\frac{216}{25}$	$\frac{96}{25}$	$\frac{6}{25}$	$\frac{-1}{2625}\delta^8$
4	$\frac{30}{137}$	$\frac{750}{137}$	$\frac{3000}{137}$	$\frac{3000}{137}$	$\frac{750}{137}$	$\frac{30}{137}$	$\frac{-1}{12659}\delta^{10}$
5	0	0	0	0	$\frac{4}{5}$	$\frac{2}{5}$	$\frac{-1}{30}\delta^3$
6	0	0	$\frac{4}{39}$	-1	0	$\frac{17}{39}$	$\frac{-19}{390}\delta^4$
7	0	0	$\frac{12}{5}$	$\frac{27}{5}$	0	$\frac{3}{5}$	$\frac{-1}{30}\delta^4$
8	0	$\frac{-9}{550}$	$\frac{228}{275}$	$\frac{1188}{275}$	$\frac{828}{275}$	$\frac{141}{550}$	$\frac{-1}{1067}\delta^7$

Column group header: A_{rs}

Iterative methods

Should it become necessary to halve the interval, because the error term is becoming significant or the number of iterations required is becoming excessive, then interpolation becomes necessary.

This interpolation, actually subtabulation to halves, is based upon previously computed values and the formulae used can take several forms. One such form is as follows

$$y_k = \frac{1}{D_r} \sum_{s=-n}^{0} A_{rs}y_s + E_r, \qquad (r = 1(1)n)$$

where $k \equiv (1 - 2r)/2$, and E_r denotes the principal error term.

$n = 2$

s \ r	0	-1	-2	D_r	E_r
1	3	6	-1	8	$\frac{-1}{16}\nabla_0^3$
2	-1	6	3	8	$\frac{1}{16}\nabla_0^3$

Column group header: A_{rs}

$n = 3$

s \ r	0	-1	-2	-3	D_r	E_r
1	5	15	-5	1	16	$\frac{-5}{128}\nabla_0^4$
2	-1	9	9	-1	16	$\frac{3}{128}\nabla_0^4$
3	1	-5	15	5	16	$\frac{-5}{128}\nabla_0^4$

Column group header: A_{rs}

DEFERRED-CORRECTOR METHODS

$n = 4$ $\diagdown$ s	0	−1	−2	−3	−4	D_r	E_r
1	35	140	−70	28	−5	128	$\dfrac{-7}{256}\, \nabla_0^5$
2	−5	60	90	−20	3	128	$\dfrac{3}{256}\, \nabla_0^5$
3	3	−20	90	60	−5	128	$\dfrac{-3}{256}\, \nabla_0^5$
4	−5	28	−70	140	35	128	$\dfrac{7}{256}\, \nabla_0^5$

The table is headed A_{rs}, with the row index r at left.

For a given "n" there will be $2n + 1$ values available at the new interval to continue the solution.

Deferred-correction methods

One of the most powerful of the iterative methods is that of "deferred correction." This is a block iteration method, a complete set of function values being obtained from a recurrence relationship, their differences formed and corrections applied from these differences.

Central difference corrections are the most useful. Let the first order differential equation be

$$y' + g(x) \cdot y = k(x)$$

The first recurrence relation, assuming an initial y only given, is

$$y_1 \left(1 + \frac{1}{2}\, hg_1\right) - y_0 \left(1 - \frac{1}{2}\, hg_0\right) = \frac{1}{2}\, h(k_0 + k_1)$$

This is used to generate y_r for both positive and negative values of r if required. When the required range of values of y_r has been covered, with sufficient additional terms to generate all the differences required, a difference table is formed and the correction terms $C(y_{\frac{1}{2}})$ tabulated from

$$C(y_{\frac{1}{2}}) \equiv \frac{1}{12}\, \delta_{\frac{1}{2}}^3 - \frac{1}{120}\, \delta_{\frac{1}{2}}^5 + \frac{1}{840}\, \delta_{\frac{1}{2}}^7 - \frac{1}{5040}\, \delta_{\frac{1}{2}}^9 \cdots$$

The correction terms $C(y_{\frac{1}{2}})$ are corrections to the recurrence relation. The corrections to the function values y_r are η_r i.e. True value = Approximate value + η

where
$$\eta_1 \left(1 + \frac{1}{2}\, hg_1\right) - \eta_0 \left(1 - \frac{1}{2}\, hg_0\right) + C(y_{\frac{1}{2}}) = 0$$

In this formula the initial η_0 is zero and the recurrence relation can be used in either direction.

New $C(y_{\frac{1}{2}})$ are then computed and the correction process repeated until there is no change in the values of $C(y_{\frac{1}{2}})$. At this point the computed values and the differences derived there-from should be checked for consistency with the differential equation. The method of deferred correction is particularly useful for linear differential equations as its convergence is extremely rapid, even for very large intervals. If more starting values are known formulae which have even faster convergence can be employed. Two such formulae are as follows: Two starting values given

DEFERRED-CORRECTOR METHODS (Continued)

Predictor $\quad y_1\left(1+\dfrac{1}{3}hg_1\right)+\dfrac{4}{3}hg_0y_0-y_{-1}\left(1-\dfrac{1}{3}hg_{-1}\right)=\dfrac{1}{3}h(k_1+4k_0+k_{-1})$

$$C(y_0)\equiv\frac{1}{180}(\delta^5_{-\frac12}+\delta^5_{\frac12})-\frac{1}{630}(\delta^7_{-\frac12}+\delta^7_{\frac12})+\frac{1}{2510}(\delta^9_{-\frac12}+\delta^9_{\frac12})\cdots$$

Corrector $\quad \eta_1\left(1+\dfrac{1}{3}hg_1\right)+\dfrac{4}{3}hg_0\eta_0-\eta_{-1}\left(1-\dfrac{1}{3}hg_{-1}\right)+C(y_0)=0.$

Three starting values given

Predictor $\quad y_1+y_0(9+6hg_0)-y_{-1}(9-6hg_{-1})-y_{-2}=6h(k_0+k_{-1})$

$$C(y_{-\frac12})\equiv-\frac{1}{10}\delta^5_{-\frac12}+\frac{1}{70}\delta^7_{-\frac12}-\frac{1}{420}\delta^9_{-\frac12}+\cdots$$

Corrector $\quad \eta_1+\eta_0(9+6hg_0)-\eta_{-1}(9-6hg_{-1})-\eta_{-2}+C(y_{-\frac12})=0$

The use of the deferred correction technique for higher order differential equations.

Second order differential equations.

Two starting values given e.g. $y''+m\cdot y'+g\cdot y=k$ where y_0 and y_{-1} are known and $y\equiv y(x);\ m\equiv m(x);\ g\equiv g(x);\ k\equiv k(x).$

Predictor $\quad y_1\left(1+\dfrac{1}{2}hm_0\right)-y_0(2-h^2g_0)+y_{-1}\left(1-\dfrac{1}{2}hm_0\right)=h^2k_0$

$$C(y_0)\equiv\left[-\frac{1}{12}\delta^4_0+\frac{1}{90}\delta^6_0-\frac{1}{560}\delta^8_0+\frac{1}{3150}\delta^{10}_0\right]$$

$$+hg_0\left[-\frac{1}{12}(\delta^3_{\frac12}+\delta^3_{-\frac12})+\frac{1}{60}(\delta^5_{\frac12}+\delta^5_{-\frac12})-\frac{1}{280}(\delta^7_{\frac12}+\delta^7_{-\frac12})+\frac{1}{1260}(\delta^9_{\frac12}+\delta^9_{-\frac12})\right].$$

Corrector $\quad \eta_1\left(1+\dfrac{1}{2}hm_0\right)-\eta_0(2-h^2g_0)+\eta_{-1}\left(1-\dfrac{1}{2}hm_0\right)+C(y_0)=0.$

Three starting values require the known functions $m(x)$, $g(x)$ $g(x)$ and $k(x)$ to be tabulated at half way points and the advantage in speed of convergence is relatively slight.

Predictor $\quad y_1\left(1-\dfrac{1}{12}hm_{-\frac12}-\dfrac{1}{8}h^2g_{-\frac12}\right)-y_0\left(1-\dfrac{9}{4}hm_{-\frac12}-\dfrac{9}{8}h^2g_{-\frac12}\right)$

$$-y_{-1}\left(1+\frac{9}{4}hm_{-\frac12}-\frac{9}{8}h^2g_{-\frac12}\right)+y_{-2}\left(1+\frac{1}{12}hm_{-\frac12}-\frac{1}{8}h^2g_{-\frac12}\right)=2h^2k_{-\frac12}$$

$$C(y_{-\frac12})\equiv\left[\frac{-5}{24}(\delta^4_0+\delta^4_{-1})+\frac{259}{5760}(\delta^6_0+\delta^6_{-1})-\frac{3229}{322560}(\delta^8_0+\delta^8_{-1})\right.$$

$$\left.+\frac{117469}{51609600}(\delta^{10}_0+\delta^{10}_{-1})\right]+hm_{-\frac12}\left[\frac{3}{320}\delta^5_{-\frac12}-\frac{5}{3584}\delta^7_{-\frac12}+\frac{35}{147456}\delta^9_{-\frac12}\right]$$

$$+h^2g_{-\frac12}\left[\frac{3}{128}(\delta^4_0+\delta^4_{-1})-\frac{5}{1024}(\delta^6_0+\delta^6_{-1})+\frac{35}{32768}(\delta^8_0+\delta^8_{-1})\right]$$

Corrector $\quad \eta_1\left(1-\dfrac{1}{12}hm_{-\frac12}-\dfrac{1}{8}h^2g_{-\frac12}\right)-\eta_0\left(1-\dfrac{9}{4}hm_{-\frac12}-\dfrac{9}{8}h^2g_{-\frac12}\right)$

$$-\eta_{-1}\left(1+\frac{9}{4}hm_{-\frac12}-\frac{9}{8}h^2g_{-\frac12}\right)+\eta_{-2}\left(1+\frac{1}{12}hm_{-\frac12}-\frac{1}{8}h^2g_{-\frac12}\right)+C(y_{-\frac12})=0$$

CHEBYSHEV METHODS

In general, for second order differential equations, recurrence relations involving an even number of known values are simpler than those involving an odd number of such values. The formulae for four starting values are given below and they are seen to be much simpler than those for three values. Further the correction terms should have more rapid convergence properties.

Predictor $\quad y_1(1 + hm_{-1}) - y_0(16 + 8hm_{-1}) + y_{-1}(30 - 12h^2g_{-1})$

$$+ y_{-2}(16 - 8hm_{-1}) + y_{-3}(1 - hm_{-1}) = -12h^2k_{-1}$$

$$C(y_{-1}) \equiv \left[-\frac{4}{30}\,\delta_{-1}^6 + \frac{3}{140}\,\delta_{-1}^8 - \frac{2}{525}\,\delta_1^{10} + \frac{1}{1386}\,\delta_{-1}^{12} \right]$$

$$+ hm_{-1}\left[-\frac{1}{5}\,(\delta_{-\frac{1}{2}}^5 + \delta_{-1\frac{1}{2}}^5) + \frac{3}{70}\,(\delta_{-\frac{1}{2}}^7 + \delta_{-1\frac{1}{2}}^7) \right.$$

$$\left. -\frac{1}{105}\,(\delta_{-\frac{1}{2}}^9 + \delta_{-1\frac{1}{2}}^9) + \frac{1}{462}\,(\delta_{-\frac{1}{2}}^{11} + \delta_{-1\frac{1}{2}}^{11}) \right].$$

Corrector $\quad \eta_1(1 + hm_{-1}) - \eta_0(16 + 8hm_{-1}) + \eta_{-1}(30 - 12h^2g_{-1})$

$$+ \eta_{-2}(16 - 8hm_{-1}) + \eta_{-3}(1 - hm_{-1}) + C(y_{-1}) = 0$$

Iterative Chebyshev

The recurrence relationships used are identical with those set up in the direct Chebyshev method. The first value of $a_0^{(s)}$ is obtained from the first term of the series for the initial value of $y^{(s)}$, all the other terms being initially set at zero. e.g. Consider the case when $a_r^{(s)}$ are required for $s = 0,1,2$ and 3. (The initial values of y, y', y'' being known at $x = -1$.) The computational sequence is as follows

Set all $a_r^{(3)} = 0$
Obtain $a_0^{(2)}$ from $y''(-1) = \frac{1}{2}a_0^{(2)}$
Use the Chebyshev recurrence formula to obtain $a_1^{(1)}$ from this value of $a_0^{(2)}$
Obtain $a_0^{(1)}$ from $y'(-1) = \frac{1}{2}a_0^{(1)} - a_1^{(1)}$
Use the Chebyshev formula again to obtain both $a_1^{(0)}$ and $a_2^{(0)}$
Obtain $a_0^{(0)}$ from $y(-1) = \frac{1}{2}a_1^{(0)} - a_1^{(0)} + a_2^{(0)}$
Now utilise the recurrence relation given by the differential equation to generate $a_0^{(3)}$.

The cycle is now repeated each series being increased by one term if desired. The determining factor being the number of significant decimals required in the result. The method is in general slower than the direct Chebyshev process but it has the merit that no predetermined knowledge of the number of terms required is necessary—further computational errors die away as the method is truly iterative, whereas in the direct approach they can nullify all the working.

Direct Chebyshev method

This method is suitable for a differential equation of any order. The range of the arguments must however be normalized to $-1 \leq x \leq 1$ (or $0 \leq x \leq 1$ if the "shifted" Chebyshev polynomials are to be used).

A polynomial approximation to the analytical solution is sought, the degree of the polynomial N being decided beforehand.

CHEBYSHEV METHODS (Continued)

Assume
$$y(x) = \tfrac{1}{2}a_0 + \sum_{r=1}^{N} a_r \cdot T_r(x)$$

$$y'(x) = \tfrac{1}{2}a'_0 + \sum_{r=1}^{N} a'_r \cdot T_r(x)$$

$$y''(x) = \tfrac{1}{2}a''_0 + \sum_{r=1}^{N} a''_r \cdot T_r(x) \qquad \text{etc.}$$

where the a's are constants.

Writing $y^{(0)}$, $y^{(1)}$, $y^{(2)}$ for $y(x)$, $y'(x)$, $y''(x)$ etc., $a_r^{(0)}$, $a_r^{(1)}$, $a_r^{(2)}$ for a_r, a'_r, a''_r, etc., and T_r for $T_r(x)$.

The recurrence relationship for the Chebyshev polynomials can be written as

$$2xT_r = T_{|r-1|} + T_{r+1} \qquad (r = 0,1,2, \ldots)$$

further
$$2 \int T_r \cdot dx = \frac{T_{r+1}}{(r+1)} - \frac{T_{r-1}}{(r-1)} \qquad (r > 1)$$

$$= \tfrac{1}{2}T_2 \qquad (r = 1)$$

$$= 2T_1 \qquad (r = 0)$$

Thus $\qquad 2r \cdot a_r^{(s)} = a_{r-1}^{(s+1)} - a_{r+1}^{(s+1)} \qquad (r > 1)$

If, in addition, the notation $C_r(x^p y^{(s)})$ is introduced to denote the coefficient of T_r in the expansion of $x^p y^{(s)}$ *and twice this coefficient when $r = 0$* then

$$C_r(y^{(0)}) = a_r$$

$$C_r(y^{(s)}) = a_r^{(s)}$$

$$C_r(x^p y^{(s)}) = \frac{1}{2^p} \sum_{k=0}^{p} \binom{p}{k} \cdot a_{|r-p+2k|}^{(s)}$$

Method of use of Chebyshev polynomials

Suppose the differential equation is

$$f(x) \cdot y'' + g(x) \cdot y' + h(x) \cdot y = 0$$

i.e.
$$fy^{(2)} + gy^{(1)} + hy^{(0)} = 0$$

where f, g and h are polynomials in x (or can be approximated to by such polynomials).
Then

$$C_r(fy^{(2)}) + C_r(gy^{(1)}) + C_r(hy^{(0)}) = 0$$

will yield a recurrence relationship based upon the differential equation. The Chebyshev polynomials themselves yield the second recurrence relationship, namely

$$2r \cdot a_r^{(s)} = a_{r-1}^{(s+1)} - a_{r+1}^{(s+1)}$$

To start the procedure, assume that

$$a_r^{(s)} = 0 \qquad r > N$$

and assign arbitrary integer values to $a_N^{(1)}$ and $a_N^{(2)}$. The recurrence relationships are used to generate $a_r^{(s)}$ for $r = N - 1$, $N - 2$, etc.

CHEBYSHEV METHODS (Continued)

The formulae for the initial conditions are

$$y^{(s)}(-1) = \tfrac{1}{2}a_0^{(s)} - a_1^{(s)} + a_2^{(s)} - a_3^{(s)} + \cdots$$
$$y^{(s)}(0) \;\;= \tfrac{1}{2}a_0^{(s)} - a_2^{(s)} + a_4^{(s)} - a_6^{(s)} + \cdots$$
$$y^{(s)}(1) \;\;= \tfrac{1}{2}a_0^{(s)} + a_1^{(s)} + a_2^{(s)} + a_3^{(s)} + \cdots$$

It will be found that the series obtained do not satisfy the given initial conditions. Therefore a second set of coefficients must be obtained by repeating the process for different arbitrary starting values and a linear combination of the two sets will yield the required solution.

$$T_0 = 1 \qquad\qquad\qquad T_{r+1} - 2xT_r + T_{r-1} = 0$$
$$T_1 = x$$
$$T_2 = 2x^2 - 1$$
$$T_3 = 4x^3 - 3x$$
$$T_4 = 8x^4 - 8x^2 + 1$$
$$T_5 = 16x^5 - 20x^3 + 5x$$
$$T_6 = 32x^6 - 48x^4 + 18x^2 - 1$$

If the "shifted" Chebyshev polynomials T_r^* are to be used then

$$y(x) = \tfrac{1}{2}a_0 + \sum_{r=1}^{N} a_r T_r^*$$

$$4r \cdot a_r^{(s)} = a_{|r-1|}^{(s+1)} - a_{r+1}^{(s+1)}$$

$$C_r(x^p y^{(s)}) = \frac{1}{2^p} \sum_{k=0}^{2p} \binom{2p}{k} a_{|r-p+k|}^{(s)}$$

with
$$y^{(s)}(0) = \tfrac{1}{2}a_0^{(s)} - a_1^{(s)} + a_2^{(s)} - a_3^{(s)} \cdots$$
$$y^{(s)}(\tfrac{1}{2}) = \tfrac{1}{2}a_0^{(s)} - a_2^{(s)} + a_4^{(s)} - a_6^{(s)} \cdots$$
$$y^{(s)}(1) = \tfrac{1}{2}a_0^{(s)} + a_1^{(s)} + a_2^{(s)} + a_3^{(s)} \cdots$$
$$T_r^*(x) = T_r(2x - 1) = \cos\{r \cdot \text{arc cos } (2x - 1)\}$$

$$T_0^* = 1 \qquad\qquad\qquad (4x - 2)T_r^* = T_{r-1}^* + T_{r+1}^*$$
$$T_1^* = 2x - 1$$
$$T_2^* = 8x^2 - 8x + 1$$
$$T_3^* = 32x^3 - 48x^2 + 18x - 1$$
$$T_4^* = 128x^4 - 256x^3 + 160x^2 - 32x + 1$$

The approach is otherwise the same.

INDIRECT METHODS

MONTE CARLO

Applicable to first order equations i.e. quadrature type, for which an upper bound can be set for the function. e.g. $y' = f(x); a \le x \le b; 0 \le f(x) < e$.

The range $[a,b]$ is subdivided into n intervals, not necessarily equal, such that $x_0 = a$ and $x_n = b$. For the sub-interval $[x_i, x_{i+1}]$ the procedure is as follows:

Set N_i equal to zero and after each trial increase N_i by unity so that it will always indicate the number of completed trials.

Set T_i equal to zero and after each trial increase T_i by unity *only if the trial was successful* otherwise allow it to retain its previous value.

A trial consists of selecting two random numbers r_1 and r_2. The first of these is selected from a uniform (rectangular) distribution in the range $[x_i, x_{i+1}]$ and the second from a uniform distribution in the range $[0,e]$. If $r_2 \le f(r_1)$ then the trial is deemed to be successful—otherwise it is a failure.

As $N_i \to \infty$,

$$\frac{T_i}{N_i} e(x_{i+1} - x_i) \to \int_{x_i}^{x_{i+1}} f(x) \cdot dx$$

and hence

$$y_{i+1} = y_i + \frac{T_i e(x_{i+1} - x_i)}{N_i} \qquad \text{as } N_i \to \infty.$$

If the function has a negative lower bound such that $-d \le f(x) \le e$ then a simple axis transformation is necessary i.e. replace $f(x)$ by $d + f(x)$ and e by $(e + d)$ in the above, giving

$$y_{i+1} = y_i + \frac{T_i(e + d)(x_{i+1} - x_i)}{N_i} \qquad \text{as } N_i \to \infty.$$

In general, the range of values for which a uniform distribution is required will not be standard and a transformation will be necessary. Such a transformation is obtained as follows:

if r^* is a random number from a uniform distribution in the range $[a,b]$ then r a random number from a uniform distribution in the range $[s,t]$ can be obtained from

$$r = \left(\frac{bs - at}{b - a}\right) - r^*\left(\frac{s - t}{b - a}\right)$$

In particular, if the given range is $[0, 1]$ then

$$r = s + r(t - s)$$

while if the given range is $[-1, -1]$ then

$$r = \tfrac{1}{2}(s + t) + \tfrac{1}{2}r(t - s).$$

In all *Monte Carlo* techniques the number of trials must be large—usually several thousand are required.

PARTIAL DIFFERENTIAL EQUATIONS

Introduction

In the section dealing with finite differences and their applications, some attention has been paid to the derivation of the formulae quoted and a few words of explanation of their use given. Formulae of interest to users of high speed digital computers have been given, as well as those for desk computation.

Physical phenomena frequently give rise to partial differential equations, rather than ordinary ones. The "field" equations of Laplace and Poisson being particular examples. The analytical solution of partial differential equations is frequently tedious, if not impossible, even in those cases where an analytical solution is feasible, a numerical treatment may well be quicker.

Partial differential equations in practice are often reduced to simultaneous equations in two dimensions, one of which is frequently time-like. It is this type of equation which will be considered here.

The classification of partial differential equations is, by analogy with the conic sections, into elliptic, parabolic and hyperbolic equations.

The physical criterion for this grouping is one of boundary conditions. It is also convenient to define the *characteristics* of the equation under consideration. If these are real and distinct then the classification is that of hyperbolic, if real and equal then it is parabolic, while if they are complex it is elliptic.

Consider partial differential equations in two dimensions.

a) Second order equation.
Notation used:

$$p = \frac{\partial u}{\partial x}; \quad q = \frac{\partial u}{\partial y}; \quad r = \frac{\partial^2 u}{\partial x^2}; \quad s = \frac{\partial^2 u}{\partial x \partial y}; \quad t = \frac{\partial^2 u}{\partial y^2}$$

A, B, C and D are functions of u, x, y, p and q.

The physical problem is determined by a second order partial differential equation, the general form of which is

$$A \cdot r + B \cdot s + C \cdot t = D$$

The geometry of the space in which the equation holds yields two more equations:

$$dp = d\left(\frac{\partial u}{\partial x}\right) = r \cdot dx + s \cdot dy; \quad \text{and similarly,} \quad dq = s \cdot dx + t \cdot dy$$

In matrix form these can be expressed as

$$\begin{bmatrix} A & B & C \\ dx & dy & 0 \\ 0 & dx & dy \end{bmatrix} \begin{bmatrix} r \\ s \\ t \end{bmatrix} = \begin{bmatrix} D \\ dp \\ dq \end{bmatrix}$$

PARTIAL DIFFERENTIAL EQUATIONS (Continued)

At any point at which the determinant of the 3×3 matrix is zero

i.e.
$$\begin{vmatrix} A & B & C \\ dx & dy & 0 \\ 0 & dx & dy \end{vmatrix} = 0,$$

a necessary condition for the equations to have a solution is that the rank of the following matrix is two.

$$\begin{bmatrix} A & B & C & D \\ dx & dy & 0 & dp \\ 0 & dx & dy & dq \end{bmatrix}$$

This condition can be stated in an alternative fashion as follows. The equations have a solution if any of the following three determinental equations are satisfied

$$\begin{vmatrix} A & B & D \\ dx & dy & dp \\ 0 & dx & dq \end{vmatrix} = 0$$

$$\begin{vmatrix} A & D & C \\ dx & dp & 0 \\ 0 & dq & dy \end{vmatrix} = 0$$

$$\begin{vmatrix} D & B & C \\ dp & dy & 0 \\ dq & dx & dy \end{vmatrix} = 0.$$

The equation
$$\begin{vmatrix} A & B & C \\ dx & dy & 0 \\ 0 & dx & dy \end{vmatrix} = 0$$

can be written in the form $\quad A \left(\dfrac{dy}{dx} \right)^2 - B \left(\dfrac{dy}{dx} \right) + C = 0$

and thus for the discriminant Δ defined by

$$\Delta \equiv B^2 - 4AC$$

PARTIAL DIFFERENTIAL EQUATIONS (Continued)

there exist three possibilities

(i) $\Delta > 0$, in which case two real distinct values can be obtained for $\dfrac{dy}{dx}$, corresponding

to real characteristics, and the equation is said to be hyperbolic.

(ii) $\Delta = 0$, when the equation is said to be parabolic.

(iii) $\Delta < 0$, when the equation is said to be elliptic.

Simple examples of these equations are

Hyperbolic
$$\frac{\partial^2 u}{\partial x^2} - \frac{\partial^2 u}{\partial y^2} = 0$$

Parabolic
$$\frac{\partial^2 u}{\partial x^2} - \frac{\partial u}{\partial y} = 0$$

Elliptic
$$\frac{\partial^2 u}{\partial x^2} + \frac{\partial^2 u}{\partial y^2} = 0$$

In the above simple forms A, B, C and D are constants while in fact they can depend upon the solution, and its first derivatives, as well as position in the region. Thus the classification of the equation *can* depend upon the solution itself.

b) Two simultaneous first order equations.

The techniques are similar to those employed in section (*a*) above.

A, B, C, D and E are functions of u, v, x, y, $\dfrac{\partial u}{\partial x}$, $\dfrac{\partial u}{\partial y}$, $\dfrac{\partial v}{\partial x}$, $\dfrac{\partial v}{\partial y}$ and the general form of the

equations are

$$A_1 \frac{\partial u}{\partial x} + B_1 \frac{\partial u}{\partial y} + C_1 \frac{\partial v}{\partial x} + D_1 \frac{\partial v}{\partial y} = E_1$$

$$A_2 \frac{\partial u}{\partial x} + B_2 \frac{\partial u}{\partial y} + C_2 \frac{\partial v}{\partial x} + D_2 \frac{\partial v}{\partial y} = E_2.$$

The geometry of the space yields, as before

$$du = \frac{\partial u}{\partial x} \cdot dx + \frac{\partial u}{\partial y} \cdot dy$$

$$dv = \frac{\partial v}{\partial x} \cdot dx + \frac{\partial v}{\partial y} \cdot dy$$

The discriminant Δ now being given by

$$\Delta \equiv (A_1 D_2 - A_2 D_1 + B_1 C_2 - B_2 C_1) - 4(A_1 C_2 - A_2 C_1)(B_1 D_2 - B_2 D_1).$$

Δ decides the class into which the two equations fall in the same manner as in the previous case.

i.e.   Hyperbolic   if $\Delta > 0$
      Parabolic   if $\Delta = 0$
      Elliptic   if $\Delta < 0$.

An elegant method for the solution of hyperbolic equations, based on the determination of the equations of the characteristics, exists but will not be discussed further here.

PARTIAL DIFFERENTIAL EQUATIONS (Continued)

Elliptic equations are best treated numerically by iteration. This enables both the interval to be adjusted arbitrarily and also the powerful convergence techniques of numerical analysis to be invoked.

Parabolic and hyperbolic equations on the other hand can be covered by step-by-step methods. These latter fall into two main groups. On the one hand, there are those methods which yield a direct solution, and, on the other, those which yield the solution implicitly.

In general, however, elliptic equations arise when the boundary conditions are specified on a contour enclosing a region, which need not be simply connected, i.e. elliptic equations are of the boundary value type.

The hyperbolic equations are of the initial value type, and require the solution over a domain having an open boundary.

For parabolic equations the boundary is also open, but in the main only in one direction, the boundary conditions themselves being mixed.

Elliptic Partial Differential Equations

A square mesh of side "h" is superimposed upon the region to enable the points to be labelled with respect to an arbitrary origin.

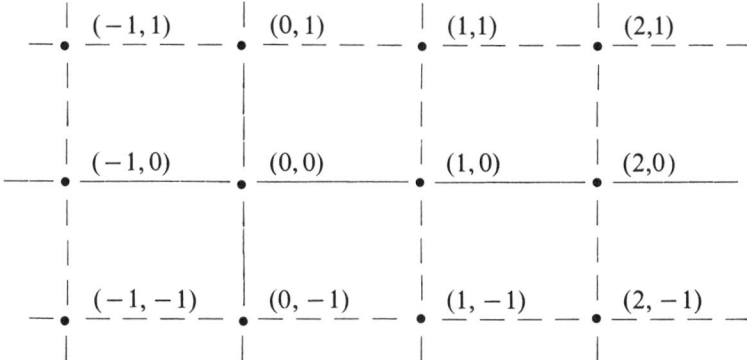

This presupposes that the boundary is formed from the sides of such a mesh. If such is not the case, the procedure must be modified at the boundary. This will be discussed at the end of this section.

The emphasis here will be on the equations of Poisson and Laplace, although the methods involved can easily be extended to any elliptic partial differential equation. In essence, the Taylor's series expansion for a number of mesh points is used to express the partial derivatives occurring in the equation at the origin, in terms of the function values at neighboring points, and higher partial derivatives at the origin. These function values are used to replace the differential equation by a finite difference equation, which is cast in the form of an iteration formula, the higher derivatives consituting the truncation error term.

Consider the equation

$$\nabla^2 u(x,y) = f(x,y)$$

where

$$\nabla^2 \equiv \frac{\partial^2}{\partial x^2} + \frac{\partial^2}{\partial y^2}$$

ELLIPTIC DIFFERENTIAL EQUATIONS

The differential equation is to be replaced by the iteration formula having the form

$$A_{00}u_{00} = \sum_{s=-n}^{n} \sum_{r=-n}^{n}{}^{*} A_{rs}u_{rs} - Bh^2f_{00} + \text{error term}$$

(the asterisk attached to the double summation indicating that the term involving u_{00} is to be omitted from the sum). In practice n will be restricted to 1 or 2.

Notation used:

$$x_r = x_0 + rh$$
$$y_r = y_0 + sh$$
$$(r,s) = (x_r,y_s)$$
$$f_{00} = f(x_0,y_0)$$
$$u_{rs} = u(x_r,y_s)$$
$$A_{rs} = \text{Integer weight associated with } u_{rs}$$
$$B = \text{Integer constant.}$$

The principal part of the error term will be of the form

$$h^4(\theta\nabla^4 + \phi\mathfrak{D}^4)u_{00}$$

where
$$\mathfrak{D}^4 \equiv \frac{\partial^4}{\partial x^2\partial y^2} \text{ and } \theta, \phi \text{ are constants.}$$

A_{rs}, B, θ and ϕ are tabulated below.

Restricting the values of the weights to the doubly symmetric case, i.e. $A_{rs} = A_{sr} = A|_r| |_s|$, and assuming the validity of the Taylor's expansion in the neighborhood of u_{00}, integer values can be obtained for A_{rs} and B, and rational fractions for θ and ϕ. However, the assumptions of the existence of the Taylor's expansion implies that $u(x,y)$ can be adequately represented by a polynomial in x and y over the region in question. Thus if a square region, centered on an arbitrary origin, is considered, the terms involving odd powers of either variable will contribute nothing to the sum providing the coordinates involved are specially selected.

The significant part of the expansion is therefore

$$u_{rs} = \left\{1 + \frac{h^2}{2!}\left(r^2\frac{\partial^2}{\partial x^2} + s^2\frac{\partial^2}{\partial y^2}\right) + \frac{h^4}{4!}\left(r^4\frac{\partial^4}{\partial x^4} + 6r^2s^2\frac{\partial^4}{\partial x^2\partial y^2} + s^4\frac{\partial^4}{\partial y^4}\right)\cdots\right\}u_{00}$$

The coordinate groupings that are used are as follows:

(i)   (0,1), (1,0), (0,−1) and (−1,0)
(ii)   (1,1), (1,−1), (−1,1) and (−1,−1)
(iii)   (0,2), (2,0), (0,−2) and (−2,0)
(iv)   (2,2), (2,−2), (−2,2) and (−2,−2)
(v)   (2,1), (1,2), (−1,2), (−2,1), (−2,−1), (−1,−2), (1,−2) and (2,−1).

ELLIPTIC DIFFERENTIAL EQUATIONS (Continued)

Group 1.   The general form is

A_{rs}

r \ s	−1	0	1
1	1	α	1
0	α	$4(1 + \alpha)$	α
−1	1	α	1

$B = (\alpha + 2)$

$\theta = -(\alpha + 2)/12$

$\phi = (\alpha - 4)/6$

in particular

A_{rs}

r \ s	−1	0	1
1	1	0	1
0	0	4	0
−1	1	0	1

$B = 2$

$\theta = -1/6$

$\phi = -2/3$

A_{rs}

r \ s	−1	0	1
1	1	2	1
0	2	12	2
−1	1	2	1

$B = 4$

$\theta = -1/3$

$\phi = -1/3$

A_{rs}

r \ s	−1	0	1
1	1	3	1
0	3	16	3
−1	1	3	1

$B = 5$

$\theta = -5/12$

$\phi = -1/6$

A_{rs}

r \ s	−1	0	1
1	1	4	1
0	4	20	4
−1	1	4	1

$B = 6$

$\theta = -1/2$

$\phi = 0$

A_{rs}

r \ s	−1	0	1
1	1	6	1
0	6	28	6
−1	1	6	1

$B = 8$

$\theta = -2/3$

$\phi = 1/3$

ELLIPTIC DIFFERENTIAL EQUATIONS (Continued)

Group 2. The general form is

s \ r	-1	0	1
1	α	1	α
0	1	$4(1+\alpha)$	1
-1	α	1	α

A_{rs}

$B = (1 + 2\alpha)$

$\theta = -(1 + 2\alpha)/12$

$\phi = (1 - 4\alpha)/6$

In particular

s \ r	-1	0	1
1	0	1	0
0	1	4	1
-1	0	1	0

A_{rs}

$B = 1$

$\theta = -1/2$

$\phi = 1/6$

s \ r	-1	0	1
1	1	1	1
0	1	8	1
-1	1	1	1

A_{rs}

$B = 3$

$\theta = -1/4$

$\phi = -1/2$

s \ r	-1	0	1
1	2	1	2
0	1	12	1
-1	2	1	2

A_{rs}

$B = 5$

$\theta = -5/12$

$\phi = -7/6$

s \ r	-1	0	1
1	4	1	4
0	1	20	1
-1	4	1	4

A_{rs}

$B = 9$

$\theta = -3/4$

$\phi = -5/3$

s \ r	-1	0	1
1	8	1	8
0	1	36	1
-1	8	1	8

A_{rs}

$B = 17$

$\theta = -17/12$

$\phi = -31/6$

ELLIPTIC DIFFERENTIAL EQUATIONS (Continued)

Group 3. The general form is

A_{rs}			
s \ r	1	0	−1
1	β	α	β
0	α	$4(\alpha + \beta)$	α
−1	β	α	β

$B = \alpha + 2\beta$

$\theta = -(\alpha + 2\beta)/12$

$\phi = (\alpha - 4\beta)/6$

In particular

A_{rs}			
s \ r	−1	0	1
1	2	3	2
0	3	20	3
−1	2	3	2

$B = 7$

$\theta = -7/2$

$\phi = -5/6$

A_{rs}			
s \ r	−1	0	1
1	2	5	2
0	5	28	5
−1	2	5	2

$B = 9$

$\theta = -3/4$

$\phi = -1/2$

A_{rs}			
s \ r	−1	0	1
1	3	4	3
0	4	28	4
−1	3	4	3

$B = 10$

$\theta = -5/6$

$\phi = -4/3$

A_{rs}			
s \ r	−1	0	1
1	3	5	3
0	5	32	5
−1	3	5	3

$B = 11$

$\theta = -11/12$

$\phi = -7/3$

A_{rs}			
s \ r	−1	0	1
1	4	5	4
0	5	36	5
−1	4	5	4

$B = 13$

$\theta = -13/12$

$\phi = -11/6$

ELLIPTIC DIFFERENTIAL EQUATIONS (Continued)

While negative weights can be used in all groups care must be taken that the subtraction of comparable terms does not reduce the number of significant decimals left in the result.

The above formulae are of the nine-point type. To increase the accuracy, twenty-five-point formulae can be used. For these the error term is taken to be

$$\{h^4(\theta\nabla^4 + \phi\mathcal{D}^4) + h^6(\eta\nabla^6 + \gamma\mathcal{D}^4\nabla^2)\}u_{00}$$

The twenty-five-point formulae which form the basic set are

A_{rs}

r \ s	−2	−1	0	1	2	
2	0	0	0	0	0	$B = 1$
1	0	0	1	0	0	$\theta = -1/12$
0	0	1	4	1	0	$\phi = 1/6$
−1	0	0	1	0	0	$\eta = -1/360$
−2	0	0	0	0	0	$\gamma = 1/120$

A_{rs}

r \ s	−2	−1	0	1	2	
2	0	0	0	0	0	$B = 2$
1	0	1	0	1	0	$\theta = -1/6$
0	0	0	4	0	0	$\phi = -2/3$
−1	0	1	0	1	0	$\eta = -1/180$
−2	0	0	0	0	0	$\gamma = -1/15$

A_{rs}

r \ s	−2	−1	0	1	2	
2	0	1	0	1	0	$B = 10$
1	1	0	0	0	1	$\theta = -17/6$
0	0	0	8	0	0	$\phi = -7/3$
−1	1	0	0	0	1	$\eta = -13/36$
−2	0	1	0	1	0	$\gamma = -7/12$

ELLIPTIC DIFFERENTIAL EQUATIONS (Continued)

A_{rs}

r \ s	-2	-1	0	1	2	
2	0	0	1	0	0	$B = 4$
1	0	0	0	0	0	$\theta = -4/3$
0	1	0	4	0	1	$\phi = 8/3$
-1	0	0	0	0	0	$\eta = -8/45$
-2	0	0	1	0	0	$\gamma = 8/15$

A_{rs}

r \ s	-2	-1	0	1	2	
2	1	0	0	0	1	$B = 8$
1	0	0	0	0	0	$\theta = -8/3$
0	0	0	4	0	0	$\phi = -32/3$
-1	0	0	0	0	0	$\eta = -16/45$
-2	1	0	0	0	1	$\gamma = -64/15$

Any linear combination of the above five sets can be used.

Group 4   The general form is

A_{rs}

r \ s	-2	-1	0	1	2	
2	μ	κ	ρ	κ	μ	$B = \alpha + 2\beta + 4\rho + 8\mu + 10\kappa$
1	κ	β	α	β	κ	$\theta = -(\alpha + 2\beta + 16\rho + 32\mu + 34\kappa)/12$
0	ρ	α	$4(\alpha + \beta + \rho + \mu + 2\kappa)$	α	ρ	$\phi = (\alpha - 4\beta + 16\rho - 64\mu - 14\kappa)/6$
-1	κ	β	α	β	κ	$\eta = -(\alpha + 2\beta + 64\rho + 128\mu + 130\kappa)/360$
-2	μ	κ	ρ	κ	μ	$\gamma = (\alpha - 8\beta + 64\rho - 512\mu - 70\kappa)/120$

In particular θ and ϕ can be reduced to zero simultaneously if either *a*) $\rho = -1$, $\alpha = 16$, $\mu = 0 = \beta = \kappa$.

A_{rs}

r \ s	-2	-1	0	1	2	
2	0	0	-1	0	0	$B = 12$
1	0	0	16	0	0	$\theta = 0$
0	-1	16	60	16	-1	$\phi = 0$
-1	0	0	16	0	0	$\eta = 2/15$
-2	0	0	-1	0	0	$\gamma = -2/5$

ELLIPTIC DIFFERENTIAL EQUATIONS (Continued)

or   b) $\mu = -1$, $\beta = 16$, $\alpha = 0 = \rho = \kappa$.

A_{rs}

r \ s	−2	−1	0	1	2	
2	−1	0	0	0	−1	$B = 24$
1	0	16	0	16	0	$\theta = 0$
0	0	0	60	0	0	$\phi = 0$
−1	0	16	0	16	0	$\eta = 4/15$
−2	−1	0	0	0	−1	$\gamma = 16/5$

or   c) $\rho = -1 = \mu$, $\alpha = 16 = \beta$.

A_{rs}

r \ s	−2	−1	0	1	2	
2	−1	0	−1	0	−1	$B = 36$
1	0	16	16	16	0	$\theta = 0$
0	−1	16	120	16	−1	$\phi = 0$
−1	0	16	16	16	0	$\eta = 3/5$
−2	−1	0	−1	0	−1	$\gamma = 14/5$

When working with digital computers it is frequently advantageous to have, as weights, powers of two. The following sets of weights yield this, and in addition the overall divisor A_{00} is also a power of two.

A_{rs}

r \ s	−2	−1	0	1	2	
2	0	1	2	1	0	$B = 14$
1	1	0	0	0	1	$\theta = -11/2$
0	2	0	16	0	2	$\phi = 3$
−1	1	0	0	0	1	$\eta = -43/60$
−2	1	1	2	1	0	$\gamma = 29/60$

A_{rs}

r \ s	−2	−1	0	1	2	
2	0	1	2	1	0	$B = 22$
1	1	4	0	4	1	$\theta = -37/6$
0	2	0	32	0	2	$\phi = 1/3$
−1	1	4	0	4	1	$\eta = -133/180$
−2	0	1	2	1	0	$\gamma = 13/60$

ELLIPTIC DIFFERENTIAL EQUATIONS (Continued)

A_{rs}					
r \ s	-2	-1	0	1	2
2	0	1	2	1	0
1	1	0	4	0	1
0	2	4	32	4	2
-1	1	0	4	0	1
-2	0	1	2	1	0

$B = 18$

$\theta = -35/6$

$\phi = 11/3$

$\eta = -131/180$

$\gamma = 31/60$

A_{rs}					
r \ s	-2	-1	0	1	2
2	0	1	2	1	0
1	1	4	8	4	1
0	2	8	64	8	2
-1	1	4	8	4	1
-2	0	1	2	1	0

$B = 34$

$\theta = -41/3$

$\phi = 5/3$

$\eta = -137/180$

$\gamma = 17/60$

A_{rs}					
r \ s	-2	-1	0	1	2
2	0	0	1	0	0
1	0	1	2	1	0
0	1	2	16	2	1
-1	0	1	2	1	0
-2	1	0	1	0	0

$B = 8$

$\theta = -5/3$

$\phi = 7/3$

$\eta = -17/90$

$\gamma = 29/60$

A_{rs}					
r \ s	-2	-1	0	1	2
2	0	1	0	1	0
1	1	1	1	1	1
0	0	1	16	1	0
-1	1	1	1	1	1
-2	0	1	0	1	0

$B = 13$

$\theta = -37/12$

$\phi = -17/6$

$\eta = -133/360$

$\gamma = -77/120$

ELLIPTIC DIFFERENTIAL EQUATIONS (Continued)

For desk machine working the value of A_{00} should be chosen so as to simplify the process of division. Some typical sets of weights in which A_{00} is 100 are

A_{rs}

r \ s	-2	-1	0	1	2	
2	1	7	10	7	1	$B = 118$
1	7	0	0	0	7	$\theta = -215/6$
0	10	0	100	0	10	$\phi = -1/6$
-1	7	0	0	0	7	$\eta = -839/180$
-2	1	7	10	7	1	$\gamma = -181/60$

A_{rs}

r \ s	-2	-1	0	1	2	
2	0	1	5	1	0	$B = 56$
1	1	8	10	8	1	$\theta = -35/3$
0	5	10	100	10	5	$\phi = 22/3$
-1	1	8	10	8	1	$\eta = -119/90$
-2	0	1	5	1	0	$\gamma = 49/30$

A_{rs}

r \ s	-2	-1	0	1	2	
2	0	5	0	5	0	$B = 70$
1	5	5	10	5	5	$\theta = -95/6$
0	0	10	100	10	0	$\phi = -40/3$
-1	5	5	10	5	5	$\eta = -67/36$
-2	0	5	0	5	0	$\gamma = -19/6$

Starting the solution

Any rough estimate can be used to start the solution. In the absence of such an estimate all the interior points can be set at zero. In the case of Laplace's equation, straight lines can be drawn through any point to cut the boundary. The estimated value of the function at that point is then obtained by simple ratio and proportion.

Continuing the solution.

A systematic sweep through the region is essential, although the actual direction of travel chosen is immaterial for all practical purposes. It is important however that once the value at a specific point has been recomputed the new value should immediately replace the old.

Refining the mesh.

Once all the values at the mesh points have converted to the degree of accuracy permitted by the interval "h," the mesh can be subdivided in the following fashion and convergence to more accurate values obtained.

ELLIPTIC DIFFERENTIAL EQUATIONS (Continued)

Fig. 1 shows the mesh of side h, near a boundary where it is required to produce a mesh of side $\frac{1}{2}h$

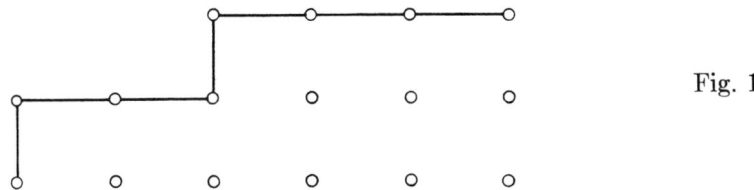

Fig. 1

The points marked with a + in Fig. 2 can be inserted by means of the first formula of Group 1.

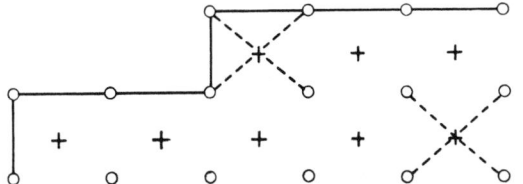

Fig. 2

The points marked with a • in Fig. 3 can then be inserted by means of the first formula of Group 2.

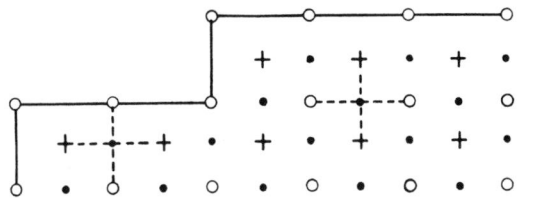

Fig. 3

Finally the boundary conditions enable the values at the new mesh points on the boundary to be inserted. These are indicated by • in Fig. 4.

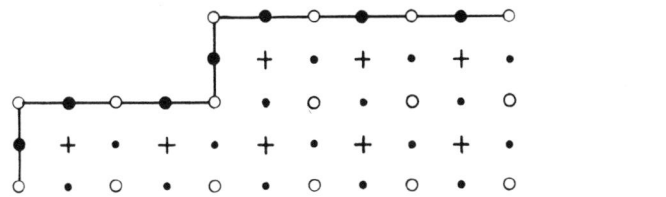

Fig. 4

Improving the numerical solution

(i) Aitken's δ^2 process.

If $u^{(1)}$, $u^{(2)}$ and $u^{(3)}$ are three successive approximations for a given h to u, then a better approximation is given by

$$u = u^{(3)} - \frac{[u^{(3} - u^{(2)}]^2}{u^{(3)} - 2u^{(2)} + u^{(1)}}$$

(ii) Richardson's deferred approach to the limit.

ELLIPTIC DIFFERENTIAL EQUATIONS (Continued)

If $u_{(1)}$ is the value obtained for a mesh size h and $u_{(2)}$ is the value when the mesh size is $\frac{1}{2}h$ then a better value for u is given by

$$u = u_{(2)} + \frac{1}{3}[u_{(2)} - u_{(1)}]$$

If, in addition, $u_{(3)}$ is the value obtained for a mesh size $\frac{1}{4}h$ then the improved value is given by

$$u = u_{(3)} + \frac{4}{9}[u_{(3)} - u_{(2)}] - \frac{1}{45}[u_{(3)} - u_{(1)}]$$

It is not necessary to refine the mesh over the entire region. In most cases only specially selected areas will need refining.

(iii) Difference correction.

The technique here is the same as is described in the section on ordinary differential equations. The derivatives in the error term are replaced by their finite difference equivalents, in both the x and y directions, and these constitute the difference correction.

Non-rectangular boundaries.

In some cases a transformation of coordinates will produce a boundary which will fit a rectangular mesh at the expense of increased complexity of the partial differential equation.

In others a mesh which is not rectangular can be employed, the usual alternatives being triangular and hexagonal.

Otherwise the rectangular mesh can be preserved for the mean body of the calculation and the iterative formula modified on the boundary. Thus two basic forms will be needed at a curved boundary.

Case 1.

$$A_0 u_0 = -B f_0 + \sum_{r=1}^{4} A_r u_r + 0(h^3)$$

$$h \geqq H_i \qquad (i = 1,2,3,4)$$

$$h_i = H_i/h$$

$$A_0 = (h_1 + h_3)(h_2 + h_4)(h_1 h_3 + h_2 h_4)$$

$$B = \tfrac{1}{2} h_1 h_2 h_3 h_4 (h_1 + h_3)(h_2 + h_4)$$

$$A_1 = h_2 h_3 h_4 (h_2 + h_4)$$

$$A_2 = h_3 h_4 h_1 (h_3 + h_1)$$

$$A_3 = h_4 h_1 h_2 (h_4 + h_2)$$

$$A_4 = h_1 h_2 h_3 (h_1 + h_3)$$

ELLIPTIC DIFFERENTIAL EQUATIONS (Continued)

Case 2

The formulae are the same as in Case 1; it is only the orientation of the mesh which is changed

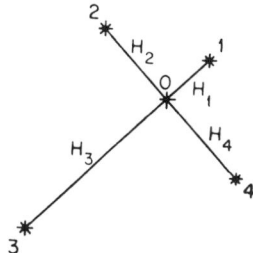

Triangular mesh formulae for Poisson's equation

The points are numbered as shown

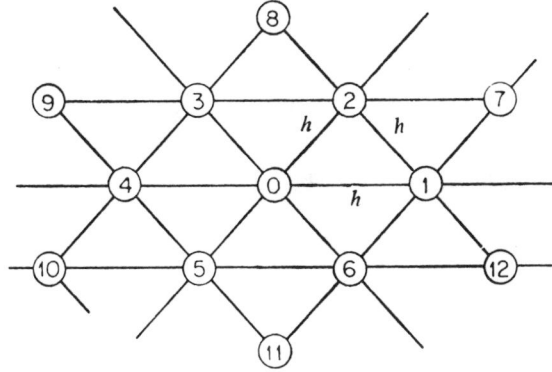

The iteration formula for the above mesh is

$$A_0 = \Sigma A_r u_r - Bh^2 f_0 + \epsilon$$

a) Summation extends over $r = 1(1)6$

$$A_0 = 6, \qquad A_r = 1, \qquad B = 3/2$$

$$\epsilon = -\frac{32}{32} h^4 \nabla_0^4$$

b) Summation extends over $r = 7(1)12$

$$A_0 = 6, \qquad A_r = 1, \qquad B = 9/2$$

$$\epsilon = -\frac{27}{32} h^4 \nabla_0^4$$

c) Summation extends over $r = 1(1)12$

$$A_0 = 48, \qquad A_r = 9 \qquad (r = 1(1)6)$$

$$B = 8 \qquad A_r = -1 \qquad (r = 7(1)12)$$

$$\epsilon = -\frac{h^6}{3840}\left(11\frac{\partial^6}{\partial x^6} + 15\frac{\partial^6}{\partial x^4 \partial y^2} + 45\frac{\partial^6}{\partial x^2 \partial y^4} + 9\frac{\partial^6}{\partial y^6}\right)u_0$$

ELLIPTIC DIFFERENTIAL EQUATIONS (Continued)

Hexagonal mesh formulae for Poisson's equation

The points are numbered as shown

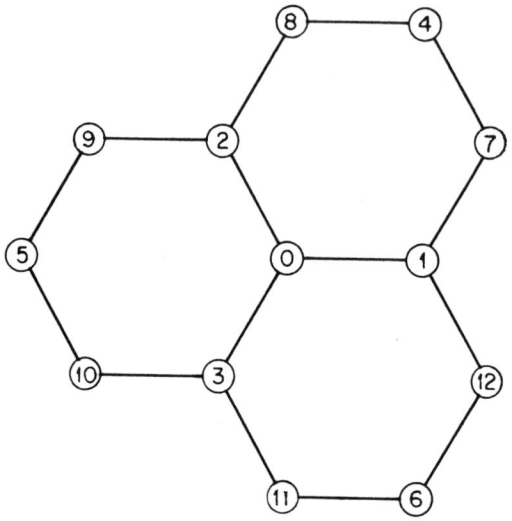

The iteration formula for the above mesh being

$$A_0 = \Sigma A_r u_r - Bh^2 f_0 + \epsilon$$

a) Summation extends over $r = 1(1)3$

$$A_0 = 3, \qquad A_r = 1, \qquad B = 3/4$$

$$\epsilon = -\frac{h^3}{8}\left(\frac{\partial^3}{\partial x^3} - 3\frac{\partial^3}{\partial x \partial y^2}\right)u_0$$

b) Summation extends over $r = 4(1)6$

$$A_0 = 3, \qquad A_r = 1, \qquad B = 3$$

$$\epsilon = -h^3\left(\frac{\partial^3}{\partial x^3} - 3\frac{\partial^3}{\partial x \partial y^2}\right)u_0$$

c) Summation extends over $r = 1(1)6$

$$A_0 = 21, \qquad A_r = 8 \qquad (r = 1(1)3)$$

$$B = 3, \qquad A_r = -1 \qquad (r = 4(1)6)$$

$$\epsilon = \frac{h^4}{8}\left(3\frac{\partial^4}{\partial x^4} + \frac{\partial^4}{\partial x^2 \partial y^2} + 3\frac{\partial^4}{\partial y^4}\right)u_0$$

PARABOLIC DIFFERENTIAL EQUATIONS

Parabolic and Hyperbolic Partial Differential Equations

While this section will be restricted to partial differential equations with two independent variables, the techniques involved can easily be extended to those with three or more.

For simplicity, a rectangular mesh will be superimposed upon the region of integration. The pivotal points will have co-ordinates (x_s, t_r) where, for the intervals "h" and "k,"

$$x_s = x_0 + sh$$

$$t_r = t_0 + rk$$

$$f_{s,r} = f(x_s, t_r).$$

If the derivatives, with respect to either x or t, are replaced by their finite difference approximations, the result will be a set of simultaneous ordinary differential equations.

If, however, all the derivatives are replaced by their relevant approximations, a difference equation corresponding to the original differential equations is obtained. It should be noted, of course, that the approximation chosen will not be unique. Some typical examples are as follows,

$$\left(\frac{\partial f}{\partial t}\right)_{s,r} = (f_{s,r+1} - f_{s,r})/k$$

or

$$= (f_{s,r} - f_{s,r-1})/k$$

or

$$= (f_{s,r+1} - f_{s,r-1})/2k$$

$$\left(\frac{\partial^2 f}{\partial x^2}\right)_{s,r} = (f_{s+1,r} - 2f_{s,r} + f_{s-1,r})/h^2$$

or

$$= (2f_{s,r} - 5f_{s-1,r} + 4f_{s-2,r} - f_{s-3,r})/h^2$$

or

$$= (11f_{s+1,r} - 20f_{s,r} + 6f_{s-1,r} + 4f_{s-2,r} - f_{s-3,r})/12h^2$$

and so forth.

Parabolic Partial Differential Equations

The examples in this section will be concerned in the main, with the simple but nevertheless typical one-dimensional heat equation given by:

$$\frac{\partial f}{\partial t} = \frac{\partial^2 f}{\partial x^2}$$

with the initial conditions $\qquad f = I(x) \qquad\qquad [x_0 \leqslant x \leqslant x_n, \, t = 0]$

and the boundary conditions $\qquad f = B(t) \qquad\qquad [t > 0, \quad x = x_0]$

$$f = B^*(t) \qquad\qquad [t > 0, \quad x = x_n]$$

PARABOLIC DIFFERENTIAL EQUATIONS (Continued)

Without loss of generality, x_0 can be replaced by 0 so that

$$x_s = sh, \quad t_r = rk,$$

and
$$I(x_s) = f_{s,0}, \quad B(t_r) = f_{0,r}, \quad B^*(t_r) = f_{n,r}.$$

Two decisions have now to be made.

(a) Is the relationship between the values of "f" at the pivotal points to be an implicit one or an explicit one? That is to say, if the solution is being determined in the direction of t increasing, is the value at $f_{s,r}$ going to involve other values for which $t = rk$, or is it only going to involve those points for which $t < rk$?

(b) How many points are going to be involved at any one time?

A small number of points will mean less computational labor, but generally at the expense of the truncation error.

The explicit formulae are more direct than the implicit ones, but may require the mesh size to be unacceptably small in order to ensure the stability of the solution. In some cases the explicit form is unstable for all meshes. On the other hand, the implicit formulae are stable but they require the solution of large numbers of simultaneous equations.

Some typical explicit formulae

i.
$$f_{s,r+1} = f_{s,r} + (k/h^2)(f_{s-1,r} - 2f_{s,r} + f_{s+1,r})$$

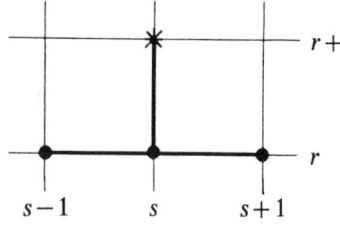

Stable if $0 < k/h^2 \leqslant 1/2$

Truncation error $= 0(k) + 0(h^2)$

In particular when $k/h^2 = 1/2$ the point pattern is simplified by the omission of the pivot $f_{s,r}$.

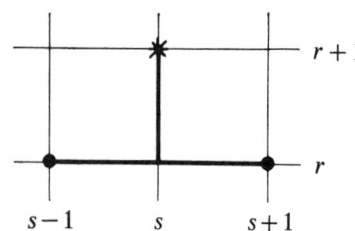

$$f_{s,r+1} = \tfrac{1}{2}(f_{s-1,r} + f_{s+1,r})$$

Milne has shown that an improved truncation error results when $k/h^2 = 1/6$

$$f_{s,r+1} = (1/6)(f_{s-1,r} + 4f_{s,r} + f_{s+1,r})$$

Truncation error $= 0(k^2) + 0(h^4)$

PARABOLIC DIFFERENTIAL EQUATIONS (Continued)

ii.
$$f_{s,r+1} = \frac{(h^2 - 2k)f_{s,r-1} + 2k(f_{s-1,r} + f_{s+1,r})}{(h^2 + 2k)}$$

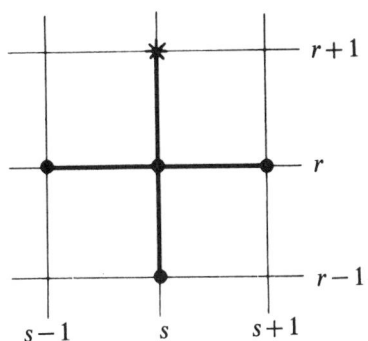

Always stable, but $f_{s,r-1}$ is required.

Truncation error $= 0(k) + 0(h^2) + 0(k/h)$

iii. $f_{s,r+1} = f_{s,r} - (1/12)(k/h^2)(f_{s-2,r} - 16f_{s-1,r} + 30f_{s,r} - 16f_{s+1,r} + f_{s+2,r})$

Stable if $0 < (k/h^2) \leq 3/8$

Truncation error $= 0(k) + 0(h^4)$

If the above mesh is used for the main body of the computation, then unsymmetric formulae are required at the ends of the range of s. The formula for the left hand side is shown below. (The formula for the right hand side is the mirror image.)

$$f_{s,r+1} = f_{s,r} + (1/12)(k/h^2)(11f_{s-1,r} - 20f_{s,r} + 6f_{s+1,r} + 4f_{s+2,r} - f_{s+3,r})$$

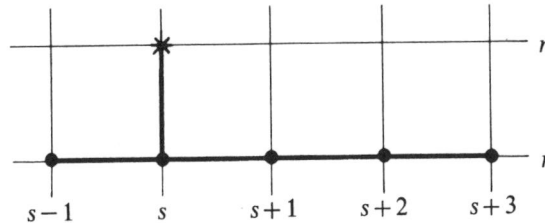

Stable if $0 < (k/h^2) \leq 2/7$

Truncation error $= 0(h^3) + 0(k)$

The truncation error of the unsymmetrical case will of course determine the overall truncation error if all three formulae are to be used in the one problem. The same observation will hold for the stability requirements.

One way of reducing the truncation error is to use additional, previously computed values; i.e., instead of using only those for which $t = rk$, increase the number of pivotal values involved by incorporating those for which $t = (r - 1)k, (r - 2)k$ etc. This method was used in example ii. However, it is generally unwise as such formulae tend toward high instability.

Some typical implicit formulae

These have the merit of stability but require the solution of a number of simultaneous equations. However, when matrix methods are used, often only one inversion is required. This simplifies the problem considerably.

PARABOLIC DIFFERENTIAL EQUATIONS (Continued)

i. $(k/h^2)(f_{s+1,r+1} + f_{s-1,r+1} + f_{s+1,r} + f_{s-1,r})$
$$- 2[1 + (k/h^2)]f_{s,r+1} + 2[1 - (k/h^2)]f_{s,r} = 0$$

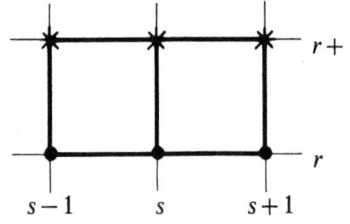

Always stable

Truncation error $= 0(k^2) + 0(h^2)$

ii. $$f_{s,r+1} - f_{s,r} = (k/h^2)(f_{s-1,r+1} - 2f_{s,r+1} + f_{s+1,r+1})$$

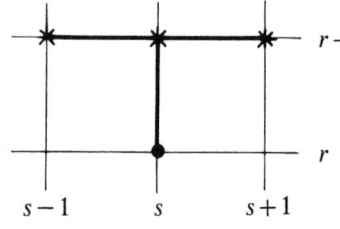

Always stable

Truncation error $= 0(k) + 0(h^2))$

iii. $12(f_{s,r+1} - f_{s,r}) + (k/h^2)(f_{s-2,r+1} - 16f_{s-1,r+1} + 30f_{s,r+1}$
$$- 16f_{s+1,r+1} + f_{s+2,r+1}) = 0$$

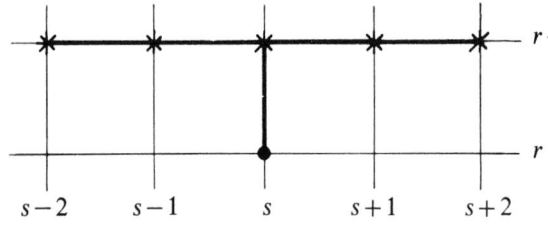

Always stable

Truncation error $= 0(k) + 0(h^4)$

As in the explicit case, unsymmetrical forms of the above formula are required at the extremities of the range. Only one will be quoted here (the other is merely a mirror image):

$$12(f_{s,r+1} - f_{s,r}) = (k/h^2)(11f_{s-1,r+1} - 20f_{s,r+1} + 6f_{s+1,r+1} + 4f_{s+2,r+1} - f_{s+3,r+1})$$

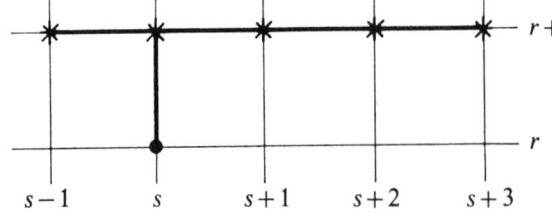

Always stable

Truncation error $= 0(k) + 0(h^3)$

HYPERBOLIC DIFFERENTIAL EQUATIONS (Continued)

iv. $[18(k/h^2) - 1](f_{s,r+1} - f_{s,r}) - [6(k/h^2) - 1](f_{s,r} - f_{s,r-1})$

$$= 12(k^2/h^4)(f_{s+1,r+1} - 2f_{s,r+1} + f_{s-1,r+1})$$

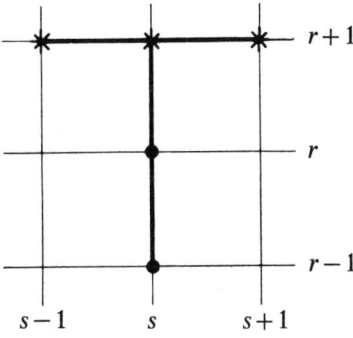

Always stable

Truncation error $= 0(k^2) + 0(h^4)$

v. An implicit method in its own right which can be used as a check on (iv) above is given by

$$(3f_{s+1,r+1} - 4f_{s+1,r} + f_{s+1,r-1}) + (30f_{s,r+1} - 40f_{s,r} + 10f_{s,r-1})$$
$$+ (3f_{s-1,r+1} - 4f_{s,r+1} + f_{s-1,r-1}) = 24(k/h^2)(f_{s+1,r+1} - 2f_{s,r+1} + f_{s-1,r+1})$$

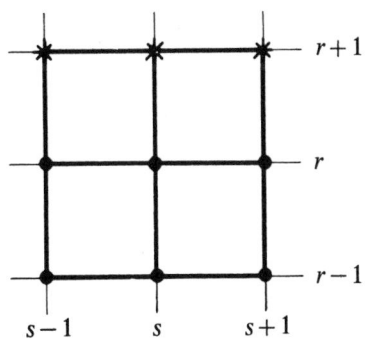

Always stable

Truncation error $= 0(k^2) + 0(h^4)$

Hyperbolic Partial Differential Equations

The methods used in the parabolic case carry over into the hyperbolic case; therefore, only one example of each will be quoted.

Consider

$$(\partial^2 f/\partial x^2) = (\partial^2 f/\partial t^2)$$

with appropriate boundary conditions.

An explicit formula:

$$f_{s,r+1} = 2f_{s,r} - f_{s,r-1} + (k^2/h)(f_{s-1,r} - 2f_{s,r} + f_{s+1,r})$$

PARABOLIC AND HYPERBOLIC DIFFERENTIAL EQUATIONS (Continued)

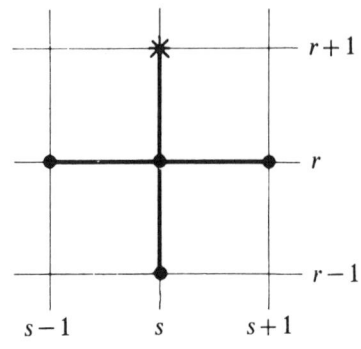

Stable if $0 < (k/h)^2 \leq 1$

Truncation error $= 0(h^4) + 0(k^4)$

An implicit formula:

$$(f_{s,r+1} - 2f_{s,r} + f_{s,r-1}) = (k/h)^2(f_{s-1,r+1} - 2f_{s,r+1} + f_{s+1,r+1})$$

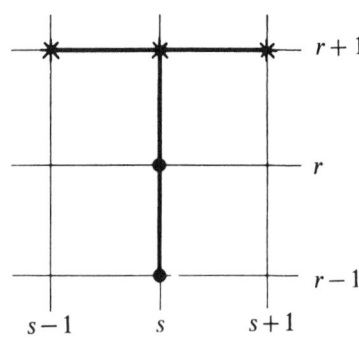

Always stable

Truncation error $= 0(h^4) + 0(k^4)$

Mixed Boundary Conditions for Parabolic and Hyperbolic Differential Equations

When the boundary conditions involve a derivative some slight modifications are necessary to take this condition into account.

Example 1
$$\frac{\partial f}{\partial t} = \frac{\partial^2 f}{\partial x^2};$$

$$f = I(x), \qquad\qquad [t = 0, \quad 0 \leq x \leq nh]$$

$$f = B(t), \qquad\qquad [t > 0, \quad x = 0]$$

$$f + A(\partial f/\partial x) = B^*(t), \qquad\qquad [t > 0, \quad x = nh]$$

The derivative can be replaced by a finite difference approximation as follows

$$f_{n,r} + \frac{A(f_{n,r} - f_{n-1,r})}{k} = B^*(t_r)$$

which can be rewritten as $f_{n,r} = \dfrac{(k/A)B^*(t_r) + f_{n-1,r}}{(1 + k/A)}$

This enables the end points to be computed. A more accurate approximation to the derivative can be used of course, e.g.,

$$f_{n,r} + \frac{A(6f_{n,r} - 10f_{n-1,r} + 5f_{n-2,r} - f_{n-3,r})}{6k} = B^*(t_r)$$

PARABOLIC AND HYPERBOLIC DIFFERENTIAL EQUATIONS (Continued)

Example 2. $\quad \dfrac{\partial f}{\partial t} = \dfrac{\partial^2 f}{\partial x^2};$ $\qquad f + A\dfrac{\partial f}{\partial t} = I(x),$ $\qquad\qquad\qquad [t = 0, 0 \leq x \leq nh]$

$$f = B(t), \qquad\qquad\qquad [t > 0, \quad x = 0]$$

$$f = B^*(t), \qquad\qquad\qquad [t > 0, \quad x = nh]$$

In this example the unconditionally stable form (ii) of the explicit set can be used. This is rewritten to give

$$f_{s,-1} = \frac{(h^2 + 2k)}{(h^2 - 2k)}\left(f_{s,1} - \frac{2k}{(h^2 + 2k)}\,(f_{s-1,0} + f_{s+1,0})\right)$$

The initial conditions yield

$$f_{s,0} + (A/2k)(f_{s,1} - f_{s-1}) = I(x_s)$$

or

$$f_{s,-1} = (2k/A)[f_{s,0} - I(x_s)] + f_{s,1}$$

Eliminating $f_{s,-1}$ from these two equations will yield an expression for $f_{s,1}[1 \leq s \leq (n-1)]$ and thereafter explicit formula (ii) can be used without modification.

MONTE CARLO TECHNIQUES FOR PARTIAL DIFFERENTIAL EQUATIONS

(*i*) *Elliptic Equations.*

The two dimensional case will be discussed here—the extension to more than two dimensions follows by increasing the number of the directions of the random walks by two for each added dimension.

The finite difference approximations

$$\frac{\partial^2 u}{\partial x^2} = \frac{u_{i+1,j} - 2u_{i,j} + u_{i-1,j}}{h_1^2}$$

and

$$\frac{\partial^2 u}{\partial y^2} = \frac{u_{i,j+1} - 2u_{i,j} + u_{i,j-1}}{h_2^2}$$

when substituted into $\nabla^2 u = 0$, yield

$$u_{i,j} = \frac{h_2^2 u_{i+1,j}}{2(h_1^2 + h_2^2)} + \frac{h_2^2 u_{i-1,j}}{2(h_1^2 + h_2^2)} + \frac{h_1^2 u_{i,j+1}}{2(h_1^2 + h_2^2)} + \frac{h_1^2 u_{i,j-1}}{2(h_1^2 + h_2^2)}$$

and, defining

$$p_1 = p_2 = \frac{h_2^2}{2(h_1^2 + h_2^2)}$$

$$p_3 = p_4 = \frac{h_1^2}{2(h_1^2 + h_2^2)}$$

It can be seen that $\sum_{i=1}^{4} p_i = 1$, which is the condition for carrying out a random walk along the four directions x increasing, x decreasing, y increasing and y decreasing. Thus to determine $u_{i,j}$ the value of u at the point with coordinates (x_i, y_j) the procedure is as follows; Set both T and N to zero initially.

For each walk completed add 1 to N.

A walk is completed when the boundary is reached and the value of u *at that point on the boundary* has been added to T. As the number of completed walks increases, $N \to \infty$ and $\frac{T}{N} \to u_{i,j}$.

For the equation $\nabla^2 u = f$ use the relationship

$$\frac{h_1^2 h_2^2}{2(h_1^2 + h_2^2)} f_{i,j} + u_{i,j} = p_1 u_{i+1,j} + p_2 u_{i-1,j} + p_3 u_{i,j+1} + p_4 u_{i,j-1}$$

As before the expression on the left hand side is the limiting value of the ratio $\frac{T}{N}$ as $N \to \infty$.

(*ii*) *Parabolic equations.*

Formula (ii) on page 717 yields, as a finite difference representation of

$$\frac{\partial f_{s,r}}{\partial t} = \frac{\partial^2 f_{s,r}}{\partial x^2}$$

$$f_{s,r+1} = \left(\frac{h^2 - 2k}{h^2 + 2k}\right) f_{s,r-1} + \left(\frac{2k}{h^2 + 2k}\right) f_{s-1,r} + \left(\frac{2k}{h^2 + 2k}\right) f_{s+1,r}$$

This can be written as

$$f_{s,r+1} = p_1 f_{s-1,r} + p_2 f_{s+1,r} + p_3 f_{s,r-1}$$

where as before $\sum_{r=1}^{3} p_r = 1$

MONTE CARLO TECHNIQUES (Continued)

for
$$p_1 = p_2 = \left(\frac{2k}{h^2 + 2k}\right); \qquad p_3 = \left(\frac{h^2 - 2k}{h^2 + 2k}\right).$$

The three directions are x increasing, x decreasing and t decreasing. In other words progress is restricted to be either towards the boundaries (along the x directions) or back towards the initial conditions along the direction of t decreasing. As before, N will be the total number of completed walks and T will be the sum of the boundary values or initial values reached.

DESCRIPTIVE STATISTICS

a) Ungrouped Data

The formulas of this section designated as *a*) apply to a random sample of size n, denoted by x_i, $i = 1, 2, \ldots, n$.

b) Grouped Data

The formulas of this section designated as *b*) apply to data grouped into a frequency distribution having class marks x_i, $i = 1, 2, \ldots, k$, and corresponding class frequencies f_i, $i = 1, 2, \ldots, k$. The total number of observations given by

$$n = \sum_{i=1}^{k} f_i$$

In the formulas that follow, c denotes the width of the class interval, x_o denotes one of the class marks taken to be the computing origin, and $u_i = \dfrac{x_i - x_o}{c}$. Then coded class marks are obtained by replacing the original class marks with the integers $\ldots, -3, -2, -1, 0, 1, 2, 3, \ldots$ where 0 corresponds to class mark x_o in the original scale.

Mean (Arithmetic Mean)

a) $\quad \bar{x} = \dfrac{1}{n} \sum_{i=1}^{n} x_i = \dfrac{x_1 + x_2 + \cdots + x_n}{n}$

b.1) $\quad \bar{x} = \dfrac{1}{n} \sum_{i=1}^{k} f_i x_i = \dfrac{f_1 x_1 + f_2 x_2 + \cdots + f_k x_k}{n}$

If data is coded

b.2) $\quad \bar{x} = x_o + c \, \dfrac{\sum\limits_{i=1}^{k} f_i u_i}{n}$

Weighted Mean (Weighted Arithmetic Mean)

If with each value x_i is associated a weighting factor $w_i \geq 0$, then $\sum\limits_{i=1}^{n} w_i$ is the total weight, and

a) $\quad \bar{x} = \dfrac{\sum\limits_{i=1}^{n} w_i x_i}{\sum\limits_{i=1}^{n} w_i} = \dfrac{w_1 x_1 + w_2 x_2 + \cdots + w_n x_n}{w_1 + w_2 + \cdots + w_n}$

Geometric Mean

a) $\quad \text{G.M.} = \sqrt[n]{x_1 \cdot x_2 \cdots x_n}$

In logarithmic form

$$\log (\text{G.M.}) = \frac{1}{n} \sum_{i=1}^{n} \log x_i = \frac{\log x_1 + \log x_2 + \cdots + \log x_n}{n}$$

b) $\text{G.M.} = \sqrt[n]{x_1^{f_1} \cdot x_2^{f_2} \cdots x_k^{f_k}}$

In logarithmic form

$$\log (\text{G.M.}) = \frac{1}{n} \sum_{i=1}^{k} f_i \log x_i = \frac{f_1 \log x_1 + f_2 \log x_2 + \cdots + f_k \log x_k}{n}$$

Harmonic Mean

a) $\text{H.M.} = \dfrac{n}{\displaystyle\sum_{i=1}^{n} \dfrac{1}{x_i}} = \dfrac{n}{\dfrac{1}{x_1} + \dfrac{1}{x_2} + \cdots + \dfrac{1}{x_n}}$

b) $\text{H.M.} = \dfrac{n}{\displaystyle\sum_{i=1}^{k} \dfrac{f_i}{x_i}} = \dfrac{n}{\dfrac{f_1}{x_1} + \dfrac{f_2}{x_2} + \cdots + \dfrac{f_k}{x_k}}$

Relation Between Arithmetic, Geometric, and Harmonic Mean

$\text{H.M.} \leq \text{G.M.} \leq \bar{x}$, (Equality sign holds only if all sample values are identical.)

Mode

a) A mode M_o of a sample of size n is a value which occurs with greatest frequency, i.e., it is the most common value. A mode may not exist, and even if it does exist it may not be unique.

b) $M_o = L + c \dfrac{\Delta_1}{\Delta_1 + \Delta_2}$,

where L is the lower class boundary of the modal class (class containing the mode),

Δ_1 is the excess of modal frequency over frequency of next lower class,

Δ_2 is the excess of modal frequency over frequency of next higher class.

Median

a) If the sample is arranged in ascending order of magnitude, then the median M_d is given by the $\dfrac{n + 1}{2}$ nd value. When n is odd, the median is the middle value of the set of ordered data; when n is even, the median is usually taken as the mean of the two middle values of the set of ordered data.

b) $M_d = L + c \dfrac{\dfrac{n}{2} - F_c}{f_m}$,

where L is lower class boundary of median class (class containing the median),

F_c is the sum of the frequencies of all classes lower than the median class,

f_m is the frequency of the median class.

Empirical Relation Between Mean, Median, and Mode

$$\text{Mean} - \text{Mode} = 3\,(\text{Mean} - \text{Median})$$

Quartiles

    a) If the data is arranged in ascending order of magnitude, the jth quartile Q_j, $j = 1$, 2, or 3, is given by the $\dfrac{j(n+1)}{4}$ th value. It may be necessary to interpolate between successive values.

    b) The jth quartile Q_j, $j = 1$, 2, or 3, is obtained from formula *b)* for the median by counting $\dfrac{jn}{4}$ cases starting at the bottom of the distribution.

Deciles

    a) If the sample is arranged in ascending order of magnitude, the jth decile D_j, $j = 1, 2, \ldots$, or 9, is given by the $\dfrac{j(n+1)}{10}$ th value. It may be necessary to interpolate between successive values.

    b) The jth decile D_j, $j = 1, 2, \ldots$, or 9, is obtained from formula *b)* for the median by counting $\dfrac{jn}{10}$ cases starting at the bottom of the distribution.

Percentiles

    a) If the sample is arranged in ascending order of magnitude, the jth percentile P_j, $j = 1. 2, \ldots$, or 99 is given by the $\dfrac{j(n+1)}{100}$ th value. It may be necessary to interpolate between successive values.

    b) The jth percentile P_j, $j = 1, 2, \ldots$, or 99, is obtained from formulas *b)* for the median by counting $\dfrac{jn}{100}$ cases starting at the bottom of the distribution.

Mean Deviation

    a) $\text{M.D.} = \dfrac{1}{n} \sum\limits_{i=1}^{n} |x_i - \bar{x}|$

or

$$\text{M.D.} = \frac{1}{n} \sum_{i=1}^{n} |x_i - M_d|$$

where $\bar{x}$ is the mean and M_d is the median of the sample.

    b) $\text{M.D.} = \dfrac{1}{n} \sum\limits_{i=1}^{k} f_i |x_i - \bar{x}|$

or

$$\text{M.D.} = \frac{1}{n} \sum_{i=1}^{k} f_i |x_i - M_d|$$

where $\bar{x}$ is the mean and M_d the median of the sample.

Standard Deviation

a) $s = \sqrt{\dfrac{\sum\limits_{i=1}^{n} (x_i - \bar{x})^2}{n - 1}}$, where $\bar{x}$ is the mean of the sample.

For computational purposes,

$$s = \sqrt{\frac{\sum\limits_{i=1}^{n} x_i^2 - n\bar{x}^2}{n - 1}}$$

$$s = \sqrt{\frac{n \sum\limits_{i=1}^{n} x_i^2 - \left(\sum\limits_{i=1}^{n} x_i\right)^2}{n(n - 1)}}$$

b) $s = \sqrt{\dfrac{\sum\limits_{i=1}^{k} f_i(x_i - \bar{x})^2}{n - 1}}$, where $\bar{x}$ is the mean of the sample.

For computational purposes

$$s = \sqrt{\frac{\sum\limits_{i=1}^{k} f_i x_i^2 - n\bar{x}^2}{n - 1}}$$

$$s = \sqrt{\frac{n \sum\limits_{i=1}^{k} f_i x_i^2 - \left(\sum\limits_{i=1}^{k} f_i x_i\right)^2}{n(n - 1)}}$$

If data is coded,

$$s = c \sqrt{\frac{n \sum\limits_{i=1}^{k} f_i u_i^2 - \left(\sum\limits_{i=1}^{k} f_i u_i\right)^2}{n(n - 1)}}$$

Variance

The variance is the square of the standard deviation.

Range

The range of a set of values is the difference between the largest and smallest values in the set.

Root Mean Square

a) $\text{R.M.S.} = \left[\dfrac{1}{n} \sum\limits_{i=1}^{n} x_i^2\right]^{\frac{1}{2}}$

b) $\text{R.M.S.} = \left[\dfrac{1}{n} \sum\limits_{i=1}^{k} f_i x_i^2\right]^{\frac{1}{2}}$

Interquartile Range

$$Q_3 - Q_1,$$

where Q_1 and Q_3 are the first and third quartiles.

Quartile Deviation (Semi-Interquartile Range)

$$\frac{Q_3 - Q_1}{2},$$

where Q_1 and Q_3 are the first and third quartiles.

Coefficient of Variation

$$V = \frac{100s}{\bar{x}},$$

where $\bar{x}$ is the mean and s the standard deviation of the sample.

Coefficient of Quartile Variation

$$V = 100 \frac{Q_3 - Q_1}{Q_3 + Q_1},$$

where Q_1 and Q_3 are the first and third quartiles.

Standardized Variable (Standard Scores)

$$z = \frac{x_i - \bar{x}}{s},$$

where $\bar{x}$ is the mean and s the standard deviation of the sample.

Moments

a) The rth moment about the origin is given by

$$m'_r = \frac{1}{n} \sum_{i=1}^{n} x_i{}^r$$

The rth moment about the mean $\bar{x}$ is given by

$$m_r = \frac{1}{n} \sum_{i=1}^{n} (x_i - \bar{x})^r$$

If $\sum_{i=1}^{n} (x_i - \bar{x})^r$ is expanded by use of the binomial theorem, moments about the mean may be expressed in terms of moments about the origin.

b) The rth moment about the origin is given by

$$m'_r = \frac{1}{n} \sum_{i=1}^{k} f_i x_i{}^r$$

The rth moment about the mean $\bar{x}$ is given by

$$m_r = \frac{1}{n} \sum_{i=1}^{k} f_i (x_i - \bar{x})^r$$

If $\sum_{i=1}^{k} f_i(x_i - \bar{x})^r$ is expanded by use of the binomial theorem, moments about the mean may be expressed in terms of moments about the origin.

If data is coded

$$m_r' = c^r \frac{\sum_{i=1}^{k} f_i u_i^r}{n}$$

Coefficient of Skewness

$$\alpha_3 = \frac{m_3}{(m_2)^{3/2}},$$

where m_2 and m_3 are the second and third moments about the mean of the sample.

Coefficient of Momental Skewness

$$\frac{\alpha_3}{2} = \frac{m_3}{2(m_2)^{3/2}},$$

where m_2 and m_3 are the second and third moments about the mean of the sample.

Pearson's First Coefficient of Skewness

$$S_{k_1} = \frac{3(\bar{x} - M_o)}{s},$$

where $\bar{x}$ is the mean, M_o the mode, and s the standard deviation of the sample.

Pearson's Second Coefficient of Skewness

$$S_{k_2} = \frac{3(\bar{x} - M_d)}{s},$$

where $\bar{x}$ is the mean, M_d the median, and s the standard deviation of the sample.

Quartile Coefficient of Skewness

$$S_{k_Q} = \frac{Q_3 - 2Q_2 + Q_1}{Q_3 - Q_1},$$

where Q_1, Q_2, and Q_3 are the first, second, and third quartiles.

Coefficient of Kurtosis

$$\alpha_4 = \frac{m_4}{(m_2)^2},$$

where m_2 and m_4 are the second and fourth moments about the mean of the sample.

Coefficient of Excess (Kurtosis)

$$\alpha_4 - 3 = \frac{m_4}{(m_2)^2} - 3,$$

where m_2 and m_4 are the second and fourth moments about the mean of the sample.

Sheppards Corrections for Grouping

Let all class intervals be of equal length c. If the distribution of x has a high order of contact with the x-axis at both tails, (i.e., if the distribution of x has tails which are very

nearly tangent to the x-axis), one may improve the grouped data approximation to the variance by adding Sheppard's correction $-\dfrac{c^2}{12}$. Thus

$$\text{corrected variance} = \text{grouped data variance} - \frac{c^2}{12}$$

Analogous corrections for grouped data sample moments

$$m'_r = \frac{1}{n} \sum_{i=1}^{k} f_i x_i{}^r \qquad \text{and} \qquad m_r = \frac{1}{n} \sum_{i=1}^{k} f_i (x_i - \bar{x})^r$$

yield improved estimates m'_{r_e} and m_{r_e} given by

$$m'_{1_e} = m'_1 \qquad\qquad\qquad m_{1_e} = m_1$$

$$m'_{2_e} = m'_2 - \frac{c^2}{12} \qquad\qquad m_{2_e} = m_2 - \frac{c^2}{12}$$

$$m'_{3_e} = m'_3 - \frac{c^2}{4} m'_1 \qquad\qquad m_{3_e} = m_3$$

$$m'_{4_e} = m'_4 - \frac{c^2}{2} m'_1 + \frac{7c^4}{240} \qquad m_{4_e} = m_4 - \frac{c^2}{2} m_2 + \frac{7c^4}{240}$$

Curve Fitting, Regression, and Correlation

The following formulas apply to a set of n ordered pairs $\{(x_i, y_i)\}$, $i = 1, 2, \ldots, n$. The assumptions of normal regression analysis are that the x's are fixed variables, and the y's are independent random variables having normal distributions with common variance σ^2. The assumptions of normal correlation analysis are that $\{(x_i, y_i)\}$ constitute a random sample from a bivariate normal population.

Curve Fitting

1. Polynomial Function

$$y = b_0 + b_1 x + b_2 x^2 + \cdots + b_m x^m$$

For a polynomial function fit by the method of least squares, the values of $b_0, b_1, \ldots, b_m$ are obtained by solving the system of $m + 1$ normal equations

$$nb_0 + b_1 \Sigma x_i + b_2 \Sigma x_i{}^2 + \cdots + b_m \Sigma x_i{}^m = \Sigma y_i$$
$$b_0 \Sigma x_i + b_1 \Sigma x_i{}^2 + b_2 \Sigma x_i{}^3 + \cdots + b_m \Sigma x_i{}^{m+1} = \Sigma x_i y_i$$
$$\cdots \cdots \cdots \cdots \cdots \cdots \cdots \cdots \cdots \cdots \cdots$$
$$b_0 \Sigma x_i{}^m + b_1 \Sigma x_i{}^{m+1} + b_2 \Sigma x_i{}^{m+2} + \cdots + b_m \Sigma x_i{}^{2m} = \Sigma x_i{}^m y_i$$

2. Straight Line

$$y = b_0 + b_1 x$$

For a straight line fit by the method of least squares, the values b_0 and b_1 are obtained by solving the normal equations

$$nb_0 + b_1 \Sigma x_i = \Sigma y_i$$
$$b_0 \Sigma x_i + b_1 \Sigma x_i{}^2 = \Sigma x_i y_i$$

The solutions of these normal equations are

$$b_1 = \frac{n\Sigma x_i y_i - (\Sigma x_i)(\Sigma y_i)}{n\Sigma x_i{}^2 - (\Sigma x_i)^2}$$

$$b_0 = \frac{\Sigma y_i}{n} - b_1 \frac{\Sigma x_i}{n} = \bar{y} - b_1 \bar{x}$$

3. Exponential Curve

$$y = ab^x$$

or

$$\log y = \log a + (\log b)x$$

For an exponential curve fit by the method of least squares, the values $\log a$ and $\log b$ are obtained by fitting a straight line to the set of ordered pairs $\{(x_i, \log y_i)\}$.

4. Power Function

$$y = ax^b$$

or

$$\log y = \log a + b \log x$$

For a power function fit by the method of least squares, the values $\log a$ and b are obtained by fitting a straight line to the set of ordered pairs $\{(\log x_i, \log y_i)\}$.

Regression and Correlation

1. Simple Linear Regression.

For a regression of y on x

$$E(y/x) = b_0 + b_1 x,$$

where $E(y/x)$ is the mean of the distribution of y for a given x.

Standard Error of Estimate

$$s_e = \sqrt{\frac{\Sigma[y_i - (b_0 + b_1 x_i)]^2}{n - 2}},$$

where b_0 and b_1 are given by

$$b_1 = \frac{n\Sigma x_i y_i - (\Sigma x_i)(\Sigma y_i)}{n\Sigma x_i^2 - (\Sigma x_i)^2}$$

$$b_0 = \frac{\Sigma y_i}{n} - b_1 \frac{\Sigma x_i}{n} = \bar{y} - b_1 \bar{x}$$

2. Correlation.

An estimate of the population correlation coefficient ρ is given by

$$r = \frac{\Sigma(x_i - \bar{x})(y_i - \bar{y})}{\sqrt{[\Sigma(x_i - \bar{x})^2][\Sigma(y_i - \bar{y})^2]}}$$

or by the computing formula

$$r = \frac{n\Sigma x_i y_i - (\Sigma x_i)(\Sigma y_i)}{\sqrt{[n\Sigma x_i^2 - (\Sigma x_i)^2][n\Sigma y_i^2 - (\Sigma y_i)^2]}}$$

For grouped data

$$r = \frac{n\Sigma f x_i y_i - (\Sigma f_x x_i)(\Sigma f_y y_i)}{\sqrt{[n\Sigma f_x x_i^2 - (\Sigma f_x x_i)^2][n\Sigma f_y y_i^2 - (\Sigma f_y y_i)^2]}}$$

where f_x and f_y denote the frequencies corresponding to the class marks x and y, and f denotes the frequency of the corresponding cell of the correlation table.

If the data is coded

$$r = \frac{n\Sigma f uv - (\Sigma f_u u)(\Sigma f_v v)}{\sqrt{[n\Sigma f_u u^2 - (\Sigma f_u u)^2][n\Sigma f_v v^2 - (\Sigma f_v v)^2]}}$$

where the u's and v's are coded class marks. The frequencies f_u and f_v are defined analogous to f_x and f_y.

PROBABILITY

Definitions

A sample space S associated with an experiment is a set S of elements such that any outcome of the experiment corresponds to one and only one element of the set. An event E is a subset of a sample space S. An element in a sample space is called a sample point or a simple event (Unit subset of S).

Definition of Probability

If an experiment can occur in n mutually exclusive and equally likely ways, and if exactly m of these ways correspond to an event E, then the probability of E is given by

$$P(E) = \frac{m}{n}.$$

If E is a subset of S, and if to each unit subset of S, a non-negative number, called its probability, is assigned, and if E is the union of two or more different simple events, then the probability of E, denoted by $P(E)$, is the sum of the probabilities of those simple events whose union is E.

Marginal and Conditional Probability

Suppose a sample space S is partioned into rs disjoint subsets where the general subset is denoted by $E_i \cap F_j$. Then the marginal probability of E_i is defined as

$$P(E_i) = \sum_{j=1}^{s} P(E_i \cap F_j)$$

and the marginal probability of F_j is defined as

$$P(F_j) = \sum_{i=1}^{r} P(E_i \cap F_j)$$

The conditional probability of E_i, given that F_j has occurred, is defined as

$$P(E_i/F_j) = \frac{P(E_i \cap F_j)}{P(F_j)} , \qquad P(F_j) \neq 0$$

and that of F_j, given that E_i has occurred, is defined as

$$P(F_j/E_i) = \frac{P(E_i \cap F_j)}{P(E_i)} , \qquad P(E_i) \neq 0 .$$

Probability Theorems

1. If ϕ is the null set, $P(\phi) = 0$.
2. If S is the sample space, $P(S) = 1$.
3. If E and F are two events

$$P(E \cup F) = P(E) + P(F) - P(E \cap F).$$

4. If E and F are mutually exclusive events,

$$P(E \cup F) = P(E) + P(F).$$

5. If E and E' are complementary events,

$$P(E) = 1 - P(E').$$

6. The conditional probability of an event E, given an event F, is denoted by $P(E/F)$ and is defined as

$$P(E/F) = \frac{P(E \cap F)}{P(F)},$$

where $P(F) \neq 0$.

7. Two events E and F are said to be independent if and only if

$$P(E \cap F) = P(E) \cdot P(F).$$

E is said to be statistically independent of F if $P(E/F) = P(E)$ and $P(F/E) = P(F)$.

8. The events $E_1, E_2, \ldots, E_n$ are called mutually independent for all combinations if and only if every combination of these events taken any number at a time is independent.

9. *Bayes Theorem.*

If $E_1, E_2, \ldots, E_n$ are n mutually exclusive events whose union is the sample space S, and E is any arbitrary event of S such that $P(E) \neq 0$, then

$$P(E_k/E) = \frac{P(E_k) \cdot P(E/E_k)}{\sum_{j=1}^{n} [P(E_j) \cdot P(E/E_j)]}$$

Random Variable

A function whose domain is a sample space S and whose range is some set of real numbers is called a random variable, denoted by $\mathbf{X}$. The function $\mathbf{X}$ transforms sample points of S into points on the x-axis. $\mathbf{X}$ will be called a discrete random variable if it is a random variable that assumes only a finite or denumerable number of values on the x-axis. $\mathbf{X}$ will be called a continuous random variable if it assumes a continuum of values on the x-axis.

Probability Function (Discrete Case)

The random variable $\mathbf{X}$ will be called a discrete random variable if there exists a function f such that $f(x_i) \geq 0$ and $\sum_i f(x_i) = 1$ for $i = 1, 2, 3, \ldots$ and such that for any event E,

$$P(E) = P[\mathbf{X} \text{ is in } E] = \sum_E f(x)$$

where $\sum_E$ means sum $f(x)$ over those values x_i that are in E and where $f(x) = P[\mathbf{X} = x]$. The probability that the value of $\mathbf{X}$ is some real number x, is given by $f(x) = P[\mathbf{X} = x]$, where f is called the probability function of the random variable $\mathbf{X}$.

Cumulative Distribution Function (Discrete Case)

The probability that the value of a random variable $\mathbf{X}$ is less than or equal to some real number x is defined as

$$F(x) = P(X \leq x)$$
$$= \Sigma f(x_i), \qquad -\infty < x < \infty,$$

where the summation extends over those values of i such that $x_i \leq x$.

Probability Density (Continuous Case)

The random variable X will be called a continuous random variable if there exists a function f such that $f(x) \geq 0$ and $\int_{-\infty}^{\infty} f(x)\, dx = 1$ for all x in interval $-\infty < x < \infty$ and such that for any event E

$$P(E) = P(X \text{ is in } E) = \int_E f(x)\, dx.$$

$f(x)$ is called the probability density of the random variable X. The probability that X assumes any given value of x is equal to zero and the probability that it assumes a value on the interval from a to b, including or excluding either end point, is equal to

$$\int_a^b f(x)\, dx.$$

Cumulative Distribution Function (Continuous Case)

The probability that the value of a random variable X is less than or equal to some real number x is defined as

$$F(x) = P(X \leq x), \qquad -\infty < x < \infty$$
$$= \int_{-\infty}^{x} f(x)\, dx.$$

From the cumulative distribution, the density, if it exists, can be found from

$$f(x) = \frac{dF(x)}{dx}.$$

From the cumulative distribution

$$P(a \leq X \leq b) = P(X \leq b) - P(X \leq a)$$
$$= F(b) - F(a)$$

Mathematical Expectation

A. EXPECTED VALUE

Let X be a random variable with density $f(x)$. Then the expected value of X, $E(X)$, is defined to be

$$E(X) = \sum_x x f(x)$$

if X is discrete and

$$E(X) = \int_{-\infty}^{\infty} x f(x)\, dx$$

if X is continuous. The expected value of a function g of a random variable X is defined as

$$E[g(X)] = \sum_x g(x) \cdot f(x)$$

if X is discrete and

$$E[g(X)] = \int_{-\infty}^{\infty} g(x) \cdot f(x)\, dx$$

if X is continuous.

Theorems

1. $E[aX + bY] = aE(X) + bE(Y)$
2. $E[X \cdot Y] = E(X) \cdot E(Y)$ if X and Y are statistically independent.

B. Moments

a. *Moments About the Origin.* The moments about the origin of a probability distribution are the expected values of the random variable which has the given distribution. The rth moment of X, usually denoted by μ'_r, is defined as

$$\mu'_r = E[X^r] = \sum_x x^r f(x)$$

if X is discrete and

$$\mu'_r = E[X^r] = \int_{-\infty}^{\infty} x^r f(x) \, dx$$

if X is continuous.

The first moment, μ'_1, is called the mean of the random variable X and is usually denoted by μ.

b. *Moments About the Mean.* The rth moment about the mean, usually denoted by μ_r, is defined as

$$\mu_r = E[(X - \mu)^r] = \sum_x (x - \mu)^r f(x)$$

if X is discrete and

$$\mu_r = E[(X - \mu)^r] = \int_{-\infty}^{\infty} (x - \mu)^r f(x) \, dx$$

if X is continuous.

The second moment about the mean, μ_2, is given by

$$\mu_2 = E[(X - \mu)^2] = \mu'_2 - \mu^2$$

and is called the variance of the random variable X, and is denoted by σ^2. The square root of the variance, σ, is called the standard deviation.

Theorems

1. $\sigma^2_{cX} = c^2 \sigma^2_X$
2. $\sigma^2_{c+X} = \sigma^2_X$
3. $\sigma^2_{aX+b} = a^2 \sigma^2_X$

c. *Factorial Moments.* The rth factorial moment of a probability distribution is defined as

$$\mu'_{(r)} = E[X^{[r]}] = \sum_x x^{[r]} f(x)$$

if X is discrete and

$$\mu'_{(r)} = E[X^{[r]}] = \int_{-\infty}^{\infty} x^{[r]} f(x) \, dx$$

if X is continuous, where the symbol $x^{[r]}$ denotes the factorial expression

$$x^{[r]} = x(x - 1)(x - 2) \cdots (x - r + 1), \, r = 1, 2, 3, \ldots .$$

C. Generating Functions

a. Moment Generating Functions. The moment generating function (m.g.f.) of the random variable X is defined as

$$m_x(t) = E(e^{tX}) = \sum_x e^{tx} f(x)$$

if X is discrete and

$$m_x(t) = E(e^{tX}) = \int_{-\infty}^{\infty} e^{tx} f(x)\, dx$$

if X is continuous.

$E(e^{tX})$ is the expected value of e^{tX}. If $m_x(t)$ and its derivatives exist, $|t| < h^2$, the rth moment about the origin is

$$\mu'_r = m_x^{(r)}(0), \qquad r = 0, 1, 2, \ldots$$

where $m_x^{(r)}(0)$ is the rth derivative of $m_x(t)$ with respect to t, evaluated at $t = 0$. For

$$
\begin{aligned}
m_x(t) &= E(e^{tX}) \\
&= E\left[1 + Xt + \frac{(Xt)^2}{2!} + \cdots\right] \\
&= 1 + \mu'_1 t + \mu'_2 \frac{t^2}{2} + \cdots
\end{aligned}
$$

Thus, the moments μ'_r appear as coefficients of $\dfrac{t^r}{r!}$, and $m_x(t)$ may be regarded as generating the moments ν_r. The moments μ_r may be generated by the generating function

$$M_x(t) = E[e^{t(X-\mu)}] = e^{-\mu t} E(e^{tX}) = e^{-\mu t} m_x(t) .$$

b. Factorial Moment Generating Function. The factorial moment generating function is defined as

$$E(t^X) = \sum_x t^x f(x) \qquad \text{(probability generation function)}$$

if X is discrete and

$$E(t^X) = \int_{-\infty}^{\infty} t^x f(x)\, dx$$

if X is continuous.

The rth factorial moment is obtained from the factorial moment generating function by differentiating it r times with respect to t and then evaluating the result when $t = 1$.

Theorems

1. If c is a constant, the m.g.f. of $c + X$ is $e^{ct} m_x(t)$.
2. If c is a constant, the m.g.f. of cX is $m_x(ct)$.
3. If $Y = \sum_{i=1}^{n} X_i$, and $m_x(t)$ is the m.g.f. of X_i, where $X_1, \ldots, X_n$ is a random sample from $f(x)$, then the m.g.f. of Y is $[m_x(t)]^n$.

D. Cumulant Generating Function

Let $m_x(t)$ be a m.g.f. If $\ln m_x(t)$ can be expanded in the form

$$c(t) = \ln m_x(t) = \kappa_1 t + \kappa_2 \frac{t^2}{2!} + \kappa_3 \frac{t^3}{3!} + \cdots + \kappa_r \frac{t^r}{r!} + \cdots,$$

then $c(t)$ is called the cumulant generating function (semi-invariant generating function) and κ_r are called the cumulants (semi-invariants) of a distribution.

$$\kappa_r = c^{(r)}(0)$$

where $c^{(r)}(0)$ is the rth derivative of $c(t)$ with respect to t evaluated at $t = 0$.

E. CHARACTERISTIC FUNCTIONS

The characteristic function of a distribution is defined as

$$\phi(t) = E(e^{itX}) = \sum_x e^{itx} \cdot f(x)$$

if **X** is discrete and

$$\phi(t) = E(e^{itX}) = \int_{-\infty}^{\infty} e^{itx} \cdot f(x) \, dx$$

if **X** is continuous.

Here t is a real number, $i^2 = -1$, and $e^{itX} = \cos(tX) + i\sin(tX)$. The characteristic function also generates moments, if they exist for

$$i^r \mu'_r = \phi^{(r)}(0)$$

where $\phi^{(r)}(0)$ is the rth derivative of $\phi(t)$ with respect to t evaluated at $t = 0$.

Multivariate Distributions

A. DISCRETE CASE

The k-dimensional random variable $(X_1, X_2, \ldots, X_k)$ is a k-dimensional discrete random variable if it assumes values only at a finite or denumerable number of points $(x_1, x_2, \ldots, x_k)$. Define

$$P[X_1 = x_1, X_2 = x_2, \ldots, X_k = x_k] = f(x_1, x_2, \ldots, x_k)$$

for every value that the random variable can assume. $f(x_1, x_2, \ldots, x_k)$ is called the joint density of the k-dimensional random variable. If E is any subset of the set of values that the random variable can assume, then

$$P(E) = P[(X_1, X_2, \ldots, X_k) \text{ is in } E] = \sum_E f(x_1, x_2, \ldots, x_k)$$

where the sum is over all those points in E. The cumulative distribution is defined as

$$F(x_1, x_2, \ldots, x_k) = \sum_{x_1} \sum_{x_2} \cdots \sum_{x_k} f(x_1, x_2, \ldots, x_k).$$

B. CONTINUOUS CASE

The k random variables $X_1, X_2, \ldots, X_k$ are said to be jointly distributed if there exists a function f such that $f(x_1, x_2, \ldots, x_k) \geq 0$ for all $-\infty < x_i < \infty$, $i = 1, 2, \ldots, k$ and such that for any event E

$$P(E) = P[(X_1, X_2, \ldots, X_k) \text{ is in } E]$$
$$= \int_E f(x_1, x_2, \ldots, x_k) \, dx_1 \, dx_2 \cdots dx_k.$$

$f(x_1, x_2, \ldots, x_k)$ is called the joint density of the random variables $X_1, X_2, \ldots, X_k$. The cumulative distribution is defined as

$$F(x_1, x_2, \ldots, x_k) = \int_{-\infty}^{x_1} \int_{-\infty}^{x_2} \cdots \int_{-\infty}^{x_k} f(x_1, x_2, \ldots, x_k) \, dx_k \cdots dx_2 \, dx_1 \, .$$

Given the cumulative distribution, the density may be found by

$$f(x_1, x_2, \ldots, x_k) = \frac{\partial}{\partial x_1} \cdot \frac{\partial}{\partial x_2} \cdots \frac{\partial}{\partial x_k} F(x_1, x_2, \ldots, x_k) \ .$$

Moments

The rth moment of X_i, say, is defined as

$$E(X_i^r) = \sum_{x_1} \sum_{x_2} \cdots \sum_{x_k} x_i^r f(x_1, x_2, \ldots, x_k)$$

if the X_i are discrete and

$$E(X_i^r) = \int_{-\infty}^{\infty} \int_{-\infty}^{\infty} \cdots \int_{-\infty}^{\infty} x_i^r f(x_1, x_2, \ldots, x_k) \, dx_k \cdots dx_2 \, dx_1$$

if the X_i are continuous.

Joint moments about the origin are defined as

$$E(X_1^{r_1} X_2^{r_2} \cdots X_k^{r_k})$$

where $r_1 + r_2 + \cdots + r_k$ is the order of the moment.

Joint moments about the mean are defined as

$$E[(X_1 - \mu_1)^{r_1}(X_2 - \mu_2)^{r_2} \cdots (X_k - \mu_k)^{r_k}].$$

Marginal and Conditional Distributions

If the random variables $X_1, X_2, \ldots, X_k$ have the joint density function $f(x_1, x_2, \ldots, x_k)$, then the marginal distribution of the subset of the random variables, say, $X_1, X_2, \ldots, X_p$ ($p < k$), is given by

$$g(x_1, x_2, \ldots, x_p) = \sum_{x_{p+1}} \sum_{x_{p+1}} \cdots \sum_{x_k} f(x_1, x_2, \ldots, x_k)$$

if the X's are discrete, and

$$g(x_1, x_2, \ldots, x_p) = \int_{-\infty}^{\infty} \int_{-\infty}^{\infty} \cdots \int_{-\infty}^{\infty} f(x_1, x_2, \ldots, x_k) \, dx_{p+1} \cdots dx_{k-1} \, dx_k$$

if the X's are continuous.

The conditional distribution of a certain subset of the random variables is the joint distribution of this subset under the condition that the remaining variables are given certain values. The conditional distribution of $X_1, X_2, \ldots, X_p$ given $X_{p+1}, X_{p+2}, \ldots, X_k$ is

$$h(x_1, x_2, \ldots, x_p | x_{p+1}, x_{p+2}, \ldots, x_k) = \frac{f(x_1, x_2, \ldots, x_k)}{g(x_{p+1}, x_{p+2}, \ldots, x_k)}$$

if $g(x_{p+1}, x_{p+2}, \ldots, x_k) \neq 0$.

The variance σ_{ii} of X_i and the covariance σ_{ij} of X_i and X_j are given by

$$\sigma_{ii} = \sigma_i^2 = E[(X_i - \mu_i)^2]$$

and

$$\sigma_{ij} = \rho_{ij}\sigma_i\sigma_j = E[(X_i - \mu_i)(X_j - \mu_j)]$$

where ρ_{ij} is the correlation coefficient and σ_i and σ_j are the standard deviations of X_i and X_j.

A joint m.g.f. is defined as

$$m(t_1, t_2, \ldots, t_k) = E[e^{t_1 \mathbf{X}_1 + t_2 \mathbf{X}_2 + \cdots + t_k \mathbf{X}_k}]$$

if it exists for all values of t_i such that $|t_i| < h^2$.

The rth moment of $\mathbf{X}_i$ may be obtained by differentiating the m.g.f. r times with respect to t_i and then evaluating the result when all t's are set equal to zero. Similarly, a joint moment would be found by differentiatins the m.g.f. r_1 times with respect to t_1, . . . , r_k times with respect to t_k, and then evaluating the result when all t's are set equal to zero.

Probability Distributions

A. DISCRETE CASE

1. *Discrete Uniform Distribution.* If the random variable $\mathbf{X}$ has a probability function given by

$$P(\mathbf{X} = x) = f(x) = \frac{1}{n}, \qquad x = x_1, x_2, \ldots, x_n,$$

then the variable $\mathbf{X}$ is said to possess a discrete uniform distribution.

Properties

When $x_i = i$ for $i = 1, 2, \ldots,$ and n

$$\text{Mean} = \mu = \frac{n + 1}{2}$$

$$\text{Variance} = \sigma^2 = \frac{n^2 - 1}{12}$$

$$\text{Standard Deviation} = \sigma = \sqrt{\frac{n^2 - 1}{12}}$$

$$\text{Moment Generating Function} = m_x(t) = \frac{e^t(1 - e^{nt})}{n(1 - e^t)}$$

2. *Binomial Distribution.* If the random variable $\mathbf{X}$ has a probability function given by

$$P(\mathbf{X} = x) = f(x) = \binom{n}{x} \theta^x (1 - \theta)^{n-x}, \qquad x = 0, 1, 2, \ldots, n$$

where

$$\binom{n}{x} = \frac{n!}{x!(n - x)!},$$

then the variable $\mathbf{X}$ is said to possess a binomial distribution. $f(x)$ is the general term of the expansion of $[\theta + (1 - \theta)]^n$.

Properties

$$\text{Mean} = \mu = n\theta$$
$$\text{Variance} = \sigma^2 = n\theta(1 - \theta)$$
$$\text{Standard Deviation} = \sigma = \sqrt{n\theta(1 - \theta)}$$
$$\text{Moment Generating Function} = m_{\mathbf{x}}(t) = [\theta e^t + (1 - \theta)]^n$$

3. *Geometric Distribution.* If the random variable $\mathbf{X}$ has a probability function given by

$$P(\mathbf{X} = x) = f(x) = \theta(1 - \theta)^{x-1}, \qquad x = 1, 2, 3, \ldots,$$

then the variable $\mathbf{X}$ is said to possess a geometric distribution.

Properties

$$\text{Mean} = \mu = \frac{1}{\theta}$$

$$\text{Variance} = \sigma^2 = \frac{1 - \theta}{\theta^2}$$

$$\text{Standard Deviation} = \sigma = \sqrt{\frac{1 - \theta}{\theta^2}}$$

$$\text{Moment Generating Function} = m_x(t) = \frac{\theta e^t}{1 - e^t(1 - \theta)}$$

4. *Multinomial Distribution.* If a set of random variables $\mathbf{X}_1$, $\mathbf{X}_2$, . . . , $\mathbf{X}_n$ has a probability function given by

$$P(\mathbf{X}_1 = x_1, \mathbf{X}_2 = x_2, \ldots, \mathbf{X}_n = x_n) = f(x_1, x_2, \ldots, x_n) = \frac{N!}{\prod_{i=1}^{n} x_i!} \prod_{i=1}^{n} \theta_i^{x_i}$$

where x_i are positive integers and each $\theta_i > 0$ for $i = 1, 2, \ldots, n$ and

$$\sum_{i=1}^{n} \theta_i = 1, \qquad \sum_{i=1}^{n} x_i = N,$$

then the joint distribution of $\mathbf{X}_1$, $\mathbf{X}_2$, . . . , $\mathbf{X}_n$ is called the multinomial distribution. $f(x_1, x_2, \ldots, x_n)$ is the general term of the expansion of $(\theta_1 + \theta_2 + \cdots + \theta_n)^N$.

Properties

$$\text{Mean of } \mathbf{X}_i = \mu_i = N\theta_i$$
$$\text{Variance of } \mathbf{X}_i = \sigma_i^2 = N\theta_i(1 - \theta_i)$$
$$\text{Covariance of } \mathbf{X}_i \text{ and } \mathbf{X}_j = \sigma_{ij}^2 = -N\theta_i\theta_j$$
$$\text{Joint Moment Generating Function} = (\theta_1 e^{t_1} + \cdots + \theta_n e^{t_n})^N$$

5. *Poisson Distribution.* If the random variable $\mathbf{X}$ has a probability function given by

$$P(\mathbf{X} = x) = f(x) = \frac{e^{-\lambda}\lambda^x}{x!}, \qquad \lambda > 0, x = 0, 1, \ldots,$$

then the variable $\mathbf{X}$ is said to possess a Poisson distribution.

Properties

$$\text{Mean} = \mu = \lambda$$
$$\text{Variance} = \sigma^2 = \lambda$$
$$\text{Standard Deviation} = \sigma = \sqrt{\lambda}$$
$$\text{Moment Generating Function} = m_x(t) = e^{\lambda(e^t - 1)}$$

6. *Hypergeometric Distribution.* If the random variable $\mathbf{X}$ has a probability function given by

$$P(\mathbf{X} = x) = f(x) = \frac{\binom{k}{x}\binom{N - k}{n - x}}{\binom{N}{n}}, \qquad x = 0, 1, 2, \ldots, [n, k],$$

where $[n, k]$ means the smaller of the two numbers n, k, then the variable $\mathbf{X}$ is said to possess a hypergeometric distribution.

Properties

$$\text{Mean} = \mu = \frac{kn}{N}$$

$$\text{Variance} = \sigma^2 = \frac{k(N-k)n(N-n)}{N^2(N-1)}$$

$$\text{Standard Deviation} = \sigma = \sqrt{\frac{k(N-k)n(N-n)}{N^2(N-1)}}$$

7. *Negative Binomial Distribution.* If the random variable **X** has a probability function given by

$$P(\mathbf{X} = x) = f(x) = \binom{x+r-1}{r-1} \theta^r (1-\theta)^x, \qquad x = 0, 1, 2, \ldots ;$$

then the variable **X** is said to possess a negative binomial distribution, known also as the Pascal or Pólya distribution.

Properties

$$\text{Mean} = \mu = \frac{r}{\theta}$$

$$\text{Variance} = \sigma^2 = \frac{r}{\theta}\left(\frac{1}{\theta} - 1\right) = \frac{r(1-\theta)}{\theta^2}$$

$$\text{Standard Deviation} = \sigma = \sqrt{\frac{r}{\theta}\left(\frac{1}{\theta} - 1\right)} = \sqrt{\frac{r(1-\theta)}{\theta^2}}$$

$$\text{Moment Generating Function} = m_x(t) = e^{tr}\theta^r[1 - (1-\theta)e^t]^{-r}$$

B. Continuous Case

1. *Uniform Distribution.* A random variable **X** is said to be distributed as the uniform distribution if the density function is given by

$$f(x) = \frac{1}{\beta - \alpha}, \qquad \alpha < x < \beta,$$

where α and β are parameters with $\alpha < \beta$.

Properties

$$\text{Mean} = \mu = \frac{\alpha + \beta}{2}$$

$$\text{Variance} = \sigma^2 = \frac{(\beta - \alpha)^2}{12}$$

$$\text{Standard Deviation} = \sigma = \sqrt{\frac{(\beta - \alpha)^2}{12}}$$

$$\text{Moment Generating Function} = m_x(t) = \frac{2}{(\beta - \alpha)t} \sin\left[\frac{(\beta - \alpha)t}{2}\right] e^{\frac{\alpha + \beta}{2}t}$$

2. *Normal Distribution.* A random variable **X** is said to be normally distributed if its density function is given by

$$f(x) = \frac{1}{\sqrt{2\pi}\,\sigma} e^{-(x-\mu)^2/2\sigma^2}, \qquad -\infty < x < \infty$$

where μ and σ are parameters, called the mean and the standard deviation or the random variable **X**, respectively.

Properties
$$\text{Mean} = \mu$$
$$\text{Variance} = \sigma^2$$
$$\text{Standard Deviation} = \sigma$$

$$\text{Moment Generating Function} = m_x(t) = e^{t\mu + \frac{\sigma^2 t^2}{2}}$$

Cumulative Distribution

$$F(x) = \int_{-\infty}^{x} \frac{1}{\sqrt{2\pi}\,\sigma} e^{-(x-\mu)^2/2\sigma^2}\, dx$$

Set $y = \dfrac{x - \mu}{\sigma}$ to obtain the cumulative standard normal.

3. *Gamma Distribution.* A random variable **X** is said to be distributed as the gamma distribution if the density function is given by

$$f(x) = \frac{1}{\Gamma(\alpha + 1)\beta^{\alpha+1}}\, x^\alpha e^{-x/\beta}, \qquad 0 < x < \infty$$

where α and β are parameters with $\alpha > -1$ and $\beta > 0$.

Properties

$$\text{Mean} = \mu = \beta(\alpha + 1)$$
$$\text{Variance} = \sigma^2 = \beta^2(\alpha + 1)$$
$$\text{Standard Deviation} = \sigma = \beta\sqrt{\alpha + 1}$$
$$\text{Moment Generating Function} = m_x(t) = (1 - \beta t)^{-(\alpha+1)}, \qquad t < \frac{1}{\beta}.$$

4. *Exponential Distribution.* A random variable **X** is said to be distributed as the exponential distribution if the density function is given by

$$f(x) = \frac{1}{\theta}\, e^{-x/\theta}, \qquad x > 0$$

where θ is a parameter and $\theta > 0$.

Properties

$$\text{Mean} = \mu = \theta$$
$$\text{Variance} = \sigma^2 = \theta^2$$
$$\text{Standard Deviation} = \sigma = \sqrt{\theta^2}$$
$$\text{Moment Generating Function} = m_x(t) = (1 - \theta t)^{-1}$$

5. *Beta Distribution.* A random variable **X** is said to be distributed as the beta distribution if the density function is given by

$$f(x) = \frac{\Gamma(\alpha + \beta + 2)}{\Gamma(\alpha + 1)\Gamma(\beta + 1)}\, x^\alpha (1 - x)^\beta, \qquad 0 < x < 1$$

where α and β are parameters with $\alpha > -1$ and $\beta > -1$.

Properties

$$\text{Mean} = \mu = \frac{\alpha + 1}{\alpha + \beta + 2}$$
$$\text{Variance} = \sigma^2 = \frac{(\alpha + 1)(\beta + 1)}{(\alpha + \beta + 2)^2(\alpha + \beta + 3)}$$
$$\text{rth moment about the origin} = \nu_r = \frac{\Gamma(\alpha + \beta + 2)\Gamma(\alpha + r + 1)}{\Gamma(\alpha + \beta + r + 2)\Gamma(\alpha + 1)}.$$

Sampling Distributions

Population—A finite or infinite set of elements of a random variable **X**.

Random Sample—If the random variables **X₁, X₂, . . . , Xₙ** have a joint density,

$$g(x_1, x_2, \ldots, x_n) = f(x_1)f(x_2) \cdots f(x_n)$$

where the density of each X_i is $f(x)$, then $X_1, X_2, \ldots, X_n$ is said to be a random sample of size n from the population with density $f(x)$.

Sampling Distributions

A random sample is selected from a population in which the form of the probability function is known, and from the joint density of the random variables a distribution, called the sampling distribution, of a function of the random variables is derived.

1. *Chi-Square Distribution.* If $Y_1, Y_2, \ldots, Y_n$ are normally and independently distributed with mean 0 and variance 1, then

$$\chi^2 = \sum_{i=1}^{n} Y_i^2$$

is distributed as Chi-Square (χ^2) with n degrees of freedom. The density function is given by

$$f(\chi^2) = \frac{(\chi^2)^{\frac{1}{2}(n-2)}}{2^{\frac{n}{2}}\Gamma\left(\frac{n}{2}\right)} e^{-\chi^2/2}, \qquad 0 < \chi^2 < \infty .$$

The transformation $w = \dfrac{mF/n}{1 + \dfrac{mF}{n}}$ transforms the F-density into a Beta density.

3. *Student's t-Distribution.* If a random variable X is normally distributed with mean 0 and variance σ^2, and if Y^2/σ^2 is distributed as χ^2 with n degrees of freedom and if X and Y are independent, then

$$t = \frac{X\sqrt{n}}{Y}$$

is distributed as Student's t with n degrees of freedom. The density function is given by

$$f(t) = \frac{\Gamma\left(\dfrac{n+1}{2}\right)}{\sqrt{n\pi}\ \Gamma\left(\dfrac{n}{2}\right)\left(1 + \dfrac{t^2}{n}\right)^{\frac{1}{2}(n+1)}}, \qquad -\infty < t < \infty .$$

Properties

$$\text{Mean} = \mu = 0$$

$$\text{Variance} = \sigma^2 = \frac{n}{n-2}, \qquad n > 2 .$$

Properties

$$\text{Mean} = \mu = n$$
$$\text{Variance} = \sigma^2 = 2n$$

Reproductive Property of χ^2 - Distribution

If χ_1^2, χ_2^2, . . . , χ_k^2 are independently distributed according to χ^2 - distributions with n_1, n_2, . . . , n_k degrees of freedom, respectively, then $\sum_{j=1}^{k} \chi_j^2$ is distributed according to a χ^2 - distribution with $n = \sum_{j=1}^{k} n_j$ degrees of freedom.

2. *Snedecor's F-Distribution.* If a random variable $\mathbf{X}$ is distributed as χ^2 with m degrees of freedom (χ_m^2) and a random variable $\mathbf{Y}$ is distributed as χ^2 with n degrees of freedom (χ_n^2) and if $\mathbf{X}$ and $\mathbf{Y}$ are independent, then $F = \dfrac{\mathbf{X}/m}{\mathbf{Y}/n}$ is distributed as Snedecor's F with m and n degrees of freedom, denoted by $F(m, n)$. The density function of the F-distribution is given by

$$f(F) = \frac{\Gamma\left(\dfrac{m+n}{2}\right)\left(\dfrac{m}{n}\right)^{m/2} F^{(m-2)/2}}{\Gamma\left(\dfrac{m}{2}\right)\Gamma\left(\dfrac{n}{2}\right)\left(1 + \dfrac{m}{n}F\right)^{(m+n)/2}}, \qquad 0 < F < \infty.$$

Properties

$$\text{Mean} = \mu = \frac{n}{n-2}, \qquad n > 2$$
$$\text{Variance} = \sigma^2 = \frac{2n^2(m+n-2)}{m(n-2)^2(n-4)}, \qquad n > 4\ .$$

THE NORMAL PROBABILITY FUNCTION
AND RELATED FUNCTIONS

This table gives values of:

a) $f(x) =$ the probability density of a standardized random variable

$$= \frac{1}{\sqrt{2\pi}} e^{-\frac{1}{2}x^2}$$

For negative values of x, one uses the fact that $f(-x) = f(x)$.

b) $F(x) =$ the cumulative distribution function of a standardized normal random variable

$$= \int_{-\infty}^{x} \frac{1}{\sqrt{2\pi}} e^{-\frac{1}{2}t^2} dt$$

For negative values of x, one uses the relationship $F(-x) = 1 - F(x)$. Values of x corresponding to a few special values of $F(x)$ are given in a separate table following the main table.

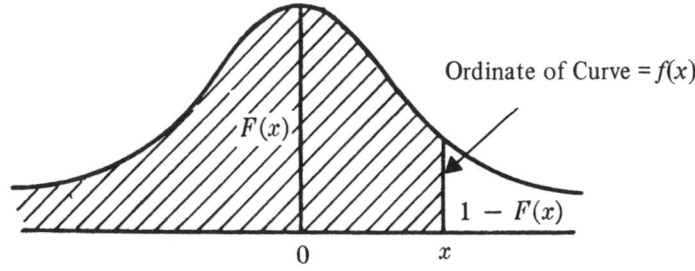

c) $f'(x) =$ the first derivative of $f(x)$ with respect to x

$$= -\frac{x}{\sqrt{2\pi}} e^{-\frac{1}{2}x^2} = -xf(x)$$

d) $f''(x) =$ the second derivative of $f(x)$ with respect to x

$$= \frac{(x^2 - 1)}{\sqrt{2\pi}} e^{-\frac{1}{2}x^2} = (x^2 - 1)f(x)$$

e) $f'''(x) =$ the third derivative of $f(x)$ with respect to x

$$= \frac{3x - x^3}{\sqrt{2\pi}} e^{-\frac{1}{2}x^2} = (3x - x^3)f(x)$$

f) $f^{iv}(x) =$ the fourth derivative of $f(x)$ with respect to x

$$= \frac{x^4 - 6x^2 + 3}{\sqrt{2\pi}} e^{-\frac{1}{2}x^2} = (x^4 - 6x^2 + 3)f(x)$$

THE NORMAL PROBABILITY FUNCTION AND
RELATED FUNCTIONS (Continued)

It should be noted that other probability integrals can be evaluated by the use of these tables. For example,

$$\int_0^x f(t)dt = \tfrac{1}{2} \operatorname{erf}\left(\frac{x}{\sqrt{2}}\right),$$

where $\operatorname{erf}\left(\dfrac{x}{\sqrt{2}}\right)$ represents the error function associated with the normal curve.

To evaluate erf (2.3) one proceeds as follows: Since $\dfrac{x}{\sqrt{2}} = 2.3$, one finds $x = (2.3)(\sqrt{2}) = 3.25$. In the entry opposite $x = 3.25$, the value 0.9994 is given. Subtracting 0.5000 from the tabular value, one finds the value 0.4994. Thus erf (2.3) = 2(0.4994) = 0.9988.

NORMAL PROBABILITY FUNCTION AND RELATED FUNCTIONS (Continued)

x	$F(x)$	$1 - F(x)$	$f(x)$	$f'(x)$	$f''(x)$	$f'''(x)$	$f^{iv}(x)$
.00	.5000	.5000	.3989	−.0000	−.3989	.0000	1.1968
.01	.5040	.4960	.3989	−.0040	−.3989	.0120	1.1965
.02	.5080	.4920	.3989	−.0080	−.3987	.0239	1.1956
.03	.5120	.4880	.3988	−.0120	−.3984	.0359	1.1941
.04	.5160	.4840	.3986	−.0159	−.3980	.0478	1.1920
.05	.5199	.4801	.3984	−.0199	−.3975	.0597	1.1894
.06	.5239	.4761	.3982	−.0239	−.3968	.0716	1.1861
.07	.5279	.4721	.3980	−.0279	−.3960	.0834	1.1822
.08	.5319	.4681	.3977	−.0318	−.3951	.0952	1.1778
.09	.5359	.4641	.3973	−.0358	−.3941	.1070	1.1727
.10	.5398	.4602	.3970	−.0397	−.3930	.1187	1.1671
.11	.5438	.4562	.3965	−.0436	−.3917	.1303	1.1609
.12	.5478	.4522	.3961	−.0475	−.3904	.1419	1.1541
.13	.5517	.4483	.3956	−.0514	−.3889	.1534	1.1468
.14	.5557	.4443	.3951	−.0553	−.3873	.1648	1.1389
.15	.5596	.4404	.3945	−.0592	−.3856	.1762	1.1304
.16	.5636	.4364	.3939	−.0630	−.3838	.1874	1.1214
.17	.5675	.4325	.3932	−.0668	−.3819	.1986	1.1118
.18	.5714	.4286	.3925	−.0707	−.3798	.2097	1.1017
.19	.5753	.4247	.3918	−.0744	−.3777	.2206	1.0911
.20	.5793	.4207	.3910	−.0782	−.3754	.2315	1.0799
.21	.5832	.4168	.3902	−.0820	−.3730	.2422	1.0682
.22	.5871	.4129	.3894	−.0857	−.3706	.2529	1.0560
.23	.5910	.4090	.3885	−.0894	−.3680	.2634	1.0434
.24	.5948	.4052	.3876	−.0930	−.3653	.2737	1.0302
.25	.5987	.4013	.3867	−.0967	−.3625	.2840	1.0165
.26	.6026	.3974	.3857	−.1003	−.3596	.2941	1.0024
.27	.6064	.3936	.3847	−.1039	−.3566	.3040	0.9878
.28	.6103	.3897	.3836	−.1074	−.3535	.3138	0.9727
.29	.6141	.3859	.3825	−.1109	−.3504	.3235	0.9572
.30	.6179	.3821	.3814	−.1144	−.3471	.3330	0.9413
.31	.6217	.3783	.3802	−.1179	−.3437	.3423	0.9250
.32	.6255	.3745	.3790	−.1213	−.3402	.3515	0.9082
.33	.6293	.3707	.3778	−.1247	−.3367	.3605	0.8910
.34	.6331	.3669	.3765	−.1280	−.3330	.3693	0.8735
.35	.6368	.3632	.3752	−.1313	−.3293	.3779	0.8556
.36	.6406	.3594	.3739	−.1346	−.3255	.3864	0.8373
.37	.6443	.3557	.3726	−.1378	−.3216	.3947	0.8186
.38	.6480	.3520	.3712	−.1410	−.3176	.4028	0.7996
.39	.6517	.3483	.3697	−.1442	−.3135	.4107	0.7803
.40	.6554	.3446	.3683	−.1473	−.3094	.4184	0.7607
.41	.6591	.3409	.3668	−.1504	−.3051	.4259	0.7408
.42	.6628	.3372	.3653	−.1534	−.3008	.4332	0.7206
.43	.6664	.3336	.3637	−.1564	−.2965	.4403	0.7001
.44	.6700	.3300	.3621	−.1593	−.2920	.4472	0.6793
.45	.6736	.3264	.3605	−.1622	−.2875	.4539	0.6583
.46	.6772	.3228	.3589	−.1651	−.2830	.4603	0.6371
.47	.6808	.3192	.3572	−.1679	−.2783	.4666	0.6156
.48	.6844	.3156	.3555	−.1707	−.2736	.4727	0.5940
.49	.6879	.3121	.3538	−.1734	−.2689	.4785	0.5721
.50	.6915	.3085	.3521	−.1760	−.2641	.4841	0.5501

NORMAL PROBABILITY FUNCTION AND RELATED FUNCTIONS (Continued)

x	$F(x)$	$1 - F(x)$	$f(x)$	$f'(x)$	$f''(x)$	$f'''(x)$	$f^{\mathrm{IV}}(x)$
.50	.6915	.3085	.3521	$-.1760$	$-.2641$	.4841	.5501
.51	.6950	.3050	.3503	$-.1787$	$-.2592$	.4895	.5279
.52	.6985	.3015	.3485	$-.1812$	$-.2543$	.4947	.5056
.53	.7019	.2981	.3467	$-.1837$	$-.2493$	.4996	.4831
.54	.7054	.2946	.3448	$-.1862$	$-.2443$	.5043	.4605
.55	.7088	.2912	.3429	$-.1886$	$-.2392$	.5088	.4378
.56	.7123	.2877	.3410	$-.1920$	$-.2341$	.5131	.4150
.57	.7157	.2843	.3391	$-.1933$	$-.2289$	.5171	.3921
.58	.7190	.2810	.3372	$-.1956$	$-.2238$	.5209	.3691
.59	.7224	.2776	.3352	$-.1978$	$-.2185$	.5245	.3461
.60	.7257	.2743	.3332	$-.1999$	$-.2133$	.5278	.3231
.61	.7291	.2709	.3312	$-.2020$	$-.2080$	.5309	.3000
.62	.7324	.2676	.3292	$-.2041$	$-.2027$	.5338	.2770
.63	.7357	.2643	.3271	$-.2061$	$-.1973$	.5365	.2539
.64	.7389	.2611	.3251	$-.2080$	$-.1919$	.5389	.2309
.65	.7422	.2578	.3230	$-.2099$	$-.1865$	.5411	.2078
.66	.7454	.2546	.3209	$-.2118$	$-.1811$	.5431	.1849
.67	.7486	.2514	.3187	$-.2136$	$-.1757$	.5448	.1620
.68	.7517	.2483	.3166	$-.2153$	$-.1702$	.5463	.1391
.69	.7549	.2451	.3144	$-.2170$	$-.1647$	.5476	.1164
.70	.7580	.2420	.3123	$-.2186$	$-.1593$	.5486	.0937
.71	.7611	.2389	.3101	$-.2201$	$-.1538$	.5495	.0712
.72	.7642	.2358	.3079	$-.2217$	$-.1483$	.5501	.0487
.73	.7673	.2327	.3056	$-.2231$	$-.1428$	.5504	.0265
.74	.7704	.2296	.3034	$-.2245$	$-.1373$	.5506	.0043
.75	.7734	.2266	.3011	$-.2259$	$-.1318$	.5505	$-.0176$
.76	.7764	.2236	.2989	$-.2271$	$-.1262$	.5502	$-.0394$
.77	.7794	.2206	.2966	$-.2284$	$-.1207$	.5497	$-.0611$
.78	.7823	.2177	.2943	$-.2296$	$-.1153$	.5490	$-.0825$
.79	.7852	.2148	.2920	$-.2307$	$-.1098$	.5481	$-.1037$
.80	.7881	.2119	.2897	$-.2318$	$-.1043$	.5469	$-.1247$
.81	.7910	.2090	.2874	$-.2328$	$-.0988$	.5456	$-.1455$
.82	.7939	.2061	.2850	$-.2337$	$-.0934$	.5440	$-.1660$
.83	.7967	.2033	.2827	$-.2346$	$-.0880$	.5423	$-.1862$
.84	.7995	.2005	.2803	$-.2355$	$-.0825$	.5403	$-.2063$
.85	.8023	.1977	.2780	$-.2363$	$-.0771$	.5381	$-.2260$
.86	.8051	.1949	.2756	$-.2370$	$-.0718$	.5358	$-.2455$
.87	.8079	.1921	.2732	$-.2377$	$-.0664$	.5332	$-.2646$
.88	.8106	.1894	.2709	$-.2384$	$-.0611$	.5305	$-.2835$
.89	.8133	.1867	.2685	$-.2389$	$-.0558$	.5276	$-.3021$
.90	.8159	.1841	.2661	$-.2395$	$-.0506$	.5245	$-.3203$
.91	.8186	.1814	.2637	$-.2400$	$-.0453$	.5212	$-.3383$
.92	.8212	.1788	.2613	$-.2404$	$-.0401$	.5177	$-.3559$
.93	.8238	.1762	.2589	$-.2408$	$-.0350$	.5140	$-.3731$
.94	.8264	.1736	.2565	$-.2411$	$-.0299$	.5102	$-.3901$
.95	.8289	.1711	.2541	$-.2414$	$-.0248$	.5062	$-.4066$
.96	.8315	.1685	.2516	$-.2416$	$-.0197$	.5021	$-.4228$
.97	.8340	.1660	.2492	$-.2417$	$-.0147$	.4978	$-.4387$
.98	.8365	.1635	.2468	$-.2419$	$-.0098$	.4933	$-.4541$
.99	.8389	.1611	.2444	$-.2420$	$-.0049$	.4887	$-.4692$
1.00	.8413	.1587	.2420	$-.2420$	.0000	.4839	$-.4839$

NORMAL PROBABILITY FUNCTION AND RELATED FUNCTIONS (Continued)

x	$F(x)$	$1 - F(x)$	$f(x)$	$f'(x)$	$f''(x)$	$f'''(x)$	$f^{\mathrm{iv}}(x)$
1.00	.8413	.1587	.2420	−.2420	.0000	.4839	−.4839
1.01	.8438	.1562	.2396	−.2420	.0048	.4790	−.4983
1.02	.8461	.1539	.2371	−.2419	.0096	.4740	−.5122
1.03	.8485	.1515	.2347	−.2418	.0143	.4688	−.5257
1.04	.8508	.1492	.2323	−.2416	.0190	.4635	−.5389
1.05	.8531	.1469	.2299	−.2414	.0236	.4580	−.5516
1.06	.8554	.1446	.2275	−.2411	.0281	.4524	−.5639
1.07	.8577	.1423	.2251	−.2408	.0326	.4467	−.5758
1.08	.8599	.1401	.2227	−.2405	.0371	.4409	−.5873
1.09	.8621	.1379	.2203	−.2401	.0414	.4350	−.5984
1.10	.8643	.1357	.2179	−.2396	.0458	.4290	−.6091
1.11	.8665	.1335	.2155	−.2392	.0500	.4228	−.6193
1.12	.8686	.1314	.2131	−.2386	.0542	.4166	−.6292
1.13	.8708	.1292	.2107	−.2381	.0583	.4102	−.6386
1.14	.8729	.1271	.2083	−.2375	.0624	.4038	−.6476
1.15	.8749	.1251	.2059	−.2368	.0664	.3973	−.6561
1.16	.8770	.1230	.2036	−.2361	.0704	.3907	−.6643
1.17	.8790	.1210	.2012	−.2354	.0742	.3840	−.6720
1.18	.8810	.1190	.1989	−.2347	.0780	.3772	−.6792
1.19	.8830	.1170	.1965	−.2339	.0818	.3704	−.6861
1.20	.8849	.1151	.1942	−.2330	.0854	.3635	−.6926
1.21	.8869	.1131	.1919	−.2322	.0890	.3566	−.6986
1.22	.8888	.1112	.1895	−.2312	.0926	.3496	−.7042
1.23	.8907	.1093	.1872	−.2303	.0960	.3425	−.7094
1.24	.8925	.1075	.1849	−.2293	.0994	.3354	−.7141
1.25	.8944	.1056	.1826	−.2283	.1027	.3282	−.7185
1.26	.8962	.1038	.1804	−.2273	.1060	.3210	−.7224
1.27	.8980	.1020	.1781	−.2262	.1092	.3138	−.7259
1.28	.8997	.1003	.1758	−.2251	.1123	.3065	−.7291
1.29	.9015	.0985	.1736	−.2240	.1153	.2992	−.7318
1.30	.9032	.0968	.1714	−.2228	.1182	.2918	−.7341
1.31	.9049	.0951	.1691	−.2216	.1211	.2845	−.7361
1.32	.9066	.0934	.1669	−.2204	.1239	.2771	−.7376
1.33	.9082	.0918	.1647	−.2191	.1267	.2697	−.7388
1.34	.9099	.0901	.1626	−.2178	.1293	.2624	−.7395
1.35	.9115	.0885	.1604	−.2165	.1319	.2550	−.7399
1.36	.9131	.0869	.1582	−.2152	.1344	.2476	−.7400
1.37	.9147	.0853	.1561	−.2138	.1369	.2402	−.7396
1.38	.9162	.0838	.1539	−.2125	.1392	.2328	−.7389
1.39	.9177	.0823	.1518	−.2110	.1415	.2254	−.7378
1.40	.9192	.0808	.1497	−.2096	.1437	.2180	−.7364
1.41	.9207	.0793	.1476	−.2082	.1459	.2107	−.7347
1.42	.9222	.0778	.1456	−.2067	.1480	.2033	−.7326
1.43	.9236	.0764	.1435	−.2052	.1500	.1960	−.7301
1.44	.9251	.0749	.1415	−.2037	.1519	.1887	−.7274
1.45	.9265	.0735	.1394	−.2022	.1537	.1815	−.7243
1.46	.9279	.0721	.1374	−.2006	.1555	.1742	−.7209
1.47	.9292	.0708	.1354	−.1991	.1572	.1670	−.7172
1.48	.9306	.0694	.1334	−.1975	.1588	.1599	−.7132
1.49	.9319	.0681	.1315	−.1959	.1604	.1528	−.7089
1.50	.9332	.0668	.1295	−.1943	.1619	.1457	−.7043

NORMAL PROBABILITY FUNCTION AND RELATED FUNCTIONS (Continued)

x	$F(x)$	$1 - F(x)$	$f(x)$	$f'(x)$	$f''(x)$	$f'''(x)$	$f^{\mathrm{IV}}(x)$
1.50	.9332	.0668	.1295	−.1943	.1619	.1457	−.7043
1.51	.9345	.0655	.1276	−.1927	.1633	.1387	−.6994
1.52	.9357	.0643	.1257	−.1910	.1647	.1317	−.6942
1.53	.9370	.0630	.1238	−.1894	.1660	.1248	−.6888
1.54	.9382	.0618	.1219	−.1877	.1672	.1180	−.6831
1.55	.9394	.0606	.1200	−.1860	.1683	.1111	−.6772
1.56	.9406	.0594	.1182	−.1843	.1694	.1044	−.6710
1.57	.9418	.0582	.1163	−.1826	.1704	.0977	−.6646
1.58	.9429	.0571	.1145	−.1809	.1714	.0911	−.6580
1.59	.9441	.0559	.1127	−.1792	.1722	.0846	−.6511
1.60	.9452	.0548	.1109	−.1775	.1730	.0781	−.6441
1.61	.9463	.0537	.1092	−.1757	.1738	.0717	−.6368
1.62	.9474	.0526	.1074	−.1740	.1745	.0654	−.6293
1.63	.9484	.0516	.1057	−.1723	.1751	.0591	−.6216
1.64	.9495	.0505	.1040	−.1705	.1757	.0529	−.6138
1.65	.9505	.0495	.1023	−.1687	.1762	.0468	−.6057
1.66	.9515	.0485	.1006	−.1670	.1766	.0408	−.5975
1.67	.9525	.0475	.0989	−.1652	.1770	.0349	−.5891
1.68	.9535	.0465	.0973	−.1634	.1773	.0290	−.5806
1.69	.9545	.0455	.0957	−.1617	.1776	.0233	−.5720
1.70	.9554	.0446	.0940	−.1599	.1778	.0176	−.5632
1.71	.9564	.0436	.0925	−.1581	.1779	.0120	−.5542
1.72	.9573	.0427	.0909	−.1563	.1780	.0065	−.5452
1.73	.9582	.0418	.0893	−.1546	.1780	.0011	−.5360
1.74	.9591	.0409	.0878	−.1528	.1780	−.0042	−.5267
1.75	.9599	.0401	.0863	−.1510	.1780	−.0094	−.5173
1.76	.9608	.0392	.0848	−.1492	.1778	−.0146	−.5079
1.77	.9616	.0384	.0833	−.1474	.1777	−.0196	−.4983
1.78	.9625	.0375	.0818	−.1457	.1774	−.0245	−.4887
1.79	.9633	.0367	.0804	−.1439	.1772	−.0294	−.4789
1.80	.9641	.0359	.0790	−.1421	.1769	−.0341	−.4692
1.81	.9649	.0351	.0775	−.1403	.1765	−.0388	−.4593
1.82	.9656	.0344	.0761	−.1386	.1761	−.0433	−.4494
1.83	.9664	.0336	.0748	−.1368	.1756	−.0477	−.4395
1.84	.9671	.0329	.0734	−.1351	.1751	−.0521	−.4295
1.85	.9678	.0322	.0721	−.1333	.1746	−.0563	−.4195
1.86	.9686	.0314	.0707	−.1316	.1740	−.0605	−.4095
1.87	.9693	.0307	.0694	−.1298	.1734	−.0645	−.3995
1.88	.9699	.0301	.0681	−.1281	.1727	−.0685	−.3894
1.89	.9706	.0294	.0669	−.1264	.1720	−.0723	−.3793
1.90	.9713	.0287	.0656	−.1247	.1713	−.0761	−.3693
1.91	.9719	.0281	.0644	−.1230	.1705	−.0797	−.3592
1.92	.9726	.0274	.0632	−.1213	.1697	−.0832	−.3492
1.93	.9732	.0268	.0620	−.1196	.1688	−.0867	−.3392
1.94	.9738	.0262	.0608	−.1179	.1679	−.0900	−.3292
1.95	.9744	.0256	.0596	−.1162	.1670	−.0933	−.3192
1.96	.9750	.0250	.0584	−.1145	.1661	−.0964	−.3093
1.97	.9756	.0244	.0573	−.1129	.1651	−.0994	−.2994
1.98	.9761	.0239	.0562	−.1112	.1641	−.1024	−.2895
1.99	.9767	.0233	.0551	−.1096	.1630	−.1052	−.2797
2.00	.9772	.0228	.0540	−.1080	.1620	−.1080	−.2700

NORMAL PROBABILITY FUNCTION AND RELATED FUNCTIONS (Continued)

x	$F(x)$	$1 - F(x)$	$f(x)$	$f'(x)$	$f''(x)$	$f'''(x)$	$f^{IV}(x)$
2.00	.9772	.0228	.0540	−.1080	.1620	−.1080	−.2700
2.01	.9778	.0222	.0529	−.1064	.1609	−.1106	−.2603
2.02	.9783	.0217	.0519	−.1048	.1598	−.1132	−.2506
2.03	.9788	.0212	.0508	−.1032	.1586	−.1157	−.2411
2.04	.9793	.0207	.0498	−.1016	.1575	−.1180	−.2316
2.05	.9798	.0202	.0488	−.1000	.1563	−.1203	−.2222
2.06	.9803	.0197	.0478	−.0985	.1550	−.1225	−.2129
2.07	.9808	.0192	.0468	−.0969	.1538	−.1245	−.2036
2.08	.9812	.0188	.0459	−.0954	.1526	−.1265	−.1945
2.09	.9817	.0183	.0449	−.0939	.1513	−.1284	−.1854
2.10	.9821	.0179	.0440	−.0924	.1500	−.1302	−.1765
2.11	.9826	.0174	.0431	−.0909	.1487	−.1320	−.1676
2.12	.9830	.0170	.0422	−.0894	.1474	−.1336	−.1588
2.13	.9834	.0166	.0413	−.0879	.1460	−.1351	−.1502
2.14	.9838	.0162	.0404	−.0865	.1446	−.1366	−.1416
2.15	.9842	.0158	.0396	−.0850	.1433	−.1380	−.1332
2.16	.9846	.0154	.0387	−.0836	.1419	−.1393	−.1249
2.17	.9850	.0150	.0379	−.0822	.1405	−.1405	−.1167
2.18	.9854	.0146	.0371	−.0808	.1391	−.1416	−.1086
2.19	.9857	.0143	.0363	−.0794	.1377	−.1426	−.1006
2.20	.9861	.0139	.0355	−.0780	.1362	−.1436	−.0927
2.21	.9864	.0136	.0347	−.0767	.1348	−.1445	−.0850
2.22	.9868	.0132	.0339	−.0754	.1333	−.1453	−.0774
2.23	.9871	.0129	.0332	−.0740	.1319	−.1460	−.0700
2.24	.9875	.0125	.0325	−.0727	.1304	−.1467	−.0626
2.25	.9878	.0122	.0317	−.0714	.1289	−.1473	−.0554
2.26	.9881	.0119	.0310	−.0701	.1275	−.1478	−.0484
2.27	.9884	.0116	.0303	−.0689	.1260	−.1483	−.0414
2.28	.9887	.0113	.0297	−.0676	.1245	−.1486	−.0346
2.29	.9890	.0110	.0290	−.0664	.1230	−.1490	−.0279
2.30	.9893	.0107	.0283	−.0652	.1215	−.1492	−.0214
2.31	.9896	.0104	.0277	−.0639	.1200	−.1494	−.0150
2.32	.9898	.0102	.0270	−.0628	.1185	−.1495	−.0088
2.33	.9901	.0099	.0264	−.0616	.1170	−.1496	−.0027
2.34	.9904	.0096	.0258	−.0604	.1155	−.1496	.0033
2.35	.9906	.0094	.0252	−.0593	.1141	−.1495	.0092
2.36	.9909	.0091	.0246	−.0581	.1126	−.1494	.0149
2.37	.9911	.0089	.0241	−.0570	.1111	−.1492	.0204
2.38	.9913	.0087	.0235	−.0559	.1096	−.1490	.0258
2.39	.9916	.0084	.0229	−.0548	.1081	−.1487	.0311
2.40	.9918	.0082	.0224	−.0538	.1066	−.1483	.0362
2.41	.9920	.0080	.0219	−.0527	.1051	−.1480	.0412
2.42	.9922	.0078	.0213	−.0516	.1036	−.1475	.0461
2.43	.9925	.0075	.0208	−.0506	.1022	−.1470	.0508
2.44	.9927	.0073	.0203	−.0496	.1007	−.1465	.0554
2.45	.9929	.0071	.0198	−.0486	.0992	−.1459	.0598
2.46	.9931	.0069	.0194	−.0476	.0978	−.1453	.0641
2.47	.9932	.0068	.0189	−.0467	.0963	−.1446	.0683
2.48	.9934	.0066	.0184	−.0457	.0949	−.1439	.0723
2.49	.9936	.0064	.0180	−.0448	.0935	−.1432	.0762
2.50	.9938	.0062	.0175	−.0438	.0920	−.1424	.0800

NORMAL PROBABILITY FUNCTION AND RELATED FUNCTIONS (Continued)

x	$F(x)$	$1 - F(x)$	$f(x)$	$f'(x)$	$f''(x)$	$f'''(x)$	$f^{iv}(x)$
2.50	.9938	.0062	.0175	$-.0438$	.0920	$-.1424$	.0800
2.51	.9940	.0060	.0171	$-.0429$	.0906	$-.1416$	.0836
2.52	.9941	.0059	.0167	$-.0420$	.0892	$-.1408$	.0871
2.53	.9943	.0057	.0163	$-.0411$	.0878	$-.1399$	.0905
2.54	.9945	.0055	.0158	$-.0403$	.0864	$-.1389$	.0937
2.55	.9946	.0054	.0155	$-.0394$	.0850	$-.1380$	.0968
2.56	.9948	.0052	.0151	$-.0386$	.0836	$-.1370$	.0998
2.57	.9949	.0051	.0147	$-.0377$	.0823	$-.1360$	.1027
2.58	.9951	.0049	.0143	$-.0369$	.0809	$-.1350$	.1054
2.59	.9952	.0048	.0139	$-.0361$	.0796	$-.1339$	.1080
2.60	.9953	.0047	.0136	$-.0353$	.0782	$-.1328$	.1105
2.61	.9955	.0045	.0132	$-.0345$	.0769	$-.1317$	.1129
2.62	.9956	.0044	.0129	$-.0338$	.0756	$-.1305$	.1152
2.63	.9957	.0043	.0126	$-.0330$	.0743	$-.1294$	.1173
2.64	.9959	.0041	.0122	$-.0323$	.0730	$-.1282$	.1194
2.65	.9960	.0040	.0119	$-.0316$	.0717	$-.1270$	.1213
2.66	.9961	.0039	.0116	$-.0309$	.0705	$-.1258$	.1231
2.67	.9962	.0038	.0113	$-.0302$	.0692	$-.1245$	.1248
2.68	.9963	.0037	.0110	$-.0295$	.0680	$-.1233$	.1264
2.69	.9964	.0036	.0107	$-.0288$	.0668	$-.1220$	.1279
2.70	.9965	.0035	.0104	$-.0281$	.0656	$-.1207$	.1293
2.71	.9966	.0034	.0101	$-.0275$	.0644	$-.1194$	.1306
2.72	.9967	.0033	.0099	$-.0269$	.0632	$-.1181$	.1317
2.73	.9968	.0032	.0096	$-.0262$	.0620	$-.1168$	.1328
2.74	.9969	.0031	.0093	$-.0256$	.0608	$-.1154$	.1338
2.75	.9970	.0030	.0091	$-.0250$	.0597	$-.1141$	.1347
2.76	.9971	.0029	.0088	$-.0244$	.0585	$-.1127$	.1356
2.77	.9972	.0028	.0086	$-.0238$	.0574	$-.1114$	.1363
2.78	.9973	.0027	.0084	$-.0233$	.0563	$-.1100$	.1369
2.79	.9974	.0026	.0081	$-.0227$	.0552	$-.1087$	.1375
2.80	.9974	.0026	.0079	$-.0222$	.0541	$-.1073$	.1379
2.81	.9975	.0025	.0077	$-.0216$	.0531	$-.1059$	.1383
2.82	.9976	.0024	.0075	$-.0211$	.0520	$-.1045$	.1386
2.83	.9977	.0023	.0073	$-.0203$	.0510	$-.1031$	.1389
2.84	.9977	.0023	.0071	$-.0201$	.0500	$-.1017$	.1390
2.85	.9978	.0022	.0069	$-.0196$	.0490	$-.1003$	.1391
2.86	.9979	.0021	.0067	$-.0191$	.0480	$-.0990$	.1391
2.87	.9979	.0021	.0065	$-.0186$	.0470	$-.0976$	.1391
2.88	.9980	.0020	.0063	$-.0182$	.0460	$-.0962$	.1389
2.89	.9981	.0019	.0061	$-.0177$	.0451	$-.0948$	.1388
2.90	.9981	.0019	.0060	$-.0173$	.0441	$-.0934$	.1385
2.91	.9982	.0018	.0058	$-.0168$	.0432	$-.0920$	.1382
2.92	.9982	.0018	.0056	$-.0164$	.0423	$-.0906$	.1378
2.93	.9983	.0017	.0055	$-.0160$	.0414	$-.0893$	.1374
2.94	.9984	.0016	.0053	$-.0156$	.0405	$-.0879$	.1369
2.95	.9984	.0016	.0051	$-.0152$	.0396	$-.0865$	.1364
2.96	.9985	.0015	.0050	$-.0148$	.0388	$-.0852$	.1358
2.97	.9985	.0015	.0048	$-.0144$	.0379	$-.0838$	.1352
2.98	.9986	.0014	.0047	$-.0140$	.0371	$-.0825$	.1345
2.99	.9986	.0014	.0046	$-.0137$	.0363	$-.0811$	.1337
3.00	.9987	.0013	.0044	$-.0133$	.0355	$-.0798$	.1330

NORMAL PROBABILITY FUNCTION AND RELATED FUNCTIONS (Continued)

x	$F(x)$	$1 - F(x)$	$f(x)$	$f'(x)$	$f''(x)$	$f'''(x)$	$f^{IV}(x)$
3.00	.9987	.0013	.0044	−.0133	.0355	−.0798	.1330
3.01	.9987	.0013	.0043	−.0130	.0347	−.0785	.1321
3.02	.9987	.0013	.0042	−.0126	.0339	−.0771	.1313
3.03	.9988	.0012	.0040	−.0123	.0331	−.0758	.1304
3.04	.9988	.0012	.0039	−.0119	.0324	−.0745	.1294
3.05	.9989	.0011	.0038	−.0116	.0316	−.0732	.1285
3.06	.9989	.0011	.0037	−.0113	.0309	−.0720	.1275
3.07	.9989	.0011	.0036	−.0110	.0302	−.0707	.1264
3.08	.9990	.0010	.0035	−.0107	.0295	−.0694	.1254
3.09	.9990	.0010	.0034	−.0104	.0288	−.0682	.1243
3.10	.9990	.0010	.0033	−.0101	.0281	−.0669	.1231
3.11	.9991	.0009	.0032	−.0099	.0275	−.0657	.1220
3.12	.9991	.0009	.0031	−.0096	.0268	−.0645	.1208
3.13	.9991	.0009	.0030	−.0093	.0262	−.0633	.1196
3.14	.9992	.0008	.0029	−.0091	.0256	−.0621	.1184
3.15	.9992	.0008	.0028	−.0088	.0249	−.0609	.1171
3.16	.9992	.0008	.0027	−.0086	.0243	−.0598	.1159
3.17	.9992	.0008	.0026	−.0083	.0237	−.0586	.1146
3.18	.9993	.0007	.0025	−.0081	.0232	−.0575	.1133
3.19	.9993	.0007	.0025	−.0079	.0226	−.0564	.1120
3.20	.9993	.0007	.0024	−.0076	.0220	−.0552	.1107
3.21	.9993	.0007	.0023	−.0074	.0215	−.0541	.1093
3.22	.9994	.0006	.0022	−.0072	.0210	−.0531	.1080
3.23	.9994	.0006	.0022	−.0070	.0204	−.0520	.1066
3.24	.9994	.0006	.0021	−.0068	.0199	−.0509	.1053
3.25	.9994	.0006	.0020	−.0066	.0194	−.0499	.1039
3.26	.9994	.0006	.0020	−.0064	.0189	−.0488	.1025
3.27	.9995	.0005	.0019	−.0062	.0184	−.0478	.1011
3.28	.9995	.0005	.0018	−.0060	.0180	−.0468	.0997
3.29	.9995	.0005	.0018	−.0059	.0175	−.0458	.0983
3.30	.9995	.0005	.0017	−.0057	.0170	−.0449	.0969
3.31	.9995	.0005	.0017	−.0055	.0166	−.0439	.0955
3.32	.9995	.0005	.0016	−.0054	.0162	−.0429	.0941
3.33	.9996	.0004	.0016	−.0052	.0157	−.0420	.0927
3.34	.9996	.0004	.0015	−.0050	.0153	−.0411	.0913
3.35	.9996	.0004	.0015	−.0049	.0149	−.0402	.0899
3.36	.9996	.0004	.0014	−.0047	.0145	−.0393	.0885
3.37	.9996	.0004	.0014	−.0046	.0141	−.0384	.0871
3.38	.9996	.0004	.0013	−.0045	.0138	−.0376	.0857
3.39	.9997	.0003	.0013	−.0043	.0134	−.0367	.0843
3.40	.9997	.0003	.0012	−.0042	.0130	−.0359	.0829
3.41	.9997	.0003	.0012	−.0041	.0127	−.0350	.0815
3.42	.9997	.0003	.0012	−.0039	.0123	−.0342	.0801
3.43	.9997	.0003	.0011	−.0038	.0120	−.0334	.0788
3.44	.9997	.0003	.0011	−.0037	.0116	−.0327	.0774
3.45	.9997	.0003	.0010	−.0036	.0113	−.0319	.0761
3.46	.9997	.0003	.0010	−.0035	.0110	−.0311	.0747
3.47	.9997	.0003	.0010	−.0034	.0107	−.0304	.0734
3.48	.9997	.0003	.0009	−.0033	.0104	−.0297	.0721
3.49	.9998	.0002	.0009	−.0032	.0101	−.0290	.0707
3.50	.9998	.0002	.0009	−.0031	.0098	−.0283	.0694

NORMAL PROBABILITY FUNCTION AND RELATED FUNCTIONS (Continued)

x	$F(x)$	$1 - F(x)$	$f(x)$	$f'(x)$	$f''(x)$	$f'''(x)$	$f^{\mathrm{iv}}(x)$
3.50	.9998	.0002	.0009	−.0031	.0098	−.0283	.0694
3.51	.9998	.0002	.0008	−.0030	.0095	−.0276	.0681
3.52	.9998	.0002	.0008	−.0029	.0093	−.0269	.0669
3.53	.9998	.0002	.0008	−.0028	.0090	−.0262	.0656
3.54	.9998	.0002	.0008	−.0027	.0087	−.0256	.0643
3.55	.9998	.0002	.0007	−.0026	.0085	−.0249	.0631
3.56	.9998	.0002	.0007	−.0025	.0082	−.0243	.0618
3.57	.9998	.0002	.0007	−.0024	.0080	−.0237	.0606
3.58	.9998	.0002	.0007	−.0024	.0078	−.0231	.0594
3.59	.9998	.0002	.0006	−.0023	.0075	−.0225	.0582
3.60	.9998	.0002	.0006	−.0022	.0073	−.0219	.0570
3.61	.9998	.0002	.0006	−.0021	.0071	−.0214	.0559
3.62	.9999	.0001	.0006	−.0021	.0069	−.0208	.0547
3.63	.9999	.0001	.0005	−.0020	.0067	−.0203	.0536
3.64	.9999	.0001	.0005	−.0019	.0065	−.0198	.0524
3.65	.9999	.0001	.0005	−.0019	.0063	−.0192	.0513
3.66	.9999	.0001	.0005	−.0018	.0061	−.0187	.0502
3.67	.9999	.0001	.0005	−.0017	.0059	−.0182	.0492
3.68	.9999	.0001	.0005	−.0017	.0057	−.0177	.0481
3.69	.9999	.0001	.0004	−.0016	.0056	−.0173	.0470
3.70	.9999	.0001	.0004	−.0016	.0054	−.0168	.0460
3.71	.9999	.0001	.0004	−.0015	.0052	−.0164	.0450
3.72	.9999	.0001	.0004	−.0015	.0051	−.0159	.0440
3.73	.9999	.0001	.0004	−.0014	.0049	−.0155	.0430
3.74	.9999	.0001	.0004	−.0014	.0048	−.0150	.0420
3.75	.9999	.0001	.0004	−.0013	.0046	−.0146	.0410
3.76	.9999	.0001	.0003	−.0013	.0045	−.0142	.0401
3.77	.9999	.0001	.0003	−.0012	.0043	−.0138	.0392
3.78	.9999	.0001	.0003	−.0012	.0042	−.0134	.0382
3.79	.9999	.0001	.0003	−.0012	.0041	−.0131	.0373
3.80	.9999	.0001	.0003	−.0011	.0039	−.0127	.0365
3.81	.9999	.0001	.0003	−.0011	.0038	−.0123	.0356
3.82	.9999	.0001	.0003	−.0010	.0037	−.0120	.0347
3.83	.9999	.0001	.0003	−.0010	.0036	−.0116	.0339
3.84	.9999	.0001	.0003	−.0010	.0034	−.0113	.0331
3.85	.9999	.0001	.0002	−.0009	.0033	−.0110	.0323
3.86	.9999	.0001	.0002	−.0009	.0032	−.0107	.0315
3.87	.9999	.0001	.0002	−.0009	.0031	−.0104	.0307
3.88	.9999	.0001	.0002	−.0008	.0030	−.0100	.0299
3.89	1.0000	.0000	.0002	−.0008	.0029	−.0098	.0292
3.90	1.0000	.0000	.0002	−.0008	.0028	−.0095	.0284
3.91	1.0000	.0000	.0002	−.0008	.0027	−.0092	.0277
3.92	1.0000	.0000	.0002	−.0007	.0026	−.0089	.0270
3.93	1.0000	.0000	.0002	−.0007	.0026	−.0086	.0263
3.94	1.0000	.0000	.0002	−.0007	.0025	−.0084	.0256
3.95	1.0000	.0000	.0002	−.0006	.0024	−.0081	.0250
3.96	1.0000	.0000	.0002	−.0006	.0023	−.0079	.0243
3.97	1.0000	.0000	.0002	−.0006	.0022	−.0076	.0237
3.98	1.0000	.0000	.0001	−.0006	.0022	−.0074	.0230
3.99	1.0000	.0000	.0001	−.0006	.0021	−.0072	.0224
4.00	1.0000	.0000	.0001	−.0005	.0020	−.0070	.0218

x	1.282	1.645	1.960	2.326	2.576	3.090
$F(x)$	.90	.95	.975	.99	.995	.999
$2[1 - F(x)]$	.20	.10	.05	.02	.01	.002

INDIVIDUAL TERMS, BINOMIAL DISTRIBUTION

The $(x + 1)^{st}$ term in the expansion of the binomial $[\theta + (1 - \theta)]^n$ is given by

$$f(x;n,\theta) = \binom{n}{x} \theta^x (1 - \theta)^{n-x}, \qquad x = 0, 1, 2, \ldots, n.$$

This is the probability of exactly x successes in n independent binomial trials with probability of success on a single trial equal to θ. This table contains the individual terms of $f(x;n,\theta)$ for specified choices of x, n, and θ.

For $\theta > 0.5$, the value of $\binom{n}{x} \theta^x (1 - \theta)^{n-x}$ is found by using the table entry for $\binom{n}{n - x} (1 - \theta)^{n-x} \theta^x$.

INDIVIDUAL TERMS, BINOMIAL DISTRIBUTION (Continued)

n	x	.05	.10	.15	.20	.25	θ .30	.35	.40	.45	.50
1	0	.9500	.9000	.8500	.8000	.7500	.7000	.6500	.6000	.5500	.5000
	1	.0500	.1000	.1500	.2000	.2500	.3000	.3500	.4000	.4500	.5000
2	0	.9025	.8100	.7225	.6400	.5625	.4900	.4225	.3600	.3025	.2500
	1	.0950	.1800	.2550	.3200	.3750	.4200	.4550	.4800	.4950	.5000
	2	.0025	.0100	.0225	.0400	.0625	.0900	.1225	.1600	.2025	.2500
3	0	.8574	.7290	.6141	.5120	.4219	.3430	.2746	.2160	.1664	.1250
	1	.1354	.2430	.3251	.3840	.4219	.4410	.4436	.4320	.4084	.3750
	2	.0071	.0270	.0574	.0960	.1406	.1890	.2389	.2880	.3341	.3750
	3	.0001	.0010	.0034	.0080	.0156	.0270	.0429	.0640	.0911	.1250
4	0	.8145	.6561	.5220	.4096	.3164	.2401	.1785	.1296	.0915	.0625
	1	.1715	.2916	.3685	.4096	.4219	.4116	.3845	.3456	.2995	.2500
	2	.0135	.0486	.0975	.1536	.2109	.2646	.3105	.3456	.3675	.3750
	3	.0005	.0036	.0115	.0256	.0469	.0756	.1115	.1536	.2005	.2500
	4	.0000	.0001	.0005	.0016	.0039	.0081	.0150	.0256	.0410	.0625
5	0	.7738	.5905	.4437	.3277	.2373	.1681	.1160	.0778	.0503	.0312
	1	.2036	.3280	.3915	.4096	.3955	.3602	.3124	.2592	.2059	.1562
	2	.0214	.0729	.1382	.2048	.2637	.3087	.3364	.3456	.3369	.3125
	3	.0011	.0081	.0244	.0512	.0879	.1323	.1811	.2304	.2757	.3125
	4	.0000	.0004	.0022	.0064	.0146	.0284	.0488	.0768	.1128	.1562
	5	.0000	.0000	.0001	.0003	.0010	.0024	.0053	.0102	.0185	.0312
6	0	.7351	.5314	.3771	.2621	.1780	.1176	.0754	.0467	.0277	.0156
	1	.2321	.3543	.3993	.3932	.3560	.3025	.2437	.1866	.1359	.0938
	2	.0305	.0984	.1762	.2458	.2966	.3241	.3280	.3110	.2780	.2344
	3	.0021	.0146	.0415	.0819	.1318	.1852	.2355	.2765	.3032	.3125
	4	.0001	.0012	.0055	.0154	.0330	.0595	.0951	.1382	.1861	.2344
	5	.0000	.0001	.0004	.0015	.0044	.0102	.0205	.0369	.0609	.0938
	6	.0000	.0000	.0000	.0001	.0002	.0007	.0018	.0041	.0083	.0156
7	0	.6983	.4783	.3206	.2097	.1335	.0824	.0490	.0280	.0152	.0078
	1	.2573	.3720	.3960	.3670	.3115	.2471	.1848	.1306	.0872	.0547
	2	.0406	.1240	.2097	.2753	.3115	.3177	.2985	.2613	.2140	.1641
	3	.0036	.0230	.0617	.1147	.1730	.2269	.2679	.2903	.2918	.2734
	4	.0002	.0026	.0109	.0287	.0577	.0972	.1442	.1935	.2388	.2734
	5	.0000	.0002	.0012	.0043	.0115	.0250	.0466	.0774	.1172	.1641
	6	.0000	.0000	.0001	.0004	.0013	.0036	.0084	.0172	.0320	.0547
	7	.0000	.0000	.0000	.0000	.0001	.0002	.0006	.0016	.0037	.0078
8	0	.6634	.4305	.2725	.1678	.1001	.0576	.0319	.0168	.0084	.0039
	1	.2793	.3826	.3847	.3355	.2670	.1977	.1373	.0896	.0548	.0312
	2	.0515	.1488	.2376	.2936	.3115	.2965	.2587	.2090	.1569	.1094
	3	.0054	.0331	.0839	.1468	.2076	.2541	.2786	.2787	.2568	.2188
	4	.0004	.0046	.0185	.0459	.0865	.1361	.1875	.2322	.2627	.2734
	5	.0000	.0004	.0026	.0092	.0231	.0467	.0808	.1239	.1719	.2188
	6	.0000	.0000	.0002	.0011	.0038	.0100	.0217	.0413	.0703	.1094
	7	.0000	.0000	.0000	.0001	.0004	.0012	.0033	.0079	.0164	.0312
	8	.0000	.0000	.0000	.0000	.0000	.0001	.0002	.0007	.0017	.0039

Linear interpolations with respect to p will in general be accurate at most to two decimal places.

INDIVIDUAL TERMS, BINOMIAL DISTRIBUTION (Continued)

n	x	.05	.10	.15	.20	θ .25	.30	.35	.40	.45	.50
9	0	.6302	.3874	.2316	.1342	.0751	.0404	.0207	.0101	.0046	.0020
	1	.2985	.3874	.3679	.3020	.2253	.1556	.1004	.0605	.0339	.0176
	2	.0629	.1722	.2597	.3020	.3003	.2668	.2162	.1612	.1110	.0703
	3	.0077	.0446	.1069	.1762	.2336	.2668	.2716	.2508	.2119	.1641
	4	.0006	.0074	.0283	.0661	.1168	.1715	.2194	.2508	.2600	.2461
	5	.0000	.0008	.0050	.0165	.0389	.0735	.1181	.1672	.2128	.2461
	6	.0000	.0001	.0006	.0028	.0087	.0210	.0424	.0743	.1160	.1641
	7	.0000	.0000	.0000	.0003	.0012	.0039	.0098	.0212	.0407	.0703
	8	.0000	.0000	.0000	.0000	.0001	.0004	.0013	.0035	.0083	.0176
	9	.0000	.0000	.0000	.0000	.0000	.0000	.0001	.0003	.0008	.0020
10	0	.5987	.3487	.1969	.1074	.0563	.0282	.0135	.0060	.0025	.0010
	1	.3151	.3874	.3474	.2684	.1877	.1211	.0725	.0403	.0207	.0098
	2	.0746	.1937	.2759	.3020	.2816	.2335	.1757	.1209	.0763	.0439
	3	.0105	.0574	.1298	.2013	.2503	.2668	.2522	.2150	.1665	.1172
	4	.0010	.0112	.0401	.0881	.1460	.2001	.2377	.2508	.2384	.2051
	5	.0001	.0015	.0085	.0264	.0584	.1029	.1536	.2007	.2340	.2461
	6	.0000	.0001	.0012	.0055	.0162	.0368	.0689	.1115	.1596	.2051
	7	.0000	.0000	.0001	.0008	.0031	.0090	.0212	.0425	.0746	.1172
	8	.0000	.0000	.0000	.0001	.0004	.0014	.0043	.0106	.0229	.0439
	9	.0000	.0000	.0000	.0000	.0000	.0001	.0005	.0016	.0042	.0098
	10	.0000	.0000	.0000	.0000	.0000	.0000	.0000	.0001	.0003	.0010
11	0	.5688	.3138	.1673	.0859	.0422	.0198	.0088	.0036	.0014	.0004
	1	.3293	.3835	.3248	.2362	.1549	.0932	.0518	.0266	.0125	.0055
	2	.0867	.2131	.2866	.2953	.2581	.1998	.1395	.0887	.0513	.0269
	3	.0137	.0710	.1517	.2215	.2581	.2568	.2254	.1774	.1259	.0806
	4	.0014	.0158	.0536	.1107	.1721	.2201	.2428	.2365	.2060	.1611
	5	.0001	.0025	.0132	.0388	.0803	.1321	.1830	.2207	.2360	.2256
	6	.0000	.0003	.0023	.0097	.0268	.0566	.0985	.1471	.1931	.2256
	7	.0000	.0000	.0003	.0017	.0064	.0173	.0379	.0701	.1128	.1611
	8	.0000	.0000	.0000	.0002	.0011	.0037	.0102	.0234	.0462	.0806
	9	.0000	.0000	.0000	.0000	.0001	.0005	.0018	.0052	.0126	.0269
	10	.0000	.0000	.0000	.0000	.0000	.0000	.0002	.0007	.0021	.0054
	11	.0000	.0000	.0000	.0000	.0000	.0000	.0000	.0000	.0002	.0005
12	0	.5404	.2824	.1422	.0687	.0317	.0138	.0057	.0022	.0008	.0002
	1	.3413	.3766	.3012	.2062	.1267	.0712	.0368	.0174	.0075	.0029
	2	.0988	.2301	.2924	.2835	.2323	.1678	.1088	.0639	.0339	.0161
	3	.0173	.0852	.1720	.2362	.2581	.2397	.1954	.1419	.0923	.0537
	4	.0021	.0213	.0683	.1329	.1936	.2311	.2367	.2128	.1700	.1208
	5	.0002	.0038	.0193	.0532	.1032	.1585	.2039	.2270	.2225	.1934
	6	.0000	.0005	.0040	.0155	.0401	.0792	.1281	.1766	.2124	.2256
	7	.0000	.0000	.0006	.0033	.0115	.0291	.0591	.1009	.1489	.1934
	8	.0000	.0000	.0001	.0005	.0024	.0078	.0199	.0420	.0762	.1208
	9	.0000	.0000	.0000	.0001	.0004	.0015	.0048	.0125	.0277	.0537
	10	.0000	.0000	.0000	.0000	.0000	.0002	.0008	.0025	.0068	.0161
	11	.0000	.0000	.0000	.0000	.0000	.0000	.0001	.0003	.0010	.0029
	12	.0000	.0000	.0000	.0000	.0000	.0000	.0000	.0000	.0001	.0002

INDIVIDUAL TERMS, BINOMIAL DISTRIBUTION (Continued)

n	x	.05	.10	.15	.20	.25	.30	.35	.40	.45	.50
13	0	.5133	.2542	.1209	.0550	.0238	.0097	.0037	.0013	.0004	.0001
	1	.3512	.3672	.2774	.1787	.1029	.0540	.0259	.9113	.0045	.0016
	2	.1109	.2448	.2937	.2680	.2059	.1388	.0836	.0453	.0220	.0095
	3	.0214	.0997	.1900	.2457	.2517	.2181	.1651	.1107	.0660	.0349
	4	.0028	.0277	.0838	.1535	.2097	.2337	.2222	.1845	.1350	.0873
	5	.0003	.0055	.0266	.0691	.1258	.1803	.2154	.2214	.1989	.1571
	6	.0000	.0008	.0063	.0230	.0559	.1030	.1546	.1968	.2169	.2095
	7	.0000	.0001	.0011	.0058	.0186	.0442	.0833	.1312	.1775	.2095
	8	.0000	.0000	.0001	.0011	.0047	.0142	.0336	.0656	.1089	.1571
	9	.0000	.0000	.0000	.0001	.0009	.0034	.0101	.0243	.0495	.0873
	10	.0000	.0000	.0000	.0000	.0001	.0006	.0022	.0065	.0162	.0349
	11	.0000	.0000	.0000	.0000	.0000	.0001	.0003	.0012	.0036	.0095
	12	.0000	.0000	.0000	.0000	.0000	.0000	.0000	.0001	.0005	.0016
	13	.0000	.0000	.0000	.0000	.0000	.0000	.0000	.0000	.0000	.0001
14	0	.4877	.2288	.1028	.0440	.0178	.0068	.0024	.0008	.0002	.0001
	1	.3593	.3559	.2539	.1539	.0832	.0407	.0181	.0073	.0027	.0009
	2	.1229	.2570	.2912	.2501	.1802	.1134	.0634	.0317	.0141	.0056
	3	.0259	.1142	.2056	.2501	.2402	.1943	.1366	.0845	.0462	.0222
	4	.0037	.0349	.0998	.1720	.2202	.2290	.2022	.1549	.1040	.0611
	5	.0004	.0078	.0352	.0860	.1468	.1963	.2178	.2066	.1701	.1222
	6	.0000	.0013	.0093	.0322	.0734	.1262	.1759	.2066	.2088	.1833
	7	.0000	.0002	.0019	.0092	.0280	.0618	.1082	.1574	.1952	.2095
	8	.0000	.0000	.0003	.0020	.0082	.0232	.0510	.0918	.1398	.1833
	9	.0000	.0000	.0000	.0003	.0018	.0066	.0183	.0408	.0762	.1222
	10	.0000	.0000	.0000	.0000	.0003	.0014	.0049	.0136	.0312	.0611
	11	.0000	.0000	.0000	.0000	.0000	.0002	.0010	.0033	.0093	.0222
	12	.0000	.0000	.0000	.0000	.0000	.0000	.0001	.0005	.0019	.0056
	13	.0000	.0000	.0000	.0000	.0000	.0000	.0000	.0001	.0002	.0009
	14	.0000	.0000	.0000	.0000	.0000	.0000	.0000	.0000	.0000	.0001
15	0	.4633	.2059	.0874	.0352	.0134	.0047	.0016	.0005	.0001	.0000
	1	.3658	.3432	.2312	.1319	.0668	.0305	.0126	.0047	.0016	.0005
	2	.1348	.2669	.2856	.2309	.1559	.0916	.0476	.0219	.0090	.0032
	3	.0307	.1285	.2184	.2501	.2252	.1700	.1110	.0634	.0318	.0139
	4	.0049	.0428	.1156	.1876	.2252	.2186	.1792	.1268	.0780	.0417
	5	.0006	.0105	.0449	.1032	.1651	.2061	.2123	.1859	.1404	.0916
	6	.0000	.0019	.0132	.0430	.0917	.1472	.1906	.2066	.1914	.1527
	7	.0000	.0003	.0030	.0138	.0393	.0811	.1319	.1771	.2013	.1964
	8	.0000	.0000	.0005	.0035	.0131	.0348	.0710	.1181	.1647	.1964
	9	.0000	.0000	.0001	.0007	.0034	.0116	.0298	.0612	.1048	.1527
	10	.0000	.0000	.0000	.0001	.0007	.0030	.0096	.0245	.0515	.0916
	11	.0000	.0000	.0000	.0000	.0001	.0006	.0024	.0074	.0191	.0417
	12	.0000	.0000	.0000	.0000	.0000	.0001	.0004	.0016	.0052	.0139
	13	.0000	.0000	.0000	.0000	.0000	.0000	.0001	.0003	.0010	.0032
	14	.0000	.0000	.0000	.0000	.0000	.0000	.0000	.0000	.0001	.0005
	15	.0000	.0000	.0000	.0000	.0000	.0000	.0000	.0000	.0000	.0000

INDIVIDUAL TERMS, BINOMIAL DISTRIBUTION (Continued)

n	x	.05	.10	.15	.20	.25	.30	.35	.40	.45	.50
16	0	.4401	.1853	.0743	.0281	.0100	.0033	.0010	.0003	.0001	.0000
	1	.3706	.3294	.2097	.1126	.0535	.0228	.0087	.0030	.0009	.0002
	2	.1463	.2745	.2775	.2111	.1336	.0732	.0353	.0150	.0056	.0018
	3	.0359	.1423	.2285	.2463	.2079	.1465	.0888	.0468	.0215	.0085
	4	.0061	.0514	.1311	.2001	.2252	.2040	.1553	.1014	.0572	.0278
	5	.0008	.0137	.0555	.1201	.1802	.2099	.2008	.1623	.1123	.0667
	6	.0001	.0028	.0180	.0550	.1101	.1649	.1982	.1983	.1684	.1222
	7	.0000	.0004	.0045	.0197	.0524	.1010	.1524	.1889	.1969	.1746
	8	.0000	.0001	.0009	.0055	.0197	.0487	.0923	.1417	.1812	.1964
	9	.0000	.0000	.0001	.0012	.0058	.0185	.0442	.0840	.1318	.1746
	10	.0000	.0000	.0000	.0002	.0014	.0056	.0167	.0392	.0755	.1222
	11	.0000	.0000	.0000	.0000	.0002	.0013	.0049	.0142	.0337	.0667
	12	.0000	.0000	.0000	.0000	.0000	.0002	.0011	.0040	.0115	.0278
	13	.0000	.0000	.0000	.0000	.0000	.0000	.0002	.0008	.0029	.0085
	14	.0000	.0000	.0000	.0000	.0000	.0000	.0000	.0001	.0005	.0018
	15	.0000	.0000	.0000	.0000	.0000	.0000	.0000	.0000	.0001	.0002
	16	.0000	.0000	.0000	.0000	.0000	.0000	.0000	.0000	.0000	.0000
17	0	.4181	.1668	.0631	.0225	.0075	.0023	.0007	.0002	.0000	.0000
	1	.3741	.3150	.1893	.0957	.0426	.0169	.0060	.0019	.0005	.0001
	2	.1575	.2800	.2673	.1914	.1136	.0581	.0260	.0102	.0035	.0010
	3	.0415	.1556	.2359	.2393	.1893	.1245	.0701	.0341	.0144	.0052
	4	.9076	.0605	.1457	.2093	.2209	.1868	.1320	.0796	.0411	.0182
	5	.0010	.0175	.0668	.1361	.1914	.2081	.1849	.1379	.0875	.0472
	6	.0001	.0039	.0236	.0680	.1276	.1784	.1991	.1839	.1432	.0944
	7	.0000	.0007	.0065	.0267	.0668	.1201	.1685	.1927	.1841	.1484
	8	.0000	.0001	.0014	.0084	.0279	.0644	.1134	.1606	.1883	.1855
	9	.0000	.0000	.0003	.0021	.0093	.0276	.0611	.1070	.1540	.1855
	10	.0000	.0000	.0000	.0004	.0025	.0095	.0263	.0571	.1008	.1484
	11	.0000	.0000	.0000	.0001	.0005	.0026	.0090	.0242	.0525	.0944
	12	.0000	.0000	.0000	.0000	.0001	.0006	.0024	.0081	.0215	.0472
	13	.0000	.0000	.0000	.0000	.0000	.0001	.0005	.0021	.0068	.0182
	14	.0000	.0000	.0000	.0000	.0000	.0000	.0001	.0004	.0016	.0052
	15	.0000	.0000	.0000	.0000	.0000	.0000	.0000	.0001	.0003	.0010
	16	.0000	.0000	.0000	.0000	.0000	.0000	.0000	.0000	.0000	.0001
	17	.0000	.0000	.0000	.0000	.0000	.0000	.0000	.0000	.0000	.0000
18	0	.3972	.1501	.0536	.0180	.0056	.0016	.0004	.0001	.0000	.0000
	1	.3763	.3002	.1704	.0811	.0338	.0126	.0042	.0012	.0003	.0001
	2	.1683	.2835	.2556	.1723	.0958	.0458	.0190	.0069	.0022	.0006
	3	.0473	.1680	.2406	.2297	.1704	.1046	.0547	.0246	.0095	.0031
	4	.0093	.0700	.1592	.2153	.2130	.1681	.1104	.0614	.0291	.0117
	5	.0014	.0218	.0787	.1507	.1988	.2017	.1664	.1146	.0666	.0327
	6	.0002	.0052	.0301	.0816	.1436	.1873	.1941	.1655	.1181	.0708
	7	.0000	.0010	.0091	.0350	.0820	.1376	.1792	.1892	.1657	.1214
	8	.0000	.0002	.0022	.0120	.0376	0811	.1327	.1734	.1864	.1669
	9	.0000	.0000	.0004	.0033	.0139	.0386	.0794	.1284	.1694	.1855
	10	.0000	.0000	.0001	.0008	.0042	.0149	.0385	.0771	.1248	.1669
	11	.0000	.0000	.0000	.0001	.0010	.0046	.0151	.0374	.0742	.1214

INDIVIDUAL TERMS, BINOMIAL DISTRIBUTION (Continued)

n	x	.05	.10	.15	.20	.25	.30	.35	.40	.45	.50
18	12	.0000	.0000	.0000	.0000	.0002	.0012	.0047	.0145	.0354	.0708
	13	.0000	.0000	.0000	.0000	.0000	.0002	.0012	.0045	.0134	.0327
	14	.0000	.0000	.0000	.0000	.0000	.0000	.0002	.0011	.0039	.0117
	15	.0000	.0000	.0000	.0000	.0000	.0000	.0000	.0002	.0009	.0031
	16	.0000	.0000	.0000	.0000	.0000	.0000	.0000	.0000	.0001	.0006
	17	.0000	.0000	.0000	.0000	.0000	.0000	.0000	.0000	.0000	.0001
	18	.0000	.0000	.0000	.0000	.0000	.0000	.0000	.0000	.0000	.0000
19	0	.3774	.1351	.0456	.0144	.0042	.0011	.0003	.0001	.0000	.0000
	1	.3774	.2852	.1529	.0685	.0268	.0093	.0029	.0008	.0002	.0000
	2	.1787	.2852	.2428	.1540	.0803	.0358	.0138	.0046	.0013	.0003
	3	.0533	.1796	.2428	.2182	.1517	.0869	.0422	.0175	.0062	.0018
	4	.0112	.0798	.1714	.2182	.2023	.1491	.0909	.0467	.0203	.0074
	5	.0018	.0266	.0907	.1636	.2023	.1916	.1468	.0933	.0497	.0222
	6	.0002	.0069	.0374	.0955	.1574	.1916	.1844	.1451	.0949	.0518
	7	.0000	.0014	.0122	.0443	.0974	.1525	.1844	.1797	.1443	.0961
	8	.0000	.0002	.0032	.0166	.0487	.0981	.1489	.1797	.1771	.1442
	9	.0000	.0000	.0007	.0051	.0198	.0514	.0980	.1464	.1771	.1762
	10	.0000	.0000	.0001	.0013	.0066	.0220	.0528	.0976	.1449	.1762
	11	.0000	.0000	.0000	.0003	.0018	.0077	.0233	.0532	.0970	.1442
	12	.0000	.0000	.0000	.0000	.0004	.0022	.0083	.0237	.0529	.0961
	13	.0000	.0000	.0000	.0000	.0001	.0005	.0024	.0085	.0233	.0518
	14	.0000	.0000	.0000	.0000	.0000	.0001	.0006	.0024	.0082	.0222
	15	.0000	.0000	.0000	.0000	.0000	.0000	.0001	.0005	.0022	.0074
	16	.0000	.0000	.0000	.0000	.0000	.0000	.0000	.0001	.0005	.0018
	17	.0000	.0000	.0000	.0000	.0000	.0000	.0000	.0000	.0001	.0003
	18	.0000	.0000	.0000	.0000	.0000	.0000	.0000	.0000	.0000	.0000
	19	.0000	.0000	.0000	.0000	.0000	.0000	.0000	.0000	.0000	.0000
20	0	.3585	.1216	.0388	.0115	.0032	.0008	.0002	.0000	.0000	.0000
	1	.3774	.2702	.1368	.0576	.0211	.0068	.0020	.0005	.0001	.0000
	2	.1887	.2852	.2293	.1369	.0669	.0278	.0100	.0031	.0008	.0002
	3	.0596	.1901	.2428	.2054	.1339	.0716	.0323	.0123	.0040	.0011
	4	.0133	.0898	.1821	.2182	.1897	.1304	.0738	.0350	.0139	.0046
	5	.0022	.0319	.1028	.1746	.2023	.1789	.1272	.0746	.0365	.0148
	6	.0003	.0089	.0454	.1091	.1686	.1916	.1712	.1244	.0746	.0370
	7	.0000	.0020	.0160	.0545	.1124	.1643	.1844	.1659	.1221	.0739
	8	.0000	.0004	.0046	.0222	.0609	.1144	.1614	.1797	.1623	.1201
	9	.0000	.0001	.0011	.0074	.0271	.0654	.1158	.1597	.1771	.1602
	10	.0000	.0000	.0002	.0020	.0099	.0308	.0686	.1171	.1593	.1762
	11	.0000	.0000	.0000	.0005	.0030	.0120	.0336	.0710	.1185	.1602
	12	.0000	.0000	.0000	.0001	.0008	.0039	.0136	.0355	.0727	.1201
	13	.0000	.0000	.0000	.0000	.0002	.0010	.0045	.0146	.0366	.0739
	14	.0000	.0000	.0000	.0000	.0000	.0002	.0012	.0049	.0150	.0370
	15	.0000	.0000	.0000	.0000	.0000	.0000	.0003	.0013	.0049	.0148
	16	.0000	.0000	.0000	.0000	.0000	.0000	.0000	.0003	.0013	.0046
	17	.0000	.0000	.0000	.0000	.0000	.0000	.0000	.0000	.0002	.0011
	18	.0000	.0000	.0000	.0000	.0000	.0000	.0000	.0000	.0000	.0002
	19	.0000	.0000	.0000	.0000	.0000	.0000	.0000	.0000	.0000	.0000
	20	.0000	.0000	.0000	.0000	.0000	.0000	.0000	.0000	.0000	.0000

CUMULATIVE TERMS, BINOMIAL DISTRIBUTION

For the binomial probability function $f(x;n,\theta)$ the probability of observing x' or more successes is given by

$$\sum_{x=x'}^{n} \binom{n}{x} \theta^x (1-\theta)^{n-x},$$

This table contains the values of $\displaystyle\sum_{x=x'}^{n} \binom{n}{x} \theta^x (1-\theta)^{n-x}$ for specified values of n, x', and

θ. If $\theta > 0.5$, the values for $\displaystyle\sum_{x=x'}^{n} \binom{n}{x} \theta^x (1-\theta)^{n-x}$ are obtained using the corresponding

results obtained from

$$1 - \sum_{x=n-x'+1}^{n} \binom{n}{x} (1-\theta)^x \theta^{n-x}$$

The cumulative binomial distribution is related to the incomplete beta function as follows:

$$\sum_{x=x'}^{n} \binom{n}{x} \theta^x (1-\theta)^{n-x} = I_\theta(x', n-x'+1),$$

$$\sum_{x=0}^{x'-1} \binom{n}{x} \theta^x (1-\theta)^{n-x} = 1 - I_\theta(x', n-x'+1)$$

$$= 1 - \int_0^\theta u^{x'-1}(1-u)^{n-x'}\, du \Big/ \int_0^1 u^{x'-1}(1-u)^{n-x'}\, du$$

The cumulative binomial distribution is related to the cumulative negative binomial distribution as follows:

$$1 - \sum_{x'=0}^{r-1} \binom{x+r}{x'} \theta^{x'}(1-\theta)^{x+r-x'} = \sum_{x'=0}^{x} \binom{x'+r-1}{r-1} \theta^r (1-\theta)^{x'}$$

or

$$\sum_{x'=r}^{x+r} \binom{x+r}{x'} \theta^{x'}(1-\theta)^{x+r-x'} = \sum_{x'=0}^{x} \binom{x'+r-1}{r-1} \theta^r (1-\theta)^{x'}.$$

CUMULATIVE TERMS, BINOMIAL DISTRIBUTION (Continued)

n	x′	.05	.10	.15	.20	.25	.30	.35	.40	.45	.50
2	1	.0975	.1900	.2775	.3600	.4375	.5100	.5775	.6400	.6975	.7500
	2	.0025	.0100	.0225	.0400	.0625	.0900	.1225	.1600	.2025	.2500
3	1	.1426	.2710	.3859	.4880	.5781	.6570	.7254	.7840	.8336	.8750
	2	.0072	.0280	.0608	.1040	.1562	.2160	.2818	.3520	.4252	.5000
	3	.0001	.0010	.0034	.0080	.0156	.0270	.0429	.0640	.0911	.1250
4	1	.1855	.3439	.4780	.5904	.6836	.7599	.8215	.8704	.9085	.9375
	2	.0140	.0523	.1095	.1808	.2617	.3483	.4370	.5248	.6090	.6875
	3	.0005	.0037	.0120	.0272	.0508	.0837	.1265	.1792	.2415	.3125
	4	.0000	.0001	.0005	.0016	.0039	.0081	.0150	.0256	.0410	.0625
5	1	.2262	.4095	.5563	.6723	.7627	.8319	.8840	.9222	.9497	.9688
	2	.0226	.0815	.1648	.2627	.3672	.4718	.5716	.6630	.7438	.8125
	3	.0012	.0086	.0266	.0579	.1035	.1631	.2352	.3174	.4069	.5000
	4	.0000	.0005	.0022	.0067	.0156	.0308	.0540	.0870	.1312	.1875
	5	.0000	.0000	.0001	.0003	.0010	.0024	.0053	.0102	.0185	.0312
6	1	.2649	.4686	.6229	.7379	.8220	.8824	.9246	.9533	.9723	.9844
	2	.0328	.1143	.2235	.3447	.4661	.5798	.6809	.7667	.8364	.8906
	3	.0022	.0158	.0473	.0989	.1694	.2557	.3529	.4557	.5585	.6562
	4	.0001	.0013	.0059	.0170	.0376	.0705	.1174	.1792	.2553	.3438
	5	.0000	.0001	.0004	.0016	.0046	.0109	.0223	.0410	.0692	.1094
	6	.0000	.0000	.0000	.0001	.0002	.0007	.0018	.0041	.0083	.0156
7	1	.3017	.5217	.6794	.7903	.8665	.9176	.9510	.9720	.9848	.9922
	2	.0444	.1497	.2834	.4233	.5551	.6706	.7662	.8414	.8976	.9375
	3	.0038	.0257	.0738	.1480	.2436	.3529	.4677	.5801	.6836	.7734
	4	.0002	.0027	.0121	.0333	.0706	.1260	.1998	.2898	.3917	.5000
	5	.0000	.0002	.0012	.0047	.0129	.0288	.0556	.0963	.1529	.2266
	6	.0000	.0000	.0001	.0004	.0013	.0038	.0090	.0188	.0357	.0625
	7	.0000	.0000	.0000	.0000	.0001	.0002	.0006	.0016	.0037	.0078
8	1	.3366	.5695	.7275	.8322	.8999	.9424	.9681	.9832	.9916	.9961
	2	.0572	.1869	.3428	.4967	.6329	.7447	.8309	.8936	.9368	.9648
	3	.0058	.0381	.1052	.2031	.3215	.4482	.5722	.6846	.7799	.8555
	4	.0004	.0050	.0214	.0563	.1138	.1941	.2936	.4059	.5230	.6367
	5	.0000	.0004	.0029	.0104	.0273	.0580	.1061	.1737	.2604	.3633
	6	.0000	.0000	.0002	.0012	.0042	.0113	.0253	.0498	.0885	.1445
	7	.0000	.0000	.0000	.0001	.0004	.0013	.0036	.0085	.0181	.0352
	8	.0000	.0000	.0000	.0000	.0000	.0001	.0002	.0007	.0017	.0039
9	1	.3698	.6126	.7684	.8658	.9249	.9596	.9793	.9899	.9954	.9980
	2	.0712	.2252	.4005	.5638	.6997	.8040	.8789	.9295	.9615	.9805
	3	.0084	.0530	.1409	.2618	.3993	.5372	.6627	.7682	.8505	.9102
	4	.0006	.0083	.0339	.0856	.1657	.2703	.3911	.5174	.6386	.7461
	5	.0000	.0009	.0056	.0196	.0489	.0988	.1717	.2666	.3786	.5000
	6	.0000	.0001	.0006	.0031	.0100	.0253	.0536	.0994	.1658	.2539
	7	.0000	.0000	.0000	.0003	.0013	.0043	.0112	.0250	.0498	.0898
	8	.0000	.0000	.0000	.0000	.0001	.0004	.0014	.0038	.0091	.0195
	9	.0000	.0000	.0000	.0000	.0000	.0000	.0001	.0003	.0008	.0020

Linear interpolation will be accurate at most to two decimal places.

CUMULATIVE TERMS, BINOMIAL DISTRIBUTION (Continued)

n	x'	.05	.10	.15	.20	.25	.30	.35	.40	.45	.50
10	1	.4013	.6513	.8031	.8926	.9437	.9718	.9865	.9940	.9975	.9990
	2	.0861	.2639	.4557	.6242	.7560	.8507	.9140	.9536	.9767	.9893
	3	.0115	.0702	.1798	.3222	.4744	.6172	.7384	.8327	.9004	.9453
	4	.0010	.0128	.0500	.1209	.2241	.3504	.4862	.6177	.7340	.8281
	5	.0001	.0016	.0099	.0328	.0781	.1503	.2485	.3669	.4956	.6230
	6	.0000	.0001	.0014	.0064	.0197	.0473	.0949	.1662	.2616	.3770
	7	.0000	.0000	.0001	.0009	.0035	.0106	.0260	.0548	.1020	.1719
	8	.0000	.0000	.0000	.0001	.0004	.0016	.0048	.0123	.0274	.0547
	9	.0000	.0000	.0000	.0000	.0000	.0001	.0005	.0017	.0045	.0107
	10	.0000	.0000	.0000	.0000	.0000	.0000	.0000	.0001	.0003	.0010
11	1	.4312	.6862	.8327	.9141	.9578	.9802	.9912	.9964	.9986	.9995
	2	.1019	.3026	.5078	.6779	.8029	.8870	.9394	.9698	.9861	.9941
	3	.0152	.0896	.2212	.3826	.5448	.6873	.7999	.8811	.9348	.9673
	4	.0016	.0185	.0694	.1611	.2867	.4304	.5744	.7037	.8089	.8867
	5	.0001	.0028	.0159	.0504	.1146	.2103	.3317	.4672	.6029	.7256
	6	.0000	.0003	.0027	.0117	.0343	.0782	.1487	.2465	.3669	.5000
	7	.0000	.0000	.0003	.0020	.0076	.0216	.0501	.0994	.1738	.2744
	8	.0000	.0000	.0000	.0002	.0012	.0043	.0122	.0293	.0610	.1133
	9	.0000	.0000	.0000	.0000	.0001	.0006	.0020	.0059	.0148	.0327
	10	.0000	.0000	.0000	.0000	.0000	.0000	.0002	.0007	.0022	.0059
	11	.0000	.0000	.0000	.0000	.0000	.0000	.0000	.0000	.0002	.0005
12	1	.4596	.7176	.8578	.9313	.9683	.9862	.9943	.9978	.9992	.9998
	2	.1184	.3410	.5565	.7251	.8416	.9150	.9576	.9804	.9917	.9968
	3	.0196	.1109	.2642	.4417	.6093	.7472	.8487	.9166	.9579	.9807
	4	.0022	.0256	.0922	.2054	.3512	.5075	.6533	.7747	.8655	.9270
	5	.0002	.0043	.0239	.0726	.1576	.2763	.4167	.5618	.6956	.8062
	6	.0000	.0005	.0046	.0194	.0544	.1178	.2127	.3348	.4731	.6128
	7	.0000	.0001	.0007	.0039	.0143	.0386	.0846	.1582	.2607	.3872
	8	.0000	.0000	.0001	.0006	.0028	.0095	.0255	.0573	.1117	.1938
	9	.0000	.0000	.0000	.0001	.0004	.0017	.0056	.0153	.0356	.0730
	10	.0000	.0000	.0000	.0000	.0000	.0002	.0008	.0028	.0079	.0193
	11	.0000	.0000	.0000	.0000	.0000	.0000	.0001	.0003	.0011	.0032
	12	.0000	.0000	.0000	.0000	.0000	.0000	.0000	.0000	.0001	.0002
13	1	.4867	.7458	.8791	.9450	.9762	.9903	.9963	.9987	.9996	.9999
	2	.1354	.3787	.6017	.7664	.8733	.9363	.9704	.9874	.9951	.9983
	3	.0245	.1339	.3080	.4983	.6674	.7975	.8868	.9421	.9731	.9888
	4	.0031	.0342	.1180	.2527	.4157	.5794	.7217	.8314	.9071	.9539
	5	.0003	.0065	.0342	.0991	.2060	.3457	.4995	.6470	.7721	.8666
	6	.0000	.0009	.0075	.0300	.0802	.1654	.2841	.4256	.5732	.7095
	7	.0000	.0001	.0013	.0070	.0243	.0624	.1295	.2288	.3563	.5000
	8	.0000	.0000	.0002	.0012	.0056	.0182	.0462	.0977	.1788	.2905
	9	.0000	.0000	.0000	.0002	.0010	.0040	.0126	.0321	.0698	.1334
	10	.0000	.0000	.0000	.0000	.0001	.0007	.0025	.0078	.0203	.0461
	11	.0000	.0000	.0000	.0000	.0000	.0001	.0003	.0013	.0041	.0112
	12	.0000	.0000	.0000	.0000	.0000	.0000	.0000	.0001	.0005	.0017
	13	.0000	.0000	.0000	.0000	.0000	.0000	.0000	.0000	.0000	.0001

CUMULATIVE TERMS, BINOMIAL DISTRIBUTION (Continued)

n	x'	.05	.10	.15	.20	.25	.30	.35	.40	.45	.50
14	1	.5123	.7712	.8972	.9560	.9822	.9932	.9976	.9992	.9998	.9999
	2	.1530	.4154	.6433	.8021	.8990	.9525	.9795	.9919	.9971	.9991
	3	.0301	.1584	.3521	.5519	.7189	.8392	.9161	.9602	.9830	.9935
	4	.0042	.0441	.1465	.3018	.4787	.6448	.7795	.8757	.9368	.9713
	5	.0004	.0092	.0467	.1298	.2585	.4158	.5773	.7207	.8328	.9102
	6	.0000	.0015	.0115	.0439	.1117	.2195	.3595	.5141	.6627	.7880
	7	.0000	.0002	.0022	.0116	.0383	.0933	.1836	.3075	.4539	.6047
	8	.0000	.0000	.0003	.0024	.0103	.0315	.0753	.1501	.2586	.3953
	9	.0000	.0000	.0000	.0004	.0022	.0083	.0243	.0583	.1189	.2120
	10	.0000	.0000	.0000	.0000	.0003	.0017	.0060	.0175	.0426	.0898
	11	.0000	.0000	.0000	.0000	.0000	.0002	.0011	.0039	.0114	.0287
	12	.0000	.0000	.0000	.0000	.0000	.0000	.0001	.0006	.0022	.0065
	13	.0000	.0000	.0000	.0000	.0000	.0000	.0000	.0001	.0003	.0009
	14	.0000	.0000	.0000	.0000	.0000	.0000	.0000	.0000	.0000	.0001
15	1	.5367	.7941	.9126	.9648	.9866	.9953	.9984	.9995	.9999	1.0000
	2	.1710	.4510	.6814	.8329	.9198	.9647	.9858	.9948	.9983	.9995
	3	.0362	.1841	.3958	.6020	.7639	.8732	.9383	.9729	.9893	.9963
	4	.0055	.0556	.1773	.3518	.5387	.7031	.8273	.9095	.9576	.9824
	5	.0006	.0127	.0617	.1642	.3135	.4845	.6481	.7827	.8796	.9408
	6	.0001	.0022	.0168	.0611	.1484	.2784	.4357	.5968	.7392	.8491
	7	.0000	.0003	.0036	.0181	.0566	.1311	.2452	.3902	.5478	.6964
	8	.0000	.0000	.0006	.0042	.0173	.0500	.1132	.2131	.3465	.5000
	9	.0000	.0000	.0001	.0008	.0042	.0152	.0422	.0950	.1818	.3036
	10	.0000	.0000	.0000	.0001	.0008	.0037	.0124	.0338	.0769	.1509
	11	.0000	.0000	.0000	.0000	.0001	.0007	.0028	.0093	.0255	.0592
	12	.0000	.0000	.0000	.0000	.0000	.0001	.0005	.0019	.0063	.0176
	13	.0000	.0000	.0000	.0000	.0000	.0000	.0001	.0003	.0011	.0037
	14	.0000	.0000	.0000	.0000	.0000	.0000	.0000	.0000	.0001	.0005
	15	.0000	.0000	.0000	.0000	.0000	.0000	.0000	.0000	.0000	.0000
16	1	.5599	.8147	.9257	.9719	.9900	.9967	.9990	.9997	.9999	1.0000
	2	.1892	.4853	.7161	.8593	.9365	.9739	.9902	.9967	.9990	.9997
	3	.0429	.2108	.4386	.6482	.8029	.9006	.9549	.9817	.9934	.9979
	4	.0070	.0684	.2101	.4019	.5950	.7541	.8661	.9349	.9719	.9894
	5	.0009	.0170	.0791	.2018	.3698	.5501	.7108	.8334	.9147	.9616
	6	.0001	.0033	.0235	.0817	.1897	.3402	.5100	.6712	.8024	.8949
	7	.0000	.0005	.0056	.0267	.0796	.1753	.3119	.4728	.6340	.7228
	8	.0000	.0001	.0011	.0070	.0271	.0744	.1594	.2839	.4371	.5982
	9	.0000	.0000	.0002	.0015	.0075	.0257	.0671	.1423	.2559	.4018
	10	.0000	.0000	.0000	.0002	.0016	.0071	.0229	.0583	.1241	.2272
	11	.0000	.0000	.0000	.0000	.0003	.0016	.0062	.0191	.0486	.1051
	12	.0000	.0000	.0000	.0000	.0000	.0003	.0013	.0049	.0149	.0384
	13	.0000	.0000	.0000	.0000	.0000	.0000	.0002	.0009	.0035	.0106
	14	.0000	.0000	.0000	.0000	.0000	.0000	.0000	.0001	.0006	.0021
	15	.0000	.0000	.0000	.0000	.0000	.0000	.0000	.0000	.0001	.0003
	16	.0000	.0000	.0000	.0000	.0000	.0000	.0000	.0000	.0000	.0000

CUMULATIVE TERMS, BINOMIAL DISTRIBUTION (Continued)

n	x'	.05	.10	.15	.20	.25	.30	.35	.40	.45	.50
17	1	.5819	.8332	.9369	.9775	.9925	.9977	.9993	.9998	1.0000	1.0000
	2	.2078	.5182	.7475	.8818	.9499	.9807	.9933	.9979	.9994	.9999
	3	.0503	.2382	.4802	.6904	.8363	.9226	.9673	.9877	.9959	.9988
	4	.0088	.0826	.2444	.4511	.6470	.7981	.8972	.9536	.9816	.9936
	5	.0012	.0221	.0987	.2418	.4261	.6113	.7652	.8740	.9404	.9755
	6	.0001	.0047	.0319	.1057	.2347	.4032	.5803	.7361	.8529	.9283
	7	.0000	.0008	.0083	.0377	.1071	.2248	.3812	.5522	.7098	.8338
	8	.0000	.0001	.0017	.0109	.0402	.1046	.2128	.3595	.5257	.6855
	9	.0000	.0000	.0003	.0026	.0124	.0403	.0994	.1989	.3374	.5000
	10	.0000	.0000	.0000	.0005	.0031	.0127	.0383	.0919	.1834	.3145
	11	.0000	.0000	.0000	.0001	.0006	.0032	.0120	.0348	.0826	.1662
	12	.0000	.0000	.0000	.0000	.0001	.0007	.0030	.0106	.0301	.0717
	13	.0000	.0000	.0000	.0000	.0000	.0001	.0006	.0025	.0086	.0245
	14	.0000	.0000	.0000	.0000	.0000	.0000	.0001	.0005	.0019	.0064
	15	.0000	.0000	.0000	.0000	.0000	.0000	.0000	.0001	.0003	.0012
	16	.0000	.0000	.0000	.0000	.0000	.0000	.0000	.0000	.0000	.0001
	17	.0000	.0000	.0000	.0000	.0000	.0000	.0000	.0000	.0000	.0000
18	1	.6028	.8499	.9464	.9820	.9944	.9984	.9996	.9999	1.0000	1.0000
	2	.2265	.5497	.7759	.9009	.9605	.9858	.9954	.9987	.9997	.9999
	3	.0581	.2662	.5203	.7287	.8647	.9400	.9764	.9918	.9975	.9993
	4	.0109	.0982	.2798	.4990	.6943	.8354	.9217	.9672	.9880	.9962
	5	.0015	.0282	.1206	.2836	.4813	.6673	.8114	.9058	.9589	.9846
	6	.0002	.0064	.0419	.1329	.2825	.4656	.6450	.7912	.8923	.9519
	7	.0000	.0012	.0118	.0513	.1390	.2783	.4509	.6257	.7742	.8811
	8	.0000	.0002	.0027	.0163	.0569	.1407	.2717	.4366	.6085	.7597
	9	.0000	.0000	.0005	.0043	.0193	.0596	.1391	.2632	.4222	.5927
	10	.0000	.0000	.0001	.0009	.0054	.0210	.0597	.1347	.2527	.4073
	11	.0000	.0000	.0000	.0002	.0012	.0061	.0212	.0576	.1280	.2403
	12	.0000	.0000	.0000	.0000	.0002	.0014	.0062	.0203	.0537	.1189
	13	.0000	.0000	.0000	.0000	.0000	.0003	.0014	.0058	.0183	.0481
	14	.0000	.0000	.0000	.0000	.0000	.0000	.0003	.0013	.0049	.0154
	15	.0000	.0000	.0000	.0000	.0000	.0000	.0000	.0002	.0010	.0038
	16	.0000	.0000	.0000	.0000	.0000	.0000	.0000	.0000	.0001	.0007
	17	.0000	.0000	.0000	.0000	.0000	.0000	.0000	.0000	.0000	.0001
	18	.0000	.0000	.0000	.0000	.0000	.0000	.0000	.0000	.0000	.0000
19	1	.6226	.8649	.9544	.9856	.9958	.9989	.9997	.9999	1.0000	1.0000
	2	.2453	.5797	.8015	.9171	.9690	.9896	.9969	.9992	.9998	1.0000
	3	.0665	.2946	.5587	.7631	.8887	.9538	.9830	.9945	.9985	.9996
	4	.0132	.1150	.3159	.5449	.7369	.8668	.9409	.9770	.9923	.9978
	5	.0020	.0352	.1444	.3267	.5346	.7178	.8500	.9304	.9720	.9904
	6	.0002	.0086	.0537	.1631	.3322	.5261	.7032	.8371	.9223	.9682
	7	.0000	.0017	.0163	.0676	.1749	.3345	.5188	.6919	.8273	.9165
	8	.0000	.0003	.0041	.0233	.0775	.1820	.3344	.5122	.6831	.8204
	9	.0000	.0000	.0008	.0067	.0287	.0839	.1855	.3325	.5060	.6762
	10	.0000	.0000	.0001	.0016	.0089	.0326	.0875	.1861	.3290	.5000

CUMULATIVE TERMS, BINOMIAL DISTRIBUTION (Continued)

n	x'	.05	.10	.15	.20	.25	.30	.35	.40	.45	.50
19	11	.0000	.0000	.0000	.0003	.0023	.0105	.0347	.0885	.1841	.3238
	12	.0000	.0000	.0000	.0000	.0005	.0028	.0114	.0352	.0871	.1796
	13	.0000	.0000	.0000	.0000	.0001	.0006	.0031	.0116	.0342	.0835
	14	.0000	.0000	.0000	.0000	.0000	.0001	.0007	.0031	.0109	.0318
	15	.0000	.0000	.0000	.0000	.0000	.0000	.0001	.0006	.0028	.0096
	16	.0000	.0000	.0000	.0000	.0000	.0000	.0000	.0001	.0005	.0022
	17	.0000	.0000	.0000	.0000	.0000	.0000	.0000	.0000	.0001	.0004
	18	.0000	.0000	.0000	.0000	.0000	.0000	.0000	.0000	.0000	.0000
	19	.0000	.0000	.0000	.0000	.0000	.0000	.0000	.0000	.0000	.0000
20	1	.6415	.8784	.9612	.9885	.9968	.9992	.9998	1.0000	1.0000	1.0000
	2	.2642	.6083	.8244	.9308	.9757	.9924	.9979	.9995	.9999	1.0000
	3	.0755	.3231	.5951	.7939	.9087	.9645	.9879	.9964	.9991	.9998
	4	.0159	.1330	.3523	.5886	.7748	.8929	.9556	.9840	.9951	.9987
	5	.0026	.0432	.1702	.3704	.5852	.7625	.8818	.9490	.9811	.9941
	6	.0003	.0113	.0673	.1958	.3828	.5836	.7546	.8744	.9447	.9793
	7	.0000	.0024	.0219	.0867	.2142	.3920	.5834	.7500	.8701	.9423
	8	.0000	.0004	.0059	.0321	.1018	.2277	.3990	.5841	.7480	.8684
	9	.0000	.0001	.0013	.0100	.0409	.1133	.2376	.4044	.5857	.7483
	10	.0000	.0000	.0002	.0026	.0139	.0480	.1218	.2447	.4086	.5881
	11	.0000	.0000	.0000	.0006	.0039	.0171	.0532	.1275	.2493	.4119
	12	.0000	.0000	.0000	.0001	.0009	.0051	.0196	.0565	.1308	.2517
	13	.0000	.0000	.0000	.0000	.0002	.0013	.0060	.0210	.0580	.1316
	14	.0000	.0000	.0000	.0000	.0000	.0003	.0015	.0065	.0214	.0577
	15	.0000	.0000	.0000	.0000	.0000	.0000	.0003	.0016	.0064	.0207
	16	.0000	.0000	.0000	.0000	.0000	.0000	.0000	.0003	.0015	.0059
	17	.0000	.0000	.0000	.0000	.0000	.0000	.0000	.0000	.0003	.0013
	18	.0000	.0000	.0000	.0000	.0000	.0000	.0000	.0000	.0000	.0002
	19	.0000	.0000	.0000	.0000	.0000	.0000	.0000	.0000	.0000	.0000
	20	.0000	.0000	.0000	.0000	.0000	.0000	.0000	.0000	.0000	.0000
21	1	.6594	.8906	.9671	.9908	.9976	.9994	.9999	1.0000	1.0000	1.0000
	2	.2830	.6353	.8450	.9424	.9810	.9944	.9996	.9997	.9999	1.0000
	3	.0849	.3516	.6295	.8213	.9255	.9729	.9914	.9976	.9994	.9999
	4	.0189	.1520	.3887	.6296	.8083	.9144	.9669	.9890	.9969	.9993
	5	.0032	.0522	.1975	.4140	.6326	.8016	.9076	.9630	.9874	.9967
	6	.0004	.0144	.0827	.2307	.4334	.6373	.7991	.9043	.9611	.9867
	7	.0000	.0033	.0287	.1085	.2564	.4495	.6433	.7998	.9036	.9608
	8	.0000	.0006	.0083	.0431	.1299	.2770	.4635	.6505	.8029	.9054
	9	.0000	.0001	.0020	.0144	.0561	.1477	.2941	.4763	.6587	.8083
	10	.0000	.0000	.0004	.0041	.0206	.0676	.1632	.3086	.4883	.6682
	11	.0000	.0000	.0001	.0010	.0064	.0264	.0772	.1744	.3210	.5000
	12	.0000	.0000	.0000	.0002	.0017	.0087	.0313	.0849	.1841	.3318
	13	.0000	.0000	.0000	.0000	.0004	.0024	.0108	.0352	.0908	.1917
	14	.0000	.0000	.0000	.0000	.0001	.0006	.0031	.0123	.0379	.0946
	15	.0000	.0000	.0000	.0000	.0000	.0001	.0007	.0036	.0132	.0392
	16	.0000	.0000	.0000	.0000	.0000	.0000	.0001	.0008	.0037	.0133
	17	.0000	.0000	.0000	.0000	.0000	.0000	.0000	.0002	.0008	.0036
	18	.0000	.0000	.0000	.0000	.0000	.0000	.0000	.0000	.0001	.0007
	19	.0000	.0000	.0000	.0000	.0000	.0000	.0000	.0000	.0000	.0001

The column header spanning is labeled θ.

CUMULATIVE TERMS, BINOMIAL DISTRIBUTION (Continued)

n	x'	.05	.10	.15	.20	θ .25	.30	.35	.40	.45	.50
21	20	.0000	.0000	.0000	.0000	.0000	.0000	.0000	.0000	.0000	.0000
	21	.0000	.0000	.0000	.0000	.0000	.0000	.0000	.0000	.0000	.0000
22	1	.6765	.9015	.9720	.9926	.9982	.9966	.9999	1.0000	1.0000	1.0000
	2	.3018	.6608	.8633	.9520	.9851	.9959	.9990	.9998	1.0000	1.0000
	3	.0948	.3800	.6618	.8455	.9394	.9793	.9399	.9984	.9997	.9999
	4	.0222	.1719	.4248	.6680	.8376	.9319	.9755	.9924	.9980	.9996
	5	.0040	.0621	.2262	.4571	.6765	.8355	.9284	.9734	.9917	.9978
	6	.0006	.0182	.0999	.2674	.4832	.6866	.8371	.9278	.9729	.9915
	7	.0001	.0044	.0368	.1330	.3006	.5058	.6978	.8416	.9295	.9738
	8	.0000	.0009	.0114	.0561	.1615	.3287	.5264	.7102	.8482	.9331
	9	.0000	.0001	.0030	.0201	.0746	.1865	.3534	.5460	.7236	.8569
	10	.0000	.0000	.0007	.0061	.0295	.0916	.2084	.3756	.5650	.7383
	11	.0000	.0000	.0001	.0016	.0100	.0387	.1070	.2281	.3963	.5841
	12	.0000	.0000	.0000	.0003	.0029	.0140	.0474	.1207	.2457	.4159
	13	.0000	.0000	.0000	.0001	.0007	.0043	.0180	.0551	.1328	.2617
	14	.0000	.0000	.0000	.0000	.0001	.0011	.0058	.0215	.0617	.1431
	15	.0000	.0000	.0000	.0000	.0000	.0002	.0015	.0070	.0243	.0669
	16	.0000	.0000	.0000	.0000	.0000	.0000	.0003	.0019	.0080	.0262
	17	.0000	.0000	.0000	.0000	.0000	.0000	.0001	.0004	.0021	.0085
	18	.0000	.0000	.0000	.0000	.0000	.0000	.0000	.0001	.0005	.0022
	19	.0000	.0000	.0000	.0000	.0000	.0000	.0000	.0000	.0001	.0004
	20	.0000	.0000	.0000	.0000	.0000	.0000	.0000	.0000	.0000	.0001
	21	.0000	.0000	.0000	.0000	.0000	.0000	.0000	.0000	.0000	.0000
	22	.0000	.0000	.0000	.0000	.0000	.0000	.0000	.0000	.0000	.0000
23	1	.6926	.9114	.9762	.9941	.9987	.9997	1.0000	1.0000	1.0000	1.0000
	2	.3206	.6849	.8796	.9602	.9884	.9970	.9993	.9999	1.0000	1.0000
	3	.1052	.4080	.6920	.8668	.9508	.9843	.9957	.9990	1.0000	1.0000
	4	.0258	.1927	.4604	.7035	.8630	.9462	.9819	.9948	.9988	.9998
	5	.0049	.0731	.2560	.4993	.7168	.8644	.9449	.9810	.9945	.9987
	6	.0008	.0226	.1189	.3053	.5315	.7312	.8691	.9460	.9814	.9947
	7	.0001	.0058	.0463	.1598	.3463	.5601	.7466	.8760	.9490	.9827
	8	.0000	.0012	.0152	.0715	.1963	.3819	.5864	.7627	.8848	.9534
	9	.0000	.0002	.0042	.0273	.0963	.2291	.4140	.6116	.7797	.8950
	10	.0000	.0000	.0010	.0089	.0408	.1201	.2592	.4438	.6364	.7976
	11	.0000	.0000	.0002	.0025	.0149	.0546	.1425	.2871	.4722	.6612
	12	.0000	.0000	.0000	.0006	.0046	.0214	.0682	.1636	.3135	.5000
	13	.0000	.0000	.0000	.0001	.0012	.0072	.0283	.0813	.1836	.3388
	14	.0000	.0000	.0000	.0000	.0003	.0021	.0100	.0349	.0937	.2024
	15	.0000	.0000	.0000	.0000	.0001	.0005	.0030	.0128	.0411	.1050
	16	.0000	.0000	.0000	.0000	.0000	.0001	.0008	.0040	.0153	.0466
	17	.0000	.0000	.0000	.0000	.0000	.0000	.0002	.0010	.0048	.0173
	18	.0000	.0000	.0000	.0000	.0000	.0000	.0000	.0002	.0012	.0053
	19	.0000	.0000	.0000	.0000	.0000	.0000	.0000	.0000	.0002	.0013
	20	.0000	.0000	.0000	.0000	.0000	.0000	.0000	.0000	.0000	.0002
	21	.0000	.0000	.0000	.0000	.0000	.0000	.0000	.0000	.0000	.0000
	22	.0000	.0000	.0000	.0000	.0000	.0000	.0000	.0000	.0000	.0000
	23	.0000	.0000	.0000	.0000	.0000	.0000	.0000	.0000	.0000	.0000

CUMULATIVE TERMS, BINOMIAL DISTRIBUTION (Continued)

n	x'	.05	.10	.15	.20	θ .25	.30	.35	.40	.45	.50
24	1	.7080	.9202	.9798	.9953	.9990	.9998	1.0000	1.0000	1.0000	1.0000
	2	.3391	.7075	.8941	.9669	.9910	.9978	.9995	.9999	1.0000	1.0000
	3	.1159	.4357	.7202	.8855	.9602	.9881	.9970	.9993	.9999	1.0000
	4	.0298	.2143	.4951	.7361	.8850	.9576	.9867	.9965	.9992	.9999
	5	.0060	.0851	.2866	.5401	.7534	.8889	.9578	.9866	.9964	.9992
	6	.0010	.0277	.1394	.3441	.5778	.7712	.8956	.9600	.9873	.9967
	7	.0001	.0075	.0572	.1889	.3926	.6114	.7894	.9040	.9636	.9887
	8	.0000	.0017	.0199	.0892	.2338	.4353	.6425	.8081	.9137	.9680
	9	.0000	.0003	.0059	.0362	.1213	.2750	.4743	.6721	.8270	.9242
	10	.0000	.0001	.0015	.0126	.0547	.1528	.3134	.5109	.7009	.8463
	11	.0000	.0000	.0003	.0038	.0213	.0742	.1833	.3498	.5461	.7294
	12	.0000	.0000	.0001	.0010	.0072	.0314	.0942	.2130	.3849	.5806
	13	.0000	.0000	.0000	.0002	.0021	.0115	.0423	.1143	.2420	.4194
	14	.0000	.0000	.0000	.0000	.0005	.0036	.0164	.0535	.1341	.2706
	15	.0000	.0000	.0000	.0000	.0001	.0010	.0055	.0217	.0648	.1537
	16	.0000	.0000	.0000	.0000	.0000	.0002	.0016	.0075	.0269	.0758
	17	.0000	.0000	.0000	.0000	.0000	.0000	.0004	.0022	.0095	.0320
	18	.0000	.0000	.0000	.0000	.0000	.0000	.0001	.0005	.0028	.0113
	19	.0000	.0000	.0000	.0000	.0000	.0000	.0000	.0001	.0007	.0033
	20	.0000	.0000	.0000	.0000	.0000	.0000	.0000	.0000	.0001	.0008
	21	.0000	.0000	.0000	.0000	.0000	.0000	.0000	.0000	.0000	.0001
	22	.0000	.0000	.0000	.0000	.0000	.0000	.0000	.0000	.0000	.0000
	23	.0000	.0000	.0000	.0000	.0000	.0000	.0000	.0000	.0000	.0000
	24	.0000	.0000	.0000	.0000	.0000	.0000	.0000	.0000	.0000	.0000
25	1	.7226	.9282	.9828	.9962	.9992	.9999	1.0000	1.0000	1.0000	1.0000
	2	.3576	.7288	.9069	.9726	.9930	.9984	.9997	.9999	1.0000	1.0000
	3	.1271	.4629	.7463	.9018	.9679	.9910	.9979	.9996	.9999	1.0000
	4	.0341	.2364	.5289	.7660	.9038	.9668	.9903	.9976	.9995	.9999
	5	.0072	.0980	.3179	.5793	.7863	.9095	.9680	.9905	.9977	.9995
	6	.0012	.0334	.1615	.3833	.6217	.8065	.9174	.9706	.9914	.9980
	7	.0002	.0095	.0695	.2200	.4389	.6593	.8266	.9264	.9742	.9927
	8	.0000	.0023	.0255	.1091	.2735	.4882	.6939	.8464	.9361	.9784
	9	.0000	.0005	.0080	.0468	.1494	.3231	.5332	.7265	.8660	.9461
	10	.0000	.0001	.0021	.0173	.0713	.1894	.3697	.5754	.7576	.8852
	11	.0000	.0000	.0005	.0056	.0297	.0978	.2288	.4142	.6157	.7878
	12	.0000	.0000	.0001	.0015	.0107	.0442	.1254	.2677	.4574	.6550
	13	.0000	.0000	.0000	.0004	.0034	.0175	.0604	.1538	.3063	.5000
	14	.0000	.0000	.0000	.0001	.0009	.0060	.0255	.0778	.1827	.3450
	15	.0000	.0000	.0000	.0000	.0002	.0018	.0093	.0344	.0960	.2122
	16	.0000	.0000	.0000	.0000	.0000	.0005	.0029	.0132	.0440	.1148
	17	.0000	.0000	.0000	.0000	.0000	.0001	.0008	.0043	.0174	.0539
	18	.0000	.0000	.0000	.0000	.0000	.0000	.0002	.0012	.0058	.0216
	19	.0000	.0000	.0000	.0000	.0000	.0000	.0000	.0003	.0016	.0073
	20	.0000	.0000	.0000	.0000	.0000	.0000	.0000	.0001	.0004	.0020
	21	.0000	.0000	.0000	.0000	.0000	.0000	.0000	.0000	.0001	.0005
	22	.0000	.0000	.0000	.0000	.0000	.0000	.0000	.0000	.0000	.0001
	23	.0000	.0000	.0000	.0000	.0000	.0000	.0000	.0000	.0000	.0000
	24	.0000	.0000	.0000	.0000	.0000	.0000	.0000	.0000	.0000	.0000

CUMULATIVE TERMS, BINOMIAL DISTRIBUTION (Continued)

n	x'	.05	.10	.15	.20	θ .25	.30	.35	.40	.45	.50
25	25	.0000	.0000	.0000	.0000	.0000	.0000	.0000	.0000	.0000	.0000
30	1	.7854	.9576	.9924	.9988	.9998	1.0000	1.0000	1.0000	1.0000	1.0000
	2	.4465	.8163	.9520	.9895	.9980	.9997	1.0000	1.0000	1.0000	1.0000
	3	.1878	.5886	.8486	.9558	.9894	.9979	.9997	1.0000	1.0000	1.0000
	4	.0608	.3526	.6783	.8773	.9626	.9907	.9981	.9997	1.0000	1.0000
	5	.0156	.1755	.4755	.7448	.9021	.9698	.9925	.9985	.9998	1.0000
	6	.0033	.0732	.2894	.5725	.7974	.9234	.9767	.9943	.9989	.9998
	7	.0006	.0258	.1526	.3930	.6519	.8405	.9414	.9828	.9960	.9993
	8	.0001	.0078	.0698	.2392	.4857	.7186	.8762	.9565	.9879	.9974
	9	.0000	.0020	.0278	.1287	.3264	.5685	.7753	.9060	.9688	.9919
	10	.0000	.0005	.0097	.0611	.1966	.4112	.6425	.8237	.9306	.9786
	11	.0000	.0001	.0029	.0256	.1057	.2696	.4922	.7085	.8650	.9506
	12	.0000	.0000	.0008	.0095	.0507	.1593	.3452	.5689	.7673	.8998
	13	.0000	.0000	.0002	.0031	.0216	.0845	.2198	.4215	.6408	.8192
	14	.0000	.0000	.0000	.0009	.0082	.0401	.1263	.2855	.4975	.7077
	15	.0000	.0000	.0000	.0002	.0027	.0169	.0652	.1754	.3552	.5722
	16	.0000	.0000	.0000	.0001	.0008	.0064	.0301	.0971	.2309	.4278
	17	.0000	.0000	.0000	.0000	.0002	.0021	.0124	.0481	.1356	.2923
	18	.0000	.0000	.0000	.0000	.0001	.0006	.0045	.0212	.0714	.1808
	19	.0000	.0000	.0000	.0000	.0000	.0002	.0014	.0083	.0334	.1002
	20	.0000	.0000	.0000	.0000	.0000	.0000	.0004	.0029	.0138	.0494
	21	.0000	.0000	.0000	.0000	.0000	.0000	.0001	.0009	.0050	.0214
	22	.0000	.0000	.0000	.0000	.0000	.0000	.0000	.0002	.0016	.0081
	23	.0000	.0000	.0000	.0000	.0000	.0000	.0000	.0000	.0004	.0026
	24	.0000	.0000	.0000	.0000	.0000	.0000	.0000	.0000	.0001	.0007
	25	.0000	.0000	.0000	.0000	.0000	.0000	.0000	.0000	.0000	.0002
	26	.0000	.0000	.0000	.0000	.0000	.0000	.0000	.0000	.0000	.0000
	27	.0000	.0000	.0000	.0000	.0000	.0000	.0000	.0000	.0000	.0000
	28	.0000	.0000	.0000	.0000	.0000	.0000	.0000	.0000	.0000	.0000
	29	.0000	.0000	.0000	.0000	.0000	.0000	.0000	.0000	.0000	.0000
	30	.0000	.0000	.0000	.0000	.0000	.0000	.0000	.0000	.0000	.0000
35	1	.8339	.9750	.9966	.9996	1.0000	1.0000	1.0000	1.0000	1.0000	1.0000
	2	.5280	.8776	.9757	.9960	.9995	.9999	1.0000	1.0000	1.0000	1.0000
	3	.2542	.6937	.9130	.9810	.9967	.9995	.9999	1.0000	1.0000	1.0000
	4	.0958	.4690	.7912	.9395	.9864	.9976	.9997	1.0000	1.0000	1.0000
	5	.0290	.2693	.6193	.8565	.9590	.9909	.9984	.9998	1.0000	1.0000
	6	.0073	.1316	.4311	.7279	.9024	.9731	.9942	.9990	.9999	1.0000
	7	.0015	.0552	.2652	.5672	.8080	.9350	.9830	.9966	.9995	.9999
	8	.0003	.0200	.1438	.4007	.6777	.8674	.9581	.9898	.9981	.9997
	9	.0000	.0063	.0689	.2550	.5257	.7659	.9110	.9740	.9943	.9991
	10	.0000	.0017	.0292	.1457	.3737	.6354	.8349	.9425	.9848	.9970
	11	.0000	.0004	.0110	.0747	.2419	.4900	.7284	.8877	.9646	.9917
	12	.0000	.0001	.0037	.0344	.1421	.3484	.5981	.8048	.9271	.9795
	13	.0000	.0000	.0011	.0142	.0756	.2271	.4577	.6943	.8656	.9552
	14	.0000	.0000	.0003	.0053	.0363	.1350	.3240	.5639	.7767	.9123
	15	.0000	.0000	.0001	.0018	.0158	.0731	.2109	.4272	.6624	.8447
	16	.0000	.0000	.0000	.0005	.0062	.0359	.1256	.2997	.5315	.7502

CUMULATIVE TERMS, BINOMIAL DISTRIBUTION (Continued)

n	x'	.05	.10	.15	.20	.25	.30	.35	.40	.45	.50
35	17	.0000	.0000	.0000	.0001	.0022	.0160	.0682	.1935	.3976	.6321
	18	.0000	.0000	.0000	.0000	.0007	.0064	.0336	.1143	.2751	.5000
	19	.0000	.0000	.0000	.0000	.0002	.0023	.0150	.0615	.1749	.3679
	20	.0000	.0000	.0000	.0000	.0001	.0008	.0061	.0300	.1016	.2498
	21	.0000	.0000	.0000	.0000	.0000	.0002	.0022	.0133	.0536	.1553
	22	.0000	.0000	.0000	.0000	.0000	.0001	.0007	.0053	.0255	.0877
	23	.0000	.0000	.0000	.0000	.0000	.0000	.0002	.0019	.0109	.0448
	24	.0000	.0000	.0000	.0000	.0000	.0000	.0001	.0006	.0042	.0205
	25	.0000	.0000	.0000	.0000	.0000	.0000	.0000	.0002	.0014	.0083
	26	.0000	.0000	.0000	.0000	.0000	.0000	.0000	.0000	.0004	.0030
	27	.0000	.0000	.0000	.0000	.0000	.0000	.0000	.0000	.0001	.0009
	28	.0000	.0000	.0000	.0000	.0000	.0000	.0000	.0000	.0000	.0003
	29	.0000	.0000	.0000	.0000	.0000	.0000	.0000	.0000	.0000	.0001
	30	.0000	.0000	.0000	.0000	.0000	.0000	.0000	.0000	.0000	.0000
	31	.0000	.0000	.0000	.0000	.0000	.0000	.0000	.0000	.0000	.0000
	32	.0000	.0000	.0000	.0000	.0000	.0000	.0000	.0000	.0000	.0000
	33	.0000	.0000	.0000	.0000	.0000	.0000	.0000	.0000	.0000	.0000
	34	.0000	.0000	.0000	.0000	.0000	.0000	.0000	.0000	.0000	.0000
	35	.0000	.0000	.0000	.0000	.0000	.0000	.0000	.0000	.0000	.0000
40	1	.8715	.9852	.9985	.9999	1.0000	1.0000	1.0000	1.0000	1.0000	1.0000
	2	.6009	.9195	.9879	.9985	.9999	1.0000	1.0000	1.0000	1.0000	1.0000
	3	.3233	.7772	.9514	.9921	.9990	.9999	1.0000	1.0000	1.0000	1.0000
	4	.1381	.5769	.8698	.9715	.9953	.9994	.9999	1.0000	1.0000	1.0000
	5	.0480	.3710	.7367	.9241	.9840	.9974	.9997	1.0000	1.0000	1.0000
	6	.0139	.2063	.5675	.8387	.9567	.9914	.9987	.9999	1.0000	1.0000
	7	.0034	.0995	.3933	.7141	.9038	.9762	.9956	.9994	.9999	1.0000
	8	.0007	.0419	.2441	.5629	.8180	.9447	.9876	.9979	.9998	1.0000
	9	.0001	.0155	.1354	.4069	.7002	.8890	.9697	.9939	.9991	.9999
	10	.0000	.0051	.0672	.2682	.5605	.8041	.9356	.9844	.9973	.9997
	11	.0000	.0015	.0299	.1608	.4161	.6913	.8785	.9648	.9926	.9989
	12	.0000	.0004	.0120	.0875	.2849	.5594	.7947	.9291	.9821	.9968
	13	.0000	.0001	.0043	.0432	.1791	.4228	.6857	.8715	.9614	.9917
	14	.0000	.0000	.0014	.0194	.1032	.2968	.5592	.7888	.9249	.9808
	15	.0000	.0000	.0004	.0079	.0544	.1926	.4279	.6826	.8674	.9597
	16	.0000	.0000	.0001	.0029	.0262	.1151	.3054	.5598	.7858	.9231
	17	.0000	.0000	.0000	.0010	.0116	.0633	.2022	.4319	.6815	.8659
	18	.0000	.0000	.0000	.0003	.0047	.0320	.1239	.3115	.5609	.7852
	19	.0000	.0000	.0000	.0001	.0017	.0148	.0699	.2089	.4349	.6821
	20	.0000	.0000	.0000	.0000	.0006	.0063	.0363	.1298	.3156	.5627
	21	.0000	.0000	.0000	.0000	.0002	.0024	.0173	.0744	.2130	.4373
	22	.0000	.0000	.0000	.0000	.0000	.0009	.0075	.0392	.1331	.3179
	23	.0000	.0000	.0000	.0000	.0000	.0003	.0030	.0189	.0767	.2148
	24	.0000	.0000	.0000	.0000	.0000	.0001	.0011	.0083	.0405	.1341
	25	.0000	.0000	.0000	.0000	.0000	.0000	.0004	.0034	.0196	.0769
	26	.0000	.0000	.0000	.0000	.0000	.0000	.0001	.0012	.0086	.0403
	27	.0000	.0000	.0000	.0000	.0000	.0000	.0000	.0004	.0034	.0192
	28	.0000	.0000	.0000	.0000	.0000	.0000	.0000	.0001	.0012	.0083
	29	.0000	.0000	.0000	.0000	.0000	.0000	.0000	.0000	.0004	.0032

CUMULATIVE TERMS, BINOMIAL DISTRIBUTION (Continued)

n	x'	.05	.10	.15	.20	θ .25	.30	.35	.40	.45	.50
40	30	.0000	.0000	.0000	.0000	.0000	.0000	.0000	.0000	.0001	.0011
	31	.0000	.0000	.0000	.0000	.0000	.0000	.0000	.0000	.0000	.0003
	32	.0000	.0000	.0000	.0000	.0000	.0000	.0000	.0000	.0000	.0001
	33	.0000	.0000	.0000	.0000	.0000	.0000	.0000	.0000	.0000	.0000
	34	.0000	.0000	.0000	.0000	.0000	.0000	.0000	.0000	.0000	.0000
	35	.0000	.0000	.0000	.0000	.0000	.0000	.0000	.0000	.0000	.0000
	36	.0000	.0000	.0000	.0000	.0000	.0000	.0000	.0000	.0000	.0000
	37	.0000	.0000	.0000	.0000	.0000	.0000	.0000	.0000	.0000	.0000
	38	.0000	.0000	.0000	.0000	.0000	.0000	.0000	.0000	.0000	.0000
	39	.0000	.0000	.0000	.0000	.0000	.0000	.0000	.0000	.0000	.0000
	40	.0000	.0000	.0000	.0000	.0000	.0000	.0000	.0000	.0000	.0000
45	1	.9006	.9913	.9993	1.0000	1.0000	1.0000	1.0000	1.0000	1.0000	1.0000
	2	.6650	.9476	.9940	.9995	1.0000	1.0000	1.0000	1.0000	1.0000	1.0000
	3	.3923	.8410	.9735	.9968	.9997	1.0000	1.0000	1.0000	1.0000	1.0000
	4	.1866	.6711	.9215	.9871	.9984	.9999	1.0000	1.0000	1.0000	1.0000
	5	.0729	.4729	.8252	.9618	.9941	.9993	.9999	1.0000	1.0000	1.0000
	6	.0239	.2923	.6858	.9098	.9821	.9974	.9997	1.0000	1.0000	1.0000
	7	.0066	.1585	.5218	.8232	.9554	.9920	.9990	.9999	1.0000	1.0000
	8	.0016	.0757	.3606	.7025	.9059	.9791	.9967	.9996	1.0000	1.0000
	9	.0003	.0320	.2255	.5593	.8275	.9529	.9909	.9988	.9999	1.0000
	10	.0001	.0120	.1274	.4120	.7200	.9066	.9780	.9964	.9996	1.0000
	11	.0000	.0040	.0651	.2795	.5911	.8353	.9531	.9906	.9987	.9999
	12	.0000	.0012	.0302	.1741	.4543	.7380	.9104	.9784	.9964	.9996
	13	.0000	.0003	.0127	.0995	.3252	.6198	.8453	.9554	.9910	.9988
	14	.0000	.0001	.0048	.0521	.2159	.4912	.7563	.9164	.9799	.9967
	15	.0000	.0000	.0017	.0250	.1327	.3653	.6467	.8570	.9591	.9920
	16	.0000	.0000	.0005	.0110	.0753	.2538	.5248	.7751	.9238	.9822
	17	.0000	.0000	.0002	.0044	.0395	.1642	.4017	.6728	.8698	.9638
	18	.0000	.0000	.0000	.0017	.0191	.0986	.2887	.5564	.7944	.9324
	19	.0000	.0000	.0000	.0006	.0085	.0549	.1940	.4357	.6985	.8837
	20	.0000	.0000	.0000	.0002	.0035	.0283	.1215	.3214	.5869	.8144
	21	.0000	.0000	.0000	.0001	.0013	.0135	.0708	.2223	.4682	.7243
	22	.0000	.0000	.0000	.0000	.0005	.0060	.0382	.1436	.3526	.6170
	23	.0000	.0000	.0000	.0000	.0001	.0024	.0191	.0865	.2494	.5000
	24	.0000	.0000	.0000	.0000	.0000	.0009	.0089	.0483	.1650	.3830
	25	.0000	.0000	.0000	.0000	.0000	.0003	.0038	.0250	.1017	.2757
	26	.0000	.0000	.0000	.0000	.0000	.0001	.0015	.0120	.0582	.1856
	27	.0000	.0000	.0000	.0000	.0000	.0000	.0005	.0053	.0308	.1163
	28	.0000	.0000	.0000	.0000	.0000	.0000	.0002	.0021	.0150	.0676
	29	.0000	.0000	.0000	.0000	.0000	.0000	.0001	.0008	.0068	.0362
	30	.0000	.0000	.0000	.0000	.0000	.0000	.0000	.0003	.0028	.0178
	31	.0000	.0000	.0000	.0000	.0000	.0000	.0000	.0001	.0010	.0080
	32	.0000	.0000	.0000	.0000	.0000	.0000	.0000	.0000	.0004	.0033
	33	.0000	.0000	.0000	.0000	.0000	.0000	.0000	.0000	.0001	.0012
	34	.0000	.0000	.0000	.0000	.0000	.0000	.0000	.0000	.0000	.0004
	35	.0000	.0000	.0000	.0000	.0000	.0000	.0000	.0000	.0000	.0001
	36	.0000	.0000	.0000	.0000	.0000	.0000	.0000	.0000	.0000	.0000

CUMULATIVE TERMS, BINOMIAL DISTRIBUTION (Continued)

n	x'	.05	.10	.15	.20	.25	.30	.35	.40	.45	.50
						θ					
45	37	.0000	.0000	.0000	.0000	.0000	.0000	.0000	.0000	.0000	.0000
	38	.0000	.0000	.0000	.0000	.0000	.0000	.0000	.0000	.0000	.0000
	39	.0000	.0000	.0000	.0000	.0000	.0000	.0000	.0000	.0000	.0000
	40	.0000	.0000	.0000	.0000	.0000	.0000	.0000	.0000	.0000	.0000
	41	.0000	.0000	.0000	.0000	.0000	.0000	.0000	.0000	.0000	.0000
	42	.0000	.0000	.0000	.0000	.0000	.0000	.0000	.0000	.0000	.0000
	43	.0000	.0000	.0000	.0000	.0000	.0000	.0000	.0000	.0000	.0000
	44	.0000	.0000	.0000	.0000	.0000	.0000	.0000	.0000	.0000	.0000
	45	.0000	.0000	.0000	.0000	.0000	.0000	.0000	.0000	.0000	.0000

INDIVIDUAL TERMS, POISSON DISTRIBUTION

The Poisson probability function is given by

$$f(x;\lambda) = \frac{\lambda^x e^{-\lambda}}{x!}, \qquad \lambda > 0, \, x = 0, 1, 2, \ldots \, .$$

This table contains the individual terms of $f(x;\lambda)$ for specified values of x and λ.

INDIVIDUAL TERMS, POISSON DISTRIBUTION (Continued)

x	0.1	0.2	0.3	0.4	0.5	0.6	0.7	0.8	0.9	1.0
0	.9048	.8187	.7408	.6703	.6065	.5488	.4966	.4493	.4066	.3679
1	.0905	.1637	.2222	.2681	.3033	.3293	.3476	.3595	.3659	.3679
2	.0045	.0164	.0333	.0536	.0758	.0988	.1217	.1438	.1647	.1839
3	.0002	.0011	.0033	.0072	.0126	.0198	.0284	.0383	.0494	.0613
4	.0000	.0001	.0003	.0007	.0016	.0030	.0050	.0077	.0111	.0153
5	.0000	.0000	.0000	.0001	.0002	.0004	.0007	.0012	.0020	.0031
6	.0000	.0000	.0000	.0000	.0000	.0000	.0001	.0002	.0003	.0005
7	.0000	.0000	.0000	.0000	.0000	.0000	.0000	.0000	.0000	.0001

x	1.1	1.2	1.3	1.4	1.5	1.6	1.7	1.8	1.9	2.0
0	.3329	.3012	.2725	.2466	.2231	.2019	.1827	.1653	.1496	.1353
1	.3662	.3614	.3543	.3452	.3347	.3230	.3106	.2975	.2842	.2707
2	.2014	.2169	.2303	.2417	.2510	.2584	.2640	.2678	.2700	.2707
3	.0738	.0867	.0998	.1128	.1255	.1378	.1496	.1607	.1710	.1804
4	.0203	.0260	.0324	.0395	.0471	.0551	.0636	.0723	.0812	.0902
5	.0045	.0062	.0084	.0111	.0141	.0176	.0216	.0260	.0309	.0361
6	.0008	.0012	.0018	.0026	.0035	.0047	.0061	.0078	.0098	.0120
7	.0001	.0002	.0003	.0005	.0008	.0011	.0015	.0020	.0027	.0034
8	.0000	.0000	.0001	.0001	.0001	.0002	.0003	.0005	.0006	.0009
9	.0000	.0000	.0000	.0000	.0000	.0000	.0001	.0001	.0001	.0002

x	2.1	2.2	2.3	2.4	2.5	2.6	2.7	2.8	2.9	3.0
0	.1225	.1108	.1003	.0907	.0821	.0743	.0672	.0608	.0550	.0498
1	.2572	.2438	.2306	.2177	.2052	.1931	.1815	.1703	.1596	.1494
2	.2700	.2681	.2652	.2613	.2565	.2510	.2450	.2384	.2314	.2240
3	.1890	.1966	.2033	.2090	.2138	.2176	.2205	.2225	.2237	.2240
4	.0992	.1082	.1169	.1254	.1336	.1414	.1488	.1557	.1622	.1680
5	.0417	.0476	.0538	.0602	.0668	.0735	.0804	.0872	.0940	.1008
6	.0146	.0174	.0206	.0241	.0278	.0319	.0362	.0407	.0455	.0504
7	.0044	.0055	.0068	.0083	.0099	.0118	.0139	.0163	.0188	.0216
8	.0011	.0015	.0019	.0025	.0031	.0038	.0047	.0057	.0068	.0081
9	.0003	.0004	.0005	.0007	.0009	.0011	.0014	.0018	.0022	.0027
10	.0001	.0001	.0001	.0002	.0002	.0003	.0004	.0005	.0006	.0008
11	.0000	.0000	.0000	.0000	.0000	.0001	.0001	.0001	.0002	.0002
12	.0000	.0000	.0000	.0000	.0000	.0000	.0000	.0000	.0000	.0001

x	3.1	3.2	3.3	3.4	3.5	3.6	3.7	3.8	3.9	4.0
0	.0450	.0408	.0369	.0334	.0302	.0273	.0247	.0224	.0202	.0183
1	.1397	.1304	.1217	.1135	.1057	.0984	.0915	.0850	.0789	.0733
2	.2165	.2087	.2008	.1929	.1850	.1771	.1692	.1615	.1539	.1465
3	.2237	.2226	.2209	.2186	.2158	.2125	.2087	.2046	.2001	.1954
4	.1734	.1781	.1823	.1858	.1888	.1912	.1931	.1944	.1951	.1954
5	.1075	.1140	.1203	.1264	.1322	.1377	.1429	.1477	.1522	.1563
6	.0555	.0608	.0662	.0716	.0771	.0826	.0881	.0936	.0989	.1042
7	.0246	.0278	.0312	.0348	.0385	.0425	.0466	.0508	.0551	.0595
8	.0095	.0111	.0129	.0148	.0169	.0191	.0215	.0241	.0269	.0298
9	.0033	.0040	.0047	.0056	.0066	.0076	.0089	.0102	.0116	.0132

INDIVIDUAL TERMS, POISSON DISTRIBUTION (Continued)

x	3.1	3.2	3.3	3.4	3.5	3.6	3.7	3.8	3.9	4.0
10	.0010	.0013	.0016	.0019	.0023	.0028	.0033	.0039	.0045	.0053
11	.0003	.0004	.0005	.0006	.0007	.0009	.0011	.0013	.0016	.0019
12	.0001	.0001	.0001	.0002	.0002	.0003	.0003	.0004	.0005	.0006
13	.0000	.0000	.0000	.0000	.0001	.0001	.0001	.0001	.0002	.0002
14	.0000	.0000	.0000	.0000	.0000	.0000	.0000	.0000	.0000	.0001

λ

x	4.1	4.2	4.3	4.4	4.5	4.6	4.7	4.8	4.9	5.0
0	.0166	.0150	.0136	.0123	.0111	.0101	.0091	.0082	.0074	.0067
1	.0679	.0630	.0583	.0540	.0500	.0462	.0427	.0395	.0365	.0337
2	.1393	.1323	.1254	.1188	.1125	.1063	.1005	.0948	.0894	.0842
3	.1904	.1852	.1798	.1743	.1687	.1631	.1574	.1517	.1460	.1404
4	.1951	.1944	.1933	.1917	.1898	.1875	.1849	.1820	.1789	.1755
5	.1600	.1633	.1662	.1687	.1708	.1725	.1738	.1747	.1753	.1755
6	.1093	.1143	.1191	.1237	.1281	.1323	.1362	.1398	.1432	.1462
7	.0640	.0686	.0732	.0778	.0824	.0869	.0914	.0959	.1002	.1044
8	.0328	.0360	.0393	.0428	.0463	.0500	.0537	.0575	.0614	.0653
9	.0150	.0168	.0188	.0209	.0232	.0255	.0280	.0307	.0334	.0363
10	.0061	.0071	.0081	.0092	.0104	.0118	.0132	.0147	.0164	.0181
11	.0023	.0027	.0032	.0037	.0043	.0049	.0056	.0064	.0073	.0082
12	.0008	.0009	.0011	.0014	.0016	.0019	.0022	.0026	.0030	.0034
13	.0002	.0003	.0004	.0005	.0006	.0007	.0008	.0009	.0011	.0013
14	.0001	.0001	.0001	.0001	.0002	.0002	.0003	.0003	.0004	.0005
15	.0000	.0000	.0000	.0000	.0001	.0001	.0001	.0001	.0001	.0002

λ

x	5.1	5.2	5.3	5.4	5.5	5.6	5.7	5.8	5.9	6.0
0	.0061	.0055	.0050	.0045	.0041	.0037	.0033	.0030	.0027	.0025
1	.0311	.0287	.0265	.0244	.0225	.0207	.0191	.0176	.0162	.0149
2	.0793	.0746	.0701	.0659	.0618	.0580	.0544	.0509	.0477	.0446
3	.1348	.1293	.1239	.1185	.1133	.1082	.1033	.0985	.0938	.0892
4	.1719	.1681	.1641	.1600	.1558	.1515	.1472	.1428	.1383	.1339
5	.1753	.1748	.1740	.1728	.1714	.1697	.1678	.1656	.1632	.1606
6	.1490	.1515	.1537	.1555	.1571	.1584	.1594	.1601	.1605	.1606
7	.1086	.1125	.1163	.1200	.1234	.1267	.1298	.1326	.1353	.1377
8	.0692	.0731	.0771	.0810	.0849	.0887	.0925	.0962	.0998	.1033
9	.0392	.0423	.0454	.0486	.0519	.0552	.0586	.0620	.0654	.0688
10	.0200	.0220	.0241	.0262	.0285	.0309	.0334	.0359	.0386	.0413
11	.0093	.0104	.0116	.0129	.0143	.0157	.0173	.0190	.0207	.0225
12	.0039	.0045	.0051	.0058	.0065	.0073	.0082	.0092	.0102	.0113
13	.0015	.0018	.0021	.0024	.0028	.0032	.0036	.0041	.0046	.0052
14	.0006	.0007	.0008	.0009	.0011	.0013	.0015	.0017	.0019	.0022
15	.0002	.0002	.0003	.0003	.0004	.0005	.0006	.0007	.0008	.0009
16	.0001	.0001	.0001	.0001	.0001	.0002	.0002	.0002	.0003	.0003
17	.0000	.0000	.0000	.0000	.0000	.0000	.0001	.0001	.0001	.0001

INDIVIDUAL TERMS, POISSON DISTRIBUTION (Continued)

x	6.1	6.2	6.3	6.4	6.5 λ	6.6	6.7	6.8	6.9	7.0
0	.0022	.0020	.0018	.0017	.0015	.0014	.0012	.0011	.0010	.0009
1	.0137	.0126	.0116	.0106	.0098	.0090	.0082	.0076	.0070	.0064
2	.0417	.0390	.0364	.0340	.0318	.0296	.0276	.0258	.0240	.0223
3	.0848	.0806	.0765	.0726	.0688	.0652	.0617	.0584	.0552	.0521
4	.1294	.1249	.1205	.1162	.1118	.1076	.1034	.0992	.0952	.0912
5	.1579	.1549	.1519	.1487	.1454	.1420	.1385	.1349	.1314	.1277
6	.1605	.1601	.1595	.1586	.1575	.1562	.1546	.1529	.1511	.1490
7	.1399	.1418	.1435	.1450	.1462	.1472	.1480	.1486	.1489	.1490
8	.1066	.1099	.1130	.1160	.1188	.1215	.1240	.1263	.1284	.1304
9	.0723	.0757	.0791	.0825	.0858	.0891	.0923	.0954	.0985	.1014
10	.0441	.0469	.0498	.0528	.0558	.0588	.0618	.0649	.0679	.0710
11	.0245	.0265	.0285	.0307	.0330	.0353	.0377	.0401	.0426	.0452
12	.0124	.0137	.0150	.0164	.0179	.0194	.0210	.0227	.0245	.0264
13	.0058	.0065	.0073	.0081	.0089	.0098	.0108	.0119	.0130	.0142
14	.0025	.0029	.0033	.0037	.0041	.0046	.0052	.0058	.0064	.0071
15	.0010	.0012	.0014	.0016	.0018	.0020	.0023	.0026	.0029	.0033
16	.0004	.0005	.0005	.0006	.0007	.0008	.0010	.0011	.0013	.0014
17	.0001	.0002	.0002	.0002	.0003	.0003	.0004	.0004	.0005	.0006
18	.0000	.0001	.0001	.0001	.0001	.0001	.0001	.0002	.0002	.0002
19	.0000	.0000	.0000	.0000	.0000	.0000	.0000	.0001	.0001	.0001

x	7.1	7.2	7.3	7.4	7.5 λ	7.6	7.7	7.8	7.9	8.0
0	.0008	.0007	.0007	.0006	.0006	.0005	.0005	.0004	.0004	.0003
1	.0059	.0054	.0049	.0045	.0041	.0038	.0035	.0032	.0029	.0027
2	.0208	.0194	.0180	.0167	.0156	.0145	.0134	.0125	.0116	.0107
3	.0492	.0464	.0438	.0413	.0389	.0366	.0345	.0324	.0305	.0286
4	.0874	.0836	.0799	.0764	.0729	.0696	.0663	.0632	.0602	.0573
5	.1241	.1204	.1167	.1130	.1094	.1057	.1021	.0986	.0951	.0916
6	.1468	.1445	.1420	.1394	.1367	.1339	.1311	.1282	.1252	.1221
7	.1489	.1486	.1481	.1474	.1465	.1454	.1442	.1428	.1413	.1396
8	.1321	.1337	.1351	.1363	.1373	.1382	.1388	.1392	.1395	.1396
9	.1042	.1070	.1096	.1121	.1144	.1167	.1187	.1207	.1224	.1241
10	.0740	.0770	.0800	.0829	.0858	.0887	.0914	.0941	.0967	.0993
11	.0478	.0504	.0531	.0558	.0585	.0613	.0640	.0667	.0695	.0722
12	.0283	.0303	.0323	.0344	.0366	.0388	.0411	.0434	.0457	.0481
13	.0154	.0168	.0181	.0196	.0211	.0227	.0243	.0260	.0278	.0296
14	.0078	.0086	.0095	.0104	.0113	.0123	.0134	.0145	.0157	.0169
15	.0037	.0041	.0046	.0051	.0057	.0062	.0069	.0075	.0083	.0090
16	.0016	.0019	.0021	.0024	.0026	.0030	.0033	.0037	.0041	.0045
17	.0007	.0008	.0009	.0010	.0012	.0013	.0015	.0017	.0019	.0021
18	.0003	.0003	.0004	.0004	.0005	.0006	.0006	.0007	.0008	.0009
19	.0001	.0001	.0001	.0002	.0002	.0002	.0003	.0003	.0003	.0004
20	.0000	.0000	.0001	.0001	.0001	.0001	.0001	.0001	.0001	.0002
21	.0000	.0000	.0000	.0000	.0000	.0000	.0000	.0000	.0001	.0001

INDIVIDUAL TERMS, POISSON DISTRIBUTION (Continued)

λ

x	8.1	8.2	8.3	8.4	8.5	8.6	8.7	8.8	8.9	9.0
0	.0003	.0003	.0002	.0002	.0002	.0002	.0002	.0002	.0001	.0001
1	.0025	.0023	.0021	.0019	.0017	.0016	.0014	.0013	.0012	.0011
2	.0100	.0092	.0086	.0079	.0074	.0068	.0063	.0058	.0054	.0050
3	.0269	.0252	.0237	.0222	.0208	.0195	.0183	.0171	.0160	.0150
4	.0544	.0517	.0491	.0466	.0443	.0420	.0398	.0377	.0357	.0337
5	.0882	.0849	.0816	.0784	.0752	.0722	.0692	.0663	.0635	.0607
6	.1191	.1160	.1128	.1097	.1066	.1034	.1003	.0972	.0941	.0911
7	.1378	.1358	.1338	.1317	.1294	.1271	.1247	.1222	.1197	.1171
8	.1395	.1392	.1388	.1382	.1375	.1366	.1356	.1344	.1332	.1318
9	.1256	.1269	.1280	.1290	.1299	.1306	.1311	.1315	.1317	.1318
10	.1017	.1040	.1063	.1084	.1104	.1123	.1140	.1157	.1172	.1186
11	.0749	.0776	.0802	.0828	.0853	.0878	.0902	.0925	.0948	.0970
12	.0505	.0530	.0555	.0579	.0604	.0629	.0654	.0679	.0703	.0728
13	.0315	.0334	.0354	.0374	.0395	.0416	.0438	.0459	.0481	.0504
14	.0182	.0196	.0210	.0225	.0240	.0256	.0272	.0289	.0306	.0324
15	.0098	.0107	.0116	.0126	.0136	.0147	.0158	.0169	.0182	.0194
16	.0050	.0055	.0060	.0066	.0072	.0079	.0086	.0093	.0101	.0109
17	.0024	.0026	.0029	.0033	.0036	.0040	.0044	.0048	.0053	.0058
18	.0011	.0012	.0014	.0015	.0017	.0019	.0021	.0024	.0026	.0029
19	.0005	.0005	.0006	.0007	.0008	.0009	.0010	.0011	.0012	.0014
20	.0002	.0002	.0002	.0003	.0003	.0004	.0004	.0005	.0005	.0006
21	.0001	.0001	.0001	.0001	.0001	.0002	.0002	.0002	.0002	.0003
22	.0000	.0000	.0000	.0000	.0001	.0001	.0001	.0001	.0001	.0001

λ

x	9.1	9.2	9.3	9.4	9.5	9.6	9.7	9.8	9.9	10
0	.0001	.0001	.0001	.0001	.0001	.0001	.0001	.0001	.0001	.0000
1	.0010	.0009	.0009	.0008	.0007	.0007	.0006	.0005	.0005	.0005
2	.0046	.0043	.0040	.0037	.0034	.0031	.0029	.0027	.0025	.0023
3	.0140	.0131	.0123	.0115	.0107	.0100	.0093	.0087	.0081	.0076
4	.0319	.0302	.0285	.0269	.0254	.0240	.0226	.0213	.0201	.0189
5	.0581	.0555	.0530	.0506	.0483	.0460	.0439	.0418	.0398	.0378
6	.0881	.0851	.0822	.0793	.0764	.0736	.0709	.0682	.0656	.0631
7	.1145	.1118	.1091	.1064	.1037	.1010	.0982	.0955	.0928	.0901
8	.1302	.1286	.1269	.1251	.1232	.1212	.1191	.1170	.1148	.1126
9	.1317	.1315	.1311	.1306	.1300	.1293	.1284	.1274	.1263	.1251
10	.1198	.1210	.1219	.1228	.1235	.1241	.1245	.1249	.1250	.1251
11	.0991	.1012	.1031	.1049	.1067	.1083	.1098	.1112	.1125	.1137
12	.0752	.0776	.0799	.0822	.0844	.0866	.0888	.0908	.0928	.0948
13	.0526	.0549	.0572	.0594	.0617	.0640	.0662	.0685	.0707	.0729
14	.0342	.0361	.0380	.0399	.0419	.0439	.0459	.0479	.0500	.0521
15	.0208	.0221	.0235	.0250	.0265	.0281	.0297	.0313	.0330	.0347
16	.0118	.0127	.0137	.0147	.0157	.0168	.0180	.0192	.0204	.0217
17	.0063	.0069	.0075	.0081	.0088	.0095	.0103	.0111	.0119	.0128
18	.0032	.0035	.0039	.0042	.0046	.0051	.0055	.0060	.0065	.0071
19	.0015	.0017	.0019	.0021	.0023	.0026	.0028	.0031	.0034	.0037

INDIVIDUAL TERMS, POISSON DISTRIBUTION (Continued)

x	9.1	9.2	9.3	9.4	9.5	9.6	9.7	9.8	9.9	10
20	.0007	.0008	.0009	.0010	.0011	.0012	.0014	.0015	.0017	.0019
21	.0003	.0003	.0004	.0004	.0005	.0006	.0006	.0007	.0008	.0009
22	.0001	.0001	.0002	.0002	.0002	.0002	.0003	.0003	.0004	.0004
23	.0000	.0001	.0001	.0001	.0001	.0001	.0001	.0001	.0002	.0002
24	.0000	.0000	.0000	.0000	.0000	.0000	.0000	.0001	.0001	.0001

λ

x	11	12	13	14	15	16	17	18	19	20
0	.0000	.0000	.0000	.0000	.0000	.0000	.0000	.0000	.0000	.0000
1	.0002	.0001	.0000	.0000	.0000	.0000	.0000	.0000	.0000	.0000
2	.0010	.0004	.0002	.0001	.0000	.0000	.0000	.0000	.0000	.0000
3	.0037	.0018	.0008	.0004	.0002	.0001	.0000	.0000	.0000	.0000
4	.0102	.0053	.0027	.0013	.0006	.0003	.0001	.0001	.0000	.0000
5	.0224	.0127	.0070	.0037	.0019	.0010	.0005	.0002	.0001	.0001
6	.0411	.0255	.0152	.0087	.0048	.0026	.0014	.0007	.0004	.0002
7	.0646	.0437	.0281	.0174	.0104	.0060	.0034	.0018	.0010	.0005
8	.0888	.0655	.0457	.0304	.0194	.0120	.0072	.0042	.0024	.0013
9	.1085	.0874	.0661	.0473	.0324	.0213	.0135	.0083	.0050	.0029
10	.1194	.1048	.0859	.0663	.0486	.0341	.0230	.0150	.0095	.0058
11	.1194	.1144	.1015	.0844	.0663	.0496	.0355	.0245	.0164	.0106
12	.1094	.1144	.1099	.0984	.0829	.0661	.0504	.0368	.0259	.0176
13	.0926	.1056	.1099	.1060	.0956	.0814	.0658	.0509	.0378	.0271
14	.0728	.0905	.1021	.1060	.1024	.0930	.0800	.0655	.0514	.0387
15	.0534	.0724	.0885	.0989	.1024	.0992	.0906	.0786	.0650	.0516
16	.0367	.0543	.0719	.0866	.0960	.0992	.0963	.0884	.0772	.0646
17	.0237	.0383	.0550	.0713	.0847	.0934	.0963	.0936	.0863	.0760
18	.0145	.0256	.0397	.0554	.0706	.0830	.0909	.0936	.0911	.0844
19	.0084	.0161	.0272	.0409	.0557	.0699	.0814	.0887	.0911	.0888
20	.0046	.0097	.0177	.0286	.0418	.0559	.0692	.0798	.0866	.0888
21	.0024	.0055	.0109	.0191	.0299	.0426	.0560	.0684	.0783	.0846
22	.0012	.0030	.0065	.0121	.0204	.0310	.0433	.0560	.0676	.0769
23	.0006	.0016	.0037	.0074	.0133	.0216	.0320	.0438	.0559	.0669
24	.0003	.0008	.0020	.0043	.0083	.0144	.0226	.0328	.0442	.0557
25	.0001	.0004	.0010	.0024	.0050	.0092	.0154	.0237	.0336	.0446
26	.0000	.0002	.0005	.0013	.0029	.0057	.0101	.0164	.0246	.0343
27	.0000	.0001	.0002	.0007	.0016	.0034	.0063	.0109	.0173	.0254
28	.0000	.0000	.0001	.0003	.0009	.0019	.0038	.0070	.0117	.0181
29	.0000	.0000	.0001	.0002	.0004	.0011	.0023	.0044	.0077	.0125
30	.0000	.0000	.0000	.0001	.0002	.0006	.0013	.0026	.0049	.0083
31	.0000	.0000	.0000	.0000	.0001	.0003	.0007	.0015	.0030	.0054
32	.0000	.0000	.0000	.0000	.0001	.0001	.0004	.0009	.0018	.0034
33	.0000	.0000	.0000	.0000	.0000	.0001	.0002	.0005	.0010	.0020
34	.0000	.0000	.0000	.0000	.0000	.0000	.0001	.0002	.0006	.0012
35	.0000	.0000	.0000	.0000	.0000	.0000	.0000	.0001	.0003	.0007
36	.0000	.0000	.0000	.0000	.0000	.0000	.0000	.0001	.0002	.0004
37	.0000	.0000	.0000	.0000	.0000	.0000	.0000	.0000	.0001	.0002
38	.0000	.0000	.0000	.0000	.0000	.0000	.0000	.0000	.0000	.0001
39	.0000	.0000	.0000	.0000	.0000	.0000	.0000	.0000	.0000	.0001

CUMULATIVE TERMS, POISSON DISTRIBUTION

This table contains the values of

$$\sum_{x=x'}^{\infty} \frac{e^{-\lambda}\lambda^x}{x!}$$

for specified values of x' and λ. The cumulative Poisson distribution and the cumulative chi-square (χ^2) distribution are related as follows:

$$\sum_{x=0}^{x'-1} \frac{e^{-\lambda}\lambda^x}{x!} = 1 - F(\chi^2)$$

$$= \frac{1}{2^{\frac{n}{2}}\Gamma\left(\frac{n}{2}\right)} \int_{\chi^2}^{\infty} x^{\frac{n}{2}-1} e^{-\frac{x}{2}} dx$$

where $\lambda = \frac{1}{2}\chi^2$ and $x' = \frac{1}{2}n$.

CUMULATIVE TERMS, POISSON DISTRIBUTION (Continued)

λ

x'	0.1	0.2	0.3	0.4	0.5	0.6	0.7	0.8	0.9	1.0
0	1.0000	1.0000	1.0000	1.0000	1.0000	1.0000	1.0000	1.0000	1.0000	1.0000
1	.0952	.1813	.2592	.3297	.3935	.4512	.5034	.5507	.5934	.6321
2	.0047	.0175	.0369	.0616	.0902	.1219	.1558	.1912	.2275	.2642
3	.0002	.0011	.0036	.0079	.0144	.0231	.0341	.0474	.0629	.0803
4	.0000	.0001	.0003	.0008	.0018	.0034	.0058	.0091	.0135	.0190
5	.0000	.0000	.0000	.0001	.0002	.0004	.0008	.0014	.0023	.0037
6	.0000	.0000	.0000	.0000	.0000	.0000	.0001	.0002	.0003	.0006
7	.0000	.0000	.0000	.0000	.0000	.0000	.0000	.0000	.0000	.0001

λ

x'	1.1	1.2	1.3	1.4	1.5	1.6	1.7	1.8	1.9	2.0
0	1.0000	1.0000	1.0000	1.0000	1.0000	1.0000	1.0000	1.0000	1.0000	1.0000
1	.6671	.6988	.7275	.7534	.7769	.7981	.8173	.8347	.8504	.8647
2	.3010	.3374	.3732	.4082	.4422	.4751	.5068	.5372	.5663	.5940
3	.0996	.1205	.1429	.1665	.1912	.2166	.2428	.2694	.2963	.3233
4	.0257	.0338	.0431	.0537	.0656	.0788	.0932	.1087	.1253	.1429
5	.0054	.0077	.0107	.0143	.0186	.0237	.0296	.0364	.0441	.0527
6	.0010	.0015	.0022	.0032	.0045	.0060	.0080	.0104	.0132	.0166
7	.0001	.0003	.0004	.0006	.0009	.0013	.0019	.0026	.0034	.0045
8	.0000	.0000	.0001	.0001	.0002	.0003	.0004	.0006	.0008	.0011
9	.0000	.0000	.0000	.0000	.0000	.0000	.0001	.0001	.0002	.0002

λ

x'	2.1	2.2	2.3	2.4	2.5	2.6	2.7	2.8	2.9	3.0
0	1.0000	1.0000	1.0000	1.0000	1.0000	1.0000	1.0000	1.0000	1.0000	1.0000
1	.8775	.8892	.8997	.9093	.9179	.9257	.9328	.9392	.9450	.9502
2	.6204	.6454	.6691	.6916	.7127	.7326	.7513	.7689	.7854	.8009
3	.3504	.3773	.4040	.4303	.4562	.4816	.5064	.5305	.5540	.5768
4	.1614	.1806	.2007	.2213	.2424	.2640	.2859	.3081	.3304	.3528
5	.0621	.0725	.0838	.0959	.1088	.1226	.1371	.1523	.1682	.1847
6	.0204	.0249	.0300	.0357	.0420	.0490	.0567	.0651	.0742	.0839
7	.0059	.0075	.0094	.0116	.0142	.0172	.0206	.0244	.0287	.0335
8	.0015	.0020	.0026	.0033	.0042	.0053	.0066	.0081	.0099	.0119
9	.0003	.0005	.0006	.0009	.0011	.0015	.0019	.0024	.0031	.0038
10	.0001	.0001	.0001	.0002	.0003	.0004	.0005	.0007	.0009	.0011
11	.0000	.0000	.0000	.0000	.0001	.0001	.0001	.0002	.0002	.0003
12	.0000	.0000	.0000	.0000	.0000	.0000	.0000	.0000	.0001	.0001

λ

x'	3.1	3.2	3.3	3.4	3.5	3.6	3.7	3.8	3.9	4.0
0	1.0000	1.0000	1.0000	1.0000	1.0000	1.0000	1.0000	1.0000	1.0000	1.0000
1	.9550	.9592	.9631	.9666	.9698	.9727	.9753	.9776	.9798	.9817
2	.8153	.8288	.8414	.8532	.8641	.8743	.8838	.8926	.9008	.9084
3	.5988	.6201	.6406	.6603	.6792	.6973	.7146	.7311	.7469	.7619
4	.3752	.3975	.4197	.4416	.4634	.4848	.5058	.5265	.5468	.5665

CUMULATIVE TERMS, POISSON DISTRIBUTION (Continued)

λ

x'	3.1	3.2	3.3	3.4	3.5	3.6	3.7	3.8	3.9	5.0
5	.2018	.2194	.2374	.2558	.2746	.2936	.3128	.3322	.3516	.3712
6	.0943	.1054	.1171	.1295	.1424	.1559	.1699	.1844	.1994	.2149
7	.0388	.0446	.0510	.0579	.0653	.0733	.0818	.0909	.1005	.1107
8	.0142	.0168	.0198	.0231	.0267	.0308	.0352	.0401	.0454	.0511
9	.0047	.0057	.0069	.0083	.0099	.0117	.0137	.0160	.0185	.0214
10	.0014	.0018	.0022	.0027	.0033	.0040	.0048	.0058	.0069	.0081
11	.0004	.0005	.0006	.0008	.0010	.0013	.0016	.0019	.0023	.0028
12	.0001	.0001	.0002	.0002	.0003	.0004	.0005	.0006	.0007	.0009
13	.0000	.0000	.0000	.0001	.0001	.0001	.0001	.0002	.0002	.0003
14	.0000	.0000	.0000	.0000	.0000	.0000	.0000	.0000	.0001	.0001

λ

x'	4.1	4.2	4.3	4.4	4.5	4.6	4.7	4.8	4.9	5.0
0	1.0000	1.0000	1.0000	1.0000	1.0000	1.0000	1.0000	1.0000	1.0000	1.0000
1	.9834	.9850	.9864	.9877	.9889	.9899	.9909	.9918	.9926	.9933
2	.9155	.9220	.9281	.9337	.9389	.9437	.9482	.9523	.9561	.9596
3	.7762	.7898	.8026	.8149	.8264	.8374	.8477	.8575	.8667	.8753
4	.5858	.6046	.6228	.6406	.6577	.6743	.6903	.7058	.7207	.7350
5	.3907	.4102	.4296	.4488	.4679	.4868	.5054	.5237	.5418	.5595
6	.2307	.2469	.2633	.2801	.2971	.3142	.3316	.3490	.3665	.3840
7	.1214	.1325	.1442	.1564	.1689	.1820	.1954	.2092	.2233	.2378
8	.0573	.0639	.0710	.0786	.0866	.0951	.1040	.1133	.1231	.1334
9	.0245	.0279	.0317	.0358	.0403	.0451	.0503	.0558	.0618	.0681
10	.0095	.0111	.0129	.0149	.0171	.0195	.0222	.0251	.0283	.0318
11	.0034	.0041	.0048	.0057	.0067	.0078	.0090	.0104	.0120	.0137
12	.0011	.0014	.0017	.0020	.0024	.0029	.0034	.0040	.0047	.0055
13	.0003	.0004	.0005	.0007	.0008	.0010	.0012	.0014	.0017	.0020
14	.0001	.0001	.0002	.0002	.0003	.0003	.0004	.0005	.0006	.0007
15	.0000	.0000	.0000	.0001	.0001	.0001	.0001	.0001	.0002	.0002
16	.0000	.0000	.0000	.0000	.0000	.0000	.0000	.0000	.0001	.0001

λ

x'	5.1	5.2	5.3	5.4	5.5	5.6	5.7	5.8	5.9	6.0
0	1.0000	1.0000	1.0000	1.0000	1.0000	1.0000	1.0000	1.0000	1.0000	1.0000
1	.9939	.9945	.9950	.9955	.9959	.9963	.9967	.9970	.9973	.9975
2	.9628	.9658	.9686	.9711	.9734	.9756	.9776	.9794	.9811	.9826
3	.8835	.8912	.8984	.9052	.9116	.9176	.9232	.9285	.9334	.9380
4	.7487	.7619	.7746	.7867	.7983	.8094	.8200	.8300	.8396	.8488
5	.5769	.5939	.6105	.6267	.6425	.6579	.6728	.6873	.7013	.7149
6	.4016	.4191	.4365	.4539	.4711	.4881	.5050	.5217	.5381	.5543
7	.2526	.2676	.2829	.2983	.3140	.3297	.3456	.3616	.3776	.3937
8	.1440	.1551	.1665	.1783	.1905	.2030	.2159	.2290	.2424	.2560
9	.0748	.0819	.0894	.0974	.1056	.1143	.1234	.1328	.1426	.1528

CUMULATIVE TERMS, POISSON DISTRIBUTION (Continued)

x	5.1	5.2	5.3	5.4	λ 5.5	5.6	5.7	5.8	5.9	6.0
10	.0356	.0397	.0441	.0488	.0538	.0591	.0648	.0708	.0772	.0839
11	.0156	.0177	.0200	.0225	.0253	.0282	.0314	.0349	.0386	.0426
12	.0063	.0073	.0084	.0096	.0110	.0125	.0141	.0160	.0179	.0201
13	.0024	.0028	.0033	.0038	.0045	.0051	.0059	.0068	.0078	.0088
14	.0008	.0010	.0012	.0014	.0017	.0020	.0023	.0027	.0031	.0036
15	.0003	.0003	.0004	.0005	.0006	.0007	.0009	.0010	.0012	.0014
16	.0001	.0001	.0001	.0002	.0002	.0002	.0003	.0004	.0004	.0005
17	.0000	.0000	.0000	.0001	.0001	.0001	.0001	.0001	.0001	.0002
18	.0000	.0000	.0000	.0000	.0000	.0000	.0000	.0000	.0000	.0001

x'	6.1	6.2	6.3	6.4	λ 6.5	6.6	6.7	6.8	6.9	7.0
0	1.0000	1.0000	1.0000	1.0000	1.0000	1.0000	1.0000	1.0000	1.0000	1.0000
1	.9978	.9980	.9982	.9983	.9985	.9986	.9988	.9989	.9990	.9991
2	.9841	.9854	.9866	.9877	.9887	.9897	.9905	.9913	.9920	.9927
3	.9423	.9464	.9502	.9537	.9570	.9600	.9629	.9656	.9680	.9704
4	.8575	.8658	.8736	.8811	.8882	.8948	.9012	.9072	.9129	.9182
5	.7281	.7408	.7531	.7649	.7763	.7873	.7978	.8080	.8177	.8270
6	.5702	.5859	.6012	.6163	.6310	.6453	.6594	.6730	.6863	.6993
7	.4098	.4258	.4418	.4577	.4735	.4892	.5047	.5201	.5353	.5503
8	.2699	.2840	.2983	.3127	.3272	.3419	.3567	.3715	.3864	.4013
9	.1633	.1741	.1852	.1967	.2084	.2204	.2327	.2452	.2580	.2709
10	.0910	.0984	.1061	.1142	.1226	.1314	.1404	.1498	.1505	.1695
11	.0439	.0514	.0563	.0614	.0668	.0726	.0786	.0849	.0916	.0985
12	.0224	.0250	.0277	.0307	.0339	.0373	.0409	.0448	.0490	.0534
13	.0100	.0113	.0127	.0143	.0160	.0179	.0199	.0221	.0245	.0270
14	.0042	.0048	.0055	.0063	.0071	.0080	.0091	.0102	.0115	.0128
15	.0016	.0019	.0022	.0026	.0030	.0034	.0039	.0044	.0050	.0057
16	.0006	.0007	.0008	.0010	.0012	.0014	.0016	.0018	.0021	.0024
17	.0002	.0003	.0003	.0004	.0004	.0005	.0006	.0007	.0008	.0010
18	.0001	.0001	.0001	.0001	.0002	.0002	.0002	.0003	.0003	.0004
19	.0000	.0000	.0000	.0000	.0001	.0001	.0001	.0001	.0001	.0001

x'	7.1	7.2	7.3	7.4	λ 7.5	7.6	7.7	7.8	7.9	8.0
0	1.0000	1.0000	1.0000	1.0000	1.0000	1.0000	1.0000	1.0000	1.0000	1.0000
1	.9992	.9993	.9993	.9994	.9994	.9995	.9995	.9996	.9996	.9997
2	.9933	.9939	.9944	.9949	.9953	.9957	.9961	.9964	.9967	.9970
3	.9725	.9745	.9764	.9781	.9797	.9812	.9826	.9839	.9851	.9862
4	.9233	.9281	.9326	.9368	.9409	.9446	.9482	.9515	.9547	.9576
5	.8359	.8445	.8527	.8605	.8679	.8751	.8819	.8883	.8945	.9004
6	.7119	.7241	.7360	.7474	.7586	.7693	.7797	.7897	.7994	.8088
7	.5651	.5796	.5940	.6080	.6218	.6354	.6486	.6616	.6743	.6866
8	.4162	.4311	.4459	.4607	.4754	.4900	.5044	.5188	.5330	.5470
9	.2840	.2973	.3108	.3243	.3380	.3518	.3657	.3796	.3935	.4075
10	.1798	.1904	.2012	.2123	.2236	.2351	.2469	.2589	.2710	.2834
11	.1058	.1133	.1212	.1293	.1378	.1465	.1555	.1648	.1743	.1841
12	.0580	.0629	.0681	.0735	.0792	.0852	.0915	.0980	.1048	.1119
13	.0297	.0327	.0358	.0391	.0427	.0464	.0504	.0546	.0591	.0638
14	.0143	.0159	.0176	.0195	.0216	.0238	.0261	.0286	.0313	.0342

CUMULATIVE TERMS, POISSON DISTRIBUTION (Continued)

x'	7.1	7.2	7.3	7.4	7.5	7.6	7.7	7.8	7.9	8.0
15	.0065	.0073	.0082	.0092	.0103	.0114	.0127	.0141	.0156	.0173
16	.0028	.0031	.0036	.0041	.0046	.0052	.0059	.0066	.0074	.0082
17	.0011	.0013	.0015	.0017	.0020	.0022	.0026	.0029	.0033	.0037
18	.0004	.0005	.0006	.0007	.0008	.0009	.0011	.0012	.0014	.0016
19	.0002	.0002	.0002	.0003	.0003	.0004	.0004	.0005	.0006	.0006
20	.0001	.0001	.0001	.0001	.0001	.0001	.0002	.0002	.0002	.0003
21	.0000	.0000	.0000	.0000	.0000	.0000	.0001	.0001	.0001	.0001

λ

x'	8.1	8.2	8.3	8.4	8.5	8.6	8.7	8.8	8.9	9.0
0	1.0000	1.0000	1.0000	1.0000	1.0000	1.0000	1.0000	1.0000	1.0000	1.0000
1	.9997	.9997	.9998	.9998	.9998	.9998	.9998	.9998	.9999	.9999
2	.9972	.9975	.9977	.9979	.9981	.9982	.9984	.9985	.9987	.9988
3	.9873	.9882	.9891	.9900	.9907	.9914	.9921	.9927	.9932	.9938
4	.9604	.9630	.9654	.9677	.9699	.9719	.9738	.9756	.9772	.9788
5	.9060	.9113	.9163	.9211	.9256	.9299	.9340	.9379	.9416	.9450
6	.8178	.8264	.8347	.8427	.8504	.8578	.8648	.8716	.8781	.8843
7	.6987	.7104	.7219	.7330	.7438	.7543	.7645	.7744	.7840	.7932
8	.5609	.5746	.5881	.6013	.6144	.6272	.6398	.6522	.6643	.6761
9	.4214	.4353	.4493	.4631	.4769	.4906	.5042	.5177	.5311	.5443
10	.2959	.3085	.3212	.3341	.3470	.3600	.3731	.3863	.3994	.4126
11	.1942	.2045	.2150	.2257	.2366	.2478	.2591	.2706	.2822	.2940
12	.1193	.1269	.1348	.1429	.1513	.1600	.1689	.1780	.1874	.1970
13	.0687	.0739	.0793	.0850	.0909	.0971	.1035	.1102	.1171	.1242
14	.0372	.0405	.0439	.0476	.0514	.0555	.0597	.0642	.0689	.0739
15	.0190	.0209	.0229	.0251	.0274	.0299	.0325	.0353	.0383	.0415
16	.0092	.0102	.0113	.0125	.0138	.0152	.0168	.0184	.0202	.0220
17	.0042	.0047	.0053	.0059	.0066	.0074	.0082	.0091	.0101	.0111
18	.0018	.0021	.0023	.0027	.0030	.0034	.0038	.0043	.0048	.0053
19	.0008	.0009	.0010	.0011	.0013	.0015	.0017	.0019	.0022	.0024
20	.0003	.0003	.0004	.0005	.0005	.0006	.0007	.0008	.0009	.0011
21	.0001	.0001	.0002	.0002	.0002	.0002	.0003	.0003	.0004	.0004
22	.0000	.0000	.0001	.0001	.0001	.0001	.0001	.0001	.0002	.0002
23	.0000	.0000	.0000	.0000	.0000	.0000	0000	.0000	.0001	.0001

λ

x'	9.1	9.2	9.3	9.4	9.5	9.6	9.7	9.8	9.9	10
0	1.0000	1.0000	1.0000	1.0000	1.0000	1.0000	1.0000	1.0000	1.0000	1.0000
1	.9999	.9999	.9999	.9999	.9999	.9999	.9999	.9999	1.0000	1.0000
2	.9989	.9990	.9991	.9991	.9992	.9993	.9993	.9994	.9995	.9995
3	.9942	.9947	.9951	.9955	.9958	.9962	.9965	.9967	.9970	.9972
4	.9802	.9816	.9828	.9840	.9851	.9862	.9871	.9880	.9889	.9897
5	.9483	.9514	.9544	.9571	.9597	.9622	.9645	.9667	.9688	.9707
6	.8902	.8959	.9014	.9065	.9115	.9162	.9207	.9250	.9290	.9329
7	.8022	.8108	.8192	.8273	.8351	.8426	.8498	.8567	.8634	.8699
8	.6877	.6990	.7101	.7208	.7313	.7416	.7515	.7612	.7706	.7798
9	.5574	.5704	.5832	.5958	.6082	.6204	.6324	.6442	.6558	.6672

CUMULATIVE TERMS, POISSON DISTRIBUTION (Continued)

x'	9.1	9.2	9.3	9.4	9.5	9.6	9.7	9.8	9.9	10
10	.4258	.4389	.4521	.4651	.4782	.4911	.5040	.5168	.5295	.5421
11	.3059	.3180	.3301	.3424	.3547	.3671	.3795	.3920	.4045	.4170
12	.2068	.2168	.2270	.2374	.2480	.2588	.2697	.2807	.2919	.3032
13	.1316	.1393	.1471	.1552	.1636	.1721	.1809	.1899	.1991	.2084
14	.0790	.0844	.0900	.0958	.1019	.1081	.1147	.1214	.1284	.1355
15	.0448	.0483	.0520	.0559	.0600	.0643	.0688	.0735	.0784	.0835
16	.0240	.0262	.0285	.0309	.0335	.0362	.0391	.0421	.0454	.0487
17	.0122	.0135	.0148	.0162	.0177	.0194	.0211	.0230	.0249	.0270
18	.0059	.0066	.0073	.0081	.0089	.0098	.0108	.0119	.0130	.0143
19	.0027	.0031	.0034	.0038	.0043	.0048	.0053	.0059	.0065	.0072
20	.0012	.0014	.0015	.0017	.0020	.0022	.0025	.0028	.0031	.0035
21	.0005	.0006	.0007	.0008	.0009	.0010	.0011	.0013	.0014	.0016
22	.0002	.0002	.0003	.0003	.0004	.0004	.0005	.0005	.0006	.0007
23	.0001	.0001	.0001	.0001	.0001	.0002	.0002	.0002	.0003	.0003
24	.0000	.0000	.0000	.0000	.0001	.0001	.0001	.0001	.0001	.0001

x'	11	12	13	14	15	16	17	18	19	20
0	1.0000	1.0000	1.0000	1.0000	1.0000	1.0000	1.0000	1.0000	1.0000	1.0000
1	1.0000	1.0000	1.0000	1.0000	1.0000	1.0000	1.0000	1.0000	1.0000	1.0000
2	.9998	.9999	1.0000	1.0000	1.0000	1.0000	1.0000	1.0000	1.0000	1.0000
3	.9988	.9995	.9998	.9999	1.0000	1.0000	1.0000	1.0000	1.0000	1.0000
4	.9951	.9977	.9990	.9995	.9998	.9999	1.0000	1.0000	1.0000	1.0000
5	.9849	.9924	.9963	.9982	.9991	.9996	.9998	.9999	1.0000	1.0000
6	.9625	.9797	.9893	.9945	.9972	.9986	.9993	.9997	.9998	.9999
7	.9214	.9542	.9741	.9858	.9924	.9960	.9979	.9990	.9995	.9997
8	.8568	.9105	.9460	.9684	.9820	.9900	.9946	.9971	.9985	.9992
9	.7680	.8450	.9002	.9379	.9626	.9780	.9874	.9929	.9961	.9979
10	.6595	.7576	.8342	.8906	.9301	.9567	.9739	.9846	.9911	.9950
11	.5401	.6528	.7483	.8243	.8815	.9226	.9509	.9696	.9817	.9892
12	.4207	.5384	.6468	.7400	.8152	.8730	.9153	.9451	.9653	.9786
13	.3113	.4240	.5369	.6415	.7324	.8069	.8650	.9083	.9394	.9610
14	.2187	.3185	.4270	.5356	.6368	.7255	.7991	.8574	.9016	.9339
15	.1460	.2280	.3249	.4296	.5343	.6325	.7192	.7919	.8503	.8951
16	.0926	.1556	.2364	.3306	.4319	.5333	.6285	.7133	.7852	.8435
17	.0559	.1013	.1645	.2441	.3359	.4340	.5323	.6250	.7080	.7789
18	.0322	.0630	.1095	.1728	.2511	.3407	.4360	.5314	.6216	.7030
19	.0177	.0374	.0698	.1174	.1805	.2577	.3450	.4378	.5305	.6186
20	.0093	.0213	.0427	.0765	.1248	.1878	.2637	.3491	.4394	.5297
21	.0047	.0116	.0250	.0479	.0830	.1318	.1945	.2693	.3528	.4409
22	.0023	.0061	.0141	.0288	.0531	.0892	.1385	.2009	.2745	.3563
23	.0010	.0030	.0076	.0167	.0327	.0582	.0953	.1449	.2069	.2794
24	.0005	.0015	.0040	.0093	.0195	.0367	.0633	.1011	.1510	.2125
25	.0002	.0007	.0020	.0050	.0112	.0223	.0406	.0683	.1067	.1568
26	.0001	.0003	.0010	.0026	.0062	.0131	.0252	.0446	.0731	.1122
27	.0000	.0001	.0005	.0013	.0033	.0075	.0152	.0282	.0486	.0779
28	.0000	.0001	.0002	.0006	.0017	.0041	.0088	.0173	.0313	.0525
29	.0000	.0000	.0001	.0003	.0009	.0022	.0050	.0103	.0195	.0343

CUMULATIVE TERMS, POISSON DISTRIBUTION (Continued)

x'	11	12	13	14	15	16	17	18	19	20
30	.0000	.0000	.0000	.0001	.0004	.0011	.0027	.0059	.0118	.0218
31	.0000	.0000	.0000	.0001	.0002	.0006	.0014	.0033	.0070	.0135
32	.0000	.0000	.0000	.0000	.0001	.0003	.0007	.0018	.0040	.0081
33	.0000	.0000	.0000	.0000	.0000	.0001	.0004	.0010	.0022	.0047
34	.0000	.0000	.0000	.0000	.0000	.0001	.0002	.0005	.0012	.0027
35	.0000	.0000	.0000	.0000	.0000	.0000	.0001	.0002	.0006	.0015
36	.0000	.0000	.0000	.0000	.0000	.0000	.0000	.0001	.0003	.0008
37	.0000	.0000	.0000	.0000	.0000	.0000	.0000	.0001	.0002	.0004
38	.0000	.0000	.0000	.0000	.0000	.0000	.0000	.0000	.0001	.0002
39	.0000	.0000	.0000	.0000	.0000	.0000	.0000	.0000	.0000	.0001
40	.0000	.0000	.0000	.0000	.0000	.0000	.0000	.0000	.0000	.0001

The λ symbol appears above the column headers, centered over the 15 column.

PERCENTAGE POINTS, STUDENT'S t-DISTRIBUTION

This table gives values of t such that

$$F(t) = \int_{-\infty}^{t} \frac{\Gamma\left(\dfrac{n+1}{2}\right)}{\sqrt{n\pi}\,\Gamma\left(\dfrac{n}{2}\right)} \left(1 + \frac{x^2}{n}\right)^{-\frac{n+1}{2}} dx$$

for n, the number of degrees of freedom, equal to 1, 2, . . . , 30, 40, 60, 120, ∞ ; and for $F(t) = 0.60, 0.75, 0.90, 0.95, 0.975, 0.99, 0.995,$ and 0.9995. The t-distribution is symmetrical, so that $F(-t) = 1 - F(t)$

n \ F	.60	.75	.90	.95	.975	.99	.995	.9995
1	.325	1.000	3.078	6.314	12.706	31.821	63.657	636.619
2	.289	.816	1.886	2.920	4.303	6.965	9.925	31.598
3	.277	.765	1.638	2.353	3.182	4.541	5.841	12.924
4	.271	.741	1.533	2.132	2.776	3.747	4.604	8.610
5	.267	.727	1.476	2.015	2.571	3.365	4.032	6.869
6	.265	.718	1.440	1.943	2.447	3.143	3.707	5.959
7	.263	.711	1.415	1.895	2.365	2.998	3.499	5.408
8	.262	.706	1.397	1.860	2.306	2.896	3.355	5.041
9	.261	.703	1.383	1.833	2.262	2.821	3.250	4.781
10	.260	.700	1.372	1.812	2.228	2.764	3.169	4.587
11	.260	.697	1.363	1.796	2.201	2.718	3.106	4.437
12	.259	.695	1.356	1.782	2.179	2.681	3.055	4.318
13	.259	.694	1.350	1.771	2.160	2.650	3.012	4.221
14	.258	.692	1.345	1.761	2.145	2.624	2.977	4.140
15	.258	.691	1.341	1.753	2.131	2.602	2.947	4.073
16	.258	.690	1.337	1.746	2.120	2.583	2.921	4.015
17	.257	.689	1.333	1.740	2.110	2.567	2.898	3.965
18	.257	.688	1.330	1.734	2.101	2.552	2.878	3.922
19	.257	.688	1.328	1.729	2.093	2.539	2.861	3.883
20	.257	.687	1.325	1.725	2.086	2.528	2.845	3.850
21	.257	.686	1.323	1.721	2.080	2.518	2.831	3.819
22	.256	.686	1.321	1.717	2.074	2.508	2.819	3.792
23	.256	.685	1.319	1.714	2.069	2.500	2.807	3.767
24	.256	.685	1.318	1.711	2.064	2.492	2.797	3.745
25	.256	.684	1.316	1.708	2.060	2.485	2.787	3.725
26	.256	.684	1.315	1.706	2.056	2.479	2.779	3.707
27	.256	.684	1.314	1.703	2.052	2.473	2.771	3.690
28	.256	.683	1.313	1.701	2.048	2.467	2.763	3.674
29	.256	.683	1.311	1.699	2.045	2.462	2.756	3.659
30	.256	.683	1.310	1.697	2.042	2.457	2.750	3.646
40	.255	.681	1.303	1.684	2.021	2.423	2.704	3.551
60	.254	.679	1.296	1.671	2.000	2.390	2.660	3.460
120	.254	.677	1.289	1.658	1.980	2.358	2.617	3.373
∞	.253	.674	1.282	1.645	1.960	2.326	2.576	3.291

* This table is abridged from the "Statistical Tables" of R. A. Fisher and Frank Yates published by Oliver & Boyd, Ltd., Edinburgh and London, 1938. It is here published with the kind permission of the authors and their publishers.

PERCENTAGE POINTS, CHI-SQUARE DISTRIBUTION

This table gives values of χ^2 such that

$$F(\chi^2) = \int_0^{\chi^2} \frac{1}{2^{\frac{n}{2}} \, \Gamma\left(\frac{n}{2}\right)} \, x^{\frac{n-2}{2}} \, e^{-\frac{x}{2}} \, dx$$

for n, the number of degrees of freedom, equal to 1, 2, . . . , 30. For $n > 30$, a normal approximation is quite accurate. The expression $\sqrt{2\chi^2} - \sqrt{2n-1}$ is approximately normally distributed as the standard normal distribution. Thus χ^2_α, the α-point of the distribution, may be computed by the formula

$$\chi^2_\alpha = \tfrac{1}{2}[x_\alpha + \sqrt{2n-1}]^2,$$

where x_α is the α-point of the cumulative normal distribution. For even values of n, $F(\chi^2)$ can be written as

$$1 - F(\chi^2) = \sum_{x=0}^{x'-1} \frac{e^{-\lambda}\lambda^x}{x!}$$

with $\lambda = \tfrac{1}{2}\chi^2$ and $x' = \tfrac{1}{2}n$. Thus the cumulative Chi-Square distribution is related to the cumulative Poisson distribution.

Another approximate formula for large n

$$\chi^2_\alpha = n\left(1 - \frac{2}{9n} + z_\alpha \sqrt{\frac{2}{9n}}\right)^3$$

n = degrees of freedom
z_α = the normal deviate, (the value of x for which $F(x)$ = the desired percentile).

x	1.282	1.645	1.960	2.326	2.576	3.090
$F(x)$	.90	.95	.975	.99	.995	.999

$\chi^2_{.99} = 60[1 - 0.00370 + 2.326(0.06086)]^3 = 88.4$ is the 99th percentile for 60 degrees of freedom.

PROBABILITY AND STATISTICS

PERCENTAGE POINTS, CHI-SQUARE DISTRIBUTION (Continued)

$$F(x^2) = \int_0^{x^2} \frac{1}{2^{\frac{n}{2}} \Gamma\left(\frac{n}{2}\right)} x^{\frac{n-2}{2}} e^{-\frac{x}{2}} \, dx$$

F / n	.005	.010	.025	.050	.100	.250	.500	.750	.900	.950	.975	.990	.995
1	.0000393	.000157	.000982	.00393	.0158	.102	.455	1.32	2.71	3.84	5.02	6.63	7.88
2	.0100	.0201	.0506	.103	.211	.575	1.39	2.77	4.61	5.99	7.38	9.21	10.6
3	.0717	.115	.216	.352	.584	1.21	2.37	4.11	6.25	7.81	9.35	11.3	12.8
4	.207	.297	.484	.711	1.06	1.92	3.36	5.39	7.78	9.49	11.1	13.3	14.9
5	.412	.554	.831	1.15	1.61	2.67	4.35	6.63	9.24	11.1	12.8	15.1	16.7
6	.676	.872	1.24	1.64	2.20	3.45	5.35	7.84	10.6	12.6	14.4	16.8	18.5
7	.989	1.24	1.69	2.17	2.83	4.25	6.35	9.04	12.0	14.1	16.0	18.5	20.3
8	1.34	1.65	2.18	2.73	3.49	5.07	7.34	10.2	13.4	15.5	17.5	20.1	22.0
9	1.73	2.09	2.70	3.33	4.17	5.90	8.34	11.4	14.7	16.9	19.0	21.7	23.6
10	2.16	2.56	3.25	3.94	4.87	6.74	9.34	12.5	16.0	18.3	20.5	23.2	25.2
11	2.60	3.05	3.82	4.57	5.58	7.58	10.3	13.7	17.3	19.7	21.9	24.7	26.8
12	3.07	3.57	4.40	5.23	6.30	8.44	11.3	14.8	18.5	21.0	23.3	26.2	28.3
13	3.57	4.11	5.01	5.89	7.04	9.30	12.3	16.0	19.8	22.4	24.7	27.7	29.8
14	4.07	4.66	5.63	6.57	7.79	10.2	13.3	17.1	21.1	23.7	26.1	29.1	31.3
15	4.60	5.23	6.26	7.26	8.55	11.0	14.3	18.2	22.3	25.0	27.5	30.6	32.8
16	5.14	5.81	6.91	7.96	9.31	11.9	15.3	19.4	23.5	26.3	28.8	32.0	34.3
17	5.70	6.41	7.56	8.67	10.1	12.8	16.3	20.5	24.8	27.6	30.2	33.4	35.7
18	6.26	7.01	8.23	9.39	10.9	13.7	17.3	21.6	26.0	28.9	31.5	34.8	37.2
19	6.84	7.63	8.91	10.1	11.7	14.6	18.3	22.7	27.2	30.1	32.9	36.2	38.6
20	7.43	8.26	9.59	10.9	12.4	15.5	19.3	23.8	28.4	31.4	34.2	37.6	40.0
21	8.03	8.90	10.3	11.6	13.2	16.3	20.3	24.9	29.6	32.7	35.5	38.9	41.4
22	8.64	9.54	11.0	12.3	14.0	17.2	21.3	26.0	30.8	33.9	36.8	40.3	42.8
23	9.26	10.2	11.7	13.1	14.8	18.1	22.3	27.1	32.0	35.2	38.1	41.6	44.2
24	9.89	10.9	12.4	13.8	15.7	19.0	23.3	28.2	33.2	36.4	39.4	43.0	45.6
25	10.5	11.5	13.1	14.6	16.5	19.9	24.3	29.3	34.4	37.7	40.6	44.3	46.9
26	11.2	12.2	13.8	15.4	17.3	20.8	25.3	30.4	35.6	38.9	41.9	45.6	48.3
27	11.8	12.9	14.6	16.2	18.1	21.7	26.3	31.5	36.7	40.1	43.2	47.0	49.6
28	12.5	13.6	15.3	16.9	18.9	22.7	27.3	32.6	37.9	41.3	44.5	48.3	51.0
29	13.1	14.3	16.0	17.7	19.8	23.6	28.3	33.7	39.1	42.6	45.7	49.6	52.3
30	13.8	15.0	16.8	18.5	20.6	24.5	29.3	34.8	40.3	43.8	47.0	50.9	53.7

PERCENTAGE POINTS, *F*-DISTRIBUTION

This table gives values of F such that

$$F(F) = \int_0^F \frac{\Gamma\left(\frac{m+n}{2}\right)}{\Gamma\left(\frac{m}{2}\right)\Gamma\left(\frac{n}{2}\right)} m^{\frac{m}{2}} n^{\frac{n}{2}} x^{\frac{m-2}{2}} (n + mx)^{-\frac{m+n}{2}} dx$$

for selected values of m, the number of degrees of freedom of the numerator of F; and for selected values of n, the number of degrees of freedom of the denominator of F. The table also provides values corresponding to $F(F) = .10, .05, .025, .01, .005, .001$ since $F_{1-\alpha}$ for m and n degrees of freedom is the reciprocal of F_α for n and m degrees of freedom. Thus

$$F_{.05}(4, 7) = \frac{1}{F_{.95}(7, 4)} = \frac{1}{6.09} = .164 .$$

PERCENTAGE POINTS, F-DISTRIBUTION (Continued)

$$F(F) = \int_0^F \frac{\Gamma\left(\dfrac{m+n}{2}\right)}{\Gamma\left(\dfrac{m}{2}\right)\Gamma\left(\dfrac{n}{2}\right)} m^{\frac{m}{2}} n^{\frac{n}{2}} x^{\frac{m}{2}-1} (n+mx)^{-\frac{m+n}{2}} \, dx = .90$$

$n \backslash m$	1	2	3	4	5	6	7	8	9	10	12	15	20	24	30	40	60	120	∞
1	39.86	49.50	53.59	55.83	57.24	58.20	58.91	59.44	59.86	60.19	60.71	61.22	61.74	62.00	62.26	62.53	62.79	63.06	63.33
2	8.53	9.00	9.16	9.24	9.29	9.33	9.35	9.37	9.38	9.39	9.41	9.42	9.44	9.45	9.46	9.47	9.47	9.48	9.49
3	5.54	5.46	5.39	5.34	5.31	5.28	5.27	5.25	5.24	5.23	5.22	5.20	5.18	5.18	5.17	5.16	5.15	5.14	5.13
4	4.54	4.32	4.19	4.11	4.05	4.01	3.98	3.95	3.94	3.92	3.90	3.87	3.84	3.83	3.82	3.80	3.79	3.78	3.76
5	4.06	3.78	3.62	3.52	3.45	3.40	3.37	3.34	3.32	3.30	3.27	3.24	3.21	3.19	3.17	3.16	3.14	3.12	3.10
6	3.78	3.46	3.29	3.18	3.11	3.05	3.01	2.98	2.96	2.94	2.90	2.87	2.84	2.82	2.80	2.78	2.76	2.74	2.72
7	3.59	3.26	3.07	2.96	2.88	2.83	2.78	2.75	2.72	2.70	2.67	2.63	2.59	2.58	2.56	2.54	2.51	2.49	2.47
8	3.46	3.11	2.92	2.81	2.73	2.67	2.62	2.59	2.56	2.54	2.50	2.46	2.42	2.40	2.38	2.36	2.34	2.32	2.29
9	3.36	3.01	2.81	2.69	2.61	2.55	2.51	2.47	2.44	2.42	2.38	2.34	2.30	2.28	2.25	2.23	2.21	2.18	2.16
10	3.29	2.92	2.73	2.61	2.52	2.46	2.41	2.38	2.35	2.32	2.28	2.24	2.20	2.18	2.16	2.13	2.11	2.08	2.06
11	3.23	2.86	2.66	2.54	2.45	2.39	2.34	2.30	2.27	2.25	2.21	2.17	2.12	2.10	2.08	2.05	2.03	2.00	1.97
12	3.18	2.81	2.61	2.48	2.39	2.33	2.28	2.24	2.21	2.19	2.15	2.10	2.06	2.04	2.01	1.99	1.96	1.93	1.90
13	3.14	2.76	2.56	2.43	2.35	2.28	2.23	2.20	2.16	2.14	2.10	2.05	2.01	1.98	1.96	1.93	1.90	1.88	1.85
14	3.10	2.73	2.52	2.39	2.31	2.24	2.19	2.15	2.12	2.10	2.05	2.01	1.96	1.94	1.91	1.89	1.86	1.83	1.80
15	3.07	2.70	2.49	2.36	2.27	2.21	2.16	2.12	2.09	2.06	2.02	1.97	1.92	1.90	1.87	1.85	1.82	1.79	1.76
16	3.05	2.67	2.46	2.33	2.24	2.18	2.13	2.09	2.06	2.03	1.99	1.94	1.89	1.87	1.84	1.81	1.78	1.75	1.72
17	3.03	2.64	2.44	2.31	2.22	2.15	2.10	2.06	2.03	2.00	1.96	1.91	1.86	1.84	1.81	1.78	1.75	1.72	1.69
18	3.01	2.62	2.42	2.29	2.20	2.13	2.08	2.04	2.00	1.98	1.93	1.89	1.84	1.81	1.78	1.75	1.72	1.69	1.66
19	2.99	2.61	2.40	2.27	2.18	2.11	2.06	2.02	1.98	1.96	1.91	1.86	1.81	1.79	1.76	1.73	1.70	1.67	1.63
20	2.97	2.59	2.38	2.25	2.16	2.09	2.04	2.00	1.96	1.94	1.89	1.84	1.79	1.77	1.74	1.71	1.68	1.64	1.61
21	2.96	2.57	2.36	2.23	2.14	2.08	2.02	1.98	1.95	1.92	1.87	1.83	1.78	1.75	1.72	1.69	1.66	1.62	1.59
22	2.95	2.56	2.35	2.22	2.13	2.06	2.01	1.97	1.93	1.90	1.86	1.81	1.76	1.73	1.70	1.67	1.64	1.60	1.57
23	2.94	2.55	2.34	2.21	2.11	2.05	1.99	1.95	1.92	1.89	1.84	1.80	1.74	1.72	1.69	1.66	1.62	1.59	1.55
24	2.93	2.54	2.33	2.19	2.10	2.04	1.98	1.94	1.91	1.88	1.83	1.78	1.73	1.70	1.67	1.64	1.61	1.57	1.53
25	2.92	2.53	2.32	2.18	2.09	2.02	1.97	1.93	1.89	1.87	1.82	1.77	1.72	1.69	1.66	1.63	1.59	1.56	1.52
26	2.91	2.52	2.31	2.17	2.08	2.01	1.96	1.92	1.88	1.86	1.81	1.76	1.71	1.68	1.65	1.61	1.58	1.54	1.50
27	2.90	2.51	2.30	2.17	2.07	2.00	1.95	1.91	1.87	1.85	1.80	1.75	1.70	1.67	1.64	1.60	1.57	1.53	1.49
28	2.89	2.50	2.29	2.16	2.06	2.00	1.94	1.90	1.87	1.84	1.79	1.74	1.69	1.66	1.63	1.59	1.56	1.52	1.48
29	2.89	2.50	2.28	2.15	2.06	1.99	1.93	1.89	1.86	1.83	1.78	1.73	1.68	1.65	1.62	1.58	1.55	1.51	1.47
30	2.88	2.49	2.28	2.14	2.05	1.98	1.93	1.88	1.85	1.82	1.77	1.72	1.67	1.64	1.61	1.57	1.54	1.50	1.46
40	2.84	2.44	2.23	2.09	2.00	1.93	1.87	1.83	1.79	1.76	1.71	1.66	1.61	1.57	1.54	1.51	1.47	1.42	1.38
60	2.79	2.39	2.18	2.04	1.95	1.87	1.82	1.77	1.74	1.71	1.66	1.60	1.54	1.51	1.48	1.44	1.40	1.35	1.29
120	2.75	2.35	2.13	1.99	1.90	1.82	1.77	1.72	1.68	1.65	1.60	1.55	1.48	1.45	1.41	1.37	1.32	1.26	1.19
∞	2.71	2.30	2.08	1.94	1.85	1.77	1.72	1.67	1.63	1.60	1.55	1.49	1.42	1.38	1.34	1.30	1.24	1.17	1.00

$F = \dfrac{s_1^2}{s_2^2} = \dfrac{S_1}{m} \bigg/ \dfrac{S_2}{n}$, where $s_1^2 = S_1/m$ and $s_2^2 = S_2/n$ are independent mean squares estimating a common variance σ^2 and based on m and n degrees of freedom, respectively.

PERCENTAGE POINTS, F-DISTRIBUTION (Continued)

$$F(F) = \int_0^F \frac{\Gamma\left(\dfrac{m+n}{2}\right)}{\Gamma\left(\dfrac{m}{2}\right)\Gamma\left(\dfrac{n}{2}\right)}\, m^{\frac{m}{2}} n^{\frac{n}{2}} x^{\frac{m}{2}-1} (n+mx)^{-\frac{m+n}{2}}\, dx = .95$$

n \ m	1	2	3	4	5	6	7	8	9	10	12	15	20	24	30	40	60	120	∞
1	161.4	199.5	215.7	224.6	230.2	234.0	236.8	238.9	240.5	241.9	243.9	245.9	248.0	249.1	250.1	251.1	252.2	253.3	254.3
2	18.51	19.00	19.16	19.25	19.30	19.33	19.35	19.37	19.38	19.40	19.41	19.43	19.45	19.45	19.46	19.47	19.48	19.49	19.50
3	10.13	9.55	9.28	9.12	9.01	8.94	8.89	8.85	8.81	8.79	8.74	8.70	8.66	8.64	8.62	8.59	8.57	8.55	8.53
4	7.71	6.94	6.59	6.39	6.26	6.16	6.09	6.04	6.00	5.96	5.91	5.86	5.80	5.77	5.75	5.72	5.69	5.66	5.63
5	6.61	5.79	5.41	5.19	5.05	4.95	4.88	4.82	4.77	4.74	4.68	4.62	4.56	4.53	4.50	4.46	4.43	4.40	4.36
6	5.99	5.14	4.76	4.53	4.39	4.28	4.21	4.15	4.10	4.06	4.00	3.94	3.87	3.84	3.81	3.77	3.74	3.70	3.67
7	5.59	4.74	4.35	4.12	3.97	3.87	3.79	3.73	3.68	3.64	3.57	3.51	3.44	3.41	3.38	3.34	3.30	3.27	3.23
8	5.32	4.46	4.07	3.84	3.69	3.58	3.50	3.44	3.39	3.35	3.28	3.22	3.15	3.12	3.08	3.04	3.01	2.97	2.93
9	5.12	4.26	3.86	3.63	3.48	3.37	3.29	3.23	3.18	3.14	3.07	3.01	2.94	2.90	2.86	2.83	2.79	2.75	2.71
10	4.96	4.10	3.71	3.48	3.33	3.22	3.14	3.07	3.02	2.98	2.91	2.85	2.77	2.74	2.70	2.66	2.62	2.58	2.54
11	4.84	3.98	3.59	3.36	3.20	3.09	3.01	2.95	2.90	2.85	2.79	2.72	2.65	2.61	2.57	2.53	2.49	2.45	2.40
12	4.75	3.89	3.49	3.26	3.11	3.00	2.91	2.85	2.80	2.75	2.69	2.62	2.54	2.51	2.47	2.43	2.38	2.34	2.30
13	4.67	3.81	3.41	3.18	3.03	2.92	2.83	2.77	2.71	2.67	2.60	2.53	2.46	2.42	2.38	2.34	2.30	2.25	2.21
14	4.60	3.74	3.34	3.11	2.96	2.85	2.76	2.70	2.65	2.60	2.53	2.46	2.39	2.35	2.31	2.27	2.22	2.18	2.13
15	4.54	3.68	3.29	3.06	2.90	2.79	2.71	2.64	2.59	2.54	2.48	2.40	2.33	2.29	2.25	2.20	2.16	2.11	2.07
16	4.49	3.63	3.24	3.01	2.85	2.74	2.66	2.59	2.54	2.49	2.42	2.35	2.28	2.24	2.19	2.15	2.11	2.06	2.01
17	4.45	3.59	3.20	2.96	2.81	2.70	2.61	2.55	2.49	2.45	2.38	2.31	2.23	2.19	2.15	2.10	2.06	2.01	1.96
18	4.41	3.55	3.16	2.93	2.77	2.66	2.58	2.51	2.46	2.41	2.34	2.27	2.19	2.15	2.11	2.06	2.02	1.97	1.92
19	4.38	3.52	3.13	2.90	2.74	2.63	2.54	2.48	2.42	2.38	2.31	2.23	2.16	2.11	2.07	2.03	1.98	1.93	1.88
20	4.35	3.49	3.10	2.87	2.71	2.60	2.51	2.45	2.39	2.35	2.28	2.20	2.12	2.08	2.04	1.99	1.95	1.90	1.84
21	4.32	3.47	3.07	2.84	2.68	2.57	2.49	2.42	2.37	2.32	2.25	2.18	2.10	2.05	2.01	1.96	1.92	1.87	1.81
22	4.30	3.44	3.05	2.82	2.66	2.55	2.46	2.40	2.34	2.30	2.23	2.15	2.07	2.03	1.98	1.94	1.89	1.84	1.78
23	4.28	3.42	3.03	2.80	2.64	2.53	2.44	2.37	2.32	2.27	2.20	2.13	2.05	2.01	1.96	1.91	1.86	1.81	1.76
24	4.26	3.40	3.01	2.78	2.62	2.51	2.42	2.36	2.30	2.25	2.18	2.11	2.03	1.98	1.94	1.89	1.84	1.79	1.73
25	4.24	3.39	2.99	2.76	2.60	2.49	2.40	2.34	2.28	2.24	2.16	2.09	2.01	1.96	1.92	1.87	1.82	1.77	1.71
26	4.23	3.37	2.98	2.74	2.59	2.47	2.39	2.32	2.27	2.22	2.15	2.07	1.99	1.95	1.90	1.85	1.80	1.75	1.69
27	4.21	3.35	2.96	2.73	2.57	2.46	2.37	2.31	2.25	2.20	2.13	2.06	1.97	1.93	1.88	1.84	1.79	1.73	1.67
28	4.20	3.34	2.95	2.71	2.56	2.45	2.36	2.29	2.24	2.19	2.12	2.04	1.96	1.91	1.87	1.82	1.77	1.71	1.65
29	4.18	3.33	2.93	2.70	2.55	2.43	2.35	2.28	2.22	2.18	2.10	2.03	1.94	1.90	1.85	1.81	1.75	1.70	1.64
30	4.17	3.32	2.92	2.69	2.53	2.42	2.33	2.27	2.21	2.16	2.09	2.01	1.93	1.89	1.84	1.79	1.74	1.68	1.62
40	4.08	3.23	2.84	2.61	2.45	2.34	2.25	2.18	2.12	2.08	2.00	1.92	1.84	1.79	1.74	1.69	1.64	1.58	1.51
60	4.00	3.15	2.76	2.53	2.37	2.25	2.17	2.10	2.04	1.99	1.92	1.84	1.75	1.70	1.65	1.59	1.53	1.47	1.39
120	3.92	3.07	2.68	2.45	2.29	2.17	2.09	2.02	1.96	1.91	1.83	1.75	1.66	1.61	1.55	1.50	1.43	1.35	1.25
∞	3.84	3.00	2.60	2.37	2.21	2.10	2.01	1.94	1.88	1.83	1.75	1.67	1.57	1.52	1.46	1.39	1.32	1.22	1.00

$F = \dfrac{s_1^2}{s_2^2} = \dfrac{S_1}{m} \Big/ \dfrac{S_2}{n}$, where $s_1^2 = S_1/m$ and $s_2^2 = S_2/n$ are independent mean squares estimating a common variance σ^2 and based on m and n degrees of freedom, respectively.

PERCENTAGE POINTS, F-DISTRIBUTION (Continued)

$$F(F) = \int_0^F \frac{\Gamma\left(\frac{m+n}{2}\right)}{\Gamma\left(\frac{m}{2}\right)\Gamma\left(\frac{n}{2}\right)} m^{\frac{m}{2}} n^{\frac{n}{2}} x^{\frac{m}{2}-1}(n+mx)^{-\frac{m+n}{2}}\,dx = .975$$

n \ m	1	2	3	4	5	6	7	8	9	10	12	15	20	24	30	40	60	120	∞
1	647.8	799.5	864.2	899.6	921.8	937.1	948.2	956.7	963.3	968.6	976.7	984.9	993.1	997.2	1001	1006	1010	1014	1018
2	38.51	39.00	39.17	39.25	39.30	39.33	39.36	39.37	39.39	39.40	39.41	39.43	39.45	39.46	39.46	39.47	39.48	39.49	39.50
3	17.44	16.04	15.44	15.10	14.88	14.73	14.62	14.54	14.47	14.42	14.34	14.25	14.17	14.12	14.08	14.04	13.99	13.95	13.90
4	12.22	10.65	9.98	9.60	9.36	9.20	9.07	8.98	8.90	8.84	8.75	8.66	8.56	8.51	8.46	8.41	8.36	8.31	8.26
5	10.01	8.43	7.76	7.39	7.15	6.98	6.85	6.76	6.68	6.62	6.52	6.43	6.33	6.28	6.23	6.18	6.12	6.07	6.02
6	8.81	7.26	6.60	6.23	5.99	5.82	5.70	5.60	5.52	5.46	5.37	5.27	5.17	5.12	5.07	5.01	4.96	4.90	4.85
7	8.07	6.54	5.89	5.52	5.29	5.12	4.99	4.90	4.82	4.76	4.67	4.57	4.47	4.42	4.36	4.31	4.25	4.20	4.14
8	7.57	6.06	5.42	5.05	4.82	4.65	4.53	4.43	4.36	4.30	4.20	4.10	4.00	3.95	3.89	3.84	3.78	3.73	3.67
9	7.21	5.71	5.08	4.72	4.48	4.32	4.20	4.10	4.03	3.96	3.87	3.77	3.67	3.61	3.56	3.51	3.45	3.39	3.33
10	6.94	5.46	4.83	4.47	4.24	4.07	3.95	3.85	3.78	3.72	3.62	3.52	3.42	3.37	3.31	3.26	3.20	3.14	3.08
11	6.72	5.26	4.63	4.28	4.04	3.88	3.76	3.66	3.59	3.53	3.43	3.33	3.23	3.17	3.12	3.06	3.00	2.94	2.88
12	6.55	5.10	4.47	4.12	3.89	3.73	3.61	3.51	3.44	3.37	3.28	3.18	3.07	3.02	2.96	2.91	2.85	2.79	2.72
13	6.41	4.97	4.35	4.00	3.77	3.60	3.48	3.39	3.31	3.25	3.15	3.05	2.95	2.89	2.84	2.78	2.72	2.66	2.60
14	6.30	4.86	4.24	3.89	3.66	3.50	3.38	3.29	3.21	3.15	3.05	2.95	2.84	2.79	2.73	2.67	2.61	2.55	2.49
15	6.20	4.77	4.15	3.80	3.58	3.41	3.29	3.20	3.12	3.06	2.96	2.86	2.76	2.70	2.64	2.59	2.52	2.46	2.40
16	6.12	4.69	4.08	3.73	3.50	3.34	3.22	3.12	3.05	2.99	2.89	2.79	2.68	2.63	2.57	2.51	2.45	2.38	2.32
17	6.04	4.62	4.01	3.66	3.44	3.28	3.16	3.06	2.98	2.92	2.82	2.72	2.62	2.56	2.50	2.44	2.38	2.32	2.25
18	5.98	4.56	3.95	3.61	3.38	3.22	3.10	3.01	2.93	2.87	2.77	2.67	2.56	2.50	2.44	2.38	2.32	2.26	2.19
19	5.92	4.51	3.90	3.56	3.33	3.17	3.05	2.96	2.88	2.82	2.72	2.62	2.51	2.45	2.39	2.33	2.27	2.20	2.13
20	5.87	4.46	3.86	3.51	3.29	3.13	3.01	2.91	2.84	2.77	2.68	2.57	2.46	2.41	2.35	2.29	2.22	2.16	2.09
21	5.83	4.42	3.82	3.48	3.25	3.09	2.97	2.87	2.80	2.73	2.64	2.53	2.42	2.37	2.31	2.25	2.18	2.11	2.04
22	5.79	4.38	3.78	3.44	3.22	3.05	2.93	2.84	2.76	2.70	2.60	2.50	2.39	2.33	2.27	2.21	2.14	2.08	2.00
23	5.75	4.35	3.75	3.41	3.18	3.02	2.90	2.81	2.73	2.67	2.57	2.47	2.36	2.30	2.24	2.18	2.11	2.04	1.97
24	5.72	4.32	3.72	3.38	3.15	2.99	2.87	2.78	2.70	2.64	2.54	2.44	2.33	2.27	2.21	2.15	2.08	2.01	1.94
25	5.69	4.29	3.69	3.35	3.13	2.97	2.85	2.75	2.68	2.61	2.51	2.41	2.30	2.24	2.18	2.12	2.05	1.98	1.91
26	5.66	4.27	3.67	3.33	3.10	2.94	2.82	2.73	2.65	2.59	2.49	2.39	2.28	2.22	2.16	2.09	2.03	1.95	1.88
27	5.63	4.24	3.65	3.31	3.08	2.92	2.80	2.71	2.63	2.57	2.47	2.36	2.25	2.19	2.13	2.07	2.00	1.93	1.85
28	5.61	4.22	3.63	3.29	3.06	2.90	2.78	2.69	2.61	2.55	2.45	2.34	2.23	2.17	2.11	2.05	1.98	1.91	1.83
29	5.59	4.20	3.61	3.27	3.04	2.88	2.76	2.67	2.59	2.53	2.43	2.32	2.21	2.15	2.09	2.03	1.96	1.89	1.81
30	5.57	4.18	3.59	3.25	3.03	2.87	2.75	2.65	2.57	2.51	2.41	2.31	2.20	2.14	2.07	2.01	1.94	1.87	1.79
40	5.42	4.05	3.46	3.13	2.90	2.74	2.62	2.53	2.45	2.39	2.29	2.18	2.07	2.01	1.94	1.88	1.80	1.72	1.64
60	5.29	3.93	3.34	3.01	2.79	2.63	2.51	2.41	2.33	2.27	2.17	2.06	1.94	1.88	1.82	1.74	1.67	1.58	1.48
120	5.15	3.80	3.23	2.89	2.67	2.52	2.39	2.30	2.22	2.16	2.05	1.94	1.82	1.76	1.69	1.61	1.53	1.43	1.31
∞	5.02	3.69	3.12	2.79	2.57	2.41	2.29	2.19	2.11	2.05	1.94	1.83	1.71	1.64	1.57	1.48	1.39	1.27	1.00

$F = \dfrac{s_1^2}{s_2^2} = \dfrac{S_1}{m} \Big/ \dfrac{S_2}{n}$, where $s_1^2 = S_1/m$ and $s_2^2 = S_2/n$ are independent mean squares estimating a common variance σ^2 and based on m and n degrees of freedom, respectively.

PERCENTAGE POINTS, F-DISTRIBUTION (Continued)

$$F(F) = \int_0^F \frac{\Gamma\left(\frac{m+n}{2}\right)}{\Gamma\left(\frac{m}{2}\right)\Gamma\left(\frac{n}{2}\right)} m^{\frac{m}{2}} n^{\frac{n}{2}} x^{\frac{m}{2}-1} (n+mx)^{-\frac{m+n}{2}} dx = .99$$

n \\ m	1	2	3	4	5	6	7	8	9	10	12	15	20	24	30	40	60	120	∞
1	4052	4999.5	5403	5625	5764	5859	5928	5982	6022	6056	6106	6157	6209	6235	6261	6287	6313	6339	6366
2	98.50	99.00	99.17	99.25	99.30	99.33	99.36	99.37	99.39	99.40	99.42	99.43	99.45	99.46	99.47	99.47	99.48	99.49	99.50
3	34.12	30.82	29.46	28.71	28.24	27.91	27.67	27.49	27.35	27.23	27.05	26.87	26.69	26.60	26.50	26.41	26.32	26.22	26.13
4	21.20	18.00	16.69	15.98	15.52	15.21	14.98	14.80	14.66	14.55	14.37	14.20	14.02	13.93	13.84	13.75	13.65	13.56	13.46
5	16.26	13.27	12.06	11.39	10.97	10.67	10.46	10.29	10.16	10.05	9.89	9.72	9.55	9.47	9.38	9.29	9.20	9.11	9.02
6	13.75	10.92	9.78	9.15	8.75	8.47	8.26	8.10	7.98	7.87	7.72	7.56	7.40	7.31	7.23	7.14	7.06	6.97	6.88
7	12.25	9.55	8.45	7.85	7.46	7.19	6.99	6.84	6.72	6.62	6.47	6.31	6.16	6.07	5.99	5.91	5.82	5.74	5.65
8	11.26	8.65	7.59	7.01	6.63	6.37	6.18	6.03	5.91	5.81	5.67	5.52	5.36	5.28	5.20	5.12	5.03	4.95	4.86
9	10.56	8.02	6.99	6.42	6.06	5.80	5.61	5.47	5.35	5.26	5.11	4.96	4.81	4.73	4.65	4.57	4.48	4.40	4.31
10	10.04	7.56	6.55	5.99	5.64	5.39	5.20	5.06	4.94	4.85	4.71	4.56	4.41	4.33	4.25	4.17	4.08	4.00	3.91
11	9.65	7.21	6.22	5.67	5.32	5.07	4.89	4.74	4.63	4.54	4.40	4.25	4.10	4.02	3.94	3.86	3.78	3.69	3.60
12	9.33	6.93	5.95	5.41	5.06	4.82	4.64	4.50	4.39	4.30	4.16	4.01	3.86	3.78	3.70	3.62	3.54	3.45	3.36
13	9.07	6.70	5.74	5.21	4.86	4.62	4.44	4.30	4.19	4.10	3.96	3.82	3.66	3.59	3.51	3.43	3.34	3.25	3.17
14	8.86	6.51	5.56	5.04	4.69	4.46	4.28	4.14	4.03	3.94	3.80	3.66	3.51	3.43	3.35	3.27	3.18	3.09	3.00
15	8.68	6.36	5.42	4.89	4.56	4.32	4.14	4.00	3.89	3.80	3.67	3.52	3.37	3.29	3.21	3.13	3.05	2.96	2.87
16	8.53	6.23	5.29	4.77	4.44	4.20	4.03	3.89	3.78	3.69	3.55	3.41	3.26	3.18	3.10	3.02	2.93	2.84	2.75
17	8.40	6.11	5.18	4.67	4.34	4.10	3.93	3.79	3.68	3.59	3.46	3.31	3.16	3.08	3.00	2.92	2.83	2.75	2.65
18	8.29	6.01	5.09	4.58	4.25	4.01	3.84	3.71	3.60	3.51	3.37	3.23	3.08	3.00	2.92	2.84	2.75	2.66	2.57
19	8.18	5.93	5.01	4.50	4.17	3.94	3.77	3.63	3.52	3.43	3.30	3.15	3.00	2.92	2.84	2.76	2.67	2.58	2.49
20	8.10	5.85	4.94	4.43	4.10	3.87	3.70	3.56	3.46	3.37	3.23	3.09	2.94	2.86	2.78	2.69	2.61	2.52	2.42
21	8.02	5.78	4.87	4.37	4.04	3.81	3.64	3.51	3.40	3.31	3.17	3.03	2.88	2.80	2.72	2.64	2.55	2.46	2.36
22	7.95	5.72	4.82	4.31	3.99	3.76	3.59	3.45	3.35	3.26	3.12	2.98	2.83	2.75	2.67	2.58	2.50	2.40	2.31
23	7.88	5.66	4.76	4.26	3.94	3.71	3.54	3.41	3.30	3.21	3.07	2.93	2.78	2.70	2.62	2.54	2.45	2.35	2.26
24	7.82	5.61	4.72	4.22	3.90	3.67	3.50	3.36	3.26	3.17	3.03	2.89	2.74	2.66	2.58	2.49	2.40	2.31	2.21
25	7.77	5.57	4.68	4.18	3.85	3.63	3.46	3.32	3.22	3.13	2.99	2.85	2.70	2.62	2.54	2.45	2.36	2.27	2.17
26	7.72	5.53	4.64	4.14	3.82	3.59	3.42	3.29	3.18	3.09	2.96	2.81	2.66	2.58	2.50	2.42	2.33	2.23	2.13
27	7.68	5.49	4.60	4.11	3.78	3.56	3.39	3.26	3.15	3.06	2.93	2.78	2.63	2.55	2.47	2.38	2.29	2.20	2.10
28	7.64	5.45	4.57	4.07	3.75	3.53	3.36	3.23	3.12	3.03	2.90	2.75	2.60	2.52	2.44	2.35	2.26	2.17	2.06
29	7.60	5.42	4.54	4.04	3.73	3.50	3.33	3.20	3.09	3.00	2.87	2.73	2.57	2.49	2.41	2.33	2.23	2.14	2.03
30	7.56	5.39	4.51	4.02	3.70	3.47	3.30	3.17	3.07	2.98	2.84	2.70	2.55	2.47	2.39	2.30	2.21	2.11	2.01
40	7.31	5.18	4.31	3.83	3.51	3.29	3.12	2.99	2.89	2.80	2.66	2.52	2.37	2.29	2.20	2.11	2.02	1.92	1.80
60	7.08	4.98	4.13	3.65	3.34	3.12	2.95	2.82	2.72	2.63	2.50	2.35	2.20	2.12	2.03	1.94	1.84	1.73	1.60
120	6.85	4.79	3.95	3.48	3.17	2.96	2.79	2.66	2.56	2.47	2.34	2.19	2.03	1.95	1.86	1.76	1.66	1.53	1.38
∞	6.63	4.61	3.78	3.32	3.02	2.80	2.64	2.51	2.41	2.32	2.18	2.04	1.88	1.79	1.70	1.59	1.47	1.32	1.00

$F = \frac{s_1^2}{s_2^2} = \frac{S_1/m}{S_2/n}$, where $s_1^2 = S_1/m$ and $s_2^2 = S_2/n$ are independent mean squares estimating a common variance σ^2 and based on m and n degrees of freedom, respectively.

PERCENTAGE POINTS, F-DISTRIBUTION (Continued)

$$F(F) = \int_0^F \frac{\Gamma\left(\frac{m+n}{2}\right)}{\Gamma\left(\frac{m}{2}\right)\Gamma\left(\frac{n}{2}\right)} m^{\frac{m}{2}} n^{\frac{n}{2}} x^{\frac{m}{2}-1} (n+mx)^{-\frac{m+n}{2}}\, dx = .995$$

n \ m	1	2	3	4	5	6	7	8	9	10	12	15	20	24	30	40	60	120	∞
1	16211	20000	21615	22500	23056	23437	23715	23925	24091	24224	24426	24630	24836	24940	25044	25148	25253	25359	25465
2	198.5	199.0	199.2	199.2	199.3	199.3	199.4	199.4	199.4	199.4	199.4	199.4	199.4	199.5	199.5	199.5	199.5	199.5	199.5
3	55.55	49.80	47.47	46.19	45.39	44.84	44.43	44.13	43.88	43.69	43.39	43.08	42.78	42.62	42.47	42.31	42.15	41.99	41.83
4	31.33	26.28	24.26	23.15	22.46	21.97	21.62	21.35	21.14	20.97	20.70	20.44	20.17	20.03	19.89	19.75	19.61	19.47	19.32
5	22.78	18.31	16.53	15.56	14.94	14.51	14.20	13.96	13.77	13.62	13.38	13.15	12.90	12.78	12.66	12.53	12.40	12.27	12.14
6	18.63	14.54	12.92	12.03	11.46	11.07	10.79	10.57	10.39	10.25	10.03	9.81	9.59	9.47	9.36	9.24	9.12	9.00	8.88
7	16.24	12.40	10.88	10.05	9.52	9.16	8.89	8.68	8.51	8.38	8.18	7.97	7.75	7.65	7.53	7.42	7.31	7.19	7.08
8	14.69	11.04	9.60	8.81	8.30	7.95	7.69	7.50	7.34	7.21	7.01	6.81	6.61	6.50	6.40	6.29	6.18	6.06	5.95
9	13.61	10.11	8.72	7.96	7.47	7.13	6.88	6.69	6.54	6.42	6.23	6.03	5.83	5.73	5.62	5.52	5.41	5.30	5.19
10	12.83	9.43	8.08	7.34	6.87	6.54	6.30	6.12	5.97	5.85	5.66	5.47	5.27	5.17	5.07	4.97	4.86	4.75	4.64
11	12.23	8.91	7.60	6.88	6.42	6.10	5.86	5.68	5.54	5.42	5.24	5.05	4.86	4.76	4.65	4.55	4.44	4.34	4.23
12	11.75	8.51	7.23	6.52	6.07	5.76	5.52	5.35	5.20	5.09	4.91	4.72	4.53	4.43	4.33	4.23	4.12	4.01	3.90
13	11.37	8.19	6.93	6.23	5.79	5.48	5.25	5.08	4.94	4.82	4.64	4.46	4.27	4.17	4.07	3.97	3.87	3.76	3.65
14	11.06	7.92	6.68	6.00	5.56	5.26	5.03	4.86	4.72	4.60	4.43	4.25	4.06	3.96	3.86	3.76	3.66	3.55	3.44
15	10.80	7.70	6.48	5.80	5.37	5.07	4.85	4.67	4.54	4.42	4.25	4.07	3.88	3.79	3.69	3.58	3.48	3.37	3.26
16	10.58	7.51	6.30	5.64	5.21	4.91	4.69	4.52	4.38	4.27	4.10	3.92	3.73	3.64	3.54	3.44	3.33	3.22	3.11
17	10.38	7.35	6.16	5.50	5.07	4.78	4.56	4.39	4.25	4.14	3.97	3.79	3.61	3.51	3.41	3.31	3.21	3.10	2.98
18	10.22	7.21	6.03	5.37	4.96	4.66	4.44	4.28	4.14	4.03	3.86	3.68	3.50	3.40	3.30	3.20	3.10	2.99	2.87
19	10.07	7.09	5.92	5.27	4.85	4.56	4.34	4.18	4.04	3.93	3.76	3.59	3.40	3.31	3.21	3.11	3.00	2.89	2.78
20	9.94	6.99	5.82	5.17	4.76	4.47	4.26	4.09	3.96	3.85	3.68	3.50	3.32	3.22	3.12	3.02	2.92	2.81	2.69
21	9.83	6.89	5.73	5.09	4.68	4.39	4.18	4.01	3.88	3.77	3.60	3.43	3.24	3.15	3.05	2.95	2.84	2.73	2.61
22	9.73	6.81	5.65	5.02	4.61	4.32	4.11	3.94	3.81	3.70	3.54	3.36	3.18	3.08	2.98	2.88	2.77	2.66	2.55
23	9.63	6.73	5.58	4.95	4.54	4.26	4.05	3.88	3.75	3.64	3.47	3.30	3.12	3.02	2.92	2.82	2.71	2.60	2.48
24	9.55	6.66	5.52	4.89	4.49	4.20	3.99	3.83	3.69	3.59	3.42	3.25	3.06	2.97	2.87	2.77	2.66	2.55	2.43
25	9.48	6.60	5.46	4.84	4.43	4.15	3.94	3.78	3.64	3.54	3.37	3.20	3.01	2.92	2.82	2.72	2.61	2.50	2.38
26	9.41	6.54	5.41	4.79	4.38	4.10	3.89	3.73	3.60	3.49	3.33	3.15	2.97	2.87	2.77	2.67	2.56	2.45	2.33
27	9.34	6.49	5.36	4.74	4.34	4.06	3.85	3.69	3.56	3.45	3.28	3.11	2.93	2.83	2.73	2.63	2.52	2.41	2.25
28	9.28	6.44	5.32	4.70	4.30	4.02	3.81	3.65	3.52	3.41	3.25	3.07	2.89	2.79	2.69	2.59	2.48	2.37	2.29
29	9.23	6.40	5.28	4.66	4.26	3.98	3.77	3.61	3.48	3.38	3.21	3.04	2.86	2.76	2.66	2.56	2.45	2.33	2.24
30	9.18	6.35	5.24	4.62	4.23	3.95	3.74	3.58	3.45	3.34	3.18	3.01	2.82	2.73	2.63	2.52	2.42	2.30	2.18
40	8.83	6.07	4.98	4.37	3.99	3.71	3.51	3.35	3.22	3.12	2.95	2.78	2.60	2.50	2.40	2.30	2.18	2.06	1.93
60	8.49	5.79	4.73	4.14	3.76	3.49	3.29	3.13	3.01	2.90	2.74	2.57	2.39	2.29	2.19	2.08	1.96	1.83	1.69
120	8.18	5.54	4.50	3.92	3.55	3.28	3.09	2.93	2.81	2.71	2.54	2.37	2.19	2.09	1.98	1.87	1.75	1.61	1.43
∞	7.88	5.30	4.28	3.72	3.35	3.09	2.90	2.74	2.62	2.52	2.36	2.19	2.00	1.90	1.79	1.67	1.53	1.36	1.00

$F = \dfrac{s_1^2}{s_2^2} = \dfrac{S_1}{m} \Big/ \dfrac{S_2}{n}$, where $s_1^2 = S_1/m$ and $s_2^2 = S_2/n$ are independent mean squares estimating a common variance σ^2 and based on m and n degrees of freedom, respectively.

PERCENTAGE POINTS, F-DISTRIBUTION (Continued)

$$F(F) = \int_0^F \frac{\Gamma\left(\frac{m+n}{2}\right)}{\Gamma\left(\frac{m}{2}\right)\Gamma\left(\frac{n}{2}\right)} m^{\frac{m}{2}} n^{\frac{n}{2}} x^{\frac{m}{2}-1}(n+mx)^{-\frac{m+n}{2}}\,dx = .999$$

m \ n	1	2	3	4	5	6	7	8	9	10	12	15	20	24	30	40	60	120	∞
1	4053*	5000*	5404*	5625*	5764*	5859*	5929*	5981*	6023*	6056*	6107*	6158*	6209*	6235*	6261*	6287*	6313*	6340*	6366*
2	998.5	999.0	999.2	999.2	999.3	999.3	999.4	999.4	999.4	999.4	999.4	999.4	999.4	999.5	999.5	999.5	999.5	999.5	999.5
3	167.0	148.5	141.1	137.1	134.6	132.8	131.6	130.6	129.9	129.2	128.3	127.4	126.4	125.9	125.4	125.0	124.5	124.0	123.5
4	74.14	61.25	56.18	53.44	51.71	50.53	49.66	49.00	48.47	48.05	47.41	46.76	46.10	45.77	45.43	45.09	44.75	44.40	44.05
5	47.18	37.12	33.20	31.09	29.75	28.84	28.16	27.64	27.24	26.92	26.42	25.91	25.39	25.14	24.87	24.60	24.33	24.06	23.79
6	35.51	27.00	23.70	21.92	20.81	20.03	19.46	19.03	18.69	18.41	17.99	17.56	17.12	16.89	16.67	16.44	16.21	15.99	15.75
7	29.25	21.69	18.77	17.19	16.21	15.52	15.02	14.63	14.33	14.08	13.71	13.32	12.93	12.73	12.53	12.33	12.12	11.91	11.70
8	25.42	18.49	15.83	14.39	13.49	12.86	12.40	12.04	11.77	11.54	11.19	10.84	10.48	10.30	10.11	9.92	9.73	9.53	9.33
9	22.86	16.39	13.90	12.56	11.71	11.13	10.70	10.37	10.11	9.89	9.57	9.24	8.90	8.72	8.55	8.37	8.19	8.00	7.81
10	21.04	14.91	12.55	11.28	10.48	9.92	9.52	9.20	8.96	8.75	8.45	8.13	7.80	7.64	7.47	7.30	7.12	6.94	6.76
11	19.69	13.81	11.56	10.35	9.58	9.05	8.66	8.35	8.12	7.92	7.63	7.32	7.01	6.85	6.68	6.52	6.35	6.17	6.00
12	18.64	12.97	10.80	9.63	8.89	8.38	8.00	7.71	7.48	7.29	7.00	6.71	6.40	6.25	6.09	5.93	5.76	5.59	5.42
13	17.81	12.31	10.21	9.07	8.35	7.86	7.49	7.21	6.98	6.80	6.52	6.23	5.93	5.78	5.63	5.47	5.30	5.14	4.97
14	17.14	11.78	9.73	8.62	7.92	7.43	7.08	6.80	6.58	6.40	6.13	5.85	5.56	5.41	5.25	5.10	4.94	4.77	4.60
15	16.59	11.34	9.34	8.25	7.57	7.09	6.74	6.47	6.26	6.08	5.81	5.54	5.25	5.10	4.95	4.80	4.64	4.47	4.31
16	16.12	10.97	9.00	7.94	7.27	6.81	6.46	6.19	5.98	5.81	5.55	5.27	4.99	4.85	4.70	4.54	4.39	4.23	4.06
17	15.72	10.66	8.73	7.68	7.02	6.56	6.22	5.96	5.75	5.58	5.32	5.05	4.78	4.63	4.48	4.33	4.18	4.02	3.85
18	15.38	10.39	8.49	7.46	6.81	6.35	6.02	5.76	5.56	5.39	5.13	4.87	4.59	4.45	4.30	4.15	4.00	3.84	3.67
19	15.08	10.16	8.28	7.26	6.62	6.18	5.85	5.59	5.39	5.22	4.97	4.70	4.43	4.29	4.14	3.99	3.84	3.68	3.51
20	14.82	9.95	8.10	7.10	6.46	6.02	5.69	5.44	5.24	5.08	4.82	4.56	4.29	4.15	4.00	3.86	3.70	3.54	3.38
21	14.59	9.77	7.94	6.95	6.32	5.88	5.56	5.31	5.11	4.95	4.70	4.44	4.17	4.03	3.88	3.74	3.58	3.42	3.26
22	14.38	9.61	7.80	6.81	6.19	5.76	5.44	5.19	4.99	4.83	4.58	4.33	4.06	3.92	3.78	3.63	3.48	3.32	3.15
23	14.19	9.47	7.67	6.69	6.08	5.65	5.33	5.09	4.89	4.73	4.48	4.23	3.96	3.82	3.68	3.53	3.38	3.22	3.05
24	14.03	9.34	7.55	6.59	5.98	5.55	5.23	4.99	4.80	4.64	4.39	4.14	3.87	3.74	3.59	3.45	3.29	3.14	2.97
25	13.88	9.22	7.45	6.49	5.88	5.46	5.15	4.91	4.71	4.56	4.31	4.06	3.79	3.66	3.52	3.37	3.22	3.06	2.89
26	13.74	9.12	7.36	6.41	5.80	5.38	5.07	4.83	4.64	4.48	4.24	3.99	3.72	3.59	3.44	3.30	3.15	2.99	2.82
27	13.61	9.02	7.27	6.33	5.73	5.31	5.00	4.76	4.57	4.41	4.17	3.92	3.66	3.52	3.38	3.23	3.08	2.92	2.75
28	13.50	8.93	7.19	6.25	5.66	5.24	4.93	4.69	4.50	4.35	4.11	3.86	3.60	3.46	3.32	3.18	3.02	2.86	2.69
29	13.39	8.85	7.12	6.19	5.59	5.18	4.87	4.64	4.45	4.29	4.05	3.80	3.54	3.41	3.27	3.12	2.97	2.81	2.64
30	13.29	8.77	7.05	6.12	5.53	5.12	4.82	4.58	4.39	4.24	4.00	3.75	3.49	3.36	3.22	3.07	2.92	2.76	2.59
40	12.61	8.25	6.60	5.70	5.13	4.73	4.44	4.21	4.02	3.87	3.64	3.40	3.15	3.01	2.87	2.73	2.57	2.41	2.23
60	11.97	7.76	6.17	5.31	4.76	4.37	4.09	3.87	3.69	3.54	3.31	3.08	2.83	2.69	2.55	2.41	2.25	2.08	1.89
120	11.38	7.32	5.79	4.95	4.42	4.04	3.77	3.55	3.38	3.24	3.02	2.78	2.53	2.40	2.26	2.11	1.95	1.76	1.54
∞	10.83	6.91	5.42	4.62	4.10	3.74	3.47	3.27	3.10	2.96	2.74	2.51	2.27	2.13	1.99	1.84	1.66	1.45	1.00

* Multiply these entries by 100.

RANDOM   UNITS

Use of Table. If one wishes to select a random sample of N items from a universe of M items, the following procedure may be applied. $(M > N.)$

1. Decide upon some arbitrary scheme of selecting entries from the table. For example, one may decide to use the entries in the first line, second column; second line, third column; third line, fourth column; etc.

2. Assign numbers to each of the items in the universe from 1 to M. Thus, if $M = 500$, the items would be numbered from 001 to 500, and therefore, each designated item is associated with a three digit number.

3. Decide upon some arbitrary scheme of selecting positional digits from each entry chosen according to Step 1. Thus, if $M = 500$, one may decide to use the first, third, and fourth digit of each entry selected, and as a consequence a three digit number is created for each entry choice.

4. If the number formed is $\leq M$, the correspondingly designated item in the universe is chosen for the random sample of N items. If a number formed is $> M$ or is a repeated number of one already chosen, it is passed over and the next desirable number is taken. This process is continued until the random sample of N items is selected.

A TABLE OF 14,000 RANDOM UNITS

Line/Col.	(1)	(2)	(3)	(4)	(5)	(6)	(7)	(8)	(9)	(10)	(11)	(12)	(13)	(14)
1	10480	15011	01536	02011	81647	91646	69179	14194	62590	36207	20969	99570	91291	90700
2	22368	46573	25595	85393	30995	89198	27982	53402	93965	34095	52666	19174	39615	99505
3	24130	48360	22527	97265	76393	64809	15179	24830	49340	32081	30680	19655	63348	58629
4	42167	93093	06243	61680	07856	16376	39440	53537	71341	57004	00849	74917	97758	16379
5	37570	39975	81837	16656	06121	91782	60468	81305	49684	60672	14110	06927	01263	54613
6	77921	06907	11008	42751	27756	53498	18602	70659	90655	15053	21916	81825	44394	42880
7	99562	72905	56420	69994	98872	31016	71194	18738	44013	48840	63213	21069	10634	12952
8	96301	91977	05463	07972	18876	20922	94595	56869	69014	60045	18425	84903	42508	32307
9	89579	14342	63661	10281	17453	18103	57740	84378	25331	12566	58678	44947	05585	56941
10	85475	36857	43342	53988	53060	59533	38867	62300	08158	17983	16439	11458	18593	64952
11	28918	69578	88231	33276	70997	79936	56865	05859	90106	31595	01547	85590	91610	78188
12	63553	40961	48235	03427	49626	69445	18663	72695	52180	20847	12234	90511	33703	90322
13	09429	93969	52636	92737	88974	33488	36320	17617	30015	08272	84115	27156	30613	74952
14	10365	61129	87529	85689	48237	52267	67689	93394	01511	26358	85104	20285	29975	89868
15	07119	97336	71048	08178	77233	13916	47564	81056	97735	85977	29372	74461	28551	90707
16	51085	12765	51821	51259	77452	16308	60756	92144	49442	53900	70960	63990	75601	40719
17	02368	21382	52404	60268	89368	19885	55322	44819	01188	65255	64835	44919	05944	55157
18	01011	54092	33362	94904	31273	04146	18594	29852	71585	85030	51132	01915	92747	64951
19	52162	53916	46369	58586	23216	14513	83149	98736	23495	64350	94738	17752	35156	35749
20	07056	97628	33787	09998	42698	06691	76988	13602	51851	46104	88916	19509	25625	58104
21	48663	91245	85828	14346	09172	30168	90229	04734	59193	22178	30421	61666	99904	32812
22	54164	58492	22421	74103	47070	25306	76468	26384	58151	06646	21524	15227	96909	44592
23	32639	32363	05597	24200	13363	38005	94342	28728	35806	06912	17012	64161	18296	22851
24	29334	27001	87637	87308	58731	00256	45834	15398	46557	41135	10367	07684	36188	18510
25	02488	33062	28834	07351	19731	92420	60952	61280	50001	67658	32586	86679	50720	94953
26	81525	72295	04839	96423	24878	82651	66566	14778	76797	14780	13300	87074	79666	95725
27	29676	20591	68086	26432	46901	20849	89768	81536	86645	12659	92259	57102	80428	25280
28	00742	57392	39064	66432	84673	40027	32832	61362	98947	96067	64760	64584	96096	98253
29	05366	04213	25669	26422	44407	44048	37937	63904	45766	66134	75470	66520	34693	90449
30	91921	26418	64117	94305	26766	25940	39972	22209	71500	64568	91402	42416	07844	69618
31	00582	04711	87917	77341	42206	35126	74087	99547	81817	42607	43808	76655	62028	76630
32	00725	69884	62797	56170	86324	88072	76222	36086	84637	93161	76038	65855	77919	88006
33	69011	65797	95876	55293	18988	27354	26575	08625	40801	59920	29841	80150	12777	48501
34	25976	57948	29888	88604	67917	48708	18912	82271	65424	69774	33611	54262	85963	03547
35	09763	83473	73577	12908	30883	18317	28290	35797	05998	41688	34952	37888	38917	88050
36	91567	42595	27958	30134	04024	86385	29880	99730	55536	84855	29080	09250	79656	73211
37	17955	56349	90999	49127	20044	59931	06115	20542	18059	02008	73708	83517	36103	42791
38	46503	18584	18845	49618	02304	51038	20655	58727	28168	15475	56942	53389	20562	87338
39	92157	89634	94824	78171	84610	82834	09922	25417	44137	48413	25555	21246	35509	20468
40	14577	62765	35605	81263	39667	47358	56873	56307	61607	49518	89656	20103	77490	18062
41	98427	07523	33362	64270	01638	92477	66969	98420	04880	45585	46565	04102	46880	45709
42	34914	63976	88720	82765	34476	17032	87589	40836	32427	70002	70663	88863	77775	69348
43	70060	28277	39475	46473	23219	53416	94970	25832	69975	94884	19661	72828	00102	66794
44	53976	54914	06990	67245	68350	82948	11398	42878	80287	88267	47363	46634	06541	97809
45	76072	29515	40980	07391	58745	25774	22987	80059	39911	96189	41151	14222	60697	59583
46	90725	52210	83974	29992	65831	38857	50490	83765	55657	14361	31720	57375	56228	41546
47	64364	67412	33339	31926	14883	24413	59744	92351	97473	89286	35931	04110	23726	51900
48	08962	00358	31662	25388	61642	34072	81249	35648	56891	69352	48373	45578	78547	81788
49	95012	68379	93526	70765	10593	04542	76463	54328	02349	17247	28865	14777	62730	92277
50	15664	10493	20492	38391	91132	21999	59516	81652	27195	48223	46751	22923	32261	85653

A TABLE OF 14,000 RANDOM UNITS (Continued)

Line/Col.	(1)	(2)	(3)	(4)	(5)	(6)	(7)	(8)	(9)	(10)	(11)	(12)	(13)	(14)
51	16408	81899	04153	53381	79401	21438	83035	92350	36693	31238	59649	91754	72772	0233
52	18629	81953	05520	91962	04739	13092	97662	24822	94730	06496	35090	04822	86772	9828
53	73115	35101	47498	87637	99016	71060	88824	71013	18735	20286	23153	72924	35165	4304
54	57491	16703	23167	49323	45021	33132	12544	41035	80780	45393	44812	12515	98931	9120
55	30405	83946	23792	14422	15059	45799	22716	19792	09983	74353	68668	30429	70735	2549
56	16631	35006	85900	98275	32388	52390	16815	69298	82732	38480	73817	32523	41961	4443
57	96773	20206	42559	78985	05300	22164	24369	54224	35083	19687	11052	91491	60383	1974
58	38935	64202	14349	82674	66523	44133	00697	35552	35970	19124	63318	29686	03387	5984
59	31624	76384	17403	53363	44167	64486	64758	75366	76554	31601	12614	33072	60332	9232
60	78919	19474	23632	27889	47914	02584	37680	20801	72152	39339	34806	08930	85001	8782
61	03931	33309	57047	74211	63445	17361	62825	39908	05607	91284	68833	25570	38818	4692
62	74426	33278	43972	10119	89917	15665	52872	73823	73144	88662	88970	74492	51805	9937
63	09066	00903	20795	95452	92648	45454	09552	88815	16553	51125	79375	97596	16296	6609
64	42238	12426	87025	14267	20979	04508	64535	31355	86064	29472	47689	05974	52468	1683
65	16153	08002	26504	41744	81959	65642	74240	56302	00033	67107	77510	70625	28725	3419
66	21457	40742	29820	96783	29400	21840	15035	34537	33310	06116	95240	15957	16572	0600
67	21581	57802	02050	89728	17937	37621	47075	42080	97403	48626	68995	43805	33386	2159
68	55612	78095	83197	33732	05810	24813	86902	60397	16489	03264	88525	42786	05269	9253
69	44657	66999	99324	51281	84463	60563	79312	93454	68876	25471	93911	25650	12682	7357
70	91340	84979	46949	81973	37949	61023	43997	15263	80644	43942	89203	71795	99533	5050
71	91227	21199	31935	27022	84067	05462	35216	14486	29891	68607	41867	14951	91696	8506
72	50001	38140	66321	19924	72163	09538	12151	06878	91903	18749	34405	56087	82790	7092
73	65390	05224	72958	28609	81406	39147	25549	48542	42627	45233	57202	94617	23772	0789
74	27504	96131	83944	41575	10573	08619	64482	73923	36152	05184	94142	25299	84387	3492
75	37169	94851	39117	89632	00959	16487	65536	49071	39782	17095	02330	74301	00275	4828
76	11508	70225	51111	38351	19444	66499	71945	05422	13442	78675	84081	66938	93654	5989
77	37449	30362	06694	54690	04052	53115	62757	95348	78662	11163	81651	50245	34971	5292
78	46515	70331	85922	38329	57015	15765	97161	17869	45349	61796	66345	81073	49106	7986
79	30986	81223	42416	58353	21532	30502	32305	86482	05174	07901	54339	58861	74818	4694
80	63798	64995	46583	09765	44160	78128	83991	42865	92520	83531	80377	35909	81250	5423
81	82486	84846	99254	67632	43218	50076	21361	64816	51202	88124	41870	52689	51275	8355
82	21885	32906	92431	09060	64297	51674	64126	62570	26123	05155	59194	52799	28225	8576
83	60336	98782	07408	53458	13564	59089	26445	29789	85205	41001	12535	12133	14645	2354
84	43937	46891	24010	25560	86355	33941	25786	54990	71899	15475	95434	98227	21824	1958
85	97656	63175	89303	16275	07100	92063	21942	18611	47348	20203	18534	03862	78095	5013
86	03299	01221	05418	38982	55758	92237	26759	86367	21216	98442	08303	56613	91511	7592
87	79626	06486	03574	17668	07785	76020	79924	25651	83325	88428	85076	72811	22717	5058
88	85636	68335	47539	03129	65651	11977	02510	26113	99447	68645	34327	15152	55230	9344
89	18039	14367	61337	06177	12143	46609	32989	74014	64708	00533	35398	58408	13261	4790
90	08362	15656	60627	36478	65648	16764	53412	09013	07832	41574	17639	82163	60859	7556
91	79556	29068	04142	16268	15387	12856	66227	38358	22478	73373	88732	09443	82558	0525
92	92608	82674	27072	32534	17075	27698	98204	63863	11951	34648	88022	56148	34925	5703
93	23982	25835	40055	67006	12293	02753	14827	22235	35071	99704	37543	11601	35503	8517
94	09915	96306	05908	97901	28395	14186	00821	80703	70426	75647	76310	88717	37890	4012
95	50937	33300	26695	62247	69927	76123	50842	43834	86654	70959	79725	93872	28117	1923
96	42488	78077	69882	61657	34136	79180	97526	43092	04098	73571	80799	76536	71255	6423
97	46764	86273	63003	93017	31204	36692	40202	35275	57306	55543	53203	18098	47625	8868
98	03237	45430	55417	63282	90816	17349	88298	90183	36600	78406	06216	95787	42579	9073
99	86591	81482	52667	61583	14972	90053	89534	76036	49199	43716	97548	04379	46370	2867
100	38534	01715	94964	87288	65680	43772	39560	12918	86537	62738	19636	51132	25739	5694

A TABLE OF 14,000 RANDOM UNITS (Continued)

Line/Col.	(1)	(2)	(3)	(4)	(5)	(6)	(7)	(8)	(9)	(10)	(11)	(12)	(13)	(14)
101	13284	16834	74151	92027	24670	36665	00770	22878	02179	51602	07270	76517	97275	45960
102	21224	00370	30420	03883	96648	89428	41583	17564	27395	63904	41548	49197	82277	24120
103	99052	47887	81085	64933	66279	80432	65793	83287	34142	13241	30590	97760	35848	91983
104	00199	50993	98603	38452	87890	94624	69721	57484	67501	77638	44331	11257	71131	11059
105	60578	06483	28733	37867	07936	98710	98539	27186	31237	80612	44488	97819	70401	95419
106	91240	18312	17441	01929	18163	69201	31211	54288	39296	37318	65724	90401	79017	62077
107	97458	14229	12063	59611	32249	90466	33216	19358	02591	54263	88449	01912	07436	50813
108	35249	38646	34475	72417	60514	69257	12489	51924	86871	92446	36607	11458	30440	52639
109	38980	46600	11759	11900	46743	27860	77940	39298	97838	95145	32378	68038	89351	37005
110	10750	52745	38749	87365	58959	53731	89295	59062	39404	13198	59960	70408	29812	83126
111	36247	27850	73958	20673	37800	63835	71051	84724	52492	22342	78071	17456	96104	18327
112	70994	66986	99744	72438	01174	42159	11392	20724	54322	36923	70009	23233	65438	59685
113	99638	94702	11463	18148	81386	80431	90628	52506	02016	85151	88598	47821	00265	82525
114	72055	15774	43857	99805	10419	76939	25993	03544	21560	83471	43989	90770	22965	44247
115	24038	65541	85788	55835	38835	59399	13790	35112	01324	39520	76210	22467	83275	32286
116	74976	14631	35908	28221	39470	91548	12854	30166	09073	75887	36782	00268	97121	57676
117	35553	71628	70189	26436	63407	91178	90348	55359	80392	41012	36270	77786	89578	21059
118	35676	12797	51434	82976	42010	26344	92920	92155	58807	54644	58581	95331	78629	73344
119	74815	67523	72985	23183	02446	63594	98924	20633	58842	85961	07648	70164	34994	67662
120	45246	88048	65173	50989	91060	89894	36063	32819	68559	99221	49475	50558	34698	71800
121	76509	47069	86378	41797	11910	49672	88575	97966	32466	10083	54728	81972	58975	30761
122	19689	90332	04315	21358	97248	11188	39062	63312	52496	07349	79178	33692	57352	72862
123	42751	35318	97513	61537	54955	08159	00337	80778	27507	95478	21252	12746	37554	97775
124	11946	22681	45045	13964	57517	59419	58045	44067	58716	58840	45557	96345	33271	53464
125	96518	48688	20996	11090	48396	57177	83867	86464	14342	21545	46717	72364	86954	55580
126	35726	58643	76869	84622	39098	36083	72505	92265	23107	60278	05822	46760	44294	07672
127	39737	42750	48968	70536	84864	64952	38404	94317	65402	13589	01055	79044	19308	83623
128	97025	66492	56177	04049	80312	48028	26408	43591	75528	65341	49044	95495	81256	53214
129	62814	08075	09788	56350	76787	51591	54509	49295	85830	59860	30883	89660	96142	18354
130	25578	22950	15227	83291	41737	79599	96191	71845	86899	70694	24290	01551	80092	82118
131	68763	69576	88991	49662	46704	63362	56625	00481	73323	91427	15264	06969	57048	54149
132	17900	00813	64361	60725	88974	61005	99709	30666	26451	11528	44323	34778	60342	60388
133	71944	60227	63551	71109	05624	43836	58254	26160	32116	63403	35404	57146	10909	07346
134	54684	93691	85132	64399	29182	44324	14491	55226	78793	34107	30374	48429	51376	09559
135	25946	27623	11258	65204	52832	50880	22273	05554	99521	73791	85744	29276	70326	60251
136	01353	39318	44961	44972	91766	90262	56073	06606	51826	18893	83448	31915	97764	75091
137	99083	88191	27662	99113	57174	35571	99884	13951	71057	53961	61448	74909	07322	80960
138	52021	45406	37945	75234	24327	86978	22644	87779	23753	99926	63898	54886	18051	96314
139	78755	47744	43776	83098	03225	14281	83637	55984	13300	52212	58781	14905	46502	04472
140	25282	69106	59180	16257	22810	43609	12224	25643	89884	31149	85423	32581	34374	70873
141	11959	94202	02743	86847	79725	51811	12998	76844	05320	54236	53891	70226	38632	84776
142	11644	13792	98190	01424	30078	28197	55583	05197	47714	68440	22016	79204	06862	94451
143	06307	97912	68110	59812	95448	43244	31262	88880	13040	16458	43813	89416	42482	33939
144	76285	75714	89585	99296	52640	46518	55486	90754	88932	19937	57119	23251	55619	23679
145	55322	07589	39600	60866	63007	20007	66819	84164	61131	81429	60676	42807	78286	29015
146	78017	90928	90220	92503	83375	26986	74399	30885	88567	29169	72816	53357	15428	86932
147	44768	43342	20696	26331	43140	69744	82928	24988	94237	46138	77426	39039	55596	12655
148	25100	19336	14605	86603	51680	97678	24261	02464	86563	74812	60069	71674	15478	47642
149	83612	46623	62876	85197	07824	91392	58317	37726	84628	42221	10268	20692	15699	29167
150	41347	81666	82961	60413	71020	83658	02415	33322	66036	98712	46795	16308	28413	05417

A TABLE OF 14,000 RANDOM UNITS (Continued)

Line/Col.	(1)	(2)	(3)	(4)	(5)	(6)	(7)	(8)	(9)	(10)	(11)	(12)	(13)	(14)
151	38128	51178	75096	13609	16110	73533	42564	59870	29399	67834	91055	89917	51096	8901
152	60950	00455	73254	96067	50717	13878	03216	78274	65863	37011	91283	33914	91303	4932
153	90524	17320	29832	96118	75792	25326	22940	24904	80523	38928	91374	55597	97567	3891
154	49897	18278	67160	39408	97056	43517	84426	59650	20247	19293	02019	14790	02852	0581
155	18494	99209	81060	19488	65596	59787	47939	91225	98768	43688	00438	05548	09443	8289
156	65373	72984	30171	37741	70203	94094	87261	30056	58124	70133	18936	02138	59372	0907
157	40653	12843	04213	70925	95360	55774	76439	61768	52817	81151	52188	31940	54273	4903
158	51638	22238	56344	44587	83231	50317	74541	07719	25472	41602	77318	15145	57515	0763
159	69742	99303	62578	83575	30337	07488	51941	84316	42067	49692	28616	29101	03013	7344
160	58012	74072	67488	74580	47992	69482	58624	17106	47538	13452	22620	24260	40155	7471
161	18348	19855	42887	08279	43206	47077	42637	45606	00011	20662	14642	49984	94509	5638
162	59614	09193	58064	29086	44385	45740	70752	05663	49081	26960	57454	99264	24142	7464
163	75688	28630	39210	52897	62748	72658	98059	67202	72789	01869	13496	14663	87645	8971
164	13941	77802	69101	70061	35460	34576	15412	81304	58757	35498	94830	75521	00603	9770
165	96656	86420	96475	86458	54463	96419	55417	41375	76886	19008	66877	35934	59801	0049
166	03363	82042	15942	14549	38324	87094	19069	67590	11087	68570	22591	65232	85915	9149
167	70366	08390	69155	25496	13240	57407	91407	49160	07379	34444	94567	66035	38918	6570
168	47870	36605	12927	16043	53257	93796	52721	73120	48025	76074	95605	67422	41646	1455
169	79504	77606	22761	30518	28373	73898	30550	76684	77366	32276	04690	61667	64798	6627
170	46967	74841	50923	15339	37755	98995	40162	89561	69199	42257	11647	47603	48779	9790
171	14558	50769	35444	59030	87516	48193	02945	00922	48189	04724	21263	20892	92955	9025
172	12440	25057	01132	38611	28135	68089	10954	10097	54243	06460	50856	65435	79377	5389
173	32293	29938	68653	10497	98919	46587	77701	99119	93165	67788	17638	23097	21468	3699
174	10640	21875	72462	77981	56550	55999	87310	69643	45124	00349	25748	00844	96831	3065
175	47615	23169	39571	56972	20628	21788	51736	33133	72696	32605	41569	76148	91544	2112
176	16948	11128	71624	72754	49084	96303	27830	45817	67867	18062	87453	17226	72904	7147
177	21258	61092	66634	70335	92448	17354	83432	49608	66520	06442	59664	20420	39201	6954
178	15072	48853	15178	30730	47481	48490	41436	25015	49932	20474	53821	51015	79841	3240
179	99154	57412	09858	65671	70655	71479	63520	31357	56968	06729	34465	70685	04184	2525
180	08759	61089	23706	32994	35426	36666	63988	98844	37533	08269	27021	45886	22835	7845
181	67323	57839	61114	62192	47547	58023	64630	34886	98777	75442	95592	06141	45096	7311
182	09255	13986	84834	20764	72206	89393	34548	93438	88730	61805	78955	18952	46436	5874
183	36304	74712	00374	10107	85061	69228	81969	92216	03568	39630	81869	52824	50937	2795
184	15884	67429	86612	47367	10242	44880	12060	44309	46629	55105	66793	93173	00480	1331
185	18745	32031	35303	08134	33925	03044	59929	95418	04917	57596	24878	61733	92834	6445
186	72934	40086	88292	65728	38300	42323	64068	98373	48971	09049	59943	36538	05976	8211
187	17626	02944	20910	57662	80181	38579	24580	90529	52303	50436	29401	57824	86039	8106
188	27117	61399	50967	41399	81636	16663	15634	79717	94696	59240	25543	97989	63306	9094
189	93995	18678	90012	63645	85701	85269	62263	68331	00389	72571	15210	20769	44686	9617
190	67392	89421	09623	80725	62620	84162	87368	29560	00519	84545	08004	24526	41252	1452
191	04910	12261	37566	80016	21245	69377	50420	85658	55263	68667	78770	04533	14513	1809
192	81453	20283	79929	59839	23875	13245	46808	74124	74703	35769	95588	21014	37078	3917
193	19480	75790	48539	23703	15537	48885	02861	86587	74539	65227	90799	58789	96257	0270
194	21456	13162	74608	81011	55512	07481	93551	72189	76261	91206	89941	15132	37738	5928
195	89406	20912	46189	76376	25538	87212	20748	12831	57166	35026	16817	79121	18929	4062
196	09866	07414	55977	16419	01101	69343	13305	94302	80703	57910	36933	57771	42546	0300
197	86541	24681	23421	13521	28000	94917	07423	57523	97234	63951	42876	46829	09781	5816
198	10414	96941	06205	72222	57167	83902	07460	69507	10600	08858	07685	44472	64220	2704
199	49942	06683	41479	58982	56288	42853	92196	20632	62045	78812	35895	51851	83534	1068
200	23995	68882	42291	23374	24299	27024	67460	94783	40937	16961	26053	78749	46704	2198

FACTORS FOR COMPUTING CONTROL LIMITS

A. Control Charts for Measurement

If the process mean and standard deviation, μ and σ, are known, and it is assumed that the underlying distribution is normal, it is possible to assert with probability $1 - \alpha$ that the mean of a random sample of size n will fall between $\bar{x} - z_{\alpha/2} \dfrac{\sigma}{\sqrt{n}}$ and $\bar{x} + z_{\alpha/2} \dfrac{\sigma}{\sqrt{n}}$. These two limits on $\bar{x}$ provide upper and lower control limits. In actual practice, μ and σ are usually unknown and it is necessary to estimate their values from a large sample taken while the process is "in control." The central line of an $\bar{x}$-chart is given by μ and the lower and upper three-sigma control limits are given by $\mu - A\sigma$ and $\mu + A\sigma$, respectively, where $A = \dfrac{3}{\sqrt{n}}$ and n is the sample size. Where the population parameters are unknown, it is necessary to estimate these parameters on the basis of preliminary samples. If k samples are used, each of size n, denote the mean of the ith sample by $\bar{x}_i$ and the grand mean of the k sample means by $\bar{\bar{x}}$, i.e.

$$\bar{\bar{x}} = \frac{1}{k} \sum_{i=1}^{k} \bar{x}_i$$

Denote the range of the ith sample by R_i and by $\bar{R}$ the mean of the k sample ranges, i.e.

$$\bar{R} = \frac{1}{k} \sum_{i=1}^{k} R_i$$

Since $\bar{\bar{x}}$ is an unbiased estimate of the population mean μ, the central line for the $\bar{x}$-chart is given by $\bar{\bar{x}}$. The statistic R does not provide an unbiased estimate of σ, but $A_2 \bar{R}$ is an unbiased estimate of $\dfrac{3\sigma}{\sqrt{n}}$. The constant multiplier A_2 depends on the assumption of normality. Thus, the central line and the lower and upper three sigma limits, LCL and UCL, for an $\bar{x}$-chart (with μ and σ estimated from past date) are given by

$$\text{central line} = \bar{\bar{x}}$$
$$\text{LCL} = \bar{\bar{x}} - A_2 \bar{R}$$
$$\text{UCL} = \bar{\bar{x}} + A_2 \bar{R}$$

The central line and control limits of an R chart are based on the distribution of the range of samples of size n from a normal population. The mean and standard deviation of the sampling distribution of R are given by $d_2\sigma$ and $d_3\sigma$, respectively, when σ is known. Here d_2 and d_3 are constants which depend on the size of the sample. The set of control chart values for an R chart (with σ known) is given by

$$\text{central line} = d_2\sigma$$
$$\text{LCL} = D_1\sigma$$
$$\text{UCL} = D_2\sigma$$

where $D_1 = d_2 - 3d_3$ and $D_2 = d_2 + 3d_3$.

If σ is unknown, the control chart values for an R chart are given by

$$\text{central line} = \bar{R}$$
$$\text{LCL} = D_3\bar{R}$$
$$\text{UCL} = D_4\bar{R},$$

where $D_3 = \dfrac{D_1}{d_2}$ and $D_4 = \dfrac{D_2}{d_2}$.

The central line and control limits of an s-chart are based on estimates obtained from the samples. A pooled estimate of the population variance is obtained from the k samples, i.e.

$$s_p^2 = \frac{\sum_i (n_i - 1)s_i^2}{\sum_i (n_i - 1)} , \qquad i = 1, 2, \ldots, k$$

If the sample sizes are all equal, the pooled estimate is

$$s_p^2 = \frac{1}{k} \sum_i s_i^2$$

The control chart values for an s-chart are given by

$$\text{central line} = C_2's_p$$
$$\text{LCL} = B_2's_p$$
$$\text{UCL} = B_4's_p$$

If one uses the biased estimator of the variance s_p', as is often done in quality control work, the control chart values are given by

$$\text{central line} = c_2s_p'$$
$$\text{LCL} = B_2s_p'$$
$$\text{UCL} = B_4s_p'$$

B. Control Charts for Attributes

Control limits for a fraction-defective chart are based on the sampling theory for proportions, using the normal curve approximation to the binomial. If k samples are taken, the estimator of p is given by

$$\bar{p} = \frac{\sum_i x_i}{\sum_i n_i} , \qquad i = 1, 2, \ldots, k$$

where x_i is the number of defectives in the ith sample of size n_i. The central line and control limits of a fraction defective chart based on analysis of past data are given by

$$\text{central line} = \bar{p}$$
$$\text{LCL} = \bar{p} - 3\sqrt{\frac{\bar{p}(1 - \bar{p})}{n_i}}$$
$$\text{UCL} = \bar{p} + 3\sqrt{\frac{\bar{p}(1 - \bar{p})}{n_i}}$$

When the sample sizes are approximately equal, n_i is replaced by $\bar{n} = \dfrac{1}{k} \sum_i n_i$.

Equivalent to the p chart for the fraction defective is the control chart for the number of defective. Here, if p is estimated by $\bar{p}$, the control chart values for a number-of-defectives chart are given by

$$\text{central line} = \bar{n}\bar{p}$$
$$\text{LCL} = \bar{n}\bar{p} - 3\sqrt{\bar{n}\bar{p}(1-\bar{p})}$$
$$\text{UCL} = \bar{n}\bar{p} + 3\sqrt{\bar{n}\bar{p}(1-\bar{p})}$$

In many cases it is necessary to control the number of defects per unit C, where C is taken to be a value of a random variable having a Poisson distribution. If k is the number of units available for estimating λ, the parameter of the Poisson distribution, and if C_i is the number of defects in the ith unit, then λ is estimated by

$$\bar{C} = \frac{1}{k}\sum_{i=1}^{k} C_i$$

and the control-chart values for the C-chart are

$$\text{central line} = \bar{C}$$
$$\text{LCL} = \bar{C} - 3\sqrt{\bar{C}}$$
$$\text{UCL} = \bar{C} + 3\sqrt{\bar{C}}$$

This table presents values of the factors for computing control limits for various sample sizes n.

Number of observations in sample, n	$\bar{X}$ chart		R chart			s chart			$\hat{\sigma}$ chart (biased)		
	Factors for control limits		Factor for central line	Factors for control limits		Factor for central line	Factors for control limits		Factor for central line	Factors for control limits	
	A	A_2	d_2	D_3	D_4	c_2'	B_2'	B_4'	c_2	B_2	B_4
2	2.121	1.880	1.128	0	3.267	0.798	0	2.298	0.5642	0	3.267
3	1.732	1.023	1.693	0	2.575	0.886	0	2.111	0.7236	0	2.568
4	1.500	0.729	2.059	0	2.282	0.921	0	1.982	0.7979	0	2.266
5	1.342	0.577	2.326	0	2.115	0.940	0	1.889	0.8407	0	2.089
6	1.225	0.483	2.534	0	2.004	0.951	0.085	1.817	0.8686	0.030	1.970
7	1.134	0.419	2.704	0.076	1.924	0.960	0.158	1.762	0.8882	0.118	1.882
8	1.061	0.373	2.847	0.136	1.864	0.965	0.215	1.715	0.9027	0.185	1.815
9	1.000	0.337	2.970	0.184	1.816	0.969	0.262	1.676	0.9139	0.239	1.761
10	0.949	0.308	3.078	0.223	1.777	0.973	0.302	1.644	0.9227	0.284	1.716
11	0.905	0.285	3.173	0.256	1.744	0.976	0.336	1.616	0.9300	0.321	1.679
12	0.866	0.266	3.258	0.284	1.716	0.977	0.365	1.589	0.9359	0.354	1.646
13	0.832	0.249	3.336	0.308	1.692	0.980	0.392	1.568	0.9410	0.382	1.618
14	0.802	0.235	3.407	0.329	1.671	0.981	0.414	1.548	0.9453	0.406	1.594
15	0.775	0.223	3.472	0.348	1.652	0.982	0.434	1.530	0.9490	0.428	1.572
16	0.750	0.212	3.532	0.364	1.636	0.984	0.454	1.514	0.9523	0.448	1.552
17	0.728	0.203	3.588	0.379	1.621	0.984	0.469	1.499	0.9551	0.466	1.534
18	0.707	0.194	3.640	0.392	1.608	0.986	0.486	1.486	0.9576	0.482	1.518
19	0.688	0.187	3.689	0.404	1.596	0.986	0.500	1.472	0.9599	0.497	1.503
20	0.671	0.180	3.735	0.414	1.586	0.987	0.513	1.461	0.9619	0.510	1.490
21	0.655	0.173	3.778	0.425	1.575	0.988	0.525	1.451	0.9638	0.523	1.477
22	0.640	0.167	3.819	0.434	1.566	0.988	0.536	1.440	0.9655	0.534	1.466
23	0.626	0.162	3.858	0.443	1.557	0.989	0.546	1.432	0.9670	0.545	1.455
24	0.612	0.157	3.895	0.452	1.548	0.989	0.556	1.422	0.9684	0.555	1.445
25	0.600	0.153	3.931	0.459	1.541	0.990	0.566	1.414	0.9696	0.565	1.435

INTEREST TABLES FROM ¼% TO 20%

SIMPLE INTEREST

If P is the principal placed at interest at a rate i (expressed as a decimal), for a period of n years

The **amount,**

$$A = P(1 + ni)$$

Present value,

$$P = \frac{A}{1 + ni}$$

COMPOUND INTEREST

At interest compounded annually the **amount,**—

$$A = P(1 + i)^n$$

At interest compounded q times per year,—

$$A = P\left(1 + \frac{i}{q}\right)^{nq}$$

At interest compounded annually the **present value,**—

$$P = \frac{A}{(1 + i)^n} = A(1 + i)^{-n} = Av^n. \quad v = \frac{1}{1 + i}$$

At interest compounded q times per year,—

$$P = A\left(1 + \frac{i}{q}\right)^{-nq}$$

* The **amount of an annuity of 1 per annum,**—

$$s_{\overline{n}|i} = \frac{(1 + i)^n - 1}{i}$$

* The **present value of an annuity,**—

$$a_{\overline{n}|i} = \frac{1 - (1 + i)^{-n}}{i}$$

The **annuity whose present value is 1,**—

$$\frac{1}{a_{\overline{n}|i}} = \frac{1}{s_{\overline{n}|i}} + i = \frac{i}{(1 - v^n)}$$

Compound amount of 1 for fractional periods,—$(1+i)^{1/p}$

* This information can be constructed by use of tables $(1 + i)^n$ and $(1 + i)^{-n}$ as may be observed from the formula structures. For example $s_{\overline{50}|.07} = \frac{(1.07)^{50} - 1}{.07}$. Here $(1.07)^{50}$ is obtained from the entries under $(1 + i)^n$, where $i = .07$ and $n = 50$ and is equal to 29.45702506. Accordingly $s_{\overline{50}|.07} = \frac{28.45702506}{.07} = 406.528929$ Similarly $a_{\overline{n}|i}$ may be evaluated by use of entries for $(1 + i)^{-n}$ and carrying out the appropriate arithmetic.

AMOUNT AT COMPOUND INTEREST $(1+i)^n$ *

The following table gives the amount after a term of n periods on unit original principal at rate of interest i.

Rate i

Periods n	0.0025 (1/4%)	0.004167 (5/12%)	0.005 (1/2%)	0.005833 (7/12%)	0.0075 (3/4%)
1	1.00250000	1.00416667	1.00500000	1.00583333	1.00750000
2	1.00500625	1.00835069	1.01002500	1.01170069	1.01505625
3	1.00751877	1.01255216	1.01507513	1.01760228	1.02266917
4	1.01003756	1.01677112	1.02015050	1.02353830	1.03033919
5	1.01256266	1.02100767	1.02525125	1.02950894	1.03806673
6	1.01509406	1.02526187	1.03037751	1.03551440	1.04585224
7	1.01763180	1.02953379	1.03552940	1.04155490	1.05369613
8	1.02017588	1.03382352	1.04070704	1.04763064	1.06159885
9	1.02272632	1.03813111	1.04591058	1.05374182	1.06956084
10	1.02528313	1.04245666	1.05114013	1.05988865	1.07758255
11	1.02784634	1.04680023	1.05639583	1.06607133	1.08566441
12	1.03041596	1.05116190	1.06167781	1.07229008	1.09380690
13	1.03299200	1.05554174	1.06698620	1.07854511	1.10201045
14	1.03557448	1.05993983	1.07232113	1.08483662	1.11027553
15	1.03816341	1.06435625	1.07768274	1.09116483	1.11860259
16	1.04075882	1.06879106	1.08307115	1.09752996	1.12699211
17	1.04336072	1.07324436	1.08848651	1.10393222	1.13544455
18	1.04596912	1.07771621	1.09392894	1.11037182	1.14396039
19	1.04858404	1.08220670	1.09939858	1.11684899	1.15254009
20	1.05120550	1.08671589	1.10489558	1.12336395	1.16118414
21	1.05383352	1.09124387	1.11042006	1.12991690	1.16989302
22	1.05646810	1.09579072	1.11597216	1.13650808	1.17866722
23	1.05910927	1.10035652	1.12155202	1.14313771	1.18750723
24	1.06175704	1.10494134	1.12715978	1.14980604	1.19641353
25	1.06441144	1.10954526	1.13279558	1.15651322	1.20538663
26	1.06707247	1.11416836	1.13845955	1.16325955	1.21442703
27	1.06974015	1.11881073	1.14415185	1.17004523	1.22353523
28	1.07241450	1.12347244	1.14987261	1.17687049	1.23271175
29	1.07509553	1.12815358	1.15562197	1.18373557	1.24195709
30	1.07778327	1.13285422	1.16140008	1.19064069	1.25127176
31	1.08047773	1.13757444	1.16720708	1.19758610	1.26065630
32	1.08317892	1.14231434	1.17304312	1.20457202	1.27011122
33	1.08588687	1.14707398	1.17890833	1.21159869	1.27963706
34	1.08860159	1.15185346	1.18480288	1.21866634	1.28923434
35	1.09132309	1.15665284	1.19072689	1.22577523	1.29890359
36	1.09405140	1.16147223	1.19668052	1.23292559	1.30864537
37	1.09678653	1.16631170	1.20266393	1.24011765	1.31846021
38	1.09952850	1.17117133	1.20867725	1.24735167	1.32834866
39	1.10227732	1.17605121	1.21472063	1.25462789	1.33831128
40	1.10503301	1.18095142	1.22079424	1.26194655	1.34834861
41	1.10779559	1.18587206	1.22689821	1.26930791	1.35846123
42	1.11056508	1.19081319	1.23303270	1.27671220	1.36864969
43	1.11334149	1.19577491	1.23919786	1.28415969	1.37891456
44	1.11612485	1.20075731	1.24539385	1.29165062	1.38925642
45	1.11891516	1.20576046	1.25162082	1.29918525	1.39967584
46	1.12171245	1.21078446	1.25787892	1.30676383	1.41017341
47	1.12451673	1.21582940	1.26416892	1.31438662	1.42074971
48	1.12732802	1.22089536	1.27048916	1.32205388	1.43140533
49	1.13014634	1.22598242	1.27684161	1.32976586	1.44214087
50	1.13297171	1.23109068	1.28322581	1.33752283	1.45295693
51	1.13580414	1.23622022	1.28964194	1.34532504	1.46385411
52	1.13864365	1.24137114	1.29609014	1.35317277	1.47483301
53	1.14149026	1.24654352	1.30257060	1.36106628	1.48589426
54	1.14434398	1.25173745	1.30908346	1.36900583	1.49703847
55	1.14720484	1.25695302	1.31562887	1.37699170	1.50826626
56	1.15007285	1.26219033	1.32220702	1.38502415	1.51957825
57	1.15294804	1.26744946	1.32881805	1.39310346	1.53097509
58	1.15583041	1.27273050	1.33546214	1.40122990	1.54245740
59	1.15871998	1.27803354	1.34213946	1.40940374	1.55402583
60	1.16161678	1.28335864	1.34885015	1.41762526	1.56568103
61	1.16452082	1.28870601	1.35559440	1.42589474	1.57742363
62	1.16743213	1.29407561	1.36237238	1.43421246	1.58925431
63	1.17035071	1.29946760	1.36918424	1.44257870	1.60117372
64	1.17327658	1.30488204	1.37603016	1.45099374	1.61318252
65	1.17620977	1.31031905	1.38291031	1.45945787	1.62528139
66	1.17915030	1.31577872	1.38982486	1.46797138	1.63747100
67	1.18209817	1.32126113	1.39677399	1.47653454	1.64975203
68	1.18505342	1.32676638	1.40375785	1.48514766	1.66212517
69	1.18801605	1.33229458	1.41077664	1.49381102	1.67459111
70	1.19098609	1.33784580	1.41783053	1.50252492	1.68715055
71	1.19396356	1.34342016	1.42491968	1.51128965	1.69980418
72	1.19694847	1.34901774	1.43204428	1.52010550	1.71255271
73	1.19994084	1.35463865	1.43920450	1.52897279	1.72539685
74	1.20294069	1.36028298	1.44640052	1.53789179	1.73833733
75	1.20594804	1.36595082	1.45363252	1.54686283	1.75137486
76	1.20896291	1.37164229	1.46090069	1.55588620	1.76451017
77	1.21198532	1.37735746	1.46820519	1.56496220	1.77774400
78	1.21501528	1.38309645	1.47554622	1.57409115	1.79107708
79	1.21805282	1.38885935	1.48292395	1.58327334	1.80451915
80	1.22109795	1.39464627	1.49033857	1.59250910	1.81804398
81	1.22415070	1.40045729	1.49779026	1.60179874	1.83167931
82	1.22721108	1.40629253	1.50527921	1.61114257	1.84541691
83	1.23027910	1.41215209	1.51280561	1.62054090	1.85925753
84	1.23335480	1.41803605	1.52036964	1.62999405	1.87320196
85	1.23643819	1.42394454	1.52797148	1.63950235	1.88725098
86	1.23952928	1.42987764	1.53561134	1.64906612	1.90140536
87	1.24262811	1.43583546	1.54328940	1.65868567	1.91566590
88	1.24573468	1.44181811	1.55100585	1.66836134	1.93003339
89	1.24884901	1.44782568	1.55876087	1.67809344	1.94450865
90	1.25197114	1.45385829	1.56655468	1.68788232	1.95909246
91	1.25510106	1.45991603	1.57438745	1.69772830	1.97378565
92	1.25823882	1.46599902	1.58225939	1.70763172	1.98859905
93	1.26138441	1.47210735	1.59017069	1.71759290	2.00350346
94	1.26453787	1.47824113	1.59812154	1.72761219	2.01852974
95	1.26769922	1.48440047	1.60611215	1.73768993	2.03366871
96	1.27086847	1.49058547	1.61414271	1.74782646	2.04892123
97	1.27404564	1.49679624	1.62221342	1.75802211	2.06428814
98	1.27723075	1.50303289	1.63032449	1.76827724	2.07977030
99	1.28042383	1.50929553	1.63847611	1.77859219	2.09536858
100	1.28362489	1.51558426	1.64666849	1.78896731	2.11108384

*The $s_{\overline{n}|}$ table may be constructed from this table by use of the formula $\dfrac{(1+i)^n - 1}{i}$ See page 805

AMOUNT AT COMPOUND INTEREST $(1 + i)^n$ (Continued)

0.0175(1 3/4%)	0.015(1 1/2%)	0.0125(1 1/4%)	0.001125(1 1/8%)	0.01(1%)	Periods n
		Rate i			
2.42245274	2.13682106	1.88428515	1.76923395	1.66107814	51
2.46484566	2.16887337	1.90783787	1.78913784	1.67768892	52
2.50798046	2.20140647	1.93168670	1.80926564	1.69446581	53
2.55187012	2.23442757	1.95583279	1.82961988	1.71141047	54
2.59652785	2.26794398	1.98028070	1.85020310	1.72852457	55
2.64196708	2.30196314	2.00503420	1.87101788	1.74580982	56
2.68820151	2.33649259	2.03002713	1.89206684	1.76326792	57
2.73524503	2.37153998	2.05547335	1.91335259	1.78090060	58
2.78311182	2.40711308	2.08116676	1.93487780	1.79870960	59
2.83181628	2.44321978	2.10718135	1.95664518	1.81669670	60
2.88137306	2.47986807	2.13352111	1.97865744	1.83486367	61
2.93179709	2.51706609	2.16019013	2.00091733	1.85321230	62
2.98310354	2.55482208	2.18719250	2.02342765	1.87174443	63
3.03530785	2.59314442	2.21453241	2.04619121	1.89046187	64
3.08842574	2.63204158	2.24221407	2.06921087	1.90936649	65
3.14247319	2.67155221	2.27024174	2.09248949	1.92846015	66
3.19746647	2.71159504	2.29861976	2.11602999	1.94774475	67
3.25342213	2.75226896	2.32735251	2.13983533	1.96722220	68
3.31035702	2.79355300	2.35644442	2.16390848	1.98689442	69
3.36828827	2.83545629	2.38589997	2.18825245	2.00676337	70
3.42723331	2.87798814	2.41572372	2.21287029	2.02683100	71
3.48720990	2.92115696	2.44592027	2.23776508	2.04709931	72
3.54823607	2.96497533	2.47649427	2.26293994	2.06757031	73
3.61033020	3.00944996	2.50745045	2.28839801	2.08824601	74
3.67351098	3.05459171	2.53879358	2.31414249	2.10912847	75
3.73779742	3.10041059	2.57052850	2.34017659	2.13021975	76
3.80320888	3.14691674	2.60266011	2.36650358	2.15152195	77
3.86976503	3.19412050	2.63519336	2.39312675	2.17303717	78
3.93748592	3.24203230	2.66813327	2.42004942	2.19476754	79
4.00639192	3.29066279	2.70148494	2.44727498	2.21671522	80
4.07650378	3.34002273	2.73525350	2.47480682	2.23888237	81
4.14784260	3.39012307	2.76944417	2.50264840	2.26127119	82
4.22042984	3.44097492	2.80406222	2.53080319	2.28388390	83
4.29428737	3.49258954	2.83911300	2.55927473	2.30672274	84
4.36943740	3.54497838	2.87460191	2.58806657	2.32978997	85
4.44590255	3.59815306	2.91053444	2.61718232	2.35308787	86
4.52370584	3.65212535	2.94691612	2.64662562	2.37661875	87
4.60287070	3.70690723	2.98375257	2.67640016	2.40038494	88
4.68342093	3.76251084	3.02104948	2.70650966	2.42438879	89
4.76538080	3.81894851	3.05881260	2.73695789	2.44863267	90
4.84877496	3.87623273	3.09704775	2.76774867	2.47311900	91
4.93362853	3.93437622	3.13576085	2.79888584	2.49785019	92
5.01996703	3.99339187	3.17495786	2.83037331	2.52282869	93
5.10781645	4.05329275	3.21464483	2.86221501	2.54805698	94
5.19720324	4.11409214	3.25482789	2.89441492	2.57353755	95
5.28815429	4.17580352	3.29551324	2.92697709	2.59927259	96
5.38069699	4.23844057	3.33670716	2.95990559	2.62526565	97
5.47485919	4.30201718	3.37841600	2.99320452	2.65151831	98
5.57066923	4.36654744	3.42064620	3.02687807	2.67803349	99
5.66815594	4.43204565	3.46340427	3.06093045	2.70481383	100

Periods n	0.01(1%)	0.001125(1 1/8%)	0.0125(1 1/4%)	0.015(1 1/2%)	0.0175(1 3/4%)
			Rate i		
1	1.01000000	1.01125000	1.01250000	1.01500000	1.01750000
2	1.02010000	1.02262656	1.02515625	1.03022500	1.03530625
3	1.03030100	1.03413111	1.03797070	1.04567838	1.05342411
4	1.04060401	1.04576509	1.05094534	1.06136355	1.07185903
5	1.05101005	1.05752994	1.06408215	1.07728400	1.09061656
6	1.06152015	1.06942716	1.07738318	1.09344326	1.10970235
7	1.07213535	1.08145821	1.09085047	1.10984491	1.12912215
8	1.08285671	1.09362462	1.10448610	1.12649259	1.14888178
9	1.09368527	1.10592789	1.11829218	1.14338998	1.16898721
10	1.10462213	1.11836958	1.13227083	1.16054083	1.18944449
11	1.11566835	1.13095124	1.14642422	1.17794894	1.21025977
12	1.12682503	1.14367444	1.16075452	1.19561817	1.23143931
13	1.13809328	1.15654078	1.17526395	1.21355244	1.25298950
14	1.14947421	1.16955186	1.18995475	1.23175573	1.27491682
15	1.16096896	1.18270932	1.20482918	1.25023207	1.29722786
16	1.17257864	1.19601480	1.21988955	1.26898555	1.31992935
17	1.18430443	1.20946997	1.23513817	1.28802033	1.34302881
18	1.19614748	1.22307650	1.25057739	1.30734064	1.36653111
19	1.20810895	1.23683611	1.26620961	1.32695075	1.39044540
20	1.22019004	1.25075052	1.28203723	1.34685501	1.41477820
21	1.23239194	1.26482146	1.29806270	1.36705783	1.43953680
22	1.24471586	1.27905071	1.31428848	1.38756370	1.46472871
23	1.25716302	1.29344003	1.33071709	1.40837715	1.49036146
24	1.26973465	1.30799123	1.34735105	1.42950281	1.51644279
25	1.28243200	1.32270613	1.36419294	1.45094535	1.54298054
26	1.29525631	1.33758657	1.38124535	1.47270953	1.56998269
27	1.30820888	1.35263442	1.39851092	1.49480018	1.59745739
28	1.32129097	1.36785156	1.41599230	1.51722218	1.62541290
29	1.33450388	1.38323989	1.43369221	1.53998051	1.65385762
30	1.34784892	1.39880134	1.45161336	1.56308022	1.68280013
31	1.36132740	1.41453785	1.46975853	1.58652642	1.71224913
32	1.37494068	1.43045140	1.48813051	1.61032432	1.74221349
33	1.38869009	1.44654398	1.50673214	1.63447918	1.77270223
34	1.40257699	1.46281760	1.52556629	1.65899637	1.80373452
35	1.41660276	1.47927430	1.54463587	1.68388132	1.83528970
36	1.43076878	1.49591613	1.56394382	1.70913954	1.86740727
37	1.44507647	1.51274519	1.58349312	1.73477663	1.90008689
38	1.45952724	1.52976357	1.60328678	1.76079828	1.93333841
39	1.47412251	1.54697341	1.62332787	1.78721018	1.96717184
40	1.48886373	1.56437687	1.64361946	1.81401841	2.00159734
41	1.50375237	1.58197611	1.66416471	1.84122868	2.03662530
42	1.51878989	1.59977334	1.68496677	1.86884712	2.07226624
43	1.53397779	1.61777079	1.70602885	1.89687982	2.10853090
44	1.54931757	1.63597071	1.72735421	1.92533302	2.14543019
45	1.56481075	1.65437538	1.74894614	1.95421301	2.18297522
46	1.58045885	1.67298710	1.77080797	1.98352621	2.22117728
47	1.59626344	1.69180821	1.79294306	2.01327910	2.26004789
48	1.61222608	1.71084105	1.81535485	2.04347829	2.29959872
49	1.62834834	1.73008801	1.83804679	2.07413046	2.33984170
50	1.64463182	1.74955150	1.86102237	2.10524242	2.38078893

AMOUNT AT COMPOUND INTEREST $(1 + i)^n$ (Continued)

Rate i Rate i

Periods n	0.02(2%)	0.0225(2 1/4%)	0.025(2 1/2%)	0.0275(2 3/4%)	Periods n	0.02(2%)	0.0225(2 1/4%)	0.025(2 1/2%)	0.0275(2 3/4%)
1	1.02000000	1.02250000	1.02500000	1.02750000	51	2.74541979	3.11049244	3.52303644	3.98908562
2	1.04040000	1.04550625	1.05062500	1.05575625	52	2.80032819	3.18047852	3.61111235	4.09878547
3	1.06120800	1.06903014	1.07689063	1.08487955	53	2.85633475	3.25203929	3.70139016	4.21150208
4	1.08243216	1.09308332	1.10381289	1.11462126	54	2.91346144	3.32521017	3.79392491	4.32721838
5	1.10408080	1.11767769	1.13140821	1.14527334	55	2.97173067	3.40002740	3.88877303	4.44631964
6	1.12616242	1.14282544	1.15969342	1.17676836	56	3.03116529	3.47652802	3.98599236	4.56859343
7	1.14868567	1.16853901	1.18868575	1.20912949	57	3.09178859	3.55474990	4.08564217	4.69422975
8	1.17165938	1.19483114	1.21840290	1.24238055	58	3.15362436	3.63473177	4.18778322	4.82332107
9	1.19509257	1.22171484	1.24886297	1.27654602	59	3.21669685	3.71651324	4.29247780	4.95596239
10	1.21899442	1.24920343	1.28008454	1.31165103	60	3.28103079	3.80013479	4.39978975	5.09225136
11	1.24337431	1.27731050	1.31208666	1.34772144	61	3.34665140	3.88563782	4.50978449	5.23228827
12	1.26824179	1.30604999	1.34488882	1.38478378	62	3.41358443	3.97306467	4.62252910	5.37617620
13	1.29360663	1.33543611	1.37851104	1.42286533	63	3.48185612	4.06245862	4.73809233	5.52402105
14	1.31947876	1.36548343	1.41297382	1.46199413	64	3.55149324	4.15386394	4.85654464	5.67593162
15	1.34586834	1.39620680	1.44829817	1.50219896	65	3.62252311	4.24732588	4.97795826	5.83201974
16	1.37278571	1.42762146	1.48450562	1.54350944	66	3.69497357	4.34289071	5.10240721	5.99240029
17	1.40024142	1.45974294	1.52161826	1.58595595	67	3.76887304	4.44060576	5.22996739	6.15719130
18	1.42824625	1.49258716	1.55965872	1.62956973	68	3.84425050	4.54051939	5.36071658	6.32651406
19	1.45681117	1.52617037	1.59865019	1.67438290	69	3.92113551	4.64268107	5.49473449	6.50049319
20	1.48594740	1.56050920	1.63861644	1.72042843	70	3.99955822	4.74714140	5.63210286	6.67925676
21	1.51566634	1.59562066	1.67958185	1.76774021	71	4.07954939	4.85395208	5.77290543	6.86293632
22	1.54597967	1.63152212	1.72157140	1.81635307	72	4.16114038	4.96316600	5.91722806	7.05166706
23	1.57689926	1.66823137	1.76461068	1.86630278	73	4.24436318	5.07483723	6.06515876	7.24558791
24	1.60843725	1.70576658	1.80872595	1.91762610	74	4.32925045	5.18902107	6.21678773	7.44484158
25	1.64060599	1.74414633	1.85394410	1.97036082	75	4.41583546	5.30577405	6.37220743	7.64957472
26	1.67341811	1.78338962	1.90029270	2.02454575	76	4.50415216	5.42515396	6.53151261	7.85993802
27	1.70688648	1.82351588	1.94780002	2.08022075	77	4.59423521	5.54721993	6.69480043	8.07608632
28	1.74102421	1.86454499	1.99649502	2.13742682	78	4.68611991	5.67203237	6.86217044	8.29817869
29	1.77584469	1.90649725	2.04640740	2.19620606	79	4.77984231	5.79965310	7.03372470	8.52637861
30	1.81136158	1.94939344	2.09756758	2.25660173	80	4.87543916	5.93014530	7.20956782	8.76085402
31	1.84758882	1.99325479	2.15000677	2.31865828	81	4.97294794	6.06357357	7.38980701	9.00177751
32	1.88454059	2.03810303	2.20375694	2.38242138	82	5.07240690	6.20000397	7.57455219	9.24932639
33	1.92223140	2.08396034	2.25885086	2.44793797	83	5.17385504	6.33950406	7.76391599	9.50368286
34	1.96067603	2.13084945	2.31532213	2.51525626	84	5.27733214	6.48214290	7.95801389	9.76503414
35	1.99988955	2.17879356	2.37320519	2.58442581	85	5.38287878	6.62799112	8.15695424	10.03357258
36	2.03988734	2.22781642	2.43253532	2.65549752	86	5.49053636	6.77712092	8.36088834	10.30949583
37	2.08068509	2.27794229	2.49334870	2.72852370	87	5.60034708	6.92960614	8.56991055	10.59300696
38	2.12229879	2.32919599	2.55568242	2.80355810	88	5.71235402	7.08552228	8.78415832	10.88421465
39	2.16474477	2.38160290	2.61957448	2.88065595	89	5.82660110	7.24494653	9.00376228	11.18363331
40	2.20803966	2.43518897	2.68506384	2.95987399	90	5.94313313	7.40795782	9.22885633	11.49118322
41	2.25220046	2.48998072	2.75219043	3.04127052	91	6.06199579	7.57463688	9.45957774	11.80719076
42	2.29724447	2.54600528	2.82099520	3.12490546	92	6.18323570	7.74506621	9.69606718	12.13188851
43	2.34318936	2.60329040	2.89152008	3.21084036	93	6.30690042	7.91933020	9.93846886	12.46551544
44	2.39005214	2.66186444	2.96380808	3.29913847	94	6.43303843	8.09751512	10.18693058	12.80831711
45	2.43785421	2.72175639	3.03790328	3.38986478	95	6.56169920	8.27970921	10.44160385	13.16054584
46	2.48661129	2.78299591	3.11385086	3.48308606	96	6.69293318	8.46600267	10.70264395	13.52246085
47	2.53634352	2.84561332	3.19169713	3.57887093	97	6.82679184	8.65648773	10.97021004	13.89432852
48	2.58707039	2.90963962	3.27148956	3.67728988	98	6.96332768	8.85125871	11.24446530	14.27642255
49	2.63881179	2.97510651	3.35327680	3.77841535	99	7.10259423	9.05041203	11.52557693	14.66902417
50	2.69158803	3.04204641	3.43710872	3.88232177	100	7.24464612	9.25404630	11.81371635	15.07242234

Rate i

Periods n	0.03(3%)	0.0325(3 1/4%)	0.035(3 1/2%)	0.0375(3 3/4%)
51	4.51542320	5.10967263	5.78039930	6.53722412
52	4.65088590	5.27573700	5.98271327	6.78237003
53	4.79041247	5.44719845	6.19210824	7.03670890
54	4.93412485	5.62423240	6.40883202	7.30058549
55	5.08214859	5.80701995	6.63314114	7.57435744
56	5.23461305	5.99574810	6.86530108	7.85839585
57	5.39165144	6.19060991	7.10558662	8.15308569
58	5.55340098	6.39180473	7.35428215	8.45882640
59	5.72000301	6.59953839	7.61168203	8.77603239
60	5.89160310	6.81402339	7.87809090	9.10513361
61	6.06835120	7.03547915	8.15382408	9.44657612
62	6.25040173	7.26413222	8.43920793	9.80082272
63	6.43791379	7.50021651	8.73458020	10.16835358
64	6.63105120	7.74397355	9.04029051	10.54966684
65	6.82998273	7.99565269	9.35670068	10.94527934
66	7.03488222	8.25551140	9.68418520	11.35572732
67	7.24592868	8.52381552	10.02313168	11.78156709
68	7.46330654	8.80083953	10.37394129	12.22337586
69	7.68720574	9.08686681	10.73702924	12.68175245
70	7.91782191	9.38218999	11.11282526	13.15731817
71	8.15535657	9.68711116	11.50177414	13.65071760
72	8.40001727	10.00194227	11.90433624	14.16261951
73	8.65201778	10.32700540	12.32098801	14.69371774
74	8.91157832	10.66263307	12.75222259	15.24473126
75	9.17892567	11.00916865	13.19855038	15.81640961
76	9.45429344	11.36696663	13.66049964	16.40952497
77	9.73792224	11.73639304	14.13861713	17.02488216
78	10.03005991	12.11782582	14.63346873	17.66331524
79	10.33096171	12.51165516	15.15456013	18.32568956
80	10.64089056	12.91828395	15.67573754	19.01290292
81	10.96011727	13.33812818	16.22438835	19.72588678
82	11.28892079	13.77161734	16.79224195	20.46560754
83	11.62758842	14.21919491	17.37997041	21.23306782
84	11.97641607	14.68131874	17.98826938	22.02930786
85	12.33570855	15.15846163	18.61785881	22.85540691
86	12.70577981	15.65111160	19.26948387	23.71248466
87	13.08695320	16.15977273	19.94391580	24.60170284
88	13.47956180	16.68496534	20.64195285	25.52426670
89	13.88394865	17.22722672	21.36442120	26.48142670
90	14.30046711	17.78711158	22.12217595	27.47448020
91	14.72948112	18.36519271	22.88610210	28.50477321
92	15.17136556	18.96206147	23.68711568	29.57370220
93	15.62650652	19.57832847	24.51616473	30.68271603
94	16.09530172	20.21462415	25.37423049	31.83331789
95	16.57816077	20.87159943	26.26232856	33.02706731
96	17.07550559	21.54992641	27.18151006	34.26558233
97	17.58777076	22.25029902	28.13286291	35.55054167
98	18.11540388	22.97343374	29.11751311	36.88368698
99	18.65886600	23.72007034	30.13662607	38.26682524
100	19.21863198	24.49007262	31.19140798	39.70183119

AMOUNT OF COMPOUND INTEREST ($S = P(1 + i)^n$) (Continued)

Rate i

Periods n	0.03(3%)	0.0325(3 1/4%)	0.035(3 1/2%)	0.0375(3 3/4%)
1	1.03000000	1.03250000	1.03500000	1.03750000
2	1.06090000	1.06605625	1.07122500	1.07640625
3	1.09272700	1.10070308	1.10871788	1.11677148
4	1.12550881	1.13647593	1.14752300	1.15865042
5	1.15927407	1.17341140	1.18768631	1.20209981
6	1.19405230	1.21154727	1.22925533	1.24711855
7	1.22987387	1.25092255	1.27227926	1.29394774
8	1.26677008	1.29157754	1.31680904	1.34247078
9	1.30477318	1.33355381	1.36289735	1.39281344
10	1.34391638	1.37689430	1.41059876	1.44504394
11	1.38423387	1.42164337	1.45996972	1.49923309
12	1.42576089	1.46784678	1.51106866	1.55545433
13	1.46853371	1.51555606	1.56395606	1.61378387
14	1.51258972	1.56480723	1.61869452	1.67430076
15	1.55796742	1.61566347	1.67534883	1.73708704
16	1.60470644	1.66817253	1.73398604	1.80222781
17	1.65284763	1.72239814	1.79467555	1.86981135
18	1.70243306	1.77836575	1.85748920	1.93992927
19	1.75350605	1.83616264	1.92250132	2.01267662
20	1.80611123	1.89583792	1.98978886	2.08815200
21	1.86029457	1.95745266	2.05943147	2.16645770
22	1.91610341	2.02106987	2.13151158	2.24769986
23	1.97358651	2.08675464	2.20611448	2.33198860
24	2.03279411	2.15457416	2.28332849	2.41943818
25	2.09377793	2.22459782	2.36324498	2.51016711
26	2.15659127	2.29689725	2.44595856	2.60429838
27	2.22128901	2.37154641	2.53156711	2.70195956
28	2.28792768	2.44862167	2.62017196	2.80328305
29	2.35656551	2.52820188	2.71187798	2.90840616
30	2.42726247	2.61036844	2.80679370	3.01747139
31	2.50008035	2.69520541	2.90503148	3.13062657
32	2.57508276	2.78279959	3.00670759	3.24802507
33	2.65233524	2.87324058	3.11194235	3.36982601
34	2.73190530	2.96662089	3.22086033	3.49619448
35	2.81386245	3.06303607	3.33359045	3.62730178
36	2.89827833	3.16258475	3.45026611	3.76332559
37	2.98522668	3.26536875	3.57102543	3.90445030
38	3.07478348	3.37149323	3.69601132	4.05086719
39	3.16702698	3.48106676	3.82537171	4.20277467
40	3.26203779	3.59420143	3.95925972	4.36037876
41	3.35989893	3.71101298	4.09783381	4.52389296
42	3.46069589	3.83162090	4.24125799	4.69353895
43	3.56451677	3.95614858	4.38970202	4.86954666
44	3.67145227	4.08472341	4.54334160	5.05215466
45	3.78159584	4.21747692	4.70233855	5.24161046
46	3.89504372	4.35454492	4.86694110	5.43817085
47	4.01189503	4.49606763	5.03728404	5.64210226
48	4.13225188	4.64218983	5.21358898	5.85368109
49	4.25621944	4.79306100	5.39606459	6.07319413
50	4.38390602	4.94883548	5.58492686	6.30093891

FINANCIAL TABLES

AMOUNT AT COMPOUND INTEREST $(1 + i)^n$ (Continued)

Rate i

Periods n	0.04(4%)	0.0425(4 1/4%)	0.045(4 1/2%)	0.0475(4 3/4%)
1	1.04000000	1.04250000	1.04500000	1.04750000
2	1.08160000	1.08680625	1.09202500	1.09725625
3	1.12486400	1.13299552	1.14116613	1.14937592
4	1.16985856	1.18114783	1.19251860	1.20397128
5	1.21665290	1.23134661	1.24618194	1.26115991
6	1.26531902	1.28367884	1.30226012	1.32106501
7	1.31593178	1.33823519	1.36086183	1.38381560
8	1.36856905	1.39511018	1.42210061	1.44954684
9	1.42331181	1.45440237	1.48609514	1.51840031
10	1.48024428	1.51621447	1.55296942	1.59052433
11	1.53945406	1.58065358	1.62285305	1.66607423
12	1.60103222	1.64783136	1.69588143	1.74521276
13	1.66507351	1.71786419	1.77219610	1.82811037
14	1.73167645	1.79087342	1.85194492	1.91494561
15	1.80094351	1.86698554	1.93528244	2.00590552
16	1.87298125	1.94633243	2.02237015	2.10118604
17	1.94790050	2.02905156	2.11337681	2.20099237
18	2.02581652	2.11528625	2.20847877	2.30553951
19	2.10684918	2.20518591	2.30786031	2.41505264
20	2.19112314	2.29890631	2.41171402	2.52976764
21	2.27876807	2.39660983	2.52024116	2.64993160
22	2.36991879	2.49846575	2.63365201	2.77580335
23	2.46471554	2.60465054	2.75216635	2.90765401
24	2.56330416	2.71534819	2.87601383	3.04576758
25	2.66583633	2.83075049	3.00543446	3.19044154
26	2.77246978	2.95105739	3.14067901	3.34198751
27	2.88336858	3.07647732	3.28200956	3.50073192
28	2.99870332	3.20722761	3.42969999	3.66701668
29	3.11865145	3.34353478	3.58403649	3.84119998
30	3.24339751	3.48563501	3.74531813	4.02365698
31	3.37313341	3.63377450	3.91385745	4.21478068
32	3.50805875	3.78820992	4.08998104	4.41498276
33	3.64838130	3.94920884	4.27403018	4.62469445
34	3.79431634	4.11705021	4.46636154	4.84436743
35	3.94608899	4.29202485	4.66734781	5.07447488
36	4.10393255	4.47443590	4.87737846	5.31551244
37	4.26808986	4.66459943	5.09686049	5.56799928
38	4.43881345	4.86284491	5.32621921	5.83247925
39	4.61636599	5.06951581	5.56589908	6.10952201
40	4.80102063	5.28497024	5.81636454	6.39972431
41	4.99306145	5.50958147	6.07810094	6.70371121
42	5.19278391	5.74373868	6.35161548	7.02213750
43	5.40049527	5.98784758	6.63743818	7.35568903
44	5.61651508	6.24233110	6.93612290	7.70508426
45	5.84117568	6.50763017	7.24824843	8.07107576
46	6.07482271	6.78420445	7.57441961	8.45445186
47	6.31781562	7.07253314	7.91526849	8.85603832
48	6.57052824	7.37311580	8.27145557	9.27667014
49	6.83334937	7.68647322	8.64367107	9.71734340

Rate i

Periods n	0.04(4%)	0.0425(4 1/4%)	0.045(4 1/2%)	0.0475(4 3/4%)
51	7.39095068	8.33570714	9.43910490	10.66241577
52	7.68658871	8.70873969	9.86386463	11.16888052
53	7.99405226	9.07886113	10.30773853	11.69940235
54	8.31381435	9.46471273	10.77158677	12.25512396
55	8.64636692	9.86696302	11.25630817	12.83724235
56	8.99222160	10.28630895	11.76284204	13.44701136
57	9.35191046	10.72347708	12.29216993	14.08574440
58	9.72598688	11.17922485	12.84531758	14.75481726
59	10.11502635	11.65434191	13.42335687	15.45567108
60	10.51596741	12.14965144	14.02740793	16.18981545
61	10.94041250	12.66601163	14.65864129	16.95883169
62	11.37802900	13.20431712	15.31828014	17.76437619
63	11.83315016	13.76550060	16.00760275	18.60818406
64	12.30647617	14.35053438	16.72794487	19.49207281
65	12.79873522	14.96043209	17.48070239	20.41794626
66	13.31068463	15.59625045	18.26733400	21.38779871
67	13.84311201	16.25909109	19.08936403	22.40371915
68	14.39683649	16.95010247	19.94838541	23.46789581
69	14.97270995	17.67048182	20.84606276	24.58262086
70	15.57161835	18.42147730	21.78413558	25.75029535
71	16.19448308	19.20439008	22.76442168	26.97343438
72	16.84226241	20.02057666	23.78882066	28.25467251
73	17.51595290	20.87145117	24.85931759	29.59676946
74	18.21659102	21.75848784	25.97798688	31.00261601
75	18.94525466	22.68322358	27.14699629	32.47524027
76	19.70306485	23.64726058	28.36861112	34.01781418
77	20.49118744	24.65226915	29.64519862	35.63366035
78	21.31083494	25.69999059	30.97923256	37.32625922
79	22.16326834	26.79224019	32.37329802	39.09925653
80	23.04979907	27.93091040	33.83009643	40.95647122
81	23.97179103	29.11797409	35.35245077	42.90190360
82	24.93066267	30.35548799	36.94331106	44.93974402
83	25.92788918	31.64559623	38.60576006	47.07438186
84	26.96500475	32.99053407	40.34301926	49.31041500
85	28.04360494	34.39263177	42.15845513	51.65265971
86	29.16534914	35.85431862	44.05558561	54.10616105
87	30.33190310	37.37812716	46.03808696	56.67620370
88	31.54524163	38.96669757	48.10980087	59.36832338
89	32.80705129	40.62278221	50.27474191	62.18831874
90	34.11933334	42.34925046	52.53710530	65.14226388
91	35.48410668	44.14909360	54.90127503	68.23652141
92	36.90347094	46.02543008	57.37183241	71.47775618
93	38.37960978	47.98151086	59.95356487	74.87294960
94	39.91479417	50.02072507	62.65147529	78.42941470
95	41.51138594	52.14660588	65.47079168	82.15481190
96	43.17184138	54.36283664	68.41697730	86.05716547
97	44.89871503	56.67325719	71.49574128	90.14488083
98	46.69466363	59.08187063	74.71304964	94.42676267
99	48.56245018	61.59285012	78.07513687	98.91203389

Rate *i*

Periods *n*	0.05(5%)	0.0525(5 1/4%)	0.055(5 1/2%)	0.0575(5 3/4%)
1	1.05000000	1.05250000	1.05500000	1.05750000
2	1.10250000	1.10775625	1.11302500	1.11830625
3	1.15762500	1.16591345	1.17424138	1.18260886
4	1.21550625	1.22712391	1.23882465	1.25060887
5	1.27628156	1.29154791	1.30696001	1.32251888
6	1.34009564	1.35935418	1.37884281	1.39856371
7	1.40710042	1.43072027	1.45467916	1.47898113
8	1.47745544	1.50583309	1.53468651	1.56402254
9	1.55132822	1.58488933	1.61909427	1.65395384
10	1.62889463	1.66809602	1.70814446	1.74905618
11	1.71033936	1.75567106	1.80209240	1.84962692
12	1.79585633	1.84784379	1.90120749	1.95598046
13	1.88564914	1.94485559	2.00577390	2.06844934
14	1.97993160	2.04696050	2.11609146	2.18738518
15	2.07892818	2.15442593	2.23247649	2.31315982
16	2.18287459	2.26753329	2.35526270	2.44616651
17	2.29201832	2.38657879	2.48480215	2.58682109
18	2.40661923	2.51187418	2.62146627	2.73556330
19	2.52695020	2.64374757	2.76564691	2.89285819
20	2.65329771	2.78254432	2.91775749	3.05919754
21	2.78596259	2.92862789	3.07823415	3.23510140
22	2.92526072	3.08238086	3.24753703	3.42111973
23	3.07152376	3.24420585	3.42615157	3.61783411
24	3.22509994	3.41452666	3.61458990	3.82585957
25	3.38635494	3.59378931	3.81339235	4.04584650
26	3.55567269	3.78246325	4.02312893	4.27848267
27	3.73345632	3.98104257	4.24440102	4.52449542
28	3.92012914	4.19004731	4.47784307	4.78465391
29	4.11613560	4.41002479	4.72412444	5.05977151
30	4.32194238	4.64155109	4.98395129	5.35070837
31	4.53803949	4.88523252	5.25806861	5.65837410
32	4.76494147	5.14170723	5.54726238	5.98373061
33	5.00318854	5.41164686	5.85236181	6.32779512
34	5.25334797	5.69575832	6.17424171	6.69164334
35	5.51601537	5.99478563	6.51382501	7.07641284
36	5.79181614	6.30951188	6.87208538	7.48330657
37	6.08140694	6.64076125	7.25005008	7.91359670
38	6.38547729	6.98940122	7.64880283	8.36862851
39	6.70475115	7.35634478	8.06948699	8.84982465
40	7.03998871	7.74255268	8.51130877	9.35868957
41	7.39198815	8.14903691	8.98154076	9.89681422
42	7.76158756	8.57686135	9.47552550	10.46588104
43	8.14966693	9.02714657	9.99667940	11.06766920
44	8.55715028	9.50107176	10.54649677	11.70406018
45	8.98500779	9.99987803	11.12655409	12.37704364
46	9.43425818	10.52487163	11.73851456	13.08872365
47	9.90597109	11.07742739	12.38413287	13.84132526
48	10.40126965	11.65899232	13.06526017	14.63720146
49	10.92133313	12.27108942	13.78384948	15.47884054
50	11.46739979	12.91532162	14.54196120	16.36887387
51	12.04076978	13.59337600	15.34176907	17.31008412
52	12.64280826	14.30702824	16.18556637	18.30541396
53	13.27494868	15.05814722	17.07577252	19.35797526
54	13.93869611	15.84869995	18.01494001	20.47105884
55	14.63563092	16.68075670	19.00576171	21.64814472
56	15.36741246	17.55649643	20.05107860	22.89291304
57	16.13578309	18.47821249	21.15388793	24.20925554
58	16.94257224	19.44831864	22.31735176	25.60128774
59	17.78970085	20.46935537	23.54480611	27.07336178
60	18.67918589	21.54399653	24.83977045	28.63008008
61	19.61314519	22.67505635	26.20595782	30.27630969
62	20.59380245	23.86549681	27.64728550	32.01719750
63	21.62349257	25.11843259	29.16788620	33.85818635
64	22.70466720	26.43715325	30.77211994	35.80503207
65	23.83990056	27.82510379	32.46458654	37.86382141
66	25.03189559	29.28592174	34.25013880	40.04099114
67	26.28349037	30.82343263	36.13389643	42.34334813
68	27.59766488	32.44166285	38.12126074	44.77809065
69	28.97754813	34.14485015	40.21793008	47.35283086
70	30.42642554	35.93745478	42.42991623	50.07561864
71	31.94774682	37.82417115	44.76356163	52.95496671
72	33.54513415	39.80994014	47.22555751	55.99987729
73	35.22239086	41.89996200	49.82296318	59.21987024
74	36.98351040	44.09971000	52.56322615	62.62501278
75	38.83268592	46.41494478	55.45420359	66.22595101
76	40.77432022	48.85172938	58.50418479	70.03394320
77	42.81303623	51.41644517	61.72191495	74.06089493
78	44.95368804	54.11580564	65.11662027	78.31939639
79	47.20137244	56.95688849	68.69803439	82.82276168
80	49.56144107	59.94712514	72.47642628	87.58507048
81	52.03951312	63.09434921	76.46262973	92.62121203
82	54.64148878	66.40680254	80.66807436	97.94693172
83	57.37356322	69.89315967	85.10481845	103.57888029
84	60.24224138	73.56255055	89.78558347	109.53466591
85	63.25435344	77.42458446	94.72379056	115.83290920
86	66.41707112	81.48937514	99.93359904	122.49330148
87	69.73792467	85.76756734	105.42994698	129.53666632
88	73.22482091	90.27036462	111.22859407	136.98502463
89	76.88606195	95.00955877	117.34616674	144.86166354
90	80.73036505	99.99756060	123.80020591	153.19120920
91	84.76688330	105.24743253	130.60921724	161.99970373
92	89.00522747	110.77292274	137.79272419	171.31468669
93	93.45548884	116.58850118	145.37132402	181.16528118
94	98.12826328	122.70939750	153.36674684	191.58228484
95	103.03467645	129.15164086	161.80191791	202.59826622
96	108.18641027	135.93210201	170.70102340	214.24766653
97	113.59573078	143.06853737	180.08957969	226.56690736
98	119.27551732	150.57963558	189.99450657	239.59450453
99	125.23929319	158.48506644	200.44420443	253.37118854
100	131.50125785	166.80553243	211.46863567	267.94003188

AMOUNT AT COMPOUND INTEREST $(1 + i)^n$ (Continued)

Periods n	0.06(6%)	0.0625(6 1/4%)	0.065(6 1/2%)	0.0675(6 3/4%)
1	1.06000000	1.06250000	1.06500000	1.06750000
2	1.12360000	1.12890625	1.13422500	1.13955625
3	1.19101600	1.19946289	1.20794963	1.21647630
4	1.26247696	1.27442932	1.28646635	1.29858845
5	1.33822558	1.35408115	1.37008666	1.38624317
6	1.41851911	1.43871123	1.45914230	1.47981458
7	1.50363026	1.52863068	1.55398655	1.57970207
8	1.59384807	1.62417009	1.65499567	1.68633195
9	1.68947896	1.72568073	1.76257039	1.80015936
10	1.79084770	1.83353577	1.87711747	1.92167012
11	1.89829856	1.94813176	1.99915140	2.05138285
12	2.01219647	2.06988999	2.12909624	2.18985119
13	2.13292826	2.19925812	2.26748750	2.33766615
14	2.26090396	2.33671175	2.41487418	2.49545861
15	2.39655819	2.48275623	2.57184101	2.66390207
16	2.54035168	2.63792850	2.73901067	2.84371546
17	2.69277279	2.80279903	2.91704637	3.03566625
18	2.85433915	2.97797397	3.10665438	3.24057373
19	3.02559950	3.16409734	3.30858691	3.45931245
20	3.20712547	3.36185342	3.52364506	3.69281604
21	3.39955360	3.57196926	3.75268199	3.94208113
22	3.60352747	3.79521734	3.99660632	4.20817160
23	3.81974966	4.03241843	4.25638573	4.49222319
24	4.04893464	4.28444458	4.53305081	4.79544825
25	4.29187072	4.55222236	4.82769911	5.11914101
26	4.54938296	4.83673626	5.14149955	5.46468303
27	4.82234594	5.13903228	5.47569702	5.83354913
28	5.11168670	5.46022180	5.83161733	6.22731370
29	5.41838790	5.80148566	6.21067245	6.64765737
30	5.74349117	6.16407851	6.61436616	7.09637424
31	6.08810064	6.54933342	7.04429996	7.57537950
32	6.45338668	6.95866676	7.50217946	8.08671762
33	6.84058988	7.39358343	7.98982113	8.63257106
34	7.25102528	7.85568239	8.50915950	9.21526961
35	7.68608679	8.34666254	9.06225487	9.83730031
36	8.14725200	8.86832895	9.65130143	10.50131808
37	8.63608712	9.42259951	10.27863603	11.21015705
38	9.15425235	10.01151198	10.94674737	11.96684265
39	9.70350749	10.63723148	11.65828595	12.77460453
40	10.28571794	11.30205845	12.41607453	13.63689033
41	10.90286101	12.00843710	13.22311938	14.55738043
42	11.55703267	12.75896442	14.08262214	15.54000361
43	12.25045463	13.55639970	14.99799258	16.58895385
44	12.98548191	14.40367468	15.97286209	17.70870824
45	13.76461083	15.30390434	17.01109813	18.90404604
46	14.59048748	16.26039837	18.11681951	20.18006915
47	15.46591673	17.27667326	19.29441278	21.54222382
48	16.39387173	18.35646534	20.54854961	22.99632392
49	17.37750403	19.50374443	21.88420533	24.54857529

Rate i

Periods n	0.06(6%)	0.0625(6 1/4%)	0.065(6 1/2%)	0.0675(6 3/4%)
51	19.52536353	22.01789898	24.82161279	27.97448297
52	20.69688534	23.39401767	26.43501762	29.86276057
53	21.93869846	24.85614377	28.15329377	31.87849691
54	23.25502037	26.40965276	29.98325786	34.03029545
55	24.65032159	28.06025606	31.93316963	36.32734039
56	26.12934089	29.81402206	34.00776065	38.77943587
57	27.69710134	31.67739844	36.21826509	41.39704779
58	29.35892742	33.65723584	38.57245233	44.19134852
59	31.12046307	35.76081308	41.07966173	47.17426454
60	32.98769085	37.99586390	43.74983974	50.35852740
61	34.96695230	40.37060539	46.59357932	53.75772800
62	37.06496944	42.89376823	49.62216198	57.38637464
63	39.28886761	45.57462874	52.84760251	61.25995492
64	41.64619967	48.42304304	56.28269667	65.39500188
65	44.14497165	51.44948323	59.94107195	69.80916451
66	46.79366994	54.66507593	63.83724163	74.52128311
67	49.60129014	58.08164318	67.9866234	79.55146972
68	52.57736755	61.71174587	72.40579539	84.92119393
69	55.73200960	65.56872999	77.11217209	90.65373452
70	59.07593018	69.66677562	82.12446327	96.77247730
71	62.62048599	74.02094909	87.46255339	103.30461952
72	66.37771515	78.64725841	93.14671936	110.27768134
73	70.36037806	83.56271206	99.20221461	117.72142483
74	74.58200074	88.78538156	105.65035856	125.66762100
75	79.05692079	94.33446791	112.51763187	134.15018542
76	83.80033603	100.23037216	119.83127794	143.20532293
77	88.82835620	106.49477042	127.62031101	152.87168223
78	94.15805757	113.15069357	135.91563122	163.19052078
79	99.80754102	120.22261191	144.75014725	174.20588094
80	105.79599348	127.73652516	154.15890683	185.96477790
81	112.14375309	135.72005798	164.17923577	198.51740041
82	118.87237828	144.20256161	174.85088609	211.91732494
83	126.00472097	153.21522171	186.21619369	226.22174437
84	133.56520423	162.79117306	198.32024628	241.49171211
85	141.57890449	172.96562138	211.21106229	257.79240268
86	150.07363875	183.77597272	224.93978134	275.19338986
87	159.07805708	195.26197101	239.56086712	293.76894368
88	168.62274050	207.46584420	255.13232349	313.59834738
89	178.74010493	220.43245946	271.71592451	334.76623582
90	189.46451123	234.20948818	289.37745961	357.36295674
91	200.83238190	248.84758119	308.18699448	381.48495632
92	212.88234282	264.40055501	328.21914912	407.23519087
93	225.65526431	280.92258970	349.55339382	434.72356626
94	239.19458017	298.48343906	372.27436441	464.06740698
95	253.54625498	317.13865400	396.47219810	495.39195695
96	268.75903028	336.95981987	422.24289098	528.83091405
97	284.88457209	358.01980861	449.68687889	564.52700074
98	301.97764642	380.39604665	478.91844302	602.63257329
99	320.09630520	404.17079957	510.04814181	643.31027199

Rate i

AMOUNT OF COMPOUND INTEREST $(1 + i)^n$ (Continued)

Rate i

Periods n	0.07(7%)	0.0725(7 1/4%)	0.075(7 1/2%)	0.0775(7 3/4%)
1	1.07000000	1.07250000	1.07500000	1.07750000
2	1.14490000	1.15025625	1.15562500	1.16100625
3	1.22504300	1.23364983	1.24229687	1.25098423
4	1.31079601	1.32308944	1.33546914	1.34793551
5	1.40255173	1.41901343	1.43562933	1.45240051
6	1.50073035	1.52189190	1.54330153	1.56496155
7	1.60578148	1.63222906	1.65904914	1.68624608
8	1.71818618	1.75056567	1.78347783	1.81693015
9	1.83845921	1.87748168	1.91723866	1.95774223
10	1.96715136	2.01359910	2.06103156	2.10946726
11	2.10485195	2.15958504	2.21560893	2.27295097
12	2.25219159	2.31615495	2.38177960	2.44910467
13	2.40984500	2.48407618	2.56041307	2.63891028
14	2.57853415	2.66417171	2.75244405	2.84342583
15	2.75903154	2.85732416	2.95887735	3.06379133
16	2.95216375	3.06448016	3.18079315	3.30123516
17	3.15881521	3.28665497	3.41935264	3.55708088
18	3.37993228	3.52493745	3.67580409	3.83275465
19	3.61652754	3.78049542	3.95148940	4.12979313
20	3.86968446	4.05458134	4.24785110	4.44985210
21	4.14056237	4.34853849	4.56643993	4.79471564
22	4.43040174	4.66380753	4.90892293	5.16630610
23	4.74052986	5.00193357	5.27709215	5.56669482
24	5.07236695	5.36457375	5.67287406	5.99811367
25	5.42743264	5.75350535	6.09833961	6.46296746
26	5.80735292	6.17063449	6.55571508	6.96384746
27	6.21386763	6.61800549	7.04739371	7.50354564
28	6.64883836	7.09781089	7.57594824	8.08050743
29	7.11425705	7.61240218	8.14414436	8.71166339
30	7.61225504	8.16430134	8.75495519	9.38681730
31	8.14511290	8.75621318	9.41157683	10.11429564
32	8.71527080	9.39103864	10.11744509	10.89815355
33	9.32533975	10.07188894	10.87625347	11.74276045
34	9.97811354	10.80210089	11.69197248	12.65282439
35	10.67658148	11.58525320	12.56887042	13.63341828
36	11.42394219	12.42518406	13.51153570	14.69000819
37	12.22361814	13.32600990	14.52490088	15.82848383
38	13.07927141	14.29214562	15.61426844	17.05519132
39	13.99482041	15.32832618	16.78533858	18.37696865
40	14.97445784	16.43962897	18.04442897	19.80118372
41	16.02266989	17.63150299	19.39755689	21.33577546
42	17.14425678	18.90978696	20.85237366	22.98929806
43	18.34435475	20.28074651	22.41630168	24.77096866
44	19.62845959	21.75110063	24.09752431	26.69071873
45	21.00245176	23.32805543	25.90483863	28.75924943
46	22.47262338	25.01933945	27.84770153	30.98809126
47	24.04570052	26.83324156	29.93627915	33.38966823
48	25.72890651	28.77865157	32.18150008	35.97736763
49	27.52992997	30.86510381	34.59511259	38.76561362
50	29.45702506	33.10282384	37.18974603	41.76994868

Rate i

Periods n	0.07(7%)	0.0725(7 1/4%)	0.075(7 1/2%)	0.0775(7 3/4%)
51	31.51901682	35.50277856	39.97897698	45.00711970
52	33.72534799	38.07673001	42.97740026	48.49517148
53	36.08612235	40.83729294	46.20070528	52.25354726
54	38.61215092	43.79799667	49.66557817	56.30319718
55	41.31500148	46.97335143	53.39069004	60.66669496
56	44.20705159	50.37891941	57.39499179	65.36836382
57	47.30154520	54.03139107	61.69961617	70.43441201
58	50.61265336	57.94866692	66.32708739	75.89307895
59	54.15553910	62.14994527	71.30161894	81.77479256
60	57.94642683	66.65581630	76.64924036	88.11233899
61	62.00267671	71.48836299	82.39793339	94.94104526
62	66.34286408	76.67126930	88.57777839	102.29897627
63	70.98686457	82.22993633	95.22111177	110.22714693
64	75.95594509	88.19160671	102.36269515	118.76975081
65	81.27286124	94.58549820	110.03989729	127.97440650
66	86.96196153	101.44294682	118.29288959	137.89242301
67	93.04929884	108.79756046	127.16485631	148.57908579
68	99.56274976	116.68538360	136.70222053	160.09396494
69	106.53214224	125.14507391	146.95488707	172.50124722
70	113.98939220	134.21809176	157.97650360	185.87009388
71	121.96864965	143.94890342	169.82474137	200.27502616
72	130.50645513	154.38519891	182.56159697	215.79634068
73	139.64190699	165.57812584	196.25371675	232.52055709
74	149.41684047	177.58253996	210.97274550	250.54090026
75	159.87601931	190.45727411	226.79570141	269.95782003
76	171.06734066	204.26542648	243.80537902	290.87955108
77	183.04205451	219.07466990	262.09078245	313.42271629
78	195.85499832	234.95758347	281.74759113	337.71297680
79	209.56484820	251.99200827	302.87866046	363.88573251
80	224.23438758	270.26142887	325.59456000	392.08687677
81	239.93079471	289.85538246	350.01415200	422.47360972
82	256.72595034	310.86989769	376.26521340	455.21531448
83	274.69676686	333.40796527	404.48510440	490.49450135
84	293.92554054	357.58004275	434.82148723	528.50782521
85	314.50032838	383.50459585	467.43309878	569.46718166
86	336.51535137	411.30867905	502.49058119	613.60088824
87	360.07142596	441.12855828	540.17737477	661.15495708
88	385.27642578	473.11037876	580.69067788	712.39446625
89	412.24577558	507.41088122	624.24247872	767.60503738
90	441.10297988	544.19817011	671.06066463	827.09442778
91	471.98018847	583.65253744	721.39021447	891.19424593
92	505.01880166	625.96734640	775.49448056	960.26179999
93	540.37011778	671.34997902	833.65656660	1034.68208949
94	578.19602602	720.02285250	896.18080910	1114.86995143
95	618.66974784	772.22450930	963.39436978	1201.27237266
96	661.97663019	828.21078623	1035.64894751	1294.37098155
97	708.31499430	888.25606823	1113.32261858	1394.68473262
98	757.89704390	952.65463317	1196.82181497	1502.77279939
99	810.94983698	1021.72209408	1286.58345109	1619.23769135
100	867.71632557	1095.79694590	1383.07720993	1744.72861243

AMOUNT AT COMPOUND INTEREST $(1 + i)^n$ (Continued)

Rate i

Periods n	0.08(8%)	0.0825(8 1/4%)	0.085(8 1/2%)	0.0875(8 3/4%)
1	1.08000000	1.08250000	1.08500000	1.08750000
2	1.16640000	1.17180625	1.17722500	1.18265625
3	1.25971200	1.26848027	1.27728912	1.28613867
4	1.36048896	1.37312989	1.38585870	1.39867581
5	1.46932808	1.48641310	1.50365569	1.52105994
6	1.58687432	1.60904218	1.63146751	1.65415268
7	1.71382427	1.74178816	1.77014225	1.79989104
8	1.85093021	1.88548569	1.92060434	1.95629401
9	1.99900463	2.04103826	2.08385571	2.12746974
10	2.15892500	2.20942391	2.26098344	2.31362334
11	2.33163900	2.39170139	2.45316703	2.51606538
12	2.51817012	2.58901675	2.66168623	2.73622110
13	2.71962373	2.80261063	2.88792956	2.97564045
14	2.93719362	3.03382601	3.13340357	3.23600898
15	3.17162911	3.28411666	3.39974288	3.51915977
16	3.42594264	3.55505628	3.68872102	3.82708625
17	3.70001805	3.84834842	4.00226231	4.16195630
18	3.99601950	4.16583717	4.34245461	4.52612747
19	4.31570106	4.50951873	4.71156325	4.92216363
20	4.66095714	4.88155403	5.11204612	5.35285295
21	5.03383372	5.28428224	5.54657005	5.82122758
22	5.43654041	5.72023552	6.01802850	6.33058499
23	5.87146365	6.19215495	6.52956092	6.88451118
24	6.34118074	6.70300774	7.08457360	7.48690591
25	6.84847520	7.25600587	7.68676236	8.14201017
26	7.39635321	7.85462636	8.34013716	8.85443606
27	7.98806147	8.50263303	9.04904881	9.62919922
28	8.62710639	9.20410026	9.81821796	10.47175415
29	9.31727490	9.96343853	10.65276649	11.38803264
30	10.06265689	10.78542221	11.55825164	12.38448649
31	10.86766944	11.67521954	12.54070303	13.46812797
32	11.73708300	12.63842515	13.60666279	14.64658917
33	12.67604964	13.68109523	14.76322913	15.92816573
34	13.69013361	14.80978558	16.01810360	17.32188023
35	14.78334429	16.03159290	17.37964241	18.83754475
36	15.96817184	17.35419931	18.85691201	20.48582991
37	17.24562558	18.78592075	20.45974953	22.27834003
38	18.62527563	20.33575921	22.19882824	24.22769478
39	20.11529768	22.01345935	24.08572865	26.34761807
40	21.72452150	23.82956975	26.13301558	28.65330466
41	23.46248322	25.79550925	28.35432190	31.16017519
42	25.33948187	27.92363876	30.76443927	33.88669052
43	27.36664042	30.22733896	33.37941660	36.85177594
44	29.55597166	32.72109442	36.21666702	40.07630633
45	31.92044939	35.42058471	39.29508371	43.58298314
46	34.47408534	38.34278295	42.63516583	47.39649416
47	37.23201217	41.50606255	46.25915492	51.54368740
48	40.21057314	44.93031271	50.19118309	56.05376005
49	43.42741899	48.63706351	54.45743365	60.95846405
50	46.90161251			

Rate i

Periods n	0.08(8%)	0.0825(8 1/4%)	0.085(8 1/2%)	0.0875(8 3/4%)
51	50.65374151	56.99321500	64.10865233	72.09290850
52	54.70604084	61.69515523	69.55788778	78.40103799
53	59.08252410	66.78500554	75.47030824	85.26112882
54	63.80912603	72.29476850	81.88528444	92.72147759
55	68.91385611	78.25908690	88.84553362	100.83460688
56	74.42696460	84.71546157	96.39740398	109.65763498
57	80.38112177	91.70448715	104.59118332	119.25267804
58	86.81161151	99.27010734	113.48143390	129.68728737
59	93.75654043	107.45989119	123.12735578	141.03492502
60	101.25706367	116.32533222	133.59318102	153.37548096
61	109.35726876	125.92217213	144.94860141	166.79583554
62	118.10623906	136.31075133	157.26923253	181.39047115
63	127.55473819	147.55638831	170.63711729	197.26213737
64	137.75911724	159.72979035	185.14127226	214.52257439
65	148.77984662	172.90749805	200.87828041	233.29329965
66	160.68223435	187.17236664	217.95293424	253.70646337
67	173.53681310	202.61408689	236.47893365	275.90577892
68	187.41978815	219.32974905	256.57964301	300.04753457
69	202.41333880	237.42445335	278.38891267	326.30169385
70	218.60640590	257.01197075	302.05197024	354.85309206
71	236.09491837	278.21545834	327.72638771	385.90273762
72	254.98251184	301.16823365	355.58313067	419.66922716
73	275.38111279	326.01461293	385.80769678	456.39028454
74	297.41160181	352.91081850	418.60135100	496.32443443
75	321.20452996	382.02596102	454.18246584	539.75282245
76	346.90089236	413.64310281	492.78797543	586.98119441
77	374.65296374	447.66040879	534.67495335	638.34204892
78	404.62520084	484.59239251	580.12232438	694.19697820
79	436.99521691	524.57126490	629.43272195	754.93921379
80	471.95483426	567.84839425	682.93450332	820.96399500
81	509.71122101	614.69588677	740.98393610	892.83357956
82	550.48811869	665.40829743	803.96757067	970.95651777
83	594.52716818	720.30448197	872.30481418	1055.91521308
84	642.08934164	779.72960173	946.45072338	1148.30779422
85	693.45648897	844.05729388	1026.89903487	1248.78472622
86	748.93300808	913.69202062	1114.18545283	1358.05338976
87	808.84764873	989.07161232	1208.89121633	1476.88306137
88	873.55546063	1070.67002034	1311.64696971	1606.11032924
89	943.43989748	1159.00029702	1423.13696214	1746.64498304
90	1018.91508928	1254.61782152	1544.10360392	1899.47641906
91	1100.42829642	1358.12379180	1675.35241025	2065.68060573
92	1188.46256013	1470.16900462	1817.75736512	2246.42765873
93	1283.53956494	1591.45794750	1972.26674116	2442.99007887
94	1386.22273014	1722.75322817	2139.90941416	2656.75171077
95	1497.12054855	1864.88036950	2321.80171436	2889.21748546
96	1616.89019244	2018.73299998	2519.15486008	3142.02401544
97	1746.24140783	2185.27847248	2733.28302319	3416.95111679
98	1885.94072046	2365.56394646	2965.61208016	3715.93433951
99	2036.81597809	2560.72297204	3217.68910698	4041.07859422

AMOUNT AT COMPOUND INTEREST $(1 + i)^n$ (Continued)

Rate i

Periods n	0.09 (9%)	0.0925 (9 1/4%)	0.095 (9 1/2%)	0.0975 (9 3/4%)
1	1.09000000	1.09250000	1.09500000	1.09750000
2	1.18810000	1.19355625	1.19902500	1.20450625
3	1.29502900	1.30396020	1.31291237	1.32194561
4	1.41158161	1.42457652	1.43766095	1.45083531
5	1.53862395	1.55634985	1.57423874	1.59229175
6	1.67710011	1.70031221	1.72379142	1.74754019
7	1.82803912	1.85759109	1.88755161	1.91792536
8	1.99256264	2.02941827	2.06686901	2.10492309
9	2.17189328	2.21713946	2.26322156	2.31015309
10	2.36736367	2.42222486	2.47822761	2.53539301
11	2.58042641	2.64628066	2.71365924	2.78259383
12	2.81266478	2.89106162	2.97145686	3.05389673
13	3.06580461	3.15848482	3.25374527	3.35165166
14	3.34172703	3.45064466	3.56285107	3.67843770
15	3.64248246	3.76982929	3.90132192	4.03708537
16	3.97030588	4.11853850	4.27194750	4.43070120
17	4.32763341	4.49950331	4.67778251	4.86269456
18	4.71712042	4.91570737	5.12217185	5.33680728
19	5.14166125	5.37041030	5.60877818	5.85714599
20	5.60441077	5.86717325	6.14161210	6.42821773
21	6.10880774	6.40988678	6.72506525	7.05496896
22	6.65860043	7.00280131	7.36394645	7.74283843
23	7.25787447	7.65056043	8.06352137	8.49775420
24	7.91108317	8.35823727	8.82955590	9.32628524
25	8.62308066	9.13137421	9.66836371	10.23579805
26	9.39915792	9.97602633	10.58685826	11.23356886
27	10.24508213	10.89880877	11.59260979	12.32884182
28	11.16713952	11.90694858	12.69300772	13.53090390
29	12.17218208	13.00834132	13.89982896	14.85016703
30	13.26767847	14.21161289	15.22031271	16.29805832
31	14.46176953	15.52618708	16.66624241	17.88711900
32	15.76332879	16.96235939	18.24953544	19.63111310
33	17.18202838	18.53137763	19.98324131	21.54514663
34	18.72841093	20.24553006	21.88164924	23.64579843
35	20.41396792	22.11824159	23.96040591	25.95126378
36	22.25122503	24.16417894	26.23664448	28.48151199
37	24.25383528	26.39936549	28.72912570	31.25845941
38	26.43668046	28.84130680	31.45839264	34.30615921
39	28.81598170	31.50912768	34.44693994	37.65100973
40	31.40942005	34.43372199	37.71939924	41.32198318
41	34.23626786	37.60791628	41.30274216	45.35087654
42	37.31753197	41.08664853	45.22650267	49.77258700
43	40.67610984	44.88716352	49.52302042	54.62541423
44	44.33695973	49.03902615	54.22770736	59.95139212
45	48.32728610	53.57535456	59.37933956	65.79665285
46	52.67674185	58.53107486	65.02037682	72.21182650
47	57.41764862	63.94519929	71.19731262	79.25247959
48	62.58523700	69.86013022	77.96105732	86.97959635
49	68.21790833	76.32219227	85.36735777	95.46010699
50	74.35752008	83.38199505	93.47725675	104.76746742

Rate i

Periods n	0.09 (9%)	0.0925 (9 1/4%)	0.095 (9 1/2%)	0.0975 (9 3/4%)
51	81.04969688	91.09482959	102.35759614	114.98229550
52	88.34416960	99.52110133	112.08156778	126.19306931
53	96.29514487	108.72680320	122.72931672	138.49689357
54	104.96170790	118.78403250	134.38860181	152.00034069
55	114.40826162	129.77155551	147.15551898	166.82037391
56	124.70500516	141.77542439	161.13529328	183.08536606
57	135.92845563	154.88965115	176.44314614	200.93618300
58	148.16201663	169.21694388	193.20524502	220.52746084
59	161.49659813	184.86951119	211.55974330	242.02888827
60	176.03129196	201.96994097	231.65791892	265.62670488
61	191.87410824	220.65216051	253.66542121	291.52530861
62	209.14277798	241.06248536	277.76363623	319.94902620
63	227.96562800	263.36076525	304.15118167	351.14405625
64	248.48253452	287.72163604	333.04554393	385.38060173
65	270.84596262	314.33588737	364.68487060	422.95521040
66	295.22209926	343.41195696	399.32993331	464.19334342
67	321.79208819	375.17756297	437.26627697	509.45219440
68	350.75337613	409.88148755	478.80657329	559.12378335
69	382.32117998	447.79552515	524.29319775	613.63835223
70	416.73008618	489.21661122	574.10105153	673.46809157
71	454.23579194	534.46914776	628.64065143	739.13123050
72	495.11701539	583.90754393	688.36151331	811.19652548
73	539.67754677	637.91899174	753.75585708	890.28818671
74	588.24852598	696.92649848	825.36266350	977.09128491
75	641.19089332	761.39219959	903.77211653	1072.35768519
76	698.89807372	831.82097805	989.63046761	1176.91255950
77	761.79890036	908.76441852	1083.64536203	1291.66153405
78	830.36080139	992.82512724	1186.59167142	1417.59853362
79	905.09272351	1084.66145150	1299.31788021	1555.81439065
80	986.55166813	1184.99263577	1422.75307883	1707.50629374
81	1075.34131826	1294.60445458	1557.91462131	1873.98815738
82	1172.12203690	1414.35536663	1705.91651034	2056.70200272
83	1277.61302022	1545.18323804	1867.97857882	2257.23044799
84	1392.59819204	1688.11268756	2045.43654381	2477.31041666
85	1517.93202933	1844.26311116	2239.75301547	2718.84818229
86	1654.54591197	2014.58744894	2452.52955194	2983.93588006
87	1803.45504404	2201.23176296	2685.51985938	3274.86962837
88	1965.76599801	2404.84570104	2940.64424602	3594.16941714
89	2142.68493783	2627.29392838	3220.00544939	3944.60093531
90	2335.52658223	2870.31861676	3525.90596708	4329.19952650
91	2545.72397464	3135.82308881	3860.86703395	4751.29648033
92	2774.83913235	3425.88672453	4227.64940218	5214.54788716
93	3024.57465426	3742.78124654	4629.27609538	5722.96630616
94	3296.78637315	4088.98851185	5069.05732445	6280.95552101
95	3593.49714673	4467.21994920	5550.61777027	6893.34868431
96	3916.91188994	4880.43779450	6077.92645844	7565.45018103
97	4269.43396003	5331.87829049	6655.32947199	8303.08157368
98	4653.68301643	5825.07703236	7287.58577183	9112.63202712
99	5072.51448791	6363.89665785	7979.90642016	10001.11364976
100	5529.04079183	6952.55709870	8737.99753007	10976.22223061

AMOUNT AT COMPOUND INTEREST $(1 + i)^n$ (Continued)

Rate i

Periods n	0.10(10%)	0.1025(10 1/4%)	0.105(10 1/2%)	0.1075(10 3/4%)
1	1.10000000	1.10250000	1.10500000	1.10750000
2	1.21000000	1.21550625	1.22102500	1.22655625
3	1.33100000	1.34009564	1.34923262	1.35841105
4	1.46410000	1.47745544	1.49090205	1.50444023
5	1.61051000	1.62889463	1.64744677	1.66616756
6	1.77156100	1.79585633	1.82042868	1.84528057
7	1.94871710	1.97993160	2.01157369	2.04364823
8	2.14358881	2.18287459	2.22278892	2.26334042
9	2.35794769	2.40661923	2.45618176	2.50664951
10	2.59374246	2.65329771	2.71408085	2.77611434
11	2.85311671	2.92526072	2.99905934	3.07454663
12	3.13842838	3.22509994	3.31396057	3.40506039
13	3.45227121	3.55567269	3.66192643	3.77110438
14	3.79749834	3.92012914	4.04642870	4.17649810
15	4.17724817	4.32194238	4.47130371	4.62547165
16	4.59497299	4.76494147	4.94079060	5.12270985
17	5.05447028	5.25334797	5.45957362	5.67340116
18	5.55991731	5.79181614	6.03282885	6.28329179
19	6.11590904	6.38547729	6.66627588	6.95874565
20	6.72749995	7.03998871	7.36623484	7.70681081
21	7.40024994	7.76158756	8.13968950	8.53529297
22	8.14027494	8.55715028	8.99435690	9.45283697
23	8.95430243	9.43425818	9.93876437	10.46901694
24	9.84973268	10.40126965	10.98233463	11.59443626
25	10.83470594	11.46739979	12.13547977	12.84083816
26	11.91817654	12.64280826	13.40970514	14.22122826
27	13.10999419	13.93869611	14.81772418	15.75001030
28	14.42099361	15.36741246	16.37358522	17.44313641
29	15.86309297	16.94257224	18.09281167	19.31827357
30	17.44940227	18.67918589	19.99255690	21.39498798
31	19.19434250	20.59380245	22.09177537	23.69494919
32	21.11377675	22.70466720	24.41141178	26.24215623
33	23.22515442	25.03189559	26.97461002	29.06318802
34	25.54766986	27.59766488	29.80694407	32.18748073
35	28.10243685	30.42642554	32.93667320	35.64763491
36	30.91268053	33.54513415	36.39502389	39.47975567
37	34.00394859	36.98351040	40.21650140	43.72382940
38	37.40434344	40.77432022	44.43923404	48.42414106
39	41.14477779	44.95368804	49.10535362	53.62973622
40	45.25925557	49.56144107	54.26141575	59.39493287
41	49.78518112	54.64148878	59.95886440	65.77988815
42	54.76369924	60.24224138	66.25454516	72.85122613
43	60.24006916	66.41707112	73.21127240	80.68273294
44	66.26407608	73.22482091	80.89845601	89.35612673
45	72.89048369	80.73036505	89.39279389	98.96191035
46	80.17953205	89.00522747	98.77903724	109.60031571
47	88.19748526	98.12826328	109.15083616	121.38234965
48	97.01723378	108.18641027	120.61167395	134.43095224
49	106.71895716	119.27551732	133.27589972	148.88227961

Rate i

Periods n	0.10(10%)	0.1025(10 1/4%)	0.105(10 1/2%)	0.1075(10 3/4%)
51	129.12993817	144.98013678	162.73320545	182.61249057
52	142.04293198	159.84060080	179.82019202	202.24333330
53	156.24722518	176.22426238	198.70131219	223.98449163
54	171.87194770	194.28724927	219.56494997	248.06282448
55	189.05914247	214.20169232	242.61926971	274.72957811
56	207.96505672	236.15736578	268.09429303	304.26300776
57	228.76156239	260.36349578	296.24419380	336.97128109
58	251.63771863	287.05075409	327.34983415	373.19569381
59	276.80149049	316.47345639	361.72156674	413.31423090
60	304.48163954	348.91198567	399.70233124	457.74551072
61	334.92980350	384.67546420	441.67107602	506.95315312
62	368.42278385	424.10469928	488.04653901	561.45061708
63	405.26506223	467.57543095	539.29142560	621.80655842
64	445.79156845	515.50191263	595.91702529	688.65076345
65	490.37072530	568.34085867	658.48831295	762.68072052
66	539.40779783	626.59579669	727.62958581	844.66889797
67	593.34857761	690.82186585	804.03069231	935.47080451
68	652.68343537	761.63110709	888.45391501	1036.03391599
69	717.95177891	839.69829557	981.74157608	1147.40756196
70	789.74695680	925.76773087	1084.82444157	1270.75387487
71	868.72165248	1020.65852638	1198.73100794	1407.35991642
72	955.59381773	1125.27602534	1324.59776377	1558.65110743
73	1051.15319950	1240.61681793	1463.68052897	1726.20610148
74	1156.26851945	1367.78004177	1617.36698451	1911.77325739
75	1271.89537140	1507.97749605	1787.19051788	2117.28888256
76	1399.08490853	1662.54518940	1974.84552226	2344.89743744
77	1538.99339939	1832.95607131	2182.20430210	2596.97391196
78	1692.89273933	2020.83406862	2411.33575382	2876.14860750
79	1862.18201326	2227.96956065	2664.52600797	3185.33458280
80	2048.40021459	2456.33644062	2944.30123880	3527.75805046
81	2253.24023604	2708.11092579	3253.45286888	3906.99204088
82	2478.56425965	2985.69229568	3595.06542011	4326.99368527
83	2726.42068561	3291.72575599	3972.54728922	4792.14550644
84	2999.06275417	3629.12764598	4389.66475459	5307.30114838
85	3298.96902959	4001.11322969	4850.57955382	5877.83602184
86	3628.86593255	4411.22733573	5359.89040697	6509.70339418
87	3991.75252581	4863.37439764	5922.67889971	7209.49650906
88	4390.92777839	5361.87439675	6544.56018417	7984.51738378
89	4830.02055623	5911.46652242	7231.73900351	8842.85300254
90	5313.02261185	6517.39184097	7991.07159888	9793.45970031
91	5844.32487303	7185.42450466	8830.13411676	10846.25661809
92	6428.75736034	7921.93051639	9757.29819902	12012.22920454
93	7071.63309637	8733.92839432	10781.81450992	13303.54384403
94	7778.79640601	9629.15605474	11913.90503346	14733.67480726
95	8556.67604661	10616.14455035	13164.86506198	16317.54484904
96	9412.34365127	11704.29936676	14547.17589348	18071.68092031
97	10353.57801640	12903.99005186	16074.62936230	20014.38661925
98	11388.93581803	14226.64903217	17762.46544534	22165.93318081
99	12527.82939984	15684.88055797	19627.52431710	24548.77099775

Rate i

Periods n	0.11(11%)	0.1125(11 1/4%)	0.115(11 1/2%)	0.1175(11 3/4%)
1	1.11000000	1.11250000	1.11500000	1.11750000
2	1.23210000	1.23765625	1.24322500	1.24880625
3	1.36763100	1.37689258	1.38619587	1.39554098
4	1.51807041	1.53179299	1.54560840	1.55951705
5	1.68505816	1.70411970	1.72335337	1.74276030
6	1.87041455	1.89583317	1.92153900	1.94753464
7	2.07616015	2.10911440	2.14251599	2.17636996
8	2.30453777	2.34638977	2.38890533	2.43209343
9	2.55803692	2.61035862	2.66362944	2.71786441
10	2.83942099	2.90402397	2.96994683	3.03721368
11	3.15175729	3.23072667	3.31149071	3.39408606
12	3.49845060	3.59418341	3.69231214	3.79289117
13	3.88328016	3.99852905	4.11692804	4.23855588
14	4.31044098	4.44836357	4.59037476	4.73658620
15	4.78458949	4.94880447	5.11826786	5.29313508
16	5.31089433	5.50554497	5.70686867	5.91507845
17	5.89509271	6.12491878	6.36315856	6.61010017
18	6.54355291	6.81397214	7.09492180	7.38678694
19	7.26334373	7.58054401	7.91083780	8.25473440
20	8.06231154	8.43335521	8.82058415	9.22466569
21	8.94916581	9.38210767	9.83495133	10.30856391
22	9.93357404	10.43759478	10.96597073	11.51982017
23	11.02626719	11.61182420	12.22705737	12.87339904
24	12.23915658	12.91815442	13.63316896	14.38602343
25	13.58546380	14.37144679	15.20098340	16.07631118
26	15.07986482	15.98823456	16.94909649	17.96535597
27	16.73864995	17.78691094	18.89824258	20.07628530
28	18.57990145	19.78793843	21.07154048	22.43524882
29	20.62369061	22.01408150	23.49476763	25.07139056
30	22.89229657	24.49066567	26.19666591	28.01727895
31	25.41044919	27.24586555	29.20928249	31.30930923
32	28.20559861	30.31102543	32.56834998	34.98815306
33	31.30821445	33.72101579	36.31371022	39.09926104
34	34.75211804	37.51463007	40.48978690	43.69342422
35	38.57485103	41.73502595	45.14611239	48.82740156
36	42.81808464	46.43021532	50.33791532	54.56462125
37	47.52807395	51.65361571	56.12677558	60.97596424
38	52.75616209	57.46464748	62.58135477	68.14064004
39	58.55933991	63.92942032	69.77821057	76.14716525
40	65.00086731	71.12148010	77.80270479	85.09445716
41	72.15096271	79.12264661	86.75001584	95.09305588
42	80.08756861	88.02394436	96.72626766	106.26643994
43	88.89720115	97.92663810	107.84978844	118.75280251
44	98.67589328	108.94338488	120.25251411	132.70625681
45	109.53024154	121.19951568	134.08155323	148.28924198
46	121.57856811	134.83446120	149.50093186	165.72440292
47	134.95221060	150.00333808	166.69323902	185.19702026
48	149.79695377	166.87871362	185.86329601	206.95767014
49	166.27461868	185.65256890	207.23757505	231.27519638
50	184.56482674	206.53848290	231.06989618	258.45003195

Rate i

Periods n	0.11(11%)	0.1125(11 1/4%)	0.115(11 1/2%)	0.1175(11 3/4%)
51	204.86695768	229.77406223	257.64293424	288.81791071
52	227.40232303	255.62364423	287.27187167	322.75401522
53	252.41657856	284.38130420	320.30813692	360.67761200
54	280.18240220	316.37420093	357.14357266	403.05723142
55	311.00246644	351.96629853	398.21508352	450.41645611
56	345.21273775	391.56250712	444.00981812	503.34038970
57	383.18613890	435.61328917	495.07094721	562.48288549
58	425.33661418	484.61978420	552.00410614	628.57462453
59	472.12364174	539.13950992	615.48457834	702.43214292
60	524.05724234	599.79270479	686.26530485	784.96791971
61	581.70353899	667.26938407	765.18581491	877.20165028
62	645.69092828	742.33718978	853.18218362	980.27284418
63	716.71693039	825.85012363	951.29813474	1095.45490337
64	795.55579274	918.75826254	1060.69742023	1224.17085452
65	883.06692994	1022.11856708	1182.67762356	1368.01092993
66	980.20429223	1137.10690587	1318.68555027	1528.75221419
67	1088.02676438	1265.03143278	1470.33438855	1708.38059936
68	1207.70970846	1407.34746897	1639.42284324	1909.11531979
69	1340.57777639	1565.67405923	1827.95647021	2133.43636986
70	1488.01913179	1741.81239089	2038.17146428	2384.11514332
71	1651.70123629	1937.7662487	2272.56118267	2664.24867266
72	1833.38837228	2155.76499192	2533.90571868	2977.29789170
73	2035.06109323	2398.28855351	2825.30487633	3327.13039397
74	2258.91781349	2668.09601578	3150.21493711	3718.06821526
75	2507.39877297	2968.25681755	3512.48965487	4154.94123056
76	2783.21263800	3302.18570953	3916.42596518	4643.14682515
77	3089.36602818	3673.68160185	4366.81495118	5188.71657710
78	3429.19079128	4086.97078206	4868.99867057	5798.39077491
79	3806.40788332	4546.75499504	5428.93351768	6479.70169096
80	4225.11275048	5058.26493198	6053.26087222	7241.06663965
81	4689.87515303	5627.31973683	6749.38587252	8091.89196981
82	5205.76141987	6260.39320722	7525.56524786	9042.68927626
83	5778.39517605	6964.68744304	8391.00525136	10105.20526622
84	6414.01864542	7748.2147038	9355.97085527	11292.56688500
85	7119.56069641	8619.88894317	10431.90750363	12619.44349399
86	7902.71237302	9589.62644928	11631.57686654	14102.22810454
87	8772.01073405	10668.45942482	12969.20820620	15759.23990682
88	9736.93191480	11868.66111011	14460.66714991	17610.95059587
89	10807.99442542	13203.88548500	16123.64387215	19680.23729088
90	11996.87381222	14689.32260206	17977.86291745	21992.66517256
91	13316.52993157	16341.87139480	20045.31715295	24576.80333034
92	14781.34822404	18180.33192671	22350.52862554	27464.57772166
93	16407.29652868	20225.66912490	24920.83941749	30691.66560395
94	18212.09914684	22501.00143617	27786.73595049	34297.93631241
95	20215.43005299	25032.36409774	30982.21058480	38327.94382912
96	22439.12735882	27848.50505873	34545.16480205	42831.47722904
97	24907.43136829	30981.46187784	38517.85875428	47864.17580346
98	27647.24881880	34466.87633910	42947.41251102	53488.21646036
99	30688.44618887	38344.39992725	47886.36494979	59773.08189446
100	34064.17526964	42658.14491906	53393.29691902	66796.41901705

FINANCIAL TABLES

AMOUNT AT COMPOUND INTEREST $(1 + i)^n$ (Continued)

Rate i

Periods n	0.12(12%)	0.1225(12 1/4%)	0.125(12 1/2%)	0.1275(12 3/4%)
1	1.12000000	1.12250000	1.12500000	1.12750000
2	1.25440000	1.26000625	1.26562500	1.27125625
3	1.40492800	1.41435702	1.42382812	1.43334142
4	1.57351936	1.58761575	1.60180664	1.61609245
5	1.76234168	1.78209868	1.80203247	1.82211424
6	1.97382269	2.00040577	2.02728653	2.05446763
7	2.21068141	2.24545547	2.28069735	2.31641225
8	2.47596318	2.52052377	2.56578451	2.61175482
9	2.77307876	2.82928793	2.88650758	2.94475356
10	3.10584821	3.17587570	3.24732103	3.32020963
11	3.47854999	3.56492048	3.65323615	3.74353636
12	3.89597599	4.00162324	4.10989067	4.22083725
13	4.36349311	4.49182208	4.62362701	4.75899400
14	4.88711229	5.04207029	5.20158038	5.36576573
15	5.47356576	5.65972390	5.85187793	6.04990086
16	6.13039365	6.35304007	6.58325017	6.82126323
17	6.86604089	7.13128748	7.40615644	7.69097429
18	7.68996580	8.00487020	8.33192600	8.67157351
19	8.61276169	8.98546680	9.37341675	9.77749913
20	9.64629309	10.08618648	10.54509384	11.02379202
21	10.80384826	11.32174433	11.86323057	12.42923550
22	12.10031006	12.70865801	13.34611439	14.01406450
23	13.55234726	14.26546861	15.01440119	15.80085773
24	15.17862893	16.01298852	16.89120134	17.81546709
25	17.00006441	17.97457961	19.00260151	20.08693914
26	19.04007214	20.17646561	21.37792670	22.64802388
27	21.32488079	22.64808265	24.05016754	25.53564693
28	23.88386649	25.42247277	27.05643848	28.79144191
29	26.74993047	28.53672569	30.43849329	32.46235075
30	29.95992212	32.03247459	34.24330495	36.60130047
31	33.55511278	35.95645272	38.52371807	41.26796628
32	37.58172631	40.36111818	43.33918283	46.52963199
33	42.09153347	45.30535516	48.75658068	52.46216006
34	47.14251748	50.85526117	54.85115327	59.15108547
35	52.79961958	57.08503066	61.70754742	66.69284887
36	59.13557393	64.07794691	69.42099085	75.19618710
37	66.23184280	71.92749541	78.09861471	84.78370095
38	74.17966394	80.73861360	87.86094155	95.59362283
39	83.08122361	90.62909377	98.84355924	107.78180974
40	93.05097044	101.73115775	111.11900415	121.52399048
41	104.21708689	114.19322458	125.09887966	137.01829926
42	116.72313732	128.18189459	140.73623962	154.48813242
43	130.72991380	143.88417667	158.32826958	174.18536930
44	146.41750346	161.50998832	178.11930327	196.39400389
45	163.98760387	181.29496188	200.38421618	221.43423939
46	183.66611634	203.50359472	225.43224320	249.66710491
47	205.70605030	228.43278507	253.61127360	281.49966078
48	230.39077633	256.41580124	285.31268280	317.39086753
49	258.03766949	287.82673689	320.97676816	357.85820315

Rate i

Periods n	0.12(12%)	0.1225(12 1/4%)	0.125(12 1/2%)	0.1275(12 3/4%)
51	323.68245261	362.66348740	406.23622220	454.92947736
52	362.52434692	407.08976461	457.01574997	512.93298573
53	406.02726855	456.95826077	514.14271872	578.33194141
54	454.75054078	512.93564771	578.41055856	652.06926394
55	509.32060567	575.77026456	650.71187838	735.20809509
56	570.43907835	646.30212197	732.05086317	828.94712721
57	638.89176776	725.47413191	823.55722107	934.63788593
58	715.55877989	814.34471307	926.50187370	1053.80421639
59	801.42583347	914.10194042	1042.31460792	1188.16425397
60	897.59693349	1026.07942812	1172.60393391	1339.65519636
61	1005.30856551	1151.77415807	1319.17942565	1510.46123389
62	1125.94559337	1292.86649243	1484.07685385	1703.04504121
63	1261.05906458	1451.24263775	1669.58646058	1920.18328397
64	1412.38615232	1629.01986088	1878.28476816	2165.00665267
65	1581.87249060	1828.57479383	2113.07036417	2441.04500089
66	1771.69718948	2052.57520608	2377.20415970	2752.27823850
67	1984.30085221	2304.01566882	2674.35467966	3103.19371391
68	2222.41695448	2586.25758825	3008.64901462	3498.85091244
69	2489.10698902	2903.07414287	3384.73014144	3944.95440377
70	2787.79982770	3258.70072531	3807.82140912	4447.93609025
71	3122.33580702	3657.89156416	4283.79908526	5015.04794176
72	3497.01610386	4105.98328077	4819.27397092	5654.46655433
73	3916.65803633	4608.96623266	5421.68321729	6375.41104001
74	4386.65700069	5173.56459616	6099.39361945	7188.27594761
75	4913.05584077	5807.32625919	6861.81782188	8104.78113094
76	5502.62254166	6518.72372594	7719.54504961	9138.14072513
77	6162.93724666	7317.26738237	8684.48818082	10303.25366758
78	6902.48971626	8213.63263671	9770.04920342	11616.91851020
79	7730.78848221	9219.80263471	10991.30535384	13098.07562025
80	8658.48310047	10349.22845746	12365.21852308	14768.08026183
81	9697.50107209	11617.00894350	13910.87083846	16651.01049522
82	10861.20120074	13040.09253908	15649.72969327	18774.01433336
83	12164.54534483	14637.50387511	17605.94590493	21167.70116086
84	13624.29078621	16430.5980981	19806.68914304	23866.58305887
85	15259.20568055	18443.34636704	22288.52528592	26909.57239887
86	17090.31036222	20702.65629700	25067.84094666	30340.54287973
87	19141.14760569	23238.73169339	28201.32106499	34208.96209690
88	21438.08531837	26085.47632583	31726.48619812	38570.60476425
89	24010.65555657	29280.94717574	35692.29697288	43448.35687169
90	26891.93422336	32867.86320477	40153.83409449	49033.12237283
91	30118.96633016	36894.17644735	45173.06335631	55284.84547537
92	33733.24228978	41413.71306215	50819.69627584	62333.66327348
93	37781.23136456	46486.89291226	57172.15831032	70281.20534085
94	42314.97912830	52181.53729402	64318.67809911	79242.05902181
95	47392.77662370	58573.77561253	72358.51286150	89345.42154709
96	53079.90981854	65749.06312507	81403.32696919	100736.96279434
97	59449.49899677	73803.32335789	91578.74284034	113580.92555062
98	66583.43887638	82844.23046923	103026.08569538	128062.49355832
99	74573.45154155	92992.64870711	115904.34640731	144390.46148701

Rate i

Periods n	0.13(13%)	0.1325(13 1/4%)	0.135(13 1/2%)	0.1375(13 3/4%)
1	1.13000000	1.13250000	1.13500000	1.13750000
2	1.27690000	1.28255625	1.28822500	1.29390625
3	1.44289700	1.45249495	1.46213537	1.47181836
4	1.63047361	1.64495053	1.65952365	1.67419338
5	1.84243518	1.86290648	1.88355934	1.90439497
6	2.08195175	2.10974159	2.13783985	2.16624928
7	2.35260548	2.38928235	2.42644824	2.46410856
8	2.65844419	2.70586226	2.75401875	2.80292349
9	3.00404194	3.06438901	3.12581128	3.18832547
10	3.39456739	3.47042055	3.54779580	3.62672022
11	3.83586115	3.93025128	4.02674823	4.12539425
12	4.33452310	4.45100957	4.57035924	4.69263596
13	4.89801110	5.04076834	5.18735774	5.33787340
14	5.53475255	5.70867015	5.88765104	6.07183099
15	6.25427038	6.46506894	6.68248393	6.90670775
16	7.06732553	7.32169057	7.58461926	7.85638007
17	7.98607785	8.29181457	8.60854286	8.93663233
18	9.02426797	9.39048001	9.77069614	10.16541928
19	10.19742280	10.63471861	11.08974012	11.56316443
20	11.52308776	12.04381882	12.58685504	13.15309953
21	13.02108917	13.63962482	14.28608047	14.96165072
22	14.71183077	15.44687510	16.21470134	17.01887769
23	16.62662877	17.49358606	18.40368602	19.35897338
24	18.78809051	19.81148621	20.88818363	22.02083222
25	21.23054227	22.43650813	23.70808842	25.04869665
26	23.99051277	25.40934546	26.90868035	28.49289243
27	27.10927943	28.77608373	30.54135220	32.41066514
28	30.63348575	32.58891482	34.66443475	36.86713160
29	34.61583890	36.90694604	39.34413344	41.93636220
30	39.11589796	41.79711639	44.65559145	47.70261200
31	44.20096469	47.33523431	50.68409630	54.26172115
32	49.94709010	53.60715286	57.52644930	61.72270781
33	56.44021181	60.71010061	65.29251996	70.20958013
34	63.77743935	68.75418894	74.10701015	79.86339740
35	72.06850647	77.86411898	84.11145652	90.84461454
36	81.43741231	88.18111474	95.46650315	103.33574904
37	92.02427591	99.86511244	108.35448108	117.54441453
38	103.98743178	113.09723984	122.98233602	133.70677153
39	117.50579791	128.08262412	139.58495138	152.09145262
40	132.78155163	145.05357182	158.42891982	173.00402735
41	150.04315335	164.27317008	179.81682400	196.79280111
42	169.54876328	186.06936512	204.09209523	223.85099227
43	191.59010251	210.68958100	231.64452809	254.63050370
44	216.49681583	238.60599048	262.91653938	289.64219796
45	244.64140189	270.22123892	298.41027220	329.46800018
46	276.44478414	306.02555308	338.69565895	374.76985021
47	312.38260608	346.57393886	384.41957291	426.30070461
48	352.99234487	392.49498576	436.31621525	484.91705149
49	398.88134970	444.50057137	495.21890431	551.59314607
50	450.73592516	503.39689708	562.07345639	627.43720366

Rate i

Periods n	0.13(13%)	0.1325(13 1/4%)	0.135(13 1/2%)	0.1375(13 3/4%)
51	509.33159543	570.09698594	637.95373300	713.70981916
52	575.54470283	645.63483658	724.07707835	811.84491930
53	650.36551420	731.18145242	821.82748393	923.47359570
54	734.91303105	828.06299487	932.77419426	1050.45121511
55	830.45172509	937.78134169	1058.69871049	1194.88825719
56	938.41044935	1062.03736946	1201.62303641	1359.18539255
57	1060.40380776	1202.75732092	1363.84214632	1546.07338403
58	1198.25630277	1362.12266594	1547.96083607	1758.65847433
59	1354.02962213	1542.60391918	1756.93554894	2000.47401455
60	1530.05347301	1746.99893847	1994.12184805	2275.53919155
61	1728.96042450	1978.47629782	2263.32829754	2588.42583039
62	1953.72527969	2240.62440728	2568.87761770	2944.33438207
63	2207.70956604	2537.50714124	2915.67609609	3349.18035960
64	2494.71180963	2873.72683746	3309.29236907	3809.69265905
65	2819.02434488	3254.49564342	3756.04683889	4333.52539966
66	3185.49750972	3685.71631617	4263.11316214	4929.38514212
67	3599.61218358	4174.07372806	4838.63343903	5607.17559916
68	4067.56177016	4727.13849703	5491.84895330	6378.16224404
69	4596.34480028	5353.48434789	6233.24856200	7255.15955260
70	5193.86962431	6062.82102398	7074.73711786	8252.74399108
71	5869.07267547	6866.14480966	8029.82662878	9387.49628986
72	6632.05212329	7775.90899694	9113.85322366	10678.27702971
73	7494.21889931	8806.21693904	10344.22340886	12146.54012130
74	8468.46735622	9973.04068346	11740.69350905	13816.68938798
75	9569.36811253	11294.46857402	13325.68720087	15716.48417882
76	10813.38596716	12790.98566008	15124.65497299	17877.50075341
77	12219.12614289	14485.79126004	17166.48339435	20335.65710701
78	13807.61254417	16405.15860199	19483.95865258	23131.80995922
79	15602.60217186	18578.84211675	22114.29307068	26312.43382861
80	17630.94045420	21040.53869722	25099.72263522	29930.39348005
81	19922.96271325	23828.41007461	28488.18519098	34045.82258355
82	22512.94786597	26985.67440949	32334.09091176	38727.12318879
83	25439.63108855	30561.27626875	36699.19236765	44052.10262725
84	28746.78313006	34610.64537436	41653.58333728	50109.26673850
85	32483.86493697	39196.55588646	47276.81708781	56999.29091504
86	36706.76737878	44390.09954142	53659.18739467	64836.69341586
87	41478.64713802	50271.78773066	60903.17769295	73751.73876054
88	46870.87126596	56932.79960497	69125.10668149	83892.60284011
89	52964.08453053	64476.39555263	78456.99608349	95427.85573063
90	59849.41551950	73019.51796335	89048.69055477	108549.16314359
91	67629.83953704	82694.60409349	101070.26377966	123474.67307583
92	76421.74867685	93651.63913588	114714.74939910	140452.44062376
93	86356.54210484	106060.48132139	130201.24055755	159764.65120953
94	97582.89257847	120113.49509647	147778.40803282	181732.29075084
95	110268.66861367	136028.53319675	167728.49311725	206720.48072908
96	124603.59553895	154052.31384532	190371.83968808	235144.54682932
97	140802.06295280	174464.24542983	216072.03804597	267476.92201836
98	159106.33113666	197580.75794928	245241.76318218	304254.99879588
99	179790.15418443	223760.20837756	278349.40121177	346090.06113031
100	203162.87422841	253408.43598758	315926.57037536	393677.44453573

AMOUNT AT COMPOUND INTEREST $(1 + i)^n$ (Continued)

Rate i

Periods n	0.14(14%)	0.1425(14 1/4%)	0.145(14 1/2%)	0.1475(14 3/4%)
51	798.26560684	892.62006668	997.88345139	1115.28896369
52	910.02279180	1019.81842618	1142.57655184	1279.79408584
53	1037.42598265	1165.14255191	1308.25015186	1468.56371350
54	1182.66562023	1331.17536556	1497.94642388	1685.17686124
55	1348.23880706	1520.86785515	1715.14865534	1933.74044827
56	1536.99224004	1737.59152451	1963.84521036	2218.96716439
57	1752.17115365	1985.19831675	2248.60276586	2546.26482114
58	1997.47511516	2268.08907689	2574.65016692	2921.83888226
59	2277.12163128	2591.12167035	2947.97444112	3352.81011739
60	2595.91865966	2960.5084762	3375.43073508	3847.34960971
61	2959.34727202	3382.42934341	3864.86819167	4414.83367714
62	3373.65589010	3864.42552484	4425.27407946	5066.02164452
63	3845.96771471	4415.10616213	5066.93882098	5813.25983708
64	4384.40319477	5044.25879024	5801.64495002	6670.71566305
65	4998.21964204	5763.06566784	6642.88346778	7654.64622335
66	5697.97039193	6584.30252551	7606.10157060	8783.76554130
67	6495.68624680	7522.56563540	8708.98629834	10079.30325614
68	7405.08232135	8594.53123844	9971.78931160	11566.00048642
69	8441.79384634	9819.25193992	11417.69876178	13271.98555817
70	9623.64498483	11218.49534136	13073.26508224	15229.60342800
71	10970.95528270	12817.13092750	14968.88851916	17475.96993363
72	12506.88902228	14643.57208467	17139.37735444	20053.67549884
73	14257.85348540	16730.28110674	19624.58707084	23011.59263492
74	16253.95297336	19114.34616445	22470.15219611	26405.80254857
75	18529.50638963	21838.14049288	25728.32426454	30300.65842448
76	21123.63728417	24950.07551312	29458.93128290	34770.00554209
77	24080.94650396	28505.46127374	33730.47631892	39898.58135955
78	27452.27901451	32567.48950524	38621.39538517	45783.62211008
79	31295.59807655	37208.35675974	44221.49771602	52536.70637132
80	35676.98180726	42510.54759800	50633.61488484	60285.87056109
81	40671.75673028	48568.30063072	57975.48904314	69178.03646885
82	46365.80555672	55489.28347060	66381.93495440	79381.79684801
83	52857.00833466	63396.50636516	76007.31552279	91090.61188309
84	60257.00090151	72430.50389660	87028.37627359	104526.47713584
85	68692.98102772	82751.85598660	99647.49083326	119944.13251338
86	78309.99837160	94543.99546469	114096.37700408	137635.89205910
87	89273.39814363	108016.51481841	130640.35166967	157937.18613782
88	101771.67388373	123408.86818004	149583.20266178	181232.92109315
89	116019.70822746	140994.63189569	171272.76704773	207964.77695439
90	132262.46737930	161086.36694083	196107.31826966	238639.58155516
91	150779.21281240	184041.17422990	224542.87941876	273838.91983454
92	171888.30260614	210267.04155766	257101.59693448	314230.16051014
93	195952.66497100	240230.09497962	294381.32848997	360579.10918538
94	223386.03806694	274462.88351422	337066.62112102	413764.52779023
95	254660.08339631	313573.84441499	385941.28118357	474794.79563929
96	290312.49507180	358258.11724413	441902.76695519	544827.02799608
97	330956.24438185	409309.89895142	505978.66816369	625189.01462550
98	377290.11859531	467636.55955200	579345.57504742	717404.39428276
99	430110.73519865	534274.76928815	663350.68342930	823221.54243947

Rate i

Periods n	0.14(14%)	0.1425(14 1/4%)	0.145(14 1/2%)	0.1475(14 3/4%)
1	1.14000000	1.14250000	1.14500000	1.14750000
2	1.29960000	1.30530625	1.31102500	1.31675625
3	1.48154400	1.49131239	1.50112362	1.51099780
4	1.68896016	1.70382441	1.71878655	1.73384702
5	1.92541458	1.94661938	1.96801060	1.98958946
6	2.19497262	2.22401265	2.25337214	2.28305390
7	2.50226879	2.54093445	2.58011110	2.61980435
8	2.85258642	2.90301761	2.95422721	3.00622550
9	3.25194852	3.31669762	3.38259015	3.44964376
10	3.70722131	3.78932703	3.87306572	3.95846621
11	4.22623230	4.32930613	4.43466025	4.54233998
12	4.81790482	4.94623225	5.07768599	5.21233512
13	5.49241149	5.65107035	5.81395046	5.98115455
14	6.26134910	6.45634787	6.65697328	6.86337485
15	7.13793798	7.37637744	7.62223440	7.87572264
16	8.13724930	8.42751123	8.72745839	9.03739193
17	9.27646420	9.62843158	9.99293985	10.37040701
18	10.57516918	11.00048308	11.44191613	11.90004204
19	12.05569287	12.56805192	13.10099397	13.65529824
20	13.74348987	14.35899932	15.00063810	15.66945474
21	15.66757845	16.40515672	17.17573062	17.98069931
22	17.86103944	18.74289155	19.66621156	20.63285246
23	20.36158496	21.41375360	22.51781224	23.67619819
24	23.21220685	24.46521349	25.78289502	27.16843743
25	26.46191581	27.95150641	29.52141479	31.17578195
26	30.16658403	31.93459607	33.80201994	35.77420979
27	34.38990579	36.48527601	38.70331283	41.05090573
28	39.20449260	41.68442784	44.31529319	47.10591432
29	44.69312156	47.62445881	50.74101070	54.05403669
30	50.95015858	54.41094419	58.09845725	62.02700710
31	58.08318078	62.16450374	66.52273355	71.17599065
32	66.21482609	71.02294552	76.16852992	81.67444927
33	75.48490175	81.14371526	87.21296676	93.72143053
34	86.05278799	92.70669468	99.85884694	107.54534154
35	98.10017831	105.91739867	114.33837974	123.40827941
36	111.83420328	121.01062798	130.91744481	141.61100063
37	127.49099173	138.25464247	149.90047430	162.49862322
38	145.33973058	157.95592902	171.63604308	186.46717015
39	165.68729286	180.46464891	196.52326932	213.97107774
40	188.88351386	206.18086138	225.01914337	245.53181171
41	215.32720580	235.56163412	257.64691916	281.74775394
42	245.47301461	269.12916699	295.00575244	323.30554764
43	279.83923665	307.48007328	337.78155220	370.99311592
44	319.01672979	351.29598372	386.75987726	425.71460052
45	363.67907196	401.35566140	442.84005947	488.50750409
46	414.59414203	458.54884315	507.05186809	560.56236095
47	472.63732191	523.89205330	580.57438896	643.24530919
48	538.80654698	598.54667090	664.75767536	738.12399229
49	614.23946356	683.83957150	761.14753829	846.99728115

		Rate i			Periods
0.1575(15 3/4%)	0.155(15 1/2%)	0.1525(15 1/4%)	0.15(15%)		n
1736.08499780	1554.82385654	1392.15514625	1246.20605782		51
2009.51838496	1795.82155431	1604.45880605	1433.13696649		52
2326.01753059	2074.17389522	1849.13877397	1648.10751147		53
2692.36529166	2395.67084898	2131.13243701	1895.32363819		54
3116.41282509	2766.99983058	2456.13013365	2179.62218392		55
3607.24784505	3195.88480431	2830.68997903	2506.56551151		56
4175.38938064	3691.24694898	3262.37020083	2882.55033823		57
4833.01320809	4263.39022608	3759.88156646	3314.93288897		58
5594.21278837	4924.21571112	4333.26360907	3812.17282231		59
6475.30130253	5687.46914634	4994.08630945	4383.99874566		60
7495.16125768	6569.02686402	5755.68447164	5041.59855751		61
8675.64915577	7587.22602795	6633.42653357	5797.83834113		62
10042.06389780	8763.24606228	7645.02387249	6667.51409230		63
11623.68896171	10121.54920193	8810.89001304	7667.64120615		64
13454.41997318	11690.38932823	10154.55074003	8817.78738707		65
15573.49111895	13502.39967411	11703.11972789	10140.45549513		66
18026.31597019	15595.27162360	13487.84548639	11661.52381940		67
20865.46073549	18012.53872525	15544.74192306	13410.75239231		68
24151.77080133	20804.48222767	17915.31506633	15422.36525115		69
27955.67470254	24029.17697296	20647.40061395	17735.72003883		70
32358.69346819	27753.69940376	23796.12920757	20396.07804465		71
37455.18768943	32055.52281135	27425.03891173	23455.48975135		72
43354.37975051	37024.12884711	31607.35734577	26973.81321405		73
50182.69456122	42762.86881841	36427.47934100	31019.88519616		74
58086.46895461	49391.11348526	41982.66994050	35672.86797558		75
67235.08788	57046.73607548	48385.02710643	41023.79817192		76
77824.61414582	65888.98016718	55763.74374016	47117.36789771		77
90081.99087379	76101.77209309	64267.71146053	54253.97308237		78
104269.90443641	87897.54676752	74068.54114626	62392.06904472		79
120692.41438514	101521.66651648	85363.99367107	71750.87940143		80
139701.46965080	117257.52482654	98382.00270590	82513.51131165		81
161704.45112080	135432.44117465	113385.25811855	94890.53800839		82
187172.90217233	156424.46955672	130676.50998163	109124.11870965		83
216652.63426447	180670.26233801	150604.67775383	125492.73651610		84
250775.42416112	208674.15300041	173571.89111129	144315.64699351		85
290272.55346650	241018.64671547	200041.60450576	165964.14404254		86
335990.48063747	278376.53695637	230547.94919289	190858.76564892		87
388908.98133788	321524.90018460	265706.51144481	219487.58048626		88
450162.14589859	371361.25971322	306226.75444014	252410.71757070		89
521062.68387762	428922.25496876	352926.33449226	290272.32520630		90
603130.05658835	495405.20448892	406747.60050233	333813.17398725		91
698123.04050101	572193.01118470	468776.60957894	383885.15008533		92
808077.41937992	660882.92791833	540265.04253973	441467.92259814		93
935349.61293226	763319.78174568	622655.46152703	507688.11098786		94
1082667.17696909	881634.34791625	717610.41940991	583841.32763603		95
1253187.25734172	1018287.67184327	827046.00836992	671417.52678144		96
1450564.25037304	1176122.26097898	953170.52464633	772130.15579865		97
1679028.11980679	1358421.21143072	1098529.02965489	887949.67916845		98
1943475.04867636	1568976.49922048	1266054.70667727	1021142.11304372		99
2249572.36884288	1812167.85657887	1459128.04944555	1174313.45070028		100

Periods		Rate i		
n	0.15(15%)	0.1525(15 1/4%)	0.155(15 1/2%)	0.1575(15 3/4%)
1	1.15000000	1.15250000	1.15500000	1.15750000
2	1.32250000	1.32825625	1.33402500	1.33980625
3	1.52087500	1.53081538	1.54079887	1.55082573
4	1.74900625	1.76426467	1.77962270	1.79508079
5	2.01135719	2.03331503	2.05546422	2.07780601
6	2.31306077	2.34339557	2.37406117	2.40506046
7	2.66001988	2.70076339	2.74204066	2.78385748
8	3.05902286	3.11262981	3.16705696	3.22231503
9	3.51787629	3.58730586	3.65795078	3.72982965
10	4.04555774	4.13437000	4.22493316	4.31727782
11	4.65239140	4.76486142	4.87979780	4.99724908
12	5.35025011	5.49150279	5.63616645	5.78431581
13	6.15278762	6.32895697	6.50977225	6.69534555
14	7.07570576	7.29412291	7.51878695	7.74986247
15	8.13706163	8.40647665	8.68419893	8.97046581
16	9.35762087	9.68846434	10.03024971	10.38236418
17	10.76126400	11.16595515	11.58493848	12.01868616
18	12.37545361	12.86876331	13.38060394	13.91162923
19	14.23177165	14.83124971	15.45459756	16.10271083
20	16.36653739	17.09301529	17.85006018	18.63888779
21	18.82151800	19.69970013	20.61681950	21.57451262
22	21.64474570	22.70390440	23.81242653	24.97249835
23	24.89145756	26.16624982	27.50335264	28.90566685
24	28.62517619	30.15660291	31.76637230	33.45830937
25	32.91895262	34.75548486	36.69016000	38.72799310
26	37.85679551	40.05569630	42.37713481	44.82765201
27	43.53531484	46.16418999	48.94559071	51.88800727
28	50.06561207	53.20422896	56.53215726	60.06036834
29	57.57545388	61.31787387	65.29464163	69.51987635
30	66.21177196	70.66884964	75.41531109	80.46925688
31	76.14353775	81.44584921	87.10468431	93.14316484
32	87.56506841	93.86634121	100.60591037	107.81321330
33	100.69982867	108.18095825	116.19982648	124.79379439
34	115.80480298	124.67855438	134.21079959	144.44881701
35	133.17552342	143.69203393	155.01347352	167.19950069
36	153.15185194	165.60506910	179.04056192	193.53342783
37	176.12462973	190.85984214	206.79184901	224.01494272
38	202.54332419	219.96596806	238.84458561	259.29729620
39	232.92482281	253.51077819	275.86549638	300.13662035
40	267.86354623	292.17171187	318.62464832	347.40813805
41	308.04307817	336.72727558	368.01146881	402.12491980
42	354.24953990	388.07818510	425.05230647	465.45959466
43	407.38697088	447.26010833	490.93649968	538.76948082
44	468.49501651	515.46727485	567.03165713	623.62567405
45	538.76926899	594.07603427	654.92176399	721.84671772
46	619.58465934	684.67262949	756.43440640	835.53757576
47	712.52235824	789.08520549	873.68173939	967.13474394
48	819.40071197	909.40069933	1009.10240900	1119.48446611
49	942.31081877	1048.10735598	1165.51528239	1295.77317452
50	1083.65744158	1207.94372776	1346.16784116	1499.85744951

FINANCIAL TABLES

AMOUNT AT COMPOUND INTEREST $(1 + i)^n$ (Continued)

Rate i — Periods $n = 51$ to 99

Periods n	0.16 (16%)	0.1625 (16 1/4%)	0.165 (16 1/2%)	0.1675 (16 3/4%)
51	1938.01641218	2162.92290447	2413.36046222	2692.16299973
52	2248.09903813	2514.39787645	2811.56493849	3143.10030218
53	2607.79488423	2922.98753137	3275.47315334	3669.56960279
54	3025.04206571	3397.97300522	3815.92622364	4284.22251126
55	3509.04879622	3950.14361857	4445.55405054	5001.82978190
56	4070.49660361	4592.04195659	5179.07046888	5839.63627037
57	4721.77606019	5338.24877453	6033.61709625	6817.77534565
58	5477.26022982	6205.71420039	7029.16391713	7959.75271605
59	6353.62186659	7214.14275796	8188.97596345	9293.01129599
60	7370.20136525	8386.44095613	9540.15697420	10849.59068807
61	8549.43358369	9749.23761500	11114.28290200	12666.89712832
62	9917.34295708	11333.48872336	12948.13958083	14788.60239731
63	11504.11783021	13175.18064091	15084.58261166	17265.69329886
64	13344.77668305	15316.14749506	17573.53874259	20157.69692642
65	15479.94095233	17805.02146300	20473.17263511	23534.11116160
66	17956.73104971	20698.33745074	23851.24611991	27476.07478116
67	20829.80854546	24061.81728649	27786.70172969	32078.31730701
68	24162.57791273	27971.86259554	32371.50751509	37451.43545593
69	28028.59037877	32517.29026732	37712.80625508	43724.55089480
70	32513.16483938	37801.34993576	43935.41928717	51048.41316968
71	37715.27121368	43944.06930032	51184.76346956	59599.02237560
72	43749.71460786	51084.98056162	59630.24944203	69581.85862351
73	50749.66894512	59386.28990288	69469.24059997	81236.81994295
74	58869.61597634	69036.56201210	80931.66529896	94843.98728340
75	68288.75453256	80255.00333907	94285.39007329	110730.35515337
76	79214.95525777	93296.44138167	109842.47943538	129277.68964156
77	91889.34809901	108457.11310619	127966.48854222	150931.70265652
78	106591.64379485	126081.39398594	149080.95915169	176212.76285148
79	123646.30680203	146569.62050866	173679.31741172	205728.40062911
80	143429.71589035	170387.18384132	202336.40478465	240187.90773448
81	166378.47043281	198075.10121553	235721.91157412	280419.38228001
82	192999.02570205	230262.30516305	274616.02698385	327389.62881191
83	223878.86981438	267679.92975205	319927.67143618	382227.39163790
84	259699.48898468	311177.91833676	372715.73722315	446250.47973725
85	301251.40722223	361744.33006648	434213.83386497	520997.43509324
86	349451.63237779	420527.78370229	505859.11645269	608264.50547136
87	405363.89355824	488863.54855391	589325.87066739	710148.81013781
88	470222.11512756	568303.87519392	686564.63932751	829098.73583589
89	545457.65517196	660653.25491293	799847.80481655	967972.77408841
90	632730.87999948	768009.40883628	931822.69261128	1130108.21374821
91	733967.82079940	892810.93777217	1085573.43689214	1319401.33955104
92	851402.67212730	1037892.71516015	1264693.05397934	1540401.06392584
93	987627.09966767	1206550.28137367	1473367.40788593	1798418.24213342
94	1145647.43561449	1402614.70209690	1716473.03018711	2099653.29769076
95	1328951.02531281	1630539.59118764	1999691.08016798	2451345.22505396
96	1541583.18936268	1895502.27475563	2329640.10839569	2861945.55025050
97	1788236.49966092	2203521.39440342	2714030.72628098	3341321.42991746
98	2074354.33960667	2561593.62099398	3161845.79611735	3900992.76942863
99	2406251.03394373	2977852.58440550	3683550.35247671	4554409.05830737

Rate i — Periods $n = 1$ to 49

Periods n	0.16 (16%)	0.1625 (16 1/4%)	0.165 (16 1/2%)	0.1675 (16 3/4%)
1	1.16000000	1.16250000	1.16500000	1.16750000
2	1.34560000	1.35140625	1.35722500	1.36305625
3	1.56089600	1.57100977	1.58116712	1.59136817
4	1.81063936	1.82629885	1.84205970	1.85792234
5	2.10034166	2.12307242	2.14599955	2.16912433
6	2.43639632	2.46807168	2.50008948	2.53245266
7	2.82621973	2.86913333	2.91260424	2.95663848
8	3.27841489	3.33536750	3.39318394	3.45187542
9	3.80296127	3.87736472	3.95305929	4.03006456
10	4.41143508	4.50743648	4.60531407	4.70510037
11	5.11726469	5.23989491	5.36519090	5.49320468
12	5.93560704	6.09137784	6.25044739	6.41331647
13	6.88579137	7.08122673	7.28177121	7.48754698
14	7.98751799	8.23192608	8.48326346	8.74171109
15	9.26552087	9.56961407	9.88300194	10.20594770
16	10.74800420	11.12467635	11.51369726	11.91544394
17	12.46768488	12.93243626	13.41345730	13.91128080
18	14.46251446	15.03395715	15.62667776	16.24142034
19	16.77651677	17.47697519	18.20507939	18.96185843
20	19.46075945	20.31698366	21.20891772	22.13796950
21	22.57448097	23.61849350	24.70838914	25.84607939
22	26.18639792	27.45649869	28.78527335	30.17529769
23	30.37622159	31.91817973	33.53484345	35.22966005
24	35.23641704	37.10488394	39.06800262	41.13062811
25	40.87424377	43.13442758	45.51432791	48.02000832
26	47.41412277	50.14377206	53.02419201	56.06335971
27	55.00038241	58.29213502	61.77318369	65.45397246
28	63.80044360	67.76460696	71.96575900	76.41751285
29	74.00851458	78.77635559	83.84010924	89.21744625
30	85.84987691	91.57751338	97.67372726	104.16136850
31	99.58585721	106.45885930	113.78989226	121.60839773
32	115.51959437	123.75842394	132.56522448	141.97780434
33	134.00272947	143.86916783	154.43848652	165.75908657
34	155.44316618	167.24790760	179.92083680	193.52373857
35	180.31407277	194.42569258	209.60777487	225.93895895
36	209.16432441	226.01986763	244.19305773	263.78373457
37	242.63061632	262.74809612	284.48491225	307.96751011
38	281.45151493	305.44466173	331.42492277	359.55206805
39	326.48375732	355.07941927	386.11003503	419.77703945
40	378.72115849	412.77982490	449.81819081	490.08969356
41	439.31654385	479.85654644	524.03819230	572.17917723
42	509.60719087	557.83333524	610.50449402	668.01981987
43	591.14434141	648.48113596	711.23773554	779.91313970
44	685.72743603	753.85932056	828.59196190	910.54859060
45	795.44382580	876.36146015	965.30963562	1063.06547952
46	922.71483793	1018.77019742	1124.58572549	1241.12894734
47	1070.34921199	1184.32035451	1310.14237020	1449.01804602
48	1241.60508591	1376.77241211	1526.31586128	1691.72856873
49	1440.26189966	1600.49792908	1778.15797839	1975.09310399

Rate *i*

Periods n	0.17(17%)	0.1725(17 1/4%)	0.175(17 1/2%)	0.1775(17 3/4%)
1	1.17000000	1.17250000	1.17500000	1.17750000
2	1.36890000	1.37475625	1.38062500	1.38650625
3	1.60161300	1.61190170	1.62223437	1.63261111
4	1.87388721	1.88995475	1.90612539	1.92239958
5	2.19244804	2.21597194	2.23969733	2.26362551
6	2.56516420	2.59822710	2.63164437	2.66541903
7	3.00124212	3.04642128	3.09218213	3.13853091
8	3.51145328	3.57192895	3.63331400	3.69562015
9	4.10840033	4.18806669	4.26914396	4.35159273
10	4.80682839	4.91053164	5.01624415	5.12400404
11	5.62398922	5.75759835	5.89408687	6.03351051
12	6.58006738	6.75078407	6.92555208	7.10445863
13	7.69867884	7.91529432	8.13752369	8.36500004
14	9.00745424	9.28068259	9.56159034	9.85037629
15	10.53872146	10.88160033	11.23486864	11.59881808
16	12.33030411	12.75867639	13.20097066	13.65760829
17	14.42645581	14.95954807	15.51114052	16.08183377
18	16.87895329	17.54007011	18.22559011	18.93635926
19	19.74837535	20.56573220	21.41506838	22.29756303
20	23.10559916	24.11332101	25.16270535	26.25538047
21	27.03355102	28.27286888	29.56617879	30.91561050
22	31.62925470	33.14993877	34.74026008	36.40324911
23	37.00622799	38.86830320	40.81980559	42.86482583
24	43.29728675	45.57308551	47.96327157	50.47333241
25	50.65782550	53.43444409	56.35684409	59.43234892
26	59.26965584	62.65188413	66.21929181	69.98159085
27	69.34549733	73.45933414	77.80766787	82.40332323
28	81.13423187	86.13106928	91.42400975	97.02991310
29	94.92705129	100.98867873	107.42321146	114.25272268
30	111.06465001	118.40922581	126.22227346	134.53258095
31	129.94564051	138.83481727	148.31117132	158.41211407
32	152.03639940	162.78382325	174.26562630	186.53026432
33	177.88258730	190.86403276	204.76211090	219.63938623
34	208.12262714	223.78807841	240.59548031	258.62537729
35	243.50347375	262.39152193	282.69968936	304.53138176
36	284.89906429	307.65405947	332.17213500	358.58570202
37	333.33190522	360.72438472	390.30225862	422.23466413
38	389.99832910	422.94934109	458.60515581	497.18131701
39	456.29804505	495.90810243	538.86105581	585.43100078
40	533.86871271	581.45225010	633.16174058	689.34500342
41	624.62639387	681.75276324	743.96504518	811.70374152
42	730.81288083	799.35511490	874.15892808	955.78115564
43	855.05107057	937.24387221	1027.13674050	1125.43231977
44	1000.40975257	1098.91844017	1206.88567009	1325.19654593
45	1170.47941051	1288.48187110	1418.09066235	1560.41893283
46	1369.46091029	1510.74499387	1666.25652826	1837.39329341
47	1602.26926504	1771.34850351	1957.85412071	2163.53060299
48	1874.65504010	2076.90612247	2300.47541933	2547.55728502
49	2193.34639691	2435.17242860	2703.05861771	2999.74870311
50	2566.21528439	2855.23967253	3176.09387581	3532.20409792

Rate *i*

Periods n	0.17(17%)	0.1725(17 1/4%)	0.175(17 1/2%)	0.1775(17 3/4%)
51	3002.47188274	3347.76851605	3731.91030408	4159.17032530
52	3512.89210280	3925.25858506	4384.99460730	4897.42305804
53	4110.08376028	4602.36569099	5152.36866357	5766.71565084
54	4808.79799952	5396.27377268	6054.03317970	6790.30767886
55	5626.29365944	6327.13099847	7113.48898614	7995.58729186
56	6582.76358155	7418.36109571	8358.34955872	9414.80403617
57	7701.83339041	8698.26288472	9821.06073150	11085.93175259
58	9011.14506678	10198.71323233	11539.74635951	13053.68463867
59	10543.03972814	11957.99126491	13559.20197242	15370.71366204
60	12335.35648192	14020.74475810	15932.06231759	18099.01533705
61	14432.36708385	16439.32322888	18720.17322317	21311.59055938
62	16885.86948810	19275.10648586	21996.20353723	25094.39788366
63	19756.46730108	22600.06223547	25845.53915624	29548.65350802
64	23115.06674226	26498.57311085	30368.50850859	34793.53950569
65	27044.62808844	31069.57697247	35682.99749759	40969.39276795
66	31642.21486348	36429.07900022	41927.52205967	48241.45998426
67	37021.39139027	42713.09512776	49264.83842011	56804.31913146
68	43315.02792662	50081.10403730	57886.18514363	66887.08577730
69	50678.58267414	58720.09448373	68016.26754376	78759.54350277
70	59293.94172875	68849.31078218	79919.11436392	92739.36247451
71	69373.91182263	80725.81689210	93904.95937761	109200.59931374
72	81167.47683248	94651.02030599	110338.32726869	128583.70569193
73	94965.94789400	110978.32130877	129647.53454071	151407.31345224
74	111110.15903598	130122.08173454	152335.85308534	178282.11159002
75	129998.88607210	152568.14083375	178994.62737527	209927.18639724
76	152098.69670436	178886.14512757	210318.68716594	247189.26198275
77	177955.47514410	209744.00516207	247124.45741998	291065.35598469
78	208207.90591859	245924.84605253	290371.23746848	342729.45667198
79	243603.24992475	288346.88199659	341186.20402547	403563.93523125
80	285015.80241196	338087.71914100	400893.78972992	475196.53773480
81	333468.48882200	396406.67819283	471050.20293266	559543.91847273
82	390158.13192173	464786.83018109	553483.98844587	658862.96400163
83	456485.01434843	544962.55838732	650343.68642390	775811.14011192
84	534087.46678766	638968.59970914	764153.83154809	913537.61748179
85	624882.33614156	749190.68315896	897880.75206900	1075666.99458481
86	731112.33283563	878426.07600389	1055009.88368108	1266597.88612361
87	855401.42994419	1029954.57411456	1239636.61332526	1491419.01091055
88	1000819.67303470	1207621.73814932	1456573.02065718	1756145.88534717
89	1170959.01745060	1415936.48798007	1711473.29927219	2067861.77999630
90	1370022.05041720	1660185.53215664	2010981.12664482	2434907.24594564
91	1602925.79898812	1946567.53645366	2362902.82380767	2867103.28210099
92	1875423.18481610	2282350.43649191	2776410.81797401	3376014.11467391
93	2194245.12623484	2676055.88678676	3262282.71111946	3975256.62002853
94	2567266.79769476	3137675.52725748	3833182.18556536	4680864.67008360
95	3003702.15330287	3678924.55570940	4503989.06803930	5511718.14902343
96	3514331.51936436	4313539.04156927	5292187.15494618	6490048.12047509
97	4111767.87765630	5057624.52623996	6218319.90706176	7642031.66185942
98	4810768.41685787	5930064.75701636	7306525.89079756	8998492.28183946
99	5628599.04772371	6953000.92760168	8585167.92168713	10595724.66186596
100	6585460.88583674	8152393.58761296	10087572.30798238	12476465.78934716

AMOUNT AT COMPOUND INTEREST $(1 + i)^n$ (Continued)

Rate i

Periods n	0.18(18%)	0.1825(18 1/4%)	0.185(18 1/2%)	0.1875(18 3/4%)
1	1.18000000	1.18250000	1.18500000	1.18750000
2	1.39240000	1.39830625	1.40422500	1.41015625
3	1.64303200	1.65349714	1.66400662	1.67456055
4	1.93877776	1.95526037	1.97184785	1.98854065
5	2.28775776	2.31209539	2.33663970	2.36139202
6	2.69955415	2.73405279	2.76891805	2.80415303
7	3.18547390	3.23301743	3.28116789	3.32993172
8	3.75885920	3.82304311	3.88818395	3.95429392
9	4.43545386	4.52074848	4.60749798	4.69572402
10	5.23383555	5.34578507	5.45988510	5.57617228
11	6.17592595	6.32139085	6.46996385	6.62170458
12	7.28559263	7.47504468	7.66690716	7.86327419
13	8.59935930	8.83924033	9.08528498	9.33763810
14	10.14724397	10.45240170	10.76606270	11.08844524
15	11.97374789	12.35996501	12.75778430	13.16752873
16	14.12902251	14.61658862	15.11797440	15.63644036
17	16.67224656	17.28301632	17.91479966	18.56827293
18	19.67325094	20.43716679	21.22903760	22.04982410
19	23.21443611	24.16694973	25.15640955	26.18416612
20	27.39303460	28.57741806	29.81034532	31.09369727
21	32.32370831	33.79279686	35.32525921	36.92376551
22	38.14206138	39.95998228	41.86043216	43.84691154
23	45.00763243	47.25677905	49.60461211	52.06827817
24	53.10900627	55.87629298	58.78146535	61.83108096
25	62.66862740	66.07371645	69.65603644	73.42440864
26	73.94890033	78.13216970	82.54240318	87.19148526
27	87.25979679	92.39129067	97.81274777	103.53988875
28	102.96656021	109.25270122	115.90810611	122.95361789
29	121.50054105	129.19131919	137.35110574	146.00742125
30	143.37013844	152.76873494	162.76106030	173.38381273
31	169.17735336	180.64902906	192.87185646	205.89327762
32	199.62927696	213.61747687	228.55314990	244.49826717
33	235.56254681	252.60266640	270.83548263	290.34169227
34	277.96380524	298.70265302	320.94004692	344.78075956
35	327.99729018	353.21588719	380.31395560	409.42715198
36	387.03680242	417.67778660	450.67203738	486.19474298
37	456.70342685	493.90398266	534.04636430	577.35625729
38	538.91004369	584.04145949	632.84494710	685.61055553
39	635.91385155	690.62902585	749.92125591	814.16253469
40	750.37834483	816.66882307	888.65668825	966.81800995
41	885.44644690	965.71088328	1053.05817558	1148.09638681
42	1044.82680734	1141.95311948	1247.87393806	1363.36445934
43	1232.89563266	1350.35956378	1478.73061660	1618.99529547
44	1454.81684654	1596.80018417	1752.29578067	1922.55691337
45	1716.68387891	1888.21621778	2076.47050010	2283.53633462
46	2025.68697712	2232.81567753	2460.61754262	2711.10564736
47	2390.31063300	2640.30453867	2915.83178800	3219.43795624
48	2820.56654694	3122.16011698	3455.26066878	3823.08257304
49	3328.26852539	3691.95433833	4094.48389250	4539.91055548

Rate i

Periods n	0.18(18%)	0.1825(18 1/4%)	0.185(18 1/2%)	0.1875(18 3/4%)
51	4634.28109475	5162.48282600	5749.57664395	6401.98324426
52	5468.45169180	6104.63594175	6813.24832308	7602.35510256
53	6452.77299633	7218.73200112	8073.69926285	9027.79668429
54	7614.27213567	8536.15059132	9567.33362648	10720.50856259
55	8984.84112009	10093.99807424	11337.29034738	12730.60391807
56	10602.11252170	11936.15272279	13434.68906164	15117.59215271
57	12510.49277561	14114.50059469	15920.10653805	17952.14068135
58	14762.38147522	16690.39695323	18865.32624759	21318.16705910
59	17419.61014076	19736.39439719	22355.41160339	25315.32338268
60	20555.13996610	23338.28637468	26491.16275002	30061.94651693
61	24255.06516000	27597.52635806	31392.02785877	35698.56148886
62	28620.97688880	32634.07170200	37199.55301264	42392.04176802
63	33772.75272878	38589.78978762	44081.47031998	50340.54959953
64	39851.84821996	45632.42642386	52236.54232918	59779.40264944
65	47025.18089955	53960.34424621	61900.30266007	70988.04064621
66	55489.71346147	63808.10707114	73351.85865219	84298.29826737
67	65477.86188454	75453.08661163	86921.95250284	100104.22919250
68	77263.87703375	89223.27491825	103002.51371587	118873.77216609
69	91171.37488803	105506.52259083	122057.97875330	141162.60444724
70	107582.22236787	124761.46296365	144638.70482267	167630.59278109
71	126947.02239409	147530.42995452	171396.86521486	199061.32892755
72	149797.48642503	174454.73342122	203105.28527961	236385.32810146
73	176761.03398153	206292.72227059	240679.76305634	280707.57712049
74	208578.02009821	243941.14408497	285205.51922176	333340.24783058
75	246122.06371589	288460.40288048	337968.54027778	395841.54429881
76	290424.03518474	341104.42640617	400492.72022917	470061.83385484
77	342700.36151800	403355.98422530	474583.87347157	558198.42770263
78	404386.42659124	476968.45134641	562381.89006381	662860.63289687
79	477175.98337766	564015.19371713	666422.53972561	787147.00156503
80	563067.66038564	666947.96655051	789710.70957485	934737.06435847
81	664419.83925505	788665.97046963	935807.19084620	1110000.26392569
82	784015.41032096	932597.51008033	1108931.52115274	1318125.31341175
83	925138.18417874	1102796.55566999	1314083.85256600	1565273.80967645
84	1091663.05733091	1304056.92707977	1557189.36529071	1858762.64899079
85	1288162.40765047	1542047.31627182	1845269.39786949	2207280.64567656
86	1520031.64102756	1823470.95149143	2186644.23647535	2621145.76674092
87	1793637.33641252	2156254.40013862	2591173.42022329	3112610.59800484
88	2116492.05696677	2549770.82816391	3070540.50296459	3696225.08513074
89	2497460.62722079	3015104.00430383	3638590.49601304	4389267.28859276
90	2947003.54012054	3565360.48508928	4311729.73777545	5212254.90520390
91	3477446.17734223	4216038.77361807	5109399.73926391	6189552.69992963
92	4103407.72926383	4985465.84980337	6054638.69102773	7350093.83116643
93	4842021.12053132	5895313.36739248	7174746.84886786	8728236.42451013
94	5713584.92222696	6971208.05694161	8502075.01590842	10364780.75410578
95	6742030.20822781	8243453.52733345	10074958.89385147	12308177.14550061
96	7955595.64570881	9747883.79607180	11938826.28921398	14615960.36028197
97	9387602.86193640	11526872.58885490	14147509.15271857	17356452.92783483
98	11077371.37708495	13630526.83632091	16764798.34597150	20610787.85180386
99	13071298.22496024	16118097.98394948	19866286.03997623	24475310.57401708

Rate i

Periods n	0.19(19%)	0.1925(19 1/4%)	0.195(19 1/2%)	0.1975(19 3/4%)	0.20(20%)
1	1.19000000	1.19250000	1.19500000	1.19750000	1.20000000
2	1.41610000	1.42205625	1.42802500	1.43400625	1.44000000
3	1.68515900	1.69580208	1.70648987	1.71722248	1.72800000
4	2.00533921	2.02224398	2.03922540	2.05637393	2.07360000
5	2.38635366	2.41152594	2.43691020	2.46250778	2.48832000
6	2.83976086	2.87574469	2.91210769	2.94885306	2.98598400
7	3.37931542	3.42932554	3.47996869	3.53125154	3.58318080
8	4.02138535	4.08947071	4.15856259	4.22867372	4.29981696
9	4.78544856	4.87669382	4.96948229	5.06383678	5.15978035
10	5.69468379	5.81545738	5.93853134	6.06394454	6.19173642
11	6.77667371	6.93493292	7.09654495	7.26157359	7.43008371
12	8.06424172	8.26990751	8.48037122	8.69573437	8.91610045
13	9.59644764	9.86186471	10.13404361	10.41314191	10.69932054
14	11.41977269	11.76027366	12.11018211	12.46973744	12.83918465
15	13.58952950	14.02412634	14.47166762	14.93251059	15.40702157
16	16.17154011	16.72377667	17.29364281	17.88168143	18.48842589
17	19.24413273	19.94309652	20.66590315	21.41331351	22.18611107
18	22.90051795	23.78214260	24.69575427	25.64244293	26.62333328
19	27.25161636	28.36020505	29.51142635	30.70682540	31.94799994
20	32.42942347	33.81954452	35.26615449	36.77142342	38.33759992
21	38.59101393	40.32980684	42.14305461	44.03377955	46.00511991
22	45.92330658	48.09329466	50.36099026	52.73045101	55.20614389
23	54.64873482	57.35125388	60.18133557	63.14471508	66.24737267
24	65.03199444	68.39137025	71.91669600	75.61579631	79.49684720
25	77.38807338	81.55670902	85.94045172	90.54991608	95.39621664
26	92.09180733	97.25637551	102.69883981	108.43352451	114.47545997
27	109.58925072	115.97822780	122.72511357	129.84914560	137.37055197
28	130.41120836	138.30403665	146.65651077	155.49543185	164.84466237
29	155.18933794	164.92756370	175.25453031	186.20448635	197.81359483
30	184.67531215	196.67611971	209.42916372	222.99987240	237.37631380
31	219.76362146	234.53627276	250.26785064	267.01839720	284.85157656
32	261.51870954	279.68450526	299.07008152	319.75453064	341.82189187
33	311.20726435	333.52377253	357.38874741	382.90605045	410.18627025
34	370.33664458	397.72709874	427.07955316	458.52999541	492.22352430
35	440.70060705	474.28956524	510.36006602	549.08966915	590.66827915
36	524.43372239	565.59030655	609.88027890	657.53487923	708.80187499
37	624.07612965	674.46644056	728.80693328	787.39801788	850.56224998
38	742.65059428	804.30123037	870.92428527	942.90912641	1020.67469998
39	883.75420719	959.12917212	1040.75452090	1129.13367888	1224.80963997
40	1051.66750656	1143.76159154	1243.70165248	1352.13758046	1469.77156797
41	1251.48633281	1363.93569791	1486.22347471	1619.18475260	1763.72588156
42	1489.26635604	1626.49313975	1776.03705228	1938.97974123	2116.47105788
43	1772.22696369	1939.59328381	2122.36427748	2321.92105513	2539.76526945
44	2108.95008679	2312.96499094	2536.22531159	2780.50046351	3047.71832334
45	2509.65060328	2758.21075169	3030.78924734	3329.64930506	3657.26198801
46	2986.48421790	3289.16632140	3621.79315058	3987.25504281	4388.71438561
47	3553.91621930	3922.33083826	4328.04281494	4774.73791376	5266.45726273
48	4229.16030097	4677.37952463	5172.01116385	5717.74865173	6319.74871528
49	5032.70075815	5577.77508312	6180.55334080	6847.00401044	7583.69845834
50	5988.91390220	6651.49678662	7385.76124226	8199.28730251	9100.43815000

Rate i

Periods n	0.19(19%)	0.1925(19 1/4%)	0.195(19 1/2%)	0.1975(19 3/4%)	0.20(20%)
51	7126.80754362	7931.90991805	8825.98468450	9818.64654475	10920.52578000
52	8480.90097691	9458.80257727	10547.05169798	11757.82923734	13104.63093600
53	10092.27216252	11279.62207339	12603.72677908	14080.00051172	15725.55712320
54	12009.80387340	13450.94932252	15061.45350100	16860.80061278	18870.66854784
55	14291.66660934	16040.25706711	17998.43693377	20190.80873380	22644.80225747
56	17007.08326512	19128.00655253	21508.13213577	24178.49345873	27173.76270890
57	20238.42908549	22810.14781389	25702.21790225	28953.74591683	32608.51525067
58	24083.73061173	27201.10126806	30714.15039318	34672.11073540	39130.21830081
59	28659.63942796	32437.31326216	36703.40971986	41519.85260564	46956.26196097
60	34104.97091927	38681.49606513	43860.57461523	49720.02349526	56347.51435317
61	40584.91539394	46127.68405767	52413.38666520	59539.72813557	67617.01722380
62	48296.04931878	55007.26323877	62633.99706491	71298.82444235	81140.42066856
63	57472.29868935	65596.16141223	74847.62649257	85380.34226971	97368.50480227
64	68392.03544033	78223.42248408	89442.91365862	102242.95986798	116842.20576272
65	81386.52217399	93281.43131227	106884.28182205	122435.94444190	140210.64691527
66	96849.96138705	111238.10683988	127726.61177735	146617.04346918	168252.77629832
67	115251.45405059	132651.44240656	152633.42654893	175573.90955434	201903.33155799
68	137149.23032020	158186.84506982	182396.94472597	210249.75669132	242283.99786959
69	163207.58408104	188637.81274576	217964.34894754	251774.08363786	290740.79744350
70	194217.02505644	224950.59169932	260467.39699230	301499.46515634	348888.95693220
71	231118.25981716	268253.58060144	311258.53940580	361045.60952472	418666.74831864
72	275030.72918242	319892.39486721	371953.95488994	432352.11740585	502400.09798237
73	327286.56772708	381471.68087915	444484.97573497	517741.66059350	602880.11757885
74	389471.01559523	454904.97944839	531159.54600329	619995.63856072	723456.14109462
75	463470.50855832	542474.18799220	634735.65747393	742444.77717646	868147.36931354
76	551529.90518440	646900.46918070	758509.11068135	889077.62066881	1041776.84317625
77	656320.58716944	771428.80949799	906418.38726421	1064670.45075090	1250132.21181149
78	781021.49871163	919928.85532635	1083169.97278074	1274942.86477420	1500158.65417319
79	929415.58349064	1097015.15997667	1294388.11747298	1526744.08056711	1800190.38500855
80	1106004.54435386	1308190.57827218	1546793.80038021	1828276.03647911	2160228.46201026
81	1316145.40778110	1560017.26458958	1848418.59145435	2189360.55368374	2592274.15441231
82	1566213.03525950	1860320.88802307	2208860.21678795	2621759.26303627	3110728.98529477
83	1863793.51195881	2218432.30121751	2639587.95906160	3139556.71748594	3732874.78235373
84	2217914.27923098	2645480.51920188	3154307.61107861	3756919.16918941	4479449.73882447
85	2639317.99228487	3154735.51914825	3769397.59523893	4502143.95510432	5375339.68658937
86	3140788.41081899	3762022.10658428	4504430.12631052	5391317.38623742	6450407.62390724
87	3737538.20887460	4486211.36210176	5382794.00094107	6456102.57001930	7740789.14868868
88	4447670.46856077	5349807.04930634	6432438.83112458	7731182.82759812	9288586.97842642
89	5292727.85758731	6379644.90629782	7686764.40319387	9258091.43604874	11146304.37411169
90	6298346.15052890	7607726.55076014	9185683.46181668	11085564.49466836	13375565.24893404
91	7495031.91912939	9072213.91178147	10976891.73687093	13276160.98236537	16050678.29872083
92	8919087.98376397	10816615.08979940	13117385.62556076	15898202.77638252	19260813.95846499
93	10613714.70067912	12901198.49458578	15675275.82254510	19038097.82471807	23112976.75015799
94	12630300.49380815	15384679.20479354	18731954.60794139	22798122.14509988	27735572.10018957
95	15030081.38763170	18346229.95171629	22384685.75648996	27300751.26875710	33282686.52022748
96	17885796.85128171	21877879.21742167	26749699.47900548	32692469.64433652	39939223.82427297
97	21284098.25302524	26089370.96677534	31965890.87741155	39149447.94909309	47927068.58912755
98	25328076.92110002	31111574.87787958	38199239.59850679	46881463.91903896	57512482.30695304
99	30140411.53610902	37100553.04187139	45648091.32021561	56140553.04304915	69014978.76834364
100	35867089.72796973	44242409.50243164	54549469.12765764	67228312.26905134	82817974.52201234

PRESENT VALUE $1/(1 + i)^n$*

The following table gives the value of unit amount due in n years at rate of interest i, compounded annually, $1/(1 + i)^n = v^n$

Rate i

n	0.0025(1/4%)	0.004167(5/12%)	0.005(1/2%)	0.005833(7/12%)	0.0075(3/4%)
1	0.99750623	0.99585062	0.99502488	0.99420050	0.99255583
2	0.99501869	0.99171846	0.99007450	0.98843463	0.98516708
3	0.99253734	0.98760345	0.98514876	0.98207220	0.97783333
4	0.99006219	0.98350551	0.98024752	0.97700301	0.97055417
5	0.98759321	0.97942457	0.97537067	0.97133688	0.96332920
6	0.98513038	0.97536057	0.97051808	0.96570361	0.95615802
7	0.98267370	0.97131343	0.96568963	0.96010301	0.94904022
8	0.98022314	0.96728308	0.96088520	0.95453489	0.94197540
9	0.97777869	0.96326946	0.95610468	0.94899906	0.93496318
10	0.97534034	0.95927249	0.95134794	0.94349534	0.92800315
11	0.97290807	0.95529211	0.94661487	0.93802354	0.92109494
12	0.97048187	0.95132824	0.94190534	0.93258347	0.91423815
13	0.96806171	0.94738082	0.93721924	0.92717495	0.90743241
14	0.96564759	0.94344978	0.93255646	0.92179779	0.90067733
15	0.96323949	0.93953505	0.92791688	0.91645182	0.89397254
16	0.96083740	0.93563657	0.92330037	0.91113686	0.88731766
17	0.95844130	0.93175426	0.91870684	0.90585272	0.88071231
18	0.95605117	0.92788806	0.91413616	0.90059922	0.87415614
19	0.95366700	0.92403790	0.90958822	0.89537619	0.86764878
20	0.95128878	0.92020372	0.90506290	0.89018346	0.86119985
21	0.94891649	0.91638544	0.90056010	0.88502084	0.85477901
22	0.94655011	0.91258301	0.89607797	0.87988815	0.84841589
23	0.94418964	0.90879636	0.89162160	0.87478524	0.84210014
24	0.94183505	0.90502542	0.88718567	0.86971192	0.83583140
25	0.93948634	0.90127013	0.88277181	0.86466802	0.82960933
26	0.93714348	0.89753042	0.87837991	0.85965338	0.82343358
27	0.93480646	0.89380623	0.87400986	0.85466782	0.81730380
28	0.93247527	0.89009749	0.86966155	0.84971117	0.81121966
29	0.93014990	0.88640414	0.86533488	0.84478327	0.80518080
30	0.92783032	0.88272611	0.86102973	0.83998394	0.79918690
31	0.92551653	0.87906335	0.85674600	0.83501303	0.79323762
32	0.92320851	0.87541578	0.85248358	0.83017037	0.78733262
33	0.92090624	0.87178335	0.84824237	0.82535580	0.78147158
34	0.91860972	0.86816599	0.84402226	0.82056914	0.77565418
35	0.91631892	0.86456365	0.83982314	0.81581025	0.76988008
36	0.91403384	0.86097624	0.83564492	0.81101896	0.76414896
37	0.91175445	0.85740373	0.83148748	0.80637510	0.75846051
38	0.90948075	0.85384604	0.82735073	0.80169853	0.75281440
39	0.90721272	0.85030311	0.82323455	0.79704907	0.74721032
40	0.90495034	0.84677488	0.81913886	0.79242659	0.74164796
41	0.90269361	0.84326129	0.81506354	0.78783091	0.73612701
42	0.90044250	0.83976228	0.81100850	0.78326188	0.73064716
43	0.89819701	0.83627779	0.80697363	0.77871935	0.72520809
44	0.89595712	0.83280776	0.80295884	0.77420316	0.71980952
45	0.89372281	0.82935212	0.79896402	0.76971317	0.71445214
46	0.89149407	0.82591083	0.79498907	0.76524922	0.70913264
47	0.88927090	0.82248381	0.79103390	0.76081115	0.70385374
48	0.88705326	0.81907102	0.78709841	0.75639883	0.69861414
49	0.88484116	0.81567238	0.78318250	0.75201209	0.69341353
50	0.88263457	0.81228785	0.77928607	0.74765079	0.68825165

Rate i

0.0075(3/4%)	0.005833(7/12%)	0.005(1/2%)	0.004167(5/12%)	0.0025(1/4%)	n
0.68312819	0.74331479	0.77540902	0.80891736	0.88043349	51
0.67804286	0.73900393	0.77155127	0.80556086	0.87823790	52
0.67299540	0.73471808	0.76771270	0.80221828	0.87604708	53
0.66798551	0.73045708	0.76389324	0.79888957	0.87386312	54
0.66301291	0.72622079	0.76009277	0.79557468	0.87168391	55
0.65807733	0.72200907	0.75631122	0.79227354	0.86951013	56
0.65317849	0.71782178	0.75254847	0.78898610	0.86734178	57
0.64831612	0.71365877	0.74880445	0.78571230	0.86517883	58
0.64348995	0.70951990	0.74507906	0.78245208	0.86302128	59
0.63869970	0.70540504	0.74137220	0.77920539	0.86086911	60
0.63394511	0.70131404	0.73768378	0.77597217	0.85872230	61
0.62922592	0.69724677	0.73401371	0.77275237	0.85658085	62
0.62454185	0.69320308	0.73036190	0.76954593	0.85444474	63
0.61989266	0.68918285	0.72672826	0.76635279	0.85231395	64
0.61527807	0.68518593	0.72311269	0.76317291	0.85018848	65
0.61069784	0.68121219	0.71951512	0.76000621	0.84806831	66
0.60615170	0.67726150	0.71593544	0.75685266	0.84595343	67
0.60163940	0.67333372	0.71237357	0.75371219	0.84384382	68
0.59716070	0.66942872	0.70882943	0.75058476	0.84173947	69
0.59271533	0.66554637	0.70530291	0.74747030	0.83964037	70
0.58830306	0.66168653	0.70179394	0.74436876	0.83754650	71
0.58392363	0.65784908	0.69830243	0.74128009	0.83545786	72
0.57957681	0.65403388	0.69482829	0.73820424	0.83337442	73
0.57526234	0.65024081	0.69137143	0.73514115	0.83129618	74
0.57097999	0.64646953	0.68793177	0.73209078	0.82922312	75
0.56672952	0.64272053	0.68450923	0.72905306	0.82715523	76
0.56251069	0.63899306	0.68110371	0.72602794	0.82509250	77
0.55832326	0.63528723	0.67771513	0.72301537	0.82303491	78
0.55416701	0.63160288	0.67434342	0.72001531	0.82098246	79
0.55004170	0.62793989	0.67098847	0.71702770	0.81893512	80
0.54594710	0.62429816	0.66765022	0.71405248	0.81689289	81
0.54188297	0.62067754	0.66432858	0.71108960	0.81485575	82
0.53784911	0.61707792	0.66102346	0.70813902	0.81282369	83
0.53384527	0.61349917	0.65773479	0.70520069	0.81079670	84
0.52987123	0.60994118	0.65446248	0.70227454	0.80877476	85
0.52592678	0.60640382	0.65120644	0.69936054	0.80675787	86
0.52201169	0.60288698	0.64796661	0.69645863	0.80474600	87
0.51812575	0.59939054	0.64474290	0.69356876	0.80273915	88
0.51426873	0.59591437	0.64153522	0.69069088	0.80073731	89
0.51044043	0.59245836	0.63834350	0.68782495	0.79874046	90
0.50664063	0.58902240	0.63516766	0.68497090	0.79674859	91
0.50286911	0.58560636	0.63200763	0.68212870	0.79476168	92
0.49912567	0.58221014	0.62886331	0.67929829	0.79277973	93
0.49541009	0.57883361	0.62573464	0.67647962	0.79080272	94
0.49172217	0.57547666	0.62262153	0.67367265	0.78883065	95
0.48806171	0.57213918	0.61952391	0.67087733	0.78686349	96
0.48442850	0.56882106	0.61644170	0.66809361	0.78490124	97
0.48082233	0.56552218	0.61337483	0.66532143	0.78294388	98
0.47724301	0.56224243	0.61032321	0.66256076	0.78099140	99
0.47369033	0.55898171	0.60728678	0.65981155	0.77904379	100

Rate i

Periods n	0.01(1%)	0.001125(1 1/8%)	0.0125(1 1/4%)	0.015(1 1/2%)	0.0175(1 3/4%)
1	0.99009901	0.98887515	0.98765432	0.98522167	0.98280098
2	0.98029605	0.97787407	0.97546106	0.97066175	0.96589777
3	0.97059015	0.96699537	0.96341833	0.95631699	0.94928528
4	0.96098034	0.95623770	0.95152428	0.94218423	0.93295851
5	0.95146569	0.94559970	0.93977706	0.92826033	0.91691254
6	0.94204524	0.93508005	0.92817488	0.91454219	0.90114254
7	0.93271805	0.92467743	0.91671593	0.90102679	0.88564378
8	0.92348322	0.91439054	0.90539845	0.88771112	0.87041157
9	0.91433982	0.90421808	0.89422069	0.87459224	0.85544135
10	0.90528695	0.89415880	0.88318093	0.86166723	0.84072860
11	0.89632372	0.88421142	0.87227746	0.84893323	0.82626889
12	0.88744923	0.87437470	0.86150860	0.83638742	0.81205788
13	0.87866260	0.86464742	0.85087269	0.82402702	0.79809128
14	0.86996297	0.85502835	0.84036809	0.81184928	0.78436490
15	0.86134947	0.84551629	0.82999318	0.79985150	0.77087459
16	0.85282126	0.83611005	0.81974635	0.78803104	0.75761631
17	0.84437749	0.82680846	0.80962602	0.77638526	0.74458605
18	0.83601731	0.81761034	0.79963064	0.76491159	0.73177990
19	0.82773992	0.80851455	0.78975866	0.75360747	0.71919401
20	0.81954447	0.79951995	0.78000855	0.74247042	0.70682458
21	0.81143017	0.79062542	0.77037881	0.73149795	0.69466789
22	0.80339621	0.78182983	0.76086796	0.72068763	0.68272028
23	0.79544179	0.77313210	0.75147453	0.71003708	0.67097817
24	0.78756613	0.76453112	0.74219707	0.69954392	0.65943800
25	0.77976844	0.75602583	0.73303414	0.68920583	0.64809632
26	0.77204796	0.74761516	0.72398434	0.67902052	0.63694970
27	0.76440392	0.73929806	0.71504626	0.66898574	0.62599479
28	0.75683557	0.73107348	0.70621853	0.65909925	0.61522829
29	0.74934215	0.72294040	0.69749978	0.64935887	0.60464697
30	0.74192292	0.71489780	0.68888867	0.63976243	0.59424764
31	0.73457715	0.70694467	0.68038387	0.63030781	0.58402716
32	0.72730411	0.69908002	0.67198407	0.62099292	0.57398247
33	0.72010307	0.69130287	0.66368797	0.61181568	0.56411053
34	0.71297334	0.68361223	0.65549429	0.60277407	0.55440839
35	0.70591420	0.67600715	0.64740177	0.59386608	0.54487311
36	0.69892495	0.66848667	0.63940916	0.58508974	0.53550183
37	0.69200490	0.66104986	0.63151522	0.57644309	0.52629172
38	0.68515337	0.65369578	0.62371873	0.56792423	0.51724002
39	0.67836967	0.64642352	0.61601850	0.55953126	0.50834400
40	0.67165314	0.63923216	0.60841334	0.55126232	0.49960098
41	0.66500311	0.63212080	0.60090206	0.54311559	0.49100834
42	0.65841892	0.62508855	0.59348352	0.53508925	0.48256348
43	0.65189992	0.61813454	0.58615656	0.52718153	0.47426386
44	0.64544546	0.61125789	0.57892006	0.51939067	0.46610699
45	0.63905492	0.60445774	0.57177290	0.51171494	0.45809040
46	0.63272764	0.59773324	0.56471597	0.50415265	0.45021170
47	0.62646301	0.59108355	0.55774219	0.49670212	0.44246850
48	0.62026041	0.58450784	0.55085649	0.48936170	0.43485848
49	0.61411921	0.57800528	0.54405579	0.48212975	0.42737934
50	0.60803882	0.57157506	0.53733905	0.47500468	0.42002883

Rate i

Periods n	0.01(1%)	0.001125(1 1/8%)	0.0125(1 1/4%)	0.0175(1 3/4%)
51	0.60201864	0.56521637	0.53070524	0.46798491
52	0.59605806	0.55892843	0.52415332	0.46106887
53	0.59015649	0.55271044	0.51768229	0.45425505
54	0.58431336	0.54656162	0.51129115	0.44754192
55	0.57852808	0.54048120	0.50497892	0.44092800
56	0.57280008	0.53446843	0.49874461	0.43441182
57	0.56712879	0.52852256	0.49258727	0.42799194
58	0.56151365	0.52264282	0.48650594	0.42166694
59	0.55595411	0.51682850	0.48049970	0.41543541
60	0.55044962	0.51107887	0.47456760	0.40929597
61	0.54499962	0.50539319	0.46870874	0.40324726
62	0.53960358	0.49977077	0.46292222	0.39728794
63	0.53426097	0.49421090	0.45720713	0.39141669
64	0.52897126	0.48871288	0.45156259	0.38563221
65	0.52373392	0.48327602	0.44598775	0.37993321
66	0.51854844	0.47789965	0.44048173	0.37431843
67	0.51341429	0.47258309	0.43504368	0.36878663
68	0.50833099	0.46732568	0.42967277	0.36333658
69	0.50329801	0.46212675	0.42436817	0.35796708
70	0.49831486	0.45698566	0.41912905	0.35267692
71	0.49338105	0.45190177	0.41395462	0.34746495
72	0.48849609	0.44687443	0.40884407	0.34233000
73	0.48365949	0.44190302	0.40379661	0.33727093
74	0.47887078	0.43698692	0.39881147	0.33228663
75	0.47412949	0.43212551	0.39388787	0.32737599
76	0.46943514	0.42731818	0.38902506	0.32253793
77	0.46478726	0.42256433	0.38422228	0.31777136
78	0.46018541	0.41786337	0.37947889	0.31307523
79	0.45562912	0.41321470	0.37479387	0.30844850
80	0.45111794	0.40861775	0.37016679	0.30389015
81	0.44665142	0.40407194	0.36559683	0.29939916
82	0.44222913	0.39957670	0.36108329	0.29497454
83	0.43785063	0.39513148	0.35662547	0.29061531
84	0.43351547	0.39073570	0.35222268	0.28632050
85	0.42922324	0.38638882	0.34787426	0.28208917
86	0.42497350	0.38209031	0.34357951	0.27792036
87	0.42076585	0.37783961	0.33933779	0.27381316
88	0.41659985	0.37363621	0.33514843	0.26976666
89	0.41247510	0.36947956	0.33101080	0.26577996
90	0.40839119	0.36536916	0.32692425	0.26185218
91	0.40434771	0.36130448	0.32288814	0.25798245
92	0.40034427	0.35728503	0.31890187	0.25416990
93	0.39638046	0.35331029	0.31496481	0.25041369
94	0.39245590	0.34937976	0.31107636	0.24671300
95	0.38857020	0.34549297	0.30723591	0.24306699
96	0.38472297	0.34164941	0.30344287	0.23947487
97	0.38091383	0.33784861	0.29969666	0.23593583
98	0.37714241	0.33409010	0.29599670	0.23244909
99	0.37340832	0.33037340	0.29234242	0.22901389
100	0.36971121	0.32669805	0.28873326	0.22562944

PRESENT VALUE 1/(1 + i)ⁿ (Continued)

Rate i

Periods n	0.02(2%)	0.0225(2 1/4%)	0.025(2 1/2%)	0.0275(2 3/4%)
1	0.98039216	0.97799511	0.97560976	0.97323601
2	0.96116878	0.95647444	0.95181440	0.94718833
3	0.94232233	0.93542732	0.92859941	0.92183779
4	0.92384543	0.91484335	0.90595064	0.89716573
5	0.90573081	0.89471232	0.88385429	0.87315400
6	0.88797138	0.87502427	0.86229687	0.84978491
7	0.87056018	0.85576946	0.84126524	0.82704128
8	0.85349037	0.83693835	0.82074657	0.80490635
9	0.83675527	0.81852161	0.80072836	0.78336385
10	0.82034830	0.80051013	0.78119840	0.76239791
11	0.80426304	0.78289499	0.76214478	0.74199310
12	0.78849318	0.76566748	0.74355589	0.72213440
13	0.77303253	0.74881905	0.72542038	0.70280720
14	0.75787502	0.73234137	0.70772720	0.68399728
15	0.74301473	0.71622628	0.69046556	0.66569078
16	0.72844581	0.70046580	0.67362493	0.64787424
17	0.71416256	0.68505212	0.65719506	0.63053454
18	0.70015937	0.66997763	0.64116591	0.61365892
19	0.68643076	0.65523484	0.62552772	0.59723496
20	0.67297133	0.64081647	0.61027094	0.58125057
21	0.65977582	0.62671538	0.59538629	0.56569398
22	0.64683904	0.61292457	0.58086467	0.55055375
23	0.63415592	0.59943724	0.56669724	0.53581874
24	0.62172149	0.58624668	0.55287535	0.52147809
25	0.60953087	0.57334639	0.53939059	0.50752126
26	0.59757928	0.56072997	0.52623472	0.49393796
27	0.58586204	0.54839117	0.51339973	0.48071821
28	0.57437455	0.53632388	0.50087778	0.46785227
29	0.56311231	0.52452213	0.48866125	0.45533068
30	0.55207089	0.51298008	0.47674269	0.44314421
31	0.54124597	0.50169201	0.46511481	0.43128391
32	0.53063330	0.49065233	0.45377055	0.41974103
33	0.52022873	0.47985558	0.44270298	0.40850708
34	0.51002817	0.46929641	0.43190534	0.39757388
35	0.50002761	0.45896960	0.42137107	0.38693314
36	0.49022315	0.44887002	0.41109372	0.37657727
37	0.48061093	0.43899268	0.40106705	0.36649856
38	0.47118719	0.42933270	0.39128492	0.35668959
39	0.46194822	0.41988528	0.38174139	0.34714316
40	0.45289042	0.41064575	0.37243062	0.33785222
41	0.44401021	0.40160954	0.36334695	0.32880995
42	0.43530413	0.39277216	0.35448463	0.32000968
43	0.42676875	0.38412925	0.34583886	0.31144495
44	0.41840074	0.37567653	0.33740376	0.30310944
45	0.41019680	0.36740981	0.32917440	0.29499702
46	0.40215373	0.35932500	0.32114576	0.28710172
47	0.39426836	0.35141809	0.31331294	0.27941773
48	0.38653761	0.34368518	0.30567116	0.27193940
49	0.37895844	0.33612242	0.29821576	0.26466122

Rate i

Periods n	0.02(2%)	0.0225(2 1/4%)	0.025(2 1/2%)	0.0275(2 3/4%)
51	0.36424302	0.32149250	0.28384606	0.25068402
52	0.35710100	0.31441810	0.27692298	0.24397471
53	0.35009902	0.30749936	0.27016876	0.23744497
54	0.34323433	0.30073287	0.26357928	0.23109000
55	0.33650425	0.29411528	0.25715052	0.22490511
56	0.32990613	0.28764330	0.25087855	0.21888575
57	0.32343738	0.28131374	0.24475956	0.21302749
58	0.31709647	0.27512347	0.23878982	0.20732603
59	0.31087791	0.26906940	0.23296568	0.20177716
60	0.30478227	0.26314856	0.22728359	0.19637679
61	0.29880614	0.25735801	0.22174009	0.19112097
62	0.29294720	0.25169487	0.21633179	0.18600585
63	0.28720314	0.24615635	0.21105541	0.18102755
64	0.28157170	0.24073971	0.20590771	0.17618253
65	0.27605069	0.23544226	0.20088557	0.17146718
66	0.27063793	0.23026138	0.19598593	0.16687804
67	0.26533130	0.22519450	0.19120578	0.16241172
68	0.26012873	0.22023912	0.18654223	0.15806493
69	0.25502817	0.21539278	0.18199241	0.15383448
70	0.25002761	0.21065309	0.17755358	0.14971726
71	0.24512511	0.20601769	0.17322300	0.14571023
72	0.24031874	0.20148429	0.16899805	0.14181044
73	0.23560661	0.19705065	0.16487615	0.13801503
74	0.23098687	0.19271458	0.16085478	0.13432119
75	0.22645771	0.18847391	0.15693149	0.13072622
76	0.22201737	0.18432657	0.15310389	0.12722747
77	0.21766408	0.18027048	0.14936965	0.12382235
78	0.21339616	0.17630365	0.14572649	0.12050837
79	0.20921192	0.17242411	0.14217218	0.11728309
80	0.20510973	0.16862993	0.13870457	0.11414412
81	0.20108797	0.16491925	0.13532153	0.11108598
82	0.19714507	0.16129022	0.13202101	0.10811598
83	0.19327948	0.15774105	0.12880098	0.10522237
84	0.18948968	0.15426997	0.12565949	0.10240620
85	0.18577420	0.15087528	0.12259463	0.09966540
86	0.18213157	0.14755528	0.11960452	0.09699795
87	0.17856036	0.14430835	0.11668733	0.09440190
88	0.17505918	0.14113286	0.11384130	0.09187533
89	0.17162665	0.13802724	0.11106468	0.08941638
90	0.16826142	0.13498997	0.10835579	0.08702324
91	0.16496217	0.13201953	0.10571296	0.08469415
92	0.16172762	0.12911640	0.10313460	0.08242740
93	0.15855649	0.12627331	0.10061912	0.08022131
94	0.15544754	0.12349468	0.09816500	0.07807427
95	0.15239955	0.12077719	0.09577073	0.07598469
96	0.14941132	0.11811950	0.09343486	0.07395104
97	0.14648169	0.11552029	0.09115596	0.07197181
98	0.14360950	0.11297828	0.08893264	0.07004556
99	0.14079363	0.11049221	0.08676355	0.06817086

Periods	Rate i				
n	0.03(3%)	0.0325(3 1/4%)	0.035(3 1/2%)	0.0375(3 3/4%)	
1	0.97087379	0.96852300	0.96618357	0.96385542	
2	0.94259591	0.93803681	0.93351070	0.92901727	
3	0.91514166	0.90851022	0.90194271	0.89543834	
4	0.88848705	0.87991305	0.87144223	0.86307310	
5	0.86260878	0.85221603	0.84197317	0.83187768	
6	0.83748426	0.82539083	0.81350064	0.80180981	
7	0.81309151	0.79941000	0.78599096	0.77282874	
8	0.78940923	0.77424698	0.75941156	0.74489517	
9	0.76641673	0.74987601	0.73373097	0.71797125	
10	0.74409391	0.72627216	0.70891881	0.69202048	
11	0.72242128	0.70341129	0.68494571	0.66700769	
12	0.70137988	0.68127002	0.66178330	0.64289898	
13	0.68095134	0.65982568	0.63940415	0.61966167	
14	0.66111781	0.63905635	0.61778179	0.59726426	
15	0.64186195	0.61894078	0.59689062	0.57567639	
16	0.62316694	0.59945838	0.57670591	0.55486881	
17	0.60501645	0.58058923	0.55720378	0.53481331	
18	0.58739461	0.56231402	0.53836114	0.51548271	
19	0.57028603	0.54461407	0.52015569	0.49685080	
20	0.55367575	0.52747125	0.50256588	0.47889234	
21	0.53754928	0.51086804	0.48557090	0.46158298	
22	0.52189250	0.49478745	0.46915063	0.44489926	
23	0.50669175	0.47921302	0.45328563	0.42881856	
24	0.49193374	0.46412884	0.43795713	0.41331910	
25	0.47760557	0.44951945	0.42314699	0.39837985	
26	0.46369473	0.43536993	0.40883767	0.38398058	
27	0.45018906	0.42166579	0.39501224	0.37010176	
28	0.43707675	0.40839302	0.38165434	0.35672459	
29	0.42434636	0.39553803	0.36874815	0.34389093	
30	0.41198676	0.38308768	0.35627841	0.33140331	
31	0.39998715	0.37102923	0.34423035	0.31942487	
32	0.38833703	0.35935035	0.33258971	0.30787940	
33	0.37702625	0.34803908	0.32134271	0.29675123	
34	0.36604490	0.33708385	0.31047605	0.28602528	
35	0.35538340	0.32647346	0.29997686	0.27568702	
36	0.35503243	0.31619706	0.28983272	0.26572242	
37	0.33498294	0.30624413	0.28003161	0.25611800	
38	0.32522615	0.29660448	0.27056194	0.24686072	
39	0.31575355	0.28726826	0.26141250	0.23793805	
40	0.30655684	0.27822592	0.25257247	0.22933788	
41	0.29762800	0.26946820	0.24403137	0.22104855	
42	0.28895922	0.26098615	0.23577010	0.21305885	
43	0.28054294	0.25277109	0.22780590	0.20535735	
44	0.27237178	0.24481462	0.22010231	0.19793535	
45	0.26443862	0.23710859	0.21265924	0.19078106	
46	0.25673653	0.22964512	0.20546787	0.18388536	
47	0.24925876	0.22241658	0.19851968	0.17723890	
48	0.24199880	0.21541558	0.19180645	0.17083268	
49	0.23495029	0.20863494	0.18532024	0.16465800	
50	0.22810708	0.20206774	0.17905337	0.15870651	

Periods	Rate i				
n	0.03(3%)	0.0325(3 1/4%)	0.035(3 1/2%)	0.0375(3 3/4%)	
51	0.22146318	0.19570725	0.17299843	0.15297013	
52	0.21501280	0.18954694	0.16714824	0.14744698	
53	0.20875029	0.18358061	0.16149589	0.14211189	
54	0.20267019	0.17780204	0.15603467	0.13697532	
55	0.19677 617	0.17220537	0.15075814	0.13202440	
56	0.19103609	0.16678486	0.14566004	0.12725243	
57	0.18547193	0.16153497	0.14073433	0.12265295	
58	0.18006984	0.15645034	0.13597520	0.11821971	
59	0.17482608	0.15152575	0.13137701	0.11394671	
60	0.16973309	0.14675617	0.12693431	0.10982815	
61	0.16478941	0.14213673	0.12264184	0.10585846	
62	0.15998972	0.13766269	0.11849453	0.10203225	
63	0.15532982	0.13332948	0.11448747	0.09834434	
64	0.15080565	0.12913267	0.11061591	0.09478972	
65	0.14641325	0.12506796	0.10687528	0.09136359	
66	0.14214879	0.12113120	0.10326114	0.08806129	
67	0.13800853	0.11731835	0.09976922	0.08487835	
68	0.13398887	0.11362552	0.09639538	0.08181046	
69	0.13008628	0.11004893	0.09313563	0.07885346	
70	0.12629736	0.10658492	0.08998612	0.07600333	
71	0.12261880	0.10322995	0.08694311	0.07325622	
72	0.11904737	0.09998058	0.08400300	0.07060841	
73	0.11557998	0.09683349	0.08116232	0.06805630	
74	0.11221157	0.09378546	0.07841770	0.06559643	
75	0.10894521	0.09083338	0.07576590	0.06322247	
76	0.10577205	0.08797422	0.07320376	0.06094022	
77	0.10269131	0.08520505	0.07072827	0.05873756	
78	0.09970030	0.08252305	0.06833650	0.05661451	
79	0.09679641	0.07992548	0.06602560	0.05456821	
80	0.09397710	0.07740966	0.06379285	0.05259586	
81	0.09123990	0.07497304	0.06163461	0.05069481	
82	0.08858243	0.07261311	0.05955131	0.04886246	
83	0.08600236	0.07032747	0.05753750	0.04709635	
84	0.08349743	0.06811377	0.05559178	0.04539407	
85	0.08106547	0.06596976	0.05371187	0.04375332	
86	0.07870434	0.06389323	0.05189553	0.04217188	
87	0.07641198	0.06188206	0.05014060	0.04064759	
88	0.07418639	0.05993420	0.04844503	0.03917840	
89	0.07202562	0.05804765	0.04680679	0.03776232	
90	0.06992779	0.05622048	0.04522395	0.03639741	
91	0.06789105	0.05445083	0.04369464	0.03508184	
92	0.06591364	0.05273688	0.04221704	0.03381383	
93	0.06399383	0.05107688	0.04079841	0.03259164	
94	0.06212993	0.04946914	0.03941006	0.03141363	
95	0.06032032	0.04791200	0.03807735	0.03027820	
96	0.05856342	0.04640387	0.03678971	0.02918380	
97	0.05685769	0.04494322	0.03554562	0.02812897	
98	0.05520164	0.04352854	0.03434359	0.02711226	
99	0.05359383	0.04215839	0.03318221	0.02613230	
100	0.05203284	0.04083137	0.03206011	0.02518776	

PRESENT VALUE $1/(1 + i)^n$ (Continued)

Rate i — Periods 1–49

Periods n	0.04(4%)	0.0425(4 1/4%)	0.045(4 1/2%)	0.0475(4 3/4%)
1	0.96153846	0.95923261	0.95693780	0.95465894
2	0.92455621	0.92012721	0.91577995	0.91136414
3	0.88899636	0.88261603	0.87629660	0.87003737
4	0.85480419	0.84663408	0.83856134	0.83058460
5	0.82192711	0.81211902	0.80245105	0.79292086
6	0.79031453	0.77901105	0.76789574	0.75696502
7	0.75991781	0.74725281	0.73482846	0.72263964
8	0.73069021	0.71678926	0.70318513	0.68987077
9	0.70258674	0.68756764	0.67290443	0.65858785
10	0.67555417	0.65953730	0.64392768	0.62872349
11	0.64958093	0.63264969	0.61619874	0.60021335
12	0.62459705	0.60685822	0.58966386	0.57299604
13	0.60057409	0.58211819	0.56427164	0.54701293
14	0.57747508	0.55838676	0.53997286	0.52220804
15	0.55526450	0.53562279	0.51672044	0.49852797
16	0.53390818	0.51378685	0.49446932	0.47592169
17	0.51337325	0.49284110	0.47317639	0.45434051
18	0.49362812	0.47274926	0.45280037	0.43373796
19	0.47464242	0.45347650	0.43330179	0.41406965
20	0.45638695	0.43499945	0.41464286	0.39529322
21	0.43883360	0.41725607	0.39678743	0.37736823
22	0.42195539	0.40024563	0.37970089	0.36025607
23	0.40572633	0.38392866	0.36335013	0.34391987
24	0.39012147	0.36827689	0.34770347	0.32832446
25	0.37511680	0.35326321	0.33273060	0.31343624
26	0.36068923	0.33886159	0.31840248	0.29922314
27	0.34681657	0.32504709	0.30469137	0.28565455
28	0.33347747	0.31179577	0.29157069	0.27270124
29	0.32065141	0.29908467	0.27901502	0.26033531
30	0.30831867	0.28689177	0.26700002	0.24853013
31	0.29646026	0.27519594	0.25550241	0.23726027
32	0.28505794	0.26397692	0.24449991	0.22650145
33	0.27409417	0.25321527	0.23397121	0.21623050
34	0.26355209	0.24289235	0.22389589	0.20642530
35	0.25341547	0.23299026	0.21425444	0.19706473
36	0.24366872	0.22349186	0.20502817	0.18812862
37	0.23429685	0.21438068	0.19619921	0.17959772
38	0.22528543	0.20564094	0.18775044	0.17134367
39	0.21662061	0.19725750	0.17966549	0.16367893
40	0.20828904	0.18921582	0.17192870	0.15625176
41	0.20027793	0.18150199	0.16452507	0.14917110
42	0.19257493	0.17410263	0.15744026	0.14240678
43	0.18516820	0.16700492	0.15066054	0.13594919
44	0.17804635	0.16019657	0.14417276	0.12978443
45	0.17119841	0.15366577	0.13796437	0.12389922
46	0.16461386	0.14740122	0.13202332	0.11828088
47	0.15828256	0.14139206	0.12633810	0.11291731
48	0.15219476	0.13562787	0.12089771	0.10779695
49	0.14634112	0.13009868	0.11569158	0.10290878

Rate i — Periods 51–99

Periods n	0.04(4%)	0.0425(4 1/4%)	0.045(4 1/2%)	0.0475(4 3/4%)
51	0.13530059	0.11970733	0.10594225	0.09378738
52	0.13009672	0.11482718	0.10138014	0.08953449
53	0.12509300	0.11014597	0.09701449	0.08547445
54	0.12028173	0.10565561	0.09283683	0.08159852
55	0.11565551	0.10134831	0.08883970	0.07789835
56	0.11120722	0.09721660	0.08501347	0.07436597
57	0.10693002	0.09325333	0.08135260	0.07099376
58	0.10281733	0.08945164	0.07784938	0.06777448
59	0.09886282	0.08580493	0.07449701	0.06470117
60	0.09506040	0.08230689	0.07128901	0.06176723
61	0.09140423	0.07895145	0.06821915	0.05896633
62	0.08788868	0.07573281	0.06528148	0.05629244
63	0.08450835	0.07264538	0.06247032	0.05373980
64	0.08125803	0.06968382	0.05978021	0.05130291
65	0.07813272	0.06684299	0.05720594	0.04897652
66	0.07512762	0.06411793	0.05474253	0.04675563
67	0.07223809	0.06150405	0.05238519	0.04463545
68	0.06945970	0.05899669	0.05012937	0.04261140
69	0.06678818	0.05659155	0.04797069	0.04067915
70	0.06421940	0.05428446	0.04590497	0.03883451
71	0.06174942	0.05207143	0.04392820	0.03707351
72	0.05937445	0.04994861	0.04203655	0.03539238
73	0.05709081	0.04791234	0.04022637	0.03378747
74	0.05489501	0.04595908	0.03849413	0.03225534
75	0.05278367	0.04408544	0.03683649	0.03079269
76	0.05075353	0.04228820	0.03525023	0.02939636
77	0.04880147	0.04056422	0.03373228	0.02806335
78	0.04692449	0.03891052	0.03227969	0.02679079
79	0.04511970	0.03732424	0.03088965	0.02557593
80	0.04338433	0.03580263	0.02955948	0.02441617
81	0.04171570	0.03434305	0.02828658	0.02330899
82	0.04011125	0.03294297	0.02706850	0.02225202
83	0.03856851	0.03159997	0.02590287	0.02124298
84	0.03708501	0.03031173	0.02478744	0.02027969
85	0.03565875	0.02907600	0.02372003	0.01936009
86	0.03428726	0.02789064	0.02269860	0.01848218
87	0.03296852	0.02675361	0.02172115	0.01764409
88	0.03170050	0.02566294	0.02078579	0.01684400
89	0.03048125	0.02461673	0.01989070	0.01608019
90	0.02930890	0.02361317	0.01903417	0.01535102
91	0.02818163	0.02265052	0.01821451	0.01465491
92	0.02709772	0.02172712	0.01743016	0.01399037
93	0.02605550	0.02084136	0.01667958	0.01335596
94	0.02505337	0.01999171	0.01596132	0.01275032
95	0.02409878	0.01917670	0.01527399	0.01217214
96	0.02316325	0.01839492	0.01461626	0.01162018
97	0.02227235	0.01764501	0.01398685	0.01109325
98	0.02141572	0.01692567	0.01338454	0.01059022
99	0.02059204	0.01623565	0.01280817	0.01010999

Rate i

Periods n	0.05(5%)	0.0525(5 1/4%)	0.055(5 1/2%)	0.0575(5 3/4%)
51	0.08305117	0.07356524	0.06518153	0.05776979
52	0.07909635	0.06989572	0.06178344	0.05462865
53	0.07532986	0.06640923	0.05856250	0.05165830
54	0.07174272	0.06309666	0.05550948	0.04884945
55	0.06832640	0.05994932	0.05261562	0.04619333
56	0.06507276	0.05695897	0.04987263	0.04368164
57	0.06197406	0.05411779	0.04727263	0.04130652
58	0.05902291	0.05141833	0.04480818	0.03906054
59	0.05621230	0.04885352	0.04247221	0.03693668
60	0.05353552	0.04641664	0.04025802	0.03492830
61	0.05098621	0.04410132	0.03815926	0.03302912
62	0.04855830	0.04190150	0.03616992	0.03123321
63	0.04624600	0.03981140	0.03428428	0.02953495
64	0.04404381	0.03782556	0.03249695	0.02792904
65	0.04194648	0.03593877	0.03080279	0.02641044
66	0.03994903	0.03414610	0.02919696	0.02497441
67	0.03804670	0.03244285	0.02767485	0.02361646
68	0.03623495	0.03082456	0.02623208	0.02233235
69	0.03450948	0.02928699	0.02486453	0.02111806
70	0.03286617	0.02782612	0.02356828	0.01996980
71	0.03130111	0.02643812	0.02233960	0.01888397
72	0.02981058	0.02511935	0.02117498	0.01785718
73	0.02839103	0.02386637	0.02007107	0.01688622
74	0.02703908	0.02267589	0.01902471	0.01596806
75	0.02575150	0.02154478	0.01803290	0.01509982
76	0.02452524	0.02047010	0.01709279	0.01427879
77	0.02335737	0.01944903	0.01620170	0.01350240
78	0.02224512	0.01847889	0.01535706	0.01276823
79	0.02118582	0.01755714	0.01455646	0.01207398
80	0.02017698	0.01668137	0.01379759	0.01141747
81	0.01921617	0.01584928	0.01307828	0.01079666
82	0.01830111	0.01505870	0.01239648	0.01020961
83	0.01742963	0.01430755	0.01175022	0.00965448
84	0.01659965	0.01359387	0.01113765	0.00912953
85	0.01580919	0.01291579	0.01055701	0.00863313
86	0.01505637	0.01227154	0.01000664	0.00816371
87	0.01433940	0.01165942	0.00948497	0.00771982
88	0.01365657	0.01107783	0.00899049	0.00730007
89	0.01300626	0.01052526	0.00852180	0.00690314
90	0.01238691	0.01000024	0.00807753	0.00652779
91	0.01179706	0.00950142	0.00765643	0.00617285
92	0.01123530	0.00902748	0.00725728	0.00583721
93	0.01070028	0.00857718	0.00687894	0.00551982
94	0.01019074	0.00814934	0.00652032	0.00521969
95	0.00970547	0.00774284	0.00618040	0.00493588
96	0.00924331	0.00735661	0.00585820	0.00466750
97	0.00880315	0.00698966	0.00555279	0.00441371
98	0.00838395	0.00664100	0.00526331	0.00417372
99	0.00798471	0.00630974	0.00498892	0.00394678
100	0.00760449	0.00599500	0.00472883	0.00373218

Rate i

Periods n	0.05(5%)	0.0525(5 1/4%)	0.055(5 1/2%)	0.0575(5 3/4%)
1	0.95238095	0.95011876	0.94786730	0.94562648
2	0.90702948	0.90272567	0.89845242	0.89420944
3	0.86383760	0.85769660	0.85161366	0.84558812
4	0.82270247	0.81491363	0.80721674	0.79961051
5	0.78352617	0.77426473	0.76513434	0.75613287
6	0.74621540	0.73564345	0.72524583	0.71501927
7	0.71068133	0.69894865	0.68743681	0.67614115
8	0.67683936	0.66408423	0.65159887	0.63937697
9	0.64460892	0.63095888	0.61762926	0.60461180
10	0.61391325	0.59948588	0.58543058	0.57173692
11	0.58467929	0.56958278	0.55491050	0.54064957
12	0.55683742	0.54117129	0.52598152	0.51125255
13	0.53032135	0.51417699	0.49856068	0.48345395
14	0.50506795	0.48852921	0.47256937	0.45716685
15	0.48101710	0.46416077	0.44793305	0.43230908
16	0.45811152	0.44100786	0.42458109	0.40880291
17	0.43629669	0.41900984	0.40244653	0.38657486
18	0.41552065	0.39810911	0.38146590	0.36555542
19	0.39573396	0.37825094	0.36157906	0.34567889
20	0.37688948	0.35938831	0.34272896	0.32688311
21	0.35894236	0.34145683	0.32486158	0.30910932
22	0.34184987	0.32442454	0.30792567	0.29230196
23	0.32557131	0.30824185	0.29187267	0.27640847
24	0.31006791	0.29286636	0.27665656	0.26137917
25	0.29530277	0.27825783	0.26223370	0.24716706
26	0.28124073	0.26437798	0.24856275	0.23372772
27	0.26784832	0.25119048	0.23560450	0.22101912
28	0.25509364	0.23866079	0.22332181	0.20900153
29	0.24294632	0.22675609	0.21167944	0.19763738
30	0.23137745	0.21544522	0.20064402	0.18689114
31	0.22035947	0.20469855	0.19018390	0.17672921
32	0.20986617	0.19448793	0.18026910	0.16711982
33	0.19987254	0.18478663	0.17087119	0.15803293
34	0.19035480	0.17556925	0.16196321	0.14944012
35	0.18129029	0.16681164	0.15341963	0.14131454
36	0.17265741	0.15849087	0.14551624	0.13363077
37	0.16443563	0.15058515	0.13793008	0.12636479
38	0.15660536	0.14307377	0.13073941	0.11949389
39	0.14914797	0.13593708	0.12392362	0.11299659
40	0.14204568	0.12915637	0.11746314	0.10685257
41	0.13528160	0.12271389	0.11133947	0.10104262
42	0.12883962	0.11659277	0.10553504	0.09554857
43	0.12270440	0.11077698	0.10003322	0.09035326
44	0.11686133	0.10525128	0.09481822	0.08544044
45	0.11129651	0.10000122	0.08987509	0.08079474
46	0.10599668	0.09501304	0.08518965	0.07640164
47	0.10094921	0.09027367	0.08074849	0.07224742
48	0.09614211	0.08577071	0.07653885	0.06831907
49	0.09156391	0.08149236	0.07254867	0.06460432
50	0.08720373	0.07742742	0.06876652	0.06109156

FINANCIAL TABLES

PRESENT VALUE $1/(1 + i)^n$ (Continued)

Rate i

Periods n	0.06(6%)	0.0625(6 1/4%)	0.065(6 1/2%)	0.0675(6 3/4%)
1	0.94339623	0.94117647	0.93896714	0.93676815
2	0.88999644	0.88581315	0.88165928	0.87753457
3	0.83961928	0.83370649	0.82784909	0.82204643
4	0.79209366	0.78466493	0.77732309	0.77006420
5	0.74725817	0.73850817	0.72988084	0.72137416
6	0.70496054	0.69506652	0.68533412	0.67576034
7	0.66505711	0.65418025	0.64350621	0.63303076
8	0.62741237	0.61569906	0.60423119	0.59300305
9	0.59189846	0.57948147	0.56735323	0.55550637
10	0.55839478	0.54539432	0.53272604	0.52038068
11	0.52678753	0.51331230	0.50021224	0.48747605
12	0.49696936	0.48311746	0.46968285	0.45665203
13	0.46883902	0.45469879	0.44101676	0.42777708
14	0.44230096	0.42795180	0.41410025	0.40072794
15	0.41726506	0.40277817	0.38882652	0.37538917
16	0.39364628	0.37908533	0.36509533	0.35165262
17	0.37135442	0.35678619	0.34281251	0.32941698
18	0.35033379	0.33579877	0.32188969	0.30858733
19	0.33051301	0.31604590	0.30224384	0.28907478
20	0.31180473	0.29745497	0.28379703	0.27079605
21	0.29415540	0.27995762	0.26647608	0.25367312
22	0.27750510	0.26348952	0.25021228	0.23763289
23	0.26179726	0.24799014	0.23494111	0.22260693
24	0.24697855	0.23340248	0.22060198	0.20853108
25	0.23299863	0.21967292	0.20713801	0.19534527
26	0.21981003	0.20675099	0.19449579	0.18299323
27	0.20736795	0.19458917	0.18262515	0.17142223
28	0.19563014	0.18314274	0.17147902	0.16058289
29	0.18455674	0.17236964	0.16101316	0.15042893
30	0.17411013	0.16223025	0.15118607	0.14091703
31	0.16425484	0.15268729	0.14195875	0.13200659
32	0.15495740	0.14370569	0.13329460	0.12365957
33	0.14618622	0.13525241	0.12515925	0.11584034
34	0.13791153	0.12729639	0.11752042	0.10851554
35	0.13010522	0.11980837	0.11034781	0.10165391
36	0.12274077	0.11276081	0.10361297	0.09522614
37	0.11579318	0.10612783	0.09728917	0.08920482
38	0.10923885	0.09988501	0.09135134	0.08356423
39	0.10305552	0.09400942	0.08577590	0.07828031
40	0.09722219	0.08847946	0.08054075	0.07333050
41	0.09171905	0.08327478	0.07562512	0.06869368
42	0.08652740	0.07837627	0.07100950	0.06435005
43	0.08162962	0.07376590	0.06667559	0.06028108
44	0.07700908	0.06942673	0.06260619	0.05646939
45	0.07265007	0.06534280	0.05878515	0.05289873
46	0.06853781	0.06149911	0.05519733	0.04955384
47	0.06465831	0.05788151	0.05182848	0.04642046
48	0.06099840	0.05447672	0.04866524	0.04348521
49	0.05754566	0.05127221	0.04569506	0.04073556

Rate i

Periods n	0.06(6%)	0.0625(6 1/4%)	0.065(6 1/2%)	0.0675(6 3/4%)
51	0.05121544	0.04541759	0.04028747	0.03574686
52	0.04831645	0.04274597	0.03782861	0.03348652
53	0.04558156	0.04023150	0.03551982	0.03136911
54	0.04300147	0.03786494	0.03335195	0.02938558
55	0.04056742	0.03563759	0.03131638	0.02752748
56	0.03827115	0.03354126	0.02940505	0.02578686
57	0.03610486	0.03156825	0.02761038	0.02415631
58	0.03406119	0.02971129	0.02592524	0.02262886
59	0.03213320	0.02796357	0.02434295	0.02119800
60	0.03031434	0.02631865	0.02285723	0.01985761
61	0.02859843	0.02477050	0.02146218	0.01860198
62	0.02697965	0.02331341	0.02015229	0.01742574
63	0.02545250	0.02194203	0.01892233	0.01632388
64	0.02401179	0.02065133	0.01776745	0.01529169
65	0.02265264	0.01943654	0.01668305	0.01432477
66	0.02137041	0.01829322	0.01566484	0.01341899
67	0.02016077	0.01721714	0.01470877	0.01257048
68	0.01901959	0.01620437	0.01381105	0.01177562
69	0.01794301	0.01525117	0.01296812	0.01103103
70	0.01692737	0.01435404	0.01217664	0.01033352
71	0.01596921	0.01350969	0.01143346	0.00968011
72	0.01506530	0.01271565	0.01073565	0.00906802
73	0.01421254	0.01196706	0.01008042	0.00849463
74	0.01340806	0.01126312	0.00946518	0.00795750
75	0.01264911	0.01060058	0.00888750	0.00745433
76	0.01193313	0.00997702	0.00834507	0.00698298
77	0.01125767	0.00939013	0.00783574	0.00654143
78	0.01062044	0.00883777	0.00735751	0.00612781
79	0.01001928	0.00831790	0.00690846	0.00574033
80	0.00945215	0.00782861	0.00648681	0.00537736
81	0.00891713	0.00736811	0.00609090	0.00503734
82	0.00841238	0.00693469	0.00571916	0.00471882
83	0.00793621	0.00652677	0.00537010	0.00442044
84	0.00748699	0.00614284	0.00504235	0.00414093
85	0.00706320	0.00578150	0.00473460	0.00387909
86	0.00666340	0.00544141	0.00444563	0.00363381
87	0.00628622	0.00512132	0.00417430	0.00340404
88	0.00593040	0.00482007	0.00391953	0.00318879
89	0.00559472	0.00453654	0.00368031	0.00298716
90	0.00527803	0.00426968	0.00345569	0.00279828
91	0.00497928	0.00401852	0.00324478	0.00262134
92	0.00469743	0.00378214	0.00304674	0.00245558
93	0.00443154	0.00355966	0.00286079	0.00230031
94	0.00418070	0.00335027	0.00268619	0.00215486
95	0.00394405	0.00315319	0.00252224	0.00201860
96	0.00372081	0.00296771	0.00236831	0.00189096
97	0.00351019	0.00279314	0.00222376	0.00177139
98	0.00331150	0.00262884	0.00208804	0.00165939
99	0.00312406	0.00247420	0.00196060	0.00155446

Rate i

Periods n	0.07(7%)	0.0725(7 1/4%)	0.075(7 1/2%)	0.0775(7 3/4%)
1	0.93457944	0.93240093	0.93023256	0.92807425
2	0.87343873	0.86937150	0.86533261	0.86132181
3	0.81629788	0.81060280	0.80496057	0.79937059
4	0.76289521	0.75580680	0.74880053	0.74187525
5	0.71298618	0.70471497	0.69655863	0.68851532
6	0.66634222	0.65707689	0.64796152	0.63899333
7	0.62274974	0.61265911	0.60275490	0.59303326
8	0.58200910	0.57124392	0.56070223	0.55037889
9	0.54393374	0.53262837	0.52158347	0.51079247
10	0.50834929	0.49662319	0.48519393	0.47405334
11	0.47509280	0.46305192	0.45134319	0.43995670
12	0.44401196	0.43175004	0.41985413	0.40831248
13	0.41496445	0.40256414	0.39056198	0.37894430
14	0.38781724	0.37535118	0.36331347	0.35168844
15	0.36244602	0.34997779	0.33796602	0.32639299
16	0.33873460	0.32631962	0.31438699	0.30291692
17	0.31657439	0.30426072	0.29245302	0.28112940
18	0.29586392	0.28369298	0.27204932	0.26090895
19	0.27650833	0.26451560	0.25306913	0.24214288
20	0.25841900	0.24663459	0.23541315	0.22472657
21	0.24151309	0.22996232	0.21898897	0.20856294
22	0.22571317	0.21441708	0.20371067	0.19356981
23	0.21094688	0.19992269	0.18949830	0.17963981
24	0.19714662	0.18640810	0.17627749	0.16671908
25	0.18424918	0.17380709	0.16397906	0.15472769
26	0.17219549	0.16205789	0.15253866	0.14359878
27	0.16093037	0.15110293	0.14189643	0.13327033
28	0.15040221	0.14088851	0.13199668	0.12368476
29	0.14056282	0.13136458	0.12278761	0.11478864
30	0.13136712	0.12248446	0.11422103	0.10653238
31	0.12277301	0.11420462	0.10625212	0.09886996
32	0.11474113	0.10648449	0.09883918	0.09175866
33	0.10723470	0.09928624	0.09194343	0.08515885
34	0.10021934	0.09257458	0.08552877	0.07903374
35	0.09366294	0.08631663	0.07956164	0.07334918
36	0.08753546	0.08048171	0.07401083	0.06807348
37	0.08180884	0.07504122	0.06884729	0.06317724
38	0.07645686	0.06996850	0.06404399	0.05863317
39	0.07145501	0.06523870	0.05957580	0.05441594
40	0.06678038	0.06082862	0.05541935	0.05050203
41	0.06241157	0.05671666	0.05155288	0.04686963
42	0.05832857	0.05288267	0.04795617	0.04349850
43	0.05451268	0.04930785	0.04461039	0.04036984
44	0.05094643	0.04597468	0.04149804	0.03746621
45	0.04761349	0.04286684	0.03860283	0.03477142
46	0.04449859	0.03996908	0.03590961	0.03227046
47	0.04158747	0.03726721	0.03340428	0.02994938
48	0.03886679	0.03474798	0.03107375	0.02779525
49	0.03632410	0.03239905	0.02890582	0.02579606
50	0.03394776	0.03020890	0.02688913	0.02394066

Rate i

Periods n	0.077(7%)	0.0725(7 1/4%)	0.075(7 1/2%)	0.0775(7 3/4%)
51	0.03172688	0.02816681	0.02501315	0.02221871
52	0.02965129	0.02626276	0.02326804	0.02062061
53	0.02771148	0.02448742	0.02164469	0.01913746
54	0.02589858	0.02283209	0.02013460	0.01776098
55	0.02420428	0.02128867	0.01872986	0.01648351
56	0.02262083	0.01984957	0.01742312	0.01529792
57	0.02114096	0.01850776	0.01620756	0.01419761
58	0.01975791	0.01725665	0.01507680	0.01317643
59	0.01846533	0.01609012	0.01402493	0.01222871
60	0.01725732	0.01500244	0.01304644	0.01134915
61	0.01612834	0.01398829	0.01213623	0.01053285
62	0.01507321	0.01304270	0.01128951	0.00977527
63	0.01408711	0.01216102	0.01050187	0.00907218
64	0.01316553	0.01133895	0.00976918	0.00841965
65	0.01230423	0.01057245	0.00908761	0.00781406
66	0.01149928	0.00985776	0.00845359	0.00725203
67	0.01074699	0.00919138	0.00786381	0.00673042
68	0.01004392	0.00857005	0.00731517	0.00624633
69	0.00938684	0.00799073	0.00680481	0.00579706
70	0.00877275	0.00745056	0.00633006	0.00538010
71	0.00819883	0.00694691	0.00588842	0.00499313
72	0.00766246	0.00647730	0.00547760	0.00463400
73	0.00716117	0.00603945	0.00509544	0.00430070
74	0.00669269	0.00563118	0.00473995	0.00399136
75	0.00625485	0.00525052	0.00440925	0.00370428
76	0.00584565	0.00489559	0.00410163	0.00343785
77	0.00546323	0.00456465	0.00381547	0.00319058
78	0.00510582	0.00425609	0.00354928	0.00296109
79	0.00477179	0.00396838	0.00330165	0.00274812
80	0.00445962	0.00370012	0.00307130	0.00255046
81	0.00416787	0.00345000	0.00285703	0.00236701
82	0.00389520	0.00321678	0.00265770	0.00219676
83	0.00364038	0.00299933	0.00247228	0.00203876
84	0.00340222	0.00279658	0.00229979	0.00189212
85	0.00317965	0.00260753	0.00213934	0.00175603
86	0.00297163	0.00243126	0.00199009	0.00162972
87	0.00277723	0.00226691	0.00185124	0.00151250
88	0.00259554	0.00211367	0.00172209	0.00140372
89	0.00242574	0.00197079	0.00160194	0.00130275
90	0.00226704	0.00183757	0.00149018	0.00120905
91	0.00211873	0.00171335	0.00138621	0.00112209
92	0.00198012	0.00159753	0.00128950	0.00104138
93	0.00185058	0.00148954	0.00119953	0.00096648
94	0.00172952	0.00138884	0.00111585	0.00089697
95	0.00161637	0.00129496	0.00103800	0.00083245
96	0.00151063	0.00120742	0.00096558	0.00077258
97	0.00141180	0.00112580	0.00089821	0.00071701
98	0.00131944	0.00104970	0.00083555	0.00066544
99	0.00123312	0.00097874	0.00077725	0.00061757
100	0.00115245	0.00091258	0.00072303	0.00057316

PRESENT VALUE $1/(1 + i)^n$ (Continued)

Rate i

Periods n	0.08(8%)	0.0825(8 1/4%)	0.085(8 1/2%)	0.0875(8 3/4%)
1	0.92592593	0.92378753	0.92165899	0.91954023
2	0.85733882	0.85338340	0.84945529	0.84555423
3	0.79383224	0.78834494	0.78290810	0.77752114
4	0.73502985	0.72826322	0.72157428	0.71496196
5	0.68058320	0.67276048	0.66504542	0.65743629
6	0.63016963	0.62148775	0.61294509	0.60453912
7	0.58349040	0.57412263	0.56492635	0.55589804
8	0.54026888	0.53036732	0.52066945	0.51117061
9	0.50024897	0.48994672	0.47987968	0.47004194
10	0.46319349	0.45260667	0.44228542	0.43222247
11	0.42888286	0.41811240	0.40763633	0.39744595
12	0.39711376	0.38624702	0.37570168	0.36546754
13	0.36769792	0.35681018	0.34626883	0.33606211
14	0.34046104	0.32961679	0.31914178	0.30902263
15	0.31524170	0.30449588	0.29413989	0.28415874
16	0.29189047	0.28128950	0.27109667	0.26129539
17	0.27026895	0.25985173	0.24985869	0.24027162
18	0.25004903	0.24004779	0.23028450	0.22093942
19	0.23171206	0.22175315	0.21224378	0.20316269
20	0.21454821	0.20485280	0.19561639	0.18681627
21	0.19865575	0.18924046	0.18029160	0.17178507
22	0.18394051	0.17481798	0.16616738	0.15796328
23	0.17031528	0.16149467	0.15314965	0.14525360
24	0.15769934	0.14918676	0.14115176	0.13356652
25	0.14601790	0.13781687	0.13009378	0.12281979
26	0.13520176	0.12731350	0.11990210	0.11293774
27	0.12518682	0.11761063	0.11050885	0.10385080
28	0.11591372	0.10864723	0.10185148	0.09549498
29	0.10732752	0.10036696	0.09387233	0.08781148
30	0.09937733	0.09271774	0.08651828	0.08074619
31	0.09201605	0.08565149	0.07974035	0.07424937
32	0.08520005	0.07912378	0.07349341	0.06827528
33	0.07888893	0.07309356	0.06773586	0.06278187
34	0.07304531	0.06752292	0.06242936	0.05773045
35	0.06763454	0.06237683	0.05753858	0.05308547
36	0.06262458	0.05762294	0.05303095	0.04881423
37	0.05798572	0.05323135	0.04887645	0.04488665
38	0.05369048	0.04917446	0.04504742	0.04127508
39	0.04971341	0.04542675	0.04151836	0.03795410
40	0.04603093	0.04196467	0.03826577	0.03490002
41	0.04262123	0.03876644	0.03526799	0.03209225
42	0.03946411	0.03581195	0.03250506	0.02951011
43	0.03654084	0.03308263	0.02995858	0.02713573
44	0.03383411	0.03056132	0.02761160	0.02495240
45	0.03132788	0.02823217	0.02544848	0.02294474
46	0.02900730	0.02608053	0.02345482	0.02109861
47	0.02685861	0.02409287	0.02161734	0.01940102
48	0.02486908	0.02225669	0.01992382	0.01784002
49	0.02302693	0.02056045	0.01836297	0.01640461
50	0.02132123	0.01899349	0.01693430	0.01508249

Rate i

Periods n	0.08(8%)	0.0825(8 1/4%)	0.085(8 1/2%)	0.0875(8 3/4%)
51	0.01974188	0.01754595	0.01559852	0.01387099
52	0.01827952	0.01620873	0.01437651	0.01275493
53	0.01692548	0.01497342	0.01325024	0.01172867
54	0.01567174	0.01383226	0.01221221	0.01078499
55	0.01451087	0.01277807	0.01125549	0.00991723
56	0.01343599	0.01180422	0.01037372	0.00911929
57	0.01244073	0.01090459	0.00956104	0.00838556
58	0.01151920	0.01007353	0.00881201	0.00771086
59	0.01066592	0.00930580	0.00812167	0.00709044
60	0.00987585	0.00859658	0.00748541	0.00651995
61	0.00914431	0.00794141	0.00689900	0.00599535
62	0.00846695	0.00733618	0.00635852	0.00551297
63	0.00783977	0.00677707	0.00586039	0.00506940
64	0.00725905	0.00626057	0.00540128	0.00466151
65	0.00672134	0.00578344	0.00497814	0.00428645
66	0.00622346	0.00534267	0.00458815	0.00394156
67	0.00576247	0.00493549	0.00422871	0.00362443
68	0.00533562	0.00455935	0.00389743	0.00333281
69	0.00494039	0.00421187	0.00359210	0.00306465
70	0.00457443	0.00389087	0.00331069	0.00281807
71	0.00423558	0.00359434	0.00305133	0.00259133
72	0.00392184	0.00332040	0.00281228	0.00238283
73	0.00363133	0.00306735	0.00259196	0.00219111
74	0.00336234	0.00283358	0.00238891	0.00201481
75	0.00311328	0.00261762	0.00220176	0.00185270
76	0.00288267	0.00241813	0.00202927	0.00170363
77	0.00266914	0.00223384	0.00187030	0.00156656
78	0.00247142	0.00206359	0.00172377	0.00144051
79	0.00228835	0.00190632	0.00158873	0.00132461
80	0.00211885	0.00176103	0.00146427	0.00121803
81	0.00196190	0.00162682	0.00134956	0.00112003
82	0.00181657	0.00150284	0.00124383	0.00102991
83	0.00168201	0.00138830	0.00114639	0.00094705
84	0.00155742	0.00128250	0.00105658	0.00087085
85	0.00144205	0.00118475	0.00097381	0.00080078
86	0.00133523	0.00109446	0.00089752	0.00073635
87	0.00123633	0.00101105	0.00082720	0.00067710
88	0.00114475	0.00093399	0.00076240	0.00062262
89	0.00105995	0.00086281	0.00070267	0.00057253
90	0.00098144	0.00079706	0.00064762	0.00052646
91	0.00090874	0.00073631	0.00059689	0.00048410
92	0.00084142	0.00068019	0.00055013	0.00044515
93	0.00077910	0.00062835	0.00050703	0.00040933
94	0.00072138	0.00058047	0.00046731	0.00037640
95	0.00066795	0.00053623	0.00043070	0.00034611
96	0.00061847	0.00049536	0.00039696	0.00031827
97	0.00057266	0.00045761	0.00036586	0.00029266
98	0.00053024	0.00042273	0.00033720	0.00026911
99	0.00049096	0.00039051	0.00031078	0.00024746

PRESENT VALUE 1/(1 + i)ⁿ (Continued)

Periods n = 1–50

Periods n	Rate i 0.09(9%)	0.0925(9 1/4%)	0.095(9 1/2%)	0.0975(9 3/4%)
1	0.91743119	0.91533181	0.91324201	0.91116173
2	0.84167999	0.83783232	0.83401570	0.83021570
3	0.77218348	0.76689457	0.76165385	0.75646077
4	0.70842521	0.70196299	0.69557429	0.68925811
5	0.64993139	0.64252906	0.63522767	0.62802561
6	0.59626733	0.58812728	0.58011659	0.57223362
7	0.54703424	0.53833161	0.52978684	0.52139672
8	0.50186628	0.49275204	0.48382360	0.47507674
9	0.46042778	0.45103162	0.44184803	0.43287175
10	0.42241081	0.41284359	0.40351419	0.39441617
11	0.38753285	0.37788887	0.36850611	0.35937692
12	0.35553473	0.34589370	0.33653626	0.32745050
13	0.32617865	0.31660751	0.30733813	0.29836036
14	0.29924647	0.28980092	0.28067410	0.27185454
15	0.27453804	0.26526400	0.25632337	0.24770346
16	0.25186976	0.24280458	0.23408527	0.22569791
17	0.23107318	0.22224675	0.21377651	0.20564730
18	0.21199374	0.20342952	0.19522969	0.18737795
19	0.19448967	0.18620551	0.17829195	0.17073162
20	0.17843089	0.17043983	0.16282370	0.15556411
21	0.16369806	0.15600900	0.14869744	0.14174407
22	0.15018171	0.14280000	0.13579675	0.12915177
23	0.13778139	0.13070938	0.12401530	0.11767815
24	0.12640494	0.11964245	0.11325598	0.10722383
25	0.11596784	0.10951254	0.10343012	0.09769825
26	0.10639251	0.10024031	0.09445673	0.08901891
27	0.09760781	0.09175315	0.08626185	0.08111062
28	0.08954845	0.08398457	0.07877795	0.07390489
29	0.08215454	0.07687375	0.07194333	0.06733931
30	0.07537114	0.07036499	0.06570167	0.06135700
31	0.06914783	0.06440731	0.06000153	0.05590615
32	0.06343838	0.05895406	0.05479592	0.05093955
33	0.05820035	0.05396253	0.05004193	0.04641417
34	0.05339481	0.04939362	0.04570039	0.04229081
35	0.04898607	0.04521155	0.04173552	0.03853377
36	0.04494135	0.04138557	0.03811463	0.03511050
37	0.04123059	0.03787970	0.03480788	0.03199134
38	0.03782623	0.03467249	0.03178802	0.02914928
39	0.03470296	0.03173684	0.02903015	0.02655971
40	0.03183758	0.02904973	0.02651156	0.02420019
41	0.02920879	0.02659015	0.02421147	0.02205029
42	0.02679706	0.02433881	0.02211093	0.02009138
43	0.02458446	0.02227808	0.02019263	0.01830650
44	0.02255455	0.02039184	0.01844076	0.01668018
45	0.02069224	0.01866530	0.01684087	0.01519834
46	0.01898371	0.01708494	0.01537979	0.01384815
47	0.01741625	0.01563839	0.01404547	0.01261790
48	0.01597821	0.01431432	0.01282692	0.01149695
49	0.01465891	0.01310235	0.01171408	0.01047558
50	0.01344854	0.01199300	0.01069779	0.00954495

Periods n = 51–100

Periods n	Rate i 0.09(9%)	0.0925(9 1/4%)	0.095(9 1/2%)	0.0975(9 3/4%)
51	0.01233811	0.01097757	0.00976967	0.00869699
52	0.01131937	0.01004882	0.00892207	0.00792437
53	0.01038474	0.00919736	0.00814801	0.00722038
54	0.00952728	0.00841864	0.00744111	0.00657893
55	0.00874063	0.00770585	0.00679553	0.00599447
56	0.00801892	0.00705341	0.00620597	0.00546193
57	0.00735681	0.00645621	0.00566755	0.00497670
58	0.00674937	0.00590957	0.00517584	0.00453458
59	0.00619208	0.00540922	0.00472680	0.00413174
60	0.00568081	0.00495123	0.00431671	0.00376468
61	0.00521175	0.00453202	0.00394220	0.00343023
62	0.00478142	0.00414830	0.00360018	0.00312550
63	0.00438663	0.00379707	0.00328784	0.00284783
64	0.00402443	0.00347558	0.00300259	0.00259484
65	0.00369214	0.00318131	0.00274209	0.00236432
66	0.00338728	0.00291195	0.00250419	0.00215427
67	0.00310760	0.00266540	0.00228694	0.00196289
68	0.00285101	0.00243973	0.00208853	0.00178851
69	0.00261560	0.00223316	0.00190733	0.00162962
70	0.00239963	0.00204408	0.00174185	0.00148485
71	0.00220150	0.00187102	0.00159073	0.00135294
72	0.00201972	0.00171260	0.00145273	0.00123275
73	0.00185296	0.00156760	0.00132669	0.00112323
74	0.00169996	0.00143487	0.00121159	0.00102345
75	0.00155960	0.00131338	0.00110647	0.00093252
76	0.00143082	0.00120218	0.00101048	0.00084968
77	0.00131268	0.00110040	0.00092281	0.00077420
78	0.00120430	0.00100723	0.00084275	0.00070542
79	0.00110486	0.00092195	0.00076963	0.00064275
80	0.00101363	0.00084389	0.00070286	0.00058565
81	0.00092994	0.00077244	0.00064188	0.00053362
82	0.00085315	0.00070704	0.00058620	0.00048622
83	0.00078271	0.00064717	0.00053534	0.00044302
84	0.00071808	0.00059238	0.00048889	0.00040366
85	0.00065879	0.00054222	0.00044648	0.00036780
86	0.00060440	0.00049631	0.00040774	0.00033513
87	0.00055449	0.00045429	0.00037237	0.00030536
88	0.00050871	0.00041583	0.00034006	0.00027823
89	0.00046670	0.00038062	0.00031056	0.00025351
90	0.00042817	0.00034839	0.00028362	0.00023099
91	0.00039282	0.00031890	0.00025901	0.00021047
92	0.00036038	0.00029190	0.00023654	0.00019177
93	0.00033063	0.00026718	0.00021602	0.00017473
94	0.00030333	0.00024456	0.00019728	0.00015921
95	0.00027828	0.00022385	0.00018016	0.00014507
96	0.00025530	0.00020490	0.00016453	0.00013218
97	0.00023422	0.00018755	0.00015026	0.00012044
98	0.00021488	0.00017167	0.00013722	0.00010974
99	0.00019714	0.00015714	0.00012531	0.00009999
100	0.00018086	0.00014383	0.00011444	0.00009111

PRESENT VALUE $1/(1+i)^n$ (Continued)

Periods 51–100 — Rate i

0.1075 (10 3/4%)	0.105 (10 1/2%)	0.1025 (10 1/4%)	0.10 (10%)	Periods n
0.00547608	0.00614503	0.00689750	0.00774414	51
0.00494454	0.00556111	0.00625623	0.00704013	52
0.00446459	0.00503268	0.00567459	0.00640011	53
0.00403124	0.00455446	0.00514702	0.00581829	54
0.00363994	0.00412168	0.00466850	0.00528935	55
0.00328663	0.00373003	0.00423446	0.00480850	56
0.00296761	0.00337559	0.00384078	0.00437136	57
0.00267956	0.00305484	0.00348370	0.00397397	58
0.00241947	0.00276456	0.00315982	0.00361270	59
0.00218462	0.00250186	0.00286605	0.00328427	60
0.00197257	0.00226413	0.00259959	0.00298570	61
0.00178110	0.00204898	0.00235791	0.00271427	62
0.00160822	0.00185428	0.00213869	0.00246752	63
0.00145211	0.00167809	0.00193986	0.00224320	64
0.00131116	0.00151863	0.00175951	0.00203927	65
0.00118390	0.00137433	0.00159593	0.00185388	66
0.00106898	0.00124373	0.00144755	0.00168535	67
0.00096522	0.00112555	0.00131297	0.00153214	68
0.00087153	0.00101860	0.00119090	0.00139285	69
0.00078693	0.00092181	0.00108018	0.00126623	70
0.00071055	0.00083422	0.00097929	0.00115112	71
0.00064158	0.00075495	0.00088867	0.00104647	72
0.00057931	0.00068321	0.00080605	0.00095134	73
0.00052307	0.00061829	0.00073111	0.00086485	74
0.00047230	0.00055954	0.00066314	0.00078623	75
0.00042646	0.00050637	0.00060149	0.00071475	76
0.00038506	0.00045825	0.00054557	0.00064978	77
0.00034769	0.00041471	0.00049485	0.00059070	78
0.00031394	0.00037530	0.00044884	0.00053700	79
0.00028347	0.00033964	0.00040711	0.00048819	80
0.00025595	0.00030737	0.00036926	0.00044381	81
0.00023111	0.00027816	0.00033493	0.00040346	82
0.00020867	0.00025173	0.00030379	0.00036678	83
0.00018842	0.00022781	0.00027555	0.00033344	84
0.00017013	0.00020616	0.00024993	0.00030313	85
0.00015362	0.00018657	0.00022669	0.00027557	86
0.00013871	0.00016884	0.00020562	0.00025052	87
0.00012524	0.00015280	0.00018650	0.00022774	88
0.00011309	0.00013828	0.00016916	0.00020704	89
0.00010211	0.00012514	0.00015344	0.00018822	90
0.00009220	0.00011325	0.00013917	0.00017111	91
0.00008325	0.00010249	0.00012623	0.00015555	92
0.00007517	0.00009275	0.00011450	0.00014141	93
0.00006787	0.00008394	0.00010385	0.00012855	94
0.00006128	0.00007596	0.00009420	0.00011687	95
0.00005534	0.00006874	0.00008544	0.00010624	96
0.00004996	0.00006221	0.00007750	0.00009658	97
0.00004511	0.00005630	0.00007029	0.00008780	98
0.00004074	0.00005095	0.00006376	0.00007982	99
				100

Periods 1–50 — Rate i

Periods n	0.10 (10%)	0.1025 (10 1/4%)	0.105 (10 1/2%)	0.1075 (10 3/4%)
1	0.90909091	0.90702948	0.90497738	0.90293454
2	0.82644628	0.82270247	0.81898405	0.81529078
3	0.75131480	0.74621540	0.74116204	0.73616204
4	0.68301346	0.67683936	0.67073487	0.66469905
5	0.62092132	0.61391325	0.60699989	0.60017973
6	0.56447393	0.55683742	0.54932116	0.54192301
7	0.51315812	0.50506795	0.49712323	0.48932100
8	0.46650738	0.45811152	0.44988527	0.44182483
9	0.42409762	0.41552065	0.40713599	0.39893890
10	0.38554329	0.37688948	0.36844886	0.36021571
11	0.35049390	0.34184987	0.33343788	0.32525121
12	0.31863082	0.31006791	0.30175374	0.29368055
13	0.28966438	0.28124073	0.27308031	0.26517431
14	0.26333125	0.25509364	0.24713150	0.23943504
15	0.23939205	0.23137745	0.22364842	0.21619417
16	0.21762914	0.20986617	0.20239676	0.19520918
17	0.19784467	0.19035480	0.18316449	0.17626111
18	0.17985879	0.17265741	0.16575972	0.15915225
19	0.16350799	0.15660536	0.15000879	0.14370406
20	0.14864363	0.14204568	0.13575456	0.12975536
21	0.13513057	0.12883962	0.12285481	0.11716059
22	0.12284597	0.11686133	0.11118082	0.10578835
23	0.11167816	0.10599668	0.10061613	0.09551995
24	0.10152560	0.09614211	0.09105532	0.08624826
25	0.09229600	0.08720373	0.08240301	0.07787654
26	0.08390545	0.07909635	0.07457286	0.07031741
27	0.07627768	0.07174272	0.06748675	0.06349202
28	0.06934335	0.06507276	0.06107398	0.05732914
29	0.06303941	0.05902291	0.05527057	0.05176446
30	0.05730855	0.05353552	0.05001861	0.04673992
31	0.05209868	0.04855830	0.04526571	0.04220309
32	0.04736244	0.04404381	0.04096445	0.03810662
33	0.04305676	0.03994903	0.03707190	0.03440779
34	0.03914251	0.03623495	0.03354923	0.03106798
35	0.03558410	0.03286617	0.03036129	0.02805235
36	0.03234918	0.02981058	0.02747628	0.02532944
37	0.02940835	0.02703908	0.02486542	0.02287082
38	0.02673486	0.02452524	0.02250264	0.02065086
39	0.02430442	0.02224512	0.02036438	0.01864637
40	0.02209493	0.02017698	0.01842930	0.01683645
41	0.02008630	0.01830111	0.01667810	0.01520221
42	0.01826027	0.01659965	0.01509330	0.01372660
43	0.01660025	0.01505637	0.01365910	0.01239423
44	0.01509113	0.01365557	0.01236118	0.01119117
45	0.01371921	0.01238691	0.01118658	0.01010490
46	0.01247201	0.01123530	0.01012361	0.00912406
47	0.01133819	0.01019074	0.00916163	0.00823843
48	0.01030745	0.00924331	0.00829107	0.00743876
49	0.00937041	0.00838395	0.00750323	0.00671672
50	0.00851855	0.00760449		

PRESENT VALUE $1/(1 + i)^n$ (Continued)

Rate i

0.1175(11 3/4%)	0.115(11 1/2%)	0.1125(11 1/4%)	0.11(11%)	Periods n
0.00346239	0.00388134	0.00435210	0.00488122	51
0.00309833	0.00348102	0.00391200	0.00439749	52
0.00277256	0.00312199	0.00351641	0.00396170	53
0.00248104	0.00279999	0.00316081	0.00356910	54
0.00222017	0.00251121	0.00284118	0.00321541	55
0.00198673	0.00225220	0.00255387	0.00289676	56
0.00177783	0.00201991	0.00229561	0.00260970	57
0.00159090	0.00181158	0.00206347	0.00235108	58
0.00142363	0.00162474	0.00185481	0.00211809	59
0.00127394	0.00145716	0.00166724	0.00190819	60
0.00113999	0.00130687	0.00149865	0.00171909	61
0.00102012	0.00117208	0.00134710	0.00154873	62
0.00091286	0.00105120	0.00121087	0.00139525	63
0.00081688	0.00094278	0.00108843	0.00125698	64
0.00073099	0.00084554	0.00097836	0.00113242	65
0.00065413	0.00075833	0.00087942	0.00102020	66
0.00058535	0.00068012	0.00079049	0.00091910	67
0.00052380	0.00060997	0.00071056	0.00082801	68
0.00046873	0.00054706	0.00063870	0.00074596	69
0.00041944	0.00049064	0.00057411	0.00067203	70
0.00037534	0.00044003	0.00051606	0.00060544	71
0.00033588	0.00039465	0.00046387	0.00054544	72
0.00030056	0.00035394	0.00041696	0.00049139	73
0.00026896	0.00031744	0.00037480	0.00044269	74
0.00024068	0.00028470	0.00033690	0.00039882	75
0.00021537	0.00025533	0.00030283	0.00035930	76
0.00019273	0.00022900	0.00027221	0.00032369	77
0.00017246	0.00020538	0.00024468	0.00029161	78
0.00015433	0.00018420	0.00021994	0.00026271	79
0.00013810	0.00016520	0.00019770	0.00023668	80
0.00012358	0.00014816	0.00017770	0.00021323	81
0.00011059	0.00013288	0.00015973	0.00019209	82
0.00009896	0.00011918	0.00014358	0.00017306	83
0.00008855	0.00010688	0.00012906	0.00015591	84
0.00007924	0.00009586	0.00011601	0.00014046	85
0.00007091	0.00008597	0.00010428	0.00012654	86
0.00006345	0.00007711	0.00009373	0.00011400	87
0.00005678	0.00006915	0.00008426	0.00010270	88
0.00005081	0.00006202	0.00007574	0.00009252	89
0.00004547	0.00005562	0.00006808	0.00008336	90
0.00004069	0.00004989	0.00006119	0.00007509	91
0.00003641	0.00004474	0.00005500	0.00006765	92
0.00003258	0.00004013	0.00004944	0.00006095	93
0.00002916	0.00003599	0.00004444	0.00005491	94
0.00002609	0.00003228	0.00003995	0.00004947	95
0.00002335	0.00002895	0.00003591	0.00004457	96
0.00002089	0.00002596	0.00003228	0.00004015	97
0.00001870	0.00002328	0.00002901	0.00003617	98
0.00001673	0.00002088	0.00002608	0.00003259	99
0.00001497	0.00001873	0.00002344	0.00002936	100

Rate i

Periods n	0.11(11%)	0.1125(11 1/4%)	0.115(11 1/2%)	0.1175(11 3/4%)
1	0.90090090	0.89887640	0.89686099	0.89485459
2	0.81162243	0.80797879	0.80435963	0.80076473
3	0.73119138	0.72627307	0.72139877	0.71656799
4	0.65873097	0.65282973	0.64699441	0.64122415
5	0.59345133	0.58681324	0.58026405	0.57380237
6	0.53464084	0.52747257	0.52041619	0.51346969
7	0.48165841	0.47413265	0.46674097	0.45948070
8	0.43392650	0.42618665	0.41860177	0.41116841
9	0.39092477	0.38308912	0.37542760	0.36793594
10	0.35218448	0.34434977	0.33670636	0.32924916
11	0.31728331	0.30952789	0.30197880	0.29463013
12	0.28584082	0.27822731	0.27083301	0.26365112
13	0.25751426	0.25009197	0.24289956	0.23592941
14	0.23199482	0.22480177	0.21784714	0.21112252
15	0.20900435	0.20206901	0.19537860	0.18892395
16	0.18829220	0.18163506	0.17522744	0.16905947
17	0.16963262	0.16326747	0.15715466	0.15128364
18	0.15282218	0.14675728	0.14094588	0.13537686
19	0.13767764	0.13191665	0.12640886	0.12114260
20	0.12403391	0.11857677	0.11337118	0.10840501
21	0.11174226	0.10658586	0.10167818	0.09700672
22	0.10066870	0.09580751	0.09119120	0.08680691
23	0.09069252	0.08611911	0.08177583	0.07767956
24	0.08170498	0.07741044	0.07335052	0.06951191
25	0.07360809	0.06958242	0.06578522	0.06220305
26	0.06631359	0.06254599	0.05900020	0.05566269
27	0.05974197	0.05622112	0.05291497	0.04981001
28	0.05382160	0.05053584	0.04745738	0.04457272
29	0.04848793	0.04542547	0.04256267	0.03988610
30	0.04368282	0.04083188	0.03817280	0.03569226
31	0.03935389	0.03670282	0.03423569	0.03193938
32	0.03545395	0.03299130	0.03070466	0.02858110
33	0.03194050	0.02965510	0.02753781	0.02557593
34	0.02877522	0.02665627	0.02469759	0.02288674
35	0.02592363	0.02396069	0.02215030	0.02048030
36	0.02335462	0.02153770	0.01986574	0.01832689
37	0.02104020	0.01935973	0.01781681	0.01639990
38	0.01895513	0.01740200	0.01597920	0.01467553
39	0.01707670	0.01564225	0.01433112	0.01313247
40	0.01538441	0.01406045	0.01285302	0.01175165
41	0.01385983	0.01263861	0.01152738	0.01051601
42	0.01248633	0.01136055	0.01033845	0.00941030
43	0.01124895	0.01021173	0.00927216	0.00842085
44	0.01013419	0.00917908	0.00831583	0.00753544
45	0.00912990	0.00825086	0.00745815	0.00674312
46	0.00822513	0.00741650	0.00668892	0.00603411
47	0.00741003	0.00666652	0.00599903	0.00539965
48	0.00667570	0.00599238	0.00538030	0.00483191
49	0.00601415	0.00538641	0.00482538	0.00432385
50	0.00541815	0.00484171	0.00432769	0.00386922

FINANCIAL TABLES

PRESENT VALUE $1/(1 + i)^n$ (Continued)

Rate i

Periods n	0.12(12%)	0.1225(12 1/4%)	0.125(12 1/2%)	0.1275(12 3/4%)
1	0.89285714	0.89086860	0.88888889	0.88691796
2	0.79719388	0.79364686	0.79012346	0.78662347
3	0.71178025	0.70703506	0.70233196	0.69767048
4	0.63551808	0.62987533	0.62429508	0.61877648
5	0.56742686	0.56113615	0.55492896	0.54880397
6	0.50663112	0.49989858	0.49327018	0.48674410
7	0.45234922	0.44534395	0.43846239	0.43170208
8	0.40388323	0.39674294	0.38974434	0.38288433
9	0.36061002	0.35344582	0.34643942	0.33958699
10	0.32197324	0.31487378	0.30794615	0.30118580
11	0.28747610	0.28051117	0.27372991	0.26712710
12	0.25667509	0.24989859	0.24331547	0.23691982
13	0.22917419	0.22262681	0.21628042	0.21012844
14	0.20461981	0.19833123	0.19224926	0.18636669
15	0.18269626	0.17668706	0.17088823	0.16529196
16	0.16312166	0.15740496	0.15190065	0.14660041
17	0.14564434	0.14022713	0.13502280	0.13002254
18	0.13003959	0.12492395	0.12002027	0.11531932
19	0.11610678	0.11129082	0.10668468	0.10227878
20	0.10366677	0.09914550	0.09483083	0.09071289
21	0.09255961	0.08832561	0.08429407	0.08045489
22	0.08264251	0.07868651	0.07492806	0.07135689
23	0.07378796	0.07009934	0.06660272	0.06328770
24	0.06588210	0.06244930	0.05920242	0.05613100
25	0.05882331	0.05563412	0.05262437	0.04978359
26	0.05252081	0.04956269	0.04677722	0.04415396
27	0.04689358	0.04415385	0.04157975	0.03916094
28	0.04186927	0.03933528	0.03695978	0.03473254
29	0.03738327	0.03504256	0.03285314	0.03080492
30	0.03337792	0.03121832	0.02920279	0.02732143
31	0.02980172	0.02781142	0.02595803	0.02423187
32	0.02660868	0.02477632	0.02307381	0.02149168
33	0.02375775	0.02207245	0.02051005	0.01906136
34	0.02121227	0.01966365	0.01823116	0.01690586
35	0.01893953	0.01751773	0.01620547	0.01499411
36	0.01691029	0.01560599	0.01440486	0.01329855
37	0.01509848	0.01390289	0.01280432	0.01179472
38	0.01348078	0.01238565	0.01138162	0.01046095
39	0.01203641	0.01103398	0.01011700	0.00927800
40	0.01074680	0.00982983	0.00899289	0.00822883
41	0.00959536	0.00875709	0.00799368	0.00729830
42	0.00856728	0.00780141	0.00710549	0.00647299
43	0.00764936	0.00695003	0.00631599	0.00574101
44	0.00682978	0.00619157	0.00561421	0.00509181
45	0.00609802	0.00551587	0.00499041	0.00451601
46	0.00544466	0.00491392	0.00443592	0.00400533
47	0.00486131	0.00437766	0.00394304	0.00355240
48	0.00434045	0.00389992	0.00350493	0.00315069
49	0.00387540	0.00347431	0.00311549	0.00279440
50	0.00346018	0.00309516	0.00276932	0.00247841

Rate i

Periods n	0.12(12%)	0.1225(12 1/4%)	0.125(12 1/2%)	0.1275(12 3/4%)
51	0.00308945	0.00275738	0.00246162	0.00219814
52	0.00275844	0.00245646	0.00218811	0.00194957
53	0.00246289	0.00218838	0.00194499	0.00172911
54	0.00219901	0.00194956	0.00172888	0.00153358
55	0.00196340	0.00173680	0.00153678	0.00136016
56	0.00175304	0.00154726	0.00136603	0.00120635
57	0.00156521	0.00137841	0.00121424	0.00106993
58	0.00139751	0.00122798	0.00107933	0.00094894
59	0.00124778	0.00109397	0.00095940	0.00084163
60	0.00111409	0.00097458	0.00085280	0.00074646
61	0.00099472	0.00086823	0.00075805	0.00066205
62	0.00088814	0.00077348	0.00067382	0.00058718
63	0.00079298	0.00068906	0.00059895	0.00052078
64	0.00070802	0.00061387	0.00053240	0.00046189
65	0.00063216	0.00054687	0.00047325	0.00040966
66	0.00056443	0.00048719	0.00042066	0.00036334
67	0.00050396	0.00043402	0.00037392	0.00032225
68	0.00044996	0.00038666	0.00033238	0.00028581
69	0.00040175	0.00034446	0.00029544	0.00025349
70	0.00035871	0.00030687	0.00026262	0.00022482
71	0.00032027	0.00027338	0.00023344	0.00019940
72	0.00028596	0.00024355	0.00020750	0.00017685
73	0.00025532	0.00021697	0.00018444	0.00015685
74	0.00022796	0.00019329	0.00016395	0.00013912
75	0.00020354	0.00017220	0.00014573	0.00012338
76	0.00018173	0.00015340	0.00012954	0.00010943
77	0.00016226	0.00013666	0.00011515	0.00009706
78	0.00014488	0.00012175	0.00010235	0.00008608
79	0.00012935	0.00010846	0.00009098	0.00007635
80	0.00011549	0.00009663	0.00008087	0.00006771
81	0.00010312	0.00008608	0.00007189	0.00006006
82	0.00009207	0.00007669	0.00006390	0.00005327
83	0.00008221	0.00006832	0.00005680	0.00004724
84	0.00007340	0.00006086	0.00005049	0.00004190
85	0.00006553	0.00005422	0.00004488	0.00003716
86	0.00005851	0.00004830	0.00003989	0.00003296
87	0.00005224	0.00004303	0.00003546	0.00002923
88	0.00004665	0.00003834	0.00003152	0.00002593
89	0.00004165	0.00003415	0.00002802	0.00002299
90	0.00003719	0.00003042	0.00002490	0.00002039
91	0.00003320	0.00002710	0.00002214	0.00001809
92	0.00002964	0.00002415	0.00001968	0.00001604
93	0.00002647	0.00002151	0.00001749	0.00001423
94	0.00002363	0.00001916	0.00001555	0.00001262
95	0.00002110	0.00001707	0.00001382	0.00001119
96	0.00001884	0.00001521	0.00001228	0.00000993
97	0.00001682	0.00001355	0.00001092	0.00000880
98	0.00001502	0.00001207	0.00000971	0.00000781
99	0.00001341	0.00001075	0.00000863	0.00000693
100	0.00001197			

Rate i

Periods n	0.13(13%)	0.1325(13 1/4%)	0.135(13 1/2%)	0.1375(13 3/4%)
1	0.88495575	0.88300221	0.88105727	0.87912088
2	0.78314668	0.77969290	0.77626191	0.77285352
3	0.69305016	0.68847055	0.68393120	0.67943167
4	0.61331873	0.60792102	0.60258255	0.59730256
5	0.54275994	0.53679560	0.53090974	0.52510115
6	0.48031853	0.47399170	0.46776188	0.46162739
7	0.42506064	0.41853572	0.41212501	0.40582628
8	0.37615986	0.36956796	0.36310573	0.35677035
9	0.33288483	0.32632933	0.31991695	0.31364427
10	0.29458835	0.28814952	0.28186515	0.27573122
11	0.26069765	0.25443666	0.24833934	0.24240107
12	0.23070589	0.22466813	0.21880118	0.21309985
13	0.20416450	0.19838246	0.19277637	0.18734052
14	0.18067655	0.17517215	0.16984702	0.16469497
15	0.15989075	0.15467739	0.14964495	0.14478678
16	0.14149624	0.13658048	0.13184577	0.12728508
17	0.12521791	0.12060086	0.11616368	0.11189898
18	0.11081231	0.10649083	0.10234685	0.09837273
19	0.09806399	0.09403164	0.09017344	0.08648152
20	0.08678229	0.08303014	0.07944796	0.07602771
21	0.07679849	0.07331580	0.06999821	0.06683754
22	0.06796327	0.06473801	0.06167243	0.05875828
23	0.06014448	0.05716381	0.05433694	0.05165563
24	0.05322521	0.05047577	0.04787396	0.04541154
25	0.04710195	0.04457022	0.04217970	0.03992224
26	0.04168314	0.03935560	0.03716273	0.03509647
27	0.03688774	0.03475108	0.03274249	0.03085404
28	0.03264402	0.03068528	0.02884801	0.02712443
29	0.02888851	0.02709517	0.02541675	0.02384565
30	0.02556505	0.02392510	0.02239361	0.02096321
31	0.02262394	0.02112591	0.01973005	0.01842920
32	0.02002119	0.01865423	0.01738331	0.01620149
33	0.01771786	0.01647172	0.01531569	0.01424307
34	0.01567953	0.01454457	0.01349400	0.01252138
35	0.01387569	0.01284289	0.01188899	0.01100781
36	0.01227937	0.01134030	0.01047488	0.00967719
37	0.01086670	0.01001351	0.00922897	0.00850742
38	0.00961655	0.00884195	0.00813125	0.00747905
39	0.00851022	0.00780746	0.00716410	0.00657499
40	0.00753117	0.00689400	0.00631198	0.00578021
41	0.00666475	0.00608742	0.00556121	0.00508151
42	0.00589801	0.00537521	0.00489975	0.00446726
43	0.00521948	0.00474632	0.00431696	0.00392726
44	0.00461901	0.00419101	0.00380349	0.00345254
45	0.00408762	0.00370067	0.00335109	0.00303520
46	0.00361736	0.00326770	0.00295250	0.00266830
47	0.00320120	0.00288539	0.00260132	0.00234576
48	0.00283292	0.00254780	0.00229192	0.00206221
49	0.00250701	0.00224972	0.00201931	0.00181293
50	0.00221859	0.00198650	0.00177913	0.00159378

Rate i

Periods n	0.13(13%)	0.1325(13 1/4%)	0.135(13 1/2%)	0.1375(13 3/4%)
51	0.00196336	0.00175409	0.00156751	0.00140113
52	0.00173748	0.00154886	0.00138107	0.00123176
53	0.00153760	0.00136765	0.00121680	0.00108287
54	0.00136071	0.00120764	0.00107207	0.00095197
55	0.00120416	0.00106635	0.00094456	0.00083690
56	0.00106563	0.00094159	0.00083221	0.00073573
57	0.00094304	0.00083142	0.00073322	0.00064680
58	0.00083455	0.00073415	0.00064601	0.00056862
59	0.00073854	0.00064825	0.00056917	0.00049988
60	0.00065357	0.00057241	0.00050147	0.00043946
61	0.00057838	0.00050544	0.00044183	0.00038634
62	0.00051184	0.00044630	0.00038928	0.00033964
63	0.00045296	0.00039409	0.00034297	0.00029858
64	0.00040085	0.00034798	0.00030218	0.00026249
65	0.00035473	0.00030727	0.00026624	0.00023076
66	0.00031392	0.00027132	0.00023457	0.00020287
67	0.00027781	0.00023957	0.00020667	0.00017834
68	0.00024585	0.00021154	0.00018209	0.00015678
69	0.00021756	0.00018679	0.00016043	0.00013783
70	0.00019253	0.00016494	0.00014135	0.00012117
71	0.00017038	0.00014564	0.00012454	0.00010652
72	0.00015078	0.00012860	0.00010972	0.00009365
73	0.00013344	0.00011356	0.00009667	0.00008233
74	0.00011809	0.00010027	0.00008517	0.00007238
75	0.00010450	0.00008854	0.00007504	0.00006363
76	0.00009248	0.00007818	0.00006612	0.00005594
77	0.00008184	0.00006903	0.00005825	0.00004917
78	0.00007242	0.00006096	0.00005132	0.00004323
79	0.00006409	0.00005382	0.00004522	0.00003800
80	0.00005672	0.00004753	0.00003984	0.00003341
81	0.00005019	0.00004197	0.00003510	0.00002937
82	0.00004442	0.00003706	0.00003093	0.00002582
83	0.00003931	0.00003272	0.00002725	0.00002270
84	0.00003479	0.00002889	0.00002401	0.00001996
85	0.00003078	0.00002551	0.00002115	0.00001754
86	0.00002724	0.00002253	0.00001864	0.00001542
87	0.00002411	0.00001989	0.00001642	0.00001356
88	0.00002134	0.00001756	0.00001447	0.00001192
89	0.00001888	0.00001551	0.00001275	0.00001048
90	0.00001671	0.00001369	0.00001123	0.00000921
91	0.00001479	0.00001209	0.00000989	0.00000810
92	0.00001309	0.00001068	0.00000872	0.00000712
93	0.00001158	0.00000943	0.00000768	0.00000626
94	0.00001025	0.00000833	0.00000677	0.00000550
95	0.00000907	0.00000735	0.00000596	0.00000484
96	0.00000803	0.00000649	0.00000525	0.00000425
97	0.00000710	0.00000573	0.00000463	0.00000374
98	0.00000629	0.00000506	0.00000408	0.00000329
99	0.00000556	0.00000447	0.00000359	0.00000289
100	0.00000492	0.00000395	0.00000317	0.00000254

PRESENT VALUE $1/(1 + i)^n$ (Continued)

Rate i

Periods n	0.14(14%)	0.1425(14 1/4%)	0.145(14 1/2%)	0.1475(14 3/4%)
1	0.87719298	0.87527352	0.87336245	0.87145969
2	0.76946753	0.76610374	0.76276196	0.75944200
3	0.67497152	0.67055032	0.66616765	0.66182309
4	0.59208028	0.58691494	0.58180581	0.57675215
5	0.51936866	0.51371111	0.50812734	0.50261625
6	0.45558655	0.44963773	0.44377934	0.43800981
7	0.39963732	0.39355600	0.38758021	0.38170789
8	0.35055905	0.34446915	0.33849800	0.33264304
9	0.30750794	0.30150472	0.29563144	0.28988501
10	0.26974381	0.26389910	0.25819340	0.25262310
11	0.23661738	0.23098390	0.22549642	0.22015085
12	0.20755910	0.20217409	0.19694010	0.19185259
13	0.18206939	0.17695763	0.17200009	0.16719180
14	0.15970999	0.15488633	0.15021842	0.14570092
15	0.14009648	0.13556790	0.13119513	0.12697248
16	0.12289165	0.11865899	0.11458090	0.11065139
17	0.10779969	0.10385908	0.10007065	0.09643823
18	0.09456113	0.09090510	0.08739795	0.08403332
19	0.08294836	0.07956683	0.07633009	0.07323165
20	0.07276172	0.06964274	0.06666383	0.06381843
21	0.06382607	0.06095644	0.05822169	0.05561519
22	0.05598778	0.05335356	0.05084863	0.04846640
23	0.04911209	0.04669896	0.04440929	0.04223651
24	0.04308078	0.04087436	0.03878540	0.03680742
25	0.03779016	0.03577625	0.03387372	0.03207618
26	0.03314926	0.03131400	0.02958403	0.02795310
27	0.02907830	0.02740832	0.02583758	0.02436000
28	0.02550728	0.02398977	0.02256557	0.02122876
29	0.02237481	0.02099761	0.01970792	0.01850001
30	0.01962702	0.01837866	0.01721216	0.01612201
31	0.01721669	0.01608635	0.01503246	0.01404968
32	0.01510236	0.01407996	0.01312878	0.01224373
33	0.01324768	0.01232381	0.01146618	0.01066992
34	0.01162077	0.01078671	0.01001414	0.00929840
35	0.01019366	0.00944132	0.00874597	0.00810318
36	0.00894181	0.00826374	0.00763840	0.00706160
37	0.00784369	0.00723303	0.00667109	0.00615390
38	0.00688043	0.00633088	0.00582628	0.00536287
39	0.00603547	0.00554125	0.00508846	0.00467353
40	0.00529427	0.00485011	0.00444407	0.00407279
41	0.00464410	0.00424517	0.00388128	0.00354927
42	0.00407377	0.00371569	0.00338976	0.00309305
43	0.00357348	0.00325224	0.00296049	0.00269547
44	0.00313463	0.00284660	0.00258558	0.00234899
45	0.00274968	0.00249156	0.00225815	0.00204705
46	0.00241200	0.00218079	0.00197218	0.00178392
47	0.00211579	0.00190879	0.00172243	0.00155462
48	0.00185595	0.00167071	0.00150431	0.00135479
49	0.00162803	0.00146233	0.00131381	0.00118064

Rate i

Periods n	0.14(14%)	0.1425(14 1/4%)	0.145(14 1/2%)	0.1475(14 3/4%)
51	0.00125272	0.00112030	0.00100212	0.00089663
52	0.00109887	0.00098057	0.00087521	0.00078138
53	0.00096392	0.00085826	0.00076438	0.00068094
54	0.00084555	0.00075122	0.00066758	0.00059341
55	0.00074171	0.00065752	0.00058304	0.00051713
56	0.00065062	0.00057551	0.00050921	0.00045066
57	0.00057057	0.00050373	0.00044472	0.00039273
58	0.00050063	0.00044090	0.00038840	0.00034225
59	0.00043915	0.00038591	0.00033922	0.00029826
60	0.00038522	0.00033777	0.00029626	0.00025992
61	0.00033791	0.00029565	0.00025874	0.00022651
62	0.00029641	0.00025877	0.00022597	0.00019739
63	0.00026001	0.00022650	0.00019736	0.00017202
64	0.00022808	0.00019825	0.00017236	0.00014991
65	0.00020007	0.00017352	0.00015054	0.00013064
66	0.00017550	0.00015188	0.00013147	0.00011385
67	0.00015395	0.00013293	0.00011482	0.00009921
68	0.00013504	0.00011635	0.00010028	0.00008646
69	0.00011846	0.00010184	0.00008758	0.00007535
70	0.00010391	0.00008914	0.00007649	0.00006566
71	0.00009115	0.00007802	0.00006681	0.00005722
72	0.00007996	0.00006829	0.00005835	0.00004987
73	0.00007014	0.00005977	0.00005096	0.00004346
74	0.00006152	0.00005232	0.00004450	0.00003787
75	0.00005397	0.00004579	0.00003887	0.00003300
76	0.00004734	0.00004008	0.00003395	0.00002876
77	0.00004153	0.00003508	0.00002965	0.00002506
78	0.00003643	0.00003071	0.00002589	0.00002184
79	0.00003195	0.00002688	0.00002261	0.00001903
80	0.00002803	0.00002352	0.00001975	0.00001659
81	0.00002459	0.00002059	0.00001725	0.00001446
82	0.00002157	0.00001802	0.00001506	0.00001260
83	0.00001892	0.00001577	0.00001316	0.00001098
84	0.00001660	0.00001381	0.00001149	0.00000957
85	0.00001456	0.00001208	0.00001004	0.00000834
86	0.00001277	0.00001058	0.00000876	0.00000727
87	0.00001120	0.00000926	0.00000765	0.00000633
88	0.00000983	0.00000810	0.00000669	0.00000552
89	0.00000862	0.00000709	0.00000584	0.00000481
90	0.00000756	0.00000621	0.00000510	0.00000419
91	0.00000663	0.00000543	0.00000445	0.00000365
92	0.00000582	0.00000476	0.00000389	0.00000318
93	0.00000510	0.00000416	0.00000340	0.00000277
94	0.00000448	0.00000364	0.00000297	0.00000242
95	0.00000393	0.00000319	0.00000259	0.00000211
96	0.00000344	0.00000279	0.00000226	0.00000184
97	0.00000302	0.00000244	0.00000198	0.00000160
98	0.00000265	0.00000214	0.00000173	0.00000139
99	0.00000232	0.00000187	0.00000151	0.00000121

Rate i

Periods n	0.15(15%)	0.1525(15 1/4%)	0.155(15 1/2%)	0.1575(15 3/4%)
51	0.00080244	0.00071831	0.00064316	0.00057601
52	0.00069777	0.00062326	0.00055685	0.00049763
53	0.00060676	0.00054079	0.00048212	0.00042992
54	0.00052761	0.00046923	0.00041742	0.00037142
55	0.00045880	0.00040714	0.00036140	0.00032088
56	0.00039895	0.00035327	0.00031290	0.00027722
57	0.00034692	0.00030653	0.00027091	0.00023950
58	0.00030167	0.00026597	0.00023456	0.00020691
59	0.00026232	0.00023077	0.00020308	0.00017876
60	0.00022810	0.00020024	0.00017583	0.00015443
61	0.00019835	0.00017374	0.00015223	0.00013342
62	0.00017248	0.00015075	0.00013180	0.00011527
63	0.00014998	0.00013080	0.00011411	0.00009958
64	0.00013042	0.00011350	0.00009880	0.00008603
65	0.00011341	0.00009848	0.00008554	0.00007433
66	0.00009861	0.00008545	0.00007406	0.00006421
67	0.00008575	0.00007414	0.00006412	0.00005547
68	0.00007457	0.00006433	0.00005552	0.00004793
69	0.00006484	0.00005582	0.00004807	0.00004140
70	0.00005638	0.00004843	0.00004162	0.00003577
71	0.00004903	0.00004202	0.00003603	0.00003090
72	0.00004263	0.00003646	0.00003120	0.00002670
73	0.00003707	0.00003164	0.00002701	0.00002307
74	0.00003224	0.00002745	0.00002338	0.00001993
75	0.00002803	0.00002382	0.00002025	0.00001722
76	0.00002438	0.00002067	0.00001753	0.00001487
77	0.00002120	0.00001793	0.00001518	0.00001285
78	0.00001843	0.00001556	0.00001314	0.00001110
79	0.00001603	0.00001350	0.00001138	0.00000959
80	0.00001394	0.00001171	0.00000985	0.00000829
81	0.00001212	0.00001016	0.00000853	0.00000716
82	0.00001054	0.00000882	0.00000738	0.00000618
83	0.00000916	0.00000765	0.00000639	0.00000534
84	0.00000797	0.00000664	0.00000553	0.00000462
85	0.00000693	0.00000576	0.00000479	0.00000399
86	0.00000603	0.00000500	0.00000415	0.00000345
87	0.00000524	0.00000434	0.00000359	0.00000298
88	0.00000456	0.00000376	0.00000311	0.00000257
89	0.00000396	0.00000327	0.00000269	0.00000222
90	0.00000345	0.00000283	0.00000233	0.00000192
91	0.00000300	0.00000246	0.00000202	0.00000166
92	0.00000260	0.00000213	0.00000175	0.00000143
93	0.00000227	0.00000185	0.00000151	0.00000124
94	0.00000197	0.00000161	0.00000131	0.00000107
95	0.00000171	0.00000139	0.00000113	0.00000092
96	0.00000149	0.00000121	0.00000098	0.00000080
97	0.00000130	0.00000105	0.00000085	0.00000069
98	0.00000113	0.00000091	0.00000074	0.00000060
99	0.00000098	0.00000079	0.00000064	0.00000051
100	0.00000085	0.00000069	0.00000055	0.00000044

Rate i

Periods n	0.15(15%)	0.1525(15 1/4%)	0.155(15 1/2%)	0.1575(15 3/4%)
1	0.86956522	0.86767896	0.86580087	0.86393089
2	0.75614367	0.75286678	0.74961114	0.74637657
3	0.65751623	0.65324666	0.64901397	0.64481778
4	0.57175325	0.56680838	0.56191686	0.55707799
5	0.49717674	0.49180771	0.48650810	0.48127688
6	0.43232760	0.42673120	0.42121914	0.41578996
7	0.37593704	0.37026568	0.36469189	0.35921379
8	0.32690177	0.32127174	0.31575056	0.31033589
9	0.28426241	0.27876073	0.27337711	0.26810876
10	0.24714471	0.24187482	0.23669014	0.23162744
11	0.21494322	0.20986969	0.20492652	0.20011010
12	0.18690715	0.18209952	0.17742556	0.17288129
13	0.16252796	0.15800392	0.15361521	0.14935749
14	0.14132866	0.13709668	0.13300018	0.12903455
15	0.12289449	0.11895590	0.11515167	0.11147690
16	0.10686477	0.10321553	0.09969841	0.09630836
17	0.09292589	0.08955795	0.08631897	0.08320377
18	0.08080512	0.07770754	0.07473504	0.07188231
19	0.07026532	0.06742520	0.06470566	0.06210134
20	0.06110028	0.05850343	0.05602222	0.05365127
21	0.05313068	0.05076219	0.04850409	0.04635099
22	0.04620059	0.04404529	0.04199488	0.04004405
23	0.04017443	0.03821717	0.03635920	0.03459529
24	0.03493428	0.03316023	0.03147983	0.02988794
25	0.03037764	0.02877244	0.02725526	0.02582112
26	0.02641534	0.02496524	0.02359763	0.02230766
27	0.02296986	0.02166181	0.02043085	0.01927228
28	0.01997379	0.01879550	0.01768905	0.01664991
29	0.01736851	0.01630846	0.01531519	0.01438438
30	0.01510305	0.01415051	0.01325991	0.01242711
31	0.01313309	0.01227810	0.01148044	0.01073616
32	0.01142008	0.01065345	0.00993977	0.00927530
33	0.00993050	0.00924377	0.00860586	0.00801322
34	0.00863522	0.00802063	0.00745097	0.00692287
35	0.00750889	0.00695933	0.00645105	0.00598088
36	0.00652947	0.00603846	0.00558533	0.00516707
37	0.00567780	0.00523945	0.00483578	0.00446399
38	0.00493722	0.00454616	0.00418682	0.00385658
39	0.00429323	0.00394461	0.00362495	0.00333182
40	0.00373324	0.00342265	0.00313849	0.00287846
41	0.00324630	0.00296976	0.00271731	0.00248679
42	0.00282287	0.00257680	0.00235265	0.00214841
43	0.00245467	0.00223584	0.00203692	0.00185608
44	0.00213449	0.00193999	0.00176357	0.00160353
45	0.00185608	0.00168329	0.00152690	0.00138534
46	0.00161398	0.00146055	0.00132199	0.00080244
47	0.00140346	0.00126729	0.00114458	0.00103398
48	0.00122040	0.00109960	0.00099098	0.00089329
49	0.00106122	0.00095410	0.00085799	0.00077174
50	0.00092280	0.00082785	0.00074285	0.00066673

PRESENT VALUE $1/(1 + i)^n$ (Continued)

Rate i — Periods $n = 1$ to 49

n	0.16 (16%)	0.1625 (16 1/4%)	0.165 (16 1/2%)	0.1675 (16 3/4%)
1	0.86206897	0.86021505	0.85836910	0.85653105
2	0.74316290	0.73996994	0.73679751	0.73364544
3	0.64065767	0.63653328	0.63244421	0.62839020
4	0.55229110	0.54755551	0.54287057	0.53823563
5	0.47611302	0.47101549	0.46598332	0.46101553
6	0.41044225	0.40517462	0.39998568	0.39487411
7	0.35382953	0.34853731	0.34333535	0.33822194
8	0.30502546	0.29981704	0.29470846	0.28969759
9	0.26295298	0.25790713	0.25296863	0.24813498
10	0.22668360	0.22185559	0.21714046	0.21253532
11	0.19541690	0.19084352	0.18638666	0.18204503
12	0.16846284	0.16416647	0.15998855	0.15592557
13	0.14522659	0.14121847	0.13732923	0.13355509
14	0.12519534	0.12147825	0.11787916	0.11438408
15	0.10792701	0.10449742	0.10118383	0.09798208
16	0.09304053	0.08989026	0.08685307	0.08392470
17	0.08020735	0.07732495	0.07455199	0.07188411
18	0.06914427	0.06651609	0.06399313	0.06157097
19	0.05960713	0.05721814	0.05492972	0.05273745
20	0.05138546	0.04921990	0.04714998	0.04517126
21	0.04429781	0.04233970	0.04047208	0.03869059
22	0.03818776	0.03642125	0.03473999	0.03313969
23	0.03292049	0.03133011	0.02981973	0.02838517
24	0.02837973	0.02695063	0.02559634	0.02431278
25	0.02446528	0.02318334	0.02197110	0.02082465
26	0.02109076	0.01994266	0.01885932	0.01783696
27	0.01818169	0.01715497	0.01618825	0.01527791
28	0.01567387	0.01475697	0.01389550	0.01308601
29	0.01351196	0.01269416	0.01192747	0.01120857
30	0.01164824	0.01091971	0.01023817	0.00960049
31	0.01004159	0.00939330	0.00878813	0.00822312
32	0.00865654	0.00808026	0.00754346	0.00704335
33	0.00746253	0.00695076	0.00647507	0.00603285
34	0.00643322	0.00597915	0.00555800	0.00516732
35	0.00554588	0.00514335	0.00477082	0.00442597
36	0.00478093	0.00442439	0.00409512	0.00379098
37	0.00412149	0.00380593	0.00351512	0.00324710
38	0.00355301	0.00327392	0.00301727	0.00278124
39	0.00306294	0.00281627	0.00258994	0.00238222
40	0.00264047	0.00242260	0.00222312	0.00204044
41	0.00227626	0.00208396	0.00190826	0.00174770
42	0.00196230	0.00179265	0.00163799	0.00149696
43	0.00169163	0.00154206	0.00140600	0.00128219
44	0.00145831	0.00132651	0.00120687	0.00109824
45	0.00125716	0.00114108	0.00103594	0.00094068
46	0.00109376	0.00098158	0.00088922	0.00080572
47	0.00093427	0.00084437	0.00076328	0.00069012
48	0.00080541	0.00072643	0.00065517	0.00059111
49	0.00069432	0.00062481	0.00056238	0.00050631

Rate i — Periods $n = 51$ to 99

n	0.16 (16%)	0.1625 (16 1/4%)	0.165 (16 1/2%)	0.1675 (16 3/4%)
51	0.00051599	0.00046234	0.00041436	0.00037145
52	0.00044482	0.00039771	0.00035567	0.00031816
53	0.00038347	0.00034212	0.00030503	0.00027251
54	0.00033057	0.00029429	0.00026206	0.00023341
55	0.00028498	0.00025316	0.00022494	0.00019993
56	0.00024567	0.00021777	0.00019308	0.00017124
57	0.00021178	0.00018733	0.00016574	0.00014668
58	0.00018257	0.00016114	0.00014226	0.00012563
59	0.00015739	0.00013862	0.00012212	0.00010761
60	0.00013568	0.00011924	0.00010482	0.00009217
61	0.00011697	0.00010257	0.00008997	0.00007895
62	0.00010083	0.00008823	0.00007723	0.00006762
63	0.00008693	0.00007590	0.00006629	0.00005792
64	0.00007494	0.00006529	0.00005690	0.00004961
65	0.00006460	0.00005616	0.00004884	0.00004249
66	0.00005569	0.00004831	0.00004193	0.00003640
67	0.00004801	0.00004156	0.00003599	0.00003117
68	0.00004139	0.00003575	0.00003089	0.00002670
69	0.00003568	0.00003075	0.00002652	0.00002287
70	0.00003076	0.00002645	0.00002276	0.00001959
71	0.00002651	0.00002276	0.00001954	0.00001678
72	0.00002286	0.00001958	0.00001677	0.00001437
73	0.00001970	0.00001684	0.00001439	0.00001231
74	0.00001699	0.00001449	0.00001236	0.00001054
75	0.00001464	0.00001246	0.00001061	0.00000903
76	0.00001262	0.00001072	0.00000910	0.00000774
77	0.00001088	0.00000922	0.00000781	0.00000663
78	0.00000938	0.00000793	0.00000671	0.00000567
79	0.00000809	0.00000682	0.00000576	0.00000486
80	0.00000697	0.00000587	0.00000494	0.00000416
81	0.00000601	0.00000505	0.00000424	0.00000357
82	0.00000518	0.00000434	0.00000364	0.00000305
83	0.00000447	0.00000374	0.00000313	0.00000262
84	0.00000385	0.00000321	0.00000268	0.00000224
85	0.00000332	0.00000276	0.00000230	0.00000192
86	0.00000286	0.00000238	0.00000198	0.00000164
87	0.00000247	0.00000205	0.00000170	0.00000141
88	0.00000213	0.00000176	0.00000146	0.00000121
89	0.00000183	0.00000151	0.00000125	0.00000103
90	0.00000158	0.00000130	0.00000107	0.00000088
91	0.00000136	0.00000112	0.00000092	0.00000076
92	0.00000117	0.00000096	0.00000079	0.00000065
93	0.00000101	0.00000083	0.00000068	0.00000056
94	0.00000087	0.00000071	0.00000058	0.00000048
95	0.00000075	0.00000061	0.00000050	0.00000041
96	0.00000065	0.00000053	0.00000043	0.00000035
97	0.00000056	0.00000045	0.00000037	0.00000030
98	0.00000048	0.00000039	0.00000032	0.00000026
99	0.00000042	0.00000034	0.00000027	0.00000022

Rate *i*

Periods n	0.17 (17%)	0.1725 (17 1/4%)	0.175 (17 1/2%)	0.1775 (17 3/4%)
51	0.00033306	0.00029871	0.00026796	0.00024043
52	0.00028467	0.00025476	0.00022805	0.00020419
53	0.00024330	0.00021728	0.00019409	0.00017341
54	0.00020795	0.00018531	0.00016518	0.00014727
55	0.00017774	0.00015805	0.00014058	0.00012507
56	0.00015191	0.00013480	0.00011964	0.00010622
57	0.00012984	0.00011497	0.00010182	0.00009020
58	0.00011097	0.00009805	0.00008666	0.00007661
59	0.00009485	0.00008363	0.00007375	0.00006506
60	0.00008107	0.00007132	0.00006277	0.00005525
61	0.00006929	0.00006083	0.00005342	0.00004692
62	0.00005922	0.00005188	0.00004546	0.00003985
63	0.00005060	0.00004425	0.00003869	0.00003384
64	0.00004326	0.00003774	0.00003293	0.00002874
65	0.00003698	0.00003219	0.00002802	0.00002441
66	0.00003160	0.00002745	0.00002385	0.00002073
67	0.00002701	0.00002341	0.00002030	0.00001760
68	0.00002309	0.00001997	0.00001728	0.00001495
69	0.00001973	0.00001703	0.00001470	0.00001270
70	0.00001687	0.00001452	0.00001251	0.00001078
71	0.00001441	0.00001239	0.00001065	0.00000916
72	0.00001232	0.00001057	0.00000906	0.00000778
73	0.00001053	0.00000901	0.00000771	0.00000660
74	0.00000900	0.00000769	0.00000656	0.00000561
75	0.00000769	0.00000655	0.00000559	0.00000476
76	0.00000657	0.00000559	0.00000475	0.00000405
77	0.00000562	0.00000477	0.00000405	0.00000344
78	0.00000480	0.00000407	0.00000344	0.00000292
79	0.00000411	0.00000347	0.00000293	0.00000248
80	0.00000351	0.00000296	0.00000249	0.00000210
81	0.00000300	0.00000252	0.00000212	0.00000179
82	0.00000256	0.00000215	0.00000181	0.00000152
83	0.00000219	0.00000183	0.00000154	0.00000129
84	0.00000187	0.00000157	0.00000131	0.00000109
85	0.00000160	0.00000133	0.00000111	0.00000093
86	0.00000137	0.00000114	0.00000095	0.00000079
87	0.00000117	0.00000097	0.00000081	0.00000067
88	0.00000100	0.00000083	0.00000069	0.00000057
89	0.00000085	0.00000071	0.00000058	0.00000048
90	0.00000073	0.00000060	0.00000050	0.00000041
91	0.00000062	0.00000051	0.00000042	0.00000035
92	0.00000053	0.00000044	0.00000036	0.00000030
93	0.00000046	0.00000037	0.00000031	0.00000025
94	0.00000039	0.00000032	0.00000026	0.00000021
95	0.00000033	0.00000027	0.00000022	0.00000018
96	0.00000028	0.00000023	0.00000019	0.00000015
97	0.00000024	0.00000020	0.00000016	0.00000013
98	0.00000021	0.00000017	0.00000014	0.00000011
99	0.00000018	0.00000014	0.00000012	0.00000009
100	0.00000015	0.00000012	0.00000010	0.00000008

Rate *i*

Periods n	0.17 (17%)	0.1725 (17 1/4%)	0.175 (17 1/2%)	0.1775 (17 3/4%)
1	0.85470085	0.85287846	0.85106383	0.72123728
2	0.73051355	0.72740168	0.72430964	0.72123728
3	0.62437056	0.62038522	0.61643374	0.61251574
4	0.53365005	0.52911320	0.52462446	0.52018322
5	0.45611115	0.45126925	0.44648890	0.44176919
6	0.38983859	0.38487783	0.37999055	0.37517553
7	0.33319538	0.32825401	0.32339622	0.31862041
8	0.28478237	0.27996078	0.27523082	0.27059058
9	0.24340374	0.23877252	0.23423900	0.22980092
10	0.20803738	0.20364394	0.19935234	0.19156001
11	0.17780973	0.17368353	0.16966156	0.16574099
12	0.15197413	0.14813094	0.14439282	0.10485668
13	0.12989242	0.12633769	0.12288751	0.11953858
14	0.11101916	0.10775070	0.10458511	0.10151896
15	0.09488817	0.09189825	0.08900861	0.08621568
16	0.08110100	0.07837804	0.07575201	0.07321926
17	0.06931709	0.06684694	0.06446979	0.06219196
18	0.05924538	0.05701231	0.05486791	0.05280846
19	0.05063708	0.04862458	0.04669609	0.04484795
20	0.04327955	0.04147085	0.03974135	0.03808743
21	0.03699107	0.03536960	0.03382243	0.03234601
22	0.03161630	0.03016597	0.02878505	0.02747008
23	0.02702248	0.02572790	0.02449791	0.02332915
24	0.02309614	0.02194278	0.02084929	0.01981244
25	0.01974029	0.01871452	0.01774407	0.01682585
26	0.01687204	0.01596121	0.01510134	0.01428947
27	0.01442055	0.01361297	0.01285220	0.01213543
28	0.01232525	0.01161021	0.01093805	0.01030610
29	0.01053440	0.00990210	0.00930898	0.00875253
30	0.00900376	0.00844529	0.00792253	0.00743314
31	0.00769553	0.00720280	0.00674258	0.00631265
32	0.00657737	0.00614312	0.00573837	0.00536106
33	0.00562169	0.00523933	0.00488372	0.00455292
34	0.00480486	0.00446851	0.00415635	0.00386660
35	0.00410672	0.00381110	0.00353732	0.00328373
36	0.00351002	0.00325040	0.00301049	0.00279973
37	0.00300001	0.00277220	0.00256212	0.00236835
38	0.00256411	0.00236435	0.00218052	0.00201134
39	0.00219155	0.00201650	0.00185577	0.00170814
40	0.00187312	0.00171983	0.00157938	0.00145065
41	0.00160096	0.00146681	0.00134415	0.00123198
42	0.00136834	0.00125101	0.00114396	0.00104626
43	0.00116952	0.00106696	0.00097358	0.00088855
44	0.00099959	0.00090999	0.00082858	0.00075461
45	0.00085435	0.00077611	0.00070517	0.00064085
46	0.00073021	0.00066193	0.00060015	0.00054425
47	0.00062411	0.00056454	0.00051076	0.00046221
48	0.00053343	0.00048149	0.00043469	0.00039253
49	0.00045592	0.00041065	0.00036995	0.00033336
50	0.00038968	0.00035023	0.00031485	0.00028311

PRESENT VALUE $1/(1 + i)^n$ (Continued)

Rate i

Periods n	0.18(18%)	0.1825(18 1/4%)	0.185(18 1/2%)	0.1875(18 3/4%)
1	0.84745763	0.84566596	0.84388186	0.84210526
2	0.71818443	0.71515092	0.71213659	0.70914127
3	0.60863087	0.60477879	0.60095915	0.59717160
4	0.51578888	0.51144084	0.50713852	0.50288135
5	0.43710922	0.43250811	0.42796500	0.42347903
6	0.37043154	0.36575738	0.36115189	0.35661392
7	0.31392503	0.30930857	0.30476953	0.30030646
8	0.26603816	0.26157173	0.25718948	0.25288965
9	0.22545607	0.22120231	0.21703753	0.21295970
10	0.19106447	0.18706326	0.18315404	0.17933449
11	0.16191904	0.15819303	0.15456037	0.15101852
12	0.13721953	0.13377846	0.13043069	0.12717349
13	0.11628773	0.11313189	0.11006809	0.10709346
14	0.09854893	0.09567179	0.09288447	0.09018397
15	0.08351604	0.08090638	0.07838352	0.07594439
16	0.07077630	0.06841977	0.06614643	0.06395317
17	0.05997992	0.05786027	0.05581977	0.05385530
18	0.05083044	0.04893046	0.04710529	0.04535184
19	0.04307664	0.04137883	0.03975130	0.03819102
20	0.03650563	0.03499266	0.03354540	0.03216086
21	0.03093698	0.02959211	0.02830836	0.02708283
22	0.02621778	0.02502504	0.02388891	0.02280659
23	0.02221845	0.02116282	0.02015942	0.01920555
24	0.01882920	0.01789668	0.01701217	0.01617310
25	0.01595695	0.01513461	0.01435626	0.01361945
26	0.01352284	0.01279883	0.01211499	0.01146901
27	0.01146003	0.01082353	0.01022362	0.00965811
28	0.00971189	0.00915309	0.00862752	0.00813315
29	0.00823042	0.00774046	0.00728061	0.00684897
30	0.00697493	0.00654584	0.00614398	0.00576755
31	0.00591096	0.00553560	0.00518479	0.00485689
32	0.00500929	0.00468126	0.00437535	0.00409001
33	0.00424516	0.00395879	0.00369228	0.00344422
34	0.00359759	0.00334781	0.00311585	0.00290039
35	0.00304881	0.00283113	0.00262941	0.00244244
36	0.00258373	0.00239419	0.00221891	0.00205679
37	0.00218960	0.00202469	0.00187250	0.00173203
38	0.00185560	0.00171221	0.00158017	0.00145855
39	0.00157254	0.00144796	0.00133347	0.00122826
40	0.00133266	0.00122449	0.00112529	0.00103432
41	0.00112937	0.00103551	0.00094962	0.00087101
42	0.00095710	0.00087569	0.00080136	0.00073348
43	0.00081110	0.00074054	0.00067626	0.00061767
44	0.00068737	0.00062625	0.00057068	0.00052014
45	0.00058252	0.00052960	0.00048159	0.00043801
46	0.00049366	0.00044787	0.00040640	0.00036885
47	0.00041836	0.00037874	0.00034296	0.00031061
48	0.00035454	0.00032029	0.00028941	0.00026157
49	0.00030046	0.00027086	0.00024423	0.00022027

Rate i

Periods n	0.18(18%)	0.1825(18 1/4%)	0.185(18 1/2%)	0.1875(18 3/4%)
51	0.00021578	0.00019371	0.00017393	0.00015620
52	0.00018287	0.00016381	0.00014677	0.00013154
53	0.00015497	0.00013853	0.00012386	0.00011077
54	0.00013133	0.00011715	0.00010452	0.00009328
55	0.00011130	0.00009907	0.00008820	0.00007855
56	0.00009432	0.00008378	0.00007443	0.00006615
57	0.00007993	0.00007085	0.00006281	0.00005570
58	0.00006774	0.00005991	0.00005301	0.00004691
59	0.00005741	0.00005067	0.00004473	0.00003950
60	0.00004865	0.00004285	0.00003775	0.00003326
61	0.00004123	0.00003624	0.00003186	0.00002801
62	0.00003494	0.00003064	0.00002688	0.00002359
63	0.00002961	0.00002591	0.00002269	0.00001986
64	0.00002509	0.00002191	0.00001914	0.00001673
65	0.00002127	0.00001853	0.00001616	0.00001409
66	0.00001802	0.00001567	0.00001363	0.00001186
67	0.00001527	0.00001325	0.00001150	0.00000999
68	0.00001294	0.00001121	0.00000971	0.00000841
69	0.00001097	0.00000948	0.00000819	0.00000708
70	0.00000930	0.00000802	0.00000691	0.00000597
71	0.00000788	0.00000678	0.00000583	0.00000502
72	0.00000668	0.00000573	0.00000492	0.00000423
73	0.00000566	0.00000485	0.00000415	0.00000356
74	0.00000479	0.00000410	0.00000351	0.00000300
75	0.00000406	0.00000347	0.00000296	0.00000253
76	0.00000344	0.00000293	0.00000250	0.00000213
77	0.00000292	0.00000248	0.00000211	0.00000179
78	0.00000247	0.00000210	0.00000178	0.00000151
79	0.00000210	0.00000177	0.00000150	0.00000127
80	0.00000178	0.00000150	0.00000127	0.00000107
81	0.00000151	0.00000127	0.00000107	0.00000090
82	0.00000128	0.00000107	0.00000090	0.00000076
83	0.00000108	0.00000091	0.00000076	0.00000064
84	0.00000092	0.00000077	0.00000064	0.00000054
85	0.00000078	0.00000065	0.00000054	0.00000045
86	0.00000066	0.00000055	0.00000046	0.00000038
87	0.00000056	0.00000046	0.00000039	0.00000032
88	0.00000047	0.00000039	0.00000033	0.00000027
89	0.00000040	0.00000033	0.00000027	0.00000023
90	0.00000034	0.00000028	0.00000023	0.00000019
91	0.00000029	0.00000024	0.00000020	0.00000016
92	0.00000024	0.00000020	0.00000017	0.00000014
93	0.00000021	0.00000017	0.00000014	0.00000011
94	0.00000018	0.00000014	0.00000012	0.00000010
95	0.00000015	0.00000012	0.00000010	0.00000008
96	0.00000013	0.00000010	0.00000008	0.00000007
97	0.00000011	0.00000009	0.00000007	0.00000006
98	0.00000009	0.00000007	0.00000006	0.00000005
99	0.00000008	0.00000006	0.00000005	0.00000004

Rate i

	0.20(20%)	0.1975(19 3/4%)	0.195(19 1/2%)	0.1925(19 1/4%)	0.19(19%)	Periods n
	0.00009157	0.00010185	0.00011330	0.00012607	0.00014032	51
	0.00007631	0.00008505	0.00009481	0.00010572	0.00011791	52
	0.00006359	0.00007102	0.00007934	0.00008866	0.00009909	53
	0.00005299	0.00005931	0.00006639	0.00007434	0.00008327	54
	0.00004416	0.00004953	0.00005556	0.00006234	0.00006997	55
	0.00003680	0.00004136	0.00004649	0.00005228	0.00005880	56
	0.00003067	0.00003454	0.00003891	0.00004384	0.00004941	57
	0.00002556	0.00002884	0.00003256	0.00003676	0.00004152	58
	0.00002130	0.00002408	0.00002725	0.00003083	0.00003489	59
	0.00001775	0.00002011	0.00002280	0.00002585	0.00002932	60
	0.00001479	0.00001680	0.00001908	0.00002168	0.00002464	61
	0.00001232	0.00001403	0.00001597	0.00001818	0.00002071	62
	0.00001027	0.00001171	0.00001336	0.00001524	0.00001740	63
	0.00000856	0.00000978	0.00001118	0.00001278	0.00001462	64
	0.00000713	0.00000817	0.00000936	0.00001072	0.00001229	65
	0.00000594	0.00000682	0.00000783	0.00000899	0.00001033	66
	0.00000495	0.00000570	0.00000655	0.00000754	0.00000868	67
	0.00000413	0.00000476	0.00000548	0.00000632	0.00000729	68
	0.00000344	0.00000397	0.00000459	0.00000530	0.00000613	69
	0.00000287	0.00000332	0.00000384	0.00000445	0.00000515	70
	0.00000239	0.00000277	0.00000321	0.00000373	0.00000433	71
	0.00000199	0.00000231	0.00000269	0.00000313	0.00000364	72
	0.00000166	0.00000193	0.00000225	0.00000262	0.00000306	73
	0.00000138	0.00000161	0.00000188	0.00000220	0.00000257	74
	0.00000115	0.00000135	0.00000158	0.00000184	0.00000216	75
	0.00000096	0.00000112	0.00000132	0.00000155	0.00000181	76
	0.00000080	0.00000094	0.00000110	0.00000130	0.00000152	77
	0.00000067	0.00000078	0.00000092	0.00000109	0.00000128	78
	0.00000056	0.00000065	0.00000077	0.00000091	0.00000108	79
	0.00000046	0.00000055	0.00000065	0.00000076	0.00000090	80
	0.00000039	0.00000046	0.00000054	0.00000064	0.00000076	81
	0.00000032	0.00000038	0.00000045	0.00000054	0.00000064	82
	0.00000027	0.00000032	0.00000038	0.00000045	0.00000054	83
	0.00000022	0.00000027	0.00000032	0.00000038	0.00000045	84
	0.00000019	0.00000022	0.00000027	0.00000032	0.00000038	85
	0.00000016	0.00000019	0.00000022	0.00000027	0.00000032	86
	0.00000013	0.00000015	0.00000019	0.00000022	0.00000027	87
	0.00000011	0.00000013	0.00000016	0.00000019	0.00000022	88
	0.00000009	0.00000011	0.00000013	0.00000016	0.00000019	89
	0.00000007	0.00000009	0.00000011	0.00000013	0.00000016	90
	0.00000006	0.00000008	0.00000009	0.00000011	0.00000013	91
	0.00000005	0.00000006	0.00000008	0.00000009	0.00000011	92
	0.00000004	0.00000005	0.00000006	0.00000008	0.00000009	93
	0.00000004	0.00000004	0.00000005	0.00000006	0.00000008	94
	0.00000003	0.00000004	0.00000004	0.00000005	0.00000007	95
	0.00000003	0.00000003	0.00000004	0.00000004	0.00000005	96
	0.00000002	0.00000003	0.00000003	0.00000004	0.00000005	97
	0.00000002	0.00000002	0.00000003	0.00000003	0.00000004	98
	0.00000001	0.00000002	0.00000002	0.00000003	0.00000003	99
	0.00000001	0.00000001	0.00000002	0.00000002	0.00000003	100

Rate i

Periods n	0.19(19%)	0.1925(19 1/4%)	0.195(19 1/2%)	0.1975(19 3/4%)	0.20(20%)
1	0.84033613	0.83857442	0.83682008	0.83507307	0.83333333
2	0.70616482	0.70320706	0.70026785	0.69734703	0.69444444
3	0.59341581	0.58969146	0.58599820	0.58233572	0.57870370
4	0.49866875	0.49450017	0.49037507	0.48629288	0.48225309
5	0.41904937	0.41467520	0.41035570	0.40609009	0.40187757
6	0.35214233	0.34773602	0.34339389	0.33911490	0.33489798
7	0.29591792	0.29160253	0.28735891	0.28318572	0.27908165
8	0.24867052	0.24453042	0.24046770	0.23648077	0.23256804
9	0.20896683	0.20505696	0.20122820	0.19747872	0.19380670
10	0.17560238	0.17195552	0.16839180	0.16490916	0.16150558
11	0.14756502	0.14419750	0.14091364	0.13771120	0.13458799
12	0.12400422	0.12092034	0.11791937	0.11499891	0.11215665
13	0.10420523	0.10140070	0.09867729	0.09603250	0.09346388
14	0.08756742	0.08503203	0.08257514	0.08019415	0.07788657
15	0.07358606	0.07130569	0.06910054	0.06696798	0.06490547
16	0.06183703	0.05979513	0.05782472	0.05592315	0.05408789
17	0.05196389	0.05014266	0.04838888	0.04669992	0.04507324
18	0.04366713	0.04204836	0.04049279	0.03899784	0.03756104
19	0.03669507	0.03526068	0.03388518	0.03256605	0.03130086
20	0.03083619	0.02956870	0.02835580	0.02719503	0.02608405
21	0.02591277	0.02479556	0.02372870	0.02270984	0.02173671
22	0.02177544	0.02079292	0.01985665	0.01896437	0.01811393
23	0.01829869	0.01743641	0.01661645	0.01583664	0.01509494
24	0.01537705	0.01462173	0.01390498	0.01322475	0.01257912
25	0.01292189	0.01226141	0.01163596	0.01104363	0.01048260
26	0.01085873	0.01028210	0.00973721	0.00922224	0.00873550
27	0.00912498	0.00862231	0.00814829	0.00770124	0.00727958
28	0.00766805	0.00723045	0.00681865	0.00643110	0.00606632
29	0.00644374	0.00606327	0.00570599	0.00537044	0.00505526
30	0.00541491	0.00508450	0.00477488	0.00448471	0.00421272
31	0.00455034	0.00426373	0.00399572	0.00374506	0.00351060
32	0.00382382	0.00357546	0.00334370	0.00312740	0.00292550
33	0.00321329	0.00299829	0.00279807	0.00261161	0.00243792
34	0.00270025	0.00251429	0.00234148	0.00218088	0.00203160
35	0.00226911	0.00210842	0.00195940	0.00182120	0.00169300
36	0.00190682	0.00176806	0.00163967	0.00152083	0.00141083
37	0.00160237	0.00148265	0.00137211	0.00127001	0.00117569
38	0.00134653	0.00124332	0.00114821	0.00106055	0.00097974
39	0.00113154	0.00104261	0.00096084	0.00088563	0.00081645
40	0.00095087	0.00087431	0.00080405	0.00073957	0.00068038
41	0.00079905	0.00073317	0.00067285	0.00061759	0.00056698
42	0.00067147	0.00061482	0.00056305	0.00051574	0.00047248
43	0.00056426	0.00051557	0.00047117	0.00043068	0.00039374
44	0.00047417	0.00043235	0.00039429	0.00035965	0.00032811
45	0.00039846	0.00036255	0.00032995	0.00030033	0.00027343
46	0.00033484	0.00030403	0.00027611	0.00025080	0.00022786
47	0.00028138	0.00025495	0.00023105	0.00020944	0.00018988
48	0.00023645	0.00021379	0.00019335	0.00017489	0.00015823
49	0.00019870	0.00017928	0.00016180	0.00014605	0.00013186
50	0.00016698	0.00015034	0.00013540	0.00012196	0.00010988

FINANCIAL TABLES

AMOUNT OF ANNUITY $[(1 + i)^n - 1]/i$ [*]

The following table gives the amount of an annuity cf unit value per period after a term of n periods at rate of interest of i per period; usually indicated as $s_{\overline{n}|i}$.

Periods	Rate i				
n	.0025 (¼%)	.004167 (₁₂%)	.005 (½%)	.005833 (₁₂%)	.0075 (¾%)
1	1.0000 0000	1.0000 0000	1.0000 0000	1.0000 0000	1.0000 0000
2	2.0025 0000	2.0041 6667	2.0050 0000	2.0058 3333	2.0075 0000
3	3.0075 0625	3.0125 1736	3.0150 2500	3.0175 3403	3.0225 5625
4	4.0150 2502	4.0250 6952	4.0301 0013	4.0351 3631	4.0452 2542
5	5.0250 6258	5.0418 4064	5.0502 5063	5.0586 7460	5.0755 6461
6	6.0376 2523	6.0628 4831	6.0755 0188	6.0881 8354	6.1136 3135
7	7.0527 1930	7.0881 1018	7.1058 7939	7.1236 9794	7.1594 8358
8	8.0703 5110	8.1176 4397	8.1414 0879	8.1652 5285	8.2131 7971
9	9.0905 2697	9.1514 6749	9.1821 1583	9.2128 8349	9.2747 7856
10	10.1132 5329	10.1895 9860	10.2280 2641	10.2666 2531	10.3443 3940
11	11.1385 3642	11.2320 5526	11.2791 6654	11.3265 1396	11.4219 2194
12	12.1663 8277	12.2788 5549	12.3355 6237	12.3925 8529	12.5075 8636
13	13.1967 9872	13.3300 1739	13.3972 4018	13.4648 7537	13.6013 9325
14	14.2297 9072	14.3855 5913	14.4642 2639	14.5434 2048	14.7034 0370
15	15.2653 6520	15.4454 9896	15.5365 4752	15.6282 5710	15.8136 7923
16	16.3035 2861	16.5098 5520	16.6142 3026	16.7194 2193	16.9322 8183
17	17.3442 8743	17.5786 4627	17.6973 0141	17.8169 5189	18.0592 7394
18	18.3876 4815	18.6518 9063	18.7857 8791	18.9208 8411	19.1947 1849
19	19.4336 1727	19.7296 0684	19.8797 1685	20.0312 5593	20.3386 7888
20	20.4822 0131	20.8118 1353	20.9791 1544	21.1481 0493	21.4912 1897
21	21.5334 0682	21.8985 2942	22.0840 1101	22.2714 6887	22.6524 0312
22	22.5872 4033	22.9897 7330	23.1944 3107	23.4013 8577	23.8222 9614
23	23.6437 0843	24.0855 6402	24.3104 0323	24.5378 9386	25.0009 6336
24	24.7028 1770	25.1859 2053	25.4319 5524	25.6810 3157	26.1884 7059
25	25.7645 7475	26.2908 6187	26.5591 1502	26.8308 3759	27.3848 8411
26	26.8289 8619	27.4004 0713	27.6919 1059	27.9873 5081	28.5902 7075
27	27.8960 5865	28.5145 7549	28.8303 7015	29.1506 1036	29.8046 9778
28	28.9657 9880	29.6333 8622	29.9745 2200	30.3206 5558	31.0282 3301
29	30.0382 1330	30.7568 5866	31.1243 9461	31.4975 2607	32.2609 4476
30	31.1133 0883	31.8850 1224	32.2800 1658	32.6812 6164	33.5029 0184
31	32.1910 9210	33.0178 6646	33.4414 1666	33.8719 0233	34.7541 7361
32	33.2715 6983	34.1554 4090	34.6086 2375	35.0694 8843	36.0148 2991
33	34.3547 4876	35.2977 5524	35.7816 6686	36.2740 6045	37.2849 4113
34	35.4406 3563	36.4448 2922	36.9605 7520	37.4856 5913	38.5645 7819
35	36.5292 3722	37.5966 8268	38.1453 7807	38.7043 2548	39.8538 1253
36	37.6205 6031	38.7533 3552	39.3361 0497	39.9301 0071	41.1527 1612
37	38.7146 1171	39.9148 0775	40.5327 8549	41.1630 2630	42.4613 6149
38	39.8113 9824	41.0811 1945	41.7354 4942	42.4031 4395	43.7798 2170
39	40.9109 2674	42.2522 9078	42.9441 2666	43.6504 9562	45.1081 7037
40	42.0132 0405	43.4283 4199	44.1588 4730	44.9051 2352	46.4464 8164
41	43.1182 3706	44.6092 9342	45.3796 4153	46.1670 7007	47.7948 3026
42	44.2260 3265	45.7951 6547	46.6065 3974	47.4363 7798	49.1532 9148
43	45.3365 9774	46.9859 7866	47.8395 7244	48.7130 9018	50.5219 4117
44	46.4499 3923	48.1817 5357	49.0787 7030	49.9972 4988	51.9008 5573
45	47.5660 6408	49.3825 1088	50.3241 6415	51.2889 0050	53.2901 1215
46	48.6849 7924	50.5882 7134	51.5757 8498	52.5880 8575	54.6897 8799
47	49.8066 9169	51.7990 5581	52.8336 6390	53.8948 4959	56.0999 6140
48	50.9312 0842	53.0148 8521	54.0978 3222	55.2092 3621	57.5207 1111
49	52.0585 3644	54.2357 8056	55.3683 2138	56.5312 9009	58.9521 1644
50	53.1886 8278	55.4617 6298	56.6451 6299	57.8610 5595	60.3942 5732

[*]For $s_{\overline{n}|i}$ where rates i = 0% to 20% are lacking in the 1/4% scaling use tables $(1 + i)^n$ and construct information by use of formula. See page 805.

AMOUNT OF ANNUITY $[(1 + i)^n - 1]/i$ (Continued)

Periods	Rate i				
n	.0025 ($\frac{1}{4}$ %)	.004167 ($\frac{5}{12}$ %)	.005 ($\frac{1}{2}$ %)	.005833 ($\frac{7}{12}$ %)	.0075 ($\frac{3}{4}$ %)
50	53.1886 828	55.4617 630	56.6451 630	57.8610 559	60.3942 573
51	54.3216 545	56.6928 537	57.9283 888	59.1985 788	61.8472 142
52	55.4574 586	57.9290 739	59.2180 307	60.5439 038	63.3110 684
53	56.5961 023	59.1704 450	60.5141 209	61.8970 766	64.7859 014
54	57.7375 925	60.4169 885	61.8166 915	63.2581 429	66.2717 956
55	58.8819 365	61.6687 260	63.1257 750	64.6271 487	67.7688 341
56	60.0291 413	62.9256 790	64.4414 038	66.0041 404	69.2771 003
57	61.1792 142	64.1878 694	65.7636 109	67.3891 646	70.7966 786
58	62.3321 622	65.4553 188	67.0924 289	68.7822 680	72.3276 537
59	63.4879 926	66.7280 493	68.4278 911	70.1834 979	73.8701 111
60	64.6467 126	68.0060 828	69.7700 305	71.5929 016	75.4241 369
61	65.8083 294	69.2894 415	71.1188 807	73.0105 269	76.9898 180
62	66.9728 502	70.5781 475	72.4744 751	74.4364 216	78.5672 416
63	68.1402 824	71.8722 231	73.8368 474	75.8706 341	80.1564 959
64	69.3106 331	73.1716 907	75.2060 317	77.3132 128	81.7576 696
65	70.4839 096	74.4765 728	76.5820 618	78.7642 065	83.3708 521
66	71.6601 194	75.7868 918	77.9649 721	80.2236 644	84.9961 335
67	72.8392 697	77.1026 706	79.3547 970	81.6916 358	86.6336 045
68	74.0213 679	78.4239 317	80.7515 710	83.1681 703	88.2833 566
69	75.2064 213	79.7506 981	82.1553 288	84.6533 180	89.9454 817
70	76.3944 374	81.0829 926	83.5661 055	86.1471 290	91.6200 729
71	77.5854 235	82.4208 384	84.9839 360	87.6496 539	93.3072 234
72	78.7793 870	83 7642 586	86.4088 557	89.1609 436	95.0070 276
73	79.9763 355	85.1132 763	87.8409 000	90.6810 491	96.7195 803
74	81.1762 763	86.4679 150	89.2801 045	92.2100 219	98.4449 771
75	82.3792 170	87.8281 980	90.7265 050	93.7479 137	100.1833 145
76	83.5851 651	89.1941 488	92.1801 375	95.2947 765	101.9346 893
77	84.7941 280	90.5657 911	93.6410 382	96.8506 627	103.6991 995
78	86.0061 133	91.9431 485	95.1092 434	98.4156 249	105.4769 435
79	87.2211 286	93.3262 450	96.5847 896	99.9897 160	107.2680 206
80	88.4391 814	94.7151 044	98.0677 136	101.5729 894	109.0725 307
81	89.6602 793	96.1097 506	99.5580 521	103.1654 985	110.8905 747
82	90.8844 300	97.5102 079	101.0558 424	104.7672 972	112.7222 540
83	92.1116 411	98.9165 004	102.5611 216	106.3784 398	114.5676 709
84	93.3419 202	100.3286 525	104.0739 272	107.9989 807	116.4269 284
85	94.5752 750	101.7466 886	105.5942 969	109.6289 748	118.3001 304
86	95.8117 132	103.1706 331	107.1222 683	111.2684 771	120.1873 814
87	97.0512 425	104.6005 108	108.6578 797	112.9175 432	122.0887 867
88	98.2938 706	106.0363 462	110.2011 691	114.5762 289	124.0044 526
89	99.5396 053	107.4781 643	111.7521 749	116.2445 902	125.9344 860
90	100.7884 543	108.9259 900	113.3109 358	117.9226 837	127.8789 947
91	102.0404 254	110.3798 483	114.8774 905	119.6105 660	129.8380 871
92	103.2955 265	111.8397 643	116.4518 779	121.3082 943	131.8118 728
93	104.5537 653	113.3057 634	118.0341 373	123.0159 260	133.8004 618
94	105.8151 497	114.7778 707	119.6243 080	124.7335 189	135.8039 653
95	107.0796 876	116.2561 118	121.2224 295	126.4611 311	137.8224 951
96	108.3473 868	117.7405 123	122.8285 417	128.1988 210	139.8561 638
97	109.6182 553	119.2310 978	124.4426 844	129.9466 475	141.9050 850
98	110.8923 009	120.7278 940	126.0648 978	131.7046 696	143.9693 731
99	112.1695 317	122.2309 269	127.6952 223	133.4729 468	146.0491 434
100	113.4499 555	123.7402 224	129.3336 984	135.2515 390	148.1445 120

AMOUNT OF ANNUITY $[(1 + i)^n - 1]/i$ (Continued)

Periods	Rate i				
n	.01 (1%)	.01125 (1⅛%)	.0125 (1¼%)	.015 (1½%)	.0175 (1¾%)
1	1.0000 0000	1.0000 0000	1.0000 0000	1.0000 0000	1.0000 0000
2	2.0100 0000	2.0112 5000	2.0125 0000	2.0150 0000	2.0175 0000
3	3.0301 0000	3.0338 7656	3.0376 5625	3.0452 2500	3.0528 0625
4	4.0604 0100	4.0680 0767	4.0756 2695	4.0909 0338	4.1062 3036
5	5.1010 0501	5.1137 7276	5.1265 7229	5.1522 6693	5.1780 8939
6	6.1520 1506	6.1713 0270	6.1906 5444	6.2295 5093	6.2687 0596
7	7.2135 3521	7.2407 2986	7.2680 3762	7.3229 9419	7.3784 0831
8	8.2856 7056	8.3221 8807	8.3588 8809	8.4328 3911	8.5075 3045
9	9.3685 2727	9.4158 1269	9.4633 7420	9.5593 3169	9.6564 1224
10	10.4622 1254	10.5217 4058	10.5816 6637	10.7027 2167	10.8253 9945
11	11.5668 3467	11.6401 1016	11.7139 3720	11.8632 6249	12.0148 4394
12	12.6825 0301	12.7710 6140	12.8603 6142	13.0412 1143	13.2251 0371
13	13.8093 2804	13.9147 3584	14.0211 1594	14.2368 2960	14.4565 4303
14	14.9474 2132	15.0712 7662	15.1963 7988	15.4503 8205	15.7095 3253
15	16.0968 9554	16.2408 2848	16.3863 3463	16.6821 3778	16.9844 4935
16	17.2578 6449	17.4235 3780	17.5911 6382	17.9323 6984	18.2816 7721
17	18.4304 4314	18.6195 5260	18.8110 5336	19.2013 5539	19.6016 0656
18	19.6147 4757	19.8290 2257	20.0461 9153	20.4893 7572	20.9446 3468
19	20.8108 9504	21.0520 9907	21.2967 6893	21.7967 1636	22.3111 6578
20	22.0190 0399	22.2889 3519	22.5629 7854	23.1236 6710	23.7016 1119
21	23.2391 9403	23.5396 8571	23.8450 1577	24.4705 2211	25.1163 8938
22	24.4715 8598	24.8045 0717	25.1430 7847	25.8375 7994	26.5559 2620
23	25.7163 0183	26.0835 5788	26.4573 6695	27.2251 4364	28.0206 5490
24	26.9734 6485	27.3769 9790	27.7880 8403	28.6335 2080	29.5110 1637
25	28.2431 9950	28.6849 8913	29.1354 3508	30.0630 2361	31.0274 5915
26	29.5256 3150	30.0076 9526	30.4996 2802	31.5139 6896	32.5704 3969
27	30.8208 8781	31.3452 8183	31.8808 7337	32.9866 7850	34.1404 2238
28	32.1290 9669	32.6979 1625	33.2793 8429	34.4814 7867	35.7378 7977
29	33.4503 8766	34.0657 6781	34.6953 7659	35.9987 0085	37.3632 9267
30	34.7848 9153	35.4490 0769	36.1290 6880	37.5386 8137	39.0171 5029
31	36.1327 4045	36.8478 0903	37.5806 8216	39.1017 6159	40.6999 5042
32	37.4940 6785	38.2623 4688	39.0504 4069	40.6882 8801	42.4121 9955
33	38.8690 0853	39.6927 9829	40.5385 7120	42.2986 1233	44.1544 1305
34	40.2576 9862	41.1393 4227	42.0453 0334	43.9330 9152	45.9271 1527
35	41.6602 7560	42.6021 5987	43.5708 6963	45.5920 8789	47.7308 3979
36	43.0768 7836	44.0814 3417	45.1155 0550	47.2759 6921	49.5661 2949
37	44.5076 4714	45.5773 5030	46.6794 4932	48.9851 0874	51.4335 3675
38	45.9527 2361	47.0900 9549	48.2629 4243	50.7198 8538	53.3336 2365
39	47.4122 5085	48.6198 5906	49.8662 2921	52.4806 8366	55.2669 6206
40	48.8863 7336	50.1668 3248	51.4895 5708	54.2678 9391	57.2341 3390
41	50.3752 3709	51.7312 0934	53.1331 7654	56.0819 1232	59.2357 3124
42	51.8789 8946	53.3131 8545	54.7973 4125	57.9231 4100	61.2723 5654
43	53.3977 7936	54.9129 5879	56.4823 0801	59.7919 8812	63.3446 2278
44	54.9317 5715	56.5307 2957	58.1883 3686	61.6888 6794	65.4531 5367
45	56.4810 7472	58.1667 0028	59.9156 9108	63.6142 0096	67.5985 8386
46	58.0458 8547	59.8210 7566	61.6646 3721	65.5684 1398	69.7815 5908
47	59.6263 4432	61.4940 6276	63.4354 4518	67.5519 4018	72.0027 3637
48	61.2226 0777	63.1858 7097	65.2283 8824	69.5652 1929	74.2627 8425
49	62.8348 3385	64.8967 1201	67.0437 4310	71.6086 9758	76.5623 8298
50	64.4631 8218	66.6268 0002	68.8817 8989	73.6828 2804	78.9022 2468

AMOUNT OF ANNUITY $[(1 + i)^n - 1]/i$ (Continued)

Periods	Rate i				
n	.01 (1 %)	.01125 (1⅛ %)	.0125 (1¼ %)	.015 (1½ %)	.0175 (1¾ %)
50	64.4631 822	66.6268 000	68.8817 899	73.6828 280	78.9022 247
51	66.1078 140	68.3763 515	70.7428 123	75.7880 705	81.2830 136
52	67.7688 921	70.1455 855	72.6270 974	77.9248 915	83.7054 663
53	69.4465 811	71.9347 233	74.5349 361	80.0937 649	86.1703 120
54	71.1410 469	73.7439 890	76.4666 228	82.2951 714	88.6782 925
55	72.8524 573	75.5736 088	78.4224 556	84.5295 989	91.2301 626
56	74.5809 819	77.4238 119	80.4027 363	86.7975 429	93.8266 904
57	76.3267 917	79.2948 298	82.4077 705	89.0995 061	96.4686 575
58	78.0900 597	81.1868 966	84.4378 676	91.4359 987	99.1568 590
59	79.8709 603	83.1002 492	86.4933 410	93.8075 386	101.8921 041
60	81.6696 699	85.0351 270	88.5745 078	96.2146 517	104.6752 159
61	83.4863 666	86.9917 722	90.6816 891	98.6578 715	107.5070 322
62	85.3212 302	88.9704 297	92.8152 102	101.1377 396	110.3884 052
63	87.1744 425	90.9713 470	94.9754 003	103.6548 057	113.3202 023
64	89.0461 869	92.9947 746	97.1625 928	106.2096 277	116.3033 058
65	90.9366 488	95.0409 659	99.3771 253	108.8027 722	119.3386 137
66	92.8460 153	97.1101 767	101.6193 393	111.4348 137	122.4270 394
67	94.7744 755	99.2026 662	103.8895 811	114.1063 359	125.5695 126
68	96.7222 202	101.3186 962	106.1882 008	116.8179 310	128.7669 791
69	98.6894 424	103.4585 315	108.5155 533	119.5701 999	132.0204 012
70	100.6763 368	105.6224 400	110.8719 978	122.3637 529	135.3307 583
71	102.6831 002	107.8106 925	113.2578 977	125.1992 092	138.6990 465
72	104.7099 312	110.0235 628	115.6736 215	128.0771 974	142.1262 798
73	106.7570 305	112.2613 278	118.1195 417	130.9983 553	145.6134 897
74	108.8246 008	114.5242 678	120.5960 360	133.9633 307	149.1617 258
75	110.9128 468	116.8126 658	123.1034 864	136.9727 806	152.7720 560
76	113.0219 753	119.1268 083	125.6422 800	140.0273 723	156.4455 670
77	115.1521 951	121.4669 849	128.2128 085	143.1277 829	160.1833 644
78	117.3037 170	123.8334 885	130.8154 686	146.2746 997	163.9865 733
79	119.4767 542	126.2266 152	133.4506 620	149.4688 202	167.8563 383
80	121.6715 217	128.6466 646	136.1187 953	152.7108 525	171.7938 242
81	123.8882 369	131.0939 396	138.8202 802	156.0015 153	175.8002 162
82	126.1271 193	133.5687 464	141.5555 337	159.3415 380	179.8767 200
83	128.3883 905	136.0713 948	144.3249 779	162.7316 611	184.0245 625
84	130.6722 744	138.6021 980	147.1290 401	166.1726 360	188.2449 924
85	132.9789 971	141.1614 727	149.9681 531	169.6652 255	192.5392 798
86	135.3087 871	143.7495 393	152.8427 550	173.2102 039	196.9087 172
87	137.6618 750	146.3667 216	155.7532 895	176.8083 569	201.3546 197
88	140.0384 937	149.0133 472	158.7002 056	180.4604 823	205.8783 256
89	142.4388 787	151.6897 474	161.6839 581	184.1673 895	210.4811 962
90	144.8632 675	154.3962 571	164.7050 076	187.9299 004	215.1646 172
91	147.3119 001	157.1332 149	167.7638 202	191.7488 489	219.9299 980
92	149.7850 191	159.9009 636	170.8608 680	195.6250 816	224.7787 729
93	152.2828 693	162.6998 495	173.9966 288	199.5594 578	229.7124 015
94	154.8056 980	165.5302 228	177.1715 867	203.5528 497	234.7323 685
95	157.3537 550	168.3924 378	180.3862 315	207.6061 425	239.8401 850
96	159.9272 926	171.2868 527	183.6410 594	211.7202 346	245.0373 882
97	162.5265 655	174.2138 298	186.9365 726	215.8960 381	250.3255 425
98	165.1518 311	177.1737 354	190.2732 798	220.1344 787	255.7062 395
99	167.8033 494	180.1669 399	193.6516 958	224.4364 959	261.1810 987
100	170.4813 829	183.1938 180	197.0723 420	228.8030 433	266.7517 679

AMOUNT OF ANNUITY $[(1 + i)^n - 1]/i$ (Continued)

Periods	Rate i				
n	.02 (2%)	.0225 (2¼%)	.025 (2½%)	.0275 (2¾%)	.03 (3%)
1	1.0000 0000	1.0000 0000	1.0000 0000	1.0000 0000	1.0000 0000
2	2.0200 0000	2.0225 0000	2.0250 0000	2.0275 0000	2.0300 0000
3	3.0604 0000	3.0680 0625	3.0756 2500	3.0832 5625	3.0909 0000
4	4.1216 0800	4.1370 3639	4.1525 1563	4.1680 4580	4.1836 2700
5	5.2040 4016	5.2301 1971	5.2563 2852	5.2826 6706	5.3091 3581
6	6.3081 2096	6.3477 9740	6.3877 3673	6.4279 4040	6.4684 0988
7	7.4342 8338	7.4906 2284	7.5474 3015	7.6047 0876	7.6624 6218
8	8.5829 6905	8.6591 6186	8.7361 1590	8.8138 3825	8.8923 3605
9	9.7546 2843	9.8539 9300	9.9545 1880	10.0562 1880	10.1591 0613
10	10.9497 2100	11.0757 0784	11.2033 8177	11.3327 6482	11.4638 7931
11	12.1687 1542	12.3249 1507	12.4834 6631	12.6444 1585	12.8077 9569
12	13.4120 8973	13.6022 2177	13.7955 5297	13.9921 3729	14.1920 2956
13	14.6803 3152	14.9082 7176	15.1404 4179	15.3769 2107	15.6177 9045
14	15.9739 3815	16.2437 0788	16.5189 5284	16.7997 8639	17.0863 2416
15	17.2934 1692	17.6091 9130	17.9319 2666	18.2617 8052	18.5989 1389
16	18.6392 8525	19.0053 9811	19.3802 2483	19.7639 7948	20.1568 8130
17	20.0120 7096	20.4330 1957	20.8647 3045	21.3074 8892	21.7615 8774
18	21.4123 1238	21.8927 6251	22.3863 4871	22.8934 4487	23.4144 3537
19	22.8405 5863	23.3853 4966	23.9460 0743	24.5230 1460	25.1168 6844
20	24.2973 6980	24.9115 2003	25.5446 5761	26.1973 9750	26.8703 7449
21	25.7833 1719	26.4720 2923	27.1832 7405	27.9178 2593	28.6764 8572
22	27.2989 8354	28.0676 4989	28.8628 5590	29.6855 6615	30.5367 8030
23	28.8449 6321	29.6991 7201	30.5844 2730	31.5019 1921	32.4528 8370
24	30.4218 6247	31.3674 0338	32.3490 3798	33.3682 2199	34.4264 7022
25	32.0302 9972	33.0731 6996	34.1577 6393	35.2858 4810	36.4592 6432
26	33.6709 0572	34.8173 1628	36.0117 0803	37.2562 0892	38.5530 4225
27	35.3443 2383	36.6007 0590	37.9120 0073	39.2807 5467	40.7096 3352
28	37.0512 1031	38.4242 2178	39.8598 0075	41.3609 7542	42.9309 2252
29	38.7922 3451	40.2887 6677	41.8562 9577	43.4984 0224	45.2188 5020
30	40.5680 7921	42.1952 6402	43.9027 0316	45.6946 0831	47.5754 1571
31	42.3794 4079	44.1446 5746	46.0002 7074	47.9512 1003	50.0026 7818
32	44.2270 2961	46.1379 1226	48.1502 7751	50.2698 6831	52.5027 5852
33	46.1115 7020	48.1760 1528	50.3540 3445	52.6522 8969	55.0778 4128
34	48.0338 0160	50.2599 7563	52.6128 8531	55.1002 2765	57.7301 7652
35	49.9944 7763	52.3908 2508	54.9282 0744	57.6154 8391	60.4620 8181
36	51.9943 6719	54.5696 1864	57.3014 1263	60.1999 0972	63.2759 4427
37	54.0342 5453	56.7974 3506	59.7339 4794	62.8554 0724	66.1742 2259
38	56.1149 3962	59.0753 7735	62.2272 9664	65.5839 3094	69.1594 4927
39	58.2372 3841	61.4045 7334	64.7829 7906	68.3874 8904	72.2342 3275
40	60.4019 8318	63.7861 7624	67.4025 5354	71.2681 4499	75.4012 5973
41	62.6100 2284	66.2213 6521	70.0876 1737	74.2280 1898	78.6632 9753
42	64.8622 2330	68.7113 4592	72.8398 0781	77.2692 8950	82.0231 9645
43	67.1594 6777	71.2573 5121	75.6608 0300	80.3941 9496	85.4838 9234
44	69.5026 5712	73.8606 4161	78.5523 2308	83.6050 3532	89.0484 0911
45	71.8927 1027	76.5225 0605	81.5161 3116	86.9041 7379	92.7198 6139
46	74.3305 6447	79.2442 6243	84.5540 3443	90.2940 3857	96.5014 5723
47	76.8171 7576	82.0272 5834	87.6678 8530	93.7771 2463	100.3965 0095
48	79.3535 1928	84.8728 7165	90.8595 8243	97.3559 9556	104.4083 9598
49	81.9405 8966	87.7825 1126	94.1310 7199	101.0332 8544	108.5406 4785
50	84.5794 0145	90.7576 1776	97.4843 4879	104.8117 0079	112.7968 6729

AMOUNT OF ANNUITY $[(1 + i)^n - 1]/i$ (Continued)

Periods	Rate i				
n	.02 (2 %)	.0225 (2¼ %)	.025 (2½ %)	.0275 (2¾ %)	.03 (3 %)
50	84.5794 015	90.7576 178	97.4843 488	104.8117 008	112.7968 673
51	87.2709 895	93.7996 642	100.9214 575	108.6940 226	117.1807 733
52	90.0164 093	96.9101 566	104.4444 939	112.6831 082	121.6961 965
53	92.8167 375	100.0906 351	108.0556 063	116.7818 937	126.3470 824
54	95.6730 722	103.3426 744	111.7569 965	120.9933 957	131.1374 949
55	98.5865 337	106.6678 846	115.5509 214	125.3207 141	136.0716 197
56	101.5582 643	110.0679 120	119.4396 944	129.7670 337	141.1537 683
57	104.5894 296	113.5444 400	123.4256 868	134.3356 272	146.3883 814
58	107.6812 182	117.0991 899	127.5113 289	139.0298 569	151.7800 328
59	110.8348 426	120.7339 217	131.6991 121	143.8531 780	157.3334 338
60	114.0515 394	124.4504 349	135.9915 900	148.8091 404	163.0534 368
61	117.3325 702	128.2505 697	140.3913 797	153.9013 917	168.9450 399
62	120.6792 216	132.1362 075	144.9011 642	159.1336 800	175.0133 911
63	124.0928 060	136.1092 722	149.5236 933	164.5098 562	181.2637 928
64	127.5746 622	140.1717 308	154.2617 856	170.0338 773	187.7017 066
65	131.1261 554	144.3255 948	159.1183 303	175.7098 089	194.3327 578
66	134.7486 785	148.5729 207	164.0962 885	181.5418 286	201.1627 406
67	138.4436 521	152.9158 114	169.1986 957	187.5342 289	208.1976 228
68	142.2125 251	157.3564 171	174.4286 631	193.6914 202	215.4435 515
69	146.0567 756	161.8969 365	179.7893 797	200.0179 343	222.9068 580
70	149.9779 111	166.5396 176	185.2841 142	206.5184 275	230.5940 637
71	153.9774 694	171.2867 590	190.9162 171	213.1976 842	238.5118 856
72	158.0570 188	176.1407 111	196.6891 225	220.0606 205	246.6672 422
73	162.2181 591	181.1038 771	202.6063 506	227.1122 876	255.0672 595
74	166.4625 223	186.1787 143	208.6715 093	234.3578 755	263.7192 773
75	170.7917 728	191.3677 354	214.8882 970	241.8027 171	272.6308 556
76	175.2076 082	196.6735 094	221.2605 045	249.4522 918	281.8097 813
77	179.7117 604	202.0986 634	227.7920 171	257.3122 298	291.2640 747
78	184.3059 956	207.6458 833	234.4868 175	265.3883 162	301.0019 969
79	188.9921 155	213.3179 157	241.3489 880	273.6864 948	311.0320 568
80	193.7719 578	219.1175 688	248.3827 126	282.2128 735	321.3630 185
81	198.6473 970	225.0477 141	255.5922 805	290.9737 275	332.0039 091
82	203.6203 449	231.1112 876	262.9820 875	299.9755 050	342.9640 264
83	208.6927 518	237.3112 916	270.5566 397	309.2248 314	354.2529 472
84	213.8666 068	243.6507 957	278.3205 557	318.7285 142	365.8805 356
85	219.1439 390	250.1329 386	286.2785 695	328.4935 484	377.8569 517
86	224.5268 178	256.7609 297	294.4355 338	338.5271 209	390.1926 602
87	230.0173 541	263.5380 506	302.7964 221	348.8366 168	402.8984 400
88	235.6177 012	270.4676 567	311.3663 327	359.4296 237	415.9853 932
89	241.3300 552	277.5531 790	320.1504 910	370.3139 384	429.4649 550
90	247.1566 563	284.7981 255	329.1542 533	381.4975 717	443.3489 037
91	253.0997 894	292.2060 834	338.3831 096	392.9887 549	457.6493 708
92	259.1617 852	299.7807 202	347.8426 873	404.7959 457	472.3788 519
93	265.3450 209	307.5257 865	357.5387 545	416.9278 342	487.5502 174
94	271.6519 214	315.4451 166	367.4772 234	429.3933 496	503.1767 240
95	278.0849 598	323.5426 318	377.6641 540	442.2016 667	519.2720 257
96	284.6466 590	331.8223 410	388.1057 578	455.3622 126	535.8501 865
97	291.3395 922	340.2883 437	398.8084 018	468.8846 734	552.9256 920
98	298.1663 840	348.9448 314	409.7786 118	482.7790 019	570.5134 628
99	305.1297 117	357.7960 901	421.0230 771	497.0554 245	588.6288 667
100	312.2323 059	366.8465 021	432.5486 540	511.7244 487	607.2877 327

FINANCIAL TABLES

AMOUNT OF ANNUITY $[(1 + i)^n - 1]/i$ (Continued)

Periods	Rate i				
n	.035 (3½ %)	.04 (4 %)	.045 (4½ %)	.05 (5 %)	.055 (5½ %)
1	1.0000 000	1.0000 000	1.0000 000	1.0000 000	1.0000 000
2	2.0350 000	2.0400 000	2.0450 000	2.0500 000	2.0550 000
3	3.1062 250	3.1216 000	3.1370 250	3.1525 000	3.1680 250
4	4.2149 429	4.2464 640	4.2781 911	4.3101 250	4.3422 664
5	5.3624 659	5.4163 226	5.4707 097	5.5256 313	5.5810 910
6	6.5501 522	6.6329 755	6.7168 917	6.8019 128	6.8880 510
7	7.7794 075	7.8982 945	8.0191 518	8.1420 085	8.2668 938
8	9.0516 868	9.2142 263	9.3800 136	9.5491 089	9.7215 730
9	10.3684 958	10.5827 953	10.8021 142	11.0265 643	11.2562 595
10	11.7313 932	12.0061 071	12.2882 094	12.5778 925	12.8753 538
11	13.1419 919	13.4863 514	13.8411 788	14.2067 872	14.5834 982
12	14.6019 616	15.0258 055	15.4640 318	15.9171 265	16.3855 907
13	16.1130 303	16.6268 377	17.1599 133	17.7129 828	18.2867 981
14	17.6769 864	18.2919 112	18.9321 094	19.5986 320	20.2925 720
15	19.2956 809	20.0235 876	20.7840 543	21.5785 636	22.4086 635
16	20.9710 297	21.8245 311	22.7193 367	23.6574 918	24.6411 400
17	22.7050 157	23.6975 124	24.7417 069	25.8403 664	26.9964 027
18	24.4996 913	25.6454 129	26.8550 837	28.1323 847	29.4812 048
19	26.3571 805	27.6712 294	29.0635 625	30.5390 039	32.1026 711
20	28.2796 818	29.7780 786	31.3714 228	33.0659 541	34.8683 180
21	30.2694 707	31.9692 017	33.7831 368	35.7192 518	37.7860 755
22	32.3289 022	34.2479 698	36.3033 780	38.5052 144	40.8643 097
23	34.4604 137	36.6178 886	38.9370 300	41.4304 751	44.1118 467
24	36.6665 282	39.0826 041	41.6891 963	44.5019 989	47.5379 983
25	38.9498 567	41.6459 083	44.5652 101	47.7270 988	51.1525 882
26	41.3131 017	44.3117 446	47.5706 446	51.1134 538	54.9659 805
27	43.7590 602	47.0842 144	50.7113 236	54.6691 264	58.9891 094
28	46.2906 273	49.9675 830	53.9933 332	58.4025 828	63.2335 105
29	48.9107 993	52.9662 863	57.4230 332	62.3227 119	67.7113 535
30	51.6226 773	56.0849 378	61.0070 697	66.4388 475	72.4354 780
31	54.4294 710	59.3283 353	64.7523 878	70.7607 899	77.4194 293
32	57.3345 025	62.7014 687	68.6662 452	75.2988 294	82.6774 979
33	60.3412 101	66.2095 274	72.7562 263	80.0637 708	88.2247 603
34	63.4531 524	69.8579 085	77.0302 565	85.0669 594	94.0771 221
35	66.6740 127	73.6522 249	81.4966 180	90.3203 074	100.2513 638
36	70.0076 032	77.5983 138	86.1639 658	95.8363 227	106.7651 888
37	73.4578 693	81.7022 464	91.0413 443	101.6281 389	113.6372 742
38	77.0288 947	85.9703 363	96.1382 048	107.7095 458	120.8873 242
39	80.7249 060	90.4091 497	101.4644 240	114.0950 231	128.5361 271
40	84.5502 777	95.0255 157	107.0303 231	120.7997 742	136.6056 141
41	88.5095 375	99.8265 363	112.8466 876	127.8397 630	145.1189 228
42	92.6073 713	104.8195 978	118.9247 885	135.2317 511	154.1004 636
43	96.8486 293	110.0123 817	125.2764 040	142.9933 387	163.5759 891
44	101.2383 313	115.4128 770	131.9138 422	151.1430 056	173.5726 685
45	105.7816 729	121.0293 920	138.8499 651	159.7001 559	184.1191 653
46	110.4840 314	126.8705 677	146.0982 135	168.6851 637	195.2457 194
47	115.3509 725	132.9453 904	153.6726 331	178.1194 218	206.9842 339
48	120.3882 566	139.2632 060	161.5879 016	188.0253 929	219.3683 668
49	125.6018 456	145.8337 343	169.8593 572	198.4266 626	232.4336 270
50	130.9979 102	152.6670 837	178.5030 283	209.3479 957	246.2174 764

AMOUNT OF ANNUITY $[(1 + i)^n - 1]/i$ (Continued)

Periods	Rate i				
n	.06 (6 %)	.065 (6½ %)	.07 (7 %)	.075 (7½ %)	.08 (8 %)
1	1.0000 000	1.0000 000	1.0000 000	1.0000 000	1.0000 000
2	2.0600 000	2.0650 000	2.0700 000	2.0750 000	2.0800 000
3	3.1836 000	3.1992 250	3.2149 000	3.2306 250	3.2464 000
4	4.3746 160	4.4071 746	4.4399 430	4.4729 219	4.5061 120
5	5.6370 930	5.6936 410	5.7507 390	5.8083 910	5.8666 010
6	6.9753 185	7.0637 276	7.1532 907	7.2440 203	7.3359 290
7	8.3938 376	8.5228 699	8.6540 211	8.7873 219	8.9228 034
8	9.8974 679	10.0768 565	10.2598 026	10.4463 710	10.6366 276
9	11.4913 160	11.7318 522	11.9779 887	12.2298 488	12.4875 578
10	13.1807 949	13.4944 225	13.8164 480	14.1470 875	14.4865 625
11	14.9716 426	15.3715 600	15.7835 993	16.2081 191	16.6454 875
12	16.8699 412	17.3707 114	17.8884 513	18.4237 280	18.9771 265
13	18.8821 377	19.4998 076	20.1406 429	20.8055 076	21.4952 966
14	21.0150 659	21.7672 951	22.5504 879	23.3659 207	24.2149 203
15	23.2759 699	24.1821 693	25.1290 220	26.1183 647	27.1521 139
16	25.6725 281	26.7540 103	27.8880 536	29.0772 421	30.3242 830
17	28.2128 798	29.4930 210	30.8402 173	32.2580 352	33.7502 257
18	30.9056 525	32.4100 674	33.9990 325	35.6773 879	37.4502 437
19	33.7599 917	35.5167 218	37.3789 648	39.3531 919	41.4462 632
20	36.7855 912	38.8253 087	40.9954 923	43.3046 813	45.7619 643
21	39.9927 267	42.3489 537	44.8651 768	47.5525 324	50.4229 214
22	43.3922 903	46.1016 357	49.0057 392	52.1189 724	55.4567 552
23	46.9958 277	50.0982 420	53.4361 409	57.0278 953	60.8932 956
24	50.8155 774	54.3546 278	58.1766 708	62.3049 874	66.7647 592
25	54.8645 120	58.8876 786	63.2490 377	67.9778 615	73.1059 400
26	59.1563 827	63.7153 777	68.6764 704	74.0762 011	79.9544 151
27	63.7057 657	68.8568 772	74.4838 233	80.6319 162	87.3507 684
28	68.5281 116	74.3325 743	80.6976 909	87.6793 099	95.3388 298
29	73.6397 983	80.1641 916	87.3465 293	95.2552 582	103.9659 362
30	79.0581 862	86.3748 640	94.4607 863	103.3994 025	113.2832 111
31	84.8016 774	92.9892 302	102.0730 414	112.1543 577	123.3458 680
32	90.8897 780	100.0335 302	110.2181 543	121.5659 345	134.2135 374
33	97.3431 647	107.5357 096	118.9334 251	131.6833 796	145.9506 204
34	104.1837 546	115.5255 308	128.2587 648	142.5596 331	158.6266 701
35	111.4347 799	124.0346 903	138.2368 784	154.2516 056	172.3168 037
36	119.1208 667	133.0969 451	148.9134 598	166.8204 760	187.1021 480
37	127.2681 187	142.7482 466	160.3374 020	180.3320 117	203.0703 198
38	135.9042 058	153.0268 826	172.5610 202	194.8569 126	220.3159 454
39	145.0584 581	163.9736 300	185.6402 916	210.4711 810	238.9412 210
40	154.7619 656	175.6319 159	199.6351 120	227.2565 196	259.0565 187
41	165.0476 836	188.0479 904	214.6095 698	245.3007 586	280.7810 402
42	175.9505 446	201.2711 098	230.6322 397	264.6983 155	304.2435 234
43	187.5075 772	215.3537 320	247.7764 965	285.5506 891	329.5830 053
44	199.7580 319	230.3517 245	266.1208 513	307.9669 908	356.9496 457
45	212.7435 138	246.3245 866	285.7493 108	332.0645 151	386.5056 174
46	226.5081 246	263.3356 848	306.7517 626	357.9693 537	418.4260 668
47	241.0986 121	281.4525 043	329.2243 860	385.8170 553	452.9001 521
48	256.5645 288	300.7469 170	353.2700 930	415.7533 344	490.1321 643
49	272.9584 006	321.2954 666	378.9989 995	447.9348 345	530.3427 374
50	290.3359 046	343.1796 720	406.5289 295	482.5299 471	573.7701 564

FINANCIAL TABLES

PRESENT VALUE OF ANNUITY $[1 - (1 + i)^{-n}]/i$ *

The following table gives the present value of an annuity of unit value per period for a term of n periods at rate of interest i per period; usually indicated as $a_{\overline{n}|i}$.

Periods	Rate i				
n	.0025 ($\frac{1}{4}$%)	.004167 ($\frac{1}{12}$%)	.005 ($\frac{1}{2}$%)	.005833 ($\frac{7}{12}$%)	.0075 ($\frac{3}{4}$%)
1	0.9975 0623	0.9958 5062	0.9950 2488	0.9942 0050	0.9925 5583
2	1.9925 2492	1.9875 6908	1.9850 9938	1.9826 3513	1.9777 2291
3	2.9850 6227	2.9751 7253	2.9702 4814	2.9653 3732	2.9555 5624
4	3.9751 2446	3.9586 7804	3.9504 9566	3.9423 4034	3.9261 1041
5	4.9627 1766	4.9381 0261	4.9258 6633	4.9136 7722	4.8894 3961
6	5.9478 4804	5.9134 6318	5.8963 8441	5.8793 8083	5.8455 9763
7	6.9305 2174	6.8847 7661	6.8620 7404	6.8394 8384	6.7946 3785
8	7.9107 4487	7.8520 5970	7.8229 5924	7.7940 1874	7.7366 1325
9	8.8885 2357	8.8153 2916	8.7790 6392	8.7430 1780	8.6715 7642
10	9.8638 6391	9.7746 0165	9.7304 1186	9.6865 1314	9.5995 7958
11	10.8367 7198	10.7298 9376	10.6770 2673	10.6245 3667	10.5206 7452
12	11.8072 5384	11.6812 2200	11.6189 3207	11.5571 2014	11.4349 1267
13	12.7753 1555	12.6286 0283	12.5561 5131	12.4842 9509	12.3423 4508
14	13.7409 6314	13.5720 5261	13.4887 0777	13.4060 9288	13.2430 2242
15	14.7042 0264	14.5115 8766	14.4166 2465	14.3225 4470	14.1369 9495
16	15.6650 4004	15.4472 2422	15.3399 2502	15.2336 8156	15.0243 1261
17	16.6234 8133	16.3789 7848	16.2586 3186	16.1395 3427	15.9050 2492
18	17.5795 3250	17.3068 6654	17.1727 6802	17.0401 3350	16.7791 8107
19	18.5331 9950	18.2309 0443	18.0823 5624	17.9355 0969	17.6468 2984
20	19.4844 8828	19.1511 0815	18.9874 1915	18.8256 9315	18.5080 1969
21	20.4334 0477	20.0674 9359	19.8879 7925	19.7107 1398	19.3627 9870
22	21.3799 5488	20.9800 7661	20.7840 5896	20.5906 0213	20.2112 1459
23	22.3241 4452	21.8888 7297	21.6756 8055	21.4653 8738	21.0533 1473
24	23.2659 7957	22.7938 9839	22.5628 6622	22.3350 9930	21.8891 4614
25	24.2054 6591	23.6951 6853	23.4456 3803	23.1997 6732	22.7187 5547
26	25.1426 0939	24.5926 9895	24.3240 1794	24.0594 2070	23.5421 8905
27	26.0774 1585	25.4865 0517	25.1980 2780	24.9140 8852	24.3594 9286
28	27.0098 9112	26.3766 0266	26.0676 8936	25.7637 9968	25.1707 1251
29	27.9400 4102	27.2630 0680	26.9330 2424	26.6085 8295	25.9758 9331
30	28.8678 7134	28.1457 3291	27.7940 5397	27.4484 6689	26.7750 8021
31	29.7933 8787	29.0247 9626	28.6507 9997	28.2834 7993	27.5683 1783
32	30.7165 9638	29.9002 1205	29.5032 8355	29.1136 5030	28.3556 5045
33	31.6375 0262	30.7719 9540	30.3515 2592	29.9390 0610	29.1371 2203
34	32.5561 1234	31.6401 6139	31.1955 4818	30.7595 7524	29.9127 7621
35	33.4724 3126	32.5047 2504	32.0353 7132	31.5753 8549	30.6826 5629
36	34.3864 6510	33.3657 0128	32.8710 1624	32.3864 6445	31.4468 0525
37	35.2982 1955	34.2231 0501	33.7025 0372	33.1928 3955	32.2052 6576
38	36.2077 0030	35.0769 5105	34.5298 5445	33.9945 3808	32.9580 8016
39	37.1149 1302	35.9272 5416	35.3530 8900	34.7915 8716	33.7052 9048
40	38.0198 6336	36.7740 2904	36.1722 2786	35.5840 1374	34.4469 3844
41	38.9225 5697	37.6172 9033	36.9872 9141	36.3718 4465	35.1830 6545
42	39.8229 9947	38.4570 5261	37.7982 9991	37.1551 0653	35.9137 1260
43	40.7211 9648	39.2933 3040	38.6052 7354	37.9338 2588	36.6389 2070
44	41.6171 5359	40.1261 3816	39.4082 3238	38.7080 2904	37.3587 3022
45	42.5108 7640	40.9554 9028	40.2071 9640	39.4777 4221	38.0731 8136
46	43.4023 7048	41.7814 0111	41.0021 8547	40.2429 9143	38.7823 1401
47	44.2916 4137	42.6038 8492	41.7932 1937	41.0038 0258	39.4861 6775
48	45.1786 9464	43.4229 5594	42.5803 1778	41.7602 0141	40.1847 8189
49	46.0635 3580	44.2386 2832	43.3635 0028	42.5122 1349	40.8781 9542
50	46.9461 7037	45.0509 1617	44.1427 8635	43.2598 6428	41.5664 4707

*For $a_{\overline{n}|i}$ where rates i = 0% to 20% are lacking in 1/4% scaling use tables $(1 + i)^{-n}$ and construct information by use of formula. See page 805.

PRESENT VALUE OF ANNUITY $[1 - (1 + i)^{-n}]/i$ (Continued)

Periods	Rate i				
n	.0025 ($\frac{1}{4}$%)	.004167 ($\frac{1}{12}$%)	.005 ($\frac{1}{2}$%)	.005833 ($\frac{7}{12}$%)	.0075 ($\frac{3}{4}$%)
50	46.9461 7037	45.0509 1617	44.1427 8635	43.2598 6428	41.5664 4707
51	47.8266 0386	45.8598 3353	44.9181 9537	44.0031 7907	42.2495 7525
52	48.7048 4176	46.6653 9439	45.6897 4664	44.7421 8301	42.9276 1812
53	49.5808 8953	47.4676 1267	46.4574 5934	45.4769 0108	43.6006 1351
54	50.4547 5265	48.2665 0224	47.2213 5258	46.2073 5816	44.2685 9902
55	51.3264 3656	49.0620 7692	47.9814 4535	46.9335 7895	44.9316 1193
56	52.1959 4669	49.8543 5046	48.7377 5657	47.6555 8802	45.5896 8926
57	53.0632 8847	50.6433 3656	49.4903 0505	48.3734 0980	46.2428 6776
58	53.9284 6730	51.4290 4885	50.2391 0950	49.0870 6856	46.8911 8388
59	54.7914 8858	52.2115 0093	50.9841 8856	49.7965 8846	47.5346 7382
60	55.6523 5769	52.9907 0632	51.7255 6075	50.5019 9350	48.1733 7352
61	56.5110 7999	53.7666 7850	52.4632 4453	51.2033 0754	48.8073 1863
62	57.3676 6083	54.5394 3087	53.1972 5824	51.9005 5431	49.4365 4455
63	58.2221 0557	55.3089 7680	53.9276 2014	52.5937 5739	50.0610 8640
64	59.0744 1952	56.0753 2959	54.6543 4840	53.2829 4024	50.6809 7906
65	59.9246 0800	56.8385 0250	55.3774 6109	53.9681 2617	51.2962 5713
66	60.7726 7631	57.5985 0871	56.0969 7621	54.6493 3836	51.9069 5497
67	61.6186 2974	58.3553 6137	56.8129 1165	55.3265 9986	52.5131 0667
68	62.4624 7355	59.1090 7357	57.5252 8522	55.9999 3358	53.1147 4607
69	63.3042 1302	59.8596 5832	58.2341 1465	56.6693 6230	53.7119 0677
70	64.1438 5339	60.6071 2862	58.9394 1756	57.3349 0867	54.3046 2210
71	64.9813 9989	61.3514 9738	59.6412 1151	57.9965 9520	54.8929 2516
72	65.8168 5774	62.0927 7748	60.3395 1394	58.5544 4427	55.4768 4880
73	66.6502 3216	62.8309 8172	61.0343 4222	59.3084 7815	56.0564 2561
74	67.4815 2834	63.5661 2287	61.7257 1366	59.9587 1896	56.6316 8795
75	68.3107 5146	64.2982 1365	62.4136 4543	60.6051 8869	57.2026 6794
76	69.1379 0670	65.0272 6670	63.0981 5466	61.2479 0922	57.7693 9746
77	69.9629 9920	65.7532 9464	63.7792 5836	61.8869 0229	58.3319 0815
78	70.7860 3411	66.4763 1002	64.4569 7350	62.5221 8952	58.8902 3141
79	71.6070 1657	67.1963 2533	65.1313 1691	63.1537 9239	59.4443 9842
80	72.4259 5169	67.9133 5303	65.8023 0539	63.7817 3229	59.9944 4012
81	73.2428 4458	68.6274 0550	66.4699 5561	64.4060 3044	60.5403 8722
82	74.0577 0033	69.3384 9511	67.1342 8419	65.0267 0798	61.0822 7019
83	74.8705 2402	70.0466 3413	67.7953 0765	65.6437 8590	61.6201 1930
84	75.6813 2072	70.7518 3482	68.4530 4244	66.2572 8507	62.1539 6456
85	76.4900 9548	71.4541 0936	69.1075 0491	66.8672 2625	62.6838 3579
86	77.2968 5335	72.1534 6991	69.7587 1135	67.4736 3007	63.2097 6257
87	78.1015 9935	72.8499 2854	70.4066 7796	68.0765 1706	63.7317 7427
88	78.9043 3850	73.5434 9730	71.0514 2086	68.6759 0759	64.2499 0002
89	79.7050 7581	74.2341 8818	71.6929 5608	69.2718 2197	64.7641 6875
90	80.5038 1627	74.9220 1313	72.3312 9958	69.8642 8033	65.2746 0918
91	81.3005 6486	75.6069 8403	72.9664 6725	70.4533 0273	65.7812 4981
92	82.0953 2654	76.2891 1272	73.5984 7487	71.0389 0910	66.2841 1892
93	82.8881 0628	76.9684 1101	74.2273 3818	71.6211 1923	66.7832 4458
94	83.6789 0901	77.6448 9063	74.8530 7282	72.1999 5284	67.2786 5467
95	84.4677 3966	78.3185 6329	75.4756 9434	72.7754 2950	67.7703 7685
96	85.2546 0315	78.9894 4062	76.0952 1825	73.3475 6869	68.2584 3856
97	86.0395 0439	79.6575 3422	76.7116 5995	73.9163 8975	68.7428 6705
98	86.8224 4827	80.3228 5566	77.3250 3478	74.4819 1193	69.2236 8938
99	87.6034 3967	80.9854 1642	77.9353 5799	75.0441 5436	69.7009 3239
100	88.3824 8346	81.6452 2797	78.5426 4477	75.6031 3607	70.1746 2272

PRESENT VALUE OF ANNUITY $[1 - (1 + i)^{-n}]/i$ (Continued)

Periods	Rate i				
n	.01 (1%)	.01125 (1⅛%)	.0125 (1¼%)	.015 (1½%)	.0175 (1¾%)
1	0.9900 9901	0.9888 7515	0.9876 5432	0.9852 2167	0.9828 0098
2	1.9703 9506	1.9667 4923	1.9631 1538	1.9558 8342	1.9486 9875
3	2.9409 8521	2.9337 4460	2.9265 3371	2.9122 0042	2.8979 8403
4	3.9019 6555	3.8899 8230	3.8780 5798	3.8543 8465	3.8309 4254
5	4.8534 3124	4.8355 8200	4.8178 3504	4.7826 4497	4.7478 5508
6	5.7954 7647	5.7706 6205	5.7460 0992	5.6971 8717	5.6489 9762
7	6.7281 9453	6.6953 3948	6.6627 2585	6.5982 1396	6.5346 4139
8	7.6516 7775	7.6097 3002	7.5681 2429	7.4859 2508	7.4050 5297
9	8.5660 1758	8.5139 4810	8.4623 4498	8.3605 1732	8.2604 9432
10	9.4713 0453	9.4081 0690	9.3455 2591	9.2221 8455	9.1012 2291
11	10.3676 2825	10.2923 1832	10.2178 0337	10.0711 1779	9.9274 9181
12	11.2550 7747	11.1666 9302	11.0793 1197	10.9075 0521	10.7395 4969
13	12.1337 4007	12.0313 4044	11.9301 8466	11.7315 3222	11.5376 4097
14	13.0037 0304	12.8863 6880	12.7705 5275	12.5433 8150	12.3220 0587
15	13.8650 5252	13.7318 8509	13.6005 4592	13.3432 3301	13.0928 8046
16	14.7178 7378	14.5679 9514	14.4202 9227	14.1312 6405	13.8504 9677
17	15.5622 5127	15.3948 0360	15.2299 1829	14.9076 4931	14.5950 8282
18	16.3982 6858	16.2124 1395	16.0295 4893	15.6725 6089	15.3268 6272
19	17.2260 0850	17.0209 2850	16.8193 0759	16.4261 6837	16.0460 5673
20	18.0455 5297	17.8204 4845	17.5993 1613	17.1686 3879	16.7528 8130
21	18.8569 8313	18.6110 7387	18.3696 9495	17.9001 3673	17.4475 4919
22	19.6603 7934	19.3929 0371	19.1305 6291	18.6208 2437	18.1302 6948
23	20.4558 2113	20.1660 3580	19.8820 3744	19.3308 6145	18.8012 4764
24	21.2433 8726	20.9305 6693	20.6242 3451	20.0304 0537	19.4606 8565
25	22.0231 5570	21.6865 9276	21.3572 6865	20.7196 1120	20.1087 8196
26	22.7952 0366	22.4342 0792	22.0812 5299	21.3986 3172	20.7457 3166
27	23.5596 0759	23.1735 0598	22.7962 9925	22.0676 1746	21.3717 2644
28	24.3164 4316	23.9045 7946	23.5025 1778	22.7267 1671	21.9869 5474
29	25.0657 8530	24.6275 1986	24.2000 1756	23.3760 7558	22.5916 0171
30	25.8077 0822	25.3424 1766	24.8889 0623	24.0158 3801	23.1858 4934
31	26.5422 8537	26.0493 6233	25.5692 9010	24.6461 4582	23.7698 7650
32	27.2695 8947	26.7484 4236	26 2412 7418	25.2671 3874	24.3438 5897
33	27.9896 9255	27.4397 4522	26.9049 6215	25.8789 5442	24.9079 6951
34	28.7026 6589	28.1233 5745	27.5604 5644	26.4817 2849	25.4623 7789
35	29.4085 8009	28.7993 6460	28.2078 5822	27.0755 9458	26.0072 5100
36	30.1075 0504	29.4678 5127	28.8472 6737	27.6606 8431	26.5427 5283
37	30.7995 0994	30.1289 0114	29.4787 8259	28.2371 2740	27.0690 4455
38	31.4846 6330	30.7825 9692	30.1025 0133	28.8050 5163	27.5862 8457
39	32.1630 3298	31.4290 2044	30.7185 1983	29.3645 8288	28.0946 2857
40	32.8346 8611	32.0682 5260	31.3269 3316	29.9158 4520	28.5942 2955
41	33.4996 8922	32.7003 7340	31.9278 3522	30.4589 6079	29.0852 3789
42	34.1581 0814	33.3254 6195	32.5213 1874	30.9940 5004	29.5678 0136
43	34.8100 0806	33.9435 9649	33.1074 7530	31.5212 3157	30.0420 6522
44	35.4554 5352	34.5548 5438	33.6863 9536	32.0406 2223	30.5081 7221
45	36.0945 0844	35.1593 1212	34.2581 6825	32.5523 3718	30.9662 6261
46	36.7272 3608	35.7570 4536	34.8228 8222	33.0564 8983	31.4164 7431
47	37.3536 9909	36.3481 2891	35.3806 2442	33.5531 9195	31.8589 4281
48	37.9739 5949	36.9326 3674	35.9314 8091	34.0425 5365	32.2938 0129
49	38.5880 7871	37.5106 4202	36.4755 3670	34.5246 8339	32.7211 8063
50	39.1961 1753	38.0822 1708	37.0128 7575	34.9996 8807	33.1412 0946

PRESENT VALUE OF ANNUITY $[1 - (1 + i)^{-n}]/i$ (Continued)

Periods	Rate i				
n	.01 (1%)	.01125 (1⅛%)	.0125 (1¼%)	.015 (1½%)	.0175 (1¾%)
50	39.1961 1753	38.0822 1708	37.0128 7575	34.9996 8807	33.1412 0946
51	39.7981 3617	38.6474 3345	37.5435 8099	35.4676 7298	33.5540 1421
52	40.3941 9423	39.2063 6188	38.0677 3431	35.9287 4185	33.9597 1913
53	40.9843 5072	39.7590 7232	38.5854 1660	36.3829 9690	34.3584 4632
54	41.5686 6408	40.3056 3394	39.0967 0776	36.8305 3882	34.7503 1579
55	42.1471 9216	40.8461 1514	39.6016 8667	37.2714 6681	35.1354 4550
56	42.7199 9224	41.3805 8358	40.1004 3128	37.7058 7863	35.5139 5135
57	43.2871 2102	41.9091 0613	40.5930 1855	38.1338 7058	35.8859 4727
58	43.8486 3468	42.4317 4896	41.0795 2449	38.5555 3751	36.2515 4523
59	44.4045 8879	42.9485 7746	41.5600 2419	38.9709 7292	36.6108 5526
60	44.9550 3841	43.4596 5633	42.0345 9179	39.3802 6889	36.9639 8552
61	45.5000 3803	43.9650 4952	42.5033 0054	39.7835 1614	37.3110 4228
62	46.0396 4161	44.4648 2029	42.9662 2275	40.1808 0408	37.6521 3000
63	46.5739 0258	44.9590 3119	43.4234 2988	40.5722 2077	37.9873 5135
64	47.1028 7385	45.4477 4407	43.8749 9247	40.9578 5298	38.3168 0723
65	47.6266 0777	45.9310 2009	44.3209 8022	41.3377 8618	38.6405 9678
66	48.1451 5621	46.4089 1975	44.7614 6195	41.7121 0461	38.9588 1748
67	48.6585 7050	46.8815 0284	45.1965 0563	42.0808 9125	39.2715 6509
68	49.1669 0149	47.3488 2852	45.6261 7840	42.4442 2783	39.5789 3375
69	49.6701 9949	47.8109 5527	46.0505 4656	42.8021 9490	39.8810 1597
70	50.1685 1435	48.2679 4094	46.4696 7562	43.1548 7183	40.1779 0267
71	50.6618 9539	48.7198 4270	46.8836 3024	43.5023 3678	40.4696 8321
72	51.1503 9148	49.1667 1714	47.2924 7431	43.8446 6677	40.7564 4542
73	51.6340 5097	49.6086 2016	47.6962 7093	44.1819 3771	41.0382 7560
74	52.1129 2175	50.0456 0708	48.0950 8240	44.5142 2434	41.3152 5857
75	52.5870 5124	50.4777 3259	48.4889 7027	44.8416 0034	41.5874 7771
76	53.0564 8638	50.9050 5077	48.8779 9533	45.1641 3826	41.8550 1495
77	53.5212 7364	51.3276 1510	49.2622 1761	45.4819 0962	42.1179 5081
78	53.9814 5905	51.7454 7847	49.6416 9640	45.7949 8485	42.3763 6443
79	54.4370 8817	52.1586 9317	50.0164 9027	46.1034 3335	42.6303 3359
80	54.8882 0611	52.5673 1092	50.3866 5706	46.4073 2349	42.8799 3474
81	55.3348 5753	52.9713 8286	50.7522 5389	46.7067 2265	43.1252 4298
82	55.7770 8666	53.3709 5957	51.1133 3717	47.0016 9720	43.3663 3217
83	56.2149 3729	53.7660 9104	51.4699 6264	47.2923 1251	43.6032 7456
84	56.6484 5276	54.1568 2674	51.8221 8532	47.5786 3301	43.8361 4237
85	57.0776 7600	54.5432 1557	52.1700 5958	47.8607 2218	44.0650 0479
86	57.5026 4951	54.9253 0588	52.5136 3909	48.1386 4254	44.2899 3099
87	57.9234 1535	55.3031 4549	52.8529 7688	48.4124 5571	44.5109 8869
88	58.3400 1520	55.6767 8169	53.1881 2531	48.6822 2237	44.7282 4441
89	58.7524 9030	56.0462 6126	53.5191 3611	48.9480 0234	44.9417 6355
90	59.1608 8148	56.4116 3041	53.8460 6035	49.2098 5452	45.1516 1037
91	59.5652 2919	56.7729 3490	54.1689 4850	49.4678 3696	45.3578 4803
92	59.9655 7346	57.1302 1992	54.4878 5037	49.7220 0686	45.5605 3860
93	60.3619 5392	57.4835 3021	54.8028 1518	49.9724 2055	45.7597 4310
94	60.7544 0982	57.8329 0997	55.1138 9154	50.2191 3355	45.9555 2147
95	61.1429 8002	58.1784 0294	55.4211 2744	50.4622 0054	46.1479 3265
96	61.5277 0299	58.5200 5235	55.7245 7031	50.7016 7541	46.3370 3455
97	61.9086 1682	58.8579 0096	56.0242 6698	50.9376 1124	46.5228 8408
98	62.2857 5923	59.1919 9106	56.3202 6368	51.1700 6034	46.7055 3718
99	62.6591 6755	59.5223 6446	56.6126 0610	51.3990 7422	46.8850 4882
100	63.0288 7877	59.8490 6251	56.9013 3936	51.6247 0367	47.0614 7304

FINANCIAL TABLES

PRESENT VALUE OF ANNUITY $[1 - (1 + i)^{-n}]/i$ (Continued)

Periods	Rate i				
n	.02 (2%)	.0225 (2¼%)	.025 (2½%)	.0275 (2¾%)	.03 (3%)
1	0.9803 9216	0.9779 9511	0.9756 0976	0.9732 3601	0.9708 7379
2	1.9415 6094	1.9344 6955	1.9274 2415	1.9204 2434	1.9134 6970
3	2.8838 8327	2.8698 9687	2.8560 2356	2.8422 6213	2.8286 1135
4	3.8077 2870	3.7847 4021	3.7619 7421	3.7394 2787	3.7170 9840
5	4.7134 5951	4.6794 5253	4.6458 2850	4.6125 8186	4.5797 0719
6	5.6014 3089	5.5544 7680	5.5081 2536	5.4623 6678	5.4171 9144
7	6.4719 9107	6.4102 4626	6.3493 9060	6.2894 0806	6.2302 8296
8	7.3254 8144	7.2471 8461	7.1701 3717	7.0943 1441	7.0196 9219
9	8.1622 3671	8.0657 0622	7.9708 6553	7.8776 7826	7.7861 0892
10	8.9825 8501	8.8662 1635	8.7520 6393	8.6400 7616	8.5302 0284
11	9.7868 4805	9.6491 1134	9.5142 0871	9.3820 6926	9.2526 2411
12	10.5753 4122	10.4147 7882	10.2577 6460	10.1042 0366	9.9540 0399
13	11.3483 7375	11.1635 9787	10.9831 8497	10.8070 1086	10.6349 5533
14	12.1062 4877	11.8959 3924	11.6909 1217	11.4910 0814	11.2960 7314
15	12.8492 6350	12.6121 6551	12.3813 7773	12.1566 9892	11.9379 3509
16	13.5777 0931	13.3126 3131	13.0550 0266	12.8045 7315	12.5611 0203
17	14.2918 7188	13.9976 8343	13.7121 9772	13.4351 0769	13.1661 1847
18	14.9920 3125	14.6676 6106	14.3533 6363	14.0487 6661	13.7535 1308
19	15.6784 6201	15.3228 9590	14.9788 9134	14.6460 0157	14.3237 9911
20	16.3514 3334	15.9637 **1237**	15.5891 6229	15.2272 5213	14.8774 7486
21	17.0112 0916	16.5904 **2775**	16.1845 4857	15.7929 4612	15.4150 2414
22	17.6580 4820	17.2033 5232	16.7654 1324	16.3434 9987	15.9369 1664
23	18.2922 0412	17.8027 8955	17.3321 1048	16.8793 1861	16.4436 0839
24	18.9139 2560	18.3890 3624	17.8849 8583	17.4007 9670	16.9355 4212
25	19.5234 5647	18.9623 8263	18.4243 7642	17.9083 1795	17.4131 4769
26	20.1210 3576	19.5231 1260	18.9506 1114	18.4022 5592	17.8768 4242
27	20.7068 9780	20.0715 0376	19.4640 1087	18.8829 7413	18.3270 3147
28	21.2812 7236	20.6078 2764	19.9648 8866	19.3508 2640	18.7641 0823
29	21.8443 8466	21.1323 4977	20.4535 4991	19.8061 5708	19.1884 5459
30	22.3964 5555	21.6453 2985	20 9302 9259	20.2493 0130	19.6004 4135
31	22.9377 0152	22.1470 2186	21.3954 0741	20.6805 8520	20.0004 2849
32	23.4683 3482	22.6376 7419	21.8491 7796	21.1003 2623	20.3887 6553
33	23.9885 6355	23.1175 2977	22.2918 8094	21.5088 3332	20.7657 9178
34	24.4985 9172	23.5868 2618	22.7237 8628	21.9064 0712	21.1318 3668
35	24.9986 1933	24.0457 9577	23.1451 5734	22.2933 4026	21.4872 2007
36	25.4888 4248	24.4946 6579	23.5562 5107	22.6699 1753	21.8322 5250
37	25.9694 5341	24.9336 5848	23.9573 1812	23.0364 1609	22.1672 3544
38	26.4406 4060	25.3629 9118	24.3486 0304	23.3931 0568	22.4924 6159
39	26.9025 8883	25.7828 7646	24.7303 4443	23.7402 4884	22.8082 1513
40	27.3554 7924	26.1935 2221	25.1027 7505	24.0781 0106	23.1147 7197
41	27.7994 8945	26.5951 3174	25.4661 2200	24.4069 1101	23.4123 9997
42	28.2347 9358	26.9879 0390	25.8206 0683	24.7269 2069	23.7013 5920
43	28.6615 6233	27.3720 3316	26.1664 4569	25.0383 6563	23.9819 0213
44	29.0799 6307	27.7477 0969	26.5038 4945	25.3414 7507	24.2542 7392
45	29.4901 5987	28.1151 1950	26.8330 2386	25.6364 7209	24.5187 1254
46	29.8923 1360	28.4744 4450	27.1541 6962	25.9235 7381	24.7754 4907
47	30.2865 8196	28.8258 6259	27.4674 8255	26.2029 9154	25.0247 0783
48	30.6731 1957	29.1695 4777	27.7731 5371	26.4749 3094	25.2667 0664
49	31.0520 7801	29.5056 7019	28.0713 6947	26.7395 9215	25.5016 5693
50	31.4236 0589	29.8343 9627	28.3623 1168	26.9971 6998	25.7297 6401

PRESENT VALUE OF ANNUITY $[1 - (1 + i)^{-n}]/i$ (Continued)

Periods	Rate i				
n	.02 (2%)	.0225 (2¼%)	.025 (2½%)	.0275 (2¾%)	.03 (3%)
50	31.4236 0589	29.8343 9627	28.3623 1168	26.9971 6998	25.7297 6401
51	31.7878 4892	30.1558 8877	28.6461 5774	27.2478 5400	25.9512 2719
52	32.1449 4992	30.4703 0687	28.9230 8072	27.4918 2871	26.1662 3999
53	32.4950 4894	30.7778 0623	29.1932 4948	27.7292 7368	26.3749 9028
54	32.8382 8327	31.0785 3910	29.4568 2876	27.9603 6368	26.5776 6047
55	33.1747 8752	31.3726 5438	29.7139 7928	28.1852 6879	26.7744 2764
56	33.5046 9365	31.6602 9768	29.9648 5784	28.4041 5454	26.9654 6373
57	33.8281 3103	31.9416 1142	30.2096 1740	28.6171 8203	27.1509 3566
58	34.1452 2650	32.2167 3489	30.4484 0722	28.8245 0806	27.3310 0549
59	34.4561 0441	32.4858 0429	30.6813 7290	29.0262 8522	27.5058 3058
60	34.7608 8668	32.7489 5285	30.9086 5649	29.2226 6201	27.6755 6367
61	35.0596 9282	33.0063 1086	31.1303 9657	29.4137 8293	27.8403 5307
62	35.3526 4302	33.2580 0573	31.3467 2836	29.5997 8879	28.0003 4279
63	35.6398 4316	33.5041 6208	31.5577 8377	29.7808 1634	28.1556 7261
64	35.9214 1486	33.7449 0179	31.7636 9148	29.9569 9887	28.3064 7826
65	36.1974 6555	33.9803 4405	31.9645 7705	30.1284 6605	28.4528 9152
66	36.4681 0348	34.2106 0543	32.1605 6298	30.2953 4409	28.5950 4031
67	36.7334 3478	34.4357 9993	32.3517 6876	30.4577 5581	28.7330 4884
68	36.9935 6351	34.6560 3905	32.5383 1099	30.6158 2074	28.8670 3771
69	37.2485 9168	34.8714 3183	32.7203 0340	30.7696 5522	28.9971 2399
70	37.4986 1929	35.0820 8492	32.8978 5698	30.9193 7247	29.1234 2135
71	37.7437 4441	35.2881 0261	33.0710 7998	31.065) 8270	29.2460 4015
72	37.9840 6314	35.4895 8691	33.2400 7803	31.2068 9314	29.3650 8752
73	38.2196 6975	35.6866 3756	33.4049 5417	31.3449 0816	29.4806 6750
74	38.4506 5662	35.8793 5214	33.5658 0895	31.4792 2936	29.5928 8107
75	38.6771 1433	36.0678 2605	33.7227 4044	31.6099 5558	29.7018 2628
76	38.8991 3170	36.2521 5262	33.8758 4433	31.7371 8304	29.8075 9833
77	39.1167 9578	36.4324 2310	34.0252 1398	31.8610 0540	29.9102 8964
78	39.3301 9194	36.6087 2675	34.1709 4047	31.9815 1377	30.0099 8994
79	39.5394 0386	36.7811 5085	34.3131 1265	32.0987 9685	30.1067 8635
80	39.7445 1359	36.9497 8079	34.4518 1722	32.2129 4098	30.2007 6345
81	39.9456 0156	37.1147 0004	34.5871 3875	32.3240 3015	30.2920 0335
82	40.1427 4663	37.2759 9026	34.7191 5976	32.4321 4613	30.3805 8577
83	40.3360 2611	37.4337 3130	34.8479 6074	32.5373 6950	30.4665 8813
84	40.5255 1579	37.5880 0127	34.9736 2023	32.6397 7469	30.5500 8556
85	40.7112 8999	37.7388 7655	35.0962 1486	32.7394 4009	30.6311 5103
86	40.8934 2156	37.8864 3183	35.2158 1938	32.8364 3804	30.7098 5537
87	41.0719 8192	38.0307 4018	35.3325 0671	32.9308 3994	30.7862 6735
88	41.2470 4110	38.1718 7304	35.4463 4801	33.0227 1527	30.8604 5374
89	41.4186 6774	38.3099 0028	35.5574 1269	33.1121 3165	30.9324 7936
90	41.5869 2916	38.4448 9025	35.6657 6848	33.1991 5489	31.0024 0714
91	41.7518 9133	38.5769 0978	35.7714 8144	33.2838 4905	31.0702 9820
92	41.9136 1895	38.7060 2423	35.8746 1604	33.3662 7644	31.1362 1184
93	42.0721 7545	38.8322 9754	35.9752 3516	33.4464 9776	31.2002 0567
94	42.2276 2299	38.9557 9221	36.0734 0016	33.5245 7202	31.2623 3560
95	42.3800 2254	39.0765 6940	36.1691 7089	33.6005 5671	31.3226 5592
96	42.5294 3386	39.1946 8890	36.2626 0574	33.6745 0775	31.3812 1934
97	42.6759 1555	39.3102 0920	36.3537 6170	33.7464 7956	31.4380 7703
98	42.8195 2505	39.4231 8748	36.4426 9434	33.8165 2512	31.4932 7867
99	42.9603 1867	39.5336 7968	36.5294 5790	33.8846 9598	31.5468 7250
100	43.0983 5164	39.6417 4052	36.6141 0526	33.9510 4232	31.5989 0534

PRESENT VALUE OF ANNUITY $[1 - (1 + i)^{-n}]/i$ (Continued)

Periods	Rate i				
n	.035 (3½%)	.04 (4%)	.045 (4½%)	.05 (5%)	.055 (5½%)
1	0.9661 8357	0.9615 3846	0.9569 3780	0.9523 8095	0.9478 6730
2	1.8996 9428	1.8860 9467	1.8726 6775	1.8594 1043	1.8463 1971
3	2.8016 3698	2.7750 9103	2.7489 6435	2.7232 4803	2.6979 3338
4	3.6730 7921	3.6298 9522	3.5875 2570	3.5459 5050	3.5051 5012
5	4.5150 5238	4.4518 2233	4.3899 7674	4.3294 7667	4.2702 8448
6	5.3285 5302	5.2421 3686	5.1578 7248	5.0756 9207	4.9955 3031
7	6.1145 4398	6.0020 5467	5.8927 0094	5.7863 7340	5.6829 6712
8	6.8739 5554	6.7327 4487	6.5958 8607	6.4632 1276	6.3345 6599
9	7.6076 8651	7.4353 3161	7.2687 9050	7.1078 2168	6.9521 9525
10	8.3166 0532	8.1108 9578	7.9127 1818	7.7217 3493	7.5376 2583
11	9.0015 5104	8.7604 7671	8.5289 1692	8.3064 1422	8.0925 3633
12	9.6633 3433	9.3850 7376	9.1185 8078	8.8632 5164	8.6185 1785
13	10.3027 3849	9.9856 4785	9.6828 5242	9.3935 7299	9.1170 7853
14	10.9205 2028	10.5631 2293	10.2228 2528	9.8986 4094	9.5896 4790
15	11.5174 1090	11.1183 8743	10.7395 4573	10.3796 5804	10.0375 8094
16	12.0941 1681	11.6522 9561	11.2340 1505	10.8377 6956	10.4621 6203
17	12.6513 2059	12.1656 6885	11.7071 9143	11.2740 6625	10.8646 0856
18	13.1896 8173	12.6592 9697	12.1599 9180	11.6895 8690	11.2460 7447
19	13.7098 3742	13.1339 3940	12.5932 9359	12.0853 2086	11.6076 5352
20	14.2124 0330	13.5903 2634	13.0079 3645	12.4622 1034	11.9503 8248
21	14.6979 7420	14.0291 5995	13.4047 2388	12.8211 5271	12.2752 4406
22	15.1671 2484	14.4511 1533	13.7844 2476	13.1630 0258	12.5831 6973
23	15.6204 1047	14.8568 4167	14.1477 7489	13.4885 7388	12.8750 4239
24	16.0583 6760	15.2469 6314	14.4954 7837	13.7986 4179	13.1516 9895
25	16.4815 1459	15.6220 7994	14.8282 0896	14.0939 4457	13.4139 3266
26	16.8903 5226	15.9827 6918	15.1466 1145	14.3751 8530	13.6624 9541
27	17.2853 6451	16.3295 8575	15.4513 0282	14.6430 3362	13.8980 9991
28	17.6670 1885	16.6630 6322	15.7428 7351	14.8981 2726	14.1214 2172
29	18.0357 6700	16.9837 1463	16.0218 8853	15.1410 7358	14.3331 0116
30	18.3920 4541	17.2920 3330	16.2888 8854	15.3724 5103	14.5337 4517
31	18.7362 7576	17.5884 9356	16.5443 9095	15.5928 1050	14.7239 2907
32	19.0688 6547	17.8735 5150	16.7888 9086	15.8026 7667	14.9041 9817
33	19.3902 0818	18.1476 4567	17.0228 6207	16.0025 4921	15.0750 6936
34	19.7006 8423	18.4111 9776	17.2467 5796	16.1929 0401	15.2370 3257
35	20.0006 6110	18.6646 1323	17.4610 1240	16.3741 9429	15.3905 5220
36	20.2904 9381	18.9082 8195	17.6660 4058	16.5468 5171	15.5360 6843
37	20.5705 2542	19.1425 7880	17.8622 3979	16.7112 8734	15.6739 9851
38	20.8410 8736	19.3678 6423	18.0499 9023	16.8678 9271	15.8047 3793
39	21.1024 9987	19.5844 8484	18.2296 5572	17.0170 4067	15.9286 6154
40	21.3550 7234	19.7927 7388	18.4015 8442	17.1590 8635	16.0461 2469
41	21.5991 0371	19.9930 5181	18.5661 0949	17.2943 6796	16.1574 6416
42	21.8348 8281	20.1856 2674	18.7235 4975	17.4232 0758	16.2629 9920
43	22.0626 8870	20.3707 9494	18.8742 1029	17.5459 1198	16.3630 3242
44	22.2827 9102	20.5488 4129	19.0183 8305	17.6627 7331	16.4578 5063
45	22.4954 5026	20.7200 3970	19.1563 4742	17.7740 6982	16.5477 2572
46	22.7009 1813	20.8846 5356	19.2883 7074	17.8800 6650	16.6329 1537
47	22.8994 3780	21.0429 3612	19.4147 0884	17.9810 1571	16.7136 6386
48	23.0912 4425	21.1951 3088	19.5356 0654	18.0771 5782	16.7902 0271
49	23.2765 6450	21.3414 7200	19.6512 9813	18.1687 2173	16.8627 5139
50	23.4556 1787	21.4821 8462	19.7620 0778	18.2559 2546	16.9315 1790

PRESENT VALUE OF ANNUITY $[1 - (1 + i)^{-n}]/i$ (Continued)

Periods	Rate i				
n	.06 (6%)	.065 (6½%)	.07 (7%)	.075 (7½%)	.08 (8%)
1	0.9433 9623	0.9389 6714	0.9345 7944	0.9302 3256	0.9259 2593
2	1.8333 9267	1.8206 2642	1.8080 1817	1.7955 6517	1.7832 6475
3	2.6730 1195	2.6484 7551	2.6243 1604	2.6005 2574	2.5770 9699
4	3.4651 0561	3.4257 9860	3.3872 1126	3.3493 2627	3.3121 2684
5	4.2123 6379	4.1556 7944	4.1001 9744	4.0458 8490	3.9927 1004
6	4.9173 2433	4.8410 1356	4.7665 3966	4.6938 4642	4.6228 7966
7	5.5823 8144	5.4845 1977	5.3892 8940	5.2966 0132	5.2063 7006
8	6.2097 9381	6.0887 5096	5.9712 9851	5.8573 0355	5.7466 3894
9	6.8016 9227	6.6561 0419	6.5152 3225	6.3788 8703	6.2468 8791
10	7.3600 8705	7.1888 3022	7.0235 8154	6.8640 8096	6.7100 8140
11	7.8868 7458	7.6890 4246	7.4986 7434	7.3154 2415	7.1389 6426
12	8.3838 4394	8.1587 2532	7.9426 8630	7.7352 7827	7.5360 7802
13	8.8526 8296	8.5997 4208	8.3576 5074	8.1258 4026	7.9037 7594
14	9.2949 8393	9.0138 4233	8.7454 6799	8.4891 5373	8.2442 3698
15	9.7122 4899	9.4026 6885	9.1079 1401	8.8271 1975	8.5594 7869
16	10.1058 9527	9.7677 6418	9.4466 4860	9.1415 0674	8.8513 6916
17	10.4772 5969	10.1105 7670	9.7632 2299	9.4339 5976	9.1216 3811
18	10.8276 0348	10.4324 6638	10.0590 8691	9.7060 0908	9.3718 8714
19	11.1581 1649	10.7347 1022	10.3355 9524	9.9590 7821	9.6035 9920
20	11.4699 2122	11.0185 0725	10.5940 1425	10.1944 9136	9.8181 4741
21	11.7640 7662	11.2849 8333	10.8355 2733	10.4134 8033	10.0168 0316
22	12.0415 8172	11.5351 9562	11.0612 4050	10.6171 9101	10.2007 4366
23	12.3033 7898	11.7701 3673	11.2721 8738	10.8066 8931	10.3710 5895
24	12.5503 5753	11.9907 3871	11.4693 3400	10.9829 6680	10.5287 5828
25	12.7833 5616	12.1978 7673	11.6535 8318	11.1469 4586	10.6747 7619
26	13.0031 6619	12.3923 7251	11.8257 7867	11.2994 8452	10.8099 7795
27	13.2105 3414	12.5749 9766	11.9867 0904	11.4413 8095	10.9351 6477
28	13.4061 6428	12.7464 7668	12.1371 1125	11.5733 7763	11.0510 7849
29	13.5907 2102	12.9074 8984	12.2776 7407	11.6961 6524	11.1584 0601
30	13.7648 3115	13.0586 7591	12.4090 4118	11.8103 8627	11.2577 8334
31	13.9290 8599	13.2006 3465	12.5318 1419	11.9166 3839	11.3497 9939
32	14.0840 4339	13.3339 2925	12.6465 5532	12.0154 7757	11.4349 9944
33	14.2302 2961	13.4590 8850	12.7537 9002	12.1074 2099	11.5138 8837
34	14.3681 4114	13.5766 0892	12.8540 0936	12.1929 4976	11.5869 3367
35	14.4982 4636	13.6869 5673	12.9476 7230	12.2725 1141	11.6545 6822
36	14.6209 8713	13.7905 6970	13.0352 0776	12.3465 2224	11.7171 9279
37	14.7367 8031	13.8878 5887	13.1170 1660	12.4153 6952	11.7751 7851
38	14.8460 1916	13.9792 1021	13.1934 7345	12.4794 1351	11.8288 6899
39	14.9490 7468	14.0649 8611	13.2649 2846	12.5389 8931	11.8785 8240
40	15.0462 9687	14.1455 2687	13.3317 0884	12.5944 0866	11.9246 1333
41	15.1380 1592	14.2211 5199	13.3941 2041	12.6459 6155	11.9672 3457
42	15.2245 4332	14.2921 6149	13.4524 4898	12.6939 1772	12.0066 9867
43	15.3061 7294	14.3588 3708	13.5069 6167	12.7385 2811	12.0432 3951
44	15.3831 8202	14.4214 4327	13.5579 0810	12.7800 2615	12.0770 7362
45	15.4558 3209	14.4802 2842	13.6055 2159	12.8186 2898	12.1084 0150
46	15.5243 6990	14.5354 2575	13.6500 2018	12.8545 3858	12.1374 0880
47	15.5890 2821	14.5872 5422	13.6916 0764	12.8879 4287	12.1642 6741
48	15.6500 2661	14.6359 1946	13.7304 7443	12.9190 1662	12.1891 3649
49	15.7075 7227	14.6816 1451	13.7667 9853	12.9479 2244	12.2121 6341
50	15.7618 6064	14.7245 2067	13.8007 4629	12.9748 1157	12.2334 8464

FINANCIAL TABLES

ANNUITY WHOSE PRESENT VALUE IS 1

$$\frac{1}{a_{\overline{n}|i}} = \frac{i}{1-(1+i)^{-n}} = \frac{i}{1-v^n} = \frac{1}{s_{\overline{n}|i}} + i$$

Rate i

Periods n	0.0025(1/4%)	0.004167(5/12%)	0.005(1/2%)	0.005833(7/12%)	0.0075(3/4%)
1	1.00250000	1.00416667	1.00500000	1.00583333	1.00750000
2	0.50187578	0.50312717	0.50375312	0.50437924	0.50563200
3	0.33500139	0.33611496	0.33667221	0.33722976	0.33834579
4	0.25156445	0.25260958	0.25313279	0.25365644	0.25470501
5	0.20150250	0.20250693	0.20300997	0.20351357	0.20452242
6	0.16812803	0.16910564	0.16959546	0.17008594	0.17106891
7	0.14428928	0.14524800	0.14572854	0.14620986	0.14717488
8	0.12641035	0.12735512	0.12782886	0.12830352	0.12925552
9	0.11250462	0.11343876	0.11390736	0.11437698	0.11531929
10	0.10138015	0.10230596	0.10277057	0.10323632	0.10417123
11	0.09227840	0.09319757	0.09365903	0.09412175	0.09505094
12	0.08469370	0.08560748	0.08606643	0.08652675	0.08745148
13	0.07827595	0.07918532	0.07964224	0.08010064	0.08102188
14	0.07277510	0.07368082	0.07413609	0.07459295	0.07551146
15	0.06800077	0.06891045	0.06936436	0.06982000	0.07073639
16	0.06383642	0.06473655	0.06518937	0.06564401	0.06655879
17	0.06015587	0.06105387	0.06150579	0.06195966	0.06287321
18	0.05688433	0.05778053	0.05823173	0.05868499	0.05959766
19	0.05395722	0.05485191	0.05530253	0.05575532	0.05666740
20	0.05132288	0.05221630	0.05266645	0.05311889	0.05403063
21	0.04893947	0.04983183	0.05028163	0.05073383	0.05164543
22	0.04677278	0.04766427	0.04811380	0.04856585	0.04947748
23	0.04479455	0.04568531	0.04613465	0.04658663	0.04749846
24	0.04298121	0.04387139	0.04432061	0.04477258	0.04568474
25	0.04131298	0.04220270	0.04265186	0.04310388	0.04401650
26	0.03977311	0.04066247	0.04111163	0.04156376	0.04247693
27	0.03834736	0.03923645	0.03968565	0.04013793	0.04105176
28	0.03702347	0.03791239	0.03836167	0.03881415	0.03972871
29	0.03579093	0.03667974	0.03712914	0.03758186	0.03849723
30	0.03464059	0.03552936	0.03597892	0.03643191	0.03734816
31	0.03356440	0.03445330	0.03490304	0.03535633	0.03627352
32	0.03255569	0.03344458	0.03389453	0.03434815	0.03526634
33	0.03160806	0.03249708	0.03294727	0.03340124	0.03432048
34	0.03071620	0.03160540	0.03205586	0.03251020	0.03343053
35	0.02987533	0.03076476	0.03121550	0.03167024	0.03259170
36	0.02908121	0.02997090	0.03042194	0.03087710	0.03179973
37	0.02833004	0.02922003	0.02967139	0.03012698	0.03105082
38	0.02761843	0.02850875	0.02896045	0.02941649	0.03034157
39	0.02694335	0.02783402	0.02828607	0.02874258	0.02966893
40	0.02630204	0.02719310	0.02764552	0.02810251	0.02903016
41	0.02569204	0.02658352	0.02703631	0.02749379	0.02842276
42	0.02511112	0.02600303	0.02645622	0.02691420	0.02784452
43	0.02455724	0.02544961	0.02590320	0.02636170	0.02729338
44	0.02402855	0.02492141	0.02537541	0.02583443	0.02676751
45	0.02352339	0.02441675	0.02487117	0.02533073	0.02626521
46	0.02304022	0.02393409	0.02438894	0.02484905	0.02578495
47	0.02257762	0.02347204	0.02392733	0.02438798	0.02532532
48	0.02213433	0.02302929	0.02348503	0.02394624	0.02488504
49	0.02170915	0.02260468	0.02306087	0.02352265	0.02446292

Rate i

Periods n	0.0025(1/4%)	0.004167(5/12%)	0.005(1/2%)	0.005833(7/12%)	0.0075(3/4%)
51	0.02090886	0.02180557	0.02226269	0.02272563	0.02366888
52	0.02053184	0.02142916	0.02188675	0.02235027	0.02329503
53	0.02016906	0.02106700	0.02152507	0.02198919	0.02293546
54	0.01981974	0.02071830	0.02117686	0.02164157	0.02258938
55	0.01948314	0.02038234	0.02081439	0.02130671	0.02225605
56	0.01915858	0.02005843	0.02051797	0.02098390	0.02193478
57	0.01884542	0.01974593	0.02020598	0.02067251	0.02162496
58	0.01854308	0.01944426	0.01990481	0.02037196	0.02132597
59	0.01825101	0.01915287	0.01961392	0.02008170	0.02103727
60	0.01796869	0.01887123	0.01933280	0.01980120	0.02075836
61	0.01769564	0.01859888	0.01906096	0.01952999	0.02048873
62	0.01743142	0.01833536	0.01879796	0.01926762	0.02022795
63	0.01717561	0.01808025	0.01854337	0.01901366	0.01997560
64	0.01692780	0.01783315	0.01829681	0.01876773	0.01973127
65	0.01668764	0.01759371	0.01805789	0.01852946	0.01949460
66	0.01645476	0.01736156	0.01782627	0.01829848	0.01926524
67	0.01622886	0.01713639	0.01760163	0.01807449	0.01904286
68	0.01600961	0.01691788	0.01738366	0.01785716	0.01882716
69	0.01579674	0.01670574	0.01717206	0.01764622	0.01861785
70	0.01558996	0.01649971	0.01696657	0.01744138	0.01841464
71	0.01538902	0.01629952	0.01676693	0.01724239	0.01821728
72	0.01519368	0.01610493	0.01657289	0.01704901	0.01802554
73	0.01500370	0.01591572	0.01638422	0.01686100	0.01783917
74	0.01481887	0.01573165	0.01620070	0.01667814	0.01765796
75	0.01463898	0.01555253	0.01602214	0.01650024	0.01748170
76	0.01446385	0.01537816	0.01584832	0.01632709	0.01731020
77	0.01429327	0.01520836	0.01567908	0.01615851	0.01714328
78	0.01412708	0.01504295	0.01551423	0.01599432	0.01698074
79	0.01396511	0.01488177	0.01535360	0.01583436	0.01682244
80	0.01380721	0.01472464	0.01519704	0.01567847	0.01666821
81	0.01365321	0.01457144	0.01504439	0.01552650	0.01651790
82	0.01350298	0.01442200	0.01489552	0.01537830	0.01637136
83	0.01335639	0.01427620	0.01475028	0.01523373	0.01622847
84	0.01321330	0.01413391	0.01460855	0.01509268	0.01608908
85	0.01307359	0.01399500	0.01447021	0.01495501	0.01595308
86	0.01293714	0.01385935	0.01433513	0.01482060	0.01582034
87	0.01280384	0.01372685	0.01420320	0.01468935	0.01569076
88	0.01267357	0.01359740	0.01407431	0.01456115	0.01556423
89	0.01254625	0.01347088	0.01394837	0.01443588	0.01544064
90	0.01242177	0.01334721	0.01382527	0.01431347	0.01531989
91	0.01230004	0.01322629	0.01370493	0.01419380	0.01520190
92	0.01218096	0.01310803	0.01358724	0.01407679	0.01508657
93	0.01206446	0.01299234	0.01347213	0.01396236	0.01497382
94	0.01195044	0.01287915	0.01335950	0.01385042	0.01486356
95	0.01183884	0.01276836	0.01324930	0.01374090	0.01475571
96	0.01172957	0.01265992	0.01314143	0.01363372	0.01465020
97	0.01162257	0.01255374	0.01303583	0.01352880	0.01454696
98	0.01151776	0.01244976	0.01293242	0.01342608	0.01444592
99	0.01141508	0.01234790	0.01283115	0.01332549	0.01434701

$$a_{\overline{n}|}^{-1} i = \frac{i}{1-v^n} = s_{\overline{n}|}^{-1} i + i \text{ (Continued)}$$

Rate i

Periods n	0.01(1%)	0.001125(1 1/8%)	0.0125(1 1/4%)	0.015(1 1/2%)	0.0175(1 3/4%)
1	1.01000000	1.01125000	1.01250000	1.01500000	1.01750000
2	0.50751244	0.50845323	0.50993441	0.51127792	0.51316295
3	0.34002211	0.34086130	0.34170117	0.34338296	0.34506746
4	0.25628109	0.25707058	0.25786102	0.25944479	0.26103237
5	0.20603980	0.20680034	0.20756211	0.20908932	0.21062142
6	0.17254837	0.17329034	0.17403381	0.17552521	0.17702256
7	0.14862828	0.14935762	0.15008872	0.15155616	0.15303059
8	0.13069029	0.13141071	0.13213314	0.13358402	0.13504292
9	0.11674036	0.11745432	0.11817055	0.11960982	0.12105813
10	0.10558208	0.10629131	0.10700307	0.10843418	0.10987534
11	0.09645408	0.09715984	0.09786839	0.09929384	0.10073038
12	0.08884879	0.08955203	0.09025831	0.09167999	0.09311377
13	0.08241482	0.08311626	0.08382100	0.08524036	0.08667283
14	0.07690117	0.07760138	0.07830515	0.07972332	0.08115562
15	0.07212378	0.07282321	0.07352646	0.07494436	0.07637739
16	0.06794460	0.06864363	0.06934672	0.07076508	0.07219958
17	0.06425806	0.06495698	0.06566023	0.06707966	0.06851623
18	0.06098205	0.06168113	0.06238479	0.06380578	0.06524492
19	0.05805175	0.05875120	0.05945548	0.06087847	0.06232061
20	0.05541531	0.05611531	0.05682039	0.05824574	0.05969122
21	0.05303075	0.05373145	0.05443749	0.05586550	0.05731464
22	0.05086372	0.05156525	0.05227238	0.05370332	0.05515638
23	0.04888584	0.04958833	0.05029666	0.05173075	0.05318796
24	0.04707347	0.04777701	0.04848665	0.04992410	0.05138565
25	0.04540675	0.04611144	0.04682247	0.04826345	0.04972952
26	0.04386888	0.04457479	0.04528729	0.04673196	0.04820269
27	0.04244553	0.04315273	0.04386677	0.04531527	0.04679079
28	0.04112444	0.04183299	0.04254863	0.04400108	0.04548151
29	0.03989502	0.04060498	0.04132228	0.04277878	0.04426424
30	0.03874811	0.03945953	0.04017854	0.04163919	0.04312975
31	0.03767573	0.03838866	0.03910942	0.04057430	0.04207005
32	0.03667089	0.03738535	0.03810791	0.03957710	0.04107812
33	0.03572744	0.03644349	0.03716786	0.03864144	0.04014779
34	0.03483997	0.03555763	0.03628387	0.03776189	0.03927363
35	0.03400368	0.03472299	0.03545111	0.03693363	0.03845082
36	0.03321431	0.03393529	0.03466533	0.03615240	0.03767507
37	0.03246805	0.03319072	0.03392270	0.03541437	0.03694257
38	0.03176150	0.03248589	0.03321983	0.03471613	0.03624990
39	0.03109160	0.03181773	0.03255365	0.03405463	0.03559399
40	0.03045560	0.03118349	0.03192141	0.03342710	0.03497209
41	0.02985102	0.03058069	0.03132063	0.03283106	0.03438170
42	0.02927563	0.03000709	0.03074906	0.03226426	0.03382057
43	0.02872737	0.02946064	0.03020466	0.03172465	0.03328666
44	0.02820441	0.02893949	0.02968557	0.03121038	0.03277810
45	0.02770505	0.02844197	0.02919012	0.03071976	0.03229321
46	0.02722775	0.02796652	0.02871675	0.03025125	0.03183043
47	0.02677111	0.02751173	0.02826406	0.02980342	0.03138836
48	0.02633384	0.02707632	0.02783075	0.02937500	0.03096569
49	0.02591474	0.02665910	0.02741563	0.02896478	0.03056124
50	0.02551273	0.02625898	0.02701763	0.02857168	0.03017391

Rate i

Periods n	0.01(1%)	0.001125(1 1/8%)	0.0125(1 1/4%)	0.015(1 1/2%)	0.0175(1 3/4%)
51	0.02512680	0.02587494	0.02663571	0.02819469	0.02980269
52	0.02475603	0.02550606	0.02626897	0.02783287	0.02944665
53	0.02439956	0.02515149	0.02591653	0.02748537	0.02910492
54	0.02405658	0.02481043	0.02557760	0.02715138	0.02877672
55	0.02372637	0.02448213	0.02525145	0.02683018	0.02846129
56	0.02340824	0.02416592	0.02493739	0.02652106	0.02815795
57	0.02310156	0.02386116	0.02463478	0.02622341	0.02786606
58	0.02280573	0.02356726	0.02434303	0.02593661	0.02758503
59	0.02252020	0.02328366	0.02406158	0.02566012	0.02731430
60	0.02224445	0.02300985	0.02378993	0.02539343	0.02705336
61	0.02197800	0.02274534	0.02352758	0.02513604	0.02680172
62	0.02172041	0.02248969	0.02327410	0.02488751	0.02655892
63	0.02147125	0.02224247	0.02302904	0.02464741	0.02632455
64	0.02123013	0.02200329	0.02279203	0.02441534	0.02609821
65	0.02099667	0.02177178	0.02256268	0.02419094	0.02587952
66	0.02077052	0.02154758	0.02234065	0.02397386	0.02566613
67	0.02055136	0.02133037	0.02212560	0.02376376	0.02546372
68	0.02033889	0.02111985	0.02191724	0.02356033	0.02526597
69	0.02013280	0.02091571	0.02171527	0.02336329	0.02507459
70	0.01993282	0.02071769	0.02151941	0.02317235	0.02488930
71	0.01973870	0.02052552	0.02132941	0.02298727	0.02470985
72	0.01955019	0.02033896	0.02114501	0.02280779	0.02453600
73	0.01936706	0.02015779	0.02096600	0.02263368	0.02436750
74	0.01918910	0.01998177	0.02079215	0.02246473	0.02420413
75	0.01901609	0.01981072	0.02062325	0.02230072	0.02404570
76	0.01884784	0.01964442	0.02045910	0.02214146	0.02389200
77	0.01868416	0.01948269	0.02029953	0.02198676	0.02374285
78	0.01852488	0.01932536	0.02014436	0.02183645	0.02359806
79	0.01836983	0.01917226	0.01999341	0.02169036	0.02345748
80	0.01821885	0.01902323	0.01984652	0.02154832	0.02332093
81	0.01807179	0.01887812	0.01970356	0.02141019	0.02318828
82	0.01792851	0.01873678	0.01956437	0.02127583	0.02305936
83	0.01778887	0.01859908	0.01942881	0.02114509	0.02293406
84	0.01765273	0.01846489	0.01929675	0.02101784	0.02281223
85	0.01751998	0.01833409	0.01916808	0.02089396	0.02269375
86	0.01739050	0.01820654	0.01904267	0.02077333	0.02257850
87	0.01726418	0.01808215	0.01892041	0.02065584	0.02246636
88	0.01714089	0.01796081	0.01880119	0.02054138	0.02235724
89	0.01702056	0.01784240	0.01868491	0.02042984	0.02225102
90	0.01690306	0.01772684	0.01857146	0.02032113	0.02214760
91	0.01678832	0.01761403	0.01846076	0.02021516	0.02204690
92	0.01667624	0.01750387	0.01835272	0.02011182	0.02194882
93	0.01656673	0.01739629	0.01824724	0.02001104	0.02185327
94	0.01645971	0.01729119	0.01814425	0.01991273	0.02176017
95	0.01635511	0.01718851	0.01804366	0.01981681	0.02166944
96	0.01625284	0.01708816	0.01794541	0.01972321	0.02158101
97	0.01615284	0.01699007	0.01784941	0.01963186	0.02149480
98	0.01605503	0.01689418	0.01775560	0.01954268	0.02141074
99	0.01595936	0.01680041	0.01766391	0.01945560	0.02132876
100	0.01586574	0.01670870	0.01757428	0.01937057	0.02124880

ANNUITY WHOSE PRESENT VALUE IS 1

$$a_{\overline{n}|i}^{-1} = \frac{i}{1 - v^n} = s_{\overline{n}|i}^{-1} + i \text{ (Continued)}$$

Rate i

Periods n	0.02(2%)	0.0225(2 1/4%)	0.025(2 1/2%)	0.0275(2 3/4%)
1	1.02000000	1.02250000	1.02500000	1.02750000
2	0.51504950	0.51693758	0.51882716	0.52071825
3	0.34675467	0.34844458	0.35013717	0.35183243
4	0.26262375	0.26421893	0.26581788	0.26742059
5	0.21215839	0.21370021	0.21524686	0.21679832
6	0.17852581	0.18003496	0.18154997	0.18307083
7	0.15451196	0.15600025	0.15749543	0.15899747
8	0.13650980	0.13798462	0.13946735	0.14095795
9	0.12251544	0.12398170	0.12545689	0.12694095
10	0.11132653	0.11278768	0.11425876	0.11573972
11	0.10217794	0.10363649	0.10510596	0.10658629
12	0.09455960	0.09601740	0.09748713	0.09896871
13	0.08811835	0.08957686	0.09104827	0.09253252
14	0.08260197	0.08406230	0.08553652	0.08702457
15	0.07782547	0.07928852	0.08076646	0.08225917
16	0.07365013	0.07511663	0.07659899	0.07809710
17	0.06996984	0.07144039	0.07292777	0.07443186
18	0.06670210	0.06817720	0.06967008	0.07118063
19	0.06378177	0.06526182	0.06676062	0.06827802
20	0.06115672	0.06264207	0.06414713	0.06567173
21	0.05878477	0.06027572	0.06178733	0.06331941
22	0.05663140	0.05812821	0.05964661	0.06118640
23	0.05466810	0.05617097	0.05769638	0.05924410
24	0.05287110	0.05438023	0.05591282	0.05746863
25	0.05122044	0.05273599	0.05427592	0.05583997
26	0.04969923	0.05122134	0.05276875	0.05434116
27	0.04829309	0.04982188	0.05137687	0.05295776
28	0.04698967	0.04852525	0.05008793	0.05167738
29	0.04577836	0.04732081	0.04889127	0.05048935
30	0.04464992	0.04619934	0.04777764	0.04938442
31	0.04359635	0.04515280	0.04673900	0.04835453
32	0.04261061	0.04417415	0.04576831	0.04739263
33	0.04168653	0.04325722	0.04485938	0.04649253
34	0.04081867	0.04239655	0.04400675	0.04564875
35	0.04000221	0.04158731	0.04320558	0.04485645
36	0.03923285	0.04082522	0.04245158	0.04411132
37	0.03850678	0.04010643	0.04174090	0.04340953
38	0.03782057	0.03942753	0.04107012	0.04274764
39	0.03717114	0.03878543	0.04043615	0.04212256
40	0.03655575	0.03817738	0.03983623	0.04153151
41	0.03597188	0.03760087	0.03926786	0.04097200
42	0.03541729	0.03705364	0.03872876	0.04044175
43	0.03488993	0.03653364	0.03821688	0.03993871
44	0.03438794	0.03603901	0.03773037	0.03946100
45	0.03390962	0.03556805	0.03726751	0.03900693
46	0.03345342	0.03511921	0.03682676	0.03857493
47	0.03301792	0.03469107	0.03640669	0.03816358
48	0.03260184	0.03428233	0.03600599	0.03777158
49	0.03220396	0.03389179	0.03562348	0.03739773

Rate i

Periods n	0.02(2%)	0.0225(2 1/4%)	0.025(2 1/2%)	0.0275(2 3/4%)
51	0.03145856	0.03316102	0.03490870	0.03670014
52	0.03110909	0.03281884	0.03457446	0.03637444
53	0.03077392	0.03249094	0.03425449	0.03606297
54	0.03045226	0.03217654	0.03394799	0.03576491
55	0.03014337	0.03187489	0.03365419	0.03547953
56	0.02984656	0.03158530	0.03337243	0.03520612
57	0.02956120	0.03130712	0.03310204	0.03494404
58	0.02928667	0.03103977	0.03284244	0.03469270
59	0.02902243	0.03078268	0.03259307	0.03445153
60	0.02876797	0.03053533	0.03235340	0.03422002
61	0.02852278	0.03029724	0.03212294	0.03399767
62	0.02828643	0.03006795	0.03190126	0.03378402
63	0.02805848	0.02984704	0.03168790	0.03357866
64	0.02783855	0.02963411	0.03148249	0.03338118
65	0.02762624	0.02942878	0.03128463	0.03319120
66	0.02742122	0.02923070	0.03109398	0.03300837
67	0.02722316	0.02903955	0.03091021	0.03283236
68	0.02703173	0.02885500	0.03073300	0.03266285
69	0.02684665	0.02867677	0.03056206	0.03249955
70	0.02666765	0.02850458	0.03039712	0.03234218
71	0.02649446	0.02833816	0.03023790	0.03219048
72	0.02632683	0.02817728	0.03008417	0.03204420
73	0.02616454	0.02802169	0.02993568	0.03190311
74	0.02600736	0.02787118	0.02979222	0.03176698
75	0.02585508	0.02772554	0.02965358	0.03163560
76	0.02570751	0.02758457	0.02951956	0.03150878
77	0.02556447	0.02744808	0.02938997	0.03138633
78	0.02542576	0.02731589	0.02926463	0.03126806
79	0.02529123	0.02718784	0.02914338	0.03115382
80	0.02516071	0.02706376	0.02902605	0.03104342
81	0.02503405	0.02694350	0.02891248	0.03093674
82	0.02491110	0.02682692	0.02880254	0.03083361
83	0.02479173	0.02671387	0.02869608	0.03073389
84	0.02467581	0.02660423	0.02859298	0.03063747
85	0.02456321	0.02649787	0.02849310	0.03054420
86	0.02445381	0.02639467	0.02839633	0.03045397
87	0.02434750	0.02629452	0.02830255	0.03036667
88	0.02424416	0.02619730	0.02821165	0.03028219
89	0.02414370	0.02610291	0.02812353	0.03020041
90	0.02404602	0.02601126	0.02803809	0.03012125
91	0.02395101	0.02592224	0.02795523	0.03004460
92	0.02385859	0.02583577	0.02787486	0.02997038
93	0.02376868	0.02575176	0.02779690	0.02989850
94	0.02368118	0.02567012	0.02772126	0.02982887
95	0.02359602	0.02559078	0.02764786	0.02976141
96	0.02351313	0.02551366	0.02757662	0.02969605
97	0.02343242	0.02543868	0.02750747	0.02963272
98	0.02335383	0.02536578	0.02744034	0.02957134
99	0.02327729	0.02529489	0.02737517	0.02951185

$$a_{\overline{n}|}^{-1} = \frac{i}{1 - v^n} = s_{\overline{n}|}^{-1} + i \text{ (Continued)}$$

Rate i

Periods n	0.03(3%)	0.0325(3 1/4%)	0.035(3 1/2%)	0.0375(3 3/4%)
1	1.03000000	1.03250000	1.03500000	1.03750000
2	0.52261084	0.52450492	0.52640049	0.52829755
3	0.35353036	0.35523095	0.35693418	0.35864005
4	0.26902705	0.27063723	0.27225114	0.27386875
5	0.21835457	0.21991560	0.22148137	0.22305189
6	0.18459750	0.18612997	0.18766821	0.18921219
7	0.16050635	0.16202204	0.16354449	0.16507370
8	0.14245639	0.14396263	0.14547665	0.14699839
9	0.12843386	0.12993555	0.13144601	0.13296517
10	0.11723051	0.11873107	0.12024137	0.12176134
11	0.10807745	0.10957936	0.11109197	0.11261521
12	0.10046209	0.10196719	0.10348395	0.10501230
13	0.09402954	0.09553925	0.09706157	0.09859642
14	0.08852634	0.09004176	0.09157073	0.09311317
15	0.08376658	0.08528858	0.08682507	0.08837595
16	0.07961085	0.08114013	0.08268483	0.08424483
17	0.07595253	0.07748966	0.07904313	0.08061280
18	0.07270870	0.07425415	0.07581684	0.07739662
19	0.06981388	0.07136804	0.07294033	0.07453058
20	0.06721571	0.06877888	0.07036108	0.07196102
21	0.06487178	0.06644424	0.06803659	0.06964862
22	0.06274739	0.06432936	0.06593207	0.06755531
23	0.06081390	0.06240555	0.06401880	0.06565339
24	0.05904742	0.06064891	0.06227283	0.06391890
25	0.05742787	0.05903933	0.06067404	0.06233169
26	0.05593829	0.05755981	0.05920540	0.06087470
27	0.05456421	0.05619588	0.05785241	0.05953343
28	0.05329323	0.05493512	0.05660265	0.05829560
29	0.05211467	0.05376682	0.05544538	0.05714991
30	0.05101926	0.05268172	0.05437133	0.05608762
31	0.04999893	0.05167172	0.05337240	0.05510046
32	0.04904662	0.05072976	0.05244150	0.05418131
33	0.04815612	0.04984961	0.05157242	0.05332395
34	0.04732196	0.04902581	0.05075966	0.05252287
35	0.04653929	0.04825348	0.04999835	0.05177320
36	0.04580379	0.04752831	0.04928416	0.05107060
37	0.04511162	0.04684645	0.04861325	0.05041122
38	0.04445934	0.04620445	0.04798214	0.04979159
39	0.04384385	0.04559920	0.04738775	0.04920860
40	0.04326238	0.04502794	0.04682728	0.04865946
41	0.04271241	0.04448814	0.04629822	0.04814164
42	0.04219167	0.04397753	0.04579828	0.04765286
43	0.04169811	0.04349403	0.04532539	0.04719106
44	0.04122985	0.04303579	0.04487768	0.04675434
45	0.04078518	0.04260108	0.04445343	0.04634098
46	0.04036254	0.04218835	0.04405148	0.04594943
47	0.03996051	0.04179616	0.04366919	0.04557824
48	0.03957777	0.04142320	0.04330646	0.04522609
49	0.03921314	0.04106828	0.04296167	0.04489179
50	0.03886549	0.04073027	0.04263371	0.04457422

Rate i

Periods n	0.03(3%)	0.0325(3 1/4%)	0.035(3 1/2%)	0.0375(3 3/4%)
51	0.03853382	0.04040817	0.04232156	0.04427235
52	0.03821718	0.04010103	0.04202429	0.04398523
53	0.03791471	0.03980797	0.04174100	0.04371199
54	0.03762558	0.03952819	0.04147090	0.04345183
55	0.03734907	0.03926095	0.04121323	0.04320398
56	0.03708447	0.03900553	0.04096730	0.04296775
57	0.03683114	0.03876131	0.04073245	0.04274249
58	0.03658848	0.03852767	0.04050810	0.04252760
59	0.03635593	0.03830405	0.04029366	0.04232251
60	0.03613296	0.03808993	0.04008862	0.04212670
61	0.03591908	0.03788483	0.03989249	0.04193967
62	0.03571385	0.03768827	0.03970480	0.04176097
63	0.03551682	0.03749983	0.03952513	0.04159016
64	0.03532760	0.03731912	0.03935308	0.04142684
65	0.03514581	0.03714574	0.03918826	0.04127063
66	0.03497110	0.03697935	0.03903031	0.04112118
67	0.03480313	0.03681962	0.03887892	0.04097816
68	0.03464159	0.03666622	0.03873375	0.04084124
69	0.03448618	0.03651886	0.03859453	0.04071013
70	0.03433663	0.03637727	0.03846095	0.04058456
71	0.03419266	0.03624117	0.03833277	0.04046426
72	0.03405404	0.03611033	0.03820973	0.04034898
73	0.03392053	0.03598451	0.03809160	0.04023848
74	0.03379191	0.03586347	0.03797816	0.04013255
75	0.03366796	0.03574702	0.03786919	0.04003098
76	0.03354849	0.03563496	0.03776450	0.03993356
77	0.03343331	0.03552709	0.03766390	0.03984011
78	0.03332224	0.03542323	0.03756721	0.03975045
79	0.03321510	0.03532323	0.03747426	0.03966442
80	0.03311175	0.03522690	0.03738489	0.03958184
81	0.03301201	0.03513411	0.03729894	0.03950258
82	0.03291576	0.03504471	0.03721628	0.03942647
83	0.03282284	0.03495855	0.03713676	0.03935340
84	0.03273313	0.03487550	0.03706025	0.03928323
85	0.03264650	0.03479545	0.03698662	0.03921582
86	0.03256284	0.03471826	0.03691576	0.03915107
87	0.03248202	0.03464383	0.03684756	0.03908887
88	0.03240393	0.03457205	0.03678190	0.03902910
89	0.03232848	0.03450281	0.03671868	0.03897166
90	0.03225556	0.03443601	0.03665781	0.03891646
91	0.03218508	0.03437156	0.03659919	0.03886340
92	0.03211694	0.03430937	0.03654273	0.03881240
93	0.03205107	0.03424935	0.03648834	0.03876336
94	0.03198737	0.03419142	0.03643594	0.03871622
95	0.03192577	0.03413550	0.03638546	0.03867088
96	0.03186619	0.03408151	0.03633682	0.03862729
97	0.03180856	0.03402939	0.03628995	0.03858537
98	0.03175281	0.03397906	0.03624478	0.03854504
99	0.03169886	0.03393045	0.03620124	0.03850626
100	0.03164667	0.03388351	0.03615927	0.03846895

ANNUITY WHOSE PRESENT VALUE IS 1

$$a_{\overline{n}|i}^{-1} = \frac{i}{1 - v^n} = s_{\overline{n}|}^{-1} + i \quad \text{(Continued)}$$

Rate i

Periods n	0.04(4%)	0.0425(4 1/4%)	0.045(4 1/2%)	0.0475(4 3/4%)
1	1.04000000	1.04250000	1.04500000	1.04750000
2	0.53019608	0.53209608	0.53399756	0.53590049
3	0.36034854	0.36205965	0.36377336	0.36548967
4	0.27549005	0.27711502	0.27874365	0.28037592
5	0.22462711	0.22620704	0.22779164	0.22938090
6	0.19076190	0.19231731	0.19387839	0.19544512
7	0.16660961	0.16815221	0.16970147	0.17125735
8	0.14852783	0.15006493	0.15160965	0.15316196
9	0.13449299	0.13602944	0.13757447	0.13912803
10	0.12329094	0.12483012	0.12637882	0.12793699
11	0.11414904	0.11569338	0.11724818	0.11881337
12	0.10655217	0.10810349	0.10966619	0.11124019
13	0.10014373	0.10170340	0.10327535	0.10485950
14	0.09466897	0.09623806	0.09782032	0.09941565
15	0.08994110	0.09152043	0.09311381	0.09472113
16	0.08582000	0.08741022	0.08901537	0.09063531
17	0.08219852	0.08380017	0.08541758	0.08705063
18	0.07899333	0.08060681	0.08223690	0.08388343
19	0.07613862	0.07776427	0.07940734	0.08106766
20	0.07358175	0.07521983	0.07687614	0.07855047
21	0.07128011	0.07293083	0.07460057	0.07628907
22	0.06919881	0.07086234	0.07254565	0.07424846
23	0.06730906	0.06898552	0.07068249	0.07239969
24	0.06558683	0.06727631	0.06898703	0.07071867
25	0.06401196	0.06571452	0.06743903	0.06918513
26	0.06256738	0.06428306	0.06602137	0.06778192
27	0.06123854	0.06296736	0.06471946	0.06649444
28	0.06001298	0.06175492	0.06352081	0.06531016
29	0.05887993	0.06063500	0.06241461	0.06421829
30	0.05783010	0.05959825	0.06139154	0.06320945
31	0.05685535	0.05863654	0.06044345	0.06227550
32	0.05594859	0.05774275	0.05956320	0.06140929
33	0.05510357	0.05691064	0.05874453	0.06060455
34	0.05431477	0.05613469	0.05798191	0.05985574
35	0.05357732	0.05540999	0.05727045	0.05915794
36	0.05288688	0.05473220	0.05660578	0.05850680
37	0.05223957	0.05409745	0.05598402	0.05789843
38	0.05163192	0.05350225	0.05540169	0.05732932
39	0.05106083	0.05294350	0.05485567	0.05679637
40	0.05052349	0.05241839	0.05434315	0.05629675
41	0.05001738	0.05192438	0.05386158	0.05582791
42	0.04954020	0.05145918	0.05340868	0.05538756
43	0.04908989	0.05102071	0.05298235	0.05497362
44	0.04866454	0.05060708	0.05258071	0.05458418
45	0.04826246	0.05021657	0.05220202	0.05421751
46	0.04788205	0.04984760	0.05184471	0.05387203
47	0.04752189	0.04949873	0.05150734	0.05354630
48	0.04718065	0.04916864	0.05118858	0.05323900
49	0.04685712	0.04885612	0.05088722	0.05294891

Rate i

Periods n	0.04(4%)	0.0425(4 1/4%)	0.045(4 1/2%)	0.0475(4 3/4%)
51	0.04625885	0.04827940	0.05033232	0.05241595
52	0.04598212	0.04801322	0.05007679	0.05217111
53	0.04571915	0.04776064	0.04983469	0.05193950
54	0.04546910	0.04752084	0.04960519	0.05172030
55	0.04523124	0.04729307	0.04938754	0.05151276
56	0.04500487	0.04707663	0.04918105	0.05131618
57	0.04478932	0.04687086	0.04898506	0.05112990
58	0.04458401	0.04667517	0.04879897	0.05095334
59	0.04438836	0.04648898	0.04862221	0.05078591
60	0.04420185	0.04631178	0.04845426	0.05062710
61	0.04402398	0.04614306	0.04829462	0.05047641
62	0.04385430	0.04598237	0.04814284	0.05033339
63	0.04369237	0.04582929	0.04799848	0.05019761
64	0.04353780	0.04568339	0.04786115	0.05006867
65	0.04339019	0.04554432	0.04773047	0.04994619
66	0.04324921	0.04541171	0.04760608	0.04982982
67	0.04311451	0.04528522	0.04748765	0.04971924
68	0.04298578	0.04516456	0.04737487	0.04961413
69	0.04286272	0.04504942	0.04726745	0.04951420
70	0.04274506	0.04493952	0.04716511	0.04941917
71	0.04263253	0.04483460	0.04706759	0.04932879
72	0.04252489	0.04473442	0.04697465	0.04924282
73	0.04242190	0.04463875	0.04688606	0.04916103
74	0.04232334	0.04454736	0.04680159	0.04908320
75	0.04222900	0.04446004	0.04672104	0.04900912
76	0.04213869	0.04437661	0.04664422	0.04893862
77	0.04205221	0.04429687	0.04657094	0.04887150
78	0.04196939	0.04422065	0.04650104	0.04880759
79	0.04189007	0.04414778	0.04643434	0.04874674
80	0.04181408	0.04407811	0.04637069	0.04868879
81	0.04174127	0.04401149	0.04630995	0.04863360
82	0.04167150	0.04394777	0.04625197	0.04858103
83	0.04160463	0.04388682	0.04619663	0.04853094
84	0.04154054	0.04382852	0.04614379	0.04848322
85	0.04147909	0.04377274	0.04609334	0.04843776
86	0.04142018	0.04371936	0.04604516	0.04839443
87	0.04136370	0.04366828	0.04599915	0.04835315
88	0.04130953	0.04361940	0.04595522	0.04831380
89	0.04125758	0.04357262	0.04591325	0.04827629
90	0.04120775	0.04352783	0.04587316	0.04824054
91	0.04115995	0.04348496	0.04583486	0.04820646
92	0.04111410	0.04344391	0.04579827	0.04817397
93	0.04107010	0.04340461	0.04576331	0.04814300
94	0.04102789	0.04336698	0.04572991	0.04811346
95	0.04098738	0.04333094	0.04569799	0.04808530
96	0.04094850	0.04329643	0.04566749	0.04805845
97	0.04091119	0.04326338	0.04563834	0.04803284
98	0.04087538	0.04323173	0.04561048	0.04800842
99	0.04084100	0.04320140	0.04558385	0.04798513

$$a_{\overline{n}|i}^{-1} = \frac{i}{1-v^n} = v^{-1}_{\overline{n}|i} + i \text{ (Continued)}$$

Rate i

n	0.0575(5 3/4%)	0.055(5 1/2%)	0.0525(5 1/4%)	0.05(5%)
51	0.06102543	0.05883495	0.05666886	0.05452867
52	0.06082266	0.05862186	0.05644528	0.05429450
53	0.06063215	0.05842130	0.05623449	0.05407334
54	0.06045310	0.05823245	0.05603566	0.05386438
55	0.06028475	0.05805458	0.05584805	0.05366686
56	0.06012642	0.05788698	0.05567096	0.05348010
57	0.05997746	0.05772900	0.05550374	0.05330343
58	0.05983728	0.05758006	0.05534579	0.05313626
59	0.05970532	0.05743959	0.05519655	0.05297802
60	0.05958107	0.05730707	0.05505549	0.05282818
61	0.05946405	0.05718202	0.05492214	0.05268627
62	0.05935381	0.05706400	0.05479604	0.05255183
63	0.05924994	0.05695258	0.05467676	0.05242442
64	0.05915206	0.05684737	0.05456391	0.05230365
65	0.05905979	0.05674800	0.05445712	0.05218915
66	0.05897281	0.05665413	0.05435605	0.05208057
67	0.05889079	0.05656544	0.05426036	0.05197758
68	0.05881344	0.05648163	0.05416976	0.05187986
69	0.05874049	0.05640242	0.05408396	0.05178715
70	0.05867166	0.05632754	0.05400269	0.05169915
71	0.05860673	0.05625675	0.05392569	0.05161563
72	0.05854546	0.05618982	0.05385275	0.05153633
73	0.05848764	0.05612652	0.05378362	0.05146103
74	0.05843306	0.05606665	0.05371811	0.05138953
75	0.05838155	0.05601002	0.05365601	0.05132161
76	0.05833292	0.05595645	0.05359714	0.05125709
77	0.05828701	0.05590577	0.05354133	0.05119580
78	0.05824367	0.05585781	0.05348841	0.05113756
79	0.05820274	0.05581243	0.05343822	0.05108222
80	0.05816409	0.05576948	0.05339063	0.05102962
81	0.05812758	0.05572884	0.05334549	0.05097963
82	0.05809311	0.05569036	0.05330267	0.05093211
83	0.05806054	0.05565395	0.05326205	0.05088694
84	0.05802978	0.05561947	0.05322351	0.05084399
85	0.05800073	0.05558683	0.05318695	0.05080316
86	0.05797328	0.05555593	0.05315226	0.05076433
87	0.05794734	0.05552667	0.05311934	0.05072740
88	0.05792284	0.05549896	0.05308810	0.05069228
89	0.05789969	0.05547273	0.05305845	0.05065888
90	0.05787781	0.05544788	0.05303032	0.05062711
91	0.05785714	0.05542435	0.05300361	0.05059689
92	0.05783761	0.05540207	0.05297826	0.05056815
93	0.05781915	0.05538096	0.05295420	0.05054080
94	0.05780171	0.05536097	0.05293136	0.05051478
95	0.05778522	0.05534204	0.05290967	0.05049003
96	0.05776964	0.05532410	0.05288908	0.05046648
97	0.05775491	0.05530711	0.05286954	0.05044407
98	0.05774099	0.05529101	0.05285098	0.05042274
99	0.05772784	0.05527577	0.05283336	0.05040245
100	0.05771540	0.05526132	0.05281664	0.05038314

Rate i

n	0.05(5%)	0.0525(5 1/4%)	0.055(5 1/2%)	0.0575(5 3/4%)
1	1.05000000	1.05250000	1.05500000	1.05750000
2	0.53780488	0.53971072	0.54161800	0.54352673
3	0.36720856	0.36893004	0.37065407	0.37238067
4	0.28201183	0.28365136	0.28529449	0.28694120
5	0.23097480	0.23257332	0.23417644	0.23578414
6	0.19701747	0.19859542	0.20017895	0.20176803
7	0.17281982	0.17438885	0.17596442	0.17754648
8	0.15472181	0.15628918	0.15786401	0.15944628
9	0.14069008	0.14226057	0.14383946	0.14542670
10	0.12950457	0.13108152	0.13266777	0.13426327
11	0.12038889	0.12197467	0.12357065	0.12517676
12	0.11282541	0.11442178	0.11602923	0.11764767
13	0.10645577	0.10806405	0.10968426	0.11131631
14	0.10102397	0.10264516	0.10427912	0.10592574
15	0.09634229	0.09797715	0.09962560	0.10128751
16	0.09226991	0.09391903	0.09558254	0.09726029
17	0.08869914	0.09036298	0.09204197	0.09373597
18	0.08554622	0.08722511	0.08891992	0.09063045
19	0.08274501	0.08443921	0.08615006	0.08787734
20	0.08024259	0.08195228	0.08367933	0.08542350
21	0.07799611	0.07972143	0.08146478	0.08322590
22	0.07597051	0.07771153	0.07947123	0.08124934
23	0.07413682	0.07589358	0.07766965	0.07946472
24	0.07247090	0.07424339	0.07603580	0.07784779
25	0.07095246	0.07274066	0.07454935	0.07637817
26	0.06956432	0.07136817	0.07319307	0.07503860
27	0.06829186	0.07011129	0.07195228	0.07381439
28	0.06712253	0.06895744	0.07081440	0.07269293
29	0.06604551	0.06789578	0.06976857	0.07166336
30	0.06505144	0.06691693	0.06880539	0.07071624
31	0.06413212	0.06601270	0.06791665	0.06984336
32	0.06328042	0.06517593	0.06709519	0.06903754
33	0.06249004	0.06440032	0.06633469	0.06829246
34	0.06175545	0.06368030	0.06562958	0.06760253
35	0.06107171	0.06301096	0.06497493	0.06696282
36	0.06043446	0.06238791	0.06436635	0.06636893
37	0.05983979	0.06180725	0.06379993	0.06581694
38	0.05928423	0.06126548	0.06327217	0.06530335
39	0.05876462	0.06075946	0.06277991	0.06482500
40	0.05827816	0.06028637	0.06232034	0.06437907
41	0.05782229	0.05984365	0.06189090	0.06396209
42	0.05739471	0.05942899	0.06148927	0.06357445
43	0.05699333	0.05904031	0.06111337	0.06321135
44	0.05661625	0.05867569	0.06076128	0.06287179
45	0.05626173	0.05833341	0.06043127	0.06255404
46	0.05592820	0.05801189	0.06012175	0.06225650
47	0.05561421	0.05770966	0.05983129	0.06197773
48	0.05531843	0.05742542	0.05955854	0.06171641
49	0.05503965	0.05715793	0.05930230	0.06147131
50	0.05477674	0.05690609	0.05906145	0.06124133

ANNUITY WHOSE PRESENT VALUE IS 1

$$a_{\overline{n}|i}^{-1} = \frac{i}{1-v^n} = s_{\overline{n}|i}^{-1} + i \quad \text{(Continued)}$$

Rate i

Periods n	0.06(6%)	0.0625(6 1/4%)	0.065(6 1/2%)	0.0675(6 3/4%)
1	1.06000000	1.06250000	1.06500000	1.06750000
2	0.54543689	0.54734848	0.54926150	0.55116540
3	0.37410981	0.37584149	0.37775570	0.37930865
4	0.28859149	0.29024534	0.29190274	0.29356367
5	0.23739640	0.23901321	0.24063454	0.24426037
6	0.20336263	0.20496273	0.20656831	0.20817934
7	0.17913502	0.18072999	0.18233137	0.18393912
8	0.16103594	0.16263296	0.16423730	0.16584891
9	0.14702224	0.14862603	0.15023803	0.15185820
10	0.13586796	0.13748179	0.13910469	0.14073662
11	0.12679294	0.12841911	0.13005521	0.13170116
12	0.11927703	0.12091722	0.12256817	0.12422978
13	0.11296011	0.11461555	0.11628256	0.11796102
14	0.10758491	0.10925653	0.11094048	0.11263666
15	0.10296276	0.10465123	0.10635278	0.10806729
16	0.09895214	0.10065795	0.10237757	0.10411086
17	0.09544480	0.09716831	0.09890633	0.10065868
18	0.09235654	0.09409799	0.09585461	0.09762621
19	0.08962086	0.09138040	0.09315575	0.09494670
20	0.08718456	0.08896227	0.09075640	0.09256670
21	0.08500455	0.08680045	0.08861333	0.09044294
22	0.08304557	0.08485962	0.08669120	0.08854002
23	0.08127848	0.08311061	0.08496078	0.08682866
24	0.07967900	0.08152909	0.08339770	0.08528446
25	0.07822672	0.08009462	0.08198148	0.08388691
26	0.07690435	0.07878989	0.08069480	0.08261865
27	0.07569717	0.07760015	0.07952288	0.08146489
28	0.07459255	0.07651276	0.07845305	0.08041294
29	0.07357961	0.07551680	0.07747440	0.07945186
30	0.07264891	0.07460284	0.07657744	0.07857215
31	0.07179222	0.07376261	0.07575393	0.07776557
32	0.07100234	0.07298892	0.07499665	0.07702486
33	0.07027293	0.07227543	0.07429924	0.07634368
34	0.06959843	0.07161653	0.07365610	0.07571641
35	0.06897386	0.07100726	0.07306226	0.07513808
36	0.06839483	0.07044324	0.07251332	0.07460428
37	0.06785743	0.06992051	0.07200534	0.07411106
38	0.06735812	0.06943557	0.07153480	0.07365492
39	0.06689377	0.06898526	0.07109854	0.07323268
40	0.06646154	0.06856675	0.07069373	0.07284150
41	0.06605886	0.06817746	0.07031779	0.07247884
42	0.06568342	0.06781509	0.06996842	0.07214236
43	0.06533312	0.06747754	0.06964352	0.07182999
44	0.06500606	0.06716290	0.06934119	0.07153981
45	0.06470050	0.06686944	0.06905968	0.07127010
46	0.06441485	0.06659557	0.06879743	0.07101928
47	0.06414768	0.06633985	0.06855300	0.07078591
48	0.06389765	0.06610096	0.06832505	0.07056869
49	0.06366356	0.06587769	0.06811240	0.07036642
50	0.06344480	0.06566964	0.06791556	0.07018097

Rate i

Periods n	0.06(6%)	0.0625(6 1/4%)	0.065(6 1/2%)	0.0675(6 3/4%)
51	0.06323880	0.06547366	0.06772861	0.07000236
52	0.06304617	0.06529092	0.06755553	0.06983865
53	0.06286551	0.06511987	0.06739382	0.06968599
54	0.06269602	0.06495970	0.06724267	0.06954358
55	0.06253696	0.06480966	0.06710137	0.06941070
56	0.06238765	0.06466908	0.06696923	0.06928669
57	0.06224744	0.06453733	0.06684563	0.06917091
58	0.06211574	0.06441382	0.06672999	0.06906281
59	0.06199200	0.06429800	0.06662177	0.06896185
60	0.06187572	0.06418938	0.06652047	0.06886754
61	0.06176642	0.06408748	0.06642564	0.06877943
62	0.06166366	0.06399187	0.06633684	0.06869710
63	0.06156704	0.06390214	0.06625367	0.06862015
64	0.06147615	0.06381792	0.06617577	0.06854822
65	0.06139066	0.06373886	0.06610280	0.06848097
66	0.06131022	0.06366463	0.06603442	0.06841810
67	0.06123454	0.06359492	0.06597034	0.06835931
68	0.06116330	0.06352945	0.06591029	0.06830433
69	0.06109625	0.06346796	0.06585400	0.06825290
70	0.06103313	0.06341019	0.06580124	0.06820480
71	0.06097370	0.06335592	0.06575177	0.06815979
72	0.06091774	0.06330492	0.06570539	0.06811769
73	0.06086505	0.06325700	0.06566190	0.06807830
74	0.06081542	0.06321196	0.06562112	0.06804144
75	0.06076867	0.06316963	0.06558287	0.06800695
76	0.06072463	0.06312985	0.06554699	0.06797467
77	0.06068315	0.06309245	0.06551335	0.06794445
78	0.06064407	0.06305729	0.06548178	0.06791618
79	0.06060724	0.06302423	0.06545217	0.06788971
80	0.06057254	0.06299315	0.06542440	0.06786493
81	0.06053984	0.06296392	0.06539833	0.06784174
82	0.06050903	0.06293644	0.06537388	0.06782003
83	0.06047998	0.06291060	0.06535094	0.06779970
84	0.06045261	0.06288630	0.06532941	0.06778067
85	0.06042681	0.06286344	0.06530921	0.06776286
86	0.06040249	0.06284195	0.06529026	0.06774618
87	0.06037956	0.06282173	0.06527247	0.06773056
88	0.06035795	0.06280271	0.06525577	0.06771593
89	0.06033757	0.06278483	0.06524010	0.06770224
90	0.06031836	0.06276800	0.06522540	0.06768941
91	0.06030025	0.06275217	0.06521160	0.06767741
92	0.06028318	0.06273728	0.06519864	0.06766616
93	0.06026708	0.06272327	0.06518649	0.06765563
94	0.06025189	0.06271010	0.06517509	0.06764577
95	0.06023758	0.06269770	0.06516436	0.06763653
96	0.06022408	0.06268603	0.06515431	0.06762788
97	0.06021135	0.06267506	0.06514487	0.06761978
98	0.06019935	0.06266474	0.06513601	0.06761219
99	0.06018803	0.06265502	0.06512769	0.06760509

ANNUITY WHOSE PRESENT VALUE IS 1

$$a_{\overline{n}|i}^{-1} = \frac{i}{1-v^n} = s_{\overline{n}|i}^{-1} + i \quad \text{(Continued)}$$

Rate i

n	0.07(7%)	0.0725(7 1/4%)	0.075(7 1/2%)	0.0775(7 3/4%)	n	0.07(7%)	0.0725(7 1/4%)	0.075(7 1/2%)	0.0775(7 3/4%)
1	1.07000000	1.07250000	1.07500000	1.07750000	51	0.07229365	0.07460128	0.07692411	0.07926108
2	0.55309179	0.55500905	0.55692771	0.55884777	52	0.07213901	0.07445540	0.07678668	0.07913174
3	0.38105167	0.38279340	0.38453763	0.38628434	53	0.07199509	0.07431990	0.07665927	0.07901209
4	0.29522812	0.29689607	0.29856751	0.30024243	54	0.07186110	0.07419400	0.07654112	0.07890137
5	0.24389069	0.24552548	0.24716472	0.24880838	55	0.07173633	0.07407700	0.07643155	0.07879888
6	0.20979580	0.21141766	0.21304489	0.21467748	56	0.07162011	0.07396824	0.07632991	0.07870401
7	0.18555322	0.18717363	0.18880032	0.19043325	57	0.07151183	0.07386711	0.07623559	0.07861616
8	0.16746776	0.16909381	0.17072702	0.17236735	58	0.07141093	0.07377308	0.07614807	0.07853481
9	0.15348647	0.15512281	0.15676716	0.15841948	59	0.07131689	0.07368561	0.07606683	0.07845946
10	0.14237750	0.14402729	0.14568593	0.14735335	60	0.07122923	0.07360424	0.07599142	0.07838966
11	0.13335690	0.13502237	0.13669747	0.13838216	61	0.07114749	0.07352854	0.07592140	0.07832499
12	0.12590199	0.12758470	0.12927783	0.13098130	62	0.07107127	0.07345809	0.07585638	0.07826506
13	0.11965085	0.12135194	0.12306420	0.12478752	63	0.07100019	0.07339253	0.07579600	0.07820953
14	0.11434494	0.11606522	0.11779737	0.11954129	64	0.07093388	0.07333150	0.07573992	0.07815806
15	0.10979462	0.11153465	0.11328724	0.11505225	65	0.07087203	0.07327469	0.07568782	0.07811036
16	0.10585765	0.10761780	0.10939116	0.11117757	66	0.07081431	0.07322180	0.07563942	0.07806614
17	0.10242519	0.10420570	0.10600003	0.10780800	67	0.07076046	0.07317256	0.07559446	0.07802514
18	0.09941260	0.10121358	0.10302896	0.10485853	68	0.07071021	0.07312670	0.07555268	0.07798713
19	0.09675301	0.09857449	0.10041090	0.10226202	69	0.07066331	0.07308399	0.07551386	0.07795189
20	0.09439293	0.09623484	0.09809219	0.09996473	70	0.07061953	0.07304422	0.07547778	0.07791921
21	0.09228900	0.09415124	0.09602937	0.09792314	71	0.07057866	0.07300717	0.07544425	0.07788891
22	0.09040577	0.09228816	0.09418687	0.09610161	72	0.07054051	0.07297267	0.07541308	0.07786081
23	0.08871393	0.09061624	0.09253528	0.09447070	73	0.07050490	0.07294052	0.07538412	0.07783474
24	0.08718902	0.08911101	0.09105008	0.09300585	74	0.07047164	0.07291057	0.07535719	0.07781057
25	0.08581052	0.08775190	0.08971067	0.09168643	75	0.07044060	0.07288267	0.07533216	0.07778815
26	0.08456103	0.08652149	0.08849961	0.09049497	76	0.07041160	0.07285668	0.07530889	0.07776735
27	0.08342573	0.08540494	0.08740204	0.08941658	77	0.07038453	0.07283245	0.07528726	0.07774806
28	0.08239193	0.08438951	0.08640520	0.08843849	78	0.07035924	0.07280989	0.07526714	0.07773017
29	0.08144865	0.08346425	0.08549811	0.08754971	79	0.07033563	0.07278885	0.07524844	0.07771357
30	0.08058640	0.08261962	0.08467124	0.08674069	80	0.07031357	0.07276926	0.07523106	0.07769817
31	0.07979691	0.08184734	0.08391628	0.08600313	81	0.07029297	0.07275099	0.07521489	0.07768388
32	0.07907292	0.08114017	0.08322599	0.08532974	82	0.07027373	0.07273397	0.07519986	0.07767062
33	0.07840807	0.08049172	0.08259397	0.08471416	83	0.07025576	0.07271811	0.07518588	0.07765833
34	0.07779674	0.07989637	0.08201461	0.08415075	84	0.07023897	0.07270332	0.07517288	0.07764692
35	0.07723396	0.07934915	0.08148291	0.08363452	85	0.07022329	0.07268954	0.07516079	0.07763633
36	0.07671531	0.07884563	0.08099447	0.08316106	86	0.07020863	0.07267670	0.07514955	0.07762651
37	0.07623685	0.07838187	0.08054533	0.08272643	87	0.07019495	0.07266472	0.07513910	0.07761740
38	0.07579505	0.07795435	0.08013197	0.08232710	88	0.07018216	0.07265357	0.07512938	0.07760894
39	0.07538676	0.07755991	0.07975124	0.08195993	89	0.07017021	0.07264316	0.07512034	0.07760110
40	0.07500914	0.07719571	0.07940031	0.08162208	90	0.07015905	0.07263347	0.07511193	0.07759381
41	0.07465962	0.07685920	0.07907663	0.08131102	91	0.07014863	0.07262443	0.07510411	0.07758706
42	0.07433591	0.07654807	0.07877789	0.08102444	92	0.07013888	0.07261601	0.07509684	0.07758079
43	0.07403590	0.07626023	0.07850201	0.08076028	93	0.07012978	0.07260815	0.07509007	0.07757497
44	0.07375769	0.07599379	0.07824710	0.08051665	94	0.07012128	0.07260083	0.07508378	0.07756958
45	0.07349957	0.07574704	0.07801146	0.08029186	95	0.07011333	0.07259401	0.07507793	0.07756457
46	0.07325996	0.07551840	0.07779354	0.08008436	96	0.07010590	0.07258764	0.07507249	0.07755992
47	0.07303744	0.07530646	0.07759190	0.07989274	97	0.07009897	0.07258171	0.07506743	0.07755561
48	0.07283070	0.07510992	0.07740527	0.07971572	98	0.07009248	0.07257618	0.07506272	0.07755161
49	0.07263853	0.07492758	0.07723247	0.07955213	99	0.07008643	0.07257103	0.07505834	0.07754789
50	0.07245985	0.07475837	0.07707241	0.07940091	100	0.07008076	0.07256622	0.07505427	0.07754444

ANNUITY WHOSE PRESENT VALUE IS 1

$$a_{\overline{n}|i}^{-1} = \frac{i}{1-v^n} = s_{\overline{n}|i}^{-1} + i \quad \text{(Continued)}$$

Rate i

Periods n	0.08(8%)	0.0825(8 1/4%)	0.085(8 1/2%)	0.0875(8 3/4%)
1	1.08000000	1.08250000	1.08500000	1.08750000
2	0.56076923	0.56269208	0.56461631	0.56654192
3	0.38803351	0.38978515	0.39153925	0.39329579
4	0.30192080	0.30360263	0.30528789	0.30697657
5	0.25045645	0.25210892	0.25376575	0.25542694
6	0.21631539	0.21795860	0.21960708	0.22126082
7	0.19207240	0.19371774	0.19536922	0.19702683
8	0.17401476	0.17566921	0.17733065	0.17899906
9	0.16007971	0.16174781	0.16342372	0.16510740
10	0.14902949	0.15071430	0.15240771	0.15410966
11	0.14007634	0.14177996	0.14349293	0.14521519
12	0.13269502	0.13441890	0.13615286	0.13789681
13	0.12652181	0.12826696	0.13002287	0.13178944
14	0.12129685	0.12306394	0.12484244	0.12663222
15	0.11682954	0.11861900	0.12042046	0.12223380
16	0.11297687	0.11478892	0.11661354	0.11845059
17	0.10962943	0.11146415	0.11331198	0.11517274
18	0.10670210	0.10855946	0.11043041	0.11231476
19	0.10412763	0.10600750	0.10790140	0.10980912
20	0.10185221	0.10375437	0.10567097	0.10760176
21	0.09983225	0.10175643	0.10369541	0.10564890
22	0.09803207	0.09997794	0.10193892	0.10391471
23	0.09642217	0.09838936	0.10037193	0.10236954
24	0.09497796	0.09696605	0.09896975	0.10098871
25	0.09367878	0.09568733	0.09771168	0.09975145
26	0.09250713	0.09453567	0.09658017	0.09864020
27	0.09144810	0.09349614	0.09556025	0.09763999
28	0.09048891	0.09255595	0.09463914	0.09673799
29	0.08961854	0.09170406	0.09380577	0.09592315
30	0.08882743	0.09093091	0.09305058	0.09518590
31	0.08810728	0.09022818	0.09236524	0.09451789
32	0.08745081	0.08958859	0.09174247	0.09391186
33	0.08685163	0.08900575	0.09117588	0.09336140
34	0.08630411	0.08847402	0.09065984	0.09286090
35	0.08580326	0.08798844	0.09018937	0.09240538
36	0.08534467	0.08754458	0.08976006	0.09199044
37	0.08492440	0.08713850	0.08936799	0.09161216
38	0.08453894	0.08676671	0.08900966	0.09126705
39	0.08418513	0.08642606	0.08868193	0.09095200
40	0.08386016	0.08611373	0.08838201	0.09066421
41	0.08356149	0.08582722	0.08810737	0.09040118
42	0.08328684	0.08556422	0.08785576	0.09016065
43	0.08303414	0.08532270	0.08762512	0.08994060
44	0.08280152	0.08510079	0.08741363	0.08973073
45	0.08258728	0.08489682	0.08721961	0.08955481
46	0.08238991	0.08470926	0.08704154	0.08938592
47	0.08220799	0.08453673	0.08687807	0.08923118
48	0.08204027	0.08437797	0.08672795	0.08908936
49	0.08188557	0.08423184	0.08659005	0.08895934
50	0.08174286	0.08409...		

Rate i

Periods n	0.08(8%)	0.0825(8 1/4%)	0.085(8 1/2%)	0.0875(8 3/4%)
51	0.08161116	0.08397339	0.08634688	0.08873078
52	0.08148959	0.08385925	0.08623983	0.08863048
53	0.08137735	0.08375409	0.08614139	0.08853844
54	0.08127370	0.08365717	0.08605087	0.08845398
55	0.08117796	0.08356784	0.08596761	0.08837645
56	0.08108952	0.08348548	0.08589101	0.08830528
57	0.08100780	0.08340955	0.08582053	0.08823994
58	0.08093227	0.08333952	0.08575568	0.08817994
59	0.08086247	0.08327494	0.08569599	0.08812484
60	0.08079795	0.08321537	0.08564106	0.08807424
61	0.08073830	0.08316041	0.08559049	0.08802776
62	0.08068314	0.08310971	0.08554393	0.08798506
63	0.08063214	0.08306292	0.08550107	0.08794583
64	0.08058497	0.08301975	0.08546160	0.08790979
65	0.08054135	0.08297991	0.08542526	0.08787668
66	0.08050099	0.08294314	0.08539179	0.08784625
67	0.08046367	0.08290920	0.08536097	0.08781829
68	0.08042914	0.08287787	0.08533258	0.08779260
69	0.08039719	0.08284895	0.08530643	0.08776898
70	0.08036764	0.08282225	0.08528234	0.08774728
71	0.08034029	0.08279760	0.08526016	0.08772733
72	0.08031498	0.08277485	0.08523972	0.08770900
73	0.08029157	0.08275383	0.08522089	0.08769214
74	0.08026989	0.08273443	0.08520354	0.08767665
75	0.08024984	0.08271652	0.08518756	0.08766241
76	0.08023128	0.08269998	0.08517284	0.08764932
77	0.08021410	0.08268470	0.08515927	0.08763729
78	0.08019820	0.08267060	0.08514677	0.08762623
79	0.08018349	0.08265757	0.08513526	0.08761606
80	0.08016987	0.08264554	0.08512465	0.08760671
81	0.08015726	0.08263443	0.08511487	0.08759811
82	0.08014559	0.08262417	0.08510586	0.08759021
83	0.08013479	0.08261469	0.08509755	0.08758295
84	0.08012479	0.08260594	0.08508990	0.08757627
85	0.08011553	0.08259786	0.08508285	0.08757012
86	0.08010696	0.08259039	0.08507636	0.08756448
87	0.08009903	0.08258350	0.08507037	0.08755929
88	0.08009168	0.08257713	0.08506485	0.08755451
89	0.08008489	0.08257124	0.08505977	0.08755012
90	0.08007863	0.08256581	0.08505508	0.08754609
91	0.08007277	0.08256079	0.08505077	0.08754238
92	0.08006737	0.08255615	0.08504679	0.08753897
93	0.08006238	0.08255187	0.08504312	0.08753583
94	0.08005775	0.08254792	0.08503974	0.08753295
95	0.08005347	0.08254426	0.08503663	0.08753030
96	0.08004951	0.08254089	0.08503375	0.08752786
97	0.08004584	0.08253777	0.08503111	0.08752562
98	0.08004244	0.08253489	0.08502867	0.08752355
99	0.08003930	0.08253223	0.08502642	0.08752166

$$a_{\overline{n}|i}^{-1} = \frac{i}{1-v^n} = s_{\overline{n}|i}^{-1} + i \text{ (Continued)}$$

Rate i

Periods n	0.09(9%)	0.0925(9 1/4%)	0.095(9 1/2%)	0.0975(9 3/4%)
1	1.09000000	1.09250000	1.09500000	1.09750000
2	0.56846890	0.57039725	0.57232697	0.57425805
3	0.39505476	0.39681615	0.39857997	0.40034619
4	0.30866866	0.31036414	0.31206300	0.31376523
5	0.25709246	0.25876229	0.26043642	0.26211482
6	0.22291978	0.22458395	0.22625328	0.22792777
7	0.19869052	0.20036026	0.20203603	0.20371779
8	0.18067438	0.18235658	0.18404561	0.18574144
9	0.16679880	0.16849786	0.17020454	0.17191878
10	0.15582009	0.15753894	0.15926615	0.16100166
11	0.14694666	0.14868726	0.15043693	0.15219558
12	0.13965066	0.14141432	0.14318771	0.14497074
13	0.13356656	0.13535414	0.13715206	0.13896022
14	0.12843317	0.13024517	0.13206809	0.13390182
15	0.12405888	0.12589556	0.12774370	0.12960315
16	0.12029991	0.12216133	0.12403470	0.12591985
17	0.11704625	0.11893232	0.12083078	0.12274145
18	0.11421229	0.11612281	0.11804610	0.11998198
19	0.11173041	0.11366506	0.11561284	0.11757352
20	0.10954648	0.11150487	0.11347670	0.11546170
21	0.10761663	0.10959832	0.11159370	0.11360248
22	0.10590499	0.10790947	0.10992784	0.11195981
23	0.10438188	0.10640860	0.10844938	0.11050389
24	0.10302256	0.10507095	0.10713351	0.10920990
25	0.10180625	0.10387569	0.10595939	0.10805698
26	0.10071536	0.10280523	0.10490940	0.10702747
27	0.09973491	0.10184456	0.10396852	0.10610635
28	0.09885205	0.10098083	0.10312389	0.10528076
29	0.09805572	0.10020298	0.10236444	0.10453963
30	0.09733635	0.09950142	0.10168058	0.10387336
31	0.09668560	0.09886781	0.10106399	0.10327363
32	0.09609619	0.09829488	0.10050739	0.10273318
33	0.09556173	0.09777625	0.10000441	0.10224565
34	0.09507660	0.09730631	0.09954945	0.10180543
35	0.09463584	0.09688010	0.09913756	0.10140762
36	0.09423505	0.09649323	0.09876437	0.10104784
37	0.09387033	0.09614182	0.09842600	0.10072224
38	0.09353820	0.09582240	0.09811901	0.10042739
39	0.09323555	0.09553188	0.09784032	0.10016023
40	0.09295961	0.09526750	0.09758819	0.09991804
41	0.09270789	0.09502678	0.09735716	0.09969838
42	0.09247814	0.09480750	0.09714803	0.09949907
43	0.09226837	0.09460768	0.09695783	0.09931817
44	0.09207675	0.09442551	0.09678478	0.09915390
45	0.09190165	0.09425938	0.09662729	0.09900471
46	0.09174160	0.09410783	0.09648390	0.09886915
47	0.09159525	0.09396953	0.09635333	0.09874597
48	0.09146139	0.09384330	0.09623439	0.09863399
49	0.09133893	0.09372806	0.09612603	0.09853218
50	0.09122687	0.09362282	0.09602728	0.09843960

Rate i

Periods n	0.09(9%)	0.0925(9 1/4%)	0.095(9 1/2%)	0.0975(9 3/4%)
51	0.09112430	0.09352670	0.09593728	0.09835540
52	0.09101041	0.09343889	0.09585523	0.09827880
53	0.09094443	0.09335865	0.09578042	0.09820911
54	0.09086570	0.09328534	0.09571220	0.09814569
55	0.09079359	0.09321833	0.09564999	0.09808799
56	0.09072754	0.09315707	0.09559325	0.09803546
57	0.09066702	0.09310108	0.09554149	0.09798766
58	0.09061157	0.09304989	0.09549426	0.09794414
59	0.09056076	0.09300307	0.09545118	0.09790452
60	0.09051419	0.09296027	0.09541187	0.09786844
61	0.09047151	0.09292112	0.09537599	0.09783560
62	0.09043240	0.09288532	0.09534325	0.09780569
63	0.09039654	0.09285257	0.09531337	0.09777846
64	0.09036366	0.09282261	0.09528611	0.09775365
65	0.09033352	0.09279521	0.09526122	0.09773107
66	0.09030589	0.09277014	0.09523850	0.09771050
67	0.09028056	0.09274721	0.09521776	0.09769176
68	0.09025732	0.09272623	0.09519883	0.09767469
69	0.09023602	0.09270703	0.09518154	0.09765915
70	0.09021649	0.09268947	0.09516576	0.09764499
71	0.09019857	0.09267339	0.09515136	0.09763209
72	0.09018214	0.09265869	0.09513821	0.09762034
73	0.09016708	0.09264523	0.09512620	0.09760964
74	0.09015326	0.09263292	0.09511524	0.09759989
75	0.09014058	0.09262165	0.09510523	0.09759101
76	0.09012896	0.09261134	0.09509609	0.09758291
77	0.09011830	0.09260190	0.09508775	0.09757554
78	0.09010852	0.09259326	0.09508013	0.09756883
79	0.09009955	0.09258536	0.09507317	0.09756271
80	0.09009132	0.09257813	0.09506682	0.09755713
81	0.09008377	0.09257151	0.09506102	0.09755206
82	0.09007685	0.09256545	0.09505572	0.09754743
83	0.09007050	0.09255990	0.09505088	0.09754321
84	0.09006467	0.09255483	0.09504647	0.09753937
85	0.09005933	0.09255018	0.09504243	0.09753587
86	0.09005443	0.09254593	0.09503875	0.09753269
87	0.09004993	0.09254204	0.09503539	0.09752978
88	0.09004581	0.09253848	0.09503232	0.09752713
89	0.09004202	0.09253522	0.09502951	0.09752472
90	0.09003855	0.09253224	0.09502695	0.09752253
91	0.09003537	0.09252951	0.09502461	0.09752053
92	0.09003245	0.09252701	0.09502248	0.09751870
93	0.09002977	0.09252472	0.09502053	0.09751704
94	0.09002731	0.09252263	0.09501874	0.09751553
95	0.09002505	0.09252071	0.09501712	0.09751415
96	0.09002298	0.09251896	0.09501563	0.09751289
97	0.09002109	0.09251735	0.09501428	0.09751174
98	0.09001934	0.09251588	0.09501304	0.09751070
99	0.09001775	0.09251454	0.09501191	0.09750975
100	0.09001628	0.09251331	0.09501087	0.09750888

ANNUITY WHOSE PRESENT VALUE IS 1

$$a_{\overline{n}|i}^{-1} = \frac{i}{1-v^n} = s_{\overline{n}|i}^{-1} + i \quad \text{(Continued)}$$

Rate i

Periods n	0.10(10%)	0.1025(10 1/4%)	0.105(10 1/2%)	0.1075(10 3/4%)
1	1.10000000	1.10250000	1.10500000	1.10750000
2	0.57619048	0.57812426	0.58005938	0.58199585
3	0.40211480	0.40388581	0.40565920	0.40743495
4	0.31547080	0.31717972	0.31889196	0.32060751
5	0.26379748	0.26548438	0.26717550	0.26887081
6	0.22960738	0.23129209	0.23298187	0.23467671
7	0.20540550	0.20709914	0.20879867	0.21050405
8	0.18744402	0.18915331	0.19086928	0.19259187
9	0.17364054	0.17536976	0.17710638	0.17885037
10	0.16274539	0.16449730	0.16625732	0.16802538
11	0.15396314	0.15573954	0.15752470	0.15931855
12	0.14676332	0.14856535	0.15037675	0.15219742
13	0.14077852	0.14260686	0.14444512	0.14629320
14	0.13574622	0.13760119	0.13946659	0.14134230
15	0.13147378	0.13335544	0.13524800	0.13715131
16	0.12781662	0.12972486	0.13164440	0.13357508
17	0.12466413	0.12659866	0.12854485	0.13050252
18	0.12193022	0.12389064	0.12586302	0.12784716
19	0.11954687	0.12153267	0.12353069	0.12554071
20	0.11745962	0.11947023	0.12149327	0.12352848
21	0.11562439	0.11765916	0.11970652	0.12176620
22	0.11400506	0.11606331	0.11813426	0.12021762
23	0.11257181	0.11465282	0.11674659	0.11885282
24	0.11129978	0.11340278	0.11551858	0.11764684
25	0.11016807	0.11229231	0.11442932	0.11657875
26	0.10915904	0.11130372	0.11346112	0.11563086
27	0.10825764	0.11042197	0.11259894	0.11478813
28	0.10745101	0.10963420	0.11182990	0.11403768
29	0.10672807	0.10892933	0.11114293	0.11336846
30	0.10607925	0.10829778	0.11052848	0.11277090
31	0.10549621	0.10773125	0.10997824	0.11223674
32	0.10497172	0.10722249	0.10948499	0.11175875
33	0.10449941	0.10676517	0.10904241	0.11133064
34	0.10407371	0.10635372	0.10864495	0.11094690
35	0.10368971	0.10598326	0.10828776	0.11060266
36	0.10334306	0.10564947	0.10796652	0.11029368
37	0.10302994	0.10534853	0.10767744	0.11001616
38	0.10274692	0.10507704	0.10741717	0.10976678
39	0.10249098	0.10483200	0.10718271	0.10954257
40	0.10225941	0.10461073	0.10697141	0.10934091
41	0.10204980	0.10441083	0.10678090	0.10915947
42	0.10185999	0.10423018	0.10660908	0.10899615
43	0.10168805	0.10406687	0.10645407	0.10884910
44	0.10153224	0.10391918	0.10631417	0.10871667
45	0.10139100	0.10378558	0.10618788	0.10859737
46	0.10126295	0.10366470	0.10607385	0.10848987
47	0.10114682	0.10355531	0.10597087	0.10839299
48	0.10104148	0.10345628	0.10587784	0.10830566
49	0.10094590	0.10336662	0.10579380	0.10822693

Rate i

Periods n	0.10(10%)	0.1025(10 1/4%)	0.105(10 1/2%)	0.1075(10 3/4%)
51	0.10078046	0.10321190	0.10564922	0.10809192
52	0.10070900	0.10314530	0.10558718	0.10803418
53	0.10064413	0.10308496	0.10553110	0.10798210
54	0.10058523	0.10303030	0.10548041	0.10793511
55	0.10053175	0.10298077	0.10543457	0.10789272
56	0.10048317	0.10293588	0.10539312	0.10785448
57	0.10043906	0.10289520	0.10535564	0.10781997
58	0.10039898	0.10285833	0.10532174	0.10778883
59	0.10036258	0.10282491	0.10529108	0.10776072
60	0.10032951	0.10279461	0.10526335	0.10773536
61	0.10029946	0.10276715	0.10523827	0.10771247
62	0.10027217	0.10274226	0.10521559	0.10769181
63	0.10024736	0.10271969	0.10519506	0.10767316
64	0.10022482	0.10269922	0.10517650	0.10765633
65	0.10020434	0.10268067	0.10515970	0.10764114
66	0.10018573	0.10266384	0.10514450	0.10762742
67	0.10016882	0.10264859	0.10513075	0.10761504
68	0.10015345	0.10263476	0.10511832	0.10760386
69	0.10013948	0.10262221	0.10510706	0.10759377
70	0.10012678	0.10261084	0.10509688	0.10758466
71	0.10011524	0.10260052	0.10508767	0.10757644
72	0.10010476	0.10259117	0.10507933	0.10756901
73	0.10009522	0.10258269	0.10507179	0.10756231
74	0.10008656	0.10257499	0.10506496	0.10755626
75	0.10007868	0.10256802	0.10505878	0.10755080
76	0.10007153	0.10256169	0.10505320	0.10754586
77	0.10006502	0.10255595	0.10504814	0.10754141
78	0.10005911	0.10255075	0.10504356	0.10753739
79	0.10005373	0.10254603	0.10503942	0.10753376
80	0.10004884	0.10254175	0.10503567	0.10753048
81	0.10004440	0.10253786	0.10503228	0.10752752
82	0.10004036	0.10253434	0.10502921	0.10752485
83	0.10003669	0.10253115	0.10502644	0.10752244
84	0.10003335	0.10252825	0.10502393	0.10752026
85	0.10003032	0.10252562	0.10502165	0.10751829
86	0.10002756	0.10252324	0.10501959	0.10751652
87	0.10002506	0.10252108	0.10501773	0.10751491
88	0.10002278	0.10251912	0.10501605	0.10751347
89	0.10002071	0.10251734	0.10501452	0.10751216
90	0.10001883	0.10251573	0.10501314	0.10751098
91	0.10001711	0.10251427	0.10501189	0.10750991
92	0.10001556	0.10251294	0.10501076	0.10750895
93	0.10001414	0.10251174	0.10500974	0.10750808
94	0.10001286	0.10251065	0.10500881	0.10750730
95	0.10001169	0.10250966	0.10500798	0.10750659
96	0.10001063	0.10250876	0.10500722	0.10750595
97	0.10000966	0.10250794	0.10500653	0.10750537
98	0.10000878	0.10250721	0.10500591	0.10750485
99	0.10000798	0.10250654	0.10500535	0.10750438

$$a_{\overline{n}|i}^{-1} = \frac{i}{1 - v^n} = s_{\overline{n}|i}^{-1} + i \quad \text{(Continued)}$$

Rate i

Periods n	0.11 (11%)	0.1125 (11 1/4%)	0.115 (11 1/2%)	0.1175 (11 3/4%)
1	1.11000000	1.11250000	1.11500000	1.11750000
2	0.58393365	0.58587278	0.58781324	0.58975502
3	0.40921307	0.41099354	0.41277636	0.41456150
4	0.32232635	0.32404848	0.32577388	0.32750254
5	0.27057031	0.27227397	0.27398177	0.27569370
6	0.23637656	0.23808142	0.23979125	0.24150602
7	0.21221527	0.21393228	0.21565505	0.21738354
8	0.19432105	0.19605678	0.19779902	0.19954772
9	0.18060166	0.18236022	0.18412597	0.18589888
10	0.16980143	0.17158539	0.17337721	0.17517682
11	0.16112101	0.16293200	0.16475144	0.16657927
12	0.15402729	0.15586625	0.15771422	0.15957110
13	0.14815099	0.15001840	0.15189530	0.15378160
14	0.14322820	0.14512417	0.14703008	0.14894582
15	0.13906524	0.14098964	0.14292436	0.14486928
16	0.13551675	0.13746923	0.13943238	0.14140603
17	0.13247148	0.13445157	0.13644259	0.13844437
18	0.12984287	0.13184994	0.13386817	0.13589736
19	0.12756250	0.12959585	0.13164053	0.13369632
20	0.12557564	0.12763448	0.12970478	0.13178629
21	0.12383793	0.12592145	0.12801648	0.13012278
22	0.12231310	0.12442041	0.12653927	0.12866939
23	0.12097118	0.12310138	0.12524311	0.12739607
24	0.11978721	0.12193938	0.12410302	0.12627781
25	0.11874024	0.12091345	0.12309803	0.12529365
26	0.11781258	0.12000589	0.12221044	0.12442588
27	0.11698916	0.11920165	0.12142521	0.12365948
28	0.11625715	0.11848788	0.12072951	0.12298163
29	0.11560547	0.11785355	0.12011230	0.12238131
30	0.11502460	0.11728914	0.11956410	0.12184907
31	0.11450627	0.11678639	0.11907667	0.12137670
32	0.11404329	0.11633815	0.11864289	0.12095709
33	0.11362938	0.11593816	0.11825653	0.12058405
34	0.11325905	0.11558096	0.11791215	0.12025218
35	0.11292749	0.11526175	0.11760499	0.11995675
36	0.11263044	0.11497633	0.11733086	0.11969361
37	0.11236416	0.11472097	0.11708610	0.11945912
38	0.11212535	0.11449240	0.11686745	0.11925006
39	0.11191107	0.11428872	0.11667204	0.11906360
40	0.11171873	0.11410436	0.11649734	0.11889724
41	0.11154601	0.11393936	0.11634111	0.11874876
42	0.11139086	0.11379275	0.11620134	0.11861621
43	0.11125146	0.11366067	0.11607628	0.11849785
44	0.11112617	0.11354221	0.11596434	0.11839214
45	0.11101354	0.11343594	0.11586413	0.11829770
46	0.11091227	0.11334059	0.11577441	0.11821331
47	0.11082119	0.11325502	0.11569405	0.11813790
48	0.11073926	0.11317821	0.11562208	0.11807051
49	0.11066556	0.11310925	0.11555761	0.11801026
50	0.11059924	0.11304734	0.11549985	0.11795640

Rate i

Periods n	0.11 (11%)	0.1125 (11 1/4%)	0.115 (11 1/2%)	0.1175 (11 3/4%)
51	0.11053957	0.11299175	0.11544809	0.11790824
52	0.11048586	0.11294183	0.11540172	0.11786519
53	0.11043752	0.11289699	0.11536015	0.11782668
54	0.11039401	0.11285672	0.11532290	0.11779225
55	0.11035484	0.11282054	0.11528952	0.11776145
56	0.11031957	0.11278805	0.11525959	0.11773391
57	0.11028782	0.11275885	0.11523276	0.11770927
58	0.11025923	0.11273262	0.11520871	0.11768723
59	0.11023348	0.11270905	0.11518715	0.11766751
60	0.11021030	0.11268788	0.11516782	0.11764988
61	0.11018943	0.11266885	0.11515049	0.11763410
62	0.11017062	0.11265175	0.11513495	0.11761999
63	0.11015369	0.11263639	0.11512101	0.11760736
64	0.11013844	0.11262258	0.11510852	0.11759606
65	0.11012471	0.11261017	0.11509732	0.11758595
66	0.11011234	0.11259902	0.11508727	0.11757691
67	0.11010119	0.11258900	0.11507827	0.11756882
68	0.11009116	0.11257999	0.11507019	0.11756158
69	0.11008212	0.11257190	0.11506295	0.11755510
70	0.11007397	0.11256462	0.11505645	0.11754931
71	0.11006664	0.11255809	0.11505063	0.11754412
72	0.11006003	0.11255221	0.11504540	0.11753948
73	0.11005408	0.11254693	0.11504072	0.11753533
74	0.11004872	0.11254218	0.11503652	0.11753161
75	0.11004389	0.11253791	0.11503275	0.11752829
76	0.11003954	0.11253408	0.11502937	0.11752531
77	0.11003562	0.11253063	0.11502634	0.11752265
78	0.11003209	0.11252753	0.11502362	0.11752027
79	0.11002891	0.11252475	0.11502119	0.11751814
80	0.11002604	0.11252225	0.11501900	0.11751623
81	0.11002346	0.11252000	0.11501704	0.11751452
82	0.11002113	0.11251797	0.11501528	0.11751300
83	0.11001904	0.11251616	0.11501371	0.11751163
84	0.11001715	0.11251452	0.11501229	0.11751041
85	0.11001545	0.11251305	0.11501102	0.11750931
86	0.11001392	0.11251173	0.11500989	0.11750833
87	0.11001254	0.11251055	0.11500887	0.11750746
88	0.11001130	0.11250948	0.11500795	0.11750667
89	0.11001018	0.11250852	0.11500713	0.11750597
90	0.11000917	0.11250766	0.11500640	0.11750534
91	0.11000826	0.11250688	0.11500574	0.11750478
92	0.11000744	0.11250619	0.11500515	0.11750428
93	0.11000670	0.11250556	0.11500461	0.11750383
94	0.11000604	0.11250500	0.11500414	0.11750343
95	0.11000544	0.11250449	0.11500371	0.11750307
96	0.11000490	0.11250404	0.11500333	0.11750274
97	0.11000442	0.11250363	0.11500299	0.11750245
98	0.11000398	0.11250326	0.11500268	0.11750220
99	0.11000358	0.11250293	0.11500240	0.11750197
100	0.11000323	0.11250264	0.11500215	0.11750176

ANNUITY WHOSE PRESENT VALUE IS 1

$$a_{\overline{n}|i}^{-1} = \frac{i}{1 - v^n} = s_{\overline{n}|i}^{-1} + i \quad \text{(Continued)}$$

Periods n	Rate i 0.12(12%)	0.1225(12 1/4%)	0.125(12 1/2%)	0.1275(12 3/4%)	Periods n	0.12(12%)	0.1225(12 1/4%)	Rate i 0.125(12 1/2%)	0.1275(12 3/4%)
1	1.12000000	1.12250000	1.12500000	1.12750000	51	0.12037188	0.12283871	0.12530846	0.12778088
2	0.59169811	0.59364252	0.59558824	0.59753525	52	0.12033193	0.12280166	0.12527411	0.12774906
3	0.41634898	0.41813877	0.41993088	0.42172528	53	0.12029088	0.12276866	0.12524360	0.12772084
4	0.32923444	0.33096957	0.33270791	0.33444946	54	0.12026446	0.12273929	0.12521648	0.12769583
5	0.27740973	0.27912985	0.28085404	0.28258228	55	0.12023607	0.12271313	0.12519239	0.12767366
6	0.24322572	0.24495031	0.24667978	0.24841410	56	0.12021073	0.12268983	0.12517099	0.12765400
7	0.21911774	0.22085759	0.22260308	0.22435416	57	0.12018812	0.12266909	0.12515197	0.12763656
8	0.20130284	0.20306434	0.20483219	0.20660632	58	0.12016794	0.12265061	0.12513506	0.12762111
9	0.18767889	0.18946595	0.19126000	0.19306101	59	0.12014992	0.12263416	0.12512004	0.12760740
10	0.17698416	0.17879917	0.18062178	0.18245193	60	0.12013384	0.12261950	0.12510669	0.12759524
11	0.16841540	0.17025977	0.17211228	0.17397287	61	0.12011949	0.12260645	0.12509483	0.12758447
12	0.16143681	0.16331125	0.16519434	0.16708598	62	0.12010667	0.12259482	0.12508428	0.12757491
13	0.15567720	0.15758197	0.15949582	0.16141865	63	0.12009523	0.12258447	0.12507491	0.12756643
14	0.15087125	0.15280625	0.15475071	0.15670450	64	0.12008502	0.12257524	0.12506659	0.12755892
15	0.14682424	0.14878911	0.15076375	0.15274802	65	0.12007591	0.12256703	0.12505918	0.12755225
16	0.14339002	0.14538419	0.14738839	0.14940246	66	0.12006777	0.12255971	0.12505260	0.12754634
17	0.14045673	0.14247949	0.14451248	0.14655552	67	0.12006051	0.12255319	0.12504676	0.12754110
18	0.13793731	0.13998783	0.14204873	0.14411980	68	0.12005402	0.12254738	0.12504156	0.12753645
19	0.13576300	0.13784037	0.13992820	0.14202627	69	0.12004823	0.12254221	0.12503694	0.12753233
20	0.13387878	0.13598200	0.13809573	0.14021974	70	0.12004306	0.12253760	0.12503284	0.12752867
21	0.13224009	0.13436815	0.13650671	0.13865551	71	0.12003845	0.12253350	0.12502919	0.12752543
22	0.13081051	0.13296234	0.13512463	0.13729709	72	0.12003432	0.12252984	0.12502594	0.12752255
23	0.12955996	0.13173450	0.13391940	0.13611437	73	0.12003065	0.12252658	0.12502306	0.12752000
24	0.12846344	0.13065960	0.13286599	0.13508230	74	0.12002736	0.12252368	0.12502050	0.12751774
25	0.12749997	0.12971667	0.13194344	0.13417996	75	0.12002443	0.12252110	0.12501822	0.12751573
26	0.12665186	0.12888804	0.13113409	0.13338968	76	0.12002181	0.12251879	0.12501619	0.12751395
27	0.12590409	0.12815870	0.13042295	0.13269652	77	0.12001947	0.12251674	0.12501440	0.12751238
28	0.12524387	0.12751587	0.12979728	0.13208774	78	0.12001739	0.12251492	0.12501280	0.12751098
29	0.12466021	0.12694860	0.12924614	0.13155246	79	0.12001552	0.12251329	0.12501137	0.12750973
30	0.12414366	0.12644748	0.12876016	0.13108133	80	0.12001386	0.12251184	0.12501011	0.12750863
31	0.12368606	0.12600436	0.12833123	0.13066629	81	0.12001238	0.12251055	0.12500899	0.12750766
32	0.12328033	0.12561221	0.12795235	0.13030037	82	0.12001105	0.12250939	0.12500799	0.12750679
33	0.12292031	0.12526490	0.12761744	0.12997755	83	0.12000987	0.12250837	0.12500710	0.12750602
34	0.12260064	0.12495711	0.12732121	0.12969256	84	0.12000881	0.12250746	0.12500631	0.12750534
35	0.12231662	0.12468418	0.12705905	0.12944085	85	0.12000786	0.12250664	0.12500561	0.12750474
36	0.12206414	0.12444204	0.12682692	0.12921842	86	0.12000702	0.12250592	0.12500499	0.12750420
37	0.12183959	0.12422712	0.12662130	0.12902178	87	0.12000627	0.12250527	0.12500443	0.12750373
38	0.12163980	0.12403627	0.12643908	0.12884787	88	0.12000560	0.12250470	0.12500394	0.12750331
39	0.12146197	0.12386674	0.12627755	0.12869402	89	0.12000500	0.12250418	0.12500350	0.12750293
40	0.12130363	0.12371611	0.12613431	0.12855788	90	0.12000446	0.12250373	0.12500311	0.12750260
41	0.12116260	0.12358222	0.12600726	0.12843737	91	0.12000398	0.12250332	0.12500277	0.12750231
42	0.12103696	0.12346319	0.12589454	0.12833068	92	0.12000356	0.12250296	0.12500246	0.12750205
43	0.12092500	0.12335734	0.12579452	0.12823621	93	0.12000318	0.12250264	0.12500219	0.12750181
44	0.12082521	0.12326319	0.12570574	0.12815253	94	0.12000284	0.12250235	0.12500194	0.12750161
45	0.12073625	0.12317944	0.12562693	0.12807840	95	0.12000253	0.12250209	0.12500173	0.12750143
46	0.12065694	0.12310493	0.12555696	0.12801273	96	0.12000226	0.12250186	0.12500154	0.12750127
47	0.12058621	0.12303862	0.12549483	0.12795455	97	0.12000202	0.12250166	0.12500136	0.12750112
48	0.12052312	0.12297961	0.12543966	0.12790298	98	0.12000180	0.12250148	0.12500121	0.12750100
49	0.12046686	0.12292709	0.12539065	0.12785728	99	0.12000161	0.12250132	0.12500108	0.12750088

Rate i

$$a_{\overline{n}|i}^{-1} = \frac{i}{1-v^n} = v_{\overline{n}|i}^{-1} + i \quad \text{(Continued)}$$

Periods n	0.13(13%)	0.1325(13 1/4%)	0.135(13 1/2%)	0.1375(13 3/4%)
1	1.13000000	1.13250000	1.13500000	1.13750000
2	0.59948357	0.60143318	0.60338407	0.60533626
3	0.42352197	0.42532095	0.42712219	0.42892571
4	0.33619420	0.33794211	0.33969319	0.34144742
5	0.28431454	0.28605082	0.28779110	0.28953534
6	0.25015323	0.25189717	0.25364587	0.25539932
7	0.22611080	0.22787298	0.22964066	0.23141380
8	0.20838672	0.21017333	0.21196611	0.21376502
9	0.19486890	0.19668364	0.19850517	0.20033343
10	0.18428956	0.18613459	0.18798698	0.18984665
11	0.17584145	0.17771797	0.17960232	0.18149445
12	0.16898608	0.17089456	0.17281132	0.17473627
13	0.16335034	0.16529079	0.16723990	0.16919756
14	0.15866750	0.16063958	0.16262063	0.16461052
15	0.15474178	0.15674489	0.15875722	0.16077862
16	0.15142624	0.15345958	0.15550232	0.15755431
17	0.14860844	0.15067106	0.15274321	0.15482473
18	0.14620085	0.14829171	0.15039216	0.15250204
19	0.14413439	0.14625235	0.14837993	0.15051693
20	0.14235379	0.14449766	0.14665113	0.14881399
21	0.14081433	0.14298291	0.14516101	0.14734841
22	0.13947948	0.14167153	0.14387300	0.14608362
23	0.13831913	0.14053343	0.14275698	0.14499453
24	0.13730826	0.13954357	0.14178795	0.14404113
25	0.13642593	0.13868104	0.14094502	0.14321773
26	0.13565451	0.13792825	0.14021061	0.14250129
27	0.13497907	0.13727029	0.13956987	0.14187749
28	0.13438693	0.13669451	0.13901017	0.14133359
29	0.13386722	0.13619009	0.13852075	0.14085887
30	0.13341065	0.13574778	0.13809239	0.14044416
31	0.13300919	0.13535959	0.13771717	0.14008159
32	0.13265593	0.13501867	0.13738826	0.13976439
33	0.13234487	0.13471906	0.13709978	0.13948672
34	0.13207081	0.13445560	0.13684661	0.13924352
35	0.13182922	0.13422382	0.13662432	0.13903042
36	0.13161616	0.13401982	0.13642908	0.13884362
37	0.13142819	0.13384021	0.13625752	0.13867981
38	0.13126229	0.13368201	0.13610672	0.13853612
39	0.13111582	0.13354263	0.13597413	0.13841004
40	0.13098648	0.13341980	0.13585753	0.13829940
41	0.13087223	0.13331152	0.13575496	0.13820228
42	0.13077129	0.13321606	0.13566472	0.13811700
43	0.13068209	0.13313189	0.13558532	0.13804213
44	0.13060326	0.13305765	0.13551543	0.13797637
45	0.13053357	0.13299216	0.13545392	0.13791861
46	0.13047196	0.13293439	0.13539977	0.13786787
47	0.13041749	0.13288342	0.13535209	0.13782330
48	0.13036933	0.13283845	0.13531012	0.13778414
49	0.13032673	0.13279876	0.13527316	0.13774973
50	0.13028906	0.13276374	0.13524061	0.13771950

Rate i

Periods n	0.13(13%)	0.1325(13 1/4%)	0.135(13 1/2%)	0.1375(13 3/4%)
51	0.13025574	0.13273282	0.13521195	0.13769293
52	0.13022627	0.13270554	0.13518670	0.13766958
53	0.13020020	0.13268146	0.13516447	0.13764906
54	0.13017713	0.13266021	0.13514488	0.13763102
55	0.13015673	0.13264144	0.13512764	0.13761517
56	0.13013868	0.13262488	0.13511244	0.13760124
57	0.13012271	0.13261026	0.13509906	0.13758899
58	0.13010858	0.13259735	0.13508727	0.13757823
59	0.13009608	0.13258595	0.13507688	0.13756877
60	0.13008502	0.13257589	0.13506773	0.13756045
61	0.13007523	0.13256700	0.13505967	0.13755314
62	0.13006657	0.13255916	0.13505257	0.13754672
63	0.13005891	0.13255224	0.13504632	0.13754107
64	0.13005213	0.13254612	0.13504081	0.13753610
65	0.13004613	0.13254073	0.13503595	0.13753174
66	0.13004082	0.13253596	0.13503167	0.13752790
67	0.13003613	0.13253175	0.13502791	0.13752453
68	0.13003197	0.13252804	0.13502459	0.13752156
69	0.13002829	0.13252475	0.13502166	0.13751895
70	0.13002503	0.13252186	0.13501908	0.13751666
71	0.13002215	0.13251930	0.13501681	0.13751465
72	0.13001960	0.13251704	0.13501481	0.13751288
73	0.13001735	0.13251505	0.13501305	0.13751132
74	0.13001535	0.13251329	0.13501150	0.13750995
75	0.13001359	0.13251173	0.13501013	0.13750875
76	0.13001202	0.13251036	0.13500893	0.13750769
77	0.13001064	0.13250915	0.13500786	0.13750676
78	0.13000942	0.13250808	0.13500693	0.13750594
79	0.13000833	0.13250713	0.13500610	0.13750523
80	0.13000737	0.13250630	0.13500538	0.13750459
81	0.13000653	0.13250556	0.13500474	0.13750404
82	0.13000577	0.13250491	0.13500418	0.13750355
83	0.13000511	0.13250434	0.13500368	0.13750312
84	0.13000452	0.13250383	0.13500324	0.13750274
85	0.13000400	0.13250338	0.13500286	0.13750241
86	0.13000354	0.13250298	0.13500252	0.13750212
87	0.13000313	0.13250264	0.13500222	0.13750186
88	0.13000277	0.13250233	0.13500195	0.13750164
89	0.13000245	0.13250206	0.13500172	0.13750144
90	0.13000217	0.13250181	0.13500152	0.13750127
91	0.13000192	0.13250160	0.13500134	0.13750111
92	0.13000170	0.13250141	0.13500118	0.13750098
93	0.13000151	0.13250125	0.13500104	0.13750086
94	0.13000133	0.13250110	0.13500091	0.13750076
95	0.13000118	0.13250097	0.13500080	0.13750067
96	0.13000104	0.13250086	0.13500071	0.13750058
97	0.13000092	0.13250076	0.13500062	0.13750051
98	0.13000082	0.13250067	0.13500055	0.13750045
99	0.13000072	0.13250059	0.13500049	0.13750040
100	0.13000064	0.13250052	0.13500043	0.13750035

ANNUITY WHOSE PRESENT VALUE IS 1

$$a_{\overline{n}|i}^{-1} = \frac{i}{1-v^n} = s_{\overline{n}|i}^{-1} + i \quad \text{(Continued)}$$

Rate i

Periods n	0.14(14%)	0.1425(14 1/4%)	0.145(14 1/2%)	0.1475(14 3/4%)
1	1.14000000	1.14250000	1.14500000	1.14750000
2	0.60728972	0.60924446	0.61120047	0.61315774
3	0.43073148	0.43253950	0.43434976	0.43616225
4	0.34320478	0.34496527	0.34672887	0.34849557
5	0.29128355	0.29303569	0.29479175	0.29655171
6	0.25715750	0.25892037	0.26068791	0.26246010
7	0.23319238	0.23497635	0.23676570	0.23856038
8	0.21557002	0.21738107	0.21919813	0.22102115
9	0.20216838	0.20400997	0.20585814	0.20771284
10	0.19171354	0.19358759	0.19546874	0.19735692
11	0.18339427	0.18530171	0.18721669	0.18913914
12	0.17666933	0.17861039	0.18055938	0.18251621
13	0.17116366	0.17313811	0.17512079	0.17711161
14	0.16660914	0.16861637	0.17063208	0.17265616
15	0.16280896	0.16484811	0.16689593	0.16895229
16	0.15961540	0.16168543	0.16376426	0.16585172
17	0.15691544	0.15901517	0.16112376	0.16324105
18	0.15462115	0.15674931	0.15888634	0.16103206
19	0.15266316	0.15481841	0.15698249	0.15915520
20	0.15098600	0.15316697	0.15535667	0.15755491
21	0.14954486	0.15175015	0.15396405	0.15618633
22	0.14830317	0.15053139	0.15276805	0.15501292
23	0.14723081	0.14948059	0.15173860	0.15400462
24	0.14630284	0.14857282	0.15085081	0.15313656
25	0.14549841	0.14778727	0.15008390	0.15238803
26	0.14480001	0.14710649	0.14942046	0.15174165
27	0.14419288	0.14651575	0.14884582	0.15118281
28	0.14366449	0.14600257	0.14834755	0.15069916
29	0.14320417	0.14555634	0.14791510	0.15028018
30	0.14280279	0.14516799	0.14753947	0.14991696
31	0.14245256	0.14482978	0.14721297	0.14960186
32	0.14214675	0.14453505	0.14692900	0.14932834
33	0.14187958	0.14427806	0.14668188	0.14909079
34	0.14164604	0.14405387	0.14646674	0.14888439
35	0.14144181	0.14385821	0.14627935	0.14870498
36	0.14126315	0.14368739	0.14611609	0.14854899
37	0.14110680	0.14353822	0.14597380	0.14841332
38	0.14096993	0.14340790	0.14584976	0.14829529
39	0.14085010	0.14329403	0.14574160	0.14819258
40	0.14074574	0.14319451	0.14564727	0.14810319
41	0.14065321	0.14310752	0.14556498	0.14802538
42	0.14057266	0.14303146	0.14549319	0.14795764
43	0.14050208	0.14296496	0.14543055	0.14789866
44	0.14044023	0.14290680	0.14537588	0.14784729
45	0.14038602	0.14285593	0.14532817	0.14780256
46	0.14033850	0.14281144	0.14528653	0.14776360
47	0.14029684	0.14277252	0.14525018	0.14772966
48	0.14026032	0.14273848	0.14521845	0.14770010
49	0.14022830	0.14270869	0.14519075	0.14767435

Rate i

Periods n	0.14(14%)	0.1425(14 1/4%)	0.145(14 1/2%)	0.1475(14 3/4%)
51	0.14017560	0.14265982	0.14514545	0.14763237
52	0.14015401	0.14263987	0.14512702	0.14761534
53	0.14013508	0.14262241	0.14511092	0.14760051
54	0.14011848	0.14260713	0.14509686	0.14758758
55	0.14010392	0.14259376	0.14508459	0.14757632
56	0.14009115	0.14258206	0.14507387	0.14756650
57	0.14007995	0.14257182	0.14506451	0.14755795
58	0.14007012	0.14256286	0.14505634	0.14755050
59	0.14006151	0.14255501	0.14504920	0.14754401
60	0.14005395	0.14254815	0.14504297	0.14753835
61	0.14004732	0.14254214	0.14503753	0.14753342
62	0.14004151	0.14253688	0.14503277	0.14752912
63	0.14003641	0.14253228	0.14502862	0.14752538
64	0.14003194	0.14252826	0.14502500	0.14752211
65	0.14002802	0.14252473	0.14502183	0.14751927
66	0.14002457	0.14252165	0.14501907	0.14751679
67	0.14002156	0.14251895	0.14501665	0.14751464
68	0.14001891	0.14251658	0.14501454	0.14751275
69	0.14001659	0.14251451	0.14501270	0.14751111
70	0.14001455	0.14251270	0.14501109	0.14750969
71	0.14001276	0.14251112	0.14500969	0.14750844
72	0.14001119	0.14250973	0.14500846	0.14750736
73	0.14000982	0.14250852	0.14500739	0.14750641
74	0.14000861	0.14250746	0.14500645	0.14750559
75	0.14000756	0.14250653	0.14500564	0.14750487
76	0.14000663	0.14250571	0.14500492	0.14750424
77	0.14000581	0.14250500	0.14500430	0.14750370
78	0.14000510	0.14250438	0.14500375	0.14750322
79	0.14000447	0.14250383	0.14500328	0.14750281
80	0.14000392	0.14250335	0.14500286	0.14750245
81	0.14000344	0.14250293	0.14500250	0.14750213
82	0.14000302	0.14250257	0.14500218	0.14750186
83	0.14000265	0.14250225	0.14500191	0.14750162
84	0.14000232	0.14250197	0.14500167	0.14750141
85	0.14000204	0.14250172	0.14500146	0.14750123
86	0.14000179	0.14250151	0.14500127	0.14750107
87	0.14000157	0.14250132	0.14500111	0.14750093
88	0.14000138	0.14250115	0.14500097	0.14750081
89	0.14000121	0.14250101	0.14500085	0.14750071
90	0.14000106	0.14250088	0.14500074	0.14750062
91	0.14000093	0.14250077	0.14500065	0.14750054
92	0.14000081	0.14250068	0.14500056	0.14750047
93	0.14000071	0.14250059	0.14500049	0.14750041
94	0.14000063	0.14250052	0.14500043	0.14750036
95	0.14000055	0.14250045	0.14500038	0.14750031
96	0.14000048	0.14250040	0.14500033	0.14750027
97	0.14000042	0.14250035	0.14500029	0.14750024
98	0.14000037	0.14250030	0.14500025	0.14750021
99	0.14000033	0.14250027	0.14500022	0.14750018

$$a_{\overline{n}|i}^{-1} = \frac{i}{1 - v^n} = s_{\overline{n}|i}^{-1} + i \quad \text{(Continued)}$$

Rate i — Periods n = 1 to 50

n	0.15 (15%)	0.1525 (15 1/4%)	0.155 (15 1/2%)	0.1575 (15 3/4%)
1	1.15000000	1.15250000	1.15500000	1.15750000
2	0.61511628	0.61707607	0.61903712	0.62099942
3	0.43797696	0.43979389	0.44161302	0.44343435
4	0.35026535	0.35203821	0.35381412	0.35559308
5	0.29831555	0.30008326	0.30185481	0.30363019
6	0.26423691	0.26601831	0.26780429	0.26959482
7	0.24036036	0.24216562	0.24397611	0.24579181
8	0.22285009	0.22468491	0.22652558	0.22837204
9	0.20957402	0.21144162	0.21331560	0.21519591
10	0.19925206	0.20115412	0.20306301	0.20497869
11	0.19106898	0.19300614	0.19495054	0.19690210
12	0.18448078	0.18645300	0.18843279	0.19042007
13	0.17911046	0.18111723	0.18313183	0.18515416
14	0.17468849	0.17672895	0.17877743	0.18083381
15	0.17101705	0.17309009	0.17517126	0.17726045
16	0.16794769	0.17005201	0.17216453	0.17428511
17	0.16536686	0.16750105	0.16964345	0.17179390
18	0.16318629	0.16534885	0.16751958	0.16969831
19	0.16133635	0.16352576	0.16572323	0.16792859
20	0.15976147	0.16197616	0.16419878	0.16642913
21	0.15841679	0.16065521	0.16290138	0.16515510
22	0.15726577	0.15952639	0.16179454	0.16407003
23	0.15627839	0.15855970	0.16084832	0.16314401
24	0.15542983	0.15773038	0.16003797	0.16235238
25	0.15469940	0.15701778	0.15934293	0.16167462
26	0.15406981	0.15640468	0.15874603	0.16109362
27	0.15352648	0.15587657	0.15823283	0.16059503
28	0.15305713	0.15542122	0.15779118	0.16016676
29	0.15265133	0.15502827	0.15741078	0.15979860
30	0.15230020	0.15468893	0.15708290	0.15948190
31	0.15199618	0.15439569	0.15680013	0.15920930
32	0.15173280	0.15414215	0.15655613	0.15897454
33	0.15150452	0.15392283	0.15634549	0.15877228
34	0.15130675	0.15373304	0.15616357	0.15859795
35	0.15113485	0.15356874	0.15600641	0.15844766
36	0.15098586	0.15342646	0.15587059	0.15831804
37	0.15085653	0.15330322	0.15575319	0.15820623
38	0.15074426	0.15319646	0.15565169	0.15810976
39	0.15064676	0.15310393	0.15556391	0.15802652
40	0.15056209	0.15302375	0.15548800	0.15795467
41	0.15048853	0.15295424	0.15542233	0.15789265
42	0.15042463	0.15289398	0.15536552	0.15783910
43	0.15036911	0.15284173	0.15531637	0.15779288
44	0.15032086	0.15279642	0.15527384	0.15775296
45	0.15027893	0.15275713	0.15523703	0.15771849
46	0.15024249	0.15272306	0.15520518	0.15768873
47	0.15021082	0.15269351	0.15517761	0.15766302
48	0.15018328	0.15266787	0.15515375	0.15764082
49	0.15015935	0.15264564	0.15513310	0.15762164
50	0.15013855	0.15262635	0.15511523	0.15760508

Rate i — Periods n = 51 to 100

n	0.15 (15%)	0.1525 (15 1/4%)	0.155 (15 1/2%)	0.1575 (15 3/4%)
51	0.15012046	0.15260962	0.15509975	0.15759077
52	0.15010474	0.15259511	0.15508636	0.15757842
53	0.15009107	0.15258252	0.15507476	0.15756774
54	0.15007918	0.15257159	0.15506473	0.15755852
55	0.15006885	0.15256211	0.15505604	0.15755056
56	0.15005987	0.15255389	0.15504852	0.15754367
57	0.15005206	0.15254676	0.15504200	0.15753773
58	0.15004526	0.15254057	0.15503636	0.15753260
59	0.15003936	0.15253520	0.15503148	0.15752816
60	0.15003422	0.15253054	0.15502726	0.15752433
61	0.15002976	0.15252650	0.15502360	0.15752102
62	0.15002588	0.15252299	0.15502043	0.15751816
63	0.15002250	0.15251995	0.15501779	0.15751569
64	0.15001957	0.15251731	0.15501532	0.15751355
65	0.15001701	0.15251502	0.15501326	0.15751171
66	0.15001479	0.15251303	0.15501148	0.15751011
67	0.15001286	0.15251131	0.15500994	0.15750874
68	0.15001119	0.15250981	0.15500861	0.15750755
69	0.15000973	0.15250851	0.15500745	0.15750652
70	0.15000846	0.15250739	0.15500645	0.15750563
71	0.15000735	0.15250641	0.15500559	0.15750487
72	0.15000640	0.15250556	0.15500484	0.15750421
73	0.15000556	0.15250482	0.15500419	0.15750363
74	0.15000484	0.15250419	0.15500362	0.15750314
75	0.15000420	0.15250363	0.15500314	0.15750271
76	0.15000366	0.15250315	0.15500272	0.15750234
77	0.15000318	0.15250273	0.15500235	0.15750202
78	0.15000276	0.15250237	0.15500204	0.15750175
79	0.15000240	0.15250206	0.15500176	0.15750151
80	0.15000209	0.15250179	0.15500153	0.15750130
81	0.15000182	0.15250155	0.15500132	0.15750113
82	0.15000158	0.15250134	0.15500114	0.15750097
83	0.15000137	0.15250117	0.15500099	0.15750084
84	0.15000119	0.15250101	0.15500086	0.15750073
85	0.15000104	0.15250088	0.15500074	0.15750063
86	0.15000090	0.15250076	0.15500063	0.15750054
87	0.15000079	0.15250066	0.15500054	0.15750047
88	0.15000068	0.15250057	0.15500047	0.15750040
89	0.15000059	0.15250050	0.15500040	0.15750035
90	0.15000052	0.15250043	0.15500035	0.15750030
91	0.15000045	0.15250037	0.15500030	0.15750026
92	0.15000039	0.15250033	0.15500026	0.15750023
93	0.15000034	0.15250028	0.15500023	0.15750019
94	0.15000030	0.15250024	0.15500020	0.15750017
95	0.15000026	0.15250021	0.15500018	0.15750015
96	0.15000022	0.15250018	0.15500015	0.15750013
97	0.15000019	0.15250016	0.15500013	0.15750011
98	0.15000017	0.15250014	0.15500011	0.15750009
99	0.15000015	0.15250012	0.15500010	0.15750008
100	0.15000013	0.15250010	0.15500009	0.15750007

ANNUITY WHOSE PRESENT VALUE IS 1

$$a_{\overline{n}|i}^{-1} = \frac{i}{1-v^n} = s_{\overline{n}|i}^{-1} + i \quad \text{(Continued)}$$

Rate i

Periods n	0.16 (16%)	0.1625 (16 1/4%)	0.165 (16 1/2%)	0.1675 (16 3/4%)
1	1.16000000	1.16250000	1.16500000	1.16750000
2	0.62296296	0.62492775	0.62689376	0.62886101
3	0.44525787	0.44708357	0.44891145	0.45074149
4	0.35737507	0.35916008	0.36094810	0.36273912
5	0.30540938	0.30719236	0.30897911	0.31076962
6	0.27138987	0.27318942	0.27499344	0.27680191
7	0.24761268	0.24943869	0.25126981	0.25310600
8	0.23022426	0.23208220	0.23394581	0.23581505
9	0.21708249	0.21897529	0.22087426	0.22277935
10	0.20690108	0.20883013	0.21076578	0.21270795
11	0.19886075	0.20082642	0.20279903	0.20477852
12	0.19241473	0.19441670	0.19642589	0.19844221
13	0.18718411	0.18922158	0.19126648	0.19331870
14	0.18289797	0.18496981	0.18704920	0.18913604
15	0.17935752	0.18146235	0.18357480	0.18569476
16	0.17641362	0.17854990	0.18069381	0.18284523
17	0.17395225	0.17611834	0.17829203	0.18047315
18	0.17188485	0.17407906	0.17628076	0.17848979
19	0.17014166	0.17236225	0.17459019	0.17682532
20	0.16866703	0.17091229	0.17316471	0.17542413
21	0.16741617	0.16968439	0.17195956	0.17424151
22	0.16635264	0.16864216	0.17093840	0.17324116
23	0.16544658	0.16775581	0.17007149	0.17239342
24	0.16467339	0.16700078	0.16933434	0.17167387
25	0.16401062	0.16635670	0.16870667	0.17106231
26	0.16344723	0.16580662	0.16817160	0.17054195
27	0.16296294	0.16533634	0.16771501	0.17009875
28	0.16254775	0.16493392	0.16732506	0.16972097
29	0.16219153	0.16458932	0.16699179	0.16939872
30	0.16188568	0.16429404	0.16670677	0.16912367
31	0.16162295	0.16404089	0.16646290	0.16888879
32	0.16139714	0.16382374	0.16625413	0.16868813
33	0.16120298	0.16363740	0.16607535	0.16851664
34	0.16103598	0.16347746	0.16592220	0.16837002
35	0.16089229	0.16334012	0.16579096	0.16824465
36	0.16076862	0.16322216	0.16567847	0.16813741
37	0.16066217	0.16312083	0.16558204	0.16804566
38	0.16057051	0.16303376	0.16549936	0.16796716
39	0.16049158	0.16295894	0.16542845	0.16789997
40	0.16042359	0.16289463	0.16536763	0.16784247
41	0.16036503	0.16283935	0.16531546	0.16779325
42	0.16031458	0.16279183	0.16527071	0.16775112
43	0.16027112	0.16275097	0.16523232	0.16771504
44	0.16023367	0.16271584	0.16519937	0.16768416
45	0.16020140	0.16268564	0.16517111	0.16765771
46	0.16017359	0.16265966	0.16514685	0.16763507
47	0.16014962	0.16263733	0.16512604	0.16761568
48	0.16012897	0.16261812	0.16510817	0.16759907
49	0.16011117	0.16260159	0.16509284	0.16758485

Rate i

Periods n	0.16 (16%)	0.1625 (16 1/4%)	0.165 (16 1/2%)	0.1675 (16 3/4%)
51	0.16008260	0.16257516	0.16506840	0.16756224
52	0.16007120	0.16256465	0.16505871	0.16755331
53	0.16006138	0.16255561	0.16505039	0.16754566
54	0.16005291	0.16254784	0.16504325	0.16753911
55	0.16004561	0.16254115	0.16503712	0.16753349
56	0.16003932	0.16253540	0.16503187	0.16752869
57	0.16003389	0.16253045	0.16502735	0.16752457
58	0.16002922	0.16252619	0.16502348	0.16752105
59	0.16002519	0.16252253	0.16502015	0.16751803
60	0.16002171	0.16251938	0.16501730	0.16751544
61	0.16001872	0.16251667	0.16501485	0.16751322
62	0.16001613	0.16251434	0.16501274	0.16751133
63	0.16001391	0.16251233	0.16501094	0.16750970
64	0.16001199	0.16251061	0.16500939	0.16750831
65	0.16001034	0.16250913	0.16500806	0.16750712
66	0.16000891	0.16250785	0.16500692	0.16750610
67	0.16000768	0.16250675	0.16500594	0.16750522
68	0.16000662	0.16250581	0.16500510	0.16750447
69	0.16000571	0.16250500	0.16500438	0.16750383
70	0.16000492	0.16250430	0.16500376	0.16750328
71	0.16000424	0.16250370	0.16500322	0.16750281
72	0.16000366	0.16250318	0.16500277	0.16750241
73	0.16000315	0.16250274	0.16500238	0.16750206
74	0.16000272	0.16250235	0.16500204	0.16750177
75	0.16000234	0.16250202	0.16500175	0.16750151
76	0.16000202	0.16250174	0.16500150	0.16750130
77	0.16000174	0.16250150	0.16500129	0.16750111
78	0.16000150	0.16250129	0.16500111	0.16750095
79	0.16000129	0.16250111	0.16500095	0.16750081
80	0.16000112	0.16250095	0.16500082	0.16750070
81	0.16000096	0.16250082	0.16500070	0.16750060
82	0.16000083	0.16250071	0.16500060	0.16750051
83	0.16000071	0.16250061	0.16500052	0.16750044
84	0.16000062	0.16250052	0.16500044	0.16750038
85	0.16000053	0.16250045	0.16500038	0.16750032
86	0.16000046	0.16250039	0.16500033	0.16750028
87	0.16000040	0.16250033	0.16500028	0.16750024
88	0.16000034	0.16250028	0.16500024	0.16750020
89	0.16000029	0.16250024	0.16500021	0.16750017
90	0.16000025	0.16250021	0.16500018	0.16750015
91	0.16000022	0.16250018	0.16500015	0.16750013
92	0.16000019	0.16250016	0.16500013	0.16750011
93	0.16000016	0.16250013	0.16500011	0.16750009
94	0.16000014	0.16250011	0.16500010	0.16750008
95	0.16000012	0.16250010	0.16500008	0.16750007
96	0.16000010	0.16250009	0.16500007	0.16750006
97	0.16000009	0.16250007	0.16500006	0.16750005
98	0.16000008	0.16250006	0.16500005	0.16750005
99	0.16000007	0.16250005	0.16500004	0.16750004

$$a_{\overline{n}|i}^{-1} = \frac{i}{1-v^n} = v^n \frac{1}{s_{\overline{n}|i}} + i \quad \text{(Continued)}$$

Rate i

Periods n	0.17 (17%)	0.1725 (17 1/4%)	0.175 (17 1/2%)	0.1775 (17 3/4%)
1	1.17000000	1.17250000	1.17500000	1.17750000
2	0.63082949	0.63279919	0.63477011	0.63674225
3	0.45257368	0.45440802	0.45624451	0.45808312
4	0.36453311	0.36633008	0.36813000	0.36993287
5	0.31256386	0.31436183	0.31616349	0.31796883
6	0.27861480	0.28043210	0.28225376	0.28407978
7	0.25494724	0.25679349	0.25864473	0.26050090
8	0.23768989	0.23957028	0.24145618	0.24334756
9	0.22469051	0.22660769	0.22853083	0.23045990
10	0.21465660	0.21661165	0.21857305	0.22054073
11	0.20676479	0.20875779	0.21075744	0.21276366
12	0.20046558	0.20249591	0.20453311	0.20657711
13	0.19537814	0.19744471	0.19951831	0.20159884
14	0.19123022	0.19333162	0.19544013	0.19755564
15	0.18782209	0.18995669	0.19209841	0.19424715
16	0.18500401	0.18717002	0.18934312	0.19152319
17	0.18266157	0.18485713	0.18705970	0.18926913
18	0.18070600	0.18292922	0.18515930	0.18739610
19	0.17906745	0.18131643	0.18357210	0.18583429
20	0.17769036	0.17996323	0.18224257	0.18452821
21	0.17653004	0.17882497	0.18112613	0.18343334
22	0.17555025	0.17786548	0.18018668	0.18251366
23	0.17472141	0.17705526	0.17939480	0.18173984
24	0.17401917	0.17637005	0.17872632	0.18108779
25	0.17342343	0.17579982	0.17816131	0.18053770
26	0.17291747	0.17529797	0.17768326	0.18007315
27	0.17248736	0.17488065	0.17727842	0.17968050
28	0.17212144	0.17452629	0.17693533	0.17934838
29	0.17180992	0.17422520	0.17664438	0.17906729
30	0.17154455	0.17396922	0.17639751	0.17882926
31	0.17131839	0.17375150	0.17618796	0.17862761
32	0.17112556	0.17356624	0.17601001	0.17845672
33	0.17096109	0.17340854	0.17585884	0.17831184
34	0.17082077	0.17327428	0.17573040	0.17818898
35	0.17070102	0.17315993	0.17562123	0.17808478
36	0.17059880	0.17306252	0.17552843	0.17799638
37	0.17051154	0.17297953	0.17544952	0.17792138
38	0.17043702	0.17290882	0.17538243	0.17785773
39	0.17037338	0.17284855	0.17532536	0.17780371
40	0.17031903	0.17279718	0.17527683	0.17775786
41	0.17027260	0.17275340	0.17523554	0.17771895
42	0.17023294	0.17271607	0.17520042	0.17768591
43	0.17019905	0.17268425	0.17517054	0.17765786
44	0.17017010	0.17265712	0.17514512	0.17763404
45	0.17014536	0.17263398	0.17512349	0.17761382
46	0.17012423	0.17261426	0.17510509	0.17759666
47	0.17010617	0.17259744	0.17508943	0.17758208
48	0.17009073	0.17258310	0.17507610	0.17756970
49	0.17007754	0.17257087	0.17506477	0.17755919
50	0.17006627	0.17256044	0.17505512	0.17755027
51	0.17005664	0.17255154	0.17504691	0.17754269
52	0.17004841	0.17254396	0.17503992	0.17753625
53	0.17004137	0.17253749	0.17503397	0.17753079
54	0.17003536	0.17253197	0.17502891	0.17752614
55	0.17003022	0.17252727	0.17502460	0.17752220
56	0.17002583	0.17252326	0.17502094	0.17751886
57	0.17002208	0.17251983	0.17501782	0.17751601
58	0.17001887	0.17251692	0.17501517	0.17751360
59	0.17001613	0.17251443	0.17501291	0.17751155
60	0.17001378	0.17251230	0.17501098	0.17750981
61	0.17001178	0.17251049	0.17500935	0.17750833
62	0.17001007	0.17250895	0.17500796	0.17750707
63	0.17000861	0.17250763	0.17500677	0.17750601
64	0.17000735	0.17250651	0.17500576	0.17750510
65	0.17000629	0.17250555	0.17500490	0.17750433
66	0.17000537	0.17250474	0.17500417	0.17750368
67	0.17000459	0.17250404	0.17500355	0.17750312
68	0.17000392	0.17250344	0.17500302	0.17750265
69	0.17000335	0.17250294	0.17500257	0.17750255
70	0.17000287	0.17250251	0.17500219	0.17750191
71	0.17000245	0.17250214	0.17500186	0.17750163
72	0.17000209	0.17250182	0.17500159	0.17750138
73	0.17000179	0.17250155	0.17500135	0.17750117
74	0.17000153	0.17250133	0.17500115	0.17750100
75	0.17000131	0.17250113	0.17500098	0.17750085
76	0.17000112	0.17250096	0.17500083	0.17750072
77	0.17000096	0.17250082	0.17500071	0.17750061
78	0.17000082	0.17250070	0.17500060	0.17750052
79	0.17000070	0.17250060	0.17500051	0.17750044
80	0.17000060	0.17250051	0.17500044	0.17750037
81	0.17000051	0.17250044	0.17500037	0.17750032
82	0.17000044	0.17250037	0.17500032	0.17750027
83	0.17000037	0.17250032	0.17500027	0.17750023
84	0.17000032	0.17250027	0.17500023	0.17750019
85	0.17000027	0.17250023	0.17500019	0.17750017
86	0.17000023	0.17250020	0.17500017	0.17750014
87	0.17000020	0.17250017	0.17500014	0.17750012
88	0.17000017	0.17250014	0.17500012	0.17750010
89	0.17000015	0.17250012	0.17500010	0.17750009
90	0.17000012	0.17250010	0.17500009	0.17750007
91	0.17000011	0.17250009	0.17500007	0.17750006
92	0.17000009	0.17250008	0.17500006	0.17750005
93	0.17000008	0.17250006	0.17500005	0.17750004
94	0.17000007	0.17250005	0.17500005	0.17750004
95	0.17000006	0.17250005	0.17500004	0.17750003
96	0.17000005	0.17250004	0.17500003	0.17750003
97	0.17000004	0.17250003	0.17500003	0.17750002
98	0.17000004	0.17250003	0.17500002	0.17750002
99	0.17000003	0.17250002	0.17500002	0.17750002
100	0.17000003	0.17250002	0.17500002	0.17750001

ANNUITY WHOSE PRESENT VALUE IS 1

$$a_{\overline{n}|i}^{-1} = \frac{i}{1-v^n} = v^{-n}s_{\overline{n}|i}^{-1} + i \quad \text{(Continued)}$$

Rate i

Periods n	0.18(18%)	0.1825(18 1/4%)	0.185(18 1/2%)	0.1875(18 3/4%)
1	1.18000000	1.18250000	1.18500000	1.18750000
2	0.63871560	0.64069015	0.64266590	0.64464286
3	0.45992386	0.46176672	0.46361168	0.46545874
4	0.37173867	0.37354739	0.37535902	0.37717354
5	0.31977784	0.32159050	0.32340678	0.32522668
6	0.28591013	0.28774478	0.28958370	0.29142688
7	0.26236200	0.26422798	0.26609881	0.26797446
8	0.24524436	0.24714655	0.24905409	0.25096694
9	0.23239482	0.23433557	0.23628208	0.23823431
10	0.22251464	0.22449471	0.22648089	0.22847311
11	0.21477639	0.21679555	0.21882106	0.22085287
12	0.20862781	0.21068513	0.21274900	0.21481932
13	0.20368621	0.20578032	0.20788107	0.20998838
14	0.19967806	0.20180726	0.20394315	0.20608562
15	0.19640278	0.19856519	0.20073426	0.20290987
16	0.19371008	0.19590369	0.19810386	0.20031049
17	0.19148527	0.19370800	0.19593717	0.19817265
18	0.18963946	0.19188923	0.19414527	0.19640744
19	0.18810284	0.19037760	0.19265842	0.19494515
20	0.18681998	0.18911773	0.19142130	0.19373054
21	0.18574643	0.18806525	0.19038962	0.19271939
22	0.18484626	0.18718429	0.18952761	0.19187604
23	0.18409020	0.18644572	0.18880622	0.19117156
24	0.18345430	0.18582566	0.18820172	0.19058231
25	0.18291883	0.18530451	0.18769459	0.19008891
26	0.18246748	0.18486607	0.18726876	0.18967539
27	0.18208672	0.18449691	0.18691091	0.18932856
28	0.18176528	0.18418587	0.18660998	0.18903747
29	0.18149377	0.18392365	0.18635679	0.18879304
30	0.18126431	0.18370249	0.18614366	0.18858769
31	0.18107030	0.18351587	0.18596419	0.18841511
32	0.18090621	0.18335835	0.18581300	0.18827003
33	0.18076737	0.18322535	0.18568560	0.18814802
34	0.18064990	0.18311303	0.18557823	0.18804541
35	0.18055046	0.18301815	0.18548772	0.18795908
36	0.18046628	0.18293799	0.18541141	0.18788644
37	0.18039499	0.18287025	0.18534706	0.18782532
38	0.18033463	0.18281301	0.18529279	0.18777388
39	0.18028350	0.18276464	0.18524702	0.18773058
40	0.18024020	0.18272374	0.18520841	0.18769414
41	0.18020352	0.18268918	0.18517585	0.18766346
42	0.18017244	0.18265995	0.18514837	0.18763763
43	0.18014612	0.18263525	0.18512519	0.18761588
44	0.18012381	0.18261436	0.18510564	0.18759758
45	0.18010491	0.18259670	0.18508914	0.18758216
46	0.18008890	0.18258177	0.18507521	0.18756919
47	0.18007534	0.18256915	0.18506347	0.18755826
48	0.18006384	0.18255847	0.18505356	0.18754906
49	0.18005410	0.18254945	0.18504519	0.18754131

Rate i

Periods n	0.18(18%)	0.1825(18 1/4%)	0.185(18 1/2%)	0.1875(18 3/4%)
51	0.18003885	0.18253536	0.18503218	0.18753929
52	0.18003292	0.18252990	0.18502716	0.18753467
53	0.18002790	0.18252528	0.18502292	0.18753077
54	0.18002364	0.18252138	0.18501934	0.18752749
55	0.18002004	0.18251808	0.18501632	0.18751749
56	0.18001698	0.18251529	0.18501377	0.18751473
57	0.18001439	0.18251293	0.18501162	0.18751240
58	0.18001219	0.18251094	0.18500981	0.18751045
59	0.18001033	0.18250925	0.18500828	0.18750880
60	0.18000876	0.18250782	0.18500698	0.18750741
61	0.18000742	0.18250661	0.18500589	0.18750624
62	0.18000629	0.18250559	0.18500497	0.18750525
63	0.18000533	0.18250473	0.18500420	0.18750442
64	0.18000452	0.18250400	0.18500354	0.18750372
65	0.18000383	0.18250338	0.18500299	0.18750314
66	0.18000324	0.18250286	0.18500252	0.18750264
67	0.18000275	0.18250242	0.18500213	0.18750222
68	0.18000233	0.18250205	0.18500180	0.18750187
69	0.18000197	0.18250173	0.18500152	0.18750158
70	0.18000167	0.18250146	0.18500128	0.18750133
71	0.18000142	0.18250124	0.18500108	0.18750112
72	0.18000120	0.18250105	0.18500091	0.18750094
73	0.18000102	0.18250088	0.18500077	0.18750079
74	0.18000086	0.18250075	0.18500065	0.18750067
75	0.18000073	0.18250063	0.18500055	0.18750056
76	0.18000062	0.18250054	0.18500046	0.18750047
77	0.18000053	0.18250045	0.18500039	0.18750040
78	0.18000045	0.18250038	0.18500033	0.18750034
79	0.18000038	0.18250032	0.18500028	0.18750028
80	0.18000032	0.18250027	0.18500023	0.18750024
81	0.18000027	0.18250023	0.18500020	0.18750020
82	0.18000023	0.18250020	0.18500017	0.18750017
83	0.18000019	0.18250017	0.18500014	0.18750014
84	0.18000016	0.18250014	0.18500012	0.18750012
85	0.18000014	0.18250012	0.18500010	0.18750010
86	0.18000012	0.18250010	0.18500008	0.18750008
87	0.18000010	0.18250008	0.18500007	0.18750007
88	0.18000009	0.18250007	0.18500006	0.18750006
89	0.18000007	0.18250006	0.18500005	0.18750005
90	0.18000006	0.18250005	0.18500004	0.18750004
91	0.18000005	0.18250004	0.18500004	0.18750004
92	0.18000004	0.18250004	0.18500003	0.18750003
93	0.18000004	0.18250003	0.18500003	0.18750003
94	0.18000003	0.18250003	0.18500002	0.18750002
95	0.18000003	0.18250002	0.18500002	0.18750002
96	0.18000002	0.18250002	0.18500002	0.18750002
97	0.18000002	0.18250002	0.18500001	0.18750001
98	0.18000002	0.18250001	0.18500001	0.18750001
99	0.18000001	0.18250001	0.18500001	0.18750001

$$a_{\overline{n}|i}^{-1} = \frac{i}{1-v^n} = v^n \cdot s_{\overline{n}|i}^{-1} + i \quad \text{(Continued)}$$

Rate i

Periods n	0.19(19%)	0.1925(19 1/4%)	0.195(19 1/2%)	0.1975(19 3/4%)	0.20(20%)
1	1.19000000	1.19250000	1.19500000	1.19750000	1.20000000
2	0.64662100	0.64860034	0.65058087	0.65256257	0.65454545
3	0.46710789	0.46915913	0.47101245	0.47286783	0.47472527
4	0.37899094	0.38081121	0.38263434	0.38446031	0.38628912
5	0.32705017	0.32887723	0.33070785	0.33254202	0.33437970
6	0.29327429	0.29512591	0.29698170	0.29884166	0.30070575
7	0.26985490	0.27174010	0.27363002	0.27552464	0.27742393
8	0.25288506	0.25480841	0.25673694	0.25867063	0.26060942
9	0.24019220	0.24215571	0.24412479	0.24609939	0.24807946
10	0.23047131	0.23247543	0.23448542	0.23650122	0.23852276
11	0.22289090	0.22493508	0.22698533	0.22904159	0.23110379
12	0.21689602	0.21897902	0.22106822	0.22316357	0.22526496
13	0.21210215	0.21422229	0.21634870	0.21848130	0.22062000
14	0.20823456	0.21038988	0.21255147	0.21471923	0.21689306
15	0.20509191	0.20728026	0.20947482	0.21167548	0.21388212
16	0.20252345	0.20474261	0.20696786	0.20919907	0.21143614
17	0.20041431	0.20266201	0.20491564	0.20717506	0.20944015
18	0.19867594	0.20094960	0.20322932	0.20551463	0.20780539
19	0.19723765	0.19953577	0.20183936	0.20414830	0.20646245
20	0.19604529	0.19836541	0.20069075	0.20302117	0.20535653
21	0.19505440	0.19739451	0.19973956	0.20208942	0.20444394
22	0.19422943	0.19658763	0.19895049	0.20131787	0.20368962
23	0.19354156	0.19591607	0.19829496	0.20067807	0.20306526
24	0.19296727	0.19535645	0.19774971	0.20014689	0.20254787
25	0.19248730	0.19488962	0.19729573	0.19970547	0.20211873
26	0.19208581	0.19449987	0.19691743	0.19933835	0.20176250
27	0.19174971	0.19417423	0.19660197	0.19903280	0.20146659
28	0.19146819	0.19390200	0.19633877	0.19877836	0.20122067
29	0.19123225	0.19367430	0.19611905	0.19856639	0.20101619
30	0.19103443	0.19348377	0.19593557	0.19838972	0.20084611
31	0.19086852	0.19332428	0.19578229	0.19824243	0.20070459
32	0.19072931	0.19319075	0.19565421	0.19811960	0.20058682
33	0.19061249	0.19307821	0.19554716	0.19801714	0.20048877
34	0.19051444	0.19298522	0.19545766	0.19793167	0.20040715
35	0.19043211	0.19290673	0.19538283	0.19786034	0.20033917
36	0.19036299	0.19284096	0.19532026	0.19780082	0.20028256
37	0.19030494	0.19278583	0.19526793	0.19775115	0.20023542
38	0.19025619	0.19273964	0.19522416	0.19770968	0.20019614
39	0.19021524	0.19270091	0.19518754	0.19767507	0.20016342
40	0.19018084	0.19266845	0.19515692	0.19764617	0.20013617
41	0.19015194	0.19264124	0.19513129	0.19762205	0.20011346
42	0.19012767	0.19261843	0.19510986	0.19760191	0.20009454
43	0.19010727	0.19259930	0.19509192	0.19758510	0.20007878
44	0.19009013	0.19258326	0.19507692	0.19757106	0.20006564
45	0.19007574	0.19256982	0.19506436	0.19755933	0.20005470
46	0.19006364	0.19255854	0.19505386	0.19754955	0.20004558
47	0.19005348	0.19254909	0.19504507	0.19754137	0.20003798
48	0.19004494	0.19254116	0.19503771	0.19753455	0.20003165
49	0.19003776	0.19253452	0.19503156	0.19752885	0.20002638
50	0.19003173	0.19252895	0.19502641	0.19752409	0.20002198

Rate i

Periods n	0.19(19%)	0.1925(19 1/4%)	0.195(19 1/2%)	0.1975(19 3/4%)	0.20(20%)
51	0.19002666	0.19252427	0.19502210	0.19752012	0.20001832
52	0.19002241	0.19252035	0.19501849	0.19751680	0.20001526
53	0.19001883	0.19251707	0.19501547	0.19751403	0.20001272
54	0.19001582	0.19251431	0.19501295	0.19751171	0.20001060
55	0.19001330	0.19251200	0.19501083	0.19750978	0.20000883
56	0.19001117	0.19251006	0.19500907	0.19750817	0.20000736
57	0.19000939	0.19250844	0.19500759	0.19750682	0.20000613
58	0.19000789	0.19250708	0.19500635	0.19750570	0.20000511
59	0.19000663	0.19250593	0.19500531	0.19750476	0.20000426
60	0.19000557	0.19250498	0.19500445	0.19750397	0.20000355
61	0.19000468	0.19250417	0.19500372	0.19750332	0.20000296
62	0.19000393	0.19250350	0.19500311	0.19750277	0.20000246
63	0.19000331	0.19250293	0.19500261	0.19750231	0.20000205
64	0.19000278	0.19250246	0.19500218	0.19750193	0.20000171
65	0.19000233	0.19250206	0.19500182	0.19750161	0.20000143
66	0.19000196	0.19250173	0.19500153	0.19750135	0.20000119
67	0.19000165	0.19250145	0.19500128	0.19750112	0.20000099
68	0.19000139	0.19250122	0.19500107	0.19750094	0.20000083
69	0.19000116	0.19250102	0.19500089	0.19750078	0.20000069
70	0.19000098	0.19250086	0.19500075	0.19750066	0.20000057
71	0.19000082	0.19250072	0.19500063	0.19750055	0.20000048
72	0.19000069	0.19250060	0.19500052	0.19750046	0.20000040
73	0.19000058	0.19250050	0.19500044	0.19750038	0.20000033
74	0.19000049	0.19250042	0.19500037	0.19750032	0.20000028
75	0.19000041	0.19250035	0.19500031	0.19750027	0.20000023
76	0.19000034	0.19250030	0.19500026	0.19750022	0.20000019
77	0.19000029	0.19250025	0.19500022	0.19750019	0.20000016
78	0.19000024	0.19250021	0.19500018	0.19750015	0.20000013
79	0.19000020	0.19250018	0.19500015	0.19750013	0.20000011
80	0.19000017	0.19250015	0.19500013	0.19750011	0.20000009
81	0.19000014	0.19250012	0.19500011	0.19750009	0.20000008
82	0.19000012	0.19250010	0.19500009	0.19750008	0.20000006
83	0.19000010	0.19250009	0.19500007	0.19750006	0.20000005
84	0.19000009	0.19250007	0.19500006	0.19750005	0.20000004
85	0.19000007	0.19250006	0.19500006	0.19750005	0.20000004
86	0.19000006	0.19250005	0.19500004	0.19750004	0.20000003
87	0.19000005	0.19250004	0.19500004	0.19750003	0.20000003
88	0.19000004	0.19250004	0.19500003	0.19750003	0.20000002
89	0.19000004	0.19250003	0.19500003	0.19750002	0.20000002
90	0.19000003	0.19250003	0.19500002	0.19750002	0.20000002
91	0.19000003	0.19250002	0.19500002	0.19750001	0.20000001
92	0.19000002	0.19250002	0.19500002	0.19750001	0.20000001
93	0.19000002	0.19250002	0.19500001	0.19750001	0.20000001
94	0.19000002	0.19250001	0.19500001	0.19750001	0.20000001
95	0.19000001	0.19250001	0.19500001	0.19750001	0.20000001
96	0.19000001	0.19250001	0.19500001	0.19750001	0.20000001
97	0.19000001	0.19250001	0.19500001	0.19750001	0.20000000
98	0.19000001	0.19250001	0.19500001	0.19750000	0.20000000
99	0.19000001	0.19250000	0.19500000	0.19750000	0.20000000
100	0.19000001	0.19250000	0.19500000	0.19750000	0.20000000

COMPOUND AMOUNT OF 1 FOR FRACTIONAL PERIODS, $(1 + i)^{1/p}$

5 1/2%	5 1/4%	5%	4 3/4%	4 1/2%	p	3/4%	7/12%	1/2%	5/12%	i = 1/4%
1.02713193	1.02591423	1.02469508	1.02347447	1.02225242	2	1.0037430	1.0029124	1.0024969	1.0020812	1.0012492
1.01800713	1.01720238	1.01639636	1.01558905	1.01478046	3	1.0024938	1.0019407	1.0016639	1.0013870	1.0008326
1.01347517	1.01287424	1.01227223	1.01166915	1.01106499	4	1.0018697	1.0014552	1.0012477	1.0010400	1.0006244
1.00896339	1.00856452	1.00816485	1.00776438	1.00736312	6	1.0012461	1.0009699	1.0008316	1.0006932	1.0004162
1.00447170	1.00427313	1.00407412	1.00387468	1.00367481	12	1.0006229	1.0004848	1.0004157	1.0003466	1.0002089
1.00412701	1.00394378	1.00376014	1.00357610	1.00339165	13	1.0005749	1.0004475	1.0003837	1.0003199	1.0001921
1.00206138	1.00196995	1.00187831	1.00178645	1.00169439	26	1.0002874	1.0002237	1.0001919	1.0001599	1.0000960
1.00103016	1.00098449	1.00093871	1.00089283	1.00084684	52	1.0001437	1.0001119	1.0000959	1.0000800	1.0000480
1.00014670	1.00014020	1.00013368	1.00012715	1.00012060	365	1.0000205	1.0000159	1.0000137	1.0000114	1.0000068

6 3/4%	6 1/2%	6 1/4%	6%	5 3/4%	p	1 3/4%	1 1/2%	1 1/4%	1 1/8%	1%
1.03319892	1.03198837	1.03077641	1.02956301	1.02834819	2	1.0087121	1.0074721	1.0062306	1.0056093	1.0049876
1.02201192	1.02121347	1.02041378	1.01961282	1.01881061	3	1.0057996	1.0049752	1.0041494	1.0037360	1.0033223
1.01646393	1.01586828	1.01527159	1.01467385	1.01407504	4	1.0043466	1.0037291	1.0031105	1.0028008	1.0024907
1.01094605	1.01055107	1.01015532	1.00975879	1.00936149	6	1.0028956	1.0024845	1.0020726	1.0018663	1.0016598
1.00545813	1.00526169	1.00506483	1.00486755	1.00466984	12	1.0014468	1.0012415	1.0010357	1.0009327	1.0008295
1.00503722	1.00485597	1.00467432	1.00449228	1.00430985	13	1.0013354	1.0011459	1.0009560	1.0008609	1.0007657
1.00251545	1.00242504	1.00233444	1.00224363	1.00215261	26	1.0006675	1.0005728	1.0004779	1.0004304	1.0003828
1.00125693	1.00121179	1.00116654	1.00112118	1.00107572	52	1.0003337	1.0002864	1.0002389	1.0002152	1.0001914
1.00017897	1.00017255	1.00016611	1.00015965	1.00015318	365	1.0000475	1.0000408	1.0000340	1.0000307	1.0000273

8%	7 3/4%	7 1/2%	7 1/4%	7%	p	3%	2 3/4%	2 1/2%	2 1/4%	2%
1.03923048	1.03802697	1.03682207	1.03561576	1.03440804	2	1.01488916	1.0136568	1.0124228	1.0111874	1.0099505
1.02598557	1.02519330	1.02439981	1.02360508	1.02280912	3	1.00990163	1.0090839	1.0082648	1.0074444	1.0066227
1.01942655	1.01883609	1.01824460	1.01765208	1.01705853	4	1.00741707	1.0068052	1.0061922	1.0055782	1.0049629
1.01290946	1.01251830	1.01212638	1.01173370	1.01134026	6	1.00493862	1.0045317	1.0041239	1.0037153	1.0033059
1.00643403	1.00623968	1.00604492	1.00584974	1.00565415	12	1.00246627	1.0022633	1.0020598	1.0018559	1.0016516
1.00593764	1.00575833	1.00557863	1.00539855	1.00521808	13	1.00227634	1.0020890	1.0019012	1.0017130	1.0015244
1.00296443	1.00287503	1.00278544	1.00269564	1.00260564	26	1.00113752	1.0010440	1.0009502	1.0008562	1.0007619
1.00148112	1.00143648	1.00139175	1.00134691	1.00130197	52	1.00056860	1.0005218	1.0004750	1.0004280	1.0003809
1.00021087	1.00020452	1.00019816	1.00019178	1.00018538	365	1.00008099	1.0000743	1.0000676	1.0000610	1.0000543

9 1/4%	9%	8 3/4%	8 1/2%	8 1/4%	p	4 1/4%	4%	3 3/4%	3 1/2%	3 1/4%
1.04522725	1.04403065	1.04283268	1.04163333	1.04043260	2	1.02102889	1.01980390	1.01857744	1.01734950	1.01612007
1.02992867	1.02914247	1.02835506	1.02756644	1.02677661	3	1.01397058	1.01315940	1.01234693	1.01153314	1.01071805
1.02236356	1.02177818	1.02119179	1.02060440	1.02001598	4	1.01045974	1.00985341	1.00924598	1.00863745	1.00802781
1.01485402	1.01446659	1.01407843	1.01368952	1.01329986	6	1.00696106	1.00655820	1.00615452	1.00575004	1.00534474
1.00739963	1.00720732	1.00701461	1.00682149	1.00662797	12	1.00347450	1.00327374	1.00307254	1.00287090	1.00266881
1.00682849	1.00665107	1.00647328	1.00629512	1.00611657	13	1.00320680	1.00302153	1.00283586	1.00264977	1.00246326
1.00340844	1.00332003	1.00323142	1.00314262	1.00305362	26	1.00160212	1.00150963	1.00141692	1.00132401	1.00123087
1.00170277	1.00165864	1.00161441	1.00157008	1.00152565	52	1.00080074	1.00075453	1.00070821	1.00066178	1.00061525
					365		1.00010087	1.00010087	1.00009435	1.00008752

COMPOUND AMOUNT OF 1 FOR FRACTIONAL PERIODS $(1 + i)^{1/p}$ (Continued)

14 1/4%	14%	13 3/4%	13 1/2%	13 1/4%	p	15 1/2%	15 1/4%	15%	14 3/4%	14 1/2%	p	16 3/4%	16 1/2%	16 1/4%	16%	15 3/4%
1.06887792	1.06770783	1.06653645	1.06536379	1.06418983	2	1.07470926	1.07354553	1.07238053	1.07121426	1.07004673	2	1.08050914	1.07935166	1.07819293	1.07703296	1.07587174
1.04540700	1.04464393	1.04387974	1.04311443	1.04234800	3	1.04920575	1.04844820	1.04768955	1.04692981	1.04616896	3	1.05297719	1.05222506	1.05147186	1.05071757	1.04996221
1.03386552	1.03329948	1.03273252	1.03216461	1.03159577	4	1.03668185	1.03612042	1.03555808	1.03499481	1.03443063	4	1.03947542	1.03891850	1.03836069	1.03780199	1.03724263
1.02245146	1.02207824	1.02170433	1.02132974	1.02095445	6	1.02430745	1.02393760	1.02356707	1.02319588	1.02282401	6	1.02614677	1.02578022	1.02541302	1.02504516	1.02467663
1.01116342	1.01097885	1.01079391	1.01060860	1.01042291	12	1.01208075	1.01189802	1.01171492	1.01153145	1.01134762	12	1.01298903	1.01280809	1.01262679	1.01244514	1.01226313
1.01030029	1.01013006	1.00995949	1.00978857	1.00961730	13	1.01114630	1.01097778	1.01080892	1.01063972	1.01047017	13	1.01198391	1.01181705	1.01164986	1.01148235	1.01131449
1.00513695	1.00505227	1.00496741	1.00488237	1.00479715	26	1.00555771	1.00547391	1.00538993	1.00530578	1.00522146	26	1.00597411	1.00589117	1.00580807	1.00572479	1.00564133
1.00256519	1.00252295	1.00248063	1.00243821	1.00239570	52	1.00277500	1.00273322	1.00269134	1.00264938	1.00260733	52	1.00298261	1.00294126	1.00289983	1.00285831	1.00281670
1.00036505	1.00035905	1.00035303	1.00034700	1.00034096	365	1.00039487	1.00038893	1.00038298	1.00037702	1.00037104	365	1.00042438	1.00041850	1.00041261	1.00040671	1.00040080

9 1/2%	9 3/4%	10%	10 1/4%	10 1/2%	p	10 3/4%	11%	11 1/4%	11 1/2%	11 3/4%	p	12%	12 1/4%	12 1/2%	12 3/4%	13%
1.04642248	1.04761634	1.04880885	1.05000000	1.05118980	2	1.05237826	1.05356538	1.05475116	1.05593560	1.05711873	2	1.05830052	1.05948101	1.06066017	1.06183803	1.06301458
1.03071368	1.03149749	1.03228012	1.03306155	1.03384181	3	1.03462089	1.03539881	1.03617555	1.03695113	1.03772555	3	1.03849882	1.03927094	1.04004191	1.04081174	1.04158044
1.02294793	1.02353131	1.02411369	1.02469508	1.02527548	4	1.02585489	1.02643333	1.02701079	1.02758727	1.02816279	4	1.02873734	1.02931094	1.02988357	1.03045525	1.03102598
1.01524070	1.01562665	1.01601187	1.01639636	1.01678012	6	1.01716316	1.01754548	1.01792708	1.01830797	1.01868815	6	1.01906762	1.01944639	1.01982445	1.02020181	1.02057848
1.00759153	1.00778304	1.00797414	1.00816485	1.00835516	12	1.00854507	1.00873459	1.00892373	1.00911247	1.00930082	12	1.00948879	1.00967638	1.00986358	1.01005040	1.01023684
1.00700553	1.00718220	1.00735849	1.00753442	1.00770998	13	1.00788517	1.00806000	1.00823447	1.00840857	1.00858231	13	1.00875570	1.00892873	1.00910140	1.00927372	1.00944569
1.00349665	1.00358467	1.00367250	1.00376014	1.00384759	26	1.00393485	1.00402191	1.00410879	1.00419548	1.00428199	26	1.00436831	1.00445444	1.00454039	1.00462616	1.00471174
1.00174680	1.00179073	1.00183457	1.00187831	1.00192195	52	1.00196549	1.00200894	1.00205229	1.00209555	1.00213871	52	1.00218177	1.00222475	1.00226763	1.00231041	1.00235310
1.00024867	1.00025492	1.00026116	1.00026738	1.00027359	365	1.00027978	1.00028596	1.00029212	1.00029828	1.00030441	365	1.00031054	1.00031665	1.00032275	1.00032883	1.00033490

COMPOUND AMOUNT OF 1 FOR FRACTIONAL PERIODS $(1 + i)^{1/p}$ (Continued)

p	19 1/2%	19 3/4%	20%
2	1.09316056	1.09430343	1.09544512
3	1.06118060	1.06192010	1.06265857
4	1.04554319	1.04608959	1.04663514
6	1.03013620	1.03049507	1.03085332
12	1.01495626	1.01513303	1.01530947
13	1.01379788	1.01396087	1.01412354
26	1.00687530	1.00695624	1.00703701
52	1.00343176	1.00347209	1.00351234
365	1.00048819	1.00049392	1.00049964

p	17%	17 1/4%	17 1/2%	17 3/4%	18%
2	1.08166538	1.08282039	1.08397417	1.08512672	1.08627805
3	1.05372824	1.05447823	1.05522715	1.05597501	1.05672181
4	1.04003143	1.04058656	1.04114080	1.04169416	1.04224664
6	1.02651266	1.02687790	1.02724250	1.02760644	1.02796975
12	1.01316961	1.01334984	1.01352972	1.01370925	1.01388843
13	1.01215044	1.01231663	1.01248251	1.01264805	1.01281328
26	1.00605687	1.00613947	1.00622190	1.00630416	1.00638625
52	1.00302387	1.00306504	1.00310612	1.00314713	1.00318804
365	1.00043024	1.00043609	1.00044193	1.00044775	1.00045357

p	18 1/4%	18 1/2%	18 3/4%	19%	19 1/4%
2	1.08742816	1.08857705	1.08972474	1.09087121	1.09201648
3	1.05746755	1.05821225	1.05895590	1.05969850	1.06044007
4	1.04279823	1.04334896	1.04389881	1.04444780	1.04499593
6	1.02833241	1.02869444	1.02905583	1.02941658	1.02977671
12	1.01406726	1.01424575	1.01442389	1.01460169	1.01477914
13	1.01297817	1.01314275	1.01330701	1.01347095	1.01363457
26	1.00646817	1.00654993	1.00663152	1.00671294	1.00679421
52	1.00322887	1.00326962	1.00331028	1.00335086	1.00339135
365	1.00045937	1.00046516	1.00047093	1.00047670	1.00048245

NOMINAL RATES CONVERTIBLE p TIMES PER YEAR
EQUIVALENT TO EFFECTIVE RATE i GIVEN IN HEADING,

$$j_p = p[(1 + i)^{\frac{1}{p}} - 1]$$

p	$\frac{1}{4}$	$\frac{5}{12}$	$\frac{1}{2}$	$\frac{7}{12}$	$\frac{3}{4}$
$\frac{1}{4}$	.0025 094	.0041 928	.0050 376	.0058 846	.0075 848
$\frac{1}{2}$	.0025 032	.0041 754	.0050 125	.0058 504	.0075 281
2	.0024 984	.0041 623	.0049 938	.0058 249	.0074 860
4	.0024 977	.0041 602	.0049 907	.0058 206	.0074 790
6	.0024 974	.0041 595	.0049 896	.0058 192	.0074 767
12	.0024 971	.0041 587	.0049 886	.0058 178	.0074 743
13	.0024 971	.0041 587	.0049 885	.0058 177	.0074 742
52	.0024 969	.0041 582	.0049 878	.0058 167	.0074 725
365	.0024 969	.0041 580	.0049 876	.0058 164	.0074 721
∞	.0024 969	.0041 580	.0049 875	.0058 164	.0074 720

p	1	$1\frac{1}{8}$	$1\frac{1}{4}$	$1\frac{1}{2}$	$1\frac{3}{4}$
$\frac{1}{4}$	.0101 510	.0114 413	.0127 363	.0153 409	.0179 648
$\frac{1}{2}$	.0100 500	.0113 133	.0125 781	.0151 125	.0176 531
2	.0099 751	.0112 185	.0124 612	.0149 442	.0174 241
4	.0099 627	.0112 029	.0124 418	.0149 164	.0173 863
6	.0099 586	.0111 976	.0124 354	.0149 071	.0173 737
12	.0099 545	.0111 924	.0124 290	.0148 979	.0173 612
13	.0099 541	.0111 920	.0124 285	.0148 971	.0173 602
52	.0099 513	.0111 884	.0124 240	.0148 907	.0173 515
365	.0099 505	.0111 874	.0124 227	.0148 889	.0173 490
∞	.0099 503	.0111 872	.0124 225	.0148 886	.0173 486

p	2	$2\frac{1}{4}$	$2\frac{1}{2}$	$2\frac{3}{4}$	3
$\frac{1}{4}$	.0206 080	.0232 708	.0259 532	.0286 553	.0313 772
$\frac{1}{2}$	.0202 000	.0227 531	.0253 125	.0278 781	.0304 500
2	.0199 010	.0223 748	.0248 457	.0273 135	.0297 783
4	.0198 517	.0223 126	.0247 690	.0272 209	.0296 683
6	.0198 353	.0222 919	.0247 435	.0271 901	.0296 317
12	.0198 190	.0222 713	.0247 180	.0271 594	.0295 952
13	.0198 177	.0222 697	.0247 161	.0271 570	.0295 924
52	.0198 064	.0222 554	.0246 985	.0271 358	.0295 672
365	.0198 032	.0222 513	.0246 934	.0271 297	.0295 600
∞	.0198 026	.0222 506	.0246 926	.0271 287	.0295 588

p	$3\frac{1}{2}$	4	$4\frac{1}{2}$	5	$5\frac{1}{2}$
$\frac{1}{4}$	.0368 808	.0424 647	.0481 297	.0538 766	.0597 062
$\frac{1}{2}$	.0356 125	.0408 000	.0460 125	.0512 500	.0565 125
2	.0346 990	.0396 078	.0445 048	.0493 902	.0542 639
4	.0345 498	.0394 136	.0442 600	.0490 889	.0539 007
6	.0345 002	.0393 492	.0441 787	.0489 891	.0537 804
12	.0344 508	.0392 849	.0440 977	.0488 895	.0536 604
13	.0344 470	.0392 799	.0440 915	.0488 818	.0536 512
52	.0344 128	.0392 355	.0440 355	.0488 131	.0535 683
365	.0344 031	.0392 228	.0440 195	.0487 934	.0535 447
∞	.0344 014	.0392 207	.0440 169	.0487 902	.0535 408

p	6	$6\frac{1}{2}$	7	$7\frac{1}{2}$	8
$\frac{1}{4}$	.0656 193	.0716 166	.0776 990	.0838 673	.0901 223
$\frac{1}{2}$	.0618 000	.0671 125	.0724 500	.0778 125	.0832 000
2	.0591 260	.0639 767	.0688 161	.0736 441	.0784 610
4	.0586 954	.0634 731	.0682 341	.0729 784	.0777 062
6	.0585 528	.0633 064	.0680 416	.0727 583	.0774 567
12	.0584 106	.0631 403	.0678 497	.0725 390	.0772 084
13	.0583 997	.0631 276	.0678 350	.0725 222	.0771 893
52	.0583 016	.0630 129	.0677 027	.0723 710	.0770 180
365	.0582 736	.0629 802	.0676 649	.0723 278	.0769 692
∞	.0582 689	.0629 748	.0676 586	.0723 207	.0769 610

AMOUNT FOR YEAR OF p DEPOSITS OF $1/p,p$ TIMES PER YEAR, i/j_p

p	¼	$1\frac{5}{2}$	½	$1\frac{7}{2}$	¾
¼	0.9962 5	0.9937 717	0.9925 312	0.9912 924	0.9888 201
½	0.9974 8	0.9979 210	0.9975 062	0.9970 918	0.9962 640
2	1.0006 246	1.0010 406	1.0012 484	1.0014 562	1.0018 715
4	1.0009 370	1.0015 611	1.0018 730	1.0021 848	1.0028 081
6	1.0010 412	1.0017 347	1.0020 813	1.0024 278	1.0031 205
12	1.0011 453	1.0019 083	1.0022 896	1.0026 708	1.0034 329
13	1.0011 533	1.0019 216	1.0023 056	1.0026 895	1.0034 569
52	1.0012 254	1.0020 418	1.0024 498	1.0028 577	1.0036 732
365	1.0012 461	1.0020 762	1.0024 911	1.0029 058	1.0037 351
∞	1.0012 495	1.0020 819	1.0024 979	1.0029 138	1.0037 453

p	1	1⅛	1¼	1½	1¾
¼	0.9851 244	0.9832 823	0.9814 441	0.9777 791	0.9741 295
½	0.9950 249	0.9944 065	0.9937 888	0.9925 558	0.9913 259
2	1.0024 938	1.0028 046	1.0031 153	1.0037 360	1.0043 618
4	1.0037 422	1.0042 089	1.0046 754	1.0056 076	1.0065 388
6	1.0041 586	1.0046 773	1.0051 958	1.0062 319	1.0072 671
12	1.0045 751	1.0051 458	1.0057 163	1.0068 565	1.0079 957
13	1.0046 071	1.0051 819	1.0057 564	1.0069 046	1.0080 518
52	1.0048 956	1.0055 063	1.0061 169	1.0073 372	1'0085 564
365	1.0049 780	1.0055 991	1.0062 199	1.0074 608	1.0087 007
∞	1.0049 917	1.0056 145	1.0062 371	1.0074 814	1.0087 247

p	2	2¼	2½	2¾	3
¼	0.9704 950	0.9668 757	0.9632 715	0.9596 824	0.9561 082
½	0.9900 990	0.9888 752	0.9876 543	0.9864 365	0.9852 217
2	1.0049 752	1.0055 937	1.0062 114	1.0068 284	1.0074 446
4	1.0074 686	1.0083 984	1.0093 268	1.0102 542	1.0111 807
6	1.0083 013	1.0093 344	1.0103 667	1.0113 979	1.0124 282
12	1.0091 339	1.0102 711	1.0114 072	1.0125 424	1.0136 766
13	1.0091 980	1.0103 431	1.0114 873	1.0126 305	1.0137 727
52	1.0097 747	1.0109 919	1.0122 082	1.0134 234	1.0146 376
365	1.0099 396	1.0111 775	1.0124 143	1.0136 502	1.0148 850
∞	1.0099 670	1.0112 083	1 0124 486	1.0136 878	1.0149 261

p	3½	4	4½	5	5½
¼	0.9490 046	0.9419 6	0.9349 7	0.9280 5	0.9211 8
½	0.9828 010	0.9803 922	0.9779 951	0.9756 098	0.9732 360
2	1.0086 748	1.0099 020	1.0111 262	1.0123 475	1.0135 660
4	1.0130 309	1.0148 774	1.0167 203	1.0185 594	1.0203 950
6	1.0144 858	1.0165 396	1.0185 895	1.0206 357	1.0226 781
12	1.0159 420	1.0182 035	1.0204 611	1.0227 148	1.0249 647
13	1.0160 541	1.0183 316	1.0206 051	1.0228 748	1.0251 407
52	1.0170 632	1.0194 847	1.0219 623	1.0243 160	1.0267 259
365	1.0173 517	1.0198 145	1.0222 733	1.0247 282	1.0271 793
∞	1.0173 997	1.0198 693	1.0223 349	1.0247 967	1.0272 546

p	6	6½	7	7½	8
¼	0.9143 7	0.9076 1	0.9009 1	0.8942 7	0.8876 8
½	0.9708 738	0.9685 230	0.9661 836	0.9638 554	0.9615 385
2	1.0147 815	1.0159 942	1.0172 040	1.0184 110	1.0196 152
4	1.0222 269	1.0240 552	1.0258 800	1.0277 013	1.0295 190
6	1.0247 168	1.0267 517	1.0287 830	1.0308 106	1.0328 346
12	1.0272 107	1.0294 529	1.0316 914	1.0339 262	1.0361 572
13	1.0274 027	1.0296 609	1.0319 154	1.0341 661	1.0364 131
52	1.0291 319	1.0315 340	1.0339 324	1.0363 270	1.0387 179
365	1.0296 265	1.0320 699	1.0345 095	1.0369 453	1.0393 774
∞	1.0297 087	1.0321 589	1.0346 053	1.0370 480	1.0394 870

COMMISSIONERS 1941 STANDARD ORDINARY MORTALITY TABLE*

x	l_x	d_x	p_x	$\overset{\circ}{e}_x$	x	l_x	d_x	p_x	$\overset{\circ}{e}_x$
0	1 023 102	23 102	.977 42	62.33	**50**	810 900	9 990	.987 68	21.37
1	1 000 000	5 770	.994 23	62.76	51	800 910	10 628	.986 73	20.64
2	994 230	4 116	.995 86	62.12	52	790 282	11 301	.985 70	19.91
3	990 114	3 347	.996 62	61.37	53	778 981	12 020	.984 57	19.19
4	986 767	2 950	.997 01	60.58	54	766 961	12 770	.983 35	18.48
5	983 817	2 715	.997 24	59.76	**55**	754 191	13 560	.982 02	17.78
6	981 102	2 561	.997 39	58.92	56	740 631	14 390	.980 57	17.10
7	978 541	2 417	.997 53	58.08	57	726 241	15 251	.979 00	16.43
8	976 124	2 255	.997 69	57.22	58	710 990	16 147	.977 29	15.77
9	973 869	2 065	.997 88	56.35	59	694 843	17 072	.975 43	15.13
10	971 804	1 914	.998 03	55.47	**60**	677 771	18 022	.973 41	14.50
11	969 890	1 852	.998 09	54.58	61	659 749	18 988	.971 22	13.88
12	968 038	1 859	.998 08	53.68	62	640 761	19 979	.968 82	13.27
13	966 179	1 913	.998 02	52.78	63	620 782	20 958	.966 24	12.69
14	964 266	1 996	.997 93	51.89	64	599 824	21 942	.963 42	12.11
15	962 270	2 069	.997 85	50.99	**65**	577 882	22 907	.960 36	11.55
16	960 201	2 103	.997 81	50.10	66	554 975	23 842	.957 04	11.01
17	958 098	2 156	.997 75	49.21	67	531 133	24 730	.953 44	10.48
18	955 942	2 199	.997 70	48.32	68	506 403	25 553	.949 54	9.97
19	953 743	2 260	.997 63	47.43	69	480 850	26 302	.945 30	9.47
20	951 483	2 312	.997 57	46.54	**70**	454 548	26 955	.940 70	8.99
21	949 171	2 382	.997 49	45.66	71	427 593	27 481	.935 73	8.52
22	946 789	2 452	.997 41	44.77	72	400 112	27 872	.930 34	8.08
23	944 337	2 531	.997 32	43.88	73	372 240	28 104	.924 50	7.64
24	941 806	2 609	.997 23	43.00	74	344 136	28 154	.918 19	7.23
25	939 197	2 705	.997 12	42.12	**75**	315 982	28 009	.911 36	6.82
26	936 492	2 800	.997 01	41.24	76	287 973	27 651	.903 98	6.44
27	933 692	2 904	.996 89	40.36	77	260 322	27 071	.896 01	6.07
28	930 788	3 025	.996 75	39.49	78	233 251	26 262	.887 41	5.72
29	927 763	3 154	.996 60	38.61	79	206 989	25 224	.878 14	5.38
30	924 609	3 292	.996 44	37.74	**80**	181 765	23 966	.868 15	5.06
31	921 317	3 437	.996 27	36.88	81	157 799	22 502	.857 40	4.75
32	917 880	3 598	.996 08	36.01	82	135 297	20 857	.845 84	4.46
33	914 282	3 767	.995 88	35.15	83	114 440	19 062	.833 43	4.18
34	910 515	3 961	.995 65	34.29	84	95 378	17 157	.820 12	3.91
35	906 554	4 161	.995 41	33.44	**85**	78 221	15 185	.805 87	3.66
36	902 393	4 386	.995 14	32.59	86	63 036	13 198	.790 63	3.42
37	898 007	4 625	.994 85	31.75	87	49 838	11 245	.774 37	3.19
38	893 382	4 878	.994 54	30.91	88	38 593	9 378	.757 00	2.98
39	888 504	5 162	.994 19	30.08	89	29 215	7 638	.738 56	2.77
40	883 342	5 459	.993 82	29.25	**90**	21 577	6 063	.719 01	2.58
41	877 883	5 785	.993 41	28.43	91	15 514	4 681	.698 27	2.39
42	872 098	6 131	.992 97	27 62	92	10 833	3 506	.676 36	2.21
43	865 967	6 503	.992 49	26.81	93	7 327	2 540	.653 34	2.03
44	859 464	6 910	.991 96	26.01	94	4 787	1 776	.629 00	1.84
45	852 554	7 340	.991 39	25.21	**95**	3 011	1 193	.603 79	1.63
46	845 214	7 801	.990 77	24.43	96	1 818	813	.552 81	1.37
47	837 413	8 299	.990 09	23.65	97	1 005	551	.451 74	1.08
48	829 114	8 822	.989 36	22.88	98	454	329	.275 33	.78
49	820 292	9 392	.988 55	22.12	99	125	125	.000 00	.50

* Reproduced by permission of the Actuarial Society of America.

COMMUTATION COLUMNS 2 1/2%
Commissioners 1941 Standard Ordinary Mortality Table*

x	D_x	N_x	C_x	M_x	$1 + a_x$	A_x
0	1 023 102.00	31 374 230	22 538.536 6	257 876.88	30.665 8	0.252 054
1	975 609.76	30 351 128	5 491.969 1	235 338.35	31.109 9	.241 222
2	946 322.43	29 375 518	3 822.115 2	229 846.38	31.041 8	.242 884
3	919 419.28	28 429 196	3 032.216 8	226 024.26	30.920 8	.245 834
4	893 962.20	27 509 776	2 607.370 2	222 992.05	30.772 9	.249 442
5	869 550.88	26 615 814	2 341.136 0	220 384.68	30.608 7	.253 447
6	846 001.18	25 746 263	2 154.480 3	218 043.54	30.432 9	.257 734
7	823 212.53	24 900 262	1 983.744 5	215 889.06	30.247 7	.262 252
8	801 150.42	24 077 050	1 805.642 5	213 905.32	30.053 1	.266 998
9	779 804.53	23 275 899	1 613.174 7	212 099.67	29.848 4	.271 991
10	759 171.73	22 496 095	1 458.745 1	210 486.50	29.632 4	.277 258
11	739 196.60	21 736 923	1 377.065 5	209 027.75	29.406 1	.282 777
12	719 790.36	20 997 726	1 348.556 5	207 650.69	29.172 0	.288 488
13	700 885.94	20 277 936	1 353.882 1	206 302.13	28.931 9	.294 345
14	682 437.28	19 577 050	1 378.169 3	204 948.25	28.687 0	.300 318
15	664 414.29	18 894 613	1 393.730 0	203 570.08	28.438 0	.306 390
16	646 815.33	18 230 198	1 382.081 2	202 176.35	28.184 5	.312 572
17	629 657.27	17 583 383	1 382.353 7	200 794.27	27.925 3	.318 895
18	612 917.42	16 953 726	1 375.535 5	199 411.91	27.660 7	.325 349
19	596 592.68	16 340 808	1 379.212 3	198 036.38	27.390 2	.331 946
20	580 662.42	15 744 216	1 376.533 1	196 657.17	27.114 2	.338 677
21	565 123.40	15 163 553	1 383.619 6	195 280.63	26.832 3	.345 554
22	549 956.28	14 598 430	1 389.541 6	193 897.01	26.544 7	.352 568
23	535 153.17	14 048 474	1 399.327 5	192 507.47	26.251 3	.359 724
24	520 701.32	13 513 320	1 407.270 0	191 108.14	25.952 2	.367 021
25	506 594.02	12 992 619	1 423.464 9	189 700.88	25.647 0	.374 463
26	492 814.61	12 486 025	1 437.519 2	188 277.41	25.336 2	.382 045
27	479 357.22	11 993 210	1 454.549 1	186 839.89	25.019 4	.389 772
28	466 211.03	11 513 853	1 478.200 3	185 385.34	24.696 7	.397 643
29	453 361.83	11 047 642	1 503.646 4	183 907.14	24.368 3	.405 652
30	440 800.58	10 594 280	1 531.158 0	182 403.50	24.034 2	.413 800
31	428 518.18	10 153 480	1 559.609 4	180 872.34	23.694 4	.422 088
32	416 506.91	9 724 962	1 592.845 3	179 312.73	23.348 9	.430 516
33	404 755.37	9 308 455	1 626.987 4	177 719.88	22.997 7	.439 080
34	393 256.29	8 903 699	1 669.050 8	176 092.90	22.641 0	.447 781
35	381 995.63	8 510 443	1 710.561 0	174 423.84	22.278 9	.456 612
36	370 968.10	8 128 447	1 759.080 1	172 713.28	21.911 4	.465 574
37	360 161.02	7 757 479	1 809.692 8	170 954.20	21.538 9	.474 660
38	349 566.90	7 397 318	1 862.134 5	169 144.51	21.161 4	.483 869
39	339 178.75	7 047 751	1 922.486 9	167 282.38	20.778 9	.493 198
40	328 983.61	6 708 573	1 983.511 0	165 359.89	20.391 8	.502 639
41	318 976.11	6 379 589	2 050.694 7	163 376.38	20.000 2	.512 190
42	309 145.51	6 060 613	2 120.338 1	161 325.68	19.604 4	.521 844
43	299 485.04	5 751 467	2 194.136 7	159 205.35	19.204 5	.531 597
44	289 986.39	5 451 982	2 274.595 1	157 011.21	18.800 8	.541 443
45	280 638.95	5 161 996	2 357.209 9	154 736.61	18.393 7	.551 373
46	271 436.89	4 881 357	2 444.154 2	152 379.40	17.983 4	.561 381
47	262 372.33	4 609 920	2 536.765 0	149 935.25	17.570 1	.571 460
48	253 436.24	4 347 548	2 630.859 4	147 398.48	17.154 4	.581 600
49	244 624.00	4 094 112	2 732.529 2	144 767.62	16.736 3	.591 796
50	235 925.04	3 849 488	2 835.622 1	142 035.10	16.316 6	.602 035

* Reproduced by permission of the Actuarial Society of America.

COMMUTATION COLUMNS 2 1/2% (Continued)
Commissioners 1941 Standard Ordinary Mortality Table*

x	D_x	N_x	C_x	M_x	$1 + a_x$	A_x
51	227 335.15	3 613 563	2 943.137 4	139 199.47	15.895 3	.612 310
52	218 847.25	3 386 227	3 053.177 2	136 256.34	15.473 0	.622 609
53	210 456.33	3 167 380	3 168.222 9	133 203.16	15.050 1	.632 925
54	202 155.03	2 956 924	3 283.812 1	130 034.94	14.627 0	.643 244
55	193 940.61	2 754 769	3 401.913 1	126 751.12	14.204 2	.653 556
56	185 808.43	2 560 828	3 522.090 1	123 349.21	13.782 1	.663 852
57	177 754.43	2 375 020	3 641.783 5	119 827.12	13 361 2	.674 116
58	169 777.17	2 197 265	3 761.696 8	116 185.34	12.942 1	.684 340
59	161 874.57	2 027 488	3 880.185 4	112 423.64	12.525 1	.694 511
60	154 046.23	1 865 614	3 996.199 9	108 543.46	12.110 7	.704 616
61	146 292.80	1 711 567	4 107.708 0	104 547.26	11.699 6	.714 644
62	138 616.97	1 565 275	4 216.676 0	100 439.55	11.292 1	.724 583
63	131 019.40	1 426 658	4 315.413 8	96 222.87	10.888 9	.734 417
64	123 508.39	1 295 638	4 407.831 2	91 907.46	10.490 3	.744 139
65	116 088.15	1 172 130	4 489.449 7	87 499.63	10.096 9	.753 734
66	108 767.29	1 056 042	4 558.728 2	83 010.18	9.709 2	.763 191
67	101 555.70	947 274.4	4 613.189 3	78 451.45	9.327 6	.772 497
68	94 465.545	845 718.7	4 650.452 1	73 838.26	8.952 7	.781 642
69	87 511.050	751 253.1	4 670.014 3	69 187.81	8.584 7	.790 618
70	80 706.625	663 742.1	4 669.226 0	64 517.79	8.224 1	.799 411
71	74 068.942	583 035.4	4 644.235 4	59 848.57	7.871 5	.808 012
72	67 618.148	508 966.5	4 595.428 1	55 204.33	7.527 1	.816 413
73	61 373.498	441 348.3	4 520.662 7	50 608.90	7.191 2	.824 605
74	55 355.921	379 974.8	4 418.249 2	46 088.24	6.864 2	.832 580
75	49 587.526	324 618.9	4 288.286 9	41 669.99	6.546 4	.840 332
76	44 089.787	275 031.4	4 130.220 2	37 381.70	6.238 0	.847 854
77	38 884.206	230 941.6	3 944.961 8	33 251.48	5.939 2	.855 141
78	33 990.850	192 057.4	3 733.725 8	29 306.52	5.650 3	.862 189
79	29 428.077	158 066.6	3 498.684 1	25 572.80	5.371 3	.868 993
80	25 211.636	128 638.5	3 243.115 8	22 074.11	5.102 3	.875 553
81	21 353.602	103 426.8	2 970.736 8	18 831.00	4.843 5	.881 865
82	17 862.047	82 073.24	2 686.402 0	15 860.26	4.594 8	.887 931
83	14 739.984	64 211.19	2 395.321 2	13 173.86	4.356 3	.893 750
84	11 985.151	49 471.21	2 103.356 1	10 778.54	4.127 7	.899 324
85	9 589.474 6	37 486.06	1 816.194 6	8 675.180	3.909 1	.904 656
86	7 539.390 5	27 896.58	1 540.039 4	6 858.986	3.700 1	.909 753
87	5 815.463 2	20 357.19	1 280.145 4	5 318.946	3.500 5	.914 621
88	4 393.477 3	14 541.73	1 041.564 6	4 038.801	3.309 8	.919 272
89	3 244.754 6	10 148.25	827.621 52	2 997.236	3.127 6	.923 717
90	2 337.992 9	6 903.496	640.937 68	2 169.615	2.952 7	.927 982
91	1 640.030 9	4 565.503	482.773 06	1 528.677	2.783 8	.932 103
92	1 117.257 1	2 925.472	352.770 63	1 045.904	2.618 4	.936 136
93	737.236 29	1 808.215	249.339 10	693.133 5	2.452 7	.940 178
94	469.915 86	1 070.979	170.088 82	443.794 4	2.279 1	.944 413
95	288.365 67	601.062 8	111.467 79	273.705 6	2.084 4	.949 162
96	169.864 58	312.697 2	74.109 795	162.237 8	1.840 9	.955 101
97	91.611 740	142.832 6	49.001 885	88.128 0	1.559 1	.961 973
98	40.375 419	51.220 9	28.545 208	39.126 1	1.268 6	.969 058
99	10.845 444	10.845 4	10.580 921	10.580 9	1.000 0	.975 610

* Reproduced by permission of the Actuarial Society of America.

COMMISSIONERS 1958 STANDARD ORDINARY
MORTALITY TABLE*

Age, x	Number Living l_x	Number Dying d_x	Deaths per 1,000	Age, x	Number Living l_x	Number Dying d_x	Deaths per 1,000
0	10,000,000	70,800	7.08	50	8,762,306	72,902	8.32
1	9,929,200	17,475	1.76	51	8,689,404	79,160	9.11
2	9,911,725	15,066	1.52	52	8,610,244	85,758	9.96
3	9,896,659	14,449	1.46	53	8,524,486	92,832	10.89
4	9,882,210	13,835	1.40	54	8,431,654	100,337	11.90
5	9,868,375	13,322	1.35	55	8,331,317	108,307	13.00
6	9,855,053	12,812	1.30	56	8,223,010	116,849	14.21
7	9,842,241	12,401	1.26	57	8,106,161	125,970	15.54
8	9,829,840	12,091	1.23	58	7,980,191	135,663	17.00
9	9,817,749	11,879	1.21	59	7,844,528	145,830	18.59
10	9,805,870	11,865	1.21	60	7,698,698	156,592	20.34
11	9,794,005	12,047	1.23	61	7,542,106	167,736	22.24
12	9,781,958	12,325	1.26	62	7,374,370	179,271	24.31
13	9,769,633	12,896	1.32	63	7,195,099	191,174	26.57
14	9,756,737	13,562	1.39	64	7,003,925	203,394	29.04
15	9,743,175	14,225	1.46	65	6,800,531	215,917	31.75
16	9,728,950	14,983	1.54	66	6,584,614	228,749	34.74
17	9,713,967	15,737	1.62	67	6,355,865	241,777	38.04
18	9,698,230	16,390	1.69	68	6,114,088	254,835	41.68
19	9,681,840	16,846	1.74	69	5,859,253	267,241	45.61
20	9,664,994	17,300	1.79	70	5,592,012	278,426	49.79
21	9,647,694	17,655	1.83	71	5,313,586	287,731	54.15
22	9,630,039	17,912	1.86	72	5,025,855	294,766	58.65
23	9,612,127	18,167	1.89	73	4,731,089	299,289	63.26
24	9,593,960	18,324	1.91	74	4,431,800	301,894	68.12
25	9,575,636	18,481	1.93	75	4,129,906	303,011	73.37
26	9,557,155	18,732	1.96	76	3,826,895	303,014	79.18
27	9,538,423	18,981	1.99	77	3,523,881	301,997	85.70
28	9,519,442	19,324	2.03	78	3,221,884	299,829	93.06
29	9,500,118	19,760	2.08	79	2,922,055	295,683	101.19
30	9,480,358	20,193	2.13	80	2,626,372	288,848	109.98
31	9,460,165	20,718	2.19	81	2,337,524	278,983	119.35
32	9,439,447	21,239	2.25	82	2,058,541	265,902	129.17
33	9,418,208	21,850	2.32	83	1,792,639	249,858	139.38
34	9,396,358	22,551	2.40	84	1,542,781	231,433	150.01
35	9,373,807	23,528	2.51	85	1,311,348	211,311	161.14
36	9,350,279	24,685	2.64	86	1,100,037	190,108	172.82
37	9,325,594	26,112	2.80	87	909,929	168,455	185.13
38	9,299,482	27,991	3.01	88	741,474	146,997	198.25
39	9,271,491	30,132	3.25	89	594,477	126,303	212.46
40	9,241,359	32,622	3.53	90	468,174	106,809	228.14
41	9,208,737	35,362	3.84	91	361,365	88,813	245.77
42	9,173,375	38,253	4.17	92	272,552	72,480	265.93
43	9,135,122	41,382	4.53	93	200,072	57,881	289.30
44	9,093,740	44,741	4.92	94	142,191	45,026	316.66
45	9,048,999	48,412	5.35	95	97,165	34,128	351.24
46	9,000,587	52,473	5.83	96	63,037	25,250	400.56
47	8,948,114	56,910	6.36	97	37,787	18,456	488.42
48	8,891,204	61,794	6.95	98	19,331	12,916	668.15
49	8,829,410	67,104	7.60	99	6,415	6,415	1,000.00

* Reproduced by permission of the Actuarial Society of America.

COMMUTATION COLUMNS 2 1/2%*
Commissioners 1958 Standard Ordinary Mortality Table

Age, x	D_x	N_x	C_x	M_x
0	10,000,000.0000	324,850,104.9680	69,073.1710	2,076,826.7172
1	9,687,024.4290	314,850,104.9680	16,632.9566	2,007,753.5462
2	9,434,122.5838	305,163,080.5390	13,990.2787	1,991,120.5896
3	9,190,031.7084	295,728,957.9552	13,090.0808	1,977,130.3109
4	8,952,794.4741	286,538,926.2468	12,228.1241	1,964,040.2301
5	8,722,205.5791	277,586,131.7727	11,487.5189	1,951,812.1060
6	8,497,981.3556	268,863,926.1936	10,778.2903	1,940,324.5871
7	8,279,935.2370	260,365,944.8380	10,178.0782	1,929,546.2968
8	8,067,807.4636	252,086,009.6010	9,681.6066	1,919,368.2186
9	7,861,350.0557	244,018,202.1374	9,279.8558	1,909,686.6120
10	7,660,329.9546	236,156,852.0817	9,042.8478	1,900,406.7562
11	7,464,449.7860	228,496,522.1271	8,957.6178	1,891,363.9084
12	7,273,432.4866	221,032,072.3411	8,940.8062	1,882,406.2906
13	7,087,090.8833	213,758,639.8545	9,126.8500	1,873,465.4844
14	6,905,108.1581	206,671,548.9712	9,364.0939	1,864,338.6344
15	6,727,326.7826	199,766,440.8131	9,582.3146	1,854,974.5405
16	6,553,663.2627	193,039,114.0305	9,846.7536	1,845,392.2259
17	6,383,971.1254	186,485,450.7678	10,090.0279	1,835,545.4723
18	6,218,174.4633	180,101,479.6424	10,252.3993	1,825,455.4444
19	6,056,259.3006	173,883,305.1791	10,280.6243	1,815,203.0451
20	5,898,264.9735	167,827,045.8785	10,300.1828	1,804,922.4208
21	5,744,104.7377	161,928,780.9050	10,255.1657	1,794,622.2380
22	5,593,749.4258	156,184,676.1673	10,150.6810	1,784,367.0723
23	5,447,165.8414	150,590,926.7415	10,044.0865	1,774,216.3913
24	5,304,263.9929	145,143,760.9001	9,883.7932	1,764,172.3048
25	5,165,007.9517	139,839,496.9072	9,725.3439	1,754,288.5116
26	5,029,306.7854	134,674,488.9555	9,617.0037	1,744,563.1677
27	4,897,023.7928	129,645,182.1701	9,507.1611	1,734,946.1640
28	4,768,076.9758	124,748,158.3773	9,442.8900	1,725,439.0029
29	4,642,339.5370	119,980,081.4015	9,420.4356	1,715,996.1129
30	4,519,691.3751	115,337,741.8645	9,392.0634	1,706,575.6773
31	4,400,062.8465	110,818,050.4894	9,401.2183	1,697,183.6139
32	4,283,343.0569	106,417,987.6429	9,402.5686	1,687,782.3956
33	4,169,468.7479	102,134,644.5860	9,437.1317	1,678,379.8270
34	4,058,337.1968	97,965,175.8381	9,502.3390	1,668,942.6953
35	3,949,851.0856	93,906,838.6413	9,672.2130	1,659,440.3563
36	3,843,840.9771	89,956,987.5557	9,900.3401	1,649,768.1433
37	3,740,188.4751	86,113,146.5786	10,217.2318	1,639,867.8032
38	3,638,747.0704	82,372,958.1035	10,685.3232	1,629,650.5714
39	3,539,311.8617	78,734,211.0331	11,222.0794	1,618,965.2482
40	3,441,765.0620	75,194,899.1714	11,853.1042	1,607,743.1688
41	3,345,966.5023	71,753,134.1094	12,535.2926	1,595,890.0646
42	3,251,822.2774	68,407,167.6071	13,229.3739	1,583,354.7720
43	3,159,280.1784	65,155,345.3297	13,962.4424	1,570,125.3981
44	3,068,262.0685	61,996,065.1513	14,727.5918	1,556,162.9557
45	2,978,698.8164	58,927,803.0828	15,547.3085	1,541,435.3639
46	2,890,500.3526	55,949,104.2664	16,440.4699	1,525,888.0554
47	2,803,559.9048	53,058,603.9138	17,395.7457	1,509,447.5855
48	2,717,784.6405	50,255,044.0090	18,427.9447	1,492,051.8398
49	2,633,069.2135	47,537,259.3685	19,523.3861	1,473,623.8951

* Reproduced by permission of the Actuarial Society of America.

COMMUTATION COLUMNS 2 1/2%* (Continued)
Commissioners 1958 Standard Ordinary Mortality Table

Age, x	D_x	N_x	C_x	M_x
50	2,549,324.6723	44,904,190.1550	20,692.9455	1,454,100.5090
51	2,466,453.0891	42,354,865.4827	21,921.2231	1,433,407.5635
52	2,384,374.4270	39,888,412.3936	23,169.1325	1,411,486.3404
53	2,303,049.8123	37,504,037.9666	24,468.5917	1,388,317.2079
54	2,222,409.2905	35,200,988.1543	25,801.7117	1,363,848.6162
55	2,142,402.4988	32,978,578.8638	27,171.9031	1,338,046.9045
56	2,062,976.8254	30,836,176.3650	28,599.9098	1,310,875.0014
57	1,984,060.3996	28,773,199.5396	30,080.3536	1,282,275.0916
58	1,905,588.3725	26,789,139.1400	31,604.8230	1,252,194.7380
59	1,827,505.7998	24,883,550.7675	33,144.7659	1,220,589.9150
60	1,749,787.7198	23,056,044.9677	34,722.7242	1,187,445.1491
61	1,672,387.2632	21,306,257.2479	36,286.6291	1,152,722.4249
62	1,595,310.6622	19,633,869.9847	37,836.1144	1,116,435.7958
63	1,518,564.5694	18,038,559.3225	39,364.2006	1,078,599.6814
64	1,442,162.1578	16,519,994.7531	40,858.9196	1,039,235.4808
65	1,366,128.5462	15,077,832.5953	42,316.6940	998,376.5612
66	1,290,491.6985	13,711,704.0491	43,738.1310	956,059.8672
67	1,215,278.1249	12,421,212.3506	45,101.6207	912,321.7362
68	1,140,535.6099	11,205,934.2257	46,378.0358	867,220.1155
69	1,066,339.5743	10,065,398.6158	47,449.5963	820,842.0797
70	992,881.7500	8,999,059.0415	48,229.7870	773,392.4834
71	920,435.3077	8,006,177.2915	48,625.9779	725,162.6964
72	849,359.6946	7,085,741.9838	48,599.8832	676,536.7185
73	780,043.7396	6,236,382.2892	48,142.0663	627,936.8353
74	712,876.2140	5,456,338.5496	47,376.6752	579,794.7690
75	648,112.3021	4,743,462.3356	46,392.1628	532,418.0938
76	585,912.5111	4,095,350.0335	45,261.0951	486,025.9310
77	526,360.8716	3,509,437.5224	44,008.9628	440,764.8359
78	469,513.8465	2,983,076.6508	42,627.3426	396,755.8731
79	415,434.9294	2,513,562.8043	41,012.5834	354,128.5305
80	364,289.7989	2,098,127.8749	39,087.3533	313,115.9471
81	316,317.3241	1,733,838.0760	36,831.6174	274,028.5938
82	271,770.6619	1,417,520.7519	34,248.4382	237,196.9764
83	230,893.6600	1,145,750.0900	31,397.0289	202,948.5382
84	193,865.0736	914,856.4300	28,372.4430	171,551.5093
85	160,764.2229	720,991.3564	25,273.7507	143,179.0663
86	131,569.3974	560,227.1335	22,183.1949	117,905.3156
87	106,177.1855	428,657.7361	19,177.1362	95,722.1207
88	84,410.3641	322,480.5506	16,326.1748	76,544.9845
89	66,025.3978	238,070.1865	13,685.6613	60,218.8097
90	50,729.3636	172,044.7887	11,291.0955	46,533.1484
91	38,200.9638	121,315.4251	9,159.6932	35,242.0529
92	28,109.5415	83,114.4613	7,292.8738	26,082.3597
93	20,131.0686	55,004.9198	5,681.8884	18,789.4859
94	13,958.1795	34,873.8512	4,312.1729	13,107.5975
95	9,305.5630	20,915.6717	3,188.7449	8,795.4246
96	5,889.8533	11,610.1087	2,301.6880	5,606.6797
97	3,444.5103	5,720.2554	1,641.3408	3,304.9917
98	1,719.1569	2,275.7451	1,120.6380	1,663.6509
99	556.5882	556.5882	543.0129	543.0129

* Reproduced by permission of the Actuarial Society of America.

ASTRODYNAMICS: BASIC ORBITAL EQUATIONS

Samuel Herrick

University of California, Los Angeles

Abstracted from *Astrodynamics* by Samuel Herrick, published by Van Nostrand Reinhold 1970. For more complete discussion refer to *Astrodynamics*.

1. Astrodynamics includes those portions of *celestial mechanics* that bear directly upon the determination of orbits and the integration of ephemerides of natural and artificial objects in interplanetary and sublunar space. For the most part, but not exclusively, it is founded upon the law of universal gravitation,

$$\mathbf{f}_{ij} = -\mathbf{f}_{ji} = k^2 m_i m_j \mathbf{r}_{ij}/r_{ij}^3 \tag{1}$$

where m_i and m_j are two masses, $\mathbf{r}_{ij}$ is the vector directed from m_i to m_j, r_{ij} is its magnitude, $\mathbf{f}_{ij}$ is the vector attraction of m_j for m_i, $\mathbf{f}_{ji}$ of m_i for m_j, and k^2 is the constant of gravitation.

The laboratory value of k^2, $G = 6.673 \times 10^{-23}$ km^3/gm sec^2, is totally inadequate to the determination of a value of k^2 that can be used in astrodynamics, and it is determined instead from planetary and satellite observations, and for the units of mass that are required by astrodynamics, as follows:

	Heliocentric Orbits		Geocentric Orbits		
Unit of length	astronomical unit (au)	km	geo-unit (gu)	km	
Unit of mass	Sun's mass (m$_\odot$)	m$_\odot$	Earth's mass (m$_\oplus$)	m$_\oplus$	
Unit of time	ephemeris day (day)	sec	ephem. sec (sec)	sec	(2)
k	0.017 202 09895	3.643×10^5	0.001 239 444	631.35	
k^2	295.912 2083 $\times 10^{-6}$	13.271×10^{10}	1.536 221 $\times 10^{-6}$	398603	

The au and gu are approximately the mean distance of the earth from the sun and the earth's equatorial radius, respectively, but are defined in such ways as to make the corresponding values of k exact. Each of these units is essential to a "canonical" set, as discussed in §2.

2. The equations of motion, for a system of n mutually attracting bodies, are derived from equations (1) and the second law of motion. Assuming that the masses are constant, we may write them in their *inertial form* as follows:

$$\left. \begin{aligned} m_1 \frac{d^2\mathbf{r}_1}{dt^2} &= \mathbf{f}_{12} + \sum_{j=3}^{n} \mathbf{f}_{1j} = k^2 m_1 m_2 \frac{\mathbf{r}_{12}}{r_{12}^3} + k^2 m_1 \sum_{j=3}^{n} m_j \frac{\mathbf{r}_{1j}}{r_{1j}^3} \\ m_2 \frac{d^2\mathbf{r}_2}{dt^2} &= \mathbf{f}_{21} + \sum_{j=3}^{n} \mathbf{f}_{2j} = -k^2 m_1 m_2 \frac{\mathbf{r}_{12}}{r_{12}^3} + k^2 m_2 \sum_{j=3}^{n} m_j \frac{\mathbf{r}_{2j}}{r_{2j}^3} \\ \cdot \ \cdot \ \cdot \ \cdot \ \cdot &\ \cdot \ \cdot \ \cdot \ \cdot \ \cdot \ \cdot \ \cdot \ \cdot \ \cdot \ \cdot \ \cdot \ \cdot \ \cdot \ \cdot \end{aligned} \right\} \tag{3}$$

From these equations we may obtain the well known ten integrals of the n-body problem, which tell us (a) that the center of mass moves uniformly in a straight line, and so may be visualized as the inertial origin, (b) that the total angular momentum of the system is constant, and (c) that the total energy of the system is constant.

The *relative motion form* of the equations of motion is derived from equations (3) and

$$\mathbf{r} = \mathbf{r}_{12} = \mathbf{r}_2 - \mathbf{r}_1 \tag{4}$$

especially for an m_1 that has, like the Sun, a dominant effect on the motion of an m_2:

$$\frac{d^2\mathbf{r}}{dt^2} = -k^2(m_1 + m_2)\frac{\mathbf{r}}{r^3} + k^2 \sum_{j=3}^{n} m_j \left(\frac{\mathbf{r}_{2j}}{r_{21}^3} - \frac{\mathbf{r}_{1j}}{r_{1j}^3}\right) \tag{5}$$

It is thus simply that $m_1 + m_2$ replaces the $m_1 m_2$ of equations (3); clearly there is no occasion for the surprise or puzzlement this replacement sometimes arouses.

The first term of equation (5) is often called the *two-body term*. The remaining terms are the *perturbations* (for relative motion and the *n*-body problem). The perturbation terms can also include the effects of thrust, drag, an equatorial bulge, the departures of relativity mechanics from Newtonian mechanics, etc. Even when we restrict the disturbing forces to those of the *n*-body problem, the perturbations can differ from those shown in equation (5), if a "two-body term" is constructed for an origin other than m_1.

The first term of equation (5) may be simplified, both theoretically and computationally, by the absorption of the gravitation-mass constant into a "canonical time,"

$$\tau = k_*(t - t_0) \tag{6}$$

and by the use of such definitions as

$$\dot{\mathbf{r}} = \frac{d\mathbf{r}}{dt} = k_*\dot{\mathbf{r}}_\tau = k_*\frac{d\mathbf{r}}{d\tau}, \qquad \ddot{\mathbf{r}} = \frac{d^2\mathbf{r}}{dt^2} = k_*^2\ddot{\mathbf{r}}_\tau = k_*^2\frac{d^2\mathbf{r}}{d\tau^2}, \text{ etc.} \tag{7}$$

where

$$k_* = k\sqrt{m_1 + m_2} \qquad \mu = k^2(m_1 + m_2) = k_*^2\mu_\tau \qquad \mu_\tau = 1 \tag{8}$$

For other forms of the equations of motion the constant μ has slightly different values.

It is best to think of τ as having the dimensions of time; the dimensions of $\sqrt{\mu}$ are "left behind" in $\mu_\tau = 1$ when the derivatives in equations hereafter are expressed with canonical units of time. When m_2 is negligible as compared with m_1, as it usually is, the canonical units of time are:

$$
\begin{aligned}
&\text{au} - \text{m}_\odot - \text{day system:} \qquad & 1 \text{ kaday} &= 58.132\ 44087 \text{ days} \\
&\text{gu} - \text{m}_\oplus - \text{sec system:} \qquad & 1 \text{ kesec} &= 806.813\ 3776 \text{ sec} \\
& & &= 13.446\ 8896 \text{ min}
\end{aligned}
\right\} \tag{9}
$$

The practical advantage of canonical units of time and distance is that they tend to keep the magnitudes of position, velocity, and acceleration vectors all in the neighborhood of unity, thus reducing, for example, the likelihood of machine errors in floating-decimal-point operations.

3. The two-body problem includes, of course, only the first term of the equations of relative motion (5), which we may now write, with the aid of equations (6), (7), (8) as follows:

$$\ddot{\mathbf{r}} = -\mu\mathbf{r}/r^3 \tag{10}$$

We seek integrals of the two-body problem first by means of

$$\mathbf{r} \times \ddot{\mathbf{r}} = 0 \tag{11}$$

of which the x component is

$$y\ddot{z} - z\ddot{y} = 0 \tag{12}$$

so that

$$\mathbf{r} \times \dot{\mathbf{r}} = \mathbf{h} = h\mathbf{W} \tag{13}$$

and

$$y\dot{z} - z\dot{y} = h_x = hW_x \tag{14}$$

where $\mathbf{W}$ is a constant unit vector normal to the orbit plane, thus established as a fixed plane, and where, with v the *true anomaly* or angle in the orbit plane measured from the perifocus to $\mathbf{r}$,

$$h = r^2 \dot{v} = \sqrt{\mu p} \tag{15}$$

expresses *Kepler's second law*, or law of areas: that the areal velocity (or angular momentum) is constant.

The orientation of the orbit plane, embodied in $\mathbf{W}$, is often expressed by the *inclination*, i, and the *longitude of the (ascending) node*, Ω.

The relationship of h to p, the *parameter* or semi latus rectum, may be established along with Kepler's first law in several different ways. When one is interested in the use as well as in the existence of integrals of the two-body problem, it is well to proceed by seeking additional functions that satisfy the differential equation (10) and so lead to additional simple integrations such as are found in equations (12) and (14). One such function is found in

$$\sqrt{\mu}\, D = r\dot{r} = \dot{\mathbf{r}} \cdot \mathbf{r} \qquad \sqrt{\mu}\, \dot{D} = \dot{s}^2 - \mu/r \qquad \ddot{D} = -\mu D/r^3 \tag{16}$$

where

$$r^2 = \mathbf{r} \cdot \mathbf{r} \qquad \dot{s}^2 = \dot{\mathbf{r}} \cdot \dot{\mathbf{r}} = \dot{r}^2 + r^2\dot{v}^2 \tag{17}$$

so that

$$\mathbf{r}\ddot{D} - D\ddot{\mathbf{r}} = 0 \tag{18}$$

$$\mathbf{r}\dot{D} - D\dot{\mathbf{r}} = \mathbf{a} = e\sqrt{\mu}\, \mathbf{P} \tag{19}$$

where $\mathbf{a}$ is a constant vector, whose relationship to e, the eccentricity, and P, a unit vector directed to the perifocus, is established by

$$\sqrt{\mu}\, (\mathbf{r} \cdot \mathbf{a}) = \sqrt{\mu}\, (r^2\dot{D} - Dr\dot{r}) = r^2(\dot{s}^2 - \dot{r}^2) - \mu r = r^4\dot{v}^2 - \mu r = h^2 - \mu r \tag{20}$$

or

$$h^2/\mu = r - (\mathbf{r} \cdot \mathbf{a})/\sqrt{\mu} = r[1 - (|\mathbf{a}|/\sqrt{\mu}) \cos (\mathbf{a},\mathbf{r})] \tag{21}$$

which is the polar equation of the conic,

$$p = r(1 - e \cos v) \tag{22}$$

so that we have established *Kepler's first law*, that the orbit is a conic with the Sun (or the Earth) at one focus. We have also established the facts that $\mathbf{a}$ must be directed to perifocus and that

$$|\mathbf{a}| = e\sqrt{\mu} \qquad h^2 = \mu p \tag{23}$$

which are the evaluations needed for equations (15) and (19).

The magnitude of $\mathbf{a}$ must not be confused with the constant a, which for the ellipse (cf. fig 1) we call the *mean distance* or *semi major axis*, and which is related to p, the *parameter*, and q, the *perifocal distance*, for all of the conics, and r_A, the *apofocal distance*, for the ellipse, by

$$q = a(1 - e) \qquad\qquad r_A = a(1 + e) \tag{24}$$

$$p = a(1 - e^2) = q(1 + e) = r_A(1 - e) \tag{25}$$

The orthogonal unit vectors $\mathbf{W}$ and $\mathbf{P}$ (cf. equations 13 and 19) are joined by the unit vector $\mathbf{Q}$, which is orthogonal to each of them, and is defined and obtained by

$$\mathbf{Q} = \mathbf{W} \times \mathbf{P} \tag{26}$$

or by one of the relationships in

$$\mathbf{b} = e\sqrt{\mu p}\, \mathbf{Q} = r\dot{H} - H\dot{\mathbf{r}} \tag{27}$$

where the latter relationship may be obtained by integration, since

$$H = r - p \qquad \dot{H} = \dot{r} \qquad \ddot{H} = -\mu H/r^3 \tag{28}$$

The orientation vectors **P** and **Q**, like **W**, are functions of i and Ω, but also of ω, the *argument of perifocus*, which is an angle measured from the node and defines the orientation of the perifocus, and of the major axis or line of apsides, in the orbit plane. They are used efficiently in the calculation of x, y, z, referred to general axes, from

$$x_\omega = r \cos v \qquad y_\omega = r \sin v \tag{29}$$

referred to orbital axes (cf. fig. 1 and §§5, 6), by means of

$$\mathbf{r} = x_\omega \mathbf{P} + y_\omega \mathbf{Q} \tag{30}$$

4. The vis-viva or energy integral may be obtained as follows:

$$2\dot{\mathbf{r}} \cdot \ddot{\mathbf{r}} = -2\mu \mathbf{r} \cdot \dot{\mathbf{r}}/r^3 = -2\mu\dot{r}/r^2 \tag{31}$$

$$\dot{s}^2 = \dot{\mathbf{r}} \cdot \dot{\mathbf{r}} = \mu(2/r + \alpha) \qquad \alpha = -1/a \tag{32}$$

where the constant α is evaluated from simple conditions known, for example, at perifocus.

Equations (15), (16), (17), (25), and (32) may now be recognized as sources of information about the nature of the conic determined by given position and velocity, **r** and $\dot{\mathbf{r}}$:

	Ellipse	Parabola	Hyperbola
General	$\dfrac{1}{a} > 0,\ 0 \le e \le 1$	$\dfrac{1}{a} = 0,\ e = 1$	$\dfrac{1}{a} < 0,\ e \ge 1$
Circular	$D = 0,\ e = 0$	—	—
Rectilinear	$\dfrac{1}{a} > 0,\ p = 0,\ e = 1$	$\dfrac{1}{a} = 0,\ p = 0,\ e = 1$	$\dfrac{1}{a} < 0,\ p = 0,\ e = 1$

$$\tag{33}$$

The vis-viva integral is used also to evaluate useful factors for converting canonical units to conventional units. When m_2 is negligible as compared with m_1, they are:

Heliocentric	Geocentric	
$V = V_s \dot{s}_\tau$	$V = V_e \dot{s}_\tau$	
$\mathbf{V} = V_s \dot{\mathbf{r}}_\tau$	$\mathbf{V} = V_e \dot{\mathbf{r}}_\tau$	

$$\left.\right\} \tag{34}$$

$V_s =$	29.785	$V_e =$	7.905	km/sec
	18.508		4.912	mi/sec
	57,897		15,367	knots
	97,720		25,936	ft/sec

$$\left.\right\} \tag{35}$$

The constants V_s and V_e may be recognized as being approximately the velocities, respectively, of the Earth in its orbit, and of a circular satellite of the Earth hypothetically at one equatorial radius or geo-unit. The velocity of escape from the Earth, in the latter circumstances, is

$$V_{pe} = V_e \sqrt{2} \tag{36}$$

Two special values of $\dot{s}$ are of interest: $\dot{s}_q$ corresponding to $r = q$ and $\dot{s}_A$ corresponding to $r = r_A$,

$$\left.
\begin{aligned}
\dot{s}_q/\sqrt{\mu} = \dot{s}_{\tau q}/\sqrt{\mu_\tau} = \sqrt{\frac{2}{q} - \frac{1}{a}} = \sqrt{\frac{1 + e}{q}} = \sqrt{\frac{1}{a}\left(\frac{1 + e}{1 - e}\right)} \\
\dot{s}_A/\sqrt{\mu} = \dot{s}_{\tau A}/\sqrt{\mu_\tau} = \sqrt{\frac{2}{r_A} - \frac{1}{a}} = \sqrt{\frac{1 - e}{r_A}} = \sqrt{\frac{1}{a}\left(\frac{1 - e}{1 + e}\right)}
\end{aligned}
\right\} \tag{37}$$

5. The ellipse has special formulae in terms of E, the *eccentric anomaly*, an extremely useful angle that is defined by fig. 1:

$$\left.\begin{array}{l} r = a(1 - e \cos E) \\ r \cos v = x_\omega = a (\cos E - e) \\ r \sin v = y_\omega = \sqrt{ap} \sin E \end{array}\right\} \tag{38}$$

From equations (6), (15), and (38) we derive

$$\frac{r^2 \dot{v}}{\sqrt{p}} = \sqrt{\mu} = a^{\frac{1}{2}}(1 - e \cos E)\dot{E} = r \sqrt{a}\, \dot{E} \tag{39}$$

and *Kepler's equation*,

$$M = M_0 + n(t - t_0) = n(t - T) = E - e \sin E \tag{40}$$

where M is the *mean anomaly*, M_0 is the *mean anomaly at the epoch*, t_0, T is the *time of perifocal passage*, and n is the *mean motion* or mean angular velocity:

$$n = \dot{M} = \sqrt{\mu}/a^{\frac{3}{2}} \tag{41}$$

We find from equations (38), (40), and (41) that the three anomalies, v, E, M are together at 0, π, 2π, . . . , and that the corresponding values of $t - T$ are 0, $\frac{1}{2}P$, P, . . . , where P is the *period* expressed in the conventional unit of time:

$$P = 2\pi/n = 2\pi a^{\frac{3}{2}}/\sqrt{\mu} \tag{42}$$

Equation (42) is an expression of *Kepler's third law*, that the squares of the periods are proportional to the cubes of the mean distances.

On next page is a table of comparative formulae and definitions.

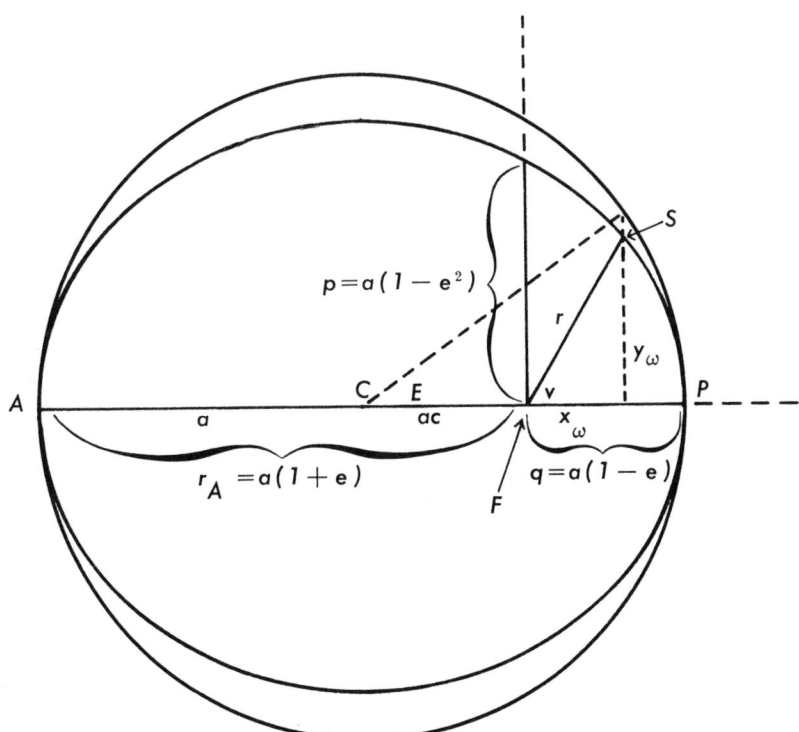

6. A table of comparative formulae and definitions:

General	Ellipse	Parabola	Hyperbola
	$0 \leq e \leq 1$	$e = 1$	$e \geq 1$
	$1/a > 0$	$1/a = 0$	$1/a < 0$
$p = q(1 + e)$	$p \leq 2q$	$p = 2q$	$p \geq 2q$
$M = M_0 + n(t - t_0)$	$\{\, n = a^{-\frac{3}{2}} \sqrt{\mu}$	$n = \sqrt{\mu}$	$n = (-a)^{-\frac{3}{2}} \sqrt{\mu}$
$= n(t - T)$	$\{\, M = E - e \sin E$	$M = qD + \frac{1}{6}D^3$	$M = e \sinh F - F$
$r = p/(1 + e \cos v)$	$r = a(1 - e \cos E)$	$r = q + \frac{1}{2}D^2$	$r = -a(e \cosh F - 1)$
$\dot{r} \sqrt{p/\mu} = e \sin v$	$D = \dfrac{r\dot{r}}{\sqrt{\mu}} = \sqrt{a}\, e \sin E$	$D = \dfrac{r\dot{r}}{\sqrt{\mu}}$	$D = \dfrac{r\dot{r}}{\sqrt{\mu}}$
		$= \sqrt{2q}\, \tan \dfrac{v}{2}$	$= \sqrt{-a}\, e \sinh F$
$r\dot{v} \sqrt{p/\mu} = 1 + e \cos v$	$r^2\dot{v} = \sqrt{\mu p}$	$r^2\dot{v} = \sqrt{2\mu q}$	$r^2\dot{v} = \sqrt{\mu p}$
	$= \sqrt{\mu a(1 - e^2)}$		$= \sqrt{-\mu a(e^2 - 1)}$
$x_\omega = r \cos v$	$x_\omega = a(\cos E - e)$	$x_\omega = q - \frac{1}{2}D^2$	$x_\omega = -a(\cosh F - e)$
$y_\omega = r \sin v$	$y_\omega = \sqrt{ap} \sin E$	$y_\omega = \sqrt{2q}\, D$	$y_\omega = \sqrt{-ap} \sinh F$
$\dot{x}_\omega \sqrt{p/\mu} = -\sin v$	$r\dot{x}_\omega = -\sqrt{\mu a} \sin E$	$r\dot{x}_\omega = -\sqrt{\mu}\, D$	$r\dot{x}_\omega = -\sqrt{-\mu a} \sinh F$
$\dot{y}_\omega \sqrt{p/\mu} = \cos v + e$	$r\dot{y}_\omega = \sqrt{\mu p} \cos E$	$r\dot{y}_\omega = \sqrt{2\mu q}$	$r\dot{y}_\omega = \sqrt{\mu p} \cosh F$

Circular Ellipse*	Rectilinear		
	Ellipse	Parabola	Hyperbola
$e = 0$	$e = 1$	$e = 1$	$e = 1$
$r = p = q = a$	$p = 2q = 0$	$p = 2q = 0$	$p = 2q = 0$
$M = E$	$M = E - \sin E$	$M = \frac{1}{6}D^3$	$M = \sinh F - F$
$\dot{s} = r\dot{v} = \sqrt{\mu/a}$	$r = a(1 - \cos E)$	$r = \frac{1}{2}D^2$	$r = -a(\cosh F - 1)$
$D = r\dot{r}/\sqrt{\mu} = 0$	$D = r\dot{r}/\sqrt{\mu} = \sqrt{a} \sin E$	$D = r\dot{r}/\sqrt{\mu}$	$D = r\dot{r}/\sqrt{\mu} = \sqrt{-a} \sinh F$
$x_\omega = a \cos E$	$x_\omega = -r$	$x_\omega = -r$	$x_\omega = -r$
$y_\omega = a \sin E$	$y_\omega = 0$	$y_\omega = 0$	$y_\omega = 0$
$\dot{x}_\omega = -\dot{s} \sin E$	$\dot{x}_\omega = -\dot{r}$	$\dot{x}_\omega = -\dot{r}$	$\dot{x}_\omega = -\dot{r}$
$\dot{y}_\omega = \dot{s} \cos E$	$\dot{y}_\omega = 0$	$\dot{y}_\omega = 0$	$\dot{y}_\omega = 0$

* $M, E, x_\omega, y_\omega, \dot{x}_\omega, \dot{y}_\omega$ are formally related as shown, but all are indeterminate!

Barker's equation, the parabolic equivalent of Kepler's equation in the foregoing table, is often written

$$\frac{\sqrt{\mu}\,(t - T)}{q^{\frac{3}{2}} \sqrt{2}} = \tan \tfrac{1}{2}v + \tfrac{1}{3} \tan^3 \tfrac{1}{2}v \tag{43}$$

but, so written, it is indeterminate for the rectilinear orbit ($q = 0$, $\tan \tfrac{1}{2}v = \infty$).

Unified variables, parameters, and formulae are designed to care for ellipses ($-1/a = \alpha < 0$), parabolas ($\alpha = 0$), and hyperbolas ($\alpha > 0$), including rectilinear ones, but not circles or nearly-circular ellipses. They are illustrated by the following table, which adds elliptic definitions for illumination but not for calculation:

Unified Formulae	*Elliptic Definitions*
$\sqrt{\mu}\,(t - T) = \tilde{M} = q\tilde{X} + e\tilde{U}$	$\tilde{X} = \sqrt{a}\,E$
$r = q + e\tilde{C}$	
$\tilde{U} = \dfrac{\tilde{X}^3}{3!} + \alpha\,\dfrac{\tilde{X}^5}{5!} + \alpha^2\,\dfrac{\tilde{X}^7}{7!} + \cdots$	$\tilde{U} = a^{\frac{3}{2}}(E - \sin E)$
$\tilde{C} = \dfrac{\tilde{X}^2}{2!} + \alpha\,\dfrac{\tilde{X}^4}{4!} + \alpha^2\,\dfrac{\tilde{X}^6}{6!} + \cdots$	$\tilde{C} = a(1 - \cos E)$
$x_\omega = q - \tilde{C}$	
$\dfrac{y_\omega}{\sqrt{p}} = -\dfrac{r\dot{x}_\omega}{\sqrt{\mu}} = \tilde{S} = \tilde{X} + \alpha\tilde{U}$	$\tilde{S} = \sqrt{a}\,\sin E$
$\dfrac{r\dot{y}_\omega}{\sqrt{\mu p}} = \tilde{K} = 1 + \alpha\tilde{C}$	$\tilde{K} = \cos E$

The definitions in terms of parabolic and hyperbolic variables may be inferred.

Universal variables, parameters, and formulae are designed to care for the foregoing and also circles and nearly-circular ellipses. They are illustrated by

Universal Formulae	*Elliptic Definitions*
$D_0 = r_0\dot{r}_0$	$D_0 = \sqrt{a}\,e\sin E_0$
$c_0 = 1 + \alpha r_0$	$c_0 = e\cos E_0$
$\sqrt{\mu}\,(t - t_0) = \hat{M} = r_0\hat{X} + D_0\hat{C} + c_0\hat{U}$	$\hat{E} = E - E_0$
$r = r_0 + D_0\hat{S} + c_0\hat{C}$	$\hat{X} = \sqrt{a}\,\hat{E}$
$\hat{U} = \dfrac{\hat{X}^3}{3!} + \alpha\,\dfrac{\hat{X}^5}{5!} + \alpha^2\,\dfrac{\hat{X}^7}{7!} + \cdots$	$\hat{U} = a^{\frac{3}{2}}(\hat{E} - \sin\hat{E})$
$\hat{C} = \dfrac{\hat{X}^2}{2!} + \alpha\,\dfrac{\hat{X}^4}{4!} + \alpha^2\,\dfrac{\hat{X}^6}{6!} + \cdots$	$\hat{C} = a(1 - \cos\hat{E})$
$\hat{S} = \hat{X} + \alpha\hat{U}$	$\hat{S} = \sqrt{a}\,\sin\hat{E}$

$$f = 1 - \hat{C}/r_0 \qquad\qquad \sqrt{\mu}\,g = \hat{M} - \hat{U}$$
$$\dot{g} = 1 - \hat{C}/r \qquad\qquad \dot{f} = -\sqrt{\mu}\,\hat{S}/rr_0$$
$$\mathbf{r} = f\mathbf{r}_0 + g\dot{\mathbf{r}}_0 \qquad\qquad \dot{\mathbf{r}} = \dot{f}\mathbf{r}_0 + \dot{g}\dot{\mathbf{r}}_0$$

It is evident that universal variables reduce to unified variables when $t_0 = T$, and $M_0 = 0$, $E_0 = 0$, $r_0 = q$, $D_0 = 0$, $c_0 = e$.

ASTRODYNAMICAL TERMINOLOGY, NOTATION, AND USAGE

SAMUEL HERRICK

University of California, Los Angeles

Abstracted from *Astrodynamics* by Samuel Herrick, published by Van Nostrand Reinhold 1970. For more complete discussion of the philosophy of selection of these symbols refer to *Astrodynamics*.

INTRODUCTION

Standardization of notation and terminology, or more properly, attention to established conventions and usage, contributes to understanding in all fields of science.

In the compilation of a standard listing of terms and symbols it is often implied, unwisely, that conformity with it is to be required thereafter of all "respectable" writing in the field. The philosophy adopted in the present listing, on the contrary, is that it should be based upon usage, that it should present alternatives sanctioned either by usage or by logical development where conflicts have come into being, and that it should be a reference list rather than a required list.

Typical of the conflicting usages in astrodynamics, encountered in celestial mechanics even before it had fully established contact with such fields as propulsion, aerodynamics, optimization, are those between v, true anomaly, and v, velocity, and between a, mean distance, and a, acceleration. In accordance with the foregoing expression of philosophy, we report all these usages but indicate that $\dot{r}$, $\dot{s}$, or V should be preferred for velocity, and that $\ddot{r}$, g, or A should be preferred for acceleration, because of the dominant use of v and a in the other senses.

The central core of astrodynamics is celestial mechanics, and an important function of the present listing is the providing of an entrée to the literature of celestial mechanics, much of which is still untapped in astrodynamical research. In consequence the present listing leans heavily upon astronomical usage, and upon the 1938 listing of the International Astronomical Union, *Transactions*, *6*, 345–348, but with departures from the latter in such matters as the following:

(1) The preferred designations for the geocentric distance (or "range") and for an increment or correction or residual are ρ and Δ rather than Δ and δ. The I.A.U. ignored long-established astronomical usage in such standard and familiar quantities as $\rho \cos \delta \, \Delta\alpha$ and $\rho\Delta\delta$, converting them into the whimsical $\Delta \cos \delta \, \delta\alpha$ and $\Delta\delta\delta$.

(2) The "direction cosines" associated with α and δ are designated as the components of a unit vector, $\mathbf{L}$, ($L_x = \cos \delta \cos \alpha$, $L_y = \cos \delta \sin \alpha$, $L_z = \sin \delta$), rather than by the l, m, n of the I.A.U. listing, or by the older sets: λ, μ, ν; α, β, γ. The use of vectors in celestial mechanics has become almost universal since 1938.

(3) The unit vector normal to the orbit plane is designated by $\mathbf{W}(W_x, W_y, W_z)$. The I.A.U. designations R_x, R_y, R_z have come into conflict with its designations for the "solar coordinates," X, Y, Z, because the vector notation for both sets would be $\mathbf{R}$, and because the two vectors sometimes appear in the same equation. Accordingly we prefer $\mathbf{R}(X, Y, Z)$ for the solar coordinates (or more generally the coordinates of the dynamical center referred to the observer).

The listing of terms and symbols is organized as follows:

(1) There is one alphabetical listing for terms and alphabetical symbols.

(2) Capital letters precede the corresponding lower case letters.

(3) Vector notation follows non-vector notation.

(4) Greek letters are alphabetized with Roman letters according to their usual trans-

literations (or the spellings of their names), thus changing the Greek order for γ, ζ, η, θ, φ, χ, ψ, ω.

(5) Vector triads are listed as groups under the first letter of triads, with cross references appearing under the other two letters.

(6) Terms are alphabetized according to spelling, and cross-referenced with notations, and vice versa.

(7) Non-alphabetical symbols are listed separately at the end. This listing makes no effort to be complete, or to include standard mathematical symbols.

(8) Terminology and definitions are primarily those that are peculiar to celestial mechanics or for which differences in usage exist, and do not include general terms such as "conic," "focus," "directrix," "least squares," "standard deviation," "celestial sphere," "ecliptic," etc., with which all users of the list may be assumed to be familiar.

(9) Alternative notations and usages are usually indicated with the author's preference or a cross reference introduced by "prefer" or by "see," "also," or "q.v." ("which see").

A

A, a	Acceleration; prefer g or A (see introduction and "g")
A, Az	Azimuth (q.v.); also Z
$A = A \left[\dfrac{km}{au} \right]$, A $[km]$	Length conversion factor, astronomical units to kilometers; au expressed in km.
A	Cross-sectional area
A, B	Constants in dynamical equation of first approximation in orbit determination: $\rho = A - B/r^3$
A, B, C	Principal moments of inertia
A_1, A_3	Ratios of sectors or time intervals, used in expressions for ratios of triangles (see "c_1, c_3"); also c_1^0, c_3^0:

$$A_1 = \tau_{23}/\tau_{13}; \quad A_3 = \tau_{12}/\tau_{13}$$

A. E.	*American Ephemeris and Nautical Almanac* or (British) *Astronomical Ephemeris*
$\mathbf{A}(A_x, A_y, A_z)$	See "**L, A, D**"
$\mathbf{A}_h(A_{xh}, A_{yh}, A_{zh})$	See "**L, A$_h$, D$_h$**"
$\mathbf{A}$, $\mathbf{B}$	$\mathbf{A} = a\mathbf{P}$; $\mathbf{B} = b\mathbf{Q}$. Used in $\mathbf{r} = \mathbf{A} (\cos E - e) + \mathbf{B} \sin E$ Not recommended in place of $a\mathbf{P}$, $b\mathbf{Q}$ because of increasing emphasis on $\dot{\mathbf{r}}$.
a	Mean distance or semi major axis of ellipse, semi transverse axis of hyperbola.
a	Altitude (q.v.); prefer h
au, $a.u.$, or A.U.	Astronomical unit, approximately equal to semi major axis of Earth's orbit, but accurately defined by Gaussian $k = k_s$.
a_e	Earth's equatorial radius
$\mathbf{a}$, $\mathbf{b}$, $\mathbf{h}$	$\mathbf{a} = e\sqrt{\mu}\,\mathbf{P}$, $\mathbf{b} = e\sqrt{\mu p}\,\mathbf{Q}$, $\mathbf{h} = \sqrt{\mu p}\,\mathbf{W}$.
α (alpha)	Right ascension
α	Azimuth (q.v.); prefer A
α	Time required for light to travel unit distance; also τ_A:

$$\alpha_s = 0.005\ 7755 \text{ day/au}$$
$$\alpha_e = 0.021\ 275 \text{ sec/gu}$$

α	Flattening; prefer f (q.v.)

α	$= -1/a$; constant of integration in vis-viva integral.
α, β	ϵ, δ (q.v.) in Lambert-Euler equation (q.v.); astronomers have usually used ϵ, δ; mathematicians starting with Whittaker have tended to use α, β
α, β, γ	See "**L, A, D**"
adjoint method	Method for obtaining the partial differential coefficients used in differential correction, rendezvous, etc. Adjoint to "linearized Encke" or "variational orbit" method.
algorithm	Algorism, misspelled because of mistakenly assumed association with the root of *arithmetic;* correctly applied to arithmetic using concept of zero; incorrectly substituted for *collection of formulae* by some programmers.
altitude (h)	Angular distance above the horizon. Also called "angular altitude," "elevation," or "angular elevation" by those who have grown up in the traditions of aeronautics rather than astronomy or navigation.
altitude (H)	Linear height above sea level; prefer "height."
angular velocity (ω)	ω should be used preferably only for earth's rotation with respect to an inertially fixed direction. Differs slightly from the rate of change of sidereal time, because the latter is referred to a moving equinox.
angular velocity $(\dot{v}, \dot{u}, \dot{l}, \dot{\theta})$	$\dot{v} = \dot{u} = \dot{l} = \dot{\theta} = \sqrt{\mu p}/r^2$ in two-body motion, and also in perturbation theory, provided the perturbations of the origins of v, u, l are absorbed in $v^\backprime = \dfrac{dv}{dt} - \dot{v}$, etc.; usually $\theta^\backprime = 0, \dfrac{d\theta}{dt} = \dot{\theta}$
anomaly	See "eccentric anomaly," "mean anomaly," "true anomaly"
apapsis, apoapsis, apex, apocenter $\Big\}$	Apofocus (q.v.)
apofocal distance (r_A)	The distance from the focus to the apofocus: $a(1 + e) = r_A$
apofocus	Point in orbit farthest from focus of attraction; the farther apsis (q.v.). Also: apogee in geocentric orbit, aphelion in heliocentric orbit, etc., apocenter, apex; avoid the incorrectly formed and misleading term "apoapsis."
apsis	Point on orbit where radius vector is maximum or minimum (apofocus or perifocus). Line of apsides: line joining apofocus and perifocus. (Say ap'-si-deez!)
argument of latitude (u)	Angle measured in orbit plane from node to object; $u = v + \omega$
argument of perifocus (ω)	Angle measured in orbit plane from node to perifocus.
associated Legendre function	See P_n^m
azimuth (A)	Angle measured in horizon plane eastward from north point: also Z, α is unacceptable; also, in infrequent astronomical usage, measured from the south point.

B

B See "A, B"

B Argument in Barker's Tables; see "Barker's equation";

$$B = \frac{\sqrt{\mu}}{k_s}\frac{t-T}{q^{\frac{3}{2}}} = \frac{\sqrt{2}}{k_s}\left(\tan \tfrac{1}{2}v + \tfrac{1}{3}\tan^3 \tfrac{1}{2}v\right)$$

B'_i Coefficients used in ratios of triangles (see "$c_1,\ c_3$")

$$B'_i = \tau_{13}^2 A_i(1 - A_i^2)/6$$

$B_1,\ B_2,\ B_3$ Coefficients used in Gibbs's expressions for the ratios of triangles (see "$c_1,\ c_3$"):

$$B_1 = (\tau_{12}^2 + \tau_{12}\tau_{23} - \tau_{23}^2)/12$$
$$B_2 = (\tau_{12}^2 + 3\tau_{12}\tau_{23} + \tau_{23}^2)/12$$
$$B_3 = (-\tau_{12}^2 + \tau_{12}\tau_{23} + \tau_{23}^2)/12$$

B   See "**A, B**"

b $= a\sqrt{1 - e^2}$; semi minor axis of ellipse.

b Latitude referred to the orbital plane.

b Heliocentric β (q.v.)

$\mathbf{b}(b_x, b_y, b_z)$ $= e\sqrt{\mu p}\ \mathbf{Q}$; see **a, b, h**. Note:

$$|\mathbf{b}| = e\sqrt{\mu p} \neq b = a\sqrt{1 - e^2}$$

β (beta)   Latitude, celestial

Barker's equation   Equation relating time, t, and true anomaly, v, for parabolic orbits (see also B):

$$\frac{\sqrt{\mu}\ (t-T)}{q^{\frac{3}{2}}\sqrt{2}} = \tan \tfrac{1}{2}v + \tfrac{1}{3}\tan^3 \tfrac{1}{2}v$$

or (see D)

$$\sqrt{\mu}\ (t-T) = qD + \tfrac{1}{6}D^3, \quad D = \sqrt{2q}\tan \tfrac{1}{2}v$$

barycenter   Center of mass of two or more bodies.

burnout   See "initial, injection, insertion."

C

C $= a_e/\sqrt{1 - e^2 \sin^2 \varphi}$, quantity tabulated in the almanacs for finding geocentric coordinates; see also S, x_c, y_c

C $= rr_0[1 - \cos (v - v_0)]$; also $C_{ij} = r_i r_j[1 - \cos (v_j - v_i)]$; see also S, K, κ, σ

C $= \cos E - e$; prefer next definition.

C $= 1 - \cos E = (r - q)/ae$

$\tilde{C}$ $= a(1 - \cos E) = -a(\cosh F - 1)$, etc., unified variable.

$\hat{C}$ $= a[1 - \cos (E - E_0)] = -a[\cosh (F - F_0) - 1]$, etc., universal variable.

C_D Shape factor for drag calculations

$\left.\begin{array}{l}C_n,\ C_{n,m} \\ \text{or } C_l,\ C_{l,m}\end{array}\right\}$ Coefficients of zonal and sectoral harmonics in the gravitational potential of a spheroid, defined under "potential of spheroid."

$c = c \left[\dfrac{\text{km}}{\text{sec}}\right] = c \left[\dfrac{\text{km}}{\text{ls}}\right]$ Velocity of light $\left[\dfrac{\text{km}}{\text{sec}}\right]$; distance conversion factor

$$\left[\dfrac{\text{kilometers}}{\text{light second}}\right]$$

c $= 1 + \alpha r = 1 - \dfrac{r}{a} = e \cos E = e \cosh F$

c Distance from center of ellipse to focus; $c = ae$.

c Length of chord; see s

c_1, c_3 Ratios of the triangles: also n_1, n_3, or n_1/n_2, n_3/n_2. May be series or closed expressions (see also "d_1, d_2, d_3"), including:

$$c_1 = \frac{\mathbf{r}_2 \times \mathbf{r}_3}{\mathbf{r}_1 \times \mathbf{r}_3} = \frac{r_2 r_3 \sin(v_3 - v_2)}{r_1 r_3 \sin(v_3 - v_1)}$$

$$c_3 = \frac{\mathbf{r}_1 \times \mathbf{r}_2}{\mathbf{r}_1 \times \mathbf{r}_3} = \frac{r_1 r_2 \sin(v_2 - v_1)}{r_1 r_3 \sin(v_3 - v_1)}$$

$$c_i = A_i + B'_i/r_2^3 \qquad i = 1, 3$$

$$c_i = A_i \frac{1 + B_i/r_i^3}{1 - B_2/r_2^3} \qquad i = 1, 3$$

The last equations are "Gibbs's expressions."

c_1^0, c_3^0 Ratios of the time intervals; see "A_1, A_3"

$\mathbf{c}$ $= \sqrt{\mu p}\,\mathbf{W}$, angular momentum vector; prefer $\mathbf{h}$ (see "$\mathbf{a}$, $\mathbf{b}$, $\mathbf{h}$")

χ (chi)   This symbol is often used in astrodynamics, but has no dominant use.

canonical time variable   See "τ"

canonical variables   Variables satisfying Hamilton's canonical equation (q.v., also "Delaunay variables").

climb angle (γ)   Flight-path angle

center of attraction   Focus of attraction (q.v.)

compression   Flattening (q.v.)

Cowell's method   Process in special perturbations in which the total acceleration of the orbiting body is numerically integrated to produce the position and velocity. The term "Cowell's method" has been applied to the "second-sum" or "Gauss-Jackson" integration formula, but Cowell did not actually use that formula. It is better to adopt the definition above, permitting the use of any integration formula with "Cowell's method," including the Runge-Kutta formulae. The term "Cowell's method" is usually, though not necessarily, limited to integrations in rectangular coordinates.

D

D "Parabolic anomaly" analogous to the eccentric and hyperbolic anomalies (see "Barker's equation"):

$$r\dot{r}/\sqrt{\mu} = D = \sqrt{2q}\tan\tfrac{1}{2}v, \quad r = q + \tfrac{1}{2}D^2$$

$D, \dot{D}, \ddot{D}$ $D = r\dot{r}/\sqrt{\mu} = \sqrt{a}\,e \sin E = \sqrt{-a}\,e \sinh F$;

$$\frac{\dot{D}}{\sqrt{\mu}} = \frac{1}{r} - \frac{1}{a}; \quad \ddot{D} = -\mu \frac{D}{r^3}$$

$\mathbf{D}(D_x, D_y, D_z)$	See "**L, A, D**"
$\mathbf{D}_h$	See "**L, A**$_h$**, D**$_h$"
d_1, d_2, d_3	Coefficients for $\dot{\mathbf{r}}_2 = -d_1\mathbf{r}_1 + d_2\mathbf{r}_2 + d_3\mathbf{r}_3$. They may be series or closed expressions (see "c_1, c_3").
Δ(delta)	Denotes an increment, residual, correction, or error: e.g., $\Delta\rho, \Delta\alpha, \Delta\delta, \Delta a, \Delta e, \Delta k_s, \Delta\mu$. Also δ; prefer δ for "virtual" increment and for numerical-analysis central-difference formulae (see "$\delta, \delta^2 \ldots$"); prefer Δ when used with α and δ (see introduction).
Δ	Topocentric distance of object; prefer $\rho = |\varrho|$; see ϱ and the introduction.
$\Delta, \Delta^2 \ldots$	Differences in numerical tables when subscript runs down a forewards diagonal
ΔL	$= \sqrt{(\Delta L_x)^2 + (\Delta L_y)^2 + (\Delta L_z)^2} = \sqrt{(\Delta\alpha \cos \delta)^2 = (\Delta\delta)^2}$ $\qquad\qquad\qquad\qquad\qquad\qquad\qquad\qquad\qquad\qquad = $ arc residual
ΔT or Δt	$=$ E.T. $-$ U.T.; time correction to eliminate irregularities of U.T., given in almanacs.
$\Delta X, \Delta Y, \Delta Z$	Corrections to solar coordinates to eliminate parallax, i.e., to translate from center of earth to point of observation. $$\Delta X = \Delta_{xy} \cos \theta; \Delta Y = \Delta_{xy} \sin \theta; \text{ and}$$ $$\Delta Z = -r_c \sin \varphi' = -x_c$$
Δ_{xy}	$\Delta_{xy} = -r_c \cos \varphi' = -y_c$; tabulated in almanacs with ΔZ, for active observatories.
δ (delta)	Declination
δ	$= h - \mathring{g}$, auxiliary quantity used in the Lambert-Euler equation (see: $\epsilon, \mathring{g}, h$); also β (see "α, β")
δ	Denotes a "virtual" increment: e.g., a virtual displacement, $\delta\mathbf{r}$. See also "Δ," "virtual increment."
$\delta, \delta^2 \ldots$	Differences in numerical tables when subscript runs horizontally
$\nabla, \nabla^2 \ldots$ (del or nabla)	Differences in numerical tables when subscript runs up a backwards diagonal
declination (δ)	Topocentric or geocentric coordinate measured north ($+$) or south ($-$) from celestial equator along an hour circle. See "right ascension."
Delaunay variables:	$l = M \qquad\qquad L = \sqrt{\mu a}$ $g = \omega \qquad\qquad G = \sqrt{\mu p}$ $h = \Omega \qquad\qquad H = \sqrt{\mu p} \cos i$
differential correction	A method of correcting the elements of an orbit by means of residuals (observation minus computation) sometimes called the Newton-Raphson process.
disturbing function	Perturbing function (q.v.)
dot-variation $\}$ dot-derivative$\}$	$= \begin{cases} \text{two-body variation} \\ \text{two-body derivative} \end{cases}$

E

E	Eccentric anomaly (q.v.)
$E = E\left[\dfrac{gm}{m_\oplus}\right]$ or $E[gm]$	Mass conversion factor, earth masses to grams; mass of the Earth in grams.

E or E_{II}	Elliptic integral of the second kind
$\hat{E}$	$= 2\hat{g} = E - E_0$
E.T., E.D.	Ephemeris Time, Ephemeris Date (q.v.)
$E(E_x,E_y,E_z)$	See "**Z, E, N**"
e	Eccentricity (q.v.)
e	Earth's meridional eccentricity; $e^2 = 2f - f^2$ where f is the flattening. See f
e	Flattening; prefer f (q.v.)
e	Subscript designating the reference orbit in Encke's method; see o
ϵ (epsilon)	Obliquity of ecliptic
ϵ	Error; mean square error
ϵ	$= h + \hat{g}$, auxiliary quantity used in the Lambert-Euler development (see δ, $\hat{g}$, h); also α (see "α, β").
ϵ	Flattening; prefer f (q.v.)
η (eta)	See "$\rho(\xi, \eta, \zeta)$"
eccentric anomaly (E)	Angle at center of ellipse between major axis and radius of auxiliary circle through a point which has same abscissa as a given point on ellipse. In connection with an ellipsoid of revolution the eccentric anomaly is also known as the "parametric," "geometric," "reduced," or "eccentric" latitude. Also u; prefer E because of notation $u = v + \omega$
eccentricity (e)	Constant ratio between the distance from a point on a conic to the focus and the distance from the point to the directrix.
ellipticity	Flattening (q.v.)
elements of orbit	Selected set of six independent constants of integration of the equations of motion.
elevation (h)	Angular distance above the horizon; prefer "altitude" (q.v.)
Encke's method	Process in special perturbations by which the perturbed departures from the reference orbit, $\rho(\xi,\eta,\zeta)$ and $\dot{\rho}(\xi,\dot{\eta},\zeta)$, are integrated from $\ddot{\rho}(\ddot{\xi},\ddot{\eta},\ddot{\zeta})$ and used to correct the reference position and velocity into the actual position and velocity. May be used to obtain partial differential coefficients, in either linearized or non-linear form.
Encke terms	The differences of the two-body terms in the equations for $\ddot{\rho}(\ddot{\xi},\ddot{\eta},\ddot{\zeta})$ in Encke's method of special perturbations: e.g.,

$$\mu\left(\frac{x_e}{r_e{}^3} - \frac{x}{r^3}\right) = \frac{\mu}{r_e{}^3}\left(fqx - \xi\right)$$

	Also called "indirect terms," but then confused with the terms of the equations of motion that represent the accelerations of the origin.
ephemeris	A table of calculated positions of an object, with equidistant dates as arguments. Plural: ephemerides. (Say ef-eh-mer'-i-deez!)

ephemeris second	Unit of time associated with Ephemeris Time;

$$1 \text{ ephemeris second} = \frac{1 \text{ tropical year } (1900.0)}{31{,}556{,}925.9747}$$

Ephemeris Time (E.T.)	$=$ U.T. $+ \Delta T$, uniform time used as independent variable in the ephemerides of the planets and other objects in space. ΔT is listed in almanacs.
Ephemeris Date (E.D.)	$=$ Julian Date $+ \Delta T - 2400\,000.^d5$
epoch (t_0)	Arbitrary instant of time for which the constants of an orbit are specified.
Eulerian angles	Orientation angles (q.v.) used for 2000 years before Euler.

F

F	Hyperbolic anomaly
F	$= \frac{1}{2}(v + v_0)$ Also: $F_{ij} = \frac{1}{2}(v_j = v_i)$
F	The negative of the Hamiltonian function, also called the force function; in astronomy usually

$$F = \Phi - T = \frac{\mu}{2a} + R$$

F or E_I	Elliptic integral of the first kind
f, g	Series or closed expressions used in the formulae:

$$\mathbf{r} = f\mathbf{r}_0 + g\dot{\mathbf{r}}_0$$
$$\mathbf{r}_j = f_j\mathbf{r}_0 + g_j\dot{\mathbf{r}}_0 = f_{ij}\mathbf{r}_i + g_{ij}\dot{\mathbf{r}}_i$$

f	Flattening; also ϵ, e, α. Prefer f, with ϵ as second choice, because of confusion with closely associated eccentricity:

$$f = 1 - \frac{b}{a} \qquad e = \sqrt{1 - \left(\frac{b}{a}\right)^2}$$

f or $\mathring{f}$	$= \frac{1}{2}(v - v_0)$. Prefer $\mathring{f}$ because of close association with primary f, g above. Also: $\mathring{f}_{ij} = \frac{1}{2}(v_j - v_i)$
f	Function (of q) used in Encke's method:

$$1 + 2q = r^2/r_e^2 \qquad fq = 1 - (1 + 2q)^{-\frac{3}{2}}$$

f	Frequency
f	True anomaly. Prefer v because of confusion with f's above.
flattening	See f; also called: oblateness, ellipticity, compression.
flight-path angle (γ)	Angle between velocity vector and plane perpendicular to radius vector; also "climb angle."
focus of attraction	Principal or dynamical focus, occupied by principal attracting mass: prefer to "center of attraction."
focus, empty	Secondary focus of conic, unoccupied.

G

G	Constant of gravitation in cgs or mks system. In astrodynamics the kilometer is preferred to the meter or the centimeter; accordingly the units of G are $km^3/gm\ sec^2$. Prefer k^2 for other systems.
G	$= \frac{1}{2}(E + E_0)$. Also: $G_{ij} = \frac{1}{2}(E_j + E_i)$
G	Velocity; see "V, v"

G	$= \sqrt{\mu p}$; prefer $\sqrt{\mu p}$ or h, except when using Delaunay variables (q.v.)
G.C.T., G.M.T.	Greenwich Civil Time, Greenwich Mean Time (q.v.)
GHA	Greenwich hour angle; also t_G; see "hour angle."
g	See "f, g"
g, g_e	Terrestrial acceleration of gravity; g_e = equatorial value.
g	Acceleration in general; prefer to a; also A.
g or $\mathring{g}$	$= \frac{1}{2}(E - E_0)$. Prefer $\mathring{g}$ to avoid confusion with primary f, g above. Also: $\mathring{g}_{ij} = \frac{1}{2}(E_j - E_0)$.
g	Argument of perifocus; prefer ω except when using "Delaunay variables" (q.v.)
gu	Geo-unit, or geocentric unit, nearly equal to the Earth's equatorial radius, a_e. Analogous to the astronomical unit of the heliocentric system.
γ (gamma)	Flight-path angle (q.v.)
γ	$= \sin i$ or $\sin \frac{1}{2}i$ in lunar and planetary theory
γ	Normal acceleration of gravity
Gauss-Jackson formula	Formula for numerically integrating second-order differential equations; also: second-sum formula, Σ^2 formula; see "Cowell's method."
geoid	The mean sea level surface of the earth. See "spheroid."
Gibb's expressions	See "c_1, c_3"
grave-variation ⎫ grave-derivative ⎭	$= \begin{cases} \text{perturbed variation} \\ \text{perturbed derivative} \end{cases}$
Greenwich Civil Time (G.C.T.)	$=$ Universal Time (U.T.)
Greenwich Mean Time (G.M.T.)	$=$ U.T. $+ 12^h$ before 1925.0 $=$ U.T. after 1925.0

H

H or h	Height above sea level, or height above the geoid; see "altitude"; prefer H.
H	$= \sqrt{\mu p} \cos i$; see "Delaunay variables."
H	Hamiltonian function
H or HA or h	Hour angle (q.v.)
h	Altitude (q.v.) or "elevation"
h	$= \sqrt{\mu p}$; angular momentum (see "$\mathbf{a}, \mathbf{b}, \mathbf{h}$"); also G, as one of the Delaunay variables (q.v.)
h	Longitude of ascending node; prefer Ω except when using Delaunay variables (q.v.)
h	Interval of argument in integration tables or in any interpolation table. Also: w.
h	Auxiliary quantity used in the Lambert-Euler formulae (see also $G, \mathring{g}, \epsilon, \delta$): $$\cos h = e \cos G$$
$\mathbf{h}(h_x, h_y, h_z)$	$= \sqrt{\mu p}\, \mathbf{W}$; angular momentum vector.
Hamiltonian function (H)	$H = \sum_s p_s \dot{q}_s - L$; also $-H = F$ (q.v.)
Hamilton's canonical equations	$\dot{q}_s = \dfrac{\partial H}{\partial p_s} \qquad \dot{p}_s = -\dfrac{\partial H}{\partial q_s}$

harmonics	Mathematical terms that indicate differences in the surface shape between a reference spheroid (e.g., for the Earth) and a sphere. "Zonal" harmonics indicate latitudinal differences; "sectoral" harmonics indicate longitudinal differences; "tesseral" harmonics include zonal and sectoral harmonics.
height (H)	Linear height above sea level; prefer to "altitude" (q.v.)
Hohmann orbit	Minimum energy heliocentric orbit tangent to the earth's orbit at one apsis and to that of the target planet at the other.
hour angle (t)	Angle measured in equator plane westward from local meridian, usually 0^h to 24^h; prefer (in order): t, HA, LHA, H; see "GHA"; the use of h for hour angle rather than angular altitude is undisciplined!
hour circles	Great circles that pass through the celestial pole, sometimes incorrectly referred to as "meridians."
hyperbolic anomaly (F)	Angle in hyperbola corresponding to E in the ellipse and D in the parabola: $F = iE$ where $i = \sqrt{-1}$, and $M = e \sinh F - F$. Also H.

I

I, J, K	$\mathbf{I}(I_x, I_y, I_z)$ is the unit vector along the x-axis in the reference plane (directed to ♈ in equatorial and ecliptic references). $\mathbf{J}$ is directed along the y-axis, $90°$ east from $\mathbf{I}$ in the reference plane. $\mathbf{K}$ forms a right-handed orthogonal set with $\mathbf{I}$, $\mathbf{J}$. Also: $\mathbf{i}$, $\mathbf{j}$, $\mathbf{k}$; prefer $\mathbf{I}$, $\mathbf{J}$, $\mathbf{K}$ in association with $\mathbf{P}$, $\mathbf{Q}$, $\mathbf{W}$ or $\mathbf{U}$, $\mathbf{V}$, $\mathbf{W}$, etc.
i	$= \sqrt{-1}$
i, I, ι (iota) ⎱ inclination ⎰	i is standard; I and ι are convenient when it has a perturbed variation; angle measured from the reference plane (ecliptic or equatorial) to the orbit plane. Limits of i: $0°$ and $180°$; or $0°$ and $90°$ if "direct" and "retrograde" are specified.
inertial axes	Axes which are fixed in direction, but which may have a moving origin (e.g., Sun or Earth) rather than an inertial one (e.g., the center of mass in the n-body problem).
indirect terms	The terms of the equations of motion (e.g., the relative-motion form) that represent the accelerations of the origin (e.g., the Sun); see "Encke terms"
initial ⎱ injection ⎰ insertion	These adjectives are sometimes used synonymously, along with burnout, launch, takeoff; writers should be careful to specify distinctions they wish to make.

J

J_n	Coefficients of zonal harmonics in the gravitational potential of a spheroid of revolution, defined under "potential of spheroid"
$J_{n,m}$	See "potential of spheroid"
J.D., J.E.D.	Julian Date, Julian Ephemeris Date (q.v.)
$\mathbf{J}(J_x, J_y, J_z)$	See "**I, J, K**"
jovicentric	Referred to the center of Jupiter; also: Jupiter-centered.
Julian Date (J.D.)	Universal Time (q.v.) expressed by a continuing day count.
Julian Ephemeris Date	Ephemeris Time (q.v.) similarly expressed:
(J.E.D.)	$$\text{J.E.D.} = \text{J.D.} + \Delta T$$

K

K	$= rr_0 \cos(v - v_0)$. See also: C, S, κ, σ.
$\tilde{K}$	$= \cos E = \cosh F$, etc., unified variable.
$\hat{K}$	$= \cos(E - E_0) = \cosh(F - F_0)$, etc., universal variable.
$\mathbf{K}(K_x, K_y, K_z)$	Unit vector perpendicular to reference plane; see "$\mathbf{I}$, $\mathbf{J}$, $\mathbf{K}$"
k, k^2	Gravitational constant, its value depending on units of time, mass and distance involved. See: k_s, k_e.
k_e	Geocentric gravitational constant:

$$k_e = 0.001\ 239\ 444[\mathrm{gu}^{\frac{3}{2}}/\mathrm{m}_{\oplus}^{\frac{1}{2}}\ \mathrm{sec}]$$

k_s or k	Gaussian or heliocentric gravitational constant:

$$k_s = 0.017\ 202\ 09895[\mathrm{au}^{\frac{3}{2}}/\mathrm{m}_{\odot}^{\frac{1}{2}}\ \mathrm{day}]$$

κ (kappa)	Auxiliary quantity used in development of closed expressions for f and g, in Lambert-Euler equation, etc.:

$$\kappa = \pm\sqrt{2(rr_0 + xx_0 + yy_0 + zz_0)} = 2\sqrt{rr_0}\cos\tfrac{1}{2}(v - v_0)$$

See also: σ, C, K, S.

kaday	The unit of $\tau = k_*(t - t_0)$ for heliocentric orbits; when k_*^2 and $\mu = k_s^2$, it is k_s^{-1} days $= 58.132\ 44087$ days
kesec	The unit of $\tau = k_*(t - t_0)$ for geocentric orbits; it has also been called the "kemin" because k_e was first based upon the minute rather than the second; when k_*^2 and $\mu = k_e^2$, it is

$$k_e^{-1}\ \mathrm{sec}\ = 13.446\ 8896\ \mathrm{min}$$

Kepler's equation	$M = E - e\sin E$, and variants thereof.
Kepler's first law	$r = p/(1 + e\cos v) = a(1 - e\cos E)$
Kepler's second law	$r^2\dot{v} = \sqrt{\mu p}$
Kepler's third law	$\mu P^2 = (2\pi)^2 a^3$ or $n^2 a^3 = \mu$

L

L, L_r	Mean longitude: $L = L_0 + n(t - t_0) = M + \omega + \Omega$; for retrograde orbits: $L_r = M + \omega - \Omega$. See "$l$, l_r" and "$\bar{\omega}$, $\bar{\omega}_r$"
L	Lagrangian function (q.v.)
L	$= \sqrt{\mu a}$; see "Delaunay variables."
L	Longitude, terrestrial (q.v.); prefer λ.
LHA	Local hour angle; also t; see "hour angle"
$\mathbf{L}$, $\mathbf{A}$, $\mathbf{D}$	$\mathbf{L}(L_x, L_y, L_z)$ is the unit vector directed from the observational reference point to the object. $\mathbf{A}$ is a unit vector perpendicular to $\mathbf{L}$, parallel to the equatorial plane, and directed with increasing right ascension, α. $\mathbf{D}$ is a unit vector such that $\mathbf{L}$, $\mathbf{A}$, $\mathbf{D}$ make up a right-handed orthogonal set, and so is directed with increasing declination, δ; so also $d\mathbf{L} = \mathbf{A}\cos\delta\,d\alpha + \mathbf{D}d\delta$:

$L_x = \cos\delta\cos\alpha$	$A_x = -\sin\alpha$	$D_x = -\sin\delta\cos\alpha$
$L_y = \cos\delta\sin\alpha$	$A_y = \cos\alpha$	$D_y = -\sin\delta\sin\alpha$
$L_z = \sin\delta$	$A_z = 0$	$D_z = \cos\delta$

Alt. to L_x, L_y, L_z: l, m, n; λ, μ, ν; α, β, γ; see introduction.

L, A_h, D_h

$L(L_{xh}, L_{yh}, L_{zh})$ is the unit vector directed from the observational reference point to the object. A_h is a unit vector perpendicular to L, parallel to the horizon plane, and directed with clockwise increasing azimuth, A. D_h is a unit vector such that L, A_h, D_h make up a left-handed orthogonal set, and so is directed with increasing altitude, h; so also $dL = A_h \cos h\, dA + D_h dh$:

$$
\begin{array}{lll}
L_{xh} = \cos h \cos A & A_{xh} = -\sin A & D_{xh} = -\sin h \cos A \\
L_{yh} = \cos h \sin A & A_{yh} = +\cos A & D_{yh} = -\sin h \sin A \\
L_{zh} = \sin h & A_{zh} = 0 & D_{zh} = +\cos h
\end{array}
$$

See "**Z, E, N**"

l, l_r

True longitude: $l = v + \omega + \Omega$; for retrograde motion: $l_r = v + \omega - \Omega$. See "$L, L_r$" and "$\bar\omega, \bar\omega_r$"

l

Mean anomaly. Prefer M, except when using Delaunay variables (q.v.).

l, m, n

Direction cosines. For preferred alternate see "**L, A, D**"

Λ (lambda)

$= E + \omega + \Omega$, to accompany $l = v + \omega + \Omega$, $L = M + \omega + \Omega$, $\bar\omega = \omega + \Omega$

λ (lambda)

Longitude, celestial (q.v.).

λ

Longitude, terrestrial (q.v.); also L

λ, μ, ν

Direction cosines. For preferred alternate see "**L, A, D**"

Lagrange's equations

$\dfrac{d}{dt}\dfrac{\partial T}{\partial \dot q_s} - \dfrac{\partial T}{\partial q_s} = Q_s$, where T denotes the kinetic energy of the body. If the forces involved have a potential function, then the equations have the form:

$$
\frac{d}{dt}\frac{\partial L}{\partial \dot q_s} - \frac{\partial L}{\partial q_s} = 0
$$

where L is the Lagrangian function.

Lagrangian function (L)

Kinetic energy minus potential energy, usually. In astronomy $L = T + \Phi$; see "potential function (Φ)"

Lambert-Euler equation

In elliptic motion often $n(t - t_0) = (\epsilon - \sin \epsilon) - (\delta - \sin \delta)$; ϵ, δ also α, β (q.v.).

Lambert's equation

In orbit determination the dynamical equation $\rho = A - B/r^3$

latitude, celestial (β)

Angle measured north or south from the ecliptic along a secondary great circle perpendicular to it; see "longitude, celestial."

latitude, terrestrial

Angle measured in a meridian plane from the Earth's equator to, e.g., the point of observation; see "$\varphi, \varphi_g, \varphi_a$" and φ'

latitude, argument of (u)

$= v + \omega$; see $U = M + \omega$, $\Upsilon = E + \omega$

launch

See "initial, injection, insertion"

Legendre polynomials

See P_n.

light time

Interval during which light travels from the observed object to the observer. See α.

line of nodes

Line formed by the intersection of the reference plane and the orbit plane.

longitude, celestial (λ)

Angle measured from vernal equinox along the ecliptic to the secondary circle passing through the object, geocentric or topocentric. See "latitude, celestial."

longitude, terrestrial (λ)	Angle measured from Greenwich meridian along the equator, east or west, to the meridian through, e.g., the point of observation. For geodesy and perturbation theory λ should be taken as positive eastward, negative westward. Also: L.
longitude, mean (L)	$= M + \omega + \Omega$; see "L, L_r" and $\Lambda = E + \omega + \Omega$
longitude, true (l)	$= v + \omega + \Omega$; see "l, l_r"
longitude of perifocus $(\tilde{\omega})$	$= \omega + \Omega$; see "$\tilde{\omega}, \tilde{\omega}_r$"

M

M, M_0	Mean anomaly (q.v.), mean anomaly at the epoch
m_1 or M	Mass at focus of attraction; prefer m_1 because of mean anomaly
m_2 or m	Mass of orbiting body
m_i, m_j	Masses of particles, planets, etc.
$m_\odot, m_\oplus, m_\mathbb{C}$, etc.	Masses of Sun, Earth, Moon, etc. See astronomical symbols at end.
m_0	Initial mass of a vehicle, before takeoff
m, m_0	See "magnitude"
μ (mu)	Mass function. In the two-body problem, $\mu = k^2(m_1 + m_2)$. More generally, $\mu = k^2(1 + m)$, where m may include some perturbation effects as well as $m_1 + m_2 - 1$.
μ	Ratio of mass of Moon to mass of Earth
$\mu, 1 - \mu$	Masses of principal bodies in restricted 3-body problem; μ is usually the smaller of the two masses.
μ	Index of refraction
μ	Mean angular motion; prefer n (q.v.)
μ_a	Ratio of the mass of the atmosphere to the mass of Earth.
magnitude (m, m_0)	Measures of the brightness of an object, often calculated from

$$m = g + 5 \log \rho + 5 \log r + C\beta^0$$

where g is a constant determined from observed values, ρ and r are geocentric and heliocentric distances, β^0 is the phase angle (in degrees), and C is a constant; for m_0: $r = a$, $\rho = a - 1$, $\beta^0 = 0$ (a hypothetical "mean" opposition).

mean anomaly (M)	Angle measured from perifocus through which a body would have travelled if it were moving uniformly at its mean angular velocity, n:

$$M = M_0 + n(t - t_0) = n(t - T)$$

where M_0 is the value of M at epoch t_0 and T is the time of perifocal passage. Also l; prefer M except when using Delaunay variables (q.v.)

mean distance (a)	Semi major axis (q.v.)
mean motion mean angular motion $\Big\}$ mean angular velocity	See "n"
meridian, celestial	The hour circle that passes through the zenith.

N

n	Mean angular motion of a body in orbit; see "mean anomaly"; also sometimes μ, but prefer n because of the notation:

$$n = \sqrt{\mu}\, a^{-\frac{3}{2}}$$

$n_1,\ n_2,\ n_3$	Ratios of the triangles (n_1,n_3), or quantities proportional to the triangles (n_1,n_2,n_3); prefer c_1, c_3 (q.v.)
ν (nu)	True anomaly; prefer v; the rather curious use of ν may come from misreading of classical French works printed from type-fonts in which there are two italic v's. One is used at the beginnings of words; the other, used internally and in equations, closely resembles the Greek ν (e.g., Tisserand, v. 1, pp. 3, 25, 26).
n-body problem	Orbit problem involving only the mutual gravitational attractions of n bodies.
node	Intersection of orbit with a reference plane.
node (Ω)	Angle measured in reference plane from the vernal equinox to the ascending node of the orbit; "node" is an abridgement of "longitude of the ascending node"; Ω_ϵ may be used for the angle in the ecliptic plane, and Ω_α for that in the equatorial plane. Note that the node symbol (Ω) is not the same as the capital omega (Ω), though the latter may be used when the type-font lacks Ω.
north celestial pole (P_n)	Point where the Earth's axis of rotation extended from the northern hemisphere intersects the celestial sphere.
north point (N)	Origin for azimuth in horizon system of coordinates, defined by an intersection of horizon with the celestial meridian, a great circle through the observer's zenith and the north celestial pole.
nutation	The periodic terms of the precession-nutation complex that describes the motion of the Earth's axis of rotation.

O

o	Subscript designating a quantity or value associated with the epoch, t_0.
o	Subscript sometimes used to designate a quantity or value associated with the Encke or other reference orbit; prefer subscript e or R to avoid confusion with the preceding use of subscript o.
Ω (omega)	See "node (Ω)"
Ω	Perturbing function; prefer R
ω (omega)	Argument of perifocus
ω	Angular velocity
$\tilde{\omega},\ \tilde{\omega}_r$	Longitude of perifocus: $\tilde{\omega} = \omega + \Omega$; for retrograde orbits $\tilde{\omega}_r = \omega - \Omega$; also π, π_r (see L, L_r). If you want to be intelligible, call $\tilde{\omega}$ "omega-tilde," not "π."
oblateness	See f and "flattening"; some would prefer to use "oblateness" for J_2, and restrict it thereto.
obliquity of the ecliptic (ϵ)	Inclination of the ecliptic plane to the equatorial plane. Its true value for a given date (varying slightly from $23\tfrac{1}{2}°$) may be found with the solar coordinates in the national ephemerides. Its mean value for a given date may be found in *Planetary Coordinates*.

orbit	A path in space; more specifically, a set of constants defining it; the set can include physical constants as well as the six elements or constants of integration; also "state vector" or "state."
orbit	Period, or revolution; this recent introduction is expressive in popular discussions or news reporting, but should be avoided, in favor of the standard terms, in precise scientific writing.
orientation angles	The elements i, Ω, ω; see "Eulerian angles"
osculating orbit	An approximation to the actual path of an object derived from the actual position and velocity at a given moment; usually a two-body orbit.

osculating variation ⎫
osculating derivative ⎭
$= \begin{Bmatrix} \text{two-body variation} \\ \text{two-body derivative} \end{Bmatrix}$ (q.v.), but are more general terms that can be used whether or not the reference solution is a two-body orbit.

P

P	Period of revolution
P_n	Legendre polynomial, used in the development of the potential function in series form:

$$P_0(x) = 1 \qquad\qquad P_1(x) = x$$
$$P_2(x) = \tfrac{1}{2}(3x^2 - 1) \qquad P_3(x) = \tfrac{1}{2}(5x^3 - 3x)$$
$$P_4(x) = \tfrac{1}{8}(35x^4 - 30x^2 + 3)$$
$$P_n(x) = \frac{2n - 1}{n}\, xP_{n-1}(x) - \frac{n - 1}{n}\, P_{n-2}(x)$$

P_n^m or P_{nm}	Associated Legendre functions defined by

$$P_n^m(x) = (1 - x^2)^{\frac{1}{2}m} \frac{d^m}{dx^m} P_n(x)$$

P, Q, W
$\mathbf{P}(P_x, P_y, P_z)$ is the unit vector directed toward the perifocus. $\mathbf{Q}$ is directed 90° from $\mathbf{P}$ in the direction of motion of the object in the orbital plane. $\mathbf{W}$ is perpendicular to the orbital plane, thus forming a right-handed orthogonal set with $\mathbf{P}$ and $\mathbf{Q}$.

p, p_i	See "parameter"
p_s	Component of generalized momentum: $p_s = \dfrac{\partial L}{\partial \dot{q}_s}$
p_α	Annual precession in right ascension:

$$p_\alpha = m^s + n^s \sin \alpha \tan \delta$$

p_δ	Annual precession in declination:

$$p_\delta = n'' \cos \alpha$$

Φ (phi)	Potential function (q.v.)
φ, φ_g, φ_a (phi)	φ is used for geodetic latitude (φ_g), which is the angle between the normal to a reference spheroid and the plane of the equator. φ is also used for astronomical latitude (φ_a), which is the angle between the direction of gravity and the plane of the equator, and which differs from the geodetic latitude by "station error" or "local anomaly." φ_g is asso-

ciated with the reference spheroid; φ_a, with the geoid. Both φ_g and φ_a are sometimes called, indiscriminately, "geographic latitude."

φ' — Geocentric latitude: angle between a radius from the center of reference spheroid and the plane of its equator.

φ — Angle of eccentricity: $\sin \varphi = e$, $\cos \varphi = \sqrt{1 - e^2}$ Convenient in logarithmic calculation, but now exists only as a confusing holdover. Used as argument in some tables.

$\Pi_\odot$ (pi) — Solar parallax, i.e., Sun's mean geocentric equatorial horizontal parallax; also $\pi_\odot$

$\Pi_\mathbb{C}$ — Moon's varying geocentric equatorial horizontal parallax; also $\pi_\mathbb{C}$

π, π_r (pi) — Longitude of perifocus: $\pi = \omega + \Omega$; for retrograde motion, $\pi_r = \omega - \Omega$. Prefer $\tilde{\omega}$, $\tilde{\omega}_r$ (q.v.)

ψ (psi) — Elongation; angle at the observational reference point between the directions of the dynamical center and the observed object, i.e., between the vectors **R** and **L**

parallax — Geocentric equatorial horizontal parallax is the angle at an object subtended by the earth's equatorial radius and is a measure of distance of objects in the solar system. Heliocentric parallax is the angle at an object subtended by the radius of the earth's orbit and is a measure of distance of objects outside the solar system: Π, π

parameter — Not generally used in its broad mathematical senses, but specialized in astrodynamics to:
(1) The semi latus rectum of a conic; usually designated by p
(2) A selected two-body element or variable (e.g., a or M), or a constant of integration in an analytic solution of some problem, used as a variable in the method of variation of parameters; sometimes designated by p_i

periapsis
pericenter — Perifocus (q.v.)

perifocal distance (q) — $= a(1 - e)$, distance between focus and perifocus

perifocus — Point in orbit nearest focus of attraction; the nearer apsis; perigee in geocentric orbit, perihelion in heliocentric orbit, etc.; also "pericenter;" "periapsis" should be avoided. See "apofocus"

perifocus, argument of (ω) — Angle measured in orbit plane from node to perifocus.

perifocus, longitude of ($\tilde{\omega}$) — $\tilde{\omega} = \omega + \Omega$; for retrograde motion, $\tilde{\omega}_r = \omega - \Omega$; also π, π_r.

perturbation (1) — Deviation from a reference orbit in force, acceleration, velocity, position, etc., because of effects not included therein. "General perturbations" involve series expansion before integration. "Special perturbations" are integrated numerically. "Secular perturbations" vary directly with time.

perturbation (2) — The engineer's term for an arbitrary variation of initial conditions, now sanctioned by time; prefer "variant" whenever there is a possibility of confusion between the two usages.

perturbed differentiation

In the method of variation of parameters, a technique (alternative to that of Hamiltonian mechanics) in which the equations for the variations are obtained by differentiations in which the "two-body derivatives" are omitted. See "perturbed variation," "two-body variation"

perturbed variation ⎱
perturbed derivative ⎰
perturbative ⎰

In the method of variation of parameters, that part of the total derivative or variation that is added by the perturbations:

$\frac{df}{dt} = \dot{f} + \acute{f}$, where $\acute{f}$ is the perturbed part and $\dot{f}$ is the two-

body part of the total derivative. Also called the "grave-derivative" (or "grave-variation"). See "perturbed differentiation," "two-body variation"

perturbing function (R)

That portion of the potential function (Φ) which takes into account perturbations caused by conservative forces, e.g.,

$\Phi = \frac{\mu}{r} + R$, where $\frac{\mu}{r}$ denotes the two-body portion of Φ.

Also: Ω; disturbing function. See "potential function (Φ)."

planetary aberration

Discrepancy between calculation and observation that results when "light time" is neglected.

precession

The secular term of the motion of the Earth's axis of rotation with respect to inertial axes.

potential function (Φ)
or "potential"

Function proportional to the potential energy, usually negatively proportional in astronomical and astrodynamical practice; also U or V; e.g., two-body potential: $\Phi = \mu/r$.

potential of spheroid

Potential function associated with, e.g.:

(a) spheroid of revolution:

$$\Phi = \frac{\mu}{r}\left[1 - \sum_{n=1}^{\infty} J_n \left(\frac{a_e}{r}\right)^n P_n (\sin \delta)\right]$$

(b) general spheroid:

$$\Phi = \frac{\mu}{r}\left\{1 + \sum_{n=1}^{\infty} \sum_{m=0}^{n} \left(\frac{a_e}{r}\right)^n P_n^m (\sin \delta)[C_{n,m} \cos m\lambda \right.$$
$$\left. + S_{n,m} \sin m\lambda]\right\}$$

where a_e is the equatorial radius, δ is the geocentric (or planetocentric) declination or latitude, and the attracted object has negligible mass. Also: $-J_n = C_{n,0} = C_n$; $C_{n,m}^2 + S_{n,m}^2 = J_{n,m}^2$; $\delta = \varphi = \beta$; $\Phi = U = V$; $\mu = k^2m$; $n,m = l,m$. See P_n, P_n^m and *IAU Trans.*, **11B** (1961), 173-174. Form (b) is often replaced by one of several forms in which the coefficients are fully normalized.

Q

Q_s

Generalized force: $Q_s = \ddot{\mathbf{r}} \cdot \dfrac{\partial \mathbf{r}}{\partial q_s}$

$\mathbf{Q}(Q_x, Q_y, Q_z)$

See "**P, Q, W**"

$\tilde{\mathbf{Q}}$	$= \sqrt{p}\,\mathbf{Q}$, a vector that is determinate for rectilinear orbits, for which $\mathbf{Q}$ is not.
q, q_2	Perifocal distance: $q = a(1 - e)$. Apofocal distance: $q_2 = a(1 + e) = r_A$; prefer r_A.
q	Auxiliary quantity used in Encke's method in special perturbations:

$$q = \xi(x_e + \tfrac{1}{2}\xi) + \eta(y_e + \tfrac{1}{2}\eta) + \zeta(z_e + \tfrac{1}{2}\zeta)/r^2 e$$

$q_\bullet$	Generalized coordinate, or angle or position variable in a canonical set (see "Hamilton's canonical equations")

R

R	Magnitude of $\mathbf{R}$; distance from point of observation to focus of attraction.
R	Geocentric distance; prefer r_c (q.v.)
R	Perturbing function (or "disturbing function")
$R = R\left[\dfrac{km}{gu}\right] = R[km]$	Length conversion factor, geo-units to kilometers; gu expressed in km.
$\mathbf{R}(X,Y,Z)$	Position vector directed from the point of observation to the focus of attraction.
$\mathbf{R}(R_x,R_y,R_z)$	See "$\mathbf{W}(W_x,W_y,W_z)$," which should be preferred because of conflict with $\mathbf{R}(X,Y,Z)$; see introduction also.
$\tilde{\mathbf{R}}(\tilde{X},\tilde{Y},\tilde{Z})$	Vector from the focus of attraction to the point of observation, used in place of $-\mathbf{R}$ when the conventional $\mathbf{R}$ orientation seems inappropriate.
r, r_i, r_j	Distance of object from focus of attraction; see "radius vector."
r_2	Distance of the object from the secondary focus of a conic.
r_A	$= a(1 + e)$; apofocal distance
r_c	$= \sqrt{x_c^2 + y_c^2}$; distance from center of Earth to a point at or near the surface; also ρ, R; prefer r_c; see "x_c, y_c"
r_{ij}	Distance from m_i to m_j.
$\mathbf{r}(x,y,z)$	Radius vector, directed from the focus of attraction to the object whose motion is under study.
ρ (rho)	Topocentric distance or "range" of any object: $\rho = |\boldsymbol{\rho}|$; also Δ (see introduction).
$\boldsymbol{\rho}(\xi,\eta,\zeta)$	Topocentric vector or similar vector directed from the point of observation to the object whose motion is under study, e.g., $\xi = x + X$
$\boldsymbol{\rho}(\xi,\eta,\zeta)$	Difference in position between the actual orbit and a reference orbit in Encke's method of special perturbations, e.g., $\xi = x - x_e$
radius vector (r)	Established mathematical term for $r = p/(1 + e\cos v)$; not a vector in the modern usage of the term; plurals: radius vectors, radii vectores.
range (ρ)	See ρ, $\boldsymbol{\rho}$
ratios of the triangles	In the orbit methods of Gauss, Olbers, et al., the ratios of the triangles formed by the radii and chords are calculated from the corresponding time intervals, with greater or less approximation; see "c_1, c_3"

ratios of sectors or time intervals	See "A_1, A_3"
ratio of sector to triangle $(\bar{y})$	$\bar{y} = \sqrt{\mu p}\ (t - t_0)/S$
rectification	The process of shifting to a new (usually osculating) reference orbit in Encke's method when the Encke terms associated with the old reference orbit become too large.
rectilinear orbit	Orbit for which $e = 1$, $p = 0$, $q = 0$.
reference orbit	An orbit, often a fixed two-body ellipse, to which perturbative effects are added to obtain the perturbed orbit; see "Encke's method," ρ
representation	Calculation of position of a body for a given date (usually the date of an observation) from a given set of elements. Usually compared with an observation to determine validity of the elements, i.e., whether a differential correction is required.
residuals	Differences between given data (O) that are observed, measured, or otherwise determined, and the corresponding "represented" data (C) that are calculated from conjectured values of the parameters. See "differential correction" and "representation."
right ascension (α)	Topocentric or geocentric coordinate measured along celestial equator eastward, usually 0^h to 24^h, from vernal equinox to hour circle through object. As a subscript α may be used to indicate equatorial coordinates. See "declination (δ)"
Runge-Kutta formulae	Formulae for the numerical integration of differential equations.

S

S	$= C(1 - e^2) = a_e(1 - e^2)/\sqrt{1 - e^2 \sin^2 \varphi}$, quantity tabulated in the almanacs for finding geocentric coordinates; see also C, x_c, y_c
S	$= rr_0 \sin (v - v_0)$, twice the area of the triangle; also $S_{ij} = r_i r_j \sin (v_j - v_i)$; see "$c_1$, c_3," "ratios of the triangles," "ratio of sector to triangle"; see also C, K, κ, σ
S	$= \sqrt{1 - e^2} \sin E$; prefer next definition.
S	$= \sin E = D/e \sqrt{a}$
$\bar{S}$	$= \sqrt{a} \sin E = \sqrt{-a} \sinh F$, unified variable.
$\hat{S}$	$= \sqrt{a} \sin (E - E_0) = \sqrt{-a} \sinh (F - F_0)$, universal variable.
$S = S\left[\dfrac{gm}{m_\odot}\right]$ or $S[gm]$	Mass conversion factor, solar masses to grams; mass of Sun in grams.
S	Determining function of a canonical transformation
$S_{n,m}$ or $S_{l,m}$	Coefficient of a sectoral harmonic; see "potential of spheroid"
S, T, W	$\mathbf{S}(S_x, S_y, S_z)$ is the tangential unit vector: $\mathbf{S} = \dot{\mathbf{r}}/\dot{s}$. The normal unit vector $\mathbf{T}$ is also the orbital plane, 90° from $\mathbf{S}$ in the same sense as the direction of motion. $\mathbf{W}$ forms a right-handed orthogonal set with $\mathbf{S}$, $\mathbf{T}$.

$\dot{s}$ Magnitude of the velocity vector, $\dot{\mathbf{r}}$:

$$\dot{s}^2 = \dot{x}^2 + \dot{y}^2 + \dot{z}^2 = \dot{\mathbf{r}} \cdot \dot{\mathbf{r}}$$

See s and "vis-viva integral"; also see "V, v"

s Length of arc between two positions on an orbit.

s Length of the chord between two positions $\mathbf{r}_0$ and $\mathbf{r}$ on an orbit; also c:

$$s^2 = (x - x_0)^2 + (y - y_0)^2 + (z - z_0)^2$$

Σ, Σ^2 (sigma) Sums in numerical integration tables and formulae; also

$$\Sigma^2 \ddot{x}_i = \Delta^{-2} \ddot{x}_{i+1} = \nabla^{-2} \ddot{x}_{i-1}, \text{ etc.}$$

Σ^2 formula See "second-sum formula."

σ (sigma) $= 2\sqrt{rr_0} \sin \frac{1}{2}(v - v_0)$; also $\sigma_{ij} = 2\sqrt{r_i r_j} \sin \frac{1}{2}(v_j - v_i)$; used in development of closed expressions for f and g, in Lambert-Euler equation, etc., see also κ, C, K, S

σ Density

σ Standard deviation

second-difference formula Formula for numerical integration of second-order differential equations; also "δ^2 formula," "Adams-Moulton formula"

second-sum formula Formula for numerical integration of second-order differential equations; also "Gauss-Jackson formula," "Σ^2 formula"

sectoral harmonics See "harmonics"

selenocentric Having the center of the moon as focus of attraction or origin of coordinates; prefer "moon-centered"

semi latus rectum (p) $= a(1 - e^2)$, one half of the chord passing through a focus and perpendicular to the major axis; also "semi-parameter" or "parameter" (q.v.)

semi major axis (a) One-half the distance from the perifocus to the apofocus of an ellipse; also "mean distance"

sidereal time (θ) The hour angle of the vernal equinox; the right ascension of the celestial meridian.

solar parallax $(\Pi_\odot)$ The angle that (in radians) is equal to the ratio of equatorial radius to the astronomical unit.

spheroid A symmetrical mathematical approximation to the geoid: e.g., an ellipsoid of revolution.

T

T Time of perifocal passage

T Period; prefer P because of preceding well-established usage

T Time measured in Julian centuries from some epoch such as 1900.0

T Kinetic energy, or K. E. per unit mass in many astrodynamic applications

$\mathbf{T}(T_x, T_y, T_z)$ See "$\mathbf{S}, \mathbf{T}, \mathbf{W}$"

t Time; true time (i.e., the time the light left the object). Distinguished from "observed time" by $t = t_{\text{obs}} - \alpha\rho$.

t Hour angle or local hour angle; also H or HA or LHA

t_0 · The epoch (q.v.)

t_{obs} · Time of observation; see t (true time)

τ (tau) · Canonical or normalized time variable: $\tau = k_*(t - t_0)$, or $\tau_j = k_*(t_j - t_0)$, where k_* may have the numerical value of $\sqrt{\mu}$, but not its dimension or units. Alternative notations are:

(a) $\tau_{ij} = k_*(t_j - t_i)$ (the "unambiguous convention")

(b) $\left.\begin{cases} \tau_1 = k_*(t_1 - t_2) \\ \tau_3 = k_*(t_3 - t_2) \end{cases}\right\}$ (the "Laplacian convention")

(c) $\left.\begin{cases} \tau_1 = k_*(t_3 - t_2) \\ \tau_2 = k_*(t_3 - t_1) \\ \tau_3 = k_*(t_2 - t_1) \end{cases}\right\}$ (the "Gaussian convention")

The unambiguous convention is to be preferred when there might be confusion between the other two.

τ_A · Time required for light to travel one astronomical unit; also α_s, α (q.v.)

θ (theta) · Sidereal time

θ_g · Greenwich sidereal time

θ · Angle measured in the orbital plane to the radius vector from an origin that is not subject to longitudinal perturbed variation

θ · Flight-path angle (q.v.); prefer γ

takeoff · See "initial, injection, insertion"

tesseral harmonics · See "harmonics"

topocentric · Referred to the point of observation

true anomaly (v) · Angle measured at the focus from the perifocal vector $\mathbf{P}$ to the radius vector $\mathbf{r}$; also f, but prefer v (see "f")

triaxial ellipsoid · Ellipsoidal figure having three orthogonal axes of symmetry

two-body variation / two-body derivative · In the method of variation of parameters, that part of the total derivative or variation that is attributed to the object at the focus of attraction:

$\dfrac{df}{dt} = \dot{f} + f^{\backprime}$, where $\dot{f}$ is the two-body part and $f^{\backprime}$ is the perturbed part of the total derivative. Also called the "dot-variation" or "osculating variation" (or " . . . derivative"). When the parameters p_i are all constants of the two body problem (or osculating solution), we may recognize

$$\dot{f} = \frac{\partial f}{\partial t} \qquad f^{\backprime} = \sum_{i=1}^{6} \frac{\partial f}{\partial p_i}\frac{dp_i}{dt} \qquad \frac{dp_i}{dt} = p_i^{\backprime}$$

When the parameters include a two-body variable such as the mean anomaly M,

$$\dot{f} = \frac{\partial f}{\partial M}\dot{M} \qquad f^{\backprime} = \sum_{i=1}^{5} \frac{\partial f}{\partial p_i}p_i^{\backprime} + \frac{\partial f}{\partial M}\dot{M}^{\backprime} \qquad \dot{M} = n$$

U

U · $= M + \omega = U_0 + n(t - t_0)$, mean argument of latitude

U	$= E - \sin E$
$\tilde{U}$	$= a^{\frac{3}{2}}(E - \sin E) = (-a)^{\frac{3}{2}}(\sinh F - F)$, etc., unified variable
$\hat{U}$	$= a^{\frac{3}{2}}(E - E_0) - \sin (E - E_0) = (-a)^{\frac{3}{2}} \sinh (F - F_0) - (F - F_0)$, etc., universal variable.
U	Potential function (q.v.)
U.T.	Universal time (q.v.)
U, V, W	$\mathbf{U}(U_x,U_y,U_z)$ is the unit vector directed along the radius vector from the dynamical center to the object. **V** is directed 90° from **U** in the direction of motion of the object in the orbital plane. **W** is perpendicular to the orbital plane, thus forming a right-handed orthogonal set with **U, V**; see "**P, Q, W**"
u	$= v + \omega$, (true) argument of latitude
u	Eccentric anomaly; prefer E because of preceding well-established usage.
Υ (upsilon)	$= E + \omega$, to accompany $u = v + \omega$, $U = M + \omega$
Υ	See "vernal equinox (Υ)"
υ (upsilon)	Generally not used because of similarity to u
Universal Time (U.T.)	$=$ G.C.T. $=$ G.M.T. after 1925.0
	$=$ G.M.T. $- 12^h$ before 1925.0
	$=$ E.T. $- \Delta$T

V

V, v	$= \dot{s} = ds/dt$, velocity per unit of t; also "G" (for Geschwindigkeit); prefer $\dot{s}$, V (see introduction)
V_c	$= \sqrt{\mu/r}$, circular velocity
V_p	$= \sqrt{2\mu/r}$, parabolic velocity, or velocity of escape
V_∞	$= \sqrt{-\mu/a}$, velocity at infinity, imaginary for elliptic orbits
V	Potential function (q.v.)
$\mathbf{V}(V_x,V_y,V_z)$	See "**U, V, W**"
$\hat{\mathbf{V}}$	$= \sqrt{p}\ \mathbf{V}$, a vector that is determinate for rectilinear orbits, for which **V** is not.
v	True anomaly; also f (q.v.)
$\dot{v}$	Angular velocity (q.v.)
variant calculations	Method of calculating the partial differential coefficients that are used in differential correction formulae, rendezvous correction, etc.; see "perturbation (2)"
variation	Used in astrodynamics as the rate of change in the value of a parameter with respect to time. It is noted that this definition is unlike the general usage of the word, in which "variation" indicates a modification or deviation. See "perturbed variation" and "two-body variation"
variation of parameters	Perturbation technique in which the constants of the 2-body orbit, or of the analytical solution of an approximation to an actual problem, are allowed to vary.
vernal equinox (Υ)	That intersection of the ecliptic and celestial equator where the Sun crosses from south to north (approximately March 21). Note that the vernal equinox symbol Υ is not the capital upsilon (Υ), which should not be used for it unless the type-font lacks Υ; distinction between Υ and Υ is more stringent than that between $\mho$ and Ω; see "node."

vertical circle	Great circle passing through the zenith.
virtual increment	An increment, as a "virtual displacement," $\delta \mathbf{r}$, that is not necessarily nor usually the same as a time-displacement along a dynamical path, e.g., as in the establishment of Lagrange's equations. Of the same character as a differential correction.
vis-viva integral	$\dot{s}^2 = \mu \left(\dfrac{2}{r} - \dfrac{1}{a} \right)$; also "energy integral"

W

$\mathbf{W}(W_x, W_y, W_z)$	Unit vector perpendicular to orbit plane; see "$\mathbf{P}, \mathbf{Q}, \mathbf{W}$"; "$\mathbf{U}, \mathbf{V}, \mathbf{W}$"; "$\mathbf{R}(R_x, R_y, R_z)$"; introduction.
w	Interval of argument in integration tables or in any interpolation table. Also: h

X, Y, Z

X, Y, Z	See "$\mathbf{R}(X,Y,Z)$"
X	$= E$ or F or D
$\tilde{X}$	$= \sqrt{a}\, E$ or $\sqrt{-a}\, F$ or D, unified variable
$\hat{X}$	$= \sqrt{a}\, (E - E_0)$ or $\sqrt{-a}\, (F - F_0)$ or $D - D_0$, universal variable
Z	Azimuth (q.v.)
$\mathbf{Z}, \mathbf{E}, \mathbf{N}$	Right-handed orthogonal set of unit vectors directed to zenith, east point, north point, useful in rotation from equatorial to horizon system: e.g.,

$$L_{xh} = \mathbf{L} \cdot \mathbf{N} \qquad L_{yh} = \mathbf{L} \cdot \mathbf{E} \qquad L_{zh} = \mathbf{L} \cdot \mathbf{Z}$$

where

$$\mathbf{Z} = \begin{Bmatrix} \cos \varphi \cos \theta \\ \cos \varphi \sin \theta \\ \sin \varphi \end{Bmatrix} \quad \mathbf{E} = \begin{Bmatrix} -\sin \theta \\ +\cos \theta \\ 0 \end{Bmatrix} \quad \mathbf{N} = \begin{Bmatrix} -\sin \varphi \cos \theta \\ -\sin \varphi \sin \theta \\ +\cos \varphi \end{Bmatrix}$$

See: "$\mathbf{L}, \mathbf{A}, \mathbf{D}$"; "$\mathbf{L}, \mathbf{A}_h, \mathbf{D}_h$"

x, y, z	See "$\mathbf{r}(x,y,z)$"
x_c, y_c	Coordinates referred to the geometrical center and major axis of an ellipse; geocentric coordinates in the plane of a meridian:

$$\left. \begin{aligned} x_c &= r_c \cos \varphi' = C \cos \varphi \\ y_c &= r_c \sin \varphi' = S \sin \varphi \end{aligned} \right\} \text{ See } C, S, \varphi, \varphi'$$

x_ω, y_ω	Coordinates referred to the focus and transverse axis of a conic: $x_\omega = r \cos v$, $y_\omega = r \sin v$
$\bar{y}$	$= \sqrt{\mu p}\, (t - t_0)/S$, ratio of sector to triangle
z	$= 90 - h$, zenith distance
ξ, η, ζ (xi, eta, zeta)	See "$\boldsymbol{\rho}(\xi, \eta, \zeta)$"
zenith	Intersection (upper) of direction of gravity and the celestial sphere
zonal harmonics	See "harmonics"

Astronomical symbols in common use in astrodynamics:

☉	Sun	♈	Vernal equinox (q.v.)
☿	Mercury	☊	Node (q.v.); also Ω
♀	Venus	☄	Comet
⊕	Earth	☽	Moon
♂	Mars		
♃ or ♃	Jupiter		
♄	Saturn		
♅ or ♅	Uranus		
♆	Neptune		
♇	Pluto		

Special uses of mathematical symbols:

˙, ¨	Derivatives with respect to τ; restricted to "two-body variations" (q.v.) in method of variation of parameters.
ˋ, ˵	"Perturbed variations" (q.v.) in method of variation of parameters.
∇	Del or nabla; listed under D

Acknowledgements for helpful suggestions and comments are due especially to J. D. Anderson, R. M. L. Baker, Jr., R. A. Broucke, C. J. Cohen, C. G. Jacchia, W. M. Kaula, D. G. King-Hele, J. D. Mulholland, C. Oesterwinter, D. A. Pierce, E. Rabe; M. S. W. Keesey was very helpful in an earlier stage of the compilation.

TABLES OF SOLID ANGLES

COMPILED BY DR. A. VICTOR MASKET

Abridged from U.S. Atomic Energy Commission Report TID-14975 (July, 1962), *Tables of Solid Angles*, by A. V. H. Masket and William C. Rodgers; composed at the Computation Center, University of North Carolina, Chapel Hill, North Carolina; abridgment prepared at General Atomic Division, General Dynamics Corporation, San Diego 12, California; reproduced with permission of the U.S. Atomic Energy Commission.

I. SOLID ANGLE SUBTENDED BY THE CIRCULAR DISC

Let the point in space at which the solid angle is subtended be 0, an origin of coordinate systems. The normal to the plane of the disc from 0 defines the z-axis and the normal to the symmetry axis of the disc defines the x-axis. *All lengths are considered normalized relative to the radius of the disc as a unit of length.* The solid angle is represented by the symbol $\Omega(1;\rho,z)$, where ρ is the distance (along the x-axis) from 0 to the symmetry axis and z is the distance (along the z-axis) from 0 to the plane of the disc. From the general expression for solid angles given by $\Omega = \iint \sin\theta\, d\theta\, d\phi$ in spherical polar coordinates, three contour integrals have been derived, which correspond to the cases with ρ less than, equal to, or greater than the radius of the disc as a unit of length.

Case 1. $\rho < 1$; the z-axis pierces the interior of the disc.

The contour integral employed for digital computation is

$$(1) \qquad \Omega(1;\rho,z) = 2 \cdot \int_0^\pi f_1^2 [1 + f_1^2 + (1 + f_1^2)^{1/2}]^{-1}\, d\phi \qquad (\rho < 1),$$

where $f_1 = S_1/z$, $S_1 = \rho\cos\phi + (1 - \rho^2 \sin^2\phi)^{1/2}$. When $\rho = 0$, $\Omega(1;0,z) = 2\pi[1 - z/(1+z^2)^{1/2}]$, exactly.

Case 2. $\rho = 1$; the z-axis touches the periphery of the disc.

$$(2) \qquad \Omega(1;1,z) = 2 \cdot \int_0^{\pi/2} f_2^2 [1 + f_2^2 + (1 + f_2^2)^{1/2}]^{-1}\, d\phi,$$

with $f_2 = (2\cos\phi)/z$. In elliptic integrals, the formula is given exactly by $\Omega(1;1,z) = \pi - kzK(k)$, where $k^2 = 4/(z^2 + 4)$ and $K(k) \equiv F(\pi/2,k)$ is the complete elliptic integral of the first kind.

Case 3. $\rho > 1$; the z-axis is external to the disc.

The computational form, where $S_2 = \rho\cos\phi - (1 - \rho^2 \sin^2\phi)^{1/2}$, is

$$(3) \qquad \Omega(1;\rho,z)_{(\rho>1)} = 2z \int_0^{\arcsin(1/\rho)} \frac{(S_1^2 - S_2^2)\, d\phi}{[(z^2 + S_1^2)(z^2 + S_2^2)]^{1/2}[(z^2 + S_1^2)^{1/2} + (z^2 + S_2^2)^{1/2}]}.$$

The solid angle subtended by the circular disc is expressed most generally in elliptic integrals. In conformity with the definitions adopted for ρ and z,

(4) $\quad \Omega(1;\rho,z) = 2\pi - 2[k'K(k)\sin\alpha + K(k)\cdot E(k',\alpha) - F(k',\alpha)\{K(k) - E(k)\}],$

where $k^2 = 4\rho/[(1+\rho)^2 + z^2]$, $(k')^2 = 1 - k^2$, $\alpha = (\pi - \phi)/2$, and $K(k)$ and $E(k)$ are the complete elliptic integrals, and $F(k',\alpha)$ and $E(k',\alpha)$ are the corresponding (incomplete) elliptic integrals of the first and second kind. The formula given by (4) is valid for all values of ρ and z; it is not convenient for computation. When $z > 100$, it is practical to use $\Omega \sim (\pi/d^2)\cdot\cos\gamma$ where d is the normalized distance from 0 to the center of the disc and γ is the projection angle. Accurate approximations are discussed in the references and literature.

II. SOLID ANGLE SUBTENDED BY THE RIGHT CIRCULAR CYLINDER

The tabulated values consist of the solid angles subtended only by the lateral surface at points in the plane of a circular flat (base) external to a cylinder of given radius and height. It will be shown that these values alone or taken in conjunction with the values of solid angles subtended by the circular disc are sufficient to cover the general case of any point in space external to the right circular cylinder. *All lengths are normalized with respect to the radius of the cylinder as a unit of length.* The variables of the table are h, the normalized height of the cylinder, and ρ, the normalized distance from the point (at which the solid angle is subtended) to the axis of the cylinder. With these definitions, the solid angle is represented by $\Omega(1,h;\rho)$.

Let the point in the plane of a flat be 0, the origin of coordinate systems. The z-axis is the normal to the plane and the x-axis is the line in the plane from 0 to the axis of the cylinder. The solid angle subtended at 0 by the lateral surface of the cylinder is given by the contour integral.

(5) $$\Omega(1,h;\rho) = 2h \int_0^{\arcsin(1/\rho)} [h^2 + S_2^2]^{-1/2}\, d\phi \qquad [\rho \geqq 1],$$

where ϕ is the azimuthal angle of the associated spherical polar system.

If a point is not located in a plane determined by a flat of the cylinder, then it is either interior or exterior to the space between the planes of the flats. In the first case, a plane through the point normal to the cylindrical axis determines two smaller cylinders and two solid angles in accordance with (5) which are added. For the second case, where a flat is viewed from 0 in addition to the lateral surface, let the normalized height of the cylinder be h and the normalized distance to the plane of the viewed flat be H. Then the total solid angle is

(6) $$\Omega = \Omega(1,h + H;\rho) - \Omega(1,H;\rho) + \Omega(1;\rho,H),$$

where ρ is the normalized distance from 0 to the axis of the cylinder. Approximations are given in the references.

III. USE OF TABLES

A. Reading the Entry Numbers (steradians)

Each entry is given to six significant figures followed by an exponent for the power of 10 as a multiplier. For example,

$$3.73950\text{--}3 \equiv 3.73950 \times 10^{-3} \equiv 0.00373950;$$
$$5.65798\text{--}0 \equiv 5.65798 \times 10^0 \equiv 5.65798.$$

B. *Solid Angle Subtended by a Disc*

To find the solid angle subtended by an end-window counter 3 cm in radius at a point 15 cm above its plane and 18 cm from its axis, we have

$$\Omega(1;\rho,z) = \Omega(1;18/3,15/3) = \Omega(1;6,5) = 0.0331611.$$

C. *Solid Angle Subtended by the Lateral Surface of a Right Circular Cylinder*

To find the solid angle subtended by a Geiger counter 3 cm in radius and 30 cm long at a point in the plane of a flat at 25.5 cm from the axis, we have

$$\Omega(1,h;\rho) = \Omega(1,30/3;25.5/3) = \Omega(1,10;8.5) = 0.186909.$$

D. *Fraction of Radiation Entering a Circular Aperture from a Distributed Plane Source*

Consider the problem of estimating the fraction of radiation entering a circular end-window counter from a thin disc source whose plane is parallel to the window. Let b be the normalized radius of the source relative to the counter, let s be the normalized distance between the (parallel) axes of the source and window, and let z be the normalized distance between the planes of the window and source.

Case 1. $s = 0$: coaxial.

Divide the source into N concentric annuli of width $\Delta\rho_i$, $i = 1,2,3, \ldots ,N$. Each point in a given annulus has subtended approximately the same solid angle $\Omega(1;\rho_i,z)$ by the window. The area of each annulus is $2\pi\rho_i\Delta\rho_i$. Hence the fraction is given by the summation

(6)
$$G_1 = \frac{1}{2\pi b^2} \sum_{i=1}^{N} \Omega(1;\rho_i,z)\rho_i\Delta\rho_i.$$

Case 2. $s \geqq b$: non-coaxial and no vertical overlap.

Divide the source into N concentric strips using the point common to the axis of the window and the plane of the source as a center. The area of each strip is $2\alpha_i\rho_i\Delta\rho_i$, where $\alpha_i = $ arc cos $[(\rho_i^2 + S^2 - b^2)/2S\rho_i]$. The fraction is given by

(7)
$$G_2 = \frac{1}{2\pi^2 b^2} \sum_{i=1}^{N} \Omega(1;\rho_i,z)\alpha_i\rho_i\Delta\rho_i.$$

Case 3. $s < b$: non-coaxial with vertical overlap. Apply Cases 1 and 2.

In the above calculations, self-absorption, scattering, non-uniformity of source strength, and non-isotropic emission have been omitted. Corrections for these effects cannot be treated here.

I. SOLID ANGLE SUBTENDED BY THE CIRCULAR DISC OF UNIT RADIUS

ρ \ z	0.2	0.4	0.6	0.8	1.0	1.2	1.4	1.6	1.8	2.0
0.0	5.05095 0	3.94967 0	3.05051 0	2.35811 0	1.84030 0	1.45631 0	1.17035 0	9.55055−1	7.90693−1	6.63334−1
0.1	5.04234 0	3.93659 0	3.03737 0	2.34716 0	1.83198 0	1.45024 0	1.16598 0	9.51907−1	7.88406−1	6.61650−1
0.2	5.01561 0	3.89649 0	2.99753 0	2.31425 0	1.80709 0	1.43213 0	1.15296 0	9.42532−1	7.81591−1	6.56633−1
0.3	4.96793 0	3.82665 0	2.92981 0	2.25924 0	1.76590 0	1.40231 0	1.13157 0	9.27131−1	7.70390−1	6.48380−1
0.4	4.89368 0	3.72227 0	2.83236 0	2.18209 0	1.70895 0	1.36136 0	1.10227 0	9.06036−1	7.55034−1	6.37049−1
0.5	4.78279 0	3.57610 0	2.70304 0	2.08304 0	1.63710 0	1.31011 0	1.06569 0	8.79705−1	7.35838−1	6.22856−1
0.6	4.61712 0	3.37830 0	2.54009 0	1.96307 0	1.55174 0	1.24970 0	1.02267 0	8.48708−1	7.13192−1	6.06068−1
0.7	4.36323 0	3.11751 0	2.34335 0	1.82425 0	1.45479 0	1.18157 0	9.74194−1	8.13717−1	6.87550−1	5.86992−1
0.8	3.95926 0	2.78525 0	2.11602 0	1.67016 0	1.34883 0	1.10741 0	9.21391−1	7.75480−1	6.59413−1	5.65969−1
0.9	3.31094 0	2.38629 0	1.86638 0	1.50600 0	1.23698 0	1.02917 0	8.65483−1	7.34795−1	6.29313−1	5.43360−1
1.00	2.40515 0	1.95112 0	1.60798 0	1.33824 0	1.12269 0	9.48851−1	8.07727−1	6.92475−1	5.97794−1	5.19535−1
1.25	7.83966−1	1.02735 0	1.02474 0	9.45919−1	8.48210−1	7.51604−1	6.63084−1	5.84636−1	5.16227−1	4.57034−1
1.50	3.30050−1	5.40110−1	6.29125−1	6.43292−1	6.19102−1	5.77621−1	5.30021−1	4.82015−1	4.36391−1	3.94380−1
1.75	1.74764−1	3.11680−1	3.97052−1	4.37844−1	4.47467−1	4.37793−1	4.17265−1	3.91356−1	3.63433−1	3.35486−1
2.00	1.05541−1	1.95924−1	2.62557−1	3.04563−1	3.25802−1	3.31582−1	3.26809−1	3.15351−1	3.00008−1	2.82710−1
2.25	6.93038−2	1.31484−1	1.81639−1	2.17930−1	2.41045−1	2.53071−1	2.56518−1	2.53750−1	2.46739−1	2.37015−1
2.50	4.82364−2	9.27336−2	1.30625−1	1.60381−1	1.81769−1	1.95484−1	2.02713−1	2.04791−1	2.02982−1	1.98380−1
2.75	3.50529−2	6.79748−2	9.70218−2	1.21083−1	1.39726−1	1.53087−1	1.61683−1	1.66228−1	1.67492−1	1.66206−1
3.00	2.63375−2	5.13818−2	7.40283−2	9.34934−2	1.09364−1	1.21567−1	1.30297−1	1.35917−1	1.38876−1	1.39646−1
3.25	2.03247−2	3.98250−2	5.77746−2	7.36211−2	8.70214−2	9.78406−2	1.06119−1	1.12032−1	1.15831−1	1.17811−1
3.50	1.60321−2	3.15170−2	4.59620−2	5.89727−2	7.02786−2	7.97380−2	8.73258−2	9.31121−2	9.72349−2	9.98737−2
3.75	1.28802−2	2.53850−2	3.71704−2	4.79510−2	5.75168−2	6.57396−2	7.25687−2	7.80213−2	8.21674−2	8.51134−2
4.00	1.05108−2	2.07566−2	3.04914−2	3.95055−2	4.76364−2	5.47745−2	6.08632−2	6.58932−2	6.98951−2	7.29297−2
4.25	8.69349−3	1.71951−2	2.53256−2	3.29283−2	3.98770−2	4.60809−2	5.14851−2	5.60685−2	5.98397−2	6.28312−2
4.50	7.27511−3	1.44086−2	2.12670−2	2.77316−2	3.37040−2	3.91096−2	4.38989−2	4.80465−2	5.15489−2	5.44214−2
4.75	6.15128−3	1.21961−2	1.80334−2	2.35721−2	2.87348−2	3.34605−2	3.77061−2	4.14456−2	4.46693−2	4.73822−2
5.00	5.24891−3	1.04165−2	1.54251−2	2.02039−2	2.46916−2	2.88383−2	3.26071−2	3.59732−2	3.89245−2	4.14597−2
5.25	4.51573−3	8.96845−3	1.32977−2	1.74477−2	2.13695−2	2.50223−2	2.83747−2	3.14042−2	3.40977−2	3.64505−2
5.50	3.91368−3	7.77790−3	1.15450−2	1.51706−2	1.86154−2	2.18459−2	2.48352−2	2.75636−2	3.00179−2	3.21920−2
5.75	3.41457−3	6.78986−3	1.00879−2	1.32731−2	1.63135−2	1.91814−2	2.18542−2	2.43144−2	2.65498−2	2.85533−2
6	2.99721−3	5.96290−3	8.86648−3	1.16792−2	1.43749−2	1.69305−2	1.93270−2	2.15491−2	2.35856−2	2.54291−2
7	1.87242−3	3.73056−3	5.56046−3	7.34874−3	9.08291−3	1.07515−2	1.23445−2	1.38533−2	1.52706−2	1.65909−2
8	1.24791−3	2.48860−3	3.71496−3	4.92012−3	6.09755−3	7.24114−3	8.34531−3	9.40506−3	1.04159−2	1.13744−2
9	8.73357−4	1.74274−3	2.60424−3	3.45403−3	4.28845−3	5.10400−3	5.89743−3	6.66576−3	7.40627−3	8.11658−3
10	6.35074−4	1.26782−3	1.89593−3	2.51716−3	3.12931−3	3.73028−3	4.31810−3	4.89090−3	5.44696−3	5.98473−3
11	4.76253−4	9.51068−4	1.42302−3	1.89070−3	2.35275−3	2.80785−3	3.25473−3	3.69220−3	4.11913−3	4.53449−3
12	3.66318−4	7.31708−4	1.09525−3	1.45604−3	1.81318−3	2.16581−3	2.51311−3	2.85426−3	3.18853−3	3.51520−3
13	2.87802−4	5.74985−4	8.60932−4	1.14503−3	1.42670−3	1.70533−3	1.98038−3	2.25129−3	2.51755−3	2.77865−3
14	2.30230−4	4.60033−4	6.88984−4	9.16665−4	1.14266−3	1.36655−3	1.58797−3	1.80653−3	2.02184−3	2.23358−3
15	1.87054−4	3.73806−4	5.59956−4	7.45206−4	9.29263−4	1.11183−3	1.29264−3	1.47142−3	1.64789−3	1.82180−3
16	1.54039−4	3.07860−4	4.61245−4	6.13980−4	7.65850−4	9.16646−4	1.06616−3	1.21420−3	1.36056−3	1.50506−3
18	1.08092−4	2.16063−4	3.23793−4	4.31162−4	5.38052−4	6.44345−4	7.49926−4	8.54683−4	9.58505−4	1.06128−3
20	7.87496−5	1.57428−4	2.35964−4	3.14288−4	3.92328−4	4.70016−4	5.47293−4	6.24061−4	7.00285−4	7.75889−4
22	5.91384−5	1.18233−4	1.77239−4	2.36113−4	2.94811−4	3.53290−4	4.11508−4	4.69421−4	5.26989−4	5.84171−4
24	4.55356−5	9.10426−5	1.36493−4	1.81857−4	2.27108−4	2.72217−4	3.17157−4	3.61899−4	4.06417−4	4.50685−4
26	3.58052−5	7.15912−5	1.07339−4	1.43030−4	1.78644−4	2.14162−4	2.49568−4	2.84841−4	3.19964−4	3.54918−4
28	2.86614−5	5.73096−5	8.59314−5	1.14514−4	1.43043−4	1.71507−4	1.99892−4	2.28186−4	2.56376−4	2.84450−4
30	2.32987−5	4.65880−5	6.98587−5	9.31014−5	1.16307−4	1.39465−4	1.62568−4	1.85607−4	2.08571−4	2.31453−4
32	1.91948−5	3.83828−5	5.75573−5	7.67115−5	9.58388−5	1.14930−4	1.33984−4	1.52990−4	1.71943−4	1.90836−4
34	1.60009−5	3.19968−5	4.79828−5	6.39537−5	7.99048−5	9.58308−5	1.11725−4	1.27587−4	1.43409−4	1.59187−4

ASTRODYNAMICS

I. SOLID ANGLE SUBTENDED BY THE CIRCULAR DISC OF UNIT RADIUS (Continued)

ρ \ z	2.2	2.4	2.6	2.8	3.0	3.2	3.4	3.6	3.8	4.0
0.0	5.63184−1	4.83322−1	4.18802−1	3.66046−1	3.22432−1	2.86011−1	2.55314−1	2.29224−1	2.06877−1	1.87600−1
0.1	5.61928−1	4.82371−1	4.18072−1	3.65479−1	3.21986−1	2.85655−1	2.55028−1	2.28991−1	2.06686−1	1.87442−1
0.2	5.58183−1	4.79535−1	4.15895−1	3.63785−1	3.20651−1	2.84592−1	2.54172−1	2.28295−1	2.06114−1	1.86969−1
0.3	5.52015−1	4.74860−1	4.12302−1	3.60987−1	3.18446−1	2.82833−1	2.52755−1	2.27142−1	2.05167−1	1.86185−1
0.4	5.43533−1	4.68421−1	4.07345−1	3.57123−1	3.15396−1	2.80399−1	2.50791−1	2.25542−1	2.03853−1	1.85096−1
0.5	5.32887−1	4.60320−1	4.01098−1	3.52243−1	3.11538−1	2.77315−1	2.48300−1	2.23511−1	2.02182−1	1.83710−1
0.6	5.20258−1	4.50686−1	3.93649−1	3.46411−1	3.06918−1	2.73615−1	2.45307−1	2.21067−1	2.00169−1	1.82038−1
0.7	5.05858−1	4.39664−1	3.85102−1	3.39700−1	3.01590−1	2.69339−1	2.41841−1	2.18232−1	1.97830−1	1.80093−1
0.8	4.89922−1	4.27418−1	3.75571−1	3.32194−1	2.95612−1	2.64529−1	2.37934−1	2.15029−1	1.95183−1	1.77888−1
0.9	4.72698−1	4.14123−1	3.65182−1	3.23982−1	2.89051−1	2.59235−1	2.33622−1	2.11487−1	1.92250−1	1.75441−1
1.00	4.54444−1	3.99960−1	3.54063−1	3.15158−1	2.81976−1	2.53507−1	2.28944−1	2.07635−1	1.89052−1	1.72768−1
1.25	4.05975−1	3.61950−1	3.23942−1	2.91052−1	2.62506−1	2.37644−1	2.15914−1	1.96749−1	1.80060−1	1.65219−1
1.50	3.56380−1	3.22360−1	2.92080−1	2.65206−1	2.41380−1	2.20250−1	2.01493−1	1.84813−1	1.69952−1	1.56679−1
1.75	3.08635−1	2.83459−1	2.60212−1	2.38952−1	2.19628−1	2.02126−1	1.86307−1	1.72020−1	1.59117−1	1.47457−1
2.00	2.64732−1	2.46887−1	2.29671−1	2.13367−1	1.98115−1	1.83967−1	1.70915−1	1.58920−1	1.47920−1	1.37847−1
2.25	2.25711−1	2.13635−1	2.01347−1	1.89221−1	1.77498−1	1.66324−1	1.55778−1	1.45895−1	1.36679−1	1.28115−1
2.50	1.91871−1	1.84146−1	1.75727−1	1.66995−1	1.58222−1	1.49599−1	1.41249−1	1.33253−1	1.25657−1	1.18484−1
2.75	1.63015−1	1.58461−1	1.52983−1	1.46922−1	1.40544−1	1.34045−1	1.27566−1	1.21210−1	1.15049−1	1.09128−1
3.00	1.38676−1	1.36366−1	1.33064−1	1.29055−1	1.24571−1	1.19798−1	1.14877−1	1.09917−1	1.04999−1	1.00181−1
3.25	1.18276−1	1.17512−1	1.15782−1	1.13313−1	1.10300−1	1.06904−1	1.03256−1	9.94607−2	9.55989−2	9.17341−2
3.50	1.01228−1	1.01499−1	1.00879−1	9.95452−2	9.76532−2	9.53378−2	9.27128−2	8.98729−2	8.68954−2	8.38425−2
3.75	8.69879−2	8.79296−2	8.80774−2	8.75641−2	8.65120−2	8.50306−2	8.32157−2	8.11498−2	7.89024−2	7.65315−2
4.00	7.50785−2	7.64353−2	7.70987−2	7.71673−2	7.67350−2	7.58888−2	7.47074−2	7.32606−2	7.16088−2	6.98043−2
4.25	6.50933−2	6.66885−2	6.76860−2	6.81579−2	6.81754−2	6.78065−2	6.71146−2	6.61575−2	6.49867−2	6.36476−2
4.50	5.66938−2	5.84071−2	5.96093−2	6.03525−2	6.06901−2	6.06747−2	6.03566−2	5.97829−2	5.89966−2	5.80367−2
4.75	4.96011−2	5.13519−2	5.26677−2	5.35858−2	5.41457−2	5.43878−2	5.43515−2	5.40748−2	5.35933−2	5.29395−2
5.00	4.35870−2	4.53227−2	4.66888−2	4.77118−2	4.84209−2	4.88467−2	4.90199−2	4.89708−2	4.87284−2	4.83198−2
5.25	3.84656−2	4.01524−2	4.15256−2	4.26035−2	4.34075−2	4.39608−2	4.42869−2	4.44101−2	4.43535−2	4.41397−2
5.50	3.40854−2	3.57030−2	3.70541−2	3.81516−2	3.90107−2	3.96487−2	4.00840−2	4.03355−2	4.04218−2	4.03613−2
5.75	3.03226−2	3.18596−2	3.31699−2	3.42622−2	3.51474−2	3.58383−2	3.63490−2	3.66942−2	3.68889−2	3.69480−2
6	2.70765−2	2.85276−2	2.97854−2	3.08556−2	3.17460−2	3.24660−2	3.30263−2	3.34383−2	3.37138−2	3.38650−2
7	1.78102−2	1.89259−2	1.99368−2	2.08432−2	2.16464−2	2.23489−2	2.29537−2	2.34649−2	2.38870−2	2.42250−2
8	1.22774−2	1.31225−2	1.39081−2	1.46332−2	1.52974−2	1.59009−2	1.64443−2	1.69288−2	1.73559−2	1.77274−2
9	8.79463−3	9.43866−3	1.00473−2	1.06194−2	1.11544−2	1.16516−2	1.21111−2	1.25329−2	1.29173−2	1.32651−2
10	6.50280−3	6.99995−3	7.47512−3	7.92743−3	8.35619−3	8.76087−3	9.14110−3	9.49667−3	9.82754−3	1.01338−2
11	4.93731−3	5.32675−3	5.70202−3	6.06247−3	6.40752−3	6.73671−3	7.04966−3	7.34608−3	7.62581−3	7.88872−3
12	3.83361−3	4.14314−3	4.44326−3	4.73345−3	5.01328−3	5.28237−3	5.54039−3	5.78708−3	6.02223−3	6.24568−3
13	3.03414−3	3.28358−3	3.52656−3	3.76273−3	3.99173−3	4.21328−3	4.42710−3	4.63298−3	4.83072−3	5.02016−3
14	2.44139−3	2.64497−3	2.84401−3	3.03824−3	3.22741−3	3.41129−3	3.58966−3	3.76235−3	3.92918−3	4.09003−3
15	1.99292−3	2.16099−3	2.32581−3	2.48717−3	2.64488−3	2.79874−3	2.94861−3	3.09433−3	3.23577−3	3.37280−3
16	1.64751−3	1.78775−3	1.92560−3	2.06091−3	2.19353−3	2.32333−3	2.45016−3	2.57392−3	2.69448−3	2.81177−3
18	1.16291−3	1.26329−3	1.36232−3	1.45992−3	1.55599−3	1.65044−3	1.74320−3	1.83419−3	1.92333−3	2.01056−3
20	8.50380−4	9.24986−4	9.98357−4	1.07080−3	1.14245−3	1.21307−3	1.28266−3	1.35118−3	1.41857−3	1.48481−3
22	6.40926−4	6.97214−4	7.52999−4	8.08242−4	8.62906−4	9.16958−4	9.70363−4	1.02309−3	1.07510−3	1.12637−3
24	4.94674−4	5.38361−4	5.81718−4	6.24722−4	6.67349−4	7.09574−4	7.51375−4	7.92729−4	8.33615−4	8.74012−4
26	3.89686−4	4.24249−4	4.58591−4	4.92695−4	5.26543−4	5.60120−4	5.93410−4	6.26397−4	6.59066−4	6.91403−4
28	3.12394−4	3.40196−4	3.67846−4	3.95329−4	4.22636−4	4.49754−4	4.76672−4	5.03379−4	5.29864−4	5.56117−4
30	2.54243−4	2.76933−4	2.99514−4	3.21977−4	3.44313−4	3.66516−4	3.88576−4	4.10485−4	4.32236−4	4.53822−4
32	2.09663−4	2.28416−4	2.47090−4	2.65679−4	2.84176−4	3.02574−4	3.20870−4	3.39055−4	3.57126−4	3.75075−4
34	1.74916−4	1.90591−4	2.06207−4	2.21760−4	2.37245−4	2.52656−4	2.67991−4	2.83245−4	2.98413−4	3.13491−4

I. SOLID ANGLE SUBTENDED BY THE CIRCULAR DISC OF
UNIT RADIUS (Continued)

ρ \ z	4.2	4.4	4.6	4.8	5.0	5.2	5.4	5.6	5.8	6.0
0.0	1.70864-1	1.56245-1	1.43405-1	1.32070-1	1.22015-1	1.13057-1	1.05042-1	9.78444-2	9.13568-2	8.54895-2
0.1	1.70732-1	1.56134-1	1.43311-1	1.31990-1	1.21947-1	1.12998-1	1.04991-1	9.78001-2	9.13181-2	8.54556-2
0.2	1.70337-1	1.55802-1	1.43031-1	1.31715-1	1.21742-1	1.12822-1	1.04839-1	9.76675-2	9.12022-2	8.53539-2
0.3	1.69683-1	1.55252-1	1.42565-1	1.31355-1	1.21403-1	1.12529-1	1.04585-1	9.74470-2	9.10096-2	8.51848-2
0.4	1.68773-1	1.54487-1	1.41917-1	1.30803-1	1.20929-1	1.12121-1	1.04232-1	9.71398-2	9.07410-2	8.49490-2
0.5	1.67615-1	1.53512-1	1.41091-1	1.30098-1	1.20325-1	1.11601-1	1.03781-1	9.67470-2	9.03975-2	8.46475-2
0.6	1.66216-1	1.52333-1	1.40092-1	1.29245-1	1.19594-1	1.10970-1	1.03234-1	9.62704-2	8.99806-2	8.42812-2
0.7	1.64586-1	1.50959-1	1.38925-1	1.28249-1	1.18738-1	1.10231-1	1.02593-1	9.57120-2	8.94919-2	8.38517-2
0.8	1.62737-1	1.49397-1	1.37598-1	1.27115-1	1.17763-1	1.09388-1	1.01862-1	9.50742-2	8.89333-2	8.33605-2
0.9	1.60681-1	1.47658-1	1.36118-1	1.25848-1	1.16673-1	1.08446-1	1.01043-1	9.43597-2	8.83070-2	8.28094-2
1.00	1.58431-1	1.45752-1	1.34494-1	1.24456-1	1.15474-1	1.07408-1	1.00140-1	9.35711-2	8.76153-2	8.22003-2
1.25	1.52054-1	1.40333-1	1.29863-1	1.20478-1	1.12039-1	1.04428-1	9.75433-2	9.12984-2	8.56186-2	8.04395-2
1.50	1.44798-1	1.34134-1	1.24540-1	1.15885-1	1.08058-1	1.00962-1	9.45137-2	8.86386-2	8.32765-2	7.83691-2
1.75	1.36909-1	1.27354-1	1.18687-1	1.10810-1	1.03639-1	9.70999-2	9.11250-2	8.56557-2	8.06400-2	7.60318-2
2.00	1.28628-1	1.20185-1	1.12459-1	1.05380-1	9.88928-2	9.29323-2	8.74532-2	8.24103-2	7.77626-2	7.34729-2
2.25	1.20174-1	1.12819-1	1.06019-1	9.97372-2	9.39249-2	8.85487-2	8.35739-2	7.89673-2	7.46983-2	7.07383-2
2.50	1.11738-1	1.05414-1	9.95043-2	9.39840-2	8.88347-2	8.40338-2	7.95591-2	7.53883-2	7.14998-2	6.78732-2
2.75	1.03474-1	9.81042-2	9.30224-2	8.82267-2	8.37106-2	7.94638-2	7.54748-2	7.17304-2	6.82170-2	6.49209-2
3.00	9.55037-2	9.09961-2	8.66758-2	8.25520-2	7.86288-2	7.49060-2	7.13801-2	6.80455-2	6.48950-2	6.19210-2
3.25	8.79142-2	8.41742-2	8.05402-2	7.70290-2	7.36525-2	7.04170-2	6.73257-2	6.43789-2	5.15745-2	5.89096-2
3.50	8.07635-2	7.76969-2	7.46722-2	7.17117-2	6.88315-2	6.60431-2	6.33540-2	6.07690-2	5.82901-2	5.59182-2
3.75	7.40847-2	7.16008-2	6.91105-2	6.66385-2	6.42035-2	6.18200-2	5.94987-2	5.72474-2	5.50709-2	5.29731-2
4.00	6.78909-2	6.59056-2	6.38787-2	6.18352-2	5.97951-2	5.77745-2	5.57858-2	5.38388-2	5.19407-2	5.00967-2
4.25	6.21797-2	6.06169-2	5.89879-2	5.73167-2	5.56236-2	5.39250-2	5.22343-2	5.05622-2	5.89176-2	4.73067-2
4.50	5.69376-2	5.57298-2	5.44393-2	5.30890-2	5.16981-2	5.02828-2	4.88567-2	4.74312-2	4.60152-2	4.46165-2
4.75	5.21432-2	5.12311-2	5.02266-2	4.91506-2	4.80209-2	4.68531-2	4.56604-2	4.44540-2	4.32434-2	4.20364-2
5.00	4.77702-2	4.71028-2	4.63381-2	4.54949-2	4.45896-2	4.36364-2	4.26481-2	4.16355-2	4.06079-2	3.95730-2
5.25	4.37897-2	4.33234-2	4.27586-2	4.21119-2	4.13980-2	4.06300-2	3.98196-2	3.89770-2	3.81114-2	3.72301-2
5.50	4.01716-2	3.98694-2	3.94702-2	3.89884-2	3.84369-2	3.78276-2	3.71713-2	3.64774-2	3.57543-2	3.50094-2
5.75	3.68860-2	3.67169-2	3.64540-2	3.61096-2	3.56953-2	3.52215-2	3.46979-2	3.41331-2	3.35351-2	3.29105-2
6	3.39038-2	3.38419-2	3.36905-2	3.34602-2	3.31611-2	3.28023-2	3.23925-2	3.19395-2	3.14505-2	3.09318-2
7	2.44839-2	2.46694-2	2.47868-2	2.48416-2	2.48393-2	2.47850-2	2.46838-2	2.45406-2	2.43598-2	2.41460-2
8	1.80456-2	1.83128-2	1.85314-2	1.87043-2	1.88341-2	1.89237-2	1.89757-2	1.89930-2	1.89782-2	1.89341-2
9	1.35769-2	1.38536-2	1.40966-2	1.43070-2	1.44862-2	1.46355-2	1.47565-2	1.48505-2	1.49192-2	1.49641-2
10	1.04157-2	1.06733-2	1.09075-2	1.11186-2	1.13073-2	1.14742-2	1.16201-2	1.17457-2	1.18520-2	1.19398-2
11	8.13482-3	8.36415-3	8.57687-3	8.77317-3	8.95332-3	9.11764-3	9.26648-3	9.40025-3	9.51941-3	9.62443-3
12	6.45734-3	6.65714-3	6.84510-3	7.02127-3	7.18572-3	7.33860-3	7.48005-3	7.61027-3	7.72949-3	7.83797-3
13	5.20118-3	5.37369-3	5.53764-3	5.69301-3	5.83979-3	5.97804-3	6.10778-3	6.22911-3	6.34215-3	6.44701-3
14	4.24474-3	4.39326-3	4.53550-3	4.67141-3	4.80096-3	4.92412-3	5.04092-3	5.15138-3	5.25553-3	5.35343-3
15	3.50533-3	3.63325-3	3.75650-3	3.87503-3	3.98878-3	4.09772-3	4.20184-3	4.30112-3	4.39557-3	4.48521-3
16	2.92568-3	3.03613-3	3.14306-3	3.24641-3	3.34614-3	3.44219-3	3.53455-3	3.62319-3	3.70811-3	3.78929-3
18	2.09582-3	2.17906-3	2.26021-3	2.33924-3	2.41611-3	2.49077-3	2.56319-3	2.63335-3	2.70123-3	2.76681-3
20	1.54983-3	1.61361-3	1.67610-3	1.73728-3	1.79711-3	1.85556-3	1.91260-3	1.96822-3	2.02239-3	2.07510-3
22	1.17687-3	1.22658-3	1.27546-3	1.32349-3	1.37065-3	1.41692-3	1.46227-3	1.50670-3	1.55016-3	1.59267-3
24	9.13900-4	9.53259-4	9.92072-4	1.03032-3	1.06799-3	1.10506-3	1.14152-3	1.17735-3	1.21253-3	1.24707-3
26	7.23392-4	7.55021-4	7.86277-4	8.17146-4	8.47617-4	8.77677-4	9.07316-4	9.36522-4	9.65289-4	9.93601-4
28	5.82128-4	6.07885-4	6.33381-4	6.58606-4	6.83550-4	7.08206-4	7.32564-4	7.56616-4	7.80358-4	8.03776-4
30	4.75233-4	4.96463-4	5.17506-4	5.38354-4	5.59000-4	5.79438-4	5.99662-4	6.19665-4	6.39445-4	6.58989-4
32	3.92897-4	4.10587-4	4.28140-4	4.45550-4	4.62812-4	4.79921-4	4.96873-4	5.13663-4	5.30285-4	5.46736-4
34	3.28475-4	3.43360-4	3.58143-4	3.72820-4	3.87386-4	4.01839-4	4.16173-4	4.30386-4	4.44474-4	4.58434-4

I. SOLID ANGLE SUBTENDED BY THE CIRCULAR DISC OF
UNIT RADIUS (Continued)

ρ \ z	6.2	6.4	6.6	6.8	7.0	7.2	7.4	7.6	7.8	8.0
0.0	8.01664-2	7.53226-2	7.09026-2	6.68585-2	6.31492-2	5.97388-2	5.65962-2	5.36942-2	5.10090-2	4.85195-2
0.1	8.01365-2	7.52962-2	7.08791-2	6.68376-2	6.31305-2	5.97221-2	5.65812-2	5.36807-2	5.09968-2	4.85085-2
0.2	8.00469-2	7.52170-2	7.08088-2	6.67750-2	6.30746-2	5.96720-2	5.65362-2	5.36402-2	5.09602-2	4.84753-2
0.3	7.98980-2	7.50852-2	7.06919-2	6.66709-2	6.29816-2	5.95887-2	5.64613-2	5.35727-2	5.08992-2	4.84201-2
0.4	7.96902-2	7.49015-2	7.05288-2	6.65256-2	6.28518-2	5.94723-2	5.63568-2	5.34785-2	5.08141-2	4.83430-2
0.5	7.94244-2	7.46662-2	7.03199-2	6.63396-2	6.26855-2	5.93233-2	5.62228-2	5.33577-2	5.07050-2	4.82442-2
0.6	7.91014-2	7.43804-2	7.00660-2	6.61133-2	6.24833-2	5.91419-2	5.60598-2	5.32107-2	5.05721-2	4.81238-2
0.7	7.87224-2	7.40448-2	6.97679-2	6.58475-2	6.22456-2	5.89288-2	5.58681-2	5.30379-2	5.04159-2	4.79822-2
0.8	7.82888-2	7.36607-2	6.94264-2	6.55430-2	6.19732-2	5.86844-2	5.56482-2	5.28396-2	5.02365-2	4.78197-2
0.9	7.78021-2	7.32292-2	6.90427-2	6.52007-2	6.16668-2	5.84095-2	5.54008-2	5.26163-2	5.00346-2	4.76365-2
1.00	7.72637-2	7.27518-2	6.86178-2	6.48214-2	6.13272-2	5.81045-2	5.61262-2	5.23685-2	4.98103-2	4.74331-2
1.25	7.57054-2	7.13679-2	6.73849-2	6.37197-2	6.03399-2	5.72172-2	5.43267-2	5.16462-2	4.91563-2	4.68396-2
1.50	7.38690-2	6.97338-2	6.59264-2	6.24141-2	5.91679-2	5.61624-2	5.33749-2	5.07853-2	4.83758-2	4.61304-2
1.75	7.17904-2	6.78799-2	6.42680-2	6.09265-2	5.78301-2	5.49562-2	5.22848-2	4.97979-2	4.74793-2	4.53147-2
2.00	6.95082-2	6.58387-2	6.24376-2	5.92809-2	5.63469-2	5.36163-2	5.10716-2	4.86969-2	4.64783-2	4.44027-2
2.25	6.70614-2	6.36438-2	6.04640-2	5.75020-2	5.47399-2	5.21614-2	4.97515-2	4.74968-2	4.53851-2	4.34049-2
2.50	6.44889-2	6.13289-2	5.83764-2	5.56152-2	5.30310-2	5.06105-2	4.83413-2	4.72121-2	4.42125-2	4.23328-2
2.75	6.18284-2	5.89266-2	5.62029-2	5.36450-2	5.12417-2	4.89825-2	4.68574-2	4.48572-2	4.29733-2	4.11975-2
3.00	5.91147-2	5.64674-2	5.39704-2	5.16150-2	4.93929-2	4.72958-2	4.53161-2	4.34465-2	4.16802-2	4.00103-2
3.25	5.63797-2	5.39798-2	5.17045-2	4.95480-2	4.75045-2	4.55682-2	4.37333-2	4.19942-2	4.03458-2	3.87827-2
3.50	5.36519-2	5.14893-2	4.94279-2	4.74643-2	4.55950-2	4.38161-2	4.21236-2	4.05136-2	3.89820-2	3.75251-2
3.75	5.09552-2	4.90178-2	4.71605-2	4.53820-2	4.36807-2	4.20543-2	4.05005-2	3.90166-2	3.75998-2	3.62475-2
4.00	4.83105-2	4.65845-2	4.49200-2	4.33174-2	4.17765-2	4.02965-2	3.88764-2	3.75146-2	3.62095-2	3.49592-2
4.25	4.57347-2	4.42054-2	4.27213-2	4.12843-2	3.98953-2	3.85546-2	3.72622-2	3.60177-2	3.48203-2	3.36689-2
4.50	4.32409-2	4.18931-2	4.05767-2	3.92943-2	3.80479-2	3.68387-2	3.56676-2	3.45349-2	3.34406-2	3.23842-2
4.75	4.08395-2	3.96580-2	3.84961-2	3.73571-2	3.62437-2	3.51578-2	3.41008-2	3.30739-2	3.20774-2	3.11117-2
5.00	3.85377-2	3.75075-2	3.64871-2	3.54803-2	3.44900-2	3.35189-2	3.25688-2	3.16412-2	3.07372-2	2.98574-2
5.25	3.63400-2	3.54468-2	3.45552-2	3.36693-2	3.27926-2	3.19278-2	3.10771-2	3.02425-2	2.94253-2	2.86266-2
5.50	3.42491-2	3.34791-2	3.27042-2	3.19286-2	3.11558-2	3.03889-2	2.96303-2	2.88821-2	2.81460-2	2.74234-2
5.75	3.22657-2	3.16061-2	3.09363-2	3.02607-2	2.95827-2	2.89055-2	2.82317-2	2.75635-2	2.69029-2	2.62513-2
6	3.03892-2	2.98280-2	2.92527-2	2.86673-2	2.80753-2	2.74800-2	2.68839-2	2.62895-2	2.56987-2	2.51131-2
7	2.39030-2	2.36346-2	2.33443-2	2.30352-2	2.27104-2	2.23724-2	2.20237-2	2.16664-2	2.13026-2	2.09340-2
8	1.88631-2	1.87676-2	1.86502-2	1.85128-2	1.83577-2	1.81868-2	1.80019-2	1.78048-2	1.75970-2	1.73801-2
9	1.49867-2	1.49886-2	1.49712-2	1.49359-2	1.48841-2	1.48173-2	1.47366-2	1.46433-2	1.45386-2	1.44236-2
10	1.20100-2	1.20634-2	1.21010-2	1.21237-2	1.21324-2	1.21279-2	1.21111-2	1.20829-2	1.20440-2	1.19953-2
11	9.71581-3	9.79407-3	9.85976-3	9.91341-3	9.95559-3	9.98686-3	1.00077-2	1.00188-2	1.00206-2	1.00137-2
12	7.93598-3	8.02381-3	8.10179-3	8.17023-3	8.22949-3	8.27989-3	8.32181-3	8.35559-3	8.38159-3	8.40019-3
13	6.54384-3	6.63280-3	6.71408-3	6.78786-3	6.85434-3	6.91375-3	6.96629-3	7.01220-3	7.05171-3	7.08506-3
14	5.44515-5	5.53078-3	5.61041-3	5.68416-3	5.75213-3	5.81447-3	5.87130-3	5.92276-3	5.96901-3	6.01019-3
15	4.57008-3	4.65020-3	4.72563-3	4.79643-3	4.86267-3	4.92441-3	4.98173-3	5.03473-3	5.08351-3	5.12814-3
16	3.86675-3	3.94050-3	4.01056-3	4.07696-3	4.13974-3	4.19892-3	4.25457-3	4.30673-3	4.35546-3	4.40082-3
18	2.83008-3	2.89102-3	2.94964-3	3.00594-3	3.05991-3	3.11158-3	3.16094-3	3.20801-3	3.25282-3	3.29539-3
20	2.12632-3	2.17605-3	2.22427-3	2.27098-3	2.31616-3	2.35983-3	2.40197-3	2.44259-3	2.48169-3	2.51927-3
22	1.63421-3	1.67476-3	1.71430-3	1.75283-3	1.79034-3	1.82682-3	1.86227-3	1.89669-3	1.93007-3	1.96240-3
24	1.28096-3	1.31416-3	1.34668-3	1.37851-3	1.40964-3	1.44006-3	1.46977-3	1.49876-3	1.52702-3	1.55456-3
26	1.02145-3	1.04883-3	1.07574-3	1.10215-3	1.12808-3	1.15351-3	1.17844-3	1.20285-3	1.22676-3	1.25014-3
28	8.26865-4	8.49621-4	8.72036-4	8.94105-4	9.15822-4	9.37180-4	9.58177-4	9.78806-4	9.99064-4	1.01895-3
30	6.78295-4	6.97359-4	7.16175-4	7.34739-4	7.53044-4	7.71089-4	7.88868-4	8.06378-4	8.23615-4	8.40575-4
32	5.63012-4	5.79109-4	5.95022-4	6.10747-4	6.26282-4	6.41622-4	6.56765-4	6.71707-4	6.68444-4	7.00975-4
34	4.72262-4	4.85955-4	4.99510-4	5.12924-4	5.26194-4	5.39318-4	5.52292-4	5.65114-4	5.77781-4	5.90291-4

I. SOLID ANGLE SUBTENDED BY THE CIRCULAR DISC OF UNIT RADIUS (Continued)

ρ \ z	8.2	8.4	8.6	8.8	9.0	9.2	9.4	9.6	9.8	10.0
0.0	4.62073-2	4.40560-2	4.20510-2	4.01794-2	3.84296-2	3.67914-2	3.52555-2	3.38135-2	3.24580-2	3.11823-2
0.1	4.61973-2	4.40468-2	4.20426-2	4.01718-2	3.84227-2	3.67850-2	3.52496-2	3.38081-2	3.24531-2	3.11777-2
0.2	4.61672-2	4.40195-2	4.20177-2	4.01490-2	3.84018-2	3.67659-2	3.52320-2	3.37919-2	3.24381-2	3.11639-2
0.3	4.61171-2	4.39739-2	4.19761-2	4.01110-2	3.83670-2	3.67340-2	3.52029-2	3.37650-2	3.24133-2	3.11409-2
0.4	4.60471-2	4.39102-2	4.19180-2	4.00579-2	3.83185-2	3.66895-2	3.51618-2	3.37273-2	3.23786-2	3.11089-2
0.5	4.59573-2	4.38285-2	4.18436-2	3.99899-2	3.82562-2	3.66323-2	3.51093-2	3.36790-2	3.23340-2	3.10677-2
0.6	4.58480-2	4.37291-2	4.17529-2	3.99070-2	3.81802-2	3.65627-2	3.50453-2	3.36201-2	3.22797-2	3.10175-2
0.7	4.57194-2	4.36120-2	4.16461-2	3.98094-2	3.80908-2	3.64806-2	3.49699-2	3.35506-2	3.22156-2	3.09584-2
0.8	4.55718-2	4.34775-2	4.15234-2	3.96972-2	3.79881-2	3.63864-2	3.48832-2	3.34708-2	3.21420-2	3.08904-2
0.9	4.54053-2	4.33260-2	4.13851-2	3.95707-2	3.78722-2	3.62800-2	3.47855-2	3.33808-2	3.20589-2	3.08136-2
1.00	4.52204-2	4.31575-2	4.12313-2	3.94301-2	3.77433-2	3.61617-2	3.46766-2	3.32805-2	3.19664-2	3.07281-2
1.25	4.46805-2	4.26654-2	4.07818-2	3.90187-2	3.73662-2	3.58153-2	3.43579-2	3.29868-2	3.16953-2	3.04775-2
1.50	4.40348-2	4.20762-2	4.02432-2	3.85254-2	3.69135-2	3.53992-2	3.39748-2	3.26335-2	3.13690-2	3.01757-2
1.75	4.32912-2	4.13969-2	3.96215-2	3.79554-2	3.63901-2	3.49176-2	3.35311-2	3.22240-2	3.09905-2	2.98253-2
2.00	4.24585-2	4.06353-2	3.89236-2	3.73148-2	3.58011-2	3.43752-2	3.30308-2	3.17618-2	3.05629-2	2.94290-2
2.25	4.15462-2	3.97997-2	3.81569-2	3.66101-2	3.51524-2	3.37771-2	3.24785-2	3.12512-2	3.00901-2	2.89906-2
2.50	4.05642-2	3.88988-2	3.73290-2	3.58482-2	3.44501-2	3.31288-2	3.18792-2	3.06964-2	2.95759-2	2.85133-2
2.75	3.95225-2	3.79414-2	3.64478-2	3.50359-2	3.37003-2	3.24357-2	3.12377-2	3.01018-2	2.90241-2	2.80006-2
3.00	3.84310-2	3.69365-2	3.55213-2	3.41805-2	3.29093-2	3.17036-2	3.05590-2	2.94720-2	2.84388-2	2.74563-2
3.25	3.73000-2	3.58931-2	3.45575-2	3.32891-2	3.20839-2	3.09383-2	2.98486-2	2.88118-2	2.78246-2	2.68842-2
3.50	3.61389-2	3.48198-2	3.35642-2	3.23687-2	3.12302-2	3.01455-2	2.91116-2	2.81258-2	2.71856-2	2.62881-2
3.75	3.49567-2	3.37247-2	3.25487-2	3.14261-2	3.03542-2	2.93306-2	2.83528-2	2.74186-2	2.65257-2	2.56719-2
4.00	3.37619-2	3.26155-2	3.15181-2	3.04675-2	2.94618-2	2.84990-2	2.75773-2	2.66946-2	2.58492-2	2.50392-2
4.25	3.25624-2	3.14995-2	3.04789-2	2.94991-2	2.85585-2	2.76558-2	2.67894-2	2.59579-2	2.51598-2	2.43935-2
4.50	3.13653-2	3.03833-2	2.94373-2	2.85264-2	2.76496-2	2.68057-2	2.59938-2	2.52127-2	2.44613-2	2.37383-2
4.75	3.01768-2	2.92726-2	2.83986-2	2.75544-2	2.67394-2	2.59530-2	2.51843-2	2.44626-2	2.37571-2	2.30767-2
5.00	2.90025-2	2.81725-2	2.73676-2	2.65877-2	2.58325-2	2.51016-2	2.43946-2	2.37110-2	2.30503-2	2.24118-2
5.25	2.78473-2	2.70880-2	2.63490-2	2.56306-2	2.49327-2	2.42553-2	2.35983-2	2.29613-2	2.23442-2	2.17463-2
5.50	2.67154-2	2.60229-2	2.53464-2	2.46865-2	2.40434-2	2.34174-2	2.28083-2	2.22163-2	2.16412-2	2.10828-2
5.75	2.56102-2	2.49805-2	2.43631-2	2.37587-2	2.31677-2	2.25906-2	2.20275-2	2.14786-2	2.09440-2	2.04236-2
6	2.45344-2	2.39636-2	2.34018-2	2.28497-2	2.23081-2	2.17775-2	2.12582-2	2.07505-2	2.02547-2	1.97707-2
7	2.05622-2	2.01886-2	1.98145-2	1.94409-2	1.90688-2	1.86992-2	1.83326-2	1.79697-2	1.76112-2	1.72572-2
8	1.71553-2	1.69240-2	1.66873-2	1.64463-2	1.62019-2	1.59549-2	1.57062-2	1.54565-2	1.52064-2	1.49563-2
9	1.42993-2	1.41667-2	1.40268-2	1.38804-2	1.37283-2	1.35713-2	1.34101-2	1.32454-2	1.30776-2	1.29076-2
10	1.19375-2	1.18713-2	1.17974-2	1.17166-2	1.16294-2	1.15364-2	1.14382-2	1.13353-2	1.12282-2	1.11176-2
11	9.99873-3	9.97597-3	9.94604-3	9.90942-3	9.86657-3	9.81795-3	9.76400-3	9.70514-3	9.64175-3	9.57422-3
12	8.41172-3	8.41656-3	8.41505-3	8.40753-3	8.39434-3	8.37582-3	9.35228-3	8.32404-3	8.29141-3	8.25465-2
13	7.11248-3	7.13422-3	7.15051-3	7.16160-3	7.16773-3	7.16912-3	7.16603-3	7.15866-3	7.14725-3	7.13201-3
14	6.04647-3	6.07800-3	6.10496-3	6.12749-3	6.14578-3	6.15998-3	6.17025-3	6.17678-3	6.17971-3	6.17921-3
15	5.16875-3	5.20542-3	5.23829-3	5.26744-3	5.29301-3	5.31510-3	5.33382-3	5.34931-3	5.36167-3	5.37102-3
16	4.44288-3	4.48170-3	4.51736-3	4.54993-3	4.57949-3	4.60612-3	4.62990-3	4.65091-3	4.66923-3	4.68495-3
18	3.33573-3	3.37388-3	3.40987-3	3.44372-3	3.47548-3	3.50518-3	3.53285-3	3.55854-3	3.58229-3	3.60413-3
20	2.55534-3	2.58992-3	2.62301-3	2.65462-3	2.68476-3	2.71347-3	2.74074-3	2.76659-3	2.79106-3	2.81414-3
22	1.99370-3	2.02396-3	2.05318-3	2.08137-3	2.10853-3	2.13466-3	2.15978-3	2.18389-3	2.20699-3	2.22910-3
24	1.57137-3	1.60744-3	1.63278-3	1.65739-3	1.68127-3	1.70441-3	1.72682-3	1.74850-3	1.76945-3	1.78968-3
26	1.27300-3	1.29534-3	1.31716-3	1.33844-3	1.35919-3	1.37941-3	1.39910-3	1.41825-3	1.43688-3	1.45496-3
28	1.03845-3	1.05757-3	1.07631-3	1.09466-3	1.11262-3	1.13019-3	1.14736-3	1.16415-3	1.18053-3	1.19651-3
30	8.57256-4	8.73654-4	8.89767-4	9.05592-4	9.21127-4	9.36371-4	9.51321-4	9.65975-4	9.80333-4	9.94393-4
32	7.15297-4	7.29406-4	7.43301-4	7.56979-4	7.70439-4	7.83678-4	7.96695-4	8.09488-4	8.22055-4	8.34397-4
34	6.02643-4	6.14833-4	6.26860-4	6.38721-4	6.50415-4	6.61941-4	6.73296-4	6.84479-4	6.95489-4	7.06326-4

I. SOLID ANGLE SUBTENDED BY THE CIRCULAR DISC OF
UNIT RADIUS (Continued)

ρ \ z	11	12	13	14	15	16	17	18	19	20
0.0	2.58037-2	2.17036-2	1.85072-2	1.59675-2	1.39163-2	1.22360-2	1.08424-2	9.67389-3	8.68443-3	7.83929-3
0.1	2.58006-2	2.17014-2	1.85056-2	1.59662-2	1.39153-2	1.22353-2	1.08419-2	9.67344-3	8.68408-3	7.83899-3
0.2	2.57911-2	2.16947-2	1.85007-2	1.59626-2	1.39126-2	1.22332-2	1.08402-2	9.67211-3	8.68300-3	7.83812-3
0.3	2.57754-2	2.16836-2	1.84926-2	1.59566-2	1.39080-2	1.22296-2	1.08374-2	9.66988-3	8.68121-3	7.83665-3
0.4	2.57534-2	2.16680-2	1.84812-2	1.59481-2	1.39016-2	1.22246-2	1.08335-2	9.66677-3	8.67869-3	7.83461-3
0.5	2.57251-2	2.16479-2	1.84667-2	1.59372-2	1.38933-2	1.22182-2	1.08285-2	9.66277-3	8.67547-3	7.83198-3
0.6	2.56907-2	2.16235-2	1.84489-2	1.59240-2	1.38832-2	1.22104-2	1.08223-2	9.65788-3	8.67153-3	7.82877-3
0.7	2.56500-2	2.15947-2	1.84279-2	1.59083-2	1.38713-2	1.22012-2	1.08151-2	9.65211-3	8.66688-3	7.82497-3
0.8	2.56033-2	2.15615-2	1.84037-2	1.58903-2	1.38576-2	1.21906-2	1.08067-2	9.64546-3	8.66151-3	7.82060-3
0.9	2.55505-2	2.15240-2	1.83763-2	1.58699-2	1.38421-2	1.21786-2	1.07973-2	9.63793-3	8.65544-3	7.81565-3
1.00	2.54916-2	2.14822-2	1.83458-2	1.58471-2	1.38247-2	1.21651-2	1.07867-2	9.62951-3	8.64865-3	7.81011-3
1.25	2.53188-2	2.13593-2	1.82561-2	1.57801-2	1.37737-2	1.21256-2	1.07556-2	9.60471-3	8.62864-3	7.79379-3
1.50	2.51101-2	2.12106-2	1.81474-2	1.56988-2	1.37117-2	1.20775-2	1.07178-2	9.57453-3	8.60427-3	7.77390-3
1.75	2.48672-2	2.10371-2	1.80202-2	1.56036-2	1.36390-2	1.20211-2	1.06734-2	9.53907-3	8.57562-3	7.75051-3
2.00	2.45914-2	2.08395-2	1.78751-2	1.54946-2	1.35556-2	1.19563-2	1.06221-2	9.49837-3	8.54272-3	7.72368-3
2.25	2.42852-2	2.06195-2	1.77132-2	1.53730-2	1.34625-2	1.18838-2	1.05649-2	9.45265-3	8.50573-3	7.69344-3
2.50	2.39506-2	2.03784-2	1.75354-2	1.52391-2	1.33599-2	1.18038-2	1.05017-2	9.40198-3	8.46471-3	7.65986-3
2.75	2.35893-2	2.01171-2	1.73420-2	1.50931-2	1.32478-2	1.17163-2	1.04324-2	9.34649-3	8.41974-3	7.62304-3
3.00	2.32037-2	1.98372-2	1.71343-2	1.49359-2	1.31266-2	1.16216-2	1.03575-2	9.28636-3	8.37096-3	7.58305-3
3.25	2.27964-2	1.95402-2	1.69131-2	1.47681-2	1.29971-2	1.15202-2	1.02770-2	9.22171-3	8.31846-3	7.53998-3
3.50	2.23696-2	1.92275-2	1.66794-2	1.45902-2	1.28596-2	1.14124-2	1.01912-2	9.15272-3	8.26236-3	7.49393-3
3.75	2.19257-2	1.89009-2	1.64344-2	1.44032-2	1.27146-2	1.12984-2	1.01004-2	9.07957-3	8.20280-3	7.44498-3
4.00	2.14672-2	1.85618-2	1.61790-2	1.42076-2	1.25627-2	1.11786-2	1.00048-2	9.00242-3	8.13992-3	7.39323-3
4.25	2.09963-2	1.82118-2	1.59143-2	1.40043-2	1.24041-2	1.10533-2	9.90500-3	8.92150-3	8.07387-3	7.33880-3
4.50	2.05153-2	1.78524-2	1.56414-2	1.37938-2	1.22396-2	1.09230-2	9.80063-3	8.83700-3	8.00477-3	7.28179-3
4.75	2.00262-2	1.74851-2	1.53611-2	1.35770-2	1.20696-2	1.07881-2	9.69227-3	8.74910-3	7.93279-3	7.22232-3
5.00	1.95314-2	1.71113-2	1.50747-2	1.33545-2	1.18945-2	1.06487-2	9.58018-3	8.65801-3	7.85808-3	7.16052-3
5.25	1.90326-2	1.67323-2	1.47829-2	1.31270-2	1.17150-2	1.05055-2	9.46466-3	8.56394-3	7.78079-3	7.09649-3
5.50	1.85318-2	1.63496-2	1.44869-2	1.28953-2	1.15315-2	1.03587-2	9.34596-3	8.46710-3	7.70107-3	7.03033-3
5.75	1.80306-2	1.59645-2	1.41875-2	1.26599-2	1.13445-2	1.02086-2	9.22437-3	8.36768-3	7.61910-3	6.96220-3
6	1.75307-2	1.55780-2	1.38856-2	1.24216-2	1.11546-2	1.00557-2	9.10016-3	8.26590-3	7.53501-3	6.89221-3
7	1.55713-2	1.40401-2	1.26691-2	1.14513-2	1.03741-2	9.42281-3	8.58240-3	7.83921-3	7.18077-3	6.59605-3
8	1.37257-2	1.25564-2	1.14713-2	1.04791-2	9.58060-3	8.77072-3	8.04325-3	7.39062-3	6.80522-3	6.27977-3
9	1.20370-2	1.11663-2	1.03261-2	9.53327-3	8.79628-3	8.11783-3	7.49719-3	6.93168-3	6.41759-3	5.95072-3
10	1.05231-2	9.89186-3	9.25505-3	8.63315-3	8.03868-3	7.47864-3	6.95626-3	6.47231-3	6.02601-3	5.61563-3
11	9.18660-3	8.74249-3	8.27073-3	7.79187-3	7.31996-3	6.86414-3	6.43004-3	6.02070-3	5.63744-3	5.28034-3
12	8.01888-3	7.71835-3	7.37790-3	7.01642-3	6.64783-3	6.28199-3	5.92569-3	5.58331-3	5.25753-3	4.94971-3
13	7.00581-3	6.81362-3	6.57595-3	6.30927-3	6.02638-3	5.73695-3	5.44809-3	5.16484-3	4.89063-3	4.62770-3
14	6.13076-3	6.01915-3	5.86083-3	5.66965-3	5.45688-3	5.23144-3	5.00025-3	4.76848-3	4.53994-3	4.31732-3
15	5.37672-3	5.32420-3	5.22639-3	5.09465-3	4.93859-3	4.76613-3	4.58366-3	4.39620-3	4.20760-3	4.02076-3
16	4.72752-3	4.71769-3	4.66549-3	4.58004-3	4.46938-3	4.34033-3	4.19862-3	4.04890-3	3.89490-3	3.73950-3
18	3.68640-3	3.72795-3	3.73463-3	3.71212-3	3.66576-3	3.60038-3	3.52028-3	3.42913-3	3.33008-3	3.22572-3
20	2.90978-3	2.97464-3	3.01202-3	3.02537-3	3.01809-3	2.99345-3	2.95448-3	2.90392-3	2.84421-3	2.77746-3
22	2.32514-3	2.39814-3	2.44991-3	2.48250-3	2.49803-3	2.49863-3	2.48638-3	2.46323-3	2.43101-3	2.39133-3
24	1.88015-3	1.95338-3	2.01033-3	2.05219-3	2.08026-3	2.09590-3	2.10051-3	2.09544-3	2.08201-3	2.06141-3
26	1.53749-3	1.60705-3	1.66415-3	1.70943-3	1.74369-3	1.76778-3	1.78263-3	1.78915-3	1.78827-3	1.78088-3
28	1.27054-3	1.33474-3	1.38935-3	1.43473-3	1.47132-3	1.49967-3	1.52037-3	1.53404-3	1.54134-3	1.54288-3
30	1.06019-3	1.11851-3	1.16939-3	1.21303-3	1.24968-3	1.27967-3	1.30337-3	1.32121-3	1.33362-3	1.34106-3
32	8.92664-4	9.45152-4	9.91852-4	1.03284-3	1.06825-3	1.09827-3	1.12315-3	1.14316-3	1.15859-3	1.16976-3
34	7.57846-4	8.04868-4	8.47346-4	8.85295-4	9.18776-4	9.47896-4	9.72800-4	9.93667-4	1.01070-3	1.02411-3

I. SOLID ANGLE SUBTENDED BY THE CIRCULAR DISC OF UNIT RADIUS (Continued)

ρ \ z	22	26	30	40	50	60	70	80	90	100
0.0	6.48085-3	4.64218-3	3.48775-3	1.96256-3	1.25626-3	8.72483-4	6.41043-4	4.90816-4	3.87815-4	3.14136-4
0.1	6.48065-3	4.64207-3	3.48769-3	1.96256-3	1.25625-3	8.72479-4	6.41041-4	4.90815-4	3.87814-4	3.14135-4
0.2	6.48005-3	4.64177-3	3.48752-3	1.96250-3	1.25623-3	8.72468-4	6.41035-4	4.90812-4	3.87812-4	3.14134-4
0.3	6.47905-3	4.64125-3	3.48723-3	1.96241-3	1.25619-3	8.72450-4	6.41026-4	4.90806-4	3.87809-4	3.14132-4
0.4	6.47765-3	4.64053-3	3.48683-3	1.96228-3	1.25614-3	8.72425-4	6.41012-4	4.90798-4	3.87804-4	3.14128-4
0.5	6.47586-3	4.63961-3	3.48630-3	1.96212-3	1.25607-3	8.72393-4	6.40995-4	4.90788-4	3.87797-4	3.14124-4
0.6	6.47366-3	4.63848-3	3.48567-3	1.96192-3	1.25599-3	8.72353-4	6.40973-4	4.90775-4	3.87790-4	3.14119-4
0.7	6.47107-3	4.63715-3	3.48492-3	1.96168-3	1.25589-3	8.72306-4	6.40948-4	4.90761-4	3.87780-4	3.14113-4
0.8	6.46808-3	4.63562-3	3.48405-3	1.96140-3	1.25578-3	8.72252-4	6.40919-4	4.90744-4	3.87770-4	3.14106-4
0.9	6.46469-3	4.63388-3	3.48306-3	1.96109-3	1.25565-3	8.72190-4	6.40886-4	4.90724-4	3.87758-4	3.14098-4
1.00	6.46089-3	4.63192-3	3.48196-3	1.96074-3	1.25551-3	8.72120-4	6.40847-4	4.90701-4	3.87743-4	3.14089-4
1.25	6.44972-3	4.62618-3	3.47871-3	1.95971-3	1.25509-3	8.71817-4	6.40738-4	4.90638-4	3.87704-4	3.14063-4
1.50	6.43610-3	4.61916-3	3.47475-3	1.95845-3	1.25457-3	8.71668-4	6.40603-4	4.90559-4	3.87654-4	3.14030-4
1.75	6.42006-3	4.61090-3	3.47007-3	1.95696-3	1.25396-3	8.71373-4	6.40444-4	4.90466-4	3.87596-4	3.13992-4
2.00	6.40164-3	4.60142-3	3.46470-3	1.95525-3	1.25327-3	8.71034-4	6.40261-4	4.90358-4	3.87529-4	3.13948-4
2.25	6.38086-3	4.59069-3	3.45861-3	1.95331-3	1.25247-3	8.70649-4	6.40053-4	4.90236-4	3.87453-4	3.13898-4
2.50	6.35778-3	4.57871-3	3.45181-3	1.95115-3	1.25154-3	8.70218-4	6.39822-4	4.90100-4	3.87368-4	3.13842-4
2.75	6.33242-3	4.56556-3	3.44434-3	1.94876-3	1.25056-3	8.69743-4	6.39565-4	4.89950-4	3.87274-4	3.13780-4
3.00	6.30482-3	4.55123-3	3.43619-3	1.94616-3	1.24949-3	8.69225-4	6.39282-4	4.89784-4	3.87171-4	3.13713-4
3.25	6.27507-3	4.53574-3	3.42736-3	1.94333-3	1.24833-3	8.68661-4	6.38977-4	4.89605-4	3.87059-4	3.13639-4
3.50	6.24321-3	4.51911-3	3.41788-3	1.94028-3	1.24706-3	8.68052-4	6.38649-4	4.89411-4	3.86938-4	3.13560-4
3.75	6.20927-3	4.50136-3	3.40773-3	1.93702-3	1.24572-3	8.67399-4	6.38296-4	4.89204-4	3.86808-4	3.13475-4
4.00	6.17334-3	4.48252-3	3.39695-3	1.93353-3	1.24428-3	8.66703-4	6.37919-4	4.88983-4	3.86670-4	3.13384-4
4.25	6.13546-3	4.46260-3	3.38553-3	1.92984-3	1.24275-3	8.65962-4	6.37517-4	4.88747-4	3.86523-4	3.13287-4
4.50	6.09570-3	4.44163-3	3.37349-3	1.92593-3	1.24114-3	8.65178-4	6.37093-4	4.88497-4	3.86366-4	3.13184-4
4.75	6.05414-3	4.41964-3	3.36083-3	1.92182-3	1.23943-3	8.64350-4	6.36644-4	4.88233-4	3.86201-4	3.13075-4
5.00	6.01086-3	4.39668-3	3.34759-3	1.91751-3	1.23764-3	8.63479-4	6.36171-4	4.87956-4	3.86027-4	3.12961-4
5.25	5.96589-3	4.37273-3	3.33375-3	1.91299-3	1.23576-3	8.62564-4	6.35675-4	4.87664-4	3.85844-4	3.12841-4
5.50	5.91932-3	4.34786-3	3.31933-3	1.90826-3	1.23379-3	8.61607-4	6.35155-4	4.87359-4	3.85654-4	3.12716-4
5.75	5.87124-3	4.32207-3	3.30436-3	1.90333-3	1.23174-3	8.60607-4	6.34612-4	4.87039-4	3.85454-4	3.12585-4
6	5.82171-3	4.29540-3	3.28885-3	1.89822-3	1.22960-3	8.59565-4	6.34047-4	4.86706-4	3.85245-4	3.12448-4
7	5.61063-3	4.18064-3	3.22162-3	1.87584-3	1.22021-3	5.54978-4	6.31551-4	4.85235-4	3.84324-4	3.11842-4
8	5.38247-3	4.05444-3	3.14684-3	1.85055-3	1.20953-3	8.49735-4	6.28692-4	4.83548-4	3.83266-4	3.11145-4
9	5.14198-3	3.91890-3	3.06552-3	1.82258-3	1.19764-3	8.43859-4	6.25477-4	4.81648-4	3.82072-4	3.10359-4
10	4.89367-3	3.77612-3	2.97879-3	1.79214-3	1.18454-3	8.37371-4	6.21917-4	4.79538-4	3.80745-4	3.09484-4
11	4.64164-3	3.62813-3	2.88741-3	1.75948-3	1.17034-3	8.30295-4	6.18020-4	4.77224-4	3.79287-4	3.08521-4
12	4.38948-1	3.47681-3	2.79265-3	1.72482-3	1.15511-3	8.22659-4	6.13800-4	4.74711-4	3.77702-4	3.07473-4
13	4.14026-3	3.32389-3	2.69539-3	1.68841-3	1.13893-3	8.14491-4	6.09266-4	4.72004-4	3.75990-4	3.06340-4
14	3.89651-3	3.17092-3	2.59653-3	1.65051-3	1.12185-3	8.05819-4	6.04431-4	4.69109-4	3.74157-4	3.05123-4
15	3.66024-3	3.01926-3	2.49689-3	1.61136-3	1.10399-3	7.96676-4	5.99310-4	4.66033-4	3.72204-4	3.03826-4
16	3.43295-3	2.87006-3	2.39723-3	1.57119-3	1.08543-3	7.87092-4	5.93915-4	4.62782-4	3.70134-4	3.02449-4
18	3.00925-3	2.58263-3	2.20044-3	1.48869-3	1.04648-3	7.66730-4	5.82360-4	4.55791-4	3.65662-4	2.99466-4
20	2.62993-3	2.31411-3	2.01048-3	1.40470-3	1.00563-3	7.44990-4	5.69882-4	4.48163-4	3.60770-4	2.96190-4
22	2.29533-3	2.06752-3	1.83037-3	1.32068-3	9.63516-4	7.22132-4	5.56601-4	4.39987-4	3.55489-4	2.92639-4
24	2.00320-3	1.84398-3	1.66202-3	1.23786-3	9.20632-4	6.98409-4	5.42637-4	4.31314-4	3.49851-4	2.88830-4
26	1.74991-3	1.64331-3	1.50644-3	1.15722-3	8.77511-4	6.74062-4	5.28109-4	4.22205-4	3.43889-4	2.84782-4
28	1.53121-3	1.46444-3	1.36392-3	1.07951-3	8.34596-4	6.49315-4	5.13133-4	4.12722-4	3.37638-4	2.80515-4
30	1.34281-3	1.30580-3	1.23426-3	1.00528-3	7.92265-4	6.24378-4	4.97820-4	4.02926-4	3.31133-4	2.76049-4
32	1.18065-3	1.16560-3	1.11692-3	9.34894-4	7.50829-4	5.99437-4	4.82275-4	3.92875-4	3.24407-4	2.71406-4
34	1.04102-3	1.04193-3	1.01112-3	8.68556-4	7.10546-4	5.74662-4	4.66596-4	3.82627-4	3.17493-4	2.66604-4

II. SOLID ANGLE SUBTENDED BY THE LATERAL SURFACE OF A RIGHT CIRCULAR CYLINDER OF UNIT RADIUS

ρ \ h	0.2	0.4	0.6	0.8	1.0	1.2	1.4	1.6	1.8	2.0
1.2	1.20776 0	1.63842 0	1.79396 0	1.86300 0	1.89875 0	1.91940 0	1.93233 0	1.94092 0	1.94691 0	1.95124 0
1.4	6.13287-1	1.01195 0	1.23118 0	1.35275 0	1.42410 0	1.46860 0	1.49786 0	1.51798 0	1.53234 0	1.54292 0
1.6	3.73447-1	6.70631-1	8.76125-1	1.01135 0	1.10050 0	1.16064 0	1.20240 0	1.23226 0	1.25419 0	1.27070 0
1.8	2.53539-1	4.73988-1	6.46727-1	7.74499-1	8.67005-1	9.33995-1	9.83056-1	1.01957 0	1.04721 0	1.06851 0
2.0	1.84468-1	3.52378-1	4.93869-1	6.07035-1	6.94977-1	7.62546-1	8.14449-1	8.54569-1	8.85882-1	9.10596-1
2.2	1.40759-1	2.72331-1	3.88319-1	4.86135-1	5.66248-1	6.30794-1	6.82443-1	7.23759-1	7.56935-1	7.83743-1
2.4	1.11208-1	2.16910-1	3.12895-1	3.96886-1	4.68412-1	5.28240-1	5.77774-1	6.18602-1	6.52243-1	6.80031-1
2.6	9.02264-2	1.76951-1	2.57326-1	3.29544-1	3.92871-1	4.47430-1	4.93885-1	5.33170-1	5.66289-1	5.94203-1
2.8	7.47567-2	1.47179-1	2.15285-1	2.77684-1	3.33637-1	3.82981-1	4.25973-1	4.63128-1	4.95086-1	5.22511-1
3.0	6.30036-2	1.24390-1	1.82744-1	2.37000-1	2.86501-1	3.30975-1	3.70462-1	4.05220-1	4.35639-1	4.62166-1
3.2	5.38531-2	1.06550-1	1.57055-1	2.04550-1	2.48476-1	2.88537-1	3.24663-1	3.56960-1	3.85650-1	4.11026-1
3.4	4.65828-2	9.23163-2	1.36428-1	1.78281-1	2.17413-1	2.53539-1	2.86539-1	3.16430-1	3.43328-1	3.67416-1
3.6	4.07061-2	8.07745-2	1.19617-1	1.56734-1	1.91744-1	2.24390-1	2.54535-1	2.82143-1	3.07265-1	3.30009-1
3.8	3.58856-2	7.12827-2	1.05736-1	1.38850-1	1.70310-1	1.99891-1	2.27452-1	2.52935-1	2.76347-1	2.97746-1
4.0	3.18806-2	6.33806-2	9.41421-2	1.23849-1	1.52241-1	1.79123-1	2.04362-1	2.27888-1	2.49682-1	2.69771-1
4.2	2.85157-2	5.67305-2	8.43592-2	1.11146-1	1.36877-1	1.61381-1	1.84538-1	2.06275-1	2.26558-1	2.45391-1
4.4	2.56606-2	5.10800-2	7.60285-2	1.00297-1	1.23708-1	1.46114-1	1.67407-1	1.87514-1	2.06397-1	2.24044-1
4.6	2.32166-2	4.62377-2	6.88760-2	9.09597-2	1.12339-1	1.32888-1	1.52512-1	1.71140-1	1.88731-1	2.05265-1
4.8	2.11080-2	4.20558-2	6.26892-2	8.28657-2	1.02459-1	1.21362-1	1.39488-1	1.56774-1	1.73177-1	1.88673-1
5.0	1.92758-2	3.84191-2	5.73018-2	7.58047-2	9.38206-2	1.11257-1	1.28039-1	1.44108-1	1.59422-1	1.73954-1
5.2	1.76735-2	3.52364-2	5.25815-2	6.96082-2	8.62255-2	1.02354-1	1.17926-1	1.32890-1	1.47204-1	1.60844-1
5.4	1.62640-2	3.24349-2	4.84223-2	6.41411-2	7.95131-2	9.44694-2	1.08951-1	1.22910-1	1.36310-1	1.49123-1
5.6	1.50174-2	2.99559-2	4.47388-2	5.92933-2	7.35522-2	8.74557-2	1.00952-1	1.13997-1	1.26558-1	1.38608-1
5.8	1.39094-2	2.77516-2	4.14609-2	5.49747-2	6.82353-2	8.11901-2	9.37934-2	1.06006-1	1.17797-1	1.29142-1
6.0	1.29202-2	2.57827-2	3.85310-2	5.11113-2	6.34731-2	7.55706-2	8.73633-2	9.88163-2	1.09901-1	1.20594-1
6.5	1.08655-2	2.16906-2	3.24357-2	4.30628-2	5.35358-2	6.38213-2	7.38892-2	8.37127-2	9.32689-2	1.02539-1
7.5	7.99611-3	1.59708-2	2.39028-2	3.17717-2	3.95575-2	4.72417-2	5.48067-2	6.22366-2	6.95169-2	7.66348-2
8.5	6.13162-3	1.22508-2	1.83452-2	2.44028-2	3.04119-2	3.63613-2	4.22402-2	4.80388-2	5.37478-2	5.93586-2
9.5	4.85156-3	9.69542-3	1.45239-2	1.93296-2	2.41050-2	2.88431-2	3.35371-2	3.81804-2	4.27670-2	4.72910-2
10.5	3.93468-3	7.86433-3	1.17840-2	1.56887-2	1.95736-2	2.34340-2	2.72654-2	3.10634-2	3.48237-2	3.85425-2
11.5	3.25539-3	6.50737-3	9.75254-3	1.29875-2	1.62091-2	1.94139-2	2.25988-2	2.57608-2	2.88969-2	3.20044-2
12.5	2.73811-3	5.47382-3	8.20474-3	1.09285-2	1.36428-2	1.63452-2	1.90336-2	2.17058-2	2.43596-2	2.69931-2
13.5	2.33509-3	4.66845-3	6.99833-3	9.32303-3	1.16408-2	1.39501-2	1.62491-2	1.85364-2	2.08103-2	2.30692-2
14.5	2.01498-3	4.02868-3	6.03980-3	8.04707-3	1.00492-2	1.20450-2	1.40332-2	1.60127-2	1.79821-2	1.99405-2
15.5	1.75649-3	3.51201-3	5.26558-3	7.01623-3	8.76301-3	1.05050-2	1.22412-2	1.39707-2	1.56926-2	1.74061-2
16.5	1.54476-3	3.08876-3	4.63127-3	6.17152-3	7.70879-3	9.24233-3	1.07714-2	1.22954-2	1.38134-2	1.53249-2
17.5	1.36914-3	2.73769-3	4.10507-3	5.47068-3	6.83395-3	8.19430-3	9.55116-3	1.09040-2	1.22522-2	1.35952-2
18.5	1.22187-3	2.44326-3	3.66373-3	4.88279-3	6.09999-3	7.31487-3	8.52697-3	9.73585-3	1.09411-2	1.21422-2
19.5	1.09715-3	2.19392-3	3.28993-3	4.38483-3	5.47822-3	6.56974-3	7.65903-3	8.74572-3	9.82945-3	1.09099-2
20.5	9.90599-4	1.98089-3	2.97057-3	3.95934-3	4.94688-3	5.93290-3	6.91710-3	7.89919-3	8.87886-3	9.85584-3
21.5	8.98856-4	1.79746-3	2.69556-3	3.59291-3	4.48925-3	5.38435-3	6.27794-3	7.16980-3	8.05967-3	8.94732-3
22.5	8.19295-4	1.63838-3	2.45705-3	3.28510-3	4.09231-3	4.90848-3	5.72341-3	6.53690-3	7.34874-3	8.15873-3
23.5	7.49852-4	1.49953-3	2.24886-3	2.99766-3	3.74577-3	4.49301-3	5.23921-3	5.98420-3	6.72781-3	7.46988-3
24.5	6.88880-4	1.37761-3	2.06605-3	2.75405-3	3.44146-3	4.12814-3	4.81394-3	5.49872-3	6.18234-3	6.86465-3
25.5	6.35054-4	1.26998-3	1.90466-3	2.53897-3	3.17278-3	3.80596-3	4.43841-3	5.06998-3	5.70056-3	6.33004-3
26	6.10478-4	1.22084-3	1.83097-3	2.44076-3	3.05009-3	3.65884-3	4.26690-3	4.87417-3	5.48052-3	6.08584-3
28	5.25174-4	1.05026-3	1.57518-3	2.09984-3	2.62417-3	3.14807-3	3.67146-3	4.19425-3	4.71638-3	5.23774-3
30	4.56578-4	9.13093-4	1.36948-3	1.82567-3	2.28161-3	2.73722-3	3.19246-3	3.64724-3	4.10152-3	4.55522-3
32	4.00597-4	8.01144-4	1.20195-3	1.60189-3	2.00200-3	2.40185-3	2.80142-3	3.20063-3	3.59946-3	3.99785-3
34	3.54315-4	7.08591-4	1.06279-3	1.41687-3	1.77080-3	2.12454-3	2.47805-3	2.83129-3	3.18422-3	3.53680-3

II. SOLID ANGLE SUBTENDED BY THE LATERAL SURFACE OF A RIGHT CIRCULAR CYLINDER OF UNIT RADIUS (Continued)

ρ \ h	2.2	2.4	2.6	2.8	3.0	3.2	3.4	3.6	3.8	4.0
1.2	1.95448 0	1.95695 0	1.95889 0	1.96043 0	1.96168 0	1.96271 0	1.96356 0	1.96427 0	1.96488 0	1.96540 0
1.4	1.55092 0	1.55710 0	1.56198 0	1.56589 0	1.56907 0	1.57169 0	1.57387 0	1.57571 0	1.57727 0	1.57861 0
1.6	1.28338 0	1.29332 0	1.30123 0	1.30763 0	1.31287 0	1.31721 0	1.32084 0	1.32392 0	1.32654 0	1.32879 0
1.8	1.08519 0	1.09845 0	1.10913 0	1.11786 0	1.12506 0	1.13106 0	1.13612 0	1.14042 0	1.14410 0	1.14727 0
2.0	9.30329-1	9.46267-1	9.59281-1	9.70018-1	9.78962-1	9.86479-1	9.92850-1	9.98291-1	1.00297 0	1.00702 0
2.2	8.05568-1	8.23482-1	8.38309-1	8.50681-1	8.61087-1	8.69905-1	8.77430-1	8.83896-1	8.89486-1	8.94347-1
2.4	7.03083-1	7.22308-1	7.38436-1	7.52051-1	7.63616-1	7.73500-1	7.81997-1	7.89345-1	7.95734-1	8.01317-1
2.6	6.17769-1	6.37724-1	6.54688-1	6.69173-1	6.81600-1	6.92314-1	7.01595-1	7.09674-1	7.16739-1	7.22945-1
2.8	5.46042-1	5.66254-1	5.83655-1	5.98680-1	6.11697-1	6.23016-1	6.32898-1	6.41557-1	6.49175-1	6.55902-1
3.0	4.85262-1	5.05365-1	5.22878-1	5.38162-1	5.51530-1	5.63253-1	5.73564-1	5.82661-1	5.90712-1	5.97861-1
3.2	4.33412-1	4.53135-1	4.70508-1	4.85822-1	4.99338-1	5.11289-1	5.21877-1	5.31282-1	5.39655-1	5.47130-1
3.4	3.88917-1	4.08069-1	4.25113-1	4.40277-1	4.53777-1	4.65806-1	4.76541-1	4.86136-1	4.94731-1	5.02444-1
3.6	3.50524-1	3.68981-1	3.85559-1	4.00437-1	4.13789-1	4.25775-1	4.36544-1	4.46231-1	4.54957-1	4.62830-1
3.8	3.17228-1	3.34912-1	3.50932-1	3.65426-1	3.78529-1	3.90375-1	4.01087-1	4.10781-1	4.19561-1	4.27523-1
4.0	2.88211-1	3.05085-1	3.20489-1	3.34528-1	3.47309-1	3.58939-1	3.69520-1	3.79150-1	3.87919-1	3.95909-1
4.2	2.62807-1	2.78859-1	2.93616-1	3.07155-1	3.19561-1	3.30918-1	3.41311-1	3.50820-1	3.59523-1	3.67491-1
4.4	2.40469-1	2.55706-1	2.69803-1	2.82817-1	2.94812-1	3.05856-1	3.16016-1	3.25359-1	3.33951-1	3.41854-1
4.6	2.20744-1	2.35188-1	2.48627-1	2.61104-1	2.72666-1	2.83368-1	2.93263-1	3.02406-1	3.10853-1	3.18654-1
4.8	2.03257-1	2.16936-1	2.29730-1	2.41669-1	2.52789-1	2.63130-1	2.72737-1	2.81655-1	2.89928-1	2.97600-1
5.0	1.87694-1	2.00643-1	2.12811-1	2.24219-1	2.34894-1	2.44866-1	2.54171-1	2.62844-1	2.70922-1	2.78444-1
5.2	1.73793-1	1.86049-1	1.97616-1	2.08507-1	2.18740-1	2.28340-1	2.37333-1	2.45749-1	2.53618-1	2.60971-1
5.4	1.61334-1	1.72935-1	1.83927-1	1.94317-1	2.04118-1	2.13348-1	2.22026-1	2.30178-1	2.37826-1	2.44998-1
5.6	1.50130-1	1.61115-1	1.71560-1	1.81469-1	1.90849-1	1.99714-1	2.08079-1	2.15962-1	2.23384-1	2.30366-1
5.8	1.40023-1	1.50429-1	1.60356-1	1.69804-1	1.78778-1	1.87286-1	1.95341-1	2.02956-1	2.10148-1	2.16934-1
6.0	1.30878-1	1.40742-1	1.50179-1	1.59188-1	1.67771-1	1.75933-1	1.83683-1	1.91033-1	1.97994-1	2.04581-1
6.5	1.11507-1	1.20161-1	1.28494-1	1.36500-1	1.44178-1	1.51528-1	1.58554-1	1.65260-1	1.71654-1	1.77743-1
7.5	8.35794-2	9.03412-2	9.69127-2	1.03288-1	1.09462-1	1.15433-1	1.21199-1	1.26759-1	1.32115-1	1.37269-1
8.5	6.48637-2	7.02563-2	7.55304-2	8.06810-2	8.57040-2	9.05959-2	9.53542-2	9.99771-2	1.04463-1	1.08813-1
9.5	5.17473-2	5.61309-2	6.04376-2	6.46633-2	6.88047-2	7.28588-2	7.68232-2	8.06957-2	8.44749-2	8.81595-2
10.5	4.22160-2	4.58407-2	4.94134-2	5.29312-2	5.63913-2	5.97915-2	6.31296-2	6.64037-2	6.96124-2	7.27542-2
11.5	3.50805-2	3.81227-2	4.11287-2	4.40962-2	4.70231-2	4.99077-2	5.27481-2	5.55429-2	5.82907-2	6.09902-2
12.5	2.96042-2	3.21910-2	3.47518-2	3.72850-2	3.97889-2	4.22621-2	4.47031-2	4.71109-2	4.94841-2	5.18218-2
13.5	2.53119-2	2.75367-2	2.97425-2	3.19279-2	3.40916-2	3.62326-2	3.83497-2	4.04420-2	4.25085-2	4.45484-2
14.5	2.18866-2	2.38194-2	2.57379-2	2.76410-2	2.95278-2	3.13975-2	3.32491-2	3.50818-2	3.68949-2	3.86876-2
15.5	1.91103-2	2.08043-2	2.24873-2	2.41586-2	2.58174-2	2.74630-2	2.90947-2	3.07118-2	3.23138-2	3.38999-2
16.5	1.68292-2	1.83256-2	1.98135-2	2.12923-2	2.27613-2	2.42200-2	2.56678-2	2.71043-2	2.85288-2	2.99409-2
17.5	1.49326-2	1.62637-2	1.75882-2	1.89054-2	2.02149-2	2.15163-2	2.28091-2	2.40928-2	2.53670-2	2.66314-2
18.5	1.33387-2	1.45304-2	1.57166-2	1.68971-2	1.80714-2	1.92392-2	2.04001-2	2.15537-2	2.26997-2	2.38377-2
19.5	1.19866-2	1.30594-2	1.41278-2	1.51916-2	1.62504-2	1.73038-2	1.83517-2	1.93937-2	2.04294-2	2.14588-2
20.5	1.08298-2	1.18006-2	1.27677-2	1.37311-2	1.46904-2	1.56454-2	1.65957-2	1.75412-2	1.84817-2	1.94168-2
21.5	9.83250-3	1.07150-2	1.15946-2	1.24710-2	1.33441-2	1.42135-2	1.50792-2	1.59409-2	1.67984-2	1.76515-2
22.5	8.96668-3	9.77238-3	1.05757-2	1.13763-2	1.21742-2	1.29691-2	1.37608-2	1.45491-2	1.53340-2	1.61152-2
23.5	8.21023-3	8.94871-3	9.68514-3	1.04194-2	1.11513-2	1.18807-2	1.26074-2	1.33313-2	1.40522-2	1.47701-2
24.5	7.54551-3	8.22480-3	8.90236-3	9.57806-3	1.02518-2	1.09234-2	1.15927-2	1.22597-2	1.29241-2	1.35860-2
25.5	6.95829-3	7.58519-3	8.21063-3	8.83449-3	9.45665-3	1.00770-2	1.06955-2	1.13119-2	1.19262-2	1.25382-2
26	6.69003-3	7.29298-3	7.89457-3	8.49470-3	9.09327-3	9.69016-3	1.02853-2	1.08785-2	1.14698-2	1.20590-2
28	5.75827-3	6.27787-3	6.79647-3	7.31399-3	7.83055-3	8.34547-3	8.85927-3	9.37168-3	9.88262-3	1.03920-2
30	5.00829-3	5.46066-3	5.91228-3	6.36307-3	6.81299-3	7.26196-3	7.70994-3	8.15687-3	8.60268-3	9.04732-3
32	4.39574-3	4.79310-3	5.18988-3	5.58603-3	5.98150-3	6.37624-3	6.77022-3	7.16338-3	7.55568-3	7.94708-3
34	3.88901-3	4.24079-3	4.59212-3	4.94296-3	5.29326-3	5.64300-3	5.99213-3	6.34063-3	6.68845-3	7.03556-3

ASTRODYNAMICS

II. SOLID ANGLE SUBTENDED BY THE LATERAL SURFACE OF A RIGHT CIRCULAR CYLINDER OF UNIT RADIUS (Continued)

ρ \ h	4.2	4.4	4.6	4.8	5.0	5.2	5.4	5.6	5.8	6.0
1.2	1.96584 0	1.96623 0	1.96657 0	1.96687 0	1.96713 0	1.96736 0	1.96757 0	1.96775 0	1.96792 0	1.96807 0
1.4	1.57977 0	1.58077 0	1.58165 0	1.58242 0	1.58310 0	1.58371 0	1.58425 0	1.58473 0	1.58517 0	1.58556 0
1.6	1.33073 0	1.33243 0	1.33392 0	1.33522 0	1.33638 0	1.33741 0	1.33833 0	1.33916 0	1.33990 0	1.34057 0
1.8	1.15002 0	1.15242 0	1.15453 0	1.15639 0	1.15805 0	1.15952 0	1.16083 0	1.16201 0	1.16308 0	1.16404 0
2.0	1.01055 0	1.01364 0	1.01636 0	1.01877 0	1.02091 0	1.02282 0	1.02453 0	1.02607 0	1.02746 0	1.02872 0
2.2	8.98599-1	9.02335-1	9.05635-1	9.08563-1	9.11171-1	9.13504-1	9.15599-1	9.17486-1	9.19192-1	9.20739-1
2.4	8.06220-1	8.10546-1	8.14380-1	8.17791-1	8.20839-1	8.23571-1	8.26030-1	8.28250-1	8.30259-1	8.32085-1
2.6	7.28420-1	7.33271-1	7.37585-1	7.41437-1	7.44887-1	7.47989-1	7.50787-1	7.53318-1	7.55615-1	7.57704-1
2.8	6.61866-1	6.67172-1	6.71909-1	6.76152-1	6.79965-1	6.83403-1	6.86512-1	6.89330-1	6.91893-1	6.94229-1
3.0	6.04229-1	6.09919-1	6.15019-1	6.19604-1	6.23737-1	6.27475-1	6.30863-1	6.33942-1	6.36749-1	6.39312-1
3.2	5.53821-1	5.59826-1	5.65230-1	5.70106-1	5.74517-1	5.78516-1	5.82152-1	5.85465-1	5.88491-1	5.91261-1
3.4	5.09382-1	5.15636-1	5.21287-1	5.26405-1	5.31049-1	5.35274-1	5.39126-1	5.42644-1	5.45866-1	5.48821-1
3.6	4.69945-1	4.76387-1	4.82231-1	4.87543-1	4.92381-1	4.96795-1	5.00831-1	5.04527-1	5.07919-1	5.11038-1
3.8	4.34752-1	4.41326-1	4.47314-1	4.52777-1	4.57768-1	4.62337-1	4.66526-1	4.70373-1	4.73913-1	4.77174-1
4.0	4.03198-1	4.09855-1	4.15941-1	4.21513-1	4.26622-1	4.31313-1	4.35627-1	4.39599-1	4.43263-1	4.46646-1
4.2	3.74791-1	3.81485-1	3.87630-1	3.93276-1	3.98469-1	3.03252-1	4.07663-1	4.11736-1	4.15501-1	4.18987-1
4.4	3.49125-1	3.55819-1	3.61986-1	3.67672-1	3.72920-1	3.77768-1	3.82251-1	3.86402-1	3.90249-1	3.93818-1
4.6	3.25862-1	3.32523-1	3.38682-1	3.44379-1	3.49654-1	3.54542-1	3.59074-1	3.63282-1	3.67191-1	3.70826-1
4.8	3.04716-1	3.11317-1	3.17440-1	3.23124-1	3.28403-1	3.33308-1	3.37869-1	3.42114-1	3.46067-1	3.49752-1
5.0	2.85445-1	2.91962-1	2.98028-1	3.03676-1	3.08938-1	3.13840-1	3.18412-1	3.22677-1	3.26658-1	3.30378-1
5.2	2.67839-1	2.74254-1	2.80244-1	2.85839-1	2.91065-1	2.95948-1	3.00513-1	3.04782-1	3.08778-1	3.12519-1
5.4	2.51720-1	2.58017-1	2.63916-1	2.69441-1	2.74616-1	2.79465-1	2.84010-1	2.88270-1	2.92266-1	2.96015-1
5.6	2.36930-1	2.43098-1	2.48893-1	2.54336-1	2.59448-1	2.64250-1	2.68761-1	2.73000-1	2.76984-1	2.80731-1
5.8	2.23333-1	2.29364-1	2.35044-1	2.40395-1	2.45432-1	2.50176-1	2.54643-1	2.58850-1	2.62814-1	2.66548-1
6.0	2.10810-1	2.16696-1	2.22256-1	2.27505-1	2.32460-1	2.37136-1	2.41550-1	2.45716-1	2.49649-1	2.53362-1
6.5	1.83538-1	1.89047-1	1.94282-1	1.99254-1	2.03974-1	2.08454-1	2.12704-1	2.16736-1	2.20561-1	2.24190-1
7.5	1.42222-1	1.46980-1	1.51545-1	1.55923-3	1.60119-1	1.64139-1	1.67987-1	1.71671-1	1.75195-1	1.78567-1
8.5	1.13026-1	1.17102-1	1.21044-1	1.24853-1	1.28530-1	1.32079-1	1.35501-1	1.38801-1	1.41980-1	1.45042-1
9.5	9.17487-2	9.52421-2	9.86398-2	1.01942-1	1.05149-1	1.08261-1	1.11281-1	1.14208-1	1.17045-1	1.19793-1
10.5	7.58282-2	7.88336-2	8.17698-2	8.46364-2	8.74333-2	9.01605-2	9.28183-2	9.54072-2	9.79275-2	1.00380-1
11.5	6.36405-2	6.62407-2	6.87901-2	7.12881-2	7.37342-2	7.61283-2	7.84701-2	8.07597-2	8.29971-2	8.51825-2
12.5	5.41231-2	5.63872-2	5.86133-2	6.08008-2	6.29492-2	6.50582-2	6.71274-2	6.91567-2	7.11457-2	7.30946-2
13.5	4.65608-2	4.85450-2	5.05005-2	5.24265-2	5.43227-2	5.61886-2	5.80238-2	5.98281-2	6.16012-2	6.33428-2
14.5	4.04594-2	4.22095-2	4.39374-2	4.56427-2	4.73248-2	4.89833-2	5.06179-2	5.22283-2	5.38141-2	5.53752-2
15.5	3.54698-2	3.70228-2	3.85585-2	4.00764-2	4.15762-2	4.30574-2	4.45197-2	4.59628-2	4.73865-2	4.87904-2
16.5	3.13402-2	3.27262-2	3.40984-2	3.54566-2	3.68004-2	3.81294-2	3.94434-2	4.07419-2	4.20249-2	4.32920-2
17.5	2.78855-2	2.91290-2	3.03616-2	3.15828-2	3.27925-2	3.39903-2	3.51759-2	3.63492-2	3.75098-2	3.86575-2
18.5	2.49675-2	2.60887-2	2.72011-2	2.83043-2	2.93981-2	3.04822-2	3.15565-2	3.26206-2	3.36745-2	3.47178-2
19.5	2.24813-2	2.34969-2	2.45053-2	2.55062-2	2.64994-2	2.74846-2	2.84618-2	2.94306-2	3.03909-2	3.13425-2
20.5	2.03464-2	1.12703-2	2.21881-2	2.30998-2	2.40052-2	2.49040-2	2.57961-2	2.66812-2	2.75593-2	2.84302-2
21.5	1.84999-2	1.93436-2	2.01824-2	2.10160-2	2.18443-2	2.26672-2	2.34844-2	2.42959-2	2.51015-2	2.59010-2
22.5	1.68925-2	1.76658-2	1.84350-2	1.91999-2	1.99603-2	2.07162-2	2.14673-2	2.22136-2	2.29549-2	2.36911-2
23.5	1.54847-2	1.61960-2	1.69038-2	1.76079-2	1.83083-2	1.90048-2	1.96973-2	2.03856-2	2.10698-2	2.17497-2
24.5	1.42451-2	1.49013-2	1.55546-2	1.62048-2	1.68518-2	1.74954-2	1.81357-2	1.87725-2	1.94057-2	2.00352-2
25.5	1.31479-2	1.37552-2	1.43599-2	1.49620-2	1.55613-2	1.61579-2	1.67515-2	1.73421-2	1.79296-2	1.85140-2
26	1.26461-2	1.32308-2	1.38133-2	1.43932-2	1.49707-2	1.55455-2	1.61176-2	1.66870-2	1.72535-2	1.78170-2
28	1.08998-2	1.14059-2	1.19103-2	1.24128-2	1.29134-2	1.34121-2	1.39087-2	1.44033-2	1.48957-2	1.53859-2
30	9.49073-3	9.93286-3	1.03737-2	1.08131-2	1.12510-2	1.16875-2	1.21224-2	1.25558-2	1.29874-2	1.34174-2
32	8.33753-3	8.72698-3	9.11541-3	9.50276-3	9.88899-3	1.02741-2	1.06579-2	1.10406-2	1.14219-2	1.18020-2
34	7.38193-3	7.72752-3	8.07230-3	8.41624-3	8.75929-3	9.10143-3	9.44263-3	9.78286-3	1.01221-2	1.04603-2

II. SOLID ANGLE SUBTENDED BY THE LATERAL SURFACE OF A RIGHT CIRCULAR CYLINDER OF UNIT RADIUS (Continued)

ρ \ h	6.2	6.4	6.6	6.8	7.0	7.2	7.4	7.6	7.8	8.0
1.2	1.96821 0	1.96833 0	1.96844 0	1.96855 0	1.96864 0	1.96873 0	1.96881 0	1.96888 0	1.96895 0	1.96901 0
1.4	1.58592 0	1.58624 0	1.58654 0	1.58681 0	1.58705 0	1.58728 0	1.58749 0	1.58768 0	1.58786 0	1.58802 0
1.6	1.34118 0	1.34173 0	1.34224 0	1.34270 0	1.34312 0	1.34351 0	1.34386 0	1.34419 0	1.34450 0	1.34478 0
1.8	1.16492 0	1.16571 0	1.16644 0	1.16710 0	1.16771 0	1.16827 0	1.16878 0	1.16926 0	1.16970 0	1.17011 0
2.0	1.02986 0	1.03090 0	1.03185 0	1.03272 0	1.03352 0	1.03425 0	1.03493 0	1.03555 0	1.03613 0	1.03667 0
2.2	9.22145-1	9.23428-1	9.24601-1	9.25676-1	9.26663-1	9.27573-1	9.28412-1	9.29188-1	9.29907-1	9.30574-1
2.4	8.33747-1	8.35265-1	8.36655-1	8.37930-1	8.39103-1	8.40184-1	8.41182-1	8.42106-1	8.42963-1	8.43758-1
2.6	7.59610-1	7.61353-1	7.62951-1	7.64419-1	7.65771-1	7.67018-1	7.68171-1	7.69239-1	7.70230-1	7.71151-1
2.8	6.96363-1	6.98318-1	7.00113-1	7.01765-1	7.03287-1	7.04694-1	7.05995-1	7.07202-1	7.08323-1	7.09365-1
3.0	6.41658-1	6.43811-1	6.45791-1	6.47615-1	6.49299-1	6.50856-1	6.52299-1	6.53638-1	6.54883-1	6.56043-1
3.2	5.93801-1	5.96137-1	5.98287-1	6.00272-1	6.02107-1	6.03806-1	6.05382-1	6.06847-1	6.08210-1	6.09480-1
3.4	5.51537-1	5.54038-1	5.56345-1	5.58478-1	5.60453-1	5.62284-1	5.63985-1	5.65567-1	5.67041-1	5.68417-1
3.6	5.13911-1	5.16561-1	5.19011-1	5.21279-1	5.23382-1	5.25334-1	5.27151-1	5.28843-1	5.30421-1	5.31895-1
4.8	4.80185-1	4.82968-1	4.85545-1	4.87934-1	4.90154-1	4.92218-1	4.94141-1	4.95934-1	4.97608-1	4.99174-1
4.0	4.49776-1	4.52676-1	4.55365-1	4.57863-1	4.60188-1	4.62352-1	4.64372-1	4.66258-1	4.68021-1	4.69672-1
4.2	4.22219-1	4.25218-1	4.28006-1	4.30600-1	4.33018-1	4.35273-1	4.37379-1	4.39349-1	4.41193-1	4.42922-1
4.4	3.97134-1	4.00219-1	4.03091-1	4.05768-1	4.08267-1	4.10602-1	4.12786-1	4.14832-1	4.16749-1	4.18549-1
4.6	3.74211-1	3.77366-1	3.80309-1	3.83057-1	3.85627-1	3.88032-1	3.90285-1	3.92397-1	3.94381-1	3.96245-1
4.8	3.53191-1	3.56402-1	3.59403-1	3.62211-1	3.64841-1	3.67306-1	3.69619-1	3.71791-1	3.73832-1	3.75753-1
5.0	3.33856-1	3.37111-1	3.40159-1	3.43015-1	3.45695-1	3.48211-1	3.50575-1	3.52798-1	3.54891-1	3.56863-1
5.2	3.16024-1	3.19310-1	3.22393-1	3.25288-1	3.28008-1	3.30566-1	3.32974-1	3.35241-1	3.37378-1	3.39393-1
5.4	2.99535-1	3.02842-1	3.05951-1	3.08875-1	3.11626-1	3.14218-1	3.16661-1	3.18965-1	3.21139-1	3.23193-1
5.6	2.84256-1	2.87574-1	2.90698-1	2.93642-1	2.96417-1	2.99034-1	3.01505-1	3.03839-1	3.06045-1	3.08130-1
5.8	2.70068-1	2.73387-1	2.76519-1	2.79474-1	2.82265-1	2.84902-1	2.87394-1	2.89751-1	2.91982-1	2.94094-1
6.0	2.56869-1	2.60182-1	2.63313-1	2.66272-1	2.69072-1	2.71720-1	2.74228-1	2.76602-1	2.78853-1	2.80987-1
6.5	2.27632-1	2.30899-1	2.33999-1	2.36941-1	2.39735-1	2.42388-1	2.44909-1	2.47304-1	2.49581-1	2.51747-1
7.5	1.81791-1	1.84875-1	1.87823-1	1.90642-1	1.93338-1	1.95916-1	1.98381-1	2.00738-1	2.02993-1	2.05150-1
8.5	1.47990-1	1.50828-1	1.53560-1	1.56188-1	1.58716-1	1.61148-1	1.63487-1	1.65737-1	1.67901-1	1.69982-1
9.5	1.22454-1	1.25029-1	1.27521-1	1.29931-1	1.32262-1	1.34516-1	1.36695-1	1.38800-1	1.40835-1	1.42802-1
10.5	1.02766-1	1.05085-1	1.07339-1	1.09530-1	1.11658-1	1.13724-1	1.15729-1	1.17676-1	1.19565-1	1.21398-1
11.5	8.73162-2	8.93986-2	9.14302-2	9.34115-2	9.53431-2	9.72257-2	9.90600-2	1.00847-1	1.02587-1	1.04281-1
12.5	7.50033-2	7.68719-2	7.87005-2	8.04895-2	8.22391-2	8.39495-2	8.56212-2	8.72546-2	8.88502-2	9.04085-2
13.5	6.50530-2	6.67316-2	6.83786-2	6.99941-2	7.15781-2	7.31308-2	7.46524-2	7.61429-2	7.76028-2	7.90322-2
14.5	5.69114-2	5.84225-2	5.99084-2	6.13691-2	6.28045-2	6.42147-2	6.55997-2	6.69595-2	6.82944-2	6.96043-2
15.5	5.01745-2	5.15384-2	5.28822-2	5.42056-2	5.55086-2	5.67911-2	5.80530-2	5.92945-2	6.05155-2	6.17160-2
16.5	4.45431-2	4.57780-2	4.69964-2	4.81984-2	4.93837-2	5.05523-2	5.17040-2	5.28390-2	5.39570-2	5.50582-2
17.5	3.97922-2	4.09137-2	4.20218-2	4.31164-2	4.41973-2	4.52645-2	4.63178-2	4.73572-2	4.83826-2	4.93940-2
18.5	3.57504-2	3.67721-2	3.77829-2	3.87824-2	3.97707-2	4.07477-2	4.17131-2	4.26669-2	4.36091-2	4.45396-2
19.5	3.22853-2	3.32191-2	3.41438-2	3.50592-2	3.59652-2	3.68618-2	3.77487-2	3.86260-2	3.94935-2	4.03511-2
20.5	2.92938-2	3.01498-2	3.09982-2	3.18389-2	3.26717-2	3.34965-2	3.43133-2	3.51220-2	3.59224-2	3.67145-2
21.5	2.63943-2	2.74814-2	2.82620-2	2.90362-2	2.98037-2	3.05645-2	3.13185-2	3.20655-2	3.28057-2	3.35387-2
22.5	2.44222-2	2.51478-2	2.58681-2	2.65829-2	2.72920-2	2.79954-2	2.86930-2	2.93848-2	3.00707-2	3.07505-2
23.5	2.24251-2	2.30960-2	2.37623-2	2.44239-2	2.50807-2	2.57326-2	2.63796-2	2.70216-2	2.76585-2	2.82902-2
24.5	2.06609-2	2.12828-2	2.19007-2	2.25146-2	2.31243-2	2.37299-2	2.43313-2	2.49283-2	2.55210-2	2.61092-2
25.5	1.90951-2	1.96729-2	2.02473-2	2.08183-2	2.13857-2	2.19494-2	2.25096-2	2.30660-2	2.36186-2	2.41674-2
26	1.83775-2	1.89350-2	1.94893-2	2.00403-2	2.05881-2	2.11325-5	2.16735-2	2.22111-2	2.27451-2	2.32755-2
28	1.58738-2	1.63594-2	1.68426-2	1.73234-2	1.78017-2	1.82775-2	1.87506-2	1.92212-2	1.96890-2	2.01541-2
30	1.38457-2	1.42722-2	1.46968-2	1.51196-2	1.55405-2	1.59594-2	1.63763-2	1.67912-2	1.72040-2	1.76147-2
32	1.21807-2	1.25580-2	1.29338-2	1.33083-2	1.36812-2	1.40526-2	1.44224-2	1.47907-2	1.51573-2	1.55222-2
34	1.07974-2	1.11334-2	1.14683-2	1.18020-2	1.21346-2	1.24659-2	1.27960-2	1.31248-2	1.34524-2	1.37786-2

II. SOLID ANGLE SUBTENDED BY THE LATERAL SURFACE OF A RIGHT CIRCULAR CYLINDER OF UNIT RADIUS (Continued)

ρ \ h	8.2	8.4	8.6	8.8	9.0	9.2	9.4	9.6	9.8	10.0
1.2	1.96907 0	1.96912 0	1.96917 0	1.96922 0	1.96926 0	1.96931 0	1.96934 0	1.96938 0	1.96941 0	1.96945 0
1.4	1.58817 0	1.58832 0	1.58845 0	1.58857 0	1.58869 0	1.58880 0	1.58890 0	1.58899 0	1.58908 0	1.58917 0
1.6	1.34504 0	1.34529 0	1.34552 0	1.34573 0	1.34593 0	1.34611 0	1.34629 0	1.34645 0	1.34660 0	1.34675 0
1.8	1.17049 0	1.17084 0	1.17117 0	1.17148 0	1.17176 0	1.17203 0	1.17228 0	1.17252 0	1.17274 0	1.17295 0
2.0	1.03717 0	1.03764 0	1.03807 0	1.03847 0	1.03885 0	1.03921 0	1.03954 0	1.03985 0	1.04014 0	1.04042 0
2.2	9.31194-1	9.31772-1	9.32311-1	9.32814-1	9.33286-1	9.33727-1	9.34141-1	9.34530-1	9.34896-1	9.35241-1
2.4	8.44499-1	8.45188-1	8.45832-1	8.46434-1	8.46997-1	8.47525-1	8.48021-1	8.48487-1	8.48925-1	8.49338-1
2.6	7.72008-1	7.72808-1	7.73555-1	7.74254-1	7.74908-2	7.75522-1	7.76098-1	7.76640-1	7.77150-1	7.77631-1
2.8	7.10337-1	7.11244-1	7.12091-1	7.12884-1	7.13628-1	7.14325-1	7.14981-1	7.15597-1	7.16178-1	7.16725-1
3.0	6.57124-1	6.58134-1	6.59078-1	6.59963-1	6.60793-1	6.61572-1	6.62304-1	6.62993-1	6.63643-1	6.64256-1
3.2	6.10666-1	6.11775-1	6.12813-1	6.13786-1	6.14698-1	6.15556-1	6.16363-1	6.17123-1	6.17840-1	6.18516-1
3.4	5.69702-1	5.70905-1	5.72032-1	5.73089-1	5.74081-1	5.75015-1	5.75893-1	5.76721-1	5.77502-1	5.78240-1
3.6	5.33274-1	5.34565-1	5.35776-1	5.36913-1	5.37982-1	5.38987-1	5.39935-1	5.40828-1	5.41671-1	5.42468-1
3.8	5.00641-1	5.02015-1	5.03306-1	5.04518-1	5.05659-1	5.06733-1	5.07745-1	5.08701-1	5.09603-1	5.10457-1
4.0	4.71219-1	4.72672-1	4.74036-1	4.75319-1	4.76528-1	4.77666-1	4.78741-1	4.79755-1	4.80715-1	4.81622-1
4.2	4.44545-1	4.46069-1	4.47502-1	4.48852-1	4.50123-1	4.51323-1	4.52456-1	4.53526-1	4.54539-1	4.55497-1
4.4	4.20240-1	4.21830-1	4.23327-1	4.24738-1	4.26069-1	4.27325-1	4.28512-1	4.29635-1	4.30698-1	4.31706-1
4.6	3.97998-1	3.99648-1	4.01204-1	4.02671-1	4.04056-1	4.05365-1	4.06603-1	4.07775-1	4.08886-1	4.09938-1
4.8	3.77562-1	3.79268-1	3.80876-1	3.82395-1	3.83831-1	3.85188-1	3.86474-1	3.87691-1	3.88846-1	3.89941-1
5.0	3.58722-1	3.60476-1	3.62132-1	3.63698-1	3.65180-1	3.66582-1	3.67911-1	3.69170-1	3.70366-1	3.71501-1
5.2	3.41296-1	3.43094-1	3.44793-1	3.46402-1	3.47924-1	3.49367-1	3.50736-1	3.52034-1	3.53267-1	3.54439-1
5.4	3.25134-1	3.26970-1	3.28707-1	3.30353-1	3.31913-1	3.33393-1	3.34798-1	3.36131-1	3.37399-1	3.38605-1
5.6	3.10104-1	3.11973-1	3.13744-1	3.15424-1	3.17017-1	3.18530-1	3.19967-1	3.21333-1	3.22632-1	3.23869-1
5.8	2.96096-1	2.97993-1	2.99793-1	3.01501-1	3.03124-1	3.04665-1	3.06132-1	3.07527-1	3.08855-1	3.10120-1
6.0	2.83010-1	2.84931-1	2.86756-1	2.88489-1	2.90137-1	2.91705-1	2.93197-1	2.94617-1	2.95971-1	2.97262-1
6.5	2.53808-1	2.55769-1	2.57637-1	2.59416-1	2.61112-1	2.62729-1	2.64272-1	2.65744-1	2.67150-1	2.68493-1
7.5	2.07215-1	2.09190-1	2.11081-1	2.12892-1	2.14626-1	2.16288-1	2.17880-1	2.19406-1	2.20869-1	2.22272-1
8.5	1.71984-1	1.73909-1	1.75761-1	1.77543-1	1.79257-1	1.80907-1	1.82494-1	1.84022-1	1.85492-1	1.86909-1
9.5	1.44702-1	1.46537-1	1.48310-1	1.50024-1	1.51679-1	1.53278-1	1.54823-1	1.56316-1	1.57758-1	1.59152-1
10.5	1.23176-1	1.24901-1	1.26574-1	1.28196-1	1.29769-1	1.31294-1	1.32773-1	1.34206-1	1.35596-1	1.36944-1
11.5	1.05930-1	1.07536-1	1.09098-1	1.10618-1	1.12096-1	1.13535-1	1.14934-1	1.16294-1	1.17618-1	1.18904-1
12.5	9.19300-2	9.34152-2	9.48648-2	9.62794-2	9.76595-2	9.90058-2	1.00319-1	1.01600-1	1.02849-1	1.04066-1
13.5	8.04315-2	8.18010-2	8.31411-2	8.44520-2	8.57343-2	8.69884-2	8.82145-2	8.94134-2	9.05852-2	9.17306-2
14.5	7.08894-2	7.21500-2	7.33863-2	7.45984-2	7.57866-2	7.69511-2	7.80923-2	7.92105-2	8.03058-2	8.13787-2
15.5	6.28961-2	6.40559-2	6.51954-2	6.63149-2	6.74144-2	6.84942-2	6.95543-2	7.05949-2	7.16163-2	7.26186-2
16.5	5.61424-2	5.72098-2	5.82604-2	5.92942-2	6.03113-2	6.13117-2	6.22956-2	6.32631-2	6.42142-2	6.51492-2
17.5	5.03913-2	5.13746-2	5.23437-2	5.32989-2	5.42399-2	5.51670-2	5.60801-2	5.69792-2	5.78646-2	5.87361-2
18.5	4.54583-2	4.63653-2	4.72604-2	4.81436-2	4.90150-2	4.98746-2	5.07223-2	5.15582-2	5.23823-2	5.31947-2
19.5	4.11989-2	4.20367-2	4.28646-2	4.36824-2	4.44902-2	4.52879-2	4.60756-2	4.68531-2	4.76206-2	4.83781-2
20.5	3.74983-2	3.82736-2	3.90404-2	3.97988-2	4.05486-2	4.12898-2	4.20224-2	4.27464-2	4.34618-2	4.41685-2
21.5	3.42647-2	3.49835-2	3.56951-2	3.63994-2	3.70964-2	3.77860-2	3.84683-2	3.91432-2	3.98106-2	4.04706-2
22.5	3.14242-2	3.20919-2	3.27533-2	3.34085-2	3.40574-2	3.47000-2	3.53363-2	3.59662-2	3.65897-2	3.72067-2
23.5	2.89167-2	2.95380-2	3.01539-2	3.07645-2	3.13696-2	3.19693-2	3.25635-2	3.31522-2	3.37353-2	3.43129-2
24.5	2.66929-2	2.72721-2	2.78467-2	2.84166-2	2.89819-2	2.95424-2	3.00982-2	3.06491-2	3.11952-2	3.17365-2
25.5	2.47122-2	2.52532-2	2.57901-2	2.63231-2	2.68519-2	2.73766-2	2.78972-2	2.84136-2	2.89258-2	2.94337-2
26	2.38023-2	2.43254-2	2.48449-2	2.53605-2	2.58723-2	2.63803-2	2.68844-2	2.73846-2	2.78809-2	2.83732-2
28	2.06165-2	2.10761-2	2.15328-2	2.19866-2	2.24375-2	2.28854-2	2.33304-2	2.37723-2	2.42112-2	2.46470-2
30	1.80232-2	1.84296-2	1.88338-2	1.92357-2	1.96353-2	2.00327-2	2.04277-2	2.08203-2	2.12106-2	2.15984-2
32	1.58855-2	1.62471-2	1.66069-2	1.69650-2	1.73212-2	1.76757-2	1.80283-2	1.83790-2	1.87278-2	1.90748-2
34	1.41035-2	1.44271-2	1.47492-2	1.50699-2	1.53892-2	1.57071-2	1.60235-2	1.63383-2	1.66517-2	1.69635-2

II. SOLID ANGLE SUBTENDED BY THE LATERAL SURFACE OF A RIGHT CIRCULAR CYLINDER OF UNIT RADIUS (Continued)

ρ \ h	11	12	13	14	15	16	17	18	19	20
1.2	1.96958 0	1.96968 0	1.96976 0	1.96983 0	1.96988 0	1.96992 0	1.96995 0	1.96998 0	1.97001 0	1.97003 0
1.4	1.58952 0	1.58979 0	1.59000 0	1.59016 0	1.59030 0	1.59041 0	1.59050 0	1.59058 0	1.59064 0	1.59069 0
1.6	1.34735 0	1.34782 0	1.34818 0	1.34846 0	1.34870 0	1.34889 0	1.34904 0	1.34917 0	1.34929 0	1.34938 0
1.8	1.17383 0	1.17450 0	1.17503 0	1.17544 0	1.17578 0	1.17606 0	1.17628 0	1.17648 0	1.17664 0	1.17678 0
2.0	1.04159 0	1.04248 0	1.04317 0	1.04372 0	1.04417 0	1.04453 0	1.04484 0	1.04509 0	1.04531 0	1.04549 0
2.2	9.36695-1	9.37807-1	9.38675-1	9.39365-1	9.39923-1	9.40381-1	9.40761-1	9.41079-1	9.41349-1	9.41580-1
2.4	8.51083-1	8.52418-1	8.53462-1	8.54292-1	8.54964-1	8.55516-1	8.55974-1	8.56358-1	8.56683-1	8.56962-1
2.6	7.79665-1	7.81223-1	7.82442-1	7.83414-1	7.84200-1	7.84846-1	7.85382-1	7.85833-1	7.86214-1	7.86541-1
2.8	7.19044-1	7.20824-1	7.22218-1	7.23330-1	7.24231-1	7.24971-1	7.25587-1	7.26103-1	7.26542-1	7.26916-1
3.0	6.66855-1	6.68852-1	6.70420-1	6.71671-1	6.72687-1	6.73521-1	6.74215-1	6.74798-1	6.75293-1	6.75716-1
3.2	6.21388-1	6.23600-1	6.25338-1	6.26728-1	6.27856-1	6.28784-1	6.29556-1	6.30205-1	6.30756-1	6.31228-1
3.4	5.81377-1	5.83798-1	5.85704-1	5.87230-1	5.88470-1	5.89490-1	5.90340-1	5.91055-1	5.91663-1	5.92183-1
3.6	5.45862-1	5.48487-1	5.50556-1	5.52216-1	5.53565-1	5.54678-1	5.55605-1	5.56385-1	5.57048-1	5.57616-1
3.8	5.14097-1	5.16920-1	5.19150-1	5.20940-1	5.22398-1	5.23600-1	5.24603-1	5.25448-1	5.26166-1	5.26782-1
4.0	4.85500-1	4.88513-1	4.90898 1	4.92816-1	4.94380-1	4.95671-1	4.96749-1	4.97658 2	4.98431-1	4.99094-1
4.2	4.59601-1	4.62799-1	4.65334-1	4.67376-1	4.69044-1	4.70422-1	4.71574-1	4.72545-1	4.73373-1	4.74082-1
4.4	4.36025-1	4.39399-1	4.42080-1	4.44243 1	4.46011-1	4.47475-1	4.48699-1	4.49732-1	4.50613-1	4.51369-1
4.6	4.14461-1	4.18004-1	4.20825-1	4.23106-1	4.24973-1	4.26520-1	4.27815-1	4.28909-1	4.29842-1	4.30643-1
4.8	3.94656-1	3.98360-1	4.01316-1	4.03710-1	4.05672-1	4.07300-1	4.08665-1	4.09819-1	4.10803-1	4.11649-1
5.0	3.76396-1	3.80253-1	3.83339-1	3.85841-1	3.87897-1	3.89604-1	3.91036-1	3.92249-1	3.93284-1	3.94174-1
5.2	3.59504-1	3.63505-1	3.66714-1	3.69322-1	3.71467-1	3.73252-1	3.74750-1	3.76020-1	3.77104-1	3.78038-1
5.4	3.43827-1	3.47965-1	3.51291-1	3.54000-1	3.56232-1	3.58091-1	3.59654-1	3.60979-1	3.62113-1	3.63089-1
5.6	3.29236-1	3.33503-1	3.36941-1	3.39746-1	3.42062-1	3.43993-1	3.45618-1	3.46998-1	3.48179-1	3.49198-1
5.8	3.15621-1	3.20008-1	3.23552-1	3.26450-1	3.28845-1	3.30846-1	3.32532-1	3.33966-1	3.35193-1	3.36252-1
6.0	3.02886-1	3.07384-1	3.11028-1	3.14014-1	3.16487-1	3.18555-1	3.20300-1	3.21785-1	3.23058-1	3.24157-1
6.5	2.74376-1	2.79120-1	2.82988-1	2.86175-1	2.88826-1	2.91051-1	2.92935-1	2.94543-1	2.95924-1	2.97120-1
7.5	2.28488-1	2.33581-1	2.37791-1	2.41298-1	2.44243-1	2.46736-1	2.48862-1	2.50686-1	2.52261-1	2.53630-1
8.5	1.93246-1	1.98524-1	2.02945-1	2.06671-1	2.09832-1	2.12530-1	2.14847-1	2.16848-1	2.18586-1	2.20103-1
9.5	1.65452-1	1.70779-1	1.75302-1	1.79157-1	1.82461-1	1.85305-1	1.87766-1	1.89906-1	1.91775-1	1.93415-1
10.5	1.43092-1	1.48367-1	1.52901-1	1.56811-1	1.60193-1	1.63131-1	1.65693-1	1.67935-1	1.69905-1	1.71643-1
11.5	1.24825-1	1.29971-1	1.34449-1	1.38352-1	1.41761-1	1.44746-1	1.47369-1	1.49681-1	1.51724-1	1.53537-1
12.5	1.09712-1	1.14680-1	1.19051-1	1.22899-1	1.26291-1	1.29286-1	1.31937-1	1.34289-1	1.36381-1	1.38246-1
13.5	9.70772-2	1.01834-1	1.06063-1	1.09821-1	1.13162-1	1.16136-1	1.18787-1	1.21154-1	1.23272-1	1.25171-1
14.5	8.64177-2	9.09463-2	9.50095-2	9.86522-2	1.01917-1	1.04846-1	1.07474-1	1.09835-1	1.11960-1	1.13875-1
15.5	7.73521-2	8.16447-2	8.55292-2	8.90399-2	9.22107-2	9.50741-2	9.76608-2	9.99992-2	1.02115-1	1.04032-1
16.5	6.95864-2	7.36430-2	7.73426-2	8.07111-2	8.37747-2	8.65597-2	8.90911-2	9.13926-2	9.34864-2	9.53927-2
17.5	6.28905-2	6.67161-2	7.02299-2	7.34510-2	7.63996-2	7.90965-2	8.15620-2	8.38159-2	8.58768-2	8.77622-2
18.5	5.70820-2	6.06853-2	6.40160-2	6.70883-2	6.99176-2	7.25201-2	7.49123-2	7.71105-2	7.91301-2	8.09861-2
19.5	5.20154-2	5.54067-2	5.85598-2	6.14847-2	6.41931-2	6.66977-2	6.90116-2	7.11481-2	7.31200-2	7.49401-2
20.5	4.75729-2	5.07639-2	5.37463-2	5.65273-2	5.91155-2	6.15207-2	6.37533-2	6.58240-2	6.77436-2	6.95226-2
21.5	4.36589-2	4.66616-2	4.94814-2	5.21232-2	5.45934-2	5.68993-2	5.90492-2	6.10517-2	6.29156-2	6.46497-2
22.5	4.01949-2	4.30213-2	4.56871-2	4.81955-2	5.05509-2	5.27589-2	5.48259-2	5.67589-2	5.85649-2	6.02515-2
23.5	3.71163-2	3.97781-2	4.22987-2	4.46797-2	4.69243-2	4.90367-2	5.10217-2	5.28849-2	5.46320-2	5.62691-2
24.5	3.43692-2	3.68778-2	3.92617-2	4.15219-2	4.36603-2	4.56799-2	4.75844-2	4.93782-2	5.10660-2	5.26528-2
25.5	3.19088-2	3.42748-2	3.65306-2	3.86764-2	4.07133-2	4.26435-2	4.44696-2	4.61952-2	4.78239-2	4.93598-2
26	3.07741-2	3.30726-2	3.52674-2	3.73584-2	3.93464-2	4.12332-2	4.30211-2	4.47131-2	4.63125-2	4.78230-2
28	2.67791-2	2.88310-2	3.08012-2	3.26887-2	3.44934-2	3.62159-2	3.78574-2	3.94197-2	4.09046-2	4.23147-2
30	2.35008-2	2.53397-2	2.71135-2	2.88210-2	3.04614-2	3.20348-2	3.35416-2	3.49826-2	3.63590-2	3.76724-2
32	2.07801-2	2.24347-2	2.40370-2	2.55855-2	2.70794-2	2.85184-2	2.99023-2	3.12314-2	3.25064-2	3.37281-2
34	1.84991-2	1.99938-2	2.14460-2	2.28543-2	2.42179-2	2.55360-2	2.68084-2	2.80350-2	2.92161-2	3.03521-2

ASTRODYNAMICS

II. SOLID ANGLE SUBTENDED BY THE LATERAL SURFACE OF A RIGHT CIRCULAR CYLINDER OF UNIT RADIUS (Continued)

ρ＼h	22	26	30	40	50	60	70	80	90	100
1.2	1.97006 0	1.97011 0	1.97014 0	1.97017 0	1.97019 0	1.97020 0	1.97021 0	1.97021 0	1.97021 0	1.97021 0
1.4	1.59078 0	1.59090 0	1.59098 0	1.59108 0	1.59112 0	1.59115 0	1.59116 0	1.59117 0	1.59118 0	1.59119 0
1.6	1.34953 0	1.34974 0	1.34987 0	1.35004 0	1.35012 0	1.35016 0	1.35019 0	1.35021 0	1.35022 0	1.35023 0
1.8	1.17700 0	1.17730 0	1.17749 0	1.17774 0	1.17786 0	1.17792 0	1.17796 0	1.17798 0	1.17800 0	1.17801 0
2.0	1.04579 0	1.04619 0	1.04644 0	1.04677 0	1.04692 0	1.04701 0	1.04706 0	1.04709 0	1.04711 0	1.04713 0
2.2	9.41951-1	9.42453-1	9.42769-1	9.43186-1	9.43380-1	9.43485-1	9.43548-1	9.43589-1	9.43617-1	9.43638-1
2.4	8.57409-1	8.58016-1	8.58397-1	8.58901-1	8.59135-1	8.59262-1	8.59339-1	8.59388-1	8.59422-1	8.59447-1
2.6	7.87066-1	7.87778-1	7.88226-1	7.88818-1	7.89093-1	7.89242-1	7.89333-1	7.89391-1	7.89431-1	7.89460-1
2.8	7.27520-1	7.28338-1	7.28853-1	7.29535-1	7.29851-1	7.30023 1	7.30127-1	7.30194-1	7.30240-1	7.30273-1
3.0	6.76398-1	6.77323-1	6.77906-1	6.78678-1	6.79036-1	6.79231-1	6.79348-1	6.79424-1	6.79477-1	6.79514-1
3.2	6.31988-1	6.33021-1	6.33672-1	6.34534-1	6.34934-1	6.35152-1	6.35283-1	6.35368-1	6.35427-1	6.35469-1
3.4	5.93021-1	5.94161-1	5.94880-1	5.95832-1	5.96275-1	5.96516-1	5.96661-1	5.96756-1	5.96820-1	5.96867-1
3.6	5.58533-1	5.59779-1	5.60566-1	5.61609-1	5.62095-1	5.62359-1	5.62518-1	5.62622-1	5.62693-1	5.62743-1
3.8	5.27776-1	5.29129-1	5.29984-1	5.31118-1	5.31646-1	5.31933-1	5.32107-1	5.32219-1	5.32297-1	5.32352-1
4.0	5.00164-1	5.01624-1	5.02546-1	5.03771-1	5.04342-1	5.04652-1	5.04840-1	5.04962-1	5.05045-1	5.05105-1
4.2	4.75229-1	4.76794-1	4.77783-1	4.79100-1	4.79713-1	4.80047-1	4.80248-1	4.80380-1	4.80469-1	4.80534-1
4.4	4.52591-1	4.54260-1	4.55317-1	4.56724-1	4.57380-1	4.57737-1	4.57953-1	4.58093-1	4.58189-1	4.58258-1
4.6	4.31940-1	4.33713-1	4.34837-1	4.36334-1	4.37032-1	4.37413-1	4.37643-1	4.37793-1	4.37895-1	4.37969-1
4.8	4.13020-1	4.14896-1	4.16086-1	4.17673-1	4.18414-1	4.18818-1	4.19063-1	4.19221-1	4.19330-1	4.19408-1
5.0	3.95617-1	3.97595-1	3.98851-1	4.00528-1	4.01312-1	4.01739-1	4.01997-1	4.02166-1	4.02281-1	4.02363-1
5.2	3.79553-1	3.81631-1	3.82953-1	3.84719-1	3.85545-1	3.85996-1	3.86268-1	3.86446-1	3.86567-1	3.86654-1
5.4	3.64674-1	3.66852-1	3.68238-1	3.70093-1	3.70962-1	3.71436-2	3.71723-1	3.71909-1	3.72037-1	3.72129-1
5.6	3.50852-1	3.53128-1	3.54579-1	3.56522-1	3.57433-1	3.57930-1	3.58231-1	3.58427-1	3.58561-1	3.58658-1
5.8	3.37975-1	3.40348-1	3.41862-1	3.43893-1	3.44846-1	3.45367-1	3.45682-1	3.45887-1	3.46028-1	3.46129-1
6.0	3.25947-1	3.28415-1	3.29993-1	3.32111-1	3.33106-1	3.33650-1	3.33979-1	3.34193-1	3.34340-1	3.34446-1
6.5	2.99070-1	3.01771-1	3.03503-1	3.05837-1	3.06936 1	3.07538-1	3.07903-1	3.08140-1	3.08303-1	3.08420-1
7.5	2.55877-1	2.59013-1	2.61041-1	2.63793-1	2.65097-1	2.65813-1	2.66248-1	2.66531-1	2.66726-1	2.66866-1
8.5	2.22609-1	2.26138-1	2.28440-1	2.31591-1	2.33094-1	2.33923-1	2.34427-1	2.34756-1	2.34982-1	2.35145-1
9.5	1.96141-1	2.00019-1	2.02572-1	2.06099-1	2.07795-1	2.08734-1	2.09307-1	2.09681-1	2.09939-1	2.10123-1
10.5	1.74552-1	1.78731-1	1.81512-1	1.85391-1	1.87273-1	1.88320-1	1.88959-1	1.89378-1	1.89667-1	1.89874-1
11.5	1.56591-1	1.61027-1	1.64010-1	1.68216-1	1.70276-1	1.71427-1	1.72133-1	1.72595-1	1.72915-1	1.73144-1
12.5	1.41411-1	1.46059-1	1.49220-1	1.53727-1	1.55956-1	1.57209-1	1.57978-1	1.58484-1	1.58834-1	1.59085-1
13.5	1.28415-1	1.33232-1	1.36547-1	1.41328-1	1.43718-1	1.45068-1	1.45901-1	1.46449-1	1.46828-1	1.47102-1
14.5	1.17169-1	1.22117-1	1.25561-1	1.30589-1	1.33130-1	1.34575-1	1.35469-1	1.36059-1	1.36467-1	1.36762-1
15.5	1.07352-1	1.12393-1	1.15943-1	1.21192-1	1.23876-1	1.25410-1	1.26364-1	1.26994-1	1.27432-1	1.27748-1
16.5	9.87155-2	1.03817-1	1.07453-1	1.12896-1	1.15712-1	1.17333-1	1.18344-1	1.19015-1	1.19481-1	1.19818-1
17.5	9.10694-2	9.62022-2	9.99031-2	1.05515-1	1.08454-1	1.10158-1	1.11224-1	1.11933-1	1.12427-1	1.12785-1
18.5	8.42621-2	8.93999-2	9.31475-2	9.89041-2	1.01956-1	1.03738-1	1.04858-1	1.05605-1	1.06126-1	1.06504-1
19.5	7.81718-2	8.32920-2	8.70693-2	9.29470-2	9.61031-2	9.79583-2	9.91302-2	9.99138-2	1.00462-1	1.00859-1
20.5	7.26993-2	7.77824-2	8.15742-2	8.75508-2	9.08012-3	9.27260-2	9.39474-2	9.47666-2	9.53407-2	9.57578-2
21.5	6.77631-2	7.27924-2	7.65849-2	8.26398-2	8.59752-2	8.79652-2	8.92341-2	9.00877-2	9.06873-2	9.11235-2
22.5	6.33951-2	6.82567-2	7.20379-2	7.81515-2	8.15629-2	8.36139-2	8.49281-2	8.58149-2	8.64392-2	8.68943-2
23.5	5.92381-2	6.41207-2	6.78797-2	7.40341-2	7.75126-2	7.96204-2	8.09777-2	8.18966-2	8.25451-2	8.30184-2
24.5	5.55437-2	6.03378-2	6.40655-2	7.02440-2	7.37812-2	7.59416-2	7.73398-2	7.82896-2	7.89615-2	7.94528-2
25.5	5.21704-2	5.68689-2	6.05571-2	6.67446-2	7.03324-2	7.25412-2	7.39780-2	7.49576-2	7.56521-1	7.61610-2
26	5.05929-2	5.52413-2	5.89072-2	6.50939-2	6.87040-2	7.09355-2	7.23909-2	7.33849-2	7.40905-2	7.46079-2
28	4.49208-2	4.93585-2	5.29206-2	5.90727-2	6.27538-2	6.50659-2	6.65901-2	6.76386-2	6.83867-2	6.89374-2
30	4.01167-2	4.43342-2	4.77750-2	5.38500-2	5.75745-2	5.99521-2	6.15364-2	6.26346-2	6.34223-2	6.40044-2
32	3.60162-2	4.00114-2	4.33199-2	4.92838-2	5.30278-2	5.54564-2	5.70926-2	5.82354-2	5.90598-2	5.96715-2
34	2.24916-2	3.62675-2	3.94376-2	4.52648-2	4.90070-2	5.14733-2	5.31534-2	5.43361-2	5.51942-2	5.58335-2

The Interstitial Sphere*
General Solution

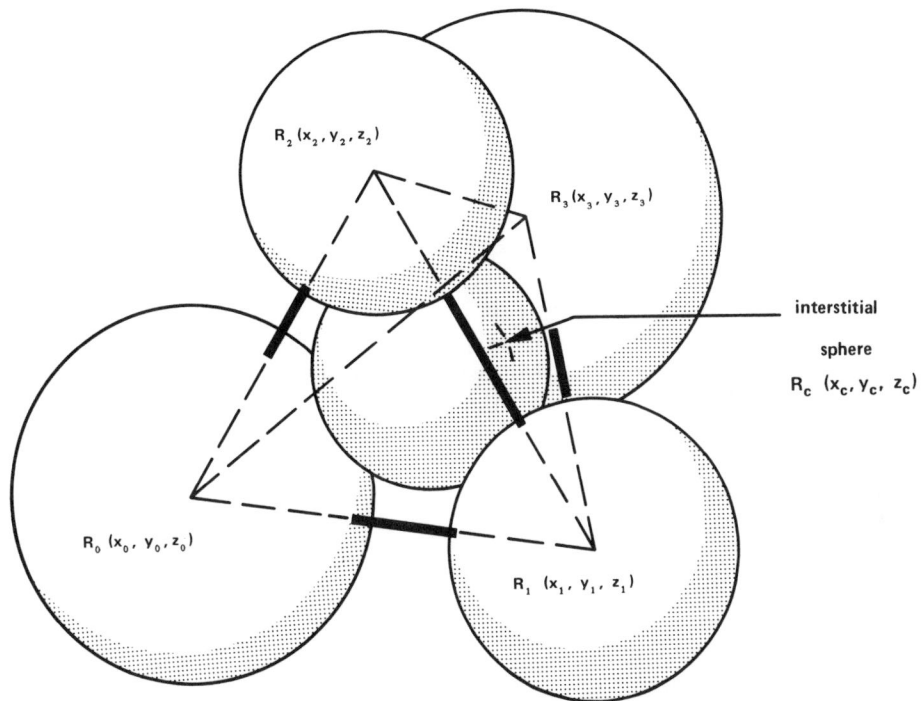

Four, noncoplanar spheres of radius R_i with centers having coordinates x_i, y_i, z_i ($i = 0,1,2,3$) may have in common tangency a fifth sphere, the interstitial sphere, of radius R_c at x_c, y_c, z_c. The simultaneous solution of four distance equations determines this condition:

$$(x_i - x_c)^2 + (y_i - y_c)^2 + (z_i - z_c)^2 = (R_i R_c)^2, \quad i = 0,1,2,3$$

A solution exists when R_c is finite definite. The solution can be expressed in closed form using seven determinants (D,E,F,G,H,P,Q) as follows:

$$x_c = \frac{E}{D} + \frac{F}{D} R_c, \qquad y_c = \frac{G}{D} + \frac{H}{D} R_c, \qquad z_c = \frac{P}{D} + \frac{Q}{D} R_c$$

where

$$R_c = \frac{U}{T} \left[1 \pm \left(1 - \frac{VT}{U^2} \right)^{1/2} \right]$$

and

$$T = \left(\frac{F}{D}\right)^2 + \left(\frac{H}{D}\right)^2 + \left(\frac{Q}{D}\right)^2 - 1$$

$$U = \left(x_0 - \frac{E}{D}\right) \frac{F}{D} + \left(y_0 - \frac{G}{D}\right) \frac{H}{D} + \left(z_0 - \frac{P}{D}\right) \frac{Q}{D} + R_0$$

$$V = \left(x_0 - \frac{E}{D}\right)^2 + \left(y_0 - \frac{G}{D}\right)^2 + \left(z_0 - \frac{P}{D}\right)^2 - R_0{}^2$$

* For further details, see Sickafus, E. N. and Mackie, N. A., *Acta Crystallogr.*, 30, 850, 1974.

$$D = \begin{vmatrix} x_0 - x_1 & x_0 - x_2 & x_3 - x_3 \\ y_0 - y_1 & y_0 - y_2 & y_0 - y_3 \\ z_0 - z_1 & z_0 - z_2 & z_0 - z_3 \end{vmatrix}$$

Set

$$C_i^2 = x_i^2 + y_i^2 + z_i^2$$

and

$$A_j = C_0^2 - C_j^2 + R_j^2 - R_0^2 \quad (j = 1,2,3)$$

then 2E, 2G, or 2P are obtained by replacing, respectively, the first, second, or third rows of D with the row $[A_1\ A_2\ A_3]$ and, similarly, F, H, and G are obtained by using the row $[(R_1-R_0)\ R_2-R_0)\ (R_3-R_0)]$ to replace, respectively, the first, second, or third rows of D, e. g.,

$$E = \tfrac{1}{2} \begin{vmatrix} A_1 & A_2 & A_3 \\ y_0 - y_1 & y_0 - y_2 & y_0 - y_3 \\ z_0 - z_1 & z_0 - z_2 & z_0 - z_3 \end{vmatrix} \qquad F = \begin{vmatrix} R_1 - R_0 & R_2 - R_0 & R_3 - R_0 \\ y_0 - y_1 & y_0 - y_2 & y_0 - y_3 \\ z_0 - z_1 & z_0 - z_2 & z_0 - z_3 \end{vmatrix}$$

Preferred Orientation Solution with $R_0 = R_1 = R_2 = R_3$.

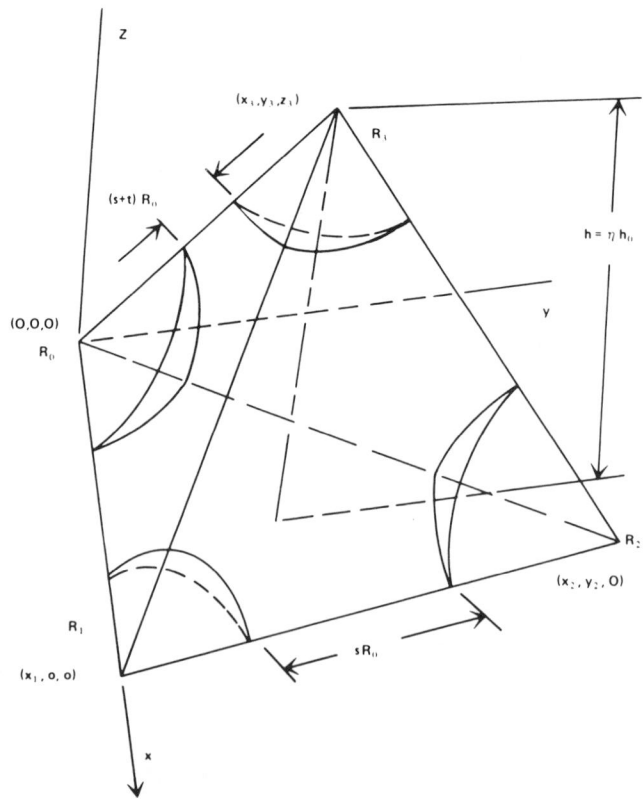

A simplified solution occurs by use of a preferred orientation of coordinates such that the sphere centers are located at: $R_0(0,0,0)$, $R_1(x_1,0,0)$, $R_2(x_2,y_2,0)$, $R_3,(x_3,y_3,z_3)$. In this case

$$F = H = Q = O, \quad T = -1, \quad U = R_0,$$

$$D = -x_1 y_2 z_3, \quad V = x_c^2 + y_c^2 + z_c^2$$

$$X_c = \frac{x_1}{2}, \quad y_c = \frac{G}{D}, \quad z_c = \frac{P}{D}, \quad R_c = \sqrt{V - R_0}$$

There always exists a uniquely defined interstitial sphere for a noncoplanar tetrahedral group of equal-radii spheres no matter how they may be arranged in space.

Parametric Variations of the Tetrahedron with Equilaterial Base

1. Altitude $h = \eta h$ were h_0 is the minimum altitude

$$\frac{R_c}{R_0} = \sqrt{\frac{2}{3}} \, \eta + \frac{1}{\sqrt{6\eta}} - 1, \quad R_0 = R_1 = R_2 = R_3$$

2. Separation S of basal spheres with R_3 (x_3,y_3,z_3) fixed

$$\frac{R_c}{R_0} = \frac{1}{2} \sqrt{\frac{3}{2}} \, S + \sqrt{\frac{3}{2}} - 1, \quad R_0 = R_1 = R_2 = R_3$$

3. Symmetrical separation of apex sphere from equilateral base

$$\frac{R_c}{R_0} = \frac{(2+t)^2}{2[\,(2+t)^2 - \frac{4}{3}\,]^{1/2}} - 1, \quad R_0 = R_1 = R_2 = R_3$$

4. Combined s,t-variations with variable apex sphere

$$R_0 = R_1 = R_2 \neq R_3 = pR_0$$

$$\frac{R_c}{R_0} = \frac{(1+s+t+p)^2 - 1 + p^2 - 2p \, \sqrt{(1+s+t+p)^2 - \frac{1}{3}(2+s)^2}}{2[1 - pt \, \sqrt{(1+s+tsp)^2 - \frac{1}{3}(2+s)^2}\,]}$$

5. Combined, p,η variation with $s = 0$, $R_0 = R_1 = R_2 \neq R_3 = pR_0$

$$\frac{R_c}{R_0} = \frac{1 + 3p^2 + \eta^2 \,[3(1+p)^2 - 41 - 6p\eta \, \sqrt{(1+p)^2 - \frac{4}{3}}}{6[1+p + \eta \sqrt{(1+p)^2 - \frac{4}{3}}\,]}$$

MATHEMATICAL SYMBOLS AND ABBREVIATIONS

Symbols and Abbreviations of Commercial Arithmetic

#	Number (if written before a numeral); pounds (weight), lb. (if written after a numeral.)	Apr.	April	Dr.	Debit, debtor, doctor
		a/s	Account sales	E	East
		Aug.	August	ea.	Each
		av.	Average	e.g.	(exempli gratia) for example
@	At, as "@ 5¢ per C," for "at 5 cents per hundred."	avoir.	Avoirdupois		
		bal.	Balance	etc.	And so forth
		bbl. *or* brl.	Barrel	ex.	Example, exercise, express
		bk.	Bank, book		
%	Per cent; per hundred.	bl.	Bale	exch.	Exchange
		B/L	Bill of lading	exp.	Expense
¢	Cents (placed after figures)	bu.	Bushel	F	Fahrenheit
		bx.	Box	Feb.	February
		C	(centum) hundred	f.o.b.	Free on board
$	Dollars, (prefixed before figures).	cd.	Cord	Fri.	Friday
		cg.	Centigram	frt.	Freight
		ch.	Chain	ft. *or* f.	Foot
£	Pounds (British currency)	chg.	Charge	gal.	Gallon
		c.i.f.	Carriage and insurance free.	gi.	Gill
✓	Check mark			gr.	Grain
		ck.	Check	gro.	Gross
&	And, as in "Smith, Jones & Co."	cm.	Centimeter	gr. gro.	Great gross
		cml.	Commercial	guar.	Guarantee
		Co.	Company, county	hf.	Half
c/o	Care of			hhd.	Hogshead
A	Acre			hr.	Hour
a/c	Account	c.o.d.	Cash on delivery	i.e.	(id est) that is
acct.	Account	coll.	Collection	in.	Inch, inches
ad val	(ad valorem), according to value	com.	Commission	ins.	Insurance
		cr.	Credit, creditor, crate	*inst.*	(instant) the present month
A.M.	(ante meridiem) in the morning, between midnight and the following noon. 12:00 A.M. is noon, better 12:00 M, 12:01 A.M. is one minute after midnight.	cs.	Case	int.	Interest
or		c. *or* ct.	Cent	inv.	Invoice
a.m.				inv'y	Inventory
		cu.	Cubic	Jan.	January
		cwt.	Hundredweight	kg.	Keg, kilogram
		d	Pence (British currency)	km.	Kilometer
		da.	Day	lb. lbs.	Pound, pounds
		Dec.	December	lp	List price
		dept.	Department	ltd.	Limited
		dft.	Draft	L.S.	(locus sigillis) place for the seal
amt.	Amount	disc.	Discount		
ans.	Answer	dm.	Decimeter	M	(mille) thousand; meridiem as in 12:00 M
ap	Apothecaries' weight or measure	do.	Ditto		
		doz.	Dozen		
		dr.	Dram	m.	Mill, meter

MATHEMATICAL SYMBOLS AND ABBREVIATIONS (Continued)

Symbols and Abbreviations of Commercial Arithmetic

Mar.	March	P.M.	(post meridiem)	Sat.	Saturday
mdse.	Merchandise	*or*	in the after-	sec.	Second
mi.	Mile	p.m.	noon, between	sec'y	Secretary
min.	Minute		noon and the	Sept.	September
mm.	Millimeter		following mid-	set.	Settlement
mo.	Month		night. 12:00	sig.	Signed, signa-
Mon.	Monday		P.M. is mid-		ture
mortg.	Mortgage		night, 12:01	sq.	Square
N, NE,	North, North-		P.M. is one	stk.	Stock
NW,	east, North-		minute after	Sun.	Sunday
etc.	west, etc.		noon.	T.	Ton
no. *or*	Number	pp.	Pages	temp.	Temperature
numb.		pr.	Pair	Thu.	Thursday
Nov.	November	*prox.*	(proximo) in the	treas.	Treasurer,
Oct.	October		following		treasury
O.K.	Correct		month	Tues.	Tuesday
oz.	Ounce	pt.	Pint, point	*ult.*	(ultimo) in the
p.	Page	pwt.	Pennyweight		last month
par.	Paragraph	(*or*		*via*	By way of
pay't	Payment	dwt.)		viz.	(videlicet)
pc.	Piece	qr.	Quire		namely
pd.	Paid	qt.	Quart	vol.	Volume
per	By, by the, as in	rd.	Rod, road	W	West
	"per C," "per	rec'd	Received	Wed.	Wednesday
	M," "per doz."	rec't	Receipt	wk.	Week
		rm.	Ream	wt.	Weight
pfd.	Preferred	S, SE,	South, South-	yd.	Yard
pk.	Peck, pecks	SW,	east, South-	yr.	Year
pkg.	Package	etc.	west, etc.		

Symbols Belonging to Plane Geometry

In blackboard presentation combined with oral discussion a variety of informal abbreviations is acceptable. But in written reports it is best to use only standard abbreviations, preferably those which are found on a typewriter. Avoid characters not sufficiently distinctive as to remain legible and unambiguous when written hurriedly. When used as nouns, the plural may be indicated by adding "s"; when used as relations the copula "is" and preposition "to" may be deleted.

A° *Angle* associated with the point or vector A. Use "rt°" for "right angle," and "st°" for "straight angle." Avoid ∠ which resembles symbol for "less than." Use "arc" rather than "⌒" to avoid confusion with bar for "line segment."

∠ Angle

⫟ Angles

MATHEMATICAL SYMBOLS AND ABBREVIATIONS (Continued)

$\odot$	Circle. $\odot$ A(B) designates the circle with center A passing through B. $\odot$ (AB) has AB as diameter, and $\odot$ (ABC) circumscribes $\triangle$ABC. $\odot$A, r has center A, radius r.
$\circledS$	Circles.
A:B(S)	Collinear. The line AB passes through the point S. Use $\overline{AB}$(S) for "S lies between A and B."
$\cong$	Congruent. (Same shape and same size).
A:B(S,r)	Point of division. "S divides AB in the ratio AS:BS = r." Use (S, −) for internal division, and (S, +) for external division.
$=$	Equal, equivalent. The quantity measured may be indicated in parenthesis at the right of the statement, as "(area)," "(vol.)," "(angle)." Avoid pictogram $\backsimeq$.
$\overline{\wedge}$	Perspective. See ABC:DEF(S) below.
$\underline{\wedge}$	Projective. See ABC::DEF below.
a/b	Fraction (with numerator a, denominator b). Same meaning as quotient "a ÷ b" (with dividend a, divisor b) and ratio a:b (with antecedent a, consequent b).
$\dot\backsim$	Homothetic (Similar and perspective). "ABC $\dot\backsim$ DEF" indicates that corresponding lines, such as BC and EF, are parallel. Use "$\dot\backsim$ (S, r)" for "the homothecy with center S and ratio r."
AB	Line, segment, vector. When further distinctions are desired, use $\overline{AB}$ (or AB) for the length of the line segment (distance between A and B), use $\overrightarrow{AB}$ for the vector (displacement from A toward B), and use A:B for the infinite line (determined by the two points).
$\parallel$	Parallel.
$\Box$	Parallelogram (vertices are named in counterclockwise order).
$\perp$	Perpendicular.
ABC::DEF	Projective (related by a sequence of perspectivities). Same meaning as pictogram "$\underline{\wedge}$."
ABC:DEF(S)	Perspective. The lines A:D and B:E and C:F are concurrent at the point S (center of perspectivity). Same meaning as pictogram "$\overline{\wedge}$."
QED	End of proof.
QEF	End of construction.
$\mathbb{R}$	Cross ratio, anharmonic ratio $\mathbb{R}$(AC, BD) = AB · CD/ AD · CB. $\mathbb{R}$ = −1 means "harmonic" and may be used for collinear points (range), concurrent lines (pencil), or cyclic quadrangle. $\mathbb{R}$(CA, BD) = 1/$\mathbb{R}$(AC, BD) = $\mathbb{R}$(AC, DB). Also $\mathbb{R}$(AB, CD) = 1 − $\mathbb{R}$(AC, BD).
$\sim$	Similar. $\triangle$ABC $\sim$ $\triangle$DEF means that A corresponds to D, B to E, and C to F, respectively.
$\Box$	Square. Use "rect" for "rectangle," "quad" for

MATHEMATICAL SYMBOLS AND ABBREVIATIONS (Continued)

	"quadrilateral" (or quadrangle), and "trap" for "trapezoid" rather than pictograms.
ABC $\stackrel{\cdot}{\sim}$ DEF(r = 1)	Displaced by translation. (The triangles are congruent and similarly placed).
$\triangle$	Triangle. Use "isos" for "isosceles triangle" (naming vertex opposite base first).
$\dot{\mathrm{B}}$	Vertex. In using triliteral symbol ABC, A is on the initial side, B is the vertex, C is on the terminal side. The vertex may be marked with a caret "ABC" or by superscript position "A^{B}C."

General Mathematical Symbols and Abbreviations

"Bold-face" or gothic type—To indicate vectors corresponding italic type indicates magnitude of the vector. In manuscript and at the blackboard, bold-faced type is variously indicated by wavy underscoring, or enclosure in a circle, or even by wavy overscoring. Some persons use German type.

Half-spaces—In writing numbers with many recorded digits, half-spaces (rather than commas or other marks) may well be used to separate convenient groups of digits. Thus $\pi = 3.14159\ 26536 -$.

Superscripts—To indicate: **1.** powers, as in x^2, $(a - x)^n$, etc. In modern practice $a^0 = 1$ always by definition (except for $a = 0$). Also in ∞', ∞^2, etc., indicating number of degrees of freedom. Wherever the context restricts the value of a to non-negative (real) values and n to positive integers, $a^{1/n}$ means the non-negative (real) nth root of a. For complex numbers, x^y is defined as $e^{y\ (\log x)}$, where the principal value of $\log x$ is to be taken. In tables 0.0^5314 may be used to indicate 0.00000314. Note special use of $\sin^n x$ for $(\sin x)^n$ except for $n = -1$, also for $\cos^n x$, etc. **2.** symbolic powers, or order of iteration, as in T^n or in $D^n\ (= d^n/dx^n)$, or in inverse functions as in $\sin^{-1}$, $\cos^{-1}$, $\sinh^{-1}$, etc. **3.** order of differentiation, as in y' ("y prime"), y'' ("y second," or "y double prime"), $\cdots$, $y^{(N)}$, $\cdots$ **4.** feet and inches, as in $3'4''$. **5.** degrees, minutes, seconds, as in $34°5'17''$. Do not omit ° for common angles. Write $0°$, $30°$, $45°$, $60°$, etc., not 0, 30, 45, 60, etc. Do not use superscript, ^{r}, for radians. Write $180° = \pi$ rad, but write $\cos (\pi/3)$ for $\cos 60°$. **6.** days, hours, minutes, seconds, as in $10^d3^h27^m5.3^s$. **7.** degrees of temperature as in $104°$. Where C (for Centigrade) or F (for Fahrenheit) is given, recent usage approves the omission of the °, thus $100C = 212F$, and $-40C = -40F$. **8.** For use with integral sign $\int$, and with vertical bar $|$, see these symbols. **9.** Vertex, as in A^BC.

Dot-accents—To indicate derivatives with respect to time, (Newton's notation), as in $\dot{x}$ for x-component of velocity, and $\ddot{x}$ for x-component of acceleration.

Subscripts—To indicate: **1.** position in a sequence, set, or matrix, as in a_1, a_2, a_3, $\cdots a_n$, $\cdots$, or $a_0x^n + a_1x^{n-1} + \cdots + a_rx^{n-r} + \cdots a_n$ or in $\begin{pmatrix} a_{11}a_{12}a_{13} \\ a_{21}a_{22}a_{23} \end{pmatrix}$. **2.** general distinguishing mark. Two subscripts may be written adjacently without commas as a_{11} and to be read "a sub one one," not "a sub eleven." A subscript is sometimes enclosed in parentheses as in $F_{(0)1}$ where such distinction seems demanded. For special uses see associated symbols.

MATHEMATICAL SYMBOLS AND ABBREVIATIONS (Continued)

Juxtaposition—To indicate: **1.** the algebraic product, as in $2bxy$. **2.** the logical product as in AB where A and B are given classes, and in symbolic logic. Also written with centrally placed dot as $A \cdot B$. **3.** the group product, as in ST (the result of performing first S, then T, or in aH, the co-set consisting for given a of all operations ah, where h is in H. **4.** general operational or functional combination as in dy/dx, $\sin x$, $\log x$, $\max y$, $\lim x_n$, etc. **5.** sequence of points or other elements determining a geometric figure, as line AB, parallelogram $ABCD$, angle ABC, etc. **6.** sum of products (in tensor notation) when index appears as subscript for one factor and superscript for another. Thus $a_i x^i$ means $\Sigma a_i x^i$, in tensor notation.

( )—Parentheses ("round brackets") to indicate: **1.** aggregation, as in $(a + b) \cdot (a - b) = a^2 - b^2$. **2.** argument of function, as in $f(x)$, $g(x,y)$, etc. **3.** sequence or set, as in $a = (a_i)$, $x = (x_{ij})$, (x,y,z), etc. **4.** matrix, as in $\begin{pmatrix} a_{11}a_{12}a_{13} \\ a_{21}a_{22}a_{23} \end{pmatrix}$ also written as $\begin{Vmatrix} a_{11}a_{12}a_{13} \\ a_{21}a_{22}a_{23} \end{Vmatrix}$. **5.** permutation (or substitution) in group theory as in $\begin{pmatrix} a_1a_2a_3 \\ b_1b_2b_3 \end{pmatrix}$ where a_i is replaced by $b_i (i = 1,2,3)$. **6.** binomial coefficient, as in $\binom{n}{r} = n!/[r!(n - r)!]$. This is also designated by $C_{n,r}$ or $_nC_r$. For n,r, positive integers, $\binom{-n}{r} = (-1)^r \binom{n + r - 1}{r}$, $\binom{n}{-r} = 0$, by definition. **7.** cycle or cylic permutation (in group theory) as in (a_1, a_2, a_3) for $\begin{pmatrix} a_1a_2a_3 \\ a_2a_3a_1 \end{pmatrix}$. **8.** greatest common divisor, as in $(30,42) = 6$, $(7,5) = 1$. **9.** inner product as in $(ab) = \Sigma_i a_i b_i$. **10.** segment or open interval, as in (a,b), for system of values of x, where $a < x < b$.

Superscript ( )—To indicate: **1.** general index as distinguished from exponent. **2.** index of order of derivative as in y, y', $\cdots$, $y^{(n)}$, $\cdots$. **3.** "factorial," as in $x^{(r)} = x(x - 1) \cdots (x - r + 1)$. By definition $x^{(-r)} = 1/[(x + 1) \cdot (x + 2) \cdots (x + r)]$.

[ ]—Brackets ("square brackets"), to indicate: **1.** aggregation. **2.** argument of function as with ( ). **3.** greatest integer in, as $[2] = 2$, $[-7/3] = -3$. **4.** inner product (for coefficients in normal equations in the method of least squares), as in $[aa]$, $[XY]$, etc. **5.** outer product of vectors. Other notations are $V\,ab$ and $a \times b$. **6.** divided difference (in formal interpolation). $[x_i] = y_i$, $[x_i, x_{i+1}] = (y_{i+1} - y_i)/(x_{i+1} - x_i)$, $\cdots$ $[x_i, x_{i+1}, \cdots, x_{i+r}] = ([x_{i+1}, \cdots, x_{i+r}] - [x_i, \cdots, x_{i+r-1}])/(x_{i+r} - x_i)$. **7.** range of points (in projective geometry) as in $[P]$. **8.** base (basis) of Abelian group, as in $[a,b, \cdots, k]$. **9.** module or ideal, as $[2] = [0, \pm 2, \pm 4, \cdots, \pm 2n, \cdots]$. **10.** Christoffel symbol, as in $\begin{bmatrix} mn \\ p \end{bmatrix} = \frac{1}{2}\left(\frac{\partial g_{pm}}{\partial x^n} + \frac{\partial g_{pn}}{\partial x^m} = \frac{\partial g_{mn}}{\partial x^p} \right)$. **11.** closed interval, as in $[a,b]$ for system of values of x where $a \leq x \leq b$.

Subscript note. The use of adjacent subscripts, rather than of indices placed directly below is recommended on account of its availability for running text, and its economy of space and of expense in type setting. Thus use $\sum_i$ rather than $\sum_{i'}$, $\int_a^b$ rather than $\int_a^b$, etc.

MATHEMATICAL SYMBOLS AND ABBREVIATIONS (Continued)

{ }—Braces ("curly brackets") to indicate: **1.**: aggregation, as in $\{(x - a)$ $(x - b)\}^2$. **2.** class of (in theory of aggregates), where the general element only is mentioned, as in $\{a_i\} = [a_1, a_2, a_3]$, $(i = 1,2,3)$. **3.** Christoffel symbol, as in $\begin{Bmatrix} m & n \\ p \end{Bmatrix} = g^{rp} \begin{bmatrix} m & n \\ p \end{bmatrix}$. **4.** the members in a uniquely determined set, as in $\{x_1, x_2, \cdots x_n\}$.

$<\ >$—Angle brackets to indicate: **1.** aggregation. **2.** closed interval as with [ ]. **3.** Angle between as in $A \cdot B = AB \cos <A, B>$. Use sparingly because of ambiguity with signs of inequality.

$|\ |$—Vertical bars, to indicate: **1.** absolute value (modulus of complex number). as $|a + ib|^2 = a^2 + b^2$. **2.** magnitude of (for vectors) as $a = |a|$. **3.** determinant, as in $\begin{vmatrix} a & b \\ c & d \end{vmatrix} = ad - bc$. The use of the notation $|a_{ij}|$ for the determinant of the matrix (a_{ij}), is common but is ambiguous. The notation det (a_{ij}) may be used for this determinant.

$\|\ \|$—Double bars, to indicate: **1.** matrix as in $\begin{Vmatrix} a_{11}a_{12}a_{13} \\ a_{21}a_{22}a_{23} \end{Vmatrix}$ or in $\|a_{ij}\|$. **2.** generalized length (for metrical spaces), as in $\|f\|^2 = \int f^2(x)dx$. **3.** To indicate the length of a vector, as in $\|X\|$.

(], [).—For intervals, as $(a,b]$, for system of values of x for which $a < x \leqq b$, and $[a,b)$, for system of values of x for which $a \leqq x < b$. Similarly $(a,b >$, and $< a,b)$ are sometimes used for these respectively.

$\langle\ \rangle$—Brackets ("bent brackets"), to indicate an ordered set of objects, as in $\langle x, y, z \rangle$.

$\vdash$—Is deducible from.

$\models$—Is valid, or is a tautology (in logic), as in $\models A$ (A is valid).

$\cup$—(is) the union, or sum or join (of), as in $A \cup B$.

$\cap$—(is) the intersection, or product (of), as in $A \cap B$.

$\supset$—**1.** contains (or containing) as proper sub-class. **2.** implies (or implying).

$\supseteq$—contains (or containing) as sub-class. (Some writers use, $\supset$, for this.)

$\subset$—(is) contained as proper sub-class within.

$\subseteq$—(is) contained as sub-class within. (Some writers use, $\subset$, for this.)

$\equiv$—**1.** (is) identical with. $\equiv_x$ indicates (is) identical with for all values of x for which both members are defined. **2.** (is) congruent to (with respect to indicated modulus) as in $a \equiv b \pmod{m}$. **3.** (is) equivalent to (in formal logic).

$=$—(is) equal (to).

$\wedge$—and (in logic).

$\vee$—or (in logic), as in $p \vee q$ (p or q), and/or

$\veebar$—exclusive or, as in $p \veebar q$ (p or q, but not both).

$<$—(is) less than.

$>$—(is greater than. Use "less than" preferably as in "$a < x < b$" rather than "$b > x > a$" since former corresponds to order of real numbers on x-axis.

$\leqq$ *or* $\leq$—(is) less than or equal to. Sometimes read (in the case of real numbers) as "(is) not greater than."

$\geqq$ *or* $\geq$—(is) greater than or equal to. Sometimes read (in the case of real numbers) as "(is) not less than."

MATHEMATICAL SYMBOLS AND ABBREVIATIONS (Continued)

$\not\equiv$—**1.** (is) not identically equal (to). (Not "identically unequal to"), is unequal to for at least one value. **2.** (is) not congruent (to).

$\neq$—(is) not equal (to).

$\lneq$—**1.** (is) not equal (to), (for real quantities). **2.** (Sometimes when explained by context) less than or greater than respectively.

$\sim$—**1.** (is) formally, asymptotically, or approximately equal to. (The context should make the meaning specific.) Do not use $\doteq$ for "approximately equal to." **2.** (is) similar (to). **3.** not (in some works on formal logic). **4.** used to indicate the equivalence of two matrices.

Use "iff" for "if and only if." Alternately "$^{(n)}$ as" (read "as" may be used for "necessary and sufficient."

$\rightarrow$—**1.** approaches (as a limit), as in $\lim_{x \to a} f(x) = b$, $f(x) \to b$, as $x \to a$, etc. (Do not use $\doteq$). Not usually employed with long expressions. **2.** leads to, validates, implies (in logic). **3.** corresponds to. **4.** "if . . . , then . . . " relation (in logic).

$\leftrightarrow$—**1.** mutually implies (in logic). **2.** in one-to-one correspondence with, corresponds reciprocally to. **3.** if and only if, also iff.

$\downarrow$—decreases monotonically to a limit.

$\uparrow$—increases monotonically to a limit.

Superscript $\rightarrow$—directed line as $\overrightarrow{AB}$.

$|$—Vertical bar, to indicate: **1.** value at, as in $f(x)|_a = f(a)$, or $f(x)|_{x=a} = f(a)$. **2.** value between as in $f(x)|_a^b = f(b) - f(a)$. **3.** is a divisor of, divides (in number theory) as $3|6$, $3/6$ for "3 divides 6" or use solidus $6/3$ to indicate that this quotient is an integer, or $(x - a)|(x^2 - a^2)$. **4.** inner product (with parentheses) as $(a|b) = \Sigma_i a_i b_i$.

$\backslash$ or $/$—Stroke, mark of cancellation as in $3x = \overset{2}{\cancel{6}}$, $x + \overset{4}{\cancel{3}} = 7$.

$/$—Solidus, or oblique rule, to indicate: **1.** actual or symbolic division, as in $3/7$, $(x - a)/(x - b)$, d/dx, dy/dx, d^2y/dx^2. Do not write ambiguously $a - b/c - d$, but $(a - b)/(c - d)$ or $a - (b/c) - d$, as may be intended. Do not write a/bc but $(a/b)c$ or $a/(bc)$ as intended. Write a proportion as $a/b = c/d$ not $a:b::c:d$. Where A, B, C, D designate displayed expressions, write the proportion as $\frac{A}{B} = \frac{C}{D}$. In commercial typing in place of $8\frac{5}{12}$, it is usual to write 8-5/12. The solidus form a/b, adapted to running text should be used where conveniently possible, rather than the displayed form $\frac{a}{b}$. **2.** quotient or factor group (in group theory) as G/H, (where H is a normal subgroup of G). **3.** per, as in ft/sec. **4.** discount symbol, as in Cash 6, 4/5, 2/30, n/90 indicating 6% discount for immediate payment, 4% discount if paid within 5 days, 2% discount if paid within 30 days, no discount thereafter, but face amount of bill is due (net) not later than the 90th day. **5.** shilling, (in British currency) as 3/6d, or 10/ $-$.

Superscript ‾‾—Vinculum. This may be regarded as obsolescent for general use as a mark of aggregation due to its unsuitability for monotype setting. In conjunction with the radical sign it is widely used, but may often be avoided. There is little logical or historical basis for using $\sqrt{2}$ rather than

MATHEMATICAL SYMBOLS AND ABBREVIATIONS (Continued)

$\sqrt{}$ 2. For a longer expression, one may write $\sqrt{(x^2 + a^2)}$ rather than $\sqrt{x^2 + a^2}$. Instead of $\sqrt{x - a}\,(x - b)$, one might write $(x - b)\sqrt{(x - a)}$. In geometry, the vinculum may be used for line segments as in $\overline{AB}$.

Superscript $\overline{}$—Bar. To indicate: **1.** complex conjugate of, as $\bar{z}$. This is somewhat inconvenient for "upper extended" letters and capitals as, $\bar{b}$, $\bar{h}$, $\bar{X}$, etc. Also indicated by *conj*, as *conj* $(x + iy) = x - iy$ or by use of a "star" as in z^*. **2.** arithmetic mean value of, as in $\bar{x}$, $= \sum_i x_i/n$. **3.** closure of (in topology), as in $\bar{E}$ (the closure of E). **4.** "least upper," as in $\overline{\lim}$, and $\bar{B}$ for least upper limit and least upper bound, respectively. See "sup." **5.** repeating decimal, as in $1.\overline{14} = 1.141414 \cdots$.

Subscript $\underline{}$—To indicate: **1.** italics (in manuscript). **2.** "greatest lower," as in $\underline{\lim}$, and $\underline{B}$, for greatest lower limit, and greatest lower bound respectively. See "inf."

$\overline{}$ —horizontal rule, sign of division, as in $\dfrac{x - a}{x + a}$. Ordinarily the solidus form, adapted to running text, is preferred, as in $(x - a)/(x + a)$. When numerator and denominator are both complicated, the displayed form using horizontal rule may be avoided by writing "A/B, where $A = \cdots$, and $B = \cdots$."

$-$ (centrally placed)—Minus sign. To indicate: **1.** subtraction as in $7 - 2 = 5$, $a^2 - b^2 = (a - b)(a + b)$. **2.** overestimate, as in $3.5-$. **3.** approach through negative values as in $-\infty$ and -0. **4.** region where variable indicated by context is negative (in graphs). **5.** logical difference (in theory of classes). **6.** in $(-)^n$, the sign expressed by $(-1)^n$.

$-$ (on line)—**1.** decimal point. In the decimal representation of a number between 0 and 1, the cipher, 0, should (except in tables) appear before the decimal point. Thus 0.314 not .314. Notation by powers of 10, ("scientific notation") is recommended, especially when recording approximate values; thus to four significant figures, 3.140×10^9 and 3.140×10^{-6}. **2.** (sometimes used in quoting bond prices) as in 95.17 for $95^{17}\!/_{32}$. **3.** (sometimes used in recording mental age) as in 12.3 for 12 yr. 3 mo. **4.** (in symbolic logic) as mark of punctuation separating terms, also as, "and."

$:$—Colon. To indicate: **1.** hours, in recording time, as in 4:10 p.m. **2.** ratio (an obsolescent form) as in $a:b$. The form a/b is preferred. **3.** (in symbolic logic) as mark of punctuation separating groups of terms, as in $p \cdot p \supset q \supset \!:\! q$. **4.** Indicates infinite line $A:B$, collinearity $A:B(S)$, and perspectivity. **5.** such that (in logic). $\cdot$ (centrally placed)—**1.** mark of algebraic multiplication, particularly where mere juxtaposition would be ambiguous, as in $\overline{AB} \cdot \overline{CD}$. **2.** (for vectors), the mark of inner or dot multiplication as in $a \cdot b = ab \cos < ab$. Other notations are (ab) and $S\,ab$.

$\cdot$ (placed above line)—to indicate repeating decimal, used in pairs, as in $1.\dot{7}3\dot{5} = 1.735735735 \cdots$.

$\cdots$ (preferably centrally placed)—"three dots" meaning "and so forth," or "and so forth up to." Particularly when the reader knows what has been omitted, as in the sequence of natural integers, etc. as in $1, 2 \cdots, n, \cdots$; or $a_0, a_1, \cdots, a_n, \cdots$, or $1, \cdots, m$.

MATHEMATICAL SYMBOLS AND ABBREVIATIONS (Continued)

$\therefore$—hence, therefore. Inverted $\because$ since.

$:.,\ ::,\ ::.,$ etc.—(in symbolic logic), marks of punctuation stronger than $\cdot$ and $:$.

$,,$—ditto.

$\circ$ (centrally placed)—indicates (in classes or sets) the composite of functions, as in $g \circ f$.

$+$ plus sign. To indicate: **1.** addition, as in $2 + 3$, $a + b$, 10^{a+1}. **2.** under-estimate, as in $3.5+$. **3.** continued fraction as in $a_0 + \dfrac{1}{a_1+}\ \dfrac{1}{a_2+}\ \cdots$ for

$a_0 + \dfrac{1}{a_1 + \dfrac{1}{a_2+}}$. **4.** approach through positive values as in $+\infty$, and in $+0$

5. region where variable indicated by the context is positive, (in graphs). **6.** logical addition (in theory of classes). **7.** " $\cdot\,\cdot$ or $\cdot\,\cdot$ or both," (in formal logic). Note: In writing series indicate sign before and after dots of

omission, as $a_0 + a_1 + \cdots + a_n$, or $1 - \dfrac{1}{2} + \dfrac{1}{3} + \cdots + (-1)^{n-1}\dfrac{1}{n}$.

8. in abstract group theory a group or co-set may be expressed as the sum of its elements.

$\oplus$—denoting a logical operation of summation between elements of a set, such as the sum of vectors.

$\pm$—**1.** "plus or minus." The repeated appearance of $\pm$ as in $\pm a \pm b \pm c$ is ambiguous. In many cases the sign $\pm$ before a term which appears repeatedly is intended to indicate the systematic use of the positive determination or of the negative determination throughout. Thus one may write $(a \pm b)^3 = a^3 \pm 3a^2b + 3ab^2 \pm b^3$. Where the context restricts the value of a to non-negative (real) values, $\sqrt{a}$ means the non-negative (real) square root of a. Hence when both signs are desired, write $\pm$ before the radical. For roots of a quadratic equation $ax^2 + bx + c = 0$, use $\pm$ as in $\dfrac{-b \pm \sqrt{b^2 - 4ac}}{2a}$. **2.** (in theory of observation), "with a probable error of." As in 17.2 ± 0.5 cm.

$\mp$—"minus or plus respectively." Used in context where $\pm$ has appeared previously, as in $a^3 \pm b^3 = (a \pm b)(a^2 \mp ab + b^2)$. Here upper signs are to be taken throughout, or else lower signs. The notation $\pm a \mp b \pm c$ is ambiguous, meaning perhaps one of the four values $\pm(a - b) \pm c$, or one of the two values $\pm(a - b + c)$.

$\times$—**1.** times, (sign of algebraic multiplication). Used chiefly in arithmetic, as in $2 \times 2 = 4$, 7.3×10^4. **2.** (for vectors) the sign of outer or cross multiplication. **3.** (for classes) the Cartesian product. Thus $A \times B$ is the class of all ordered pairs (a,b) where a is an element of A, and b of B.

$\otimes$—denoting a logical operation of multiplication between elements of a set, such as the product of vectors.

$\div$—sign of division. Used chiefly in arithmetic. Should be replaced by solidus, $/$, where convenient.

$\sqrt{\ }\ \sqrt[n]{\ }$—square root of, nth root of. (See discussion under "superscript," and under "vinculum"). By custom, for a positive, $\sqrt{(-a)}$ means usually $i\sqrt{a}$, rather than $-i\sqrt{a}$, but the latter unambiguous forms are preferred.

$!$—"factorial," as in $3! = 1 \cdot 2 \cdot 3 = 6$. $0! = 1$, (by definition). The ele-

MATHEMATICAL SYMBOLS AND ABBREVIATIONS (Continued)

mentary arithmetic definition of factorial n, may be replaced in favor of the definition as a special case of the Gamma function $\Gamma(x)$. For $-1 < n$,

$$n! = \Gamma(n + 1), = \int_0^\infty x^n e^{-x} dx.$$ For n a large natural number, Stirling's

asymptotic formula (extended) yields $n! \sim \sqrt{2n\pi}\,(n/e)^n \left(1 + \dfrac{1}{12n} + \right.$

$\left. \dfrac{1}{288n^2} - \dfrac{139}{51840n^3} - \cdots \right).$ Note: Do not use the obsolescent form $\lfloor n$ for $n!$

$\int, \int_a^b, \int_a^x, \int\int, \int_c$ —Integral signs. (use preferably bold-face type)

$$\int_a^b \int_c^d f(x,y)\,dx\,dy \text{ denotes } \int_a^b \left(\int_c^d f(x,y)\,dx\right)dy, = \int_a^b dy \int_c^d dx\,f(x,y).$$

$\oint$—curvilinear integral over closed path free from singularities. (Use preferably bold-face type.)

§—section, or article.

❡ *or* ¶—paragraph.

$\propto$ —varies as. Instead of $y \propto x$ one may write $y = kx$, k being the constant factor of proportionality.

∇—nabla—To indicate: **1.** linear vector operator $\left(\dfrac{\partial}{\partial x}, \dfrac{\partial}{\partial y}, \dfrac{\partial}{\partial z}\right)$ as used also in

divergence, gradient, and curl (or rotation). **2.** backward difference (in interpolation theory) $\nabla a_n = a_n - a_{n-1}$.

∇^2—Laplace operator. Sometimes written Δ.

⊡—Four dimensional differential operator of D'Alembert and Poincare [= point carré].

°, ′, ″, ‴, $\cdots$, $(N) \cdots$, (superscript)—superscript numbers. See "superscripts."

∞—infinity. Use $+\infty$ or $-\infty$ respectively, where direction of approach along real numbers is to be indicated. Otherwise use ∞ rather than $\pm\infty$. Note: "$n \to \infty$," may be read "as n increases without bound." Lim $f(x) = \infty$ means "Lim $1/f(x) = 0$," so that whenever one variable "becomes infinite" the meaning is that its reciprocal "becomes zero."

$\in$—(is) a member (of), as in $x \in A$. Several objects can be denoted as members in a set A by $x_1, x_2, \cdots x_n \in A$.

$\notin$—(is) not a member (of).

$\mathcal{P}$—denotes a power set, as in $\mathcal{P}(A)$ which denotes the set of all subsets of a set A.

ℵ—Aleph (initial Hebrew letter) transfinite cardinal number, in particular that of all real numbers. $\aleph_0$ (aleph null) first transfinite cardinal. Use of Hebrew letters for transfinite numerals is recommended: "aleph" (omit the null) for the cardinal of the set of integers; ℶ "beth" for the cardinal of the continuum (number of points on a line); and ℷ "gimel" for the cardinal of functions of a real variable.

𝔉—the Farey series. $\mathfrak{F}_n$ denotes the Farey series of order n.

α—Alpha. To indicate: **1.** (in analytic geometry of 3 dimensions), direction angle with X-axis. **2.** angular acceleration. **3.** (in statistics) $\alpha_0 = 1$, $\alpha_1 = 0$, $\alpha_2 = 1$, $\alpha_3 = \mu_3/\sigma^3$, $\alpha_4 = \mu_4/\sigma^4 = \mu_4/\mu_2^2$. **4.** (in mathematical astronomy), right ascension (also indicated by R.A.) **5.** angle of triangle

MATHEMATICAL SYMBOLS AND ABBREVIATIONS (Continued)

at A, opposite side a.   **6.** root of algebraic equation as in $a(x - \alpha)(x - \beta)$ $(x - \gamma) = 0$.

B—(Greek Beta)—$B(m,n) = \Gamma(m)\Gamma(n)/\Gamma(m + n)$, (Eulerian Beta-function).

β—Beta.   To indicate: **1.** (in analytic geometry of 3 dimensions), direction angle with Y-axis.   **2.** (in statistics), $\beta_1 = \alpha_3{}^2 = \mu_3{}^2/\mu_2{}^3$, $\beta_2 = \alpha_4 = \mu_4/\mu_2{}^2$. **3.** angle of triangle at B, opposite side b.   **4.** root of algebraic equation. See α.

Γ—$\Gamma(x)$ Gamma-function.   See "!"   Among numerous definitions equivalent for positive real values of x, are the two following: (i) $\Gamma(x) = \lim\limits_{n \to \infty}$

$$\frac{1 \cdot 2 \cdots n}{x(x + 1) \cdots (x + n - 1)} n^{x-1}, x > 0. \quad \text{(ii)} \ \Gamma(x) = \int_0^\infty e^{-t} t^{x-1} dt, R(x) > 0.$$

γ—Gamma.   To indicate: **1.** (in analytic geometry of 3 dimensions) direction angle with Z-axis.   **2.** Euler or Mascheroni constant.   (Also indicated by C.) $\gamma = \lim\limits_{n \to \infty} \left(\frac{1}{1} + \frac{1}{2} + \cdots + \frac{1}{n} - \log n \right) = 0.57721 \quad 56649 \quad 01532$ $86060 \ 65120 \cdots$ **3.** angle of triangle at C, opposite side c.   **4.** radius of geodesic curvature.   **5.** universal constant of gravitation $= 6.670 \times 10^{-8}$ $\text{cm}^3/(\text{gm. sec}^2)$.   **6.** root of algebraic equation, see α.

Δ—Delta.   To indicate: **1.** triangle (in plane geometry).   (For right triangle, write rtΔ, not $\angle$).   Also area of triangle.   **2.** increment, as in Δx, Δf, $f(x + \Delta x)$, etc.   **3.** forward difference (interpolation theory). $\Delta a_n = a_{n+1} - a_n$.   **4.** Laplacian operator $\frac{\partial^2}{\partial x^2} + \frac{\partial^2}{\partial y^2}$, or $\frac{\partial^2}{\partial x^2} + \frac{\partial^2}{\partial y^2} + \frac{\partial^2}{\partial z^2}$, also designated by ∇^2.   **5.** selected square root of the discriminant of a given polynomial, as in $\Delta^2 = b^2 - 4ac$ for the polynomial $ax^2 + bx + c$.   **6.** triangular number, (of form $(n^2 - n)/2$).   **7.** Legendre's radical, $\Delta(\varphi)^2 = 1 - k^2 \sin^2 \varphi$.

δ—Delta.   To indicate: **1.** positive constant dependent upon ϵ that may be chosen initially as near to zero as desired.   (In theory of limits, of continuity, etc.)   **2.** variation of.   **3.** (in interpolational theory) central difference $\delta y_{c+i+\frac{1}{2}} = y_{c+i+1} - y_{c+i}$.   **4.** (in mathematical astronomy) apparent declination.   **5.** number of double points, or nodes (Plücker number). **6.** (in statistics) deviation.   **7.** force of interest, $e^\delta = 1 + i$, (in mathematics of finance).   **8.** Kronecker Delta, $\delta_{ij} = 0$ for $i \neq j$, $= 1$ for $i = j$. In tensor notation, also $\delta_i{}^j$.   One has $\delta_{ij} = \begin{pmatrix} o \\ i - j \end{pmatrix}$ or $C_{0, i-i}$.   **9.** unit elongation (in strength of materials).

∂—curly d.   To indicate: **1.** partial differentiation as in $\partial f(x,y)/\partial x$.   **2.** The Jacobian operator, as in $\partial(u,v,w)/\partial(x,y,z)$.   This is variously represented, sometimes as $J\left(\frac{u,v,w}{x,y,z}\right)$ etc.   **3.** a specified square root of the discriminant D.   (also sometimes as Δ.)

ϵ—Epsilon.   To indicate: **1.** positive constant, that may be chosen initially independently as near to zero as desired.   (In theory of limits, of continuity etc.)   **2.** primitive root of unity.   **3.** (is) member of, (relation of element to containing class).   **4.** eccentricity of conic section, usually better designated by e.   **5.** (in mathematical astronomy) obliquity of ecliptic. **6.** an ϵ-number is a transfinite ordinal or a certain limiting type.   Note: Do not use ϵ or ε for Napierian base except in engineering.   See e.

MATHEMATICAL SYMBOLS AND ABBREVIATIONS (Continued)

э—(Inverted Epsilon). Such that.

∉—(is not a member of.)

ζ—Zeta. To indicate: **1.** Riemann Zeta-function $\zeta(s) = \Sigma_{n=1}^{\infty} n^{-s}$ (for $s > 1$). **2.** (in statistics) a test of linearity. $\zeta = \eta^2 - r^2$.

η—Eta. To indicate: **1.** general variable or unknown constant, analogous to y as in case of moving system of coordinates, etc. Used in ordered set (ξ, η, ζ). **2.** a confocal coordinate. See ξ. **3.** (in statistics), correlation ratio. **4.** order-type of the aggregate of all rational numbers.

Θ—Theta. To indicate: **1.** Theta-function. See ϑ. **2.** absolute temperature (where t is used for time).

θ—Theta. To indicate: **1.** general angular displacement (in trigonometry and analytic geometry). **2.** (in plane polar coordinates $(r \text{ cis } \theta)$) angle from initial ray to radius vector, $x = r \cos \theta$, $y = r \sin \theta$. **3.** (in cylindrical coordinates $(r\ \theta\ z)$) angle from initial radial half-plane to radial half-plane containing radius vector. **4.** (in spherical coordinates (r, θ, φ)) co-latitude (measured from zenith) and (in astronomy) zenith distance. This notation is traditional in mathematical physics. In texts on analytic geometry, usage varies, θ being employed frequently for the longitude. See φ. **5.** Theta-function. See ϑ. **6.** (in formal theory of operations) a displacement operator. **7.** ordinary temperature (when t is used for time).

ϑ—Theta-function. Definitions and notations vary widely. For elliptic Theta-functions the notation given here is that followed by Whittaker and Watson. Here ϑ_i designates the value of $\vartheta_i(o,q)$, ϑ_i', the value of $d\vartheta_i(z,q)/dz$. $(i = 1,2,3,4)$. These are defined by $\vartheta_1(z,q) = 2q^{\frac{1}{4}} \sin Z - 2q^{\frac{9}{4}} \sin 3z + 2q^{\frac{25}{4}} \sin 5z - \cdots \vartheta_2(z,q) = 2q^{\frac{1}{4}} \sin z + 2q^{\frac{9}{4}} \sin 3z + 2q^{\frac{25}{4}} \sin 5z + \cdots \vartheta_3(z,q) = 1 + 2q \cos 2z + 2q^4 \cos 4z + 2q^9 \cos 6z + \cdots \vartheta_4(z,q) = 1 - 2q \cos 2z + 2q^4 \cos 4z - 2q^9 \cos 6z + \cdots$.

ι—Iota, number of inflexions (a Plücker number).

ɩ—inverted Iota, (in formal logic) the unique element fulfilling description stated.

κ—Kappa, number of cusps. (A Plücker number).

Λ—Lambda, sometimes used for null-class.

λ—Lambda. To indicate: **1.** general linear parameter (e.g., in a pencil), as in $F + \lambda G$. **2.** running index, as in $x_\lambda (\lambda = 1, 2, \cdots)$. **3.** longitude (in mathematical astronomy). **4.** characteristic value (as in λ_i) in theory of linear differential equations of second order, linear integral equations, etc. **5.** order-type of the aggregate of all real numbers. **6.** In solid analytic geometry (λ, μ, ν) are direction cosines.

μ—Mu. To indicate: **1.** running index, usually used with λ, as in $x_\lambda y_\mu$. **2.** general linear parameter, when used with λ, as in $\lambda F + \mu G$. **3.** (in statistics) moment, about the arithmetic mean, as in $\mu_k = \Sigma_i f_i (x_i - \bar{x})^k$, $\mu_2 = \sigma^2 =$ variance. **4.** μ_x, force of mortality $= -d(\log_e l_x)/dx$. **5.** (in number theory) inversion function of Moebius and Mertens. **6.** Various physical constants such as permeability, reduced mass. **7.** Integrating factor which converts integrable expression into exact differential form.

ν—Nu. To indicate: **1.** running index, usually with λ and μ. **2.** (in statistics) moment about arbitrary origin A (in "short method") as in $\nu_k = \Sigma_i f_i (x_i - A)^k$. **3.** Frequency.

ξ—Xi. To indicate: **1.** general variable, or unknown constant analogous to

MATHEMATICAL SYMBOLS AND ABBREVIATIONS (Continued)

x, as in moving systems of coordinates, etc. **2.** a confocal coordinate as in (i) confocal ellipses and hyperbolas, $\frac{x^2}{a^2 - \lambda} + \frac{y^2}{b^2 - \lambda} = 1$, $-\infty < \xi < b^2 <$ $\eta < a^2$. (ii) confocal ellipsoids and hyperboloids of revolution, $\frac{x^2}{a^2 - \lambda} +$ $\frac{y^2 + z^2}{b^2 - \lambda} = 1$, $-\infty < \xi < b^2 < \eta < a^2$. (iii) confocal parabolas, $y^2 + 2\lambda$. $(x - \lambda) = 0$, $-\infty < \xi < 0 < \eta < +\infty$. (iv) confocal paraboloids of revolution, $y^2 + z^2 + 2\lambda(x - \lambda) = 0$, $-\infty < \xi < 0 < \eta < +\infty$. (v) confocal ellipsoids and hyperboloids, $\frac{x^2}{a^2 - \lambda} + \frac{y^2}{b^2 - \lambda} + \frac{z^2}{c^2 - \lambda} = 1$, $-\infty < \xi <$ $c^2 < \eta < b^2 < \zeta < a^2$. (vi) confocal paraboloids, $\frac{x^2}{a^2 - \lambda} + \frac{y^2}{b^2 - \lambda} = 2z - \lambda$, $-\infty < \xi < b^2 < \eta < a^2 < \zeta < +\infty$. (ξ, η, ζ), Xi, eta, zeta, are used as alternates for rectangular coordinates (x, y, z).

Π, $\Pi_i \Pi_{i=m}^{n}$, $\Pi_{(R)}$ or Π—**1.** product of terms with index i, or j, etc. ranging from m to n, or over R. Do not use $\prod_i$, $\prod_{i=m}^{n}$, etc. (Bold-faced type preferred.) **2.** (in some formal logical treatments) "for every."

Π_{ij}, Π_{ijk}, $\cdots$ —$\Pi_i \Pi_j$, $\Pi_i \Pi_j \Pi_k$, etc.

π—Pi. **1.** the ratio of the length of circumference of a circle, to the diameter. $\pi = 3.14159\ 26535\ 89793\ 23846 \cdots$ **2.** general notation for plane, projectivity, projective, period, etc.

ρ—Rho. **1.** radius of geodesic curvature. **2.** proportionality factor, as in $\rho X_i = \Sigma_j a_{ij} x_j$.

$\sum$, $\sum_i$, $\sum_{i=m}^{n}$, $\sum_{(R)}$ or $\sum_{(R)}$ —Sigma. **1.** summation, sum of terms of index i, or j, etc., ranging from m to n, or over range R. Do not use $\sum_i$, $\sum_{i=m}^{n}$, etc. (bold-faced type preferred). **2.** (on some formal logical treatments) "for at least one." **3.** (in number theory) $\Sigma_{d/n}$ summation extended over all divisors of n. **4.** (in mathematical astronomy) Σ-pt is the intersection of the meridian with the equator.

Σ_{ij}, Σ_{ijk} $\cdots$ —$\Sigma_i \Sigma_j$, $\Sigma_i \Sigma_j \Sigma_k$, etc.

σ—Sigma. To indicate: **1.** radius of torsion. **2.** (in statistics) standard deviation $\sigma^2 N = \Sigma_i (x_i - \bar{x})^2 f_i$. **3.** (in number theory), $\sigma_k(n) = $ sum of kth powers of divisors of n. **4.** any one of several analogous Sigma-functions. The simplest elliptic Sigma-function $\sigma(x)$ is related to the Weierstrassian $\wp$ function by $\wp u = -d^2 \log \sigma u / du^2$. One has $\sigma u = u \left\{ 1 - \frac{g_2}{2} \frac{u^4}{5!} \right.$ $- 6g_3 \frac{u^6}{7!} - \frac{9}{4} g_2^2 \frac{u^8}{9!} - 18 g_2 g_3 \frac{u^{10}}{11!} - \cdots \left. \right\}$ **5.** proportionality factor, usually used with ρ.

τ—Tau. To indicate: **1.** number of bitangents (a Plücker number). **2.** time (when t is used for temperature). **3.** torsion (of curve in space).

Υ—Upsilon. (In mathematical astronomy) vernal equinox.

ϕ—Phi. **1.** Used to indicate the Golden Ratio or Section, $\phi = 1.61803\ 39887$ $49894 \cdots$. **2.** Used to denote Euler's function, where $\phi(m)$ is the number

MATHEMATICAL SYMBOLS AND ABBREVIATIONS (Continued)

of positive integers not greater than and prime to m.   **3.** The null (or empty) set containing no elements.

φ—Phi.   To indicate: **1.** general functional symbol, especially for polynomials. **2.** (in spherical coordinates, (r,θ,φ), longitude from x to y in right-handed system.   In some astronomical work the z-axis points to the zenith, θ is the zenith-distance, and φ is the latitude.   In some works on analytic geometry the roles of θ and φ are interchanged, although the system given is traditional mathematical physics. $x = r \sin \theta \cos \varphi$, $y = r \sin \theta \sin \varphi$, $z = r \cos \theta$.   **3.** (in geocentric coordinates, (r,φ,λ), φ = latitude (not co-latitude as with spherical coordinates).   **4.** (in plane polar coordinates (r,φ).)   Used chiefly as specialized case of spherical coordinates $(r,\pi/2,\varphi)$.   See θ.   **5.** inclination of plane curve, $\tan \varphi = dy/dx = m$.   **6.** (in number theory.) Euler's function or indicatrix. $\varphi(n)$ is the number of positive integers not exceeding n and prime to n.   **7.** $\varphi_i(x)$, characteristic function, see λ_i.   **8.** argument in Legendre's elliptic integrals. $E(k,\varphi) = \int_0^\varphi \Delta(\varphi)d\varphi$, $F(k,\varphi) = \int_0^\varphi d\varphi/\Delta(\varphi)$.   **9.** the normal probability function of Laplace and Gauss in the form $\varphi(t) = \dfrac{1}{\sqrt{2\pi}}e^{\frac{-t^2}{2}}$.   **10.** $\varphi_n(x)$, sometimes used for Bernoulli polynomial.   See $B_n(x)$.

χ—Chi.   (In statistical theory) χ^2 is a measure of goodness of fit, devised by Karl Pearson. $\chi^2 = \Sigma(f_i - Np_i)^2/(Np_i)$ for N items, with p_i the probability of appearances and f_i the frequency for items in an ith class.

ψ—Psi.   To indicate: **1.** general functional symbol (usually with φ).   **2.** angle from radius vector to tangent of plane curve.   **3.** (with geocentric coordinates in mathematical astronomy), co-latitude.   See φ.

Ω—Omega.   To indicate: **1.** a certain annihilator in the theory of binary concomitants.   **2.** (with subscript) transfinite ordinals of certain minimal type. **3.** (in geometry of the triangle) Ω,Ω', the Brocard points.

ω—Omega.   To indicate: **1.** angular velocity.   **2.** first transfinite ordinal, order-type of the aggregate of all natural numbers.   **3.** imaginary cube root of unity, related to i, by $\omega = (-1 + i\sqrt{3})/2$.   **4.** ω_1, ω_2, ω_3, half-periods of Weierstrassian $\wp$-function.   **5.** (in geometry of the triangle) Brocard angle. $\cot \omega = \cot A + \cot B + \cot C$.

A—**1.** A vertex, and the associated angle of $\triangle ABC$.   See α.   **2.** A_{ij}, algebraic complement of a_{ij} in determinant, D. $A_{ij} = dD/da_{ij}$.   **3.** (in astronomy) azimuth.   **4.** (in astronomy) astronomical unit, mean geocentric distance to the sun.   **5.** acres.   **6.** area.

$\overset{\circ}{A}$—ångstrom.

$\mathbf{V}_x$—For every x.

AM—arithmetic mean.   See also superscript $^-$.

Ans.—answer.

AP—arithmetic progression.

Ax—axiom.

a—**1.** (in elementary algebra) initial term in arithmetic or geometric progression.   **2.** (with subscript) coefficient in Fourier series, $(a_0/2) + \Sigma_{n=1}^\infty (a_n \cos nx + b_n \sin nx)$.   **3.** (with two indices) element in matrix or determinant, as in $\begin{pmatrix} a_{11} & a_{12} & a_{13} \\ a_{21} & a_{22} & a_{23} \end{pmatrix}$ or $\begin{vmatrix} a_{11} & a_{12} \\ a_{21} & a_{22} \end{vmatrix}$.   **4.** (in elementary geometry) apothegm.   **5.** (in

MATHEMATICAL SYMBOLS AND ABBREVIATIONS (Continued)

geometry or triangle) first side-line, also length of first side of the triangle.
6. (in elementary analytic geometry) x-intercept. **7.** (in elementary analytic geometry) semi-major axis of ellipse or semi-transverse axis of hyperbola, etc. Thus latus rectum of central conic is $2p = 2b^2/a$, eccentricity $e = c/a$. For central conics and quadrics the a is sometimes associated with x, as in $(x^2/a^2) + (y^2/b^2) = 1$, even when a may be less than b, or as in $-(x^2/a^2) + (y^2/b^2) = 1$, where a is the semi-conjugate axis.

abs—absolute value of.

acc—acceleration.

am—amplitude function. $\varphi = \text{am } u$, where $u = F = \int_0^\varphi d\varphi/\Delta(\varphi)$.

amp—amplitude of vibration.

antilog—antilogarithm.

approx—approximate(ly).

arc (in "arc sin" etc.)—inverse. Also written $\sin^{-1}$ etc. Do not use "arc" for inverse of hyperbolic functions. Write $\sinh^{-1}$, etc.

arg—argument. Angle in polar coordinates r cis θ, and in complex number. $re^{i\theta}$ for r and θ real. Better than "arc" and more legible than superscript -1 to indicate inverse hyperbolic functions, though "$\sinh^{-1} x$" is often used.

av—average.

B—**1.** (With subscripts) Bernoulli numbers and polynomials. To indicate what usage among many is being followed in any given case, authors would do well to list the values of the first few Bernoulli numbers as for example, $B_1 = \frac{1}{2}$, $B_2 = \frac{1}{6}$, $B_3 = 0$, $B_4 = -\frac{1}{30}$, etc. The Bernoulli polynomials, are defined as $B_n(x) = \Sigma_{r=0}^n \binom{n}{r} B_r x^{n-r}$, and satisfy $B_n(x + 1) - B_n(x) = nx^{n-1}$ with the choice of notation for Bernoulli numbers given above. (Also designated by $\varphi_n(x)$.) See page 613 for a second definition of Bernoulli numbers. **2.** bound (general symbol). $\bar{B}$, $\underline{B}$ designate least upper, and greatest lower bound respectively. Preferred notations are "sup" and "inf" respectively. **3.** a vertex and the associated angle of $\triangle ABC$. See β. **4.** (in elementary solid geometry), area of base of a solid.

b—**1.** (in elementary geometry) length of base of plane figure. b, b', parallel bases of trapezoid. **2.** (in elementary analytic geometry) y-intercept. **3.** (in elementary analytic geometry) semi-axis. See a. **4.** (in geometry of the triangle) second side-line, also length of second side of the triangle.

bei(z)—Thomson-Bessel function, $\text{bei}(z) = \dfrac{(\frac{1}{2}z)^2}{(2!)^2} - \dfrac{(\frac{1}{2}z)_6}{(6!)^2} + \dfrac{(\frac{1}{2}z)^{10}}{(10!)^2} - \cdots$

$\text{ber}(z) \pm i\,\text{bei}(z) = J_0(zi\sqrt{} \pm i) = I_0(z\sqrt{} \pm i)$.

ber(z)—Thomson-Bessel function. (See bei(z).) $\text{ber}(z) = 1 - \dfrac{(\frac{1}{2}z)^4}{(4!)^2} + \dfrac{(\frac{1}{2}z)^8}{(8!)^2} - $

$\cdots$.

(B)-space—A Banach space.

B_m^s—An s-dimensional Betti group modulo m (m prime).

B_0^s—An s-dimensional Betti group relative to the group of integers.

C—**1.** arbitrary constant of integration. **2.** (in elementary geometry) circumference of circle; also, circle. **3.** general symbol for curve. **4.** (with subscripts) combination, as in $C_{n,r}$ or $_nC_r$, the number of combinations of n things taken r at a time (without repetitions). The form $_nC_r$ or even ^nC_r is

MATHEMATICAL SYMBOLS AND ABBREVIATIONS (Continued)

widely used but the notation $C_{n,r}$ or $C(n,r)$ or $\binom{n}{r}$ is to be preferred. **5.** Roman numeral for "hundred." **6.** Euler or Mascheroni constant. Also designated by γ. (See γ.) **7.** (chiefly as subscript) contour of integration. **8.** Centigrade, degree Centigrade, as $-52C$.

C_I—(in topology) class of spaces satisfying first axiom of countability, or property of satisfying first axiom of countability.

C_{II}—Same as above for second axiom of countability.

$\underline{C}$—(underlined) the set of complex numbers.

$\underset{\sim}{C}$—(wavy underline) indicates congruence of two n-square matrices.

Ci—cosine integral function, $Ci(x) = \int_{\infty}^{x} (\cos u/u)du$.

c—**1.** (in geometry of triangle) third side-line, also length of third side of triangle. **2.** (in elementary analytic geometry), z-intercept. **3.** (in elementary analytic geometry) semi-axis. (See a.)

cis—$\text{cis } \theta = \cos \theta + i \sin \theta = e^{i\theta} = exp(i\theta)$. Used to distinguish polar coordinates $r \text{ cis } \theta$ from rectangular coordinates. Using Gaussian coordinates, $r \text{ cis } \theta = x + iy$. In de Moivres' formula $\text{cis}^n \theta = \text{cis } n\theta$.

cn—cosine amplitude function. (Jacobian elliptic function.)

colog—cologarithm, $= \log$ of reciprocal $=$ negative of log (especially with base 10).

conj—(complex) conjugate (of). See superscript —.

cos—cosine $=$ sine of the complementary angle.

$\cos^{-1}$—inverse cosine (of). Also written arc cos. $\theta = \cos^{-1} x$ means $\cos \theta = x$. Arc cos x (with capital A) indicates principal value, $0 < \theta < \pi$.

cosh—hyperbolic cosine (of). Do not write Cos nor $\mathfrak{Cof}$ (in German letters).

$\cosh^{-1}$—inverse hyperbolic cosine of. Also written as arg cosh.

covers—coversed sine or coversine.

csc—cosecant (of). Reciprocal of sine.

$\csc^{-1}$—inverse cosecant (of). Also written arc csc.

ctn also cot—cotangent (of). Reciprocal of tangent.

ctn^{-1}—inverse cotangent (of). Also written as $\cot^{-1}$, arc cot, or arc ctn.

ctnh—hyperbolic cotangent (of). Also written as coth.

ctnh^{-1}—inverse hyperbolic cotangent of. Also written as arg coth or arg ctnh.

cu—cubic. In arithmetic "cubic feet" is written "cu ft" but "ft^3" is better.

cum—cumulative.

D—**1.** differential operator, as in $Dy = y'$, $d_x f(x,y) = \partial f/\partial x$. **2.** Roman numeral for "five hundred." **3.** general symbol for denominator, or for determinant. **4.** discriminant of binary form, or of polynomial. **5.** (in statistical theory), (with subscripts 0, 1, $\cdots$, 10), decile marks. **6.** $D(a_1, a_1, \cdots, a_n)$ sometimes designates the Vandermonde determinant.

$$\begin{vmatrix} 1 a_1 & \cdots & a_1^{n-1} \\ \cdot & \cdots & \cdot \\ 1 a_n & \cdots & a_n^{n-1} \end{vmatrix}$$

Def—definition.

Dem—demonstration, proof.

d—**1.** (in elementary algebra), common difference in arithmetic progression. **2.** differential operator, as in d^2y/dx^2. **3.** (in elementary geometry) diameter. **4.** (as superscript) days, as in $2^d3^h17^m$. **5.** (British currency) pence.

MATHEMATICAL SYMBOLS AND ABBREVIATIONS (Continued)

deg—degree, degrees. In navigation use 3 digits measured clockwise from north, so that 090 is due east. In trigonometry use cis θ to indicate direction measured counterclockwise from the positive x-axis, so that cis 90 is the direction of the positive y-axis.

det—determinant of, as in det (a_{ii}).

div—divergence of, also indicated by $\nabla \cdot$ (with nabla and dot).

dn—dn(z), a Jacobian elliptic function.

$\exists$—(there) exists.

$\exists|$—there exist uniquely.

E—**1.** E,F,G fundamental differential quantities of first order for surfaces. **2.** $E(k,\varphi)$, Legendre's normal elliptic integral, of the second kind, $E = E(k,\varphi)$ $\int_0^\varphi \Delta(\varphi)d\varphi$. **3.** east. **4.** (in Euler's polyhedral formula) number of edges of polyhedron. **5.** displacement operator, $E(f(x)) = f(x + 1)$. **6.** (in mathematical astronomy) equation of time.

Ei—exponential integral function $Ei(x) = \int_{-\infty}^x \dfrac{e^v dv}{v}$.

Eq—equation.

Ex—exercise.

e—**1.** base of natural (or Napierian) logarithms. In place of e^A one may write exp A. $e = 2.71828\ 18284\ 59045\ 23536 \cdots \log_{10} e = M = 0.43429\ 44819$ $03251\ 82765 \cdots \log_e 10 = 1/M = 2.30258\ 50929\ 94045\ 68402$. In some engineering work, where e is used otherwise, the base of natural logarithms is designated by ϵ. **2.** eccentricity of a conic. **3.** $e_1 = \wp(\omega_1)$, $e_2 = \wp(\omega_2)$, $e_3 = \wp(\omega_3)$, for Weierstrassian elliptic functions. **4.** (in mathematical astronomy) eccentricity of earth's orbit. **5.** (in elementary solid geometry) length of lateral edge (of right pyramid, prism, etc.).

eq—equivalent to.

erf—error function, $\mathrm{erf}(x) = \dfrac{2}{\sqrt{\pi}} \int_0^x e^{-v^2}dv$.

erfc—complementary function to error function, $\mathrm{erfc}(x) = 1 - \mathrm{erf}(x) = \dfrac{2}{\sqrt{\pi}} \int_x^\infty e^{-v^2}dv$.

exp—exponential function of, as in $\exp(a^2 + b^2)$ for $e^{a^2+b^2}$. One could also write this "e^u where $u = a^2 + b^2$."

exsec—Exsecant

F—Force.

F—**1.** general symbol for function or functional. **2.** the second fundamental differential quantity of first order for surfaces. See E. **3.** (in Euler's polyhedral formula) number of faces of polyhedron. **4.** $F(k,\varphi)$, Legendre's normal elliptic integral of the first kind, $F = F(k,\varphi) \int_0^\varphi d\varphi/\Delta(\varphi)$. See Δ and E. φ is here the amplitude of F, $\varphi = \mathrm{am}\ F$. **5.** $F(a, b; c: x)$, hypergeometric function. **6.** Fahrenheit, degree Fahrenheit, as in 70F. **7.** falsity (in logic).

FS—Fourier series.

Fig.—figure.

Fr—frontier set of.

f—**1.** general symbol for function or functional. **2.** f_i, frequency of X_i in

MATHEMATICAL SYMBOLS AND ABBREVIATIONS (Continued)

univariate table. **3.** frequency of vibration. **4.** feet as in f/s, feet per second. Preferable ft/sec.

ft—feet. See also f and $'$.

G—**1.** general symbol for group. **2.** the third fundamental differential quantity of first order for surfaces. **3.** $G(x_1, \cdots, x_n; \xi_1, \cdots, \xi_n)$ Green's function for two points in n-space. **4.** (constant) linear group of points on an algebraic curve. See g. **5.** gravitational constant.

G.C.T.—Greenwich civil time.

GCD—greatest common divisor.

GCS—greatest common subgroup.

GF—Galois field, as in $\mathrm{GF}(p^n)$.

GM—geometric mean.

GP—geometric progression.

g—**1.** general function symbol, used with f. **2.** (terrestrial) gravitational attraction. **3.** (variable) linear group of points on an algebraic curve. See G. **4.** g_i, frequency of y_i in bivariate table. **5.** general coefficient in tensor, as in $g_{ij}^k x^i y^i z_k$.

gd—Gudermannian. $e^u = \tan\left(\dfrac{\pi}{4} + \dfrac{1}{2}\,\mathrm{gd}\ u\right)$. If $\theta = \mathrm{gd}\ u$ then

$$\sin\theta = \tanh u, \qquad \cos\theta = \operatorname{sech} u$$
$$\tan\theta = \sinh u, \qquad \cot\theta = \operatorname{csch} u$$
$$\sec\theta = \cosh u, \qquad \csc\theta = \coth u$$

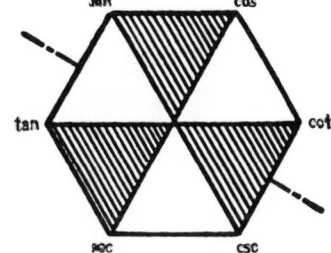

and corresponds to flipping the trigonometric hexagon on an axis perpendicular to cos-sec diagonal. Every vertex of the hexagon is the product of its adjacent vertices, (exhibiting 6 products, and 12 quotients, such as tan/sec = sin) opposite vertices are reciprocals, and in each shaded sector the Pythagorean identity holds. These identities also hold for hyperbolic functions except that Pythagorean sum is at right (so that $\tanh^2 + \operatorname{sech}^2 = 1$).

grad—gradient of. Also written ∇.

H—**1.** general symbol for subgroup, as in G/H, particularly for normal (or self-conjugate) subgroup. **2.** Hessian, as $H(f) = \det\dfrac{\partial^2 f}{\partial x_i \partial x_j}$. **3.** $H_n(x)$, nth Hermite polynomial, $H_n(x) = e^{x^2} D^n e^{-x^2}$. **4.** $H(P_1, P_3; P_2, P_4)$ is the proposition that P_1 and P_3 separate harmonically P_2 and P_4. **5.** orthocenter of triangle where altitudes meet. **6.** $H(q_1, \cdots, q_n, t, p_1, \cdots, p_n)$ Hamiltonian function (in mathematical physics). **7.** mean curvature of surface, $H = EG - F^2$. **8.** (in mathematical astronomy) hour-angle. Also designated by t. **9.** Hilbert space, also $\mathfrak{H}$.

$\mathfrak{H}$—Hilbert space.

HCF—highest common factor.

MATHEMATICAL SYMBOLS AND ABBREVIATIONS (Continued)

HM—harmonic mean.

HP—(in elementary algebra) harmonic progression.

Hyp.—hypothesis.

h—**1.** (in interpolation theory), distance, between uniformly spaced ordinates. **2.** class interval, in x. **3.** increment of x. Also Δx. **4.** (as superscript) hours as in $8^h 15^m$. **5.** (terminal) hyperbolic, as in sinh, $\tanh^{-1}$, etc. **6.** altitude ("height").

hav—haversine (of). hav $x = (\text{vers } x)/2 = (1 - \cos x)/2$.

I—**1.** general symbol for interval, and for definite integral. **2.** Roman numeral for "one." Write IV not IIII, IX not VIIII. **3.** $I(\ )$, imaginary part of, also designated by $\mathfrak{I}(\ )$, or Im$(\ )$. **4.** $I_n(z)$, the Bessel function "of imaginary argument," $I_n(z) = \sum_{m=0}^{\infty} \dfrac{(\frac{1}{2})z^{n+2m}}{m!\Gamma(n+m+1)}$. **5.** (in geometry of triangle) in center where angle bisectors meet. **6.** sometimes used for the identity as an operation in a group.

$\mathfrak{I}$—(Black letter) imaginary part of. See I.

Im—imaginary part of. See I.

i—**1.** running index, as in a_i, $i = 1, \cdots, n$. **2.** one of the two imaginary square roots of -1. (In electrical engineering, when it is used for the current, j is used for this imaginary unit.)

$\boldsymbol{i}$—$\boldsymbol{i}, \boldsymbol{j}, \boldsymbol{k}$, unit vectors in a right-handed rectangular system. $\boldsymbol{i} \times \boldsymbol{j} = \boldsymbol{k}$, $\boldsymbol{j} \times \boldsymbol{k} = \boldsymbol{i}, \boldsymbol{k} \times \boldsymbol{i} = \boldsymbol{j}$.

inf.—("infimum") greatest lower bound.

J—**1.** Jacobian as in $J\left(\dfrac{u,v,w}{x,y,z,}\right)$, also designated by $\partial(u,v,w)/\partial(x,y,z)$. **2.** $J_n(z)$, Bessel coefficient of order n. **3.** Jacobian curve. **4.** Jacobian group of points in a linear series of groups of points on an algebraic curve.

j—**1.** running index, with i. **2.** (sometimes in electrical engineering) $\sqrt{(-1)}$. See i.

$\boldsymbol{j}$—a unit vector. See $\boldsymbol{i}$.

K—**1.** specific curvature of surface. **2.** kernel of integral equation, as in $u(x) = f(x) + \lambda \int_a^b \bar{K}(x,t)u(t)dt$. K_n, the nth iterated kernel is then defined recursively by $K_1 \equiv K$, $K_n(x,y) = \int_a^b K_{n-1}(x,t)K(t,y)dt$. Also designated by $K^{(n)}$. **3.** K, iK', periods for Jacobian elliptic functions. **4.** Symmedian (Lemoine) center of triangle. **5.** $K_n(z)$, the Bessel function ("second solution") $\lim_{\nu \to n} \dfrac{(-1)^n}{2}\left[\dfrac{I_{-\nu}(z) - I_\nu(z)}{\nu - n}\right]$

k—**1.** proportionality factor for variation. Do not use $y \propto x$. **2.** running index, used with h. **3.** k,k', modulus and complementary modulus respectively of Jacobian elliptic functions. **4.** class interval, in y. **5.** increment in y. Also Δy.

$\boldsymbol{k}$—a unit vector. See $\boldsymbol{i}$.

kei, ker—Bessel functions defined as real for real z and satisfying, ker$(z) + i$ kei$(z) = K_0(z\sqrt{\pm i})$.

L—**1.** general symbol for linear function. **2.** general symbol for linear system, or linear space. **3.** limit, as in $\underset{n \to \infty}{L}\ e^{-n} = 0$. See "lim." **4.** Roman nu-

MATHEMATICAL SYMBOLS AND ABBREVIATIONS (Continued)

meral for "fifty." **5.** length. Also designated by l. **6.** first fundamental differential quantity of second order for surfaces. **7.** Lexis ratio, $\sigma/\sqrt{pq/s}$, for sets of s objects each. **8.** $L_n(x)$, nth Laguerre polynomial, $L_n(x)e^{-x}n! = D^n(e^{-x}x^n)$.

LCD—lowest common denominator.

LCM—lowest (or least) common multiple.

l—**1.** running index. **2.** (in elementary algebra) last term (of arithmetic or geometric progression). **3.** $l = \cos\alpha$, directional cosine, (with x-axis). **4.** length. Also designated by L.

lat.—latitude.

li—logarithmic integral or integral logarithm function, $li(x) = \int_0^x du/\log u$.

lim—limit ( ), $\overline{\lim}$, least upper limit, $\underline{\lim}$, greatest lower limit.

ln—(Sometimes) natural logarithm of.

log—logarithm (of). In theoretical work, the natural base, e, is understood; in numerical computation with tables, the base 10 is understood unless otherwise specified. Some writers use "ln" for natural logarithm of. Where ambiguity is otherwise likely, indicate the base, thus $\log_b x$, $\log_{10} x$, $\log_b x$.

long—longitude.

M—**1.** Roman numeral, thousand. **2.** arithmetic mean. Also designated by superscript bar, as X, or by AM. **3.** centroid (in geometry of triangle) where medians meet. **4.** second fundamental differential quantity of second order for surfaces.

M.D.—mean deviation.

Md—median.

Mm—mid-mean, arithmetic mean of data in range Q_1 to Q_3.

Mo—mode.

m—**1.** general symbol for natural number, or integer, usually used with n. **2.** slope of line, dy/dx. **3.** $m = \cos\beta$, directional cosine (with y-axis). **4.** m_a, m_b, m_c, median lines, lengths of medians of triangle. **5.** (as subscript) meridian measurement. **6.** class of an algebraic plane curve (a Plücker number). **7.** (superscript) minutes, as in $10^d13^h5^m$. **8.** meters.

max—maximum (of).

meas—measure (of).

mi—miles.

min—**1.** minimum (of). **2.** minutes. **3.** mi. n. = nautical miles (at equator each minute of longitude corresponds to one nautical mile).

mod—**1.** modulus (of), as in $\mathrm{mod}(re^{i\theta}) = r$. **2.** modulo as in $7 \equiv -3(\mathrm{mod}\ 5)$.

N—**1.** third fundamental differential quantity of second order for surfaces. **2.** north. **3.** total frequency in a statistical distribution.

n—**1.** general symbol for natural number or integer. **2.** $n = \cos\gamma$, directional cosine (with z-axis). **3.** order or degree of plane algebraic curve (a Plücker number). **4.** (in elementary algebra) number of terms in finite progression. **5.** (sometimes) total frequency. See N. **6.** outward normal to surface, as in $\cos(\theta, n)$.

O—**1.** origin of coordinates. **2.** circumcenter of triangle where the perpendicular bisectors of the sides meet. **3.** of comparable order with, as $\Sigma_{n=0}^{N}n = O(N)^2$.

o—of inferior order to, as $\log n = o(n)$.

MATHEMATICAL SYMBOLS AND ABBREVIATIONS (Continued)

ord—order.

P—**1.** general symbol for polynomial, in particular the interpolational polynomial. **2.** product moment. Also expressed by p. **3.** general symbol for point. The common notation indicating the coordinate system used as $P(x,y,z)$, $P(r,\theta,\varphi)$, etc., is not recommended. **4.** general probability distribution function, in particular any one of Pearson's standard types, or Poisson's forms. **5.** $P_n(x)$, Legendre polynomial, $2^n n! P_n(x) = D^n(x^2 - 1)^n$. **6.** total force due to pressure. **7.** function, as in $Pdx + Qdy$, and in $y' + P(x)y = Q(x)$. **8.** $P_{n,r}$ or $_nP_r$, or $P(n,r)$, number of permutations of n distinct things taken r at a time (without repetitions), $n!/(n - r)!$. **9.** general potential due to finite number of particles. In Newtonian case $P = \Sigma_i m_i/r_i$. See U and W. **10.** horizontal parallax. **11.** north celestial pole.

PE—probable error. See $\pm$.

$P(E)$—Probability of E.

$P(E \wedge F)$—Probability of both E and F.

$P(E\backslash F)$—Probability of E, given F.

$P(E \veebar F)$—Probability of E or F, but not both.

$P(E \vee F)$—Probability of E or F or both.

Post.—postulate.

Prob.—**1.** problem. **2.** probability.

Prop.—proposition.

PS—power series.

Pt.—point.

$\wp$—Weierstrassian elliptic function.

p—**1.** general symbol for prime number. **2.** semi-latus rectum. **3.** probability ratio. **4.** genus (or deficiency) of a plane algebraic curve (a Plücker number). **5.** perpendicular distance from origin to given line or plane.

6. p_n, numerator of nth convergent of continued fraction $a_0 + \cfrac{1}{a_1+} \cfrac{1}{a_2+}$

$\cdots$ $(p_{-1} = 0, \; p_0 = 1)$, $p_1 = a_0$, $p_{n+1} = a_n p_n + p_{n-1}$. **7.** p_{12}, p_{13}, p_{14}, p_{23}, p_{24}, p_{34}, line coordinates (point system). **8.** sometimes "per," as in "rpm," revolutions per minute. This use is not recommended. **9.** perimeter. Use s for semiperimeter. **10.** $p(n)$, total number of partitions of n. **11.** p_i, impulse component. **12.** the genus of an orientable surface.

p—page. pp—pages.

pos.—positive.

Q—**1.** general symbol for quadratic form or quadratic manifold. **2.** Q_1, Q_3 first and third quartile marks. (Q_2 is the median, Md.) **3.** function, as in $Pdx + Qdy$, and in $y' + P(x)y = Q(x)$. **4.** $Q(P_1, P_2, P_3; P_4, P_5, P_6)$, quadrangular set of six points.

$\underline{Q}$—(underlined) the set of rational numbers.

$\underline{Q}^+$—(underlined) the set of positive rational numbers.

QD—quartile deviation.

Q.E.D.—("Quod erat demonstrandum") which was to be proved.

Q.E.F.—("Quod erat faciendum") which was to be constructed.

q—**1.** complementary probability, $q = 1 - p$. **2.** q_n, denominator of nth convergent of continued fraction, $a_0 + \cfrac{1}{a_1+} \cfrac{1}{a_2+} \cdots (q_0 = 0)$, $q_1 = 1$, $q_{n+1} = a_n q_n + q_{n-1}$. **3.** q_{12}, q_{13}, q_{14}, q_{23}, q_{24}, q_{34}, line coordinates (plane sys-

MATHEMATICAL SYMBOLS AND ABBREVIATIONS (Continued)

tem). **4.** q_1, q_2, quartile distances from the median. **5.** q_i, force component. **6.** the number of cross-caps on a non-orientable surface.

R—**1.** general symbol for remainder. $R_n(x)$, remainder after n terms in power-series in x. **2.** radius, in particular circumradius of triangle. **3.** real part of. Also indicated by **ℝ** (Black letter), and Re. **4.** general symbol for range of variable, as in $\int_{(R)}$.

R—(underlined) the set of real numbers.

R^+—(underlined) the set of positive real numbers.

$\Re$ —(Black letter) real value of. See R.

R. A.—right ascension. Also designated by α.

R_m^s—An s-dimensional Betti number modulo m (m prime).

R_0^s—An s-dimensional Betti number relative to the group of integers.

Re—real value of. See R.

RMS—root-mean-square. $\sqrt{(\Sigma_{i=1}^n x^2/n)}$.

r—**1.** general running index, as in rth term. **2.** radius (see R), in particular in radius of triangle. **3.** coefficient of linear correlation, correlation coefficient. **4.** (in elementary algebra) common ratio between successive terms in a geometric progression. **5.** distance, in polar and in spherical coordinates; projected distances in cylindrical coordinates. **6.** (sometimes) revolutions, as in r.p.m. (revolutions per minute). **7.** (sometimes) (superscript) radians, as in $2\pi^{(r)}$. (This usage is not recommended.) **8.** the number of boundary curves on a surface.

rad—**1.** radius. **2.** radians. Where no units are indicated angles are measured in radians, sin 30 means "sine of 30 radians," not sin 30°. Do not write sin a^r or sin $a^{(r)}$ for sin a (where a is measured in radians), since superscript r is sometimes interpreted as "revolutions."

rot—rotation or curl of vector. Also designated by $\nabla \times$ (nabla and cross).

S—**1.** general symbol for space, as S_n, space of n dimension. See L. **2.** general symbol for sum, as in S_n, sum of first n terms of given sequence or series. See s. **3.** south. **4.** standard error of estimate. **5.** radius of spherical curvature of curve. **6.** a set (any collection of distinguishable objects).

∂S—Boundary of a set S.

Si—1st sine-integral function $Si(x) = \int_0^x (\sin u/u)du$. See si.

S.T.—sidereal time.

s.—**1.** general running index. Used with r. **2.** general symbol for sum, as in s_n sum of first n terms of sequence or series. See S. **3.** (in elementary algebra), sum of arithmetic or of geometric progression. **4.** $s_k(n)$, sum of kth powers of first n natural numbers. **5.** s_k, sum of the kth powers of the roots of an algebraic equation. **6.** arc length. **7.** slant height. **8.** (usually as superscript) seconds. **9.** semi-interquartile range. **10.** semi-perimeter of triangle, $s = (a + b + c)/2$. **11.** (sometimes) number of individuals in sample. **12.** root-mean-square deviation about arbitrarily assumed origin, (in "short method").

sec—secant (of). Reciprocal of cosine.

sec^{-1}—inverse secant (of). Also designated by arc sec.

sech—hyperbolic secant (of). Do not use Sec or $\mathfrak{Sec}$ (in German letters).

$sech^{-1}$—inverse hyperbolic secant of. Also written as arg sech.

MATHEMATICAL SYMBOLS AND ABBREVIATIONS (Continued)

si—2nd sine-integral function, $\beta_i(x) = \int_{\infty}^{x} (\sin u/u)du$. See Si.

sgn—(signum) sign (of), more generally for z complex, sgn $z = z/|z|$.

Use $\sigma_1 = \begin{pmatrix} + & + \\ - & - \end{pmatrix}$ for the signum of the sine (in the corresponding quadrant).

Use $\sigma_2 = \begin{pmatrix} - & + \\ - & + \end{pmatrix}$ for the signum of the cosine.

and $\sigma_3 = \begin{pmatrix} - & + \\ + & - \end{pmatrix}$ for the signum of the tangent.

Thus $d(\text{arc sin } x)/dx = \sigma_2/\sqrt{1 - x^2}$;
$d(\text{arc cos } x)/dx = -\sigma_1/\sqrt{1 - x^2}$

and $\sigma_1/\sigma_2 = \sigma_1\sigma_2 = \sigma_3$.

sin—sine (of). Do not use Sin. In general triangle sin $A = a/d$ where d is circumdiameter. Identity $d = a/\sin A = b/\sin B = c/\sin C$ is the "law of sines."

sin⁻¹—inverse sine (of). Also designated arc sin.

sinh—hyperbolic sine (of).

sinh⁻¹—inverse hyperbolic sine of—also written as arg sinh.

sk—skewness of frequency distribution.

sn—(Jacobian elliptic function), sine amplitude.

sq—square.

sup—(supremum) least upper bound. Sometimes designated by L.U.B., or l.u.b.

T—**1.** total time, (as in time of flight of projectile). **2.** clock time. **3.** general symbol for transformation, T^n, nth iterate of T. **4.** tons. **5.** (in logic), true or truth. **6.** absolute temperature.

Th—theorem.

t—**1.** general variable or parameter. **2.** time. (In navigation) use 4 digits 0230 for 2:30 a.m., and 1430 for 2:30 p.m. See τ. See "dot accent." **3.** ordinary temperature. See T, τ, θ.

tan—tangent (of).

tan⁻¹—inverse tangent (of). Also designated by arc tan.

tanh—hyperbolic tangent (of). Do not use Tan or $\mathfrak{Tan}$ (in German letters).

tanh⁻¹—inverse hyperbolic tangent (of). Do not use arc tanh. Also written as arg tanh.

T_0-space—A topological space such that for distinct x and y there is either a neighborhood of x not containing y or a neighborhood of y not containing x.

T_1-space—A topological space such that for distinct x and y there is a neighborhood of x not containing y.

T_2-space—A Hausdorff topological space.

T_3-space—A T_2-space which is regular.

T_4-space—A T_2-space which is normal.

U-general (line surface or volume) potential. In Newtonian case, $U = \int_{(L)} \frac{\mu dL}{r}$, or $\int_{(S)} \frac{\mu dS}{r}$, or $\int_{(V)} \frac{\mu dV}{r}$. See P and W.

u—**1.** general variable, especially dependent variable or real part thereof. See w. **2.** u_n, Lucas' function $u_n = (\alpha^n - \beta^n)/(\alpha - \beta)$, α, β, roots of given quadratic.

V—**1.** Roman numeral, five. **2.** (in Euler's polyhedral formula) number of

MATHEMATICAL SYMBOLS AND ABBREVIATIONS (Continued)

vertices. **3.** general harmonic function. **4.** volume. **5.** coefficient of variation.

v—(linear) velocity.

v—**1.** general variable, especial dependent variable, used with u, or coefficient of pure imaginary part thereof. See w. **2.** v_n, Lucas' function $\alpha^n + \beta^n$, α, β, roots of given quadratic. See u_n. **3.** speed.

vers—versed sine or versine.

W—**1.** west. **2.** general potential of double layer. In Newtonian case,

$$W = \int_{(S)} v \frac{\partial}{\partial n}\left(\frac{1}{r}\right) dS, = -\int_{(S)} \frac{v}{r^2} \cos (r,n)\, dS.$$ See P and U. **3.** Wronskian,

$$W = \begin{vmatrix} y_1 & y_1' & \cdots & y_1^{(n-1)} \\ \cdots & \cdots & \cdots & \cdots \\ y_n & y_n' & \cdots & y_n^{(n-1)} \end{vmatrix}.$$

4. total weight. Also designated by Wt. **5.** work (or energy). Also designated by Wk.

Wt.—weight. See W.

w—**1.** general symbol for variable, particularly dependent variable. Used with u and v as in $J\left(\frac{u,v,w}{x,y,z}\right)$, etc. **2.** dependent complex variable, $w = u + iv$, or $w(z) = u(x,y) + iv(x,y)$ where $z = x + iy$, x,y,u,v, real.

X—**1.** Roman numeral, ten; as in XCIII, etc. **2.** X_i, original numerical data for x-variates, (previous to change of origin or scale). **3.** general symbol for variable point, particularly on x-axis. **4.** function, as in $X dx + Y dy + Z dz$ or $\frac{dx}{X} = \frac{dy}{Y} = \frac{dz}{Z}$.

x—**1.** general symbol for independent variable or unknown. **2.** first rectangular coordinate. In space a right-handed coordinate system such as indicated

by $\begin{array}{c} Z \\ | \\ /O\!\!-\!\!Y \\ X/ \end{array}$ or $\begin{array}{c} Y \\ | \\ /O\!\!-\!\!X \\ Z/ \end{array}$ is recommended. The former with OZ

directed to the zenith is more common. **3.** real part of independent complex variable $z = x + iy$.

Y—**1.** Y_i, original numerical data for y-variates (previous to change of origin or scale). **2.** function as in $X dx + Y dy + Z dz$, or $\frac{dx}{X} = \frac{dy}{Y} = \frac{dz}{Z}$.

y—**1.** general symbol for dependent (real) variable. **2.** general symbol for second independent variable, r unknown. **3.** second rectangular coordinate. See x. **4.** pure imaginary coefficient, in independent complex variable, $z = x + iy$.

Z—zenith.

Z—(underlined) the set of integers.

Z^+—(underlined) the set of positive integers.

Z.T.—zone time.

z—**1.** independent complex variable, $z = x + iy$. **2.** general symbol for third independent variable or unknown. **3.** third rectangular coordinate. See x. **4.** axial coordinate in cylindrical coordinates (r, θ, z). **5.** zenith distance, $(90^\circ - h)$. **6.** Fisher's z statistic.

MATHEMATICAL SYMBOLS AND ABBREVIATIONS (Continued)

Selected Symbols Used in Financial and Actuarial Theory

α—net premium in first policy year.

β—net premium in each policy year after the first.

δ—force of interest (and of discount) $e^\delta = 1 + i$.

ω—terminal recorded age in mortality table, "limiting" age.

A_x—commutation symbol, present value of net single premium for whole life policy on (x), $= M_x/D_x$.

$a_{\overline{n}|i}$—present value of annuity for unit periodic payment, $= (1 - v^n)/i$.

$a_{\overline{n}|i}^{(p)}$—present value of an annuity of 1 per annum at interest rate i, payable p times a year (in installments of $1/p$ each).

a_x—commutation symbol, present value of (ordinary) whole life annuity on (x) of unit annual payment.

$a_x^{(m)}$—present value of whole life annuity on (x), of unit annual payment, payable m times a year.

$n|a_x$—present value of whole life annuity, on (x), deferred n years for unit annual payment.

$a_{x\overline{n}|}$—present value of temporary life annuity, on (x), for n years, for unit annual payment.

$a_{\infty i}$—present value of perpetuity at rate of interest, i.

$a_{\infty i}$—present value of perpetuity due at rate of interest, i.

a_x—commutation symbol present value of whole life annuity due, on (x), of unit annual payment.

$a_{\overline{n}|i}$—present value of an annuity due, for unit periodic payments at interest rate i.

B—book value.

B_k—book value, after k years.

C—**1.** original cost. **2.** capitalized cost.

C_x—commutation symbol, $= v^{x+1}d_x$.

c_x—natural premium at age x, $= C_x/D_x$.

D—total simple discount.

D_b—total bank discount.

D_c—cash discount, where for example, "terms 4/10, 2/30, n/90" designates 4% discount for payment within 10 days, 2% thereafter but within 30 days, payable net in 90 days.

D_t—trade discount.

D_x—commutation symbol, $= v^x l_x$.

d—rate of simple discount, $= 1 - v = (1 + i)^{-1} = i/(1 + i)$.

d_x—number dying between ages x and $x + 1$, according to mortality table (for 100,000 alive at age 10).

E—present value of expectation.

$_nE_x$—present value of an n-year pure endowment to (x), $= v^n l_{x+n}/l_x$.

e_x—curtate expectation of life for (x), $= (l_x + \cdots + l_\omega)/l_x$.

$\overset{o}{e}_x$—complete expectation of life, for (x), $= e_x + \frac{1}{2}$.

F—**1.** net-cost-rate factor. **2.** face value of bond.

I—total interest (ordinary simple).

I'—total interest (exact, simple).

i—rate of interest (effective).

MATHEMATICAL SYMBOLS AND ABBREVIATIONS (Continued)

$j_{(p)}$—nominal rate of interest convertible p times a year corresponding to effective annual rate i, $= p[(1 + i)^{1/p} - 1]$.

k_x—valuation symbol, $= C_x/D_{x+1}$.

$_nk_x$—valuation symbol, $= (M_x - M_{x+n})/D_{x+n}$, $[_1k_x = k_x]$, accumulated cost of insurance.

L—**1.** list price (for trade discount). **2.** salvage value.

l_x—number living at age x according to mortality table.

N_x—("open bar N"), commutation symbol, $= D_x + D_{x+1} + \cdots + D\omega$.

n—number of conversion periods (for compound interest).

P—principal.

P_b—bank proceeds.

P_x—net annual premium for ordinary whole life policy, on (x), for unit annual payment $= A_x/(1 + a_x)$.

$_rP_x$—net annual premium for r-payment life policy, $= M_x/(\mathrm{N}_x - \mathrm{N}_{x+r})$.

p—**1.** probability of success. **2.** interest period/payment interval.

p_x—probability of living for another year for a person of age x (according to mortality table).

$_np_x$—probability that a person aged x will live n years, $= l_{x+n}/l_x$.

p_{xy}—the probability that (x) and (y) will survive jointly for one year.

$_np_{xy}$—the probability that (x) and (y) will survive jointly for n years.

q—probability of failure, $= 1 - p$.

q_x—probability of dying within a year for a person of age x (according to mortality table).

$|_nq_x$—probability that (x) will die within n years.

$_n|q_x$—the probability that (x) will die between ages $x + n$ and $x + n + 1$.

R—**1.** periodic payment or "rent." **2.** replacement cost. **3.** repair charge (annual).

S—amount.

S—**1.** scrap value. **2.** amount of sinking fund. **3.** subscription price. **4.** amount (at simple interest).

s—amount (at compound interest) for unit principal $= (1 + i)^n$.

$s_{\overline{n}|i}$—amount of annuity for unit periodic payment, $= [(1 + i)^n - 1]/i$.

$s_{\infty i}$—amount of perpetuity at interest rate i.

s_∞—amount of perpetuity due.

$s_{\overline{n}|i}$—amount of an annuity due, for unit periodic payments.

$s_{\overline{n}|i}^{(p)}$—amount at end of n years of annuity of 1 per annum at interest rate i, payable p times a year (in installments of $1/p$ each).

u_x—valuation symbol, $= D_x/D_{x+1}$.

$_nu_x$—valuation symbol, $(\mathrm{N}_x - \mathrm{N}_{x+n})/D_{x+n}$, $[_1u_x = u_x]$, accumulated value of individual survivors payments.

V—purchase price (of bond).

$_tV_x$—terminal reserve of tth policy year on policy on (x) of unit annual payment.

v—present value (at compound interest) for unit principal, $= (1 + i)^{-1}$.

W—wearing value, $=$ original cost minus scrap value.

x—age of insured (to nearest year).

(x)—a person aged x (for use with mortality table).

$x]$—where $[x] + t$ indicates a life, now aged $x + t$, who was accepted for insurance t years ago at age x.

INDEX

Q

R

S